PAPERBA[illegible]

Paperback

Oxford English Dictionary

Edited by

CATHERINE SOANES

OXFORD
UNIVERSITY PRESS

OXFORD
UNIVERSITY PRESS

Great Clarendon Street, Oxford OX2 6DP

Oxford University Press is a department of the University of Oxford.
It furthers the University's objective of excellence in research, scholarship, and education by publishing worldwide in

Oxford New York

Auckland Bangkok Buenos Aires Cape Town Chennai
Dar es Salaam Delhi Hong Kong Istanbul Karachi Kolkata
Kuala Lumpur Madrid Melbourne Mexico City Mumbai Nairobi
São Paulo Shanghai Taipei Tokyo Toronto

Oxford is a registered trade mark of Oxford University Press in the UK and in certain other countries

Published in the United States
by Oxford University Press Inc., New York

Dictionary text first published as the *New Pocket Oxford Dictionary*, 2001

British Library Cataloguing in Publication Data

Data available

Library of Congress Cataloging in Publication Data

Data available

ISBN 0-19-860454-8

5

Typeset in Nimrod and Arial
by Interactive Sciences Ltd.
Printed in Great Britain by
Clays Ltd, Bungay, Suffolk

Contents

Preface

The *Paperback Oxford English Dictionary* is part of the range of new generation dictionaries based on the *New Oxford Dictionary of English*. It is a handy all-in-one reference book that provides up-to-date and accessible information on the core vocabulary of current English, together with over 4,700 factual entries on important people, places, historical events, etc. Its priorities are clear explanations of meaning, informative encyclopedic entries, and help with spelling, pronunciation, and usage.

The dictionary text is directly informed by the evidence of how the language is actually used today, based on the analysis of hundreds of millions of words of real English carried out for *NODE*. This information is presented in a clear and concise way; definitions focus on the central meanings of words and are immediately accessible, avoiding the use of difficult and over-technical vocabulary. Boxed usage notes within the text give clear guidance on points of grammar and usage. An open layout, with each new section of an entry (phrases, derivatives, usage notes, and etymologies) on a new line, ensures that finding individual sections and entries is easy to do.

The encyclopedic entries cover a wide range of important people, places, historical events, mythological characters, and other proper names, giving useful facts, figures, and points of interest. They are highlighted within the text by special design features, making them easy to find. In addition, there is a set of Appendices providing a wealth of information on subjects such as countries and currencies, prime ministers, and weights and measures.

Pronunciations are given using a simple system, making them very easy to understand. Greater clarity has also been introduced into etymologies, which are written in a non-technical style to focus on root words, with language names written out in full.

The editor would like to thank Clare Collinson for editorial work on encyclopedic entries, Bill Trumble for scientific advice, and Susan Wilkin for providing pronunciations.

Guide to the use of the dictionary

1. Structure of entries

The *Paperback Oxford English Dictionary* is designed to be as straightforward as possible and the use of special dictionary symbols and conventions has been kept to a minimum. Those that are used are explained below.

Headword

Verb inflections

bathe /bay*th*/ ● v. (**bathes, bathing, bathed**) **1** wash by immersing one's body in water. **2** Brit. take a swim. **3** soak or wipe gently with liquid to clean or soothe. ● n. a swim.
– DERIVATIVES **bather** n.
– ORIGIN Old English.

Label (showing regional distribution)

● Introduces new part of speech

Pronunciation (for selected words)

Subject label

apogee /ap-uh-jee/ ● n. **1** Astron. the point in the orbit of the moon or a satellite at which it is furthest from the earth. **2** the highest point: *his creative activity reached its apogee in 1910.*
– ORIGIN from Greek *apogaion diastēma*, 'distance away from earth'.

Sense number

Example of use (taken from real evidence)

buck[1] ● n. **1** the male of some animals, e.g. deer and rabbits. **2** a vertical jump performed by a horse. **3** archaic a fashionable young man. ● v. **1** (of a horse) perform a buck. **2** go against: *the shares bucked the market trend.* **3** (**buck up**) informal make or become more cheerful.
ORIGIN Old English.

Label (showing currency)

Typical pattern (in bold)

Homonym number (indicates different word with the same spelling)

Label (showing level of formality)

buck[2] ● n. N. Amer. & Austral./NZ informal a dollar.
– ORIGIN unknown.

Variant spelling

centralize (also **centralise**) ● v. (**centralizes, centralizing, centralized**) bring under the control of a central authority.
– DERIVATIVES **centralism** n. **centralist** n. & adj. **centralization** (also **centralisation**) n.

Derivatives (in alphabetical order)

Part of speech

Grammatical information (in round brackets)

him ● pron. (third person sing.) used as the object of a verb or preposition to refer to a male person or animal previously mentioned.
– ORIGIN Old English.

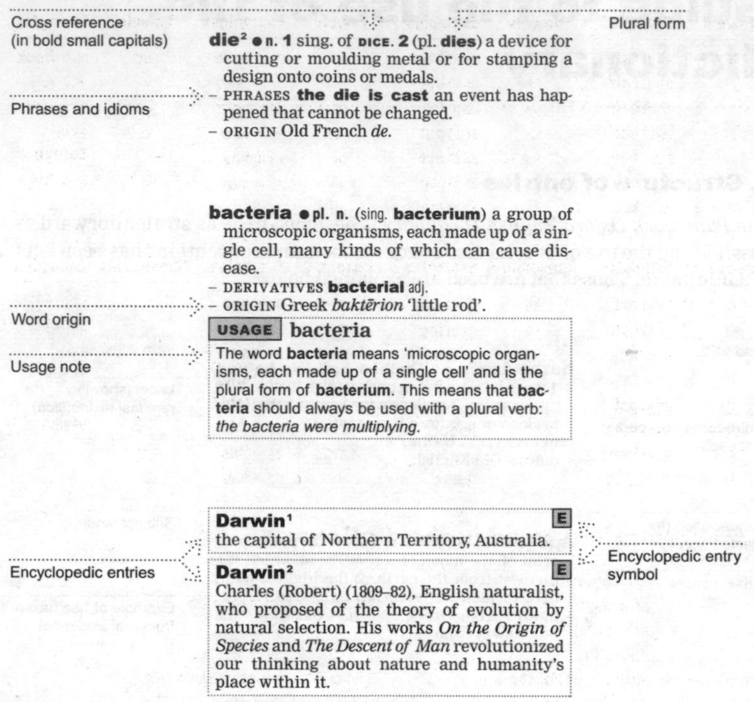

Cross reference (in bold small capitals)
Plural form
die[2] ● n. 1 sing. of DICE. 2 (pl. **dies**) a device for cutting or moulding metal or for stamping a design onto coins or medals.
Phrases and idioms
– PHRASES **the die is cast** an event has happened that cannot be changed.
– ORIGIN Old French *de*.
bacteria ● pl. n. (sing. **bacterium**) a group of microscopic organisms, each made up of a single cell, many kinds of which can cause disease.
– DERIVATIVES **bacterial** adj.
Word origin
– ORIGIN Greek *baktērion* 'little rod'.
Usage note
USAGE bacteria
The word **bacteria** means 'microscopic organisms, each made up of a single cell' and is the plural form of **bacterium.** This means that **bacteria** should always be used with a plural verb: *the bacteria were multiplying.*
Darwin[1] E
the capital of Northern Territory, Australia.
Encyclopedic entries
Encyclopedic entry symbol
Darwin[2] E
Charles (Robert) (1809–82), English naturalist, who proposed of the theory of evolution by natural selection. His works *On the Origin of Species* and *The Descent of Man* revolutionized our thinking about nature and humanity's place within it.

2. Pronunciation system used in the dictionary

The *Paperback Oxford English Dictionary* uses a respelling system for pronunciations in which special symbols are avoided. The dictionary's policy is to give a pronunciation for any word which might cause difficulty; it does not provide pronunciations for everyday words assumed to be familiar to everyone, such as *table* or *large*. Foreign pronunciations are always anglicized, e.g. /kor-don **bler**/ (cordon bleu).

Hyphens have been used to divide pronunciations approximately into syllables. The main stress is shown in bold, e.g. /**ab**-duh-muhn/ (abdomen). Secondary stresses are not given.

An apostrophe has been used instead of the sound /uh/ in cases where this is too heavy, or where the sound is a syllabic consonant (a consonant that is a whole syllable), as in /**ay**-*zh*'n/ (Asian) or /**har**-k'n/ (hearken).

A consonant is sometimes doubled to avoid misinterpretation, for example, -ss- is given whenever -s- might be pronounced as -z-, as in /**cha**-liss/ (chalice).

'I' occurs in initial segments of words and in stand-alone segments (e.g. /I-uh-**tol**-luh/ (ayatollah), /**cat**-I-uhn/ (cation)). All other instances of 'I' are represented with 'y'.

A rhyming pronunciation is given where the alternative respelling involves odd-looking word groups, as in aisle /*rhymes with* mile/.

List of Respelling Symbols

Vowels	Examples	Vowels	Examples	Vowels	Examples	Vowels	Examples
a	as in **cat**	eer	as in **beer**	oo	as in **soon**	uu	as in **book**
ah	as in **calm**	er	as in **her**	oor	as in **poor**	y	as in **cry**
air	as in **hair**	ew	as in **few**	or	as in **corn**	yoo	as in **unit**
ar	as in **bar**	i	as in **pin**	ow	as in **cow**	yoor	as in **Europe**
aw	as in **law**	I	as in **eye**	oy	as in **boy**	yr	as in **fire**
ay	as in **say**	o	as in **top**	u	as in **cup**		
e	as in **bed**	oh	as in **most**	uh	as in **along**		
ee	as in **meet**	oi	as in **join**				

Consonants	Examples	Consonants	Examples	Consonants	Examples	Consonants	Examples
b	as in **bat**	kh	as in **loch**	p	as in **pen**	w	as in **will**
ch	as in **chin**	l	as in **leg**	r	as in **red**	y	as in **yes**
d	as in **day**	m	as in **man**	s	as in **sit**	z	as in **zebra**
f	as in **fat**	n	as in **not**	sh	as in **shop**	*zh*	as in **vision**
g	as in **get**	ng	as in **sing, finger**	t	as in **top**		
h	as in **hat**			th	as in **thin**		
j	as in **jam**	nk	as in **thank**	*th*	as in **this**		
k	as in **king**			v	as in **van**		

3. Abbreviations used in the dictionary

abbrev.	abbreviation	Med.	Medicine
adj.	adjective	Meteorol.	Meteorology
adv.	adverb	Mil.	Military
Anat.	Anatomy	n.	noun
Amer. Football	American Football	N. Amer.	North American
Archit.	Architecture	Naut.	Nautical
Astron.	Astronomy	N. Engl.	Northern English
Austral.	Australian	NZ	New Zealand
b.	born	opp.	opposite of
Biochem.	Biochemistry	offens.	offensive
Biol.	Biology	part.	participle
Bot.	Botany	Philos.	Philosophy
Chem.	Chemistry	Phonet.	Phonetics
comb. form	combining form	Physiol.	Physiology
contr.	contraction	pl.	plural
d.	died	predet.	predeterminer
derog.	derogatory	prep.	preposition
det.	determiner	pres.	present
Electron.	Electronics	pronunc.	pronunciation
Engl. Law	English Law	Rom. Myth.	Roman Mythology
esp.	especially	S. Afr.	South African
euphem.	euphemistic	Sc.	Scottish
exclam.	exclamation	sing.	singular
fem.	feminine	Stat.	Statistics
Geol.	Geology	symb.	symbol
Gk Myth.	Greek Mythology	tech.	technical
hist.	historical	usu.	usually
Ind.	Indian	v.	verb
Ir.	Irish	var.	variant
Math.	Mathematics	Zool.	Zoology

Note on trademarks and proprietary status

This dictionary includes some words which have, or are asserted to have, proprietary status as trademarks or otherwise. Their inclusion does not imply that they have acquired for legal purposes a non-proprietary or general significance, nor any other judgement concerning their legal status. In cases where the editorial staff have some evidence that a word has proprietary status this is indicated in the entry for that word by the label trademark, but no judgement concerning the legal status of such words is made or implied thereby.

Aa

A[1] (also **a**) ● **n.** (pl. **As** or **A's**) **1** the first letter of the alphabet. **2** referring to the first, best, or most important item in a group. **3** Music the sixth note of the scale of C major.
– PHRASES **from A to B** from one's starting point to one's finishing point.

A[2] ● **abbrev.** **1** ampere(s). **2** (**Å**) ångstrom(s). **3** answer.

a[1] ● **det.** **1** used when mentioning someone or something for the first time; the indefinite article. **2** one single: *a hundred*. **3** per.
– ORIGIN Old English.

a[2] ● **abbrev.** **1** (in travel timetables) arrives. **2** (used before a date) before. [ORIGIN Latin *ante*.]

a-[1] (often **an-** before a vowel) ● **prefix** not; without: *atheistic*.
– ORIGIN Greek.

a-[2] ● **prefix** **1** to; towards: *aside*. **2** in the process of: *a-hunting*. **3** in a specified state: *aflutter*.
– ORIGIN Old English.

a-[3] ● **prefix** **1** of: *anew*. **2** utterly: *abash*.
– ORIGIN Old French.

A1 ● **adj.** informal excellent.

AA ● **abbrev.** **1** Alcoholics Anonymous. **2** Automobile Association.

aardvark /ard-vark/ ● **n.** an African mammal with a tubular snout and a long tongue, feeding on ants and termites.
– ORIGIN South African Dutch, 'earth pig'.

> **Aaron** [E]
> /air-uhn/ (in the Bible) the brother of Moses and traditional founder of the Jewish priesthood.

ab- (also **abs-**) ● **prefix** away; from: *abdicate*.
– ORIGIN Latin.

aback ● **adv.** (in phr. **take aback**) shock or surprise (someone).
– ORIGIN Old English.

abacus /ab-uh-kuhss/ ● **n.** (pl. **abacuses**) a frame with rows of wires along which beads are slid, used for counting.
– ORIGIN Greek *abax* 'slab'.

abaft /uh-bahft/ ● **adv. & prep.** Naut. in or behind the stern of a ship.
– ORIGIN from archaic *baft* 'in the rear'.

abandon ● **v.** **1** leave permanently. **2** give up (an action or practice) completely. **3** (**abandon oneself to**) give in to (a desire) completely. ● **n.** complete lack of self-consciousness or self-control.
– DERIVATIVES **abandonment** n.
– ORIGIN Old French *abandoner*.

abandoned ● **adj.** wild; uncontrolled.

abase /uh-bayss/ ● **v.** (**abases**, **abasing**, **abased**) (**abase oneself**) behave in a way that causes others to think less of one.
– DERIVATIVES **abasement** n.
– ORIGIN Old French *abaissier* 'to lower'.

abashed ● **adj.** embarrassed or ashamed.
– ORIGIN Old French *esbair* 'utterly astound'.

abate /uh-bayt/ ● **v.** (**abates**, **abating**, **abated**) (of something bad) become less severe or widespread.
– DERIVATIVES **abatement** n.
– ORIGIN Old French *abatre* 'to fell'.

abattoir /ab-uh-twar/ ● **n.** a slaughterhouse.
– ORIGIN French.

> **Abbas** [E]
> /uh-bass/, Ferhat (1899–1989), Algerian nationalist leader, first President of independent Algeria in 1962.

abbess /ab-biss/ ● **n.** a woman who is the head of an abbey of nuns.

abbey ● **n.** (pl. **abbeys**) a building occupied by a community of monks or nuns.
– ORIGIN Old French *abbeie*.

abbot ● **n.** a man who is the head of an abbey of monks.
– ORIGIN Greek *abbas* 'father'.

abbreviate /uh-bree-vi-ayt/ ● **v.** (**abbreviates**, **abbreviating**, **abbreviated**) shorten (a word, phrase, or text).
– ORIGIN Latin *abbreviare*.

abbreviation ● **n.** a shortened form of a word or phrase.

> **USAGE** abbreviation
> What is the difference between an **abbreviation**, an **acronym**, a **contraction**, and an **initialism**? An **abbreviation** is a shortened form of a word or phrase (for example, *miss* is an abbreviation of *mistress*). An **acronym** is a word formed from the first letters of other words (for example, *laser* is an acronym formed from the initial letters of the words *light amplification by stimulated emission of radiation*). A **contraction** is a shortened form of a word or words, often joined by an apostrophe (for example *I'll* is a contraction of either *I shall* or *I will*). Finally, an **initialism** is an abbreviation consisting of initial letters pronounced separately (for example, *BBC* is an initialism for the *British Broadcasting Corporation*).

ABC ● **n.** **1** the alphabet. **2** a guide to something arranged in alphabetical order. **3** the basic facts of a subject.

abdicate /ab-di-kayt/ ● **v.** (**abdicates**, **abdicating**, **abdicated**) **1** give up the role of king or queen. **2** fail to carry out (a duty).
– DERIVATIVES **abdication** n.
– ORIGIN Latin *abdicare* 'renounce'.

abdomen /ab-duh-muhn/ ● **n.** **1** the part of the body containing the digestive and reproductive organs; the belly. **2** the rear part of the body of an insect, spider, or crustacean.
– DERIVATIVES **abdominal** adj.
– ORIGIN Latin.

abduct ● **v.** take (someone) away by force or trickery.
– DERIVATIVES **abductee** n. **abduction** n. **abductor** n.
– ORIGIN Latin *abducere*.

a

Abdul Hamid II E
/ab-duul ha-**mid**/ (1842–1918), the last sultan of Turkey 1876–1909.

Abdullah ibn Hussein E
/ab-duul-luh i-b'n huu-**sayn**/ (1882–1951), king of Jordan 1946–51. Emir of Transjordan from 1921, he became king of Jordan on its independence.

Abdul Rahman E
/ab-duul **rah**-muhn/, Tunku (1903–90), first Prime Minister of independent Malaya 1957–63 and of Malaysia 1963–70.

Abel E
/**ay**-b'l/ (in the Bible) the second son of Adam and Eve, murdered by his brother Cain.

Abelard E
/**ab**-uh-lard/, Peter (1079–1142), French scholar, theologian, and philosopher, famous for his tragic love affair with his pupil Héloïse (see **Héloïse**).

Aberdeen[1] E
a city and seaport in NE Scotland, a centre of the offshore North Sea oil industry.

Aberdeen[2], E
George Hamilton Gordon, 4th Earl of (1784–1860), British Conservative statesman, Prime Minister 1852–5.

Aberdeen Angus • n. a Scottish breed of black beef cattle.

Aberdeenshire E
an administrative region and former county of NE Scotland.

Aberfan E
/a-ber-**van**/ a village in South Wales where, in 1966, a slag heap collapsed, overwhelming houses and a school and killing 28 adults and 116 children.

aberrant /uh-**berr**-uhnt/ • adj. not normal or acceptable.

aberration /a-buh-**ray**-sh'n/ • n. an action, event, or way of behaving that is not normal or acceptable.
– ORIGIN Latin.

Abertawe E
/a-ber-**tow**-i/ Welsh name for **Swansea**.

abet /uh-**bet**/ • v. (**abets, abetting, abetted**) (usu. in phr. **aid and abet**) encourage or help (someone) to do something wrong.
– ORIGIN Old French *abeter*.

abeyance /uh-**bay**-uhnss/ • n. (in phr. **in/into abeyance**) temporarily not occurring or in use.
– ORIGIN Old French *abeer* 'aspire after'.

abhor /uhb-**hor**/ • v. (**abhors, abhorring, abhorred**) detest; hate.
– ORIGIN Latin *abhorrere*.

abhorrent • adj. disgusting or hateful.
– DERIVATIVES **abhorrence** n.

abide • v. (**abides, abiding, abided**) **1** (**abide by**) accept or obey (a rule or decision). **2** informal put up with: *he could not abide conflict.* **3** (of a feeling or memory) last for a long time.
– ORIGIN Old English, 'wait'.

abiding • adj. lasting; enduring.

ability • n. (pl. **abilities**) **1** the power or capacity to do something. **2** skill or talent.
– ORIGIN Latin *habilitas*.

abject /**ab**-jekt/ • adj. **1** extremely unpleasant and wretched: *abject poverty.* **2** completely without pride or dignity: *an abject apology.*
– DERIVATIVES **abjectly** adv.
– ORIGIN Latin *abjectus* 'rejected'.

abjure /uhb-**joor**/ • v. (**abjures, abjuring, abjured**) formal swear to give up (a belief or claim).
– ORIGIN Latin *abjurare*.

ablaze • adj. burning fiercely.

able • adj. (**abler, ablest**) **1** having the power, skill, or means to do something. **2** skilful and capable.
– DERIVATIVES **ably** adv.
– ORIGIN Latin *habilis* 'handy'.

-able • suffix forming adjectives meaning: **1** able to be: *calculable.* **2** subject to; relevant to: *taxable.* **3** having the quality to: *suitable.*
– DERIVATIVES **-ability** suffix **-ably** suffix.

able-bodied • adj. physically fit; not disabled.

ablutions /uh-**bloo**-shuhnz/ • pl. n. formal or humorous the act of washing oneself.
– ORIGIN Latin.

abnegate /**ab**-ni-gayt/ • v. (**abnegates, abnegating, abnegated**) formal give up or reject (something desired or valuable).
– DERIVATIVES **abnegation** n.
– ORIGIN Latin.

abnormal • adj. not normal.
– DERIVATIVES **abnormally** adv.
– ORIGIN Greek *anōmalos* 'uneven'.

abnormality • n. (pl. **abnormalities**)**1** a feature or event which is not normal. **2** the state of being abnormal.

Abo /**ab**-oh/ • n. (pl. **Abos**) Austral. informal, offens. an Aboriginal.

aboard • adv. & prep. on or into (a ship, train, or other vehicle).

abode • n. formal or literary a house or home.
– ORIGIN from **abide**.

abolish • v. put an end to (a system, law, or custom).
– ORIGIN Latin *abolere* 'destroy'.

abolition • n. the ending of a system, law, or custom.

abolitionist • n. a person who supports the abolition of something.

A-bomb • n. = **atom bomb**.

abominable • adj. **1** very unpleasant and causing disgust. **2** informal very bad.
– DERIVATIVES **abominably** adv.
– ORIGIN Latin *abominabilis*.

Abominable Snowman • n. a yeti.

abominate /uh-**bom**-i-nayt/ • v. (**abominates, abominating, abominated**) formal hate.

abomination • n. **1** a thing that causes disgust or hatred. **2** a feeling of hatred.

aboriginal • adj. **1** existing in a land from the earliest times or from before the arrival of colonists. **2** (**Aboriginal**) having to do with the Australian Aboriginals. • n. **1** an inhabitant of a land from the earliest times. **2** (**Aboriginal**) a member of one of the original peoples of Australia.

aborigine /ab-uh-**ri**-ji-nee/ (also **Aborigine**)

● **n.** an original inhabitant of a land, especially an Australian Aboriginal.
– ORIGIN from Latin *ab origine* 'from the beginning'.

abort ● **v. 1** carry out the abortion of (a fetus). **2** bring to an early end because of a problem or fault.
– ORIGIN Latin *aboriri* 'miscarry'.

abortion ● **n. 1** the deliberate bringing to an end of a human pregnancy. **2** the natural ending of a pregnancy before the fetus is able to survive on its own.

abortionist ● **n.** derog. a person who carries out abortions.

abortive ● **adj.** failing to achieve the intended result; unsuccessful.

abound ● **v. 1** exist in large numbers or amounts. **2** (**abound in/with**) have in large numbers or amounts.
– ORIGIN Latin *abundare* 'overflow'.

about ● **prep. & adv. 1** on the subject of; concerning. **2** used to indicate movement within an area or position in a place: *she looked about the room.* **3** approximately.
– PHRASES **be about to** be on the point of.
– ORIGIN Old English.

about-turn (also esp. N. Amer. **about-face**) ● **n.** Brit. **1** Mil. a turn made so as to face the opposite direction. **2** informal a complete change of opinion or policy.

above ● **prep. & adv. 1** at a higher level than. **2** rather or more than: *he valued safety above comfort.* **3** (in printed text) mentioned earlier.
– PHRASES **above board** lawful and honest. **above oneself** arrogant and self-important. **not be above** be capable of doing (something unworthy).
– ORIGIN Old English.

abracadabra ● **exclam.** a word said by magicians when performing a trick.
– ORIGIN Latin.

abrade /uh-brayd/ ● **v.** (**abrades, abrading, abraded**) scrape or wear away.
– ORIGIN Latin *abradere.*

> **Abraham** E
> /ay-bruh-ham/ (in the Bible) the Hebrew patriarch from whom all Jews trace their descent.

abrasion /uh-bray-*zh*'n/ ● **n. 1** the action or process of scraping or wearing away. **2** an area of scraped skin.

abrasive /uh-bray-siv/ ● **adj. 1** able to polish or clean a hard surface by rubbing or grinding. **2** harsh or rough in manner.

abreast ● **adv. 1** side by side and facing the same way. **2** (**abreast of**) up to date with.

abridge ● **v.** (**abridges, abridging, abridged**) shorten (a text or film).
– ORIGIN Old French *abregier.*

abridgement (also **abridgment**) ● **n.** a shortened version of a larger work.

abroad ● **adv. 1** in or to a foreign country or countries. **2** over a wide area: *millions of seeds are scattered abroad.* **3** at large: *there is a new spirit abroad.*

abrogate /ab-ruh-gayt/ ● **v.** (**abrogates, abrogating, abrogated**) formal cancel or do away with (a law or agreement).
– ORIGIN Latin *abrogare* 'repeal'.

abrupt ● **adj. 1** sudden and unexpected. **2** brief to the point of rudeness. **3** steep.
– DERIVATIVES **abruptly** adv. **abruptness** n.
– ORIGIN Latin *abruptus* 'broken off, steep'.

abscess ● **n.** a swelling containing pus.
– ORIGIN Latin *abscessus.*

abscond /uhb-skond/ ● **v.** leave quickly and secretly to escape from custody or avoid arrest.
– ORIGIN Latin *abscondere* 'hide'.

abseil /ab-sayl/ ● **v.** climb down a rock-face using a rope wrapped round the body and fixed at a higher point.
– ORIGIN German *abseilen.*

absence ● **n. 1** the state of being away from a place or person: *the letter had arrived in his absence.* **2** (**absence of**) the non-existence or lack of.

absent ● **adj.** /ab-s'nt/ **1** not present. **2** not paying attention. ● **v.** /uhb-sent/ (**absent oneself**) stay or go away.
– DERIVATIVES **absently** adv.
– ORIGIN Latin *abesse* 'to be away'.

absentee ● **n.** a person who is absent.

absenteeism ● **n.** frequent absence from work or school without good reason.

absent-minded ● **adj.** inattentive or forgetful.
– DERIVATIVES **absent-mindedly** adv.

absinthe /ab-sinth/ ● **n** a green aniseed-flavoured liqueur.
– ORIGIN French.

absolute ● **adj. 1** complete; total. **2** having unlimited power: *an absolute ruler.* **3** not related or compared to anything else: *absolute moral principles.*
– ORIGIN Latin *absolutus* 'freed'.

absolutely ● **adv. 1** completely; entirely. **2** used for emphasis or to express agreement.

absolute majority ● **n.** a majority over all rivals considered as a group; more than half.

absolute pitch ● **n.** Music **1** the ability to recognize the pitch of a note or produce any given note. **2** a fixed standard of pitch defined by the frequency of the sound vibration.

absolute temperature ● **n.** a temperature measured from absolute zero in kelvins.

absolute zero ● **n.** the lowest temperature theoretically possible (zero kelvins, −273.15°C).

absolution ● **n.** formal forgiveness of a person's sins.
– ORIGIN Latin.

absolutism ● **n.** the principle that those in government should have unlimited power.
– DERIVATIVES **absolutist** n. & adj.

absolve /uhb-zolv/ ● **v.** (**absolves, absolving, absolved**) declare (someone) free from guilt, blame, or sin.
– ORIGIN Latin *absolvere* 'set free, acquit'.

absorb /uhb-zorb/ ● **v. 1** soak up (liquid or another substance). **2** take in (information). **3** take over (something less powerful). **4** use up (time or resources). **5** reduce the effect or strength of (sound or an impact): *buffers absorbed most of the shock.* **6** hold the attention of.
– DERIVATIVES **absorbable** adj. **absorber** n.
– ORIGIN Latin *absorbere* 'suck in'.

absorbent ● **adj.** able to soak up liquid easily.
– DERIVATIVES **absorbency** n.

absorption • n. the process of absorbing or the action of being absorbed.

abstain • v. **1** (**abstain from**) stop oneself from (doing something enjoyable). **2** formally choose not to vote.
– DERIVATIVES **abstainer** n.
– ORIGIN Latin *abstinere* 'hold from'.

abstemious /uhb-**stee**-mi-uhss/ • adj. taking care to limit one's intake of food or alcohol.
– ORIGIN Latin *abstemius*.

abstention /uhb-**sten**-sh'n/ • n. **1** a deliberate decision not to vote. **2** abstinence.

abstinence /**ab**-sti-nuhnss/ • n. the avoidance of something enjoyable, such as food or alcohol.
– DERIVATIVES **abstinent** adj.
– ORIGIN Latin *abstinentia*.

abstract • adj. /**ab**-strakt/ **1** having to do with ideas or qualities rather than physical things. **2** (of art) using colour and shapes to create an effect rather than attempting to represent real life accurately. • v. /uhb-**strakt**/ take out or remove. • n. /**ab**-strakt/ a summary of a book or article.
– DERIVATIVES **abstractly** adv.
– ORIGIN Latin *abstrahere* 'draw away'.

abstracted • adj. not paying attention to what is happening; preoccupied.

abstraction • n. **1** the quality of being abstract. **2** something which exists only as an idea. **3** a preoccupied state. **4** the action of removing something.

abstruse /uhb-**strooss**/ • adj. difficult to understand.
– ORIGIN Latin *abstrusus* 'concealed'.

absurd • adj. completely illogical or ridiculous.
– DERIVATIVES **absurdity** n. **absurdly** adv.
– ORIGIN Latin *absurdus* 'out of tune'.

Abu Dhabi E
/a-boo **dah**-bi/ the largest of the seven member states of the United Arab Emirates; capital, Abu Dhabi.

Abuja E
/uh-**boo**-juh/ a newly built city in Nigeria, capital since 1991.

abundance /uh-**bun**-duhnss/ • n. **1** a very large quantity. **2** the state of having a very large quantity: *vines grew in abundance*.
– ORIGIN Latin *abundantia*.

abundant • adj. **1** existing in large quantities; plentiful. **2** (**abundant in**) having plenty of.
– DERIVATIVES **abundantly** adv.

abuse • v. /uh-**byooz**/ (**abuses, abusing, abused**) **1** use badly or wrongly. **2** treat cruelly or violently. **3** speak to in an insulting and offensive way. • n. /uh-**byooss**/ **1** the wrong use of something. **2** cruel and violent treatment. **3** insulting and offensive language.
– DERIVATIVES **abuser** n.
– ORIGIN Latin *abuti* 'misuse'.

Abu Simbel E
/a-boo **sim**-b'l/ the site of two huge temples cut out of cliffs in southern Egypt, built in the 13th century BC.

abusive • adj. **1** extremely offensive and insulting. **2** involving cruelty and violence.
– DERIVATIVES **abusively** adv.

abut /uh-**but**/ • v. (**abuts, abutting, abutted**) be next to or touching.
– ORIGIN Old French *abouter*.

abysmal /uh-**biz**-m'l/ • adj. informal extremely bad.
– DERIVATIVES **abysmally** adv.
– ORIGIN Old French *abisme* 'abyss'.

abyss /uh-**biss**/ • n. a very deep hole.
– ORIGIN Greek *abussos* 'bottomless'.

Abyssinia E
/a-bi-**sin**-i-uh/ former name for **ETHIOPIA**.

AC • abbrev. alternating current.

a/c • abbrev. account.

acacia /uh-**kay**-shuh/ • n. a tree or shrub with yellow or white flowers, found in warm climates.
– ORIGIN Greek *akakia*.

academia /a-kuh-**dee**-mi-uh/ • n. the academic environment or community.

academic • adj. **1** having to do with education or study. **2** not related to a real situation and so not important. • n. a teacher or scholar in a university or college.
– DERIVATIVES **academically** adv.

Académie française E
/uh-ka-duh-mi fron-**sayz**/ a French literary academy responsible for the standard form of the French language.

academy • n. (pl. **academies**) **1** a place of study or training in a special field. **2** a society or institution of scholars, artists, or scientists. **3** US & Sc. a secondary school.
– ORIGIN Greek *akadēmeia*.

Academy award • n. an award given by the Academy of Motion Picture Arts and Sciences for achievement in the film industry; an Oscar.

Acadia E
/uh-**kay**-di-uh/ a former French colony established in 1604 in the territory now forming Nova Scotia in Canada.

acanthus /uh-**kan**-thuhss/ • n. a plant or shrub with spiny leaves.
– ORIGIN Greek *akanthos*.

a cappella /a kuh-**pel**-luh/ • adj. & adv. (of music) sung without being accompanied by instruments.
– ORIGIN Italian, 'in chapel style'.

Acapulco E
/a-kuh-**puul**-koh/ a port and resort in southern Mexico.

accede /uhk-**seed**/ • v. (**accedes, acceding, acceded**) (usu. **accede to**) formal **1** agree to a demand or request. **2** take up an office or position.
– ORIGIN Latin *accedere* 'come to'.

accelerate /uhk-**sel**-uh-rayt/ • v. (**accelerates, accelerating, accelerated**) **1** begin or cause to move more quickly. **2** increase in amount or scale.
– DERIVATIVES **acceleration** n.
– ORIGIN Latin *accelerare*.

accelerator • n. **1** a foot pedal which controls the speed of a vehicle. **2** Physics an apparatus for causing charged particles to move at high speeds.

accent • n. /**ak**-s'nt, **ak**-sent/ **1** a way of pronouncing a language. **2** an emphasis given to a syllable, word, or note. **3** a mark on a letter or word showing how a sound is pronounced

or stressed. **4** a particular emphasis: *the accent is on participation.* ● **v.** /ak-sent/ **1** (**accented**) spoken with a particular accent. **2** emphasize.
– ORIGIN Latin *accentus* 'tone, signal, or intensity'.

accentuate /uhk-sen-tyuu-ayt/ ● **v.** (**accentuates, accentuating, accentuated**) make more noticeable.
– DERIVATIVES **accentuation** n.

accept ● **v. 1** agree to receive or do (something offered or proposed). **2** regard favourably. **3** believe or receive as valid or correct. **4** admit responsibility for. **5** put up with.
– DERIVATIVES **acceptance** n. **acceptor** n.
– ORIGIN Latin *acceptare*.

acceptable ● **adj. 1** able to be accepted. **2** adequate.
– DERIVATIVES **acceptability** n. **acceptably** adv.

access ● **n. 1** the means or opportunity to approach or enter a place. **2** the right or opportunity to use something or see someone. ● **v. 1** obtain (data) from a computer. **2** enter (a place).
– ORIGIN Latin *accessus*.

accessible ● **adj. 1** able to be reached or used. **2** friendly and easy to talk to. **3** easily understood or enjoyed.
– DERIVATIVES **accessibility** n.

accession ● **n. 1** the gaining of an important position or rank. **2** a new item added to a library or museum collection.

accessorize (also **accessorise**) ● **v.** (**accessorizes, accessorizing, accessorized**) add a fashion accessory to (a garment).

accessory ● **n.** (pl. **accessories**) **1** a thing which can be added to or worn with something else to make it more useful or attractive. **2** Law a person who helps someone commit a crime without taking part in it.
– ORIGIN Latin *accessorius* 'additional thing'.

accident ● **n. 1** an unpleasant incident that happens unexpectedly. **2** an incident that happens by chance.
– ORIGIN Latin *accidere* 'fall or happen'.

accidental ● **adj.** happening by accident. ● **n.** Music a sign attached to a note indicating a momentary departure from the key signature.
– DERIVATIVES **accidentally** adv.

acclaim ● **v.** praise enthusiastically and publicly. ● **n.** enthusiastic public praise.
– ORIGIN Latin *acclamare*.

acclamation ● **n.** loud and enthusiastic approval or praise.

acclimatize (also **acclimatise**) ● **v.** (**acclimatizes, acclimatizing, acclimatized**) make or become used to a new climate or new conditions.
– DERIVATIVES **acclimatization** (also **acclimatisation**) n.
– ORIGIN French *acclimater*.

accolade /ak-kuh-layd/ ● **n.** something given as a special honour or as a reward for excellence.
– ORIGIN first meaning 'a touch on a person's shoulders with a sword when knighting them': from Provençal *acolada* 'embrace around the neck'.

accommodate ● **v.** (**accommodates, accommodating, accommodated**) **1** provide lodging or space for. **2** adapt to or fit in with.
– ORIGIN Latin *accommodare*.

accommodating ● **adj.** willing to help or fit in with someone's wishes.

accommodation ● **n. 1** a place where someone may live or stay. **2** a settlement or compromise.

accompaniment ● **n. 1** a musical part which accompanies an instrument, voice, or group. **2** something that accompanies something else.

accompanist ● **n.** a person who plays a musical accompaniment.

accompany ● **v.** (**accompanies, accompanying, accompanied**) **1** go somewhere with (someone). **2** be present or occur at the same time as. **3** play musical support or backing for (an instrument, voice, or group).
– ORIGIN Old French *accompagner*.

accomplice /uh-kum-pliss/ ● **n.** a person who helps another commit a crime.
– ORIGIN Old French *complice*.

accomplish ● **v.** achieve or complete (something) successfully.
– ORIGIN Old French *acomplir*.

accomplished ● **adj.** highly skilled

accomplishment ● **n. 1** an activity that one can do well. **2** something that has been achieved successfully.

accord ● **v. 1** give (power or recognition) to. **2** (**accord with**) be in agreement or consistent with. ● **n. 1** agreement in opinion. **2** an official agreement or treaty.
– PHRASES **of one's own accord** willingly.
– ORIGIN Old French *acorder* 'reconcile, be of one mind'.

accordance ● **n.** (in phr. **in accordance with**) in a way conforming with.

according ● **adv.** (**according to**) **1** as stated by. **2** following or agreeing with: *cook the rice according to the instructions.*

accordingly ● **adv. 1** in a way that is appropriate. **2** therefore.

accordion /uh-kor-di-uhn/ ● **n.** a musical instrument played by stretching and squeezing with the hands to work a bellows, the notes being sounded by buttons or keys.
– DERIVATIVES **accordionist** n.
– ORIGIN German *Akkordion*.

accost ● **v.** approach and speak to boldly or aggressively.
– ORIGIN French *accoster*.

account ● **n. 1** a description of an event. **2** a record of money spent and received. **3** a service through a bank or firm by which funds are held on behalf of a customer or goods or services are supplied on credit. **4** importance: *money was of no account to her.* ● **v.** regard in a particular way.
– PHRASES **account for 1** supply or make up (an amount). **2** give a satisfactory explanation of. **call to account** require (someone) to explain poor performance. **on someone's account** for someone's benefit. **on account of** because of. **on no account** under no circumstances. **take account of** take into consideration.
– ORIGIN Old French *acont*.

accountable ● **adj.** responsible for one's actions and expected to explain them.
– DERIVATIVES **accountability** n.

accountant ● **n.** a person who keeps or inspects financial accounts.

a

a

– DERIVATIVES **accountancy** n.

accounting ● n. the keeping of financial accounts.

accoutrement /uh-koo-truh-muhnt, uh-koo-ter-muhnt/ (US **accouterment**) ● n. an extra item of dress or equipment.
– ORIGIN French *accoutrer* 'clothe, equip'.

Accra E
/uh-**krah**/ the capital of Ghana.

accredit ● v. (**accredits**, **accrediting**, **accredited**) **1** (**accredit to**) give (someone) the credit for (something). **2** give official authorization to.
– ORIGIN French *accréditer*.

accretion /uh-kree-sh'n/ ● n. **1** growth or increase by a gradual build-up of layers. **2** a thing formed or added in this way.
– ORIGIN Latin *accrescere* 'grow'.

accrue /uh-kroo/ ● v. (**accrues**, **accruing**, **accrued**) **1** (of money) be received in regular or increasing amounts. **2** collect or receive (payments or benefits).
– DERIVATIVES **accrual** n.
– ORIGIN Old French *acreistre* 'increase'.

accumulate /uh-kyoo-myuu-layt/ ● v. (**accumulates**, **accumulating**, **accumulated**) **1** gather together a number or quantity of. **2** increase.
– DERIVATIVES **accumulation** n.
– ORIGIN Latin *accumulare* 'heap up'.

accumulator ● n. Brit. **1** a large rechargeable electric cell. **2** a bet placed on a series of events, the winnings and stake from each being placed on the next.

accurate /ak-kyuu-ruht/ ● adj. **1** correct in all details. **2** reaching an intended target.
– DERIVATIVES **accuracy** n. **accurately** adv.
– ORIGIN Latin *accurare* 'do with care'.

accursed /uh-ker-sid, uh-**kerst**/ ● adj. literary under a curse.

accusation ● n. a claim that someone has done something illegal or wrong.

accusative /uh-kyoo-zuh-tiv/ ● adj. (of a grammatical case) used for the object of a verb.
– ORIGIN from Latin *casus accusativus* 'the case showing cause'.

accusatory /uh-kyoo-zuh-tuh-ri/ ● adj. suggesting that one believes a person has done something wrong.

accuse ● v. (**accuses**, **accusing**, **accused**) say that (someone) has done something wrong or has committed a crime: *he was accused of murder.*
– DERIVATIVES **accuser** n.
– ORIGIN Latin *accusare* 'call to account'.

accustom ● v. **1** (**accustom to**) make used to. **2** (**be accustomed to**) be used to. **3** (**accustomed**) usual.
– ORIGIN Old French *acostumer*.

AC/DC ● adj. alternating current/direct current.

ace ● n. **1** a playing card with a single spot on it, usually the highest card in its suit. **2** informal a person who is very good at a particular activity. **3** Tennis a service that an opponent is unable to return. ● adj. informal very good.
– PHRASES **ace up one's sleeve** a plan or piece of information kept secret until needed. **hold all the aces** have all the advantages.
– ORIGIN Latin *as* 'unity, a unit'.

acellular /ay-sel-yuu-ler/ ● adj. Biol. **1** not divided into or containing cells. **2** consisting of one cell only.

acerbic /uh-ser-bik/ ● adj. sharp and direct: *acerbic comments.*
– DERIVATIVES **acerbity** n.
– ORIGIN Latin *acerbus* 'sour-tasting'.

acetate /a-si-tayt/ ● n. **1** Chem. a salt or ester of acetic acid. **2** fibre or plastic made from a substance produced from cellulose.

acetic acid /uh-see-tik/ ● n. the acid that gives vinegar its characteristic taste.
– ORIGIN Latin *acetum* 'vinegar'.

acetone /a-si-tohn/ ● n. a colourless liquid used as a solvent.
– ORIGIN from **ACETIC ACID**.

acetylene /uh-set-i-leen/ ● n. a gas which burns with a bright flame, used in welding.
– ORIGIN from **ACETIC ACID**.

ache ● n. a continuous or long-lasting dull pain. ● v. (**aches**, **aching**, **ached**) **1** suffer from an ache. **2** (**ache for/to do**) feel great desire for or to do.
– ORIGIN Old English.

Achebe E
/uh-**chay**-bi/, Chinua (b.1930), Nigerian novelist, poet, and short-story writer.

Achernar E
/ay-kuh-nar/ the ninth-brightest star in the sky and the brightest in the constellation Eridanus.

achieve ● v. (**achieves**, **achieving**, **achieved**) succeed in doing by effort, skill, or courage.
– DERIVATIVES **achievable** adj. **achiever** n.
– ORIGIN Old French *achever* 'come or bring to a head'.

achievement ● n. **1** a thing that is achieved. **2** the action of achieving something.

Achilles E
/uh-**kil**-leez/ Gk Myth. a hero of the Trojan War. His mother plunged him in the river Styx when he was a baby, making his body invulnerable except for the heel by which she held him.

Achilles heel ● n. a weak point.
– ORIGIN see **ACHILLES**.

Achilles tendon ● n. the tendon connecting calf muscles to the heel.

achromatic /a-kroh-mat-ik/ ● adj. **1** transmitting light without separating it into colours. **2** without colour.

achy (also **achey**) ● adj. suffering from an ache or aches.

acid ● n. **1** a substance with chemical properties including turning litmus red, neutralizing alkalis, and dissolving some metals. **2** informal the drug LSD. ● adj. **1** having the properties of an acid; having a pH of less than 7. **2** sharp-tasting or sour. **3** (of a remark) bitter or cutting.
– DERIVATIVES **acidic** adj. **acidly** adv.
– ORIGIN Latin *acidus*.

acidify ● v. (**acidifies**, **acidifying**, **acidified**) make or become acid.

acidity ● n. **1** the level of acid in something. **2** bitterness or sharpness in a person's remarks or tone.

acid rain ● n. rainfall made acidic by pollution.

a

acid test • n. a decisive test of success or value.
– ORIGIN from the use of an acid to test whether or not a metal is gold.

acknowledge • v. (**acknowledges**, **acknowledging**, **acknowledged**) **1** accept that (something) exists or is true. **2** confirm that one has received or is grateful for (something). **3** greet with words or gestures.
– ORIGIN from the former verb *knowledge* (in the same sense).

acknowledgement (also **acknowledgment**) • n. **1** the action of acknowledging. **2** something done or given in gratitude.

acme /ak-mi/ • n. the highest point of achievement or excellence.
– ORIGIN Greek *akmē*.

acne • n. a skin condition causing red pimples.
– ORIGIN Greek *aknas*.

acolyte /ak-uh-lyt/ • n. an assistant or follower.
– ORIGIN Greek *akolouthos*.

Aconcagua E
/a-kon-**kah**-gwuh/ an extinct volcano in the Andes, at 6,960 m (22,834 ft), the highest mountain in the western hemisphere.

acorn • n. the fruit of the oak, a smooth oval nut in a cup-like base.
– ORIGIN Old English.

acoustic /uh-koo-stik/ • adj. **1** having to do with sound or hearing. **2** not electrically amplified: *an acoustic guitar*. • n. (**acoustics**) **1** the aspects of a room or building that affect how well it transmits sound. **2** the branch of physics concerned with the properties of sound.
– DERIVATIVES **acoustical** adj.
– ORIGIN Greek *akoustikos*.

acquaint • v. **1** (**acquaint with**) make (someone) aware of or familiar with. **2** (**be acquainted with**) know personally.
– ORIGIN Latin *accognitare*.

acquaintance • n. **1** a person one knows slightly. **2** familiarity with or knowledge of someone or something.

acquiesce /ak-wi-ess/ • v. (**acquiesces**, **acquiescing**, **acquiesced**) accept something without protest.
– ORIGIN Latin *acquiescere*.

acquiescent • adj. ready to accept or do something without protest.
– DERIVATIVES **acquiescence** n.

acquire • v. (**acquires**, **acquiring**, **acquired**) **1** come to have. **2** learn or develop (a skill or quality).
– DERIVATIVES **acquirement** n. **acquirer** n.
– ORIGIN Latin *acquirere* 'get in addition'.

acquisition /ak-wi-zi-sh'n/ • n. **1** something that has recently been acquired. **2** the action of acquiring.

acquisitive • adj. too interested in gaining money or material things.
– DERIVATIVES **acquisitiveness** n.

acquit • v. (**acquits**, **acquitting**, **acquitted**) **1** formally state that (someone) is not guilty of a criminal charge. **2** (**acquit oneself**) behave or perform in a particular way.
– ORIGIN Latin *acquitare* 'pay a debt'.

acquittal • n. a judgement that a person is not guilty of the crime with which they have been charged.

acre /ay-ker/ • n. a unit of land area equal to 4,840 square yards (0.405 hectare).
– DERIVATIVES **acreage** n.
– ORIGIN Old English.

acrid /ak-rid/ • adj. unpleasantly bitter or sharp.
– ORIGIN Latin *acer*.

acrimonious /ak-ri-moh-ni-uhss/ • adj. angry and bitter.

acrimony /ak-ri-muh-ni/ • n. bitterness or ill feeling.
– ORIGIN Latin *acrimonia*.

acrobat • n. an entertainer who performs spectacular gymnastic feats.
– ORIGIN Greek *akrobatēs*.

acrobatic • adj. involving or skilled at spectacular gymnastic feats. • n. (**acrobatics**) spectacular gymnastic feats.

acronym /ak-ruh-nim/ • n. a word formed from the first letters of other words (e.g. *laser*).
– ORIGIN from Greek *akron* 'end' + *onoma* 'name'.

acropolis /uh-krop-uh-liss/ • n. the citadel of an ancient Greek city, built on high ground.
– ORIGIN Greek.

across • prep. & adv. from one side to the other of (something).
– PHRASES **across the board** applying to all.
– ORIGIN from Old French *a croix*, *en croix* 'in or on a cross'.

acrostic /uh-kross-tik/ • n. a poem or puzzle in which certain letters in each line form a word or words.
– ORIGIN Greek *akrostikhis*.

acrylic • adj. (of a synthetic fabric, plastic, or paint) made from a particular organic acid.
– ORIGIN from Latin *acer* 'pungent' + *oleum* 'oil'.

act • v. **1** do something. **2** take effect or have a particular effect. **3** behave in a particular way. **4** (**act as**) perform the function of. **5** (**act for/on behalf of**) represent the interests of. **6** (**acting**) temporarily doing the duties of another. **7** perform a role in a play or film. • n. **1** a thing done. **2** a law passed formally by a parliament. **3** a pretence: *putting on an act*. **4** a main division of a play, ballet, or opera. **5** a set performance or performing group.
– PHRASES **act of God** an event caused by natural forces beyond human control. **act up** informal behave badly. **get in on the act** informal become involved in an activity to share its benefits.
– ORIGIN Latin *actus* 'event, thing done'.

actinium /ak-tin-i-uhm/ • n. a rare radioactive metallic chemical element found in uranium ores.
– ORIGIN Greek *aktis* 'ray'.

action • n. **1** the process of doing something to achieve an aim. **2** a thing done. **3** the effect of something such as a chemical. **4** a lawsuit. **5** armed conflict. **6** the way in which something works or moves. • v. deal with.
– PHRASES **in action** performing an activity. **out of action** not working.

actionable • adj. Law giving cause for legal action.

action replay • n. Brit. a playback of part of a television broadcast.

a

action stations ● pl. n. esp. Brit. the positions taken up by soldiers in preparation for action.

Actium, Battle of E
/ak-ti-uhm/ a naval battle which took place in 31 BC off the coast of western Greece, in the course of which Octavian defeated Mark Antony.

activate ● v. (**activates**, **activating**, **activated**) cause (something) to act or work.
– DERIVATIVES **activation** n. **activator** n.

active ● adj. **1** moving or tending to move about often or energetically. **2** (of a person's mind) alert and lively. **3** doing something regularly: *sexually active men.* **4** functioning. **5** Grammar (of verbs) in which the subject is the person or thing performing the action and which can take a direct object (e.g. *she loved him* as opposed to the passive form *he was loved*).
– DERIVATIVES **actively** adv.
– ORIGIN Latin *activus.*

active service ● n. direct involvement in military operations as a member of the armed forces.

activist ● n. a person who campaigns for political or social change.
– DERIVATIVES **activism** n.

activity ● n. (pl. **activities**) **1** a condition in which things are happening or being done. **2** busy or energetic action or movement. **3** an action or pursuit: *sporting activities.*

actor ● n. a person whose profession is acting.

actress ● n. a female actor.

actual ● adj. existing in fact or reality.
– ORIGIN Latin *actualis.*

actuality ● n. (pl. **actualities**) actual reality or fact, as opposed to what was intended or expected.

actualize (also **actualise**) ● v. (**actualizes**, **actualizing**. **actualized**) make a reality of.

actually ● adv. in truth; in reality.

actuary /ak-choo-uh-ri/ ● n. (pl. **actuaries**) a person who compiles and analyses statistics in order to calculate insurance risks and premiums.
– ORIGIN Latin *actuarius* 'bookkeeper'.

actuate /ak-choo-ayt/ ● v. (**actuates**, **actuating**, **actuated**) **1** cause (a machine) to function. **2** motivate (someone) to act in a particular way.

acuity /uh-kyoo-i-ti/ ● n. sharpness of thought, vision, or hearing.
– ORIGIN Latin *acuitas.*

acumen /ak-yoo-muhn/ ● n. the ability to make good judgements and take quick decisions.
– ORIGIN Latin, 'sharpness, point'.

acupuncture /ak-yoo-pungk-cher/ ● n. the insertion of very thin needles into the skin as a medical treatment.
– DERIVATIVES **acupuncturist** n.
– ORIGIN from Latin *acu* 'with a needle' + **PUNCTURE**.

acute ● adj. **1** (of something bad) serious. **2** (of an illness) coming sharply to a crisis. **3** sharp-witted; shrewd. **4** (of a physical sense or faculty) highly developed. **5** (of an angle) less than 90°.
– DERIVATIVES **acutely** adv. **acuteness** n.
– ORIGIN Latin *acutus* 'sharpened'.

acute accent ● n. a mark (´) placed over a letter to indicate pronunciation (e.g. in *fiancée*).

-acy ● suffix forming nouns of state or quality: *celibacy.*
– ORIGIN Latin *-atia* or Greek *-ateia.*

AD ● abbrev. Anno Domini (used to indicate that a date comes the specified number of years after the traditional date of Christ's birth).
– ORIGIN Latin, 'in the year of the Lord'.

USAGE AD
AD is normally written in small capitals and should be placed **before** the numerals, as in AD *375*. However, when the date is spelled out, you should write *the third century* AD.

ad ● n. informal an advertisement.

adage /ad-ij/ ● n. a proverb or saying expressing a general truth.
– ORIGIN Latin *adagium.*

adagio /uh-dah-ji-oh/ Music ● adv. & adj. in slow time. ● n. (pl. **adagios**) a passage in slow time.
– ORIGIN Italian.

Adam[1] E
(in the Bible and the Koran) the name of the first man. According to the Book of Genesis, Adam was created by God and lived with Eve in the garden of Eden.

Adam[2], E
Robert (1728–92), Scottish architect. Assisted by his brother **James**, he introduced a light, neoclassical style of architecture to late 18th-century Britain.

adamant ● adj. refusing to be persuaded or to change one's mind.
– DERIVATIVES **adamantly** adv.
– ORIGIN Greek *adamas* 'invincible'.

Adams[1], E
John (1735–1826), American Federalist statesman, 2nd President of the US 1797–1801. He helped draft the Declaration of Independence (1776).

Adams[2], E
John Quincy (1767–1848), American statesman, 6th President of the US 1825–9. He was the son of John Adams, the 2nd President of the US.

Adam's apple ● n. the projection of cartilage at the front of the neck.
– ORIGIN from the belief that a piece of the forbidden fruit became lodged in Adam's throat.

adapt ● v. **1** make suitable for a new use or purpose. **2** become adjusted to new conditions.
– DERIVATIVES **adaptive** adj.
– ORIGIN Latin *adaptare.*

adaptable ● adj. able to adjust to or be altered for new conditions or uses.
– DERIVATIVES **adaptability** n.

adaptation (also **adaption**) ● n. **1** the action of adapting something. **2** a film or play adapted from a written work.

adaptor (also **adapter**) ● n. **1** a device for connecting pieces of equipment. **2** Brit. a device for connecting more than one plug at a time or plugs of a non-standard type to an electrical socket.

add • v. **1** join to or put with something else. **2** put together (two or more numbers or amounts) to find their total value. **3 (add up)** increase in amount, number, or degree. **4** say as a further remark. **5 (add up)** informal make sense.
– ORIGIN Latin *addere.*

addendum /uh-**den**-duhm/ • n. (pl. **addenda** /uh-**den**-duh/) an extra item added at the end of a book or text.
– ORIGIN Latin, 'that which is to be added'.

adder • n. a poisonous snake with a dark zig-zag pattern on its back.
– ORIGIN Old English, 'serpent, adder'.

addict • n. a person who is addicted to something.

addicted • adj. **1** physically dependent on a particular substance. **2** devoted to a particular interest or activity.
– ORIGIN Latin *addicere* 'assign'.

addiction • n. the fact or condition of being addicted.
– DERIVATIVES **addictive** adj.

Addington E
Henry, 1st Viscount Sidmouth (1757–1844), British Tory statesman, Prime Minister 1801–4.

Addis Ababa E
/ad-diss **ab**-uh-buh/ the capital of Ethiopia.

addition • n. **1** the action or process of adding. **2** a person or thing added.

additional • adj. added; extra.
– DERIVATIVES **additionally** adv.

additive • n. a substance added to improve or preserve something.

addle • v. (**addles, addling, addled**) **1** confuse. **2 (addled)** (of an egg) rotten.
– ORIGIN Old English, 'liquid filth'.

address • n. **1** the details of where a building is or where someone lives. **2** Computing a number indicating where to find a piece of information in a data storage system or computer memory. **3** a formal speech. • v. **1** write someone's name and address on (an envelope or parcel). **2** speak formally to. **3** think about and begin to deal with.
– DERIVATIVES **addressee** n.
– ORIGIN from Latin *ad* 'towards' + *directus* 'direct'.

adduce /uh-**dyooss**/ • v. (**adduces, adducing, adduced**) refer to as evidence.
– ORIGIN Latin *adducere.*

Adelaide E
/**ad**-uh-layd/ a city in Australia, the capital and chief port of the state of South Australia.

Aden E
/**ay**-duhn/ a port in Yemen at the mouth of the Red Sea, under British rule until 1967.

Adenauer E
/**ad**-i-now-er/, Konrad (1876–1967), German statesman, first Chancellor of the Federal Republic of Germany 1949–63.

adenoids /**ad**-uh-noydz/ • pl. n. a mass of tissue between the back of the nose and the throat.
– ORIGIN Greek *adēn* 'gland'.

adept • adj. /**ad**-ept, uh-**dept**/ very skilled or able. • n. /**ad**-ept/ a person who is very skilled at something.
– DERIVATIVES **adeptly** adv. **adeptness** n.
– ORIGIN Latin *adipisci* 'obtain, attain'.

adequate • adj. satisfactory or acceptable.
– DERIVATIVES **adequacy** n. **adequately** adv.
– ORIGIN Latin *adaequare* 'make equal to'.

adhere /uhd-**heer**/ • v. (**adheres, adhering, adhered**) (**adhere to**) stick firmly to.
– DERIVATIVES **adherence** n.
– ORIGIN Latin *adhaerere.*

adherent • n. a person who supports a particular party, person, or set of ideas. • adj. sticking firmly to something.

adhesion /uhd-**hee**-*zh*'n/ • n. the action or process of adhering.

adhesive /uhd-**hee**-siv/ • adj. sticky. • n. a substance which causes things to stick together.
– DERIVATIVES **adhesiveness** n.

ad hoc /ad **hok**/ • adj. & adv. created or done for a particular purpose only.
– ORIGIN Latin, 'to this'.

adieu /uh-**dyoo**/ • exclam. literary goodbye.
– ORIGIN Old French.

Adi Granth E
/ah-di **gruunt**/ the principal sacred scripture of Sikhism.

ad infinitum /ad in-fi-**ny**-tuhm/ • adv. endlessly; forever.
– ORIGIN Latin, 'to infinity'.

adipose /**ad**-i-pohss/ • adj. tech. having to do with fatty body tissue.
– ORIGIN Latin *adiposus.*

adjacent /uh-**jay** s'nt/ • adj. near or next to something else.
– ORIGIN Latin *adjacere* 'lie near to'.

adjective • n. Grammar a word used to describe a noun or to make its meaning clearer, such as *sweet, red,* or *technical.*
– DERIVATIVES **adjectival** adj.
– ORIGIN Old French *adjectif.*

adjoin • v. be next to and joined with.
– ORIGIN Old French *ajoindre.*

adjourn /uh-**jern**/ • v. **1** break off (a meeting) until later. **2** postpone (a decision).
– DERIVATIVES **adjournment** n.
– ORIGIN Old French *ajorner.*

adjudge • v. (**adjudges, adjudging, adjudged**) (of a law court or judge) decide to be the case: *he was adjudged guilty.*
– ORIGIN Latin *adjudicare.*

adjudicate /uh-**joo**-di-kayt/ • v. (**adjudicates, adjudicating, adjudicated**) **1** make a formal judgement on an undecided matter. **2** judge a competition.
– DERIVATIVES **adjudication** n. **adjudicator** n.
– ORIGIN Latin *adjudicare* 'adjudge'.

adjunct /**a**-jungkt/ • n. **1** an additional part. **2** Grammar a word or phrase that adds meaning to the verb in a sentence or clause (e.g. *on the table* in *we left some flowers on the table*).
– ORIGIN Latin *adjungere* 'adjoin'.

adjure /uh-**joor**/ • v. (**adjures, adjuring, adjured**) formal solemnly urge to do something.
– ORIGIN Latin *adjurare.*

adjust • v. **1** alter slightly. **2** become used to a new situation. **3** decide (the amount to be paid for loss or damages) when settling an

insurance claim.
– DERIVATIVES **adjustable** adj. **adjuster** n. **adjustment** n.
– ORIGIN Old French *ajoster* 'to approximate'.

adjutant /a-juu-tuhnt/ ● n. a military officer who assists a senior officer with administrative work.
– ORIGIN Latin *adjutare.*

Adler E
/**ad**-ler/, Alfred (1870–1937), Austrian psychologist and psychiatrist, who introduced the concept of the inferiority complex.

ad-lib ● v. (**ad-libs**, **ad-libbing**, **ad-libbed**) speak or perform in public without preparing beforehand. ● adv. & adj. spoken without having been prepared. ● n. an unprepared remark or speech.
– ORIGIN from Latin *ad libitum* 'according to pleasure'.

administer ● v. (**administers**, **administering**, **administered**) **1** organize or put into effect. **2** give out or apply (a drug or remedy).
– ORIGIN Latin *administrare.*

administrate ● v. (**administrates**, **administrating**, **administrated**) manage the affairs of (an organization or company).
– DERIVATIVES **administrative** adj. **administrator** n.

administration ● n. **1** the organization and running of a business or system. **2** the action of giving out or applying something. **3** the government in power. **4** esp. N. Amer. the term of office of a political leader or government.

admirable /ad-mi-ruh-b'l/ ● adj. deserving respect and approval.
– DERIVATIVES **admirably** adv.

admiral ● n. **1** the most senior commander of a fleet or navy. **2** (**Admiral**) a naval officer of the second most senior rank.
– ORIGIN Old French *amiral.*

Admiralty ● n. (in the UK) the government department formerly in charge of the Royal Navy.

admire ● v. (**admires**, **admiring**, **admired**) **1** greatly approve of or respect. **2** look at with pleasure.
– DERIVATIVES **admiration** n. **admirer** n.
– ORIGIN Latin *admirari* 'wonder at'.

admissible ● adj. acceptable or valid.

admission ● n. **1** a confession. **2** the process or fact of being allowed to enter a place. **3** a person received into hospital for treatment.

admit ● v. (**admits**, **admitting**, **admitted**) **1** confess to be true or to be the case. **2** allow to enter. **3** receive into a hospital for treatment. **4** accept as valid.
– ORIGIN Latin *admittere* 'let into'.

admittance ● n. the process of entering or the fact of being allowed to enter.

admixture ● n. tech. a mixture.

admonish ● v. **1** reprimand firmly. **2** urge or warn seriously.
– DERIVATIVES **admonishment** n. **admonition** n. **admonitory** adj.
– ORIGIN Latin *admonere.*

ad nauseam /ad naw-zi-am/ ● adv. to an annoyingly excessive extent.
– ORIGIN Latin, 'to sickness'.

ado ● n. trouble; fuss.
– ORIGIN from dialect *at do* 'to do'.

adobe /uh-**doh**-bi/ ● n. a kind of clay used to make sun-dried bricks.
– ORIGIN Spanish *adobar* 'to plaster'.

adolescent ● adj. in the process of developing from a child into an adult. ● n. an adolescent boy or girl.
– DERIVATIVES **adolescence** n.
– ORIGIN Latin *adolescere* 'to mature'.

Adonis /uh-**doh**-niss/ ● n. an extremely handsome young man.
– ORIGIN from the name of a beautiful youth in Greek myth.

adopt ● v. **1** legally take (another's child) and bring it up as one's own. **2** choose to take up or follow (an option or course of action). **3** take on (an attitude or position): *he adopted a patronizing tone.*
– DERIVATIVES **adoptee** n. **adopter** n. **adoption** n.
– ORIGIN Latin *adoptare.*

adoptive ● adj. (of a child or parent) in that relationship by adoption.

adorable ● adj. very lovable or charming.
– DERIVATIVES **adorably** adv.

adore ● v. (**adores**, **adoring**, **adored**) love and respect deeply.
– DERIVATIVES **adoration** n. **adorer** n.
– ORIGIN Latin *adorare* 'to worship'.

adorn ● v. make more attractive or beautiful; decorate.
– DERIVATIVES **adornment** n.
– ORIGIN Latin *adornare.*

adrenal /uh-**dree**-n'l/ ● adj. having to do with a pair of glands found above the kidneys which produce adrenalin and other hormones.

adrenalin /uh-**dre**-nuh-lin/ (also **adrenaline**) ● n. a hormone produced in response to stress, that increases rates of blood circulation, breathing, and metabolism.

Adrian IV E
(*c.*1100–59; born *Nicholas Breakspear*). He was pope from 1154 to 1159, the only Englishman to have held this office.

Adriatic Sea E
an arm of the Mediterranean Sea between the Balkans and the Italian peninsula.

adrift ● adj. & adv. **1** (of a boat) drifting without control. **2** Brit. informal no longer fixed in position.

adroit /uh-**droyt**/ ● adj. clever or skilful in using the hands or mind.
– ORIGIN from French *à droit* 'according to right, properly'.

adsorb /uhd-**zorb**/ ● v. (of a solid) hold (molecules of a gas or liquid) in a layer on its surface.
– DERIVATIVES **adsorption** n.

adsorbent ● n. a substance which adsorbs another.

adulation /ad-yuu-**lay**-sh'n/ ● n. excessive admiration.
– DERIVATIVES **adulatory** adj.
– ORIGIN Latin.

adult /ad-ult, uh-**dult**/ ● n. a person who is fully grown and developed. ● adj. **1** fully grown and developed. **2** suitable for or typical of adults.
– DERIVATIVES **adulthood** n.
– ORIGIN Latin *adultus.*

adulterate /uh-dul-tuh-rayt/ • v. (**adulterates, adulterating, adulterated**) make poorer in quality by adding another substance.
– DERIVATIVES **adulteration** n.
– ORIGIN Latin *adulterare* 'to corrupt'.

adulterer • n. (fem. **adulteress**) a person who has committed adultery.
– ORIGIN Latin *adulterare* 'to corrupt'.

adultery • n. sexual intercourse between a married person and a person who is not their husband or wife.
– DERIVATIVES **adulterous** adj.

adumbrate /ad-um-brayt/ • v. (**adumbrates, adumbrating, adumbrated**) formal **1** give a faint or general idea of. **2** be a warning of.
– ORIGIN Latin *adumbrare* 'shade, overshadow'.

advance • v. (**advances, advancing, advanced**) **1** move forwards. **2** make or cause to make progress. **3** put forward (a theory or suggestion). **4** hand over (payment) to (someone) as a loan or before it is due. • n. **1** a forward movement. **2** a development or improvement. **3** an amount of money advanced. **4** (**advances**) approaches made to someone with the aim of beginning a sexual or romantic relationship. • adj. done, sent, or supplied beforehand.
– ORIGIN Old French *avancer*.

advanced • adj. **1** far on in progress or life. **2** complex; not basic.

advanced level • n. = **A LEVEL**.

advanced subsidiary level • n. (in the UK except Scotland) an examination at a level between GCSE and advanced level.

advancement • n. **1** the process of helping the progress of a cause or plan. **2** the raising of a person to a higher rank or status. **3** a development or improvement.

advantage • n. **1** something that puts one in a favourable position. **2** Tennis a score marking a point between deuce and winning the game.
– PHRASES **take advantage of 1** make unfair use of for one's own benefit. **2** make good use of the opportunities offered.
– DERIVATIVES **advantageous** adj.
– ORIGIN Old French *avantage*.

advent /ad-vent/ • n. **1** the arrival of an important person or thing. **2** (**Advent**) (in Christian belief) the coming or second coming of Christ. **3** (**Advent**) (in the Christian Church) the period of time leading up to Christmas.
– ORIGIN Latin *adventus*.

Adventist • n. a member of a Christian sect which believes that the second coming of Christ is about to happen.

adventitious /ad-vuhn-ti-shuhss/ • adj. happening by chance.
– ORIGIN Latin *adventicius* 'coming to us from abroad'.

adventure • n. **1** an unusual, exciting, and daring experience. **2** excitement which is the result of danger or risk.
– DERIVATIVES **adventuresome** adj.
– ORIGIN Latin *adventurus* 'about to happen'.

adventurer • n. (fem. **adventuress**) **1** a person willing to take risks or use dishonest methods for personal gain: *a political adventurer.* **2** a person who enjoys or seeks adventure.

adventurous • adj. open to or involving new or exciting experiences.

adverb • n. Grammar a word or phrase that adds more information about place, time, manner, or degree to an adjective, verb, other adverb, or a sentence (e.g *gently, very, fortunately*).
– DERIVATIVES **adverbial** adj.
– ORIGIN Latin *adverbium*.

adversarial /ad-ver-sair-i-uhl/ • adj. having to do with conflict or opposition.

adversary /ad-ver-suh-ri/ • n. (pl. **adversaries**) an opponent or enemy.
– ORIGIN Latin *adversarius* 'opposed, opponent'.

adverse /ad-verss/ • adj. harmful; unfavourable.
– DERIVATIVES **adversely** adv.
– ORIGIN Latin *adversus* 'against, opposite'.

adversity • n. (pl. **adversities**) difficulty; misfortune.

advert /ad-vert/ • n. Brit. informal an advertisement.

advertise • v. (**advertises, advertising, advertised**) **1** present or describe (a product, service, or event) in a publication or on television in order to increase sales. **2** seek to fill (a vacancy) by placing a notice in a newspaper or other publication. **3** make (a fact) known.
– DERIVATIVES **advertiser** n. **advertising** n.
– ORIGIN Old French *advertir*.

advertisement • n. a notice or display advertising something.

advice • n. guidance or recommendations offered about future action.
– ORIGIN Old French *avis*.

> **USAGE** advice
>
> Do not confuse **advice** and **advise**. **Advice** is a noun meaning 'guidance or recommendations about future action', as in *friends always asked his advice*, whereas **advise** is a verb that chiefly means 'recommend a course of action', as in *I advised him to go home*.

advisable • adj. to be recommended; sensible.
– DERIVATIVES **advisability** n.

advise • v. (**advises, advising, advised**) **1** recommend (a course of action). **2** inform about a fact or situation. **3** offer advice to.
– DERIVATIVES **adviser** (also **advisor**) n.
– ORIGIN Old French *aviser*.

advised • adj. behaving as someone would recommend; sensible.
– DERIVATIVES **advisedly** adv.

advisory • adj. having the power to make recommendations but not to make sure that they are carried out.

advocaat /ad-vuh-kah/ • n. a liqueur made with eggs, sugar, and brandy.
– ORIGIN Dutch, 'advocate'.

advocate • n. /ad-vuh-kuht/ **1** a person who publicly supports or recommends a particular cause or policy. **2** a person who pleads a case on someone else's behalf. **3** Sc. = **BARRISTER**. • v. /ad-vuh-kayt/ (**advocates, advocating, advocated**) publicly recommend or support.
– DERIVATIVES **advocacy** n.

a

– ORIGIN Latin *advocare* 'call to one's aid'.

adze /adz/ (US **adz**) ● **n.** a tool similar to an axe, with an arched blade.
– ORIGIN Old English.

Aegean Sea E
a part of the Mediterranean Sea lying between Greece and Turkey.

aegis /ee-jiss/ ● **n.** the protection, backing, or support of someone.
– ORIGIN Greek *aigis* 'shield of Zeus'.

Aeneas E
/i-nee-uhss/ Gk & Rom. Myth. a Trojan leader and legendary ancestor of the Romans. The story of his travels after Troy was defeated is told in Virgil's *Aeneid*.

aeon /ee-on/ (US or tech. also **eon**) ● **n. 1** an extremely long period of time. **2** a major division of time in geology, subdivided into eras.
– ORIGIN Greek *aiōn* 'age'.

aerate /air-ayt/ ● **v.** (**aerates, aerating, aerated**) introduce air into.
– DERIVATIVES **aeration** n. **aerator** n.
– ORIGIN Latin *aer* 'air'.

aerial ● **n.** a structure that sends out or receives radio or television signals. ● **adj. 1** existing or taking place in the air. **2** involving the use of aircraft.
– ORIGIN Greek *aēr* 'air'.

aerie ● **n.** US = **EYRIE**.

aero- /air-oh/ ● **comb. form 1** relating to air: *aerobic*. **2** relating to aircraft: *aerodrome*.
– ORIGIN Greek *aēr* 'air'.

aerobatics ● **n.** exciting and skilful movements performed in an aircraft for display.
– DERIVATIVES **aerobatic** adj.

aerobic /air-oh-bik/ ● **adj. 1** relating to physical exercise intended to improve the intake of oxygen and its movement around the body. **2** Biol. using oxygen from the air. ● **n.** (**aerobics**) aerobic exercises.
– DERIVATIVES **aerobically** adv.
– ORIGIN from **AERO-** + Greek *bios* 'life'.

aerodrome ● **n.** Brit. a small airport or airfield.

aerodynamic ● **adj. 1** relating to aerodynamics. **2** (of an object) having a shape which enables it to move through the air quickly. ● **n.** (**aerodynamics**) **1** the science concerned with the movement of solid bodies through the air. **2** the aspects of an object which make it good or bad at moving through the air.

aerofoil ● **n.** Brit. a curved structure, such as a wing, designed to give an aircraft lift in flight.

aeronautics ● **n.** the study or practice of travel through the air.
– DERIVATIVES **aeronautical** adj.
– ORIGIN from Greek *aēr* 'air' + *nautēs* 'sailor'.

aeroplane ● **n.** esp. Brit. a powered flying vehicle with fixed wings and a weight greater than that of the air it passes through.
– ORIGIN from French *aéro-* 'air' + Greek *-planos* 'wandering'.

aerosol ● **n.** a substance sealed in a container under pressure and released as a fine spray.
– ORIGIN from **AERO-** + **SOLUTION**.

aerospace ● **n.** the technology and industry concerned with flight.

Aeschylus E
/ee-ski-luhss/ (*c.*525–*c.*456 BC), Greek tragic dramatist, best known for his trilogy the *Oresteia*.

Aesop E
/ee-sop/ (6th century BC), Greek storyteller associated with moral animal fables.

aesthete /eess-theet/ (US also **esthete**) ● **n.** a person who appreciates art and beauty.

aesthetic /eess-thet-ik/ (US also **esthetic**) ● **adj. 1** concerned with beauty or the appreciation of beauty. **2** having a pleasant appearance. ● **n. 1** a set of principles behind the work of a particular artist or artistic movement. **2** (**aesthetics**) the branch of philosophy that deals with questions of beauty and artistic taste.
– DERIVATIVES **aesthetically** (US also **esthetically**) adv.
– ORIGIN Greek *aisthētikos*.

aether ● **n.** var. of **ETHER** (in sense 2).

afar ● **adv.** literary at or to a distance.

affable ● **adj.** good-natured and friendly.
– DERIVATIVES **affability** n. **affably** adv.
– ORIGIN Latin *affabilis*.

affair ● **n. 1** an event of a particular kind or that has previously been referred to **2** a matter that is a particular person's responsibility. **3** a love affair. **4** (**affairs**) matters of public interest and importance.
– ORIGIN from Old French *à faire* 'to do'.

affect[1] /uh-fekt/ ● **v. 1** make a difference to; have an effect on. **2** touch the feelings of.
– ORIGIN Latin *afficere* 'affect'.

USAGE affect
For an explanation of the difference between **affect** and **effect**, see the note at **EFFECT**.

affect[2] /uh-fekt/ ● **v. 1** pretend to have or feel. **2** use, wear, or assume in a false way or in order to impress: *I affected an interest in his stories.*
– ORIGIN Latin *affectare* 'aim at'.

affectation /af-fek-tay-sh'n/ ● **n.** behaviour, speech, or writing that is false and designed to impress.

affected ● **adj.** false and designed to impress.
– DERIVATIVES **affectedly** adv.

affection ● **n.** a feeling of fondness or liking.

affectionate ● **adj.** readily showing affection.
– DERIVATIVES **affectionately** adv.

affidavit /af-fi-day-vit/ ● **n.** Law a written statement for use as evidence in court, sworn on oath to be true.
– ORIGIN Latin, 'he has stated on oath'.

affiliate ● **v.** /uh-fil-i-ayt/ (**affiliates, affiliating, affiliated**) officially link (a person or group) to a larger organization. ● **n.** /uh-fil-i-uht/ a person or group linked to a larger organization.
– DERIVATIVES **affiliation** n.
– ORIGIN Latin *affiliare* 'adopt as a son'.

affinity ● **n.** (pl. **affinities**) **1** a natural liking or sympathy. **2** a close relationship based on similar origin or structure. **3** the tendency of a substance to combine with another.
– ORIGIN Latin *affinitas*.

affirm ● **v.** state firmly or publicly.
– DERIVATIVES **affirmation** n.

– ORIGIN Latin *affirmare*.

affirmative • adj. agreeing with or to a statement or request. • n. a statement or word indicating agreement.

affix • v. /uh-**fiks**/ attach or fasten to something else. • n. /**af**-fiks/ Grammar a letter or letters added to a word in order to alter its meaning or create a new word.

– ORIGIN Latin *affixare*.

afflict • v. cause pain or suffering to.

– DERIVATIVES **affliction** n.

– ORIGIN Latin *afflictare* 'harass' or *affligere* 'knock down'.

affluent • adj. wealthy.

– DERIVATIVES **affluence** n.

– ORIGIN Latin *affluere* 'flow towards, flow freely'.

afford • v. **1** (**can/could afford**) have enough money or time for. **2** provide (an opportunity or facility): *the rooftop terrace affords beautiful views*.

– DERIVATIVES **affordable** adj.

– ORIGIN Old English, 'promote, perform'.

afforest /uh-**forr**-ist/ • v. convert (land) into forest.

– DERIVATIVES **afforestation** n.

affray • n. Law, dated a breach of the peace by fighting in a public place.

– ORIGIN Old French *afrayer* 'disturb'.

affront • n. an action or remark that causes offence. • v. offend.

– ORIGIN Old French *afronter* 'to slap in the face, insult'.

Afghan /**af**-gan/ • n. a person from Afghanistan. • adj. relating to Afghanistan.

– ORIGIN Pashto (the language of Afghanistan).

Afghan hound • n. a silky-haired breed of dog used for hunting.

> **Afghanistan** [E]
> /af-**gan**-i-stahn, af-**gan**-i-stan/ a mountainous republic in central Asia; capital, Kabul.

aficionado /uh-fi-shuh-**nah**-doh/ • n. (pl. **aficionados**) a person who knows a lot about and is very keen on an activity or subject.

– ORIGIN Spanish.

afield • adv. to or at a distance.

aflame • adj. in flames.

afloat • adj. & adv. **1** floating in water. **2** on board a ship or boat. **3** out of debt or difficulty.

afoot • adv. & adj. in preparation or progress.

afore • prep. archaic or dialect before.

aforementioned • adj. referring to a thing or person previously mentioned.

afraid • adj. fearful or anxious.

– PHRASES **I'm afraid** expressing polite regret.

– ORIGIN Old French *afrayer* 'disturb'.

afresh • adv. in a new or different way.

> **Africa** [E]
> the second-largest continent, divided roughly in two by the equator and surrounded by sea except where the Isthmus of Suez joins it to Asia.

African • n. **1** a person from Africa, especially a black person. **2** a person of black African descent. • adj. relating to Africa or Africans.

African American esp. US • n. an American of African origin. • adj. relating to African Americans.

> **African National Congress** [E]
> a South African political party and black nationalist organization. Banned by the South African government 1960–90, it was victorious in the country's first democratic elections in 1994 when its leader Nelson Mandela became president.

Afrikaans /af-ri-**kahnz**/ • n. a language of southern Africa derived from Dutch.

– ORIGIN Dutch, 'African'.

Afrikaner /af-ri-**kah**-ner/ • n. an Afrikaans-speaking white person in South Africa.

Afro • n. a hairstyle consisting of a mass of very tight curls all round the head.

Afro- • comb. form African: *Afro-American*.

Afro-American • adj. & n. = **African American**.

Afro-Caribbean • n. a person of African descent living in or coming from the Caribbean. • adj. relating to Afro-Caribbeans.

aft /ahft/ • adv. & adj. at, near, or towards the stern of a ship or tail of an aircraft.

– ORIGIN prob. related to **abaft**.

after • prep. **1** in the time following (an event or another period of time). **2** behind. **3** in pursuit of. **4** next to and following in order or importance. **5** in reference to: *they named her Pauline, after Barbara's mother*. • conj. & adv. in the time following (an event).

– PHRASES **after all** in spite of any suggestion otherwise. **after hours** after normal working or opening hours.

– ORIGIN Old English.

afterbirth • n. the placenta and other material discharged from the womb after a birth.

aftercare • n. care of a person after a stay in hospital or on release from prison.

after-effect • n. an effect that occurs some time after its cause has gone.

afterglow • n. light remaining in the sky after the sun has set.

afterlife • n. (in some religions) life after death.

aftermath • n. the consequences of an unpleasant event.

– ORIGIN from dialect *math* 'mowing'.

afternoon • n. the time from noon or lunchtime to evening.

afters • pl. n. Brit. informal the dessert course of a meal.

aftershave • n. a scented lotion for applying to the skin after shaving.

aftershock • n. a smaller earthquake following a large earthquake.

aftertaste • n. a strong or unpleasant taste lingering in the mouth after eating or drinking.

afterthought • n. something thought of or added later.

afterwards (US also **afterward**) • adv. at a later or future time.

afterword • n. a section at the end of a book, usually by a person other than the author.

Ag • symb. the chemical element silver.

– ORIGIN Latin *argentum*.

again /uh-**gen**, uh-**gayn**/ • adv. **1** once more. **2** returning to a previous position or condition. **3** in addition to what has already been mentioned.

– ORIGIN Old English.

against • prep. **1** so as to oppose: *the fight*

a

against crime. **2** so as to resist: *he turned up his collar against the wind.* **3** so as to anticipate and prepare for (a difficulty). **4** so as to reduce, cancel, or secure (money owed, due, or lent). **5** in or into contact with. **6** (in betting) in anticipation of the failure of.

Agamemnon E
/ag-uh-**mem**-non/ Gk Myth. king of Mycenae and commander-in-chief of the Greek expedition against Troy.

agape /uh-gayp/ • **adj.** (of a person's mouth) wide open.

Agassi E
/ag-uh-si/, André (b.1970), American tennis player. His men's singles titles include Wimbledon (1992), the French Open and the US Open (both 1999), and the Australian Open (2000 and 2001).

agate /ag-uht/ • **n.** an ornamental form of quartz with a banded appearance.
– ORIGIN Greek *akhatēs.*

agave /uh-gay-vi/ • **n.** an American plant with narrow spiny leaves.
– ORIGIN from *Agauē,* one of the daughters of Cadmus in Greek mythology.

age • **n. 1** the length of time that a person or thing has existed. **2** a particular stage in someone's life: *children of primary school age.* **3** old age. **4** a distinct period of history: *the Elizabethan age.* **5** Geology a subdivision of an epoch. • **v.** (**ages**, **ageing** or **aging**, **aged**) grow or cause to appear old or older.
– PHRASES **come of age** reach adult status (in UK law at 18).
– ORIGIN Old French.

-age • **suffix** forming nouns referring to: **1** an action or its result: *leverage.* **2** a number of: *mileage.* **3** a place or dwelling: *vicarage.* **4** fees payable for: *postage.*
– ORIGIN Latin *-aticum.*

aged • **adj. 1** /ayjd/ of a specified age. **2** /ay-jid/ old.

ageism • **n.** prejudice or discrimination on the grounds of age.
– DERIVATIVES **ageist** adj.

ageless • **adj.** not ageing or appearing to age.

agency • **n. 1** an organization or government department providing a particular service. **2** action or intervention: *channels carved by the agency of running water.*

agenda • **n. 1** a list of items to be discussed at a meeting. **2** a list of matters to be dealt with.
– ORIGIN Latin, 'things to be done'.

agent • **n. 1** a person who provides a particular service: *a travel agent.* **2** a spy. **3** a person or thing that takes an active role or produces a particular effect.
– ORIGIN Latin *agere* 'to do'.

agent noun • **n.** a noun which refers to a person or thing that performs the action of a verb, usually ending in *-er* or *-or,* e.g. *worker, accelerator.*

agent provocateur /a-*zh*on pruh-vo-kuh-ter/ • **n.** (pl. **agents provocateurs** /a-*zh*on pruh-vo-kuh-ter/) a person who tempts suspected criminals to commit a crime and therefore be convicted.
– ORIGIN French, 'provocative agent'.

age of consent • **n.** the age at which a person can legally agree to have sexual intercourse.

age-old • **adj.** very old.

agglomerate • **v.** /uh-glom-uh-rayt/ (**agglomerates**, **agglomerating**, **agglomerated**) collect or form into a mass. • **n.** /uh-glom-uh-ruht/ a mass or collection of things.
– DERIVATIVES **agglomeration** n.
– ORIGIN Latin *agglomerare* 'add to'.

agglutinate /uh-gloo-ti-nayt/ • **v.** (**agglutinates**, **agglutinating**, **agglutinated**) firmly stick together to form a mass.
– DERIVATIVES **agglutination** n.
– ORIGIN Latin *agglutinare.*

aggrandize /uh-gran-dyz/ (also **aggrandise**) • **v.** (**aggrandizes**, **aggrandizing**, **aggrandized**) **1** increase the power, status, or wealth of. **2** artificially improve the reputation of.
– DERIVATIVES **aggrandizement** (also **aggrandisement**) n.
– ORIGIN French *agrandir.*

aggravate • **v.** (**aggravates**, **aggravating**, **aggravated**) **1** make worse. **2** informal annoy.
– DERIVATIVES **aggravation** n.
– ORIGIN Latin *aggravare* 'make heavy'.

aggregate • **n.** /ag-gri-guht/ a whole formed by combining several different elements. • **adj.** /ag-gri-guht/ formed or calculated by combining many separate items. • **v.** /ag-gri-gayt/ (**aggregates**, **aggregating**, **aggregated**) combine into a whole.
– ORIGIN Latin *aggregare* 'herd together'.

aggression • **n.** hostile or violent behaviour or attitudes.
– ORIGIN Latin.

aggressive • **adj. 1** very angry or hostile. **2** excessively forceful.
– DERIVATIVES **aggressively** adv. **aggressiveness** n.

aggressor • **n.** a person or country that attacks without being provoked.

aggrieved • **adj.** resentful because of unfair treatment.
– ORIGIN Old French *agrever* 'make heavier'.

aghast /uh-gahst/ • **adj.** filled with horror or shock.
– ORIGIN from former *gast* 'frighten'.

agile • **adj. 1** able to move quickly and easily. **2** quick-witted or shrewd.
– DERIVATIVES **agility** n.
– ORIGIN Latin *agilis.*

Agincourt, Battle of E
/aj-in-kor, aj-in-kort/ a battle in northern France in 1415 during the Hundred Years War, in which the English under Henry V defeated a large French army.

agitate • **v.** (**agitates**, **agitating**, **agitated**) **1** make troubled or nervous. **2** campaign to arouse public concern about an issue. **3** stir or disturb (a liquid) briskly.
– DERIVATIVES **agitation** n.
– ORIGIN Latin *agitare* 'agitate, drive'.

agitator • **n.** a person who urges others to protest or rebel.

AGM • **abbrev.** annual general meeting.

Agnes, St E
(died *c.*304), Christian martyr, patron saint of virgins, whose emblem is a lamb. Feast day, 21 January.

a

Agnesi E
/an-yay-zi/, Maria Gaetana (1718–99), Italian mathematician and philosopher, regarded as the first female mathematician of the Western world.

agnostic /ag-noss-tik/ • **n.** a person who believes that one cannot know whether or not God exists.
– DERIVATIVES **agnosticism** n.

ago • **adv.** before the present (used with a measurement of time).
– ORIGIN from former *ago* 'to pass'.

agog • **adj.** very eager to hear or see something.
– ORIGIN from Old French *en* 'in' + *gogue* 'fun'.

agonize (also **agonise**) • **v.** (**agonizes, agonizing, agonized**) **1** worry greatly. **2** cause agony to.

agony • **n.** (pl. **agonies**) extreme suffering.
– ORIGIN Greek *agōnia*.

agony aunt • **n.** Brit. informal a person who answers letters in an agony column.

agony column • **n.** Brit. informal a column in a newspaper or magazine offering advice on readers' personal problems.

agoraphobia /ag-uh-ruh-**foh**-bi-uh/ • **n.** abnormal fear of open or public places.
– DERIVATIVES **agoraphobic** adj. & n.
– ORIGIN Greek *agora* 'marketplace'.

Agra E
/ah-gruh/ a city on the River Jumna in northern India, site of the Taj Mahal.

agrarian /uh-**grair**-i-uhn/ • **adj.** having to do with agriculture.
– ORIGIN Latin *agrarius*.

agree • **v.** (**agrees, agreeing, agreed**) **1** have the same opinion about something. **2** (**be agreed**) (of two or more people) hold the same opinion. **3** (**agree to**) consent to do something which has been suggested by another person. **4** esp. Brit. (of two or more people) decide on. **5** (**agree with**) be consistent with: *your body language does not agree with what you are saying.* **6** be good for.
– ORIGIN Old French *agreer*.

agreeable • **adj.** **1** pleasant. **2** willing to agree to something. **3** acceptable.
– DERIVATIVES **agreeably** adv.

agreement • **n.** **1** the sharing of opinion or feeling. **2** an arrangement or contract agreed between people. **3** consistency between two things.

agriculture • **n.** the science or practice of farming.
– DERIVATIVES **agricultural** adj.
– ORIGIN Latin *ager* 'field'.

Agrippa E
/uh-**grip**-puh/, Marcus Vipsanius (63–12 BC), Roman general. Augustus' adviser and son-in-law, he played an important part in the naval victories over Mark Antony.

agronomy /uh-**gron**-uh-mi/ • **n.** the science of soil management and crop production.
– DERIVATIVES **agronomic** adj, **agronomist** n.
– ORIGIN French.

aground • **adj. & adv.** (with reference to a ship) on or on to the bottom in shallow water.

ague /ay-gyoo/ • **n.** archaic malaria or an other illness involving fever and shivering.
– ORIGIN from Latin *acuta febris* 'acute fever'.

ahead • **adv.** **1** further forward in space or time. **2** in advance. **3** in the lead.
– PHRASES **ahead of** **1** before. **2** earlier than planned or expected.

Ahern E
/uh-**hern**/, Bertie (b.1951), Irish Fianna Fáil statesman, Taoiseach (Prime Minister) since 1997.

ahoy • **exclam.** Naut. a call to attract attention.

AI • **abbrev.** artificial intelligence.

aid • **n.** **1** help or support. **2** food or money given to a country in need. • **v.** help.
– ORIGIN Old French *aide*.

Aidan, St E
/ay-d'n/ (d. AD 651), Irish missionary, who founded a monastery at Lindisfarne in 635 whose monks were important in promoting Christianity in northern England.

aide /ayd/ • **n.** an assistant to a political leader.

aide-de-camp /ayd-duh-**kom**/ • **n.** (pl. **aides-de-camp** /ayd-duh-**kom**/) a military officer acting as a personal assistant to a senior officer.
– ORIGIN French.

Aids • **n.** a disease, caused by the HIV virus and transmitted in body fluids, which breaks down the sufferer's natural defences against infection.
– ORIGIN from *acquired immune deficiency syndrome.*

aikido /I-kee-doh/ • **n.** a Japanese martial art that uses locks, holds, throws, and the opponent's own movements.
– ORIGIN Japanese, 'way of adapting the spirit'.

ail • **v.** archaic cause trouble or suffering to.
– ORIGIN Old English.

aileron /ayl-uh-ron/ • **n.** a hinged part of an aircraft's wing, used to control the balance of the aircraft.
– ORIGIN French, 'small wing'.

ailing • **adj.** in poor health.

ailment • **n.** a minor illness.

aim • **v.** **1** point (a weapon or camera) at a target. **2** direct (something) at someone or something. **3** try to achieve something. • **n.** **1** a purpose or intention. **2** the aiming of a weapon or missile.
– PHRASES **take aim** point a weapon or camera at a target.
– ORIGIN Old French *amer*.

aimless • **adj.** without purpose or direction.

ain't • **contr.** informal **1** am not; are not; is not. **2** has not; have not.

USAGE ain't
Ain't is not good English and should not be used when writing or speaking in a formal situation.

Aintree E
/ayn-tree/ a suburb of Liverpool, site of a racecourse over which the Grand National is run.

air • **n.** **1** the invisible mixture of gases surrounding the earth. **2** the open space above the surface of the earth. **3** (before another noun) using aircraft: *air travel.* **4** a tune or short tuneful composition. **5** (**an air of**) an impres-

sion of: *she answered with a faint air of boredom.* **6** (**airs**) an affected and condescending manner. ● v. **1** express (an opinion or complaint) publicly. **2** broadcast (a programme) on radio or television. **3** expose (laundry or a place) to fresh or warm air.
– PHRASES **airs and graces** affected behaviour intended to impress. **in the air** noticeable all around. **on** (or **off**) **the air** being (or not being) broadcast on radio or television. **up in the air** unresolved. **walk on air** feel extremely pleased or happy.
– DERIVATIVES **airless** adj.
– ORIGIN Greek *aēr*.

air bag ● n. a safety device in a vehicle, that fills rapidly with air when there is a sudden impact and cushions the driver or passenger.

airbase ● n. a base for military aircraft.

airborne ● adj. **1** carried or spread through the air. **2** (of an aircraft) flying.

airbrick ● n. Brit. a brick pierced with small holes in order to let air pass through.

airbrush ● n. an artist's device for spraying paint by means of compressed air. ● v. **1** paint with an airbrush. **2** alter (a photograph) using an airbrush.

air conditioning ● n. a system for controlling the temperature and circulation of the air in a building or vehicle.
– DERIVATIVES **air-conditioned** adj.

air corridor ● n. a route over a foreign country which aircraft must take.

aircraft ● n. (pl. **aircraft**) an aeroplane, helicopter, or other machine capable of flight.

aircraft carrier ● n. a large warship from which aircraft can take off and land.

aircrew ● n. (pl. **aircrews**) the crew of an aircraft.

Airedale ● n. a large rough-coated black-and-tan breed of terrier.
– ORIGIN from *Airedale*, a district in Yorkshire.

airer ● n. Brit. a frame or stand for airing or drying laundry.

airfield ● n. an area of land set aside for the take-off, landing, and repairing of aircraft.

air force ● n. a branch of the armed forces concerned with fighting or defence in the air.

air gun ● n. **1** a gun which uses compressed air to fire pellets. **2** a tool using very hot air to strip paint.

airhead ● n. informal a stupid person.

air hostess ● n. Brit. a stewardess in a passenger aircraft.

airing ● n. **1** an act of exposing laundry or a place to warm or fresh air. **2** a public statement of an opinion or discussion of a subject.

air kiss ● n. an embrace in which the lips are pursed as if kissing but without making contact.

air letter ● n. a sheet of light paper folded and sealed to form a letter for sending by airmail.

airlift ● n. an act of transporting supplies by aircraft.

airline ● n. an organization which provides regular flights for public use.

airliner ● n. a large passenger aircraft.

airlock ● n. **1** a stoppage of the flow in a pump or pipe, caused by an air bubble. **2** a compartment with controlled pressure and airtight doors at each end, to allow movement between areas at different pressures.

airmail ● n. a system of transporting mail overseas by air.

airman (or **airwoman**) ● n. a pilot or member of the crew of an aircraft in an air force.

air mile ● n. **1** a nautical mile used as a measure of distance flown by aircraft. **2** (**Air Miles**) trademark points (equivalent to miles of free air travel) collected by buyers of airline tickets and other products.

air pistol (or **air rifle**) ● n. a gun which uses compressed air to fire pellets.

airplane ● n. N. Amer. an aeroplane.

airplay ● n. broadcasting time devoted to a particular record, performer, or type of music.

air pocket ● n. **1** a hollow space containing air. **2** an area of low pressure causing an aircraft to lose height suddenly.

airport ● n. a complex of runways and buildings for the take-off, landing, and repairing of commercial aircraft.

air quality ● n. the degree to which the air is pollution-free.

air raid ● n. an attack in which bombs are dropped from aircraft on to a target on the ground.

air-sea rescue ● n. a rescue from the sea using aircraft.

airship ● n. a power-driven aircraft kept in the air by a body of gas which is lighter than air.

airspace ● n. the part of the air above and subject to the laws of a particular country.

airspeed ● n. the speed of an aircraft in relation to the air through which it is moving.

airstream ● n. a current of air.

airstrip ● n. a strip of ground for the take-off and landing of aircraft.

airtight ● adj. **1** not allowing air to escape or pass through. **2** unable to be questioned: *an airtight alibi.*

airtime ● n. time during which a broadcast is being transmitted.

air traffic control ● n. the ground-based people and equipment concerned with controlling and observing air traffic within a particular area.

airwaves ● pl. n. the radio frequencies used for broadcasting.

airway ● n. **1** the passage by which air reaches the lungs. **2** a recognized route followed by aircraft.

airworthy ● adj. (of an aircraft) safe to fly.

> **Airy**, E
> Sir George Biddell (1801–92), English scientist, who as Astronomer Royal (1835–81) completely re-equipped the Royal Greenwich Observatory and modernized its system of astronomical measurements.

airy ● adj. (**airier**, **airiest**) **1** spacious and well ventilated. **2** casual; dismissive: *her airy unconcern for economy.*
– DERIVATIVES **airily** adv. **airiness** n.

airy-fairy ● adj. informal, esp. Brit. vague and unrealistic or impractical.

aisle /*rhymes with* mile/ ● n. a passage between rows of seats in a church or other public building or between shelves in a shop.
– ORIGIN Latin *ala* 'wing'.

aitch • n. the letter H.
– PHRASES **drop one's aitches** fail to pronounce the letter *h* at the beginning of words.
– ORIGIN Old French *ache*.

Aix-en-Provence E
/eks-on-pro-**vonss**/ a city in Provence in southern France.

ajar • adv. & adj. (of a door or window) slightly open.
– ORIGIN Old English, 'a turn'.

Ajax E
/**ay**-jaks/ Gk Myth. a Greek hero of the Trojan war, famous for his size and strength.

Ajman E
/aj-**mahn**/ one of the seven member states of the United Arab Emirates.

aka • abbrev. also known as.

Akbar E
/**ak**-bar/, Jalaludin Muhammad (1542–1605), Mogul emperor of India 1556–1605. He expanded the Mogul empire, encouraged education and culture, and established an enlightened administration.

Akihito E
/a-ki-**hee**-toh/ (b.1933), son of Emperor Hirohito, emperor of Japan since 1989.

akimbo /uh-**kim**-boh/ • adv. with hands on the hips and elbows turned outwards.
– ORIGIN prob. from Old Norse.

akin • adj. **1** of similar character. **2** related by blood.
– ORIGIN from *of kin*.

Akmola E
/ak-**mo**-la/ former name for **ASTANA**.

-al • suffix **1** (forming adjectives) relating to; of the kind of: *tidal*. **2** forming nouns chiefly referring to the action of a verb: *arrival*.
– ORIGIN Latin *-alis*.

Alabama E
/al-uh-**bam**-uh/ a state in the south-eastern US, on the Gulf of Mexico; capital, Montgomery.
– DERIVATIVES **Alabaman** adj. & n.

alabaster /al-uh-bah-ster, al-uh-bass-ter/ • n. a white, semi-transparent form of the mineral gypsum, often carved into ornaments. • adj. literary smooth and white: *pale, alabaster skin*.
– ORIGIN Greek *alabastos, alabastros*.

à la carte /ah lah **kart**/ • adj. & adv. (of a menu or meal) offering or ordered as dishes that are separately priced, rather than part of a set meal.
– ORIGIN French, 'according to the card'.

alacrity • n. brisk eagerness or enthusiasm.
– ORIGIN Latin *alacritas*.

Aladdin E
the hero of a story in the *Arabian Nights*, who finds an old lamp which, when rubbed, summons a genie who obeys the will of the owner.

Aladdin's cave • n. a place filled with a great number of interesting or precious items.
– ORIGIN from **ALADDIN**.

Alamein E
see **EL ALAMEIN, BATTLE OF**.

Alamo E
/al-uh-moh/ (**the Alamo**) a mission in San Antonio, Texas, site of a siege in 1836 by Mexican forces, in which all 180 defenders were killed.

à la mode /ah lah **mohd**/ • adv. & adj. up to date; fashionable.
– ORIGIN French.

alarm • n. **1** anxious or frightened awareness of danger. **2** a warning of danger. **3** a warning sound or device. • v. **1** frighten or disturb. **2** (**be alarmed**) be fitted with an alarm.
– ORIGIN from Italian *all' arme!* 'to arms!'

alarm clock • n. a clock that can be set to sound an alarm at a particular time.

alarmist • n. a person who exaggerates a danger, so causing needless alarm. • adj. causing needless alarm.

alas • exclam. literary or humorous an expression of grief, pity, or concern.
– ORIGIN from Old French *a las, a lasse*.

Alaska E
the largest state of the US, in the extreme north-west of North America; capital, Juneau.
– DERIVATIVES **Alaskan** adj. & n.

Alban, St E
(3rd century), the first British Christian martyr. He was put to death at Verulamium (now St Albans). Feast day, 22 June.

Albania E
/al-**bay**-ni-uh/ a republic in SE Europe; capital, Tirana.

Albanian • n. **1** a person from Albania. **2** the language of Albania. • adj. relating to Albania.

albatross /al-buh-tross/ • n. (pl. **albatrosses**) a very large seabird with long narrow wings, found chiefly in the southern oceans.
– ORIGIN Arabic, 'the diver'.

Albee E
/**awl**-bee, **al**-bee/, Edward Franklin (b.1928), American dramatist, best known for *Who's Afraid of Virginia Woolf?*

albeit /awl-**bee**-it/ • conj. though.
– ORIGIN from *all be it*.

Albert, Prince E
Albert Francis Charles Augustus Emmanuel (1819–61), consort to Queen Victoria and prince of Saxe-Coburg-Gotha.

Alberta E
a prairie province in western Canada; capital, Edmonton.

Alberti E
/al-**bair**-ti/, Leon Battista (1404–72), Italian architect and writer. He was an influential figure in the reawakening of interest in classical architecture during the Renaissance.

albino /al-**bee**-noh/ • n. (pl. **albinos**) a person or animal born without pigment in the skin and hair (which are white) and the eyes (which are usually pink).

a

– ORIGIN Latin *albus* 'white'.

Albinoni E
/al-bi-**noh**-ni/, Tomaso (1671–1751), Italian composer. The *Adagio in G* with which he is associated was in fact composed by Remo Giazotto, based on a manuscript fragment by Albinoni.

Albion ● **n.** literary Britain or England.
– ORIGIN Latin.

album ● **n. 1** a blank book for displaying photographs, stamps, or other items forming a collection. **2** a collection of musical recordings issued as a single item.
– ORIGIN Latin, 'blank tablet'.

albumen /al-byuu-muhn/ ● **n.** egg white, or the protein contained in it.
– ORIGIN Latin.

albumin /al-byuu-min/ ● **n.** a form of protein that is soluble in water and is found especially in blood and egg white.

Albuquerque E
/al-buh-ker-ki/ the largest city in the state of New Mexico.

Alcatraz E
/al-kuh-traz/ a rocky island in San Francisco Bay, California, the site of a top-security federal prison from 1934 to 1963.

alchemy /al-kuh-mi/ ● **n.** the medieval forerunner of chemistry, concerned particularly with attempts to convert common metals into gold.
– DERIVATIVES **alchemical** adj. **alchemist** n.
– ORIGIN Greek *khēmia*, *khēmeia* 'art of transforming metals'.

Alcock E
/awl-kok/, Sir John William (1892–1919), English aviator, who with Sir Arthur Whitten Brown made the first non-stop transatlantic flight in 1919.

alcohol ● **n. 1** a colourless flammable liquid which is the intoxicating ingredient in drinks such as wine, beer, and spirits. **2** drink containing this. **3** Chem. any organic compound containing a group –OH: *propyl alcohol.*
– ORIGIN Arabic, 'the kohl'.

alcoholic ● **adj.** relating to alcohol. ● **n.** a person suffering from alcoholism.

alcoholism ● **n.** addiction to alcoholic drink.

alcopop ● **n.** Brit. informal a ready-mixed fizzy drink containing alcohol.

Alcott E
/awl-kot/, Louisa May (1832–88), American novelist, author of *Little Women.*

alcove ● **n.** a recess in the wall of a room.
– ORIGIN French.

Alcuin E
/al-kwin/ (*c.*735–804), English scholar and theologian. As head of Charlemagne's palace school, he played a central role in fostering the cultural revival known as the Carolingian Renaissance.

aldehyde /al-di-hyd/ ● **n.** Chem. a compound made by oxidation of an alcohol.
– ORIGIN from Latin *alcohol dehydrogenatum* 'alcohol deprived of hydrogen'.

al dente /al **den**-tay/ ● **adj. & adv.** (of food) cooked so as to be still firm when bitten.
– ORIGIN Italian, 'to the tooth'.

alder ● **n.** a tree of the birch family, which bears catkins and has toothed leaves.
– ORIGIN Old English.

alderman ● **n. 1** hist. a member of an English county or borough council, next in status to the Mayor. **2** (also **alderwoman**) N. Amer. & Austral. an elected member of a city council.
– ORIGIN Old English, 'chief, patriarch'.

Alderney E
/awl-der-ni/ an island in the English Channel, to the north-east of Guernsey.

Aldiss E
/awl-diss/, Brian (Wilson) (b.1925), English novelist and critic, best known for his works of science fiction.

Aldrin E
/awl-drin/, Buzz (b.1930; full name *Edwin Eugene Aldrin*), American astronaut, who in 1969 was the second person to set foot on the moon, after Neil Armstrong.

ale ● **n.** esp. Brit. beer other than lager, stout, or porter.
– ORIGIN Old English.

aleatory /ay-lee-uh-tri/ (also **aleatoric**) ● **adj.** depending on the throw of a dice or on chance.
– ORIGIN Latin *aleator* 'dice player'.

Aleppo E
/a-lep-poh/ a city in northern Syria, important as a commercial entre.

alert ● **adj. 1** quick to notice and respond to danger or change. **2** having an active mind. ● **n. 1** the state of being alert. **2** a warning of danger. ● **v.** warn of a danger or problem.
– DERIVATIVES **alertly** adv. **alertness** n.
– ORIGIN from Italian *all' erta* 'to the watchtower'.

Aleutian Islands E
/uh-**lyoo**-sh'n, uh-**loo**-sh'n/ (also **the Aleutians**) a chain of volcanic islands in US possession, extending south-west from the Alaska Peninsula.

A level ● **n.** (in the UK except Scotland) the higher of the two main levels of the GCE examination.
– ORIGIN from **ADVANCED LEVEL**.

Alexander Nevsky E
/nyef-ski/ (also **Nevski**) (*c.*1220–63), Russian prince, who defeated the Swedes in 1240. Feast day, 30 August or 23 November.

Alexander technique ● **n.** a system designed to promote well-being through the control of posture.
– ORIGIN named after its originator, the Australian-born actor Frederick Matthias *Alexander* (1869–1955).

Alexander the Great E
(356–323 BC), king of Macedon 336–323. He conquered Persia, Egypt, Syria, Mesopotamia, Bactria, and the Punjab, and in Egypt founded the city of Alexandria.

Alexandria E
/a-lig-**zahn**-dri-uh/ the chief port of Egypt, formerly a major centre of Hellenistic culture.

alexandrine /a-lig-**zahn**-dryn/ ● **adj.** (of a line of verse) having six iambic feet.
– ORIGIN French.

alfalfa /al-**fal**-fuh/ ● **n.** a plant with clover-like leaves and bluish flowers, used as fodder.
– ORIGIN Spanish.

Alfonso XIII E
/al-**fon**-soh/ (1886–1941), king of Spain 1886–1931, forced into exile after elections indicating a preference for a republic.

Alfred the Great E
(849–99), king of Wessex 871–99. He saved SW England from Viking occupation and is credited with the foundation of the English navy.

alfresco /al-**fress**-koh/ ● **adv. & adj.** in the open air.
– ORIGIN from Italian *al fresco*.

algae /**al**-jee, **al**-gee/ ● **pl. n.** (sing. **alga** /**al**-guh/) simple plants lacking true stems, roots, and leaves, e.g. seaweed.
– ORIGIN Latin *alga* 'seaweed'.

Algarve E
/al-**garv**/ (**the Algarve**) the southernmost province of Portugal, on the Atlantic coast.

algebra /**al**-ji-bruh/ ● **n.** the branch of mathematics in which letters and other symbols are used to represent numbers and quantities.
– DERIVATIVES **algebraic** /al-ji-**bray**-ik/ adj.
– ORIGIN Latin.

Algeria E
/al-**jeer**-i-uh/ a republic on the Mediterranean coast of North Africa; capital, Algiers.
– DERIVATIVES **Algerian** adj. & n.

Algiers E
/al-**jeerz**/ the capital of Algeria.

algorithm /**al**-guh-ri-*th*'m/ ● **n.** a process or set of rules used in calculations or other problem-solving operations.
– ORIGIN Latin *algorismus*.

Ali, E
Muhammad, see **MUHAMMAD ALI**.

alias /**ay**-li-uhss/ ● **adv.** also known as. ● **n. 1** a false identity. **2** Computing an identifying label used to access a file, command, or address.
– ORIGIN Latin, 'at another time, otherwise'.

Ali Baba E
/a-li **bah**-buh/ the hero of a story supposed to be from the *Arabian Nights,* who discovered the magic formula ('Open Sesame!') which opened a cave where forty thieves kept their treasure.

alibi /**a**-li-by/ ● **n.** (pl. **alibis**) a piece of evidence that one was elsewhere when a crime was committed.
– ORIGIN Latin, 'elsewhere'.

Alicante E
/a-li-**kan**-ti/ a seaport on the Mediterranean coast of SE Spain.

Alice Springs E
a town and railway terminus serving the outback of Northern Territory, Australia.

alien ● **adj. 1** belonging to a foreign country. **2** unfamiliar or unacceptable: *principles that are alien to them.* **3** relating to beings from other worlds. ● **n. 1** a foreigner. **2** a being from another world.
– DERIVATIVES **alienness** n.
– ORIGIN Latin *alienus*.

alienate ● **v.** (**alienates, alienating, alienated**) **1** cause to feel isolated. **2** lose the support or sympathy of.
– DERIVATIVES **alienation** n.

Alighieri E
/a-li-**gyair**-i/, Dante, see **DANTE**.

alight¹ ● **v. 1** formal, esp. Brit. get down from a vehicle. **2** (**alight on**) happen to notice.
– ORIGIN Old English.

alight² ● **adv. & adj. 1** on fire. **2** shining brightly.

align ● **v. 1** place in a straight line or in the correct position in relation to others. **2** (**align oneself with**) be on the side of.
– DERIVATIVES **alignment** n.
– ORIGIN French *aligner*.

alike ● **adj.** similar. ● **adv.** in a similar way.
– ORIGIN Old English.

alimentary canal ● **n.** the passage along which food passes through the body.
– ORIGIN Latin *alimentum* 'nourishment'.

alimony /**a**-li-muh-ni/ ● **n.** esp. N. Amer. financial support for a husband or wife after separation or divorce.
– ORIGIN Latin *alimonia* 'nutriment'.

A-line ● **adj.** (of a garment) slightly flared.

aliquot /**a**-li-kwot/ ● **n.** a portion or sample taken for analysis or treatment.
– ORIGIN Latin, 'some, so many'.

alive ● **adj. 1** living; not dead. **2** continuing in existence or use: *keeping hope alive.* **3** alert and active. **4** having interest and meaning. **5** (**alive with**) teeming with.

alkali /**al**-kuh-ly/ ● **n.** (pl. **alkalis** or US also **alkalies**) a substance with particular chemical properties that include turning litmus blue and neutralizing acids.
– ORIGIN Arabic, 'fry, roast'.

alkaline ● **adj.** having the properties of an alkali; having a pH greater than 7.
– DERIVATIVES **alkalinity** n.

alkane /**al**-kayn/ ● **n.** Chem. any of the series of saturated hydrocarbons whose simplest members are methane and ethane.
– ORIGIN German *Alkohol* 'alcohol'.

alkene /**al**-keen/ ● **n.** Chem. any of the series of unsaturated hydrocarbons containing a double bond, of which the simplest member is ethylene.
– ORIGIN German *Alkohol* 'alcohol'.

all ● **det. & predet. 1** the whole quantity or extent of. **2** any whatever: *he denied all knowledge.* **3** the greatest possible: *with all speed.* ● **pron.** everything or everyone. ● **adv. 1** completely. **2** indicating an equal score: *one-all.*
– PHRASES **all along** from the beginning. **all and sundry** everyone. **all but 1** very nearly. **2** all except. **all for** informal strongly in favour of. **all in** informal exhausted. **all in all** on the whole. **all out** using all one's effort. **all over** informal **1** everywhere. **2** informal typical of the person mentioned. **all round 1** in all respects. **2** for or by each person: *drinks all round.* **all told** in total. **at all** in any way. **in all** in total. **on all fours** on hands and knees. **one's all** one's fullest effort.
– ORIGIN Old English.

a

Allah /al-luh/ • n. the name of God among Muslims (and Arab Christians).
– ORIGIN Arabic.

Allahabad E
/al-luh-huh-bad/ a city and place of Hindu pilgrimage in north central India, situated at the confluence of the sacred Jumna and Ganges Rivers.

allay /uh-lay/ • v. reduce or end (fear, concern, or difficulty).
– ORIGIN Old English, 'lay down or aside'.

All Blacks E
the New Zealand international rugby union team.

all-clear • n. a signal that danger or difficulty is over.

allegation • n. a claim that someone has done something illegal or wrong.

allege /uh-lej/ • v. (**alleges**, **alleging**, **alleged**) claim that someone has done something illegal or wrong.
– DERIVATIVES **alleged** adj. **allegedly** adv.
– ORIGIN Old French *esligier*.

Allegheny Mountains E
/al-luh-gay-ni/ a mountain range of the Appalachian system in the eastern US.

allegiance /uh-lee-juhnss/ • n. loyalty to a person of higher status or to a group or cause.
– ORIGIN Old French *ligeance*.

allegory /al-li-guh-ri/ • n. (pl. **allegories**) a story, poem, or picture which contains a hidden meaning.
– DERIVATIVES **allegorical** adj.
– ORIGIN Greek *allēgoria*.

allegretto /al-li-gret-toh/ • adv. & adj. Music at a fairly brisk speed.
– ORIGIN Italian.

allegro /uh-lay-groh/ Music • adv. & adj. at a brisk speed. • n. (pl. **allegros**) an allegro passage.
– ORIGIN Italian, 'lively'.

alleluia /al-li-loo-yuh/ • exclam. & n. var. of HALLELUJAH.

Allen, E
Woody (b.1935; born *Allen Stewart Konigsberg*), American film director, writer, and actor, known for films such as *Annie Hall* and *Hannah and her Sisters*.

Allende E
/a-yen-di/, Salvador (1908–73), Chilean Marxist statesman, President 1970–3. He was killed in a military coup led by General Pinochet.

Allen key • n. trademark a spanner designed to turn an Allen screw.

Allen screw • n. trademark a screw with a hexagonal socket in the head.
– ORIGIN from the *Allen* Manufacturing Company, Connecticut.

allergen /al-ler-juhn/ • n. a substance that causes an allergic reaction.

allergenic /al-ler-jen-ik/ • adj. likely to cause an allergic reaction.

allergic • adj. **1** caused by an allergy. **2** having an allergy.

allergy • n. (pl. **allergies**) a medical condition in which the body reacts badly when it comes into contact with a particular substance.
– ORIGIN Greek *allos* 'other'.

alleviate /uh-lee-vi-ayt/ • v. (**alleviates**, **alleviating**, **alleviated**) make (pain or difficulty) less severe.
– DERIVATIVES **alleviation** n.
– ORIGIN Latin *alleviare* 'lighten'.

alley • n. (pl. **alleys**) **1** a narrow passageway between or behind buildings. **2** a path in a park or garden. **3** a long, narrow area in which skittles and bowling are played.
– ORIGIN Old French *alee* 'walking, passage'.

alleyway • n. an alley between or behind buildings.

alliance • n. **1** a relationship formed between countries or organizations for a joint purpose. **2** the state of being joined or associated.

allied • adj. **1** joined by an alliance. **2** (**Allied**) relating to Britain and its allies in the First and Second World Wars. **3** (**allied to/with**) combined with: *skilled craftsmanship allied to advanced technology.*

alligator • n. a large reptile similar to a crocodile but with a broader and shorter head.
– ORIGIN from Spanish *el lagarto* 'the lizard'.

all-in • adj. Brit. (especially of a price) including everything.

all-in wrestling • n. esp. Brit. wrestling with few or no restrictions.

alliteration /uh-lit-uh-ray-sh'n/ • n. the occurrence of the same letter or sound at the beginning of words next to or close to each other.
– DERIVATIVES **alliterative** adj.
– ORIGIN Latin.

allocate • v. (**allocates**, **allocating**, **allocated**) give (resources or duties) to.
– DERIVATIVES **allocation** n.
– ORIGIN Latin *allocare*.

allot • v. (**allots**, **allotting**, **allotted**) give out as a share to.
– ORIGIN Old French *aloter*.

allotment • n. **1** Brit. a small plot of rented land for growing vegetables or flowers. **2** the action of allotting. **3** an amount of something allotted.

allotrope /al-luh-trohp/ • n. Chem. each of two or more different physical forms in which a particular element exists.
– DERIVATIVES **allotropic** adj.
– ORIGIN Greek *allotropos* 'of another form'.

allow • v. **1** permit to do something. **2** accept as legal or proper. **3** (**allow for**) take into consideration. **4** provide or set aside: *allow an hour or so for driving.* **5** admit the truth of.
– DERIVATIVES **allowable** adj.
– ORIGIN Old French *alouer*.

allowance • n. **1** the amount of something allowed. **2** a sum of money paid regularly to a person. **3** an amount of money that can be earned free of tax.
– PHRASES **make allowances for 1** take into consideration. **2** treat (someone) less harshly because of their difficult circumstances.

alloy • n. /al-loy/ **1** a mixture of two or more metals. **2** an inferior metal mixed with a precious one. • v. /uh-loy/ **1** mix (metals) to make an alloy. **2** spoil by adding something inferior.
– ORIGIN Old French *aloier*, *aleier* 'combine'.

all right • adj. **1** satisfactory; acceptable.

2 permitted. ● **adv.** fairly well. ● **exclam.** expressing or asking for agreement or acceptance.

all-round (US **all-around**) ● **adj. 1** having a wide range of abilities: *an all-round athlete.* **2** including many different subjects or features.

all-rounder ● **n.** Brit. a person with a wide range of skills.

All Saints' Day ● **n.** a Christian festival in honour of all the saints, held (in the Western Church) on 1 November.

All Souls' Day ● **n.** a Catholic festival with prayers for the souls of the dead in purgatory, held on 2 November.

allspice ● **n.** the dried fruit of a Caribbean tree, used as a spice in cookery.

all-time ● **adj.** not having been bettered or beaten: *the all-time record.*

allude /uh-lood/ ● **v.** (**alludes**, **alluding**, **alluded**) (**allude to**) **1** hint at. **2** mention in passing.
– ORIGIN Latin *alludere.*

allure ● **n.** powerful attractiveness or charm.
– ORIGIN Old French *aleurier.*

alluring ● **adj.** attractive; tempting.

allusion ● **n.** an indirect reference to something.

alluvium /uh-loo-vi-uhm, uh-lyoo-vi-uhm/ ● **n.** a fertile deposit of clay, silt, and sand left by flood water.
– DERIVATIVES **alluvial** adj.
– ORIGIN Latin.

ally ● **n.** /al-ly/ (pl. **allies**) **1** a person, organization, or country that cooperates with another. **2** (**the Allies**) the countries that fought with Britain in the First and Second World Wars. ● **v.** /uh-ly/ (**allies**, **allying**, **allied**) (**ally to/with**) **1** combine (a resource) with (another) in a way that benefits both: *he allied his racing experience with his father's business skills.* **2** (**ally oneself with**) side with.
– ORIGIN Old French *alier.*

alma mater /al-muh **mah**-ter (or **may**-ter)/ ● **n.** the school, college, or university that one once attended.
– ORIGIN Latin, 'bountiful mother'.

almanac /al-muh-nak/ (also **almanack**) ● **n. 1** a calendar giving important dates and information such as the phases of the moon. **2** an annual handbook containing information of general or specialist interest.
– ORIGIN Greek *almenikhiaka.*

almighty ● **adj. 1** having unlimited or very great power. **2** informal enormous. ● **n.** (**the Almighty**) a name or title for God.

almond ● **n.** the oval nut-like kernel of the almond tree.
– ORIGIN Old French *alemande.*

almost ● **adv.** very nearly.
– ORIGIN Old English.

alms /ahmz/ ● **pl. n.** hist. charitable donations of money or food to the poor.
– ORIGIN Greek *eleēmosunē* 'compassion'.

almshouse ● **n.** a house founded by charity, offering accommodation for the poor.

aloe /a-loh/ ● **n.** a tropical plant with thick tapering leaves.
– ORIGIN Greek *aloē.*

aloe vera /a-loh veer-uh/ ● **n.** a jelly-like substance obtained from an aloe, used as a soothing treatment for the skin.
– ORIGIN Latin, 'true aloe'.

aloft ● **adj. & adv.** up in or into the air.
– ORIGIN Old Norse.

alone ● **adj. & adv. 1** on one's own. **2** isolated and lonely. **3** only; exclusively.
– PHRASES **leave alone 1** abandon or desert. **2** stop interfering with.
– ORIGIN from **ALL** + **ONE**.

along ● **prep. & adv. 1** moving in a constant direction on: *we were driving along a narrow road.* **2** extending in a horizontal line on. **3** in or into company with others: *he had brought along a friend.*
– PHRASES **along with** in company with or at the same time as. **be** (or **come**) **along** arrive.
– ORIGIN Old English.

alongside (N. Amer. also **alongside of**) ● **prep. 1** close to the side of; next to. **2** at the same time as.

aloof ● **adj.** cool and distant.
– DERIVATIVES **aloofness** n.
– ORIGIN from **LUFF**.

alopecia /a-luh-pee-shuh/ ● **n.** Med. abnormal loss of hair.
– ORIGIN Greek *alōpekia* 'fox mange'.

aloud ● **adv.** so as to be heard; audibly.

alpaca /al-pak-uh/ ● **n.** (pl. **alpaca** or **alpacas**) a long-haired South American mammal related to the llama.
– ORIGIN Spanish.

alpha /al-fuh/ ● **n. 1** the first letter of the Greek alphabet (Α, α). **2** Brit. a first-class mark given for a piece of work.
– PHRASES **alpha and omega** the beginning and the end.
– ORIGIN Greek.

alphabet ● **n.** an ordered set of letters or symbols used to represent the basic speech sounds of a language.
– ORIGIN from Greek *alpha* and *bēta*, the first two letters of the Greek alphabet.

alphabetical ● **adj.** in the order of the letters of the alphabet.
– DERIVATIVES **alphabetically** adv.

Alpha Centauri E
/al-fuh sen-**tor**-I/ the third-brightest star in the sky, in the constellation Centaurus.

alphanumeric /al-fuh-nyoo-**me**-rik/ ● **adj.** using both letters and numerals.

alpha particle (also **alpha ray**) ● **n.** Physics a helium nucleus, especially as given out by some radioactive substances.

alpine ● **adj. 1** relating to or growing on high mountains. **2** (**Alpine**) relating to the Alps. ● **n.** an alpine plant.

Alps E
a mountain system extending in a curve from the coast of SE France through NW Italy, Switzerland, Liechtenstein, and southern Germany into Austria.

already ● **adv. 1** before the time in question. **2** expressing surprise that something has happened so soon or early.

alright ● **adj., adv., & exclam.** var. of **ALL RIGHT**.

USAGE alright
When writing, use the spelling **all right** rather than **alright**.

Alsace E
/al-sass/ a region of NE France, on the borders with Germany and Switzerland.

Alsatian • n. Brit. a German shepherd dog.
– ORIGIN Latin *Alsatia* 'Alsace'.

also • adv. in addition.
– ORIGIN Old English.

also-ran • n. a loser in a race or contest.

Altai Mountains E
/al-ty/ a mountain system of central Asia extending from Kazakhstan into western Mongolia and northern China.

Altamira E
/al-tuh-**meer**-uh/ the site of a cave in northern Spain with Palaeolithic rock paintings.

altar • n. **1** the table in a Christian church at which the bread and wine are consecrated in communion services. **2** a table on which religious offerings are made.
– ORIGIN Latin.

altar boy • n. a boy who acts as a priest's assistant during a service.

altarpiece • n. a work of art set above and behind an altar.

Altdorfer E
/**alt**-dor-fer/, Albrecht (*c.*1485–1538), German painter and engraver, one of the first modern European landscape painters.

alter • v. make or become different; change.
– DERIVATIVES **alteration** n.
– ORIGIN Latin *alterare.*

altercation /awl-ter-**kay**-sh'n/ • n. a noisy disagreement.
– ORIGIN Latin.

alter ego /awl-ter ee-goh/ • n. **1** a person's alternative personality. **2** a close friend who is very like oneself.
– ORIGIN Latin, 'other self'.

alternate • v. /awl-ter-nayt/ (**alternates, alternating, alternated**) **1** occur or do in turn repeatedly. **2** change repeatedly between two contrasting states. • adj. /awl-**ter**-nuht/ **1** every other. **2** (of two things) each following and succeeded by the other in a regular pattern.
– DERIVATIVES **alternately** adv. **alternation** n.
– ORIGIN Latin *alternare* 'do by turns'.

alternate angles • pl. n. two equal angles on opposite sides of a line crossing two parallel lines.

alternating current • n. an electric current that reverses its direction many times a second. Compare with DIRECT CURRENT.

alternative • adj. **1** (of one or more things) available as another possibility: *an alternative approach to the problem.* **2** departing from traditional practices. • n. one of two or more available possibilities.
– DERIVATIVES **alternatively** adv.

alternative energy • n. energy produced by fuels that do not use up natural resources or harm the environment.

alternative medicine • n. medical treatment that does not follow the usual practices of Western medicine, e.g. herbalism.

alternator • n. a dynamo that generates an alternating current.

although • conj. **1** in spite of the fact that. **2** but.

altimeter /al-ti-mee-ter/ • n. an instrument which indicates the altitude reached by an aircraft.

altitude • n. the height of an object or point above sea level or ground level.
– ORIGIN Latin *altitudo.*

alto /al-toh/ • n. (pl. **altos**) **1** the highest adult male or lowest female singing voice. **2** (before another noun) referring to the second or third highest instrument in a family: *an alto sax.*
– ORIGIN from Italian *alto canto* 'high song'.

altogether • adv. **1** completely. **2** in total. **3** on the whole.
– PHRASES **in the altogether** informal naked.

altruism /al-troo-i-z'm/ • n. unselfish concern for others.
– DERIVATIVES **altruist** n. **altruistic** adj.
– ORIGIN Italian *altrui* 'somebody else'.

alum /al-uhm/ • n. a compound of aluminium and potassium, used in dyeing and tanning.
– ORIGIN Latin *alumen.*

aluminium /al-yoo-**min**-i-uhm/ (US **aluminum** /uh-**loo**-mi-nuhm/) • n. a lightweight silvery-grey metallic element that resists corrosion.

alumnus /uh-**lum**-nuhss/ • n. (pl. **alumni** /uh-**lum**-ny/; fem. **alumna** /uh-**lum**-nuh/, pl. **alumnae** /uh-**lum**-nee/) a former student of a particular school, college, or university.
– ORIGIN Latin, 'pupil'.

Alvarez E
/al-**vah**-rez/, Luis Walter (1911–88), American physicist, who discovered iridium in sediment from the time when the Cretaceous period ended and the Tertiary period began, and proposed that this was due to a catastrophic meteorite impact that may have resulted in the extinction of the dinosaurs.

always • adv. **1** at all times. **2** forever. **3** repeatedly. **4** if all else fails.

Alzheimer's disease /alts-hy-merz/ • n. a disorder which causes mental deterioration in middle or old age.
– ORIGIN named after the German neurologist Alois *Alzheimer* (1864–1915).

AM • abbrev. amplitude modulation.

am 1st person sing. present of BE.

a.m. • abbrev. before noon.
– ORIGIN from Latin *ante meridiem.*

Amal E
/uh-**mahl**/ a Lebanese Shiite Muslim organization founded in 1975.

amalgam /uh-**mal**-guhm/ • n. **1** a mixture or blend. **2** Chem. an alloy of mercury with another metal.
– ORIGIN Greek *malagma* 'an emollient'.

amalgamate /uh-**mal**-guh-mayt/ • v. (**amalgamates, amalgamating, amalgamated**) **1** combine to form one organization or structure. **2** Chem. mix (a metal) with mercury to make an alloy.
– DERIVATIVES **amalgamation** n.

amanuensis /uh-man-yoo-**en**-siss/ • n. (pl. **amanuenses** /uh-man-yoo-**en**-seez/) a literary assistant.
– ORIGIN Latin.

amaryllis /am-uh-**ril**-liss/ • n. a plant with large trumpet-shaped flowers.
– ORIGIN Greek *Amarullis,* a girl's name in poetry.

amass • v. build up over time.

– ORIGIN Latin *amassare*.

amateur • n. **1** a person who takes part in a sport or other activity without being paid. **2** a person who is incompetent at a particular activity. • adj. **1** non-professional. **2** unskilful.
– DERIVATIVES **amateurism** n.
– ORIGIN French, 'lover'.

amateurish • adj. incompetent; unskilful.

Amati E
/uh-mah-ti/ a family of Italian violin-makers, working in the 16th and 17th centuries.

amatory /am-uh-tuh-ri/ • adj. having to do with sexual love or desire.
– ORIGIN Latin *amatorius*.

amaze • v. (**amazes, amazing, amazed**) surprise greatly; astonish.
– DERIVATIVES **amazement** n.
– ORIGIN Old English.

Amazon[1] E
/am-uh-z'n/ a river in South America, flowing over 6,683 km (4,150 miles) through Peru, Colombia, and Brazil into the Atlantic Ocean. It is the largest river in the world in terms of water flow.
– DERIVATIVES **Amazonian** adj.

Amazon[2] /am-uh-zuhn/ • n. **1** a member of a legendary race of female warriors. **2** a very tall, strong woman.
– DERIVATIVES **Amazonian** adj.
– ORIGIN Greek.

ambassador • n. **1** a diplomat sent by a state as its permanent representative in a foreign country. **2** a representative of an activity.
– ORIGIN Italian *ambasciator*.

amber • n. **1** hard clear fossilized resin used in jewellery. **2** a honey-yellow colour.
– ORIGIN Old French *ambre*.

ambergris /am-ber-greess/ • n. a wax-like substance produced by sperm whales, used in perfume manufacture.
– ORIGIN from Old French *ambre gris* 'grey amber'.

ambidextrous /am-bi-dek-struhss/ • adj. able to use the right and left hands equally well.
– ORIGIN from Latin *ambi-* 'on both sides' + *dexter* 'right-handed'.

ambience /am-bi-uhnss/ (also **ambiance**) • n. the character and atmosphere of a place.

ambient /am-bi-uhnt/ • adj. surrounding: *there was no ambient light*.
– ORIGIN Latin.

ambiguity /am-bi-gyoo-i-ti/ • n. (pl. **ambiguities**) uncertain or inexact meaning.

ambiguous /am-big-yoo-uhss/ • adj. **1** (of language) having more than one meaning. **2** not clear or decided.
– DERIVATIVES **ambiguously** adv.
– ORIGIN Latin *ambiguus* 'doubtful'.

ambit • n. the scope or extent of something.
– ORIGIN Latin *ambitus* 'circuit'.

ambition • n. **1** a strong desire to do or achieve something. **2** desire for success, wealth, or fame.
– ORIGIN Latin.

ambitious • adj. **1** having or showing determination to succeed. **2** intended to meet a high standard and therefore difficult to achieve: *an ambitious enterprise*.
– DERIVATIVES **ambitiously** adv.

ambivalent /am-biv-uh-luhnt/ • adj. having mixed feelings about something or someone.
– DERIVATIVES **ambivalence** n.
– ORIGIN from Latin *ambi-* 'on both sides' + *valere* 'be worth'.

amble • v. (**ambles, ambling, ambled**) walk at a leisurely pace. • n. a leisurely walk.
– ORIGIN Latin *ambulare* 'to walk'.

Ambrose, St E
/am-brohz/ (*c*.339–97), Christian theologian and bishop of Milan. Feast day, 7 December.

ambrosia • n. **1** Gk & Rom. Myth. the food of the gods. **2** something very pleasing to taste or smell.
– DERIVATIVES **ambrosial** adj.
– ORIGIN Greek, 'elixir of life'.

ambulance • n. a vehicle for taking sick or injured people to and from hospital.
– ORIGIN French.

ambulatory /am-byoo-luh-tri/ • adj. **1** relating to walking or able to walk. **2** movable; mobile.

ambush • n. a surprise attack by people lying in wait in a hidden position. • v. attack in such a way.
– ORIGIN Old French *embusche*.

ameba • n. (pl. **amebae** or **amebas**) US = AMOEBA.

ameliorate /uh-mee-li-uh-rayt/ • v. (**ameliorates, ameliorating, ameliorated**) formal make (something) better.
– ORIGIN Latin *meliorare*.

amen /ah-men, ay-men/ • exclam. said at the end of a prayer or hymn, meaning 'so be it'.
– ORIGIN Greek.

amenable /uh-meen-uh-b'l/ • adj. **1** willing to be persuaded. **2** (**amenable to**) able to be affected by.
– DERIVATIVES **amenability** n.
– ORIGIN Old French *amener* 'bring to'.

amend • v. make minor improvements to.
– ORIGIN Latin *emendare* 'to correct'.

amendment • n. a minor improvement.

amends • pl. n. (in phr. **make amends**) make up for a wrongdoing.

amenity /uh-meen-i-ti/ • n. (pl. **amenities**) a useful or desirable feature of a place.
– ORIGIN Latin *amoenitas*.

America[1] E
(also **the Americas**) a land mass consisting of the continents of North and South America joined by the Isthmus of Panama.

America[2] E
the United States.

American • adj. relating to the United States or to the continents of America. • n. a person from the United States or any of the countries of North, South, or Central America.

American Civil War E
the war between the northern US states (usually known as the Union) and the Confederate states of the South, 1861–5. The Union states, who opposed slavery, were eventually victorious.

American dream • n. the ideal of equality of opportunity associated with the US.

American football • n. a kind of football played in the US with an oval ball on a field marked out as a gridiron.

a

American Independence, War of E
the war of 1775–83 in which the American colonists won independence from British rule. Called the **American Revolution** in the US and Canada.

American Indian • n. a member of the native peoples of America.

Americanism • n. a word or phrase originating in the US.

American Samoa E
an unincorporated overseas territory of the US comprising a group of islands in the southern Pacific Ocean, to the east of Samoa; capital, Fagatogo.

America's Cup E
an international yachting race held every three to four years.

americium /am-uh-riss-i-uhm/ • n. a radioactive metallic chemical element made by high-energy atomic collisions.
– ORIGIN from *America*.

Amerindian /am-uh-rin-di-uhn/ (also **Amerind** /am-uh-rind/) • n. & adj. = AMERICAN INDIAN.

amethyst /am-uh-thist/ • n. a precious stone consisting of a violet or purple variety of quartz.
– ORIGIN Greek *amethustos* 'not drunken' (because the stone was believed to prevent drunkenness).

amiable • adj. friendly and pleasant in manner.
– DERIVATIVES **amiability** n. **amiably** adv.
– ORIGIN Old French.

amicable /am-i-kuh-b'l/ • adj. friendly and without disagreement.
– DERIVATIVES **amicably** adv.
– ORIGIN Latin *amicabilis*.

amid • prep. in the middle of.

amidships (US also **amidship**) • adv. & adj. in the middle of a ship.

amidst • prep. literary = AMID.

amigo /uh-mee-goh/ • n. (pl. **amigos**) informal, esp. N. Amer. a friend.
– ORIGIN Spanish.

Amin E
/a-meen/, Idi (1925–2003), Ugandan soldier and head of state 1971–9. He was overthrown after a regime characterized by the murder of political opponents and the expulsion of non-Africans.

amino acid /uh-mee-noh/ • n. any of about twenty organic compounds which form the basic constituents of proteins.
– ORIGIN from AMMONIA.

amir /uh-meer/ • n. var. of EMIR.

Amis[1] E
/ay-miss/, Sir Kingsley (1922–95), English novelist, author of *Lucky Jim* and *The Old Devils*.

Amis[2] E
/ay-miss/, Martin (Louis) (b.1949), English novelist, author of *Money* and *Time's Arrow*. He is the son of Sir Kingsley Amis.

amiss • adj. not quite right; inappropriate. • adv. wrongly or inappropriately.
– PHRASES **not go amiss** be welcome and useful. **take amiss** be offended by.
– ORIGIN prob. from Old Norse, 'so as to miss'.

amity /am-i-ti/ • n. friendly relations.
– ORIGIN Old French *amitie*.

Amman E
/uh-mahn/ the capital of Jordan.

ammeter /am-mi-ter/ • n. an instrument for measuring electric current in amperes.

ammo • n. informal ammunition.

ammonia /uh-moh-ni-uh/ • n. a colourless, strong-smelling gas that forms a very alkaline solution in water, which is used as a cleaning fluid.
– ORIGIN first referring to a salt obtained near the temple of Jupiter *Ammon* in Egypt.

ammonite /am-uh-nyt/ • n. an extinct sea creature with a spiral shell, found as a fossil.
– ORIGIN from Latin *cornu Ammonis* 'horn of Ammon'.

ammunition /am-yuu-ni-sh'n/ • n. **1** a supply of bullets and shells. **2** points used to support one's case in argument.
– ORIGIN from French *la munition* 'the fortification'.

amnesia /am-nee-zi-uh/ • n. loss of memory.
– ORIGIN Greek, 'forgetfulness'.

amnesiac /am-nee-zi-ak/ • n. a person who has lost their memory.

amnesty • n. (pl. **amnesties**) **1** an official pardon for people convicted of political offences. **2** a period during which people admitting to particular offences are not prosecuted.
– ORIGIN Greek *amnēstia* 'forgetfulness'.

Amnesty International E
an independent international organization in support of human rights, especially for prisoners of conscience.

amniotic fluid • n. the fluid surrounding a fetus before birth.
– ORIGIN from Greek *amnion* 'membrane surrounding an embryo'.

amoeba /uh-mee-buh/ (US also **ameba**) • n. (pl. **amoebas** or **amoebae** /uh-mee-bee/) a microscopic animal that is made up of a single cell and can change its shape.
– ORIGIN Greek *amoibē* 'change'.

amok /uh-mok/ (also **amuck**) • adv. (in phr. **run amok**) behave in an uncontrolled and disorderly way.
– ORIGIN Malay.

among (also **amongst**) • prep. **1** surrounded by. **2** included or occurring in. **3** shared by; between.
– ORIGIN Old English.

amoral /ay-mo-ruhl/ • adj. without morals; not concerned about right or wrong.
– DERIVATIVES **amorality** n.

amorous • adj. showing or feeling sexual desire.
– ORIGIN Latin *amor* 'love'.

amorphous /uh-mor-fuhss/ • adj. without a definite shape or form.
– ORIGIN Greek *amorphos*.

amortize /uh-mor-tyz/ (also **amortise**) • v. (**amortizes**, **amortizing**, **amortized**) gradually pay off (a debt).
– ORIGIN Old French *amortir*.

amount ● n. **1** the total number, size, or value of something. **2** a quantity. ● v. (**amount to**) **1** add up to (a total). **2** be the equivalent of.
– ORIGIN Old French *amont* 'upward'.

amperage /am-puh-rij/ ● n. the strength of an electric current, measured in amperes.

ampere /am-pair/ ● n. the base unit of electric current in the SI system.
– ORIGIN named after the French physicist André-Marie *Ampère* (1775–1836).

ampersand /am-per-sand/ ● n. the sign &, standing for *and*.
– ORIGIN from *and per se and* '& by itself is *and*'.

amphetamine /am-fet-uh-meen/ ● n. a drug used illegally as a stimulant.
– ORIGIN from its chemical name.

amphibian ● n. a cold-blooded animal such as a frog or toad, which lives in the water when young and on the land as an adult.
– ORIGIN from Greek *amphi* 'both' + *bios* 'life'.

amphibious /am-fib-i-uhss/ ● adj. **1** living in or suited for both land and water. **2** (of a military operation) involving forces landed from the sea.

amphitheatre (US **amphitheater**) ● n. a round building consisting of tiers of seats surrounding a central space for dramatic or sporting events.
– ORIGIN from Greek *amphi* 'on both sides' + *theatron* 'theatre'.

ample ● adj. (**ampler**, **amplest**) **1** enough or more than enough; plentiful. **2** large.
– DERIVATIVES **amply** adv.
– ORIGIN Latin *amplus*.

amplifier ● n. an electronic device for increasing the strength of electrical signals.

amplify ● v. (**amplifies**, **amplifying**, **amplified**) **1** increase the strength of (sound or electrical signals). **2** add details to (a story).
– DERIVATIVES **amplification** n.
– ORIGIN Latin *amplificare*.

amplitude ● n. **1** Physics the maximum amount by which an alternating current or electromagnetic wave can vary from its average level. **2** great size or extent.

amplitude modulation ● n. the modification of a radio wave by varying its amplitude, used as a means of broadcasting an audio signal.

ampoule /am-pool/ (US also **ampule** /am-pyool/) ● n. a small sealed glass capsule containing a measured quantity of liquid ready for injecting.
– ORIGIN Latin *ampulla* 'flask'.

amputate /am-pyoo-tayt/ ● v. (**amputates**, **amputating**, **amputated**) cut off (a limb) in a surgical operation.
– DERIVATIVES **amputation** n.
– ORIGIN Latin *amputare*.

amputee ● n. a person who has had a limb amputated.

Amritsar E
/um-rit-ser/ a city in the state of Punjab in NW India, the centre of the Sikh faith and the site of its holiest temple.

Amsterdam E
the capital and largest city of the Netherlands.

amuck /uh-muk/ ● adv. var. of AMOK.

Amu Darya E
/ah-moo dah-ri-uh/ a river of central Asia (known in classical times as the Oxus), rising in the Pamir mountains and flowing into the Aral Sea.

amulet /am-yoo-lit/ ● n. an ornament or small piece of jewellery worn as protection against evil.
– ORIGIN Latin *amuletum*.

Amundsen E
/ah-muund-s'n/ , Roald (1872–1928), Norwegian explorer, the first to reach the South Pole (1911).

Amur E
/uh-moor/ a river of NE Asia, which forms for the greater part of its length the boundary between Russia and China.

amuse ● v. (**amuses**, **amusing**, **amused**) **1** make (someone) laugh or smile. **2** give (someone) something enjoyable or interesting to do.
– ORIGIN Old French *amuser* 'entertain, deceive'.

amusement ● n. **1** the state of being amused. **2** Brit. a fairground ride or game machine.

an ● det. the form of the indefinite article 'a' used before words beginning with a vowel sound.

an- ● prefix var. of A-[1] before a vowel.

Anabaptist /an-uh-bap-tist/ ● n. a member of a Protestant religious group believing that only adults should be baptized.
– ORIGIN from Greek *ana-* 'again' + *baptismos* 'baptism'.

anabolic steroid /an-uh-bol-ik/ ● n. a synthetic hormone used to build up muscle.

anabolism /uh-nab-uh-li-z'm/ ● n. the formation of complex molecules from simpler ones in living organisms. together with the storage of energy. Opp. CATABOLISM.
DERIVATIVES **anabolic** adj.
– ORIGIN Greek *anabolē* 'ascent'.

anachronism /uh-nak-ruh-ni-z'm/ ● n. a thing belonging to a period other than the one in which it exists.
– DERIVATIVES **anachronistic** adj.
– ORIGIN from Greek *ana-* 'backwards' + *khronos* 'time'.

anaconda /an-uh-kon-duh/ ● n. a very large snake of the boa family, found in tropical South America.
– ORIGIN Sinhalese, 'whip snake'.

anaemia /uh-nee-mi-uh/ (US **anemia**) ● n. a shortage of red cells or haemoglobin in the blood, causing tiredness.
– ORIGIN from Greek *an-* 'without' + *haima* 'blood'.

anaemic (US **anemic**) ● adj. **1** suffering from anaemia. **2** lacking spirit or energy.

anaerobic /an-air-oh-bik/ ● adj. (of an organism) not using oxygen from the air.

anaesthetic /an-iss-thet-ik/ (US **anesthetic**) ● n. a drug or gas that causes a loss of sensitivity to pain.
– ORIGIN Greek *anaisthētos* 'unconscious'

anaesthetist /uh-neess-thuh-tist/ (US **anesthetist**) ● n. a medical specialist who gives anaesthetics.

anaesthetize /uh-neess-thuh-tyz/ (also

a

anaesthetise, US **anesthetize**) • v. (**anaesthetizes**, **anaesthetizing**, **anaesthetized**) give an anaesthetic to.

anagram /an-uh-gram/ • n. a word or phrase formed by rearranging the letters of another.
– ORIGIN from Greek *ana-* 'back, anew' + *gramma* 'letter'.

anal /ay-n'l/ • adj. having to do with the anus.

analgesic /an-uhl-jee-zik/ • n. a pain-relieving drug.
– ORIGIN from Greek *an-* 'not' + *algeein* 'feel pain'.

analogous /uh-nal-uh-guhss/ • adj. alike or comparable in some ways.
– ORIGIN Greek *analogos* 'proportionate'.

analogue /an-uh-log/ (US also **analog**) • n. a person or thing that is like or comparable to another. • adj. (also **analog**) having to do with electronic information or signals represented by a varying physical effect (e.g. voltage, the position of a pointer, etc.) rather than by a digital display.

analogy /uh-nal-uh-ji/ • n. (pl. **analogies**) **1** a way of explaining something by comparing it to something else. **2** a partial similarity.
– DERIVATIVES **analogical** adj.

analyse (US **analyze**) • v. (**analyses**, **analysing**, **analysed**; US **analyzes**, **analyzing**, **analyzed**) **1** examine (something) in detail so as to explain it or to find out its structure or composition. **2** psychoanalyse.

analysis /uh-nal-i-siss/ • n. (pl. **analyses** /uh-nal-i-seez/) **1** a detailed examination of the elements or structure of something. **2** the separation of something into its component parts. **3** psychoanalysis.
– ORIGIN Greek *analuein* 'unloose'.

analyst • n. a person who carries out analysis.

analytical (also **analytic**) • adj. having to do with analysis.
– DERIVATIVES **analytically** adv.

analyze • v. US = **ANALYSE**.

anarchic /uh-nar-kik/ • adj. with no controlling rules or principles.

anarchist • n. a person who believes that government should be abolished and that society should be organized on a cooperative basis.
– DERIVATIVES **anarchism** n. **anarchistic** adj.

anarchy • n. a state of disorder due to lack of government or control.
– ORIGIN from Greek *an-* 'without' + *arkhos* 'ruler'.

anathema /uh-na-thuh-muh/ • n. something that one hates: *racism was anathema to her.*
– ORIGIN Greek, 'thing devoted to evil'.

anathematize /uh-na-thuh-muh-tyz/ (also **anathematise**) • v. (**anathematizes**, **anathematizing**, **anathematized**) curse; condemn.

> **Anatolia** E
> /an-uh-toh-li-uh/ the western peninsula of Asia, bounded by the Black Sea, the Aegean, and the Mediterranean, that forms the greater part of Turkey.

anatomical /an-uh-tom-i-k'l/ • adj. having to do with bodily structure or the study of it.
– DERIVATIVES **anatomically** adv.

anatomy • n. (pl. **anatomies**) **1** the scientific study of bodily structure. **2** the bodily structure of a person, animal, or plant. **3** a detailed examination or analysis.
– DERIVATIVES **anatomist** n.
– ORIGIN from Greek *ana-* 'up' + *tomia* 'cutting'.

ANC • abbrev. African National Congress.

-ance • suffix forming nouns referring to: **1** a quality or state: *perseverance.* **2** an action: *utterance.*
– ORIGIN French.

ancestor • n. **1** a person from whom one is descended. **2** something from which a later species or version has developed.
– DERIVATIVES **ancestress** n.
– ORIGIN Latin *antecessor.*

ancestral /an-sess-truhl/ • adj. having to do with or inherited from an ancestor or ancestors: *their ancestral home.*

ancestry • n. (pl. **ancestries**) a person's ancestors or ethnic origins.

anchor • n. a heavy metal object used to moor a ship to the sea bottom. • v. **1** moor with an anchor. **2** fix firmly in position.
– ORIGIN Greek *ankura.*

> **Anchorage** E
> the largest city in Alaska.

anchorage • n. a place where ships may anchor safely.

anchorite /ang-kuh-ryt/ • n. hist. a person who lives apart from others for religious reasons.
– ORIGIN Greek *anakhōrein* 'retire'.

anchorman (or **anchorwoman**) • n. a person who presents a live television or radio programme and coordinates the contributions of participants.

anchovy /an-chuh-vi/ • n. (pl. **anchovies**) a small fish of the herring family, with a strong flavour.
– ORIGIN Spanish and Portuguese *anchova.*

ancien régime /on-si-an ray-*zheem*/ • n. (pl. **anciens régimes** /on-si-an ray-*zheem*/) a political or social system that has been replaced by a more modern one.
– ORIGIN French, 'old rule'.

ancient • adj. **1** belonging to the very distant past. **2** very old. • pl. n. (**the ancients**) the people of ancient times.
– DERIVATIVES **anciently** adv.
– ORIGIN Old French *ancien.*

ancillary /an-sil-luh-ri/ • adj. **1** providing support to the main activities of an organization. **2** additional; extra: *laboratories with ancillary rooms.*
– ORIGIN Latin *ancilla* 'female servant'.

-ancy • suffix forming nouns referring to a quality or state: *expectancy.*
– ORIGIN Latin *-antia.*

and • conj. **1** used to connect words, clauses, or sentences. **2** used to connect two identical words to show gradual change, continuing action, or great extent: *getting better and better.* **3** (connecting two numbers) plus. **4** informal (after a verb) to: *try and do it.*
– ORIGIN Old English.

> **Andalusia** E
> /an-duh-loo-si-uh/ the southernmost region of Spain; capital, Seville.

Andaman and Nicobar Islands E
/an-duh-muhn, **nik**-uh-bar/ two groups of islands in the Bay of Bengal, constituting a Union Territory in India; capital, Port Blair.

andante /an-**dan**-tay/ • adv. & adj. Music in a moderately slow tempo.
– ORIGIN Italian, 'going'.

Andersen, E
Hans Christian (1805–75), Danish author, famous for his fairy tales, such as 'The Ugly Duckling' and 'The Little Match Girl'.

Anderson[1], E
Elizabeth Garrett (1836–1917), English physician, the first English woman doctor and the first woman elected to the BMA (1873).

Anderson[2], E
Marian (1902–93), American operatic contralto, the first black singer to perform at the New York Metropolitan Opera (1955).

Andes E
/**an**-deez/ a major mountain system running the length of the Pacific coast of South America.

Andhra Pradesh E
/ahn-druh pruh-**desh**/ a state in SE India, on the Bay of Bengal; capital, Hyderabad.

Andorra E
/an-**dor**-ruh/ a small autonomous principality in the southern Pyrenees, between France and Spain; capital, Andorra la Vella.
– DERIVATIVES **Andorran** adj. & n.

Andrew, Prince, E
Andrew Albert Christian Edward, Duke of York (b.1960), second son of Elizabeth II.

Andrew, St, E
an Apostle, patron saint of Scotland and Russia. Feast day, 30 November.

Androcles E
/**an**-druh-kleez/ a runaway slave in a Roman legend, who extracted a thorn from the paw of a lion, which later refrained from attacking him when he faced it in the arena.

androgynous /an-**dro**-ji-nuhss/ • adj. partly male and partly female.
– DERIVATIVES **androgyny** n.
– ORIGIN from Greek *anēr* 'man' + *gunē* 'woman'.

android /an-droyd/ • n. (in science fiction) a robot with a human appearance.
– ORIGIN from Greek *anēr* 'man'.

Andromeda E
/an-**drom**-i-duh/ Gk Myth. an Ethiopian princess, who was fastened to a rock as a sacrifice to a sea monster, and was rescued by Perseus.

Andropov E
/an-**drop**-off/ , Yuri (Vladimirovich) (1914–84), Soviet statesman, General Secretary of the Communist Party of the USSR 1982–4 and President 1983–4. He initiated reforms carried through by his successor, Mikhail Gorbachev.

anecdotal /an-ik-**doh**-t'l/ • adj. (of a story) not necessarily true because not backed up by facts.

anecdote /an-ik-doht/ • n. a short entertaining story about a real incident or person.
– ORIGIN Greek *anekdota* 'things unpublished'.

anemia • n. US = ANAEMIA.

anemic • adj. US = ANAEMIC.

anemometer /an-i-**mom**-i-ter/ • n. an instrument for measuring the speed of the wind.
– ORIGIN Greek *anemos* 'wind'.

anemone /uh-**nem**-uh-ni/ • n. a plant having brightly coloured flowers with dark centres.
– ORIGIN Greek, 'windflower'.

aneroid barometer /an-uh-royd/ • n. a barometer that measures air pressure by the action of air on the flexible lid of a box containing a vacuum.
– ORIGIN from Greek *a-* 'without' + *nēros* 'water'.

anesthetic etc. • n. US = ANAESTHETIC etc.

aneurysm /an-yuu-ri-z'm/ (also **aneurism**) • n. Med. an excessive swelling of the wall of an artery.
– ORIGIN Greek *aneurusma* 'widening'.

anew • adv. **1** in a new or different way. **2** once more; again.

angel • n. **1** a spiritual being acting as an attendant or messenger of God, pictured as being of human form with wings. **2** a very beautiful, kind, or good person. **3** informal a person who gives financial backing to a theatrical production.
– ORIGIN Greek *angelos* 'messenger'.

Angel Falls E
a waterfall in SE Venezuela, at 978 m (3,210 ft) the highest in the world.

angelfish • n. a tropical fish with large fins, often vividly coloured or patterned.

angelic • adj. **1** having to do with angels. **2** very beautiful, innocent, or kind.

angelica /an-**jel**-li-kuh/ • n. the stalks of a sweet-smelling plant, preserved in sugar and used in cake decoration.
– ORIGIN from Latin *herba angelica* 'angelic herb'.

Angelico E
/an-**jel**-i-koh/ , Fra (*c.*1400–55), Italian painter and Dominican friar, whose works include the frescoes in the convent of San Marco, Florence.

Angelou E
/**an**-juh-loo/ , Maya (b.1928), American novelist and poet, known especially for the first volume of her autobiography, *I Know Why the Caged Bird Sings*.

angelus /an-juh-luhss/ • n. a Roman Catholic prayer commemorating the Incarnation of Jesus, said at morning, noon, and sunset.
– ORIGIN from Latin *Angelus domini* 'the angel of the Lord'.

anger • n. a strong feeling of extreme displeasure. • v. (**angers**, **angering**, **angered**) make angry.
– ORIGIN Old Norse, 'grief'.

angina /an-jy-nuh/ (also **angina pectoris** /**pek**-tuh-riss/) • n. severe pain in the chest caused by an inadequate supply of blood to the heart.
– ORIGIN from Greek *ankhonē* 'strangling' + Latin *pectoris* 'of the chest'.

a

angiosperm /an-ji-oh-sperm/ ● **n.** a plant of a large group that have flowers and produce seeds enclosed in a carpel, including herbaceous plants, shrubs, grasses, and most trees.

Angkor E
/ang-kor/ the capital of the ancient kingdom of Khmer in NW Cambodia, noted for its temples.

Angle ● **n.** a member of an ancient Germanic people who founded kingdoms in the north and east of England in the 5th century AD.
– ORIGIN Latin *Anglus* 'inhabitant of *Angul*' (in northern Germany).

angle[1] ● **n.** **1** the space between two lines or surfaces that meet. **2** a position from which something is viewed: *he was filmed from a variety of camera angles.* **3** a way of considering something: *a fresh angle on life.* ● **v.** (**angles, angling, angled**) **1** move or place in a slanting position. **2** present (information) from a particular point of view.
– ORIGIN Latin *angulus* 'corner'.

angle[2] ● **v.** (**angles, angling, angled**) **1** fish with a rod and line. **2** try to get something by indirectly prompting someone to offer it: *she was angling for sympathy.*
– DERIVATIVES **angler** n.
– ORIGIN Old English.

Anglesey E
/ang-g'l-si/ an island and county of NW Wales. Welsh name **Ynys Môn**.

Anglican ● **adj.** relating to the Church of England or any Church associated with it. ● **n.** a member of the Anglican Church.
– DERIVATIVES **Anglicanism** n.
– ORIGIN Latin *Anglicanus*.

Anglicism ● **n.** a word or phrase that is peculiar to British English.

anglicize (also **anglicise**) ● **v.** (**anglicizes, anglicizing, anglicized**) make English in form or character.
– DERIVATIVES **anglicization** (also **anglicisation**) n.

Anglo- ● **comb. form** **1** English: *Anglophile.* **2** English or British and ...: *Anglo-Indian.*
– ORIGIN Latin *Anglus* 'English'.

Anglo-Catholic ● **n.** a member of a section of the Church of England which is close to Catholicism in its beliefs and worship.

Anglo-Indian ● **adj.** **1** having to do with both Britain and India. **2** of mixed British and Indian parentage. **3** hist. of British descent or birth but having lived long in India. ● **n.** an Anglo-Indian person.

Anglo-Irish ● **adj.** **1** having to do with both Britain and Ireland. **2** of mixed English and Irish parentage. **3** of English descent but born or living in Ireland.

Anglophile ● **n.** a person who greatly admires England or Britain.

Anglo-Saxon ● **n.** **1** a Germanic inhabitant of England between the 5th century and the Norman Conquest. **2** a person of English descent. **3** the Old English language.

Angola E
/ang-goh-luh/ a republic on the west coast of southern Africa; capital, Luanda.
– DERIVATIVES **Angolan** adj. & n.

angora /ang-gor-uh/ ● **n.** **1** a cat, goat, or rabbit of a long-haired breed. **2** fabric made from the hair of the angora goat or rabbit.
– ORIGIN from *Angora* (former name for **Ankara**).

angostura /ang-guh-styoor-uh/ ● **n.** the bitter bark of a South American tree, used as a flavouring.
– ORIGIN from *Angostura* (now Ciudad Bolívar) in Venezuela.

angry ● **adj.** (**angrier, angriest**) **1** feeling or showing anger. **2** (of a wound or sore) red and inflamed.
– DERIVATIVES **angrily** adv.

angst /angst/ ● **n.** a strong feeling of anxiety about life in general.
– ORIGIN German, 'fear'.

angstrom /ang-struhm/ ● **n.** Physics a unit of length equal to one hundred-millionth of a centimetre.
– ORIGIN named after the Swedish physicist A. J. *Ångström* (1814–74).

Anguilla E
/ang-gwil-luh/ the most northerly of the Leeward Islands in the Caribbean; capital, The Valley.
– DERIVATIVES **Anguillan** adj. & n.

anguish ● **n.** severe mental or physical pain or suffering.
– DERIVATIVES **anguished** adj.
– ORIGIN Latin *angustia* 'tightness'.

angular /ang-gyuu-ler/ ● **adj.** **1** having angles or sharp corners. **2** lean and bony. **3** placed or directed at an angle. **4** Physics measured by means of an angle.
– DERIVATIVES **angularity** n.

Angus E
/ang-guhss/ an administrative region of NE Scotland, formerly known as Forfarshire.

anhydrous /an-hy-druhss/ ● **adj.** Chem. containing no water.
– ORIGIN from Greek *an-* 'without' + *hudōr* 'water'.

aniline /an-i-leen/ ● **n.** an oily liquid found in coal tar, used in making dyes, drugs, and plastics.
– ORIGIN Arabic, 'indigo'.

animadvert /an-im-uhd-vert/ ● **v.** (**animadvert on/upon/against**) formal speak out against; criticize.
– DERIVATIVES **animadversion** n.
– ORIGIN from Latin *animus* 'mind' + *advertere* 'to turn'.

animal ● **n.** **1** a living organism that can move about of its own accord and has specialized sense organs and nervous system. **2** a mammal, as opposed to a bird, reptile, fish, or insect. **3** a very cruel, violent, or uncivilized person. **5** a particular type of person or thing: *a political animal.* ● **adj.** **1** having to do with animals. **2** physical rather than spiritual or intellectual: *animal lust.*
– ORIGIN Latin *animalis* 'having breath'.

animality ● **n.** physical and instinctive human behaviour, like that of animals.

animate ● **v.** /an-i-mayt/ (**animates, animating, animated**) **1** bring life or vigour to. **2** make (drawings or models) into an animated film. ● **adj.** /an-i-muht/ alive; having life.
– DERIVATIVES **animator** n.
– ORIGIN Latin *anima* 'life, soul'.

animated • adj. **1** lively. **2** (of a film) made using animation.
– DERIVATIVES **animatedly** adv.

animation • n. **1** liveliness or vigour. **2** the technique of filming a sequence of drawings or positions of models to give the appearance of movement. **3** (also **computer animation**) the creation of moving images by means of a computer.

animism /an-i-mi-z'm/ • n. the belief that all things in nature, such as plants, winds, and hills, have a soul.
– DERIVATIVES **animist** n. **animistic** adj.
– ORIGIN Latin *anima* 'life, soul'.

animosity /an-i-moss-i-ti/ • n. (pl. **animosities**) hatred or strong dislike.
– ORIGIN Latin *animositas*.

animus /an-i-muhss/ • n. hatred or strong dislike.
– ORIGIN Latin, 'spirit, mind'.

anion /an-I-uhn/ • n. Chem. an ion with a negative charge. Opp. **CATION**.
– ORIGIN from **ANODE** + **ION**.

aniseed • n. the seed of the plant anise, used as a flavouring.
– ORIGIN Greek *anison* 'anise, dill'.

Anjou E
/on-*zhoo*/ a former province of western France, on the river Loire.

Ankara E
/ang-kuh-ruh/ the capital of Turkey.

ankle • n. **1** the joint connecting the foot with the leg. **2** the narrow part of the leg between this joint and the calf.
– ORIGIN Old English.

anklet • n. a chain or band worn round the ankle.

annals /an-nuhlz/ • pl. n. a historical record of events year by year.
– ORIGIN from Latin *annales libri* 'yearly books'.

Annan E
/an-an, an-nuhn/, Kofi (b.1938), Ghanaian diplomat, Secretary General of the United Nations since 1997.

Annapurna E
/an-nuh-per-nuh/ a ridge of the Himalayas, in north central Nepal.

Anne E
(1665–1714), queen of England and Scotland (known as Great Britain from 1707) and Ireland 1702–14. She was the last of the Stuart monarchs and by the Act of Settlement (1701) the throne passed to the House of Hanover on her death.

Anne, Princess, E
Anne Elizabeth Alice Louise, the Princess Royal (b.1950), daughter of Elizabeth II.

anneal /uh-neel/ • v. heat (metal or glass) and allow it to cool slowly, so as to toughen it.
– ORIGIN Old English, 'set on fire'.

Anne Boleyn E
see **BOLEYN**.

annelid /an-ni-lid/ • n. a worm with a body made up of segments, such as an earthworm.
– ORIGIN Latin *annelus* 'small ring'.

Anne of Cleves E
/kleevz/ (1515–57), fourth wife of Henry VIII. The marriage, arranged for political purposes, was dissolved after only six months.

Anne, St, E
traditionally the mother of the Virgin Mary, patron saint of Brittany and the province of Quebec in Canada. Feast day, 26 July.

annex • v. /an-neks/ **1** seize (territory) and add it to one's own. **2** add (something) to something more important. • n. /an-neks/ (esp. Brit. also **annexe**) (pl. **annexes**) **1** a building attached or near to a main building, used for additional space. **2** an addition to a document.
– DERIVATIVES **annexation** n.
– ORIGIN Latin *annectere* 'connect'.

annihilate /uh-ny-i-layt/ • v. (**annihilates, annihilating, annihilated**) **1** destroy completely. **2** informal defeat completely.
– DERIVATIVES **annihilation** n.
– ORIGIN Latin *annihilare* 'reduce to nothing'.

anniversary • n. (pl. **anniversaries**) the date on which an event took place in a previous year.
– ORIGIN Latin *anniversarius* 'returning yearly'.

Anno Domini /an-noh dom-i-ny/ • adv. full form of **AD**.

annotate /an-nuh-tayt/ • v. (**annotates, annotating, annotated**) add explanatory notes to.
– DERIVATIVES **annotation** n.
– ORIGIN Latin *annotare* 'to mark'.

announce • v. (**announces, announcing, announced**) **1** make a public statement about. **2** be a sign of: *lilies announce the arrival of summer.*
– DERIVATIVES **announcer** n.
– ORIGIN Latin *annuntiare*.

announcement • n. **1** a public statement. **2** the action of announcing.

annoy • v. **1** make slightly angry. **2** be troublesome to; harass.
– DERIVATIVES **annoyance** n.
– ORIGIN from Latin *mihi in odio est* 'it is hateful to me'.

annual • adj. **1** happening once a year. **2** calculated over or covering a year: *his annual income.* **3** (of a plant) living for a year or less. • n. a book published once a year under the same title but with different contents.
– DERIVATIVES **annually** adv.
– ORIGIN Latin *annus* 'year'.

annuity /uh-nyoo-i-ti/ • n. (pl. **annuities**) a fixed sum of money paid to someone each year.
– ORIGIN Latin *annuitas*.

annul /uh-nul/ • v. (**annuls, annulling, annulled**) declare (a law, marriage, or other legal contract) to be no longer valid.
– DERIVATIVES **annulment** n.
– ORIGIN Latin *annullare*.

annular /an-yuu-ler/ • adj. tech. ring-shaped.
– ORIGIN Latin *anulus* 'small ring'.

Annunciation • n. (**the Annunciation**) the announcement by the angel Gabriel to the Virgin Mary that she was to be the mother of Christ.

anode /an-ohd/ • n. an electrode with a positive charge. Opp. **CATHODE**.

a

– ORIGIN Greek *anodos* 'way up'.

anodized /an-uh-dyzd/ (also **anodised**) ● **adj.** (of metal) coated with a protective layer by electrolysis.

anodyne /an-uh-dyn/ ● **adj.** unlikely to cause offence or disagreement; bland. ● **n.** a pain-killing drug or medicine.
– ORIGIN Greek *anōdunos* 'painless'.

anoint ● **v.** smear or rub with oil, especially as part of a religious ceremony.
– ORIGIN Old French *enoindre*.

anomalous ● **adj.** differing from what is standard or normal.
– ORIGIN from Greek *an-* 'not' + *homalos* 'even'.

anomaly /uh-nom-uh-li/ ● **n.** (pl. **anomalies**) something that departs from what is standard or normal.

anomie /an-uh-mi/ ● **n.** lack of the usual standards of good behaviour.
– ORIGIN Greek *anomos* 'lawless'.

anon ● **adv.** archaic or informal soon; shortly.
– ORIGIN Old English, 'in or into one'.

anonymity /an-uh-nim-iti/ ● **n.** the state of being anonymous.

anonymous ● **adj.** **1** with a name that is not known or not made known. **2** having no outstanding or individual features: *her anonymous flat.*
– DERIVATIVES **anonymously** adv.
– ORIGIN Greek *anōnumos* 'nameless'.

anorak ● **n.** a waterproof jacket with a hood.
– ORIGIN Eskimo.

anorexia /an-uh-rek-si-uh/ (also **anorexia nervosa** /ner-voh-suh/) ● **n.** a psychological disorder in which a person refuses to eat because they are afraid of becoming fat.
– ORIGIN from Greek *an-* 'without' + *orexis* 'appetite'.

anorexic (also **anorectic**) ● **adj.** having to do with anorexia. ● **n.** a person with anorexia.

another ● **det. & pron.** **1** one more. **2** different from the one already mentioned.

Anouilh E
/on-wee/, Jean (1910–87), French dramatist, best known for his reworking of the Greek myth of Antigone in *Antigone*.

Anselm, St E
/an-selm/ (*c.*1033–1109), Italian-born philosopher and theologian, Archbishop of Canterbury 1093–1109. Feast day, 21 April.

answer ● **n.** **1** something said or written in reaction to a question or statement. **2** the solution to a problem. ● **v.** (**answers, answering, answered**) **1** give an answer. **2** (**answer back**) give a cheeky reply. **3** (**answer to/for**) be responsible to (someone) or for (something). **4** meet (a need).
– ORIGIN Old English.

answerable ● **adj.** (**answerable to/for**) responsible to or for.

answering machine ● **n.** a machine which gives a recorded answer to a telephone call and can record a message from the caller.

ant ● **n.** a small insect, usually wingless, living with many others in a highly organized group.
– ORIGIN Old English.

-ant ● **suffix** **1** (forming adjectives) having a quality: *arrogant.* **2** (forming nouns) performing a function: *deodorant.*
– ORIGIN Latin.

antacid /an-tass-id/ ● **adj.** (of a medicine) reducing excess acid in the stomach.

antagonism /an-tag-uh-ni-z'm/ ● **n.** open hostility or opposition.

antagonist ● **n.** an opponent or enemy.
– DERIVATIVES **antagonistic** adj.
– ORIGIN Greek *antagōnizesthai* 'struggle against'.

antagonize (also **antagonise**) ● **v.** (**antagonizes, antagonizing, antagonized**) make (someone) hostile.

Antananarivo E
/an-tuh-nan-uh-ree-voh/ the capital of Madagascar.

Antarctic ● **adj.** relating to Antarctica.
– ORIGIN Greek *antarktikos* 'opposite to the north'.

Antarctica E
a continent around the South Pole, situated mainly within the Antarctic Circle and almost entirely covered by ice sheets.

Antarctic Circle E
the parallel of latitude 66° 33′ south of the equator.

Antarctic Ocean E
the sea surrounding Antarctica, consisting of parts of the South Atlantic, the South Pacific, and the southern Indian Ocean. Also called **SOUTHERN OCEAN**.

ante /an-ti/ ● **n.** a stake put up by a player in poker or brag before receiving cards.
– PHRASES **up** (or **raise**) **the ante** increase what is at stake.
– ORIGIN Latin, 'before'.

ante- ● **prefix** before; preceding: *antecedent.*

anteater ● **n.** a mammal with a long snout, feeding on ants and termites.

antecedent /an-ti-see-duhnt/ ● **n.** **1** a thing that occurs or exists before another. **2** (**antecedents**) a person's ancestors and background. **3** Grammar an earlier word, phrase, or clause to which a following pronoun refers back. ● **adj.** coming before in time or order.
– ORIGIN Latin *antecedere* 'go before'.

antedate ● **v.** (**antedates, antedating, antedated**) **1** come before in time. **2** indicate that (a document or event) belongs to an earlier date.

antediluvian /an-ti-di-loo-vi-uhn/ ● **adj.** **1** belonging to the time before the biblical Flood. **2** esp. humorous ridiculously old-fashioned.
– ORIGIN from **ANTE-** + Latin *diluvium* 'deluge'.

antelope ● **n.** a swift deer-like animal with long horns, found in Africa and Asia.
– ORIGIN Greek *antholops*.

antenatal ● **adj.** before birth; during or relating to pregnancy.

antenna /an-ten-nuh/ ● **n.** (pl. **antennae** /an-ten-nee/) **1** each of a pair of long, thin growths on the heads of some insects, shellfish, etc., used for feeling. **2** (pl. also **antennas**) an aerial.
– ORIGIN Latin *antemna* 'yard' (of a ship's mast).

antepenultimate ● **adj.** last but two in a series.

anterior • adj. tech. at or nearer the front. Opp. **POSTERIOR**.
– ORIGIN Latin.

ante-room • n. a small room leading to a more important one.

anthem • n. **1** an uplifting song chosen by a country to express patriotic feelings. **2** a musical setting of a religious text to be sung by a choir during a church service.
– ORIGIN Latin *antiphona* 'antiphon'.

anther • n. the part of a flower's stamen that contains the pollen.
– ORIGIN Greek *anthos* 'flower'.

anthill • n. a mound-shaped nest built by ants or termites.

anthology • n. (pl. **anthologies**) a collection of poems or other pieces of writing or music.
– ORIGIN Greek *anthos* 'flower'.

Anthony, St E
(also **Antony**) (*c.*251–356), Egyptian hermit, the founder of monasticism. Feast day, 17 January.

anthracite /an-thruh-syt/ • n. hard coal that burns with little flame and smoke.
– ORIGIN Greek *anthrax* 'coal'.

anthrax /an-thraks/ • n. a serious disease of sheep and cattle, able to be transmitted to humans.
– ORIGIN Greek, 'coal, boil'.

anthropoid • adj. having to do with apes that are like humans in form, such as gorillas or chimpanzees.
– ORIGIN Greek *anthrōpos* 'human being'.

anthropology /an-thruh-**pol**-uh-ji/ • n. the study of human origins, societies, and cultures.
DERIVATIVES **anthropological** adj. **anthropologist** n.
– ORIGIN Greek *anthrōpos* 'human being'.

anthropomorphic /an-thruh-puh-**mor**-fik/ • adj. (of a god, animal or object) treated as if having human feelings.

anti- • prefix **1** opposed to; against: *antisocial*. **2** preventing or relieving: *antibiotic*. **3** the opposite of: *anticlimax*.
– ORIGIN Greek.

antibiotic • n. a medicine that destroys bacteria or slows down their growth.
– ORIGIN from Greek *biōtikos* 'fit for life'.

antibody • n. (pl. **antibodies**) a protein produced in the blood in reaction to harmful substances, which it then destroys.

Antichrist • n. an enemy of Christ believed by the early Church to appear before the end of the world.

anticipate • v. (**anticipates**, **anticipating**, **anticipated**) **1** be aware of (a future event) and prepare for it. **2** expect. **3** look forward to. **4** do something earlier than (someone else).
– DERIVATIVES **anticipatory** adj.
– ORIGIN Latin *anticipare*.

anticipation • n. the action of anticipating; expectation.

anticlimax • n. a disappointing end to an exciting series of events.
– DERIVATIVES **anticlimactic** adj.

anticline • n. a land formation in which strata are folded so as to slope down on opposite sides of a ridge.
– ORIGIN from Greek *klinein* 'lean'.

anticlockwise • adv. & adj. Brit. in the opposite direction to the way in which the hands of a clock move round.

antics • pl. n. foolish, outrageous, or amusing behaviour.
– ORIGIN Italian *antico* 'antique'.

anticyclone • n. an area of high atmospheric pressure around which air slowly circulates, usually resulting in calm, fine weather.

antidote • n. **1** a medicine taken to counteract a poison. **2** a thing that counteracts something unpleasant: *laughter is a good antidote to stress*.
– ORIGIN from Greek *didonai* 'give'.

antifreeze • n. a liquid added to water to prevent it from freezing, used in the radiator of a motor vehicle.

antigen /an-ti-jen/ • n. a harmful substance which causes the body to produce antibodies.

Antigone E
/an-tig-uh-ni/ Gk Myth. the daughter of Jocasta by her son Oedipus; she is the subject of a tragedy by Sophocles.

Antigua and Barbuda E
/an-tee-guh, bar-**boo**-duh/ a country consisting of three islands (Antigua, Barbuda, and Redonda) in the Leeward Islands in the Eastern Caribbean; capital, St John's (on Antigua).
– DERIVATIVES **Antiguan** adj. & n.

anti-hero (or **anti-heroine**) • n. a central character in a story, film, or play who lacks typical heroic qualities.

antihistamine • n. a drug that counteracts the effects of histamine, used in treating allergies.

Antilles E
/an-til-leez/ a group of islands, forming the greater part of the West Indies. See also **GREATER ANTILLES**, **LESSER ANTILLES**, **NETHERLANDS ANTILLES**.

antilogarithm • n. the number of which a given number is the logarithm.

antimacassar /an-ti-muh-**kass**-er/ • n. a piece of cloth put over the back of a chair to protect it from grease and dirt.
– ORIGIN from **ANTI-** + *Macassar*, a kind of hair oil formerly used by men.

antimatter • n. matter consisting of the antiparticles of the particles making up normal matter.

antimony /an-ti-muh-ni/ • n. a brittle silvery-white metallic element.
– ORIGIN Latin *antimonium*.

Antioch E
/an-ti-ok/ a city in southern Turkey, formerly the capital of ancient Syria.

antioxidant • n. a substance that counteracts oxidation.

antiparticle • n. a subatomic particle with the same mass as a corresponding particle but an opposite electric charge or magnetic effect.

antipathy /an-**ti**-puh-thi/ • n. (pl. **antipathies**) a strong feeling of dislike.
– DERIVATIVES **antipathetic** adj.
– ORIGIN from Greek *anti-* 'against' + *pathos* 'feeling'.

a

antiperspirant • n. a substance applied to the skin to prevent or reduce sweating.

antiphon /an-ti-fuhn/ • n. a short chant sung before or after a psalm or canticle.
– ORIGIN Greek *antiphōna* 'harmonies'.

antiphonal /an-tif-fuh-n'l/ • adj. sung or recited alternately between two groups.

Antipodes /an-**ti**-puh-deez/ • pl. n. (**the Antipodes**) Australia and New Zealand (because situated on the opposite side of the earth from Europe).
– DERIVATIVES **Antipodean** adj. & n.
– ORIGIN Greek, 'having the feet opposite'.

antiquarian /an-ti-**kwair**-i-uhn/ • adj. relating to the collection or study of antiques, rare books, or antiquities. • n. (also **antiquary**) a person who studies or collects antiquarian items.

antiquated • adj. old-fashioned or outdated.

antique • n. a decorative object or piece of furniture that is valuable because of its age. • adj. **1** valuable because of its age. **2** old-fashioned or outdated.
– ORIGIN Latin *antiquus* 'former, ancient'.

antiquity • n. (pl. **antiquities**) **1** the distant past, especially before the Middle Ages. **2** an object from the distant past. **3** great age.

antirrhinum /an-ti-**ry**-nuhm/ • n. (pl. **antirrhinums**) a snapdragon.
– ORIGIN from Greek *anti-* 'imitating' + *rhis* 'nose'.

anti-Semitism • n. hostility to or prejudice against Jews.
– DERIVATIVES **anti-Semite** n. **anti-Semitic** adj.

antiseptic • adj. preventing the growth of micro-organisms that cause disease or infection. • n. an antiseptic substance.

antisocial • adj. **1** acting in a way that conflicts with accepted behaviour and causes annoyance. **2** not wanting to mix with other people.

antithesis /an-ti-thuh-siss/ • n. (pl. **antitheses** /an-ti-thuh-seez/) **1** a person or thing that is the direct opposite of another. **2** the putting together of contrasting ideas or words to produce an effect in writing or speaking.
– ORIGIN Greek *antitithenai* 'set against'.

antithetical /an-ti-**thet**-i-k'l/ • adj. opposed to or incompatible with each other.

antivivisectionist • n. a person who is opposed to using live animals for scientific research.

antler • n. each of a pair of branched horns on the head of an adult male deer.
– ORIGIN Old French *antoillier*.

Antony, E
Mark (*c.*83–30 BC; Latin name *Marcus Antonius*), Roman general. He ruled the Roman empire with Octavian and Lepidus from 43 BC, during which time he began a relationship with Cleopatra. Quarrels with Octavian led to his defeat at the battle of Actium and to his suicide.

Antony, St E
see **ANTHONY, ST**.

antonym /an-tuh-nim/ • n. a word opposite in meaning to another.
– ORIGIN from Greek *anti-* 'against' + *onoma* 'a name'.

Antrim E
one of the Six Counties of Northern Ireland.

Antwerp E
/an-twerp/ a port in northern Belgium.

anus /ay-nuhss/ • n. the opening at the end of the digestive system through which solid waste leaves the body.
– ORIGIN Latin.

anvil • n. an iron block on which metal can be hammered and shaped.
– ORIGIN Old English.

anxiety • n. (pl. **anxieties**) an anxious feeling or state.

anxious • adj. **1** experiencing worry or unease. **2** very eager: *she was anxious to leave.*
– DERIVATIVES **anxiously** adv.
– ORIGIN Latin *anxius*.

any • det. & pron. **1** one or some, no matter how much or how many. **2** whichever or whatever one chooses. • adv. at all: *he wasn't any good at football.*
– ORIGIN Old English.

anybody • pron. anyone.

anyhow • adv. **1** anyway. **2** in a careless or disorderly way.

anyone • pron. any person or people.

anything • pron. a thing of any kind, no matter what.
– PHRASES **anything but** not at all.

anyway • adv. **1** used to emphasize something just said or change the subject. **2** nevertheless.

anywhere • adv. in or to any place. • pron. any place.

Anzus E
/an-zuhss/ an alliance between Australia, New Zealand, and the US, established in 1951 to protect those countries in the Pacific area from armed attack.

Aorangi E
/ow-rang-i/ Maori name for Mount Cook (see **COOK, MOUNT**).

aorta /ay-or-tuh/ • n. the main artery supplying blood from the heart to the rest of the body.
– ORIGIN Greek *aortē*.

apace • adv. literary quickly.

Apache /uh-pa-chi/ • n. (pl. **Apache** or **Apaches**) a member of an American Indian people living chiefly in New Mexico and Arizona.
– ORIGIN prob. from an American Indian word meaning 'enemy'.

apart • adv. **1** separated by a distance. **2** into pieces.
– PHRASES **apart from 1** except for. **2** as well as.
– ORIGIN from Latin *a parte* 'at the side'.

apartheid /uh-par-tayt/ • n. the official system of segregation or discrimination on racial grounds formerly in force in South Africa.
– ORIGIN Afrikaans, 'separateness'.

apartment • n. **1** esp. N. Amer. a flat. **2** (**apartments**) a private set of rooms in a very large house.
– ORIGIN French *appartement*.

apathetic • adj. not interested or enthusiastic.

apathy /ap-uh-thi/ ● **n.** lack of interest or enthusiasm.
– ORIGIN Greek *apathēs* 'without feeling'.

apatosaurus /uh-pa-tuh-**sor**-uhss/ ● **n.** a huge plant-eating dinosaur with a long neck and tail. Also called **BRONTOSAURUS**.
– ORIGIN from Greek *apatē* 'deceit' + *sauros* 'lizard'.

ape ● **n.** an animal like a monkey but without a tail, such as a chimpanzee or gorilla. ● **v.** (**apes, aping, aped**) imitate.
– ORIGIN Old English.

Apennines [E]
/**ap**-in-nynz/ a mountain range running down the length of Italy.

aperitif /uh-pe-ri-teef, uh-pe-ri-**teef**/ ● **n.** an alcoholic drink taken before a meal to stimulate the appetite.
– ORIGIN French.

aperture /a-per-cher/ ● **n. 1** an opening, hole, or gap. **2** the variable opening by which light enters a camera.
– ORIGIN Latin *apertura*.

apex /ay-peks/ ● **n.** (pl. **apexes** or **apices** /ay-pi-seez/) the top or highest point.
– ORIGIN Latin, 'peak, tip'.

aphelion /ap-**hee**-li-uhn/ ● **n.** (pl. **aphelia** /ap-**hee**-li-uh/) the point in a planet's orbit at which it is furthest from the sun. Opp. **PERIHELION**.
– ORIGIN from Greek *aph' hēlion* 'from the sun'.

aphid /ay-fid/ ● **n.** a greenfly or similar small insect feeding on the sap of plants.
– ORIGIN Greek *aphis*.

aphorism /af-uh-ri-z'm/ ● **n.** a short witty remark which contains a general truth.
– ORIGIN Greek *aphorismos* 'definition'.

aphrodisiac /af-ruh-**diz**-i-ak/ ● **n.** a food, drink, or drug that arouses sexual desire.
– ORIGIN from **APHRODITE**.

Aphrodite [E]
/af-ruh-**dy**-ti/ the Greek goddess of beauty, fertility, and sexual love. Roman equivalent **VENUS**[1].

Apia [E]
/ap-i-uh/ the capital of Western Samoa.

apiary /ay-pee-uh-ri/ ● **n.** (pl. **apiaries**) a place where bees are kept.
– DERIVATIVES **apiarist** n.
– ORIGIN Latin *apis* 'bee'.

apical /ay-pi-k'l/ ● **adj.** tech. relating to or forming an apex.

apices pl. of **APEX**.

apiece ● **adv.** to, for, or by each one: *tickets were a pound apiece.*

aplenty ● **adj.** in abundance: *he has work aplenty.*

aplomb /uh-**plom**/ ● **n.** calm self-confidence.
– ORIGIN from French *à plomb* 'straight as a plumb line'.

apocalypse /uh-**pok**-uh-lips/ ● **n. 1** an event involving great destruction. **2** (**the Apocalypse**) the final destruction of the world, as described in the biblical book of Revelation.
– ORIGIN Greek *apokaluptein* 'reveal'.

apocalyptic ● **adj.** having far-reaching or disastrous consequences.

Apocrypha /uh-**pok**-ri-fuh/ ● **n.** those books of the Old Testament not accepted as part of Hebrew scripture and excluded from the Protestant Bible at the Reformation.
– ORIGIN from Latin *apocrypha scripta* 'hidden writings'.

apocryphal ● **adj. 1** widely circulated but unlikely to be true: *an apocryphal story.* **2** having to do with the Apocrypha.

apogee /ap-uh-jee/ ● **n. 1** Astron. the point in the orbit of the moon or a satellite at which it is furthest from the earth. **2** the highest point: *his creative activity reached its apogee in 1910.*
– ORIGIN from Greek *apogaion diastēma*, 'distance away from earth'.

apolitical ● **adj.** not interested or involved in politics.

Apollinaire [E]
/uh-pol-li-**nair**/, Guillaume (1880–1918; pen name of *Wilhelm Apollinaris de Kostrowitzki*), French poet. He coined the term *surrealist* and was regarded by the surrealist poets as their forerunner.

Apollo[1] [E]
a Greek god associated with the sun, music, poetic inspiration, prophecy, and medicine.

Apollo[2] [E]
the American space programme for landing astronauts on the moon, which achieved its object with *Apollo 11* in 1969.

Apollonius [E]
/a-puh-**loh**-ni-uhss/ (*c.*260–190 BC), Greek mathematician, who was the first to use the terms *ellipse*, *parabola*, and *hyperbola* for these classes of curve.

apologetic ● **adj.** admitting and showing regret for a wrongdoing. ● **n.** (**apologetics**) reasoned arguments defending a theory or belief.
– DERIVATIVES **apologetically** adv.

apologia /ap-uh-**loh**-ji-uh/ ● **n.** a formal written defence of one's opinions or behaviour.
– ORIGIN Latin.

apologist ● **n.** a person who offers an argument in defence of something controversial.

apologize (also **apologise**) ● **v.** (**apologizes, apologizing, apologized**) say sorry for a wrongdoing.

apology ● **n.** (pl. **apologies**) **1** an expression of regret for a wrongdoing. **2** (**an apology for**) a very poor example of.
– ORIGIN Greek *apologia* 'a speech in one's own defence'.

apophthegm /ap-uh-them/ ● **n.** a concise saying stating a general truth.
– ORIGIN Greek *apophthengesthai* 'speak out'.

apoplectic /a-puh-**plek**-tik/ ● **adj. 1** informal overcome with anger. **2** dated relating to apoplexy (stroke).

apoplexy /a-puh-plek-si/ ● **n.** (pl. **apoplexies**) dated unconsciousness or inability to feel or move, caused by a stroke.
– ORIGIN Greek *apoplēssein* 'disable by a stroke'.

apostasy /uh-poss-tuh-si/ ● **n.** abandonment of a belief or principle.
– ORIGIN Greek *apostasis* 'desertion'.

apostate /ap-uh-stayt/ ● **n.** a person who

a

abandons a belief or principle.

apostle ● **n. 1** (**Apostle**) each of the twelve chief disciples of Jesus Christ. **2** an enthusiastic supporter of an idea or cause.
– ORIGIN Greek *apostolos* 'messenger'.

apostolic /a-puh-**stol**-ik/ ● **adj. 1** relating to the Apostles. **2** relating to the Pope, seen as the successor to St Peter.

apostrophe /uh-**poss**-truh-fi/ ● **n.** a punctuation mark (') used to indicate either possession or the omission of letters or numbers.
– ORIGIN Greek *apostrephein* 'turn away'.

USAGE apostrophe

An apostrophe is used in two ways: first, it is used to show that a thing or person belongs to somebody and is called the *possessive*. It is formed by adding *'s* to singular nouns (*my friend's sister*) and by adding an apostrophe after the *s* for plural nouns ending in *s* (*the students' books*). When a plural noun does not end in *s*, then the possessive is formed by adding *'s* (*the children's coats*).

The second use of the apostrophe is to show that letters or numbers have been omitted, such as in *I'm* (short for *I am*) and *June '99* (short for *June 1999*).

apothecary /uh-**poth**-uh-kuh-ri/ ● **n.** (pl. **apothecaries**) archaic a person who prepared and sold medicines.
– ORIGIN Greek *apothēkē* 'storehouse'.

apotheosis /uh-po-thi-**oh**-siss/ ● **n.** (pl. **apotheoses** /uh-po-thi-**oh**-seez/) **1** the highest point: *science is the apotheosis of the intellect.* **2** the raising of someone to the rank of a god.
– ORIGIN Greek *apotheoun* 'make a god of'.

appal (US **appall**) ● **v.** (**appals**, **appalling**, **appalled**) **1** greatly dismay or horrify. **2** (**appalling**) informal very bad.
– ORIGIN Old French *apalir* 'grow pale'.

Appalachian Mountains E /ap-puh-**lay**-sh'n, ap-puh-**lay**-chi-uhn/ a mountain system of eastern North America, stretching from Quebec and Maine to Georgia and Alabama.

apparatchik /ap-puh-**raht**-chik/ ● **n.** (pl. **apparatchiks** or **apparatchiki** /ap-puh-**raht**-chi-kee/) **1** esp. hist. a member of the administrative system of a communist party. **2** derog. or humorous an official in a large political organization.
– ORIGIN Russian.

apparatus /ap-puh-**ray**-tuhss/ ● **n.** (pl. **apparatuses**) **1** the equipment needed for a particular activity or purpose. **2** a complex structure within an organization: *the apparatus of government.*
– ORIGIN Latin.

apparel /uh-**pa**-ruhl/ ● **n.** formal clothing.
– ORIGIN Old French *apareillier.*

apparent ● **adj. 1** clearly seen or understood; obvious. **2** seeming real, but not necessarily so.
– DERIVATIVES **apparently** adv.
– ORIGIN Latin *apparere* 'appear'.

apparition ● **n.** a remarkable thing that makes a sudden appearance, especially a ghost.

appeal ● **v. 1** make a serious or earnest request. **2** be attractive or interesting: *activities that appeal to all.* **3** ask a higher court of law to reverse the decision of a lower court. **4** Cricket (of the bowler or fielders) call on the umpire to declare a batsman out. ● **n. 1** an act of appealing. **2** attractiveness or interest.
– ORIGIN Latin *appellare* 'to address'.

appealing ● **adj.** attractive or interesting.

appear ● **v. 1** come into view or existence: *smoke appeared on the horizon.* **2** seem. **3** present oneself publicly or formally, especially as a performer or in a law court.
– ORIGIN Latin *apparere.*

appearance ● **n. 1** the way that someone or something looks or seems. **2** an act of appearing.
– PHRASES **keep up appearances** keep up an impression of wealth or well-being.

appease ● **v.** (**appeases**, **appeasing**, **appeased**) make (someone) calm or less hostile by agreeing to their demands.
– DERIVATIVES **appeasement** n.
– ORIGIN Old French *apaisier.*

appellation /ap-puh-**lay**-sh'n/ ● **n.** formal a name or title.
– ORIGIN Latin *appellare* 'to address'.

append ● **v.** add to the end of a document or piece of writing.
– ORIGIN Latin *appendere* 'hang on'.

appendage ● **n.** a thing attached to or projecting from something larger or more important.

appendicitis ● **n.** inflammation of the appendix.

appendix ● **n.** (pl. **appendices** or **appendixes**) **1** a small tube of tissue attached to the lower end of the large intestine. **2** a section of additional information at the end of a book.
– ORIGIN Latin.

appertain /ap-per-**tayn**/ ● **v. 1** (**appertain to**) relate to. **2** be appropriate.
– ORIGIN Latin *appertinere.*

appetite ● **n. 1** a natural desire to satisfy a bodily need, especially for food. **2** a liking or inclination: *my appetite for study had gone.*
– ORIGIN Latin *appetitus.*

appetizer (also **appetiser**) ● **n.** a small dish of food or a drink taken before a meal to stimulate the appetite.

appetizing (also **appetising**) ● **adj.** stimulating the appetite.

applaud ● **v. 1** show approval by clapping. **2** express approval of: *the world applauded his courage.*
– ORIGIN Latin *applaudere.*

applause ● **n.** approval shown by clapping.

apple ● **n.** a round fruit that grows on a tree, with green or red skin and crisp flesh.
– PHRASES **the apple of one's eye** a person of whom one is extremely fond and proud. [ORIGIN formerly referring to the pupil of the eye.] **a rotten** (or **bad**) **apple** informal a corrupt person in a group, likely to have a bad influence on the others. **upset the apple cart** spoil a plan.
– ORIGIN Old English.

apple-pie order ● **n.** perfect order.

Appleton, E Sir Edward Victor (1892–1965), English physicist, who discovered a region of ionized gases (the Appleton layer) in the atmosphere.

appliance ● **n.** a device designed to perform a specific task.

applicable • adj. able to be applied; appropriate.
– DERIVATIVES **applicability** n.

applicant • n. a person who applies for something.

application • n. **1** a formal request to an authority. **2** the action of applying something. **3** practical use or relevance. **4** continued effort. **5** a computer program designed to fulfil a particular purpose.

applicator • n. a device for putting something into or on to something.

applied • adj. practical rather than theoretical: *applied chemistry.*

appliqué /uh-plee-kay/ • n. decorative needlework in which fabric shapes are sewn or fixed on to a fabric background.
– ORIGIN French, 'applied'.

apply • v. (**applies, applying, applied**) **1** make a formal request for something: *he applied for a job as a carpenter.* **2** bring into operation or use. **3** be relevant. **4** put (a substance) on a surface. **5** (**apply oneself**) put all one's efforts into a task.
– ORIGIN Latin *applicare* 'fold, fasten to'.

appoint • v. **1** give a job or role to. **2** decide on (a time or place). **3** (**appointed**) equipped or furnished: *a luxuriously appointed lounge.*
– DERIVATIVES **appointee** n.
– ORIGIN Old French *apointer.*

appointment • n. **1** an arrangement to meet. **2** a job or position. **3** the appointing of someone to a job. **4** (**appointments**) furniture or fittings.

apportion • v. share out.
– DERIVATIVES **apportionment** n.
– ORIGIN Latin *apportionare.*

apposite /ap-puh-zit/ • adj. appropriate.
– ORIGIN Latin *appositus* 'applied'.

apposition • n. Grammar a relationship in which a word or phrase is placed next to another so as to qualify or explain it (e.g. *my friend Sue*).

appraisal • n. **1** the action of assessing. **2** a formal assessment of an employee's performance.

appraise • v. (**appraises, appraising, appraised**) assess the quality, value, or nature of.
– ORIGIN from APPRISE.

appreciable • adj. large or important enough to be noticed.
– DERIVATIVES **appreciably** adv.

appreciate /uh-pree-shi-ayt/ • v. (**appreciates, appreciating, appreciated**) **1** recognize the value of. **2** understand (a situation) fully. **3** be grateful for. **4** rise in value or price.
– ORIGIN Latin *appretiare* 'appraise'.

appreciation • n. **1** recognition of the value or importance of something. **2** gratitude. **3** a favourable written assessment of a person or their work. **4** increase in value.

appreciative • adj. feeling or showing gratitude or pleasure.
– DERIVATIVES **appreciatively** adv.

apprehend • v. **1** seize or arrest (someone) for doing something unlawful or wrong. **2** grasp the meaning of; understand.
– ORIGIN Latin *prehendere* 'lay hold of'.

apprehension • n. **1** worry or fear about what might happen. **2** understanding. **3** the action of arresting someone.

apprehensive • adj. worried or afraid about what might happen.
– DERIVATIVES **apprehensively** adv.

apprentice • n. a person learning a skilled practical trade from an employer. • v. (**apprentices, apprenticing, apprenticed**) employ as an apprentice.
– DERIVATIVES **apprenticeship** n.
– ORIGIN Old French *apprendre* 'to learn'.

apprise • v. (**apprises, apprising, apprised**) inform: *I apprised him of what had happened.*
– ORIGIN French *apprendre* 'learn, teach'.

approach • v. **1** come near to in distance, time, or quality. **2** go to (someone) with a proposal or request. **3** start to deal with in a certain way. • n. **1** a way of dealing with something. **2** an initial proposal or request. **3** the action of approaching. **4** a way leading to a place.
– ORIGIN Old French *aprochier.*

approachable • adj. **1** friendly and easy to talk to. **2** able to be reached from a particular direction or by a particular means.

approbation • n. approval.
– ORIGIN Latin *approbare* 'approve'.

appropriate • adj. /uh-proh-pri-uht/ suitable; proper. • v. /uh-proh-pri-ayt/ (**appropriates, appropriating, appropriated**) **1** take for one's own use without permission. **2** set aside (money) for a special purpose.
– DERIVATIVES **appropriately** adv. **appropriateness** n. **appropriation** n.
– ORIGIN Latin *appropriare.*

approval • n. **1** the opinion that something is good. **2** official acceptance that something is satisfactory.
– PHRASES **on approval** (of goods) able to be returned to a supplier if unsatisfactory.

approve • v. (**approves, approving, approved**) **1** believe that someone or something is good or acceptable: *he approved of stiff punishments for criminals.* **2** officially accept as satisfactory.
– ORIGIN Latin *approbare.*

approximate • adj. /uh-prok-si-muht/ almost but not completely accurate. • v. /uh-prok-si-mayt/ (**approximates, approximating, approximated**) come close or be similar to.
– DERIVATIVES **approximately** adv.
– ORIGIN Latin *approximatus.*

approximation /uh-prok-si-may-sh'n/ • noun **1** an approximate figure or result. **2** the action of estimating something fairly accurately.

appurtenances /uh-per-ti-nuhn-siz/ • pl. n. accessories associated with a particular activity.
– ORIGIN Old French *apertenance.*

APR • abbrev. annual (or annualized) percentage rate.

après-ski • n. social activities following a day's skiing.
– ORIGIN French.

apricot • n. an orange-yellow fruit resembling a small peach.
– ORIGIN Portuguese *albricoque* or Spanish *albaricoque.*

April • n. the fourth month of the year.
– ORIGIN Latin *Aprilis.*

April Fool's Day • n. 1 April, traditionally an occasion for playing tricks.

a priori /ay pry-or-I/ • adj. & adv. based on theoretical reasoning rather than actual observation.
– ORIGIN Latin, 'from what is before'.

apron • n. **1** a protective garment covering the front of one's clothes. **2** an area on an airfield used for manoeuvring or parking aircraft. **3** (also **apron stage**) a strip of stage extending in front of the curtain.
– PHRASES **tied to someone's apron strings** be dominated or excessively influenced by someone.
– ORIGIN Old French *naperon* 'small tablecloth'.

apropos /a-pruh-poh/ • prep. (**apropos of**) with reference to.
– ORIGIN from French *à propos*.

apse /apss/ • n. a large recess with a domed or arched roof at the eastern end of a church.
– ORIGIN Greek *apsis* 'arch, vault'.

apt • adj. **1** appropriate; suitable. **2** (**apt to**) having a tendency to. **3** quick to learn.
– DERIVATIVES **aptly** adv.
– ORIGIN Latin *aptus* 'fitted'.

aptitude • n. a natural ability or tendency.

Apuleius E
/ap-yuu-lee-uhss/ (2nd century AD), Roman writer, author of *Metamorphoses* (*The Golden Ass*).

Aqaba E
/ak-uh-buh/ Jordan's only port, at the head of the Gulf of Aqaba, the north-east arm of the Red Sea.

aqualung • n. a portable breathing apparatus for divers, consisting of cylinders of compressed air attached to a mouthpiece or mask.
– ORIGIN Latin *aqua* 'water'.

aquamarine • n. **1** a light bluish-green precious stone. **2** a light bluish-green colour.
– ORIGIN from Latin *aqua marina* 'seawater'.

aquaplane • v. (**aquaplanes**, **aquaplaning**, **aquaplaned**) (of a vehicle) slide uncontrollably on a wet surface.
– ORIGIN from Latin *aqua* 'water' + **PLANE**[1].

aquarium • n. (pl. **aquaria** or **aquariums**) a water-filled glass tank for keeping fish and other water creatures and plants.
– ORIGIN Latin.

Aquarius /uh-kwair-i-uhss/ • n. a constellation (the Water Carrier) and sign of the zodiac, which the sun enters about 21 January.

aquatic /uh-kwat-ik/ • adj. **1** relating to water. **2** living in or near water.

aqueduct /ak-wuh-dukt/ • n. a long channel or raised bridge-like structure, used for carrying water across country.
– ORIGIN from Latin *aquae ductus* 'conduit'.

aqueous /ay-kwee-uhss/ • adj. relating to or containing water.
– ORIGIN Latin *aqua* 'water'.

aqueous humour • n. the clear fluid in the eyeball in front of the lens.

aquifer /ak-wi-fer/ • n. a body of rock that holds water or through which water flows.
– ORIGIN Latin, 'water-bearing'.

aquiline /ak-wi-lyn/ • adj. **1** (of a nose) curved like an eagle's beak. **2** like an eagle.
– ORIGIN Latin *aquila* 'eagle'.

Aquinas, St Thomas E
/uh-kwy-nuhss/ (1225–74), Italian philosopher, theologian, and Dominican friar. He introduced the work of Aristotle to Christian western Europe and devised the official tenets of the Roman Catholic Church. Feast day, 28 January.

Aquitaine[1] E
/ak-wi-tayn/ a region and former province of SW France.

Aquitaine[2], E
Eleanor of, see **ELEANOR OF AQUITAINE**.

Arab • n. **1** a member of a Semitic people inhabiting much of the Middle East and North Africa. **2** a breed of horse originating in Arabia.
– ORIGIN Arabic.

arabesque /a-ruh-besk/ • n. **1** a ballet posture in which one leg is extended horizontally backwards and the arms are outstretched. **2** an ornamental design of intertwined flowing lines.
– ORIGIN Italian *arabesco* 'in the Arabic style'.

Arabia E
/uh-ray-bi-uh/ (also **Arabian peninsula**) a peninsula of SW Asia, between the Red Sea and the Persian Gulf and bounded on the north by Jordan and Iraq.
– DERIVATIVES **Arabian** adj.

Arabian Nights E
a collection of stories and romances written in Arabic, including the tales of Aladdin and Sinbad the Sailor.

Arabic • n. the Semitic language of the Arabs, written from right to left. • adj. relating to the Arabs or Arabic.

Arabic numeral • n. any of the numerals 0, 1, 2, 3, 4, 5, 6, 7, 8, and 9.

arable /a-ruh-b'l/ • adj. (of land) able to be ploughed and used for growing crops.
– ORIGIN Latin *arare* 'to plough'.

arachnid /uh-rak-nid/ • n. an animal of a class of including spiders, scorpions, mites, and ticks.
– ORIGIN Greek *arakhnē* 'spider'.

arachnophobia /uh-rak-nuh-foh-bi-uh/ • n. extreme fear of spiders.
– ORIGIN from Greek *arakhnē* 'spider'.

Arafat E
/a-ruh-fat/ , Yasser (b.1929), Palestinian statesman, chairman of the Palestine Liberation Organization from 1968 and Palestinian President since 1996.

Aragon[1] E
/a-ruh-guhn/ an autonomous region of NE Spain; capital, Saragossa.

Aragon[2], E
Catherine of, see **CATHERINE OF ARAGON**.

Aral Sea E
/a-ruhl/ an inland sea in central Asia, on the border between Kazakhstan and Uzbekistan.

Aramaic /a-ruh-may-ik/ • n. an ancient Semitic language still spoken in parts of the Middle East.

– ORIGIN Greek *Aramaios* 'of *Aram*' (the biblical name of Syria).

Aran Islands E
a group of three islands, Inishmore, Inishmaan, and Inisheer, off the west coast of the Republic of Ireland.

Ararat, Mount E
/a-ruh-rat/ a pair of volcanic peaks in eastern Turkey, the higher of which is the traditional site of the resting place of Noah's ark after the Flood.

arbiter /ar-bi-ter/ ● n. **1** a person who settles a dispute. **2** a person who has influence in a particular area: *an arbiter of taste.*
– ORIGIN Latin, 'judge, supreme ruler'.

arbitrary /ar-bi-truh-ri, ar-bi-tri/ ● adj. **1** based on random choice or impulse. **2** (of power or authority) used without restraint.
– DERIVATIVES **arbitrarily** adv.
– ORIGIN Latin *arbitrarius.*

arbitrate ● v. (**arbitrates**, **arbitrating**, **arbitrated**) act as an arbitrator to settle a dispute.
– ORIGIN Latin *arbitrari* 'give judgement'.

arbitration ● n. the use of an arbitrator to settle a dispute.

arbitrator ● n. an independent person or body officially appointed to settle a dispute.

arboreal /ar-bor-i-uhl/ ● adj. **1** relating to trees. **2** living in trees.
– ORIGIN Latin *arbor* 'tree'.

arboretum /ar-buh-ree-tuhm/ ● n. (pl. **arboretums** or **arboreta**) a botanical garden devoted to trees.
– ORIGIN Latin.

arbour (US **arbor**) ● n. a shady place in a garden, with a canopy of trees or climbing plants.
– ORIGIN Latin *herba* 'grass, herb', influenced by *arbor* 'tree'.

arc ● n. **1** a curve forming part of the circumference of a circle. **2** a curving passage through the air. **3** a glowing electrical discharge between two points. ● v. (**arcs**, **arcing**, **arced**) move in or form an arc.
– ORIGIN Latin *arcus* 'bow, curve'.

arcade ● n. **1** a covered passage with arches along one or both sides. **2** esp. Brit. a covered walk with shops along one or both sides.
– ORIGIN French.

Arcadia E
/ar-kay-di-uh/ a mountainous district in southern Greece, represented in classical and Renaissance literature as a rural paradise.

Arcadian ● adj. literary rural in an unrealistically pleasant way.
– ORIGIN see **ARCADIA**.

arcana /ar-kay-nuh, ar-kah-nuh/ ● pl. n. (sing. **arcanum**) hidden things; mysteries.
– ORIGIN Latin.

arcane /ar-kayn/ ● adj. understood by few; mysterious.
– ORIGIN Latin *arcere* 'shut up'.

Arc de Triomphe E
/ark duh tree-omf/ a ceremonial arch at the top of the Champs Élysées in Paris, commissioned by Napoleon and completed in 1836.

arch¹ ● n. **1** a curved structure spanning an opening or supporting the weight of a bridge, roof, or wall. **2** the inner side of the foot. ● v. form or cause to form an arch.
– ORIGIN Latin *arcus* 'bow'.

arch² ● adj. self-consciously playful or teasing.
– ORIGIN from the use of **ARCH-** in nouns such as *arch-scoundrel.*

arch- ● comb. form **1** chief: *archbishop.* **2** most extreme: *an arch-enemy.*
– ORIGIN Greek *arkhos* 'chief'.

archaeology (US also **archeology**) ● n. the study of ancient history by examining objects dug up from the ground.
– DERIVATIVES **archaeological** (US also **archeological**) adj. **archaeologist** (US also **archeologist**) n.
– ORIGIN Greek *arkhaios* 'ancient'.

archaeopteryx /ar-ki-op-tuh-riks/ ● n. the oldest known fossil bird, which had feathers and wings like a bird, but teeth and a bony tail like a dinosaur.
– ORIGIN from Greek *arkhaios* 'ancient' + *pterux* 'wing'.

archaic /ar-kay-ik/ ● adj. **1** very old or old-fashioned. **2** belonging to former or ancient times.
– ORIGIN Greek *arkhaios* 'ancient'.

archaism ● n. an old or old-fashioned word or style.

Archangel E
/ark-ayn-j'l/ a port of NW Russia, on the White Sea.

archangel /ark-ayn-j'l/ ● n. an angel of high rank.

archbishop ● n. a bishop of the highest rank.

archdeacon ● n. a senior Christian priest ranking immediately below a bishop.

archduke ● n. a chief duke, especially (hist.) a son of the Emperor of Austria.

archeology ● n. US = **ARCHAEOLOGY**.

archer ● n. a person who shoots with a bow and arrows.
– DERIVATIVES **archery** n.
– ORIGIN Latin *arcus* 'bow'.

archetype /ar-ki-typ/ ● n. **1** a very typical example: *he looked the archetype of the old sailor.* **2** an original model which others follow.
– DERIVATIVES **archetypal** adj.
– ORIGIN from Greek *arkhe-* 'primitive' + *tupos* 'a model'.

Archimedes E
/ar-ki-mee-deez/ (*c.*287–212 BC), Greek mathematician and inventor, famous for his discovery of Archimedes' principle, a law stating that a body immersed in a fluid is subject to an upward force equal in magnitude to the weight of fluid it displaces. Legend has it that he made this discovery while taking a bath, and ran through the streets shouting 'Eureka!'.

archipelago /ar-ki-pel-uh-goh/ ● n. (pl. **archipelagos** or **archipelagoes**) a group of many islands.
– ORIGIN from Greek *arkhi-* 'chief' + *pelagos* 'sea'.

architect ● n. **1** a person who designs buildings and supervises their construction. **2** a creator or originator.
– ORIGIN Greek *arkhitektōn* 'chief builder'.

architectonic /ar-ki-tek-ton-ik/ ● adj. relat-

a

ing to architecture or architects. • n. (**architectonics**) the scientific study of architecture.

architecture • n. **1** the design and construction of buildings. **2** the style in which a building is designed and constructed: *Gothic architecture.* **3** the complex structure of something.
– DERIVATIVES **architectural** adj.

architrave /ar-ki-trayv/ • n. **1** (in classical architecture) a main beam resting across the tops of columns. **2** the frame around a doorway or window.
– ORIGIN French.

archive /ar-kyv/ • n. a collection of historical documents or records. • v. (**archives, archiving, archived**) **1** place in an archive. **2** Computing transfer (data) to a less frequently used storage medium.
– DERIVATIVES **archival** adj.
– ORIGIN Greek *arkheia* 'public records'.

archivist /ar-ki-vist/ • n. a person who is in charge of archives.

archway • n. a curved structure forming a passage or entrance.

arc lamp (also **arc light**) • n. a light source using an electric arc.

Arctic • adj. **1** relating to the regions around the North Pole. **2** (**arctic**) informal (of weather) very cold.
– ORIGIN Greek *arktos* 'constellation of the Great Bear'.

Arctic Circle E
the parallel of latitude 66° 33′ north of the equator.

Arctic Ocean E
the sea that surrounds the North Pole, lying within the Arctic Circle.

Arcturus E
/ark-**tyuu**-uh-ruhss/ the fourth-brightest star in the sky, and the brightest in the constellation Boötes.

Ardennes E
/ar-**den**/ a forested upland region extending over parts of SE Belgium, NE France, and Luxembourg.

ardent • adj. **1** very enthusiastic; passionate. **2** archaic burning; glowing.
– DERIVATIVES **ardently** adv.
– ORIGIN Latin *ardere* 'to burn'.

ardour (US **ardor**) • n. great enthusiasm; passion.
– ORIGIN Latin *ardor.*

arduous • adj. difficult and tiring.
– ORIGIN Latin *arduus* 'steep, difficult'.

are 2nd person sing. present and 1st, 2nd, 3rd person pl. present of **BE**.

area • n. **1** a part of a place, object, or surface. **2** the extent or measurement of a surface. **3** a subject or range of activity. **4** a sunken enclosure leading to a basement.
– ORIGIN Latin, 'piece of level ground'.

arena • n. **1** a level area surrounded by seating, in which sports and other public events are held. **2** an area of activity: *conflicts within the political arena.*
– ORIGIN Latin *harena, arena* 'sand, sand-covered place of combat'.

aren't • contr. **1** are not. **2** am not (only in questions): *I'm right, aren't I?*

areola /uh-ree-uh-luh/ • n. (pl. **areolae** /uh-ree-uh-lee/) the circular area of darker skin surrounding a human nipple.
– ORIGIN Latin, 'small open space'.

Ares E
/**air**-eez/ the Greek god of war. Roman equivalent **MARS**[1].

arête /uh-ret/ • n. a sharp mountain ridge.
– ORIGIN French.

Argentina E
/ar-juhn-**tee**-nuh/ a republic occupying much of the southern part of South America; capital, Buenos Aires.
– DERIVATIVES **Argentine** (also **Argentinian**) adj. & n.

argon /ar-gon/ • n. an inert gaseous element, present in small amounts in the air.
– ORIGIN Greek *argos* 'idle'.

Argonauts E
/ar-guh-nawts/ Gk Myth. a group of heroes who accompanied Jason on board the ship *Argo* in the quest for the Golden Fleece.

argot /ar-goh/ • n. the jargon or slang of a particular group.
– ORIGIN French.

arguable • adj. able to be argued or disagreed with.
– DERIVATIVES **arguably** adv.

argue • v. (**argues, arguing, argued**) **1** exchange conflicting views heatedly. **2** give reasons or evidence in support of something.
– PHRASES **argue the toss** informal, esp. Brit. question a decision already made.
– ORIGIN Latin *arguere* 'accuse'.

argument • n. **1** a heated exchange of conflicting views. **2** a set of reasons given in support of something.

argumentation • n. systematic reasoning in support of something.

argumentative • adj. apt to argue.

Argyll and Bute E
/ar-**gyl**, byoot/ an administrative region in the west of Scotland.

aria /ah-ri-uh/ • n. an accompanied song for a solo voice in an opera.
– ORIGIN Italian.

arid • adj. **1** very dry because having little or no rain. **2** lacking in interest: *arid verse.*
– DERIVATIVES **aridity** n.
– ORIGIN Latin *aridus.*

Aries /air-eez/ • n. a constellation (the Ram) and sign of the zodiac, which the sun enters about 20 March.
– ORIGIN Latin.

Ariosto E
/a-ri-**oss**-toh/, Ludovico (1474–1533), Italian poet, noted for his romantic epic *Orlando Furioso.*

arise • v. (**arises, arising, arose**; past part. **arisen**) **1** come into being or come to notice. **2** (**arise from/out of**) occur as a result of. **3** formal get or stand up.

aristocracy • n. (pl. **aristocracies**) the highest social class, consisting of people with hereditary titles.
– ORIGIN Greek *aristokratia* 'rule by the best'.

aristocrat • n. a member of the aristocracy.
– DERIVATIVES **aristocratic** adj.

Aristophanes E
/a-ri-**stof**-fuh-neez/ (*c.*450–*c.*385 BC), Greek comic dramatist. His works, including *Lysistrata* and the *Birds*, are notable for his satirical treatment of contemporary figures.

Aristotle E
/a-ri-sto-t'l/ (384–322 BC), Greek philosopher and scientist. His surviving works, covering a wide range of subjects including logic, ethics, politics, and metaphysics, are among the most influential in the history of Western thought.

arithmetic • n. /uh-**rith**-muh-tik/ **1** the branch of mathematics concerned with numbers. **2** the use of numbers in counting and calculation. • adj. /a-rith-**met**-ik/ relating to arithmetic.
– DERIVATIVES **arithmetical** adj.
– ORIGIN from Greek *arithmētikē tekhnē* 'art of counting'.

arithmetic progression • n. a sequence of numbers in which each differs from the next by a constant quantity (e.g. 9, 7, 5, 3, etc.).

Arizona E
a state of the south-western US; capital, Phoenix.
– DERIVATIVES **Arizonan** adj. & n.

ark • n. **1** (in the Bible) the ship built by Noah to save his family and two of every kind of animal from the Flood. **2** (also **Holy Ark**) a chest or cupboard housing the Torah scrolls in a synagogue. **3** (**Ark of the Covenant**) the chest which contained the laws of the ancient Israelites.
– ORIGIN Latin *arca* 'chest'.

Arkansas E
/ar-kuhn-saw/ a state of the south central US; capital, Little Rock.
– DERIVATIVES **Arkansan** n. & adj.

Ark of the Covenant E
the wooden chest which contained the tablets of the laws of the ancient Israelites. Carried by the Israelites on their wanderings in the wilderness, it was later placed by Solomon in the Temple at Jerusalem.

Arkwright, E
Sir Richard (1732–92), English inventor and industrialist, who in 1767 patented a water-powered spinning machine.

arm[1] • n. **1** each of the two upper limbs of the human body from the shoulder to the hand. **2** a side part of a chair supporting a sitter's arm. **3** a strip of water or land extending from a larger body. **4** a branch or division of an organization.
– PHRASES **cost an arm and a leg** informal be extremely expensive. **in arms** (of a baby) too young to walk. **keep at arm's length** avoid close or friendly contact with. **with open arms** with great warmth or enthusiasm.
– ORIGIN Old English.

arm[2] • v. **1** supply with weapons. **2** make (a bomb) ready to explode. **3** provide with essential equipment or information.
– ORIGIN Latin *arma* 'armour, arms'.

armada /ar-**mar**-duh/ • n. **1** a fleet of warships. **2** (**the (Spanish) Armada**) a Spanish naval force sent to invade England in 1588, but defeated by the English fleet.
– ORIGIN Spanish.

armadillo /ar-muh-**dil**-loh/ • n. (pl. **armadillos**) an insect-eating mammal of Central and South America, with a body covered in bony plates.
– ORIGIN Spanish, 'little armed man'.

Armageddon /ar-muh-**ged**-duhn/ • n. **1** (in the New Testament) the last battle between good and evil before the Day of Judgement. **2** a catastrophic conflict.
– ORIGIN Hebrew, 'hill of Megiddo' (Book of Revelation, chapter 16).

Armagh E
/ar-**mah**/ one of the Six Counties of Northern Ireland; chief town, Armagh.

armament /ar-muh-muhnt/ • n. **1** (also **armaments**) military weapons and equipment. **2** the equipping of military forces for war.

Armani E
/ar-**mah**-ni/, Giorgio (b.1935), Italian fashion designer.

armature /ar-muh-cher/ • n. **1** the rotating coil of a dynamo or electric motor. **2** a piece of iron placed across the poles of a magnet to preserve its power.
– ORIGIN Latin *armatura* 'armour'.

armchair • n. an upholstered chair with side supports for the sitter's arms. • adj. reading about or watching something rather than doing it: *an armchair traveller.*

armed • adj. carrying or having to do with a firearm.

armed forces • pl. n. a country's army, navy, and air force.

Armenia E
/ar-**mee**-ni-uh/ a country in the Caucasus of SE Europe; capital, Yerevan.
– DERIVATIVES **Armenian** n. & adj.

armistice /ar-miss-tiss/ • n. a truce.
– ORIGIN from Latin *arma* 'arms' + *-stitium* 'stoppage'.

armorial • adj. relating to coats of arms.

armour (US **armor**) • n. **1** the metal coverings formerly worn to protect the body in battle. **2** (also **armour plate**) the tough metal layer covering a military vehicle or ship. **3** the protective layer or shell of some animals and plants.
– DERIVATIVES **armoured** (US **armored**) adj.
– ORIGIN Old French *armure.*

armourer (US **armorer**) • n. **1** a maker or supplier of weapons or armour. **2** an official in charge of the arms of a warship or regiment.

armoury (US **armory**) • n. (pl. **armouries**) a store or supply of arms.

armpit • n. a hollow under the arm at the shoulder.

arms • pl. n. **1** guns and other weapons. **2** the heraldic emblems on a coat of arms.
– PHRASES **up in arms** protesting vigorously.
– ORIGIN Latin *arma.*

arms race • n. a situation in which nations compete for superiority in developing and stockpiling weapons.

a

Armstrong[1], E
(Daniel) Louis (1900–71; known as **Satchmo**), American jazz trumpeter and singer.

Armstrong[2], E
Neil (Alden) (b.1930), American astronaut, the first man to set foot on the moon (20 July 1969).

arm-wrestling ● n. a contest in which two seated people engage hands and try to force each other's arm down.

army ● n. (pl. **armies**) **1** an organized military force equipped for fighting on land. **2** a large number: *an army of researchers.*
– ORIGIN Old French *armee.*

Arne E
/arn/, Thomas (1710–78), English composer noted for 'Rule, Britannia'.

Arnhem E
/arn-uhm/ a town in the eastern Netherlands, site of a heavy defeat of Allied airborne forces during the Second World War (1944).

Arno E
/ar-noh/ a river which rises in the Apennines of northern Italy and flows through Florence and Pisa to the Ligurian Sea.

Arnold[1], E
Sir Malcolm (Henry) (b.1921), English composer and trumpeter, noted especially for his orchestral works and film scores.

Arnold[2], E
Matthew (1822–88), English poet, essayist, and social critic. His works include *Culture and Anarchy* and the poem 'Dover Beach'.

aroma ● n. a pleasant smell.
– ORIGIN Greek, 'spice'.

aromatherapy ● n. the use of aromatic oils extracted from plants for healing or to promote well-being.
– DERIVATIVES **aromatherapist** n.

aromatic ● adj. **1** having an aroma. **2** Chem. (of an organic compound such as benzene) containing a flat ring of atoms in its molecule.

arose past of **ARISE**.

around ● adv. & prep. **1** on every side. **2** in or to many places throughout an area. ● adv. **1** so as to face in the opposite direction. **2** approximately. **3** available or present. **4** without purpose.

arouse ● v. (**arouses**, **arousing**, **aroused**) **1** bring about (a feeling or response) in someone. **2** excite sexually. **3** awaken from sleep.
– DERIVATIVES **arousal** n.

Arp E
/arp/ , Jean (1887–1966), French painter, sculptor, and poet, co-founder of the Dada movement.

arpeggio /ar-pej-ji-oh/ ● n. (pl. **arpeggios**) the notes of a musical chord played in rapid succession.
– ORIGIN Italian.

arraign /uh-rayn/ ● v. call (someone) before a court to answer a criminal charge.
– DERIVATIVES **arraignment** n.
ORIGIN Old French *araisnier.*

arrange ● v. (**arranges**, **arranging**, **arranged**) **1** put tidily or in a particular order. **2** organize or plan. **3** adapt (a piece of music) for performance with different instruments or voices.
– DERIVATIVES **arranger** n.
– ORIGIN Old French *arangier.*

arrangement ● n. **1** something made up of things placed in an attractive or ordered way. **2** a plan for a future event. **3** an arranged piece of music.

arrant /a-ruhnt/ ● adj. utter; complete.
– ORIGIN from **ERRANT**.

array ● n. **1** an impressive display or range: *a bewildering array of choices.* **2** an ordered arrangement of troops. **3** literary elaborate or beautiful clothing. ● v. **1** display or arrange in a neat or impressive way. **2** (**be arrayed in**) be clothed in.
– ORIGIN Old French *arei.*

arrears ● pl. n. money owed that should already have been paid.
– PHRASES **in arrears 1** behind with paying money that is owed. **2** (of wages or rent) paid at the end of each period of work or occupation.
– ORIGIN Old French *arere.*

arrest ● v. **1** seize (someone) by legal authority and take them into custody. **2** stop or check (progress). **3** (**arresting**) attracting attention. ● n. **1** the action of arresting someone. **2** a sudden stop: *a cardiac arrest.*
– ORIGIN Latin *restare* 'remain, stop'.

Arrhenius E
/uh-ray-ni-uhss/, Svante August (1859–1927), Swedish chemist, one of the founders of modern physical chemistry, noted for his work on electrolytes.

arrival ● n. **1** the action or process of arriving. **2** a person or thing that has just arrived.

arrive ● v. (**arrives**, **arriving**, **arrived**) **1** reach a destination. **2** (of a particular moment) come about. **3** (**arrive at**) reach (a conclusion or decision). **4** informal become successful and well known.
– ORIGIN Old French *ariver.*

arriviste /a-ri-veest/ ● n. usu. derog. a person who has recently become wealthy or risen in social status.
– ORIGIN French.

arrogant ● adj. having too great a sense of one's own importance or abilities.
– DERIVATIVES **arrogance** n. **arrogantly** adv.
– ORIGIN Latin *arrogare* 'claim for oneself'.

arrogate /a-ruh-gayt/ ● v. (**arrogates**, **arrogating**, **arrogated**) take or claim for oneself without justification.
– ORIGIN Latin *arrogare.*

arrow ● n. **1** a stick with a sharp pointed head, that is shot from a bow. **2** a symbol resembling this, used to show direction or position.
– ORIGIN Old Norse.

arrowroot ● n. a powdery starch used in cookery, obtained from a Caribbean plant.
– ORIGIN from a word in a South American language meaning 'meal of meals'.

arse ● n. Brit. vulgar a person's bottom.
– ORIGIN Old English.

arsenal ● n. a store of weapons and ammunition.
– ORIGIN Arabic, 'house of industry'.

arsenic ● n. a brittle grey element with many highly poisonous compounds.

– ORIGIN Greek *arsenikon*.

arson • n. the criminal act of deliberately setting fire to property.
– DERIVATIVES **arsonist** n.
– ORIGIN Old French.

art[1] • n. **1** the expression of creative skill in a visual form such as painting or sculpture. **2** paintings, drawings, and sculpture as a whole. **3** (**the arts**) creative activities such as painting, music, and drama. **4** (**arts**) subjects of study concerned with human culture. **5** a skill: *the art of conversation*.
ORIGIN Latin *ars*.

art[2] archaic or dialect 2nd person sing. present of BE.

art deco • n. a decorative style of the 1920s and 1930s, characterized by geometric shapes.
– ORIGIN French *art décoratif* 'decorative art'.

artefact /ar-ti-fakt/ (US **artifact**) • n. a useful or decorative man-made object.
– ORIGIN from Latin *arte* 'using art' + *factum* 'something made'.

Artemis E
/ar-ti-miss/ the Greek goddess of the moon and hunting. Roman equivalent DIANA.

arterial /ar-teer-i-uhl/ • adj. **1** relating to an artery or arteries. **2** relating to an important transport route.

arteriosclerosis /ar-teer-i-oh-skluh-roh-siss/ • n. Med. thickening and hardening of the walls of the arteries.

artery • n. (pl. **arteries**) **1** any of the tubes through which blood flows from the heart around the body. **2** an important transport route.
– ORIGIN Greek *artēria*.

artesian well /ar-tee-zh'n/ • n. a well that is bored vertically into a layer of water-bearing rock, the water coming to the surface through natural pressure.
– ORIGIN from *Artois*, a region in France.

artful • adj. cunningly clever.
– DERIVATIVES **artfully** adv.

arthritis /ar-thry-tiss/ • n. painful inflammation and stiffness of the joints.
– DERIVATIVES **arthritic** adj. & n.
– ORIGIN Greek *arthron* 'joint'.

arthropod /ar-thruh-pod/ • n. an animal with a body divided into segments and an external skeleton, such as an insect, spider, crab, or lobster.
– ORIGIN from Greek *arthron* 'joint' + *pous* 'foot'.

Arthur[1] E
a legendary king of Britain and leader of the knights of the Round Table at his court in Camelot; historically he was perhaps a 5th- or 6th-century Romano-British chieftain.
– DERIVATIVES **Arthurian** /ar-thyoor-i-uhn/ adj.

Arthur[2], E
Chester Alan (1830–86), American Republican statesman, 21st President of the US 1881–5.

artichoke • n. (also **globe artichoke**) a vegetable consisting of the unopened flower head of a thistle-like plant.
– ORIGIN Italian *articiocco*.

article • n. **1** a particular object. **2** a piece of writing in a newspaper or magazine. **3** a clause or paragraph of a legal document. **4** (**articles**) a period of professional training as a solicitor, architect, etc. • v. (**be articled**) (of a solicitor, architect, etc.) be employed under contract as a trainee.
– PHRASES **article of faith** a firmly held belief.
– ORIGIN Latin *articulus* 'small connecting part'.

articled clerk • n. a law student employed as a trainee.

articular • adj. Anat. relating to a joint.

articulate • adj. /ar-tik-yuu-luht/ **1** fluent and clear in speech. **2** having joints or jointed segments. • v. /ar-tik-yuu-layt/ (**articulates, articulating, articulated**) **1** pronounce (words) distinctly. **2** clearly express (an idea or feeling). **3** (**articulated**) having sections connected by a flexible joint or joints.
– DERIVATIVES **articulacy** n. **articulately** adv. **articulation** n.
– ORIGIN Latin *articulare*.

artifact • n. US = ARTEFACT.

artifice /ar-ti-fiss/ • n. the use of cunning or skill so as to deceive.
– ORIGIN from Latin *ars* 'art' + *facere* 'make'.

artificer /ar-ti-fi-ser/ • n. a person skilled in making or planning things.

artificial • adj. **1** made as a copy of something natural. **2** not sincere; affected: *she gave an artificial smile*.
– DERIVATIVES **artificiality** n. **artificially** adv.

artificial insemination • n. the procedure of injecting semen into the vagina or womb of a woman or female animal.

artificial intelligence • n. the performance by computers of tasks normally requiring human intelligence.

artificial respiration • n. the forcing of air into and out of a person's lungs to make them begin breathing again.

artillery /ar-til-luh-ri/ • n. **1** large guns used in warfare on land. **2** a branch of the armed forces that uses artillery.
– ORIGIN Old French *atillier* 'equip, arm'.

artisan • n. a skilled worker who makes things by hand.
– DERIVATIVES **artisanal** adj.
– ORIGIN French.

artist • n. **1** a person who paints or draws. **2** a person who practises or performs any of the creative arts.
– DERIVATIVES **artistry** n.

artiste /ar-teest/ • n. a professional singer or dancer.
– ORIGIN French.

artistic • adj. **1** having creative skill. **2** having to do with art or artists.
– DERIVATIVES **artistically** adv.

artless • adj. sincere and straightforward.

art nouveau /ar noo-voh, art noo-voh/ • n. a style of art and architecture of the late 19th and early 20th centuries, having intricate designs and flowing curves.
– ORIGIN French, 'new art'.

artwork • n. illustrations for inclusion in a publication.

arty (N. Amer. also **artsy**) • adj. (**artier, artiest**) informal interested or involved in the arts in an affected way.
– DERIVATIVES **artiness** (N. Amer. also **artsiness**) n.

a

Arunachal Pradesh E
/ah-ruh-nah-chuhl pruh-**desh**/ a mountainous state in the far north-east of India; capital, Itanagar.

-ary ● suffix **1** forming adjectives: *budgetary.* **2** forming nouns: *dictionary.*

Aryan /air-i-uhn/ ● n. **1** a member of an ancient people speaking an Indo-European language. **2** (in Nazi ideology) a white person not of Jewish descent. ● adj. relating to Aryans.
– ORIGIN Sanskrit, 'noble'.

as ● adv. used in comparisons to refer to extent or amount. ● conj. **1** while. **2** in the way that. **3** because. **4** even though. ● prep. **1** in the role of; being: *a job as a cook.* **2** while; when.
– PHRASES **as for** with regard to. **as yet** until now or that time.
– ORIGIN Old English, 'similarly'.

asap ● abbrev. as soon as possible.

asbestos ● n. a fibrous mineral used in fire-resistant and insulating materials.
– ORIGIN Greek, 'unquenchable'.

ascend ● v. go up; climb or rise.
– ORIGIN Latin *ascendere.*

ascendant ● adj. **1** rising in power or status. **2** (of a planet or sign of the zodiac) just above the eastern horizon.
– DERIVATIVES **ascendancy** n.

ascension ● n. **1** the action of ascending in status. **2** (**the Ascension**) the ascent of Christ into heaven after the Resurrection.

Ascension Island E
a small island in the South Atlantic, incorporated with St Helena, with which it is a dependency of the UK.

ascent ● n. **1** an instance of ascending. **2** an upward slope.

ascertain /ass-er-**tayn**/ ● v. find out for certain.
– ORIGIN Old French *acertener.*

ascetic /uh-set-ik/ ● adj. strictly self-disciplined and avoiding any pleasures or luxuries. ● n. an ascetic person.
– DERIVATIVES **asceticism** n.
– ORIGIN Greek *askētēs* 'monk'.

ASCII /ass-ki/ ● abbrev. Computing American Standard Code for Information Interchange.

Asclepius E
/uh-sklee-pi-uhss/ the Greek god of healing.

ascorbic acid /uh-skor-bik/ ● n. vitamin C.
– ORIGIN Latin *scorbutus* 'scurvy'.

Ascot E
a town in southern England, south-west of Windsor. Its racecourse is the site of an annual race meeting.

ascribe ● v. (**ascribes, ascribing, ascribed**) (**ascribe to**) regard as caused by: *he ascribed his breakdown to exhaustion.*
– DERIVATIVES **ascription** n.
– ORIGIN Latin *ascribere.*

aseptic /ay-sep-tik/ ● adj. free from harmful bacteria, viruses, and other micro-organisms.

asexual ● adj. **1** without sex or sexual organs. **2** (of reproduction) not involving the fusion of gametes. **3** not having or causing sexual feelings.
– DERIVATIVES **asexually** adv.

ash[1] ● n. **1** the powder remaining after something has been burned. **2** (**ashes**) the remains of a human body after cremation. **3** (**the Ashes**) a cricket trophy awarded for winning a test match series between England and Australia.
– ORIGIN Old English.

ash[2] ● n. a tree with winged fruits and hard pale wood.
– ORIGIN Old English.

ashamed ● adj. feeling embarrassed or guilty.

Ashcroft, E
Dame Peggy (1907–91; born *Edith Margaret Emily Ashcroft*), English stage and film actress, known for her Shakespearean roles.

Ashe, E
Arthur (Robert) (1943–93), American tennis player. He was the first black male player to achieve world rankings.

ashen ● adj. very pale from shock, fear, or illness.

Ashgabat E
/ash-guh-bat/ (also **Ashkhabad**) the capital of Turkmenistan.

Ashkenazi /ash-kuh-**nah**-zi/ ● n. (pl. **Ashkenazim** /ash-kuh-**nah**-zim/) a Jew of central or eastern European descent.
– ORIGIN from *Ashkenaz*, a grandson of Noah.

Ashkenazy E
/ash-kuh-**nah**-zi/, Vladimir (Davidovich) (b.1937), Russian-born pianist, who left the Soviet Union in 1963 and later settled in Iceland.

ashlar /ash-ler/ ● n. large square-cut stones used as the surface layer of a wall.
– ORIGIN Old French *aisselier.*

ashore ● adv. to or on the shore or land.

ashram /ash-ruhm/ ● n. a Hindu religious retreat or community.
– ORIGIN Sanskrit, 'hermitage'.

Ashton, E
Sir Frederick (William Mallandaine) (1904–88), British ballet dancer, choreographer, and director.

Ash Wednesday ● n. the first day of Lent in the Christian Church.

Asia E
the largest of the world's continents, forming nearly one third of the land mass, lying entirely north of the equator except for some SE Asian islands.

Asia Minor E
the western peninsula of Asia, which now forms the bulk of modern Turkey.

Asian /ay-*zh*'n/ ● n. a person from Asia or a person of Asian descent. ● adj. relating to Asia.

Asiatic /ay-zi-at-ik/ ● adj. relating to Asia.

aside ● adv. **1** to one side; out of the way. **2** in reserve. ● n. **1** an actor's remark spoken to the audience rather than the other characters. **2** a remark that is not directly related to the main subject.
– PHRASES **aside from** apart from.

Asimov E
/az-i-moff/, Isaac (1920–92), Russian-born American writer and scientist, known for his works of science fiction (such as *I, Robot*) and for his books on science for non-scientists.

asinine /ass-i-nyn/ • **adj.** extremely stupid or foolish.
– ORIGIN Latin *asinus* 'ass'.

ask • **v. 1** say something so as to get an answer or some information. **2** say that one wants someone to do, give, or allow something. **3** (**ask for**) request to speak to. **4** expect (something) of someone. **5** invite (someone) to a social occasion. **6** (**ask out**) invite (someone) out on a date. **7** (**ask after**) enquire about the well-being of (someone).
– PHRASES **for the asking** for little or no effort or cost.
– ORIGIN Old English.

askance /uh-skanss, uh-skahnss/ • **adv.** with a suspicious or disapproving look.
– ORIGIN unknown.

askew /uh-skyoo/ • **adv. & adj.** not straight or level.

asking price • **n.** the price at which something is offered for sale.

aslant • **adv. & prep.** at or across at a slant.

asleep • **adj. & adv.** in or into a state of sleep.

Asmara E
/ass-**mah**-ruh/ the capital of Eritrea.

asp /asp/ • **n.** a small viper with an upturned snout.
– ORIGIN Greek *aspis*.

asparagus /uh-spa-ruh-guhss/ • **n.** a vegetable consisting of the tender young shoots of a tall plant.
– ORIGIN Greek *asparagos*.

aspect • **n. 1** a particular part or feature of a matter. **2** a particular appearance or quality: *the air of desertion lent the place a sinister aspect.* **3** the side of a building facing a particular direction.
– ORIGIN Latin *aspectus*.

Aspen E
a ski resort in south central Colorado.

aspen • **n.** a poplar tree with small rounded leaves.
– ORIGIN dialect.

asperity /uh-spe-ri-ti/ • **n.** harshness of tone or manner.
– ORIGIN Latin *asperitas*.

aspersions /uh-sper-sh'nz/ • **pl. n.** critical remarks about someone's character or reputation.
– ORIGIN Latin *aspergere* 'sprinkle'.

asphalt /ass-falt/ • **n.** a dark tar-like substance used in surfacing roads or waterproofing buildings.
– ORIGIN Greek *asphalton*.

asphodel /ass-fuh-del/ • **n.** a plant with clusters of yellow or white flowers on a long stem.
– ORIGIN Greek *asphodelos*.

asphyxia /uh-**sfik**-si-uh/ • **n.** a condition caused by the body being deprived of oxygen, leading to unconsciousness or death.
– ORIGIN from Greek *a-* 'without' + *sphuxis* 'pulse'.

asphyxiate • **v.** (**asphyxiates**, **asphyxiating**, **asphyxiated**) kill or be killed by asphyxia; suffocate.
– DERIVATIVES **asphyxiation** n.

aspic • **n.** a savoury jelly made with meat stock.
– ORIGIN French, 'asp', the colours of the jelly being compared to the snake.

aspidistra /ass-pi-**diss**-truh/ • **n.** a plant of the lily family with broad tapering leaves.
– ORIGIN Greek *aspis* 'shield'.

aspirant /ass-pi-ruhnt/ • **n.** a person with ambitions to do or be something.

aspirate • **v.** /ass-pi-rayt/ (**aspirates**, **aspirating**, **aspirated**) pronounce with the sound of *h* at the start of a word. • **n.** /ass-pi-ruht/ the sound of *h*.
– ORIGIN Latin *aspirare*.

aspiration • **n.** a hope or ambition.
– DERIVATIVES **aspirational** adj.

aspire • **v.** (**aspires**, **aspiring**, **aspired**) have ambitions. *she aspired to be an actress.*
– ORIGIN Latin *aspirare*.

aspirin • **n.** (pl. **aspirin** or **aspirins**) a medicine used to relieve pain and reduce fever and inflammation.
– ORIGIN from its chemical name.

Asquith E
/ass-kwith/, Herbert Henry, 1st Earl of Oxford and Asquith (1852–1928), British Liberal statesman, Prime Minister 1908–16.

ass[1] • **n. 1** a donkey or related small wild horse. **2** informal a stupid person.
– ORIGIN Latin *asinus*.

ass[2] • **n.** N. Amer. = **ARSE**.

Assad E
/ass-ad/, Hafiz al- (1928–2000), Syrian Baath statesman, President 1971–2000.

assail • **v. 1** attack violently. **2** (of an unpleasant feeling) disturb (someone).
– ORIGIN Latin *assalire*.

assailant • **n.** an attacker.

Assam E
/as-**sam**/ a state in NE India, noted for tea production; capital, Dispur.

assassin • **n.** a person who assassinates someone.
– ORIGIN Arabic, 'hashish-eater' (referring to fanatical Muslims at the time of the Crusades who were said to use hashish before murdering people).

assassinate • **v.** (**assassinates**, **assassinating**, **assassinated**) murder (a political or religious leader).
– DERIVATIVES **assassination** n.

assault • **n. 1** a violent attack. **2** a determined attempt: *an assault on Everest.* • **v.** make an assault on.
– ORIGIN Old French *assauter*.

assault course • **n.** Brit. a demanding obstacle course for training soldiers.

assay /uh-say, ass-ay/ • **n.** the testing of a metal or ore to determine its quality. • **v.** test (a metal or ore).
– ORIGIN Old French *assai*, *essai* 'trial'.

assegai /ass-uh-gy/ • **n.** (pl. **assegais**) an iron-tipped spear used by southern African peoples.
– ORIGIN Arabic, 'the spear'.

assemblage • **n. 1** a collection or gathering. **2** something made of pieces fitted together.

a

assemble • v. (**assembles**, **assembling**, **assembled**) **1** come or bring together. **2** fit together the parts of.
– DERIVATIVES **assembler** n.
– ORIGIN Old French *asembler*.

assembly • n. (pl. **assemblies**) **1** a group of people gathered or meeting together. **2** a body of people with law-making powers. **3** the assembling of parts.

assembly line • n. a series of machines by which identical items are assembled in successive stages.

assent /uh-sent/ • n. approval or agreement. • v. agree.
– ORIGIN Latin *assentire*.

assert • v. **1** state (a fact or belief) confidently. **2** (**assert oneself**) be confident and forceful. **3** cause others to recognize: *cyclists asserted their rights to use the road.*
– ORIGIN Latin *asserere* 'claim, affirm'.

assertion • n. **1** a confident and forceful statement. **2** the action of asserting.

assertive • adj. confident and forceful.
– DERIVATIVES **assertively** adv. **assertiveness** n.

assess • v. evaluate or estimate the value, importance, or quality of.
– DERIVATIVES **assessment** n. **assessor** n.
– ORIGIN Latin *assidere* 'sit by, levy tax'.

asset • n. **1** a useful or valuable thing or person. **2** (**assets**) property owned by a person or company.
– ORIGIN Old French *asez* 'enough'.

asset-stripping • n. the taking over of a company in financial difficulties and selling its assets separately at a profit.

asseveration /uh-sev-uh-ray-sh'n/ • n. formal a solemn or emphatic declaration.
– ORIGIN Latin *asseverare*.

assiduity /ass-i-**dyoo**-i-ti/ • n. constant or close attention to what one is doing.

assiduous /uh-**sid**-yoo-uhss/ • adj. showing great care and thoroughness.
– DERIVATIVES **assiduously** adv.
– ORIGIN Latin *assiduus*.

assign • v. **1** allocate (a task or duty). **2** give a job or task to. **3** regard as being caused by or belonging to: *she assigned the text to the sixteenth century.*
– ORIGIN Latin *assignare*.

assignation • n. **1** a secret arrangement to meet. **2** the action of assigning.

assignment • n. **1** a task allocated to someone. **2** the action of assigning.

assimilate • v. (**assimilates**, **assimilating**, **assimilated**) **1** take in and understand (information). **2** absorb and incorporate (people or ideas) into a wider society or culture. **3** absorb and digest (food or nutrients). **4** regard as similar.
– DERIVATIVES **assimilation** n.
– ORIGIN Latin *assimilare*.

assist • v. help (someone).
– ORIGIN Latin *assistere* 'stand by'.

assistance • n. help or support.

assistant • n. **1** a person who ranks below a senior person. **2** a person who helps in particular work.

assize /uh-syz/ (also **assizes**) • n. hist. a court which sat at intervals in each county of England and Wales.
– ORIGIN Old French *assise*.

associate • v. /uh-soh-shi-ayt/ (**associates**, **associating**, **associated**) **1** connect in the mind. **2** frequently meet or have dealings. **3** (**be associated with** or **associate oneself with**) be involved with. • n. /uh-**soh**-shi-uht/ a work partner or colleague. • adj. /uh-**soh**-shi-uht/ **1** connected with an organization. **2** belonging to an association but not having full membership.
– DERIVATIVES **associative** adj.
– ORIGIN Latin *associare*.

association • n. **1** a group of people organized for a joint purpose. **2** a connection or link.
– DERIVATIVES **associational** adj.

Association Football • n. formal = **SOCCER**.

assonance /ass-uh-nuhnss/ • n. rhyming of vowel sounds only (e.g. *hide, time*) or of consonants but not vowels (e.g. *cold, killed*).
– ORIGIN Latin *assonare* 'respond to'.

assorted • adj. of various sorts put together.
– ORIGIN Old French *assorter*.

assortment • n. a varied collection.

assuage /uh-swayj/ • v. (**assuages**, **assuaging**, **assuaged**) **1** make (an unpleasant feeling) less intense. **2** satisfy (an appetite or desire).
– ORIGIN Old French *assouagier*.

assume • v. (**assumes**, **assuming**, **assumed**) **1** accept as true without proof. **2** take (responsibility or control). **3** begin to have: *the island has recently assumed increased importance.* **4** pretend to have or feel.
– ORIGIN Latin *assumere*.

assuming • conj. based on the assumption that.

assumption • n. **1** a thing assumed to be true. **2** the assuming of responsibility or control. **3** (**Assumption**) the taking up of the Virgin Mary into heaven, according to Roman Catholic doctrine.

assurance • n. **1** a statement or promise intended to give confidence. **2** self-confidence. **3** Brit. life insurance.

assure • v. (**assures**, **assuring**, **assured**) **1** declare confidently to. **2** make certain. **3** Brit. cover by assurance.
– ORIGIN Old French *assurer*.

assured • adj. **1** confident. **2** protected against change or ending: *an assured tenancy.*
– DERIVATIVES **assuredly** adv.

Assyria E
/uh-si-ri-uh/ an ancient country in what is now northern Iraq, the centre of a succession of empires from the early part of the 2nd millennium BC until its fall in 612 BC.

Astaire E
/uh-**stair**/, Fred (1899–1987; born *Frederick Austerlitz*), American dancer and singer. He is famous for his roles in film musicals and for his dancing partnership with Ginger Rogers.

Astana E
/a-**stah**-nuh/ the capital of Kazakhstan. Former name **AKMOLA**.

astatine /ass-tuh-teen/ • n. a very unstable radioactive chemical element belonging to the halogen group.
– ORIGIN Greek *astatos* 'unstable'.

asterisk • n. a symbol (*) used as a pointer to

a note.
– ORIGIN Greek *asteriskos* 'small star'.

astern • adv. behind or towards the rear of a ship or aircraft.

asteroid /ass-tuh-royd/ • n. a small rocky planet orbiting the sun.
– ORIGIN Greek *asteroeidēs* 'starlike'.

asthma /ass-muh/ • n. a medical condition causing difficulty in breathing.
– DERIVATIVES **asthmatic** adj. & n.
– ORIGIN Greek.

astigmatism /uh-stig-muh-ti-z'm/ • n. a defect in an eye or lens, preventing proper focusing.
– ORIGIN from **A-**[1] + Greek *stigma* 'point'.

astir • adj. **1** in a state of excited movement. **2** awake and out of bed.

Aston, E
Francis William (1877–1945), English physicist, who invented the mass spectrograph (with J. J. Thomson).

astonish • v. surprise or impress greatly.
– DERIVATIVES **astonishment** n.
– ORIGIN Old French *estoner* 'stun'.

Astor, E
Nancy Witcher Langhorne, Viscountess (1879–1964), American-born British Conservative politician, the first woman to sit in the House of Commons (1919).

astound • v. shock or greatly surprise.
– ORIGIN related to **ASTONISH**.

astrakhan /ass-truh-kan/ • n. the dark curly fleece of a type of young lamb from central Asia.
– ORIGIN named after the Russian city of *Astrakhan*.

astral /ass-truhl/ • adj. relating to the stars.
– ORIGIN Latin *astrum* 'star'.

astray • adv. away from the correct course.
– ORIGIN Old French *estraie*.

astride • prep. & adv. **1** with a leg on each side of. **2** (as adv.) (of a person's legs) apart.

astringent /uh-strin-juhnt/ • adj. **1** causing body tissue to contract. **2** sharp or severe. • n. an astringent lotion used medically or as a cosmetic.
– DERIVATIVES **astringency** n.
– ORIGIN Latin *astringere* 'pull tight'.

astrolabe /ass-truh-layb/ • n. an instrument formerly used for measuring the altitudes of stars and calculating latitude in navigation.
– ORIGIN Greek *astrolabos* 'star-taking'.

astrology • n. the study of the supposed influence of stars and planets on human affairs.
– DERIVATIVES **astrologer** n. **astrological** adj.
– ORIGIN Greek *astron* 'star'.

astronaut • n. a person trained to travel in a spacecraft.
– ORIGIN from Greek *astron* 'star' + *nautēs* 'sailor'.

astronomical • adj. **1** relating to astronomy. **2** informal extremely large: *astronomical fees*.
– DERIVATIVES **astronomic** adj. **astronomically** adv.

astronomy • n. the science of stars, planets, and the universe.
– DERIVATIVES **astronomer** n.
– ORIGIN Greek *astron* 'star'.

astrophysics • n. the branch of astronomy concerned with the physical nature of stars and planets.
– DERIVATIVES **astrophysicist** n.

Asturias E
/a-styuu-ri-uhss/ an autonomous region and former principality of NW Spain; capital, Oviedo.

astute /uh-styoot/ • adj. good at making accurate judgements; shrewd.
– DERIVATIVES **astutely** adv.
– ORIGIN Latin *astutus*.

Asunción E
/uh-suun-syon/ the capital and chief port of Paraguay.

asunder • adv. literary apart.
– ORIGIN Old English.

Aswan E
/ass-wan/ a city in southern Egypt, near which are two dams across the Nile.

asylum • n. **1** protection from danger, especially for those who leave their own country because of persecution for their political beliefs. **2** dated an institution for people who are mentally ill.
– ORIGIN Greek *asulon* 'refuge'.

asymmetrical • adj. lacking symmetry.

asymmetry /ay-sim-mi-tri/ • n. (pl. **asymmetries**) lack of symmetry.

asynchronous • adj. not existing or occurring at the same time.

at • prep. used to express: **1** location, arrival, or time. **2** a value, rate, or point on a scale. **3** a state or condition. **4** direction towards. **5** the means by which something is done.
– PHRASES **at that** in addition.
ORIGIN Old English.

Atatürk E
/at-uh-terk/ , Kemal (1881–1938), Turkish general and statesman, President 1923–38. As first President of the Turkish republic, his policies were designed to transform Turkey into a modern secular state.

atavistic /at-uh-viss-tik/ • adj. returning to something ancient or inherited from a remote ancestor: *atavistic fears*.
– DERIVATIVES **atavism** n.
– ORIGIN Latin *atavus* 'forefather'.

ate past of **EAT**.

-ate[1] • suffix forming nouns referring to: **1** status, office, or function: *doctorate*. **2** a group: *electorate*. **3** Chem. a salt or ester: *chlorate*. **4** a product of a chemical process: *filtrate*.
– ORIGIN Old French *-at* or Latin *-atus*.

-ate[2] • suffix forming adjectives, nouns, and verbs: *associate*.
– ORIGIN Latin *-atus*.

atelier /uh-tel-i-ay/ • n. a workshop or studio.
– ORIGIN French.

atheism /ay-thi-i-z'm/ • n. the belief that God does not exist.
– DERIVATIVES **atheist** n. **atheistic** adj.
– ORIGIN from Greek *a-* 'without' + *theos* 'god'.

Athelstan E
/ath-uhl-stuhn/ (895–939), king of England 925–39, who ruled Wessex and Mercia before effectively becoming the first king of all England.

a

Athene E
/uh-**thee**-ni/ (also **Athena**) the Greek goddess of wisdom and patron goddess of Athens. Also called **PALLAS**. Roman equivalent **MINERVA**.

Athens E
the capital of Greece.
– DERIVATIVES **Athenian** adj. & n.

athlete • n. **1** a person who is good at sports. **2** a person who competes in track and field events.
– ORIGIN Greek *athlētēs*.

athlete's foot • n. a form of ringworm infection affecting the feet.

athletic • adj. **1** fit and good at sport. **2** relating to athletics. • n. (**athletics**) Brit. the sport of competing in track and field events.
– DERIVATIVES **athletically** adv. **athleticism** n.

Athos, Mount E
/a-thoss, ay-thoss/ a mountainous peninsula in NE Greece, projecting into the Aegean Sea. It is inhabited by monks of the Orthodox Church, who forbid women to set foot on the peninsula.

athwart /uh-**thwort**/ • prep. & adv. across from side to side.

-ation • suffix (forming nouns) referring to an action or its result: *exploration*.
– ORIGIN French or Latin.

Atlantic • adj. having to do with the Atlantic Ocean.
– ORIGIN first referring to Mount Atlas in Libya; named after the god *Atlas* (see **ATLAS**).

Atlantic Ocean E
the ocean lying between Europe and Africa to the east and North and South America to the west.

Atlantis E
a legendary island, beautiful and prosperous, which was overwhelmed by the sea.

Atlas E
Gk Myth. one of the Titans, who was punished for his part in their revolt against Zeus by being made to support the heavens.

atlas • n. a book of maps or charts.
– ORIGIN named after **ATLAS**, shown on early atlases as supporting the heavens.

Atlas Mountains E
a range of mountains in North Africa extending from Morocco to Tunisia.

ATM • abbrev. automated teller machine.

atmosphere • n. **1** the gases surrounding the earth or another planet. **2** the quality of the air in a place. **3** an overall tone or mood: *the hotel has a friendly atmosphere.* **4** a unit of pressure equal to the pressure of the atmosphere at sea level, 101,325 pascals.
– ORIGIN from Greek *atmos* 'vapour' + *sphaira* 'globe'.

atmospheric • adj. **1** relating to the atmosphere of a planet. **2** creating a distinctive mood: *atmospheric lighting.* • n. (**atmospherics**) electrical disturbances in the atmosphere, especially as causing interference with telecommunications.

atoll /a-tol/ • n. a ring-shaped coral reef or chain of islands.
– ORIGIN Maldivian (the language of the Maldives).

atom • n. **1** the smallest particle of a chemical element that can exist. **2** a very small amount: *she did not have an atom of strength left.*
– ORIGIN Greek *atomos* 'indivisible'.

atom bomb (also **atomic bomb**) • n. a bomb whose explosive power comes from the fission of atomic nuclei.

atomic • adj. **1** relating to an atom or atoms. **2** relating to nuclear energy or weapons.

atomic mass unit • n. a unit of mass used for atomic and molecular weights, equal to one twelfth of the mass of an atom of carbon-12.

atomic number • n. the number of protons in the nucleus of the atom of a chemical element.

atomic weight • n. = **RELATIVE ATOMIC MASS**.

atomize (also **atomise**) • v. (**atomizes, atomizing, atomized**) convert into very fine particles or droplets.
– DERIVATIVES **atomizer** (also **atomiser**) n.

atonal /ay-**toh**-n'l/ • adj. not written in any musical key.

atone • v. (**atones, atoning, atoned**) (**atone for**) make amends for.
– ORIGIN from *at one*.

atonement • n. **1** amends for a wrong. **2** (**the Atonement**) the reconciliation of God and humankind through the death of Jesus Christ.

atop • prep. literary on the top of.

atrium /ay-tri-uhm/ • n. (pl. **atria** /ay-tri-uh/ or **atriums**) **1** a central hall rising through several storeys and having a glazed roof. **2** an open central court in an ancient Roman house. **3** each of the two upper cavities of the heart.
– ORIGIN Latin.

atrocious /uh-**troh**-shuhss/ • adj. **1** horrifyingly wicked. **2** informal very bad or unpleasant.
– ORIGIN Latin *atrox* 'cruel'.

atrocity /uh-**tross**-i-ti/ • n. (pl. **atrocities**) an extremely wicked or cruel act.

atrophy /a-truh-fi/ • v. (**atrophies, atrophying, atrophied**) **1** (of body tissue or an organ) waste away. **2** gradually become weaker. • n. the condition or process of atrophying.
– ORIGIN Greek *atrophia* 'lack of food'.

attach • v. **1** fasten; join. **2** regard something as being: *the country attaches importance to human rights.* **3** appoint (someone) for special or temporary duties. **4** (**attached to**) very fond of.
– DERIVATIVES **attachable** adj.
– ORIGIN Old French *atachier*.

attaché /uh-**tash**-ay/ • n. a person attached to an ambassador's staff in a specific field of activity: *a military attaché.*
– ORIGIN French, 'attached'.

attaché case • n. a small, flat briefcase for carrying documents.

attachment • n. **1** an extra part attached to something to perform a particular function. **2** the action of attaching or the state of being attached.

attack • v. **1** take violent action against. **2** act harmfully on. **3** criticize fiercely. **4** tackle

(something) with determination. **5** (in sport) try to score goals or points. ● **n. 1** an instance of attacking. **2** a sudden short spell of an illness.
– DERIVATIVES **attacker** n.
– ORIGIN Italian *attaccare.*

attain ● **v. 1** succeed in doing. **2** reach: *he attained the grand old age of 47.*
– DERIVATIVES **attainable** adj.
– ORIGIN Latin *attingere.*

attainment ● **n. 1** the achieving of something. **2** an achievement.

attar /at-tar/ ● **n.** a sweet-smelling oil made from rose petals.
– ORIGIN Arabic, 'perfume, essence'.

attempt ● **v.** make an effort to do. ● **n.** an act of attempting.
– ORIGIN Latin *attemptare.*

Attenborough[1] E
/at-t'n-buh-ruh/, Sir David (Frederick) (b.1926), English naturalist and broadcaster, brother of Richard Attenborough.

Attenborough[2] E
/at-t'n-buh-ruh/, Richard (Samuel), Baron Attenborough of Richmond-upon-Thames (b.1923), English film actor, producer, and director of films including *Gandhi* and *Shadowlands.* He is the brother of David Attenborough.

attend ● **v. 1** be present at or go regularly to. **2** (**attend to**) deal with or pay attention to. **3** accompany as a result of: *the work was attended by many difficulties.* **4** escort and wait on (an important person).
– DERIVATIVES **attendee** n. **attender** n.
– ORIGIN Latin *attendere.*

attendance ● **n. 1** the action of attending. **2** the number of people present.

attendant ● **n. 1** a person employed to provide a service. **2** an assistant to an important person. ● **adj.** accompanying: *the sea and its attendant attractions.*

attention ● **n. 1** the faculty of considering or taking notice. **2** special care or consideration. **3** (**attentions**) attentive treatment or sexual approaches. **4** an erect position taken up by a soldier, with the feet together and the arms straight down the sides of the body.

attentive ● **adj. 1** paying close attention. **2** considerate and courteous.
– DERIVATIVES **attentively** adv. **attentiveness** n.

attenuate /uh-ten-yoo-ayt/ ● **v.** (**attenuates, attenuating, attenuated**) **1** make weaker. **2** make thin or thinner.
– DERIVATIVES **attenuation** n.
– ORIGIN Latin *attenuare.*

attest /uh-test/ ● **v. 1** provide or act as clear evidence of. **2** declare to be true: *I can attest to his tremendous energy.*
– DERIVATIVES **attestation** n.
– ORIGIN Latin *attestari.*

attic ● **n.** a space or room inside the roof of a building.
– ORIGIN Latin *Atticus* 'relating to Athens or Attica' (see ATTICA).

Attica E
/at-ti-kuh/ a triangular promontory of eastern Greece.

Attila E
/uh-til-luh/ (406–53), king of the Huns 434–53, who ravaged vast areas between the Rhine and the Caspian Sea.

attire ● **n.** clothes of a particular kind: *business attire.* ● **v.** (**attires, attiring, attired**) (**be attired**) be dressed in clothes of a particular kind.
– ORIGIN Old French *atirer* 'equip'.

attitude ● **n. 1** a way of thinking or feeling about someone or something. **2** a posture of the body. **3** informal self-confident or hostile behaviour.
– ORIGIN Latin *aptitudo* 'suitability'.

attitudinize /at-ti-tyoo-di-nyz/ (also **attitudinise**) ● **v.** (**attitudinizes, attitudinizing, attitudinized**) adopt an attitude just for effect.

Attlee, E
Clement Richard, 1st Earl Attlee (1883–1967), British Labour statesman, Prime Minister 1945–51. His term saw the creation of the modern welfare state and the nationalization of major industries.

attorney /uh-ter-ni/ ● **n.** (pl. **attorneys**) **1** a person appointed to act for another in legal matters. **2** esp. US a lawyer.
– ORIGIN Old French *atorner* 'assign'.

Attorney General ● **n.** (pl. **Attorneys General**) the principal legal officer in some countries.

attract ● **v. 1** draw in by offering something interesting or worthwhile. **2** cause (a reaction). **3** cause to have a liking for or interest in: *boys are attracted to video games with action.* **4** draw (something) closer by an unseen force.
– DERIVATIVES **attractor** n.
– ORIGIN Latin *attrahere* 'draw near'.

attraction ● **n. 1** the action or power of attracting. **2** something interesting or appealing.

attractive ● **adj. 1** pleasing in appearance. **2** arousing interest.
– DERIVATIVES **attractively** adv. **attractiveness** n.

attribute ● **v.** /uh-trib-yoot/ (**attributes, attributing, attributed**) (**attribute to**) regard as belonging to, made, or caused by: *the moth's scarcity is attributed to pollution.* ● **n.** /at-tri-byoot/ **1** a characteristic quality. **2** an object traditionally associated with a person or thing: *the hourglass is an attribute of Father TIme.*
– DERIVATIVES **attributable** /uh-trib-yuu-tuh-b'l/ adj. **attribution** n.
– ORIGIN Latin *attribuere* 'assign to'.

attributive /uh-trib-yuu-tiv/ ● **adj.** Grammar (of an adjective) coming before the word that it describes, as *old* in *the old dog*.

attrition /uh-tri-sh'n/ ● **n. 1** gradual wearing down through prolonged attack or pressure. **2** wearing away by friction.
– ORIGIN Latin *atterere* 'to rub'.

attune ● **v.** (**attunes, attuning, attuned**) adjust or accustom to a situation.

Atwood, E
Margaret (Eleanor) (b.1939), Canadian novelist, poet, and critic. Her novels include *Cat's Eye* and *The Blind Assassin.*

a

atypical • adj. not typical.

Au • symb. the chemical element gold.
– ORIGIN Latin *aurum*.

aubergine /oh-ber-*zheen*/ • n. esp. Brit. a purple egg-shaped vegetable.
– ORIGIN French.

aubretia /aw-**bree**-shuh/ (also **aubrietia**) • n. a trailing plant with purple, pink, or white flowers.
– ORIGIN named after the French botanist Claude *Aubriet* (1668–1743).

Aubrey E
/aw-bri/, John (1626–97), English antiquarian and author, known for *Brief Lives*, a collection of biographies.

auburn /aw-bern/ • n. a reddish-brown colour.
– ORIGIN Old French *auborne*.

Auckland E
/awk-luhnd/ the largest city and chief seaport of New Zealand, on North Island.

auction /awk-sh'n/ • n. a public sale in which goods or property are sold to the highest bidder. • v. sell at an auction.
– ORIGIN Latin, 'increase, auction'.

auctioneer • n. a person who conducts auctions.

audacious /aw-day-shuhss/ • adj. willing to take bold risks.
– DERIVATIVES **audaciously** adv. **audacity** n.
– ORIGIN Latin *audax* 'bold'.

Auden E
/aw-d'n/, W. H. (1907–73; full name *Wystan Hugh Auden*), British-born poet, US citizen from 1946. His collections of poetry include *Look, Stranger!* and *The Age of Anxiety*.

audible • adj. able to be heard.
– DERIVATIVES **audibility** n. **audibly** adv.
– ORIGIN Latin *audire* 'hear'.

audience • n. **1** the people gathered to see or listen to a play, concert, film, etc. **2** a formal interview with a person in authority.
– ORIGIN Latin *audire* 'hear'.

audio- • comb. form relating to hearing or sound: *audio-visual*.
– ORIGIN Latin *audire* 'hear'.

audio frequency • n. a frequency capable of being perceived by the human ear.

audio tape • n. magnetic tape on which sound can be recorded.

audio typist • n. a typist who types documents from recorded dictation.

audio-visual • adj. using both sight and sound.

audit /aw-dit/ • n. an official inspection of an organization's accounts. • v. (**audits**, **auditing**, **audited**) make an audit of.
– ORIGIN Latin *audire* 'hear'.

audition • n. an interview for a performer in which they give a practical demonstration of their skill. • v. assess or be assessed by an audition.

auditor • n. **1** a person who carries out an audit. **2** a listener.

auditorium • n. (pl. **auditoriums** or **auditoria**) the part of a theatre or hall in which the audience sits.
– ORIGIN Latin.

auditory • adj. relating to hearing.

Audubon E
/aw-duh-buhn/, John James (1785–1851), American naturalist and artist, author of *The Birds of America*.

au fait /oh fay/ • adj. (**au fait with**) having a thorough knowledge of.
– ORIGIN French, 'to the point'.

auger /aw-ger/ • n. a tool resembling a large corkscrew, for boring holes.
– ORIGIN Old English.

aught /awt/ (also **ought**) • pron. archaic anything at all.
– ORIGIN Old English.

augment /awg-**ment**/ • v. make greater by adding.
– DERIVATIVES **augmentation** n.
– ORIGIN Latin *augmentare*.

au gratin /oh gra-tan/ • adj. sprinkled with breadcrumbs or grated cheese and browned.
– ORIGIN French, 'by grating'.

augur /aw-ger/ • v. be a sign of (a likely outcome).
– ORIGIN Latin, 'person who interprets omens'.

augury /aw-gyuu-ri/ • n. (pl. **auguries**) a sign that shows what will happen in the future.

August • n. the eighth month of the year.
– ORIGIN named after the emperor **Augustus**.

august /aw-**gust**/ • adj. inspiring respect and admiration.
– ORIGIN Latin *augustus* 'venerable'.

Augustine of Hippo, St E
/aw-**guss**-tin/ (354–430), Christian theologian and bishop of Hippo in North Africa. His writings, such as *Confessions* and the *City of God*, dominated subsequent Western Christian theology. Feast day, 28 August.

Augustine, St E
/aw-**guss**-tin/ (died *c.*604), Italian churchman, who led England's conversion to Christianity and became the first archbishop of Canterbury (597). Feast day, 26 May.

Augustus E
/aw-**guss**-tuhss/ (63 BC–AD 14; born *Gaius Octavius*; also called, until 27 BC, **Octavian**), the first Roman emperor. He gained supreme power by his defeat of Antony in 31 BC and in 27 BC he was given the title Augustus ('venerable')

auk /awk/ • n. a black and white seabird with short wings.
– ORIGIN Old Norse.

auld lang syne /awld lang **syn**/ • n. times long past.
– ORIGIN Scots, 'old long since'.

Aung San Suu Kyi E
/awng san soo **tsee**/ (b.1945), Burmese political leader, leader of the National League for Democracy (NLD) since 1988.

aunt • n. the sister of one's father or mother or the wife of one's uncle.
– ORIGIN Old French *ante*.

au pair /oh **pair**/ • n. a foreign girl employed to look after children and help with housework in exchange for board and lodging.
– ORIGIN French, 'on equal terms'.

aura /aw-ruh/ • n. (pl. **aurae** /aw-ree/ or **auras**) **1** the distinctive atmosphere of a place, person, or thing. **2** a supposed invisible

force surrounding a creature.
– ORIGIN Greek, 'breeze, breath'.

aural /aw-ruhl/ • **adj.** having to do with the ear or hearing.
– DERIVATIVES **aurally** adv.
– ORIGIN Latin *auris* 'ear'.

aureole /aw-ri-ohl/ • **n. 1** (in paintings) a bright circle surrounding a person to show that they are holy. **2** a circle of light around the sun or moon.
– ORIGIN from Latin *aureola corona* 'golden crown'.

au revoir /aw ruh-**vwar**/ • **exclam.** goodbye.
– ORIGIN French, 'to the seeing again'.

auricle /o-ri-k'l/ • **n. 1** the external part of the ear. **2** an upper cavity of the heart.
– ORIGIN Latin *auricula* 'little ear'.

aurora australis /uh-raw-ruh oss-**tray**-liss/ • **n.** the southern lights, streamers of coloured light seen in the sky near the South Pole.
– ORIGIN Latin.

aurora borealis /uh-raw-ruh bo-ri-**ay**-liss/ • **n.** the northern lights, streamers of coloured light seen in the sky near the North Pole.
– ORIGIN Latin.

Auschwitz E
/ow-shvits/ a Nazi concentration camp in the Second World War, near the town of Oświęcim (Auschwitz) in Poland.

auspice /awss-piss/ • **n.** archaic an omen.
– PHRASES **under the auspices of** with the support or protection of.
– ORIGIN Latin *auspicium*.

auspicious /aw-**spi**-shuhss/ • **adj.** suggesting that there is a good chance of success.

Aussie (also **Ozzie**) • **n.** (pl. **Aussies**) & **adj.** informal Australia or Australian.

Austen E
/oss-tin, aw-stin/, Jane (1775–1817), English novelist, known for her skilful characterization, wit, and social observation. Her major novels include *Sense and Sensibility, Pride and Prejudice*, and *Emma*.

austere /oss-**teer**/ • **adj.** (**austerer, austerest**) **1** severe or strict in appearance or manner. **2** lacking comforts, luxuries, or decoration.
– ORIGIN Greek *austēros* 'severe'.

austerity /oss-**te**-ri-ti/ • **n.** (pl. **austerities**) **1** strictness or severity. **2** difficult economic conditions, in which public spending is cut back.

Austerlitz, Battle of E
/**ow**-ster-lits/ a battle in 1805 near the town of Austerlitz (now in the Czech Republic), in which Napoleon defeated the Austrians and Russians.

Austin E
/oss-tin, aw-stin/, Herbert, 1st Baron Austin of Longbridge (1866–1941), British motor manufacturer. His factory produced the Austin Seven ('Baby Austin').

Australasia E
the region consisting of Australia, New Zealand, New Guinea, and the neighbouring islands of the Pacific.
– DERIVATIVES **Australasian** adj.

Australia E
an island country and continent of the southern hemisphere, in the SW Pacific; capital, Canberra.
– DERIVATIVES **Australian** adj. & n.

Australian Capital Territory E
a federal territory in Australia, forming an enclave in New South Wales; it includes the national capital, Canberra.

Australian Rules • **n.** a form of football played on an oval field with an oval ball by teams of eighteen players.

Austria E
a republic in central Europe; capital, Vienna.
– DERIVATIVES **Austrian** adj. & n.

Austria-Hungary E
(also **Austro-Hungarian empire**) the dual monarchy established in 1867 by the Austrian emperor Franz Josef, according to which Austria and Hungary became autonomous states under a common sovereign.

autarky (also **autarchy**) • **n.** (pl. **autarkies**) **1** economic independence or self-sufficiency. **2** an economically independent state or society.
– ORIGIN Greek *autarkēs*.

authentic • **adj.** of undisputed origin; genuine.
– DERIVATIVES **authentically** adv. **authenticity** n.
– ORIGIN Greek *authentikos*.

authenticate • **v.** (**authenticates, authenticating, authenticated**) prove or show to be authentic.
– DERIVATIVES **authentication** n.

author /aw-ther/ • **n. 1** a writer of a book or article. **2** the inventor of something.
– DERIVATIVES **authoress** n. **authorial** /aw-**thor**-i-uhl/ adj. **authorship** n.
– ORIGIN Latin *auctor*.

authoritarian /aw-tho-ri-**tair**-i-uhn/ • **adj.** in favour of or demanding strict obedience to authority. • **n.** an authoritarian person.

authoritative /aw-**tho**-ri-tuh-tiv/ • **adj.** **1** true or accurate and so able to be trusted. **2** commanding and self-confident. **3** supported by authority; official.
– DERIVATIVES **authoritatively** adv.

authority • **n.** (pl. **authorities**) **1** the power to give orders and enforce obedience. **2** a person or organization having official power. **3** recognized knowledge or expertise. **4** an authoritative person or book.
– ORIGIN Old French *autorite*.

authorize (also **authorise**) • **v.** (**authorizes, authorizing, authorized**) give official permission for.
– DERIVATIVES **authorization** (also **authorisation**) n.

Authorized Version • **n.** an English translation of the Bible published in 1611.

autism /aw-ti-z'm/ • **n.** a mental condition in which a person has great difficulty in communicating with others.
– DERIVATIVES **autistic** adj. & n.
– ORIGIN Greek *autos* 'self'.

auto • **adj.** & **n.** = AUTOMATIC.

auto- • **comb. form 1** self: *autocrat*. **2** one's own:

a

autograph. **3** automatic; spontaneous: *autoxidation.*
– ORIGIN Greek *autos* 'self'.

autobiography • n. (pl. **autobiographies**) an account of a person's life written by that person.
– DERIVATIVES **autobiographer** n. **autobiographical** adj.

autoclave /or-toh-klayv/ • n. a strong heated container used for processes using high pressures and temperatures, e.g. steam sterilization.
– ORIGIN from **AUTO-** + Latin *clavis* 'key'.

autocracy /aw-tok-ruh-si/ • n. (pl. **autocracies**) **1** a system of government in which one person has total power. **2** a state governed in this way.
– ORIGIN from Greek *autos* 'self' + *kratos* 'power'.

autocrat • n. **1** a ruler who has absolute power. **2** a domineering person.
– DERIVATIVES **autocratic** adj.

autodidact /aw-toh-dy-dakt/ • n. a self-taught person.
– ORIGIN Greek *autodidaktos* 'self-taught'.

autograph • n. **1** a celebrity's signature written for an admirer. **2** a manuscript or musical score in an author's or composer's own handwriting. • v. write one's signature on.
– ORIGIN Greek *autographos* 'written with one's own hand'.

autoimmune • adj. (of disease) caused by antibodies or lymphocytes produced by the body to counteract substances naturally present in it.

automate • v. (**automates**, **automating**, **automated**) convert (a process or facility) so that it can operate automatically.

automated teller machine • n. a machine that provides banking services when a special card is inserted.

automatic • adj. **1** operating by itself without human control. **2** (of a firearm) self-loading and able to fire continuously. **3** done or happening without conscious thought. **4** (of a punishment) applied without question because of a fixed rule.
– DERIVATIVES **automatically** adv.
– ORIGIN Greek *automatos.*

automatic pilot • n. a device for keeping an aircraft on a set course.
– PHRASES **on automatic pilot** doing something out of habit and without concentration.

automation /aw-tuh-may-sh'n/ • n. the use of automatic equipment instead of manual labour.

automaton /aw-tom-uh-tuhn/ • n. (pl. **automata** /aw-tom-uh-tuh/ or **automatons**) **1** a moving mechanical device resembling a human being. **2** a machine which operates according to coded instructions.

automobile • n. N. Amer. a motor car.

automotive /aw-tuh-moh-tiv/ • adj. having to do with motor vehicles.

autonomous • adj. self-governing or independent.
– DERIVATIVES **autonomously** adv.

autonomy /aw-ton-uh-mi/ • n. **1** self-government. **2** freedom of action.
– ORIGIN Greek *autonomia.*

autopilot • n. = **AUTOMATIC PILOT**.

autopsy /aw-top-si/ • n. (pl. **autopsies**) an examination of a dead body to discover the cause of death.
– ORIGIN Greek *autopsia.*

autumn • n. esp. Brit. the season after summer and before winter.
– DERIVATIVES **autumnal** adj.
– ORIGIN Latin *autumnus.*

Auvergne E
/oh-vairn/ a region of south central France.

auxiliary /awg-zil-yuh-ri/ • adj. providing extra help and support. • n. (pl. **auxiliaries**) an auxiliary person or thing.
– ORIGIN Latin *auxilium* 'help'.

auxiliary verb • n. Grammar a verb used in forming the tenses, moods, and voices of other verbs (e.g. *be*, *do*, and *have*).

avail • v. (**avail oneself of**) use or take advantage of. • n. use or benefit: *his protests were to little avail.*
– ORIGIN Latin *valere* 'be strong'.

available • adj. **1** able to be used or obtained. **2** not occupied.
– DERIVATIVES **availability** n.

avalanche /av-uh-lahnsh/ • n. **1** a mass of snow and ice falling rapidly down a mountainside. **2** an overwhelming amount: *an avalanche of crime.*
– ORIGIN French.

Avalon E
/av-uh-lon/ (in Arthurian legend) the place to which Arthur was taken after his death.

avant-garde /a-von gard/ • adj. (in the arts) new and experimental.
– ORIGIN French, 'vanguard'.

avarice • n. extreme greed for wealth or material things.
– ORIGIN Latin *avarus* 'greedy'.

avaricious /av-uh-ri-shuhss/ • adj. very greedy for wealth or material things.

avatar /av-uh-tar/ • n. Hinduism a god or goddess appearing in bodily form on earth.
– ORIGIN Sanskrit, 'descent'.

Avebury E
/ayv-buh-ri/ a village in Wiltshire, site of a major late-Neolithic monument consisting of circles of standing stones.

Ave Maria /ah-vay muh-ree-uh/ • n. a prayer to the Virgin Mary used in Catholic worship.
– ORIGIN the opening words in Latin, 'hail, Mary!'

avenge • v. (**avenges**, **avenging**, **avenged**) cause harm in return for (a wrong).
– DERIVATIVES **avenger** n.
– ORIGIN Old French *avengier.*

avenue • n. **1** a broad road or path. **2** a means of achieving something.
– ORIGIN French.

aver /uh-ver/ • v. (**avers**, **averring**, **averred**) formal declare to be the case.
– ORIGIN Old French *averer.*

average • n. **1** the result obtained by adding several amounts together and then dividing the total by the number of amounts. **2** a usual amount or level. • adj. **1** being an average: *the average temperature was 4°C below normal.* **2** usual or ordinary. • v. (**averages**, **averaging**, **averaged**) **1** amount to or achieve as an average. **2** calculate the average of.
– ORIGIN French *avarie* 'damage to ship or

cargo'; the modern meaning comes from the sharing of the costs of things lost at sea.

averse ● adj. (**averse to**) strongly disliking or opposed to.
– ORIGIN Latin *avertere* 'turn away from'.

aversion ● n. a strong dislike.

avert ● v. **1** turn away (one's eyes). **2** prevent (an unpleasant event).
– ORIGIN Latin *vertere* 'to turn'.

avian /ay-vi-uhn/ ● adj. having to do with birds.
– ORIGIN Latin *avis* 'bird'.

aviary /ay-vi-uh-ri/ ● n. (pl. **aviaries**) a large enclosure for keeping birds in.

aviation ● n. the activity of operating and flying aircraft.
– ORIGIN Latin *avis* 'bird'.

aviator ● n. dated a pilot.

Avicenna E
/a-vi-**sen**-nuh/ (980–1037), Persian philosopher and physician. His *Canon of Medicine* was a standard medieval medical text and his philosophical system greatly influenced the development of scholasticism.

avid ● adj. keenly interested or enthusiastic.
– DERIVATIVES **avidly** adv.
– ORIGIN Latin *avere* 'crave'.

Avignon E
/**av**-i-nyon/ a city on the Rhône in SE France. From 1309 until 1377 it was the residence of the popes during their exile from Rome.

avionics ● n. electronics used in aviation.

avocado ● n. (pl. **avocados**) a pear-shaped fruit with pale green flesh and a large stone.
– ORIGIN Spanish.

avocet /av-uh-set/ ● n. a wading bird with long legs and an upturned bill.
– ORIGIN French.

Avogadro E
/a-vuh-**gah**-droh/, Amedeo (1776–1856), Italian chemist and physicist. He proposed that equal volumes of gases at the same temperature and pressure contain the same numbers of molecules, a hypothesis which is used in determining molecular weights.

avoid ● v. **1** keep away or refrain from. **2** prevent from doing or happening.
– DERIVATIVES **avoidable** adj. **avoidance** n.
– ORIGIN Old French *evuider* 'clear out'.

avoirdupois /av-war-dyoo-**pwah**/ ● n. a system of weights based on a pound of 16 ounces or 7,000 grains. Compare with **TROY**.
– ORIGIN from Old French *aveir de peis* 'goods of weight'.

Avon E
a former county of SW England, replaced in 1996 by unitary councils of NW Somerset, Bristol, South Gloucestershire, and Bath and NE Somerset.

avow ● v. assert or confess openly.
– DERIVATIVES **avowal** n.
– ORIGIN Old French *avouer* 'acknowledge'.

avuncular /uh-vung-kyuu-ler/ ● adj. like an uncle in being friendly towards a younger person.
– ORIGIN Latin *avunculus* 'maternal uncle'.

await ● v. wait for.

awake ● v. (**awakes**, **awaking**, **awoke**; past part. **awoken**) **1** stop sleeping. **2** make or become active again. ● adj. not asleep.

awaken ● v. **1** awake. **2** stir up (a feeling).

awakening ● n. **1** an act of becoming suddenly aware of something. **2** the beginning of a feeling or belief.

award ● v. give officially as a prize or reward. ● n. **1** something awarded. **2** the action of awarding.
– ORIGIN Old French *esguarder* 'consider'.

aware ● adj. having knowledge of a situation or fact.
– DERIVATIVES **awareness** n.
– ORIGIN Old English.

awash ● adj. covered or flooded with water.

away ● adv. **1** to or at a distance. **2** into a place for storage. **3** until disappearing: *the sound died away.* **4** constantly or continuously. ● adj. (of a sports fixture) played at the opponents' ground.
– ORIGIN Old English.

Awdry E
/aw-dri/, Reverend W. (1911–97), English author, creator of the *Thomas the Tank Engine* series of children's books.

awe ● n. a feeling of great respect mixed with fear. ● v. (**awes**, **awing**, **awed**) fill with awe.
– ORIGIN Old English.

awesome ● adj. **1** inspiring awe. **2** informal excellent.

awful ● adj. **1** very bad or unpleasant. **2** used for emphasis: *an awful lot.*
– DERIVATIVES **awfulness** n.

awfully ● adv. **1** informal very or very much: *I'm awfully sorry.* **2** very badly or unpleasantly.

awhile ● adv. for a short time.

awkward ● adj. **1** hard to do or deal with. **2** causing or feeling embarrassment. **3** inconvenient. **4** clumsy.
– DERIVATIVES **awkwardly** adv. **awkwardness** n.
– ORIGIN Old Norse.

awl /awl/ ● n. a small pointed tool used for making holes.
– ORIGIN Old English.

awn /awn/ ● n. Bot. a stiff bristle growing from the ear or flower of barley, rye, and grasses.
– ORIGIN Old Norse.

awning ● n. a sheet of canvas on a frame, used for shelter.
– ORIGIN unknown.

awoke past of **AWAKE**.

awoken past part. of **AWAKE**.

AWOL /ay-wol/ ● adj. Mil. absent but without intent to desert.
– ORIGIN from *absent without* (*official*) *leave*.

awry /uh-ry/ ● adv. & adj. away from the expected course or position.
– ORIGIN from **WRY**.

axe (US also **ax**) ● n. a tool with a heavy blade, used for chopping wood. ● v. (**axes**, **axing**, **axed**) cancel or dismiss suddenly and ruthlessly.
– PHRASES **have an axe to grind** have a private reason for doing something.
– ORIGIN Old English.

axes pl. of **AXIS**.

axial /ak-si-uhl/ ● adj. forming or having to do with an axis.

axil /ak-sil/ ● n. Bot. the upper angle where a leaf joins a stem.

– ORIGIN Latin *axilla*.

axiom /ak-si-uhm/ ● **n.** a statement regarded as obviously true.
– DERIVATIVES **axiomatic** adj.
– ORIGIN Greek *axiōma* 'what is thought fitting'.

axis /ak-siss/ ● **n.** (pl. **axes** /ak-seez/) **1** an imaginary line through a body, about which it rotates. **2** an imaginary line about which a regular figure is symmetrically arranged. **3** Math. a fixed reference line for the measurement of coordinates.
– ORIGIN Latin, 'axle, pivot'.

axle /ak-s'l/ ● **n.** a rod passing through the centre of a wheel or group of wheels.
– ORIGIN Old Norse.

ayatollah /I-uh-tol-luh/ ● **n.** a religious leader in Iran.
– ORIGIN Arabic, 'token of God'.

Ayatollah Khomeini E
see **KHOMEINI**.

Ayckbourn E
/ayk-born/, Sir Alan (b.1939), English dramatist, known for comedies dealing with suburban and middle-class life, such as *A Chorus of Disapproval*.

aye /*rhymes with* my/ (also **ay**) ● **exclam.** archaic or dialect yes. ● **n.** a vote in favour of something.
– ORIGIN prob. from *I*, first person personal pronoun.

Ayers Rock E
/airz/ a red rock mass in Northern Territory, Australia. The largest such mass in the world, it is 348 m (1,143 ft) high and about 9 km (6 miles) in circumference. Aboriginal name **ULURU**.

Ayrshire E
/air-sheer, air-sher/ a former county of SW Scotland, now divided into the administrative regions of **North Ayrshire**, **East Ayrshire**, and **South Ayrshire**.

azalea /uh-zay-li-uh/ ● **n.** a shrub with brightly coloured flowers.
– ORIGIN Greek *azaleos* 'dry' (because the shrubs flourish in dry soil).

Azerbaijan E
/az-er-by-jahn/ a country in SE Europe, on the western shore of the Caspian Sea; capital, Baku.
– DERIVATIVES **Azerbaijani** n. & adj.

Azikiwe E
/ah-zi-kee-way/, (Benjamin) Nnamdi (1904–96), Nigerian statesman, the first Governor General of an independent Nigeria 1960–3 and its first President 1963–6.

azimuth /az-i-muhth/ ● **n.** Astron. the horizontal direction of a celestial object, measured from the north or south point of the horizon.
– ORIGIN Arabic, 'the way, direction'.

Azores E
/uh-zorz/ a group of partially autonomous Portuguese islands in the Atlantic Ocean, west of Portugal; capital, Ponta Delgada.

Azov, Sea of E
/az-off/ an inland sea of southern Russia and Ukraine, separated from the Black Sea by the Crimea and linked to it by a narrow strait.

Aztec /az-tek/ ● **n.** a member of the American Indian people dominant in Mexico before the Spanish conquest.
– ORIGIN from a Central American language.

azure /az-yuur/ ● **adj.** bright blue in colour like a cloudless sky. ● **n.** a bright blue colour.
– ORIGIN Old French *azur*.

Bb

B[1] (also **b**) ● **n.** (pl. **Bs** or **B's**) **1** the second letter of the alphabet. **2** referring to the second item in a set. **3** Music the seventh note of the scale of C major.

B[2] ● **abbrev.** **1** (in chess) bishop. **2** black (used in describing grades of pencil lead).

b. ● **abbrev.** born.

BA ● **abbrev.** Bachelor of Arts.

baa ● **v.** (**baas**, **baaing**, **baaed**) (of a sheep or lamb) bleat. ● **n.** the cry of a sheep or lamb.

Baader-Meinhof Group E
/bah-der myn-hoff/ = **RED ARMY FACTION**.

Baalbek E
/bahl-bek/ a town in eastern Lebanon, site of the ancient city of Heliopolis.

Babbage E
/bab-bij/, Charles (1791–1871), English mathematician, inventor, and pioneer of machine computing.

babble ● **v.** (**babbles**, **babbling**, **babbled**) talk rapidly in a thoughtless or confused way. ● **n.** thoughtless or confused talk.
– ORIGIN prob. from German *babbelen*.

babe ● **n.** **1** literary a baby. **2** informal a sexually attractive young woman.

babel /bay-b'l/ ● **n.** a confused noise made by a number of people speaking together.
– ORIGIN from *Babel* (see **TOWER OF BABEL**), where God confused the languages of the builders.

Babel, Tower of E
see **TOWER OF BABEL**.

baboon ● n. a large monkey with a long snout, large teeth, and a pink rump.
– ORIGIN Latin *babewynus*.

Babur E
/**bah**-boor/ (1483–1530), first Mogul emperor of India *c.*1526–30. A descendent of Tamerlane, he invaded India in *c.*1525 and conquered the territory from the Oxus to Patna.

baby ● n. (pl. **babies**) **1** a child or animal that is newly or recently born. **2** a timid or childish person. **3** informal an affectionate way of talking about a person one is in love with. ● adj. small or very young: *baby carrots.* ● v. (**babies**, **babying**, **babied**) treat (someone) too protectively.
– PHRASES **be left holding the baby** informal be given something to do that one does not want to do.
– DERIVATIVES **babyhood** n. **babyish** adj.

baby boom ● n. informal a temporary sharp rise in the birth rate, especially the one following the Second World War.

Babylon E
/**bab**-i-lon/ an ancient city in Mesopotamia. It was the capital of Babylonia in the 2nd millennium BC and was famous for its Hanging Gardens.

Babylonia E
/ba-bi-**loh**-ni-uh/ an ancient region and powerful kingdom of Mesopotamia.
– DERIVATIVES **Babylonian** adj. & n.

babysit ● v. (**babysits**, **babysat**, **babysitting**) look after a child or children while the parents are out.
– DERIVATIVES **babysitter** n.

Bacall E
/buh-**kawl**/, Lauren (b.1924), American actress. She co-starred with her husband, Humphrey Bogart, in a number of thrillers, including *The Big Sleep*.

baccalaureate /ba-kuh-**lor**-i-uht/ ● n. **1** an examination taken to qualify for higher education. **2** a university degree of bachelor.
– ORIGIN Latin *baccalaureus* 'bachelor'.

baccarat /**bak**-kuh-rah/ ● n. a gambling card game in which players bet against a banker.
– ORIGIN French *baccara*.

bacchanalian /bak-kuh-**nay**-li-uhn/ ● adj. (of a party or celebration) drunken and wild.
– ORIGIN from the god **Bacchus**.

Bacchus E
/**bak**-kuhss/ the Greek and Roman god of wine. Also called **Dionysus**.

Bach E
/bahkh/, Johann Sebastian (1685–1750), German baroque composer. He produced works ranging from violin concertos, suites, and the six *Brandenburg Concertos* to sacred cantatas and large-scale choral works such as the *Mass in B minor*.

Bacharach E
/**bak**-uh-rak/, Burt (b.1929), American writer of popular songs, including 'Walk On By', and 'Raindrops Keep Falling on my Head'.

bachelor ● n. **1** a man who has never been married. **2** a person who holds a first degree from a university.
– DERIVATIVES **bachelorhood** n.
– ORIGIN Old French *bacheler* 'a young man wishing to become a knight'.

bacillus /buh-**sil**-luhss/ ● n. (pl. **bacilli** /buh-**sil**-lee/) a rod-shaped bacterium.
– ORIGIN Latin, 'little stick'.

back ● n. **1** the rear surface of a person's body from the shoulders to the hips. **2** the upper part of an animal's body, equivalent to a person's back. **3** the side or part of something that is furthest from the front or that is not normally seen or used. **4** a player in a team game who plays in a defensive position behind the forwards. ● adv. **1** in the opposite direction from that in which one is facing or travelling. **2** so as to return to an earlier or normal position or state. **3** into the past. **4** in return. ● v. **1** give support to. **2** walk or drive backwards. **3** bet money on (a person or animal) to win a race or contest. **4** (**back on/on to**) (of a building) have its back facing or next to. **5** cover the back of (an object). **6** provide musical backing to (a singer or musician). **7** (of the wind) change direction anticlockwise. ● adj. **1** at or towards the back. **2** in a remote or less important position. **3** relating to the past.
– PHRASES **back and forth** to and fro. **the back of beyond** a very remote place. **back down** give in. **back off** draw back from opposing someone. **back out** withdraw from something one has promised to do. **back to front** Brit. with the back at the front and the front at the back. **back up** Computing make a spare copy of (data or a disk). **behind someone's back** without a person knowing. **get** (or **put**) **someone's back up** annoy someone. **put one's back into** tackle (a task) in a determined and energetic way. **turn one's back on** ignore; reject. **with one's back to** (or **up against**) **the wall** in a very difficult situation.
– DERIVATIVES **backer** n. **backless** adj.
– ORIGIN Old English.

backbencher ● n. a member of parliament who does not hold a government or opposition post and who sits behind the front benches in the House of Commons.
– DERIVATIVES **backbench** adj.

backbiting ● n. spiteful talk about a person who is not present.

backbone ● n. **1** the spine. **2** the chief support of a system or organization. **3** strength of character.

back-breaking ● adj. (of manual labour) physically demanding.

back burner ● n. (in phr. **on the back burner**) set aside because not very important.

backchat ● n. Brit. informal rude or cheeky remarks.

backcomb ● v. esp. Brit. comb (the hair) towards the scalp to make it look thicker.

backdate ● v. (**backdates**, **backdating**, **backdated**) Brit. make valid from an earlier date.

back-door ● adj. done in an underhand or secret way.

backdrop ● n. **1** a painted cloth hung at the back of a theatre stage as part of the scenery. **2** the setting or background for a scene or event.

b

backfire • v. (**backfires**, **backfiring**, **backfired**) **1** (of a vehicle or its engine) make a bang as a result of a mistimed explosion. **2** (of a plan or action) produce the opposite effect to what was meant.

backgammon • n. a board game in which two players move their pieces around triangular points according to the throw of dice.
– ORIGIN from BACK + an Old English word meaning 'game'.

background • n. **1** part of a scene or description that forms a setting for the main figures or events. **2** information or circumstances that influence or explain something. **3** a person's education, experience, and social circumstances.

backhand • n. (in tennis and similar games) a stroke played with the back of the hand facing in the direction of the stroke.

backhanded • adj. **1** made with the back of the hand facing in the direction of movement. **2** seeming favourable but not really so: *a backhanded compliment.*

backhander • n. **1** a backhand stroke or blow. **2** Brit. informal a bribe.

backing • n. **1** support. **2** a layer of material that forms or strengthens the back of something. **3** music or singing that accompanies a pop singer.

backlash • n. **1** a strong and angry reaction by a large number of people. **2** recoil or freedom of movement between parts of a machine.

backlog • n. a build-up of things needing to be dealt with.

backpack • n. a rucksack. • v. travel carrying one's belongings in a rucksack.
– DERIVATIVES **backpacker** n.

back-pedal • v. (**back-pedals**, **back-pedalling**, **back-pedalled**) **1** move the pedals of a bicycle backwards. **2** go back on something said or done.

back-seat driver • n. informal a passenger in a car who gives the driver unwanted advice.

backside • n. informal a person's bottom.

backslapping • n. the offering of hearty congratulations or praise.

backslide • v. (**backslides**, **backsliding**, **backslid**) return to bad ways.

backspin • n. a backward spin given to a moving ball, making it stop more quickly or bounce back at a steeper angle.

backstage • adv. & adj. behind the stage in a theatre.

backstreet • n. a less important street. • adj. secret, especially because illegal: *backstreet abortions.*

backstroke • n. a swimming stroke in which the swimmer lies on their back and lifts their arms alternately out of the water in a backward circular movement.

back-to-back • adj. **1** esp. Brit. (of houses) built in a terrace backing on to another terrace, with a wall or an alley between. **2** following one after the other.

backtrack • v. **1** retrace one's steps. **2** change one's opinion to the opposite of what it was.

back-up • n. **1** support. **2** a person or thing kept ready to be used when needed.

backward • adj. **1** directed towards the back. **2** having made less progress than is normal or expected. • adv. (also **backwards**) **1** towards one's back. **2** back towards the starting point. **3** opposite to the usual direction or order.
– PHRASES **bend over backwards** informal try one's hardest to be fair or helpful. **know something backwards** know something very fully.
– DERIVATIVES **backwardly** adv. **backwardness** n.

backwash • n. waves flowing outwards behind a ship.

backwater • n. **1** a stretch of stagnant water on a river. **2** a place or state which always stays the same.

backwoods • pl. n. esp. N. Amer. **1** uncleared forested land in a remote region. **2** a region that is remote or has few inhabitants.
– DERIVATIVES **backwoodsman** n.

backyard • n. **1** Brit. a yard at the back of a house. **2** N. Amer. a back garden. **3** informal the area close to where one lives.

Bacon[1], E
Francis, Baron Verulam and Viscount St Albans (1561–1626), English statesman, philosopher, and scientist. His emphasis on the observation and classification of the natural world laid the basis of the inductive method of scientific research.

Bacon[2], E
Francis (1909–92), Irish painter. His work depicts human figures in grotesquely distorted postures.

bacon • n. salted or smoked meat from the back or sides of a pig.
– PHRASES **bring home the bacon** informal make money or achieve success.
– ORIGIN Old French.

bacteria • pl. n. (sing. **bacterium**) a group of microscopic organisms, each made up of a single cell, many kinds of which can cause disease.
– DERIVATIVES **bacterial** adj.
– ORIGIN Greek *baktērion* 'little rod'.

USAGE bacteria
The word **bacteria** means 'microscopic organisms, each made up of a single cell' and is the plural form of **bacterium**. This means that **bacteria** should always be used with a plural verb: *the bacteria were multiplying.*

bacteriology /bak-teer-i-ol-uh-ji/ • n. the study of bacteria.
– DERIVATIVES **bacteriological** adj. **bacteriologist** n.

Bactrian camel /bak-tri-uhn/ • n. a camel with two humps, found in central Asia.
– ORIGIN from the ancient empire of *Bactria* in central Asia.

bad • adj. (**worse**, **worst**) **1** poor in quality; well below standard. **2** unpleasant. **3** severe; serious. **4** wicked or evil. **5** (**bad for**) harmful to. **6** injured, ill, or diseased. **7** (of food) decayed. **8** N. Amer. informal good; excellent.
– DERIVATIVES **badness** n.
– ORIGIN perh. from an Old English word meaning 'womanish man'.

bad debt • n. a debt that will not be repaid.

bade /bayd/ past of BID[2].

Baden-Powell E
/bay-d'n-**poh**-uhl/, Robert (Stephenson Smyth), 1st Baron Baden-Powell of Gilwell (1857–1941), English soldier and founder of the Boy Scout movement.

badge • n. a small flat object that a person wears to show who they are or what they do.
– ORIGIN unknown.

badger • n. a heavily built mammal with a grey and black coat and a white-striped head, which lives underground. • v. (**badgers, badgering, badgered**) pester (someone) to do something.
– ORIGIN perh. from BADGE, because of the animal's head markings.

badinage /**bad**-i-nahzh/ • n. witty conversation.
– ORIGIN French.

badlands • pl. n. poor land with very little soil.

badly • adv. (**worse, worst**) **1** in a way that is below acceptable standards. **2** severely; seriously. **3** very much.
– PHRASES **badly off** poor.

badminton • n. a game with rackets in which a shuttlecock is hit across a high net.
– ORIGIN named after *Badminton* in SW England.

bad-mouth • v. informal criticize spitefully.

bad-tempered • adj. easily angered.

Baez E
/**by**-ez/, Joan (b.1941), American folk singer.

Baffin Island E
a large island in the Canadian Arctic, situated at the mouth of Hudson Bay.

baffle • v. (**baffles, baffling, baffled**) make (someone) feel puzzled. • n. a device for controlling or stopping the flow of sound, light, gas, or a fluid.
– DERIVATIVES **bafflement** n.
– ORIGIN perh. from French *bafouer* 'ridicule'.

bag • n. **1** a flexible container with an opening at the top. **2** (**bags**) loose folds of skin under a person's eyes. **3** (**bags of**) Brit. informal plenty of. **4** informal an unpleasant or unattractive woman. • v. (**bags, bagging, bagged**) **1** put in a bag. **2** manage to kill or catch (an animal). **3** informal manage to get.
– PHRASES **in the bag** informal sure to be gained.
– ORIGIN perh. from Old Norse.

bagatelle /ba-guh-**tel**/ • n. **1** a game in which small balls are hit into numbered holes on a board. **2** something unimportant.
– ORIGIN Italian *bagatella*.

bagel /**bay**-g'l/ • n. a ring-shaped bread roll with a heavy texture.
– ORIGIN Yiddish.

baggage • n. **1** luggage packed with belongings for travelling. **2** a person's past experiences or opinions seen as a burden: *emotional baggage*.
– ORIGIN Old French *bagage*.

baggy • adj. (**baggier, baggiest**) loose and hanging in bulges or folds.

Baghdad E
/bag-**dad**/ the capital of Iraq.

bag lady • n. informal a homeless woman who carries her possessions in shopping bags.

bagpipe (also **bagpipes**) • n. a musical instrument with pipes that are sounded by wind squeezed from a bag.
– DERIVATIVES **bagpiper** n.

baguette /ba-**get**/ • n. a long, narrow French loaf of bread.
– ORIGIN French.

Bahamas E
a country consisting of an archipelago off the SE coast of Florida, part of the West Indies; capital, Nassau.
– DERIVATIVES **Bahamian** /buh-**hay**-mi-uhn/ adj. & n.

Bahrain E
/bah-**rayn**/ a sheikhdom consisting of a group of islands in the Persian Gulf; capital, Manama.
– DERIVATIVES **Bahraini** adj. & n.

Baikal, Lake E
/by-**kahl**/ a large lake in southern Siberia. It is the largest freshwater lake in Europe and Asia and, with a depth of 1,743 m (5,714 ft), the deepest lake in the world.

bail[1] • n. **1** setting an accused person free before they are tried, often on condition that a sum of money is promised to the court to make sure they attend the trial. **2** money paid by or for such a person. • v. set free (an accused person) on payment of bail.
– ORIGIN Old French, 'custody'.

bail[2] • n. **1** Cricket either of the two crosspieces resting on the stumps. **2** a bar on a typewriter or computer printer which holds the paper steady. **3** a bar separating horses in an open stable.
– ORIGIN Old French *baile* 'enclosure'.

bail[3] (Brit. also **bale**) • v. **1** scoop water out of (a ship or boat). **2** (**bail out**) make an emergency jump out of an aircraft, using a parachute. **3** (**bail out**) rescue from a difficulty.
– ORIGIN French *baille* 'bucket'.

Baile Átha Cliath E
/blah a-thuh **kleer**/ Irish name for DUBLIN.

bailey • n. (pl. **baileys**) the outer wall of a castle.
– ORIGIN prob. from Old French *baile* 'enclosure'.

bailiff • n. **1** esp. Brit. a sheriff's officer who delivers writs, seizes property to clear rent that is owed, and carries out arrests. **2** Brit. the agent of a landlord.
– ORIGIN Old French *baillif*.

bailiwick /**bay**-li-wik/ • n. **1** Law a district over which a bailiff has authority. **2** (**one's bailiwick**) the field in which one operates or in which one is interested.
– ORIGIN from BAILIFF.

Bainbridge, E
Dame Beryl (b. 1934), English novelist. Her works include *An Awfully Big Adventure*.

Baird E
/baird/, John Logie (1888–1946), Scottish pioneer of television, who gave the first public demonstration of a television image in 1926 and made the first transatlantic transmission in 1928.

bairn ● n. Sc. & N. Engl. a child.
– ORIGIN Old English.

bait ● n. **1** food put on a hook or in a trap to attract fish or other animals. **2** var. of **BATE**. ● v. **1** taunt or tease. **2** (**baiting**) setting dogs on an animal (such as a badger or bear) that is trapped or tied up. **3** put bait on or in (a trap or hook).
– PHRASES **rise to the bait** react to taunting or temptation exactly as someone planned.
– ORIGIN Old Norse, 'pasture, food'.

baize ● n. a thick green material, used for covering billiard and card tables.
– ORIGIN French *bai* 'chestnut-coloured'.

bake ● v. (**bakes**, **baking**, **baked**) **1** cook (food) by dry heat in an oven. **2** heat (something) so as to dry or harden it. **3** informal be or become very hot in hot weather. ● n. a dish in which a number of ingredients are mixed together and baked.
– ORIGIN Old English.

Baker[1], E
Dame Janet (Abbott) (b.1933), English operatic mezzo-soprano.

Baker[2], E
Josephine (1906–75), American dancer. A star of the Folies-Bergère, she was famed for her exotic dancing and risqué clothing.

baker ● n. a person whose trade is making bread and cakes.
– PHRASES **baker's dozen** a group of thirteen.
– DERIVATIVES **bakery** n. (pl. **bakeries**).

baking powder ● n. a mixture of sodium bicarbonate and cream of tartar, used to make cakes rise.

baking soda ● n. sodium bicarbonate.

baksheesh /bak-**sheesh**/ ● n. (in India and some other eastern countries) money given as charity, a tip, or a bribe.
– ORIGIN Persian.

Baku E
/ba-**koo**/ the capital of Azerbaijan.

balaclava /ba-luh-**klah**-vuh/ ● n. a close-fitting woollen hat covering the head and neck except for the face.
– ORIGIN named after *Balaclava*, site of a battle in the Crimean War.

balance ● n. **1** a state in which weight is evenly distributed, ensuring that a person or object does not wobble or fall over. **2** a situation in which different parts are in the correct proportions: *political balance in broadcasting.* **3** a device for weighing. **4** an amount that is the difference between money received and money spent in an account: *a healthy bank balance.* **5** an amount still owed when part of a debt has been paid. ● v. (**balances**, **balancing**, **balanced**) **1** be or put in a steady position. **2** compare the value of (one thing) with another. **3** make (something) have a balance of proportions or parts: *she managed to balance work and family life.*
– PHRASES **be** (or **hang**) **in the balance** be in an uncertain state. **on balance** when everything is taken into account.
– DERIVATIVES **balancer** n.
– ORIGIN from Latin *libra bilanx* 'balance having two scale-pans'.

balance of payments ● n. the difference in total value between payments into and out of a country over a period.

balance of power ● n. **1** a situation in which states of the world have roughly equal power. **2** the power held by a small group when larger groups are of equal strength.

balance of trade ● n. the difference in value between a country's imports and exports.

balance sheet ● n. a written statement of what a business owns and what it owes.

Balanchine E
/**ba**-luhn-sheen/, George (1904–83), Russian-born American ballet dancer and choreographer, who worked with Diaghilev and later co-founded the company which became the New York City Ballet.

Balboa E
/bal-**boh**-uh/, Vasco Núñez de (1475–1519), Spanish explorer. In 1513 he reached the western coast of the isthmus of Darien (Panama), becoming the first European to see the Pacific Ocean.

balcony ● n. (pl. **balconies**) **1** an enclosed platform projecting from the outside of a building. **2** the highest level of seats in a theatre or cinema.
– ORIGIN Italian *balcone*.

bald ● adj. **1** having no hair on the head. **2** (of an animal) not covered by the usual fur, hair, or feathers. **3** (of a tyre) having the tread worn away. **4** plain or blunt: *the bald facts.*
– DERIVATIVES **baldness** n.
– ORIGIN prob. from a former word meaning 'white patch'.

balderdash ● n. nonsense.
– ORIGIN unknown.

balding ● adj. going bald.

Baldwin, E
Stanley, 1st Earl Baldwin of Bewdley (1867–1947), British Conservative statesman, Prime Minister 1923–4, 1924–9, and 1935–7.

bale[1] ● n. a large quantity of paper, hay, or cotton, tied or wrapped in a bundle. ● v. (**bales**, **baling**, **baled**) make up into bales.
– DERIVATIVES **baler** n.
– ORIGIN prob. from Dutch.

bale[2] ● n. & v. Brit. = **BAIL**[3].

Balearic Islands E
/ba-li-a-rik, buh-**leer**-ik/ (also **the Balearics**) a group of islands in the western Mediterranean forming an autonomous region of Spain, with four large islands (Majorca, Minorca, Ibiza, Formentera) and seven smaller ones; capital, Palma (on Majorca).

baleen /buh-**leen**/ ● n. whalebone.
– ORIGIN Latin *balaena* 'whale'.

baleen whale ● n. any of the kinds of whale that have plates of whalebone in the mouth for straining plankton from the water.

baleful ● adj. causing or threatening to cause harm.
– DERIVATIVES **balefully** adv.
– ORIGIN Old English.

Balfour E
/**bal**-fer/, Arthur James, 1st Earl of Balfour (1848–1930), British Conservative statesman, Prime Minister 1902–5. In 1917 (as Foreign

Secretary) Balfour issued the Balfour Declaration in favour of a Jewish national home in Palestine.

Bali E
/bah-li/ a mountainous island of Indonesia.

balk • v. & n. esp. US = **BAULK**.

Balkanize (also **Balkanise**) • v. (**Balkanizes**, **Balkanizing**, **Balkanized**) divide (a region or body) into smaller states or groups who oppose each other.
– DERIVATIVES **Balkanization** (also **Balkanisation**) n.

Balkans E
/bawl-kuhnz/ the countries occupying the peninsula in SE Europe bounded by the Adriatic and Ionian Seas in the west, the Aegean and Black Seas in the east, and the Mediterranean in the south.
– DERIVATIVES **Balkan** adj.

Ball, E
John (d.1381), English priest and rebel. He was excommunicated and imprisoned for heresy, and following the Peasants' Revolt was hanged as a traitor.

ball[1] • n. **1** a rounded object that is kicked, thrown, or hit in a game. **2** a single throw or kick of the ball in a game. **3** a rounded part or thing: *the ball of the foot.* • v. squeeze or form into a ball.
– PHRASES **the ball is in your court** it is up to you to make the next move. **on the ball** alert. **play ball** informal cooperate. **start** (or **set**) **the ball rolling** make a start.
– ORIGIN Old Norse.

ball[2] • n. a formal party for dancing.
– PHRASES **have a ball** informal really enjoy oneself.
– ORIGIN French *bal* 'a dance'.

ballad • n. **1** a poem or song telling a popular story. **2** a slow sentimental or romantic song.
– ORIGIN Provençal *balada* 'dance, song to dance to'.

ball-and-socket joint • n. a joint in which a rounded end lies in a socket, allowing movement in all directions.

Ballarat E
/bal-luh-rat/ a city in Victoria, Australia, formerly the centre of a rich gold-mining industry.

Ballard, E
J. G. (b.1930; full name *James Graham Ballard*), British novelist, known for his autobiographical novel *Empire of the Sun* and for his works of science fiction.

ballast • n. **1** a heavy substance carried by a ship or hot-air balloon to keep it stable. **2** gravel or coarse stone used to form the base of a railway track or road.
– ORIGIN prob. German or Scandinavian.

ball bearing • n. **1** a bearing in which the parts are separated by a ring of small metal balls which reduce rubbing. **2** a ball used in such a bearing.

ballboy (or **ballgirl**) • n. a boy (or girl) who fetches balls that go out of play during a tennis match or baseball game.

ballcock • n. a valve which automatically tops up a cistern when liquid is drawn from it.

ballerina • n. a female ballet dancer.

Ballesteros E
/bal-luh-stair-oss/, Severiano (b.1957), Spanish golfer. He won the British Open three times and in 1980 was the youngest-ever winner of the US Masters.

ballet • n. **1** an artistic form of dancing performed to music, using set steps and gestures. **2** a creative work of this form.
– DERIVATIVES **balletic** adj.
– ORIGIN Italian *balletto* 'a little dance'.

ballistic /buh-liss-tik/ • adj. having to do with to the flight through the air of missiles, bullets, or similar objects. • n. (**ballistics**) the science of missiles and firearms.
– PHRASES **go ballistic** informal fly into a rage.
– ORIGIN Greek *ballein* 'to throw'.

ballistic missile • n. a missile which is powered and guided when first launched, but falls under gravity on to its target.

balloon • n. **1** a small rubber bag which is inflated and used as a toy or a decoration. **2** a large bag filled with hot air or gas to make it rise in the air, with a basket for passengers attached to it. **3** a rounded outline in which the words or thoughts of characters in a comic strip are written. • v. **1** swell outwards. **2** increase rapidly. **3** (**ballooning**) travelling by hot-air balloon.
– DERIVATIVES **balloonist** n.
– ORIGIN French *ballon* 'large ball'.

ballot • n. **1** a way of voting on something secretly, usually by means of paper slips placed in a box. **2** (**the ballot**) the total number of such votes recorded. • v. (**ballots**, **balloting**, **balloted**) ask for a secret vote from.
– ORIGIN Italian *ballotta* 'little ball' (from the former practice of voting by placing a ball in a container).

ballpark esp. N. Amer. • n. **1** a baseball ground. **2** informal a particular area or range. • adj. informal approximate: *a ballpark figure.*

ballpoint pen • n. a pen with a tiny ball as its writing point.

ballroom • n. a large room for formal dancing.

ballroom dancing • n. formal dancing in couples.

balls • pl. n. vulgar **1** testicles. **2** courage to do something. **3** Brit. nonsense.

balls-up vulgar • n. Brit. a bungled task or action. • v. (**balls up**) bungle (something).

ballsy • adj. informal bold and confident.

ballyhoo • n. informal excessive publicity or fuss.
– ORIGIN unknown.

balm • n. **1** a sweet-smelling ointment used to heal or soothe the skin. **2** something that soothes or heals.
– ORIGIN Latin *balsamum* 'balsam'.

Balmoral Castle E
a Scottish castle used by the British royal family as a holiday residence.

balmy • adj. (of the weather) pleasantly warm.

baloney /buh-loh-ni/ • n. informal nonsense.
– ORIGIN perh. from **BOLOGNA**.

balsa /bawl-suh/ (also **balsa wood**) • n. very lightweight wood from a tropical American

tree, used for making models.
– ORIGIN Spanish, 'raft'.

balsam /bawl-suhm/ ● n. a scented resin obtained from some trees and shrubs, used in perfumes and medicines.
– DERIVATIVES **balsamic** adj.
– ORIGIN Greek *balsamon*.

balsamic vinegar /bawl-sam-ik/ ● n. dark, sweet Italian vinegar.

balti /bawl-ti, bal-ti/ ● n. (pl. **baltis**) a spicy Pakistani dish that is cooked in a small two-handled pan.
– ORIGIN Urdu, 'pail'.

Baltic /bawl-tik/ ● adj. relating to the Baltic Sea or those states on its eastern shores.

Baltic Sea E
an almost landlocked sea of northern Europe, between Sweden, Finland, Russia, Poland, Germany, and Denmark.

Baltimore E
/bawl-ti-mor, bol-ti-mor/ a seaport in north Maryland, USA.

baluster /ba-luh-ster/ ● n. a short pillar forming part of a series supporting a rail.
– ORIGIN Italian *balaustra* 'wild pomegranate flower'.

balustrade /ba-luh-strayd/ ● n. a railing supported by balusters.

Balzac E
/bal-zak/, Honoré de (1799–1850), French novelist, remembered for his series of ninety-one interconnected novels and stories known collectively as *La Comédie humaine*.

Bamako E
/bam-uh-koh/ the capital of Mali.

bamboo ● n. a giant tropical grass with hollow woody stems.
– ORIGIN Malay.

bamboozle ● v. (**bamboozles**, **bamboozling**, **bamboozled**) informal **1** cheat or deceive. **2** confuse.
– ORIGIN unknown.

ban ● v. (**bans**, **banning**, **banned**) forbid officially. ● n. an official order forbidding something.
– ORIGIN Old English, 'call for by a public proclamation'.

banal /buh-nahl/ ● adj. boring because not new or unusual.
– DERIVATIVES **banality** n. (pl. **banalities**).
– ORIGIN first meaning 'compulsory': from French *ban* 'proclamation'.

banana ● n. a long curved fruit of a tropical tree, with yellow skin and soft flesh.
– PHRASES **go** (or **be**) **bananas** informal become (or be) mad or angry.
– ORIGIN from an African language.

band[1] ● n. **1** a flat, thin strip or loop of material used as a fastener, for strengthening, or as decoration. **2** a stripe or strip of a different colour or nature from its surroundings: *a band of cloud*. **3** a range of values or frequencies within a series: *the lower-rate tax band*. ● v. **1** put a band on or round. **2** mark with a stripe or stripes. **3** put in a range or category.
– ORIGIN Old English.

band[2] ● n. **1** a small group of musicians and singers who play pop, jazz, or rock music. **2** a group of musicians who play brass, wind, or percussion instruments. **3** a group of people with the same aim or a shared feature. ● v. form a group to follow a common aim.
– ORIGIN Old French *bande*.

Banda E
/ban-duh/, Hastings Kamuzu (1906–97), Malawian statesman, Prime Minister 1964–94 and the first President of the Republic of Malawi 1966–94.

bandage ● n. a strip of material used to tie around a wound or to protect an injury. ● v. (**bandages**, **bandaging**, **bandaged**) tie a bandage around.
– ORIGIN French.

bandanna /ban-dan-nuh/ (also **bandana**) ● n. a large coloured handkerchief.
– ORIGIN Hindi.

Bandaranaike E
/ban-duh-ruh-ny-kuh/, Sirimavo Ratwatte Dias (1916–2000), Sinhalese stateswoman, Prime Minister of Sri Lanka 1960–5, 1970–7, and 1994–2000. She was the world's first woman Prime Minister.

Bandar Seri Begawan E
/ban-duh se-ri buh-gah-wuhn/ the capital of Brunei.

B. & B. ● abbrev. bed and breakfast.

bandeau /ban-doh/ ● n. (pl. **bandeaux** /ban-dohz/) **1** a narrow band worn round the head. **2** a woman's strapless top.
– ORIGIN Old French *bandel* 'small band'.

bandicoot /ban-di-koot/ ● n. an insect-eating marsupial found in Australia and New Guinea.
– ORIGIN from a word in an Indian language, meaning 'pig-rat'.

bandit /ban-dit/ ● n. (pl. **bandits** or **banditti** /ban-dee-ti/) a member of a gang of armed robbers.
– DERIVATIVES **banditry** n.
– ORIGIN Italian *bandito* 'banned'.

bandolier /ban-duh-leer/ (also **bandoleer**) ● n. a shoulder belt with loops or pockets for cartridges.
– ORIGIN French *bandoulière*.

bandsaw ● n. a power saw consisting of an endless moving steel belt with a toothed edge.

bandstand ● n. a covered outdoor platform for a band to play on.

bandwagon ● n. an activity or cause that has suddenly become fashionable or popular: *the company is jumping on the Green bandwagon*.

bandwidth ● n. **1** a range of frequencies used in telecommunications. **2** the ability of a computer network or other telecommunication system to transmit signals.

bandy[1] ● adj. (of a person's legs) curved outwards so that the knees are wide apart.
– ORIGIN perh. from a former word meaning 'curved hockey stick'.

bandy[2] ● v. (**bandies**, **bandying**, **bandied**) use (an idea, term, or name) frequently in casual talk.
– PHRASES **bandy words** exchange angry remarks.
– ORIGIN perh. from French *bander* 'take sides at tennis'.

bane ● n. a cause of great distress or annoyance.
– ORIGIN Old English.

bang ● n. **1** a sudden loud sharp noise. **2** a sudden painful blow. ● v. **1** hit or put down forcefully and noisily. **2** make or cause to make a bang. ● adv. informal, esp. Brit. exactly: *bang on time*.
– PHRASES **bang away at** informal do in a stubbornly determined way. **bang on** Brit. informal exactly right. **bang on about** informal talk about boringly for a long time. **bang up** Brit. informal put in prison.

Bangalore E
/bang-guh-**lor**/ a city in south central India, capital of the state of Karnataka.

banger ● n. esp. Brit. **1** informal a sausage. **2** informal an old car. **3** a loud explosive firework.

Bangkok E
/bang-**kok**/ the capital and chief port of Thailand.

Bangladesh E
/bang-gluh-**desh**/ a country of the Indian subcontinent, in the Ganges delta; capital, Dhaka.
– DERIVATIVES **Bangladeshi** adj. & n.

bangle ● n. a rigid band worn around the arm as jewellery.
– ORIGIN Hindi.

Bangui E
/**bang**-gee/ the capital of the Central African Republic.

banish ● v. **1** make (someone) leave a place, especially as an official punishment. **2** get rid of; drive away.
– DERIVATIVES **banishment** n.
– ORIGIN Old French *banir*.

banister (also **bannister**) ● n. **1** the upright posts and handrail at the side of a staircase. **2** a single upright post at the side of a staircase.
– ORIGIN from **BALUSTER**.

banjo ● n. (pl. **banjos** or **banjoes**) a musical instrument like a guitar, with five strings, a circular body, and a long neck.
– DERIVATIVES **banjoist** n.
– ORIGIN from *bandore*, a kind of lute.

Banjul E
/ban-**jool**/ the capital of Gambia.

bank[1] ● n. **1** the land alongside a river or lake. **2** a long, high slope, mound, or mass: *mud banks*. **3** a set of similar things grouped together in rows. ● v. **1** make or form into a bank. **2** (of an aircraft or vehicle) tilt sideways in making a turn.
– ORIGIN Old Norse.

bank[2] ● n. **1** an organization offering financial services, especially loans and the safekeeping of customers' money. **2** a stock or supply available for use: *a blood bank*. **3** a site or container where something may be left for recycling: *a paper bank*. ● v. **1** place in a bank. **2** have an account at a bank. **3** (**bank on**) rely on.
– PHRASES **break the bank** informal cost more than one can afford.
– ORIGIN Latin *banca* 'bench' (first meaning a money dealer's table).

bankable ● adj. certain to bring profit and success.
– DERIVATIVES **bankability** n.

bank card ● n. a cheque card.

banker ● n. a person who manages or owns a bank.

bank holiday ● n. Brit. a public holiday, when banks are officially closed.

banking ● n. the business activity of a bank.

banknote ● n. a piece of paper money issued by a central bank.

Bank of England E
the central bank of England and Wales, which issues legal tender, manages the national debt, administers exchange rate policy, and sets interest rates.

bank rate ● n. = **BASE RATE** or **DISCOUNT RATE**.

bankroll ● n. N. Amer. available funds. ● v. informal give funds to.

bankrupt ● adj. **1** declared in law as not having the money to pay one's debts. **2** completely lacking in a particular good quality or value: *morally bankrupt*. ● n. a bankrupt person. ● v. make bankrupt.
– DERIVATIVES **bankruptcy** n. (pl. **bankruptcies**).
– ORIGIN from Italian *banca rotta* 'broken bench' or 'broken bank'.

banner ● n. a long strip of cloth with a slogan or design, hung up or carried on poles.
– ORIGIN Old French *baniere*.

Bannister, E
Sir Roger (Gilbert) (b.1929), British athlete and neurologist. In 1954 he became the first person to run a mile in under 4 minutes, with a time of 3 minutes 59.4 seconds.

bannister ● n. = **BANISTER**.

Bannockburn, Battle of E
/ban-nuhk-bern/ a battle which took place near Stirling in central Scotland in 1314, in which the English army of Edward II was defeated by the Scots under Robert the Bruce.

banns ● pl. n. a public announcement of an intended marriage read out in a parish church.
– ORIGIN plural of **BAN**.

banquet /bang-kwit/ ● n. a formal meal for many people. ● v. (**banquets**, **banqueting**, **banqueted**) give or take part in a banquet.
– ORIGIN French, 'little bench'.

banquette /bang-**ket**/ ● n. a padded bench along a wall.
– ORIGIN Italian *banchetta* 'little bench'.

banshee ● n. (in Irish legend) a female spirit whose wailing warns that someone in the house has died.
– ORIGIN from Old Irish *ben side* 'woman of the fairies'.

bantam ● n. a chicken of a small breed.
– ORIGIN prob. named after the province of *Bantam* in Java.

bantamweight ● n. a weight in boxing and other sports, coming between flyweight and featherweight.

banter ● n. friendly teasing between people. ● v. (**banters**, **bantering**, **bantered**) make friendly teasing remarks.
– ORIGIN unknown.

b

Banting, E
Sir Frederick Grant (1891–1941), Canadian physiologist and surgeon. His discovery of insulin in 1921–2 (with C. H. Best) revolutionized the treatment of diabetes, which was previously a fatal disease.

Bantu /ban-too/ ● n. (pl. **Bantu** or **Bantus**) **1** a member of a large group of peoples living in central and southern Africa. **2** the group of languages spoken by these peoples.
– ORIGIN Bantu, 'people'.

USAGE Bantu
Bantu is a very offensive word in South African English, especially when used to refer to individual black people.

banyan /ban-yan/ ● n. an Indian fig tree with spreading branches from which roots grow downwards to the ground and form new trunks.
– ORIGIN Gujarati, 'trader' (because first used by Europeans to refer to a tree under which traders had built a pagoda).

banzai /ban-zy/ ● exclam. a cry used by the Japanese when going into battle or in greeting their emperor.
– ORIGIN Japanese, 'ten thousand years (of life to you)'.

baobab /bay-oh-bab/ ● n. a short African tree with a very thick trunk and large fruit.
– ORIGIN prob. from an African language.

bap ● n. Brit. a soft, round, flattish bread roll.
– ORIGIN unknown.

baptism ● n. the Christian ceremony of sprinkling a person with water or dipping them in it, as a sign that they have been cleansed of sin and have entered the Church.
– PHRASES **baptism of fire** a difficult new experience.
– DERIVATIVES **baptismal** adj.
– ORIGIN Greek *baptizein*.

Baptist ● n. a member of a Protestant group believing that only adults should be baptized and that this should be by total immersion in water.

baptistery (also **baptistry**) ● n. (pl. **baptisteries**) a building or part of a church used for baptism.

baptize (also **baptise**) ● v. (**baptizes, baptizing, baptized**) **1** perform the ceremony of baptism on. **2** give a name or nickname to.

bar[1] ● n. **1** a long rigid piece of wood, metal, etc. **2** a counter, room, or place where alcohol or food and drink is served. **3** a small shop or counter serving food and drink or providing a service: *a snack bar.* **4** something that stops or delays progress: *her beginnings were no bar to becoming head of state.* **5** any of the short units into which a piece of music is divided, shown on a sheet of music by vertical lines. **6** (**the bar**) the place in a court room where an accused person stands during a trial. **7** (**the Bar**) the profession of barrister. **8** (**the Bar**) barristers or (in America) lawyers as a group. **9** Brit. a metal strip added to a medal as an additional honour. ● v. (**bars, barring, barred**) **1** fasten with a bar or bars. **2** forbid or prevent. ● prep. esp. Brit. except for.
– PHRASES **be called** (or **go**) **to the Bar** Brit. be allowed to practise as a barrister. **behind bars** in prison.
– ORIGIN Old French *barre*.

bar[2] ● n. a unit of pressure equivalent to 100,000 newtons per square metre.
– ORIGIN Greek *baros* 'weight'.

barb ● n. **1** a backward-pointing part of an arrowhead, fish hook, or similar object, that makes it difficult to take out from something it has pierced. **2** a spiteful remark.
– ORIGIN Latin *barba* 'beard'.

Barbados E
an island of the West Indies, part of the Windward Islands group; capital, Bridgetown.
– DERIVATIVES **Barbadian** adj. & n.

barbarian /bar-bair-i-uhn/ ● n. **1** (in ancient times) a member of a people not belonging to the Greek, Roman, or Christian civilizations. **2** an uncivilized or cruel person. ● adj. uncivilized or cruel.
– ORIGIN Greek *barbaros* 'foreign'.

barbaric /bar-ba-rik/ ● adj. **1** savagely cruel. **2** lacking culture; coarse.

barbarism /bar-buh-ri-z'm/ ● n. **1** great cruelty. **2** an uncivilized or primitive state: *the barbarism of the Dark Ages.*
– DERIVATIVES **barbarity** n. (pl. **barbarities**).

barbarous /bar-buh-ruhss/ ● adj. **1** very cruel. **2** primitive; uncivilized.

barbecue ● n. **1** an outdoor meal or party at which food is grilled over a charcoal fire. **2** a grill used at a barbecue. ● v. (**barbecues, barbecuing, barbecued**) cook (food) on a barbecue.
– ORIGIN Spanish *barbacoa* 'wooden frame'.

barbed ● adj. **1** having a barb or barbs. **2** (of a remark) spiteful.

barbed wire ● n. wire with clusters of short, sharp spikes along it.

barbel /bar-b'l/ ● n. **1** a long, thin growth hanging from the mouth or snout of some fish. **2** a large freshwater fish with barbels.
– ORIGIN Latin *barbellus* 'small barbel'.

barbell /bar-bel/ ● n. a long metal bar to which discs of different weights are attached at each end, used for weightlifting.

barber ● n. a person whose job is cutting men's hair and shaving or trimming their beards.
– ORIGIN Old French *barbe* 'beard'.

barbican /bar-bi-kuhn/ ● n. a double tower above a gate or drawbridge of a castle or fortified city.
– ORIGIN Old French *barbacane*.

barbiturate /bar-bit-yuu-ruht/ ● n. a kind of sedative drug.
– ORIGIN German *Barbitursäure*.

Barbuda E
see **ANTIGUA AND BARBUDA**.
– DERIVATIVES **Barbudan** adj. & n.

Barcelona E
a city on the coast of NE Spain, capital of Catalonia.

bar chart (also **bar graph**) ● n. a diagram in which different quantities are shown by rectangles of varying height.

bar code ● n. a set of stripes printed on a product, able to be read by a computer to provide information on prices and quantities in stock.

bard ● n. **1** archaic or literary a poet. **2** (**the Bard**) Shakespeare. **3** (**Bard**) the winner of a prize

for Welsh verse at an Eisteddfod.
– DERIVATIVES **bardic** adj.
– ORIGIN Celtic.

Bardot E
/bar-**doh**/, Brigitte (b.1934; born *Camille Javal*), French actress.

bare • adj. **1** not wearing clothes. **2** without the proper or usual covering or contents: *a big, bare room.* **3** without detail; basic. **4** only just enough: *a bare majority.* • v. (**bares**, **baring**, **bared**) uncover or reveal.
– PHRASES **with one's bare hands** without using tools or weapons.
– DERIVATIVES **barely** adv. **bareness** n.
– ORIGIN Old English.

bareback • adv. & adj. on a horse without a saddle.

barefaced • adj. done openly and without shame: *a barefaced lie.*

Barenboim E
/**ba**-ruhn-boym/, Daniel (b.1942), Israeli pianist and conductor, musical director of the Chicago Symphony Orchestra since 1991. He was married to the cellist Jacqueline du Pré.

Barents Sea E
/**ba**-ruhnts/ a part of the Arctic Ocean to the north of Norway and Russia.

bargain • n. **1** an agreement made between people saying what each will do for the other. **2** a thing bought or put on sale at a low price. • v. **1** discuss the terms of an agreement. **2** (**bargain for/on**) expect.
– PHRASES **drive a hard bargain** press hard for a deal in one's favour. **into the bargain** as well.
– ORIGIN Old French *bargaine*.

barge • n. a long flat-bottomed boat for carrying goods on canals and rivers. • v. (**barges**, **barging**, **barged**) **1** move forcefully or roughly. **2** (**barge in**) burst in on (someone) rudely or awkwardly.
– ORIGIN Old French.

bargee /bar-**jee**/ • n. esp. Brit. a person in charge of or working on a barge.

bargepole • n. a long pole used to push a barge along.
– PHRASES **would not touch with a bargepole** informal would not want to have anything to do with.

bar graph • n. a bar chart.

baritone • n. a man's singing voice between tenor and bass. • adj. relating to a musical instrument that is second lowest in pitch in its family: *a baritone sax.*
– ORIGIN from Greek *barus* 'heavy' + *tonos* 'tone'.

barium /**bair**-i-uhm/ • n. a soft white metallic chemical element.
– ORIGIN Greek *barus* 'heavy'.

barium meal • n. a substance containing barium, which is swallowed so that the stomach or intestines can be seen on an X-ray.

bark[1] • n. the sharp sudden cry of a dog, fox, or seal. • v. **1** give a bark. **2** say (a command or question) suddenly or fiercely.
– PHRASES **one's bark is worse than one's bite** one is not as fierce as one seems. **be barking up the wrong tree** informal be doing or thinking something that is incorrect.
– ORIGIN Old English.

bark[2] • n. the tough outer covering of the trunk and branches of a tree. • v. scrape the skin off (one's shin) by accidentally hitting it.
– ORIGIN Old Norse.

barker • n. informal a person at a fair who calls out to passers-by to persuade them to visit a sideshow.

barking • adj. Brit. informal completely mad.

barley • n. a type of cereal plant with bristly heads, the grains of which are used in brewing and animal feed.
– ORIGIN Old English.

barley sugar • n. an orange sweet made of boiled sugar.

barmaid • n. a woman who serves drinks in a bar or public house.

barman • n. esp. Brit. a man who serves drinks in a bar or public house.

bar mitzvah /bar **mits**-vuh/ • n. a religious ceremony in which a Jewish boy aged 13 takes on the responsibilities of an adult under Jewish law.
– ORIGIN Hebrew, 'son of the commandment'.

barmy • adj. (**barmier**, **barmiest**) Brit. informal mad.
– ORIGIN Old English, 'froth on fermenting malt liquor'.

barn • n. a large farm building used for storing hay or grain or housing livestock.
– ORIGIN Old English, 'barley house'.

Barnabas, St E
/**bar**-nuh-buhss/ (died *c.*61), a Cypriot Apostle. He accompanied St Paul on the first missionary journey to Cyprus and Asia Minor. Feast day, 11 June.

barnacle /**bar**-nuh-k'l/ • n. a small shellfish which fixes itself to rocks and other underwater surfaces.
– ORIGIN Latin *bernaca*.

barnacle goose • n. a goose with a white face and black neck.
– ORIGIN because the bird was once thought to hatch from barnacles.

Barnard E
/**bar**-nard/, Christiaan (Neethling) (1922–2001), South African surgeon, who performed the first human heart transplant in 1967.

Barnardo E
/buh-**nar**-doh/, Thomas (John) (1845–1905), Irish-born doctor and philanthropist, founder of homes for destitute children.

barn dance • n. **1** a party with country dancing. **2** a dance for a number of couples moving round a circle.

barnet /**bar**-nit/ • n. Brit. informal a person's hair.
– ORIGIN from rhyming slang *barnet fair* (a horse fair held at *Barnet*, Herts).

barney • n. (pl. **barneys**) Brit. informal a noisy quarrel.
– ORIGIN unknown.

barn owl • n. a pale-coloured owl with a heart-shaped face.

barnstorm • v. esp. N. Amer. **1** tour country districts putting on shows or giving displays of flying. **2** make a rapid tour as part of a political campaign.

barnstorming • adj. done in a very showy,

forceful, and successful way.

Barnum E
/bar-nuhm/, P. T. (1810–91; full name *Phineas Taylor Barnum*), American showman, who opened his first circus in 1871 and combined it with that of Anthony Bailey ten years later.

barograph /ba-ruh-grahf/ ● n. a barometer that records its readings on a moving chart.

barometer /buh-rom-i-ter/ ● n. **1** an instrument that measures the pressure of the atmosphere, used to forecast the weather. **2** something that indicates change: *furniture is a barometer of changing tastes.*
– DERIVATIVES **barometric** adj.
– ORIGIN Greek *baros* 'weight'.

baron ● n. **1** a man belonging to the lowest rank of the British nobility. **2** (in the middle ages) a man who held lands or property from the sovereign or an overlord. **3** a powerful person in business or industry: *a press baron.*
– DERIVATIVES **baronial** adj.
– ORIGIN Latin *baro* 'man, warrior'.

baroness ● n. **1** the wife or widow of a baron. **2** a woman holding the rank of baron.

baronet ● n. a man who holds a title below that of baron.

baronetcy ● n. (pl. **baronetcies**) the rank of a baronet.

barony ● n. (pl. **baronies**) the rank and lands of a baron.

baroque /buh-rok/ ● n. a very ornate style of European architecture, art, and music of the 17th and 18th centuries. ● adj. **1** having to do with this style or period. **2** showy and very ornate.
– ORIGIN French.

barque /bark/ ● n. **1** a sailing ship with three masts. **2** literary a boat.
– ORIGIN Latin *barca* 'ship's boat'.

barrack[1] ● v. provide (soldiers) with somewhere to stay. ● n. (**barracks**) a large building or group of buildings for housing soldiers.
– ORIGIN Spanish *barraca* 'soldier's tent'.

barrack[2] ● v. **1** Brit. & Austral./NZ shout loud insulting comments at (a performer or speaker). **2** (**barrack for**) Austral./NZ support and encourage.
– ORIGIN prob. from Northern Irish dialect.

barracuda /ba-ruh-koo-duh/ ● n. (pl. **barracuda** or **barracudas**) a large, slender fish that preys on other fish and is found in tropical seas.
– ORIGIN unknown.

barrage /ba-rahzh/ ● n. **1** a continuous attack by heavy guns over a wide area. **2** an overwhelming number of questions or complaints coming one after the other. **3** Brit. a barrier placed across a river to control the water level.
– ORIGIN French.

barre /bar/ ● n. a horizontal bar at waist level used by ballet dancers during exercises.
– ORIGIN French.

barrel ● n. **1** a large cylindrical container bulging out in the middle and with flat ends. **2** a measure of capacity for oil and beer (36 imperial gallons for beer and 35 for oil). **3** a tube forming part of an object such as a gun.
– PHRASES **over a barrel** informal in a very weak position.
– ORIGIN Latin *barriclus* 'small cask'.

barrel organ ● n. a small pipe organ that plays a set tune when a handle is turned.

barren ● adj. **1** (of land) too poor to produce vegetation. **2** (of a female animal) unable to bear young. **3** bleak and lifeless.
– DERIVATIVES **barrenness** n.
– ORIGIN Old French *barhaine*.

Barrett, E
Elizabeth, see **BROWNING**[1].

barricade /ba-ri-kayd/ ● n. a makeshift barrier used to block a road or entrance. ● v. (**barricades**, **barricading**, **barricaded**) block or defend with a barricade.
– ORIGIN French.

Barrie, E
Sir J. M. (1860–1937; full name *James Matthew Barrie*), Scottish dramatist and novelist, best known for the play *Peter Pan*.

barrier ● n. **1** an obstacle that prevents movement or access. **2** an obstacle to communication or progress: *a language barrier.*
– ORIGIN Old French *barriere*.

barrier cream ● n. Brit. a cream used to protect the skin from damage or infection.

barrier reef ● n. a coral reef close to the shore but separated from it by a channel of deep water.

barring ● prep. except for; if not for.

barrister /ba-riss-ter/ ● n. esp. Brit. a lawyer qualified to argue a case in court. Compare with **SOLICITOR**.
– ORIGIN from **BAR**[1].

barrow[1] ● n. Brit. a two-wheeled handcart used by street traders.
– ORIGIN Old English.

barrow[2] ● n. an ancient burial mound.
– ORIGIN Old English.

Barry, E
Sir Charles (1795–1860), English architect, designer of the Houses of Parliament.

Barrymore E
an American family of film and stage actors, notably **Lionel** (1878–1954), his sister **Ethel** (1879–1959), and their brother **John** (1882–1942).

bartender ● n. a person serving drinks at a bar.

barter ● v. (**barters**, **bartering**, **bartered**) exchange (goods or services) for other goods or services. ● n. trading by bartering.
– ORIGIN prob. from Old French *barater* 'deceive'.

Bartholomew, St E
/bar-thol-uh-myoo/ an Apostle, the patron saint of tanners. Feast day, 24 August.

Bartók E
/bar-tok/, Béla (1881–1945), Hungarian composer. His work includes six string quartets, three piano concertos, and the *Concerto for Orchestra*.

Barton, E
Sir Edmund (1849–1920), Australian statesman, first Prime Minister of Australia 1901–3.

Baryshnikov E
/buh-reesh-ni-koff/, Mikhail (Nikolaevich) (b.1948), Latvian-born American ballet dancer.

basal /bay-s'l/ • **adj.** forming or belonging to a base.

basalt /ba-sawlt/ • **n.** a dark fine-grained volcanic rock.
– ORIGIN Latin *basaltes*.

base[1] • **n.** **1** the lowest or supporting part of something. **2** a foundation, support, or starting point: *the town's economic base collapsed.* **3** the main place where a person works or stays. **4** a centre of operations: *a military base.* **5** a main element to which others are added. **6** Chem. a substance able to react with an acid to form a salt and water. **7** Math. the number on which a system of counting is based, e.g. 10 in conventional notation. **8** Baseball each of the four stations that must be reached in turn to score a run. • **v.** (**bases, basing, based**) **1** use something as the foundation for. **2** put at a centre of operations.
– ORIGIN Greek *basis* 'base, pedestal'.

base[2] • **adj.** **1** bad or immoral. **2** archaic of low social class.
– ORIGIN Latin *bassus* 'short'.

baseball • **n.** a game played with a bat and ball on a diamond-shaped circuit of four bases, around all of which a batsman must run to score.

baseball cap • **n.** a cotton cap with a large peak.

baseless • **adj.** not based on fact; untrue.

baseline • **n.** **1** (in tennis, volleyball, etc.) the line marking each end of a court. **2** a starting point for comparisons.

basement • **n.** a room or floor below ground level.

base metal • **n.** a common non-precious metal such as copper or tin.

base rate • **n.** the interest rate set by the Bank of England for lending to other banks, used as the basis for interest rates generally.

bases pl. of **BASE**[1] and **BASIS**.

bash informal • **v.** hit hard and violently. • **n.** **1** a heavy blow. **2** a party. **3** Brit. an attempt: *she'll have a bash at anything.*
– ORIGIN perh. from **BANG** and **SMASH**.

bashful • **adj.** shy and easily embarrassed.
– DERIVATIVES **bashfully** adv. **bashfulness** n.
– ORIGIN from **ABASH**.

BASIC • **n.** a high-level computer programming language.
– ORIGIN from *Beginners' All-purpose Symbolic Instruction Code.*

basic • **adj.** **1** forming an essential foundation; fundamental. **2** consisting of the minimum needed or offered: *a basic wage.* **3** Chem. containing or having the properties of a base; alkaline. • **n.** (**basics**) essential facts or principles.

basically • **adv.** **1** in the most fundamental respects. **2** in fact; essentially: *I basically did the same thing every day.*

Basie E
/bay-si/, Count (1904–84; born *William Basie*), American jazz pianist, organist, and bandleader, who formed the Count Basie Orchestra.

basil • **n.** a herb with leaves that are used in cookery.
– ORIGIN Greek *basilikos* 'royal'.

Basil, St E
(*c.*330–79), bishop of Caesarea. His monastic rule forms the basis of monasticism in the Eastern Church. Feast day, 14 June.

basilica /buh-zil-i-kuh/ • **n.** **1** a large ancient Roman building with two rows of columns and a domed recess at one end. **2** a Christian church of a similar design.
– ORIGIN Latin, 'royal palace'.

basilisk /baz-i-lisk/ • **n.** **1** a mythical reptile whose gaze or breath was deadly. **2** a long, slender Central American lizard.
– ORIGIN Greek *basiliskos* 'little king, serpent'.

basin • **n.** **1** a large bowl or open container for preparing food or holding liquid. **2** a circular valley or natural depression. **3** an area drained by a river and its tributaries. **4** an enclosed area of water for mooring boats.
– ORIGIN Latin *bacinus*.

basis /bay-siss/ • **n.** (pl. **bases** /bay-seez/) **1** the foundation of a theory or process. **2** the principles according to which an activity is carried on: *she needs coaching on a regular basis.*
– ORIGIN Greek, 'step, pedestal'.

bask • **v.** **1** lie in warmth and sunlight for pleasure. **2** (**bask in**) take great pleasure in.
– ORIGIN perh. from Old Norse, 'bathe'.

basket • **n.** **1** a container for carrying things, made from strips of cane or wire. **2** a net fixed on a hoop, used as the goal in basketball.
– ORIGIN Old French.

basketball • **n.** a team game in which goals are scored by throwing a ball through a netted hoop.

basket case • **n.** informal a useless person or thing.
– ORIGIN first referring to a soldier who had lost all four limbs.

basking shark • **n.** a large shark which feeds on plankton and swims slowly close to the surface.

Basle E
/bahl/ a commercial and industrial city in NW Switzerland.

Basque /bask, bahsk/ • **n.** **1** a member of a people living in the western Pyrenees in France and Spain. **2** the language of this people.
– ORIGIN Latin *Vasco* 'inhabitant of Vasconia'.

basque /bask/ • **n.** a woman's close-fitting bodice.
– ORIGIN from **BASQUE**, referring to traditional Basque dress.

bas-relief /bass-ri-leef/ • **n.** Art low relief.
– ORIGIN Italian *basso-rilievo*.

bass[1] /bayss/ • **n.** **1** the lowest adult male singing voice. **2** informal a bass guitar or double bass. **3** the low-frequency output of transmitted or reproduced sound. • **adj.** relating to a musical instrument that is the lowest in pitch in its family: *a bass clarinet.*
– DERIVATIVES **bassist** n.
– ORIGIN from **BASE**[2].

bass[2] /bass/ • **n.** (pl. **bass** or **basses**) the common freshwater perch.
– ORIGIN Germanic.

bass clef • **n.** Music a clef placing F below middle C on the second-highest line of the stave.

basset (also **basset hound**) ● **n.** a breed of hunting dog with a long body, short legs, and long, drooping ears.
– ORIGIN French.

Basseterre E
/bass-**tair**/ the capital of St Kitts and Nevis in the Leeward Islands, on the island of St Kitts.

Bassey, E
Dame Shirley (Veronica) (b.1937), Welsh popular music singer.

bassoon ● **n.** a large bass woodwind instrument of the oboe family.
– DERIVATIVES **bassoonist** n.
– ORIGIN Italian *bassone*.

Bass Strait E
/bass/ a channel separating Tasmania from the mainland of Australia.

bastard /bah-sterd/ ● **n. 1** archaic or derog. a person born of unmarried parents. **2** informal an unpleasant person. ● **adj.** no longer in its pure or original form.
– ORIGIN Latin *bastardus*.

bastardize (also **bastardise**) ● **v.** (**bastardizes, bastardizing, bastardized**) make impure by adding new elements.

baste[1] ● **v.** (**bastes, basting, basted**) pour fat or juices over (meat) during cooking.
– ORIGIN unknown.

baste[2] /*rhymes with* taste/ ● **v.** (**bastes, basting, basted**) sew with long, loose stitches in preparation for permanent sewing.
– ORIGIN Old French *bastir* 'sew lightly'.

Bastille E
/ba-**steel**/ a fortress and prison in Paris. Its storming by the mob on 14 July 1789 marked the start of the French Revolution.

bastion /bass-ti-uhn/ ● **n. 1** a projecting part of a fortification allowing an increased angle of fire. **2** something protecting or preserving particular principles or activities: *the town was a bastion of Conservatism.*
– ORIGIN Italian *bastione*.

bat[1] ● **n.** an implement with a handle and a solid surface, used in sports for hitting the ball. ● **v.** (**bats, batting, batted**) **1** (in sport) take the role of hitting rather than throwing the ball. **2** hit with the flat of one's hand.
– PHRASES **off one's own bat** Brit. informal of one's own accord.
– ORIGIN Old English, 'club, stick, staff'.

bat[2] ● **n. 1** a winged mammal that is active at night. **2** (**old bat**) informal an unattractive and unpleasant woman.
– PHRASES **have bats in the belfry** informal be eccentric or mad.
– ORIGIN Scandinavian; sense 2 is from an old slang term for 'prostitute', or from BATTLE-AXE.

bat[3] ● **v.** (**bats, batting, batted**) flutter (one's eyelashes).
– PHRASES **not bat an eyelid** informal show no surprise or concern.
– ORIGIN Old French *batre* 'beat'.

batch ● **n. 1** a quantity of goods produced or dispatched at one time. **2** a group of people or things.
– ORIGIN Old English, related to BAKE.

bated ● **adj.** (in phr. **with bated breath**) in great suspense.
– ORIGIN from ABATE.

Bates, E
H. E. (1905–74; full name *Herbert Ernest Bates*), English novelist and short-story writer. His novels include *The Darling Buds of May.*

Bateson, E
William (1861–1926), English geneticist, who coined the term *genetics* in its current sense and publicized the work of Mendel.

Bath E
a spa town in SW England, founded by the Romans (as Aquae Sulis), and fashionable in the 18th and early 19th centuries.

bath ● **n. 1** a large tub that is filled with water for washing one's body. **2** an act of washing in a bath. **3** (also **baths**) a building containing a public swimming pool or washing facilities. ● **v.** wash in a bath.
– ORIGIN Old English.

bathe /bay*th*/ ● **v.** (**bathes, bathing, bathed**) **1** wash by immersing one's body in water. **2** Brit. take a swim. **3** soak or wipe gently with liquid to clean or soothe. ● **n.** a swim.
– DERIVATIVES **bather** n.
– ORIGIN Old English.

bathos /bay-thoss/ ● **n.** (in literature) a change in mood from the important and serious to the trivial or ridiculous.
– ORIGIN Greek, 'depth'.

bathrobe ● **n.** a dressing gown made of towelling.

bathroom ● **n. 1** a room containing a bath and usually also a washbasin and toilet. **2** N. Amer. a room containing a toilet.

bath salts ● **pl. n.** crystals that are dissolved in bathwater to soften or perfume it.

Bathsheba E
/bath-shee-buh, **bath**-shi-buh/ (in the Bible) one of the wives of David and the mother of Solomon.

batik /ba-teek/ ● **n.** a method of producing coloured designs on cloth by waxing the parts not to be dyed.
– ORIGIN Javanese, 'painted'.

Batista E
/ba-tee-stuh/, Fulgencio (1901–73), Cuban soldier and statesman, President 1940–4 and 1952–9.

batman ● **n.** dated (in the British armed forces) an officer's personal attendant.
– ORIGIN Old French *bat* 'packsaddle'.

baton ● **n. 1** a thin stick used to conduct an orchestra or choir. **2** a short stick passed from runner to runner in a relay race. **3** a stick carried and twirled by a drum major.
– ORIGIN Latin *bastum* 'stick'.

batsman ● **n.** a player who bats in cricket.

battalion /buh-tal-i-uhn/ ● **n.** a large body of troops, forming part of a brigade.
– ORIGIN French *bataillon*.

Batten, E
Jean (1909–82), New Zealand aviator, the first woman to fly from England to Australia and back (1934–5).

batten ● **n.** a long wooden or metal strip for

strengthening or securing something.
– PHRASES **batten down the hatches 1** secure a ship's tarpaulins. **2** prepare for a difficulty or crisis.
– ORIGIN Old French *batre* 'to beat'.

Battenberg • n. Brit. an oblong marzipan-covered sponge cake in two colours.
– ORIGIN named after the town of *Battenberg* in Germany.

batter[1] • v. (**batters**, **battering**, **battered**) hit repeatedly with hard blows.
– DERIVATIVES **batterer** n.
– ORIGIN Old French *batre* 'to beat'.

batter[2] • n. a mixture of flour, egg, and milk or water, used for making pancakes or coating food before frying.
– ORIGIN Old French *batre* 'to beat'.

battered • adj. (of food) coated in batter and fried.

battering ram • n. a heavy object swung or rammed against a door to break it down.

battery • n. (pl. **batteries**) **1** a device containing one or more electrical cells, for use as a source of power. **2** an extensive series: *a battery of tests.* **3** Brit. a series of small cages for the intensive rearing of poultry. **4** Law the crime of physically attacking another person. **5** a group of heavy guns.
– ORIGIN Latin *battuere* 'to beat'.

battle • n. **1** a prolonged fight between organized armed forces. **2** a long and difficult struggle: *a battle of wits.* • v. (**battles**, **battling**, **battled**) fight or struggle with determination.
– ORIGIN Old French *bataille.*

battleaxe • n. **1** a large axe used in ancient warfare. **2** informal an aggressive older woman.

battledress • n. combat dress worn by soldiers.

battlefield (also **battleground**) • n. the piece of ground on which a battle is fought.

battlement • n. a parapet with gaps for firing from, forming part of a fortification.
– ORIGIN Old French *bataillier* 'fortify'.

Battle of Actium, Battle of Bannockburn, etc. E
see **Actium, Battle of**; **Bannockburn, Battle of**, etc.

battleship • n. a heavily armoured warship with large guns.

batty • adj. (**battier**, **battiest**) informal mad.
– ORIGIN from **bat**[2].

bauble /baw-b'l/ • n. a small, showy trinket or decoration.
– ORIGIN Old French *baubel* 'child's toy'.

baud /*rhymes with* code/ • n. (pl. **baud** or **bauds**) Computing a unit of transmission speed for electronic signals, corresponding to one information unit or event per second.
– ORIGIN named after the French engineer Jean *Baudot* (1845–1903).

Baudelaire E
/boh-duh-**lair**/, Charles (Pierre) (1821–67), French poet and critic, known for his series of poems *Les Fleurs du mal.*

Bauhaus E
/**bow**-howss/ a school of functionalist architecture and design established by Walter Gropius in Weimar in 1919.

baulk /bawlk/ (esp. US also **balk**) • v. **1** (**baulk at**) hesitate to accept (an idea). **2** thwart or hinder.
– ORIGIN Old Norse, 'partition'.

bauxite /**bawk**-syt/ • n. a clay-like rock from which aluminium is obtained.
– ORIGIN from *Les Baux*, a village in SE France, where it was first found.

Bavaria E
/buh-**vair**-i-uh/ a state of southern Germany; capital, Munich.
– DERIVATIVES **Bavarian** n. & adj.

bawdy • adj. (**bawdier**, **bawdiest**) indecent in an amusing way.
– DERIVATIVES **bawdiness** n.
– ORIGIN Old French *baude* 'shameless'.

bawl • v. **1** shout out noisily. **2** (**bawl out**) criticize angrily. **3** weep noisily. • n. a loud shout.

bay[1] • n. a broad curved inlet of the sea.
– ORIGIN Old French *baie.*

bay[2] (also **bay laurel**) • n. an evergreen Mediterranean shrub, with leaves that are used in cookery.
– ORIGIN Old French *baie.*

bay[3] • n. **1** a window area that projects outwards from a wall. **2** an area allocated for a purpose: *a loading bay.*
– ORIGIN Old French *baie.*

bay[4] • adj. (of a horse) reddish-brown with black points. • n. a bay horse.
– ORIGIN Old French *bai.*

bay[5] • v. (of a dog) howl loudly.
– PHRASES **at bay** trapped or cornered. **hold** (or **keep**) **at bay** prevent from approaching or having an effect.
– ORIGIN Old French *abaiier* 'to bark'.

Bayeux Tapestry E
/by-**yer**/ a embroidered cloth, about 70 metres (230 feet) long, illustrating events leading up to the Norman Conquest and made between 1066 and 1077.

Bay of Bengal, Bay of Biscay, etc. E
see **Bengal, Bay of**, **Biscay, Bay of**; etc.

bayonet • n. a long blade fixed to a rifle for hand-to-hand fighting. • v. (**bayonets**, **bayoneting**, **bayoneted**) stab with a bayonet.
– ORIGIN French *baïonnette* 'dagger', named after the French town of *Bayonne*, where they were first made.

Bayreuth E
/by-**royt**/ a town in Bavaria where Wagner is buried and where regular festivals of his operas are held.

bay window • n. a window built to project outwards from a wall.

bazaar /buh-**zar**/ • n. **1** a market in a Middle-Eastern country. **2** a sale of goods to raise funds.
– ORIGIN Persian, 'market'.

bazooka • n. a short-range rocket launcher used against tanks.
– ORIGIN prob. from US slang *bazoo* 'kazoo'.

BBC • abbrev. British Broadcasting Corporation.

BC • abbrev. before Christ (used to indicate that a date is before the Christian era).

USAGE **BC**
BC is normally written in small capitals and placed **after** the numerals, as in *72* BC.

BCE ● **abbrev.** before the Common Era (indicating dates before the Christian era, used especially by non-Christians).

be ● **v.** (sing. present **am**; **are**; **is**; pl. present **are**; 1st and 3rd sing. past **was**; 2nd sing. past and pl. past **were**; present subjunctive **be**; past subjunctive **were**; present part. **being**; past part. **been**) **1** exist; be present. **2** happen. **3** have the specified state, nature, or role: *I want to be a teacher.* **4** come; go; visit. ● **auxiliary verb 1** used with a present participle to form continuous tenses: *they are coming.* **2** used with a past participle to form the passive voice: *it is said.* **3** used to show something that is due to, may, or should happen.
– PHRASES **the be-all and end-all** informal the most important aspect.
– ORIGIN Old English.

be- ● **prefix** forming verbs: **1** all over; all round: *bespatter.* **2** thoroughly; excessively: *bewilder.* **3** expressing action: *bemoan.* **4** affect with or cause to be: *befog.* **5** (forming adjectives ending in *-ed*) having; covered with: *bejewelled.*
– ORIGIN Old English.

beach ● **n.** a shore of sand or pebbles at the edge of the sea or a lake. ● **v.** bring or come on to a beach from the water.
– ORIGIN perh. from Old English, 'brook'.

beachcomber ● **n.** a person who searches beaches for valuable things.

beachhead ● **n.** a fortified position on a beach taken by landing forces.

beacon ● **n. 1** a fire lit on the top of a hill as a signal. **2** a light acting as a signal for ships or aircraft.
– ORIGIN Old English, 'sign'.

bead ● **n. 1** a small piece of glass, stone, etc., threaded in a string with others to make a necklace or rosary. **2** a drop of a liquid on a surface. ● **v.** decorate or cover with beads.
– ORIGIN Old English, 'prayer' (each bead on a rosary representing a prayer).

beadle ● **n.** Brit. **1** a ceremonial officer of a church, college, etc. **2** hist. a parish officer dealing with petty offenders.
– ORIGIN Old English, 'a person who makes a proclamation'.

beady ● **adj.** (of a person's eyes) small, round, and observant.

beagle ● **n.** a small short-legged breed of hound.
– ORIGIN perh. from Old French *beegueule* 'open-mouthed'.

beak ● **n. 1** a bird's horny projecting jaws; a bill. **2** Brit. informal a magistrate or schoolmaster.
– ORIGIN Latin *beccus.*

beaker ● **n.** Brit. **1** a tall plastic cup. **2** a cylindrical glass container used in laboratories.
– ORIGIN Old Norse.

beam ● **n. 1** a long piece of timber or metal used as a support in building. **2** a narrow horizontal length of timber for balancing on in gymnastics. **3** a ray or shaft of light or particles. **4** a radiant smile. **5** a ship's breadth at its widest point. ● **v. 1** transmit (a radio signal). **2** shine brightly. **3** smile radiantly.
– PHRASES **off beam** informal on the wrong track.
– ORIGIN Old English.

bean ● **n. 1** an edible seed growing in long pods on certain plants. **2** the hard seed of a coffee or cocoa plant. **3** informal a very small amount or nothing at all: *there is not a bean of truth in the report.*
– PHRASES **full of beans** informal lively; in high spirits. **old bean** Brit. informal, dated a friendly form of address.
– ORIGIN Old English.

beanbag ● **n. 1** a small bag filled with dried beans and used in children's games. **2** a large cushion filled with polystyrene beads, used as a seat.

beanfeast ● **n.** Brit. informal a party.
– ORIGIN first referring to an annual dinner given to employees, which always featured beans and bacon.

beano ● **n.** (pl. **beanos**) Brit. informal a party.
– ORIGIN from BEANFEAST.

bear[1] ● **v.** (**bears**, **bearing**, **bore**; past part. **borne**) **1** carry. **2** have as a quality or visible mark. **3** support (a weight). **4** (**bear oneself**) behave in a specified manner: *she bore herself with dignity.* **5** tolerate: *I can't bear it.* **6** give birth to (a child). **7** (of a tree or plant) produce (fruit or flowers). **8** turn and go in a specified direction: *bear left.*
– PHRASES **bear down on** approach in a purposeful or threatening manner. **bear fruit** have good results. **bear someone a grudge** feel resentment against someone. **bear in mind** remember and take into account. **bear on** relate to. **bear out** support or confirm. **bear up** remain cheerful in difficult circumstances. **bear with** be patient with. **bear witness** (or **testimony**) **to** provide evidence of. **bring to bear** prepare and use effectively.
– ORIGIN Old English.

bear[2] ● **n.** a large mammal with thick fur and a very short tail.
– ORIGIN Old English.

bearable ● **adj.** able to be accepted.
– DERIVATIVES **bearably** adv.

beard ● **n.** a growth of hair on the chin and lower cheeks of a man's face. ● **v.** boldly confront or challenge (someone formidable).
– DERIVATIVES **bearded** adj.
– ORIGIN Old English.

Beardsley, **E**
Aubrey (Vincent) (1872–98), English artist and illustrator, known for his original style of art nouveau illustrations.

bearer ● **n. 1** a person or thing that carries something. **2** a person who presents a cheque or other order to pay money.

bear hug ● **n.** a rough, tight embrace.

bearing ● **n. 1** a person's way of standing, moving, or behaving. **2** relation; relevance: *the case has no bearing on the issues.* **3** (**bearings**) a device that allows two parts to rotate or move in contact with each other. **4** direction or position relative to a fixed point. **5** (**one's bearings**) awareness of one's position relative to one's surroundings.

bearish ● **adj.** resembling a bear.

beast ● **n. 1** an animal, especially a large or dangerous mammal. **2** a very cruel or wicked person.
– ORIGIN Latin *bestia.*

beastly ● **adj.** Brit. informal very unpleasant.
– DERIVATIVES **beastliness** n.

beast of burden ● n. an animal used for carrying loads.

beat ● v. (**beats**, **beating**, **beat**; past part. **beaten**) **1** strike (someone) repeatedly and violently. **2** strike (something) repeatedly. **3** defeat or be better than: *he beat his own world record.* **4** informal baffle. **5** (of the heart) pulsate. **6** (of a bird) move (the wings) up and down. **7** stir (cooking ingredients) vigorously. ● n. **1** a main accent in music or poetry. **2** a pulsation of the heart. **3** a movement of a bird's wings. **4** a brief pause. **5** an area patrolled by a police officer. ● adj. informal completely exhausted.
– PHRASES **beat about the bush** discuss a matter without coming to the point. **beat it** informal leave. **beat up** attack (someone) and hit them repeatedly. **off the beaten track** isolated.
– ORIGIN Old English.

beatific /bee-uh-tif-ik/ ● adj. feeling or expressing blissful happiness.
– DERIVATIVES **beatifically** adv.

beatify /bi-at-i-fy/ ● v. (**beatifies**, **beatifying**, **beatified**) (in the Roman Catholic Church) announce that (a dead person) is in a state of bliss, the first step towards making them a saint.
– ORIGIN Latin *beatus* 'blessed'.

Beatles E
a pop and rock group from Liverpool, consisting of George Harrison, John Lennon, Paul McCartney, and Ringo Starr, who had a major impact on pop culture in the 1960s.

beatnik ● n. a young person in the 1950s and early 1960s who rejected conventional society.

Beaton, E
Sir Cecil (Walter Hardy) (1904–80), English photographer, famous for his fashion features and portraits of celebrities.

beat-up ● adj. informal worn out by overuse.

beau /boh/ ● n. (pl. **beaux** or **beaus** /bohz, boh/) dated a boyfriend.
– ORIGIN French, 'handsome'.

Beau Brummell E
see **BRUMMELL**.

Beaufort scale /boh-fert/ ● n. a scale of wind speed ranging from force 0 (less than 1 knot or 1 kph) to force 12 (64 knots or 118 kph and above).
– ORIGIN named after the English admiral Sir Francis *Beaufort* (1774–1857).

Beaujolais /boh-*zh*uh-lay/ ● n. a light red wine produced in the Beaujolais district of SE France.

Beaumarchais E
/boh-mar-shay/, Pierre Augustin Caron de (1732–99), French dramatist, who wrote the comedies *The Barber of Seville* and *The Marriage of Figaro*, which inspired operas by Rossini and Mozart.

beauteous ● adj. literary beautiful.

beautician ● n. a person whose job is to give beauty treatments.

beautiful ● adj. **1** very pleasing to the senses. **2** of a very high standard.
– DERIVATIVES **beautifully** adv.

beautify ● v. (**beautifies**, **beautifying**, **beautified**) make beautiful.

beauty ● n. (pl. **beauties**) **1** a combination of qualities that delights the senses. **2** a beautiful woman. **3** an excellent example. **4** an attractive feature or advantage.
– ORIGIN Old French *beaute.*

beauty queen ● n. the winner of a contest to choose the most beautiful woman.

beauty salon (also **beauty parlour**) ● n. a place in which hairdressing and cosmetic treatments are carried out.

Beauvoir, E
Simone de, see **DE BEAUVOIR**.

beaux pl. of **BEAU**.

beaver ● n. (pl. **beaver** or **beavers**) a large rodent that lives partly in water. ● v. (**beavers**, **beavering**, **beavered**) (**beaver away**) informal work hard.
– ORIGIN Old English.

Beaverbrook, E
Max Aitken, 1st Baron (1879–1964; full name *William Maxwell Aitken*), Canadian-born British Conservative politician and newspaper proprietor.

becalm ● v. (**be becalmed**) (of a sailing ship) be unable to move through lack of wind.

became past part. of **BECOME**.

because ● conj. for the reason that.
– PHRASES **because of** by reason of.
– ORIGIN from *by cause.*

beck ● n. (in phr. **at someone's beck and call**) always having to be ready to obey someone's orders.
– ORIGIN from **BECKON**.

Beckenbauer E
/bek-uhn-bow-er/, Franz (b.1945), German footballer, captain of Germany when they won the World Cup in 1974 and manager of the national team that won the World Cup again in 1990.

Becker E
/bek-er/, Boris (b.1967), German tennis player, who in 1985 became the youngest man and first unseeded player to win the men's singles at Wimbledon.

Becket, St Thomas à E
/bek-it/ (*c.*1118–70), English prelate and statesman, Archbishop of Canterbury 1162–70. His open opposition to Henry II led to his assassination in Canterbury cathedral. Feast day, 29 December.

Beckett E
/bek-it/, Samuel (Barclay) (1906–89), Irish dramatist, novelist, and poet, author of the influential play *Waiting for Godot*.

beckon ● v. **1** make a movement to encourage or tell someone to approach or follow. **2** seem appealing: *the wide open spaces of Australia beckoned.*
– ORIGIN Old English.

become ● v. (**becomes**, **becoming**, **became**; past part. **become**) **1** begin to be. **2** turn into. **3** (**become of**) happen to. **4** (of clothing) look good when worn by (someone).
– ORIGIN from **BE-** + **COME**.

becoming ● adj. (of clothing) looking good on someone.

b

becquerel /bek-kuh-rel/ ● **n.** Physics a unit of radioactivity in the SI system.
– ORIGIN named after the French physicist A-H. *Becquerel* (1852–1908).

BEd ● **abbrev.** Bachelor of Education.

bed ● **n.** **1** a piece of furniture with a surface for sleeping on. **2** informal a bed as a place for sexual activity. **3** an area of ground where flowers and plants are grown. **4** a flat base or foundation. ● **v.** (**beds**, **bedding**, **bedded**) **1** provide with or settle in sleeping accommodation. **2** (**bed in/down**) fix or be fixed firmly. **3** informal have sexual intercourse with.
– PHRASES **a bed of roses** a comfortable or easy situation or activity.
– ORIGIN Old English.

bed and breakfast ● **n.** **1** sleeping accommodation and breakfast in a guest house or hotel. **2** a guest house.

bedbug ● **n.** a bug which sucks the blood of sleeping humans.

bedclothes ● **pl. n.** coverings for a bed, such as sheets and blankets.

bedding ● **n.** **1** bedclothes. **2** straw or other material for animals to sleep on.

bedding plant ● **n.** a plant produced for planting in a bed in the spring.

Bede, St E
/beed/ (*c.*673–735; known as **the Venerable Bede**), English monk, theologian, and historian, who wrote *The Ecclesiastical History of the English People* (731), a valuable source for early English history. Feast day, 27 May.

bedevil ● **v.** (**bedevils**, **bedevilling**, **bedevilled**; US **bedevils**, **bedeviling**, **bedeviled**) cause continual trouble to.

Bedfordshire E
a county of south central England; county town, Bedford.

bedlam /bed-luhm/ ● **n.** a scene of great confusion and noise.
– ORIGIN from the name of the hospital of St Mary of Bethlehem in London, used as an asylum for the insane.

bedlinen ● **n.** sheets, pillowcases, and duvet covers.

Bedouin /bed-oo-in/ ● **n.** (pl. **Bedouin**) an Arab living as a nomad in the desert.
– ORIGIN Old French.

bedpan ● **n.** a container used as a toilet by a bedridden patient.

bedraggled ● **adj.** untidy.

bedridden ● **adj.** unable to get out of bed because of sickness or old age.

bedrock ● **n.** **1** solid rock underlying soil. **2** the central principles on which something is based.

bedroom ● **n.** a room for sleeping in.

Beds. ● **abbrev.** Bedfordshire.

bedside manner ● **n.** the way in which a doctor attends a patient.

bedsit ● **n.** Brit. informal a rented room used for both living and sleeping.

bedsore ● **n.** a sore caused by lying in bed in one position for a long time.

bedspread ● **n.** a decorative cloth used to cover a bed.

bedstead ● **n.** the framework of a bed.

bed-wetting ● **n.** urinating while asleep.

bee ● **n.** a winged insect with a sting, which collects nectar and pollen from flowers and makes wax and honey.
– PHRASES **the bee's knees** informal an outstandingly good person or thing. **have a bee in one's bonnet** informal be obsessed with something.
– ORIGIN Old English.

beech ● **n.** a large tree with grey bark and pale wood.
– ORIGIN Old English.

Beecham, E
Sir Thomas (1879–1961), English conductor and impresario, founder of the London Philharmonic and the Royal Philharmonic orchestras.

beef ● **n.** **1** the flesh of a cow, bull, or ox, used as food. **2** informal a complaint. ● **v.** informal (**beef up**) make stronger or larger.
– ORIGIN Old French *boef*.

beefburger ● **n.** a fried or grilled cake of minced beef eaten in a bun.

beefcake ● **n.** informal men with well-developed muscles.

beefeater ● **n.** a Yeoman Warder or Yeoman of the Guard in the Tower of London.

beefsteak ● **n.** a thick slice of steak.

beefy ● **adj.** informal muscular or strong.

beehive ● **n.** a structure in which bees are kept.

bee-keeping ● **n.** the owning and breeding of bees for their honey.
– DERIVATIVES **bee-keeper** n.

beeline ● **n.** (in phr. **make a beeline for**) hurry straight to.

Beelzebub /bi-el-zi-bub/ ● **n.** the Devil.
– ORIGIN Hebrew, 'lord of flies'.

been past part. of **BE**.

beep ● **n.** a short, high-pitched sound made by electronic equipment or the horn of a vehicle. ● **v.** produce a beep.
– DERIVATIVES **beeper** n.

beer ● **n.** an alcoholic drink made from fermented malt flavoured with hops.
– ORIGIN Latin *biber* 'a drink'.

beer belly (also **beer gut**) ● **n.** informal a man's stomach that sticks out because of excessive drinking of beer.

beer mat ● **n.** a small cardboard mat for resting glasses on in a public house.

beery ● **adj.** informal smelling or tasting of beer.

beeswax ● **n.** wax produced by bees to make honeycombs, used for wood polishes and candles.

beet ● **n.** a plant with a fleshy root, grown as food and for making into sugar.
– ORIGIN Latin *beta*.

Beethoven E
/bayt-hoh-vuhn/, Ludwig van (1770–1827), German composer. Despite increasing deafness he produced many works, including nine symphonies, thirty-two piano sonatas, sixteen string quartets, the opera *Fidelio*, and the Mass in D (the *Missa Solemnis*).

beetle ● **n.** an insect with a hard case on its back, covering its wings.
– ORIGIN Old English, 'biter'.

beetle-browed ● **adj.** having large or bushy eyebrows.
– ORIGIN uncertain.

b

Beeton, Mrs Isabella Mary (1836–65), English author, noted for her *Book of Cookery and Household Management*. E

beetroot • n. Brit. the edible dark-red root of a kind of beet.

befall • v. (**befalls**, **befalling**, **befell**; past part. **befallen**) literary (of something bad) happen to.

befit • v. (**befits**, **befitting**, **befitted**) be appropriate for.

before • prep., conj., & adv. **1** during the time preceding. **2** in front of. **3** rather than.
– ORIGIN Old English.

beforehand • adv. in advance.

befriend • v. become a friend to.

befuddle • v. (**befuddles**, **befuddling**, **befuddled**) muddle or confuse.

beg • v. (**begs**, **begging**, **begged**) **1** ask humbly or solemnly for something. **2** ask for food or money as charity.
– PHRASES **beg the question 1** (of a fact or action) invite a question or point that has not been dealt with. **2** assume the truth of something without arguing it. **go begging** be available because unwanted by others.
– ORIGIN prob. Old English.

began past of **BEGIN**.

begat archaic past of **BEGET**.

beget /bi-get/ • v. (**begets**, **begetting**, **begot**; past part. **begotten**) archaic or literary **1** produce (a child). **2** cause.
– ORIGIN Old English.

beggar • n. **1** a person who lives by begging for food or money. **2** informal a person of a certain type: *lucky beggar!* • v. reduce to poverty.
– PHRASES **beggar belief** be too extraordinary to be believed or described.

beggarly • adj. meagre and ungenerous.

Begin /bay-gin, beg-in/, Menachem (1913–92), Israeli statesman, Prime Minister 1977–83. He shared the Nobel Peace Prize (1978) with President Sadat of Egypt for his part in the negotiations that led to a peace treaty between Israel and Egypt. E

begin • v. (**begins**, **beginning**, **began**; past part. **begun**) **1** carry out or experience the first part of (an action or activity). **2** come into being. **3** have as its starting point. **4** (**begin on/upon**) set to work on. **5** informal have any chance of doing.
– DERIVATIVES **beginner** n. **beginning** n.
– ORIGIN Old English.

begonia /bi-goh-ni-uh/ • n. a plant with brightly coloured flowers.
– ORIGIN named after the French botanist Michel *Bégon* (1638–1710).

begot past of **BEGET**.

begotten past part. of **BEGET**.

begrudge • v. (**begrudges**, **begrudging**, **begrudged**) **1** feel envious that (someone) possesses or enjoys (something). **2** give reluctantly or resentfully.

beguile • v. (**beguiles**, **beguiling**, **beguiled**) charm or trick.

begun past part. of **BEGIN**.

behalf • n. (in phr. **on behalf of** or **on someone's behalf**) **1** in the interests of a person, group, or principle. **2** as a representative of.
– ORIGIN from former *on his halve* and *bihalve him*, both meaning 'on his side'.

behave • v. (**behaves**, **behaving**, **behaved**) **1** act in a certain way. **2** (also **behave oneself**) act in a polite or proper way.

behaved • adj. acting in a certain way: *a well-behaved child.*

behaviour (US **behavior**) • n. the way in which someone or something behaves.

behead • v. execute (someone) by cutting off their head.

beheld past and past part. of **BEHOLD**.

behemoth /bi-hee-moth/ • n. a huge creature or monster.
– ORIGIN Hebrew, 'monstrous beast'.

behest /bi-hest/ • n. (in phr. **at the behest of**) literary at the request or order of.
– ORIGIN Old English.

behind • prep. & adv. **1** at or to the back or far side of. **2** further back than other members of a group. **3** in support of. **4** responsible for (an event or plan). **5** less advanced than. **6** late in doing something. • n. informal a person's bottom.
– ORIGIN Old English.

Behn /bayn, ben/, Aphra (1640–89), English novelist and dramatist. the first professional woman writer in England. Her works include the comic play *The Rover* and the novel *Oroonoko, or the History of the Royal Slave*. E

behold • v. (**behold**, **beholding**, **beheld**) archaic or literary see or observe.
– ORIGIN Old English.

beholden • adj. (**beholden to**) having a duty to (someone) in return for a favour.

behove /bi-hohv/ • v. (**it behoves someone to do**) formal it is right or necessary for someone to do.
ORIGIN Old English.

beige • n. a pale sandy colour.
– ORIGIN French.

Beijing /bay-**jing**/ (also **Peking**) the capital of China. E

being • n. **1** existence. **2** the nature of a person. **3** a living creature: *alien beings.*

Beirut /bay-**root**/ the capital of Lebanon. E

bejewelled (US **bejeweled**) • adj. decorated with jewels.

belabour (US **belabor**) • v. attack.

Belarus /bel-uh-**rooss**/ a country in eastern Europe; capital, Minsk. Also called **BELORUSSIA**. E
– DERIVATIVES **Belarusian** (also **Belarussian**) adj. & n.

belated • adj. coming late or too late.
– DERIVATIVES **belatedly** adv.

Belau /buh-low/ var. of **PALAU**. E

belch • v. **1** noisily expel wind from the stomach through the mouth. **2** give out (smoke or flames) with great force. • n. an act of belching.

– ORIGIN Old English.

beleaguered • adj. **1** under siege. **2** in difficulties; harassed.
– ORIGIN Dutch *belegeren* 'camp round'.

Belfast E
the capital and chief port of Northern Ireland.

belfry • n. (pl. **belfries**) the place in a bell tower or steeple in which bells are housed.
– ORIGIN Old French *belfrei*.

Belgium E
a low-lying country in western Europe on the south shore of the North Sea and English Channel; capital, Brussels.
– DERIVATIVES **Belgian** adj. & n.

Belgrade E
/bel-**grayd**/ the capital of Serbia and the federal capital of Yugoslavia.

belie • v. (**belies, belying, belied**) **1** fail to give a true idea of. **2** show to be untrue or unjustified.
– ORIGIN Old English, 'deceive by lying'.

belief • n. **1** a feeling that something exists or is true, especially one without proof. **2** a firmly held opinion. **3** (**belief in**) trust or confidence in. **4** religious faith.
– PHRASES **beyond belief** incredible.
– ORIGIN Old English.

believe • v. (**believes, believing, believed**) **1** accept that (something) is true or (someone) is telling the truth. **2** (**believe in**) have faith in the truth or existence of. **3** think or suppose. **4** have religious faith.
– DERIVATIVES **believable** adj. **believer** n.

belittle • v. (**belittles, belittling, belittled**) dismiss as unimportant.

Belize E
/be-**leez**/ a country on the Caribbean coast of Central America; capital, Belmopan. Former name (until 1973) **British Honduras**.
– DERIVATIVES **Belizean** adj. & n.

Bell, E
Alexander Graham (1847–1922), Scottish-born American scientist, the inventor of the telephone (first demonstrated in 1876) and the gramophone.

bell • n. **1** a deep metal cup held upside down, that sounds a clear musical note when struck. **2** a device that buzzes or rings to give a signal. • v. call or show with a bell.
– PHRASES **give someone a bell** Brit. informal telephone someone. **ring a bell** informal sound vaguely familiar.
– ORIGIN Old English.

belladonna /bel-luh-**don**-nuh/ • n. a drug made from deadly nightshade.
– ORIGIN from Italian *bella donna* 'fair lady'.

belle /bel/ • n. a beautiful woman.
– ORIGIN French.

bellicose /bel-li-kohss/ • adj. aggressive and ready to fight.
– ORIGIN Latin *bellicosus*.

belligerence /buh-li-juh-ruhnss/ • n. aggressive or warlike behaviour.

belligerent • adj. **1** hostile and aggressive. **2** engaged in a war or conflict.
– DERIVATIVES **belligerently** adv.
– ORIGIN Latin *belligerare* 'wage war'.

Bellini[1] E
/bel-**lee**-ni/, a family of Italian painters in Venice; **Jacopo** (*c.*1400–70) and his sons **Gentile** (*c.*1429–1507) and **Giovanni** (*c.*1430–1516).

Bellini[2] E
/bel-**lee**-ni/, Vincenzo (1801–35), Italian composer, noted for operas such as *Norma* and *I Puritani*.

Belloc E
/**bel**-lok/ (Joseph) Hilaire (Pierre René) (1870–1953), French-born British writer, historian, and poet, author of *Cautionary Tales*.

Bellow, E
Saul (b.1915), Canadian-born American novelist, author of *The Adventures of Augie March* and *Herzog*.

bellow • v. **1** give a deep roar of pain or anger. **2** shout or sing very loudly. • n. a deep shout or noise.
– ORIGIN perh. from Old English.

bellows • pl. n. a device consisting of a bag with two handles, used for blowing air into a fire.
– ORIGIN prob. from Old English, 'belly'.

bell-ringing • n. the activity or hobby of ringing church bells or handbells.

belly • n. (pl. **bellies**) **1** the front part of the human body below the ribs, containing the stomach and bowels. **2** a person's stomach. **3** the rounded underside of a ship or aircraft.
– PHRASES **go belly up** informal go bankrupt.
– ORIGIN Old English, 'bag'.

bellyache • v. (**bellyaches, bellyaching, bellyached**) informal complain noisily or often.

belly button • n. informal a person's navel.

bellyflop • n. informal a dive into water, landing flat on one's front.

belly laugh • n. a loud unrestrained laugh.

Belmopan E
/bel-moh-**pan**/ the capital of Belize.

belong • v. **1** be rightly put into a particular position or class. **2** fit or be acceptable in a particular place or situation. **3** (**belong to**) be a member of. **4** (**belong to**) be the property of.

belongings • pl. n. a person's movable possessions.

Belorussia E
/be-loh-**ruh**-shuh/ (also **Byelorussia**) = **Belarus**.
– DERIVATIVES **Belorussian** (also **Byelorussian**) adj. & n.

beloved • adj. dearly loved.

below • prep. & adv. **1** at a lower level than. **2** (in printed text) mentioned further down.

Belsen E
/**bel**-s'n/ a Nazi concentration camp in the Second World War, in NW Germany.

belt • n. **1** a strip of material worn round the waist to support or hold in clothes or to carry weapons. **2** a continuous band in machinery that transfers motion from one wheel to another. **3** a strip or encircling area: *the asteroid belt*. • v. **1** fasten or secure with a belt. **2** beat

or hit very hard. **3** (**belt out**) informal sing or play (something) loudly and forcefully. **5** (**belt up**) informal be quiet.
– PHRASES **below the belt** unfair; against the rules. [ORIGIN from the idea of an illegal blow in boxing.] **tighten one's belt** cut one's spending. **under one's belt** achieved or acquired.
– ORIGIN Latin *balteus*.

beluga /buh-loo-guh/ ● n. (pl. **beluga** or **belugas**) **1** a small whale of Arctic waters. **2** a very large sturgeon from which caviar is obtained.
– ORIGIN Russian, 'white'.

belying pres. part. of BELIE.

BEM ● abbrev. British Empire Medal.

bemoan ● v. express sadness for.

bemuse ● v. (**bemuses**, **bemusing**, **bemused**) confuse or bewilder.
– DERIVATIVES **bemusement** n.

Ben Bella E
/ben bel-**luh**/, (Muhammad) Ahmed (b.1916), Algerian statesman, first Prime Minister of independent Algeria (1962–3) and its first President (1963–5).

bench ● n. **1** a long seat for more than one person. **2** a long work table in a workshop or laboratory. **3** (**the bench**) the office of judge or magistrate. **4** (**the bench**) a seat at the side of a sports field for coaches and players not taking part in a game.
– ORIGIN Old English.

benchmark ● n. a standard or point of reference.

bench press ● n. an exercise in which one lies on a bench with feet on the floor and raises a weight with both arms.

bend ● v. (**bends**, **bending**, **bent**) **1** give or have a curved or angled shape, form, or course. **2** lean or curve the body downwards; stoop. **3** force or be forced to give in. **4** change (a rule) to suit oneself. ● n. **1** a curved or angled part or course. **2** a kind of knot used to join two ropes together, or one rope to another object. **3** (**the bends**) decompression sickness.
– PHRASES **round the bend** informal mad.
– DERIVATIVES **bendy** adj.
– ORIGIN Old English.

bender ● n. informal a drinking bout.

beneath ● prep. & adv. extending or directly underneath. ● prep. of lower status or worth than.
– ORIGIN Old English.

Benedict, St E
(*c.*480–*c.*550), Italian hermit, the founder of Western monasticism. Feast day, 11 July.

Benedictine /ben-i-**dik**-teen/ ● n. a monk or nun of a Christian religious order following the rule of St Benedict.

benediction ● n. **1** the speaking of a blessing. **2** the state of being blessed.
– ORIGIN Latin *benedicere* 'bless'.

benefaction /ben-i-**fak**-sh'n/ ● n. formal a donation.
– ORIGIN Latin.

benefactor ● n. a person who gives money or other help.

benefice /ben-i-fiss/ ● n. a Church office in which a member of the clergy receives accommodation and income in return for their duties.
– ORIGIN Latin *beneficium* 'favour'.

beneficial ● adj. having a good effect; favourable.

beneficiary ● n. (pl. **beneficiaries**) a person who benefits from something.

benefit ● n. **1** advantage or profit. **2** a payment made by the state or an insurance scheme to someone entitled to receive it. **3** a public performance to raise money for a charity. ● v. (**benefits**, **benefiting**, **benefited**; also **benefits**, **benefitting**, **benefitted**) **1** receive an advantage; profit. **2** bring advantage to.
– PHRASES **the benefit of the doubt** acceptance that a person must be regarded as correct or innocent if the opposite has not been proven.
– ORIGIN Latin *benefactum* 'good deed'.

Benelux E
/ben-i-luks/ the countries of Belgium, the Netherlands, and Luxembourg as an economic union.

benevolent /bi-nev-uh-luhnt/ ● adj. **1** well meaning and kindly. **2** (of an organization) charitable rather than profit-making.
– DERIVATIVES **benevolence** n.
– ORIGIN Old French *benivolent*.

Bengal E
/beng-**gawl**/ a region and former province in the north-east of the Indian subcontinent. In 1947 the province was divided into West Bengal, which has remained a state of India, and East Bengal, now Bangladesh.

Bengal, Bay of E
a part of the Indian Ocean lying between India to the west and Burma (Myanmar) and Thailand to the east.

Bengali /ben-gaw-li/ ● n. (pl. **Bengalis**) **1** a person from Bengal. **2** the language of Bangladesh and West Bengal. ● adj. relating to Bengal.
– ORIGIN Hindi.

Ben-Gurion E
/ben-**goo**-ri-uhn/, David (1886–1973), Israeli statesman, who served as Israel's first Prime Minister 1948–53 and again in 1955–63.

benighted ● adj. ignorant or primitive.

benign ● adj. **1** cheerful and kindly. **2** favourable; not harmful. **3** (of a tumour) not malignant.
– ORIGIN Latin *benignus*.

Benin E
/be-**neen**/ a country of West Africa; capital, Porto Novo. Former name (until 1975) DAHOMEY.
– DERIVATIVES **Beninese** /ben-i-**neez**/ adj. & n.

Bennett[1], E
Alan (b.1934), English dramatist and actor. His works include *Beyond the Fringe* and *Talking Heads*.

Bennett[2], E
(Enoch) Arnold (1867–1931), English novelist, dramatist, and critic, known for his novels set in the Potteries ('the Five Towns'), such as *Anna of the Five Towns*.

b

Ben Nevis E
/ben **nev**-iss/ a mountain in western Scotland. Rising to 1,343 m (4,406 ft), it is the highest in the British Isles.

bent past and past part. of BEND. ● adj. **1** having an angle or sharp curve. **2** Brit. informal dishonest; corrupt. **3** Brit. informal, derog. homosexual. **4** (**bent on**) determined to do or have. ● n. a natural talent or inclination.

Bentham E
/**ben**-thuhm/, Jeremy (1748–1832), English philosopher and jurist, founder of utilitarianism.

Benz E
/benz/, Karl Friedrich (1844–1929), German engineer and motor manufacturer, who in 1885 built the first vehicle to be driven by an internal-combustion engine.

benzene /**ben**-zeen/ ● n. a liquid hydrocarbon present in coal tar and petroleum.
– ORIGIN French *benjoin*, referring to a resin obtained from a tree.

benzine /**ben**-zeen/ ● n. a mixture of liquid hydrocarbons obtained from petroleum.

bequeath /bi-**kweeth**/ ● v. **1** leave (property) to someone by a will. **2** hand down or pass on.
– ORIGIN Old English.

bequest ● n. **1** the action of bequeathing. **2** something that is bequeathed.

berate ● v. (**berates**, **berating**, **berated**) scold or criticize angrily.

Berber /**ber**-ber/ ● n. a member of a people native to North Africa.
– ORIGIN Greek *barbaros* 'foreigner'.

bereave ● v. (**bereaves**, **bereaving**, **bereaved**) (**be bereaved**) be deprived of a close relation or friend through their death.
– DERIVATIVES **bereavement** n.
– ORIGIN Old English.

bereft ● adj. **1** (**bereft of**) deprived of; without. **2** lonely and abandoned.
– ORIGIN from BEREAVE.

beret /**be**-ray/ ● n. a flat round cap of felt or cloth.
– ORIGIN French.

Berg E
/**bairg**/, Alban (Maria Johannes) (1885–1935), Austrian composer. His works include the operas *Wozzeck* and *Lulu*.

bergamot /**ber**-guh-mot/ ● n. **1** an oily substance extracted from Seville oranges, used as flavouring in Earl Grey tea. **2** a herb of the mint family.
– ORIGIN from *Bergamo* in Italy.

Bergen E
/**bair**-g'n/ a seaport in SW Norway, a centre of the fishing and North Sea oil industries.

Bergman[1] E
/**bairg**-muhn/, (Ernst) Ingmar (b.1918), Swedish film and theatre director, noted for the films *The Seventh Seal* and *Wild Strawberries*.

Bergman[2] E
/**berg**-muhn/, Ingrid (1915–82), Swedish actress. She starred in a number of classic films, including *Casablanca*.

beriberi /**be**-ri-**be**-ri/ ● n. a disease causing inflammation of the nerves and heart failure, due to a lack of vitamin B_1.
– ORIGIN Sinhalese.

Bering E
/**bair**-ing/, Vitus (Jonassen) (1681–1741), Danish navigator and explorer, who led several Russian expeditions aimed at discovering whether Asia and North America were connected by land.

Bering Sea E
an arm of the North Pacific lying between NE Siberia and Alaska. It is linked to the Arctic Ocean by the Bering Strait.

Bering Strait E
a narrow sea passage which separates the eastern tip of Siberia from Alaska and links the Arctic Ocean with the Bering Sea, about 85 km (53 miles) wide at its narrowest point.

berk /berk/ ● n. Brit. informal a stupid person.
– ORIGIN from *Berkeley* or *Berkshire Hunt*, rhyming slang for 'cunt'.

Berkeley[1] E
/**berk**-li/ a city in western California, on San Francisco Bay, site of a campus of the University of California.

Berkeley[2] E
/**berk**-li/, Busby (1895–1976; born *William Berkeley Enos*), American choreographer and film director, famous for his spectacular sequences in which huge casts of dancers formed kaleidoscopic patterns on the screen.

Berkeley[3] E
/**bark**-li/, George (1685–1753), Irish philosopher and bishop. He argued that material objects exist solely by being perceived, so there are only minds and mental events.

berkelium /ber-**kee**-li-uhm/ ● n. a radioactive metallic chemical element made by high-energy atomic collisions.
– ORIGIN from BERKELEY[1].

Berks. ● abbrev. Berkshire.

Berkshire E
/**bark**-sheer, **bark**-sher/ a former county of southern England, west of London, divided in 1998 into six unitary authorities.

Berlin[1] E
/ber-**lin**/ the capital of Germany. At the end of the Second World War the city was divided into two parts: **West Berlin**, a state of the Federal Republic of Germany despite forming an enclave within the German Democratic Republic, and **East Berlin**, the capital of the German Democratic Republic; the two parts were reunited in 1990.

Berlin[2] E
/ber-**lin**/, Irving (1888–1989; born *Israel Baline*), Russian-born American songwriter, noted for the songs 'White Christmas' and 'God Bless America'.

Berlin Wall E
a fortified and heavily guarded wall built in 1961 by the communist authorities on the boundary between East and West Berlin. It

was opened in November 1989 after the collapse of the communist regime in East Germany and later dismantled.

Berlioz E
/**bair**-li-ohz/, Hector (Louis) (1803–69), French composer. His works include the opera *Les Troyens* and the symphony *Symphonie fantastique*.

Bermuda E
/ber-**myoo**-duh/ a country consisting of about 150 small islands off the coast of North Carolina; capital, Hamilton. It is a British dependency with full internal self-government.
– DERIVATIVES **Bermudan** (also **Bermudian**) adj. & n.

Bermuda shorts • pl. n. casual knee-length shorts.

Bermuda Triangle E
an area of the western Atlantic Ocean where a large number of ships and aircraft are said to have mysteriously disappeared.

Bernadette, St E
(1844–79; born *Marie Bernarde Soubirous*), French peasant girl. Her visions of the Virgin Mary in Lourdes in 1858 led to the town's establishment as a centre of pilgrimage. Feast day, 18 February.

Bernard, St E
(*c*.996–*c*.1081), French monk who founded two hospices for travellers in the Alps. St Bernard dogs are named after him. Feast day, 28 May.

Berne E
/bern, bairn/ (also **Bern**) the capital of Switzerland.

Berners-Lee, E
Tim (b.1955), English computer engineer, who proposed the World Wide Web in 1989 and designed its first software.

Bernhardt E
/**bern**-hart/, Sarah (1844–1923), French actress, best known for her portrayal of Marguerite in *La Dame aux Camélias* and Cordelia in *King Lear*.

Bernini E
/bair-**nee**-ni/, Gian Lorenzo (1598–1680), Italian baroque sculptor, painter, and architect. His work includes the colonnade round the piazza at St Peter's, Rome.

Bernstein E
/**bern**-steen, **bern**-styn/, Leonard (1918–90), American composer, conductor, and pianist, best known for the score for the musical *West Side Story* and the operetta *Candide*.

Berry, E
Chuck (b.1931; born *Charles Edward Berry*), American rock-and-roll singer, guitarist, and songwriter, whose songs include 'Johnny B Goode'.

berry • n. (pl. **berries**) **1** a small round juicy fruit without a stone. **2** Bot. a fruit that has its seeds enclosed in a fleshy pulp, e.g. a banana.
– ORIGIN Old English.

berserk /buh-**zerk**/ • adj. out of control with anger or excitement.
– ORIGIN Old Norse.

berth • n. **1** a place for a ship to moor at a wharf. **2** a bunk on a ship or train. • v. moor in a berth.
– PHRASES **give a wide berth** stay well away from.
– ORIGIN prob. from **BEAR**[1] + **-TH**[2].

Bertolucci E
/bair-tuh-**loo**-chi/, Bernardo (b.1940), Italian film director. His films include *Last Tango in Paris* and *The Last Emperor*.

beryl • n. a transparent pale green, blue, or yellow gemstone.
– ORIGIN Greek *bērullos*.

beryllium /buh-**ril**-li-uhm/ • n. a hard, grey, lightweight metallic element.

beseech • v. (**beseeches**, **beseeching**, **besought** or **beseeched**) literary ask in a pleading way.
– ORIGIN Old English.

beset • v. (**besets**, **besetting**, **beset**) trouble or worry continuously.
– ORIGIN Old English.

beside • prep. **1** at the side of; next to. **2** compared with. **3** (also **besides**) as well as. • adv. (**besides**) as well.
– PHRASES **beside oneself** frantic with worry.

besiege • v. (**besieges**, **besieging**, **besieged**) **1** surround (a place) with armed forces so as to force it to surrender. **2** worry or overwhelm with requests or complaints.

besmirch /bi-**smerch**/ • v. damage (someone's reputation).

besom /**bee**-zuhm/ • n. a broom made of twigs tied round a stick.
– ORIGIN Old English.

besotted /bi-**sot**-tid/ • adj. in love in an irrational and intense way.
– ORIGIN from **SOT**.

besought past and past part. of **BESEECH**.

bespeak • v. (**bespeaks**, **bespeaking**, **bespoke**; past part. **bespoken**) **1** be evidence of. **2** formal order in advance.

bespoke • adj. Brit. made to a customer's requirements.

Best[1], E
Charles Herbert (1899–1978), American-born Canadian physiologist, who assisted F. G. Banting in research leading to the discovery of insulin in 1922.

Best[2], E
George (b.1946), Northern Irish footballer, named European Footballer of the Year in 1968.

best • adj. **1** of the highest quality. **2** most suitable or sensible. • adv. **1** to the highest degree or standard; most. **2** most suitably or sensibly. • n. **1** (**the best**) that which is best. **2** (**one's best**) the highest standard one can reach.
– PHRASES **at best** taking the most optimistic view. **the best of three** (or **five** etc.) victory achieved by winning the majority of a specified odd number of games. **the best part of** most of. **get the best of** overcome. **had best**

b

find it most sensible to. **make the best of** get what limited advantage one can from. **six of the best** Brit. six strokes of the cane as a punishment.
– ORIGIN Old English.

bestial /bess-ti-uhl/ ● **adj.** savagely cruel or wicked.
– ORIGIN Latin *bestia* 'beast'.

bestiality ● **n. 1** savagely cruel behaviour. **2** sexual intercourse between a person and an animal.

bestir ● **v.** (**bestirs**, **bestirring**, **bestirred**) (**bestir oneself**) rouse oneself to action.

best man ● **n.** a man chosen by a bridegroom to assist him at his wedding.

bestow ● **v.** award (an honour, right, or gift).
– ORIGIN Old English.

bestride ● **v.** (**bestrides**, **bestriding**, **bestrode**; past part. **bestridden**) stand astride over.

best-seller ● **n.** a book or other product that sells in very large numbers.

bet ● **v.** (**bets**, **betting**, **bet** or **betted**) **1** risk money or property against someone else's on the outcome of an unpredictable event such as a race. **2** informal feel sure. ● **n. 1** an act of betting or the money betted. **2** informal a candidate or option with a specified chance of success: *Allen looked a good bet for victory.* **3** (**one's bet**) informal one's opinion.
– PHRASES **you bet** informal certainly.
– DERIVATIVES **bettor** (also **better**) n.
– ORIGIN perh. from a former word meaning 'abetting'.

beta /bee-tuh/ ● **n. 1** the second letter of the Greek alphabet (Β, β). **2** Brit. a second-class grade or mark.
– ORIGIN Greek.

beta blocker ● **n.** a drug used to treat angina and reduce high blood pressure.

betake ● **v.** (**betakes**, **betaking**, **betook**; past part. **betaken**) (**betake oneself to**) literary go to.

beta particle ● **n.** Physics a fast-moving electron given off by some radioactive substances.

betel /bee-t'l/ ● **n.** the leaf of an Asian plant, chewed as a mild stimulant.
– ORIGIN Portuguese.

Betelgeuse E
/bee-t'l-jerz/ the tenth-brightest star in the sky, in the constellation Orion.

bête noire /bet nwar/ ● **n.** (pl. **bêtes noires** /bet **nwar**/) a person or thing that one particularly dislikes.
– ORIGIN French, 'black beast'.

Bethlehem E
/**beth**-li-hem/ a small town near Jerusalem; it was the native city of King David and the reputed birthplace of Jesus.

betide ● **v.** (**betide**, **betiding**, **betided**) literary happen or happen to.

betimes ● **adv.** literary in good time.

Betjeman E
/**bet**-chuh-muhn/, Sir John (1906–84), English poet and writer, noted for his gently satirical poems. He was Poet Laureate 1972–84.

betoken ● **v.** literary be a sign of.

betook past of BETAKE.

betray ● **v. 1** act treacherously towards (one's country) by helping an enemy. **2** be disloyal to. **3** reveal (something) without meaning to.
– DERIVATIVES **betrayal** n. **betrayer** n.
– ORIGIN Latin *tradere* 'hand over'.

betrothed /bi-**troh***thd*/ formal ● **adj.** engaged to be married. ● **n.** (**one's betrothed**) the person to whom one is engaged.
– DERIVATIVES **betrothal** n.

better ● **adj. 1** more satisfactory or suitable. **2** partly or fully recovered from illness or injury. ● **adv. 1** in a better way **2** to a greater degree; more. ● **n. 1** something that is better. **2** (**one's betters**) dated or humorous people who are more important or skilled than oneself. ● **v. 1** improve on. **2** (**better oneself**) improve one's social status.
– PHRASES **better off** in a more favourable position. **the better part of** most of. **get the better of** defeat. **had better** would find it wiser to.
– ORIGIN Old English.

better half ● **n.** informal a person's husband or wife.

betterment ● **n.** improvement.

between ● **prep. & adv. 1** at, into, or across the space separating (two things). **2** in the period separating (two points in time). **3** (as prep.) indicating a connection or relationship. **4** (as prep.) shared by; together with.
– PHRASES **between ourselves** (or **you and me**) in confidence.
– ORIGIN Old English.

betwixt ● **prep. & adv.** archaic between.
– ORIGIN Old English.

Bevan E
/**bev**-uhn/, Nye (1897–1960; full name *Aneurin Bevan*), British Labour politician. As Minister of Health 1945–51, he was responsible for the creation of the National Health Service (1948).

bevel /*rhymes with* level/ ● **n. 1** (in carpentry) a sloping surface or edge. **2** (also **bevel square**) a tool for marking angles in carpentry and stonework. ● **v.** (**bevels**, **bevelling**, **bevelled**; US **bevels**, **beveling**, **beveled**) cut a bevel on.
– ORIGIN Old French.

beverage ● **n.** a drink other than water.
– ORIGIN Old French *bevrage*.

Beveridge E
/**bev**-uh-rij/, William Henry, 1st Baron (1879–1963), British economist and social reformer, born in India. His report formed the basis of much of the legislation on which the welfare state in the UK is founded.

Beverly Hills E
a city in California, on the NW side of Los Angeles, the home of many film stars.

Bevin E
/**bev**-in/, Ernest (1881–1951), British Labour statesman and trade unionist. He was one of the founders of the Transport and General Workers' Union and a leading organizer of the General Strike (1926).

bevy /*rhymes with* heavy/ ● **n.** (pl. **bevies**) a large group.
– ORIGIN unknown.

bewail • v. express great regret or sorrow over.

beware • v. be cautious and alert to risks.
– ORIGIN from *be ware* 'be aware'.

bewilder • v. (**bewilders**, **bewildering**, **bewildered**) puzzle or confuse.
– DERIVATIVES **bewilderment** n.
– ORIGIN from a former word meaning 'lead or go astray'.

bewitch • v. **1** cast a spell over. **2** attract and delight.

beyond • prep. & adv. **1** at or to the further side of. **2** outside the range or limits of. **3** to or in a state where something is impossible: *the radio was beyond repair.* **4** happening or continuing after. **5** except.
– ORIGIN Old English.

bezique /bi-zeek/ • n. a card game for two players.
– ORIGIN French *bésigue*.

Bhagavadgita E
/bug-uh-vuhd-**gee**-tuh/ a poem composed between the 2nd century BC and the 2nd century AD, part of the epic poem the Mahabharata and the most famous religious text of Hinduism.

bhaji /**bah**-ji/ (also **bhajia** /**bah**-juh/) • n. (pl. **bhajis**, **bhajia**) an Indian dish of vegetables fried in batter.
– ORIGIN Hindi.

bhang /bang/ (also **bang**) • n. the leaves and flower-tops of cannabis, used as a narcotic in India.
– ORIGIN Hindi.

Bharat E
/**bu**-ruht/ Hindi name for **INDIA**.

Bhopal E
/boh-**pahl**/ a city in central India, the capital of the state of Madhya Pradesh.

b.h.p. • abbrev. brake horsepower.

Bhutan E
/boo-**tahn**/ a small independent kingdom on the south-eastern slopes of the Himalayas, a protectorate of the Republic of India; capital, Thimphu.
– DERIVATIVES **Bhutanese** /boo-tuh-**neez**/ adj. & n.

Bhutto[1] E
/**boo**-toh/, Benazir (b.1953), Pakistani stateswoman, Prime Minister 1988–90 and 1993–6, daughter of Zulfikar Ali Bhutto. She was the first woman Prime Minister of a Muslim country.

Bhutto[2] E
/**boo**-toh/, Zulfikar Ali (1928–79), Pakistani statesman, President 1971–3 and Prime Minister 1973–7. He was executed for conspiring to murder a political rival.

bi- (also **bin-** before a vowel) • comb. form **1** two; having two: *biathlon.* **2** occurring twice in every one or once in every two: *bicentennial.* **3** lasting for two: *biennial.*
– ORIGIN Latin.

Biafra E
/bi-**af**-ruh/ a state proclaimed in 1967, when part of eastern Nigeria declared independence. In the ensuing civil war the new state's troops were defeated, and by 1970 it had ceased to exist.
– DERIVATIVES **Biafran** adj. & n.

biannual • adj. occurring twice a year.

bias /**by**-uhss/ • n. **1** an opinion or tendency to be strongly for or against a person or thing. **2** a slanting direction across the grain of a fabric. **3** Electron. a steady voltage, applied to an electronic device, that can be adjusted to change the way the device operates. • v. (**biases**, **biasing**, **biased**) cause to feel bias: *the courts were biased towards the police.*
– ORIGIN French *biais*.

bias binding • n. a narrow strip of fabric cut on the bias, used to bind edges.

biathlon /by-**ath**-lon/ • n. a sporting event combining cross-country skiing and rifle shooting.
– ORIGIN from Greek *athlon* 'contest'.

bib • n. **1** a piece of cloth or plastic fastened under a child's chin to protect its clothes. **2** the part of an apron or pair of dungarees that covers the chest.
– PHRASES **one's best bib and tucker** informal one's smartest clothes.
– ORIGIN prob. from Latin *bibere* 'to drink'.

Bible • n. **1** the Christian scriptures, consisting of the Old and New Testaments. **2** the Jewish scriptures. **3** (**bible**) informal a book seen as thorough and reliable.
– ORIGIN Greek *biblion* 'book'.

biblical • adj. having to do with or found in the Bible.

bibliography /bib-li-**og**-ruh-fi/ • n. (pl. **bibliographies**) **1** a list of the books referred to in a scholarly work. **2** a list of books on a particular subject or by a particular author. **3** the study of books and their production.
– DERIVATIVES **bibliographer** n. **bibliographic** adj.
– ORIGIN from Greek *biblion* 'book'.

bibliophile /**bib**-li-oh-fyl/ • n. a person who collects or loves books.

bibulous /**bib**-yuu-luhss/ • adj. formal very fond of drinking alcohol.
– ORIGIN Latin *bibulus* 'freely drinking'.

bicameral /by-**kam**-uh-ruhl/ • adj. (of a law-making body) having two chambers.
– ORIGIN from Latin *camera* 'chamber'.

bicarbonate • n. Chem. a compound containing HCO_3 negative ions together with a metallic element.

bicarbonate of soda • n. sodium bicarbonate.

bicentenary • n. (pl. **bicentenaries**) a two-hundredth anniversary.
– DERIVATIVES **bicentennial** n. & adj.

biceps /**by**-seps/ • n. (pl. **biceps**) a large muscle in the upper arm which flexes the arm and forearm.
– ORIGIN Latin, 'two-headed'.

bicker • v. (**bickers**, **bickering**, **bickered**) argue about unimportant things.
– ORIGIN unknown.

bicuspid /by-**kuss**-pid/ • adj. having two cusps or points. • n. a tooth with two cusps.

bicycle • n. a two-wheeled vehicle propelled by pedals. • v. (**bicycles**, **bicycling**, **bicycled**) ride a bicycle.
– DERIVATIVES **bicyclist** n.
– ORIGIN from Greek *kuklos* 'wheel'.

bid[1] ● v. (**bids**, **bidding**, **bid**) **1** offer (a price) for something. **2** (**bid for**) try to get or do. ● n. an act of bidding.
– DERIVATIVES **bidder** n. **bidding** n.
– ORIGIN Old English.

b

bid[2] ● v. (**bids**, **bidding**, **bid** or **bade**; past part. **bid**) **1** say (a greeting or farewell) to. **2** archaic command.
– ORIGIN Old English.

biddable ● adj. obedient.

biddy ● n. (pl. **biddies**) informal an old woman.
– ORIGIN unknown.

bide ● v. (**bides**, **biding**, **bided**) archaic or dialect stay in a place.
– PHRASES **bide one's time** wait patiently for a good opportunity.
– ORIGIN Old English.

bidet /bee-day/ ● n. a low basin used for washing one's genital area.
– ORIGIN French, 'pony'.

biennial /by-en-ni-uhl/ ● adj. **1** taking place every other year. **2** (of a plant) living for two years.
– ORIGIN from Latin *annus* 'year'.

bier /beer/ ● n. a movable platform on which a coffin or corpse is placed before burial.
– ORIGIN Old English.

biff ● v. informal strike hard with the fist.

bifocal ● adj. (of a lens) made in two sections, one with a focus for seeing distant things and one for seeing things that are close. ● n. (**bifocals**) a pair of glasses with bifocal lenses.

big ● adj. (**bigger**, **biggest**) **1** large in size, amount, or extent. **2** very important or serious. **3** older or grown-up: *my big sister.* **4** informal very popular.
– PHRASES **the big screen** informal the cinema. **talk big** informal talk confidently or boastfully. **think big** informal be ambitious. **too big for one's boots** informal conceited.
– DERIVATIVES **biggish** adj. **bigness** n.
– ORIGIN unknown.

bigamy /bi-guh-mi/ ● n. the crime of marrying someone while already married to another person.
– DERIVATIVES **bigamist** n. **bigamous** adj.
– ORIGIN from **BI-** + Greek *-gamos* 'married'.

Big Apple E
informal New York City.

big bang ● n. the rapid expansion of extremely dense matter which marked the origin of the universe according to current theories.

Big Ben E
the great clock tower of the Houses of Parliament in London and its bell.

Big Brother ● n. a person or organization exercising total control over people's lives.
– ORIGIN the name of the head of state in George Orwell's novel *Nineteen Eighty-four.*

big end ● n. the larger end of the connecting rod in a piston engine.

big-head ● n. informal a conceited person.

bight /*rhymes with* light/ ● n. a long inward curve in a coastline.
– ORIGIN Old English.

big mouth ● n. informal a person who boasts or cannot keep secrets.

bigot /bi-guht/ ● n. a person with prejudiced views who does not tolerate the opinions of other people.
– DERIVATIVES **bigoted** adj. **bigotry** n.
– ORIGIN French.

big top ● n. the main tent in a circus.

big wheel ● n. a Ferris wheel.

bigwig ● n. informal an important person.

Bihar E
/bi-har/ a state in NE India; capital, Patna.

bijou /bee-*zh*oo/ ● adj. small and elegant.
– ORIGIN French, 'jewel'.

bike informal ● n. a bicycle or motorcycle. ● v. (**bikes**, **biking**, **biked**) ride a bicycle or motorcycle.
– DERIVATIVES **biker** n.

Bikini E
an atoll in the Marshall Islands, in the western Pacific, used by the US between 1946 and 1958 as a site for testing nuclear weapons.

bikini ● n. (pl. **bikinis**) a women's two-piece swimsuit.
– ORIGIN named after **BIKINI** (the garment's devastating effect being compared to that of the atom bomb tested there).

Biko E
/bee-koh/, Steve (1946–77), South African radical leader. After his death in police custody he became a symbol of heroic resistance to apartheid.

bilateral ● adj. **1** having two sides. **2** involving two parties.
– DERIVATIVES **bilaterally** adv.

Bilbao E
/bil-bow/ a seaport and industrial city in northern Spain.

bilberry ● n. (pl. **bilberries**) the small blue edible berry of a shrub found on high ground.
– ORIGIN prob. Scandinavian.

bile ● n. **1** a bitter fluid which is produced by the liver and aids digestion. **2** anger; irritability.
– ORIGIN Latin *bilis*.

bile duct ● n. the tube which conveys bile from the liver and the gall bladder to the duodenum.

bilge ● n. **1** the bottom of a ship's hull. **2** (also **bilge water**) dirty water that collects in the bilge. **3** informal nonsense.
– ORIGIN prob. from **BULGE**.

bilingual ● adj. **1** speaking two languages fluently. **2** expressed in two languages.

bilious ● adj. **1** affected by sickness; nauseous. **2** relating to bile. **3** bad-tempered.

bilk ● v. informal cheat or defraud.
– ORIGIN perh. from **BAULK**.

Bill ● n. (**the Bill** or **the Old Bill**) Brit. informal the police.
– ORIGIN familiar form of the man's name *William.*

bill[1] ● n. **1** a written statement of charges for goods or services. **2** a draft of a proposed law presented to parliament for discussion. **3** a programme of entertainment at a theatre or cinema. **4** an advertising poster. **5** N. Amer. a banknote. ● v. **1** list (a person or event) in a programme. **2** (**bill as**) describe as. **3** send a statement of charges to.
– PHRASES **a clean bill of health** a statement confirming good health or condition. **fit the bill** be suitable.

– DERIVATIVES **billing** n.
– ORIGIN Old French *bille*.

bill[2] ● n. **1** the beak of a bird. **2** a narrow piece of land projecting into the sea: *Portland Bill*.
– PHRASES **bill and coo** informal behave in a loving and sentimental way.
– ORIGIN Old English.

billabong ● n. Austral. a branch of a river forming a backwater or stagnant pool.
– ORIGIN from an Aboriginal word.

billboard ● n. a hoarding.

billet /*rhymes with* fillet/ ● n. a civilian house where soldiers are lodged temporarily. ● v. (**billets**, **billeting**, **billeted**) lodge in a billet.
– ORIGIN Old French *billette* 'small document'.

billet-doux /bil-li-doo/ ● n. (pl. **billets-doux** /bil-li-**dooz**/) dated or humorous a love letter.
– ORIGIN French, 'sweet note'.

billhook ● n. a tool with a curved blade, used for pruning.

billiards ● n. a game played on a table with pockets at the sides and corners, into which balls are struck with a cue.
– ORIGIN French *billard*.

Billingsgate E
a large London fish market originally situated near London Bridge and now located at the Isle of Dogs in the East End.

billion ● cardinal number (pl. **billions** or (with numeral or quantifying word) **billion**) **1** a thousand million; 1,000,000,000 or 10^9. **2** Brit. dated a million million (1,000,000,000,000 or 10^{12}). **3** (**billions**) informal a very large number or amount.
– DERIVATIVES **billionth** ordinal number.
– ORIGIN French.

billionaire ● n. a person owning money and property worth at least a billion pounds or dollars.

bill of rights ● n. a statement of the rights of a country's citizens.

billow ● v. **1** (of smoke, cloud, or steam) roll outward. **2** fill with air and swell out: *her dress billowed out behind her*. ● n. a large rolling mass of cloud, smoke, or steam.
– DERIVATIVES **billowy** adj.
– ORIGIN Old Norse.

billy (also **billycan**) ● n. (pl. **billies**) a metal cooking pot with a lid and handle, used in camping.
– ORIGIN perh. from an Aboriginal word meaning 'water'.

billy goat ● n. a male goat.
– ORIGIN *Billy*, familiar form of the man's name *William*.

Billy the Kid E
see **BONNEY**.

bimbo ● n. (pl. **bimbos**) informal, derog. an attractive but unintelligent woman.
– ORIGIN Italian, 'little child'.

bin Brit. ● n. **1** a container for rubbish. **2** a large storage container. ● v. (**bins**, **binning**, **binned**) throw away.
– ORIGIN Old English.

binary /by-nuh-ri/ ● adj. **1** composed of or involving two things. **2** having to do with a system of numbers with two as its base, using the digits 0 and 1.
– ORIGIN Latin *binarius*.

bind ● v. (**binds**, **binding**, **bound**) **1** tie or fasten; tie up. **2** wrap or encircle tightly: *her hair was bound up in a towel*. **3** hold together in a united group or mass. **4** (**be bound by**) be hampered or restricted by. **5** require (someone) to do something by law or because of a contract. **6** (**bind over**) (of a court of law) require (someone) to do something: *he was bound over to keep the peace*. **7** fix together and enclose (the pages of a book) in a cover. **8** trim (the edge of a piece of material) with a fabric strip. ● n. informal an annoying or difficult situation.
– ORIGIN Old English.

binder ● n. **1** a cover for holding magazines or loose papers together. **2** a reaping machine that binds grain into sheaves. **3** a person who binds books.
– DERIVATIVES **bindery** n. (pl. **binderies**).

binding ● n. **1** a strong covering holding the pages of a book together. **2** fabric in a strip, used for binding the edges of material. ● adj. (of an agreement) putting someone under a legal obligation.

bindweed ● n. a plant that twines itself round things.

binge informal ● n. a short period of uncontrolled eating or drinking. ● v. (**binges**, **bingeing**, **binged**) do something, especially eat, uncontrollably.
– ORIGIN unknown.

bingo ● n. a game in which players mark off randomly called numbers on cards, the winner being the first to mark off all their numbers. ● exclam. **1** a call by someone who wins a game of bingo. **2** said to express satisfaction at a sudden good event.
– ORIGIN unknown.

binnacle ● n. a casing to hold a ship's compass.
– ORIGIN Spanish *bitácula*, *bitácora* or Portuguese *bitacola*.

binocular /bi-nok-yuu-ler/ ● adj. for or using both eyes. ● n. (**binoculars**) an instrument with a separate lens for each eye, used for viewing distant objects.
– ORIGIN from Latin *bini* 'two together' + *oculus* 'eye'.

binomial /by-noh-mi-uhl/ ● n. Math. an algebraic expression consisting of two terms linked by a plus or minus sign.
– ORIGIN from Latin *bi-* 'having two' + Greek *nomos* 'part'.

bint ● n. Brit. informal, derog. a girl or woman.
– ORIGIN Arabic.

bio- ● comb. form **1** having to do with life or living beings: *biosynthesis*. **2** biological; relating to biology: *biohazard*.
– ORIGIN Greek *bios* 'human life'.

biochemistry ● n. the branch of science concerned with the chemical processes which occur within living organisms.
– DERIVATIVES **biochemical** adj. **biochemist** n.

biodegradable ● adj. capable of being decomposed by bacteria or other living organisms.

biodiversity ● n. the variety of plant and animal life in the world or in a habitat.

bioengineering ● n. **1** genetic engineering. **2** the use of artificial tissues or organs in the body. **3** the use of organisms or biological processes in industry.

biography ● n. (pl. **biographies**) an account of a person's life written by someone else.
– DERIVATIVES **biographer** n. **biographical** adj.

biohazard ● n. a risk to human health or the environment arising from biological research.

biological ● adj. **1** relating to biology or living organisms. **2** (of a parent or child) related by blood. **3** (of warfare) using harmful micro-organisms. **4** (of a detergent) containing enzymes.
– DERIVATIVES **biologically** adv.

biological clock ● n. a natural mechanism that controls certain regularly recurring physical processes in an organism.

biology ● n. the scientific study of living organisms.
– DERIVATIVES **biologist** n.

bionic ● adj. having to do with the use of electronically powered artificial body parts.

biopsy /by-op-si/ ● n. (pl. **biopsies**) an examination of tissue taken from the body, to discover the presence or cause of a disease.
– ORIGIN from Greek *bios* 'life' + *opsis* 'sight'.

biorhythm ● n. a recurring cycle in the functioning of an organism, such as the daily cycle of sleeping and waking.

biosphere ● n. the parts of the earth occupied by living organisms.

biosynthesis ● n. the production of complex molecules within living organisms or cells.
– DERIVATIVES **biosynthetic** adj.

biotechnology ● n. the use of micro-organisms in industry and medicine for the production of antibiotics, hormones, etc.

biotin /by-uh-tin/ ● n. a vitamin of the B complex, found in egg yolk, liver, and yeast.
– ORIGIN from Greek *bios* 'life'.

bipartisan ● adj. involving the cooperation of two political parties.

bipartite ● adj. **1** involving two separate parties. **2** tech. consisting of two parts.

biped /by-ped/ ● n. an animal that walks on two feet.
– DERIVATIVES **bipedal** /by-pee-d'l/ adj.
– ORIGIN from Latin *bi-* 'having two' + *pes* 'foot'.

biplane ● n. an early type of aircraft with two pairs of wings, one above the other.

bipolar ● adj. having to do with two poles or outer limits.

birch ● n. **1** a slender tree with thin, peeling bark. **2** (**the birch**) a former punishment in which a person was beaten with a bundle of birch twigs.
– ORIGIN Old English.

bird ● n. **1** a warm-blooded animal with feathers and wings, that lays eggs and is usually able to fly. **2** informal a person of a particular kind: *she's a sharp old bird.* **3** Brit. informal a young woman or girlfriend.
– PHRASES **the birds and the bees** informal basic facts about sex.
– ORIGIN Old English.

birdbrain ● n. informal a stupid person.

birdie ● n. (pl. **birdies**) **1** informal a little bird. **2** Golf a score of one stroke under par at a hole.

birdlime ● n. a sticky substance spread on to twigs to trap small birds.

bird of paradise ● n. (pl. **birds of paradise**) a tropical bird, the male of which has brightly coloured plumage.

bird of prey ● n. (pl. **birds of prey**) a bird that feeds on animal flesh, such as an eagle, hawk, or owl.

Birdseye, E
Clarence (1886–1956), American pioneer of the frozen food industry.

bird's-eye view ● n. a general view from above.

birdwatching ● n. the hobby of observing birds in their natural environment.

biretta /bi-ret-tuh/ ● n. a square cap worn by Roman Catholic clergymen.
– ORIGIN Italian *berretta* or Spanish *birreta*.

biriani /bi-ri-**ah**-ni/ (also **biryani**) ● n. an Indian dish made with seasoned rice and meat, fish, or vegetables.
– ORIGIN Persian, 'fried, grilled'.

Birmingham E
an industrial city in west central England.

biro ● n. (pl. **biros**) Brit. trademark a ballpoint pen.
– ORIGIN named after the Hungarian inventor László József *Biró* (1899–1985).

birth ● n. **1** the emergence of a baby or other young from the body of its mother. **2** the beginning of something. **3** origin or ancestry: *he is of noble birth.*
– PHRASES **give birth** bear a child or young.
– ORIGIN Old Norse.

birth certificate ● n. an official document recording a person's name, their place and date of birth, and the names of their parents.

birth control ● n. the use of contraception to prevent unwanted pregnancies.

birthday ● n. the annual anniversary of the day on which a person was born.

birthmark ● n. a coloured mark on the body which is there from birth.

birthplace ● n. the place where a person was born.

birth rate ● n. the number of live births per thousand of population per year.

birthright ● n. **1** a right or privilege that a person has through being born into a particular family, class, or place. **2** a natural right possessed by everyone.

Birtwistle E
/**bert**-wis-s'l/, Sir Harrison (Paul) (b.1934), English composer. His works include the opera *The Mask of Orpheus.*

biryani ● n. var. of **BIRIANI**.

Biscay, Bay of E
/**biss**-kay/ a part of the North Atlantic between the north coast of Spain and the west coast of France, noted for its strong currents and storms.

biscuit ● n. **1** Brit. a small, flat, crisp cake. **2** a light brown colour.
– PHRASES **take the biscuit** (or **cake**) informal be the most surprising or annoying thing that has happened.
– ORIGIN from Latin *bis* 'twice' + *coquere* 'to cook'.

bisect ● v. divide into two parts.
– DERIVATIVES **bisection** n. **bisector** n.
– ORIGIN from **BI-** + Latin *secare* 'to cut'.

bisexual ● adj. **1** sexually attracted to both

men and women. **2** Biol. having characteristics of both sexes. ● **n.** a bisexual person.
– DERIVATIVES **bisexuality** n.

Bishkek E
/bish-**kek**/ the capital of Kyrgyzstan.

bishop ● **n. 1** a senior member of the Christian clergy in charge of a diocese. **2** a chess piece with a top shaped like a mitre, that can move diagonally in any direction.
– ORIGIN Greek *episkopos* 'overseer'.

bishopric ● **n.** the position or diocese of a bishop.

Bismarck E
/**biz**-mark/, Otto Eduard Leopold von, Prince of Bismarck, Duke of Lauenburg (1815–98), Prussian minister and German statesman, Chancellor of the German Empire 1871–90. He was the driving force behind the unification of Germany.

bismuth /biz-muhth/ ● **n.** a brittle reddish-grey metallic element resembling lead.
– ORIGIN German *Wismut*.

bison ● **n.** (pl. **bison**) a shaggy-haired wild ox with a humped back.
– ORIGIN Latin.

bisque[1] /bisk/ ● **n.** a rich soup made from lobster or other shellfish.
– ORIGIN French.

bisque[2] ● **n.** = BISCUIT (in sense 2).

Bissau E
/bi-**sow**/ the capital of Guinea-Bissau.

bistro /bee-stroh/ ● **n.** (pl. **bistros**) a small, inexpensive restaurant.
– ORIGIN French.

bit[1] ● **n. 1** a small piece or quantity. **2** (**a bit**) a short time or distance.
– PHRASES **a bit** rather; slightly. **bit by bit** gradually. **bit of stuff** (or **fluff**) informal a girl or young woman. **bit on the side** informal a person with whom one is unfaithful to one's partner. **do one's bit** informal make a useful contribution. **to bits 1** into pieces. **2** informal very much.
– ORIGIN Old English, 'bite, mouthful'.

bit[2] past of BITE.

bit[3] ● **n. 1** a metal mouthpiece attached to a bridle, used to control a horse. **2** a tool or piece for boring or drilling.
– PHRASES **get the bit between one's teeth** make a determined start on a task.
– ORIGIN Old English, 'biting, a bite'.

bit[4] ● **n.** Computing a unit of information expressed as either a 0 or 1 in binary notation.
– ORIGIN from BINARY and DIGIT.

bitch ● **n. 1** a female dog, wolf, fox, or otter. **2** informal a spiteful or unpleasant woman. **3** (**a bitch**) informal something difficult or unpleasant: *life's a bitch.* ● **v.** informal make spiteful comments.
– ORIGIN Old English.

bitchy ● **adj.** (**bitchier**, **bitchiest**) informal spiteful.
– DERIVATIVES **bitchiness** n.

bite ● **v.** (**bites**, **biting**, **bit**; past part. **bitten**) **1** cut into with the teeth. **2** (of a snake, insect, or spider) wound with a sting or fangs. **3** (of a fish) take a bait or lure into the mouth. **4** (of a tool, tyre, etc.) grip a surface. **5** take effect, with unpleasant consequences: *the cuts in education were starting to bite.* **6** (**bite back**) stop oneself saying. ● **n. 1** an act of biting or a piece bitten off. **2** informal a quick snack. **3** a feeling of cold in the air.
– PHRASES **bite the bullet** make oneself do something difficult. **bite the dust** informal die or be killed. **bite the hand that feeds one** deliberately hurt a person who is trying to help. **bite off more than one can chew** take on a responsibility one cannot fulfil. **bite one's tongue** stop oneself saying something.
– DERIVATIVES **biter** n.
– ORIGIN Old English.

biting ● **adj. 1** (of a wind) painfully cold. **2** (of wit or criticism) cruel.

bitmap ● **n.** the information used to control an image or display on a computer screen, in which each item corresponds to one or more bits of information.

bit part ● **n.** a small acting role in a play or a film.

bitten past part. of BITE.

bitter ● **adj. 1** having a sharp taste or smell; not sweet. **2** painful or distressing. **3** feeling deep resentment. **4** (of a conflict) intense and full of hatred: *a bitter row broke out.* **5** intensely cold. ● **n. 1** Brit. bitter-tasting beer that is strongly flavoured with hops. **2** (**bitters**) bitter-tasting liquor used in cocktails.
– PHRASES **to the bitter end** to the very end, in spite of harsh difficulties.
– DERIVATIVES **bitterly** adv. **bitterness** n.
– ORIGIN Old English.

bittern ● **n.** a bird found in marshland, noted for the male's booming call.
– ORIGIN Old French *butor*.

bittersweet ● **adj. 1** sweet with a bitter aftertaste. **2** pleasant but with a touch of sadness.

bitty ● **adj.** informal, esp. Brit. made up of small unrelated parts.

bitumen /bit-yuu-muhn/ ● **n.** a black sticky substance obtained naturally or from petroleum, used for road surfacing.
– ORIGIN Latin.

bituminous /bi-tyoo-mi-nuhss/ ● **adj.** having to do with or containing bitumen.

bivalve ● **n.** a mollusc that lives in water and has two hinged shells, such as an oyster or mussel.

bivouac /bi-voo-ak/ ● **n.** a temporary camp without tents. ● **v.** (**bivouacs**, **bivouacking**, **bivouacked**) stay in such a camp.
– ORIGIN French.

bizarre /bi-zar/ ● **adj.** very strange or unusual.
– DERIVATIVES **bizarrely** adv.
– ORIGIN Italian *bizzarro* 'angry'.

Bizet E
/**bee**-zay/, Georges (1838–75; born *Alexandre César Léopold Bizet*), French composer. He is best known for the opera *Carmen*.

blab ● **v.** (**blabs**, **blabbing**, **blabbed**) informal reveal secrets by indiscreet talk.

blabber ● **v.** (**blabbers**, **blabbering**, **blabbered**) informal talk indiscreetly or excessively.

black ● **adj. 1** of the very darkest colour. **2** relating to the human group having dark-coloured skin. **3** (of coffee or tea) served without milk. **4** marked by disaster or despair: *the future looks black.* **5** (of humour) pre-

b

senting distressing situations in comic terms. **6** full of anger or hatred. ● **n. 1** black colour. **2** a black person. ● **v. 1** make black. **2** Brit. dated refuse to deal with (someone or something) as a form of industrial action.
– PHRASES **black out 1** make (a room or building) dark by switching off lights and covering windows. **2** faint. **in the black** not owing any money.
– DERIVATIVES **blackish** adj. **blackly** adv. **blackness** n.
– ORIGIN Old English.

black and white ● **adj.** involving clear-cut opposing opinions or issues.

black art (also **black arts**) ● **n.** black magic.

blackball ● **v.** reject (a candidate for membership of a private club).
– ORIGIN from the practice of voting against something by placing a black ball in a box.

black belt ● **n.** a black belt worn by an expert in judo, karate, and other martial arts.

blackberry ● **n.** (pl. **blackberries**) the purple-black edible fruit of a prickly climbing shrub.

blackbird ● **n.** a type of thrush, the male of which has black plumage and a yellow bill.

blackboard ● **n.** a board with a dark surface for writing on with chalk.

black box ● **n.** a flight recorder in an aircraft.

Black Country E
a district of the Midlands with much heavy industry.

blackcurrant ● **n.** the small round edible black berry of a shrub.

Black Death E
the great epidemic of bubonic plague that killed a large proportion of the population of Europe in the mid 14th century.

black economy ● **n.** the part of a country's economy which is not recorded or taxed by its government.

blacken ● **v. 1** become or make black or dark. **2** damage or destroy (someone's reputation).

black eye ● **n.** an area of bruised skin around the eye.

blackfly ● **n.** a black or dark green flying insect which attacks crops.

Black Forest E
a hilly wooded region of SW Germany, lying to the east of the Rhine valley.

blackguard /blag-gerd/ ● **n.** dated a man who behaves in a dishonourable or contemptible way.
– ORIGIN first referring to a group of kitchen servants.

blackhead ● **n.** a lump of oily matter blocking a pore in the skin.

black hole ● **n.** a region of space having a gravitational field so intense that no matter or radiation can escape.

Black Hole of Calcutta E
a dungeon 6 metres (20 feet) square in Fort William, Calcutta (Kolkata), where perhaps as many as 146 English prisoners were imprisoned overnight after the capture of the city by the nawab (governor) of Bengal in 1756. Only twenty-three of them were alive the next morning.

black ice ● **n.** transparent ice on a road.

blackleg ● **n.** Brit. derog. a person who continues working when fellow workers are on strike.

blacklist ● **n.** a list of people or groups seen as unacceptable or untrustworthy. ● **v.** put on a blacklist.

black magic ● **n.** magic involving the summoning of evil spirits.

blackmail ● **n. 1** the demanding of money from someone in return for not revealing information that could disgrace them. **2** the use of threats or other pressure to influence someone: *emotional blackmail*. ● **v.** use blackmail on.
– DERIVATIVES **blackmailer** n.
– ORIGIN Old Norse, 'speech, agreement'.

Black Maria ● **n.** informal a police vehicle for transporting prisoners.

black mark ● **n.** informal a record of disapproval for a misdeed.

black market ● **n.** an illegal trade in officially controlled or scarce goods.
– DERIVATIVES **black marketeer** n.

black mass ● **n.** a blasphemous imitation of the Roman Catholic Mass, performed in worship of the Devil.

Blackmore, E
R. D. (1825–1900; full name *Richard Doddridge Blackmore*), English novelist and poet, known for his romantic novel *Lorna Doone*.

blackout ● **n. 1** a period when all lights must be turned out during an enemy air raid. **2** a sudden failure of electric lights. **3** a short loss of consciousness. **4** an official restriction on publishing information: *a total news blackout*.

Blackpool E
a seaside resort in NW England.

Black Prince E
(1330–76), the name given to *Edward, Prince of Wales and Duke of Cornwall*, eldest son of Edward III of England. He was responsible for a number of English victories in the Hundred Years War, including that at Poitiers in 1356.

black pudding ● **n.** Brit. a black sausage containing pork, dried pig's blood, and suet.

Black Rod (in full **Gentleman Usher of the Black Rod**) ● **n.** the chief usher of the House of Lords and the Lord Chamberlain's department.

Black Sea E
a tideless almost landlocked sea bounded by Ukraine, Russia, Georgia, Turkey, Bulgaria, and Romania.

black sheep ● **n.** informal a person seen as as a disgrace to their family.

blackshirt ● **n.** a member of a Fascist organization, especially in Italy before and during the Second World War.

blacksmith ● **n.** a person who makes and repairs things made of iron.

black spot ● **n.** Brit. a place marked by a particular problem: *an accident black spot*.

blackthorn ● **n.** a thorny shrub with white flowers and blue-black fruits (sloes).

black tie ● **n.** men's formal evening wear.

black widow ● **n.** a highly poisonous American spider having a black body with red markings.

bladder • n. **1** a sac in the abdomen which stores urine for excretion. **2** an inflated or hollow flexible bag.
– ORIGIN Old English.

blade • n. **1** the flat cutting edge of a knife or other tool or weapon. **2** the broad flat part of an oar, leaf, or other object. **3** a long narrow leaf of grass. **4** a shoulder bone in a joint of meat.
– ORIGIN Old English.

blag Brit. informal • v. (**blags**, **blagging**, **blagged**) **1** steal in a violent robbery. **2** get by clever talk or lying. • n. a violent robbery.
– DERIVATIVES **blagger** n.
– ORIGIN perh. from French *blaguer* 'tell lies'.

Blair, E
Tony (b.1953; full name *Anthony Charles Lynton Blair*), British Labour statesman, Prime Minister since 1997.
– DERIVATIVES **Blairism** n. **Blairite** n. & adj.

Blake, E
William (1757–1827), English artist and poet. His books of poems include *Songs of Innocence* and *Songs of Experience*; often mystical and using powerful imagery, they mark the beginning of romanticism.

blame • v. (**blames**, **blaming**, **blamed**) hold responsible and criticize for doing wrong: *the terrorists were blamed for the bombings.* • n. **1** responsibility for a fault. **2** criticism for doing wrong.
– DERIVATIVES **blameworthy** adj.
– ORIGIN Old French *blasmer.*

blameless • adj. innocent of wrongdoing.

blanch /blahnch/ • v. **1** make or become white or pale. **2** prepare (vegetables) by putting them briefly in boiling water.
– ORIGIN Old French *blanchir.*

blancmange /bluh-**monzh**/ • n. a sweet jelly-like dessert made with cornflour and milk.
– ORIGIN from Old French *blanc* 'white' + *mangier* 'eat'.

bland • adj. **1** lacking strong qualities and therefore uninteresting: *the pasta tasted a little bland.* **2** showing little emotion: *his voice was bland, uninvolved.*
– DERIVATIVES **blandly** adv. **blandness** n.
– ORIGIN Latin *blandus* 'soft, smooth'.

blandishments • pl. n. flattery intended to persuade or coax.

blank • adj. **1** not marked or decorated; bare or plain. **2** not understanding or reacting. **3** complete; absolute: *a blank refusal.* • n. **1** a space left to be filled in a document. **2** an empty space or period of time. **3** a cartridge containing gunpowder but no bullet. • v. **1** hide or block out: *she blanked out her memories of him.* **2** Brit. informal deliberately ignore.
– PHRASES **draw a blank** fail to obtain a favourable response.
– DERIVATIVES **blankly** adv. **blankness** n.
– ORIGIN Old French *blanc* 'white'.

blank cheque • n. **1** a cheque with the amount left for the person cashing it to fill in. **2** an unlimited freedom of action.

blanket • n. **1** a large piece of woollen material used as a warm covering. **2** a thick mass or layer: *a blanket of cloud.* • adj. covering all cases; total: *a blanket ban.* • v. (**blankets**, **blanketing**, **blanketed**) cover with a thick layer.
– ORIGIN Old French *blanc* 'white'.

blanket stitch • n. a looped stitch used on the edges of material too thick to be hemmed.

blank verse • n. verse without rhyme.

blare • v. (**blares**, **blaring**, **blared**) sound loudly and harshly. • n. a loud, harsh sound.
– ORIGIN Dutch or German *blaren.*

blarney • n. talk intended to be charming or flattering.
– ORIGIN named after the *Blarney* Stone in Ireland, said to give persuasive speech to anyone who kisses it.

blasé /blah-zay/ • adj. unimpressed with something because of over-familiarity.
– ORIGIN French.

blaspheme /blass-feem/ • v. (**blasphemes**, **blaspheming**, **blasphemed**) speak irreverently about God or sacred things.
– DERIVATIVES **blasphemer** n.
– ORIGIN Greek *blasphēmein.*

blasphemous /blass-fuh-muhss/ • adj. irreverent about God or sacred things.

blasphemy /blass-fuh-mi/ • n. (pl. **blasphemies**) irreverent talk about God or sacred things.

blast • n. **1** an explosion, or the destructive wave of air spreading outwards from it. **2** a strong gust of wind or air. **3** a single loud note of a horn or whistle. • v. **1** blow up with explosives. **2** (**blast off**) (of a rocket or spacecraft) take off. **3** produce loud music or noise. **4** strike (a ball) hard. **5** informal criticize fiercely. **6** (**blasted**) informal expressing annoyance. • exclam. Brit. informal expressing annoyance.
– PHRASES **(at) full blast** at maximum power or intensity.
– DERIVATIVES **blaster** n.
– ORIGIN Old English.

blast furnace • n. a smelting furnace using blasts of hot compressed air.

blatant • adj. open and unashamed: *a blatant act of racism.*
– DERIVATIVES **blatancy** n. **blatantly** adv.
– ORIGIN perh. from Scots *blatand* 'bleating'.

blather • v. (**blathers**, **blathering**, **blathered**) talk at length without making much sense. • n. rambling talk.
– ORIGIN Old Norse.

blaze • n. **1** a very large or fierce fire. **2** a very bright light or display of colour. **3** an outburst: *he left in a blaze of glory.* **4** a white stripe down the face of a horse or other animal. • v. (**blazes**, **blazing**, **blazed**) **1** burn or shine fiercely or brightly. **2** shoot repeatedly or wildly. **3** present (news) in a prominent way.
– PHRASES **blaze a trail 1** mark out a path. **2** be the first to do something.
– ORIGIN Old English; sense 3 of the verb is from German or Dutch *blāzen* 'to blow'.

blazer • n. **1** a jacket worn by schoolchildren or sports players as part of a uniform. **2** a man's smart jacket not forming part of a suit.

blazon /blay-zuhn/ • v. **1** display or describe prominently: *their company name was blazoned all over the media.* **2** Heraldry depict (a

coat of arms). ● n. a coat of arms.
– ORIGIN Old French *blason* 'shield'.

b

bleach ● v. lighten by chemicals or sunlight. ● n. a chemical used to lighten things and also to sterilize drains, sinks, etc.
– ORIGIN Old English.

bleak ● adj. **1** bare and exposed to the weather. **2** dreary and unwelcoming: *a bleak little room.* **3** (of a situation) not hopeful.
– DERIVATIVES **bleakly** adv. **bleakness** n.
– ORIGIN Old English, 'white, shining'.

bleary ● adj. (**blearier**, **bleariest**) (of the eyes) dull and not focusing properly.
– DERIVATIVES **blearily** adv.
– ORIGIN prob. from German *blerre* 'blurred vision'.

bleat ● v. **1** (of a sheep or goat) make a weak, wavering cry. **2** speak or complain in a weak or foolish way. ● n. a bleating sound.
– ORIGIN Old English.

bleed ● v. (**bleeds**, **bleeding**, **bled**) **1** lose blood from the body. **2** take blood from (someone) as a former medical treatment. **3** informal drain of money or resources. **4** (of dye or colour) seep into an adjoining colour or area. **5** allow (fluid or gas) to escape from a closed system through a valve. ● n. an instance of bleeding.
– ORIGIN Old English.

bleeding ● adj. Brit. informal used for emphasis or to express annoyance.

bleeding heart ● n. informal, derog. a person considered to be too liberal or soft-hearted.

bleep ● n. a short high-pitched sound made by an electronic device. ● v. **1** make a bleep. **2** call with a device that makes a bleep.
– DERIVATIVES **bleeper** n.

blemish ● n. a small mark or flaw. ● v. spoil the appearance of.
– ORIGIN Old French *blesmir* 'make pale'.

blench ● v. flinch suddenly through fear or pain.
– ORIGIN Old English, 'deceive'.

blend ● v. **1** mix and combine with something else. **2** merge well: *a bodyguard has to blend in.* ● n. a mixture.
– ORIGIN prob. Scandinavian.

blender ● n. an electric device for liquidizing or chopping food.

Blenheim E
/blen-im/ a battle in 1704 in Bavaria, near the village of Blindheim, in which the English, under the Duke of Marlborough, defeated the French and the Bavarians.

Blériot E
/ble-ri-oh/, Louis (1872–1936), French aviation pioneer, who in July 1909 became the first to fly the English Channel in a monoplane.

bless ● v. **1** make holy. **2** call on God to favour. **3** (**be blessed with**) be granted (something desired).
– PHRASES **bless you!** said to a person who has just sneezed.
– ORIGIN Old English.

blessed /bless-id, blest/ ● adj. **1** holy or favoured by God. **2** bringing welcome pleasure or relief: *blessed sleep.* **3** informal expressing mild annoyance.
– DERIVATIVES **blessedly** adv.

blessing ● n. **1** God's favour and protection. **2** a prayer asking for this. **3** something for which one is very grateful: *it's a blessing we're alive.* **4** a person's approval or support.

blew past of BLOW[1].

Bligh E
/bly/, William (1754–1817), British naval officer. He was the captain of HMS *Bounty*, whose crew mutinied in 1789.

blight ● n. **1** a plant disease, especially one caused by fungi. **2** a thing that spoils or damages: *divorce is a great blight on your life.* ● v. **1** infect with blight. **2** spoil or destroy.
– ORIGIN unknown.

blighter ● n. Brit. informal a person regarded with scorn or pity.

Blighty ● n. Brit. informal (used by soldiers serving abroad) Britain or England.
– ORIGIN Urdu, 'foreign, European'.

blimey ● exclam. Brit. informal expressing surprise or alarm.
– ORIGIN from *God blind* (or *blame*) *me!*

blind ● adj. **1** lacking the power of sight. **2** done without being able to see or without certain information. **3** lacking awareness, judgement, or reason. **4** concealed, closed, or blocked off: *a blind alley.* **5** informal the slightest: *it didn't do a blind bit of good.* ● v. **1** make blind. **2** cause to lose understanding or judgement: *he was blinded by rage.* **3** (**blind with**) confuse or overawe (someone) with (something hard to understand). ● n. **1** a screen for a window. **2** something meant to hide one's plans. ● adv. without being able to see clearly.
– PHRASES **blind drunk** informal extremely drunk. **turn a blind eye** pretend not to notice.
– DERIVATIVES **blindly** adv. **blindness** n.
– ORIGIN Old English.

blind date ● n. a meeting with a person one has not met before, with a romantic aim.

blinder ● n. Brit. informal an excellent performance.

blindfold ● n. a piece of cloth tied around the head to cover someone's eyes. ● v. deprive of sight with a blindfold. ● adv. with a blindfold covering the eyes.
– ORIGIN Old English.

blinding ● adj. **1** (of light) very bright. **2** suddenly very obvious. **3** informal very skilful and exciting.

blind man's buff (US also **blind man's bluff**) ● n. a game in which a blindfold player tries to catch others while being pushed about by them.
– ORIGIN from the former word *buff* 'a blow'.

blind spot ● n. **1** a small area of the retina in the eye that is insensitive to light. **2** an area where a person's view is obstructed. **3** an area where understanding is lacking: *he had a blind spot where ethics were concerned.*

blindworm ● n. = SLOW-WORM.

blink ● v. **1** shut and open the eyes quickly. **2** (of a light) flash on and off. ● n. an act of blinking.
– PHRASES **on the blink** informal out of order.
– ORIGIN from BLENCH.

blinker ● n. (**blinkers**) esp. Brit. **1** a pair of small screens attached to a horse's bridle to prevent it from seeing sideways. **2** a thing that prevents complete understanding. ● v. (**blinkers**, **blinkering**, **blinkered**) **1** put blinkers on (a horse). **2** cause to have a narrow outlook.

blinking ● **adj.** Brit. informal used to express annoyance.

blip ● **n. 1** a very short high-pitched sound made by an electronic device. **2** a small flashing point of light on a radar screen. **3** an unexpected and temporary departure from an overall trend: *a minor blip in the firm's growth rate.* ● **v. (blips, blipped, blipping)** make a blip.

bliss ● **n. 1** perfect happiness. **2** a state of spiritual blessedness.
– ORIGIN Old English.

blissful ● **adj.** extremely happy.
– DERIVATIVES **blissfully** adv.

blister ● **n. 1** a small bubble on the skin filled with watery liquid. **2** a similar swelling, filled with air or fluid, on a surface. ● **v.** form or cause to form blisters.
– ORIGIN perh. from Old French *blestre*.

blistering ● **adj. 1** (of heat) intense. **2** very fierce or forceful.

blithe /bly*th*/ ● **adj. 1** without thought or care: *a blithe ignorance of the facts.* **2** literary happy.
– DERIVATIVES **blithely** adv.
– ORIGIN Old English.

blithering ● **adj.** informal complete: *a blithering idiot.*
– ORIGIN from **BLATHER**.

BLitt ● **abbrev.** Bachelor of Letters.
– ORIGIN from Latin *Baccalaureus Litterarum*.

blitz ● **n. 1** an intensive or sudden military attack. **2** (**the Blitz**) the German air raids on Britain in the Second World War. **3** informal a sudden and concentrated effort. ● **v. 1** attack in a blitz. **2** overwhelm or completely defeat.
– ORIGIN German *Blitzkrieg* 'lightning war'.

blizzard ● **n.** a severe snowstorm with high winds.
– ORIGIN unknown.

bloat ● **v.** cause to swell with fluid or gas.
– ORIGIN perh. from Old Norse, 'soft'.

bloater ● **n.** a salted and smoked herring.

blob ● **n. 1** a drop of a thick liquid or sticky substance. **2** a roundish mass or shape.
– DERIVATIVES **blobby** adj.

bloc ● **n.** a group of countries or political parties who have formed an alliance.
– ORIGIN French, 'block'.

block ● **n. 1** a large solid piece of material with flat surfaces on each side. **2** esp. Brit. a large single building subdivided into flats or offices. **3** a group of buildings bounded by four streets. **4** a large quantity of things regarded as a unit: *a block of shares.* **5** an obstacle. **6** (also **cylinder block** or **engine block**) a large metal moulding containing the cylinders of an internal-combustion engine. **7** a pulley or system of pulleys mounted in a case. ● **v. 1** prevent movement or flow in. **2** hinder or prevent: *the government tried to block the agreement.*
– PHRASES **knock someone's block off** informal hit someone about the head.
– DERIVATIVES **blocker** n.
– ORIGIN Dutch.

blockade ● **n.** an act of sealing off a place to prevent goods or people from entering or leaving. ● **v. (blockades, blockading, blockaded)** set up a blockade of.

blockage ● **n.** an obstruction.

block and tackle ● **n.** a lifting mechanism consisting of ropes, a pulley block, and a hook.

blockbuster ● **n.** informal a film or book that is a great commercial success.

block capitals ● **pl. n.** plain capital letters.

blockhead ● **n.** informal a very stupid person.

blockhouse ● **n.** a reinforced concrete shelter used as an observation point.

Bloemfontein E
/**bloom**-fon-tayn, **bluum**-fon-tayn/ the capital of Free State province and judicial capital of South Africa.

bloke ● **n.** Brit. informal a man.
– DERIVATIVES **blokeish** (also **blokish**) adj.
– ORIGIN Shelta (a language used by Irish and Welsh gypsies).

blonde ● **adj.** (also **blond**) **1** (of hair) fair or pale yellow. **2** having fair hair and a light complexion. ● **n.** a woman with blonde hair.
– ORIGIN French.

blood ● **n. 1** the red liquid that circulates in the arteries and veins, carrying oxygen and carbon dioxide. **2** family background: *she must have Irish blood.* **3** passionate temperament. ● **v.** initiate in an activity.
– PHRASES **first blood 1** the first shedding of blood in a fight. **2** the first advantage gained in a contest. **have blood on one's hands** be responsible for someone's death. **in one's blood** fundamental to one's character. **make someone's blood boil** informal make someone very angry. **new** (or **fresh**) **blood** new members admitted to a group.
– ORIGIN Old English.

bloodbath ● **n.** an event in which many people are killed violently.

blood brother ● **n.** a man who has sworn to treat another man as a brother.

blood count ● **n.** a calculation of the number of corpuscles in a particular quantity of blood.

blood-curdling ● **adj.** horrifying.

blood group ● **n.** any of the various types into which human blood is classified.

bloodhound ● **n.** a large hound with a very keen sense of smell, used in tracking.

bloodless ● **adj. 1** without violence or killing: *a bloodless coup.* **2** (of the skin) drained of colour. **3** lacking in vitality; feeble.

bloodletting ● **n. 1** hist. the surgical removal of some of a patient's blood. **2** violence during a war or conflict.

bloodline ● **n.** a pedigree or set of ancestors.

blood money ● **n. 1** money paid to compensate the family of someone who has been killed. **2** money paid to a hired killer.

blood poisoning ● **n.** a diseased state that results when harmful micro-organisms have infected the blood.

blood pressure ● **n.** the pressure of the blood in the circulatory system.

blood relation (also **blood relative**) ● **n.** a person who is related to another by birth.

bloodshed ● **n.** the killing or wounding of people.

bloodshot ● **adj.** (of the eyes) inflamed or tinged with blood.

blood sport ● **n.** a sport involving the hunting, wounding, or killing of animals.

bloodstream ● **n.** the blood circulating through the body.

blood sugar • n. the concentration of glucose in the blood.

bloodthirsty • adj. taking pleasure in killing and violence.

blood vessel • n. a vein, artery, or capillary carrying blood through the body.

bloody • adj. (**bloodier**, **bloodiest**) **1** covered with or containing blood. **2** involving much violence or cruelty. **3** Brit. informal used to express anger or shock, or for emphasis. • v. (**bloodies**, **bloodying**, **bloodied**) cover or stain with blood.

bloody-minded • adj. Brit. informal deliberately unhelpful.

bloom • v. **1** produce flowers; be in flower. **2** be or become very healthy. • n. **1** a flower. **2** the state or period of blooming: *the apple trees were in bloom.* **3** a healthy glow in a person's complexion. **4** a fine powder on the surface of fruit.
– ORIGIN Old Norse.

bloomers • pl. n. **1** women's loose-fitting knee-length knickers. **2** hist. women's loose-fitting trousers, gathered at the knee or ankle.
– ORIGIN named after the American social reformer Mrs Amelia J. *Bloomer* (1818–94).

blooming • adj. Brit. informal used to express annoyance or for emphasis.

Bloomsbury Group E
a group of influential modernist writers, artists, and philosophers living in or associated with Bloomsbury in London in the early 20th century. The group's members included Virginia Woolf, Lytton Strachey, and John Maynard Keynes.

blossom • n. **1** a flower or a mass of flowers on a tree or bush. **2** the state or period of flowering. • v. **1** produce blossom. **2** develop in a promising or healthy way: *our friendship blossomed into love.*
– ORIGIN Old English.

blot • n. **1** a spot or stain made by ink. **2** a thing that spoils something good: *the hotel is a blot on the coastline.* • v. (**blots**, **blotting**, **blotted**) **1** dry with an absorbent material. **2** mark or spoil. **3** (**blot out**) obscure (a view). **4** (**blot out**) keep from one's mind: *they wanted to blot out the bad news.*
– PHRASES **blot one's copybook** Brit. spoil one's good reputation.
– ORIGIN prob. Scandinavian.

blotch • n. a large irregular mark.
– DERIVATIVES **blotchy** adj.
– ORIGIN from **BLOT** + **BOTCH**.

blotter • n. a pad of blotting paper.

blotting paper • n. absorbent paper used for soaking up excess ink when writing.

blotto • adj. informal extremely drunk.

blouse • n. a woman's upper garment resembling a shirt.
– ORIGIN French.

blouson /bloo-zon/ • n. a short loose-fitting jacket.
– ORIGIN French.

blow[1] • v. (**blows**, **blowing**, **blew**; past part. **blown**) **1** (of wind) move or be moving. **2** send out air through pursed lips. **3** force air through the mouth into (a musical instrument). **4** (of an explosion) force out of place: *the blast blew the windows out of the van.* **5** burst or burn out through pressure or overheating. **6** informal spend (money) recklessly. **7** informal reveal (something secret): *his cover was blown.* **8** informal waste (an opportunity). • n. **1** an act of blowing. **2** a strong wind.
– PHRASES **blow a fuse** informal lose one's temper. **blow hot and cold** keep changing one's mind. **blow someone's mind** informal impress or affect someone very strongly. **blow over** (of trouble) fade away without serious consequences. **blow one's top** informal lose one's temper. **blow up 1** explode. **2** begin to develop or become public.
– ORIGIN Old English.

blow[2] • n. **1** a powerful stroke with a hand or weapon. **2** a sudden shock or disappointment.
– PHRASES **come to blows** start fighting after a disagreement.
– ORIGIN unknown.

blow-by-blow • adj. (of a description of an event) giving all the details in order.

blower • n. **1** a device that creates a current of air to dry or heat something. **2** Brit. informal a telephone.

blowfly • n. a bluebottle or similar large fly which lays its eggs on meat and carcasses.

blowhole • n. **1** the nostril of a whale or dolphin on the top of its head. **2** a hole in ice for breathing or fishing through.

blow job • n. vulgar an act of fellatio.

blowlamp • n. Brit. a blowtorch.

blown past part. of **BLOW[1]**.

blowout • n. **1** an occasion when a vehicle tyre bursts or an electric fuse melts. **2** informal a large meal.

blowpipe • n. a weapon consisting of a long tube through which an arrow or dart is blown.

blowsy /*rhymes with* drowsy/ (also **blowzy**) • adj. (of a woman) coarse, untidy, and red-faced.
– ORIGIN from a former word meaning 'beggar's female companion'.

blowtorch • n. a portable device producing a hot flame, used to burn off paint.

blowy • adj. windy or windswept.

blub • v. (**blubs**, **blubbing**, **blubbed**) informal sob noisily.
– ORIGIN from **BLUBBER[2]**.

blubber[1] • n. the fat of sea mammals, especially whales and seals.
– DERIVATIVES **blubbery** adj.

blubber[2] • v. (**blubbers**, **blubbering**, **blubbered**) informal sob noisily and uncontrollably.

bludgeon • n. a thick stick with a heavy end, used as a weapon. • v. **1** hit with a bludgeon. **2** bully into doing something.
– ORIGIN unknown.

blue[1] • adj. (**bluer**, **bluest**) **1** of the colour of the sky on a sunny day. **2** informal sad or depressed. **3** informal with sexual or pornographic content: *a blue movie.* **4** Brit. informal politically conservative. • n. **1** blue colour or material. **2** Brit. a person who has represented Cambridge University or Oxford University in a particular sport.
– PHRASES **once in a blue moon** informal very rarely. **out of the blue** informal unexpectedly.
– DERIVATIVES **blueness** n.
– ORIGIN Old French *bleu.*

blue[2] • v. (**blues**, **bluing** or **blueing**, **blued**)

Brit. informal, dated spend in a reckless or wasteful way.
– ORIGIN perh. from **BLOW**[1].

bluebell ● **n.** a woodland plant having clusters of blue bell-shaped flowers.

blueberry ● **n.** (pl. **blueberries**) the small blue-back berry of a North American shrub.

blue-blooded ● **adj.** of noble birth.

bluebottle ● **n.** a common blowfly with a metallic-blue body.

blue cheese ● **n.** cheese containing veins of blue mould, such as Stilton.

blue-chip ● **adj.** (of a company or shares) considered to be a reliable investment.
– ORIGIN from the *blue chip* used in gambling, which has a high value.

blue-collar ● **adj.** esp. N. Amer. relating to manual work or workers.

blue-eyed boy ● **n.** Brit. informal, derog. a person held in high regard and treated with special favour.

blueish ● **adj.** var. of **BLUISH**.

Blue Nile E
one of the two main headwaters of the Nile, rising in NW Ethiopia and meeting the White Nile at Khartoum.

blueprint ● **n.** **1** a design plan or other technical drawing. **2** something which acts as a plan or model.

blue ribbon ● **n.** (also **blue riband**) a blue silk ribbon given to the winner of a competition.

Blue Ridge Mountains E
a range of the Appalachian Mountains in the eastern US, stretching from southern Pennsylvania to northern Georgia.

blues ● **n.** **1** slow, sad music of black American folk origin. **2** (**the blues**) informal feelings of sadness or depression.
– DERIVATIVES **bluesy** adj.
– ORIGIN from *blue devils* 'depression'.

blue-sky ● **adj.** informal not yet capable of being achieved or making a profit.

bluestocking ● **n.** usu. derog. an intellectual or literary woman.
– ORIGIN in reference to literary parties held in 18th-century London by society ladies, where some of the men wore blue worsted stockings.

blue tit ● **n.** a common titmouse with a blue cap and yellow underparts.

blue whale ● **n.** a bluish-grey whale which is the largest living animal.

bluff[1] ● **n.** an attempt to deceive someone into believing that one can or will do something. ● **v.** try to deceive someone as to what one can or is going to do.
– PHRASES **call someone's bluff** challenge someone to prove something, in the belief that they are bluffing.
– ORIGIN Dutch *bluffen* 'brag'.

bluff[2] ● **adj.** frank and direct in a good-natured way.
– ORIGIN from **BLUFF**[3].

bluff[3] ● **n.** a steep cliff or slope.
– ORIGIN unknown.

bluish (also **blueish**) ● **adj.** having a blue tinge.

blunder ● **n.** a stupid or careless mistake. ● **v.** (**blunders**, **blundering**, **blundered**) **1** make a blunder. **2** move clumsily or as if unable to see.
– ORIGIN prob. Scandinavian.

blunderbuss ● **n.** hist. a gun with a short, wide barrel, firing balls or lead bullets.
– ORIGIN Dutch *donderbus* 'thunder gun'.

Blunt, E
Anthony (Frederick) (1907–83), British art historian and Foreign Office official, who confessed in 1965 that he had been a Soviet agent since the 1930s.

blunt ● **adj.** **1** lacking a sharp edge or point. **2** very frank and direct: *a blunt statement of fact.* ● **v.** **1** make or become blunt. **2** reduce the force of.
– DERIVATIVES **bluntly** adv. **bluntness** n.
– ORIGIN perh. Scandinavian.

blur ● **v.** (**blurs**, **blurring**, **blurred**) make or become unclear or less distinct. ● **n.** something that cannot be seen, heard, or recalled clearly.
– DERIVATIVES **blurry** adj.
– ORIGIN perh. from **BLEARY**.

blurb ● **n.** a short description written to promote a book, film, or other product.
– ORIGIN coined by the American humorist Gelett Burgess (died 1951).

blurt ● **v.** say suddenly and without thinking.

blush ● **v.** become red in the face through shyness or embarrassment. ● **n.** **1** an instance of blushing. **2** literary a pink tinge.
– ORIGIN Old English.

blusher ● **n.** a cosmetic used to give a warm reddish tinge to the cheeks.

bluster ● **v.** (**blusters**, **blustering**, **blustered**) **1** talk in a loud or aggressive way with little effect. **2** (of wind or rain) blow or beat fiercely and noisily. ● **n.** loud and empty talk.
– DERIVATIVES **blustery** adj.

Blyton, E
Enid (1897–1968), English writer of children's fiction, author of the *Famous Five* and *Secret Seven* adventures and creator of Noddy.

BM ● **abbrev.** Bachelor of Medicine.

BMA ● **abbrev.** British Medical Association.

B-movie ● **n.** a low budget film supporting a main film in a cinema programme.

BMX ● **abbrev.** bicycle motocross (referring to sturdy bicycles designed for cross-country racing).

boa ● **n.** **1** a large snake which winds itself round its prey and crushes it to death. **2** a long, thin stole of feathers or fur worn around a woman's neck.
– ORIGIN Latin.

Boadicea E
/boh-di-see-uh/ = **BOUDICCA**.

boar ● **n.** (pl. **boar** or **boars**) **1** (also **wild boar**) a wild pig with tusks. **2** an uncastrated male pig.
– ORIGIN Old English.

board ● **n.** **1** a long, thin, flat piece of wood used in building. **2** a thin, flat, rectangular piece of stiff material used for games, displaying notices, and other purposes. **3** the decision-making body of an organization. **4** the provision of regular meals in return for payment. ● **v.** **1** get on or into (a ship, aircraft, or other vehicle). **2** receive meals and accommodation in return for payment. **3** (of a pupil)

live in school during term time. **4** (**board up/over**) cover or seal with pieces of wood.
– PHRASES **go by the board** (of a plan or principle) be abandoned or rejected. [ORIGIN from nautical use meaning 'fall overboard'.] **on board** on or in a ship, aircraft, or other vehicle. **take on board** informal fully consider or accept (a new idea). **tread the boards** informal appear on stage as an actor.
– ORIGIN Old English.

boarder ● n. **1** a pupil who lives in school during term time. **2** a person who forces their way on to a ship in an attack.

board game ● n. a game that involves the movement of counters or other objects around a board.

boarding house ● n. a private house providing food and lodging for paying guests.

boarding school ● n. a school in which the pupils live during term time.

boardroom ● n. a room in which a board of directors meets regularly.

boast ● v. **1** talk about oneself with excessive pride. **2** possess (a feature that is a source of pride): *the hotel boasts high standards of comfort.* ● n. an act of boasting.
– ORIGIN unknown.

boastful ● adj. showing excessive pride in oneself.

boat ● n. **1** a vehicle for travelling on water. **2** a boat-shaped serving jug for sauce or gravy.
– PHRASES **be in the same boat** informal be in the same difficult circumstances as others. **miss the boat** informal be too slow to take advantage of something. **push the boat out** Brit. informal be extravagant. **rock the boat** informal disturb an existing situation.
– ORIGIN Old English.

boater ● n. a flat-topped straw hat with a brim.

boathook ● n. a long pole with a hook and a spike at one end, used for moving boats.

boating ● n. the activity of using a small boat for pleasure.

boatman ● n. a person who provides transport by boat.

boat people ● pl. n. refugees who have left a country by sea.

boatswain /boh-s'n/ (also **bo'sun** or **bosun**) ● n. a ship's officer in charge of equipment and the crew.

Bob ● n. (in phr. **Bob's your uncle**) Brit. informal said when a person thinks a task will be easy to complete.

bob[1] ● v. (**bobs**, **bobbing**, **bobbed**) make or cause to make a quick, short movement up and down. ● n. a quick, short movement up and down.
– ORIGIN unknown.

bob[2] ● n. **1** a short hairstyle hanging evenly all round. **2** a weight on a pendulum, plumb line, or kite-tail. **3** a bobsleigh. ● v. (**bobs**, **bobbing**, **bobbed**) cut (hair) in a bob.
– ORIGIN unknown.

bob[3] ● n. (pl. **bob**) Brit. informal a shilling.
– ORIGIN unknown.

bobbin ● n. a cylinder, cone, or reel holding thread.
– ORIGIN French *bobine*.

bobble ● n. a small ball made of strands of wool.
– DERIVATIVES **bobbly** adj.
– ORIGIN from BOB[2].

bobby ● n. (pl. **bobbies**) Brit. informal, dated a police officer.
– ORIGIN pet form of *Robert*, from Sir Robert PEEL.

bobsleigh (N. Amer. **bobsled**) ● n. a sledge with brakes and a steering mechanism, used for racing down an ice-covered run.

Boccaccio E
/buh-**kach**-i-oh/, Giovanni (1313–75), Italian writer, poet, and humanist, famous for the collection of stories known as the *Decameron*.

Boche /bosh/ ● n. (**the Boche**) informal, dated German soldiers as a group.
– ORIGIN French, 'rascal'.

bod ● n. informal **1** a body. **2** esp. Brit. a person.

bode ● v. (**bodes**, **boding**, **boded**) (**bode well/ill**) be a sign of a good or bad outcome: *the film's success bodes well for similar projects.*
– ORIGIN Old English, 'proclaim, foretell'.

bodge ● v. (**bodges**, **bodging**, **bodged**) Brit. informal make or repair badly or clumsily.
– ORIGIN from BOTCH.

bodice ● n. **1** the upper part of a woman's dress. **2** a woman's sleeveless undergarment.
– ORIGIN formerly *bodies*, plural of BODY.

bodily ● adj. relating to the body. ● adv. by taking hold of a person's body with force.

bodkin ● n. a thick, blunt needle with a large eye, used for drawing tape or cord through a hem.
– ORIGIN perh. Celtic.

Bodrum E
/**bod**-ruhm/ a resort town on the coast of western Turkey, site of the ancient Greek city of Halicarnassus.

body ● n. (pl. **bodies**) **1** the whole physical structure of a person or an animal. **2** the main part of the body, apart from the head and limbs. **3** the main or central part: *the body of the aircraft was filled with smoke.* **4** a mass or collection. **5** an organized group set up for a particular purpose: *a regulatory body.* **6** tech. an object: *the path taken by the falling body.* **7** fullness of flavour, texture, etc. **8** a bodysuit.
– PHRASES **keep body and soul together** stay alive in difficult circumstances. **over my dead body** informal used to express strong opposition.
– ORIGIN Old English.

body blow ● n. **1** a heavy punch to the body. **2** a severe setback.

bodybuilder ● n. a person who strengthens and enlarges their muscles through exercise.

body clock ● n. a person's biological clock.

bodyguard ● n. a person employed to protect a rich or famous person.

body language ● n. the conveying of one's feelings by the movement or position of one's body.

body politic ● n. the people of a nation or society considered as an organized group of citizens.

body stocking ● n. a woman's one-piece

undergarment covering the torso and legs.

bodysuit • n. a woman's close-fitting stretch garment for the upper body.

bodywork • n. the metal outer shell of a vehicle.

Boer /*rhymes with* more *or* mower/ • n. an early Dutch or Huguenot settler of southern Africa. • adj. relating to the Boers.
– ORIGIN Dutch, 'farmer'.

Boer Wars E
two wars (1880–1 and 1899–1902) fought by Great Britain against the Boer settlers in southern Africa.

boffin • n. Brit. informal a scientist.
– ORIGIN unknown.

bog • n. **1** an area of soft, wet, muddy ground. **2** Brit. informal a toilet. • v. (**bogs, bogging, bogged**) (**bog down**) hinder the progress of.
– DERIVATIVES **boggy** adj.
– ORIGIN Irish or Scottish Gaelic, 'soft'.

Bogarde E
/**boh**-gard/, Sir Dirk (1921–99; born *Derek Niven van den Bogaerde*), British actor and writer, of Dutch descent. His films include *Death in Venice*.

Bogart E
/**boh**-gart/, Humphrey (DeForest) (1899–1957), American actor. His many films include *Casablanca* and *The Big Sleep*.

bogey[1] • n. (pl. **bogeys**) Golf a score of one stroke over par at a hole.
– ORIGIN perh. from BOGEY[2], referring to the Devil as an imaginary player.

bogey[2] (also **bogy**) • n. (pl. **bogeys**) **1** an evil or mischievous spirit. **2** a cause of fear or alarm: *the bogey of recession.* **3** Brit. informal a piece of mucus in the nose.
– ORIGIN formerly a name for the Devil.

bogeyman (also **bogyman**) • n. an evil spirit.

boggle • v. (**boggles, boggling, boggled**) informal **1** be astonished or baffled: *the mind boggles at the complexity of the system.* **2** (**boggle at**) hesitate to do.
– ORIGIN prob. related to BOGEY[2].

bogie /**boh**-gi/ • n. (pl. **bogies**) esp. Brit. a supporting frame with wheels, fitted on a pivot beneath the end of a railway vehicle.
– ORIGIN unknown.

Bogotá E
/bog-uh-**tah**/ the capital of Colombia. Official name **SANTA FÉ DE BOGOTÁ**.

bog-standard • adj. informal, derog. ordinary; basic.

bogus • adj. not genuine or true.
– ORIGIN unknown.

bogy • n. (pl. **bogies**) var. of BOGEY[2].

Bohemia E
/boh-**hee**-mi-uh/ a region forming the western part of the Czech Republic.

Bohemian /boh-**hee**-mi-uhn/ • n. **1** a person from Bohemia. **2** a person who does not conform to accepted standards of behaviour. [ORIGIN because gypsies were thought to come from Bohemia.] • adj. **1** having to do with Bohemia. **2** unconventional.
– DERIVATIVES **Bohemianism** n.

Bohr E
/bor/, Niels Hendrik David (1885–1962), Danish physicist and pioneer in quantum physics, whose theory of the structure of the atom incorporated quantum theory for the first time.

bohrium /**bor**-iuhm/ • n. a very unstable chemical element made by high-energy atomic collisions.
– ORIGIN from BOHR.

boil[1] • v. **1** (with reference to a liquid) reach or cause to reach the temperature at which it bubbles and turns to vapour. **2** (with reference to food) cook or be cooked by immersing in boiling water. **3** (**boil down to**) amount to. • n. **1** the action or process of boiling; boiling point. **2** a state of vigorous activity or excitement: *the team have gone off the boil this season.*
– ORIGIN Latin *bullire* 'to bubble'.

boil[2] • n. an inflamed pus-filled swelling on the skin.
– ORIGIN Old English.

boiler • n. a fuel-burning device for heating water.

boiler suit • n. Brit. a one-piece suit worn as overalls for manual work.

boiling • adj. **1** at or near boiling point. **2** informal extremely hot.

boiling point • n. the temperature at which a liquid boils.

boisterous • adj. noisy, lively, and high-spirited.
– ORIGIN unknown.

Bokassa E
/buh-**kass**-uh/, Jean Bédel (1921–96), African statesman and military leader, President 1972–6 of the Central African Republic, self-styled emperor 1976–9.

bold • adj. **1** confident and courageous. **2** dated lacking respect or shame. **3** (of a colour or design) strong or vivid. **4** (of type) having thick strokes.
– PHRASES **as bold as brass** so confident as to be cheeky or disrespectful.
– DERIVATIVES **boldly** adv. **boldness** n.
– ORIGIN Old English.

bole • n. a tree trunk.
– ORIGIN Old Norse.

bolero /buh-**lair**-oh/ • n. (pl. **boleros**) **1** a Spanish dance. **2** /**bol**-uh-roh/ a woman's short open jacket.
– ORIGIN Spanish.

Boleyn E
/buh-**lin**/, Anne (1507–36), second wife of Henry VIII and mother of Elizabeth I. She fell from favour when she failed to provide Henry with a male heir and was executed following her alleged adultery.

Bolger E
/**bol**-jer/, James (Brendan) (b.1935), New Zealand National Party statesman, Prime Minister 1990–7.

Bolívar E
/**bol**-i-var/, Simón (1783–1830), Venezuelan patriot and statesman. He freed Venezuela, Colombia, Peru, and Ecuador from Spanish rule.

Bolivarian Republic of Venezuela E
official name for **VENEZUELA**.

Bolivia E
/buh-**liv**-i-uh/ a landlocked country in South America; capital, La Paz.
– DERIVATIVES **Bolivian** adj. & n.

boll /*rhymes with* hole/ • **n.** the rounded seed capsule of plants such as cotton.
– ORIGIN Dutch *bolle* 'rounded object'.

bollard • **n.** **1** Brit. a short post used to prevent traffic from entering an area. **2** a short post on a ship or quayside for securing a rope.
– ORIGIN perh. from Old Norse, 'bole'.

bollocking (also **ballocking**) • **n.** Brit. vulgar a severe reprimand.

bollocks (also **ballocks**) • **pl. n.** Brit. vulgar **1** the testicles. **2** nonsense.
– ORIGIN Germanic.

Bologna E
/buh-**lon**-yuh/ a city in northern Italy, capital of Emilia-Romagna region. Its university (founded 1088) is the oldest in Europe.

Bolshevik /**bol**-shi-vik/ • **n.** hist. **1** a member of the majority group within the Russian Social Democratic Party, which seized power in the Revolution of 1917. **2** a person with revolutionary or radical political views.
– DERIVATIVES **Bolshevism** n.
– ORIGIN Russian *bol'she* 'greater'.

bolshie (also **bolshy**) • **adj.** Brit. informal hostile and uncooperative.
– ORIGIN from **BOLSHEVIK**.

Bolshoi Ballet E
/**bol**-shoy/ a Moscow ballet company, founded in 1776.

bolster • **n.** a long, firm pillow. • **v.** (**bolsters, bolstering, bolstered**) support or strengthen: *campaigns to bolster the president's image.*
– ORIGIN Old English.

Bolt, E
Robert (Oxton) (1924–95), English dramatist, who wrote the play *A Man for All Seasons*.

bolt • **n.** **1** a long metal pin with a head that screws into a nut, used to fasten things together. **2** a bar that slides into a socket to fasten a door or window. **3** a short, heavy arrow shot from a crossbow. **4** a flash of lightning. **5** a roll of fabric. • **v.** **1** fasten with a bolt. **2** run away suddenly. **3** eat (food) quickly. **4** (of a plant) grow quickly upwards and stop flowering as seeds develop.
– PHRASES **a bolt from** (or **out of**) **the blue** a sudden and unexpected event. **bolt upright** with the back very straight. **have shot one's bolt** informal have done everything possible but still not succeeded. **make a bolt for** try to escape by running suddenly towards.
– ORIGIN Old English.

bolt hole • **n.** esp. Brit. a place where a person can escape to and hide.

Boltzmann E
/**bolts**-man/, Ludwig (1844–1906), Austrian physicist, who made major contributions to the kinetic theory of gases.

bomb • **n.** **1** a container of material capable of exploding or causing a fire. **2** (**the bomb**) nuclear weapons collectively. **3** (**a bomb**) Brit. informal a large sum of money. • **v.** **1** attack with a bomb or bombs. **2** Brit. informal move very quickly. **3** informal fail badly.
– PHRASES **go like a bomb** Brit. informal **1** be very successful. **2** move very fast.
– ORIGIN French *bombe*.

bombard /bom-**bard**/ • **v.** **1** attack continuously with bombs or other missiles. **2** direct a continuous flow of questions or information at. **3** Physics direct a stream of high-speed particles at (a substance).
– DERIVATIVES **bombardment** n.
– ORIGIN French *bombarder*.

bombardier /bom-buh-**deer**/ • **n.** **1** a rank of non-commissioned officer in some artillery regiments, equivalent to corporal. **2** a member of a bomber crew in the US air force responsible for releasing bombs.
– ORIGIN French.

bombast /**bom**-bast/ • **n.** language that sounds impressive but has little meaning.
– DERIVATIVES **bombastic** adj.
– ORIGIN Old French *bombace* 'cotton used as padding'.

Bombay E
a city and port on the west coast of India, capital of the state of Maharashtra. Official name (from 1995) **MUMBAI**.

bombazine /**bom**-buh-zeen/ • **n.** a twill dress fabric of worsted and silk or cotton.
– ORIGIN Latin *bombycinus* 'silken'.

bombed • **adj.** informal intoxicated by drink or drugs.

bomber • **n.** **1** an aircraft that drops bombs. **2** a person who plants bombs.

bomber jacket • **n.** a short jacket gathered at the waist and cuffs by elasticated bands and having a zip front.

bombshell • **n.** **1** something that comes as a great surprise and shock. **2** informal a very attractive woman.

bona fide /boh-nuh **fy**-di/ • **adj.** genuine; real.
– ORIGIN Latin, 'with good faith'.

bona fides /boh-nuh **fy**-deez/ • **n.** evidence proving that a person is what they claim to be; credentials.
– ORIGIN Latin, 'good faith'.

Bonaire E
/bo-**nair**/ one of the two principal islands of the Netherlands Antilles (the other is Curaçao); chief town, Kralendijk.

bonanza • **n.** a source of wealth, profit, or good fortune.
– ORIGIN Spanish, 'fair weather'.

bonbon • **n.** a sweet.
– ORIGIN French *bon* 'good'.

bonce • **n.** Brit. informal a person's head.
– ORIGIN unknown.

bond • **n.** **1** a thing used to tie or fasten things together. **2** (**bonds**) ropes or chains used to hold someone prisoner. **3** a force or feeling that links people: *the bonds between mother and daughter.* **4** an agreement with legal force. **5** a certificate issued by a government or a public company promising to repay money lent to it at a fixed rate of interest and at a specified time. **6** (also **chemical bond**) a strong force of attraction holding atoms to-

gether in a molecule. ● v. **1** join or be joined securely to something else. **2** establish a relationship based on shared feelings or experiences.
– ORIGIN from **BAND**[1].

bondage ● n. **1** the state of being a slave or feudal serf. **2** sexual practice that involves the tying up of one partner.

Bondi E
/bon-dy/ a coastal resort in New South Wales, Australia, a suburb of Sydney.

bond paper ● n. high-quality writing paper.

bone ● n. **1** any of the pieces of hard, whitish tissue making up the skeleton in vertebrates. **2** the hard material of which bones consist. **3** a thing made or formerly made of bone, such as a strip of stiffening for an undergarment. ● v. (**bones, boning, boned**) **1** remove the bones from (meat or fish) before cooking. **2** (**bone up on**) informal study (a subject) intensively.
– PHRASES **bone of contention** a source of continuing disagreement. **close to the bone** **1** (of a remark) accurate to the point of causing discomfort. **2** (of a joke or story) near the limit of decency. **have a bone to pick with** informal have reason to quarrel with. **in one's bones** felt or believed deeply or instinctively. **make no bones about** be direct in stating or dealing with. **work one's fingers to the bone** work very hard.
– DERIVATIVES **boneless** adj.
– ORIGIN Old English.

bone china ● n. white porcelain containing the mineral residue of burnt bones.

bone dry ● adj. very dry.

bonehead ● n. informal a stupid person.

bone idle ● adj. extremely idle.

bonemeal ● n. ground bones used as a fertilizer.

boneshaker ● n. Brit. informal an old vehicle with poor suspension.

bonfire ● n. a large open-air fire lit to burn rubbish or as a celebration.
– ORIGIN first referring to a fire on which bones were burnt, or for burning heretics.

bongo ● n. (pl. **bongos** or **bongoes**) each of a pair of small drums, held between the knees and played with the fingers.
– ORIGIN Latin American Spanish.

bonhomie /bon-uh-mee/ ● n. good-natured friendliness.
– ORIGIN French.

Boniface, St E
/bon-i-fayss/ (680–754; born *Wynfrith*), Anglo-Saxon missionary, who was appointed Primate of Germany in 732. Feast day, 5 June.

Bonington E
/bon-ing-tuhn/, Chris (b.1934; full name *Christian John Storey Bonington*), English mountaineer, who made the first British ascent of the north face of the Eiger in 1962.

bonito /buh-nee-toh/ ● n. (pl. **bonitos**) a small tuna with dark stripes.
– ORIGIN Spanish.

bonk informal ● v. **1** hit. **2** Brit. have sexual intercourse. ● n. **1** a hit or knock. **2** Brit. an act of sexual intercourse.

bonkers ● adj. informal mad.
– ORIGIN unknown.

bon mot /bon moh/ ● n. (pl. **bons mots** /bon moh, bon mohz/) a clever or witty remark.
– ORIGIN French, 'good word'.

Bonn E
a city in the state of North Rhine-Westphalia in Germany, the capital of the Federal Republic of Germany from 1949 until the reunification of Germany in 1990.

Bonnard E
/bon-nar/, Pierre (1867–1947), French painter and graphic artist. His works continue and develop the Impressionist tradition.

bonnet ● n. **1** a woman's or child's hat tied under the chin and with a brim framing the face. **2** a soft brimless hat like a beret, worn by men and boys in Scotland. **3** Brit. the hinged metal cover over the engine of a motor vehicle.
– ORIGIN Old French *bonet*.

Bonney E
William H. (1859–81 ; known as **Billy the Kid**), American outlaw, a notorious murderer.

Bonnie Prince Charlie E
see **STUART**[1].

bonny (also **bonnie**) ● adj. (**bonnier, bonniest**) esp. Sc. & N. Engl. **1** physically attractive; healthy-looking. **2** considerable: *it's worth a bonny sum.*
– ORIGIN perh. from Old French *bon* 'good'.

bonsai /bon-sy/ ● n. the art of growing ornamental trees or shrubs in small pots so as to greatly restrict their growth.
– ORIGIN Japanese, 'tray planting'.

bonus ● n. **1** a sum of money added to a person's wages for good performance. **2** an unexpected and welcome thing.
– ORIGIN Latin, 'good'.

bon vivant /bon vee-von/ ● n. (pl. **bon vivants** or **bons vivants** /bon vee-von/) a person who enjoys a sociable and luxurious lifestyle.
– ORIGIN French.

bon viveur /bon vee-ver/ ● n. (pl. **bon viveurs** or **bons viveurs** /bon vee-ver/) = **BON VIVANT**.
– ORIGIN French.

bon voyage /bon voy-*yahzh*/ ● exclam. have a good journey.
– ORIGIN French.

bony ● adj. (**bonier, boniest**) **1** having to do with or containing bones. **2** so thin that the bones can be seen.

bonzer ● adj. Austral./NZ informal excellent.
– ORIGIN perh. from **BONANZA**.

boo ● exclam. **1** said suddenly to surprise someone. **2** said to show disapproval or contempt. ● v. (**boos, booing, booed**) say 'boo' to show disapproval or contempt.

boob[1] Brit. informal ● n. an embarrassing mistake. ● v. make such a mistake.
– ORIGIN from **BOOBY**[1].

boob[2] ● n. informal a woman's breast.
– ORIGIN from **BOOBY**[2].

boo-boo ● n. informal a mistake.
– ORIGIN from **BOOB**[1].

boob tube ● n. Brit. informal a woman's tight-fitting strapless top.

booby[1] • n. (pl. **boobies**) **1** informal a stupid person. **2** a large tropical seabird of the gannet family.
– ORIGIN prob. from Spanish *bobo*.

booby[2] • n. (pl. **boobies**) informal a woman's breast.
– ORIGIN dialect *bubby*.

booby prize • n. a prize given to the person who comes last in a contest.

booby trap • n. an object containing a hidden explosive device designed to explode when someone touches it.

boodle • n. informal money.
– ORIGIN Dutch *boedel, boel* 'possessions'.

boogie • n. (also **boogie-woogie**) (pl. **boogies**) **1** a style of blues played on the piano with a strong, fast beat. **2** informal a dance to pop or rock music. • v. (**boogies, boogieing, boogied**) informal dance to pop or rock music.
– ORIGIN unknown.

book • n. **1** a written or printed work consisting of pages fastened together along one side and bound in covers. **2** a main division of a literary work or of the Bible. **3** a bound set of blank sheets for writing in: *an exercise book*. **4** (**books**) a set of records or accounts. **5** a set of tickets, stamps, etc., bound together. • v. **1** reserve (accommodation, a ticket, etc.). **2** (**book in**) register one's arrival at a hotel. **3** engage (a performer or guest) for an event. **4** (**be booked up**) have all places or dates reserved. **5** make an official note of (someone who has broken a law or rule).
– PHRASES **bring someone to book** make someone explain their behaviour. **by the book** strictly according to the rules. **in someone's bad** (or **good**) **books** in disfavour (or favour) with someone. **on the books** contained in a list of members, employees, or clients. **take a leaf out of someone's book** imitate someone in a particular way. **throw the book at** informal reprimand or punish severely.
– ORIGIN Old English, 'grant by charter'.

bookcase • n. an open cabinet containing shelves on which to keep books.

book club • n. an organization which sells its members selected books at reduced prices.

bookend • n. a support placed at the end of a row of books to keep them upright.

Booker Prize E
an annual literary prize awarded to a novel published by a British or Commonwealth citizen during the previous year.

bookie • n. (pl. **bookies**) informal a bookmaker.

booking • n. **1** an act of reserving accommodation, a ticket, etc. **2** Soccer an instance of a player being cautioned by the referee for foul play.

bookish • adj. devoted to reading and studying.

bookkeeping • n. the activity of keeping records of financial dealings.

booklet • n. a small, thin book with paper covers.

bookmaker • n. a person whose job is to take bets, calculate odds, and pay out winnings.

bookmark • n. **1** a strip of leather or card used to mark a place in a book. **2** Computing a record of the address of a file, Internet page, etc., enabling quick access by a user.

Book of Common Prayer E
the official service book of the Church of England, compiled by Thomas Cranmer and others, first issued in 1549 and largely unchanged since being revised in 1662.

bookworm • n. informal a person who greatly enjoys reading.

Boolean /boo-li-uhn/ • adj. Computing (of a system of notation) used to represent logical operations by means of the binary digits 0 (false) and 1 (true).
– ORIGIN named after the English mathematician George *Boole* (1815–64).

boom[1] • n. **1** a loud, deep sound. **2** a period of rapid economic growth. • v. **1** make a loud, deep sound. **2** experience a period of rapid economic growth.
– ORIGIN perh. from Dutch *bommen* 'to hum, buzz'.

boom[2] • n. **1** a pivoted spar to which the foot of a vessel's sail is attached. **2** a movable arm carrying a microphone or film camera. **3** a floating beam used to contain oil spills or to form a barrier across the mouth of a harbour.
– ORIGIN Dutch, 'beam, tree, pole'.

boomerang • n. a curved flat piece of wood that can be thrown so as to return to the thrower, used by Australian Aboriginals for hunting.
– ORIGIN from an Aboriginal language.

boon • n. a thing that is helpful or beneficial.
– ORIGIN Old Norse, 'a request'.

boon companion • n. a close friend.
– ORIGIN *boon* from Old French *bon* 'good'.

Boone, E
Daniel (*c.*1734–1820), American pioneer, who made trips west into the unexplored area of Kentucky.

boor /boor/ • n. a rough and bad-mannered person.
– DERIVATIVES **boorish** adj.
– ORIGIN German *būr* or Dutch *boer* 'farmer'.

boost • v. help or encourage to improve: *a range of measures to boost tourism*. • n. a source of help or encouragement.
– ORIGIN unknown.

booster • n. **1** a thing that helps increase something. **2** a dose of a vaccine that increases or renews the effect of an earlier one. **3** the part of a rocket or spacecraft used to give acceleration after lift-off.

boot[1] • n. **1** an item of footwear covering the foot and ankle, and sometimes the lower leg. **2** Brit. a space at the back of a car for luggage. **3** informal a hard kick. • v. **1** kick hard. **2** (**boot out**) informal force (someone) to leave. **3** start up (a computer) by loading a program with a few instructions that enable the rest of the program to be introduced from an input device. [ORIGIN from **BOOTSTRAP**.]
– PHRASES **the boot is on the other foot** the situation is now reversed. **give** (or **get**) **the boot** informal dismiss (or be dismissed) from a job. **old boot** informal an ugly or disliked old woman. **put the boot in** Brit. informal kick or attack someone when they are on the ground.
– ORIGIN Old French *bote*.

boot[2] • n. (in phr. **to boot**) as well.
– ORIGIN Old English, 'advantage'.

bootee (also **bootie**) ● **n. 1** a baby's woollen shoe. **2** a woman's short boot.

Booth, E
William (1829–1912), English religious leader, founder and first general of the Salvation Army.

booth ● **n. 1** a small temporary structure used for selling goods or staging shows at a market or fair. **2** an enclosed compartment allowing privacy when telephoning, voting, etc.
– ORIGIN Old Norse, 'dwell'.

bootleg ● **adj.** (of alcoholic drink or a recording) made or distributed illegally. ● **n.** an illegal musical recording.
– DERIVATIVES **bootlegger** n. **bootlegging** n.
– ORIGIN from a practice among smugglers of hiding bottles in their boots.

bootstrap ● **n.** a loop at the back of a boot, used to pull it on.
– PHRASES **pull oneself up by one's bootstraps** improve one's position by one's own efforts.

booty ● **n.** valuable stolen goods.
– ORIGIN German *būte, buite* 'exchange'.

booze informal ● **n.** alcoholic drink. ● **v.** (**boozes**, **boozing**, **boozed**) drink large quantities of alcohol.
– DERIVATIVES **boozy** adj.
– ORIGIN Dutch *būsen*.

boozer ● **n.** informal **1** a person who drinks large quantities of alcohol. **2** Brit. a pub.

booze-up ● **n.** informal a heavy drinking session.

bop[1] informal ● **n.** a dance to pop music. ● **v.** (**bops**, **bopping**, **bopped**) dance to pop music.
– DERIVATIVES **bopper** n.

bop[2] informal ● **v.** (**bops, bopping, bopped**) hit or punch quickly. ● **n.** a quick blow or punch.

boracic /buh-rass-ik/ ● **adj.** having to do with boric acid.

borax /bor-aks/ ● **n.** a white mineral that is a compound of boron, used in making glass and as a flux in soldering or smelting.
– ORIGIN Latin.

Bordeaux E
/bor-**doh**/ a port of SW France on the River Garonne, capital of Aquitaine and a centre of the wine trade.

Border, E
Allan (Robert) (b.1955), Australian cricketer, who captained the national team and scored 11,174 runs in test matches (a world record).

border ● **n. 1** a boundary between two countries or other areas. **2** a decorative band around the edge of something. **3** a strip of ground along the edge of a lawn for planting flowers or shrubs. ● **v.** (**borders**, **bordering**, **bordered**) **1** form a border around or along. **2** (of a country or area) be next to (another). **3** (**border on**) come close to: *his demands bordered on the impossible.*
– ORIGIN Old French *bordeure*.

borderline ● **n.** a boundary. ● **adj.** on the boundary between two qualities or categories: *the borderline area between sleep and wakening.*

bore[1] ● **v.** (**bores**, **boring**, **bored**) make (a hole) in something with a drill or other tool. ● **n. 1** the hollow part inside a gun barrel or other tube. **2** the diameter of this: *a small-bore rifle.*
– DERIVATIVES **borer** n.
– ORIGIN Old English.

bore[2] ● **n.** a dull and uninteresting person or activity. ● **v.** (**bores, boring, bored**) make (someone) feel tired and unenthusiastic by being dull and uninteresting.
– ORIGIN unknown.

bore[3] ● **n.** a high wave caused by the meeting of two tides or by a tide rushing up a narrow estuary.
– ORIGIN perh. from Old Norse, 'a wave'.

bore[4] past of BEAR[1].

bored ● **adj.** feeling tired and impatient because one is doing something dull or one has nothing to do.

USAGE bored
Use **bored by** or **bored with** rather than **bored of.** Although **bored of** is often used in speech, you should not use it in writing.

boredom ● **n.** the state of being bored.

borehole ● **n.** a deep, narrow hole in the ground made to find water or oil.

Borg, E
Björn (Rune) (b.1956), Swedish tennis player, who won five consecutive men's singles titles at Wimbledon (1976–80).

Borges E
/bor-khes/, Jorge Luis (1899–1986), Argentinian poet, short-story writer, and essayist. His volume of short stories *A Universal History of Infamy* is a founding work of magic realism (literature combining realistic and fantasy elements).

Borgia[1] E
/bor-*zhuh*/, Cesare (*c.*1476–1507), Italian statesman, cardinal, and general, the illegitimate son of Pope Alexander VI and brother of Lucrezia Borgia. He was made captain general of the papal army in 1499.

Borgia[2] E
/bor-*zhuh*/, Lucrezia (1480–1519), Italian noblewoman and patron of the arts.

boric acid ● **n.** Chem. a compound derived from boron, used as a mild antiseptic.

boring ● **adj.** causing tiredness or impatience because not interesting.

Bormann E
/bor-muhn/, Martin (1900–*c.*1945), German Nazi politician and Hitler's closest collaborator. He disappeared in 1945.

Born E
/born/, Max (1882–1970), German theoretical physicist, a founder of quantum mechanics.

born ● **adj. 1** existing as a result of birth. **2** (**born of**) existing as a result of (a situation or feeling). **3** having a particular natural ability: *a born engineer.* **4** (**-born**) having a particular nationality.
– PHRASES **born and bred** by birth and upbringing. **I** (or **she**, etc.) **wasn't born yesterday** I am (or she, etc. is) not easily deceived.
– ORIGIN Old English, from BEAR[1].

born-again ● **adj. 1** having to do with a person who has converted to a personal faith in

Christ. **2** showing the great enthusiasm of a person newly converted to a cause: *born-again environmentalists.*

borne past part. of **BEAR**[1]. ● **adj.** (**-borne**) carried by the thing specified: *water-borne bacteria.*

Borneo E
/bor-ni-oh/ a large island of the Malay Archipelago.
– DERIVATIVES **Bornean** adj. & n.

Borodin E
/bo-ruh-din/, Aleksandr (Porfirevich) (1833–87), Russian composer, who composed the epic opera *Prince Igor.*

boron /bor-on/ ● **n.** a crystalline chemical element used in making alloy steel and in nuclear reactors.
– ORIGIN from **BORAX**.

borough /*rhymes with* thorough/ ● **n. 1** Brit. a town with a corporation and privileges granted by a royal charter. **2** an administrative division of London or of New York City.
– ORIGIN Old English, 'fortress, citadel'.

borrow ● **v. 1** take and use (something belonging to someone else) with the intention of returning it. **2** have (money) on a loan from a person or bank.
– DERIVATIVES **borrower** n.
– ORIGIN Old English.

borstal /bor-st'l/ ● **n.** Brit. hist. a prison for young offenders.
– ORIGIN named after the village of *Borstal* in southern England.

borzoi /bor-zoy/ ● **n.** (pl. **borzois**) a breed of large Russian dog with a narrow head and silky coat.
– ORIGIN Russian *borzyĭ* 'swift'.

Bosch E
/bosh/, Hieronymus (*c.*1450–1516), Dutch painter, known for his highly detailed works full of half-human, half-animal creatures, and grotesque demons.

Bose E
/bohss/, Satyendra Nath (1894–1974), Indian physicist, who with Einstein described the fundamental particles later known as *bosons.*

bosh ● **n.** informal nonsense.
– ORIGIN Turkish *boş* 'empty, worthless'.

bosky /boss-ki/ ● **adj.** literary covered by trees or bushes.
– ORIGIN from **BUSH**[1].

Bosnia–Herzegovina E
/boz-ni-uh herts-uh-**gov**-i-nuh/ a country in the Balkans, formerly a constituent republic of Yugoslavia; capital, Sarajevo.
– DERIVATIVES **Bosnian** adj. & n.

bosom ● **n. 1** a woman's breast or chest. **2** loving care or protection: *he went home to the bosom of his family.* ● **adj.** (of a friend) very close.
– DERIVATIVES **bosomy** adj.
– ORIGIN Old English.

Bosporus E
/boss-puh-ruhss/ (also **Bosphorus** /boss-fuh-ruhss/) a strait connecting the Black Sea with the Sea of Marmara, with Istanbul at its south end.

boss[1] informal ● **n.** a person who is in charge of an employee or organization. ● **v.** give orders in a domineering manner.
– ORIGIN Dutch *baas* 'master'.

boss[2] ● **n.** a projecting knob or stud on the centre of a shield, propeller, etc.
– ORIGIN Old French *boce.*

bossa nova /bos-suh **noh**-vuh/ ● **n.** a Brazilian dance like the samba.
– ORIGIN Portuguese, 'new tendency'.

boss-eyed ● **adj.** Brit. informal cross-eyed.
– ORIGIN unknown.

bossy ● **adj.** (**bossier**, **bossiest**) informal fond of giving orders; domineering.

Boston E
the state capital of Massachusetts.
– DERIVATIVES **Bostonian** n. & adj.

Boston Tea Party E
a violent demonstration in 1773 by American colonists who threw cargoes of tea into Boston harbour in protest at the imposition of a tax on tea by the British Parliament.

bosun /**boh**-suhn/ (also **bo'sun**) ● **n.** var. of **BOATSWAIN**.

Boswell, E
James (1740–95), Scottish author, companion and biographer of Samuel Johnson.

Bosworth Field E
(also **Battle of Bosworth**) a battle of the Wars of the Roses fought in 1485 near Market Bosworth in Leicestershire. The Yorkist king Richard III was killed by Henry Tudor, who took the throne as Henry VII.

botanical ● **adj.** relating to botany.
– DERIVATIVES **botanic** adj. **botanically** adv.

botanical garden (also **botanic garden**) ● **n.** a place where plants are grown for scientific study and display to the public.

botany /**bot**-uh-ni/ ● **n.** the scientific study of plants.
– DERIVATIVES **botanist** n.
– ORIGIN Greek *botanē* 'plant'.

Botany Bay E
a bay in New South Wales, Australia, just south of Sydney, the site of Captain James Cook's landing in 1770.

botch informal ● **v.** do badly or carelessly. ● **n.** a badly performed action or task.
– ORIGIN unknown.

both ● **det., predet. & pron.** two people or things, regarded together. ● **adv.** applying equally to each of two alternatives: *it won favour with both young and old.*
– ORIGIN Old Norse.

Botha[1] E
/**boh**-tuh/, Louis (1862–1919), South African soldier and statesman, first Prime Minister of the Union of South Africa 1910–19.

Botha[2] E
/**boh**-tuh/, P. W. (b.1916; full name *Pieter Willem Botha*), South African statesman, Prime Minister 1978–84, State President 1984–9. He introduced limited reforms to the apartheid system, but his resistance to more radical change led to his fall from power.

Botham E
/**boh**-thuhm/, Ian (Terence) (b.1955), English all-round cricketer, who in 1978 became the first player to score 100 runs and take eight wickets in a single test match.

bother • v. (**bothers**, **bothering**, **bothered**) **1** take the trouble: *the driver didn't bother to ask why.* **2** worry, disturb, or upset. **3** (**bother with/about**) feel concern about or interest in. • n. **1** trouble and fuss. **2** (**a bother**) a cause of trouble or fuss. • exclam. esp. Brit. used to express mild irritation.
– ORIGIN Anglo-Irish.

bothersome • adj. annoying; troublesome.

Bothwell E
/**both**-wel/, James Hepburn, 4th Earl of (c.1536–78), Scottish nobleman and third husband of Mary, Queen of Scots. He was tried for his involvement in the murder of Mary's previous husband, Lord Darnley, but acquitted.

Botswana E
/bot-**swah**-nuh/ a landlocked country in southern Africa; capital, Gaborone.
– DERIVATIVES **Botswanan** adj. & n.

Botticelli E
/bot-ti-**chel**-li/, Sandro (1445–1510), Italian painter, best known for his mythological works such as *The Birth of Venus*.

bottle • n. **1** a container with a narrow neck, used for storing liquids. **2** Brit. informal courage or confidence. • v. (**bottles**, **bottling**, **bottled**) **1** place in bottles for storage. **2** (**bottle up**) control and hide (one's feelings). **3** (**bottle out**) Brit. informal lose one's nerve and decide not to do something.
– PHRASES **hit the bottle** informal start to drink alcohol heavily.
– ORIGIN Latin *butticula* 'small cask'.

bottle bank • n. Brit. a place where used glass bottles may be left for recycling.

bottle green • adj. dark green.

bottleneck • n. a narrow section of road where traffic flow is restricted.

bottom • n. **1** the lowest or furthest point or part. **2** the lowest position in a competition or ranking: *life at the bottom of society.* **3** esp. Brit. a person's buttocks. **4** (also **bottoms**) the lower half of a two-piece garment. • adj. in the lowest or furthest position. • v. (**bottom out**) (of a situation) reach the lowest point before stabilizing or improving.
– PHRASES **at bottom** basically. **the bottom falls** (or **drops**) **out of something** something suddenly fails or collapses. **bottoms up!** informal said as a toast before drinking. **get to the bottom of** find an explanation for.
– DERIVATIVES **bottomless** adj.
– ORIGIN Old English.

bottom drawer • n. Brit. dated household linen and other items stored by a woman in preparation for her marriage.

bottom line • n. informal **1** the final total of an account or balance sheet. **2** the underlying and most important factor.

botulism /**bot**-yuu-li-z'm/ • n. a dangerous form of food poisoning caused by a bacterium.
– ORIGIN German *Botulismus* 'sausage poisoning'.

Boucher E
/**boo**-shay/, François (1703–70), French rococo painter and decorative artist.

bouclé /**boo**-klay/ • n. yarn with a looped or curled strand.
– ORIGIN French, 'buckled, curled'.

Boudicca E
/boo-**dik**-kuh/ (d. AD 62; also known as **Boadicea**), queen of the Iceni tribe in eastern England, who led her forces in revolt against the Romans.

boudoir /**boo**-dwar/ • n. a woman's bedroom or small private room.
– ORIGIN French, 'sulking-place'.

bouffant /**boo**-fon/ • adj. (of hair) styled so as to stand out from the head in a rounded shape.
– ORIGIN French, 'swelling'.

bougainvillea /boo-guhn-**vil**-li-uh/ (also **bougainvillaea**) • n. a tropical climbing plant with brightly coloured modified leaves (bracts) surrounding the flowers.
– ORIGIN named after the French explorer L. A. de *Bougainville* (1729–1811).

bough • n. a main branch of a tree.
– ORIGIN Old English, 'bough, shoulder'.

bought past and past part. of **BUY**.

USAGE **bought**
Do not confuse **bought** and **brought**. **Bought** is the past tense and past participle of **buy** (as in *she bought a bar of chocolate*), whereas **brought** is the past tense and past participle of **bring** (as in *the article brought a massive response*).

bouillon /**boo**-yon/ • n. thin soup or stock.
– ORIGIN French.

boulder • n. a large rock.
– ORIGIN Scandinavian.

boule /bool/ (also **boules** /bool/) • n. a French game similar to bowls, played with metal balls.
– ORIGIN French, 'bowl'.

boulevard /**boo**-luh-vard/ • n. a wide street, typically one lined with trees.
– ORIGIN French, 'rampart'.

Boulez E
/**boo**-lez/, Pierre (b.1925), French composer and conductor.

Boulogne E
/buu-**loyn**/ a ferry port and fishing town in northern France.

Boult E
/bohlt/, Sir Adrian (Cedric) (1889–1983), English conductor, principal conductor of the London Philharmonic Orchestra 1950–7.

bounce • v. (**bounces**, **bouncing**, **bounced**) **1** move quickly up or away from a surface after hitting it. **2** move or jump up and down repeatedly. **3** (**bounce back**) recover well after a setback. **4** informal (of a cheque) be returned by a bank when there is not enough money in an account for it to be paid. • n. **1** an act of bouncing. **2** high-spirited self-confidence: *the bounce was back in Jenny's step.* **3** body in a person's hair.
– ORIGIN perh. from German *bunsen* 'beat' or Dutch *bons* 'a thump'.

b

bouncer ● **n.** a person employed by a nightclub to prevent troublemakers entering or to remove them from the building.

bouncing ● **adj.** (of a baby) vigorous and healthy.

bouncy ● **adj.** (**bouncier**, **bounciest**) **1** able to bounce or making something bounce. **2** confident and lively.

bound[1] ● **v.** walk or run with leaping strides. ● **n.** a leaping movement towards or over something.
– ORIGIN French *bondir* 'resound'.

bound[2] ● **n.** a boundary or limit: *her grief knew no bounds.* ● **v. 1** form the boundary of. **2** restrict.
– PHRASES **out of bounds 1** (in sport) beyond the field of play. **2** beyond permitted limits.
– ORIGIN Latin *bodina*.

bound[3] ● **adj.** going towards somewhere: *a train bound for Edinburgh.*
– ORIGIN Old Norse, 'get ready'.

bound[4] past and past part. of **BIND**. ● **adj. 1** (**-bound**) restricted to or by a place or situation: *his job kept him city-bound.* **2** certain to be, do, or have: *there is bound to be a change of plan.* **3** obliged to do.
– PHRASES **I'll be bound** I am sure.

boundary ● **n.** (pl. **boundaries**) **1** a line marking the limits of an area. **2** Cricket a hit crossing the limits of the field, scoring four or six runs.
– ORIGIN from **BOUND**[2].

bounden /bown-d'n/ ● **adj.** (in phr. **one's bounden duty**) a duty that one feels is morally right.
– ORIGIN from **BIND**.

bounder ● **n.** Brit. informal, dated a dishonourable man.

boundless ● **adj.** unlimited.

bounteous ● **adj.** archaic bountiful.
– ORIGIN Old French *bontif* 'benevolent'.

bountiful ● **adj. 1** plentiful. **2** giving generously.

bounty ● **n.** (pl. **bounties**) **1** a reward paid for killing or capturing someone. **2** hist. a sum paid by the state to encourage trade or to encourage people to join the army or navy. **3** literary something provided in generous amounts. **4** literary generosity: *people along the Nile depend on its bounty.*
– ORIGIN Old French *bonte* 'goodness'.

bouquet /boo-kay, boh-kay/ ● **n. 1** a bunch of flowers. **2** the characteristic scent of a wine or perfume.
– ORIGIN French.

> **Bourbon** E
> /boor-b'n, **bor**-bon/ the surname of a branch of the French royal family, who ruled France from 1589 until the monarchy was overthrown in 1848. Members of this family have also been kings of Spain (1700–1931 and since 1975).

bourbon /ber-buhn/ ● **n.** an American whisky made from maize and rye.
– ORIGIN named after *Bourbon* County, Kentucky.

bourgeois /boor-*zh*wah/ (also **bourgeoise** /boor-*zh*wahz/) ● **adj.** having to do with the middle class, especially in being conventional and concerned with wealth.
– ORIGIN French.

bourgeoisie /boor-*zh*wah-zee/ ● **n.** the middle class.
– ORIGIN French.

> **Bourguiba** E
> /boor-gee-buh/, Habib ibn Ali (1903–2000), Tunisian nationalist and statesman, the first President of independent Tunisia 1957–87.

> **Bournemouth** E
> a resort on the south coast of England, a unitary council formerly in Dorset.

bout /bowt/ ● **n. 1** a short period of illness or intense activity. **2** a wrestling or boxing match.
– ORIGIN dialect *bought* 'bend, loop'.

boutique /boo-teek/ ● **n.** a small shop selling fashionable clothes.
– ORIGIN French.

> **Boutros-Ghali** E
> /boo-tross **gah**-li/, Boutros (b.1922), Egyptian diplomat and politician, Secretary General of the United Nations 1992–7.

bovine /boh-vyn/ ● **adj. 1** having to do with cattle. **2** sluggish or stupid.
– ORIGIN Latin *bovinus*.

bovine spongiform encephalopathy ● **n.** see **BSE**.

> **Bow** E
> /boh/, Clara (1905–65), American actress. One of the most popular stars and sex symbols of the 1920s, she was known as the 'It Girl'.

bow[1] /*rhymes with* toe/ ● **n. 1** a knot tied with two loops and two loose ends. **2** a weapon for shooting arrows, made of curved wood joined at both ends by a taut string. **3** a rod with horsehair stretched along its length, used for playing some stringed instruments.
– PHRASES **have another string to one's bow** Brit. have a further resource available.
– ORIGIN Old English.

bow[2] /*rhymes with* cow/ ● **v. 1** bend the head or upper body as a sign of respect, greeting, or shame. **2** bend with age or under a heavy weight. **3** give in to pressure. **4** (**bow out**) withdraw or retire from an activity. ● **n.** an act of bowing.
– PHRASES **bow and scrape** behave in a servile way. **take a bow** acknowledge applause by bowing.
– ORIGIN Old English, 'bend'.

bow[3] /*rhymes with* cow/ (also **bows**) ● **n.** the front end of a ship.
– ORIGIN German *boog* or Dutch *boeg*.

bowdlerize /bowd-luh-ryz/ (also **bowdlerise**) ● **v.** (**bowdlerizes**, **bowdlerizing**, **bowdlerized**) remove indecent or offensive material from (a text).
– ORIGIN from Dr Thomas *Bowdler* (1754–1825), who published a censored edition of Shakespeare.

bowel /*rhymes with* towel/ ● **n. 1** the intestine. **2** (**bowels**) the deepest inner parts of something.
– ORIGIN Latin *botellus* 'little sausage'.

bowel movement ● **n.** an act of defecation.

> **Bowen** E
> /boh-in/, Elizabeth (Dorothea Cole) (1899–1973), British novelist and short-story writer, born in Ireland. Her novels include *The Heat of the Day.*

b

bower /*rhymes with* tower/ ● **n.** **1** a pleasant shady place under trees. **2** literary a lady's private room.
– ORIGIN Old English.

bowerbird ● **n.** an Australasian bird noted for the male's habit of building an elaborate bower to attract the female.

Bowie[1] E
/*rhymes with* snowy/, David (b.1947; born *David Robert Jones*), English rock singer, songwriter, and actor, known for his unconventional stage personae.

Bowie[2] E
/*rhymes with* snowy/, Jim (1799–1836), American frontiersman. He shared command of the garrison that resisted the Mexican attack on the Alamo, where he died.

bowie knife /*rhymes with* snowy/ ● **n.** a long knife with a blade double-edged at the point.
– ORIGIN named after Jim *Bowie* (see **BOWIE**[2]).

bowl[1] ● **n.** **1** a round, deep dish or basin. **2** a rounded, hollow part of an object. **3** esp. N. Amer. a stadium for sporting or musical events.
– ORIGIN Old English.

bowl[2] ● **v.** **1** roll (a round object) along the ground. **2** Cricket (of a bowler) throw (the ball) towards the wicket, or dismiss (a batsman) by hitting the wicket with a ball. **3** move rapidly and smoothly. **4** (**bowl over**) knock down. **5** (**bowl over**) informal completely overwhelm or astonish. ● **n.** a heavy ball used in bowls or tenpin bowling.
– ORIGIN Old French *boule*.

bow-legged ● **adj.** having legs that curve outwards at the knee.

bowler[1] ● **n.** **1** Cricket a member of the fielding side who bowls. **2** a player at bowls or tenpin bowling.

bowler[2] ● **n.** a man's hard felt hat with a round dome-shaped crown.
– ORIGIN named after the 19th-century English hatter William *Bowler*.

bowline /**boh**-lin/ ● **n.** a simple knot for forming a non-slipping loop at the end of a rope.

bowling ● **n.** the game of bowls, tenpin bowling, or skittles.

bowling alley ● **n.** a long narrow track along which balls are rolled in skittles or tenpin bowling.

bowling green ● **n.** an area of very short grass on which the game of bowls is played.

bowls /bohlz/ ● **n.** a game played with wooden bowls, the object of which is to roll one's bowl as close as possible to a small white ball (the jack).

bowsprit /**boh**-sprit/ ● **n.** a pole projecting from a ship's bow, to which the ropes supporting the front mast are fastened.

bow tie ● **n.** a necktie in the form of a bow.

bow window ● **n.** a curved bay window.

box[1] ● **n.** **1** a container with a flat base and sides and a lid. **2** an area within straight lines on a page or computer screen. **3** an enclosed area reserved for a group of people in a theatre, sports ground, or law court. **4** a small booth or building used for a particular purpose: *a telephone box.* **5** a service at a newspaper office for receiving replies to an advertisement, or at a post office for keeping letters until collected. **6** Brit. a shield for protecting a man's genitals in sport. **7** (**the box**) informal, esp. Brit. television. ● **v.** **1** put in a box. **2** (**box in**) restrict or confine.
– ORIGIN Old English.

box[2] ● **v.** fight an opponent with the fists in padded gloves as a sport. ● **n.** a slap on the side of a person's head.
– PHRASES **box clever** Brit. informal outwit someone. **box someone's ears** slap someone on the side of the head.
– DERIVATIVES **boxing** n.
– ORIGIN unknown.

box[3] ● **n.** an evergreen shrub with small glossy leaves and hard wood.
– ORIGIN Greek *puxos*.

boxer ● **n.** **1** a person who boxes as a sport. **2** a medium-sized breed of dog with a brown coat and pug-like face.

boxer shorts ● **pl. n.** men's underpants resembling shorts.

Boxing Day ● **n.** esp. Brit. a public holiday on the first day after Christmas Day.
– ORIGIN from the former custom of giving tradespeople a Christmas gift on this day.

box junction ● **n.** Brit. a road area at a junction marked with a yellow grid, which a vehicle should enter only if its exit is clear.

box number ● **n.** a number identifying an advertisement in a newspaper, used as an address for replies.

box office ● **n.** a place at a theatre, cinema, etc. where tickets are sold.

box pleat ● **n.** a pleat consisting of two parallel creases forming a raised band.

boxroom ● **n.** Brit. a very small room.

boxy ● **adj.** (**boxier**, **boxiest**) **1** squarish in shape. **2** (of a room) cramped.

boy ● **n.** a male child or youth.
– DERIVATIVES **boyhood** n. **boyish** adj.
– ORIGIN unknown.

boycott ● **v.** refuse to have dealings with (a person, organization, or country) as a punishment or protest. ● **n.** an act of boycotting.
– ORIGIN from Captain Charles C. *Boycott*, an Irish land agent so treated in 1880 in an attempt to get rents reduced.

Boyd, E
Arthur (Merric Bloomfield) (1920–99), Australian painter, potter, and ceramic artist, famous for his pictures inspired by his travels among Aboriginals.

boyfriend ● **n.** a person's regular male companion in a romantic or sexual relationship.

Boyle, E
Robert (1627–91), Irish-born scientist. His experiments with the air pump led to the law (**Boyle's law**) which states that the pressure of a gas is inversely proportional to its volume at a constant temperature.

Boyne, Battle of the E
/boyn/ a battle fought near the River Boyne in Ireland in 1690, in which the Protestant army of William III defeated the Catholic army led by the recently deposed James II.

boyo /**boy**-o/ ● **n.** (pl. **boyos**) Welsh & Ir. informal a boy or man.

Boy Scout ● **n.** dated = **SCOUT** (in sense 2).

Boz E
/boz/ the pen name used by Charles Dickens.

bozo /**boh**-zoh/ ● n. (pl. **bozos**) informal, esp. N. Amer. a stupid person.
– ORIGIN unknown.

bra ● n. a woman's undergarment worn to support the breasts.
– ORIGIN short for **BRASSIERE**.

Brabham E
/**brab**-uhm/, Sir Jack (b.1926; full name *John Arthur Brabham*), Australian motor-racing driver. He won the Formula One world championship three times (1959, 1960, 1966).

brace ● n. **1** (**braces**) Brit. a pair of straps passing over the shoulders and fastening to the top of trousers to hold them up. **2** a strengthening or supporting part. **3** a wire device used to straighten the teeth. **4** (also **brace and bit**) a drilling tool with a crank handle and a socket to hold a bit. **5** (pl. **brace**) a pair: *a brace of grouse.* **6** either of two connecting marks { and }, used in printing and music. ● v. (**braces**, **bracing**, **braced**) **1** make stronger or firmer with a brace. **2** press (one's body) firmly against something to stay balanced. **3** (**brace oneself**) prepare for something difficult or unpleasant.
– ORIGIN Old French *bracier* 'embrace'.

bracelet ● n. an ornamental band or chain worn on the wrist or arm.
– ORIGIN Old French.

bracing ● adj. fresh and invigorating.

bracken ● n. a tall fern with coarse fronds.
– ORIGIN Scandinavian.

bracket ● n. **1** each of a pair of marks ( ) [ ] { } < > used to enclose words or figures. **2** a category of similar people or things: *a high income bracket.* **3** a right-angled support projecting from a wall. ● v. (**brackets, bracketing**, **bracketed**) **1** enclose (words or figures) in brackets. **2** place in the same category. **3** hold or attach by means of a bracket.
– ORIGIN Spanish *bragueta* 'codpiece, bracket'.

brackish ● adj. (of water) slightly salty.
– ORIGIN German or Dutch *brac.*

bract ● n. Bot. a leaf with a flower in the angle where it meets the stem.
– ORIGIN Latin *bractea* 'thin metal plate'.

brad ● n. a nail with a rectangular cross section and a small head.
– ORIGIN Old Norse.

bradawl /**brad**-awl/ ● n. a tool for boring holes, resembling a screwdriver.

Bradbury, E
Ray (b.1920; full name *Raymond Douglas Bradbury*), American science-fiction writer, author of the novel *Fahrenheit 451.*

Bradford E
an industrial city in northern England, a unitary council formerly in Yorkshire.

Bradman, E
Don (1908–2001; full name *Sir Donald George Bradman*), Australian cricketer, who holds the record for the highest Australian test score against England (334 in 1930).

brae /bray/ ● n. Sc. a steep bank or hillside.
– ORIGIN Old Norse, 'eyelash'.

brag ● v. (**brags**, **bragging**, **bragged**) say something boastfully. ● n. **1** an act of bragging. **2** a simplified form of poker.
– ORIGIN unknown.

braggart /**brag**-gert/ ● n. a person who brags.
– ORIGIN French *bragard.*

Brahe E
/**brah**-i/, Tycho (1546–1601), Danish astronomer, who measured the positions of stars and the motions of planets and comets with unprecedented precision.

Brahma E
/**brah**-muh/ the creator god in Hinduism.

Brahman /**brah**-muhn/ (also **Brahmin** /**brah**-min/) ● n. (pl. **Brahmans**) a member of the highest Hindu caste, that of the priesthood.
– ORIGIN Sanskrit.

Brahmaputra E
/brah-muh-**poo**-truh/ a river of southern Asia, rising in the Himalayas and flowing through Tibet, NE India, and Bangladesh, to join the Ganges at the Bay of Bengal.

Brahms E
/brahmz/, Johannes (1833–97), German composer and pianist. His works include four symphonies, four concertos, chamber and piano music, choral works, and nearly 200 songs.
– DERIVATIVES **Brahmsian** adj.

braid ● n. **1** threads woven into a decorative band. **2** a plaited length of hair. ● v. **1** form a braid with (hair). **2** trim with braid.
– ORIGIN Old English, 'interweave'.

Braille /brayl/ ● n. a written language for the blind using raised dots.
– ORIGIN named after the French educationist Louis *Braille* (1809–52).

brain ● n. **1** an organ of soft tissue contained in the skull, that is the centre of the nervous system. **2** intellectual ability: *success requires brain as well as brawn.* **3** (**the brains**) informal the main organizer within a group. ● v. informal hit hard on the head with an object.
– PHRASES **have on the brain** informal be obsessed with.
– ORIGIN Old English.

brainchild ● n. informal an idea or invention thought up by a particular person.

brain death ● n. irreversible brain damage causing the end of independent breathing.
– DERIVATIVES **brain-dead** adj.

brain drain ● n. informal the emigration of highly skilled or qualified people from a country.

brainless ● adj. stupid; very foolish.

brainstorm ● n. **1** informal a moment in which one is suddenly unable to think clearly. **2** a group discussion to produce ideas. ● v. have a discussion to produce ideas.

brain-teaser ● n. informal a tricky problem or puzzle.

brainwash ● v. cause (someone) to change completely their attitudes and beliefs using repetition or mental pressure.

brainwave ● n. **1** an electrical impulse in the brain. **2** informal a sudden clever idea.

brainy ● adj. (**brainier**, **brainiest**) informal intelligent.

braise ● v. (**braises**, **braising**, **braised**) fry (food) lightly and then stew slowly in a closed container.

– ORIGIN French *braiser*.

brake • n. a device for slowing or stopping a moving vehicle. • v. (**brakes**, **braking**, **braked**) slow or stop a vehicle with a brake.
– ORIGIN unknown.

brake drum • n. a broad, short cylinder attached to a wheel, against which the brake shoes press to cause braking.

brake horsepower • n. an imperial unit equal to one horsepower, used in expressing the power available at the shaft of an engine.

brake shoe • n. a long curved block which presses on to a brake drum.

bramble • n. **1** a prickly shrub of the rose family, especially a blackberry. **2** esp. Brit. the fruit of the blackberry.
– ORIGIN Old English.

bran • n. pieces of grain husk separated from flour after milling.
– ORIGIN Old French.

Branagh E
/bran-uh/, Kenneth (Charles) (b.1960), English actor, producer, and director, noted for his Shakespearean roles and for directing and starring in films such as *Hamlet*.

branch • n. **1** a part of a tree which grows out from the trunk or a bough. **2** a river, road, or railway extending out from a main one. **3** a division of a larger group. • v. **1** divide into one or more branches. **2** (**branch out**) extend one's activities in a new direction.
– ORIGIN Old French *branche*.

Brancusi E
/brang-koo-zi/, Constantin (1876–1957), Romanian sculptor. His work reduces forms to an almost abstract simplicity.

brand • n. **1** a type of product made by a company under a particular name. **2** a brand name. **3** a mark burned on livestock with a hot iron. **4** a piece of smouldering wood. • v. **1** mark with a branding iron. **2** mark out as having a particular shameful quality: *she was branded a liar.* **3** give a brand name to.
– ORIGIN Old English, 'burning'.

brandish • v. wave (something) as a threat or in anger or excitement.
– ORIGIN Old French *brandir*.

brand name • n. a name given by the maker to a product.

brand new • adj. completely new.
– ORIGIN from the idea of a brand being 'straight from the fire'.

Brando, E
Marlon (b.1924), American actor, star of such films as *A Streetcar Named Desire*, *On the Waterfront*, and *The Godfather*.

Brands Hatch E
a motor-racing circuit near Farningham in Kent.

Brandt E
/brant/, Willy (1913–92; born *Karl Herbert Frahm*), German statesman, Chancellor of West Germany 1969–74. His active pursuit of a policy of détente led to the opening of relations with the countries of the Eastern bloc.

brandy • n. (pl. **brandies**) a strong alcoholic spirit distilled from wine or fermented fruit juice.
– ORIGIN from Dutch *branden* 'burn, distil' + *wijn* 'wine'.

Branson, E
Sir Richard (b.1950), English businessman, who made his name with the company Virgin Records and later established Virgin Atlantic Airways and Virgin Trains.

Braque E
/brak/, Georges (1882–1963), French painter, who collaborated with Picasso in the development of cubism.

brash • adj. self-confident in a rude, noisy, or overbearing way.
– DERIVATIVES **brashly** adv. **brashness** n.
– ORIGIN perh. from **RASH**[1].

Brasilia E
/bruh-zil-i-uh/ the capital of Brazil.

brass • n. **1** a yellow alloy of copper and zinc. **2** (also **horse brass**) a flat brass ornament for the harness of a draught horse. **3** Brit. a brass memorial plaque in the wall or floor of a church. **4** brass wind instruments forming a section of an orchestra. **5** (also **top brass**) informal people in authority. **6** Brit. informal money.
– PHRASES **brassed off** Brit. informal annoyed. **get down to brass tacks** informal start to consider the basic facts.
– ORIGIN Old English.

brass band • n. a group of musicians playing brass instruments.

brasserie /brass-uh-ri/ • n. (pl. **brasseries**) an inexpensive French or French-style restaurant.
– ORIGIN French, 'brewery'.

brassica /brass-ik-uh/ • n. a plant of a family that includes cabbage, swede, and rape.
– ORIGIN Latin, 'cabbage'.

brassiere /braz-i-er/ • n. formal = **BRA**.
– ORIGIN French, 'bodice, child's vest'.

brass rubbing • n. reproduction of the design on an engraved brass by rubbing chalk over paper laid on it.

brassy • adj. (**brassier**, **brassiest**) **1** resembling brass in colour. **2** harsh or blaring like a brass instrument. **3** tastelessly showy.

brat • n. informal a badly behaved child.
– DERIVATIVES **brattish** adj.
– ORIGIN perh. from Old French *brachet* 'hound, bitch'.

Bratislava E
/brat-i-slah-vuh/ the capital of Slovakia.

Braun E
/brown/, Wernher Magnus Maximilian von (1912–77), German-born American rocket engineer, who pioneered the work which resulted in the US space programme.

bravado • n. boldness intended to impress or intimidate.
– ORIGIN Spanish *bravada*.

brave • adj. having or showing courage. • n. dated an American Indian warrior. • v. (**braves**, **braving**, **braved**) face (unpleasant conditions) with courage.
– DERIVATIVES **bravely** adv. **bravery** n.
– ORIGIN Italian or Spanish *bravo* 'bold'.

bravo /brah-voh/ • exclam. shouted to express approval for a performer.

– ORIGIN Italian, 'bold'.

bravura /bruh-vyoor-uh/ ● n. great skill and enthusiasm.
– ORIGIN Italian.

brawl ● n. a rough or noisy fight. ● v. take part in a brawl.
– DERIVATIVES **brawler** n.

brawn ● n. physical strength as opposed to intelligence.
– DERIVATIVES **brawny** adj.
– ORIGIN Old French *braon* 'fleshy part of the leg'.

bray ● n. the loud, harsh cry of a donkey. ● v. make such a sound.
– ORIGIN Old French *braire* 'to cry'.

braze ● v. (**brazes, brazing, brazed**) solder with an alloy of copper and zinc.
– ORIGIN French *braser* 'solder'.

brazen ● adj. bold and shameless. ● v. (**brazen it out**) endure a difficult situation with an apparent lack of shame.
– DERIVATIVES **brazenly** adv.
– ORIGIN Old English, 'made of brass'.

brazier /bray-zi-er/ ● n. a portable heater holding lighted coals.
– ORIGIN French *brasier.*

Brazil E
the largest country in South America; capital, Brasilia.
– DERIVATIVES **Brazilian** adj. & n.

brazil nut ● n. the large three-sided nut of a South American tree.

Brazzaville E
/braz-zuh-vil/ the capital of the Republic of the Congo.

breach ● v. **1** make a hole in; break through. **2** break (a rule or agreement). ● n. **1** a gap made in a wall or barrier. **2** an act of breaking a rule or agreement. **3** a break in relations.
– PHRASES **breach of the peace** Brit. the criminal offence of behaving in a violent or noisy way in public. **step into the breach** replace someone who is suddenly unable to do a job.
– ORIGIN Old French *breche.*

bread ● n. **1** food made of flour, water, and yeast mixed together and baked. **2** informal money.
– PHRASES **bread and butter** a person's main source of income. **break bread** celebrate the Eucharist. **know which side one's bread is buttered** informal know where one's advantage lies.
– ORIGIN Old English.

breadcrumb ● n. a small fragment of bread.

breaded ● adj. (of food) coated with breadcrumbs and fried.

breadfruit ● n. a large round starchy fruit of a tropical tree, used as a vegetable.

breadline ● n. (usu. in phr. **on the breadline**) Brit. the poorest condition in which it is acceptable to live.

breadth ● n. **1** the distance from side to side of something. **2** wide range: *breadth of experience.*
– ORIGIN related to **BROAD**.

breadwinner ● n. a person who supports their family with the money they earn.

break ● v. (**breaks, breaking, broke**; past part. **broken**) **1** separate into pieces as a result of a blow or strain. **2** stop working. **3** interrupt (a sequence or course). **4** fail to observe (a rule or agreement). **5** crush the spirit of. **6** beat (a record). **7** work out (a code). **8** make a rush or dash. **9** soften (a fall). **10** suddenly make or become public. **11** (of a person's voice) falter and change tone. **12** (of a boy's voice) become deeper at puberty. **13** (of the weather) change suddenly. **14** (of a storm, the dawn, or a day) begin. ● n. **1** a pause, gap, or short rest. **2** an instance of breaking, or the point where something is broken. **3** a sudden rush or dash. **4** informal a chance: *his big break had finally come.* **5** (also **break of serve** or **service break**) Tennis the winning of a game against an opponent's serve. **6** Snooker & Billiards an uninterrupted series of successful shots.
– PHRASES **break away** escape. **break one's back** work hard to achieve something. **break the back of** accomplish the main part of. **break down 1** suddenly stop functioning. **2** lose control of one's emotions when upset. **break in 1** force entry to a building. **2** interrupt with a statement. **3** make (a horse) used to being ridden. **4** make (new shoes) comfortable by wearing them. **break into** burst into (laughter, song, a run, etc.). **break off** stop suddenly. **break out 1** (of something undesirable) start suddenly. **2** escape. **3** informal open and start using: *break out the champagne.* **break out in** suddenly be affected by: *she broke out in spots.* **break up** (of a gathering or relationship) end or part. **break wind** release gas from the anus. **break with** go against (a tradition). **give someone a break** informal stop putting pressure on someone.
– DERIVATIVES **breakable** adj.
– ORIGIN Old English.

breakage ● n. **1** the action of breaking something or the fact of being broken. **2** a thing that has been broken.

breakaway ● n. **1** a departure from something long-standing: *rock was a breakaway from pop.* **2** (in sport) a sudden attack or forward movement.

break-dancing ● n. an energetic and acrobatic style of street dancing.

breakdown ● n. **1** a failure or collapse. **2** an analysis of costs or figures.

breaker ● n. **1** a heavy sea wave that breaks on the shore. **2** a person that breaks up old machinery.

breakfast ● n. the first meal of the day. ● v. eat this meal.
– ORIGIN from **BREAK** + **FAST**[2].

break-in ● n. an illegal forced entry in order to steal something.

breakneck ● adj. dangerously fast.

breakthrough ● n. a sudden important development or success.

breakwater ● n. a barrier built out into the sea to protect a coast or harbour from the force of waves.

bream ● n. (pl. **bream**) a greenish-bronze freshwater fish.
– ORIGIN Old French *bresme.*

breast ● n. **1** either of the two organs on a woman's chest which produce milk after pregnancy. **2** a person's or animal's chest region. ● v. **1** face and move forwards against or through: *I watched him breast the wave.* **2** reach the top of (a hill).

– ORIGIN Old English.

breastbone • n. a thin flat bone running down the centre of the chest and connecting the ribs.

breastfeed • v. (**breastfeeds, breastfeeding, breastfed**) feed (a baby) with milk from the breast.

breastplate • n. a piece of armour covering the chest.

breaststroke • n. a style of swimming in which the arms are pushed forwards and then swept back while the legs are tucked in and kicked out.

breath • n. **1** air taken into or sent out of the lungs. **2** an instance of breathing in or out. **3** a slight movement of air. **4** a sign or hint: *he avoided the slightest breath of scandal.*

– PHRASES **take someone's breath away** astonish or inspire someone. **under one's breath** in a very quiet voice.

– DERIVATIVES **breathable** adj.

– ORIGIN Old English, 'smell, scent'.

breathalyse (US **breathalyze**) • v. (**breathalyses, breathalysing, breathalysed**; US **breathalyzes, breathalyzing, breathalyzed**) use a breathalyser to measure how much alcohol (a driver) has consumed.

breathalyser (US trademark **Breathalyzer**) • n. a device for measuring the amount of alcohol in a driver's breath.

– ORIGIN from **BREATH** and **ANALYSE**.

breathe • v. (**breathes, breathing, breathed**) **1** take air into the lungs and send it out again. **2** say quietly. **3** let air or moisture in or out.

– PHRASES **breathe down someone's neck** **1** follow closely behind someone. **2** constantly check up on someone.

breather • n. informal a brief pause for rest.

breathing space • n. an opportunity to relax or decide what to do next.

breathless • adj. **1** gasping for breath. **2** feeling or causing great excitement, fear, etc.

– DERIVATIVES **breathlessly** adv. **breathlessness** n.

breathtaking • adj. astonishing or impressive.

breath test • n. a test in which a driver is made to blow into a breathalyser.

breathy • adj. having the sound of breathing: *a breathy laugh.*

breccia /bre-chi-uh/ • n. rock consisting of angular fragments cemented by finer chalky material.

– ORIGIN Italian, 'gravel'.

Brecht E
/brekht/, (Eugen) Bertolt (Friedrich) (1898–1956), German dramatist and poet. He is noted for works such as *The Threepenny Opera*, a combination of drama and music written in collaboration with Kurt Weill, and the plays *Mother Courage* and *The Caucasian Chalk Circle*.
– DERIVATIVES **Brechtian** adj.

bred past and past part. of **BREED**.

breech • n. the back part of a rifle or gun barrel.

– ORIGIN Old English, 'garment covering the loins and thighs'.

breech birth • n. a birth in which the baby's buttocks or feet are delivered first.

breeches • pl. n. short trousers fastened just below the knee.

breed • v. (**breeds, breeding, bred**) **1** (of animals) mate and produce offspring. **2** keep (animals) for the purpose of producing young. **3** bring up in a particular way: *she'd had rebellion bred into her.* **4** produce: *familiarity breeds contempt.* • n. **1** a particular type within a species of animals or plants. **2** a type: *a new breed of businessman.*

– DERIVATIVES **breeder** n.

– ORIGIN Old English.

breeding • n. upper class good manners seen as being passed on from one generation to another.

breeze • n. **1** a gentle wind. **2** informal something easy to do. • v. (**breezes, breezing, breezed**) informal come or go in a casual way.

– ORIGIN prob. from Spanish and Portuguese *briza*.

breeze block • n. Brit. a lightweight building brick made from cinders, sand, and cement.

– ORIGIN French *braise* 'live coals'.

breezy • adj. (**breezier, breeziest**) **1** pleasantly windy. **2** relaxed and cheerily brisk: *a breezy matter-of-fact manner.*

Bremen E
/bray-muhn/ a state of NE Germany; capital, Bremen.

Brest[1] E
/brest/ a port and naval base in France, on the Atlantic coast of Brittany.

Brest[2] E
/brest/ a river port and industrial city in Belarus. The peace treaty between Germany and Russia was signed there in March 1918.

brethren archaic pl. of **BROTHER**. • pl. n. fellow Christians or members of a male religious order.

Breton[1] /bre-tuhn/ • n. **1** a person from Brittany. **2** the language of Brittany.

– ORIGIN Old French, 'Briton'.

Breton[2] E
/bre-tuhn/, André (1896–1966), French poet, essayist, and critic, who launched the surrealist movement.

Breughel E
var. of **BRUEGEL**.

breve /*rhymes with* sleeve/ • n. Music a note twice as long as a semibreve.

– ORIGIN from **BRIEF**.

breviary /bree-vi-uh-ri/ • n. (pl. **breviaries**) a book containing the service for each day, used in the Roman Catholic Church.

– ORIGIN Latin *breviarium* 'summary'.

brevity /brev-i-ti/ • n. **1** concise and exact use of words. **2** shortness of time.

– ORIGIN Latin *brevitas*.

brew • v. **1** make (beer) by soaking, boiling, and fermentation. **2** make (tea or coffee) by mixing it with hot water. **3** begin to develop: *trouble is brewing.* • n. something brewed.

– DERIVATIVES **brewer** n.

– ORIGIN Old English.

brewery • n. (pl. **breweries**) a place where beer is made.

b

Brezhnev E
/**brezh**-nef/, Leonid (Ilich) (1906–82), Soviet statesman, General Secretary of the Communist Party of the USSR 1966–82 and President 1977–82. He was largely responsible for the invasion of Czechoslovakia (1968).

briar (also **brier**) • n. a prickly shrub, especially a wild rose.
– ORIGIN Old English.

bribe • v. (**bribes, bribing, bribed**) dishonestly pay (someone) to act in one's favour. • n. something offered in an attempt to bribe.
– DERIVATIVES **bribery** n.
– ORIGIN Old French *briber* 'beg'.

bric-a-brac • n. various objects of little value.
– ORIGIN French.

brick • n. **1** a small rectangular block of fired clay, used in building. **2** Brit. informal, dated a helpful and reliable person. • v. block or enclose with a wall of bricks.
– PHRASES **bricks and mortar** buildings.
– ORIGIN German or Dutch *bricke, brike*.

brickbat • n. a critical remark.

bricklayer • n. a person whose job is to build structures with bricks.

bridal • adj. relating to a bride or a newly married couple.

bride • n. a woman on her wedding day or just before and after the event.
– ORIGIN Old English.

bridegroom • n. a man on his wedding day or just before and after the event.
– ORIGIN Old English, 'bride man'.

bridesmaid • n. a girl or woman who accompanies a bride on her wedding day.

Bride, St E
/bree-duh, bryd/ see **BRIDGET, ST**[1].

bridge[1] • n. **1** a structure carrying a road, path, or railway across a river, road, etc. **2** the platform on a ship from which the captain and officers direct its course. **3** the upper bony part of a person's nose. **4** a false tooth or teeth held in place by natural teeth on either side. **5** the part on a stringed instrument over which the strings are stretched. • v. (**bridges, bridging, bridges**) be or make a bridge over or between.
– ORIGIN Old English.

bridge[2] • n. a card game played by two teams, each of two players.
– ORIGIN unknown.

bridgehead • n. a strong position gained by an army inside enemy territory.

Bridges, E
Robert (Seymour) (1844–1930), English poet and literary critic, Poet Laureate 1913–30.

Bridget, St[1] E
(also **Bride** or **Brigid**) (6th century), Irish abbess and a patron saint of Ireland. Feast day, 1 February.

Bridget, St[2] E
(also **Birgitta** /beer-git-tuh/) (*c*.1303–73), Swedish nun and patron saint of Sweden. Feast day, 23 July.

Bridgetown E
the capital of Barbados.

bridging loan • n. esp. Brit. a sum of money lent by a bank to cover the period of time between the buying of one thing and the selling of another.

bridle • n. the headgear used to control a horse. • v. (**bridles, bridling, bridled**) **1** put a bridle on. **2** bring under control. **3** show resentment or anger.
– ORIGIN Old English.

bridleway (also **bridle path**) • n. Brit. a path along which horse riders have right of way.

Brie /bree/ • n. a kind of soft, mild, creamy cheese.
– ORIGIN named after *Brie* in northern France.

brief • adj. **1** lasting a short time. **2** using few words. **3** (of clothing) not covering much of the body. • n. **1** esp. Brit. a summary of the facts in a case given to a barrister to argue in court. **2** informal a solicitor or barrister. **3** esp. Brit. a set of instructions about a task. • v. instruct (someone) before a task.
– DERIVATIVES **briefly** adv.
– ORIGIN Old French.

briefcase • n. a flat rectangular case for carrying books and documents.

briefing • n. a meeting for giving information or instructions.

briefs • pl. n. short underpants.

brier • n. var. of **BRIAR**.

brig • n. a square-rigged sailing ship with two masts.
– ORIGIN from **BRIGANTINE**.

brigade • n. **1** a subdivision of an army, made up of battalions and forming part of a division. **2** informal, usu. derog. a particular group of people: *the anti-smoking brigade*.
– ORIGIN French.

brigadier /bri-guh-**deer**/ • n. a rank of officer in the British army, above colonel.

brigand /**brig**-uhnd/ • n. a member of a gang of bandits.
– ORIGIN Italian *brigante* '(person) contending'.

brigantine /**brig**-uhn-teen/ • n. a sailing ship with two masts.
– ORIGIN Italian *brigantino*.

bright • adj. **1** giving out or filled with light. **2** (of colour) vivid and bold. **3** intelligent and quick-witted. **4** cheerfully lively. **5** (of prospects) good.
– DERIVATIVES **brightly** adv. **brightness** n.
– ORIGIN Old English.

brighten • v. **1** make or become brighter. **2** make or become more cheerful.

Brighton E
a resort on the south coast of England, noted for its Regency architecture. It became a city (with Hove) in 2000.

bright spark • n. ironic a clever person.

Brigid, St E
/bri-jid/ see **BRIDGET, ST**[1].

brill • n. a flatfish similar to the turbot.
– ORIGIN unknown.

brilliance (also **brilliancy**) • n. **1** intense brightness. **2** great talent or intelligence.

brilliant • adj. **1** (of light or colour) very bright or vivid. **2** extremely clever or talented. **3** Brit. informal excellent.
– DERIVATIVES **brilliantly** adv.

– ORIGIN French *brillant.*

brim • **n. 1** the projecting edge around the bottom of a hat. **2** the lip of a cup, bowl, etc. • **v.** (**brims, brimming, brimmed**) fill or be full to the point of overflowing.
– DERIVATIVES **brimful** adj.
– ORIGIN perh. from German *Bräme* 'trimming'.

brimstone /brim-stohn/ • **n.** archaic sulphur.
– ORIGIN Old English.

brindle (also **brindled**) • **adj.** (of an animal) brownish with streaks of another colour.
– ORIGIN prob. Scandinavian.

brine • **n.** water with a high salt content.
– ORIGIN Old English.

bring • **v.** (**brings, bringing, brought**) **1** carry or accompany to a place. **2** cause to be in a particular position or state. **3** cause (someone) to receive: *his first novel brought him a great deal of money.* **4** (**bring oneself to do**) force oneself to do (something unpleasant). **5** begin (legal action).
– PHRASES **bring about** cause to happen. **bring forward** move (something planned) to an earlier time. **bring the house down** make an audience laugh or applaud very enthusiastically. **bring off** achieve successfully. **bring on** cause (something unpleasant) to occur. **bring out 1** produce and launch: *the band are bringing out a video.* **2** emphasize (a feature). **bring round 1** make conscious again. **2** persuade (someone) to adopt a point of view. **bring to bear** apply (influence or pressure). **bring to pass** literary cause to happen. **bring up 1** look after (a child) until it is an adult. **2** raise (a matter) for discussion.
– DERIVATIVES **bringer** n.
– ORIGIN Old English.

Brink, E
André (b.1935), South African novelist and dramatist. His novels include *A Dry White Season* and *A Chain of Voices.*

brink • **n. 1** the edge of land before a steep slope or a body of water. **2** the point where a new or unpleasant situation is about to begin: *on the brink of a crisis.*
– ORIGIN Scandinavian.

brinkmanship /bringk-muhn-ship/ (US also **brinksmanship**) • **n.** the pursuing of a dangerous course of action to the limits of safety before stopping.

briny /*rhymes with* tiny/ • **adj.** salty. • **n.** (**the briny**) Brit. informal the sea.

brio /bree-oh/ • **n.** energy or liveliness.
– ORIGIN Italian.

brioche /bree-osh/ • **n.** a small, round, sweet French roll.
– ORIGIN French.

briquette /bri-ket/ (also **briquet**) • **n.** a block of compressed coal dust or peat used as fuel.
– ORIGIN French, 'small brick'.

Brisbane E
/briz-buhn/ the capital of Queensland, Australia.

brisk • **adj. 1** active and energetic. **2** slightly abrupt: *a brisk, businesslike tone.*
– DERIVATIVES **briskly** adv.
– ORIGIN prob. from French *brusque* 'lively, fierce'.

brisket • **n.** meat from the breast of a cow.
– ORIGIN perh. from Old Norse, 'cartilage, gristle'.

bristle • **n.** a short, stiff hair. • **v.** (**bristles, bristling, bristled**) **1** (of hair or fur) stand upright away from the skin. **2** react angrily or defensively. **3** (**bristle with**) be covered with.
– DERIVATIVES **bristly** adj.
– ORIGIN Old English.

Bristol E
a city and port on the River Avon in SW England.

Bristol Channel E
a wide inlet of the Atlantic between South Wales and the south-western peninsula of England, narrowing into the estuary of the River Severn.

Brit • **n.** informal a British person.

Britain E
the island containing England, Wales, and Scotland, and including the small adjacent islands. See also **GREAT BRITAIN, UNITED KINGDOM.**

Britain, Battle of E
a series of air battles fought over Britain (August–October 1940), in which the RAF successfully resisted raids by the larger German air force.

Britannia /bri-tan-yuh/ • **n.** a woman wearing a helmet and carrying a shield and trident, used to represent Britain.
– ORIGIN Latin, 'Britain'.

British • **adj.** relating to Great Britain.
– DERIVATIVES **Britishness** n.
– ORIGIN Old English.

British Antarctic Territory E
that part of Antarctica claimed by Britain, designated in 1962 from territory that was formerly part of the Falkland Islands Dependencies.

British Broadcasting Corporation E
a public corporation (established in 1927) for radio and television broadcasting in Britain.

British Columbia E
a province on the west coast of Canada; capital, Victoria.

British Empire E
a former empire consisting of Great Britain and its colonies, territories, and dependencies, which reached its peak around 1920, when over 600 million people were ruled from London.

British Honduras E
former name for **BELIZE.**

British Isles E
a group of islands lying off the coast of NW Europe, including Britain, Ireland, the Isle of Man, the Hebrides, the Orkney Islands, the Shetland Islands, the Scilly Isles, and the Channel Islands.

British Library E
the national library and main copyright library of Britain.

b

British Museum E
a national museum of antiquities in London, established with public funds in 1753.

British Summer Time E
time as advanced one hour ahead of Greenwich Mean Time for daylight saving in the UK between March and October.

British Virgin Islands E
see **Virgin Islands**.

Briton • n. **1** a British person. **2** a native of southern Britain before and during Roman times.

Brittany E
/brit-tuh-ni/ a region of NW France, forming a peninsula between the Bay of Biscay and the English Channel.

Britten E
/brit-t'n/, (Edward) Benjamin, Lord Britten of Aldeburgh (1913–76), English composer, pianist, and conductor. His works include the operas *Peter Grimes* and *A Midsummer Night's Dream*. He was a co-founder of the Aldeburgh festival with the tenor Peter Pears (1948).

brittle • adj. **1** hard but likely to break easily. **2** sharp or artificial: *a brittle laugh*.
– ORIGIN from Old English, 'break up'.

Brno E
/ber-noh/ an industrial city in the Czech Republic, the capital of Moravia.

broach • v. **1** raise (a subject) for discussion. **2** pierce or open (a container) to draw out liquid.
– ORIGIN Old French *brochier*.

broad • adj. **1** larger than usual from side to side; wide. **2** of a specified distance wide. **3** large in area or range: *a broad expanse of paddy fields*. **4** without detail: *a broad outline*. **5** (of a hint) clear and unmistakable. **6** (of an accent) very strong. • n. N. Amer. informal a woman.
– PHRASES **broad daylight** full daylight.
– DERIVATIVES **broadly** adv.
– ORIGIN Old English.

broad bean • n. a large flat green bean.

broadcast • v. (**broadcasts, broadcasting, broadcast**; past part. **broadcast** or **broadcasted**) **1** transmit by radio or television. **2** tell to many people. **3** scatter (seeds). • n. a radio or television programme.
– DERIVATIVES **broadcaster** n.

broadcloth • n. a fine cloth of wool or cotton.

broaden • v. make or become broader.

broadleaved (also **broadleaf**) • adj. having fairly wide flat leaves.

broadloom • n. carpet woven in wide widths.

broad-minded • adj. tolerant or open-minded.

Broads E
(also **the Norfolk Broads**) a network of shallow freshwater lakes, linked by slow-moving rivers, in Norfolk and Suffolk.

broadsheet • n. a newspaper printed on large sheets of paper.

broadside • n. **1** a strongly worded critical attack. **2** hist. a firing of all the guns from one side of a warship.

Broadway E
a street running through the length of Manhattan in New York, famous for its theatres.

brocade • n. a rich fabric woven with a raised pattern.
– ORIGIN Spanish and Portuguese *brocado*.

broccoli /brok-kuh-li/ • n. a vegetable with heads of small green or purplish flower buds.
– ORIGIN Italian.

brochure /broh-sher/ • n. a magazine containing information about a product or service.
– ORIGIN French, 'something stitched'.

broderie anglaise /broh-duh-ri ong-glayz/ • n. open embroidery on fine white cotton or linen.
– ORIGIN French, 'English embroidery'.

brogue • n. **1** a strong outdoor shoe with perforated patterns in the leather. **2** a noticeable Irish or Scottish accent when speaking English.
– ORIGIN Scottish Gaelic and Irish *bróg*.

broil • v. esp. N. Amer. grill (meat or fish).
– ORIGIN Old French *bruler* 'to burn'.

broiler • n. a young chicken suitable for roasting, grilling, or barbecuing.

broke past of **break**. • adj. informal having no money.
– PHRASES **go for broke** informal risk everything in one determined effort.

broken past part. of **break**. • adj. (of a language) spoken hesitantly and with many mistakes.

broken-down • adj. in a bad condition or not working.

broken-hearted • adj. overwhelmed by grief or disappointment.

broken home • n. a family in which the parents are divorced or separated.

broker • n. a person who buys and sells goods or shares for others. • v. (**brokers, brokering, brokered**) arrange (a deal or plan).
– DERIVATIVES **brokerage** n.
– ORIGIN Old French *brocour*.

brolly • n. (pl. **brollies**) Brit. informal an umbrella.

bromide /broh-myd/ • n. Chem. a compound of bromine with another element or group.

bromine /broh-meen/ • n. a dark red liquid chemical element.
– ORIGIN Greek *brōmos* 'a stink'.

bronchi pl. of **bronchus**.

bronchial /brong-ki-uhl/ • adj. relating to the bronchi or to the smaller tubes into which they divide.

bronchitis • n. inflammation of the bronchial tubes.

bronchus /brong-kuhss/ • n. (pl. **bronchi** /brong-kee/) any of the major air passages of the lungs which spread out from the windpipe.
– ORIGIN Greek *bronkhos* 'windpipe'.

bronco • n. (pl. **broncos**) a wild or half-tamed horse of the western US.
– ORIGIN Spanish, 'rough, rude'.

Brontë E
/bron-ti/ the name of three English novelists: **Charlotte** (1816–55), author of *Jane Eyre*; **Emily** (1818–48), author of *Wuthering Heights*; and **Anne** (1820–49), author of *Agnes Grey*.

brontosaurus /bron-tuh-sor-uhss/ ● **n.** former term for **APATOSAURUS**.
– ORIGIN from Greek *brontē* 'thunder' + *sauros* 'lizard'.

Bronx E
/brongks/ (**the Bronx**) a borough in the north-east of New York City.

bronze ● **n. 1** a yellowish-brown alloy of copper and tin. **2** a yellowish-brown colour. **3** an object made of bronze. ● **v.** (**bronzes, bronzing, bronzed**) make suntanned.
– ORIGIN Italian *bronzo*.

Bronze Age ● **n.** a period that came after the Stone Age and before the Iron Age, when weapons and tools were made of bronze.

bronze medal ● **n.** a medal made of or coloured bronze, awarded for third place in a competition.

brooch ● **n.** an ornament fastened to clothing with a hinged pin and catch.
– ORIGIN Old French *broche* 'spit for roasting'.

brood ● **n. 1** a family of young animals produced at one hatching or birth. **2** informal all the children in a family. ● **v. 1** think deeply about an unpleasant subject. **2** (**brooding**) darkly menacing: *the brooding moorland*. **3** (of a bird) sit on (eggs) to hatch them.
– ORIGIN Old English.

broody ● **adj. 1** (of a hen) wishing to hatch eggs. **2** informal (of a woman) having a strong desire to have a baby. **3** thoughtful and unhappy.

brook[1] ● **n.** a small stream.
– ORIGIN Old English.

brook[2] ● **v.** formal tolerate: *she would brook no criticism*.
– ORIGIN Old English 'use, possess'.

Brooke, E
Rupert (Chawner) (1887–1915), English poet, known for his wartime poetry.

Brooklyn E
a borough of New York City.

Brookner E
/bruuk-ner/, Anita (b.1928), English novelist, author of *Hotel du Lac*.

Brooks, E
Mel (b.1927; born *Melvin Kaminsky*), American film director and comic actor, who directed *The Producers* and *Blazing Saddles*.

broom ● **n. 1** a long-handled brush used for sweeping. **2** a shrub with yellow flowers and small or few leaves.
– ORIGIN Old English.

broomstick ● **n.** the handle of a broom, on which witches are said to fly.

Bros ● **pl. n.** brothers.

broth ● **n.** soup made of meat or vegetable chunks cooked in stock.
– ORIGIN Old English.

brothel ● **n.** a house where men visit prostitutes.
– ORIGIN related to Old English 'degenerate, deteriorate'.

brother ● **n. 1** a man or boy in relation to other children of his parents. **2** a male colleague or friend. **3** (pl. also **brethren**) a (male) fellow Christian. **4** a member of a religious order of men: *a Benedictine brother*.
– DERIVATIVES **brotherly** adj.
– ORIGIN Old English.

brotherhood ● **n. 1** the relationship between brothers. **2** a feeling of fellowship and closeness. **3** a group of people linked by a shared interest or belief: *a religious brotherhood*.

brother-in-law ● **n.** (pl. **brothers-in-law**) **1** the brother of one's wife or husband. **2** the husband of one's sister or sister-in-law.

brougham /broo-uhm/ ● **n.** hist. a horse-drawn carriage with a roof and an open driver's seat in front.
– ORIGIN named after Lord *Brougham* (1778–1868), its designer.

brought past and past part. of **BRING**.

USAGE brought
For an explanation of the difference between **brought** and **bought**, see the note at **BOUGHT**.

brouhaha /broo-hah-hah/ ● **n.** a noisy and overexcited reaction.
– ORIGIN French.

brow ● **n. 1** a person's forehead. **2** an eyebrow. **3** the highest point of a hill or pass.
– ORIGIN Old English.

browbeat ● **v.** (**browbeats, browbeating, browbeat**; past part. **browbeaten**) bully or frighten with words or looks.

Brown[1], E
Sir Arthur Whitten (1886–1948), Scottish aviator, who with Sir John William Alcock made the first non-stop transatlantic flight in 1919.

Brown[2], E
James (b.1928), American soul and funk singer and songwriter, a leading figure in the development of funk in the 1960s.

Brown[3], E
John (1800–59), American anti-slavery campaigner. He was executed after raiding a government arsenal at Harpers Ferry in Virginia, intending to arm black slaves and start a revolt.

Brown[4], E
Lancelot (1716–83; known as **Capability Brown**), English landscape gardener, noted for his natural-looking landscaped parks.

brown ● **adj. 1** of a colour produced by mixing red, yellow, and blue, as of rich soil. **2** dark-skinned or suntanned. ● **n.** brown colour or material. ● **v. 1** make or become brown. **2** (**be browned off**) informal be irritated or depressed.
– DERIVATIVES **brownish** adj.
– ORIGIN Old English.

Brownian motion ● **n.** Physics the irregular movement of tiny particles in a fluid, caused by the surrounding molecules striking against them.
– ORIGIN named after the Scottish botanist Robert *Brown* (1773–1858).

Brownie ● **n.** (pl. **Brownies**) **1** (Brit. also

b

Brownie Guide) a member of the junior branch of the Guides Association. **2** (**brownie**) a small square of rich chocolate cake.
– PHRASES **brownie point** informal an imaginary mark given for an attempt to please.

Browning[1], E
Elizabeth Barrett (1806–61; born *Elizabeth Barrett*), English poet, known for *Sonnets from the Portuguese*. In 1846 she eloped to Italy with Robert Browning.

Browning[2], E
Robert (1812–89), English poet, known for his collection *Dramatic Lyrics*, containing the poems 'The Pied Piper of Hamelin' and 'My Last Duchess'.

brown owl ● n. = TAWNY OWL.

brown rice ● n. unpolished rice with only the husk of the grain removed.

brownstone ● n. N. Amer. a building faced with a reddish-brown sandstone.

brown sugar ● n. unrefined or partially refined sugar.

brown trout ● n. (pl. **trout**) the common trout of European lakes and rivers.

browse ● v. (**browses**, **browsing**, **browsed**) **1** look at goods or text in a leisurely way. **2** Computing look at (data files) via a network. **3** (of an animal) feed on leaves, twigs, etc. ● n. an act of browsing.
– DERIVATIVES **browsable** adj.
– ORIGIN Old French *brost* 'young shoot'.

browser ● n. **1** a person or animal that browses. **2** a program used to navigate the Internet.

Bruce[1], E
Robert the, see **ROBERT I**.

Bruce[2], E
Lenny (1925–66; born *Leonard Alfred Schneider*), American comedian, notorious for his risqué humour.

Bruckner E
/**bruuk**-ner/, Anton (1824–96), Austrian composer and organist. He wrote ten symphonies, four masses, and a *Te Deum*.

Bruegel E
/**broy**-g'l/ (also **Breughel** or **Brueghel**), Pieter (*c*.1525–69; known as **Pieter Bruegel the Elder**), Flemish artist, who produced landscapes, religious allegories, and satires of peasant life.

Bruges E
/broo*zh*/ a city in NW Belgium, capital of the province of West Flanders.

bruise ● n. **1** an area of discoloured skin on the body, caused by a blow bursting underlying blood vessels. **2** a similar area of damage on a fruit, vegetable, or plant. ● v. (**bruises**, **bruising**, **bruised**) cause or develop a bruise.
– ORIGIN Old English.

bruiser ● n. informal, derog. a tough, aggressive person.

bruit /*rhymes with* fruit/ ● v. spread (a report or rumour) widely.
– ORIGIN Old French *bruire* 'to roar'.

Brummell E
/**brum**-m'l/, George Bryan (1778–1840; known as **Beau Brummell**), English dandy, who greatly influenced British fashion in the early years of the 19th century.

Brummie (also **Brummy**) Brit. informal ● n. (pl. **Brummies**) a person from Birmingham. ● adj. relating to Birmingham.

brunch ● n. a late morning meal eaten instead of breakfast and lunch.

Brunei E
/broo-**ny**/ a sultanate on the NW coast of Borneo; capital, Bandar Seri Begawan.
– DERIVATIVES **Bruneian** /broo-**ny**-uhn/ adj. & n.

Brunel E
/bruu-**nel**/, Isambard Kingdom (1806–59), English engineer. He was chief engineer of the Great Western Railway and designer of the Clifton suspension bridge (Bristol) and the first transatlantic steamship, the *Great Western* (1838).

Brunelleschi E
/broo-nuh-**less**-ki/, Filippo (1377–1446), Italian architect, noted for the engineering feat of building the massive dome of Florence cathedral.

brunette (US also **brunet**) ● n. a woman or girl with dark brown hair.
– ORIGIN French *brun* 'brown'.

Bruno, St E
/**broo**-noh/ (*c*.1032–1101), German-born French churchman, founder of the Carthusian religious order. Feast day, 6 October.

Brunswick E
/**brunz**-wik/ an industrial city and former duchy and state of northern Germany.

brunt ● n. the chief impact of something bad: *education will bear the brunt of the cuts*.
– ORIGIN unknown.

brush[1] ● n. **1** an implement with a handle and a block of bristles, hair, or wire. **2** an act of brushing. **3** a brief encounter with something bad. **4** the bushy tail of a fox. ● v. **1** clean, smooth, or apply with a brush. **2** touch lightly. **3** (**brush off**) dismiss curtly. **4** (**brush up on** or **brush up**) work to regain (a former skill).
– ORIGIN Old French *broisse*.

brush[2] ● n. N. Amer. & Austral./NZ undergrowth, small trees, and shrubs.
– ORIGIN Old French *broce*.

brushed ● adj. (of fabric) having soft raised fibres.

brushwood ● n. undergrowth, twigs, and small branches.

brusque /bruusk/ ● adj. abrupt or offhand.
– DERIVATIVES **brusquely** adv.
– ORIGIN French, 'lively, fierce'.

Brussels E
the capital of Belgium and home of the headquarters of the European Commission.

Brussels sprout (also **Brussel sprout**) ● n. the bud of a variety of cabbage, eaten as a vegetable.

brut /*rhymes with* loot/ ● adj. (of sparkling wine) very dry.

– ORIGIN French, 'raw, rough'.

brutal • adj. **1** savagely violent. **2** not attempting to hide unpleasantness: *brutal honesty.*
– DERIVATIVES **brutality** n. **brutally** adv.

brutalize (also **brutalise**) • v. (**brutalizes, brutalizing, brutalized**) **1** make brutal by frequent exposure to violence. **2** treat in a cruel way.

brute • n. **1** a violent person or animal. **2** informal a cruel person. • adj. involving physical strength rather than reasoning: *brute force.*
– DERIVATIVES **brutish** adj.
– ORIGIN Latin *brutus* 'dull, stupid'.

Bruton E
/broo-t'n/, John (Gerard) (b.1947), Irish Fine Gael statesman, Taoiseach (Prime Minister) 1994–7.

Brutus, E
Marcus Junius (85–42 BC), Roman senator who, with Cassius, led the conspirators who assassinated Julius Caesar in 44.

bryony /bry-uh-ni/ • n. (pl. **bryonies**) a climbing hedgerow plant with red berries.
– ORIGIN Greek *bruōnia.*

BS • abbrev. **1** Bachelor of Surgery. **2** British Standard(s).

BSc • abbrev. Bachelor of Science.

BSE • abbrev. bovine spongiform encephalopathy, a fatal disease of cattle which is believed to be related to Creutzfeldt–Jakob disease in humans.

BSI • abbrev. British Standards Institution.

BST • abbrev. British Summer Time.

BT • abbrev. British Telecom.

bubble • n. **1** a thin sphere of liquid enclosing a gas. **2** an air- or gas-filled sphere in a liquid or a solidified liquid such as glass. **3** a transparent dome. • v. (**bubbles, bubbling, bubbled**) **1** (of a liquid) contain rising bubbles of gas. **2** (**bubble with**) be filled with: *she was bubbling with enthusiasm.*

bubble and squeak • n. Brit. a dish of cooked cabbage fried with cooked potatoes.

bubble bath • n. sweet-smelling liquid added to bathwater to make it foam.

bubblegum • n. chewing gum that can be blown into bubbles.

bubbly • adj. **1** containing bubbles. **2** cheerful and high-spirited. • n. informal champagne.

bubonic plague • n. a form of plague passed on by rat fleas, causing swellings in the groin or armpits.
– ORIGIN Greek *boubōn* 'groin or swelling in the groin'.

buccaneer /buk-kuh-neer/ • n. **1** hist. a pirate. **2** a recklessly adventurous person.
– ORIGIN French *boucanier.*

Buchan E
/buk-k'n/, John, 1st Baron Tweedsmuir (1875–1940), Scottish novelist, known for his adventure stories including *The Thirty-Nine Steps.*

Buchanan E
/byoo-**kan**-nuhn/, James (1791–1868), American Democratic statesman, 15th President of the US 1857–61.

Bucharest E
/boo-kuh-**rest**/ the capital of Romania.

Buchenwald E
/**boo**-kuhn-vald/ a Nazi concentration camp in the Second World War, near the village of Buchenwald in eastern Germany.

buck[1] • n. **1** the male of some animals, e.g. deer and rabbits. **2** a vertical jump performed by a horse. **3** archaic a fashionable young man. • v. **1** (of a horse) perform a buck. **2** go against: *the shares bucked the market trend.* **3** (**buck up**) informal make or become more cheerful.
– ORIGIN Old English.

buck[2] • n. N. Amer. & Austral./NZ informal a dollar.
– ORIGIN unknown.

buck[3] • n. an object placed in front of a poker player whose turn it is to deal.
– PHRASES **the buck stops here** informal the responsibility for something cannot be avoided. **pass the buck** informal shift responsibility to someone else.
– ORIGIN unknown.

bucket • n. **1** an open container with a handle, used to carry liquids. **2** (**buckets**) informal large quantities of liquid. • v. (**buckets, bucketing, bucketed**) Brit. informal (**bucket down**) rain heavily.
– DERIVATIVES **bucketful** n.
– ORIGIN Old French *buquet.*

bucket shop • n. Brit. a travel agency that sells cheap air tickets.

Buckingham Palace E
the London home of the British sovereign since 1837.

Buckinghamshire E
a county of central England; county town, Aylesbury

buckle • n. a flat frame with a hinged pin, used as a fastener. • v. (**buckles, buckling, buckled**) **1** fasten with a buckle. **2** bend and give way under pressure. **3** (**buckle down**) tackle a task with determination.
– ORIGIN Latin *buccula* 'cheek strap of a helmet'; sense 2 is from French *boucler* 'to bulge'.

buckram • n. coarse cloth stiffened with paste, used in binding books.
– ORIGIN Old French *boquerant.*

Bucks • abbrev. Buckinghamshire.

buckshee • adj. informal, esp. Brit. free of charge.
– ORIGIN from BAKSHEESH.

buckshot • n. coarse lead shot used in shotgun shells.

buckskin • n. soft leather made from the skin of deer or sheep.

buck-teeth • pl. n. teeth that project over the lower lip.
– DERIVATIVES **buck-toothed** adj.

buckthorn • n. a thorny shrub which bears black berries.

buckwheat • n. the starchy seeds of a plant, used for fodder or making flour.
– ORIGIN Dutch *boecweite* 'beech wheat'.

bucolic /byoo-kol-ik/ • adj. relating to country life.
– ORIGIN Greek *boukolikos.*

bud • n. a growth on a plant which develops into a leaf, flower, or shoot. • v. (**buds, budding, budded**) form a bud or buds.

– ORIGIN unknown.

Budapest E
/boo-duh-**pest**/ the capital of Hungary.

Buddha E
/**buud**-duh/ (also **the Buddha**) a title given to the founder of Buddhism, Siddartha Gautama (*c.*563–*c.*460 BC). Born an Indian prince, he renounced wealth and family and after achieving enlightenment while meditating, taught all who came to learn from him.

Buddhism /**buud**-di-z'm/ ● n. a religion founded by Buddha, which has no god and teaches that all existence is suffering; freedom from this (nirvana) may be achieved by following the 'eightfold path' that combines ethical behaviour, wisdom, and mental discipline (including meditation).
– DERIVATIVES **Buddhist** n. & adj.

budding ● adj. beginning and showing signs of promise: *their budding relationship.*

buddleia /**bud**-dli-uh/ ● n. a shrub with clusters of lilac, white, or yellow flowers.
– ORIGIN named after the English botanist Adam *Buddle* (d. 1715).

buddy ● n. (pl. **buddies**) N. Amer. informal a close friend.
– ORIGIN perh. from BROTHER.

Budge, E
Don (1915–2000; born *John Donald Budge*), American tennis player. He was the first to win the four major singles championships—Australia, France, Britain, and the US—in one year (1938).

budge ● v. (**budges**, **budging**, **budged**) **1** make or cause to make the slightest movement. **2** change or cause to change an opinion.
– ORIGIN French *bouger* 'to stir'.

budgerigar ● n. a small Australian parakeet.
– ORIGIN Aboriginal.

budget ● n. **1** an estimate of income and spending for a set period of time. **2** the amount of money needed or available for a purpose. **3** (**Budget**) a regular estimate of national income and spending put forward by a finance minister. ● v. (**budgets**, **budgeting**, **budgeted**) allow for in a budget. ● adj. inexpensive.
– DERIVATIVES **budgetary** adj.
– ORIGIN Old French *bougette* 'little leather bag'.

budgie ● n. (pl. **budgies**) informal = BUDGERIGAR.

Buenos Aires E
/bway-nuhss **I**-reez/ the capital and chief port of Argentina.

buff[1] ● n. a yellowish-beige colour. ● v. polish.
– PHRASES **in the buff** informal naked.
– ORIGIN prob. from French *buffle* 'buffalo'.

buff[2] ● n. informal a person who knows a lot about a particular subject: *a film buff.*
– ORIGIN from BUFF[1], first referring to people who watched fires in New York, because of the firemen's buff uniforms.

buffalo ● n. (pl. **buffalo** or **buffaloes**) **1** a heavily built wild ox with backward-curving horns. **2** the North American bison.
– ORIGIN Latin *bufalus.*

Buffalo Bill E
(1846–1917; born *William Frederick Cody*), American showman, who toured with his Wild West Show.

buffer ● n. **1** (**buffers**) Brit. shock-absorbing devices at the end of a railway track or on a railway vehicle. **2** a person or thing that lessens the impact of harmful effects: *friends can provide a buffer against stress.* **3** (also **buffer solution**) Chem. a solution which resists changes in pH when acid or alkali is added to it.
– ORIGIN prob. from former *buff* 'deaden the force of something'.

buffet[1] /**boo**-fay, **buf**-fay/ ● n. **1** a meal made up of several dishes from which guests serve themselves. **2** a room or counter selling light meals or snacks.
– ORIGIN Old French *bufet* 'stool'.

buffet[2] /**buf**-fit/ ● v. (**buffets**, **buffeting**, **buffeted**) (especially of wind or waves) strike repeatedly and violently.
– ORIGIN Old French *buffeter.*

buffoon /buh-**foon**/ ● n. a ridiculous but amusing person.
– DERIVATIVES **buffoonery** n.
– ORIGIN French *bouffon.*

bug ● n. **1** an insect of an order including aphids. **2** informal any small insect. **3** informal an illness caused by a harmful micro-organism: *he'd just recovered from a flu bug.* **4** informal an enthusiasm for something: *the sailing bug.* **5** a microphone used for secret recording. **6** an error in a computer program or system. ● v. (**bugs**, **bugging**, **bugged**) **1** hide a microphone in (a room or telephone). **2** informal annoy.
– ORIGIN unknown.

bugbear ● n. a cause of anxiety or irritation.
– ORIGIN prob. from former *bug* 'evil spirit' + BEAR[2].

bug-eyed ● adj. with bulging eyes.

bugger Brit. vulgar ● n. **1** derog. a person who commits buggery. **2** a person regarded with contempt or pity. **3** an annoyingly awkward thing. ● v. **1** practise buggery with. **2** cause serious harm or trouble to. **3** (**bugger off**) go away. ● exclam. used to express annoyance.
– PHRASES **bugger about/around** act stupidly. **bugger all** nothing.
– ORIGIN Old French *bougre* 'heretic'.

buggery ● n. anal intercourse.

buggy ● n. (pl. **buggies**) **1** a small motor vehicle with an open top. **2** hist. a light horse-drawn vehicle for one or two people.
– ORIGIN unknown.

bugle ● n. a brass instrument like a small trumpet.
– DERIVATIVES **bugler** n.
– ORIGIN Latin *buculus* 'little ox'.

build ● v. (**builds**, **building**, **built**) **1** construct by putting parts together. **2** (often **build up**) increase over time. **3** (**build on**) use as a basis for further development. **4** (**build in/into**) make (something) a permanent part of (a larger structure). ● n. the size or form of someone or something: *she was of slim build.*
– DERIVATIVES **builder** n.
– ORIGIN Old English.

building ● n. **1** a structure with a roof and walls. **2** the process or trade of building houses and other structures.

building society ● n. Brit. a financial organization which pays interest on members' investments and lends money for mortgages.

build-up ● n. **1** a gradual increase. **2** a period of excitement and preparation before an event.

built past and past part. of **BUILD**. ● adj. of a particular physical build: *a slightly built woman.*

built-in ● adj. included as part of a larger structure: *a worktop with a built-in cooker.*

built-up ● adj. (of an area) covered by many buildings.

Bujumbura E
/boo-juhm-**boor**-uh/ the capital of Burundi. Former name (until 1962) **USUMBURA**.

Bulawayo E
/buul-uh-**way**-oh/ an industrial city in western Zimbabwe.

bulb ● n. **1** the rounded base of the stem of some plants, from which the roots grow. **2** a light bulb.
– ORIGIN Greek *bolbos* 'onion'.

bulbous ● adj. **1** round or bulging. **2** (of a plant) growing from a bulb.

Bulgaria E
/buul-**gair**-i-uh, bul-**gair**-i-uh/ a country in SE Europe on the western shores of the Black Sea; capital, Sofia.
– DERIVATIVES **Bulgarian** adj. & n.

bulge ● n. **1** a rounded swelling on a flat surface. **2** informal a temporary increase: *a bulge in the birth rate.* ● v. (**bulges**, **bulging**, **bulged**) **1** swell or stick out. **2** be full of: *a briefcase bulging with documents.*
– DERIVATIVES **bulgy** adj.
– ORIGIN Latin *bulga* 'leather bag'.

bulimia /buu-**lim**-i-uh/ (also **bulimia nervosa** /ner-**voh**-suh/) ● n. a disorder which causes bouts of overeating, followed by fasting or self-induced vomiting.
– DERIVATIVES **bulimic** adj. & n.
– ORIGIN Greek *boulimia* 'ravenous hunger'.

bulk ● n. **1** the mass or size of something large. **2** the greater part. **3** a large mass or shape. ● adj. large in quantity: *bulk orders.* ● v. **1** be very important. **2** (**bulk up/out**) make (something) appear bigger than it really is.
– PHRASES **in bulk** (of goods) in large quantities.
– ORIGIN prob. from Old Norse, 'cargo'.

bulkhead ● n. a barrier between separate areas inside a ship, aircraft, etc.

bulky ● adj. (**bulkier**, **bulkiest**) large and awkward to handle.

bull[1] ● n. **1** an uncastrated male animal of the cattle family. **2** a large male animal, e.g. a whale or elephant. **3** Brit. a bullseye.
– PHRASES **like a bull in a china shop** behaving clumsily in a delicate situation. **take the bull by the horns** deal decisively with a difficult situation.
– ORIGIN Old Norse.

bull[2] ● n. an order or announcement issued by the Pope.
– ORIGIN Latin *bulla* 'bubble, seal'.

bulldog ● n. a short breed of dog with a powerful lower jaw and a flat wrinkled face.

bulldog clip ● n. Brit. trademark a metal device with two flat plates held together by a spring, used to hold papers together.

bulldoze ● v. (**bulldozes**, **bulldozing**, **bulldozed**) **1** clear or destroy with a bulldozer. **2** informal use force to deal with or persuade.
– ORIGIN from **BULL**[1] + *-doze*, from **DOSE**.

bulldozer ● n. a tractor with a broad curved blade at the front for clearing ground.

bullet ● n. **1** a small missile fired from a gun. **2** a solid circle printed before each item in a list.
– ORIGIN French *boulet* 'small ball'.

bulletin ● n. **1** a short official statement or summary of news. **2** a regular newsletter or report.
– ORIGIN Italian *bullettino* 'little passport'.

bulletin board ● n. **1** N. Amer. a noticeboard. **2** a site on a computer system where any user can read or write messages.

bullfighting ● n. the sport of baiting and killing a bull for public entertainment.
DERIVATIVES **bullfight** n. **bullfighter** n.

bullfinch ● n. a finch with grey and black plumage and a pink breast.

bullfrog ● n. a very large frog with a deep croak.

bullion /**buul**-li-uhn/ ● n. gold or silver in bulk before being made into coins.
– ORIGIN Old French *bouillon*.

bullish ● adj. aggressively confident.

bullock ● n. a castrated male animal of the cattle family, raised for beef.
– ORIGIN Old English.

bullring ● n. an arena where bullfights are held.

bullrush ● n. var. of **BULRUSH**.

bullseye ● n. the centre of the target in sports such as archery and darts.

bullshit vulgar ● n. nonsense. ● v. (**bullshits**, **bullshitting**, **bullshitted**) talk nonsense in an attempt to deceive.
– DERIVATIVES **bullshitter** n.

bull terrier ● n. a dog that is a cross-breed of bulldog and terrier.

bully ● n. (pl. **bullies**) a person who intimidates or frightens weaker people. ● v. (**bullies**, **bullying**, **bullied**) intimidate.
– PHRASES **bully for you!** ironic an expression of admiration or approval.
– ORIGIN prob. from Dutch *boele* 'lover'.

bulrush (also **bullrush**) ● n. a tall waterside plant with a long brown head.
– ORIGIN prob. from **BULL**[1] in the sense 'large, coarse'.

bulwark /**buul**-werk/ ● n. **1** a defensive wall. **2** an extension of a ship's sides above deck level.
– ORIGIN German and Dutch *bolwerk*.

bum[1] ● n. Brit. informal a person's bottom.
– ORIGIN unknown.

bum[2] informal ● n. N. Amer. **1** a homeless person or beggar. **2** a lazy or worthless person. ● v. (**bums**, **bumming**, **bummed**) get by asking or begging. ● adj. bad: *not one bum note was played.*
– ORIGIN prob. from **BUMMER**.

bumbag ● n. Brit. informal a small pouch on a belt, worn round the hips.

bumble ● v. (**bumbles**, **bumbling**, **bumbled**) move or speak in an awkward or confused way.
– DERIVATIVES **bumbler** n.
– ORIGIN from **BOOM**[1].

b

bumblebee ● n. a large hairy bee with a loud hum.

bumf (also **bumph**) ● n. informal, esp. Brit. useless or dull printed information.
– ORIGIN from slang *bum-fodder*.

bummer ● n. informal an annoying or disappointing thing.
– ORIGIN perh. from German *Bummler* 'loafer'.

bump ● n. **1** a light blow or collision. **2** a hump or swelling on a level surface. ● v. **1** knock or run into with a jolt. **2** move with much jolting. **3** (**bump into**) meet by chance. **4** (**bump off**) informal murder. **5** (**bump up**) informal make (something) larger or seem larger.
– DERIVATIVES **bumpy** adj. (**bumpier**, **bumpiest**).
– ORIGIN perh. Scandinavian.

bumper ● n. a bar fixed across the front or back of a motor vehicle to reduce damage in a collision. ● adj. exceptionally large or successful: *a bumper crop*.

bumph ● n. var. of BUMF.

bumpkin ● n. an unsophisticated person from the countryside.
– ORIGIN perh. from Dutch *boomken* 'little tree' or *bommekijn* 'little barrel'.

bumptious ● adj. self-confident or proud in an annoying way.
– ORIGIN from BUMP.

bun ● n. **1** a small cake or bread roll. **2** a tight coil of hair at the back of the head.
– PHRASES **have a bun in the oven** informal be pregnant.
– ORIGIN unknown.

bunch ● n. **1** a number of things grouped or held together. **2** informal a group of people. ● v. collect or form into a bunch.
– ORIGIN unknown.

Bundesbank E
/buun-duhz-bangk/ the central bank of Germany.

Bundestag E
/buun-duhz-tahg/ the Lower House of Parliament in Germany.

bundle ● n. **1** a group of things or a quantity of material tied or wrapped up together. **2** informal a large amount of money. ● v. (**bundles**, **bundling**, **bundled**) **1** tie or roll up in a bundle. **2** (**be bundled up**) be dressed in many warm clothes. **3** informal push or carry forcibly.
– ORIGIN perh. from Old English, 'a binding'.

bunfight ● n. Brit. informal, humorous a grand party or other function.

bung[1] ● n. a stopper for a hole in a container. ● v. **1** close with a bung. **2** (**bung up**) block up.
– ORIGIN Dutch *bonghe*.

bung[2] Brit. informal ● v. put or throw somewhere casually. ● n. a bribe.

bungalow ● n. a house with only one storey.
– ORIGIN Hindi, 'belonging to Bengal'.

bungee /bun-ji/ (also **bungee cord** or **rope**) ● n. a long rubber band encased in nylon, used for securing luggage and in bungee jumping.
– ORIGIN unknown.

bungee jumping ● n. the sport of leaping from a high place, held by a bungee around the ankles.

bungle ● v. (**bungles**, **bungling**, **bungled**) perform (a task) clumsily or unskilfully. ● n. a mistake or failure.
– DERIVATIVES **bungler** n.
– ORIGIN unknown.

bunion ● n. a painful swelling on the big toe.
– ORIGIN Old French *buignon*.

bunk[1] ● n. a narrow shelf-like bed.
– ORIGIN unknown.

bunk[2] ● v. Brit. informal be absent from school or work without permission.
– PHRASES **do a bunk** leave hurriedly.
– ORIGIN unknown.

bunk bed ● n. a structure made up of two beds, one above the other.

bunker ● n. **1** a large container for storing fuel. **2** an underground shelter for use in wartime. **3** a hollow filled with sand on a golf course.
– ORIGIN Scots 'seat or bench'.

bunkum ● n. informal, dated nonsense.
– ORIGIN named after *Buncombe* County in North Carolina.

bunny ● n. (pl. **bunnies**) informal **1** a child's term for a rabbit. **2** (also **bunny girl**) a nightclub hostess wearing a skimpy costume with ears and a tail.
– ORIGIN dialect *bun* 'squirrel, rabbit'.

Bunsen burner /bun-s'n/ ● n. a small gas burner used in laboratories.
– ORIGIN named after the German chemist Robert *Bunsen* (1811–99).

bunting[1] ● n. a songbird with brown streaked plumage and a boldly marked head.
– ORIGIN unknown.

bunting[2] ● n. flags and streamers used as decorations.
– ORIGIN unknown.

Buñuel E
/buun-wel/, Luis (1900–83), Spanish film director. Influenced by surrealism, he collaborated with Salvador Dali on his first film, *Un Chien andalou*; other films include *The Discreet Charm of the Bourgeoisie*.

Bunyan E
/bun-yuhn/, John (1628–88), English writer and Nonconformist preacher, author of *The Pilgrim's Progress*, which he began while in prison for unlicensed preaching.

buoy /boy/ ● n. a floating object that marks safe channels for boats. ● v. **1** keep afloat. **2** (often **be buoyed up**) make or remain cheerful and confident.
– ORIGIN prob. from Dutch *boye*, *boeie*; the verb is from Spanish *boyar* 'to float'.

buoyant ● adj. **1** able to keep afloat. **2** cheerful and optimistic.
– DERIVATIVES **buoyancy** n.

BUPA /boo-puh/ ● abbrev. British United Provident Association, a private health insurance organization.

bur ● n. see BURR.

Burbage E
/ber-bij/, Richard (*c*.1567–1619), English actor, the first performer of most of Shakespeare's great tragic roles: Hamlet, Othello, Lear, and Richard III.

burble ● v. (**burbles**, **burbling**, **burbled**) **1** make a continuous murmuring noise. **2** speak at length in a way that is hard to understand. ● n. **1** continuous murmuring noise. **2** rambling speech.

burden ● n. **1** a heavy load. **2** a cause of hardship, worry, or grief. **3** the main responsibility for a task. ● v. **1** load heavily. **2** cause worry, hardship, or grief.
– ORIGIN Old English.

burdensome ● adj. troublesome.

burdock ● n. a plant with large leaves and prickly flowers.
– ORIGIN from **BUR** + **DOCK**[3].

bureau /byoor-oh/ ● n. (pl. **bureaux** or **bureaus**) **1** Brit. a writing desk with an angled top opening downwards to form a writing surface. **2** N. Amer. a chest of drawers. **3** an office for carrying out particular business: *a news bureau*. **4** a government department.
– ORIGIN French.

bureaucracy /byuu-rok-ruh-si/ ● n. (pl. **bureaucracies**) **1** a system of government in which most decisions are taken by state officials rather than by elected representatives. **2** excessively complicated administrative procedure.

bureaucrat ● n. an official seen as being excessively concerned with following guidelines rigidly.
– DERIVATIVES **bureaucratic** adj.

bureau de change /byoo-roh duh shon*zh*/ ● n. (pl. **bureaux de change** /byoo-roh duh shon*zh*/) a place where one can exchange foreign money.
– ORIGIN French, 'office of exchange'.

burette /byuu-ret/ (US also **buret**) ● n. a glass tube with measurements on it and a tap at one end, for delivering known amounts of a liquid.
– ORIGIN French.

burgeon /ber-juhn/ ● v. grow or increase rapidly.
– ORIGIN Old French *bourgeonner* 'put out buds'.

burger ● n. a hamburger.

Burgess[1], E
Anthony (1917–93; pen name of *John Anthony Burgess Wilson*), English novelist, author of *A Clockwork Orange* and *Earthly Powers*.

Burgess[2], E
Guy (Francis de Moncy) (1911–63), British Foreign Office official and spy. A Soviet agent from the 1930s, he was charged with espionage in 1951 and fled to the USSR with Donald Maclean.

burgher /ber-guh/ ● n. archaic a citizen of a town or city.
– ORIGIN from **BOROUGH**.

burglar ● n. a person who commits burglary.
– ORIGIN Old French *burgier* 'pillage'.

burglary ● n. (pl. **burglaries**) illegal entry into a building in order to steal its contents.

burgle ● v. (**burgles**, **burgling**, **burgled**) commit burglary in (a building).

Burgundy E
/ber-guhn-di/ a region and former duchy of east central France, noted for its wine.

burgundy /ber-guhn-di/ ● n. (pl. **burgundies**) **1** a red wine from Burgundy. **2** a deep red colour.

burial ● n. the burying of a dead body.

Burke[1], E
Edmund (1729–97), British writer and Whig politician. He wrote in support of political moderation and emancipation, especially in respect of Roman Catholics and the American colonies.

Burke[2], E
Robert O'Hara (1820–61), Irish explorer, who in 1860–1 led the first expedition by white men from south to north across Australia, but died on the return journey.

Burkina Faso E
/ber-kee-nuh fas-soh/ a landlocked country in western Africa; capital, Ouagadougou. Former name (until 1984) **UPPER VOLTA**.
– DERIVATIVES **Burkinan** adj. & n.

burlap /ber-lap/ ● n. coarse canvas woven from jute or hemp.
– ORIGIN unknown.

burlesque /ber-lesk/ ● n. **1** a comically exaggerated imitation. **2** N. Amer. a variety show. ● v. (**burlesques**, **burlesquing**, **burlesqued**) imitate in a comically exaggerated way.
– ORIGIN French.

burly ● adj. (**burlier**, **burliest**) (of a person) large and strong.
– DERIVATIVES **burliness** n.
– ORIGIN prob. from Old English 'stately'.

Burma E
/ber-muh/ a country in SE Asia, on the Bay of Bengal; capital, Rangoon. Official name **UNION OF MYANMAR**.

Burmese ● n. (pl. **Burmese**) **1** a member of the largest ethnic group of Burma. **2** a person from Burma. ● adj. relating to Burma or the Burmese.

burn[1] ● v. (**burns**, **burning**, **burned** or esp. Brit. **burnt**) **1** (of a fire) flame or glow while using up a fuel. **2** be or cause to be harmed by fire. **3** use (a fuel) as a source of heat or energy. **4** (of the skin) become red and painful through exposure to the sun. **5** (**be burning with**) be entirely possessed by (a desire or emotion). **6** (**burn out**) become exhausted through overwork. ● n. an injury caused by burning.
– PHRASES **burn one's boats** (or **bridges**) do something which makes turning back impossible. **burn the candle at both ends** go to bed late and get up early. **burn the midnight oil** work late into the night.
– ORIGIN Old English.

burn[2] ● n. Sc. & N. Engl. a small stream.
– ORIGIN Old English.

Burne-Jones, E
Sir Edward (Coley) (1833–98), English Pre-Raphaelite painter and designer of tapestry and stained glass.

burner ● n. **1** a part of a cooker, lamp, etc. that gives out a flame. **2** a device for burning something.

Burnett E
/ber-net/, Frances (Eliza) Hodgson (1849–1924), British-born American novelist. She is best known for her children's novels, including *Little Lord Fauntleroy* and *The Secret Garden*.

b

Burney, E
Fanny (1752–1840; born *Frances Burney*), English novelist. Her works include *Evelina*, *Cecilia*, and *Letters and Diaries*.

burning ● adj. **1** very deeply felt. **2** of urgent interest and importance: *the burning issues of the day.*

burnish ● v. polish by rubbing. ● n. the shine on a polished surface.
– ORIGIN Old French *brunir* 'make brown'.

burnous /ber-nooss/ (US also **burnoose**) ● n. a long hooded cloak worn by Arabs.
– ORIGIN Arabic.

burnout ● n. physical or mental collapse.

Burns, E
Robert (1759–96), Scottish poet, best known for poems such as 'Tam o' Shanter', and for the old Scottish songs he collected, including 'Auld Lang Syne'. Burns Night is celebrated on his birthday, 25 January.

burnt (also **burned**) past and past part. of BURN[1].

burp informal ● v. **1** belch. **2** make (a baby) belch after feeding. ● n. a belch.

burr ● n. **1** a whirring sound. **2** a strong pronunciation of the letter *r.* **3** (also **bur**) a prickly seed case or flower head that clings to clothing and animal fur. ● v. make a whirring sound.
– ORIGIN prob. Scandinavian.

Burroughs[1] E
/bur-rohz/ , Edgar Rice (1875–1950), American novelist, known for his adventure stories about Tarzan.

Burroughs[2] E
/bur-rohz/, William (Seward) (1914–97), American novelist, who wrote *The Naked Lunch*.

burrow ● n. a hole or tunnel dug by a small animal as a home. ● v. **1** make a burrow. **2** hide underneath or delve into something.
– DERIVATIVES **burrower** n.
– ORIGIN from BOROUGH.

bursar ● n. esp. Brit. a person who manages the financial affairs of a college or school.
– ORIGIN Latin *bursarius.*

bursary ● n. (pl. **bursaries**) esp. Brit. a grant for study.

burst ● v. (**bursts**, **bursting**, **burst**) **1** break suddenly and violently apart. **2** be very full. **3** move or be opened suddenly and forcibly. **4** (**be bursting with**) feel full of (an emotion). **5** suddenly do something as a result of strong emotion: *she burst out crying.* ● n. **1** an instance of bursting. **2** a sudden brief outbreak: *a burst of activity.* **3** a period of continuous effort.
– ORIGIN Old English.

Burton[1], E
Richard (1925–84; born *Richard Jenkins*), Welsh actor. His films include *Who's Afraid of Virginia Woolf?*, in which he co-starred with Elizabeth Taylor (to whom he was twice married).

Burton[2], E
Sir Richard (Francis) (1821–90), English explorer, anthropologist, and translator, who with John Hanning Speke was the first European to see Lake Tanganyika (1858).

burton ● n. (in phr. **go for a burton**) Brit. informal be ruined, destroyed, or killed.
– ORIGIN perh. referring to *Burton* ale, from Burton-upon-Trent.

Burundi E
/buu-ruun-di/ a central African country on the east side of Lake Tanganyika; capital, Bujumbura.
– DERIVATIVES **Burundian** adj. & n.

bury ● v. (**buries**, **burying**, **buried**) **1** put underground. **2** place (a dead body) in the earth or a tomb. **3** cause to disappear or become unnoticeable. **4** (**bury oneself**) involve oneself deeply in something.
– ORIGIN Old English.

bus ● n. (pl. **buses**; US also **busses**) a large motor vehicle carrying customers along a fixed route. ● v. (**buses**, **busing**, **bused**; also **busses**, **bussing**, **bussed**) transport or travel in a bus.
– ORIGIN from OMNIBUS.

Busby, E
Sir Matt (1909–94), Scottish-born footballer and manager of Manchester United 1945–69.

busby ● n. (pl. **busbies**) a tall fur hat worn by certain military regiments.
– ORIGIN unknown.

Bush[1], E
George (Herbert Walker) (b.1924), American Republican statesman, 41st President of the US 1989–93.

Bush[2], E
George W(alker) (b.1946), American Republican statesman, 43rd President of the US (since 2001). He is the son of George Bush, the 41st President of the US.

bush[1] ● n. **1** a shrub or clump of shrubs. **2** (**the bush**) (in Australia and Africa) wild or uncultivated country.
– ORIGIN Old French *bois* 'wood'.

bush[2] ● n. Brit. **1** a metal lining for a hole in which something fits or revolves. **2** a sleeve that protects an electric cable.
– ORIGIN Dutch *busse.*

bushbaby ● n. (pl. **bushbabies**) a small African mammal with very large eyes.

bushed ● adj. informal exhausted.

bushel ● n. **1** Brit. a measure of capacity equal to 8 gallons (equivalent to 36.4 litres). **2** US a measure of capacity equal to 64 US pints (equivalent to 35.2 litres).
– ORIGIN Old French *boissel.*

Bushman ● n. **1** a member of any of several aboriginal peoples of southern Africa. **2** (**bushman**) a person who lives or travels in the Australian bush.

bush telegraph ● n. an informal network by which information is spread quickly.

bushy ● adj. (**bushier**, **bushiest**) **1** growing thickly. **2** covered with bush or bushes.

business ● n. **1** a person's regular occupation. **2** work to be done or matters to be attended to. **3** a person's concern. **4** commercial activity. **5** a commercial organization. **6** informal a difficult matter. **7** (**the business**) informal an excellent person or thing.
– PHRASES **mind one's own business** avoid

interfering in other people's affairs.
– ORIGIN Old English, 'anxiety'.

businesslike • adj. efficient and practical.

businessman (or **businesswoman**) • n. a person who works in commerce.

busk • v. play music in the street in order to be given money by passers-by.
– DERIVATIVES **busker** n.
– ORIGIN from former French *busquer* 'seek'.

busman's holiday • n. leisure time spent doing the same thing that one does at work.

bust[1] • n. **1** a woman's breasts. **2** a sculpture of a person's head, shoulders, and chest.
– ORIGIN French *buste*.

bust[2] informal • v. (**busts, busting, busted** or **bust**) **1** break, split, or burst. **2** esp. N. Amer. raid, search, or arrest. • n. **1** a period of economic difficulty. **2** a police raid. • adj. **1** damaged; broken. **2** bankrupt.
– ORIGIN from BURST.

bustard /buss-terd/ • n. a large swift-running bird of open country.
– ORIGIN perh. from Old French *bistarde* and *oustarde*.

buster • n. informal, esp. N. Amer. a form of address to a man or boy.

bustier /buss-ti-ay/ • n. a close-fitting strapless top for women.
– ORIGIN French.

bustle[1] • v. (**bustles, bustling, bustled**) **1** move energetically or noisily. **2** (of a place) be full of activity. • n. excited activity and movement.
– DERIVATIVES **bustling** adj.
– ORIGIN perh. from former *busk* 'prepare'.

bustle[2] • n. hist. a pad or frame worn under a skirt to puff it out behind.
– ORIGIN unknown.

bust-up • n. informal a serious quarrel or fight.

busty • adj. informal having large breasts.

busy • adj. (**busier, busiest**) **1** having a great deal to do. **2** currently occupied with an activity. **3** excessively detailed. • v. (**busies, busying, busied**) (**busy oneself**) keep occupied.
– DERIVATIVES **busily** adv. **busyness** n.
– ORIGIN Old English.

busybody • n. an interfering or nosy person.

busy Lizzie • n. Brit. a plant with many red, pink, or white flowers.

but • conj. **1** in spite of that; however. **2** on the contrary. **3** other than; otherwise than: *one cannot but sympathize.* **4** archaic without it being the case that: *it never rains but it pours.* • prep. except; apart from: *the last but one.* • adv. only. • n. an objection: *no buts - just get out of here!*
– PHRASES **but for 1** except for. **2** if it were not for. **but then** on the other hand.
– ORIGIN Old English, 'outside, except'.

butane /byoo-tayn/ • n. a flammable gas present in petroleum and natural gas, used as a fuel.
– ORIGIN Latin *butyrum* 'butter'.

butch • adj. informal aggressively masculine.
– ORIGIN perh. from BUTCHER.

butcher • n. **1** a person who cuts up and sells meat as a trade. **2** a person who slaughters animals for food. **3** a person who kills brutally or at random. • v. (**butchers, butchering, butchered**) **1** slaughter or cut up (an animal) for food. **2** kill (someone) brutally. **3** spoil (something) by doing it badly: *the film was butchered by the studio.*
– DERIVATIVES **butchery** n.
– ORIGIN Old French *bochier*.

> **Bute** E
> /byoot/, John Stuart, 3rd Earl of (1713–92), British Tory statesman, Prime Minister 1762–3.

> **Butler**, E
> Samuel (1835–1902), English novelist, author of *Erewhon* and the semi-autobiographical *The Way of All Flesh*.

butler • n. the chief manservant of a house.
– ORIGIN Old French *bouteillier* 'cup-bearer'.

butt[1] • v. **1** hit with the head or horns. **2** (**butt in**) interrupt a conversation or activity. • n. a rough push with the head.
– ORIGIN Old French *boter*.

butt[2] • n. **1** an object of criticism or ridicule. **2** a target or range in archery or shooting.
– ORIGIN Old French *but*.

butt[3] • n. **1** the thicker end of a tool or a weapon. **2** the stub of a cigar or a cigarette. **3** N. Amer. informal a person's bottom. • v. be next to or against.
– ORIGIN Dutch *bot* 'stumpy'.

butter • n. a pale yellow fatty substance made by churning cream. • v. (**butters, buttering, buttered**) **1** spread with butter. **2** (**butter up**) informal flatter (someone).
– PHRASES **look as if butter wouldn't melt in one's mouth** informal appear innocent while being the opposite.
– ORIGIN Latin *butyrum*.

butter bean • n. a large flat edible bean.

buttercream • n. a mixture of butter and icing sugar used in cake making.

buttercup • n. a plant with bright yellow cup-shaped flowers.

butterfat • n. the natural fat found in milk and dairy products.

butterfingers • n. informal a person who often drops things.

butterfly • n. **1** an insect with two pairs of large wings, which feeds on nectar. **2** a showy or frivolous person: *a social butterfly.* **3** (**butterflies**) informal a fluttering sensation felt in the stomach when one is nervous. **4** a stroke in swimming in which both arms are raised out of the water and lifted forwards together.
– ORIGIN Old English.

butter icing • n. = BUTTERCREAM.

buttermilk • n. the slightly sour liquid left after butter has been churned.

butterscotch • n. a sweet made with butter and brown sugar.

buttery[1] • adj. containing, tasting like, or covered with butter.

buttery[2] • n. (pl. **butteries**) Brit. a room in a college where food is kept and sold to students.
– ORIGIN Old French *boterie* 'butt-store'.

buttie • n. (pl. **butties**) var. of BUTTY.

buttock • n. either of the two round fleshy parts of the human body that form the bottom.
– ORIGIN Old English.

button • n. **1** a small disc sewn on to a garment to fasten it by being pushed through a buttonhole. **2** a knob on a piece of equipment

which is pressed to operate it. ● v. fasten or be fastened with buttons.
– PHRASES **button one's lip** informal stop oneself from talking.
– ORIGIN Old French *bouton*.

buttonhole ● n. **1** a slit made in a garment to receive a button for fastening. **2** Brit. a flower or spray worn in a lapel buttonhole. ● v. (**buttonholes**, **buttonholing**, **buttonholed**) informal stop and hold (someone) in conversation.

button mushroom ● n. a young unopened mushroom.

buttress /but-triss/ ● n. **1** a projecting support built against a wall. **2** a projecting part of a hill or mountain. ● v. support or strengthen.
– ORIGIN from Old French *ars bouterez* 'thrusting arch'.

butty (also **buttie**) ● n. (pl. **butties**) Brit. informal a sandwich.
– ORIGIN from BUTTER.

buxom /buk-suhm/ ● adj. (of a woman) attractively plump and large-breasted.
– ORIGIN Old English, 'to bend'.

buy ● v. (**buys**, **buying**, **bought**) **1** get in return for payment. **2** get (something) by sacrifice or great effort. **3** informal accept the truth of. ● n. informal a purchase.
– PHRASES **buy out** pay (someone) to give up a share in something. **buy time** delay an event so as to have longer to improve one's own position. **have bought it** informal be killed.
– ORIGIN Old English.

buyer ● n. **1** a person who buys. **2** a person employed to buy stock for a business.

buyer's market ● n. a situation in which goods or shares are plentiful and buyers can keep prices down.

buyout ● n. the purchase of a controlling share in a company.

buzz ● n. **1** a low, continuous humming sound. **2** the sound of a buzzer or telephone. **3** an atmosphere of excitement and activity. **4** informal a thrill. **5** informal a rumour. ● v. **1** make a humming sound. **2** signal with a buzzer. **3** move quickly. **4** (**buzz off**) informal go away. **5** have an air of excitement or activity.

buzzard /buz-zerd/ ● n. **1** a large bird of prey which soars in wide circles. **2** N. Amer. a vulture.
– ORIGIN Old French *busard*.

buzzer ● n. an electrical device that makes a buzzing noise to attract attention.

buzzword ● n. informal a technical word or phrase that has become fashionable.

by ● prep. **1** through the action or means of. **2** indicating an amount or the size of a margin: *the shot missed her by miles.* **3** showing multiplication. **4** indicating the end of a time period. **5** beside. **6** past and beyond. **7** during. **8** according to. ● adv. so as to go past. ● n. (pl. **byes**) var. of BYE[1].
– PHRASES **by and by** before long. **by the by** in passing. **by and large** on the whole. [ORIGIN first describing the handling of a ship both to the wind and off it.]
– ORIGIN Old English.

by- (also **bye-**) ● prefix less important; secondary: *by-election.*

bye[1] ● n. **1** the moving of a competitor straight to the next round of a competition because they have no opponent. **2** Cricket a run scored from a ball that passes the batsman without being hit.
– ORIGIN from BY.

bye[2] ● exclam. informal goodbye.

by-election ● n. Brit. an election held during a government's term of office to fill a vacant seat.

Byelorussia E
/byel-uh-ruush-uh/ = BELORUSSIA.

bygone ● adj. belonging to an earlier time.
– PHRASES **let bygones be bygones** forget past disagreements.

by-law (also **bye-law**) ● n. **1** Brit. a rule made by a local authority. **2** a rule made by a company or society to control its members.
– ORIGIN prob. from former *byrlaw* 'local law or custom'.

byline ● n. **1** a line in a newspaper naming the writer of an article. **2** (also **byeline**) (in soccer) the part of the goal line to either side of the goal.

bypass ● n. **1** a road passing round a town. **2** an operation to help the circulation of blood by directing it through a new passage. ● v. go past or round.

by-product ● n. a product produced in the making of something else.

Byrd[1] E
/berd/, Richard (Evelyn) (1888–1957), American explorer, naval officer, and aviator, the first to fly over the South Pole (1929).

Byrd[2] E
/berd/, William (1543–1623), English composer, noted for his Latin masses and his Anglican Great Service.

byre /*rhymes with* fire/ ● n. Brit. a cowshed.
– ORIGIN Old English.

Byron E
/by-ruhn/, George Gordon, 6th Baron (1788–1824), English poet. His work, such as *Childe Harold's Pilgrimage* and *Don Juan*, greatly influenced Romanticism.

Byronic /by-ron-ik/ ● adj. **1** referring to Lord Byron. **2** (of a man) interestingly mysterious and moody.

bystander ● n. a person who is present at an event but does not take part.

byte /*rhymes with* white/ ● n. a unit of information stored in a computer, equal to eight bits.
– ORIGIN from BIT[4] and BITE.

byway ● n. a minor road or path.

byword ● n. **1** a notable example of something: *his name became the byword for luxury.* **2** a saying.

Byzantine /bi-zan-tyn/ ● adj. **1** relating to Byzantium, the Byzantine Empire, or the Eastern Orthodox Church. **2** excessively complicated. **3** very crafty or underhand.

Byzantine Empire E
the empire in SE Europe and Asia Minor formed from the eastern part of the Roman Empire in AD 395. It came to an end with the loss of Constantinople (formerly Byzantium) to the Ottoman Turks in 1453.

Byzantium E
/bi-**zan**-ti-uhm, by-**zan**-ti-uhm/ an ancient Greek city, founded in the 7th century BC, at the southern end of the Bosporus. It was rebuilt by Constantine the Great as Constantinople (modern Istanbul).

C[1] (also **c**) ● n. (pl. **Cs** or **C's**) **1** the third letter of the alphabet. **2** referring to the third item in a set. **3** Music the first note of the scale of C major. **4** the Roman numeral for 100. [ORIGIN from Latin *centum* 'hundred'.]

C[2] ● abbrev. **1** Celsius or centigrade. **2** (©) copyright. **3** Physics coulomb(s). ● symb. the chemical element carbon.

c ● abbrev. **1** cent(s). **2** (before a date or amount) circa. **3** (**c.**) century or centuries.

Ca ● symb. the chemical element calcium.

ca. ● abbrev. (before a date or amount) circa.

CAB ● abbrev. Citizens' Advice Bureau.

cab ● n. **1** (also **taxi cab**) a taxi. **2** the driver's compartment in a truck, bus, or train.
ORIGIN from CABRIOLET.

cabal /kuh-**bal**/ ● n. a secret political group.
– ORIGIN Latin *cabala* 'Kabbalah'.

cabaret /**kab**-uh-ray/ ● n. entertainment held in a nightclub or restaurant while the audience sit at tables.
– ORIGIN Old French, 'inn'.

cabbage ● n. a vegetable with thick green or purple leaves around a core of young leaves.
– ORIGIN Old French *caboche* 'head'.

cabby (also **cabbie**) ● n. (pl. **cabbies**) informal a taxi driver.

caber /**kay**-ber/ ● n. a roughly trimmed tree trunk that is thrown in the Scottish Highland sport of tossing the caber.
– ORIGIN Scottish Gaelic *cabar* 'pole'.

cabin ● n. **1** a private compartment on a ship. **2** the passenger compartment in an aircraft. **3** a small wooden shelter or house.
– ORIGIN Old French *cabane*.

cabin cruiser ● n. a motor boat with a living area.

cabinet ● n. **1** a cupboard with drawers or shelves for storing articles. **2** a piece of furniture housing a radio, television, or speaker. **3** (also **Cabinet**) a committee of senior government ministers.
– ORIGIN from CABIN.

cabinetmaker ● n. a skilled joiner who makes furniture.

cable ● n. **1** a thick rope of wire or fibre. **2** a wire or wires for transmitting electricity or telecommunication signals.
– ORIGIN Old French *chable*.

cable car ● n. a small carriage hung from a moving cable and travelling up and down a mountainside.

cable television ● n. a system in which television programmes are transmitted by cable.

caboodle ● n. (in phr. **the whole caboodle** or **the whole kit and caboodle**) informal the whole number of people or things in question.
– ORIGIN uncertain.

Cabot E
/**kab**-uht/, John (*c.*1450–*c.*1498; Italian name *Giovanni Caboto*), Italian explorer and navigator, who sailed from Bristol in 1497 in search of Asia, but in fact discovered the mainland of North America.

cabriolet /**kab**-ri-oh-lay/ ● n. **1** a car with a roof that folds down. **2** a light two-wheeled carriage with a hood, drawn by one horse.
– ORIGIN French.

cacao /kuh-**kah**-oh/ ● n. the bean-like seeds of a tropical American tree, from which cocoa and chocolate are made.
– ORIGIN Nahuatl (a language of Central America).

cache /kash/ ● n. a hidden store of things.
– ORIGIN French.

cachet /**ka**-shay/ ● n. the state of being respected or admired; prestige.
– ORIGIN French.

cack ● n. Brit. informal excrement.
– ORIGIN Old English.

cack-handed ● adj. Brit. informal clumsy

cackle ● n. a noisy clucking cry. ● v. (**cackles**, **cackling**, **cackled**) give a cackle.
– ORIGIN prob. from German *kākelen*.

cacophony /kuh-**koff**-uh-ni/ ● n. (pl. **cacophonies**) a harsh mixture of sounds.
– DERIVATIVES **cacophonous** adj.
– ORIGIN Greek *kakophōnia*.

cactus /**kak**-tuhss/ ● n. (pl. **cacti** /**kak**-ty/ or **cactuses**) a plant with a thick fleshy stem bearing spines but no leaves.
– ORIGIN Greek *kaktos* 'cardoon'.

cad ● n. dated or humorous a man who behaves dishonourably.
– DERIVATIVES **caddish** adj.
– ORIGIN from CADDIE or CADET.

cadaver /kuh-**da**-ver/ ● n. Med. or literary a corpse.
– ORIGIN Latin.

cadaverous ● adj. like a corpse in being very pale and thin.

Cadbury, George (1839–1922) and Richard (1835–99), English Quaker chocolate manufacturers and social reformers. E

caddie (also **caddy**) • n. (pl. **caddies**) a person who carries a golfer's clubs during a match. • v. (**caddies**, **caddying**, **caddied**) work as a caddie.
– ORIGIN French *cadet*.

caddis /kad-iss/ (also **caddis fly**) • n. a small winged insect having larvae that live in water and build cases of sticks, stones, etc.
– ORIGIN unknown.

caddy • n. (pl. **caddies**) a small storage container.
– ORIGIN Malay, referring to a unit of weight of 1⅓ lb (0.61 kg).

cadence /kay-duhnss/ • n. **1** the rise and fall in pitch of a person's voice. **2** a sequence of notes or chords making up the close of a musical phrase. **3** rhythm.
– ORIGIN Italian *cadenza*.

cadenza /kuh-den-zuh/ • n. a difficult solo passage in a musical work.
– ORIGIN Italian.

cadet • n. a young trainee in the armed services or police.
– ORIGIN French.

cadge • v. (**cadges**, **cadging**, **cadged**) informal ask for or get (something to which one is not entitled).
– DERIVATIVES **cadger** n.
– ORIGIN northern English and Scottish *cadger*, 'travelling dealer'.

Cadiz /kuh-diz/ a city and port on the coast of SW Spain. E

cadmium /kad-mi-uhm/ • n. a silvery-white metallic chemical element resembling zinc.
– ORIGIN Latin *cadmia* 'calamine'.

cadre /kah-der/ • n. a small group of people trained for a particular purpose or at the centre of a political organization.
– ORIGIN French.

caecum /see-kuhm/ (US **cecum**) • n. (pl. **caeca** /see-kuh/) a pouch connected to the join between the small and large intestines.
– DERIVATIVES **caecal** (US **cecal**) adj.
– ORIGIN from Latin *intestinum caecum* 'blind gut'.

Caerdydd /kyr-di*th*/ Welsh name for **CARDIFF**. E

Caernarfon /ker-nar-v'n/ (also **Caernarvon**) a town in NW Wales on the shore of the Menai Strait, the administrative centre of Gwynedd. E

Caesar /see-zer/ • n. a title of Roman emperors.
– ORIGIN family name of the Roman statesman Gaius **JULIUS CAESAR**.

Caesarea /see-zuh-ree-uh/ an ancient port on the Mediterranean coast of Israel, one of the chief cities of Roman Palestine. E

Caesarean section /si-zair-i-uhn/ • n. an operation for delivering a child by cutting through the wall of the mother's abdomen.
– ORIGIN from the story that Julius Caesar was delivered by this method.

caesium /see-zi-uhm/ (US **cesium**) • n. a soft, silvery, extremely reactive metallic chemical element.
– ORIGIN Latin *caesius* 'greyish-blue'.

caesura /si-zyoor-uh/ • n. a pause near the middle of a line of verse.
– ORIGIN Latin.

cafe /ka-fay/ • n. a small restaurant selling light meals and drinks.
– ORIGIN French, 'coffee or coffee house'.

cafeteria /ka-fuh-teer-i-uh/ • n. a self-service restaurant.
– ORIGIN Latin American Spanish, 'coffee shop'.

cafetière /ka-fuh-tyair/ • n. a coffee pot containing a plunger with which the grounds are pushed to the bottom.
– ORIGIN French.

caffeine /kaf-feen/ • n. a substance found in tea and coffee plants which stimulates the central nervous system.
– DERIVATIVES **caffeinated** adj.
– ORIGIN French *caféine*.

caftan • n. var. of **KAFTAN**.

Cage, John (Milton) (1912–92), American composer, an experimentalist and pioneer of the use of chance in music. E

cage • n. **1** a structure of bars or wires in which animals are confined. **2** any similar structure. • v. (**cages**, **caging**, **caged**) enclose in a cage.
– ORIGIN Old French.

cagey (also **cagy**) • adj. informal cautiously reluctant to speak.
– DERIVATIVES **cagily** adv.
– ORIGIN unknown.

Cagliari /ka-li-ah-ri/ the capital of Sardinia. E

Cagney, James (1899–1986), American actor, remembered for playing gangster roles in films such as *The Public Enemy*. E

cagoule /kuh-gool/ • n. a light waterproof jacket with a hood.
– ORIGIN French, 'cowl'.

cahoots /kuh-hoots/ • pl. n. (in phr. **in cahoots**) informal making secret plans together.
– ORIGIN unknown.

caiman /kay-muhn/ (also **cayman**) • n. a tropical American reptile similar to an alligator.
– ORIGIN Carib.

Caine, Sir Michael (b.1933; born *Maurice Micklewhite*), English film actor, star of such films as *Alfie* and *Hannah and Her Sisters*. E

cairn • n. a mound of rough stones built as a memorial or landmark.
– ORIGIN Scottish Gaelic *carn*.

Cairngorm Mountains a mountain range in northern Scotland. E

Cairo /ky-roh/ the capital of Egypt. E

cajole /kuh-johl/ • v. (**cajoles**, **cajoling**, **cajoled**) persuade (someone) to do something using flattery.
– ORIGIN French *cajoler*.

Cajun /kay-juhn/ ● n. a member of a French-speaking community in areas of southern Louisiana.
– ORIGIN from *Acadian* (see **ACADIA**).

cake ● n. **1** an item of soft sweet food made from baking a mixture of flour, fat, eggs, and sugar. **2** a flat, round item of savoury food that is baked or fried. ● v. (**cakes**, **caking**, **caked**) (of a thick or sticky substance) cover and become encrusted on.
– PHRASES **a piece of cake** informal something easily achieved. **sell like hot cakes** informal be sold quickly and in large amounts.
– ORIGIN Scandinavian.

Cal ● abbrev. large calorie(s).

cal ● abbrev. small calorie(s).

calabash /kal-uh-bash/ ● n. a water container made from the dried shell of a gourd.
– ORIGIN Spanish *calabaza*.

calabrese /kal-uh-breez/ ● n. a bright green variety of broccoli.
– ORIGIN Italian.

Calabria E
/kuh-**lab**-ri-uh/ a region of SW Italy, forming the 'toe' of the Italian peninsula.

Calais E
/ka-lay/ a ferry port in northern France.

calamine /kal-uh-myn/ ● n. a pink powder used to make a soothing lotion.
– ORIGIN Latin *calamina*.

calamity ● n. (pl. **calamities**) a sudden event causing great damage or distress.
– DERIVATIVES **calamitous** adj.
– ORIGIN Latin *calamitas*.

calcareous /kal-kair-i-uhss/ ● adj. containing calcium carbonate; chalky.
– ORIGIN Latin *calcarius*.

calciferol /kal-si-fuh-rol/ ● n. vitamin D_2, essential for the storing of calcium in bones.

calcify /kal-si-fy/ ● v. (**calcifies**, **calcifying**, **calcified**) harden by a deposit of calcium salts.

calcine /kal-syn/ ● v. (**calcines**, **calcining**, **calcined**) reduce, oxidize, or dry (a substance) by strong heat.
– ORIGIN Latin *calcinare*.

calcite /kal-syt/ ● n. a mineral consisting of calcium carbonate.
– ORIGIN German *Calcit*.

calcium ● n. a soft grey metallic chemical element.
– ORIGIN Latin *calx* 'lime'.

calcium carbonate ● n. a white compound found as chalk, limestone, and marble.

calculate ● v. (**calculates**, **calculating**, **calculated**) **1** find out by using mathematics. **2** intend (an action) to have a particular effect.
– DERIVATIVES **calculable** adj.
– ORIGIN Latin *calculare* 'count'.

calculated ● adj. done with awareness of the likely effect.

calculating ● adj. craftily planning things so as to benefit oneself.

calculation ● n. **1** an act of finding something out by using mathematics. **2** an assessment of the results of a course of action.

calculator ● n. a small electronic device used for making mathematical calculations.

calculus /kal-kyuu-luhss/ ● n. (pl. **calculi** /kal-kyuu-ly/ or **calculuses**) the branch of mathematics concerned with problems involving rates of variation.
– ORIGIN Latin, 'small pebble'.

Calcutta E
/kal-**kut**-tuh/ a port in eastern India, capital of the state of West Bengal and the second-largest city in India. Official name (from 2000) **KOLKATA**.

caldron ● n. US = **CAULDRON**.

Caledonian /ka-li-**doh**-ni-uhn/ ● adj. relating to Scotland or the Scottish Highlands.
– ORIGIN from *Caledonia*, the Latin name for northern Britain.

calendar /ka-lin-der/ ● n. **1** a chart or series of pages showing the days, weeks, and months of a particular year. **2** a system by which the beginning, length, and subdivisions of the year are fixed. **3** a list of special events.
– ORIGIN Latin *kalendarium* 'account book'.

calf[1] ● n. (pl. **calves**) **1** a young cow or bull. **2** the young of some other large mammals, e.g. elephants.
– ORIGIN Old English.

calf[2] ● n. (pl. **calves**) the back of a person's leg below the knee.
– ORIGIN Old Norse.

calibrate /ka-li-brayt/ ● v. (**calibrates**, **calibrating**, **calibrated**) **1** mark (a gauge or instrument) with a standard scale of readings. **2** compare the readings of (an instrument) with those of a standard.
– DERIVATIVES **calibration** n.
– ORIGIN from **CALIBRE**.

calibre /ka-li-ber/ (US **caliber**) ● n. **1** the quality of a person's ability: *musicians of the highest calibre.* **2** the diameter of the inside of a gun barrel, or of a bullet or shell.
– ORIGIN French.

calico /ka-li-koh/ ● n. (pl. **calicoes** or US also **calicos**) **1** Brit. a type of plain white or unbleached cotton cloth. **2** N. Amer. printed cotton fabric.
– ORIGIN from *Calicut*, a seaport in SW India where the fabric originated.

California E
a state of the US, on the Pacific coast; capital, Sacramento.
– DERIVATIVES **Californian** adj. & n.

californium /ka-li-for-ni-uhm/ ● n. a radioactive metallic chemical element made by high-energy atomic collisions.
– ORIGIN from *California* University.

Caligula E
/kuh-lig-yuu-luh/ (AD 12–41; born *Gaius Julius Caesar Germanicus*), Roman emperor 37–41, notorious for his cruel and tyrannical reign.

caliper /ka-li-per/ (also **calliper**) ● n. **1** (also **calipers**) a measuring instrument with two hinged legs. **2** a metal support for a person's leg.
– ORIGIN prob. from **CALIBRE**.

caliph /kay-lif/ ● n. hist. the chief Muslim ruler.
– ORIGIN Arabic, 'deputy of God'.

calisthenics ● pl. n. US = **CALLISTHENICS**.

calk ● n. & v. US = **CAULK**.

call ● v. **1** cry out to (someone) so as to summon them or attract their attention. **2** order

C

(someone) to go or come somewhere. **3** telephone. **4** give a particular name or description to. **5** pay a brief visit. **6** fix a date or time for: *call an election.* **7** predict the result of (a vote or contest). **8** (of a bird or animal) make its typical cry. ● **n. 1** an act or instance of calling. **2** the typical cry of a bird or animal. **3** (**call for**) demand or need for: *there is little call for antique furniture.*
– PHRASES **call for** require. **call in** demand payment of (a loan). **call off** cancel. **call on/upon** turn to for help. **call of nature** euphem. a need to go to the toilet. **call the shots** (or **tune**) control a situation. **call up 1** summon (someone) to serve in the army or to play in a team. **2** bring (something stored) into use. **on call** available to provide a service if necessary.
– DERIVATIVES **caller** n.
– ORIGIN Old Norse.

Callaghan E
/**kal**-luh-han/, (Leonard) James, Baron Callaghan of Cardiff (b.1912), British Labour statesman, Prime Minister 1976–9.

Callas E
/**kal**-luhss/, Maria (1923–77; born *Maria Cecilia Anna Kalageropoulos*), American-born operatic soprano, of Greek parentage.

call centre ● **n.** an office in which large numbers of telephone calls are handled for an organization.

call girl ● **n.** a female prostitute who accepts appointments by telephone.

calligraphy /kuh-**lig**-ruh-fi/ ● **n.** decorative handwriting.
– DERIVATIVES **calligrapher** n. **calligraphic** adj.
– ORIGIN Greek *kalligraphia*.

calling ● **n. 1** a profession or occupation. **2** a vocation.

calliper ● **n.** var. of CALIPER.

callisthenics /kal-liss-**then**-iks/ (US **calisthenics**) ● **pl. n.** gymnastic exercises to achieve fitness and grace of movement.
– ORIGIN from Greek *kallos* 'beauty' + *sthenos* 'strength'.

callous /**kal**-luhss/ ● **adj.** insensitive and cruel.
– DERIVATIVES **callously** adv. **callousness** n.
– ORIGIN Latin *callosus* 'hard-skinned'.

calloused (also **callused**) ● **adj.** having hardened skin.

callow ● **adj.** (of a young person) inexperienced and immature.
– ORIGIN Old English, 'bald'.

callus /**kal**-luhss/ ● **n.** an area of thickened and hardened skin.
– ORIGIN Latin, 'hardened skin'.

calm ● **adj. 1** not nervous, angry, or excited. **2** peaceful and undisturbed. ● **n.** a calm state or period. ● **v.** (often **calm down**) make or become calm.
– DERIVATIVES **calmly** adv. **calmness** n.
– ORIGIN Greek *kauma* 'heat of the day'.

Calor gas /**ka**-ler/ ● **n.** Brit. trademark liquefied butane stored under pressure in containers, for domestic use.
– ORIGIN Latin *calor* 'heat'.

caloric /kuh-**lo**-rik/ ● **adj.** N. Amer. or tech. relating to heat.

calorie ● **n.** (pl. **calories**) **1** (also **large calorie**) a unit of energy equal to the energy needed to raise the temperature of 1 kilogram of water through 1 °C (4.1868 kilojoules). **2** (also **small calorie**) a unit of energy equal to one-thousandth of a large calorie.
– ORIGIN Latin *calor* 'heat'.

calorific ● **adj.** esp. Brit. relating to the amount of energy contained in food or fuel.

calorimeter /ka-luh-**rim**-i-ter/ ● **n.** a device for measuring the amount of heat involved in a chemical reaction or other process.

calumny /**ka**-luhm-ni/ ● **n.** (pl. **calumnies**) the making of false and damaging statements about someone.
– ORIGIN Latin *calumnia*.

Calvary E
/**kal**-vuh-ri/ the hill outside Jerusalem on which Christ was crucified.

calve ● **v.** (**calves, calving, calved**) give birth to a calf.
– ORIGIN Old English.

calves pl. of CALF[1], CALF[2].

Calvin, E
John (1509–64), French Protestant theologian and leader of the Reformation. On becoming a Protestant he fled to Switzerland, where he established the first Presbyterian government, in Geneva.

Calvinism ● **n.** the form of Protestantism of John Calvin, centring on the belief that God has decided everything that happens in advance.
– DERIVATIVES **Calvinist** n. **Calvinistic** adj.

calypso /kuh-**lip**-soh/ ● **n.** (pl. **calypsos**) a kind of West Indian song with improvised words on a topical theme.
– ORIGIN unknown.

calyx /**kay**-liks/ ● **n.** (pl. **calyces** /**kay**-li-seez/ or **calyxes**) the sepals of a flower, forming a protective layer around a bud.
– ORIGIN Greek *kalux* 'husk'.

cam ● **n. 1** a projecting part on a wheel or shaft, designed to come into contact with another part while rotating and cause it to move. **2** a camshaft.
– ORIGIN Dutch *kam* 'comb'.

camaraderie /kam-uh-**rah**-duh-ri/ ● **n.** trust and friendship between people.
– ORIGIN French.

Camargue E
/kuh-**marg**/ (**the Camargue**) a region of the Rhône delta in SE France, characterized by many shallow salt lagoons and known for its white horses.

camber /**kam**-ber/ ● **n.** a slightly arched shape of a horizontal surface e.g. a road.
– ORIGIN Old French *chambre* 'arched'.

cambium /**kam**-bi-uhm/ ● **n.** (pl. **cambia** /**kam**-bi-uh/ or **cambiums**) Bot. a layer of cells in a plant stem from which new tissue grows by the division of cells.
– ORIGIN Latin, 'change, exchange'.

Cambodia E
/kam-**boh**-di-uh/ a country in SE Asia between Thailand and southern Vietnam; capital, Phnom Penh. Also officially called the KHMER REPUBLIC (1970–5) and KAMPUCHEA (1976–89).
– DERIVATIVES **Cambodian** adj. & n.

Cambrian /kam-bri-uhn/ • adj. **1** Welsh. **2** Geol. relating to the first period in the Palaeozoic era (about 570 to 510 million years ago).
– ORIGIN Latin *Cambria*.

cambric /kam-brik/ • n. a light, closely woven white linen or cotton fabric.
– ORIGIN named after the town of *Cambrai* in northern France.

Cambridge[1] E
a city in eastern England, site of Cambridge University.

Cambridge[2] E
a city in eastern Massachusetts in the US, site of Harvard University and the Massachusetts Institute of Technology.

Cambridgeshire E
a county of eastern England; county town, Cambridge.

Cambs. • abbrev. Cambridgeshire.

camcorder • n. a portable combined video camera and video recorder.

came past tense of **COME**.

camel • n. a large mammal of desert countries, with a long neck and either one or two humps on the back.
– ORIGIN Greek *kamēlos*.

camellia /kuh-mee-li-uh/ • n. a shrub with showy flowers and shiny leaves.
– ORIGIN named after the botanist Joseph *Kamel* (1661–1706).

Camelot E
/kam-uh-lot/ (in Arthurian legend) the place where King Arthur held his court.

Camembert /kam-uhm-bair/ • n. a rich, soft cheese originally made near Camembert in Normandy.

cameo /kam-i-oh/ • n. (pl. **cameos**) **1** a piece of jewellery consisting of a carving of a head shown in outline against a differently coloured background. **2** a short descriptive written sketch. **3** a small part in a play or film for a well-known actor.
– ORIGIN Latin *cammaeus*.

camera • n. a device for taking photographs or recording moving images.
– PHRASES **in camera** Law in the private rooms of a judge, without the press and public being present.
– ORIGIN Latin, 'vault, arched chamber'.

camera obscura /ob-skyoor-uh/ • n. a darkened box or building with a lens or opening for casting the image of an outside object on to a screen inside.
– ORIGIN Latin, 'dark chamber'.

Cameron, E
James (b. 1954), Canadian film director and scriptwriter, whose films include *The Terminator*, *Aliens*, and *Titanic*.

Cameroon E
/kam-uh-roon/ a country on the west coast of Africa between Nigeria and Gabon; capital, Yaoundé.
– DERIVATIVES **Cameroonian** adj. & n.

camiknickers • pl. n. Brit. a woman's one-piece undergarment which combines a camisole and a pair of French knickers.

camisole /kam-i-sohl/ • n. a woman's loose-fitting undergarment for the upper body.
– ORIGIN French.

camomile • n. var. of **CHAMOMILE**.

camouflage /kam-uh-flahzh/ • n. **1** the painting or covering of soldiers and military equipment to make them blend in with their surroundings. **2** clothing or materials used for such a purpose. **3** the natural colouring or form of an animal which allows it to blend in with its surroundings. • v. (**camouflages**, **camouflaging**, **camouflaged**) hide by means of camouflage.
– ORIGIN French.

camp[1] • n. **1** a place where tents are temporarily set up. **2** a complex of buildings for soldiers, holidaymakers, or people held in custody. **3** the supporters of a particular party or set of beliefs regarded as a group. • v. stay in a tent or caravan while on holiday.
– ORIGIN Latin *campus* 'level ground'.

camp[2] informal • adj. **1** (of a man) effeminate in an exaggerated way. **2** deliberately exaggerated and theatrical in style. • n. camp behaviour or style. • v. (**camp it up**) behave in a camp way.
– ORIGIN unknown.

campaign • n. **1** a series of military operations intended to achieve a particular aim. **2** an organized course of action to achieve a goal. • v. work in an organized way towards a goal.
– DERIVATIVES **campaigner** n.
– ORIGIN French *campagne* 'open country'.

campanile /kam-puh-nee-lay/ • n. a bell tower.
– ORIGIN Italian.

campanology /kam-puh-nol-uh-ji/ • n. the art of bell-ringing.
– ORIGIN Latin *campana* 'bell'.

camp bed • n. Brit. a folding portable bed.

Campbell E
Sir Malcolm (1885–1948), English motor-racing driver, who in 1935 became the first to exceed a land speed of 300 mph (483 kph). His son Donald (1921–67) held the world records on land and water, and was killed attempting to break his own water speed record.

Campbell-Bannerman, E
Sir Henry (1836–1908), British Liberal statesman, Prime Minister 1905–8.

Camp David E
the retreat of the President of the US, in the Appalachian Mountains in Maryland. President Carter hosted talks there between the leaders of Israel and Egypt which resulted in the Camp David agreements (1978) and the Egypt–Israel peace treaty of 1979.

camper • n. **1** a person who spends a holiday in a tent or holiday camp. **2** (also **camper van**) a large motor vehicle with a living area.

campfire • n. an open-air fire in a camp.

camp follower • n. **1** a civilian attached to a military camp. **2** a person who associates with a group without being a full member of it.

camphor /kam-fer/ • n. a substance with a sweet smell and bitter taste, occurring in

certain essential oils.
– ORIGIN Latin *camphora*.

campsite ● n. a place used for camping.

campus ● n. (pl. **campuses**) the grounds and buildings of a university or college.
– ORIGIN Latin, 'level ground'.

camshaft /**kam**-shahft/ ● n. a shaft with one or more cams attached to it.

Camus E
/**ka**-moo/, Albert (1913–60), French novelist, dramatist, and essayist. His works include the novels *The Outsider* and *The Plague*, which give expression to his view that the universe and life are meaningless.

can[1] ● modal verb (3rd sing. present **can**; past **could**) **1** be able to. **2** used to express doubt or surprise: *he can't have finished.* **3** used to indicate that something is often the case: *he could be very moody.* **4** be permitted to.
– ORIGIN Old English, 'know'.

USAGE **can**
The verb **can** is mainly used to mean 'be able to', as in the sentence *can he move?* = is he physically able to move? When asking to be allowed to do something, it is better to say **may** (*may we leave now?* rather than *can we leave now?*), as **can** is thought to be less correct or less polite in such cases.

can[2] ● n. a cylindrical metal container. ● v. (**cans**, **canning**, **canned**) preserve in a can.
– PHRASES **a can of worms** a complex matter that is full of possible problems.
– ORIGIN Old English.

Canaan E
/**kay**-nuhn/ the biblical name for the area of ancient Palestine west of the River Jordan which the Israelites conquered and occupied.

Canada E
the second-largest country in the world, covering the entire northern half of North America with the exception of Alaska; capital, Ottawa.
– DERIVATIVES **Canadian** n. & adj.

canal ● n. **1** a waterway cut through land for the passage of boats or for conveying water for irrigation. **2** a tubular passage in a plant or animal carrying food, liquid, or air.
– ORIGIN Latin *canalis* 'pipe, channel'.

Canaletto E
/ka-nuh-**let**-toh/ (1697–1768; born *Giovanni Antonio Canale*), Italian painter, known for his paintings of Venetian festivals and scenery.

canalize /**kan**-uh-lyz/ (also **canalise**) ● v. (**canalizes**, **canalizing**, **canalized**) **1** convert (a river) into a canal. **2** convey through a duct or channel.

canapé /**kan**-uh-pay/ ● n. a small piece of bread or pastry with a savoury topping.
– ORIGIN French, 'sofa, couch'.

canard /ka-**nard**/ ● n. an unfounded rumour or story.
– ORIGIN French, 'duck, hoax'.

canary ● n. (pl. **canaries**) a bright yellow finch with a tuneful song.
– ORIGIN from the **CANARY ISLANDS**, to which one species of the bird is native.

Canary Islands E
a group of islands in the Atlantic Ocean, off the NW coast of Africa, forming an autonomous region of Spain; capital, Las Palmas (on Gran Canaria). The main islands are Tenerife, Gran Canaria, Fuerteventura, Lanzarote, Gomera, La Palma, and Hierro.

Canaveral, Cape E
/kuh-**nav**-uh-ruhl/ a cape on the east coast of Florida (known as Cape Kennedy 1963–73), the site of the John F. Kennedy Space Center, from which the Apollo space missions were launched.

Canberra E
/**kan**-buh-ruh/ the capital of Australia and seat of the federal government, in Australian Capital Territory.

cancan ● n. a lively, high-kicking stage dance originating in 19th-century Parisian music halls.
– ORIGIN French.

cancel ● v. (**cancels**, **cancelling**, **cancelled**; US also **cancels**, **canceling**, **canceled**) **1** decide that (a planned event) will not take place. **2** withdraw from or end (an agreement). **3** (**cancel out**) have an equal but opposite effect on. **4** mark (a stamp, ticket, etc.) to show that it has been used.
– DERIVATIVES **cancellation** n.
– ORIGIN Latin *cancellare*.

Cancer ● n. a constellation (the Crab) and sign of the zodiac, which the sun enters about 21 June.
– ORIGIN Latin, 'crab'.

cancer ● n. **1** a disease caused by an uncontrolled division of abnormal cells in a part of the body. **2** a harmful growth or tumour resulting from such a division of cells. **3** something evil or destructive that is hard to contain or destroy.
– DERIVATIVES **cancerous** adj.
– ORIGIN Latin, 'crab, ulcer'.

Cancún E
/kan-**koon**/ a resort in SE Mexico, on the NE coast of the Yucatán Peninsula.

candela /kan-**dee**-luh/ ● n. Physics the SI unit of luminous intensity.
– ORIGIN Latin, 'candle'.

candelabrum /kan-di-**lah**-bruhm/ ● n. (pl. **candelabra** /kan-di-**lah**-bruh/) a large branched candlestick or holder for several candles or lamps.
– ORIGIN Latin.

candid ● adj. truthful and straightforward; frank.
– DERIVATIVES **candidly** adv.
– ORIGIN Latin *candidus* 'white'.

candidate /**kan**-di-duht/ ● n. **1** a person who applies for a job or is nominated for election. **2** a person taking an examination. **3** a person or thing seen as suitable for a particular fate, treatment, or position: *she was the perfect candidate for a biography.*
– DERIVATIVES **candidacy** n.
– ORIGIN Latin *candidatus* 'white-robed'.

candied ● adj. (of fruit) preserved in a sugar syrup.

candle ● n. a stick of wax with a central wick which is lit to produce light as it burns.
– ORIGIN Latin *candela*.

Candlemas /kan-d'l-mass/ • n. a Christian festival held on 2 February to commemorate the purification of the Virgin Mary and the presentation of Christ in the Temple.

candlestick • n. a support or holder for a candle.

candlewick • n. a thick, soft cotton fabric with a raised, tufted pattern.

candour (US **candor**) • n. the quality of being open and honest.
– ORIGIN Latin *candor* 'whiteness, purity'.

candy • n. (pl. **candies**) (also **sugar candy**) N. Amer. sweets.
– ORIGIN from French *sucre candi* 'crystallized sugar'.

candyfloss • n. Brit. a mass of pink or white fluffy spun sugar wrapped round a stick.

candy-striped • adj. patterned with alternating stripes of white and another colour.

cane • n. **1** the hollow jointed stem of tall reeds, grasses, etc. **2** the slender, flexible stem of plants such as rattan. **3** a woody stem of a raspberry or related plant. **4** a length of cane used as a support for plants, a walking stick, or for hitting children as a punishment. • v. (**canes, caning, caned**) beat with a cane as a punishment.
– ORIGIN Greek *kanna, kannē*.

canine /kay-nyn/ • adj. having to do with a dog or dogs. • n. **1** a dog or other animal of the dog family. **2** (also **canine tooth**) a pointed tooth next to the incisors.
– ORIGIN Latin *caninus*.

canister • n. a round or cylindrical container.
– ORIGIN Greek *kanastron* 'wicker basket'.

canker • n. **1** a destructive disease of trees and plants, caused by a fungus. **2** a condition in animals that causes open sores.
– ORIGIN Latin *cancer* 'crab, ulcer'.

cannabis • n. a drug obtained from the hemp plant.
– ORIGIN Greek *kannabis*.

canned • adj. **1** preserved in a can. **2** informal, esp. derog. (of music, applause, etc.) prerecorded.

cannelloni /kan-nuh-loh-ni/ • pl. n. rolls of pasta stuffed with a meat or vegetable mixture, cooked in a cheese sauce.
– ORIGIN Italian, 'large tubes'.

cannery • n. (pl. **canneries**) a factory where food is canned.

> **Cannes** E
> /kan/ a resort on the Mediterranean coast of France, site of an annual international film festival.

cannibal • n. a person who eats the flesh of other human beings.
– DERIVATIVES **cannibalism** n. **cannibalistic** adj.
– ORIGIN Spanish *Caribes*, a West Indian people said to eat humans.

cannibalize (also **cannibalise**) • v. (**cannibalizes, cannibalizing, cannibalized**) use (a machine) as a source of spare parts for others.

> **Canning**, E
> George (1770–1827), British Tory statesman, Prime Minister 1827. He died shortly after taking office.

cannon • n. (pl. **cannon** or **cannons**) **1** a large, heavy gun formerly used in warfare. **2** an automatic heavy gun that fires shells from an aircraft or tank.
– ORIGIN Italian *cannone* 'large tube'.

cannonade /kan-nuh-**nayd**/ • n. a period of continuous heavy gunfire.

cannonball • n. a metal or stone ball fired from a cannon.

cannon fodder • n. soldiers seen only as a resource to be used up in war.

cannot • contr. can not.

canny • adj. (**cannier, canniest**) shrewd, especially in financial matters.
– DERIVATIVES **cannily** adv.
– ORIGIN from CAN[1].

canoe • n. a shallow narrow boat with pointed ends, propelled with a paddle. • v. (**canoes, canoed, canoeing**) travel in a canoe.
– DERIVATIVES **canoeist** n.
– ORIGIN Spanish *canoa*.

canon • n. **1** a general rule or principle by which something is judged: *his designs break the canons of fashion.* **2** a Church decree or law. **3** the authentic works of a particular author or artist. **4** a list of literary works considered to be permanently established as being of the highest quality. **5** a member of the clergy on the staff of a cathedral. **6** a piece of music in which a theme is taken up by two or more parts that overlap.
– ORIGIN Greek *kanōn* 'rule'.

canonical /kuh-non-i-k'l/ • adj. **1** according to the laws of the Christian Church. **2** accepted as being authentic or established as a standard: *the canonical works of science fiction.* • n. (**canonicals**) the official clothing of the clergy.

canonize (also **canonise**) • v. (**canonizes, canonizing, canonized**) (in the Roman Catholic Church) officially declare (a dead person) to be a saint.
– DERIVATIVES **canonization** (also **canonisation**) n.

canon law • n. the laws of the Christian Church.

canoodle • v. (**canoodles, canoodling, canoodled**) informal kiss and cuddle lovingly.
– ORIGIN unknown.

> **Canopus** E
> /kuh-**noh**-puhss/ the second-brightest star in the sky and the brightest in the constellation Carina.

canopy • n. (pl. **canopies**) **1** a cloth covering hung or held up over a throne or bed. **2** a rooflike covering or shelter. **3** the expanding, umbrella-like part of a parachute. • v. (**canopies, canopying, canopied**) provide with a canopy.
– ORIGIN Latin *conopeum* 'mosquito net over a bed'.

cant[1] /*rhymes with* rant/ • n. **1** insincere talk about moral or religious matters. **2** derog. the language typical of a particular group: *thieves' cant.*
– ORIGIN prob. from Latin *cantare* 'to sing'.

cant[2] /*rhymes with* rant/ • v. be or cause to be in a slanting position; tilt. • n. a slope or tilt.
– ORIGIN German *kant, kante* or Dutch *cant* 'point, side, edge'.

can't ● contr. cannot.

Cantab. /kan-tab/ ● abbrev. having to do with Cambridge University.
– ORIGIN Latin *Cantabrigia* 'Cambridge'.

cantabile /kan-tah-bi-lay/ ● adv. & adj. Music in a smooth singing style.
– ORIGIN Italian, 'singable'.

cantaloupe /kan-tuh-loop/ ● n. a small round melon with orange flesh.
– ORIGIN from *Cantaluppi* near Rome.

cantankerous /kan-tang-kuh-ruhss/ ● adj. bad-tempered and uncooperative.
– ORIGIN perh. from Anglo-Irish *cant* 'auction' and *rancorous*.

cantata /kan-tah-tuh/ ● n. a sung musical composition based on a narrative work and usually accompanied by a chorus and orchestra.
– ORIGIN from Italian *cantata aria* 'sung air'.

canteen ● n. **1** a restaurant in a workplace or educational establishment. **2** Brit. a case containing a set of cutlery. **3** a small water bottle, as used by soldiers or campers.
– ORIGIN Italian *cantina* 'cellar'.

canter ● n. a pace of a horse between a trot and a gallop. ● v. (**canters**, **cantering**, **cantered**) move at a canter.
– ORIGIN from *Canterbury pace*, the easy pace at which medieval pilgrims travelled to Canterbury.

Canterbury E
a city in Kent, SE England, the seat of the Archbishop of Canterbury.

canticle /kan-ti-k'l/ ● n. a hymn or chant forming a regular part of a church service.
– ORIGIN Latin *canticulum* 'little song'.

cantilever /kan-ti-lee-ver/ ● n. a long projecting beam or girder fixed at only one end, used in bridge construction.
– ORIGIN unknown.

canto /kan-toh/ ● n. (pl. **cantos**) one of the sections into which some long poems are divided.
– ORIGIN Italian, 'song'.

Canton E
/kan-ton/ var. of **GUANGZHOU**.

canton /kan-ton/ ● n. a political or administrative subdivision of a country, especially in Switzerland.
– ORIGIN Old French, 'corner'.

cantonment /kan-ton-muhnt/ ● n. a military station in British India.
– ORIGIN French *cantonnement*.

cantor /kan-tor/ ● n. **1** an official who leads the prayers in a Jewish synagogue. **2** a person who sings solo verses to which the choir or congregation respond in a Christian service.
– ORIGIN Latin, 'singer'.

Canute E
/kuh-nyoot/ (also **Cnut** or **Knut**) (d.1035), Danish king of England 1017–35, Denmark 1018–35, and Norway 1028–35. He is remembered for ordering the incoming tide to go back, as a lesson to his flattering courtiers that kings are only human and have limited powers.

canvas ● n. (pl. **canvases** or **canvasses**) **1** a strong, coarse cloth used to make sails, tents, etc. **2** an oil painting on canvas.
– PHRASES **under canvas** in a tent or tents.
– ORIGIN Old French *canevas*.

canvass ● v. **1** visit (someone) to seek their vote in an election. **2** question (someone) to find out their opinion. **3** Brit. propose for discussion.
– DERIVATIVES **canvasser** n.
– ORIGIN first meaning 'toss in a canvas sheet' (as a sport or punishment).

canyon ● n. a deep gorge.
– ORIGIN Spanish *cañón* 'tube'.

CAP ● abbrev. Common Agricultural Policy.

cap ● n. **1** a soft, flat hat with a peak. **2** a soft, close-fitting head covering worn for a particular purpose: *a shower cap*. **3** esp. Brit. a cap awarded to members of a national sports team. **4** a lid or cover. **5** an upper limit set on spending or borrowing. **6** Brit. informal a contraceptive diaphragm. **7** a small amount of explosive powder in a metal or paper case that explodes when struck. ● v. (**caps**, **capping**, **capped**) **1** put or form a cap, lid, or cover on. **2** provide a fitting end to. **3** place a limit on (prices, spending, etc.). **4** (**be capped**) esp. Brit. be chosen as a member of a national sports team.
– PHRASES **cap in hand** humbly asking for a favour. **set one's cap at** dated (of a woman) try to attract (a man).
– ORIGIN Latin *cappa*.

capability ● n. (pl. **capabilities**) the power or ability to do something.

Capability Brown E
see **BROWN**[4].

capable ● adj. **1** (**capable of**) having the necessary ability or quality to do. **2** able to achieve whatever one has to do.
– DERIVATIVES **capably** adv.
– ORIGIN Latin *capere* 'take or hold'.

capacious ● adj. having a lot of space inside.
– ORIGIN Latin *capax* 'capable'.

capacitance /kuh-pass-i-tuhnss/ ● n. the ability to store electric charge.

capacitor ● n. a device used to store electric charge.

capacity ● n. (pl. **capacities**) **1** the maximum amount that something can contain or produce: *the room was filled to capacity*. **2** (before another noun) fully occupying the available space: *a capacity crowd*. **3** the ability or power to do something. **4** a specified role or position: *I'm here in an official capacity*.
– ORIGIN Latin *capere* 'take or hold'.

caparison /kuh-pa-ri-s'n/ ● v. (**be caparisoned**) be clothed in rich decorative coverings.
– ORIGIN Spanish *caparazón* 'saddlecloth'.

cape[1] ● n. a short cloak.
– DERIVATIVES **caped** adj.
– ORIGIN Latin *cappa* 'head-covering'.

cape[2] ● n. a piece of land that projects into the sea.
– ORIGIN Latin *caput* 'head'.

Cape Cod E
a sandy peninsula in SE Massachusetts, USA.

Capella E
/kuh-pel-luh/ the sixth-brightest star in the sky, and the brightest in the constellation Auriga.

Cape of Good Hope E
a mountainous promontory south of Cape Town, South Africa, near the southern tip of Africa.

Cape Province E
a former province of South Africa; it was divided in 1994 into the provinces of Northern Cape, Western Cape, and Eastern Cape.

caper[1] ● v. (**capers**, **capering**, **capered**) skip or dance about in a lively or playful way. ● n. **1** a playful skipping movement. **2** informal a light-hearted or dishonest activity.
– ORIGIN Latin *capreolus* 'little goat'.

caper[2] ● n. a flower bud of a southern European shrub, pickled for use in cooking.
– ORIGIN Greek *kapparis*.

capercaillie /kap-er-kay-li/ ● n. (pl. **capercaillies**) a large turkey-like grouse of forests in northern Europe.
– ORIGIN from Scottish Gaelic *capull coille*, 'horse of the wood'.

Cape Town E
the legislative capital of South Africa and administrative capital of the province of Western Cape.

Cape Verde Islands E
/verd/ a country consisting of a group of islands in the Atlantic off the coast of Senegal; capital, Praia.
– DERIVATIVES **Cape Verdean** adj. & n.

capillarity ● n. the tendency of a liquid in a narrow tube or pore to rise or fall as a result of surface tension.

capillary /kuh-pil-luh-ri/ ● n. **1** any of the fine branching blood vessels that form a network between the arteries and veins. **2** (also **capillary tube**) a tube with an internal diameter of hair-like thinness.
– ORIGIN Latin *capillus* 'hair'.

capillary action ● n. = CAPILLARITY.

capital[1] ● n. **1** the most important city or town of a country or region. **2** wealth owned by a person or organization or invested, lent, or borrowed. **3** a capital letter. ● adj. **1** (of an offence) punishable by death. **2** (of a letter of the alphabet) large in size and of the form used to begin sentences and names. **3** informal, dated excellent.
– PHRASES **make capital out of** use to advantage.
– ORIGIN Latin *caput* 'head'.

capital[2] ● n. the top part of a pillar.
– ORIGIN Latin *capitellum* 'little head'.

capital gain ● n. a profit from the sale of property or an investment.

capital goods ● pl. n. goods that are used in producing other goods.

capitalism ● n. an economic and political system in which a country's trade and industry are controlled by private owners for profit.
– DERIVATIVES **capitalist** n. & adj.

capitalize (also **capitalise**) ● v. (**capitalizes**, **capitalizing**, **capitalized**) **1** (**capitalize on**) take advantage of. **2** convert into or provide with financial capital. **3** write or print (a word or letter) in capital letters or with a capital initial letter.
– DERIVATIVES **capitalization** (also **capitalisation**) n.

capital punishment ● n. the punishment of a crime by death.

capital sum ● n. a lump sum of money payable to an insured person or paid as an initial fee or investment.

capitation ● n. the payment of a fee or grant to a doctor, school, etc., the amount being determined by the number of people involved.
– ORIGIN Latin.

Capitol E
/kap-i-t'l/ (**the Capitol**) the seat of the US Congress in Washington DC.

capitulate /kuh-pit-yuu-layt/ ● v. (**capitulates**, **capitulating**, **capitulated**) give in to an opponent or an unwelcome demand.
– DERIVATIVES **capitulation** n.
– ORIGIN Latin *capitulare* 'draw up under headings'.

capon /kay-pon/ ● n. a domestic cock that has been castrated and fattened for eating.
– ORIGIN Latin *capo*.

Capone E
/kuh-pohn/, Al (1899–1947; full name *Alphonse Capone*), American gangster. He was indirectly responsible for many murders, including the St Valentine's Day Massacre, a shooting of rival gang members which took place on 14th February 1929.

Capote E
/kuh-poh-ti/, Truman (1924–84; born *Truman Streckfus Persons*), American writer, author of *Breakfast at Tiffany's* and *In Cold Blood*.

cappuccino /kap-puh-chee-noh/ ● n. (pl. **cappuccinos**) coffee made with milk that has been frothed up with pressurized steam.
– ORIGIN Italian, 'Capuchin' (because the colour of the coffee resembles that of a Capuchin monk's habit).

Capra E
/kap-ruh/, Frank (1897–1991), Italian-born American film director, known for comedies such as *It Happened One Night* and *It's a Wonderful Life*.

Capri E
/kuh-pree/ an island off the west coast of Italy, south of Naples.

caprice /kuh-preess/ ● n. a sudden change of mood or behaviour.
– ORIGIN Italian *capriccio* 'sudden start'.

capricious /kuh-pri-shuhss/ ● adj. prone to sudden changes of mood or behaviour.

Capricorn /kap-ri-korn/ ● n. a constellation and sign of the zodiac (the Goat), which the sun enters about 21 December.
– ORIGIN Latin *capricornus*.

capri pants /kuh-pree/ ● pl. n. close-fitting tapered trousers for women.
– ORIGIN named after CAPRI.

capsicum /kap-si-kuhm/ ● n. (pl. **capsicums**) a sweet pepper or chilli pepper.
– ORIGIN Latin.

capsize ● v. (**capsizes**, **capsizing**, **capsized**) (of a boat) overturn in the water.
– ORIGIN perh. from Spanish *capuzar* 'sink (a ship) by the head'.

capstan /kap-stuhn/ ● n. a broad revolving cylinder with a vertical axis, used for wind-

ing a rope or cable.
– ORIGIN Provençal *cabestan*.

capsule ● n. **1** a small case of gelatin containing a dose of medicine, that dissolves after it is swallowed. **2** a small case or container. **3** a dry fruit that releases its seeds by bursting open when ripe.
– ORIGIN Latin *capsula*.

captain ● n. **1** the person in command of a ship or civil aircraft. **2** a rank of naval officer above commander. **3** a rank of officer in the army above lieutenant. **4** a leader of a team. ● v. be the captain of.
– DERIVATIVES **captaincy** n.
– ORIGIN Old French *capitain* 'chief'.

caption ● n. **1** a title or brief explanation printed with an illustration or cartoon. **2** a piece of text appearing on screen as part of a film or television broadcast. ● v. provide with a caption.
– ORIGIN Latin, 'taking'.

captious /kap-shuhss/ ● adj. formal prone to petty fault-finding.
– ORIGIN Latin *captiosus*.

captivate ● v. (**captivates**, **captivating**, **captivated**) attract and hold the interest of; charm.

captive ● n. a person who has been captured or held in confinement. ● adj. **1** confined. **2** not free to choose an alternative: *advertisements at the cinema reach a captive audience*.
– DERIVATIVES **captivity** n.
– ORIGIN Latin *captivus*.

captor ● n. a person who captures another.

capture ● v. (**captures**, **capturing**, **captured**) **1** take or get by force. **2** take prisoner. **3** record accurately in words or pictures: *photographers tried to capture her soulful blue eyes*. **4** cause (data) to be stored in a computer. ● n. the action of capturing or the state of being captured.
– ORIGIN Latin *capere* 'seize, take'.

Capuchin /kap-uh-chin/ ● n. **1** a friar belonging to a strict branch of the Franciscan order. **2** (**capuchin**) a South American monkey with a hood-like cap of hair on the head.
– ORIGIN Italian *cappuccino* 'small hood'.

capybara /ka-pi-bah-ruh/ ● n. (pl. **capybara** or **capybaras**) a large South American rodent resembling a long-legged guinea pig.
– ORIGIN from an American Indian word meaning 'grass-eater'.

car ● n. **1** a powered road vehicle designed to carry a small number of people. **2** a railway carriage or (N. Amer.) wagon.
– ORIGIN Latin *carrus* 'two-wheeled vehicle'.

Caracalla E
/ka-ruh-kal-luh/ (188–217; later called *Marcus Aurelius Severus Antoninus Augustus*), Roman emperor 211–17.

Caracas E
/kuh-rak-uhss/ the capital of Venezuela.

Caractacus E
/kuh-rak-tuh-kuhss/ var. of CARATACUS.

carafe /kuh-raf/ ● n. an open-topped glass flask used for serving wine in a restaurant.
– ORIGIN French.

carambola /ka-ruhm-boh-luh/ ● n. a golden-yellow fruit which is shaped like a star when cut through.
– ORIGIN Portuguese.

caramel ● n. **1** sugar or syrup heated until it turns brown, used as a flavouring or colouring for food. **2** a soft toffee made with sugar and butter.
– ORIGIN Spanish *caramelo*.

caramelize /ka-ruh-muh-lyz/ (also **caramelise**) ● v. (**caramelizes**, **caramelizing**, **caramelized**) turn or be turned into caramel.

carapace /ka-ruh-payss/ ● n. the hard upper shell of a tortoise, lobster, or related animal.
– ORIGIN Spanish *carapacho*.

carat /ka-ruht/ ● n. **1** a unit of weight for precious stones and pearls, equivalent to 200 milligrams. **2** (US also **karat**) a measure of the purity of gold, pure gold being 24 carats.
– ORIGIN Greek *keration* 'fruit of the carob'.

Caratacus E
/kuh-rat-uh-kuhss/ (also **Caractacus** /kuh-rak-tuh-kuhss/) (1st century AD), British chieftain, who took part in the resistance to the Roman invasion of AD 43.

Caravaggio E
/ka-ruh-vaj-i-oh/, Michelangelo Merisi da (*c.*1571–1610), Italian painter, known for his dramatic use of light and shade.

caravan ● n. **1** Brit. a vehicle equipped for living in, designed to be towed by a vehicle or a horse. **2** a group of people with vehicles or animals who are travelling together.
– DERIVATIVES **caravanner** n. **caravanning** n.
– ORIGIN Persian.

caravanserai /ka-ruh-van-suh-ry/ (US also **caravansary**) ● n. (pl. **caravanserais** or **caravansaries**) **1** hist. an inn with a central courtyard in the desert regions of Asia or North Africa. **2** a group of people travelling together; a caravan.
– ORIGIN Persian, 'caravan palace'.

caravel /ka-ruh-vel/ (also **carvel**) ● n. hist. a small, fast Spanish or Portuguese ship of the 15th–17th centuries.
– ORIGIN Portuguese *caravela*.

caraway /ka-ruh-way/ ● n. the seeds of a plant of the parsley family, used for flavouring.
– ORIGIN Latin *carui*.

carbide ● n. Chem. a compound of carbon with a metal or other element.

carbine ● n. a light automatic rifle.
– ORIGIN French *carabine*.

carbohydrate ● n. any of a large group of compounds (including sugars and starch) which contain carbon, hydrogen, and oxygen, found in food and used to give energy.

carbolic acid (also **carbolic**) ● n. phenol, used as a disinfectant.

carbon ● n. a non-metallic chemical element which has two main pure forms (diamond and graphite), and is present in all organic compounds.
– ORIGIN Latin *carbo* 'coal, charcoal'.

carbonaceous /kar-buh-nay-shuhss/ ● adj. consisting of or containing carbon or its compounds.

carbonate /kar-buh-nayt/ ● n. a compound containing CO_3 negative ions together with a metallic element.

carbonated ● adj. (of a drink) containing dissolved carbon dioxide.

carbon copy • n. **1** a copy made with carbon paper. **2** a person or thing identical to another.

carbon dating • n. a method of finding out the age of an organic object by measuring the amount of radioactive carbon-14 that it contains.

carbon dioxide • n. a gas produced by burning carbon and by breathing, and absorbed by plants in photosynthesis.

carbonic acid • n. a very weak acid formed when carbon dioxide dissolves in water.

Carboniferous /kar-buh-**nif**-uh-ruhss/ • adj. Geol. relating to the fifth period in the Palaeozoic era (about 363 to 290 million years ago), when extensive coal-bearing strata were formed.

carbonize (also **carbonise**) • v. (**carbonizes, carbonizing, carbonized**) convert into carbon, by heating or burning.
– DERIVATIVES **carbonization** (also **carbonisation**) n.

carbon monoxide • n. a poisonous flammable gas formed by incomplete burning of carbon.

carbon paper • n. thin paper coated with carbon, used for making a copy as a document is being written or typed.

car boot sale • n. Brit. a sale at which people sell things from the boots of their cars.

carborundum /kar-buh-**run**-duhm/ • n. a very hard black solid consisting of silicon and carbon, used for grinding, smoothing, and polishing.
– ORIGIN from CARBON and CORUNDUM.

carboy • n. a large rounded glass bottle with a narrow neck, used for holding acids.
– ORIGIN Persian.

carbuncle /**kar**-bung-k'l/ • n. **1** a severe abscess or multiple boil in the skin. **2** a polished garnet.
– ORIGIN Latin *carbunculus* 'small coal'.

carburettor /kar-buh-**ret**-ter/ (US also **carburetor**) • n. a device in an internal combustion engine for mixing air with a fine spray of liquid fuel.
– ORIGIN from archaic *carburet* 'combine or fill with carbon'.

carcass (Brit. also **carcase**) • n. **1** the dead body of an animal. **2** the remains of a cooked bird after all the edible parts have been removed. **3** the structural framework or remains of something.
– ORIGIN Old French *carcois*.

Carcassonne E
/kar-kuh-**son**/ a walled city in SW France.

carcinogen /kar-**sin**-uh-juhn/ • n. a substance capable of causing cancer.
– DERIVATIVES **carcinogenic** adj.

carcinoma /kar-si-**noh**-muh/ • n. (pl. **carcinomas** or **carcinomata** /kar-si-**noh**-muh-tuh/) a cancer arising in the tissues of the skin or of the lining of the internal organs.
– ORIGIN from Greek *karkinos* 'crab'.

card[1] • n. **1** thick, stiff paper or thin cardboard. **2** a piece of card for writing on or printed with information: *a business card*. **3** a small rectangular piece of plastic containing personal details in a form that can be read by a computer: *a credit card*. **4** a playing card. **5** (**cards**) a game played with playing cards. **6** informal, dated or N. Amer. an odd or amusing person.
– PHRASES **a card up one's sleeve** Brit. a plan or asset that is kept secret until needed. **give someone their cards** (or **get one's cards**) Brit. informal dismiss someone (or be dismissed) from employment. **on the cards** informal likely. **play the —— card** make use of a particular issue to gain an advantage: *he played the race card*. **play one's cards right** make the best use of one's assets and opportunities. **put one's cards on the table** state one's plans openly.
– ORIGIN Greek *khartēs* 'papyrus leaf'.

card[2] • v. comb and clean (raw wool or similar material) with a sharp-toothed instrument to disentangle the fibres. • n. a toothed implement or machine for this purpose.
– ORIGIN Latin *carduus* 'thistle'.

cardamom /**kar**-duh-muhm/ • n. the seeds of a SE Asian plant, used as a spice.
– ORIGIN from Greek *kardamon* 'cress' + *amōmon*, a kind of spice plant.

cardboard • n. thin board made from layers of paper pasted together or from paper pulp. • adj. not realistic: *the novel's cardboard characters*.

card-carrying • adj. registered as a member of a political party or trade union.

cardiac /**kar**-di-ak/ • adj. having to do with the heart.
– ORIGIN Greek *kardia* 'heart'.

Cardiff E
the capital of Wales. Welsh name CAERDYDD.

cardigan • n. a knitted jumper fastening with buttons down the front.
– ORIGIN named after the 7th Earl of *Cardigan* (1797–1868), whose troops first wore such garments.

Cardiganshire E
a former county of SW Wales, which became part of Dyfed in 1974. The area became a county once more in 1996, but was renamed Ceredigion.

Cardin E
/**kar**-dan/, Pierre (b.1922). French fashion designer.

cardinal • n. a leading Roman Catholic clergyman, nominated by and having the power to elect the Pope. • adj. most important; chief.
– ORIGIN Latin *cardinalis*.

cardinal number • n. a number expressing quantity (one, two, three, etc.), rather than order (first, second, third, etc.).

cardinal point • n. each of the four main points of the compass (north, south, east, and west).

cardiograph /**kar**-di-uh-grahf/ • n. an instrument for recording heart movements.

cardiology /kar-di-**ol**-uh-ji/ • n. the branch of medicine concerned with diseases and abnormalities of the heart.
– DERIVATIVES **cardiologist** n.
– ORIGIN Greek *kardia* 'heart'.

cardiovascular /kar-di-oh-**vass**-kyuu-ler/ • adj. having to do with the heart and blood vessels.

cardoon /kar-**doon**/ • n. a tall thistle-like plant related to the globe artichoke, with

edible leaves and roots.
– ORIGIN Latin *carduus* 'thistle'.

card sharp (also **card sharper**) ● **n.** a person who cheats at cards.

care ● **n. 1** the provision of welfare and protection: *the care of the elderly.* **2** Brit. the taking over of a child's welfare and protection by a local authority: *he was taken into care.* **3** serious attention to avoid damage, risk, or error: *handle with care.* **4** a feeling of or cause for anxiety. ● **v.** (**cares**, **caring**, **cared**) **1** feel concern or interest: *he doesn't really care about anybody.* **2** feel affection or liking. **3** (**care for/to do**) like to have or be willing to do. **4** (**care for**) look after and provide for the needs of.
– PHRASES **care of** at the address of. **take care 1** be careful. **2** make sure (to do). **take care of** look after or deal with.
– ORIGIN Old English.

careen /kuh-reen/ ● **v. 1** (with reference to a ship) tilt to one side. **2** move in an uncontrolled way; career.
– ORIGIN Latin *carina* 'a keel'.

career ● **n.** an occupation undertaken for a substantial period of a person's life. ● **adj.** (of a woman) choosing to pursue a profession rather than devoting herself to childcare or housekeeping. ● **v.** (**careers**, **careering**, **careered**) move along swiftly and in an uncontrolled way.
– ORIGIN French *carrière* 'racecourse'.

careerist ● **n.** a person whose main concern is to progress in their career.
– DERIVATIVES **careerism** n.

carefree ● **adj.** free from anxiety or responsibility.

careful ● **adj. 1** taking care to avoid harm or trouble; cautious. **2** (**careful with**) sensible in the use of. **3** done with or showing thought and attention.
– DERIVATIVES **carefully** adv.

careless ● **adj. 1** not giving enough attention or thought to avoiding harm or mistakes. **2** (**careless of/about**) not concerned about.
– DERIVATIVES **carelessly** adv. **carelessness** n.

carer ● **n.** Brit. a family member or paid helper who cares for a sick, elderly, or disabled person.

caress ● **v.** touch or stroke gently or lovingly. ● **n.** a gentle or loving touch.
– ORIGIN French *caresser.*

caretaker ● **n.** Brit. a person employed to look after a public building. ● **adj.** holding power temporarily: *a caretaker government.*

careworn ● **adj.** tired and unhappy because of prolonged worry.

> **Carey,** E
> George (Leonard) (b.1935), English Anglican churchman, Archbishop of Canterbury since 1991.

cargo ● **n.** (pl. **cargoes** or **cargos**) goods carried on a ship, aircraft, or truck.
– ORIGIN Spanish.

Carib /ka-rib/ ● **n. 1** a member of a people living mainly in coastal regions of north-east South America. **2** the language of the Carib.
– ORIGIN Spanish *caribe.*

Caribbean /ka-rib-**bee**-uhn/ ● **adj.** relating to the region consisting of the Caribbean Sea, its islands, and the surrounding coasts.

> **Caribbean Sea** E
> the part of the Atlantic Ocean lying between the Antilles and the mainland of Central and South America.

caribou /ka-ri-boo/ ● **n.** (pl. **caribou**) N. Amer. a reindeer.
– ORIGIN Canadian French.

caricature /ka-ri-kuh-tyoor/ ● **n.** a picture in which a person's distinctive features are exaggerated for comic effect. ● **v.** (**caricatures**, **caricaturing**, **caricatured**) make a caricature of.
– DERIVATIVES **caricaturist** n.
– ORIGIN Italian *caricare* 'exaggerate'.

caries /kair-eez/ ● **n.** decay and crumbling of a tooth or bone.
– ORIGIN Latin.

carillon /ka-ril-lyuhn/ ● **n.** a set of bells sounded from a keyboard or by an automatic mechanism.
– ORIGIN Old French *quarregnon* 'peal of four bells'.

> **Carlisle** E
> /kar-lyl/ a city in NW England, the county town of Cumbria.

> **Carlyle** E
> /kar-lyl/, Thomas (1795–1881), Scottish historian and political philosopher, noted for his *History of the French Revolution*. Other writings include *Sartor Resartus*, a semi-autobiographical philosophical work.

> **Carmarthenshire** E
> a county of South Wales; administrative centre, Carmarthen.

Carmelite /kar-muh-lyt/ ● **n.** a friar or nun of an order founded at Mount Carmel in Israel during the Crusades.

carmine /kar-myn/ ● **n.** a vivid crimson colour.
– ORIGIN French *carmin.*

carnage /kar-nij/ ● **n.** the killing of a large number of people.
– ORIGIN Latin *caro* 'flesh'.

carnal ● **adj.** relating to sexual urges and activities.
– DERIVATIVES **carnality** n.
– ORIGIN Latin *caro* 'flesh'.

carnation ● **n.** a cultivated variety of pink, with double pink, white, or red flowers.
– ORIGIN perh. from a misreading of an Arabic word.

> **Carnegie** E
> /kar-**nay**-gi, kar-**nee**-gi/, Andrew (1835–1919), Scottish-born American industrialist and philanthropist.

carnelian /kar-nee-li-uhn/ (also **cornelian**) ● **n.** a dull red or pink semi-precious variety of chalcedony.
– ORIGIN Old French *corneline.*

carnival ● **n. 1** an annual public festival involving processions, music, and dancing. **2** N. Amer. a travelling funfair or circus.
– ORIGIN Italian *carnevale.*

carnivore /kar-ni-vor/ ● **n.** an animal that eats meat.

carnivorous /kar-**niv**-uh-ruhss/ ● **adj.** (of an animal) eating meat.
– ORIGIN from Latin *caro* 'flesh'.

carob /ka-ruhb/ ● n. the edible pod of an Arabian tree, from which a substitute for chocolate is made.
– ORIGIN Old French *carobe*.

carol ● n. a religious song or popular hymn associated with Christmas. ● v. (**carols**, **carolling**, **carolled**; US **carols**, **caroling**, **caroled**) **1** (**go carolling**) sing carols in the streets. **2** sing or say happily.
– DERIVATIVES **caroller** (US **caroler**) n.
– ORIGIN Old French *carole*.

Caroline Islands E
a group of islands in the western Pacific Ocean, forming the Federated States of Micronesia.

carotene /ka-ruh-teen/ ● n. an orange or red substance found in carrots and many other plants, important in the formation of vitamin A.
– ORIGIN from Latin *carota* 'carrot'.

carotid /kuh-rot-id/ ● adj. relating to the two main arteries carrying blood to the head and neck.
– ORIGIN Latin *carotides*.

carouse /kuh-rowz/ ● v. (**carouses**, **carousing**, **caroused**) drink alcohol and enjoy oneself with others in a noisy, lively way.
– DERIVATIVES **carousal** n.
– ORIGIN from German *gar aus trinken* 'drink heavily'.

carousel /ka-ruh-sel/ ● n. **1** a merry-go-round at a fair. **2** a rotating device, such as a conveyor system for baggage collection at an airport.
– ORIGIN Italian *carosello* 'tournament for knights on horseback'.

carp[1] ● n. (pl. **carp**) an edible freshwater fish.
– ORIGIN Latin *carpa*.

carp[2] ● v. complain continually.
– ORIGIN Old Norse, 'brag'.

carpal /kar-p'l/ ● adj. relating to the bones in the wrist. ● n. a bone in the wrist.

Carpathian Mountains E
/kar-pay-thi-uhn/ a mountain system extending south-eastwards from southern Poland and Slovakia into Romania.

carpel /kar-p'l/ ● n. the female reproductive organ of a flower, consisting of an ovary, a stigma, and usually a style.
– ORIGIN Greek *karpos* 'fruit'.

Carpentaria, Gulf of E
/kar-puhn-tair-i-uh/ a large bay on the north coast of Australia.

carpenter ● n. a person who makes wooden objects and structures.
– DERIVATIVES **carpentry** n.
– ORIGIN from Latin *carpentarius artifex* 'carriage-maker'.

carpet ● n. **1** a floor covering made from thick woven fabric. **2** a thick or soft layer: *a carpet of bluebells.* ● v. (**carpets**, **carpeting**, **carpeted**) **1** cover with a carpet. **2** Brit. informal reprimand severely.
– PHRASES **sweep under the carpet** conceal or ignore (a problem) in the hope that it will be forgotten.
– ORIGIN Old French *carpite* 'woollen covering for a table or bed'.

carpet bag ● n. a travelling bag originally made of carpet-like fabric.

carpetbagger ● n. derog., esp. N. Amer. **1** a politician who tries to get elected in an area where they have no local connections. **2** a person who exploits a situation unscrupulously.

carpet-bomb ● v. bomb (an area) intensively.

carpeting ● n. material for carpets or carpets in general.

carpet slipper ● n. a soft slipper with an upper of wool or thick cloth.

carport ● n. an open-sided shelter for a car, projecting from the side of a house.

carpus /kar-puhss/ ● n. (pl. **carpi** /kar-py/) the group of small bones in the wrist.
– ORIGIN Greek *karpos* 'wrist'.

carrel /ka-ruhl/ ● n. a small cubicle with a desk for a reader in a library.
– ORIGIN prob. from **CAROL** in the former sense 'a ring or enclosure'.

Carreras E
/kuh-rair-uhss/, José (b.1946), Spanish operatic tenor.

carriage ● n. **1** a four-wheeled horse-drawn vehicle for passengers. **2** Brit. a passenger vehicle in a train. **3** Brit. the carrying of goods from one place to another. **4** a person's bearing or deportment. **5** a moving part of a machine that carries other parts into the required position: *a typewriter carriage.* **6** a wheeled support for moving a gun.
– ORIGIN Old French *cariage*.

carriage clock ● n. Brit. a portable clock in a rectangular case with a handle on top.

carriageway ● n. Brit. **1** each of the two sides of a dual carriageway or motorway. **2** the part of a road intended for vehicles.

carrier ● n. **1** a person or thing that carries or holds something. **2** a company that transports goods or people for payment. **3** a person or animal that transmits a disease to others without suffering from it themselves.

carrier bag ● n. Brit. a plastic or paper bag with handles, for carrying shopping.

carrier pigeon ● n. a homing pigeon trained to carry messages.

carrion ● n. the decaying flesh of dead animals.
– ORIGIN Old French *caroine, charoigne*.

Carroll, E
Lewis (1832–98; pen name of *Charles Lutwidge Dodgson*), English writer, author of the children's classics *Alice's Adventures in Wonderland* and *Through the Looking Glass*.

carrot ● n. **1** a tapering orange root vegetable. **2** something tempting offered as a means of persuasion: *training that relies more on the carrot than on the stick.*
– ORIGIN Greek *karōton*.

carroty ● adj. (of a person's hair) orange-red.

carry ● v. (**carries**, **carrying**, **carried**) **1** move or take from one place to another. **2** have with one wherever one goes: *I never carry money.* **3** support the weight of. **4** assume or accept (responsibility or blame). **5** have as a feature or result: *the bike carries a ten-year guarantee.* **6** take or develop (an idea or activity) to a particular point: *he carried the criticism much further.* **7** publish or broadcast. **8** (of a sound or voice) travel: *his voice carried clearly across the room.* **9** approve (a proposal) by a majority of votes. **10** (**carry**

oneself) stand and move in a specified way. **11** be pregnant with. ● **n.** (pl. **carries**) an act of carrying.
– PHRASES **be/get carried away** lose self-control. **carry the can** Brit. informal take responsibility for a mistake. **carry forward** transfer (figures) to a new page or account. **carry off 1** take away by force. **2** succeed in doing. **carry on 1** continue. **2** take part in. **3** informal, esp. Brit. have a love affair. **carry out** perform (a task). **carry over 1** keep to use or deal with in a new situation. **2** postpone. **carry through** bring to completion. **carry weight** be influential.
– ORIGIN Old French *carier*.

carrycot ● **n.** Brit. a small portable baby's cot.

carry-on ● **n.** Brit. informal **1** a fuss. **2** (also **carryings-on**) improper behaviour.

Carson, E
Rachel (Louise) (1907–64), American zoologist, noted for *Silent Spring*, an attack on the indiscriminate use of pesticides.

cart ● **n. 1** an open horse-drawn vehicle with two or four wheels, for carrying loads or passengers. **2** a shallow open container on wheels, pulled or pushed by hand. ● **v. 1** carry in a cart or similar vehicle. **2** informal carry (a heavy object) with difficulty. **3** convey or remove roughly: *the demonstrators were carted off by the police*.
– PHRASES **put the cart before the horse** reverse the proper order of doing something.
– ORIGIN Old Norse.

carte blanche /kart **blahnsh**/ ● **n.** complete freedom to act as one wishes.
– ORIGIN French, 'blank paper'.

cartel /kar-**tel**/ ● **n.** an association of manufacturers or suppliers formed to maintain high prices and restrict competition.
– ORIGIN German *Kartell*.

Carter[1], E
Howard (1874–1939), English archaeologist, who discovered the tomb of the Egyptian pharaoh Tutankhamen in 1922.

Carter[2], E
Jimmy (b.1924; full name *James Earl Carter*), American Democratic statesman, 39th President of the US 1977–81.

Cartesian /kar-**tee**-zi-uhn/ ● **adj.** relating to the French philosopher Descartes and his ideas.
– ORIGIN from *Cartesius*, Latin form of DESCARTES.

Cartesian coordinates ● **pl. n.** a system for locating a point by reference to its distance from axes intersecting at right angles.

Carthage E
/**kar**-thij/ an ancient city on the coast of North Africa near present-day Tunis. Founded by the Phoenicians *c.*814 BC, Carthage became a major force in the Mediterranean, and came into conflict with Rome in the Punic Wars, at the end of which it was destroyed in 146 BC.
– DERIVATIVES **Carthaginian** n. & adj.

carthorse ● **n.** Brit. a large, strong horse suitable for heavy work.

Carthusian /kar-**thyoo**-zi-uhn/ ● **n.** a monk or nun of a strict order founded by St Bruno at Chartreuse in France in 1084.
– ORIGIN Latin *Carthusia* 'Chartreuse'.

Cartier E
/**kar**-ti-ay/, Jacques (1491–1557), French explorer. The first to establish France's claim to North America, he made three voyages to Canada between 1534 and 1541.

cartilage /**kar**-ti-lij/ ● **n.** firm, flexible tissue which covers the ends of joints and forms structures such as the external ear.
– ORIGIN Latin *cartilago*.

cartilaginous /kar-ti-**laj**-i-nuhss/ ● **adj.** made of cartilage.

Cartland, E
Dame (Mary) Barbara (Hamilton) (1901–2000), English author of light romantic fiction.

cartography /kar-**tog**-ruh-fi/ ● **n.** the science or practice of drawing maps.
– DERIVATIVES **cartographer** n. **cartographic** adj.
– ORIGIN French *carte* 'card, map'.

carton ● **n.** a light cardboard box or container.
– ORIGIN Italian *cartone* 'cartoon'.

cartoon ● **n. 1** a humorous drawing in a newspaper or magazine. **2** (also **cartoon strip**) a sequence of such drawings that tell a story. **3** an animated film made from a sequence of drawings. **4** a full-size drawing made as a preliminary design for a painting or other work of art.
– DERIVATIVES **cartoonist** n.
– ORIGIN Italian *cartone*.

cartouche /kar-**toosh**/ ● **n. 1** a carved decoration or drawing in the form of a scroll with rolled-up ends. **2** an oval or oblong containing Egyptian hieroglyphs representing the name and title of a monarch.
– ORIGIN French.

cartridge ● **n. 1** a container holding film, a quantity of ink, or other item or substance, to be inserted into a mechanism. **2** a casing containing a charge and a bullet or shot for a gun.
– ORIGIN from CARTOUCHE.

cartridge paper ● **n.** thick, rough-textured drawing paper.

cartwheel ● **n.** a circular sideways handspring with the arms and legs extended. ● **v.** perform cartwheels.

Caruso E
/kuh-**roo**-soh/, Enrico (1873–1921), Italian operatic tenor, the first major tenor to be recorded on gramophone records.

carve ● **v.** (**carves**, **carving**, **carved**) **1** cut into or shape (a hard material) to produce an object or design. **2** produce by carving. **3** cut (cooked meat) into slices for eating. **4** (**carve out**) develop (a career, reputation, etc.) through great effort. **5** (**carve up**) divide up ruthlessly.
– ORIGIN Old English.

carvel /**kar**-v'l/ ● **n.** var. of CARAVEL.

carver ● **n. 1** a person or tool that carves. **2** Brit. the principal chair, with arms, in a set of dining chairs.

carvery ● **n.** (pl. **carveries**) esp. Brit. a buffet or restaurant where cooked joints are carved as required.

carving ● **n.** an object or design carved from wood or stone as a work of art.

Casablanca /kass-uh-**blang**-kuh/ the largest city of Morocco, a seaport on the Atlantic coast.

Casanova /kass-uh-**noh**-vuh/ • n. a man who has sexual relationships with many women.
– ORIGIN named after the Italian Giovanni Jacopo *Casanova* (1725–98), who described his sexual encounters in his memoirs.

casbah • n. var. of **KASBAH**.

cascade • n. **1** a small waterfall, especially one in a series. **2** a mass of something that falls, hangs, or occurs in large quantities: *a cascade of blossoms.* • v. (**cascades**, **cascading**, **cascaded**) pour downwards rapidly and in large quantities.
– ORIGIN Italian *cascata*.

case[1] • n. **1** an instance of something occurring: *a case of mistaken identity.* **2** an incident being investigated by the police. **3** a legal action that is to be or has been decided in a court of law. **4** a set of facts or arguments supporting one side of a debate or lawsuit. **5** a person or their situation as a subject of medical or welfare attention. **6** Grammar a form of a noun, adjective, or pronoun expressing the relationship of the word to others in the sentence: *the possessive case.*
– PHRASES **be the case** be so. **in case** so as to provide for the possibility of something happening.
– ORIGIN Latin *casus* 'fall, chance'.

case[2] • n. **1** a container or protective covering. **2** Brit. a suitcase. **3** a box containing twelve bottles of wine or other drink, sold as a unit. • v. (**cases**, **casing**, **cased**) **1** enclose within a case. **2** informal look around (a place) before carrying out a robbery.
– ORIGIN Latin *capsa*.

case history • n. a record of a person's background or medical history kept by a doctor or social worker.

casein /kay-seen/ • n. the main protein present in milk and cheese.
– ORIGIN from Latin *caseus* 'cheese'.

casement • n. a window set on a hinge at the side, so that it opens like a door.
– ORIGIN Latin *cassimentum*.

case study • n. **1** a detailed study of the development of a person, group, or situation over a period of time. **2** a particular instance used to illustrate a general principle.

casework • n. social work concerned with a person's family history and their personal circumstances.

Cash, Johnny (1932–2003), American country music singer and songwriter.

cash • n. **1** money in coins or notes. **2** money as available for use: *he was always short of cash.* • v. **1** give or obtain notes or coins for (a cheque or money order). **2** (**cash in**) convert (an insurance policy, savings account, etc.) into money. **3** (**cash in on**) informal take advantage of.
– PHRASES **cash in hand** payment in cash rather than by cheque or other means.
– DERIVATIVES **cashless** adj.
– ORIGIN Old French *casse* 'box for money'.

cash and carry • n. a system of wholesale trading in which goods are paid for in full and taken away by the purchaser.

cashback • n. **1** a cash refund offered as an incentive to buyers. **2** a service offered by a shop whereby a customer may withdraw cash when buying goods with a debit card.

cash book • n. a book in which amounts of money paid and received are recorded.

cash card • n. Brit. a plastic card issued by a bank or building society which enables the holder to withdraw money from a cash dispenser.

cash crop • n. a crop produced for sale rather than for use by the grower.

cash dispenser • n. Brit. an automated teller machine.

cashew /ka-shoo/ • n. (also **cashew nut**) the edible kidney-shaped nut of a tropical American tree.
– ORIGIN from an American Indian language.

cash flow • n. the total amount of money passing into and out of a business.

cashier[1] • n. a person whose job is to pay out and receive money in a shop, bank, or business.
– ORIGIN French *caissier*.

cashier[2] • v. (**cashiers**, **cashiering**, **cashiered**) dismiss from the armed forces because of serious wrongdoing.
– ORIGIN French *casser* 'revoke, dismiss'.

cashmere • n. fine soft wool, originally that from a breed of Himalayan goat.
– ORIGIN early spelling of **KASHMIR**.

cashpoint • n. Brit. an automated teller machine.

cash register • n. a machine used in shops for totalling and recording the amount of each sale and storing the money received.

casing • n. a cover or shell that protects or encloses something.

casino • n. (pl. **casinos**) a public building or room for gambling.
– ORIGIN Italian, 'little house'.

cask • n. a large barrel for storing alcoholic drinks.
– ORIGIN French *casque* or Spanish *casco* 'helmet'.

casket • n. **1** a small ornamental box or chest for holding valuable objects. **2** esp. N. Amer. a coffin.
– ORIGIN perh. from Old French *cassette* 'little box'.

Caspian Sea /kass-pi-uhn/ a large landlocked salt lake, bounded by Russia, Kazakhstan, Turkmenistan, Azerbaijan, and Iran. It is the world's largest body of inland water with an area of about 371,800 sq. km (143,550 sq. miles).

Cassandra /kuh-san-druh/ • n. a person who makes gloomy predictions.
– ORIGIN from *Cassandra* in Greek mythology, whose prophecies were not believed.

cassava /kuh-sah-vuh/ • n. the starchy root of a tropical American tree, used as food.
– ORIGIN from an extinct Caribbean language.

casserole • n. **1** a large dish with a lid, used for cooking food slowly in an oven. **2** a kind of stew cooked slowly in an oven. • v. (**casseroles**, **casseroling**, **casseroled**) cook in a casserole.
– ORIGIN French.

cassette • n. a sealed plastic case containing audio tape, videotape, film, etc., to be inserted

into a recorder, camera, or other device.
– ORIGIN French, 'little box'.

Cassius E
/kass-i-uhss/, Gaius (d.42 BC), Roman general, one of the leaders of the conspiracy in 44 BC to assassinate Julius Caesar.

C

cassock • n. a long garment worn by some Christian clergy and members of church choirs.
– ORIGIN Italian *casacca* 'riding coat'.

cassowary /kass-uh-wuh-ri/ • n. (pl. **cassowaries**) a very large flightless bird, native mainly to New Guinea.
– ORIGIN Malay.

cast • v. (**casts**, **casting**, **cast**) **1** throw forcefully. **2** cause (light or shadow) to appear on a surface. **3** direct (one's eyes or thoughts) towards something. **4** express: *journalists cast doubt on this account.* **5** register (a vote). **6** give a part to (an actor) or allocate parts in (a play or film). **7** leave aside or shed: *Sam jumped in, casting caution to the wind.* **8** shape (metal or other material) by pouring it into a mould while molten. **9** produce by casting: *a figure cast in bronze.* **10** cause (a magic spell) to take effect. • n. **1** the actors taking part in a play or film. **2** an object made by casting metal or other material. **3** (also **plaster cast**) a bandage stiffened with plaster of Paris, moulded to support and protect a broken limb. **4** appearance or character: *minds of a philosophical cast.*
– PHRASES **be cast away** be stranded after a shipwreck. **be cast down** feel depressed. **cast about** (or **around** or **round**) search far and wide. **cast off 1** Knitting take the stitches off the needle by looping each over the next. **2** set a boat or ship free from its moorings. **cast on** Knitting make the first row of loops on the needle.
– ORIGIN Old Norse.

castanets • pl. n. a pair of small curved pieces of wood, clicked together by the fingers to accompany Spanish dancing.
– ORIGIN Spanish *castañeta* 'little chestnut'.

castaway • n. a person who has been shipwrecked in an isolated place.

caste • n. each of the hereditary classes of Hindu society.
– ORIGIN Spanish and Portuguese *casta* 'lineage, breed'.

castellated /kass-tuh-lay-tid/ • adj. having battlements.
– ORIGIN Latin *castellum* 'little fort'.

caster • n. **1** a person or machine that casts. **2** var. of **CASTOR**.

caster sugar (also **castor sugar**) • n. Brit. white sugar in fine granules.

castigate /kass-ti-gayt/ • v. (**castigates**, **castigating**, **castigated**) reprimand severely.
– DERIVATIVES **castigation** n.
– ORIGIN Latin *castigare.*

Castile E
/ka-steel/ a region of central Spain, formerly an independent Spanish kingdom.

casting • n. an object made by casting molten metal or other material.

casting vote • n. an extra vote used by a chairperson to decide an issue when votes on each side are equal.

cast iron • n. a hard alloy of iron and carbon which can be cast in a mould. • adj. firm and unchangeable: *a cast-iron guarantee.*

castle • n. **1** a large fortified building or group of buildings of the medieval period. **2** Chess, informal dated = **ROOK²**.
– PHRASES **castles in the air** (or **in Spain**) schemes existing in the imagination that will never be achieved.
– ORIGIN Latin *castellum* 'little fort'.

cast-off • adj. abandoned or discarded. • n. a cast-off garment.

castor /kah-ster/ (also **caster**) • n. **1** each of a set of small swivelling wheels fixed to the legs or base of a piece of furniture. **2** a small container with holes in the top, used for sprinkling salt, sugar, etc.
– ORIGIN from **CASTER**.

Castor and Pollux E
/kah-ster, pol-luhks/ Gk Myth. the twin sons of Leda. Castor was the mortal son of Leda and her husband Tyndareus; his brother Pollux was the immortal son of Leda and Zeus.

castor oil • n. an oil obtained from the seeds of an African shrub, used as a laxative.
– ORIGIN Greek *kastōr* 'beaver'; perh. because an oily substance produced by a beaver was formerly used as a laxative.

castor sugar • n. var. of **CASTER SUGAR**.

castrate • v. (**castrates**, **castrating**, **castrated**) **1** remove the testicles of. **2** deprive of power or vigour.
– DERIVATIVES **castration** n.
– ORIGIN Latin *castrare.*

Castro E
/ka-stroh/, Fidel (b.1927), Cuban statesman, Prime Minister 1959–76 and President since 1976. After overthrowing President Batista he set up a long-lasting communist regime in Cuba.

casual • adj. **1** relaxed and unconcerned. **2** lacking care or thought: *a casual remark.* **3** not regular or firmly established; occasional or temporary: *casual jobs.* **4** happening by chance. **5** informal. • n. **1** a temporary or occasional worker. **2** (**casuals**) informal clothes or shoes.
– DERIVATIVES **casually** adv.
– ORIGIN Latin *casualis.*

casualty • n. (pl. **casualties**) **1** a person killed or injured in a war or accident. **2** a person or thing badly affected by an event or situation: *the firm was one of the casualties of the recession.*

casuistry /kazh-oo-iss-tri/ • n. the use of clever but false reasoning.
– DERIVATIVES **casuist** n.
– ORIGIN Latin *casus* 'fall, chance'.

cat • n. **1** a small furry mammal that is kept as a pet. **2** a wild animal related to or resembling this, e.g. a lion.
– PHRASES **the cat's whiskers** informal an excellent person or thing. **let the cat out of the bag** informal reveal a secret by mistake. **like a cat on a hot tin roof** informal very anxious. **put** (or **set**) **the cat among the pigeons** Brit. do something likely to cause trouble.
– ORIGIN Old English.

cata- (also **cat-**) • prefix **1** down; downwards: *catabolism.* **2** wrongly; badly: *catatonia.* **3** completely: *cataclysm.* **4** against; alongside:

catechize.
– ORIGIN Greek *kata.*

catabolism /kuh-**tab**-uh-li-z'm/ • **n.** the breakdown of complex molecules in living organisms to form simpler ones, together with the release of energy. Opp. **ANABOLISM**.
– DERIVATIVES **catabolic** adj.
– ORIGIN Greek *katabolē* 'throwing down'.

cataclysm /**kat**-uh-kli-z'm/ • **n.** a violent upheaval or disaster.
– DERIVATIVES **cataclysmic** adj.
– ORIGIN Greek *kataklusmos* 'deluge'.

catacomb /**kat**-uh-koom/ • **n.** an underground cemetery consisting of tunnels with recesses for tombs.
– ORIGIN Latin *catacumbas*, the name of an underground cemetery near Rome.

catafalque /**kat**-uh-falk/ • **n.** a decorated wooden framework to support a coffin.
– ORIGIN Italian *catafalco*.

Catalan /**kat**-uh-lan/ • **n. 1** a person from Catalonia. **2** the language of Catalonia. • **adj.** relating to Catalonia.

catalepsy /**kat**-uh-lep-si/ • **n.** a medical condition in which a person suffers a loss of consciousness and their body becomes rigid.
– DERIVATIVES **cataleptic** adj. & n.
– ORIGIN Greek *katalambanein* 'seize upon'.

catalogue (US also **catalog**) • **n. 1** a list of items arranged in alphabetical or other systematic order. **2** a publication containing details of items for sale. **3** a series of bad things: *a catalogue of failures.* • **v.** (**catalogues**, **cataloguing**, **catalogued**; US also **catalogs**, **cataloging**, **cataloged**) list in a catalogue.
– ORIGIN Greek *katalogos*.

Catalonia E
/kat-uh-**loh**-ni-uh/ an autonomous region of NE Spain; capital, Barcelona.
– DERIVATIVES **Catalonian** adj. & n.

catalyse /**kat**-uh-lyz/ (US **catalyze**) • **v.** (**catalyses**, **catalysing**, **catalysed**; US **catalyzes**, **catalyzing**, **catalyzed**) cause or speed up (a reaction) by acting as a catalyst.

catalysis /kuh-**tal**-i-siss/ • **n.** the speeding up of a chemical reaction by a catalyst.
– DERIVATIVES **catalytic** /kat-uh-**lit**-ik/ adj.
– ORIGIN Greek *katalusis* 'dissolving'.

catalyst /**kat**-uh-list/ • **n. 1** a substance that increases the rate of a chemical reaction while remaining unchanged itself. **2** a person or thing that triggers an event.

catalytic converter • **n.** a device in the exhaust system of a motor vehicle, containing a catalyst for converting pollutant gases into less harmful ones.

catamaran /**kat**-uh-muh-ran/ • **n.** a boat with twin parallel hulls.
– ORIGIN Tamil, 'tied wood'.

catapult • **n. 1** esp. Brit. a forked stick with an elastic band fastened to the two prongs, used for shooting small stones. **2** a former machine for throwing large stones at buildings. **3** a mechanical device for launching a glider or aircraft. • **v. 1** throw forcefully: *the explosion catapulted the car along the road.* **2** move suddenly or very fast.
– ORIGIN Latin *catapulta*.

cataract /**kat**-uh-rakt/ • **n. 1** a large waterfall. **2** a medical condition in which the lens of the eye becomes cloudy, resulting in blurred vision.
– ORIGIN Greek *kataraktēs* 'down-rushing'.

catarrh /kuh-**tar**/ • **n.** excessive mucus in the nose or throat.
– ORIGIN Greek *katarrhein* 'flow down'.

catastrophe /kuh-**tass**-truh-fi/ • **n.** a sudden event causing great damage or suffering.
– DERIVATIVES **catastrophic** adj.
– ORIGIN Greek *katastrophē* 'overturning'.

catatonia /kat-uh-**toh**-ni-uh/ • **n.** a form of schizophrenia in which a person experiences periods of unconsciousness or overactivity.
– DERIVATIVES **catatonic** adj.
– ORIGIN from Greek *tonos* 'tone'.

cat burglar • **n.** a thief who enters a building by climbing to an upper storey.

catcall • **n.** a shrill whistle or shout of mockery or disapproval. • **v.** make a catcall.

catch • **v.** (**catches**, **catching**, **caught**) **1** seize and hold (something moving). **2** capture (a person or animal). **3** be in time to board (a vehicle) or to see (a person or event). **4** entangle or become entangled: *she caught her foot in the bedspread.* **5** surprise (someone) in the act of doing something wrong or embarrassing. **6** (**be caught in**) unexpectedly find oneself in (an unwelcome situation) **7** gain (a person's interest). **8** see, hear, or understand: *he said something Jess couldn't catch.* **9** hit. **10** become infected with (an illness). **11** start burning. **12** Cricket dismiss (a batsman) by catching the ball before it touches the ground. • **n. 1** an act of catching. **2** a device for fastening a door, window, etc. **3** a hidden problem. **4** a break in a person's voice caused by emotion. **5** an amount of fish caught.
– PHRASES **catch one's breath 1** breathe in sharply to express an emotion. **2** recover one's breath after exercise. **catch someone's eye 1** be noticed by someone. **2** attract someone's attention. **catch on** informal **1** become popular. **2** understand. **catch out** Brit. **1** discover that (someone) has done something wrong. **2** take unawares: *you might get caught out by the weather.* **catch the sun 1** be in a sunny position. **2** Brit. become tanned or sunburnt. **catch up 1** succeed in reaching a person ahead. **2** do tasks which one should have done earlier.
– DERIVATIVES **catcher** n.
– ORIGIN Latin *capture* 'try to catch'.

catch-all • **n.** a term or category intended to cover all possibilities.

catching • **adj.** informal (of a disease) infectious.

catchment (also **catchment area**) • **n. 1** the area from which a hospital's patients or a school's pupils are drawn. **2** the area from which rainfall flows into a river, lake, or reservoir.

catchpenny • **adj.** outwardly attractive so as to sell quickly.

catchphrase • **n.** a well-known sentence or phrase.

catch-22 • **n.** a difficult situation from which there is no escape because it involves conditions which conflict with each other.
– ORIGIN the title of a novel by Joseph Heller.

catchword • **n.** a word or phrase commonly used to sum up a particular idea.

catchy • **adj.** (**catchier**, **catchiest**) (of a tune or phrase) appealing and easy to remember.

C

C

catechism /kat-i-ki-z'm/ • n. a summary of the principles of Christian religion in the form of questions and answers, used for teaching.

catechist • n. a Christian teacher.

catechize (also **catechise**) • v. (**catechizes**, **catechizing**, **catechized**) teach by using a catechism.
– ORIGIN Greek *katēkhein* 'instruct orally'.

categorical (also **categoric**) • adj. completely clear and direct.
– DERIVATIVES **categorically** adv.

categorize (also **categorise**) • v. (**categorizes**, **categorizing**, **categorized**) place in a category.
– DERIVATIVES **categorization** (also **categorisation**) n.

category • n. (pl. **categories**) a class or group of people or things with shared characteristics.
– ORIGIN Greek *katēgoria* 'statement'.

cater • v. (**caters**, **catering**, **catered**) **1** Brit. (**cater for**) provide food and drink at (a social event). **2** (**cater for/to**) provide with what is needed or required. **3** (**cater for**) take into account. **4** (**cater to**) satisfy (a need or demand).
– DERIVATIVES **caterer** n.
– ORIGIN Old French *acater* 'buy'.

caterpillar • n. **1** the larva of a butterfly or moth. **2** (also **caterpillar track** or **tread**) trademark a steel band passing round the wheels of a vehicle for travel on rough ground.
– ORIGIN perh. from Old French *chatepelose* 'hairy cat'.

caterwaul /kat-er-wawl/ • v. make a shrill howling or wailing noise.

catfish • n. a freshwater or marine fish with whisker-like growths round the mouth.

catgut • n. material used for the strings of musical instruments and for sewing up wounds, made of the dried intestines of sheep or horses.
– ORIGIN uncertain.

catharsis /kuh-thar-siss/ • n. the release of pent-up emotions.
– DERIVATIVES **cathartic** adj.
– ORIGIN Greek *kathairein* 'cleanse'.

Cathay E
/ka-**thay**/ the name by which China was known to medieval Europe.

cathedral • n. the principal church of a diocese.
– ORIGIN Greek *kathedra* 'seat'.

Cather E
/ka-*th*er/, Willa (Sibert) (1876–1974), American novelist and short-story writer, author of *O Pioneers!*

Catherine, St E
(died *c*.307), early Christian martyr, who is said to have been tortured on a spiked wheel and beheaded. Feast day, 25 November.

Catherine de' Medici E
(1519–89), queen of France, wife of Henry II of France. She acted as regent (1560–74) for her three sons, Francis II, Charles IX, and Henry III, during which time the Huguenots were massacred at the Massacre of St Bartholomew (1572).

Catherine of Aragon E
(1485–1536), first wife of Henry VIII, mother of Mary I. Henry's wish to annul his marriage to Catherine (due to her failure to produce a male heir) led eventually to England's break with the Roman Catholic Church.

Catherine the Great E
(1729–96), empress of Russia, reigned 1762–96. She formed alliances with Prussia and Austria, and made territorial advances at the expense of the Turks and Tartars.

Catherine wheel • n. Brit. a firework in the form of a spinning coil.
– ORIGIN named after St *Catherine* (see **CATHERINE, ST**).

catheter /kath-i-ter/ • n. a flexible tube inserted into the bladder or another body cavity, for removing fluid.
– ORIGIN Greek *kathienai* 'send down'.

cathode /kath-ohd/ • n. an electrode with a negative charge. Opp. **ANODE**.
– ORIGIN Greek *kathodos* 'way down'.

cathode ray tube • n. a vacuum tube in which beams of electrons produce a luminous image on a fluorescent screen, used in televisions and visual display units.

catholic • adj. **1** including a wide variety of things: *catholic tastes.* **2** (**Catholic**) Roman Catholic. • n. (**Catholic**) a Roman Catholic.
– DERIVATIVES **Catholicism** n.
– ORIGIN Greek *katholikos* 'universal'.

cation /kat-I-uhn/ • n. Chem. an ion with a positive charge. Opp. **ANION**.
– ORIGIN from **CATHODE** + **ION**.

catkin • n. a spike of small soft flowers hanging from trees such as the willow.
– ORIGIN former Dutch *katteken* 'kitten'.

catnap • n. a short sleep during the day. • v. (**catnaps**, **catnapping**, **catnapped**) have a catnap.

cat-o'-nine-tails • n. hist. a rope whip with nine knotted cords.

cat's cradle • n. a game in which patterns are formed in a loop of string held between the fingers of each hand.

catseye • n. Brit. trademark each of a series of reflective studs marking the lanes of a road.

Catskill Mountains E
a range of mountains in the state of New York, part of the Appalachian system.

cat's paw • n. a person used by another to carry out an unpleasant task.

catsuit • n. esp. Brit. a woman's close-fitting one-piece garment with trouser legs.

cattery • n. (pl. **catteries**) a place where cats are bred or kept while their owners are away.

cattle • pl. n. cows, bulls, and oxen.
– ORIGIN Old French *chatel* 'chattel'.

cattle grid • n. Brit. a metal grid covering a trench across a road, allowing vehicles to pass over but not animals.

catty • adj. (**cattier**, **cattiest**) spiteful.

Catullus E
/kuh-**tul**-luhss/, Gaius Valerius (*c*.84–*c*.54 BC), Roman poet, best known for his love poems.

catwalk • n. **1** a raised narrow walkway. **2** a

narrow platform along which models walk to display clothes.

Caucasian /kaw-**kay**-*zh*'n/ ● adj. **1** relating to a division of humankind covering peoples from Europe, western Asia, and parts of India and North Africa. **2** white-skinned; of European origin. **2** relating to the Caucasus. ● n. a Caucasian person.

> **Caucasus** E
> /kaw-kuh-suhss/ a mountainous region of SE Europe, lying between the Black Sea and the Caspian Sea, in Georgia, Armenia, Azerbaijan, and SE Russia.

caucus /kaw-kuhss/ ● n. (pl. **caucuses**) **1** a meeting of a policy-making committee of a political party. **2** a group of people with shared concerns within a larger organization.
– ORIGIN perh. from an American Indian word meaning 'adviser'.

caudal /kaw-duhl/ ● adj. having to do with the tail or the rear part of the body.
– ORIGIN Latin *cauda* 'tail'.

caught past and past part. of **CATCH**.

caul /*rhymes with* ball/ ● n. a membrane enclosing a fetus, part of which is sometimes found on a baby's head at birth.
– ORIGIN perh. from Old French *cale* 'head covering'.

cauldron (US **caldron**) ● n. a large metal cooking pot.
– ORIGIN Old French *caudron*.

cauliflower ● n. a variety of cabbage with a large white flower head.
– ORIGIN from former French *chou fleuri* 'flowered cabbage'.

caulk /kawk/ (US also **calk**) ● n. a waterproof substance used to fill cracks and seal joins. ● v. seal with caulk.
– ORIGIN Latin *calcare* 'to tread'.

causal ● adj. relating to or being a cause: *a causal connection between smoking and lung cancer.*
– DERIVATIVES **causally** adv.

causality ● n. the relationship between a cause and the effect it produces.

causation ● n. **1** the causing of an effect. **2** = **CAUSALITY**.

causative ● adj. causing an effect: *HIV is the causative agent of Aids.*

cause ● n. **1** a person or thing that produces an effect. **2** a good reason for thinking or doing something: *cause for concern.* **3** a principle or movement which one is prepared to support. **4** a lawsuit. ● v. (**causes, causing, caused**) make (something) happen.
– ORIGIN Latin *causa*.

cause célèbre /kohz se-**leb**-ruh/ ● n. (pl. **causes célèbres** /kohz se-**leb**-ruh/) a matter causing great public interest and discussion.
– ORIGIN French, 'famous case'.

causeway ● n. a raised road or track across low or wet ground.

caustic /kaw-stik/ ● adj. **1** able to burn through or wear away living tissue by chemical action. **2** sarcastic in a hurtful way.
– ORIGIN Greek *kaustikos*.

caustic soda ● n. sodium hydroxide.

cauterize /kaw-tuh-ryz/ (also **cauterise**) ● v. (**cauterizes, cauterizing, cauterized**) burn the skin or flesh of (a wound) to stop bleeding or prevent infection.
– ORIGIN Greek *kautēriazein*.

caution ● n. **1** care taken to avoid danger or mistakes. **2** warning. **3** Engl. Law a formal warning given to someone who has committed a minor offence. ● v. **1** warn or advise. **2** Engl. Law give a caution to.
– PHRASES **throw caution to the wind** act in a reckless way.
– ORIGIN Latin *cavere* 'take heed'.

cautionary ● adj. acting as a warning.

cautious ● adj. careful to avoid possible problems or dangers.
– DERIVATIVES **cautiously** adv.

cavalcade /ka-vuhl-**kayd**/ ● n. a procession of vehicles or riders.
– ORIGIN Italian *cavalcare* 'to ride'.

cavalier ● n. (**Cavalier**) a supporter of King Charles I in the English Civil War. ● adj. showing a lack of proper concern: *the cavalier treatment of mental illness.*
– ORIGIN Italian *cavaliere* 'knight, gentleman'.

cavalry ● n. (pl. **cavalries**) soldiers who formerly fought on horseback, but who now normally use armoured vehicles.
– DERIVATIVES **cavalryman** n.

> **Cavan** E
> /*rhymes with* cavern/ a county of the Republic of Ireland; county town, Cavan.

cave ● n. a large natural hollow in the side of a hill or cliff, or underground. ● v. (**caves, caving, caved**) **1** (**caving**) exploring caves as a sport. **2** (**cave in**) give way or collapse. **3** (**cave in**) give in because forced to do so.
– DERIVATIVES **caver** n.
– ORIGIN Latin *cavus* 'hollow'.

caveat /ka-vi-at/ ● n. a warning.
– ORIGIN Latin, 'let a person beware'.

> **Cavell** E
> /ka-vuhl/, Edith (Louisa) (1865–1915), English nurse, who helped Allied soldiers to escape from occupied Belgium during the First World War. She was executed by the Germans and became a heroine of the Allied cause.

> **Cavendish** F
> /kav-uhn-dish/, Henry (1731–1810), English chemist and physicist, who identified hydrogen, established that water is a compound, and determined the density of the earth.

cavern ● n. a large cave.
– ORIGIN Latin *caverna*.

cavernous /kav-er-nuhss/ ● adj. like a cavern in being huge or gloomy.

caviar /ka-vi-ar/ (also **caviare**) ● n. the pickled roe of the sturgeon.
– ORIGIN French.

cavil /ka-vuhl/ ● v. (**cavils, cavilling, cavilled**; US **cavils, caviling, caviled**) make petty objections. ● n. a petty objection.
– ORIGIN Latin *cavillari*.

cavity ● n. (pl. **cavities**) **1** a hollow space within a solid object. **2** a decayed part of a tooth.
– ORIGIN Latin *cavitas*.

cavity wall ● n. a wall formed from two layers of bricks with a space between them.

cavort ● v. jump or dance around excitedly.
– ORIGIN perh. from **CURVET**.

Cavour E
/kuh-**voor**/, Camillo Benso, Conte di (1810–61), Italian statesman, first Premier of a united Italy (1861).

cavy /**kay**-vi/ ● n. (pl. **cavies**) a guinea pig or related South American rodent.
– ORIGIN Latin *cavia*.

caw ● v. (of a rook, crow, etc.) make a harsh cry.

Cawley, E
Evonne (Fay) (b.1951; born *Evonne Fay Goolagong*), Australian tennis player. She won two Wimbledon singles titles (1971; 1980) and was Australian singles champion three times.

Caxton, E
William (*c.*1422–91), the first English printer, who printed the first book in English in 1474.

Cayenne E
/kay-**en**/ the capital and chief port of French Guiana.

cayenne /kay-**en**/ (also **cayenne pepper**) ● n. a hot-tasting red powder made from dried chillies.
– ORIGIN from a South American language.

Cayley E
/**kay**-li/, Sir George (1773–1857), British engineer and pioneer of British aeronautics, who built the first manned glider (1853).

cayman ● n. var. of **CAIMAN**.

Cayman Islands E
/**kay**-muhn/ a British dependency consisting of a group of three islands in the Caribbean Sea, south of Cuba; capital, George Town.

CB ● abbrev. **1** Citizens' Band. **2** (in the UK) Companion of the Order of the Bath.

CBE ● abbrev. (in the UK) Commander of the Order of the British Empire.

CBI ● abbrev. Confederation of British Industry.

cc (also **c.c.**) ● abbrev. **1** carbon copy (showing that a copy has been or should be sent to another person). **2** cubic centimetre(s).

CCTV ● abbrev. closed-circuit television.

CD ● abbrev. compact disc.

cd ● abbrev. candela.

CD-ROM ● n. a compact disc used in a computer as a read-only device for displaying data.

CE ● abbrev. Church of England.

cease ● v. (**ceases**, **ceasing**, **ceased**) come or bring to an end; stop.
– ORIGIN Latin *cessare*.

ceasefire ● n. a temporary period when fighting in a war stops.

ceaseless ● adj. never stopping.
– DERIVATIVES **ceaselessly** adv.

Ceauşescu E
/chow-**shess**-koo/, Nicolae (1918–89), Romanian communist statesman, first President of the Socialist Republic of Romania 1974–89. A popular uprising in December 1989 resulted in the downfall of his totalitarian regime and in his execution.

Cecilia, St E
(2nd or 3rd century), Roman martyr, patron saint of church music. Feast day, 22 November.

cecum ● n. (pl. **ceca**) US = **CAECUM**.

cedar ● n. a tall coniferous tree with hard, sweet-smelling wood.
– ORIGIN Greek *kedros*.

cede /seed/ ● v. (**cedes**, **ceding**, **ceded**) give up (power or territory).
– ORIGIN Latin *cedere*.

cedilla /si-**dil**-luh/ ● n. a mark (¸) written under the letter *c* to show that it is pronounced like an *s* (e.g. *soupçon*).
– ORIGIN Spanish *zedilla* 'little "z"'.

ceilidh /**kay**-li/ ● n. a social event with Scottish or Irish folk music and dancing.
– ORIGIN Old Irish *céilide* 'visit, visiting'.

ceiling ● n. **1** the upper inside surface of a room. **2** an upper limit set on prices, wages, or spending.
– ORIGIN from former *ceil* 'line or plaster the roof of (a building)'.

celandine /**sel**-uhn-dyn/ ● n. a yellow-flowered plant of the buttercup family.
– ORIGIN Greek *khelidōn* 'swallow' (because the plant flowers at the time swallows arrive).

Celebes E
/sel-i-beez/ former name for **SULAWESI**.

Celebes Sea E
a part of the western Pacific between the Philippines and Sulawesi.

celebrant /**sel**-i-bruhnt/ ● n. a person who performs a religious ceremony, especially a priest who leads Holy Communion.

celebrate ● v. (**celebrates**, **celebrating**, **celebrated**) **1** mark (an important occasion) by doing something special and enjoyable. **2** honour or praise publicly. **3** perform (a religious ceremony).
– DERIVATIVES **celebration** n. **celebratory** adj.
– ORIGIN Latin *celebrare*.

celebrity ● n. (pl. **celebrities**) **1** a famous person. **2** the state of being famous.

celeriac /suh-**lair**-i-ak/ ● n. a variety of celery which forms a large edible root.

celerity /si-**le**-ri-ti/ ● n. archaic or literary speed of movement.
– ORIGIN Latin *celeritas*.

celery ● n. a vegetable with crisp juicy stalks.
– ORIGIN Greek *selinon* 'parsley'.

celestial /si-**less**-ti-uhl/ ● adj. **1** having to do with heaven. **2** having to do with the sky or outer space.
– ORIGIN Latin *caelum* 'heaven'.

celibate /**sel**-i-buht/ ● adj. not marrying or having sexual relations, often for religious reasons. ● n. a person who is celibate.
– DERIVATIVES **celibacy** n.
– ORIGIN Latin *caelibatus* 'unmarried state'.

cell ● n. **1** a small room for a prisoner, monk, or nun. **2** the smallest unit of a living organism that is able to reproduce and perform other functions. **3** a small compartment in a larger structure. **4** a small active political group that is part of a larger organization. **5** a device for producing electricity by chemical action or light.
– ORIGIN Latin *cella* 'storeroom'.

cellar ● n. **1** a storage space or room below ground level in a building. **2** a stock of wine.
– ORIGIN Latin *cellarium* 'storehouse'.

Cellini E
/chel-lee-ni/, Benvenuto (1500–71), Italian goldsmith and sculptor.

cello /chel-loh/ ● n. (pl. **cellos**) an instrument like a large violin, held upright on the floor between the legs of the seated player.
– DERIVATIVES **cellist** n.
– ORIGIN from **VIOLONCELLO**.

cellophane /sel-luh-fayn/ ● n. trademark a thin transparent wrapping material.
– ORIGIN from **CELLULOSE**.

cellphone ● n. a mobile phone.

cellular /sel-yuu-ler/ ● adj. **1** relating to or made up of cells. **2** relating to a mobile telephone system that uses a number of short-range radio stations to cover the area it serves.

cellulite /sel-yuu-lyt/ ● n. fat that builds up under the skin, causing a dimpled effect.
– ORIGIN French.

celluloid ● n. a kind of transparent plastic formerly used for cinema film.

cellulose /sel-yuu-lohz/ ● n. a substance found in all plant tissues, used in making paint, plastics, and man-made fibres.
– ORIGIN French.

Celsius /sel-si-uhss/ ● adj. having to do with a scale of temperature on which water freezes at 0° and boils at 100°.
– ORIGIN named after the Swedish astronomer Anders *Celsius* (1701–44).

Celt /kelt/ ● n. **1** a member of a people inhabiting much of Europe and Asia Minor in pre-Roman times. **2** a person from a modern region in which a Celtic language is (or was) spoken.
– ORIGIN Greek *Keltoi* 'Celts'.

Celtic /kel-tik/ ● n. a group of languages including Irish, Scottish Gaelic, Welsh, Breton, Manx, and Cornish. ● adj. relating to Celtic or to the Celts.

cement ● n. **1** a powdery substance made by strongly heating lime and clay, used in making mortar and concrete. **2** a soft glue that hardens on setting. ● v. **1** fix with cement. **2** strengthen: *the occasion cemented our friendship.*
– ORIGIN Latin *caementum* 'quarry stone'.

cemetery ● n. (pl. **cemeteries**) a large burial ground.
– ORIGIN Greek *koimētērion* 'dormitory'.

cenotaph /sen-uh-tahf/ ● n. a memorial to members of the armed forces killed in a war.
– ORIGIN from Greek *kenos* 'empty' + *taphos* 'tomb'.

Cenozoic /see-nuh-zoh-ik/ ● adj. Geol. relating to the era following the Mesozoic era (from about 65 million years ago to the present).
– ORIGIN from Greek *kainos* 'new' + *zōion* 'animal'.

censer ● n. a container in which incense is burnt.
– ORIGIN Old French *censier.*

censor ● n. an official who examines material that is to be published and bans anything considered offensive or a threat to security. ● v. ban unacceptable parts of (a book, film, etc).
– DERIVATIVES **censorship** n.
– ORIGIN Latin.

censorious /sen-sor-i-uhss/ ● adj. severely critical.

censure /sen-sher/ ● v. (**censures**, **censuring**, **censured**) criticize strongly. ● n. strong disapproval or criticism.
– ORIGIN Latin *censura* 'judgement'.

census ● n. (pl. **censuses**) an official count or survey of a population.
– ORIGIN Latin.

cent ● n. a unit of money equal to one hundredth of a dollar or other decimal currency unit.
– ORIGIN Latin *centum* 'hundred'.

centaur /sen-tor/ ● n. Gk Myth. a creature with a man's head, arms, and upper body and a horse's lower body and legs.
– ORIGIN Greek *kentauros.*

centenarian /sen-ti-nair-i-uhn/ ● n. a person who is a hundred or more years old.

centenary /sen-tee-nuh-ri/ ● n. (pl. **centenaries**) esp. Brit. the hundredth anniversary of an event.
– ORIGIN Latin *centenarius* 'containing a hundred'.

centennial ● adj. relating to a hundredth anniversary. ● n. a hundredth anniversary.

center ● n. US = **CENTRE**.

centerboard ● n. US = **CENTREBOARD**.

centerfold ● n. US = **CENTREFOLD**.

centerpiece ● n. US = **CENTREPIECE**.

centi- ● comb. form **1** one hundredth: *centilitre.* **2** hundred: *centipede.*
– ORIGIN Latin *centum* 'hundred'.

centigrade ● adj. relating to the Celsius scale of temperature.
– ORIGIN from Latin *centum* 'a hundred' + *gradus* 'step'.

centilitre (US **centiliter**) ● n. a metric unit equal to one hundredth of a litre.

centime /son-teem/ ● n. a unit of money of Switzerland and some other countries, equal to one hundredth of a franc or other decimal currency unit.
– ORIGIN French.

centimetre (US **centimeter**) ● n. a metric unit equal to one hundredth of a metre.

centipede ● n. an insect-like creature with a long thin body made up of many segments, most of which have a pair of legs.
– ORIGIN from Latin *centum* 'a hundred' + *pes* 'foot'.

central ● adj. **1** in or near the centre. **2** very important.
– DERIVATIVES **centrality** n. **centrally** adv.

Central African Republic E
a country of central Africa; capital, Bangui. Former name (until 1958) **UBANGHI SHARI**.

Central America E
the southernmost part of North America, linking the continent to South America and consisting of the countries of Guatemala, Belize, Honduras, El Salvador, Nicaragua, Costa Rica, and Panama.
– DERIVATIVES **Central American** adj. & n.

central bank ● n. a national bank that provides services for its country's government and commercial banking system, and issues currency.

central heating ● n. a system for warming

a building by heating water or air in one place and circulating it through pipes and radiators or vents.

Central Intelligence Agency E
a federal agency in the US responsible for coordinating government intelligence activities.

centralize (also **centralise**) • v. (**centralizes**, **centralizing**, **centralized**) bring under the control of a central authority.
– DERIVATIVES **centralism** n. **centralist** n. & adj. **centralization** (also **centralisation**) n.

central nervous system • n. the complex of nerve tissues that controls the activities of the body, consisting of the brain and spinal cord in vertebrates.

central processing unit • n. the part of a computer in which operations are controlled and carried out.

central reservation • n. Brit. the strip of land between the carriageways of a motorway or dual carriageway.

centre (US **center**) • n. **1** a point or part in the middle of something. **2** a place where particular activities are brought together: *a conference centre.* **3** a point from which something spreads or to which something is directed: *the city was a centre of discontent.* **4** a moderate political group. • v. (**centres, centring, centred**; US **centers, centering, centered**) **1** place in the centre. **2** (**centre on/around**) have as a major concern or theme.
– ORIGIN Latin *centrum*.

centre back • n. Soccer a defender who plays in the middle of the field.

centreboard (US **centerboard**) • n. a board lowered through the keel of a sailing boat to reduce sideways movement.

centrefold (US **centerfold**) • n. the two middle pages of a magazine, containing illustrations or a special feature.

centre forward • n. Sport an attacker who plays in the middle of the field.

centre half • n. Soccer a centre back.

centre of gravity • n. the central point in an object, about which its mass is evenly balanced.

centrepiece (US **centerpiece**) • n. an object or item that is meant to attract attention.

-centric • comb. form **1** having a specified centre: *geocentric.* **2** coming from a specified viewpoint: *Eurocentric.*

centrifugal /sen-tri-**fyoo**-g'l/ • adj. Physics moving away from a centre.
– ORIGIN from Latin *centrum* 'centre' + *-fugus* 'fleeing'.

centrifugal force • n. Physics a force which appears to cause a body travelling round a central point to fly outwards from its circular path.

centrifuge /sen-tri-fyooj/ • n. a machine with a rapidly rotating container, used to separate liquids from solids.

centripetal /sen-tri-**pee**-t'l/ • adj. Physics moving towards a centre.
– ORIGIN from Latin *centrum* 'centre' + *-petus* 'seeking'.

centripetal force • n. Physics a force which causes a body travelling round a central point to move inwards from its circular path.

centrist • n. a person having moderate political views or policies.
– DERIVATIVES **centrism** n.

centurion • n. the commander of a hundred men in the ancient Roman army.
– ORIGIN Latin.

century • n. (pl. **centuries**) **1** a period of one hundred years. **2** a batsman's score of a hundred runs in cricket.
– ORIGIN Latin *centuria*.

CEO • abbrev. chief executive officer.

cephalic /si-fal-ik/ • adj. relating to the head.
– ORIGIN Greek *kephalē* 'head'.

Cephalonia E
/sef-fuh-**loh**-ni-uh, kef-fuh-**loh**-ni-uh/ a Greek island in the Ionian Sea.

cephalopod /**sef**-uh-luh-pod/ • n. a mollusc of a group including octopuses and squids.
– ORIGIN from Greek *kephalē* 'head' + *pous* 'foot'.

ceramic • adj. made of clay that is permanently hardened by heat. • n. (**ceramics**) the art of making ceramic articles.
– DERIVATIVES **ceramicist** n.
– ORIGIN Greek *keramos* 'pottery'.

Cerberus E
/**ser**-buh-ruhss/ Gk Myth. a monstrous watchdog with three (or in some stories fifty) heads, which guarded the entrance to Hades.

cereal • n. **1** a grass producing an edible grain, such as wheat, maize, or rye. **2** a breakfast food made from a cereal grain or grains.
– ORIGIN from **Ceres**.

cerebellum /se-ri-**bel**-luhm/ • n. (pl. **cerebellums** or **cerebella**) the part of the brain at the back of the skull, which coordinates muscular activity.
– DERIVATIVES **cerebellar** adj.
– ORIGIN Latin, 'little brain'.

cerebral /suh-ree-bruhl/ • adj. **1** relating to the cerebrum of the brain. **2** intellectual rather than emotional or physical: *cerebral pursuits such as chess.*

cerebral palsy • n. a condition in which a person has difficulty in controlling or moving their muscles, caused by brain damage before or at birth.

cerebration /se-ri-**bray**-sh'n/ • n. formal the working of the brain; thinking.

cerebrospinal /suh-ree-broh-**spy**-n'l/ • adj. relating to the brain and spine.

cerebrum /se-ri-bruhm/ • n. (pl. **cerebra** /se-ri-bruh/) the main part of the brain, located in the front of the skull.
– ORIGIN Latin, 'brain'.

Ceredigion E
/ke-ruh-**dig**-i-uhn/ a county of western mid Wales; administrative centre, Aberaeron.

ceremonial • adj. having to do with ceremonies. • n. = **ceremony**.
– DERIVATIVES **ceremonially** adv.

ceremonious • adj. done in a way appropriate to a grand and formal occasion.
– DERIVATIVES **ceremoniously** adv.

ceremony • n. (pl. **ceremonies**) **1** a formal religious or public occasion celebrating an event. **2** the set procedures followed at such occasions.

– PHRASES **stand on ceremony** insist on formal behaviour.
– ORIGIN Latin *caerimonia* 'religious worship'.

Ceres E
/*rhymes with* series/ the Roman goddess of agriculture. Greek equivalent **DEMETER**.

cerise /suh-reess/ • **n.** a light, clear red colour.
– ORIGIN French, 'cherry'.

cerium /seer-i-uhm/ • **n.** a silvery-white metallic chemical element.
– ORIGIN named after the asteroid *Ceres*.

cert • **n.** Brit. informal **1** an event that is certain to happen. **2** a competitor, candidate, etc. that is certain to win.

certain • **adj. 1** able to be relied on to happen or be the case. **2** completely sure about something. **3** specific but not directly named or stated: *he raised certain personal problems.* • **pron.** (**certain of**) some but not all.
– ORIGIN Latin *certus* 'settled, sure'.

certainly • **adv. 1** without doubt; definitely. **2** yes.

certainty • **n.** (pl. **certainties**) **1** the state of being certain. **2** a fact that is true or an event that is definitely going to take place.

certifiable • **adj.** able or needing to be certified.

certificate • **n. 1** an official document recording a particular fact, event, or achievement. **2** an official classification given to a cinema film, indicating its suitability for a particular age group.
– DERIVATIVES **certification** n.

certify • **v.** (**certifies**, **certifying**, **certified**) **1** declare or confirm in a certificate or other official document. **2** officially declare insane.
– ORIGIN Latin *certificare*.

certitude • **n.** a feeling of complete certainty.

cerulean /si-roo-li-uhn/ • **adj.** deep blue in colour like a clear sky.
– ORIGIN Latin *caeruleus*.

Cervantes E
/ser-van-teez/, Miguel de (1547–1616), Spanish novelist and dramatist, author of *Don Quixote*.

cervical /ser-vi-k'l, ser-vy-k'l/ • **adj.** relating to the cervix.

cervical smear • **n.** Brit. a specimen of cells from the neck of the womb, spread on a microscope slide for examination for signs of cancer.

cervix /ser-viks/ • **n.** (pl. **cervices** /ser-vi-seez/) the narrow neck-like passage forming the lower end of the womb.
– ORIGIN Latin.

cesium • **n.** US = **CAESIUM**.

cessation • **n.** the action or an instance of stopping.
– ORIGIN Latin.

cession • **n.** the formal giving up of rights or territory by a state.
– ORIGIN Latin.

cesspool (also **cesspit**) • **n.** an underground tank or covered pit where liquid waste and sewage is stored before disposal.
– ORIGIN prob. from Old French *souspirail* 'air hole'.

cetacean /si-tay-sh'n/ Zool. • **n.** a sea mammal of a group including whales and dolphins.
– ORIGIN Greek *kētos* 'whale'.

Ceylon E
former name for **SRI LANKA**.

Cézanne E
/say-zan/, Paul (1839–1906), French post-Impressionist painter. His typical subjects were landscapes and still lifes and his later work had an important influence on cubism.

cf • **abbrev.** compare with.
– ORIGIN Latin *confer* 'compare'.

CFC • **abbrev.** chlorofluorocarbon, a gas that is a compound of carbon, hydrogen, chlorine, and fluorine, used in refrigerators and aerosols and harmful to the ozone layer.

CFE • **abbrev.** (in the UK) College of Further Education.

CH • **abbrev.** (in the UK) Companion of Honour.

ch. • **abbrev.** chapter.

Chablis /shab-lee/ • **n.** a dry white wine from Chablis in France.

cha-cha • **n.** a modern ballroom dance performed to a Latin American rhythm.
– ORIGIN Latin American Spanish.

Chad E
/chad/ a landlocked country in northern central Africa; capital, N'Djamena.
– DERIVATIVES **Chadian** adj. & n.

chador /chah-dor/ • **n.** a piece of dark cloth worn by Muslim women around the head and upper body, so that only part of the face can be seen.
– ORIGIN Persian.

Chadwick, E
Sir James (1891–1974), English physicist, who discovered the neutron.

chafe • **v.** (**chafes**, **chafing**, **chafed**) **1** make or become sore or worn by rubbing against something. **2** rub (a part of the body) to warm it. **3** become impatient because one is prevented from acting freely.
– ORIGIN Old French *chaufer* 'make hot'.

chafer • **n.** a large flying beetle.
– ORIGIN Old English.

chaff[1] /chahf/ • **n. 1** husks of grain separated from the seed by winnowing or threshing. **2** hay and straw cut up as food for cattle.
– PHRASES **separate** (or **sort**) **the wheat from the chaff** pick out what is valuable from what is worthless.
– ORIGIN Old English.

chaff[2] /chaff/ • **v.** tease.
– ORIGIN perh. from **CHAFE**.

chaffinch • **n.** a finch, the male of which has a bluish head, pink underparts, and dark wings.
– ORIGIN Old English.

Chagall E
/sha-gal/, Marc (1887–1985), Russian-born French painter and graphic artist. His work is notable for its rich colour and use of images from Russian folklore.

chagrin /sha-grin, sha-grin/ • **n.** annoyance or shame at having failed. • **v.** (**be chagrined**) feel annoyed or ashamed.
– ORIGIN French, 'rough skin'.

C

chain • n. **1** a series of connected metal links. **2** a connected series, set, or sequence: *a chain of superstores.* **3** a measure of length equal to 66 ft. • v. fasten or restrain with a chain.
– ORIGIN Old French *chaine.*

chain gang • n. a group of convicts chained together while working outside the prison.

chain letter • n. a letter sent to a number of people, all of whom are asked to make copies and send these to other people, who then do the same.

chain mail • n. hist. armour made of small metal rings linked together.

chain reaction • n. **1** a chemical reaction in which the products of the reaction cause other changes. **2** a series of events, each caused by the previous one.

chainsaw • n. a power-driven saw with teeth set on a moving chain.

chain-smoke • v. (**chain-smokes**, **chain-smoking**, **chain-smoked**) smoke cigarettes one after the other.

chain store • n. one of a series of shops owned by one firm and selling the same goods.

chair • n. **1** a separate seat for one person, with a back and four legs. **2** the person in charge of a meeting or an organization. **3** a post as professor. • v. act as chairperson of.
– ORIGIN Old French *chaiere.*

chairlift • n. a series of chairs hung from a moving cable, used for carrying passengers up and down a mountain.

chairman (or **chairwoman**) • n. a person in charge of a meeting or organization.

chairperson • n. a chairman or chairwoman.

chaise /shayz/ • n. esp. hist. a two-wheeled horse-drawn carriage for one or two people.
– ORIGIN French.

chaise longue /shayz **long**/ • n. (pl. **chaises longues** /shayz **long**/) a sofa with a backrest at only one end.
– ORIGIN French, 'long chair'.

chalcedony /kal-**sed**-uh-ni/ • n. (pl. **chalcedonies**) a type of quartz with very small crystals, such as onyx.
– ORIGIN Greek *khalkēdōn.*

chalet /**sha**-lay/ • n. **1** a wooden house with overhanging eaves, found in the Swiss Alps. **2** a small wooden cabin used by holidaymakers.
– ORIGIN Old French *chasel* 'farmstead'.

chalice /**cha**-liss/ • n. **1** hist. a goblet. **2** the wine cup used in Holy Communion.
– ORIGIN Latin *calix* 'cup'.

chalk • n. **1** a white soft limestone formed from the skeletons of sea creatures. **2** a similar substance made into sticks and used for drawing or writing. • v. draw or write with chalk.
– PHRASES **as different as chalk and cheese** Brit. completely different. **by a long chalk** Brit. by far. **chalk up** achieve (something noteworthy).
– DERIVATIVES **chalky** adj.
– ORIGIN Latin *calx* 'lime'.

challenge • n. **1** a call to someone to take part in a contest. **2** a call to prove something. **3** a demanding task or situation. • v. (**challenges**, **challenging**, **challenged**) **1** raise doubt as to whether (something) is true or genuine. **2** call on (someone) to do something difficult or take part in a fight. **3** (of a sentry) call on (someone) to prove their identity.
– DERIVATIVES **challenger** n.
– ORIGIN Old French *chalenge.*

challenging • adj. presenting a test of one's abilities: *the most challenging job in medicine.*

chalybeate /kuh-**lib**-i-uht/ • adj. (of a natural mineral spring) containing iron salts.
– ORIGIN Latin *chalybeatus.*

chamber • n. **1** a large room used for formal or public events. **2** one of the parts of a parliament. **3** (**chambers**) Law, Brit. rooms used by a barrister or barristers. **4** archaic a bedroom. **5** a space or cavity within something. **6** the part of a gun bore that contains the charge.
– ORIGIN Old French *chambre.*

Chamberlain, E
(Arthur) Neville (1869–1940), British Conservative statesman, Prime Minister 1937–40. He tried to avoid war with Germany but was forced to abandon this policy following Hitler's invasion of Czechoslovakia and Poland in 1939.

chamberlain /**chaym**-ber-lin/ • n. hist. an officer who managed the household of a monarch or noble.
– ORIGIN Old French.

chambermaid • n. a woman who cleans rooms in a hotel.

chamber music • n. instrumental music played by a small group of players, such as a string quartet.

Chamber of Commerce • n. a local association to promote the interests of the business community.

chamber pot • n. a bowl kept in a bedroom and used as a toilet.

chambray /**sham**-bray/ • n. a fabric with a white weft and a coloured warp.
– ORIGIN from the French town of *Cambrai.*

chameleon /kuh-**mee**-li-uhn/ (also **chamaeleon**) • n. a small lizard that can change colour according to its surroundings.
– ORIGIN from Greek *khamai* 'on the ground' + *leōn* 'lion'.

chamfer /**sham**-fer/ • v. (**chamfers**, **chamfering**, **chamfered**) Carpentry cut away (a right-angled edge or corner) to make a symmetrical sloping edge.
– ORIGIN from French *chant* 'point, edge' + *fraint* 'broken'.

chamois • n. (pl. **chamois**) **1** /**sham**-wah/ (pl. /**sham**-wah, **sham**-wahz/) an agile wild antelope found in mountainous areas of southern Europe. **2** /**sham**-mi/ (pl. /**sham**-miz/) (also **chamois leather**) soft pliable leather made from the skin of sheep, goats, or deer.
– ORIGIN French.

chamomile /**kam**-uh-myl/ (also **camomile**) • n. a plant with white and yellow flowers, used in herbal medicine.
– ORIGIN Greek *khamaimēlon* 'earth-apple'.

champ[1] • v. munch noisily.
– PHRASES **champ at the bit** be very impatient.

champ[2] • n. informal a champion.

champagne /sham-**payn**/ • n. a white sparkling wine from the Champagne region of France.

champion ● **n. 1** a person who has won a sporting contest or other competition. **2** a person who argues or fights for a cause or another person. ● **v.** strongly support the cause of: *priests who championed human rights.* ● **adj.** Brit. informal or dialect excellent.
– ORIGIN Latin *campion* 'fighter'.

championship ● **n. 1** a sporting contest for the position of champion. **2** the strong support of a person or cause.

Champlain E
/sham-**playn**/, Samuel de (1567–1635), French explorer and colonial statesman, who established a settlement at Quebec in 1608.

Champs Élysées E
/shonz ay-lee-zay/ an avenue in Paris, leading from the Place de la Concorde to the Arc de Triomphe.

chance ● **n. 1** a possibility of something happening. **2** (**chances**) the probability of something happening. **3** an opportunity. **4** the way in which things happen without any obvious plan or cause: *they met by chance at a youth hostel.* ● **v.** (**chances**, **chancing**, **chanced**) **1** happen or do something by chance. **2** informal risk.
– PHRASES **by any chance** possibly. **chance one's arm** Brit. informal risk doing something. **on the off chance** just in case. **stand a chance** have a likelihood of success. **take a chance** (or **chances**) take a risk.
– ORIGIN Old French *cheance*.

chancel /**chahn**-s'l/ ● **n.** the part of a church near the altar, reserved for the clergy and choir.
– ORIGIN Latin *cancelli* 'crossbars'.

chancellery /**chahn**-suh-luh-ri/ ● **n.** (pl. **chancelleries**) the post or department of a chancellor.

chancellor ● **n. 1** a senior state or legal official of various kinds. **2** (**Chancellor**) the head of the government in some European countries.
– ORIGIN Latin *cancellarius* 'porter'.

Chancellor of the Exchequer ● **n.** the finance minister of the United Kingdom.

chancer ● **n.** Brit. informal a person who makes the most of any opportunity.

Chancery (also **Chancery Division**) ● **n.** (pl. **Chanceries**) (in the UK) the Lord Chancellor's court, a division of the High Court of Justice.
– ORIGIN from CHANCELLERY.

chancre /**shang**-ker/ ● **n.** a painless ulcer that develops on the genitals in venereal disease.
– ORIGIN French.

chancy ● **adj.** informal risky.

chandelier ● **n.** a large hanging light with branches for several light bulbs or candles.
– ORIGIN French.

Chandigarh E
/chun-di-**gar**/ a city in Chandigargh Union Territory in NW India, the capital of the states of Punjab and Haryana.

Chandler E
/**chahnd**-ler/, Raymond (Thornton) (1888–1959), American novelist, the creator of the private detective Philip Marlowe.

chandler /**chahnd**-ler/ (also **ship chandler**) ● **n.** a dealer in supplies and equipment for ships.
– DERIVATIVES **chandlery** n.
– ORIGIN Old French *chandelier* 'candlemaker or candle seller'.

Chanel E
/shuh-**nel**/, Coco (1883–1971; born *Gabrielle Bonheur Chanel*), French fashion designer and perfume maker, known for her simple but sophisticated garments.

change ● **v.** (**changes**, **changing**, **changed**) **1** make or become different. **2** exchange for another. **3** move from one to (another): *he changed jobs frequently.* **4** (**change over**) move from one system or situation to another. **5** exchange (a sum of money) for the same sum in a different currency or denomination. ● **n. 1** the action or an instance of changing. **2** money returned as the balance of the sum paid or money given in exchange for the same sum in larger units. **3** coins as opposed to banknotes. **4** a clean garment or garments as replacement clothing.
– PHRASES **change hands** pass to a different owner. **change one's tune** express a very different attitude. **ring the changes** vary the ways of doing something.
– DERIVATIVES **changeless** adj. **changer** n.
– ORIGIN Old French *changer*.

changeable ● **adj. 1** liable to unpredictable change. **2** able to be changed.

changeling ● **n.** a child believed to have been secretly exchanged by fairies for the parents' real child.

changeover ● **n.** a change from one system or situation to another.

channel ● **n. 1** a wide stretch of water joining two seas: *the English Channel.* **2** a passage along which liquid or a watercourse may flow. **3** a means of communication: *they didn't apply through the proper channels.* **4** a band of frequencies used in radio and television transmission. **5** an electric circuit which acts as a path for a signal. **6** a passage that boats can pass through in a stretch of water. ● **v.** (**channels**, **channelling**, **channelled**; US **channels**, **channeling**, **channeled**) **1** direct towards a particular purpose. **2** pass along or through a particular channel.
– ORIGIN Latin *canalis* 'pipe, channel'.

Channel Islands E
a group of islands in the English Channel off the NW coast of France, of which the largest are Jersey, Guernsey, and Alderney.

Channel Tunnel E
a railway tunnel under the English Channel, linking the coasts of England and France, opened in 1994 and 49 km (31 miles) long.

chant ● **n. 1** a repeated rhythmic phrase, shouted or sung together by a group. **2** a tune to which the words of psalms or other works with irregular rhythm are fitted by singing several syllables or words to the same note. ● **v.** say, shout, or sing in a chant.
– ORIGIN Old French *chanter* 'sing'.

Chanukkah /**khan**-uu-kuh, **han**-uu-kuh/ ● **n.** var. of HANUKKAH.

chaos ● **n.** complete disorder and confusion.
– ORIGIN Greek *khaos* 'vast chasm, void'.

chaotic /kay-ot-ik/ ● adj. in a state of complete confusion and disorder.
– DERIVATIVES **chaotically** adv.

chap ● n. Brit. informal a man.
– ORIGIN from former *chapman*, 'pedlar'.

chapatti /chuh-pah-ti/ ● n. (pl. **chapattis**) (in Indian cookery) a flat cake of wholemeal bread.
– ORIGIN Hindi.

chapel ● n. **1** a small building or room for Christian worship. **2** a part of a large church with its own altar.
– ORIGIN Old French *chapele*.

chaperone /shap-uh-rohn/ ● n. dated an older woman in charge of an unmarried girl at social occasions. ● v. (**chaperones**, **chaperoning**, **chaperoned**) accompany and look after.
– ORIGIN French.

chaplain ● n. a member of the clergy attached to a chapel in a private house or an institution, or to a military unit.
– DERIVATIVES **chaplaincy** n.
– ORIGIN Old French *chapelain*.

chaplet ● n. an ornamental circular band worn on the head.
– ORIGIN Old French *chapelet* 'little hat'.

Chaplin, E
Charlie (1889–1977; full name *Sir Charles Spencer Chaplin*), English film actor and director. He directed and starred in many short silent comedies, mostly playing a bowler-hatted tramp.

chapped ● adj. (of the skin) cracked and sore through exposure to cold weather.
– ORIGIN unknown.

Chappell, E
Greg (b.1948; full name *Gregory Stephen Chappell*), Australian cricketer. He was the first Australian to score more than 7,000 test-match runs.

chapter ● n. **1** a main division of a book. **2** a particular period in history or in a person's life. **3** the governing body of a cathedral or other religious community. **4** esp. N. Amer. a local branch of a society.
– PHRASES **chapter and verse** an exact reference or authority. **a chapter of accidents** a series of unfortunate events.
– ORIGIN Old French *chapitre*.

char[1] ● v. (**chars**, **charring**, **charred**) partially burn so as to blacken the surface.
– ORIGIN prob. from **CHARCOAL**.

char[2] Brit. informal ● n. a charwoman. ● v. (**chars**, **charring**, **charred**) work as a charwoman.

char[3] ● n. Brit. informal tea.
– ORIGIN Chinese.

charabanc /sha-ruh-bang/ ● n. Brit. an early form of bus.
– ORIGIN French *char-à-bancs* 'carriage with benches'.

character ● n. **1** the particular qualities that make a person or thing different from others: *running away was not in keeping with her character.* **2** strength and originality in a person's nature. **3** a person's good reputation. **4** a person in a novel, play, or film. **5** informal an eccentric or amusing person. **6** a printed or written letter or symbol.
– DERIVATIVES **characterful** adj. **characterless** adj.
– ORIGIN Greek *kharaktēr* 'a stamping tool'.

characteristic ● adj. typical of a particular person, place, or thing: *he began with a characteristic attack on extremism.* ● n. a quality typical of a person or thing.
– DERIVATIVES **characteristically** adv.

characterize (also **characterise**) ● v. (**characterizes**, **characterizing**, **characterized**) **1** describe the character of. **2** be typical of: *the rugged hills that characterize this part of Wales.*
– DERIVATIVES **characterization** (also **characterisation**) n.

charade /shuh-rahd/ ● n. **1** an absurd pretence. **2** (**charades**) a game of guessing a word or phrase from written or acted clues.
– ORIGIN Provençal *charrado* 'conversation'.

charcoal ● n. **1** a black form of carbon obtained when wood is heated in the absence of air. **2** a dark grey colour.
– ORIGIN prob. related to **COAL**.

chard /chard/ (also **Swiss chard**) ● n. a variety of beet with edible broad white leaf stalks and green blades.
– ORIGIN French *carde*.

charge ● v. (**charges**, **charging**, **charged**) **1** ask (an amount) as a price. **2** accuse (someone) formally of something. **3** rush forward in attack. **4** rush in a particular direction. **5** entrust with a task. **6** store electrical energy in (a battery). **7** load or fill (a container, gun, etc.). **8** fill with a quality or emotion: *the air was charged with menace.* ● n. **1** a price asked. **2** a formal accusation made against a prisoner brought to trial. **3** responsibility for care or control. **4** a person or thing entrusted to someone's care. **5** a headlong rush forward. **6** a property of matter that is responsible for electrical phenomena, existing in a positive or negative form. **7** energy stored chemically in a battery for conversion into electricity. **8** a quantity of explosive needed to fire a gun or similar weapon.
– DERIVATIVES **chargeable** adj.
– ORIGIN Old French *charger*.

charge card ● n. a credit card issued by a chain store or other organization.

chargé d'affaires /shar-*zh*ay da-fair/ ● n. (pl. **chargés d'affaires** /shar-*zh*ay da-fair/) **1** an ambassador's deputy. **2** the diplomatic representative of a state in a minor country.
– ORIGIN French.

charger ● n. **1** a device for charging a battery. **2** a horse ridden by a knight or cavalryman.

chargrill ● v. grill (food) quickly at a very high heat.

chariot ● n. a two-wheeled horse-drawn vehicle, used in ancient warfare and racing.
– DERIVATIVES **charioteer** n.
– ORIGIN Old French.

charisma /kuh-riz-muh/ ● n. **1** attractiveness or charm that can inspire admiration or enthusiasm in other people. **2** (pl. **charismata** /kuh-riz-muh-tuh/) (in Christian belief) a special gift given by God.
– ORIGIN Greek *kharisma*.

charismatic ● adj. **1** having charisma. **2** (of a Christian movement) that emphasizes special gifts from God, such as healing the sick.

charitable ● adj. **1** relating to the assistance of those in need. **2** tolerant in judging others.

– DERIVATIVES **charitably** adv.

charity ● n. (pl. **charities**) **1** an organization set up to help those in need. **2** the voluntary giving of money or other help to those in need. **3** help or money given in this way. **4** tolerance in judging others.
– ORIGIN Latin *caritas* 'affection'.

charlatan /shar-luh-tuhn/ ● n. a person who falsely claims to have a particular skill.
– DERIVATIVES **charlatanism** n.
– ORIGIN Italian *ciarlatano* 'babbler'.

Charlemagne E
/**shar**-luh-mayn/ (742–814), king of the Franks 768–814 and the first Holy Roman emperor (as Charles I) 800–14. He promoted the arts and education and his court became the centre of the cultural revival known as the Carolingian Renaissance.

Charles, E
Ray (b.1930; born *Ray Charles Robinson*), American pianist and singer, who drew on blues, jazz, and country music for songs such as 'Georgia On My Mind'.

Charles I E
(1600–49), son of James I, king of England, Scotland, and Ireland 1625–49. His reign was dominated by the religious and constitutional crisis that resulted in the English Civil War 1642–9, which ended in his defeat and execution.

Charles II E
(1630–85), son of Charles I, king of England, Scotland, and Ireland 1660–85. Charles was restored to the throne after the collapse of Cromwell's regime, but his reign was dominated by continuing religious and political strife.

Charles, Prince, E
Charles Philip Arthur George, Prince of Wales (b.1948), eldest son of Elizabeth II and heir to the throne. He was married to Lady Diana Spencer (1981–96); the couple had two children, Prince William Arthur Philip Louis (b.1982) and Prince Henry Charles Albert David (b.1984).

Charleston[1] E
the state capital of West Virginia.

Charleston[2] E
a city and port in South Carolina. The bombardment by Confederate troops in 1861 of Fort Sumter, in the harbour, marked the beginning of the American Civil War.

charleston ● n. a lively dance of the 1920s which involved turning the knees inwards and kicking out the lower legs.
– ORIGIN named after *Charleston* (see CHARLESTON[2]).

charlie ● n. (pl. **charlies**) informal **1** Brit. a fool. **2** cocaine.
– ORIGIN from the man's name *Charles*.

Charlton, E
Bobby (b.1937; full name *Sir Robert Charlton*), English footballer, who scored a record forty-nine goals for England and was a member of the side that won the World Cup in 1966. His brother **Jack** (b.1935) also played for England and later managed the Republic of Ireland national side.

charm ● n. **1** the power or quality of delighting or fascinating others: *he was captivated by her youthful charm.* **2** a small ornament worn on a necklace or bracelet. **3** an object, act, or saying believed to have magic power. ● v. **1** delight greatly. **2** use one's charm in order to influence someone: *he charmed her into going out.* **3** (**charmed**) unusually lucky as if protected by magic.
– DERIVATIVES **charmer** n. **charmless** adj.
– ORIGIN Old French *charme*.

charming ● adj. **1** delightful; attractive. **2** very polite, friendly, and likeable.

charnel house ● n. hist. a building in which corpses or bones were kept.
– ORIGIN Latin *carnalis* 'relating to flesh'.

Charon E
/**kair**-uhn/ Gk Myth. an old man who ferried the souls of the dead across the Rivers Styx and Acheron to Hades.

chart ● n. **1** a sheet of information in the form of a table, graph, or diagram. **2** a geographical map used for navigation by sea or air. **3** (**the charts**) a weekly listing of the current best-selling pop records. ● v. **1** make a map of. **2** plot or record on a chart.
– ORIGIN Greek *khartēs* 'papyrus leaf'.

charter ● n. **1** a document granted by a ruler or government, by which an institution such as a university is created or its rights are defined. **2** a written constitution or description of an organization's functions. **3** the hiring of an aircraft, ship, or motor vehicle. ● v. (**charters**, **chartering**, **chartered**) **1** hire (an aircraft, ship, or motor vehicle). **2** grant a charter to.
– ORIGIN Latin *chartula* 'little paper'.

chartered ● adj. Brit. (of an accountant, engineer, etc.) qualified as a member of a professional body that has a royal charter.

charter flight ● n. a flight by an aircraft chartered for a specific journey.

Chartism ● n. a UK movement (1837–48) for social and parliamentary reform, the principles of which were set out in *The People's Charter*.
– DERIVATIVES **Chartist** n. & adj.

Chartres E
/**shar**-truh/ a city in northern France, noted for its Gothic cathedral.

chartreuse /shar-trerz/ ● n. a pale green or yellow liqueur.
– ORIGIN named after *La Grande Chartreuse*, a monastery near Grenoble where the liqueur was first made.

charwoman ● n. Brit. dated a woman employed as a cleaner in a house or office.
– ORIGIN from former *char* or *chare* 'a chore'.

chary /chair-i/ ● adj. cautiously reluctant: *leaders are chary of reform.*
– ORIGIN Old English, 'sorrowful'.

Charybdis E
/kuh-**rib**-diss/ Gk Myth. a dangerous whirlpool in a narrow channel of the sea, opposite the cave of the sea monster Scylla.

chase[1] ● v. (**chases**, **chasing**, **chased**) **1** pursue in order to catch. **2** hurry or cause to hurry. **3** try to get: *the company employs*

people to chase up debts. ● **n. 1** an act of chasing. **2** (**the chase**) hunting as a sport.
– PHRASES **give chase** go in pursuit.
– ORIGIN Old French *chacier.*

chase[2] ● **v.** (**chases**, **chasing**, **chased**) engrave (metal, or a design on metal).
– ORIGIN prob. from Old French *enchasser* 'enclose'.

C

chaser ● **n. 1** a person or thing that chases. **2** informal a strong alcoholic drink taken after a weaker one.

chasm ● **n. 1** a deep crack or opening in the earth. **2** a marked difference between people, opinions, etc.
– ORIGIN Greek *khasma.*

chassis /shas-si/ ● **n.** (pl. **chassis** /shas-siz/) the base frame of a vehicle.
– ORIGIN French.

chaste ● **adj. 1** not having sexual intercourse outside marriage or at all. **2** without unnecessary decoration.
– ORIGIN Latin *castus* 'morally pure'.

chasten /chay-s'n/ ● **v.** cause to feel subdued or ashamed: *they were chastened by the bitter lessons of life.*
– ORIGIN Old French *chastier.*

chastise ● **v.** (**chastises**, **chastising**, **chastised**) reprimand severely.
– DERIVATIVES **chastisement** n.

chastity ● **n.** the state of not having sexual intercourse.

chasuble /chaz-yuu-b'l/ ● **n.** a sleeveless outer garment worn by a priest when celebrating Mass.
– ORIGIN Latin *casula* 'hooded cloak, little cottage'.

chat ● **v.** (**chats**, **chatting**, **chatted**) **1** talk in an informal way. **2** (**chat up**) informal talk flirtatiously to. ● **n.** an informal conversation.
– ORIGIN from **CHATTER**.

chateau /sha-toh/ ● **n.** (pl. **chateaux** pronunc. /sha-toh/ or /sha-tohz/) a large French country house or castle.
– ORIGIN French.

Chateaubriand E
/sha-toh-bree-on/, François-René, Vicomte de (1768–1848), French writer and diplomat. He was an important figure in early French romanticism.

chatelaine /sha-tuh-layn/ ● **n.** dated a woman in charge of a large house.
– ORIGIN French.

chatline ● **n.** a telephone service which allows conversation among a number of separate callers.

chat room ● **n.** an area on the Internet where users can communicate.

chat show ● **n.** Brit. a television or radio programme in which celebrities talk informally to a presenter.

chattel /chat-t'l/ ● **n.** a personal possession.
– ORIGIN Old French *chatel.*

chatter ● **v.** (**chatters**, **chattering**, **chattered**) **1** talk at length about unimportant matters. **2** (of a person's teeth) click together from cold or fear. ● **n. 1** continuous unimportant talk. **2** a series of short quick high-pitched sounds.

chatterbox ● **n.** informal a person who chatters.

chatty ● **adj.** (**chattier**, **chattiest**) **1** fond of chatting. **2** (of a conversation, letter, etc.) informal and lively.

Chaucer E
/chaw-ser/, Geoffrey (*c.*1342–1400), English poet, author of the *Canterbury Tales*, a cycle of linked tales told by a group of pilgrims.
– DERIVATIVES **Chaucerian** /chaw-seer-i-uhn/ adj. & n.

chauffeur ● **n.** a person employed to drive a car. ● **v.** be a driver for.
– ORIGIN French, 'stoker'.

chauvinism /shoh-vin-i-z'm/ ● **n. 1** extreme or aggressive support for one's country. **2** extreme or unreasonable support for one's own cause, group, or sex: *the club is a bastion of male chauvinism.*
– ORIGIN named after Nicolas *Chauvin*, a 19th-century French soldier noted for his extreme patriotism.

chauvinist ● **n.** a person displaying extreme or unreasonable support for their own country, cause, group, or sex. ● **adj.** having to do with chauvinists or chauvinism.
– DERIVATIVES **chauvinistic** adj.

cheap ● **adj. 1** low in price. **2** charging low prices. **3** low in price and quality. **4** worthless because achieved in a regrettable way: *her moment of cheap triumph.* ● **adv.** at or for a low price.
– DERIVATIVES **cheaply** adv. **cheapness** n.
– ORIGIN Old English 'bargaining, trade'.

cheapen ● **v.** lower the price or worth of.

cheapskate ● **n.** informal a miserly person.

cheat ● **v. 1** act dishonestly or unfairly to gain an advantage. **2** deprive (someone) of something by trickery or unfair means. **3** avoid by luck or skill: *she cheated death in a spectacular crash.* ● **n. 1** a person who cheats. **2** an act of cheating.
– ORIGIN from former *escheat* 'return of property to the state on the owner's dying without heirs'.

Chechnya E
/chech-nyah/ an autonomous republic in the Caucasus in SW Russia; capital, Grozny. Also called **CHECHEN REPUBLIC**.

check[1] ● **v. 1** examine the accuracy, quality, or condition of. **2** stop or slow the progress of. **3** Chess move a piece or pawn to a square where it directly attacks (the opposing king). ● **n. 1** an act of checking accuracy, quality, or condition. **2** an act of checking progress. **3** a control or restraint. **4** Chess an act of checking the opposing king. **5** N. Amer. the bill in a restaurant.
– PHRASES **check in 1** register at a hotel or airport. **2** have (one's baggage) weighed and loaded onto an aircraft. **check out 1** settle one's hotel bill before leaving. **2** find out about. **check up on** investigate. **in check** under control.
– DERIVATIVES **checker** n.
– ORIGIN Persian, 'king'.

check[2] ● **n.** a pattern of small squares. ● **adj.** (also **checked**) having a pattern of small squares.
– ORIGIN prob. from **CHEQUER**.

check[3] ● **n.** US = **CHEQUE**.

checker ● **n. & v.** US = **CHEQUER**.

checklist ● **n.** a list of items to be done or considered.

checkmate • n. **1** Chess a position of check from which a king cannot escape. **2** a final defeat or deadlock. • v. (**checkmates, checkmating, checkmated**) **1** Chess put into checkmate. **2** defeat or thwart.
– ORIGIN Persian, 'the king is dead'.

checkout • n. a point at which goods are paid for in a supermarket or similar store.

checkpoint • n. a barrier where security checks are carried out on travellers.

check-up • n. a thorough medical or dental examination to detect any problems.

Cheddar • n. a kind of firm smooth cheese originally made in Cheddar in SW England.

cheek • n. **1** either side of the face below the eye. **2** either of the buttocks. **3** impertinent or bold behaviour: *he had the cheek to complain.* • v. speak impertinently to.
– PHRASES **cheek by jowl** close together. **turn the other cheek** stop oneself from retaliating to an attack. [ORIGIN Gospel of Matthew, chapter 5.]
– ORIGIN Old English.

cheekbone • n. the bone below the eye.

cheeky • adj. (**cheekier, cheekiest**) showing a cheerful lack of respect.
– DERIVATIVES **cheekily** adv. **cheekiness** n.

cheep • n. **1** a shrill squeaky cry made by a young bird. **2** informal the slightest sound: *there wasn't a cheep from anybody.* • v. make a cheep.

cheer • v. **1** shout for joy or in praise or encouragement. **2** praise or encourage with shouts. **3** (**cheer up**) make or become less miserable. **4** give comfort to. • n. **1** a shout of joy, encouragement, or praise. **2** (also **good cheer**) cheerfulness; optimism. **3** food and drink provided for a festive occasion.
– ORIGIN first meaning 'face, expression, mood': from Old French *chiere* 'face'.

cheerful • adj. **1** noticeably happy and optimistic. **2** bright and pleasant: *a cheerful, flower-filled garden.*
– DERIVATIVES **cheerfully** adv. **cheerfulness** n.

cheerio • exclam. Brit. informal goodbye.

cheerleader • n. (in North America) a girl belonging to a group that performs organized chanting and dancing at sporting events.

cheerless • adj. gloomy; depressing.

cheers • exclam. informal **1** expressing good wishes before drinking. **2** Brit. said to express thanks or on parting.

cheery • adj. (**cheerier, cheeriest**) happy and optimistic.

cheese[1] • n. a food made from the pressed curds of milk.
– ORIGIN Latin *caseus.*

cheese[2] • v. (**be cheesed off**) Brit. informal be irritated or bored.
– ORIGIN unknown.

cheesecake • n. **1** a rich sweet tart made with cream and soft cheese on a biscuit base. **2** informal pictures of women posed in a sexually attractive way.

cheesecloth • n. thin, loosely woven cotton cloth.

cheese-paring • n. excessive care with money; meanness.

cheesy • adj. (**cheesier, cheesiest**) **1** like cheese in taste or smell. **2** informal lacking quality or taste: *a cheesy plastic purse.*

cheetah /chee-tuh/ • n. a large swift-running spotted cat found in Africa and parts of Asia.
– ORIGIN Hindi.

chef • n. a professional cook in a restaurant or hotel.
– ORIGIN French, 'head'.

> **Chekhov** E
> /chek-off/, Anton (Pavlovich) (1860–1904), Russian dramatist and short-story writer. His plays combine naturalism and symbolism and include *Uncle Vanya, The Three Sisters,* and *The Cherry Orchard.*

> **Chelsea** E
> a residential district of London, on the north bank of the River Thames.

> **Cheltenham** E
> a town in western England, in Gloucestershire, a fashionable spa in the 19th century.

chemical • adj. relating to chemistry or chemicals. • n. a compound or substance which has been artificially prepared or purified.
– DERIVATIVES **chemically** adv.
– ORIGIN French *chimique.*

chemical engineering • n. the branch of engineering concerned with the design and operation of industrial chemical plants.

chemise /shuh-meez/ • n. a woman's loose-fitting dress, nightdress, or undergarment, hanging straight from the shoulders.
– ORIGIN Latin *camisia* 'shirt'.

chemist • n. **1** Brit. a person who is authorized to dispense medicinal drugs. **2** Brit. a shop where medicinal drugs are dispensed and toiletries and cosmetics are sold. **3** a person engaged in chemical research or experiments.
– ORIGIN Latin *alchimista* 'alchemist'.

chemistry • n. **1** the branch of science concerned with the nature and properties of substances and how they react with each other. **2** attraction or interaction between two people: *their affair was triggered by sexual chemistry.*

chemotherapy /kee-moh-the-ruh-pi/ • n. the treatment of disease, especially cancer, by the use of chemicals.

chenille /shuh-neel/ • n. fabric with a long velvety pile.
– ORIGIN French, 'hairy caterpillar'.

> **Chennai** E
> /chin-ny/ official name (since 1995) for **MADRAS**.

> **Cheops** E
> /kee-ops/ (*fl.* early 26th century BC; Egyptian name **Khufu**), Egyptian pharaoh of the 4th dynasty, who commissioned the building of the Great Pyramid at Giza.

cheque (US **check**) • n. a written order to a bank to pay a stated sum from an account to a specified person.
– ORIGIN from **CHECK**[1], in the former sense 'means of checking an amount'.

cheque card • n. Brit. a card issued by a bank to guarantee payment of a customer's cheques.

chequer (US **checker**) • n. **1** (**chequers**) a pattern of alternately coloured squares.

2 (**checkers**) N. Amer. the game of draughts. ● v. **1** (**be chequered**) be divided into or marked with chequers. **2** (**chequered**) marked by periods of varied fortune: *a chequered career.*
– ORIGIN from **EXCHEQUER**.

Chequers E
a mansion in Buckinghamshire, the country residence of the British Prime Minister.

Cherbourg E
/**sher**-boorg/ a seaport and naval base in Normandy, northern France.

cherish ● v. **1** protect and care for lovingly. **2** keep in one's mind: *I will always cherish memories of those days.*
– ORIGIN Old French *cherir.*

Chernenko E
/cher-**nyeng**-koh/, Konstantin (Ustinovich) (1911–85), Soviet statesman, General Secretary of the Communist Party of the USSR and President 1984–5.

Chernobyl E
/cher-**no**-bil, cher-**noh**-bil/ a town near Kiev in Ukraine, site of a serious accident at a nuclear power station in 1986.

Cherokee /che-ruh-kee/ ● n. (pl. **Cherokee** or **Cherokees**) a member of an American Indian people formerly inhabiting much of the southern US.
– ORIGIN the Cherokees' name for themselves.

cheroot /shuh-**root**/ ● n. a cigar with both ends open.
– ORIGIN Tamil, 'roll of tobacco'.

cherry ● n. (pl. **cherries**) **1** the small, round bright or dark red fruit with a stone. **2** a bright deep red colour.
– PHRASES **a bite at the cherry** an attempt or opportunity.
– ORIGIN Greek *kerasos.*

cherry-pick ● v. choose (the best things or people) from those available.

cherry tomato ● n. a miniature tomato.

cherub ● n. **1** (pl. **cherubim** or **cherubs**) a type of angel, shown in art as a chubby child with wings. **2** (pl. **cherubs**) a beautiful or innocent-looking child.
– DERIVATIVES **cherubic** /chuh-**roo**-bik/ adj.
– ORIGIN Hebrew.

chervil /**cher**-vil/ ● n. a herb with an aniseed flavour, used in cooking.
– ORIGIN Greek *khairephullon.*

Ches. ● abbrev. Cheshire.

Chesapeake Bay E
/**chess**-uh-peek/ a large inlet of the North Atlantic on the US coast, extending 320 km (200 miles) northwards through the states of Virginia and Maryland.

Cheshire[1] E
/**che**-sher, **che**-sheer/ a county of west central England; county town, Chester.

Cheshire[2] ● n. a kind of firm crumbly cheese, originally made in Cheshire.

chess ● n. a board game for two players, the object of which is to put the opponent's king under a direct attack, leading to checkmate.
– ORIGIN Persian, 'king'.

chessboard ● n. a square board divided into sixty-four chequered squares, used for playing chess or draughts.

chest ● n. **1** the front surface of a person's body between the neck and the stomach. **2** a large strong box for storage or transport.
– PHRASES **get something off one's chest** informal say something that one has wanted to say for a long time. **keep** (or **play**) **one's cards close to one's chest** informal be extremely secretive about one's plans.
– ORIGIN Greek *kistē* 'box'.

Chester E
a town in NW England, the county town of Cheshire.

chesterfield ● n. a sofa with a back of the same height as the arms.
– ORIGIN named after an Earl of *Chesterfield.*

Chesterton, E
G. K. (1874–1936; full name *Gilbert Keith Chesterton*), English novelist and critic, author of a series of detective stories featuring Father Brown.

chestnut ● n. **1** a glossy brown edible nut. **2** (also **sweet chestnut** or **Spanish chestnut**) the large tree that produces these nuts. **3** a deep reddish-brown colour. **4** a reddish- or yellowish-brown horse. **5** (**old chestnut**) a joke or story that has become uninteresting because repeated too often.
– ORIGIN from Greek *kastanea* + **NUT**.

chest of drawers ● n. a piece of furniture consisting of an upright frame fitted with a set of drawers.

chesty ● adj. Brit. informal having a lot of catarrh in the lungs.

Chevalier E
/shuh-**val**-i-ay/, Maurice (1888–1972), French singer and actor, whose films include *Gigi.*

Cheviot Hills E
/**che**-vi-uht, **chee**-vi-uht/ a range of hills on the border between England and Scotland.

chevron ● n. a V-shaped line or stripe, especially one on the sleeve of a soldier's or police officer's uniform to show rank.
– ORIGIN Old French.

chew ● v. **1** bite and work (food) in the mouth to make it easier to swallow. **2** (**chew over**) discuss or consider at length. ● n. **1** an act of chewing. **2** a thing meant for chewing.
– PHRASES **chew the fat** informal chat in a leisurely way.
– DERIVATIVES **chewable** adj. **chewer** n.
– ORIGIN Old English.

chewing gum ● n. flavoured gum for chewing.

chewy ● adj. needing to be chewed a lot.

Chiang Kai-shek E
/chang ky **shek**/ (also **Jiang Jie Shi**) (1887–1975), Chinese statesman and general, President of China 1928–31 and 1943–9 and of Taiwan 1950–75. He was defeated by the communists on mainland China and in 1949 set up a separate Nationalist Chinese State in Taiwan.

Chianti /ki-**an**-ti/ ● n. (pl. **Chiantis**) a dry red Italian wine.
– ORIGIN named after the *Chianti* Mountains, Italy.

chiaroscuro /ki-ah-ruh-**skoor**-oh/ • **n.** the treatment of light and shade in drawing and painting.
– ORIGIN Italian.

chic /sheek/ • **adj.** (**chicer**, **chicest**) elegant and fashionable. • **n.** stylishness and elegance.
– ORIGIN French.

Chicago E
a major city and port in Illinois, on Lake Michigan.
– DERIVATIVES **Chicagoan** n. & adj.

chicane /shi-**kayn**/ • **n.** a sharp double bend created to form an obstacle on a motor-racing track.
– ORIGIN French *chicaner* 'quibble'.

chicanery • **n.** the use of trickery to achieve one's aims.

Chichén Itzá E
/chi-chen **it**-sah/ a site in northern Yucatán, Mexico, the centre of the Mayan empire after AD 918.

Chichester E
/**chi**-chi-ster/, Sir Francis (Charles) (1901–72), English yachtsman, who in 1966–7 was the first person to sail alone round the world in his yacht *Gipsy Moth IV.*

chick • **n.** **1** a young bird that is newly hatched. **2** informal a young woman.
– ORIGIN from **CHICKEN**.

chicken • **n.** **1** a domestic fowl kept for its eggs or meat. **2** informal a coward. • **adj.** informal cowardly. • **v.** (**chicken out**) informal be too scared to do something.
– ORIGIN Old English.

chicken feed • **n.** informal a very small sum of money.

chickenpox • **n.** a disease causing a mild fever and itchy inflamed pimples.

chickpea • **n.** a yellowish seed eaten as a vegetable.
– ORIGIN Latin *cicer.*

chickweed • **n.** a small white-flowered plant, often growing as a garden weed.

chicory /**chi**-kuh-ri/ • **n.** (pl. **chicories**) **1** a plant with a root which is added to or used instead of coffee. **2** N. Amer. = **ENDIVE**.
– ORIGIN Greek *kikhorion.*

chide /chyd/ • **v.** (**chides**, **chiding**, **chided** or **chid**) scold or rebuke.
– ORIGIN Old English.

chief • **n.** **1** a leader or ruler of a people. **2** the head of an organization. • **adj.** **1** having the highest rank or authority. **2** most important: *the chief reason.*
– ORIGIN Old French.

chief constable • **n.** Brit. the head of the police force of a county or other region.

chiefly • **adv.** mainly; mostly.

chief of staff • **n.** the senior staff officer of an armed service or command.

chieftain • **n.** the leader of a people or clan.
– ORIGIN Old French.

chiffchaff • **n.** a common warbler with brownish plumage.

chiffon • **n.** a light, see-through fabric of silk or nylon.
– ORIGIN French.

Chifley E
/**chiff**-li/, Joseph Benedict (1885–1951), Australian Labor statesman, Prime Minister 1945–9.

chignon /**sheen**-yon/ • **n.** a knot or coil of hair arranged on the back of a woman's head.
– ORIGIN French, 'nape of the neck'.

chihuahua /chi-**wah**-wuh/ • **n.** a very small breed of dog with smooth hair and large eyes.
– ORIGIN named after *Chihuahua* in northern Mexico.

chilblain • **n.** a painful, itching swelling on a hand or foot caused by poor circulation in the skin when exposed to cold.
– ORIGIN from **CHILL** + an Old English word meaning 'inflamed swelling'.

child • **n.** (pl. **children**) **1** a young human being below the age of full physical development. **2** a son or daughter of any age.
– PHRASES **child's play** an easy task. **with child** archaic pregnant.
– DERIVATIVES **childless** adj.
– ORIGIN Old English.

childbirth • **n.** the action of giving birth to a child.

childhood • **n.** the state or period of being a child.

childish • **adj.** **1** like or appropriate to a child. **2** silly and immature.

childlike • **adj.** (of an adult) having the good qualities, such as innocence, associated with a child.

childminder • **n.** Brit. a person who is paid to look after children in their own house.

children pl. of **CHILD**.

Chile E
/**chi**-li/ a country on the Pacific coast of South America; capital, Santiago.
– DERIVATIVES **Chilean** adj. & n.

chill • **n.** **1** an unpleasant feeling of coldness. **2** a feverish cold. • **v.** **1** make cold. **2** frighten. **3** informal relax: *chilling out in a hammock.* • **adj.** chilly.
– ORIGIN Old English.

chiller • **n.** a cold cabinet or refrigerator for keeping stored food a few degrees above freezing point.

chilli • **n.** (pl. **chillies**) **1** (also **chilli pepper**) a small hot-tasting pod of a kind of pepper, used in cooking and as a spice. **2** chilli con carne.
– ORIGIN from a Central American Indian language.

chilli con carne /chil-li kon **kar**-ni/ • **n.** a stew of minced beef and beans flavoured with chilli.
– ORIGIN Spanish *chile con carne.*

chilly • **adj.** (**chillier**, **chilliest**) **1** unpleasantly cold. **2** unfriendly.

Chiltern Hills E
/**chil**-tern/ a range of chalk hills in southern England, north of the River Thames.

Chiltern Hundreds E
(in the UK) a Crown manor, whose administration is a nominal office for which an MP applies as a way of resigning from the House of Commons.

chime • n. **1** a tuneful ringing sound. **2** a bell or a metal bar used in a set to produce chimes when struck. • v. (**chimes**, **chiming**, **chimed**) **1** (of a bell or clock) make a tuneful ringing sound. **2** (**chime in**) interrupt a conversation with a remark.
– ORIGIN prob. from **CYMBAL**.

chimera /ky-meer-uh/ (also **chimaera**) • n. **1** Gk Myth. a female monster with a lion's head, a goat's body, and a serpent's tail. **2** an impossible idea or hope.
– ORIGIN Greek *khimaira*.

chimerical /ky-me-ri-k'l/ • adj. impossible to achieve: *chimerical projects*.

chimney • n. (pl. **chimneys**) a vertical pipe which takes smoke and gases up from a fire or furnace.
– ORIGIN Old French *cheminee*.

chimney breast • n. a part of an inside wall that comes out to surround a chimney.

chimney pot • n. a pipe at the top of a chimney.

chimney stack • n. the part of a chimney that sticks up above a roof.

chimp • n. informal a chimpanzee.

chimpanzee • n. an ape native to west and central Africa.
– ORIGIN from a language of the Congo.

chin • n. the part of the face below the mouth.
– PHRASES **keep one's chin up** informal remain cheerful in difficult circumstances. **take it on the chin** informal accept misfortune without complaint.
– ORIGIN Old English.

China E
a country in east Asia; capital, Beijing. Official name **PEOPLE'S REPUBLIC OF CHINA**.

china • n. **1** a fine white ceramic material. **2** household objects made from china.
– ORIGIN Persian, 'relating to China'.

China, Republic of E
official name for **TAIWAN**.

china clay • n. = **KAOLIN**.

China Sea E
the part of the Pacific Ocean off the coast of China.

chinchilla /chin-chil-luh/ • n. a small South American rodent with soft grey fur and a long bushy tail.
– ORIGIN from South American Indian languages.

chine /chyn/ • n. the backbone of an animal, or a joint of meat containing part of it.
– ORIGIN Old French *eschine*.

Chinese • n. (pl. **Chinese**) **1** the language of China. **2** a person from China. • adj. relating to China.

Chinese leaves • pl. n. a kind of cabbage which does not form a firm heart.

Chink (also **Chinky**) • n. informal, offens. a Chinese person.

chink[1] • n. **1** a narrow opening or crack. **2** a beam of light entering through a chink.
– ORIGIN Old English.

chink[2] • v. make a light, high-pitched ringing sound. • n. a high-pitched ringing sound.

chinless • adj. **1** lacking a well-defined chin. **2** informal lacking strength of character.

chino /chee-noh/ • n. **1** a cotton twill fabric. **2** (**chinos**) casual trousers made from such fabric.
– ORIGIN Latin American Spanish, 'toasted' (referring to the typical colour of the fabric).

chinoiserie /shin-wah-zuh-ri/ • n. **1** the use of Chinese styles in Western art, furniture, and architecture. **2** objects or decorations in this style.
– ORIGIN French.

chintz • n. multicoloured shiny cotton fabric, used for curtains and upholstery.
– ORIGIN Hindi, 'spattering, stain'.

chintzy • adj. **1** decorated or covered with chintz. **2** colourful but fussy and tasteless.

chinwag • n. Brit. informal a chat.

Chios E
/ky-oss/ a Greek island in the Aegean Sea.

chip • n. **1** a small, thin piece cut or broken off from a hard material. **2** a mark left by the removal of such a piece. **3** Brit. a long rectangular piece of deep-fried potato. **4** a microchip. **5** a counter used in some gambling games to represent money. **6** (in football or golf) a short high kick or shot. • v. (**chips**, **chipping**, **chipped**) **1** cut or break (a chip) from a hard material. **2** (**chip away**) gradually make something smaller or weaker. **3** (in football or golf) strike (the ball) to produce a short high shot or pass.
– PHRASES **chip in 1** give one's share of a joint activity. **2** Brit. informal interrupt with a remark. **a chip off the old block** informal someone who resembles their mother or father. **a chip on one's shoulder** informal a long-held grievance. **when the chips are down** informal when a very serious situation arises.
– ORIGIN Old English.

chipboard • n. material made from compressed wood chips and resin.

chipmunk • n. a burrowing squirrel with light and dark stripes running down the body.
– ORIGIN from an American Indian language.

chipolata • n. Brit. a small thin sausage.
– ORIGIN Italian *cipollata* 'dish of onions'.

Chippendale, E
Thomas (1718–79), English furniture-maker and designer, who produced furniture in a neoclassical style with Chinese and Gothic elements.

chipper • adj. informal cheerful and lively.
– ORIGIN perh. from northern English dialect *kipper* 'lively'.

chipping • n. Brit. a small fragment of stone, wood, or similar material.

chippy (also **chippie**) • n. Brit. informal (pl. **chippies**) **1** a fish-and-chip shop. **2** a carpenter.

Chirac E
/sheer-ak/, Jacques (René) (b.1932), French statesman, Prime Minister 1974–6 and 1986–8 and President since 1995.

Chirico E
/ki-ri-koh/, Giorgio de (1888–1978), Greek-born Italian painter, whose work had a significant influence on surrealism.

chiropody /ki-rop-uh-di/ • n. the medical

treatment of the feet.
– DERIVATIVES **chiropodist** n.
– ORIGIN from Greek *kheir* 'hand' + *pous* 'foot'.

chiropractic /ky-roh-prak-tik/ • n. a system of complementary medicine based on the manipulation of the joints, especially those of the spinal column.
– DERIVATIVES **chiropractor** n.
– ORIGIN from Greek *kheir* 'hand' + *praktikos* 'practical'.

chirp • v. (of a small bird) make a short, high-pitched sound. • n. a chirping sound.

chirpy • adj. informal cheerful and lively.

chisel • n. a hand tool with a long blade, used to cut or shape wood, stone, or metal. • v. (**chisels**, **chiselling**, **chiselled**; US **chisels**, **chiseling**, **chiseled**) **1** cut or shape with a chisel. **2** (**chiselled**) (of a man's facial features) strongly defined.
– ORIGIN Old French.

Chişinău E
/ki-shi-now/ the capital of Moldova.

chit[1] • n. derog. an impudent young woman.
– ORIGIN perh. from dialect, 'sprout'.

chit[2] • n. a short official note recording a sum owed.
– ORIGIN Hindi, 'note, pass'.

chit-chat informal • n. trivial conversation. • v. (**chit-chats**, **chit-chatting**, **chit-chatted**) talk about trivial things.

chitin /ky-tin/ • n. a fibrous substance which forms the external skeletons of some insects, spiders, and crustaceans.
– ORIGIN Greek *khitōn* 'tunic'.

chivalrous • adj. (of a man) polite and gallant, especially towards women.

chivalry • n. **1** the medieval knightly system with its religious, moral, and social code. **2** polite behaviour, especially that of a man towards women.
– ORIGIN Old French *chevalerie*.

chives • pl. n. a small plant having tubular leaves with an onion taste, used as a herb in cooking.
– ORIGIN Old French.

chivvy • v. (**chivvies**, **chivvying**, **chivvied**) tell (someone) repeatedly to do something.
– ORIGIN first meaning 'a hunting cry'.

chloral /klor-uhl/ • n. Chem. a liquid used as a sedative.
– ORIGIN French.

chlorate • n. Chem. a compound containing ClO_3 negative ions together with a metallic element: *sodium chlorate*.

chloride /klor-yd/ • n. a compound of chlorine with another element or group.

chlorinate /klor-in-ayt/ • v. (**chlorinates**, **chlorinating**, **chlorinated**) fill or treat with chlorine.

chlorine /klor-een/ • n. a poisonous green gaseous chemical element.
– ORIGIN Greek *khlōros* 'green'.

chlorofluorocarbon /klor-oh-floor-oh-kar-b'n/ • n. see **CFC**.

chloroform • n. a liquid used as a solvent and formerly as an anaesthetic. • v. make unconscious with this substance.
– ORIGIN from **CHLORINE** + **FORMIC ACID**.

chlorophyll /klo-ruh-fil/ • n. a green pigment which is responsible for the absorption of light by plants to provide energy for photosynthesis.
– ORIGIN from Greek *khlōros* 'green' + *phullon* 'leaf'.

chloroplast /klo-ruh-plahst/ • n. a structure in green plant cells which contains chlorophyll and in which photosynthesis takes place.
– ORIGIN from Greek *khlōros* 'green' + *plastos* 'formed'.

choc ice • n. Brit. a bar of ice cream with a coating of chocolate.

chock • n. a wedge or block placed against a wheel to prevent it from moving.
– ORIGIN Old French *çoche*.

chock-a-block • adj. informal crammed full.
– ORIGIN first referring to blocks in tackle running close together.

chock-full • adj. informal filled to overflowing.
– ORIGIN unknown.

chocoholic • n. informal a person who is very fond of chocolate.

chocolate • n. **1** a food made from roasted cacao seeds, eaten as a sweet, or mixed with milk or water to make a drink. **2** a sweet covered with chocolate. **3** a deep brown colour.
– ORIGIN Nahuatl (a language of Central America).

chocolate-box • adj. (of a place) pretty in an unreal way.

choice • n. **1** an act of choosing. **2** the right or ability to choose. **3** a range from which to choose: *a choice of over forty fabrics*. **4** something chosen. • adj. of very good quality.
– ORIGIN Old French *chois*.

choir • n. an organized group of singers.
– ORIGIN Old French *quer*.

choirboy (or **choirgirl**) • n. a boy (or girl) who sings in a church choir.

choke • v. (**chokes**, **choking**, **choked**) **1** prevent (someone) from breathing by squeezing or blocking the throat or depriving them of air. **2** have trouble breathing. **3** (**be choked with**) (of a space) be filled or blocked with. • n. a valve in the carburettor of a petrol engine used to reduce the amount of air in the fuel mixture.
– ORIGIN Old English.

choker • n. a close-fitting necklace or ornamental neckband.

cholecalciferol /ko-li-kal-sif-uh-rol/ • n. vitamin D_3, produced naturally in the skin by the action of sunlight.

cholera /kol-uh-ruh/ • n. an infectious disease of the small intestine, causing severe vomiting and diarrhoea.
– ORIGIN Latin, 'diarrhoea, bile'.

choleric /kol-uh-rik/ • adj. irritable.
– ORIGIN from *choler*, a bodily substance in medieval medicine associated with an irritable temperament.

cholesterol /kuh-less-tuh-rol/ • n. a compound which occurs normally in most body tissues and is believed to cause disease of the arteries if present in high concentrations in the blood.
– ORIGIN from Greek *kholē* 'bile' + *stereos* 'stiff'.

chomp • v. munch or chew noisily or vigorously.

Chomsky E
/**chom**-ski/, (Avram) Noam (b.1928), American theoretical linguist, noted for his theory of generative grammar and for demonstrating that all languages share the same underlying grammatical base.

Chongqing E
/chuung-**ching**/ (also **Chungking**) a city in Sichuan province in central China, the capital of China 1938–46.

choose • v. (**chooses, choosing, chose**; past part. **chosen**) **1** pick out as being the best of the available alternatives. **2** decide on a course of action.
– ORIGIN Old English.

USAGE choose
Do not confuse **choose** and **chose**. **Choose** is the present tense of the verb, used in such sentences as *I choose my casual clothes with great care.* **Chose** is the past tense of **choose**, as in *he chose a seat facing the door.*

choosy • adj. (**choosier, choosiest**) informal very careful in making a choice.

chop[1] • v. (**chops, chopping, chopped**) **1** cut with repeated heavy blows of an axe or knife. **2** strike with a short, heavy blow. **3** reduce by a large amount. • n. **1** a downward cutting blow or movement. **2** (**the chop**) Brit. informal dismissal, cancellation, or killing. **3** a thick slice of meat, especially pork or lamb, next to and usually including a rib.
– ORIGIN from CHAPPED.

chop[2] • v. (**chops, chopping, chopped**) (in phr. **chop and change**) Brit. informal repeatedly change one's opinions or behaviour.

chop-chop • adv. & exclam. quickly.
– ORIGIN pidgin English.

Chopin E
/**shoh**-pan/, Frédéric (François) (1810–49), Polish-born French composer and pianist. His works include nocturnes, preludes, and two piano concertos.

chopper • n. **1** Brit. a short axe with a large blade. **2** informal a helicopter. **3** (**choppers**) informal teeth.

choppy • adj. (of the sea) having many small waves.

chops • pl. n. informal a person's or animal's mouth, jaws, or cheeks.
– ORIGIN unknown.

chopstick • n. each of a pair of thin, tapered sticks held in one hand and used as eating utensils by the Chinese and Japanese.
– ORIGIN pidgin English.

chop suey /chop **soo**-i/ • n. a Chinese-style dish of meat with bean sprouts, bamboo shoots, and onions.
– ORIGIN Chinese, 'mixed bits'.

choral • adj. having to do with or sung by a choir or chorus.

chorale • n. choral composition using a simple, stately hymn tune.
– ORIGIN from Latin *cantus choralis.*

chord[1] • n. a group of three or more notes sounded together in harmony.
– ORIGIN from ACCORD.

chord[2] • n. a straight line joining the ends of an arc.
– PHRASES **strike a chord** affect or stir someone's emotions.
– ORIGIN from CORD.

chore • n. a routine or boring task, especially a household one.
– ORIGIN from former *char* or *chare* 'an odd job'.

choreograph /**ko**-ri-uh-grahf/ • v. compose the sequence of steps and moves for (a dance performance).

choreographer /ko-ri-**og**-ruh-fer/ • n. a person who designs the steps and moves for a dance.

choreography /ko-ri-**og**-ruh-fi/ • n. **1** the sequence of steps and movements in dance. **2** the practice of designing such sequences.
– ORIGIN Greek *khoreia* 'dancing together'.

chorister • n. a choirboy or choirgirl.
– ORIGIN Old French *cueriste.*

chortle • v. (**chortles, chortling, chortled**) laugh loudly.
– ORIGIN coined by Lewis Carroll in *Through the Looking Glass.*

chorus • n. (pl. **choruses**) **1** a part of a song which is repeated after each verse. **2** something said at the same time by many people. **3** a large group of singers performing with an orchestra. **4** a group of singers or dancers in a musical or an opera. • v. (**choruses, chorusing, chorused**) (of a group of people) say the same thing at the same time.
– ORIGIN Latin.

chorus girl • n. a young woman who sings or dances in the chorus of a musical.

chose past of CHOOSE.

chosen past part. of CHOOSE.

Chou En-lai E
/choh en-**ly**/ var. of **ZHOU ENLAI**.

chough /chuff/ • n. a black bird of the crow family with a red or yellow bill.

choux pastry /shoo/ • n. very light pastry made with egg, used for eclairs and profiteroles.
– ORIGIN French.

chow /chow/ • n. **1** informal food. **2** a Chinese breed of dog with a tail curled over its back.
– ORIGIN from pidgin English *chow chow* 'mixed pickle'.

chow mein /chow **mayn**/ • n. a Chinese-style dish of fried noodles with shredded meat or seafood and vegetables.
– ORIGIN Chinese, 'stir-fried noodles'.

Chrétien E
/**kray**-tyan/, (Joseph-Jacques) Jean (b.1934), Canadian Liberal statesman, Prime Minister 1993–2003.

Christ • n. the title given to Jesus. • exclam. used to express irritation, dismay, or surprise.
– ORIGIN Greek *Khristos* 'anointed one'.

Christchurch E
a city on South Island, New Zealand.

christen • v. **1** name (a baby) at baptism to mark their entry into a Christian Church. **2** informal use for the first time.
– DERIVATIVES **christening** n.
– ORIGIN Old English 'make Christian'.

Christendom • n. dated the worldwide body of Christians.

Christian • adj. relating to or believing in

Christianity or its teachings. ● n. a person who has received Christian baptism or is a believer in Christianity.

Christiania E
/kriss-ti-**ah**-ni-uh/ former name for **Oslo**.

Christianity ● n. the religion based on the teaching and works of Jesus Christ.

Christian name ● n. a forename, especially one given at baptism.

Christian Science ● n. the beliefs and practices of the Church of Christ Scientist, a Christian sect.
– DERIVATIVES **Christian Scientist** n.

Christie[1], E
Dame Agatha (1890–1976), English writer of detective fiction, including the novel *Murder on the Orient Express* and the play *The Mousetrap*.

Christie[2], E
Linford (b.1960), Jamaican-born British sprinter, winner of the 100 metres Olympic gold medal (1992) and the World Championship title (1993).

Christmas ● n. (pl. **Christmases**) **1** (also **Christmas Day**) the annual Christian festival celebrating Christ's birth, held on 25 December. **2** the period immediately before and after this.
– ORIGIN Old English, 'Mass of Christ'.

Christmas box ● n. Brit. a present given at Christmas to tradespeople and employees.

Christmas cake ● n. Brit. a rich fruit cake covered with marzipan and icing, eaten at Christmas.

Christmas pudding ● n. Brit. a rich pudding eaten at Christmas, made with flour, suet, and dried fruit.

Christmas tree ● n. an evergreen tree decorated with lights and ornaments at Christmas.

Christopher, St E
a legendary Christian martyr, the patron saint of travellers.

chromatic ● adj. **1** (of a musical scale) rising or falling by semitones. **2** relating to or produced by colour.
– ORIGIN Greek *khrōmatikos*.

chromatography /kroh-muh-**tog**-ruh-fi/ ● n. Chem. a technique for separating a mixture by passing it through a medium in which the components move at different rates.
– DERIVATIVES **chromatographic** adj.
– ORIGIN from Greek *khrōma* 'colour' (early separations being displayed as coloured bands or spots).

chrome ● n. a hard shiny metal coating made from chromium.
– ORIGIN Greek *khrōma* 'colour'.

chromium ● n. a hard white metallic chemical element used in stainless steel and other alloys.

chromosome ● n. Biol. a thread-like structure in a cell nucleus, carrying the genes.
– ORIGIN from Greek *khrōma* 'colour' + *sōma* 'body'.

chronic ● adj. **1** (of an illness or problem) lasting for a long time. **2** having a long-lasting illness or bad habit. **3** Brit. informal very bad.
– DERIVATIVES **chronically** adv.
– ORIGIN Greek *khronikos* 'of time'.

chronicle ● n. a written account of historical events in the order in which they occurred. ● v. (**chronicles**, **chronicling**, **chronicled**) record (a series of events) in detail.
– DERIVATIVES **chronicler** n.
– ORIGIN Greek *khronika* 'annals'.

chronograph ● n. an instrument for recording time very accurately.

chronological ● adj. **1** (of a number of events) starting with the earliest and following the order in which they occurred. **2** relating to the establishment of dates of past events.
– DERIVATIVES **chronologically** adv.

chronology /kruh-**nol**-uh-ji/ ● n. (pl. **chronologies**) **1** the study of records to establish the dates of past events. **2** the arrangement of events in the order in which they occurred.
– ORIGIN Greek *khronos* 'time'.

chronometer /kruh-**nom**-i-ter/ ● n. an instrument for measuring time accurately in spite of motion or varying conditions.

chrysalis /**kriss**-uh-liss/ ● n. (pl. **chrysalises**) **1** an insect pupa, especially of a butterfly or moth. **2** the hard case enclosing this.
– ORIGIN Greek *khrusallis*.

chrysanthemum /kri-**santh**-i-muhm/ ● n. (pl. **chrysanthemums**) a garden plant with brightly coloured flowers.
– ORIGIN from Greek *khrusos* 'gold' + *anthemon* 'flower'.

chub ● n. a thick-bodied river fish.
– ORIGIN unknown.

Chubb ● n. trademark a lock with a device for fixing the bolt to prevent it from being picked.
– ORIGIN named after the London locksmith Charles *Chubb* (1773–1845).

chubby ● adj. (**chubbier**, **chubbiest**) plump and rounded.
– ORIGIN from **chub**.

chuck[1] ● v. informal throw (something) carelessly or casually.
– ORIGIN from **chuck**[2].

chuck[2] ● v. touch playfully under the chin.
– ORIGIN prob. from Old French *chuquer* 'to knock, bump'.

chuck[3] ● n. **1** a device for holding a workpiece in a lathe or a tool in a drill. **2** a cut of beef extending from the neck to the ribs.
– ORIGIN from **chock**.

chuckle ● v. (**chuckles**, **chuckling**, **chuckled**) laugh quietly or inwardly. ● n. a quiet laugh.
– ORIGIN from a former word meaning 'to cluck'.

chuff ● v. (of a steam engine) move with a regular puffing sound.

chuffed ● adj. Brit. informal delighted.
– ORIGIN dialect *chuff* 'plump, pleased'.

chug ● v. (**chugs**, **chugging**, **chugged**) move with or give out a series of muffled explosive sounds, as of an engine running slowly.

chukka ● n. each of six periods into which play in a game of polo is divided.
– ORIGIN Sanskrit, 'circle or wheel'.

chum informal ● n. a close friend.
– DERIVATIVES **chummy** adj.
– ORIGIN Oxford University slang for a roommate: prob. from *chamber-fellow*.

chump ● n. **1** informal, dated a foolish person. **2** Brit. the thick end of a loin of lamb.
– ORIGIN prob. from **chunk**[1] and **lump**[1].

C

chunder informal, esp. Austral./NZ ● **v.** (**chunders, chundering, chundered**) vomit. ● **n.** vomit.
– ORIGIN prob. from rhyming slang *Chunder Loo* 'spew'.

chunk ● **n.** **1** a thick, solid piece. **2** a large amount.
– ORIGIN prob. from **CHUCK**[3].

chunky ● **adj.** (**chunkier, chunkiest**) **1** (of a person) short and sturdy. **2** containing chunks.

church ● **n.** **1** a building used for public Christian worship. **2** (**Church**) a particular Christian organization. **3** organized Christian religion as a political or social force.
– ORIGIN from Greek *kuriakon dōma* 'Lord's house'.

Churchill, E
Sir Winston (Leonard Spencer) (1874–1965), British Conservative statesman, Prime Minister 1940–5 and 1951–5. He became Prime Minister of a coalition government in 1940 and led Britain throughout the Second World War.
– DERIVATIVES **Churchillian** adj.

churchman (or **churchwoman**) ● **n.** a member of the Christian clergy or of a Church.

Church of England ● **n.** the English branch of the Western Christian Church, which rejects the Pope's authority and has the monarch as its head.

Church of Scotland ● **n.** the national (Presbyterian) Christian Church in Scotland.

churchwarden ● **n.** either of two people in an Anglican parish who are elected to represent the congregation.

churchyard ● **n.** an enclosed area surrounding a church.

churl ● **n.** a rude or bad-tempered person.
– ORIGIN Old English.

churlish ● **adj.** rude or bad-tempered.
– DERIVATIVES **churlishly** adv.

churn ● **n.** **1** a machine for making butter by shaking milk or cream. **2** Brit. a large metal milk can. ● **v.** **1** shake (milk or cream) in a churn to produce butter. **2** (of liquid) move about vigorously. **3** (**churn out**) produce mechanically and in large quantities.
– ORIGIN Old English.

chute (also **shoot**) ● **n.** **1** a sloping channel for moving things to a lower level. **2** a water slide into a swimming pool.
– ORIGIN French, 'fall'.

chutney ● **n.** (pl. **chutneys**) a spicy sauce made of fruits or vegetables with vinegar and sugar.
– ORIGIN Hindi.

chutzpah /khuuts-puh/ ● **n.** informal shameless self-confidence.
– ORIGIN Yiddish.

chyle /kyl/ ● **n.** a milky fluid which drains from the small intestine into the lymphatic system during digestion.
– ORIGIN Greek *khūlos*.

chyme /kym/ ● **n.** the fluid which passes from the stomach to the small intestine, consisting of gastric juices and partly digested food.
– ORIGIN Greek *khūmos*.

Ci ● **abbrev.** curie.

CIA ● **abbrev.** Central Intelligence Agency.

ciabatta /chuh-bah-tuh/ ● **n.** a flat Italian bread made with olive oil.
– ORIGIN Italian, 'slipper' (from its shape).

ciao /chow/ ● **exclam.** informal hello or goodbye.
– ORIGIN Italian.

cicada /si-kah-duh/ ● **n.** a large insect with long wings, which makes a continuous high sound after dark.
– ORIGIN Latin.

cicatrix /sik-uh-triks/ (also **cicatrice** /sik-uh-triss/) ● **n.** (pl. **cicatrices** /sik-uh-try-seez/) a scar.
– ORIGIN Latin.

Cicero E
/si-suh-roh/, Marcus Tullius (106–43 BC), Roman statesman, orator, and writer. His writings and speeches established a model for Latin prose.

CID ● **abbrev.** (in the UK) Criminal Investigation Department.

Cid, El E
/el sid/, Count of Bivar (*c.*1043–99; born *Rodrigo Díaz de Vivar*), Spanish soldier, a champion of Christianity against the Moors.

-cide ● **comb. form** **1** referring to a person or thing that kills: *insecticide*. **2** referring to an act of killing: *suicide*.
– ORIGIN Latin *-cida*, *-cidium*.

cider ● **n.** Brit. an alcoholic drink made from apple juice.
– ORIGIN Old French *sidre*.

cigar ● **n.** a cylinder of tobacco rolled in tobacco leaves for smoking.
– ORIGIN French.

cigarette ● **n.** a cylinder of finely cut tobacco rolled in paper for smoking.
– ORIGIN French, 'little cigar'.

cigarillo /sig-uh-ril-loh/ ● **n.** (pl. **cigarillos**) a small cigar.
– ORIGIN Spanish.

cilium /si-li-uhm/ ● **n.** (pl. **cilia** /si-li-uh/) Biol. a microscopic hair-like structure, occurring on the surface of certain cells.
– ORIGIN Latin.

C.-in-C. ● **abbrev.** Commander-in-Chief.

cinch ● **n.** informal **1** a very easy task. **2** a certainty.
– ORIGIN Spanish *cincha* 'girth'.

cinchona /sing-koh-nuh/ ● **n.** a medicinal drug obtained from the bark of a South American tree, containing quinine.
– ORIGIN named after the Countess of *Chinchón* (d.1641).

Cincinnati E
/sin-sin-na-ti/ an industrial city in Ohio, on the Ohio River.

cinder ● **n.** a piece of partly burnt coal or wood.
– ORIGIN Old English.

cine ● **adj.** having to do with film-making.

cinema ● **n.** esp. Brit. **1** a theatre where films are shown. **2** the production of films as an art or industry.
– ORIGIN Greek *kinēma* 'movement'.

cinematic ● **adj.** relating to films and film-making.

cinematography ● **n.** the art of photography and camerawork in film-making.
– DERIVATIVES **cinematographer** n.

cinnabar /sin-nuh-bar/ ● **n.** a bright red mineral consisting of mercury sulphide.
– ORIGIN Greek *kinnabari*.

cinnamon ● n. a spice made from the dried and rolled bark of an Asian tree.
– ORIGIN Greek *kinnamōmon*.

cinquefoil /singk-foyl/ ● n. a plant with leaves made up of five small leaves.
– ORIGIN from Latin *quinque* 'five' + *folium* 'leaf'.

Cinque Ports E
/singk/ a group of ports in SE England, which from the 11th to the 16th centuries were allowed trading privileges in exchange for providing the bulk of England's navy. The five original ports were Hastings, Sandwich, Dover, Romney, and Hythe.

cipher (also **cypher**) ● n. **1** a code. **2** a key to a code. **3** an unimportant person or thing.
– ORIGIN Old French *cifre*.

circa /ser-kuh/ ● prep. approximately.
– ORIGIN Latin.

circadian /ser-kay-di-uhn/ ● adj. (of biological processes) happening on a twenty-four-hour cycle.
– ORIGIN from Latin *circa* 'about' + *dies* 'day'.

Circe E
/ser-si/ Gk Myth. an enchantress who detained Odysseus on her island and changed his companions into pigs.

circle ● n. **1** a round plane figure whose boundary is made up of points at an equal distance from the centre. **2** a group of people or things forming a circle. **3** a curved upper tier of seats in a theatre. **4** a group of people with a shared job, interests, or friends. ● v. (**circles**, **circling**, **circled**) **1** move or be placed all the way around. **2** draw a line around.
– PHRASES **come full circle** return to a previous position. **go** (or **run**) **round in circles** informal do something for a long time without achieving anything.
– ORIGIN Latin *circulus* 'small ring'.

circlet ● n. a circular band worn on the head as an ornament.

circuit ● n. **1** a roughly circular line, route, or movement. **2** Brit. a track used for motor racing. **3** a system of components forming a complete path for an electric current. **4** a series of sporting events or entertainments. **5** a regular journey by a judge around a district to hear court cases. ● v. move all the way around.
– ORIGIN Latin *circuitus*.

circuit-breaker ● n. an automatic safety device for stopping the flow of current in an electric circuit.

circuitous /ser-kyoo-i-tuhss/ ● adj. (of a route) longer than the most direct way.

circuitry ● n. (pl. **circuitries**) electric circuits as a whole.

circular ● adj. **1** having the form of a circle. **2** (of an argument) false because it uses as evidence the point which is to be proved. **3** (of a letter or advertisement) for distribution to a large number of people. ● n. a circular letter or advertisement.

circular saw ● n. a power saw with a quickly turning toothed disc.

circulate ● v. (**circulates**, **circulating**, **circulated**) **1** move continuously through a closed system or area. **2** pass from place to place or person to person.

circulation ● n. **1** movement around something. **2** the continuous motion of blood round the body. **3** the public availability of something. **4** the number of copies sold of a newspaper or magazine.

circum- ● prefix about; around: *circumnavigate*.
– ORIGIN Latin *circum* 'round'.

circumambulate /ser-kuhm-am-byuu-layt/ ● v. (**circumambulates**, **circumambulating**, **circumambulated**) formal walk all the way round.

circumcise ● v. (**circumcises**, **circumcising**, **circumcised**) **1** cut off the foreskin of (a young boy or man). **2** cut off the clitoris of (a girl or young woman).
– DERIVATIVES **circumcision** n.
– ORIGIN Latin *circumcidere* 'cut around'.

circumference ● n. **1** the boundary which encloses a circle. **2** the distance around something.
– ORIGIN Latin *circumferentia*.

circumflex ● n. a mark (ˆ) placed over a vowel in some languages to show a change in its sound.
– ORIGIN Latin *circumflexus*.

circumlocution /ser-kuhm-luh-kyoo-sh'n/ ● n. the use of many words where fewer would do.
– ORIGIN Latin.

circumnavigate ● v. (**circumnavigates**, **circumnavigating**, **circumnavigated**) sail all the way around.
– DERIVATIVES **circumnavigation** n.

circumscribe ● v. (**circumscribes**, **circumscribing**, **circumscribed**) **1** restrict; limit. **2** Geom. draw (a figure) round another, touching it at points but not cutting it.
– ORIGIN Latin *circumscribere*.

circumspect ● adj. cautious or sensible.
– ORIGIN Latin *circumspectus*.

circumstance ● n. **1** a fact or condition connected with an event or action. **2** unforeseen events outside one's control: *a victim of circumstance*. **3** (**circumstances**) a person's situation in life, especially the money they have.
– PHRASES **under** (or **in**) **the circumstances** given the difficult nature of the situation. **under** (or **in**) **no circumstances** never.
– ORIGIN Latin *circumstantia*.

circumstantial ● adj. (of evidence) consisting of facts that strongly suggest something but do not prove it.

circumvent /ser-kuhm-vent/ ● v. find a way around (an obstacle).
– ORIGIN Latin *circumvenire*.

circus ● n. (pl. **circuses**) **1** a travelling company of acrobats, trained animals, and clowns. **2** informal a scene of frantic activity: *a media circus*.
– ORIGIN Latin.

cirque /serk/ ● n. a steep-sided hollow at the head of a valley or on a mountainside.
– ORIGIN French.

cirrhosis /si-roh-siss/ ● n. a liver disease marked by degeneration of cells and thickening of tissue.
– ORIGIN Greek *kirrhos* 'tawny' (the colour of the liver in many cases).

cirrus /sir-ruhss/ ● n. (pl. **cirri** /sir-ry/) cloud in the form of wispy streaks high in the sky.

– ORIGIN Latin, 'a curl'.
CIS • abbrev. Commonwealth of Independent States.
Cistercian /si-ster-sh'n/ • n. a monk or nun of an order that is a stricter branch of the Benedictines.
– ORIGIN from *Cîteaux* in France, where the order was founded.
cistern • n. **1** a water storage tank, especially as part of a flushing toilet. **2** an underground reservoir for rainwater.
– ORIGIN Latin *cisterna*.
citadel • n. a fortress protecting or overlooking a city.
– ORIGIN French *citadelle* or Italian *cittadella*.
citation /sy-tay-sh'n/ • n. **1** a quotation from or reference to a book or author. **2** a mention of a praiseworthy act in an official report. **3** a note accompanying an award, giving reasons for it.
cite • v. (**cites**, **citing**, **cited**) quote (a book or author) as evidence for an argument.
– ORIGIN Latin *citare*.
citizen • n. **1** a person who is legally recognized as a member of a country. **2** an inhabitant of a town or city.
– DERIVATIVES **citizenship** n.
– ORIGIN Old French *citezein*.
Citizens' Band • n. a range of radio frequencies which are able to be used for local communication by private individuals.
citric acid • n. a sharp-tasting acid present in the juice of lemons and other sour fruits.
citron • n. the lemon-like fruit of an Asian tree.
– ORIGIN Latin *citrus* 'citron tree'.
citrus (also **citrus fruit**) • n. (pl. **citruses**) a fruit of a group that includes lemons, limes, oranges, and grapefruit.
– ORIGIN Latin.
city • n. (pl. **cities**) **1** a large town, in particular (Brit.) a town created a city by charter and containing a cathedral. **2** (**the City** or **the City of London**) the part of London governed by the Lord Mayor and the Corporation, especially with regard to its financial and commercial institutions.
– ORIGIN Old French *cite*.
cityscape • n. a city landscape.
city slicker • n. informal a person with the sophisticated tastes or values associated with people who live in a city.
city state • n. a city and surrounding territory that forms an independent state.
City Technology College • n. (in the UK) a type of secondary school set up to teach technology and science in inner-city areas.
civet /siv-it/ • n. **1** a cat native to Africa and Asia. **2** a strong perfume obtained from the civet.
– ORIGIN Arabic.
civic • adj. having to do with a city or town.
– ORIGIN Latin *civicus*.
civic centre • n. **1** the area of a town where municipal offices are situated. **2** a building containing municipal offices.
civics • n. the study of the rights and duties of citizenship.
civil • adj. **1** relating to ordinary citizens, rather than to military or church matters. **2** Law non-criminal: *a civil court*. **3** polite.
– ORIGIN Latin *civilis*.
civil disobedience • n. the refusal to obey certain laws or to pay taxes, as a political protest.
civil engineer • n. an engineer who designs roads, bridges, dams, etc.
civilian • n. a person not in the armed services or the police force. • adj. relating to a civilian.
– ORIGIN Old French *civilien*.
civility • n. (pl. **civilities**) politeness.
civilization (also **civilisation**) • n. **1** an advanced stage or system of human social development. **2** the process of achieving this. **3** a civilized nation or area.
civilize (also **civilise**) • v. (**civilizes**, **civilizing**, **civilized**) **1** bring to an advanced stage of social development. **2** (**civilized**) polite and good-mannered.
civil law • n. law concerned with ordinary citizens.
civil liberty • n. **1** freedom of action and speech subject to laws established for the good of the community. **2** (**civil liberties**) one's rights to this.
Civil List • n. (in the UK) an annual allowance voted by Parliament for the royal family's household expenses.
civil rights • pl. n. the rights of citizens to political and social freedom.
civil servant • n. a member of the civil service.
civil service • n. the branches of state administration, excluding military and legal branches and elected politicians.
civil war • n. a war between people of the same country.
CJD • abbrev. Creutzfeldt–Jakob disease.
cl • abbrev. centilitre.
clack • v. make a sharp sound as of a hard object striking another. • n. a clacking sound.

Clackmannan E
/klak-man-nuhn/ (also **Clackmannanshire**) an administrative region and former county of central Scotland; administrative centre, Alloa.

clad archaic or literary past part. of CLOTHE. • adj. clothed.
cladding • n. a covering or coating on a structure or material.
claim • v. **1** state as being true, without being able to give proof. **2** demand (something) to which one has a right. **3** call for (someone's attention). **4** ask for (money) under the terms of an insurance policy. **5** cause the loss of (someone's life). • n. **1** a statement that something is true. **2** a demand for something to which one has a right. **3** a request for compensation under the terms of an insurance policy.
– ORIGIN Latin *clamare* 'call out'.
claimant • n. a person who makes a claim.
clairvoyance /klair-voy-uhnss/ • n. the supposed ability to see events in the future or beyond normal contact.
– ORIGIN from French *clair* 'clear' + *voir* 'to see'.
clairvoyant • n. a person claiming to have clairvoyance.
clam • n. a large sea mollusc with two shells of equal size. • v. (**clams**, **clamming**,

clammed) (**clam up**) informal stop talking suddenly.
– ORIGIN Old English 'bond, bondage'.

clamber • v. (**clambers**, **clambering**, **clambered**) climb or move in an awkward and laborious way.
– ORIGIN prob. from CLIMB.

clammy • adj. (**clammier**, **clammiest**) **1** damp and sticky. **2** (of air) cold and damp.
– ORIGIN dialect *clam* 'to be sticky'.

clamour (US **clamor**) • n. **1** a loud and confused noise. **2** a strong protest or demand. • v. (of a group) make a clamour.
– DERIVATIVES **clamorous** adj.
– ORIGIN Latin *clamor*.

clamp • n. a brace, band, or clasp for strengthening or holding things together. • v. **1** fasten in place or together with a clamp. **2** (**clamp down**) take strict action to prevent something. **3** fit a wheel clamp to (an illegally parked car).
– ORIGIN prob. from Dutch.

clampdown • n. informal a determined attempt to prevent something.

clan • n. a group of related families, especially in the Scottish Highlands.
– ORIGIN Scottish Gaelic, 'offspring'.

clandestine /klan-dess-tin/ • adj. secretive.
– ORIGIN Latin *clandestinus*.

clang • n. a loud metallic sound. • v. make a clang.

clanger • n. informal a mistake.

clangour /klang-ger/ (US **clangor**) • n. a continuous clanging sound.
– ORIGIN Latin *clangor*.

clank • n. a sharp sound as of pieces of metal being struck together. • v. make a clank.

clannish • adj. (of a group) excluding others outside the group.

clap[1] • v. (**claps**, **clapping**, **clapped**) **1** strike the palms of (one's hands) together repeatedly, especially to applaud. **2** slap encouragingly on the back. **3** place (a hand) briefly over one's face to show dismay. • n. **1** an act of clapping. **2** an explosive sound of thunder.
– ORIGIN Old English.

clap[2] • n. informal gonorrhoea.
– ORIGIN Old French *clapoir*.

clapped-out • adj. informal worn out.

clapper • n. the striker of a bell.
– PHRASES **like the clappers** Brit. informal very fast or hard.

clapperboard • n. hinged boards that are struck together at the beginning of filming so that the picture and sound machinery can be synchronized.

claptrap • n. nonsense.
– ORIGIN first referring to something designed to make people applaud.

claque /klak/ • n. **1** a group of people hired to applaud or heckle a performer. **2** a group of flattering followers.
– ORIGIN French.

Clare E
a county on the west coast of the Republic of Ireland; county town, Ennis.

claret /kla-ruht/ • n. **1** a red wine, especially from Bordeaux in France. **2** a purplish red colour.
– ORIGIN from Latin *claratum vinum* 'clarified wine'.

clarify • v. (**clarifies**, **clarifying**, **clarified**) **1** make easier to understand. **2** melt (butter) to separate out the impurities.
– DERIVATIVES **clarification** n.
– ORIGIN Old French *clarifier*.

clarinet • n. a woodwind instrument with holes stopped by keys and a mouthpiece with a single reed.
– DERIVATIVES **clarinettist** (US **clarinetist**) n.
– ORIGIN French *clarinette*.

clarion /kla-ri-uhn/ • adj. loud and clear.
– PHRASES **clarion call** a strongly expressed demand for action.
– ORIGIN Latin, 'war trumpet'.

clarity • n. **1** the state or quality of being clear and easily understood. **2** transparency or purity.
– ORIGIN Latin *claritas*.

Clark[1], E
Helen (b.1950), New Zealand Labour Stateswoman, Prime Minister of New Zealand from 1999.

Clark[2], E
William (1770–1838), American explorer. With Meriwether Lewis, he commanded an expedition (1804–6) across the North American continent.

Clarke, E
Sir Arthur C. (b.1917; full name *Arthur Charles Clarke*), English writer of science fiction.

clash • v. **1** (of opposing groups) come into violent conflict. **2** disagree or be at odds. **3** (of colours) not go well together. **4** (of dates or events) occur inconveniently at the same time. **5** strike together, producing a loud harsh sound. • n. an act or sound of clashing.

clasp • v. **1** grasp tightly with one's hand. **2** place (one's arms) around something so as to hold it tightly. **3** fasten with a clasp. • n. **1** a device with interlocking parts used for fastening. **2** an act of clasping.
– ORIGIN unknown.

clasp knife • n. a knife with a blade that folds into the handle.

class • n. **1** a group of things having a common characteristic. **2** a system that divides members of a society into sets based on social or economic status. **3** a set in a society ordered by social or economic status. **4** a group of students or pupils who are taught together. **5** a lesson. **6** Biol. a category into which animals and plants with similar characteristics are divided, ranking above order and below phylum. **7** informal impressive stylishness. • v. put in a category.
– ORIGIN Latin *classis*.

classic • adj. **1** judged over a period of time to be of the highest quality. **2** typical. • n. **1** a work of art which is generally agreed to be of high quality. **2** (**Classics**) the study of ancient Greek and Latin literature, philosophy, and history. **3** (**the classics**) the works of ancient Greek and Latin writers.
– ORIGIN Latin *classicus*.

classical • adj. **1** relating to ancient Greek or Latin literature, art, or culture. **2** (of a form of art or a language) representing the highest standard within a long-established form. **3** (of music) written in the European tradition between approximately 1750 and 1830.

– DERIVATIVES **classically** adv.

classicism • n. the following of ancient Greek or Roman principles and style in art and literature.

classicist • n. a person who studies Classics.

classification • n. **1** the action of classifying. **2** a category into which something is put.

classified • adj. **1** (of newspaper or magazine advertisements) organized in categories. **2** (of information or documents) officially secret. • n. (**classifieds**) classified advertisements.

classify • v. (**classifies**, **classifying**, **classified**) **1** arrange (a group) in classes. **2** put in a class or category. **3** make (documents or information) officially secret.

– DERIVATIVES **classifiable** adj. **classifier** n.

classless • adj. **1** not divided into social classes. **2** not showing characteristics of a particular social class.

classroom • n. a room in which a class of pupils or students is taught.

classy • adj. (**classier**, **classiest**) informal stylish and sophisticated.

clatter • n. a loud rattling sound as of hard objects striking each other. • v. (**clatters**, **clattering**, **clattered**) make a clatter.

– ORIGIN Old English.

Claude Lorraine E
/clawd luh-rayn/ (1600–82; born *Claude Gellée*), French painter, noted for his landscapes.

Claudius E
/klaw-di-uhss/ (10 BC–AD 54; full name *Tiberius Claudius Drusus Nero Germanicus*), Roman emperor 41–54. His reign was noted its expansion of the Empire, including the invasion of Britain in AD 43.

clause • n. **1** a group of words that includes a subject and a verb, forming a sentence or part of a sentence. **2** a particular and separate item of a treaty, bill, or contract.

– ORIGIN Old French.

claustrophobia /kloss-truh-foh-bi-uh/ • n. extreme fear of being in an enclosed place.

– DERIVATIVES **claustrophobic** adj.

– ORIGIN Latin *claustrum* 'lock'.

clavichord /klav-i-kord/ • n. a small early keyboard instrument with a soft tone.

– ORIGIN Latin *clavichordium*.

clavicle • n. tech. the collarbone.

– ORIGIN Latin *clavicula* 'small key'.

claw • n. **1** a curved horny nail on each digit of the foot in birds, lizards, and some mammals. **2** the pincer of a shellfish. • v. **1** scratch or tear at with the claws or fingernails. **2** (**claw one's way**) haul oneself forward with one's hands. **3** (**claw back**) get back (something lost) with difficulty.

– ORIGIN Old English.

claw hammer • n. a hammer with one side of the head split and curved.

Clay, E
Cassius, see **MUHAMMAD ALI**.

clay • n. a heavy, sticky earth that can be moulded when wet and baked to make bricks and pottery.

– ORIGIN Old English.

claymore • n. hist. a type of large sword used in Scotland.

– ORIGIN Scottish Gaelic, 'great sword'.

clay pigeon • n. a saucer-shaped piece of baked clay thrown up in the air as a target for shooting.

clean • adj. **1** free from dirt or harmful substances. **2** not obscene or immoral. **3** showing or having no record of offences or crimes: *a clean driving licence*. **4** done according to the rules: *a good clean fight*. **5** having a smooth and regular surface: *a clean fracture*. **6** (of an action) smoothly and skilfully done. • adv. **1** so as to be free from dirt. **2** informal completely: *he got clean away*. • v. **1** make clean. **2** (**clean out**) informal use up or take (all someone's money or resources). **3** (**clean up**) informal make a large gain or profit. • n. esp. Brit. an act of cleaning.

– PHRASES **come clean** informal fully confess something. **make a clean breast of it** fully confess something.

– ORIGIN Old English.

clean-cut • adj. (of a person) clean and neat.

cleaner • n. a person or thing that cleans.

cleanliness /klen-li-nuhss/ • n. the state of being clean or the habit of keeping clean.

cleanly /kleen-li/ • adv. in a clean way.

cleanse • v. (**cleanses**, **cleansing**, **cleansed**) **1** make thoroughly clean. **2** rid of something unpleasant or unwanted.

– ORIGIN Old English.

clean-shaven • adj. (of a man) without a beard or moustache.

clear • adj. **1** easy to see, hear, or understand. **2** leaving or feeling no doubt. **3** transparent. **4** free of marks, obstructions, or unwanted objects. **5** (of a period of time) free of commitments. **6** free from disease or guilt. **7** (**clear of**) not touching. **8** complete: *seven clear days' notice*. • adv. **1** so as to be out of the way of or unobstructed by. **2** so as to be easily heard or seen. • v. **1** make or become clear. **2** get past or over (something) safely or without touching it. **3** show or declare to be innocent. **4** give official approval to. **5** cause people to leave (a building or place). **6** (of a cheque) be paid into a person's account.

– PHRASES **clear the air 1** make the air less humid. **2** improve a tense situation by frank discussion. **clear off** informal go away. **clear out** informal **1** empty. **2** leave quickly. **clear up 1** make tidy. **2** solve or explain. **3** (of an illness or other medical condition) become cured. **4** (of the weather) become fine. **in the clear** no longer in danger or under suspicion.

– ORIGIN Old French *cler*.

clearance • n. **1** the action or an act of clearing. **2** official authorization for something to take place. **3** clear space allowed for a thing to move past or under another.

clear-cut • adj. easy to see or understand.

clearing • n. an open space in a forest.

clearing house • n. a bankers' establishment where cheques and bills from member banks are exchanged.

clearly • adv. **1** in a clear way. **2** without doubt.

clear-sighted • adj. thinking clearly.

clearway • n. Brit. a main road other than a motorway on which vehicles are not allowed to stop.

cleat • n. **1** a T-shaped projection to which a

rope may be attached. **2** a projecting piece of rubber or metal on the sole of a shoe, to prevent a person from slipping.
– ORIGIN Germanic.

cleavage ● n. **1** the space between a woman's breasts. **2** a sharp division; a split.

cleave[1] ● v. (**cleaves**, **cleaving**, **clove** or **cleft** or **cleaved**; past part. **cloven** or **cleft** or **cleaved**) **1** split along a natural grain or line. **2** divide; split.
– ORIGIN Old English.

cleave[2] ● v. (**cleaves**, **cleaving**, **cleaved**) (**cleave to**) literary **1** stick fast to. **2** become emotionally attached to.
– ORIGIN Old English.

cleaver ● n. a tool with a heavy broad blade, used for chopping meat.

Cleese E
/kleez/, John (Marwood) (b.1939), English comic actor and writer, famous for *Monty Python's Flying Circus* and the situation comedy *Fawlty Towers*.

clef ● n. Music any of several symbols placed on a stave to show the pitch of the notes written on the stave.
– ORIGIN French.

cleft past part. of CLEAVE[1]. ● adj. split, divided, or partly divided into two. ● n. a split, crack, or partial division in the ground or part of a person's body.

cleft palate ● n. a split in the roof of the mouth which is present from birth.

clematis /klem-uh-tiss/ ● n. a climbing plant with white, pink, or purple flowers.
– ORIGIN Greek *klēmatis*.

clement ● adj. **1** (of weather) mild. **2** merciful.
– DERIVATIVES **clemency** n.
– ORIGIN Latin *clemens*.

clementine /klem-uhn-tyn/ ● n. an orange-red variety of tangerine.
– ORIGIN French, from the man's name *Clément*.

clench ● v. **1** (of one's fist or teeth) close tightly, in response to stress or anger. **2** (of a set of muscles) contract sharply. **3** grasp tightly.
– ORIGIN Old English.

Cleopatra E
/klee-uh-pat-ruh/ (69–30 BC), queen of Egypt 47–30. She formed a political and romantic alliance with Mark Antony which led to conflict with Rome. She is said to have killed herself after the battle of Actium in 31 by allowing an asp to bite her.

clerestory /kleer-stor-i/ ● n. (pl. **clerestories**) the upper part of the nave, choir, and transepts of a large church, with windows which allow light into the building.
– ORIGIN from CLEAR + STOREY.

clergy /kler-ji/ ● n. the body of people ordained for religious duties in the Christian Church.
– ORIGIN Latin *clericus* 'clergyman'.

clergyman (or **clergywoman**) ● n. a priest or minister of a Christian church.

cleric /kle-rik/ ● n. a priest or religious leader.
– ORIGIN Latin *clericus*.

clerical ● adj. **1** relating to the work of an office clerk. **2** relating to the clergy.

clerical collar ● n. a stiff white collar worn by the clergy in some churches.

clerk ● n. **1** a person employed in an office or bank to keep records or accounts and to undertake other administrative duties. **2** a person in charge of the records of a local council or court.
– ORIGIN Latin *clericus* 'clergyman'.

Cleveland, E
(Stephen) Grover (1837–1908), American Democratic statesman, 22nd and 24th President of the US 1885–9 and 1893–7.

clever ● adj. (**cleverer**, **cleverest**) **1** quick to understand, learn, or have good ideas. **2** skilled at doing something.
– ORIGIN perh. Dutch or German.

cliché /klee-shay/ (also **cliche**) ● n. a phrase or idea that has been overused and has become uninteresting or stale.
– DERIVATIVES **clichéd** (also **cliched**) adj.
– ORIGIN French.

click ● n. **1** a short, sharp sound as of two hard objects coming into contact. **2** Computing an act of pressing one of the buttons on a mouse. ● v. **1** make or cause to make a click. **2** move with a click. **3** Computing press (a mouse button). **4** informal become suddenly clear. **5** informal become friendly.

client ● n. a person using the services of a professional person or organization.
– ORIGIN Latin *cliens*.

clientele /klee-on-tel/ ● n. clients or customers collectively.
– ORIGIN French.

cliff ● n. a steep rock face at the edge of the sea.
– ORIGIN Old English.

cliffhanger ● n. a story or event that is exciting because its outcome is uncertain.

climacteric /kly-mak-tuh-rik/ ● n. the period of life when fertility is in decline; (in women) the menopause.
– ORIGIN Greek *klimaktēr*.

climactic /kly-mak-tik/ ● adj. forming an exciting climax.

climate ● n. **1** the general weather conditions in an area over a long period. **2** a widespread trend or public attitude: *the current economic climate*.
– ORIGIN Greek *klima* 'zone'.

climatic /kly-mat-ik/ ● adj. relating to climate.

climax ● n. **1** the most intense, exciting, or important point of something. **2** an orgasm. ● v. reach or bring to a climax.
– ORIGIN Greek *klimax* 'ladder, climax'.

climb ● v. **1** go or come up to a higher position. **2** go up (a hill, rock face, etc.) **3** move with effort into or out of a confined space. **4** increase in scale, amount, or power. **5** (**climb down**) withdraw from a position taken up in argument or negotiation. ● n. **1** an act of climbing. **2** a route up a mountain or cliff.
– ORIGIN Old English.

climber ● n. a person who climbs rocks or mountains as a sport.

climbing frame ● n. Brit. a structure of joined bars for children to climb on.

clime ● n. literary a region considered in terms of its climate: *sunnier climes*.

– ORIGIN Greek *klima*.

clinch • v. **1** completely settle (a contract or contest). **2** settle (something uncertain). • n. **1** a tight hold in boxing. **2** an embrace.
– ORIGIN from CLENCH.

C

clincher • n. informal a fact, argument, or event that fully settles a matter.

cling • v. (**clings**, **clinging**, **clung**) (**cling to/on to**) **1** hold on tightly to. **2** stick to. **3** remain faithful to (a belief or hope). **4** be emotionally dependent on.
– ORIGIN Old English.

cling film • n. Brit. a clinging plastic film used to wrap or cover food.

clingy • adj. (**clingier**, **clingiest**) likely to cling; clinging.

clinic • n. a place where specialized medical treatment or advice is given.
– ORIGIN from Greek *klinikē tekhnē* 'bedside art'.

clinical • adj. **1** relating to the observation and treatment of patients (rather than theoretical studies). **2** calm and without feeling or sympathy. **3** (of a place) very clean and plain.

clinician • n. a doctor having direct contact with and responsibility for treating patients.

clink • n. a sharp ringing sound, as when metal or glass are struck. • v. make or cause to make a clink.
– ORIGIN Dutch *klinken*.

clinker • n. the stony remains from burnt coal or from a furnace.

Clinton[1], E
Bill (b.1946; full name *William Jefferson Clinton*), American Democratic statesman, 42nd President of the US 1993–2001.

Clinton[2], E
Hillary (Diane) Rodham (b.1947), American Democratic stateswoman, New York Senator from 2000. She is the wife of Bill Clinton, 42nd President of the US, and is the first American first lady to hold elected office.

clip[1] • n. **1** a flexible or spring-loaded device for holding an object or objects together or in place. **2** a piece of jewellery that can be fastened on to a garment with a clip. • v. (**clips**, **clipping**, **clipped**) fasten with a clip.
– ORIGIN Old English.

clip[2] • v. (**clips**, **clipping**, **clipped**) **1** cut or cut out with shears or scissors. **2** trim the hair or wool of (an animal). **3** strike sharply or with a glancing blow. • n. **1** an act of clipping. **2** a short sequence taken from a film or broadcast. **3** informal a sharp blow.
– ORIGIN Old Norse.

clipboard • n. a small board with a clip at the top, for holding papers and providing support for writing.

clipped • adj. (of speech) having short, sharp vowel sounds and clear pronunciation.

clipper • n. **1** (**clippers**) a tool for clipping. **2** a fast sailing ship of the 19th century.

clipping • n. **1** a small piece trimmed from something: *hedge clippings*. **2** an article cut from a newspaper or magazine.

clique /*rhymes with* seek/ • n. a small group of people who spend time together and do not allow others to join them.
– ORIGIN French.

clitoris /**kli**-tuh-riss/ • n. a small sensitive part of the female genitals at the front end of the vulva.
– DERIVATIVES **clitoral** adj.
– ORIGIN Greek *kleitoris*.

Clive, E
Robert, 1st Baron Clive of Plassey (1725–74; known as **Clive of India**), British general and colonial administrator. He was responsible for securing British control over south-east India, especially by his defeat of the nawab (governor) of Bengal in 1757.

cloak • n. **1** an outer garment that hangs loosely from the shoulders over the arms to the knees or ankles. **2** something that hides or covers: *a cloak of secrecy*. • v. cover or hide.
– ORIGIN Old French *cloke*.

cloak-and-dagger • adj. having to do with intrigue and secrecy.

cloakroom • n. **1** a room in a public building where outdoor clothes and bags may be left. **2** Brit. a room that contains a toilet or toilets.

clobber informal • n. Brit. clothing and personal belongings. • v. (**clobbers**, **clobbering**, **clobbered**) **1** hit hard. **2** defeat heavily.

cloche /klosh/ • n. **1** a glass or plastic cover for protecting or forcing outdoor plants. **2** (also **cloche hat**) a woman's bell-shaped hat.
– ORIGIN French, 'bell'.

clock • n. **1** an instrument that measures and indicates the time. **2** informal a measuring device such as a speedometer. • v. informal **1** reach or show (a specified time, distance, or speed). **2** (**clock in/out** or Brit. **on/off**) register one's arrival at or departure from work by means of an automatic recording clock. **3** Brit. see or watch.
– PHRASES **round the clock** all day and all night. **turn** (or **put**) **back the clock** return to the past or to an earlier way of doing things.
– ORIGIN Latin *clocca* 'bell'.

clockwise • adv. & adj. in the direction of the movement of the hands of a clock.

clockwork • n. a mechanism with a spring and toothed gearwheels, used to drive a mechanical clock or other device.
– PHRASES **like clockwork** very smoothly and easily.

clod • n. **1** a lump of earth. **2** informal a stupid person.
– ORIGIN from CLOT.

clodhopper • n. informal **1** a large, heavy shoe. **2** a stupid or clumsy person.

clog • n. a shoe with a thick wooden sole. • v. (**clogs**, **clogging**, **clogged**) block or become blocked.
– ORIGIN unknown.

cloister /**kloy**-ster/ • n. a covered passage round an open court in a convent, monastery, college, or cathedral.
– ORIGIN Old French *cloistre*.

cloistered • adj. **1** having or enclosed by a cloister. **2** sheltered from the outside world.

clomp • v. walk with a heavy tread.

clone • n. **1** Biol. an animal or plant produced from the cells of another, to which it is genetically identical. **2** a person or thing regarded as identical to another. • v. (**clones**, **cloning**, **cloned**) **1** create as a clone. **2** make an iden-

tical copy of.
– ORIGIN Greek *klōn* 'twig'.

clop ● n. a sound made by a horse's hooves on a hard surface. ● v. (**clops**, **clopping**, **clopped**) move with such a sound.

close[1] /*rhymes with* dose/ ● adj. **1** only a short distance away or apart in space or time. **2** (of a connection or likeness) strong. **3** (of a person) part of a person's immediate family. **4** (of a relationship or the people in it) very affectionate or intimate. **5** (of observation or examination) done in a careful and thorough way. **6** uncomfortably humid or airless. ● adv. so as to be very near. ● n. Brit. **1** a residential street without through access. **2** the grounds surrounding a cathedral.
– PHRASES **close-knit** (of a group of people) united or bound together by strong relationships and common interests. **at** (or **from**) **close quarters** (or **range**) very near. **close-run** (of a contest or objective) won or lost by a very small margin. **close shave** (also **close call**) informal a narrow escape from danger or disaster.
– DERIVATIVES **closely** adv. **closeness** n.
– ORIGIN Old French *clos*.

close[2] /*rhymes with* nose/ ● v. (**closes**, **closing**, **closed**) **1** move so as to cover an opening. **2** (also **close up**) bring two parts of (something) together. **3** (**close on/in on/up on**) gradually get nearer to or surround. **4** (**close in**) (of bad weather or darkness) gradually surround one. **5** (**close around/over**) encircle and hold. **6** bring or come to an end. **7** finish speaking or writing. **8** (often **close down/up**) (with reference to a business or other organization) stop or cause to stop trading or operating. **9** bring (a deal or arrangement) to a conclusion. ● n. the end of a period of time or an activity.
– ORIGIN Old French *clore*.

closed ● adj. **1** not open or allowing access. **2** not communicating with or influenced by others.
– PHRASES **behind closed doors** in private.

closed-circuit television ● n. a television system in which the signals are sent by cable to a restricted set of monitors.

closed shop ● n. a place of work where all employees must belong to a particular trade union.

close season (also **closed season**) ● n. **1** a period when fishing or the killing of particular game is officially forbidden. **2** Brit. a part of the year when a particular sport is not played.

closet ● n. esp. N. Amer. a cupboard or wardrobe. ● adj. secret. ● v. (**closets**, **closeting**, **closeted**) shut away in private to talk to someone or to be alone.
– PHRASES **in** (or **out of**) **the closet** not admitting (or admitting) that one is a homosexual.
– ORIGIN Old French.

close-up ● n. a photograph or film sequence taken at close range.

closure ● n. **1** an act or the process of closing. **2** a device that closes or seals.

clot ● n. **1** a thick mass of a semi-liquid substance, especially blood. **2** Brit. informal a foolish or clumsy person. ● v. (**clots**, **clotting**, **clotted**) form into clots.
– ORIGIN Old English.

cloth ● n. (pl. **cloths**) **1** fabric made by weaving or knitting a soft fibre such as wool or cotton. **2** a piece of cloth for a particular purpose. **3** (**the cloth**) Christian priests as a group.
– ORIGIN Old English.

clothe ● v. (**clothes**, **clothing**, **clothed**) **1** provide with clothes. **2** (**be clothed in**) be dressed in.
– ORIGIN Old English.

clothes ● pl. n. things worn to cover the body.

clothes horse ● n. a frame on which washed clothes are hung to dry.

clothes peg ● n. Brit. a clip or forked device for securing washed clothes to a rope or wire.

clothier /kloh-*thi*-er/ ● n. a person who makes or sells clothes or cloth.

clothing ● n. clothes as a whole.

clotted cream ● n. esp. Brit. thick cream made by heating milk slowly and then allowing it to cool while the cream rises to the top in lumps.

cloud ● n. **1** a white or grey mass of condensed watery vapour floating in the atmosphere. **2** a mass of smoke, dust, etc. **3** a large number of insects or birds moving together. **4** a state or cause of gloom or anxiety: *inflation is a cloud on the horizon*. ● v. **1** (**cloud over**) (of the sky) become full of clouds. **2** make or become less clear. **3** (of someone's face or eyes) show sadness, anxiety, or anger.
– PHRASES **have one's head in the clouds** be full of unrealistic thoughts. **on cloud nine** extremely happy. **under a cloud** under suspicion of having done wrong.
– DERIVATIVES **cloudy** adj. (**cloudier**, **cloudiest**).
– ORIGIN Old English, 'mass of rock'.

cloudburst ● n. a sudden violent rainstorm.

cloud cuckoo land ● n. a state of unrealistic fantasy.
– ORIGIN Greek *Nephelokokkugia*, a city built by the birds in Aristophanes' comedy *Birds*.

clout informal ● n. **1** a heavy blow. **2** influence or power. ● v. hit hard.
– ORIGIN Old English, 'a patch or metal plate'.

clove[1] ● n. the dried flower bud of a tropical tree, used as a spice.
– ORIGIN Old French.

clove[2] ● n. any of the small bulbs making up a compound bulb of garlic, shallot, etc.
– ORIGIN Old English.

clove[3] past of CLEAVE[1].

clove hitch ● n. a knot by which a rope is secured to a spar or another rope.
– ORIGIN *clove*, past tense of CLEAVE[1].

cloven past part. of CLEAVE[1].

cloven hoof ● n. the divided hoof of animals such as cattle, sheep, goats, and deer.

clover ● n. a plant with round white or pink flowers and leaves with three rounded parts.
– PHRASES **in clover** in ease and luxury.
– ORIGIN Old English.

clown ● n. **1** a comic entertainer in a circus, wearing a traditional costume and exaggerated make-up. **2** a playful, outgoing person. ● v. act comically or playfully.
– DERIVATIVES **clownish** adj.
– ORIGIN German.

cloying ● adj. disgusting or sickening because excessively sweet or sentimental.

– ORIGIN Old French *encloyer* 'drive a nail into.'

club¹ • n. **1** an association dedicated to a particular activity. **2** an organization where members can meet, eat meals, or stay overnight. **3** a nightclub with dance music. • v. (**clubs**, **clubbing**, **clubbed**) (**club together**) combine with others to do something.
– DERIVATIVES **clubber** n.
– ORIGIN from CLUB².

club² • n. **1** a heavy stick with a thick end, used as a weapon. **2** (also **golf club**) a club used to hit the ball in golf. **3** (**clubs**) one of the four suits in a conventional pack of playing cards, represented by a black trefoil. • v. (**clubs**, **clubbing**, **clubbed**) beat with a club or similar implement.
– ORIGIN Old Norse.

clubbable • adj. sociable and popular.

club class • n. Brit. the class of seating on an aircraft designed for business travellers.

club foot • n. a deformed foot which is twisted so that the sole cannot be placed flat on the ground.

clubhouse • n. a building having a bar and other facilities for club members.

club sandwich • n. a sandwich consisting typically of chicken and bacon, tomato, and lettuce, layered between three slices of bread.

cluck • n. the short sound made by a hen. • v. **1** make a cluck. **2** (**cluck over/around**) express fussy concern about.

clue • n. a fact or piece of evidence that helps to clear up a mystery or solve a problem. • v. (**clues**, **clueing**, **clued**) (**clue in**) informal inform.
– PHRASES **not have a clue** informal be confused or incompetent.
– ORIGIN first meaning a ball of thread, as used to guide a person out of a maze.

clued-up • adj. informal well informed.

clueless • adj. informal having no knowledge, understanding, or ability.

clump • n. **1** a small group of trees or plants growing closely together. **2** a mass or lump of something. • v. form into a clump or mass.
– ORIGIN from CLUB².

clumpy • adj. (of shoes or boots) heavy and clumsy.

clumsy • adj. (**clumsier**, **clumsiest**) **1** awkward in movement or performance. **2** difficult to use. **3** tactless.
– ORIGIN prob. Scandinavian.

clung past and past part. of CLING.

clunk • n. a dull, heavy sound as of thick pieces of metal striking together. • v. move with or make a clunk.

cluster • n. a group of similar things placed or occurring closely together. • v. (**cluster**, **clustering**, **clustered**) form a cluster.
– ORIGIN Old English.

clutch¹ • v. grasp tightly. • n. **1** a tight grasp. **2** (**clutches**) power; control. **3** a mechanism for connecting and disconnecting the engine and the transmission system in a vehicle.
– ORIGIN Old English.

clutch² • n. **1** a group of eggs fertilized at the same time and laid in a single session. **2** a brood of chicks.
– ORIGIN Old Norse.

clutter • n. **1** things lying about untidily. **2** an untidy state. • v. (**clutters**, **cluttering**, **cluttered**) cover or fill with clutter.
– ORIGIN dialect *clotter* 'to clot'.

Clwyd E
/kloo-id/ a former county of NE Wales, replaced in 1996 by Denbighshire and Flintshire.

Clyde E
a river in western central Scotland which flows from SE Strathclyde to the Firth of Clyde.

Clyde, Firth of E
the estuary of the River Clyde in western Scotland.

Clytemnestra E
/kly-tem-ness-truh/ Gk Myth. wife of Agamemnon, who murdered her husband, and was murdered in revenge by her son Orestes.

cm • abbrev. centimetre or centimetres.

CMG • abbrev. (in the UK) Companion of St Michael and St George (or Companion of the Order of St Michael and St George).

CND • abbrev. Campaign for Nuclear Disarmament.

Cnut E
var. of CANUTE.

CO • abbrev. Commanding Officer.

Co. • abbrev. **1** company. **2** county.

c/o • abbrev. care of.

co- • prefix **1** (forming nouns) joint; mutual; common: *co-driver.* **2** (forming adjectives) jointly; mutually: *coequal.* **3** (forming verbs) together with another or others: *co-produce.*
– ORIGIN Latin.

coach¹ • n. **1** esp. Brit. a single-decker bus with comfortable seats, used for longer journeys. **2** a railway carriage.
– ORIGIN French *coche.*

coach² • n. **1** an instructor or trainer in sport. **2** a tutor who gives private or specialized teaching. • v. train or teach as a coach.
– ORIGIN from COACH¹.

coachwork • n. the bodywork of a road or railway vehicle.

coagulant /koh-ag-yuu-luhnt/ • n. a substance that causes a fluid to change to a solid or semi-solid state.

coagulate /koh-ag-yuu-layt/ • v. (**coagulates**, **coagulating**, **coagulated**) (of a fluid, especially blood) change to a solid or semi-solid state.
– DERIVATIVES **coagulation** n.
– ORIGIN Latin *coagulare* 'curdle'.

coal • n. **1** a black rock consisting mainly of carbonized plant matter and used as fuel. **2** Brit. a piece of coal.
– PHRASES **haul over the coals** reprimand severely.
– ORIGIN Old English.

coalesce /koh-uh-less/ • v. (**coalesces**, **coalescing**, **coalesced**) come or bring together to form a mass or whole.
– ORIGIN Latin *coalescere.*

coalface • n. an exposed surface of coal in a mine.

coalfield • n. a large area rich in underground coal.

coalition /koh-uh-li-sh'n/ • n. a temporary

alliance, especially one enabling political parties to form a government.
– ORIGIN Latin.

coal tar • n. a thick black liquid distilled from coal, containing organic chemicals.

coal tit • n. a small titmouse with a grey back, and a black cap and throat.

coaming • n. a raised border round the cockpit or hatch of a boat to keep out water.
– ORIGIN unknown.

coarse • adj. **1** rough or harsh in texture. **2** consisting of large grains or particles. **3** rude or vulgar in behaviour or speech.
– ORIGIN perh. from **COURSE**.

coarse fish • n. (pl. **coarse fish**) Brit. any freshwater fish other than salmon and trout.

coarsen • v. make or become coarse.

coast • n. land next to or near the sea. • v. **1** move easily without using power. **2** achieve something without making much effort: *United coasted to victory.*
– PHRASES **the coast is clear** there is no danger of being observed or caught.
– DERIVATIVES **coastal** adj.
– ORIGIN Latin *costa* 'rib, side'.

coaster • n. **1** a small mat for a glass. **2** a ship carrying cargo along the coast from port to port.

coastguard • n. an organization or person that keeps watch over coastal waters.

coastline • n. a stretch of coast: *a rugged coastline.*

coat • n. **1** a full-length outer garment with sleeves. **2** an animal's covering of fur or hair. **3** an enclosing or covering layer or structure. **4** a single application of paint or similar material. • v. provide with or form a layer or covering.
– ORIGIN Old French *cote*.

coating • n. a thin layer or covering.

coat of arms • n. a heraldic design or shield that is the symbol of a person, family, corporation, or country.

coat of mail • n. hist. a jacket made of metal rings or plates, serving as armour.

coat-tail • n. each of the flaps formed by the back of a tailcoat.
– PHRASES **on someone's coat-tails** benefiting from another's success.

coax /kohks/ • v. **1** persuade gradually or by flattery to do something. **2** move carefully into a particular situation or position.
– ORIGIN unknown.

coaxial /koh-ak-si-uhl/ • adj. **1** having a common axis. **2** (of a cable or line) transmitting by means of two concentric conductors separated by an insulator.

cob • n. **1** Brit. a loaf of bread. **2** a corncob. **3** (also **cobnut**) a hazelnut or filbert.
– ORIGIN unknown.

cobalt /koh-bolt/ • n. a silvery-white metallic chemical element.
– ORIGIN German *Kobalt* 'imp, demon' (from the belief that cobalt was harmful to the ores with which it occurred).

cobber • n. Austral./NZ informal a companion or friend.
– ORIGIN perh. from English dialect *cob* 'take a liking to'.

cobble[1] • n. (also **cobblestone**) a small round stone used to cover road surfaces.
– DERIVATIVES **cobbled** adj.
– ORIGIN from **COB**.

cobble[2] • v. (**cobbles, cobbling, cobbled**) (**cobble together**) roughly assemble from available parts.
– ORIGIN from **COBBLER**.

cobbler • n. **1** a person whose job is mending shoes. **2** (**cobblers**) Brit. informal nonsense. [ORIGIN rhyming slang *cobbler's awls* 'balls'.]
– ORIGIN unknown.

cobra /koh-bruh/ • n. a poisonous snake native to Africa and Asia.
– ORIGIN from Portuguese *cobra de capello* 'snake with hood'.

cobweb • n. a spider's web, especially an old or dusty one.
– ORIGIN from former *coppe* 'spider'.

coca /koh-kuh/ • n. a tropical American shrub grown for its leaves, which are the source of cocaine.
– ORIGIN Spanish.

cocaine /koh-kayn/ • n. an addictive drug made from coca, used as an illegal stimulant and sometimes in medicine as a local anaesthetic.

coccus /kok-kuhss/ • n. (pl. **cocci** /kok-ky/) Biol. any rounded bacterium.
– ORIGIN Greek *kokkos* 'berry'.

coccyx /kok-siks/ • n. (pl. **coccyges** /kok-si-jeez/ or **coccyxes**) a small triangular bone at the base of the spinal column in humans.
– ORIGIN Greek *kokkux* 'cuckoo' (because the bone resembles a cuckoo's bill).

cochineal /koch-i-neel/ • n. a scarlet dye used for colouring food, made from the crushed bodies of an insect.
– ORIGIN French *cochenille* or Spanish *cochinilla*.

cochlea /kok-li-uh/ • n. (pl. **cochleae** /kok-li-ee/) the spiral cavity of the inner ear.
– ORIGIN Latin, 'snail shell or screw'.

cock • n. **1** a male bird, especially of a domestic fowl. **2** vulgar a man's penis. **3** a firing lever in a gun which can be raised to be released by the trigger. • v. **1** tilt or bend (something) in a particular direction. **2** raise the cock of (a gun) to make it ready for firing.
– ORIGIN Latin *coccus*.

cockade /kok-ayd/ • n. a rosette or knot of ribbons worn in a hat as a badge of office or as part of a uniform.
– ORIGIN French *cocarde*.

cock-a-hoop • adj. extremely pleased.
– ORIGIN from *set cock a hoop*, prob. referring to the action of turning on a tap and allowing liquor to flow.

cock and bull story • n. informal an unbelievable story.

cockatoo /kok-uh-too/ • n. a crested parrot.
– ORIGIN Dutch *kaketoe*.

Cockcroft, E
Sir John Douglas (1897–1967), English physicist. In 1932, with E. T. S. Walton, he split the atom, ushering in the field of nuclear and particle physics.

cockcrow • n. literary dawn.

cockerel • n. a young domestic cock.

cocker spaniel • n. a small breed of spaniel with a silky coat.
– ORIGIN from **COCK**, because the dog was bred to flush game birds.

cock-eyed • adj. informal **1** crooked or askew;

C

not level. **2** absurd; impractical.

cockfighting ● n. the sport (illegal in the UK) of setting two cocks to fight each other.

cockle ● n. an edible shellfish with a ribbed shell.
– PHRASES **warm the cockles of one's heart** give one a feeling of contentment.
– ORIGIN Old French *coquille* 'shell'.

cockney /kok-ni/ ● n. (pl. **cockneys**) **1** a person from of the East End of London. **2** the dialect or accent used in this area.
– ORIGIN uncertain.

cockpit ● n. **1** a compartment for the pilot and crew in an aircraft or spacecraft. **2** the driver's compartment in a racing car.
– ORIGIN from **COCK** + **PIT**[1].

cockroach ● n. a beetle-like insect with long antennae and legs.
– ORIGIN Spanish *cucaracha*.

cocksure ● adj. arrogantly confident.
– ORIGIN from archaic *cock* (a euphemism for *God*) + **SURE**.

cocktail ● n. **1** an alcoholic drink consisting of a spirit mixed with other ingredients. **2** a dish consisting of a mixture of small pieces of food. **3** a mixture of different substances or factors: *a cocktail of chemicals.* ● adj. relating to cocktail drinking or formal social occasions: *a cocktail dress.*
– ORIGIN first meaning a horse with a docked tail.

cock-up ● n. Brit. informal something done badly. ● v. (**cock up**) Brit. informal spoil or ruin.

cocky ● adj. (**cockier**, **cockiest**) conceited in a bold or cheeky way.
– ORIGIN from **COCK**.

cocoa ● n. **1** a powder made from roasted and ground cacao seeds. **2** a hot drink made from cocoa powder.
– ORIGIN from **CACAO**.

cocoa butter ● n. a fatty substance obtained from cocoa beans.

coconut ● n. **1** the large brown seed of a tropical palm, consisting of a woody husk lined with edible white flesh and containing a clear liquid. **2** the white flesh of a coconut.
– ORIGIN Spanish and Portuguese *coco* 'grinning face'.

coconut shy ● n. Brit. a fairground sideshow where balls are thrown at coconuts in an attempt to knock them off stands.

cocoon /kuh-koon/ ● n. **1** a silky case spun by the larvae of many insects for protection before becoming adults. **2** something that envelops in a protective or comforting way. ● v. wrap in a cocoon.
– ORIGIN French *cocon*.

Cocos Islands E
/koh-kuhss/ a group of twenty-seven small islands in the Indian Ocean, an external territory of Australia since 1955. Also called **KEELING ISLANDS**.

Cocteau E
/kok-toh/, Jean (1889–1963), French dramatist, novelist, and film director. His works include the novel *Les Enfants terribles*.

cod[1] ● n. (pl. **cod**) a large sea fish which is important as a food fish.
– ORIGIN perh. from Old English 'bag'.

cod[2] ● adj. Brit. informal fake.
– ORIGIN uncertain.

coda /koh-duh/ ● n. Music the concluding passage of a piece or movement.
– ORIGIN Italian.

coddle ● v. (**coddles**, **coddling**, **coddled**) treat in an overprotective way.
– ORIGIN uncertain.

code ● n. **1** a system of words, figures, or symbols used to represent others, especially for the purposes of secrecy. **2** (also **dialling code**) a sequence of numbers dialled to connect a telephone line with another exchange. **3** Computing program instructions. **4** a set of principles or rules of behaviour. **5** a systematic collection of laws or statutes: *the penal code.* ● v. (**codes**, **coding**, **coded**) **1** convert into a code. **2** (**coded**) expressed in an indirect way.
– ORIGIN Latin *codex* 'block of wood'.

codeine /koh-deen/ ● n. a sleep-inducing and painkilling drug obtained from morphine.
– ORIGIN Greek *kōdeia* 'poppy head'.

codex /koh-deks/ ● n. (pl. **codices** /koh-di-seez/ or **codexes**) an ancient manuscript text in book form.
– ORIGIN Latin, 'block of wood'.

codger ● n. informal, derog. an elderly man.
– ORIGIN perh. from **CADGE**.

codicil /koh-di-sil/ ● n. an addition or supplement that explains, alters, or cancels a will or part of one.
– ORIGIN Latin *codicillus* 'little book'.

codify /koh-di-fy/ ● v. (**codifies**, **codifying**, **codified**) organize (procedures or rules) into a system.

cod liver oil ● n. oil pressed from the fresh liver of cod, which is rich in vitamins D and A.

codpiece ● n. a pouch to cover the genitals on a pair of man's breeches, worn in the 15th and 16th centuries.
– ORIGIN from former *cod* 'scrotum'.

codswallop ● n. Brit. informal nonsense.
– ORIGIN perh. named after Hiram *Codd*, who invented a bottle for fizzy drinks (1875).

Cody E
/koh-di/, William Frederick, see **BUFFALO BILL**.

co-education ● n. the education of pupils of both sexes together.
– DERIVATIVES **co-educational** adj.

coefficient /koh-i-fi-sh'nt/ ● n. **1** Math. a quantity multiplying the variable in an algebraic expression (e.g. *4* in $4x^2$). **2** Physics a multiplier or factor that measures a particular property.

coelacanth /seel-uh-kanth/ ● n. a large sea fish with a tail fin in three rounded parts.
– ORIGIN from Greek *koilos* 'hollow' + *akantha* 'spine'.

coelenterate /see-len-tuh-ruht/ ● n. Zool. a member of a group of invertebrate sea animals, including jellyfish, corals, and sea anemones.
– ORIGIN from Greek *koilos* 'hollow' + *enteron* 'intestine'.

coerce /koh-erss/ ● v. (**coerces**, **coercing**, **coerced**) persuade (an unwilling person) to do something by using force or threats.
– DERIVATIVES **coercion** n. **coercive** adj.
– ORIGIN Latin *coercere* 'restrain'.

Coetzee E
/koot-**seer**, koot-**see**/, J. M. (b.1940; full name *John Maxwell Coetzee*), South African novelist. His novels include *Life and Times of Michael K* and *Disgrace*.

coeval /koh-**ee**-vuhl/ • **adj.** having the same age or date of origin; contemporary. • **n.** a person of roughly the same age as oneself; a contemporary.
– ORIGIN Latin *coaevus*.

coexist • **v. 1** exist at the same time or in the same place. **2** exist in harmony.
– DERIVATIVES **coexistence** n.

C. of E. • **abbrev.** Church of England.

coffee • **n. 1** a hot drink made from the roasted and ground seeds of a tropical shrub. **2** the seeds used to make this drink.
– ORIGIN Arabic.

coffee table • **n.** a small, low table.

coffee-table book • **n.** a large book with many illustrations.

coffer • **n. 1** a small chest for holding valuables. **2** (**coffers**) the funds or financial reserves of an institution.
– ORIGIN Old French *coffre*.

coffin • **n.** a long box in which a dead body is buried or cremated.
– ORIGIN Old French *cofin* 'little basket'.

cog • **n. 1** a wheel or bar with projections on its edge, which transfers motion by engaging with projections on another wheel or bar. **2** any one of these projections.
– ORIGIN prob. Scandinavian.

cogent /**koh**-juhnt/ • **adj.** (of an argument) clear, logical, and convincing.
– DERIVATIVES **cogency** n. **cogently** adv.
– ORIGIN Latin *cogere* 'compel'.

cogitate /**koj**-i-tayt/ • **v.** (**cogitates, cogitating, cogitated**) formal think deeply.
– DERIVATIVES **cogitation** n.
– ORIGIN Latin *cogitare* 'to consider'.

cognac /**kon**-yak/ • **n.** a high-quality brandy made in Cognac in France.

cognition /kog-**ni**-sh'n/ • **n.** the process of obtaining knowledge through thought, experience, and the senses.
– ORIGIN Latin.

cognitive /**kog**-ni-tiv/ • **adj.** having to do with cognition.

cognizance /**kog**-ni-zuhnss/ (also **cognisance**) • **n.** formal knowledge or awareness.
– ORIGIN Old French *conoisance*.

cognoscenti /kon-yuh-**shen**-ti/ • **pl. n.** people who are well informed about a particular subject.
– ORIGIN Italian.

cohabit • **v.** (**cohabits, cohabiting, cohabited**) **1** live together and have a sexual relationship without being married. **2** coexist.
– DERIVATIVES **cohabitation** n.
– ORIGIN Latin *cohabitare*.

cohere /koh-**heer**/ • **v.** (**coheres, cohering, cohered**) hold firmly together; form a whole.
– ORIGIN Latin *cohaerere*.

coherent /coh-**heer**-uhnt/ • **adj. 1** (of an argument or theory) logical and consistent. **2** able to speak clearly and logically.

cohesion /koh-**hee**-*zh*'n/ • **n.** the action of holding together or forming a whole.

cohesive • **adj. 1** forming a whole. **2** causing cohesion.

cohort /**koh**-hort/ • **n. 1** an ancient Roman military unit equal to one tenth of a legion. **2** a group of people with a shared feature.
– ORIGIN Latin *cohors* 'yard, retinue'.

coif /koyf/ • **n.** a close-fitting cap worn by nuns under a veil. • **v.** /kwuhf/ (**coifs, coiffed, coiffing**) style or arrange (someone's hair).
– ORIGIN Old French *coife*.

coiffure /kwah-**fyoor**/ • **n.** a person's hairstyle.

coil • **n. 1** a length of something wound in a joined sequence of loops. **2** a contraceptive device in the form of a coil, placed in the womb. **3** an electrical device consisting of a coiled wire, for converting the level of a voltage, producing a magnetic field, or adding inductance to a circuit. • **v.** arrange or form into a coil.
– ORIGIN Old French *coillir*.

coin • **n.** a flat disc or piece of metal used as money. • **v. 1** make (coins) by stamping metal. **2** invent (a new word or phrase).
– ORIGIN Old French 'wedge, die'.

coinage • **n. 1** coins as a whole. **2** the action or process of producing coins. **3** a system of coins in use. **4** a newly invented word or phrase.

coincide /koh-in-**syd**/ • **v.** (**coincides, coinciding, coincided**) **1** happen at the same time or place. **2** be the same or similar.
– ORIGIN Latin *coincidere*.

coincidence /koh-**in**-si-duhnss/ • **n. 1** a remarkable occurrence of events or circumstances at the same time but without apparent connection. **2** the fact of two or more things happening at the same time or being the same.
– DERIVATIVES **coincidental** adj.

coir /**koy**-uh/ • **n.** fibre from the outer husk of the coconut, used in potting compost and for making ropes and matting.
– ORIGIN from a language of southern India.

coitus /**koh**-i-tuhss/ • **n.** tech. sexual intercourse.
– DERIVATIVES **coital** adj.
– ORIGIN Latin.

coitus interruptus /koh-i-tuhss in-ter-**rup**-tuhss/ • **n.** sexual intercourse in which the man withdraws his penis before ejaculation.

coke[1] • **n.** a solid fuel made by heating coal in the absence of air.
– ORIGIN unknown.

coke[2] • **n.** informal cocaine.

Col. • **abbrev.** Colonel.

col • **n.** the lowest point between two peaks of a mountain ridge.
– ORIGIN French, 'neck'.

colander /**kol**-uhn-der/ • **n.** a bowl with holes in it, used for draining food.
– ORIGIN Latin *colare* 'to strain'.

cold • **adj. 1** of or at a low or relatively low temperature. **2** not feeling, showing, or affected by emotion: *cold statistics*. **3** (of a colour) containing pale blue or grey and giving no impression of warmth. **4** (of a scent or trail) no longer fresh and easy to follow. **5** without preparation; unawares: *going into the test cold*. • **n. 1** cold weather or surroundings. **2** an infection causing running at the nose and sneezing.
– PHRASES **get cold feet** lose one's nerve. **the cold shoulder** deliberate unfriendliness or

rejection. **in cold blood** without mercy; deliberately cruel.
– DERIVATIVES **coldly** adv. **coldness** n.
– ORIGIN Old English.

cold-blooded • adj. **1** (of reptiles and fish) having a body whose temperature varies with that of the environment. **2** without emotion or pity.

cold-call • v. visit or telephone (someone) without their agreement in an attempt to sell goods or services.

cold cream • n. a cream for cleansing and softening the skin.

cold frame • n. a frame with a glass top in which small plants are grown and protected.

cold-hearted • adj. lacking affection or warmth; unfeeling.

Colditz E
/kohl-dits/ a medieval castle near Leipzig, used as a top-security camp for Allied prisoners in the Second World War.

cold sore • n. an inflamed blister in or near the mouth, caused by a virus.

cold sweat • n. a state of sweating caused by nervousness or illness.

cold turkey • n. informal the unpleasant state caused by abrupt withdrawal from a drug to which one is addicted.

cold war • n. a state of hostility between the countries allied to the former Soviet Union and the Western powers after the Second World War.

Cole, E
Nat King (1919–65; born *Nathaniel Adams Coles*), American singer and pianist, the first black man to have his own radio (1948–9) and television (1956–7) series.

Coleridge E
/**koh**-luh-rij/, Samuel Taylor (1772–1834), English poet and critic. His *Lyrical Ballads*, written with William Wordsworth and including 'The Rime of the Ancient Mariner', was a major influence on English romanticism. Other poems include 'Kubla Khan'.

coleslaw • n. a salad dish of shredded raw cabbage and carrots mixed with mayonnaise.
– ORIGIN Dutch *koolsla*.

Colette E
(1873–1954; born *Sidonie Gabrielle Claudine*), French novelist, whose novels include *Chéri*.

colic • n. severe pain in the abdomen caused by wind or obstruction in the intestines.
– DERIVATIVES **colicky** adj.
– ORIGIN Latin *colicus*.

collaborate /kuh-lab-uh-rayt/ • v. (**collaborates**, **collaborating**, **collaborated**) **1** work jointly on an activity or project. **2** betray one's country by cooperating with an enemy.
– DERIVATIVES **collaboration** n. **collaborative** adj. **collaborator** n.
– ORIGIN Latin *collaborare*.

collage /kol-lah*zh*/ • n. **1** a form of art in which various materials are arranged and stuck to a backing. **2** a combination of various things.
– ORIGIN French, 'gluing'.

collagen /kol-luh-juhn/ • n. a protein found in animal tissue.
– ORIGIN French *collagène*.

collapse • v. (**collapses**, **collapsing**, **collapsed**) **1** suddenly fall down or give way. **2** (of a person) fall down as a result of illness. **3** fail suddenly and completely. • n. **1** an instance of a structure collapsing. **2** a sudden failure or breakdown.
– ORIGIN Latin *collabi*.

collapsible • adj. able to be folded down.

collar • n. **1** a band of material around the neck of a shirt or other garment. **2** a band put around the neck of a domestic animal. • v. informal seize or arrest (someone).
– ORIGIN Latin *collare*.

collarbone • n. either of the pair of bones joining the breastbone to the shoulder blades.

collate /kuh-layt/ • v. (**collates**, **collating**, **collated**) **1** collect and combine (texts or information). **2** compare (two or more sources of information).
– DERIVATIVES **collation** n.
– ORIGIN Latin *collatus* 'brought together'.

collateral /kuh-lat-uh-ruhl/ • n. something promised to someone if one cannot repay a loan. • adj. additional but less important.
– ORIGIN Latin *collateralis*.

colleague • n. a person with whom one works.
– ORIGIN Latin *collega*.

collect[1] /kuh-lekt/ • v. **1** bring or come together. **2** buy or find (items of a particular kind) as a hobby. **3** call for and take away; fetch. **4** win or receive.
– ORIGIN Latin *colligere*.

collect[2] /kol-lekt/ • n. (in the Christian Church) a short prayer, especially one used on a particular day.
– ORIGIN Latin *collecta* 'a gathering'.

collectable (also **collectible**) • adj. worth collecting as a hobby. • n. an item valued by collectors.

collected • adj. **1** calm. **2** (of works) brought together in one volume or edition.

collection • n. **1** the action of collecting. **2** a regular removal of mail or of refuse. **3** a group of things that have been collected.

collective • adj. **1** done by or belonging to all the members of a group. **2** taken as a whole. • n. a business owned or operated cooperatively.

collective bargaining • n. negotiation of wages and other conditions of employment by an organized body of employees.

collective farm • n. a farm or group of farms owned by the state and run by a group of people.

collective noun • n. a noun that refers to a group of individuals (e.g. *staff*, *family*).

USAGE collective noun

A **collective noun** is one that refers to a group of people or things. Such nouns can be used with either a singular verb (*my family was always hard-working*) or a plural verb (*his family were disappointed in him*). It is important to remember that, if the verb is singular, any following pronouns (words such as 'he', 'she', or 'they') must be too: *the government is prepared to act, but not until it knows the outcome of the talks* (not *... until they know the outcome...*).

collectivism • n. the ownership of land,

business, and industry by the people or the state.

collector • n. a person who collects things of a particular type.

colleen /kol-leen/ • n. Ir. a girl or young woman.
– ORIGIN Irish *cailin*.

college • n. **1** an educational establishment providing higher education or specialized training. **2** (in Britain) any of the independent institutions into which some universities are separated.
– ORIGIN Latin *collegium* 'partnership'.

collegiate /kuh-lee-ji-uht/ • adj. **1** having to do with a college or college students. **2** (of a university) composed of different colleges.

collide • v. (**collides**, **colliding**, **collided**) **1** hit by accident when moving. **2** come into conflict.
– ORIGIN Latin *collidere*.

collie • n. (pl. **collies**) a breed of sheepdog with a pointed nose and long hair.
– ORIGIN perh. from **COAL** (the breed originally being black).

collier /kol-li-er/ • n. esp. Brit. **1** a coal miner. **2** a ship carrying coal.

colliery • n. (pl. **collieries**) a coal mine.

collinear /kol-lin-i-er/ • adj. Geom. (of points) lying in the same straight line.

Collins[1], E
Michael (1890–1922), Irish nationalist leader and member of Parliament for Sinn Fein, who was one of the negotiators of the Anglo-Irish Treaty of 1921.

Collins[2], E
(William) Wilkie (1824–89), English novelist, noted for his detective stories *The Woman in White* and *The Moonstone*.

collision • n. an instance of colliding.

collocation • n. **1** the frequent occurrence of a word with another word or words. **2** a word or group of words that very often occur together (e.g. *heavy drinker*).
– ORIGIN Latin.

colloid /kol-loyd/ • n. a homogeneous substance consisting of submicroscopic particles of one substance dispersed in another, as in an emulsion or gel.
– DERIVATIVES **colloidal** adj.
– ORIGIN Greek *kolla* 'glue'.

colloquial /kuh-loh-kwi-uhl/ • adj. (of language) used in ordinary conversation; not formal or literary.
– DERIVATIVES **colloquially** adv.
– ORIGIN Latin *colloquium* 'conversation'.

colloquialism • n. an informal word or phrase.

colloquium /kuh-loh-kwi-uhm/ • n. (pl. **colloquiums** or **colloquia** /kuh-loh-kwi-uh/) an academic conference or seminar.
– ORIGIN Latin.

colloquy /kol-luh-kwi/ • n. (pl. **colloquies**) formal a conference or conversation.
– ORIGIN Latin *colloquium*.

collude /kuh-lood/ • v. (**colludes**, **colluding**, **colluded**) come to a secret understanding; conspire.
– ORIGIN Latin *colludere*.

collusion • n. secret cooperation in order to cheat or deceive.

colobus /kol-uh-buhss/ • n. (pl. **colobus**) a slender African monkey with silky fur.
– ORIGIN Greek *kolobos* 'curtailed' (referring to its shortened thumbs).

Cologne E
/kuh-lohn/ an industrial and university city in western Germany, in the state of North Rhine-Westphalia.

cologne /kuh-lohn/ • n. eau de cologne or similarly scented toilet water.

Colombia E
/kuh-lom-bi-uh/ a country in the extreme NW of South America; capital, Bogotá.
– DERIVATIVES **Colombian** adj. & n.

Colombo E
/kuh-lum-boh/ the capital and chief port of Sri Lanka.

colon[1] /koh-luhn, koh-lon/ • n. a punctuation mark (:) used before a list, a quotation, or an explanation.
– ORIGIN Greek *kōlon* 'limb, clause'.

colon[2] /koh-luhn, koh-lon/ • n. the main part of the large intestine, which passes from the caecum to the rectum.
– DERIVATIVES **colonic** adj.
– ORIGIN Greek *kolon* 'food, meat'.

colonel /ker-nuhl/ • n. a rank of officer in the army and in the US air force, above a lieutenant colonel.
– ORIGIN Italian *colonnello* 'column of soldiers'.

colonial • adj. having to do with a colony or colonialism. • n. a person who lives in a colony.

colonialism • n. the practice of acquiring control over another country, occupying it with settlers, and exploiting it economically.
– DERIVATIVES **colonialist** n. & adj.

colonist • n. an inhabitant of a colony.

colonize (also **colonise**) • v. (**colonizes**, **colonizing**, **colonized**) **1** make a colony in (a place). **2** take over (a place) for one's own use.
– DERIVATIVES **colonization** (also **colonisation**) n.

colonnade /kol-uh-nayd/ • n. a row of evenly spaced columns supporting a roof.
– ORIGIN French.

colony • n. (pl. **colonies**) **1** a country or area under the control of another country and occupied by settlers from that country. **2** a group of people of one nationality or race living in a foreign place. **3** a place where a group of people with a common interest live together: *a nudist colony.* **4** a community of animals or plants of one kind living close together.
– ORIGIN Latin *colonia*.

color • n. & v. US = **COLOUR**.

Colorado[1] E
/ko-luh-rah-doh/ a river which rises in the Rocky Mountains of northern Colorado and flows to the Gulf of California, passing through the Grand Canyon.

Colorado[2] E
/ko-luh-rah-doh/ a state in the central US; capital, Denver.
– DERIVATIVES **Coloradan** n. & adj.

C

C

Colorado beetle • n. an American beetle whose larvae are very destructive to potato plants.
– ORIGIN from *Colorado* (see **COLORADO²**).

coloration (also **colouration**) • n. colouring.

coloratura /kol-uh-ruh-**tyoor**-uh/ • n. elaborate ornamentation of a vocal melody, e.g. in opera.
– ORIGIN Italian, 'colouring'.

colossal • adj. extremely large.

colossus /kuh-**loss**-uhss/ • n. (pl. **colossi** /kuh-**loss**-I/ or **colossuses**) a person or thing of enormous size.
– ORIGIN Latin.

colostomy /kuh-**loss**-tuh-mi/ • n. (pl. **colostomies**) a surgical operation in which the colon is shortened and the cut end diverted to an opening in the abdominal wall.
– ORIGIN from **COLON²** + Greek *stoma* 'mouth'.

colour (US **color**) • n. **1** an object's property of producing different sensations on the eye as a result of the way it reflects or gives out light. **2** one, or any mixture, of the parts into which light can be separated. **3** the use of all colours in photography or television. **4** the shade of the skin as an indication of someone's race. **5** redness of the complexion. **6** interest and excitement: *a town full of colour and character.* • v. **1** give a colour to. **2** blush. **3** influence, especially in a bad way: *the experiences had coloured her whole life.*
– ORIGIN Latin *color*.

colouration • n. var. of **COLORATION**.

colour-blind • adj. unable to tell the difference between certain colours.

coloured (US **colored**) • adj. **1** having a colour or colours. **2** dated or offens. wholly or partly of non-white descent. • n. dated or offens. a person who is wholly or partly of non-white descent.

colour-fast • adj. dyed in colours that will not fade or be washed out.

colourful (US **colorful**) • adj. **1** having many or varied colours. **2** lively and exciting; vivid.
– DERIVATIVES **colourfully** (US **colorfully**) adv.

colouring (US **coloring**) • n. **1** the process or art of applying colour. **2** the appearance of something with regard to colour. **3** the natural hues of a person's skin, hair, and eyes. **4** a substance used to colour something.

colourist (US **colorist**) • n. an artist or designer who uses colour in a special or skilful way.

colourless (US **colorless**) • adj. **1** without colour. **2** lacking character or interest; dull.

colour scheme • n. an arrangement or combination of colours.

colt /kohlt/ • n. **1** a young uncastrated male horse. **2** a member of a junior sports team.
– ORIGIN Old English.

coltish • adj. energetic but awkward in one's movements or behaviour.

Coltrane E
/kol-**trayn**/, John (William) (1926–67), American jazz saxophonist.

Columba, St E
/kuh-**lum**-buh/ (*c.*521–97), Irish abbot and missionary, who established a monastery at Iona in *c.*563 and converted the Picts to Christianity. Feast day, 9 June.

Columbia, District of E
see **DISTRICT OF COLUMBIA**.

columbine /**kol**-uhm-byn/ • n. a plant with purplish-blue flowers.
– ORIGIN Latin *columba* 'dove' (from the flower's resemblance to a cluster of doves).

Columbus, E
Christopher (1451–1506; Spanish name *Cristóbal Colón*), Italian-born Spanish explorer. In 1492 he reached the New World (in fact various Caribbean islands); in 1498 he was the first European to reach the South American mainland.

column • n. **1** an upright pillar supporting a structure or standing alone as a monument. **2** a line of people or vehicles moving in the same direction. **3** a vertical division of a page. **4** a regular section of a newspaper or magazine on a particular subject or by a particular person.
– ORIGIN Latin *columna*.

columnist /**kol**-uhm-ist/ • n. a journalist who writes a column in a newspaper or magazine.

com- (also **co-**, **col-**, **con-**, or **cor-**) • prefix with; together; altogether: *combine*.
– ORIGIN Latin *cum*.

coma /**koh**-muh/ • n. a state of long-lasting deep unconsciousness.
– ORIGIN Greek *kōma* 'deep sleep'.

Comanche /kuh-**man**-chi/ • n. (pl. **Comanche** or **Comanches**) a member of an American Indian people of the south-western US.
– ORIGIN the Comanches' name for themselves.

comatose /**koh**-muh-tohss/ • adj. in a state of coma.

comb • n. **1** an object with a row of narrow teeth, used for arranging the hair. **2** a device for separating and dressing textile fibres. **3** the red fleshy crest on the head of a domestic fowl. • v. **1** arrange (the hair) by drawing a comb through it. **2** prepare (wool, flax, or cotton) for manufacture with a comb. **3** search in an organized way.
– ORIGIN Old English.

combat • n. fighting, especially between armed forces. • v. (**combats**, **combating**, **combated**; also **combats**, **combatting**, **combatted**) take action to reduce or prevent (something undesirable).
– ORIGIN Latin *combattere*.

combatant /**kom**-buh-tuhnt/ • n. a person or nation engaged in fighting during a war.

combative /**kom**-buh-tiv/ • adj. ready or eager to fight or argue.

combat trousers • pl. n. loose trousers with large pockets halfway down each leg.

combe /koom/ • n. Brit. a short valley or hollow on a hillside or coastline.
– ORIGIN Old English.

combination • n. **1** the action of combining different things. **2** something made up of distinct elements. **3** a sequence of numbers or letters used to open a combination lock.

combination lock • n. a lock that is opened using a specific sequence of letters or numbers.

combine • v. /kuhm-**byn**/ (**combines**, **com-**

bining, **combined**) **1** join or mix together. **2** do at the same time: *combine shopping and sightseeing.* ● n. /**kom**-byn/ a group acting together for a commercial purpose.
– ORIGIN Latin *combinare.*

combine harvester ● n. a farming machine that reaps, threshes, and cleans a cereal crop in one operation.

combining form ● n. a form of a word used in combination with another element to form a word (e.g. *bio-* 'life' in *biology*).

combo ● n. (pl. **combos**) informal a small jazz, rock, or pop band.

combust /kuhm-**bust**/ ● v. burn or be burnt by fire.
– ORIGIN Latin *comburere* 'burn up'.

combustible ● adj. able to catch fire and burn easily.

combustion ● n. **1** the process of burning. **2** rapid chemical combination with oxygen, involving the production of heat.

come ● v. (**comes**, **coming**, **came**; past part. **come**) **1** move or reach towards or into a place: *Jess came into the kitchen.* **2** arrive. **3** happen. **4** have or achieve a certain position: *she came second.* **5** pass into a certain condition or state of mind: *his shirt came undone.* **6** be sold or available in a particular form: *they come in three sizes.* **7** (**coming**) likely to be successful in the future: *a coming man.* **8** informal have an orgasm. ● prep. informal when a specified time is reached.
– PHRASES **come about** happen. **come across 1** give a particular impression. **2** meet or find by chance. **come back** reply vigorously. **come by** manage to get. **come down to** be dependent on (a factor). **come from** originate in. **come in** prove to be: *it came in handy.* **come into** inherit (money or property). **come of** result from. **come off 1** succeed. **2** proceed in a specified way. **come off it** informal said when expressing strong disbelief. **come on 1** (of a state or condition) begin. **2** (also **come upon**) meet or find by chance. **come out 1** (of a fact) become known. **2** declare oneself as being for or against something. **come out with** say in a sudden or incautious way. **come round** esp. Brit. **1** recover consciousness. **2** be converted to another person's opinion. **come to 1** recover consciousness. **2** (of an expense) amount to. **come up** (of a situation or problem) arise. **come what may** no matter what happens. **have it coming (to one)** informal be due to face the unpleasant consequences of one's behaviour.
– ORIGIN Old English.

comeback ● n. **1** a return to fame or popularity. **2** informal a quick reply.

comedian ● n. (fem. **comedienne**) **1** an entertainer whose act is intended to make people laugh. **2** a comic actor.

comedown ● n. informal **1** a loss of status or importance. **2** a feeling of disappointment or depression.

comedy ● n. (pl. **comedies**) **1** entertainment consisting of jokes and sketches intended to make people laugh. **2** an amusing film, play, or programme. **3** a humorous play in which the characters finally triumph over difficult situations.
– DERIVATIVES **comedic** /kuh-mee-dik/ adj.
– ORIGIN Greek *kōmōidia.*

come-hither ● adj. informal flirtatious.

comely /kum-li/ ● adj. (**comelier**, **comeliest**) archaic pleasant to look at.
– ORIGIN prob. from former *becomely* 'becoming'.

come-on ● n. informal a gesture or remark intended to attract someone sexually.

comestible /kuh-mess-ti-b'l/ formal ● n. an item of food.
– ORIGIN Latin *comestibilis.*

comet /kom-it/ ● n. a mass of ice and dust with a long tail, moving around the solar system.
– ORIGIN Greek *komētēs* 'long-haired star'.

comeuppance ● n. informal a punishment or fate that someone deserves.

comfort ● n. **1** a state of physical ease. **2** (**comforts**) things that contribute to comfort. **3** consolation for grief or anxiety: *a few words of comfort.* ● v. make less unhappy.
– ORIGIN Old French *confort.*

comfortable ● adj. **1** giving or enjoying physical comfort. **2** free from financial worry. **3** (of a victory) easily achieved.
– DERIVATIVES **comfortably** adv.

comforter ● n. a person or thing that comforts.

comfy ● adj. (**comfier**, **comfiest**) informal comfortable.

comic ● adj. **1** causing or meant to cause laughter. **2** having to do with comedy: *a comic actor.* ● n. **1** a comedian. **2** a children's periodical containing comic strips.
– ORIGIN Greek *kōmikos.*

comical ● adj. causing laughter, especially through being ridiculous.

comic strip ● n. a sequence of drawings in boxes that tell an amusing story.

comity /kom-i-ti/ ● n. (pl. **comities**) formal considerate behaviour towards others.
– ORIGIN Latin *comitas.*

comma ● n. a punctuation mark (,) showing a pause between parts of a sentence or separating items in a list.
– ORIGIN Greek *komma.*

command ● v. **1** give an order. **2** be in charge of (a military unit). **3** be in a position to receive: *emeralds command a high price.* ● n. **1** an order. **2** authority: *the officer in command.* **3** a group of officers having control over a particular group or operation. **4** the ability to use or control something: *his command of English.* **5** an instruction causing a computer to perform one of its basic functions.
– ORIGIN Latin *commandare.*

commandant /kom-muhn-dant/ ● n. an officer in charge of a force or institution.

commandeer /kom-muhn-deer/ ● v. (**commandeers**, **commandeering**, **commandeered**) officially take possession of (something) for military purposes.
– ORIGIN Afrikaans *kommandeer.*

commander ● n. **1** a person in command. **2** a rank of naval officer next below captain.

commander-in-chief ● n. (pl. **commanders-in-chief**) an officer in charge of all of the armed forces of a country.

commanding ● adj. **1** indicating or expressing authority; imposing. **2** having or giving superior strength: *a commanding lead.*

commandment ● n. a law given by God, especially one of the Ten Commandments.

commando • n. (pl. **commandos**) **1** a soldier trained for carrying out raids. **2** a unit of such troops.
– ORIGIN Portuguese.

command performance • n. a presentation of a play, concert, or film at the request of royalty.

commemorate • v. (**commemorates, commemorating, commemorated**) honour the memory of.
– DERIVATIVES **commemoration** n.
– ORIGIN Latin *commemorare.*

commemorative /kuh-mem-muh-ruh-tiv/ • adj. acting to honour the memory of an event or person.

commence • v. (**commences, commencing, commenced**) begin.
– ORIGIN Old French *commencier.*

commencement • n. the beginning of something.

commend • v. **1** praise formally or officially. **2** present as suitable or good; recommend.
– DERIVATIVES **commendation** n.
– ORIGIN Latin *commendare.*

commendable • adj. deserving praise.

commensal /kuh-men-s'l/ • adj. Biol. (of two organisms) having an association in which one benefits and the other derives neither benefit nor harm.
– ORIGIN Latin *commensalis.*

commensurable /kuh-men-shuh-ruh-b'l/ • adj. measurable by the same standard: *the finite is not commensurable with the infinite.*
– ORIGIN Latin *commensurabilis.*

commensurate /kuh-men-shuh-ruht/ • adj. corresponding in size or degree; in proportion: *salary will be commensurate with age and experience.*

comment • n. **1** a remark expressing an opinion or reaction. **2** discussion of an issue or event. • v. express an opinion or reaction.
– ORIGIN Latin *commentum* 'contrivance'.

commentary • n. (pl. **commentaries**) **1** the expression of opinions about an event or situation. **2** a broadcast spoken account of a sports match or other event as it happens. **3** a set of explanatory notes on a text.

commentate • v. (**commentates, commentating, commentated**) provide a commentary on a sports match or other event.

commentator • n. a person who broadcasts or writes a commentary.

commerce • n. the activity of buying and selling, especially on a large scale.
– ORIGIN Latin *commercium.*

commercial • adj. **1** concerned with or engaged in commerce. **2** making or intended to make a profit. **3** (of radio or television) funded by broadcast advertisements. • n. a television or radio advertisement.
– DERIVATIVES **commercially** adv.

commercialism • n. emphasis on making as much profit as possible.

commercialize (also **commercialise**) • v. (**commercializes, commercializing, commercialized**) manage in a way designed to make a profit.
– DERIVATIVES **commercialization** (or **commercialisation**) n.

Commie • n. (pl. **Commies**) informal, derog. a communist.

commingle /kom-ming-g'l/ • v. (**commingles, commingling, commingled**) literary mix; blend.

commiserate /kuh-miz-uh-rayt/ • v. (**commiserates, commiserating, commiserated**) express sympathy or pity; sympathize.
– DERIVATIVES **commiseration** n.
– ORIGIN Latin *commiserari.*

commissar /kom-mi-sar/ • n. a Communist official responsible for political education.
– ORIGIN Russian *komissar.*

commissariat /kom-mi-sair-i-uht/ • n. a military department for the supply of food and equipment.

commission • n. **1** an instruction, command, or duty. **2** an order for something to be produced specially. **3** a group of people given official authority to do something. **4** payment to an agent for selling goods or services. **5** a warrant conferring the rank of military officer. • v. **1** order or authorize the production of. **2** bring into working order.
– PHRASES **in** (or **out of**) **commission** in (or not in) use or working order.
– ORIGIN Latin.

commissionaire /kuh-mi-shuh-nair/ • n. esp. Brit. a uniformed door attendant at a hotel, theatre, or other building.
– ORIGIN French.

commissioner • n. **1** a person appointed by, or as a member of, a commission. **2** a representative of the highest authority in an area.

commit • v. (**commits, committing, committed**) **1** do (something wrong or illegal). **2** (**commit oneself**) promise to do something: *they were reluctant to commit themselves to an opinion.* **3** dedicate to a particular use. **4** set aside for safekeeping. **5** send to prison or psychiatric hospital.
– ORIGIN Latin *committere.*

commitment • n. **1** dedication to a cause or policy. **2** a promise. **3** an engagement or duty that restricts freedom of action: *business commitments.*

committal • n. the sending of someone to prison or psychiatric hospital, or for trial.

committed • adj. dedicated to a cause, activity, job, etc.

committee • n. a group of people appointed for a particular function by a larger group.

commode • n. a piece of furniture containing a concealed chamber pot.
– ORIGIN French, 'convenient, suitable'.

commodify /kuh-mod-i-fy/ • v. (**commodifies, commodifying, commodified**) turn into or treat as a mere commodity: *art has become commodified.*
– DERIVATIVES **commodification** n.

commodious /kuh-moh-di-uhss/ • adj. formal roomy and comfortable.
– ORIGIN Latin *commodus* 'convenient'.

commodity /kuh-mod-i-ti/ • n. (pl. **commodities**) **1** a raw material or agricultural product that can be bought and sold. **2** something useful or valuable.
– ORIGIN Latin *commoditas.*

commodore /kom-muh-dor/ • n. **1** a naval rank above captain and below rear admiral. **2** the president of a yacht club.
– ORIGIN prob. from Dutch *komandeur.*

common • adj. (**commoner, commonest**)

1 occurring, found, or done often; not rare. **2** without special qualities or position; ordinary. **3** showing a lack of refinement supposedly typical of the lower classes. **4** shared by two or more people or things. **5** belonging to or affecting the whole of a community: *common land.* ● n. a piece of open land for public use.
– PHRASES **common or garden** Brit. informal of the usual or ordinary type. **in common** shared.
– ORIGIN Latin *communis.*

commonality ● n. (pl. **commonalities**) the sharing of features.

common denominator ● n. **1** Math. a common multiple of the denominators of several fractions. **2** a feature shared by all members of a group.

commoner ● n. one of the ordinary or common people, as opposed to the aristocracy.

common ground ● n. views shared by each of two or more parties.

common law ● n. law derived from custom and precedent rather than created in a law-making body.

common-law husband (or **wife**) ● n. a man or woman who has lived with a person long enough to be recognized as a husband or wife, but has not been married in a civil or religious ceremony.

commonly ● adv. usually.

common market ● n. **1** a group of countries imposing few duties on trade with one another. **2** (**the Common Market**) the European Economic Community or European Union.

common noun ● n. a noun referring to a thing (e.g. *tree*) as opposed to a particular person, place, etc.

commonplace ● adj. ordinary. ● n. **1** a usual or ordinary thing. **2** a cliche.

common room ● n. esp. Brit. a room in an educational institution for use of students or staff outside teaching hours.

Commons ● pl. n. (**the Commons**) the House of Commons.

common sense ● n. good sense and sound judgement in practical matters.

commonsensical ● adj. having or showing common sense.

common time ● n. Music a rhythm in which there are two or four beats in a bar.

commonwealth ● n. **1** an independent state or community. **2** (**the Commonwealth** or **the Commonwealth of Nations**) an association consisting of the UK together with states that were previously part of the British Empire, and dependencies.

Commonwealth Games E
an amateur sports competition held every four years between countries of the Commonwealth.

Commonwealth of Independent States E
a confederation of independent states, formerly republics within the Soviet Union, established in 1991.

commotion ● n. noisy confusion or disturbance.
– ORIGIN Latin.

communal /kuh-myoo-n'l/ ● adj. shared or done by all members of a community.
– DERIVATIVES **communally** adv.
– ORIGIN Latin *communalis.*

commune[1] /kom-myoon/ ● n. a group of people living together and sharing possessions and responsibilities.

commune[2] /kuh-myoon/ ● v. (**communes, communing, communed**) (**commune with**) share one's intimate thoughts or feelings with.
– ORIGIN Old French *comuner.*

communicable ● adj. (of a disease) able to be communicated to others.

communicant ● n. a person who receives Holy Communion.

communicate ● v. (**communicates, communicating, communicated**) **1** share or exchange information. **2** pass on or convey (an emotion, disease, heat, etc.). **3** (**communicating**) (of two rooms) having a common connecting door.
– ORIGIN Latin *communicare.*

communication ● n. **1** the action of communicating. **2** a letter or message. **3** (**communications**) means of sending or receiving information, such as telephone lines or computers.

communication cord ● n. Brit. a cord which a train passenger may pull in an emergency, causing the train to brake.

communicative ● adj. willing or eager to talk or give information.

communion ● n. **1** the sharing of intimate thoughts and feelings. **2** (also **Holy Communion**) the service of Christian worship at which bread and wine are made sacred and shared; the Eucharist.

communiqué /kuh-myoo-ni-kay/ ● n. an official announcement or statement.
– ORIGIN French, 'communicated'.

communism ● n. **1** a political system whereby all property is owned by the community and each person contributes and receives according to their ability and needs. **2** a system of this kind derived from Marxism.
– ORIGIN French *communisme.*

communist ● n. a supporter of communism. ● adj. having to do with communism.

community ● n. (pl. **communities**) **1** a group of people living together in one place. **2** (**the community**) society. **3** a group of people with a common religion, race, or profession: *the scientific community.* **4** the holding of attitudes or interests in common. **5** a group of animals or plants living or growing in the same place.
– ORIGIN Old French *comunete.*

community care ● n. long-term care for mentally ill, elderly, and disabled people within the community rather than in hospitals or institutions.

community centre ● n. a place providing educational or recreational activities for a neighbourhood.

community service ● n. socially useful work that an offender is required to do instead of going to prison.

commutate /kom-yuu-tayt/ ● v. (**commutates, commutating, commutated**) regulate the direction of (an alternating electric

C

current), especially to make it a direct current.
– DERIVATIVES **commutation** n.

commutative /kuh-myoo-tuh-tiv/ • **adj.** Math. unchanged in result by altering the order of quantities, such that for example $a \times b = b \times a$.

commutator /kom-yuu-tay-ter/ • **n.** an attachment which ensures that electric current flows as direct current.

commute • **v.** (**commutes**, **commuting**, **commuted**) **1** travel some distance between one's home and place of work on a regular basis. **2** reduce (a judicial sentence) to a less severe one.
– DERIVATIVES **commuter** n.
– ORIGIN Latin *commutare*; sense 1 is from *commutation ticket*, the US term for a season ticket.

Como, Lake E
/koh-moh/ a lake in the foothills of the Alps in northern Italy.

Comoros E
/kom-uh-rohz/ a country consisting of a group of islands in the Indian Ocean north of Madagascar; capital, Moroni.
– DERIVATIVES **Comoran** adj. & n.

compact[1] • **adj.** /kuhm-pakt/ **1** closely and neatly packed together; dense. **2** having all the necessary components fitted into a small space. • **v.** /kuhm-pakt/ press firmly together. • **n.** /kom-pakt/ a small case containing face powder, a mirror, and a powder puff.
– ORIGIN Latin *compingere* 'fasten together'.

compact[2] /kom-pakt/ • **n.** a formal agreement.
– ORIGIN Latin *compactum*.

compact disc • **n.** a small disc on which music or other digital information is stored.

companion • **n. 1** a person with whom one spends time or travels. **2** each of a pair of things intended to complement or match each other.
– DERIVATIVES **companionship** n.
– ORIGIN Old French *compaignon* 'one who breaks bread with another'.

companionable • **adj.** friendly.

companionway • **n.** a set of steps leading from a ship's deck down to a cabin or lower deck.
– ORIGIN from former Dutch *kompanje* 'quarterdeck'.

company • **n.** (pl. **companies**) **1** a commercial business. **2** the fact of being with others in an enjoyable way: *she is excellent company.* **3** a guest or guests: *we're expecting company.* **4** a number of people gathered together. **5** a division of an infantry battalion. **6** a group of actors, singers, or dancers who perform together.
– PHRASES **keep someone company** spend time with someone to prevent them feeling lonely or bored.
– ORIGIN Old French *compainie*.

comparable /kom-puh-ruh-b'l/ • **adj.** able to be likened to another; similar.

comparative /kuhm-pa-ruh-tiv/ • **adj. 1** measured or judged by comparison; relative. **2** involving comparison between two or more subjects. **3** (of an adjective or adverb) expressing a higher degree of a quality (e.g. *braver*), but not the highest possible. Contrasted with **POSITIVE**, **SUPERLATIVE**.

comparatively • **adv.** as compared to something else.

comparator /kuhm-pa-ruh-ter/ • **n.** a device for comparing something measurable with a reference or standard.

compare • **v.** (**compares**, **comparing**, **compared**) **1** (often **compare to/with**) estimate, measure, or note the similarity or difference between. **2** (**compare to**) point out or describe the resemblances of (something) with. **3** (usu. **compare with**) be similar to or have a specified relationship with another thing or person.
– ORIGIN Latin *comparare*.

comparison • **n. 1** the action or an instance of comparing. **2** the quality of being similar or equivalent.

compartment • **n. 1** a separate section of a structure or container. **2** a division of a railway carriage marked by partitions.
– ORIGIN French *compartiment*.

compartmentalize (also **compartmentalise**) • **v.** (**compartmentalizes**, **compartmentalizing**, **compartmentalized**) divide into categories or sections.

compass • **n. 1** an instrument containing a magnetized pointer which shows the direction of magnetic north. **2** (also **compasses**) an instrument for drawing circles, consisting of two arms linked by a movable joint. **3** range or scope.
– ORIGIN Old French *compas*.

compassion • **n.** sympathetic pity and concern for the sufferings of others.
– ORIGIN Latin.

compassionate • **adj.** feeling or showing compassion.

compatible • **adj. 1** able to exist or be used together without conflict. **2** (of two people) able to have a good relationship; well suited. **3** (usu. **compatible with**) consistent or in keeping.
– DERIVATIVES **compatibility** n.
– ORIGIN Latin *compatibilis*.

compatriot /kuhm-pat-ri-uht/ • **n.** a person from the same country.
– ORIGIN French.

compel • **v.** (**compels**, **compelling**, **compelled**) **1** force to do something. **2** bring about by force or pressure.
– ORIGIN Latin *compellere*.

compelling • **adj.** attracting much attention or admiration.

compendious • **adj.** formal presenting facts in a comprehensive but concise way.
– ORIGIN Latin *compendiosus*.

compendium /kuhm-pen-di-uhm/ • **n.** (pl. **compendiums** or **compendia** /kuhm-pen-di-uh/) **1** a collection of concise but detailed information about a subject. **2** a collection of similar items.
– ORIGIN Latin, 'profit, saving'.

compensate • **v.** (**compensates**, **compensating**, **compensated**) **1** give (someone) something to reduce or balance the bad effect of loss, suffering, or injury. **2** (**compensate for**) make up for (something undesirable) by exerting an opposite force or effect.
– ORIGIN Latin *compensare* 'weigh against'.

compensation ● n. **1** something given to compensate for loss, suffering, or injury. **2** something that compensates for an undesirable situation.

compère /**kom**-pair/ Brit. ● n. a person who introduces the acts in a variety show. ● v. (**compères**, **compèring**, **compèred**) act as a compère for.
– ORIGIN French, 'godfather'.

compete ● v. (**competes**, **competing**, **competed**) try to gain or win something by defeating others.
– ORIGIN Latin *competere*.

competence (also **competency**) ● n. the quality of being competent.

competent ● adj. **1** having the necessary skill or knowledge to do something successfully. **2** satisfactory, though not outstanding: *she spoke quite competent French*.
– DERIVATIVES **competently** adv.
– ORIGIN Latin *competere*.

competition ● n. **1** the activity of competing against others. **2** an event or contest in which people compete. **3** the person or people with whom one is competing.

competitive ● adj. **1** having to do with competition. **2** strongly wanting to be more successful than others. **3** as good as or better than others of a similar nature.
– DERIVATIVES **competitively** adv. **competitiveness** n.

competitor ● n. **1** a person who takes part in a sporting contest. **2** an organization competing with others in business.

compilation ● n. **1** the action of compiling. **2** a thing, especially a book or record, compiled from different sources.

compile ● v. (**compiles**, **compiling**, **compiled**) **1** produce (a book, report, etc.) by assembling material from other sources. **2** gather (material) to produce a book, report, etc.
– DERIVATIVES **compiler** n.
– ORIGIN Latin *compilare* 'plunder'.

complacent /kuhm-**play**-s'nt/ ● adj. uncritically satisfied with oneself; smug.
– DERIVATIVES **complacency** n.
– ORIGIN Latin *complacere* 'to please'.

complain ● v. **1** express dissatisfaction or annoyance. **2** (**complain of**) state that one is suffering from (a symptom of illness).
– ORIGIN Old French *complaindre*.

complainant ● n. Law a person who brings a case against another in certain lawsuits.

complaint ● n. **1** an act of complaining. **2** a reason for dissatisfaction. **3** the expression of dissatisfaction: *a letter of complaint*. **4** an illness or medical condition, especially a minor one.

complaisant /kuhm-**play**-z'nt/ ● adj. willing to please others or to accept their behaviour without protest.
– ORIGIN French.

complement ● n. /**kom**-pli-muhnt/ **1** a thing that contributes extra features to something else so as to improve it. **2** the number or quantity that makes something complete. **3** a word or words used with a verb to complete the meaning of the subject (e.g. *happy* in the sentence *we are happy*). ● v. /**kom**-pli-ment/ act as a complement to.
– ORIGIN Latin *complementum*.

> **USAGE complement**
>
> Do not confuse **complement** and **compliment**. As a verb, **complement** means 'add to in a way that improves' (as in *she selected a green sweater to complement her blonde hair*), while **compliment** means 'politely congratulate or praise' (as in *he complimented her on her appearance*).

complementary ● adj. **1** combining so as to form a complete whole or to improve each other. **2** having to do with complementary medicine.

complementary angle ● n. either of two angles whose sum is 90°.

complementary medicine ● n. medical therapy that is not part of scientific medicine but may be used alongside it, e.g. acupuncture.

complete ● adj. **1** having all the necessary parts; entire. **2** having run its course; finished. **3** to the greatest extent or degree; total. ● v. (**completes**, **completing**, **completed**) **1** finish making or doing. **2** provide with the items necessary to make (something) complete. **3** write the required information on (a form).
– ORIGIN Latin *complere*.

completely ● adv. totally; utterly.

completion ● n. the action of completing or the state of being completed.

complex ● adj. **1** consisting of many different and connected parts. **2** hard to understand; complicated. ● n. **1** a group of similar buildings or facilities on the same site. **2** an interlinked system; a network. **3** a group of repressed feelings which lead to abnormal mental states or behaviour.
– DERIVATIVES **complexity** n.
– ORIGIN Latin *complexus*.

complexion ● n. **1** the condition of the skin of a person's face. **2** the general character of something.
– ORIGIN Latin, 'combination'.

complex number ● n. Math. a number containing both a real and an imaginary part.

compliance /kuhm-**ply**-uhnss/ ● n. the action or fact of complying.

compliant ● adj. **1** tending to be excessively obedient or ready to accept something. **2** complying with rules.

complicate ● v. (**complicates**, **complicating**, **complicated**) make more intricate or confusing.
– ORIGIN Latin *complicare* 'fold together'.

complicated ● adj. **1** consisting of many connected elements; intricate. **2** involving many confusing aspects.

complication ● n. **1** a circumstance that complicates something; a difficulty. **2** an involved or confused state. **3** Med. a secondary disease or condition which makes an already existing one worse.

complicity ● n. involvement with others in an unlawful activity.
– DERIVATIVES **complicit** adj.
– ORIGIN Old French *complice* 'an associate'.

compliment ● n. /**kom**-pli-muhnt/ **1** an expression of praise or admiration. **2** (**compliments**) formal greetings. ● v. /**kom**-pli-ment/ politely congratulate or praise.
– PHRASES **with the compliments of some-**

C

one given without charge.
– ORIGIN Italian *complimento.*

> **USAGE** **compliment**
> For an explanation on the difference between **compliment** and **complement**, see the note at **COMPLEMENT**.

complimentary • adj. **1** praising or approving. **2** given free of charge.

comply /kuhm-**ply**/ • v. (**complies, complying, complied**) (often **comply with**) act in accordance with a wish, law, rule, or command.
– ORIGIN Latin *complere.*

component /kuhm-**poh**-nuhnt/ • n. a part of a larger whole. • adj. being part of a larger whole.
– ORIGIN Latin *componere* 'put together'.

comport /kuhm-**port**/ • v. (**comport oneself**) formal behave in a particular way.
– ORIGIN Latin *comportare.*

compose • v. (**composes, composing, composed**) **1** create (a work of art, especially music or poetry). **2** make up (a whole). **3** arrange in an orderly or artistic way. **4** (**composed**) calm and in control of one's feelings.
– ORIGIN Old French *composer.*

composer • n. a person who writes music.

composite /**kom**-puh-zit/ • adj. **1** made up of various parts. **2** /**kom**-puh-zyt/ (of a plant) having flower heads consisting of numerous small flowers. • n. a thing made up of several parts.
– ORIGIN Latin *componere* 'put together'.

composition • n. **1** the way in which something is made up from different elements: *the molecular composition of cells.* **2** a work of music, literature, or art. **3** a thing composed of various elements. **4** the action of composing. **5** the arrangement of the parts of a picture.

compos mentis /kom-poss **men**-tiss/ • adj. having full control of one's mind.
– ORIGIN Latin.

compost • n. decayed organic material used as a fertilizer.
– ORIGIN Latin *composita* 'something put together'.

composure • n. the state of being calm and self-controlled.

compound[1] • n. /**kom**-pownd/ **1** a thing composed of two or more separate elements. **2** a substance formed from two or more elements chemically united in fixed proportions. **3** a word made up of two or more existing words. • adj. /**kom**-pownd/ **1** made up or consisting of several parts. **2** (of interest) payable on both capital and the accumulated interest. Compare with **SIMPLE**. • v. /kuhm-**pownd**/ **1** make up (a whole). **2** make (something bad) worse.
– ORIGIN Latin *componere* 'put together'.

compound[2] /**kom**-pownd/ • n. a large open area enclosed by a fence.
– ORIGIN Malay.

compound fracture • n. an injury in which a broken bone pierces the skin.

comprehend /kom-pri-**hend**/ • v. grasp mentally; understand.
– ORIGIN Latin *comprehendere.*

comprehensible • adj. able to be understood.

comprehension • n. **1** the action of understanding. **2** the ability to understand: *mysteries beyond human comprehension.*

comprehensive • adj. **1** including or dealing with all or nearly all aspects of something. **2** Brit. (of a system of secondary education) in which children of all abilities are educated in one school. **3** (of motor-vehicle insurance) providing cover for most risks. **4** (of a victory or defeat) by a large margin. • n. Brit. a comprehensive school.

compress • v. /kuhm-**press**/ **1** force into a smaller space. **2** squeeze or press (two things) together. • n. /**kom**-press/ an absorbent pad pressed on to part of the body to relieve inflammation or stop bleeding.
– ORIGIN Old French *compresser.*

compressed air • n. air that is at more than atmospheric pressure.

compression • n. **1** the action of compressing or the state of being compressed. **2** the reduction in volume (causing an increase in pressure) of the fuel mixture in an internal-combustion engine before ignition.

compressor • n. **1** a device for compressing something. **2** a machine used to supply air at increased pressure.

comprise • v. (**comprises, comprising, comprised**) **1** be made up of. **2** (also **be comprised of**) make up.
– ORIGIN French, 'comprised'.

compromise • n. **1** an agreement reached by each side making concessions. **2** something that is halfway between different elements: *a compromise between greed and caution.* • v. (**compromises, compromising, compromised**) **1** settle a dispute by each side making concessions. **2** accept standards that are lower than is desirable for practical reasons. **3** bring into disrepute or danger by reckless behaviour.
– ORIGIN Old French *compromis.*

compromising • adj. revealing an embarrassing or incriminating secret.

> **Compton**, E
> Arthur Holly (1892–1962), American physicist, who showed that the wavelength of X-rays increased when scattered by electrons (the **Compton effect**).

> **Compton-Burnett** E
> /komp-tuhn ber-**net**, **ber**-nit/, Dame Ivy (1884–1969), English novelist, whose novels include *Brothers and Sisters.*

comptroller /kuhn-**troh**-ler, komp-**troh**-ler/ • n. a controller (used in the title of some financial officers).
– ORIGIN from **CONTROLLER**.

compulsion • n. **1** pressure forcing someone to do something. **2** an irresistible urge to do something.

compulsive • adj. **1** resulting from or acting on an irresistible urge. **2** irresistibly exciting.

compulsory • adj. required by law or a rule; obligatory.

compunction • n. a feeling of guilt that prevents or follows wrongdoing: *he felt no compunction in letting her worry.*
– ORIGIN Latin.

computation • n. **1** mathematical calculation. **2** the use of computers.

– DERIVATIVES **computational** adj.

compute • v. (**computes, computing, computed**) calculate (a figure or amount).
– ORIGIN Latin *computare*.

computer • n. an electronic device capable of storing and processing information in accordance with a set of instructions.

computerize (also **computerise**) • v. (**computerizes, computerizing, computerized**) convert to a system which is controlled, stored, or processed by computer.

computing • n. the use or operation of computers.

comrade • n. **1** (among men) a companion who shares one's activities or is a fellow member of an organization. **2** (also **comrade-in-arms**) a fellow soldier.
– DERIVATIVES **comradeship** n.
– ORIGIN Spanish *camarada* 'room-mate'.

Comte E
/comt/, Auguste (1798–1857), French philosopher, one of the founders of sociology.

con¹ informal • v. (**cons, conning, conned**) deceive (someone) into doing or believing something by lying. • n. a deception of this kind.
– ORIGIN from *confidence trick*.

con² • n. (in plur. **pros and cons**) a disadvantage of or argument against something.
– ORIGIN Latin *contra* 'against'.

con- • prefix var. of **COM-**.

Conakry E
/kon-uh-kri/ the capital of Guinea.

Conan Doyle E
/koh-nuhn **doyl**/ see **DOYLE**.

concatenation /kon-ka-ti-nay-sh'n/ • n. a series of interconnected things.
– ORIGIN Latin *concatenare* 'link together'.

concave /kon-kayv/ • adj. having an outline or surface that curves inwards. Compare with **CONVEX**.
– ORIGIN Latin *concavus*.

conceal • v. prevent from being seen or known.
– DERIVATIVES **concealment** n.
– ORIGIN Latin *concelare*.

concede • v. (**concedes, conceding, conceded**) **1** finally admit that something is true. **2** give up (a possession, advantage, or right). **3** admit defeat in (a match or contest). **4** fail to prevent an opponent scoring (a goal or point).
– ORIGIN Latin *concedere*.

conceit • n. **1** excessive pride in oneself. **2** an artistic effect. **3** a complicated metaphor.
– ORIGIN from **CONCEIVE**.

conceited • adj. excessively proud of oneself.

conceivable • adj. capable of being imagined or understood.
– DERIVATIVES **conceivably** adv.

conceive • v. (**conceives, conceiving, conceived**) **1** become pregnant with (a child). **2** imagine.
– ORIGIN Latin *concipere*.

concentrate • v. (**concentrates, concentrating, concentrated**) **1** focus all one's attention on something. **2** gather together in numbers or a mass at one point. **3** focus on: *concentrate your energy on breathing*. **4** increase the strength of (a solution). • n. a concentrated substance or solution.
– ORIGIN from Latin *con-* 'together' + *centrum* 'centre'.

concentration • n. **1** the action or power of concentrating. **2** a close gathering of people or things. **3** the amount of a particular substance within a solution or mixture.

concentration camp • n. a camp for holding political prisoners.

concentric • adj. (of circles or arcs) sharing the same centre.
– ORIGIN Latin *concentricus*.

concept • n. an abstract idea.
– ORIGIN Latin *conceptum*.

conception • n. **1** the action of conceiving a child or of one being conceived. **2** the forming of a plan or idea. **3** a concept. **4** ability to imagine or understand.

conceptual • adj. having to do with mental concepts.

conceptualize (also **conceptualise**) • v. (**conceptualizes, conceptualizing, conceptualized**) form a concept of.

concern • v. **1** relate to; be about. **2** affect or involve: *many thanks to all concerned*. **3** make anxious or worried. • n. **1** worry; anxiety. **2** a matter of interest or importance. **3** a business.
– ORIGIN Latin *concernere*.

concerned • adj. worried or anxious.

concerning • prep. about.

concert /kon-sert/ • n. a musical performance given in public.
– PHRASES **in concert** acting jointly.
– ORIGIN Italian *concerto*.

concerted /kuhn-ser-tid/ • adj. **1** jointly arranged or carried out: *a concerted campaign*. **2** determined: *a concerted effort*.

concertina /kon-ser-tee-nuh/ • n. a small musical instrument with bellows, the notes being sounded by buttons. • v. (**concertinas, concertinaing, concertinaed**) compress in folds like those of a concertina.

concerto /kuhn-cher-toh/ • n. (pl. **concertos** or **concerti** /kuhn-cher-ti/) a musical composition for an orchestra and one or more solo instruments.
– ORIGIN Italian.

concession • n. **1** a thing given up or allowed to settle a dispute. **2** a reduction in price for a certain kind of person. **3** the right to use land or other property for a particular purpose, granted by a government. **4** a commercial operation set up within a larger business.
– DERIVATIVES **concessionary** adj.
– ORIGIN Latin.

conch /konch/ • n. (pl. **conchs** or **conches** /kon-chiz/) a mollusc of tropical seas, with a spiral shell.
– ORIGIN Greek *konkhē*.

concierge /kon-si-airzh/ • n. **1** (especially in France) a resident caretaker of a block of flats or small hotel. **2** a hotel employee who makes entertainment bookings for guests.
– ORIGIN French.

conciliate /kuhn-sil-i-ayt/ • v. (**conciliates, conciliating, conciliated**) **1** make calm and content. **2** mediate in a dispute.
– DERIVATIVES **conciliation** n. **conciliator** n. **conciliatory** adj.

C

– ORIGIN Latin *conciliare* 'combine'.

concise ● adj. giving a lot of information clearly and in few words.
– DERIVATIVES **concisely** adv. **concision** n.
– ORIGIN Latin *concisus* 'cut up'.

conclave /kong-klayv/ ● n. **1** a private meeting. **2** (in the Roman Catholic Church) the assembly of cardinals for the election of a pope.
– ORIGIN Latin, 'lockable room'.

conclude ● v. (**concludes**, **concluding**, **concluded**) **1** bring or come to an end. **2** arrive at an opinion by reasoning. **3** formally settle or arrange (an agreement).
– ORIGIN Latin *concludere*.

conclusion ● n. **1** an end or finish. **2** the summing-up of an argument or text. **3** a decision reached by reasoning.

conclusive ● adj. decisive or convincing.
– DERIVATIVES **conclusively** adv.

concoct /kuhn-kokt/ ● v. **1** make (a dish or meal) by combining ingredients. **2** invent (a story or plan).
– DERIVATIVES **concoction** n.
– ORIGIN Latin *concoquere*.

concomitant /kuhn-kom-i-tuhnt/ formal ● adj. naturally accompanying or associated. ● n. a concomitant thing.
– ORIGIN Latin *concomitari*.

concord ● n. agreement; harmony.
– ORIGIN Latin *concordia*.

concordance /kuhn-kor-duhnss/ ● n. an alphabetical list of the important words in a text.

concordat /kuhn-kor-dat/ ● n. an agreement between the Roman Catholic Church and a state.

concourse ● n. a large open area inside or in front of a public building.
– ORIGIN Latin *concursus*.

concrete ● adj. **1** existing in a physical form; not abstract. **2** definite: *concrete proof.* ● n. a building material made from gravel, sand, cement, and water, forming a stone-like mass when dry. ● v. (**concretes**, **concreting**, **concreted**) cover with concrete.
– ORIGIN Latin *concretus* 'grown together'.

concretion ● n. a hard solid mass.

concubine /kong-kyuu-byn/ ● n. esp. hist. (in societies in which a man may have more than one wife) a woman who lives with a man but has lower status than his wife or wives.
– ORIGIN Latin *concubina*.

concur /kuhn-ker/ ● v. (**concurs**, **concurring**, **concurred**) **1** (often **concur with**) agree. **2** happen at the same time.
– ORIGIN Latin *concurrere*.

concurrent ● adj. existing or happening at the same time.
– DERIVATIVES **concurrence** n. **concurrently** adv.

concussion ● n. **1** temporary unconsciousness or confusion caused by a blow on the head. **2** a violent shock as from a heavy blow.
– DERIVATIVES **concussed** adj.
– ORIGIN Latin.

condemn ● v. **1** express complete disapproval of. **2** (usu. **condemn to**) sentence to a punishment. **3** force (someone) to endure something unpleasant. **4** officially declare to be unfit for use.
– DERIVATIVES **condemnation** n. **condemnatory** adj.
– ORIGIN Latin *condemnare*.

condensation ● n. **1** water from humid air collecting as droplets on a cold surface. **2** the conversion of a vapour or gas to a liquid.

condense ● v. (**condenses**, **condensing**, **condensed**) **1** make more concentrated. **2** change from a gas or vapour to a liquid. **3** express (a piece of writing or speech) in fewer words.
– ORIGIN Latin *condensare*.

condensed milk ● n. milk that has been thickened by evaporation and sweetened.

condescend ● v. **1** behave as if one is better than other people. **2** do something that one believes to be below one's dignity: *he condescended to see me at my hotel.*
– DERIVATIVES **condescension** n.
– ORIGIN Latin *condescendere*.

condescending ● adj. behaving as if one is better than other people.

condiment ● n. a seasoning or relish for food, such as salt or mustard.
– ORIGIN Latin *condimentum*.

condition ● n. **1** the state of something or someone, with regard to appearance, fitness, or working order. **2** (**conditions**) circumstances affecting something. **3** a state of affairs that must exist before something else is possible: *for a country to borrow money, three conditions must be met.* **4** an illness or medical problem. ● v. **1** influence. **2** bring into a good or desirable state or condition. **3** train to become used to something or to behave in a certain way: *the child is conditioned to dislike food.*
– PHRASES **in** (or **out of**) **condition** in a fit (or unfit) physical state.
– ORIGIN Latin *condicion* 'agreement'.

conditional ● adj. **1** subject to one or more conditions. **2** (of a clause, phrase, conjunction, or verb form) expressing a condition. ● n. the conditional form of a verb (e.g. *should* in *if I should die*).
– DERIVATIVES **conditionally** adv.

conditioner ● n. a thing used to improve the condition of something.

condo ● n. (pl. **condos**) N. Amer. informal = **CONDOMINIUM** (in sense 2).

condole /kuhn-dohl/ ● v. (**condoles**, **condoling**, **condoled**) (**condole with**) express sympathy for.
– ORIGIN Latin *condolere*.

condolence ● n. an expression of sympathy.

condom ● n. a rubber sheath worn on the penis during sexual intercourse as a contraceptive or to protect against infection.
– ORIGIN unknown.

condominium /kon-duh-min-i-uhm/ ● n. (pl. **condominiums**) **1** the joint control of a state's affairs by other states. **2** N. Amer. a building containing a number of individually owned flats.
– ORIGIN Latin.

condone /kuhn-dohn/ ● v. (**condones**, **condoning**, **condoned**) accept or forgive (an offence or wrongdoing).
– ORIGIN Latin *condonare* 'refrain from punishing'.

condor ● n. a very large South American vulture with a bare head and black plumage.

– ORIGIN Spanish.

conducive ● adj. (**conducive to**) contributing or helping towards.

conduct ● n. /**kon**-dukt/ **1** the way in which a person behaves. **2** management or direction: *the conduct of foreign affairs.* ● v. /kuhn-**dukt**/ **1** organize and carry out. **2** direct the performance of (an orchestra or choir). **3** guide to or around a place. **4** (**conduct oneself**) behave in a particular way. **5** transmit (heat, electricity, etc.) by conduction.
– ORIGIN Latin *conducere* 'bring together'.

conductance ● n. the degree to which a material conducts electricity.

conduction ● n. the transmission of heat or electricity directly through a substance.

conductivity ● n. the degree to which a particular material conducts electricity or heat.

conductor ● n. **1** a person who conducts an orchestra or choir. **2** a material or device that conducts heat or electricity. **3** a person who collects fares on a bus.

conduit /**kon**-dit, **kon**-dyuu-it/ ● n. **1** a channel for carrying fluid from one place to another. **2** a tube or trough protecting electric wiring.
– ORIGIN Old French.

cone ● n. **1** an object which tapers from a circular base to a point. **2** (also **traffic cone**) a plastic cone used to separate off sections of a road. **3** the dry fruit of a conifer. **4** a type of light-sensitive cell in the eye, responsible for sharpness of vision and colour perception. Compare with ROD.
– ORIGIN Greek *konos*.

coney /**koh**-ni/ ● n. (pl. **coneys**) Brit. a rabbit.
– ORIGIN Old French *conin*.

confab ● n. informal an informal conversation.

confabulate /kuhn-**fab**-yuu-layt/ ● v. (**confabulates, confabulating, confabulated**) formal have a conversation.
– DERIVATIVES **confabulation** n.
– ORIGIN Latin *confabulari*.

confection ● n. **1** an elaborate sweet dish or delicacy. **2** an elaborately constructed thing.
– ORIGIN Latin, 'making'.

confectioner ● n. a person who makes or sells confectionery.

confectionery ● n. sweets and chocolates.

confederacy ● n. (pl. **confederacies**) an alliance, especially of confederate states.

confederate ● adj. /kuhn-**fed**-uh-ruht/ **1** joined by an agreement or treaty. **2** (**Confederate**) having to do with the southern states which separated from the US in 1860–1. ● n. /kuhn-**fed**-uh-ruht/ an accomplice. ● v. /kuhn-**fed**-uh-rayt/ (**confederates, confederating, confederated**) bring into an alliance.
– ORIGIN Latin *confoederatus*.

confederation ● n. **1** an alliance of a number of groups. **2** a union of states with some political power belonging to a central authority.

confer /kuhn-**fer**/ ● v. (**confers, conferring, conferred**) **1** grant (a title, degree, or right). **2** have discussions.
– ORIGIN Latin *conferre* 'bring together'.

conference ● n. a formal meeting for discussion or debate.

confess ● v. **1** admit to a crime or wrongdoing. **2** acknowledge reluctantly. **3** declare one's sins formally to a priest.
– ORIGIN Old French *confesser*.

confession ● n. **1** an act of confessing, especially a statement admitting to a crime. **2** an account of one's sins given privately to a priest.

confessional ● n. **1** an enclosed stall in a church, in which a priest sits to hear confessions. **2** a confession.

confessor ● n. a priest who hears confessions.

confetti ● n. small pieces of coloured paper traditionally thrown over a bride and groom after a marriage ceremony.
– ORIGIN Italian, 'sweets'.

confidant /**kon**-fi-dant/ ● n. (fem. **confidante** /**kon**-fi-dant/) a person in whom one confides.

confide /kuhn-**fyd**/ ● v. (**confides, confiding, confided**) tell someone about a secret or private matter in confidence.
– ORIGIN Latin *confidere*.

confidence ● n. **1** faith in someone or something. **2** self-assurance arising from a belief in one's own ability to achieve things. **3** a feeling of trust that someone will keep secret information private.
– PHRASES **in someone's confidence** in a position of trust with someone.

confidence trick ● n. an act of cheating someone by gaining their trust.

confident ● adj. **1** feeling confidence in oneself. **2** feeling certainty about something.
– DERIVATIVES **confidently** adv.

confidential ● adj. intended to be kept secret.
– DERIVATIVES **confidentiality** n. **confidentially** adv.

configuration /kuhn-fi-guh-**ray**-sh'n/ ● n. an arrangement of parts in a particular form or figure.

configure ● v. (**configures, configuring, configured**) **1** arrange in a particular way. **2** arrange (a computer system) so as to fit it for a particular task.
– ORIGIN Latin *configurare*.

confine ● v. /kuhn-**fyn**/ (**confines, confining, confined**) **1** (**confine to**) restrict (someone or something) within certain limits of (space, scope, or time). **2** (**be confined to**) be unable to leave (one's bed, home, etc.) due to illness or disability. **3** (**be confined**) dated (of a woman) remain in bed for a period before, during, and after giving birth. ● n. /**kon**-fynz/ (**confines**) boundaries.
– DERIVATIVES **confinement** n.
– ORIGIN Latin *confinis*.

confined ● adj. (of a space) small and enclosed.

confirm ● v. **1** establish the truth or correctness of. **2** state with assurance that something is true. **3** make definite or valid. **4** (**confirm in**) reinforce (someone) in (an opinion or feeling). **5** (usu. **be confirmed**) administer the religious rite of confirmation to.
– ORIGIN Latin *confirmare*.

confirmation ● n. **1** the action of confirming. **2** the rite at which a baptized person is admitted as a full member of the Christian Church.

confirmed ● adj. firmly established in a habit

or way of life: *a confirmed bachelor.*

confiscate /kon-fi-skayt/ ● v. (**confiscates**, **confiscating**, **confiscated**) take or seize (property) with authority.
– DERIVATIVES **confiscation** n.
– ORIGIN Latin *confiscare* 'put in a chest'.

C

conflagration /kon-fluh-gray-sh'n/ ● n. a large and destructive fire.
– ORIGIN Latin.

conflate ● v. (**conflates**, **conflating**, **conflated**) combine into one.
– ORIGIN Latin *conflare* 'kindle, fuse'.

conflict ● n. /kon-flikt/ **1** a serious disagreement. **2** a long-lasting armed struggle. **3** a lack of agreement between opinions, principles, etc.: *a conflict of interests.* ● v. /kuhn-flikt/ be different or in opposition.
– ORIGIN Latin *conflictus.*

confluence /kon-floo-uhnss/ ● n. the junction of two rivers.
– ORIGIN Latin *confluere.*

conform ● v. **1** comply with rules or standards. **2** be similar in form or type.
– ORIGIN Latin *conformare.*

conformation ● n. the shape or structure of something.

conformist ● n. a person who conforms to accepted behaviour or established practices. ● adj. conventional.

conformity ● n. compliance with conventions, rules, or laws.

confound ● v. **1** surprise or bewilder. **2** prove wrong. **3** defeat (a plan).
– ORIGIN Latin *confundere* 'mix up'.

confounded ● adj. informal, dated used to express annoyance.

confraternity ● n. (pl. **confraternities**) an association with a religious or charitable purpose.
– ORIGIN Latin *confraternitas.*

confront ● v. **1** meet face to face in hostility or defiance. **2** (of a problem) present itself to. **3** face up to and deal with (a problem). **4** force to face something.
– ORIGIN Latin *confrontare.*

confrontation /kon-fruhn-tay-sh'n/ ● n. a situation of angry disagreement or opposition.
– DERIVATIVES **confrontational** adj.

Confucius E
/kuhn-fyoo-shuhss/ (551–479 BC), Chinese philosopher. His ideas about the importance of practical moral values formed the basis of the philosophy of Confucianism.

confuse ● v. (**confuses**, **confusing**, **confused**) **1** make bewildered or perplexed. **2** make less easy to understand. **3** mistake (one for another).
– ORIGIN Latin *confusus.*

confused ● adj. **1** bewildered. **2** lacking order and so difficult to understand.

confusion ● n. **1** the state of being confused. **2** a situation of panic or disorder. **3** the mistaking of one person or thing for another.

confute ● v. (**confutes**, **confuting**, **confuted**) formal prove to be wrong.
– ORIGIN Latin *confutare.*

conga /kong-guh/ ● n. a dance performed by people in single file.
– ORIGIN Spanish.

congeal /kuhn-jeel/ ● v. become semi-solid, especially on cooling.
– ORIGIN Latin *congelare.*

congenial /kuhn-jee-ni-uhl/ ● adj. **1** pleasant because of qualities or interests similar to one's own: *congenial company.* **2** suited to one's taste.

congenital /kuhn-jen-i-t'l/ ● adj. **1** (of a disease or abnormality) present from birth. **2** having a trait as part of one's character.
– ORIGIN Latin *congenitus.*

conger /kong-ger/ (also **conger eel**) ● n. a large eel of coastal waters.
– ORIGIN Greek *gongros.*

congested ● adj. **1** so crowded as to make freedom of movement difficult or impossible. **2** abnormally full of blood. **3** blocked with mucus.
– DERIVATIVES **congestion** n.
– ORIGIN Latin *congerere* 'heap up'.

conglomerate ● n. /kuhn-glom-muh-ruht/ **1** something consisting of a number of different and distinct things. **2** a large corporation formed by the merging of separate firms.
– DERIVATIVES **conglomeration** n.
– ORIGIN Latin *conglomerare.*

Congo[1] E
/kong-goh/ a major river of central Africa, which rises in northern Zaire (Democratic Republic of Congo) and forms the border with the Congo before flowing into the Atlantic. Also called **Zaire River**.

Congo[2] E
/kong-goh/ (also **the Congo**) an equatorial country on the west coast of Africa; capital, Brazzaville.
– DERIVATIVES **Congolese** adj. & n.

Congo, Democratic Republic of E
official name (since 1997) for **Zaire**.

congratulate ● v. (**congratulates**, **congratulating**, **congratulated**) **1** express good wishes or praise at the happiness or success of. **2** (**congratulate oneself**) think oneself lucky or clever.
– DERIVATIVES **congratulatory** adj.
– ORIGIN Latin *congratulari.*

congratulation ● n. **1** (**congratulations**) praise or good wishes on a special occasion. **2** the action of congratulating.

congregate ● v. (**congregates**, **congregating**, **congregated**) gather into a crowd or mass.
– ORIGIN Latin *congregare.*

congregation ● n. **1** a group of people gathered for religious worship. **2** a gathering of people or things.

congress ● n. **1** a formal meeting or series of meetings between delegates. **2** (**Congress**) a national law-making body.
– DERIVATIVES **congressional** adj.
– ORIGIN Latin *congressus.*

congressman (or **congresswoman**) ● n. a male (or female) member of the US Congress.

Congreve E
/kong-greev/, William (1670–1729), English dramatist, known for such comedies as *The Way of the World.*

congruent /kong-groo-uhnt/ ● adj. **1** in agreement or harmony. **2** Geom. (of figures)

identical in form.
– DERIVATIVES **congruence** n.
– ORIGIN Latin *congruere* 'agree'.

conic /kon-ik/ • adj. of a cone.

conical • adj. shaped like a cone.

conic section • n. the figure of a circle, ellipse, parabola, or hyperbola formed by the intersection of a plane and a circular cone.

conifer /kon-i-fer/ • n. a tree bearing cones and evergreen needle-like or scale-like leaves.
– DERIVATIVES **coniferous** adj.
– ORIGIN Latin, 'cone-bearing'.

conjecture /kuhn-**jek**-cher/ • n. an opinion based on incomplete information; a guess. • v. (**conjectures**, **conjecturing**, **conjectured**) guess.
– DERIVATIVES **conjectural** adj.
– ORIGIN Latin *conjectura*.

conjoin • v. formal join; combine.

conjugal /kon-juu-g'l/ • adj. relating to marriage or the relationship between husband and wife.
– ORIGIN Latin *conjugalis*.

conjugate /kon-juu-gayt/ • v. (**conjugates**, **conjugating**, **conjugated**) give the different forms of (a verb).
– DERIVATIVES **conjugation** n.
– ORIGIN Latin *conjugare* 'yoke together'.

conjunction • n. **1** a word used to connect words or clauses (e.g. *and*, *if*). **2** an instance of two or more events occurring together.

USAGE conjunction

A **conjunction** is used to connect words or clauses of a sentence together, as in the sentence *it was Monday morning and I was in bed.* Some people believe that it is wrong to start a sentence with a conjunction such as **and**, **because**, or **but**, but it is possible to do this as a way of creating a particular effect, for example: *What are the government's chances of winning in court? And what are the consequences?*

conjunctiva /kon-jungk-ty-vuh/ • n. the mucous membrane that covers the front of the eye and lines the inside of the eyelids.
– ORIGIN from Latin *membrana conjunctiva* 'linking membrane'.

conjunctivitis /kuhn-jungk-ti-vy-tiss/ • n. inflammation of the conjunctiva.

conjure /kun-jer/ • v. (**conjures**, **conjuring**, **conjured**) (usu. **conjure up**) **1** cause to appear as if by magic. **2** call to the mind. **3** call upon (a spirit) to appear by magic.
– ORIGIN Latin *conjurare* 'conspire'.

conjuring • n. the performance of seemingly magical tricks.

conjuror (also **conjurer**) • n. a performer of conjuring tricks.

conk[1] • v. (**conk out**) informal (of a machine) break down.
– ORIGIN unknown.

conk[2] • n. Brit. informal a person's nose.
– ORIGIN perh. from CONCH.

conker • n. Brit. **1** the dark brown nut of a horse chestnut tree. **2** (**conkers**) a children's game in which each has a conker on a string and tries to break another's with it.
– ORIGIN dialect, 'snail shell' (with which the game was originally played).

con man • n. informal a man who cheats others using confidence tricks.

Connacht E
/kon-nawt/ (also **Connaught**) a province in the south-west of the Republic of Ireland.

connect • v. **1** bring together so as to establish a link. **2** join together so as to provide access and communication. **3** (**be connected**) be related in some way. **4** (of a train, bus, etc.) arrive at its destination just before another leaves so that passengers can transfer.
– DERIVATIVES **connector** n.
– ORIGIN Latin *connectere*.

Connecticut E
/kuh-**net**-i-kuht/ a state in the north-eastern US, on the Atlantic coast; capital, Hartford.

connection (Brit. also **connexion**) • n. **1** a link or relationship. **2** the action of connecting. **3** (**connections**) influential people with whom one has contact or to whom one is related.
– PHRASES **in connection with** concerning.

connective • adj. connecting.

connective tissue • n. bodily tissue that connects, supports, binds, or separates other tissues or organs.

Connemara E
/kon-ni-**mah**-ruh/ a mountainous coastal region of Galway, in the west of the Republic of Ireland.

Connery, E
Sir Sean (b.1930; born *Thomas Connery*), Scottish film actor, best known for his portrayal of James Bond.

conning tower • n. a raised structure on a submarine, containing the periscope.

connive /kuh-nyv/ • v. (**connives**, **conniving**, **connived**) **1** (**connive at/in**) secretly allow (a wrongdoing). **2** (often **connive with**) conspire.
– DERIVATIVES **connivance** n.
– ORIGIN Latin *connivere* 'shut the eyes (to)'.

connoisseur /kon-nuh-ser/ • n. an expert judge in matters of taste.
– ORIGIN French.

Connors, E
Jimmy (b.1952; full name *James Scott Connors*), American tennis player. He won Wimbledon in 1974 and 1982 and the US Open championship five times.

connotation /kon-nuh-tay-sh'n/ • n. an idea or feeling suggested by a word in addition to its primary meaning.

connote /kuh-noht/ • v. (**connotes**, **connoting**, **connoted**) (of a word) suggest in addition to its primary meaning.
– ORIGIN Latin *connotare*.

connubial /kuh-nyoo-bi-uhl/ • adj. literary conjugal.
– ORIGIN Latin *connubialis*.

conquer • v. (**conquers**, **conquering**, **conquered**) **1** overcome and take control of by military force. **2** successfully overcome (a problem) or climb (a mountain).
– DERIVATIVES **conqueror** n.
– ORIGIN Latin *conquirere*.

conquest • n. **1** the action of conquering. **2** a conquered territory. **3** a person whose affection has been won.

conquistador /kon-kwiss-tuh-dor/ • n. (pl.

conquistadores /kon-kwiss-tuh-**dor**-ayz/ or **conquistadors**) a Spanish conqueror of Mexico or Peru in the 16th century.
– ORIGIN Spanish.

Conrad, Joseph (1857–1924), Polish-born British novelist. Much of his work, including his story *Heart of Darkness* and the novel *Nostromo*, explores the darker side of human nature.

consanguinity /kon-sang-**gwin**-i-ti/ ● **n.** descent from the same ancestor.
– DERIVATIVES **consanguineous** adj.
– ORIGIN Latin *consanguineus* 'of the same blood'.

conscience ● **n.** a person's moral sense of right and wrong.
– ORIGIN Latin *conscientia*.

conscientious /kon-shi-en-shuhss/ ● **adj.** **1** careful and thorough in carrying out one's work or duty. **2** relating to a person's conscience.

conscientious objector ● **n.** a person who refuses to serve in the armed forces for reasons of conscience.

conscious ● **adj.** **1** aware of and responding to one's surroundings. **2** (usu. **conscious of**) aware. **3** deliberate.
– DERIVATIVES **consciously** adv.
– ORIGIN Latin *conscius*.

consciousness ● **n.** **1** the state of being conscious. **2** one's awareness of something.

conscript ● **v.** /kuhn-**skript**/ call up for compulsory military service. ● **n.** /**kon**-skript/ a conscripted person.
– DERIVATIVES **conscription** n.
– ORIGIN Latin *conscriptus*.

consecrate /kon-si-krayt/ ● **v.** (**consecrates**, **consecrating**, **consecrated**) **1** make or declare sacred. **2** ordain (a priest). **3** (in Christian belief) make (bread or wine) into the body and blood of Christ.
– DERIVATIVES **consecration** n.
– ORIGIN Latin *consecrare*.

consecutive /kuhn-**sek**-yuu-tiv/ ● **adj.** following in unbroken sequence.
– DERIVATIVES **consecutively** adv.
– ORIGIN Latin *consecutivus*.

consensual /kuhn-**sen**-syoo-uhl/ ● **adj.** relating to or involving consent.

consensus /kuhn-**sen**-suhss/ ● **n.** general agreement.
– ORIGIN Latin, 'agreement'.

consent ● **n.** permission or agreement. ● **v.** **1** give permission. **2** agree to do.
– ORIGIN Latin *consentire*.

consequence ● **n.** **1** a result or effect. **2** importance or relevance: *the past is of no consequence*.
– ORIGIN Latin *consequentia*.

consequent ● **adj.** following as a consequence.
– DERIVATIVES **consequential** adj. **consequently** adv.

conservancy /kuhn-**ser**-vuhn-si/ ● **n.** (pl. **conservancies**) an organization concerned with the preservation of natural resources.

conservation ● **n.** **1** preservation or restoration of the natural environment. **2** preservation and repair of archaeological and historical sites and objects. **3** careful use of a resource.
– DERIVATIVES **conservationist** n.

conservative ● **adj.** **1** opposed to change and holding traditional values. **2** (in politics) favouring free enterprise and private ownership. **3** (**Conservative**) relating to a Conservative Party. **4** (of an estimate) purposely low for the sake of caution. ● **n.** **1** a conservative person. **2** (**Conservative**) a supporter or member of a Conservative Party.
– DERIVATIVES **conservatism** n.

conservatoire /kuhn-**ser**-vuh-twar/ ● **n.** a college for the study of classical music.
– ORIGIN French.

conservatory ● **n.** (pl. **conservatories**) Brit. a room with a glass roof and walls, attached to a house.

conserve /kuhn-**serv**/ ● **v.** (**conserves**, **conserving**, **conserved**) protect from harm or overuse. ● **n.** /also **kon**-serv/ fruit jam.
– ORIGIN Latin *conservare*.

consider ● **v.** (**considers**, **considering**, **considers**) **1** think carefully about. **2** believe or think. **3** take into account when making a judgement.
– ORIGIN Latin *considerare*.

considerable ● **adj.** great in size, amount, or importance.
– DERIVATIVES **considerably** adv.

considerate ● **adj.** careful not to harm or inconvenience others.

consideration ● **n.** **1** careful thought. **2** a fact taken into account when making a decision. **3** thoughtfulness towards others. **4** a payment or reward.

considering ● **prep.** & **conj.** taking into consideration.

consign /kuhn-**syn**/ ● **v.** **1** deliver to someone's possession or care. **2** send (goods) by a public carrier. **3** (**consign to**) put (someone or something) in (a place) so as to be rid of them.
– ORIGIN Latin *consignare* 'mark with a seal'.

consignment ● **n.** a batch of goods consigned.

consist ● **v.** **1** (**consist of**) be composed of. **2** (**consist in**) have as an essential feature.
– ORIGIN Latin *consistere* 'stand firm'.

consistency ● **n.** (pl. **consistencies**) **1** the state of being consistent. **2** the degree of thickness of a substance.

consistent ● **adj.** **1** conforming to a regular pattern; unchanging. **2** (usu. **consistent with**) in agreement.
– DERIVATIVES **consistently** adv.

consolation /kon-suh-**lay**-sh'n/ ● **n.** **1** comfort received after a loss or disappointment. **2** a source of such comfort.

consolation prize ● **n.** a prize given to a competitor who just fails to win.

console[1] /kuhn-**sohl**/ ● **v.** (**consoles**, **consoling**, **consoled**) comfort in a time of grief or disappointment.
– ORIGIN Latin *consolari*.

console[2] /**kon**-sohl/ ● **n.** **1** a panel or unit containing a set of controls. **2** (also **games console**) a small machine for playing computerized video games.
– ORIGIN French.

consolidate /kuhn-**sol**-i-dayt/ ● **v.** (**consolidates**, **consolidating**, **consolidated**) **1** make stronger or more solid. **2** combine into a single unit.

– DERIVATIVES **consolidation** n.
– ORIGIN Latin *consolidare.*

consommé /kuhn-**som**-may/ ● n. a clear soup made with concentrated stock.
– ORIGIN French.

consonance /**kon**-suh-nuhnss/ ● n. agreement or compatibility.

consonant /**kon**-suh-nuhnt/ ● n. **1** a speech sound in which the breath is partly or completely obstructed. **2** a letter representing such a sound (e.g. *c, t*).
– ORIGIN Latin *consonare* 'sound together'.

consort ● n. /**kon**-sort/ a wife, husband, or companion. ● v. /kuhn-**sort**/ (**consort with**) habitually associate with.
– ORIGIN Latin *consors* 'sharing'.

consortium /kuhn-**sor**-ti-uhm/ ● n. (pl. **consortia** /kuhn-**sor**-ti-uh/ or **consortiums**) an association of several companies.
– ORIGIN Latin, 'partnership'.

conspicuous /kuhn-**spik**-yoo-uhss/ ● adj. **1** clearly visible. **2** attracting notice: *conspicuous bravery.*
– DERIVATIVES **conspicuously** adv.
– ORIGIN Latin *conspicuus.*

conspiracy ● n. (pl. **conspiracies**) **1** a secret plan by a group to do something unlawful or harmful. **2** the action of conspiring.

conspire ● v. (**conspires**, **conspiring**, **conspired**) **1** jointly make secret plans to commit a wrongful act. **2** (of circumstances) seem to be acting together in bringing about an unfortunate result.
– DERIVATIVES **conspirator** n. **conspiratorial** adj.
– ORIGIN Latin *conspirare.*

Constable, E
John (1776–1837), English painter. His best-known works include *Flatford Mill* and *The Hay Wain*, inspired by the landscape of his native Suffolk.

constable ● n. Brit. a police officer of the lowest rank.
– ORIGIN Old French *conestable* 'chief court officer'.

constabulary /kuhn-**stab**-yuu-luh-ri/ ● n. (pl. **constabularies**) esp. Brit. a police force.

constant ● adj. **1** occurring continuously. **2** remaining the same. **3** faithful and dependable. ● n. **1** an unchanging situation. **2** Math. & Physics a number or quantity that does not change its value.
– DERIVATIVES **constancy** n. **constantly** adv.
– ORIGIN Old French.

Constantine E
/**kon**-stuhn-tyn/ (*c.*274–337; known as **Constantine the Great**), Roman emperor, the first to become a Christian. In 330 he moved his capital from Rome to Byzantium, renaming it Constantinople.

Constantinople E
/kon-stan-ti-**noh**-p'l/ the former name for Istanbul from AD 330 to the capture of the city by the Turks in 1453.

constellation ● n. a group of stars forming a recognized pattern.
– ORIGIN Latin.

consternation ● n. anxiety or dismay.
– ORIGIN Latin.

constipate ● v. (**be constipated**) be affected with constipation.
– ORIGIN Latin *constipare* 'to crowd'.

constipation ● n. difficulty in emptying the bowels.

constituency /kuhn-**stit**-yoo-uhn-si/ ● n. (pl. **constituencies**) **1** a body of voters in an area who elect a representative to a law-making body. **2** esp. Brit. the area represented in this way.

constituent ● adj. being a part of a whole. ● n. **1** a voter in a constituency. **2** a component part.

constitute /**kon**-sti-tyoot/ ● v. (**constitutes**, **constituting**, **constituted**) **1** be (a part) of a whole. **2** be or be equivalent to. **3** (**be constituted**) be established by law.
– ORIGIN Latin *constituere.*

constitution ● n. **1** a body of principles according to which a state or organization is governed. **2** composition or formation. **3** a person's physical or mental state.

constitutional ● adj. **1** relating to or in accordance with a constitution. **2** relating to a person's physical or mental state. ● n. dated a walk taken regularly to maintain good health.
– DERIVATIVES **constitutionally** adv.

constrain ● v. **1** force to do something. **2** (**constrained**) appearing forced or unnatural. **3** severely restrict the scope or activity of.
– ORIGIN Old French *constraindre.*

constraint ● n. **1** a limitation or restriction. **2** strict control of one's behaviour.

constrict ● v. **1** make or become narrower or tighter. **2** deprive of freedom of movement.
– DERIVATIVES **constriction** n.
– ORIGIN Latin *constringere.*

constrictor ● n. a snake that kills by squeezing and choking its prey.

construct ● v. /kuhn-**strukt**/ build or erect. ● n. /**kon**-strukt/ **1** an idea or theory containing various elements. **2** a thing constructed.
– ORIGIN Latin *construere.*

construction ● n. **1** the action or process of constructing. **2** a building or other structure. **3** the industry of erecting buildings. **4** an interpretation.

constructive ● adj. serving a useful purpose.

construe ● v. (**be construed**) be interpreted in a particular way.
– ORIGIN Latin *construere* 'build'.

consul /**kon**-s'l/ ● n. **1** a state official living in a foreign city and protecting the state's citizens and interests there. **2** (in ancient Rome) one of two elected magistrates who ruled for a year.
– DERIVATIVES **consular** /**kon**-syuu-ler/ adj.
– ORIGIN Latin.

consulate ● n. the place where a consul works.

consult ● v. **1** seek information or advice from. **2** seek permission or approval from.
– DERIVATIVES **consultation** n. **consultative** adj.
– ORIGIN Latin *consultare.*

consultancy ● n. (pl. **consultancies**) a professional practice giving expert advice in a particular field.

consultant ● n. **1** a person who provides expert advice professionally. **2** Brit. a hospital doctor of senior rank.

consume • v. (**consumes**, **consuming**, **consumed**) **1** eat or drink. **2** use up. **3** (especially of a fire) completely destroy. **4** (of a feeling) absorb all of the attention and energy of: *she was consumed with guilt.*
– DERIVATIVES **consumable** adj.
– ORIGIN Latin *consumere*.

C

consumer • n. a person who buys a product or service for personal use.

consumerism • n. **1** the protection of the interests of consumers. **2** the preoccupation of society with buying goods.
– DERIVATIVES **consumerist** adj. & n.

consummate • v. /kon-syuu-mayt/ (**consummates**, **consummating**, **consummated**) **1** make (a marriage or relationship) complete by having sexual intercourse. **2** complete (a transaction). • adj. /kuhn-**sum**-muht/ showing great skill and flair.
– DERIVATIVES **consummation** n.
– ORIGIN Latin *consummare*.

consumption • n. **1** the action or process of consuming. **2** an amount consumed. **3** dated tuberculosis.
– DERIVATIVES **consumptive** adj. & n. (dated).

contact • n. /**kon**-takt/ **1** the state of touching something. **2** the state of communicating or meeting. **3** a meeting or communication set up with someone. **4** a person who may be asked for information or assistance. **5** a connection for the passage of an electric current from one thing to another. • adj. /**kon**-takt/ caused by or operating through physical touch: *contact dermatitis.* • v. /**kon**-takt, kuhn-**takt**/ get in touch with.
– ORIGIN Latin *contactus*.

contact lens • n. a plastic lens placed on the surface of the eye to correct visual defects.

contagion /kuhn-**tay**-juhn/ • n. the communication of disease from one person to another by close contact.
– ORIGIN Latin.

contagious • adj. **1** (of a disease) spread by direct or indirect contact between people or organisms. **2** having a contagious disease.

contain • v. **1** have or hold within. **2** control or restrain. **3** prevent (a problem) from becoming worse.
– ORIGIN Latin *continere*.

container • n. **1** a box, cylinder, or similar object for holding something. **2** a large metal box for the transport of goods.

containment • n. the action of keeping something harmful under control.

contaminate • v. (**contaminates**, **contaminating**, **contaminated**) make impure by exposure to a poisonous or polluting substance.
– DERIVATIVES **contamination** n.
– ORIGIN Latin *contaminare*.

contemplate /**kon**-tuhm-playt/ • v. (**contemplates**, **contemplating**, **contemplated**) **1** look at thoughtfully. **2** think about. **3** think deeply and at length.
– ORIGIN Latin *contemplari*.

contemplation • n. **1** the action of contemplating. **2** religious meditation.

contemplative /kuhn-**tem**-pluh-tiv/ • adj. showing or involving contemplation.

contemporaneous /kuhn-tem-puh-**ray**-ni-uhss/ • adj. existing at or occurring in the same period of time.
– DERIVATIVES **contemporaneity** n.
– ORIGIN Latin.

contemporary /kuhn-**tem**-puh-ruh-ri, kuhn-**tem**-puh-ri/ • adj. **1** living or occurring at the same time. **2** belonging to or occurring in the present. **3** modern in style. • n. (pl. **contemporaries**) **1** a person or thing existing at the same time as another. **2** a person of roughly the same age as another.
– ORIGIN Latin *contemporarius*.

contempt • n. **1** the feeling that a person or a thing is worthless or beneath consideration. **2** (also **contempt of court**) the offence of being disobedient to or disrespectful of a court of law.
– PHRASES **beneath contempt** utterly worthless.
– ORIGIN Latin *contemptus*.

contemptible • adj. deserving contempt.

contemptuous • adj. showing contempt.

contend • v. **1** (**contend with/against**) struggle to deal with (a difficulty). **2** (**contend for**) engage in a struggle to achieve. **3** assert as a position in an argument.
– DERIVATIVES **contender** n.
– ORIGIN Latin *contendere*.

content[1] /kuhn-**tent**/ • adj. happy or satisfied. • v. satisfy; please. • n. happiness or satisfaction.
– DERIVATIVES **contentment** n.
– ORIGIN Latin *contentus*.

content[2] /**kon**-tent/ • n. **1** (**contents**) the things that are contained in something. **2** the amount of a particular thing occurring in a substance: *soya milk has a low fat content.* **3** (**contents** or **table of contents**) a list of chapters at the front of a book or periodical. **4** the material dealt with in a speech or text as distinct from its form or style.
– ORIGIN Latin *contentum*.

contented • adj. happy or satisfied.

contention • n. **1** heated disagreement. **2** an assertion.
– PHRASES **in contention** having a good chance of success in a contest.
– ORIGIN Latin.

contentious • adj. **1** causing or likely to cause disagreement or controversy. **2** liking to cause arguments.

contest • n. /**kon**-test/ an event in which people compete to see who is the best. • v. /kuhn-**test**/ **1** compete to achieve (a position of power). **2** take part in (a competition or election). **3** challenge or dispute.
– ORIGIN Latin *contestari* 'call to witness'.

contestant • n. a person who takes part in a contest.

context • n. **1** the circumstances that form the setting for an event, statement, or idea. **2** the parts that immediately come before and after a word or passage and clarify its meaning.
– DERIVATIVES **contextual** adj.
– ORIGIN Latin *contextus*.

contiguous /kuhn-**tig**-yoo-uhss/ • adj. **1** sharing a border. **2** next or together in sequence.
– DERIVATIVES **contiguity** n.
– ORIGIN Latin *contiguus* 'touching'.

continent[1] • n. **1** any of the world's main

continuous expanses of land (Europe, Asia, Africa, North and South America, Australia, Antarctica). **2** (also **the Continent**) the mainland of Europe as distinct from the British Isles.
– ORIGIN from Latin *terra continens* 'continuous land'.

continent[2] ● adj. **1** able to control movements of the bowels and bladder. **2** exercising self-restraint.
– DERIVATIVES **continence** n.
– ORIGIN Latin *continere.*

continental ● adj. **1** forming or belonging to a continent. **2** (also **Continental**) coming from or typical of mainland Europe. ● n. (also **Continental**) a person from mainland Europe.

continental drift ● n. the gradual movement of the continents across the earth's surface through geological time.

continental shelf ● n. an area of seabed around a large land mass where the sea is relatively shallow.

contingency /kuhn-tin-juhn-si/ ● n. (pl. **contingencies**) **1** a future event which is possible but cannot be predicted with certainty. **2** a plan for such an event.

contingent /kuhn-tin-juhnt/ ● adj. **1** subject to chance. **2** (**contingent on/upon**) dependent on. ● n. a group of people with a common feature, forming part of a larger group.
– ORIGIN Latin *contingere* 'befall'.

continual ● adj. **1** constantly or often occurring. **2** having no interruptions.
– DERIVATIVES **continually** adv.

continuation ● n. **1** the action of continuing or the state of being continued. **2** a part that is attached to and is an extension of something else.

continue ● v. (**continues, continuing, continued**) **1** keep happening without stopping. **2** remain in existence, operation, or a particular state. **3** carry on with. **4** carry on travelling in the same direction. **5** start again.
– ORIGIN Latin *continuare.*

continuity /kon-ti-nyoo-i-ti/ ● n. (pl. **continuities**) **1** the uninterrupted and unchanged existence or operation of something. **2** a connection.

continuous ● adj. **1** without interruption. **2** forming a series with no exceptions or reversals.
– DERIVATIVES **continuously** adv.

continuous assessment ● n. Brit. the evaluation of a pupil's progress throughout a course of study, rather than by examination.

continuum ● n. (pl. **continua**) a continuous sequence in which the elements next to each other are very similar, but the last and the first are very different.
– ORIGIN Latin.

contort ● v. twist or bend out of its normal shape.
– DERIVATIVES **contortion** n.
– ORIGIN Latin *contorquere.*

contortionist ● n. an entertainer who twists and bends their body into unnatural positions.

contour ● n. **1** an outline of the shape or form of something. **2** (also **contour line**) a line on a map joining points of equal height. ● v. **1** mould into a shape. **2** (**contoured**) (of a map) marked with contours.
– ORIGIN French.

contra- ● prefix against; opposite: *contraception.*
– ORIGIN Latin *contra.*

contraband /kon-truh-band/ ● n. **1** goods that have been imported or exported illegally. **2** trade in smuggled goods.
– ORIGIN Italian *contrabando.*

contraception ● n. the use of contraceptives.

contraceptive ● adj. **1** preventing pregnancy. **2** relating to contraception. ● n. a device or drug used to prevent pregnancy.

contract ● n. /kon-trakt/ **1** a written or spoken agreement intended to be enforceable by law. **2** informal an arrangement for someone to be killed by a hired assassin. ● v. /kuhn-trakt/ **1** decrease in size, number, or range. **2** (of a muscle) become shorter and tighter in order to move part of the body. **3** enter into a legally binding agreement. **4** catch (a disease).
– DERIVATIVES **contractual** adj.
– ORIGIN Latin *contractus.*

contract bridge ● n. the standard form of the card game bridge.

contractible ● adj. able to be shrunk or capable of contracting.

contractile /kuhn-trak-tyl/ ● adj. tech. able to contract or or produce contraction.

contraction ● n. **1** the process of contracting. **2** a shortening of the muscles of the womb occurring at intervals during childbirth. **3** a shortened form of a word or words.

contractor ● n. a person who undertakes a contract to provide materials or labour for a job.

contradict ● v. **1** deny the truth of (a statement) by saying the opposite. **2** challenge (someone) by making a statement opposing one made by them.
– ORIGIN Latin *contradicere.*

contradiction ● n. **1** a combination of things which are opposed to one another. **2** the action of contradicting something.

contradictory ● adj. **1** opposed to something else. **2** containing opposing elements.

contradistinction ● n. distinction made by contrasting the different qualities of two things.

contraflow ● n. Brit. an arrangement by which the lanes of a dual carriageway or motorway normally carrying traffic in one direction become two-directional.

contralto /kuhn-tral-toh/ ● n. (pl. **contraltos**) the lowest female singing voice.
– ORIGIN Italian.

contraption ● n. a machine or device that appears strange or unnecessarily complicated.
– ORIGIN perh. from **CONTRIVE**.

contrapuntal /kon-truh-pun-t'l/ ● adj. Music relating to or in counterpoint.
– ORIGIN Italian *contrapunto.*

contrariwise /kuhn-trair-i-wyz/ ● adv. in the opposite way.

contrary /kon-truh-ri/ ● adj. **1** opposite in nature, direction, or meaning. **2** (of two or more statements, beliefs, etc.) opposed to one another. **3** /kuhn-trair-i/ deliberately inclined

to do the opposite of what is expected or desired. ● n. (**the contrary**) the opposite.
– ORIGIN Latin *contrarius*.

contrast ● n. /kon-trahst/ **1** the state of being noticeably different from something else when put or considered together. **2** a thing or person noticeably different from another. **3** the amount of difference between tones in a television picture, photograph, etc. ● v. /kuhn-**trahst**/ **1** differ noticeably. **2** compare so as to emphasize differences.
– DERIVATIVES **contrastive** adj.
– ORIGIN Latin *contrastare*.

contravene /kon-truh-veen/ ● v. (**contravenes, contravening, contravened**) **1** commit an act that is not allowed by (a law, treaty, etc.). **2** conflict with (a right, principle, etc.).
– DERIVATIVES **contravention** n.
– ORIGIN Latin *contravenire*.

contretemps /kon-truh-ton/ ● n. (pl. **contretemps** /kon-truh-ton/ or /kon-truh-tonz/) a minor disagreement.
– ORIGIN French.

contribute /kuhn-trib-yoot/ ● v. (**contributes, contributing, contributed**) **1** give in order to help achieve or provide something. **2** (**contribute to**) help to cause.
– DERIVATIVES **contribution** n. **contributor** n.
– ORIGIN Latin *contribuere* 'bring together'.

contributory /kuhn-trib-yuu-tuh-ri/ ● adj. **1** playing a part in bringing something about. **2** (of a pension or insurance scheme) operated by means of a fund into which people pay.

con trick ● n. informal a confidence trick.

contrite /kuhn-tryt, kon-tryt/ ● adj. very sorry for having done wrong.
– DERIVATIVES **contrition** n.
– ORIGIN Latin *contritus*.

contrivance ● n. **1** the action of contriving. **2** a clever device or scheme.

contrive /kuhn-tryv/ ● v. (**contrives, contriving, contrived**) **1** devise or plan using skill and subtlety. **2** manage to do something foolish.
– ORIGIN Old French *controver*.

contrived ● adj. deliberately created rather than arising naturally.

control ● n. **1** the power to influence people's behaviour or the course of events. **2** the restriction of something: *crime control*. **3** a means of limiting or regulating something: *exchange controls*. **4** a person or thing used as a standard of comparison for checking the results of a survey or experiment. ● v. (**controls, controlling, controlled**) **1** have power over. **2** limit or regulate.
– DERIVATIVES **controllable** adj. **controller** n.
– ORIGIN Old French *contreroller* 'keep a copy of a roll of accounts'.

control tower ● n. a tall building from which the movements of air traffic are controlled.

controversial ● adj. causing or likely to cause controversy.

controversy /kon-truh-ver-si, kuhn-trov-er-si/ ● n. (pl. **controversies**) public debate about a matter which arouses strongly opposing opinions.
– ORIGIN Latin *controversia*.

contumely /kon-tyoom-li/ ● n. archaic insulting language or treatment.
– ORIGIN Latin *contumelia*.

contusion /kuhn-tyoo-*zh*'n/ ● n. Med. a bruise.
– ORIGIN Latin.

conundrum /kuh-nun-druhm/ ● n. (pl. **conundrums**) **1** a confusing and difficult problem or question. **2** a riddle.
– ORIGIN unknown.

conurbation /kon-er-bay-sh'n/ ● n. an extended urban area, consisting of several towns merging with the suburbs of a central city.
– ORIGIN Latin *urbs* 'city'.

convalesce /kon-vuh-less/ ● v. (**convalesces, convalescing, convalesced**) gradually recover one's health after an illness or medical treatment.
– ORIGIN Latin *convalescere*.

convalescent ● adj. recovering from an illness or medical treatment. ● n. a convalescent person.
– DERIVATIVES **convalescence** n.

convection ● n. transference of mass or heat within a fluid caused by the tendency of warmer material to rise.
– DERIVATIVES **convective** adj.
– ORIGIN Latin.

convector ● n. a heating appliance that circulates warm air by convection.

convene /kuhn-veen/ ● v. (**convenes, convening, convened**) **1** call people together for (a meeting). **2** assemble for a common purpose.
– ORIGIN Latin *convenire*.

convener (also **convenor**) ● n. a person who convenes meetings of a committee.

convenience ● n. **1** freedom from effort or difficulty. **2** a useful device or situation. **3** Brit. a public toilet.
– PHRASES **at one's convenience** when or where it suits one.
– ORIGIN Latin *convenientia*.

convenience food ● n. a food that has been pre-prepared commercially and so requires little preparation by the consumer.

convenient ● adj. **1** fitting in well with a person's needs, activities, and plans. **2** involving little trouble or effort.
– DERIVATIVES **conveniently** adv.

convenor ● n. var. of **CONVENER**.

convent ● n. a Christian community of nuns living under monastic vows.
– ORIGIN Old French.

convention ● n. **1** a way in which something is usually done. **2** socially acceptable behaviour. **3** an agreement between countries. **4** a large meeting or conference.
– ORIGIN Latin.

conventional ● adj. **1** based on or following convention. **2** following social conventions; not individual or adventurous. **3** (of weapons or power) non-nuclear.
– DERIVATIVES **conventionally** adv.

converge /kuhn-verj/ ● v. (**converges, converging, converged**) **1** come together from different directions so as eventually to meet. **2** (**converge on/upon**) come from different directions and meet at.
– DERIVATIVES **convergent** adj.
– ORIGIN Latin *convergere*.

conversant ● adj. (**conversant with**) familiar with or knowledgeable about.

conversation ● n. an informal spoken ex-

change between two or more people.
– DERIVATIVES **conversational** adj.

conversationalist • n. a person who is good at or fond of engaging in conversation.

converse[1] /kuhn-verss/ • v. (**converses, conversing, conversed**) hold a conversation.
– ORIGIN Latin *conversari* 'keep company with'.

converse[2] /kon-verss/ • n. (**the converse**) the opposite of a fact or statement. • adj. opposite.
– DERIVATIVES **conversely** adv.
– ORIGIN Latin *conversus* 'turned about'.

conversion • n. **1** the action of converting. **2** Brit. a building that has been converted to a new purpose. **3** Rugby a successful kick at goal after a try.

convert • v. /kuhn-vert/ **1** change in form, character, or function. **2** change (money or units) into others of a different kind. **3** adapt (a building) for a new purpose. **4** change one's religious faith or other beliefs. • n. /kon-vert/ a person who has changed their religious faith or other beliefs.
– ORIGIN Latin *convertere* 'turn about'.

convertible • adj. **1** able to be converted. **2** (of a car) having a folding or detachable roof. • n. a convertible car.

convex /kon-veks/ • adj. having an outline or surface that curves outwards. Compare with **CONCAVE**.
– ORIGIN Latin *convexus* 'vaulted, arched'.

convey /kuhn-vay/ • v. **1** transport to a place. **2** communicate (an idea or feeling).
– ORIGIN Latin *conviare*.

conveyance • n. **1** the action of conveying. **2** formal a means of transport. **3** the legal process of transferring property from one owner to another.
– DERIVATIVES **conveyancing** n.

conveyor belt • n. a continuous moving band used for transporting objects from one place to another.

convict • v. /kuhn-vikt/ declare to be guilty of a criminal offence by the verdict of a jury or the decision of a judge. • n. /kon-vikt/ a person convicted of a criminal offence and serving a sentence of imprisonment.
– ORIGIN Latin *convictus* 'demonstrated').

conviction • n. **1** an instance of being convicted of a criminal offence. **2** the action of convicting. **3** a firmly held belief or opinion. **4** the quality of showing that one is convinced of what one believes or says.

convince • v. (**convinces, convincing, convinced**) **1** cause to believe firmly in the truth of something. **2** persuade to do something.
– ORIGIN Latin *convincere* 'overcome'.

convincing • adj. **1** able to convince. **2** (of a victory or a winner) leaving no margin of doubt.

convivial /kuhn-viv-i-uhl/ • adj. **1** (of an atmosphere or event) friendly and lively. **2** (of a person) cheerfully sociable.
– ORIGIN Latin *convivium* 'a feast'.

convocation /kon-vuh-kay-sh'n/ • n. a large formal assembly of people.
– ORIGIN Latin.

convoke /kuhn-vohk/ • v. (**convokes, convoking, convoked**) formal call together (an assembly or meeting).
– ORIGIN Latin *convocare*.

convoluted /kon-vuh-loo-tid/ • adj. **1** (of an argument, statement, etc.) extremely complex. **2** folded or twisted in a complex way.

convolution • n. **1** a coil or twist. **2** a complex argument, statement, etc.
– ORIGIN Latin.

convolvulus /kuhn-volv-yuu-luhss/ • n. (pl. **convolvuluses**) a twining plant with trumpet-shaped flowers.
– ORIGIN Latin.

convoy /kon-voy/ • n. a group of ships or vehicles travelling together under armed protection.
– PHRASES **in convoy** travelling as a group.
– ORIGIN French *convoyer*.

convulse /kuhn-vulss/ • v. (**convulses, convulsing, convulsed**) **1** suffer convulsions. **2** (**be convulsed**) make sudden, uncontrollable movements because of laughter or emotion.
– DERIVATIVES **convulsive** adj.
– ORIGIN Latin *convellere* 'pull violently'.

convulsion • n. **1** a sudden, irregular movement of the body caused by involuntary contraction of muscles. **2** (**convulsions**) uncontrollable laughter. **3** a violent social or natural upheaval.

coo • v. (**coos, cooing, cooed**) **1** (of a pigeon or dove) make a soft murmuring sound. **2** (of a person) speak in a soft gentle voice. • n. a cooing sound.

Cook, E
Captain James (1728–79), English explorer. During his voyages to the Pacific he charted the coast of New Zealand and explored the east coast of Australia, claiming it for Britain.

cook • v. **1** prepare (food or a meal) by heating the ingredients. **2** (with reference to food) heat or be heated so as to reach an edible state. **3** informal alter dishonestly. **4** (**cook up**) informal invent (a story or plan). • n. a person who cooks.
– ORIGIN Latin *coquus* 'a cook'.

Cook, Mount E
the highest peak in New Zealand, in the Southern Alps on South Island, rising to a height of 3,764 m (12,349 ft). Maori name **AORANGI**.

cooker • n. Brit. an appliance for cooking food.

cookery • n. the practice or skill of preparing and cooking food.

cookie • n. (pl. **cookies**) **1** N. Amer. a sweet biscuit. **2** informal a person of a specified kind: *she's a tough cookie.*
– ORIGIN Dutch *koekje* 'little cake'.

Cook Islands E
a group of fifteen islands in the SW Pacific Ocean, a self-governing territory in free association with New Zealand; capital, Avarua, on Rarotonga.

Cookson, E
Dame Catherine (Anne) (1906–98), English writer, a prolific author of romantic fiction.

cool • adj. **1** of or at a fairly low temperature. **2** keeping one from becoming too hot. **3** unfriendly or unenthusiastic. **4** free from

anxiety or excitement: *he kept a cool head.* **5** informal fashionably attractive or impressive. **6** informal excellent. ● **n.** (**the cool**) a fairly low temperature: *the cool of the day.* ● **v.** make or become cool.
– PHRASES **keep** (or **lose**) **one's cool** informal stay (or fail to stay) calm and controlled.
– DERIVATIVES **coolly** adv. **coolness** n.
– ORIGIN Old English.

coolant ● **n.** a fluid used to cool an engine or other device.

cooler ● **n.** a device or container for keeping things cool.

Coolidge E
/koo-lij/, (John) Calvin (1872–1933), American Republican statesman, 30th President of the US 1923–9.

coolie /koo-li/ ● **n.** (pl. **coolies**) dated, offens. an unskilled native labourer in some Asian countries.
– ORIGIN Hindi.

cooling-off period ● **n.** **1** an interval during which the parties in a dispute can try to settle their differences before taking further action. **2** an interval after a sale contract is agreed during which the purchaser can decide to cancel without loss.

cooling tower ● **n.** an open-topped cylindrical tower, used for cooling water or condensing steam from an industrial process.

coombe (also **coomb**) ● **n.** var. of **COMBE**.

coon ● **n.** **1** N. Amer. = **RACCOON**. **2** informal, offens. a black person. [ORIGIN from an earlier meaning of sense 1, '(sly) fellow'.]

coop /koop/ ● **n.** a cage or pen for poultry. ● **v.** (**coop up**) confine in a small space.
– ORIGIN Latin *cupa* 'cask, tub'.

Cooper[1], E
Gary (1901–61; born *Frank James Cooper*), American actor, noted for his performances in such westerns as *High Noon*.

Cooper[2], E
James Fenimore (1789–1851), American novelist, known for *The Last of the Mohicans*.

cooper ● **n.** a person who makes or repairs casks and barrels.
– ORIGIN Latin *cupa* 'cask, tub'.

cooperate /koh-op-uh-rayt/ (also **co-operate**) ● **v.** (**cooperates**, **cooperating**, **cooperated**) **1** work together towards the same end. **2** comply with a request.
– DERIVATIVES **cooperation** (also **co-operation**) n.
– ORIGIN Latin *cooperari*.

cooperative (also **co-operative**) ● **adj.** **1** involving cooperation. **2** willing to be of assistance. **3** (of a farm, business, etc.) owned and run jointly by its members, with profits or benefits shared among them. ● **n.** a cooperative organization.
– DERIVATIVES **cooperatively** (also **co-operatively**) adv.

co-opt ● **v.** **1** appoint to membership of a committee or other body by invitation of the existing members. **2** divert to a role different from the usual or original one. **3** adopt (an idea or policy) for one's own use.
– DERIVATIVES **co-optation** n.
– ORIGIN Latin *cooptare*.

coordinate (also **co-ordinate**) ● **v.** /koh-or-di-nayt/ (**coordinates**, **coordinating**, **coordinated**) **1** bring the different elements of (a complex activity or organization) into an efficient relationship. **2** (**coordinate with**) negotiate with (others) in order to work together effectively. **3** match or harmonize attractively. ● **n.** /koh-**or**-di-nuht/ **1** Math. each of a group of numbers used to indicate the position of a point, line, or plane. **2** (**coordinates**) matching items of clothing.
– DERIVATIVES **coordinator** (also **co-ordinator**) n.
– ORIGIN Latin *ordinare* 'put in order'.

coordination (also **co-ordination**) ● **n.** **1** the action of coordinating. **2** the ability to move different parts of the body smoothly and at the same time.

coot ● **n.** (pl. **coot** or **coots**) a black waterbird with a white bill.
– ORIGIN prob. Dutch or German.

cop informal ● **n.** a police officer. ● **v.** (**cops**, **copping**, **copped**) **1** catch or arrest (an offender). **2** incur (something unwelcome). **3** (**cop off**) have a sexual encounter. **4** (**cop out**) avoid doing something that one ought to do.
– PHRASES **cop hold of** Brit. take hold of. **cop it** Brit. **1** get into trouble. **2** be killed. **not much cop** Brit. not very good.
– ORIGIN perh. from Old French *caper* 'seize'.

cope[1] ● **v.** (**copes**, **coping**, **coped**) deal effectively with something difficult.
– ORIGIN Old French *coper* 'to strike'.

cope[2] ● **n.** a long cloak worn by a priest on ceremonial occasions.
– ORIGIN Latin *cappa* 'head-covering'.

copeck ● **n.** var. of **KOPEK**.

Copenhagen E
/koh-puhn-**hay**-g'n, koh-puhn-**hah**-g'n/ the capital and chief port of Denmark.

Copernican system /kuh-**per**-ni-kuhn/ (also **Copernican theory**) ● **n.** the theory proposed by Nicolaus Copernicus that the sun is the centre of the solar system, with the planets orbiting round it. Compare with **PTOLEMAIC SYSTEM**.

Copernicus E
/kuh-**per**-ni-kuhss/, Nicolaus (1473–1543), Polish astronomer, who proposed that the planets orbit the sun, rejecting the established view that the Earth was the centre of the universe.
– DERIVATIVES **Copernican** adj.

copier ● **n.** a machine that makes exact copies of something.

co-pilot ● **n.** a second pilot in an aircraft.

coping ● **n.** the top layer of a brick or stone wall.
– ORIGIN from **COPE**[2].

copious ● **adj.** abundant; plentiful.
– DERIVATIVES **copiously** adv.
– ORIGIN Latin *copia* 'plenty'.

Copland E
/**kohp**-luhnd/, Aaron (1900–90), American composer, pianist, and conductor, of Lithuanian descent. He established a distinctive American style in his compositions which include *Appalachian Spring* and *Fanfare for the Common Man*.

copper[1] ● **n.** **1** a red-brown metallic chemical

element which is used for electrical wiring and as a component of brass and bronze. **2** (**coppers**) Brit. coins made of copper or bronze. **3** a reddish-brown colour.
– ORIGIN from Latin *cyprium aes* 'Cyprus metal'.

copper[2] ● n. Brit. informal a police officer.
– ORIGIN from COP.

copper-bottomed ● adj. Brit. thoroughly reliable.
– ORIGIN with reference to copper covering applied to the bottom of a ship.

copperplate ● n. a neat style of handwriting with slanted letters.
– ORIGIN the copybooks for this were originally printed from copper plates.

copper sulphate ● n. a blue solid used in electroplating and as a fungicide.

coppice ● n. an area of woodland in which the trees or shrubs are periodically cut back to ground level.
– ORIGIN Old French *copeiz*.

Coppola E
/kop-puh-luh/, Francis Ford (b.1939), American film director, writer, and producer. His films include *The Godfather* and its two sequels, and *Apocalypse Now*.

copra /kop-ruh/ ● n. dried coconut kernels, from which oil is obtained.
– ORIGIN Portuguese and Spanish.

copse ● n. a small group of trees.
– ORIGIN from COPPICE.

Copt /kopt/ ● n. **1** a native Egyptian in the periods of Greek and Roman domination. **2** a member of the Coptic Church, the native Christian Church in Egypt.
– ORIGIN Latin *Coptus*.

copulate /kop-yuu-layt/ ● v. (**copulates**, **copulating**, **copulated**) have sexual intercourse.
– DERIVATIVES **copulation** n.
– ORIGIN Latin *copulare* 'fasten together'.

copy ● n. (pl. **copies**) **1** a thing made to be similar or identical to another. **2** a single example of a particular book, record, etc. **3** matter to be printed in a book, newspaper, or magazine. ● v. (**copies**, **copying**, **copied**) **1** make a copy of. **2** imitate the behaviour or style of.
– ORIGIN Latin *copia* 'abundance'.

copybook ● n. a book containing models of handwriting for learners to imitate. ● adj. exactly following established standards: *a copybook landing*.

copycat ● n. informal a person who copies another. ● adj. (of an action) carried out in imitation of another: *copycat attacks*.

copyist ● n. a person who makes copies.

copyright ● n. the exclusive legal right to publish, perform, film, or record literary, artistic, or musical material.

copywriter ● n. a person who writes the text of advertisements or publicity material.

coquette /ko-ket/ ● n. a woman who flirts.
– DERIVATIVES **coquetry** n. **coquettish** adj.
– ORIGIN French.

coracle /ko-ruh-k'l/ ● n. a small, round boat made of wickerwork covered with a watertight material, propelled with a paddle.
– ORIGIN Welsh *corwgl*.

coral ● n. **1** a hard substance secreted by certain sea animals as an external skeleton. **2** precious red coral, used in jewellery. **3** the pinkish-red colour of red coral.
– ORIGIN Greek *korallion*, *kouralion*.

Coral Sea E
a part of the western Pacific lying between Australia, New Guinea, and Vanuatu.

C

cor anglais /kor ong-glay/ ● n. (pl. **cors anglais** /kor ong-glay/) a woodwind instrument of the oboe family, sounding a fifth lower than the oboe.
– ORIGIN French, 'English horn'.

corbel /kor-b'l/ ● n. a projection jutting out from a wall to support a structure above it.
– ORIGIN Old French 'little crow'.

cord ● n. **1** thin string or rope made from several twisted strands. **2** a length of cord. **3** a structure in the body resembling a cord. **4** an electric flex. **5** corduroy. **6** (**cords**) corduroy trousers.
– ORIGIN Greek *khordē*.

cordial ● adj. **1** warm and friendly. **2** deeply felt: *a cordial loathing*. ● n. **1** Brit. a sweet fruit-flavoured drink, sold as a concentrate.
– ORIGIN Latin *cordialis*.

cordite ● n. a smokeless explosive.
– ORIGIN from CORD.

cordless ● adj. (of an electrical appliance) working without connection to a mains supply or central unit.

Cordoba E
/kor-duh-buh/ (also **Cordova**) a city in Andalusia in southern Spain, renowned for its Moorish architecture.

cordon /kor-d'n/ ● n. a line or circle of police, soldiers, or guards forming a barrier. ● v. (**cordon off**) close off by means of a cordon.
– ORIGIN Italian *cordone* and French *cordon*.

cordon bleu /kor-don bler/ ● adj. Cookery of the highest class.
– ORIGIN French, 'blue ribbon'.

Cordova E
/kor-duh-vuh/ English name for CORDOBA.

corduroy /kor-duh-roy/ ● n. a thick cotton fabric with velvety ribs.
– ORIGIN prob. from CORD + *duroy*, a former kind of lightweight fabric.

core ● n. **1** the tough central part of various fruits. **2** the central or most important part. **3** the dense central region of a planet. **4** the central part of a nuclear reactor. ● v. (**cores**, **coring**, **cored**) remove the core from (a fruit).
– ORIGIN unknown.

Corelli E
/kuh-rel-li/, Arcangelo (1653–1713), Italian violinist and composer. He is known for his trio and solo sonatas for the violin and his concerti grossi, especially the 'Christmas' concerto.

co-respondent (also **corespondent**) ● n. a person named in a divorce case as having committed adultery with the husband or wife of the person who wants a divorce.

Corfu E
/kor-foo/ one of the Ionian Islands, off the west coast of mainland Greece.

corgi (also **Welsh corgi**) ● n. (pl. **corgis**) a

breed of dog with short legs and a foxlike head.
– ORIGIN Welsh.

coriander /ko-ri-an-der/ ● **n.** a herb of the parsley family, used in cookery.
– ORIGIN Old French *coriandre*.

Corinth E
/ko-rinth/ a city on the north coast of the Peloponnese, Greece.

Cork E
a county of the Republic of Ireland, on the south coast in the province of Munster; county town, Cork.

cork ● **n.** **1** the buoyant, brown substance obtained from the bark of a kind of oak tree. **2** a bottle stopper made of cork. ● **v.** **1** close or seal (a bottle) with a cork. **2** (**corked**) (of wine) spoilt by a faulty cork.
– ORIGIN Dutch and German *kork*.

corkage ● **n.** a charge made by a restaurant for serving wine that has been brought in by a customer.

corker ● **n.** informal an excellent person or thing.
– DERIVATIVES **corking** adj.

corkscrew ● **n.** a device with a spiral metal rod, used for pulling corks from bottles. ● **v.** move or twist in a spiral.

corm ● **n.** an underground storage organ present in some plants.
– ORIGIN Greek *kormos* 'trunk stripped of its boughs'.

cormorant /kor-muh-ruhnt/ ● **n.** a diving seabird with a long hooked bill and black plumage.
– ORIGIN Old French *cormaran*.

corn[1] ● **n.** **1** esp. Brit. the chief cereal crop of a district, especially (in England) wheat or (in Scotland) oats. **2** N. Amer. & Austral./NZ maize.
– ORIGIN Old English.

corn[2] ● **n.** a painful area of thickened skin on the toes or foot, caused by pressure.
– ORIGIN Latin *cornu* 'horn'.

corncob ● **n.** the central part of an ear of maize, to which the grains are attached.

corn dolly ● **n.** Brit. a model of a human figure, made of plaited straw.

cornea /kor-ni-uh/ ● **n.** the transparent layer forming the front of the eye.
– ORIGIN from Latin *cornea tela* 'horny tissue'.

corned beef ● **n.** Brit. beef preserved in brine, chopped and pressed and sold in tins.

Corneille E
/kor-**nay**/, Pierre (1606–84), French dramatist, the founder of classical French tragedy. His plays include *Le Cid*, *Cinna*, and *Polyeucte*.

cornelian /kor-nee-li-uhn/ ● **n.** var. of **CARNELIAN**.

corner ● **n.** **1** a place or angle where two or more sides or edges meet. **2** a place where two streets meet. **3** a secluded or remote region or area. **4** a difficult or awkward position. **5** (also **corner kick**) Soccer a free kick taken by the attacking side from a corner of the field. ● **v.** (**corners**, **cornering**, **cornered**) **1** force into a place or situation from which it is hard to escape. **2** control (a market) by dominating the supply of particular goods. **3** go round a bend in a road.
– ORIGIN Latin *cornu* 'horn, corner'.

corner shop ● **n.** Brit. a small shop selling groceries and general goods in a residential area.

cornerstone ● **n.** **1** a stone that forms the base of a corner of a building. **2** a vital part: *sugar was the cornerstone of the economy.*

cornet /kor-nit/ ● **n.** **1** a brass instrument resembling a trumpet but shorter and wider. **2** Brit. a cone-shaped wafer for holding ice cream.
– ORIGIN Old French, 'little horn'.

cornflakes ● **pl. n.** a breakfast cereal consisting of toasted flakes made from maize flour.

cornflour ● **n.** Brit. ground maize flour, used for thickening sauces.

cornflower ● **n.** a plant of the daisy family with deep blue flowers.

cornice /kor-niss/ ● **n.** **1** a moulding round the wall of a room just below the ceiling. **2** a horizontal moulded projection crowning a building or structure.
– ORIGIN Italian.

Cornish ● **adj.** relating to Cornwall. ● **n.** the ancient Celtic language of Cornwall.

Cornish pasty ● **n.** Brit. a pasty containing seasoned meat and vegetables.

Corn Laws E
a series of laws introduced in Britain in the early 19th century to protect farmers from foreign competition. They had the unintended effect of forcing up bread prices and were eventually repealed in 1846.

cornucopia /kor-nyuu-**koh**-pi-uh/ ● **n.** **1** an abundant supply of good things. **2** a symbol of plenty consisting of a goat's horn overflowing with flowers, fruit, and corn.
– ORIGIN from Latin *cornu copiae* 'horn of plenty'.

Cornwall E
a county occupying the extreme south-western peninsula of England; county town, Truro.

Cornwell, E
Patricia (b.1956), American crime writer, author of *Postmortem* and *Cruel and Unusual*.

corny ● **adj.** (**cornier**, **corniest**) informal trivial or very sentimental.
– ORIGIN from **CORN**[1].

corolla /kuh-rol-luh/ ● **n.** the petals of a flower.
– ORIGIN Latin, 'little crown'.

corollary /kuh-rol-luh-ri/ ● **n.** (pl. **corollaries**) **1** a logical proposition that follows from one already proved. **2** a direct consequence or result.
– ORIGIN Latin *corollarium* 'gratuity'.

corona /kuh-roh-nuh/ ● **n.** (pl. **coronae** /kuh-**roh**-nee/) **1** the gaseous envelope of the sun or a star. **2** a small circle of light seen round the sun or moon.
– ORIGIN Latin, 'crown'.

coronary /ko-ruh-nuh-ri/ ● **adj.** relating to the arteries which surround and supply the heart. ● **n.** (pl. **coronaries**) (also **coronary thrombosis**) a blockage of the flow of blood to the heart, caused by a blood clot in a coronary artery.
– ORIGIN Latin *coronarius* 'resembling or forming a crown'.

coronation • n. the ceremony of crowning a sovereign.
– ORIGIN Latin.

coroner /ko-ruh-ner/ • n. an official who holds inquests into violent, sudden, or suspicious deaths.
– ORIGIN Old French *coruner.*

coronet /ko-ruh-net/ • n. **1** a small or simple crown. **2** a decorative band encircling the head.
– ORIGIN Old French *coronete.*

Corot E
/ko-roh/, (Jean-Baptiste) Camille (1796–1875), French landscape painter, who had a significant influence on the Impressionists.

corpora pl. of **CORPUS**.

corporal[1] • n. a rank of non-commissioned officer in the army, below sergeant.
– ORIGIN Italian *caporale.*

corporal[2] • adj. relating to the human body.
– ORIGIN Latin *corporalis.*

corporal punishment • n. physical punishment, such as caning.

corporate • adj. **1** relating to a business corporation. **2** of or shared by all members of a group: *corporate responsibility.*
– ORIGIN Latin *corporare* 'form into a body'.

corporation • n. **1** a large company or group of companies, recognized by law as a single unit. **2** Brit. a group of people elected to govern a city, town, or borough.

corporation tax • n. tax paid by companies on their profits.

corporeal /kor-por-i-uhl/ • adj. relating to a person's body; physical rather than spiritual.
– ORIGIN Latin *corporealis.*

corps /kor/ • n. (pl. **corps** /korz/) **1** a main subdivision of an army in the field. **2** a branch of an army assigned to a particular kind of work. **3** a group of people engaged in a particular activity: *the press corps.*
– ORIGIN French.

corps de ballet /kor duh bal-lay/ • n. the members of a ballet company who dance together as a group.

corpse • n. a dead body of a human.
– ORIGIN Latin *corpus.*

corpulent /kor-pyuu-luhnt/ • adj. (of a person) fat.
– ORIGIN Latin *corpulentus.*

corpus /kor-puhss/ • n. (pl. **corpora** /kor-puh-ruh/ or **corpuses**) a collection of written texts.
– ORIGIN Latin, 'body'.

corpuscle /kor-pus-s'l/ • n. a red or white blood cell.
– ORIGIN Latin *corpusculum* 'small body'.

corral /kuh-rahl/ • n. N. Amer. a pen for livestock on a farm or ranch. • v. (**corrals**, **corralling**, **corralled**) **1** N. Amer. put or keep (livestock) in a corral. **2** gather (a group) together.
– ORIGIN Spanish and Portuguese.

correct • adj. **1** free from error; true; right. **2** following accepted social standards. • v. **1** put right. **2** mark the errors in (a text). **3** tell (someone) that they are in error.
– DERIVATIVES **correctly** adv. **correctness** n.
– ORIGIN Latin *corrigere.*

correction • n. **1** the action of correcting. **2** a change that corrects something wrong.

corrective • adj. designed to correct something undesirable. • n. a corrective measure.

Correggio E
/ko-rej-i-oh/, Antonio Allegri da (*c.*1494–1534), Italian painter. His soft, sensual style influenced the development of rococo in the 18th century.

correlate /ko-ruh-layt/ • v. (**correlates**, **correlating**, **correlated**) have or bring into a relationship in which one thing affects or depends on another.

correlation • n. **1** a relationship in which one thing affects or depends on another. **2** the process of correlating two or more things.

correlative /kuh-rel-uh-tiv/ • adj. having a correlation.
– ORIGIN Latin *correlativus.*

correspond • v. **1** match or agree almost exactly. **2** be comparable or equivalent in character or form. **3** communicate by exchanging letters.
– ORIGIN Latin *correspondere.*

correspondence • n. **1** the action or fact of corresponding. **2** letters sent or received.

correspondence course • n. a course of study in which student and tutors communicate by post.

correspondent • n. **1** a person who writes letters. **2** a journalist reporting on a particular subject.

corridor • n. **1** a passage in a building or train, with doors leading into rooms or compartments. **2** a belt of land linking two other areas or following a road or river.
– PHRASES **the corridors of power** the senior levels of government or administration.
– ORIGIN Italian *corridore.*

corroborate /kuh-rob-uh-rayt/ • v. (**corroborates**, **corroborating**, **corroborated**) confirm or give support to (a statement or theory).
– DERIVATIVES **corroboration** n.
– ORIGIN Latin *corroborare* 'strengthen'.

corrode /kuh-rohd/ • v. (**corrodes**, **corroding**, **corroded**) **1** (with reference to metal or other hard material) wear or be worn away slowly by chemical action. **2** gradually weaken or destroy: *the affair corroded her self-esteem.*
– ORIGIN Latin *corrodere.*

corrosion /kuh-roh-*zh*'n/ • n. **1** the process of corroding. **2** the damage caused by this process.

corrosive • adj. causing corrosion.

corrugate /ko-ruh-gayt/ • v. (**corrugates**, **corrugating**, **corrugated**) **1** contract into wrinkles or folds. **2** (**corrugated**) shaped into alternate ridges and grooves.
– DERIVATIVES **corrugation** n.
– ORIGIN Latin *corrugare.*

corrupt • adj. **1** willing to act dishonestly in return for money or personal gain. **2** evil or immoral. **3** (of a text or computer data) made unreliable by errors or alterations. • v. make corrupt.
– DERIVATIVES **corruptible** adj.
– ORIGIN Latin *corrumpere* 'bribe, destroy'.

corruption • n. **1** dishonest or illegal behaviour. **2** the action of corrupting someone or

the state of being morally corrupt.
corsage /kor-**sahzh**/ ● **n.** a spray of flowers worn pinned to a woman's clothes.
– ORIGIN French.
corsair /kor-**sair**/ ● **n.** archaic a pirate.
– ORIGIN French *corsaire*.
corset ● **n. 1** a woman's tight-fitting undergarment extending from below the chest to the hips, worn to shape the figure. **2** a similar garment worn to support a weak or injured back.
– DERIVATIVES **corsetry** n.
– ORIGIN Old French, 'little body'.

Corsica E
/**kor**-si-kuh/ an island off the west coast of Italy, a region of France; chief towns, Bastia and Ajaccio.

cortège /kor-**tezh**/ ● **n.** a solemn funeral procession.
– ORIGIN Italian *corteggio* 'entourage'.

Cortés E
/kor-**tez**/ (also **Cortez**), Hernando (1485–1547), Spanish conquistador, who overthrew the Aztec empire, destroying its capital in 1521.

cortex /**kor**-teks/ ● **n.** (pl. **cortices** /**kor**-ti-seez/) the outer layer of a bodily organ or structure, especially the outer, folded layer of the brain (**cerebral cortex**).
– DERIVATIVES **cortical** adj.
– ORIGIN Latin, 'bark of a tree'.
cortisone /**kor**-ti-zohn/ ● **n.** a steroid hormone used to treat inflammation and allergy.
– ORIGIN from its chemical name.
corundum /kuh-**run**-duhm/ ● **n.** an extremely hard form of aluminium oxide, used for grinding, smoothing, and polishing.
– ORIGIN Tamil.

Corunna E
/kuh-**run**-nuh/ a port in NW Spain, the point of departure for the Armada in 1588 and the site of a battle in 1809 in the Peninsular War, at which British forces defeated the French.

coruscating /**ko**-ruh-skay-ting/ ● **adj.** literary flashing or sparkling.
– ORIGIN Latin *coruscare* 'glitter'.
corvette /kor-**vet**/ ● **n.** a small warship used to escort convoys.
– ORIGIN French.

Cos E
var. of **Kos**.

cos[1] /koss/ ● **n.** a variety of lettuce with crisp narrow leaves.
– ORIGIN named after **Cos**.
cos[2] /koz/ ● **abbrev.** cosine.
cosec /**koh**-sek/ ● **abbrev.** cosecant.
cosecant /koh-see-kuhnt, koh-**sek**-uhnt/ ● **n.** (in a right-angled triangle) the ratio of the hypotenuse to the side opposite an acute angle.
cosh Brit. ● **n.** a thick heavy stick or bar used as a weapon. ● **v.** hit with a cosh.
– ORIGIN unknown.

Cosimo de' Medici E
/koz-i-moh duh **med**-i-chi/ (1389–1464), Italian statesman and banker, who laid the foundations for the Medici family's power in Florence, becoming the city's ruler in 1434.

cosine /**koh**-syn/ ● **n.** (in a right-angled triangle) the ratio of the side adjacent to a particular acute angle to the hypotenuse.
cosmetic ● **adj. 1** relating to treatment intended to improve a person's appearance. **2** improving something only outwardly: *the reforms were merely a cosmetic exercise.* ● **n.** (**cosmetics**) cosmetic substances for the face and body.
– DERIVATIVES **cosmetically** adv.
– ORIGIN Greek *kosmein* 'arrange'.
cosmic ● **adj.** relating to the universe.
cosmogony /koz-**mog**-uh-ni/ ● **n.** (pl. **cosmogonies**) the branch of science concerned with the origin of the universe, especially the solar system.
– ORIGIN from Greek *kosmos* 'order or world' + *-gonia* '-creating'.
cosmology ● **n.** (pl. **cosmologies**) the science of the origin and development of the universe.
– DERIVATIVES **cosmological** adj. **cosmologist** n.
cosmonaut ● **n.** a Russian astronaut.
– ORIGIN from **cosmos** + Greek *nautēs* 'sailor'.
cosmopolitan /koz-muh-**pol**-i-tuhn/ ● **adj. 1** consisting of people from many different countries: *Barcelona is a cosmopolitan city.* **2** familiar with and at ease in many different countries. ● **n.** a cosmopolitan person.
– ORIGIN from Greek *kosmos* 'world' + *politēs* 'citizen'.
cosmos ● **n.** the universe seen as a well-ordered whole.
– ORIGIN Greek *kosmos* 'order or world'.
Cossack /**koss**-ak/ ● **n.** a member of a people of southern Russia, Ukraine, and Siberia, noted for their horsemanship and military skill.
– ORIGIN Russian *kazak* 'nomad'.
cosset ● **v.** (**cossets**, **cosseting**, **cosseted**) care for and protect in an excessively soft-hearted way.
– ORIGIN uncertain.
cost ● **v.** (**costs**, **costing**, **cost**) **1** be obtainable for (a specific price). **2** involve the loss of: *his heroism cost him his life.* **3** (**costs**, **costing**, **costed**) estimate the cost of. ● **n. 1** an amount given or required as payment. **2** the effort or loss necessary to achieve something: *the cuts came at the cost of customer service.* **3** (**costs**) legal expenses.
– PHRASES **to someone's cost** with loss or disadvantage to someone.
– ORIGIN Latin *constare* 'stand firm'.

Costa Blanca E
/koss-tuh **blang**-kuh/ a resort region on the Mediterranean coast of SE Spain.

Costa Brava E
/koss-tuh **brah**-vuh/ a resort region to the north of Barcelona, on the Mediterranean coast of NE Spain.

Costa del Sol E
/koss-tuh del **sol**/ a resort region on the Mediterranean coast of southern Spain.

co-star ● **n.** a performer appearing with another or others of equal importance. ● **v. 1** appear in a production as a co-star. **2** (of a production) include (someone) as a co-star.

Costa Rica E
/koss-tuh ree-kuh/ a republic in Central America on the Isthmus of Panama; capital, San José.
– DERIVATIVES **Costa Rican** adj. & n.

cost-effective (also **cost-efficient**) ● **adj.** effective or productive in relation to its cost.

costermonger /koss-ter-mung-ger/ ● **n.** Brit. dated a person who sells fruit and vegetables from a handcart in the street.
– ORIGIN from *Costard* (a type of apple) + **-MONGER**.

costing ● **n.** the estimated cost of producing or doing something.

costly ● **adj.** (**costlier**, **costliest**) **1** expensive. **2** causing suffering, loss, or disadvantage: *her most costly mistake.*

cost price ● **n.** the price at which goods are bought by a retailer.

costume ● **n. 1** a set of clothes in a style typical of a particular country or historical period. **2** a set of clothes worn by an actor or performer for a role. ● **v.** (**costumes**, **costuming**, **costumed**) dress in a costume.
– ORIGIN Italian, 'custom, fashion'.

costume jewellery ● **n.** jewellery made with inexpensive materials or imitation gems.

costumier /koss-tyoo-mi-er/ ● **n.** a maker or supplier of theatrical or fancy-dress costumes.

cosy (US **cozy**) ● **adj.** (**cosier**, **cosiest**) **1** comfortable, warm, and secure. **2** not difficult or demanding: *the cosy belief that man is master.* ● **n.** (pl. **cosies**) a cover to keep a teapot or a boiled egg hot. ● **v.** (**cosies**, **cosying**, **cosied**) informal (**cosy up to**) try to gain the favour of.
– DERIVATIVES **cosily** (US **cozily**) adv. **cosiness** (US **coziness**) n.
– ORIGIN unknown.

cot[1] ● **n.** Brit. a small bed with high barred sides for a baby or very young child.
– ORIGIN Hindi, 'bedstead, hammock'.

cot[2] ● **abbrev.** cotangent.

cotangent /koh-tan-juhnt/ ● **n.** (in a right-angled triangle) the ratio of the side (other than the hypotenuse) adjacent to a particular acute angle to the side opposite the angle.

cot death ● **n.** Brit. the unexplained death of a baby in its sleep.

coterie /koh-tuh-ri/ ● **n.** (pl. **coteries**) a small exclusive group of people with shared interests or tastes.
– ORIGIN French.

Cotopaxi E
/kot-uh **pak**-si/ an active volcano in the Andes of central Ecuador, at 5,896 m (19,142 ft) the highest in the world.

Cotswold Hills E
a range of limestone hills in SW England, largely in the county of Gloucestershire.

cottage ● **n.** a small house, typically one in the country.
– ORIGIN Latin *cotagium*.

cottage cheese ● **n.** soft, lumpy white cheese made from the curds of skimmed milk.

cottage industry ● **n.** a business or manufacturing activity carried on in people's homes.

cottage pie ● **n.** Brit. a dish of minced meat topped with mashed potato.

cottager ● **n.** a person living in a cottage.

cotter pin ● **n. 1** a metal pin used to fasten two parts of a mechanism together. **2** a split pin that is opened out after being passed through a hole.
– ORIGIN unknown.

cotton ● **n.** the soft white fibres which surround the seeds of a tropical and subtropical plant, used to make cloth or thread for sewing. ● **v.** (**cotton on**) informal begin to understand.
– DERIVATIVES **cottony** adj.
– ORIGIN Arabic.

cotton wool ● **n.** Brit. fluffy soft material, used for applying or removing cosmetics or bathing wounds.

cotyledon /ko-ti-lee-duhn/ ● **n.** the first leaf to grow from a germinating seed.
– ORIGIN Greek *kotulēdōn* 'cup-shaped cavity'.

couch /kowch/ ● **n. 1** a long padded piece of furniture for several people to sit on. **2** a long seat with a headrest at one end on which a psychoanalyst's subject or doctor's patient lies during treatment. ● **v.** express in language of a particular style: *some warnings are couched in general terms.*
– ORIGIN Old French *couche*.

couch potato ● **n.** informal a person who spends a great deal of time watching television.

cougar /koo-ger/ ● **n.** N. Amer. = **PUMA**.
– ORIGIN French *couguar*.

cough ● **v. 1** send out air from the lungs with a sudden sharp sound. **2** (**cough up**) informal give (money or information required) reluctantly. ● **n. 1** an act or sound of coughing. **2** an illness of the throat or lungs causing coughing.

could ● **modal verb** past of **CAN**[1].

couldn't ● **contr.** could not.

coulomb /koo-lom/ ● **n.** the unit of electric charge in the SI system.
– ORIGIN named after the French military engineer Charles-Augustin de *Coulomb* (1736–1806).

council ● **n. 1** an assembly of people meeting regularly to advise on, discuss, or organize something. **2** a group of people elected to manage the affairs of a city, county, or district. ● **adj.** Brit. (of housing) provided by a local council.
– ORIGIN Latin *concilium* 'assembly'.

councillor (US also **councilor**) ● **n.** a member of a council.

council tax ● **n.** (in the UK) a tax charged on households by local authorities, based on the estimated value of a property.

counsel ● **n. 1** advice. **2** (pl. **counsel**) a barrister or other legal adviser conducting a case. ● **v.** (**counsels**, **counselling**, **counselled**; US **counsels**, **counseling**, **counseled**) **1** advise or recommend. **2** give professional help and advice to (someone with psychological or personal problems).
– PHRASES **keep one's own counsel** not reveal one's plans or opinions.
– ORIGIN Latin *consilium* 'advice'.

counsellor (US **counselor**) ● **n. 1** a person trained to give advice on personal or psychological problems. **2** a senior officer in the diplomatic service.

count[1] ● v. **1** find the total number of. **2** recite numbers in ascending order. **3** take into account: *the staff has shrunk to five, if you count the director.* **4** regard or be regarded as being: *people she had counted as her friends.* **5** be important. **6** (**count on/upon**) rely on. **7** (**count in** or **out**) include (or not include) in an activity. **8** (**count out**) complete a count of ten seconds over (a fallen boxer) to indicate defeat. ● n. **1** an act of counting. **2** a total found by counting: *a low pollen count.* **3** a point for discussion or consideration. **4** Law each of the charges against an accused person.
– PHRASES **keep** (or **lose**) **count** take note of (or forget) the number or amount when counting. **out for the count 1** Boxing defeated by being knocked to the ground and unable to rise within ten seconds. **2** unconscious or asleep.
– DERIVATIVES **countable** adj.
– ORIGIN Latin *computare.*

count[2] ● n. a foreign nobleman whose rank corresponds to that of an earl.
– ORIGIN Old French *conte.*

countdown ● n. **1** an act of counting backwards to zero to launch a rocket. **2** the final moments before a significant event.

countenance /kown-tuh-nuhnss/ ● n. a person's face or facial expression. ● v. (**countenances**, **countenancing**, **countenanced**) tolerate or allow.
– ORIGIN Old French *contenance* 'bearing'.

counter[1] ● n. **1** a long flat surface over which goods are sold or served or across which business is conducted with customers. **2** a small disc used in board games for keeping the score or as a place marker. **3** a person or thing that counts something.
– PHRASES **over the counter** by ordinary sale in a shop. **under the counter** (or **table**) (with reference to goods bought or sold) secretly and illegally.
– ORIGIN Old French *conteor.*

counter[2] ● v. (**counters**, **countering**, **countered**) speak or act in opposition or response to: *he helped to counter an invasion.* ● adv. (**counter to**) in the opposite direction or in opposition to. ● adj. opposing. ● n. an act which opposes something else.
– ORIGIN Latin *contra* 'against'.

counter- ● prefix **1** against, opposing, or done in return: *counter-attack.* **2** corresponding: *counterpart.*

counteract ● v. act against (something) so as to reduce its force or cancel it out: *meditation can counteract the effects of stress.*

counter-attack ● n. an attack made in response to an attack. ● v. attack in response.

counterbalance ● n. /kown-ter-bal-uhnss/ **1** a weight that balances another. **2** a factor that counters another. ● v. /kown-ter-bal-uhnss/ (**counterbalances**, **counterbalancing**, **counterbalanced**) have an opposing and balancing effect on.

counter-espionage ● n. activities designed to prevent spying by an enemy.

counterfeit /kown-ter-fit/ ● adj. made in exact imitation of something valuable so as to deceive or defraud. ● n. a forgery. ● v. **1** imitate fraudulently. **2** pretend to feel or possess: *no pretence could have counterfeited such terror.*
– DERIVATIVES **counterfeiter** n.
– ORIGIN Old French *contrefait* 'made in opposition'.

counterfoil ● n. Brit. the part of a cheque, ticket, etc. that is kept as a record by the person issuing it.

countermand /kown-ter-mahnd/ ● v. cancel (an order).
– ORIGIN Latin *contramandare.*

countermeasure ● n. an action taken to counteract a danger or threat.

counterpane ● n. a bedspread.
– ORIGIN Old French *contrepointe.*

counterpart ● n. a person or thing that corresponds to another.

counterpoint ● n. **1** the technique of writing or playing a melody or melodies together with another. **2** a melody played together with another. **3** an idea or theme contrasting with the main element. ● v. contrast with.

counterpoise ● n. a counterbalance. ● v. (**counterpoises**, **counterpoising**, **counterpoised**) counterbalance.

counterproductive ● adj. having the opposite of the desired effect.

Counter-Reformation E
the reform of the Roman Catholic Church in the 16th and 17th centuries, to counter the spread of the Protestant Reformation.

countersign ● v. sign (a document already signed by another person).

countersink ● v. (**countersinks**, **countersinking**, **countersunk**) **1** enlarge the rim of (a drilled hole) so that a screw or bolt can be inserted level with the surface. **2** drive (a screw or bolt) into such a hole.

countertenor ● n. the highest male adult singing voice.

countervail /kown-ter-vayl/ ● v. counteract (something) with something else of equal force: *he did all he could to countervail the impression.*
– ORIGIN from Latin *contra valere* 'be of worth against'.

countess ● n. **1** the wife or widow of a count or earl. **2** a woman holding the rank of count or earl.

counting ● prep. taking account of; including.

countless ● adj. too many to be counted; very many.

count noun ● n. a noun that can form a plural and, in the singular, can be used with *a*, e.g. *books*, *a book*. Contrasted with **MASS NOUN**.

countrified ● adj. characteristic of the country or country life.

country ● n. (pl. **countries**) **1** a nation with its own government, occupying a particular territory. **2** districts outside large city areas. **3** an area with regard to its physical features: *hill country.*
– PHRASES **across country** not keeping to roads.
– ORIGIN Old French *cuntree.*

country and western ● n. country music.

country club ● n. a club in a country area with sporting and social facilities.

country dance ● n. a traditional type of English dance, performed by couples facing each other in long lines.

countryman (or **countrywoman**) ● n. **1** a person living or born in the country. **2** a person from the same country as someone else.

country music ● n. a form of popular music originating in the rural southern US, featuring ballads and dance tunes accompanied by a guitar.

countryside ● n. the land and scenery of a rural area.

county ● n. (pl. **counties**) **1** each of the main areas into which some countries are divided for the purposes of local government. **2** US a political and administrative division of a state.
– ORIGIN Old French *conte* 'land of a count'.

county council ● n. (in the UK) the elected governing body of a county.

county court ● n. (in England and Wales) a local court for civil cases.

County Durham E
see **DURHAM**.

county town ● n. the town that is the administrative capital of a county.

coup /koo/ ● n. (pl. **coups** /kooz/) **1** a coup d'état. **2** a successful move: *the deal is a major coup for the company.*
– ORIGIN French.

coup de grâce /koo duh **grahss**/ ● n. (pl. **coups de grâce** /koo duh **grahss**/) a final blow or shot given to kill a wounded person or animal.
– ORIGIN French, 'stroke of grace'.

coup d'état /koo day-**tah**/ ● n. (pl. **coups d'état** /koo day-**tah**/) a sudden violent seizure of power from a government.
– ORIGIN French, 'blow of state'.

coupé /**koo**-pay/ (also **coupe** /koop/) ● n. a car with a fixed roof, two doors, and a sloping back.
– ORIGIN from French *carrosse coupé* 'cut carriage'.

couple ● n. **1** two people or things of the same sort considered together. **2** two people who are married or in a romantic or sexual relationship. **3** informal an indefinite small number. ● v. (**couples, coupling, coupled**) **1** connect or combine. **2** have sexual intercourse.
– DERIVATIVES **coupler** n.
– ORIGIN Latin *copula* 'connection'.

couplet ● n. a pair of successive rhyming lines of verse.

coupling ● n. a device for connecting railway vehicles or parts of machinery together.

coupon ● n. **1** a voucher entitling the holder to receive a discount or a quantity of something rationed. **2** a detachable form used to send for a purchase or information or to enter a competition.
– ORIGIN French, 'piece cut off'.

courage ● n. **1** the ability to do something that frightens one. **2** strength in the face of pain or grief.
– PHRASES **have the courage of one's convictions** act on one's beliefs despite danger or disapproval.
– ORIGIN Old French *corage*.

courageous ● adj. brave.

Courbet E
/**koor**-bay/, Gustave (1819–77), French realist painter, known for such works as *Burial at Ornans* and *Painter in his Studio.*

courgette /koor-**zhet**/ ● n. Brit. a variety of small vegetable marrow.
– ORIGIN French, 'little gourd'.

courier /**kuu**-ri-er/ ● n. **1** a messenger who carries goods or documents. **2** a person employed to guide and assist a group of tourists.
– ORIGIN Old French *coreor.*

course ● n. **1** a direction taken or intended: *the aircraft changed course.* **2** the way in which something progresses or develops: *the course of history.* **3** a procedure adopted to deal with a situation. **4** a dish forming one of the successive parts of a meal. **5** a series of lectures or lessons in a particular subject. **6** a series of repeated treatments or doses of medication. **7** an area of land or water prepared for racing, golf, or another sport. ● v. (**courses, coursing, coursed**) **1** flow. **2** (**coursing**) hunting game, especially hares, with greyhounds using sight rather than scent.
– PHRASES **in (the) course of 1** in the process of. **2** during. **of course 1** as expected. **2** certainly; yes.
– ORIGIN Latin *cursus* 'running'.

coursework ● n. work done during a course of study, counting towards a final mark.

court ● n. **1** (also **court of law**) the judge, jury, and law officers before whom legal cases are heard. **2** the place where this body meets. **3** a quadrangular area marked out for ball games such as tennis. **4** a quadrangle surrounded by a building or group of buildings. **5** the residence, councillors, and household staff of a sovereign. ● v. **1** dated try to win the love of (someone) with a view to marriage. **2** try to win the support of. **3** behave in a way that makes oneself vulnerable to: *he often courted controversy.*
– PHRASES **hold court** be the centre of attention. **out of court** before a legal hearing can take place. **pay court to** pay flattering attention to.
– ORIGIN Old French *cort*.

court card ● n. Brit. a playing card that is a king, queen, or jack of a suit.

courteous /**ker**-ti-uhss/ ● adj. polite and considerate.
– DERIVATIVES **courteously** adv.
– ORIGIN Old French *corteis* 'having manners fit for a royal court'.

courtesan /kor-ti-**zan**/ ● n. a prostitute with wealthy or upper-class clients.
– ORIGIN French *courtisane.*

courtesy /**ker**-tuh-si/ ● n. (pl. **courtesies**) **1** courteous behaviour. **2** a polite speech or action.
– PHRASES **(by) courtesy of** given or allowed by.

courthouse ● n. a building in which a court of law is held.

courtier /**kor**-ti-er/ ● n. a sovereign's companion or adviser.

courtly ● adj. (**courtlier, courtliest**) very dignified and polite.

court martial ● n. (pl. **courts martial** or **court martials**) a court for trying members

C

of the armed services accused of breaking military law. ● v. (**court-martial**) (**court-martials**, **court-martialling**, **court-martialled**; US **court-martials**, **court-martialing**, **court-martialed**) try by court martial.

Court of St James's E
the court of the British monarch.

court order ● n. a direction issued by a court or a judge requiring a person to do or not do something.

courtship ● n. **1** a period during which a couple develop a romantic relationship. **2** the action of courting a person to win their support.

court shoe ● n. Brit. a woman's plain shoe with a low-cut upper and no fastening.

courtyard ● n. an open area enclosed by walls or buildings.

couscous /kuuss-kuuss, **kooss**-kooss/ ● n. a North African dish of steamed or soaked semolina, served with spicy meat or vegetables.
– ORIGIN Arabic.

cousin ● n. **1** (also **first cousin**) a child of one's uncle or aunt. **2** a person of a similar people or nation.
– PHRASES **second cousin** a child of one's parent's first cousin.
– ORIGIN Old French *cosin*.

Cousteau E
/koo-stoh/, Jacques-Yves (1910–97), French oceanographer and film director, known for his feature films and popular television series on marine life.

couture /koo-tyoor/ ● n. the design and manufacture of fashionable clothes to a client's specific requirements.
– ORIGIN French, 'dressmaking'.

couturier /koo-tyoo-ri-ay/ ● n. (fem. **couturière** /koo-tyoo-ri-**air**/) a person who designs and sells couture clothes.

cove ● n. a small sheltered bay.
– ORIGIN Old English, 'chamber, cave'.

coven /**kuv**-uhn/ ● n. a group of witches who meet regularly.
– ORIGIN Latin *convenire* 'come together'.

covenant /**kuv**-uh-nuhnt/ ● n. **1** a formal agreement. **2** a contract by which one agrees to make regular payments to a charity. **3** an agreement believed to be the basis of a relationship of commitment between God and his people. ● v. agree or pay by covenant.
– ORIGIN Old French, 'agreeing'.

Covent Garden E
a district in central London, the site until 1974 of London's chief fruit and vegetable market, and the home of the national opera and ballet companies, based at the Royal Opera House.

Coventry E
an industrial city in the west Midlands of England.
– PHRASES **send someone to Coventry** esp. Brit. refuse to associate with or speak to someone.

cover ● v. (**covers**, **covering**, **covered**) **1** put something over or in front of (someone or something) so as to protect or conceal. **2** spread or extend over: *the grounds covered eight acres.* **3** deal with or report on: *the course will cover a range of subjects.* **4** travel (a specified distance). **5** (of money) be enough to pay for. **6** (of insurance) protect against a loss or accident. **7** (**cover up**) try to hide or deny the fact of (a wrongful action). **8** (**cover for**) temporarily take over the job of. ● n. **1** something that covers or protects. **2** a thick protective outer part or page of a book or magazine. **3** shelter: *they ran for cover.* **4** a means of concealing an illegal or secret activity: *his neat office was a cover for his real work.* **5** Brit. protection by insurance. **6** (also **cover version**) a recording or performance of a song previously recorded by a different artist.
– PHRASES **break cover** suddenly leave shelter when being chased. **under cover of** concealed by.
– DERIVATIVES **covering** n.
– ORIGIN Old French *covrir*.

coverage ● n. **1** the treatment of a subject by the media. **2** the extent to which something is covered.

cover charge ● n. a service charge per person added to the bill in a restaurant.

Coverdale E
/**kuv**-er-dayl/, Miles (1488–1568), English biblical scholar, who translated the first complete printed English Bible (1535).

covering letter ● n. a letter explaining the contents of an accompanying enclosure.

coverlet ● n. a bedspread.
– ORIGIN from Old French *covrir* 'to cover' + *lit* 'bed'.

cover note ● n. Brit. a temporary certificate showing that a person has a current insurance policy.

covert ● adj. /**kuv**-ert, **koh**-vert/ not done openly; secret. ● n. /**kuv**-ert/ a thicket in which game can hide.
– DERIVATIVES **covertly** adv.
– ORIGIN Old French, 'covered'.

cover-up ● n. an attempt to conceal a mistake or crime.

covet /**kuv**-it/ ● v. (**covets**, **coveting**, **coveted**) long to possess (something belonging to someone else).
– ORIGIN Old French *cuveitier*.

covetous ● adj. longing to possess something.

covey /**kuv**-i/ ● n. (pl. **coveys**) a small flock of game birds.
– ORIGIN Old French *cover* 'sit on, hatch'.

cow[1] ● n. **1** a mature female animal of a domesticated breed of ox. **2** the female of certain other large animals, such as the elephant. **3** informal, derog. a woman.
– ORIGIN Old English.

cow[2] ● v. frighten into giving in to one's wishes.
– ORIGIN prob. from Old Norse, 'oppress'.

Coward, E
Sir Noel (Pierce) (1899–1973), English dramatist, actor, and composer, remembered for witty comedies, such as *Private Lives*, and for songs such as 'Mad Dogs and Englishmen'.

coward ● n. a person who lacks the courage to do dangerous or unpleasant things.
– DERIVATIVES **cowardly** adj.

– ORIGIN Old French *couard*.

cowardice /kow-er-diss/ ● n. lack of courage.

cowboy ● n. **1** a man on horseback who herds cattle in the western US. **2** informal a dishonest or unqualified tradesman.

cower ● v. (**cowers**, **cowering**, **cowered**) crouch down or shrink back in fear.
– ORIGIN German *kūren* 'lie in wait'.

> **Cowes** E
> a town on the Isle of Wight, southern England, famous as a yachting centre.

cowl ● n. **1** a large loose hood forming part of a monk's habit. **2** a covering for a chimney or ventilation shaft.
– ORIGIN Latin *cucullus* 'hood of a cloak'.

cowling ● n. a removable cover for a vehicle or aircraft engine.

cowpat ● n. a flat, round piece of cow dung.

cowrie /kow-ri/ ● n. (pl. **cowries**) a sea mollusc having a glossy shell with a long, narrow opening.
– ORIGIN Hindi.

cowslip ● n. a wild plant with clusters of sweet-smelling yellow flowers.
– ORIGIN Old English, 'cow slime'.

cox ● n. a coxswain. ● v. act as a coxswain for.

coxcomb /koks-kohm/ ● n. archaic a vain and conceited man; a dandy.
– ORIGIN from **COCKSCOMB**.

coxswain /kok-suhn/ ● n. the steersman of a boat.
– ORIGIN from former *cock* 'small boat' + **SWAIN**.

coy ● adj. (**coyer**, **coyest**) **1** pretending to be shy or modest. **2** reluctant to give details about something sensitive: *he's coy about his age.*
– DERIVATIVES **coyly** adv. **coyness** n.
– ORIGIN Old French *coi*.

coyote /koy-oh-ti/ ● n. (pl. **coyote** or **coyotes**) a wolf-like wild dog found in North America.
– ORIGIN from a North American Indian language.

coypu /koy-pyoo/ ● n. (pl. **coypus**) a large beaver-like South American rodent, farmed for its fur.
– ORIGIN from a Chilean language.

cozen /kuz-uhn/ ● v. literary deceive.
– ORIGIN perh. from former Italian *cozzonare* 'to cheat'.

cozy ● adj. US = **COSY**.

CPS ● abbrev. (in the UK) Crown Prosecution Service.

cps (also **c.p.s.**) ● abbrev. **1** Computing characters per second. **2** cycles per second.

CPU ● abbrev. Computing central processing unit.

crab ● n. a marine shellfish with a broad shell and five pairs of legs.
– PHRASES **catch a crab** make a faulty stroke in rowing in which the oar is jammed under the water or misses the water completely.
– ORIGIN Old English.

crab apple ● n. a small, sour kind of apple.
– ORIGIN perh. from Scots and northern English *scrab*.

crabbed ● adj. **1** (of writing) hard to read. **2** bad-tempered.

crabby ● adj. (**crabbier**, **crabbiest**) bad-tempered.

crabwise ● adv. & adj. sideways.

crack ● n. **1** a narrow opening between two parts of something which has split or been broken. **2** a sudden sharp noise. **3** a sharp blow. **4** informal a joke. **5** informal an attempt or chance to do something. **6** (also **crack cocaine**) a very strong form of cocaine. ● v. **1** break with little or no separation of the parts: *take care not to crack the glass.* **2** give way under pressure or strain. **3** make a sudden sharp sound. **4** hit hard. **5** (of a person's voice) suddenly change in pitch. **6** informal solve or decipher: *the code will help you crack the messages.* ● adj. very good or skilful: *a crack shot.*
– PHRASES **crack down on** informal take severe measures against. **crack of dawn** daybreak. **crack of the whip** Brit. informal a chance to try or take part in something. **crack on** informal proceed or progress quickly. **crack up** informal **1** suffer an emotional breakdown. **2** (**be cracked up to be**) be said to be. **get cracking** informal get busy on something.
– ORIGIN Old English.

crackbrained ● adj. informal extremely foolish.

crackdown ● n. a series of severe measures against undesirable or illegal behaviour.

cracked ● adj. informal crazy.

cracker ● n. **1** a paper cylinder which, when pulled apart, makes a sharp noise and releases a small novelty. **2** a firework that explodes with a crack. **3** a thin dry biscuit. **4** Brit. informal a very good example of something.

crackers ● adj. Brit. informal crazy.

cracking ● adj. Brit. informal **1** excellent. **2** fast: *a cracking pace.*

crackle ● v. (**crackles**, **crackling**, **crackled**) make a series of slight cracking noises. ● n. a crackling sound.
– DERIVATIVES **crackly** adj.

crackling ● n. the crisp fatty skin of roast pork.

crackpot informal ● n. an eccentric or foolish person. ● adj. eccentric; impractical.

> **Cracow** E
> /kra-koff, kra-kow/ an industrial and university city in southern Poland.

-cracy ● comb. form referring to a particular form of government or rule: *democracy.*
– ORIGIN Greek *-kratia* 'power, rule'.

cradle ● n. **1** a baby's bed on rockers. **2** a place in which something originates or flourishes: *the Middle East is believed to be the cradle of agriculture.* **3** a supporting framework. ● v. (**cradles**, **cradling**, **cradled**) hold gently and protectively.
– ORIGIN Old English.

craft ● n. **1** an activity involving skill in making things by hand. **2** skill in carrying out one's work. **3** (**crafts**) things made by hand. **4** cunning. **5** (pl. **craft**) a boat, ship, or aircraft. ● v. make (something) skilfully.
– ORIGIN Old English.

craftsman (or **craftswoman**) ● n. a worker skilled in a particular craft.
– DERIVATIVES **craftsmanship** n.

crafty ● adj. (**craftier**, **craftiest**) skilled in deceiving people; cunning.

– DERIVATIVES **craftily** adv. **craftiness** n.

crag ● n. a steep or rugged rock face.
– DERIVATIVES **craggy** adj.
– ORIGIN Celtic.

cram ● v. (**crams**, **cramming**, **crammed**) **1** force (too many people or things) into a space. **2** fill (something) to the point of overflowing. **3** study hard just before an examination.
– ORIGIN Old English.

crammer ● n. Brit. a college that gives students concentrated preparation for examinations.

cramp ● n. painful involuntary tightening of a muscle or muscles. ● v. restrict the development of: *tighter rules will cramp economic growth.*
– ORIGIN German and Dutch *krampe.*

cramped ● adj. **1** uncomfortably small or crowded. **2** (of handwriting) small and difficult to read.

crampon /kram-pon/ ● n. a plate with spikes, fixed to a boot for climbing on ice or rock.
– ORIGIN Old French.

cranberry ● n. (pl. **cranberries**) a small sour-tasting red berry used in cooking.
– ORIGIN German *Kranbeere* 'crane-berry'.

crane ● n. **1** a tall machine used for moving heavy objects by suspending them from a projecting arm. **2** a grey or white wading bird with long legs and a long neck. ● v. (**cranes**, **craning**, **craned**) stretch out (one's neck) to see something.
– ORIGIN Old English.

crane fly ● n. a fly with very long legs; a daddy-long-legs.

cranial /kray-ni-uhl/ ● adj. relating to the skull or cranium.

cranium /kray-ni-uhm/ ● n. (pl. **craniums** or **crania** /kray-ni-uh/) the part of the skull enclosing the brain.
– ORIGIN Latin.

crank[1] ● n. a right-angled part of an axle or shaft, for converting linear to circular motion or vice versa. ● v. **1** turn a crankshaft or handle. **2** (**crank up**) informal increase the intensity of. **3** (**crank out**) informal produce regularly and routinely: *researchers cranked out worthy studies.*
– ORIGIN Old English.

crank[2] ● n. an eccentric person.
– ORIGIN from **CRANKY**.

crankshaft ● n. a shaft driven by a crank.

cranky ● adj. (**crankier**, **crankiest**) informal **1** eccentric. **2** esp. N. Amer. bad-tempered.
– ORIGIN perh. from Dutch or German *krank* 'sick'.

Cranmer, E
Thomas (1489–1556), English priest and martyr, the first Protestant Archbishop of Canterbury and chief compiler of the Book of Common Prayer. He was tried for treason and heresy and burnt at the stake in the reign of Mary I.

cranny ● n. (pl. **crannies**) a small, narrow space or opening.
– ORIGIN Latin *crena* 'notch'.

crap vulgar ● n. **1** excrement. **2** nonsense. ● v. (**craps**, **crapping**, **crapped**) defecate. ● adj. extremely poor in quality.
– DERIVATIVES **crappy** adj.
– ORIGIN from Dutch *krappe* 'chaff'.

crape ● n. black silk, formerly used for mourning clothes.
– ORIGIN from **CRÊPE**.

craps ● n. a North American gambling game played with two dice.
– ORIGIN perh. from **CRAB** or *crab's eyes*, referring to a throw of two ones.

crapulous /krap-yuu-luhss/ ● adj. literary relating to the drinking of alcohol or to drunkenness.
– DERIVATIVES **crapulent** adj.
– ORIGIN Latin *crapulentus* 'very drunk'.

crash ● v. **1** (of a vehicle) collide violently with an obstacle or another vehicle. **2** (of an aircraft) fall from the sky and hit the land or sea. **3** move with force and sudden loud noise: *huge waves crashed down on us.* **4** (of shares) fall suddenly in value. **5** Computing fail suddenly. **6** (also **crash out**) informal fall deeply asleep. ● n. an instance or sound of crashing. ● adj. rapid and concentrated: *a crash course in Italian.*

crash helmet ● n. a helmet worn by a motorcyclist to protect the head.

crashing ● adj. informal complete; total: *a crashing bore.*

crash-land ● v. (of an aircraft) land roughly in an emergency.

crass ● adj. very thoughtless and stupid.
– ORIGIN Latin *crassus* 'solid, thick'.

-crat ● comb. form referring to a member or supporter of a particular form of government or rule: *democrat.*
– ORIGIN Greek *-kratia* 'power, rule'.

crate ● n. **1** a wooden case for transporting goods. **2** a square container divided into sections for holding bottles. **3** informal an old and ramshackle vehicle. ● v. (**crates**, **crating**, **crated**) pack in a crate.
– ORIGIN perh. from Dutch *krat* 'tailboard of a wagon'.

crater ● n. a large bowl-shaped hollow, caused by an explosion or impact or forming the mouth of a volcano.
– ORIGIN Greek *kratēr* 'mixing bowl'.

-cratic ● comb. form referring to a particular form of government or rule: *democratic.*

cravat /kruh-vat/ ● n. a strip of fabric worn by men round the neck and tucked inside a shirt.
– ORIGIN French *cravate.*

crave ● v. (**craves**, **craving**, **craved**) **1** feel a powerful desire for. **2** archaic ask for: *I must crave your indulgence.*
– ORIGIN Old English.

craven ● adj. cowardly.
– ORIGIN perh. from Old French *cravanter* 'crush'.

craving ● n. a powerful desire for something.

craw ● n. dated the crop of a bird.
– ORIGIN Dutch *crāghe* or German *krage* 'neck'.

Crawford, E
Joan (1908–77; born *Lucille le Sueur*), American actress, star of such films as *Mildred Pierce* and *Whatever Happened to Baby Jane?*

crawl ● v. **1** move forward on the hands and knees or with the body close to the ground. **2** move along very slowly. **3** (**be crawling with**) be unpleasantly covered or crowded with: *the place was crawling with journalists.*

4 informal behave in a servile way to win someone's favour. ● n. **1** an act of crawling. **2** a very slow rate of movement. **3** a swimming stroke involving alternate overarm movements and rapid kicks of the legs.
– DERIVATIVES **crawler** n.
– ORIGIN perh. from Swedish *kravla* and Danish *kravle.*

crayfish ● n. (pl. **crayfish**) a freshwater or marine shellfish resembling a small lobster.
– ORIGIN Old French *crevice.*

crayon ● n. a stick of coloured chalk or wax, used for drawing. ● v. draw with a crayon or crayons.
– ORIGIN French.

craze ● n. a widespread but short-lived enthusiasm for something. ● v. (**crazes, crazing, crazed**) **1** (**crazed**) wildly insane. **2** (**be crazed**) (of a surface) be covered with a network of fine cracks.
– ORIGIN perh. Scandinavian.

crazy ● adj. (**crazier, craziest**) **1** insane. **2** very enthusiastic or fond: *I'm crazy about Cindy.* **3** foolish or ridiculous.
– PHRASES **like crazy** to a great degree.
– DERIVATIVES **crazily** adv. **craziness** n.

crazy paving ● n. Brit. paving made of irregular pieces of flat stone.

creak ● v. make or move with a harsh high sound. ● n. a creaking sound.
– DERIVATIVES **creaky** adj.

cream ● n. **1** the thick fatty liquid which rises to the top when milk is left to stand. **2** a food containing cream or having a creamy texture. **3** a thick liquid cosmetic or medical substance. **4** the very best of a group: *the cream of Paris society.* **5** a very pale yellow or off-white colour. ● v. **1** work (butter) to form a smooth soft paste. **2** mash (a cooked vegetable) with milk or cream. **3** (**cream off**) take away the best of.
– ORIGIN Old French *cresme.*

cream cheese ● n. soft cheese made from unskimmed milk and cream.

creamer ● n. a cream or milk substitute for adding to coffee or tea.

creamery ● n. (pl. **creameries**) a factory that produces butter and cheese.

creamy ● adj. (**creamier, creamiest**) resembling or containing a lot of cream.

crease ● n. **1** a line or ridge produced on paper or cloth by folding or pressing. **2** Cricket any of a number of lines marked on the pitch at specified places. ● v. (**creases, creasing, creased**) **1** make or become crumpled. **2** (**crease up**) Brit. informal burst out laughing.
– ORIGIN prob. from CREST.

create ● v. (**creates, creating, created**) **1** bring into existence. **2** cause to happen; produce: *he wanted to create a good impression.* **3** Brit. informal make a fuss; complain.
– ORIGIN Latin *creare.*

creation ● n. **1** the action of creating. **2** a thing which has been made or invented. **3** (**the Creation**) the creating of the universe regarded as an act of God. **4** (**Creation**) literary the universe.

creative ● adj. involving the use of the imagination or original ideas in order to create something.
– DERIVATIVES **creatively** adv. **creativity** n.

creator ● n. **1** a person or thing that creates. **2** (**the Creator**) God.

creature ● n. **1** a living being, in particular an animal as distinct from a person. **2** a person viewed in a particular way: *the poor creature!*
– ORIGIN Latin *creatura* 'thing created'.

creature comforts ● pl. n. things that make one's life comfortable, such as good food.

crèche /kresh/ ● n. Brit. a day nursery for babies and young children.
– ORIGIN French.

Crécy, Battle of E
/kress-i/ a battle in 1346 near the village of Crécy-en-Ponthieu in Picardy in which the English defeated the French, the first major English victory of the Hundred Years War.

credence /kree-duhnss/ ● n. belief in something as true: *he gave no credence to the witness's statement.*
– ORIGIN Latin *credentia.*

credential /kri-den-sh'l/ ● n. **1** a qualification, achievement, or quality, used to indicate a person's suitability for something: *his academic credentials cannot be doubted.* **2** (**credentials**) documents proving a person's identity or qualifications.

credible ● adj. able to be believed; convincing.
– DERIVATIVES **credibility** n. **credibly** adv.
– ORIGIN Latin *credere* 'believe'.

credit ● n. **1** the system of doing business by trusting that a customer will pay at a later date for goods or services supplied. **2** public recognition or praise. **3** a source of pride: *the fans are a credit to the club.* **4** an entry in an account recording a sum received. **5** a written acknowledgement of a contributor's role displayed at the beginning or end of a film or programme. **6** a unit of study counting towards a degree or diploma. ● v. (**credits, crediting, credited**) **1** (**credit with**) attribute (something) to: *he has been credited with changing Texan politics.* **2** believe. **3** add (an amount of money) to an account.
– PHRASES **be in credit** (of an account) have money in it. **do someone credit** make someone worthy of praise or respect.
– ORIGIN Latin *creditum.*

creditable ● adj. deserving recognition and praise.
– DERIVATIVES **creditably** adv.

credit card ● n. a plastic card allowing the holder to make purchases on credit.

creditor ● n. a person or company to whom money is owed.

creditworthy ● adj. considered suitable to receive financial credit.

credo /kree-doh/ ● n. (pl. **credos**) a statement of a person's beliefs or aims.
– ORIGIN Latin, 'I believe'.

credulity /kri-dyoo-li-ti/ ● n. the tendency to be too ready to believe things.

credulous /kred-yuu-luhss/ ● adj. too ready to believe things.
– ORIGIN Latin *credulus.*

creed ● n. **1** a system of religious belief; a faith. **2** a statement of beliefs or principles: *liberalism was more than a political creed.*
– ORIGIN Latin *credo* 'I believe'.

creek ● n. **1** an inlet in a shoreline. **2** N. Amer. &

Austral./NZ a stream or small river.
– PHRASES **up the creek** informal in severe difficulty.
– ORIGIN Old French *crique*.

creel ● n. a large basket for carrying fish.
– ORIGIN unknown.

C

creep ● v. (**creeps**, **creeping**, **crept**) **1** move slowly and cautiously. **2** progress or develop gradually: *interest rates are creeping up.* **3** (**creeping**) (of a plant) growing along the ground or another surface. **4** (**creep to**) informal behave in a servile way towards. ● n. **1** informal a person who behaves in a servile way to win favour. **2** slow and gradual movement.
– PHRASES **give someone the creeps** informal make someone feel disgust or fear.
– ORIGIN Old English.

creeper ● n. a plant that grows along the ground or another surface.

creepy ● adj. (**creepier**, **creepiest**) informal causing an unpleasant feeling of fear or unease.

creepy-crawly ● n. (pl. **creepy-crawlies**) informal a spider or small insect.

cremate ● v. (**cremates**, **cremating**, **cremated**) dispose of (a corpse) by burning it to ashes.
– DERIVATIVES **cremation** n.
– ORIGIN Latin *cremare* 'burn'.

crematorium /kre-muh-tor-i-uhm/ ● n. (pl. **crematoria** or **crematoriums**) a building where the dead are cremated.

crème de la crème /krem duh la **krem**/ ● n. the best person or thing of a particular kind.
– ORIGIN French, 'cream of the cream'.

crenellated /kren-uhl-lay-tid/ (also **crenelated**) ● adj. (of a building) having battlements.
– ORIGIN Latin *crena* 'notch'.

crenellations ● pl. n. battlements.

Creole ● n. **1** a person of mixed European and black descent. **2** a descendant of European settlers in the Caribbean or Central or South America. **3** a descendant of French settlers in the southern US. **4** a language formed from a combination of a European language and an African language.
– ORIGIN French.

creosote /kree-uh-soht/ ● n. **1** a dark brown oil obtained from coal tar, used as a wood preservative. **2** a liquid obtained from wood tar, used as an antiseptic.
– ORIGIN from Greek *kreas* 'flesh' + *sōtēr* 'preserver'.

crêpe /krayp/ (also **crape**) ● n. **1** a light, thin fabric with a wrinkled surface. **2** hard-wearing wrinkled rubber used for the soles of shoes. **3** /also krep/ a thin pancake.
– ORIGIN Old French *crespe* 'curled'.

crêpe paper ● n. thin, crinkled paper used for making decorations.

crept past and past part. of **CREEP**.

crepuscular /kri-pus-kyuu-ler/ ● adj. literary resembling or relating to twilight.
– ORIGIN Latin *crepusculum* 'twilight'.

crescendo /kri-shen-doh/ ● n. **1** (pl. **crescendos** or **crescendi** /kri-shen-di/) a gradual increase in loudness in a piece of music. **2** a climax: *the hysteria reached a crescendo before the festival.* ● adv. & adj. Music gradually becoming louder.
– ORIGIN Italian.

crescent /krez-uhnt/ ● n. **1** the form of the waxing or waning moon, seen as a narrow curved shape tapering to a point at each end. **2** something of this shape: *a crescent of golden sand.*
– ORIGIN Old French *creissant*.

cress ● n. a plant with hot-tasting leaves, some kinds of which are eaten in salads.
– ORIGIN Old English.

crest ● n. **1** a tuft or growth of feathers, fur, or skin on the head of a bird or animal. **2** a plume of feathers on a helmet. **3** the top of a ridge, wave, etc. **4** a distinctive heraldic design representing a family or organization. ● v. **1** reach the top of: *she crested a hill and saw the valley.* **2** (**crested**) having a crest.
– ORIGIN Latin *crista*.

crestfallen ● adj. sad and disappointed.

Cretaceous /kri-tay-shuhss/ ● adj. Geol. relating to the last period of the Mesozoic era (about 146 to 65 million years ago), at the end of which dinosaurs and many other organisms died out.
– ORIGIN from Latin *creta* 'chalk'.

Crete E
/kreet/ a Greek island in the eastern Mediterranean; capital, Heraklion.
– DERIVATIVES **Cretan** adj. & n.

cretin /kret-in/ ● n. **1** a stupid person. **2** Med., dated a person who is physically and mentally handicapped because of a lack of thyroid hormone.
– ORIGIN Swiss French *crestin* 'Christian', prob. to convey a reminder that handicapped people are human.

cretinous ● adj. very stupid.

cretonne /kri-ton/ ● n. a heavy cotton fabric with a floral pattern, used for upholstery.
– ORIGIN French.

Creutzfeldt–Jakob disease /kroyts-felt-yak-ob/ ● n. a fatal disease affecting nerve cells in the brain, a form of which is possibly linked to BSE.
– ORIGIN named after the German neurologists H. G. *Creutzfeldt* (1885–1964) and A. *Jakob* (1882–1927).

crevasse /kri-vass/ ● n. a deep open crack in a glacier or ice field.
– ORIGIN Old French *crevace* 'crevice'.

crevice /kre-viss/ ● n. a narrow opening or crack in a rock or wall.
– ORIGIN Old French *crevace*.

crew[1] ● n. **1** a group of people who work on a ship, aircraft, or train. **2** such a group other than the officers. **3** a group of people who work together. **4** informal, usu. derog. a group of people considered together. ● v. **1** provide with a crew. **2** act as a member of a crew.
– ORIGIN Old French *creue* 'increase'.

crew[2] past of **CROW**[2].

crew cut ● n. a very short haircut for men and boys.

crew neck ● n. a close-fitting round neckline.

crib ● n. **1** esp. N. Amer. a child's cot. **2** a rack for animal fodder. **3** informal a translation of a text for use by students. **4** informal something copied from another person's work. **5** cribbage. ● v. (**cribs**, **cribbing**, **cribbed**) informal copy (some-

thing) dishonestly or without acknowledgement.
– ORIGIN Old English.

cribbage • n. a card game for two players, in which the objective is to reach a certain number of points.
– ORIGIN from **CRIB**.

Crick, E
Francis Harry Compton (b.1916), English biophysicist, who with J. D. Watson proposed the double helix structure of the DNA molecule.

crick • n. a painful stiff feeling in the neck or back. • v. twist or strain (one's neck or back), causing painful stiffness.
– ORIGIN unknown.

cricket[1] • n. an open-air game played with a bat, ball, and wickets, between two teams of eleven players.
– PHRASES **not cricket** Brit. informal not fair or honourable.
– DERIVATIVES **cricketer** n.
– ORIGIN unknown.

cricket[2] • n. an insect like a grasshopper, the male of which produces a shrill chirping sound.
– ORIGIN Old French *criquet*.

cri de cœur /kree duh **ker**/ • n. (pl. **cris de cœur** /kree duh **ker**/) a passionate appeal or complaint.
– ORIGIN French, 'cry from the heart'.

cried past and past part. of **CRY**.

crikey • exclam. Brit. informal an expression of surprise.
– ORIGIN euphemism for **CHRIST**.

crime • n. **1** an offence against an individual or the state which is punishable by law. **2** such actions as a whole: *the fight against organized crime*. **3** informal something disgraceful or regrettable.
– ORIGIN Latin *crimen* 'judgement'.

Crimea E
/kry-**mee**-uh/ (usu. **the Crimea**) a peninsula of Ukraine lying between the Sea of Azov and the Black Sea.

Crimean War E
a war (1853–6) between Russia and an alliance of Great Britain, France, Sardinia, and Turkey.

criminal • n. a person who has committed a crime. • adj. **1** relating to crime or a crime. **2** informal disgraceful and regrettable.
– DERIVATIVES **criminality** n. **criminally** adv.

criminology /kri-mi-**nol**-uh-ji/ • n. the scientific study of crime and criminals.
– DERIVATIVES **criminologist** n.

crimp • v. press into small folds or ridges.
– ORIGIN Old English.

crimplene /**krimp**-leen/ • n. trademark a synthetic crease-resistant fabric.
– ORIGIN prob. from **CRIMP** + **TERYLENE**.

crimson /**krim**-z'n/ • n. a deep red colour.
– ORIGIN Arabic.

cringe /krinj/ • v. (**cringes**, **cringing**, **cringed**) **1** shrink back or cower in fear or in a servile way. **2** have a sudden feeling of embarrassment or disgust.
– ORIGIN Old English, 'bend'.

crinkle • v. (**crinkle**, **crinkling**, **crinkled**) form small creases or wrinkles. • n. a small crease or wrinkle.
– DERIVATIVES **crinkly** adj.
– ORIGIN from **CRINGE**.

crinoline /**krin**-uh-lin/ • n. a petticoat stiffened with hoops, formerly worn to make a long skirt stand out.
– ORIGIN French.

Crippen, E
Hawley Harvey (1862–1910; known as **Doctor Crippen**), American-born British murderer, who poisoned his wife and sailed to Canada with his former secretary. His arrest in Canada was achieved through a message sent by radio-telegraphy, the first case of its use in catching a criminal.

cripple • n. archaic or offens. a person who is unable to walk or move properly through disability or injury. • v. (**cripples**, **crippling**, **crippled**) **1** make (someone) unable to move or walk properly. **2** severely damage or weaken.
– ORIGIN Old English.

crisis • n. (pl. **crises**) **1** a time of severe difficulty or danger. **2** a time when a difficult or important decision must be made: *she's having a mid-life crisis*.
– ORIGIN Greek *krisis* 'decision'.

crisp • adj. **1** firm, dry, and brittle. **2** (of the weather) cool and fresh. **3** brisk and decisive: *her answer was crisp*. • n. (also **potato crisp**) Brit. a thin slice of fried potato eaten as a snack. • v. make or become crisp.
– DERIVATIVES **crisply** adv. **crispness** n.
– ORIGIN Latin *crispus* 'curled'.

crispbread • n. a thin crisp biscuit made from rye or wheat.

crispy • adj. (**crispier**, **crispiest**) firm and brittle; crisp.

criss-cross • adj. with a pattern of crossing lines. • v. **1** form a criss-cross pattern on. **2** travel around (a place) by going back and forth repeatedly.

criterion /kry-**teer**-i-uhn/ • n. (pl. **criteria** /kry-**teer**-i-uh/) a standard by which something may be judged or decided.
– ORIGIN Greek *kritērion*.

USAGE criterion
The singular form is **criterion** and the plural form is **criteria**. Do not use **criteria** as if it were a singular, as in *a further criteria needs to be considered*; you should say *a further criterion needs to be considered*.

critic • n. **1** a person who finds fault with something. **2** a person who assesses literary or artistic works.
– ORIGIN Greek *kritēs* 'a judge'.

critical • adj. **1** expressing disapproving comments. **2** expressing or involving an assessment of a literary or artistic work. **3** having a decisive importance. **4** at a point of danger or crisis: *the floods were rising and the situation was critical*. **5** (of a nuclear reactor or fuel) maintaining a chain reaction that can sustain itself.
– DERIVATIVES **critically** adv.

criticism • n. **1** expression of disapproval. **2** the critical assessment of literary or artistic works.

criticize (also **criticise**) • v. (**criticizes**, **criticizing**, **criticized**) **1** express disapproval of. **2** assess (a literary or artistic work).

critique /kri-teek/ • n. a critical assessment.
– ORIGIN French.

croak • n. a deep hoarse sound, like that made by a frog. • v. **1** utter a croak. **2** informal die.
– DERIVATIVES **croaky** adj.

Croatia E
/kroh-ay-shuh/ a country in SE Europe, formerly a republic of Yugoslavia; capital, Zagreb.
– DERIVATIVES **Croatian** adj. & n.

crochet /kroh-shay/ • n. a handicraft in which yarn is looped into a fabric of connected stitches by means of a hooked needle. • v. (**crochets** /kroh-shayz/, **crocheting** /kroh-shay-ing/, **crocheted** /kroh-shayd/) make (an article) in this way.
– ORIGIN French, 'little hook'.

croci pl. of **CROCUS**.

crock[1] • n. informal **1** an old person considered to be feeble and useless. **2** Brit. an old worn-out vehicle.
– ORIGIN prob. from **CRACK**.

crock[2] • n. an earthenware pot or jar.
– ORIGIN Old English.

crockery • n. plates, dishes, cups, etc., made of earthenware or china.

Crockett, E
Davy (1786–1836), American frontiersman, soldier, and politician, who took up the cause of Texan independence and was killed at the siege of the Alamo.

crocodile • n. **1** a large tropical reptile living partly in water, with long jaws and a long tail. **2** Brit. informal a line of schoolchildren walking in pairs.
– ORIGIN Greek *krokodilos* 'worm of the stones'.

crocodile tears • pl. n. false tears or sorrow.
– ORIGIN from a belief that crocodiles wept while eating or luring their prey.

crocus /kroh-kuhss/ • n. (pl. **crocuses** or **croci** /kroh-kee/) a small plant with bright yellow, purple, or white flowers.
– ORIGIN Greek *krokos*.

Croesus /kree-suhss/ • n. a person of great wealth.
– ORIGIN the name of a wealthy king of Lydia *c.*560–546 BC.

croft • n. a small rented farm in Scotland or northern England.
– DERIVATIVES **crofter** n.
– ORIGIN Old English.

croissant /krwass-on/ • n. a crescent-shaped flaky bread roll.
– ORIGIN French, 'crescent'.

cromlech /krom-lek/ • n. **1** (in Wales) an ancient tomb consisting of a large flat stone laid on upright ones. **2** (in Brittany) a circle of standing stones.
– ORIGIN Welsh, 'arched flat stone'.

Crompton[1], E
Richmal (1890–1969; pen name of *Richmal Crompton Lamburn*), English writer, who wrote a number of children's stories about a mischievous schoolboy, William Brown.

Crompton[2], E
Samuel (1753–1827), English inventor, known for his invention of the spinning mule.

Cromwell[1], E
Oliver (1599–1658), English general and statesman, Lord Protector of the Commonwealth 1653–8. Cromwell was the leader of the victorious Parliamentary forces (or Roundheads) in the English Civil War.

Cromwell[2], E
Thomas (*c.*1485–1540), English statesman, chief minister to Henry VIII 1531–40. He fell from favour over Henry's marriage to Anne of Cleves and was executed on a charge of treason.

crone • n. an ugly old woman.
– ORIGIN Old French *caroigne* 'carrion'.

Cronin E
/kroh-nin/, A. J. (1896–1981; full name *Archibald Joseph Cronin*), Scottish novelist, author of *The Citadel* and *Dr Finlay's Casebook*.

Cronus E
/kroh-nuhss/ (also **Kronos**) Gk Myth. the youngest son of Uranus (Heaven) and Gaia (Earth), who overthrew his father and was the supreme god until dethroned by his son Zeus. Roman equivalent **SATURN**.

crony /kroh-ni/ • n. (pl. **cronies**) informal, usu. derog. a close friend or companion.
– ORIGIN Greek *khronios* 'long-lasting'.

cronyism • n. derog. the improper appointment of friends and associates to positions of authority.

crook • n. **1** a shepherd's or bishop's hooked staff. **2** a bend at a person's elbow. **3** informal a criminal or dishonest person. • v. bend (a finger or leg). • adj. Austral./NZ informal **1** bad or unwell. **2** dishonest; illegal.
– ORIGIN Old Norse, 'hook'.

crooked /kruu-kid/ • adj. **1** bent or twisted out of shape or position. **2** informal dishonest or illegal.
– DERIVATIVES **crookedly** adv. **crookedness** n.

croon • v. hum, sing, or speak in a soft, low voice.
– DERIVATIVES **crooner** n.
– ORIGIN German and Dutch *krōnen* 'groan'.

crop • n. **1** a plant grown for food or other use. **2** an amount of a crop harvested at one time. **3** an amount of people or things appearing at one time: *the current crop of politicians.* **4** a very short hairstyle. **5** a riding crop. **6** a pouch in a bird's throat where food is stored or prepared for digestion. • v. (**crops**, **cropping**, **cropped**) **1** cut very short. **2** (of an animal) bite off and eat the tops of (plants). **3** (**crop up**) occur unexpectedly. **4** produce (a crop).
– ORIGIN Old English.

crop circle • n. crops which have been flattened in the form of a circle or other pattern by unexplained means.

cropper • n. (in phr. **come a cropper**) informal fall or fail heavily.

croquet /kroh-kay/ • n. a game played on a lawn, in which wooden balls are driven through hoops with a mallet.
– ORIGIN perh. from French *crochet* 'hook'.

croquette /kroh-ket/ • n. a small cake or roll of vegetables, meat, or fish, fried in breadcrumbs.
– ORIGIN French.

Crosby, Bing (1904–77; born *Harry Lillis Crosby*), American singer and actor, famous for the song 'White Christmas'. E

crosier /kroh-zi-er/ • n. var. of CROZIER.

cross • n. **1** a mark, object, or shape formed by two short intersecting lines or pieces (+ or ×). **2** a cross-shaped medal or monument. **3** a thing that has to be endured: *she's just a cross we have to bear.* **4** an animal or plant resulting from cross-breeding. **5** a mixture of two things. **6** Soccer a pass of the ball across the field towards the centre. • v. **1** go or extend across or to the other side of. **2** pass in an opposite or different direction. **3** place crosswise: *Michele crossed her legs.* **4** oppose or stand in the way of. **5** draw a line or lines across; mark with a cross. **6** Brit. mark (a cheque) with a pair of parallel lines to indicate that it must be paid into a named bank account. **7** Soccer pass (the ball) across the field towards the centre. **8** cause (an animal) to interbreed with another of a different species or breed. • adj. annoyed.
– PHRASES **at cross purposes** misunderstanding one another. **cross off** delete (an item) from a list. **cross oneself** make the sign of the cross in front of one's chest as a sign of Christian reverence or to call on God for protection. **cross out/through** delete (a word or phrase) by drawing a line through it. **cross swords** have an argument or dispute. **crossed line** a telephone connection that has been wrongly made with the result that another call can be heard. **get one's wires crossed** have a misunderstanding.
– ORIGIN Latin *crux*.

crossbar • n. **1** a horizontal bar between the two upright posts of a football goal. **2** a bar between the handlebars and saddle on a bicycle.

cross-bencher • n. a member of the House of Lords who is independent of any political party.

crossbow • n. a bow fixed across a wooden support, with a mechanism for drawing and releasing the string.

cross-breed • n. an animal or plant produced by crossing two different species, breeds, or varieties. • v. (**cross-breeds**, **cross-breeding**, **cross-bred**) breed in this way.

cross-check • v. check (information) by using an alternative source or method.

cross-country • adj. **1** across fields or countryside, rather than keeping to roads or tracks. **2** across a region or country.

cross-dressing • n. the wearing of clothing typical of the opposite sex.

cross-examine • v. (**cross-examines**, **cross-examining**, **cross-examined**) question (a witness called by the other party) in a court of law to check their testimony.
– DERIVATIVES **cross-examination** n.

cross-eyed • adj. having one or both eyes turned inwards towards the nose.

cross-fertilize (also **cross-fertilise**) • v. (**cross-fertilizes**, **cross-fertilizing**, **cross-fertilized**) **1** fertilize (a plant) using pollen from another plant of the same species. **2** stimulate the development of (something) with an exchange of ideas.
– DERIVATIVES **cross-fertilization** (also **cross-fertilisation**) n.

crossfire • n. gunfire from two or more directions passing through the same area.

cross-hatch • v. shade (an area) with many intersecting parallel lines.

crossing • n. **1** a place where roads or railway lines cross. **2** a place at which one may safely cross a street or railway line.

cross-legged • adj. & adv. (of a seated person) with the legs crossed at the ankles and the knees bent outwards.

crossover • n. **1** a point or place of crossing. **2** the production of work in a new style or in a combination of styles, especially in popular music: *a perfect dance/soul crossover.*

cross ownership • n. the ownership by one corporation of different companies with related interests or commercial aims.

cross-question • v. question in great detail.

cross reference • n. a reference to another text or part of a text, given to provide further information.

crossroads • n. a place where two or more roads cross each other.

cross section • n. **1** a surface exposed by making a straight cut through a solid object at right angles to its length. **2** a typical sample of a larger group.

crosswind • n. a wind blowing across one's direction of travel.

crosswise (also **crossways**) • adv. **1** in the form of a cross. **2** diagonally.

crossword • n. a puzzle consisting of a grid of squares and blanks into which words crossing vertically and horizontally are written according to clues.

crotch • n. the part of the human body between the legs where they join the torso.
– ORIGIN partly from CRUTCH.

crotchet /kro-chit/ • n. **1** esp. Brit. a musical note having the time value of half a minim, shown by a large solid dot with a plain stem. **2** an odd or unfounded belief.
– ORIGIN Old French *crochet* 'little hook'.

crotchety • adj. irritable.

crouch • v. bend the knees and bring the upper body forward and down. • n. a crouching position.
– ORIGIN perh. from Old French *crochir* 'be bent'.

croup[1] /kroop/ • n. inflammation of the throat in children, causing coughing and breathing difficulties.
– ORIGIN dialect, 'to croak'.

croup[2] /kroop/ • n. the rump of a horse.
– ORIGIN Old French.

croupier /kroo-pi-ay/ • n. the person in charge of a gambling table, gathering in and paying out money or tokens.
– ORIGIN French.

crouton /kroo-ton/ • n. a small piece of fried or toasted bread served with soup or used as a garnish.
– ORIGIN French.

crow[1] • n. a large black bird with a harsh call.
– PHRASES **as the crow flies** in a straight line across country.
– ORIGIN Old English.

crow[2] ● v. (**crows**, **crowing**, **crowed** or **crew**) **1** (of a cock) make its loud shrill cry. **2** express pride or triumph in a gloating way. ● n. the cry of a cock.
– ORIGIN Old English.

crowbar ● n. an iron bar with a flattened end, used as a lever.

C

crowd ● n. **1** a large number of people gathered together. **2** informal, usu. derog. a group of people with a shared quality: *he hangs around with a fancy writing crowd.* ● v. **1** fill (a space) almost completely. **2** move or come together as a crowd. **3** move or stand too close to. **4** (**crowd out**) keep (someone or something) out by taking their place.
– DERIVATIVES **crowded** adj.
– ORIGIN Old English, 'press, hasten'.

crown ● n. **1** a circular ornamental headdress worn by a monarch as a symbol of authority. **2** (**the Crown**) the monarchy or reigning monarch. **3** a wreath of leaves or flowers worn as an emblem of victory. **4** an award gained by a victory: *the world heavyweight crown.* **5** the top or highest part of something, such as a person's head or a hat. **6** an artificial replacement or covering for the upper part of a tooth. **7** a former British coin worth five shillings (25 pence). ● v. **1** place a crown on the head of (someone) to formally declare them to be a monarch. **2** rest on or form the top of. **3** be the triumphant conclusion of: *his ride crowned an amazing sporting comeback.*
– ORIGIN Latin *corona.*

Crown Colony ● n. a British colony controlled by the Crown.

Crown Court ● n. (in England and Wales) a court which deals with serious cases referred from the magistrates' courts.

Crown jewels ● pl. n. the crown and other jewellery worn or carried by the sovereign on state occasions.

Crown prince ● n. (in some countries) a male heir to a throne.

Crown princess ● n. **1** the wife of a Crown prince. **2** (in some countries) a female heir to a throne.

Crown Prosecution Service E
(in England and Wales) an independent organization which decides whether cases brought by the police proceed to the criminal court.

crow's foot ● n. a branching wrinkle at the outer corner of a person's eye.

crow's-nest ● n. a platform for a lookout at the masthead of a ship.

crozier /kroh-zi-er/ (also **crosier**) ● n. a hooked staff carried by a bishop.
– ORIGIN Old French *croisier* 'cross-bearer'.

cruces pl. of CRUX.

crucial /kroo-sh'l/ ● adj. **1** decisive or critical: *negotiations were at a crucial stage.* **2** informal very important. **3** informal excellent.
– DERIVATIVES **crucially** adv.
– ORIGIN Latin *crux* 'cross'.

crucible /kroo-si-b'l/ ● n. a container in which metals or other substances may be melted or subjected to very high temperatures.
– ORIGIN Latin *crucibulum.*

cruciferous /kroo-sif-uh-ruhss/ ● adj. Bot. of the cabbage family, with four equal petals arranged in a cross.
– ORIGIN from Latin *crux* 'cross' + *-fer* 'bearing'.

crucifix /kroo-si-fiks/ ● n. a model of a cross with a figure of Christ on it.
– ORIGIN from Latin *cruci fixus* 'fixed to a cross'.

crucifixion ● n. **1** the execution of a person by crucifying them. **2** (**the Crucifixion**) the killing of Jesus Christ in such a way.

cruciform /kroo-si-form/ ● adj. having the shape of a cross.

crucify /kroo-si-fy/ ● v. (**crucifies**, **crucifying**, **crucified**) **1** put (someone) to death by nailing or binding them to a cross. **2** informal criticize severely.
– ORIGIN from Latin *crux* 'cross' + *figere* 'fix'.

crud ● n. informal **1** an unpleasantly dirty or messy substance. **2** nonsense.
– DERIVATIVES **cruddy** adj.
– ORIGIN from CURD.

crude ● adj. **1** in a natural state; not yet processed: *crude oil.* **2** rough or simple: *a pair of crude huts.* **3** coarse or vulgar. ● n. natural mineral oil.
– DERIVATIVES **crudely** adv. **crudity** n.
– ORIGIN Latin *crudus* 'raw, rough'.

crudités /kroo-di-tay/ ● pl. n. mixed raw vegetables served with a sauce into which they may be dipped.
– ORIGIN French *crudité* 'rawness'.

cruel ● adj. (**crueller**, **cruellest** or **crueler**, **cruelest**) **1** taking pleasure in the suffering of others. **2** causing pain or suffering.
– DERIVATIVES **cruelly** adv.
– ORIGIN Latin *crudelis.*

cruelty ● n. (pl. **cruelties**) cruel behaviour or attitudes.

cruet /kroo-it/ ● n. **1** a small container for salt, pepper, oil, or vinegar for use at a dining table. **2** Brit. a stand holding such containers.
– ORIGIN Old French, 'small pot'.

Cruikshank E
/kruuk-shangk/, George (1792–1878), English painter, illustrator, and caricaturist, known for exposing the private life of the Prince Regent (the future George IV).

cruise ● v. (**cruises**, **cruising**, **cruised**) **1** move slowly around without a precise destination. **2** travel smoothly at a moderate speed that is economical on fuel. **3** achieve an objective with ease: *United cruised to a 2-0 win.* ● n. a voyage on a ship taken as a holiday, calling in at several places.
– ORIGIN prob. from Dutch *kruisen* 'to cross'.

cruise missile ● n. a low-flying missile which is guided to its target by an on-board computer.

cruiser ● n. **1** a large fast warship. **2** a yacht or motor boat with passenger accommodation.

cruiserweight ● n. esp. Brit. = LIGHT HEAVYWEIGHT.

crumb ● n. **1** a small fragment of bread, cake, or biscuit. **2** a very small amount: *the Budget provided few crumbs of comfort.*
– ORIGIN Old English.

crumble ● v. (**crumbles**, **crumbling**, **crumbled**) **1** break or fall apart into small fragments. **2** gradually decline or fall apart. ● n. Brit. a baked pudding made with fruit and a crumbly topping.

– ORIGIN Old English.

crumbly • adj. easily crumbling.

crummy • adj. informal bad or unpleasant.

crumpet • n. **1** a soft, flat cake with an open texture, eaten toasted and buttered. **2** Brit. informal women regarded as objects of sexual desire.

– ORIGIN unknown.

crumple • v. (**crumples**, **crumpling**, **crumpled**) **1** crush so as to become creased. **2** collapse. • n. a crease or wrinkle.

– ORIGIN Old English, 'bent, crooked'.

crunch • v. **1** crush (something hard or brittle) with the teeth. **2** move with a noisy grinding sound. • n. **1** a crunching sound. **2** (**the crunch**) informal the crucial point of a situation.

– DERIVATIVES **crunchy** (**crunchier**, **crunchiest**) adj.

crupper /krup-per/ • n. a strap at the back of a saddle and looped under a horse's tail, to prevent the saddle or harness from slipping.

– ORIGIN Old French *cropiere*.

crusade • n. **1** any of a series of medieval military expeditions made by Europeans to recover the Holy Land from the Muslims. **2** an energetic organized campaign: *a crusade against crime*. • v. (**crusades**, **crusading**, **crusaded**) lead or take part in a crusade.

– DERIVATIVES **crusader** n.

– ORIGIN French *croisée* 'the state of being marked with the cross'.

crush • v. **1** press so as to squash, crease, or break up. **2** defeat or subdue completely: *he sent in the army to crush the militants*. • n. **1** a crowd of people pressed closely together. **2** informal an intense infatuation: *she had a crush on Dr Jones*. **3** a drink made from the juice of pressed fruit.

– DERIVATIVES **crusher** n.

– ORIGIN Old French *cruissir* 'to crack'.

crust • n. **1** the tough outer part of a loaf of bread. **2** informal a living or livelihood: *I've been earning a crust where I can*. **3** a hardened layer, coating, or deposit. **4** the outermost rocky layer of the earth. **5** a layer of pastry covering a pie. • v. form into or cover with a crust.

– ORIGIN Latin *crusta*.

crustacean /kruss-tay-sh'n/ • n. an animal with a hard shell, usually living in water, such as a crab or lobster.

– ORIGIN Latin *crusta* 'shell, crust'.

crusty • adj. (**crustier**, **crustiest**) **1** having or consisting of a crust. **2** easily irritated. • n. (pl. **crusties**) informal a young person of a group having a shabby appearance and a wandering lifestyle.

crutch • n. **1** a long stick with a crosspiece at the top, used as a support by a lame person. **2** a person's crotch.

– ORIGIN Old English.

crux /kruks/ • n. (pl. **cruxes** or **cruces** /kroo-seez/) (**the crux**) the most important point under discussion.

– ORIGIN Latin, 'cross'.

Cruyff E
/kroyff/, Johan (b.1947), Dutch footballer and football manager. He was a member of the Ajax team that won three European Cup Finals (1971–3). He went on to manage Barcelona 1988–96.

cry • v. (**cries**, **crying**, **cried**) **1** shed tears. **2** shout or scream loudly. **3** (of a bird or other animal) make a distinctive call. **4** (**cry out for**) demand: *the scheme cries out for reform*. **5** (**cry off**) informal fail to keep to an arrangement. • n. (pl. **cries**) **1** a spell of shedding tears. **2** a loud shout or scream. **3** a distinctive call of a bird or other animal.

– ORIGIN Old French *crier*.

crying • adj. very great: *it would be a crying shame*.

cryogenics /kry-uh-jen-iks/ • n. the branch of physics concerned with the production and effects of very low temperatures.

– DERIVATIVES **cryogenic** adj.

– ORIGIN from Greek *kruos* 'frost'.

crypt • n. an underground room or vault beneath a church, used as a chapel or burial place.

– ORIGIN Greek *kruptē*.

cryptic • adj. mysterious or obscure in meaning: *he gave us a cryptic message to pass on*.

– DERIVATIVES **cryptically** adv.

– ORIGIN Greek *kruptos* 'hidden'.

cryptogram /krip-tuh-gram/ • n. a text written in code.

cryptography • n. the art of writing or solving codes.

– DERIVATIVES **cryptographer** n. **cryptographic** adj.

crystal • n. **1** a transparent mineral, especially quartz. **2** a piece of a solid substance with a regular internal structure and plane faces arranged symmetrically. **3** very clear glass. • adj. completely clear: *the crystal waters of the lake*.

– ORIGIN Greek *krustallos* 'ice, crystal'.

crystal ball • n. a solid globe of glass or crystal, used for predicting the future.

crystalline /kriss-tuh-lyn/ • adj. **1** having the structure and form of a crystal. **2** literary very clear.

crystallize (also **crystallise**) • v. (**crystallizes**, **crystallizing**, **crystallized**) **1** form crystals. **2** make or become definite and clear: *his book helped me to crystallize my thoughts*. **3** (**crystallized**) (of fruit) coated with and preserved in sugar.

– DERIVATIVES **crystallization** (also **crystallisation**) n.

crystallography /kriss-tuh-log-ruh-fi/ • n. the branch of science concerned with the structure and properties of crystals.

– DERIVATIVES **crystallographer** n. **crystallographic** adj.

Crystal Palace E
a large building of iron and glass, designed by Joseph Paxton for the Great Exhibition of 1851 in London. It burned down in 1936.

c/s • abbrev. cycles per second.

CS gas • n. a powerful form of tear gas used in the control of riots.

– ORIGIN from the initials of the American chemists Ben B. *Corson* (b.1896) and Roger W. *Stoughton* (1906–57).

ct • abbrev. **1** carat. **2** cent.

CTC • abbrev. City Technology College.

Cu • symb. the chemical element copper.

– ORIGIN Latin *cuprum*.

cu. • abbrev. cubic.

C

cub • n. **1** the young of a fox, bear, lion, or other carnivorous mammal. **2** (also **Cub Scout**) a member of the junior branch of the Scout Association, for boys aged about 8 to 11.
– ORIGIN unknown.

Cuba E
a Caribbean country, the largest and furthest west of the islands of the West Indies; capital, Havana.
– DERIVATIVES **Cuban** adj. & n.

cubbyhole • n. a small enclosed space or room.
– ORIGIN from dialect *cub* 'pen, hutch'.

cube • n. **1** a three-dimensional shape with six equal square faces. **2** Math. the product of a number multiplied by itself twice. • v. **1** cut (food) into small cubes. **2** Math. find the cube of (a number).
– ORIGIN Greek *kubos*.

cube root • n. the number which produces a given number when cubed.

cubic /kyoo-bik/ • adj. **1** having the shape of a cube. **2** esp. Math. related to a cube: *a cubic metre*.

cubicle • n. a small area of a room that is partitioned off for privacy.
– ORIGIN Latin *cubiculum* 'bedroom'.

cubism • n. an early 20th-century style of painting in which objects are shown as made up of geometric shapes.
– DERIVATIVES **cubist** n. & adj.

cubit /kyoo-bit/ • n. an ancient measure of length, approximately equal to the length of a forearm.
– ORIGIN Latin *cubitum* 'elbow, cubit'.

cuboid /kyoo-boyd/ • adj. having the shape of a cube. • n. a solid which has six rectangular faces at right angles to each other.

cuckold /kuk-ohld/ • n. derog. a man whose wife has committed adultery. • v. make (a married man) a cuckold.
– ORIGIN Old French *cucu* 'cuckoo' (from the cuckoo's habit of laying its egg in another bird's nest).

cuckoo • n. a grey or brown bird with a two-note call, known for laying its eggs in the nests of other birds. • adj. informal crazy.
– ORIGIN Old French *cucu*.

cucumber • n. a long, green fruit with watery flesh, eaten as a vegetable in salads.
– ORIGIN Latin *cucumis*.

cud • n. partly digested food returned from the first stomach of cattle or similar animals to the mouth for further chewing.
– ORIGIN Old English.

cuddle • v. (**cuddles**, **cuddling**, **cuddled**) **1** hold closely and lovingly in one's arms. **2** (often **cuddle up to**) lie or sit close. • n. an affectionate hug.
– ORIGIN unknown.

cuddly • adj. (**cuddlier**, **cuddliest**) pleasantly soft or plump.

cudgel /ku-juhl/ • n. a short thick stick used as a weapon. • v. (**cudgels**, **cudgelling**, **cudgelled**; US **cudgels**, **cudgeling**, **cudgeled**) beat with a cudgel.
– PHRASES **take up the cudgels** start to defend someone or something strongly.
– ORIGIN Old English.

cue[1] • n. **1** a signal to an actor to enter or to begin their speech or performance. **2** a signal or prompt for action. • v. (**cues**, **cueing** or **cuing**, **cued**) **1** give a cue to or for. **2** set a piece of audio or video equipment in readiness to play (a particular part of a recording).
– PHRASES **on cue** at the correct moment.
– ORIGIN unknown.

cue[2] • n. a long tapering wooden rod for striking the ball in snooker, billiards, or pool. • v. (**cues**, **cueing** or **cuing**, **cued**) use a cue to strike the ball.
– ORIGIN from QUEUE.

cuff[1] • n. the end part of a sleeve, where the material is turned back or a separate band is sewn on.
– PHRASES **off the cuff** informal without preparation.
– ORIGIN unknown.

cuff[2] • v. strike with an open hand. • n. a blow given with an open hand.
– ORIGIN unknown.

cufflink • n. a device for fastening together the sides of a shirt cuff.

cuirass /kwi-rass/ • n. hist. a piece of armour consisting of breastplate and a similar plate at the back.
– ORIGIN Old French *cuirace*.

cuisine /kwi-zeen/ • n. a style of cooking, especially as typical of a country or region: *classic French cuisine*.
– ORIGIN French, 'kitchen'.

cul-de-sac /kul-duh-sak/ • n. (pl. **culs-de-sac** /kul-duh-sak/) a street or passage closed at one end.
– ORIGIN French, 'bottom of a sack'.

culinary /cul-i-nuh-ri/ • adj. having to do with cooking.
– ORIGIN Latin *culina* 'kitchen'.

cull • v. **1** reduce the numbers of (animals) by selective slaughter. **2** select from a wide range or large quantity: *anecdotes culled from Roman history*. • n. a selective slaughter of animals.
– ORIGIN Latin *colligere* 'gather together'.

Culloden, Battle of E
/kuh-lod-d'n/ the final battle of the Jacobite uprising of 1745–6, fought near Inverness. The Jacobite army of Charles Edward Stuart was defeated by the English and German forces led by the Duke of Cumberland.

culminate /kul-mi-nayt/ • v. (**culminates**, **culminating**, **culminated**) reach a climax or point of highest development: *the disorders which culminated in World War II*.
– DERIVATIVES **culmination** n.
– ORIGIN Latin *culminare*.

culottes /kyuu-lots/ • pl. n. women's knee-length trousers, cut with full legs to resemble a skirt.
– ORIGIN French.

culpable /kul-puh-b'l/ • adj. deserving blame.
– DERIVATIVES **culpability** n.
– ORIGIN Latin *culpabilis*.

Culpeper E
/kul-pep-er/, Nicholas (1616–54), English herbalist, whose *Complete Herbal* was important in the development of botany and pharmacology.

culprit • n. a person who is responsible for an

offence or misdeed.
– ORIGIN perh. from *cul. prist*, the abbreviation for Old French *Culpable: prest d'averrer notre bille* '(You are) guilty: (We are) ready to prove our charge'.

cult ● n. **1** a system of religious worship directed towards a particular person or object. **2** a small religious group regarded as strange or imposing excessive control over members. **3** something popular or fashionable among a particular group of people: *the series has become a cult in the UK.*
– DERIVATIVES **cultish** adj. **cultist** n.
– ORIGIN Latin *cultus* 'worship'.

cultivar /**kul**-ti-var/ ● n. a plant variety that has been produced by selective breeding.

cultivate ● v. (**cultivates**, **cultivating**, **cultivated**) **1** prepare and use (land) for crops or gardening. **2** grow (plants or crops). **3** try to develop or gain: *he cultivated an air of detachment.* **4** try to win the friendship or favour of. **5** (**cultivated**) refined and well educated.
– DERIVATIVES **cultivable** adj. **cultivation** n.
– ORIGIN Latin *cultivare.*

cultivator ● n. a mechanical implement for breaking up the ground.

cultural ● adj. **1** relating to the culture of a society. **2** relating to the arts and to intellectual achievements.
– DERIVATIVES **culturally** adv.

Cultural Revolution E
a political upheaval in China 1966–8, intended to bring about a return to revolutionary Maoist beliefs. It resulted in attacks on intellectuals and the appearance of a personality cult around Mao Zedong, and was gradually ended by premier Zhou Enlai.

culture ● n. **1** the arts, customs, and institutions of a nation, people, or group. **2** the arts and other instances of human intellectual achievement regarded as a whole: *museums of culture.* **3** a refined understanding or appreciation of this. **4** the growing of plants or the breeding of animals. **5** a preparation of cells or bacteria grown in an artificial medium. ● v. (**cultures**, **culturing**, **cultured**) grow (cells, bacteria, etc.) in an artificial medium.
– ORIGIN Latin *cultura* 'growing'.

cultured ● adj. **1** refined and well educated. **2** (of a pearl) formed round a foreign body inserted into an oyster.

culvert /**kul**-vert/ ● n. a tunnel carrying a stream or open drain under a road or railway.
– ORIGIN unknown.

cum /kum/ ● prep. combined with: *a study-cum-bedroom.*
– ORIGIN Latin.

Cumberland[1] E
a former county of NW England, united with Westmorland and part of Lancashire to form the county of Cumbria in 1974.

Cumberland[2], E
William Augustus, Duke of (1721–65), English military commander, third son of George II, known for the severity of his suppression of the Jacobite clans in the aftermath of his victory at the Battle of Culloden (1746).

cumbersome ● adj. **1** difficult to carry or use through size or weight. **2** complicated and therefore time-consuming: *cumbersome business processes.*
– ORIGIN from **ENCUMBER**.

Cumbria E
a county of NW England; county town, Carlisle.
– DERIVATIVES **Cumbrian** adj. & n.

cumbrous /**kum**-bruhss/ ● adj. literary cumbersome.

cumin /**kum**-in, **kyoo**-min/ (also **cummin**) ● n. the seeds of a plant, used as a spice.
– ORIGIN Greek *kuminon.*

cummerbund /**kum**-mer-bund/ ● n. a sash worn around the waist, especially as part of a man's formal evening suit.
– ORIGIN Urdu and Persian.

cummings, E
e. e. (1894–1962; full name *Edward Estlin Cummings*), American poet, whose poems are notable for their experimental typography, frank vocabulary, and wordplay.

cumulative /**kyoo**-myuu-luh-tiv/ ● adj. increasing by successive additions: *the cumulative effect of years of drought.*
– ORIGIN Latin *cumulus* 'a heap'.

cumulonimbus /kyoo-myuu-loh-**nim**-buhss/ ● n. (pl. **cumulonimbi** /kyoo-myuu-loh-**nim**-by/) cloud forming a towering mass with a flat base, as in thunderstorms.

cumulus /**kyoo**-myuu-luhss/ ● n. (pl. **cumuli** /**kyoo**-myuu-lee/) cloud forming rounded masses heaped on a flat base.
– ORIGIN Latin, 'heap'.

Cunard E
/kyoo-**nard**/, Sir Samuel (1787–1865), Canadian-born British shipowner, a pioneer of the regular transatlantic passenger service.

cuneiform /**kyoo**-ni-form, kyoo-**nay**-i-form/ ● adj. relating to the wedge-shaped characters used in the ancient writing systems of Mesopotamia, Persia, and Ugarit in Syria. ● n. cuneiform writing.
– ORIGIN from Latin *cuneus* 'wedge'.

cunnilingus /kun-ni-**ling**-guhss/ ● n. stimulation of a woman's genitals using the tongue or lips.
– ORIGIN from Latin *cunnus* 'vulva' + *lingere* 'lick'.

cunning ● adj. **1** skilled at deceiving people. **2** skilful or clever. ● n. craftiness.
– ORIGIN perh. from Old Norse, 'knowledge'.

cunt ● n. vulgar **1** a woman's genitals. **2** an unpleasant or stupid person.
– ORIGIN Germanic.

cup ● n. **1** a small bowl-shaped container with a handle for drinking from. **2** a cup-shaped trophy with a stem and two handles, awarded as a prize in a sports contest. **3** either of the two parts of a bra shaped to contain or support one breast. ● v. (**cups**, **cupping**, **cupped**) **1** form (one's hand or hands) into the curved shape of a cup. **2** place one's curved hand or hands around.
– PHRASES **not one's cup of tea** informal not what one likes or finds interesting.
– ORIGIN Latin *cuppa.*

cupboard ● n. a piece of furniture or small recess with a door, used for storage.

cupboard love ● n. false affection that is

pretended so as to obtain something.

Cupid • n. **1** the Roman god of love, represented as a naked winged boy with a bow and arrows. Greek equivalent **Eros**. **2** (also **cupid**) a picture or statue of a naked winged child carrying a bow.

cupidity /kyoo-**pid**-i-ti/ • n. greed for money or possessions.
– ORIGIN Latin *cupiditas*.

cupola /**kyoo**-puh-luh/ • n. a rounded dome forming or decorating a roof or ceiling.
– ORIGIN Latin *cupula* 'small cask'.

cupro-nickel • n. an alloy of copper and nickel, especially as used in 'silver' coins.

cur /ker/ • n. an aggressive mongrel dog.
– ORIGIN perh. from Old Norse, 'grumbling'.

Curaçao E
/kyoo-ruh-**soh**/ the largest island of the Netherlands Antilles, situated north of the Venezuelan coast.

curacy • n. (pl. **curacies**) the position of a curate.

curare /kyuu-**rah**-ri/ • n. a paralysing poison obtained from South American plants.
– ORIGIN Carib.

curate /**kyoor**-uht/ • n. a member of the clergy engaged as assistant to a parish priest.
– ORIGIN Latin *curatus*.

curative • adj. able to cure disease.

curator • n. a keeper of a museum or other collection.
– DERIVATIVES **curatorial** adj.
– ORIGIN Latin.

curb • n. **1** a check or restraint: *curbs on pollution*. **2** a type of bit with a strap or chain attached which passes under a horse's lower jaw, used as a check. **3** US = **kerb**. • v. keep in check.
– ORIGIN Old French *courber* 'to bend'.

curd (also **curds**) • n. a soft, white substance formed when milk coagulates, used for making cheese.
– ORIGIN unknown.

curd cheese • n. a soft cheese made from skimmed milk curd.

curdle • v. (**curdles**, **curdling**, **curdled**) form or cause to form curds or lumps.

cure • v. (**cures**, **curing**, **cured**) **1** make (a person who is ill) well again. **2** end (a disease, condition, or problem) by treatment or appropriate action. **3** preserve (meat, fish, etc.) by salting, drying, or smoking. • n. **1** a remedy. **2** the healing of a person who is ill.
– DERIVATIVES **curable** adj. **curer** n.
– ORIGIN Latin *cura* 'care'.

curfew /**ker**-fyoo/ • n. **1** a regulation requiring people to remain indoors between specified hours of the night. **2** the time at which such a restriction begins.
– ORIGIN first meaning a regulation requiring that fires be put out at a particular time: from Old French *cuevrefeu*.

Curia /**kyoor**-i-uh/ • n. the papal court at the Vatican, by which the Roman Catholic Church is governed.
– ORIGIN Latin.

Curie E
/**kyoor**-i/, Marie (1867–1934), Polish-born French physicist, and Pierre (1859–1906), French physicist, who discovered the elements polonium and radium.

curie /**kyoor**-i/ • n. (pl. **curies**) a unit of radioactivity.
– ORIGIN named after Pierre and Marie **Curie**.

curio /**kyoor**-i-oh/ • n. (pl. **curios**) an object that is interesting because it is rare or unusual.

curiosity • n. (pl. **curiosities**) **1** a strong desire to know or learn something. **2** a unusual or interesting object.

curious • adj. **1** eager to know or learn something. **2** strange; unusual.
– DERIVATIVES **curiously** adv.
– ORIGIN Latin *curiosus* 'careful'.

curium /**kyoor**-i-uhm/ • n. a radioactive metallic chemical element made by high-energy atomic collisions.
– ORIGIN named after Marie and Pierre **Curie**.

curl • v. **1** form or cause to form a curved or spiral shape. **2** move in a spiral or curved course: *smoke curled into the air.* • n. something in the shape of a spiral or coil.
– DERIVATIVES **curly** adj.
– ORIGIN Dutch *krul*.

curler • n. a roller around which a lock of hair is wrapped to curl it.

curlew /**ker**-lyoo/ • n. (pl. **curlew** or **curlews**) a large wading bird with a long bill that curves downwards and brown streaked plumage.
– ORIGIN Old French *courlieu*.

curlicue /**ker**-li-kyoo/ • n. a decorative curl or twist.
– ORIGIN from *curly* + **cue**[2].

curling • n. a game played on ice, in which large circular flat stones are slid across the surface towards a mark.

curmudgeon /ker-**muj**-uhn/ • n. a bad-tempered person.
– DERIVATIVES **curmudgeonly** adj.
– ORIGIN unknown.

currant • n. **1** a dried fruit made from a small seedless variety of grape. **2** a shrub producing small edible black, red, or white berries.
– ORIGIN from Old French *raisins de Corauntz* 'grapes of Corinth'.

currency • n. (pl. **currencies**) **1** a system of money in general use in a country. **2** the state or period of being current: *the term has gained new currency.*

current • adj. **1** happening or being used or done now: *current events*. **2** in common or general use. • n. **1** a body of water or air moving in a particular direction. **2** a flow of electrically charged particles.
– ORIGIN Latin *currere* 'run'.

current account • n. Brit. an account with a bank or building society from which money may be withdrawn without notice.

currently • adv. at the present time.

curriculum /kuh-**rik**-yuu-luhm/ • n. (pl. **curricula** or **curriculums**) the subjects included in a course of study in a school or college.
– DERIVATIVES **curricular** adj.
– ORIGIN Latin, 'course, racing chariot'.

curriculum vitae /kuh-**rik**-yuu-luhm **vee**-ty/ • n. (pl. **curricula vitae**) a brief account of a person's qualifications and previous occupations, sent with a job application.
– ORIGIN Latin, 'course of life'.

curried • adj. made as a curry with a hot,

spicy sauce.

curry[1] ● n. (pl. **curries**) a dish of meat, vegetables, or fish, cooked in a hot, spicy sauce of Indian origin.
– ORIGIN Tamil.

curry[2] ● v. (**curries, currying, curried**) esp. N. Amer. groom (a horse) with a curry-comb.
– PHRASES **curry favour** try to win favour by flattery and servile behaviour.
– ORIGIN Old French *correier*.

curry-comb ● n. a hand-held device with serrated ridges, used for grooming horses.

curse ● n. **1** an appeal to a supernatural power to harm someone or something. **2** a cause of harm or misery: *impatience is the curse of our time.* **3** an offensive word or phrase used to express anger or annoyance. ● v. (**curses, cursing, cursed**) **1** use a curse against. **2** (**be cursed with**) be afflicted with. **3** say offensive words.
– ORIGIN Old English.

cursive /ker-siv/ ● adj. (of handwriting) written with the characters joined.
– ORIGIN Latin *cursivus* 'running'.

cursor ● n. **1** a movable indicator on a computer screen identifying the point where input from the user will take effect. **2** the sliding part, bearing a hairline, used to locate points on a slide rule.
– ORIGIN Latin, 'runner'.

cursory /ker-suh-ri/ ● adj. hasty and therefore not thorough.

curt ● adj. rudely brief.
– DERIVATIVES **curtly** adv.
– ORIGIN Latin *curtus* 'cut short'.

curtail /ker-tayl/ ● v. reduce or restrict.
– DERIVATIVES **curtailment** n.
– ORIGIN French *courtault* 'horse with a docked tail'.

curtain ● n. **1** a piece of material suspended at the top to form a screen, hung at a window or between the stage and auditorium of a theatre. **2** (**the curtain**) the rise or fall of a stage curtain between acts or scenes. **3** (**curtains**) informal a disastrous end: *it's curtains for the bank.* ● v. provide or screen with a curtain or curtains.
– ORIGIN Latin *cortina*.

curtain call ● n. the appearance of one or more performers on stage after a performance to acknowledge the audience's applause.

curtain-raiser ● n. an event happening just before a longer or more important one.

Curtin, E
John (Joseph Ambrose) (1885–1945), Australian Labor statesman, Prime Minister 1941–5.

Curtiss, E
Glenn (Hammond) (1878–1930), American air pioneer and aircraft designer, who in 1908 made the first public American flight of 1.0 km (0.6 miles).

curtsy (also **curtsey**) ● n. (pl. **curtsies** or **curtseys**) a woman's or girl's respectful greeting, made by bending the knees with one foot in front of the other. ● v. (**curtsies, curtsying, curtsied**; also **curtseys, curtseying, curtseyed**) perform a curtsy.
– ORIGIN from **COURTESY**.

curvaceous /ker-vay-shuhss/ ● adj. having an attractively curved shape.

curvature /ker-vuh-cher/ ● n. the fact of being curved or the degree to which something is curved: *curvature of the spine.*

curve ● n. **1** a line which gradually turns from a straight course. **2** a line on a graph showing how one quantity varies with respect to another. ● v. (**curves, curving, curved**) form a curve.
– ORIGIN Latin *curvus* 'bent'.

curvet /ker-vet/ ● v. (**curvets, curvetting, curvetted**; also **curvets, curveting, curveted**) (of a horse) make a short energetic leap.
– ORIGIN Italian *corvetta* 'little curve'.

curvilinear /ker-vi-lin-i-er/ ● adj. contained by or consisting of a curved line or lines: *a curvilinear building.*

curvy ● adj. (**curvier, curviest**) **1** having many curves. **2** informal curvaceous.

cushion ● n. **1** a bag of cloth stuffed with soft material, used to provide comfort when sitting. **2** a means of protection against impact or something unpleasant. **3** the inner sides of a billiard table, from which the balls rebound. ● v. **1** soften the effect of an impact on. **2** lessen the unpleasant effects of: *he relied on his savings to cushion the blow of losing his job.*
– ORIGIN Old French *cuissin*.

cushy ● adj. (**cushier, cushiest**) informal easy and undemanding: *a cushy job.*
– ORIGIN Urdu, 'pleasure'.

cusp /kusp/ ● n. **1** a pointed end where two curves meet, such as each of the ends of a crescent moon. **2** a cone-shaped projection on the surface of a tooth. **3** the initial point of an astrological sign or house. **4** a point of changing from one state to another: *those on the cusp of adulthood.*
– ORIGIN Latin *cuspis* 'point or apex'.

cuss informal ● n an annoying or stubborn person or animal. ● v. swear or curse.

cussed /kuss-id/ ● adj. informal stubborn and awkward.
– DERIVATIVES **cussedness** n.

custard ● n. **1** a sweet sauce made with milk and eggs, or milk and flavoured cornflour. **2** a baked dessert made from eggs and milk.
– ORIGIN first meaning a pie containing meat or fruit in a sauce: from Old French *crouste* 'crust'.

Custer, E
George (Armstrong) (1839–76), American cavalry general, who served with courage in the American Civil War but led his men to their deaths in a clash (known as Custer's Last Stand) with the Sioux at Little Bighorn in Montana.

custodial /kuss-toh-di-uhl/ ● adj. having to do with custody.

custodian /kuss-toh-di-uhn/ ● n. a person who has responsibility for or looks after something.

custody /kuss-tuh-di/ ● n. **1** protective care. **2** Law parental responsibility as allocated to one of two parents who are getting divorced. **3** imprisonment: *he was taken into custody.*
– ORIGIN Latin *custos* 'guardian'.

custom ● n. **1** a traditional way of behaving or doing something that is specific to a society, place, or time: *the English custom of dancing round the maypole.* **2** esp. Brit. regular

C

dealings with a shop or business by customers.
– ORIGIN Old French *coustume*.

customary ● adj. in accordance with custom; usual.
– DERIVATIVES **customarily** adv.

C

custom-built (also **custom-made**) ● adj. made to a particular customer's order.

customer ● n. **1** a person who buys goods or services from a shop or business. **2** a person or thing of a specified kind that one has to deal with: *he's a tough customer.*

customize (also **customise**) ● v. (**customizes**, **customizing**, **customized**) modify (something) to suit a person or task.

customs ● pl. n. **1** the duties charged by a government on imported goods. **2** the official department that administers and collects such duties.

cut ● v. (**cuts**, **cutting**, **cut**) **1** make an opening or wound in (something) with a sharp implement. **2** make, shorten, divide, or remove with a sharp implement: *she cut his photo out of the paper.* **3** make or design (a garment) in a particular way: *an impeccably cut suit.* **4** reduce the amount or quantity of: *I should cut down my salt intake.* **5** end or interrupt the provision of (a supply). **6** go across or through: *is it illegal to cut across a mini roundabout?* **7** move to another shot in a film. **8** divide a pack of playing cards by lifting a portion from the top. ● n. **1** an act of cutting. **2** a result of cutting: *a cut on his jaw.* **3** a reduction. **4** the style in which a garment or the hair is cut. **5** a piece of meat cut from a carcass. **6** informal a share of profits. **7** a version of a film after editing.
– PHRASES **be cut out for** (or **to be**) informal have exactly the right qualities for (a role). **a cut above** informal better than. **cut and dried** decided or planned in advance. **cut and run** informal make a speedy departure from a difficult situation. **cut and thrust** a difficult or competitive situation. **cut both ways 1** (of a point) serve both sides of an argument. **2** have both good and bad effects. **cut corners** do something with a lack of thoroughness to save time or money. **cut a dash** be stylish or impressive. **cut dead** completely ignore (someone). **cut in 1** interrupt. **2** pull in too closely in front of another vehicle. **3** (of a machine) begin operating automatically. **cut it out** informal stop it. **cut the mustard** informal reach the required standard. **cut no ice** informal have no influence or effect. **cut off 1** block the usual means of access to (a place). **2** deprive of a supply. **3** break a telephone connection with (someone). **cut out 1** exclude (someone). **2** (of an engine) suddenly stop operating. **cut one's teeth** get initial experience of an activity. **cut a tooth** (of a baby) have a tooth appear through the gum. **cut up** informal very upset. **cut up rough** Brit. informal behave in an aggressive or awkward way.
– ORIGIN prob. Germanic.

cutaneous /kyoo-tay-ni-uhss/ ● adj. having to do with the skin.
– ORIGIN Latin *cutis* 'skin'.

cutback ● n. a reduction.

cute ● adj. **1** charmingly pretty; sweet. **2** informal, esp. N. Amer. clever; shrewd.
– DERIVATIVES **cutely** adv. **cuteness** n.
– ORIGIN from ACUTE.

cut glass ● n. glass with decorative patterns cut into it.

cuticle /kyoo-ti-k'l/ ● n. **1** the dead skin at the base of a fingernail or toenail. **2** the epidermis of the body.
– ORIGIN Latin *cuticula* 'little skin'.

cutlass /kut-luhss/ ● n. a short sword with a slightly curved blade, formerly used by sailors.
– ORIGIN Latin *cultellus* 'small knife'.

cutler ● n. a maker or seller of cutlery.
– ORIGIN Latin *cultellus* 'small knife'.

cutlery ● n. knives, forks, and spoons used for eating or serving food.

cutlet ● n. **1** a lamb or veal chop from just behind the neck. **2** a flat cake of minced meat, nuts, etc., covered in breadcrumbs and fried.
– ORIGIN French *côtelette.*

cut-off ● n. **1** a point or level marking a set limit. **2** a device for interrupting a power or fuel supply. **3** (**cut-offs**) shorts made by cutting off the legs of a pair of jeans.

cut-out ● n. **1** a shape cut out of board or paper. **2** a device that automatically breaks an electric circuit for safety.

cut-price ● adj. for sale at a reduced price; cheap.

cutter ● n. **1** a person or thing that cuts. **2** a light, fast patrol boat or sailing boat. **3** a ship's boat used for carrying light stores or passengers.

cut-throat ● adj. ruthless and fierce: *cut-throat competition.* ● n. dated a murderer or other violent criminal.

cut-throat razor ● n. Brit. a razor with a long blade which folds like a penknife.

cutting ● n. **1** a piece cut off, especially an article cut from a newspaper or a piece cut from a plant to grow a new one. **2** an open passage excavated through higher ground for a railway, road, or canal. ● adj. **1** capable of cutting. **2** hurtful: *a cutting remark.*

cutting edge ● n. the most advanced stage; the forefront. ● adj. (**cutting-edge**) innovative; pioneering.

cuttlefish ● n. a marine mollusc resembling a squid, that squirts out a black liquid when attacked.
– ORIGIN Old English.

Cuvier E
/koo-vi-ay/, Georges Léopold Chrétien Frédéric Dagobert, Baron (1769–1832), French naturalist, founder of the science of palaeontology.

Cuzco E
/kuus-koh/ a city in the Andes in southern Peru, capital of the Inca empire until the Spanish conquest in 1533.

CV ● abbrev. curriculum vitae.

CVO ● abbrev. (in the UK) Commander of the Royal Victorian Order.

cwt. ● abbrev. hundredweight.
– ORIGIN from Latin *centum* 'a hundred'.

cyan /sy-uhn/ ● n. a greenish-blue colour.
– ORIGIN Greek *kuaneos* 'dark blue'.

cyanide /sy-uh-nyd/ ● n. a highly poisonous compound containing a metal combined with carbon and nitrogen atoms.

cyanocobalamin /sy-uh-noh-kuh-bal-uh-min/ ● n. vitamin B_{12}, found in liver, fish,

and eggs.
– ORIGIN from Greek *kuanos* 'dark blue' + **COBALT** and **VITAMIN**.

cyanosis /sy-uh-**noh**-siss/ ● **n.** a bluish discoloration of the skin due to poor circulation or a lack of oxygen in the blood.
– ORIGIN Greek *kuanōsis* 'blueness'.

cyber- /sy-ber/ ● **comb. form** relating to information technology, the Internet, and virtual reality: *cyberspace.*
– ORIGIN from **CYBERNETICS**.

cybernetics ● **n.** the science of communications and automatic control systems in both machines and living things.
– DERIVATIVES **cybernetic** adj.
– ORIGIN Greek *kubernētēs* 'steersman'.

cyberphobia ● **n.** extreme or irrational fear of computers or technology.

cyberspace ● **n.** the hypothetical environment in which communication over computer networks occurs.

cybersquatting ● **n.** the registering of well-known names as Internet domain names, in the hope of selling them to the owner at a profit.

cyborg /sy-borg/ ● **n.** (in science fiction) a person having mechanical elements built into the body to extend their normal physical abilities.
– ORIGIN from **CYBER-** and **ORGANISM**.

Cyclades E
/sik-luh-deez/ a large group of islands in the southern Aegean Sea.

cyclamen /sik-luh-muhn/ ● **n.** (pl. **cyclamen** or **cyclamens**) a plant having pink, red, or white flowers with backward-curving petals.
– ORIGIN Greek *kuklaminos.*

cycle ● **n. 1** a series of events that are regularly repeated in the same order: *the cycle of birth and death.* **2** a complete sequence of changes associated with a recurring phenomenon such as an alternating electric current. **3** a series of musical or literary works composed around a particular theme. **4** a bicycle. ● **v.** (**cycles**, **cycling**, **cycled**) ride a bicycle.
– ORIGIN Greek *kuklos* 'circle'.

cyclic /syk-lik, sik-lik/ ● **adj. 1** occurring in cycles. **2** Chem. having a molecular structure containing one or more closed rings of atoms.
– DERIVATIVES **cyclical** adj.

cyclist ● **n.** a person who rides a bicycle.

cyclone /sy-klohn/ ● **n. 1** a system of winds rotating inwards to an area of low atmospheric pressure. **2** a violent tropical storm.
– DERIVATIVES **cyclonic** adj.
– ORIGIN prob. from Greek *kuklōma* 'wheel, coil of a snake'.

cyclopean /sy-kluh-**pee**-uhn, sy-**kloh**-pi-uhn/ ● **adj.** relating to a Cyclops.

Cyclops /sy-klops/ ● **n.** (pl. **Cyclops** or **Cyclopes** /sy-**kloh**-peez/) Gk Myth. a member of a race of one-eyed giants.
– ORIGIN Greek *Kuklōps* 'round-eyed'.

cyclotron /sy-kluh-tron/ ● **n.** an apparatus for accelerating charged atomic and subatomic particles by making them move spirally in a magnetic field.

cygnet /sig-nit/ ● **n.** a young swan.
– ORIGIN Old French.

cylinder /si-lin-der/ ● **n. 1** a three-dimensional shape with straight parallel sides and circular or oval ends. **2** a piston chamber in a steam or internal-combustion engine. **3** a cylindrical container for liquefied gas under pressure.
– ORIGIN Greek *kulindros* 'roller'.

cylindrical /si-**lin**-dri-k'l/ ● **adj.** having the shape of a cylinder.

cymbal /**sim**-buhl/ ● **n.** a musical instrument consisting of a round brass plate which is either struck against another one or hit with a stick.
– ORIGIN Greek *kumbalon.*

cyme /sym/ ● **n.** a flower cluster with a central stem bearing a single flower on the end that develops first. Compare with **RACEME**.
– ORIGIN Latin *cyma* 'summit'.

Cymru E
/**kum**-ree/ Welsh name for **WALES**.

cynic /si-nik/ ● **n. 1** a person who believes that people always act from selfish motives. **2** a person who raises doubts about something. **3** (**Cynic**) a member of an ancient Greek school of philosophers who despised wealth and pleasure.
– DERIVATIVES **cynicism** n.
– ORIGIN Greek *kunikos.*

cynical ● **adj. 1** believing that people always act from selfish motives. **2** doubtful or sneering. **3** concerned only with one's own interests: *a cynical professional foul.*
– DERIVATIVES **cynically** adv.

cynosure /sin-uh-zyoor/ ● **n.** a person or thing that is the centre of attention or admiration.
– ORIGIN Greek *kunosoura* 'dog's tail', also 'Ursa Minor' (the constellation contains the pole star, which was used as a guide by sailors).

cypher ● **n.** var. of **CIPHER**.

cypress ● **n.** an evergreen coniferous tree with small dark leaves.
– ORIGIN Greek *kuparissos.*

Cyprus E
/sy-pruhss/ an island in the eastern Mediterranean, south of the Turkish coast; capital, Nicosia.
– DERIVATIVES **Cypriot** adj. & n.

Cyrillic /si-ril-lik/ ● **adj.** having to do with the alphabet used for Russian, Ukrainian, Bulgarian, and related languages.
– ORIGIN named after the Greek missionary St *Cyril* (826–69), who is said to have invented it.

Cyrus the Great E
/sy-ruhss/ (died *c.*530 BC), king of Persia 559–530 BC. He conquered Asia Minor, Babylonia, Syria, Palestine, and most of the Iranian plateau, and founded a dynasty that ruled Persia until 330 BC.

cyst /sist/ ● **n.** a thin-walled abnormal sac or cavity in the body, containing fluid.
– ORIGIN Greek *kustis* 'bladder'.

cystic ● **adj. 1** having to do with cysts. **2** relating to the urinary bladder or the gall bladder.

cystic fibrosis ● **n.** a hereditary disorder in which the production of abnormally thick mucus leads to the blockage of the pancreatic ducts, intestines, and bronchi.

cystitis /si-sty-tiss/ • n. inflammation of the urinary bladder.

cytology /sy-tol-uh-ji/ • n. the branch of biology concerned with the structure and function of cells.
– DERIVATIVES **cytological** adj. **cytologist** n.

cytoplasm /sy-toh-pla-z'm/ • n. the material of a living cell, excluding the nucleus.
– DERIVATIVES **cytoplasmic** adj.

czar etc. • n. var. of TSAR etc.

Czech /chek/ • n. **1** a person from the Czech Republic or (formerly) Czechoslovakia. **2** the Slavic language spoken in the Czech Republic. • adj. relating to the Czech Republic.
– ORIGIN Czech.

Czechoslovak /chek-uh-**sloh**-vak/ (also **Czechoslovakian**) • n. a person from the former country of Czechoslovakia, now divided between the Czech Republic and Slovakia. • adj. relating to the former country of Czechoslovakia.

Czechoslovakia E
/chek-uh-sluh-**vak**-i-uh/ a former country in central Europe, now divided between the Czech Republic and Slovakia.

Czech Republic E
a country in central Europe; capital, Prague.

Dd

D[1] (also **d**) • n. (pl. **Ds** or **D's**) **1** the fourth letter of the alphabet. **2** referring to the fourth item in a set. **3** Music the second note of the scale of C major. **4** the Roman numeral for 500.

D[2] • abbrev. **1** depth (in the sense of the dimension of an object from front to back). **2** (with a numeral) dimension(s) or dimensional.

d • abbrev. **1** deci-. **2** (in travel timetables) departs. **3** (**d.**) died (used to indicate a date of death). **4** Brit. penny or pence (of pre-decimal currency). [ORIGIN Latin *denarius* 'penny'.]

'd • contr. **1** had. **2** would.

DA • abbrev. US district attorney.

dab[1] • v. (**dabs**, **dabbing**, **dabbed**) **1** press lightly with a cloth, sponge, etc. **2** apply with light quick strokes. • n. a small amount lightly applied.

dab[2] • n. a small North Atlantic flatfish.
– ORIGIN unknown.

dabble • v. (**dabbles**, **dabbling**, **dabbled**) **1** move (one's hands or feet) around gently in water. **2** take part in an activity in a casual way.
– DERIVATIVES **dabbler** n.
– ORIGIN from former Dutch *dabbelen* or from DAB[1].

dab hand • n. Brit. informal a person who is very skilled in a particular activity.
– ORIGIN unknown.

Dacca E
var. of **DHAKA**.

dace /dayss/ • n. (pl. **dace**) a small freshwater fish related to the carp.
– ORIGIN Old French *dars*.

dacha /da-chuh/ • n. (in Russia) a house or cottage in the country, used as a holiday home.
– ORIGIN Russian.

Dachau E
/da-kow/ a Nazi concentration camp in southern Bavaria, from 1933 to 1945.

dachshund /dak-suhnd/ • n. a breed of dog with a long body and very short legs.
– ORIGIN German, 'badger dog'.

dactyl /dak-til/ • n. Poetry a metrical foot consisting of one stressed syllable followed by two unstressed syllables.
– ORIGIN Greek *daktulos* 'finger'.

dad • n. informal one's father.

Dada /dah-dah/ • n. an early 20th-century movement in the arts which mocked conventions and emphasized the illogical and absurd.
– ORIGIN French, 'hobby horse'.

daddy • n. (pl. **daddies**) informal one's father.

daddy-long-legs • n. Brit. informal a crane fly.

dado /day-doh/ • n. (pl. **dados**) the lower part of the wall of a room, when decorated differently from the upper part.
– ORIGIN Italian, 'dice or cube'.

Daedalus E
/dee-duh-luhss/ Gk Myth. a craftsman who built the labyrinth for Minos, king of Crete. Minos imprisoned him and his son Icarus, but they escaped using wings which Daedalus made and fastened with wax. Icarus, however, flew too near the sun and was killed.

daffodil • n. a plant bearing bright yellow flowers with a long trumpet-shaped centre.
– ORIGIN Latin *asphodilus* 'asphodel'.

daffy • adj. informal silly.
– ORIGIN northern English dialect *daff* 'simpleton'.

daft • adj. informal, esp. Brit. silly; foolish.
– ORIGIN Old English, 'mild, meek'.

da Gama E
/duh **gah**-muh/, Vasco (*c.*1469–1524), Portuguese explorer. He led the first European expedition round the Cape of Good Hope in 1497, before crossing the Indian Ocean and arriving in Calicut in SW India in 1498. He also established colonies in Mozambique.

Dagestan E
/dag-i-stahn, **dag**-i-stan/ an autonomous republic in SW Russia, on the western shore of the Caspian Sea; capital, Makhachkala.

dagger ● n. a short pointed knife, used as a weapon.
– ORIGIN perh. from former *dag* 'pierce'.

dago /day-goh/ ● n. (pl. **dagos** or **dagoes**) informal, offens. a Spanish, Portuguese, or Italian-speaking person.
– ORIGIN from the Spanish man's name *Diego* 'James'.

Daguerre E
/duh-**gair**/, Louis-Jacques-Mandé (1789–1851), French physicist, inventor of the first practical photographic process (1839).

daguerreotype /duh-ger-ruh-typ/ (also **daguerrotype**) ● n. an early kind of photograph produced using silver-coated copper plate and mercury vapour.
– ORIGIN named after L.-J.-M. **Daguerre**.

Dahl E
/dahl/, Roald (1916–90), British writer, of Norwegian descent. He is known for his children's books such as *Charlie and the Chocolate Factory.*

dahlia /day-li-uh/ ● n. a garden plant with brightly coloured flowers.
– ORIGIN named after the Swedish botanist Andreas *Dahl* (1751–89).

Dahomey E
/duh-**hoh**-mi/ former name for **Benin**.

Dáil E
/doyl/ (in full **Dáil Éireann** /air-uhn/) the lower House of Parliament in the Republic of Ireland, composed of 166 members.

daily ● adj. done, happening, or produced every day or every weekday. ● adv. every day. ● n. (pl. **dailies**) informal a newspaper published every day except Sunday.

Daimler E
/**daym**-ler/, Gottlieb (1834–1900), German engineer and motor manufacturer. He produced one of the first high-speed internal-combustion engines suitable for road vehicles (1885) and went on to found the Daimler motor company (1890)

dainty ● adj. (**daintier**, **daintiest**) delicately small and pretty. ● n. (pl. **dainties**) a small appetizing item of food.
– DERIVATIVES **daintily** adv. **daintiness** n.
– ORIGIN Old French *daintie* 'choice morsel, pleasure'.

daiquiri /dy-ki-ri, da-ki-ri/ ● n. (pl. **daiquiris**) a cocktail containing rum and lime juice.
– ORIGIN *Daiquiri*, a district in Cuba.

dairy ● n. (pl. **dairies**) a building for treating and distributing milk and milk products. ● adj. **1** made from milk. **2** involved in milk production.
– ORIGIN Old English, 'female servant'.

dais /day-iss/ ● n. a low platform for a lectern or throne.
– ORIGIN Old French *deis*.

daisy ● n. (pl. **daisies**) a small plant having flowers with a yellow centre and white petals.
– ORIGIN Old English, 'day's eye'.

daisy wheel ● n. a disc bearing spokes with printing characters on the ends, used in word processors and typewriters.

Dakar E
/da-kar/ the capital of Senegal.

Dalai Lama /da-ly lah-muh/ ● n. the spiritual head of Tibetan Buddhism.
– ORIGIN Tibetan, 'ocean monk'.

dale ● n. (in northern England) a valley.
– ORIGIN Old English.

Dali E
/**dah**-li/, Salvador (1904–89), Spanish surrealist painter, who depicted dream images with almost photographic realism against backgrounds of arid landscapes.

Dallas E
/**dal**-luhss/ a city and centre of the oil industry in NE Texas.

dally ● v. (**dallies**, **dallying**, **dallied**) **1** do something in a leisurely way. **2** (**dally with**) have casual sexual relations with.
– DERIVATIVES **dalliance** n.
– ORIGIN Old French *dalier* 'to chat'.

Dalmatia E
/dal-**may**-shuh/ a region in SW Croatia which once formed part of the ancient Roman province of Illyricum.

Dalmatian /dal-may-sh'n/ ● n. a breed of large dog with short white hair and dark spots.
– ORIGIN from **Dalmatia**.

Dalton E
/**dawl**-t'n/, John (1766–1844), English chemist, who formulated modern atomic theory. He defined an atom as the smallest part of a substance that could participate in a chemical reaction and produced the first table of comparative atomic weights.

dam[1] ● n. a barrier built across a river to hold back water. ● v. (**dams**, **damming**, **dammed**) build a dam across.
– ORIGIN German or Dutch.

dam[2] ● n. the female parent of an animal.
– ORIGIN from **dame**.

damage ● n. **1** physical harm reducing the value or usefulness of something. **2** (**damages**) financial compensation for a loss or injury. ● v. (**damages**, **damaging**, **damaged**) cause harm to.
– ORIGIN Old French.

damaging ● adj. harmful or undesirable: *the damaging effects of the sun.*

Damascus E
/duh-**mass**-kuhss/ the capital of Syria, established over 4,000 years ago and one of the oldest cities in the world.

damask /dam-uhsk/ ● n. a rich heavy fabric with a pattern woven into it.
– ORIGIN from **Damascus**, where the fabric was first produced.

dame ● n. **1** (**Dame**) (in the UK) the title of a woman awarded a knighthood, equivalent to *Sir.* **2** N. Amer. informal a woman. **3** (also **pantomime dame**) Brit. a comic female character in pantomime, played by a man.
– ORIGIN Old French.

damn /dam/ ● v. **1** (**be damned**) (in Christian belief) be condemned by God to eternal punishment in hell. **2** strongly criticize. ● exclam. informal expressing anger. ● adj. informal used to emphasize anger.

– PHRASES **damn with faint praise** praise without enthusiasm, suggesting a critical attitude.
– ORIGIN Latin *dampnare* 'inflict loss on'.

damnable /dam-nuh-b'l/ • **adj.** very bad or unpleasant.
– DERIVATIVES **damnably** adv.

damnation /dam-nay-sh'n/ • **n.** condemnation to eternal punishment in hell. • **exclam.** expressing anger.

damned /damd/ • **adj.** used to emphasize anger.
– PHRASES **do one's damnedest** do one's utmost.

damning /dam-ing/ • **adj.** strongly suggesting guilt.

Damocles E
/dam-uh-kleez/ a legendary courtier who flattered Dionysius I, ruler of Syracuse (*c.*430–367 BC), so much that the king made him feast sitting under a sword suspended by a single hair, to show him how precarious the king's good fortune was.

damp • **adj.** slightly wet. • **n.** moisture in the air, on a surface, or in a solid. • **v. 1** make damp. **2** (**damp down**) control (a feeling or situation).
– DERIVATIVES **dampness** n.
– ORIGIN Germanic.

damp course (also **damp-proof course**) • **n.** a layer of waterproof material in a wall near the ground, to prevent rising damp.

dampen • **v. 1** make damp. **2** make less strong or intense.
– DERIVATIVES **dampener** n.

damper • **n. 1** a pad for silencing a piano string. **2** a movable metal plate used to regulate the air flow in a chimney.
– PHRASES **put a damper on** informal have a subduing effect on.

damp squib • **n.** Brit. something that turns out to be much less impressive than expected.

damsel /dam-z'l/ • **n.** archaic a young unmarried woman.
– ORIGIN Old French *dameisele.*

damselfly • **n.** a slender insect related to the dragonflies.

damson /dam-zuhn/ • **n.** a small purple-black plum-like fruit.
– ORIGIN from Latin *damascenum prunum* 'plum of Damascus'.

dan • **n. 1** any of ten degrees of advanced skill in judo or karate. **2** a person who has achieved a dan.
– ORIGIN Japanese.

Danae E
/dan-ay-ee/ Gk Myth. the daughter of the king of Argos. She was imprisoned by her father when an oracle foretold that she would bear a son who would kill him, but Zeus visited her in the form of a shower of gold and she conceived Perseus, who killed her father by accident.

dance • **v.** (**dances**, **dancing**, **danced**) **1** move rhythmically to music. **2** move in a quick and lively way. • **n. 1** a series of steps and movements that match the rhythm of a piece of music. **2** a social gathering at which people dance. **3** (also **dance music**) music for dancing to.
– PHRASES **dance attendance on** try hard to please. **lead someone a merry dance** Brit. cause someone a great deal of trouble.
– DERIVATIVES **dancer** n. **dancing** n.
– ORIGIN Old French *dancer.*

dandelion • **n.** a weed with large bright yellow flowers followed by rounded heads of seeds with downy tufts.
– ORIGIN French *dent-de-lion* 'lion's tooth'.

dander • **n.** (in phr. **get one's dander up**) informal lose one's temper.
– ORIGIN unknown.

dandified • **adj.** (of a man) too concerned about personal appearance.

dandle • **v.** (**dandles**, **dandling**, **dandled**) gently bounce (a young child) on one's knees or in one's arms.
– ORIGIN unknown.

dandruff • **n.** flakes of dead skin on a person's scalp and in the hair.
– ORIGIN uncertain.

dandy • **n.** (pl. **dandies**) a man who is too concerned with a stylish and fashionable appearance. • **adj.** N. Amer. informal excellent.
– DERIVATIVES **dandyish** adj.
– ORIGIN an informal form of the man's name *Andrew.*

Dane • **n.** a person from Denmark.
– ORIGIN Old English.

Danelaw E
/dayn-law/ the part of northern and eastern England occupied or administered by Danes from the late 9th century until after the Norman Conquest.

danger • **n. 1** the possibility of suffering harm or of experiencing something unpleasant. **2** a cause of harm.
– ORIGIN Old French *dangier.*

dangerous • **adj.** likely to cause harm or problems.
– DERIVATIVES **dangerously** adv.

dangle • **v.** (**dangles**, **dangling**, **dangled**) **1** hang so as to swing freely. **2** offer (an incentive) to someone.
– DERIVATIVES **dangly** adj.

Daniel E
a Hebrew prophet (6th century BC), who spent his life as a captive at the court of Babylon. In the Bible he interpreted the dreams of Nebuchadnezzar and was saved by God from the lions' den.

Danish /day-nish/ • **adj.** relating to Denmark or the Danes. • **n.** the language of Denmark.

Danish pastry • **n.** a cake of sweetened yeast pastry topped with icing, fruit, or nuts.

dank • **adj.** damp and cold.
– ORIGIN prob. Scandinavian.

Dante E
/dan-tay/ (1265–1321; full name *Dante Alighieri*), Italian poet. He is famous for *The Divine Comedy,* an epic poem describing his spiritual journey through Hell and Purgatory and finally to Paradise.

Danton E
/dan-ton/, Georges (Jacques) (1759–94), French revolutionary. He won great popularity at the start of the Revolution, but his growing moderation brought him into conflict with Robespierre and he was executed.

Danube
/**dan**-yoob/ a river which rises in the Black Forest in SW Germany and flows about 2,850 km (1,770 miles) through Austria, Hungary, and Serbia, then forming the border between Bulgaria and Romania before reaching the Black Sea. It is the second-longest river in Europe.

Daphne
Gk Myth. a nymph who was turned into a laurel bush to save her from the amorous pursuit of Apollo.

daphnia /daf-ni-uh/ • n. (pl. **daphnia**) a minute semi-transparent freshwater crustacean.
– ORIGIN Latin.

dapper • adj. (of a man) neat in dress and appearance.
– ORIGIN prob. from German or Dutch, 'strong, stout'.

dapple • v. (**dapples**, **dappling**, **dappled**) mark with spots or small patches.
– ORIGIN perh. from Old Norse, 'spot'.

dapple grey • adj. (of a horse) grey or white with darker ring-like markings.

Dardanelles
/dar-duh-**nelz**/ a narrow strait between Europe and Asiatic Turkey (called the Hellespont in classical times), linking the Sea of Marmara with the Aegean Sea.

dare • v. (**dares**, **daring**, **dared**) **1** have the courage to do. **2** challenge to do. • n. a challenge to do something brave or risky.
– ORIGIN Old English.

daredevil • n. a person who enjoys doing dangerous things.

Dar es Salaam
/dahr ess suh-**lahm**/ the chief port and former capital of Tanzania.

daring • adj. **1** willing to do dangerous or risky things. **2** involving risk or danger. • n. adventurous courage.
– DERIVATIVES **daringly** adv.

Darius I
/duh-ry-uhss/ (*c.*550–486 BC; known as **Darius the Great**), king of Persia 521–486 BC. After a revolt by the Greek cities in Ionia (499–494 BC) he invaded Greece but was defeated at Marathon (490 BC).

dark • adj. **1** with little or no light. **2** of a deep colour. **3** (of skin, hair, or eyes) brown or black. **4** mysterious: *a dark secret.* **5** (**darkest**) humorous most remote or uncivilized. **6** unpleasant and gloomy: *the dark days of the war.* **7** evil. • n. **1** (**the dark**) the absence of light. **2** nightfall.
– PHRASES **in the dark** in a state of ignorance. **a shot** (or **stab**) **in the dark** a wild guess.
– DERIVATIVES **darkly** adv. **darkness** n.
– ORIGIN Old English.

Dark Ages • pl. n. the period in Europe between the fall of the Roman Empire and the Middle Ages, *c.*500–1100, seen as a time when culture and learning were in decline.

darken • v. **1** make or become darker. **2** make or become unhappy or angry.
– PHRASES **never darken someone's door** keep away from someone's home.

dark horse • n. a person who is secretive about themselves.

darkroom • n. a room for developing photographs, from which normal light is excluded.

Darling,
Grace (1815–42), English heroine, who came to fame in 1838 when she and her father rowed through a storm to rescue the survivors of a wrecked ship.

darling • n. **1** used as an affectionate form of address. **2** a lovable person. **3** a person popular with a particular group: *he became the darling of the art crowd.* • adj. **1** beloved. **2** charming.
– ORIGIN Old English.

Darling River
a river of SE Australia which rises in the Great Dividing Range and flows southwestward to join the Murray River.

darn[1] • v. mend (knitted material) by interweaving yarn across it.
– DERIVATIVES **darning** n.
– ORIGIN perh. from Old English, 'to hide'.

darn[2] • v., adj., & exclam. informal euphemism for DAMN.

darned • adj. informal euphemism for DAMNED.

Darnley,
Henry Stewart (or Stuart), Lord (1545–67), Scottish nobleman, second husband of Mary, Queen of Scots and father of James I of England. He was involved in the murder of his wife's secretary Rizzio in 1566, and was later killed in a mysterious explosion.

dart • n. **1** a small pointed missile thrown or fired as a weapon. **2** a small pointed missile used in the game of darts. **3** (**darts**) an indoor game in which darts are thrown at a dartboard. **4** a sudden rapid movement. **5** a tapered tuck in a garment. • v. move suddenly or rapidly.
– ORIGIN Old French.

dartboard • n. a circular board used as a target in the game of darts.

Dartmoor
a moorland district in Devon that was a royal forest in Saxon times, now a national park.

Darwin[1]
the capital of Northern Territory, Australia.

Darwin[2],
Charles (Robert) (1809–82), English naturalist, who proposed of the theory of evolution by natural selection. His works *On the Origin of Species* and *The Descent of Man* revolutionized our thinking about nature and humanity's place within it.

Darwinism • n. the theory of the evolution of species by natural selection, proposed by Charles Darwin.
– DERIVATIVES **Darwinian** n. & adj. **Darwinist** n. & adj.

dash • v. **1** run or travel in a great hurry. **2** strike or throw with great force. **3** destroy: *his hopes were dashed.* **4** (**dash off**) write (something) hurriedly. • n. **1** an act of dashing. **2** N. Amer. a sprint. **3** a small amount added: *a dash of soda.* **4** impressive style; flair. **5** a horizontal stroke in writing, marking a pause or omission. **6** the longer of the signals used in Morse code.

dashboard • n. the panel of instruments and controls facing the driver of a vehicle.
– ORIGIN first referring to a board in front of a carriage, to keep out mud.

dashing • adj. excitingly attractive and stylish.

dastardly /dass-terd-li/ • adj. dated or humorous wicked and cruel.
– ORIGIN from archaic *dastard* 'despicable person'.

d

DAT • abbrev. digital audio tape.

data /day-tuh/ • n. **1** facts or statistics used for reference or analysis. **2** the quantities, characters, or symbols operated on by a computer.
– ORIGIN Latin, plural of **DATUM**.

USAGE data
The word **data** is the plural of Latin **datum** and in scientific use it is treated as a plural noun, taking a plural verb (for example, *the data were classified*). In everyday use, however, **data** is often treated as a singular noun and sentences such as *data was collected over a number of years* are now widely accepted.

databank • n. a large store of data in a computer.

database • n. a structured set of data held in a computer.

datable (also **dateable**) • adj. able to be dated to a particular time.

data capture • n. Computing the process of gathering data and putting it into a form accessible by computer.

data protection • n. Brit. legal control over access to data stored in computers.

date[1] • n. **1** the day of the month or year as specified by a number. **2** a day or year when a particular event occurred or will occur. **3** informal a social or romantic appointment. **4** a musical or theatrical performance. • v. (**dates**, **dating**, **dated**) **1** establish the date of. **2** mark with a date. **3** (**date back to**) originate at (a particular time in the past). **4** (**dated**) old-fashioned. **5** N. Amer. informal go on a date or regular dates with.
– PHRASES **to date** until now.
– ORIGIN Latin *data* 'given'.

date[2] • n. the sweet, dark brown, oval fruit of a palm tree of North Africa and western Asia.
– ORIGIN Greek *daktulos* 'finger'.

dateable • adj. var. of **DATABLE**.

Date Line E
(also **International Date Line**) an imaginary North–South line through the Pacific Ocean (chiefly along longitude 180°), to the east of which the date is a day earlier than it is to the west.

dating agency • n. a service which arranges introductions for people seeking romantic partners or friends.

dative /day-tiv/ • adj. Grammar (in Latin, Greek, German, etc.) referring to the case of nouns and pronouns indicating an indirect object or the person or thing affected by a verb.
– ORIGIN from Latin *casus dativus* 'case of giving'.

datum /day-tuhm/ • n. (pl. **data**) a piece of information.
– ORIGIN Latin, 'something given'.

daub /dawb/ • v. **1** smear carelessly or heavily with a thick substance. **2** spread (a thick substance) on a surface. • n. **1** plaster, clay, or a similar substance, used in building. **2** a smear of a thick substance. **3** an unskilful painting.
– DERIVATIVES **dauber** n.
– ORIGIN Old French *dauber*.

daughter • n. **1** a girl or woman in relation to her parents. **2** a female descendant.
– ORIGIN Old English.

daughter-in-law • n. (pl. **daughters-in-law**) the wife of one's son.

daunt /dawnt/ • v. (usu. **be daunted**) cause to feel nervous or discouraged.
– DERIVATIVES **daunting** adj.
– ORIGIN Old French *danter*.

dauntless • adj. fearless and determined.

dauphin /doh-fan/ • n. hist. the eldest son of the King of France.
– ORIGIN French.

David[1] E
/day-vid/ (died *c.*962 BC), king of Judah and Israel *c.*1000–*c.*962 BC. In the biblical account he killed the Philistine Goliath and became king on Saul's death.

David[2] E
/day-vid/, Elizabeth (1913–92), British cookery writer, whose books introduced Mediterranean cuisine to Britain in the 1950s and 1960s.

David[3] E
/da-veed/, Jacques-Louis (1748–1825), French painter, famous for neoclassical paintings such as *The Oath of the Horatii*.

David, St E
(6th century; Welsh name **Dewi**), Welsh bishop and patron saint of Wales. Feast day, 1 March.

Davies[1], E
Sir Peter Maxwell (b.1934), English composer and conductor. His work is influenced by serialism and early English music.

Davies[2], E
(William) Robertson (1913–95), Canadian novelist, dramatist, and journalist, known for his Deptford trilogy of novels.

da Vinci, E
Leonardo, see **LEONARDO DA VINCI**.

Davis[1], E
Bette (1908–89; born *Ruth Elizabeth Davis*), American actress, famous for playing strong, independent female characters in such films as *Dangerous*.

Davis[2], E
Miles (Dewey) (1926–91), American jazz trumpeter, composer, and bandleader, who in the 1950s introduced a style known as 'cool' jazz.

Davis Cup E
an annual tennis championship for men, played between teams from different countries.

davit /da-vit/ • n. a small crane on a ship.
– ORIGIN Old French *daviot*.

Davy, E
Sir Humphry (1778–1829), English chemist. He discovered the elements sodium, potassium, magnesium, calcium, strontium, and barium. In 1815 he invented a safety lamp for miners.

dawdle • v. (**dawdles, dawdling, dawdled**) move slowly; take one's time.
– ORIGIN from dialect *daddle* 'dally'.

Dawkins, E
Richard (b.1941), English biologist. Dawkins's book *The Selfish Gene* tried to show the biological basis of social behaviour, while *The Blind Watchmaker* discussed how evolution by natural selection could explain the origin of life.

dawn • n. **1** the first appearance of light in the sky in the morning. **2** the beginning of something: *the dawn of civilization.* • v. **1** (of a day) begin. **2** come into existence. **3** (**dawn on**) become evident to.
– ORIGIN Old English.

dawn chorus • n. the early-morning singing of birds.

Day, E
Doris (b.1924; born *Doris Kappelhoff*), American actress and singer. She starred in musicals and comedies such as *Calamity Jane* and *Pillow Talk*.

day • n. **1** a period of twenty-four hours, reckoned from midnight to midnight. **2** the time between sunrise and sunset. **3** a particular period of the past: *laws were strict in those days.* **4** (**the day**) the present time or the time in question. **5** (**one's day**) the youthful or successful period of one's life.
– PHRASES **any day** informal at any time or under any circumstances. **call it a day** decide to stop doing something. **day by day** gradually. **day in, day out** continuously or repeatedly over a long period. **that will be the day** informal that is very unlikely. **these days** at present.
– ORIGIN Old English.

day boy (or **day girl**) • n. Brit. a boy (or girl) who lives at home and attends a school that also takes boarders.

daybreak • n. dawn.

day centre (also **day-care centre**) • n. a place providing daytime care and social facilities for elderly or disabled people.

daydream • n. a series of pleasant thoughts that distract one's attention from the present. • v. have a daydream.
– DERIVATIVES **daydreamer** n.

Day Lewis, E
Cecil (1904–72), English poet and critic, whose early verse reflects the influence of revolutionary ideas. He was Poet Laureate 1968–72.

daylight • n. **1** the natural light of the day. **2** dawn. **3** visible distance between one person or thing and another.
– PHRASES **beat** (or **knock** etc.) **the living daylights out of** hit or beat very hard.

daylight robbery • n. Brit. informal blatant and unfair overcharging.

day release • n. Brit. a system in which employees are granted days off work to go on educational courses.

day return • n. Brit. a ticket at a reduced rate for a return journey on public transport within one day.

day school • n. **1** a school for pupils who live at home. **2** a short educational course.

daytime • n. **1** the time between sunrise and sunset. **2** the period of time corresponding to normal working hours.

day-to-day • adj. **1** happening regularly every day. **2** ordinary.

day trip • n. a journey or outing completed in one day.
– DERIVATIVES **day tripper** n.

daze • v. (**dazes, dazing, dazed**) stun or bewilder. • n. a state of stunned confusion or bewilderment.
– ORIGIN Old Norse, 'weary'.

dazzle • v. (**dazzles, dazzling, dazzled**) **1** (of a bright light) blind temporarily. **2** amaze with an impressive quality: *I was dazzled by her beauty.* • n. blinding brightness.
– DERIVATIVES **dazzler** n.
– ORIGIN from DAZE.

dB • abbrev. decibel(s).

DBE • abbrev. (in the UK) Dame Commander of the Order of the British Empire.

DC • abbrev. **1** direct current. **2** District of Columbia.

DCB • abbrev. (in the UK) Dame Commander of the Order of the Bath.

DCM • abbrev. (in the UK) Distinguished Conduct Medal.

DCMG • abbrev. (in the UK) Dame Commander of the Order of St Michael and St George.

DD • abbrev. Doctor of Divinity.

D-Day • n. the day (6 June 1944) in the Second World War on which Allied forces invaded northern France.
– ORIGIN from *D* for *day* + DAY.

DDR • abbrev. hist. German Democratic Republic.
– ORIGIN short for German *Deutsche Demokratische Republik*.

DDT • abbrev. dichlorodiphenyltrichloroethane, a compound used as an insecticide but now banned in many countries.

DE • abbrev. (in the UK) Department of Employment.

de- • prefix forming or added to verbs or their derivatives: **1** down; away: *deduct.* **2** completely: *denude.* **3** indicating removal or reversal: *de-ice.*
– ORIGIN Latin *de* 'off, from' or *dis-*.

deacon /dee-kuhn/ • n. **1** (in Catholic, Anglican, and Orthodox Churches) a minister ranking below a priest. **2** (in some Protestant Churches) a lay officer assisting a minister.
– ORIGIN Greek *diakonos* 'servant'.

deaconess • n. a woman with duties similar to those of a deacon.

deactivate • v. (**deactivates, deactivating, deactivated**) make (equipment or a virus) inactive by disconnecting or destroying it.

dead • adj. **1** no longer alive. **2** (of a part of the body) numb. **3** displaying no emotion: *a cold, dead voice.* **4** no longer current. **5** lacking activity or excitement. **6** (of equipment) not functioning. **7** complete: *dead silence.* • adv. **1** completely; exactly: *dead on time.* **2** directly: *dead ahead.* **3** Brit. informal very.
– PHRASES **dead and buried** finished. **the dead of night** the quietest, darkest part of

the night. **the dead of winter** the coldest part of winter. **from the dead** from being dead.
– DERIVATIVES **deadness** n.
– ORIGIN Old English.

deadbeat • adj. (**dead beat**) informal completely exhausted. • n. informal an idle or unreliable person.

dead duck • n. informal an unsuccessful or useless person or thing.

deaden • v. **1** make less strong or intense. **2** make numb.

dead end • n. an end of a road or passage from which no exit is possible.

dead hand • n. an undesirable long-lasting influence: *the dead hand of discrimination.*

dead heat • n. a race in which two or more competitors are exactly level.

dead letter • n. a law or treaty which is no longer applied in practice.

deadline • n. the latest time or date by which something should be completed.

deadlock • n. **1** a situation in which no progress can be made. **2** Brit. a lock operated by a key. • v. cause to reach a deadlock.

dead loss • n. an unproductive or useless person or thing.

deadly • adj. (**deadlier**, **deadliest**) **1** causing or able to cause death. **2** (of a voice, glance, etc.) filled with hate. **3** extremely accurate or effective. **4** informal extremely boring. • adv. **1** as if dead. **2** extremely: *she was deadly serious.*

deadly nightshade • n. a poisonous plant with purple flowers and round black fruit.

deadly sin • n. (in Christian tradition) a sin seen as leading to damnation.

deadpan • adj. not showing any emotion; expressionless.

dead reckoning • n. a way of finding out one's position by estimating the direction and distance travelled.

dead ringer • n. a person or thing very like another.

Dead Sea E
a salt lake in the Jordan valley, on the Israel–Jordan border. At 400 m (1,300 ft) below sea level, it is the lowest point in the world.

Dead Sea scrolls E
a collection of Hebrew and Aramaic manuscripts discovered in caves near the north-western shore of the Dead Sea between 1947 and 1956. The scrolls include texts of many books of the Old Testament, some 1,000 years older than previously known versions.

deadweight • n. **1** the weight of a motionless person or thing. **2** the total weight which a ship can carry.

dead wood • n. useless or unproductive people or things.

deaf • adj. **1** wholly or partially unable to hear. **2** (**deaf to**) unwilling to listen to.
– PHRASES **fall on deaf ears** be ignored.
– DERIVATIVES **deafness** n.
– ORIGIN Old English.

deafen • v. **1** make deaf. **2** (**deafening**) extremely loud.

deaf mute • n. offens. a person who is deaf and unable to speak.

deal[1] • v. (**deals**, **dealing**, **dealt**) **1** give out (cards) to players for a game or round. **2** (**deal out**) distribute. **3** buy and sell a product commercially. **4** informal buy and sell illegal drugs. **5** inflict (a blow) on. • n. **1** an agreement between two or more parties. **2** a particular form of treatment given or received: *working mothers get a bad deal.*
– PHRASES **a big deal** informal an important thing. **a deal of** a large amount of. **deal with** **1** do business with. **2** take action to put right. **3** cope with. **4** have as a subject. **a good** (or **great**) **deal** **1** a large amount. **2** much; a lot. **a square deal** a fair bargain or treatment.
– ORIGIN Old English.

deal[2] • n. fir or pine wood (as a building material).
– ORIGIN German and Dutch *dele* 'plank'.

dealer • n. **1** a person who buys and sells goods. **2** a person who sells illegal drugs. **3** a player who deals cards in a card game.
– DERIVATIVES **dealership** n.

dealt past part. of DEAL[1].

Dean, E
James (1931–55; born *James Byron*), American actor. He starred in only three films before dying in a car accident, but became a cult figure closely identified with the title role of *Rebel Without a Cause.*

dean • n. **1** the head of the governing body of a cathedral. **2** the head of a university department or of a medical school. **3** a college officer who deals with discipline and welfare.
– ORIGIN Old French *deien.*

deanery • n. (pl. **deaneries**) the official house of a dean.

dear • adj. **1** much loved. **2** used in the polite introduction to a letter. **3** expensive. • n. **1** a lovable person. **2** used as an affectionate form of address. • adv. at a high cost. • exclam. used in expressions of surprise or dismay.
– ORIGIN Old English.

dearly • adv. **1** very much. **2** at great cost.

dearth /derth/ • n. a lack: *a dearth of evidence.*
– ORIGIN from DEAR.

death • n. **1** the action or fact of dying. **2** an instance of a person or an animal dying. **3** the state of being dead. **4** the end of something.
– PHRASES **at death's door** so ill that one may die. **catch one's death (of cold)** informal catch a severe cold. **die a death** fail or come to an end. **do to death** repeat to the point of boredom. **put to death** execute. **to death** used for emphasis: *sick to death of him.*
– DERIVATIVES **deathless** adj.
– ORIGIN Old English.

deathbed • n. the bed where someone is dying or has died.

death certificate • n. an official statement of a person's death.

death duty • n. dated = INHERITANCE TAX.

death knell • n. **1** the tolling of a bell to mark a death. **2** an event that signals the end of something.

deathly • adj. suggesting death: *a deathly hush.*

death penalty • n. punishment by execution.

death rate • n. the number of deaths per one thousand people per year.

death row • n. a prison block for convicts

who are sentenced to death.

death toll • n. the number of deaths resulting from a particular cause.

death trap • n. a dangerous building, vehicle, etc.

Death Valley E
a deep arid desert basin below sea level in SE California and SW Nevada, the hottest and driest part of North America.

death-watch beetle • n. a beetle whose larvae bore into dead wood and structural timbers.
– ORIGIN so-called because it makes a sound like a watch ticking, formerly believed to be an omen of death.

death wish • n. an unconscious wish for one's own death.

debacle /day-**bah**-k'l/ • n. a complete failure or disaster.
– ORIGIN French.

debar • v. (**debars**, **debarring**, **debarred**) prevent officially from doing something.
– ORIGIN Old French *desbarrer* 'unbar'.

debark • v. leave a ship or aircraft.
– ORIGIN French *débarquer*.

debase /di-**bayss**/ • v. (**debases**, **debasing**, **debased**) lower the quality, value, or character of.
– DERIVATIVES **debasement** n.

debatable • adj. open to discussion or argument.

debate • n. **1** a formal discussion in which opposing arguments are presented. **2** an argument. • v. (**debates**, **debating**, **debated**) **1** discuss or argue about. **2** consider (a course of action).
– DERIVATIVES **debater** n.
– ORIGIN Old French.

debauch /di-**bawch**/ • v. corrupt morally.
– ORIGIN Old French *desbaucher* 'turn away from one's duty'.

debauchery • n. excessive indulgence in sex, alcohol, and drugs.

de Beauvoir E
/duh **bow**-vwahr/, Simone (1908–86), French existentialist philosopher, novelist, and feminist, famous for *The Second Sex*, an influential feminist work. She had a lifelong association with Jean-Paul Sartre.

debenture /di-**ben**-cher/ • n. Brit. a certificate issued by a company acknowledging that it has borrowed money on which interest is being paid.
– ORIGIN Latin *debentur* 'are owing'.

debilitate /di-**bil**-i-tayt/ • v. (**debilitates**, **debilitating**, **debilitated**) severely weaken.
– DERIVATIVES **debilitation** n.
– ORIGIN Latin *debilitare*.

debility • n. (pl. **debilities**) physical weakness.

debit • n. **1** an entry in an account recording a sum owed. **2** a payment made or owed. • v. (**debits**, **debiting**, **debited**) (of a bank) remove (money) from a customer's account.
– ORIGIN French.

debit card • n. a card allowing the holder to remove money from a bank account electronically when making a purchase.

debonair /deb-uh-**nair**/ • adj. (of a man) confident, stylish, and charming.
– ORIGIN from Old French *de bon aire* 'of good disposition'.

debouch /di-**bowch**/ • v. emerge from a confined space into a wide, open area.
– ORIGIN French.

debrief • v. question in detail about a completed mission.

debris /**deb**-ree/ • n. scattered pieces of rubbish or the remains of something that has been destroyed.
– ORIGIN French.

de Broglie E
/duh **broh**-li/, Louis-Victor, Prince (1892–1987), French physicist. He was the first to suggest that subatomic particles can have the properties of waves.

debt • n. **1** a sum of money owed. **2** the state of owing money. **3** a feeling of gratitude for a favour or service.
– ORIGIN Latin *debitum*.

debtor • n. a person who owes money.

debug • v. (**debugs**, **debugging**, **debugged**) remove errors from (computer hardware or software).

debunk • v. reveal (a widely held opinion or reputation) to be false.

deburr /dee-**ber**/ (also **debur**) • v. (**deburs**, **deburring**, **deburred**) smooth the rough edges of.

Debussy E
/duh-**boo**-si/, (Achille) Claude (1862–1918), French composer. His music, such as *Prélude à l'après midi d'un faune*, reflects the influence of Impressionist art and was influential in freeing 20th-century music from the restrictions of classical form.

debut /**day**-byoo/ • n. a person's first appearance in a role. • v. make a debut.
– ORIGIN French.

debutant /**deb**-yoo-ton(t)/ • n. a person making a debut.

debutante /**deb**-yuh-tahnt/ • n. a young upper-class woman making her first appearance in society.

Dec. • abbrev. December.

deca- (also **dec-** before a vowel) • comb. form ten; having ten: *decahedron*.
– ORIGIN Greek *deka* 'ten'.

decade /**dek**-ayd/ • n. a period of ten years.
– ORIGIN Old French.

decadent • adj. having low moral standards and interested only in pleasure.
– DERIVATIVES **decadence** n. **decadently** adv.
– ORIGIN French.

decaffeinated /dee-**kaf**-fi-nay-tid/ • adj. (of tea or coffee) having had most or all of its caffeine removed.

decagon /**dek**-uh-guhn/ • n. a plane figure with ten straight sides and angles.

decahedron /dek-uh-**hee**-druhn/ • n. (pl. **decahedra** or **decahedrons**) a solid figure with ten plane faces.

decalitre (US **decaliter**, **dekaliter**) • n. a unit of volume, equal to 10 litres.

Decalogue /**dek**-uh-log/ • n. the Ten Commandments.
– ORIGIN from Greek *dekalogos biblos* 'book of the Ten Commandments'.

decametre (US **decameter**, **dekameter**) • n. a unit of length, equal to 10 metres.

decamp • v. leave suddenly or secretly.

decanal /di-kay-nuhl/ • adj. having to do with a dean or deanery.
– ORIGIN Latin *decanalis*.

decant /di-kant/ • v. pour (liquid) from one container into another.
– ORIGIN Latin *decanthare*.

decanter • n. a glass container with a stopper, into which wine or spirit is decanted.

d

decapitate /di-kap-i-tayt/ • v. (**decapitates**, **decapitating**, **decapitated**) cut off the head of.
– DERIVATIVES **decapitation** n.
– ORIGIN Latin *decapitare*.

decapod /dek-uh-pod/ • n. a crustacean, such as a crab, with five pairs of walking legs.
– ORIGIN from Greek *deka* 'ten' + *pous* 'foot'.

decarbonize (also **decarbonise**) • v. (**decarbonizes**, **decarbonizing**, **decarbonized**) remove carbon deposits from (an engine).

decathlon /di-kath-lon/ • n. an athletic event in which each competitor takes part in the same ten events.
– DERIVATIVES **decathlete** n.
– ORIGIN from Greek *deka* 'ten' + *athlon* 'contest'.

decay • v. **1** rot. **2** become less powerful or good. **3** Physics (of a radioactive substance, particle, etc.) undergo change to a different form by giving out radiation. • n. **1** the state or process of decaying. **2** rotten matter or tissue.
– ORIGIN Old French *decair*.

decease • n. formal or Law death.
– ORIGIN Latin *decessus*.

deceased formal or Law • n. (**the deceased**) the recently dead person in question. • adj. recently dead.

deceit • n. **1** the action of deceiving. **2** a deceitful act or statement.

deceitful • adj. acting to deceive others.
– DERIVATIVES **deceitfully** adv.

deceive • v. (**deceives**, **deceiving**, **deceived**) **1** deliberately cause (someone) to believe something false. **2** (of a thing) give a mistaken impression.
– DERIVATIVES **deceiver** n.
– ORIGIN Old French *deceivre*.

decelerate /dee-sel-uh-rayt/ • v. (**decelerates**, **decelerating**, **decelerated**) begin to move more slowly.
– DERIVATIVES **deceleration** n.

December • n. the twelfth month of the year.
– ORIGIN Latin.

decency • n. (pl. **decencies**) **1** decent behaviour. **2** (**decencies**) standards of acceptable behaviour.

decennial /di-sen-ni-uhl/ • adj. lasting for or recurring every ten years.
– ORIGIN from Latin *decem* 'ten' + *annus* 'year'.

decent • adj. **1** following accepted moral standards. **2** of an acceptable quality. **3** Brit. informal kind or generous.
– DERIVATIVES **decently** adv.
– ORIGIN Latin *decere* 'to be fit'.

decentralize (also **decentralise**) • v. (**decentralizes**, **decentralizing**, **decentralized**) transfer (authority) from central to local government.

deception • n. **1** the action of deceiving. **2** a thing that deceives.

deceptive • adj. giving a misleading impression.

deceptively • adv. **1** to a lesser extent than appears the case: *a deceptively smooth surface.* **2** to a greater extent than appears the case: *a deceptively spacious room.*

deci- • comb. form one tenth: *decilitre.*
– ORIGIN Latin *decimus* 'tenth'.

decibel /dess-i-bel/ • n. a unit of measurement expressing the intensity of a sound or the power of an electrical signal.
– ORIGIN from **DECI-** + *bel*, a unit (= 10 decibels) named after Alexander Graham **BELL**.

decide • v. (**decides**, **deciding**, **decided**) **1** consider and make a judgement or decision. **2** settle (an issue or contest). **3** give a judgement concerning a legal case.
– ORIGIN Latin *decidere* 'determine'.

decided • adj. definite; clear: *a decided improvement.*
– DERIVATIVES **decidedly** adv.

decider • n. a contest that settles the winner of a series of contests.

deciduous /di-sid-yoo-uhss/ • adj. **1** (of a tree or shrub) shedding its leaves annually. Contrasted with **EVERGREEN**. **2** (of teeth or horns) shed after a time.
– ORIGIN Latin *deciduus*.

decilitre (US **deciliter**) • n. a unit of volume, equal to one tenth of a litre.

decimal • adj. having to do with a system of numbers based on the number ten. • n. a fraction whose denominator is a power of ten, expressed by numbers placed to the right of a decimal point.
– ORIGIN Latin *decimus* 'tenth'.

decimal place • n. the position of a digit to the right of a decimal point.

decimal point • n. a full point placed after the figure representing units in a decimal fraction.

decimate /dess-i-mayt/ • v. (**decimates**, **decimating**, **decimated**) **1** kill or destroy a large proportion of. **2** severely reduce the strength of.
– DERIVATIVES **decimation** n.
– ORIGIN Latin *decimare* 'take as a tenth'.

decimetre (US **decimeter**) • n. a unit of length, equal to one tenth of a metre.

decipher /di-sy-fer/ • v. (**deciphers**, **deciphering**, **deciphered**) **1** convert from code into normal language. **2** succeed in understanding (something hard to interpret).

decision • n. **1** a conclusion reached after consideration. **2** the action of deciding. **3** decisiveness.

decisive • adj. **1** settling an issue quickly: *decisive evidence.* **2** able to make decisions quickly.
– DERIVATIVES **decisively** adv.

deck • n. **1** a floor of a ship. **2** a floor or platform. **3** esp. N. Amer. a pack of cards. **4** a piece of sound-reproduction equipment, made up of a player or recorder for discs or tapes. • v. decorate (something) for a special occasion.
– PHRASES **hit the deck** informal fall to the ground.
– ORIGIN Dutch *dec* 'covering, roof'.

deckchair • n. a folding chair with a wooden frame and a canvas seat.

decking ● n. material used in making a deck.

declaim ● v. speak or recite in a dramatic or passionate way.
– ORIGIN Latin *declamare.*

declamation ● n. the action or art of declaiming.
– DERIVATIVES **declamatory** adj.

declaration ● n. **1** a formal statement or announcement. **2** the action of declaring.

> **Declaration of Independence** [E]
> a document declaring the US to be independent of the British Crown, signed on 4 July 1776.

declarative /di-kla-ruh-tiv/ ● adj. **1** making a declaration: *declarative statements.* **2** Grammar (of a sentence or phrase) taking the form of a simple statement.

declare ● v. (**declares**, **declaring**, **declared**) **1** announce solemnly or officially. **2** (**declare oneself**) reveal one's intentions or identity. **3** (**declared**) having stated something openly: *a declared atheist.* **4** state that one has (income or goods on which tax or duty should be paid). **5** Cricket close an innings voluntarily with wickets remaining.
– ORIGIN Latin *declarare.*

declassify ● v. (**declassifies**, **declassifying**, **declassified**) officially declare (information or documents) to be no longer secret.

declension /di-klen-sh'n/ ● n. the changes in the form of a noun, pronoun, or adjective that identify its grammatical case, number, and gender.
– ORIGIN Old French *decliner* 'to decline'.

declination /dek-li-nay-sh'n/ ● n. **1** Astron. the position of a point in the sky equivalent to latitude on the earth. **2** the angular deviation of a compass needle from true north.

decline ● v. (**declines**, **declining**, **declined**) **1** become smaller, weaker, or worse: *the birth rate continued to decline.* **2** politely refuse. **3** Grammar form (a noun, pronoun, or adjective) according to case, number, and gender. ● n. a gradual and continuous loss of strength, numbers, or value.
– ORIGIN Latin *declinare* 'bend down'.

declivity /di-kliv-i-ti/ ● n. (pl. **declivities**) a downward slope.
– ORIGIN Latin *declivitas.*

decoction ● n. the concentrated essence of a substance, produced by heating or boiling.
– ORIGIN Latin.

decode ● v. (**decodes**, **decoding**, **decoded**) **1** convert (a coded message) into understandable language. **2** convert (audio or video signals) from analogue to digital.
– DERIVATIVES **decoder** n.

décolletage /day-kol-*tahzh*/ ● n. a low neckline on a woman's garment.
– ORIGIN French.

décolleté /day-kol-tay/ ● adj. having a low neckline.
– ORIGIN French.

decommission ● v. **1** take (a ship) out of service. **2** dismantle and make safe (a nuclear reactor or weapon).

decompose ● v. (**decomposes**, **decomposing**, **decomposed**) **1** decay. **2** break down (a substance) into its elements.
– DERIVATIVES **decomposition** n.

decompress /dee-kuhm-press/ ● v. **1** reduce pressure on. **2** expand (compressed computer data) to its normal size.
– DERIVATIVES **decompressor** n.

decompression ● n. **1** reduction in air pressure. **2** a gradual reduction of air pressure on a person who has been experiencing high pressure while diving. **2** the process of decompressing computer data.

decompression sickness ● n. a serious condition that results when too rapid decompression by a diver causes nitrogen bubbles to form in the tissues of the body.

decongestant /dee-kuhn-jess-tuhnt/ ● adj. (of a medicine) used to relieve a blocked nose.

deconstruct /dee-kuhn-strukt/ ● v. dismantle.

decontaminate ● v. (**decontaminates**, **decontaminating**, **decontaminated**) remove dangerous substances from.
– DERIVATIVES **decontamination** n.

decor /day-kor, dek-or/ ● n. the furnishing and decoration of a room.
– ORIGIN French.

decorate ● v. (**decorates**, **decorating**, **decorated**) **1** make more attractive by adding ornamentation. **2** apply paint or wallpaper to. **3** give an award or medal to.
– ORIGIN Latin *decorare* 'embellish'.

decoration ● n. **1** the process or art of decorating. **2** a decorative object or pattern. **3** the way in which something is decorated. **4** a medal or award given as an honour.

decorative /dek-uh-ruh-tiv/ ● adj. **1** making something look more attractive. **2** having to do with decoration: *a decorative artist.*
– DERIVATIVES **decoratively** adv.

decorator ● n. Brit. a person whose job is to paint interior walls or hang wallpaper.

decorous /dek-uh-ruhss/ ● adj. in good taste; polite and restrained.
– DERIVATIVES **decorously** adv.
– ORIGIN Latin *decorus* 'seemly'.

decorum /di-kor-uhm/ ● n. polite and socially acceptable behaviour.
– ORIGIN Latin, 'seemly thing'.

decoupage /day-koo-pah*zh*, dek-oo-pah*zh*/ ● n. the decoration of a surface with paper cut-outs.
– ORIGIN French.

decoy ● n. /dee-koy/ **1** a real or imitation bird or mammal, used by hunters to lure game. **2** a person or thing used to mislead or lure someone into a trap. ● v. /di-**koy**/ lure by means of a decoy.
– ORIGIN Dutch *de kooi.*

decrease ● v. /di-kreess/ (**decreases**, **decreasing**, **decreased**) make or become smaller or fewer in size, amount, or strength. ● n. /dee-kreess/ **1** the amount by which something decreases. **2** the process of decreasing.
– ORIGIN Latin *decrescere.*

decree ● n. **1** an official order that has the force of law. **2** a judgement of certain law courts. ● v. (**decrees**, **decreeing**, **decreed**) order by decree.
– ORIGIN Latin *decretum* 'something decided'.

decree absolute ● n. (pl. **decrees absolute**) Engl. Law a final order by a court of law which officially ends a marriage.

decree nisi /di-kree ny-sy/ ● **n.** (pl. **decrees nisi**) Engl. Law an order by a court of law that states the date on which a marriage will end, unless a good reason to prevent a divorce is produced.
– ORIGIN Latin *nisi* 'unless'.

decrepit /di-krep-it/ ● **adj. 1** worn out or ruined because of age or neglect. **2** elderly and infirm.
– DERIVATIVES **decrepitude** n.
– ORIGIN Latin *decrepitus*.

d

decriminalize (also **decriminalise**) ● **v.** (**decriminalizes, decriminalizing, decriminalized**) cease to treat (something) as illegal.

decry /di-kry/ ● **v.** (**decries, decrying, decried**) publicly declare to be wrong.
– ORIGIN French *décrier* 'cry down'.

decrypt /dee-kript/ ● **v.** convert (a coded or unclear message) into understandable language.

dedicate ● **v.** (**dedicates, dedicating, dedicated**) **1** devote to a particular subject, task, or purpose. **2** address (a book) to a person as a sign of respect or affection. **3** hold a ceremony to devote (a building) to a god, goddess, or saint.
– DERIVATIVES **dedicatory** adj.
– ORIGIN Latin *dedicare*.

dedicated ● **adj. 1** devoted to a task or purpose. **2** used or designed for one particular purpose only.

dedication ● **n. 1** devotion to a purpose or task. **2** the action of dedicating. **3** the words with which something is dedicated.

deduce ● **v.** (**deduces, deducing, deduced**) arrive at (an opinion) by reasoning.
– ORIGIN Latin *deducere* 'lead away'.

deduct ● **v.** take away from a total.
– ORIGIN Latin *deducere*.

deductible ● **adj.** able to be deducted.

deduction ● **n. 1** the action of deducting. **2** an amount that is or may be deducted. **3** a method of reasoning in which a general rule or principle is used to draw a particular conclusion.
– DERIVATIVES **deductive** adj.

Dee E
a river in NE Scotland, which rises in the Grampian Mountains and flows into the North Sea at Aberdeen.

deed ● **n. 1** an action that is performed deliberately. **2** (usu. **deeds**) a legal document.
– ORIGIN Old English.

deed of covenant ● **n.** Brit. an agreement to pay a regular amount of money.

deed poll ● **n.** Engl. Law a legal deed made and carried out by one party only.

deejay ● **n.** informal a disc jockey.

deem ● **v.** formal consider in a specified way.
– ORIGIN Old English.

deep ● **adj. 1** extending far down or in from the top or surface. **2** extending a specified distance from the top, surface, or outer edge. **3** (of sound) low in pitch. **4** (of colour) dark. **5** very intense, serious, or extreme: *a deep sleep.* **6** difficult to understand. **7** (in ball games) far down or across the field. ● **n.** (**the deep**) literary the sea. ● **adv.** far down or in; deeply.
– PHRASES **go off the deep end** informal give way suddenly to an outburst of emotion. **in deep water** informal in trouble. **jump** (or **be thrown**) **in at the deep end** informal face a difficult situation with little experience.
– ORIGIN Old English.

deepen ● **v.** make or become deep or deeper.

deep freeze ● **n.** (also **deep freezer**) a freezer.

deep-frozen ● **adj.** stored at a very low temperature.

deep-fry ● **v.** (**deep-fries, deep-frying, deep-fried**) fry (food) in enough fat or oil to cover it completely.

deeply ● **adv. 1** far down or in. **2** intensely.

deep-seated (also **deep-rooted**) ● **adj.** firmly established.

deer ● **n.** (pl. **deer**) a hoofed animal, the male of which usually has antlers.
– ORIGIN Old English.

deerstalker ● **n.** a soft cloth cap, with peaks in front and behind and ear flaps which can be tied together over the top.

deface ● **v.** (**defaces, defacing, defaced**) spoil the appearance of.

de facto /day fak-toh/ ● **adj.** existing in fact, whether legally accepted or not.
– ORIGIN Latin, 'of fact'.

defame ● **v.** (**defames, defaming, defamed**) damage the good reputation of.
– DERIVATIVES **defamation** n. **defamatory** adj.
– ORIGIN Latin *diffamare* 'spread evil rumour'.

default ● **n. 1** failure to fulfil an obligation, especially to repay a loan. **2** a pre-selected option adopted by a computer program or other mechanism when no alternative is specified. ● **v. 1** fail to fulfil an obligation. **2** (**default to**) go back automatically to (a pre-selected option).
– PHRASES **by default** because of a lack of opposition or positive action.
– DERIVATIVES **defaulter** n.
– ORIGIN Old French *defaillir* 'to fail'.

defeat ● **v. 1** win a victory over. **2** prevent from achieving an aim. **3** reject or block (a proposal or motion). ● **n.** an instance of defeating or the state of being defeated.
– ORIGIN Old French *desfaire*.

defeatist ● **n.** a person who gives in to failure too readily. ● **adj.** showing ready acceptance of failure.
– DERIVATIVES **defeatism** n.

defecate /def-i-kayt/ ● **v.** (**defecates, defecating, defecated**) discharge waste matter from the bowels.
– DERIVATIVES **defecation** n.
– ORIGIN Latin *defaecare*.

defect[1] /dee-fekt/ ● **n.** a shortcoming, imperfection, or lack.
– ORIGIN Latin *defectus*.

defect[2] /di-fekt/ ● **v.** abandon one's country or cause in favour of an opposing one.
– DERIVATIVES **defection** n. **defector** n.
– ORIGIN Latin *deficere*.

defective ● **adj.** imperfect or faulty.

defence (US **defense**) ● **n. 1** the action of defending against attack. **2** military measures or resources for protecting a country. **3** (**defences**) fortifications against attack. **4** attempted justification: *he spoke in defence of his actions.* **5** the case presented by the party being accused or sued in a lawsuit. **6** (**the defence**) the counsel for the defendant in a lawsuit. **7** (in sport) the players who prevent the other team from scoring.

defenceless (US **defenseless**) ● **adj.** completely vulnerable.

defend ● **v. 1** protect from attack or danger. **2** act as a lawyer for (the party being accused or sued) in a lawsuit. **3** attempt to justify. **4** compete to hold on to (a title or seat) in a contest or election. **5** (in sport) prevent the other team from scoring.
– DERIVATIVES **defendable** adj. **defender** n.
– ORIGIN Latin *defendere*.

defendant ● **n.** a person sued or accused in a court of law. Compare with **PLAINTIFF**.

defensible ● **adj. 1** justifiable by argument. **2** able to be protected.

defensive ● **adj. 1** used or intended to defend or protect. **2** very anxious to challenge or avoid criticism.
– PHRASES **on the defensive** expecting or resisting criticism or attack.
– DERIVATIVES **defensively** adv. **defensiveness** n.

defer[1] /di-fer/ ● **v.** (**defers**, **deferring**, **deferred**) put off to a later time.
– DERIVATIVES **deferment** n. **deferral** n.
– ORIGIN Latin *differre*.

defer[2] /di-fer/ ● **v.** (**defers**, **deferring**, **deferred**) (**defer to**) accept or give in humbly to.
– ORIGIN Latin *deferre* 'carry away, refer'.

deference ● **n.** humble respect.

deferential ● **adj.** respectful.
– DERIVATIVES **deferentially** adv.

defiance ● **n.** bold disobedience.
– ORIGIN Old French.

defiant ● **adj.** showing defiance.
– DERIVATIVES **defiantly** adv.

deficiency ● **n.** (pl. **deficiencies**) **1** a lack or shortage. **2** a failing or shortcoming.

deficient /di-fi-sh'nt/ ● **adj. 1** not having enough of a specified quality or ingredient. **2** inadequate.
– ORIGIN Latin.

deficit /def-i-sit/ ● **n. 1** the amount by which something falls short. **2** an excess of money spent over money earned.
– ORIGIN Latin, 'it is lacking'.

defile[1] /di-fyl/ ● **v.** (**defiles**, **defiling**, **defiled**) **1** make dirty. **2** treat (something holy) with disrespect.
– ORIGIN Old French *defouler* 'trample down'.

defile[2] /dee-fyl/ ● **n.** a steep-sided narrow gorge or mountain pass.
– ORIGIN French.

define ● **v.** (**defines**, **defining**, **defined**) **1** describe the exact nature of. **2** give the meaning of (a word or phrase). **3** mark out the limits or outline of.
– DERIVATIVES **definable** adj.
– ORIGIN Latin *definire*.

definite ● **adj. 1** clearly stated or decided. **2** (of a person) certain about something. **3** known to be true or real. **4** having exact and measurable physical limits.
– DERIVATIVES **definiteness** n.

definite article ● **n.** Grammar the word *the*.

definitely ● **adv.** without doubt; certainly.

definition ● **n. 1** a statement of the exact meaning of a word or the nature of something. **2** the action of defining. **3** the degree of sharpness in outline of an object or image.
– PHRASES **by definition** by its very nature.

definitive ● **adj. 1** (of a conclusion or agreement) final and with authority. **2** (of a text) the most accurate and trusted of its kind.
– DERIVATIVES **definitively** adv.

deflate ● **v.** (**deflates**, **deflating**, **deflated**) **1** let air or gas out of (a tyre, balloon, etc.). **2** cause to feel suddenly low in spirits. **3** reduce price levels in (an economy).

deflation ● **n. 1** the action of deflating. **2** reduction of the general level of prices in an economy.
– DERIVATIVES **deflationary** adj.

deflect ● **v.** turn aside from a straight course or intended purpose.
– DERIVATIVES **deflection** n.
– ORIGIN Latin *deflectere*.

deflower ● **v.** (**deflowers**, **deflowering**, **deflowered**) literary deprive (a woman) of her virginity.

Defoe E
/di-foh/, Daniel (1660–1731), English novelist and journalist. He is best known as the author of *Robinson Crusoe*, which has a claim to being the first English novel. His other novels include *Moll Flanders*.

defoliant ● **n.** a chemical used to remove the leaves from trees and plants.

defoliate /dee-foh-li-ayt/ ● **v.** (**defoliates**, **defoliating**, **defoliated**) remove leaves from (trees or plants).
– DERIVATIVES **defoliation** n.
– ORIGIN Latin *defoliare*.

De Forest, E
Lee (1873–1961), American electrical engineer, who designed a triode valve that was crucial to the development of radio communication and electronics.

deforest ● **v.** clear of trees.
– DERIVATIVES **deforestation** n.

deform ● **v.** change or spoil the usual shape of.

deformed ● **adj.** misshapen.

deformity ● **n.** (pl. **deformities**) **1** a deformed part. **2** the state of being deformed.

defraud ● **v.** illegally obtain money from (someone) by deception.
ORIGIN Latin *defraudare*.

defray ● **v.** provide money to pay (a cost).
– ORIGIN French *défrayer*.

defrock ● **v.** officially remove (a Christian priest) from their job because of a wrongdoing.

defrost ● **v. 1** free of ice. **2** thaw (frozen food).

deft ● **adj.** quick and neatly skilful.
– DERIVATIVES **deftly** adv. **deftness** n.
– ORIGIN from **DAFT**.

defunct /di-fungkt/ ● **adj.** no longer existing or functioning.
– ORIGIN Latin *defunctus* 'dead'.

defuse ● **v.** (**defuses**, **defusing**, **defused**) **1** remove the fuse from (an explosive device) in order to prevent it from exploding. **2** reduce the danger or tension in (a difficult situation).

defy ● **v.** (**defies**, **defying**, **defied**) **1** openly resist or refuse to obey. **2** challenge to do or prove something.

– ORIGIN Old French *desfier.*

Degas E
/**day**-gah/, (Hilaire Germain) Edgar (1834–1917), French Impressionist painter and sculptor, best known for his paintings of ballet dancers.

de Gaulle E
/duh **gohl**/, Charles (André Joseph Marie) (1890–1970), French general and statesman, head of government 1944–6, President 1959–69. He is remembered for his assertive foreign policy and for quelling the student uprisings and strikes of May 1968.

degenerate ● adj. /di-**jen**-uh-ruht/ having very low moral standards. ● n. /di-**jen**-uh-ruht/ a morally degenerate person. ● v. /di-**jen**-uh-rayt/ (**degenerates**, **degenerating**, **degenerated**) become worse or weaker.
– DERIVATIVES **degeneracy** n. **degeneration** n.
– ORIGIN Latin *degeneratus* 'no longer of its kind'.

degenerative ● adj. (of a disease) causing gradual deterioration.

degradation /deg-ruh-**day**-sh'n/ ● n. **1** the state of being humiliated. **2** the action of being broken down or made worse.

degrade ● v. (**degrades**, **degrading**, **degraded**) **1** cause (someone) to suffer a loss of dignity. **2** make worse in quality. **3** cause to break down or deteriorate chemically.
– DERIVATIVES **degradable** adj.

degrading ● adj. causing a loss of self-respect; humiliating.

degree n. **1** the amount, level, or extent to which something happens or is present: *a degree of caution is wise.* **2** a unit of measurement of angles, equivalent to one ninetieth of a right angle. **3** a stage in a scale, e.g. of temperature. **4** an academic rank awarded by a college or university after examination or completion of a course.
– PHRASES **by degrees** gradually.
– ORIGIN Old French.

de Havilland E
/duh **hav**-i-land/, Sir Geoffrey (1882–1965), English aircraft designer and manufacturer, whose aircraft include the Mosquito of the Second World War.

dehisce /di-**hiss**/ ● v. (**dehisces**, **dehiscing**, **dehisced**) tech. gape or burst open.
– DERIVATIVES **dehiscence** n.
– ORIGIN Latin *dehiscere.*

dehumanize (also **dehumanise**) ● v. (**dehumanizes**, **dehumanizing**, **dehumanized**) deprive of good human qualities.

dehumidify ● v. (**dehumidifies**, **dehumidifying**, **dehumidified**) remove moisture from (the air or a gas).
– DERIVATIVES **dehumidifier** n.

dehydrate /dee-hy-**drayt**/ ● v. (**dehydrates**, **dehydrating**, **dehydrated**) **1** cause (someone) to lose a large amount of water from their body. **2** remove water from (food) in order to preserve it.
– DERIVATIVES **dehydration** n.
– ORIGIN Greek *hudros* 'water'.

de-ice ● v. (**de-ices**, **de-icing**, **de-iced**) remove ice from.
– DERIVATIVES **de-icer** n.

deify /**day**-i-fy/ ● v. (**deifies**, **deifying**, **deified**) make into or worship as a god.
– DERIVATIVES **deification** n.
– ORIGIN Latin *deificare.*

Deighton E
/**day**-t'n/, Len (b.1929; full name *Leonard Cyril Deighton*), English writer, noted for his spy thrillers.

deign /dayn/ ● v. (**deign to do**) do something that one considers to be beneath one's dignity.
– ORIGIN Latin *dignare* 'consider worthy'.

deism /**day**-i-z'm, **dee**-i-z'm/ ● n. belief in the existence of an all-powerful creator who does not intervene in the universe. Compare with **THEISM**.
– DERIVATIVES **deist** n.

deity /**day**-i-ti, **dee**-i-ti/ ● n. (pl. **deities**) **1** a god or goddess. **2** divine status or nature.
– ORIGIN Latin *deitas.*

déjà vu /day-*zhah* **voo**/ ● n. a feeling of having already experienced the present situation.
– ORIGIN French, 'already seen'.

dejected ● adj. sad and dispirited.

dejection ● n. sadness or low spirits.
– ORIGIN Latin.

de jure /day **joo**-ray/ ● adv. rightfully; by right. ● adj. rightful.
– ORIGIN Latin, 'of law'.

de Klerk E
/duh **klairk**/, F. W. (b.1936; full name *Frederik Willem de Klerk*), South African statesman, State President 1989–94. He freed Nelson Mandela in 1990, lifted the ban on the ANC, and opened the negotiations that led to South Africa's first democratic elections in 1994.

de Kooning E
/duh **koo**-ning/, Willem (1904–97), Dutch-born American painter. He was a leading exponent of abstract expressionism (abstract art that uses spontaneous freedom of expression to convey the artist's emotions).

Delacroix E
/del-uh-**krwah**/, (Ferdinand Victor) Eugène (1798–1863), French romantic painter, noted for his use of vivid colour and exotic or dramatic subject matter.

de la Mare E
/duh la **mair**/, Walter (John) (1873–1956), English poet, known for his verse for children.

Delaunay E
/duh **law**-nay/, Robert (1885–1941), French painter, who created some of the first purely abstract pictures.

Delaware E
/**del**-uh-wair/ a state of the US on the Atlantic coast; capital, Dover.

delay ● v. **1** make late or slow. **2** put off to a later time. ● n. **1** the amount of time for which someone or something is delayed.**2** the action of delaying.
– ORIGIN Old French *delayer.*

delectable ● adj. lovely, delightful, or delicious.
– DERIVATIVES **delectably** adv.

delectation /dee-lek-tay-sh'n/ ● **n.** formal, humorous pleasure and delight.
– ORIGIN Latin.

delegate ● **n.** /del-i-guht/ **1** a person sent to represent others. **2** a member of a committee. ● **v.** /del-i-gayt/ (**delegates**, **delegating**, **delegated**) **1** give (a task or responsibility) to a less important person. **2** authorize (someone) to act as a representative.
– ORIGIN Latin *delegare* 'send away'.

delegation ● **n. 1** a body of delegates. **2** the action of delegating.

delete ● **v.** (**deletes**, **deleting**, **deleted**) remove or erase (text).
– DERIVATIVES **deletion** n.
– ORIGIN Latin *delere*.

deleterious /del-i-teer-i-uhss/ ● **adj.** causing harm or damage.
– ORIGIN Greek *dēlētērios* 'harmful'.

delft /delft/ ● **n.** glazed earthenware, decorated in blue on a white background.
– ORIGIN named after the town of *Delft* in the Netherlands.

Delhi E
/del-i/ a Union Territory in north central India, containing the cities of Old Delhi and New Delhi (the capital of India).

deli ● **n.** (pl. **delis**) informal a delicatessen.

deliberate ● **adj.** /di-lib-uh-ruht/ **1** done on purpose. **2** careful and unhurried: *a deliberate worker*. ● **v.** /di-lib-uh-rayt/ (**deliberates**, **deliberating**, **deliberated**) consider carefully and for a long time.
– DERIVATIVES **deliberately** adv.
– ORIGIN Latin *deliberare*.

deliberation ● **n. 1** long and careful consideration. **2** slow and careful action.

deliberative ● **adj.** having to do with consideration or discussion: *a deliberative assembly*.

Delibes E
/duh-leeb/, (Clément Philibert) Léo (1836–91), French composer, best known for the ballets *Coppélia* and *Sylvia*.

delicacy ● **n.** (pl. **delicacies**) **1** delicate quality or structure. **2** discretion and tact. **3** a high-quality or expensive food.

delicate ● **adj. 1** very fine in quality or structure. **2** easily broken or damaged. **3** tending to become ill easily. **4** requiring tact and discretion: *a delicate issue*. **5** skilful; deft. **6** (of colours or flavours) light and pleasant.
– DERIVATIVES **delicately** adv.
– ORIGIN Latin *delicatus*.

delicatessen /de-li-kuh-tess-uhn/ ● **n.** a shop selling cooked meats, cheeses, and unusual or foreign prepared foods.
– ORIGIN German or Dutch.

delicious ● **adj. 1** very pleasant to the taste. **2** delightful: *a delicious irony*.
– DERIVATIVES **deliciously** adv. **deliciousness** n.
– ORIGIN Latin *deliciosus*.

delight ● **v. 1** please greatly. **2** (**delight in**) take great pleasure in. ● **n. 1** great pleasure. **2** a source of great pleasure.
– DERIVATIVES **delighted** adj.
– ORIGIN Latin *delectare* 'to charm'.

delightful ● **adj.** very pleasing.
– DERIVATIVES **delightfully** adv.

Delilah E
/di-ly-luh/ (in the Bible) a woman who betrayed Samson to the Philistines by revealing to them that the secret of his strength lay in his long hair.

delimit /di-lim-it/ ● **v.** (**delimits**, **delimiting**, **delimited**) determine the limits or boundaries of.

delineate /di-lin-i-ayt/ ● **v.** (**delineates**, **delineating**, **delinetated**) describe or indicate precisely.
– DERIVATIVES **delineation** n.
– ORIGIN Latin *delineare*.

delinquency ● **n.** (pl. **delinquencies**) **1** minor crime. **2** formal neglect of one's duty.

delinquent /di-ling-kwuhnt/ ● **adj. 1** tending to commit crime. **2** formal failing in one's duty. ● **n.** a delinquent person.
– ORIGIN Latin *delinquere* 'to offend'.

deliquescence /del-i-kwess-uhnss/ ● **n.** tech. or literary the process of becoming liquid.
– DERIVATIVES **deliquescent** adj.
– ORIGIN Latin *deliquescere*.

delirious ● **adj. 1** suffering from delirium. **2** extremely excited or happy.
– DERIVATIVES **deliriously** adv.

delirium /di-li-ri-uhm/ ● **n.** a disturbed state of mind marked by restlessness, illusions, and incoherent thought and speech.
– ORIGIN Latin.

delirium tremens /di-li-ri-uhm tree-menz/ ● **n.** a condition in which alcoholics who are trying to give up alcohol experience tremors and hallucinations.
– ORIGIN Latin, 'trembling delirium'.

Delius E
/dee-li-uhss/, Frederick (1862–1934), English composer, known for pastoral works such as *Brigg Fair*.

deliver ● **v.** (**delivers**, **delivering**, **delivered**) **1** bring and hand over (something) to the person who is to receive it. **2** provide (something promised or expected). **3** save or set free. **4** present in a formal way. **5** assist in the birth of. **6** (also **be delivered of**) give birth to. **7** launch or aim (a blow).
– DERIVATIVES **deliverable** adj. **deliverer** n.
– ORIGIN Old French *delivrer*.

deliverance ● **n.** the process of being rescued or set free.

delivery ● **n.** (pl. **deliveries**) **1** the action of delivering something. **2** the process of giving birth. **3** an act of throwing or bowling a ball. **4** the manner or style of giving a speech.

dell ● **n.** literary a small valley.
– ORIGIN Old English.

della Francesca E
see **PIERO DELLA FRANCESCA**.

Delphi E
/del-fi, del-fy/ one of the most important religious sanctuaries of ancient Greece, situated on the slopes of Mount Parnassus. It was the seat of the Delphic Oracle whose riddling responses to questions were delivered by the Pythia (the priestess of Apollo).

Delphic /del-fik/ ● **adj.** deliberately difficult to understand: *Delphic utterances*.
– ORIGIN from the oracle at **DELPHI**.

delphinium /del-fin-i-uhm/ ● **n.** (pl. **delphin-**

iums) a garden plant bearing tall spikes of blue flowers.
– ORIGIN Greek *delphinion* 'larkspur' (a similar plant).

delta ● n. **1** the fourth letter of the Greek alphabet (Δ, δ). **2** a triangular area of land where a river has split into several channels just before entering the sea.
– ORIGIN Greek.

d

delude /di-**lood**/ ● v. (**deludes, deluding, deluded**) persuade (someone) to believe something incorrect.
– ORIGIN Latin *deludere* 'to mock'.

deluge /**del**-yooj/ ● n. **1** a severe flood or very heavy fall of rain. **2** a large number of things arriving at the same time: *a deluge of complaints.* ● v. (**deluges, deluging, deluged**) **1** overwhelm with a large number of things. **2** flood.
– ORIGIN Old French.

delusion ● n. a belief or impression that is not real.
– DERIVATIVES **delusional** adj.

de luxe /di **luks**/ ● adj. of a high quality.
– ORIGIN French, 'of luxury'.

delve ● v. (**delves, delving, delved**) **1** reach inside a container and search for something. **2** research something very thoroughly.
– ORIGIN Old English.

demagnetize (also **demagnetise**) ● v. (**demagnetizes, demagnetizing, demagnetized**) remove magnetic properties from.

demagogue /**dem**-uh-gog/ ● n. a political leader who appeals to the desires and prejudices of the public.
– DERIVATIVES **demagogic** /dem-uh-**gog**-ik/ adj.
– ORIGIN Greek *dēmagōgos.*

demand ● n. **1** a very firm and forceful request. **2** (**demands**) urgent requirements. **3** the desire of consumers for a particular product or service. ● v. **1** ask or ask for very firmly; insist on having. **2** need.
– PHRASES **in demand** sought after.
– ORIGIN Latin *demandare* 'hand over'.

demanding ● adj. requiring much skill or effort.

demarcate /**dee**-mar-kayt/ ● v. (**demarcates, demarcating, demarcated**) set the boundaries of.

demarcation ● n. **1** the action of fixing boundaries. **2** a dividing line.
– ORIGIN Spanish *demarcación.*

dematerialize (also **dematerialise**) ● v. (**dematerializes, dematerializing, dematerialized**) become no longer physically present.

de Maupassant, E
Guy, see **MAUPASSANT**.

demean /di-**meen**/ ● v. **1** cause to suffer a loss of dignity or respect. **2** (**demean oneself**) do something that is beneath one's dignity.
– DERIVATIVES **demeaning** adj.
– ORIGIN from **DE-** + **MEAN**[2].

demeanour (US **demeanor**) ● n. outward behaviour or bearing.
– ORIGIN Old French *demener* 'to lead'.

de' Medici[1], E
Catherine, see **CATHERINE DE' MEDICI**.

de' Medici[2], E
Cosimo, see **COSIMO DE' MEDICI**.

de' Medici[3], E
Lorenzo, see **LORENZO DE' MEDICI**.

demented ● adj. **1** suffering from dementia. **2** informal wild and irrational.
– DERIVATIVES **dementedly** adv.
– ORIGIN Latin *demens* 'insane'.

dementia /di-**men**-shuh/ ● n. a mental disorder marked by memory failures, personality changes, and impaired reasoning.
– ORIGIN Latin.

demerara sugar /dem-uh-**rair**-uh/ ● n. light brown cane sugar coming originally from Demerara in Guyana.

demerit ● n. something deserving blame or criticism.

demersal /di-**mer**-s'l/ ● adj. living close to the seabed.
– ORIGIN Latin *demergere* 'sink'.

demesne /di-**mayn**/ ● n. **1** hist. land attached to a manor. **2** archaic a domain.
– ORIGIN Old French *demeine* 'belonging to a lord'.

Demeter E
/di-**mee**-ter/ the Greek goddess of agriculture, mother of Persephone. Roman equivalent **CERES**.

demi- ● prefix **1** half: *demisemiquaver.* **2** partially: *demigod.*
– ORIGIN Latin *dimidius* 'half'.

demigod (or **demigoddess**) ● n. a lesser or partial god (or goddess).

demijohn ● n. a narrow-necked bottle holding from 3 to 10 gallons of liquid.
– ORIGIN prob. from French *dame-jeanne* 'Lady Jane'.

demilitarize (also **demilitarise**) ● v. (**demilitarizes, demilitarizing, demilitarized**) remove all military forces from (an area).
– DERIVATIVES **demilitarization** (also **demilitarisation**) n.

de Mille E
/duh **mil**/, Cecil B.(1881–1959; full name *Cecil Blount de Mille*), American film producer and director, famous for his spectacular epics, including *The Ten Commandments.*

demi-monde /dem-i-**mond**/ ● n. a group considered to be on the fringes of respectable society.
– ORIGIN French, 'half-world'.

demise /di-**myz**/ ● n. **1** a person's death. **2** the end or failure of something.
– ORIGIN Old French.

demisemiquaver /**dem**-i-sem-i-kway-ver/ ● n. Music, esp. Brit. a note having the time value of half a semiquaver.

demist /dee-**mist**/ ● v. Brit. clear condensation from.
– DERIVATIVES **demister** n.

demo informal ● n. (pl. **demos**) **1** = **DEMONSTRATION**. **2** a demonstration recording or piece of software. ● v. (**demos, demoing, demoed**) give a demonstration of.

demob /dee-**mob**/ ● v. (**demobs, demobbing, demobbed**) Brit. informal demobilize.

demobilize /dee-**moh**-bi-lyz/ (also **demobilise**) ● v. (**demobilizes, demobilizing, demobilized**) take (troops) out of active service.

democracy /di-**mok**-ruh-si/ ● n. (pl. **democracies**) **1** a form of government in which the people have a say in who should hold power and how it should be used. **2** a state governed in such a way. **3** control of a group by the majority of its members.
– ORIGIN Greek *dēmokratia*.

democrat ● n. **1** a supporter of democracy. **2** (**Democrat**) (in the US) a member of the Democratic Party.

democratic ● adj. **1** relating to or supporting democracy. **2** open to anyone: *cycling is a very democratic activity.* **3** (**Democratic**) (in the US) relating to the Democratic Party.
– DERIVATIVES **democratically** adv.

Democratic Party E
one of the two main US political parties (the other being the Republican Party), which follows a broadly liberal programme.

democratize (also **democratise**) ● v. (**democratizes**, **democratizing**, **democratized**) introduce a democratic system or democratic ideas to.
– DERIVATIVES **democratization** (also **democratisation**) n.

Democritus E
/di-**mok**-ri-tuhss/ (*c.*460–*c.*370 BC), Greek philosopher. His atomic theory explained natural phenomena in terms of the arrangement and rearrangement of atoms moving in a void.

demodulate ● v. (**demodulates**, **demodulating**, **demodulated**) Electron. reverse the modulation of.

demography /di-**mog**-ruh-fi/ ● n. the study of the structure of human populations using records of the numbers of births, deaths, instances of disease, etc.
– DERIVATIVES **demographer** n. **demographic** adj.

demolish /di-**mol**-ish/ ● v. **1** pull or knock down (a building). **2** thoroughly defeat. **3** humorous eat (food) quickly.
– ORIGIN Latin *demoliri*.

demolition /de-muh-**li**-shuhn/ ● n. the action of demolishing.

demon ● n. **1** an evil spirit or devil. **2** usu. humorous an evil or destructive person or thing. ● adj. forceful or skilful: *a demon cook*.
– ORIGIN Greek *daimōn* 'deity, spirit'.

demonetize /dee-**mun**-i-tyz/ (also **demonetise**) ● v. (**demonetizes**, **demonetizing**, **demonetized**) make (a coin or precious metal) no longer valid as money.
– ORIGIN French *démonétiser*.

demoniac /di-**moh**-ni-ak/ ● adj. demonic.

demonic /di-**mon**-ik/ ● adj. having to do with demons or evil spirits.
– DERIVATIVES **demonically** adv.

demonize (also **demonise**) ● v. (**demonizes**, **demonizing**, **demonized**) portray as wicked and threatening.
– DERIVATIVES **demonization** (also **demonisation**) n.

demonology ● n. the study of demons or belief in demons.

demonstrable /di-**mon**-struh-b'l/ ● adj. clearly apparent or able to be proved.
– DERIVATIVES **demonstrably** adv.

demonstrate ● v. (**demonstrates**, **demonstrating**, **demonstrated**) **1** clearly show that (something) exists or is true. **2** show and explain (how something works). **3** express (a feeling or quality) by one's actions. **4** take part in a public demonstration.
– DERIVATIVES **demonstrator** n.
– ORIGIN Latin *demonstrare* 'point out'.

demonstration ● n. **1** the action or an instance of demonstrating. **2** a public meeting or march expressing an opinion on an issue.

demonstrative /di-**mon**-struh-tiv/ ● adj. **1** tending to show one's feelings openly. **2** serving to demonstrate something. **3** Grammar (of a determiner or pronoun) indicating the person or thing referred to (e.g. *this*, *that*, *those*).
– DERIVATIVES **demonstratively** adv.

demoralize (also **demoralise**) ● v. (**demoralizes**, **demoralizing**, **demoralized**) cause to lose confidence or hope.
– ORIGIN French *démoraliser* 'to corrupt'.

Demosthenes E
/di-**moss**-thuh-neez/ (384–322 BC), Athenian orator and statesman, known for his political speeches (the *Philippics*) opposing Philip II of Macedon.

demote ● v. (**demotes**, **demoting**, **demoted**) reduce to a less senior position.
– DERIVATIVES **demotion** n.
– ORIGIN from **DE-** + **PROMOTE**.

demotic /di-**mot**-ik/ ● adj. (of language) used by ordinary people.
– ORIGIN Greek *dēmotikos*.

demotivate ● v. (**demotivates**, **demotivating**, **demotivated**) make less eager to work or make an effort.
– DERIVATIVES **demotivation** n.

Dempsey, E
Jack (1895–1983; full name *William Harrison Dempsey*), American boxer, world heavyweight champion 1919–26.

demur /di-**mer**/ ● v. (**demurs**, **demurring**, **demurred**) raise objections; show reluctance. ● n. the action of demurring: *they accepted without demur.*
– DERIVATIVES **demurral** n.
– ORIGIN Old French *demourer*.

demure /di-**myoor**/ ● adj. (of a woman) reserved, modest, and shy.
– DERIVATIVES **demurely** adv.
– ORIGIN perh. from Old French *demourer* 'remain'.

demystify ● v. (**demystifies**, **demystifying**, **demystified**) make (a subject) less difficult to understand.
– DERIVATIVES **demystification** n.

den ● n. **1** a wild animal's lair or home. **2** informal a person's private room. **3** a place where people meet to do something immoral or forbidden: *an opium den*.
– ORIGIN Old English.

Denali E
/di-**nah**-li/ = Mount McKinley (see **McKinley, Mount**).

denationalize (also **denationalise**) ● v. (**denationalizes**, **denationalizing**, **denationalized**) transfer from public to private ownership.

denature /dee-**nay**-cher/ ● v. (**denatures**, **denaturing**, **denatured**) **1** alter the natural qualities of. **2** make (alcohol) unfit for drinking by adding poisonous or foul-tasting substances.

Denbighshire E
/**den**-bi-sheer, **den**-bi-sher/ a county of North Wales; administrative centre, Ruthin.

Dench, E
Dame Judi (b.1934; full name *Judith Olivia Dench*), English actress.

d

dendrite /**den**-dryt/ • n. a short outgrowth of a nerve cell, that carries impulses to the cell body.
– DERIVATIVES **dendritic** /den-**dri**-tik/ adj.
– ORIGIN Greek *dendritēs* 'tree-like'.

dene /deen/ • n. Brit. a deep, narrow, wooded valley.
– ORIGIN Old English.

Deng Xiaoping E
/deng show-**ping**/ (also **Teng Hsiao-p'ing**) (1904–97), Chinese communist statesman, Vice-Premier 1973–6 and 1977–80; Vice-Chairman of the Central Committee of the Chinese Communist Party 1977–80. As effective leader of China from 1977, he worked to modernize the economy and improve relations with the West.

deniable • adj. able to be denied.
– DERIVATIVES **deniability** n.

denial • n. **1** the action of denying. **2** Psychol. refusal to acknowledge an unacceptable truth or emotion.

denier /**den**-yer/ • n. a unit by which the fineness of yarn is measured.
– ORIGIN Latin *denarius*, a Roman coin.

denigrate /**den**-i-grayt/ • v. (**denigrates**, **denigrating**, **denigrated**) criticize unfairly.
– DERIVATIVES **denigration** n.
– ORIGIN Latin *denigrare* 'make dark'.

denim • n. **1** a hard-wearing cotton twill fabric. **2** (**denims**) jeans or other clothes made of such fabric.
– ORIGIN from French *serge de Nîmes*, referring to serge from the town of *Nîmes*.

De Niro E
/duh **neer**-oh/, Robert (b.1943), American actor, known for his performances in films such as *The Godfather Part II* and *Raging Bull*.

Denis, St E
(also **Denys**) (died *c.*250), Italian-born French bishop, patron saint of France. Feast day, 9 October.

denizen /**den**-i-zuhn/ • n. formal or humorous an inhabitant or occupant.
– ORIGIN Old French *deinz* 'within'.

Denmark E
a Scandinavian country consisting of the greater part of the Jutland peninsula and several neighbouring islands, between the North Sea and the Baltic; capital, Copenhagen.

denominate /di-**nom**-i-nayt/ • v. (**denominates**, **denominating**, **denominated**) formal call; name.
– ORIGIN Latin *denominare*.

denomination • n. **1** a recognized branch of a church or religion. **2** the face value of a banknote, coin, postage stamp, etc.

denominational • adj. relating to a particular religious denomination.

denominator • n. Math. the number below the line in a fraction.

denote /di-**noht**/ • v. (**denotes**, **denoting**, **denoted**) **1** be a sign of. **2** (of a word or phrase) mean.
– DERIVATIVES **denotation** n.
– ORIGIN Latin *denotare*.

denouement /day-**noo**-mon/ • n. the final part of a play, film, or story, in which matters are explained or settled.
– ORIGIN French.

denounce • v. (**denounces**, **denouncing**, **denounced**) publicly declare to be wrong or evil.
– ORIGIN Latin *denuntiare* 'give official information'.

dense • adj. **1** closely packed in substance. **2** containing parts crowded closely together: *a dense cluster of stars*. **3** informal stupid.
– DERIVATIVES **densely** adv.
– ORIGIN Latin *densus*.

density • n. (pl. **densities**) **1** the degree to which a substance is dense; mass per unit volume. **2** the quantity of people or things in a particular area.

dent • n. a slight hollow in a surface made by a blow or pressure. • v. **1** mark with a dent. **2** have a bad effect on: *the experience dented his enthusiasm*.
– ORIGIN from **DINT**.

dental • adj. relating to the teeth or to dentistry.
– ORIGIN Latin *dentalis*.

dentine /**den**-teen/ (US **dentin** /**den**-tin/) • n. hard dense bony tissue forming the main part of a tooth.

dentist • n. a person who is qualified to treat the diseases and conditions that affect the teeth and gums.
– DERIVATIVES **dentistry** n.

dentition /den-**ti**-sh'n/ • n. the arrangement or condition of the teeth in a particular species.

denture /**den**-cher/ • n. a removable plate or frame holding one or more false teeth.

denude • v. (**denudes**, **denuding**, **denuded**) make bare: *the land is denuded of trees to create fields*.
– ORIGIN Latin *denudare*.

denunciation /di-nun-si-**ay**-sh'n/ • n. the action of denouncing.

Denver E
the state capital of Colorado.

deny • v. (**denies**, **denying**, **denied**) **1** refuse to admit the truth or existence of. **2** refuse to give (something desired) to. **3** (**deny oneself**) go without.
– ORIGIN Old French *deneier*.

Denys, St E
see **DENIS, ST**.

deodorant /di-**oh**-duh-ruhnt/ • n. a substance which removes or conceals unpleasant bodily smells.
– ORIGIN Latin *odor* 'smell'.

deodorize (also **deodorise**) • v. (**deodorizes**, **deodorizing**, **deodorized**) remove or conceal an unpleasant smell in.

deoxygenate /dee-**ok**-si-juh-nayt/ • v. (**deoxygenates**, **deoxygenating**, **deoxygen-**

ated) remove oxygen from.

deoxyribonucleic acid /di-ok-si-ry-boh-nyoo-klay-ik/ ● **n.** see **DNA**.

depart ● **v. 1** leave. **2** (**depart from**) do something different from (a usual course of action).
– ORIGIN Old French *departir*.

departed ● **adj.** dead.

department ● **n. 1** a division of a large organization or building, dealing with a specific area of activity. **2** an administrative district, especially in France. **3** (**one's department**) informal an area of special skill or responsibility.
– DERIVATIVES **departmental** adj.

department store ● **n.** a large shop stocking many types of goods in different departments.

departure ● **n.** the action or an instance of departing.

depend ● **v.** (**depend on**) **1** be determined or influenced by. **2** rely on.
– ORIGIN Latin *dependere* 'hang down'.

dependable ● **adj.** trustworthy and reliable.
– DERIVATIVES **dependability** n.

dependant (also **dependent**) ● **n.** a person who relies on another for financial support.

USAGE dependant

The correct spelling of the noun is either **dependant** or **dependent**. However, the adjective is always spelled **dependent** (as in *we were dependent on his good will*).

dependency ● **n.** (pl. **dependencies**) **1** a country or province controlled by another. **2** the state of being dependent.

dependent ● **adj. 1** (**dependent on**) determined or influenced by. **2** relying on someone or something for support. **3** (**dependent on**) unable to do without. ● **n.** var. of DEPENDANT.
– DERIVATIVES **dependence** n. **dependently** adv.

depict /di-pikt/ ● **v. 1** represent by a drawing, painting, or other art form. **2** describe in words.
– DERIVATIVES **depiction** n.
– ORIGIN Latin *depingere*.

depilate /dep-i-layt/ ● **v.** (**depilates, depilating, depilated**) remove the hair from.
– ORIGIN Latin *depilare*.

depilatory /di-pil-uh-tri/ ● **adj.** used to remove unwanted hair. ● **n.** (pl. **depilatories**) a cream or lotion used to remove unwanted hair.

deplete /di-pleet/ ● **v.** (**depletes, depleting, depleted**) **1** reduce the number or quantity of. **2** use up (supplies).
– DERIVATIVES **depletion** n.
– ORIGIN Latin *deplere* 'empty out'.

deplorable /di-plor-uh-b'l/ ● **adj.** shockingly bad.
– DERIVATIVES **deplorably** adv.

deplore ● **v.** (**deplores, deploring, deplored**) feel or express strong disapproval of.
– ORIGIN Latin *deplorare*.

deploy /di-ploy/ ● **v. 1** bring or move into position for military action. **2** use effectively.
– DERIVATIVES **deployment** n.
– ORIGIN French *déployer*.

depoliticize (also **depoliticise**) ● **v.** (**depoliticizes, depoliticizing, depoliticized**) remove from political influence.

depopulate ● **v.** (**depopulates, depopulating, depopulated**) greatly reduce the population of.
– DERIVATIVES **depopulation** n.

deport ● **v.** expel (a foreigner or immigrant) from a country.
– DERIVATIVES **deportation** n. **deportee** n.
– ORIGIN Latin *deportare*.

deportment ● **n. 1** Brit. the way a person stands and walks. **2** N. Amer. a person's behaviour or manners.

depose ● **v.** (**deposes, deposing, deposed**) remove from power suddenly and forcefully.
– ORIGIN Old French *deposer*.

deposit ● **n. 1** a sum of money placed in a bank or other account. **2** a payment made as a first instalment in buying something. **3** a returnable sum paid to cover possible loss or damage when renting something. **4** a layer of collected matter. ● **v.** (**deposits, depositing, deposited**) **1** put down in a specific place. **2** store with someone for safekeeping. **3** pay as a deposit. **4** lay down (matter) as a layer or covering.
– DERIVATIVES **depositor** n.
– ORIGIN Latin *depositum*.

deposit account ● **n.** Brit. a bank account that pays interest on money placed in it.

deposition /dep-uh-zi-shuhn/ ● **n. 1** the action of removing someone from power. **2** a sworn statement to be used as evidence in a court of law. **3** the action of depositing.

depository ● **n.** (pl. **depositories**) a place where things are stored.

depot /dep-oh/ ● **n. 1** a place for the storage of large quantities of goods. **2** a place where vehicles are housed and repaired.
– ORIGIN French.

deprave /di-prayv/ ● **v.** (**depraves, depraving, depraved**) lead away from what is natural or right; corrupt.
– DERIVATIVES **depravity** /di-prav-i-ti/ n.
– ORIGIN Latin *depravare*.

deprecate /dep-ri-kayt/ ● **v.** (**deprecates, deprecating, deprecated**) express disapproval of.
– DERIVATIVES **deprecation** n. **deprecatory** adj.
– ORIGIN Latin *deprecari* 'pray to ward off evil'.

depreciate /di-pree-shi-ayt/ ● **v.** (**depreciates, depreciating, depreciated**) **1** reduce in value over time. **2** dismiss as unimportant.
– DERIVATIVES **depreciation** n.
– ORIGIN Latin *depreciare*.

depredations /dep-ri-day-sh'nz/ ● **pl. n.** acts that cause harm or damage.
– ORIGIN Latin.

depress ● **v. 1** cause to feel very unhappy. **2** reduce the level of activity in: *alcohol depresses the nervous system.* **3** push or pull down.
– ORIGIN Latin *depressare*.

depressant ● **adj.** reducing activity in bodily processes.

depressed ● **adj. 1** very unhappy, and without hope. **2** suffering the effects of an economic slump: *depressed rural areas.*

depression ● **n. 1** a mental state in which a

person has feelings of great unhappiness and hopelessness. **2** a long and severe slump in an economy or market. **3** a sunken place or hollow. **4** Meteorol. an area of low pressure which may bring rain.

depressive ● **adj.** tending to causing depression. ● **n.** a person who tends to suffer from depression.

deprivation /dep-ri-vay-sh'n/ ● **n. 1** hardship resulting from the lack of basic necessities. **2** the action of depriving.

deprive ● **v.** (**deprives, depriving, deprived**) prevent from having, using, or enjoying something: *the city was deprived of its water supply.*
– ORIGIN Latin *deprivare.*

deprived ● **adj.** suffering a damaging lack of the basic necessities for life.

Dept ● **abbrev.** Department.

depth ● **n. 1** the distance from the top or surface down, or from front to back. **2** complex or meaningful thought: *the book has unexpected depth.* **3** extensive and detailed study. **4** strength of emotion. **5** (**the depths**) the deepest, lowest, or inmost part.
– PHRASES **out of one's depth 1** in water too deep to stand in. **2** in a situation beyond one's ability to cope.
– DERIVATIVES **depthless** adj.
– ORIGIN from **DEEP**.

depth charge ● **n.** a charge designed to explode under water, used for attacking submarines.

deputation ● **n.** a group of people who are appointed to act on behalf of a larger group.

depute /di-pyoot/ ● **v.** (**deputes, deputing, deputed**) **1** appoint (someone) to perform a task for which one is responsible. **2** delegate (authority or a task).
– ORIGIN Latin *deputare* 'assign'.

deputize /dep-yuu-tyz/ (also **deputise**) ● **v.** (**deputizes, deputizing, deputized**) temporarily act on behalf of someone else.

deputy ● **n.** (pl. **deputies**) a person appointed to perform the duties of a more senior person in that person's absence.

De Quincey E
/duh **kwin**-si/, Thomas (1785–1859), English essayist and critic, known for his *Confessions of an English Opium Eater*, a study of his addiction to opium.

derail ● **v. 1** cause (a train) to leave the tracks. **2** obstruct (a process) by diverting it from its intended course: *an attempt to derail the negotiations.*
– DERIVATIVES **derailment** n.

derange ● **v.** (**deranges, deranging, deranged**) **1** make insane. **2** throw into disorder.
– DERIVATIVES **derangement** n.
– ORIGIN French *déranger.*

Derby[1] E
Edward George Geoffrey Smith Stanley, 14th Earl of (1799–1869), British Conservative statesman, Prime Minister 1852, 1858–9, and 1866–8.

Derby[2] /dar-bi/ ● **n.** (pl. **Derbies**) **1** an annual flat race at Epsom in Surrey for three-year-old horses, founded by the 12th Earl of Derby. **2** (**derby**; also **local derby**) a sports match between two rival teams from the same area.

Derbyshire E
/dar-bi-sheer, dar-bi-sher/ a county of north central England; county town, Matlock.

deregulate ● **v.** (**deregulates, deregulating, deregulated**) remove regulations or restrictions from.
– DERIVATIVES **deregulation** n.

derelict /de-ri-likt/ ● **adj.** in a very poor condition as a result of disuse and neglect. ● **n.** a person without a home, job, or property.
– ORIGIN Latin *derelinquere* 'to abandon'.

dereliction ● **n. 1** the state of having been abandoned and become run down. **2** (**dereliction of duty**) shameful failure to fulfil one's duty.

deride /di-ryd/ ● **v.** (**derides, deriding, derided**) express contempt for; ridicule.
– ORIGIN Latin *deridere* 'scoff at'.

de rigueur /duh ri-ger/ ● **adj.** required by etiquette or current fashion: *large bathroom suites are de rigueur.*
– ORIGIN French, 'in strictness'.

derision /di-ri-*zh*'n/ ● **n.** scornful ridicule or mockery.
– ORIGIN Latin.

derisive /di-ry-siv/ ● **adj.** expressing contempt or ridicule.
– DERIVATIVES **derisively** adv.

derisory /di-ry-suh-ri/ ● **adj. 1** ridiculously small or inadequate. **2** = **DERISIVE**.

derivation ● **n. 1** the deriving of something from a source. **2** the formation of a word from another word or from a root in the same or another language.

derivative /di-riv-uh-tiv/ ● **adj.** esp. derog. copied from the work of another artist, writer, etc. ● **n. 1** something which is derived from another source. **2** Math. an expression representing the rate of change of one quantity in relation to another.

derive /di-ryv/ ● **v.** (**derives, deriving, derived**) (**derive from**) **1** obtain (something) from (a source). **2** arise or originate from.
– ORIGIN Latin *derivare* 'draw off water'.

dermatitis /der-muh-ty-tiss/ ● **n.** inflammation of the skin as a result of irritation or an allergic reaction.
– ORIGIN Greek *derma* 'skin'.

dermatology ● **n.** the branch of medicine concerned with skin disorders.
– DERIVATIVES **dermatological** adj. **dermatologist** n.

dermis /der-miss/ ● **n.** Anat. the thick layer of the skin below the epidermis.
– ORIGIN Latin.

derogate /der-uh-gayt/ ● **v.** (**derogates, derogating, derogated**) formal **1** (**derogate from**) deviate from (a set of rules). **2** speak critically of.
– DERIVATIVES **derogation** n.
– ORIGIN Latin *derogare* 'abrogate'.

derogatory /di-rog-uh-tri/ ● **adj.** critical or disrespectful.

derrick /derr-ik/ ● **n. 1** a kind of crane with a movable pivoted arm. **2** the framework over an oil well, holding the drilling machinery.
– ORIGIN from *Derrick*, the surname of a 17th-century hangman.

derring-do /derr-ing-doo/ ● **n.** dated or humorous action displaying heroic courage.
– ORIGIN from former *dorryng do* 'daring to do'.

Derry
see **LONDONDERRY**.

dervish /der-vish/ ● n. a member of a Muslim religious group vowed to poverty and known for their wild rituals.
– ORIGIN Persian, 'religious beggar'.

de Sade,
Marquis, see **SADE**.

desalinate /dee-sal-i-nayt/ ● v. (**desalinates**, **desalinating**, **desalinated**) remove salt from (seawater).
– DERIVATIVES **desalination** n.

descant /dess-kant/ ● n. an independent melody sung or played above a basic melody.
– ORIGIN Latin *discantus* 'part song'.

Descartes
/day-kart/, René (1596–1650), French philosopher, mathematician, and scientist. He believed that everything was open to doubt except his own conscious experience and his existence as a necessary condition of this: '*Cogito, ergo sum*' (I think, therefore I am).

descend ● v. **1** move down or downwards. **2** slope or lead downwards. **3** (**descend to**) lower oneself to commit (a shameful act). **4** (**descend on**) make a sudden attack on or unwelcome visit to. **5** (**be descended from**) be a blood relative of (an ancestor).
– ORIGIN Latin *descendere* 'climb down'.

descendant ● n. a person, animal, etc. that is descended from a particular ancestor.

descent ● n. **1** an act or the action of descending. **2** a downward slope. **3** a person's origin or nationality.

describe ● v. (**describes**, **describing**, **described**) **1** give a detailed account in words of. **2** mark out or draw (a shape).
– DERIVATIVES **describable** adj.
– ORIGIN Latin *describere* 'write down'.

description ● n. **1** a spoken or written account. **2** the action of describing. **3** a sort, kind, or class: *people of any description*.

descriptive ● adj. **1** giving a description. **2** describing without expressing judgement.
– DERIVATIVES **descriptively** adv.

descry /di-skry/ ● v. (**descries**, **descrying**, **descried**) literary catch sight of.
– ORIGIN perh. from **DESCRIBE**.

desecrate /dess-i-krayt/ ● v. (**desecrates**, **desecrating**, **desecrated**) treat (something sacred) with violent disrespect.
– DERIVATIVES **desecration** n.
– ORIGIN from **DE-** + **CONSECRATE**.

desegregate ● v. (**desegregates**, **desegregating**, **desegregated**) end racial segregation in.
– DERIVATIVES **desegregation** n.

deselect ● v. Brit. reject (an existing MP) as a candidate in a forthcoming election.
– DERIVATIVES **deselection** n.

desensitize (also **desensitise**) ● v. (**desensitizes**, **desensitizing**, **desensitized**) **1** make less sensitive. **2** make (someone) less likely to be distressed by cruelty or suffering.
– DERIVATIVES **desensitization** (also **desensitisation**) n.

desert[1] /di-zert/ ● v. **1** leave (someone) without help or support. **2** leave (a place), causing it to appear empty. **3** illegally run away from military service.
– DERIVATIVES **desertion** n.
– ORIGIN Latin *desertare*.

desert[2] /dez-ert/ ● n. a waterless, empty area of land with little or no vegetation.
– ORIGIN Latin *desertum* 'something left waste'.

deserter ● n. a member of the armed forces who deserts.

deserts /di-zerts/ ● pl. n. (usu. in phr. **get** or **receive one's just deserts**) the reward or punishment that a person deserves.
– ORIGIN Old French *desert*.

deserve ● v. (**deserves**, **deserving**, **deserved**) do something or show qualities worthy of (a reward or punishment).
– DERIVATIVES **deservedly** adv.
– ORIGIN Latin *deservire* 'serve well'.

deserving ● adj. worthy of favourable treatment or help.

déshabillé /day-za-bee-yay/ (also **dishabille** /diss-uh-beel/) ● n. the state of being only partly or scantily clothed.
– ORIGIN French, 'undressed'.

desiccate /dess-i-kayt/ ● v. (**desiccates**, **desiccating**, **desiccated**) remove the moisture from.
– ORIGIN Latin *desiccare*.

desideratum /di-zi-duh-rah-tuhm/ ● n. (pl. **desiderata** /di-zi-duh-rah-tuh/) something that is needed or wanted.
– ORIGIN Latin.

design ● n. **1** a plan or drawing produced to show the appearance and workings of something before it is made. **2** the action of producing such a plan or drawing. **3** a decorative pattern. **4** underlying purpose or planning: *the appearance of design in the universe*. ● v. **1** produce a design for. **2** intend for a purpose.
– PHRASES **by design** on purpose. **have designs on** aim to obtain.
– ORIGIN Latin *designare* 'mark out'.

designate ● v. /dez-ig-nayt/ (**designates**, **designating**, **designated**) **1** officially give a particular status or name to: *certain schools are designated 'science schools'*. **2** appoint to a particular job. ● adj. /dez-ig-nuht/ (after a noun) appointed to a position but not yet having taken it up: *the Director designate*.
– ORIGIN Latin *designare*.

designation ● n. **1** the action of designating. **2** an official title or description.

designer ● n. a person who designs things. ● adj. made by a famous fashion designer.

designing ● adj. cunning and deceitful.

desirable ● adj. **1** wished for as being attractive, useful, or necessary. **2** (of a person) arousing sexual desire.
– DERIVATIVES **desirability** n.

desire ● n. **1** a strong feeling of wanting to have something or wishing for something to happen. **2** strong sexual appetite. ● v. (**desires**, **desiring**, **desired**) **1** strongly wish for or want. **2** want sexually.
– ORIGIN Latin *desiderare*.

desirous /di-zy-ruhss/ ● adj. strongly wishing to have: *the pope was desirous of peace*.

desist /di-sisst/ ● v. stop doing (something).
– ORIGIN Latin *desistere*.

desk ● n. **1** a piece of furniture with a flat or

sloping surface on which one can work. **2** a counter in a hotel, bank, airport, etc. **3** a particular section of a news organization: *the sports desk.*
– ORIGIN Latin *discus* 'plate'.

desktop ● **n. 1** the working surface of a desk. **2** a microcomputer suitable for use at an ordinary desk. **3** the working area of a computer screen seen as representing a desktop.

d

desolate ● **adj.** /dess-uh-luht/ **1** bleak and empty. **2** very unhappy. ● **v.** /dess-uh-layt/ (**desolates**, **desolating**, **desolated**) make very unhappy.
– DERIVATIVES **desolation** n.
– ORIGIN Latin *desolare* 'abandon'.

despair ● **n.** the complete loss or absence of hope. ● **v.** lose or be without hope.
– ORIGIN Latin *desperare.*

despatch ● **v. & n.** var. of **DISPATCH**.

desperado /dess-puh-**rah**-doh/ ● **n.** (pl. **desperadoes** or **desperados**) dated a desperate or reckless criminal.
– ORIGIN pseudo-Spanish.

desperate ● **adj. 1** completely without hope. **2** done when all else has failed: *fare cutting is a desperate attempt to increase business.* **3** extremely serious. **4** having a great need for something.
– DERIVATIVES **desperately** adv. **desperation** n.
– ORIGIN Latin *desperatus.*

despicable /di-**spik**-uh-b'l/ ● **adj.** deserving hatred and contempt.
– DERIVATIVES **despicably** adv.
– ORIGIN Latin *despicabilis.*

despise /di-**spyz**/ ● **v.** (**despise**, **despising**, **despised**) hate or feel disgusted by.
– ORIGIN Latin *despicere* 'look down'.

despite /di-**spyt**/ ● **prep.** in spite of.
– ORIGIN Latin *despectus* 'looking down on'.

despoil /di-**spoyl**/ ● **v.** literary steal valuable possessions from.
– ORIGIN Latin *despoliare* 'rob, plunder'.

despondent ● **adj.** in low spirits from loss of hope or courage.
– DERIVATIVES **despondency** n. **despondently** adv.
– ORIGIN Latin *despondere* 'give up'.

despot /dess-pot/ ● **n.** a ruler with total power, especially one who uses it in a cruel way.
– DERIVATIVES **despotic** adj. **despotism** n.
– ORIGIN Greek *despotēs.*

dessert /di-**zert**/ ● **n.** the sweet course eaten at the end of a meal.
– ORIGIN French.

dessertspoon ● **n.** a spoon used for dessert, smaller than a tablespoon and larger than a teaspoon.

destabilize (also **destabilise**) ● **v.** (**destabilizes**, **destabilizing**, **destabilized**) make unstable.
– DERIVATIVES **destabilization** (also **destabilisation**) n.

destination ● **n.** the place to which someone or something is going or being sent.

destine ● **v.** (**destines**, **destining**, **destined**) (**be destined**) **1** be intended for a particular purpose: *he was destined to be an engineer.* **2** bound for a particular destination.
– ORIGIN Latin *destinare* 'make firm'.

destiny ● **n.** (pl. **destinies**) **1** the events that will happen to a person, seen as unable to be changed. **2** the hidden power believed to control what will happen in the future.
– ORIGIN Latin *destinata.*

destitute /dess-ti-tyoot/ ● **adj.** extremely poor and lacking the means to provide for oneself.
– DERIVATIVES **destitution** n.
– ORIGIN Latin *destituere* 'forsake'.

destroy ● **v. 1** cause (something) to cease to exist by badly damaging it. **2** kill (an animal) by humane means.
– ORIGIN Latin *destruere.*

destroyer ● **n. 1** a person or thing that destroys. **2** a small fast warship.

destructible ● **adj.** able to be destroyed.

destruction ● **n. 1** the action of destroying or the state of being destroyed. **2** a cause of someone's ruin: *gambling was his destruction.*
– ORIGIN Latin.

destructive ● **adj.** causing destruction.
– DERIVATIVES **destructively** adv. **destructiveness** n.

desuetude /dess-wi-tyood/ ● **n.** formal a state of disuse.
– ORIGIN Latin *desuetudo.*

desultory /dess-uhl-tuh-ri/ ● **adj. 1** lacking purpose or enthusiasm. **2** going from one subject to another in a half-hearted way: *they had a desultory conversation.*
– DERIVATIVES **desultorily** adv.
– ORIGIN Latin *desultorius* 'superficial'.

detach ● **v. 1** disconnect (something) and remove it. **2** (**detach oneself from**) distance oneself from (a group or situation). **3** (**be detached**) (of a group of soldiers) be sent on a separate mission.
– DERIVATIVES **detachable** adj.
– ORIGIN French *détacher.*

detached ● **adj. 1** separate or disconnected. **2** not interested or involved.

detachment ● **n. 1** the state of being uninvolved: *he felt a sense of detachment from what was going on.* **2** a group of troops, ships, etc. sent on a separate mission. **3** the action of detaching.

detail ● **n. 1** a small individual item or fact. **2** small items or facts as a group: *attention to detail.* **3** a small detachment of troops or police officers given a special duty. ● **v. 1** describe item by item. **2** order to undertake a task.
– ORIGIN French *détail.*

detailed ● **adj.** having many details.

detailing ● **n.** small decorative features on a building, garment, or work of art.

detain ● **v. 1** keep from going somewhere. **2** keep in official custody.
– DERIVATIVES **detainment** n.
– ORIGIN Latin *detinere.*

detainee /dee-tay-**nee**/ ● **n.** a person kept in custody, especially for political reasons.

detect ● **v. 1** discover the presence of: *cancer may soon be detected in its earliest stages.* **2** discover or investigate (a crime or criminal). **3** notice.
– DERIVATIVES **detectable** adj. **detection** n.
– ORIGIN Latin *detegere* 'uncover'.

detective ● **n.** a person whose occupation is to investigate crimes.

detector ● **n.** a device designed to discover the presence of something and to send out a signal.

détente /day-**tahnt**/ • **n.** the easing of hostility or unfriendly relations between countries.
– ORIGIN French, 'loosening, relaxation'.

detention • **n.** **1** the action of detaining or the state of being detained. **2** the punishment of being kept in school after hours.

detention centre • **n.** an institution where people are detained for short periods.

deter /di-**ter**/ • **v.** (**deters, deterring, deterred**) **1** discourage from doing something through fear of the consequences. **2** prevent the occurrence of.
– ORIGIN Latin *deterrere*.

detergent • **n.** a chemical substance used for removing dirt, grease, etc.
– ORIGIN Latin *detergere* 'wipe away'.

deteriorate /di-**teer**-i-uh-rayt/ • **v.** (**deteriorates, deteriorating, deteriorated**) become gradually worse.
– DERIVATIVES **deterioration** n.
– ORIGIN Latin *deteriorare*.

determinant /di-**ter**-mi-nuhnt/ • **n.** **1** a factor which determines the nature or outcome of something. *force of will was the main determinant of his success.* **2** Math. a quantity obtained by adding products of the elements of a square matrix according to a given rule.

determinate /di-**ter**-mi-nuht/ • **adj.** having fixed and definite limits.

determination • **n.** **1** firmness of purpose. **2** the action of establishing something exactly.

determine • **v.** (**determines, determining, determined**) **1** be the main factor in: *it is biological age that determines our looks.* **2** firmly decide. **3** establish by research or calculation.
– DERIVATIVES **determinable** adj.
– ORIGIN Latin *determinare* 'limit, fix'.

determined • **adj.** having firmness of purpose; resolute.
– DERIVATIVES **determinedly** adv.

determiner • **n.** **1** a person or thing that determines. **2** Grammar a word that comes before a noun to determine its meaning, such as *a*, *the*, *every*.

determinism • **n.** the belief that people are not free to do as they wish because their lives are determined by factors outside their control.
– DERIVATIVES **determinist** n. & adj.

deterrent /di-**terr**-uhnt/ • **n.** a thing that deters or is intended to deter.
– DERIVATIVES **deterrence** n.

detest • **v.** dislike intensely.
– ORIGIN Latin *detestari* 'denounce, hate'.

detestable • **adj.** deserving intense dislike.

detestation /dee-tess-**tay**-sh'n/ • **n.** intense dislike.

dethrone • **v.** (**dethrones, dethroning, dethroned**) remove (a monarch) from power.

detonate /**det**-uh-nayt/ • **v.** (**detonates, detonating, detonated**) explode.
– DERIVATIVES **detonation** n.
– ORIGIN Latin *detonare*.

detonator • **n.** a device used to detonate an explosive.

detour /**dee**-toor/ • **n.** a long or roundabout route taken to avoid something or to visit something along the way. • **v.** take a detour.
– ORIGIN French, 'change of direction'.

detox informal • **n.** /**dee**-toks/ detoxification. • **v.** /dee-**toks**/ detoxify.

detoxify • **v.** (**detoxifies, detoxifying, detoxified**) **1** remove harmful or poisonous substances from. **2** stop taking or help to stop taking drink or drugs.
– DERIVATIVES **detoxification** n.

DETR • **abbrev.** (in the UK) Department of the Environment, Transport, and the Regions.

detract • **v.** (**detract from**) cause (something) to seem less valuable or impressive.
– ORIGIN Latin *detrahere* 'draw away'.

detractor • **n.** a person who criticizes someone or something.

detriment /**det**-ri-muhnt/ • **n.** harm or damage: *she fasted to the detriment of her health.*
– DERIVATIVES **detrimental** adj.
– ORIGIN Latin *detrimentum*.

detritus /di-**try**-tuhss/ • **n.** debris or waste material.
– ORIGIN Latin.

Detroit E
/di-**troyt**/ a major industrial city and Great Lakes port in SE Michigan.

de trop /duh **troh**/ • **adj.** unwelcome.
– ORIGIN French, 'excessive'.

deuce[1] /dyooss/ • **n.** Tennis the score of 40 all in a game, at which two consecutive points are needed to win the game.
– ORIGIN Old French *deus*.

deuce[2] /dyooss/ • **exclam.** (**the deuce**) informal used as a euphemism for 'devil'.
– ORIGIN German *duus*.

deus ex machina /day-uuss eks **mak**-i-nuh/ • **n.** an unexpected event saving a seemingly hopeless situation.
– ORIGIN Latin, 'god from the machinery'.

deuterium /dyoo-**teer**-i-uhm/ • **n.** Chem. a stable isotope of hydrogen with a mass approximately twice that of the usual isotope.
– ORIGIN Latin.

Deutschmark /**doych**-mark/ • **n.** the former basic unit of money of Germany.
– ORIGIN from German *deutsche Mark* 'German mark'.

de Valera E
/duh vuh-**lair**-uh/, Eamon (1882–1975), American-born Irish statesman, Taoiseach (Prime Minister) 1937–48, 1951–4, and 1957–9 and President of the Republic of Ireland 1959–73. He was the founder of the Fianna Fáil Party (1926), and as President of the Irish Free State (1932–7) devised the new constitution of 1937 which created the state of Eire.

de Valois E
/duh **val**-wah/, Dame Ninette (1898–2001; *born Edris Stannus*), Irish choreographer, ballet dancer, and teacher. She founded the Vic-Wells Ballet (which became the Royal Ballet).

devalue • **v.** (**devalues, devaluing, devalued**) **1** reduce the worth of: *people seem to devalue my achievement.* **2** reduce the official value of (a currency) in relation to other currencies.
– DERIVATIVES **devaluation** n.

devastate /**dev**-uh-stayt/ • **v.** (**devastates, devastating, devastated**) **1** destroy or ruin. **2** overwhelm with shock or grief.
– DERIVATIVES **devastation** n.

– ORIGIN Latin *devastare*.

devastating ● adj. **1** highly destructive. **2** extremely distressing. **3** informal very impressive or attractive.

– DERIVATIVES **devastatingly** adv.

develop ● v. (**develops**, **developing**, **developed**) **1** become or make larger or more advanced. **2** start to exist, experience, or possess. **3** convert (land) to a new purpose. **4** treat (a photographic film) with chemicals to make a visible image.

– DERIVATIVES **developer** n.

– ORIGIN French *développer*.

developing country ● n. a poor agricultural country that is seeking to become more advanced.

development ● n. **1** the action of developing or the state of being developed. **2** a new product or idea. **3** a new stage in a changing situation. **4** an area of land with new buildings on it.

– DERIVATIVES **developmental** adj.

Devi E
/day-vi/ the supreme Hindu goddess.

deviant ● adj. departing from normal standards. ● n. a deviant person.

– DERIVATIVES **deviance** n.

deviate /dee-vi-ayt/ ● v. (**deviates**, **deviating**, **deviated**) depart from an established course or from normal standards.

– DERIVATIVES **deviation** n.

– ORIGIN Latin *deviare* 'turn out of the way'.

device ● n. **1** a thing made for a particular purpose. **2** a plan, scheme, or trick: *a clever marketing device.* **3** a drawing or design.

– PHRASES **leave someone to their own devices** leave someone to do as they wish.

– ORIGIN Old French *devis*.

devil ● n. **1** (**the Devil**) (in Christian and Jewish belief) the most powerful spirit of evil. **2** an evil spirit. **3** a very wicked or cruel person. **4** a mischievously clever person: *the old devil is up to something.* **5** informal a person with specified characteristics: *the poor devil.* **6** (**the devil**) expressing surprise or annoyance.

– PHRASES **between the devil and the deep blue sea** caught in a dilemma. **devil-may-care** cheerful and reckless. **the devil to pay** serious trouble to be dealt with. **speak** (or **talk**) **of the devil** said when a person appears just after being mentioned.

– ORIGIN Greek *diabolos* 'accuser'.

devilish ● adj. **1** evil and cruel. **2** mischievous: *a devilish grin.*

– DERIVATIVES **devilishly** adv.

devilment ● n. reckless mischief.

devilry ● n. **1** wicked activity. **2** reckless mischief.

devil's advocate ● n. a person who expresses an unpopular opinion in order to provoke debate.

Devil's Island E
a rocky island off the coast of French Guiana, used as a French prison colony (1852–1953).

devious /dee-vi-uhss/ ● adj. **1** skilful in using underhand tactics. **2** (of a route or journey) indirect.

– DERIVATIVES **deviously** adv. **deviousness** n.

– ORIGIN Latin *devius* 'out of the way'.

devise /di-vyz/ ● v. (**devises**, **devising**, **devised**) plan or invent (a complex procedure or device).

– ORIGIN Old French *deviser*.

devoid /di-voyd/ ● adj. (**devoid of**) completely lacking in: *her voice was devoid of emotion.*

– ORIGIN Old French *devoidier* 'cast out'.

devolution /dee-vuh-loo-sh'n/ ● n. the transferring of power by central government to local or regional governments.

devolve /di-volv/ ● v. (**devolves**, **devolving**, **devolved**) **1** transfer (power) to a lower level. **2** (**devolve on/to**) (of responsibility) pass to (a deputy or successor).

– ORIGIN Latin *devolvere* 'roll down'.

Devon E
(also **Devonshire**) a county of SW England; county town, Exeter.

Devonian /di-voh-ni-uhn/ ● adj. Geol. relating to the fourth period of the Palaeozoic era (about 409 to 363 million years ago), when the first amphibians appeared.

devote ● v. (**devotes**, **devoting**, **devoted**) (**devote to**) give (time or resources) to.

– ORIGIN Latin *devovere* 'consecrate'.

devoted ● adj. very loving or loyal.

– DERIVATIVES **devotedly** adv.

devotee /dev-uh-tee/ ● n. **1** a person who is very enthusiastic about someone or something. **2** a follower of a particular religion or god.

devotion ● n. **1** great love or loyalty. **2** religious worship. **3** (**devotions**) prayers or religious observances.

– DERIVATIVES **devotional** adj.

devour /di-vow-er/ ● v. **1** eat greedily. **2** (of a force) consume destructively: *fire devoured the old house.* **3** read quickly and eagerly. **4** (**be devoured**) be totally absorbed by an emotion.

– ORIGIN Latin *devorare*.

devout /di-vowt/ ● adj. **1** deeply religious. **2** earnestly sincere: *my devout hope.*

– DERIVATIVES **devoutly** adv.

– ORIGIN Latin *devotus* 'devoted'.

dew ● n. tiny drops of moisture that form on cool surfaces at night, when water vapour in the air condenses.

– ORIGIN Old English.

Dewar[1] E
/dyoo-er/, Donald (1937–2000), Scottish Labour statesman, first First Minister of the Scottish Parliament 1999–2000.

Dewar[2] E
/dyoo-er/, Sir James (1842–1923), Scottish chemist and physicist, who achieved temperatures close to absolute zero and made other advances in cryogenics. He also invented the vacuum flask.

Dewi E
/de-wi/ Welsh name for St David (see **David, St**).

dewlap ● n. a fold of loose skin hanging from the neck or throat of an animal or bird.

dewy ● adj. wet with dew.

dewy-eyed ● adj. having eyes moist with tears because one is feeling emotional.

dexterity /dek-ste-ri-ti/ ● n. skill in performing tasks.

– ORIGIN Latin *dexteritas*.

dexterous /dek-stuh-ruhss/ (also **dextrous** /dek-struhss/) • **adj.** showing neat skill.
– DERIVATIVES **dexterously** (also **dextrously**) adv.

DFC • **abbrev.** (in the UK) Distinguished Flying Cross.

DFE • **abbrev.** Department for Education.

DFM • **abbrev.** (in the UK) Distinguished Flying Medal.

DG • **abbrev.** director general.

Dhaka E
/da-kuh/ (also **Dacca**) the capital of Bangladesh.

dhal /dahl/ (also **dal**) • **n.** (in Indian cookery) split pulses.
– ORIGIN Hindi.

dharma /dar-muh/ • **n.** (in Indian religion) the eternal law of the universe.
– ORIGIN Sanskrit, 'decree or custom'.

dhow /dow/ • **n.** a sailing ship with one or two masts, used in the Arabian region.
– ORIGIN Arabic.

di- • **comb. form** two-; double: *dioxide*.
– ORIGIN Greek *dis* 'twice'.

dia- (also **di-** before a vowel) • **prefix** **1** through; across: *diameter*. **2** apart: *diaeresis*.
– ORIGIN Greek *dia* 'through'.

diabetes /dy-uh-bee-teez/ • **n.** a disorder of the metabolism in which a lack of the hormone insulin results in a failure to absorb sugar and starch properly.
– ORIGIN Greek, 'siphon'.

diabetic • **adj.** having to do with diabetes. • **n.** a person with diabetes.

diabolical • **adj.** **1** (also **diabolic**) of or like the Devil. **2** informal very bad: *an absolutely diabolical voice*.
– DERIVATIVES **diabolically** adv.
– ORIGIN Greek *diabolos* 'accuser'.

diaconal /dy-ak-uh-nuhl/ • **adj.** relating to a deacon or deacons.
– ORIGIN Latin *diaconus* 'deacon'.

diacritic /dy-uh-krit-ik/ • **n.** a sign written above or below a letter to indicate a difference in pronunciation from the same letter when unmarked.
– ORIGIN Greek *diakritikos*.

diadem /dy-uh-dem/ • **n.** a jewelled crown or headband worn as a symbol of royalty.
– ORIGIN Greek *diadēma*.

diaeresis /dy-eer-i-siss/ (US **dieresis**) • **n.** (pl. **diaereses** /dy-eer-i-seez/) a mark (¨) placed over a vowel to indicate that it is sounded separately, as in *naïve*.
– ORIGIN Greek *diairesis* 'separation'.

Diaghilev E
/di-ag-i-leff/, Sergei (Pavlovich) (1872–1929), Russian ballet impresario. He founded the Ballets Russes, a ballet company which transformed the European ballet scene.

diagnose /dy-uhg-nohz/ • **v.** (**diagnoses**, **diagnosing**, **diagnosed**) identify the nature of (an illness or problem) by examining the symptoms.

diagnosis • **n.** (pl. **diagnoses**) the identification of the nature of an illness or problem by examination of the symptoms.
– ORIGIN Greek.

diagnostic /dy-uhg-noss-tik/ • **adj.** having to do with diagnosis.
– DERIVATIVES **diagnostically** adv.

diagonal /dy-ag-uh-n'l/ • **adj.** **1** (of a straight line) joining opposite corners of a rectangle, square, or other figure. **2** (of a line) straight and at an angle; slanting. • **n.** a diagonal line.
– DERIVATIVES **diagonally** adv.
– ORIGIN Greek *diagōnios* 'from angle to angle'.

diagram • **n.** a simplified drawing showing the appearance or structure of something.
– DERIVATIVES **diagrammatic** adj.
– ORIGIN Greek *diagramma*.

dial • **n.** **1** a disc marked to show the time on a clock or to indicate a measurement by means of a pointer. **2** a disc with numbered holes on a telephone, turned to make a call. **3** a disc turned to select a setting on a radio, cooker, etc. • **v.** (**dials**, **dialling**, **dialled**; US **dials**, **dialing**, **dialed**) call (a telephone number) by turning a dial or using a keypad.
– ORIGIN Latin *diale*.

dialect /dy-uh-lekt/ • **n.** a form of a language used in a particular region or by a particular social group.
– DERIVATIVES **dialectal** adj.
– ORIGIN Greek *dialektos* 'discourse'.

dialectic /dy-uh-lek-tik/ (also **dialectics**) • **n.** Philos. the art of investigating or debating the truth of opinions.
– DERIVATIVES **dialectical** adj.
– ORIGIN from Greek *dialektikē tekhnē* 'art of debate'.

dialling code • **n.** Brit. a sequence of numbers dialled to connect a telephone to an exchange in another area or country.

dialling tone • **n.** a sound produced by a telephone that indicates that a caller may start to dial.

dialog box (Brit. also **dialogue box**) • **n.** a small area on a computer screen in which the user is prompted to provide information or select commands.

dialogue (US also **dialog**) • **n.** **1** conversation between two or more people as a feature of a book, play, or film. **2** a discussion intended to explore a subject or to resolve a problem.
– ORIGIN Greek *dialogos*.

dialysis /dy-al-i-siss/ • **n.** (pl. **dialyses** /dy-al-i-seez/) **1** Chem. the separation of particles in a liquid on the basis of differences in their ability to pass through a membrane. **2** the purifying of blood by this technique, as a substitute for the normal function of the kidney.
– ORIGIN Greek *dialusis*.

diamanté /dy-uh-mon-tay/ • **adj.** decorated with artificial jewels.
– ORIGIN French, 'set with diamonds'.

diameter /dy-am-i-ter/ • **n.** a straight line passing from side to side through the centre of a circle or sphere.
– ORIGIN from Greek *diametros grammē* 'line measuring across'.

diametrical /dy-uh-met-ri-k'l/ • **adj.** **1** (of opposites) complete. **2** having to do with a diameter.
– DERIVATIVES **diametric** adj. **diametrically** adv.

diamond • **n.** **1** a precious stone consisting of a clear, colourless form of pure carbon, the hardest naturally occurring substance. **2** a

figure with four straight sides of equal length forming two opposite acute angles and two opposite obtuse angles. **3** (**diamonds**) one of the four suits in a pack of playing cards.
– ORIGIN Old French *diamant*.

diamond jubilee • **n.** the sixtieth anniversary of a notable event.

diamond wedding • **n.** the sixtieth anniversary of a wedding.

d

diamorphine /dy-mor-feen/ • **n.** tech. heroin.
– ORIGIN short for *diacetylmorphine*.

Diana E
a Roman goddess associated with hunting, virginity, and the moon. Greek equivalent **ARTEMIS**.

Diana, Princess of Wales E
(1961–97; title before marriage *Lady Diana Frances Spencer*), daughter of the 8th Earl Spencer and wife of Prince Charles (1981–1996). Her death in a car crash in Paris gave rise to intense national mourning.

diaper /dy-uh-per/ • **n.** N. Amer. a baby's nappy.
– ORIGIN Greek *diaspros*.

diaphanous /dy-af-fuh-nuhss/ • **adj.** light, delicate, and semi-transparent.
– ORIGIN Greek *diaphanēs*.

diaphragm /dy-uh-fram/ • **n.** **1** a muscular partition separating the thorax from the abdomen in mammals. **2** a taut flexible membrane in mechanical or sound systems. **3** a thin contraceptive cap fitting over the cervix.
– ORIGIN Latin *diaphragma*.

diarist • **n.** a person who writes a diary.

diarrhoea /dy-uh-ree-uh/ (US **diarrhea**) • **n.** a condition in which there are frequent discharges of liquid faeces from the bowels.
– ORIGIN Greek *diarrhoia*.

diary • **n.** (pl. **diaries**) **1** a book in which one keeps a daily record of one's experiences. **2** a book marked with each day's date, in which to note appointments.
– ORIGIN Latin *diarium*.

Dias E
/dee-ass/ (also **Diaz**), Bartolomeu (*c.*1450–1500), Portuguese navigator and explorer, the first European to round the Cape of Good Hope (1488).

diaspora /dy-ass-puh-ruh/ • **n.** **1** (**the diaspora**) the dispersion of the Jews beyond Israel. **2** the dispersion of any people from their traditional homeland.
– ORIGIN Greek.

diastole /dy-ass-tuh-li/ • **n.** the phase of the heartbeat when the heart muscle relaxes and the chambers fill with blood. Often contrasted with **SYSTOLE**.
– DERIVATIVES **diastolic** adj.
– ORIGIN Greek, 'separation, expansion'.

diatom /dy-uh-tuhm/ • **n.** a single-celled alga which has a cell wall of silica.
– ORIGIN Greek *diatomos* 'cut in two'.

diatomic /dy-uh-tom-ik/ • **adj.** Chem. consisting of two atoms.

diatonic /dy-uh-ton-ik/ • **adj.** Music involving only the notes of the major or minor scale, without additional sharps, flats, etc.
– ORIGIN Greek *diatonikos* 'at intervals of a tone'.

diatribe /dy-uh-tryb/ • **n.** a harsh and forceful verbal attack.
– ORIGIN Greek, 'discourse'.

Diaz E
var. of **DIAS**.

dice • **n.** (pl. **dice**; sing. also **die**) a small cube with faces bearing from one to six spots, used in games of chance. • **v.** (**dices**, **dicing**, **diced**) **1** cut (food) into small cubes. **2** (**dice with**) take great risks with: *he enjoyed dicing with death.*
– ORIGIN Old French *des*.

dicey • **adj.** (**dicier**, **diciest**) informal difficult or risky.

dichotomy /dy-kot-uh-mi/ • **n.** (pl. **dichotomies**) a separation or contrast between two things: *the false dichotomy between education and entertainment.*
– DERIVATIVES **dichotomous** adj.
– ORIGIN Greek *dikhotomia* 'a cutting in two'.

dick • **n.** vulgar **1** a penis. **2** Brit. a stupid person.
– ORIGIN familiar form of the man's name *Richard*.

Dickens, E
Charles (John Huffam) (1812–70), English novelist. His novels, such as *Oliver Twist*, *Nicholas Nickleby*, *A Christmas Carol*, *David Copperfield*, and *Great Expectations*, are notable for their satirical humour and treatment of social problems.

dickens • **n.** informal used to express annoyance or surprise.
– ORIGIN a euphemism for 'devil'.

Dickensian /di-ken-zi-uhn/ • **adj.** like the novels of Dickens, especially in terms of the urban poverty that they portray.

dicker • **v.** (**dickers**, **dickering**, **dickered**) **1** argue or bargain in a petty way. **2** toy or fiddle with something.
– ORIGIN perh. from former *dicker* 'set of ten hides'.

dickhead • **n.** vulgar a stupid man.

Dickinson, E
Emily (Elizabeth) (1830–86), American poet, who lived as a recluse. Her poems are characterized by their striking imagery and the use of assonance and alliteration rather than rhyme.

dicky • **adj.** Brit. informal not strong, healthy, or functioning reliably.
– ORIGIN perh. from the man's name *Dick*, in the old saying *as queer as Dick's hatband*.

dicotyledon /dy-kot-i-lee-duhn/ • **n.** a plant with an embryo bearing two cotyledons (seed leaves).

dicta pl. of **DICTUM**.

dictate • **v.** /dik-tayt/ (**dictates**, **dictating**, **dictated**) **1** state or order with the force of authority. **2** say or read aloud (words to be typed or written down). **3** control or determine: *choice is often dictated by availability.* • **n.** /**dik**-tayt/ an order or principle that must be obeyed: *the dictates of fashion.*
– DERIVATIVES **dictation** n.
– ORIGIN Latin *dictare*.

dictator /dik-tay-ter/ • **n.** a ruler with total power over a country.
– DERIVATIVES **dictatorial** adj.

dictatorship • **n.** **1** government by a dictator. **2** a country governed by a dictator.

diction ● n. **1** the choice and use of words in speech or writing: *poetic diction*. **2** a person's way of pronouncing words.
– ORIGIN Latin.

dictionary ● n. (pl. **dictionaries**) a book that lists the words of a language and gives their meaning, or their equivalent in a different language.
– ORIGIN from Latin *dictionarium manuale* or *dictionarius liber* 'manual or book of words'.

dictum /dik-tuhm/ ● n. (pl. **dicta** /dik-tuh/ or **dictums**) **1** a formal statement from an authoritative source. **2** a short statement that expresses a general principle.
– ORIGIN Latin, 'something said'.

did past of DO[1].

didactic /dy-**dak**-tik/ ● adj. intended to teach or give moral instruction.
– DERIVATIVES **didacticism** n.
– ORIGIN Greek *didaskein* 'teach'.

diddle ● v. (**diddles, diddling, diddled**) informal cheat or swindle.
– ORIGIN prob. from Jeremy *Diddler*, a character in a farce.

Diderot E
/dee-duh-roh/, Denis (1713–84), French philosopher, writer, and critic. A leading figure of the Enlightenment, he was chief editor of the *Encyclopédie*, through which he spread and popularized philosophy and scientific knowledge.

didgeridoo /di-juh-ri-**doo**/ ● n. an Australian Aboriginal wind instrument in the form of a long wooden tube, blown to produce a deep resonant sound.
– ORIGIN from an Aboriginal language.

didn't ● contr. did not.

Dido E
/dy-doh/ the legendary queen and founder of Carthage, who fell in love with the shipwrecked Aeneas and killed herself when he deserted her.

die[1] ● v. (**dies, dying, died**) **1** stop living. **2** (**die out**) become extinct. **3** become less loud or strong: *the noise died down*. **4** (**be dying for/to do**) informal be very eager for.
– PHRASES **die hard** disappear or change very slowly. **never say die** do not give up hope. **to die for** informal extremely good or desirable.
– ORIGIN Old Norse.

die[2] ● n. **1** sing. of DICE. **2** (pl. **dies**) a device for cutting or moulding metal or for stamping a design onto coins or medals.
– PHRASES **the die is cast** an event has happened that cannot be changed.
– ORIGIN Old French *de*.

die-cast ● adj. formed by pouring molten metal into a mould.

diehard ● n. a person who obstinately supports something in spite of opposition or changing circumstances: *diehard Marxists*.

dielectric /dy-i-**lek**-trik/ Physics ● adj. that does not conduct electricity; insulating. ● n. an insulator.

Dieppe E
/di-**ep**/ a channel port in northern France.

dieresis ● n. US = DIAERESIS.

diesel /dee-z'l/ ● n. **1** an internal-combustion engine in which the heat of compressed air is used to ignite the fuel. **2** a form of petroleum used to fuel diesel engines.
– ORIGIN named after the German engineer Rudolf *Diesel* (1858–1913).

diet[1] ● n. **1** the kinds of food that a person, animal, or community usually eats. **2** a restricted range of food, followed in order to lose weight or for medical reasons. ● adj. with reduced fat or sugar content: *diet drinks*. ● v. (**diets, dieting, dieted**) restrict oneself to a diet to lose weight.
– DERIVATIVES **dieter** n.
– ORIGIN Greek *diaita* 'a way of life'.

diet[2] ● n. **1** a law-making assembly in certain countries. **2** hist. a regular meeting of the states of a confederation.
– ORIGIN Latin *dieta* 'day's work'.

dietary /dy-uh-tri/ ● adj. **1** having to do with diets or dieting. **2** provided by one's diet: *dietary fibre*.

dietetics /dy-uh-**tet**-iks/ ● n. the branch of knowledge concerned with the diet and its effects on health.
– DERIVATIVES **dietetic** adj.

dietitian /dy-uh-**ti**-sh'n/ (also **dietician**) ● n. an expert on diet and nutrition.

Dietrich E
/**dee**-trikh/, Marlene (1901–92; born *Maria Magdelene von Losch*), German-born American actress and singer. She was famous for her part in the film *The Blue Angel*, and later as an international cabaret star.

differ ● v. (**differs, differing, differed**) **1** be unlike: *the second set of data differed from the first*. **2** disagree.
– ORIGIN Latin *differre* 'differ, defer'.

difference ● n. **1** a way in which people or things are unlike. **2** the state of being unlike: *there is little difference between his public and private self*. **3** a disagreement or dispute. **4** the remainder left after one value is subtracted from another.
– PHRASES **make a** (or **no**) **difference** have an effect (or no effect).

different ● adj. **1** not the same as another or each other. **2** separate. **3** informal new and unusual.
– DERIVATIVES **differently** adv.

USAGE different
Different can be followed by **from, to,** or **than.** In British English **different from** is generally thought of as the correct use, while **different than** is largely found in North America.

differential /dif-fuh-**ren**-sh'l/ ● adj. tech. having to do with or depending on a difference: *the differential achievements of boys and girls*. ● n. **1** Brit. a difference in wages between industries or between categories of employees in the same industry. **2** Math. a minute difference between successive values of a variable. **3** a gear allowing a vehicle's driven wheels to revolve at different speeds in cornering.
– DERIVATIVES **differentially** adv.

differential calculus ● n. Math. the part of calculus concerned with the derivatives of functions.

differential equation ● n. an equation involving derivatives of a function or functions.

differentiate /dif-fuh-**ren**-shi-ayt/ ● v. (**differentiates, differentiating, differenti-**

ated) **1** recognize as different; distinguish. **2** cause to appear different: *little differentiates the firm's products from its rivals.* **3** Math. transform (a function) into its derivative.
– DERIVATIVES **differentiation** n.

difficult ● adj. **1** needing much effort or skill to do or understand. **2** causing or full of problems: *a difficult economic climate.* **3** not easy to please or satisfy.

d

difficulty ● n. (pl. **difficulties**) **1** the state of being difficult. **2** a difficult or dangerous thing or situation.
– ORIGIN Latin *difficultas*.

diffident ● adj. lacking in self-confidence.
– DERIVATIVES **diffidence** n. **diffidently** adv.
– ORIGIN Latin *diffidere* 'fail to trust'.

diffraction ● n. Physics the process by which a beam of light or other system of waves is spread out as a result of passing through a narrow opening or across an edge.
– DERIVATIVES **diffract** v.
– ORIGIN Latin *diffringere* 'break into pieces'.

diffuse ● v. /dif-**fyooz**/ (**diffuses**, **diffusing**, **diffused**) **1** spread over a wide area: *technologies diffuse rapidly.* **2** Physics (with reference to a gas or liquid) become or cause to become intermingled with a substance by movement. ● adj. /dif-**fyooss**/ **1** spread out over a large area; not concentrated. **2** not clear or concise: *the second argument is more diffuse.*
– DERIVATIVES **diffusely** /dif-**fyooss**-li/ adv. **diffuser** n.
– ORIGIN Latin *diffundere* 'pour out'.

diffusion ● n. **1** the action of spreading over a wide area. **2** Physics the intermingling of substances by the natural movement of their particles.
– DERIVATIVES **diffusive** adj.

dig ● v. (**digs**, **digging**, **dug**) **1** break up and turn over or move earth. **2** remove or do by digging. **3** push or poke sharply: *he dug his hands into his pockets.* **4** (**dig into**/**through**) search or rummage in. **5** (**dig out**/**up**) discover (facts). **6** (**dig in**) begin eating heartily. **7** informal, dated like: *I really dig heavy rock.* ● n. **1** an act of digging. **2** an archaeological excavation. **3** a sharp push or poke. **4** informal a critical remark. **5** (**digs**) Brit. informal lodgings.
– PHRASES **dig in one's heels** stubbornly refuse to compromise.
– ORIGIN perh. from Old English, 'ditch'.

digest ● v. /dy-**jest**/ **1** break down (food) in the stomach and intestines into substances that can be absorbed by the body. **2** reflect on and absorb (information). ● n. /**dy**-jest/ a summary or collection of material or information.
– DERIVATIVES **digestible** adj.
– ORIGIN Latin *digerere* 'distribute'.

digestion ● n. **1** the process of digesting food. **2** a person's capacity to digest food: *he suffered with his digestion.*

digestive ● adj. relating to the digestion of food. ● n. Brit. a semi-sweet biscuit made with wholemeal flour.

digger ● n. **1** a person or machine that digs earth. **2** Austral./NZ informal a friendly form of address for a man.

digit /**di**-jit/ ● n. **1** any of the numerals from 0 to 9. **2** a finger or thumb.
– ORIGIN Latin *digitus* 'finger, toe'.

digital ● adj. **1** having to do with information represented as a series of binary digits, as in a computer. **2** (of a clock or watch) showing the time by means of displayed digits. **3** having to do with a finger or fingers.
– DERIVATIVES **digitally** adv.

digital audiotape ● n. audio tape on which sound is recorded digitally.

digitalis /di-ji-**tay**-liss/ ● n. a drug prepared from foxglove leaves, used to stimulate the heart muscle.
– ORIGIN Latin genus name of the foxglove.

digitize (also **digitise**) ● v. (**digitizes**, **digitizing**, **digitized**) convert (pictures or sound) into a digital form that can be processed by a computer.
– DERIVATIVES **digitizer** (also **digitiser**) n.

dignified ● adj. having or showing dignity.

dignify ● v. (**dignifies**, **dignifying**, **dignified**) make impressive or worthy of respect: *they dignified their departure with a ceremony.*
– ORIGIN Latin *dignificare*.

dignitary /**dig**-ni-tuh-ri/ ● n. (pl. **dignitaries**) a person holding high rank or office.

dignity ● n. (pl. **dignities**) **1** the state of being worthy of respect. **2** a calm or serious manner. **3** a sense of pride in oneself: *it was beneath his dignity to shout.*
– PHRASES **stand on one's dignity** insist on being treated with respect.
– ORIGIN Latin *dignitas*.

digraph /**dy**-grahf/ ● n. a combination of two letters representing one sound, as in *ph*.

digress /dy-**gress**/ ● v. leave the main subject temporarily in speech or writing.
– DERIVATIVES **digression** n.
– ORIGIN Latin *digredi* 'step away'.

dihedral /dy-**hee**-druhl/ ● adj. having or contained by two plane faces.

Dijon E
/**dee**-*zh*on/ an industrial city in east central France.

dike[1] ● n. var. of DYKE[1].

dike[2] ● n. var. of DYKE[2].

diktat /**dik**-tat/ ● n. a decree imposed by someone in power without popular consent.
– ORIGIN German.

dilapidated /di-**lap**-i-day-tid/ ● adj. in a state of disrepair or ruin.
– DERIVATIVES **dilapidation** n.
– ORIGIN Latin *dilapidare* 'demolish'.

dilate /dy-**layt**/ ● v. (**dilates**, **dilating**, **dilated**) make or become wider, larger, or more open.
– DERIVATIVES **dilation** n.
– ORIGIN Latin *dilatare* 'spread out'.

dilatory /**di**-luh-tri/ ● adj. **1** slow to act. **2** intended to cause delay.
– ORIGIN Latin *dilatorius*.

dildo ● n. (pl. **dildos** or **dildoes**) an object shaped like an erect penis, used for sexual stimulation.
– ORIGIN unknown.

dilemma /di-**lem**-muh/ ● n. **1** a situation in which a difficult choice has to be made between alternatives that are equally undesirable. **2** informal a difficult situation or problem.
– ORIGIN Greek.

dilettante /di-li-**tan**-tay/ ● n. (pl. **dilettanti** /di-li-**tan**-ti/ or **dilettantes**) a person who dabbles in a subject for enjoyment but without serious study.

– DERIVATIVES **dilettantism** n.
– ORIGIN Italian, 'person loving the arts'.

diligent • adj. careful and conscientious in a task or duties.
– DERIVATIVES **diligence** n. **diligently** adv.
– ORIGIN Latin *diligens.*

dill • n. a herb, the leaves and seeds of which are used in cookery or for medicinal purposes.
– ORIGIN Old English.

dilly-dally • v. (**dilly-dallies**, **dilly-dallying**, **dilly-dallied**) informal dawdle or be indecisive.
– ORIGIN from DALLY.

dilute /dy-lyoot/ • v. (**dilutes**, **diluting**, **diluted**) **1** make (a liquid) thinner or weaker by adding water or another solvent. **2** weaken by modifying or adding other elements. • adj. /also **dy**-lyoot/ (of a liquid) containing little dissolved matter; weak.
– DERIVATIVES **dilution** n.
– ORIGIN Latin *diluere* 'wash away'.

dim • adj. (**dimmer**, **dimmest**) **1** not shining brightly. **2** not clearly seen or remembered; indistinct: *a dim figure in the dark kitchen.* **3** not able to see clearly. **4** informal stupid. • v. (**dims**, **dimming**, **dimmed**) make or become dim.
– PHRASES **take a dim view of** regard with disapproval.
– DERIVATIVES **dimly** adv. **dimness** n.
– ORIGIN Old English.

DiMaggio E
/di **maj**-ji-oh/, Joe (1914–99; full name *Joseph Paul DiMaggio*), American baseball player with the New York Yankees (1936–51).

Dimbleby, E
(Frederick) Richard (1913–65), English broadcaster, the BBC's first news correspondent (1936). His sons **David** (b.1938) and **Jonathan** (b.1944) have both followed their father into careers in broadcasting.

dime /dym/ • n. N. Amer. a ten-cent coin.
– ORIGIN Old French *disme* 'tenth part'.

dimension /di-men-sh'n/ • n. **1** a measurable extent, such as length, breadth, or height. **2** an aspect or feature: *we modern types lack a spiritual dimension.*
– DERIVATIVES **dimensional** adj.
– ORIGIN Latin.

diminish • v. make or become less.
– ORIGIN Latin *deminuere.*

diminuendo /di-min-yoo-**en**-doh/ • adv. & adj. Music with a decrease in loudness.
– ORIGIN Italian, 'diminishing'.

diminution /di-mi-**nyoo**-sh'n/ • n. a reduction.

diminutive /di-**min**-yuh-tiv/ • adj. **1** extremely or unusually small. **2** (of a word, name, or suffix) used to convey smallness (e.g. *-let* in *booklet*). • n. a shortened form of a name, used informally.
– ORIGIN Latin *diminutivus.*

dimmer • n. (also **dimmer switch**) a device for varying the brightness of an electric light.

dimple • n. **1** a small depression formed in the fleshy part of the cheeks when one smiles. **2** any small depression in a surface. • v. (**dimples**, **dimpling**, **dimpled**) produce a dimple or dimples in the surface of.
– ORIGIN Germanic.

dimwit • n. informal a stupid person.
– DERIVATIVES **dim-witted** adj.

DIN • n. any of a series of international technical standards, used for electrical connections, film speeds, etc.
– ORIGIN from German *Deutsche Industrie-Norm* 'German Industrial Standard'.

din • n. a prolonged loud and unpleasant noise. • v. (**dins**, **dinning**, **dinned**) (**din into**) repeat (information) constantly to make (someone) remember it.
– ORIGIN Old English.

dinar /dee-nar/ • n. the basic unit of money of Yugoslavia and some Middle Eastern and North African countries.
– ORIGIN Arabic and Persian.

dine • v. (**dines**, **dining**, **dined**) **1** eat dinner. **2** (**dine out on**) regularly entertain friends with (an amusing story).
– ORIGIN Old French *disner.*

diner • n. **1** a person who dines. **2** a dining car on a train. **3** N. Amer. a small roadside restaurant.

dinette /dy-net/ • n. a small room or part of a room used for eating meals.

ding-dong • n. Brit. **1** the sound of a bell ringing with alternate chimes. **2** informal a fierce argument or fight.

dinghy /ding-gi, ding-i/ • n. (pl. **dinghies**) **1** a small open sailing boat. **2** a small inflatable rubber boat.
– ORIGIN Hindi, 'rowing boat'.

dingle • n. literary a deep wooded valley.
– ORIGIN unknown.

dingo /ding-goh/ • n. (pl. **dingoes** or **dingos**) a wild Australian dog.
– ORIGIN from an Aboriginal language.

dingy /din-ji/ • adj. (**dingier**, **dingiest**) gloomy and drab.
– ORIGIN perh. from Old English, 'dung'.

dining car • n. a railway carriage equipped as a restaurant.

dinkum /ding kuhm/ • adj. Austral./NZ informal genuine.
– PHRASES **fair dinkum** used for emphasis or to query whether something is true.
– ORIGIN unknown.

dinky • adj. (**dinkier**, **dinkiest**) Brit. informal attractively small and neat.
– ORIGIN Scots and northern English *dink* 'neat, trim'.

dinner • n. **1** the main meal of the day, eaten either around midday or in the evening. **2** a formal evening meal.
– ORIGIN Old French *disner* 'to dine'.

dinner jacket • n. a man's short jacket, worn for formal evening occasions.

dinosaur /dy-nuh-sor/ • n. **1** an extinct reptile of the Mesozoic era, often reaching an enormous size. **2** a person or thing that is outdated.
– ORIGIN from Greek *deinos* 'terrible' + *sauros* 'lizard'.

dint • n. (in phr. **by dint of**) by means of.
– ORIGIN Old English, 'a blow'.

diocese /dy-uh-siss/ • n. (pl. **dioceses** /dy-uh-seez, dy-uh-seez-iz/) (in the Christian church) a district for which a bishop is responsible.
– DERIVATIVES **diocesan** /dy-oss-i-z'n/ adj.
– ORIGIN Latin *diocesis.*

d

Diocletian E
/dy-uh-**klee**-sh'n/ (245–313; full name *Gaius Aurelius Valerius Diocletianus*), Roman emperor 284–305, noted for his persecution of the Christians.

diode /**dy**-ohd/ ● **n.** a semiconductor device with two terminals, allowing the flow of current in one direction only.
– ORIGIN from **DI-** + **ELECTRODE**.

Diogenes E
/dy-**oj**-i-neez/ (*c*.400–*c*.325 BC), Greek Cynic philosopher, who believed that a person only needed to satisfy their natural needs in the simplest way in order to be happy.

Dionysian /dy-uh-**niss**-i-uhn/ (also **Dionysiac** /dy-uh-**niss**-i-ak/) ● **adj. 1** relating to the Greek god Dionysus. **2** wild and uninhibited.

Dionysus E
/dy-uh-**ny**-suhss/ a Greek god associated with wild religious rites, and later a god of wine who inspires creativity in music and poetry. Also called **BACCHUS**.

dioptric ● **adj.** relating to the refraction of light.

Dior E
/**dee**-or/, Christian (1905–57), French fashion designer. In 1947 he introduced a style which became known as the New Look, featuring narrow-waisted tightly fitted bodices and full pleated skirts.

diorama /dy-uh-**rah**-muh/ ● **n.** a model representing a scene with three-dimensional figures against a painted background.
– ORIGIN French.

diorite /**dy**-uh-ryt/ ● **n.** a speckled, coarse-grained igneous rock.
– ORIGIN French.

dioxide /dy-**ok**-syd/ ● **n.** Chem. an oxide with two atoms of oxygen to one of a metal or other element.

dioxin /dy-**ok**-sin/ ● **n.** a highly poisonous organic compound produced as a by-product in some manufacturing processes.

dip ● **v.** (**dips**, **dipping**, **dipped**) **1** (**dip in/into**) put or lower briefly in or into. **2** sink, drop, or slope downwards. **3** (of a level or amount) temporarily become lower or smaller. **4** lower briefly: *the plane dipped its wings.* **5** (**dip into**) reach into (a bag or container) to take something out. **6** (**dip into**) spend from (one's financial resources). ● **n. 1** an act of dipping. **2** a thick sauce in which pieces of food are dipped before eating. **3** a brief swim. **4** a brief downward slope followed by an upward one.
– ORIGIN Old English.

diphtheria /dip-**theer**-i-uh/ ● **n.** a serious infectious disease causing inflammation of the mucous membranes, especially in the throat.
– ORIGIN Greek *diphthera* 'skin, hide'.

diphthong /**dif**-thong/ ● **n.** a sound formed by the combination of two vowels in a single syllable (as in *coin*).
– ORIGIN from Greek *di-* 'twice' + *phthongos* 'sound'.

diploid /**dip**-loyd/ ● **adj.** Genetics (of a cell or nucleus) containing two complete sets of chromosomes, one from each parent. Compare with **HAPLOID**.
– ORIGIN Greek *diplous* 'double'.

diploma ● **n.** a certificate awarded by an educational establishment for successfully completing a course of study.
– ORIGIN Greek, 'folded paper'.

diplomacy ● **n. 1** the profession or skill of managing international relations. **2** skill and tact in dealing with people.
– ORIGIN French *diplomatie*.

diplomat ● **n.** an official representing a country abroad.

diplomatic ● **adj. 1** having to do with diplomacy. **2** tactful.
– DERIVATIVES **diplomatically** adv.

dipole /**dy**-pohl/ ● **n. 1** Physics a pair of equal and oppositely charged or magnetized poles separated by a distance. **2** an aerial consisting of a horizontal metal rod with a connecting wire at its centre.
– DERIVATIVES **dipolar** adj.

dipper ● **n. 1** a songbird able to dive into fast-flowing streams to feed. **2** a ladle.

dippy ● **adj.** informal foolish or eccentric.
– ORIGIN unknown.

dipsomania /dip-suh-**may**-ni-uh/ ● **n.** alcoholism.
– DERIVATIVES **dipsomaniac** n.
– ORIGIN Greek *dipsa* 'thirst'.

dipstick ● **n.** a rod for measuring the depth of a liquid.

diptych /**dip**-tik/ ● **n.** a painting on two hinged wooden panels, forming an altarpiece.
– ORIGIN Greek *diptukha* 'pair of writing tablets'.

Dirac E
/di-**rak**/, Paul Adrian Maurice (1902–84), English theoretical physicist, who described the properties of the electron by applying Einstein's theory of relativity to quantum mechanics.

dire ● **adj. 1** extremely serious or urgent. **2** informal of a very poor quality.
– ORIGIN Latin *dirus* 'fearful'.

direct /di-**rekt**, dy-**rekt**/ ● **adj. 1** going from one place to another without changing direction or stopping. **2** with nothing or no one in between: *he relied on direct contact with the leaders.* **3** frank. **4** clear and explicit. ● **adv.** in a direct way or by a direct route. ● **v. 1** aim towards: *comics directed at adolescent males.* **2** tell or show (someone) the way. **3** control the operations of. **4** supervise and control (a film, play, or other production). **5** give an order to.
– DERIVATIVES **directness** n.
– ORIGIN Latin *directus*.

direct action ● **n.** the use of public forms of protest rather than negotiation to achieve one's aims.

direct current ● **n.** an electric current flowing in one direction only. Compare with **ALTERNATING CURRENT**.

direct debit ● **n.** Brit. an arrangement with a bank that allows money to be taken from a person's account to pay a particular person or organization.

direction /di-**rek**-sh'n, dy-**rek**-sh'n/ ● **n. 1** a course along which someone or something moves, or which leads to a destination. **2** a point to or from which a person or thing moves or faces: *a house with views in all directions.* **3** the action of directing or managing people. **4** (**directions**) instructions on how to reach a destination or how to do something.

directional ● adj. **1** having to do with or indicating direction. **2** operating or sending radio signals in one direction only: *a directional microphone.*

directive ● n. an official instruction.

directly ● adv. **1** in a direct way. **2** exactly in a specified position: *the house directly opposite.* **3** immediately. ● conj. Brit. as soon as.

direct mail ● n. advertising literature mailed to possible customers without them having asked for it.

direct object ● n. a person or thing that is directly affected by the action of a transitive verb (e.g. *the dog* in *I fed the dog*).

director ● n. **1** a person who is in charge of a department, organization, or activity. **2** a member of the managing board of a business. **3** a person who directs a film, play, etc.
– DERIVATIVES **directorial** adj. **directorship** n.

directorate ● n. **1** the board of directors of a company. **2** a section of a government department in charge of a particular activity.

director-general ● n. (pl. **directors-general**) esp. Brit. the chief executive of a large organization.

directory ● n. (pl. **directories**) a book listing people or organizations with details such as addresses and telephone numbers.

direct speech ● n. the reporting of speech by repeating the actual words of a speaker, for example *'I'm going', she said.* Contrasted with **REPORTED SPEECH**.

direct tax ● n. a tax, such as income tax, which is charged on the income or profits of the person who pays it, rather than on goods or services.

dirge /derj/ ● n. **1** a lament for the dead. **2** a mournful song or piece of music.
– ORIGIN Latin *dirige!* 'direct!', the first word of a psalm used in a religious service for the dead.

dirigible /di-ri-ji-b'l/ ● n. an airship.
– ORIGIN Latin *dirigere* 'to direct'.

dirk /derk/ ● n. a short dagger formerly carried by Scottish Highlanders.
– ORIGIN unknown.

dirndl /dern-d'l/ (also **dirndl skirt**) ● n. a full, wide skirt gathered into a tight waistband.
– ORIGIN German dialect, 'little girl'.

dirt ● n. **1** a substance that causes uncleanliness. **2** soil. **3** informal excrement. **4** informal scandalous or damaging information: *what's the dirt on Jack?*
– ORIGIN Old Norse.

dirt cheap ● adj. & adv. extremely cheap.

dirt track ● n. a racing track made of earth or rolled cinders.

dirty ● adj. (**dirtier**, **dirtiest**) **1** covered or marked with dirt; not clean. **2** obscene. **3** dishonest; dishonourable. **4** (of weather) rough and unpleasant. ● adv. Brit. informal used for emphasis: *a dirty great stone.* ● v. (**dirties**, **dirtying**, **dirtied**) make dirty.
– PHRASES **do the dirty on** Brit. informal cheat or betray. **play dirty** informal act in a dishonest or unfair way.

dirty look ● n. informal a look expressing disapproval, disgust, or anger.

dirty weekend ● n. Brit. informal a weekend spent away with a lover.

dirty word ● n. **1** an offensive or indecent word. **2** a subject regarded with dislike or disapproval.

dirty work ● n. unpleasant or dishonest activities that are passed to someone else.

dis- ● prefix expressing: **1** not; the reverse of: *disadvantage.* **2** separation or removal: *disperse.*
– ORIGIN Latin.

disability ● n. (pl. **disabilities**) **1** a physical or mental condition that limits a person's movements, senses, or activities. **2** a disadvantage.

disable ● v. (**disables**, **disabling**, **disabled**) **1** (of a disease, injury, or accident) limit (someone) in their movements, senses, or activities. **2** put out of action.
– DERIVATIVES **disablement** n.

disabled ● adj. having a physical or mental disability.

disabuse /diss-uh-byooz/ ● v. (**disabuses**, **disabusing**, **disabused**) persuade (someone) that an idea or belief is mistaken: *he disabused her of this idea.*

disadvantage ● n. an unfavourable circumstance or condition. ● v. (**disadvantages**, **disadvantaging**, **disadvantaged**) **1** put in an unfavourable position. **2** (**disadvantaged**) less wealthy and having fewer opportunities than most people.
– DERIVATIVES **disadvantageous** adj.

disaffected ● adj. discontented through having lost one's feelings of loyalty.
– DERIVATIVES **disaffection** n.

disagree ● v. (**disagrees**, **disagreeing**, **disagreed**) **1** have a different opinion. **2** be inconsistent: *results which disagree with the findings reported so far.* **3** (**disagree with**) make slightly unwell.
– DERIVATIVES **disagreement** n.

disagreeable ● adj. **1** unpleasant. **2** bad-tempered.

disallow ● v. declare to be invalid.

disappear ● v. **1** cease to be visible. **2** cease to exist.
– DERIVATIVES **disappearance** n.

disappoint ● v. **1** fail to fulfil the hopes of. **2** prevent (hopes) from becoming a reality.
– ORIGIN Old French *desappointer.*

disappointed ● adj. sad or displeased because one's hopes have not been fulfilled.

disappointment ● n. **1** sadness or displeasure felt when one's hopes are not fulfilled. **2** a person or thing that causes such a feeling.

disapprobation /diss-ap-ruh-bay-sh'n/ ● n. strong disapproval.

disapprove ● v. (**disapproves**, **disapproving**, **disapproved**) think that someone or something is wrong or bad: *Bob disapproved of drinking and driving.*
– DERIVATIVES **disapproval** n.

disarm ● v. **1** take a weapon or weapons away from. **2** (of a country or force) give up or reduce its armed forces or weapons. **3** remove the fuse from (a bomb). **4** win over (a hostile or suspicious person).

disarmament /diss-arm-uh-muhnt/ ● n. the reduction or withdrawal of military forces and weapons.

disarming ● adj. removing suspicion or hostility.

disarrange ● v. (**disarranges**, **disarran-**

ging, **disarranged**) make untidy or disordered.

disarray ● n. a state of disorder or confusion.

disassociate ● v. = DISSOCIATE.

disaster ● n. **1** a sudden accident or a natural catastrophe that causes great damage or loss of life. **2** a sudden misfortune: *a string of personal disasters.*

– ORIGIN Italian *disastro* 'unlucky event'.

disastrous ● adj. **1** causing great damage. **2** informal very unsuccessful.

– DERIVATIVES **disastrously** adv.

disavow ● v. deny any responsibility or support for.

– DERIVATIVES **disavowal** n.

disband ● v. (with reference to an organized group) break up or cause to break up: *the team was disbanded.*

disbar ● v. (**disbars**, **disbarring**, **disbarred**) expel (a barrister) from the Bar.

disbelief ● n. inability or refusal to accept that something is true or real.

disbelieve ● v. (**disbelieves**, **disbelieving**, **disbelieved**) be unable to believe.

disburse /diss-berss/ ● v. (**disburses**, **disbursing**, **disbursed**) pay out (money from a fund).

– DERIVATIVES **disbursement** n.

– ORIGIN Old French *desbourser.*

disc (US also **disk**) ● n. **1** a flat, thin, round object. **2** (**disk**) an information storage device for a computer, on which data is stored either magnetically or optically. **3** a layer of cartilage separating vertebrae in the spine. **4** dated a gramophone record.

– ORIGIN Greek *diskos* 'discus'.

discard ● v. /diss-kard/ get rid of as useless or unwanted. ● n. /diss-kard/ a discarded item.

– ORIGIN from DIS- + CARD[1].

discern /di-sern/ ● v. **1** recognize or be aware of. **2** see or hear with difficulty.

– DERIVATIVES **discernible** adj.

– ORIGIN Latin *discernere.*

discerning ● adj. having or showing good judgement.

– DERIVATIVES **discernment** n.

discharge ● v. /diss-charj/ (**discharges**, **discharging**, **discharged**) **1** dismiss or allow to leave: *he was discharged from the RAF.* **2** send out (a liquid, gas, or other substance). **3** fire (a gun or missile). **4** fulfil (a responsibility). **5** Physics release or neutralize the electric charge of. ● n. /diss-charj, diss-charj/ **1** the action of discharging: *my discharge from hospital.* **2** a substance that has been discharged. **3** a flow of electricity through the air or other gas.

– ORIGIN Old French *descharger* 'unload'.

disciple /di-sy-p'l/ ● n. **1** a follower of Christ during his life, especially one of the twelve Apostles. **2** a follower of a teacher, leader, or philosophy.

– ORIGIN Latin *discipulus* 'learner'.

disciplinarian ● n. a person who enforces firm discipline.

disciplinary /diss-i-plin-uh-ri/ ● adj. having to do with discipline.

discipline ● n. **1** the training of people to obey rules or a code of behaviour. **2** controlled behaviour resulting from such training: *he maintained discipline among his men.* **3** a branch of academic study. ● v. (**disciplines**, **disciplining**, **disciplined**) **1** train to be obedient or self-controlled. **2** punish or rebuke formally for an offence. **3** (**disciplined**) behaving in a controlled way.

– ORIGIN Latin *disciplina* 'instruction'.

disc jockey ● n. a person who introduces and plays recorded popular music on radio or at a club.

disclaim ● v. deny responsibility for or knowledge of (something).

disclaimer ● n. a statement disclaiming responsibility for something.

disclose ● v. (**discloses**, **disclosing**, **disclosed**) **1** make (secret or new information) known. **2** allow to be seen.

disclosure ● n. **1** the disclosing of information. **2** a secret that is disclosed.

disco ● n. (pl. **discos**) informal a club or party at which people dance to pop music.

discolour (US **discolor**) ● v. make or become stained or otherwise changed in colour.

– DERIVATIVES **discoloration** (also **discolouration**) n.

discomfit /diss-kum-fit/ ● v. (**discomfits**, **discomfiting**, **discomfited**) make uneasy or embarrassed.

– DERIVATIVES **discomfiture** n.

– ORIGIN Old French *desconfire* 'defeat'.

discomfort ● n. **1** slight pain. **2** slight anxiety or embarrassment. ● v. cause discomfort to.

discompose ● v. (**discomposes**, **discomposing**, **discomposed**) disturb or agitate.

– DERIVATIVES **discomposure** n.

disconcert /diss-kuhn-sert/ ● v. unsettle; upset.

– ORIGIN former French *desconcerter.*

disconnect ● v. **1** break the connection of or between. **2** detach (an electrical device) from a power supply.

– DERIVATIVES **disconnection** n.

disconnected ● adj. lacking a logical sequence.

disconsolate /diss-kon-suh-luht/ ● adj. very unhappy and unable to be comforted.

discontent ● n. lack of contentment or satisfaction.

– DERIVATIVES **discontented** adj. **discontentment** n.

discontinue ● v. (**discontinues**, **discontinuing**, **discontinued**) stop doing, providing, or making: *he discontinued his visits.*

– DERIVATIVES **discontinuation** n.

discontinuous /diss-kuhn-tin-yoo-uhss/ ● adj. having intervals or gaps; not continuous.

– DERIVATIVES **discontinuity** n.

discord ● n. **1** lack of agreement or harmony: *those who promote racial discord.* **2** lack of harmony between musical notes sounding together.

– ORIGIN Latin *discors* 'discordant'.

discordant ● adj. **1** not in harmony or agreement: *discordant opinions.* **2** (of a sound) harsh and unpleasant.

discotheque /diss-kuh-tek/ ● n. a disco.

– ORIGIN French.

discount ● n. /diss-kownt/ a deduction from the usual cost of something. ● v. /diss-kownt/ **1** deduct a discount from (the usual price of something). **2** disregard because unlikely: *she'd heard rumours, but discounted them.*

discourage ● v. (**discourages, discouraging, discouraged**) **1** cause (someone) to lose confidence or enthusiasm. **2** prevent by persuasion or showing disapproval: *we want to discourage children from smoking.*
– DERIVATIVES **discouragement** n.
– ORIGIN Old French *descouragier.*

discourse ● n. /diss-korss/ **1** written or spoken communication or debate. **2** a formal discussion of a topic. ● v. /diss-**korss**/ (**discourses, discoursing, discoursed**) speak or write authoritatively about a topic.
– ORIGIN Latin *discursus* 'running to and fro'.

discourteous ● adj. rude and lacking consideration for others.

discourtesy ● n. (pl. **discourtesies**) **1** rude and inconsiderate behaviour. **2** an impolite act or remark.

discover ● v. (**discovers, discovering, discovered**) **1** find unexpectedly or in the course of a search. **2** gain knowledge or become aware of. **3** be the first to find or observe (a place, substance, or scientific phenomenon).
– DERIVATIVES **discoverer** n.

discovery ● n. (pl. **discoveries**) **1** the action of discovering. **2** a person or thing discovered.

discredit ● v. (**discredits, discrediting, discredited**) **1** harm the good reputation of. **2** cause (something) to seem false or unreliable. ● n. loss or lack of reputation.

discreditable ● adj. bringing discredit, shameful.

discreet ● adj. careful not to attract attention or give offence: *we made some discreet inquiries.*
– DERIVATIVES **discreetly** adv.
– ORIGIN Old French *discret.*

discrepancy /diss-krep-uhn-si/ ● n. (pl. **discrepancies**) a difference between things expected to be the same.
– ORIGIN Latin *discrepantia.*

discrete ● adj. individually separate and distinct.
– DERIVATIVES **discretely** adv.
– ORIGIN Latin *discretus* 'separate'.

discretion ● n. **1** the quality of being discreet. **2** the freedom to decide what should be done in a particular situation: *funds for use at your own discretion.*

discretionary ● adj. done or used at a person's discretion.

discriminate /diss-krim-i-nayt/ ● v. (**discriminates, discriminating, discriminated**) **1** recognize a difference. **2** make an unjust distinction in the treatment of different groups of people on the grounds of race, sex, or age.
– DERIVATIVES **discriminative** adj.
– ORIGIN Latin *discriminare.*

discriminating ● adj. having or showing good taste or judgement.

discrimination ● n. **1** the action of discriminating against people. **2** recognition of the difference between one thing and another. **3** good judgement or taste.

discriminatory ● adj. showing discrimination or prejudice.

discursive /diss-ker-siv/ ● adj. wandering from subject to subject.
– ORIGIN Latin *discursivus* 'running to and fro'.

discus ● n. (pl. **discuses**) a heavy disc thrown in athletic contests.
– ORIGIN Greek *diskos.*

discuss ● v. **1** talk about (something) so as to reach a decision. **2** talk or write about (a topic) in detail.
– ORIGIN Latin *discutere* 'dash to pieces'.

discussion ● n. **1** the action or an act of discussing something. **2** a detailed treatment of a topic in speech or writing.

disdain ● n. the feeling that someone or something is unworthy of one's consideration or respect. ● v. consider or treat with disdain.
– DERIVATIVES **disdainful** adj.
– ORIGIN Old French *desdeign.*

disease ● n. a disorder in a human, animal, or plant, caused by infection, diet, or by faulty functioning of a process.
– DERIVATIVES **diseased** adj.
– ORIGIN Old French *desaise* 'lack of ease'.

disembark ● v. leave a ship, aircraft, or train.
– DERIVATIVES **disembarkation** n.

disembodied ● adj. **1** separated from or existing without the body. **2** (of a sound) coming from a person who cannot be seen.

disembowel ● v. (**disembowels, disembowelling, disembowelled**; US **disembowels, disemboweling, disemboweled**) cut open and remove the internal organs of.

disempower ● v. (**disempowers, disempowering, disempowered**) make less powerful or confident.

disenchant ● v. make disillusioned: *those who are disenchanted with science.*
– DERIVATIVES **disenchantment** n.

disenfranchise ● v. (**disenfranchises, disenfranchising, disenfranchised**) deprive of a right, especially the right to vote.

disengage ● v. (**disengages, disengaging, disengaged**) **1** release or detach: *I disengaged his hand from mine.* **2** remove (troops) from an area of conflict.
– DERIVATIVES **disengagement** n.

disentangle ● v. (**disentangles, disentangling, disentangled**) free from entanglement.

disestablish ● v. deprive (a national Church) of its official status.
– DERIVATIVES **disestablishment** n.

disfavour (US **disfavor**) ● n. **1** disapproval or dislike. **2** the state of being disliked.

disfigure ● v. (**disfigures, disfiguring, disfigured**) spoil the appearance of.
– DERIVATIVES **disfigurement** n.

disgorge ● v. (**disgorges, disgorging, disgorged**) **1** cause to pour out: *a bus disgorged a group of youths.* **2** bring up (food).
– ORIGIN Old French *desgorger.*

disgrace ● n. **1** loss of reputation as the result of a dishonourable action. **2** a shameful person or thing: *he's a disgrace to the legal profession.* ● v. (**disgraces, disgracing, disgraced**) bring disgrace on.

disgraceful ● adj. shockingly unacceptable.
– DERIVATIVES **disgracefully** adv.

disgruntled ● adj. angry or dissatisfied.
– ORIGIN from dialect *gruntle* 'grumble'.

disguise ● v. (**disguises, disguising, dis-**

guised) **1** alter in appearance or nature so as to conceal the identity of: *he was disguised as a priest.* **2** hide (a feeling or situation). ● **n. 1** a means of disguising one's identity. **2** the state of being disguised.
– ORIGIN Old French *desguisier.*

disgust ● **n.** revulsion or strong disapproval. ● **v.** cause disgust in.
– ORIGIN from **DIS-** + Latin *gustus* 'taste'.

d

disgusting ● **adj.** arousing revulsion or strong disapproval.

dish ● **n. 1** a shallow container for cooking or serving food. **2** (**the dishes**) all the crockery and utensils used for a meal. **3** a particular kind of food: *a simple pork dish.* **4** a shallow, concave object. **5** informal a sexually attractive person. ● **v. 1** (**dish out/up**) put (food) on to a plate or plates before a meal. **2** (**dish out**) distribute in a casual or random way.
– ORIGIN Greek *diskos* 'discus'.

disharmony ● **n.** lack of harmony.

dishearten ● **v.** cause (someone) to lose determination or confidence.

dishevelled /di-shev-v'ld/ (US **disheveled**) ● **adj.** untidy; disordered: *a greasy, dishevelled man.*
– ORIGIN Old French *deschevele.*

dishonest ● **adj.** not honest, trustworthy, or sincere.
– DERIVATIVES **dishonesty** n.

dishonour (US **dishonor**) ● **n.** a state of shame or disgrace. ● **v. 1** bring dishonour to. **2** fail to keep (an agreement).

dishonourable (US **dishonorable**) ● **adj.** bringing shame or disgrace.

dishwasher ● **n.** a machine for washing dishes automatically.

dishy ● **adj.** (**dishier**, **dishiest**) informal, esp. Brit. sexually attractive.

disillusion ● **n.** disappointment from discovering that one's beliefs are mistaken or unrealistic. ● **v.** cause (someone) to experience disillusion.
– DERIVATIVES **disillusionment** n.

disincentive ● **n.** a factor that discourages a particular action: *rising house prices are a disincentive to development.*

disinclination ● **n.** a reluctance to do something.

disinclined ● **adj.** reluctant; unwilling.

disinfect ● **v.** make free from infection with a chemical disinfectant.
– DERIVATIVES **disinfection** n.

disinfectant ● **n.** a chemical liquid that destroys bacteria.

disinformation ● **n.** information which is intended to mislead.

disingenuous /diss-in-jen-yoo-uhss/ ● **adj.** not sincere, especially in pretending ignorance about something.
– DERIVATIVES **disingenuously** adv.

disinherit ● **v.** (**disinherits**, **disinheriting**, **disinherited**) deprive (someone) of an inheritance.

disintegrate ● **v.** (**disintegrates**, **disintegrating**, **disintegrated**) break up into small parts as a result of impact or decay.
– DERIVATIVES **disintegration** n.

disinter /diss-in-ter/ ● **v.** (**disinters**, **disinterring**, **disinterred**) dig up (something buried).

disinterest ● **n. 1** impartiality. **2** lack of interest.

disinterested ● **adj.** not influenced by personal feelings; impartial.

USAGE disinterested
Do not confuse **disinterested** and **uninterested**. **Disinterested** means 'impartial' (as in *a banker is under an obligation to give disinterested advice*), while **uninterested** means 'not interested' (as in *a man uninterested in money*).

disjointed ● **adj.** lacking coherence; disconnected.

disjunction ● **n.** a difference between things expected to be similar.

disk ● **n.** US & Computing = **DISC**.

disk drive ● **n.** a device which allows a computer to read from and write on to computer disks.

diskette ● **n.** = **FLOPPY**.

dislike ● **v.** (**dislike**, **disliking**, **disliked**) feel distaste for or hostility towards. ● **n. 1** a feeling of distaste or hostility. **2** a thing that is disliked.
– DERIVATIVES **dislikable** (also **dislikeable**) adj.

dislocate /diss-luh-kayt/ ● **v.** (**dislocates**, **dislocating**, **dislocated**) **1** displace (a bone) from its proper position in a joint. **2** disrupt.
– DERIVATIVES **dislocation** n.

dislodge ● **v.** (**dislodges**, **dislodging**, **dislodged**) remove from a fixed position.

disloyal ● **adj.** not loyal or faithful.
– DERIVATIVES **disloyalty** n.

dismal ● **adj. 1** causing or showing gloom or depression. **2** informal shockingly bad.
– DERIVATIVES **dismally** adv.
– ORIGIN from Latin *dies mali* 'evil days'.

dismantle ● **v.** (**dismantles**, **dismantling**, **dismantled**) take to pieces.
– DERIVATIVES **dismantlement** n.
– ORIGIN Old French *desmanteler.*

dismay ● **n.** discouragement and distress. ● **v.** cause (someone) to feel dismay.
– ORIGIN Old French.

dismember ● **v.** (**dismembers**, **dismembering**, **dismembered**) **1** tear or cut the limbs from. **2** divide up (a territory or organization).
– DERIVATIVES **dismemberment** n.
– ORIGIN Old French *desmembrer.*

dismiss ● **v. 1** order or allow to leave. **2** order (an employee) to leave a job. **3** treat as unworthy of consideration. **4** refuse further hearing to (a legal case). **5** Cricket end the innings of (a batsman or side).
– DERIVATIVES **dismissal** n.
– ORIGIN Latin *dimittere* 'send away'.

dismissive ● **adj.** showing that something is unworthy of consideration.
– DERIVATIVES **dismissively** adv.

dismount ● **v.** get off or down from a horse or bicycle.

Disney, E
Walt (1901–66; full name *Walter Elias Disney*), American animator and film producer. He was the creator of cartoon characters such as Mickey Mouse, Donald Duck, and Pluto.

disobedient ● **adj.** failing or refusing to be obedient.
– DERIVATIVES **disobedience** n.

disobey ● **v.** fail or refuse to obey.

disorder ● n. **1** a lack of order; confusion. **2** the disruption of peaceful and law-abiding behaviour. **3** an illness or disease. ● v. (**disorders, disordering, disordered**) bring disorder to.

disorderly ● adj. **1** untidy or disorganized. **2** involving a breakdown of peaceful and law-abiding behaviour.

disorganized (also **disorganised**) ● adj. **1** not properly planned and controlled. **2** not able to plan one's activities efficiently.
– DERIVATIVES **disorganization** (also **disorganisation**) n.

disorientate ● v. (**disorientates, disorientating, disorientated**) confuse (someone) so that they lose their bearings.
– DERIVATIVES **disorientation** n.

disown ● v. refuse to have anything further to do with (someone).

disparage /di-spa-rij/ ● v. (**disparages, disparaging, disparaged**) speak of (someone or something) as being of little worth.
– DERIVATIVES **disparagement** n.
– ORIGIN Old French *desparagier* 'marry someone of unequal rank'.

disparate /diss-puh-ruht/ ● adj. **1** very different in kind. **2** containing elements very different from one another: *a culturally disparate country.*
– ORIGIN Latin *disparatus* 'separated'.

disparity ● n. (pl. **disparities**) a great difference.

dispassionate ● adj. not influenced by strong emotion; rational and impartial.
– DERIVATIVES **dispassionately** adv.

dispatch (also **despatch**) ● v. **1** send off to a destination or for a purpose. **2** deal with (a task or problem) quickly and efficiently. **3** kill. ● n. **1** the action of dispatching. **2** an official report on the latest situation in state or military affairs. **3** a report sent in from abroad by a journalist. **4** promptness and efficiency: *proceed with dispatch.*
– DERIVATIVES **dispatcher** (also **despatcher**) n.
– ORIGIN Italian *dispacciare* or Spanish *despachar* 'expedite'.

dispel ● v. (**dispels, dispelling, dispelled**) make (a doubt, feeling, or belief) disappear.
– ORIGIN Latin *dispellere* 'drive apart'.

dispensable ● adj. able to be replaced or done without.

dispensary ● n. (pl. **dispensaries**) a room where medicines are prepared and provided.

dispensation ● n. **1** exemption from a rule or usual requirement. **2** a religious or political system prevailing at a particular time: *the capitalist dispensation.* **3** the action of dispensing.

dispense ● v. (**dispenses, dispensing, dispensed**) **1** distribute or supply to a number of people. **2** (of a chemist) prepare and supply (medicine) according to a prescription. **3** (**dispense with**) get rid of or manage without.
– DERIVATIVES **dispenser** n.
– ORIGIN Latin *dispensare* 'continue to weigh out'.

disperse ● v. (**disperses, dispersing, dispersed**) **1** go or distribute in different directions or over a wide area: *the crowd dispersed.* **2** (of gas, smoke, etc.) thin out and eventually disappear.
– DERIVATIVES **dispersal** n.
– ORIGIN Latin *dispergere.*

dispersion ● n. **1** the action of dispersing. **2** the action of splitting light into components with different wavelengths.

dispirited ● adj. disheartened or depressed.
– DERIVATIVES **dispiriting** adj.

displace ● v. (**displaces, displacing, displaced**) **1** move from the proper or usual position. **2** take over the position or role of.

displacement ● n. **1** the action of displacing. **2** the amount by which something is displaced. **3** the volume or weight of water displaced by a floating ship, used as a measure of the ship's size.

display ● v. **1** put on show in a noticeable and attractive way. **2** show (data or an image) on a screen. **3** show (a quality or feeling). ● n. **1** a performance, show, or event for public entertainment. **2** a collection of objects being displayed. **3** the action or an instance of displaying: *a display of emotion.* **4** the data or images shown on a screen.
– ORIGIN Old French *despleier* 'unfold'.

displease ● v. (**displeases, displeasing, displeased**) annoy or upset.

displeasure ● n. annoyance or dissatisfaction.

disport ● v. (**disport oneself**) enjoy oneself without restraint.
– ORIGIN Old French *desporter* 'carry away'.

disposable ● adj. **1** (of an article) intended to be used once and then thrown away. **2** (of income or financial assets) available for use as required.

disposal ● n. the action of disposing.
– PHRASES **at one's disposal** available for one to use whenever or however one wishes.

dispose ● v. (**disposes, disposing, disposed**) **1** (**dispose of**) get rid of. **2** arrange in a particular position. **3** incline (someone) to do or think something: *I was disposed to quarrel with this.* **4** (**disposed**) having a specified attitude: *they were favourably disposed towards him.*
– DERIVATIVES **disposer** n.
– ORIGIN Old French *disposer.*

disposition ● n. **1** a person's natural qualities of character: *a lady of a kindly disposition.* **2** an inclination or tendency. **3** the arrangement of something.

dispossess ● v. deprive (someone) of a possession.
– DERIVATIVES **dispossession** n.

disproportionate ● adj. too large or too small in comparison with something else.
– DERIVATIVES **disproportionately** adv.

disprove ● v. (**disproves, disproving, disproved**) prove to be false.

disputable ● adj. open to question.

disputation ● n. debate or argument.

disputatious ● adj. fond of arguing.

dispute ● v. /diss-pyoot/ (**disputes, disputing, disputed**) **1** argue about. **2** question the truth or validity of. **3** compete for. ● n. /diss-pyoot, diss-pyoot/ **1** an argument or disagreement. **2** a disagreement between management and employees.
– ORIGIN Latin *disputare* 'to estimate'.

disqualify ● v. (**disqualifies, disqualifying, disqualified**) **1** ban (someone) from a job or

activity because of a breach of the law or rules. **2** make unsuitable for a job or activity: *a heart complaint disqualified him for military service.*
– DERIVATIVES **disqualification** n.

disquiet • n. a feeling of anxiety. • v. make anxious.

disquisition /diss-kwi-zi-sh'n/ • n. a long or complex discussion of a subject in speech or writing.
– ORIGIN Latin, 'investigation'.

d

Disraeli E
/diz-ray-li/, Benjamin, 1st Earl of Beaconsfield (1804–81), British Tory statesman, Prime Minister 1868 and 1874–80. He ensured that Britain bought a controlling interest in the Suez Canal (1875) and was largely responsible for the introduction of the second Reform Act (1867).

disregard • v. pay no attention to. • n. the action of disregarding: *his disregard for truth.*

disrepair • n. a poor condition due to neglect.

disreputable • adj. not respectable in appearance or character.

disrepute • n. the state of having a bad reputation.

disrespect • n. lack of respect or courtesy.
– DERIVATIVES **disrespectful** adj.

disrobe • v. (**disrobes**, **disrobing**, **disrobed**) undress.

disrupt • v. interrupt or disturb (an activity or process).
– DERIVATIVES **disruption** n.
– ORIGIN Latin *disrumpere* 'break apart'.

disruptive • adj. causing disruption.

dissatisfied • adj. not content or happy.
– DERIVATIVES **dissatisfaction** n.

dissect /di-sekt, dy-sekt/ • v. **1** methodically cut up (a body, part, or plant) in order to study its internal parts. **2** analyse in great detail.
– DERIVATIVES **dissection** n.
– ORIGIN Latin *dissecare.*

dissemble • v. (**dissembles**, **dissembling**, **dissembled**) hide or disguise one's motives or feelings.
– ORIGIN Latin *dissimulare.*

disseminate • v. (**disseminates**, **disseminating**, **disseminated**) spread (information) widely.
– DERIVATIVES **dissemination** n.
– ORIGIN Latin *disseminare* 'scatter'.

dissension • n. disagreement within a group.
– ORIGIN Latin.

dissent • v. **1** express disagreement with a widely held view. **2** disagree with the doctrine of an established Church. • n. disagreement with a widely held view.
– DERIVATIVES **dissenter** n.
– ORIGIN Latin *dissentire.*

dissertation • n. a long essay, especially one written for a university degree or diploma.
– ORIGIN Latin *dissertare* 'continue to discuss'.

disservice • n. a harmful action.

dissident • n. a person who opposes official policy. • adj. opposing official policy.
– DERIVATIVES **dissidence** n.
– ORIGIN Latin *dissidere* 'sit apart'.

dissimilar • adj. not similar; different.
– DERIVATIVES **dissimilarity** n.

dissimulate • v. (**dissimulates**, **dissimulating**, **dissimulated**) hide or disguise one's thoughts or feelings.
– DERIVATIVES **dissimulation** n.
– ORIGIN Latin *dissimulare.*

dissipate • v. (**dissipates**, **dissipating**, **dissipated**) **1** be or cause to be dispersed: *the steam dissipated in the air.* **2** waste (money, energy, or resources). **3** (**dissipated**) overindulgent in physical pleasures.
– ORIGIN Latin *dissipare.*

dissipation • n. **1** dissipated living. **2** the action of dissipating.

dissociate • v. (**dissociates**, **dissociating**, **dissociated**) **1** disconnect or separate. **2** (**dissociate oneself from**) declare that one is not connected with (someone or something).
– DERIVATIVES **dissociation** n.
– ORIGIN Latin *dissociare.*

dissolute /diss-uh-loot/ • adj. overindulgent in physical pleasures.
– ORIGIN Latin *dissolutus* 'loose'.

dissolution • n. **1** the formal closing down or ending of an official body or agreement. **2** the action of dissolving or decomposing. **3** dissolute living.

dissolve • v. (**dissolves**, **dissolving**, **dissolved**) **1** (with reference to a solid) disperse or cause to disperse in a liquid so as to form a solution. **2** close down or end (an assembly or agreement). **3** (**dissolve into/in**) give way to (strong emotion).
– ORIGIN Latin *dissolvere.*

dissonant • adj. lacking harmony; discordant.
– DERIVATIVES **dissonance** n.
– ORIGIN Latin *dissonare* 'be discordant'.

dissuade /dis-swayd/ • v. (**dissuades**, **dissuading**, **dissuaded**) persuade or advise not to do: *they tried to dissuade him from going.*
– DERIVATIVES **dissuasion** n.
– ORIGIN Latin *dissuadere.*

distaff /diss-tahf/ • n. a stick or spindle on to which wool or flax is wound for spinning.
– ORIGIN Old English.

distaff side • n. the female side of a family.

distance • n. **1** the length of the space between two points: *I cycled the short distance home.* **2** the state of being distant. **3** a far-off point or place. **4** an interval of time. **5** the full length or time of a race or other contest. • v. (**distances**, **distancing**, **distanced**) **1** make distant. **2** (**distance oneself from**) dissociate oneself from.
– ORIGIN Latin *distantia.*

distant • adj. **1** far away in space or time. **2** at a specified distance: *the star is 15 light years distant from Earth.* **3** far apart in resemblance or relationship: *a distant acquaintance.* **4** aloof or reserved.
– DERIVATIVES **distantly** adv.

distaste • n. dislike.

distasteful • adj. unpleasant or offensive.

distemper • n. **1** a kind of paint made of powdered pigment mixed with glue or size, used on walls. **2** a disease affecting dogs, causing fever and coughing.
– ORIGIN Latin *distemperare* 'soak'.

distend • v. swell because of internal pressure.
– DERIVATIVES **distension** n.

– ORIGIN Latin *distendere*.

distil (US **distill**) ● v. (**distils, distilling, distilled**; US **distills, distilling, distilled**) **1** purify (a liquid) by heating it so that it vaporizes, then condensing the vapour and collecting the resulting liquid. **2** make (spirits) in this way. **3** extract the most important aspects of: *my notes were distilled into a book.*
– DERIVATIVES **distillation** n.
– ORIGIN Latin *distillare*.

distiller ● n. a person or company that manufactures spirits.
– DERIVATIVES **distillery** n. (pl. **distilleries**).

distinct ● adj. **1** noticeably different: *there are two distinct types of the disease.* **2** able to be perceived clearly by the senses.
– DERIVATIVES **distinctly** adv. **distinctness** n.
– ORIGIN Latin *distinctus*.

distinction ● n. **1** a noticeable difference or contrast. **2** the action of distinguishing. **3** outstanding excellence. **4** a special honour or recognition.

distinctive ● adj. characteristic of a person or thing, so distinguishing it from others: *the car's distinctive design.*
– DERIVATIVES **distinctively** adv. **distinctiveness** n.

distinguish ● v. **1** recognize or treat as different: *she can distinguish reality from fantasy.* **2** manage to see or hear. **3** be a distinctive characteristic of: *what distinguishes sport from games?* **4** (**distinguish oneself**) make oneself worthy of respect.
– DERIVATIVES **distinguishable** adj.
– ORIGIN Latin *distinguere*.

distinguished ● adj. **1** dignified in appearance. **2** commanding great respect.

distort ● v. **1** pull or twist out of shape. **2** give a misleading account of.
– DERIVATIVES **distortion** n.
– ORIGIN Latin *distorquere* 'twist apart'.

distract ● v. **1** prevent (someone) from giving their full attention to something. **2** divert (attention) from something.
– ORIGIN Latin *distrahere* 'draw apart'.

distraction ● n. **1** a thing that distracts someone's attention. **2** a thing offering entertainment. **3** mental agitation.

distraught ● adj. very worried and upset.
– ORIGIN Latin *distructus* 'pulled apart'.

distress ● n. **1** extreme anxiety, pain, or exhaustion. **2** the state of a ship or aircraft when in danger or difficulty. ● v. cause distress to.
– ORIGIN Old French *destresce*.

distribute ● v. (**distributes, distributing, distributed**) **1** hand or share out to a number of people. **2** (**be distributed**) be spread over an area. **3** supply (goods) to retailers.
– DERIVATIVES **distributable** adj.
– ORIGIN Latin *distribuere* 'divide up'.

distribution ● n. **1** the action of distributing. **2** the way in which something is distributed: *the uneven distribution of wealth.*

distributive ● adj. relating to distribution.

distributor ● n. **1** an agent who supplies goods to retailers. **2** a device in a petrol engine for passing electric current to each spark plug in turn.

district ● n. an area of a town or region, regarded as a unit for administrative purposes or because of a particular feature.
– ORIGIN Latin *districtus* 'territory of jurisdiction'.

district attorney ● n. (in the US) a public official who acts as prosecutor for the state or the federal government in court in a particular district.

district nurse ● n. (in the UK) a nurse who treats patients in their homes, operating within a particular district.

District of Columbia E
a federal district of the US, extending over the same area as the city of Washington.

distrust ● n. lack of trust. ● v. have little trust in.
– DERIVATIVES **distrustful** adj.

disturb ● v. **1** interrupt the sleep, relaxation, or privacy of. **2** interfere with the normal arrangement or functioning of. **3** make anxious. **4** (**disturbed**) having emotional or mental problems.
– ORIGIN Latin *disturbare*.

disturbance ● n. **1** the action of disturbing or the state of being disturbed. **2** a breakdown of peaceful behaviour.

disunited ● adj. lacking unity.
– DERIVATIVES **disunity** n.

disuse ● n. the state of not being used; neglect.
– DERIVATIVES **disused** adj.

ditch ● n. a narrow channel dug to hold or carry water. ● v. **1** make or repair ditches. **2** (with reference to an aircraft) bring or come down in a forced landing on the sea. **3** informal get rid of; give up.
– ORIGIN Old English.

dither ● v. (**dithers, dithering, dithered**) be indecisive. ● n. informal a state of agitation or indecision.
– DERIVATIVES **dithery** adj.
– ORIGIN from dialect *didder* 'tremble'.

ditto ● n. **1** the same thing again (used in lists). **2** (also **ditto mark**) a symbol consisting of two apostrophes („) placed under the item to be repeated.
– ORIGIN Italian *detto* 'said'.

ditty ● n. (pl. **ditties**) a short simple song.
– ORIGIN Old French *dite* 'composition'.

diuretic /dy-uh-ret-ik/ Med. ● adj. (of a drug) causing increased passing of urine.
– ORIGIN Greek *diourein* 'urinate'.

diurnal /dy-er-nuhl/ ● adj. **1** of or during the daytime. **2** daily.
– ORIGIN Latin *diurnalis*.

diva /dee-vuh/ ● n. a famous female opera singer.
– ORIGIN Latin, 'goddess'.

Divali ● n. var. of **DIWALI**.

divan /di-van/ ● n. **1** a bed consisting of a base and mattress but no footboard or headboard. **2** a long, low sofa without a back or arms.
– ORIGIN Persian, 'bench, court'.

dive ● v. (**dives, diving, dived**; US past and past part. also **dove** /*rhymes with* rove/) **1** plunge head first into water. **2** (of a submarine or diver) go under water. **3** plunge steeply downwards through the air. **4** move quickly or suddenly downwards or under cover: *he dived into an office building.* ● n. **1** an act of diving. **2** informal a disreputable nightclub or bar.
– ORIGIN Old English.

dive-bomb ● v. bomb (a target) while diving steeply in an aircraft.

diver ● n. **1** a person who dives under water as a sport or for their work. **2** a large diving waterbird.

diverge ● v. (**diverges**, **diverging**, **diverged**) **1** (of a route or line) separate from another route and go in a different direction. **2** (**diverge from**) be different from.
– DERIVATIVES **divergence** n.
– ORIGIN Latin *divergere*.

divergent ● adj. different.

divers /dy-verz/ ● adj. archaic various; several: *in divers places.*

diverse /dy-verss/ ● adj. widely varied.
– ORIGIN Latin *diversus*.

diversify ● v. (**diversifies**, **diversifying**, **diversified**) **1** make or become more varied. **2** (of a company) expand its range of products or field of operation.
– DERIVATIVES **diversification** n.

diversion ● n. **1** the action or an instance of diverting something: *the diversion of the country's largest river.* **2** Brit. an alternative route for use when the usual road is closed. **3** something intended to distract attention. **4** a recreation or pastime.
– DERIVATIVES **diversionary** adj.

diversity ● n. (pl. **diversities**) **1** the state of being varied. **2** a range of different things.

divert /dy-vert/ ● v. **1** change the direction or course of. **2** distract (someone or their attention). **3** amuse or entertain.
– ORIGIN Latin *divertere* 'turn in separate ways'.

divertissement /dee-vair-teess-mon/ ● n. a minor entertainment.
– ORIGIN French.

divest /dy-vest/ ● v. **1** (**divest of**) deprive of. **2** (**divest oneself of**) free oneself of.
– ORIGIN Old French *desvestir*.

divide ● v. (**divides**, **dividing**, **divided**) **1** separate into parts. **2** share out. **3** cause to disagree: *the question had divided the French for years.* **4** form a boundary between. **5** Math. find how many times (a number) contains another. ● n. a wide difference between two groups: *the North-South divide.*
– ORIGIN Latin *dividere* 'force apart'.

dividend ● n. **1** a sum of money that is divided among a number of people, such as the part of a company's profits paid to its shareholders. **2** (**dividends**) benefits: *persistence pays dividends.* **3** Math. a number to be divided by another number.
– ORIGIN Latin *dividendum* 'something to be divided'.

divider ● n. **1** a screen or piece of furniture that divides a room into separate parts. **2** (**dividers**) a measuring compass.

divination ● n. the practice of seeking knowledge of the future or the unknown by supernatural means.

divine[1] ● adj. **1** having to do with God or a god: *divine forces.* **2** informal excellent.
– DERIVATIVES **divinely** adv.
– ORIGIN Latin *divinus*.

divine[2] ● v. (**divines**, **divining**, **divined**) **1** discover by guesswork or intuition. **2** have supernatural insight into (the future).
– DERIVATIVES **diviner** n.
– ORIGIN Latin *divinare* 'predict'.

diving board ● n. a board projecting over a swimming pool, from which people dive in.

diving suit ● n. a watertight suit with a helmet and an air supply, worn for working or exploring deep under water.

divinity ● n. (pl. **divinities**) **1** the state of being divine. **2** a god or goddess. **3** the study of religion; theology.

divisible ● adj. **1** capable of being divided. **2** Math. (of a number) containing another number a number of times without a remainder.

division ● n. **1** the action of dividing or the state of being divided. **2** each of the parts into which something is divided. **3** a major section of an organization. **4** a number of sports teams grouped together for competitive purposes. **5** a partition.
– DERIVATIVES **divisional** adj.

division sign ● n. the sign ÷, placed between two numbers to show that the first is to be divided by the second.

divisive /di-vy-siv/ ● adj. causing disagreement or hostility between people.

divisor ● n. Math. a number by which another number is to be divided.

divorce ● n. the legal ending of a marriage. ● v. (**divorces**, **divorcing**, **divorced**) **1** legally end one's marriage with. **2** (**divorce from**) separate from: *jazz has become divorced from its origins.*
– ORIGIN Old French.

divorcee /di-vor-see/ ● n. a divorced person.

divot /di-vuht/ ● n. a piece of turf cut out of the ground.
– ORIGIN unknown.

divulge /dy-vulj/ ● v. (**divulges**, **divulging**, **divulged**) reveal (information).
– ORIGIN Latin *divulgare* 'publish widely'.

Diwali /di-wah-li/ (also **Divali**) ● n. a Hindu festival with lights, held in October and November to celebrate the end of the monsoon.
– ORIGIN Sanskrit, 'row of lights'.

DIY ● n. esp. Brit. the activity of decorating and making repairs in the home oneself rather than employing a professional.
– ORIGIN from *do-it-yourself*.

dizzy ● adj. (**dizzier**, **dizziest**) **1** having a sensation of spinning around and losing one's balance. **2** informal (of a woman) silly but attractive. ● v. (**dizzies**, **dizzying**, **dizzied**) make unsteady or confused.
– DERIVATIVES **dizzily** adv. **dizziness** n.
– ORIGIN Old English, 'foolish'.

DJ ● n. **1** a disc jockey. **2** a person who uses samples of recorded music to make techno or rap music.

Djakarta E
/juh-kar-tuh/ (also **Jakarta**) the capital of Indonesia, situated in NW Java.

djellaba /jel-luh-buh/ ● n. a loose woollen hooded cloak traditionally worn by Arabs.
– ORIGIN Arabic.

Djibouti E
/ji-boo-ti/ (also **Jibuti**) a country on the NE coast of Africa; capital, Djibouti.
– DERIVATIVES **Djiboutian** adj. & n.

dl ● abbrev. decilitre(s).

DLitt ● abbrev. Doctor of Letters.
– ORIGIN Latin *Doctor Litterarum*.

DM (also **D-mark**) ● abbrev. Deutschmark.

dm ● abbrev. decimetre(s).

DMA ● abbrev. Computing direct memory access.

DMus ● abbrev. Doctor of Music.

DNA ● n. deoxyribonucleic acid, a substance carrying genetic information that is found in the cell nuclei of nearly all organisms.

DNA fingerprinting ● n. = **GENETIC FINGERPRINTING**.

Dnieper E
/dnee-per/ a river of eastern Europe, rising in Russia west of Moscow and flowing southwards through Ukraine to the Black Sea.

do[1] ● v. (**does**, **doing**, **did**; past part. **done**) **1** carry out or complete (an action, duty, or task). **2** act or progress in a specified way: *the team were doing badly.* **3** work on (something) to bring it to a required state. **4** make or provide. **5** have a particular effect on: *the walk will do me good.* **6** work at for a living or take as one's subject of study. **7** be suitable or acceptable: *if he's like you, he'll do.* **8** (**be/have done with**) give up concern for. **9** informal swindle. ● auxiliary verb **1** used before a verb in questions and negative statements. **2** used to refer back to a verb already mentioned: *he looks better than he did before.* **3** used in commands, or to give emphasis to a verb: *do sit down.* ● n. (pl. **dos** or **do's**) Brit. informal a party or other social event.
– PHRASES **be done up** be dressed elaborately. **can** (or **could**) **do with** informal would find useful or would like. **do away with** informal put an end to; kill. **do for 1** informal defeat or kill. **2** be good enough for. **do in** informal **1** kill. **2** (**be done in**) be tired out. **dos and don'ts** rules of behaviour. **do up 1** fasten, wrap, or arrange. **2** informal renovate or redecorate.
– DERIVATIVES **doable** adj. (informal) **doer** n.
– ORIGIN Old English.

do[2] ● n. var. of **DOH**.

Dobermann /doh-ber-muhn/ (also **Doberman** or **Dobermann pinscher** /pin-sher/) ● n. a large breed of dog with powerful jaws.
– ORIGIN named after the 19th-century German dog-breeder Ludwig *Dobermann* + German *Pinscher* 'terrier'.

docile ● adj. willing to accept control or instruction; submissive.
– DERIVATIVES **docilely** adv. **docility** n.
– ORIGIN Latin *docilis* 'easily taught'.

dock[1] ● n. an enclosed area of water in a port for the loading, unloading, and repair of ships. ● v. **1** (with reference to a ship) come or bring into a dock. **2** (of a spacecraft) join with a space station or another spacecraft in space.
– ORIGIN Dutch or German *docke*.

dock[2] ● n. the enclosure in a criminal court for a person on trial.
– ORIGIN prob. from Flemish *dok* 'chicken coop'.

dock[3] ● n. a weed with broad leaves.
– ORIGIN Old English.

dock[4] ● v. **1** deduct (money) from a person's wages. **2** cut short (an animal's tail).
– ORIGIN uncertain.

docker ● n. a person employed in a port to load and unload ships.

docket ● n. Brit. a document accompanying a batch of goods that lists its contents, certifies payment of duty, or entitles the holder to delivery.
– ORIGIN perh. from **DOCK**[4].

dockyard ● n. an area with docks and equipment for repairing and building ships.

doctor ● n. **1** a person who is qualified to practise medicine. **2** (**Doctor**) a person who holds the highest university degree. ● v. **1** change in order to deceive; falsify. **2** add a harmful or strong ingredient to (a food or drink). **3** Brit. remove the sexual organs of (an animal).
– ORIGIN Latin, 'teacher'.

doctoral ● adj. relating to a doctorate.

doctorate ● n. the highest degree awarded by a university.

doctrinaire /dok-tri-**nair**/ ● adj. very strict in applying beliefs or principles.
– ORIGIN French.

doctrine /**dok**-trin/ ● n. a set of beliefs or principles held and taught by a religious, political, or other group.
– DERIVATIVES **doctrinal** /dok-**try**-n'l/ adj.
– ORIGIN Latin *doctrina* 'teaching'.

docudrama ● n. a television film based on a dramatized version of real events.

document ● n. /**dok**-yoo-muhnt/ a piece of written, printed, or electronic matter that provides information or evidence. ● v. /**dok**-yoo-ment/ record in written or other form.
– ORIGIN Latin *documentum* 'lesson'.

documentary ● adj. **1** consisting of documents and other material. **2** using film, photographs, and sound recordings of real events to provide a factual report. ● n. (pl. **documentaries**) a documentary film or television or radio programme.

documentation ● n. **1** documents providing official information or evidence. **2** written specifications or instructions for a computer.

dodder ● v. (**dodders**, **doddering**, **doddered**) be slow and unsteady.
– DERIVATIVES **doddery** adj.
– ORIGIN from **DITHER**.

doddle ● n. Brit. informal a very easy task.
– ORIGIN unknown.

dodecagon /doh-**dek**-uh-guhn/ ● n. a plane figure with twelve straight sides and angles.

dodecahedron /doh-de-kuh-**hee**-druhn/ ● n. (pl. **dodecahedra** /doh-de-kuh-**hee**-druh/ or **dodecahedrons**) a three-dimensional shape with twelve plane faces.
– ORIGIN Greek *dōdekaedros* 'twelve-faced'.

Dodecanese E
/doh-di-kuh-**neez**/ a group of twelve islands in the SE Aegean, of which the largest is Rhodes.

dodge ● v. (**dodges**, **dodging**, **dodged**) **1** avoid by a sudden quick movement. **2** avoid in a cunning or dishonest way. ● n. an act of avoiding something.
– ORIGIN unknown.

dodgem ● n. a small electric car with rubber bumpers, driven at a funfair with the aim of bumping other such cars.
– ORIGIN US trademark, from *dodge them*.

dodger ● n. informal a person who avoids something that is required of them: *a tax dodger.*

Dodgson, E
Charles Lutwidge, see **CARROLL**.

dodgy ● adj. (**dodgier**, **dodgiest**) Brit. informal **1** dishonest. **2** risky. **3** not good or reliable.

dodo /doh-doh/ ● n. (pl. **dodos** or **dodoes**) a large extinct flightless bird formerly found on Mauritius.
– ORIGIN Portuguese *doudo* 'simpleton'.

Dodoma E
/doh-**doh**-muh/ the capital of Tanzania.

DoE ● abbrev. (formerly in the UK) Department of the Environment.

d

doe ● n. **1** a female deer or reindeer. **2** the female of some other animals, such as a rabbit or hare.
– ORIGIN Old English.

does 3rd person sing. present of **DO**[1].

doesn't ● contr. does not.

doff ● v. remove (one's hat) when greeting someone.
– ORIGIN from *do off*.

dog ● n. **1** a four-legged meat-eating mammal, kept as a pet or used for work or hunting. **2** any member of the dog family, such as the wolf. **3** the male of an animal of the dog family. ● v. (**dogs**, **dogging**, **dogged**) **1** follow closely and persistently. **2** cause continual trouble for: *he was dogged by ankle problems.*
– PHRASES **a dog in the manger** a person who prevents others from having things that they do not need themselves. [ORIGIN from the fable of the dog that lay in a manger to prevent the ox and horse from eating the hay.] **go to the dogs** informal get much worse.
– ORIGIN Old English.

dog collar ● n. informal a white upright collar worn by the Christian clergy.

dog days ● pl. n. the hottest period of the year (formerly reckoned from the first time Sirius, the Dog Star, rose at the same time as the sun).

doge /dohj/ ● n. hist. the chief magistrate of Venice or Genoa.
– ORIGIN Italian *doze*.

dog-eared ● adj. having worn or battered corners.

dog-end ● n. informal a cigarette end.

dogfight ● n. a close combat between military aircraft.

dogfish ● n. a small shark with a long tail, living close to the seabed.

dogged /dog-gid/ ● adj. very persistent.
– DERIVATIVES **doggedly** adv.

doggerel /dog-guh-ruhl/ ● n. badly written verse.
– ORIGIN prob. from **DOG**.

doggo ● adv. (in phr. **lie doggo**) Brit. informal remain still and quiet to avoid being found.
– ORIGIN uncertain.

doggy ● adj. **1** having to do with dogs. **2** fond of dogs.

doggy bag ● n. a bag used to take home leftover food from a restaurant.

doggy-paddle ● n. a simple swimming stroke like that of a dog.

doghouse ● n. N. Amer. a dog's kennel.
– PHRASES **in the doghouse** informal in disgrace.

dog-leg ● n. a sharp bend.

dogma ● n. a principle or principles laid down by an authority and intended to be accepted without question.
– ORIGIN Greek, 'opinion'.

dogmatic ● adj. firmly putting forward one's opinions as true.
– DERIVATIVES **dogmatically** adv. **dogmatism** n.

do-gooder ● n. a well-meaning but unrealistic or interfering person.

dog rose ● n. a wild rose with pink or white flowers.

dogsbody ● n. (pl. **dogsbodies**) Brit. informal a person who is given boring, menial tasks.

dog-tired ● adj. extremely tired.

dog-tooth ● n. a small check pattern with notched corners.

dogwood ● n. a shrub or small tree with red stems, colourful berries, and hard wood.
– ORIGIN from the use of the wood to make 'dogs' (i.e. skewers).

DoH ● abbrev. (in the UK) Department of Health.

doh /doh/ (also **do**) ● n. Music the first note of a major scale, coming before 'ray'.
– ORIGIN Italian *do*.

Doha E
/doh-har/ the capital of Qatar.

doily ● n. (pl. **doilies**) a small ornamental mat made of lace or paper.
– ORIGIN from *Doiley* or *Doyley*, a 17th-century London draper.

doings ● pl. n. a person's actions or activities.

Doisneau E
/dwa-noh/, Robert (1912–94), French photographer, famous for his photos of Paris life.

Dolby /dol-bi/ ● n. trademark **1** a noise-reduction system used in tape recording. **2** an electronic system providing stereophonic sound for cinemas and televisions.
– ORIGIN named after the American engineer Ray M. *Dolby* (b.1933).

doldrums /dol-druhmz/ ● pl. n. (**the doldrums**) **1** a state of inactivity or depression. **2** a region of the Atlantic Ocean where the wind is erratic or scarce.
– ORIGIN perh. from **DULL**.

dole ● n. Brit. informal benefit paid by the state to unemployed people: *I ended up on the dole.* ● v. (**doles**, **doling**, **doled**) (**dole out**) distribute.
– ORIGIN Old English, 'division or share'.

doleful ● adj. sad or depressing.
– DERIVATIVES **dolefully** adv.
– ORIGIN Old French *doel* 'mourning'.

dolerite /dol-luh-ryt/ ● n. a dark igneous rock.
– ORIGIN Greek *doleros* 'deceptive' (because it resembles diorite).

doll ● n. a small model of a human figure, used as a child's toy. ● v. (**be dolled up**) informal be dressed smartly and attractively.
– ORIGIN from the woman's name *Dorothy*.

dollar ● n. the basic unit of money of the US, Canada, Australia, and some other countries.
– ORIGIN German *Thaler*, referring to a silver coin.

dollar sign (also **dollar mark**) ● n. the sign $, representing a dollar.

dollop informal ● n. a shapeless mass or lump. ● v. (**dollops**, **dolloping**, **dolloped**) add or serve out (a mass of something) casually.
– ORIGIN perh. Scandinavian.

dolly bird ● n. Brit. informal, dated an attractive and fashionable young woman.

dolman sleeve /dol-muhn/ ● n. a loose sleeve cut in one piece with the body of a garment.
– ORIGIN Turkish *dolama* 'open robe'.

dolmen /dol-men/ ● n. a prehistoric tomb with a large flat stone laid on upright ones.
– ORIGIN Cornish, 'hole of a stone'.

dolomite /dol-uh-myt/ ● n. a mineral or rock consisting chiefly of a carbonate of calcium and magnesium.
– ORIGIN named after the French geologist M. *Dolomieu* (1750–1801).

Dolomite Mountains E
/dol-uh-myt/ a range of the Alps in northern Italy.

dolour /dol-er/ (US **dolor**) ● n. literary great sorrow or distress.
– DERIVATIVES **dolorous** adj.
– ORIGIN Latin *dolor* 'pain, grief'.

dolphin ● n. a small whale with a beak-like snout and a curved fin on the back.
– ORIGIN Greek *delphin*.

dolphinarium /dol-fi-nair-i-uhm/ ● n. (pl. **dolphinariums** or **dolphinaria**) an aquarium in which dolphins are kept and trained for public entertainment.

dolt /dohlt/ ● n. a stupid person.
– ORIGIN perh. from DULL.

-dom ● suffix forming nouns referring to: **1** a state or condition: *freedom*. **2** status: *earldom*. **3** a place or area: *kingdom*. **4** a class of people: *officialdom*.
– ORIGIN Old English, 'decree'.

domain /doh-mayn/ ● n. **1** an area controlled by a ruler or government. **2** an area of activity or knowledge. **3** a subset of the Internet with addresses sharing a common suffix.
– ORIGIN Old French *demeine* 'belonging to a lord'.

dome ● n. **1** a rounded roof of a building, with a circular base. **2** a stadium or other building with a rounded roof.
– ORIGIN Italian *duomo* 'cathedral, dome'.

domestic ● adj. **1** relating to a home or family. **2** for use in the home. **3** (of an animal) tame and kept by humans. **4** existing or occurring within a country; not foreign. ● n. a person employed to do household tasks.
– DERIVATIVES **domestically** adv.
– ORIGIN Latin *domesticus*.

domesticate ● v. (**domesticates, domesticating, domesticated**) **1** tame (an animal) and keep it as a pet or for farm produce. **2** grow (a plant) for food.
– DERIVATIVES **domestication** n.

domesticity ● n. home or family life.

domicile /dom-i-syl/ formal or Law ● n. **1** the country in which a person lives permanently. **2** a person's home. ● v. (**domiciles, domiciling, domiciled**) (**be domiciled**) be living in a particular country or place.
– ORIGIN Latin *domicilium* 'dwelling'.

domiciliary /dom-i-sil-i-uh-ri/ ● adj. in someone's home: *a domiciliary visit*.

dominant ● adj. **1** most important, powerful, or influential: *a dominant position in the market*. **2** (of a high place or object) overlooking others. **3** (of a gene) appearing in offspring even if a contrary gene is also inherited. Compare with RECESSIVE.
– DERIVATIVES **dominance** n. **dominantly** adv.

dominate ● v. (**dominates, dominating, dominated**) **1** have a very strong influence over. **2** be the most important or noticeable person or thing in: *the race was dominated by the 1999 champion*.
– DERIVATIVES **domination** n.
– ORIGIN Latin *dominari* 'rule'.

domineering ● adj. arrogant and overbearing.
– ORIGIN Latin *dominari* 'rule'.

Domingo E
/duh-ming-goh/, Plácido (b.1941), Spanish-born tenor.

Dominic, St E
(*c*.1170–1221), Spanish priest and friar. In 1216 he founded the Order of Friars Preachers at Toulouse in France; its members became known as Dominicans. Feast day, 8 August.

Dominica E
/dom-i-nee-kuh, duh-min-i-kuh/ an island in the Caribbean, the northernmost and largest of the Windward Islands, capital, Roseau.

Dominican /duh-min-i-kuhn/ ● n. a member of an order of friars founded by St Dominic, or of a corresponding order of nuns.

Dominican Republic E
/duh-min-i-kuhn/ a country in the Caribbean occupying the eastern part of the island of Hispaniola; capital, Santo Domingo.

dominion ● n. **1** supreme power or control. **2** the territory of a sovereign or government.
– ORIGIN Latin *dominium*.

Domino, E
Fats (b.1928; born *Antoine Domino*), American pianist, singer, and songwriter. His music forms part of the transition from rhythm and blues to rock and roll.

domino ● n. (pl. **dominoes**) any of 28 small oblong pieces marked with 0–6 pips in each half, used in the game of **dominoes**.
– ORIGIN prob. from Latin *dominus* 'lord'.

domino effect ● n. an effect compared to a row of dominoes falling, when a political event in one country seems to cause similar events elsewhere.

Domitian E
/duh-mi-sh'n/ (AD 51–96; full name *Titus Flavius Domitianus*), son of Vespasian, Roman emperor 81–96.

Don E
a river in Russia which rises near Tula, south-east of Moscow, and flows generally south to the Sea of Azov.

don[1] ● n. a university teacher, especially at Oxford or Cambridge.
– ORIGIN Spanish.

don[2] ● v. (**dons, donning, donned**) put on (an item of clothing).
– ORIGIN from *do on*.

donate ● v. (**donates, donating, donated**) **1** give (something) to a good cause. **2** allow (blood or an organ) to be removed from one's body and given to another person.
– ORIGIN Latin *donare*.

Donatello E
/don-uh-**tel**-loh/ (1386–1466; born *Donato di Betto Bardi*), Italian sculptor, famous for his lifelike sculptures and a pioneer of scientific perspective.

donation ● n. something that is given to a charity.

Doncaster E
an industrial town and unitary council in northern England.

d

done past part. of DO[1]. ● adj. **1** cooked thoroughly. **2** no longer happening or existing. **3** informal socially acceptable: *the done thing.* ● exclam. (in response to an offer) I accept.

Donegal E
/don-i-**gawl**/ a county in the extreme northwest of the Republic of Ireland; capital, Lifford.

doner kebab /**don**-er/ ● n. a Turkish dish of spiced lamb cooked on a spit and served in slices.
– ORIGIN from Turkish *döner* 'rotating' and *kebap* 'roast meat'.

Donizetti E
/don-i-**tzet**-ti/, Gaetano (1797–1848), Italian composer. His operas include tragedies such as *Lucia di Lammermoor* and comedies such as *Don Pasquale.*

donjon /**don**-juhn/ ● n. the great tower or innermost keep of a castle.
– ORIGIN from DUNGEON.

Don Juan /don **hwahn**, don **joo**-uhn/ ● n. a man who seduces many women.
– ORIGIN named after a legendary Spanish nobleman.

donkey ● n. (pl. **donkeys**) **1** a domesticated mammal of the horse family with long ears and a braying call. **2** informal a foolish person.
– PHRASES **donkey's years** informal a very long time. **talk the hind leg off a donkey** Brit. informal talk continuously.
– ORIGIN perh. from DUN[1], or from the man's name *Duncan.*

donkey jacket ● n. Brit. a heavy jacket with a patch of waterproof material across the shoulders.

donkey work ● n. informal the part of a job that is demanding or boring.

Donne E
/dun/, John (1572–1631), English metaphysical poet and priest, noted for his *Satires, Elegies,* and love poems. As dean of St Paul's from 1621, he was a celebrated preacher.

donnish ● adj. like a college don, particularly in having a fussy manner.

donor ● n. a person who donates something.

don't ● contr. do not.

donut ● n. US = DOUGHNUT.

doodle ● v. (**doodles**, **doodling**, **doodled**) scribble absent-mindedly. ● n. a drawing made absent-mindedly.
– ORIGIN German *dudeldopp* 'simpleton'.

doolally /doo-**lal**-li/ ● adj. informal temporarily insane.
– ORIGIN from *Deolali* (a town near Bombay) + Urdu *tap* 'fever'.

doom ● n. death, destruction, or another terrible fate. ● v. (**be doomed**) be fated to fail or be destroyed.
– ORIGIN Old English, 'decree'.

doomsday ● n. **1** the last day of the world's existence. **2** (in religious belief) the day of the Last Judgement.

door ● n. **1** a movable barrier at the entrance to a building, room, or vehicle, or as part of a cupboard. **2** the distance from one building in a row to another: *he lived two doors away.*
– PHRASES **out of doors** in or into the open air.
– ORIGIN Old English.

doorbell ● n. a bell in a building which can be rung by visitors outside.

do-or-die ● adj. showing or requiring a determination not to be deterred.

doorman ● n. a man who is on duty at the entrance to a large building.

doormat ● n. **1** a mat placed in a doorway for wiping the shoes. **2** informal a person who allows other to control them.

doornail ● n. (in phr. **dead as a doornail**) completely dead.

doorstep ● n. a step leading up to the outer door of a house. ● v. (**doorsteps**, **doorstepping**, **doorstepped**) Brit. informal (of a journalist) wait uninvited outside the home of (someone) for an interview or photograph.

doorstop ● n. an object that keeps a door open or in place.

dope ● n. **1** informal an illegal drug, especially cannabis. **2** a drug used to improve the performance of an athlete, racehorse, or greyhound. **3** informal a stupid person. ● v. (**dopes**, **doping**, **doped**) give a drug to.
– ORIGIN Dutch *doop* 'sauce'.

dopey (also **dopy**) ● adj. (**dopier**, **dopiest**) informal **1** in a semi-conscious state from sleepiness or a drug. **2** stupid.

doppelgänger /**dop**-puhl-geng-er, **dop**-puhl-gang-er/ ● n. a ghost or double of a living person.
– ORIGIN German, 'double-goer'.

Doppler effect /**dop**-pler/ ● n. Physics an increase (or decrease) in the apparent frequency of sound, light, or other waves as the source and the observer move towards (or away from) each other.
– ORIGIN named after the Austrian physicist Johann Christian *Doppler* (1803–53).

Dordogne E
/dor-**doyn**/ a river of western France which rises in the Auvergne and flows westwards to meet the River Garonne and form the Gironde estuary north of Bordeaux.

dork ● n. informal a worthless or stupid person.
– ORIGIN perh. from DIRK.

dormant ● adj. **1** (of an animal) in or as if in a deep sleep. **2** (of a plant or bud) alive but not growing. **3** (of a volcano) temporarily inactive.
– ORIGIN Old French, 'sleeping'.

dormer (also **dormer window**) ● n. a window set vertically into a sloping roof.
– ORIGIN Old French *dormir* 'to sleep'.

dormitory ● n. (pl. **dormitories**) a bedroom for a number of people in an institution. ● adj. referring a place from which people travel to work in a nearby city.
– ORIGIN Latin *dormitorium.*

dormouse ● n. (pl. **dormice**) a small mouse-

like rodent with a bushy tail.
– ORIGIN unknown.

dorsal ● adj. tech. having to do with the upper side or back. Compare with VENTRAL.
– ORIGIN Latin *dorsum* 'back'.

Dorset E
a county of SW England; county town, Dorchester.

dory /*rhymes with* story/ ● n. (pl. **dories**) a narrow marine fish with a large mouth.
– ORIGIN French *dorée* 'gilded'.

DOS ● abbrev. Computing disk operating system.

dosage ● n. the size of a dose of medicine or radiation.

dose ● n. **1** a quantity of a medicine or drug taken at one time. **2** an amount of radiation received or absorbed at one time. ● v. (**doses, dosing, dosed**) give a dose of medicine to.
– ORIGIN Greek *dosis* 'gift'.

dosh ● n. Brit. informal money.
– ORIGIN unknown.

doss ● v. Brit. informal **1** sleep in rough or makeshift conditions. **2** spend time idly.
– DERIVATIVES **dosser** n.
– ORIGIN perh. from Latin *dorsum* 'back'.

dossier /doss-i-er, doss-i-ay/ ● n. a collection of documents about a person or subject.
– ORIGIN French.

Dostoevsky E
/doss-toy-eff-ski/ (also **Dostoyevsky**), Fyodor (Mikhailovich) (1821–81), Russian novelist. He is best known for such novels as *Crime and Punishment* and *The Brothers Karamazov*, which reveal his psychological insight and savage humour.

DoT ● abbrev. (in Canada and formerly in the UK) Department of Transport.

dot ● n. **1** a small round mark or spot. **2** the shorter signal of the two used in Morse code. ● v. (**dots, dotting, dotted**) **1** mark with a dot or dots. **2** scatter over (an area).
– PHRASES **on the dot** informal exactly on time. **the year dot** Brit. informal a very long time ago.
– ORIGIN Old English, 'head of a boil'.

dotage /doh-tij/ ● n. the period of life in which a person is old and weak.
– ORIGIN from DOTE.

dotard /doh-terd/ ● n. a person who is weak or senile from old age.

dot-com ● n. a company that conducts its business on the Internet.
– ORIGIN from '.com' in an Internet address, indicating a commercial site.

dote ● v. (**dotes, doting, doted**) (**dote on/upon**) be excessively fond of.
– ORIGIN Dutch *doten* 'be silly'.

dotty ● adj. (**dottier, dottiest**) Brit. informal slightly mad or eccentric.
– ORIGIN perh. from former *dote* 'fool'.

double ● adj. **1** consisting of two equal, identical, or similar parts or things. **2** having twice the usual size, quantity, or strength: *a double brandy.* **3** designed to be used by two people. **4** having two different roles or interpretations: *she began a double life.* **5** (of a flower) having more than one circle of petals. ● adv. twice the amount or quantity. ● n. **1** a thing which is twice as large as usual or is made up of two parts. **2** a person who looks exactly like another. **3** (**doubles**) a game involving sides made up of two players. ● pron. an amount twice as large as usual: *he paid double and had his own room.* ● v. (**doubles, doubling, doubled**) **1** make or become double. **2** fold or bend over on itself. **3** (**double up**) bend over or curl up with pain or laughter. **4** (**double (up) as**) be used in or play a different role: *the van doubled as a mobile kitchen.* **5** (**double back**) go back in the direction one has come.
– PHRASES **at the double** very fast.
– DERIVATIVES **doubly** adv.
– ORIGIN Latin *duplus*.

double agent ● n. an agent who pretends to act as a spy for one country while in fact acting for its enemy.

double-barrelled ● adj. Brit. (of a surname) having two parts joined by a hyphen.

double bass ● n. the largest and lowest-pitched instrument of the violin family.

double-book ● v. mistakenly reserve (something) for two different customers at the same time.

double-breasted ● adj. (of a jacket or coat) having a large overlap at the front and two rows of buttons.

double-check ● v. check again.

double chin ● n. a roll of flesh below a person's chin.

double cream ● n. Brit. thick cream with a high fat content.

double-cross ● v. betray (a person one is supposedly helping).

double-dealing ● n. deceitful behaviour.

double-decker ● n. a bus with two levels.

double Dutch ● n. Brit. informal language that is hard to understand.

double-edged ● adj. having two opposing aspects or possible outcomes.

double entendre /doo-b'l on-ton-druh/ ● n. (pl. **double entendres** /doo-b'l on-ton-druh/) a word or phrase with two meanings, one of which is usually indecent.
– ORIGIN from former French, 'double understanding'.

double figures ● pl. n. a number from 10 to 99 inclusive.

double glazing ● n. windows having two layers of glass with a space between them.

double helix ● n. a pair of parallel helices with a common axis, especially that in the structure of DNA.

double-jointed ● adj. (of a person) having unusually flexible joints.

double negative ● n. Grammar a negative statement containing two negative elements (e.g. *didn't say nothing*).

USAGE double negative
If you say *I don't know nothing*, this is not good English. The structure is called a **double negative** because it is the use of two negative words in the same clause to convey a single negative. This is bad English because the two negative elements cancel each other out to give a positive statement, so that *I don't know nothing* would be taken to mean *I know something*; you should therefore say *I don't know anything* to avoid confusion.

double pneumonia ● n. pneumonia affecting both lungs.

doublespeak ● n. language that is deliber-

ately unclear or has more than one meaning.
– ORIGIN see **DOUBLETHINK**.

double standard • n. a rule or principle applied unfairly in different ways to different people.

doublet • n. hist. a man's short close-fitting padded jacket.
– ORIGIN Old French, 'something folded'.

double take • n. a delayed reaction to something unexpected.

doublethink • n. the acceptance of conflicting opinions or beliefs at the same time.
– ORIGIN coined by George Orwell in his novel *Nineteen Eighty-Four*.

double time • n. a rate of pay equal to double the standard rate.

doubloon /dub-loon/ • n. hist. a Spanish gold coin.
– ORIGIN Spanish *doblón*.

doubt • n. a feeling of uncertainty. • v. **1** feel uncertain about. **2** question the truth of.
– PHRASES **no doubt** certainly; probably.
– DERIVATIVES **doubter** n.
– ORIGIN Latin *dubius* 'doubtful'.

doubtful • adj. **1** feeling uncertain. **2** causing uncertainty. **3** unlikely.
– DERIVATIVES **doubtfully** adv.

doubting Thomas • n. a person who refuses to believe something without proof.
– ORIGIN referring to the apostle Thomas (Gospel of John, Chapter 20).

doubtless • adv. very probably.

douche /doosh/ • n. **1** a shower of water. **2** a jet of liquid applied to part of the body for cleansing or medicinal purposes. • v. (**douches**, **douching**, **douched**) spray with or use a douche.
– ORIGIN French.

dough • n. **1** a thick mixture of flour and liquid, for baking into bread or pastry. **2** informal money.
– DERIVATIVES **doughy** adj.
– ORIGIN Old English.

doughnut (also US **donut**) • n. a small fried cake or ring of sweetened dough.

doughty /dow-ti/ • adj. archaic or humorous brave and resolute.
– ORIGIN Old English.

Douglas E
the capital of the Isle of Man.

Douglas-Home E
/dug-luhss **hyoom**/, Sir Alec, Baron Home of the Hirsel of Coldstream (1903–95; born *Alexander Frederick Douglas-Home*), British Conservative statesman, Prime Minister 1963–4.

dour /*rhymes with* tower/ • adj. very severe, stern, or gloomy.
– ORIGIN prob. from Scottish Gaelic *dúr* 'dull, obstinate'.

Douro E
/**door**-oh/ a river of the Iberian peninsula, rising in central Spain and flowing west through Portugal to the Atlantic Ocean near Oporto.

douse /dowss/ (also **dowse**) • v. (**douses**, **dousing**, **doused**; also **dowses**, **dowsing**, **dowsed**) **1** drench with liquid. **2** extinguish (a fire or light).
– ORIGIN perh. from Dutch and German *dossen* 'strike, beat'.

dove[1] /duv/ • n. **1** a bird with a small head and a cooing voice, very similar to a pigeon. **2** a person who favours a policy of peace and negotiation.
– ORIGIN Old Norse.

dove[2] /dohv/ N. Amer. past of **DIVE**.

dovecote /duv-kot/ • n. a shelter with nest holes for domesticated pigeons.
– ORIGIN Old English.

Dover E
a ferry port in Kent, on the coast of the English Channel. It is mainland Britain's nearest point to the Continent, being only 35 km (22 miles) from Calais.

dovetail • n. a wedge-shaped joint formed by interlocking two pieces of wood. • v. **1** join by means of a dovetail. **2** fit together easily or conveniently: *flights that dovetail with the working day.*

dowager /dow-uh-jer/ • n. **1** a widow who holds a title or property from her late husband. **2** informal a dignified elderly woman.
– ORIGIN Old French *douagiere*.

dowdy • adj. (**dowdier**, **dowdiest**) (especially of a woman) unfashionable and dull in appearance.

dowel /*rhymes with* towel/ • n. a headless peg used for holding together components.
– ORIGIN perh. from German *dovel*.

dower /*rhymes with* tower/ • n. a widow's share for life of her late husband's estate.
– ORIGIN Old French *douaire*.

Dow Jones index E
/dow **johnz**/ (also **Dow Jones average**) an index of figures indicating the relative price of shares on the New York Stock Exchange, based on the average price of selected stocks.

Down E
one of the Six Counties of Northern Ireland; chief town, Downpatrick.

down[1] • adv. **1** towards, in, or at a lower place, position, or level: *he put his glass down | output was down by 20%.* **2** to a smaller amount or size, or a more basic state. **3** in or into a weaker or worse position or condition. **4** away from a central place or the north: *they're living down south.* **5** from an earlier to a later point in time or order: *farms were passed down within the family.* **6** in or into writing. **7** (of a computer system) out of action. • prep. **1** from a higher to a lower point of. **2** at a point further along the course of: *he lived down the street.* **3** along. **4** informal at or to. • adj. **1** directed or moving downwards. **2** unhappy. • v. informal **1** knock or bring to the ground. **2** consume (a drink).
– PHRASES **be down to 1** be caused by. **2** be left with only (the specified amount). **down in the mouth** informal unhappy. **down with ——** expressing strong dislike.
– ORIGIN Old English.

down[2] • n. soft fine feathers or hairs.
– ORIGIN Old Norse.

down[3] • n. **1** a gently rolling hill. **2** (**the Downs**) an area of chalk and limestone hills in southern England.
– ORIGIN Old English.

down and out • adj. homeless and without money; destitute. • n. (**down-and-out**) a destitute person.

down at heel • **adj.** esp. Brit. shabby because of lack of money.

downbeat • **adj.** **1** gloomy. **2** relaxed and low-key. • **n.** Music an accented beat, usually the first of the bar.

downcast • **adj.** **1** (of eyes) looking downwards. **2** downhearted.

downer • **n.** informal **1** a tranquillizing or depressant drug. **2** something depressing.

downfall • **n.** a loss of power, wealth, or status.

downgrade • **v.** (**downgrades**, **downgrading**, **downgraded**) reduce to a lower rank or level of importance.

downhearted • **adj.** feeling sad or discouraged.

downhill /down-**hil**/ • **adv. & adj.** **1** towards the bottom of a slope. **2** into a steadily worsening situation: *the business is going downhill.*

Downing Street [E]
a street in Westminster, London. No. 10 is the official residence of the Prime Minister; No. 11 is the home of the Chancellor of the Exchequer.

download • **v.** copy (data) from one computer system to another or to a disk.

downmarket • **adj.** esp. Brit. cheap and of poor quality.

down payment • **n.** an initial payment made when buying on credit.

downplay • **v.** make (something) appear less important than it really is.

downpour • **n.** a heavy fall of rain.

downright • **adj.** utter; complete. • **adv.** extremely.

downriver • **adv. & adj.** towards or at a point nearer the mouth of a river.

downside • **n.** the negative aspect of something.

downsize • **v.** (**downsizes**, **downsizing**, **downsized**) **1** make (an organization) smaller by shedding staff. **2** (of an organization) shed staff.

Down's syndrome • **n.** a medical disorder arising from a genetic defect, causing mental and physical abnormalities.
– ORIGIN named after the English physician John L. H. *Down* (1828–96).

downstairs • **adv. & adj.** down a flight of stairs; to a lower floor. • **n.** the ground floor or lower floors of a building.

downstream • **adv. & adj.** in the direction in which a stream or river flows.

down-to-earth • **adj.** practical and realistic.

downtown • **adj. & adv.** esp. N. Amer. in, to, or towards the central area of a city.

downtrodden • **adj.** treated badly by people in power.

downturn • **n.** a decline in economic or other activity.

down under • **n.** informal Australia and New Zealand.

downward • **adv.** (also **downwards**) towards a lower point or level. • **adj.** moving towards a lower point or level.

downwind • **adv. & adj.** in the direction in which the wind is blowing.

downy • **adj.** covered with fine soft hair or feathers.

dowry /dow-ri/ • **n.** (pl. **dowries**) property or money brought by a bride to her husband on their marriage.
– ORIGIN Old French *dowarie.*

dowse[1] /dowz/ • **v.** (**dowses**, **dowsing**, **dowsed**) search for underground water or minerals with a pointer which is supposedly moved by unseen influences.
– DERIVATIVES **dowser** n.
– ORIGIN unknown.

dowse[2] • **v.** var. of DOUSE.

doxology /dok-**sol**-uh-ji/ • **n.** (pl. **doxologies**) a set form of prayer praising God.
– ORIGIN Greek *doxologia.*

doyen /doy-yen/ • **n.** (fem. **doyenne** /doy-**yen**/) the most respected or prominent person in a particular field: *he was the doyen of British physicists.*
– ORIGIN French.

Doyle, [E]
Sir Arthur Conan (1859–1930), Scottish novelist and short-story writer. He created the private detective Sherlock Holmes, who, with his friend Dr Watson, featured in more than fifty stories and in novels such as *The Hound of the Baskervilles.*

D'Oyly Carte [E]
/doy-li **kart**/, Richard (1844–1901), English impresario and producer, who brought together Sir W. S. Gilbert and Sir Arthur Sullivan, producing many of their operettas in London's Savoy Theatre.

doze • **v.** (**dozes**, **dozing**, **dozed**) sleep lightly. • **n.** a short light sleep.
– ORIGIN perh. from Danish *døse* 'make drowsy'.

dozen • **n.** **1** (pl. **dozen**) a group or set of twelve. **2** (**dozens**) a lot.
– PHRASES **talk nineteen to the dozen** Brit. talk fast and continuously.
– DERIVATIVES **dozenth** adj.
– ORIGIN Old French *dozeine.*

dozy • **adj.** **1** feeling drowsy and lazy. **2** Brit. informal stupid.

DP • **abbrev.** data processing.

DPhil • **abbrev.** Doctor of Philosophy.

DPP • **abbrev.** (in the UK) Director of Public Prosecutions.

Dr • **abbrev.** (as a title) Doctor.

drab • **adj.** (**drabber**, **drabbest**) dull and uninteresting. • **n.** a dull light brown colour.
– ORIGIN prob. from Old French *drap* 'cloth'.

drachm /dram/ • **n.** hist. a unit of measure equivalent to one eighth of an ounce or one eighth of a fluid ounce.
– ORIGIN see DRACHMA.

drachma /drak-muh/ • **n.** (pl. **drachmas** or **drachmae** /**drak**-mee/) the former basic unit of money in Greece.
– ORIGIN Greek *drakhmē*, referring to an ancient weight and coin.

draconian /druh-**koh**-ni-uhn, dray-**koh**-ni-uhn/ • **adj.** (of laws) excessively harsh.
– ORIGIN named after the ancient Athenian legislator *Draco.*

draft • **n.** **1** a preliminary version of a piece of writing. **2** a written order requesting a bank to pay a specified sum. **3** (**the draft**) US compulsory recruitment for military service. **4** US = DRAUGHT. • **v.** **1** prepare a preliminary version of (a text). **2** select for a particular pur-

pose: *he was drafted in to oversee security.* **3** US conscript for military service.
– ORIGIN from **DRAUGHT**.

draftsman ● n. N. Amer. = **DRAUGHTSMAN**.

drafty ● adj. US = **DRAUGHTY**.

drag ● v. (**drags**, **dragging**, **dragged**) **1** pull along forcefully, roughly, or with difficulty. **2** trail along the ground. **3** (of time) pass slowly. **4** (**drag out**) prolong (something) unnecessarily. **5** (**drag up**) informal deliberately mention (something unwelcome). **6** search the bottom of (an area of water) with grapnels or nets. **7** (**drag on**) informal inhale the smoke from (a cigarette). **8** move (an image) across a computer screen using a mouse. ● n. **1** the action of dragging. **2** informal a boring or tiresome person or thing. **3** informal women's clothing worn by a man. **4** informal an act of inhaling smoke from a cigarette. **5** the force exerted by air or water to slow down a moving object.
– PHRASES **drag one's feet** be slow or reluctant.
– ORIGIN Old English.

dragnet ● n. **1** a net drawn through water or across ground to trap fish or game. **2** a systematic search for criminals.

dragon ● n. **1** a mythical monster like a giant reptile, able to breathe out fire. **2** derog. a fierce and frightening woman.
– ORIGIN Greek *drakōn* 'serpent'.

dragonfly ● n. a long-bodied insect with two pairs of large transparent wings.

dragoon /druh-**goon**/ ● n. a member of any of several British cavalry regiments. ● v. force into doing something.
– ORIGIN French *dragon* 'dragon'.

drag queen ● n. informal a man who dresses up in showy women's clothes.

drag race ● n. a short race between two cars to see which can accelerate fastest from a standstill.

drain ● v. **1** cause the liquid in (something) to run out. **2** (of liquid) run off or out. **3** become dry as liquid runs off. **4** exhaust of strength or resources: *the hospital bills are draining my income.* **5** drink the entire contents of. ● n. **1** a channel or pipe carrying off surplus liquid. **2** a thing that uses up a resource or one's strength.
– PHRASES **go down the drain** informal be totally wasted.
– ORIGIN Old English.

drainage ● n. **1** the action of draining. **2** a system of drains.

draining board ● n. Brit. a sloping surface next to a sink, on which crockery is left to drain.

drainpipe ● n. **1** a pipe for carrying off rainwater from a building. **2** (**drainpipes** or **drainpipe trousers**) trousers with very narrow legs.

> **Drake,** E
> Sir Francis (*c.*1540–96), English sailor and explorer, who was the first Englishman to sail round the world (1577–80), in his ship the *Golden Hind*. He also played an important part in the defeat of the Spanish Armada.

drake ● n. a male duck.
– ORIGIN Germanic.

DRAM ● abbrev. Computing dynamic random-access memory.

dram ● n. **1** a small drink of spirits. **2** = **DRACHM**.
– ORIGIN Greek *drakhmē* 'drachma'.

drama ● n. **1** a play. **2** plays as a literary form. **3** an exciting series of events.
– ORIGIN Greek.

dramatic ● adj. **1** relating to drama. **2** sudden and striking: *a dramatic increase.* **3** exciting or impressive. ● n. (**dramatics**) **1** the practice of acting in and producing plays. **2** exaggerated or overemotional behaviour.
– DERIVATIVES **dramatically** adv.

dramatis personae /dra-muh-tiss per-**soh**-ny/ ● pl. n. the characters of a play or novel.
– ORIGIN Latin.

dramatist ● n. a person who writes plays.

dramatize (also **dramatise**) ● v. (**dramatizes**, **dramatizing**, **dramatized**) **1** present (a novel, event, etc.) as a play. **2** exaggerate the excitement or seriousness of.
– DERIVATIVES **dramatization** (also **dramatisation**) n.

drank past of **DRINK**.

drape ● v. (**drapes**, **draping**, **draped**) **1** arrange (cloth or clothing) loosely on or round something. **2** rest (a part of one's body) on something in a relaxed way. ● n. (**drapes**) long curtains.
– ORIGIN from **DRAPERY**.

draper ● n. Brit. dated a person who sells fabrics.

drapery ● n. (pl. **draperies**) cloth or clothing hanging in loose folds.
– ORIGIN Old French *drap* 'cloth'.

drastic ● adj. having a strong or far-reaching effect.
– DERIVATIVES **drastically** adv.
– ORIGIN Greek *drastikos*.

drat ● exclam. used to express mild annoyance.
– ORIGIN from *od rat*, a euphemism for *God rot*.

draught (US **draft**) ● n. **1** a current of cool air indoors. **2** an act of drinking or breathing in. **3** archaic a quantity of a medicinal liquid. **4** the depth of water needed to float a particular ship: *the shallow draught provides a flat cabin floor.* **5** (**draughts**) Brit. a game for two players using 24 pieces, played on a chequered board. ● v. var. of **DRAFT**. ● adj. **1** (of beer) served from a cask. **2** (of an animal) used for pulling heavy loads.
– ORIGIN Old Norse.

draughtsman (or **draughtswoman**) ● n. **1** a person who makes detailed technical plans or drawings. **2** an artist skilled in drawing.
– DERIVATIVES **draughtsmanship** n.

draughty (US **drafty**) ● adj. uncomfortable because of draughts of cold air.

draw ● v. (**draws**, **drawing**, **drew**; past part. **drawn**) **1** produce (a picture or diagram) by making lines and marks on paper. **2** pull or drag (a vehicle) so as to make it follow behind. **3** pull or move in a specified direction: *the train drew into the station.* **4** pull (curtains) shut or open. **5** arrive at a point in time: *the campaign drew to a close.* **6** take from a container or source: *he drew his gun.* **7** be the cause of (a specified response). **8** attract to a place or an event. **9** persuade to reveal something: *he refused to be drawn on what would happen.* **10** reach (a conclusion).

11 finish (a contest or game) with an even score. **12** take in (a breath). ● **n. 1** a selection of names at random for prizes, sporting fixtures, etc. **2** a game or match that ends with the scores even. **3** a person or thing that is very attractive or interesting. **4** an act of inhaling smoke from a cigarette.
– PHRASES **draw someone's fire** attract hostile criticism away from a more important target. **draw in** (of successive days) become shorter. **draw the line at** refuse to do or tolerate. **draw on 1** (of a period of time) pass by and approach its end. **2** suck smoke from (a cigarette or pipe). **draw out 1** make (something) last longer. **2** persuade to be more talkative. **draw up 1** come to a halt. **2** prepare (a plan or document).
– ORIGIN Old English.

drawback ● **n.** a disadvantage.

drawbridge ● **n.** a bridge which is hinged at one end so that it can be raised.

drawer ● **n. 1** /draw/ a storage compartment made to slide horizontally in and out of a desk or chest. **2** (**drawers**) /drawz/ dated knickers or underpants. **3** /draw-er/ a person who draws something.

drawing ● **n.** a picture or diagram made with a pencil, pen, or crayon.

drawing board ● **n.** a board on which paper can be spread for artists or designers to work on.
– PHRASES **back to the drawing board** a plan has failed and a new one is needed.

drawing pin ● **n.** Brit. a short flat-headed pin for fastening paper to a surface.

drawing room ● **n.** a room in a private house in which guests can be received.
– ORIGIN from *withdrawing-room* 'a room to withdraw to'.

drawl ● **v.** speak in a slow, lazy way with prolonged vowel sounds. ● **n.** a drawling accent.
– ORIGIN German or Dutch *dralen* 'delay'.

drawn past part. of DRAW. ● **adj.** looking strained from illness or exhaustion.

drawn-out ● **adj.** lasting longer than is necessary.

drawstring ● **n.** a string in the seam of a garment or bag, which can be pulled to tighten or close it.

dray ● **n.** a low truck or cart without sides, for delivering barrels or other heavy loads.
– ORIGIN perh. from Old English, 'dragnet'.

dread ● **v.** think about with great fear or anxiety. ● **n.** great fear or anxiety.
– ORIGIN Old English.

dreadful ● **adj. 1** extremely bad or serious. **2** used for emphasis: *he's a dreadful flirt.*
– DERIVATIVES **dreadfully** adv.

dreadlocks ● **pl. n.** a Rastafarian hairstyle in which the hair is twisted into tight braids or ringlets.
– DERIVATIVES **dreadlocked** adj.

dream ● **n. 1** a series of images and feelings occurring in a person's mind during sleep. **2** a long-held ambition or wish. **3** informal a wonderful or perfect person or thing. ● **v.** (**dreams**, **dreaming**, **dreamed** or **dreamt** /dremt/) **1** experience dreams during sleep. **2** have daydreams. **3** think of as possible: *I never dreamed she'd take offence.* **4** (**dream up**) invent.
– PHRASES **like a dream** informal very easily or successfully.
– DERIVATIVES **dreamer** n.
– ORIGIN Germanic.

dreamy ● **adj.** (**dreamier**, **dreamiest**) **1** dreamlike. **2** tending to daydream.

dreary ● **adj.** (**drearier**, **dreariest**) dull, bleak, and depressing.
– ORIGIN Old English, 'gory, melancholy'.

dredge ● **v.** (**dredges**, **dredging**, **dredged**) **1** clean out the bed of (a harbour, river, etc.) with a dredge. **2** (**dredge up**) bring (something unwelcome and forgotten) to people's attention. ● **n.** an apparatus for bringing up objects from a river or seabed by scooping or dragging.
– DERIVATIVES **dredger** n.
– ORIGIN perh. from Dutch *dregghe* 'grappling hook'.

dregs ● **n. 1** the last drops of a liquid left in a container, together with any sediment. **2** the most worthless parts: *the dregs of society.*
– ORIGIN prob. from Scandinavian.

drench ● **v. 1** wet thoroughly. **2** cover liberally with something.
– ORIGIN Old English.

Dresden
/drez-duhn/ a city in eastern Germany, the capital of Saxony. Famous for its baroque architecture, it was almost totally destroyed by Allied bombing in 1945.

dress ● **v. 1** (also **get dressed**) put on one's clothes. **2** put clothes on (someone). **3** wear clothes in a particular way or of a particular type: *she dresses well.* **4** decorate or arrange in an attractive way. **5** clean and cover (a wound). **6** clean and prepare (food) for cooking or eating. ● **n. 1** a one-piece garment for a woman or girl that covers the body and extends down over the legs. **2** clothing of a specified kind.
– PHRASES **dress down** informal wear informal clothes. **dress up** dress in smart clothes or in a special costume.
– ORIGIN Old French *dresser* 'arrange'.

dressage /dress-ah*zh*/ ● **n.** the training of a horse to perform a set of controlled movements at the rider's command.
– ORIGIN French.

dress circle ● **n.** the first level of seats above the ground floor in a theatre.

dresser ● **n. 1** a sideboard with shelves above for storing and displaying crockery. **2** a person who dresses in a particular way.

dressing ● **n. 1** a sauce for salads, usually consisting of oil and vinegar with flavourings. **2** a piece of material placed on a wound to protect it.

dressing-down ● **n.** informal a severe reprimand.

dressing gown ● **n.** a long robe worn after getting out of bed or bathing.

dressing room ● **n. 1** a room in which actors or other performers change clothes. **2** a room attached to a bedroom for storing clothes.

dressing table ● **n.** a table with a mirror and drawers, used while dressing or applying make-up.

dress rehearsal ● **n.** a final rehearsal in which everything is done as it would be in a real performance.

dress shirt ● n. a man's white shirt worn with a bow tie on formal occasions.

dressy ● adj. (**dressier**, **dressiest**) (of clothes) smart or formal.

drew past of DRAW.

Dreyfus E
/dray-fuhss/, Alfred (1859–1935), French army officer, of Jewish descent, who was falsely accused of spying for Germany (1894); his trial and imprisonment caused a major political crisis in France. He was officially declared innocent in 1906.

dribble ● v. (**dribbles**, **dribbling**, **dribbled**) **1** (of a liquid) fall slowly in drops or a thin stream. **2** allow saliva to run from the mouth. **3** (in sport) take (the ball) forward with slight touches or (in basketball) by continuous bouncing. ● n. a thin stream of liquid.
– ORIGIN from DRIP.

dribs and drabs ● pl. n. (in phr. **in dribs and drabs**) informal in small amounts over a period of time.

dried past and past part. of DRY.

drier[1] ● n. var. of DRYER.

drier[2] ● adj. comparative of DRY.

drift ● v. **1** be carried slowly by a current of air or water. **2** walk or move slowly or casually. **3** (of snow, leaves, etc.) be blown into heaps by the wind. ● n. **1** a continuous slow movement from one place to another. **2** the general meaning of someone's remarks: *he got her drift*. **3** a large mass of snow, leaves, etc. piled up by the wind.
– ORIGIN Old Norse.

drifter ● n. a person who is continually moving from place to place, without any fixed home or job.

drift net ● n. a large fishing net allowed to drift in the sea.

driftwood ● n. pieces of wood floating on the sea or washed ashore.

drill[1] ● n. **1** a tool or machine for boring holes. **2** training in military exercises. **3** instruction by means of repeated exercises. **4** (**the drill**) informal the correct procedure. ● v. **1** bore (a hole) with a drill. **2** give military training or other thorough instruction to.
– ORIGIN Dutch *drillen*.

drill[2] ● n. a machine which makes small furrows, sows seed in them, and then covers the sown seed.
– ORIGIN perh. from DRILL[1].

drill[3] ● n. a strong cotton fabric woven with parallel diagonal lines.
– ORIGIN Latin *trilix* 'triple-twilled'.

drily /dry-li/ (also **dryly**) ● adv. in a matter-of-fact or ironically humorous way.

drink ● v. (**drinks**, **drinking**, **drank**; past part. **drunk**) **1** take (a liquid) into the mouth and swallow it. **2** consume alcohol. ● n. **1** a liquid for drinking. **2** a quantity of liquid swallowed at one time. **3** alcohol or an alcoholic drink.
– DERIVATIVES **drinkable** adj. **drinker** n.
– ORIGIN Old English.

drink-driving ● n. Brit. the crime of driving a vehicle after drinking too much alcohol.

drinking chocolate ● n. a mixture of cocoa powder and sugar used to make a chocolate drink.

drip ● v. (**drips**, **dripping**, **dripped**) fall or let fall in small drops of liquid. ● n. **1** a small drop of a liquid. **2** an apparatus which slowly passes a substance into a patient's body through a vein. **3** informal a weak or foolish person.
– ORIGIN Old English.

drip-dry ● adj. (of a garment) that will dry without creases if hung up when wet.

drip-feed ● v. (**drip-feeds**, **drip-feeding**, **drip-fed**) put (fluid) into something drop by drop.

dripping ● n. Brit. fat that has melted and dripped from roasting meat. ● adj. extremely wet.

drippy ● adj. informal weak, silly, or very sentimental.

drive ● v. (**drives**, **driving**, **drove**; past part. **driven**) **1** operate (a motor vehicle). **2** carry in a motor vehicle. **3** carry or urge along. **4** compel to act in a particular way. **5** provide the energy to keep (an engine or machine) in motion. ● n. **1** a journey in a car. **2** (also **driveway**) a short private road leading to a house. **3** an inborn desire or urge. **4** an organized effort to achieve a particular purpose. **5** determination and ambition.
– PHRASES **what someone is driving at** what someone is trying to say.
– DERIVATIVES **driver** n.
– ORIGIN Old English.

drive-in ● adj. N. Amer. (of a cinema, restaurant, etc.) that one can visit without leaving one's car.

drivel /driv-uhl/ ● n. nonsense.
– ORIGIN Old English.

driven past part. of DRIVE.

driving ● adj. **1** having a controlling influence: *the driving force behind the plan*. **2** being blown by the wind with great force.
– PHRASES **in the driving seat** in control.

drizzle ● n. light rain falling in fine drops. ● v. (**drizzles**, **drizzling**, **drizzled**) **1** (**it drizzles**, **it is drizzling**, etc.) rain lightly. **2** Cookery pour a thin stream of (a liquid ingredient) over a dish.
– ORIGIN prob. from Old English, 'to fall'.

droll /drohl/ ● adj. amusing in a strange or unexpected way.
– DERIVATIVES **drollery** n.
– ORIGIN French.

dromedary /drom-i-duh-ri/ ● n. (pl. **dromedaries**) an Arabian camel, with one hump.
– ORIGIN from Latin *dromedarius camelus* 'swift camel'.

drone ● v. (**drones**, **droning**, **droned**) **1** make a low continuous humming sound. **2** (**drone on**) talk for a long time in a boring way. ● n. **1** a low continuous humming sound. **2** a male bee which does no work but can fertilize a queen.
– ORIGIN Old English, 'male bee'.

drool ● v. (**drools**, **drooling**, **drooled**) **1** drop saliva uncontrollably from the mouth. **2** (**drool over**) informal show great pleasure or desire for.
– ORIGIN from DRIVEL, in the earlier sense 'spittle'.

droop ● v. bend, hang, or move downwards limply, especially from tiredness. ● n. an act of drooping.
– ORIGIN Old Norse.

droopy ● adj. (**droopier**, **droopiest**) **1** hanging down limply. **2** lacking strength or spirit.

drop ● v. (**drops**, **dropping**, **dropped**) **1** fall or cause to fall. **2** sink to the ground. **3** make or become lower or less: *he dropped his voice.* **4** abandon (a course of action). **5** (often **drop off**) set down or unload (a passenger or goods). **6** place or leave (something) without ceremony: *just drop it in the post.* **7** lose (a point, a match, etc.). ● n. **1** a small round or pear-shaped amount of liquid. **2** an instance of dropping. **3** a small drink: *a drop of water.* **4** an abrupt fall or slope. **5** a sweet.
– PHRASES **drop by/in** visit informally and briefly. **drop a line** informal send (someone) a short letter. **drop off** fall asleep. **drop out** **1** stop participating. **2** pursue an alternative lifestyle.
– ORIGIN Old English.

drop goal ● n. Rugby a goal scored by a drop kick over the crossbar.

drop kick ● n. a kick made by dropping a ball and kicking it as it bounces.

droplet ● n. a very small drop of a liquid.

dropout ● n. a person who has dropped out of society or a course of study.

dropper ● n. a short glass tube with a rubber bulb at one end, for measuring out drops of liquid.

droppings ● pl. n. the excrement of animals.

dropsy /drop-si/ ● n. dated = OEDEMA.
– ORIGIN from former *hydropsy.*

dross ● n. rubbish.
– ORIGIN Old English.

drought /drowt/ ● n. a very long period of little or no rainfall.
– ORIGIN Old English, 'dryness'.

drove[1] past of DRIVE.

drove[2] ● n. **1** a flock of animals being driven. **2** a large number of people doing the same thing: *tourists arrived in droves.*
– DERIVATIVES **drover** n.
– ORIGIN Old English.

drown ● v. **1** die or kill through submersion in water. **2** flood (an area). **3** (usu. **drown out**) make impossible to hear by being much louder.
– ORIGIN Old Norse, 'be drowned'.

drowsy ● adj. sleepy
– DERIVATIVES **drowsily** adv. **drowsiness** n.
ORIGIN prob. from Old English, 'be slow'.

drubbing ● n. informal a thorough defeat in a match or contest.
– ORIGIN prob. from Arabic.

drudge ● n. a person made to do hard, menial, or dull work.
– ORIGIN unknown.

drudgery ● n. hard, menial, or dull work.

drug ● n. **1** a substance used as a medicine. **2** an illegal substance taken for the effects it has on the body. ● v. (**drugs**, **drugging**, **drugged**) affect (someone) by administering a drug.
– ORIGIN Old French *drogue.*

druggy informal ● adj. caused by or involving drugs. ● n. (also **druggie**) (pl. **druggies**) a drug addict.

drugstore ● n. N. Amer. a pharmacy which also sells toiletries and other articles.

Druid /droo-id/ ● n. a priest in the ancient Celtic religion.
– ORIGIN Gaulish (the language of the ancient Gauls).

drum ● n. **1** a percussion instrument with a skin stretched across a frame, sounded by being struck with sticks or the hands. **2** a cylindrical container or part. ● v. (**drums**, **drumming**, **drummed**) **1** play on a drum. **2** make a continuous rhythmic noise. **3** (**drum into**) instruct someone in (something) by constant repetition. **4** (**drum up**) try hard to get (support or business).
– ORIGIN Dutch or German *tromme.*

drumbeat ● n. a stroke or pattern of strokes on a drum.

drum kit ● n. a set of drums, cymbals, and other percussion instruments.

drum majorette ● n. the female leader of a marching band.

drummer ● n. a person who plays a drum or drums.

drum roll ● n. a rapid succession of drumbeats.

drumstick ● n. **1** a stick used for beating a drum. **2** the lower joint of the leg of a cooked chicken or similar bird.

drunk past part. of DRINK. ● adj. affected by alcohol to the extent of losing control of oneself. ● n. a person who is drunk or who often drinks to excess.

drupe /droop/ ● n. Bot. a fleshy fruit with a central stone, e.g. a plum or olive.
– ORIGIN Latin *drupa* 'overripe olive'.

dry ● adj. (**drier**, **driest**) **1** free from moisture or liquid. **2** without grease or other lubrication: *his throat was dry and sore.* **3** serious and boring. **4** (of humour) subtle and expressed in a matter-of-fact way. **5** (of wine) not sweet. ● v. (**dries**, **drying**, **dried**) **1** make or become dry. **2** preserve by evaporating the moisture from. **3** (**dry up**) (of a supply) decrease and stop.
– DERIVATIVES **dryness** n.
– ORIGIN Old English.

dryad /dry-uhd, dry-ad/ ● n. (in Greek mythology) a nymph living in a tree or wood.
– ORIGIN Greek *druas.*

dry cell (also **dry battery**) ● n. an electric cell (or battery) in which the electrolyte is in the form of a paste.

dry clean ● v. clean (a garment) with a chemical.

Dryden E
/dry-d'n/, John (1631–1700), English poet, critic, and dramatist. He is best known for the comedy *Marriage à la mode* and the tragedy *All for Love.*

dryer (also **drier**) ● n. a machine or device for drying something.

dry ice ● n. **1** solid carbon dioxide. **2** white mist produced with this as a theatrical effect.

dryly ● adv. var. of DRILY.

dry rot ● n. a fungus causing decay of wood in poorly ventilated conditions.

dry run ● n. informal a rehearsal.

drystone ● adj. Brit. (of a stone wall) built without using mortar.

DSC ● abbrev. (in the UK) Distinguished Service Cross.

DSM ● abbrev. (in the UK) Distinguished Service Medal.

DSO ● abbrev. (in the UK) Distinguished Service Order.

DSS • **abbrev.** (in the UK) Department of Social Security.

DTI • **abbrev.** (in the UK) Department of Trade and Industry.

DTP • **abbrev.** desktop publishing.

DTs • **pl. n.** informal delirium tremens.

dual • **adj.** consisting of two parts or aspects.
– ORIGIN Latin *dualis*.

d

dual carriageway • **n.** Brit. a road consisting of two or more lanes in each direction.

dualism • **n. 1** division into two opposed aspects, such as good and evil. **2** duality.
– DERIVATIVES **dualist** n. & adj.

duality • **n.** (pl. **dualities**) the state of having two parts or aspects.

dub[1] • **v.** (**dubs, dubbing, dubbed**) **1** give an unofficial name to. **2** knight (someone) by the touching of the shoulder with a sword.
– ORIGIN Old French *adober* 'equip with armour'.

dub[2] • **v.** (**dubs, dubbing, dubbed**) **1** provide (a film) with a soundtrack in a different language from the original. **2** add (sound effects or music) to a film or a recording. • **n.** an instance of dubbing sound effects or music.
– ORIGIN from **DOUBLE**.

Dubai E
/doo-**by**/ a member state of the United Arab Emirates; capital, Dubai.

dubbin /**dub**-bin/ • **n.** Brit. prepared grease used for softening and waterproofing leather.
– ORIGIN from **DUB**[1].

Dubček E
/**duub**-chek/, Alexander (1921–92), Czechoslovak statesman, First Secretary of the Czechoslovak Communist Party 1968–9. His political reforms prompted the Soviet invasion of Czechoslovakia in 1968 and his removal from office. He returned to public life after the collapse of communism in 1989.

dubiety /dyoo-**by**-i-ti/ • **n.** formal uncertainty.

dubious /**dyoo**-bi-uhss/ • **adj. 1** hesitating or doubting. **2** not to be relied upon. **3** of questionable value.
– DERIVATIVES **dubiously** adv.
– ORIGIN Latin *dubiosus*.

Dublin[1] E
the capital city of the Republic of Ireland. Irish name **BAILE ÁTHA CLIATH**.

Dublin[2] E
a county of the Republic of Ireland; county town, Dublin.

dubnium /**dub**-ni-uhm/ • **n.** a very unstable chemical element made by high-energy atomic collisions.
– ORIGIN from *Dubna* in Russia.

Du Bois E
/doo **boyz**/, W. E. B. (1868–1963; full name *William Edward Burghardt Du Bois*), American writer, sociologist, and political activist. He was an important figure in campaigning for equality for black Americans and co-founded the National Association for the Advancement of Colored People in 1909.

Dubrovnik E
/duu-**brov**-nik/ a port and resort on the Adriatic coast of Croatia.

ducal /**dyoo**-k'l/ • **adj.** relating to a duke or dukedom.

ducat /**duk**-uht/ • **n.** a former European gold coin.
– ORIGIN Italian *ducato*.

Duchamp E
/dyoo-**shon**/, Marcel (1887–1968), French-born American artist, a leading figure of the Dada movement.

duchess • **n. 1** the wife or widow of a duke. **2** a woman holding a rank equivalent to duke.
– ORIGIN Old French.

duchy /**duch**-i/ • **n.** (pl. **duchies**) the territory of a duke or duchess.
– ORIGIN Old French *duche*.

duck[1] • **n.** (pl. **duck** or **ducks**) **1** a waterbird with a broad bill, short legs, and webbed feet. **2** the female of such a bird.
– PHRASES **like water off a duck's back** (of a critical remark) having no effect.
– ORIGIN Old English.

duck[2] • **v. 1** lower oneself quickly to avoid being hit or seen. **2** push (someone) under water. **3** informal avoid (an unwelcome duty). • **n.** a quick lowering of the head.
– ORIGIN Germanic.

duck[3] • **n.** Cricket a batsman's score of nought.
– ORIGIN short for *duck's egg*, used for the figure 0.

duck-billed platypus • **n.** see **PLATYPUS**.

duckboards • **pl. n.** wooden slats joined together to form a path over muddy ground.

ducking stool • **n.** hist. a chair on the end of a pole, in which offenders were plunged into a pond or river as a punishment.

duckling • **n.** a young duck.

duct • **n. 1** a tube or passageway for air, cables, etc. **2** a tube in the body through which fluid passes. • **v.** convey through a duct.
– ORIGIN Latin *ductus* 'leading'.

ductile /**duk**-tyl/ • **adj.** (of a metal) able to be drawn out into a thin wire.
– DERIVATIVES **ductility** n.

ductless • **adj.** Anat. (of a gland) producing secretions directly into the bloodstream.

dud informal • **n.** a thing that fails to work properly. • **adj.** failing to work or meet a standard.
– ORIGIN unknown.

dude /dyood/ • **n.** N. Amer. informal a man.
– ORIGIN prob. from German dialect *Dude* 'fool'.

dudgeon /**duj**-uhn/ • **n.** (in phr. **in high dudgeon**) angry or resentful.
– ORIGIN unknown.

Dudley E
Robert, Earl of Leicester (*c.*1532–88), English nobleman, military commander, and favourite of Elizabeth I.

due • **adj. 1** needing to be paid; owing. **2** expected at a certain time. **3** at a point where something is owed or deserved: *he was due for a rise.* **4** proper: *due process of law.* • **n. 1** (**one's due/dues**) a person's right. **2** (**dues**) fees. • **adv.** (with reference to a point of the compass) directly: *head due south.*
– PHRASES **due to 1** caused by. **2** because of. **in due course** at the appropriate time.
– ORIGIN Old French *deu* 'owed'.

duel ● n. **1** hist. a pre-arranged contest with deadly weapons between two people to settle a point of honour. **2** a contest between two parties. ● v. (**duels**, **duelling**, **duelled**; US **duels**, **dueling**, **dueled**) fight a duel.
– ORIGIN Latin *duellum* 'war'.

duet ● n. **1** a performance by two singers, musicians, or dancers. **2** a musical composition for two performers. ● v. (**duets**, **duetting**, **duetted**) perform a duet.
– ORIGIN Italian *duetto*.

duff[1] ● adj. Brit. informal worthless or false.
– ORIGIN unknown.

duff[2] ● v. informal (**duff up**) Brit. beat (someone) up.
– ORIGIN uncertain.

duffel bag (also **duffle bag**) ● n. a cylinder-shaped canvas bag closed by a drawstring.

duffel coat (also **duffle coat**) ● n. a hooded coat made of a coarse woollen material.
– ORIGIN named after the Belgian town of *Duffel*.

duffer ● n. informal an incompetent or stupid person.
– ORIGIN Scots *dowfart*.

Dufy E
/dyoo-fi/, Raoul (1877–1953), French painter and textile designer. His characteristic style involved rapidly drawn outlines sketched on backgrounds of bright, thinly applied colours.

dug[1] past and past part. of DIG.

dug[2] ● n. the udder, teat, or nipple of a female animal.
– ORIGIN perh. from Old Norse.

dugong /dyoo-gong/ ● n. (pl. **dugong** or **dugongs**) a large plant-eating mammal found in the Indian Ocean.
– ORIGIN Malay.

dugout ● n. **1** a trench that is roofed over as a shelter for troops. **2** a low shelter at the side of a sports field for a team's coaches and substitutes.

duke ● n. **1** a man holding the highest hereditary title in Britain and certain other countries. **2** hist. (in parts of Europe) a male ruler of a small independent state.
– DERIVATIVES **dukedom** n.
– ORIGIN Old French *duc*.

dulcet /dul-sit/ ● adj. usu. ironic (of a sound) sweet and soothing.
– ORIGIN Old French *doucet*.

dulcimer /dul-si-mer/ ● n. a musical instrument with strings which are struck with hand-held hammers.
– ORIGIN Old French *doulcemer*.

dull ● adj. **1** lacking interest. **2** lacking brightness. **3** (of the weather) overcast. **4** slow to understand. ● v. make or become dull.
– DERIVATIVES **dullness** n. **dully** adv.
– ORIGIN Old English.

dullard /dul-lerd/ ● n. a slow or stupid person.

duly ● adv. in accordance with what is required or expected.

Dumas[1] E
/dyoo-mah/ Alexandre (1802–70; known as **Dumas** *père*), author of the historical adventure novels *The Three Musketeers* and *The Count of Monte Cristo*.

Dumas[2] E
/dyoo-mah/ Alexandre (1824–95; known as **Dumas** *fils*), son of Dumas *père*. He wrote the novel (and play) *La Dame aux camélias*.

Du Maurier E
/dyoo mo-ri-ay/, Dame Daphne (1907–89), English novelist. She is known for her novels set in the West Country of England, including *Jamaica Inn* and *Rebecca*.

d

dumb ● adj. **1** offens. unable to speak; lacking the power of speech. **2** temporarily unable or unwilling to speak. **3** N. Amer. informal, stupid. ● v. (**dumb down**) informal make or become less intellectually challenging.
– DERIVATIVES **dumbly** adv.
– ORIGIN Old English.

Dumbartonshire E
var. of DUNBARTONSHIRE.

dumb-bell ● n. a short bar with a weight at each end, used for exercise.
– ORIGIN first referring to an object similar to that used to ring a church bell (but without the bell, so 'dumb').

dumbfound ● v. astonish greatly.
– ORIGIN from DUMB and CONFOUND.

dumbo ● n. (pl. **dumbos**) informal a stupid person.

dumbshow ● n. gestures used to communicate something without speech.

dumbstruck ● adj. so shocked or surprised as to be unable to speak.

dumb waiter ● n. a small lift for carrying food and crockery between floors.

dumdum (also **dumdum bullet**) ● n. a kind of soft-nosed bullet that expands on impact.
– ORIGIN from *Dum Dum*, a town in India.

Dumfries and Galloway E
/dum-freess, gal-luh-way/ an administrative region in SW Scotland, formed in 1975; administrative centre, Dumfries.

dummy ● n. (pl. **dummies**) **1** a model of a human being. **2** an object designed to resemble and take the place of the real one. **3** Brit. a rubber or plastic teat for a baby to suck on. **4** (in sport) a pretended pass or kick. ● v. (**dummies**, **dummying**, **dummied**) pretend to pass or kick the ball.
– ORIGIN from DUMB.

dummy run ● n. a practice or trial.

dump ● n. **1** a site for depositing rubbish or waste. **2** a heap of rubbish left at a dump. **3** informal an unpleasant or dull place. **4** Mil. a temporary store of weapons or provisions. ● v. **1** deposit or dispose of (rubbish). **2** put down (something) carelessly. **3** informal abandon (someone).
– ORIGIN perh. from Old Norse.

dumper ● n. **1** a person or thing that dumps something. **2** (also **dumper truck**) Brit. a truck with a body that tilts or opens at the back for unloading.

dumpling ● n. a small savoury ball of dough boiled in water or in a stew.
– ORIGIN perh. from former *dump* 'of the consistency of dough'.

dumps ● pl. n. (in phr. (**down**) **in the dumps**) informal depressed or unhappy.
– ORIGIN prob. from Dutch *domp* 'haze'.

dumpy ● adj. (**dumpier**, **dumpiest**) short and

rather fat.

dun ● n. a dull greyish-brown colour.
– ORIGIN Old English.

Dunbartonshire E
(also **Dumbartonshire**) an administrative region and former county of west central Scotland, on the Clyde, divided into **East Dunbartonshire** and **West Dunbartonshire**.

d

Duncan, E
Isadora (1878–1927), American dancer and teacher, famous for her 'free' barefoot dancing. She died through being accidentally strangled when her scarf became entangled in the wheels of a car.

dunce ● n. a person who is slow at learning.
– ORIGIN from the name of the Scottish theologian John *Duns* Scotus (*c.*1265–1308), whose followers were ridiculed.

dunce's cap ● n. a paper cone formerly put on the head of a dunce at school as a mark of disgrace.

Dundee E
a city in eastern Scotland, on the north side of the Firth of Tay.

dunderhead ● n. informal a stupid person.
– ORIGIN perh. from former Scots *dunder, dunner* 'resounding noise'.

dune ● n. a mound or ridge of sand formed by the wind.
– ORIGIN Dutch.

Dunedin E
/dun-ee-din/ a city and port in South Island, New Zealand.

dung ● n. manure.
– ORIGIN Old English.

dungarees /dung-guh-**reez**/ ● pl. n. a garment consisting of trousers held up by straps over the shoulders.
– ORIGIN Hindi.

dung beetle ● n. a beetle whose larvae feed on dung.

dungeon ● n. a strong underground prison cell.
– ORIGIN Old French.

dunghill ● n. a heap of dung or refuse.

dunk ● v. **1** dip (food) into a drink or soup before eating it. **2** immerse in water.
– ORIGIN German *tunken*.

Dunkirk E
/dun-**kerk**/ a port in northern France, scene of the evacuation of 335,000 Allied troops by ships and small boats in 1940.

Dun Laoghaire E
/dun **leer**-i, dun lair-**uh**/ a ferry port and resort town in the Republic of Ireland, near Dublin.

dunlin ● n. (pl. **dunlin** or **dunlins**) a sandpiper with a downcurved bill and (in winter) greyish-brown upper parts.
– ORIGIN prob. from DUN + -LING.

Dunlop, E
John Boyd (1840–1921), Scottish inventor. He developed the first successful pneumatic bicycle tyre (1888), manufactured by the company named after him.

Dunnet Head E
a headland on the north coast of Scotland, between Thurso and John o'Groats. It is the most northerly point on the British mainland.

dunnock /**dun**-nuhk/ ● n. a songbird with a grey head and a reddish-brown back.
– ORIGIN prob. from DUN.

dunny ● n. (pl. **dunnies**) Austral./NZ informal a toilet.
– ORIGIN prob. from DUNG + former slang *ken* 'house'.

duo ● n. (pl. **duos**) **1** a pair of people or things, especially in music or entertainment. **2** Music a duet.
– ORIGIN Latin, 'two'.

duodecimal /dyoo-oh-**dess**-i-m'l/ ● adj. relating to a system of counting that has twelve as a base.
– ORIGIN Latin *duodecimus* 'twelfth'.

duodenum /dyoo-uh-**dee**-nuhm/ ● n. (pl. **duodenums** or **duodena** /dyoo-uh-**dee**-nuh/) the first part of the small intestine immediately beyond the stomach.
– DERIVATIVES **duodenal** adj.
– ORIGIN Latin.

duopoly /dyoo-**op**-uh-li/ ● n. (pl. **duopolies**) a situation in which two suppliers dominate a market.

dupe ● v. (**dupes**, **duping**, **duped**) deceive; trick. ● n. a victim of deception.
– ORIGIN French dialect, 'hoopoe'.

duple /**dyoo**-p'l/ ● adj. Music (of rhythm) based on two main beats to the bar.
– ORIGIN Latin *duplus*.

duplex /**dyoo**-pleks/ ● n. **1** N. Amer. a residential building divided into two apartments. **2** N. Amer. & Austral. a semi-detached house.
– ORIGIN Latin.

duplicate ● adj. /**dyoo**-pli-kuht/ **1** exactly like something else. **2** having two corresponding parts. **3** twice the number or quantity. ● n. /**dyoo**-pli-kuht/ one of two or more identical things. ● v. /**dyoo**-pli-kayt/ (**duplicates**, **duplicating**, **duplicated**) **1** make or be an exact copy of. **2** multiply by two. **3** do (something) again unnecessarily.
– DERIVATIVES **duplication** n.
– ORIGIN Latin *duplicare*.

duplicator ● n. a machine for copying something.

duplicitous ● adj. deceitful.

duplicity /dyoo-**pli**-si-ti/ ● n. deceitfulness.

du Pré E
/dyoo **pray**/, Jacqueline (1945–87), English cellist. Her performing career was halted in 1972 by multiple sclerosis.

durable ● adj. **1** hard-wearing. **2** (of goods) not for immediate consumption and so able to be kept.
– DERIVATIVES **durability** n.
– ORIGIN Latin *durabilis*.

dura mater /dyoo-ruh **may**-ter/ ● n. the tough outermost membrane enclosing the brain and spinal cord.
– ORIGIN Latin, 'hard mother'.

duration ● n. the time during which something continues.
– ORIGIN Latin.

Durban E
a seaport and resort in South Africa, on the coast of KwaZulu/Natal.

Dürer E
/**dyoor**-er/, Albrecht (1471–1528), German engraver and painter, important for his technically advanced woodcuts and copper engravings.

duress /dyuu-**ress**/ ● **n.** threats or violence used to force a person to do something: *confessions extracted under duress.*
– ORIGIN Latin *durus* 'hard'.

Durham E
(also **County Durham**) a county of NE England; county town, Durham.

during ● **prep. 1** throughout the course of. **2** at a particular point in the course of.
– ORIGIN Latin *durare* 'endure'.

Durkheim E
/**derk**-hym/, Émile (1858–1917), French sociologist, a founder of modern sociology.

Durrell[1] E
/**dur**-ruhl/, Gerald (Malcolm) (1925–95), English zoologist and writer, younger brother of Lawrence Durrell. He founded a zoo devoted to the conservation of endangered species.

Durrell[2] E
/**dur**-ruhl/, Lawrence (George) (1912–90), English novelist, poet, and travel writer, brother of Gerald Durrell. His works include the four novels of the *Alexandria Quartet*.

durum wheat /**dyoo**-ruhm/ ● **n.** a kind of hard wheat, yielding flour that is used to make pasta.
– ORIGIN Latin.

Dushanbe E
/doo-**shan**-bay/ the capital of Tajikistan. Former name (1929–61) **STALINABAD**.

dusk ● **n.** the darker stage of twilight.
– ORIGIN Old English, 'dark, swarthy'.

dusky ● **adj.** (**duskier**, **duskiest**) darkish in colour.

Düsseldorf E
/**duus**-s'l-dorf/ an industrial city of NW Germany, on the Rhine, capital of the state of North Rhine-Westphalia.

dust ● **n. 1** fine, dry powder made up of tiny particles of earth or waste matter. **2** any material in the form of tiny particles: *coal dust.* ● **v. 1** remove dust from the surface of. **2** cover lightly with a powdered substance.
– ORIGIN Old English.

dustbin ● **n.** Brit. a large container for household rubbish.

dust bowl ● **n.** an area where vegetation has been lost and soil reduced to dust and eroded.

dustcart ● **n.** Brit. a vehicle used for collecting household rubbish.

dust cover ● **n.** a dust jacket or dust sheet.

duster ● **n.** Brit. a cloth for dusting furniture.

dust jacket ● **n.** a removable paper cover on a book.

dustman ● **n.** Brit. a man employed to remove household rubbish from dustbins.

dustpan ● **n.** a hand-held container into which dust and waste can be swept.

dust sheet ● **n.** Brit. a sheet for covering furniture to protect it from dust or while decorating.

dust-up ● **n.** informal a fight or quarrel.

dusty ● **adj.** (**dustier**, **dustiest**) **1** covered with or resembling dust. **2** solemn and uninteresting.

Dutch ● **adj.** relating to the Netherlands or its language. ● **n.** the language of the Netherlands.
– PHRASES **go Dutch** share the cost of a meal equally.
ORIGIN Dutch *dutsch*.

Dutch courage ● **n.** confidence gained from drinking alcohol.

Dutch East Indies E
former name for **INDONESIA**.

Dutch elm disease ● **n.** a disease of elm trees, caused by a fungus.

Dutch Guiana E
former name for **SURINAME**.

Dutch oven ● **n.** a covered earthenware container for cooking casseroles.

dutiable /**dyoo**-ti-uh-b'l/ ● **adj.** on which customs or other duties have to be paid.

dutiful ● **adj.** conscientiously doing one's duty.
– DERIVATIVES **dutifully** adv.

duty ● **n.** (pl. **duties**) **1** something one has to do because it is morally or legally necessary. **2** a task required as part of one's job. **3** a payment charged on the import, export, manufacture, or sale of goods.
– PHRASES **on** (or **off**) **duty** engaged (or not engaged) in one's regular work.
– ORIGIN Old French *duete*.

duty-bound ● **adj.** morally or legally obliged.

duty-free ● **adj. & adv.** not requiring payment of duty.

Duvalier E
/dyoo-**val**-i-ay/ François (1907–71; known as **Papa Doc**), Haitian statesman, President 1957–71. His regime was noted for its oppressive nature. He was succeeded by his son Jean-Claude (b.1951; known as **Baby Doc**), who was overthrown by a mass uprising in 1986.

duvet /**doo**-vay/ ● **n.** esp. Brit. a thick quilt used instead of an upper sheet and blankets.
– ORIGIN French, 'down'.

DVD ● **abbrev.** digital versatile disc.

DVLA ● **abbrev.** Driver and Vehicle Licensing Agency.

Dvořák E
/**dvor**-*zhahk*/, Antonín (1841–1904), Czech composer, who is famous for his ninth symphony ('From the New World').

dwarf ● **n.** (pl. **dwarfs** or **dwarves**) **1** a member of a mythical race of short human-like creatures. **2** an abnormally small person. ● **v.** cause to seem small in comparison. ● **adj.** (of an animal or plant) much smaller than is usual for its type or species: *a dwarf conifer.*
– ORIGIN Old English.

dwarfism ● **n.** unusually low stature or small size.

dwell ● v. (**dwells**, **dwelling**, **dwelt** or **dwelled**) **1** formal live in or at a place. **2** (**dwell on/upon**) think at length about.
– DERIVATIVES **dweller** n.
– ORIGIN Old English.

dwelling ● n. formal a house or other place of residence.

dwindle ● v. (**dwindles**, **dwindling**, **dwindled**) gradually lessen or fade.
– ORIGIN Scots and dialect *dwine*.

dye ● n. a natural or synthetic substance used to colour something. ● v. (**dyes**, **dyeing**, **dyed**) make (something) a particular colour with dye.
– PHRASES **dyed in the wool** unchanging in a particular belief.
– ORIGIN Old English.

dyestuff ● n. a substance used as or yielding a dye.

dying pres. part. of DIE[1].

dyke[1] (also **dike**) ● n. **1** a barrier built to prevent flooding from the sea. **2** a ditch or watercourse. **3** Geol. an intrusion of igneous rock cutting across existing strata.
– ORIGIN Old Norse.

dyke[2] (also **dike**) ● n. informal a lesbian.
– ORIGIN unknown.

Dylan, E
Bob (b.1941; born *Robert Allen Zimmerman*), American singer and songwriter. He led an urban folk-music revival in the 1960s. becoming known for his political songs.

dynamic ● adj. **1** (of a process) constantly changing or active. **2** full of energy and new ideas. **3** Physics relating to forces producing motion. Often contrasted with STATIC. ● n. an energizing force.
– DERIVATIVES **dynamical** adj. **dynamically** adv.
– ORIGIN Greek *dunamikos*.

dynamic range ● n. the range of sound that occurs in a piece of music or that can be handled by a piece of equipment.

dynamics ● n. **1** the branch of mechanics concerned with the motion of bodies under the action of forces. **2** the forces which stimulate change within a process. **3** the varying levels of volume of sound in a musical performance.

dynamism ● n. the quality of being dynamic.

dynamite ● n. **1** a high explosive made of nitroglycerine. **2** informal an extremely impressive or dangerous person or thing. ● v. (**dynamites**, **dynamiting**, **dynamited**) blow up with dynamite.
– ORIGIN Greek *dunamis* 'power'.

dynamo ● n. (pl. **dynamos**) esp. Brit. a machine for converting mechanical energy into electrical energy.
– ORIGIN from *dynamo-electric machine*.

dynast /dy-nuhst, dy-nast/ ● n. a member of a dynasty, especially a hereditary ruler.

dynasty /di-nuh-sti/ ● n. (pl. **dynasties**) **1** a line of hereditary rulers. **2** a succession of powerful people from the same family.
– DERIVATIVES **dynastic** adj.
– ORIGIN Greek *dunasteia* 'lordship'.

dyne /dyn/ ● n. Physics force required to give a mass of one gram an acceleration of one centimetre per second per second.
– ORIGIN Greek *dunamis* 'force, power'.

dys- ● comb. form bad; difficult: *dyspepsia*.
– ORIGIN Greek *dus-*.

dysentery /diss-uhn-tri/ ● n. a disease in which the intestines are infected, resulting in severe diarrhoea.
– ORIGIN Greek *dusenteria*.

dysfunctional ● adj. **1** not operating properly. **2** unable to deal with normal social relations.
– DERIVATIVES **dysfunction** n.

dyslexia /diss-lek-si-uh/ ● n. a disorder involving difficulty in learning to read words, letters, and other symbols.
– DERIVATIVES **dyslexic** adj. & n.
– ORIGIN Greek *lexis* 'speech'.

dysmenorrhoea /diss-men-uh-ree-uh/ (US **dysmenorrhea**) ● n. Med. painful menstruation.

dyspepsia /diss-pep-si-uh/ ● n. indigestion.
– ORIGIN Greek *duspepsia*.

dyspeptic ● adj. **1** relating to or suffering from dyspepsia. **2** irritable.

dysprosium /diss-proh-zi-uhm/ ● n. a soft silvery-white metallic chemical element.
– ORIGIN Greek *dusprositos* 'hard to get at'.

dystopia /diss-toh-pi-uh/ ● n. an imaginary place or society in which everything is bad.
– DERIVATIVES **dystopian** adj. & n.
– ORIGIN from DYS- + UTOPIA.

dystrophy /diss-truh-fi/ ● n. Med. a disorder in which an organ or tissue of the body wastes away. See also MUSCULAR DYSTROPHY.
– ORIGIN from Greek *-trophia* 'nourishment'.

Ee

E[1] (also **e**) ● n. (pl. **Es** or **E's**) **1** the fifth letter of the alphabet. **2** Music the third note of the scale of C major.

E[2] ● abbrev. **1** East or Eastern. **2** informal the drug Ecstasy or a tablet of Ecstasy. **3** Physics energy.

each ● det. & pron. every one of two or more people or things, regarded separately. ● adv. to, for, or by every one of a group.
– ORIGIN Old English.

each other ● pron. the other one or ones.

eager ● adj. **1** strongly wanting to do or have. **2** keenly expectant or interested.
– DERIVATIVES **eagerly** adv. **eagerness** n.

– ORIGIN Old French *aigre* 'keen'.

eagle • n. a large keen-sighted bird of prey with long broad wings.
– ORIGIN Old French *aigle*.

eagle-eyed • adj. sharp-sighted and very observant.

ear[1] • n. **1** the organ of hearing and balance in humans and other vertebrates. **2** an ability to recognize and appreciate music or language. **3** willingness to listen: *a sympathetic ear.*
– PHRASES **be all ears** informal be listening attentively. **keep one's ear to the ground** be well informed about events. **be out on one's ear** informal be forced to leave a job. **up to one's ears in** informal very busy with.
– ORIGIN Old English.

ear[2] • n. the seed-bearing head of a cereal plant.
– ORIGIN Old English.

earache • n. pain inside the ear.

eardrum • n. the membrane of the middle ear, which vibrates in response to sound waves.

earful • n. informal a lengthy reprimand.

> **Earhart** E
> /air-hart/, Amelia (1898–1937), American aviator, who in 1932 became the first woman to fly across the Atlantic solo. Her aircraft disappeared over the Pacific Ocean during a later round-the-world flight.

earhole • n. the external opening of the ear.

earl • n. a British nobleman ranking above a viscount and below a marquess.
– DERIVATIVES **earldom** n.
– ORIGIN Old English.

ear lobe • n. the rounded fleshy part at the lower edge of the external ear.

early • adj. **(earlier, earliest)** & adv. **1** before the usual or expected time. **2** near the beginning of a particular time, period, or sequence.
– PHRASES **at the earliest** not before the time or date specified. **early** (or **earlier**) **on** at an early (or earlier) stage.
– DERIVATIVES **earliness** n.
– ORIGIN Old English.

earmark • n. a mark on the ear of a domesticated animal indicating its owner or identity. • v. **(be earmarked)** be chosen for a particular purpose.

earmuffs • pl. n. a pair of fabric coverings worn over the ears to protect them from cold or noise.

earn • v. **1** obtain (money) in return for labour or services. **2** gain as the reward for hard work or merit. **3** (of money invested) gain (money) as interest or profit.
– DERIVATIVES **earner** n.
– ORIGIN Old English.

earnest /er-nist/ • adj. very serious.
– PHRASES **in earnest** with sincere and serious intention.
– DERIVATIVES **earnestly** adv. **earnestness** n.
– ORIGIN Old English.

earnings • pl. n. money or income earned.

> **Earp** E
> /erp/, Wyatt (Berry Stapp) (1848–1929), American gambler and marshal, famous for the gunfight at the OK Corral at Tombstone, Arizona (1881).

earphone • n. an electrical device worn on the ear to receive communications or to listen to a radio or recorded sound.

earpiece • n. the part of a telephone, radio receiver, or other device for listening that is applied to the ear during use.

ear-piercing • adj. loud and shrill.

earplug • n. a piece of wax, cotton wool, etc., placed in the ear as protection against noise or water.

earring • n. a piece of jewellery worn on the lobe or edge of the ear.

earshot • n. the distance over which one can hear or be heard.

ear-splitting • adj. extremely loud.

earth • n. **1** (also **Earth**) the planet on which we live. **2** the substance of the land surface; soil. **3** Brit. electrical connection to the ground, regarded as having zero electrical potential. **4** the underground lair of a badger or fox. • v. Brit. connect (an electrical device) to earth.
– PHRASES **come back** (or **down**) **to earth** return to reality. **the earth** esp. Brit. a very large amount: *her hat cost the earth.* **on earth** used for emphasis: *what on earth are you doing?*
– ORIGIN Old English.

earthen • adj. **1** made of compressed earth. **2** (of a pot) made of baked clay.

earthenware • n. pottery made of baked clay.

earthling • n. (in science fiction) a person from the earth.

earthly • adj. **1** relating to the earth or human life on the earth. **2** material; worldly. **3** informal used for emphasis; *there was no earthly reason to rush.*

earthquake • n. a sudden violent shaking of the ground, caused by movements within the earth's crust.

earth sciences • pl. n. the branches of science concerned with the physical composition of the earth and its atmosphere.

earth-shattering • adj. informal very important or shocking.

earthwork • n. a large man-made bank of soil.

earthworm • n. a burrowing worm that lives in the soil.

earthy • adj. **(earthier, earthiest) 1** resembling soil. **2** direct and not embarrassed about sexual subjects or bodily functions.

earwax • n. the protective waxy substance produced in the passage of the outer ear.

earwig • n. a small insect with a pair of pincers at its rear end.
– ORIGIN Old English.

ease • n. **1** absence of difficulty or effort. **2** freedom from problems. • v. **(eases, easing, eased) 1** make or become less serious. **2** move carefully or gradually. **3 (ease off/up)** do something with more moderation.
– ORIGIN Old French *aise*.

easel /ee-z'l/ • n. a wooden frame on legs for holding an artist's work in progress.
– ORIGIN Dutch *ezel* 'ass'.

easily • adv. **1** without difficulty or effort. **2** without doubt.

east • n. **1** the direction in which the sun rises at the equinoxes, on the right-hand side of a person facing north. **2** the eastern part of a place. **3 (the East)** the regions or countries lying to the east of Europe. **4 (the East)** hist. the former communist states of eastern Eur-

ope. • **adj. 1** lying towards or facing the east. **2** (of a wind) blowing from the east. • **adv.** to or towards the east.
– DERIVATIVES **eastbound** adj. & adv.
– ORIGIN Old English.

East Anglia E
a region of eastern England consisting of the counties of Norfolk, Suffolk, and parts of Essex and Cambridgeshire.

Eastbourne E
a resort town on the south coast of England, in East Sussex.

Easter (also **Easter Day** or **Easter Sunday**) • **n.** the festival of the Christian Church celebrating the resurrection of Christ.
– ORIGIN Old English.

Easter egg • **n.** a chocolate egg or decorated hard-boiled egg given as a gift at Easter.

Easter Island E
an island in the SE Pacific west of Chile and administered by that country, famous for its large statues of human heads.

easterly • **adj. & adv. 1** towards or facing the east. **2** (of a wind) blowing from the east.

eastern • **adj. 1** situated in or facing the east. **2** (**Eastern**) coming from or characteristic of the regions to the east of Europe.

Eastern Cape E
a province of south-eastern South Africa; capital, Bisho.

Eastern Church • **n.** = **ORTHODOX CHURCH**.

easterner • **n.** a person from the east of a region.

Easter Rising E
the uprising in Dublin and other cities in Ireland against British rule, Easter 1916. It ended with the surrender of the protesters, but contributed to the establishment of the Irish Free State (1921).

East India Company E
a trading company formed in 1600 to develop commerce in the newly colonized areas of SE Asia and India. In the 18th century it took administrative control of parts of India, and held it until the British Crown took over in 1858.

East Indies E
the islands of SE Asia, especially the Malay Archipelago.

East Lothian E
an administrative region and former county of east central Scotland.

east-north-east • **n.** the direction halfway between east and north-east.

East Riding of Yorkshire E
a unitary council in NE England, formerly one of the traditional ridings (divisions) of the county of Yorkshire.

east-south-east • **n.** the direction halfway between east and south-east.

East Sussex E
a county of SE England; county town, Lewes.

East Timor E
the eastern part of the island of Timor in the southern Malay Archipelago; chief town, Dili.
– DERIVATIVES **East Timorese** n. & adj.

eastward • **adj.** in an easterly direction. • **adv.** (also **eastwards**) towards the east.

Eastwood, E
Clint (b.1930), American film actor and director, known for his roles in films such as *Dirty Harry* and for directing the western *Unforgiven*.

easy • **adj.** (**easier**, **easiest**) **1** achieved without great effort; presenting few difficulties. **2** free from worry or problems. **3** lacking anxiety or awkwardness: *his easy and agreeable manner.*
– PHRASES **take it easy** relax.

easy chair • **n.** a large, comfortable chair.

easy-going • **adj.** relaxed and open-minded.

easy listening • **n.** popular music that is tuneful and undemanding.

eat • **v.** (**eats**, **eating**, **ate** /et, ayt/; past part. **eaten**) **1** put (food) into the mouth and chew and swallow it. **2** (**eat away**) gradually wear away or destroy (something). **3** (**eat up**) use (resources) in very large quantities. • **n.** (**eats**) informal light food or snacks.
– PHRASES **eat one's words** admit that what one said before was wrong.
– DERIVATIVES **eater** n.
– ORIGIN Old English.

eatable • **adj.** fit to be consumed as food. • **n.** (**eatables**) items of food.

eatery • **n.** (pl. **eateries**) informal a restaurant or cafe.

eau de cologne /oh duh kuh-**lohn**/ • **n.** (pl. **eaux de cologne** /oh duh kuh-**lohn**/) = **COLOGNE**.
– ORIGIN French, 'water of Cologne'.

eau de toilette /oh duh twah-**let**/ • **n.** (pl. **eaux de toilette** /oh duh twah-**let**/) a dilute form of perfume; toilet water.
– ORIGIN French.

eaves • **pl. n.** the part of a roof that meets or overhangs the walls of a building.
– ORIGIN Old English.

eavesdrop • **v.** (**eavesdrops**, **eavesdropping**, **eavesdropped**) secretly listen to a conversation.
– DERIVATIVES **eavesdropper** n.
– ORIGIN from former *eavesdrop* 'the ground on to which water drips from the eaves'.

ebb • **n.** the movement of the tide out to sea. • **v. 1** (of tidewater) move away from the land. **2** gradually become less or weaker: *my enthusiasm was ebbing away.*
– PHRASES **at a low ebb** in a poor state.
– ORIGIN Old English.

ebony /eb-uh-ni/ • **n. 1** heavy blackish or very dark brown wood from a tree of tropical and warm regions. **2** a very dark brown or black colour.
– ORIGIN Greek *ebenos* 'ebony tree'.

Ebro E
/ee-broh, **eb**-roh/ the chief river of NE Spain, rising in the north and flowing southeastwards into the Mediterranean Sea.

ebullient /i-**bul**-yuhnt/ • **adj.** cheerful and full of energy.

– DERIVATIVES **ebullience** n.
– ORIGIN Latin *ebullire* 'boil up'.

EC • **abbrev.** European Community.

eccentric /ik-sen-trik/ • **adj. 1** unconventional and slightly strange. **2** tech. not placed centrally or not having its axis placed centrally. • **n.** an eccentric person.
– DERIVATIVES **eccentrically** adv.
– ORIGIN Greek *ekkentros.*

eccentricity /ek-sen-triss-i-ti/ • **n.** (pl. **eccentricities**) **1** the quality of being eccentric. **2** an eccentric act or habit.

ecclesiastic • **n.** formal a Christian priest.

ecclesiastical /i-klee-zi-ass-ti-k'l/ • **adj.** relating to the Christian Church or its clergy.
– ORIGIN Greek *ekklēsiastikos.*

ECG • **abbrev.** electrocardiogram or electrocardiograph.

echelon /esh-uh-lon/ • **n.** a level or rank in an organization, profession, or society.
– ORIGIN French *échelon.*

echinoderm /i-ky-nuh-derm/ • **n.** Zool. a marine invertebrate of a large group including starfishes and sea urchins.
– ORIGIN from Greek *ekhinos* 'hedgehog, sea urchin' + *derma* 'skin'.

echo • **n.** (pl. **echoes**) **1** a sound caused by the reflection of sound waves from a surface back to the listener. **2** a reflected radio or radar beam. **3** something suggestive of or similar to something else. • **v.** (**echoes**, **echoing**, **echoed**) **1** (of a sound) reverberate or be repeated after the original sound has stopped. **2** have a continued significance or influence. **3** repeat (someone's words or opinions).
– DERIVATIVES **echoey** adj.
– ORIGIN Greek *ēkhō.*

echo chamber • **n.** an enclosed space for producing echoes.

echoic /e-koh-ik/ • **adj.** of or like an echo.

echolocation /e-koh-loh-kay-sh'n/ • **n.** the location of objects by reflected sound, used by animals such as dolphins and bats.

echo sounder • **n.** a device for determining the depth of the seabed or detecting objects in water by measuring the time taken for echoes to return to the listener.

eclair /i-klair/ • **n.** a long cake of choux pastry filled with cream and topped with chocolate icing.
– ORIGIN French, 'lightning'.

eclampsia /i-klamp-si-uh/ • **n.** Med. a condition in which a pregnant woman suffering from high blood pressure experiences convulsions.
– ORIGIN Greek *eklampsis* 'sudden development'.

éclat /ay-klah/ • **n.** a notably brilliant or successful effect.
– ORIGIN French.

eclectic /i-klek-tik/ • **adj.** deriving ideas or style from a wide range of sources.
– DERIVATIVES **eclecticism** n.
– ORIGIN Greek *eklektikos.*

eclipse /i-klips/ • **n. 1** an occasion when the moon, a planet, etc. blocks out the light from a similar object. **2** a sudden loss of significance or power. • **v.** (**eclipses**, **eclipsing**, **eclipsed**) **1** (of a planet, the moon, etc.) obscure the light from or to (a similar object). **2** deprive of significance or power.
– ORIGIN Greek *ekleipsis.*

ecliptic /i-klip-tik/ • **n.** Astron. the sun's apparent circular path among the stars during the year.

eco- /ee-koh/ • **comb. form** = **ECOLOGY.**

eco-friendly • **adj.** not harmful to the environment.

E. coli /ee **koh**-ly/ • **n.** the bacterium *Escherichia coli*, some strains of which can cause severe food poisoning.

ecology /i-kol-uh-ji/ • **n.** the branch of biology concerned with the relations of organisms to one another and to their surroundings.
– DERIVATIVES **ecological** adj. **ecologist** n.
– ORIGIN Greek *oikos* 'house'.

e-commerce • **n.** commercial transactions conducted on the Internet.

economic /ee-kuh-nom-ik, ek-uh-**nom**-ik/ • **adj. 1** relating to economics or the economy of a country or region. **2** profitable, or having to do with profitability.

economical • **adj. 1** giving good value in relation to the resources used or money spent. **2** careful in the use of resources or money.
– DERIVATIVES **economically** adv.

economics • **n.** the branch of knowledge concerned with the production, consumption, and transfer of wealth.

economist • **n.** an expert in economics.

economize (also **economise**) • **v.** (**economizes**, **economizing**, **economized**) spend less; be economical.

economy • **n.** (pl. **economies**) **1** the state of a country or region in terms of the production and consumption of goods and services and the supply of money. **2** careful management of resources. **3** a financial saving. **4** (also **economy class**) the cheapest class of air or rail travel. • **adj.** offering good value for money: *an economy pack.*
– ORIGIN Greek *oikonomia* 'household management'.

ecosystem • **n.** a biological community of interacting organisms and their environment.

ecotourism • **n.** tourism directed towards unspoilt natural environments and intended to support conservation efforts.

eco-warrior • **n.** a person who engages in protest activities aimed at protecting the environment from damage.

ecru /ek-roo/ • **n.** a light cream or beige colour.
– ORIGIN French, 'unbleached'.

ecstasy /ek-stuh-si/ • **n.** (pl. **ecstasies**) **1** an overwhelming feeling of great happiness or joyful excitement. **2** an emotional or religious frenzy. **3** (**Ecstasy**) an illegal amphetamine-based drug.
– ORIGIN Greek *ekstasis* 'standing outside oneself'.

ecstatic /ik-stat-ik/ • **adj.** very happy, excited, or enthusiastic.

ectopic pregnancy • **n.** a pregnancy in which the fetus develops outside the womb.
– ORIGIN Greek *ektopos* 'out of place'.

ectoplasm /ek-toh-pla-z'm/ • **n.** a substance that supposedly comes out of the body of a medium during a trance.

ecu /ek-yoo/ (also **ECU**) • **n.** (pl. **ecu** or **ecus**) former term for **EURO.**

– ORIGIN acronym from *European currency unit*.

Ecuador E
/ek-wuh-dor/ a republic in South America, on the Pacific coast; capital, Quito.
– DERIVATIVES **Ecuadorean** adj. & n.

ecumenical /ee-kyoo-men-i-k'l, ek-yoo-men-i-k'l/ • **adj. 1** representing a number of different Christian Churches. **2** promoting unity among the world's Christian Churches.
– ORIGIN Greek *oikoumenikos*.

e

ecumenism /i-kyoo-muh-ni-z'm/ • **n.** the aim of promoting unity among the world's Christian Churches.

eczema /eks-(i)-muh/ • **n.** a condition in which patches of skin become rough and inflamed, causing itching and bleeding.
– ORIGIN Greek *ekzema*.

-ed[1] • **suffix** forming adjectives: **1** having; affected by: *talented*. **2** from phrases consisting of adjective and noun: *bad-tempered*.
– ORIGIN Old English.

-ed[2] • **suffix** forming: **1** the past tense and past participle of weak verbs: *landed*. **2** participial adjectives: *wounded*.

Edam /ee-dam/ • **n.** a round yellow cheese with a red wax coating.
– ORIGIN from *Edam* in the Netherlands.

Eddington, E
Sir Arthur Stanley (1882–1944), English astronomer, considered the founder of astrophysics.

eddy • **n.** (pl. **eddies**) a circular movement of water causing a small whirlpool. • **v.** (**eddies, eddying, eddied**) (of water, air, etc.) move in a circular way.
– ORIGIN prob. from Old English, 'again, back'.

edelweiss /ay-duhl-vyss/ • **n.** a mountain plant with small flowers.
– ORIGIN German.

edema • **n.** US = **OEDEMA**.

Eden[1], E
(Robert) Anthony, 1st Earl of Avon (1897–1977), British Conservative statesman, Prime Minister 1955–7. He resigned after widespread opposition to Britain's role in the Suez Crisis of 1956.

Eden[2] E
(also **Garden of Eden**) the place where Adam and Eve lived in the biblical account of the Creation, from which they were expelled for disobediently eating the fruit of the tree of knowledge.

Edgar E
(944–75), king of England 959–75. King of Northumbria and Mercia from 957, he succeeded to the throne of England on the death of his brother Edwy.

edge • **n. 1** the outside limit of an object, area, or surface. **2** the line along which two surfaces of a solid meet. **3** the sharpened side of a blade. **4** a slight advantage over close rivals. • **v.** (**edges, edging, edged**) **1** provide with an edge or border. **2** move gradually and carefully.
– PHRASES **on edge** tense or irritable.
– ORIGIN Old English.

Edgehill, Battle of E
the first battle of the English Civil War (1642), fought between the Royalists and Parliamentarians at the village of Edgehill in the west Midlands; it ended with no clear winner.

edgeways (also **edgewise**) • **adv.** with the edge uppermost or towards the viewer.
– PHRASES **get a word in edgeways** manage to break into a conversation.

edging • **n.** something forming an edge or border.

edgy • **adj.** (**edgier, edgiest**) tense, nervous, or irritable.
– DERIVATIVES **edgily** adv. **edginess** n.

edible • **adj.** fit to be eaten. • **n.** (**edibles**) items of food.
– ORIGIN Latin *edibilis*.

edict /ee-dikt/ • **n.** an official order or proclamation.
– ORIGIN Latin *edictum*.

edifice /ed-i-fiss/ • **n.** a large, impressive building.
– ORIGIN Latin *aedificium*.

edify /ed-i-fy/ • **v.** (**edifies, edifying, edified**) improve the mind or character of (someone) by teaching.
– DERIVATIVES **edification** n.
– ORIGIN Latin *aedificare* 'build'.

Edinburgh E
/ed-in-buh-ruh/ the capital of Scotland.

Edinburgh, Duke of E
see **PHILIP, PRINCE**.

Edison E
/ed-i-suhn/, Thomas (Alva) (1847–1931), American inventor. His inventions include automatic telegraph systems, the phonograph (1877), and the carbon filament lamp.

edit • **v.** (**edits, editing, edited**) **1** prepare (written material) for publication by correcting, shortening, or improving it. **2** prepare material for (a recording or broadcast). **3** be editor of (a newspaper or magazine). • **n.** a change made as a result of editing.
– ORIGIN from **EDITOR**.

edition • **n. 1** a particular form of a published text. **2** the total number of copies of a book, newspaper, etc. issued at one time. **3** a particular instance of a regular television or radio programme.
– ORIGIN Latin.

editor • **n. 1** a person who is in charge of a newspaper or magazine. **2** a person who prepares or selects texts or recorded material for publication or broadcasting.
– DERIVATIVES **editorship** n.
– ORIGIN Latin.

editorial • **adj.** relating to the selecting or preparing of material for publication. • **n.** a newspaper article giving the editor's opinion on an issue.

editorialize (also **editorialise**) • **v.** (**editorializes, editorializing, editorialized**) (of a newspaper or editor) express opinions rather than just report news.

Edmonton E
/ed-muhn-tuhn/ the capital of Alberta, Canada.

Edmund I E
(921–46), king of England 939–46.

Edmund II E
(*c.*980–1016; known as **Edmund Ironside**), son of Ethelred the Unready, king of England 1016. He was forced to divide the kingdom with Canute, who became king of all England on Edmund's death.

educate /ed-yuu-kayt/ ● v. (**educates**, **educating**, **educated**) **1** give intellectual or moral instruction to. **2** give training in a particular subject.
– DERIVATIVES **educative** adj. **educator** n.
– ORIGIN Latin *educare* 'lead out'.

educated guess ● n. a guess based on knowledge and experience.

education ● n. **1** the process of teaching or learning. **2** the theory and practice of teaching. **3** training in a particular subject.
– DERIVATIVES **educational** adj. **educationist** n.

Edward I E
(1239–1307; known as **the Hammer of the Scots**), son of Henry III, king of England 1272–1307. He established English rule over Wales, but failed to conquer Scotland.

Edward II E
(1284–1327), son of Edward I, king of England 1307–27. His reign ended when he was deposed by his wife, Isabella of France, and her lover, Roger de Mortimer, and murdered.

Edward III E
(1312–77), son of Edward II, king of England 1327–77. In 1330 he banished his mother Isabella and executed her lover Mortimer. His claim to the French throne started the Hundred Years War.

Edward IV E
(1442–83), son of Richard, Duke of York, king of England 1461–83. He became king after defeating the Lancastrian Henry VI.

Edward V E
(1470–*c.*1483), son of Edward IV, king of England 1483 but not crowned. Edward and his brother Richard (known as the Princes in the Tower) were probably murdered and the throne was taken by their uncle, Richard III.

Edward VI E
(1537–53), son of Henry VIII, king of England 1547–53. His reign saw the establishment of Protestantism as the state religion.

Edward VII E
(1841–1910), son of Queen Victoria, king of Great Britain and Ireland 1901–10. His popularity helped revitalize the monarchy.

Edward VIII E
(1894–1972), son of George V, king of the United Kingdom 1936 but not crowned. He abdicated eleven months after coming to the throne in order to marry the American divorcee Mrs Wallis Simpson.

Edward, Prince, E
Edward Antony Richard Louis, Earl of Wessex (b.1964), third son of Elizabeth II.

Edwardian /ed-wor-di-uhn/ ● adj. relating to the reign of King Edward VII (1901–10).

Edward the Confessor, St E
(*c.*1003–66), son of Ethelred the Unready, king of England 1042–66. He founded Westminster Abbey. Feast day, 13 October.

Edward the Martyr, St E
(*c.*963–78), son of Edgar, king of England 975–8. He was murdered by supporters of his half-brother, Ethelred. Feast day, 18 March.

Edwy E
/ed-wi/ (also **Eadwig**) (d.959), king of England 955–7. After Mercia and Northumbria renounced him in favour of his brother Edgar, he ruled over only the lands south of the Thames.

-ee ● suffix forming nouns: **1** referring to the person affected by the action of a verb: *employee*. **2** referring to a person described as or concerned with: *absentee*.
– ORIGIN Old French *-é*.

EEC ● abbrev. European Economic Community.

eel ● n. a snake-like fish with a very long thin body and small fins.
– ORIGIN Old English.

e'er /air/ ● adv. literary = **EVER**.

eerie /eer-i/ ● adj. (**eerier**, **eeriest**) strange and frightening.
– ORIGIN prob. from Old English, 'cowardly'.

efface /i-fayss/ ● v. (**effaces**, **effacing**, **effaced**) **1** rub off (a mark) from a surface. **2** (**efface oneself**) make oneself appear unimportant.
– ORIGIN French *effacer*.

effect ● n. **1** a change which is a result of an action or other cause. **2** the state of being or becoming operative: *the ban is to take effect in six months*. **3** the extent to which something succeeds: *wind power can be used to great effect*. **4** (**effects**) personal belongings. **5** (**effects**) the lighting, sound, or scenery used in a play or film. **6** Physics a physical phenomenon, named after its discoverer: *the Doppler effect*. ● v. bring about (a result).
– PHRASES **in effect** in practice, even if not formally acknowledged.
– ORIGIN Latin *effectus*.

USAGE effect
Do not confuse **affect** and **effect**. **Affect** is a verb meaning 'make a difference to', as in *the changes will affect everyone*. **Effect** is used both as a noun meaning 'a result' (e.g. *the substance has a pain-killing effect*) and as a verb meaning 'bring about (a result)', as in *she effected a cost-cutting exercise*.

effective ● adj. **1** producing an intended result. **2** (of a law or policy) operative. **3** existing in fact, though not formally acknowledged as such: *he is in effective control of the military*.
– DERIVATIVES **effectively** adv. **effectiveness** n.

effectual /i-fek-choo-uhl/ ● adj. effective.
– DERIVATIVES **effectually** adv.

effeminate /i-fem-i-nuht/ ● adj. (of a man) having characteristics regarded as typical of a woman.
– DERIVATIVES **effeminacy** n.

– ORIGIN Latin *effeminare* 'make feminine'.

effervesce • v. (**effervesces, effervescing, effervesced**) (of a liquid) give off bubbles.

effervescent • adj. **1** (of a liquid) giving off bubbles; fizzy. **2** lively and enthusiastic.
– DERIVATIVES **effervescence** n.
– ORIGIN Latin *effervescere* 'boil up'.

effete /i-feet/ • adj. **1** no longer effective; weak. **2** (of a man) effeminate.
– ORIGIN Latin *effetus* 'worn out by bearing young'.

efficacious /ef-fi-kay-shuhss/ • adj. formal effective.
– ORIGIN Latin *efficere* 'accomplish'.

efficacy /ef-fi-kuh-si/ • n. formal the ability to produce an intended result.

efficiency • n. (pl. **efficiencies**) the quality of being efficient.

efficient • adj. working productively with no waste of money or effort.
– ORIGIN Latin *efficere* 'accomplish'.

effigy /ef-fi-ji/ • n. (pl. **effigies**) a sculpture or model of a person.
– ORIGIN Latin *effigies*.

efflorescence /ef-fluh-ress-uhnss/ • n. literary a very high stage of development.
– ORIGIN Latin *efflorescere*.

effluent • n. liquid waste or sewage discharged into a river or the sea.
– ORIGIN Latin *effluere* 'flow out'.

effluvium /i-floo-vi-uhm/ • n. (pl. **effluvia** /i-floo-vi-uh/) an unpleasant or harmful smell or discharge.
– ORIGIN Latin.

effort • n. **1** a vigorous or determined attempt. **2** strenuous exertion.
– ORIGIN French.

effortless • adj. done or achieved without effort; natural and easy.
– DERIVATIVES **effortlessly** adv.

effrontery /i-frun-tuh-ri/ • n. insolence or impertinence.
– ORIGIN French *effronterie*.

effusion • n. **1** an instance of giving off a liquid, light, or smell. **2** an instance of unrestrained speech or writing.
– ORIGIN Latin.

effusive • adj. expressing pleasure or approval in an unrestrained way.

e.g. • abbrev. for example.
– ORIGIN from Latin *exempli gratia* 'for the sake of example'.

egalitarian /i-gal-i-tair-i-uhn/ • adj. believing that all people are equal and deserve equal rights and opportunities. • n. an egalitarian person.
– DERIVATIVES **egalitarianism** n.
– ORIGIN French *égalitaire*.

Egbert E
(d.839), king of Wessex 802–39. By 829 he had established the supremacy of Wessex, laying the foundations for a united England.

egg¹ • n. **1** an oval or round object laid by a female bird, reptile, fish, or invertebrate and containing an ovum which if fertilized can develop into a new organism. **2** an ovum. **3** informal, dated a person of a specified kind: *you're a good egg.*
– PHRASES **with egg on one's face** informal appearing foolish.
– DERIVATIVES **eggy** adj.
– ORIGIN Old English.

egg² • v. (**egg on**) urge to do something foolish or risky.
– ORIGIN Old Norse.

egghead • n. informal a very studious person.

eggplant • n. N. Amer. = **AUBERGINE**.

eggshell • n. the fragile outer layer of an egg. • adj. **1** (of china) extremely thin and delicate. **2** referring to an oil-based paint that dries with a slight sheen.

egg white • n. the clear substance round the yolk of an egg that turns white when cooked or beaten.

Egmont, Mount E
a volcanic peak in North Island, New Zealand, rising to a height of 2,518 m (8,260 ft). Maori name **TARANAKI**.

ego /ee-goh/ • n. (pl. **egos**) **1** a person's sense of self-esteem. **2** Psychoanalysis the part of the mind that is responsible for the interpretation of reality and the sense of self. Compare with **ID** and **SUPEREGO**.
– ORIGIN Latin, 'I'.

egocentric • adj. self-centred.
– DERIVATIVES **egocentricity** n.

egoism • n. = **EGOTISM**.
– DERIVATIVES **egoist** n.

egomania • n. obsessive egotism.

egotism • n. the quality of being excessively conceited or absorbed in oneself.
– DERIVATIVES **egotist** n. **egotistical** adj.

ego trip • n. informal something that a person does to make them feel important.

egregious /i-gree-juhss/ • adj. outstandingly bad.
– ORIGIN Latin *egregius* 'illustrious'.

egress /ee-gress/ • n. formal **1** the action of going out of or leaving a place. **2** a way out.
– ORIGIN Latin *egressus*.

egret /ee-grit/ • n. a heron with mainly white plumage.
– ORIGIN Old French *aigrette*.

Egypt E
a country in NE Africa bordering on the Mediterranean Sea; capital, Cairo.

Egyptian • n. **1** a person from Egypt. **2** the language used in ancient Egypt. • adj. relating to Egypt.

Ehrlich E
/air-lik/, Paul (1854–1915), German medical scientist, one of the founders of modern immunology and chemotherapy.

Eid /eed/ (also **Id**) • n. **1** (in full **Eid ul-Fitr** /eed uul fee-truh/) the Muslim festival marking the end of the fast of Ramadan. **2** (in full **Eid ul-Adha** /eed uul aa-duh/) the festival marking the culmination of the annual pilgrimage to Mecca.
– ORIGIN Arabic, 'feast'.

eider /I-der/ • n. (pl. **eider** or **eiders**) **1** (also **eider duck**) a northern sea duck with black-and-white plumage. **2** (also **eider down**) soft feathers from the breast of the female eider duck.
– ORIGIN Old Norse.

eiderdown • n. esp. Brit. a quilt filled with down (originally from the eider) or some other soft material.

Eiffel Tower E
/I-fuhl/ a wrought-iron structure 300 metres (984 ft) high, designed by the French engineer Alexandre Gustave Eiffel (1832–1923) and erected in Paris for the World Exhibition of 1889.

Eiger E
/I-ger/ a mountain peak in the Bernese Alps in central Switzerland, which rises to 3,970 m (13,101 ft).

eight • **cardinal number 1** one more than seven; 8. (Roman numeral: **viii** or **VIII**.) **2** an eight-oared rowing boat or its crew.
– ORIGIN Old English.

eighteen • **cardinal number** one more than seventeen; 18. (Roman numeral: **xviii** or **XVIII**.)
– DERIVATIVES **eighteenth** ordinal number.

eighth • **ordinal number 1** that is number eight in a sequence; 8th. **2** (**an eighth/one eighth**) each of eight equal parts into which something is divided.

eighty • **cardinal number** (pl. **eighties**) ten less than ninety; 80. (Roman numeral: **lxxx** or **LXXX**.)
– DERIVATIVES **eightieth** ordinal number.

Eilat E
/ay-lat/ (also **Elat**) a port and resort in Israel, at the head of the Gulf of Aqaba. It is Israel's only outlet to the Red Sea.

Einstein E
/yn-styn/, Albert (1879–1955), German-born American theoretical physicist, originator of the theory of relativity. He influenced the decision to build an atom bomb but after the Second World War he was a strong opponent of nuclear weapons.
– DERIVATIVES **Einsteinian** adj.

einsteinium /yn-sty-ni-uhm/ • **n.** an unstable radioactive chemical element made by high-energy atomic collisions.
– ORIGIN named after Albert EINSTEIN.

Eire E
/air-uh/ the Gaelic name for Ireland, the official name of the Republic of Ireland from 1937 to 1949.

Eisenhower E
/I-z'n-how-er/, Dwight David (1890–1969; known as **Ike**), American general and Republican statesman, 34th President of the US 1953–61. As President he adopted a hard line towards communism.

Eisenstein E
/I-z'n-styn/, Sergei (Mikhailovich) (1898–1948), Soviet film director, best known for *The Battleship Potemkin*.

eisteddfod /I-ste*th*-vod/ • **n.** (pl. **eisteddfods** or **eisteddfodau** /I-ste*th*-vod-I/) a competitive festival of music and poetry in Wales.
– ORIGIN Welsh, 'session'.

either /I-*ther*, ee-*ther*/ • **conj. & adv. 1** used before the first of two alternatives specified. **2** (adv.) used to indicate a similarity or link with a statement just made: *You don't like him, do you? I don't either.* **3** for that matter; moreover. • **det. & pron. 1** one or the other of two people or things. **2** each of two.
– ORIGIN Old English.

ejaculate • **v.** /i-jak-yuu-layt/ (**ejaculates**, **ejaculating**, **ejaculated**) **1** (of a man or male animal) eject semen from the penis at the moment of orgasm. **2** dated say something suddenly.
– DERIVATIVES **ejaculation** n.
– ORIGIN Latin *ejaculari* 'dart out'.

eject • **v. 1** force or throw out violently or suddenly. **2** (of a pilot) escape from an aircraft by means of an ejection seat. **3** force (someone) to leave a place.
– DERIVATIVES **ejection** n. **ejector** n.
– ORIGIN Latin *eicere*.

ejection seat (also **ejector seat**) • **n.** an aircraft seat that can throw its occupant from the craft in an emergency.

eke /eek/ • **v.** (**ekes**, **eking**, **eked**) (**eke out**) **1** use sparingly. **2** make (a living) with difficulty.
– ORIGIN Old English, 'increase'.

elaborate • **adj.** /i-lab-uh-ruht/ involving many carefully arranged parts; complicated. • **v.** /i-lab-uh-rayt/ (**elaborates**, **elaborating**, **elaborated**) **1** develop or present in detail. **2** (**elaborate on**) add more detail to (something already said).
– DERIVATIVES **elaborately** adv. **elaboration** n.
– ORIGIN Latin *elaborare* 'work out'.

El Alamein, Battle of E
/el al-uh-mayn/ a battle of the Second World War fought in 1942 at El Alamein in Egypt, in which British forces under Montgomery defeated German troops led by Rommel.

elan /ay-lan/ • **n.** energy and flair.
– ORIGIN French.

eland /ee-luhnd/ • **n.** an African antelope with spiral horns.
– ORIGIN Dutch, 'elk'.

elapse • **v.** (**elapses**, **elapsing**, **elapsed**) (of time) pass.
– ORIGIN Latin *elabi* 'slip away'.

elastic /i-lass-tik/ • **adj. 1** able to return to normal size or shape after being stretched or squeezed. **2** flexible. • **n.** cord or fabric which returns to its original size or shape after being stretched.
– DERIVATIVES **elasticity** /i-lass-tiss-i-ti/ n.
– ORIGIN Greek *elastikos* 'propulsive'.

elasticated • **adj.** esp. Brit. (of a garment or material) made elastic with rubber thread or tape.

elastic band • **n.** a rubber band.

elastomer /i-lass-tuh-mer/ • **n.** a natural or synthetic polymer having elastic properties, e.g. rubber.

Elat E
var. of EILAT.

elated /i-lay-tid/ • **adj.** extremely happy and excited.
– ORIGIN Latin *elatus* 'raised'.

elation /i-lay-sh'n/ • **n.** great happiness and excitement.

Elba E
/el-buh/ a small island off the west coast of Italy, the place of Napoleon's first exile (1814–15).

Elbe E
/elb, el-buh/ a river of central Europe, flowing generally north-westwards from the Czech Republic through Germany to the North Sea.

Elbert, Mount E
/el-bert/ a mountain in Colorado, the highest peak in the Rocky Mountains at a height of 4,399 m (14,431 ft).

elbow • **n.** the joint between the forearm and the upper arm. • **v.** strike or push with one's elbow.
– ORIGIN Old English.

elbow grease • **n.** informal hard physical work, especially vigorous cleaning.

elbow room • **n.** informal enough space to move or work in.

Elbrus E
/el-brooss/ a peak in the Caucasus mountains, on the border between Russia and Georgia. Rising to 5,642 m (18,481 ft), it is the highest mountain in Europe.

El Cid, E
see **CID, EL**.

elder[1] • **adj.** (of one or more out of a group of people) of a greater age. • **n. 1** (**one's elder**) a person older than oneself. **2** a leader or senior figure in a community.
– ORIGIN Old English.

elder[2] • **n.** a small tree or shrub with white flowers and bluish-black or red berries.
– ORIGIN Old English.

elderberry • **n.** the berry of the elder, used for making jelly or wine.

elderflower • **n.** the flower of the elder, used to make wines and cordials.

elderly • **adj.** old or ageing.

eldest • **adj.** (of one out of a group of people) oldest.

El Dorado /el duh-rah-doh/ • **n.** (pl. **El Dorados**) a place of great wealth.
– ORIGIN Spanish, 'the golden one', first referring to a legendary South American country or city rich in gold.

Eleanor of Aquitaine E
(*c.*1122–1204), daughter of the Duke of Aquitaine, queen of France 1137–52 and of England 1154–89. In 1152 her marriage to Louis VII of France was annulled and she married the future Henry II of England.

elect • **v. 1** choose (someone) to hold a public position by voting. **2** choose to do something. • **adj. 1** chosen or singled out. **2** elected to a position but not yet in office: *the President Elect.*
– ORIGIN Latin *eligere.*

election • **n. 1** a procedure whereby a person is elected. **2** the action of electing or the fact of being elected.

electioneering • **n.** the action of campaigning to be elected to a political position.

elective • **adj. 1** relating to or appointed by election. **2** (of a course of study, treatment, etc.) chosen by the person concerned; not compulsory.

elector • **n.** a person who has the right to vote in an election.

electoral • **adj.** relating to elections or electors.
– DERIVATIVES **electorally** adv.

electoral college • **n.** a group of people chosen to represent the members of a political party in the election of a leader.

electoral roll (also **electoral register**) • **n.** an official list of the people in a district who are entitled to vote in an election.

electorate /i-lek-tuh-ruht/ • **n.** the group of people in a country or area who are entitled to vote in an election.

Electra E
/i-lek-truh/ Gk Myth. the daughter of Agamemnon and Clytemnestra. She persuaded her brother Orestes to kill Clytemnestra and her lover in revenge for the murder of Agamemnon.

electric • **adj. 1** having to do with, using, or producing electricity. **2** very exciting. • **n.** (**electrics**) Brit. the system of electric wiring in a house or vehicle.
– ORIGIN Greek *ēlektron* 'amber'.

electrical • **adj.** having to do with, using, or producing electricity.
– DERIVATIVES **electrically** adv.

electric blanket • **n.** an electrically wired blanket used for heating a bed.

electric blue • **n.** a steely or brilliant light blue.

electric chair • **n.** a chair in which convicted criminals are executed by electrocution.

electric eel • **n.** a large eel-like South American fish which uses pulses of electricity to kill its prey.

electric guitar • **n.** a guitar with a built-in pickup which converts sound vibrations into electrical signals.

electrician • **n.** a person who installs and repairs electrical equipment.

electricity • **n. 1** a form of energy resulting from the existence of charged particles, either statically as a build-up of charge or dynamically as a current. **2** the supply of electric current to a building for heating, lighting, etc. **3** great excitement.

electric shock • **n.** a sudden discharge of electricity through a part of the body.

electric storm • **n.** a thunderstorm or other violent disturbance of the electrical condition of the atmosphere.

electrify • **v.** (**electrifies**, **electrifying**, **electrified**) **1** charge with electricity. **2** convert to the use of electrical power. **3** (**electrifying**) causing great excitement.
– DERIVATIVES **electrification** n.

electroconvulsive • **adj.** referring to the treatment of mental illness by applying electric shocks to the brain.

electrocute • **v.** (**electrocutes**, **electrocuting**, **electrocuted**) injure or kill by electric shock.
– DERIVATIVES **electrocution** n.

electrode /i-lek-trohd/ • **n.** a conductor through which electricity enters or leaves something.
– ORIGIN from **ELECTRIC** + Greek *hodos* 'way'.

electrolysis /i-lek-trol-i-siss/ • **n. 1** chemical decomposition produced by passing an electric current through a conducting liquid. **2** the breaking up and removal of hair roots or small blemishes on the skin by means of an

electric current.
– DERIVATIVES **electrolytic** /i-lek-truh-lit-ik/ adj.

electrolyte /i-lek-truh-lyt/ • n. a liquid or gel which contains ions and can be decomposed by electrolysis, e.g. that present in a battery.
– ORIGIN Greek *lutos* 'released'.

electromagnet • n. a metal core made into a magnet by the passage of electric current through a surrounding coil.

electromagnetic • adj. relating to the interrelation of electric currents or fields and magnetic fields.
– DERIVATIVES **electromagnetism** n.

electromagnetic radiation • n. radiation in which electric and magnetic fields vary at the same time.

electromotive /i-lek-truh-moh-tiv/ • adj. tending to produce an electric current.

electromotive force • n. a difference in potential that tends to give rise to an electric current.

electron • n. Physics a negatively charged subatomic particle found in all atoms and acting as the primary carrier of electricity in solids.

electronic • adj. **1** having components such as microchips and transistors that control and direct electric currents. **2** relating to electrons or electronics. **3** relating to or carried out by means of a computer: *electronic shopping*.
– DERIVATIVES **electronically** adv.

electronics • n. **1** the branch of physics and technology concerned with the behaviour and movement of electrons. **2** circuits or devices using transistors, microchips, etc.

electron microscope • n. a microscope with high magnification and resolution, employing electron beams in place of light.

electroplate /i-lek-troh-playt/ • v. (**electroplates**, **electroplating**, **electroplated**) coat (a metal object) with another metal using electrolysis.

electroscope • n. an instrument for detecting and measuring electric charge.

electrostatic • adj. relating to stationary electric charges or fields as opposed to electric currents.

elegant • adj. **1** graceful and stylish. **2** pleasingly clever but simple.
– DERIVATIVES **elegance** n. **elegantly** adv.
– ORIGIN Latin *elegans* 'discriminating'.

elegiac /el-i-jy-uhk/ • adj. **1** relating to or like an elegy. **2** sad.

elegy /el-i-ji/ • n. (pl. **elegies**) a sad poem, especially for someone who has died.
– ORIGIN Greek *elegos*.

element • n. **1** a basic part of something. **2** (also **chemical element**) each of more than one hundred substances that cannot be chemically changed or broken down. **3** any of the four substances (earth, water, air, and fire) formerly believed to be the basic constituents of all matter. **4** a trace: *an element of danger*. **5** a distinct group within a larger group. **6** (**the elements**) the weather. **7** a part in an electric device through which an electric current is passed to provide heat.
– PHRASES **in one's element** in a situation in which one feels happy or relaxed.
– ORIGIN Latin *elementum* 'principle'.

elemental /el-i-men-t'l/ • adj. **1** fundamental. **2** having to do with the primitive forces of nature: *elemental hatred*.

elementary • adj. **1** relating to the most basic aspects of a subject. **2** straightforward and uncomplicated.

elephant • n. (pl. **elephant** or **elephants**) a very large mammal with a trunk, curved tusks, and large ears, found in Africa and southern Asia.
– ORIGIN Greek *elephas*.

elephantine /el-i-fan-tyn/ • adj. like an elephant.

elevate /el-i-vayt/ • v. (**elevates**, **elevating**, **elevated**) **1** lift to a higher position. **2** raise to a higher level or status.
– ORIGIN Latin *elevare*.

elevated • adj. having a high intellectual or moral level.

elevation • n. **1** the action of elevating or the fact of being elevated. **2** height above a given level. **3** the angle of something with the horizontal.

elevator • n. N. Amer. = LIFT (in sense 1).

eleven • cardinal number **1** one more than ten; 11. (Roman numeral: **xi** or **XI**.) **2** a sports team of eleven players.
– ORIGIN Old English.

eleven-plus • n. (in the UK, especially formerly) an examination taken at the age of 11–12 to determine the type of secondary school a child should enter.

elevenses • pl. n. Brit. informal a break for light refreshments taken at about eleven o'clock in the morning.

eleventh • ordinal number **1** that is number eleven in a sequence; 11th. **2** (**an eleventh**/**one eleventh**) each of eleven equal parts into which something is divided.
– PHRASES **the eleventh hour** the latest possible moment.

elf • n. (pl. **elves**) a supernatural creature of folk tales, shown as a small human figure with pointed ears.
– ORIGIN Old English.

elfin • adj. like an elf, especially in being small and delicate.

Elgar E
/el-gar/, Sir Edward (William) (1857–1934), British composer. His works include the *Enigma Variations*, the oratorio *The Dream of Gerontius*, and the *Pomp and Circumstance* marches.

Elgin Marbles E
a collection of classical Greek marble sculptures, chiefly from the Parthenon in Athens, brought to England between 1803 and 1812 by Thomas Bruce, the 7th Earl of Elgin. They are currently housed in the British Museum, but the Greek government has requested their return.

El Greco E
/el grek-oh/ (1541–1614; born *Domenikos Theotokopoulos*), Cretan-born Spanish painter. His works are characterized by distorted perspective and elongated figures.

elicit /i-liss-it/ • v. (**elicits**, **eliciting**, **elicited**) produce or draw out (a response or reaction).

– ORIGIN Latin *elicere* 'draw out by trickery'.

elide /i-lyd/ • v. (**elides**, **eliding**, **elided**) **1** omit (a sound or syllable) when speaking. **2** join together.
– ORIGIN Latin *elidere* 'crush out'.

eligible /el-i-ji-b'l/ • adj. **1** satisfying the conditions to do or receive something: *you may be eligible for a refund.* **2** desirable as a wife or husband.
– ORIGIN Latin *eligibilis.*

Elijah E
/i-ly-juh/ (9th century BC), a Hebrew prophet in the time of Jezebel who strengthened the worship of God (Jehovah) and opposed that of pagan gods.

eliminate /i-lim-i-nayt/ • v. (**eliminates**, **eliminating**, **eliminated**) **1** completely remove or get rid of. **2** exclude (a competitor) from a sporting competition by beating them.
– DERIVATIVES **elimination** n.
– ORIGIN Latin *eliminare* 'turn out of doors'.

Eliot[1], E
George (1819–80; pen name of *Mary Ann Evans*), English novelist. She is noted for her novels of provincial life, including *The Mill on the Floss* and *Middlemarch*.

Eliot[2], E
T. S. (1888–1965; full name *Thomas Stearns Eliot*), American-born British poet, critic, and dramatist. He was a leading figure of literary modernism, especially as evidenced by the long poem *The Waste Land*.

elision /i-li-*zh*'n/ • n. the omission of a sound or syllable in speech.
– ORIGIN Latin.

elite /i-leet/ • n. a group of people regarded as the best in a particular society or organization.
– ORIGIN French, 'selection'.

elitism • n. **1** the belief that a society should be run by an elite. **2** the feeling of being superior to others associated with an elite.
– DERIVATIVES **elitist** adj. & n.

elixir /i-lik-seer/ • n. a magical potion, especially one supposedly able to make people live forever.
– ORIGIN Arabic.

Elizabeth I E
(1533–1603), daughter of Henry VIII, queen of England and Ireland 1558–1603. Succeeding her Catholic sister Mary I, Elizabeth re-established Protestantism as the state religion. Her reign was dominated by conflict with Spain.

Elizabeth II E
(b.1926; born *Princess Elizabeth Alexandra Mary*), daughter of George VI, queen of the United Kingdom from 1952.

Elizabeth, the Queen Mother E
(1900–2002; born *Lady Elizabeth Angela Marguerite Bowes-Lyon*), wife of George VI, mother of Elizabeth II and Princess Margaret.

Elizabethan /i-liz-uh-bee-thuhn/ • adj. relating to the reign of Queen Elizabeth I (1558–1603).

elk /elk/ • n. (pl. **elk** or **elks**) a large northern deer with a growth of skin hanging from the neck.
– ORIGIN prob. from Old English.

Ellice Islands E
/el-liss/ former name for **TUVALU**.

Ellington, E
Duke (1899–1974; born *Edward Kennedy Ellington*), American jazz pianist, composer, and bandleader.

ellipse /i-lips/ • n. a regular oval shape resulting when a cone is cut by an oblique plane which does not intersect the base.

ellipsis /i-lip-siss/ • n. (pl. **ellipses** /i-lip-seez/) **1** the omission of words from speech or writing. **2** a set of dots indicating such an omission.
– ORIGIN Greek *elleipsis.*

elliptic • adj. relating to or having the form of an ellipse.

elliptical • adj. **1** = **ELLIPTIC**. **2** (of speech or writing) having a word or words deliberately omitted.

Ellis, E
(Henry) Havelock (1859–1939), English psychologist and writer, pioneer of the scientific study of sex.

elm • n. a tall deciduous tree with rough leaves.
– ORIGIN Old English.

El Niño /el neen-yoh/ • n. (pl. **El Niños**) a complex cycle of climatic changes affecting the Pacific region.
– ORIGIN Spanish, 'the Christ child', so called because the signs of an El Niño appear around Christmas time.

elocution /el-uh-kyoo-sh'n/ • n. the skill of clear and expressive speech.
– ORIGIN Latin.

elongate /ee-long-gayt/ • v. (**elongates**, **elongating**, **elongated**) make or become longer.
– ORIGIN Latin *elongare* 'place at a distance'.

elope • v. (**elopes**, **eloping**, **eloped**) run away secretly in order to get married.
– DERIVATIVES **elopement** n.
– ORIGIN Old French *aloper.*

eloquence /el-uh-kwuhnss/ • n. fluent or persuasive speaking or writing.
– ORIGIN Latin *eloquentia.*

eloquent • adj. **1** showing eloquence. **2** clearly expressive.
– DERIVATIVES **eloquently** adv.

El Salvador E
/el sal-vuh-dor/ a country in Central America, on the Pacific coast; capital, San Salvador.
– DERIVATIVES **Salvadorean** adj. & n.

else • adv. **1** in addition. **2** different.
– PHRASES **or else** used to introduce the second of two alternatives.
– ORIGIN Old English.

elsewhere • adv. in, at, or to some other place or other places. • pron. some other place.

elucidate /i-loo-si-dayt/ • v. (**elucidates**, **elucidating**, **elucidated**) make clear; explain.
– DERIVATIVES **elucidation** n.
– ORIGIN Latin *elucidare.*

elude /i-lood/ • v. (**eludes**, **eluding**,

eluded) **1** evade or escape cleverly from. **2** fail to be understood by: *the logic of this eluded her.*
– ORIGIN Latin *eludere.*

elusive ● **adj.** difficult to find, catch, or achieve.
– ORIGIN Latin *eludere* 'elude'.

elver /el-ver/ ● **n.** a young eel.
– ORIGIN from dialect *eel-fare* 'the passage of young eels up a river'.

elves pl. of **ELF**.

Elysée Palace E
/ay-lee-zay/ a building in Paris which is the official residence of the French President.

Elysian /i-liz-i-uhn/ ● **adj. 1** relating to Elysium. **2** relating to or like paradise.

Elysium E
/i-liz-i-uhm/ (also **the Elysian Fields**) Gk Myth. the place at the ends of the earth to which heroes were taken by the gods after death.

em- ● **prefix** var. of **EN-**[1], **EN-**[2].

emaciated /i-may-si-ay-tid/ ● **adj.** abnormally thin and weak.
– DERIVATIVES **emaciation** n.
– ORIGIN Latin *emaciare* 'make thin'.

email ● **n.** the sending of electronic messages from one computer user to another via a network. ● **v.** mail or send using email.
– ORIGIN from *electronic mail.*

emanate /em-uh-nayt/ ● **v.** (**emanates, emanating, emanated**) **1** (**emanate from**) come or spread out from (a source). **2** give out: *he emanated a brooding air.*
– ORIGIN Latin *emanare* 'flow out'.

emanation ● **n. 1** something which comes from a source. **2** the action of emanating.

emancipate /i-man-si-payt/ ● **v.** (**emancipates, emancipating, emancipated**) **1** free from legal, social, or political restrictions. **2** free from slavery.
– DERIVATIVES **emancipation** n.
– ORIGIN Latin *emancipare* 'transfer as property'.

emasculate /i-mass-kyuu-layt/ ● **v.** (**emasculates, emaculating, emasculated**) **1** make weaker or less effective. **2** deprive (a man) of his male role or identity.
– DERIVATIVES **emasculation** n.
– ORIGIN Latin *emasculare* 'castrate'.

embalm /im-bahm/ ● **v.** treat (a corpse) to preserve it from decay.
– DERIVATIVES **embalmer** n.
– ORIGIN Old French *embaumer.*

embankment ● **n. 1** a wall or bank built to prevent flooding by a river. **2** a bank of earth or stone built to carry a road or railway over low ground.

embargo /em-bar-goh, im-bar-goh/ ● **n.** (pl. **embargoes**) an official ban, especially on trade with a particular country. ● **v.** (**embargoes, embargoing, embargoed**) put an embargo on.
– ORIGIN Spanish.

embark ● **v. 1** go on board a ship or aircraft. **2** (**embark on/upon**) begin (a new project or course of action).
– DERIVATIVES **embarkation** n.
– ORIGIN French *embarquer.*

embarrass /im-ba-ruhss, em-ba-ruhss/ ● **v. 1** cause to feel awkward or ashamed. **2** (**be embarrassed**) be in financial difficulties. **3** (**embarrassing**) causing shame or awkwardness.
– DERIVATIVES **embarrassment** n.
– ORIGIN French *embarrasser.*

embassy ● **n.** (pl. **embassies**) the official residence or offices of an ambassador.
– ORIGIN Old French *ambasse.*

embattled ● **adj. 1** surrounded by enemy forces. **2** beset by difficulties: *the embattled Chancellor.*

embed (also **imbed**) ● **v.** (**embeds, embedding, embedded**; also **imbeds, imbedding, imbedded**) **1** fix firmly in a surrounding mass. **2** implant (an idea or feeling).

embellish ● **v. 1** make more attractive; decorate. **2** add details to (a story).
– DERIVATIVES **embellishment** n.
– ORIGIN Old French *embellir.*

ember /em-ber/ ● **n.** a piece of burning wood or coal in a dying fire.
– ORIGIN Old English.

embezzle ● **v.** (**embezzles, embezzling, embezzled**) steal (money placed in one's trust or under one's control).
– DERIVATIVES **embezzler** n.
– ORIGIN Old French *embesiler.*

embitter ● **v.** (**embitters, embittering, embittered**) make bitter or resentful.

emblazon /im-blay-zuhn/ ● **v.** display (a design) on something in a noticeable way.

emblem /em-bluhm/ ● **n. 1** a heraldic design or symbol as a badge of a nation, organization, or family. **2** something which represents a quality or an idea.
– ORIGIN Greek *emblēma* 'insertion'.

emblematic ● **adj.** representing a particular quality or idea.

embody ● **v.** (**embodies, embodying, embodied**) **1** give a tangible or visible form to (an idea or quality). **2** include as a part.
– DERIVATIVES **embodiment** n.

embolden ● **v.** give courage or confidence to.

embolism /em-buh-li-z'm/ ● **n.** Med. obstruction of an artery by a clot of blood or an air bubble.
– ORIGIN Greek *embolismos.*

emboss ● **v.** make a raised design on.
– ORIGIN from former French *embosser.*

embrace ● **v.** (**embraces, embracing, embraced**) **1** hold closely in one's arms as a sign of affection. **2** include or contain. **3** accept or support (a belief or change) willingly. ● **n.** an act of embracing.
– ORIGIN Old French *embracer.*

embrocation /em-bruh-kay-sh'n/ ● **n.** a liquid medication rubbed on the body to relieve pain from strains.
– ORIGIN Latin.

embroider ● **v.** (**embroiders, embroidering, embroidered**) **1** sew decorative needlework patterns on. **2** add false or exaggerated details to.
– ORIGIN Old French *enbrouder.*

embroidery ● **n.** (pl. **embroideries**) **1** the art of embroidering. **2** embroidered cloth.

embroil ● **v.** involve deeply in a conflict or difficult situation.
– ORIGIN French *embrouiller* 'to muddle'.

embryo /em-bri-oh/ ● **n.** (pl. **embryos**) **1** an unborn or unhatched offspring in the process of development, especially an unborn human in the first eight weeks from conception. Com-

pare with FETUS. **2** the part of a seed which develops into a new plant.
– ORIGIN Greek *embruon*.

embryonic /em-bri-on-ik/ ● adj. **1** relating to an embryo. **2** in an early stage of development.

emend /i-mend/ ● v. correct and revise (a text).
– DERIVATIVES **emendation** n.
– ORIGIN Latin *emendare*.

emerald ● n. **1** a green gem variety of beryl. **2** a bright green colour.
– ORIGIN Old French *esmeraud*.

emerge ● v. (**emerges**, **emerging**, **emerged**) **1** become gradually visible. **2** (of facts) become known. **3** survive a difficult period.
– DERIVATIVES **emergence** n.
– ORIGIN Latin *emergere*.

emergency ● n. (pl. **emergencies**) a serious, unexpected, and potentially dangerous situation requiring immediate action. ● adj. arising from or used in an emergency: *an emergency exit*.
– ORIGIN Latin *emergentia*.

emergent ● adj. in the process of coming into being.

emeritus /i-me-ri-tuhss/ ● adj. having retired but allowed to keep a title as an honour: *an emeritus professor*.
– ORIGIN Latin.

Emerson E
/em-er-s'n/, Ralph Waldo (1803–82), American philosopher and poet. He was a central figure of the idealistic social and philosophical movement known as Transcendentalism.

emery board ● n. a strip of thin wood or card coated with a hard rough substance and used as a nail file.
– ORIGIN Old French *esmeri*.

emetic /i-met-ik/ ● adj. (of a substance) causing vomiting.
– ORIGIN Greek *emetikos*.

emf ● abbrev. electromotive force.

emigrant ● n. a person who emigrates.

emigrate /em-i-grayt/ ● v. (**emigrates**, **emigrating**, **emigrated**) leave one's own country in order to settle permanently in another.
– DERIVATIVES **emigration** n.
– ORIGIN Latin *emigrare*.

émigré /em-i-gray/ ● n. a person who has emigrated.
– ORIGIN French.

eminence /em-i-nuhnss/ ● n. **1** the quality of being highly accomplished and respected in a particular area. **2** an important person.
– ORIGIN Latin *eminentia*.

eminent ● adj. **1** distinguished. **2** outstanding or obvious: *the eminent reasonableness of their claim*.
– DERIVATIVES **eminently** adv.

emir /e-meer/ (also **amir**) ● n. a title of various Muslim rulers.
– ORIGIN Arabic, 'commander'.

emirate /em-i-ruht/ ● n. the lands or rank of an emir.

emissary /em-i-suh-ri/ ● n. (pl. **emissaries**) a person sent as a diplomatic representative on a special mission.
– ORIGIN Latin *emissarius* 'scout, spy'.

emission /i-mi-sh'n/ ● n. **1** the action of emitting something. **2** a substance which is emitted.

emit ● v. (**emits**, **emitting**, **emitted**) **1** discharge; send forth or give out. **2** make (a sound).
– ORIGIN Latin *emittere*.

emollient /i-mol-li-uhnt/ ● adj. **1** having a softening or soothing effect on the skin. **2** attempting to avoid confrontation; calming.
– DERIVATIVES **emollience** n.
– ORIGIN Latin *emollire* 'make soft'.

emolument /i-mol-yuu-muhnt/ ● n. formal a salary or fee.
– ORIGIN Latin *emolumentum*.

emote /i-moht/ ● v. (**emotes**, **emoting**, **emoted**) show emotion in an exaggerated way.

emotion ● n. **1** a strong feeling, such as joy or anger. **2** instinctive feeling as distinguished from reasoning.
– ORIGIN Latin *emovare* 'disturb'.

emotional ● adj. **1** relating to the emotions. **2** arousing emotion. **3** readily showing emotion.
– DERIVATIVES **emotionally** adv.

emotive ● adj. arousing strong feeling.

empathize (also **empathise**) ● v. (**empathizes**, **empathizing**, **empathized**) understand and share the feelings of another.

empathy /em-puh-thi/ ● n. the ability to empathize.
– DERIVATIVES **empathetic** adj. **empathic** adj.
– ORIGIN Greek *empatheia*.

emperor ● n. the ruler of an empire.
– ORIGIN Latin *imperator* 'military commander'.

emperor penguin ● n. the largest kind of penguin, found in the Antarctic and with a yellow patch on each side of the head.

emphasis /em-fuh-siss/ ● n. (pl. **emphases** /em-fuh-seez/) **1** special importance or value given to something. **2** stress given to a word or words in speaking.
– ORIGIN Greek.

emphasize (also **emphasise**) ● v. (**emphasizes**, **emphasizing**, **emphasized**) give special importance to.

emphatic ● adj. **1** showing or giving emphasis. **2** definite and clear.

emphysema /em-fi-see-muh/ (also **pulmonary emphysema**) ● n. Med. a condition in which the air sacs of the lungs are damaged and enlarged, causing breathlessness.
– ORIGIN Greek *emphusēma*.

empire ● n. **1** a large group of states ruled over by a single monarch or ruling authority. **2** a large commercial organization under the control of one person or group.
– ORIGIN Latin *imperium*.

Empire State Building E
a skyscraper on Fifth Avenue, New York City, which at 449 m (1,472 ft) was once the tallest building in the world.

empirical (also **empiric**) ● adj. based on observation or experience rather than theory or logic.
– DERIVATIVES **empirically** adv.
– ORIGIN Greek *empeirikos*.

empiricism /em-pi-ri-si-z'm/ ● n. the theory that all knowledge is derived from experience and observation.

– DERIVATIVES **empiricist** n. & adj.

emplacement • n. a structure or platform where a gun is placed for firing.

employ • v. **1** give work to (someone) and pay them for it. **2** make use of. **3** keep occupied.
– ORIGIN Old French *employer.*

employee • n. a person employed for wages or salary.

employer • n. a person or organization that employs people.

employment • n. **1** the action of employing or the state of being employed. **2** a person's work or profession.

emporium /em-**por**-i-uhm/ • n. (pl. **emporia** /em-**por**-i-uh/ or **emporiums**) a large store selling a wide variety of goods.
– ORIGIN Greek *emporion.*

empower • v. (**empowers**, **empowering**, **empowered**) **1** give authority or power to **2** give strength and confidence to.
– DERIVATIVES **empowerment** n.

empress /em-priss/ • n. **1** a female emperor. **2** the wife or widow of an emperor.

empty • adj. (**emptier**, **emptiest**) **1** containing nothing; not filled or occupied. **2** having no meaning or likelihood of fulfilment: *an empty threat.* • v. (**empties**, **emptying**, **emptied**) **1** make or become empty. **2** (of a river) flow into the sea or a lake. • n. (pl. **empties**) informal a bottle or glass left empty of its contents.
– DERIVATIVES **emptily** adv. **emptiness** n.
– ORIGIN Old English, 'at leisure'.

empty-handed • adj. having failed to get or achieve what one wanted.

empty-headed • adj. foolish.

empyrean /em-py-ree-uhn/ • n. literary (**the empyrean**) heaven or the sky.
– ORIGIN Greek *empurios.*

EMS • abbrev. European Monetary System.

EMU • abbrev. Economic and Monetary Union.

emu • n. a flightless Australian bird similar to an ostrich.
– ORIGIN Portuguese *ema.*

emulate /em-yuu-layt/ • v. (**emulates**, **emulating**, **emulated**) try to equal or be better than.
– DERIVATIVES **emulation** n. **emulator** n.
– ORIGIN Latin *aemulari.*

emulsifier • n. a substance that stabilizes an emulsion, especially one used to stabilize processed foods.

emulsify /i-mul-si-fy/ • v. (**emulsifies**, **emulsifying**, **emulsified**) make into or become an emulsion.

emulsion • n. **1** a liquid in which particles of one liquid are evenly distributed in another. **2** a type of matt paint for walls. **3** a light-sensitive coating for photographic film.
– ORIGIN Latin.

en-[1] (also **em-**) • prefix forming verbs: **1** put into or on: *engulf.* **2** bring into the condition of: *enliven.* **3** in, into, or on: *ensnare.*
– ORIGIN French.

en-[2] (also **em-**) • prefix inside: *energy.*
– ORIGIN Greek.

-en[1] • suffix forming verbs from adjectives or nouns referring to the intensification of a quality: *widen.*
– ORIGIN Old English.

-en[2] • suffix (also **-n**) forming adjectives from nouns: **1** made or consisting of: *earthen.* **2** resembling: *golden.*
– ORIGIN Old English.

-en[3] (also **-n**) • suffix forming past participles of strong verbs: *spoken.*
– ORIGIN Old English.

enable • v. (**enables**, **enabling**, **enabled**) **1** provide with the ability or means to do something. **2** make possible.

enact • v. **1** make (a bill or other proposal) law. **2** act out (a role or play).

enactment • n. the process of enacting.

enamel • n. **1** a coloured shiny substance applied to metal, glass, or pottery for decoration or protection. **2** the hard substance that covers the crown of a tooth. **3** a paint that dries to give a hard coat. • v. (**enamels**, **enamelling**, **enamelled**; US **enamels**, **enameling**, **enameled**) coat or decorate with enamel.
– ORIGIN Old French *enamailler.*

enamour /i-nam-er/ (US **enamor**) • v. (**be enamoured of/with**) be filled with love or admiration for.
– ORIGIN Old French *enamourer.*

en bloc /on blok/ • adv. all together or all at once.
– ORIGIN French.

encamp • v. settle in or establish a camp.

encampment • n. a place where a camp is set up.

encapsulate /in-kap-syuu-layt/ • v. (**encapsulates**, **encapsulating**, **encapsulated**) **1** enclose in or as if in a capsule. **2** express clearly and in few words.

encase • v. (**encases**, **encasing**, **encased**) enclose or cover in a case.

encephalitis /en-sef-uh-ly-tiss/ • n. inflammation of the brain.
– ORIGIN Greek *enkephalos* 'brain'.

enchant • v. **1** delight, charm. **2** put under a spell.
– DERIVATIVES **enchanter** n. **enchantress** n.
– ORIGIN French *enchanter.*

enchanting • adj. delightfully charming or attractive.

enchantment • n. **1** the state of being under a magic spell. **2** delight or fascination.

encircle • v. (**encircles**, **encircling**, **encircled**) form a circle around.

enclave /en-klayv/ • n. **1** a small territory surrounded by a larger territory whose inhabitants are of a different culture or nationality. **2** a group that is different from those surrounding it: *a male enclave.*
– ORIGIN Old French *enclaver* 'enclose'.

enclose • v. (**encloses**, **enclosing**, **enclosed**) **1** surround or close off on all sides. **2** place in an envelope together with a letter.
– ORIGIN Old French *enclore.*

enclosure • n. **1** an enclosed area. **2** a document or object placed in an envelope together with a letter.

encode • v. (**encodes**, **encoding**, **encoded**) convert into a coded form.
– DERIVATIVES **encoder** n.

encomium /en-koh-mi-uhm/ • n. (pl. **encomiums** or **encomia** /en-koh-mi-uh/) formal a speech or piece of writing expressing praise.
– ORIGIN Greek *enkōmion.*

encompass /in-kum-puhss/ • v. **1** surround or cover. **2** include a wide range of.

encore /ong-kor/ • n. a repeated or additional performance at the end of a concert, as called for by an audience. • exclam. again!
– ORIGIN French.

encounter • v. (**encounters**, **encountering**, **encountered**) unexpectedly meet or be faced with. • n. **1** an unexpected or casual meeting. **2** a confrontation.
– ORIGIN Old French *encontrer.*

encourage • v. (**encourages**, **encouraging**, **encouraged**) **1** give support, confidence, or hope to. **2** help the development of.
– DERIVATIVES **encouragement** n. **encouraging** adj.
– ORIGIN French *encourager.*

e

encroach • v. **1** (**encroach on/upon**) gradually intrude on (a person's territory, rights, etc.). **2** advance gradually beyond acceptable limits: *the sea has encroached all round the coast.*
– ORIGIN Old French *encrochier* 'seize'.

encrust • v. cover with a hard crust.
– DERIVATIVES **encrustation** n.

encrypt /en-kript/ • v. convert into code.
– DERIVATIVES **encryption** n.
– ORIGIN Greek *kruptos* 'hidden'.

encumber /in-kum-ber/ • v. (**encumbers**, **encumbering**, **encumbered**) be a burden or hindrance to.
– ORIGIN Old French *encombrer* 'block up'.

encumbrance • n. a burden or impediment.

encyclical /en-sik-li-k'l/ • n. a letter sent by the pope to all bishops of the Roman Catholic Church.
– ORIGIN Greek *enkuklios* 'circular'.

encyclopedia /en-sy-kluh-pee-di-uh/ (also **encyclopaedia**) • n. a book or set of books giving information on many subjects.
– ORIGIN from Greek *enkuklios paideia* 'all-round education'.

encyclopedic /en-sy-kluh-pee-dik/ (also **encyclopaedic**) • adj. **1** comprehensive: *an encyclopedic knowledge of food.* **2** relating to encyclopedias.

end • n. **1** the final part of something. **2** the furthest part. **3** the stopping of a state or situation: *they called for an end to violence.* **4** a person's death or downfall. **5** a goal or desired result. **6** a part of an activity: *your end of the deal.* • v. **1** come or bring to an end. **2** (**end in**) have as its result. **3** (**end up**) eventually reach or come to a particular state or place.
– PHRASES **in the end** eventually. **make ends meet** earn just enough money to live on. **on end** continuously.
– ORIGIN Old English.

endanger • v. (**endangers**, **endangering**, **endangered**) **1** put in danger. **2** (**endangered**) in danger of becoming extinct.

endear /in-deer/ • v. cause to be loved or liked.

endearing • adj. inspiring love or affection.
– DERIVATIVES **endearingly** adv.

endearment • n. **1** love or affection. **2** a word or phrase expressing affection.

endeavour /in-dev-er/ (US **endeavor**) • v. try hard to do or achieve something. • n. **1** a serious effort to achieve something. **2** hard work; effort.
– ORIGIN from former *put oneself in devoir* 'do one's utmost'.

endemic /en-dem-ik/ • adj. **1** (of a disease or condition) regularly found among particular people or in a certain area. **2** (of a plant or animal) native or restricted to a certain area.
– ORIGIN Greek *endēmios.*

ending • n. an end or final part.

endive /en-dyv/ • n. a plant with bitter curly or smooth leaves, eaten in salads.
– ORIGIN Old French.

endless • adj. **1** having or seeming to have no end. **2** (of a belt, chain, or tape) having the ends joined to allow for continuous action.

endo- • comb. form internal; within: *endoskeleton.*
– ORIGIN Greek *endon.*

endocrine /en-duh-krin/ • adj. (of a gland) secreting hormones or other products directly into the blood.
– ORIGIN Greek *krinein* 'sift'.

endorphin /en-dor-fin/ • n. any of a group of hormones produced within the brain and nervous system and having a painkilling effect.
– ORIGIN from *endogenous* 'having an internal cause' and **MORPHINE**.

endorse /in-dorss/ • v. (**endorses**, **endorsing**, **endorsed**) **1** declare one's public approval of. **2** sign (a cheque) on the back so that it can be paid into another person's account.
– ORIGIN Latin *indorsare.*

endorsement • n. **1** an act or the action of endorsing. **2** (in the UK) a note on a driving licence recording the penalty points for a driving offence.

endoskeleton • n. an internal skeleton. Compare with **EXOSKELETON**.

endosperm • n. the part of a seed which acts as a food store for the developing plant embryo.

endothermic • adj. Chem. (of a reaction) absorbing heat. Opp. **EXOTHERMIC**.

endow /in-dow/ • v. **1** give or leave an income or property to. **2** provide with a quality or asset: *he was endowed with tremendous physical strength.* **3** establish (a post, prize, or project) by donating funds.
– ORIGIN Old French *endouer.*

endowment • n. **1** the action of endowing. **2** a quality or ability possessed or inherited by someone. **3** an income or property given or left to someone.

endowment mortgage • n. Brit. a mortgage linked to an endowment insurance policy which is intended to repay the sum borrowed when the policy reaches the end of its term.

endowment policy • n. a form of life insurance policy in which the insured person is paid a fixed sum on a specified date.

endpaper • n. a leaf of paper at the beginning or end of a book, fixed to the inside of the cover.

endurance • n. the fact or power of enduring something painful and long-lasting.

endure /in-dyoor/ • v. (**endures**, **enduring**, **endured**) **1** suffer (something painful and long-lasting) patiently. **2** tolerate. **3** remain in existence: *these cities have endured through time.*
– DERIVATIVES **endurable** adj.

– ORIGIN Latin *indurare* 'harden'.

ENE ● abbrev. east-north-east.

enema /en-i-muh/ ● n. (pl. **enemas** or **enemata** /i-nem-uh-tuh/) a medical procedure in which fluid is injected into the rectum to empty it.
– ORIGIN Greek.

enemy ● n. (pl. **enemies**) **1** a person who is actively opposed or hostile to someone or something. **2** (**the enemy**) a hostile nation or its armed forces in time of war. **3** a thing that harms or weakens something.
– ORIGIN Old French *enemi*.

energetic ● adj. showing or involving great energy.
– DERIVATIVES **energetically** adv.
– ORIGIN Greek *energein* 'operate'.

energize (also **energise**) ● v. (**energizes, energizing, energized**) give energy and enthusiasm to: *people were energized by his ideas.*

energy ● n. (pl. **energies**) **1** the strength and vitality required to keep active. **2** (**energies**) a person's physical and mental powers. **3** power derived from physical or chemical resources to provide light and heat or to work machines. **4** Physics the capacity of matter or radiation to perform work.
– ORIGIN Greek *energeia*.

enervate /en-er-vayt/ ● v. (**enervates, enervating, enervated**) cause to feel drained of energy.
– ORIGIN Latin *enervare* 'weaken'.

enfant terrible /on-fon te-ree-bluh/ ● n. (pl. **enfants terribles** /on-fon te-ree-bluh/) a person whose controversial attitude shocks others.
– ORIGIN French, 'terrible child'.

enfeeble ● v. (**enfeebles, enfeebling, enfeebled**) weaken.

enfilade /en-fi-layd/ ● n. a volley of gunfire directed along a line from end to end.
– ORIGIN French.

enfold ● v. envelop: *silence enfolded them.*

enforce ● v. (**enforces, enforcing, enforced**) **1** make sure (a law, rule, or obligation) is obeyed or fulfilled. **2** force (something) to happen.
– DERIVATIVES **enforceable** adj. **enforcement** n. **enforcer** n.

enfranchise /in-fran-chyz/ ● v. (**enfranchises, enfranchising, enfranchised**) **1** give the right to vote to. **2** hist. free (a slave).
– DERIVATIVES **enfranchisement** n.

engage ● v. (**engages, engaging, engaged**) **1** attract or involve (someone's interest or attention). **2** (**engage in/with**) become involved in. **3** esp. Brit. employ. **4** enter into a contract to do. **5** enter into combat with. **6** (with reference to a part of a machine or engine) move into position so as to begin to operate: *the clutch will not engage.*
– ORIGIN French *engager*.

engaged ● adj. **1** occupied: *I was otherwise engaged.* **2** Brit. (of a telephone line) unavailable because already in use. **3** having formally agreed to marry.

engagement ● n. **1** a formal agreement to get married. **2** an appointment. **3** the state of being involved in something. **4** a battle between armed forces.

engaging ● adj. charming and attractive.
– DERIVATIVES **engagingly** adv.

> **Engels** E
> /eng-g'lz/, Friedrich (1820–95), German socialist and political philosopher, who collaborated with Marx in the writing of the *Communist Manifesto*.

engender /in-jen-der/ ● v. (**engenders, engendering, engendered**) give rise to.
– ORIGIN Old French *engendrer*.

engine ● n. **1** a machine with moving parts that converts power into motion. **2** (also **railway engine**) a locomotive.
– ORIGIN Latin *ingenium* 'talent, device'.

engineer ● n. **1** a person qualified in engineering. **2** a person who maintains or controls an engine or machine. ● v. (**engineers, engineering, engineered**) **1** design and build. **2** skilfully arrange for (something) to occur: *she engineered a meeting with him.*

engineering ● n. the branch of science and technology concerned with the design, building, and use of engines, machines, and structures.

> **England** E
> a country forming the largest and southernmost part of Great Britain and of the United Kingdom, and containing the capital, London.

English ● n. the language of England, now used in many varieties throughout the world. ● adj. relating to England.
– DERIVATIVES **Englishness** n.
– ORIGIN Old English.

> **English Channel** E
> the sea channel separating southern England from northern France, 35 km (22 miles) wide at its narrowest point.

> **English Civil War** E
> the war between Charles I and his supporters (the Royalists or Cavaliers) and his Parliamentary opponents (the Roundheads), 1642–9. It started after Charles refused to give in to a series of demands made by Parliament and ended with Charles's execution in 1649.

engorge /in-gorj/ ● v. (**engorges, engorging, engorged**) (often **be engorged**) swell or cause to swell with a fluid.
– ORIGIN Old French *engorgier* 'feed to excess'.

engrain ● v. var. of **INGRAIN**.

engrained ● adj. var. of **INGRAINED**.

engrave ● v. (**engraves, engraving, engraved**) **1** carve (words or a design) on a hard surface. **2** carve words or a design on. **3** (**be engraved on** or **in**) be permanently fixed in (one's mind).
– DERIVATIVES **engraver** n.
– ORIGIN from **EN-**[1] + former *grave* 'engrave'.

engraving ● n. **1** a print made from an engraved plate or block. **2** the process or art of carving a design on a hard surface.

engross /in-grohss/ ● v. (**be engrossed in**) be completely involved in.
– ORIGIN from Latin *in grosso* 'wholesale'.

engulf ● v. (of a natural force) sweep over so as to completely surround or cover.

enhance /in-hahnss/ ● v. (**enhances, enhancing, enhanced**) increase the quality,

value, or extent of.
– DERIVATIVES **enhancement** n. **enhancer** n.
– ORIGIN Old French *enhauncer*.

enigma /i-nig-muh/ ● n. a mysterious or puzzling person or thing.
– DERIVATIVES **enigmatic** adj. **enigmatically** adv.
– ORIGIN Greek *ainigma* 'riddle'.

enjoin ● v. instruct or urge to do.
– ORIGIN Old French *enjoindre*.

enjoy ● v. **1** take pleasure in. **2** (**enjoy oneself**) have a pleasant time. **3** possess and benefit from: *these professions enjoy high status.*
– DERIVATIVES **enjoyment** n.
– ORIGIN Old French *enjoier* 'give joy to' or *enjoïr* 'enjoy'.

enjoyable ● adj. giving pleasure.
– DERIVATIVES **enjoyably** adv.

enlarge ● v. (**enlarges**, **enlarging**, **enlarged**) **1** make or become bigger. **2** (**enlarge on/upon**) speak or write about in greater detail.
– DERIVATIVES **enlarger** n.

enlargement ● n. **1** the action of enlarging or the state of being enlarged. **2** a photograph that is larger than the original negative or than an earlier print.

enlighten ● v. **1** give greater knowledge and understanding to. **2** (**enlightened**) reasonable, tolerant, and well-informed: *a most enlightened body of men.*

enlightenment ● n. **1** knowledge and understanding. **2** (**the Enlightenment**) a European intellectual movement of the late 17th and 18th centuries emphasizing reason and individualism.

enlist ● v. **1** enrol or be enrolled in the armed services. **2** engage (a person or their help).
– DERIVATIVES **enlistment** n.

enliven ● v. **1** make (something) more interesting. **2** make (someone) more cheerful or lively.

en masse /on mass/ ● adv. all together.
– ORIGIN French, 'in a mass'.

enmesh ● v. (usu. **be enmeshed in**) involve in complicated circumstances.

enmity ● n. (pl. **enmities**) hostility.
– ORIGIN Old French *enemistie*.

ennoble ● v. (**ennobles**, **ennobling**, **ennobled**) **1** give a noble rank or title to. **2** give greater dignity to: *ennoble the mind and uplift the spirit.*

ennui /on-wee/ ● n. listlessness and dissatisfaction arising from boredom.
– ORIGIN French.

enormity ● n. (pl. **enormities**) **1** (**the enormity of**) the extreme seriousness of (something bad). **2** great size or scale: *the enormity of Einstein's intellect.* **3** a serious crime or sin.
– ORIGIN Latin *enormitas*.

enormous ● adj. very large.
– DERIVATIVES **enormously** adv.

enough ● det. & pron. as much or as many as is necessary or desirable. ● adv. **1** to the required degree. **2** to a moderate degree.
– ORIGIN Old English.

enquire ● v. (**enquires**, **enquiring**, **enquired**) **1** ask for information. **2** (**enquire after**) ask about the well-being of. **3** (**enquire into**) investigate.
– DERIVATIVES **enquirer** n.
– ORIGIN Latin *inquirere*.

enquiry ● n. (pl. **enquiries**) **1** an act of asking for information. **2** an official investigation.

enrage ● v. (**enrages**, **enraging**, **enraged**) make very angry.

enrapture ● v. (**enraptures**, **enrapturing**, **enraptured**) give great pleasure to.

enrich ● v. **1** improve the quality or value of. **2** make wealthier.
– DERIVATIVES **enrichment** n.

enrol /in-rohl/ (US **enroll**) ● v. (**enrols**, **enrolling**, **enrolled**; US **enrolls**, **enrolling**, **enrolled**) officially register or recruit as a member or student.
– DERIVATIVES **enrolment** (US **enrollment**) n.
– ORIGIN Old French *enroller*.

en route /on root/ ● adv. on the way.
– ORIGIN French.

ensconce /in-skonss/ ● v. (**ensconces**, **ensconcing**, **ensconced**) establish in a comfortable, safe, or secret place.
– ORIGIN from archaic *sconce*, referring to a small fort.

ensemble /on-som-b'l/ ● n. **1** a group of musicians, actors, or dancers who perform together. **2** a passage for a whole choir or group of instruments. **3** a group of items viewed as a whole: *her ensemble of tweed and cashmere.*
– ORIGIN French.

enshrine ● v. (**enshrines**, **enshrining**, **enshrined**) **1** place (a precious or holy object) in an appropriate receptacle. **2** preserve (a right, tradition, or idea) in a form that ensures it will be respected: *rights enshrined in the constitution.*

enshroud /in-shrowd/ ● v. literary cover completely and hide from view.

ensign /en-syn/ ● n. **1** a flag showing a ship's nationality. **2** the lowest rank of commissioned officer in the US and some other navies.
– ORIGIN Old French *enseigne*.

enslave ● v. (**enslaves**, **enslaving**, **enslaved**) **1** make (someone) a slave. **2** cause (someone) to lose freedom of choice or action.
– DERIVATIVES **enslavement** n.

ensnare ● v. (**ensnares**, **ensnaring**, **ensnared**) catch in or as in a trap.

ensue ● v. (**ensues**, **ensuing**, **ensued**) happen afterwards or as a result.
– ORIGIN Old French *ensivre*.

en suite /on sweet/ ● adj. & adv. Brit. (of a bathroom) immediately next to a bedroom and forming a single unit with it.
– ORIGIN French, 'in sequence'.

ensure /in-shoor/ ● v. (**ensures**, **ensuring**, **ensured**) **1** make certain that (something) will occur or be so. **2** (**ensure against**) make sure that (a problem) does not occur.
– ORIGIN Old French *enseurer*.

entail ● v. involve (something) that is unavoidable.
– ORIGIN Old French *taille* 'notch, tax'.

entangle ● v. (**entangles**, **entangling**, **entangled**) (usu. **be entangled in/with**) **1** make tangled. **2** involve in complicated circumstances.
– DERIVATIVES **entanglement** n.

Entebbe E
/en-**teb**-bi/ a town in southern Uganda, on Lake Victoria. It was the capital of Uganda during British rule, from 1894 to 1962.

entente /on-**tont**/ (also **entente cordiale** /on-tont kor-di-**ahl**/) • **n.** a friendly understanding between states.
– ORIGIN from French *entente cordiale* 'friendly understanding'.

enter • **v.** (**enters**, **entering**, **entered**) **1** come or go into. **2** (often **enter into/on**) begin to be involved in or do. **3** join (an institution or profession). **4** register as a participant in. **5** (**enter into**) undertake to be bound by (an agreement). **6** record (information) in a book, computer, etc.
– ORIGIN Old French *entrer*.

enteric /en-**terr**-ik/ • **adj.** having to do with the intestines.
– ORIGIN Greek *enterikos*.

enterprise • **n. 1** a project or undertaking. **2** bold resourcefulness: *success was the result of talent and enterprise.* **3** a business or company.
– ORIGIN Old French.

enterprising • **adj.** showing initiative and resourcefulness.

entertain • **v. 1** provide with amusement or enjoyment. **2** receive (someone) as a guest and give them food and drink. **3** give consideration to: *he entertained little hope of success.*
– ORIGIN French *entretenir*.

entertainer • **n.** a person whose job is to entertain others.

entertaining • **adj.** providing amusement or enjoyment.
– DERIVATIVES **entertainingly** adv.

entertainment • **n. 1** the action of entertaining. **2** an event, performance, or activity designed to entertain others.

enthral /in-**thrawl**/ (US **enthrall**) • **v.** (**enthrals**, **enthralling**, **enthralled**; US **enthralls**, **enthralling**, **enthralled**) fascinate (someone) and hold their attention.

enthrone • **v.** (**enthrones**, **enthroning**, **enthroned**) place (a monarch or bishop) on a throne in a ceremony to mark the beginning of their reign or period of office.
– DERIVATIVES **enthronement** n.

enthuse /in-**thyooz**/ • **v.** (**enthuses**, **enthusing**, **enthused**) **1** (often **enthuse over**) express one's great enthusiasm for something. **2** make enthusiastic.

enthusiasm • **n.** great enjoyment, interest, or approval.
– ORIGIN Greek *enthous* 'possessed by a god'.

enthusiast • **n.** a person who is full of enthusiasm for something.

enthusiastic • **adj.** having or showing great enthusiasm.
– DERIVATIVES **enthusiastically** adv.

entice /in-**tyss**/ • **v.** (**entices**, **enticing**, **enticed**) attract by offering something pleasant or beneficial.
– DERIVATIVES **enticement** n.
– ORIGIN Old French *enticier*.

entire /in-**tyr**/ • **adj.** with no part left out; whole.
– ORIGIN Old French *entier*.

entirely • **adv. 1** wholly; completely. **2** solely; just.

entirety • **n.** (**the entirety**) the whole.
– PHRASES **in its entirety** as a whole.

entitle • **v.** (**entitles**, **entitling**, **entitled**) **1** give (someone) a right to do or have. **2** give a title to (a book, play, etc.).
– DERIVATIVES **entitlement** n.

entity /**en**-ti-ti/ • **n.** (pl. **entities**) a thing which exists separately from other things.
– ORIGIN French *entité*.

entomb • **v. 1** place in a tomb. **2** bury in or under something.

entomology /en-tuh-**mol**-uh-ji/ • **n.** the scientific study of insects.
– DERIVATIVES **entomological** adj. **entomologist** n.
– ORIGIN Greek *entomon* 'insect'.

entourage /**on**-toor-ahzh/ • **n.** a group of people accompanying an important person.
– ORIGIN French.

entrails • **pl. n.** a person's or animal's intestines or internal organs.
– ORIGIN Latin *intralia* 'internal things'.

entrance¹ /**en**-truhnss/ • **n. 1** an opening through which one may enter a place. **2** an act of entering. **3** the right, means, or opportunity to enter: *fifty people attempted to gain entrance.*

entrance² /in-**trahnss**/ • **v.** (**entrances**, **entrancing**, **entranced**) **1** fill with wonder and delight. **2** cast a spell on.

entrant • **n.** a person who enters, joins, or takes part in something.

entrap • **v.** (**entraps**, **entrapping**, **entrapped**) **1** catch in a trap. **2** (of a police officer) deceive (someone) into committing a crime in order to have them prosecuted.
– DERIVATIVES **entrapment** n.

entreat • **v.** ask (someone) earnestly or anxiously.
– ORIGIN Old French *entraitier*.

entreaty • **n.** (pl. **entreaties**) an earnest request.

entrée /**on**-tray/ • **n. 1** the main course of a meal. **2** the right to enter a place or social group: *an entrée into fashionable society.*
– ORIGIN French.

entrench • **v. 1** establish (something) so firmly that change is difficult: *prejudice is entrenched in our society.* **2** establish (a military force) in fortified positions.
– DERIVATIVES **entrenchment** n.

entrepreneur /on-truh-pruh-**ner**/ • **n.** a person who makes money by starting new businesses.
– ORIGIN French.

entrepreneurial /on-truh-pruh-**ner**-i-uhl/ • **adj.** having to do with an entrepreneur.

entropy /**en**-truh-pi/ • **n.** Physics a quantity expressing how much of a system's thermal energy is unavailable for conversion into mechanical work.
– DERIVATIVES **entropic** /en-**trop**-ik/ adj.
– ORIGIN Greek *tropē* 'transformation'.

entrust • **v. 1** (**entrust with**) give a responsibility to. **2** (**entrust to**) put (something) into someone's care.

entry • **n.** (pl. **entries**) **1** an act or the action of entering. **2** an entrance. **3** the right, means, or opportunity to enter. **4** an item entered in a list, reference book, etc.

entry-level • **adj.** suitable for a beginner or

first-time user.

entwine ● v. (**entwines**, **entwining**, **entwined**) wind or twist together.

E-number ● n. Brit. a code number beginning with the letter E, given to food additives.

enumerate /i-nyoo-muh-rayt/ ● v. (**enumerates**, **enumerating**, **enumerated**) mention (a number of things) one by one.
– DERIVATIVES **enumeration** n.
– ORIGIN Latin *enumerare* 'count out'.

enunciate /i-nun-si-ayt/ ● v. (**enunciates**, **enunciating**, **enunciated**) **1** pronounce clearly. **2** set out precisely: *a document enunciating this policy.*
– DERIVATIVES **enunciation** n.
– ORIGIN Latin *enuntiare* 'announce'.

envelop /in-vel-uhp/ ● v. (**envelops**, **enveloping**, **enveloped**) wrap up, cover, or surround completely.
– ORIGIN Old French *envoluper.*

envelope /en-vuh-lohp/ ● n. **1** a flat paper container with a sealable flap, used to enclose a letter or document. **2** a structure or layer that covers or encloses something.
– ORIGIN French *envelopper* 'envelop'.

enviable /en-vi-uh-b'l/ ● adj. desirable, and so arousing envy.
– DERIVATIVES **enviably** adv.

envious ● adj. feeling or showing envy.
– DERIVATIVES **enviously** adv.

environment ● n. **1** the surroundings or conditions in which a person, animal, or plant lives or operates. **2** (**the environment**) the natural world.
– DERIVATIVES **environmental** adj. **environmentally** adv.

environmentalist ● n. a person who is concerned with the protection of the environment.
– DERIVATIVES **environmentalism** n.

environs ● pl. n. the surrounding area or district.
– ORIGIN French.

envisage /in-viz-ij/ ● v. (**envisages**, **envisaging**, **envisaged**) **1** see as a possibility. **2** form a mental picture of.
– ORIGIN French *envisager.*

envision ● v. visualize; envisage.

envoy /en-voy/ ● n. a messenger or representative.
– ORIGIN French *envoyé* 'sent'.

envy ● n. (pl. **envies**) **1** discontented longing for something belonging to another that one cannot have. **2** (**the envy of**) a person or thing that inspires such a feeling. ● v. (**envies**, **envying**, **envied**) feel envy of.
– ORIGIN Old French *envie.*

enzyme /en-zym/ ● n. a substance produced by a living organism and acting as a catalyst to promote a particular reaction.
– ORIGIN modern Greek *enzumos* 'leavened'.

Eocene /ee-oh-seen/ ● adj. Geol. relating to the second epoch of the Tertiary period (56.5 to 35.4 million years ago).
– ORIGIN from Greek *ēōs* 'dawn' + *kainos* 'new'.

eon ● n. US and tech. var. of **AEON**.

EP ● abbrev. **1** (of a record or compact disc) extended-play. **2** European Parliament.

ep- ● prefix var. of **EPI-**.

epaulette /e-puh-let/ (US also **epaulet**) ● n. an ornamental shoulder piece on a military uniform.
– ORIGIN French, 'little shoulder'.

ephemera /i-fem-uh-ruh/ ● pl. n. items of short-lived interest or usefulness.
– ORIGIN Greek, 'things lasting only a day'.

ephemeral ● adj. lasting or living for a very short time.

Ephesus E
/ef-fi-suhss/ an ancient Greek city on the west coast of Asia Minor, in present-day Turkey, site of the temple of Diana, one of the Seven Wonders of the World.

epi- (also **ep-**) ● prefix **1** upon: *epigraph.* **2** above: *epidermis.*
– ORIGIN Greek *epi.*

epic ● n. **1** a long poem describing the actions of heroic figures or the past history of a nation. **2** a long film, book, etc. portraying heroic actions or covering a long period of time. ● adj. **1** having to do with an epic. **2** heroic or grand: *an epic journey around the world.*
– ORIGIN Greek *epikos.*

epicene /e-pi-seen/ ● adj. having male and female characteristics or no characteristics of either sex.
– ORIGIN Greek *epikoinos.*

epicentre (US **epicenter**) ● n. the point on the earth's surface directly above the origin of an earthquake.

epicure /e-pi-kyoor/ ● n. a person who takes particular pleasure in good food and drink.
– DERIVATIVES **epicurean** n. & adj.
– ORIGIN from **EPICURUS**.

Epicurus E
/e-pi-**kyoor**-uhss/ (341–270 BC), Greek philosopher, founder of Epicureanism, a school of philosophy based on the belief that pleasure was the only worthwhile aim in life.

epidemic ● n. **1** a widespread occurrence of an infectious disease in a community at a particular time. **2** a sudden, widespread occurrence of something undesirable: *an epidemic of violent crime.*
– ORIGIN Greek *epidēmia.*

epidemiology /e-pi-dee-mi-ol-uh-ji/ ● n. the study of the spread and control of diseases.
– DERIVATIVES **epidemiologist** n.

epidermis /e-pi-der-miss/ ● n. **1** the surface layer of an animal's skin, overlying the dermis. **2** the outer layer of tissue in a plant.
– DERIVATIVES **epidermal** adj.
– ORIGIN Greek.

epidural /e-pi-dyoor-uhl/ ● n. an anaesthetic put into the space around the outermost membrane of the spinal cord.

epiglottis /e-pi-glot-tiss/ ● n. a flap of cartilage at the root of the tongue, that descends during swallowing to cover the opening of the windpipe.
– ORIGIN Greek.

epigram /e-pi-gram/ ● n. **1** a concise and witty saying. **2** a short witty poem.
– DERIVATIVES **epigrammatic** adj.
– ORIGIN Greek *epigramma.*

epigraph /e-pi-grahf/ ● n. **1** an inscription on a building, statue, or coin. **2** a short quotation introducing a book or chapter.
– ORIGIN Greek *epigraphein* 'write on'.

epilepsy /e-pi-lep-si/ ● n. a disorder of the nervous system causing periodic loss of con-

sciousness or convulsions.
– DERIVATIVES **epileptic** adj. & n.
– ORIGIN Greek *epilēpsia*.

epilogue /e-pi-log/ (US also **epilog**) ● n. a section at the end of a book or play which comments on what has happened.
– ORIGIN Greek *epilogos*.

epiphany /i-pif-uh-ni/ ● n. (pl. **epiphanies**) **1** (**Epiphany**) the occasion when Christ appeared to the Magi (Gospel of Matthew, chapter 2). **2** (**Epiphany**) the festival commemorating this, on 6 January.
– ORIGIN Greek *epiphainein* 'reveal'.

episcopacy /i-piss-kuh-puh-si/ ● n. (pl. **episcopacies**) **1** government of a Church by bishops. **2** (**the episcopacy**) the bishops of a region or church as a group.

episcopal /i-piss-kuh-puhl/ ● adj. having to do with a bishop or bishops.
– ORIGIN Latin *episcopus* 'bishop'.

Episcopal Church E
the Anglican Church in Scotland and the US.

episcopalian /i-piss-kuh-pay-li-uhn/ ● adj. having to do with the government of a Church by bishops. ● n. a supporter of government of a Church by bishops.
– DERIVATIVES **episcopalianism** n.

episcopate /i-piss-kuh-puht/ ● n. **1** the position or period of office of a bishop. **2** (**the episcopate**) the bishops of a church or region as a group.

episode ● n. **1** an event or a group of events occurring as part of a sequence. **2** each of the parts into which a serialized story or programme is divided.
– ORIGIN Greek *epeisodion*.

episodic /e-pi-sod-ik/ ● adj. **1** made up of a series of separate events. **2** occurring at irregular intervals: *volcanic activity is highly episodic in nature.*

epistemology /i-piss-ti-mol-uh-ji/ ● n. the branch of philosophy that deals with knowledge.
– DERIVATIVES **epistemological** adj.
– ORIGIN Greek *epistēmē* 'knowledge'.

epistle /i-piss-uhl/ ● n. **1** formal or humorous a letter. **2** (**Epistle**) a book of the New Testament in the form of a letter from an Apostle.
– ORIGIN Greek *epistolē*.

epistolary /i-piss-tuh-luh-ri/ ● adj. **1** relating to the writing of letters. **2** (of a literary work) in the form of letters.

epitaph /e-pi-tahf/ ● n. words written in memory of a person who has died.
– ORIGIN Greek *epitaphion* 'funeral oration'.

epithet /e-pi-thet/ ● n. a word or phrase used to describe the most important quality of a person or thing.
– ORIGIN Greek *epitheton*.

epitome /i-pit-uh-mi/ ● n. (**the epitome of**) a perfect example of (a quality or type).
– ORIGIN Greek.

epitomize (also **epitomise**) ● v. (**epitomizes, epitomizing, epitomized**) be a perfect example of.

epoch /ee-pok/ ● n. **1** a period of time in history or a person's life: *the Victorian epoch.* **2** the beginning of a period of history. **3** Geol. a division of time that is a subdivision of a period and is itself subdivided into ages.
– ORIGIN Greek *epokhē* 'fixed point of time'.

epoch-making ● adj. of major importance; historic.

eponym /e-puh-nim/ ● n. **1** a word or name derived from the name of a person. **2** a person after whom something is named.

eponymous /i-pon-i-muhss/ ● adj. **1** (of a person) giving their name to something. **2** (of a thing) named after a particular person.
– ORIGIN Greek *epōnumos*.

epoxy /i-pok-si/ (also **epoxy resin**) ● n. (pl. **epoxies**) a type of strong glue made from synthetic polymers.
– ORIGIN from **EPI-** + **OXYGEN**.

Epsom E
a town in Surrey, SE England. The annual Derby and Oaks horse races are held at its racecourse.

Epsom salts ● pl. n. crystals of magnesium sulphate used as a laxative.
– ORIGIN named after **EPSOM**.

Epstein E
/ep-styn/, Sir Jacob (1880–1959), American-born British sculptor. His early sculptures were often attacked for their modernism, but his later portrait busts of famous people gained wide approval.

equable /ek-wuh-b'l/ ● adj. **1** calm and even-tempered. **2** not varying greatly: *an equable climate.*
– ORIGIN Latin *aequabilis*.

equal ● adj. **1** the same in quantity, size, degree, value, or status. **2** evenly balanced. **3** (**equal to**) having the ability to meet (a challenge). ● n. a person or thing that is equal to another. ● v. (**equals, equalling, equalled**; US **equals, equaling, equaled**) **1** be equal to. **2** match or rival.
– ORIGIN Latin *aequalis*.

equality ● n. the state of being equal.

equalize (also **equalise**) ● v. (**equalizes, equalizing, equalized**) **1** make or become equal. **2** level the score in a match by scoring a goal.
– DERIVATIVES **equalization** (also **equalisation**) n.

equalizer (also **equaliser**) ● n. **1** a thing that has an equalizing effect. **2** a goal that levels the score in a match.

equally ● adv. **1** in an equal way or to an equal extent. **2** in amounts that are equal.

USAGE equally
You should not use the words **equally as** together, as in the sentence *follow-up discussion is equally as important*: just say **equally** or **as** on its own.

equals sign (also **equal sign**) ● n. the symbol =.

equanimity /ek-wuh-nim-i-ti/ ● n. calmness; evenness of temper.
– ORIGIN Latin *aequanimitas*.

equate /i-kwayt/ ● v. (**equates, equating, equated**) (often **equate to/with**) **1** consider (one thing) as equal to another. **2** make (two or more things) the same: *we must equate supply and demand.*

equation /i-kway-*zh*'n/ ● n. **1** Math. a statement that the values of two mathematical expressions are equal (indicated by the sign =). **2** Chem. a formula representing the changes which occur in a chemical reaction. **3** the process of equating one thing with another.

equator /i-kway-ter/ ● **n.** an imaginary line around the earth at equal distances from the poles, dividing the earth into northern and southern hemispheres.
– ORIGIN Latin *aequator*.

equatorial /ek-wuh-tor-i-uhl/ ● **adj.** having to do with the equator.

Equatorial Guinea E
a small country on the coast of West Africa, comprising several offshore islands and a settlement between Cameroon and Gabon; capital, Malabo (on the island of Bioko).
– DERIVATIVES **Equatorial Guinean** adj & n.

e

equerry /ek-wuh-ri/ ● **n.** (pl. **equerries**) an officer of the British royal household who assists members of the royal family.
– ORIGIN Old French *esquierie* 'company of squires'.

equestrian /i-kwess-tri-uhn/ ● **adj.** relating to horse riding. ● **n.** (fem. **equestrienne** /i-kwess-tri-**en**/) a person on horseback.
– ORIGIN Latin *equester*.

equestrianism ● **n.** the skill or sport of horse riding.

equi- /ee-kwi, ek-wi/ ● **comb. form** equal; equally: *equidistant*.
– ORIGIN Latin *aequus* 'equal'.

equidistant ● **adj.** at equal distances.

equilateral ● **adj.** having all its sides of the same length: *an equilateral triangle*.

equilibrium /ee-kwi-**lib**-ri-uhm, ek-wi-**lib**-ri-uhm/ ● **n.** (pl. **equilibria** /ee-kwi-**lib**-ri-uh, ek-wi-**lib**-ri-uh/) **1** a state in which opposing forces are balanced. **2** the state of being physically balanced. **3** a calm state of mind.
– ORIGIN Latin *aequilibrium*.

equine /ek-wyn/ ● **adj. 1** relating to horses or other members of the horse family. **2** resembling a horse.
– ORIGIN Latin *equinus*.

equinoctial /ee-kwi-**nok**-sh'l, ek-wi-**nok**-sh'l/ ● **adj. 1** having to do with the equinox. **2** at or near the equator.

equinox /ee-kwi-noks, ek-wi-noks/ ● **n.** the time or date (twice each year, about 22 September and 20 March) when day and night are of equal length.
– ORIGIN Latin *aequinoctium*.

equip ● **v.** (**equips**, **equipping**, **equipped**) **1** supply with the items needed for a purpose. **2** prepare (someone) mentally for a situation or task: *he is not equipped for the modern age*.
– ORIGIN French *équiper*.

equipment ● **n. 1** the items needed for a particular purpose. **2** the supply of these items.

equipoise /ek-wi-poyz/ ● **n.** balance of forces or interests: *this temporary equipoise of power*.

equitable /ek-wi-tuh-b'l/ ● **adj.** treating everyone equally; fair.
– DERIVATIVES **equitably** adv.

equitation /ek-wi-tay-sh'n/ ● **n.** formal the art and practice of horse riding.
– ORIGIN Latin.

equity /ek-wi-ti/ ● **n.** (pl. **equities**) **1** the quality of being fair and impartial. **2** Law a branch of law based on natural justice, to be used when existing laws would be unfair or inappropriate. **3** the value of the shares issued by a company. **4** (**equities**) stocks and shares that do not pay a fixed amount of interest.
– ORIGIN Latin *aequitas*.

equivalent /i-kwiv-uh-luhnt/ ● **adj.** equal in value, amount, meaning, etc.: *a brightness equivalent to a billion suns*. ● **n.** a person or thing that is equivalent to another.
– DERIVATIVES **equivalence** n. **equivalently** adv.
– ORIGIN Latin *aequivalere* 'be of equal worth'.

equivocal /i-kwiv-uh-k'l/ ● **adj.** unclear because able to be understood in more than one way.
– DERIVATIVES **equivocally** adv.
– ORIGIN from Latin *aequus* 'equal' + *vocare* 'to call'.

equivocate /i-kwiv-uh-kayt/ ● **v.** (**equivocates, equivocating, equivocated**) use language that can be understood in more than one way in order to avoid the truth.
– DERIVATIVES **equivocation** n.

ER ● **abbrev. 1** Queen Elizabeth. [ORIGIN from Latin *Elizabetha Regina*.] **2** N. Amer. emergency room.

-er[1] ● **suffix** referring to: **1** a person or thing that performs a specified action or activity: *farmer*. **2** a person or thing that has a specified quality or form: *two-wheeler*. **3** a person concerned with a specified thing: *milliner*. **4** a person belonging to a specified place or group: *city-dweller*.
– ORIGIN Old English.

-er[2] ● **suffix** forming the comparative of adjectives (as in *bigger*) and adverbs (as in *faster*).
– ORIGIN Old English.

era /eer-uh/ ● **n. 1** a long and distinct period of history. **2** Geol. a major division of time that is a subdivision of an aeon and is itself subdivided into periods.
– ORIGIN Latin *aera* 'counters'.

eradicate /i-rad-i-kayt/ ● **v.** (**eradicates, eradicating, eradicated**) remove or destroy completely.
– DERIVATIVES **eradication** n. **eradicator** n.
– ORIGIN Latin *eradicare* 'tear up by the roots'.

erase /i-rayz/ ● **v.** (**erases, erasing, erased**) **1** rub out. **2** remove all traces of.
– DERIVATIVES **erasable** adj. **erasure** n.
– ORIGIN Latin *eradere* 'scrape away'.

eraser ● **n.** a piece of rubber or plastic used to rub out something written.

Erasmus E
/i-raz-muhss/, Desiderius (*c.*1469–1536), Dutch humanist and scholar, who paved the way for the Reformation with his satires on the Church.

erbium /er-bi-uhm/ ● **n.** a soft silvery-white metallic chemical element.
– ORIGIN from *Ytterby* in Sweden.

ere /air/ ● **prep. & conj.** archaic before (in time).
– ORIGIN Old English.

Erebus, Mount E
/e-ri-buhss/ a volcanic peak on Ross Island, Antarctica, the world's most southerly active volcano.

erect ● **adj. 1** rigidly upright. **2** (of a body part) enlarged and rigid. ● **v. 1** build. **2** create or establish: *the party that erected the welfare state*.
– DERIVATIVES **erector** n.
– ORIGIN Latin *erigere* 'set up'.

erectile /i-rek-tyl/ ● **adj.** able to become

erect.

erection ● n. **1** the action of erecting a structure or object. **2** a building or other upright structure. **3** an erect state of the penis.

erg /erg/ ● n. Physics a unit of work or energy.
– ORIGIN Greek *ergon* 'work'.

ergo /er-goh/ ● adv. therefore.
– ORIGIN Latin.

ergonomics /er-guh-nom-iks/ ● n. the study of people's efficiency in their working environment.
– DERIVATIVES **ergonomic** adj.
– ORIGIN Greek *ergon* 'work'.

ergot /er-got/ ● n. a disease of rye and other cereals, caused by a fungus.
– ORIGIN French.

Ericsson E
/e-rik-s'n/ (also **Ericson** or **Eriksson**), Leif, Norse explorer, son of Eric the Red. He sailed westward from Greenland (*c.*1000) and discovered land (which has been identified as Labrador, Newfoundland, or New England).

Eric the Red E
(*c.*940–*c.*1010), Norse explorer, who in 982 explored Greenland and later established a Norse settlement there.

Erie, Lake E
/eer-i/ one of the five Great Lakes of North America, situated on the border between Canada and the US.

Erin /e-rin/ ● n. archaic or literary Ireland.
– ORIGIN Irish.

Eritrea E
/e-ri-tray-uh/ an independent state in NE Africa, on the Red Sea; capital, Asmara.
– DERIVATIVES **Eritrean** adj. & n.

ERM ● abbrev. Exchange Rate Mechanism.

ermine /er-min/ ● n. (pl. **ermine** or **ermines**) **1** a stoat. **2** the white winter fur of the stoat.
– ORIGIN Old French *hermine*.

Ernst E
/ernst, airnst/, Max (1891–1976), German artist, a leader of the Dada movement and later a major figure of surrealism.

erode /i-rohd/ ● v. (**erodes, eroding, eroded**) **1** gradually wear or be worn away. **2** gradually destroy: *this humiliation has eroded Jean's confidence.*
– ORIGIN Latin *erodere*.

erogenous /i-roj-i-nuhss/ ● adj. (of a part of the body) sensitive to sexual stimulation.
– ORIGIN from **Eros**.

Eros E
/eer-oss/ the Greek god of love, son of Aphrodite. Roman equivalent **Cupid**.

erosion /i-roh-*zh*'n/ ● n. the process of eroding or the result of being eroded.

erotic /i-rot-ik/ ● adj. having to do with sexual desire or excitement.
– DERIVATIVES **erotically** adv.
– ORIGIN Greek *erōtikos*.

erotica ● n. erotic literature or art.

eroticism ● n. **1** the quality of being erotic. **2** sexual desire or excitement.

eroticize (also **eroticise**) ● v. (**eroticizes, eroticizing, eroticized**) give erotic qualities to.

err /er/ ● v. **1** make a mistake. **2** do wrong: *he had erred as a husband.*
– PHRASES **err on the side of** display more rather than less of (a quality): *it is best to err on the side of caution.*
– ORIGIN Latin *errare* 'to stray'.

errand ● n. a short journey made to deliver or collect something.
– ORIGIN Old English, 'message, mission'.

errant /e-ruhnt/ ● adj. **1** formal or humorous straying from the accepted course or standards. **2** archaic travelling in search of adventure: *a knight errant.*
– ORIGIN sense 1 from Latin *errare* 'err'; sense 2 from Old French, 'travelling'.

erratic /i-rat-ik/ ● adj. not even or regular in pattern or movement.
– DERIVATIVES **erratically** adv.

erratum /e-rah-tuhm, e-ray-tuhm/ ● n. (pl. **errata** /e-rah-tuh, e-ray-tuh/) an error in printing or writing.
– ORIGIN Latin.

erroneous /i-roh-ni-uhss/ ● adj. incorrect.
– DERIVATIVES **erroneously** adv.
– ORIGIN Latin *erroneus*.

error ● n. **1** a mistake. **2** the state of being wrong in behaviour or judgement: *the money was paid in error.*
– ORIGIN Latin.

ersatz /er-sats/ ● adj. **1** (of a product) made or used as a poor-quality substitute for something else. **2** not genuine: *ersatz emotion.*
– ORIGIN German, 'replacement'.

Erse /erss/ ● n. the Scottish or Irish Gaelic language.
– ORIGIN early Scots form of **Irish**.

erstwhile ● adj. former.
– ORIGIN Old English.

erudite /e-roo-dyt/ ● adj. having or showing knowledge or learning.
– DERIVATIVES **erudition** n.
– ORIGIN Latin *eruditus*.

erupt ● v. **1** (of a volcano) become active and throw out lava, ash, and gases. **2** break out suddenly: *noise erupted from the next room.* **3** give vent to feelings in a sudden and noisy way. **4** (of a spot or rash) suddenly appear on the skin.
– ORIGIN Latin *erumpere* 'break out'.

eruption ● n. an act or the action or erupting.

-ery (also **-ry**) ● suffix forming nouns referring to: **1** a class or kind: *greenery.* **2** an occupation, a state, or behaviour: *archery.* **3** a place set aside for an activity or a grouping of things or animals: *rookery.*
– ORIGIN Latin *-arius* and *-ator*.

erythrocyte /i-rith-ruh-syt/ ● n. a red blood cell.
– ORIGIN Greek *eruthros* 'red'.

Esbjerg E
/ess-byerg/ a port in Denmark, on the west coast of Jutland.

escalate /ess-kuh-layt/ ● v. (**escalates, escalating, escalated**) **1** increase rapidly. **2** become or make more serious.
– DERIVATIVES **escalation** n.
– ORIGIN from **escalator**.

escalator ● n. a moving staircase consisting of a circulating belt of steps driven by a motor.

– ORIGIN French *escalade*, referring to a former method of military attack using ladders.

escalope /i-ska-luhp/ • **n.** a thin slice of meat, coated in breadcrumbs and fried.
– ORIGIN Old French, 'shell'.

escapade /ess-kuh-payd/ • **n.** an incident involving daring and adventure.

escape • **v.** (**escapes**, **escaping**, **escaped**) **1** break free from imprisonment or control. **2** get free from (someone). **3** succeed in avoiding (something bad). **4** fail to be noticed or remembered by: *his name escapes me.* • **n.** **1** an act of escaping. **2** a means of escaping.
– DERIVATIVES **escapee** n. **escaper** n.
– ORIGIN Old French *eschaper.*

escape clause • **n.** a clause in a contract which details the conditions under which one party can be freed from an obligation.

escapement /i-skayp-muhnt/ • **n.** a mechanism that connects and regulates the movement of a clock or watch.

escapism • **n.** the seeking of relief from unpleasant realities by engaging in entertainment or fantasy.
– DERIVATIVES **escapist** n. & adj.

escapologist /ess-kuh-**pol**-uh-jist/ • **n.** an entertainer who specializes in breaking free from ropes, handcuffs, and chains.

escarpment /i-**skarp**-muhnt/ • **n.** a long, steep slope that separates an area of high ground from an area of lower ground.
– ORIGIN French *escarpement.*

eschatology /ess-kuh-**tol**-uh-ji/ • **n.** the part of theology concerned with death, judgement, and destiny.
– ORIGIN Greek *eskhatos* 'last'.

eschew /iss-**choo**/ • **v.** deliberately avoid doing (something).
– ORIGIN Old French *eschiver.*

Escoffier E
/e-**skof**-fi-ay/, Georges-Auguste (1846–1935), French chef, who gained an international reputation while working in London at the Savoy and Carlton Hotels.

escort • **n.** /ess-kort/ **1** a person, vehicle, or group accompanying another to provide protection or as a mark of rank. **2** a person who accompanies a member of the opposite sex to a social event. • **v.** /i-**skort**/ accompany as an escort.
– ORIGIN French *escorte.*

escritoire /ess-kri-**twar**/ • **n.** a small writing desk with drawers and compartments.
– ORIGIN French.

escudo /ess-**kyoo**-doh/ • **n.** (pl. **escudos**) the former basic unit of money of Portugal.
– ORIGIN Portuguese.

escutcheon /i-sku-chuhn/ • **n.** a shield or emblem bearing a coat of arms.
– ORIGIN Old French *escuchon.*

ESE • **abbrev.** east-south-east.

-ese • **suffix** forming adjectives and nouns: **1** referring to an inhabitant or language of a country or city: *Chinese.* **2** usu. derog. referring to character or style: *journalese.*
– ORIGIN Latin *-ensis.*

Eskimo • **n.** (pl. **Eskimo** or **Eskimos**) **1** a member of a people inhabiting northern Canada, Alaska, Greenland, and eastern Siberia. **2** the language of this people. • **adj.** having to do with Eskimos.
– ORIGIN a North American Indian word.

USAGE Eskimo
Some people believe that it is better to use the term **Inuit** rather than **Eskimo**, because they think that **Eskimo** could be seen as offensive. The term **Eskimo**, however, is the only term that correctly covers both the Inuit (people of northern Canada and parts of Greenland and Alaska) and the Yupik (people of Siberia, the Aleutian Islands, and Alaska), and is still widely used.

esophagus • **n.** US = **OESOPHAGUS**.

esoteric /e-suh-te-rik/ • **adj.** intended for or understood by only a small number of people with a specialized knowledge.
– ORIGIN Greek *esōterikos.*

ESP • **abbrev.** extrasensory perception.

espadrille /ess-puh-dril/ • **n.** a light canvas shoe with a plaited fibre sole.
– ORIGIN French.

especial • **adj.** **1** special: *it was of especial interest to me.* **2** for or belonging chiefly to one person or thing.
– ORIGIN Latin *specialis* 'special'.

especially • **adv.** **1** in particular. **2** to a great extent: *he didn't especially like dancing.* **3** particularly; very.

USAGE especially
Although the words **especially** and **specially** can both mean 'particularly', they are not exactly the same. **Especially** also means 'in particular, chiefly', as in *he hated them all, especially Thomas,* while **specially** also means 'for a special purpose', as in *the car was specially made for the occasion.*

Esperanto /ess-puh-**ran**-toh/ • **n.** an artificial language invented as a means of international communication.
– ORIGIN from *Dr Esperanto,* a pen name of the inventor of the language, Ludwik L. Zamenhof (1858–1917).

espionage /ess-pi-uh-nah*zh*/ • **n.** the practice of spying or of using spies.
– ORIGIN French.

esplanade /ess-pluh-nayd/ • **n.** a long, level area along which people may walk for pleasure.
– ORIGIN French.

espousal /i-**spow**-z'l/ • **n.** the action of espousing.

espouse /i-**spowz**/ • **v.** (**espouses**, **espousing**, **espoused**) adopt or support (a cause, belief, or way of life).
– ORIGIN Old French *espouser.*

espresso /ess-**press**-oh/ (also **expresso** /ex-**press**-oh/) • **n.** (pl. **espressos**) strong black coffee made by forcing steam through ground coffee beans.
– ORIGIN from Italian *caffè espresso* 'pressed out coffee'.

esprit de corps /e-spree duh **kor**/ • **n.** a feeling of pride and loyalty uniting the members of a group.
– ORIGIN French, 'spirit of the body'.

espy /i-**spy**/ • **v.** (**espies**, **espying**, **espied**) literary catch sight of.
– ORIGIN Old French *espier.*

Esq. • **abbrev.** Esquire.

-esque • **suffix** (forming adjectives) in the style of: *Kafkaesque.*
– ORIGIN French.

esquire /i-skwyr/ • n. **1** (**Esquire**) Brit. a polite title placed after a man's name when no other title is used. **2** hist. a young nobleman who acted as an attendant to a knight.
– ORIGIN Old French *esquier.*

-ess • suffix forming nouns referring to females: *abbess.*
– ORIGIN French *-esse.*

essay • n. /ess-ay/ **1** a piece of writing on a particular subject. **2** formal an attempt or effort. • v. /e-say/ formal attempt: *Donald essayed a smile.*
– DERIVATIVES **essayist** n.
– ORIGIN Old French *essai* 'trial'; the verb is from **ASSAY**.

Essen E
/ess-uhn/ an industrial city in the Ruhr valley, in NW Germany.

essence • n. **1** the quality which determines the character of something: *conflict is the essence of drama.* **2** an extract obtained from a plant or other substance and used for flavouring or scent.
– PHRASES **in essence** basically. **of the essence** very important.
– ORIGIN Latin *essentia.*

essential • adj. **1** absolutely necessary. **2** central to the nature of: *the essential weakness of the case.* • n. (**essentials**) **1** things that are absolutely necessary. **2** the basic elements.
– DERIVATIVES **essentially** adv.

essential oil • n. a natural oil extracted from a plant.

Essex E
a county of eastern England; county town, Chelmsford.

-est • suffix forming the superlative of adjectives (such as *shortest*) and of adverbs (such as *soonest*).
– ORIGIN Old English.

establish • v. **1** set up on a firm or permanent basis. **2** start or bring about: *establish diplomatic relations.* **3** (**be established**) be settled in a particular place or role. **4** show to be true by finding out the facts. **5** (**established**) recognized by the state as the national Church or religion.
– ORIGIN Old French *establir.*

establishment • n. **1** the action of establishing or the state of being established. **2** an organization, institution, or hotel. **3** (**the Establishment**) a group in a society who have power and influence in matters of policy or opinion, and who oppose change.

estate • n. **1** a property consisting of a large house and extensive grounds. **2** Brit. an area of land and modern buildings used for housing, industrial, or business purposes. **3** a property where crops such as coffee are grown or where wine is produced. **4** all the money and property owned by a person at the time of their death. **5** (also **estate of the realm**) (in Britain) one of the three groups which make up Parliament, the Lords spiritual (the heads of the Church), the Lords temporal (the peerage), and the Commons.
– ORIGIN Old French *estat.*

estate agency • n. Brit. a business that sells and rents out buildings and land for clients.
– DERIVATIVES **estate agent** n.

estate car • n. Brit. a car which has a large carrying area behind the seats and an extra door at the rear.

esteem • n. respect and admiration. • v. respect and admire.
– ORIGIN Latin *aestimare* 'to estimate'.

ester /ess-ter/ • n. Chem. an organic compound formed by a reaction between an acid and an alcohol.

Esther E
(in the Bible) a beautiful woman chosen by the Persian king Ahasuerus (believed to be Xerxes I) to be his queen. She used her influence with him to save the Israelites from persecution.

esthete • n. US = **AESTHETE**.

esthetic • adj. US = **AESTHETIC**.

estimable • adj. worthy of great respect.
– DERIVATIVES **estimably** adv.

estimate • n. /ess-ti-muht/ **1** an approximate calculation. **2** a written statement giving the likely price that will be charged for specified work. **3** a judgement. • v. /ess-ti-mayt/ (**estimates, estimating, estimated**) form an estimate of.
– DERIVATIVES **estimation** n.
– ORIGIN Latin *aestimare* 'determine'.

Estonia E
/i-stoh-ni-uh/ a country with a coastline on the Baltic Sea; capital, Tallinn.
– DERIVATIVES **Estonian** adj. & n.

Estoril E
/ess-tuh-ril/ a resort on the Atlantic coast of Portugal.

estrange • v. (**estranges, estranging, estranged**) **1** cause to feel less close or friendly. **2** (**estranged**) (of a husband or wife) no longer living with their husband or wife.
– DERIVATIVES **estrangement** n.
– ORIGIN Old French *estranger.*

estrogen • n. US = **OESTROGEN**.

estrus • n. US = **OESTRUS**.

estuary /ess-tyuh-ri/ • n. (pl. **estuaries**) the mouth of a large river where it becomes affected by tides.
– ORIGIN Latin *aestuarium* 'tidal part of a shore'.

ETA[1] /ee-tee-ay/ • abbrev. estimated time of arrival.

ETA[2] E
/et-uh/ a Basque separatist movement in Spain, which since 1959 has waged a terrorist campaign for an independent Basque state.

e-tailer • n. a retailer who sells goods over the Internet.

et al. /et al/ • abbrev. and others.
– ORIGIN Latin *et alii.*

etc. • abbrev. et cetera.

et cetera /et set-uh-ruh/ (also **etcetera**) • adv. and other similar things; and so on.
– ORIGIN Latin.

etch • v. **1** engrave (metal, glass, or stone) by drawing on a protective coating with a needle, and then covering it with acid to attack the exposed parts. **2** cut (a text or design) on a surface. **3** make clearly defined: *names forever etched in the memory.*
– ORIGIN Dutch *etsen.*

etching • n. **1** the art or process of etching.

2 a print produced by etching.

eternal • adj. **1** lasting or existing forever. **2** valid for all time: *eternal truths*.
– PHRASES **eternal triangle** a relationship between three people involving sexual rivalry.
– DERIVATIVES **eternally** adv.
– ORIGIN Latin *aeternalis*.

eternity • n. (pl. **eternities**) **1** unending time: *their love was sealed for eternity*. **2** (**an eternity**) informal an undesirably long period of time.

ethane /ee-thayn/ • n. Chem. a flammable hydrocarbon gas, present in petroleum and natural gas.
– ORIGIN from **ETHER**.

ethanol /eth-uh-nol/ • n. = **ALCOHOL** (in sense 1).

Ethelred I E
(d.871), king of Wessex and Kent 865–71, elder brother of Alfred. His reign was marked by the continuing struggle against the invading Danes.

Ethelred II E
(*c.*969–1016; known as **Ethelred the Unready**), king of England 978–1016. He tried to prevent the Danes from attacking England by paying them. His mishandling of policy earned him the title *Unready* meaning 'badly advised'.

ether /ee-ther/ • n. **1** a highly flammable liquid used as an anaesthetic and as a solvent. **2** (also **aether**) esp. literary the sky or the upper regions of air.
– ORIGIN Greek *aithēr* 'upper air'.

ethereal /i-theer-i-uhl/ (also **etherial**) • adj. **1** extremely delicate and light: *she has a weirdly ethereal voice*. **2** heavenly or spiritual.

Ethernet • n. Computing a system for connecting a number of computer systems to form a local area network.
– ORIGIN from **ETHER** and **NETWORK**.

ethic • n. a set of moral principles: *the puritan ethic*.
– ORIGIN Latin *ethice*.

ethical • adj. **1** having to do with moral principles. **2** morally correct.
– DERIVATIVES **ethically** adv.

ethics • n. **1** the moral principles that govern a person's behaviour or how an activity is conducted: *medical ethics*. **2** the branch of knowledge concerned with moral principles.

Ethiopia E
/ee-thi-**oh**-pi-uh/ a country in NE Africa, on the Red Sea; capital, Addis Ababa. Former name **ABYSSINIA**.
– DERIVATIVES **Ethiopian** adj. & n.

ethnic • adj. **1** having to do with a group of people who have a common national or cultural tradition. **2** referring to origin by birth rather than by present nationality: *ethnic Albanians*. **3** belonging to a non-Western cultural tradition.
– DERIVATIVES **ethnically** adv. **ethnicity** n.
– ORIGIN Greek *ethnikos* 'heathen'.

ethnic cleansing • n. the expelling or killing of members of one ethnic or religious group in an area by those of another.

ethnic minority • n. a group within a community which has a different ethnic origin from the main population.

ethnography • n. the scientific description of peoples and cultures.

ethnology /eth-**nol**-uh-ji/ • n. the study of the characteristics of different peoples and the differences and relationships between them.

ethos /ee-thoss/ • n. the characteristic spirit of a culture, era, or community.
– ORIGIN Greek *ēthos* 'nature'.

ethyl /eth-yl/ • n. Chem. a radical ($-C_2H_5$) derived from ethane, present in alcohol and ether.
– ORIGIN German.

ethyl alcohol • n. = **ALCOHOL** (in sense 1).

ethylene /eth-i-leen/ • n. Chem. a flammable hydrocarbon gas, present in natural gas and coal gas.

etiolated /ee-ti-uh-lay-tid/ • adj. (of a plant) pale and weak due to a lack of light.
– ORIGIN French *étioler*.

etiquette /et-i-ket/ • n. the code of polite behaviour in a society.
– ORIGIN French, 'list of ceremonial observances of a court'.

Etna, Mount E
/et-nuh/ a volcano in eastern Sicily. Rising to 3,323 m (10,902 ft), it is the highest and most active volcano in Europe.

Eton College E
a boys' public school near Windsor in southern England, founded in 1440 by Henry VI.

Etruria E
/i-troo-ri-uh/ an ancient state of western Italy, corresponding roughly to modern Tuscany and parts of Umbria. It was the centre of the Etruscan civilization, which was at its height *c.*500 BC.
– DERIVATIVES **Etrurian** n. & adj.

Etruscan /i-truss-k'n/ • n. **1** a person from Etruria. **2** the language of Etruria. • adj. relating to Etruria.
– ORIGIN Latin *Etruscus*.

et seq. • adv. and what follows (used in page references).
– ORIGIN from Latin *et sequens*.

-ette • suffix forming nouns referring to: **1** small size: *kitchenette*. **2** an imitation or substitute: *leatherette*. **3** female gender: *suffragette*.
– ORIGIN Old French.

étude /ay-tyood/ • n. a short musical composition or exercise.
– ORIGIN French, 'study'.

etymology /et-i-mol-uh-ji/ • n. (pl. **etymologies**) an account of the origins and the developments in meaning of a word.
– DERIVATIVES **etymological** adj. **etymologist** n.
– ORIGIN Greek *etumologia*.

EU • abbrev. European Union.

eucalyptus /yoo-kuh-**lip**-tuhss/ (also **eucalypt**) • n. (pl. **eucalyptuses** or **eucalypti** /yoo-kuh-**lip**-ty/) an evergreen Australasian tree valued for its wood, oil, gum, and resin.
– ORIGIN Latin.

Eucharist /yoo-kuh-rist/ • n. **1** the Christian ceremony commemorating the Last Supper, in which consecrated bread and wine are consumed. **2** the consecrated bread and wine used in this ceremony.
– DERIVATIVES **Eucharistic** adj.

– ORIGIN Greek *eukharistia* 'thanksgiving'.

Euclid E
/**yoo**-klid/ (*c*.300 BC), Greek mathematician. His *Elements of Geometry* was the standard work on the subject until the 19th century.

eugenics /yoo-**jen**-iks/ ● **n.** the science of improving a population by controlled breeding to increase the occurrence of desirable characteristics which are able to be inherited.
– ORIGIN from Greek *eu* 'well' + *genēs* 'born'.

Euler E
/**oy**-ler/, Leonhard (1707–83), Swiss mathematician, who made major contributions to geometry, number theory, and the study of infinite series.

eulogize /**yoo**-luh-jyz/ (also **eulogise**) ● **v.** (**eulogizes**, **eulogizing**, **eulogized**) praise highly.

eulogy /**yoo**-luh-ji/ ● **n.** (pl. **eulogies**) a speech or piece of writing that praises someone highly.
– ORIGIN Greek *eulogia* 'praise'.

eunuch /**yoo**-nuhk/ ● **n.** a man who has been castrated.
– ORIGIN Greek *eunoukhos* 'bedroom guard'.

euphemism /**yoo**-fuh-mi-z'm/ ● **n.** a less direct word used instead of one that is harsh or blunt when referring to something unpleasant or embarrassing.
– DERIVATIVES **euphemistic** adj. **euphemistically** adv.
– ORIGIN Greek *euphēmismos*.

euphonious /yoo-**foh**-ni-uhss/ ● **adj.** sounding pleasant.
– DERIVATIVES **euphoniously** adv.

euphonium /yoo-**foh**-ni-uhm/ ● **n.** a brass musical instrument resembling a small tuba.
– ORIGIN Greek *euphōnos* 'having a pleasing sound'.

euphony /**yoo**-fuh-ni/ ● **n.** the quality of having a pleasant sound.
– DERIVATIVES **euphonic** adj.

euphoria /yoo-**for**-i-uh/ ● **n.** a feeling of great happiness.
– DERIVATIVES **euphoric** adj.
– ORIGIN Greek.

Euphrates E
/yoo-**fray**-teez/ a river of SW Asia which rises in the mountains of eastern Turkey and flows through Syria and Iraq to join the Tigris.

Eurasia E
/yoor-**ay**-*zh*uh/ the continental land mass of Europe and Asia as a whole.

Eurasian ● **adj.** **1** of mixed European (or European-American) and Asian parentage. **2** relating to Eurasia.

eureka /yoo-**ree**-kuh/ ● **exclam.** a cry of joy or satisfaction when one finds or discovers something.
– ORIGIN Greek *heurēka* 'I have found it'.

Euripides E
/yoo-**rip**-i-deez/ (480–*c*.406 BC), Greek dramatist. His surviving tragedies include *Medea*, *Electra*, and *Bacchae*.

euro ● **n.** the single European currency, which replaced the national currencies of France, Germany, Spain, Italy, Greece, Portugal, Luxembourg, Austria, Finland, Ireland, Belgium, and the Netherlands in 2002.

Europa E
/yoo-**roh**-puh/ Gk Myth. a princess of Tyre who was courted by Zeus in the form of a bull and was carried off by him to Crete.

Europe E
a continent of the northern hemisphere, separated from Africa to the south by the Mediterranean Sea and from Asia to the east roughly by the Bosporus, the Caucasus Mountains, and the Ural Mountains.

Europe, Council of E
an association of European states founded in 1949 to protect the political and cultural heritage of Europe and promote economic and social cooperation.

European ● **n.** **1** a person from Europe. **2** a person who is white or of European parentage. ● **adj.** having to do with Europe or the European Union.

European Commission E
a group which initiates action in the European Union and safeguards its treaties.

European Community E
an economic and political association of certain European countries formed in 1967 and incorporated since 1993 in the European Union.

European Economic Community E
an institution of the European Union, an economic association of western European countries set up by the Treaty of Rome (1957). The original members were France, West Germany, Italy, Belgium, the Netherlands, and Luxembourg.

European Monetary Union E
a European Union programme intended to work towards full economic unity in Europe based on the phased introduction of a common currency (the euro).

European Parliament E
the Parliament of the European Community, established in 1952 and meeting in Strasbourg. Since the Single European Act (1987) it has had a degree of sovereignty over national parliaments.

European Union E
an economic and political association of certain European countries created in 1993, with free trade between member countries.

europium /yoo-**roh**-pi-uhm/ ● **n.** a soft silvery-white metallic element.
– ORIGIN from **Europe**.

Eurydice E
/yoo-**rid**-i-si/ Gk Myth. the wife of Orpheus. After she died Orpheus was allowed to rescue her from the underworld on the condition that he did not look back at her, but he did look back and she had to remain there.

Eustachian tube /yoo-**stay**-sh'n/ ● **n.** Anat. a narrow passage leading from the pharynx to the cavity of the middle ear, which equalizes the pressure on each side of the eardrum.
– ORIGIN named after the Italian anatomist Bartolomeo *Eustachio* (d.1574).

euthanasia /yoo-thuh-nay-zi-uh/ • n. the painless killing of a patient suffering from an incurable disease or in an irreversible coma.
– ORIGIN from Greek *eu* 'well' + *thanatos* 'death'.

evacuate • v. (**evacuates**, **evacuating**, **evacuated**) **1** remove from a place of danger to a safer place. **2** leave (a dangerous place). **3** tech. remove the contents from (a container). **4** empty (the bowels).
– DERIVATIVES **evacuation** n.
– ORIGIN Latin *evacuare*.

evacuee • n. a person evacuated from a place of danger.

evade • v. (**evades**, **evading**, **evaded**) **1** escape or avoid. **2** avoid giving a direct answer to (a question). **3** escape paying (tax or duty).
– ORIGIN Latin *evadere*.

evaluate • v. (**evaluates**, **evaluating**, **evaluated**) form an idea of the amount or value of.
– DERIVATIVES **evaluation** n. **evaluative** adj. **evaluator** n.

evanescent /ev-uh-ness-uhnt/ • adj. literary soon passing out of sight, memory, or existence: *an evanescent bubble*.
– DERIVATIVES **evanescence** n.
– ORIGIN Latin *evanescere* 'disappear'.

evangelical • adj. **1** having to do with the teaching of the gospel or Christianity. **2** relating to a tradition within Protestant Christianity which emphasizes Biblical authority and personal conversion. **3** showing passionate support for something: *evangelical feminists*. • n. a member of the evangelical tradition in the Christian Church.
– DERIVATIVES **evangelicalism** n.
– ORIGIN Greek *euangelos* 'bringing good news'.

evangelist • n. **1** a person who seeks to convert others to the Christian faith. **2** the writer of one of the four Gospels. **3** a passionate supporter of something.
– DERIVATIVES **evangelism** n. **evangelistic** adj.

evangelize (also **evangelise**) • v. (**evangelizes**, **evangelizing**, **evangelized**) **1** convert or try to convert (someone) to Christianity. **2** preach the gospel.

Evans[1], E
Sir Arthur (John) (1851–1941), English archaeologist, whose excavations at Knossos (1899–1935) resulted in the discovery of the Bronze Age civilization of Crete.

Evans[2], E
Dame Edith (Mary) (1888–1976), English stage and film actress.

evaporate • v. (**evaporates**, **evaporating**, **evaorated**) **1** turn from liquid into vapour. **2** cease to exist: *my goodwill evaporated*.
– DERIVATIVES **evaporation** n.
– ORIGIN Latin *evaporare*.

evaporated milk • n. thick sweetened milk that has had some of the liquid removed by evaporation.

evasion • n. the action or an act of evading.

evasive • adj. **1** avoiding a direct answer to a question. **2** intended to avoid or escape something: *evasive action*.
– DERIVATIVES **evasively** adv. **evasiveness** n.

Eve E
(in the Bible) the first woman, companion of Adam and mother of Cain and Abel.

eve • n. **1** the day or period of time immediately before an event. **2** literary evening.
– ORIGIN from **EVEN[2]**.

Evelyn E
/eev-lin/, John (1620–1706), English diarist and writer, known for his *Diary*, which includes descriptions of the Great Plague and the Fire of London.

even[1] • adj. **1** flat and smooth; level. **2** equal in number, amount, or value. **3** regular: *an even pace*. **4** equally balanced. **5** placid; calm: *an even temper*. **6** (of a number) able to be divided by two without a remainder. • v. make or become even. • adv. used for emphasis: *he knows even less than I do*.
– PHRASES **even as** at the very same time as. **even if** despite the possibility that. **even so** nevertheless. **even though** despite the fact that.
– DERIVATIVES **evenly** adv. **evenness** n.
– ORIGIN Old English.

even[2] • n. archaic evening.

even-handed • adj. fair and impartial.

evening • n. the period of time at the end of the day.
– ORIGIN Old English.

evening primrose • n. a plant with pale yellow flowers that open in the evening, used for a medicinal oil.

evening star • n. (**the evening star**) the planet Venus, seen shining in the western sky after sunset.

even money • n. (in betting) odds offering an equal chance of winning or losing.

evens • pl. n. Brit. even money.

evensong • n. (in the Anglican Church) a service of evening prayers, psalms, and canticles.

event • n. **1** a thing that happens. **2** a public or social occasion. **3** each of several contests making up a sports competition.
– PHRASES **in any event** (or **at all events**) whatever happens or may have happened. **in the event 1** as it turned out. **2** (**in the event of/that**) if the specified thing happens.
– ORIGIN Latin *eventus*.

eventful • adj. marked by interesting or exciting events.

eventide • n. archaic evening.

eventing • n. a riding competition in which competitors must take part in each of several contests.
– DERIVATIVES **eventer** n.

eventual • adj. occurring at the end of a process or period of time.
– DERIVATIVES **eventually** adv.

eventuality • n. (pl. **eventualities**) a possible event or outcome.

ever • adv. **1** at any time. **2** used in comparisons for emphasis: *better than ever*. **3** always. **4** increasingly: *ever larger sums*.
– ORIGIN Old English.

Everest, Mount E
a mountain in the Himalayas, on the border between Nepal and Tibet. Rising to 8,848 m (29,028 ft), it is the highest mountain in the world.

Everglades E
a vast area of marshland and coastal mangrove in southern Florida.

evergreen ● adj. **1** (of a plant) having green leaves throughout the year. Contrasted with DECIDUOUS. **2** having a lasting freshness or success: *this symphony is an evergreen favourite.* ● n. an evergreen plant.

everlasting ● adj. lasting forever or a very long time.
– DERIVATIVES **everlastingly** adv.

evermore ● adv. literary forever.

Evert, E
Chris (b.1954; full name *Christine Marie Evert*), American tennis player, who won both the US and French Open championships six times and three Wimbledon titles (1974; 1976; 1981).

every ● det. **1** used to refer to all the members of a set without exception. **2** used to indicate something happening at specified intervals: *every thirty minutes.* **3** all possible: *every effort was made.*

everybody ● pron. every person.

everyday ● adj. **1** daily. **2** ordinary: *everyday activities.*

Everyman ● n. an ordinary or typical human being.

everyone ● pron. every person.

every one ● pron. each one.

everything ● pron. **1** all things, or all the things of a group. **2** the most important thing: *money isn't everything.*

everywhere ● adv. **1** in or to all places. **2** in many places: *sandwich bars are everywhere.*

evict ● v. force (someone) legally to leave a property.
– DERIVATIVES **eviction** n.
– ORIGIN Latin *evincere* 'overcome'.

evidence ● n. **1** information indicating whether something is true or valid. **2** information used to establish facts in a legal investigation or to support a case in a law court. ● v. (**evidences**, **evidencing**, **evidenced**) be or show evidence of: *his popularity was evidenced by a large turnout.*
– PHRASES **in evidence** noticeable.
– ORIGIN Latin *evidentia.*

evident ● adj. plain or obvious.
– DERIVATIVES **evidently** adv.

evidential ● adj. formal having to do with evidence.

evil ● adj. **1** very immoral and wicked. **2** extremely unpleasant: *an evil smell.* ● n. **1** extreme wickedness. **2** something harmful or undesirable: *unpleasant social evils.*
– PHRASES **the evil eye** a gaze superstitiously believed to cause harm.
– DERIVATIVES **evilly** adv.
– ORIGIN Old English.

evince ● v. (**evinces**, **evincing**, **evinced**) formal reveal the presence of: *his letters evince the excitement he felt.*
– ORIGIN Latin *evincere* 'overcome'.

eviscerate /i-viss-uh-rayt/ ● v. (**eviscerates**, **eviscerating**, **eviscerated**) formal remove the intestines of.
– ORIGIN Latin *eviscerare.*

evocative /i-vok-uh-tiv/ ● adj. bringing strong images or feelings to mind.

evoke /i-vohk/ ● v. (**evokes**, **evoking**, **evoked**) **1** bring to the mind. **2** obtain (a response).
– DERIVATIVES **evocation** n.
– ORIGIN Latin *evocare* 'call on (a spirit)'.

evolution ● n. **1** the process by which different kinds of living organism develop from earlier forms. **2** gradual development.
– DERIVATIVES **evolutionary** adj.
– ORIGIN Latin, 'unrolling'.

evolutionist ● n. a person who believes in the theories of evolution and natural selection.

evolve ● v. (**evolves**, **evolving**, **evolved**) **1** develop gradually. **2** (of an organism) develop from earlier forms by evolution.
– ORIGIN Latin *evolvere.*

ewe ● n. a female sheep.
– ORIGIN Old English.

ewer /yoo-er/ ● n. a large jug with a wide mouth.
– ORIGIN Old French *aiguiere.*

ex[1] ● prep. not including.

ex[2] ● n. informal a former husband, wife, or partner in a relationship.

ex- (also **e-**; **ef-** before *f*) ● prefix **1** out: *exclude.* **2** upward: *extol.* **3** thoroughly: *excruciating.* **4** giving rise to: *exasperate.* **5** former: *ex-husband.*
– ORIGIN Latin or Greek.

exacerbate /ig-zass-er-bayt/ ● v. (**exacerbates**, **exacerbating**, **exacerbated**) make (something bad) worse.
– DERIVATIVES **exacerbation** n.
– ORIGIN Latin *exacerbare* 'make harsh'.

exact ● adj. **1** precise. **2** correct in all details. ● v. **1** demand and obtain (something) from someone. **2** inflict (revenge) on someone.
– DERIVATIVES **exactness** n.
– ORIGIN Latin *exigere* 'enforce'.

exacting ● adj. making great demands on one's endurance or skill.

exaction ● n. formal **1** the action of demanding payment. **2** a sum of money demanded.

exactitude ● n. the quality of being exact.

exactly ● adv. **1** in an exact way. **2** used to confirm or agree with what has just been said.

exaggerate ● v. (**exaggerates**, **exaggerating**, **exaggerated**) **1** make (something) seem greater than in reality. **2** (**exaggerated**) larger or more noticeable than normal.
– DERIVATIVES **exaggeration** n.
– ORIGIN Latin *exaggerare* 'heap up'.

exalt /ig-zawlt/ ● v. **1** praise highly. **2** raise to a higher rank or position.
– ORIGIN Latin *exaltare.*

exaltation ● n. **1** extreme happiness. **2** the action of exalting.

exalted ● adj. **1** at a high level: *her exalted position.* **2** (of an idea) noble.

exam ● n. = EXAMINATION (in sense 2).

examination ● n. **1** a detailed inspection. **2** a formal test of knowledge or ability in a subject or skill. **3** the action of examining.

examine ● v. (**examines**, **examining**, **examined**) **1** inspect closely to find out the nature or condition of. **2** test the knowledge or ability of. **3** Law formally question (a person on trial or witness) in court.
– DERIVATIVES **examinee** n. **examiner** n.
– ORIGIN Latin *examinare* 'weigh, test'.

example ● n. **1** a thing typical of its kind or

illustrating a general rule. **2** a person or thing seen in terms of their suitability to be copied: *public figures should set an example.*
– PHRASES **for example** used to introduce something chosen as a typical case. **make an example of** punish as a warning to others.
– ORIGIN Latin *exemplum.*

exasperate /ig-zass-puh-rayt/ • **v.** (**exasperates**, **exasperating**, **exasperated**) greatly irritate.
– DERIVATIVES **exasperation** n.
– ORIGIN Latin *exasperare.*

e

excavate • **v.** (**excavates**, **excavating**, **excavated**) **1** make (a hole or channel) by digging. **2** dig out (material) from the ground. **3** carefully remove earth from (an area) in order to find buried remains.
– DERIVATIVES **excavation** n.
– ORIGIN Latin *excavare* 'hollow out'.

exceed • **v. 1** be greater in number or size than. **2** go beyond what is set down by (a limit). **3** be better than: *they exceeded expectations.*
– ORIGIN Latin *excedere.*

exceedingly • **adv.** extremely.

excel • **v.** (**excels**, **excelling**, **excelled**) **1** be very good at something. **2** (**excel oneself**) perform exceptionally well.
– ORIGIN Latin *excellere.*

Excellency • **n.** (pl. **Excellencies**) (**His**, **Your**, etc. **Excellency**) a title or form of address for certain high officials of state or of the Roman Catholic Church.

excellent • **adj.** extremely good; outstanding.
– DERIVATIVES **excellence** n.

except • **prep.** not including. • **conj.** used before a statement that is not included in one just made. • **v.** exclude: *present company excepted.*
– ORIGIN Latin *excipere* 'take out'.

excepting • **prep.** except for.

exception • **n.** a person or thing that is not included in a general statement or that does not follow a rule.
– PHRASES **take exception to** object strongly to.

exceptionable • **adj.** formal causing disapproval or offence.

exceptional • **adj. 1** unusual. **2** unusually good.
– DERIVATIVES **exceptionally** adv.

excerpt • **n.** /ek-serpt/ a short extract from a film or piece of music or writing. • **v.** /ik-serpt/ take (a short extract) from a piece of writing.
– ORIGIN Latin *excerpere* 'pluck out'.

excess /ik-sess/ • **n. 1** an amount that is more than necessary, allowed, or desirable. **2** (**excesses**) outrageous behaviour: *the worst excesses of the French Revolution.* **3** Brit. a part of an insurance claim to be paid by the person insured. • **adj.** usu. /ek-sess/ exceeding an allowed or desirable amount: *excess fat.*
– ORIGIN Latin *excessus.*

excess baggage • **n.** luggage weighing more than the limit allowed on an aircraft, liable to an extra charge.

excessive • **adj.** more than is necessary, normal, or desirable.
– DERIVATIVES **excessively** adv.

exchange • **v.** (**exchanges**, **exchanging**, **exchanged**) give something and receive something else in return. • **n. 1** an act or the action of exchanging. **2** a short conversation or argument. **3** the giving of money for its equivalent in the currency of another country. **4** a building used for financial trading. **5** a set of equipment that connects telephone lines during a call.
– DERIVATIVES **exchangeable** adj. **exchanger** n.
– ORIGIN Old French *eschangier.*

exchange rate • **n.** the value at which one currency may be exchanged for another.

exchequer /iks-chek-er/ • **n. 1** a royal or national treasury. **2** (**Exchequer**) the account at the Bank of England into which public money is paid.
– ORIGIN Old French *eschequier.*

excise[1] /ek-syz/ • **n.** a tax charged on certain goods, such as alcohol.
– ORIGIN Dutch *excijs.*

excise[2] /ik-syz/ • **v.** (**excises**, **excising**, **excised**) **1** cut out surgically. **2** remove (a section) from a piece of writing or music.
– DERIVATIVES **excision** n.
– ORIGIN Latin *excidere* 'cut out'.

excitable • **adj.** easily excited.
– DERIVATIVES **excitability** n. **excitably** adv.

excite • **v.** (**excites**, **exciting**, **excited**) **1** cause strong feelings of enthusiasm and eagerness in. **2** arouse sexually. **3** give rise to: *the report excited great controversy.* **4** increase the energy or activity in (a physical or biological system).
– DERIVATIVES **excitation** n.
– ORIGIN Latin *excitare.*

excitement • **n. 1** a feeling of great enthusiasm and eagerness. **2** something that arouses such a feeling. **3** sexual arousal.

exciting • **adj.** causing excitement.
– DERIVATIVES **excitingly** adv.

exclaim • **v.** cry out suddenly.
– ORIGIN Latin *exclamare.*

exclamation • **n.** a sudden cry or remark.
– DERIVATIVES **exclamatory** adj.

exclamation mark • **n.** a punctuation mark (!) indicating an exclamation.

exclude • **v.** (**excludes**, **excluding**, **excluded**) **1** prevent from entering or taking part in something. **2** remove from consideration: *these figures exclude this month's sales.*
– DERIVATIVES **excluder** n.
– ORIGIN Latin *excludere.*

excluding • **prep.** except.

exclusion • **n.** the process of excluding or the state of being excluded.
– DERIVATIVES **exclusionary** adj.

exclusive • **adj. 1** excluding or not admitting other things. **2** restricted to the person, group, or area concerned: *a problem exclusive to London.* **3** catering for or available to a select group. **4** not published or broadcast elsewhere. • **n.** an exclusive story or broadcast.
– DERIVATIVES **exclusively** adv. **exclusiveness** n. **exclusivity** n.
– ORIGIN Latin *exclusivus.*

excommunicate /eks-kuh-myoo-ni-kayt/ • **v.** (**excommunicates**, **excommunicating**, **excommunicated**) officially bar (someone) from the sacraments and services of the Christian Church.

– DERIVATIVES **excommunication** n.
– ORIGIN Latin *excommunicare*.

excoriate /ik-skor-i-ayt/ ● **v.** (**excoriates, excoriating, excoriated**) **1** Med. damage or remove part of the surface of (the skin). **2** formal criticize severely.
– DERIVATIVES **excoriation** n.
– ORIGIN Latin *excoriare* 'to skin'.

excrement /eks-kri-muhnt/ ● **n.** waste matter discharged from the bowels.
– ORIGIN Latin *excrementum*.

excrescence /iks-kress-uhnss/ ● **n.** an abnormal growth protruding from a body or plant.
– ORIGIN Latin *excrescentia*.

excreta /ik-skree-tuh/ ● **n.** waste discharged from the body.
– ORIGIN Latin.

excrete ● **v.** (**excretes, excreting, excreted**) discharge (a substance) from the body as waste.
– DERIVATIVES **excretion** n. **excretory** adj.
– ORIGIN Latin *excernere* 'sift out'.

excruciating ● **adj. 1** very painful. **2** very embarrassing, awkward, or tedious.
– ORIGIN Latin *excruciare* 'torment'.

exculpate /eks-kul-payt/ ● **v.** (**exculpates, exculpating, exculpated**) formal show or declare to be not guilty of wrongdoing.
– ORIGIN Latin *exculpare*.

excursion ● **n.** a short journey or trip taken for pleasure.
– ORIGIN Latin.

excuse ● **v.** /ik-skyooz/ (**excuses, excusing, excused**) **1** justify or try to justify (a fault or offence). **2** release from a duty. **3** forgive (a fault or a person committing one). **4** allow (someone) to leave a room or gathering. **5** (**excuse oneself**) say politely that one is leaving. ● **n.** /ik-skyooss/ **1** a reason put forward to justify a fault or offence. **2** something said to conceal the real reason for an action. **3** informal a poor example of: *that pathetic excuse for a man.*
– PHRASES **excuse me** a polite apology.
– DERIVATIVES **excusable** adj.
– ORIGIN Latin *excusare* 'free from blame'.

ex-directory ● **adj.** Brit. not listed in a telephone directory at one's own request.

execrable /ek-si-kruh-b'l/ ● **adj.** extremely bad or unpleasant.
– ORIGIN Latin *execrabilis*.

execrate /ek-si-krayt/ ● **v.** (**execrates, execrating, execrated**) feel or express great hatred for.
– DERIVATIVES **execration** n.
– ORIGIN Latin *exsecrari* 'curse'.

execute ● **v.** (**executes, executing, executed**) **1** carry out (a plan, order, etc.). **2** carry out a sentence of death on (a condemned person). **3** perform (an action or manoeuvre). **4** Computing run (a file or program).
– ORIGIN Latin *executare*.

execution ● **n. 1** the carrying out or performance of something. **2** the killing of a condemned person. **3** the way in which something is produced or carried out.

executioner ● **n.** an official who executes condemned criminals.

executive /ig-zek-yuu-tiv/ ● **adj.** having the power to put plans, actions, or laws into effect. ● **n. 1** a senior manager in a business. **2** (**the executive**) the branch of a government responsible for putting plans or laws into effect. **3** an executive committee within an organization.

executor /ig-zek-yuu-ter/ ● **n.** Law a person appointed by someone to carry out the terms of their will.

executrix /ig-zek-yoo-triks/ ● **n.** (pl. **executrices** /ig-zek-yoo-tri-seez/ or **executrixes**) Law a female executor.

exegesis /ek-si-jee-siss/ ● **n.** (pl. **exegeses** /ek-si-jee-seez/) critical explanation or interpretation of a text.
– DERIVATIVES **exegetical** adj.
– ORIGIN Greek.

exemplar /ig-zem-pler/ ● **n.** a person or thing serving as a typical example or appropriate model.
– ORIGIN Latin *exemplarium*.

exemplary ● **adj. 1** representing the best of its kind: *exemplary behaviour.* **2** (of a punishment) serving as a warning.

exemplify /ig-zem-pli-fy/ ● **v.** (**exemplifies, exemplifying, exemplified**) be or give a typical example of.
– DERIVATIVES **exemplification** n.

exempt /ig-zempt/ ● **adj.** free from an obligation or requirement imposed on others: *these patients are exempt from all charges.* ● **v.** make exempt.
– DERIVATIVES **exemption** n.
– ORIGIN Latin *exemptus* 'taken out'.

exercise ● **n. 1** activity requiring physical effort carried out for the sake of health and fitness. **2** a task set to practise or test a skill. **3** an activity carried out for a purpose: *a public relations exercise.* **4** (**exercises**) military drills or training manoeuvres. **5** the use of a power, right, or quality: *the exercise of authority.* ● **v.** (**exercises, exercising, exercised**) **1** use (a power, right, or quality). **2** engage in or subject to physical exercise. **3** worry or puzzle.
– ORIGIN Latin *exercitium*.

exercise book ● **n.** Brit. a booklet with blank pages for students to write in.

exert /ig-zert/ ● **v. 1** apply or bring to bear (a force, influence, or quality). **2** (**exert oneself**) make a physical or mental effort.
– DERIVATIVES **exertion** n.
– ORIGIN Latin *exserere* 'put forth'.

Exeter E
the county town of Devon.

exeunt /ek-si-uhnt/ ● **v.** (as a stage direction) (actors) leave the stage.
– ORIGIN Latin, 'they go out'.

exfoliate /iks-foh-li-ayt/ ● **v.** (**exfoliates, exfoliating, exfoliated**) **1** shed or be shed from a surface in scales or layers. **2** rub (the skin) with a rough substance to remove dead cells.
– DERIVATIVES **exfoliation** n. **exfoliator** n.
– ORIGIN Latin *exfoliare* 'strip of leaves'.

ex gratia /eks gray-shuh/ ● **adv. & adj.** (of payment) given as a gift or favour rather than because of any legal requirement.
– ORIGIN Latin, 'from favour'.

exhale ● **v.** (**exhales, exhaling, exhaled**) **1** breathe out. **2** give off (vapour or fumes).
– DERIVATIVES **exhalation** n.
– ORIGIN Latin *exhalare*.

exhaust ● **v. 1** tire out completely. **2** use up

(resources) completely. **3** explore (a subject) thoroughly. ● **n. 1** waste gases that are sent out from an engine. **2** the system through which such gases are sent out.
– DERIVATIVES **exhaustible** adj.
– ORIGIN Latin *exhaurire* 'drain out'.

exhaustion ● **n.** the action of exhausting or the state of being exhausted.

exhaustive ● **adj.** covering all aspects fully.
– DERIVATIVES **exhaustively** adv.

exhibit ● **v. 1** publicly display (an item) in an art gallery or museum. **2** show: *they exhibited great humility.* ● **n. 1** an object or collection on display in an art gallery or museum. **2** Law an object produced in a court as evidence.
– ORIGIN Latin *exhibere* 'hold out'.

exhibition ● **n. 1** a public display of items in an art gallery or museum. **2** a display or demonstration of a skill or quality.
– PHRASES **make an exhibition of oneself** behave very foolishly in public.

exhibitionism ● **n.** behaviour that is intended to attract attention to oneself.
– DERIVATIVES **exhibitionist** n.

exhilarate /ig-zil-uh-rayt/ ● **v.** (**exhilarates**, **exhilarating**, **exhilarated**) cause to feel very happy or lively.
– DERIVATIVES **exhilaration** n.
– ORIGIN Latin *exhilarare.*

exhort /ig-zort/ ● **v.** strongly urge (someone) to do something.
– ORIGIN Latin *exhortari.*

exhortation ● **n.** a speech or statement strongly urging someone to do something.

exhume /ek-syoom/ ● **v.** (**exhumes**, **exhuming**, **exhumed**) dig out (something buried) from the ground.
– ORIGIN Latin *exhumare.*

exigency /ek-si-juhn-si/ ● **n.** (pl. **exigencies**) urgent need or demand.
– ORIGIN Latin *exigentia.*

exigent /ek-si-juhnt/ ● **adj.** formal pressing: *exigent demands.*

exiguous /ig-zig-yoo-uhss/ ● **adj.** formal very small.
– ORIGIN Latin *exiguus* 'scanty'.

exile ● **n. 1** the state of being barred from one's native country. **2** a person who lives in exile. ● **v.** (**exiles**, **exiling**, **exiled**) expel and bar (someone) from their native country.
– ORIGIN Latin *exilium* 'banishment'.

exist ● **v. 1** be real or present. **2** live.

existence ● **n. 1** the fact or state of existing. **2** a way of living: *a rural existence.*
– ORIGIN Latin *existentia.*

existent ● **adj.** existing.

existential /eg-zi-sten-sh'l/ ● **adj. 1** having to do with existence. **2** concerned with existentialism.
– DERIVATIVES **existentially** adv.

existentialism ● **n.** a philosophical theory which emphasizes the existence of the individual person as a free agent, responsible for their own development.
– DERIVATIVES **existentialist** n. & adj.

exit ● **n. 1** a way out of a building, room, or passenger vehicle. **2** an act of leaving. **3** a place for traffic to leave a major road or roundabout. ● **v.** (**exits**, **exiting**, **exited**) **1** go out of or leave a place. **2** Computing end a process or program.
– ORIGIN Latin, 'he or she goes out'.

exit poll ● **n.** a poll of people leaving a polling station, asking how they voted.

> **Exmoor** E
> an area of moorland and national park in north Devon and west Somerset, SW England.

exo- ● **prefix** external: *exoskeleton.*
– ORIGIN Greek *exō* 'outside'.

exocrine /ek-soh-kryn/ ● **adj.** (of a gland) secreting hormones or other products through ducts rather than directly into the blood.
– ORIGIN Greek *krinein* 'sift'.

exodus ● **n.** a mass departure of people.
– ORIGIN Greek *exodos.*

ex officio /eks uh-fish-i-oh/ ● **adv. & adj.** as a result of one's position or status: *an ex officio member of the committee.*
– ORIGIN from Latin *ex* 'out of' + *officium* 'duty'.

exonerate /ig-zon-uh-rayt/ ● **v.** (**exonerates**, **exonerating**, **exonerated**) officially declare free from blame.
– DERIVATIVES **exoneration** n.
– ORIGIN Latin *exonerare* 'free from a burden'.

exorbitant /ig-zor-bi-tuhnt/ ● **adj.** (of an amount charged) unreasonably high.
– DERIVATIVES **exorbitantly** adv.
– ORIGIN Latin *exorbitare* 'go off the track'.

exorcize /ek-sor-syz/ (also **exorcise**) ● **v.** (**exorcizes**, **exorcizing**, **exorcizes**) drive out (a supposed evil spirit) from a person or place.
– DERIVATIVES **exorcism** n. **exorcist** n.
– ORIGIN Greek *exorkizein.*

exoskeleton ● **n.** the rigid outer covering of the body in some invertebrate animals.

exothermic /ek-soh-ther-mik/ ● **adj.** Chem. (of a reaction) releasing heat. Opp. **ENDOTHERMIC**.

exotic ● **adj. 1** coming from or characteristic of a distant foreign country. **2** strikingly colourful or unusual: *an exotic outfit.*
– DERIVATIVES **exotically** adv. **exoticism** n.
– ORIGIN Greek *exōtikos* 'foreign'.

expand ● **v. 1** make or become larger or more extensive. **2** (**expand on**) give a fuller account of.
– DERIVATIVES **expandable** adj. **expander** n.
– ORIGIN Latin *expandere* 'spread out'.

expanse ● **n.** a wide continuous area of something: *the green expanse of forest.*

expansion ● **n. 1** the action or an instance of expanding. **2** extension of a state's territory by advancing gradually into that of other nations.
– DERIVATIVES **expansionary** adj.

expansive ● **adj. 1** covering a wide area. **2** relaxed, friendly, and communicative.
– DERIVATIVES **expansively** adv.

expat ● **n.** informal = **EXPATRIATE**.

expatiate /ik-spay-shi-ayt/ ● **v.** (**expatiates**, **expatiating**, **expatiated**) (**expatiate on**) speak or write at length or in detail about.
– ORIGIN Latin *exspatiari* 'move beyond one's usual bounds'.

expatriate ● **n.** /eks-pat-ri-uht/ a person who lives outside their native country.
– DERIVATIVES **expatriation** n.
– ORIGIN Latin *expatriare.*

expect ● **v. 1** regard as likely to happen. **2** regard (someone) as likely to do or be some-

thing. **3** believe that (someone) will arrive soon. **4** require or demand (something) because it is a person's duty or responsibility: *we expect great things of you.* **5** (**be expecting**) informal be pregnant.
– DERIVATIVES **expectable** adj.
– ORIGIN Latin *exspectare* 'look out for'.

expectancy • n. (pl. **expectancies**) hope or anticipation that something will happen.

expectant • adj. **1** hoping or anticipating that something is about to happen. **2** (of a woman) pregnant.
– DERIVATIVES **expectantly** adv.

expectation • n. **1** belief that something will happen or be the case. **2** a thing that is expected to happen.

expectorant • n. a medicine which helps to bring up phlegm from the air passages, used to treat coughs.

expectorate /ik-spek-tuh-rayt/ • v. (**expectorates**, **expectorating**, **expectorated**) cough or spit out (phlegm) from the throat or lungs.
– ORIGIN Latin *expectorare* 'expel from the chest'.

expedient /ik-spee-di-uhnt/ • adj. necessary to achieve something, though not always right or fair. • n. a means of achieving something.
– DERIVATIVES **expediency** n.
– ORIGIN Latin.

expedite /eks-pi-dyt/ • v. (**expedites**, **expediting**, **expedited**) cause to happen sooner or be done more quickly: *he promised to expedite economic reforms.*
– ORIGIN Latin *expedire* 'extricate'.

expedition • n. a journey undertaken by a group of people with a particular purpose.
– DERIVATIVES **expeditionary** adj.

expeditious /eks-pi-di-shuhss/ • adj. quick and efficient.
– DERIVATIVES **expeditiously** adv.

expel • v. (**expels**, **expelling**, **expelled**) **1** force out. **2** force (a pupil) to leave a school.
– ORIGIN Latin *expellere*.

expend • v. spend or use up (a resource).
– ORIGIN Latin *expendere*.

expendable • adj. **1** suitable to be used once only. **2** able to be sacrificed because of little importance when compared to an overall purpose.

expenditure /ik-spen-di-cher/ • n. **1** the action of spending funds. **2** the amount of money spent.

expense • n. **1** the cost of something. **2** (**expenses**) money spent in the carrying out of a job or task. **3** something on which money must be spent.
– PHRASES **at the expense of 1** paid for by. **2** so as to cause harm to.
– ORIGIN Old French.

expense account • n. an arrangement under which money spent in the course of business is later repaid by one's employer.

expensive • adj. costing a lot of money.
– DERIVATIVES **expensively** adv.

experience • n. **1** practical contact with and observation of facts or events. **2** knowledge or skill gained over time. **3** an event which leaves an impression on one: *a learning experience.* • v. (**experiences**, **experiencing**, **experienced**) **1** have (an event or situation) happen to or affect one. **2** feel (an emotion).
– ORIGIN Latin *experientia*.

experienced • adj. having knowledge or skill in a particular field gained over time.

experiential /ik-speer-i-en-sh'l/ • adj. having to do with experience and observation: *experiential learning.*

experiment • n. **1** a scientific procedure undertaken to make a discovery, test a theory, or demonstrate a known fact. **2** a new course of action adopted without being sure of the outcome. • v. **1** perform a scientific experiment. **2** try out new things.
– DERIVATIVES **experimentation** n. **experimenter** n.
– ORIGIN Latin *experimentum*.

experimental • adj. **1** based on new, untested ideas and not yet finalized. **2** having to do with scientific experiments. **3** (of art, music, etc.) not following tradition; original.
– DERIVATIVES **experimentally** adv.

expert • n. a person who has great knowledge or skill in a particular area. • adj. having or involving such knowledge or skill: *an expert witness.*
– DERIVATIVES **expertly** adv.
– ORIGIN Latin *expertus*.

expertise /ek-sper-teez/ • n. great skill or knowledge in a particular field.

expiate /ek-spi-ayt/ • v. (**expiates**, **expiating**, **expiated**) make amends for (guilt or sin).
– DERIVATIVES **expiation** n.
– ORIGIN Latin *expiare* 'appease by sacrifice'.

expire /ik-spyr/ • v. (**expires**, **expiring**, **expired**) **1** (of a document or agreement) cease to be valid. **2** (of a period of time) come to an end. **3** (of a person) die. **4** tech. breath out (air) from the lungs.
– ORIGIN Latin *exspirare*.

expiry • n. the end of the period for which something is valid.

explain • v. **1** make clear by giving a detailed description. **2** give a reason for. **3** (**explain oneself**) justify one's motives or behaviour. **4** (**explain away**) give an excuse for (something).
– DERIVATIVES **explainable** adj. **explanation** n.
– ORIGIN Latin *explanare*.

explanatory /ik-splan-uh-tuh-ri/ • adj. explaining something.

expletive /ik-splee-tiv/ • n. a swear word.
– ORIGIN Latin *expletivus* 'acting to fill out'.

explicable /ik-splik-uh-b'l/ • adj. able to be explained.
– ORIGIN Latin *explicare* 'unfold'.

explicate /eks-pli-kayt/ • v. (**explicates**, **explicating**, **explicated**) analyse and explain (something) in detail.
– DERIVATIVES **explication** n.
– ORIGIN Latin *explicare* 'unfold'.

explicit /ik-spli-sit/ • adj. **1** clear and detailed, with no room for confusion. **2** graphically showing or describing sexual activity.
– DERIVATIVES **explicitly** adv. **explicitness** n.
– ORIGIN Latin *explicare* 'unfold'.

explode • v. (**explodes**, **exploding**, **exploded**) **1** burst or shatter violently as a result of the release of internal energy. **2** show sudden violent emotion. **3** increase suddenly

in number or extent: *the use of this drug exploded in the nineties.* **4** show (a belief) to be false.
– DERIVATIVES **exploder** n.
– ORIGIN Latin *explodere* 'drive out by clapping'.

exploit ● v. /ik-sployt/ **1** make good use of (a resource). **2** treat or use unfairly. ● n. /ek-sployt/ a daring feat.
– DERIVATIVES **exploitable** adj. **exploitation** n. **exploiter** n.
– ORIGIN Old French *esploit* 'success'.

exploitative ● adj. treating someone unfairly so as to make money or gain an advantage.

explore ● v. (**explores**, **exploring**, **explored**) **1** travel through (an unfamiliar area) in order to learn about it. **2** inquire into or discuss in detail. **3** examine by searching through or touching.
– DERIVATIVES **exploration** n. **exploratory** adj. **explorer** n.
– ORIGIN Latin *explorare* 'search out'.

explosion ● n. an act or the action of exploding.

explosive ● adj. **1** able or likely to explode. **2** likely to cause an outburst of anger or controversy: *the idea was politically explosive.* **3** (of an increase) sudden and dramatic. ● n. a substance which can be made to explode.
– DERIVATIVES **explosively** adv. **explosiveness** n.

exponent /ik-spoh-nuhnt/ ● n. **1** a promoter of an idea or theory. **2** a person who does a particular thing skilfully. **3** Math. a raised figure beside a number indicating how many times that number is to be multiplied by itself (e.g. 3 in $2^3 = 2 \times 2 \times 2$).
– ORIGIN Latin.

exponential /eks-puh-nen-sh'l/ ● adj. **1** (of an increase) becoming more and more rapid. **2** having to do with a mathematical exponent.
– DERIVATIVES **exponentially** adv.

export ● v. /ik-sport/ **1** send (goods or services) to another country for sale. **2** introduce (ideas or customs) to another country. ● n. /ek-sport/ **1** the exporting of goods or services. **2** an exported product or service.
– DERIVATIVES **exportation** n. **exporter** n.
– ORIGIN Latin *exportare.*

expose ● v. (**exposes**, **exposing**, **exposed**) **1** uncover and make visible. **2** reveal the true nature of. **3** (**exposed**) unprotected from the weather. **4** (**expose to**) make vulnerable to. **5** subject (photographic film) to light. **6** (**expose oneself**) publicly display one's genitals.
– DERIVATIVES **exposer** n.
– ORIGIN Latin *exponere* 'to present'.

exposé /ik-spoh-zay/ ● n. a report in the media that reveals something discreditable.
– ORIGIN French, 'shown'.

exposition ● n. **1** a full description and explanation of a theory. **2** a large public exhibition of art or trade goods. **3** Music the part of a movement in which the principal themes are first presented.
– ORIGIN Latin.

expositor /ik-spoz-i-ter/ ● n. a person or thing that explains complicated ideas or theories.
– DERIVATIVES **expository** adj.

expostulate /ik-sposs-tyoo-layt/ ● v. (**expostulates**, **expostulating**, **expostulated**) express strong disapproval or disagreement.
– DERIVATIVES **expostulation** n.
– ORIGIN Latin *expostulare* 'demand'.

exposure ● n. **1** the state of being exposed to something harmful. **2** a physical condition resulting from being exposed to severe weather conditions. **3** the quantity of light reaching a photographic film. **4** the revealing of something secret. **5** the publicizing of information or an event: *the meetings received regular exposure in the media.*

expound ● v. present and explain (a theory or idea) systematically.
– ORIGIN Latin *exponere* 'present'.

express[1] /ik-spress/ ● v. **1** convey (a thought or feeling) in words or by gestures and behaviour. **2** squeeze out (liquid or air).
– ORIGIN Old French *expresser.*

express[2] /ik-spress/ ● adj. **1** operating at high speed. **2** (of a delivery service) using a special messenger. ● adv. by express train or delivery service. ● n. (also **express train**) a train that stops at few stations and so travels quickly. ● v. send by express messenger or delivery.
– ORIGIN Latin *expressus* 'distinctly presented'.

express[3] /ik-spress/ ● adj. **1** stated clearly. **2** excluding anything else.
– DERIVATIVES **expressly** adv.

expression ● n. **1** the action of expressing. **2** the look on someone's face. **3** a word or phrase expressing an idea. **4** Math. a collection of symbols expressing a quantity.
– DERIVATIVES **expressionless** adj.

expressionism ● n. a style in art, music, or drama in which the artist or writer tries to express the inner world of emotion rather than external reality.
– DERIVATIVES **expressionist** n. & adj.

expressive ● adj. **1** effectively conveying thought or feeling. **2** (**expressive of**) conveying (a quality or idea).
– DERIVATIVES **expressively** adv. **expressiveness** n.

expresso ● n. var. of **ESPRESSO**.

expressway ● n. N. Amer. an urban motorway.

expropriate /iks-proh-pri-ayt/ ● v. (**expropriates**, **expropriating**, **expropriated**) (of the state) take (property) from its owner for public use or benefit.
– DERIVATIVES **expropriation** n.
– ORIGIN Latin *expropriare.*

expulsion ● n. the action of expelling.
– ORIGIN Latin.

expunge /ik-spunj/ ● v. (**expunges**, **expunging**, **expunged**) remove completely.
– ORIGIN Latin *expungere* 'mark for deletion by means of points'.

expurgate /eks-per-gayt/ ● v. (**expurgates**, **expurgating**, **expurgated**) remove matter seen as obscene or unsuitable from (a text).
– DERIVATIVES **expurgation** n.
– ORIGIN Latin *expurgare* 'cleanse thoroughly'.

exquisite /ik-skwi-zit, ek-skwi-zit/ ● adj. **1** very beautiful and delicate. **2** highly refined: *exquisite taste.* **3** intensely felt.
– DERIVATIVES **exquisitely** adv.
– ORIGIN Latin *exquirere* 'seek out'.

extant /ik-stant, ek-stuhnt/ ● adj. still in existence.

– ORIGIN Latin.

extempore /ik-stem-puh-ri/ ● **adj.** & **adv.** spoken or done without preparation: *extempore public speaking.*
– ORIGIN from Latin *ex tempore* 'on the spur of the moment'.

extemporize /ik-stem-puh-ryz/ (also **extemporise**) ● **v.** (**extemporizes**, **extemporizing**, **extemporized**) improvise: *he extemporized at the piano.*

extend ● **v. 1** make larger in area. **2** cause to last longer. **3** occupy a specified area or continue for a specified distance. **4** hold out (a part of one's body) towards someone. **5** offer: *she extended an invitation to her to stay.*
– DERIVATIVES **extendable** adj. **extender** n. **extendible** adj. **extensible** adj.
– ORIGIN Latin *extendere* 'stretch out'.

extended family ● **n.** a family which extends beyond the nuclear family to include relatives living close by.

extension ● **n. 1** the action of extending. **2** a part added to a building to make it bigger. **3** an additional period of time. **4** (also **extension lead** or **cable**) an extra length of electric cable which can be plugged into a fixed socket and has another socket on the end. **5** a secondary telephone.
– ORIGIN Latin.

extensive ● **adj. 1** covering a large area. **2** large in amount or scale.
– DERIVATIVES **extensively** adv.

extensor /ik-sten-ser/ ● **n.** Anat. a muscle which causes a part of the body to extend.

extent ● **n. 1** the area covered by something. **2** size or scale: *the extent of global warming.* **3** the degree to which something is the case: *everyone compromises to some extent.*
– ORIGIN Old French *extente.*

extenuating /ik-sten-yoo-ay-ting/ ● **adj.** showing reasons why an offence should be treated less seriously.
– ORIGIN Latin *extenuare* 'make thin'.

exterior ● **adj. 1** having to do with the outside of something. ● **n.** the outer surface or structure of something.
– ORIGIN Latin.

exterminate /ik-ster-mi-nayt/ ● **v.** (**exterminates**, **exterminating**, **exterminated**) destroy completely.
– DERIVATIVES **extermination** n. **exterminator** n.
– ORIGIN Latin *exterminare* 'drive out'.

external ● **adj. 1** having to do with the outside of something. **2** coming from a source outside the subject affected: *external authority.* **3** having to do with another country: *external affairs.* ● **n.** (**externals**) the outward features of something.
– DERIVATIVES **externally** adv.
– ORIGIN Latin.

externalize (also **externalise**) ● **v.** (**externalizes**, **externalizing**, **externalized**) express (a thought or feeling) in words or actions.

extinct ● **adj. 1** (of a species or other large group) having no living members. **2** no longer in existence. **3** (of a volcano) not having erupted in recorded history.
– ORIGIN Latin *exstinguere* 'extinguish'.

extinction ● **n.** the state or process of being or becoming extinct.

extinguish ● **v. 1** put out (a fire or light). **2** put an end to.
– DERIVATIVES **extinguisher** n.
– ORIGIN Latin *exstinguere.*

extirpate /ek-ster-payt/ ● **v.** (**extirpates**, **extirpating**, **extirpated**) search out and destroy completely.
– DERIVATIVES **extirpation** n.
– ORIGIN Latin *exstirpare.*

extol /ik-stohl/ ● **v.** (**extols**, **extolling**, **extolled**) praise enthusiastically.
– ORIGIN Latin *extollere.*

extort /ik-stort/ ● **v.** obtain by force, threats, or other unfair means.
– DERIVATIVES **extortion** n.
– ORIGIN Latin *extorquere.*

extortionate /ik-stor-shuh-nuht/ ● **adj.** (of a price) much too high.
– DERIVATIVES **extortionately** adv.

extra ● **adj.** added to an existing or usual amount or number. ● **adv. 1** to a greater extent than usual. **2** in addition. ● **n. 1** an additional item, for which an extra charge is made. **2** a person employed to take part in a crowd scene in a film or play.
– ORIGIN prob. from EXTRAORDINARY.

extra- ● **prefix 1** outside: *extramarital.* **2** beyond the scope of: *extra-curricular.*
– ORIGIN Latin *extra.*

extract ● **v.** /ik-strakt/ **1** remove with care or effort. **2** obtain (something) from someone unwilling to give it: *I tried to extract a promise from him.* **3** obtain (a substance or resource) from something by a special method. **4** select (a passage from a text, film, or piece of music) for quotation, performance, or reproduction. ● **n.** /ek-strakt/ **1** a short passage taken from a text, film, or piece of music. **2** the concentrated form of the active ingredient of a substance.
– DERIVATIVES **extractable** adj. **extractive** adj.
– ORIGIN Latin *extrahere* 'draw out'.

extraction ● **n. 1** the action of extracting. **2** the ethnic origin of someone's family.

extractor ● **n.** a machine or device used to extract something.

extra-curricular ● **adj.** (of an activity at a school or college) done in addition to the normal curriculum.

extradite /ek-struh-dyt/ ● **v.** (**extradites**, **extraditing**, **extradited**) hand over (a person accused or convicted of committing a crime in a foreign state) to the legal authority of that state.
– DERIVATIVES **extradition** n.
– ORIGIN French *extradition.*

extramarital /eks-truh-ma-ri-t'l/ ● **adj.** occurring outside marriage.

extramural /eks-truh-myoor-uhl/ ● **adj.** Brit. (of a course of study) arranged for people who are not full-time members of an educational establishment.
– ORIGIN from Latin *extra muros* 'outside the walls'.

extraneous /ik-stray-ni-uhss/ ● **adj.** unrelated to the subject being dealt with.
– ORIGIN Latin *extraneus.*

extraordinaire /ek-struh-or-di-nair/ ● **adj.** outstanding in a particular area: *a gardener extraordinaire.*
– ORIGIN French.

extraordinary ● **adj. 1** very unusual or re-

markable. **2** (of a meeting) held for a particular reason rather than being one of a regular series.
– DERIVATIVES **extraordinarily** adv.
– ORIGIN Latin *extraordinarius.*

extrapolate /ik-strap-uh-layt/ ● v. (**extrapolates**, **extrapolating**, **extrapolated**) use (a fact valid for one situation) to make conclusions about a different or wider situation.
– DERIVATIVES **extrapolation** n.
– ORIGIN from **EXTRA-** + **INTERPOLATE**.

e

extrasensory perception /eks-truh-sen-suh-ri/ ● n. the supposed ability to perceive things by means other than the known senses, e.g. by telepathy.

extraterrestrial /eks-truh-tuh-ress-tri-uhl/ ● adj. having to do with things outside the earth or its atmosphere. ● n. a fictional being from outer space.

extravagant /ik-strav-uh-guhnt/ ● adj. **1** lacking restraint in spending money or using resources. **2** costing a great deal. **3** exceeding what is reasonable: *extravagant claims.*
– DERIVATIVES **extravagance** n. **extravagantly** adv.
– ORIGIN Latin *extravagari* 'diverge greatly'.

extravaganza /ik-stra-vuh-**gan**-zuh/ ● n. an elaborate and spectacular entertainment.
– ORIGIN Italian *estravaganza* 'extravagance'.

extra virgin ● adj. referring to a very high grade of olive oil made from the first pressing of the olives.

extreme ● adj. **1** to the highest degree; very great. **2** highly unusual: *extreme cases.* **3** very severe or serious. **4** not moderate: *extreme socialists.* **5** furthest from the centre or a given point. **6** (of a sport) performed in a dangerous environment. ● n. **1** either of two abstract things that are as different from each other as possible. **2** the most extreme degree: *extremes of temperature.*
– DERIVATIVES **extremely** adv.
– ORIGIN Latin *extremus* 'outermost'.

extremist ● n. a person who holds extreme political or religious views.
– DERIVATIVES **extremism** n.

extremity /ik-strem-i-ti/ ● n. (pl. **extremities**) **1** the furthest point or limit. **2** (**extremities**) the hands and feet. **3** severity: *the extremity of the violence.* **4** extreme hardship.

extricate /eks-tri-kayt/ ● v. (**extricates**, **extricating**, **extricated**) free from a difficulty.
– ORIGIN Latin *extricare* 'unravel'.

extrinsic /eks-trin-sik/ ● adj. **1** not essential. **2** coming from outside.
– DERIVATIVES **extrinsically** adv.
– ORIGIN Latin *extrinsecus* 'outward'.

extrovert /ek-struh-vert/ ● n. an outgoing, socially confident person. ● adj. having to do with an extrovert.
– ORIGIN from **EXTRA-** + Latin *vertere* 'to turn'.

extrude /ik-strood/ ● v. (**extrudes**, **extruding**, **extruded**) thrust or force out.
– DERIVATIVES **extrusion** n.
– ORIGIN Latin *extrudere.*

exuberant /ig-zyoo-buh-ruhnt/ ● adj. lively and cheerful.
– DERIVATIVES **exuberance** n. **exuberantly** adv.
– ORIGIN Latin *exuberare* 'be abundantly fruitful'.

exude /ig-zyood/ ● v. (**exudes**, **exuding**, **exuded**) **1** discharge or be discharged slowly and steadily. **2** display (an emotion or quality) strongly and openly.
– DERIVATIVES **exudation** n.
– ORIGIN Latin *exsudare.*

exult ● v. show or feel triumphant joy.
– DERIVATIVES **exultant** adj. **exultantly** adv. **exultation** n.
– ORIGIN Latin *exsultare.*

eye ● n. **1** the organ of sight in humans and animals. **2** a round, dark spot on a potato from which a new shoot grows. **3** the small hole in a needle through which the thread is passed. **4** a small metal loop into which a hook is fitted as a fastener on a garment. **5** the calm region at the centre of a storm. **6** a person's opinion or feelings: *to European eyes, the city seems overcrowded.* ● v. (**eyes**, **eyeing** or **eying**, **eyed**) **1** look at closely or with interest. **2** (**eye up**) informal look at (someone) in a way that reveals a sexual interest.
– PHRASES **be all eyes** be watching eagerly. **an eye for an eye and a tooth for a tooth** doing the same thing in return is the appropriate way to deal with an offence or crime. **have an eye for** be able to recognize and judge wisely. **have one's eye on** aim to acquire. **have** (or **with**) **an eye to** have (or having) as one's objective. **make eyes at** look at in a way that indicates sexual interest. **one in the eye for** a setback for. **see eye to eye** be in full agreement. **a twinkle** (or **gleam**) **in someone's eye** something that is as yet no more than an idea or dream. **up to one's eyes** informal extremely busy.
– ORIGIN Old English.

eyeball ● n. the round part of the eye of a vertebrate, within the eyelids and socket.
– PHRASES **eyeball to eyeball** face to face with someone.

eyebrow ● n. the strip of hair growing on the ridge above a person's eye socket.
– PHRASES **raise one's eyebrows** show surprise or mild disapproval.

eye-catching ● adj. immediately appealing or noticeable.

eyeful ● n. informal **1** a long steady look. **2** an eye-catching person or thing.

eyeglass ● n. a single lens for correcting defective eyesight.

eyelash ● n. each of the short hairs growing on the edges of the eyelids.

eyelet ● n. **1** a small round hole made in leather or cloth, used for threading a lace, string, or rope through. **2** a metal ring strengthening such a hole.
– ORIGIN Old French *oillet.*

eyelid ● n. each of the upper and lower folds of skin which cover the eye when closed.

eyeliner ● n. a cosmetic applied as a line round the eyes.

eye-opener ● n. informal an unexpectedly revealing event or situation.

eyepiece ● n. the lens that is closest to the eye in a microscope or other optical instrument.

eyeshadow ● n. a coloured cosmetic applied to the eyelids or to the skin around the eyes.

eyesight ● n. a person's ability to see.

eye socket ● n. the cavity in the skull which encloses an eyeball with its surrounding muscles.

eyesore ● n. a thing that is very ugly.

eye tooth ● n. a canine tooth.
– PHRASES **give one's eye teeth for** (or **to be** or **to do**) do anything in order to have or to be or do.

eyewitness ● n. a person who has seen something happen and so can give a first-hand description of it.

Eyre, Lake E
/air/ a lake in South Australia, Australia's largest salt lake.

eyrie /eer-i, I-ri/ (US also **aerie**) ● n. a large nest of a bird of prey.
– ORIGIN prob. from Old French *aire*.

Eysenck E
/I-sengk/, Hans (Jürgen) (1916–97), German-born British psychologist, noted for his opposition to Freudian psychoanalysis and for his ideas concerning the assessment of intelligence and personality.

Ezekiel E
/i-zee-ki-uhl/ a Hebrew prophet of the 6th century BC who prophesied the destruction of Jerusalem and the Jewish nation and the future restoration of a Jewish state.

F[1] (also **f**) ● n. (pl. **Fs** or **F's**) **1** the sixth letter of the alphabet. **2** Music the fourth note of the scale of C major.

F[2] ● abbrev. **1** Fahrenheit. **2** farad(s). **3** female. **4** Brit. fine (used in describing grades of pencil lead). **5** Franc(s). ● symb. **1** the chemical element fluorine. **2** Physics force.

f ● abbrev. **1** Grammar feminine. **2** (in textual references) folio. **3** Music forte. ● symb. Electron. frequency.

FA ● abbrev. (in the UK) Football Association.

fa ● n. var. of FAH.

fab ● adj. informal fabulous.

Fabergé E
/fab-er-*zhay*/, Peter Carl (1846–1920), Russian goldsmith and jeweller, famous for the intricate jewelled Easter eggs that he made.

Fabian /fay-bi-uhn/ ● n. a supporter of the Fabian Society, an organization aiming to achieve socialism by non-revolutionary methods. ● adj. relating to the Fabians.
– ORIGIN from Roman general Quintus *Fabius* Maximus Verrucosus (d.203 BC), known for his delaying tactics.

fable ● n. **1** a short story with a moral. **2** a supernatural story containing elements of myth and legend.
– ORIGIN Old French.

fabled ● adj. **1** famous: *a fabled art collection.* **2** mythical.

fabric ● n. **1** cloth. **2** the walls, floor, and roof of a building. **3** the essential structure of a system or organization: *the fabric of society.*
– ORIGIN Latin *fabrica* 'something skilfully produced'.

fabricate ● v. (**fabricates**, **fabricating**, **fabricated**) **1** invent (false information). **2** construct or manufacture (an industrial product).
– DERIVATIVES **fabrication** n. **fabricator** n.
– ORIGIN Latin *fabricare.*

fabulous ● adj. **1** great; extraordinary. **2** informal excellent. **3** mythical.
– DERIVATIVES **fabulously** adv.
– ORIGIN Latin *fabulosus* 'celebrated in fable'.

facade /fuh-sahd/ ● n. **1** the face of a building. **2** a deceptive outward appearance.
– ORIGIN French.

face ● n. **1** the front part of the head from the forehead to the chin. **2** an expression on someone's face. **3** the main surface of something. **4** a vertical or sloping side of a mountain or cliff. **5** an aspect: *the hidden face of American politics.* ● v. (**faces**, **facing**, **faced**) **1** be positioned with the face or front towards or in a specified direction. **2** confront and deal with. **3** have (a difficulty) ahead of one. **4** cover the surface of (something) with a layer of a different material.
– PHRASES **someone's face fits** Brit. someone has the necessary qualities for something. **face the music** be confronted with the unpleasant consequences of one's actions. **in the face of** when confronted with. **lose** (or **save**) **face** suffer (or avoid) humiliation. **on the face of it** apparently. **to one's face** openly in one's presence.
– ORIGIN Latin *facies* 'form, face'.

facecloth ● n. (Brit. also **face flannel**) a small towelling cloth for washing one's face.

faceless ● adj. remote and impersonal: *faceless bureaucrats.*

facelift ● n. an operation to remove unwanted wrinkles by tightening the skin of the face.

face mask ● n. **1** a protective mask covering the face or part of the face. **2** a face pack.

face pack ● n. esp. Brit. a cream or gel which is spread over the face and then removed, designed to clean the skin.

face-saving ● adj. preserving one's reputation or dignity.

facet /fa-set/ ● n. **1** one side of something many-sided. **2** an aspect: *different facets of the truth.*
– DERIVATIVES **faceted** adj.
– ORIGIN French *facette* 'little face'.

facetious /fuh-see-shuhss/ ● adj. treating serious issues with inappropriate humour.
– DERIVATIVES **facetiously** adv. **facetiousness** n.
– ORIGIN French *facétieux.*

face value ● n. **1** the value printed or shown on a coin, postage stamp, etc. **2** the apparent value or nature of something.

facia ● n. esp. Brit. var. of **FASCIA**.

facial /fay-sh'l/ ● adj. having to do with the face. ● n. a beauty treatment for the face.
– DERIVATIVES **facially** adv.

facile /fa-syl/ ● adj. **1** lacking careful thought. **2** too easily achieved.
– ORIGIN Latin *facilis* 'easy'.

facilitate /fuh-sil-i-tayt/ ● v. (**facilitates, facilitating, facilitated**) make easy or easier.
– DERIVATIVES **facilitation** n. **facilitator** n.
– ORIGIN French *faciliter*.

facility ● n. (pl. **facilities**) **1** a building, service, or piece of equipment provided for a particular purpose. **2** a natural ability to do something well and easily.

f

facing ● n. **1** a piece of material sewn to the inside edge of a garment at the neck, armhole, etc., used to strengthen the edge. **2** an outer layer covering the surface of a wall. ● adj. positioned so as to face.

facsimile /fak-sim-i-li/ ● n. **1** an exact copy of written or printed material. **2** a fax.
– ORIGIN from Latin *fac!* 'make!' and *simile* 'like'.

fact ● n. **1** a thing that is known to be true. **2** (**facts**) information used as evidence or as part of a report.
– PHRASES **before** (or **after**) **the fact** Law before (or after) the committing of a crime. **a fact of life** something that must be accepted, even if unpleasant. **the facts of life** information about sexual matters. **in fact** in reality.
– ORIGIN Latin *factum* 'an act'.

faction ● n. a small group within a larger one that disagrees with some of its beliefs.
– DERIVATIVES **factional** adj.
– ORIGIN Latin *facere* 'do, make'.

factious /fak-shuhss/ ● adj. having to do with opposition or disagreement.
– ORIGIN Latin *factiosus*.

factitious /fak-ti-shuhss/ ● adj. not genuine; made up.
– ORIGIN Latin *facticius* 'made by art'.

factor ● n. **1** a circumstance, fact, or influence that contributes to a result. **2** Math. a number or quantity that when multiplied with another produces a given number or expression. **3** any of a number of substances in the blood which are involved in clotting. **4** a business or land agent. ● v. (**factor in/out**) include (or exclude) as relevant when making a decision.
– ORIGIN Latin *facere* 'do'.

factorial ● n. Math. the product of a whole number and all the whole numbers below it, e.g. 4 × 3 × 2 × 1 (*factorial 4*, written as *4!* and equal to 24).

factorize (also **factorise**) ● v. (**factorizes, factorizing, factorized**) Math. break down or be able to be broken down into factors.
– DERIVATIVES **factorization** (also **factorisation**) n.

factory ● n. (pl. **factories**) a building where goods are manufactured or assembled chiefly by machine.
– ORIGIN Latin *factorium* 'oil press'.

factory farming ● n. a system of rearing poultry, pigs, or cattle indoors under strictly controlled conditions.

factory floor ● n. the workers in a company or industry, rather than the management.

factotum /fak-toh-tuhm/ ● n. (pl. **factotums**) an employee who does all kinds of work.
– ORIGIN from Latin *fac!* 'do!' + *totum* 'the whole thing'.

factual ● adj. based on or concerned with fact or facts.
– DERIVATIVES **factually** adv.

faculty ● n. (pl. **faculties**) **1** a basic mental or physical power. **2** an ability for doing something. **3** esp. Brit. a group of university departments concerned with a particular area of knowledge. **4** N. Amer. the teaching or research staff of a university or college.
– ORIGIN Latin *facultas*.

fad ● n. **1** a craze. **2** a fussy like or dislike.
– DERIVATIVES **faddish** adj.
– ORIGIN uncertain.

faddy ● adj. Brit. having many fussy likes and dislikes about food.

fade ● v. (**fades, fading, faded**) **1** gradually grow faint and disappear. **2** lose or cause to lose colour. **3** (of a film or video image or recorded sound) become more or less clear or loud. ● n. an act of fading.
– ORIGIN Old French *fader*.

faeces /fee-seez/ (US **feces**) ● pl. n. waste matter remaining after food has been digested, discharged from the bowels.
– DERIVATIVES **faecal** /fee-k'l/ (US **fecal**) adj.
– ORIGIN Latin, 'dregs'.

Faeroe Islands E
var. of **FAROE ISLANDS**.

faff ● v. (**faff about/around**) Brit. informal bustle about without achieving much.
– ORIGIN dialect, 'blow in gusts'.

fag[1] Brit. informal ● n. **1** a tiring or unwelcome task. **2** a junior pupil at a public school who does minor chores for a senior pupil. ● v. (**fags, fagging, fagged**) **1** (of a public-school pupil) act as a fag. **2** (**fagged out**) exhausted.
– ORIGIN unknown.

fag[2] ● n. N. Amer. informal, derog. a male homosexual.
– ORIGIN from **FAGGOT** (in sense 3).

fag[3] ● n. Brit. informal a cigarette.
– ORIGIN from **FAG END**.

fag end ● n. informal, esp. Brit. **1** a cigarette end. **2** an unimportant remaining part.
– ORIGIN from former *fag* 'a flap'.

faggot /fag-guht/ ● n. **1** Brit. a ball of seasoned chopped liver, baked or fried. **2** (US **fagot**) a bundle of sticks tied together as fuel. **3** N. Amer. informal, derog. a male homosexual.
– ORIGIN Greek *phakelos* 'bundle'.

fah (also **fa**) ● n. Music the fourth note of a major scale, coming between 'me' and 'soh'.
– ORIGIN the first syllable of *famuli*, taken from a Latin hymn.

Fahrenheit /fa-ruhn-hyt/ ● adj. having to do with a scale of temperature on which water freezes at 32° and boils at 212°.
– ORIGIN named after the German physicist Gabriel Daniel *Fahrenheit* (1686–1736).

fail ● v. **1** be unsuccessful in achieving something. **2** be unable to meet the standards set by (a test). **3** neglect to do: *the firm failed to give adequate warnings*. **4** stop working properly. **5** become weaker or less good. **6** desert or let down: *her nerve failed her*. ● n. a mark which is not high enough to pass an examination or test.
– PHRASES **without fail** whatever happens.

– ORIGIN Latin *fallere* 'deceive'.

failing ● n. a weakness in a person's character. ● prep. if not.

fail-safe ● adj. **1** causing machinery to return to a safe condition in the event of a breakdown. **2** unlikely to fail.

failure ● n. **1** lack of success. **2** an unsuccessful person or thing. **3** the ceasing of something to function. **4** the non-performance of something required: *failure to comply with the rules.*

fain archaic ● adj. **1** willing or obliged to do. ● adv. gladly.

– ORIGIN Old English, 'happy'.

faint ● adj. **1** not clearly seen, heard, or smelt. **2** slight: *a faint chance.* **3** close to losing consciousness. ● v. briefly lose consciousness. ● n. a sudden loss of consciousness.

– DERIVATIVES **faintly** adv. **faintness** n.

– ORIGIN Old French *faindre* 'feign'.

faint-hearted ● adj. timid.

fair[1] ● adj. **1** treating people equally. **2** just or appropriate in the circumstances. **3** considerable in size or amount: *he did a fair bit of coaching.* **4** moderately good. **5** (of hair or complexion) light; blonde. **6** (of weather) fine and dry. **7** archaic beautiful. ● adv. in a fair way.

– PHRASES **fair and square 1** with absolute accuracy. **2** honestly and straightforwardly. **fair enough** informal that is reasonable. **the fair sex** (also **the fairer sex**) dated or humorous women.

– DERIVATIVES **fairness** n.

– ORIGIN Old English.

fair[2] ● n. **1** a gathering of stalls and amusements for public entertainment. **2** a periodic gathering for the sale of goods. **3** an exhibition to promote particular products: *a fine art fair.*

– ORIGIN Latin *feriae* 'holy days'.

Fairbanks, E
Douglas (1909–2000; known as **Douglas Fairbanks Jr**), American actor, famous for his swashbuckling film roles.

fair copy ● n. a copy of written or printed matter produced after final correction.

Fairfax, E
Thomas, 3rd Baron Fairfax of Cameron (1612–71), English general and leader of the Parliamentary Army, who defeated Charles I at the Battle of Naseby.

fair game ● n. a person or thing regarded as an acceptable target for criticism or ridicule.

fairground ● n. an outdoor area where a fair is held.

fairing ● n. an external structure added to increase streamlining on a vehicle, boat, or aircraft.

Fair Isle ● n. a traditional multicoloured geometric design used in knitwear.

– ORIGIN from *Fair Isle*, one of the Shetland Islands.

fairly ● adv. **1** with justice. **2** moderately.

fair play ● n. respect for the rules or equal treatment for all.

fairway ● n. **1** the part of a golf course between a tee and a green. **2** a channel in a river or harbour which can be used by shipping.

fair-weather friend ● n. a person who stops being a friend in times of difficulty.

fairy ● n. (pl. **fairies**) **1** a small imaginary being of human form that has magical powers. **2** informal, derog. a male homosexual.

– ORIGIN Old French *fae.*

fairy godmother ● n. a female character in fairy stories who helps the hero or heroine.

fairy lights ● pl. n. Brit. small electric lights used to decorate a Christmas tree.

fairy ring ● n. a ring of dark grass caused by fungi, once believed to have been made by fairies dancing.

fairy story ● n. **1** a children's tale about magical and imaginary beings and lands. **2** an untrue account.

fairy tale ● n. a fairy story. ● adj. magical or wonderful: *a fairy-tale romance.*

Faisalabad E
/fy-zuh-luh-bad/ an industrial city in Punjab, Pakistan. Former name (until 1979) **Lyallpur**.

fait accompli /fayt uh-kom-pli/ ● n. a thing that has been done or decided and cannot now be altered.

– ORIGIN French, 'accomplished fact'.

faith ● n. **1** complete trust or confidence. **2** strong belief in a religion. **3** a system of religious belief.

– ORIGIN Latin *fides.*

faithful ● adj. **1** remaining loyal. **2** remaining sexually loyal to a lover, husband or wife. **3** true to the facts or the original: *a faithful copy of a painting.* ● n. (**the faithful**) the believers in a particular religion.

– DERIVATIVES **faithfully** adv. **faithfulness** n.

faith healing ● n. healing achieved by religious faith and prayer.

faithless ● adj. disloyal, especially to a lover, husband, or wife.

fake ● adj. not genuine: *fake designer clothing.* ● n. a person or thing that is not genuine. ● v. (**fakes**, **faking**, **faked**) **1** make (something) that seems genuine, in order to deceive. **2** pretend to feel or have (an emotion or illness).

– DERIVATIVES **faker** n. **fakery** n.

– ORIGIN uncertain.

fakir /fay-keer/ ● n. a Muslim (or Hindu) holy man who lives by begging.

– ORIGIN Arabic, 'needy man'.

falcon /fawl-k'n/ ● n. a fast-flying bird of prey with long pointed wings.

– ORIGIN Latin *falco* 'hawk'.

falconry ● n. the keeping of birds of prey and training them to hunt.

– DERIVATIVES **falconer** n.

Faldo E
/fal-doh/, Nick (b.1957; full name *Nicholas Alexander Faldo*), English golfer. He won the British Open championship twice and the US Masters Tournament three times (1989, 1990, and 1996).

Falkland Islands E
/fawlk-luhnd/ a group of islands in the South Atlantic, forming a British Crown Colony; capital, Stanley (on East Falkland).

Falkland Islands Dependencies E
an overseas territory of the UK in the South Atlantic, consisting of the South Sandwich Islands and South Georgia, which is administered from the Falkland Islands.

Falklands War E
an armed conflict between Britain and Argentina in 1982. Argentina had long refused to recognize British sovereignty of the islands and sent forces to invade them. Britain responded with a task force of ships and aircraft and the Argentinians surrendered six weeks after its arrival.

fall • v. (**falls**, **falling**, **fell**; past part. **fallen**) **1** move downwards quickly and without control. **2** collapse to the ground. **3** hang or slope down: *the land fell away in a steep bank*. **4** become less or lower. **5** become: *he fell silent*. **6** happen; come about. **7** (of someone's face) show dismay. **8** be captured or defeated in a battle or contest. • n. **1** an act of falling. **2** a thing which falls or has fallen. **3** a waterfall. **4** a drop in size or number. **5** a defeat or downfall. **6** N. Amer. autumn.
– PHRASES **fall back** retreat. **fall back on** turn to (something) for help. **fall for** informal **1** fall in love with. **2** be tricked by. **fall foul of** come into conflict with. **fall in line** do what one is told or what others do. **fall in with 1** meet and become involved with. **2** agree to. **fall on** (or **upon**) **1** attack fiercely or unexpectedly. **2** be the duty of. **fall out** have an argument. **fall short** (**of**) fail to reach a required standard or target. **fall through** fail. **fall to** become the duty of.
– ORIGIN Old English.

Falla E
/fy-uh/, Manuel de (1876–1946), Spanish composer and pianist, known for his ballet *The Three-Cornered Hat*.

fallacious /fuh-lay-shuhss/ • adj. based on a mistaken belief: *a fallacious explanation*.

fallacy /fal-luh-si/ • n. (pl. **fallacies**) **1** a mistaken belief. **2** a mistake in reasoning which makes an argument invalid.
– ORIGIN Latin *fallere* 'deceive'.

fallback • n. an alternative plan for use in an emergency.

fallen past part. of FALL.

fall guy • n. informal a person who is blamed for something that is not their fault; a scapegoat.

fallible /fal-li-b'l/ • adj. capable of making mistakes or being wrong.
– DERIVATIVES **fallibility** n.
– ORIGIN Latin *fallibilis*.

falling star • n. a meteor or shooting star.

Fallopian tube /fuh-loh-pi-uhn/ • n. either of a pair of tubes along which eggs travel from the ovaries to the uterus of a female mammal.
– ORIGIN named after the Italian anatomist Gabriello *Fallopio* (1523–62).

fallout • n. **1** radioactive particles that are spread over a wide area after a nuclear explosion. **2** the unfavourable side effects of a situation.

fallow • adj. **1** (of farmland) ploughed but left for a period without being planted with crops. **2** when very little is done or achieved.
– ORIGIN Old English.

fallow deer • n. a small deer that has a white-spotted reddish-brown coat in summer.
– ORIGIN Old English, 'pale brown'.

false • adj. **1** not in accordance with the truth or facts. **2** fake; artificial: *false eyelashes*. **3** seeming but not actually so: *a false sense of security*. **4** disloyal.
– DERIVATIVES **falsely** adv. **falsity** n.
– ORIGIN Latin *falsum* 'fraud'.

false alarm • n. a warning given about something that fails to take place.

falsehood • n. **1** the state of being untrue. **2** a lie.

false move • n. an unwise action that could have dangerous consequences.

false pretences • pl. n. behaviour intended to deceive.

false step • n. **1** a slip or stumble. **2** a mistake.

falsetto /fawl-set-toh/ • n. (pl. **falsettos**) a high-pitched voice above one's natural range, used by male singers.
– ORIGIN Italian.

falsify /fawl-si-fy/ • v. (**falsifies**, **falsifying**, **falsified**) alter so as to mislead: *they had falsified evidence*.
– DERIVATIVES **falsification** n.

falter /fawl-ter/ • v. (**falters**, **faltering**, **faltered**) **1** lose strength or momentum. **2** move or speak hesitantly.
– ORIGIN perh. from FOLD[1].

fame • n. the state of being famous.

famed • adj. famous; well known.

familial /fuh-mil-i-uhl/ • adj. having to do with a family.

familiar • adj. **1** well known. **2** often encountered; common. **3** (**familiar with**) having a good knowledge of. **4** friendly. **5** more friendly or informal than is proper. • n. (also **familiar spirit**) a spirit supposedly attending and obeying a witch.
– DERIVATIVES **familiarly** adv.
– ORIGIN Latin *familiaris*.

familiarity • n. the state of being familiar.

familiarize (also **familiarise**) • v. (**familiarizes**, **familiarizing**, **familiarized**) **1** (**familiarize with**) give (someone) knowledge or understanding of. **2** make better known or easier to understand.
– DERIVATIVES **familiarization** (also **familiarisation**) n.

family • n. (pl. **families**) **1** a group consisting of parents and their children. **2** a group of people related by blood or marriage. **3** the children of a person or couple. **4** all the descendants of a common ancestor: *the house has been in the family for years*. **5** a group of things that are alike in some way. **6** a group of related plants or animals. • adj. suitable for children as well as adults.
– PHRASES **in the family way** informal pregnant.
– ORIGIN Latin *familia* 'household servants, family'.

family credit • n. (in the UK) a regular payment by the state to a family with an income below a certain level.

family name • n. a surname.

family planning • n. the control of the number of children in a family by means of contraception.

family tree • n. a diagram showing the relationship between people in several generations of a family.

famine • n. extreme scarcity of food.
– ORIGIN Latin *fames* 'hunger'.

famished • adj. informal very hungry.

– ORIGIN Latin *fames* 'hunger'.

famous ● **adj.** **1** known about by many people. **2** informal excellent.

– DERIVATIVES **famously** adv.

– ORIGIN Latin *fama* 'fame'.

fan[1] ● **n.** **1** a device with rotating blades that creates a current of air. **2** a hand-held folding device that is waved so as to cool the user. ● **v.** (**fans**, **fanning**, **fanned**) **1** drive a current of air towards: *he fanned himself with his hat.* **2** strengthen (a belief or emotion). **3** (**fan out**) spread out from a central point to cover a wide area.

– ORIGIN Latin *vannus*.

fan[2] ● **n.** a person who has a strong interest in or admiration for a sport, art form, or celebrity.

– ORIGIN from **FANATIC**.

fanatic ● **n.** **1** a person filled with excessive enthusiasm for an extreme political or religious cause. **2** informal a person with an extreme enthusiasm for a pastime or hobby.

– DERIVATIVES **fanatical** adj. **fanaticism** n.

– ORIGIN Latin *fanaticus* 'of a temple'.

fan belt ● **n.** a belt driving the fan that cools the radiator of a motor vehicle.

fanciable ● **adj.** informal sexually attractive.

fancier ● **n.** a person who has a special interest in or breeds a particular animal: *a pigeon fancier.*

fanciful ● **adj.** **1** existing only in the imagination. **2** highly ornamental or imaginative: *lavish and fanciful costumes.*

– DERIVATIVES **fancifully** adv.

fancy ● **v.** (**fancies**, **fancying**, **fancied**) **1** Brit. informal want or want to do. **2** Brit. informal find sexually attractive. **3** think: *he fancied he could smell roses.* **4** regard as a likely winner. ● **adj.** (**fancier**, **fanciest**) elaborate or highly decorated. ● **n.** (pl. **fancies**) **1** a brief feeling of attraction. **2** the power of imagining things. **3** something that is imagined.

– PHRASES **take someone's fancy** appeal to someone. **take a fancy to** become fond of.

– ORIGIN from **FANTASY**.

fancy dress ● **n.** a costume worn to make someone look like a famous person, fictional character, or an animal.

fancy-free ● **adj.** not in love.

fancy man (or **woman**) ● **n.** informal, usu. derog. a lover.

fandango /fan-dang-goh/ ● **n.** (pl. **fandangoes** or **fandangos**) a lively Spanish dance for two people.

– ORIGIN Spanish.

fanfare ● **n.** a short tune played on brass instruments to announce someone or something.

– ORIGIN French.

fang ● **n.** **1** a canine tooth of a dog or wolf. **2** a tooth with which a snake injects poison.

– ORIGIN Old Norse, 'capture, grasp'.

> **Fangio** E
> /fan-ji-oh/, Juan Manuel (1911–95), Argentinian motor-racing driver. He first won the world championship in 1951 and then held the title from 1954 until 1957.

fanlight ● **n.** a small semicircular window over a door or another window.

fanny ● **n.** (pl. **fannies**) **1** Brit. vulgar a woman's genitals. **2** N. Amer. informal a person's bottom.

– ORIGIN unknown.

fantasia /fan-tay-zi-uh/ ● **n.** **1** a musical composition that does not follow a conventional form. **2** a musical composition based on several familiar tunes.

– ORIGIN Italian, 'fantasy'.

fantasize (also **fantasise**) ● **v.** (**fantasizes**, **fantasizing**, **fantasized**) imagine something desired: *he fantasized about emigrating.*

– DERIVATIVES **fantasist** n.

fantastic ● **adj.** **1** hard to believe; fanciful. **2** strange or exotic. **3** informal very good or large.

– DERIVATIVES **fantastical** adj. **fantastically** adv.

fantasy ● **n.** (pl. **fantasies**) **1** the imagining of improbable or impossible things. **2** a fanciful product of the imagination reflecting a person's desires: *fantasies about the lives we'd live.* **3** a type of imaginative fiction involving magic and adventure.

– ORIGIN Greek *phantasia* 'imagination'.

fanzine /fan-zeen/ ● **n.** a magazine for fans.

– ORIGIN from **FAN[2]** and **MAGAZINE**.

FAQ ● **abbrev.** Computing frequently asked questions.

far ● **adv.** (**further**, **furthest** or **farther**, **farthest**) **1** at, to, or by a great distance. **2** over a long time. **3** by a great deal: *he's functioning far better than usual.* ● **adj.** **1** situated at a great distance. **2** distant from the centre. **3** more distant than another object of the same kind.

– PHRASES **as far as** to the extent that. **be a far cry from** be very different to. **far and away** by a very large amount. **far and wide** over a large area. **far gone** in a bad or worsening state. **go far 1** achieve a great deal. **2** be worth much. **go too far** go beyond what is acceptable.

– ORIGIN Old English.

farad /fa-rad/ ● **n.** the SI unit of electrical capacitance.

– ORIGIN named after Michael **FARADAY**.

> **Faraday** E
> /fa-ruh-day/, Michael (1791–1867), English physicist and chemist, who made major contributions to the fields of electricity and magnetism, including the discovery of electromagnetic induction.

faraway ● **adj.** **1** distant in space or time. **2** remote from one's present situation: *a faraway look.*

farce ● **n.** **1** a comedy involving horseplay and ridiculously improbable situations. **2** an absurd event.

– ORIGIN French, 'stuffing' (from the former practice of 'stuffing' comic passages into religious plays).

farcical ● **adj.** absurd or ridiculous.

fare ● **n.** **1** the money a passenger on public transport has to pay. **2** a range of food: *English fare.* ● **v.** (**fares**, **faring**, **fared**) perform in a specified way: *the party fared badly in the elections.*

– ORIGIN Old English.

Far East ● **n.** China, Japan, and other countries of east Asia.

farewell ● **exclam.** archaic goodbye. ● **n.** an act of leaving or of marking someone's departure.

far-fetched ● **adj.** far from reality and therefore unlikely: *a far-fetched plot.*

far-flung • adj. distant or remote.

farinaceous /fa-ri-**nay**-shuhss/ • adj. containing or resembling starch.
– ORIGIN Latin *farina* 'flour'.

farm • n. **1** an area of land and its buildings used for growing crops and rearing animals. **2** a farmhouse. **3** a place for breeding or growing something: *a fish farm.* • v. **1** make one's living by growing crops or keeping livestock. **2** breed or grow (a type of livestock or crop) commercially. **3** (**farm out**) send out or subcontract (work) to others.
– DERIVATIVES **farming** n.
– ORIGIN Old French *ferme* 'fixed payment'.

f

farmer • n. a person who owns or manages a farm.

farmhouse • n. the main house on a farm.

farmstead • n. a farm and its buildings.

Farne Islands E
/*rhymes with* barn/ a group of seventeen small islands off the coast of Northumberland, noted for their wildlife.

Faro E
/**fah**-roo/ a seaport on the south coast of Portugal, capital of the Algarve.

Faroe Islands E
/*rhymes with* pharaoh/ (also **Faeroe Islands**) a group of islands in the North Atlantic between Iceland and the Shetland Islands, belonging to Denmark but partly autonomous; capital, Tórshavn.

Farouk E
/fa-**rook**/ (1920–65), king of Egypt, reigned 1936–52. He was forced to abdicate in favour of his infant son, Fuad, following a military coup.

far out • adj. **1** unconventional. **2** informal, dated excellent.

Farquhar E
/**far**-ker/, George (1678–1707), Irish dramatist. His comedies include *The Recruiting Officer* and *The Beaux' Stratagem.*

farrago /fuh-**rah**-goh/ • n. (pl. **farragos** or US **farragoes**) a confused mixture.
– ORIGIN Latin, 'mixed fodder'.

far-reaching • adj. having wide and important effects or implications.

farrier /**fa**-ri-er/ • n. a smith who shoes horses.
– ORIGIN Old French *ferrier.*

farrow • n. a litter of pigs. • v. (of a sow) give birth to (piglets).
– ORIGIN Old English, 'young pig'.

far-seeing • adj. having great foresight.

Farsi /**far**-see/ • n. the modern form of the Persian language.
– ORIGIN Persian, 'Persia'.

far-sighted • adj. far-seeing.

fart informal • v. **1** discharge wind from the anus. **2** (**fart about/around**) waste time on silly or unimportant things. • n. **1** a discharge of wind from the anus. **2** a boring or unpleasant person.
– ORIGIN Old English.

farther • adv. & adj. var. of FURTHER.

USAGE **farther**
For an explanation of the difference between **farther** and **further**, see the note at **FURTHER**.

farthermost • adj. var. of FURTHERMOST.

farthest • adj. & adv. var. of FURTHEST.

farthing • n. a former coin of the UK, worth a quarter of an old penny.
– ORIGIN Old English.

farthingale /**far**-*th*ing-gayl/ • n. a hooped petticoat or circular pad of fabric around the hips, formerly worn under women's skirts to extend them.
– ORIGIN French *verdugale.*

fascia /**fay**-shuh/ (Brit. also **facia**) • n. **1** a board covering the ends of rafters or other fittings. **2** a signboard on a shopfront. **3** esp. Brit. the dashboard of a motor vehicle.
– ORIGIN Latin, 'band, door frame'.

fascinate • v. (**fascinates**, **fascinating**, **fascinated**) interest or charm greatly.
– ORIGIN Latin *fascinare* 'bewitch'.

fascinating • adj. extremely interesting or attractive.

fascination • n. **1** the quality of being fascinating: *the fascination of science.* **2** a strong feeling of interest.

fascism /**fash**-i-z'm/ • n. **1** a right-wing system of government characterized by extreme nationalistic beliefs and strict obedience to a leader or the state. **2** extreme right-wing or intolerant views or behaviour.
– DERIVATIVES **fascist** n. & adj. **fascistic** adj.
– ORIGIN Italian *fascismo.*

fashion • n. **1** a popular trend, especially in dress. **2** the production and marketing of new styles of clothing and cosmetics. **3** a way of doing something: *the work was done in a casual fashion.* • v. make or shape.
– PHRASES **after a fashion** to a certain extent but not perfectly.
– ORIGIN Old French *façon.*

fashionable • adj. in or adopting a style that is currently popular.
– DERIVATIVES **fashionability** n. **fashionably** adv.

Fassbinder E
/**fass**-bin-der/, Rainer Werner (1946–82), German film director, known for *The Bitter Tears of Petra von Kant.*

fast[1] • adj. **1** moving or capable of moving at high speed. **2** taking place or acting rapidly. **3** (of a clock or watch) ahead of the correct time. **4** firmly fixed or attached: *he made a rope fast to each corner.* **5** (of a dye) not fading in light or when washed. **6** devoting oneself to pleasurable or immoral activities. • adv. **1** quickly. **2** firmly or securely.
– PHRASES **fast asleep** in a deep sleep. **pull a fast one** informal try to gain an unfair advantage.
– ORIGIN Old English.

fast[2] • v. go without food or drink, especially for religious reasons. • n. an act or period of fasting.
– ORIGIN Old English.

fast breeder • n. a nuclear reactor using high-speed neutrons.

fasten • v. **1** close or do up securely. **2** fix or hold in place. **3** (**fasten on/upon**) pick out and concentrate on.
– ORIGIN Old English, 'make sure'.

fastener (also **fastening**) ● **n.** a device for fastening something.

fast food ● **n.** cooked food sold in snack bars and restaurants as a quick meal.

fastidious /fa-stid-i-uhss/ ● **adj. 1** very careful about accuracy and detail. **2** very concerned about cleanliness.
– DERIVATIVES **fastidiously** adv. **fastidiousness** n.
– ORIGIN Latin *fastidium* 'loathing'.

fastness ● **n. 1** a secure place well protected by natural features. **2** the ability of a dye to maintain its colour.

fast track ● **n.** a rapid method. ● **v.** (**fast-track**) speed up the progress of.

fat ● **n. 1** a natural oily substance found in animal bodies. **2** such a substance, or a similar one made from plants, used in cooking. ● **adj.** (**fatter, fattest**) **1** (of a person or animal) having much excess fat. **2** (of food) containing much fat. **3** informal large: *fat profits.* **4** informal very little: *fat chance.*
– PHRASES **live off the fat of the land** have the best of everything.
– DERIVATIVES **fatness** n.
– ORIGIN Old English.

Fatah, Al E
/al fa-tuh/ a Palestinian political and military organization founded in 1958 by Yasser Arafat and others to bring about the establishment of a Palestinian state. It is the dominant force within the Palestine Liberation Organization.

fatal ● **adj. 1** causing death. **2** leading to failure or disaster: *the strategy contained three fatal flaws.*
– DERIVATIVES **fatally** adv.
– ORIGIN Latin *fatalis.*

fatalism ● **n.** the belief that all events are decided in advance by a supernatural power and humans have no control over them.
– DERIVATIVES **fatalist** n. **fatalistic** adj.

fatality ● **n.** (pl. **fatalities**) an occurrence of death by accident, in war, or from disease.

fat cat ● **n.** derog. a wealthy and powerful businessperson.

fate ● **n. 1** the development of events outside a person's control, regarded as decided in advance by a supernatural power. **2** the course or unavoidable outcome of a person's life. **3** (**the Fates**) Gk & Rom. Myth. the three goddesses (Clotho, Lachesis, and Atropos) who control people's lives. ● **v.** (**be fated**) be destined to happen in a particular way: *they were fated to meet again.*
– ORIGIN Latin *fatum* 'that which has been spoken'.

fateful ● **adj.** having far-reaching, often unpleasant, consequences.

fathead ● **n.** informal a stupid person.

father ● **n. 1** a male parent. **2** an important figure in the origin and early history of something: *Pasteur, the father of microbiology.* **3** literary a male ancestor. **4** (often as a title or form of address) a priest. **5** (**the Father**) (in Christian belief) God. ● **v.** (**fathers, fathering, fathered**) be the father of.
– DERIVATIVES **fatherhood** n.
– ORIGIN Old English.

Father Christmas ● **n.** an imaginary old man said to bring presents for children on Christmas Eve.

father-in-law ● **n.** (pl. **fathers-in-law**) the father of one's husband or wife.

fatherland ● **n.** a person's native country.

fatherly ● **adj.** protective and affectionate.

fathom ● **n.** a unit of length equal to six feet (1.8 metres), used in measuring the depth of water. ● **v.** understand after much thought: *I can't fathom him out.*
– ORIGIN Old English, 'something which embraces' (the original measurement was based on the span of a person's outstretched arms).

fatigue ● **n. 1** extreme tiredness. **2** brittleness in metal or other materials caused by repeated stress. **3** (**fatigues**) loose-fitting clothing of a sort worn by soldiers. ● **v.** (**fatigues, fatiguing, fatigued**) make extremely tired.
– ORIGIN Latin *fatigare.*

Fatima E
/fat-i-muh/ (c.606–32 AD), youngest daughter of the prophet Muhammad and wife of the fourth caliph, Ali. The descendants of Muhammad trace their lineage through her.

fatten ● **v.** make or become fat or fatter.

fatty ● **adj.** (**fattier, fattiest**) containing a large amount of fat. ● **n.** (pl. **fatties**) informal a fat person.

fatty acid ● **n.** Chem. an organic acid whose molecule contains a hydrocarbon chain.

fatuity /fuh-tyoo-i-ti/ ● **n.** (pl. **fatuities**) **1** foolishness. **2** a foolish act.

fatuous ● **adj.** silly and pointless.
– DERIVATIVES **fatuously** adv.
– ORIGIN Latin *fatuus.*

fatwa /fat-wah/ ● **n.** an authoritative ruling on a point of Islamic law.
– ORIGIN Arabic.

faucet /faw-sit/ ● **n.** N. Amer. a tap.
– ORIGIN Old French *fausset.*

Faulkner F
/fawlk-ner/, William (1897–1962), American novelist. His works, set in a semi-imaginary world in the American South, include *The Sound and the Fury* and *Absalom! Absalom!*.

fault ● **n. 1** a defect or mistake. **2** responsibility for an accident or misfortune: *it's not my fault that she left.* **3** (in tennis) a service that breaks the rules. **4** an extended break in the continuity of layers of rock, caused by movement of the earth's crust. ● **v.** criticize for being unsatisfactory.
– PHRASES **find fault** make a criticism or objection. —— **to a fault** to an excessive extent: *you're generous to a fault.*
– DERIVATIVES **faultless** adj.
– ORIGIN Latin *fallere* 'deceive'.

faulty ● **adj.** (**faultier, faultiest**) having or displaying faults.

faun /fawn/ ● **n.** Rom. Myth. a lustful god of woods and fields, in the form of a man with a goat's horns, ears, legs, and tail.
– ORIGIN Latin *Faunus.*

fauna /faw-nuh/ ● **n.** the animals of a particular region, habitat, or geological period. Compare with **FLORA**.
– ORIGIN Latin *Fauna*, a rural goddess.

Fauré E
/for-ay/, Gabriel (Urbain) (1845–1924), French composer and organist, known for his choral *Requiem.*

Faust E
/fowsst/ (also **Faustus** /fowss-tuhss/) (died *c.*1540), German astronomer and magician, who was said to have sold his soul to the Devil.
– DERIVATIVES **Faustian** adj.

faux pas /foh pah/ ● n. (pl. **faux pas**) an embarrassing blunder in a social situation.
– ORIGIN French, 'false step'.

favour (US **favor**) ● n. **1** approval or liking. **2** an act of kindness beyond what is due or usual: *I've come to ask you a favour.* **3** special treatment given to one person at the expense of another. ● v. **1** regard or treat with favour. **2** work to the advantage of: *natural selection has favoured bats.* **3** (**favour with**) give (something desired) to.
– PHRASES **in favour of 1** to be replaced by. **2** in support or to the advantage of.
– ORIGIN Latin *favor.*

favourable (US **favorable**) ● adj. **1** expressing approval or agreement. **2** advantageous or helpful.
– DERIVATIVES **favourably** (US **favorably**) adv.

favourite (US **favorite**) ● adj. preferred to all others of the same kind. ● n. **1** a favourite person or thing. **2** the competitor thought most likely to win.

favouritism (US **favoritism**) ● n. the unfair favouring of one person or group at the expense of another.

Fawkes E
/fawks/, Guy (1570–1606), English conspirator, hanged for his part in the plot to blow up the Houses of Parliament on 5 November 1605. The occasion is marked annually on Bonfire Night with fireworks, bonfires, and the burning of a guy.

fawn[1] ● n. **1** a young deer in its first year. **2** a light brown colour.
– ORIGIN Old French *faon.*

fawn[2] ● v. try to gain favour by servile flattery or attentive behaviour.
– ORIGIN Old English, 'make or be glad'.

fax ● n. **1** an exact copy of a document made by electronic scanning and sent by telecommunications links. **2** the making or sending of such documents. **3** (also **fax machine**) a machine for sending and receiving such documents. ● v. **1** send (a document) by fax. **2** contact by fax.
– ORIGIN from FACSIMILE.

faze ● v. (**fazes**, **fazing**, **fazed**) informal disturb or unsettle.
– ORIGIN Old English, 'drive off'.

FBI ● abbrev. (in the US) Federal Bureau of Investigation.

FC ● abbrev. Football Club.

FCO ● abbrev. (in the UK) Foreign and Commonwealth Office.

FE ● abbrev. (in the UK) further education.

Fe ● symb. the chemical element iron.
– ORIGIN Latin *ferrum.*

fealty /fee-uhl-ti/ ● n. hist. the loyalty sworn to a feudal lord by his tenant.
– ORIGIN Old French *feaulte.*

fear ● n. **1** an unpleasant emotion caused by the threat of danger, pain, or harm. **2** the likelihood of something unwelcome happening. ● v. **1** be afraid of. **2** (**fear for**) be anxious about.
– PHRASES **without fear or favour** in a fair and impartial way.
– ORIGIN Old English, 'danger'.

fearful ● adj. **1** showing or causing fear. **2** informal very great.
– DERIVATIVES **fearfully** adv.

fearless ● adj. lacking fear; brave.
– DERIVATIVES **fearlessly** adv.

fearsome ● adj. frightening.

feasible ● adj. **1** able to be done easily. **2** informal likely.
– DERIVATIVES **feasibility** n. **feasibly** adv.
– ORIGIN Old French *faisible.*

feast ● n. **1** a large meal marking a special occasion. **2** an annual religious celebration. ● v. **1** have a feast. **2** (**feast on**) eat large quantities of.
– PHRASES **feast one's eyes on** gaze at with pleasure.
– ORIGIN Latin *festa.*

feat ● n. an achievement requiring great courage, skill, or strength.
– ORIGIN Old French *fait.*

feather ● n. any of the flat structures growing from a bird's skin, consisting of a partly hollow shaft fringed with fine strands. ● v. (**feathers**, **feathering**, **feathered**) **1** (**feathered**) covered or decorated with feathers. **2** turn (an oar) so that the blade passes through the air edgeways.
– PHRASES **a feather in one's cap** an achievement to be proud of. **feather one's nest** make money dishonestly.
– DERIVATIVES **feathery** adj.
– ORIGIN Old English.

feather bed ● n. a bed with a mattress stuffed with feathers. ● v. (**feather-bed**) (**feather-beds**, **feather-bedding**, **feather-bedded**) provide with very favourable conditions.

feather-brained ● adj. silly or absent-minded.

featherweight ● n. **1** a weight in boxing between bantamweight and lightweight. **2** a person or thing of little or no importance.

feature ● n. **1** a distinctive element or aspect: *the software has some welcome new features.* **2** a distinctive part of the face, such as the mouth. **3** a newspaper or magazine article or a broadcast programme on a particular topic. **4** (also **feature film**) a full-length film forming the main item in a cinema programme. ● v. (**features**, **featuring**, **featured**) **1** have as a feature: *the hotel features a restaurant and a sauna.* **2** take an important part in. **3** have as an important actor or participant.
– DERIVATIVES **featureless** adj.
– ORIGIN Old French *faiture* 'form'.

Feb. ● abbrev. February.

febrile /fee-bryl/ ● adj. **1** having or showing the symptoms of a fever. **2** over-active and excitable: *her febrile imagination.*
– ORIGIN Latin *febris* 'fever'.

February /feb-yuu-ri, feb-ruu-uh-ri/ ● n. (pl. **Februaries**) the second month of the year.
– ORIGIN Latin *februarius.*

feces ● n. US = FAECES.

feckless ● adj. **1** lacking determination or purpose; feeble. **2** irresponsible.
– ORIGIN from EFFECT.

fecund /fek-uhnd/ ● adj. highly fertile.
– DERIVATIVES **fecundity** n.

– ORIGIN Latin *fecundus*.
fed past and past part. of **FEED**.
federal • adj. **1** relating to a system of government in which several states unite under a central authority but remain independent in internal affairs. **2** having to do with the central government of a federation: *federal laws*. **3** (**Federal**) US hist. having to do with the Northern States in the Civil War.
– DERIVATIVES **federally** adv.
– ORIGIN Latin *foedus* 'league, covenant'.

Federal Bureau of Investigation E
a US federal government agency that deals with internal security and counterintelligence and that also carries out investigations in federal law enforcement.

federalism • n. the federal principle or system of government.
– DERIVATIVES **federalist** n. & adj.

Federal Republic of Germany E
former name for West Germany (see **GERMANY**).

Federal Reserve E
(in the US) the banking authority that performs the functions of a central bank and is used to implement the country's monetary policy.

federate /fed-uh-rayt/ • v. (**federates**, **federating**, **federated**) (of states) unite on a federal basis.

Federated States of Micronesia E
full name for **MICRONESIA²**.

federation • n. **1** a group of states with a central government but independence in internal affairs. **2** an organization within which smaller divisions have some internal independence.
fedora /fi-dor-uh/ • n. a soft felt hat with a curled brim and the crown creased lengthways.
ORIGIN *Fédora*, a drama written by the French dramatist V. Sardou (1831–1908).
fed up • adj. informal annoyed or bored.
fee • n. **1** a payment given for professional advice or services. **2** a sum payable to be allowed to do something: *an admission fee*.
– ORIGIN Old French *feu* 'an estate held on condition of feudal service'.
feeble • adj. (**feebler**, **feeblest**) **1** lacking strength. **2** failing to convince or impress: *a feeble excuse*.
– DERIVATIVES **feebleness** n. **feebly** adv.
– ORIGIN Latin *flebilis* 'lamentable'.
feeble-minded • adj. foolish; stupid.
feed • v. (**feeds**, **feeding**, **fed**) **1** give food to. **2** provide enough food for. **3** eat. **4** supply with material, power, information, etc. **5** pass (something) gradually through a confined space. • n. **1** an act of feeding or of being fed. **2** food for domestic animals. **3** a device for supplying material to a machine. **4** the supply of raw material to a machine.
– ORIGIN Old English.
feedback • n. **1** comments about a product or a person's performance, used as a basis for improvement. **2** the return of a fraction of the output of an amplifier, microphone, or other device to the input of the same device, causing distortion or a whistling sound.
feeder • n. **1** a person or animal that eats a particular food or in a particular way. **2** a thing that feeds or supplies something. **3** a road or rail route linking outlying districts with a main system.
feel • v. (**feels**, **feeling**, **felt**) **1** be aware of, examine, or search by touch. **2** be aware of through physical sensation. **3** give a sensation when touched: *the wool feels soft*. **4** experience (an emotion or sensation). **5** be affected by. **6** have a belief or opinion. **7** (**feel up to**) have the strength or energy to. • n. **1** an act of feeling. **2** the sense of touch. **3** an impression: *the restaurant has a bistro feel*.
– PHRASES **get a feel for** become used to. **have a feel for** have a sensitive appreciation of.
– ORIGIN Old English.
feeler • n. **1** an organ such as an antenna, used by some animals for testing things by touch. **2** a cautious proposal intended to find out someone's attitude or opinion.
feeling • n. **1** an emotional state or reaction: *a feeling of joy*. **2** (**feelings**) the emotional side of a person's character. **3** strong emotion. **4** the capacity to feel. **5** the sensation of touching or being touched: *the feeling of water against your skin*. **6** a belief or opinion. **7** (**feeling for**) an understanding of.
– DERIVATIVES **feelingly** adv.
feet pl. of **FOOT**.
feign • v. pretend to feel or have: *she feigned nervousness*.
– ORIGIN Old French *feindre*.
feint¹ /faynt/ • n. a deceptive or pretended attacking movement in boxing or fencing. • v. make a feint.
– ORIGIN French *feindre* 'pretend'.
feint² /faynt/ • adj. (of paper) printed with faint lines as a guide for handwriting.
– ORIGIN from **FAINT**.
feisty /fy-sti/ • adj. (**feistier**, **feistiest**) informal spirited and lively.
– ORIGIN from former *feist* 'small dog'.
feldspar /feld-spar/ (also **felspar**) • n. a mineral forming igneous rocks, consisting chiefly of aluminium silicates.
– ORIGIN German *Feldspat* 'field spar'.
felicitations • pl. n. congratulations.
felicitous /fuh-liss-i-tuhss/ • adj. well chosen or appropriate.
felicity • n. (pl. **felicities**) **1** great happiness. **2** the ability to express oneself in an appropriate or pleasing way. **3** an appropriate or well-chosen feature of a work of literature.
– ORIGIN Latin *felicitas*.
feline /fee-lyn/ • adj. having to do with a cat or cats. • n. a cat or other animal of the cat family.
– ORIGIN Latin *feles* 'cat'.
fell¹ past of **FALL**.
fell² • v. **1** cut down (a tree). **2** knock down.
– ORIGIN Old English.
fell³ • n. a hill or stretch of high moorland in northern England.
– ORIGIN Old Norse.
fell⁴ • adj. literary extremely evil or fierce.
– PHRASES **in** (or **at**) **one fell swoop** all in one go.
– ORIGIN Old French *fel*.
fellatio /fe-lay-shi-oh/ • n. stimulation of a man's penis using the tongue or lips.
– ORIGIN Latin *fellare* 'to suck'.

Fellini E
/fuh-lee-ni/, Federico (1920–93), Italian film director, whose films include *8½* and *La Dolce vita*.

fellow ● n. **1** informal a man or boy. **2** a person in the same situation, activity, or otherwise associated with another: *the rebel was murdered by his fellows*. **3** a thing of the same kind as another. **4** a member of a learned society. **5** Brit. a member of the governing body of certain colleges. ● adj. sharing a particular situation or condition: *a fellow sufferer*.
– ORIGIN Old English, 'partner'.

fellow feeling ● n. sympathy based on shared experiences.

fellowship ● n. **1** friendliness and companionship based on shared interests. **2** a group of people meeting to pursue a shared interest or aim. **3** the position of a fellow of a college or society.

fellow-traveller ● n. a person who sympathizes with the Communist Party but is not a member of it.

felon /fe-luhn/ ● n. a person who has committed a felony.
– ORIGIN Old French, 'wicked person'.

felonious /fi-**loh**-ni-uhss/ ● adj. having to do with crime.

felony ● n. (pl. **felonies**) (in the US and formerly also in English Law) a serious crime.

felspar /fel-spar/ ● n. var. of FELDSPAR.

felt[1] ● n. cloth made by rolling and pressing wool accompanied by the application of moisture or heat, which causes the fibres to become matted.
– ORIGIN Old English.

felt[2] past and past part. of FEEL.

female ● adj. **1** referring to the sex that can bear offspring or produce eggs. **2** having to do with women: *a female name*. **3** (of a plant or flower) having a pistil but no stamens. **4** (of a fitting) manufactured hollow so that a corresponding male part can be inserted. ● n. a female person, animal, or plant.
– ORIGIN Latin *femina* 'woman'.

feminine ● adj. **1** having qualities associated with women, especially delicacy and prettiness. **2** female. **3** Grammar (of a gender of nouns and adjectives in certain languages) treated as female.
– DERIVATIVES **femininity** n.
– ORIGIN Latin *femina* 'woman'.

feminism ● n. a movement or theory supporting women's rights on the grounds of equality of the sexes.
– DERIVATIVES **feminist** n. & adj.

feminize (also **feminise**) ● v. (**feminizes**, **feminizing**, **feminized**) make more feminine or female.
– DERIVATIVES **feminization** (also **feminisation**) n.

femme fatale /fam fuh-**tahl**/ ● n. (pl. **femmes fatales** /fam fuh-**tahl**/) an attractive and seductive woman.
– ORIGIN French, 'disastrous woman'.

femur /fee-mer/ ● n. (pl. **femurs** or **femora** /fem-uh-ruh/) the bone of the thigh.
– DERIVATIVES **femoral** /fem-uh-ruhl/ adj.
– ORIGIN Latin, 'thigh'.

fen ● n. a low and marshy or frequently flooded area of land.
– ORIGIN Old English.

fence ● n. **1** a barrier enclosing an area, consisting of posts connected by wire, wood, etc. **2** a large upright obstacle in steeplechasing, showjumping, or cross-country. **3** informal a dealer in stolen goods. ● v. (**fences**, **fencing**, **fenced**) **1** surround or protect with a fence. **2** informal deal in (stolen goods). **3** practise the sport of fencing.
– PHRASES **sit on the fence** avoid making a decision.
– DERIVATIVES **fencer** n.
– ORIGIN from DEFENCE.

fencing ● n. **1** the sport of fighting with blunted swords in order to score points. **2** fences or material for making fences.

fend ● v. **1** (**fend for oneself**) look after and provide for oneself. **2** (**fend off**) defend oneself from.
– ORIGIN from DEFEND.

fender ● n. **1** a low frame around a fireplace to keep in falling coals. **2** a cushioning device hung over a ship's side to protect it against impact. **3** N. Amer. the mudguard or area around the wheel well of a vehicle.

feng shui /feng **shoo**-i, fung **shway**/ ● n. an ancient Chinese system of designing buildings and positioning objects inside buildings to ensure a favourable flow of energy.
– ORIGIN Chinese, 'wind' and 'water'.

fennel /fen-n'l/ ● n. a plant, the leaves and seeds of which are used as a herb, and the base of which is eaten as a vegetable.
– ORIGIN Latin *faeniculum*.

fenugreek /fen-yuu-greek/ ● n. a plant with seeds that are used as a spice.
– ORIGIN from Latin *faenum graecum* 'Greek hay'.

feral /fe-ruhl/ ● adj. **1** (of an animal or plant) wild, especially after having been domesticated. **2** fierce.
– ORIGIN Latin *ferus* 'wild'.

Ferdinand E
/fer-di-nand/ of Aragon (1452–1516), king of Castile 1474–1516 and of Aragon 1479–1516. He ruled Castile and Aragon with his wife Isabella, and their capture of Granada from the Moors in 1492 effectively united Spain.

Fermanagh E
/fer-**man**-uh/ one of the Six Counties of Northern Ireland; chief town, Enniskillen.

Fermat E
/fer-mah/, Pierre de (1601–65), French mathematician. His work on curves led directly to the general methods of calculus introduced by Newton and Leibniz. He is also recognized as the founder of the theory of numbers.

ferment ● v. /fer-**ment**/ **1** undergo or cause to undergo fermentation. **2** stir up (disorder). ● n. /fer-ment/ social unrest or disorder.
– ORIGIN Latin *fermentum* 'yeast'.

fermentation ● n. the chemical breakdown of a substance by bacteria, yeasts, or other micro-organisms, such as when sugar is converted into alcohol.

Fermi E
/fair-mi, fer-mi/, Enrico (1901–54), Italian-born American atomic physicist, who directed the first controlled nuclear chain reaction in 1942.

fermium /fer-mi-uhm/ ● **n.** an unstable radioactive chemical element made by high-energy atomic collisions.
– ORIGIN named after Enrico **Fermi**.

fern ● **n.** (pl. **fern** or **ferns**) a flowerless plant which has feathery or leafy fronds and reproduces by means of spores.
– DERIVATIVES **ferny** adj.
– ORIGIN Old English.

ferocious /fuh-roh-shuss/ ● **adj.** savagely fierce, cruel, or violent.
– DERIVATIVES **ferociously** adv.
– ORIGIN Latin *ferox* 'fierce'.

ferocity /fuh-ross-i-ti/ ● **n.** the state of being ferocious.

-ferous (usu. **-iferous**) ● **comb. form** having or containing: *Carboniferous*.
– ORIGIN Latin *-fer* 'producing'.

Ferrari E
/fuh-rah-ri/, Enzo (1898–1988), Italian car designer and manufacturer, who in 1929 founded the company named after him, producing a range of sports and racing cars.

ferret /fe-rit/ ● **n.** a domesticated albino or brown polecat, used for catching rabbits. ● **v.** (**ferrets**, **ferreting**, **ferreted**) **1** (**ferreting**) hunting with ferrets. **2** search for something in a place or container. **3** (**ferret out**) discover by determined searching.
– DERIVATIVES **ferrety** adj.
– ORIGIN Old French *fuiret*.

ferric /fe-rik/ ● **adj.** Chem. relating to iron with a valency of three.
– ORIGIN Latin *ferrum* 'iron'.

Ferrier E
/fe-ri-er/, Kathleen (1912–53), English contralto.

Ferris wheel ● **n.** a fairground ride consisting of a giant vertical revolving wheel with passenger cars hanging from its outer edge.
– ORIGIN named after the American engineer George W. G. *Ferris* (1859–96).

ferroconcrete ● **n.** concrete reinforced with steel.

ferrous /fe-ruhss/ ● **adj.** **1** (of metals) containing iron. **2** Chem. relating to iron with a valency of two.

ferrule /fe-rool/ ● **n.** a metal ring or cap which strengthens the end of a handle, stick, or tube.
– ORIGIN Old French *virelle*.

ferry ● **n.** (pl. **ferries**) a boat that transports passengers and goods as a regular service. ● **v.** (**ferries**, **ferrying**, **ferried**) carry by ferry or other transport.
– ORIGIN Old Norse.

fertile ● **adj.** **1** (of soil or land) producing abundant vegetation or crops. **2** (of a person, animal, or plant) able to conceive young or produce seed. **3** productive in generating ideas: *a fertile debate*.
– DERIVATIVES **fertility** n.
– ORIGIN Latin *fertilis*.

fertilize (also **fertilise**) ● **v.** (**fertilizes**, **fertilizing**, **fertilized**) **1** introduce sperm or pollen into (an egg, female animal, or plant) to develop a new individual. **2** add fertilizer to.
– DERIVATIVES **fertilization** (also **fertilisation**) n.

fertilizer (also **fertiliser**) ● **n.** a chemical or natural substance added to soil to increase its fertility.

fervent /fer-vuhnt/ ● **adj.** very passionate.
– DERIVATIVES **fervently** adv.
– ORIGIN Latin *fervere* 'to boil'.

fervid ● **adj.** fervent.
– ORIGIN Latin *fervidus*.

fervour (US **fervor**) ● **n.** passionate feeling.

Fès E
var. of **Fez**.

festal ● **adj.** relating to a festival.
– ORIGIN Latin *festa* 'feast'.

fester ● **v.** (**festers**, **festering**, **festered**) **1** (of a wound or sore) become septic. **2** become rotten. **3** become worse: *tensions began to fester between Rose and Nick*.
– ORIGIN Old French *festrir*.

festival ● **n.** **1** a day or period of celebration. **2** an organized series of concerts, films, etc.
– ORIGIN Latin *festa* 'feast'.

Festival of Britain E
a festival celebrated with exhibitions and shows throughout Britain in 1951 to mark the centenary of the Great Exhibition of 1851.

festive ● **adj.** relating to or suitable for a festival: *the festive season*.

festivity ● **n.** (pl. **festivities**) **1** joyful celebration. **2** (**festivities**) activities or events celebrating a special occasion.

festoon /fess-toon/ ● **n.** an ornamental chain of flowers, leaves, or ribbons, hung in a curve. ● **v.** decorate with festoons or other decorations.
– ORIGIN Italian *festone* 'festive ornament'.

feta /fet-uh/ ● **n.** a salty Greek cheese made from the milk of ewes or goats.
– ORIGIN modern Greek *pheta*.

fetal /fee-t'l/ ● **adj.** relating to a fetus.

fetch ● **v.** **1** go for and bring back. **2** sell for (a particular price). **3** (**fetch up**) informal arrive or come to rest somewhere. **4** (**fetching**) attractive.
– PHRASES **fetch and carry** run errands for someone in a servile way.
– ORIGIN Old English.

fête /fayt/ ● **n.** Brit. an outdoor public event to raise funds for charity, involving entertainment and the sale of goods. ● **v.** (**fêtes**, **fêting**, **fêted**) honour or entertain lavishly.
– ORIGIN French.

fetid /fet-id/ (also **foetid**) ● **adj.** smelling very unpleasant.
– ORIGIN Latin *fetidus*.

fetish ● **n.** **1** an object worshipped for its supposed magical powers. **2** a form of sexual desire in which satisfaction is focused abnormally on an object, part of the body, etc. **3** something to which a person is obsessively devoted: *he had a fetish about purity*.
– DERIVATIVES **fetishism** n. **fetishist** n.
– ORIGIN French *fétiche*.

fetlock ● **n.** a joint of a horse's leg between the knee and the hoof.
– ORIGIN Germanic.

fetor /fee-ter/ ● **n.** a strong, foul smell.
– ORIGIN Latin.

fetter ● **n.** **1** a chain or shackle placed around a prisoner's ankles. **2** (**fetters**) restraints or controls. ● **v.** (**fetters**, **fettering**, **fettered**) **1** restrain with fetters. **2** (**be fettered**) be restricted.

– ORIGIN Old English.

fettle ● n. condition: *the three horses were in fine fettle.*

– ORIGIN Old English, 'strip of material'.

fettuccine /fet-tuh-chee-ni/ ● pl. n. pasta made in ribbons.

– ORIGIN Italian, 'little ribbons'.

fetus /fee-tuhss/ (Brit. (in non-technical use) also **foetus**) ● n. (pl. **fetuses**) an unborn offspring of a mammal, in particular an unborn human more than eight weeks after conception.

– ORIGIN Latin, 'pregnancy, birth'.

feud ● n. a long-lasting and bitter dispute. ● v. take part in a feud.

– ORIGIN Old French *feide* 'hostility'.

feudal ● adj. having to do with feudalism.

– ORIGIN Latin *feodum* 'fee'.

feudalism ● n. the dominant social system in medieval Europe, in which the nobility held lands from the Crown in exchange for military service, and lower orders of society held lands from and worked for the nobles.

fever ● n. **1** an abnormally high body temperature. **2** a state of nervous excitement or agitation.

– DERIVATIVES **feverish** adj.

– ORIGIN Latin *febris.*

fevered ● adj. **1** affected with fever. **2** nervously excited or agitated.

feverfew ● n. a plant with daisy-like flowers, used as a herbal remedy for headaches.

– ORIGIN from Latin *febris* 'fever' + *fugare* 'drive away'.

fever pitch ● n. a state of extreme excitement.

few ● det., pron., & adj. **1** (**a few**) a small number of; some. **2** not many: *he had few friends.* ● n. (**the few**) a small group of people with special powers or privileges.

– PHRASES **a good few** Brit. a fairly large number of. **quite a few** a fairly large number.

– ORIGIN Old English.

USAGE few

Many people use the words **fewer** and **less** incorrectly. The rule is that **fewer** should be used with plural nouns, as in *eat fewer cakes* or *there are fewer people here today.* Use **less** with nouns referring to things that cannot be counted, as in *there is less blossom on this tree.* It is wrong to use **less** with a plural noun (*less people, less cakes*).

fey /fay/ ● adj. **1** unworldly and vague. **2** able to see into the future.

– ORIGIN Old English.

Feydeau E
/fay-doh/, Georges (1862–1921), French dramatist, famous for farces such as *Hotel Paradiso* and *Le Dindon.*

Feynman E
/fyn-muhn/, Richard Phillips (1918–88), American theoretical physicist, who introduced important new methods for studying the electromagnetic interactions between subatomic particles.

Fez E
(also **Fès**) a city in northern Morocco.

fez ● n. (pl. **fezzes**) a flat-topped conical red hat, worn by men in some Muslim countries.

– ORIGIN named after **FEZ**.

ff. ● abbrev. following pages.

fiancé /fi-on-say/ ● n. (fem. **fiancée** /fi-on-say/) a person to whom another is engaged to be married.

– ORIGIN French.

fiasco /fi-ass-koh/ ● n. (pl. **fiascos**) a ridiculous or humiliating failure.

– ORIGIN from Italian *far fiasco* 'fail in a performance' (literally 'make a bottle').

fiat /fy-at/ ● n. an official order or authorization.

– ORIGIN Latin, 'let it be done'.

fib ● n. a trivial lie. ● v. (**fibs, fibbing, fibbed**) tell a fib.

– DERIVATIVES **fibber** n.

– ORIGIN perh. from **FABLE**.

fiber ● n. US = **FIBRE**.

fiberboard ● n. US = **FIBREBOARD**.

fiberglass ● n. US = **FIBREGLASS**.

Fibonacci series /fi-buh-nah-chi/ ● n. Math. a series of numbers in which each number (**Fibonacci number**) is the sum of the two preceding numbers (e.g. the series 1, 1, 2, 3, 5, 8, etc.).

– ORIGIN named after the Italian mathematician Leonardo *Fibonacci* (*c.*1170–*c.*1250).

fibre (US **fiber**) ● n. **1** a thread or strand from which a plant or animal tissue, mineral substance, or textile is formed. **2** a substance formed of fibres. **3** substances in vegetables, fruit, and some other foods, that are difficult to digest and therefore help the passage of food through the body. **4** strength of character: *he's lacking in moral fibre.*

– ORIGIN Latin *fibra* 'fibre, entrails'.

fibreboard (US **fiberboard**) ● n. a building material made of compressed wood fibres.

fibreglass (US **fiberglass**) ● n. **1** a reinforced plastic material containing glass fibres. **2** a textile fabric made from woven glass fibres.

fibre optics ● n. the use of thin flexible transparent fibres to transmit light signals, used for telecommunications or for internal inspection of the body.

– DERIVATIVES **fibre-optic** adj.

fibril /fy-bril/ ● n. tech. a small or slender fibre.

– ORIGIN Latin *fibrilla.*

fibrin /fy-brin/ ● n. an insoluble protein formed as a fibrous mesh during the clotting of blood.

fibroid ● adj. relating to fibres or fibrous tissue. ● n. a non-cancerous tumour of fibrous tissues, developing in the womb.

fibrosis /fy-broh-siss/ ● n. Med. the thickening and scarring of connective tissue, as a result of injury.

fibrous ● adj. having to do with or made of fibres.

fibula /fib-yuu-luh/ ● n. (pl. **fibulae** /fib-yuu-lee/ or **fibulas**) the outer of the two bones between the knee and the ankle, parallel with the tibia.

– ORIGIN Latin, 'brooch'.

fickle ● adj. changeable in one's loyalties.

– ORIGIN Old English, 'deceitful'.

fiction ● n. **1** literature in prose form. describing imaginary events and people. **2** a false belief or statement.

– ORIGIN Latin.

fictional ● adj. having to do with fiction.

fictionalize (also **fictionalise**) ● v. (**fictionalizes, fictionalizing, fictionalized**) make into a fictional story.

fictitious /fik-tish-uhss/ ● adj. **1** imaginary or invented; not real. **2** referring to fiction.

fiddle informal ● n. **1** a violin. **2** Brit. an act of fraud or cheating. ● v. (**fiddles, fiddling, fiddled**) **1** touch or handle something restlessly or nervously. **2** esp. Brit. falsify: *everyone is fiddling their expenses.*
– PHRASES **fit as a fiddle** in very good health. **play second fiddle to** take a less important role to.
– DERIVATIVES **fiddler** n.
– ORIGIN Old English.

fiddlesticks ● exclam. informal, dated nonsense.

fiddly ● adj. Brit. informal complicated and awkward to do or use.

fidelity /fi-del-i-ti/ ● n. **1** continuing faithfulness to a person, cause, or belief. **2** the degree of exactness with which something is copied or reproduced.
– ORIGIN Latin *fidelis* 'faithful'.

fidget /fi-jit/ ● v. (**fidgets, fidgeting, fidgeted**) make small movements through nervousness or impatience. ● n. a person who fidgets.
– DERIVATIVES **fidgety** adj.
– ORIGIN from former *fidge* 'to twitch'.

fief /feef/ ● n. **1** hist. an estate of land held on condition of feudal service. **2** a person's area of operation or control.
– DERIVATIVES **fiefdom** n.
– ORIGIN Old French.

field ● n. **1** an area of open land, planted with crops or used for grazing animals. **2** a piece of land used for a sport or game. **3** a subject of study or area of activity. **4** a space within which a particular property has an effect: *a magnetic field.* **5** a range within which objects are visible. **6** (**the field**) all the participants in a contest or sport. ● v. **1** Cricket & Baseball attempt to catch or stop the ball and return it after it has been hit. **2** select (someone) to play in a game or to stand in an election. **3** try to deal with: *we frantically fielded phone calls.* ● adj. **1** carried out or working in the natural environment, rather than in a laboratory or office. **2** (of military equipment) light and mobile for use on campaign.
– PHRASES **in the field 1** (of troops) engaged in combat or manoeuvres. **2** engaged in practical work in the natural environment. **play the field** informal have a series of casual sexual relationships.
– DERIVATIVES **fielder** n.
– ORIGIN Old English.

field day ● n. an opportunity to do something without being hindered.

field events ● pl. n. athletic sports other than races, such as throwing and jumping events.

fieldfare ● n. a large thrush with a grey head.
– ORIGIN Old English.

field glasses ● pl. n. binoculars.

> **Fielding**, **E**
> Henry (1707–54), English novelist, author of *Tom Jones*. Fielding was also responsible for the formation of the police force known as the Bow Street Runners (1749).

field marshal ● n. the highest rank of officer in the British army.

field mouse ● n. a common dark brown mouse with a long tail and large eyes.

field officer ● n. a major, lieutenant colonel, or colonel.

> **Fields[1]**, **E**
> Dame Gracie (1898–1979; born *Grace Stansfield*), English singer and comedienne, famous for her music-hall appearances.

> **Fields[2]**, **E**
> W. C. (1880–1946; born *William Claude Dukenfield*), American comedian and actor.

field sports ● pl. n. the sports of hunting, shooting, and fishing.

field test (also **field trial**) ● n. a test carried out in the place in which a product is to be used.

fieldwork ● n. practical work carried out by a researcher in the field.

fiend /feend/ ● n. **1** an evil spirit. **2** a very wicked or cruel person. **3** informal an enthusiast: *an exercise fiend.*
– ORIGIN Old English, 'an enemy'.

fiendish ● adj. **1** extremely cruel or unpleasant. **2** extremely difficult.
– DERIVATIVES **fiendishly** adv.

fierce ● adj. **1** violent or aggressive. **2** intense or powerful: *fierce opposition.*
– DERIVATIVES **fiercely** adv. **fierceness** n.
– ORIGIN Latin *ferus* 'untamed'.

fiery ● adj. (**fierier, fieriest**) **1** consisting of or resembling fire. **2** quick-tempered or passionate.

fiesta /fi-ess-tuh/ ● n. (in Spanish-speaking countries) a religious festival.
– ORIGIN Spanish.

FIFA /fee-fuh/ ● abbrev. Fédération Internationale de Football Association, the international governing body of soccer.

> **Fife** **E**
> an administrative region of east central Scotland; administrative centre, Glenrothes.

fife ● n. a small high-pitched flute played in military bands.
– ORIGIN German *Pfeife* 'pipe'.

fifteen ● cardinal number **1** one more than fourteen; 15. (Roman numeral: **xv** or **XV**.) **2** a Rugby Union team of fifteen players.
– DERIVATIVES **fifteenth** ordinal number.
– ORIGIN Old English.

fifth ● ordinal number **1** that is number five in a sequence; 5th. **2** (**a fifth/one fifth**) each of five equal parts into which something is divided. **3** a musical interval spanning five consecutive notes in a scale.

fifth column ● n. a group within a country at war who are working for its enemies.
– DERIVATIVES **fifth columnist** n.
– ORIGIN from a general in the Spanish Civil War, who while leading four columns of troops towards Madrid, said that he had a fifth column inside the city.

fifty ● cardinal number (pl. **fifties**) ten less than sixty; 50. (Roman numeral: **l** or **L**.)
– DERIVATIVES **fiftieth** ordinal number.
– ORIGIN Old English.

fifty-fifty ● adj. & adv. with equal shares or chances.

fig[1] ● n. a soft sweet pear-shaped fruit with

many small seeds.
– ORIGIN Latin *ficus*.

fig[2] ● **n.** (in phr. **in full fig**) informal wearing the complete set of clothes appropriate to a particular occasion or profession.
– ORIGIN from former *feague* 'liven up'.

fight ● **v.** (**fights**, **fighting**, **fought**) **1** take part in a violent struggle involving physical force or weapons. **2** take part in (a war or contest). **3** (**fight off**) defend oneself against an attack by. **4** struggle to overcome or prevent: *she fought racial discrimination.* **5** (**fight for**) try very hard to obtain or do. ● **n.** an act of fighting.
– PHRASES **fight shy of** avoid through unwillingness. **fight one's way** move forward with difficulty.
– ORIGIN Old English.

fighter ● **n. 1** a person or animal that fights. **2** a fast military aircraft designed for attacking other aircraft.

fighting chance ● **n.** a possibility of success if great effort is made.

fighting fit ● **adj.** in excellent health.

fig leaf ● **n.** a leaf of a fig tree, used to conceal the genitals of naked people in art.

figment /fig-muhnt/ ● **n.** a thing that exists only in the imagination.
– ORIGIN Latin *figmentum*.

figurative ● **adj. 1** not using words in their literal sense; metaphorical. **2** (of art) representing people or things as they appear in real life.
– DERIVATIVES **figuratively** adv.

figure ● **n. 1** a number or numerical symbol. **2** a person's bodily shape, especially that of a woman. **3** an important or distinctive person: *senior figures in politics.* **4** a geometrical or decorative shape defined by one or more lines. **5** a diagram or illustrative drawing. **6** a short succession of musical notes from which longer passages are developed. ● **v.** (**figures**, **figuring**, **figured**) **1** play an important part: *nuclear policy figured prominently in the talks.* **2** calculate arithmetically. **3** (**figure out**) informal understand. **4** N. Amer. informal think; consider.
– ORIGIN Latin *figura*.

figurehead ● **n. 1** a carved bust or full-length figure at the prow of an old-fashioned sailing ship. **2** a leader without real power.

figure of speech ● **n.** a word or phrase used in a non-literal sense to add interest to speech or writing.

figure skating ● **n.** the sport of skating in set patterns.

figurine /fi-guh-reen/ ● **n.** a small statue of a human form.
– ORIGIN Italian *figurina* 'small figure'.

Fiji E
/fee-jee/ a country in the South Pacific consisting of a group of some 840 islands; capital, Suva.
– DERIVATIVES **Fijian** n. & adj.

filament /fil-uh-muhnt/ ● **n. 1** a slender thread-like object. **2** a metal wire in an electric light bulb, which glows white-hot when an electric current is passed through it.
– ORIGIN Latin *filamentum*.

filbert ● **n.** a cultivated hazelnut.
– ORIGIN from French *noix de filbert* (because it ripens around 20 August, the feast day of St Philibert).

filch ● **v.** informal steal.
– ORIGIN unknown.

file[1] ● **n. 1** a folder or box for keeping loose papers together and in order. **2** Computing a collection of data or programs stored under a single identifying name. **3** a line of people or things one behind another. ● **v.** (**files**, **filing**, **filed**) **1** place in a file. **2** place (a legal document, application, or charge) on record. **3** walk one behind the other.
– ORIGIN Latin *filum* 'a thread'.

file[2] ● **n.** a tool with a roughened surface or surfaces, used for smoothing or shaping. ● **v.** (**files**, **filing**, **filed**) smooth or shape with a file.
– ORIGIN Old English.

filial /fil-i-uhl/ ● **adj.** having to do with a son or daughter.
– ORIGIN Latin *filialis*.

filibuster /fil-i-buss-ter/ ● **n.** prolonged speaking which obstructs progress in a law-making assembly. ● **v.** (**filibusters**, **filibustering**, **filibustered**) obstruct legislation with a filibuster.
– ORIGIN French *flibustier*, first referring to pirates in the West Indies.

filigree /fil-i-gree/ ● **n.** delicate ornamental work of fine gold, silver, or copper wire.
– DERIVATIVES **filigreed** adj.
– ORIGIN from Latin *filum* 'thread' + *granum* 'seed'.

filings ● **pl. n.** small particles rubbed off by a file.

Filipino /fi-li-pee-noh/ ● **n.** (pl. **Filipinos**; fem. **Filipina**, pl. **Filipinas**) **1** a person from the Philippines. **2** the national language of the Philippines. ● **adj.** relating to the Philippines or to Filipinos.
– ORIGIN Spanish.

fill ● **v. 1** make or become full. **2** block up (a hole, gap, etc.). **3** appoint a person to (a vacant post). **4** hold and perform the duties of (a position or role). **5** occupy (time). ● **n.** (**one's fill**) as much as one wants or can bear.
– PHRASES **fill in 1** complete (a form). **2** inform (someone) more fully of a matter. **3** act as a substitute. **fill out** put on weight.
– ORIGIN Old English.

filler ● **n.** something used to fill a gap or cavity, or to increase bulk.

fillet ● **n. 1** a boneless piece of meat from near the loins or the ribs of an animal. **2** a boned side of a fish. **3** a band or ribbon binding the hair. ● **v.** (**fillets**, **filleting**, **filleted**) remove the bones from (a fish).
– ORIGIN Old French *filet* 'thread'.

filling ● **n.** a quantity or piece of material used to fill something. ● **adj.** (of food) leaving one with a pleasantly full feeling.

filling station ● **n.** a petrol station.

fillip /fil-lip/ ● **n.** a stimulus or boost.

Fillmore, E
Millard (1800–74), American Whig statesman, 13th President of the US 1850–3.

filly ● **n.** (pl. **fillies**) **1** a young female horse. **2** humorous a lively girl or young woman.
– ORIGIN Old Norse.

film ● **n. 1** a thin flexible strip of plastic or other material coated with light-sensitive material, used in a camera to make photographs

or motion pictures. **2** a story or event recorded by a camera and shown in a cinema or on television. **3** motion pictures considered as an art or industry: *feminist writings on film.* **4** material in the form of a very thin flexible sheet. **5** a thin layer covering a surface. ● **v.** make a film of.
– ORIGIN Old English, 'membrane'.

film star ● **n.** a well-known film actor or actress.

filmy ● **adj. 1** thin and almost transparent: *a filmy black dress.* **2** covered with a thin film.

filo /fee-loh/ (also **phyllo**) ● **n.** a kind of Greek flaky pastry in the form of very thin sheets.
– ORIGIN modern Greek *phullo* 'leaf'.

Filofax /fy-loh-faks/ ● **n.** trademark a loose-leaf notebook for recording appointments, addresses, and notes.

filter ● **n. 1** a device or substance that allows liquid or gas to pass through it, but holds back any solid particles. **2** a screen, plate, or layer which absorbs some of the light passing through it. **3** Brit. an arrangement at a junction whereby vehicles may turn while traffic waiting to go straight ahead is stopped by a red light. ● **v.** (**filters**, **filtering**, **filtered**) **1** pass through a filter. **2** move gradually in or out of somewhere. **3** (of information) gradually become known.
– ORIGIN Latin *filtrum* 'felt used as a filter'.

filter tip ● **n.** a filter attached to a cigarette that traps impurities from the smoke.

filth ● **n. 1** disgusting dirt. **2** obscene and offensive language or printed material.
– ORIGIN Old English.

filthy ● **adj.** (**filthier**, **filthiest**) **1** disgustingly dirty. **2** obscene and offensive. **3** informal very unpleasant. ● **adv.** informal extremely: *he ended up filthy rich.*

filtrate /fil-trayt/ ● **n.** a liquid which has passed through a filter.

filtration /fil-tray-sh'n/ ● **n.** the action of passing something through a filter.

fin ● **n. 1** a flattened part that projects from the body of a fish, dolphin, etc., used for swimming and balancing. **2** a part that projects from an aircraft, rocket, or car, for providing stability.
– ORIGIN Old English.

final ● **adj. 1** coming at the end; last. **2** allowing no further doubt or dispute: *the decision of the judges is final.* ● **n. 1** the last game in a tournament, which will decide the overall winner. **2** (**finals**) Brit. a series of examinations at the end of a degree course.
– ORIGIN Latin *finalis.*

finale /fi-nah-li/ ● **n.** the last part of a piece of music, an entertainment, or a public event.
– ORIGIN Italian.

finalist ● **n.** a person or team competing in a final.

finality ● **n.** the fact or quality of being final.

finalize (also **finalise**) ● **v.** (**finalizes**, **finalizing**, **finalized**) decide on or complete (a plan or agreement).

finally ● **adv. 1** after a long time and much difficulty. **2** as a final point.

finance /fy-nanss/ ● **n. 1** the management of large amounts of money by governments or large companies. **2** funds to support an enterprise. **3** (**finances**) the money available to a state, organization, or person. ● **v.** (**finances**, **financing**, **financed**) provide funding for.
– ORIGIN Old French.

finance company (also **finance house**) ● **n.** a company concerned mainly with providing money, e.g. for hire-purchase transactions.

financial ● **adj.** relating to finance.
– DERIVATIVES **financially** adv.

financial year ● **n.** a year as reckoned for taxing or accounting purposes, especially the British tax year reckoned from 6 April.

financier /fy-nan-si-er/ ● **n.** a person who manages the finances of large organizations.
– ORIGIN French.

finch ● **n.** a songbird of a large group including the chaffinch, goldfinch, etc., most of which have short stubby bills.
– ORIGIN Old English.

find ● **v.** (**finds**, **finding**, **found**) **1** discover by chance or by searching. **2** recognize or discover to be present or to be the case. **3** work out or confirm by research or calculation. **4** (of a law court) officially declare to be the case: *he was found guilty of speeding.* **5** reach or arrive at (a state or point) by a natural or normal process: *water finds its own level.* ● **n.** a valuable or interesting discovery.
– PHRASES **find one's feet** become confident in a new situation. **find out 1** discover (information). **2** discover that (someone) has lied or been dishonest.
– ORIGIN Old English.

finder ● **n. 1** a person who finds someone or something. **2** a viewfinder in a camera.

finding ● **n.** a conclusion reached as a result of an inquiry, investigation, or trial.

fine[1] ● **adj. 1** of very high quality. **2** satisfactory. **3** in good health and feeling well. **4** (of the weather) bright and clear. **5** (of a thread, strand, or hair) thin. **6** consisting of small particles: *fine sand.* **7** of delicate or complex workmanship. **8** difficult to distinguish because precise or subtle: *the ear makes fine distinctions between different noises.* ● **adv.** informal in a satisfactory or pleasing manner.
– PHRASES **cut it fine** allow only just enough time for something. **not to put too fine a point on it** to speak bluntly.
– DERIVATIVES **finely** adv. **fineness** n.
ORIGIN Old French *fin.*

fine[2] ● **n.** a sum of money imposed as a punishment by a court of law or other authority. ● **v.** (**fines**, **fining**, **fined**) punish by a fine.
– ORIGIN Old French *fin* 'end, payment'.

fine art ● **n.** art intended to appeal to the sense of beauty, such as painting or sculpture.

fine print ● **n.** = SMALL PRINT.

finery /fy-nuh-ri/ ● **n.** showy clothes or decoration.

finesse /fi-ness/ ● **n. 1** elegant or delicate skill: *his acting showed dignity and finesse.* **2** subtle skill in handling people or situations. ● **v.** (**finesses**, **finessing**, **finessed**) do in a skilful and delicate manner.
– ORIGIN French.

fine-tooth comb (also **fine-toothed comb**) ● **n.** (in phr. **with a fine-tooth comb**) with a very thorough search or examination.

fine-tune ● **v.** (**fine-tunes**, **fine-tuning**, **fine-tuned**) make small adjustments to (something) so as to improve performance.

finger ● n. **1** each of the four jointed parts attached to either hand (or five, if the thumb is included). **2** a measure of liquor in a glass, based on the breadth of a finger. **3** an object with the long, narrow shape of a finger. ● v. (**fingers**, **fingering**, **fingered**) touch or feel with the fingers.
– PHRASES **be all fingers and thumbs** Brit. informal be clumsy. **have a finger in the pie** be involved in a matter. **lay a finger on** touch (someone) with the intention of harming them. **pull one's finger out** Brit. informal stop hesitating and start to act. **put one's finger on** identify exactly.
– ORIGIN Old English.

fingerboard ● n. a flat strip on the neck of a stringed instrument, against which the strings are pressed in order to vary the pitch.

finger bowl ● n. a small bowl holding water for rinsing the fingers at a meal.

fingering ● n. a way or technique of using the fingers to play a musical instrument.

fingernail ● n. the nail on the upper surface of the tip of each finger.

fingerprint ● n. a mark made on a surface by a person's fingertip, used for identification. ● v. record the fingerprints of.

fingertip ● adj. using or operated by the fingers.
– PHRASES **at one's fingertips** (of information) readily available.

finial /fin-i-uhl/ ● n. an ornamental top or end of a roof or object.
– ORIGIN Latin *finis* 'end'.

finicky ● adj. **1** fussy. **2** excessively detailed or elaborate.

finish ● v. **1** bring or come to an end: *they were too exhausted to finish the job.* **2** eat or drink the whole or the remainder of (food or drink). **3** (**finish with**) have nothing more to do with. **4** reach the end of a race or other sporting competition. **5** (**finish off**) kill or completely defeat. **6** complete the manufacture or decoration of (something) by giving it an attractive surface appearance. ● n. **1** an end or final stage. **2** the place at which a race or competition ends. **3** the way in which a manufactured article is finished.
– DERIVATIVES **finisher** n.
– ORIGIN Latin *finire.*

finishing school ● n. a private college where girls are taught how to behave correctly in fashionable society.

finishing touch ● n. a detail that completes and improves a piece of work.

Finisterre, Cape E
/fin-i-**stair**/ a promontory of NW Spain, forming the westernmost point of the mainland.

finite /fy-nyt/ ● adj. limited in size or extent: *every computer has a finite amount of memory.*
– DERIVATIVES **finitely** adv.
– ORIGIN Latin *finitus* 'finished'.

Finland E
a country on the Baltic Sea, between Sweden and Russia; capital, Helsinki.

Finn ● n. a person from Finland.

Finnish ● n. the language of the Finns. ● adj. relating to the Finns.

fiord ● n. var. of FJORD.

fir ● n. an evergreen coniferous tree with upright cones and needle-shaped leaves.
– ORIGIN prob. Old Norse.

fire ● n. **1** the state of burning, in which substances combine with oxygen from the air and give out light, heat, and smoke. **2** an instance of burning in which buildings or their contents are destroyed. **3** wood or coal burnt in a hearth or stove for heating or cooking. **4** (also **electric fire** or **gas fire**) Brit. a heater for a room that uses electricity or gas as fuel. **5** passionate emotion or enthusiasm. **6** the firing of guns: *a burst of machine-gun fire.* ● v. (**fires**, **firing**, **fired**) **1** send (a bullet, shell, or missile) explosively from a gun or other weapon. **2** informal dismiss (an employee) from a job. **3** direct a rapid series of (questions or statements) towards someone. **4** supply (a furnace, power station, etc.) with fuel. **5** set fire to. **6** stimulate: *the idea fired his imagination.* **7** bake or dry (pottery or bricks) in a kiln.
– PHRASES **catch fire** begin to burn. **fire away** informal go ahead. **set fire to** (or **set on fire**) cause to burn. **set the world on fire** do something remarkable or sensational. **under fire** being shot at or strongly criticized.
– ORIGIN Old English.

fire alarm ● n. a device making a loud noise that gives warning of a fire.

firearm ● n. a rifle, pistol, or other portable gun.

firebomb ● n. a bomb intended to cause a fire.

firebrand ● n. a person who passionately supports a particular cause and often stirs up unrest.

firebreak ● n. a strip of open space in a forest to stop a fire from spreading.

fire brigade ● n. esp. Brit. an organized body of people trained and employed to put out fires.

firecracker ● n. a firework that makes a loud bang.

fire door ● n. a door made of fire-resistant material to prevent the spread of fire.

fire drill ● n. a practice of the emergency procedures to be used in case of fire.

fire engine ● n. a vehicle carrying firefighters and their equipment.

fire escape ● n. a staircase or ladder used for escaping from a building if there is a fire.

fire extinguisher ● n. a portable device that discharges a jet of liquid, foam, or gas to put out a fire.

firefighter ● n. a person whose job is to put out fires.

firefly ● n. a kind of beetle which glows in the dark.

fireguard ● n. a protective screen or grid placed in front of an open fire.

firelighter ● n. Brit. a piece of flammable material used to help start a fire.

fireman ● n. a male firefighter.

Fire of London E
the huge fire which destroyed some 13,000 houses over 400 acres of London between 2 and 6 September 1666, having started in a bakery.

fireplace ● n. a partially enclosed space at the base of a chimney for a domestic fire.

firepower ● n. the destructive capacity of guns, missiles, or a military force.

fireproof • adj. able to withstand fire or great heat.

fireside • n. the part of a room round a fireplace.

fire station • n. the headquarters of a fire brigade.

firestorm • n. a very fierce fire, fanned by strong currents of air drawn in from the surrounding area.

firetrap • n. a building without enough fire exits in case of fire.

firewall • n. a part of a computer system or network that blocks unauthorized access to a network while allowing outward communication.

firewater • n. informal strong alcoholic liquor.

firewood • n. wood that is burnt as fuel.

firework • n. **1** a device containing chemicals that is ignited to produce spectacular effects and explosions. **2** (**fireworks**) an outburst of anger or a display of skill.

firing line • n. **1** the front line of troops in a battle. **2** a position where one is likely to be criticized.

firing squad • n. a group of soldiers ordered to shoot a condemned person.

firm[1] • adj. **1** having a surface or structure that does not give way or sink under pressure. **2** solidly in place and stable. **3** having steady power or strength: *a firm grip.* **4** showing determination and strength of character. **5** fixed or definite: *she had no firm plans.* • v. make firm. • adv. in a determined manner: *she stood firm against the proposal.*
– DERIVATIVES **firmly** adv. **firmness** n.
ORIGIN Latin *firmus.*

firm[2] • n. a business organization.
– ORIGIN Latin *firmare* 'settle'.

firmament /fer-muh-muhnt/ • n. literary the heavens; the sky.
ORIGIN Latin *firmamentum.*

firmware • n. Computing permanent software programmed into a read-only memory.

first • ordinal number **1** coming before all others in time, order, or importance; 1st. **2** before doing something else. **3** informal something never previously done or occurring: *travelling by air was a first for us.* **4** Brit. a place in the top grade in an examination for a degree.
– PHRASES **at first** at the beginning. **first thing** early in the morning; before anything else. **of the first order** excellent or considerable of its kind.
– ORIGIN Old English.

first aid • n. emergency medical help given to a sick or injured person before full treatment is available.

firstborn • n. the first child to be born to someone.

first class • n. **1** a set of people or things grouped together as the best. **2** the best accommodation in an aircraft, train, or ship. **3** Brit. the highest division in the results of the examinations for a university degree. • adj. & adv. (**first-class**) having to do with to the first class.

first-day cover • n. an envelope with one or more stamps postmarked on their day of issue.

first-degree • adj. Med. (of burns) affecting only the surface of the skin and causing reddening.

first-foot • v. be the first person to cross someone's threshold in the New Year. • n. (also **first-footer**) the first person to cross a threshold in such a way.

first-hand • adj. & adv. from the original source or personal experience; direct.
– PHRASES **at first hand** directly.

first lady • n. the wife of the President of the United States.

firstly • adv. first (used to introduce a first point).

first mate • n. the officer second in command to the master of a merchant ship.

first name • n. a personal name given to someone at birth or baptism and used before a surname.
– PHRASES **on first-name terms** having a friendly relationship.

first night • n. the first public performance of a play or show.

first officer • n. **1** the first mate on a merchant ship. **2** the second in command to the captain on an aircraft.

first person • n. see PERSON (sense 3).

first-rate • adj. excellent.

First World War E
a war (1914–18) in which the Central Powers (Germany and Austria-Hungary, joined later by Turkey and Bulgaria) were defeated by an alliance of Britain, France, Russia, and others, joined later by Italy and the US.

firth • n. a narrow inlet of the sea, especially in Scotland.
– ORIGIN Old Norse.

fiscal /fiss-k'l/ • adj. relating to the income received by a government, especially as raised through taxes.
– ORIGIN Latin *fiscalis.*

Fischer-Dieskau L
/fi-sher dee-skow/, Dietrich (b.1925), German baritone.

fish[1] • n. (pl. **fish** or **fishes**) **1** a cold-blooded animal with a backbone, gills and fins, living in water. **2** the flesh of fish as food. • v. **1** catch or try to catch fish. **2** (**fish out**) pull or take out of water or a container. **3** (**fish for**) search or feel for something hidden. **4** (**fish for**) try to obtain by indirect means: *I was not fishing for compliments.*
– PHRASES **a big fish** an important person. **a fish out of water** a person who feels out of place in their surroundings. **have other** (or **bigger**) **fish to fry** have more important matters to attend to.
– DERIVATIVES **fishing** n.
– ORIGIN Old English.

USAGE fish
When referring to more than one fish, the normal plural is **fish**, as in *he caught two fish*. When you want to talk about different kinds of fish, however, you can use **fishes**: *freshwater fishes of the British Isles.*

fish[2] (also **fishplate**) • n. a flat piece fixed across a joint to strengthen or connect it.
– ORIGIN prob. from French *ficher* 'to fix'.

fish cake • n. a flattened round cake of shredded fish and mashed potato.

fisherman • n. a person who catches fish for

a living or for sport.

fishery ● n. (pl. **fisheries**) **1** a place where fish are reared for food, or caught in numbers. **2** the industry of catching or rearing fish.

fisheye ● n. a very wide-angle lens for a camera.

fish finger ● n. Brit. a small oblong piece of flaked or minced fish coated in batter or breadcrumbs.

fishing line ● n. a long thread of silk or nylon attached to a baited hook and used for catching fish.

fishing rod ● n. a long, tapering rod to which a fishing line is attached.

f

fishmonger ● n. a person who sells fish for food.

fishnet ● n. an open mesh fabric resembling a fishing net.

fishtail ● n. an object which is forked like a fish's tail. ● v. travel with a side-to-side motion.

fishwife ● n. a coarse-mannered woman with a loud voice.

fishy ● adj. (**fishier**, **fishiest**) **1** having to do with or like a fish or fish. **2** informal causing feelings of doubt or suspicion.

fissile /fiss-yl/ ● adj. **1** (of an atom or element) able to undergo nuclear fission. **2** (of rock) easily split.
– ORIGIN Latin *fissilis*.

fission /fi-sh'n/ ● n. **1** the action of splitting into two or more parts. **2** a reaction in which an atomic nucleus splits in two, releasing much energy. **3** Biol. reproduction by means of a cell dividing into two or more new cells.

fissure /fi-sher/ ● n. a long, narrow crack.
– ORIGIN Latin *fissura*.

fist ● n. a person's hand when the fingers are bent in towards the palm and held there tightly.
– PHRASES **make a —— fist of** informal do something to the specified degree of success: *she was making a poor fist of hiding her disgust.*
– DERIVATIVES **fistful** n.
– ORIGIN Old English.

fisticuffs ● pl. n. fighting with the fists.

fit[1] ● adj. (**fitter**, **fittest**) **1** of a suitable quality or type to meet the required purpose: *the meat is fit for human consumption.* **2** in good health. **3** (**fit to do**) informal on the point of doing: *he was laughing fit to bust.* ● v. (**fits**, **fitting**, **fitted**) **1** be the right shape and size for. **2** be able to occupy a particular position or space. **3** fix into place. **4** provide with a component or article. **5** be in harmony with; match: *the punishment should fit the crime.* **6** make (someone) suitable for a role or task: *an MSc fits the student for a professional career.* **7** try clothing on (someone) in order to alter it to the correct size. ● n. the way in which something fits.
– PHRASES **fit in** be well suited or in harmony. **fit out** (or **up**) provide with necessary items. **fit up** Brit. informal produce false evidence against (someone) so as to make it seem they have committed a crime. **see** (or **think**) **fit** consider it correct or acceptable.
– DERIVATIVES **fitness** n.
– ORIGIN unknown.

fit[2] ● n. **1** a sudden attack when a person makes violent, uncontrolled movements and often loses consciousness. **2** a sudden attack of coughing, fainting, etc. **3** a sudden burst of strong feeling.
– PHRASES **in** (or **by**) **fits and starts** with irregular bursts of activity.
– ORIGIN Old English, 'conflict'.

fitful ● adj. active or occurring irregularly: *a few hours' fitful sleep.*
– DERIVATIVES **fitfully** adv.

fitment ● n. esp. Brit. a fixed item of furniture or piece of equipment.

fitted ● adj. **1** made to fill a space or to cover something closely. **2** esp. Brit. (of a room) equipped with matching units of furniture.

fitter ● n. **1** a person who fits together or installs machinery. **2** a person who fits clothes.

fitting ● n. **1** an attachment. **2** (**fittings**) items which are fixed in a building but can be removed when the owner moves. **3** an occasion when one tries on a garment that is being made or altered. ● adj. appropriate.
– DERIVATIVES **fittingly** adv.

Fittipaldi E
/fit-ti-pal-di/, Emerson (b.1946), Brazilian motor-racing driver. He was the Formula One world champion in 1972 and 1974.

FitzGerald[1], E
Ella (1917–96), American jazz singer.

FitzGerald[2], E
F. Scott (1896–1940; full name *Francis Scott Key FitzGerald*), American novelist. His novels, in particular *The Great Gatsby*, provide a vivid portrait of the US during the 1920s.

five ● cardinal number one more than four; 5. (Roman numeral: **v** or **V**.)
– DERIVATIVES **fivefold** adj. & adv.
– ORIGIN Old English.

five o'clock shadow ● n. a slight growth of beard on a man's chin several hours after he has shaved.

Five Pillars of Islam E
the five duties expected of every Muslim – profession of the faith in a prescribed form, observance of ritual prayer, giving alms to the poor, fasting during the month of Ramadan, and performing a pilgrimage to Mecca.

fiver ● n. Brit. informal a five-pound note.

fix ● v. **1** attach or position securely. **2** repair or restore. **3** decide or settle on. **4** make arrangements for. **5** make unchanging or permanent: *the rate of interest is fixed for five years.* **6** (**fix on**) direct (a look or the eyes) steadily toward. **7** informal influence the outcome of (something) in an underhand way: *the club attempted to fix the match.* ● n. **1** an act of fixing. **2** informal a difficult or awkward situation. **3** informal a dose of a narcotic drug to which one is addicted.
– PHRASES **be fixed for** informal be provided with: *How are you fixed for money?* **fix up** **1** arrange or organize. **2** informal provide with something. **get a fix on** find out the position, nature, or facts of.
– DERIVATIVES **fixer** n.
– ORIGIN Latin *fixus* 'fixed'.

fixate /fik-sayt/ ● v. (**fixates**, **fixating**, **fixated**) (**fixate on** or **be fixated on**) be interested in (someone or something) to an excessive extent.

fixation ● n. **1** an excessive interest in someone or something. **2** the process by which some plants and micro-organisms combine chemically with nitrogen or carbon dioxide in the air to form solid compounds.

fixative /fiks-uh-tiv/ ● **n.** a substance used to fix, protect, or stabilize something.

fixings ● **pl. n.** Brit. screws, bolts, or other items used to fix or assemble building material, furniture, or equipment.

fixity ● **n.** the state of being permanent.

fixture ● **n. 1** a piece of equipment or furniture which is fixed in position. **2** (**fixtures**) articles attached to a house or land and considered legally part of it so that they normally remain in place when an owner moves. **3** Brit. a sporting event which takes place on a particular date. **4** informal a person or thing that has become firmly established.

fizz ● **v.** make a hissing sound, as when gas escapes in bubbles from a liquid. ● **n. 1** the sound of fizzing. **2** informal a fizzy drink. **3** liveliness.

fizzle ● **v.** (**fizzles, fizzling, fizzled**) **1** make a weak hissing sound. **2** (**fizzle out**) end or fail in a weak or disappointing way.

fizzy ● **adj.** (**fizzier, fizziest**) (of a drink) containing bubbles of gas.
– DERIVATIVES **fizziness** n.

fjord /fyord, fee-ord/ (also **fiord**) ● **n.** a long, narrow, deep inlet of the sea between high cliffs, especially in Norway.
– ORIGIN Norwegian.

fl. ● **abbrev. 1** floruit. **2** fluid.

flab ● **n.** informal excess fat on a person's body.

flabbergast /flab-ber-gahst/ ● **v.** informal (**be flabbergasted**) be very surprised.
– ORIGIN unknown.

flabby ● **adj.** (**flabbier, flabbiest**) **1** (of a part of a person's body) fat and floppy. **2** weak or unsuccessful because not tightly controlled: *a flabby documentary epic.*
– DERIVATIVES **flabbiness** n.
– ORIGIN from FLAP.

flaccid /flass-id, flak-sid/ ● **adj.** soft and limp.
– DERIVATIVES **flaccidity** n.
– ORIGIN Latin *flaccus* 'flabby'.

flag[1] ● **n. 1** a piece of cloth that is attached to a pole or rope and used as a symbol of a country or organization or as a signal. **2** a small paper badge given to people who donate to a charity appeal. ● **v.** (**flags, flagging, flagged**) **1** mark for attention. **2** (**flag down**) signal to (a driver) to stop.
– PHRASES **put the flags out** celebrate.
– ORIGIN unknown.

flag[2] (also **flagstone**) ● **n.** a flat rectangular or square stone slab, used for paving.
– DERIVATIVES **flagged** adj.
– ORIGIN prob. Scandinavian.

flag[3] ● **n.** a plant of the iris family.
– ORIGIN unknown.

flag[4] ● **v.** (**flags, flagging, flagged**) **1** become tired or less enthusiastic. **2** (**flagging**) losing vigour or strength: *a flagging business.*
– ORIGIN related to FLAG[1].

flagellate[1] /fla-juh-layt/ ● **v.** (**flagellates, flagellating, flagellated**) whip (someone), either as a form of religious punishment or for sexual pleasure.
– DERIVATIVES **flagellation** n.
– ORIGIN Latin *flagellare.*

flagellate[2] /fla-juh-luht/ ● **adj.** (of a single-celled organism) having one or more flagella used for swimming.

flagellum /fluh-jel-luhm/ ● **n.** (pl. **flagella** /fluh-jel-luh/) Biol. a long thin projection which enables many single-celled organisms to swim.
– ORIGIN Latin, 'little whip'.

flageolet /fla-juh-lay/ ● **n.** a very small flute-like instrument resembling a recorder.
– ORIGIN French.

flagon /fla-guhn/ ● **n.** a large bottle or other container in which wine, cider, or beer is sold or served.
– ORIGIN Latin *flasco.*

flagpole (also **flagstaff**) ● **n.** a pole used for flying a flag.

flagrant /flay-gruhnt/ ● **adj.** very obvious and unashamed: *a flagrant violation of the law.*
– DERIVATIVES **flagrantly** adv.
– ORIGIN Latin *flagrare* 'blaze'.

flagship ● **n. 1** the ship in a fleet which carries the commanding admiral. **2** the best or most important thing owned or produced by an organization.

flail /flayl/ ● **v. 1** swing wildly. **2** (**flail around/about**) struggle to make one's way. ● **n.** a tool or machine with a swinging action, used for threshing grain.
– ORIGIN Latin *flagellum* 'little whip'.

flair ● **n. 1** a natural ability or talent. **2** stylishness.
– ORIGIN French.

flak ● **n. 1** anti-aircraft fire. **2** strong criticism.
– ORIGIN from German *Fliegerabwehrkanone* 'aviator-defence gun'.

flake[1] ● **n.** a small, flat, very thin piece of something. ● **v.** (**flakes, flaking, flaked**) **1** come away from a surface in flakes. **2** separate into flakes.
– ORIGIN prob. Germanic.

flake[2] ● **v.** (**flakes, flaking, flaked**) (**flake out**) informal fall asleep or drop from exhaustion.
– ORIGIN from FLAG[1].

flak jacket ● **n.** a sleeveless jacket reinforced with metal, worn as protection against bullets and shrapnel.

flaky ● **adj.** (**flakier, flakiest**) breaking or separating easily into flakes.

flambé /flom-bay/ ● **v.** (**flambés, flambéing, flambéed**) cover (food) with spirits and set it alight briefly.
– ORIGIN French, 'singed'.

flamboyant /flam-boy-uhnt/ ● **adj. 1** confident and lively in a noticeable way. **2** brightly coloured or highly decorated.
– DERIVATIVES **flamboyance** n. **flamboyantly** adv.
– ORIGIN French, 'flaming, blazing'.

flame ● **n. 1** a hot glowing body of ignited gas produced by something on fire. **2** a brilliant orange-red colour. ● **v.** (**flames, flaming, flamed**) **1** give off flames. **2** (of a strong emotion) appear suddenly. **3** Computing, informal send insulting or hostile email messages to.
– PHRASES **old flame** informal a former lover.
– ORIGIN Latin *flamma.*

flamenco /fluh-meng-koh/ ● **n.** a lively style of Spanish guitar music accompanied by singing and dancing.
– ORIGIN Spanish, 'like a gypsy, Flemish'.

f

flame-thrower ● n. a weapon that sprays out burning fuel.

flaming ● adj. **1** sending out flames. **2** very hot. **3** (of an argument) passionate. **4** informal expressing annoyance.

flamingo /fluh-ming-goh/ ● n. (pl. **flamingos** or **flamingoes**) a wading bird with mainly pink or scarlet plumage and a long neck and legs.
– ORIGIN Spanish *flamengo*.

flammable /flam-muh-b'l/ ● adj. easily set on fire.

flan ● n. a baked dish consisting of an open pastry case with a savoury or sweet filling.
– ORIGIN Old French *flaon*.

f

Flanders E
/flahn-derz/ a region in the south-western part of the Low Countries, now divided between Belgium, France, and the Netherlands.

flange /flanj/ ● n. a projecting flat rim on an object, for strengthening it or attaching it to something.
– DERIVATIVES **flanged** adj.
– ORIGIN perh. from Old French *flanchir* 'to bend'.

flank ● n. **1** the side of the body between the ribs and the hip. **2** the side of something such as a building or mountain. **3** the left or right side of a group of people. ● v. be on each or on one side of: *the hall was flanked by two towers*.
– ORIGIN Old French *flanc*.

flanker ● n. Rugby a wing forward.

flannel ● n. **1** a kind of soft-woven woollen or cotton fabric. **2** (**flannels**) men's trousers made of woollen flannel. **3** Brit. a small piece of towelling for washing oneself. **4** Brit. informal empty or flattering talk used to avoid a difficult subject. ● v. (**flannels**, **flannelling**, **flannelled**) Brit. informal use empty or flattering talk to avoid a difficult subject.
– ORIGIN prob. from Welsh *gwlanen* 'woollen article'.

flannelette /flan-nuh-let/ ● n. a cotton fabric resembling flannel.

flap ● v. (**flaps**, **flapping**, **flapped**) **1** move up and down or from side to side. **2** informal be agitated. ● n. **1** a piece of something attached on one side only, that covers an opening. **2** a moveable section of an aircraft wing, used to control upward movement. **3** a single flapping movement. **4** informal a panic.

flapjack ● n. Brit. a soft thick biscuit made from oats and butter.
– ORIGIN from FLAP (in the dialect sense 'toss a pancake') + JACK[1].

flapper ● n. informal a fashionable and unconventional young woman of the 1920s.

flare ● n. **1** a sudden brief burst of flame or light. **2** a device producing a very bright flame as a signal or marker. **3** a gradual widening towards the hem of a garment. **4** (**flares**) trousers of which the legs widen from the knees down. ● v. (**flares**, **flaring**, **flared**) **1** burn or shine with a sudden intensity. **2** suddenly become stronger or violent: *in 1943 the Middle East crisis flared up again*. **3** gradually become wider at one end.
– ORIGIN unknown.

flash ● v. **1** shine with a bright but brief or irregular light. **2** move, pass, or send swiftly in a particular direction: *the scenery flashed by*. **3** display or be displayed briefly or repeatedly. **4** informal display in an obvious way so as to impress: *they flash their money about*. **5** informal (of a man) show one's genitals in public. ● n. **1** a sudden brief burst of bright light. **2** a camera attachment that produces a flash of light, for taking photographs in poor light. **3** a sudden or brief occurrence: *a flash of inspiration*. **4** Brit. a coloured patch on a uniform, used to identify a regiment, country, etc. ● adj. informal stylish or expensive in a showy way.
– PHRASES **flash in the pan** a sudden but brief success.
– DERIVATIVES **flasher** n.

flashback ● n. **1** a scene in a film or novel set in a time earlier than the main story. **2** a sudden vivid memory of a past event.

flashbulb ● n. a bulb for a flashgun.

flash flood ● n. a sudden local flood resulting from very heavy rainfall.

flashgun ● n. a device which gives a brief flash of light, used for taking photographs in poor light.

flashing ● n. a strip of metal used to seal the junction of a roof with another surface.

flashlight ● n. **1** an electric torch with a strong beam. **2** a flashgun.

flashpoint ● n. **1** a point or place at which anger or violence flares up. **2** the temperature at which a flammable compound gives off enough vapour to ignite in air.

flashy ● adj. (**flashier**, **flashiest**) attractive in a showy or cheap way.
– DERIVATIVES **flashily** adv.

flask ● n. **1** a conical or round bottle with a narrow neck. **2** Brit. a vacuum flask.
– ORIGIN Latin *flasca* 'cask or bottle'.

flat[1] ● adj. (**flatter**, **flattest**) **1** having a level and even surface. **2** not sloping; horizontal. **3** with a level surface and little height: *a flat cap*. **4** lacking liveliness or interest: *a flat voice*. **5** (of a sparkling drink) no longer fizzy. **6** (of something kept inflated) having lost some or all of its air. **7** Brit. (of a battery) having used up its charge. **8** (of a charge or price) fixed. **9** definite and firm: *his statement was a flat denial*. **10** (of musical sound) below true or normal pitch. **11** (of a note or key) lower by a semitone than a specified note or key: *E flat*. ● adv. **1** in or into a flat position or state. **2** informal completely; absolutely: *she turned him down flat*. **3** emphasizing speed. ● n. **1** the flat part of something. **2** (**flats**) an area of low level ground near water. **3** (**the Flat**) Brit. flat racing. **4** a musical note that is a semitone lower than the corresponding one of natural pitch, shown by the sign ♭.
– PHRASES **fall flat** fail to produce the intended effect. **flat out** as fast or as hard as possible.
– DERIVATIVES **flatly** adv. **flatness** n.
– ORIGIN Old Norse.

flat[2] ● n. esp. Brit. a set of rooms forming an individual home within a larger building.
– DERIVATIVES **flatlet** n.
– ORIGIN Germanic.

flatbed ● n. **1** a vehicle with a flat load-carrying area. **2** Computing a scanner, plotter, or other device which keeps paper flat during use.

flat feet ● pl. n. feet with arches that are lower than usual.

flatfish • n. a sea fish, such as a plaice, that swims on its side and has both eyes on the upper side of its flattened body.

flat-footed • adj. **1** having flat feet. **2** informal clumsy.

flat iron • n. hist. an iron heated on a hotplate or fire.

flatmate • n. Brit. a person with whom one shares a flat.

flat race • n. a horse race over a course with no jumps.

flatten • v. **1** make or become flat or flatter. **2** informal knock down.

flatter • v. (**flatters**, **flattering**, **flattered**) **1** compliment (someone) excessively or without meaning what one says. **2** (**be flattered**) feel honoured and pleased. **3** make (someone) appear attractive: *a green dress that flattered her skin.* **4** paint or draw (someone) so that they appear more attractive than in reality.
– DERIVATIVES **flatterer** n.
– ORIGIN Old French *flater.*

flattery • n. (pl. **flatteries**) excessive or false praise.

flatulent /flat-yuu-luhnt/ • adj. suffering from a build-up of gas in the intestines or stomach.
– DERIVATIVES **flatulence** n.
– ORIGIN Latin *flatus* 'blowing'.

flatworm • n. a type of worm, such as a tapeworm, with a simple flattened body.

Flaubert E
/**floh**-bair/, Gustave (1821–80), French realist novelist and short-story writer, author of *Madame Bovary.*

flaunt • v. display proudly or obviously: *she flaunted her wealth.*
– ORIGIN unknown.

flautist /flaw-tist/ • n. a flute player.
– ORIGIN Italian *flautista.*

flavour (US **flavor**) • n. **1** the distinctive taste of a food or drink. **2** a particular quality: *balconies gave the building a Spanish flavour.* • v. give flavour to.
– PHRASES **flavour of the month** a person or thing that is currently popular.
– ORIGIN Old French *flaor* 'a smell'.

flavouring (US **flavoring**) • n. a substance used to give a better or different flavour to food or drink.

flaw • n. **1** a mark or fault that spoils something. **2** a weakness or mistake. • v. spoil or weaken.
– DERIVATIVES **flawless** adj.
– ORIGIN perh. from Old Norse, 'stone slab'.

flax • n. **1** a blue-flowered plant that is grown for its seed (linseed) and for textile fibre. **2** textile fibre made from the stalks of this plant.
– ORIGIN Old English.

flaxen • adj. literary (of hair) pale yellow.

flay • v. **1** strip the skin from (a body or carcass). **2** whip or beat very harshly. **3** criticize harshly.
– ORIGIN Old English.

flea • n. a small wingless jumping insect which feeds on the blood of mammals and birds.
– PHRASES **a flea in one's ear** a sharp reprimand.
– ORIGIN Old English.

flea market • n. a street market selling second-hand goods.

fleapit • n. esp. Brit. a run-down or dirty cinema.

fleck • n. **1** a very small patch of colour or light. **2** a small particle. • v. mark or dot with flecks.
– ORIGIN perh. from Old Norse.

fled past and past part. of FLEE.

fledge /flej/ • v. (**fledges**, **fledging**, **fledged**) **1** (of a young bird) develop wing feathers that are large enough for flight. **2** (**fledged**) having just taken on the role specified: *a newly fledged Detective Inspector.*
– ORIGIN Old English, 'ready to fly'.

fledgling (also **fledgeling**) • n. a young bird that has just fledged. • adj. new and inexperienced: *fledgling democracies.*

flee • v. (**flees**, **fleeing**, **fled**) run away.
– ORIGIN Old English.

fleece • n. **1** the wool coat of a sheep. **2** a soft, warm fabric with a pile, or a garment made from this. • v. (**fleeces**, **fleecing**, **fleeced**) informal swindle (someone) by charging them too much money.
– DERIVATIVES **fleecy** adj.
– ORIGIN Old English.

fleet[1] • n. **1** a group of ships, vehicles, or aircraft travelling together or having the same owner. **2** (**the fleet**) a country's navy.
– ORIGIN Old English.

fleet[2] • adj. fast and nimble.
– ORIGIN prob. from Old Norse.

fleeting • adj. lasting for a very short time.
– DERIVATIVES **fleetingly** adv.

Fleet Street E
a street in central London in which the offices of national newspapers were located until the mid 1980s (often used to refer to the British Press).

Fleming[1], E
Sir Alexander (1881–1955), Scottish bacteriologist, who discovered the antibiotic effect of penicillin on bacteria in 1928.

Fleming[2], E
Ian (Lancaster) (1908–64), English novelist, known for his spy novels whose hero is the secret agent James Bond.

Flemish /flem-ish/ • n. **1** (**the Flemish**) the people of Flanders. **2** the Dutch language as spoken in Flanders. • adj. relating to Flanders or the Flemish.
– ORIGIN Dutch *Vlāmisch.*

flesh • n. **1** the soft substance in the body consisting of muscle and fat. **2** the edible soft part of a fruit or vegetable. **3** (**the flesh**) the physical aspects and needs of the body: *pleasures of the flesh.* • v. (**flesh out**) make more detailed.
– PHRASES **in the flesh** in person or (of a thing) in its actual state. **make someone's flesh creep** cause someone to feel fear, horror, or disgust.
– ORIGIN Old English.

fleshly • adj. relating to the body and its needs.

fleshpots • pl. n. places where people can satisfy their sexual desires.
– ORIGIN from the *fleshpots of Egypt* mentioned in the Bible (Book of Exodus).

flesh wound ● n. a wound that breaks the skin but does not damage bones or vital organs.

fleshy ● adj. (**fleshier**, **fleshiest**) **1** having much flesh; plump. **2** (of leaves or fruit) soft and thick.

fleur-de-lis /fler-duh-lee/ (also **fleur-de-lys**) ● n. (pl. **fleurs-de-lis** /fler-duh-lee/) a design showing a lily made up of three petals bound together near their bases.
– ORIGIN Old French *flour de lys* 'flower of the lily'.

flew past of FLY[1].

flex[1] ● v. **1** bend (a limb or joint). **2** tighten (a muscle). **3** warp or bend and then return to shape.
– ORIGIN Latin *flectere*.

flex[2] ● n. esp. Brit. a flexible insulated cable used for carrying electric current to an appliance.
– ORIGIN from FLEXIBLE.

flexible ● adj. **1** able to bend easily without breaking. **2** able to change or be changed to adapt to different circumstances.
– DERIVATIVES **flexibility** n. **flexibly** adv.

flexion /flek-sh'n/ ● n. the action of bending or the state of being bent.

flexitime ● n. a system allowing some flexibility as to working hours.

flibbertigibbet /flib-ber-ti-**jib**-bit/ ● n. a person who is not interested in serious things.

flick ● n. **1** a sudden sharp movement up and down or from side to side. **2** informal (**the flicks**) the cinema. ● v. **1** make a sudden sharp movement. **2** hit or remove with a quick light movement. **3** (**flick through**) look quickly through (a book, magazine, etc.).

flicker ● v. (**flickers**, **flickering**, **flickered**) **1** shine or burn unsteadily. **2** appear briefly: *amusement flickered in his eyes.* **3** make small, quick movements. ● n. **1** a flickering movement or light. **2** a brief occurrence of a feeling.
– ORIGIN Old English, 'to flutter'.

flick knife ● n. Brit. a knife with a blade that springs out from the handle when a button is pressed.

flier ● n. var. of FLYER.

flight ● n. **1** the action of flying. **2** a journey made in an aircraft or in space. **3** the path of something through the air. **4** the action of running away: *the enemy were in flight.* **5** a highly imaginative idea or story: *a flight of fancy.* **6** a group of birds or aircraft flying together. **7** a series of steps between floors or levels. **8** the tail of an arrow or dart.
– ORIGIN Old English.

flight deck ● n. **1** the cockpit of a large aircraft. **2** the deck of an aircraft carrier, used as a runway.

flightless ● adj. (of a bird or insect) naturally unable to fly.

flight recorder ● n. an electronic device in an aircraft that records technical details during a flight.

flighty ● adj. (**flightier**, **flightiest**) unreliable and uninterested in serious things.

flimsy ● adj. (**flimsier**, **flimsiest**) **1** weak and fragile. **2** (of clothing) light and thin. **3** not convincing: *a flimsy excuse.*
– ORIGIN uncertain.

flinch ● v. **1** make a quick, nervous movement as a reaction to fear or pain. **2** (**flinch from**) avoid (something) through fear or anxiety.
– ORIGIN Old French *flenchir* 'turn aside'.

Flinders, Matthew (1774–1814), English explorer. He circumnavigated Australia (1801–3) for the Royal Navy, charting much of the west coast of the continent for the first time. E

fling ● v. (**flings**, **flinging**, **flung**) **1** throw or move forcefully: *she flung the tray against the wall.* **2** (**fling on/off**) put on or take off (clothes) carelessly and rapidly. ● n. **1** a short period of enjoyment or wild behaviour. **2** a short sexual relationship.
– ORIGIN perh. from Old Norse, 'flog'.

flint ● n. **1** a hard grey rock consisting of nearly pure silica. **2** a piece of flint or a metal alloy, used to produce a spark in a cigarette lighter.
– ORIGIN Old English.

flintlock ● n. an old-fashioned type of gun fired by a spark from a flint.

Flintshire a county of NE Wales; administrative centre, Mold. E

flinty ● adj. **1** having to do with or like flint. **2** grim and hard: *a flinty stare.*

flip ● v. (**flips**, **flipping**, **flipped**) **1** turn over with a quick, smooth movement. **2** move or throw with a sudden sharp movement: *he flipped a switch.* **3** (also **flip one's lid**) informal suddenly become very angry or lose one's self-control. ● n. a flipping action or movement. ● adj. not serious or respectful.
– ORIGIN prob. from FILLIP.

flip-flop ● n. a light sandal with a thong that passes between the big and second toes.

flippant ● adj. not showing the proper seriousness or respect.
– DERIVATIVES **flippancy** n.
– ORIGIN from FLIP.

flipper ● n. **1** a broad, flat limb without fingers, used for swimming by sea animals such as turtles. **2** each of a pair of flat rubber attachments worn on the feet for underwater swimming.

flip side ● n. informal **1** the less important side of a pop single. **2** the reverse or unwelcome aspect of a situation.

flirt ● v. **1** behave as if trying to attract someone sexually but without serious intentions. **2** (**flirt with**) show a casual interest in. **3** (**flirt with**) deliberately risk (danger or death). ● n. a person who likes to flirt.
– DERIVATIVES **flirtation** n. **flirty** adj.

flirtatious /fler-tay-shuhss/ ● adj. liking to flirt.

flit ● v. (**flits**, **flitting**, **flitted**) move quickly and lightly. ● n. Brit. informal an act of leaving one's home in secrecy.
– ORIGIN Old Norse.

flitter ● v. (**flitters**, **flittering**, **flittered**) move quickly here and there.
– ORIGIN from FLIT.

float ● v. **1** rest on the surface of a liquid without sinking. **2** move or be held up in a liquid or the air: *clouds floated across the sky.* **3** put forward (an idea) as a suggestion. **4** (**floating**) unsettled in one's opinions, where one lives, etc. **5** offer the shares of (a company) for sale on the stock market for the first time. **6** allow (a currency) to have a variable rate of ex-

change against other currencies. ● n. **1** a lightweight object or device designed to float on water. **2** Brit. a small vehicle powered by electricity: *a milk float*. **3** a platform mounted on a truck and carrying a display in a procession. **4** Brit. a sum of money available for minor expenses or to provide change.
– DERIVATIVES **floater** n.
– ORIGIN Old English.

floatation ● n. var. of **FLOTATION**.

floating voter ● n. a person who does not vote for the same party all the time.

floaty ● adj. esp. Brit. (of a woman's garment or a fabric) light and flimsy.

flocculent /flok-kyuu-luhnt/ ● adj. looking like tufts of wool.
– ORIGIN Latin *flocculus* 'tuft of wool'.

flock[1] ● n. **1** a number of birds, sheep, or goats moving or kept together. **2** (**a flock/flocks**) a large number or crowd. **3** a Christian congregation under the charge of a particular minister. ● v. gather or move in a flock.
– ORIGIN Old English.

flock[2] ● n. a soft material for stuffing cushions and quilts, made of wool refuse or torn-up cloth.
– ORIGIN Latin *floccus* 'tuft of wool'.

flock wallpaper ● n. wallpaper with a raised pattern made from powdered cloth.

Flodden, Battle of E
/flod-d'n/ (also **Flodden Field**) a decisive battle of the Anglo-Scottish war of 1513, at Flodden in Northumbria. An army under James IV of Scotland was defeated by the English forces and James was killed.

floe /floh/ ● n. a sheet of floating ice.
– ORIGIN prob. from Norwegian *flo* 'layer'.

flog ● v. (**flogs, flogging, flogged**) **1** beat with a whip or stick as a punishment. **2** Brit. informal sell.
– PHRASES **flog a dead horse** waste energy on something that can never be successful.
– ORIGIN perh. from Latin *flagellare* 'to whip'.

flood ● n. **1** an overflow of a large amount of water over dry land. **2** (**the Flood**) the flood described in the Bible, brought by God because of the wickedness of the human race. **3** an overwhelming quantity or outpouring: *a flood of complaints*. **4** the rising of the tide. ● v. **1** cover or become covered with water in a flood. **2** (of a river) fill up and overflow its banks. **3** arrive in very large numbers. **4** fill completely.
– ORIGIN Old English.

floodgate ● n. **1** a gate that can be opened or closed to control a flow of water. **2** (**floodgates**) controls holding back something powerful: *success could open the floodgates for similar mergers*.

floodlight ● n. a large, powerful lamp used to light up a stage, sports ground, etc. ● v. (**floodlights, floodlighting, floodlit**) light up with floodlights.

flood plain ● n. an area of low-lying ground next to a river that is subject to flooding.

flood tide ● n. an incoming tide.

floor ● n. **1** the lower surface of a room. **2** a storey of a building. **3** the bottom of the sea, a cave, etc. **4** (**the floor**) the part of a law-making body in which members sit. **5** (**the floor**) the right to speak next in a debate: *other speakers have the floor*. ● v. **1** provide (a room) with a floor. **2** informal knock to the ground. **3** informal baffle completely.
– ORIGIN Old English.

floorboard ● n. a long plank making up part of a wooden floor.

flooring ● n. the boards or other material of which a floor is made.

floor show ● n. an entertainment presented on the floor of a nightclub or restaurant.

floozy (also **floozie**) ● n. (pl. **floozies**) informal, derog. a girl or woman who has many sexual partners.
– ORIGIN uncertain.

flop ● v. (**flops, flopping, flopped**) **1** hang or swing loosely. **2** sit or lie down heavily. **3** informal fail totally. ● n. **1** a heavy and clumsy fall. **2** informal a total failure.
– ORIGIN from **FLAP**.

floppy ● adj. not firm or rigid. ● n. (pl. **floppies**) (also **floppy disk**) Computing a flexible removable magnetic disk used for storing data.

flora ● n. (pl. **floras** or **florae**) **1** the plants of a particular area or period of time. Compare with **FAUNA**. **2** the bacteria found naturally in the intestines.
– ORIGIN Latin *flos* 'flower'.

floral ● adj. having to do with flowers.

Florence E
a city in west central Italy, the capital of Tuscany. Florence was a leading centre of the Italian Renaissance from the 14th to the 16th century.
– DERIVATIVES **Florentine** adj. & n.

floret /flo-rit/ ● n. **1** one of the small flowers making up a composite flower head. **2** one of the flowering stems making up a head of cauliflower or broccoli.
– ORIGIN Latin *flos* 'flower'.

Florey E
/flor-i/, Howard Walter, Baron (1898–1968), Australian pathologist, who, with the British biochemist Ernst Chain (1906–79), established the therapeutic use of penicillin as an antibiotic.

florid /flo-rid/ ● adj. **1** having a red or flushed complexion. **2** over-elaborate: *florid prose*.
– ORIGIN Latin *floridus*.

Florida E
/flo-ri-duh/ a state forming a peninsula of the south-eastern US; capital, Tallahassee.
– DERIVATIVES **Floridian** adj. & n.

Florida Keys E
a chain of small islands off the tip of the Florida peninsula, extending south-westwards over a distance of 160 km (100 miles).

florin /flo-rin/ ● n. a former British coin worth two shillings.
– ORIGIN Italian *fiorino* 'little flower'.

florist ● n. a person who sells and arranges cut flowers.
– DERIVATIVES **floristry** n.

floruit /flo-ruu-it/ ● v. used to indicate when a historical figure lived, worked, or was most active.
– ORIGIN Latin, 'he or she flourished'.

floss ● n. **1** untwisted silk thread used in embroidery. **2** (also **dental floss**) a soft thread used to clean between the teeth. ● v. clean between (one's teeth) with dental floss.

– DERIVATIVES **flossy** adj.
– ORIGIN Old French *flosche* 'down'.

flotation /floh-tay-sh'n/ (also **floatation**) ● n. **1** the action of floating. **2** the process of offering a company's shares for sale on the stock market for the first time.

flotilla /fluh-til-luh/ ● n. a small fleet of ships or boats.
– ORIGIN Spanish.

flotsam /flot-suhm/ ● n. wreckage found floating on the sea.
– PHRASES **flotsam and jetsam** useless or discarded objects.
– ORIGIN Old French *floteson*.

f

flounce[1] ● v. (**flounces**, **flouncing**, **flounced**) move in a way that emphasizes one's anger or impatience. ● n. an exaggerated action expressing annoyance or impatience.
– ORIGIN perh. from Norwegian *flunsa* 'hurry'.

flounce[2] ● n. a wide strip of material gathered and sewn to a skirt or dress.
– DERIVATIVES **flouncy** adj.
– ORIGIN Old French *fronce* 'a fold.'

flounder[1] ● v. (**flounders**, **floundering**, **floundered**) **1** stagger clumsily in mud or water. **2** have trouble doing or understanding something.
– ORIGIN perh. from **FOUNDER**[3] and **BLUNDER**.

flounder[2] ● n. a small flatfish of shallow coastal waters.
– ORIGIN Old French *flondre*.

flour ● n. a powder produced by grinding grain, used to make bread, cakes, and pastry. ● v. sprinkle with flour.
– ORIGIN from **FLOWER** in the sense 'the best part' (of ground wheat).

flourish ● v. **1** grow or develop in a healthy or vigorous way. **2** be successful during a specified period. **3** wave about in a noticeable way. ● n. **1** a bold or unrestrained gesture. **2** an ornamental flowing curve in handwriting. **3** a fanfare played by brass instruments.
– ORIGIN Old French *florir*.

floury ● adj. **1** covered with flour. **2** (of a potato) soft and fluffy when cooked.

flout /flowt/ ● v. openly fail to follow (a rule, law, or custom).
– ORIGIN perh. from Dutch *fluiten* 'play the flute, hiss derisively'.

flow ● v. **1** move steadily and continuously in a current or stream. **2** move steadily and freely: *people flowed into the courtyard.* **3** hang loosely and elegantly. **4** (of the sea) move towards the land. ● n. **1** the action of flowing. **2** a steady, continuous stream. **3** the rise of a tide.
– PHRASES **in full flow** talking or performing easily and enthusiastically.
– ORIGIN Old English.

flow chart (also **flow diagram**) ● n. a diagram showing a sequence of stages making up a complex process or computer program.

flower ● n. **1** the part of a plant from which the seed or fruit develops, usually having brightly coloured petals. **2** the state or period in which a plant is flowering. **3** (**the flower of**) the best of (a group). ● v. (**flowers**, **flowering**, **flowered**) **1** produce flowers. **2** develop fully and richly: *she flowered into a striking beauty.*
– ORIGIN Old French *flour*, *flor*.

flower head ● n. a compact mass of flowers at the top of a stem.

flowerpot ● n. an earthenware or plastic container in which to grow a plant.

flowery ● adj. **1** full of, decorated with, or like flowers. **2** (of speech or writing) elaborate.

flown past part. of **FLY**[1].

flu ● n. influenza.

fluctuate /fluk-chuu-ayt/ ● v. (**fluctuates**, **fluctuating**, **fluctuated**) rise and fall irregularly in number or amount.
– DERIVATIVES **fluctuation** n.
– ORIGIN Latin *fluctuare* 'undulate'.

flue /floo/ ● n. **1** a passage in a chimney for smoke and waste gases. **2** a pipe or passage for conveying heat.
– ORIGIN unknown.

fluent /floo-uhnt/ ● adj. **1** speaking or writing in a clear and natural manner. **2** (of a language) used easily and accurately. **3** smoothly graceful and easy: *a runner in fluent motion.*
– DERIVATIVES **fluency** n. **fluently** adv.
– ORIGIN Latin *fluere* 'to flow'.

fluff ● n. **1** soft fibres gathered in small light clumps. **2** the soft fur or feathers of a young mammal or bird. **3** informal a mistake. ● v. **1** (**fluff up/out**) make fuller and softer by shaking or patting. **2** informal fail to do properly: *he fluffed his only line.*
– ORIGIN prob. from Flemish *vluwe*.

fluffy ● adj. (**fluffier**, **fluffiest**) **1** like or covered with fluff. **2** (of food) light in texture.
– DERIVATIVES **fluffily** adv. **fluffiness** n.

flugelhorn /floo-g'l-horn/ ● n. a brass musical instrument like a cornet but with a broader tone.
– ORIGIN German.

fluid ● n. a substance, such as a liquid or gas, that has no fixed shape and gives way to outside pressure. ● adj. **1** able to flow easily. **2** not stable: *a fluid political situation.* **3** graceful.
– DERIVATIVES **fluidity** n. **fluidly** adv.
– ORIGIN Latin *fluidus*.

fluid ounce ● n. Brit. one twentieth of a pint (approximately 0.028 litre).

fluke[1] ● n. a lucky chance occurrence.
– DERIVATIVES **fluky** (also **flukey**) adj.
– ORIGIN perh. dialect.

fluke[2] ● n. a parasitic flatworm.
– ORIGIN Old English.

flume /floom/ ● n. **1** an artificial channel carrying water. **2** a water slide at a swimming pool or amusement park.
– ORIGIN Latin *flumen* 'river'.

flummery /flum-muh-ri/ ● n. empty talk or compliments.
– ORIGIN Welsh *llymru*.

flummox /flum-muhks/ ● v. informal baffle (someone) completely.
– ORIGIN prob. dialect.

flung past and past part. of **FLING**.

flunk ● v. informal, esp. N. Amer. fail (an examination).
– ORIGIN perh. from **FUNK**[1].

flunkey (also **flunky**) ● n. (pl. **flunkeys** or **flunkies**) esp. derog. **1** a uniformed manservant or footman. **2** a person who performs menial tasks.
– ORIGIN perh. from **FLANK**.

fluoresce /fluu-uh-ress/ ● v. (**fluoresces**, **fluorescing**, **fluoresced**) shine or glow brightly due to fluorescence.

fluorescence ● n. **1** light given out by a substance when it is exposed to radiation such as ultraviolet light or X-rays. **2** the property of giving out light in this way.
– ORIGIN from **FLUORSPAR**.

fluorescent ● adj. **1** having or showing fluorescence. **2** (of lighting) based on fluorescence from a substance lit by ultraviolet light. **3** vividly colourful.

fluoridate /fluu-uh-ri-dayt/ ● v. (**fluoridates**, **fluoridating**, **fluoridated**) add traces of fluorides to.
– DERIVATIVES **fluoridation** n.

fluoride /fluu-uh-ryd/ ● n. **1** Chem. a compound of fluorine with another element or group. **2** a fluorine-containing salt added to water supplies or toothpaste to reduce tooth decay.

fluorine /fluu-uh-reen/ ● n. a poisonous, extremely reactive, pale yellow gas.
ORIGIN from Latin *fluor* 'a flow'.

fluorite ● n. a mineral form of calcium fluoride.

fluorspar /fluu-uh-spar/ ● n. = **FLUORITE**.
– ORIGIN from Latin *fluor* 'a flow' + **SPAR**[3].

flurried ● adj. agitated or nervous.

flurry ● n. (pl. **flurries**) **1** a small swirling mass of snow, leaves, etc. moved by a gust of wind. **2** a sudden short spell of activity or excitement. **3** a number of things arriving suddenly and at the same time.
– ORIGIN from former *flurr* 'fly up'.

flush[1] ● v. **1** (of a person's skin or face) become red and hot. **2** glow or cause to glow with warm colour or light. **3** (**be flushed with**) be very pleased by: *he was flushed with success.* **4** clean (something) by passing large quantities of water through it. **5** remove by flushing with water. **6** force (a person or animal) into the open: *their task was to flush out the rebels.* ● n. **1** a reddening of the face or skin. **2** a sudden rush of strong emotion. **3** a period of freshness and vigour: *the first flush of youth.* **4** an act of flushing.

flush[2] ● adj. **1** completely level with another surface. **2** informal having plenty of money.
– ORIGIN prob. from **FLUSH**[1].

flush[3] ● n. (in poker or brag) a hand of cards all of the same suit.
– ORIGIN French *flux*.

fluster ● v. (**fluster**, **flustering**, **flustered**) make (someone) agitated or confused. ● n. a flustered state.
– ORIGIN perh. Scandinavian.

flute ● n. **1** a high-pitched wind instrument consisting of a tube with holes along it. **2** a tall, narrow wine glass. ● v. (**flutes**, **fluting**, **fluted**) speak in a tuneful way.
– ORIGIN Old French *flahute*.

fluted ● adj. (of an object) having a series of decorative grooves.

flutter ● v. (**flutters**, **fluttering**, **fluttered**) **1** fly unsteadily by flapping the wings quickly and lightly. **2** move or fall with a light trembling motion. **3** (of a pulse or heartbeat) beat irregularly. ● n. **1** an act of fluttering. **2** a state of nervous excitement. **3** Brit. informal a small bet.
– DERIVATIVES **fluttery** adj.
– ORIGIN Old English.

fluvial /floo-vi-uhl/ ● adj. Geol. having to do with a river.
– ORIGIN Latin *fluvialis*.

flux /fluks/ ● n. **1** continuous change. **2** an abnormal discharge from or within the body. **3** Physics the total amount of radiation, or of electric or magnetic field lines, passing through an area. **4** a substance mixed with a solid to lower the melting point, used in soldering or smelting.
– ORIGIN Latin *fluxus*.

fly[1] ● v. (**flies**, **flying**, **flew**; past part. **flown**) **1** (of a winged creature or aircraft) move through the air. **2** control the flight of or transport in (an aircraft). **3** move quickly through the air. **4** go or move quickly. **5** flutter in the wind. **6** (of a flag) be displayed on a flagpole. **7** (**fly into**) suddenly go into (a rage or temper). **8** (**fly at**) attack. **9** archaic run away. ● n. (pl. **flies**) **1** (Brit. also **flies**) an opening at the crotch of a pair of trousers, closed with a zip or buttons. **2** a flap of material covering the opening of a tent.
– PHRASES **fly in the face of** be the opposite of (what is usual or expected). **fly off the handle** informal lose one's temper suddenly.
– ORIGIN Old English.

fly[2] ● n. (pl. **flies**) **1** a flying insect with a single pair of transparent wings and sucking or piercing mouthparts. **2** used in names of other flying insects, e.g. **dragonfly**. **3** a fishing bait consisting of a natural or artificial flying insect.
– PHRASES **a fly in the ointment** a minor irritation that spoils something. **fly on the wall** an unnoticed observer. **there are no flies on ——** the person specified is quick and shrewd.
– ORIGIN Old English.

fly[3] ● adj. Brit. informal knowing and clever.
– ORIGIN unknown.

flyaway ● adj. (of hair) fine and difficult to control.

flyblown ● adj. contaminated by contact with flies.

fly-by-night ● adj. unreliable or untrustworthy.

flycatcher ● n. a perching bird that catches flying insects.

flyer (also **flier**) ● n. **1** a person or thing that flies. **2** informal a fast-moving person or thing. **3** a small handbill advertising an event or product. **4** a flying start.

fly-fishing ● n. the sport of fishing using a rod and an artificial fly as bait.

fly half ● n. Rugby = **STAND-OFF HALF**.

flying ● adj. **1** able to fly. **2** brief: *a flying visit.*
– PHRASES **with flying colours** particularly well.

flying fish ● n. a fish of warm seas which leaps out of the water and uses its wing-like fins to glide.

flying picket ● n. Brit. a person who travels to picket a workplace where there is a strike.

flying saucer ● n. a disc-shaped flying craft supposedly piloted by aliens.

flying squad n. ● n. Brit. a division of a police force which is capable of reaching an incident quickly.

flying start ● n. **1** a start of a race in which the competitors are already moving at speed as they pass the starting point. **2** a good beginning giving an advantage over competitors.

flyleaf ● n. (pl. **flyleaves**) a blank page at the beginning or end of a book.

Flynn, E
Errol (1909–59; born *Leslie Thomas Flynn*), Australian-born American actor, famous for his roles as a swashbuckling hero in romantic costume dramas.

flyover ● n. esp. Brit. a bridge carrying one road or railway line over another.

flypaper ● n. sticky, poison-treated strips of paper that are hung indoors to catch and kill flies.

fly-past ● n. Brit. a ceremonial flight of aircraft past a person or a place.

fly-post ● v. Brit. put up (advertising posters) in places where they are not permitted.

flysheet ● n. Brit. a fabric cover pitched over a tent to keep the rain out.

fly-tipping ● n. Brit. the illegal dumping of waste.

flyweight ● n. a weight in boxing and other sports coming between light flyweight and bantamweight.

flywheel ● n. a heavy revolving wheel in a machine which is used to increase the machine's momentum and thereby make it more stable or provide it with a reserve of available power.

FM ● abbrev. frequency modulation.

FO ● abbrev. Foreign Office.

Fo E
/*rhymes with* go/, Dario (b.1926), Italian dramatist, noted for his political satire *Accidental Death of an Anarchist*.

foal ● n. a young horse or related animal. ● v. (of a mare) give birth to a foal.
– ORIGIN Old English.

foam ● n. **1** a mass of small bubbles formed on or in liquid. **2** a liquid substance containing many small bubbles: *shaving foam.* **3** a lightweight form of rubber or plastic made by solidifying foam. ● v. form or produce foam.
– DERIVATIVES **foamy** adj.
– ORIGIN Old English.

fob[1] ● n. **1** a chain attached to a watch for carrying in a waistcoat or waistband pocket. **2** a tab on a key ring.
– ORIGIN prob. from German dialect *Fuppe* 'pocket'.

fob[2] ● v. (**fobs, fobbing, fobbed**) **1** (**fob off**) try to deceive (someone) into accepting excuses or something inferior. **2** (**fob off on**) give (something) inferior to.
– ORIGIN perh. from German *foppen* 'deceive, banter'.

fob watch ● n. a pocket watch.

focal /foh-k'l/ ● adj. relating to a focus.

focal point ● n. **1** the point at which rays or waves from a lens or mirror meet, or the point from which rays or waves going in different directions appear to proceed. **2** the centre of interest or activity.

fo'c's'le /fohk-s'l/ ● n. var. of **FORECASTLE**.

focus /foh-kuhss/ ● n. (pl. **focuses** or **foci** /foh-sy/) **1** the centre of interest or activity. **2** the state of having or producing a clear and defined image: *his face is out of focus.* **3** the point at which an object must be situated in order for a lens or mirror to produce a clear image of it. **4** a focal point. **5** the point of origin of an earthquake. Compare with **EPICENTRE**. **6** Geom. a fixed point with reference to which an ellipse, parabola, or other curve is drawn. ● v. (**focuses, focusing, focused** or **focusses, focussing, focussed**) **1** adapt to the available level of light and become able to see clearly. **2** adjust the focus of (a telescope, camera, etc.). **3** (of rays or waves) meet or cause to meet at a single point. **4** (**focus on**) pay particular attention to.
– DERIVATIVES **focuser** n.
– ORIGIN Latin, 'domestic hearth'.

focus group ● n. a group of people assembled to assess a new product, political campaign, etc.

fodder ● n. **1** food for cattle and other livestock. **2** people or things regarded only as material to satisfy a need: *young people ending up as factory fodder.*
– ORIGIN Old English.

foe ● n. literary an enemy or opponent.
– ORIGIN Old English, 'hostile'.

foetid ● adj. var. of **FETID**.

foetus ● n. Brit. var. of **FETUS**.
– DERIVATIVES **foetal** adj.

fog ● n. **1** a thick cloud of tiny water droplets suspended in the atmosphere at or near the earth's surface which reduces visibility. **2** a state or cause of confusion: *a fog of detail.* ● v. (**fogs, fogging, fogged**) **1** cover or become covered with steam. **2** confuse.
– ORIGIN perh. from **FOGGY**.

fogey /foh-gi/ (also **fogy**) ● n. (pl. **fogeys** or **fogies**) a very old-fashioned or conservative person.
– ORIGIN unknown.

foggy ● adj. (**foggier, foggiest**) full of fog.
– PHRASES **not have the foggiest (idea)** informal, esp. Brit. have no idea at all.
– ORIGIN perh. from Norwegian *fogg* 'grass which grows in a field after a crop of hay has been cut'.

foghorn ● n. a device making a loud, deep sound as a warning to ships in fog.

foible /foy-b'l/ ● n. a minor weakness or eccentricity.
– ORIGIN French.

foie gras /fwah grah/ ● n. = **PÂTÉ DE FOIE GRAS**.

foil[1] ● v. prevent the success of.
– ORIGIN perh. from Old French *fouler* 'to trample'.

foil[2] ● n. **1** metal hammered or rolled into a thin flexible sheet. **2** a person or thing that contrasts with and so emphasizes the qualities of another.
– ORIGIN Latin *folium* 'leaf'.

foil[3] ● n. a light, blunt-edged fencing sword with a button on its point.
– ORIGIN unknown.

foist /foysst/ ● v. (**foist on**) impose (an unwelcome person or thing) on.
– ORIGIN Dutch dialect *vuisten* 'take in the hand'.

Fokine E
/foh-keen/, Michel (1880–1942), Russian-born American dancer and choreographer. As Diaghilev's chief choreographer, he had a major influence on the development of modern ballet.

Fokker E
/*rhymes with* locker/, Anthony Herman Gerard (1890–1939), Dutch-born American aircraft designer, who designed fighter planes used by the Germans in the First World War.

fold[1] • v. **1** bend (something) over on itself so that one part of it covers another. **2** be able to be folded into a flatter shape. **3** use (a flexible material) to wrap something. **4** affectionately clasp in one's arms. **5** informal (of a company) go out of business. **6** (**fold in/into**) mix (an ingredient) gently with (another). • n. **1** a folded part or thing. **2** a line produced by folding.
– PHRASES **fold one's arms** cross one's arms over one's chest.
– DERIVATIVES **foldable** adj.
– ORIGIN Old English.

fold[2] • n. **1** a pen or enclosure for livestock. **2** (**the fold**) a group with shared aims and values.
– ORIGIN Old English.

-fold • suffix forming adjectives and adverbs from cardinal numbers: **1** in an amount multiplied by: *threefold*. **2** consisting of so many parts: *twofold*.
– ORIGIN Old English.

folder • n. **1** a folding cover or wallet for storing loose papers. **2** Computing a directory containing related files.

foliage /foh-li-ij/ • n. the leaves of plants.
– ORIGIN Old French *feuillage*.

folic acid /foh-lik/ • n. a vitamin of the B complex found especially in leafy green vegetables, liver, and kidney.
– ORIGIN Latin *folium* 'leaf'.

Folies-Bergère E
/fo-li bair-**zhair**/ a variety theatre in Paris, known for its lavish productions featuring nude and semi-nude female performers.

folio /foh-li-oh/ • n. (pl. **folios**) **1** a sheet of paper folded once to form two leaves (four pages) of a book. **2** a book made up of such sheets.
– ORIGIN Latin *folium* 'leaf'.

folk /fohk/ • pl. n. **1** (also **folks**) informal people in general. **2** (**one's folks**) one's family. **3** (also **folk music**) traditional music of unknown authorship, passed on by word of mouth. • adj. originating from the beliefs, culture, and customs of ordinary people: *folk wisdom*.
– ORIGIN Old English.

folk dance • n. a traditional dance of a particular people or area.

Folkestone E
/**fohk**-stuhn/ a seaport and resort in Kent, on the SE coast of England.

folklore • n. the traditional beliefs, stories, and customs of a community, passed on by word of mouth.

folksy • adj. traditional and homely: *the shop's folksy, small-town image*.
– DERIVATIVES **folksiness** n.

folk tale • n. a traditional story originally passed on by word of mouth.

follicle /fol-li-k'l/ • n. a small cavity in the body, especially one in which the root of the hair develops.
– DERIVATIVES **follicular** /fol-**lik**-yuu-ler/ adj.
– ORIGIN Latin *folliculus* 'little bag'.

follow • v. **1** move behind. **2** go after (someone) so as to observe them. **3** go along (a route). **4** come after in time or order. **5** be a logical consequence. **6** (also **follow on from**) occur as a result of. **7** act according to (an instruction or example). **8** understand or pay close attention to. **9** practise or undertake (a career or course of action). **10** (**follow through**) continue (an action or task) to its end. **11** (**follow up**) pursue further.
– PHRASES **follow one's nose 1** trust to one's instincts. **2** go straight ahead. **follow suit 1** do the same as someone else. **2** (in card games) play a card of the suit led.
– ORIGIN Old English.

follower • n. **1** a person who follows. **2** a supporter, fan, or disciple.

following • prep. coming after or as a result of. • n. a group of supporters or admirers. • adj. next in time or order.

follow-through • n. the continuing of an action or task to its end.

follow-up • n. **1** an activity carried out to check or further develop earlier work. **2** a work that follows or builds on an earlier work.

folly • n. (pl. **follies**) **1** foolishness. **2** a foolish act or idea. **3** an ornamental building with no practical purpose.
– ORIGIN Old French *folie* 'madness'.

foment /foh-ment/ • v. stir up (revolution or conflict).
– ORIGIN Latin *fomentare*.

fond • adj. **1** (**fond of**) having an affection or liking for. **2** affectionate: *fond memories*. **3** (of a hope or belief) unlikely to be fulfilled.
– DERIVATIVES **fondly** adv. **fondness** n.
– ORIGIN unknown.

Fonda, E
Henry (1905–82), American actor, noted for his roles in such films as *The Grapes of Wrath* and *Twelve Angry Men*. His daughter **Jane** (b.1937) is known for films such as *Klute* and *The China Syndrome*.

fondant /fon-duhnt/ • n. a thick paste made of sugar and water, used in making sweets and icing cakes.
– ORIGIN French, 'melting'.

fondle • v. (**fondles, fondling, fondled**) stroke or caress lovingly or sexually. • n. an act of fondling.
– ORIGIN from **FOND**.

fondue /fon-dyoo/ • n. a dish in which small pieces of food are dipped into melted cheese or a hot sauce.
– ORIGIN French, 'melted'.

font[1] • n. a large stone bowl in a church for the water used in baptism.
– ORIGIN Latin *fons* 'fountain'.

font[2] (Brit. also **fount**) • n. Printing a set of type of a particular size and design.
– ORIGIN French *fonte* 'casting'.

fontanelle /fon-tuh-nel/ (US **fontanel**) • n. a soft area between the bones of the skull in a baby or fetus.
– ORIGIN Old French, 'little fountain'.

Fonteyn E
/fon-tayn/, Dame Margot (1919–91; born *Margaret Hookham*), English ballet dancer.

food • n. any substance that people or animals eat or drink or that plants absorb to maintain life and growth.
– PHRASES **food for thought** something that gives rise to serious consideration.
– ORIGIN Old English.

food chain • n. a series of organisms, each of which depend on the next as a source of food.

foodie • n. (pl. **foodies**) informal a person with a strong interest in food.

food poisoning • n. illness caused by food contaminated by bacteria or other organisms.

f

foodstuff • n. a substance suitable to be eaten as food.

fool[1] • n. **1** a person who acts unwisely. **2** hist. a jester or clown. • v. **1** trick or deceive (someone). **2** (**fool about/around**) act in a joking or silly way.
– DERIVATIVES **foolery** n.
– ORIGIN Old French *fol.*

fool[2] • n. esp. Brit. a cold dessert made of puréed fruit mixed with cream or custard.
– ORIGIN perh. from FOOL[1].

foolhardy • adj. bold in a reckless way.
– DERIVATIVES **foolhardiness** n.
– ORIGIN Old French *folhardi.*

foolish • adj. silly or unwise.
– DERIVATIVES **foolishly** adv. **foolishness** n.

foolproof • adj. incapable of going wrong or being wrongly used.

foolscap /foolz-kap/ • n. Brit. a size of paper, about 330 × 200 (or 400) mm.
– ORIGIN perh. from a former watermark of a fool's cap.

fool's gold • n. pyrites, a brassy yellow mineral that can be mistaken for gold.

fool's paradise • n. a state of happiness based on not knowing about or ignoring possible trouble.

foot • n. (pl. **feet**) **1** the part of the leg below the ankle, on which a person walks. **2** the bottom of something vertical. **3** the end of a bed. **4** a unit of length equal to 12 inches (30.48 cm). **5** Poetry a group of syllables making up a basic unit of metre. • v. informal pay (a bill).
– PHRASES **get** (or **start**) **off on the right** (or **wrong**) **foot** make a good (or bad) start. **have** (or **keep**) **one's feet on the ground** be (or remain) practical and sensible. **have** (or **get**) **a foot in the door** have (or gain) a first introduction to a profession or organization. **land** (or **fall**) **on one's feet** have good luck or success. **on** (or **by**) **foot** walking. **put one's best foot forward** begin with as much effort and determination as possible. **put one's foot down** informal be firm when faced with opposition or disobedience. **put one's foot in it** informal say or do something tactless. **put a foot wrong** make a mistake. **under one's feet** in one's way.
– DERIVATIVES **footless** adj.
– ORIGIN Old English.

footage • n. **1** part of a film made for cinema or television. **2** size or length measured in feet.

foot-and-mouth disease • n. a disease caused by a virus in cattle and sheep, causing ulcers on the hoofs and around the mouth.

football • n. **1** a team game involving kicking a ball, in particular (in the UK) soccer or (in the US) American football. **2** a large inflated ball used in football.
– DERIVATIVES **footballer** n.

footbrake • n. a foot-operated brake lever in a motor vehicle.

footbridge • n. a bridge for pedestrians.

footer /fuut-er/ • n. **1** a person or thing of a specified number of feet in length or height: *she was a strapping six-footer.* **2** a line of text appearing at the foot of each page of a book or document.

footfall • n. the sound of a footstep or footsteps.

foot fault • n. (in tennis, squash, etc.) an act of overstepping the baseline when serving, not allowed by the rules.

foothill • n. a low hill at the base of a mountain or mountain range.

foothold • n. **1** a place where one can lodge a foot to give secure support while climbing. **2** a secure position from which further progress may be made.

footing • n. **1** (**one's footing**) a secure grip with one's feet. **2** the basis on which something is established or operates.

footlights • pl. n. a row of spotlights along the front of a stage at the level of the actors' feet.

footling /foot-ling/ • adj. unimportant and irritating.

footloose • adj. free to do as one pleases.

footman • n. a uniformed servant whose duties include admitting visitors and waiting at table.

footmark • n. a footprint.

footnote • n. an additional piece of information printed at the bottom of a page.

footpad • n. hist. a highwayman who operated on foot.

footpath • n. a path for people to walk along.

footprint • n. the mark left by a foot or shoe on the ground.

footsie /fuut-si/ • n. (in phr. **play footsie**) informal touch someone's feet lightly and playfully with one's own to express romantic interest.

footsore • adj. having sore feet from much walking.

footstep • n. a step taken in walking.
– PHRASES **follow in someone's footsteps** do as another person did before.

footstool • n. a low stool for resting the feet on when sitting.

footwear • n. shoes, boots, and other coverings for the feet.

footwork • n. the manner in which one moves one's feet in dancing and sport.

fop • n. a man who is too concerned about his clothes and appearance.
– DERIVATIVES **foppish** adj.
– ORIGIN uncertain.

for • prep. **1** affecting or relating to: *tickets for the show.* **2** in favour or on behalf of. **3** because of: *I could dance for joy.* **4** so as to get, have, or do: *shall we go for a walk?* **5** in place of or in exchange for. **6** in the direction of. **7** over (a distance) or during (a period). **8** so as to happen at. • conj. literary because.

– ORIGIN Old English.

fora pl. of **FORUM** (in sense 2).

forage /fo-rij/ ● v. (**forages**, **foraging**, **foraged**) **1** search for food. **2** obtain by searching. ● n. food for horses and cattle.
– DERIVATIVES **forager** n.
– ORIGIN Old French *fourrager*.

forage cap ● n. a soldier's peaked cap.

foray /fo-ray/ ● n. **1** a sudden attack or move into enemy territory. **2** a brief but spirited attempt to become involved in a new activity.
– ORIGIN Old French *forrier* 'forager'.

forbade (also **forbad**) past of **FORBID**.

forbear[1] /for-bair/ ● v. (**forbears**, **forbearing**, **forbore**; past part. **forborne**) stop oneself from doing something.
– ORIGIN Old English.

forbear[2] /for-bair/ ● n. var. of **FOREBEAR**.

forbearance ● n. patient self-control.

forbearing ● adj. patient and self-controlled.

forbid /for-bid/ ● v. (**forbids**, **forbidding**, **forbade** /for-bad, for-bayd/ or **forbad**; past part. **forbidden**) **1** refuse to allow. **2** order not to do.
– ORIGIN Old English.

forbidding ● adj. appearing unfriendly or threatening.
– DERIVATIVES **forbiddingly** adv.

forbore past of **FORBEAR**[1].

forborne past part. of **FORBEAR**[1].

force ● n. **1** physical strength or energy accompanying action or movement. **2** Physics a measurable influence that causes something to move. **3** pressure to do something backed by the use or threat of violence. **4** influence or power. **5** a person or thing having influence: *a force for peace*. **6** an organized group of soldiers, police, or workers. **7** (**the forces**) Brit. informal the army, navy, and air force. ● v. (**forces**, **forcing**, **forced**) **1** make a way through or into by force. **2** push into position using force. **3** achieve by effort: *force a smile*. **4** make (someone) do something against their will. **5** (**force on/upon**) impose (something) on. **6** artificially cause (a plant) to develop or mature quickly.
– PHRASES **force someone's hand** make someone do something. **in force 1** in great strength or numbers. **2** (**in/into force**) in or into effect.
– ORIGIN Old French.

force-feed ● v. (**force-feeds**, **force-feeding**, **force-fed**) force to eat food.

forceful ● adj. powerful and confident.
– DERIVATIVES **forcefully** adv. **forcefulness** n.

forcemeat ● n. a mixture of chopped and seasoned meat or vegetables used as a stuffing or garnish.

forceps /for-seps/ ● pl. n. **1** a pair of pincers used in surgery or in a laboratory. **2** a large instrument of such a type with broad blades, used to help in the delivery of a baby.
– ORIGIN Latin.

forcible ● adj. done by force.
– DERIVATIVES **forcibly** adv.

Ford[1], E
Gerald (Rudolph) (b.1913), American Republican statesman, 38th President of the US 1974–7. He became President on the resignation of Richard Nixon.

Ford[2], E
Harrison (b.1942), American actor, known for his roles in such films as *Star Wars* and *Raiders of the Lost Ark*.

Ford[3], E
Henry (1863–1947), American motor manufacturer. A pioneer of large-scale mass production, he founded the Ford Motor Company, which in 1909 produced the famous Model T.

Ford[4], E
John (1586–*c*.1639), English dramatist, whose plays include *'Tis Pity She's a Whore*.

Ford[5], E
John (1895–1973; born *Sean Aloysius O'Feeney*), American film director, known for westerns such as *Stagecoach* and *She Wore a Yellow Ribbon*.

ford ● n. a shallow place in a river or stream where it can be crossed. ● v. cross at a ford.
– ORIGIN Old English.

fore ● adj. found or placed in front.
– PHRASES **to the fore** in or to a noticeable or leading position.
– ORIGIN Old English.

fore- ● comb. form **1** before; in advance: *forebode*. **2** in front of: *forecourt*.

forearm[1] /for-arm/ ● n. the part of a person's arm from the elbow to the wrist.

forearm[2] /for-arm/ ● v. (**be forearmed**) be prepared in advance for danger or attack.

forebear (also **forbear**) ● n. an ancestor.
– ORIGIN from **FORE** + former *bear* 'someone who exists'.

forebode ● v. (**forebodes**, **foreboding**, **foreboded**) archaic or literary act as an advance warning of (something bad).

foreboding ● n. a feeling that something bad will happen. ● adj. suggesting that something bad will happen.

forecast ● v. (**forecasts**, **forecasting**, **forecast** or **forecasted**) predict or estimate (a future event or trend). ● n. a prediction or estimate.
– DERIVATIVES **forecaster** n.

forecastle /fohk-s'l/ (also **fo'c's'le**) ● n. the front part of a ship below the deck.

foreclose ● v. (**forecloses**, **foreclosing**, **foreclosed**) **1** take possession of a mortgaged property as a result of someone's failure to keep up their mortgage payments. **2** rule out or prevent (a course of action).
– DERIVATIVES **foreclosure** n.
– ORIGIN Old French *forclore* 'shut out'.

forecourt ● n. an open area in front of a large building or petrol station.

forefather (or **foremother**) ● n. an ancestor.

forefinger ● n. the finger next to the thumb.

forefoot ● n. (pl. **forefeet**) each of the two front feet of a four-footed animal.

forefront ● n. the leading position.

forego[1] ● v. var. of **FORGO**.

forego[2] ● v. (**foregoes**, **foregoing**, **forewent**; past part. **foregone**) archaic come before in place or time.

foregoing ● adj. previously mentioned.

foregone past part. of **FOREGO**[2].
– PHRASES **a foregone conclusion** a result that can be easily predicted.

foreground ● n. **1** the part of a view or picture nearest to the observer. **2** the most important position.

forehand ● n. (in racket sports) a stroke played with the palm of the hand facing in the direction of the stroke.

forehead /for-hed, fo-rid/ ● n. the part of the face above the eyebrows.

foreign /fo-rin/ ● adj. **1** having to do with a country or language other than one's own. **2** dealing with other countries: *foreign policy.* **3** coming from outside: *a foreign influence.* **4** (**foreign to**) not known to or typical of: *cruelty is foreign to him.*
– ORIGIN Old French *forein, forain.*

Foreign and Commonwealth Office (also **Foreign Office**) ● n. the British government department dealing with foreign affairs.

foreign body ● n. a piece of unwanted matter that has entered the body from outside.

foreigner ● n. **1** a person from a foreign country. **2** informal a stranger or outsider.

foreign exchange ● n. the currency of other countries.

Foreign Legion ● n. a military formation of the French army made up chiefly of non-Frenchmen.

Foreign Secretary ● n. (in the UK) the government minister who heads the Foreign and Commonwealth Office.

foreknowledge ● n. awareness of something before it happens or exists.

foreland ● n. **1** an area of land in front of a particular feature. **2** a piece of land that projects into the sea.

forelock ● n. a lock of hair growing just above the forehead.

Foreman, E
George (b.1948), American boxer. He won the world heavyweight title in 1973–4, regaining it in 1994–5 to become the oldest world heavyweight champion.

foreman (or **forewoman**) ● n. **1** a worker who supervises other workers. **2** (in a law court) a person who is head of a jury and speaks on its behalf.

foremast ● n. the mast of a ship nearest the bow.

foremost ● adj. highest in importance or position. ● adv. in the first place.

forename ● n. = **FIRST NAME**.

forensic /fuh-ren-sik/ ● adj. **1** having to do with the use of scientific methods in the investigation of crime. **2** having to do with a court of law.
– ORIGIN Latin *forensis* 'in open court'.

forensic medicine ● n. medical knowledge used in the investigation of crime.

foreplay ● n. sexual activity that occurs before intercourse.

forerunner ● n. a person or thing which comes before and influences someone or something else.

foresail /for-sayl, for-s'l/ ● n. the main sail on a foremast.

foresee ● v. (**foresees**, **foreseeing**, **foresaw**; past part. **foreseen**) be aware of beforehand.
– DERIVATIVES **foreseeable** adj.

foreshadow ● v. be a warning or indication of (a future event).

foreshore ● n. the part of a shore between high- and low-water marks, or between the water and land that has been cultivated or built on.

foreshorten ● v. **1** portray (an object or view) as closer or shallower than it really is. **2** reduce in time or scale.

foresight ● n. the ability to predict and prepare for future events and needs.

foreskin ● n. the roll of skin covering the end of the penis.

forest ● n. **1** a large area covered thickly with trees and plants. **2** a large number of tangled or upright objects: *a forest of flags.* ● v. plant with trees.
– DERIVATIVES **forestation** n.
– ORIGIN from Latin *forestis silva* 'outside wood'.

forestall /for-stawl/ ● v. prevent or delay (something) by taking action before it happens.
– ORIGIN Old English, 'an ambush'.

Forester, E
C. S. (1899–1966; pen name of *Cecil Lewis Troughton Smith*), English novelist, known for his seafaring novels featuring Captain Horatio Hornblower.

forester ● n. a person in charge of a forest or skilled in forestry.

forestry ● n. the science or practice of planting, managing, and caring for forests.

foretaste ● n. a sample of something that lies ahead.

foretell ● v. (**foretells**, **foretelling**, **foretold**) predict.

forethought ● n. careful consideration of what will be necessary or may happen in the future.

foretold past and past part. of **FORETELL**.

forever ● adv. **1** (also **for ever**) for all future time. **2** a very long time. **3** continually: *she is forever complaining.*

forewarn ● v. warn in advance.

forewent past of **FOREGO**[1], **FOREGO**[2].

foreword ● n. a short introduction to a book.

forfeit /for-fit/ ● v. (**forfeits**, **forfeiting**, **forfeited**) **1** lose (property or a right) as a punishment for wrongdoing. **2** lose or give up as a necessary result: *forfeit a night's sleep for a night on the town.* ● n. a punishment for wrongdoing.
– ORIGIN Old French *forfet* 'crime'.

forgave past of **FORGIVE**.

forge[1] ● v. (**forges**, **forging**, **forged**) **1** make or shape (a metal object) by heating and hammering the metal. **2** create: *they forged a close relationship.* **3** produce a copy of (a banknote, work of art, signature, etc.) for the purpose of deception. ● n. **1** a blacksmith's workshop. **2** a furnace for melting or refining metal.
– DERIVATIVES **forger** n.
– ORIGIN Old French *forger.*

forge[2] ● v. (**forges**, **forging**, **forged**) **1** move forward gradually or steadily. **2** (**forge ahead**) make progress.
– ORIGIN perh. from **FORCE**.

forgery ● n. (pl. **forgeries**) **1** the action of forging a banknote, work of art, etc. **2** a forged or copied item.

forget ● v. (**forgets**, **forgetting**, **forgot**; past

part. **forgotten** or US **forgot**) **1** fail to remember. **2** fail to remember to do something. **3** no longer think of. **4** (**forget oneself**) behave inappropriately.
– DERIVATIVES **forgettable** adj.
– ORIGIN Old English.

forgetful • **adj.** tending or likely not to remember.
– DERIVATIVES **forgetfully** adv. **forgetfulness** n.

forget-me-not • **n.** a low-growing plant with bright blue flowers.

forgive • **v.** (**forgives**, **forgiving**, **forgave**; past part. **forgiven**) **1** stop feeling angry or resentful towards (someone) for an offence or mistake. **2** excuse (an offence, flaw, or mistake).
– DERIVATIVES **forgivable** adj.
– ORIGIN Old English.

forgiveness • **n.** the action of forgiving or the state of being forgiven.

forgo (also **forego**) • **v.** (**forgoes**, **forgoing**, **forwent**; past part. **forgone**) go without (something desirable).
– ORIGIN Old English.

forgot past of FORGET.

forgotten past part. of FORGET.

fork • **n. 1** a small tool with two or more prongs used for lifting or holding food. **2** a larger similar-shaped farm or garden tool used for digging or lifting. **3** the point where a road, path, or river divides into two parts. **4** either of two such parts. • **v. 1** divide into two parts. **2** take one route or the other at a fork. **3** dig or lift with a fork. **4** (**fork out/up**) informal pay money for something.
– ORIGIN Latin *furca* 'pitchfork'.

forked • **adj.** having a divided or fork-shaped end.

forked lightning • **n.** lightning in the form of a zigzag or branching line across the sky.

forklift truck • **n.** a vehicle with a forked device in front for lifting and carrying heavy loads.

forlorn /fuh-lorn/ • **adj. 1** very sad and lonely. **2** unlikely to succeed or be achieved: *a forlorn attempt to escape.*
– DERIVATIVES **forlornly** adv.
– ORIGIN Old English, 'depraved, lost'.

form • **n. 1** the visible shape or arrangement of something. **2** a particular way in which a thing exists: *passages in the form of poems.* **3** a type. **4** what is usually done: *the Englishman knew the form.* **5** a printed document with blank spaces for information to be filled in. **6** esp. Brit. a class or year in a school. **7** the current standard of play of a sports player. **8** details of previous performances by a racehorse or greyhound. **9** a person's mood and state of health: *she was on good form.* • **v. 1** bring together parts to create (something). **2** go to make up. **3** establish or develop. **4** make or be made into a certain form.
– DERIVATIVES **formless** adj.
– ORIGIN Latin *forma* 'a mould or form'.

formal • **adj. 1** following rules of custom or polite behaviour. **2** officially recognized: *a formal complaint.* **3** (of language) very correct and used in official situations. **4** arranged in a precise or regular way: *a formal garden.*
– DERIVATIVES **formally** adv.

formaldehyde /for-mal-di-hyd/ • **n.** Chem. a colourless strong-smelling gas, used in solution as a preservative and disinfectant.
– ORIGIN from FORMIC ACID and ALDEHYDE.

formalin /for-muh-lin/ • **n.** a solution of formaldehyde in water.

formalism • **n.** (in art, music, literature, etc.) excessive concern with rules and outward form rather than the content of something.
– DERIVATIVES **formalist** n.

formality • **n.** (pl. **formalities**) **1** the rigid following of rules or customs. **2** a thing done simply to follow customs or rules. **3** (**a formality**) a thing done or occurring as a matter of course.

formalize (also **formalise**) • **v.** (**formalizes**, **formalizing**, **formalized**) **1** give (something) legal or formal status. **2** give (something) a definite shape: *formalize our thoughts.*
– DERIVATIVES **formalization** (also **formalisation**) n.

format • **n. 1** the way in which something is arranged or presented. **2** the shape, size, and presentation of a book, document, etc. **3** the medium in which a sound recording is made available: *LP and CD formats.* **4** Computing a structure for the processing, storage, or display of data. • **v.** (**formats**, **formatting**, **formatted**) put into a particular shape or arrangement.
– ORIGIN from Latin *formatus liber* 'shaped book'.

formation • **n. 1** the action of forming or the process of being formed. **2** a structure or arrangement: *a cloud formation.* **3** a formal arrangement of aircraft in flight or troops.

formative • **adj.** having a strong influence in the development of something.

Formby E
/form-bi/, George (1904–61; born *George Booth*), English comedian, known for his film musicals in which he accompanied his songs on the ukulele.

former[1] • **adj. 1** having been previously. **2** in the past: *in former times.* **3** (**the former**) referring to the first of two things mentioned.
– ORIGIN Old English.

former[2] • **n. 1** a person or thing that forms something. **2** Brit. a person in a particular school year: *a fifth-former.*

formerly • **adv.** in the past.

Formica /for-my-kuh/ • **n.** trademark a hard, strong plastic material used for worktops, cupboard doors, etc.
– ORIGIN unknown.

formic acid /for-mik/ • **n.** Chem. an acid present in the fluid discharged by some ants.
– ORIGIN Latin *formica* 'ant'.

formidable /for-mi-duh-b'l, for-**mid**-uh-b'l/ • **adj.** causing fear or respect through being very large, powerful, or capable.
– DERIVATIVES **formidably** adv.
– ORIGIN Latin *formidabilis.*

Formosa E
/for-**moh**-suh/ former name for TAIWAN.

formula /for-myuu-luh/ • **n.** (pl. **formulae** /for-myuu-lee/ (in senses 1 and 2) or **formulas**) **1** a mathematical relationship or rule expressed in symbols. **2** (also **chemical formula**) a set of chemical symbols showing the elements present in a compound and the amounts in which they are present. **3** a fixed

form of words used in particular situations. **4** a method for achieving something. **5** a list of ingredients with which something is made. **6** a classification of racing car: *formula one.*
– ORIGIN Latin, 'small shape or mould'.

formulaic /for-myuu-lay-ik/ ● **adj. 1** containing a set form of words. **2** made by closely following a rule or style: *much romantic fiction is formulaic.*

formulate /for-myuu-layt/ ● **v. (formulates, formulating, formulated) 1** create or prepare methodically. **2** express (an idea) in a brief or orderly way.

formulation ● **n. 1** the action of creating or preparing something. **2** a mixture prepared according to a formula.

fornicate ● **v. (fornicates, fornicating, fornicated)** formal or humorous have sexual intercourse with someone one is not married to.
– DERIVATIVES **fornication** n. **fornicator** n.
– ORIGIN Latin.

forsake ● **v. (forsakes, forsaking, forsook**; past part. **forsaken)** literary **1** abandon. **2** give up.
– ORIGIN Old English.

forsooth /fer-sooth/ ● **adv.** archaic or humorous indeed.

Forster, E. M. (1879–1970; full name *Edward Morgan Forster*), English novelist and literary critic, whose novels include *A Room with a View* and *A Passage to India*. E

forswear ● **v. (forswears, forswearing, forswore**; past part. **forsworn)** formal **1** agree to give up or do without. **2 (forswear oneself/ be forsworn)** give false evidence in a court of law.

Forsyth /for-**syth**/, Frederick (b.1938), English novelist, known for political thrillers such as *The Day of the Jackal*. E

forsythia /for-sy-thi-uh/ ● **n.** a shrub whose bright yellow flowers appear before its leaves.
– ORIGIN named after the Scottish botanist William *Forsyth* (1737–1804).

fort ● **n.** a building or position constructed or established to defend against attack.
– PHRASES **hold the fort** be responsible for something temporarily.
– ORIGIN Latin *fortis* 'strong'.

Fort-de-France /for duh **frahnss**/ the capital of Martinique. E

forte[1] /for-tay/ ● **n.** a thing for which someone has a particular talent.
– ORIGIN French, 'strong'.

forte[2] /for-tay/ ● **adv. & adj.** Music loud or loudly.
– ORIGIN Italian.

Forth a river that rises in central Scotland and flows eastwards through Stirling into the North Sea. E

forth ● **adv.** esp. archaic **1** out from a starting point and forwards or into view. **2** onwards in time.
– PHRASES **and so forth** and so on.
– ORIGIN Old English.

forthcoming ● **adj. 1** about to happen or appear. **2** made available when required: *help was not forthcoming.* **3** willing to reveal information.

Forth, Firth of the estuary of the River Forth. E

forthright ● **adj.** direct and outspoken.
– DERIVATIVES **forthrightly** adv. **forthrightness** n.
– ORIGIN Old English.

forthwith ● **adv.** without delay.

fortify /for-ti-fy/ ● **v. (fortifies, fortifying, fortified) 1** strengthen (a place) with defensive structures as protection against attack. **2** invigorate or encourage. **3** strengthen (an alcoholic drink) with extra alcohol: *fortified wine.* **4** make (food) more nutritious by adding vitamins.
– DERIVATIVES **fortification** n.
– ORIGIN Latin *fortificare.*

fortissimo /for-tiss-i-moh/ ● **adv. & adj.** Music very loud or loudly.
– ORIGIN Italian.

fortitude /for-ti-tyood/ ● **n.** courage and strength when facing pain or trouble.
– ORIGIN Latin *fortitudo.*

Fort Knox a US military reservation in Kentucky, the site of the depository which holds the bulk of the nation's gold bullion in its vaults. E

Fort Lamy /lah-mi/ former name for **N'DJAMENA**. E

fortnight ● **n.** esp. Brit. a period of two weeks.
– ORIGIN Old English, 'fourteen nights'.

fortnightly esp. Brit. ● **adj.** happening or produced every two weeks. ● **adv.** every two weeks.

fortress ● **n.** a building or town which has been strengthened against attack.
– ORIGIN Old French *forteresse* 'strong place'.

fortuitous /for-tyoo-i-tuhss/ ● **adj. 1** happening by chance. **2** lucky.
– DERIVATIVES **fortuitously** adv.
– ORIGIN Latin *fortuitus.*

fortunate ● **adj. 1** involving good luck. **2** advantageous or favourable: *a most fortunate match for our daughter.*

fortunately ● **adv.** it is fortunate that.

fortune ● **n. 1** chance as an external force affecting people's lives. **2** luck: *a piece of good fortune.* **3 (fortunes)** the success or failure of a person or undertaking. **4** a large amount of money or property.
– PHRASES **a small fortune** informal a large amount of money.
– ORIGIN Latin *Fortuna*, a goddess of luck or chance.

fortune-teller ● **n.** a person who predicts what will happen in people's lives.
– DERIVATIVES **fortune-telling** n.

forty ● **cardinal number** (pl. **forties)** ten less than fifty; 40. (Roman numeral: **xl** or **XL.**)
– PHRASES **forty winks** informal a short daytime sleep.
– DERIVATIVES **fortieth** ordinal number.
– ORIGIN Old English.

forum /for-uhm/ ● **n.** (pl. **forums) 1** a meeting or opportunity for an exchange of views. **2** (pl. **fora** /for-uh/) (in ancient Roman cities) a square or marketplace used for public business.

– ORIGIN Latin, 'what is out of doors'.

forward • adv. (also **forwards**) **1** in the direction that one is facing or travelling. **2** towards a successful end. **3** ahead in time. **4** in or near the front of a ship or aircraft. • adj. **1** towards the direction that one is facing or travelling. **2** relating to the future. **3** bold or over-familiar in manner. **4** situated in or near the front of a ship or aircraft. • n. an attacking player in a sport. • v. **1** send (a letter) on to a further destination. **2** send.
– DERIVATIVES **forwardly** adv. **forwardness** n.
– ORIGIN Old English.

forward-looking • adj. open to new ideas and developments.

forwent past of **FORGO**.

fossil /foss-uhl/ • n. **1** the remains or impression of a prehistoric plant or animal that have become hardened into rock. **2** humorous a very out-of-date person or thing.
– ORIGIN French *fossile.*

fossil fuel • n. a natural fuel such as coal or gas, formed from the remains of animals and plants.

fossilize (also **fossilise**) • v. (**fossilizes, fossilizing, fossilized**) (usu. **be fossilized**) preserve (an animal or plant) so that it becomes a fossil.
– DERIVATIVES **fossilization** (also **fossilisation**) n.

Foster[1], E
Jodie (b.1962; born *Alicia Christian Foster*), American film actress. Her films include *The Accused* and *Silence of the Lambs*.

Foster[2], E
Sir Norman (Robert), Baron Foster of Thames Bank (b.1935), English architect. His work is notable for its sophisticated engineering approach and technological style.

foster • v. (**fosters, fostering, fostered**) **1** encourage the development of. **2** bring up (a child that is not one's own by birth).
– ORIGIN Old English, 'feed, nourish'.

Foucault E
/foo-koh/, Jean Bernard Léon (1819–68), French physicist, who used a pendulum to demonstrate the rotation of the earth. He also invented the gyroscope and was the first to measure the velocity of light accurately.

fought past and past part. of **FIGHT**.

foul • adj. **1** having a disgusting smell or taste. **2** very unpleasant. **3** wicked or obscene. **4** not allowed by the rules of a sport. **5** polluted. • n. (in sport) a piece of play that is unfair or not allowed by the rules. • v. **1** make foul or dirty. **2** (in sport) commit a foul against. **3** (**foul up**) make a mistake with. **4** cause (a cable, anchor, etc.) to become entangled or jammed.
– ORIGIN Old English.

foul-mouthed • adj. regularly using bad language.

foul play • n. **1** unfair play in a game or sport. **2** criminal or violent activity.

found[1] past and past part. of **FIND**.

found[2] • v. **1** establish (an institution or organization). **2** (**be founded on/upon**) be based on (a particular idea).
– ORIGIN Old French *fonder.*

found[3] • v. **1** melt and mould (metal). **2** make (an object) by melting and moulding metal.
– ORIGIN French *fondre.*

foundation • n. **1** the lowest weight-bearing part of a building. **2** an underlying basis for something. **3** reason: *there was no foundation for the claim.* **4** the action of founding an institution or organization. **5** an institution so established. **6** a cream or powder applied to the face as a base for other make-up.
– DERIVATIVES **foundational** adj.

foundation stone • n. a stone laid at a ceremony to celebrate the founding of a building.

founder[1] • n. a person who founds an institution or settlement.

founder[2] • n. the owner or operator of a foundry.

founder[3] • v. (**founders, foundering, foundered**) **1** (of a ship) fill with water and sink. **2** (of a plan or undertaking) fail or break down.
– ORIGIN Old French *fondrer* 'to collapse'.

founding father • n. **1** a founder. **2** (**Founding Father**) a member of the group of men that drew up the constitution of the US in 1787.

foundling • n. a young child that has been abandoned by its parents and is discovered and cared for by others.

foundry • n. (pl. **foundries**) a workshop or factory for casting metal.

fount[1] • n. **1** a source of a desirable quality. **2** literary a spring or fountain.

fount[2] • n. Brit. var. of **FONT**[2].

fountain • n. **1** a decorative structure in a pool or lake from which a jet of water is pumped into the air. **2** literary a natural spring of water. **3** a source of something desirable.
– ORIGIN Old French *fontaine.*

fountainhead • n. an original source of something.

fountain pen • n. a pen with a container from which ink flows continuously to the nib.

four • cardinal number **1** one more than three; 4. (Roman numeral: **iv** or **IV**.) **2** Cricket a hit that reaches the boundary after first striking the ground, scoring four runs. **3** a four-oared rowing boat or its crew.
– DERIVATIVES **fourfold** adj. & adv.
– ORIGIN Old English.

four-letter word • n. any of several short words seen as coarse or offensive.

four-poster (also **four-poster bed**) • n. a bed with a post at each corner supporting a canopy.

foursome • n. a group of four people.

four-square • adj. **1** (of a building) having a square shape and solid appearance. **2** firm and resolute. • adv. firmly and resolutely.

fourteen • cardinal number one more than thirteen; 14. (Roman numeral: **xiv** or **XIV**.)
– DERIVATIVES **fourteenth** ordinal number.

fourth • ordinal number **1** that is number four in a sequence; 4th. **2** (**a fourth/one fourth**) esp. N. Amer. a quarter. **3** Music an interval spanning four consecutive notes in a scale.
– PHRASES **the fourth estate** the press.
– DERIVATIVES **fourthly** adv.

four-wheel drive • n. a system which provides power directly to all four wheels of a vehicle.

f

fowl ● n. (pl. **fowl** or **fowls**) **1** (also **domestic fowl**) a domesticated bird kept for its eggs or meat, such as chicken. **2** birds as a group.
– ORIGIN Old English.

Fowles E
John (Robert) (b.1926), English novelist. His works include the psychological thriller *The Collector* and the semi-historical novel *The French Lieutenant's Woman*.

Fox, E
George (1624–91), English preacher and founder of the Society of Friends (Quakers).

f

fox ● n. **1** an animal with a pointed muzzle, bushy tail, and a reddish coat. **2** informal a sly or crafty person. ● v. informal baffle or deceive.
– ORIGIN Old English.

foxglove ● n. a tall plant with flowers shaped like the fingers of gloves growing up the stem.

foxhole ● n. a hole in the ground used by troops as a shelter against enemy fire or as a firing point.

foxhound ● n. a breed of dog trained to hunt foxes in packs.

fox-hunting ● n. the sport of hunting a fox across country with a pack of hounds.

foxtrot ● n. a ballroom dance which involves switching between slow and quick steps.

foxy ● adj. (**foxier**, **foxiest**) **1** like a fox. **2** informal crafty or sly.

foyer /foy-ay/ ● n. a large entrance hall in a hotel or theatre.
– ORIGIN French, 'hearth, home'.

Fr ● abbrev. Father (as a title of priests).
– ORIGIN French *frère* 'brother'.

fr. ● abbrev. franc(s).

fracas /fra-kah/ ● n. (pl. **fracas** /fra-kah or fra-kahz/) a noisy disturbance or quarrel.
– ORIGIN French.

fraction ● n. **1** a number that is not a whole number (e.g. ½, 0.5). **2** a very small part or amount. **3** Chem. each of the parts into which a mixture may be separated by fractionation.
– ORIGIN Latin.

fractional ● adj. **1** having to do with a fraction. **2** very small in amount.
– DERIVATIVES **fractionally** adv.

fractionation ● n. Chem. separation of a mixture into its constituent parts by using the fact that they condense or vaporize at different temperatures.

fractious /frak-shuhss/ ● adj. **1** bad-tempered. **2** difficult to control.
– ORIGIN from **FRACTION**.

fracture ● n. **1** the cracking or breaking of a hard object or material. **2** a crack or break. ● v. (**fractures**, **fracturing**, **fractured**) **1** break or cause to break. **2** (of a group) break up.
– ORIGIN Latin *fractura*.

fragile ● adj. **1** easily broken or damaged. **2** (of a person) delicate and vulnerable.
– DERIVATIVES **fragility** n.
– ORIGIN Latin *fragilis*.

fragment ● n. /frag-muhnt/ **1** a small part broken or separated off. **2** an incomplete part: *a fragment of conversation*. ● v. /frag-ment/ break into fragments.
– DERIVATIVES **fragmentary** adj. **fragmentation** n.
– ORIGIN Latin *fragmentum*.

Fragonard E
/frag-uh-nar/, Jean-Honoré (1732–1806), French painter, known for his landscapes and for erotic canvases such as *The Swing*.

fragrance /fray-gruhnss/ ● n. **1** a pleasant, sweet smell. **2** a perfume or aftershave.

fragrant ● adj. having a pleasant, sweet smell.
– ORIGIN Latin.

frail ● adj. **1** weak and delicate. **2** easily damaged or broken.
– ORIGIN Old French *fraile*.

frailty ● n. (pl. **frailties**) **1** the condition of being frail. **2** weakness in character or morals: *human frailty*.

Frame, E
Janet (Paterson) (b.1924), New Zealand novelist. Her works include *Intensive Care*.

frame ● n. **1** a rigid structure surrounding a picture, door, etc. **2** (**frames**) a metal or plastic structure holding the lenses of a pair of glasses. **3** the rigid supporting structure of something such as a building or car. **4** the structure of a person's body: *her slim frame*. **5** the underlying structure that supports a system or idea. **6** a single complete picture in a series forming a cinema or video film. **7** a single game of snooker. ● v. (**frames**, **framing**, **framed**) **1** place (a picture) in a frame. **2** surround so as to create an attractive image: *hair cut to frame the face*. **3** create or develop (a plan or system). **4** informal produce false evidence against (an innocent person) in order to make them appear guilty of a crime.
– PHRASES **frame of mind** a particular mood.
– ORIGIN Old English, 'be useful'.

frame of reference ● n. a set of values according to which judgements can be made.

frame-up ● n. informal a plot to make an innocent person appear guilty of a crime.

framework ● n. a supporting or underlying structure.

franc /frangk/ ● n. the basic unit of money of Switzerland and several other countries, formerly also of France, Belgium, and Luxembourg.
– ORIGIN Old French.

France E
a country in western Europe; capital, Paris.

franchise /fran-chyz/ ● n. **1** a licence granted by a government or company to a person or group allowing them to use or sell certain products. **2** a business or service granted such a franchise. **3** the right to vote in public elections. ● v. (**franchises**, **franchising**, **franchised**) grant a franchise to (someone) or for (goods or a service).
– ORIGIN Old French.

Francis, E
Dick (b.1920; full name *Richard Stanley Francis*), English jockey and writer, known for his thrillers set in the world of horse racing.

Franciscan /fran-siss-kuhn/ ● n. a monk or nun of a Christian religious order following the rule of St Francis of Assisi. ● adj. having to do with St Francis or the Franciscans.

Francis of Assisi, St E
(*c.*1181–1226), Italian monk, founder of the Franciscan order in 1209. He was known for his simple faith, humility, and love of nature. Feast day, 4 October.

Francis Xavier, St, E
see **XAVIER, ST FRANCIS**.

francium /fran-si-uhm/ • **n.** an unstable radioactive chemical element of the alkali-metal group.
– ORIGIN from **FRANCE**.

Franck E
/frongk/, César (Auguste) (1822–90), Belgian-born French composer and organist, whose best-known compositions include the D minor Symphony and the *String Quartet*.

Franco, F
Francisco (1892–1975), Spanish general and statesman, head of state 1939–75. He led the Nationalists to victory in the Civil War and in 1939 established a dictatorship that ruled Spain until his death.

Franco-Prussian War E
the war of 1870–1 between France and Prussia, in which Prussian armies advanced into France and decisively defeated the French at Sedan.

frangible /fran-ji-b'l/ • **adj.** fragile; brittle.
– ORIGIN Latin *frangibilis*.

franglais /frong-glay/ • **n.** a blend of French and English.
– ORIGIN from French *français* 'French' and *anglais* 'English'.

Frank[1], E
Anne (1929–45), German Jewish girl. She is known for her diary, which records the experiences of her family living in hiding from the Nazis in occupied Amsterdam. They were eventually betrayed and Anne died in a concentration camp.

Frank[2] • **n.** a member of a Germanic people that conquered Gaul in the 6th century.
– DERIVATIVES **Frankish** adj. & n.
– ORIGIN Old English *Franca*.

frank[1] • **adj. 1** honest and direct. **2** open or undisguised: *frank admiration*.
– DERIVATIVES **frankness** n.
– ORIGIN Latin *francus* 'free'.

frank[2] • **v.** stamp an official mark on (a letter or parcel) to indicate that postage has been paid or does not need to be paid. • **n.** a franking mark on a letter or parcel.
– ORIGIN from **FRANK**[1], in the former sense 'free of obligation'.

Frankenstein /frang-kuhn-styn/ (also **Frankenstein's monster**) • **n.** a thing that becomes terrifying or destructive to its maker.
– ORIGIN from Victor *Frankenstein*, a scientist in a novel (1818) by Mary Shelley.

Frankfurt E
/frangk-fert/ a commercial city in western Germany. Full name **FRANKFURT AM MAIN** /am **myn**/.

frankfurter • **n.** a seasoned smoked sausage made of beef and pork.
– ORIGIN from German *Frankfurter Wurst* 'Frankfurt sausage'.

frankincense /frang-kin-senss/ • **n.** a kind of sweet-smelling gum obtained from an African tree and burnt as incense.
– ORIGIN from Old French *franc encens* 'high-quality incense'.

Franklin[1], E
Aretha (b.1942), American soul and gospel singer.

Franklin[2], E
Benjamin (1706–90), American statesman and scientist, one of the authors of the American Declaration of Independence. His scientific achievements included a demonstration of the electrical nature of lightning, and he invented several devices, including the lightning conductor.

Franklin[3], E
(Stella Maria Sarah) Miles (1879–1954), Australian novelist, author of *My Brilliant Career*, regarded as the first true Australian novel.

frankly • **adv. 1** in a frank way. **2** to be frank.

frantic • **adj. 1** agitated due to fear, anxiety, etc. **2** done in a hurried and confused way.
– DERIVATIVES **frantically** adv.
– ORIGIN Old French *frenetique* 'violently mad'.

Franz Josef E
/frants **yoh**-zef/ (1830–1916), emperor of Austria 1848–1916 and king of Hungary 1867–1916. The assassination in Sarajevo of his heir apparent, Archduke Franz Ferdinand, triggered the First World War.

Fraser[1], E
Dawn (b.1937), Australian swimmer, who won the Olympic gold medal for the 100-metres freestyle in 1956, 1960, and 1964.

Fraser[2], E
(John) Malcolm (b.1930), Australian Liberal statesman, Prime Minister 1975–83.

fraternal /fruh-ter-n'l/ • **adj. 1** like a brother. **2** having to do with a fraternity. **3** (of twins) developed from separate ova and therefore not identical.
– ORIGIN Latin *fraternalis*.

fraternity /fruh-ter-ni-ti/ • **n.** (pl. **fraternities**) **1** a group of people sharing a common profession or interests. **2** friendship and shared support within a group.

fraternize /frat-er-nyz/ (also **fraternise**) • **v.** (**fraternizes**, **fraternizing**, **fraternized**) be on friendly terms.
– DERIVATIVES **fraternization** (also **fraternisation**) n.

fratricide /frat-ri-syd/ • **n. 1** the killing of one's brother or sister. **2** the accidental killing of one's own forces in war.
– DERIVATIVES **fratricidal** adj.
– ORIGIN from Latin *frater* 'brother'.

Frau /frow/ • **n.** (pl. **Frauen** /frow-uhn/) a form of address for a married or widowed German woman.
– ORIGIN German.

fraud /frawd/ • **n. 1** criminal deception intended to gain money or personal advantage. **2** a person intending to deceive.
– DERIVATIVES **fraudster** n.
– ORIGIN Old French *fraude*.

fraudulent /fraw-dyuu-luhnt/ ● **adj.** **1** involving fraud. **2** deceitful or dishonest.
– DERIVATIVES **fraudulently** adv.

fraught /frawt/ ● **adj.** **1** (**fraught with**) filled with (something undesirable). **2** causing or feeling anxiety or stress.
– ORIGIN from Dutch *uracht* 'ship's cargo'.

Fräulein /froy-lyn/ ● **n.** a form of address for a young German woman.
– ORIGIN German.

fray[1] ● **v.** **1** (of a fabric, rope, or cord) unravel or become worn at the edge. **2** (of a person's nerves or temper) show the effects of strain.
– ORIGIN Old French *freiier.*

fray[2] ● **n.** (**the fray**) **1** a very competitive situation. **2** a battle or fight.
– ORIGIN Old French *afrayer* 'disturb'.

Frazer, E
Sir James George (1854–1941), Scottish anthropologist, author of *The Golden Bough*, in which he proposed that human beliefs followed an evolutionary progression from magic and religion to modern science.

Frazier E
/fray-zi-er/, Joe (b.1944; full name *Joseph Frazier*), American boxer, who was world heavyweight champion 1968–73.

frazzle ● **n.** (**a frazzle**) informal **1** an exhausted state. **2** a burnt state.
– ORIGIN perh. from **FRAY**[1] and former *fazle* 'ravel out'.

frazzled ● **adj.** informal completely exhausted.

freak ● **n.** **1** (also **freak of nature**) a person, animal, or plant which is abnormal or deformed. **2** a very unusual and unexpected event. **3** informal a person who is obsessed with a particular interest: *a fitness freak.* ● **v.** (usu. **freak out**) informal behave or cause to behave in a wild and irrational way.
– DERIVATIVES **freakish** adj.
– ORIGIN prob. from a dialect word.

freaky ● **adj.** (**freakier**, **freakiest**) informal very strange.

freckle ● **n.** a small light brown spot on the skin. ● **v.** (**freckles**, **freckling**, **freckled**) cover or become covered with freckles.
– DERIVATIVES **freckly** adj.
– ORIGIN Old Norse.

Frederick I E
(*c.*1123–90; known as **Frederick Barbarossa**, 'Redbeard'), king of Germany and Holy Roman emperor 1152–90. He came into opposition with the pope when he attempted to strengthen his empire in Italy, and was eventually defeated in 1176.

Frederick II E
(1712–86; known as **Frederick the Great**), king of Prussia 1740–86. His campaigns in the War of the Austrian Succession (1740–8) and the Seven Years War (1756–63) considerably strengthened Prussia's position.

free ● **adj.** (**freer**, **freest**) **1** not under the control of anyone else; able to do what one wants. **2** not confined, obstructed, or fixed. **3** not having or filled with things to do: *free time.* **4** not in use. **5** (**free of/from**) not containing or affected by. **6** available without charge. **7** (**free with**) giving things or behaving without restraint. ● **adv.** without cost or payment. ● **v.** (**frees**, **freeing**, **freed**) make free.
– PHRASES **free and easy** informal and relaxed. **a free hand** freedom to do exactly as one wishes. **a free ride** a situation in which someone benefits without contributing fairly.
– ORIGIN Old English.

freebie ● **n.** informal a thing given free of charge.

freebooter ● **n.** a person who behaves in a lawless way for their own gain.
– DERIVATIVES **freebooting** n.
– ORIGIN Dutch *vrijbuiter.*

freeborn ● **adj.** not born in slavery.

Free Church ● **n.** a Christian Church which has separated from an established Church.

freedom ● **n.** **1** the power or right to act, speak, or think freely. **2** the state of being free. **3** (**freedom from**) the state of not being subject to or affected by (something undesirable). **4** a special privilege or right of access: *freedom of the City of Glasgow.*

freedom fighter ● **n.** a person who takes part in a struggle to achieve political freedom.

free enterprise ● **n.** an economic system in which private businesses compete with each other with little state control.

free fall ● **n.** **1** downward movement under the force of gravity. **2** a sudden drop or decline that cannot be stopped: *her career was about to go into free fall.*

free-for-all ● **n.** a disorganized situation or event in which everyone may take part.

free-form ● **adj.** not in a regular or formal structure.

freehand ● **adj.** & **adv.** done by hand without the aid of instruments such as rulers.

freehold ● **n.** permanent and unlimited ownership of land or property with the freedom to sell it when one wishes.
– DERIVATIVES **freeholder** n.

free house ● **n.** Brit. a public house not controlled by a brewery and therefore not restricted to selling that brewery's products.

free kick ● **n.** (in soccer and rugby) an unopposed kick of the ball awarded when the opposing team breaks the rules.

freelance /free-lahnss/ ● **adj.** self-employed and hired to work for different companies on particular jobs. ● **n.** (also **freelancer**) a freelance worker. ● **v.** (**freelances**, **freelancing**, **freelanced**) earn one's living as a freelance.

freeloader ● **n.** informal a person who takes advantage of other people's generosity without giving anything in return.
– DERIVATIVES **freeload** v.

free love ● **n.** dated the practice of having sexual relations without being faithful to one partner.

freely ● **adv.** **1** not under the control of another. **2** without restriction. **3** in abundant amounts. **4** openly and honestly. **5** willingly and readily.

Freeman, E
Cathy, (b.1973), Australian athlete. She became the first Aboriginal to represent Australia at the Olympic Games in 1992, and won the Olympic gold medal in the 400 metres in 2000.

freeman ● **n.** **1** a person who has been given the freedom of a city or borough. **2** hist. a person who is not a slave or serf.

free market • n. an economic system in which prices are determined by supply and demand rather than controlled by a government.

Freemason • n. a member of an international order established for help and fellowship between members, which holds secret ceremonies.
– DERIVATIVES **Freemasonry** n.

free port • n. **1** a port open to all traders. **2** a port area where goods being transported are not subject to customs duty.

free radical • n. Chem. a highly reactive molecule with an unpaired electron.

free-range • adj. (of livestock or eggs) kept or produced in natural conditions, where the animals may move around freely.

freesia /free-zi-uh/ • n. a plant with sweet smelling, colourful flowers, native to southern Africa.
– ORIGIN named after the German physician Friedrich H. T. *Freese* (d. 1876).

free-standing • adj. not attached to or supported by another structure.

Free State E
a province in central South Africa; capital, Bloemfontein. Former name (until 1995) **Orange Free State**.

freestyle • adj. referring to a contest, race, or type of sport in which there are few restrictions on the style or technique that competitors use.

freethinker • n. a person who questions or rejects accepted opinions.

Freetown E
the capital and chief port of Sierra Leone.

free trade • n. international trade left to its natural course without interference such as tariffs or quotas.

free verse • n. poetry that does not rhyme or have a regular rhythm.

free vote • n. esp. Brit. a vote in which members of parliament cast their votes independently of party policy.

freeway • n. N. Amer. a dual-carriageway main road.

freewheel • n. a bicycle wheel which is able to turn freely when no power is being applied to the pedals. • v. ride a bicycle without using the pedals.

free will • n. the power to act according to one's own wishes.

freeze • v. (**freezes**, **freezing**, **froze**; past part. **frozen**) **1** (with reference to a liquid) turn or be turned into a solid as a result of extreme cold. **2** become or make blocked or rigid with ice. **3** be or make very cold. **4** preserve (something) by storing it at a very low temperature. **5** become suddenly motionless with fear or shock. **6** (of a computer screen) suddenly become locked. **7** keep or stop at a fixed level or in a fixed state. **8** (**freeze out**) informal cause (someone) to feel left out by treating them in a cold or hostile way. • n. **1** an act of freezing. **2** informal a period of very cold weather.
– ORIGIN Old English.

freeze-dry • v. (**freeze-dries**, **freeze-drying**, **freeze-dried**) preserve (something) by rapidly freezing it and then removing the ice in a vacuum.

freeze-frame • n. the facility or process of stopping a film or videotape to obtain a single still image.

freezer • n. a refrigerated cabinet or room for preserving food at very low temperatures.

freezing • adj. **1** having a temperature below 0°C. **2** informal very cold. **3** (of fog or rain) consisting of droplets which freeze rapidly on contact with a surface. • n. the freezing point of water (0°C).

freezing point • n. the temperature at which a liquid turns into a solid when cooled.

Frege E
/fray-guh/, Gottlob (1848–1925), German philosopher and mathematician, the founder of modern logic.

freight /frayt/ • n. **1** transport of goods in bulk by truck, train, ship, or aircraft. **2** goods transported by freight. • v. transport by freight.
– ORIGIN Dutch and German *vrecht*.

freighter • n. a large ship or aircraft designed to carry freight.

Fremantle E
/free-man-t'l/ the chief port of Western Australia, part of the Perth metropolitan area.

French • adj. having to do with France or its people or language. • n. the language of France, also used in parts of Belgium, Switzerland, Canada, and elsewhere.
– ORIGIN Old English.

French bean • n. Brit. an edible green bean.

French bread • n. white bread in a long, crisp loaf.

French Canadian • n. a Canadian whose native language is French.

French dressing • n. a salad dressing of vinegar, oil, and seasonings.

French fries • pl. n. esp. N. Amer. chips.

French Guiana E
an overseas department of France, in northern South America; capital, Cayenne.

French horn • n. a brass instrument with a coiled tube, valves, and a wide bell.

French kiss • n. a kiss with contact between tongues.

French polish • n. a kind of polish that produces a high gloss on wood. • v. (**french-polish**) treat (wood) with French polish.

French Polynesia E
an overseas territory of France in the South Pacific, comprising the Society Islands, the Gambier Islands, the Tuamotu Archipelago, the Tubuai Islands, and the Marquesas; capital, Papeete (on Tahiti).

French Revolution E
the overthrow of the monarchy in France (1789–99). The Revolution began with the meeting of the law-making body (the States General) in May 1789 and the Bastille was stormed in July of the same year. The execution of Louis XVI in 1793 was followed by Robespierre's Reign of Terror, and after several forms of administration the Revolution ended when Napoleon seized power in 1799.

French Sudan E
former name for **Mali**.

French Wars of Religion E
a series of religious and political conflicts in France (1562–98) involving the Protestant Huguenots on one side and Catholic groups on the other. The wars were complicated by interventions from Spain, Rome, England, the Netherlands, and elsewhere.

French window • **n.** each of a pair of glazed doors in an outside wall.

frenetic /fruh-net-ik/ • **adj.** fast and energetic in a disorganized way.
– DERIVATIVES **frenetically** adv.
– ORIGIN Old French *frenetique* 'violently mad'.

frenzy • **n.** (pl. **frenzies**) a state or period of uncontrolled excitement or wild behaviour.
– DERIVATIVES **frenzied** adj. **frenziedly** adv.
– ORIGIN Latin *phrenesia*.

frequency • **n.** (pl. **frequencies**) **1** the rate at which something occurs in a given period or sample. **2** the state of being frequent. **3** the number of cycles per second of a sound, light, or radio wave. **4** the particular waveband at which radio signals are transmitted.

frequency modulation • **n.** the varying of the frequency of a wave, used as a means of broadcasting an audio signal by radio.

frequent • **adj.** /free-kwuhnt/ **1** occurring or done many times at short intervals. **2** doing something often: *a frequent visitor.* • **v.** /fri-kwent/ visit (a place) often.
– DERIVATIVES **frequenter** n. **frequently** adv.
– ORIGIN Latin *frequens* 'crowded'.

fresco /fress-koh/ • **n.** (pl. **frescoes** or **frescos**) a painting done on wet plaster on a wall or ceiling, in which the colours become fixed as the plaster dries.
– ORIGIN Italian, 'cool, fresh'.

fresh • **adj.** **1** new or different. **2** (of food) recently made or obtained. **3** recently created and not faded: *the memory was fresh in their minds.* **4** (of water) not salty. **5** (of the wind) cool and fairly strong. **6** pleasantly clean and cool: *fresh air.* **7** full of energy and vigour. **8** informal over-familiar in a sexual way. • **adv.** newly; recently.
– DERIVATIVES **freshly** adv. **freshness** n.
– ORIGIN Old English.

freshen • **v.** **1** make or become fresh. **2** esp. N. Amer. top up (a drink).

fresher • **n.** Brit. informal a first-year student at college or university.

freshman • **n.** a first-year student at university or (N. Amer.) at high school.

freshwater • **adj.** having to do with or found in fresh water.

fret[1] • **v.** (**frets**, **fretting**, **fretted**) be constantly or visibly anxious.
– ORIGIN Old English, 'devour, consume'.

fret[2] • **n.** each of a sequence of ridges on the fingerboard of some stringed instruments, used for fixing the positions of the fingers.
– ORIGIN unknown.

fretful • **adj.** anxious or irritated.

fretsaw • **n.** a saw with a narrow blade for cutting designs in thin wood or metal.

fretwork • **n.** decorative patterns cut in wood.
– ORIGIN Old French *frete* 'trelliswork'.

Freud[1] E
/froyd/, Lucian (b.1922), German-born British painter, grandson of Sigmund Freud. His subjects, chiefly portraits and nudes, are painted in a powerful naturalistic style.

Freud[2] E
/froyd/, Sigmund (1856–1939), Austrian neurologist and psychotherapist, founder of psychoanalysis and pioneer in the study of the influence that the unconscious element of the mind has on consciousness.

Freudian /froy-di-uhn/ • **adj.** having to do with Sigmund Freud and his methods of psychoanalysis.

Fri. • **abbrev.** Friday.

friable /fry-uh-b'l/ • **adj.** easily crumbled.
– ORIGIN Latin *friabilis*.

friar • **n.** a member of certain religious orders of men.
– ORIGIN Old French *frere*.

friary • **n.** (pl. **friaries**) a building or community occupied by friars.

fricassée /fri-kuh-say/ • **n.** a dish of stewed or fried pieces of meat served in a thick white sauce.
– ORIGIN French.

friction • **n.** **1** the resistance that one surface or object encounters when moving over another. **2** the action of one surface or object rubbing against another. **3** conflict or disagreement.
– DERIVATIVES **frictional** adj. **frictionless** adj.
– ORIGIN Latin.

Friday • **n.** the day of the week before Saturday and following Thursday.
– ORIGIN Old English, named after the goddess **Frigga**.

fridge • **n.** a refrigerator.

fridge-freezer • **n.** esp. Brit. an upright unit made up of a separate refrigerator and freezer.

fried past and past part. of **fry**[1].

Friedan E
/free-d'n/, Betty (b.1921), American feminist and writer, known for *The Feminine Mystique*, which presented femininity as an artificial construct.

Friedman E
/freed-muhn/, Milton (b.1912), American economist, a principal exponent of monetarism.

friend • **n.** **1** a person that one likes and knows well. **2** a familiar or helpful thing. **3** a person who supports a particular cause or organization. **4** (**Friend**) a Quaker.
– DERIVATIVES **friendless** adj. **friendship** n.
– ORIGIN Old English.

friendly • **adj.** (**friendlier**, **friendliest**) **1** kind and pleasant. **2** (in combination) not harmful to a specified thing: *environment-friendly.* **3** Mil. having to do with one's own forces. • **n.** (pl. **friendlies**) Brit. a game not forming part of a serious competition.
– DERIVATIVES **friendliness** n.

Friendly Islands E
= **Tonga**.

friendly society • **n.** (in the UK) an association owned by its members and providing sickness benefits, life assurance, and pensions.

Friends of the Earth E
an international pressure group established in 1971 to campaign on environmental issues.

Friesian /free-*zh*'n/ ● **n.** Brit. an animal of a black-and-white breed of dairy cattle.

frieze /freez/ ● **n.** a broad horizontal band of sculpted or painted decoration.
– ORIGIN Latin *frisium*.

frigate /fri-guht/ ● **n.** a warship with mixed weapons and equipment.
– ORIGIN Italian *fregata*.

Frigga E
/frig-guh/ Scand. Myth. the wife of Odin and goddess of married love and of the hearth.

fright ● **n.** **1** a sudden strong feeling of fear. **2** a shock.
– PHRASES **look a fright** informal look ridiculous or grotesque.
– ORIGIN Old English.

frighten ● **v.** **1** cause to be afraid. **2** (**frighten off**) drive away by fear.
– DERIVATIVES **frightened** adj. **frightening** adj.

frightener ● **n.** (in phr. **put the frighteners on**) Brit. informal threaten or intimidate.

frightful ● **adj.** **1** very unpleasant, serious, or shocking. **2** informal awful.
– DERIVATIVES **frightfully** adv.

frigid /fri-jid/ ● **adj.** **1** very cold. **2** (of a woman) unable to be sexually aroused.
– DERIVATIVES **frigidity** n. **frigidly** adv.
– ORIGIN Latin *frigidus*.

frill ● **n.** **1** a strip of gathered or pleated material used as a decorative edging. **2** a frill-like fringe of feathers, hair, skin, etc. on an animal. **3** (**frills**) unnecessary extra features.
– DERIVATIVES **frilled** adj. **frilly** adj.
– ORIGIN Flemish *frul*.

fringe ● **n.** **1** a border of threads, tassels, or twists, used to edge clothing or material. **2** esp. Brit. the front part of someone's hair, cut so as to hang over the forehead. **3** a natural border of hair or fibres in an animal or plant. **4** the outer part of something. ● **adj.** not part of the mainstream: *fringe theatre*. ● **v.** (**fringes**, **fringing**, **fringed**) provide with or form a fringe.
– ORIGIN Old French *frenge*.

fringe benefit ● **n.** an additional benefit.

Frink, E
Dame Elisabeth (1930–93), English sculptor and graphic artist, known for her bronze figures.

frippery ● **n.** (pl. **fripperies**) **1** showy or unnecessary ornament. **2** a frivolous thing.
– ORIGIN Old French *freperie* 'second-hand clothes'.

frisbee ● **n.** trademark a plastic disc designed for skimming through the air as an outdoor game.
– ORIGIN said to be named after the pie tins of the *Frisbie* bakery in Connecticut.

Frisian Islands E
a chain of islands lying off the coast of NW Europe, extending from the IJsselmeer in the Netherlands to Jutland.

frisk ● **v.** **1** pass the hands over (someone) in a search for hidden weapons or drugs. **2** skip or move playfully.
– ORIGIN Old French *frisque* 'alert'.

frisky ● **adj.** (**friskier**, **friskiest**) playful and full of energy.

frisson /free-son/ ● **n.** a thrill.
– ORIGIN French.

fritillary /fri-til-luh-ri/ ● **n.** **1** a plant with hanging bell-like flowers. **2** a butterfly with orange-brown wings chequered with black.
– ORIGIN Latin *fritillaria*.

fritter[1] ● **v.** (**fritters**, **frittering**, **frittered**) (**fritter away**) waste (time, money, or energy) on unimportant matters.
– ORIGIN from former *fitter* 'break into fragments'.

fritter[2] ● **n.** a piece of food that is coated in batter and deep-fried.
– ORIGIN Old French *friture*.

frivolous ● **adj.** **1** not having any serious purpose or value. **2** (of a person) carefree and not serious.
– DERIVATIVES **frivolity** n. **frivolously** adv.
– ORIGIN Latin *frivolus* 'silly, trifling'.

frizz ● **v.** (of hair) form into a mass of tight curls. ● **n.** a mass of tightly curled hair.
– ORIGIN French *friser*.

frizzy ● **adj.** (**frizzier**, **frizziest**) made up of a mass of small, tight, wiry curls.

fro ● **adv.** see **TO AND FRO**.
– ORIGIN Old Norse.

Frobisher E
/froh-bi-sher/, Sir Martin (*c.*1535–94), English explorer, who led an unsuccessful expedition in search of the North-West Passage in 1576. He also played a leading role in the defeat of the Armada.

frock ● **n.** **1** esp. Brit. a dress. **2** a loose outer garment, worn by priests.
– ORIGIN Old French *froc*.

frock coat ● **n.** a man's double-breasted, long-skirted coat.

Froebel E
/froh-b'l, frer-b'l/, Friedrich (Wilhelm August) (1782–1852), German educationist, who opened the first kindergarten for young children in 1837.

frog[1] ● **n.** **1** a tailless amphibian with a short body and very long hind legs for leaping. **2** (**Frog**) informal, derog. a French person.
– PHRASES **have a frog in one's throat** informal find it hard to speak because of hoarseness.
– DERIVATIVES **froggy** adj.
– ORIGIN Old English: sense 2 is partly from the reputation of the French for eating frogs' legs.

frog[2] ● **n.** **1** a thing used to hold or fasten something. **2** an ornamental coat fastener consisting of a spindle-shaped button and a loop.
– ORIGIN perh. from **FROG**[1].

frog[3] ● **n.** a horny pad in the sole of a horse's hoof.
– ORIGIN perh. from **FROG**[1].

frogman ● **n.** a diver equipped with a rubber suit, flippers, and breathing equipment.

frogmarch ● **v.** force (someone) to walk forward by pinning their arms from behind.

frogspawn ● **n.** a mass of frogs' eggs surrounded by transparent jelly.

frolic • v. (**frolics**, **frolicking**, **frolicked**) play or move about in a cheerful and lively way. • n. a playful action or activity.
– ORIGIN Dutch *vrolijk* 'merry, cheerful'.

frolicsome • adj. lively and playful.

from • prep. **1** indicating the point at which a journey, process, or action starts. **2** indicating the source of something. **3** indicating the starting point of a range. **4** indicating separation, removal, or prevention. **5** indicating a cause. **6** indicating a difference.
– PHRASES **from time to time** occasionally.
– ORIGIN Old English.

fromage frais /from-ah*zh* fray/ • n. a type of smooth soft fresh cheese.
– ORIGIN French, 'fresh cheese'.

frond • n. the leaf or leaf-like part of a palm, fern, or similar plant.
– ORIGIN Latin *frons*.

front • n. **1** the part of an object that presents itself to view or that is normally seen first. **2** the position directly ahead. **3** the forward-facing part of a person's body. **4** a face of a building: *the west front of the Cathedral.* **5** the furthest position that an army has reached. **6** Meteorol. the forward edge of an advancing mass of air. **7** a particular situation or sphere: *good news on the jobs front.* **8** an organized political group. **9** a false appearance or way of behaving. **10** a person or organization serving as a cover for secret or illegal activities. **11** boldness and confidence of manner. • adj. having to do with the front. • v. **1** have the front facing towards. **2** place or be at the front of. **3** provide with a front or facing. **4** be at the forefront of. **5** present (a television or radio programme). **6** act as a front for.
– PHRASES **front of house** the parts of a theatre in front of the stage. **in front of** in the presence of.
– ORIGIN Latin *frons* 'forehead, front'.

frontage • n. **1** the front of a building. **2** a strip of land next to a street or waterway.

frontal • adj. having to do with the front.
– DERIVATIVES **frontally** adv.

front bencher • n. a member of the cabinet or shadow cabinet, who sits in the front benches in the House of Commons.
– DERIVATIVES **frontbench** adj.

frontier • n. **1** a border separating two countries. **2** the extreme limit of settled land beyond which lies wilderness. **3** the extreme limit of understanding or achievement in a particular area.
– ORIGIN Old French *frontiere*.

frontispiece /frun-tiss-peess/ • n. an illustration facing the title page of a book.
– ORIGIN Latin *frontispicium* 'facade'.

front line • n. the part of an army that is closest to the enemy.

frontman • n. a person who acts as a representative of a group or organization.

front-runner • n. the contestant that is leading in a competition.

front-wheel drive • n. a system that provides power to the front wheels of a motor vehicle.

Frost, E
Robert (Lee) (1874–1963), American poet. His poetry, mostly concerned with country life in New England, is noted for its ironic tone and simple language.

frost • n. **1** a deposit of white ice crystals formed on surfaces when the temperature falls below freezing. **2** a period of cold weather when frost forms. • v. freeze.
– ORIGIN Old English.

frostbite • n. injury to body tissues caused by exposure to extreme cold.

frosted • adj. **1** covered with frost. **2** (of glass) having a semi-transparent textured surface.

frosting • n. N. Amer. icing.

frosty • adj. (**frostier**, **frostiest**) **1** (of the weather) very cold with frost forming on surfaces. **2** cold and unfriendly.
– DERIVATIVES **frostily** adv. **frostiness** n.

froth • n. **1** a mass of small bubbles in liquid. **2** worthless talk, ideas, or activities. • v. form or contain froth.
– DERIVATIVES **frothy** adj.
– ORIGIN Old Norse.

frown • v. **1** furrow one's brow to show disapproval, displeasure, or concentration. **2** (**frown on/upon**) disapprove of. • n. a facial expression of this type.
– ORIGIN Old French *froignier*.

frowsty • adj. Brit. having a stale, warm, and stuffy atmosphere.
– ORIGIN from FROWZY.

frowzy /frow-zi/ (also **frowsy**) • adj. scruffy, dingy, and neglected in appearance.
– ORIGIN unknown.

froze past of FREEZE.

frozen past part. of FREEZE.

fructose /fruk-tohz/ • n. Chem. a simple sugar found chiefly in honey and fruit.
– ORIGIN Latin *fructus* 'fruit'.

frugal /froo-g'l/ • adj. sparing with money or food.
– DERIVATIVES **frugality** n. **frugally** adv.
– ORIGIN Latin *frugalis*.

fruit • n. **1** the sweet and fleshy product of a plant that contains seed and can be eaten as food. **2** Bot. the seed-bearing part of a plant, e.g. an acorn. **3** the result of work or activity. • v. produce fruit.
– PHRASES **bear fruit** have good results.
– ORIGIN Latin *fructus* 'enjoyment of produce'.

fruit bat • n. a large bat which feeds chiefly on fruit or nectar.

fruitcake • n. informal an eccentric or mad person.

fruiterer • n. esp. Brit. a person who sells fruit.

fruit fly • n. a small fly which feeds on fruit.

fruitful • adj. **1** producing much fruit. **2** producing good results.
– DERIVATIVES **fruitfully** adv. **fruitfulness** n.

fruiting body • n. the spore-producing organ of a fungus, often seen as a toadstool.

fruition /fruu-i-sh'n/ • n. the fulfilment of a plan or project.
– ORIGIN Latin.

fruitless • adj. failing to achieve the desired results.
– DERIVATIVES **fruitlessly** adv.

fruit machine • n. Brit. a coin-operated gambling machine that generates combinations of symbols, certain combinations winning money for the player.

fruit salad • n. a mixture of different types of chopped fruit served in syrup or juice.

fruity • adj. (**fruitier**, **fruitiest**) **1** having to do with fruit. **2** (of a voice) deep and rich. **3** Brit.

informal sexually suggestive.
– DERIVATIVES **fruitiness** n.

frump ● n. an unattractive woman who wears old-fashioned clothes.
– DERIVATIVES **frumpy** adj.
– ORIGIN prob. from Dutch *verrompelen* 'wrinkle'.

frustrate ● v. (**frustrates, frustrating, frustrated**) **1** prevent (a plan or action) from progressing or succeeding. **2** prevent (someone) from doing or achieving something. **3** cause to feel dissatisfied.
– DERIVATIVES **frustration** n.
– ORIGIN Latin *frustrare* 'disappoint'.

Fry E
Elizabeth (1780–1845), English Quaker and a leading prison reformer.

fry[1] ● v. (**fries, frying, fried**) cook or be cooked in hot fat or oil. ● n. (**fries**) N. Amer. = **FRENCH FRIES**.
– ORIGIN Old French *frire*.

fry[2] ● pl. n. young fish.
– ORIGIN Old Norse.

fryer ● n. a large, deep container for frying food.

frying pan ● n. a shallow pan with a long handle, used for frying food.
– PHRASES **out of the frying pan into the fire** from a bad situation to one that is worse.

fry-up ● n. Brit. informal a dish of fried food.

ft ● abbrev. foot or feet.

FTSE index (also **FT index**) ● n. a figure (published by the *Financial Times*) indicating the relative prices of shares on the London Stock Exchange.
– ORIGIN short for *Financial Times Stock Exchange*.

Fuchs[1] E
/*rhymes with* books/, (Emil) Klaus (Julius) (1911–88), German-born physicist. He became a British citizen and worked on the development of the atom bomb in the US and Britain in the 1940s, during which time he passed vital information to the USSR.

Fuchs[2] E
/*rhymes with* books/, Sir Vivian (Ernest) (1908–99), English geologist and explorer, who led the Commonwealth Trans-Antarctic Expedition (1955–8), making the first overland crossing of the Antarctic.

fuchsia /fyoo-shuh/ ● n. **1** an ornamental shrub with drooping tubular flowers. **2** a vivid purplish-red colour.
– ORIGIN named after the German botanist Leonhard *Fuchs* (1501–66).

fuck vulgar ● v. **1** have sexual intercourse with. **2** damage or ruin. ● n. an act of sexual intercourse. ● exclam. a strong expression of annoyance or contempt.
– PHRASES **fuck about** (or **around**) spend time doing unimportant things. **fuck off** go away. **fuck up 1** damage emotionally. **2** do badly.
– DERIVATIVES **fucker** n.
– ORIGIN Germanic.

fuddled ● adj. confused or dazed.
– ORIGIN unknown.

fuddy-duddy ● n. (pl. **fuddy-duddies**) informal a person who is very old-fashioned and pompous.
– ORIGIN unknown.

fudge ● n. **1** a soft sweet made from sugar, butter, and milk or cream. **2** an attempt to present an issue in a vague way. ● v. **1** present in a vague way. **2** manipulate (facts or figures) so as to present a desired picture.
– ORIGIN prob. from former *fadge* 'to fit'.

fuehrer ● n. var. of **FÜHRER**.

fuel ● n. **1** material such as coal, gas, or oil that is burned to produce heat or power. **2** food, drink, or drugs as a source of energy. **3** something that stirs up argument or strong emotion. ● v. (**fuels, fuelling, fuelled**; US **fuels, fueling, fueled**) **1** supply or power with fuel. **2** stir up (feeling or activity).
– ORIGIN Old French *fouaille*.

fuel injection ● n. the direct introduction of fuel into the cylinders of an internal-combustion engine.

fug ● n. Brit. informal a warm, stuffy atmosphere.
– DERIVATIVES **fuggy** adj.
– ORIGIN unknown.

Fugard E
/foo-gard/, Athol (b.1932), South African dramatist. His plays, including *Blood Knot* and *The Road to Mecca*, explore the racial tensions and inequalities of South African life under apartheid.

fugitive /fyoo-ji-tiv/ ● n. a person who has escaped from captivity or is in hiding. ● adj. quick to disappear: *a fugitive memory*.
– ORIGIN Latin *fugitivus*.

fugue /fyoog/ ● n. Music a composition in which a short melody or phrase is introduced by one part and successively taken up by others.
– ORIGIN Latin *fuga* 'flight'.

führer /fyoo-uh-ruh/ (also **fuehrer**) ● n. the title used by Hitler as leader of Germany.
– ORIGIN German, 'leader'.

Fujairah C
/foo-jy-ruh/ (also **Al Fujayrah**) one of the seven member states of the United Arab Emirates.

Fuji, Mount E
/foo-ji/ a dormant volcano in Japan, on the island of Honshu. Rising to 3,776 m (12,385 ft), it is Japan's highest mountain.

-ful ● suffix **1** (forming adjectives) full of: *sorrowful*. **2** (forming adjectives from verbs) accustomed to: *forgetful*. **3** forming nouns referring to the amount needed to fill the specified container: *bucketful*.

fulcrum /fuul-kruhm/ ● n. (pl. **fulcra** /fuul-kruh/ or **fulcrums**) the point on which a lever turns or is supported.
– ORIGIN Latin, 'post of a couch'.

fulfil (US **fulfill**) ● v. (**fulfils, fulfilling, fulfilled**; US **fulfills, fulfilling, fulfilled**) **1** achieve or realize (something desired, promised, or predicted). **2** meet (a requirement). **3** (**fulfil oneself**) gain satisfaction by fully developing one's abilities.
– ORIGIN Old English, 'fill up, make full'.

fulfilment (US **fulfillment**) ● n. **1** satisfaction as a result of fully developing one's abilities. **2** the action of fulfilling.

full[1] ● adj. **1** holding as much or as many as possible. **2** (**full of**) having a large number or quantity of. **3** complete: *full details on request*.

4 (**full of**) unable to stop talking or thinking about. **5** plump or rounded. **6** (of flavour, sound, or colour) strong or rich. ● **adv. 1** straight. **2** very.
– PHRASES **full of oneself** excessively proud of oneself. **full on 1** running at or providing maximum power or capacity. **2** so as to make a direct impact. **full steam** (or **speed**) **ahead** proceeding with as much speed or energy as possible. **full up** filled to capacity. **to the full** to the greatest possible extent.
– ORIGIN Old English.

full[2] ● **v.** clean, shrink, and thicken (cloth) using heat, pressure, and moisture.
– ORIGIN prob. from **FULLER**.

f

fullback ● **n.** a player in a defensive position near the goal in a game such as soccer.

full-blooded ● **adj.** wholehearted and enthusiastic.

full-blown ● **adj.** fully developed.

full board ● **n.** Brit. provision of accommodation and all meals at a hotel or guest house.

full-bodied ● **adj.** rich and satisfying in flavour or sound.

Fuller, E
R. Buckminster (1895–1983; full name *Richard Buckminster Fuller*), American designer and architect, best known for his invention of the geodesic dome.

fuller ● **n.** a person whose occupation is fulling cloth.
– ORIGIN Old English *fullere*.

full-frontal ● **adj.** fully exposing the genitals.

full house ● **n. 1** a theatre or meeting that is filled to capacity. **2** a winning card at bingo.

full moon ● **n.** the phase of the moon in which its whole disc is lit up.

fullness (also **fulness**) ● **n.** the state of being full.
– PHRASES **in the fullness of time** after a due length of time has gone by.

full-scale ● **adj. 1** (of a model or plan) of the same size as the thing represented. **2** complete and thorough: *a full-scale invasion*.

full stop ● **n.** a punctuation mark (.) used at the end of a sentence or an abbreviation.

full-time ● **adj.** using the whole of a person's available working time. ● **adv.** on a full-time basis. ● **n.** (**full time**) the end of a sports match.
– DERIVATIVES **full-timer** n.

fully ● **adv. 1** completely. **2** no less or fewer than: *fully 65 per cent*.

-fully ● **suffix** forming adverbs corresponding to adjectives ending in *-ful*: *sorrowfully*.

fully fledged ● **adj.** Brit. completely developed or established: *a fully-fledged pilot*.

fulmar /fuul-mer/ ● **n.** a grey and white northern seabird.
– ORIGIN Old Norse, 'stinking gull'.

fulminate /fuul-mi-nayt/ ● **v.** (**fulminates**, **fulminating**, **fulminated**) express strong protest.
– DERIVATIVES **fulmination** n.
– ORIGIN Latin *fulminare* 'strike with lightning'.

fulness ● **n.** var. of **FULLNESS**.

fulsome ● **adj. 1** excessively flattering. **2** of large size or quantity: *fulsome details*.
– DERIVATIVES **fulsomely** adv.

Fulton, E
Robert (1765–1815), American pioneer of the steamship, who in 1806 built the first successful paddle steamer.

fumble ● **v.** (**fumbles**, **fumbling**, **fumbled**) **1** use the hands clumsily while doing something. **2** (of the hands) do something clumsily. **3** (**fumble about/around**) move about clumsily using the hands to find one's way. **4** express oneself or deal with something clumsily or nervously. ● **n.** an act of fumbling.
– ORIGIN German *fommeln* or Dutch *fommelen*.

fume ● **n.** a gas or vapour that smells strongly or is dangerous to breathe in. ● **v.** (**fumes**, **fuming**, **fumed**) **1** send out fumes. **2** feel great anger.
– ORIGIN Latin *fumus* 'smoke'.

fumigate /fyoo-mi-gayt/ ● **v.** (**fumigates**, **fumigating**, **fumigated**) disinfect with the fumes of certain chemicals.
– DERIVATIVES **fumigation** n.
– ORIGIN Latin *fumigare*.

fun ● **n. 1** light-hearted pleasure. **2** a source of this. **3** playfulness: *she's full of fun*. ● **adj.** informal enjoyable.
– PHRASES **make fun of** laugh at in a mocking way.
– ORIGIN unknown.

Funafuti E
/foo-nuh-**foo**-ti/ the capital of Tuvalu, situated on an island of the same name.

Funchal E
/fuun-**shahl**/ the capital and chief port of Madeira.

function ● **n. 1** an activity that is natural to or the purpose of a person or thing. **2** a large or formal social event. **3** a basic task of a computer. **4** Math. a relationship between one element and another, or between several elements and one another. ● **v. 1** operate in a proper or particular way. **2** (**function as**) fulfil the purpose of.
– ORIGIN French *fonction*.

functional ● **adj. 1** having to do with a function. **2** designed to be practical and useful. **3** working or operating.
– DERIVATIVES **functionality** n. **functionally** adv.

functionalism ● **n.** the theory that the design of an object should be governed by its use rather than a pleasant appearance.
– DERIVATIVES **functionalist** n. & adj.

functionary ● **n.** (pl. **functionaries**) an official.

fund ● **n. 1** a sum of money saved or made available for a purpose. **2** (**funds**) financial resources. **3** a large stock. ● **v.** provide with a fund.
– DERIVATIVES **funding** n.
– ORIGIN Latin *fundus* 'bottom'.

fundamental ● **adj.** of basic importance. ● **n.** a basic rule or principle: *the fundamentals of navigation*.
– DERIVATIVES **fundamentally** adv.
– ORIGIN Latin *fundamentum* 'foundation'.

fundamentalism ● **n. 1** a form of Protestant Christianity which promotes the belief that the Bible is literally true. **2** the strict following of the fundamental doctrines of any religion or system of thought.

– DERIVATIVES **fundamentalist** n. & adj.

fundamental note ● **n.** Music the lowest note of a chord.

fund-raiser ● **n. 1** a person who raises money for an organization or cause. **2** an event held to raise money for an organization or cause.
– DERIVATIVES **fund-raising** n.

funeral ● **n.** a ceremony in which a dead person is buried or cremated.
– ORIGIN Latin *funeralia*.

funeral director ● **n.** an undertaker.

funeral parlour (also **funeral home**) ● **n.** an establishment where the dead are prepared for burial or cremation.

funerary /fyoo-nuh-ruh-ri/ ● **adj.** having to do with a funeral or the remembrance of the dead.

funereal /fyoo-neer-i-uhl/ ● **adj.** having the solemn character appropriate to a funeral.

funfair ● **n.** esp. Brit. a fair consisting of rides, sideshows, and other amusements.

fungi pl. of **FUNGUS**.

fungicide /fun-ji-syd, fung-gi-syd/ ● **n.** a chemical that destroys fungus.
– DERIVATIVES **fungicidal** adj.

fungus /fung-guhss/ ● **n.** (pl. **fungi** /fung-gy/) a spore-producing organism, such as a mushroom, that has no leaves or flowers and grows on other plants or on decaying matter.
– DERIVATIVES **fungal** adj.
– ORIGIN Latin.

funicular /fuh-nik-yuu-ler/ ● **adj.** (of a railway on a steep slope) operated by cable attached to cars which balance each other while one goes up and the other down.
– ORIGIN Latin *funiculus* 'little rope'.

Funk, E
Casimir (1884–1967), Polish-born American biochemist. He showed that certain diseases, including scurvy and rickets, were each caused by the deficiency of a particular dietary component, and coined the term *vitamins* for the chemicals concerned.

funk[1] informal ● **n.** (also **blue funk**) a state of panic or depression. ● **v.** avoid out of fear.
– ORIGIN perh. from **FUNK**[2] in the informal sense 'tobacco smoke'.

funk[2] ● **n.** a style of popular dance music of US black origin, having a strong rhythm.
– ORIGIN perh. from French dialect *funkier* 'blow smoke on'.

funky ● **adj.** (**funkier**, **funkiest**) informal **1** (of music) having a strong dance rhythm. **2** strikingly stylish and unusual.
– DERIVATIVES **funkily** adv. **funkiness** n.

funnel ● **n. 1** a utensil that is wide at the top and narrow at the bottom, used for guiding liquid or powder into a small opening. **2** a metal chimney on a ship or steam engine. ● **v.** (**funnels**, **funnelling**, **funnelled**; US **funnels**, **funneling**, **funneled**) move through a funnel or narrow space.
– ORIGIN Provençal *fonilh*.

funny ● **adj.** (**funnier**, **funniest**) **1** causing laughter or amusement. **2** strange. **3** suspicious: *something funny is going on.* **4** informal slightly unwell.
– DERIVATIVES **funnily** adv.

funny bone ● **n.** informal the part of the elbow over which a very sensitive nerve passes.

fun run ● **n.** informal an uncompetitive run held to raise money for charity.

fur ● **n. 1** the short, soft hair of some animals. **2** the skin of an animal with fur on it, used in making garments. **3** a coat made from fur. **4** a coating formed on the tongue as a sign of illness. ● **v.** (**furs**, **furring**, **furred**) Brit. coat or clog with a deposit.
– ORIGIN Old French *forrer* 'to line'.

furbelow ● **n. 1** a flounce on a skirt or petticoat. **2** (**furbelows**) showy trimmings.
– ORIGIN French *falbala* 'trimming'.

furious ● **adj. 1** extremely angry. **2** full of anger or energy: *he drove at a furious speed.*
– DERIVATIVES **furiously** adv.
– ORIGIN Latin *furiosus*.

furl ● **v.** roll or fold up neatly and securely.
– ORIGIN French *ferler*.

furlong ● **n.** an eighth of a mile, 220 yards.
– ORIGIN from the Old English words for 'furrow' + 'long'.

furlough /fer-loh/ ● **n.** permission to leave one's duties or job for a period of time.
– ORIGIN Dutch *verlof*.

furnace ● **n. 1** an enclosed chamber in which material can be heated to very high temperatures. **2** a very hot place.
– ORIGIN Latin *fornax*.

Furneaux Islands E
/fer-noh/ a group of islands off the coast of NE Tasmania, in the Bass Strait.

furnish ● **v. 1** provide (a room or building) with furniture and fittings. **2** (**furnish with**) supply with (equipment or information). **3** provide.
– ORIGIN Old French *furnir*.

furnishings ● **pl. n.** furniture and fittings in a room or building.

furniture ● **n.** the movable objects that are used to make a room or building suitable for living or working in.
– ORIGIN French *fourniture*.

furore /fyoo-ror-i/ (US **furor** /fyoo-ror/) ● **n.** an outbreak of public anger or excitement.
– ORIGIN Italian.

furrier /fu-ri-er/ ● **n.** a person who prepares or deals in furs.

furrow ● **n. 1** a long, narrow trench made in the ground by a plough. **2** a rut or groove. **3** a deep wrinkle on a person's face. ● **v.** make a furrow in.
– ORIGIN Old English.

furry ● **adj.** (**furrier**, **furriest**) covered with or like fur.

further ● **adv.** (also **farther**) **1** at or to a greater distance. **2** for a longer way: *he had walked further than intended.* **3** beyond the point already reached. **4** at or to a more advanced stage. **5** in addition. ● **adj. 1** (also **farther**) more distant in space. **2** additional. ● **v.** (**furthers**, **furthering**, **furthered**) help the progress of.
– PHRASES **further to** formal following on from.
– ORIGIN comparative of **FAR**.

USAGE further
When should you use **further** and when is it better to say **farther**? When talking about distance, either form can be used: *she moved further down the train* and *she moved farther down the train* are both correct. However, you should use **further** when you mean 'beyond or in addition to

what has already been done' (*I won't trouble you any further*) or when you mean 'additional' (*phone for further information*).

furtherance • n. the action of helping a plan or interest to progress.

further education • n. Brit. education below degree level for people above school age.

furthermore • adv. in addition.

furthest (also **farthest**) • adj. **1** situated at the greatest distance. **2** covering the greatest area or distance. • adv. **1** at or by the greatest distance. **2** over the greatest distance or area. **3** to the most extreme or advanced point.

furtive • adj. trying to avoid being noticed in a secretive or guilty way.
– DERIVATIVES **furtively** adv.
– ORIGIN Latin *furtivus*.

fury • n. (pl. **furies**) **1** extreme anger. **2** extreme strength or violence: *the fury of a gathering storm.* **3** (**Furies**) Gk Myth. three goddesses (Alecto, Megaera, and Tisiphone) who punished people for wrongdoing.
– ORIGIN Latin *furia*.

furze • n. = **GORSE**.
– ORIGIN Old English.

fuse[1] • v. (**fuses, fusing, fused**) **1** join or become combined to form a whole. **2** melt (a material or object) with intense heat, so as to join it with something else. **3** Brit. (of an electrical appliance) stop working when a fuse melts. **4** provide (a circuit or electrical appliance) with a fuse. • n. a safety device consisting of a strip of wire that melts and breaks an electric circuit if the current goes beyond a safe level.
– ORIGIN Latin *fundere* 'pour, melt'.

fuse[2] (US also **fuze**) • n. **1** a length of material along which a small flame moves to explode a bomb or firework. **2** a device in a bomb that controls the timing of the explosion. • v. (**fuses**, **fusing**, **fused**; US **fuzes**, **fuzing**, **fuzed**) fit a fuse to (a bomb).
– ORIGIN Latin *fusus* 'spindle'.

fuse box • n. a box containing the fuses for electrical circuits in a building.

fuselage /fyoo-zuh-lah*zh*/ • n. the main body of an aircraft.
– ORIGIN French.

fusible • adj. able to be melted easily.

Fusilier /fyoo-zi-leer/ • n. a member of any of several British regiments formerly armed with fusils (a type of light musket).
– ORIGIN French.

fusillade /fyoo-zi-layd/ • n. a series of shots fired at the same time or quickly one after the other.
– ORIGIN French.

fusion • n. **1** the process or result of joining two or more things together to form a whole. **2** a reaction in which light atomic nuclei fuse to form a heavier nucleus, releasing much energy.
– ORIGIN Latin.

fuss • n. **1** a display of unnecessary excitement, activity, or interest. **2** a protest or complaint. • v. **1** show unnecessary concern about something. **2** treat with excessive attention or affection.
– PHRASES **not be fussed** Brit. informal not have strong feelings about something.
– ORIGIN perh. Anglo-Irish.

fusspot • n. informal a fussy person.

fussy • adj. (**fussier**, **fussiest**) **1** hard to please. **2** full of unnecessary detail.
– DERIVATIVES **fussily** adv. **fussiness** n.

fustian /fuss-ti-uhn/ • n. a thick, hard-wearing cloth woven with parallel diagonal lines.
– ORIGIN from Latin *pannus fustaneus* 'cloth from *Fostat*', a suburb of Cairo.

fusty • adj. **1** smelling stale, damp, or stuffy. **2** old-fashioned.
– ORIGIN Old French *fuste* 'smelling of the cask'.

futile • adj. pointless.
– DERIVATIVES **futilely** adv. **futility** n.
– ORIGIN Latin *futilis*.

futon /foo-ton/ • n. a Japanese padded mattress that can be rolled up.
– ORIGIN Japanese.

future • n. **1** (**the future**) time that is still to come. **2** events or conditions occurring or existing in time still to come. **3** a prospect of success or happiness: *I might have a future as an artist.* **4** Grammar a tense of verbs expressing events that have not yet happened. • adj. **1** existing or occurring in the future. **2** destined to hold a specified position: *his future wife.* **3** Grammar (of a tense) expressing an event yet to happen.
– PHRASES **in future** from now onward.
– ORIGIN Latin *futurus* 'going to be'.

future perfect • n. Grammar a tense of verbs expressing an action that will be completed in the future, as in English *will have done.*

Futurism • n. an early 20th-century artistic movement which strongly rejected traditional forms and embraced modern technology.
– DERIVATIVES **Futurist** n. & adj.

futuristic • adj. **1** having or involving very modern technology or design. **2** (of a film or book) set in the future.

futurity /fyoo-tyoor-i-ti/ • n. (pl. **futurities**) **1** the future time. **2** a future event.

fuze • n. US = **FUSE**[2].

fuzz[1] • n. a frizzy mass of hair or fibre.
– ORIGIN prob. German or Dutch.

fuzz[2] • n. (**the fuzz**) informal the police.
– ORIGIN unknown.

fuzzy • adj. (**fuzzier**, **fuzziest**) **1** having a frizzy texture or appearance. **2** not clear: *the picture is very fuzzy.*
– DERIVATIVES **fuzzily** adv. **fuzziness** n.

F-word • n. euphem. the word 'fuck'.

FX • abbrev. visual or sound effects.
– ORIGIN from the pronunciation of *effects*.

-fy • suffix forming verbs meaning to make, transform, or become: *petrify* | *horrify.*
– ORIGIN Latin *-ficare*.

FYI • abbrev. for your information.

Gg

G[1] (also **g**) ● n. (pl. **Gs** or **G's**) **1** the seventh letter of the alphabet. **2** Music the fifth note in the scale of C major.

G[2] ● abbrev. **1** giga- (10^9). **2** N. Amer. informal grand (a thousand dollars). **3** the force exerted by the earth's gravitational field.

g ● abbrev. **1** Chem. gas. **2** gram(s). ● symb. Physics the acceleration due to gravity (9.81 m s^{-2}).

gab informal ● v. (**gabs**, **gabbing**, **gabbed**) talk at length. ● n. chatter.
– PHRASES **the gift of the gab** the ability to speak fluently and persuasively.
– ORIGIN from GOB[1].

gabardine ● n. var. of GABERDINE.

gabble ● v. (**gabbles**, **gabbling**, **gabbled**) talk quickly and in a way that is difficult to understand. ● n. talk that is rapid and difficult to understand.
– DERIVATIVES **gabbler** n.
– ORIGIN Dutch *gabbelen*.

gabbro /gab-broh/ ● n. (pl. **gabbros**) a dark, coarse-grained igneous rock.
– ORIGIN Italian.

gaberdine /ga-ber-**deen**/ ● n. **1** a smooth, hard-wearing worsted or cotton cloth. **2** Brit. a raincoat made of gaberdine.
– ORIGIN Old French *gauvardine*.

Gable, E
(William) Clark (1901–60), American actor, star of such films as *It Happened One Night* and *Gone with the Wind*.

gable ● n. the triangular upper part of a wall at the end of a ridged roof.
– ORIGIN Old Norse.

Gabon E
/guh **bon**/ a country in West Africa, on the Atlantic coast; capital, Libreville.
– DERIVATIVES **Gabonese** /gab-uh-**neez**/ adj. & n.

Gaborone E
/gab-uh-**roh** ni/ the capital of Botswana.

Gabriel E
/gay-bri-uhl/ (in the Bible) the archangel who foretold the birth of Jesus to the Virgin Mary; (in Islam) the archangel who revealed the Koran to the Prophet Muhammad.

gad ● v. (**gads**, **gadding**, **gadded**) (**gad about/around**) informal go from one place to another in search of pleasure.
– ORIGIN Germanic.

gadabout ● n. informal a person who gads about.

Gaddafi E
/guh-**dah**-fi/ (also **Qaddafi**), Mu'ammer Muhammad al (b.1942), Libyan colonel, head of state since 1970. He led the coup which overthrew King Idris in 1969 and established the Libyan Arab Republic.

gadfly ● n. **1** a fly that bites livestock. **2** an annoying person.
– ORIGIN from GAD, or former *gad* 'goad'.

gadget ● n. a small mechanical device.
– DERIVATIVES **gadgetry** n.
– ORIGIN prob. from French *gâchette* 'lock mechanism'.

gadolinium /gad-uh-**lin**-i-uhm/ ● n. a soft silvery-white metallic chemical element.
– ORIGIN named after the Finnish mineralogist Johan *Gadolin* (1760–1852).

Gael /gayl/ ● n. a Gaelic-speaking person.
– ORIGIN Scottish Gaelic.

Gaelic ● n. **1** /ga-lik/ (also **Scottish Gaelic**) a Celtic language spoken in western Scotland. **2** /gay-lik/ (also **Irish Gaelic**) the Celtic language of Ireland.

gaff[1] ● n. a stick with a hook for landing large fish.
– ORIGIN Provençal *gaf* 'hook'.

gaff[2] ● n. (in phr. **blow the gaff**) Brit. informal reveal a plot or secret.
– ORIGIN unknown.

gaff[3] ● n. Brit. informal a person's house, flat, or shop.
– ORIGIN unknown.

gaffe /gaf/ (also **gaff**) ● n. an embarrassing blunder.
– ORIGIN French.

gaffer ● n. Brit. **1** informal a boss. **2** informal an old man. **3** the chief electrician on a film or television set.
– ORIGIN prob. from GODFATHER.

gag[1] ● n. **1** a piece of cloth put in or over a person's mouth to prevent them from speaking. **2** a restriction on free speech. ● v. (**gags**, **gagging**, **gagged**) **1** put a gag on. **2** choke or retch.

gag[2] ● n. a joke or funny story or act.
– ORIGIN unknown.

gaga /**gah**-gah/ ● adj. informal rambling in speech or thought; senile.
– ORIGIN French.

Gagarin E
/guh-**gah**-rin/, Yuri (Alekseevich) (1934–68), Russian cosmonaut, who in 1961 made the first manned space flight.

gage[1] /gayj/ ● n. archaic **1** a valued object deposited as a guarantee of good faith. **2** a glove or other object thrown down as a challenge to fight.
– ORIGIN Old French.

gage[2] ● n. & v. var. of GAUGE.

gaggle ● n. **1** a flock of geese. **2** informal a disorderly group of people.

Gaia hypothesis E
/gy-uh/ the theory, put forward by James Lovelock, that the part of the earth occupied by life acts as a self-regulating organism, like the human body.

gaiety (US also **gayety**) ● n. (pl. **gaieties**)

1 the state or quality of being light-hearted and cheerful. **2** merrymaking.
– ORIGIN French *gaieté*.

gaily • **adv. 1** in a light-hearted and cheerful manner. **2** without thinking of the consequences. **3** with a bright appearance.

gain • **v. 1** obtain or secure: *they fought to gain control of the island.* **2** reach: *we gained the ridge.* **3** (**gain on**) come closer to (a person or thing being chased). **4** increase the amount or rate of (weight, speed, etc.). **5** increase in value. **6** (**gain in**) increase in (a quality). **7** (of a clock or watch) become fast. • **n. 1** a thing that is gained. **2** an increase in wealth or resources.
– ORIGIN Old French *gagnier*.

gainful • **adj.** (of employment) paid; profitable.

gainsay /gayn-say/ • **v.** (**gainsays, gainsaying; gainsaid**) formal deny or contradict; speak against.
– ORIGIN from former *gain-* 'against' + SAY.

Gainsborough E
/gaynz-buh-ruh/, Thomas (1727–88), English painter, famous for his society portraits, including *Mr and Mrs Andrews*, and also for landscapes such as *The Watering Place*.

gait /gayt/ • **n. 1** a person's manner of walking. **2** a way in which a horse moves along, such as a trot.
– ORIGIN Old Norse, 'street'.

gaiter • **n.** a covering of cloth or leather for the ankle and lower leg.
– ORIGIN French *guêtre*.

Gaitskell E
/gayt-skil/, Hugh (Todd Naylor) (1906–63), British Labour statesman, Chancellor of the Exchequer 1950–1 and leader of the Labour Party 1955–63.

gal • **n.** informal, esp. N. Amer. a girl or young woman.

gal. • **abbrev.** gallon(s).

gala /gah-luh, gay-luh/ • **n. 1** a festive entertainment or performance. **2** Brit. a special sports event, especially a swimming competition.
– ORIGIN Old French *gale* 'rejoicing'.

galactic /guh-lak-tik/ • **adj.** relating to a galaxy or galaxies.

Galahad E
/gal-uh-had/ (also **Sir Galahad**) (in Arthurian legend) the purest of King Arthur's knights, destined to find the Holy Grail.

Galapagos Islands E
/guh-lap-uh-guhss/ a Pacific archipelago west of Ecuador, to which it belongs. The islands are noted for their abundant wildlife, including giant tortoises and many other endemic species.

galaxy • **n.** (pl. **galaxies**) **1** a system of millions or billions of stars. **2** (**the Galaxy**) the galaxy of which the solar system is a part; the Milky Way.
– ORIGIN from Greek *galaxias kuklos* 'milky vault' (referring to the Milky Way).

Galba E
/gal-buh/ (*c.*3 BC–AD 69; full name *Servius Sulpicius Galba*), Roman emperor AD 68–9. He aroused hostility by his severity and was murdered.

Galbraith E
/gal-brayth/, John Kenneth (b.1908), Canadian-born American economist, known for his criticism of consumerism and of the power of large multinational corporations.

gale • **n. 1** a very strong wind. **2** an outburst of laughter.
– ORIGIN perh. from Old Norse, 'mad, frantic'.

Galen E
/gay-luhn/ (129–99), Greek physician, who made important discoveries in anatomy and physiology, and whose works dominated medieval medicine.

Galicia E
/guh-li-si-uh, guh-li-shuh/ an autonomous region and former kingdom of NW Spain; capital, Santiago de Compostela.

Galilee E
/ga-li-lee/ a northern region of ancient Palestine, associated with the life of Jesus. It is now part of Israel.

Galilee, Sea of E
a lake in northern Israel, through which the River Jordan flows from north to south. Also called LAKE TIBERIAS, LAKE KINNERET.

Galileo Galilei E
/ga-li-lay-oh ga-li-lay-ee/ (1564–1642), Italian astronomer and physicist, who discovered the constancy of a pendulum's swing and the uniform acceleration of falling bodies. He also pioneered the use of the telescope and observed craters on the moon, sunspots, Jupiter's moons, and the phases of Venus.

gall[1] /gawl/ • **n. 1** bold and impudent behaviour. **2** bitterness or cruelty.
– ORIGIN Old English.

gall[2] /gawl/ • **n. 1** annoyance; irritation. **2** a sore on the skin made by chafing. • **v. 1** annoy; irritate. **2** make sore by chafing.
– ORIGIN Old English.

gall[3] /gawl/ • **n.** an abnormal growth caused by the presence of insect larvae, mites, or fungi on plants and trees.
– ORIGIN Latin *galla*.

gall. • **abbrev.** gallon(s).

gallant /gal-luhnt/ • **adj. 1** brave; heroic. **2** /guh-lant/ (of a man) charming; chivalrous. • **n.** /guh-lant/ a man who is charmingly attentive to women.
– DERIVATIVES **gallantly** adv.
– ORIGIN Old French *galant*.

gallantry • **n.** (pl. **gallantries**) **1** courageous behaviour. **2** polite attention or respect given by men to women.

gall bladder • **n.** a small sac-shaped organ beneath the liver, in which bile is stored.

galleon • **n.** hist. a large square-rigged sailing ship with three or more decks and masts.
– ORIGIN French *galion* or Spanish *galeón*.

gallery • **n.** (pl. **galleries**) **1** a room or building in which works of art are displayed or sold. **2** a balcony or upper floor projecting

from a back or side wall inside a hall or church. **3** the highest balcony in a theatre, having the cheapest seats. **4** a horizontal underground passage in a mine.
– PHRASES **play to the gallery** aim to attract popular attention.
– ORIGIN Italian *galleria*.

galley • n. (pl. **galleys**) **1** hist. a low, flat ship with one or more sails and up to three banks of oars. **2** a narrow kitchen in a ship or aircraft.
– ORIGIN Greek *galaia*.

Gallic /gal-lik/ • adj. having to do with France or the French.
– ORIGIN Latin *Gallicus*.

gallimaufry /gal-li-maw-fri/ • n. a jumble or medley.
– ORIGIN archaic French *galimafrée* 'unappetizing dish'.

Gallipoli E
/guh-li-puh-li/ a major campaign (1915–16) of the First World War on the Gallipoli peninsula, on the European side of the Dardanelles. The Allied troops were withdrawn after each side suffered heavy casualties.

gallium /gal-li-uhm/ • n. a soft, silvery-white metallic chemical element.
– ORIGIN Latin *Gallia* 'France' or *gallus* 'cock'.

gallivant /gal-li-vant/ • v. informal go from place to place seeking pleasure and entertainment.
– ORIGIN perh. from **GALLANT**.

gallon /gal-luhn/ • n. **1** Brit. a unit of volume for liquid measure equal to eight pints (4.55 litres). **2** (**gallons**) informal large quantities.
– ORIGIN Old French *galon*.

gallop • n. **1** the fastest pace of a horse, with all the feet off the ground together in each stride. **2** a ride on a horse at a gallop. • v. (**gallops**, **galloping**, **galloped**) **1** go or cause to go at the pace of a gallop. **2** go at great speed.
– ORIGIN Old French *galoper*.

gallows • pl. n. **1** a structure consisting of two uprights and a crosspiece, used for hanging a person. **2** (**the gallows**) execution by hanging.
– ORIGIN Old English.

gallows humour • n. grim humour in a desperate or hopeless situation.

gallstone /gawl-stohn/ • n. a hard mass of crystals formed abnormally in the gall bladder or bile ducts from bile pigments, cholesterol, and calcium salts.

Gallup poll /gal-luhp/ • n. trademark an assessment of public opinion by the questioning of a representative sample.
– ORIGIN from the name of the American statistician George H. *Gallup* (1901–84).

galore • adj. in abundance: *there were prizes galore*.
– ORIGIN from Irish *go leor* 'to sufficiency'.

galosh /guh-losh/ • n. a waterproof rubber overshoe.
– ORIGIN from Latin *gallica solea* 'Gallic shoe'.

Galsworthy E
/gawlz-wer-*thi*/, John (1867–1933), English novelist and dramatist, noted for his series of novels *The Forsyte Saga*.

galumph /guh-lumf/ • v. informal move in a clumsy or noisy way.
– ORIGIN coined by Lewis Carroll in *Through the Looking Glass*.

Galvani E
/gal-vah-ni/, Luigi (1737–98), Italian anatomist, who showed, by the twitching of frogs' legs in an electric field, that electricity is involved in the processes of life.

galvanic /gal-van-ik/ • adj. having to do with electric currents produced by chemical action.
– ORIGIN French *galvanique*.

galvanize /gal-vuh-nyz/ (also **galvanise**) • v. (**galvanizes**, **galvanizing**, **galvanized**) **1** shock or excite into action. **2** (**galvanized**) (of iron or steel) coated with a protective layer of zinc.
– ORIGIN named after Luigi **GALVANI**.

galvanometer /gal-vuh-nom-i-ter/ • n. an instrument for detecting and measuring small electric currents.

Galway E
/gawl-way/ a county in the west of the Republic of Ireland; county town, Galway.

Galway Bay E
an inlet of the Atlantic Ocean on the west coast of Ireland.

Gama, Vasco da E
see **DA GAMA**.

Gambia E
/gam-bi-uh/ (also **the Gambia**) a country on the coast of West Africa; capital, Banjul.
– DERIVATIVES **Gambian** adj. & n.

gambit • n. an action or remark intended to gain an advantage.
– ORIGIN Italian *gambetto* 'tripping up'.

gamble • v. (**gambles**, **gambling**, **gambled**) **1** play games of chance for money. **2** bet (a sum of money). **3** take risky action in the hope of a desired result. • n. **1** an act of gambling. **2** a risky undertaking.
– DERIVATIVES **gambler** n.
– ORIGIN from former *gamel* 'play games', or from **GAME**[1].

gambol • v. (**gambols**, **gambolling**, **gambolled**; US **gambols**, **gamboling**, **gamboled**) run or jump about playfully.
– ORIGIN Italian *gambata* 'trip up'.

game[1] • n. **1** an activity that one does for amusement. **2** a form of competitive activity or sport played according to rules. **3** a complete period of play, ending in a final result. **4** a part of a tennis match, forming a unit of scoring. **5** (**games**) a meeting for sporting contests. **6** the equipment used in playing a board game, computer game, etc. **7** a type of activity or business regarded as a game. **8** wild mammals or birds hunted for sport or food. • adj. eager and willing to do something new or challenging: *they were game for anything*. • v. (**games**, **gaming**, **gamed**) play at games of chance for money.
– PHRASES **the game is up** the deception or crime is revealed or foiled. **on the game** Brit. informal working as a prostitute.
– DERIVATIVES **gamely** adv.
– ORIGIN Old English.

game[2] • adj. (of a person's leg) lame.
– ORIGIN unknown.

g

game bird • n. a bird shot for sport or food.

gamekeeper • n. a person employed to breed and protect game for a large estate.

game plan • n. a plan for success in sport, politics, or business.

gamer • n. a participant in a computer or role-playing game.

game show • n. a programme on television in which people compete to win prizes.

gamesmanship • n. the art of winning games by using ploys to gain a psychological advantage.

gamete /gam-eet/ • n. Biol. a cell which is able to unite with another of the opposite sex in sexual reproduction to form a zygote.
– ORIGIN Greek, 'wife'.

gamey • adj. var. of **GAMY**.

gamine /ga-**meen**/ • adj. (of a girl) having a mischievous, boyish charm.
– ORIGIN French.

gamma /gam-muh/ • n. the third letter of the Greek alphabet (Γ, γ).
– ORIGIN Greek.

gamma rays (also **gamma radiation**) • pl. n. electromagnetic radiation of shorter wavelength than X-rays.

gammon • n. **1** ham which has been cured like bacon. **2** the bottom piece of a side of bacon, including a hind leg.
– ORIGIN Old French *gambon*.

gammy • adj. Brit. informal (especially of a leg) unable to function normally because of injury or pain.
– ORIGIN dialect form of **GAME**[2].

gamut /gam-uht/ • n. **1** the complete range or scope of something. **2** a complete scale of musical notes.
– PHRASES **run the gamut** experience or perform the complete range of something.
– ORIGIN from Latin *gamma ut*, the lowest note in the medieval scale.

gamy (also **gamey**) • adj. (of meat) having the strong flavour or smell of game when it is high.

Ganapati E
/gun-uh-**put**-i/ Hinduism = **GANESH**.

gander /gan-der/ • n. **1** a male goose. **2** informal a look.
– ORIGIN Old English.

Gandhi[1] E
/gan-di/, Mrs Indira (1917–84), Indian stateswoman, Prime Minister 1966–77 and 1980–4. The daughter of Jawaharlal Nehru, she sought to establish a secular state and was assassinated by her own Sikh bodyguards.

Gandhi[2] E
/gan-di/, Mahatma (1869–1948), Indian nationalist and spiritual leader. He became prominent in the opposition to British rule in India, pursuing a policy of non-violent civil disobedience. He was assassinated by a Hindu following his agreement to the creation of the state of Pakistan.

Gandhi[3] E
/gan-di/, Rajiv (1944–91), Indian statesman, Prime Minister 1984–9. The son of Indira Gandhi, he was assassinated during an election campaign.

Ganesh E
/guh-**naysh**/ an elephant-headed Hindu god, son of Shiva and Parvati. Also called **GANAPATI**.

gang • n. **1** an organized group of criminals or rowdy young people. **2** informal a group of people who regularly meet and do things together. **3** an organized group of people doing manual work. • v. **1** (**gang together**) form a group or gang. **2** (**gang up**) join together in opposition to someone.
– ORIGIN Old Norse, 'course, going'.

gang bang • n. informal **1** a gang rape. **2** a sexual orgy.

Ganges E
/gan-jeez/ a river of northern India and Bangladesh, which rises in the Himalayas and flows south-east to the Bay of Bengal. The river is regarded by Hindus as sacred.

gangling (also **gangly**) • adj. (of a person) tall, thin, and awkward.
– ORIGIN Old English, 'go'.

ganglion /gang-gli-uhn/ • n. (pl. **ganglia** /gang-gli-uh/ or **ganglions**) **1** a structure containing a number of nerve cells, often forming a swelling on a nerve fibre. **2** a harmless swelling on a tendon.
– ORIGIN Greek.

gangplank • n. a movable plank used to board or leave a ship or boat.

gang rape • n. the rape of one person by a group of other people.

gangrene /gang-green/ • n. the death of body tissue, resulting from either obstructed circulation or infection.
– ORIGIN Greek *gangraina*.

gangster • n. a member of an organized gang of violent criminals.

gangway • n. **1** a raised platform or walkway providing a passage. **2** a movable bridge linking a ship to the shore. **3** Brit. a passage between rows of seats.

ganja /gan-juh/ • n. cannabis.
– ORIGIN Hindi.

gannet /gan-nit/ • n. **1** a large seabird with mainly white plumage. **2** Brit. informal a greedy person.
– ORIGIN Old English.

gantry • n. (pl. **gantries**) a bridge-like overhead structure supporting equipment such as a crane or railway signals.
– ORIGIN prob. from **GALLON** + **TREE**.

gaol • n. Brit. var. of **JAIL**.

gap • n. **1** a break or hole in an object or between two objects. **2** a space, interval, or break.
– DERIVATIVES **gappy** adj.
– ORIGIN Old Norse, 'chasm'.

gape • v. (**gapes**, **gaping**, **gaped**) **1** be or become wide open. **2** stare with one's mouth open wide in amazement. • n. **1** a wide opening. **2** an open-mouthed stare.
– ORIGIN Old Norse.

gap year • n. a period taken by a student as a break from education between leaving school and starting a university or college course.

garage /ga-rahj/ • n. **1** a building for housing a motor vehicle or vehicles. **2** an establishment which sells fuel or which repairs and sells motor vehicles. • v. (**garages**, **garaging**, **garaged**) put or keep (a motor ve-

hicle) in a garage.
– ORIGIN French.

garb ● n. clothing or dress of a particular kind. ● v. (**be garbed**) be dressed in particular clothes.
– ORIGIN French.

garbage ● n. esp. N. Amer. **1** domestic rubbish or waste. **2** something worthless or meaningless.
– ORIGIN Old French.

garble ● v. (**garbles**, **garbling**, **garbled**) reproduce (a message or transmission) in a confused and distorted way.
– ORIGIN Arabic, 'sift'.

Garbo, E
Greta (1905–90; born *Greta Gustafsson*), Swedish-born American actress, known for such films as *Mata Hari* and *Anna Karenina*.

García Lorca E
see **Lorca**.

García Márquez E
/gar-see-uh **mar**-kez/, Gabriel (b.1928), Colombian novelist. He is best known for *One Hundred Years of Solitude*, a major example of magic realism (literature combining realistic and fantasy elements).

Garda, Lake E
/**gar**-duh/ a lake in NE Italy.

garden ● n. **1** esp. Brit. a piece of ground next to a house, with a lawn or flowers. **2** (**gardens**) ornamental grounds laid out for public enjoyment. ● v. cultivate or work in a garden.
– DERIVATIVES **gardener** n.
– ORIGIN Old French *jardin*.

garden centre ● n. a place that sells plants and gardening equipment.

garden city ● n. a new town built on a plan incorporating open space and greenery.

gardenia /gar-**dee**-ni-uh/ ● n. a tree or shrub with large white or yellow flowers.
– ORIGIN named after the Scottish naturalist Dr Alexander *Garden* (1730–91).

Garden of Eden E
see **Eden**[2].

garden party ● n. a social event held on a lawn in a garden.

Gardner, E
Ava (Lavinia) (1922–90), American actress, known for such films such as *Bhowani Junction* and *The Night of the Iguana*.

Garfield, E
James Abram (1831–81), American Republican statesman, 20th President of the US March–September 1881. He was assassinated soon after becoming President.

gargantuan /gar-**gan**-tyuu-uhn/ ● adj. enormous.
– ORIGIN from *Gargantua*, a giant in a book by Rabelais.

gargle ● v. (**gargles**, **gargling**, **gargled**) wash one's mouth and throat with a liquid that is kept in motion by breathing through it.
– ORIGIN French *gargouiller* 'to gurgle'.

gargoyle /**gar**-goyl/ ● n. a grotesque face or figure carved on the gutter of a building.
– ORIGIN Old French *gargouille*.

Garibaldi E
/ga-ri-**bawl**-di/, Giuseppe (1807–82), Italian patriot and military leader. His capture of Sicily and southern Italy from the Austrians in 1860–1 played a key role in forming a united kingdom of Italy.

garish /**gair**-ish/ ● adj. unpleasantly bright and showy; lurid.
– DERIVATIVES **garishly** adv. **garishness** n.
– ORIGIN unknown.

Garland, E
Judy (1922–69; born *Frances Gumm*), American singer and actress, famous for her roles in such films as *The Wizard of Oz* and *A Star is Born*.

garland ● n. a wreath of flowers and leaves, worn on the head or hung as a decoration. ● v. decorate with a garland.
– ORIGIN Old French *garlande*.

garlic ● n. the strong-smelling bulb of a plant of the onion family, used in cookery.
– ORIGIN Old English.

garment ● n. an item of clothing.
– ORIGIN Old French *garnement* 'equipment'.

garner ● v. (**garners**, **garnering**, **garnered**) gather or collect.
– ORIGIN Old French *gernier*.

garnet /**gar**-nit/ ● n. a red semi-precious stone.
– ORIGIN Old French *grenat*.

garnish ● v. **1** decorate (food). ● n. a decoration for food.
– ORIGIN Old French *garnir* 'equip'.

Garonne E
/ga-**ron**/ a river of SW France which rises in the Pyrenees and flows north-west to join the Dordogne at the Gironde estuary north of Bordeaux.

garret ● n. a top-floor or attic room.
– ORIGIN Old French *garite* 'watchtower'.

Garrick, E
David (1717–79), English actor and theatre manager.

garrison ● n. a body of troops stationed in a fortress or town to defend it. ● v. provide (a place) with a garrison.
– ORIGIN Old French *garison*.

garrotte /guh-**rot**/ (US **garrote**) ● v. (**garrottes**, **garrotting**, **garrotted**; US **garrotes**, **garroting**, **garroted**) kill by strangulation. ● n. a wire or cord used for garrotting.
– ORIGIN Spanish *garrote*.

garrulous /**ga**-rjuh-luhss/ ● adj. extremely talkative.
– DERIVATIVES **garrulity** /guh-**roo**-li-ti/ n.
– ORIGIN Latin *garrulus*.

garter ● n. **1** a band worn around the leg to keep up a stocking or sock. **2** N. Amer. a suspender for a sock or stocking.
– ORIGIN Old French *gartier*.

gas ● n. (pl. **gases** or esp. US **gasses**) **1** an air-like fluid substance which expands to fill any space available. **2** a flammable substance of this type used as a fuel. **3** a gas used as an anaesthetic. **4** N. Amer. informal petrol. ● v. (**gases**, **gassing**, **gassed**) **1** harm or kill with gas. **2** informal chatter.
– ORIGIN invented by the Belgian chemist J. B. van Helmont (1577–1644).

gasbag ● **n.** informal a person who chatters too much.

gas chamber ● **n.** an airtight room that can be filled with poisonous gas to kill people or animals.

Gascony E
/gass-kuh-ni/ a region and former province of SW France, in the northern foothills of the Pyrenees.

gaseous /gass-i-uhss/ ● **adj.** relating to or like a gas.

gash ● **n.** a long slash, cut, or wound. ● **v.** make a gash in.
– ORIGIN Old French *garcer* 'to crack'.

Gaskell, E
Mrs Elizabeth (Cleghorn) (1810–65), English novelist, whose works, including *Cranford* and *North and South*, reflect her interest in social concerns.

g

gasket /gass-kit/ ● **n.** a sheet or ring of rubber sealing the junction between two surfaces in an engine or other device.
– ORIGIN perh. from French *garcette* 'thin rope'.

gaslight ● **n.** light from a gas lamp.
– DERIVATIVES **gaslit** adj.

gas mask ● **n.** a protective mask used to cover the face as a defence against poison gas.

gasoline (also **gasolene**) ● **n.** N. Amer. petrol.

gasometer /gass-om-i-ter/ ● **n.** a large tank in which gas is stored before being distributed to consumers.

gasp ● **v. 1** catch one's breath with an open mouth, from pain, breathlessness, or astonishment. **2** (**gasp for**) strain to obtain (air) by gasping. **3** (**be gasping for**) informal be desperate to have. ● **n.** a sudden catching of breath.
– ORIGIN Old Norse, 'to yawn'.

gassy ● **adj.** (**gassier**, **gassiest**) resembling or full of gas.

gastric ● **adj.** having to do with the stomach.
– ORIGIN Greek *gastēr* 'stomach'.

gastric flu ● **n.** a short-lived stomach disorder of unknown cause.

gastric juice ● **n.** an acidic substance produced by the stomach glands which aids digestion.

gastritis /gass-try-tiss/ ● **n.** inflammation of the lining of the stomach.

gastro-enteritis ● **n.** inflammation of the stomach and intestines, causing vomiting and diarrhoea.

gastronomy /gass-tron-uh-mi/ ● **n.** the practice or art of choosing, cooking, and eating good food.
– DERIVATIVES **gastronomic** adj.
– ORIGIN Greek *gastronomia*.

gastropod /gass-truh-pod/ ● **n.** Zool. any of a large class of molluscs including snails and slugs.
– ORIGIN from Greek *gastēr* 'stomach' + *pous* 'foot'.

gas turbine ● **n.** a turbine driven by expanding hot gases produced by burning fuel, as in a jet engine.

gasworks ● **pl. n.** a place where gas is manufactured and processed.

gate ● **n. 1** a hinged barrier used to close an opening in a wall, fence, or hedge. **2** an exit from an airport building to an aircraft. **3** a hinged or sliding barrier for controlling the flow of water. **4** the number of people who pay to enter a sports ground for an event. **5** an electric circuit with an output which depends on the combination of several inputs.
– ORIGIN Old English.

gateau /gat-oh/ ● **n.** (pl. **gateaus** or **gateaux** /gat-ohz/) Brit. a rich cake having layers of cream or fruit.
– ORIGIN French.

gatecrash ● **v.** enter (a party) without an invitation or ticket.
– DERIVATIVES **gatecrasher** n.

gatefold ● **n.** an oversized page in a book or magazine, intended to be opened out for reading.

gatehouse ● **n.** a house standing by the gateway to a country estate.

gatekeeper ● **n.** an attendant at a gate.

gateleg table ● **n.** a table with hinged legs that may be swung out from the centre to support folding leaves.

gatepost ● **n.** a post on which a gate is hinged or against which it shuts.

Gates, E
Bill (b.1955; full name *William Henry Gates*), American computer entrepreneur, co-founder of the software company Microsoft.

gateway ● **n. 1** an opening that can be closed by a gate. **2** a frame built around or over a gate.

gather ● **v.** (**gathers**, **gathering**, **gathered**) **1** come or bring together; assemble. **2** harvest (a crop). **3** collect plants, fruits, etc., for food. **4** draw together or towards oneself: *she gathered the child in her arms.* **5** increase in speed, force, etc. **6** infer; understand. **7** pull and hold together (fabric) in a series of folds by drawing thread through it. ● **n.** (**gathers**) a series of folds in fabric, formed by gathering.
– DERIVATIVES **gatherer** n.
– ORIGIN Old English.

gathering ● **n.** an assembly of people.

gauche /gohsh/ ● **adj.** socially awkward or unsophisticated.
– ORIGIN French, 'left'.

gaucho /gow-choh/ ● **n.** (pl. **gauchos**) a cowboy from the South American plains.
– ORIGIN Latin American Spanish.

Gaudí E
/gow-dee/, Antonio (1853–1926; full name *Antonio Gaudí y Cornet*), Spanish architect. A leading exponent of art nouveau, he is famous for his ornate church of the Sagrada Familia in Barcelona.

gaudy ● **adj.** (**gaudier**, **gaudiest**) excessively or tastelessly bright or showy.
– DERIVATIVES **gaudily** adv.
– ORIGIN prob. from Old French *gaudir* 'rejoice'.

gauge /gayj/ (US also **gage**) ● **n. 1** an instrument that measures and gives a visual display of the amount, level, or contents of something. **2** the thickness, size, or capacity of a wire, tube, etc. **3** the distance between the rails of a railway track. ● **v.** (**gauges**, **gauging**, **gauged**; US **gages**, **gaging**, **gaged**) **1** estimate or measure the amount or level of. **2** judge (a situation, mood, etc.).
– ORIGIN Old French.

Gauguin E
/goh-gan/, (Eugène Henri) Paul (1848–1903), French painter. From 1891 he lived mainly in Tahiti, painting in a post-Impressionist style that was influenced by primitive art.

Gaul[1] E
/gawl/ an ancient region of Europe, corresponding to modern France, Belgium, the south Netherlands, SW Germany, and northern Italy.

Gaul[2] /gawl/ • n. a person from ancient Gaul.
– ORIGIN Latin *Gallus*.

Gaulle, E
Charles de, see **DE GAULLE**.

Gaunt, E
John of, see **JOHN OF GAUNT**.

gaunt • adj. **1** lean and haggard. **2** (of a place) grim or desolate.
– ORIGIN unknown.

gauntlet[1] • n. **1** a strong glove with a long loose wrist. **2** a glove worn as part of medieval armour.
– PHRASES **take up** (or **throw down**) **the gauntlet** accept (or give) a challenge.
– ORIGIN Old French *gantelet*.

gauntlet[2] (US also **gantlet**) • n. (in phr. **run the gauntlet**) go through an intimidating crowd or experience in order to reach a goal.
– ORIGIN from Swedish *gata* 'lane' + *lopp* 'course'.

Gauss E
/gowss/, Karl Friedrich (1777–1855), German mathematician, astronomer, and physicist. He laid the foundations of number theory and contributed to the development of geometry and electromagnetism.

Gauteng F
/khow-teng, khow-uh-teng/ a province of north-eastern South Africa; capital, Johannesburg. Former name (until 1995) **PRETORIA-WITWATERSRAND VEREENIGING**.

gauze /gawz/ • n. **1** a thin transparent fabric. **2** Med. thin cloth used for dressing and swabbing wounds. **3** (also **wire gauze**) a fine wire mesh.
– DERIVATIVES **gauzy** adj.
– ORIGIN French *gaze*.

Gavaskar E
/gav-uh-sker, gav-uh-skar/, Sunil Manohar (b.1949), Indian cricketer. He captained India, and in 1987 became the first batsman to score 10,000 runs in Test cricket.

gave past of **GIVE**.

gavel /gav-uhl/ • n. a small hammer with which an auctioneer or judge hits a surface to call for attention or order.
– ORIGIN unknown.

gavotte /guh-vot/ • n. a medium-paced French dance, popular in the 18th century.
– ORIGIN Provençal *gavoto* 'dance of the mountain people'.

gawk • v. stare openly and stupidly.
– ORIGIN perh. from Old Norse 'to heed'.

gawky • adj. (**gawkier**, **gawkiest**) nervously awkward and ungainly.
– ORIGIN perh. from **GAPE**.

gawp • v. Brit. informal stare openly in a stupid or rude manner.

gay • adj. (**gayer**, **gayest**) **1** (especially of a man) homosexual. **2** relating to homosexuals. **3** dated light-hearted and carefree. **4** dated brightly coloured. • n. a homosexual person, especially a man.
– ORIGIN Old French *gai*.

Gaye, E
Marvin (1939–84), American soul singer, composer, and musician.

gayety • n. US = **GAIETY**.

Gaza Strip E
/gah-zuh/ a strip of territory in Palestine, on the SE Mediterranean coast, including the town of Gaza. Administered by Egypt from 1949, and occupied by Israel from 1967, it became a self-governing enclave in 1994.

gaze • v. (**gazes**, **gazing**, **gazed**) look steadily and intently. • n. a steady intent look.
– DERIVATIVES **gazer** n.
– ORIGIN perh. from **GAWK**.

gazebo /guh-zee-boh/ • n. (pl. **gazebos** or **gazeboes**) a summer house offering a wide view of the surrounding area.
– ORIGIN perh. from **GAZE**.

gazelle • n. a small antelope with curved horns and white underparts.
– ORIGIN French.

gazette • n. a journal or newspaper.
– ORIGIN from Venetian *gazeta de la novità* 'a halfpennyworth of news'.

gazetteer /ga-zuh-teer/ • n. a geographical index or dictionary.

gazump /guh-zump/ • v. Brit. informal deprive (someone whose offer to purchase a house has already been accepted) from proceeding with the purchase by offering or accepting a higher figure.
– ORIGIN Yiddish, 'overcharge'.

GB • abbrev. **1** Great Britain. **2** (also **Gb**) Computing gigabyte(s).

GBE • abbrev. Knight or Dame Grand Cross of the Order of the British Empire.

GBH • abbrev. Brit. grievous bodily harm.

GC • abbrev. George Cross.

GCB • abbrev. Knight or Dame Grand Cross of the Order of the Bath.

GCE • abbrev. General Certificate of Education.

GCMG • abbrev. Knight or Dame Grand Cross of the Order of St Michael and St George.

GCSE • abbrev. (in the UK except Scotland) General Certificate of Secondary Education (the lower of the two main levels of the GCE examination).

GCVO • abbrev. Knight or Dame Grand Cross of the Royal Victorian Order.

Gdańsk E
/guh-dansk/ an industrial port and shipbuilding centre in northern Poland, on an inlet of the Baltic Sea.

GDP • abbrev. gross domestic product.

gear • n. **1** a toothed wheel that works with others to alter the relation between the speed of an engine and the speed of the driven parts. **2** a particular setting of engaged gears. **3** informal equipment or clothing. • v. **1** design or adjust gears to give a specified speed or power output. **2** (**gear up**) equip or prepare.

– PHRASES **in** (or **out of**) **gear** with a gear (or no gear) engaged.
– ORIGIN Scandinavian.

gearbox ● n. a set of gears with its casing, especially in a motor vehicle.

gear lever (also **gearstick**) ● n. Brit. a lever used to engage or change gear in a motor vehicle.

gearwheel ● n. **1** a toothed wheel in a set of gears. **2** (on a bicycle) a cogwheel driven directly by the chain.

gecko /gek-koh/ ● n. (pl. **geckos** or **geckoes**) a lizard of warm regions, with adhesive pads on the feet.
– ORIGIN Malay.

gee ● exclam. **1** (**gee up**) a command to a horse to go faster. **2** (also **gee whiz**) N. Amer. informal a mild expression of surprise, enthusiasm, or sympathy.
– ORIGIN unknown.

g

geek /geek/ ● n. informal **1** a person who is socially uncomfortable or unfashionable. **2** an obsessive enthusiast.
– DERIVATIVES **geeky** adj.
– ORIGIN from dialect *geck* 'fool'.

geese pl. of **GOOSE**.

geezer /gee-zer/ ● n. informal a man.
– ORIGIN from former *guiser* 'mummer'.

Gehry E
/*rhymes with* dairy/, Frank (Owen) (b.1929), Canadian-born American architect and designer, whose buildings include the Guggenheim Museum in Bilbao.

Geiger E
/gy-ger/, Hans (Johann) Wilhelm (1882–1945), German nuclear physicist, who developed a prototype radiation counter for detecting alpha particles (1908).

Geiger counter ● n. a device for measuring radioactivity.
– ORIGIN named after Hans **GEIGER**.

G8 ● abbrev. Group of Eight.

geisha /gay-shuh/ ● n. (pl. **geisha** or **geishas**) a Japanese hostess trained to entertain men with conversation, dance, and song.
– ORIGIN Japanese.

gel[1] /jel/ ● n. **1** a jelly-like substance, used cosmetically on the hair or skin. **2** Chem. a semi-solid suspension of a solid dispersed in a liquid.
– ORIGIN from **GELATIN**.

gel[2] /jel/ ● v. var. of **JELL**.

gelatin /jel-uh-tin/ (also **gelatine** /jel--uh-teen/) ● n. **1** a water-soluble protein used in food preparation, in photographic processing, and for making glue. **2** a high explosive consisting chiefly of a gel of nitroglycerine with added cellulose nitrate.
– DERIVATIVES **gelatinous** adj.
– ORIGIN French *gélatine*.

geld ● v. castrate (a male animal).
– ORIGIN Old Norse, 'barren'.

gelding ● n. a castrated animal, especially a male horse.

gelid /jel-id/ ● adj. very cold; icy.
– ORIGIN Latin *gelidus*.

gelignite /jel-ig-nyt/ ● n. a high explosive made from nitroglycerine in a base of wood pulp and sodium.
– ORIGIN prob. from **GELATIN** + Latin *lignis* 'wood'.

Gell-Mann E
/gel-**man**/, Murray (b.1929), American theoretical physicist. He coined the word *quark* and proposed the concept of strangeness in quarks.

gem ● n. **1** a precious or semi-precious stone. **2** an outstanding person or thing.
– ORIGIN Latin *gemma* 'bud, jewel'.

Gemini ● n. a constellation (the Twins) and sign of the zodiac, which the sun enters about 21 May.
– ORIGIN Latin, 'twins'.

gemstone ● n. a gem used in a piece of jewellery.

gen /jen/ Brit. informal ● n. information. ● v. (**gens, genning, genned**) (**gen up**) provide with or obtain information.
– ORIGIN perh. from *general information*.

gendarme /*zhon*-darm/ ● n. a police officer in French-speaking countries.
– ORIGIN French.

gender ● n. **1** Grammar a class (usually masculine, feminine, common, or neuter) into which nouns and pronouns are placed in some languages. **2** the state of being male or female (with reference to social or cultural differences). **3** the members of one or other sex.
– ORIGIN Old French *gendre*.

gene /jeen/ ● n. Biol. a distinct sequence of DNA forming part of a chromosome, by which offspring inherit characteristics from a parent.
– ORIGIN German *Gen*.

genealogy /jee-ni-al-uh-ji/ ● n. (pl. **genealogies**) **1** a line of descent traced from an ancestor. **2** the study of lines of descent.
– DERIVATIVES **genealogical** adj. **genealogist** n.
– ORIGIN Greek *genealogia*.

gene pool ● n. the stock of different genes in an interbreeding population.

genera pl. of **GENUS**.

general ● adj. **1** affecting or concerning all or most people or things. **2** involving only the main features or elements; not detailed. **3** chief: *the general manager.* ● n. a commander of an army, or an army officer ranking above lieutenant general.
– PHRASES **in general 1** usually; mainly. **2** as a whole.
– ORIGIN Latin *generalis*.

general anaesthetic ● n. an anaesthetic that affects the whole body and causes a loss of consciousness.

general election ● n. the election of representatives to a law-making body from constituencies throughout the country.

generalist ● n. a person competent in several different fields or activities.

generality ● n. (pl. **generalities**) **1** a statement that is general rather than specific. **2** the state of being general. **3** (**the generality**) the majority.

generalize (also **generalise**) ● v. (**generalizes, generalizing, generalized**) **1** make a general or broad statement based on specific cases. **2** make more common or more widely applicable. **3** (**generalized**) Med. (of a disease) affecting much or all of the body.

– DERIVATIVES **generalization** (also **generalisation**) n.

generally ● adv. **1** in most cases or by most people. **2** without regard to exceptions.

general meeting ● n. a meeting open to all members of an organization.

general practice ● n. a community medical practice treating patients with minor or long-lasting illnesses.

general practitioner ● n. a community doctor who treats patients with minor or long-lasting illnesses.

general staff ● n. the staff assisting a military commander.

general strike ● n. a strike of workers in all or most industries.

generate ● v. (**generates, generating, generated**) **1** cause to arise or come about. **2** produce (energy).

– ORIGIN Latin *generare*.

generation ● n. **1** all of the people born and living at about the same time. **2** the average period in which children grow up and have children of their own (usually reckoned as about thirty years). **3** a set of members of a family regarded as a single stage in descent. **4** the action of producing or generating.

– DERIVATIVES **generational** adj.

generation gap ● n. a difference in attitudes between people of different generations.

generative ● adj. capable of producing something.

generator ● n. **1** a person or thing that generates. **2** a dynamo or similar machine for converting mechanical energy into electricity.

generic /ji-ne-rik/ ● adj. **1** referring to a class or group; not specific. **2** (of goods) having no brand name. **3** Biol. relating to a genus.

– DERIVATIVES **generically** adv.

– ORIGIN Latin *genus* 'stock, race'.

generous ● adj. **1** freely giving more than is necessary or expected. **2** kind towards others. **3** larger or more plentiful than is usual: *a generous sprinkle of pepper.*

– DERIVATIVES **generosity** n. **generously** adv.

– ORIGIN Latin *generosus* 'noble'.

genesis /jen-i-siss/ ● n. the origin of something.

– ORIGIN Greek.

Genet E
/*zh*uh-nay/, Jean (1910–86), French novelist, poet, and dramatist, best known for his play *The Maids* and for his novel *Our Lady of the Flowers.*

gene therapy ● n. the introduction of normal genes into cells in order to correct genetic disorders.

genetic ● adj. **1** relating to genes or heredity. **2** relating to genetics.

– DERIVATIVES **genetical** adj. **genetically** adv.

genetically modified ● adj. (of an organism) containing genetic material that has been artificially altered so as to produce a desired characteristic.

genetic code ● n. the means by which DNA and RNA molecules carry genetic information.

genetic engineering ● n. the deliberate alteration of an organism by manipulating its genetic material.

genetic fingerprinting (also **genetic profiling**) ● n. the analysis of DNA from samples of body tissues or fluids in order to identify individuals.

genetics ● n. the study of heredity and the variation of inherited characteristics.

– DERIVATIVES **geneticist** n.

Geneva E
/ji-nee-vuh/ a city in SW Switzerland, on Lake Geneva.

Geneva, Lake E
a lake in SW central Europe, on the border between France and Switzerland.

Geneva Convention E
an international agreement first made at Geneva in 1864 and later revised, governing the status and treatment of captured and wounded military personnel and civilians in wartime.

Genghis Khan E
/geng-giss **kahn**/ (1162–1227; born *Temujin*), founder of the Mongol empire. He united the Mongol tribes, and by the time of his death his empire extended from China to the Black Sea.

genial /jee-ni-uhl/ ● adj. friendly and cheerful.

– DERIVATIVES **geniality** n. **genially** adv.

– ORIGIN Latin *genialis* 'productive'.

-genic ● comb. form **1** producing or produced by: *carcinogenic.* **2** well suited to: *photogenic.*

genie /jee-ni/ ● n. (pl. **genii** /jee-ni-I/ or **genies**) (in Arabian folklore) a spirit.

– ORIGIN Latin *genius* (see **GENIUS**).

genital ● adj. referring to the human or animal reproductive organs. ● n. (**genitals**) a person or animal's external reproductive organs.

– ORIGIN Latin *genitalis*.

genitalia /jen-i-tay-li-uh/ ● pl. n. formal or tech. the genitals.

– ORIGIN Latin.

genitive /jen-i-tiv/ ● adj. (of a grammatical case) showing possession.

– ORIGIN from Latin *genitivus casus* 'case of production or origin'.

genius /jee-ni-uhss/ ● n. (pl. **geniuses**) **1** exceptional natural ability. **2** an exceptionally intelligent or able person.

– ORIGIN Latin.

Genoa E
/jen-oh-uh/ a seaport on the NW coast of Italy, capital of Liguria region.
– DERIVATIVES **Genoese** /jen-oh-eez/ adj. & n.

genocide /jen-uh-syd/ ● n. the deliberate killing of a very large number of people from a particular ethnic group or nation.

– DERIVATIVES **genocidal** adj.

– ORIGIN from Greek *genos* 'race' + **-CIDE**.

genome /jee-nohm/ ● n. Biol. **1** the full set of the chromosomes of an organism. **2** the complete set of genetic material of an organism.

– ORIGIN from **GENE** and **CHROMOSOME**.

genotype /jen-uh-typ/ ● n. Biol. the genetic make-up of an individual organism.

genre /*zh*on-ruh/ ● n. a style or category of art or literature.

– ORIGIN French.

g

gent ● n. informal **1** a gentleman. **2** **(the Gents)** Brit. a men's public toilet.

genteel ● adj. polite and refined in an exaggerated way.
– ORIGIN French *gentil* 'well-born'.

gentian /jen-sh'n/ ● n. a plant with violet or blue trumpet-shaped flowers.
– ORIGIN Latin *gentiana*.

Gentile /jen-tyl/ ● adj. not Jewish. ● n. a person who is not Jewish.
– ORIGIN Latin *gentilis* 'of a family or nation'.

gentility ● n. polite and refined behaviour.
– ORIGIN Old French *gentil* 'high-born'.

gentle ● adj. **(gentler, gentlest)** **1** mild or kind; not rough or violent. **2** not harsh or severe: *a gentle breeze*.
– DERIVATIVES **gentleness** n. **gently** adv.
– ORIGIN Old French *gentil* 'high-born'.

g

gentlefolk ● pl. n. archaic people of noble birth or good social position.

gentleman ● n. **1** a courteous or honourable man. **2** a man of good social position. **3** (in polite or formal use) a man.

gentleman's agreement ● n. an arrangement which is based on trust rather than being legally binding.

gentrify ● v. **(gentrifies, gentrifying, gentrified)** renovate (a house or district) so that it follows middle-class taste.
– DERIVATIVES **gentrification** n.

gentry ● n. **(the gentry)** people of the class next below the nobility.
– ORIGIN Old French *genterie*.

genuflect /jen-yuu-flekt/ ● v. lower one's body briefly by bending one knee to the ground in worship or as a sign of respect.
– DERIVATIVES **genuflection** n.
– ORIGIN Latin *genuflectere*.

genuine ● adj. **1** truly what it is said to be; authentic: *the book is bound in genuine leather.* **2** honest.
– DERIVATIVES **genuinely** adv.
– ORIGIN Latin *genuinus*.

genus /jee-nuhss/ ● n. (pl. **genera** /jen-uh-ruh/) **1** a category in scientific classification that ranks above species and below family. **2** a class of things which have common characteristics.
– ORIGIN Latin, 'race, stock'.

geo- /jee-oh/ ● comb. form relating to the earth: *geology*.
– ORIGIN Greek *gē* 'earth'.

geode /jee-ohd/ ● n. **1** a small cavity in rock lined with crystals. **2** a rock containing such a cavity.
– ORIGIN Greek *geōdēs* 'earthy'.

geodesic /jee-oh-dess-ik/ ● adj. **1** referring to the shortest possible line between two points on a curved surface. **2** (of a dome) constructed from struts which follow geodesic lines.

geodesy /ji-od-i-si/ ● n. the branch of mathematics concerned with the shape and area of the earth.
– ORIGIN Greek *geōdaisia*.

geographical ● adj. relating to geography.
– DERIVATIVES **geographic** adj. **geographically** adv.

geography ● n. **1** the study of the physical features of the earth and of human activity as it relates to these. **2** the arrangement of places and physical features: *the geography of your college.*
– DERIVATIVES **geographer** n.

geology ● n. **1** the science which deals with the physical structure and substance of the earth. **2** the geological features of a district.
– DERIVATIVES **geological** adj. **geologist** n.

geometric /ji-uh-met-rik/ ● adj. **1** relating to geometry. **2** (of a design) decorated with regular lines and shapes.
– DERIVATIVES **geometrical** adj. **geometrically** adv.

geometric mean ● n. the central number in a geometric progression (e.g. 9 in 3, 9, 27).

geometric progression (also **geometric series**) ● n. a sequence of numbers with a constant ratio between each number and the one before (e.g. 1, 3, 9, 27, 81).

geometry /ji-om-uh-tri/ ● n. (pl. **geometries**) **1** the branch of mathematics concerned with the properties and relations of points, lines, surfaces, and solids. **2** the shape and relative arrangement of the parts of something.
– ORIGIN Greek.

geomorphology /jee-oh-mor-fol-uh-ji/ ● n. the study of the physical features of the surface of the earth and their relation to its geological structures.

geophysics ● n. the physics of the earth.
– DERIVATIVES **geophysical** adj. **geophysicist** n.

Geordie ● n. Brit. informal a person from Tyneside.
– ORIGIN from the man's name *George*.

George I E
(1660–1727), king of Great Britain and Ireland 1714–27, Elector of Hanover 1698–1727. The great-grandson of James I, he succeeded to the British throne as a result of the Act of Settlement (1701).

George II E
(1683–1760), son of George I, king of Great Britain and Ireland 1727–60, Elector of Hanover 1727–60. He was the last English king to lead his troops in battle, during the War of the Austrian Succession (1740–8).

George III E
(1738–1820), grandson of George II, king of Great Britain and Ireland 1760–1820, Elector of Hanover 1760–1815, and king of Hanover 1815–20. He suffered bouts of mental illness, as a result of which his son was made regent in 1811.

George IV E
(1762–1830), son of George III, king of Great Britain and Ireland 1820–30. He was a leader of fashion and patron of the arts, but became unpopular when he attempted to divorce his wife Caroline of Brunswick in 1820.

George V E
(1865–1936), son of Edward VII, king of Great Britain and Ireland 1910–36 (of the United Kingdom from 1920). He exercised a restrained but important influence in British politics.

George VI E
(1894–1952), son of George V, king of the United Kingdom 1936–52. He came to the throne on the abdication of his elder brother Edward VIII.

George, St, E
patron saint of England, who according to legend killed a dragon. Feast day, 23 April.

Georgetown E
the capital of Guyana.

George Town E
the capital of the Cayman Islands, on the island of Grand Cayman.

georgette /jor-**jet**/ ● n. a thin silk or crêpe dress material.
– ORIGIN named after the French dressmaker *Georgette* de la Plante (*c.*1900).

Georgia[1] E
a country of SE Europe, on the eastern shore of the Black Sea; capital, Tbilisi.
– DERIVATIVES **Georgian** adj. & n.

Georgia[2] E
a state of the south-eastern US, on the Atlantic coast; capital, Atlanta.
– DERIVATIVES **Georgian** adj. & n.

Georgian ● adj. **1** relating to the reigns of the British Kings George I–IV (1714–1830). **2** relating to British neoclassical architecture of this period.

geostationary ● adj. (of an artificial satellite) orbiting in such a way that it appears to be stationary above a fixed point on the earth's surface.

geothermal ● adj. relating to or produced by the internal heat of the earth.

geranium ● n. a garden plant with red, white, or pink flowers.
– ORIGIN Greek *geranion.*

gerbil ● n. a mouse-like desert rodent.
– ORIGIN Latin *gerbillus* 'little jerboa'.

geriatric /je-ri-**at**-rik/ ● adj. relating to old people. ● n. an old person, especially one receiving special care.
– ORIGIN from Greek *gēras* 'old age' + *iatros* 'doctor'.

geriatrics ● n. the branch of medicine or social science concerned with the health and care of old people.

Géricault E
/*zhe*-ri-koh/, (Jean Louis André) Théodore (1791–1824), French painter. His best-known work, *The Raft of the Medusa*, depicts the survivors of a famous shipwreck.

germ ● n. **1** a micro-organism, especially one which causes disease. **2** a portion of an organism capable of developing into a new one or part of one. **3** an initial stage from which something may develop: *the germ of an idea.*
– ORIGIN Latin *germen* 'seed, sprout'.

German ● n. **1** a person from Germany. **2** the language of Germany, Austria, and parts of Switzerland. ● adj. relating to Germany or German.

German Democratic Republic E
former name for East Germany (see **GERMANY**).

germane /jer-**mayn**/ ● adj. relevant to a subject under consideration.
– ORIGIN Latin *germanus* 'genuine'.

Germanic ● adj. **1** referring to the language family that includes English, German, Dutch, and the Scandinavian languages. **2** referring to the peoples of ancient northern and western Europe speaking such languages. **3** having to do with Germans or Germany. ● n. **1** the Germanic languages as a whole. **2** the ancient language from which these developed.

germanium /jer-**may**-ni-uhm/ ● n. a grey crystalline element with semiconducting properties, resembling silicon.
– ORIGIN Latin *Germanus* 'German'.

German measles ● pl. n. = **RUBELLA**.

German shepherd ● n. a large breed of dog often used as guard dogs; an Alsatian.

Germany E
a country in central Europe; capital, Berlin; seat of government, Bonn. After its defeat in the Second World War Germany was divided into two parts: the Federal Republic of Germany (or West Germany) and the German Democratic Republic (or East Germany). The two countries were reunited on 3 October 1990, after the collapse of communism in eastern Europe.

germicide ● n. a substance which destroys harmful micro-organisms.
– DERIVATIVES **germicidal** adj.

germinal ● adj. **1** relating to a gamete or embryo. **2** in the earliest stage of development.
– ORIGIN Latin *germen* 'sprout, seed'.

germinate ● v. (**germinates**, **germinating**, **germinated**) (of a seed or spore) begin to grow and put out shoots after a period of being dormant.
– DERIVATIVES **germination** n.
– ORIGIN Latin *germinare.*

germ warfare ● n. the use of disease-spreading micro-organisms as a military weapon.

Geronimo E
/juh-**ron**-i-moh/ (*c.*1829–1909), Apache chief, who led his people in raids on settlers and US troops before surrendering in 1886.

gerontology /je-ruhn-**tol**-uh-ji/ ● n. the scientific study of old age and old people.

gerrymander ● v. (**gerrymanders**, **gerrymandering**, **gerrymandered**) alter the boundaries of (an electoral constituency) so as to favour one party.
– ORIGIN from Governor Elbridge *Gerry* of Massachusetts + **SALAMANDER**, from the similarity between a salamander and the shape of a voting district created when he was in office (1812).

Gershwin, E
George (1898–1937; born *Jacob Gershovitz*), American composer and pianist. He composed the orchestral work *Rhapsody in Blue*, the opera *Porgy and Bess*, and many songs and musicals.

gerund /je-ruhnd/ ● n. Grammar a verb form which functions as a noun, in English ending in *-ing* (e.g. *asking* in *do you mind my asking you?*).
– ORIGIN Latin *gerundum.*

Gestapo /ge-**stah**-poh/ ● n. the German secret police under Nazi rule.
– ORIGIN German.

gestation /jess-**tay**-sh'n/ ● n. **1** the process of

g

developing in the womb between conception and birth. **2** the development of a plan or idea over a period of time.
– ORIGIN Latin.

gesticulate /jess-**tik**-yuu-layt/ • v. (**gesticulates**, **gesticulating**, **gesticulated**) gesture dramatically in place of or to emphasize speech.
– DERIVATIVES **gesticulation** n.
– ORIGIN Latin *gesticulari*.

gesture • n. **1** a movement of part of the body to express an idea or meaning. **2** an action performed to show one's feelings or intentions: *people sharing food is a gesture of hospitality.* • v. (**gestures**, **gesturing**, **gestured**) make a gesture.
– ORIGIN Latin *gestura*.

get • v. (**gets**, **getting**, **got**; past part. **got**, N. Amer. **gotten**) **1** come to have or hold; receive. **2** succeed in achieving or experiencing. **3** experience or suffer: *I got a sudden pain in my eye.* **4** fetch. **5** bring or come into a specified state: *it's getting late.* **6** catch or thwart. **7** come or go eventually. **8** move or come into a specified position. **9** travel by or catch (a form of transport). **10** begin to be or do something.
– PHRASES **get across** manage to communicate (an idea) clearly. **get at 1** reach. **2** informal mean. **get away with** escape blame or punishment for. **get back at** take revenge on. **get by** manage with difficulty to live or do something. **get down to** begin to do or give serious attention to. **get off** informal escape a punishment. **get on 1** make progress with a task. **2** esp. Brit. have a friendly relationship. **3** (**be getting on**) informal be old. **get over 1** recover from (an illness or an unpleasant experience). **2** manage to communicate (an idea or theory). **get one's own back** informal have one's revenge. **get round** esp. Brit. persuade (someone) to do or allow something. **get round to** esp. Brit. deal with (a task) in due course. **get through 1** pass or endure (a difficult experience or period). **2** esp. Brit. use up (a large amount of something). **3** make contact by telephone. **4** succeed in communicating with someone.
– ORIGIN Old Norse.

getaway • n. an escape or quick departure.

get-together • n. an informal gathering.

Getty, E
Jean Paul (1892–1976), American industrialist. He made a large fortune in the oil industry and was also a noted art collector.

Gettysburg, Battle of E
a decisive battle of the American Civil War, fought near the town of Gettysburg in Pennsylvania in 1863. A Union army defeated the Confederate army of General Lee, forcing him to abandon his invasion of the north.

get-up • n. informal an outfit, especially an unusual one.

gewgaw /**gyoo**-gor/ • n. a showy thing, especially one that is worthless.
– ORIGIN unknown.

geyser /**gee**-zer, **gy**-zer/ • n. a hot spring in which water intermittently boils, sending a column of water and steam into the air.
– ORIGIN named after a particular spring in Iceland.

Ghana E
/**gah**-nuh/ a country of West Africa on the Atlantic Ocean; capital, Accra. Former name (until 1957) **Gold Coast**.
– DERIVATIVES **Ghanaian** /gah-**nay**-uhn/ adj. & n.

ghastly • adj. (**ghastlier**, **ghastliest**) **1** causing great horror or fear. **2** informal very unpleasant.
– DERIVATIVES **ghastliness** n.
– ORIGIN Old English, 'terrify'.

Ghats E
/*rhymes with* parts/ two mountain ranges in central and southern India, known as **the Eastern Ghats** and **the Western Ghats**.

Ghent E
/gent/ a city in Belgium, capital of the province of East Flanders.

gherkin /**ger**-kin/ • n. a small pickled cucumber.
– ORIGIN Dutch *gurkje*.

ghetto /**get**-toh/ • n. (pl. **ghettos** or **ghettoes**) **1** a part of a city occupied by a minority group. **2** hist. the Jewish quarter in a city.
– ORIGIN perh. from Italian *getto* 'foundry' (because the first ghetto was established on the site of a foundry in Venice).

ghetto blaster • n. informal a large portable radio and cassette or CD player.

ghost • n. **1** an apparition of a dead person which is believed to appear to the living. **2** a faint trace: *the ghost of a smile.*
– ORIGIN Old English, 'spirit, soul'.

ghosting • n. the appearance of a secondary image on a television or other display screen.

ghostly • adj. (**ghostlier**, **ghostliest**) like a ghost; eerie.

ghost town • n. a town with few or no remaining inhabitants.

ghost writer • n. a person employed to write material for another person, who is the named author.

ghoul /gool/ • n. **1** an evil spirit believed to rob graves and eat corpses. **2** a person with an unhealthy interest in death or disaster.
– DERIVATIVES **ghoulish** adj.
– ORIGIN Arabic.

GHQ • abbrev. General Headquarters.

GI • n. (pl. **GIs**) a private soldier in the US army.
– ORIGIN from *government* (or *general*) *issue* (referring to military equipment).

Giacometti E
/ja-kuh-**met**-ti/, Alberto (1901–66), Swiss sculptor and painter, known for his sculptures of emaciated and extremely elongated human forms.

giant • n. **1** an imaginary being of human form but superhuman size. **2** an abnormally tall or large person, animal, or plant. • adj. very large.
– ORIGIN Old French *geant*.

giant-killer • n. a person or team that defeats a more powerful opponent.

Giant's Causeway E
a geological formation of basalt columns, dating from the Tertiary period, on the north coast of Northern Ireland.

gibber /jib-ber/ ● v. (**gibbers, gibbering, gibbered**) speak rapidly in a way that is difficult to understand.

gibberish /jib-buh-rish/ ● n. speech or writing that is difficult to understand or meaningless.

gibbet /jib-bit/ ● n. hist. **1** a gallows. **2** an upright post with an arm on which the bodies of executed criminals were left hanging.
– ORIGIN Old French *gibet* 'little cudgel, gallows'.

Gibbon, E
Edward (1737–94), English historian, best known for his multi-volume work *The History of the Decline and Fall of the Roman Empire*.

gibbon ● n. a small ape with long, powerful arms, native to the forests of SE Asia.
– ORIGIN French.

Gibbons, E
Grinling (1648–1721), Dutch-born English sculptor. He is famous for his decorative carvings in wood, as in St Paul's Cathedral, London.

gibbous /gib-buhss/ ● adj. (of the moon) having the illuminated part greater than a semicircle and less than a circle.
– ORIGIN Latin *gibbosus*.

Gibbs, E
James (1682–1754), Scottish architect, who developed Wren's ideas for London's city churches.

gibe /jib/ ● n. & v. var. of JIBE[1].

giblets /jib-lits/ ● pl. n. the liver, heart, gizzard, and neck of a chicken or other fowl.
– ORIGIN Old French *gibelet* 'game bird stew'.

Gibraltar E
/ji-brawl-ter/ a British dependency near the southern tip of the Iberian peninsula, at the eastern end of the Strait of Gibraltar.
DERIVATIVES **Gibraltarian** /ji-brawl-tair-i-uhn/ adj. & n.

Gibraltar, Strait of E
a sea passage between the southern tip of the Iberian peninsula and North Africa (24 km (15 miles) wide at its narrowest point), forming the only outlet of the Mediterranean Sea to the Atlantic.

Gibson[1], E
Althea (1927–2003), American tennis player. She was the first black player to succeed at the highest level of tennis, winning all the major singles titles in the late 1950s.

Gibson[2], E
Mel (Columcille Gerard) (b.1956), American-born Australian actor and director, who starred in films such as *Mad Max* and *Braveheart*, which he also directed.

giddy ● adj. (**giddier, giddiest**) **1** having or causing a sensation of whirling and a tendency to fall; dizzy. **2** not interested in serious things.
– ORIGIN Old English, 'insane'.

Gide E
/zheed/, André (Paul Guillaume) (1869–1951), French novelist, essayist, and critic, known for his novels *The Immoralist*, *La Porte étroite*, and *The Counterfeiters*.

Gielgud E
/geel-guud/, Sir (Arthur) John (1904–2000), English actor and director, famous as a Shakespearean actor and also for his film and television roles.

GIF ● n. Computing **1** a format for image files, with built-in data compression. **2** (also **gif**) a file in this format.
– ORIGIN from *graphic interchange format*.

gift ● n. **1** a thing given willingly to someone without payment; a present. **2** a natural ability or talent. **3** informal a very easy task. ● v. **1** give as a gift, especially formally. **2** (**gifted**) having exceptional talent or ability.
– ORIGIN Old Norse.

gift token (also **gift voucher**) ● n. Brit. a voucher given as a gift which is exchangeable for goods.

gift-wrap ● v. (**gift-wraps, gift-wrapping, gift-wrapped**) wrap (a gift) in decorative paper.

gig[1] /gig, jig/ ● n. esp. hist. a light two-wheeled carriage pulled by one horse.
– ORIGIN perh. from former *gig* 'a flighty girl'.

gig[2] /gig/ informal ● n. a live performance by a musician or other performer.
– ORIGIN unknown.

giga- /gig-uh, jig-uh/ ● comb. form **1** referring to a factor of one thousand million (10^9). **2** Computing referring to a factor of 2^{30}.
– ORIGIN Greek *gigas* 'giant'.

gigabyte /gig-uh-byt, jig-uh-byt/ ● n. Computing a unit of information equal to one thousand million (10^9) or (strictly) 2^{30} bytes.

gigantic ● adj. very large.
– ORIGIN Latin *gigas* 'giant'.

giggle ● v. (**giggles, giggling, giggled**) laugh lightly in a nervous or silly manner. ● n. **1** a nervous or silly laugh. **2** informal an amusing person or thing.
– DERIVATIVES **giggly** adj.

gigolo /jig-uh-loh/ ● n. (pl. **gigolos**) a young man paid by an older woman to be her escort or lover.
– ORIGIN French.

Gilbert, E
Sir W. S. (1836–1911; full name *William Schwenck Gilbert*), English dramatist. He wrote the librettos for light operas by Sir Arthur Sullivan, including *HMS Pinafore* and *The Mikado*.

Gilbert Islands E
a group of islands in the central Pacific, forming part of Kiribati. They were formerly part of the British colony of the Gilbert and Ellice Islands.

gild ● v. **1** cover thinly with gold. **2** (**gilded**) wealthy and privileged: *gilded youth*.
– DERIVATIVES **gilding** n.
– ORIGIN Old English.

gilet /zhi-lay/ ● n. (pl. **gilets** /zhi-lay/) a light sleeveless padded jacket.
– ORIGIN French, 'waistcoat'.

gill[1] /gil/ ● n. **1** the respiratory organ of fishes and some amphibians. **2** the plates on the underside of mushrooms and many toadstools.

– ORIGIN Old Norse.

gill² /jil/ ● **n.** a unit of liquid measure, equal to a quarter of a pint.
– ORIGIN Old French *gille* 'measure or container for wine'.

Gillespie E
/gi-**less**-pi/, Dizzy (1917–93; born *John Birks Gillespie*), American jazz trumpet player and bandleader.

gillie /**gil**-li/ ● **n.** (in Scotland) an attendant on a hunting or fishing expedition.
– ORIGIN Scottish Gaelic *gille* 'lad'.

gilt ● **adj.** covered thinly with gold leaf or gold paint. ● **n. 1** gold leaf or gold paint applied in a thin layer to a surface. **2** (**gilts**) fixed-interest loan securities issued by the UK government.
– ORIGIN from **GILD**.

g

gilt-edged ● **adj.** referring to stocks or securities (such as gilts) that are regarded as extremely reliable investments.

gimcrack /**jim**-krak/ ● **adj.** showy but flimsy or poorly made.
– ORIGIN unknown.

gimlet /**gim**-lit/ ● **n.** a T-shaped tool with a screw-tip for boring holes.
– ORIGIN Old French *guimbelet* 'little drill'.

gimmick ● **n.** a trick or device intended to attract attention rather than fulfil a useful purpose.
– DERIVATIVES **gimmickry** n. **gimmicky** adj.
– ORIGIN unknown.

gin¹ ● **n.** a clear alcoholic spirit flavoured with juniper berries.
– ORIGIN from *genever*, a kind of Dutch gin.

gin² ● **n. 1** a machine for separating cotton from its seeds. **2** a machine for raising and moving heavy weights. **3** a trap for catching small game.
– ORIGIN Old French *engin* 'engine'.

ginger ● **n. 1** a hot spice made from the root of a SE Asian plant. **2** a light reddish-yellow colour. ● **verb** (**ginger up**) (**gingers**, **gingering**, **gingered**) make more active or exciting.
– DERIVATIVES **gingery** adj.
– ORIGIN Latin *gingiber*.

ginger ale (also **ginger beer**) ● **n.** a fizzy drink flavoured with ginger.

gingerbread ● **n.** cake made with treacle or syrup and flavoured with ginger.

gingerly ● **adv.** in a careful or cautious manner.
– ORIGIN perh. from Old French *gensor* 'delicate'.

gingham /**ging**-uhm/ ● **n.** lightweight cotton cloth with a checked pattern.
– ORIGIN Malay, 'striped'.

gingivitis /jin-ji-**vy**-tiss/ ● **n.** Med. inflammation of the gums.
– ORIGIN Latin *gingiva* 'gum'.

ginormous ● **adj.** Brit. informal extremely large.
– ORIGIN from **GIANT** and **ENORMOUS**.

Ginsberg E
/**ginz**-berg/, Allen (1926–97), American poet, a leading figure of the beat generation, a movement of the 1950s and early 1960s which rejected conventional society and valued free self-expression.

ginseng /**jin**-seng/ ● **n.** the tuber of an east Asian and North American plant, supposed to have medicinal properties.
– ORIGIN from Chinese 'man' + the name of a kind of herb.

Giotto E
/**jot**-toh/ (*c.*1267–1337; full name *Giotto di Bondone*), Italian painter. His work shows a rejection of the flat, linear style of Byzantine art in favour of a naturalistic style showing human expression.

gip ● **n.** var. of **GYP¹**.

gipsy ● **n.** var. of **GYPSY**.

giraffe ● **n.** (pl. **giraffe** or **giraffes**) a large mammal with a very long neck and legs, the tallest living animal.
– ORIGIN French *girafe*.

gird ● **v.** (**girds**, **girding**, **girded**; past part. **girded** or **girt**) literary **1** encircle or secure with a belt or band. **2** (often in phr. **gird one's loins**) prepare and strengthen oneself for what is to come.
– ORIGIN Old English.

girder ● **n.** a large metal beam used in building bridges and large buildings.
– ORIGIN from **GIRD** in the archaic sense 'brace, strengthen'.

girdle ● **n. 1** a belt or cord worn round the waist. **2** a woman's elasticated corset extending from waist to thigh. ● **v.** (**girdles**, **girdling**, **girdled**) encircle with a girdle or belt.
– ORIGIN Old English.

girl ● **n. 1** a female child. **2** a young woman. **3** a person's girlfriend.
– DERIVATIVES **girlish** adj.
– ORIGIN perh. from German *gör* 'child'.

girlfriend ● **n. 1** a person's regular female companion in a romantic or sexual relationship. **2** N. Amer. a woman's female friend.

Girl Guide ● **n.** a member of the Guides Association.

girlie informal ● **n.** (also **girly**) (pl. **girlies**) a girl or young woman. ● **adj. 1** (usu. **girly**) usu. derog. like a girl. **2** showing nude young women in erotic poses: *girlie magazines*.

giro ● **n.** (pl. **giros**) **1** a system of electronic credit transfer involving banks, post offices, and public utilities. **2** a cheque or payment by giro.
– ORIGIN Italian, 'circulation (of money)'.

girt past part. of **GIRD**.

girth ● **n. 1** the measurement around the middle of something. **2** a band attached to a saddle and fastened around a horse's belly.
– ORIGIN Old Norse.

Gisborne E
/**giz**-bern/ a port and resort on the east coast of North Island, New Zealand.

Giscard d'Estaing E
/*zhee*-skar de-**stan**/, Valéry (b.1926), French statesman, President 1974–81.

gist /jist/ ● **n.** the substance or essence of a speech or text.
– ORIGIN from Old French *cest action gist* 'this action lies', meaning that there were enough grounds to proceed in a legal case.

git ● **n.** Brit. informal an unpleasant or contemptible person.
– ORIGIN from dialect *get* 'a stupid or unpleasant person'.

give ● **v.** (**gives**, **giving**, **gave**; past part. **given**)

1 cause (someone) to have, get, or experience. **2** carry out (an action) or make (a sound). **3** show: *he gave no sign of life.* **4** put forward (information or argument). **5** have as a result. **6** (**give off/out**) send out (a smell, heat, etc). **7** admit that (someone) deserves recognition for (something): *to give him his due, he tried.* **8** bend under pressure. ● **n.** the ability of something to bend under pressure.
– PHRASES **give and take** willingness on both sides of a relationship to make allowances. **give away** reveal (something secret). **give in** stop opposing something. **give out** stop operating. **give rise to** make happen. **give up** **1** stop making an effort and accept that one has failed. **2** stop doing, eating, or drinking (something) regularly. **3** hand over (a wanted person).
– ORIGIN Old English.

giveaway ● **n.** informal **1** something given free, especially for promotional purposes. **2** something that makes an inadvertent revelation: *the shape of the parcel was a dead giveaway.*

given past part. of **GIVE**. ● **adj. 1** specified or stated. **2** (**given to**) inclined to. ● **prep.** taking into account. ● **noun** an established fact.

given name ● **n.** = **FIRST NAME**.

Giza E
/**gee**-zer/ a city south-west of Cairo, on the west bank of the Nile, site of the Pyramids and the Sphinx.

gizmo ● **n.** (pl. **gizmos**) informal a gadget, especially one the speaker cannot name.
– ORIGIN unknown.

gizzard ● **n. 1** a muscular part of a bird's stomach for grinding food. **2** a muscular stomach of some fish, insects, and other invertebrates.
– ORIGIN Old French.

glacé /**gla**-say/ ● **adj.** (of fruit) having a glossy surface due to preservation in sugar.
– ORIGIN French, 'iced'.

glacé icing ● **n.** icing made with icing sugar and water.

glacial /**glay**-si-uhl/ ● **adj. 1** relating to ice, especially in the form of glaciers. **2** extremely cold or unfriendly.
– ORIGIN Latin *glacialis* 'icy'.

glacial period ● **n.** an ice age.

glaciation ● **n.** the state or result of being covered by glaciers.

glacier /**glay**-si-er/ ● **n.** a slowly moving mass of ice formed by the accumulation of snow on mountains or near the poles.
– ORIGIN French.

glad ● **adj.** (**gladder**, **gladdest**) **1** pleased; delighted. **2** (often **glad of**) grateful. **3** causing happiness: *glad tidings.*
– ORIGIN Old English, 'bright, shining'.

gladden ● **v.** make glad.

glade ● **n.** an open space in a wood or forest.
– ORIGIN unknown.

gladiator ● **n.** (in ancient Rome) a man trained to fight with weapons against other men or wild animals in an arena.
– DERIVATIVES **gladiatorial** adj.
– ORIGIN Latin.

gladiolus /glad-i-**oh**-luhss/ ● **n.** (pl. **gladioli** /glad-i-**oh**-ly/ or **gladioluses**) a plant with sword-shaped leaves and tall stems carrying brightly coloured flowers.
– ORIGIN Latin.

glad rags ● **pl. n.** informal clothes for a party or special occasion.

Gladstone, E
William Ewart (1809–98), British Liberal statesman, Prime Minister 1868–74, 1880–5, 1886, and 1892–4. His ministries saw reforms in education and the legal system and his campaign in favour of Home Rule for Ireland.

glamorize (also **glamorise**) ● **v.** (**glamorizes**, **glamorizing**, **glamorized**) make (something bad) seem glamorous or desirable.

glamorous ● **adj.** having glamour.
– DERIVATIVES **glamorously** adv.

glamour (US also **glamor**) ● **n.** an attractive and exciting quality.
– ORIGIN first meaning 'magic': from **GRAMMAR**, with reference to the magical practices associated with learning in medieval times.

glance ● **v.** (**glances**, **glancing**, **glanced**) **1** take a brief or hurried look. **2** strike and bounce off at an angle. ● **n.** a brief or hurried look.
– ORIGIN Old French *glacier* 'to slip'.

gland ● **n. 1** an organ of the body which secretes particular chemical substances. **2** a lymph node.
– ORIGIN Latin *glandulae* 'throat glands'.

glandular ● **adj.** relating to or affecting a gland or glands.

glandular fever ● **n.** an infectious disease characterized by swelling of the lymph glands and persistent lack of energy.

glare ● **v.** (**glares**, **glaring**, **glared**) **1** stare in an angry way. **2** shine with a dazzling light. **3** (**glaring**) extremely obvious: *a glaring omission.* ● **n. 1** an angry stare. **2** dazzling light.
– ORIGIN Dutch and German *glaren.*

Glasgow E
the largest city in Scotland, on the River Clyde.

glasnost /**glaz**-nosst/ ● **n.** (in the former Soviet Union) the policy or practice of more open government.
– ORIGIN Russian.

Glass, E
Philip (b.1937), American minimalist composer, known for such works as the opera *Einstein on the Beach* and *Low Symphony.*

glass ● **n. 1** a hard transparent substance made by fusing sand with soda and lime. **2** a drinking container made of glass. **3** esp. Brit. a mirror. ● **v.** cover or enclose with glass.
– DERIVATIVES **glassware** n.
– ORIGIN Old English.

glass-blowing ● **n.** the craft of making glassware by blowing semi-liquid glass through a long tube.

glass ceiling ● **n.** an imaginary barrier to progress in a profession, especially affecting women and members of minorities.

glasses ● **pl. n.** a pair of lenses set in a frame that rests on the nose and ears, used to correct eyesight.

glass fibre ● **n.** esp. Brit. a strong material containing embedded glass filaments for reinforcement.

glasshouse • **n.** Brit. a greenhouse.

glasspaper • **n.** paper covered with powdered glass, used for smoothing and polishing.

glass wool • **n.** glass in the form of fine fibres, used for packing and insulation.

glassy • **adj.** (**glassier, glassiest**) **1** resembling glass. **2** (of a person's eyes or expression) showing no interest.

Glaswegian /glaz-wee-j'n/ • **n.** a person from Glasgow. • **adj.** relating to Glasgow.

glaucoma /glaw-**koh**-muh/ • **n.** Med. a condition of increased pressure within the eyeball, causing gradual loss of sight.
– ORIGIN Greek *glaukōma*.

glaze • **v.** (**glazes**, **glazing**, **glazed**) **1** fit panes of glass into (a window frame or similar structure). **2** enclose or cover with glass. **3** cover with a glaze. **4** lose brightness and animation: *her eyes glazed over.* • **n. 1** a glass-like substance fused on to the surface of pottery to form a hard coating. **2** a thin topcoat of transparent paint used to alter the tone of an underlying colour. **3** a liquid such as milk or beaten egg, used to form a shiny coating on food.
– ORIGIN from **GLASS**.

glazier /**glay**-zi-er/ • **n.** a person whose trade is fitting glass into windows and doors.

gleam • **v.** shine brightly with reflected light. • **n. 1** a faint or brief light. **2** a brief or faint show of a quality or emotion: *the gleam of hope vanished.*
– ORIGIN Old English.

glean • **v. 1** collect gradually from various sources. **2** hist. gather (leftover grain) after a harvest.
– ORIGIN Latin *glennare*.

gleanings • **pl. n.** things gathered from various sources.

glebe /gleeb/ • **n.** hist. a piece of land serving as part of a clergyman's benefice and providing income.
– ORIGIN Latin *gleba* 'land, soil'.

glee • **n. 1** great delight. **2** a song for men's voices in three or more parts.
– ORIGIN Old English, 'entertainment, music'.

gleeful • **adj.** exuberantly or triumphantly joyful.
– DERIVATIVES **gleefully** adv.

glen • **n.** a narrow valley, especially in Scotland or Ireland.
– ORIGIN Scottish Gaelic and Irish *gleann*.

Glencoe, Massacre of E
a massacre in 1692 of members of the Jacobite MacDonald clan by Campbell soldiers, which took place near Glencoe in the Scottish Highlands.

Glendower E
/glen-**dow**-er/ (also **Glyndwr**), Owen (*c.*1354–*c.*1417), Welsh chief, who proclaimed himself Prince of Wales and led a national uprising against Henry IV.

glib • **adj.** (**glibber**, **glibbest**) able to express oneself well, but not meaning what one says.
– DERIVATIVES **glibly** adv.
– ORIGIN Germanic.

glide • **v.** (**glides, gliding, glided**) **1** move with a smooth, quiet motion. **2** fly without power or in a glider. • **n.** an instance of gliding.
– ORIGIN Old English.

glider • **n.** a light aircraft designed to fly without using an engine.

glimmer • **v.** (**glimmers**, **glimmering**, **glimmered**) shine faintly with a wavering light. • **n. 1** a faint or wavering light. **2** a faint sign of a feeling or quality: *a glimmer of hope.*
– ORIGIN prob. from Scandinavian.

glimpse • **n.** a brief or partial view. • **v.** (**glimpses**, **glimpsing**, **glimpsed**) see briefly or partially.
– ORIGIN prob. Germanic.

Glinka E
/**gling**-kuh/, Mikhail (Ivanovich) (1804–57), Russian composer, best known for his opera *Russlan and Ludmilla*.

glint • **v.** give out or reflect small flashes of light. • **n.** a small flash of reflected light.
– ORIGIN prob. from Scandinavian.

glissando /glis-**san**-doh/ • **n.** (pl. **glissandi** /glis-**san**-di/ or **glissandos**) Music a slide upwards or downwards between two notes.
– ORIGIN Italian.

glisten • **v.** (of something wet or greasy) shine or sparkle. • **n.** a sparkling light reflected from something wet.
– ORIGIN Old English.

glitch • **n.** informal **1** a sudden fault or irregularity of equipment. **2** an unexpected setback in a plan.
– ORIGIN unknown.

glitter • **v.** (**glitters**, **glittering**, **glittered**) **1** shine with a shimmering reflected light. **2** (**glittering**) impressively successful or glamorous: *a glittering career.* • **n. 1** shimmering reflected light. **2** tiny pieces of sparkling material used for decoration. **3** an attractive but superficial quality.
– DERIVATIVES **glittery** adj.
– ORIGIN Old Norse.

glitterati /glit-tuh-**rah**-ti/ • **pl. n.** informal fashionable people involved in show business or other glamorous activity.
– ORIGIN from **GLITTER** and **LITERATI**.

glitz • **n.** informal showy but superficial display.
– ORIGIN from **GLITTER**.

gloaming • **n.** (**the gloaming**) literary twilight; dusk.
– ORIGIN Old English.

gloat • **v.** be smug or pleased about one's own success or another's misfortune. • **n.** an act of gloating.
– DERIVATIVES **gloating** adj.
– ORIGIN uncertain.

glob • **n.** informal a lump of a semi-liquid substance.
– ORIGIN perh. from **BLOB** and **GOB**[2].

global • **adj. 1** relating to the whole world; worldwide. **2** relating to or including the whole of something, or of a group of things. **3** Computing operating or applying through the whole of a file or program.
– DERIVATIVES **globally** adv.

globalize (also **globalise**) • **v.** (**globalizes**, **globalizing**, **globalized**) develop or operate worldwide.
– DERIVATIVES **globalization** (also **globalisation**) n.

global warming • **n.** the gradual increase in the overall temperature of the earth's atmosphere due to increased levels of carbon dioxide and other pollutants.

globe ● n. **1** a spherical or rounded object. **2** (**the globe**) the earth. **3** a spherical model of the earth with a map on the surface.
– ORIGIN Latin *globus*.

globetrotter ● n. informal a person who travels widely.
– DERIVATIVES **globetrotting** n. & adj.

globular ● adj. **1** spherical. **2** composed of globules.

globule ● n. a small round particle of a substance; a drop.
– ORIGIN Latin *globulus* 'little globe'.

globulin /glob-yuu-lin/ ● n. Biochem. any of a group of simple proteins found in blood serum.

glockenspiel /glok-uhn-shpeel/ ● n. a musical instrument containing metal pieces which are struck with small hammers.
– ORIGIN German, 'bell play'.

gloom ● n. **1** partial or total darkness. **2** a state of depression or despair.
– ORIGIN unknown.

gloomy ● adj. (**gloomier**, **gloomiest**) **1** dark or poorly lit. **2** causing or feeling depression or despair.
– DERIVATIVES **gloomily** adv.

gloop ● n. informal sloppy or sticky semi-fluid matter.
– DERIVATIVES **gloopy** adj.

glorify ● v. (**glorifies**, **glorifying**, **glorified**) **1** represent as admirable. **2** (**glorified**) made to appear more important than is the case: *a glorified courier.* **3** praise and worship (God).
– DERIVATIVES **glorification** n.

glorious ● adj. **1** having or bringing glory. **2** very beautiful or impressive: *a glorious autumn day.*
– DERIVATIVES **gloriously** adv.

Glorious Revolution E
the events (1688–9) that led to the replacement of James II by his daughter Mary II and her husband William of Orange (who became William III) as joint monarchs. The bloodless 'revolution' marked the establishment of a constitutional form of government.

glory ● n. (pl. **glories**) **1** fame or honour won by notable achievements. **2** magnificence; great beauty. **3** a very beautiful or impressive thing: *the glories of Paris.* **4** worship and thanksgiving offered to God. ● v. (**glories**, **glorying**, **gloried**) (**glory in**) take great pride or pleasure in.
– ORIGIN Latin *gloria*.

Glos. ● abbrev. Gloucestershire.

gloss[1] ● n. **1** the shine on a smooth surface. **2** a type of paint which dries to a bright shiny surface. **3** a superficially attractive appearance. ● v. **1** give a shiny appearance to. **2** (**gloss over**) try to conceal or pass over (something) by mentioning it briefly or misleadingly.
– ORIGIN unknown.

gloss[2] ● n. a translation or explanation of a word, phrase, or passage. ● v. provide a gloss for.
– ORIGIN Old French *glose*.

glossary ● n. (pl. **glossaries**) an alphabetical list of words relating to a specific subject or text, with explanations.
– ORIGIN Latin *glossarium*.

glossy ● adj. (**glossier**, **glossiest**) **1** shiny and smooth. **2** superficially attractive and stylish. ● n. (pl. **glossies**) informal a magazine printed on shiny paper with many colour photographs.

glottal ● adj. relating to or produced by the glottis.

glottal stop ● n. a consonant formed by the audible release of the airstream after complete closure of the glottis.

glottis /glot-tiss/ ● n. the part of the larynx made up of the vocal cords and the slit-like opening between them.
– ORIGIN Greek.

Gloucester E
/*rhymes with* foster/ a city in SW England, the county town of Gloucestershire.

Gloucestershire E
a county of SW England; county town, Gloucester.

glove ● n. **1** a covering for the hand having separate parts for each finger. **2** a padded covering for the hand used in boxing and other sports.
– ORIGIN Old English.

glove compartment (also **glovebox**) ● n. a small recess for storage in the dashboard of a motor vehicle.

glove puppet ● n. esp. Brit. a cloth puppet fitted on the hand and worked by the fingers.

glow ● v. **1** give out steady light without flame. **2** have a strong, warm colour. **3** convey deep pleasure through one's expression. ● n. **1** a steady radiance of light or heat. **2** a feeling or appearance of warmth. **3** a strong feeling of pleasure or well-being.
– ORIGIN Old English.

glower /glow-er/ ● v. (**glowers**, **glowering**, **glowered**) have an angry or sullen look on one's face. ● n. an angry or sullen look.
– ORIGIN perh. from Scandinavian.

glowing ● adj. expressing great praise: *a glowing report.*

glow-worm ● n. a beetle whose wingless female glows to attract males.

gloxinia /glok-sin-i-uh/ ● n. a tropical plant with large, bell-shaped flowers.
– ORIGIN named after the 18th-century German botanist Benjamin P. *Gloxin*.

Gluck E
/*rhymes with* look/, Christoph Willibald von (1714–87), German composer. His works include the opera *Orfeo ed Euridice*.

glucose /gloo-kohz/ ● n. a simple sugar which is an important energy source in living organisms.
– ORIGIN Greek *gleukos* 'sweet wine'.

glue ● n. an adhesive substance used for sticking things together. ● v. (**glues**, **gluing** or **glueing**, **glued**) **1** fasten or join with glue. **2** (**be glued to**) informal be paying very close attention to.
– ORIGIN Latin *glus*.

glue ear ● n. blocking of the Eustachian tube by mucus, occurring especially in children and causing impaired hearing.

glue-sniffing ● n. the practice of inhaling intoxicating fumes from adhesives.

glug ● v. informal (**glugs**, **glugging**, **glugged**) pour or drink (liquid) with a gurgling sound.

glum ● **adj.** (**glummer**, **glummest**) dejected; morose.
– DERIVATIVES **glumly** adv.
– ORIGIN from **GLOOM**.

glut ● **n.** an excessively large supply. ● **v.** (**gluts**, **glutting**, **glutted**) supply or fill to excess.
– ORIGIN prob. from Latin *gluttire* 'to swallow'.

glutamate /gloo-tuh-mayt/ ● **n.** Biochem. a salt or ester of an amino acid which is a constituent of many proteins.
– ORIGIN from *glutamic acid*, from **GLUTEN** + **AMINE**.

gluten /gloo-tuhn/ ● **n.** a protein present in cereal grains, which is responsible for the elastic texture of dough.
– ORIGIN Latin, 'glue'.

g

glutinous /gloo-ti-nuhss/ ● **adj.** like glue in texture; sticky.
– ORIGIN Latin *glutinosus*.

glutton ● **n.** **1** an extremely greedy eater. **2** a person who enjoys doing unpleasant or difficult things: *a glutton for punishment*.
– ORIGIN Latin *glutto*.

gluttony ● **n.** the habit of eating too much.

glycerine /gli-suh-reen/ (US **glycerin** /gli-suh-rin/) ● **n.** = **GLYCEROL**.
– ORIGIN French *glycerin*.

glycerol /gli-suh-rol/ ● **n.** a liquid formed as a by-product in soap manufacture, used as a softening agent and laxative.

glycogen /gly-kuh-juhn/ ● **n.** a substance deposited in bodily tissues as a store of carbohydrates.

Glyndwr E
/glin-**duur**/ Welsh form of **GLENDOWER**.

GM ● **abbrev.** **1** genetically modified. **2** George Medal. **3** (of a school) grant-maintained.

gm ● **abbrev.** gram(s).

GMT ● **abbrev.** Greenwich Mean Time.

gnarled (also **gnarly**) ● **adj.** knobbly, rough, and twisted.
– ORIGIN from former *knarre* 'rugged rock'.

gnash /nash/ ● **v.** grind (one's teeth) together, especially as a sign of anger.
– ORIGIN perh. from Old Norse.

gnashers ● **pl. n.** Brit. informal teeth.

gnat /nat/ ● **n.** a small two-winged fly resembling a mosquito.
– ORIGIN Old English.

gnaw /naw/ ● **v.** **1** bite at or nibble persistently. **2** cause persistent anxiety or pain: *doubts continued to gnaw at me*.
– ORIGIN Old English.

gneiss /nyss/ ● **n.** a metamorphic rock with a banded or layered structure, typically consisting of feldspar, quartz, and mica.
– ORIGIN German.

gnome ● **n.** a legendary dwarfish creature supposed to guard the earth's treasures underground.
– ORIGIN Latin *gnomus*.

gnomic /noh-mik/ ● **adj.** in the form of short, clever sayings that are often difficult to understand.
– ORIGIN Greek *gnōmē* 'thought, opinion'

Gnosticism /noss-ti-si-z'm/ ● **n.** a former heretical movement of the Christian Church, teaching that mystical knowledge (gnosis) of the supreme divine being enabled the human spirit to be saved.
– DERIVATIVES **Gnostic** adj.
– ORIGIN Greek *gnosis* 'knowledge'.

GNP ● **abbrev.** gross national product.

gnu /noo/ ● **n.** a large African antelope with a long head and a beard and mane.
– ORIGIN from a southern African language.

GNVQ ● **abbrev.** General National Vocational Qualification.

go ● **v.** (**goes**, **going**, **went**; past part. **gone**) **1** move to or from a place. **2** pass into or be in a particular state: *her mind went blank*. **3** lie or extend in a certain direction. **4** come to an end. **5** disappear or be used up. **6** (of time) pass. **7** pass time in a particular way: *they went for months without talking*. **8** engage in a specified activity. **9** have a particular outcome: *it all went off smoothly*. **10** (**be going to be/do**) used to express a future tense. **11** function or operate. **12** match: *the earrings and the scarf don't really go*. **13** be acceptable or allowed. **14** fit into or be regularly kept in a particular place. **15** make a specified sound. ● **n.** (pl. **goes**) informal **1** an attempt. **2** a turn to do or use something. **3** spirit or energy.
– PHRASES **go about** begin or carry on work at. **go along with** agree to. **go back on** fail to keep (a promise). **go down 1** be defeated in a contest. **2** obtain a specified reaction: *the show went down well*. **go for 1** decide on. **2** attempt to gain. **3** attack. **go in for 1** enter (a contest). **2** like. **going!, gone!** an auctioneer's announcement that bidding is closing or closed. **go into 1** investigate or enquire into. **2** (of a whole number) be capable of dividing another. **go off 1** (of a gun or bomb) explode or fire. **2** esp. Brit. (of food) begin to decompose. **3** informal, esp. Brit. begin to dislike. **go on 1** continue. **2** take place. **go out 1** be extinguished. **2** carry on a regular romantic relationship with someone. **go over** examine or check the details of. **go round** esp. Brit. be enough to supply everybody present. **go through 1** undergo (a difficult experience). **2** examine carefully. **3** informal use up or spend. **go without** suffer lack or hardship. **have a go at** esp. Brit. attack or criticize. **make a go of** informal be successful in. **on the go** informal very active or busy.
– ORIGIN Old English.

Goa E
/**goh**-uh/ a state on the west coast of India; capital, Panaji.
– DERIVATIVES **Goan** (also **Goanese**) adj. & n.

goad /gohd/ ● **n.** **1** a spiked stick used for driving cattle. **2** a thing that stimulates someone into action. ● **v.** provoke to action.
– ORIGIN Old English.

go-ahead informal ● **n.** (**the go-ahead**) permission to proceed. ● **adj.** enterprising and ambitious: *a go-ahead managing director*.

goal ● **n.** **1** (in soccer, rugby, etc.) a pair of posts linked by a crossbar and forming a space into or over which the ball has to be sent to score. **2** an instance of sending the ball into or over a goal. **3** an aim or desired result.
– DERIVATIVES **goalless** adj.
– ORIGIN unknown.

goal difference ● **n.** Soccer the difference between the number of goals scored for and against a team in a series of matches.

goalie • n. informal a goalkeeper.
goalkeeper • n. a player in soccer or field hockey whose role is to stop the ball from entering the goal.
goal kick • n. **1** Soccer a free kick taken by the defending side after attackers send the ball over the byline. **2** Rugby an attempt to kick a goal.
goal line • n. a line across a football or hockey field on which the goal is placed or which acts as the boundary beyond which a try or touchdown is scored.
goalpost • n. either of the two upright posts of a goal.
goat • n. **1** a hardy domesticated mammal that has backward-curving horns and (in the male) a beard. **2** a wild mammal related to this.
– PHRASES **get someone's goat** informal irritate someone.
– ORIGIN Old English.
goatee /goh-tee/ • n. a small pointed beard like that of a goat.
goatherd • n. a person who looks after goats.
gob[1] • n. Brit. informal a person's mouth.
– ORIGIN perh. from Scottish Gaelic.
gob[2] informal • n. a lump or clot of a slimy substance. • v. (**gobs**, **gobbing**, **gobbed**) Brit. spit.
– ORIGIN Old French *gobe* 'mouthful'.
gobbet /gob-bit/ • n. a piece of flesh, food, or other matter.
– ORIGIN Old French *gobet*.

Gobbi E
/gob-bi/, Tito (1915–84), Italian operatic baritone.

gobble • v. (**gobbles**, **gobbling**, **gobbled**) **1** eat hurriedly and noisily. **2** (often **gobble up**) use a large amount of (something) very quickly. **3** (of a turkey) make a swallowing sound in the throat.
– ORIGIN prob. from **GOB**[2].
gobbledegook /gob-b'l-di-gook/ (also **gobbledygook**) • n. informal complicated language that is difficult to understand.
go-between • n. an intermediary or negotiator.

Gobi Desert E
/goh-bi/ a barren plateau of southern Mongolia and northern China.

goblet • n. **1** a drinking glass with a foot and a stem. **2** Brit. a container forming part of a liquidizer.
– ORIGIN Old French *gobelet* 'little cup'.
goblin • n. a mischievous, dwarf-like creature of folklore.
– ORIGIN Old French *gobelin*.
gobsmacked • adj. Brit. informal utterly astonished.
gobstopper • n. esp. Brit. a hard round sweet.
goby /goh-bi/ • n. (pl. **gobies**) a small sea fish, typically with a sucker on the underside.
– ORIGIN Greek *kōbios*.
go-cart • n. = **GO-KART**.
God • n. **1** (in Christianity and other religions which believe in only one God) the creator and supreme ruler of the universe. **2** (**god**) a superhuman being or spirit: *a moon god.* **3** (**god**) a greatly admired or influential person. • exclam. used to express surprise, anger, etc. or for emphasis.
– DERIVATIVES **godlike** adj.
– ORIGIN Old English.

Godard E
/god-ar/, Jean-Luc (b.1930), French film director, known for such films as *Breathless* and *Alphaville.*

godchild • n. (pl. **godchildren**) a person in relation to a godparent.

Goddard, E
Robert Hutchings (1882–1945), American rocket pioneer, who designed and built the first successful liquid-fuelled rocket.

god-daughter • n. a female godchild.
goddess • n. a female god.
godfather • n. **1** a male godparent. **2** the male head of the Mafia.
God-fearing • adj. earnestly religious.
godforsaken • adj. lacking any merit or attraction.
godhead • n. **1** (**the Godhead**) God. **2** divine nature.

Godiva E
/guh-dy-vuh/, Lady (d.1080), English noblewoman, wife of Leofric, Earl of Mercia. According to a medieval legend, she rode naked on horseback through Coventry after her husband stated that he would reduce unpopular taxes if she did so.

godless • adj. **1** not believing in a god or God. **2** wicked.
godly • adj. very religious.
– DERIVATIVES **godliness** n.
godmother • n. a female godparent.
godparent • n. a person who presents a child at baptism and promises to be responsible for their religious education.
godsend • n. something very helpful or welcome at a particular time.
godson • n. a male godchild.

Godthåb E
/god-hawb/ former name for **NUUK**.

Godunov E
/god-uu-noff/, Boris (1550–1605), tsar of Russia 1598–1605.

Goebbels E
/ger-b'lz/ (also **Göbbels**), (Paul) Joseph (1897–1945), German Nazi leader and politician, Hitler's Minister of Propaganda from 1933.

goer • n. a person who regularly attends a particular place or event: *a theatre-goer.*

Goering E
/ger-ing/, Hermann Wilhelm (1893–1946), German Nazi leader and politician, the founder of the Gestapo.

goes 3rd person sing. present of **GO**[1].

Goethe E
/ger-tuh/, Johann Wolfgang von (1749–1832), German poet, dramatist, and scholar. His wide range of works includes the plays *Tasso* and *Faust* and the novel *The Sorrows of Young Werther,* as well as poetry and scientific writings.

go-getter • n. informal an energetic and very enterprising person.
– DERIVATIVES **go-getting** adj.

goggle • v. (**goggles**, **goggling**, **goggled**) **1** look with wide open eyes. **2** (of the eyes) stick out or open wide. • n. (**goggles**) close-fitting protective glasses.

go-go • adj. referring to an erotic style of dancing to popular music.

Gogol E
/goh-gol/, Nikolai (Vasilevich) (1809–52), Russian novelist, dramatist, and short-story writer. His works include the play *The Government Inspector* and the novel *Dead Souls*.

going • n. **1** the condition of the ground viewed in terms of suitability for horse racing or walking. **2** conditions for an activity: *the going gets tough*. • adj. **1** esp. Brit. existing or available: *any jobs going?* **2** (of a price) usual or current.

going concern • n. a thriving business.

going-over • n. informal **1** a thorough cleaning or inspection. **2** a beating.

goings-on • pl. n. informal strange or dishonest activities.

goitre /goy-ter/ • n. a swelling of the neck resulting from enlargement of the thyroid gland.
– ORIGIN French.

go-kart (also **go-cart**) • n. a small racing car with a lightweight body.

Gokhale E
/goh-kuh-lay/, Gopal Krishna (1866–1915), Indian political leader and social reformer, president of the Indian National Congress from 1905. He was a leading advocate of Indian self-government through constitutional or moderate means.

Golan Heights E
/goh-**lahn**, **goh**-luhn/ a range of hills on the border between Syria and Israel, north-east of the Sea of Galilee. Formerly under Syrian control, the area was occupied by Israel in 1967 and annexed in 1981.

gold • n. **1** a yellow precious metal, used as an ornament and as money. **2** a deep yellow or yellow-brown colour. **3** articles made of gold.
– ORIGIN Old English.

Gold Coast E
former name for **Ghana**.

goldcrest • n. a very small warbler with a yellow or orange crest.

gold-digger • n. informal a woman who forms relationships with men purely for financial gain.

gold disc • n. a golden disc awarded to a recording artist or group for sales above a specified figure.

gold dust • n. **1** fine particles of gold. **2** something rare and very valuable.

golden • adj. **1** made of or resembling gold. **2** (of a period) very happy and prosperous. **3** excellent.

golden age • n. the period when a specified art or activity is at its peak: *the golden age of cinema*.

golden boy (or **golden girl**) • n. informal a very popular or successful young man or woman.

golden eagle • n. a large eagle with yellow-tipped head feathers.

Golden Fleece E
Gk Myth. the fleece of a golden ram, guarded by a dragon that never slept, and sought and won by Jason.

Golden Gate E
a deep channel connecting San Francisco Bay with the Pacific Ocean, spanned by the Golden Gate suspension bridge (completed 1937).

golden handshake • n. informal a payment given to someone who is made redundant or retires early.

golden jubilee • n. the fiftieth anniversary of an important event.

golden mean • n. the ideal middle position between two extremes.

golden retriever • n. a breed of retriever with a thick golden-coloured coat.

goldenrod • n. a plant with tall stems carrying spikes of bright yellow flowers.

golden rule • n. a principle which should always be followed.

golden syrup • n. Brit. a pale treacle.

golden wedding • n. the fiftieth anniversary of a wedding.

goldfield • n. a district in which gold is found as a mineral.

goldfinch • n. a brightly coloured finch with a yellow patch on each wing.

goldfish • n. a small reddish-golden carp popular in ponds and aquaria.

goldfish bowl • n. esp. Brit. **1** a round glass container for goldfish. **2** a place or situation without privacy.

Golding, E
Sir William (Gerald) (1911–93), English novelist, author of *Lord of the Flies* and *Rites of Passage*.

gold leaf • n. gold beaten into a very thin sheet, used in gilding.

gold medal • n. a medal made of or coloured gold, awarded for first place in a race or competition.

gold mine • n. **1** a place where gold is mined. **2** a source of great wealth or resources.

gold plate • n. **1** a thin layer of gold applied as a coating to another metal. **2** plates, dishes, etc. made of or plated with gold.

gold rush • n. a rapid movement of people to a newly discovered goldfield.

Goldsmith, E
Oliver (1728–74), Irish novelist, poet, essayist, and dramatist, noted for the novel *The Vicar of Wakefield* and the comedy *She Stoops to Conquer*.

goldsmith • n. a person who makes gold articles.

gold standard • n. hist. the system by which the value of a currency was defined in terms of gold.

golf • n. a game played on an outdoor course, the aim of which is to strike a small ball with a club into a series of small holes.
– DERIVATIVES **golfer** n.
– ORIGIN perh. from Dutch *kolf* 'club'.

golf club • n. see CLUB² (sense 2).

Goliath E
/guh-ly-uhth/ (in the Bible) a Philistine giant killed by David, according to one account.

golliwog • n. a soft doll with a black face and fuzzy hair.
– ORIGIN from *Golliwogg*, a doll character in books by the US writer Bertha Upton (d. 1912).

golly • exclam. informal used to express surprise or delight.
– ORIGIN from **GOD**.

Gomorrah E
/guh-morr-uh/ a town in ancient Palestine, probably south of the Dead Sea. According to the Old Testament it was destroyed by God, along with Sodom, to punish the wickedness of its inhabitants.

gonad /goh-nad/ • n. a bodily organ that produces gametes; a testis or ovary.
– ORIGIN Latin *gonades*.

gondola /gon-duh-luh/ • n. **1** a flat-bottomed boat used on Venetian canals, worked by one oar at the stern. **2** a cabin on a ski lift, or hanging from an airship or balloon.
– ORIGIN Venetian Italian.

gondolier /gon-duh-leer/ • n. a person who propels and steers a gondola.

gone past part. of **GO**¹. • adj. no longer present or in existence. • prep. Brit. (of time) past.

goner /gon-er/ • n. informal a person or thing that cannot be saved.

gong • n. **1** a metal disc with a turned rim, giving a resonant note when struck. **2** Brit. informal a medal or decoration.
– ORIGIN Malay.

gonorrhoea /gon-uh-ree-uh/ (US **gonorrhea**) • n. a sexually transmitted disease causing discharge from the urethra or vagina.
– ORIGIN Greek *gonorrhoia*.

goo • n. informal a sticky or slimy substance.
– ORIGIN perh. from *burgoo*, a nautical slang term for porridge.

good • adj. (**better**, **best**) **1** having the right qualities; of a high standard. **2** behaving in a way that is right, polite, or obedient. **3** enjoyable or satisfying: *a good time*. **4** appropriate. **5** (**good for**) of benefit to. **6** thorough: *a really good clear-up*. **7** at least. • n. **1** that which is right or of benefit. **2** (**goods**) products or possessions: *luxury goods*. **3** (**goods**) Brit. freight.
– PHRASES **as good as** —— very nearly ——. **for good** forever. **the Good Book** the Bible. **a good word** words in favour of or defending a person. **in good time 1** with no risk of being late. **2** (also **all in good time**) in due course but without haste. **make good 1** compensate for (loss, damage, or expense). **2** fulfil (a promise or claim).
– ORIGIN Old English.

goodbye (US also **goodby**) • exclam. used to express good wishes when parting or ending a conversation.
– ORIGIN from *God be with you!*

good faith • n. honesty or sincerity of intention.

good-for-nothing • adj. worthless.

Good Friday • n. the Friday before Easter Sunday, on which the Crucifixion of Christ is commemorated in the Christian Church.

Good Hope, Cape of E
see **CAPE OF GOOD HOPE**.

good-humoured • adj. friendly or cheerful.

goodie • n. var. of **GOODY**.

goodish • adj. **1** fairly good. **2** fairly large: *a goodish portion*.

good-looking • adj. attractive.

goodly • adj. dated considerable in size or quantity.

Goodman, E
Benny (1909–86; full name *Benjamin David Goodman*), American jazz clarinettist and bandleader.

goodness • n. **1** the quality of being good. **2** the nutritious element of food. • exclam. expressing surprise or anger.

goods and chattels • pl. n. all kinds of personal possessions.

good-tempered • adj. not easily angered.

goodwill • n. friendly or helpful feelings or attitude.

goody • n. (also **goodie**) (pl. **goodies**) informal **1** Brit. a good person, especially a hero in a story or film. **2** (**goodies**) tasty things to eat. • exclam. expressing childish delight.

Goodyear, E
Charles (1800–60), American inventor, who developed the process of vulcanizing rubber, making possible its development as a commercial product.

goody-goody • n. informal a smug person who behaves well so as to impress others.

gooey • adj. (**gooier**, **gooiest**) informal soft and sticky.

goof informal, esp. N. Amer. • n. a mistake. • v. **1** fool around. **2** make a mistake.
– ORIGIN unknown.

goofy • adj. (**goofier**, **goofiest**) informal **1** esp. N. Amer. foolish. **2** having front teeth that stick out.

Goolagong E
/goo-luh-gong/, Evonne, see **CAWLEY**.

goolie (also **gooly**) • n. (pl. **goolies**) Brit. informal a testicle.
– ORIGIN perh. from Hindi, 'bullet, ball'.

goon • n. informal **1** a foolish person. **2** N. Amer. a thug.
– ORIGIN perh. from dialect *gooney* 'stupid person'.

goose • n. (pl. **geese**) **1** a large waterbird with a long neck and webbed feet. **2** the female of such a bird. **3** informal a foolish person. • v. (**gooses**, **goosing**, **goosed**) informal poke (someone) in the bottom.
– ORIGIN Old English.

gooseberry • n. (pl. **gooseberries**) **1** an edible yellowish-green berry with a hairy skin. **2** Brit. informal a third person in the company of two lovers.
– ORIGIN perh. from **GOOSE**, or perh. from Old French *groseille*.

gooseflesh • n. a pimply state of the skin with the hairs erect, produced by cold or fright.

goose pimples • pl. n. gooseflesh.

goose step • n. a military marching step in which the legs are kept straight. • v. (**goose-step**) (**goose-steps**, **goose-stepping**,

g

goose-stepped) march with such a step.

gopher /goh-fer/ ● n. (also **pocket gopher**) a burrowing American rodent with pouches on its cheeks.
– ORIGIN perh. from Canadian French *gaufre* 'honeycomb' (because the gopher 'honeycombs' the ground with its burrows).

Gorbachev E
/gor-buh-choff/, Mikhail (Sergeevich) (b.1931), Soviet statesman, General Secretary of the Communist Party of the USSR 1985–91 and President 1988–91. He introduced major reforms in the USSR and his foreign policy brought about an end to the cold war.

Gordian knot /gor-di-uhn/ ● n. (in phr. **cut the Gordian knot**) solve a difficult problem in a forceful or direct way.
– ORIGIN from the legendary knot tied by King *Gordius* and cut through by Alexander the Great in response to the prophecy that whoever untied it would rule Asia.

Gordimer E
/gor-di-mer/, Nadine (b.1923), South African novelist and short-story writer, author of *The Conservationist.*

Gordon, E
Charles George (1833–85), British general and colonial administrator, famous for crushing the Taiping Rebellion (1863–4) in China. In 1884 he fought forces in Sudan led by Muhammad Ahmad (1843–85, known as the *Mahdi*) but was trapped at Khartoum and killed.

gore[1] ● n. blood that has been shed.
– ORIGIN Old English, 'dung, dirt'.

gore[2] ● v. (**gores, goring, gored**) (of an animal such as a bull) pierce or stab with a horn or tusk.
– ORIGIN unknown.

gore[3] ● n. a triangular piece of material used in making a garment, sail, or umbrella.
– ORIGIN Old English, 'triangular piece of land'.

Górecki E
/guh-ret-ski/, Henryk (Mikołaj) (b.1933), Polish composer. His works include the Third Symphony, known as the *Symphony of Sorrowful Songs.*

gorge ● n. **1** a narrow valley or ravine. **2** archaic the contents of the stomach. ● v. (**gorges, gorging, gorged**) eat a large amount in a greedy way.
– ORIGIN Old French 'throat'.

gorgeous ● adj. **1** beautiful. **2** informal very pleasant.
– ORIGIN Old French *gorgias* 'fine'.

gorgon /gor-guhn/ ● n. **1** Gk Myth. each of three sisters with snakes for hair, who had the power to turn anyone who looked at them to stone. **2** a frightening or repulsive woman.
– ORIGIN Greek *Gorgō.*

Gorgonzola /gor-guhn-zoh-luh/ ● n. a strong-flavoured Italian cheese with bluish-green veins.
– ORIGIN named after the Italian village of *Gorgonzola.*

gorilla ● n. **1** a powerfully built great ape of central Africa, the largest living primate. **2** informal a heavily built aggressive-looking man.
– ORIGIN Greek.

Gorky[1] E
/gor-ki/ former name for **NIZHNI NOVGOROD**.

Gorky[2] E
/gor-ki/, Maxim (1868–1936; pen name of *Aleksei Maksimovich Peshkov*), Russian writer and revolutionary, a founder of socialist realism. His works include the play *The Lower Depths.*

gormless ● adj. Brit. informal stupid or slow-witted.
– ORIGIN from dialect *gaum* 'understanding'.

gorse ● n. a yellow-flowered shrub with thin prickly leaves.
– ORIGIN Old English.

gory ● adj. **1** involving violence and bloodshed. **2** covered in blood.

gosh ● exclam. informal used to express surprise or give emphasis.
– ORIGIN euphemism for **GOD**.

goshawk /goss-hawk/ ● n. a short-winged hawk resembling a large sparrowhawk.
– ORIGIN Old English, 'goose-hawk'.

gosling ● n. a young goose.
– ORIGIN Old Norse.

gospel ● n. **1** the teachings of Christ. **2** (**Gospel**) the record of Christ's life and teaching in the first four books of the New Testament. **3** (**Gospel**) each of these books. **4** (also **gospel truth**) something absolutely true. **5** (also **gospel music**) a style of black American religious singing.
– ORIGIN Old English, 'good news'.

gossamer ● n. a fine substance consisting of cobwebs spun by small spiders. ● adj. very fine and insubstantial.
– ORIGIN prob. from **GOOSE** + **SUMMER**, perh. from the time of year around St Martin's day (11 November) when geese were eaten and gossamer is often seen.

gossip ● n. **1** casual conversation or unproven reports about other people. **2** derog. a person who likes talking about other people's private lives. ● v. (**gossips, gossiping, gossiped**) engage in gossip.
– ORIGIN Old English.

gossip column ● n. a section of a newspaper devoted to gossip about well-known people.

got past and past part. of **GET**.

Goth /goth/ ● n. a member of a Germanic people that invaded the Roman Empire between the 3rd and 5th centuries.
– ORIGIN Greek *Gothoi.*

Gothenburg E
/goth-uhn-berg/ a seaport in SW Sweden, the second-largest city in Sweden.

Gothic ● adj. **1** having to do with the ancient Goths. **2** of the style of architecture common in western Europe in the 12th–16th centuries. **3** very gloomy or horrifying. ● n. **1** the language of the Goths. **2** Gothic architecture.

gotten N. Amer. past part. of **GET**.

gouache /goo-ash/ ● n. **1** a method of painting using opaque pigments ground in water and thickened with a glue-like substance. **2** paint of this kind.
– ORIGIN French.

Gouda /gow-duh/ ● n. a flat round Dutch cheese with a yellow rind.
– ORIGIN first made in *Gouda* in the Netherlands.

gouge /gowj/ ● v. (**gouges**, **gouging**, **gouged**) **1** make (a rough hole) in a surface. **2** (**gouge out**) cut or force out roughly. ● n. **1** a chisel with a concave blade. **2** a hole or groove made by gouging.
– ORIGIN Old French.

goulash /goo-lash/ ● n. a rich Hungarian stew of meat and vegetables.
– ORIGIN from Hungarian *gulyás* 'herdsman' + *hús* 'meat'.

Gould E
/goold/, Stephen Jay (1941–2002), American palaeontologist. He proposed that evolution may take place in bursts rather than smoothly and continuously, and investigated the influence of social context on scientific theory.

Gounod E
/goo-noh/, Charles François (1818–93), French composer, conductor, and organist, best known for his opera *Faust*.

gourd /gord/ ● n. **1** the large hard-skinned fleshy fruit of a climbing or trailing plant. **2** a container made from the hollowed skin of a gourd.
– ORIGIN Old French *gourde*.

gourmand /gor-muhnd/ ● n. **1** a person who enjoys eating, sometimes to excess. **2** a person who is knowledgeable about good food.
– ORIGIN Old French.

gourmet /gor-may/ ● n. a person who is knowledgeable about good food. ● adj. (of food or a meal) high quality.
– ORIGIN French.

gout /gowt/ ● n. **1** a disease causing the joints to swell and become painful. **2** literary a drop or spot.
– DERIVATIVES **gouty** adj.
– ORIGIN Latin *gutta*.

govern ● v. **1** conduct the policy and affairs of (a state, organization, or people). **2** control or influence.
– ORIGIN Old French *governer*.

governance ● n. the action or manner of governing.

governess ● n. a woman employed to teach children in a private household.

government ● n. **1** the group of people who govern a state. **2** the system by which a state or community is governed. **3** the action or manner of governing a state: *she believed in strong government*.
– DERIVATIVES **governmental** adj.

governor ● n. **1** an official appointed to govern a town or region. **2** the elected executive head of a US state. **3** the representative of the British Crown in a colony or in a Commonwealth state that regards the monarch as head of state. **4** the head of a public institution. **5** a member of a group of people who govern a school or other institution.
– DERIVATIVES **governorship** n.

Governor General ● n. (pl. **Governors General**) the chief representative of the Crown in a Commonwealth country of which the British monarch is head of state.

gown ● n. **1** a long dress worn on formal occasions. **2** a protective garment worn in hospital by surgical staff or patients. **3** a loose cloak showing one's profession or status, worn by a lawyer, teacher, academic, or university student.
– ORIGIN Old French *goune*.

Goya E
/goy-uh/ (1746–1828; full name *Francisco José de Goya y Lucientes*), Spanish painter and etcher, famous for his works dealing with the horrors of war during the French occupation of Spain.

Gozo E
/goh-zoh/ a Maltese island, to the north-west of Malta.

GP ● abbrev. general practitioner.

gr. ● abbrev. **1** grain(s). **2** gram(s). **3** gross.

grab ● v. (**grabs**, **grabbed**, **grabbing**) **1** seize suddenly and roughly. **2** informal obtain quickly or when an opportunity arises. **3** informal impress: *how does that grab you?* ● n. a sudden attempt to seize.
– PHRASES **up for grabs** informal available.
– ORIGIN German and Dutch *grabben*.

Grace, E
W. G. (1848–1915; full name *William Gilbert Grace*), English cricketer. During his long career he made 126 centuries, scored 54,896 runs, and took 2,864 wickets.

grace ● n. **1** elegance of movement. **2** polite good will: *she had the grace to look sheepish*. **3** (**graces**) attractive qualities or behaviour: *a horrible character with no saving graces*. **4** (in Christian belief) the unearned favour of God. **5** a person's favour. **6** a period officially allowed an obligation to be met: *three days' grace*. **7** a short prayer of thanks said before or after a meal. **8** (**His**, **Her**, or **Your Grace**) used as forms of description or address for a duke, duchess, or archbishop. ● v. (**graces**, **gracing**, **graced**) **1** lend honour to by one's presence. **2** be an attractive presence in or on.
– PHRASES **with good** (or **bad**) **grace** in a willing (or reluctant) manner.
– ORIGIN Latin *gratia*.

graceful ● adj. having or showing grace or elegance.
– DERIVATIVES **gracefully** adv. **gracefulness** n.

graceless ● adj. lacking grace or charm.

grace note ● n. Music an extra note added to ornament a melody.

gracious ● adj. **1** polite, kind, and pleasant. **2** showing the elegance associated with high social status or wealth. ● exclam. expressing polite surprise.
– DERIVATIVES **graciously** adv.

gradation ● n. **1** a scale of successive changes, stages, or degrees. **2** a stage in a such a scale.

grade ● n. **1** a specified level of rank, quality, ability, or value. **2** a mark indicating the quality of a student's work. ● v. (**grades**, **grading**, **graded**) **1** arrange in or allocate to grades. **2** pass gradually from one level to another.
– PHRASES **make the grade** informal succeed.
– ORIGIN Latin *gradus* 'step'.

gradient /gray-di-uhnt/ ● n. **1** a sloping part of a road or railway. **2** the degree to which the ground slopes.
– ORIGIN from GRADE.

gradual ● adj. **1** taking place in stages over an extended period. **2** (of a slope) not steep.

g

– DERIVATIVES **gradually** adv.
– ORIGIN Latin *gradualis*.

graduate ● n. /grad-yuu-uht/ a person who has been awarded a first academic degree. ● v. /grad-yoo-ayt/ (**graduates**, **graduating**, **graduated**) **1** successfully complete a degree or course. **2** (**graduate to**) move up to (something more advanced). **3** arrange or mark out in gradations. **4** change gradually.
– DERIVATIVES **graduation** n.
– ORIGIN Latin *graduare* 'take a degree'.

Graeco- /gree-koh/ (also **Greco-**) ● comb. form Greek; Greek and ...: *Graeco-Roman*.
– ORIGIN Latin *Graecus*.

Graf E
/grahf/, Steffi (b.1969; full name *Stephanie Graf*), German tennis player. Her titles include seven Wimbledon and five US Open singles championships.

graffiti /gruh-fee-ti/ ● n. unauthorized writing or drawings on a surface in a public place.
– ORIGIN Italian.

graft[1] ● n. **1** a shoot from one plant inserted into another to form a new growth. **2** a piece of living bodily tissue that is transplanted surgically to replace diseased or damaged tissue. ● v. **1** insert or transplant as a graft. **2** add to something else, especially inappropriately.
– ORIGIN Old French *grafe*.

graft[2] Brit. informal ● n. hard work. ● v. work hard.
– ORIGIN perh. from *spade's graft* 'the amount of earth that one stroke of a spade will move'.

graft[3] informal ● n. bribery and other corrupt measures pursued for gain in politics or business.
– ORIGIN unknown.

Grafton E
/grahf-tuhn/, Augustus Henry Fitzroy, 3rd Duke of (1735–1811), British Whig statesman, Prime Minister 1768–70.

Graham[1], E
Martha (1893–1991), American dancer and choreographer, who developed a new style of dance using more flexible movements intended to express psychological and emotional states.

Graham[2], E
Billy (b.1918; full name *William Franklin Graham*), American evangelical preacher.

Grahame, E
Kenneth (1859–1932), Scottish writer, author of the children's classic *The Wind in the Willows*.

Grail (also **Holy Grail**) ● n. (in medieval legend) the cup or platter used by Christ at the Last Supper, especially as the object of quests by knights.
– ORIGIN Old French *graal*.

grain ● n. **1** wheat or other cultivated cereal used as food. **2** a single seed or fruit of a cereal. **3** a small, hard particle of a substance such as sand. **4** the smallest unit of weight in the troy and avoirdupois systems. **5** the smallest possible amount: *there wasn't a grain of truth in it*. **6** the lengthwise arrangement of fibres, particles, or layers in wood, paper, rock, etc.
– PHRASES **against the grain** conflicting with one's nature or instinct.
– ORIGIN Old French.

Grainger E
/grayn-jer/, (George) Percy (Aldridge) (1882–1961), Australian-born American composer and pianist. From 1901 he lived in London, where he collected, edited, and arranged English folk songs.

grainy ● adj. (**grainier**, **grainiest**) **1** (of a photograph) showing visible grains of emulsion. **2** consisting of grains; granular.

gram (Brit. also **gramme**) ● n. a metric unit of mass equal to one thousandth of a kilogram.
– ORIGIN French *gramme*.

-gram ● comb. form forming nouns referring to something written or recorded: *anagram*.
– ORIGIN Greek *gramma* 'thing written'.

grammar ● n. **1** the whole structure of a language, including the rules for the way words are formed and their relationship to each other in sentence. **2** knowledge and use of the rules of grammar: *bad grammar*. **3** a book on grammar.
– ORIGIN from Greek *grammatikē tekhnē* 'art of letters'.

grammarian /gruh-mair-i-uhn/ ● n. a person who studies and writes about grammar.

grammar school ● n. (in the UK, especially formerly) a state secondary school to which pupils are admitted on the basis of ability.

grammatical /gruh-mat-i-k'l/ ● adj. having to do with or in accordance with the rules of grammar.
– DERIVATIVES **grammatically** adv.

gramme ● n. var. of GRAM.

gramophone ● n. Brit. dated a record player.
– ORIGIN formed by reversing the elements of *phonogram* 'sound recording'.

gramophone record ● n. = RECORD (in sense 3).

Grampian Mountains E
a mountain range in north central Scotland.

grampus /gram-puhss/ ● n. (pl. **grampuses**) a killer whale or other dolphin-like sea animal.
– ORIGIN Old French *grapois*.

gran ● n. Brit. informal one's grandmother.

Granada E
/gruh-nah-duh/ a city in Andalusia in southern Spain, the former capital of the Moorish kingdom of Granada (1238–1429).

granary ● n. (pl. **granaries**) a storehouse for grain.
– ORIGIN Latin *granarium*.

granary bread ● n. Brit. trademark a type of brown bread containing whole grains of wheat.

Gran Canaria E
/gran kuh-nair-i-uh/ one of the Canary Islands; chief town, Las Palmas.

grand ● adj. **1** magnificent and impressive. **2** large or ambitious in scale: *his grand design for peace*. **3** of the highest importance or rank. **4** dignified, noble, or proud. **5** informal excellent. ● n. **1** (pl. **grand**) informal a thousand dollars or pounds. **2** a grand piano.

– DERIVATIVES **grandly** adv.
– ORIGIN Latin *grandis* 'great'.

grandad (also **granddad**) • n. informal one's grandfather. • adj. (of a shirt) having a collar in the form of a narrow upright band.

Grand Canyon E
a deep gorge in Arizona, formed by the Colorado River. It is about 440 km (277 miles) long, 8 to 24 km (5 to 15 miles) wide, and, in places, 1,800 m (6,000 ft) deep.

grandchild • n. a child of one's son or daughter.

granddaughter • n. a daughter of one's son or daughter.

grand duke • n. (in Europe, especially formerly) a prince or nobleman ruling over a small independent state.

Grande Comore E
/grond kuh-**mor**/ the largest of the islands of the Comoros; chief town (and capital of the Comoros), Moroni.

grande dame /grond **dam**/ • n. a woman who is influential within a particular area.
– ORIGIN French, 'grand lady'.

grandee /gran-**dee**/ • n. **1** a Spanish or Portuguese nobleman of the highest rank. **2** a high-ranking or important man.
– ORIGIN Spanish and Portuguese *grande* 'grand'.

grandeur /gran-dyer/ • n. **1** splendour and impressiveness. **2** high rank or social importance.

grandfather • n. **1** the father of one's father or mother. **2** a founder or originator: *the grandfather of liberalism.*

grandfather clock • n. a clock in a tall wooden case.

grandiloquent /gran-**dil**-uh-kwuhnt/ • adj. using long or difficult words in order to impress.
– ORIGIN Latin *grandiloquus* 'grand-speaking'.

grandiose /**gran**-di-ohss/ • adj. impressive or magnificent, especially in a way which is intended to impress.
– ORIGIN Italian *grandioso.*

grand jury • n. US Law a jury selected to examine the validity of an accusation prior to trial.

grandma • n. informal one's grandmother.

grand mal /gron **mal**/ • n. a serious form of epilepsy with prolonged loss of consciousness. Compare with **PETIT MAL**.
– ORIGIN French, 'great sickness'.

grand master • n. (also **grandmaster**) a chess player of the highest class.

grandmother • n. the mother of one's father or mother.

Grand National • n. an annual steeplechase held at Aintree, Liverpool.

grandpa • n. informal one's grandfather.

grandparent • n. a grandmother or grandfather.

grand piano • n. a large piano which has the body, strings, and soundboard arranged horizontally.

Grand Prix /gron **pree**/ • n. (pl. **Grands Prix** /gron **pree**/) a race forming part of a motor-racing or motorcycling world championship.
– ORIGIN French, 'great or chief prize'.

grandsire • n. archaic = **GRANDFATHER**.

grand slam • n. the winning of each of a group of major championships or matches in a particular sport in the same year.

grandson • n. the son of one's son or daughter.

grandstand • n. the main stand at a racecourse or sports ground.

grand total • n. the final amount after everything is added up.

grand tour • n. a cultural tour of Europe formerly undertaken by upper-class young men.

grange • n. Brit. **1** a country house with farm buildings attached. **2** archaic a barn.
– ORIGIN Old French.

granite /**gran**-it/ • n. a very hard rock made up of quartz, mica, and feldspar.
– DERIVATIVES **granitic** adj.
– ORIGIN Italian *granito* 'grained'.

granny (also **grannie**) • n. (pl. **grannies**) informal one's grandmother.

granny flat • n. informal a part of a house made into self-contained accommodation suitable for an elderly relative.

granny knot • n. a reef knot with the ends crossed the wrong way and therefore liable to slip.

Grant[1], E
Cary (1904–86; born *Alexander Archibald Leach*), British-born American actor. His many films include *Holiday* and *The Philadelphia Story.*

Grant[2], E
Ulysses S. (1822–85; full name *Ulysses Simpson Grant*), American general and 18th President of the US 1869–77. As supreme commander of the Unionist armies in the American Civil War, he was successful in defeating the Confederate forces and bringing the war to an end.

grant • v. **1** agree to give or allow (something requested) to. **2** give (something) formally or legally to. **3** admit to (someone) that (something) is true. • n. a sum of money given by a government or public body for a particular purpose.
PHRASES **take for granted 1** fail to appreciate through over-familiarity. **2** assume that (something) is true.
– ORIGIN Old French *granter* 'consent to support'.

granted • adv. it is true. • conj. (**granted that**) even assuming that.

grant-maintained • adj. Brit. (of a school) funded by central rather than local government, and self-governing.

gran turismo /gran tuu-**riz**-moh/ • n. (pl. **gran turismos**) a high-performance model of car.
– ORIGIN Italian, 'great touring'.

granular • adj. **1** resembling or consisting of granules. **2** having a roughened surface.

granulated • adj. in the form of granules.
– DERIVATIVES **granulation** n.

granule /**gran**-yool/ • n. a small compact particle of a substance.
– ORIGIN Latin *granulum* 'little grain'.

Granville-Barker, E
Harley (1877–1946), English dramatist, critic, and theatre director, who wrote *The Voysey Inheritance.*

grape ● n. a green, purple, or black berry growing on a vine, eaten as fruit and used in making wine.
– ORIGIN Old French, 'bunch of grapes'.

grapefruit ● n. (pl. **grapefruit**) a large yellow citrus fruit with an acid juicy pulp.
– ORIGIN from **GRAPE** + **FRUIT**.

grapeshot ● n. hist. ammunition consisting of a number of small iron balls fired together from a cannon.

grapevine ● n. **1** a vine bearing grapes. **2** (**the grapevine**) informal the circulation of rumours and unofficial information.

graph ● n. a diagram showing the relation between variable quantities, typically of two variables measured along a pair of lines at right angles.
– ORIGIN from *graphic formula*.

g

-graph ● comb. form **1** referring to something written or drawn in a specified way: *autograph*. **2** referring to an instrument that records: *seismograph*.
– ORIGIN Greek *graphos* 'written'.

graphic ● adj. **1** relating to visual art, especially involving drawing, engraving, or lettering. **2** giving vividly explicit detail: *a graphic description*. **3** in the form of a graph. ● n. **1** Computing a visual image displayed on a screen or stored as data. **2** (**graphics**) the use of drawings, designs, or pictures to illustrate books, magazines, etc.
– DERIVATIVES **graphically** adv.
– ORIGIN Greek *graphikos*.

graphic design ● n. the art of combining words and pictures in advertisements, magazines, or books.

graphic equalizer ● n. a device for controlling the strength and quality of selected frequency bands.

graphic novel ● n. a novel in comic-strip format.

graphite ● n. a grey form of carbon used as a solid lubricant and as pencil lead.
– ORIGIN Greek *graphein* 'write'.

graphology ● n. the study of handwriting to analyse a person's character.
– DERIVATIVES **graphologist** n.
– ORIGIN Greek *graphē* 'writing'.

graph paper ● n. paper printed with a network of small squares to assist the drawing of graphs or other diagrams.

-graphy ● comb. form forming nouns meaning: **1** a descriptive science: *geography*. **2** a technique of producing images: *radiography*. **3** a style of writing or drawing: *calligraphy*. **4** writing about (a specified subject): *hagiography*. **5** a list: *bibliography*.
– DERIVATIVES **-graphic** comb. form
– ORIGIN Greek *-graphia* 'writing'.

grapnel /grap-nuhl/ ● n. a grappling hook.
– ORIGIN Old French *grapon*.

> **Grappelli** E
> /gruh-pel-li/, Stephane (1908–97), French jazz violinist.

grapple ● v. (**grapples**, **grappling**, **grappled**) **1** engage in a close fight or struggle without weapons. **2** (**grapple with**) struggle to deal with or understand. ● n. an act of grappling.
– ORIGIN Old French *grapil* 'small hook'.

grappling hook (also **grappling iron**) ● n. a device with iron claws, attached to a rope and used for dragging or grasping.

grasp ● v. **1** seize and hold firmly. **2** understand fully. ● n. **1** a firm grip. **2** a person's capacity to achieve or understand something: *meanings that are beyond my grasp*.
– ORIGIN perh. from **GROPE**.

grasping ● adj. greedy.

> **Grass** E
> /grahss/, Günter (Wilhelm) (b.1927), German novelist, poet, and dramatist, author of such novels as *The Tin Drum* and *Cat and Mouse*, which often reflect his socialist views.

grass ● n. **1** vegetation consisting of short plants with long narrow leaves. **2** ground covered with grass. **3** informal cannabis. **4** Brit. informal a police informer. ● v. **1** cover with grass. **2** Brit. informal inform the police of someone's criminal activity.
– ORIGIN Old English.

grasshopper ● n. an insect with long hind legs which are used for jumping and for producing a chirping sound.

grass roots ● pl. n. the most basic level of an activity or organization.

grass snake ● n. a harmless grey-green snake with a yellowish band around the neck.

grass widow ● n. a woman whose husband is away often or for a long time.
– ORIGIN first referring to an unmarried woman with a child: perh. from the idea of a couple having lain on the grass rather than a bed.

grassy ● adj. covered with or resembling grass.

grate[1] ● v. (**grates**, **grating**, **grated**) **1** reduce (food) to small shreds by rubbing it on a grater. **2** make an unpleasant scraping sound. **3** have an irritating effect: *he grated on her nerves*.
– ORIGIN Old French *grater*.

grate[2] ● n. a metal frame preventing fuel from falling out of a fireplace or furnace.
– ORIGIN Old French.

grateful ● adj. feeling or showing gratitude.
– DERIVATIVES **gratefully** adv.
– ORIGIN Latin *gratus* 'thankful'.

grater ● n. a device having a surface covered with sharp-edged holes, used for grating food.

gratify ● v. (**gratifies**, **gratifying**, **gratified**) **1** give pleasure or satisfaction: *he was gratified to be alone*. **2** indulge or satisfy (a desire).
– DERIVATIVES **gratification** n.
– ORIGIN Latin *gratificari* 'give or do as a favour'.

gratin /gra-tan/ ● n. a dish with a browned crust of breadcrumbs or melted cheese.
– ORIGIN French.

grating[1] ● adj. **1** sounding harsh and unpleasant. **2** irritating.

grating[2] ● n. a framework of parallel or crossed bars that cover an opening.

gratis /grah-tiss/ ● adv. & adj. free of charge.
– ORIGIN Latin.

gratitude ● n. thankfulness; appreciation of kindness.
– ORIGIN Latin *gratitudo*.

gratuitous /gruh-tyoo-i-tuhss/ ● adj. done

without good reason or purpose: *gratuitous violence.*
– ORIGIN Latin *gratuitus* 'given freely'.

gratuity /gruh-tyoo-i-ti/ ● **n.** (pl. **gratuities**) formal a tip given to a waiter, porter, etc.
– ORIGIN Latin *gratuitas* 'gift'.

grave[1] ● **n. 1** a hole dug in the ground for a coffin or corpse. **2** (**the grave**) death.
– PHRASES **turn in one's grave** (of a dead person) be likely to have been angry or distressed about something had they been alive.
– ORIGIN Old English.

grave[2] ● **adj. 1** giving cause for alarm or concern. **2** solemn.
– DERIVATIVES **gravely** adv.
– ORIGIN Old French.

grave accent /grahv/ ● **n.** a mark (`) placed over a vowel to indicate pronunciation.
– ORIGIN French *grave* 'serious'.

gravel ● **n.** a loose mixture of small stones and coarse sand, used for paths and roads.
– ORIGIN Old French.

gravelly ● **adj. 1** containing or made of gravel. **2** (of a voice) deep and rough-sounding.

> **Graves,** E
> Robert (Ranke) (1895–1985), English poet, novelist, and critic. He is known for the historical novel *I, Claudius* and his autobiography *Goodbye to All That.*

gravestone ● **n.** an inscribed headstone marking a grave.

graveyard ● **n.** a burial ground beside a church.

gravid /gra-vid/ ● **adj. 1** tech. pregnant. **2** literary full of a specified quality.
– ORIGIN Latin *gravidus.*

gravitas /gra-vi-tass/ ● **n.** dignity or solemnity of manner.
– ORIGIN Latin.

gravitate /gra-vi-tayt/ ● **v.** (**gravitates, gravitating, gravitated**) be drawn towards a place, person, or thing.

gravitation ● **n. 1** movement, or a tendency to move, towards a centre of gravity. **2** Physics gravity.

gravity ● **n. 1** the force that attracts a body towards the centre of the earth, or towards any other physical body having mass. **2** extreme importance or seriousness: *crimes of the utmost gravity.* **3** solemnity of manner.
– ORIGIN Latin *gravitas.*

gravy ● **n.** (pl. **gravies**) **1** the fat and juices that come out of meat during cooking. **2** a sauce made from these juices together with stock and other ingredients.
– ORIGIN perh. from Old French *grané.*

gravy boat ● **n.** a narrow jug used for serving gravy.

gravy train ● **n.** informal a situation in which someone can easily make a lot of money.

> **Gray,** E
> Thomas (1716–71), English poet, best known for 'Elegy Written in a Country Church-Yard'.

gray ● **adj.** US = **GREY**.

graze[1] ● **v.** (**grazes, grazing, grazed**) (of cattle, sheep, etc.) eat grass in a field.
– ORIGIN Old English.

graze[2] ● **v.** (**grazes, grazing, grazed**) **1** scrape and break the skin on (part of the body). **2** touch (something) lightly in passing. ● **n.** a superficial injury caused by grazing the skin.
– ORIGIN perh. from **GRAZE**[1].

grazing ● **n.** grassland suitable for use as pasture.

grease ● **n. 1** a thick oily substance, especially one used to lubricate machinery. **2** animal fat produced in cooking. ● **v.** (**greases, greasing, greased**) smear or lubricate with grease.
– ORIGIN Old French *graisse.*

grease monkey ● **n.** informal a mechanic.

greasepaint ● **n.** a waxy substance used as make-up by actors.

greaseproof ● **adj.** not allowing grease to pass through it.

greasy ● **adj.** (**greasier, greasiest**) **1** covered with or resembling grease. **2** extremely polite in an unpleasantly insincere way.

greasy spoon ● **n.** informal a cheap cafe or restaurant serving fried foods.

great ● **adj. 1** considerably above average in amount, extent, or strength. **2** much above average in ability, quality, or importance. **3** informal excellent. **4** particularly deserving a specified description: *I was a great fan of Hank's.* **5** (**Greater**) (of a city) including adjacent urban areas. ● **n.** a famous and successful person.
– DERIVATIVES **greatness** n.
– ORIGIN Old English.

great ape ● **n.** a large ape of a family closely related to humans, including the gorilla and chimpanzees.

great-aunt ● **n.** an aunt of one's father or mother.

> **Great Australian Bight** E
> a wide bay on the south coast of Australia.

> **Great Barrier Reef** E
> a coral reef in the western Pacific, off the coast of Queensland, Australia. With a length of about 2,000 km (1,250 miles), it is the largest coral reef in the world.

> **Great Bear** E
> the constellation Ursa Major.

> **Great Britain** E
> England, Wales, and Scotland considered as a unit. The name is also often used loosely to refer to the United Kingdom.

great circle ● **n.** a circle on the surface of a sphere which lies in a plane passing through the sphere's centre.

greatcoat ● **n.** a long heavy overcoat.

Great Dane ● **n.** a very large breed of dog with short hair.

> **Great Dividing Range** E
> a mountain system in eastern Australia, extending from eastern Victoria to northern Queensland.

> **Greater Antilles** E
> the part of the Antilles extending roughly east to west and comprising Cuba, Jamaica, Hispaniola (Haiti and the Dominican Republic), and Puerto Rico.

Greater London E
a metropolitan area comprising central London and the surrounding regions. It is divided administratively into the City of London, thirteen inner London boroughs, and twenty outer London boroughs.

Greater Manchester E
a metropolitan county of NW England including the city of Manchester and adjacent areas.

Great Exhibition E
the first international exhibition of the products of industry, held in the Crystal Palace in London in 1851.

Great Lakes E
a group of five large interconnected lakes in central North America, consisting of Lakes Superior, Michigan, Huron, Erie, and Ontario, and forming the largest area of fresh water in the world.

greatly • **adv.** very much.

Great Plague E
a serious outbreak of bubonic plague in England in 1665–6, in which about one fifth of the population of London died.

Great Plains E
a vast area of plains to the east of the Rocky Mountains in North America, extending from the valleys of the Mackenzie River in Canada to southern Texas.

Great Rift Valley E
a large system of rift valleys running for some 4,285 km (3,000 miles) from the Jordan valley in Syria into Mozambique in eastern Africa, forming the most extensive such system in the world.

Great Salt Lake E
a salt lake in northern Utah, near Salt Lake City. With an area of some 2,590 sq. km (1,000 sq. miles), it is the largest salt lake in North America.

Great Slave Lake E
a large lake in the Northwest Territories in Canada. With a depth of 615 m (2,015 ft), it is the deepest lake in North America.

great-uncle • **n.** an uncle of one's mother or father.

Great Wall of China E
a fortified defensive wall in northern China, extending some 2,400 km (1,500 miles) from Kansu province in the north-west to the Yellow Sea north of Beijing. The present wall dates mostly from the Ming dynasty (14th to 15th century).

Great War • **n.** the First World War.

greave • **n.** hist. a piece of armour for the shin.
– ORIGIN Old French *greve* 'shin, greave'.

grebe /greeb/ • **n.** a diving waterbird with a long neck and a very short tail.
– ORIGIN French.

Grecian /gree-sh'n/ • **adj.** relating to ancient Greece.

Greco, El E
see **El Greco**.

Greece E
a country in SE Europe; capital, Athens.

greed • **n.** strong and selfish desire for food, wealth, or power.

greedy • **adj.** (**greedier**, **greediest**) having or showing greed.
– DERIVATIVES **greedily** adv. **greediness** n.
– ORIGIN Old English.

Greek • **n.** **1** a person from Greece. **2** the ancient or modern language of Greece. • **adj.** relating to Greece.
– ORIGIN Greek *Graikoi*.

Greek cross • **n.** a cross of which all four arms are of equal length.

Greek Orthodox Church • **n.** the national church of Greece.

green • **adj.** **1** of the colour between blue and yellow in the spectrum; coloured like grass. **2** covered with grass or other vegetation. **3** (**Green**) concerned with or supporting protection of the environment. **4** in an untreated or original state; not cured, seasoned, etc. **5** inexperienced or naive: *a green recruit*. • **n.** **1** green colour or material. **2** a piece of common grassy land. **3** an area of very short grass surrounding a hole on a golf course. **4** (**greens**) green vegetables. **5** (**Green**) a member or supporter of an environmentalist group or party. • **v.** make or become green.
– ORIGIN Old English.

Greenaway[1], E
Kate (1846–1901; full name *Catherine Greenaway*), English artist, best known for her illustrations of children's books.

Greenaway[2], E
Peter (b.1942), English film director. His films include *The Draughtsman's Contract* and *The Cook, The Thief, His Wife, and Her Lover*.

green belt • **n.** an area of open land around a city, on which building is restricted.

Greene, E
(Henry) Graham (1904–91), English novelist. His works reflect his concern with moral dilemmas and divided allegiances, and include *Brighton Rock*, *The Power and the Glory*, and *The Third Man*.

greenery • **n.** green leaves or plants.

greenfield • **adj.** (of a site) previously undeveloped.

greenfinch • **n.** a large finch with green and yellow plumage.

green fingers • **pl. n.** Brit. informal natural ability in growing plants.

greenfly • **n.** esp. Brit. a green aphid.

greengage • **n.** a sweet greenish fruit resembling a small plum.
– ORIGIN named after the English botanist Sir William *Gage* (1657–1727).

greengrocer • **n.** Brit. a person who sells fruit and vegetables.

greenhouse • **n.** a glass building in which plants are kept to protect them from cold weather.

greenhouse effect • **n.** the trapping of the sun's warmth in the earth's lower atmosphere, due to the greater transparency of the atmosphere to visible radiation from the sun than to infrared radiation coming from the planet's surface.

greenhouse gas ● n. a gas, such as carbon dioxide, that contributes to the greenhouse effect by absorbing infrared radiation.

Greenland E
a large island lying to the north-east of North America and mostly within the Arctic Circle; capital, Nuuk.
– DERIVATIVES **Greenlander** n.

green light ● n. **1** a green traffic light giving permission to proceed. **2** permission to go ahead with a project.

Greenpeace E
an international organization that campaigns for conservation of the environment and the preservation of endangered species.

green pepper ● n. the unripe fruit of a sweet pepper.

green room ● n. a room in a theatre or studio in which performers can relax when they are not performing.

greensward /green-sword/ ● n. archaic grass-covered ground.

green tea ● n. tea made from unfermented leaves, produced mainly in China and Japan.

Greenwich Mean Time ● n. the mean solar time at the Greenwich meridian, used as the standard time in a zone that includes the British Isles.
– ORIGIN from *Greenwich* in London, former site of the Royal Observatory.

Greenwich meridian ● n. the meridian of zero longitude, passing through Greenwich.

greenwood ● n. archaic a wood or forest in leaf.

Greer, E
Germaine (b.1939), Australian feminist and writer, author of the influential book *The Female Eunuch*.

greet ● v. **1** give a word or sign of welcome when meeting (someone). **2** receive or acknowledge in a specified way: *everyone greeted the idea warmly.* **3** (of a sight or sound) become apparent to (a person arriving somewhere).
– ORIGIN Old English.

greeting ● n. **1** a word or sign of welcome or recognition. **2** (**greetings**) a formal expression of good wishes.

greetings card (N. Amer. **greeting card**) ● n. a decorative card sent to convey good wishes.

gregarious /gri-gair-i-uhss/ ● adj. **1** fond of company; sociable. **2** (of animals) living in flocks or colonies.
– ORIGIN Latin *gregarius.*

Gregorian chant /gri-gor-i-uhn/ ● n. medieval church plainsong.
– ORIGIN named after St *Gregory* (see **GREGORY, ST**).

Gregory, St E
(*c.*540–604; known as **St Gregory the Great**), pope (as Gregory I) 590–604. An important reformer, he did much to establish the temporal power of the papacy. Feast day, 12 March.

gremlin ● n. a mischievous sprite regarded as responsible for unexplained mechanical or electrical faults.
– ORIGIN perh. from **GOBLIN**.

Grenada E
/gruh-nay-duh/ a country in the Caribbean, consisting of the island of Grenada (one of the Windward Islands) and the southern Grenadine Islands; capital, St George's.
– DERIVATIVES **Grenadian** adj. & n.

grenade /gruh-nayd/ ● n. a small bomb thrown by hand or launched mechanically.
– ORIGIN from Old French *pome grenate* 'pomegranate'.

grenadier /gren-uh-deer/ ● n. **1** hist. a soldier armed with grenades. **2** (**Grenadiers** or **Grenadier Guards**) the first regiment of the royal household infantry.

Grenadine Islands E
/gren-uh-deen/ a chain of small islands in the Caribbean, part of the Windward Islands. They are divided administratively between St Vincent and Grenada.

Grenoble E
/gruh-noh-b'l/ an industrial city in SE France.

Grenville, E
George (1712–70), British Whig statesman, Prime Minister 1763–5.

Gretna Green E
a village in Scotland just north of the English border near Carlisle, formerly a popular place for runaway couples from England to be married without parental consent.

Gretzky E
/gret-ski/, Wayne (b.1961), Canadian ice hockey player, the all-time leading point-scorer in the National Hockey League.

grew past of **GROW**.

Grey[1], E
Charles, 2nd Earl (1764–1845), British statesman, Prime Minister 1830–4. His government passed the first Reform Act (1832) and the Act abolishing slavery throughout the British Empire.

Grey[2], E
Lady Jane (1537–54), niece of Henry VIII, queen of England 9–19 July 1553. Edward VI was persuaded to name Jane, a Protestant, as his successor, but she was quickly deposed by forces loyal to Edward's (Catholic) sister Mary, and later executed.

grey (US **gray**) ● adj. **1** of a colour between black and white, as of ashes. **2** (of hair) turning grey or white with age. **3** (of the weather) cloudy and dull. **4** lacking interest or character: *grey, faceless men.* **5** not accounted for in official statistics: *the grey economy.* ● n. grey colour. ● v. (of hair) become grey with age.
– ORIGIN Old English.

grey area ● n. an area of activity that does not easily fit into an existing category and is difficult to deal with.

greyhound ● n. a swift, slender breed of dog used in racing.
– ORIGIN Old English.

greylag ● n. a large goose with mainly grey plumage.

g

– ORIGIN prob. from dialect *lag* 'goose'.

grey matter ● n. **1** the darker tissue of the brain and spinal cord. **2** informal intelligence.

grey seal ● n. a large North Atlantic seal with a spotted greyish coat.

grey squirrel ● n. a tree squirrel with mainly grey fur.

grid ● n. **1** a framework of spaced bars that are parallel to or cross each other. **2** a network of lines that cross each other to form a series of squares or rectangles. **3** a network of cables or pipes for distributing electricity or gas.
– ORIGIN from **GRIDIRON**.

griddle ● n. a circular iron plate that is heated and used for cooking food. ● v. (**griddles, griddling, griddled**) cook on a griddle.
– ORIGIN Old French *gredil*.

g

gridiron /grid-I-uhn/ ● n. **1** a frame of parallel metal bars used for grilling meat or fish over an open fire. **2** a field for American football, marked with regularly spaced parallel lines.
– ORIGIN from former *gredile* 'griddle'.

gridlock ● n. a traffic jam affecting a whole network of linked streets.
– DERIVATIVES **gridlocked** adj.

grief ● n. **1** deep sorrow, especially caused by someone's death. **2** informal trouble or annoyance.
– ORIGIN Old French.

Grieg E
/greeg/, Edvard (1843–1907), Norwegian composer, conductor, and violinist, known for his Piano Concerto in A minor and the incidental music to Ibsen's play *Peer Gynt*.

grievance ● n. a cause for complaint.

grieve ● v. (**grieves, grieving, grieved**) **1** suffer grief. **2** cause great distress to.
– ORIGIN Old French *grever* 'burden'.

grievous ● adj. formal (of something bad) very severe or serious: *his death was a grievous blow.*
– DERIVATIVES **grievously** adv.

grievous bodily harm ● n. Law serious physical injury inflicted on a person by the deliberate action of another.

griffin (also **gryphon** or **griffon**) ● n. a mythical creature with the head and wings of an eagle and the body of a lion.
– ORIGIN Old French *grifoun*.

Griffith[1], E
Arthur (1872–1922), Irish nationalist leader, President of the Irish Free State 1922. He founded Sinn Fein (1905) and led the Irish delegation that negotiated the Anglo-Irish Treaty (1921).

Griffith[2], E
D. W. (1875–1948; full name *David Lewelyn Wark Griffith*), American film director, who pioneered many cinematic techniques in films such as *The Birth of a Nation* and *Intolerance*.

griffon /grif-fuhn/ ● n. a small dog resembling a terrier.
– ORIGIN from **GRIFFIN**.

grill ● n. Brit. **1** a device on a cooker that directs heat downwards for cooking food. **2** a gridiron used for cooking food on an open fire. **3** a dish of food cooked using a grill. **4** a restaurant serving grilled food. **5** var. of **GRILLE**. ● v. **1** cook with a grill. **2** informal subject to intense questioning; interrogate.
– ORIGIN Old French *graille* 'grille'.

grille (also **grill**) ● n. a grating or screen of metal bars or wires.
– ORIGIN French.

grilse /grilss/ ● n. a salmon that has returned to fresh water after a single winter at sea.
– ORIGIN unknown.

grim ● adj. (**grimmer, grimmest**) **1** very serious or gloomy. **2** horrifying, depressing, or unappealing: *the grim prospect of dearer mortgages.*
– DERIVATIVES **grimly** adv. **grimness** n.
– ORIGIN Old English.

grimace /gri-mayss, gri-muhss/ ● n. a twisted expression on a person's face, expressing disgust, pain, or wry amusement. ● v. (**grimaces, grimacing, grimaced**) make a grimace.
– ORIGIN French.

grime ● n. dirt ingrained on a surface. ● v. (**grimes, griming, grimed**) blacken or make dirty with grime.
– ORIGIN German and Dutch.

Grimm, E
Jacob (Ludwig Carl) (1785–1863) and Wilhelm (Carl) (1786–1859), German scholars and writers. They jointly initiated a historical dictionary of German and compiled an anthology of German fairy tales.

grimy ● adj. (**grimier, grimiest**) covered with grime.

grin ● v. (**grins, grinning, grinned**) smile broadly. ● n. a broad smile.
– PHRASES **grin and bear it** suffer pain or misfortune without complaining.
– ORIGIN Old English.

grind ● v. (**grinds, grinding, ground**) **1** reduce to small particles or powder by crushing. **2** sharpen, smooth, or produce by crushing or friction. **3** rub together or move gratingly. **4** (**grind down**) wear (someone) down with harsh treatment. **5** (**grind out**) produce (something) slowly and with effort. **6** (**grinding**) (of a difficult situation) seemingly endless: *grinding poverty.* ● n. hard dull work: *the daily grind.*
– ORIGIN Old English.

grindstone ● n. a revolving disc of abrasive material used for sharpening or polishing metal objects.
– PHRASES **keep one's nose to the grindstone** work hard and continuously.

gringo /gring-goh/ ● n. (pl. **gringos**) informal (in Latin America) a white English-speaking person.
– ORIGIN Spanish, 'foreign'.

grip ● v. (**grips, gripping, gripped**) **1** take and keep a firm hold of. **2** deeply affect: *she was gripped by a feeling of excitement.* **3** hold the attention or interest of. ● n. **1** a firm hold. **2** understanding. **3** a part or attachment by which something is held in the hand.
– PHRASES **come** (or **get**) **to grips with** begin to deal with or understand. **lose one's grip** become unable to understand or control one's situation.
– ORIGIN Old English.

gripe ● v. (**gripes, griping, griped**) **1** informal express a trivial complaint; grumble. **2** affect with stomach pain. ● n. **1** informal a trivial complaint. **2** pain in the stomach.

– ORIGIN Old English, 'grasp, clutch'.

grisly /griz-li/ • adj. (**grislier**, **grisliest**) causing horror or revulsion.
– ORIGIN Old English.

grist • n. corn that is ground to make flour.
– PHRASES **grist to the mill** useful experience or knowledge.
– ORIGIN Old English, 'grinding'.

gristle /griss-uhl/ • n. cartilage, especially when found as tough inedible tissue in meat.
– DERIVATIVES **gristly** adj.
– ORIGIN Old English.

grit • n. **1** small loose particles of stone or sand. **2** (also **gritstone**) a coarse sandstone. **3** courage and determination: *the true grit of the navy pilot.* • v. (**grits**, **gritting**, **gritted**) **1** clench (the teeth) with determination. **2** spread grit on (an icy road).
– ORIGIN Old English.

gritty • adj. (**grittier**, **grittiest**) **1** containing or covered with grit. **2** showing courage and determination. **3** tough and uncompromising: *a gritty look at urban life.*
– DERIVATIVES **grittily** adv. **grittiness** n.

grizzle • v. (**grizzles**, **grizzling**, **grizzled**) Brit. informal (of a child) cry or whimper fretfully.
– ORIGIN unknown.

grizzled • adj. having grey or grey-streaked hair.
– ORIGIN Old French *gris* 'grey'.

grizzly bear • n. a large variety of brown bear often having white-tipped fur.
– ORIGIN from **GRIZZLED**.

groan • v. **1** make a deep sound of pain or despair. **2** make a low creaking sound when pressure or weight is applied. • n. a groaning sound.
– ORIGIN Old English.

groat • n. hist. an English silver coin worth four old pence.
– ORIGIN Dutch *groot* or German *grote* 'great, thick'.

grocer • n. a person who sells food and small household goods.
– ORIGIN Old French *grossier*.

grocery • n. (pl. **groceries**) **1** a grocer's shop or business. **2** (**groceries**) items of food sold in a grocer's shop or supermarket.

Groening E
/gray-ning/, Matt (b. 1954), American cartoonist and writer, creator of the television cartoon series *The Simpsons*.

grog • n. **1** spirits (originally rum) mixed with water. **2** informal alcoholic drink.
– ORIGIN said to be from the nickname of Admiral Vernon (1684–1757), who ordered diluted rum to be served out to sailors.

groggy • adj. dazed and unsteady after drunkenness, sleep, etc.

groin[1] • n. **1** the area between the abdomen and the thigh. **2** informal the region of the genitals. **3** Archit. a curved edge formed by two intersecting roof arches.
– ORIGIN perh. from Old English, 'depression, abyss'.

groin[2] • n. US = **GROYNE**.

grommet /grom-mit/ • n. **1** a protective eyelet in a hole that a rope or cable passes through. **2** a tube implanted in the eardrum to drain fluid from the middle ear.
– ORIGIN from former French *gourmer* 'to curb'.

Gromyko E
/gruh-mee-koh/, Andrei (Andreevich) (1909–89), Soviet statesman, Foreign minister 1957–1985, President of the USSR 1985–8.

groom • v. **1** brush and clean the coat of (a horse or dog). **2** give a neat and tidy appearance to. **3** prepare or train for a particular purpose or activity: *pupils who are groomed for higher things.* • n. **1** a person employed to take care of horses. **2** a bridegroom.
– ORIGIN unknown.

groove • n. **1** a long, narrow cut or depression in a hard material. **2** a spiral track cut in a gramophone record. **3** an established routine or habit. • v. (**grooves**, **grooving**, **grooved**) **1** make a groove or grooves in. **2** informal dance to or play popular or jazz music.
– ORIGIN Dutch *groeve* 'furrow, pit'.

groovy • adj. (**groovier**, **grooviest**) informal, dated fashionable and exciting.

grope • v. (**gropes**, **groping**, **groped**) **1** feel about or search blindly or uncertainly with the hands. **2** informal fondle (someone) for sexual pleasure. • n. informal an act of groping someone.
– ORIGIN Old English.

Gropius E
/groh-pi-uhss/, Walter (1883–1969), German-born American architect. An influential figure in modern architecture and design, he founded the Bauhaus School of Design and was its first director (1919–28).

grosgrain /groh-grayn/ • n. a heavy ribbed fabric of silk or rayon.
– ORIGIN French, 'coarse grain'.

gross • adj. **1** unattractively large. **2** vulgar; coarse. **3** informal very unpleasant. **4** complete; blatant: *a gross exaggeration.* **5** (of income, profit, or interest) without deduction of tax or other contributions; total. **6** (of weight) including contents or other variable items. • adv. without tax or other contributions having been deducted. • v. produce or earn (an amount of money) as gross profit or income. • n. **1** (pl. **gross**) an amount equal to twelve dozen; 144. **2** (pl. **grosses**) a gross profit or income.
– DERIVATIVES **grossly** adv. **grossness** n.
– ORIGIN Old French *gros*.

gross domestic product • n. the total value of goods produced and services provided within a country during one year.

gross national product • n. the total value of goods produced and services provided by a country during one year, equal to the gross domestic product plus the net income from foreign investments.

grotesque /groh-tesk/ • adj. **1** comically or repulsively ugly or distorted. **2** shocking. • n. a grotesque person or picture.
– DERIVATIVES **grotesquely** adv.
– ORIGIN Italian *grottesca*.

grotesquerie /groh-tesk-uh-ri/ • n. (pl. **grotesqueries**) grotesque quality or things.

grotto • n. (pl. **grottoes** or **grottos**) a small artificial cave in a park or garden.
– ORIGIN Italian *grotta*.

grotty • adj. (**grottier**, **grottiest**) Brit. informal **1** unpleasant and of poor quality. **2** unwell.
– ORIGIN from **GROTESQUE**.

g

grouch /growch/ • **n.** informal **1** a person who is often grumpy. **2** a complaint or grumble.
– ORIGIN Old French *grouchier* 'to grumble, murmur'.

grouchy • **adj.** irritable and bad-tempered; grumpy.

ground[1] • **n. 1** the solid surface of the earth. **2** land of a specified kind: *marshy ground.* **3** an area of land or sea with a specified use: *fishing grounds.* **4** (**grounds**) an area of enclosed land surrounding a large house. **5** (**grounds**) factors forming a good reason for doing or thinking something: *there are some grounds for optimism.* • **v. 1** ban or prevent (a pilot or aircraft) from flying. **2** run (a ship) aground. **3** (**be grounded in/on**) have as a basis. **4** informal (of a parent) refuse to allow (a child) to go out socially, as a punishment.
– PHRASES **be thick** (or **thin**) **on the ground** exist in large (or small) numbers or amounts. **break new ground** achieve or create something new. **get off the ground** start happening or functioning successfully. **give** (or **lose**) **ground** retreat or lose one's advantage. **hold** (or **stand**) **one's ground** not retreat or lose one's advantage.
– ORIGIN Old English.

ground[2] past and past part. of **GRIND**.

ground-breaking • **adj.** completely new; pioneering.

ground control • **n.** the personnel and equipment that monitor and direct the flight and landing of aircraft or spacecraft.

ground floor • **n.** Brit. the floor of a building at ground level.

ground frost • **n.** Brit. frost formed on the surface of the ground or in the top layer of soil.

ground glass • **n. 1** glass with a smooth ground surface that makes it non-transparent. **2** glass ground into an abrasive powder.

groundhog • **n.** N. Amer. = **WOODCHUCK**.

grounding • **n.** basic training or instruction in a subject.

groundless • **adj.** not based on any good reason.

groundnut • **n.** = **PEANUT**.

ground rent • **n.** Brit. rent paid by the owner of a building to the owner of the land on which it is built.

ground rules • **pl. n.** basic rules controlling the way in which something is done.

groundsel /grownd-s'l/ • **n.** a plant of the daisy family with small yellow flowers.
– ORIGIN Old English.

groundsheet • **n.** a waterproof sheet spread on the ground inside a tent.

groundsman (N. Amer. **groundskeeper**) • **n.** Brit. a person who maintains a sports ground or the grounds of a large building.

ground squirrel • **n.** a burrowing squirrel of a large group including the chipmunks.

groundswell /grownd-swel/ • **n.** a build-up of opinion in a large section of the population.

groundwater • **n.** water held underground in the soil or in rock.

groundwork • **n.** preliminary or basic work.

group • **n. 1** a number of people or things gathered or classed together. **2** a number of musicians who play popular music together. **3** Chem. a set of elements occupying a column in the periodic table. • **v.** place in or form a group or groups.
– ORIGIN Italian *gruppo*.

groupie • **n.** informal a young woman who follows a pop group or celebrity.

grouping • **n.** a group of people with a common interest or aim, especially within a larger organization.

Group of Eight E
the eight leading industrial nations (the US, Japan, Germany, France, the UK, Italy, Russia, and Canada) whose heads of government meet regularly to discuss economic and political matters.

group therapy • **n.** a form of psychiatric therapy in which patients meet to discuss their problems.

grouse[1] • **n.** (pl. **grouse**) a game bird with a plump body and feathered legs.
– ORIGIN perh. from Latin *gruta* or Old French *grue* 'crane'.

grouse[2] • **v.** (**grouses**, **grousing**, **groused**) complain pettily; grumble. • **n.** a grumble or complaint.
– ORIGIN unknown.

grout /growt/ • **n.** (also **grouting**) a mortar or paste for filling crevices, especially the gaps between tiles. • **v.** fill in with grout.
– ORIGIN perh. from French dialect *grouter* 'grout a wall'.

grove • **n.** a small orchard or group of trees.
– ORIGIN Old English.

grovel • **v.** (**grovels**, **grovelling**, **grovelled**; US **grovels**, **groveling**, **groveled**) **1** crouch or crawl on the ground. **2** act in a very humble way to obtain forgiveness or favour.
– ORIGIN Old Norse, 'face downwards'.

grow • **v.** (**grows**, **growing**, **grew**; past part. **grown**) **1** (of a living thing) develop by increasing in size and changing physically. **2** (of a plant) germinate and develop. **3** become larger or greater over time. **4** become gradually or increasingly: *we grew braver.* **5** (**grow up**) become an adult. **6** (**grow on**) become gradually more appealing to.
– DERIVATIVES **grower** n.
– ORIGIN Old English.

growbag • **n.** Brit. a bag containing potting compost, in which plants such as tomatoes can be grown.

growing pains • **pl. n. 1** pains occurring in the limbs of young children. **2** difficulties experienced in the early stages of an enterprise.

growl • **v. 1** (especially of a dog) make a low sound of hostility in the throat. **2** say something in a low voice. **3** make a rumbling sound. • **n.** a growling sound.

grown past part. of **GROW**.

grown-up • **adj.** adult. • **n.** informal an adult.

growth • **n. 1** the process of growing. **2** something that has grown or is growing. **3** a tumour or other formation which is not normal.

growth hormone • **n.** a hormone which promotes growth in animal or plant cells.

growth industry • **n.** an industry that is developing particularly quickly.

groyne (US **groin**) • **n.** a low wall built out into

the sea from a beach to prevent erosion and drifting.
– ORIGIN Latin *gronium* 'pig's snout'.

Grozny E
/groz-ni/ the capital of Chechnya.

grub • n. **1** the larva of an insect. **2** informal food. • v. (**grubs**, **grubbing**, **grubbed**) **1** dig shallowly in soil. **2** search clumsily and unmethodically: *I began grubbing about in the waste-paper basket.*
– ORIGIN perh. from Dutch *grobbelen.*

grubby • adj. (**grubbier**, **grubbiest**) **1** dirty; grimy. **2** not respectable; sordid.

grudge • n. a long-lasting feeling of ill will resulting from a past insult or injury. • v. (**grudges**, **grudging**, **grudged**) **1** be unwilling to grant or allow (something). **2** feel resentful that (someone) has achieved (something).
– ORIGIN from GROUCH.

grudging • adjective given or allowed only reluctantly or resentfully: *a grudging apology.*

gruel • n. a thin liquid food of oatmeal or other meal boiled in milk or water.
– ORIGIN Old French.

gruelling (US **grueling**) • adj. extremely tiring and demanding.
– ORIGIN from former *gruel* 'exhaust'.

gruesome • adj. **1** causing disgust or horror. **2** informal extremely unpleasant.
– ORIGIN Scottish *grue* 'feel horror'.

gruff • adj. **1** (of a voice) rough and low in pitch. **2** abrupt in manner.
– DERIVATIVES **gruffly** adv.
– ORIGIN Flemish and Dutch *grof* 'rude'.

grumble • v. (**grumbles**, **grumbling**, **grumbled**) **1** complain in a bad-tempered way. **2** make a low rumbling sound. • n. an instance of grumbling; a complaint.
– ORIGIN prob. from Germanic.

grump informal • n. a grumpy person.

grumpy • adj. bad-tempered and sulky.
– DERIVATIVES **grumpily** adv.

grunge • n. **1** N. Amer. grime; dirt. **2** a style of rock music with a loud and harsh guitar sound.
– DERIVATIVES **grungy** adj.
– ORIGIN perh. from GRUBBY and DINGY.

grunt • v. **1** (of an animal) make a low, short sound. **2** make a low sound to express effort or indicate agreement. • n. a grunting sound.
– ORIGIN Old English.

Gruyère /groo-yair/ • n. a tangy Swiss cheese.
– ORIGIN named after *Gruyère*, a district in Switzerland.

gryphon • n. var. of GRIFFIN.

gsm • abbrev. grams per square metre.

Gstaad E
/guh-**shtaht**/ a winter-sports resort in western Switzerland.

G-string • n. a skimpy undergarment covering the genitals, consisting of a narrow strip of cloth attached to a waistband.

GT • n. a high-performance car.
– ORIGIN short for GRAN TURISMO.

guacamole /gwa-kuh-**moh**-lay/ • n. a dish of mashed avocado.
– ORIGIN from a Central American Indian language.

Guadeloupe E
/gwah-duh-**loop**/ a group of islands in the Lesser Antilles, forming an overseas department of France; capital, Basse-Terre.
– DERIVATIVES **Guadeloupian** adj. & n.

Guam E
/gwahm/ the largest and southernmost of the Mariana Islands, administered as an unincorporated territory of the US; capital, Agaña.
– DERIVATIVES **Guamanian** /gwah-**may**-ni-uhn/ adj. & n.

Guangdong E
/gwang-**duung**/ (also **Kwangtung**) a province of southern China, on the South China Sea; capital, Guangzhou.

Guangzhou E
/gwang-**joh**/ (also **Kwangchow**) an industrial and commercial city in southern China, the capital of Guangdong province. Also called CANTON.

guano /**gwah**-noh/ • n. (pl. **guanos**) the excrement of seabirds, used as a fertilizer.
– ORIGIN from a language of Peru.

guarantee • n. **1** an assurance that certain conditions will be fulfilled, especially that a product will be of a specified quality. **2** something that makes an outcome certain. **3** var. of GUARANTY. • v. (**guarantees**, **guaranteeing**, **guaranteed**) **1** provide a guarantee for something. **2** promise with certainty. **3** provide financial security for.
– ORIGIN perh. from Spanish *garante.*

guarantor /ga-ruhn-**tor**/ • n. a person or organization that gives or acts as a guarantee.

guaranty /ga-ruhn-ti/ (also **guarantee**) • n. (pl. **guaranties**) **1** a promise to pay a debt or carry out a duty for another person should they fail to do so. **2** a thing serving as security for such a promise.

guard • v. **1** watch over in order to protect or control. **2** (**guard against**) take precautions against. • n. **1** a person who guards or keeps watch. **2** a body of soldiers guarding a place or person. **3** (**Guards**) the troops of the British army whose original duty was to protect the monarch. **4** a defensive posture adopted in a fight. **5** a state of vigilance: *she was on guard.* **6** a device worn or fitted to prevent injury or damage: *a blade guard.* **7** Brit. an official who rides on and is in general charge of a train.
– ORIGIN Old French *garder.*

guarded • adj. cautious and having possible reservations: *a guarded welcome.*

guardhouse (also **guardroom**) • n. a building used to house a military guard or to detain military prisoners.

guardian • n. **1** a defender, protector, or keeper. **2** a person legally responsible for someone unable to manage their own affairs.
– DERIVATIVES **guardianship** n.
– ORIGIN Old French *garden.*

guardian angel • n. a spirit believed to watch over and protect a person.

guardsman • n. **1** (in the UK) a soldier of a regiment of Guards. **2** (in the US) a member of the National Guard.

Guatemala E
/gwah-tuh-**mah**-luh/ a country in Central America, mainly bordering on the Pacific Ocean; capital, Guatemala City.
– DERIVATIVES **Guatemalan** adj. & n.

Guatemala City E
the capital of Guatemala.

guava /**gwah**-vuh/ • n. a tropical fruit with pink juicy flesh.
– ORIGIN prob. from a Caribbean language.

gubbins • pl. n. Brit. informal **1** miscellaneous items. **2** a gadget.
– ORIGIN Old French.

gubernatorial /goo-ber-nuh-**tor**-i-uhl/ • adj. having to do with a governor of a US state.
– ORIGIN Latin *gubernator* 'governor'.

g

gudgeon[1] /**guj**-uhn/ • n. a small freshwater fish often used as bait by anglers.
– ORIGIN Old French *goujon*.

gudgeon[2] /**guj**-uhn/ • n. **1** a pivot or spindle on which something swings or rotates. **2** the tubular part of a hinge into which the pin fits.
– ORIGIN Old French *goujon*.

guelder rose /**gel**-der/ • n. a shrub with creamy-white flowers followed by semi-transparent red berries.
– ORIGIN from Dutch *geldersche roos* 'rose of *Gelderland*' (a province of the Netherlands).

Guernsey[1] E
/**gern**-zi/ the second-largest of the Channel Islands; capital, St Peter Port.

Guernsey[2] /**gern**-zi/ • n. (pl. **Guernseys**) an animal of a breed of dairy cattle from Guernsey.

guerrilla /guh-**ril**-luh/ (also **guerilla**) • n. a member of a small independent group fighting against the government or regular forces.
– ORIGIN Spanish, 'little war'.

guess • v. **1** estimate or suppose (something) without enough information to be sure of being correct. **2** correctly estimate. • n. an estimate.
– ORIGIN perh. from Dutch *gissen*.

guesstimate /**gess**-ti-muht/ • n. informal an estimate based on a mixture of guesswork and calculation.

guesswork • n. the process or results of guessing.

guest • n. **1** a person invited to visit someone's home or take part in an event. **2** a visiting performer invited to take part in an entertainment. **3** a person staying at a hotel or boarding house.
– ORIGIN Old Norse.

guest house • n. a private house offering accommodation to paying guests.

guest worker • n. a person with temporary permission to work in another country.

Guevara E
/guh-**vah**-ruh/, Che (1928–67; full name *Ernesto Guevara de la Serna*), Argentinian revolutionary and guerrilla leader. He played an important part in the Cuban revolution (1956–9) and became a government minister under Castro.

guff • n. informal trivial or worthless talk or ideas.

guffaw /guhf-**faw**/ • n. a loud and lively laugh. • v. laugh in such a way.

Guggenheim E
/**guug**-guhn-hym/, Solomon (1861–1949), American industrialist, who set up a foundation providing support for the arts, including the Guggenheim Museums in New York and Bilbao.

Guiana E
/gi-**ah**-nuh, gy-**an**-nuh/ a region in northern South America, made up of Guyana, Suriname, French Guiana, and the Guiana Highlands (a mountainous plateau in SE Venezuela and northern Brazil).

guidance • n. advice or information aimed at solving a problem.

guide • n. **1** a person who advises or shows the way to others. **2** something which helps a person make a decision or form an opinion. **3** a book providing information on a subject. **4** a structure or marking which directs the movement or positioning of something. **5** (**Guide**) a member of the Guides Association, a girls' organization corresponding to the Scouts, founded by Lord Baden-Powell with his wife and sister. • v. (**guides, guiding, guided**) **1** show the way to. **2** direct the positioning or course of. **3** (**guided**) directed by remote control or internal equipment.
– ORIGIN Old French.

guidebook • n. a book of information about a place for visitors or tourists.

guide dog • n. a dog that has been trained to lead a blind person.

guideline • n. a general rule, principle, or piece of advice.

guild • n. **1** a medieval association of craftsmen or merchants. **2** an association of people for a common purpose.
– ORIGIN Old English.

guilder /**gil**-der/ • n. (pl. **guilder** or **guilders**) the former basic unit of money of the Netherlands.
– ORIGIN Dutch.

guildhall • n. **1** the meeting place of a guild or corporation. **2** Brit. a town hall.

guile /gyl/ • n. sly or cunning intelligence.
– DERIVATIVES **guileful** adj.
– ORIGIN Old French.

guileless • adj. very honest and sincere.
– DERIVATIVES **guilelessly** adv.

guillemot /**gil**-li-mot/ • n. an auk (seabird) with a narrow pointed bill.
– ORIGIN French.

guillotine /**gil**-luh-teen/ • n. **1** a machine with a heavy blade that slides down a frame, used for beheading people. **2** a device with a descending or sliding blade used for cutting paper or sheet metal. • v. (**guillotines, guillotining, guillotined**) execute by guillotine.
– ORIGIN named after the French physician Joseph-Ignace *Guillotin* (1738–1814), who recommended its use for executions.

guilt • n. **1** the fact of having committed an offence or crime. **2** a feeling of having done something wrong.
– ORIGIN Old English.

guiltless • adj. having no guilt; innocent.

guilty • adj. (**guiltier, guiltiest**) **1** (often **guilty of**) responsible for a specified wrong-

doing, fault, or error. **2** having or showing a feeling of guilt.
– DERIVATIVES **guiltily** adv.

Guinea E
/gi-ni/ a country on the west coast of Africa; capital, Conakry.
– DERIVATIVES **Guinean** adj. & n.

guinea /gi-ni/ ● n. Brit. **1** the sum of £1.05 (21 shillings in pre-decimal currency), used for professional fees and auction prices. **2** a former British gold coin with a value of 21 shillings.
– ORIGIN named after **GUINEA** (the source of the gold for the first guineas).

Guinea, Gulf of E
a large inlet of the Atlantic Ocean bordering on the southern coast of West Africa.

Guinea-Bissau E
/gi-ni bis-**sow**/ a country on the west coast of Africa, between Senegal and Guinea; capital, Bissau.

guineafowl ● n. (pl. **guineafowl**) a large African game bird with slate-coloured, white-spotted plumage.

guinea pig ● n. **1** a tailless South American rodent. **2** a person or thing used as a subject for experiment.

Guinevere E
/**gwin**-i-veer/ (in Arthurian legend) the wife of King Arthur and lover of Lancelot.

Guinness E
/**gin**-niss/, Sir Alec (1914–2000), English actor. His many films include *Bridge on the River Kwai* and *Star Wars*.

guise /gyz/ ● n. an external form, appearance, or manner of presentation: *in the guise of an inspector.*
– ORIGIN Old French.

guitar ● n. a stringed musical instrument with six strings, played by plucking or strumming.
– DERIVATIVES **guitarist** n.
– ORIGIN Spanish *guitarra*.

Gujarat E
/guu-juh **raht**/ a state in western India; capital, Gandhinagar.

Gulag /goo-lag/ ● n. (**the Gulag**) a system of harsh labour camps in the former Soviet Union.
– ORIGIN Russian.

Gulbenkian E
/guul-**beng**-ki-uhn/, Calouste Sarkis (1869–1955), Turkish-born British oil magnate and philanthropist. He founded the Gulbenkian Foundation, to which he left his large fortune and art collection.

gulch /gulch/ ● n. N. Amer. a narrow, steep-sided ravine.
– ORIGIN perh. from dialect *gulch* 'to swallow'.

gulf ● n. **1** a deep inlet of the sea almost surrounded by land, with a narrow mouth. **2** a deep ravine. **3** a large difference between two people, concepts, or situations: *a wide gulf between theory and practice.*
– ORIGIN Italian *golfo*.

Gulf of Carpentaria, Gulf of Mexico, etc. E
see **CARPENTARIA, GULF OF; MEXICO, GULF OF**; etc.

Gulf States E
the states bordering on the Persian Gulf (Iran, Iraq, Kuwait, Saudi Arabia, Bahrain, Qatar, the United Arab Emirates, and Oman).

Gulf Stream E
a warm ocean current which flows from the Gulf of Mexico towards Newfoundland, continuing across the Atlantic Ocean towards NW Europe.

Gulf War E
the war of January and February 1991 in which an international coalition of forces under the authority of the UN drove out Iraqi forces from Kuwait, which they had invaded in August 1990.

gull[1] ● n. a long-winged seabird having white plumage with a grey or black back.
– ORIGIN Celtic.

gull[2] ● v. fool or deceive (someone).
– ORIGIN unknown.

gullet ● n. the passage by which food passes from the mouth to the stomach.
– ORIGIN Old French *goulet* 'little throat'.

gullible ● adj. easily persuaded to believe something.
– DERIVATIVES **gullibility** n.
– ORIGIN from **GULL**[2].

gully (also **gulley**) ● n. (pl. **gullies** or **gulleys**) a ravine or deep channel caused by the action of running water.
– ORIGIN French *goulet*.

gulp ● v. **1** swallow (drink or food) quickly or in large mouthfuls. **2** swallow with difficulty in response to strong emotion: *she gulped back the tears.* ● n. **1** an act of gulping. **2** a large mouthful of liquid hastily drunk.
– ORIGIN prob. from Dutch *gulpen*.

gum[1] ● n. **1** a sticky substance produced by some trees and shrubs. **2** glue used for sticking paper or other light materials together. **3** chewing gum or bubble gum. ● v. (**gums, gumming, gummed**) **1** cover or fasten with gum or glue. **2** (**gum up**) clog up (a mechanism).
– ORIGIN Old French *gomme*.

gum[2] ● n. the firm area of flesh around the roots of the teeth.
– ORIGIN Old English.

gum arabic ● n. a gum produced by some kinds of acacia and used as glue and in incense.

gumboil ● n. a small swelling formed on the gum at the root of a tooth.

gumboot ● n. Brit. dated a wellington boot.

gumdrop ● n. a firm, jelly-like sweet.

gummy[1] ● adj. sticky.

gummy[2] ● adj. toothless: *a gummy grin.*

gumption /**gump**-sh'n/ ● n. informal initiative and resourcefulness.
– ORIGIN unknown.

gumshield ● n. a pad or plate used by a sports player to protect the teeth and gums.

gun ● n. **1** a weapon with a metal tube from which bullets or shells are propelled by explo-

g

sive force. **2** a device for discharging something in a required direction: *a glue gun*. ● **v.** (**guns, gunning, gunned**) (**gun down**) shoot with a gun.
– PHRASES **jump the gun** informal act before the proper or right time. **stick to one's guns** informal refuse to compromise or change.
– ORIGIN perh. from the Scandinavian name *Gunnhildr*, meaning 'war'.

gunboat ● **n.** a small ship armed with guns.

gunboat diplomacy ● **n.** foreign policy supported by the use or threat of military force.

gun carriage ● **n.** a wheeled support for a piece of artillery.

gun dog ● **n.** a dog trained to collect game that has been shot.

gunge ● **n.** Brit. informal sticky and unpleasantly messy material.
– ORIGIN perh. from **GOO** and **GUNK**.

gung-ho /gung-**hoh**/ ● **adj.** unthinkingly enthusiastic and eager, especially about taking part in fighting.
– ORIGIN Chinese, 'work together'.

gunk ● **n.** informal unpleasantly sticky or messy matter.
– ORIGIN the trademark of a US detergent.

gunman ● **n.** a man who uses a gun to commit a crime.

gunmetal ● **n. 1** a grey corrosion-resistant form of bronze containing zinc. **2** a dull bluish-grey colour.

gunnel ● **n.** var. of **GUNWALE**.

gunner ● **n. 1** a person who operates a gun. **2** a British artillery soldier.

gunnery ● **n.** the design, manufacture, or firing of heavy guns.

gunpoint ● **n.** (in phr. **at gunpoint**) while threatening or being threatened with a gun.

gunpowder ● **n.** an explosive consisting of a powdered mixture of saltpetre, sulphur, and charcoal.

Gunpowder Plot E
a conspiracy by a small group of Catholic extremists to blow up James I and his Parliament on 5 November 1605.

gunrunner ● **n.** a person engaged in the illegal sale or importing of firearms.
– DERIVATIVES **gunrunning** n.

gunship ● **n.** a heavily armed helicopter.

gunsight ● **n.** a device on a gun enabling it to be aimed accurately.

gunslinger ● **n.** informal a man who carries a gun.

gunsmith ● **n.** a person who makes and sells small firearms.

gunwale /gun-n'l/ (also **gunnel**) ● **n.** the upper edge or planking of the side of a boat.
– ORIGIN from **GUN** + **WALE** (because it was formerly used to support guns).

Guomindang E
/gwoh-min-**dang**/ var. of **KUOMINTANG**.

guppy /gup-pi/ ● **n.** (pl. **guppies**) a small freshwater fish native to tropical America.
– ORIGIN named after the Trinidadian clergyman R. J. Lechmere *Guppy* (1836–1916), who discovered the first specimen.

gurgle ● **v.** (**gurgles, gurgling, gurgled**) make or move with a hollow bubbling sound. ● **n.** a gurgling sound.
– ORIGIN perh. from Latin *gurgulio* 'gullet'.

Gurkha /ger-kuh/ ● **n. 1** a member of a people of Nepal noted for their ability as soldiers. **2** a member of a regiment in the British army for Nepalese recruits.
– ORIGIN a Nepalese place name.

gurn /gern/ (also **girn**) ● **v.** Brit. pull a grotesque face.
– ORIGIN from **GRIN**.

gurnard /ger-nerd/ ● **n.** a small sea fish with three finger-like bony parts to its fins.
– ORIGIN Old French *gornart* 'grunter'.

guru /guu-roo/ ● **n. 1** a Hindu spiritual teacher. **2** each of the ten first leaders of the Sikh religion. **3** an influential teacher or popular expert: *a management guru*.
– ORIGIN Sanskrit, 'weighty, grave'.

gush ● **v. 1** send out or flow in a rapid and strong stream. **2** express approval in an unrestrained way. ● **n.** a rapid and strong stream.

gushing (also **gushy**) ● **adj.** expressing approval in an overenthusiastic way.

gusset /guss-it/ ● **n.** a piece of material sewn into a garment to strengthen or enlarge a part of it.
– ORIGIN Old French *gousset*.

gust ● **n. 1** a brief, strong rush of wind. **2** a burst of rain, sound, emotion, etc. ● **v.** blow in gusts.
– DERIVATIVES **gusty** adj.
– ORIGIN Old Norse.

gusto ● **n.** enjoyment or vigour.
– ORIGIN Italian.

gut ● **n. 1** the stomach or belly. **2** Med. & Biol. the intestine. **3** (**guts**) the internal parts or essence of something. **4** (**guts**) informal courage and determination. ● **v.** (**guts, gutting, gutted**) **1** take out the internal organs of (a fish or other animal) before cooking. **2** remove or destroy the internal parts of: *the fire gutted most of the factory*. ● **adj.** informal instinctive: *a gut feeling*.
– ORIGIN Old English.

Gutenberg E
/goo-t'n-berg/, Johannes (*c.*1400–68), German printer, the first in the West to print using movable type (*c.* 1448) and the first to use a press.

Guthrie E
/guth-ri/, Woody (1912–1967; full name *Woodrow Wilson Guthrie*), American folk singer and songwriter, whose songs were inspired by his radical politics.

gutless ● **adj.** informal lacking courage or determination.

gutsy ● **adj.** (**gutsier, gutsiest**) informal showing courage and determination.

gutted ● **adj.** Brit. informal bitterly disappointed or upset.

gutter ● **n. 1** a shallow trough beneath the edge of a roof, or a channel at the side of a street, for carrying off rainwater. **2** (**the gutter**) a very poor or squalid environment. ● **v.** (**gutters, guttering, guttered**) (of a flame) flicker and burn unsteadily.
– ORIGIN Old French *gotiere*.

guttering ● **n.** esp. Brit. the gutters of a building.

gutter press ● **n.** newspapers engaging in sensational journalism.

guttersnipe ● **n.** a street urchin.

guttural /gut-tuh-ruhl/ ● **adj.** **1** (of a speech sound) produced in the back of the throat. **2** (of speech) characterized by guttural sounds.
– ORIGIN Latin *gutturalis*.

guv (also **guv'nor**) ● **n.** Brit. informal (as a form of address) sir.

guy[1] ● **n.** **1** informal a man. **2** (**guys**) N. Amer. informal people of either sex. **3** Brit. a figure representing Guy Fawkes, burnt on a bonfire on 5 November. ● **v.** ridicule.

guy[2] ● **n.** a rope or line fixed to the ground to secure a tent.
– ORIGIN prob. from German.

Guyana E
/gy-an-nuh/ a country on the NE coast of South America; capital, Georgetown.
– DERIVATIVES **Guyanese** /gy-uh-neez/ adj. & n.

guzzle ● **v.** (**guzzles**, **guzzling**, **guzzled**) eat or drink greedily.
– ORIGIN perh. from Old French *gosillier* 'chatter, vomit'.

Gwynedd E
/gwin-ne*th*/ a county of NW Wales; administrative centre, Caernarfon.

Gwynn, E
Nell (1650–87; full name *Eleanor Gwynn*), English actress and a mistress of Charles II.

gybe /jyb/ (US **jibe**) Sailing ● **v.** (**gybes**, **gybing**, **gybed**) change course by swinging the sail across a following wind. ● **n.** an act of gybing.
– ORIGIN from former Dutch *gijben*.

gym ● **n.** informal **1** a gymnasium. **2** gymnastics.

gymkhana /jim-kah-nuh/ ● **n.** an event consisting of a series of competitions on horseback.
– ORIGIN Urdu, 'racket court'.

gymnasium /jim-nay-zi-uhm/ ● **n.** (pl. **gymnasiums** or **gymnasia** /jim-nay-zi-uh/) a hall or building equipped for gymnastics and other physical exercise.
– ORIGIN Latin.

gymnast ● **n.** a person trained in gymnastics.

gymnastics ● **n.** **1** exercises involving physical agility, flexibility, and coordination. **2** physical or mental agility or skill: *vocal gymnastics*.
– DERIVATIVES **gymnastic** adj.

gymnosperm /jim-noh-sperm/ ● **n.** a plant of a large group that have seeds unprotected by an ovary or fruit, including conifers.
– ORIGIN Greek *gumnos* 'naked'.

gymslip ● **n.** Brit. dated a sleeveless belted tunic reaching from the shoulder to the knee, worn by schoolgirls doing physical education.

gynaecology /gy-ni-kol-uh-ji/ (US **gynecology**) ● **n.** the branch of medicine concerned with conditions and diseases specific to women and girls.
– DERIVATIVES **gynaecological** (US **gynecological**) adj. **gynaecologist** (US **gynecologist**) n.
– ORIGIN Greek *gunē* 'woman, female'.

gyp /jip/ (also **gip**) ● **n.** Brit. informal pain or discomfort.
– ORIGIN uncertain.

gypsophila /jip-sof-fi-luh/ ● **n.** a garden plant with small pink or white flowers.
– ORIGIN Latin.

gypsum /jip-suhm/ ● **n.** a soft white or grey mineral used to make plaster of Paris and in the building industry.
– ORIGIN Latin.

Gypsy (also **gypsy** or **gipsy**) ● **n.** (pl. **Gypsies** or **gipsies**) a member of a travelling people speaking the Romany language.
– ORIGIN from EGYPTIAN (because gypsies were believed to have come from Egypt).

gyrate /jy-rayt/ ● **v.** (**gyrates**, **gyrating**, **gyrated**) **1** move in a circle or spiral. **2** dance in a wild manner.
– DERIVATIVES **gyration** n.
– ORIGIN Latin *gyrare* 'revolve'.

gyrfalcon /jer-fawl-kuhn/ ● **n.** a large arctic falcon, with mainly grey or white plumage.
– ORIGIN prob. from German *gēr* 'spear'.

gyro /jy-roh/ ● **n.** (pl. **gyros**) a gyroscope or gyrocompass.

gyrocompass ● **n.** a compass in which the direction of true north is maintained by a gyroscope rather than magnetism.
– ORIGIN Greek *guros* 'a ring'.

gyroscope ● **n.** a device, used to provide stability or maintain a fixed direction, consisting of a wheel or disc spinning rapidly about an axis which is itself free to alter in direction.

H[1] (also **h**) ● **n.** (pl. **Hs** or **H's**) the eighth letter of the alphabet.

H[2] ● **abbrev.** **1** (of a pencil lead) hard. **2** height. **3** Physics henry(s). ● **symb.** the chemical element hydrogen.

h ● **abbrev.** hour(s).

ha ● **abbrev.** hectare(s).

habeas corpus /hay-bi-uhss kor-puhss/ ● **n.** Law a written order that an arrested person be brought before a judge or into court, to decide whether their detention is lawful.
– ORIGIN Latin, 'you shall have the body (in court)'.

haberdasher /hab-er-dash-er/ ● **n.** **1** Brit. a dealer in dressmaking and sewing goods. **2** N. Amer. a dealer in men's clothing.
– DERIVATIVES **haberdashery** n.
– ORIGIN prob. from Old French *hapertas*.

habiliment /huh-**bil**-i-muhnt/ • **n.** archaic clothing.
– ORIGIN Old French *habillement*.

habit • **n. 1** something that a person does often. **2** informal an addiction to drugs. **3** a long, loose garment worn by a member of a religious order.
– ORIGIN Latin *habitus* 'condition'.

habitable • **adj.** suitable to live in.
– ORIGIN Latin *habitabilis*.

habitat • **n.** the natural home or environment of an animal or plant.
– ORIGIN Latin, 'it inhabits'.

habitation • **n. 1** the state of living somewhere. **2** formal a house or home.

habit-forming • **adj.** (of a drug) addictive.

habitual /huh-**bit**-yuu-uhl/ • **adj. 1** done often or as a habit. **2** regular; usual: *his habitual dress*.
– DERIVATIVES **habitually** adv.

h

habituate • **v.** (**habituates**, **habituating**, **habituated**) make or become used to something.

habitué /huh-**bit**-yuu-ay/ • **n.** a resident of or frequent visitor to a place.
– ORIGIN French, 'accustomed'.

Habsburg E
/**haps**-berg/ (also **Hapsburg**) one of the main dynasties of central Europe from medieval to modern times, who provided rulers for Spain, Austria, and Hungary, and secured the title of Holy Roman emperor from 1452–1806.

hachures /ha-**shyoorz**/ • **pl. n.** parallel lines used on maps to shade in hills.
– ORIGIN French.

hacienda /ha-si-**en**-duh/ • **n.** (in Spanish-speaking countries) a large estate with a house.
– ORIGIN Spanish.

hack[1] • **v. 1** cut with rough or heavy blows. **2** kick wildly or roughly. **3** use a computer to gain unauthorized access to data. • **n.** a rough cut or blow.
– DERIVATIVES **hacker** n.
– ORIGIN Old English.

hack[2] • **n. 1** a writer producing dull, unoriginal work. **2** a horse for ordinary riding, or one that is inferior.
– ORIGIN short for HACKNEY.

hacking cough • **n.** a dry, frequent cough.

hackles • **pl. n.** hairs along an animal's back which rise when it is angry or alarmed.
– PHRASES **make someone's hackles rise** make someone angry.
– ORIGIN Germanic.

hackney • **n.** (pl. **hackneys**) hist. a horse-drawn vehicle kept for hire.
– ORIGIN prob. from *Hackney* in East London, where horses were pastured.

hackney carriage • **n.** Brit. the official term for a taxi.

hackneyed • **adj.** (of a phrase or idea) unoriginal and dull.
– ORIGIN from former *hackney* 'use a horse for general purposes'.

hacksaw • **n.** a saw with a narrow blade set in a frame.

had past and past part. of HAVE.

haddock • **n.** (pl. **haddock**) a silvery-grey edible fish of North Atlantic coastal waters.
– ORIGIN Old French *hadoc*.

Hades /**hay**-deez/ • **n.** Gk Myth. **1** the underworld. **2** = PLUTO[1].
– ORIGIN Greek *Haidēs*.

Hadlee E
/**had**-li/, Sir Richard (John) (b.1951), New Zealand cricketer, who took 431 test wickets during his career.

hadn't • **contr.** had not.

Hadrian E
/**hay**-dri-uhn/ (AD 76–138; full name *Publius Aelius Hadrianus*), Roman emperor 117–138.

Hadrian's Wall E
a fortified Roman wall across northern England, stretching from the Solway Firth in the west to the mouth of the River Tyne in the east, begun in AD 122 and built to defend Britain against attack from tribes from the north.

haematite /**hee**-muh-tyt/ (US **hematite**) • **n.** a reddish-black mineral consisting of ferric oxide.
– ORIGIN from Greek *haimatitēs lithos* 'blood-like stone'.

haematology /hee-muh-**tol**-uh-ji/ (US **hematology**) • **n.** the scientific study of the blood.
– DERIVATIVES **haematologist** (US **hematologist**) n.
– ORIGIN Greek *haima* 'blood'.

haemoglobin /hee-muh-**gloh**-bin/ (US **hemoglobin**) • **n.** a red protein responsible for transporting oxygen in the blood.
– ORIGIN from Greek *haima* 'blood' + GLOBULE.

haemophilia /hee-muh-**fil**-i-uh/ (US **hemophilia**) • **n.** a medical condition in which the ability of the blood to clot is severely reduced, causing severe bleeding from even a slight injury.

haemophiliac (US **hemophiliac**) • **n.** a person with haemophilia.

haemorrhage /**hem**-uh-rij/ (US **hemorrhage**) • **n. 1** an escape of blood from a burst blood vessel. **2** a damaging loss of something valuable. • **v.** (**haemorrhages**, **haemorrhaging**, **haemorrhaged**; US **hemorrhages**, **hemorrhaging**, **hemorrhaged**) **1** suffer a haemorrhage. **2** use or spend in large amounts: *the business was haemorrhaging cash*.
– ORIGIN Greek *haimorrhagia*.

haemorrhoid /**hem**-uh-royd/ (US **hemorrhoid**) • **n.** a swollen vein in the region of the anus.
– ORIGIN from Greek *haimorrhoides phlebes* 'bleeding veins'.

hafnium /**haf**-ni-uhm/ • **n.** a hard silver-grey metal resembling zirconium.
– ORIGIN from *Hafnia*, the Latin form of *Havn*, a former name of Copenhagen.

haft /hahft/ • **n.** the handle of a knife, axe, or spear.
– ORIGIN Old English.

hag • **n. 1** an ugly old woman. **2** a witch.
– ORIGIN perh. from Old English.

Haggard, E
Sir (Henry) Rider (1856–1925), English novelist, famous for adventure novels such as *King Solomon's Mines* and *She*.

haggard • **adj.** looking exhausted and un-

well: *the haggard faces of the women.*
– ORIGIN French *hagard*.

haggis • n. (pl. **haggis**) a Scottish dish consisting of seasoned sheep's or calf's offal mixed with suet and oatmeal.
– ORIGIN prob. from Old Norse, 'hack'.

haggle • v. (**haggles**, **haggling**, **haggled**) bargain persistently over a price.
– ORIGIN Old Norse.

hagiography /ha-gi-og-ruh-fi/ • n. **1** the writing of the lives of saints. **2** a biography idealizing its subject.
– DERIVATIVES **hagiographer** n.

hag-ridden • adj. suffering from nightmares or anxieties.

Hague E
/hayg/ (**The Hague**) the seat of government and administrative centre of the Netherlands.

ha-ha • n. a ditch with a wall below ground level, forming a boundary to a garden without interrupting the view.
– ORIGIN perh. from the cry of surprise made on meeting such an obstacle.

Hahn E
/hahn/, Otto (1879–1968), German chemist, co-discoverer with Lise Meitner (1878–1968) of nuclear fission.

Haifa E
/hy-fuh/ the chief port of Israel, in the north-west of the country.

Haig, E
Douglas, 1st Earl Haig of Bemersyde (1861–1928), British Field Marshal, Commander-in-Chief of British forces in France during the First World War.

haiku /hy-koo/ • n. (pl. **haiku** or **haikus**) a Japanese poem of seventeen syllables.
– ORIGIN Japanese.

hail[1] • n. **1** pellets of frozen rain falling in showers. **2** a large number of things hurled forcefully through the air: *a hail of bullets.* • v. (**it hails**, **it is hailing**, **it hailed**) hail falls.
– ORIGIN Old English.

hail[2] • v. **1** call out to (someone) to attract attention. **2** describe enthusiastically: *he has been hailed as the new James Dean.* **3** (**hail from**) have one's home or origins in.
– ORIGIN from former *hail* 'healthy'.

Haile Selassie E
/hy-li suh-las-si/ (1892–1975; born *Tafari Makonnen*), emperor of Ethiopia 1930–74. He was exiled during the Italian occupation of Ethiopia (1936–41), regained power with the aid of the Allies, and ruled until deposed by a military coup.

Hail Mary • n. (pl. **Hail Marys**) a prayer to the Virgin Mary used chiefly by Roman Catholics.

hailstone • n. a pellet of hail.

Hainan E
/hy-nan/ an island in the South China Sea, forming an autonomous region of China; capital, Haikou.

hair • n. **1** any of the fine thread-like strands growing from the skin of mammals and other animals, or from a plant. **2** strands of hair.
– PHRASES **hair of the dog** informal an alcoholic drink taken to cure a hangover. [ORIGIN from *hair of the dog that bit you*, formerly thought to be a remedy for the bite of a mad dog.] **a hair's breadth** a very small margin. **let one's hair down** informal behave wildly or in a very relaxed way. **split hairs** make excessively fine distinctions.
– ORIGIN Old English.

hairband • n. a band for fixing or tying back one's hair.

hairbrush • n. a brush for smoothing one's hair.

haircut • n. **1** the style in which someone's hair is cut. **2** an act of cutting someone's hair.

hairdo • n. (pl. **hairdos**) informal the style of a person's hair.

hairdresser • n. a person who cuts and styles hair.
– DERIVATIVES **hairdressing** n.

hairdryer (also **hairdrier**) • n. an electrical device for drying the hair with warm air.

hairgrip • n. Brit. a flat hairpin with the ends close together.

hairline • n. the edge of a person's hair. • adj. very thin or fine: *a hairline fracture.*

hairnet • n. a fine net for holding the hair in place.

hairpiece • n. a piece of false hair used to add to a person's natural hair.

hairpin • n. a U-shaped pin for fastening the hair.

hairpin bend • n. Brit. a sharp U-shaped bend in a road.

hair-raising • adj. very frightening.

hair shirt • n. a shirt made of stiff cloth woven from horsehair, formerly worn as a form of punishing oneself.

hairslide • n. Brit. a clip for keeping a woman's hair in position.

hairspray • n. a solution sprayed on to hair to keep it in place.

hairspring • n. a flat coiled spring regulating the movement of the balance wheel in a watch.

hairstyle • n. a way in which someone's hair is cut or arranged.
– DERIVATIVES **hairstylist** n.

hair trigger • n. a firearm trigger set for release at the slightest pressure.

hairy • adj. (**hairier**, **hairiest**) **1** covered with or resembling hair. **2** informal alarming and difficult: *a hairy mountain road.*
– DERIVATIVES **hairiness** n.

Haiti E
/hay-ti/ a country in the Caribbean, situated on the western third of the island of Hispaniola; capital, Port-au-Prince.
– DERIVATIVES **Haitian** n. & adj.

Haitink E
/hy-tingk/, Bernard (Johann Herman) (b.1929), Dutch conductor, musical director of Glyndebourne (1977–87) and Covent Garden (from 1987).

hajj /haj/ (also **haj**) • n. the pilgrimage to Mecca which all Muslims are expected to make at least once.
– ORIGIN Arabic.

haka /hah-kuh/ • n. a ceremonial Maori war dance.
– ORIGIN Maori.

hake • n. a long food fish with strong teeth.
– ORIGIN perh. from Old English, 'hook'.

halal /huh-lahl/ • adj. (of meat) prepared according to Muslim law.
– ORIGIN Arabic.

halberd /hal-berd/ • n. hist. a combined spear and battleaxe.
– ORIGIN German *helmbarde*.

halcyon /hal-si-uhn/ • adj. (of a past time) extremely happy and peaceful: *halcyon days*.
– ORIGIN Greek *alkuōn* 'kingfisher' (first referring to a mythical bird said to calm the sea).

hale • adj. (of an old person) strong and healthy.
– ORIGIN Old English, 'whole'.

Haley E
/hay-li/, Bill (1925–81; full name *William John Clifton Haley*), American rock-and-roll singer, famous for such songs as 'Rock Around the Clock'.

h

half • n. (pl. **halves**) **1** either of two equal or matching parts into which something is or can be divided. **2** either of two equal periods into which a match or performance is divided. **3** Brit. informal half a pint of beer. • **predet. & pron.** an amount equal to a half: *half an hour.* • **adj.** forming a half. • **adv. 1** to the extent of half. **2** partly: *half-cooked*.
– PHRASES **at half mast** (of a flag) flown halfway down its mast, as a mark of respect for a person who has died. **not do things by halves** do things thoroughly. **not half 1** not nearly. **2** Brit. informal to an extreme degree: *she didn't half flare up.* **too —— by half** excessively ——: *too superstitious by half.*
– ORIGIN Old English.

half-and-half • adv. & adj. in equal parts.

half-arsed • adj. vulgar done without skill or effort.

halfback • n. a player in a ball game whose position is between the forwards and fullbacks.

half-baked • adj. poorly planned or considered.

half board • n. Brit. the providing of bed, breakfast, and a main meal at a hotel or guest house.

half-breed • n. offens. a person of mixed race.

half-brother (or **half-sister**) • n. a brother (or sister) with whom one has only one parent in common.

half-caste • n. offens. a person of mixed race.

half-crown (also **half a crown**) • n. a former British coin equal to two shillings and sixpence (12½p).

half-cut • adj. Brit. informal drunk.

half-dozen (also **half a dozen**) • n. a group of six.

half-hearted • adj. without enthusiasm or energy.

half hitch • n. a knot formed by passing the end of a rope round itself and then through the loop created.

half holiday • n. a half day taken as a holiday.

half-hour • n. (also **half an hour**) a period of thirty minutes.
– DERIVATIVES **half-hourly** adj. & adv.

half-life • n. the time taken for the radioactivity of a substance to fall to half its original value.

half-light • n. dim light, as at dusk.

half measure • n. an inadequate action or policy.

half-moon • n. **1** the moon when only half its surface is visible from the earth. **2** a semicircular or crescent-shaped object.

halfpenny /hayp-ni/ (also **ha'penny**) • n. (pl. **halfpennies** (for separate coins); **halfpence** /hay-p'nss/ (for a sum of money)) a former British coin equal to half an old or new penny.

half-term • n. Brit. a short holiday halfway through a school term.

half-timbered • adj. (of a building) having walls with a timber frame and a brick or plaster filling.

half-time • n. (in sport) a short gap between two halves of a match.

half-volley • n. (in sport) a strike or kick of the ball immediately after it bounces.

halfway • adv. & adj. **1** at or to a point equal in distance between two others. **2** to some extent: *halfway decent*.

halfway house • n. **1** the halfway point in a process. **2** a compromise.

halfwit • n. informal a stupid person.
– DERIVATIVES **half-witted** adj.

halibut /ha-li-buht/ • n. (pl. **halibut**) a large marine flatfish, used as food.
– ORIGIN from former *haly* 'holy' + *butt* 'flatfish' (because it was often eaten on holy days).

halide /hay-lyd/ • n. Chem. a compound of a halogen and another element or group: *silver halide*.

Halifax E
the capital of Nova Scotia, Canada.

halitosis /ha-li-toh-siss/ • n. unpleasant-smelling breath.
– ORIGIN Latin *halitus* 'breath'.

hall • n. **1** the room or space just inside the front entrance of a house. **2** a large room for meetings, concerts, etc. **3** (also **hall of residence**) Brit. a university building in which students live. **4** the dining room of a college, university, or school. **5** Brit. a large country house.
– ORIGIN Old English.

Hallé E
/hal-lay/, Sir Charles (1819–95; born *Karl Halle*), German-born pianist and conductor. He settled in Manchester, where he founded the Hallé Orchestra (1858).

hallelujah /hal-li-loo-yuh/ (also **alleluia**) • exclam. God be praised.
– ORIGIN Hebrew, 'praise ye the Lord'.

Halley's Comet /hal-liz/ E
a periodical comet with an orbital period of about 76 years, its reappearance in 1758–9 having been predicted by the English astronomer Edmond Halley (1656–1742).

hallmark • n. **1** an official mark stamped on articles of gold, silver, or platinum to certify their purity. **2** a distinctive feature: *the hallmark of fine champagnes.* • v. stamp with a hallmark.
– ORIGIN from *Goldsmiths' Hall* in London, where articles were tested and stamped.

hallo ● exclam. var. of **HELLO**.

hallowed /hal-lohd/ ● adj. **1** made holy. **2** greatly respected: *the hallowed turf of Wimbledon.*
– ORIGIN Old English.

Halloween (also **Hallowe'en**) ● n. the night of 31 October, the eve of All Saints' Day.
– ORIGIN from *All Hallow Even.*

hallucinate /huh-loo-si-nayt/ ● v. (**hallucinates**, **hallucinating**, **hallucinated**) see something which is not actually present.
– DERIVATIVES **hallucination** n. **hallucinatory** adj.
– ORIGIN Latin *hallucinari* 'go astray in thought'.

hallucinogen /huh-loo-si-nuh-juhn/ ● n. a drug causing hallucinations.
– DERIVATIVES **hallucinogenic** adj.

hallway ● n. = **HALL** (in sense 1).

halo /hay-loh/ ● n. (pl. **haloes** or **halos**) **1** (in a painting) a circle of light surrounding the head of a holy person. **2** a circle of light round the sun or moon, caused by refraction through ice crystals in the atmosphere.
– ORIGIN Greek *halōs* 'disc of the sun or moon'.

halogen /hal-uh-juhn/ ● n. Chem. any of the group of reactive elements fluorine, chlorine, bromine, iodine, and astatine. ● adj. using a filament surrounded by halogen vapour: *a halogen bulb.*
– ORIGIN Greek *hals* 'salt'.

Hals [E]
/halss/, Frans (*c.*1580–1666), Dutch painter, best known for portraits such as *The Laughing Cavalier.*

halt[1] ● v. bring or come to a sudden stop. ● n. **1** a stopping of movement or activity. **2** Brit. a minor stopping place on a railway line.
– ORIGIN German *halten* 'to hold'.

halt[2] ● adj. archaic lame.
– ORIGIN Old English.

halter ● n. a rope or strap placed around the head of an animal and used to lead it or tie it to something.
– ORIGIN Old English.

halter neck ● n. a style of neckline in which a strap passes around the neck to hold a woman's sleeveless dress or top in position.

halting ● adj. slow and hesitant.

halve ● v. (**halves**, **halving**, **halved**) **1** divide into two parts of equal size. **2** reduce or be reduced by half.

halves pl. of **HALF**.

halyard /hal-yerd/ ● n. a rope used for raising and lowering a sail, yard, or flag on a ship.
– ORIGIN Old French *haler* 'haul'.

ham[1] ● n. **1** meat from the upper part of a pig's leg salted and dried or smoked. **2** (**hams**) the back of the thigh or the thighs and buttocks.
– ORIGIN Germanic, 'be crooked'.

ham[2] ● n. **1** a poor actor, especially one who overacts. **2** (also **radio ham**) informal an amateur radio operator. ● v. (**hams**, **hamming**, **hammed**) informal overact.
– DERIVATIVES **hammy** adj.
– ORIGIN perh. from **AMATEUR**.

Hamas [E]
/ha-**mass**/ a Palestinian Islamic fundamentalist movement.

Hamburg [E]
a port in northern Germany, on the River Elbe. It is the country's largest port.

hamburger ● n. a small cake of minced beef, fried or grilled and typically served in a bread roll.
– ORIGIN German.

ham-fisted ● adj. informal clumsy; awkward.

ham-handed ● adj. = **HAM-FISTED**.

Hamilton[1] [E]
the capital of Bermuda.

Hamilton[2], [E]
Lady Emma (*c.*1765–1815; born *Amy Lyon*), English beauty and mistress of Lord Nelson.

hamlet ● n. a small village.
– ORIGIN Old French *hamelet.*

hammer ● n. **1** a tool consisting of a heavy metal head mounted at the end of a handle, used for breaking things and driving in nails. **2** an auctioneer's mallet. **3** a part of a mechanism that hits another, e.g. one exploding the charge in a gun. **4** a heavy metal ball attached to a wire for throwing in an athletic contest. ● v. (**hammers**, **hammering**, **hammered**) **1** hit repeatedly. **2** (**hammer away**) work hard and persistently. **3** (**hammer in/into**) make (something) stick in someone's mind by constantly repeating it. **4** (**hammer out**) work out (the details of a plan or agreement).
– ORIGIN Old English.

hammer and sickle ● n. the symbols of the industrial worker and the peasant used as the emblem of the former USSR.

hammer drill ● n. a power drill that delivers a rapid succession of blows.

hammerhead ● n. a shark with flattened blade-like extensions on either side of the head.

Hammerstein [E]
/**ham**-mer-styn/, Oscar (1895–1960; full name *Oscar Hammerstein II*), American librettist, known for his collaboration with Richard Rodgers on such musicals as *Oklahoma!*, *South Pacific,* and *The Sound of Music.*

hammer toe ● n. a toe that is bent permanently downwards.

Hammett [E]
/**ham**-mit/, (Samuel) Dashiell (1894–1961), American novelist, author of such detective novels as *The Maltese Falcon* and *The Thin Man.*

hammock ● n. a wide strip of canvas or rope mesh suspended by two ends, used as a bed.
– ORIGIN from an extinct Caribbean language.

Hammond, [E]
Dame Joan (1912–96), Australian operatic soprano, born in New Zealand.

Hammurabi [E]
/ham-muu-**rah**-bi/ (d.1750 BC), king of Babylonia 1792–1750 BC. He extended the Babylonian empire and drew up one of the earliest known collections of laws.

hamper[1] ● n. **1** a basket used for food, cutlery, etc. on a picnic. **2** Brit. a box containing food and drink for a special occasion.
– ORIGIN Old French *hanaper* 'case for a

goblet'.

hamper[2] • v. (**hampers**, **hampering**, **hampered**) slow down or prevent the movement or progress of.
– ORIGIN perh. from German *hemmen* 'restrain'.

Hampshire E
a county on the coast of southern England; county town, Winchester.

Hampton Court E
a palace on the north bank of the Thames in the borough of Richmond-upon-Thames, London. Its gardens contain a well-known maze.

hamster • n. a burrowing rodent with a short tail and large cheek pouches.
– ORIGIN German *hamustro* 'corn-weevil'.

hamstring • n. any of five tendons at the back of a person's knee. • v. (**hamstrings**, **hamstringing**, past and past part. **hamstrung**) **1** cripple by cutting the hamstrings. **2** severely restrict.

Hancock, E
Tony (1924–68; full name *Anthony John Hancock*), English comedian, famous for the radio series (later also a television programme) *Hancock's Half Hour*.

hand • n. **1** the end part of the arm beyond the wrist. **2** a pointer on a clock or watch indicating the passing of time. **3** (**hands**) a person's power or control: *taking the law into their own hands*. **4** an active role. **5** help in doing something. **6** a person who does physical work. **7** informal a round of applause. **8** the set of cards dealt to a player in a card game. **9** a unit of measurement of a horse's height, equal to 4 inches (10.16 cm). • v. give to. • adj. **1** operated by or held in the hand: *hand luggage*. **2** done or made by hand.
– PHRASES **at hand** near; easy to reach. **get** (or **keep**) **one's hand in** become (or remain) practised in something. **hand in glove** in close association. (**from**) **hand to mouth** meeting only one's immediate needs because of lack of money. **hands-on** involving or offering active participation. **in hand 1** in progress; needing immediate attention. **2** ready for use if needed. **on hand** present and available. **on one's hands** as one's responsibility. **on the one** (or **the other**) **hand** used to present reasons for (and against). **out of hand 1** not under control. **2** without taking time to think: *it was rejected out of hand*. **to hand** within easy reach.
– ORIGIN Old English.

handbag • n. Brit. a small bag used by a woman to carry everyday personal items.

handball • n. **1** a game in which the ball is hit with the hand in a walled court. **2** Soccer unlawful touching of the ball with the hand or arm.

handbill • n. a small printed advertisement or other notice distributed by hand.

handbook • n. a book giving basic information or instructions.

handbrake • n. a brake operated by hand, used to hold an already stationary vehicle.

handcrafted • adj. made skilfully by hand.

handcuff • n. (**handcuffs**) a pair of lockable linked metal rings for securing a prisoner's wrists. • v. put handcuffs on.

Handel E
/han-d'l/, George Frederick (1685–1759), German-born composer and organist, resident in England from 1712. His many works include the choral oratorio *Messiah* and the orchestral *Water Music* suite.

handful • n. **1** a quantity that fills the hand. **2** a small number or amount. **3** informal a person who is difficult to deal with or control.

hand grenade • n. a hand-thrown grenade.

handgun • n. a gun designed for use by one hand.

handhold • n. something for a hand to grip on.

handicap • n. **1** a condition that restricts a person's ability to function physically, mentally, or socially. **2** a disadvantage given to a superior competitor in sports in order to make the chances more equal, such as the extra weight given to a racehorse. **3** the number of strokes by which a golfer normally exceeds par for a course. • v. (**handicaps**, **handicapping**, **handicapped**) act as a handicap to; place at a disadvantage.
– ORIGIN from *hand in cap*, a game in which players showed that they agreed or disagreed with the valuation of an object by bringing their hands either full or empty out of a cap in which forfeit money had been placed.

handicapped • adj. having a handicap.

handicraft • n. **1** a particular skill of making decorative objects by hand. **2** an object made using a skill of this kind.

handiwork • n. **1** (**one's handiwork**) something that one has made or done. **2** the making of things by hand.

handkerchief /hang-ker-cheef/ • n. (pl. **handkerchiefs** or **handkerchieves**) a square of material for wiping one's nose.

handle • v. (**handles**, **handling**, **handled**) **1** feel or move with the hands. **2** control (a vehicle or animal). **3** deal or cope with. **4** control or manage commercially. **5** (**handle oneself**) behave in a particular way. • n. **1** the part by which a thing is held, carried, or controlled. **2** a means of understanding or controlling a person or situation. **3** informal the name of a person or place.

handlebar (also **handlebars**) • n. the steering bar of a bicycle, motorbike, or similar vehicle.

handler • n. **1** a person who handles a particular type of article or commodity. **2** a person who trains or has charge of an animal.

handmade • adj. made by hand rather than machine.

handmaid (also **handmaiden**) • n. archaic a female servant.

hand-me-down • n. a piece of clothing or other item that has been passed on from another person.

handout • n. **1** an amount of money or other aid given to a needy person or organization. **2** a piece of printed information provided free of charge.

handover • n. esp. Brit. an act of handing something over.

hand-pick • v. select carefully.

handset • n. **1** the part of a telephone that is held up to speak into and listen to. **2** a hand-held control device for a piece of electronic equipment.

handshake • n. an act of shaking a person's hand.

handsome • adj. (**handsomer**, **handsomest**) **1** (of a man) good-looking. **2** (of a woman) striking and impressive rather than pretty. **3** (of a thing) well made and of obvious quality. **4** (of an amount) large: *a handsome majority.*
– DERIVATIVES **handsomely** adv.
– ORIGIN from **HAND** + **-SOME**[1], first meaning 'easy to handle or use'.

handspring • n. a jump through the air on to one's hands followed by another on to one's feet.

handstand • n. an act of balancing upside down on one's hands.

hand-to-hand • adj. (of fighting) at close quarters.

handwriting • n. **1** writing with a pen or pencil rather than by typing or printing. **2** a person's particular style of writing.

handwritten • adj. written with a pen or pencil.

handy • adj. (**handier**, **handiest**) **1** convenient to handle or use; useful. **2** in a convenient place or position.
– DERIVATIVES **handily** adv.

handyman • n. a person employed to do general decorating or domestic repairs.

hang • v. (**hangs**, **hanging**, past and past part. **hung** except in sense 2) **1** suspend or be suspended from above with the lower part not attached. **2** (past and past part. **hanged**) kill (someone) by suspending them from a rope tied around the neck. **3** attach so as to allow free movement about the point of attachment: *hanging a door.* **4** (of fabric or a garment) fall or drape in a specified way. **5** attach (meat or game) to a hook and leave it until dry, tender, or high.
– PHRASES **get the hang of** informal learn how to operate or do. **hang around** wait around. **hang on 1** hold tightly. **2** informal wait for a short time. **hang out** informal spend time relaxing or enjoying oneself. **hang up** end a telephone conversation by cutting the connection.
– ORIGIN Old English.

USAGE hang
Hang has two past tense and past participle forms: **hanged** and **hung**. You should use **hung** in general situations, as in *they hung out the washing*, while **hanged** should only be used when talking about executing someone by hanging, as in *the prisoner was hanged*.

hangar /hang-er/ • n. a large building for housing aircraft.
– ORIGIN French.

hangdog • adj. having a sad or guilty appearance; shamefaced.

hanger • n. **1** a person who hangs something. **2** (also **coat hanger**) a shaped piece of wood, plastic, or metal with a hook at the top, for hanging clothes from a rail.

hanger-on • n. (pl. **hangers-on**) a person who tries to be friends with a rich or powerful person in order to benefit from the relationship.

hang-glider • n. an unpowered flying apparatus consisting of a frame with fabric stretched over it from which the operator is suspended.
– DERIVATIVES **hang-gliding** n.

hanging • n. **1** the practice of hanging criminals as a form of capital punishment. **2** a decorative piece of fabric hung on the wall of a room or around a bed.

Hanging Gardens of Babylon E
legendary terraced gardens in ancient Babylon, one of the Seven Wonders of the World.

hanging valley • n. a valley that ends in a very steep descent to a main valley, the main valley having been deepened by glacial erosion.

hangman • n. an executioner who hangs condemned people.

hangnail • n. a piece of torn skin at the root of a fingernail.
– ORIGIN Old English.

hang-out • n. informal a place one lives in or visits often.

hangover • n. **1** a severe headache or other after-effects caused by drinking too much alcohol. **2** a thing that has survived from the past.

Hang Seng index E
/hang seng/ a figure indicating the relative price of shares on the Hong Kong Stock Exchange.

hang-up • n. informal an emotional problem or inhibition.

hank • n. a coil or length of wool, hair, or other material.
– ORIGIN Old Norse.

hanker • v. (**hankers**, **hankering**, **hankered**) (**hanker after/for/to do**) feel a strong desire for or to do.
– ORIGIN prob. from **HANG**.

Hanks, F
Tom (b.1956; full name *Thomas J. Hanks*), American actor. His films include *Philadelphia* and *Forrest Gump.*

hanky (also **hankie**) • n. (pl. **hankies**) informal a handkerchief.

hanky-panky • n. informal, humorous slightly improper or dishonest behaviour.
– ORIGIN uncertain.

Hannibal E
/han-ni-b'l/ (247–182 BC), Carthaginian general. In the second Punic War he attacked Italy via the Alps, repeatedly defeating the Romans, but failed to take Rome itself.

Hanoi E
/ha-**noy**/ the capital of Vietnam.

Hanover[1] E
/han-oh-ver/ an industrial city in NW Germany.

Hanover[2] E
/han-oh-ver/ a former German state whose ruler succeeded to the British throne as George I in 1714. It was also the name of the British royal house 1714–1901.
– DERIVATIVES **Hanoverian** adj. & n.

Hansard /han-sard/ • n. the official record of debates in the British, Canadian, Australian, or New Zealand parliament.

– ORIGIN named after the English printer Thomas C. *Hansard* (1776–1833).

Hanseatic League E
/han-si-at-ik/ a medieval association of north German cities, formed in 1241 as a trading alliance and developing into an independent political power in the later Middle Ages.

hansom /han-suhm/ (also **hansom cab**) ● **n.** hist. a two-wheeled horse-drawn cab for two passengers, with the driver seated behind.
– ORIGIN named after the English architect Joseph A. *Hansom* (1803–82).

Hants ● **abbrev.** Hampshire.

Hanukkah /han-uu-kuh/ (also **Chanukkah**) ● **n.** a Jewish festival of lights held in December, commemorating the rededication of the Jewish Temple in Jerusalem.
– ORIGIN Hebrew, 'consecration'.

ha'penny ● **n.** var. of **HALFPENNY**.

haphazard ● **adj.** lacking order or organization.
– DERIVATIVES **haphazardly** adv.

hapless ● **adj.** unlucky.

haploid /hap-loyd/ ● **adj.** Genetics (of a cell or nucleus) having a single set of unpaired chromosomes. Compare with **DIPLOID**.

happen ● **v. 1** take place by chance or as a result of something. **2** (**happen on**) come across by chance. **3** (**happen to**) be experienced by. **4** (**happen to**) become of: *I don't care what happens to the money.*
– ORIGIN Old Norse, 'chance'.

happening ● **n.** an event or occurrence. ● **adj.** informal fashionable.

happy ● **adj.** (**happier, happiest**) **1** feeling or showing pleasure. **2** willing to do something. **3** fortunate and convenient: *a happy coincidence.*
– DERIVATIVES **happily** adv. **happiness** n.
– ORIGIN Old Norse, 'luck'.

happy-go-lucky ● **adj.** cheerfully unconcerned about the future.

happy hour ● **n.** a period of the day when drinks are sold at reduced prices in a bar.

Hapsburg E
/haps-berg/ var. of **HABSBURG**.

hara-kiri /ha-ruh-ki-ri/ ● **n.** (formerly, in Japan) ritual suicide by removing one's own intestines with a sword.
– ORIGIN Japanese, 'belly-cutting'.

harangue /huh-rang/ ● **v.** (**harangues, haranguing, harangued**) criticize at length in an aggressive manner. ● **n.** a forceful and aggressive speech.
– ORIGIN Latin *harenga.*

Harare E
/huh-rah-ri/ the capital of Zimbabwe. Former name (until 1982) **SALISBURY**.

harass /ha-ruhss, huh-rass/ ● **v. 1** torment (someone) by subjecting them to constant interference or bullying. **2** make repeated small-scale attacks on (an enemy) in order to wear down resistance.
– DERIVATIVES **harassment** n.
– ORIGIN French *harasser.*

harbinger /har-bin-jer/ ● **n.** a person or thing that announces or signals the approach of something: *the harbingers of spring.*
– ORIGIN Old French *herbergere.*

harbour (US **harbor**) ● **n.** a place on the coast where ships may moor in shelter. ● **v. 1** keep (a thought or feeling) secretly in one's mind. **2** give a refuge or shelter to. **3** carry the germs of (a disease).
– ORIGIN Old English, 'shelter'.

hard ● **adj. 1** solid, firm, and rigid. **2** requiring a great deal of endurance or effort; difficult. **3** (of a person) tough. **4** (of information or a subject of study) concerned with precise facts that can be proved: *hard science.* **5** harsh or unpleasant to the senses. **6** done with a great deal of force or strength: *a hard whack.* **7** (of liquor) strongly alcoholic. **8** (of a drug) very addictive. **9** (of water) containing mineral salts. ● **adv. 1** with a great deal of effort or force. **2** so as to be solid or firm.
– PHRASES **hard and fast** (of a rule) fixed and definitive. **hard done by** Brit. harshly or unfairly treated. **hard feelings** feelings of resentment. **hard up** informal short of money.
– DERIVATIVES **hardness** n.
– ORIGIN Old English.

hardback ● **n.** a book bound in stiff covers.

hardbitten ● **adj.** tough and cynical.

hardboard ● **n.** stiff board made of compressed wood pulp.

hard-boiled ● **adj. 1** (of an egg) boiled until solid. **2** (of a person) tough and cynical.

hard cash ● **n.** coins and banknotes as opposed to other forms of payment.

hard copy ● **n.** a printed version on paper of data held in a computer.

hard core ● **n. 1** the most committed or uncompromising members of a group. **2** very explicit pornography.

hard disk (also **hard drive**) ● **n.** Computing a rigid magnetic disk with a large data storage capacity.

harden ● **v.** make or become hard or harder.

hard-headed ● **adj.** tough and realistic.

hard-hearted ● **adj.** unfeeling.

Hardie, E
(James) Keir (1856–1915), Scottish Labour politician, the first leader of the Labour Party (1906).

Harding, E
Warren (Gamaliel) (1865–1923), American Republican statesman, 29th President of the US 1921–3.

hard labour ● **n.** heavy physical work as a punishment.

hard line ● **n.** an uncompromising support for a firm policy.
– DERIVATIVES **hardliner** n.

hardly ● **adv. 1** scarcely; barely. **2** only with great difficulty. **3** no or not: *I hardly think so.*

hard-nosed ● **adj.** informal realistic and tough-minded.

hard-on ● **n.** vulgar an erection of the penis.

hard palate ● **n.** the bony front part of the roof of the mouth.

hard-pressed ● **adj.** in difficulties or under pressure.

hard sell ● **n.** a policy or technique of aggressive selling or advertising.

hardship ● **n.** severe suffering.

hard shoulder ● **n.** Brit. a hardened strip alongside a motorway for use in an emergency.

hardware ● n. **1** the machines, wiring, and other physical parts of a computer. **2** tools and other items used in the home and in activities such as gardening. **3** heavy military equipment such as tanks and missiles.

hardwood ● n. the wood from a broadleaved tree as distinguished from that of conifers.

Hardy[1], E
Oliver, see **LAUREL AND HARDY**.

Hardy[2], E
Thomas (1840-1928), English novelist and poet. His novels, set in Dorset, include *The Mayor of Casterbridge, Tess of the D'Urbervilles*, and *Jude the Obscure*.

hardy ● adj. (**hardier, hardiest**) **1** capable of surviving difficult conditions. **2** (of a plant) able to survive outside during winter.
– DERIVATIVES **hardiness** n.
– ORIGIN Old French *hardi*.

Hare, E
Sir David (b.1947), English dramatist and director, noted for his political dramas, such as *Plenty* and *Pravda*.

hare ● n. a fast-running mammal resembling a large rabbit, with very long hind legs. ● v. (**hares, haring, hared**) run very fast.
– ORIGIN Old English.

harebell ● n. a plant with pale blue bell-shaped flowers.

hare-brained ● adj. foolish; ill-judged.

Hare Krishna /ha-ri **krish**-nuh/ ● n. a member of a religious sect based on the worship of the Hindu god Krishna.
– ORIGIN Sanskrit.

harelip ● n. offens. = **CLEFT LIP**.
– ORIGIN from a resemblance to the mouth of a hare.

harem /**hah**-reem/ ● n. **1** the separate part of a Muslim household reserved for women. **2** the women living in this area.
– ORIGIN Arabic, 'prohibited place'.

Hargreaves, E
James (1720–78), English inventor of the spinning jenny (*c.*1764), which played an important part in mechanizing the cotton industry.

haricot /ha-ri-koh/ ● n. a variety of French bean with small white seeds, which can be dried and used as a vegetable.
– ORIGIN French.

hark ● v. **1** literary listen. **2** (**hark back**) recall an earlier period.
– ORIGIN Germanic.

harken ● v. var. of **HEARKEN**.

Harlem E
/**har**-luhm/ a district of New York City, in NE Manhattan. In the 1920s and 1930s it was noted for its nightclubs and jazz bands.

harlequin /har-li-kwin/ ● n. (**Harlequin**) a character in traditional pantomime, wearing a mask and a diamond-patterned costume.
– ORIGIN French.

Harley Street E
a street in central London where many medical specialists have consulting rooms.

harlot ● n. archaic a prostitute or a woman who has many brief sexual relationships.
– ORIGIN Old French, 'young man'.

harm ● n. **1** deliberate injury to a person. **2** damage. **3** a bad effect: *I can't see any harm in it.* ● v. **1** injure. **2** have a bad effect on.
– ORIGIN Old English.

harmful ● adj. causing or likely to cause harm.
– DERIVATIVES **harmfully** adv.

harmless ● adj. not able or likely to cause harm.
– DERIVATIVES **harmlessly** adv.

harmonic /har-mon-ik/ ● adj. having to do with harmony. ● n. Music a tone produced by vibration of a string in any of certain fractions (half, third, etc.) of its length.
– DERIVATIVES **harmonically** adv.

harmonica ● n. a small rectangular wind instrument with a row of metal reeds that produce different notes.

harmonious ● adj. **1** tuneful. **2** forming a pleasing combination of things. **3** free from conflict: *harmonious relationships*.
– DERIVATIVES **harmoniously** adv.

harmonium ● n. a keyboard instrument in which the notes are produced by air driven through metal reeds by foot-operated bellows.
– ORIGIN Greek *harmonios* 'harmonious'.

harmonize (also **harmonise**) ● v. (**harmonizes, harmonizing, harmonized**) **1** Music add notes to (a melody) to produce harmony. **2** make or be harmonious.

harmony ● n. (pl. **harmonies**) **1** the combination of musical notes sounded at the same time to produce chords with a pleasing effect. **2** the quality of forming a pleasing combination of things. **3** agreement.
– ORIGIN Latin *harmonia* 'joining'.

harness ● n. **1** a set of straps by which a horse or other animal is fastened to a cart, plough, etc. and is controlled by its driver. **2** a similar arrangement of straps, such as those for fastening a parachute to a person's body. ● v. **1** fit with a harness. **2** control and make use of (resources): *attempts to harness solar energy*.
– ORIGIN Old French *harneis* 'military equipment'.

Harold I E
(d.1040; known as **Harold Harefoot**), king of England 1035–40.

Harold II E
(*c.*1019–66), king of England 1066, the last Anglo-Saxon king of England. He resisted an invasion led by his half-brother Tostig and the Norse king Harald Hardrada, but was defeated and killed by William the Conqueror at the Battle of Hastings.

harp ● n. a musical instrument consisting of a frame supporting a series of strings of different lengths, played by plucking with the fingers. ● v. (**harp on**) keep talking about something in a boring way.
– DERIVATIVES **harpist** n.
– ORIGIN Old English.

harpoon ● n. a barbed spear-like missile used for catching whales and other large sea creatures. ● v. spear with a harpoon.
– ORIGIN French *harpon*.

harpsichord ● n. a keyboard instrument with horizontal strings plucked by points operated by pressing the keys.

– ORIGIN from Latin *harpa* 'harp' + *chorda* 'string'.

harpy ● n. (pl. **harpies**) **1** Gk & Rom. Myth. a monster with a woman's head and body and a bird's wings and claws. **2** a cruel or greedy woman.
– ORIGIN Greek *harpuiai* 'snatchers'.

harridan ● n. a bossy or aggressive old woman.
– ORIGIN perh. from French *haridelle* 'old horse'.

harrier[1] ● n. a breed of hound used for hunting hares.
– ORIGIN from **HARE**.

harrier[2] ● n. a long-winged bird of prey with low hunting flight.
– ORIGIN from **HARRY**.

Harris E
the southern part of the island of Lewis and Harris in the Outer Hebrides.

Harrison[1], E
Benjamin (1833–1901), American Republican statesman, 23rd President of the US 1889–93.

Harrison[2], E
George (1943–2001), English rock and pop guitarist, the lead guitarist of the Beatles.

Harrison[3], E
Sir Rex (1908–90; full name *Reginald Carey Harrison*), English actor, whose films include *My Fair Lady* and *Dr Dolittle*.

Harrison[4], E
William Henry (1773–1841), American Whig statesman, 9th President of the US, 1841.

harrow ● n. an implement consisting of a heavy frame set with teeth which is dragged over ploughed land to break up or spread the soil. ● v. **1** draw a harrow over. **2** (**harrowing**) very distressing.
– ORIGIN Old Norse.

Harrow School E
a boys' public school in NW London, founded under Queen Elizabeth I in 1571.

harry ● v. (**harries, harrying, harried**) **1** persistently carry out attacks on (an enemy). **2** persistently harass: *he harried them to pay up*.
– ORIGIN Old English.

harsh ● adj. **1** unpleasantly rough or jarring to the senses. **2** cruel or severe. **3** (of climate or conditions) difficult to survive in.
– ORIGIN German *harsch*.

hart ● n. an adult male deer.
– ORIGIN Old English.

hartebeest /har-ti-beest/ ● n. a large African antelope with a long head and sloping back.
– ORIGIN from Dutch *hert* 'hart' + *beest* 'beast'.

Hartley, E
L. P. (1895–1972; full name *Leslie Poles Hartley*), English novelist and short-story writer, author of *The Go-Between*.

harum-scarum ● adj. reckless.
– ORIGIN from **HARE** and **SCARE**.

Harvard University E
/har-verd/ the oldest American university, founded in 1636 at Cambridge, Massachusetts.

harvest ● n. **1** the process or period of gathering in crops. **2** the season's yield or crop. ● v. gather as a harvest.
– DERIVATIVES **harvester** n.
– ORIGIN Old English, 'autumn'.

harvest mouse ● n. a small mouse with a tail which it can use for grasping.

Harvey, E
William (1578–1657), English physician. who described the motion of the heart and discovered the circulation of the blood.

Haryana E
/hu-ri-**ah**-nuh/ a state of northern India; capital, Chandigarh.

has 3rd person sing. present of **HAVE**.

has-been ● n. informal a person or thing that is old-fashioned or no longer important.

hash[1] ● n. a dish of diced cooked meat reheated with potatoes.
– PHRASES **make a hash of** informal make a mess of.
– ORIGIN French *hacher*.

hash[2] ● n. informal = **HASHISH**.

hash[3] ● n. the symbol #.
– ORIGIN prob. from **HATCH**[3].

Hashemite Kingdom of Jordan E
official name for **JORDAN**[1].

hashish /ha-**sheesh**/ ● n. cannabis.
– ORIGIN Arabic, 'dry herb'.

hasn't ● contr. has not.

hasp ● n. a hinged metal plate that forms part of a fastening and is fitted over a metal loop and secured by a pin or padlock.
– ORIGIN Old English.

hassium /hass-i-uhm/ ● n. a very unstable chemical element made by high-energy atomic collisions.
– ORIGIN from *Hassias*, the Latin name for the German state of *Hesse*.

hassle informal ● n. **1** annoying inconvenience. **2** deliberate harassment. ● v. (**hassles, hassling, hassled**) harass.
– ORIGIN unknown.

hassock ● n. esp. Brit. a cushion for kneeling on in church.
– ORIGIN Old English, 'clump of grass'.

haste ● n. excessive speed or urgency when doing something.
– ORIGIN Old French.

hasten ● v. **1** be quick to do something. **2** cause to happen sooner than expected.

Hastings, E
Warren (1732–1818), British colonial administrator, the first Governor General of India (1774–1784).

Hastings, Battle of E
a decisive battle in 1066 near the town of Hastings, East Sussex, in which William the Conqueror defeated the forces of king Harold II.

hasty ● adj. (**hastier, hastiest**) done or acting with haste; hurried.
– DERIVATIVES **hastily** adv.

hat ● n. a shaped covering for the head, typically with a brim and a crown.
– PHRASES **keep something under one's hat** keep something a secret. **pass the hat round** collect contributions of money. **take one's hat off to** used to express admiration or

praise for.
– ORIGIN Old English.

hatband • n. a decorative ribbon around a hat.

hatch[1] • n. **1** a small opening in a floor, wall, or roof allowing access from one area to another. **2** a door in an aircraft, spacecraft, or submarine.
– ORIGIN Old English.

hatch[2] • v. **1** (with reference to a young bird, fish, or reptile) come out or cause to come out from its egg. **2** (of an egg) open and produce a young animal. **3** create (a plot or plan).
– ORIGIN unknown.

hatch[3] • v. (in drawing) shade with closely drawn parallel lines.
– ORIGIN Old French *hacher*.

hatchback • n. a car with a door across the full width at the back end that opens upwards.

hatchet • n. a small axe with a short handle.
– PHRASES **bury the hatchet** end a quarrel. [ORIGIN referring to an American Indian custom.]
– ORIGIN Old French *hachette* 'little axe'.

hatchet job • n. informal a fierce spoken or written attack.

hatchet man • n. informal a person who carries out unpleasant tasks on behalf of an employer.

hatchling • n. a newly hatched young animal.

hatchway • n. an opening or hatch, especially in a ship's deck.

hate • v. (**hates**, **hating**, **hated**) feel very strong dislike for. • n. **1** very strong dislike. **2** informal a disliked thing.
– ORIGIN Old English.

hateful • adj. arousing or deserving of hatred: *this hateful place*.

Hathaway, Anne (*c.*1557–1623), the wife of Shakespeare. C

hatred • n. very strong hate.

hatter • n. a person who makes and sells hats.
– PHRASES **(as) mad as a hatter** informal completely insane.

hat-trick • n. three successes of the same kind, especially (in soccer) a player scoring three goals in a game or (in cricket) a bowler taking three wickets with successive balls.
– ORIGIN first referring to the presentation of a new hat to a bowler taking a hat-trick.

haughty • adj. (**haughtier**, **haughtiest**) behaving arrogantly because one feels one is better than others.
– DERIVATIVES **haughtily** adv.
– ORIGIN Old French *hault* 'high'.

haul • v. **1** pull or drag with effort. **2** transport in a truck or cart. • n. **1** a quantity of something obtained illegally. **2** a number of fish caught at one time.
– ORIGIN Old French *haler*.

haulage • n. the commercial transport of goods.

haulier • n. Brit. a person or company employed in the commercial transport of goods by road.

haunch • n. **1** the buttock and thigh of a human or animal. **2** the leg and loin of an animal, as food.
– ORIGIN Old French *hanche*.

haunt • v. **1** (of a ghost) appear regularly at (a place). **2** (of a person) visit (a place) frequently. **3** be persistently and disturbingly present in the mind. • n. a place that a particular person often visits: *a favourite haunt of pickpockets*.
– ORIGIN Old French *hanter*.

haunted • adj. **1** (of a place) visited by a ghost. **2** having or showing signs of mental suffering: *haunted eyes*.

haunting • adj. beautiful or sad in a way that is hard to forget.
– DERIVATIVES **hauntingly** adv.

haute couture /oht kuu-**tyoor**/ • n. the designing and making of high-quality clothes by leading fashion houses.
– ORIGIN French 'high dressmaking'.

haute cuisine /oht kwi-**zeen**/ • n. high-quality cooking in the traditional French style.
– ORIGIN French, 'high cookery'.

hauteur /oh-**ter**/ • n. proud haughtiness of manner.
– ORIGIN French.

Havana /huh-**van**-uh/ the capital of Cuba. F

have • v. (**has**, **having**, **had**) **1** possess or own. **2** experience: *have difficulty*. **3** be able to make use of: *how much time have I got?* **4** (**have to**) be obliged to; must. **5** perform an action: *he had a look round*. **6** show (a personal characteristic). **7** suffer from (an illness or disability). **8** cause to be or be done: *I want to have everything ready*. **9** place, hold, or keep in a particular position. **10** eat or drink. • auxiliary verb used with a past participle to form the perfect, pluperfect, and future perfect tenses, and the conditional mood.
– PHRASES **have had it** informal be beyond repair. **have on** Brit. informal try to make (someone) believe something untrue.
– ORIGIN Old English.

have-a-go • adj. Brit. informal (of a member of the public) stepping in to stop a criminal during the course of a crime.

Havel /**hah**-v'l/, Václav (b.1936), Czech dramatist and statesman, President of Czechoslovakia 1989–92 and of the Czech Republic since 1993. An active campaigner for human rights, he was in the vanguard of the peaceful revolution that caused the overthrow of the Communist regime and was elected president in the same year. E

haven • n. **1** a place of safety. **2** a harbour or small port.
– ORIGIN Old English.

haven't • contr. have not.

haver /**hay**-ver/ • v. (**havers**, **havering**, **havered**) **1** Sc. talk foolishly. **2** Brit. be hesitant.
– ORIGIN unknown.

haversack • n. a small, sturdy bag carried on the back or over the shoulder.
– ORIGIN from former German *Habersack* 'bag used to carry oats'.

havoc • n. **1** widespread destruction. **2** great confusion or disorder.
– ORIGIN Old French *havot*.

haw • n. the red fruit of the hawthorn.

– ORIGIN Old English.

Hawaii E
/huh-wy-ee/ a state of the US consisting of a group of over twenty islands (including Hawaii and Oahu) in the North Pacific; capital, Honolulu (on Oahu). Former name **SANDWICH ISLANDS**.
– DERIVATIVES **Hawaiian** n. & adj.

hawk[1] • n. **1** a fast-flying bird of prey with broad rounded wings and a long tail. **2** any bird used in falconry. **3** a person who favours aggressive policies in foreign affairs. • v. esp. hist. hunt game with a trained hawk.
– DERIVATIVES **hawkish** adj.
– ORIGIN Old English.

hawk[2] • v. carry about and offer (goods) for sale in the street.
– ORIGIN prob. from **HAWKER**.

hawk[3] • v. **1** clear the throat noisily. **2** (**hawk up**) bring (phlegm) up from the throat.

h

Hawke, E
Bob (b.1929; full name *Robert James Lee Hawke*), Australian Labor statesman, Prime Minister 1983–91.

hawker • n. a person who travels about selling goods.
– ORIGIN prob. from German or Dutch.

Hawking, E
Stephen (William) (b.1942), English theoretical physicist, noted for his work on space-time, quantum mechanics, and black holes, and for his book *A Brief History of Time*.

Hawks, E
Howard (Winchester) (1896–1977), American film director, producer, and screenwriter, who directed such films as *The Big Sleep* and *Gentlemen Prefer Blondes*.

Hawksmoor, E
Nicholas (1661–1736), English architect, who worked with Sir Christopher Wren and Vanbrugh, and later designed six London churches.

hawser /haw-zer/ • n. a thick rope or cable for mooring or towing a ship.
– ORIGIN Old French *haucier* 'to hoist'.

hawthorn • n. a thorny shrub or tree with white, pink, or red blossom and small dark red fruits.
– ORIGIN Old English.

Hawthorne, E
Nathaniel (1804–64), American novelist and short-story writer, best known as the author of *The Scarlet Letter*.

hay • n. grass that has been mown and dried for use as fodder.
– PHRASES **make hay (while the sun shines)** make good use of an opportunity while it lasts.
– ORIGIN Old English.

haycock • n. a cone-shaped heap of hay left in the field to dry.

Haydn E
/*rhymes with* widen/, Franz Joseph (1732–1809), Austrian classical composer. His works include 108 symphonies, 67 string quartets, 12 masses, and the oratorio *The Creation*.

Hayek E
/hy-ek/, Friedrich August von (1899–1992), Austrian-born British economist, a leading advocate of the free market.

Hayes, E
Rutherford (Birchard) (1822–93), American Republican statesman, 19th President of the US 1877–81.

hay fever • n. an allergy to pollen or dust, causing sneezing and watery eyes.

haystack (also **hayrick**) • n. a large packed pile of hay.

haywire • adj. informal out of control.
– ORIGIN from **HAY** + **WIRE**, referring to the use of hay-baling wire in makeshift repairs.

Hayworth, E
Rita (1918–87; born *Margarita Carmen Cansino*), American actress and dancer. Her films include *The Lady from Shanghai*.

hazard • n. a danger. • v. **1** dare to say. **2** put at risk.
– ORIGIN Old French *hasard*.

hazard lights • pl. n. flashing lights on a vehicle, used to warn that the vehicle is not moving or is unexpectedly slow.

hazardous • adj. dangerous.

haze • n. **1** a thin mist caused by fine particles of dust, pollutants, etc. **2** a state of mental confusion: *he went to bed in an alcoholic haze*.

hazel • n. **1** a shrub or small tree bearing catkins in spring and nuts in autumn. **2** a rich reddish-brown colour.
– ORIGIN Old English.

hazelnut • n. the round brown edible nut of the hazel.

hazy • adj. (**hazier**, **haziest**) **1** covered by a haze. **2** vague or unclear: *hazy memories*.
– ORIGIN unknown.

HB • abbrev. **1** half board. **2** hard black (as a grade of pencil lead).

H-bomb • n. = **HYDROGEN BOMB**.

He • symb. the chemical element helium.

he • pron. (third person sing.) **1** used to refer to a man, boy, or male animal previously mentioned or easily identified. **2** used to refer to a person or animal of unspecified sex.
– ORIGIN Old English.

USAGE he
In the past, **he** was used to talk about both males and females when a person's sex was not specified: *every child needs to know that he is loved*. Many people now think of this as outdated and sexist. One solution is to use **he or she**, but this can be awkward if used a lot. An alternative solution is to use **they**, especially where it occurs after an indefinite pronoun such as **everyone** or **someone** (as in *everyone needs to feel that they matter*).

head • n. **1** the upper part of the body, containing the brain, mouth, and sense organs. **2** a person in charge. **3** the front, forward, or upper part of something. **4** the cutting or striking end of a tool or mechanism. **5** a person considered as a unit: *fifty pounds per head*. **6** (treated as pl.) a number of cattle or sheep: *seventy head of cattle*. **7** a compact mass of leaves or flowers at the top of a stem.

8 a part of a computer or a tape or video recorder which transfers information to and from a tape or disk. **9** the source of a river or stream. **10** (**heads**) the side of a coin bearing the image of a head. **11** pressure of water or steam in an enclosed space: *a good head of steam.* ● **adj.** chief. ● **v. 1** be or act as the head of: *the mayor headed the procession.* **2** give a heading to. **3** move in a specified direction. **4** (**head off**) obstruct and turn aside. **5** Soccer hit (the ball) with the head.
– PHRASES **come to a head** reach a crisis. **go to someone's head 1** (of alcohol) make someone slightly drunk. **2** (of success) make someone feel too proud. **a head for** a talent for or ability to cope with: *a head for heights.* **head over heels** madly in love. **a head start** an advantage gained at the beginning. **make head or tail of** understand at all. **off** (or **out of**) **one's head** informal crazy. **off the top of one's head** without careful thought.
– DERIVATIVES **headless** adj.
– ORIGIN Old English.

headache ● **n. 1** a continuous pain in the head. **2** informal something that causes worry.

headband ● **n.** a band of fabric worn around the head as a decoration or to keep the hair off the face.

headboard ● **n.** an upright panel at the head of a bed.

headbutt ● **v.** attack (someone) by hitting them hard with the head. ● **n.** an act of headbutting.

head case ● **n.** informal a mentally unstable person.

headcount ● **n.** a count of the number of people present.

headdress ● **n.** an ornamental covering for the head.

header ● **n. 1** Soccer a shot or pass made with the head. **2** informal a headlong fall or dive. **3** a line of text at the top of each page of a book or document.

head first ● **adj. & adv. 1** with the head in front of the rest of the body. **2** without thinking beforehand.

headgear ● **n.** items worn on the head.

headhunting ● **n. 1** the practice among some peoples of collecting the heads of dead enemies as trophies. **2** the practice of approaching people already employed elsewhere to fill a business position.
– DERIVATIVES **headhunt** v. **headhunter** n.

heading ● **n. 1** a title at the top of a page or section of a book. **2** a direction or bearing.

headland ● **n.** a narrow piece of land that juts out into the sea.

headlight (also **headlamp**) ● **n.** a powerful light at the front of a motor vehicle or railway engine.

headline ● **n. 1** a heading at the top of a newspaper or magazine article. **2** (**the headlines**) a summary of the most important items of news. ● **v.** (**headlines, headlining, headlined**) **1** provide with a headline. **2** appear as the star performer at (a concert).
– DERIVATIVES **headliner** n.

headlock ● **n.** a method of restraining someone by holding an arm firmly around their head.

headlong ● **adv. & adj. 1** with the head first. **2** in a rush.

headman ● **n.** the leader of a tribe.

headmaster (or **headmistress**) ● **n.** esp. Brit. a male (or female) head teacher.

head of state ● **n.** the official leader of a country, who may also be the head of government.

head-on ● **adj. & adv. 1** with or involving the front of a vehicle. **2** with or involving direct confrontation.

headphones ● **pl. n.** a pair of earphones joined by a band placed over the head.

headpiece ● **n.** a device worn on the head.

headquarters ● **n. 1** the centre of an organization from which operations are directed. **2** the premises of a military commander and their staff.

headrest ● **n.** a padded support for the head on the back of a seat.

headroom ● **n.** the space between the top of a vehicle or a person's head and the ceiling or other structure above.

headscarf ● **n.** (pl. **headscarves**) a square of fabric worn as a covering for the head.

headset ● **n.** a set of headphones with a microphone attached.

headship ● **n. 1** the position of leader. **2** esp. Brit. the position of head teacher in a school.

headstone ● **n.** a stone slab set up at the head of a grave.

headstrong ● **adj.** very wilful and determined.

head teacher ● **n.** the teacher in charge of a school.

head-to-head ● **adj. & adv.** involving two parties confronting each other.

headwaters ● **pl. n.** streams forming the source of a river.

headway ● **n.** forward progress.

headwind ● **n.** a wind blowing from directly in front.

headword ● **n.** a word which begins a separate entry in a reference work.

heady ● **adj.** (**headier, headiest**) **1** (of alcohol) strong. **2** having a strong or exciting effect: *a heady, exotic perfume.*

heal ● **v. 1** make or become sound or healthy again. **2** put right.
– DERIVATIVES **healer** n.
– ORIGIN Old English.

health ● **n. 1** the state of being free from illness or injury. **2** a person's mental or physical condition.
– ORIGIN Old English.

health centre ● **n.** an establishment housing local medical services or the practice of a group of doctors.

health farm ● **n.** an establishment where people stay so as to improve their health by dieting, exercise, and treatment.

health food ● **n.** natural food that is thought to have health-giving qualities.

healthful ● **adj.** having or helping towards good health.

health service ● **n.** a public service providing medical care.

health visitor ● **n.** Brit. a nurse who visits the homes of patients who are ill for a long time or parents with very young children.

healthy ● **adj.** (**healthier, healthiest**) **1** having or helping towards good health. **2** normal, sensible, or desirable: *maintain a healthy*

h

balance between work and home. **3** of a very satisfactory size or amount: *a healthy profit.*
– DERIVATIVES **healthily** adv. **healthiness** n.

Heaney E
/hee-ni/, Seamus (Justin) (b.1939), Irish poet. His works include *North* and *The Spirit Level.*

heap • n. **1** a pile of a substance or of a number of objects. **2** informal a large amount or number: *heaps of room.* **3** informal an untidy or broken-down place or vehicle. • v. **1** put in or form a heap. **2** (**heap with**) load heavily with. **3** (**heap on**) give (much praise, criticism, etc) to: *the press heaped abuse on him.*
– ORIGIN Old English.

hear • v. (**hears**, **hearing**, **heard**) **1** perceive (a sound) with the ear. **2** be told of. **3** (**have heard of**) be aware of the existence of. **4** (**hear from**) receive a letter or phone call from. **5** listen to. **6** Law listen to and judge (a case or person bringing a case).
– PHRASES **hear! hear!** used to show agreement with something said in a speech.
– DERIVATIVES **hearer** n.
– ORIGIN Old English.

hearing • n. **1** the ability to perceive sounds. **2** the range within which sounds may be heard. **3** an opportunity to state one's case: *a fair hearing.* **4** an act of listening to evidence.

hearing aid • n. a small device worn on the ear by a partially deaf person, which amplifies sounds.

hearken /har-k'n/ (also **harken**) • v. (usu. **hearken to**) archaic listen.
– ORIGIN Old English.

hearsay • n. information received from other people which cannot be assumed to be true.

hearse /herss/ • n. a vehicle for conveying the coffin at a funeral.
– ORIGIN Old French *herce* 'harrow'.

heart • n. **1** a hollow muscular organ that pumps the blood around the body. **2** the central or innermost part: *the heart of the city.* **3** a person's feeling of or capacity for love or compassion. **4** mood or feeling: *a change of heart.* **5** courage or enthusiasm. **6** a shape representing a heart with two equal curves meeting at a point at the bottom and a cusp at the top. **7** (**hearts**) one of the four suits in a pack of playing cards.
– PHRASES **after one's own heart** sharing one's tastes. **at heart** in one's real nature. **break someone's heart** make someone deeply sad. **by heart** from memory. **from the** (or **the bottom of one's**) **heart** with sincere feeling. **have a heart** be merciful. **have a heart of gold** have a very kind nature. **have one's heart in one's mouth** be very alarmed or anxious. **take to heart** be greatly affected by (criticism). **wear one's heart on one's sleeve** show one's feelings openly.
– ORIGIN Old English.

heartache • n. worry or grief.

heart attack • n. a sudden failure of the heart to function normally.

heartbeat • n. **1** a pulsation of the heart. **2** a very brief moment of time: *I'd go there in a heartbeat.*

heartbreak • n. extreme distress.
– DERIVATIVES **heartbreaking** adj. **heartbroken** adj.

heartburn • n. a form of indigestion felt as a burning sensation in the chest.

hearten • v. make more cheerful or confident.

heart failure • n. severe failure of the heart to function properly.

heartfelt • adj. deeply felt.

hearth /harth/ • n. the floor or surround of a fireplace.
– ORIGIN Old English.

hearthrug • n. a rug laid in front of a fireplace.

heartily • adv. **1** in a hearty way. **2** very: *I'm heartily sick of them.*

heartland • n. the central or most important part of a country or area.

heartless • adj. unfeeling or inconsiderate.
– DERIVATIVES **heartlessly** adv.

heart-rending • adj. very sad or distressing.

heart-searching • n. thorough examination of one's feelings and motives.

heart-throb • n. informal a man whom women find very attractive.

heart-to-heart • adj. (of a conversation) intimate and personal.

heart-warming • adj. emotionally rewarding or uplifting.

heartwood • n. the dense inner part of a tree trunk, where the hardest wood is to be found.

hearty • adj. (**heartier**, **heartiest**) **1** enthusiastic and friendly. **2** strong and healthy. **3** heartfelt. **4** (of a meal) wholesome and filling.

heat • n. **1** the quality of being hot. **2** heat as a form of energy produced by the movement of molecules. **3** a source of heat for cooking. **4** strength of feeling. **5** (**the heat**) informal very great and unwelcome pressure: *the heat is on.* **6** a preliminary round in a race or contest. • v. **1** make or become hot or warm. **2** (**heat up**) become more intense and exciting. **3** (**heated**) passionate: *a heated argument.*
– PHRASES **on heat** (of a female mammal) in the mating period of the sexual cycle.
– DERIVATIVES **heatedly** adv.
– ORIGIN Old English.

heater • n. a device for heating something.

Heath, E
Sir Edward (Richard George) (b.1916), British Conservative statesman, Prime Minister 1970–4. He negotiated Britain's entry into the European Economic Community.

heath • n. **1** esp. Brit. an area of open uncultivated land, usually covered with heather, gorse, and coarse grasses. **2** a shrub with small pink or purple bell-shaped flowers, found on heaths and moors.
– ORIGIN Old English.

heathen /hee-*th*uhn/ • n. derog. a person who does not belong to a widely held religion, as seen by those who do.
– DERIVATIVES **heathenism** n.
– ORIGIN Old English.

heather • n. a shrub with small purple flowers, found on moors and heaths.
– ORIGIN Old English.

heating • n. equipment used to provide heat.

heat-seeking • adj. (of a missile) able to detect and home in on heat sent out by a target, such as the exhaust vent of a jet aircraft.

heatstroke • n. a feverish condition, resulting from the body's being exposed to very high temperatures.

heatwave • n. a period of unusually hot weather.

heave • v. (**heaves**, **heaving**, **heaved** or Naut. **hove**) **1** lift or drag with great effort. **2** produce (a sigh) noisily. **3** informal throw (something heavy). **4** rise and fall: *his shoulders heaved.* **5** try to vomit. **6** (**heave to**) Naut. come to a stop. • n. an act of heaving.
– ORIGIN Old English.

heave-ho • n. (**the heave-ho**) informal dismissal from a position or contest.

heaven • n. **1** (in various religions) the place where God or the gods live and where good people go after death. **2** (**the heavens**) literary the sky. **3** informal a place or state of extreme happiness: *lying in the sun is my idea of heaven.*
– PHRASES **in seventh heaven** very happy. **move heaven and earth to do** make extraordinary efforts to do.
– ORIGIN Old English.

heavenly • adj. **1** having to do with heaven. **2** having to do with the sky. **3** informal wonderful.

heavenly body • n. a planet, star, or other celestial body.

heaven-sent • adj. occurring at a very favourable time.

heaving • adj. Brit. informal extremely crowded.

heavy • adj. (**heavier**, **heaviest**) **1** of great weight. **2** thick or dense. **3** of more than the usual size, amount, or force. **4** doing something to excess: *a heavy smoker.* **5** forceful: *a heavy blow.* **6** not delicate or graceful. **7** needing much physical effort. **8** very important. **9** informal serious or difficult. **10** (of ground) muddy or full of clay. • n. (pl. **heavies**) informal a large, strong man.
– DERIVATIVES **heavily** adv. **heaviness** n.
– ORIGIN Old English.

heavy-duty • adj. designed to withstand a lot of use or wear.

heavy-handed • adj. clumsy, insensitive, or too forceful.

heavy industry • n. the making of large, heavy articles and materials in large quantities.

heavy metal • n. a type of very loud harsh-sounding rock music with a strong beat.

heavy petting • n. sexual activity between two people that stops short of intercourse.

heavyweight • n. **1** the heaviest weight in boxing and other sports. **2** informal an influential person. • adj. **1** of above-average weight. **2** informal serious or influential: *heavyweight news coverage.*

hebdomadal /heb-dom-uh-duhl/ • adj. formal weekly.
– ORIGIN Greek *hebdomas* 'the number seven, seven days'.

Hebraic /hi-bray-ik/ • adj. having to do with the Hebrew language or people.

Hebrew /hee-broo/ • n. **1** a member of an ancient people living in what is now Israel and Palestine, who established the kingdoms of Israel and Judah. **2** the language of the Hebrews.
– ORIGIN Greek *Hebraios*.

Hebrew Bible E
the sacred writings of Judaism, called by Christians the Old Testament, and comprising the Law (Torah), the Prophets, and the Hagiographa or Writings.

Hebrides E
/heb-ri-deez/ a group of about 500 islands off the NW coast of Scotland. The **Inner Hebrides** include the islands of Skye, Mull, Jura, Islay, Iona, and Tiree, while the **Outer Hebrides** include the islands of Lewis and Harris, North and South Uist, and the isolated St Kilda group. Also called **WESTERN ISLES**.
– DERIVATIVES **Hebridean** n. & adj.

Hebron E
/heb-ron/ a Palestinian city on the West Bank of the Jordan. As the home of Abraham it is a holy city of both Judaism and Islam.

Hecate E
/hek-uh-ti/ a Greek goddess of dark places, often associated with ghosts and sorcery.

heck • exclam. used for emphasis, or to express surprise, annoyance, etc.
– ORIGIN from **HELL**.

heckle • v. (**heckles**, **heckling**, **heckled**) interrupt (a public speaker) with comments or abuse.
– DERIVATIVES **heckler** n.
– ORIGIN first meaning 'dress flax or hemp with a comb': from **HACKLE**.

hectare /hek-tair/ • n. a unit of area, equal to 10,000 square metres (2.471 acres).
– ORIGIN Greek *hekaton* 'hundred'.

hectic • adj. full of constant or frantic activity.
– DERIVATIVES **hectically** adv.
– ORIGIN Greek *hektikos* 'habitual'.

Hector E
Gk Myth. a Trojan warrior and son of Priam, who was killed by Achilles.

hector /hek-ter/ • v. talk to in a bullying way.
– ORIGIN from **HECTOR**.

he'd • contr. **1** he had. **2** he would.

hedge • n. a fence formed by closely growing bushes. • v. (**hedges**, **hedging**, **hedged**) **1** surround with a hedge. **2** qualify (something) by making conditions or exceptions. **3** avoid making a definite statement or decision.
– ORIGIN Old English.

hedgehog • n. a small insect-eating mammal with a spiny coat, able to roll itself into a ball for defence.

hedgerow • n. a hedge of wild bushes and trees bordering a field.

hedging • n. **1** the planting or trimming of hedges. **2** bushes planted to form hedges.

hedonism /hee-duh-ni-z'm/ • n. the pursuit of pleasure.
– DERIVATIVES **hedonist** n. **hedonistic** adj.
– ORIGIN Greek *hēdonē* 'pleasure'.

heebie-jeebies • pl. n. (**the heebie-jeebies**) informal a state of nervous fear or anxiety.
– ORIGIN unknown.

heed • v. pay attention to.

– PHRASES **pay** (or **take**) **heed** pay careful attention.
– ORIGIN Old English.

heedless ● adj. showing a reckless lack of care or attention.

hee-haw ● n. the loud, harsh cry of a donkey or mule.

heel[1] ● n. **1** the back part of the foot below the ankle. **2** the part of a shoe or boot supporting the heel. **3** the part of the palm of the hand next to the wrist. ● v. renew a heel on (a shoe or boot).
– PHRASES **bring to heel** bring under control. **cool** (or Brit. **kick**) **one's heels** be kept waiting. **take to one's heels** run away.
– ORIGIN Old English.

heel[2] ● v. (of a ship) lean over to one side. ● n. an instance of heeling, or the amount that a ship heels.
– ORIGIN Germanic.

h

heft ● v. **1** lift or carry (something heavy). **2** lift (something) to test its weight.
– ORIGIN prob. from HEAVE.

hefty ● adj. (**heftier**, **heftiest**) **1** large, heavy, and powerful. **2** (of a number or amount) considerable.

Hegel E
/hay-g'l/, Georg Wilhelm Friedrich (1770–1831), German philosopher. He believed that each stage of history is composed of a thesis, which is contradicted by an antithesis, out of whose conflict there emerges a new thesis, which is opposed by a new antithesis, and so on.
– DERIVATIVES **Hegelian** /hay-gee-li-uhn, hi-gay-li-uhn/ adj. & n.

hegemony /hi-jem-uh-ni, hi-gem-uh-ni/ ● n. dominance of one group or state over another.
– ORIGIN Greek *hēgemonia*.

Heidegger E
/hy-deg-ger/, Martin (1889–1976), German philosopher. His investigation of the nature of Being influenced existentialist philosophers such as Sartre.

Heidelberg E
/hy-d'l-berg/ a city in SW Germany, whose university is the oldest in Germany.

heifer /hef-fer/ ● n. a cow that has not borne a calf, or has borne only one calf.
– ORIGIN Old English.

height ● n. **1** the measurement of someone or something from head to foot or from base to top. **2** the distance of something above ground or sea level. **3** the quality of being tall or high. **4** a high place. **5** the most intense part: *the height of the attack.* **6** an extreme example of something: *the height of folly.*
– ORIGIN Old English.

heighten ● v. **1** make higher. **2** make or become more intense.

Heine E
/hy-nuh/, (Christian Johann) Heinrich (1797–1856), German poet, best known for his early lyric poetry.

heinous /hay-nuhss, hee-nuhss/ ● adj. very wicked: *a heinous crime.*
– ORIGIN Old French *haineus*.

heir /air/ ● n. **1** a person who has the legal right to inherit the property or rank of another on that person's death. **2** a person who continues the work of someone earlier.
– ORIGIN Old French.

heir apparent ● n. (pl. **heirs apparent**) **1** an heir whose claim cannot be set aside by the birth of another heir. **2** a person who is most likely to take the job or role of another.

heiress ● n. a female heir.

heirloom ● n. a valuable object that has belonged to a family for several generations.
– ORIGIN from HEIR + LOOM[1].

heir presumptive ● n. (pl. **heirs presumptive**) an heir whose claim may be set aside by the birth of another heir.

Heisenberg E
/hy-z'n-berg/, Werner Karl (1901–76), German mathematical physicist. He developed a system of quantum mechanics in which he states his uncertainty principle (the principle that the momentum and position of a particle cannot both be precisely determined at the same time).

heist /hysst/ ● n. informal, esp. N. Amer. a robbery.
– ORIGIN from HOIST.

held past and past part. of HOLD[1].

Helen E
Gk Myth. the wife of Menelaus, king of Sparta. Her abduction by Paris led to the Trojan War.

helical /hel-i-k'l/ ● adj. in the shape of a helix.

helices pl. of HELIX.

Helicon, Mount E
/hel-i-k'n/ a mountain in central Greece, believed by the ancient Greeks to be the home of the Muses.

helicopter ● n. a type of aircraft with one or two sets of horizontally revolving blades.
– ORIGIN French *hélicoptère*.

heliograph /hee-li-uh-grahf/ ● n. a device which reflects sunlight in flashes from a movable mirror, used to send signals.
– ORIGIN Greek *hēlios* 'sun'.

helipad ● n. a landing and take-off area for helicopters.

heliport ● n. an airport or landing place for helicopters.

helium /hee-li-uhm/ ● n. a light colourless gas that does not burn.
– ORIGIN Greek *hēlios* 'sun'.

helix /hee-liks/ ● n. (pl. **helices** /hee-li-seez/) an object in the shape of a spiral.
– ORIGIN Greek.

hell ● n. **1** (in various religions) a place of evil and suffering where wicked people are sent after death. **2** a state or place of great suffering.
– PHRASES **come hell or high water** whatever difficulties may occur. **for the hell of it** informal just for fun. **hell for leather** as fast as possible. **like hell** informal very fast, much, hard, etc. **play hell** informal create havoc or cause damage. **there will be hell to pay** informal serious trouble will result.
– ORIGIN Old English.

he'll ● contr. he shall or he will.

hell-bent ● adj. determined to achieve something at all costs.

Hellenic /hel-len-ik/ • adj. Greek.
– ORIGIN named after *Hellen*, the mythical ancestor of all the Greeks.

Hellenism • n. **1** the national character or culture of Greece. **2** the study or imitation of ancient Greek culture.

Hellenistic • adj. having to do with Greek culture from 323BC to 31BC.

Heller, E
Joseph (1923–99), American novelist, author of *Catch-22*, a black comedy satirizing war and the source of the expression 'catch-22'.

Hellespont E
/hel-liss-pont/ the ancient name for the Dardanelles.

hellfire • n. the fire regarded as existing in hell.

hellhole • n. a very unpleasant place.

hellish • adj. **1** relating to or like hell. **2** informal very difficult or unpleasant.
– DERIVATIVES **hellishly** adv.

hello (also **hallo** or **hullo**) • exclam. **1** used as a greeting. **2** Brit. used to express surprise or to attract someone's attention.
– ORIGIN from French *ho* 'ho!' + *là* 'there'.

hellraiser • n. a person who causes trouble by violent, drunken, or outrageous behaviour.

Hell's Angel • n. a member of a male motorcycle gang known for their lawless behaviour.

helm • n. **1** a tiller or wheel for steering a ship or boat. **2** (**the helm**) a position of leadership.
– ORIGIN Old English.

helmet • n. a hard or padded protective hat.
– ORIGIN Old French, 'little helmet'.

helmsman • n. a person who steers a boat.

Héloïse E
/el-oo-eez/ (1098–1164), French abbess, known for her tragic love affair with Peter Abelard which began after she became his pupil. Her uncle disapproved, forcing the lovers to separate; Héloïse became a nun.

helot /hel-uht/ • n. a member of a class in ancient Sparta, having a status in between slaves and citizens.
– ORIGIN Greek *Heilōtes*.

help • v. **1** make it easier for (someone) to do something. **2** improve (a situation or problem). **3** (**help someone to**) serve someone with (food or drink). **4** (**help oneself**) take something without asking for it first. **5** (**can/could not help**) cannot or could not stop oneself doing. • n. **1** the action of helping. **2** a person or thing that helps: *the map is a help in locating the house.*
– DERIVATIVES **helper** n.
– ORIGIN Old English.

helpful • adj. **1** giving or ready to give help. **2** useful.
– DERIVATIVES **helpfully** adv. **helpfulness** n.

helping • n. a portion of food served to one person at one time.

helpless • adj. **1** unable to defend oneself or to act without help. **2** uncontrollable: *helpless laughter.*
– DERIVATIVES **helplessly** adv. **helplessness** n.

helpline • n. a telephone service providing help with problems.

helpmate (also **helpmeet**) • n. a helpful companion.

Helsinki E
/hel-sing-ki/ the capital of Finland.

helter-skelter • adj. & adv. in disorderly haste or confusion. • n. Brit. a tall slide winding around a tower at a fair.
– ORIGIN uncertain.

hem • n. the edge of a piece of cloth or clothing which has been turned under and sewn. • v. (**hems, hemming, hemmed**) **1** turn under and sew the edge of. **2** (**hem in**) surround and restrict the space or movement of.
– ORIGIN Old English.

he-man • n. informal a very well-built, masculine man.

hematite etc. • adj. US = **HAEMATITE** etc.

hemi- • prefix half: *hemisphere.*
– ORIGIN Greek *hēmi-*.

Hemingway, E
Ernest (Miller) (1899–1961), American novelist, short-story writer, and journalist, author of *A Farewell to Arms, For Whom the Bell Tolls,* and *The Old Man and the Sea.*

hemisphere • n. **1** a half of a sphere. **2** a half of the earth.
– DERIVATIVES **hemispherical** adj.

hemline • n. the level of the lower edge of a garment such as a skirt or coat.

hemlock • n. **1** a highly poisonous plant with fern-like leaves and small white flowers. **2** a poison obtained from hemlock.
– ORIGIN Old English.

hemp • n. **1** (also **Indian hemp**) the cannabis plant. **2** the fibre of this plant, used to make rope, strong fabrics, paper, etc. **3** the drug cannabis.
– ORIGIN Old English.

hen • n. **1** a female bird, especially of a domestic fowl. **2** (**hens**) domestic fowls of either sex.
– ORIGIN Old English.

hence • adv. **1** for this reason. **2** from now.
– ORIGIN Old English.

henceforth (also **henceforward**) • adv. from this or that time on.

henchman • n. esp. derog. a faithful follower or assistant.
– ORIGIN from Old English, 'male horse' + **MAN**.

Hendrix, E
Jimi (1942–70; full name *James Marshall Hendrix*), American rock guitarist and singer. His songs include 'Purple Haze' and 'All Along the Watchtower'.

henge /henj/ • n. a prehistoric monument consisting of a circle of stone or wooden uprights.
– ORIGIN from **STONEHENGE**.

henna • n. the powdered leaves of a tropical shrub, used as a reddish-brown dye.
– ORIGIN Arabic.

hen night • n. Brit. informal a celebration held for a woman who is about to get married, attended only by women.

hen party • n. informal a social gathering of

women.

henpecked • **adj.** (of a man) continually criticized by his wife.

henry • **n.** (pl. **henries** or **henrys**) Physics the SI unit of inductance.
– ORIGIN named after the American physicist Joseph *Henry* (1797–1878).

Henry I E
(1068–1135), son of William I, king of England 1100–35. The death of his only son led to the accession of Henry's nephew Stephen and a period of civil war between Stephen and Henry's daughter Matilda.

Henry II E
(1133–89), son of Matilda, king of England 1154–89. Opposition to his policies on reducing the power of the Church was led by Thomas à Becket, who was eventually murdered by four of Henry's knights.

Henry III E
(1207–72), son of John, king of England 1216–72. His ineffectual government caused widespread discontent, ending in Simon de Montfort's defeat and capture of Henry in 1264.

Henry IV E
(1367–1413; known as **Henry Bolingbroke**), son of John of Gaunt, king of England 1399–1413. He overthrew Richard II, establishing the Lancastrian dynasty. His reign was marked by rebellion in Wales and the north.

Henry V E
(1387–1422), son of Henry IV, king of England 1413–22. He renewed the Hundred Years War soon after coming to the throne and defeated the French at Agincourt in 1415.

Henry VI E
(1387–1422), son of Henry IV, king of England 1422–61 and 1470–1. After intermittent civil war with the House of York (the Wars of the Roses), Henry was deposed in 1461 by Edward IV. He briefly regained his throne following a Lancastrian uprising.

Henry VII E
(1457–1509), son of Edmund Tudor, Earl of Richmond, king of England 1485–1509. He defeated Richard III at Bosworth Field and eventually established a Tudor dynasty.

Henry VIII E
(1491–1547), son of Henry VII, king of England 1509–47. Henry had six wives; his divorce from Catherine of Aragon was opposed by the Pope, leading to England's break with the Roman Catholic Church.

hepatic /hi-pat-ik/ • **adj.** having to do with the liver.
– ORIGIN Greek *hēpatikos.*

hepatitis /hep-uh-ty-tiss/ • **n.** a disease in which the liver becomes inflamed, mainly transmitted by viruses in blood or food.

Hepburn[1] E
/**hep**-bern/ , Audrey (1929–93), British actress. Her films include *Roman Holiday* and *My Fair Lady.*

Hepburn[2] E
/**hep**-bern/, Katharine (b.1909), American actress, star of such films as *The African Queen* and *On Golden Pond.*

Hephaestus E
/hi-fee-stuhss/ the Greek god of fire and of craftsmen. Roman equivalent **VULCAN**.

Hepplewhite E
/**hep**-p'l-wyt/, George (d.1786), English cabinetmaker and designer of neoclassical furniture.

hepta- • **comb. form** seven: *heptathlon.*
– ORIGIN Greek.

heptagon /**hep**-tuh-guhn/ • **n.** a plane figure with seven straight sides and angles.

heptathlon /hep-**tath**-lon/ • **n.** an athletic contest for women that consists of seven separate events.
– DERIVATIVES **heptathlete** n.
– ORIGIN from **HEPTA-** + Greek *athlon* 'contest'.

Hepworth, E
Dame (Jocelyn) Barbara (1903–75), English sculptor, noted for her abstract sculptures in landscape and architectural settings.

her • **pron.** (third person sing.) **1** used as the object of a verb or preposition to refer to a female person or animal previously mentioned. **2** referring to a ship, country, or other thing regarded as female. • **possess. det. 1** belonging to or associated with a female person or animal previously mentioned. **2** (**Her**) used in titles.
– ORIGIN Old English.

Hera E
/**heer**-uh/ a Greek goddess, the queen of heaven and wife and sister of Zeus. Roman equivalent **JUNO**.

Heraklion E
/hi-**rak**-li-uhn/ the capital of Crete.

herald • **n. 1** hist. a person who carried official messages, made announcements, and oversaw tournaments. **2** a sign that something is about to happen. **3** (in the UK) an official who oversees matters concerning state ceremonies, orders of rank, and coats of arms. • **v. 1** signal the future arrival of. **2** announce.
– ORIGIN Old French *herault.*

heraldic /hi-**ral**-dik/ • **adj.** having to do with heraldry.

heraldry • **n.** the system by which coats of arms are drawn up and controlled.

herb • **n. 1** a plant with leaves, seeds, or flowers used for flavouring, food, medicine, or perfume. **2** Bot. a seed-bearing plant which does not have a woody stem and dies down to the ground after flowering.
– ORIGIN Latin *herba.*

herbaceous /her-**bay**-shuhss/ • **adj.** relating to herbs (in the botanical sense).

herbaceous border • **n.** a garden border containing mainly flowering plants which live for several years.

herbage • **n.** herbaceous plants.

herbal • **adj.** relating to or made from herbs. • **n.** a book that describes herbs and their uses.

herbalism • **n.** the study or practice of using plants in medicine and cookery.

– DERIVATIVES **herbalist** n.

herbarium /her-**bair**-i-uhm/ ● **n.** (pl. **herbaria** /her-**bair**-i-uh/) an ordered collection of dried plants.

Herbert, E
George (1593–1633), English metaphysical poet and clergyman, whose poems reflect the spiritual conflicts he experienced before submitting his will to God.

herbicide /**her**-bi-syd/ ● **n.** a substance used to destroy unwanted plants.

herbivore /**her**-bi-vor/ ● **n.** an animal that feeds on plants.
– DERIVATIVES **herbivorous** /her-**biv**-uh-ruhss/ adj.

Hercegovina E
var. of **HERZEGOVINA**.

Herculaneum E
/her-kyuu-**lay**-ni-uhm/ an ancient Roman town, near Naples, on the lower slopes of Vesuvius. It was buried under volcanic ash when Vesuvius erupted in AD 79.

Herculean /her-kyuu-**lee**-uhn/ ● **adj.** requiring or having great strength or effort.
– ORIGIN from **HERCULES**.

Hercules E
/**her**-kyuu-leez/ Gk & Rom. Myth. a hero of superhuman strength and courage who performed twelve immense tasks or 'labours' imposed on him.

herd ● **n. 1** a large group of animals that live or are kept together. **2** derog. a large group of people. ● **v. 1** move in a large group. **2** look after (livestock).
– ORIGIN Old English.

herdsman ● **n.** the owner or keeper of a herd of animals.

here ● **adv. 1** in, at, or to this place or position. **2** (usu. **here is/are**) used when introducing or handing over something or someone. **3** used when indicating a time, point, or situation that has arrived or is happening.
– PHRASES **here and now** at the present time. **here and there** in various places. **neither here nor there** of no importance.
– ORIGIN Old English.

hereabouts (also **hereabout**) ● **adv.** near this place.

hereafter ● **adv.** formal **1** from now on or at some time in the future. **2** after death. ● **n.** (**the hereafter**) life after death.

hereby ● **adv.** formal as a result of this.

hereditary /hi-**red**-i-tuh-ri/ ● **adj. 1** having to do with the inheriting of something. **2** (of a characteristic or disease) able to be passed on from parents to their offspring.

heredity /hi-**red**-i-ti/ ● **n. 1** the passing on of physical or mental characteristics from one generation to another. **2** the inheriting of a title, office, or right.
– ORIGIN Latin *hereditas* 'heirship'.

Herefordshire E
a county of west central England; administrative centre, Hereford.

herein ● **adv.** formal in this document, book, or matter.

heresy /**he**-ri-si/ ● **n.** (pl. **heresies**) **1** belief or opinion which goes against traditional religious doctrine. **2** opinion greatly at odds with what is generally accepted.
– ORIGIN Greek *hairesis* 'choice, sect'.

heretic /**he**-ri-tik/ ● **n.** a person believing in or practising heresy.
– DERIVATIVES **heretical** /hi-**ret**-i-k'l/ adj.

hereto ● **adv.** formal to this matter or document.

heretofore ● **adv.** formal before now.

hereupon ● **adv.** archaic after or as a result of this.

Hereward the Wake E
/**he**-ri-werd/ (11th century), semi-legendary Anglo-Saxon rebel leader. He is thought to have led an uprising centred on the Isle of Ely in 1070 against William I's Norman regime.

herewith ● **adv.** formal with this letter.

heritable ● **adj.** able to be inherited.

heritage ● **n. 1** property that is or may be inherited. **2** valued things such as historic buildings that have been passed down from previous generations.
– ORIGIN Old French.

hermaphrodite /her-**maf**-ruh-dyt/ ● **n. 1** a person or animal having both male and female sex organs. **2** Bot. a plant having stamens and pistils in the same flower.
– DERIVATIVES **hermaphroditic** adj.
– ORIGIN Greek *hermaphroditos*.

Hermes E
/**her**-meez/ Gk Myth. the messenger of the gods, and god of merchants, thieves, and oratory. Roman equivalent **MERCURY**[1].

hermetic /her-**met**-ik/ ● **adj.** (of a seal or closure) complete and airtight.
– DERIVATIVES **hermetically** adv.
– ORIGIN from Latin *Hermes Trismegistus*, the mythical founder of alchemy and astrology.

hermit ● **n. 1** a person who lives alone for religious reasons. **2** a person who prefers to live alone.
– ORIGIN Greek *erēmitēs*.

hermitage ● **n.** the home of a hermit.

hermit crab ● **n.** a crab with a soft abdomen, which lives in a cast-off shell.

hernia /**her**-ni-uh/ ● **n.** (pl. **hernias** or **herniae** /**her**-ni-ee/) a condition in which part of an organ protrudes through the wall of the cavity containing it.
– ORIGIN Latin.

Hero E
Gk Myth. a priestess whose lover Leander swam across the Hellespont nightly to visit her. She threw herself into the sea after he drowned one stormy night.

hero ● **n.** (pl. **heroes**) **1** a person who is admired for their courage or outstanding achievements. **2** the chief male character in a book, play, or film.
– ORIGIN Greek *hērōs*.

Herod Antipas E
/**he**-ruhd **an**-ti-pas/ (22 BC–c.40 AD), son of Herod the Great, governor of Galilee and Peraea 4 BC–AD 40. He was responsible for the beheading of John the Baptist, who had denounced his marriage to Herodias, the wife of Herod's brother.

Herodotus E
/hi-**rod**-uh-tuhss/ (5th century BC), Greek historian, the first historian to collect his materials systematically, test their accuracy, and arrange them in a well-constructed narrative.

Herod the Great E
/**he**-ruhd/ (*c.*74–4 BC), ruled Palestine 37–4 BC. According to the New Testament, Jesus was born during his reign, and he ordered the massacre of the innocents.

heroic • adj. **1** very brave. **2** grand in scale or planning. • n. (**heroics**) behaviour or talk that is bold or dramatic.
– DERIVATIVES **heroically** adv.

heroin • n. a highly addictive illegal drug.
– ORIGIN German.

heroine • n. **1** a woman admired for her courage or outstanding achievements. **2** the chief female character in a book, play, or film.

h

heroism • n. great bravery.

heron • n. a large fish-eating bird with long legs, a long neck, and a long pointed bill.
– ORIGIN Old French.

hero worship • n. excessive admiration for someone. • v. (**hero-worship**) (**hero-worships**, **hero-worshipping**, **hero-worshipped**) admire excessively.

herpes /her-peez/ • n. a disease caused by a virus, affecting the skin or the nervous system.
– ORIGIN Greek *herpēs* 'shingles'.

Herr /hair/ • n. (pl. **Herren** /**he**-ruhn/) a form of address for a German-speaking man.
– ORIGIN German *hērro* 'more exalted'.

Herrick, E
Robert (1591–1674), English poet, best known for his collection *Hesperides*.

herring • n. a silvery edible fish which is abundant in coastal waters.
– ORIGIN Old English.

herringbone • n. a zigzag pattern consisting of columns of short parallel lines, with all the lines in one column sloping one way and all the lines in the next column sloping the other way.

herring gull • n. a common northern gull with grey black-tipped wings.

Herriot E
/**he**-ri-uht/, James (1916–1995; pen name of *James Alfred Wight*), English writer and veterinary surgeon. His experiences as a vet inspired a series of stories including *All Creatures Great and Small*.

hers • possess. pron. used to refer to a thing or things belonging to or associated with a female person or animal previously mentioned.

Herschel E
/**her**-sh'l/, Sir (Frederick) William (1738–1822), German-born British astronomer. His cataloguing of the skies resulted in the discovery of the planet Uranus and he put forward the idea that the sun belongs to the star system of the Milky Way.

herself • pron. (third person sing.) **1** used as the object of a verb or preposition to refer to a female person or animal previously mentioned as the subject of the clause. **2** she or her personally.

Hertfordshire E
a county of SE England; county town, Hertford.

Herts. /harts/ • abbrev. Hertfordshire.

Hertz E
/herts/, Heinrich Rudolf (1857–94), German physicist and pioneer of radio communication, the first to broadcast and receive radio waves. He also showed that light and radiant heat were electromagnetic in nature.

hertz /herts/ • n. (pl. **hertz**) the SI unit of frequency, equal to one cycle per second.
– ORIGIN named after H. R. **HERTZ**.

Herzegovina E
/herts-uh-**gov**-i-nuh, herts-uh-guh-**vee**-nuh/ (also **Hercegovina**) a region in the Balkans forming the southern part of Bosnia–Herzegovina; chief town, Mostar.
– DERIVATIVES **Herzegovinian** (also **Hercegovinian**) adj. & n.

Herzl E
/**hert**-s'l/, Theodor (1860–1904), Hungarian-born journalist and founder of the Zionist movement (1897).

he's • contr. **1** he is. **2** he has.

Hesiod E
/**hee**-si-uhd/ (*c.*700 BC), one of the earliest known Greek poets, he wrote the *Theogony* and *Works and Days*.

hesitant • adj. slow to act or speak through indecision or reluctance.
– DERIVATIVES **hesitancy** n. **hesitantly** adv.

hesitate • v. (**hesitates**, **hesitating**, **hesitated**) **1** pause indecisively. **2** be reluctant to do something.
– DERIVATIVES **hesitation** n.
– ORIGIN Latin *haesitare* 'stick fast'.

Hess, E
(Walther Richard) Rudolf (1894–1987), German Nazi politician, deputy leader of the Nazi Party 1934–41. In 1941 he secretly parachuted into Scotland to negotiate peace with Britain. He was imprisoned for life in Spandau prison, Berlin, where he died.

Hesse E
/hess, **hess**-uh/, Hermann (1877–1962), German-born Swiss novelist and poet. His works reflect his interest in Eastern religion, and include *Der Steppenwolf* and *The Glass Bead Game*.

hessian • n. a strong, coarse fabric made from hemp or jute.
– ORIGIN from the German state of *Hesse*.

hetero- • comb. form different: *heterosexual*.
– ORIGIN Greek *heteros* 'other'.

heterodox /het-uh-ruh-doks/ • adj. not following traditional standards or beliefs.
– DERIVATIVES **heterodoxy** n.
– ORIGIN Greek *doxa* 'opinion'.

heterogeneous /het-uh-ruh-**jee**-ni-uhss/ • adj. varied: *a heterogeneous collection*.
– DERIVATIVES **heterogeneity** /het-uh-ruh-juh-**nee**-i-ti/ n.
– ORIGIN Greek *genos* 'a kind'.

heterosexual • adj. **1** sexually attracted to

the opposite sex. **2** having to do with such sexual attraction. ● **n.** a heterosexual person.
– DERIVATIVES **heterosexuality** n.

het up ● **adj.** informal angry and agitated.
– ORIGIN from dialect *het* 'heated, hot'.

heuristic /hyuu-uh-riss-tik/ ● **adj.** allowing a person to discover or learn something for themselves.
– ORIGIN Greek *heuriskein* 'to find'.

hew /hyoo/ ● **v.** (**hews**, **hewing**, **hewed**, past part. **hewn** or **hewed**) **1** chop or cut (wood, coal, etc.) with an axe or other tool. **2** (**be hewn**) be cut or formed from a hard material such as wood or stone.
– ORIGIN Old English.

hexa- (also **hex-** before a vowel) ● **comb. form** six: *hexagon*.
– ORIGIN Greek *hex*.

hexagon /hek-suh-guhn/ ● **n.** a plane figure with six straight sides and angles.
– DERIVATIVES **hexagonal** adj.

hexagram ● **n.** a six-pointed star formed by two intersecting equilateral triangles.

hexameter /hek-sam-i-ter/ ● **n.** a line of verse made up of six metrical feet.

heyday ● **n.** (**one's heyday**) the period of one's greatest success, activity, or energy.

Heyer E
/hay-er/, Georgette (1902–74), English historical novelist.

Hezbollah E
/hez-buh-lah/ (also **Hizbullah**) an extremist Shiite Muslim group active especially in Lebanon.

HF ● **abbrev.** Physics high frequency.

Hg ● **symb.** the chemical element mercury.
– ORIGIN from Latin *hydrargyrum*.

HGV ● **abbrev.** Brit. heavy goods vehicle.

hi ● **exclam.** informal used as a friendly greeting.

hiatus /hy-ay-tuhss/ ● **n.** (pl. **hiatuses**) a pause or gap in a series or sequence.
– ORIGIN Latin, 'gaping'.

hibernate ● **v.** (**hibernates**, **hibernating**, **hibernated**) (of an animal) spend the winter in a state like deep sleep.
– DERIVATIVES **hibernation** n.
– ORIGIN Latin *hibernare*.

Hibernian /hy-ber-ni-uhn/ ● **adj.** Irish. ● **n.** an Irish person.
– ORIGIN Latin *Hibernia*.

hibiscus /hi-biss-kuhss/ ● **n.** a plant with large brightly coloured flowers.
– ORIGIN Greek *hibiskos* 'marsh mallow'.

hiccup (also **hiccough** /hik-kup/) ● **n.** **1** a gulping sound in the throat caused by an uncontrollable movement of the diaphragm. **2** a minor setback. ● **v.** (**hiccups**, **hiccuping**, **hiccuped**; also **hiccoughs**, **hiccoughing**, **hiccoughed**) make the sound of a hiccup or hiccups.

hick ● **n.** informal, esp. N. Amer. an unsophisticated person from the country.
– ORIGIN informal form of the man's name *Richard*.

Hickok, E
James Butler (1837–76; known as **Wild Bill Hickok**), American frontiersman and marshal.

hickory ● **n.** a chiefly North American tree which has tough, heavy wood and edible nuts.
– ORIGIN from an American Indian language.

hid past of **HIDE**[1].

hidden past part. of **HIDE**[1].

hidden agenda ● **n.** a secret motive or plan.

hide[1] ● **v.** (**hides**, **hiding**, **hid**; past part. **hidden**) **1** put or keep out of sight. **2** conceal oneself. **3** keep secret. ● **n.** Brit. a concealed shelter used to observe wildlife at close quarters.
– PHRASES **hide one's light under a bushel** keep quiet about one's talents. [ORIGIN with biblical reference to the Gospel of Matthew, chapter 15.]
– ORIGIN Old English.

hide[2] ● **n.** the skin of an animal.
– ORIGIN Old English.

hideaway ● **n.** a hiding place.

hidebound ● **adj.** unwilling or unable to change because of tradition or convention.

hideous ● **adj.** **1** extremely ugly. **2** extremely unpleasant.
– DERIVATIVES **hideously** adv. **hideousness** n.
– ORIGIN Old French *hidos*, *hideus*.

hideout ● **n.** a hiding place.

hiding[1] ● **n.** **1** a physical beating. **2** informal a severe defeat.
– PHRASES **be on a hiding to nothing** Brit. be unlikely to succeed.
– ORIGIN from **HIDE**[2].

hiding[2] ● **n.** the action of hiding or the state of being hidden.

hierarchy /hy-uh-rar-ki/ ● **n.** (pl. **hierarchies**) **1** a system in which people are ranked one above the other according to status or authority. **2** a classification of things according to their relative importance.
– DERIVATIVES **hierarchical** adj.
– ORIGIN Greek *hierarkhia*.

hieroglyph /hy-ruh-glif/ ● **n.** a picture of an object representing a word, syllable, or sound, especially as found in the ancient Egyptian writing system.

hieroglyphic ● **n.** (**hieroglyphics**) writing consisting of hieroglyphs. ● **adj.** having to do with hieroglyphs.
– ORIGIN Greek *hieroglyphikos*.

hi-fi informal ● **adj.** having to do with high fidelity sound. ● **n.** (pl. **hi-fis**) a set of equipment for reproducing high-fidelity sound.

higgledy-piggledy ● **adv. & adj.** in confusion or disorder.
– ORIGIN prob. with reference to the irregular herding together of pigs.

high ● **adj.** **1** extending far upwards: *a high mountain*. **2** of a specified height. **3** far above ground or sea level. **4** large in amount, value, size, or intensity: *a high temperature*. **5** (of a period or movement) at its peak: *high summer*. **6** great in status. **7** morally good. **8** (of a sound or note) not deep or low. **9** informal under the influence of drugs or alcohol. **10** (of food) strong-smelling because beginning to go bad. ● **n.** **1** a high point, level, or figure. **2** an area of high atmospheric pressure. **3** informal a state of high spirits. ● **adv.** **1** at or to a high or specified level or position: *the sculpture stood about five feet high*. **2** (of a sound) at or to a high pitch.
– PHRASES **high and dry 1** stranded by the sea as it retreats. **2** in a difficult position. **high**

and low in many different places. **high and mighty** informal arrogant. **it is high time that ——** it is past the time when something should have happened. **on one's high horse** informal behaving arrogantly or pompously.
– ORIGIN Old English.

highball • n. N. Amer. a long drink consisting of a spirit and a mixer, served with ice.

highbrow • adj. usu. derog. intellectual or refined in taste.

high chair • n. a small chair with long legs for an infant, fitted with a tray and used at mealtimes.

High Church • n. a tradition within the Anglican Church which gives an important place to ritual and the authority of bishops and priests.

high colour • n. a flushed complexion.

high command • n. the commander-in-chief and senior staff of an army, navy, or air force.

h

high commission • n. an embassy of one Commonwealth country in another.
– DERIVATIVES **high commissioner** n.

high court • n. a supreme court of justice.

Higher • n. (in Scotland) the more advanced of the two main levels of the Scottish Certificate of Education.

higher education • n. education to degree level or equivalent, provided at universities or colleges.

highest common factor • n. Math. the highest number that can be divided exactly into each of two or more numbers.

high explosive • n. a powerful chemical explosive of the kind used in shells and bombs.

highfalutin /hy-fuh-loo-tin/ • adj. informal affectedly grand or self-important.
– ORIGIN perh. from **HIGH** + *fluting*.

high fidelity • n. the reproduction of sound with little distortion.

high five • n. a gesture of celebration or greeting in which two people slap each other's palms with their arms raised.

high-flown • adj. grand-sounding.

high-flyer (also **high-flier**) • n. a very successful person.

high frequency • n. (in radio) a frequency of 3–30 megahertz.

high-handed • adj. using authority without considering the feelings of others.

high-impact • adj. **1** (of a material) able to withstand great impact without breaking. **2** (of exercises) that place a great deal of stress on the body.

high jinks • pl. n. high-spirited fun.

high jump • n. (**the high jump**) an athletic event in which competitors jump as high as possible over a bar which is raised after each round.

highland • n. (also **highlands**) **1** an area of high or mountainous land. **2** (**the Highlands**) the mountainous northern part of Scotland.
– DERIVATIVES **highlander** n.

Highland fling • n. a lively solo Scottish dance consisting of a series of complex steps.

Highland Region, E
a local government region of northern Scotland; administrative centre, Inverness.

high-level • adj. of high importance.

high life • n. an extravagant social life as enjoyed by the wealthy.

highlight • n. **1** an outstanding part of an event or period of time. **2** a bright area in a picture or design. **3** (**highlights**) bright tints in the hair, produced by bleaching or dyeing. • v. **1** draw attention to. **2** mark with a highlighter. **3** create highlights in (hair).

highlighter • n. **1** a broad marker pen used to mark transparent fluorescent colour on a part of a text or plan. **2** a powder or cream used to emphasize facial features.

highly • adv. **1** to a high degree or level. **2** favourably.

highly strung • adj. Brit. very nervous and easily upset.

high-minded • adj. having strong moral principles.

highness • n. **1** (**His, Your**, etc. **Highness**) a title given to a person of royal rank. **2** the state of being high.

high-octane • adj. **1** (of petrol) having a high octane number and therefore allowing an engine to run smoothly. **2** powerful or dynamic.

high-powered • adj. informal (of a person) dynamic and forceful.

high priest • n. **1** a chief priest of a non-Christian religion. **2** (also **high priestess**) the leader of a cult or movement.

high-rise • adj. (of a building) having many storeys.

high road • n. a main road.

high school • n. **1** N. Amer. a secondary school. **2** (in the UK except Scotland) a grammar school or independent secondary school.

high seas • pl. n. (**the high seas**) the areas of the sea that are not under the control of any one country.

high season • n. Brit. the most popular time of year for a holiday, when prices are highest.

high sheriff • n. see **SHERIFF**.

Highsmith, E
Patricia (1921–95; born *Patricia Plangman*), American writer of detective fiction featuring the amoral anti-hero Tom Ripley.

high spirits • pl. n. lively and cheerful behaviour or mood.
– DERIVATIVES **high-spirited** adj.

high spot • n. the most enjoyable or significant part of an experience or period of time.

high street • n. Brit. the main street of a town. • adj. (**high-street**) catering to the needs of the ordinary public: *high-street fashion*.

hightail • v. informal, esp. N. Amer. move or travel fast.

high tea • n. Brit. a meal eaten in the late afternoon or early evening.

high-tech (also **hi-tech**) • adj. having to do with high technology.

high technology • n. advanced technology.

high-tensile • adj. (of metal) very strong under tension.

high tide • n. the state of the tide when at its highest level.

high treason • n. see **TREASON**.

high water • n. high tide.

high-water mark • n. the level reached by the sea at high tide, or by a lake or river in time of flood.

highway • **n.** **1** esp. N. Amer. a main road. **2** a public road.

highwayman • **n.** hist. a man who held up and robbed travellers.

high wire • **n.** a high tightrope.

hijack • **v.** **1** illegally seize control of (an aircraft, ship, etc.) while it is travelling somewhere. **2** take over (something) and use it for a different purpose. • **n.** an instance of hijacking.
– DERIVATIVES **hijacker** n.
– ORIGIN unknown.

hike • **n.** **1** a long walk or walking tour. **2** a sharp increase. • **v.** (**hikes**, **hiking**, **hiked**) **1** go on a hike. **2** pull or lift up (clothing). **3** increase (a price) sharply.
– DERIVATIVES **hiker** n.
– ORIGIN unknown.

hilarious /hi-lair-i-uhss/ • **adj.** extremely funny or merry.
– DERIVATIVES **hilariously** adv. **hilarity** n.
– ORIGIN Greek *hilaros* 'cheerful'.

Hill[1], E
Benny (1925–92; born *Alfred Hawthorne*), English comedian, known for his risqué humour.

Hill[2], E
(Norman) Graham (1929–75), English motor-racing driver, Formula One world champion in 1962 and 1975. His son **Damon** (b.1960) is also a racing driver, and won the Formula One championship in 1996.

Hill[3], E
Sir Rowland (1795–1879), English educationist, administrator, and inventor, who introduced the penny postage-stamp system in 1840.

hill • **n.** a naturally raised area of land, not as high as a mountain.
– PHRASES **over the hill** informal old and past one's best.
– ORIGIN Old English.

Hillary, E
Sir Edmund (Percival) (b.1919), New Zealand mountaineer and explorer who, with Tenzing Norgay, was the first to reach the summit of Mount Everest (1953).

hillbilly • **n.** (pl. **hillbillies**) N. Amer. informal, esp. derog. an unsophisticated country person.
– ORIGIN from HILL + *Billy* (informal form of the man's name *William*).

hillock • **n.** a small hill or mound.

hillwalking • **n.** the pastime of walking in hilly country.

hilly • **adj.** (**hillier**, **hilliest**) having many hills.

hilt • **n.** the handle of a sword, dagger, or knife.
– PHRASES **to the hilt** completely.
– ORIGIN Old English.

him • **pron.** (third person sing.) used as the object of a verb or preposition to refer to a male person or animal previously mentioned.
– ORIGIN Old English.

Himachal Pradesh E
/hi-mah-chuhl pruh-**desh**/ a mountainous state in northern India; capital, Shimla.

Himalayas E
/him-uh-**lay**-uhz/ a vast mountain system in southern Asia, extending 2,400 km (1,500 miles) from Kashmir eastwards to Assam. The system includes the world's highest mountain, Mount Everest.

Himmler E
/**him**-ler/, Heinrich (1900–45), German Nazi leader, chief of the SS (1929–45) and of the Gestapo (1936–45). He directed the systematic genocide of over 6 million Jews. Captured by British forces in 1945, he committed suicide.

himself • **pron.** (third person sing.) **1** used as the object of a verb or preposition to refer to a male person or animal previously mentioned as the subject of the clause. **2** he or him personally.

hind[1] • **adj.** situated at the back.
– ORIGIN perh. from Old English.

hind[2] • **n.** a female deer.
– ORIGIN Old English.

Hindemith E
/**hin**-duh-mit/, Paul (1895–1963), German neoclassical composer, who believed that music should have a social purpose. His works include the opera *Mathis der Maler.*

Hindenburg E
/**hin**-duhn-berg/, Paul Ludwig von Beneckendorff und von (1847–1934), German Field Marshal and statesman, President of the Weimar Republic 1925–34. He was chief of the general staff in the First World War, and as President appointed Hitler as Chancellor (1933).

hinder[1] /**hin**-der/ • **v.** (**hinders**, **hindering**, **hindered**) delay or obstruct: *health problems have hindered his development.*
– ORIGIN Old English, 'damage'.

hinder[2] /**hyn**-der/ • **adj.** situated at or towards the back.
– ORIGIN perh. from Old English.

Hindi /**hin**-di/ • **n.** a language of northern India derived from Sanskrit.
– ORIGIN Urdu.

hindmost • **adj.** furthest back.

hindquarters • **pl. n.** the hind legs and adjoining parts of a four-legged animal.

hindrance /**hin**-druhnss/ • **n.** a thing that hinders.

hindsight • **n.** understanding of a situation or event after it has happened.

Hindu /**hin**-doo/ • **n.** (pl. **Hindus**) a follower of Hinduism. • **adj.** relating to Hinduism.
– ORIGIN Urdu.

Hinduism • **n.** a major religious and cultural tradition of the Indian subcontinent, including belief in reincarnation and the worship of a large number of gods and goddesses.

Hindu Kush E
/hin-doo **kuush**/ a range of high mountains in northern Pakistan and Afghanistan, forming a westward continuation of the Himalayas.

Hindustani /hin-duu-**stah**-ni/ • **n.** a group of languages and dialects spoken in NW India, principally Hindi and Urdu.

hinge • **n.** a movable joint or mechanism by which a door, gate, or lid opens and closes or which connects linked objects. • **v.** (**hinges**,

h

hingeing or **hinging**, **hinged**) **1** attach or join with a hinge. **2** (**hinge on**) depend entirely on.
– ORIGIN from **HANG**.

hint • n. **1** a slight or indirect suggestion. **2** a very small trace. **3** a small item of practical information. • v. **1** suggest indirectly. **2** (**hint at**) be a slight suggestion of.
– ORIGIN prob. from Old English, 'grasp'.

hinterland /hin-ter-land/ • n. **1** the remote areas of a country, away from the coast and major rivers. **2** the area around a major town or port.
– ORIGIN German.

hip[1] • n. **1** a projection formed by the pelvis and upper thigh bone on each side of the body. **2** (**hips**) the measurement around the body at the buttocks.
– ORIGIN Old English.

hip[2] • n. the fruit of a rose.
– ORIGIN Old English.

h

hip[3] • adj. (**hipper**, **hippest**) informal fashionable.
– DERIVATIVES **hipness** n.
– ORIGIN unknown.

hip bath • n. a bath shaped to sit rather than lie down in.

hip bone • n. a large bone forming the main part of the pelvis on each side of the body.

hip flask • n. a small flask for spirits, carried in a hip pocket.

hip hop • n. a style of popular music of US black and Hispanic origin, featuring rap with an electronic backing.
– ORIGIN prob. from **HIP**[3].

hippie • n. var. of **HIPPY**.

hippo • n. (pl. **hippo** or **hippos**) informal a hippopotamus.

Hippocrates E
/hi-pok-ruh-teez/ (*c.*460–377 BC), Greek physician, the father of medicine. His name is traditionally associated with the Hippocratic oath, although he was probably not the author of the ancient Greek medical writings attributed to him.

Hippocratic oath /hip-puh-krat-ik/ • n. an oath (formerly taken by medical doctors) to observe a code of professional behaviour.
– ORIGIN from **HIPPOCRATES**.

hippodrome /hip-puh-drohm/ • n. **1** a theatre or concert hall. **2** (in ancient Greece or Rome) a course for chariot or horse races.
– ORIGIN Greek *hippodromos*.

hippopotamus /hip-puh-pot-uh-muhss/ • n. (pl. **hippopotamuses** or **hippopotami** /hip-puh-pot-uh-my/) a large African mammal with a thick skin and massive jaws, living partly on land and partly in water.
– ORIGIN Greek *hippopotamos*.

hippy (also **hippie**) • n. (pl. **hippies**) (especially in the 1960s) a young person who supported peace and free love and dressed unconventionally.
– ORIGIN from **HIP**[3].

hipster Brit. • adj. (of a garment) having the waistline at the hips rather than the waist. • n. (**hipsters**) trousers with such a waistline.
– ORIGIN from **HIP**[1].

hire • v. (**hires, hiring, hired**) **1** esp. Brit. obtain the temporary use of (something) in return for payment. **2** (**hire out**) grant the temporary use of (something) in return for payment. **3** employ (someone) for wages. **4** temporarily employ (someone) to do a particular job. • n. the action of hiring.
– PHRASES **for** (or **on**) **hire** available to be hired.
– ORIGIN Old English.

hireling • n. esp. derog. a person who is hired to do menial or unpleasant work.

hire purchase • n. Brit. a system by which someone pays for a thing in regular instalments while having the use of it.

Hirohito E
/hi-ruh-hee-toh/ (1901–89; full name *Michinomiya Hirohito*), emperor of Japan 1926–89. Following Japan's surrender at the end of the Second World War he renounced his status as a god and became a constitutional monarch (1946).

Hiroshima E
/hi-rosh-i-muh/ a city in Japan, on the island of Honshu. It was the target of the first atom bomb, which was dropped by the United States on 6 August 1945.

Hirst, E
Damien (b.1965), English artist, known particularly for using the bodies of dead animals in his work.

hirsute /her-syoot/ • adj. hairy.
– ORIGIN Latin *hirsutus*.

his • possess. det. **1** belonging to or associated with a male person or animal previously mentioned. **2** (**His**) used in titles. • possess. pron. used to refer to a thing belonging to or associated with a male person or animal previously mentioned.
– ORIGIN Old English.

Hispanic /hi-span-ik/ • adj. having to do with Spain or the Spanish-speaking countries of Central and South America. • n. a Spanish-speaking person living in the US.
– ORIGIN Latin *Hispanicus*.

Hispaniola E
/hi-span-yoh-luh/ an island of the Greater Antilles in the Caribbean, divided into the states of Haiti and the Dominican Republic.

hiss • v. **1** make a sharp sound as of the letter *s*, often as a sign of disapproval or mockery. **2** whisper something in an urgent or angry way. • n. a hissing sound.

histamine /hiss-tuh-meen/ • n. a substance which is released by cells in response to injury and in allergic and inflammatory reactions.
– ORIGIN from Greek *histos* 'web' and *amine* (a compound containing an amino group).

histology /hi-stol-uh-ji/ • n. the branch of biology concerned with the microscopic structure of tissues.
– DERIVATIVES **histological** adj. **histologist** n.

historian • n. an expert in history.

historic • adj. **1** famous or important in history, or likely to be seen as such in the future. **2** Grammar (of a tense) used in describing past events.

historical • adj. **1** having to do with history. **2** belonging to or set in the past. **3** (of the study of a subject) looking at its development

over a period.
– DERIVATIVES **historically** adv.

historiography /hi-sto-ri-og-ruh-fi/ ● n. **1** the study of the writing of history and of written histories. **2** the writing of history.
– DERIVATIVES **historiographical** adj.

history ● n. (pl. **histories**) **1** the study of past events. **2** the past considered as a whole. **3** the past events connected with someone or something. **4** a continuous record of past events or trends.
– ORIGIN Greek *historia*.

histrionic /hiss-tri-on-ik/ ● adj. excessively dramatic. ● n. (**histrionics**) exaggerated behaviour intended to attract attention.
– ORIGIN Latin *histrionicus*.

hit ● v. (**hits**, **hitting**, **hit**) **1** strike with one's hand or a tool, bat, etc. **2** (of something moving) come into contact with (someone or something not moving) quickly and forcefully. **3** strike (a target). **4** cause harm or distress to. **5** (**hit out**) criticize or attack strongly. **6** be suddenly realized by: *it hit me that I was successful*. **7** (**hit on**) suddenly discover or think of. ● n. **1** an instance of hitting or being hit. **2** a successful film, pop record, etc. **3** Computing an instance of picking out an item of data which matches the requirements of a search. **4** informal, esp. N. Amer. a murder carried out by a criminal organization. **5** informal a dose of an addictive drug.
– PHRASES **hit-and-miss** done or occurring at random. **hit-and-run** (of a road accident) from which the driver responsible leaves rapidly without helping others involved. **hit someone below the belt 1** Boxing give one's opponent an illegal low blow. **2** behave unfairly towards someone. **hit someone for six** Brit. affect someone very severely. [ORIGIN with reference to a forceful hit that scores six runs in cricket.] **hit it off** informal be naturally well suited. **hit the nail on the head** be exactly right.
– ORIGIN Old Norse, 'come upon'.

hitch ● v. **1** move into a different position with a jerk. **2** fasten with a rope. **3** informal travel or obtain (a lift) by hitch-hiking. ● n. **1** a temporary difficulty. **2** a temporary knot used to fasten one thing to another.
– PHRASES **get hitched** informal get married.
– ORIGIN unknown.

Hitchcock, E
Sir Alfred (Joseph) (1899–1980), English film director, known for his films of suspense such as *Psycho* and *The Birds*.

hitch-hike ● v. (**hitch-hikes**, **hitch-hiking**, **hitch-hiked**) travel by getting free lifts in passing vehicles.
– DERIVATIVES **hitch-hiker** n.

hither ● adv. archaic to or towards this place.
– ORIGIN Old English.

hither and thither (also **hither and yon**) ● adv. to and fro.

hitherto ● adv. until this point in time.

Hitler, E
Adolf (1889–1945), Austrian-born Nazi leader, Chancellor of Germany 1933–45. He co-founded the National Socialist German Workers' (Nazi) Party in 1919. As Chancellor he established the Third Reich, his intended expansion of which into Czechoslovakia and Poland led to the Second World War. His fanatical anti-Semitism culminated in the Holocaust.
– DERIVATIVES **Hitlerian** adj.

hit list ● n. a list of people to be killed for criminal or political reasons.

hit man ● n. informal a person paid to kill someone.

HIV ● abbrev. human immunodeficiency virus (the virus causing Aids).

hive ● n. **1** a beehive. **2** a place full of people working hard.
– PHRASES **hive off** chiefly Brit. transfer (part of a business) to new ownership.
– ORIGIN Old English.

hives ● pl. n. a rash of round, red, itchy weals on the skin, caused by an allergy.
– ORIGIN unknown.

HK ● abbrev. Hong Kong.

HM ● abbrev. (in the UK) Her or His Majesty or Majesty's.

HMS ● abbrev. Her or His Majesty's Ship.

HMSO ● abbrev. (in the UK) Her or His Majesty's Stationery Office, which publishes government documents.

HNC ● abbrev. (in the UK) Higher National Certificate.

HND ● abbrev. (in the UK) Higher National Diploma.

hoard ● n. a store of money or valued objects. ● v. collect (something) over time and store it away.
– DERIVATIVES **hoarder** n.
– ORIGIN Old English.

hoarding ● n. Brit. **1** a large board used to display advertisements. **2** a temporary board fence around a building site.
– ORIGIN prob. from Old French *hourd*.

hoar frost ● n. a greyish-white feathery deposit of frost.
– ORIGIN from HOARY.

hoarse ● adj. (of a voice) rough and harsh.
– DERIVATIVES **hoarsely** adv. **hoarseness** n.
– ORIGIN Old English.

hoary ● adj. (**hoarier**, **hoariest**) **1** having grey hair. **2** old and unoriginal: *a hoary old adage*.
– ORIGIN Old English.

hoax ● n. a humorous or cruel trick. ● v. deceive with a hoax.
– DERIVATIVES **hoaxer** n.
– ORIGIN prob. from HOCUS-POCUS.

hob ● n. Brit. the flat top part of a cooker, with hotplates or burners.
– ORIGIN from HUB.

Hobart E
/hoh-bart/ the capital and chief port of Tasmania.

Hobbes E
/*rhymes with* jobs/, Thomas (1588–1679), English materialist philosopher. He believed that human action was motivated wholly by selfish concerns, especially the fear of death, and in *Leviathan* argued that absolute monarchy was the most rational and desirable form of government.

hobble ● v. (**hobbles**, **hobbling**, **hobbled**) **1** walk with difficulty or painfully. **2** strap together the legs of (a horse) to stop it wandering away.

– ORIGIN prob. from Dutch *hobbelen* 'rock from side to side'.

hobby ● n. (pl. **hobbies**) an activity done regularly in one's leisure time for pleasure.
– ORIGIN from an informal form of the man's name *Robin*.

hobby horse ● n. **1** a child's toy consisting of a stick with a model of a horse's head at one end. **2** a rocking horse. **3** a person's favourite topic of conversation: *the scheme became her favourite hobby horse.*

hobgoblin ● n. a mischievous imp.
– ORIGIN from *hob*, informal form of the names *Robin* and *Robert*, used in the sense 'country fellow'.

hobnail ● n. a short heavy-headed nail used to strengthen the soles of boots.
– DERIVATIVES **hobnailed** adj.

hobnob ● v. (**hobnobs**, **hobnobbing**, **hobnobbed**) informal spend time socially with rich or important people.
– ORIGIN from former *hob or nob*, or *hob and nob*, prob. meaning 'give and take'.

hobo ● n. (pl. **hoboes** or **hobos**) N. Amer. a homeless person.
– ORIGIN unknown.

Hobson's choice ● n. a choice of taking what is offered or nothing at all.
– ORIGIN named after Thomas *Hobson* (1554–1631), who hired out horses, making the customer take the one nearest the door or none at all.

Ho Chi Minh E
/hoh chee **min**/, (1890–1969; born *Nguyen That Thanh*), Vietnamese communist statesman, President of North Vietnam 1954–69. He led the Vietminh in the fight to gain independence from the French (1945–54), leaving him in control of North Vietnam. He then committed his forces in the struggle to unite North and South Vietnam that became the Vietnam War.

Ho Chi Minh City E
official name for **SAIGON**.

hock¹ ● n. the joint in the back leg of a four-legged animal, between the knee and the fetlock.
– ORIGIN Old English, 'heel'.

hock² ● n. Brit. a dry white wine from the German Rhineland.
– ORIGIN from German *Hochheimer Wein* 'wine from Hochheim'.

hock³ ● v. informal pawn (an object).
– PHRASES **in hock 1** having been pawned. **2** in debt.
– ORIGIN Dutch *hok* 'prison, debt'.

hockey /hok-ki/ ● n. a game played between two teams of eleven players each, using hooked sticks to drive a small hard ball towards a goal.
– ORIGIN unknown.

Hockney, E
David (b.1937), English painter and draughtsman, known for his association with pop art and for his Californian work of the mid 1960s.

hocus-pocus ● n. meaningless talk used to deceive.
– ORIGIN from *hax pax max Deus adimax*, a pseudo-Latin phrase used by magicians.

hod ● n. **1** a builder's V-shaped open trough attached to a short pole, used for carrying bricks. **2** a metal container for storing coal.
– ORIGIN Old French *hotte* 'pannier'.

hodgepodge ● n. N. Amer. = **HOTCHPOTCH**.

Hodgkin's disease ● n. a cancerous disease causing enlargement of the lymph nodes, liver, and spleen.
– ORIGIN named after the English physician Thomas *Hodgkin* (1798–1866).

hoe ● n. a long-handled gardening tool with a thin metal blade. ● v. (**hoes**, **hoeing**, **hoed**) use a hoe to turn (earth) or cut through (weeds).
– ORIGIN Old French *houe*.

Hoffman, E
Dustin (Lee) (b.1937), American actor. His many films include *The Graduate*, *Kramer vs Kramer*, and *Rain Man*.

hog ● n. a castrated male pig reared for slaughter. ● v. (**hogs**, **hogging**, **hogged**) informal take or hoard selfishly.
– PHRASES **go the whole hog** informal do something fully.
– ORIGIN Old English.

Hogarth E
/**hoh**-garth/, William (1697–1764), English painter and engraver. His works include *A Rake's Progress* and *Marriage à la Mode*, which satirize the vices of life in 18th-century England.

Hogmanay /**hog**-muh-nay/ ● n. (in Scotland) New Year's Eve.
– ORIGIN perh. from Old French *aguillanneuf* 'last day of the year'.

hogshead ● n. **1** a large cask. **2** a measure of liquid volume equal to 52.5 imperial gallons (238.7 litres) for wine or 54 imperial gallons (245.5 litres) for beer.

hogwash ● n. informal nonsense.
– ORIGIN first meaning 'kitchen scraps for pigs'.

hoick ● v. Brit. informal lift or pull with a jerk.
– ORIGIN perh. from **HIKE**.

hoi polloi /hoy puh-**loy**/ ● pl. n. derog. the common people.
– ORIGIN Greek, 'the many'.

hoist ● v. **1** raise by means of ropes and pulleys. **2** haul or lift up. ● n. **1** an act of hoisting. **2** an apparatus for hoisting.
– ORIGIN prob. from Dutch *hijsen* or German *hiesen*.

hoity-toity ● adj. snobbish.
– ORIGIN from former *hoit* 'romp'.

Hokkaido E
/hok-**ky**-doh/ the most northerly of the four main islands of Japan; capital, Sapporo.

hokum /**hoh**-kuhm/ ● n. informal **1** nonsense. **2** overused or sentimental material in a film, book, etc.
– ORIGIN unknown.

Hokusai E
/**hoh**-kuu-sy, hoh-kuu-**sy**/, Katsushika (1760–1849), Japanese painter and wood engraver. He represented aspects of Japanese everyday life in his woodcuts and strongly influenced European Impressionist artists.

Holbein E
/hol-byn/, Hans (1497–1543; known as **Holbein the Younger**), German painter and engraver, best known as a portrait artist who worked at the court of Henry VIII.

hold[1] ● v. (**holds**, **holding**, **held**) **1** grasp, carry, or support. **2** keep or detain. **3** have, own, or occupy. **4** contain or be able to contain. **5** stay or keep at a certain level. **6** (**hold to**) stick or cause to stick to (a commitment). **7** continue to follow (a course). **8** arrange and take part in (a meeting or conversation). **9** (**hold in**) regard (someone or something) with (a specified feeling). ● n. **1** a grip. **2** a place where one can grip while climbing. **3** a degree of control.
– PHRASES **get hold of 1** grasp. **2** informal find or contact. **hold against** continue to feel resentful for (a past action). **hold back** hesitate. **hold down** informal succeed in keeping (a job). **hold fast 1** remain tightly secured. **2** stick to a principle. **hold forth** talk at length. **hold it** informal wait or stop doing something. **hold off 1** resist (an attacker or challenge). **2** postpone. **3** (of bad weather) fail to occur. **hold on 1** wait. **2** keep going in difficult circumstances. **hold out 1** resist difficult circumstances. **2** continue to be sufficient. **hold out for** continue to demand. **hold over** postpone. **hold up 1** delay the progress of. **2** rob using the threat of violence. **3** present as an example. **4** remain strong. **no holds barred** without restrictions. **on hold** waiting to be dealt with or connected by telephone. **take hold** start to have an effect.
– DERIVATIVES **holder** n.
– ORIGIN Old English.

hold[2] ● n. a storage space in the lower part of a ship or aircraft.
– ORIGIN from **HOLE**.

holdall ● n. Brit. a large bag with handles and a shoulder strap.

holding ● n. **1** an area of land held by lease. **2** (**holdings**) stocks and property owned by a person or organization.

hold-up ● n. **1** a cause of delay. **2** a robbery carried out with the threat of violence.

hole ● n. **1** a hollow space in a solid object or surface. **2** an opening in or passing through something. **3** a cavity on a golf course into which the ball must be hit. **4** informal an awkward or unpleasant place or situation. ● v. (**holes**, **holing**, **holed**) **1** make a hole or holes in. **2** Golf hit (the ball) into a hole. **3** (**hole up**) informal hide oneself.
– DERIVATIVES **holey** adj.
– ORIGIN Old English.

hole in the heart ● n. an abnormal opening present from birth in the wall between the chambers of the heart.

Holiday, E
Billie (1915–59; born *Eleanora Fagan*), American jazz singer.

holiday esp. Brit. ● n. **1** an extended period of leisure. **2** a day of national or religious celebration when no work is done. ● v. spend a holiday.
– ORIGIN Old English, 'holy day'.

holidaymaker ● n. Brit. a tourist.

holier-than-thou ● adj. offensively certain that one is morally superior.

holiness ● n. **1** the state of being holy. **2** (**His/Your Holiness**) the title of the Pope, Orthodox patriarchs, and the Dalai Lama.

holistic /hoh-liss-tik/ ● n. Med. treating the whole person rather than just the symptoms of a disease.
– DERIVATIVES **holism** n.
– ORIGIN Greek *holos* 'whole'.

Holland E
= **NETHERLANDS**.

holler informal ● v. (**hollers**, **hollering**, **hollered**) give a loud shout. ● n. a loud shout.
– ORIGIN from *halloo*, a call used to urge on dogs during a hunt.

hollow ● adj. **1** having empty space inside. **2** curving inwards: *hollow cheeks*. **3** (of a sound) echoing. **4** worthless or insincere: *a hollow promise*. ● n. **1** a hole. **2** a small valley. ● v. (**hollow out**) **1** make hollow. **2** form by making a hole.
– DERIVATIVES **hollowness** n.
– ORIGIN Old English, 'cave'.

Holly, E
Buddy (1936–59; born *Charles Hardin Holley*), American rock-and-roll singer, guitarist, and songwriter, known for such songs as 'That'll be the Day'.

holly ● n. an evergreen shrub with prickly dark green leaves and red berries.
– ORIGIN Old English.

hollyhock ● n. a tall plant with large showy flowers.
– ORIGIN from **HOLY** + former *hock* 'mallow'.

Hollywood E
a district of Los Angeles, the main centre of the American film industry.

holmium /hohl-mi-uhm/ ● n. a soft silvery-white metallic element.
– ORIGIN from *Holmia*, Latin form of **STOCKHOLM**.

holocaust /hol-uh-kawst/ ● n. **1** destruction or slaughter on a mass scale. **2** (**the Holocaust**) the mass murder of Jews under the German Nazi regime in World War II.
– ORIGIN from Greek *holos* 'whole' + *kaustos* 'burnt'.

Holocene /hol-uh-seen/ ● adj. Geol. having to do with the present epoch (from about 10,000 years ago).
– ORIGIN French.

hologram /hol-uh-gram/ ● n. a photographic image formed in such a way that, when lit up, a three-dimensional image is seen.
– DERIVATIVES **holographic** adj.

Holst E
/hohlst/, Gustav (Theodore) (1874–1934), English composer, best known for the orchestral suite *The Planets*.

holster /hohl-ster/ ● n. a holder for carrying a handgun.
– ORIGIN unknown.

holy ● adj. (**holier**, **holiest**) **1** dedicated to God or a religious purpose. **2** very good in a moral and religious way.
– ORIGIN Old English.

holy day ● n. a religious festival.

Holy Father ● n. the Pope.

Holy Island E
= **Lindisfarne**.

Holy Land E
a region in what is now Israel and Palestine, regarded as holy by Christians as the place in which Christ lived and taught, by Jews as the land given to the people of Israel, and by Muslims.

Holyoake E
/**hoh**-li-ohk/, Sir Keith (Jacka) (1904–83), New Zealand statesman, Prime Minister 1957 and 1960–72, Governor General 1977–80.

holy of holies • n. **1** hist. the inner chamber of the sanctuary in the Jewish Temple in Jerusalem. **2** a place seen as most sacred.

holy orders • pl. n. see **order** (in sense 10 of the noun).

Holy Roman Empire E
the western part of the Roman empire, as revived by Charlemagne in 800. Created as an attempt by the medieval popes to unite Christendom under one rule, at times it included Germany, Austria, Switzerland, and parts of Italy and the Netherlands.

Holy See • n. the office of or the court surrounding the Pope.

Holy Spirit (or **Holy Ghost**) • n. (in Christianity) God as spiritually active in the world.

Holy Week • n. the week before Easter.

homage /**hom**-ij/ • n. honour shown to someone in public.
– origin Old French.

homburg /**hom**-berg/ • n. a man's felt hat with a narrow curled brim and a dented crown.
– origin named after the German town of *Homburg*.

home • n. **1** the place where one lives. **2** an institution for people needing professional care. **3** a place where something flourishes or from which it originated. **4** (in games) the place where a player is free from attack. • adj. **1** relating to one's home. **2** made, done, or intended for use in the home. **3** relating to one's own country. **4** (in sport) referring to a team's own ground. • adv. **1** to or at one's home. **2** to the end of something. **3** to the intended position: *slide the bolt home*. • v. (**homes**, **homing**, **homed**) **1** (of an animal) return by instinct to its territory. **2** (**home in on**) move or be aimed towards.
– phrases **at home 1** comfortable and at ease. **2** ready to receive visitors. **bring home to** make aware of the significance of. **close to home** (of a remark) uncomfortably accurate. **home and dry** esp. Brit. having achieved one's objective.
– origin Old English.

homecoming • n. an instance of returning home.

Home Counties E
the English counties surrounding London, consisting chiefly of Essex, Kent, Surrey, and Hertfordshire.

home economics • n. the study of cookery and household management.

home-grown • adj. grown in one's own garden or country.

Home Guard • n. the British volunteer force organized in 1940 to defend the UK against invasion.

home help • n. Brit. a person employed to help with household work.

homeland • n. **1** a person's native land. **2** hist. any of ten partially self-governing areas in South Africa assigned to particular black African peoples.

homeless • adj. not having anywhere to live.
– derivatives **homelessness** n.

homely • adj. (**homelier**, **homeliest**) **1** Brit. simple but comfortable. **2** unsophisticated.

homemaker • n. a person who manages a home.

Home Office • n. the British government department dealing with law and order, immigration, etc. in England and Wales.

homeopathy /hoh-mi-**op**-uh-thi/ (also **homoeopathy**) • n. a system of complementary medicine in which disease is treated by tiny doses of natural substances that in large quantities would produce symptoms of the disease.
– derivatives **homeopath** (also **homoeopath**) n. **homeopathic** (also **homoeopathic**) adj.
– origin from Greek *homoios* 'like' + *patheia* 'feeling'.

homeostasis /hoh-mi-uh-**stay**-siss/ (also **homoeostasis**) • n. (pl. **homeostases** /hoh-mi-uh-**stay**-seez/) the tendency of the body to keep its own temperature, blood pressure, etc. at a constant level.
– derivatives **homeostatic** (also **homoeostatic**) adj.
– origin from Greek *homoios* 'like' + *stasis* 'stoppage'.

home page • n. Computing an individual's or organization's introductory document on the World Wide Web.

Homer E
(8th century BC), Greek poet, traditionally regarded as the author of the epic poems the *Iliad* (telling of the climax of the Trojan War) and the *Odyssey*, describing the adventures of Odysseus.
– derivatives **Homeric** adj.

home rule • n. the government of a place by its own citizens.

home run • n. Baseball a hit that allows the batter to make a run around all the bases.

Home Secretary • n. (in the UK) the Secretary of State in charge of the Home Office.

homesick • adj. feeling upset because one is missing one's home.

homespun • adj. **1** simple and unsophisticated. **2** (of cloth or yarn) made or spun at home.

homestead • n. a house with surrounding land and outbuildings.
– derivatives **homesteader** n.

home straight (also **home stretch**) • n. the final stretch of a racecourse.

home truth • n. an unpleasant fact about oneself.

homeward • adv. (also **homewards**) towards home. • adj. going or leading towards home.

homework • n. **1** school work that a pupil is

required to do at home. **2** preparation for an event or situation. **3** paid work done in one's own home.

homicide /hom-i-syd/ ● **n.** murder.
– DERIVATIVES **homicidal** adj.
– ORIGIN Old French.

homiletic /hom-i-let-ik/ ● **adj.** having to do with or like a homily.

homily /hom-i-li/ ● **n.** (pl. **homilies**) **1** a talk on a religious subject, intended to be uplifting rather than to instruct. **2** a dull talk on a moral issue.
– ORIGIN Greek *homilia* 'discourse'.

homing ● **adj.** **1** (of an animal) able to return home from a great distance. **2** (of a weapon) able to find and hit a target electronically.

hominid /hom-i-nid/ ● **n.** Zool. a member of a family of primates which includes humans and their prehistoric ancestors.
– ORIGIN Latin *homo* 'man'.

homo /hoh-moh/ ● **n.** (pl. **homos**) informal, derog. a homosexual man.

homo- ● **comb. form** **1** same: *homogeneous*. **2** having to do with homosexual love: *homoerotic*.
– ORIGIN Greek *homos* 'same'.

homoeopathy ● **n.** var. of **HOMEOPATHY**.

homoeostasis ● **n.** var. of **HOMEOSTASIS**.

homoerotic /hoh-moh-i-rot-ik, hom-oh-i-rot-ik/ ● **adj.** concerning sexual desire centred on a person of the same sex.

homogeneous /hom-uh-jee-ni-uhss/ ● **adj.** **1** alike. **2** made up of parts of the same kind.
– DERIVATIVES **homogeneity** /hom-uh-ji-nee-i-ti/ n.
– ORIGIN Greek *homogenēs*.

homogenize (also **homogenise**) ● **v.** (**homogenizes**, **homogenizing**, **homogenized**) **1** treat (milk) so that the particles of fat are broken down and cream does not separate. **2** make alike.
– DERIVATIVES **homogenization** (also **homogenisation**) n.

homograph ● **n.** each of two or more words having the same spelling but different meanings and origins and often different pronunciations (e.g. **BOW**[1] and **BOW**[2] in this dictionary).

homologous /huh-mol-uh-guhss/ ● **adj.** having a related or similar position or structure; corresponding.
– DERIVATIVES **homology** n.
– ORIGIN Greek *homologos* 'agreeing'.

homonym /hom-uh-nim/ ● **n.** each of two or more words having the same spelling and pronunciation but different meanings and origins (e.g. **CAN**[1] and **CAN**[2] in this dictionary).
– ORIGIN Greek *homōnumos* 'having the same name'.

homophobia ● **n.** an extreme hatred or fear of homosexuality and homosexuals.
– DERIVATIVES **homophobe** n. **homophobic** adj.

homophone ● **n.** each of two or more words having the same pronunciation but different meanings, origins, or spelling (e.g. *new* and *knew*).
– ORIGIN Greek *phōnē* 'sound, voice'.

Homo sapiens /hoh-moh sap-i-enz/ ● **n.** the species to which modern humans belong.
– ORIGIN Latin, 'wise man'.

homosexual ● **adj.** feeling or involving sexual attraction to people of one's own sex. ● **n.** a homosexual person.
– DERIVATIVES **homosexuality** n.

Hon ● **abbrev.** **1** (in official job titles) Honorary. **2** (in titles of the British nobility and members of parliament) Honourable.

honcho /hon-choh/ ● **n.** (pl. **honchos**) informal a leader.
– ORIGIN Japanese, 'group leader'.

Honda, E
Soichiro (1906–92), Japanese motor manufacturer.

Honduras E
/hon-dyoo-ruhss/ a country of Central America, mainly bordering on the Caribbean Sea; capital, Tegucigalpa.
– DERIVATIVES **Honduran** adj. & n.

hone /hohn/ ● **v.** (**hones**, **honing**, **honed**) **1** sharpen (a tool) with a stone. **2** make sharper or more efficient.
– ORIGIN Old English, 'stone'.

Honecker E
/hon-i-ker/, Erich (1912–94), East German communist statesman, head of state 1976–89. He was ousted in 1989 as communism collapsed throughout eastern Europe.

honest ● **adj.** **1** truthful and sincere. **2** fairly earned: *an honest living*. **3** simple and straightforward: *good, honest food*. ● **adv.** informal really.
– ORIGIN Latin *honestus*.

honestly ● **adv.** **1** in an honest way. **2** really (used for emphasis).

honesty ● **n.** the quality of being honest.

honey ● **n.** (pl. **honeys**) **1** a sweet, sticky yellowish-brown fluid made by bees from flower nectar. **2** esp. N. Amer. darling.
– ORIGIN Old English.

honeybee ● **n.** the common bee.

honeycomb ● **n.** **1** a structure of six-sided cells of wax, made by bees to store honey and eggs. **2** a structure like a bee's honeycomb.

honeydew ● **n.** a sweet, sticky substance produced by small insects feeding on the sap of plants.

honeyed ● **adj.** **1** containing or coated with honey. **2** having a warm yellow colour. **3** soothing and soft: *honeyed words*.

honeymoon ● **n.** **1** a holiday taken by a newly married couple. **2** an initial period of enthusiasm or goodwill. ● **v.** spend a honeymoon.
– DERIVATIVES **honeymooner** n.
– ORIGIN first referring to affection waning like the moon.

honeypot ● **n.** a place to which many people are attracted.

honeysuckle ● **n.** a climbing shrub with sweet-smelling yellow and pink flowers.

Hong Kong E
a former British dependency on the SE coast of China, returned to China in 1997; capital, Victoria.

honk ● **n.** **1** the cry of a goose. **2** the sound of a car horn. ● **v.** make or cause to make a honk.

honky-tonk ● **n.** informal **1** N. Amer. a cheap bar or club, or one with a bad reputation. **2** rag-

time piano music.
– ORIGIN unknown.

Honolulu E
/hon-uh-loo-loo/ the state capital and principal port of Hawaii, on the island of Oahu.

honor • n. & v. US = HONOUR.
honorable • adj. US = HONOURABLE.
honorarium /on-uh-rair-i-uhm/ • n. (pl. **honorariums** or **honoraria** /on-uh-rair-i-uh/) a voluntary payment for professional services which are offered without charge.
– ORIGIN Latin.
honorary • adj. **1** (of a title or position) given as an honour. **2** Brit. (of a position or its holder) unpaid.
honorific • adj. given as a mark of respect.
honour (US **honor**) • n. **1** high respect. **2** something that is a privilege or pleasure. **3** a clear sense of what is morally right. **4** a person or thing that brings credit. **5** an award or title given as a reward for achievement. **6** (**honours**) a course of degree studies more specialized than for an ordinary pass. **7** (**His, Your**, etc. **Honour**) a title of respect for a judge. • v. **1** regard with great respect. **2** pay public respect to. **3** fulfil (an obligation) or keep (an agreement).
– ORIGIN Latin *honor*.
honourable (US **honorable**) • adj. **1** bringing or worthy of honour. **2** (**Honourable**) a title given to certain high officials, members of the nobility, and MPs.
– DERIVATIVES **honourably** (US **honorably**) adv.

Honshu E
/hon-shoo/ the largest of the four main islands of Japan.

hooch /hooch/ (also **hootch**) • n. informal strong alcoholic drink.
– ORIGIN from *Hoochinoo*, an Alaskan Indian people who made liquor.
hood[1] • n. **1** a covering for the head and neck with an opening for the face. **2** Brit. a folding waterproof cover of a vehicle or pram. **3** N. Amer. the bonnet of a vehicle. **4** a protective cover. • v. put a hood on or over.
– DERIVATIVES **hooded** adj.
– ORIGIN Old English.
hood[2] • n. informal, esp. N. Amer. a gangster or violent criminal.
– ORIGIN from HOODLUM.
-hood • suffix forming nouns referring to: **1** a condition or quality: *womanhood*. **2** a collection or group: *brotherhood*.
– ORIGIN Old English.
hoodlum /hood-luhm/ • n. a gangster or violent criminal.
– ORIGIN unknown.
hoodoo • n. **1** voodoo. **2** a run or cause of bad luck.
– ORIGIN from VOODOO.
hoodwink • v. deceive or trick.
– ORIGIN from HOOD[1] + WINK in the former sense 'close the eyes'.
hooey • n. informal nonsense.
– ORIGIN unknown.
hoof • n. (pl. **hoofs** or **hooves**) the horny part of the foot of a horse, cow, etc. • v. informal (**hoof it**) go on foot.
– DERIVATIVES **hoofed** adj.
– ORIGIN Old English.
hoo-ha • n. informal a fuss or commotion.
– ORIGIN unknown.
hook • n. **1** a piece of curved metal or other material for catching hold of things or hanging things on. **2** a curved cutting instrument. **3** a short punch made with the elbow bent and rigid. • v. **1** be or become attached or fastened with a hook. **2** (**hook up**) link to electronic equipment. **3** bend into the shape of a hook. **4** catch with a hook. **5** (**be hooked**) informal be addicted. **6** (in sport) hit (the ball) in a curving path.
– PHRASES **by hook or by crook** by any possible means. **hook, line, and sinker** completely. **off the hook 1** informal no longer in trouble. **2** (of a telephone receiver) not on its rest.
– DERIVATIVES **hooked** adj.
– ORIGIN Old English.
hookah /huuk-uh/ • n. an oriental tobacco pipe with a long tube which draws the smoke through water in a bowl.
– ORIGIN Urdu.
hook and eye • n. a small metal hook and loop used to fasten a garment.

Hooke, E
Robert (1635–1703), English scientist. His achievements included the formulation of the law of elasticity (stating that the strain in a solid is proportional to the applied stress, within the elastic limit) and the introduction of the term *cell* to biology.

hooker • n. **1** Rugby the player in the middle of the front row of the scrum. **2** informal a prostitute.

Hook of Holland E
a cape and port of the Netherlands, near The Hague.

hook-up • n. a connection to mains electricity, a communications system, etc.
hookworm • n. a worm which can infest the intestines and feeds by attaching itself with hook-like mouthparts.
hooligan • n. a violent young troublemaker.
– DERIVATIVES **hooliganism** n.
– ORIGIN perh. from *Hooligan*, the surname of a fictional rowdy Irish family.
hoop • n. **1** a rigid circular band. **2** a large ring used as a toy or for circus performers to jump through. **3** esp. Brit. a metal arch through which the balls are hit in croquet. • v. surround with a hoop or hoops.
– ORIGIN Old English.
hoopla /hoop-lah/ • n. Brit. a game in which rings are thrown in an attempt to encircle a prize.
hoopoe /hoo-poo, hoo-poh/ • n. a salmon-pink bird with a long downcurved bill, a large crest, and black-and-white wings and tail.
– ORIGIN Latin *upupa*.
hooray • exclam. hurrah.
hoot • n. **1** a low sound made by owls or a similar sound made by a horn, siren, etc. **2** a short laugh or mocking shout. **3** (**a hoot**) informal an amusing person or thing. • v. make or cause to make a hoot.
– PHRASES **not give a hoot** (or **two hoots**) informal not care at all.
hootch • n. var. of HOOCH.

hooter • n. **1** Brit. a siren, steam whistle, or horn. **2** informal a person's nose.

Hoover[1], E
Herbert (Clark) (1874–1964), American Republican statesman, 31st President of the US 1929–33.

Hoover[2], E
J. Edgar (1895–1972; full name *John Edgar Hoover*), American lawyer and director of the FBI 1924–72, who reorganized the FBI into a scientific law-enforcement agency.

Hoover[3] Brit. • n. trademark a vacuum cleaner. • v. (**hoover**) (**hoovers**, **hoovering**, **hoovered**) clean with a vacuum cleaner.
– ORIGIN named after the American industrialist William H. *Hoover* (1849–1942).

hooves pl. of **HOOF**.

hop[1] • v. (**hops**, **hopping**, **hopped**) **1** jump along on one foot. **2** (of a bird or animal) jump along with two or all feet at once. **3** informal move or go quickly. **4** (**hop it**) Brit. informal go away. • n. **1** a hopping movement. **2** a short journey or distance.
– PHRASES **hopping mad** informal extremely angry. **on the hop** Brit. informal unprepared.
– ORIGIN Old English.

hop[2] • n. a climbing plant whose dried flowers (**hops**) are used in brewing to give beer a bitter flavour.
– ORIGIN German or Dutch.

Hope, E
Bob (1903–2003; born *Leslie Townes Hope*), British-born American comedian, famous for his series of *Road* films.

hope • n. **1** a feeling of expectation and desire for something to happen. **2** a person or thing that gives cause for hope. • v. (**hopes**, **hoping**, **hoped**) **1** expect and want something to happen. **2** intend if possible to do something.
– ORIGIN Old English.

hopeful • adj. feeling or inspiring hope. • n. a person likely or hoping to succeed.
– DERIVATIVES **hopefulness** n.

hopefully • adv. **1** in a hopeful way. **2** it is to be hoped that.

USAGE hopefully
The traditional sense of **hopefully** is 'in a hopeful way'. The newer use, meaning 'it is to be hoped that' (as in *hopefully, we'll see you tomorrow*), is now the most common, although some people still think that it is incorrect.

hopeless • adj. **1** feeling or causing despair. **2** very bad or unskilful.
– DERIVATIVES **hopelessly** adv. **hopelessness** n.

Hopkins[1], E
Sir Anthony (Philip) (b.1937), Welsh-born American actor, star of such films as *The Silence of the Lambs* and *The Remains of the Day*.

Hopkins[2], E
Gerard Manley (1844–89), English poet. He invented the poetic metre known as 'sprung rhythm' (a combination of regular stress patterns with freely varying numbers of syllables). His poems include 'Windhover', 'Pied Beauty', and 'The Wreck of the Deutschland'.

Hopper, E
Edward (1882–1967), American realist painter, known for his works depicting isolated figures in bleak urban scenes.

hopper • n. a container that tapers downwards and empties its contents at the bottom.

hopscotch • n. a children's game of hopping into and over squares marked on the ground to retrieve a marker.
– ORIGIN from **HOP[1]** + **SCOTCH** in the sense 'put an end to'.

Horace E
/ho-riss/ (65–8 BC; full name *Quintus Horatius Flaccus*), Roman poet, best known for his *Odes* and *Satires*.

horde • n. esp. derog. a large group of people.
– ORIGIN Polish *horda*.

horizon • n. **1** the line at which the earth's surface and the sky appear to meet. **2** the limit of a person's understanding, experience, or interest.
– PHRASES **on the horizon** about to happen.
– ORIGIN Greek *horizōn* 'limiting'.

horizontal • adj. parallel to the ground, at right angles to the vertical. • n. a horizontal line or surface.
– DERIVATIVES **horizontally** adv.

hormone • n. a substance produced by a living thing and carried by blood or sap to specific cells or tissues to stimulate them into action.
– DERIVATIVES **hormonal** adj.
– ORIGIN Greek *hormōn* 'setting in motion'.

hormone replacement therapy • n. treatment with certain hormones to make symptoms of the menopause or osteoporosis less severe.

Hormuz, Strait of E
/hor-**muuz**/ a strait linking the Persian Gulf with the Gulf of Oman, separating Iran from Arabia.

horn • n. **1** a hard bony outgrowth found in pairs on the heads of cattle, sheep, and other animals. **2** the substance of which horns are made. **3** a brass wind instrument, shaped like a cone or wound into a spiral. **4** an instrument sounding a signal.
– PHRASES **on the horns of a dilemma** faced with a decision involving equally unfavourable alternatives.
– DERIVATIVES **horned** adj.
– ORIGIN Old English.

Horn, Cape E
the southernmost point of South America, on a Chilean island south of Tierra del Fuego. Until the opening of the Panama Canal (1914) it was the only sea route between the Atlantic and Pacific Oceans.

hornbeam • n. a tree with hard pale wood.
– ORIGIN from the tree's hard wood.

hornbill • n. a tropical bird with a horn-like structure on its large curved bill.

hornblende /horn-blend/ • n. a dark brown, black, or green mineral present in many rocks.
– ORIGIN German.

hornet • n. a kind of large wasp.
– PHRASES **stir up a hornets' nest** cause difficulties or angry feelings to arise.

– ORIGIN Old English.

Horn of Africa E
a peninsula of NE Africa, comprising Somalia and parts of Ethiopia.

hornpipe • n. **1** a lively solo dance traditionally performed by sailors. **2** a piece of music for such a dance.

horn-rimmed • adj. (of glasses) having rims made of horn or a similar substance.

horny • adj. (**hornier**, **horniest**) **1** made of or like horn. **2** hard and rough. **3** informal sexually aroused or arousing.

horology /ho-rol-uh-ji/ • n. **1** the study and measurement of time. **2** the art of making clocks and watches.
– ORIGIN Greek *hōra* 'time'.

horoscope • n. a forecast of a person's future based on the positions of the stars and planets at the time of their birth.
– ORIGIN Greek *hōroskopos.*

h

Horowitz E
/ho-ruh-vits/, Vladimir (1904–89), Russian pianist, a leading international virtuoso who settled in the US.

horrendous /huh-ren-duhss/ • adj. extremely unpleasant or horrifying.
– DERIVATIVES **horrendously** adv.
– ORIGIN Latin *horrendus.*

horrible • adj. **1** causing or likely to cause horror. **2** informal very unpleasant.
– DERIVATIVES **horribly** adv.

horrid • adj. **1** causing horror. **2** informal very unpleasant.

horrific • adj. causing horror.
– DERIVATIVES **horrifically** adv.

horrify • v. (**horrifies**, **horrifying**, **horrified**) fill with horror.
– ORIGIN Latin *horrificare.*

horror • n. **1** a strong feeling of fear, shock, or disgust. **2** a thing causing such a feeling. **3** very great dismay. **4** informal a badly behaved child.
– ORIGIN Latin.

hors d'oeuvre /or derv/ • n. (pl. **hors d'oeuvre** or **hors d'oeuvres** /or derv, or dervz/) a small item of savoury food eaten before a meal.
– ORIGIN French, 'outside the work'.

horse • n. **1** a large four-legged mammal with a flowing mane and tail, used for riding and for pulling heavy loads. **2** an adult male horse. **3** cavalry. **4** a structure on which something is mounted or supported: *a clothes horse.* • v. (**horses**, **horsing**, **horsed**) (**horse around/about**) informal fool about.
– PHRASES **from the horse's mouth** from a person directly concerned. **hold one's horses** informal wait a moment.
– ORIGIN Old English.

horseback • n. (in phr. **on horseback**) mounted on a horse.

horsebox • n. Brit. a vehicle or trailer for transporting one or more horses.

horse chestnut • n. **1** a large tree producing nuts (conkers) enclosed in a spiny case. **2** a conker.

horseflesh • n. horses as a group.

horsefly • n. a large fly that inflicts painful bites on horses and other large mammals.

horsehair • n. hair from the mane or tail of a horse, used in furniture for padding.

horse laugh • n. a loud, coarse laugh.

horseman (or **horsewoman**) • n. a rider on horseback.

horseplay • n. rough, high-spirited play.

horsepower • n. (pl. **horsepower**) an imperial unit of power equal to 550 foot-pounds per second (about 750 watts).

horseradish • n. a plant grown for its strong-tasting root which is often made into a sauce.

horse sense • n. informal common sense.

horseshoe • n. a U-shaped iron shoe for a horse.

horsewhip • n. a long whip used for controlling horses. • v. (**horsewhips**, **horsewhipping**, **horsewhipped**) beat with such a whip.

horsey (also **horsy**) • adj. **1** having to do with or like a horse. **2** very interested in horses or horse racing.

horst • n. Geol. a raised elongated block of the earth's crust lying between two faults.
– ORIGIN German, 'heap'.

Horta E
/or-tuh/, Victor (1861–1947), Belgian architect. He was a leading figure in art nouveau architecture and his work was notable for its innovative use of iron and glass.

hortatory /hor-tuh-tuh-ri/ • adj. formal intended to strongly urge someone to do something.
– ORIGIN Latin *hortatorius.*

horticulture /hor-ti-kul-cher/ • n. the art or practice of cultivating and managing gardens.
– DERIVATIVES **horticultural** adj. **horticulturist** (also **horticulturalist**) n.
– ORIGIN Latin *hortus* 'garden'.

hosanna (also **hosannah**) • n. & exclam. a biblical cry of praise or joy.
– ORIGIN Greek.

hose • n. **1** (Brit. also **hosepipe**) a flexible tube conveying water. **2** stockings, socks, and tights. • v. (**hoses**, **hosing**, **hosed**) wash or spray with a hose.
– ORIGIN Old English.

hosiery /hoh-zi-uh-ri/ • n. stockings, socks, and tights.

hospice • n. **1** a home providing care for the sick or terminally ill. **2** archaic a lodging for travellers.
– ORIGIN French.

hospitable /hoss-pit-uh-b'l/ • adj. **1** friendly and welcoming to strangers or guests. **2** (of an environment) pleasant and favourable for living in.
– DERIVATIVES **hospitably** adv.

hospital • n. an institution providing medical treatment and nursing care for sick or injured people.
– ORIGIN Latin *hospitale.*

hospitality • n. the friendly and generous treatment of guests or strangers.

hospitalize (also **hospitalise**) • v. (**hospitalizes**, **hospitalizing**, **hospitalized**) admit or cause to be admitted to hospital for treatment.
– DERIVATIVES **hospitalization** (also **hospitalisation**) n.

host[1] • n. **1** a person who receives or enter-

tains guests. **2** the presenter of a television or radio programme. **3** a person, place, or organization that holds an event to which others are invited. **4** Biol. an animal or plant on or in which a parasite lives. ● **v.** act as host at (an event) or for (a television or radio programme).
– ORIGIN Old French *hoste*.

host² ● **n.** **(a host/hosts of)** a large number of.
– ORIGIN Latin *hostis* 'stranger, enemy'.

host³ ● **n.** **(the Host)** the bread used in the Christian Eucharist.
– ORIGIN Latin *hostia* 'victim'.

hostage ● **n.** a person held in order to try to make others agree to a demand or condition.
– PHRASES **a hostage to fortune** an act or remark regarded as unwise because it invites trouble in the future.
– ORIGIN Old French.

hostel ● **n.** an establishment which provides cheap food and lodging for a particular group of people.
– ORIGIN Old French.

hostelry ● **n.** (pl. **hostelries**) archaic or humorous an inn or pub.
– ORIGIN Old French *hostelerie*.

hostess ● **n.** **1** a female host. **2** a woman employed to welcome and entertain customers at a nightclub or bar. **3** a stewardess on an aircraft, train, etc.

hostile ● **adj.** **1** unfriendly and aggressive. **2** having to do with a military enemy. **3** (of a takeover bid) opposed by the company to be bought.
– ORIGIN Latin *hostilis*.

hostility /hoss-til-i-ti/ ● **n.** (pl. **hostilities**) **1** hostile behaviour. **2** **(hostilities)** acts of warfare.

hot ● **adj.** **(hotter, hottest)** **1** having a high temperature. **2** feeling or producing an uncomfortable sensation of heat. **3** very exciting or intense. **4** currently popular or interesting. **5** informal (of goods) stolen. **6** **(hot on)** informal very knowledgeable about. **7** **(hot on)** informal strict about. ● **v.** **(hots, hotting, hotted)** **(hot up)** Brit. informal become more exciting or intense.
– PHRASES **have the hots for** informal be sexually attracted to. **hot under the collar** informal angry or annoyed. **in hot water** informal in trouble.
– DERIVATIVES **hotly** adv.
– ORIGIN Old English.

hot air ● **n.** informal empty or boastful talk.

hotbed ● **n.** a place where a particular activity happens or flourishes: *a hotbed of crime.*

hot-blooded ● **adj.** passionate.

hotchpotch (N. Amer. **hodgepodge**) ● **n.** a confused mixture.
– ORIGIN Old French *hochepot*.

hot cross bun ● **n.** a bun marked with a cross, traditionally eaten on Good Friday.

hot dog ● **n.** a hot sausage served in a long, soft roll.

hotel ● **n.** an establishment providing accommodation and meals for travellers and tourists.
– ORIGIN French.

hotelier /hoh-tel-i-er/ ● **n.** a person who owns or manages a hotel.

hot flush (also **hot flash**) ● **n.** a sudden feeling of heat in the skin or face.

hotfoot ● **adv.** in eager haste. ● **v.** **(hotfoots, hotfooting, hotfooted)** **(hotfoot it)** hurry eagerly.

hothead ● **n.** a rash or quick-tempered person.
– DERIVATIVES **hot-headed** adj.

hothouse ● **n.** **1** a heated greenhouse. **2** an environment that encourages rapid development.

hotline ● **n.** a direct telephone line set up for a specific purpose.

hot pants ● **pl. n.** women's tight, brief shorts.

hotplate ● **n.** a flat heated metal or ceramic surface on an electric cooker.

hotpot (also **Lancashire hotpot**) ● **n.** Brit. a casserole of meat and vegetables with a covering layer of sliced potato.

hot potato ● **n.** informal a controversial and difficult issue.

hot rod ● **n.** a motor vehicle that has been specially adapted to give it extra power and speed.

hot seat ● **n.** **(the hot seat)** informal the position of a person who carries full responsibility for something.

hotshot ● **n.** informal an important or extremely able person.

hot spot ● **n.** **1** a small area with a high temperature in comparison to its surroundings. **2** a place where there is a lot of activity or danger.

hot stuff ● **n.** informal **1** a person or thing of outstanding talent or interest. **2** a sexually exciting person, book, etc.

hot-tempered ● **adj.** easily angered.

Hottentot /hot tuhn tot/ ● **n. & adj.** offens. formerly used to refer to the Khoikhoi peoples of South Africa and Namibia.
– ORIGIN Dutch.

hot ticket ● **n.** informal a person or thing that is in great demand.

hot tub ● **n.** a large tub filled with hot bubbling water.

hot-water bottle (US also **hot-water bag**) ● **n.** a rubber container that is filled with hot water and used for warming a bed or part of the body.

hot-wire ● **v.** **(hot-wires, hot-wiring, hot-wired)** informal start the engine of (a vehicle) without using the ignition switch.

> **Houdini** E
> /hoo-dee-ni/, Harry (1874–1926; born *Erik Weisz*), Hungarian-born American magician and escape artist, famous for his ability to escape from all kinds of bonds and containers.

houmous ● **n.** var. of HUMMUS.

hound ● **n.** a hunting dog. ● **v.** harass.
– ORIGIN Old English.

hour ● **n.** **1** a period of 60 minutes, one of the twenty-four parts that a day is divided into. **2** a point in time: *you can't tun him away at this hour.* **3** a period set aside for a particular purpose or activity: *leisure hours.*
– ORIGIN Greek *hōra*.

hourglass ● **n.** a device with two connected glass bulbs containing sand that takes an hour to fall from the upper to the lower bulb. ● **adj.** shaped like an hourglass.

hourly ● **adj.** **1** done or occurring every hour.

2 calculated hour by hour: *hourly rates.* • **adv.** **1** every hour. **2** by the hour.

house • **n.** /howss/ **1** a building for people to live in. **2** a building in which animals live or in which things are kept: *a reptile house.* **3** a building devoted to a particular activity: *a house of prayer.* **4** a firm or institution: *a fashion house.* **5** a religious community that occupies a particular building. **6** esp. Brit. a group of pupils living in the same building at a boarding school. **7** a law-making assembly. **8** a dynasty. **9** (also **house music**) a style of fast popular dance music. • **adj. 1** (of an animal or plant) kept in or infesting buildings. **2** having to do with medical staff who have living quarters at a hospital. **3** having to do with a firm or institution. • **v.** /howz/ (**houses, housing, housed**) **1** provide with accommodation. **2** provide space for. **3** enclose (something).
– PHRASES **on the house** at the management's expense.
– ORIGIN Old English.

h

house arrest • **n.** the state of being kept as a prisoner in one's own house.

houseboat • **n.** a boat that people can live in.

housebound • **adj.** unable to leave one's house because of illness or old age.

housebreaking • **n.** the action of breaking into a building to commit a crime.

housecoat • **n.** a woman's long, loose robe worn casually around the house.

housefly • **n.** a common small fly often found in houses.

household • **n.** a house and its occupants.
– DERIVATIVES **householder** n.

household name (also **household word**) • **n.** a famous person or thing.

house-hunting • **n.** the process of seeking a house to buy or rent.

house husband • **n.** a man who lives with a partner and carries out the household duties traditionally done by a housewife.

housekeeper • **n.** a person employed to manage a household.
– DERIVATIVES **housekeeping** n.

house lights • **pl. n.** the lights in the part of a theatre where the audience sits.

housemaid • **n.** a female employee who carries out household tasks.

housemaid's knee • **n.** swelling of the fluid-filled cavity covering the kneecap.

house martin • **n.** a black-and-white bird which nests on buildings.

housemaster (or **housemistress**) • **n.** a teacher in charge of a house at a boarding school.

House of Commons • **n.** the part of Parliament in the UK whose members have been elected by voters.

House of Keys • **n.** the part of Tynwald, the parliament of the Isle of Man, whose members have been elected by voters.

House of Lords • **n.** the part of Parliament in the UK whose members are peers and bishops and have not been elected by voters.

House of Representatives • **n.** the lower house of the US Congress.

house-proud • **adj.** very concerned with the cleanliness and appearance of one's home.

Houses of Parliament • **pl. n.** the Houses of Lords and Commons in the UK regarded together.

house-train • **v.** esp. Brit. train (a pet) to urinate and defecate outside the house.

house-warming • **n.** a party celebrating a move to a new home.

housewife • **n.** (pl. **housewives**) a woman whose main occupation is caring for her family and running the household.
– DERIVATIVES **housewifery** /howss-**wif**-uh-ri/ n.

housework • **n.** cleaning, cooking, and other work done in running a home.

housing • **n. 1** houses and flats as a whole. **2** a casing for a piece of equipment.

housing estate • **n.** Brit. a number of houses in an area planned and built as a unit.

Housman, E
A. E. (1859–1936; full name *Alfred Edward Housman*), English poet and classical scholar, best known for the poems collected in *A Shropshire Lad*.

Houston E
/**hoo**-stuhn, **hyoo**-stuhn/ an inland port of Texas, the site of the NASA Space Centre.

hove Naut. past tense of **HEAVE**.

hovel • **n.** a small dirty or run-down dwelling.
– ORIGIN unknown.

hover • **v.** (**hovers, hovering, hovered**) **1** remain in one place in the air. **2** wait about uncertainly. **3** remain at or near a particular level: *inflation will hover around the 4 per cent mark.*
– ORIGIN unknown.

hovercraft • **n.** (pl. **hovercraft**) a vehicle that travels over land or water on a cushion of air.

how • **adv. 1** in what way or by what means. **2** in what condition. **3** to what extent or degree. **4** the way in which.
– PHRASES **how about?** would you like? **how do you do?** said when one meets someone for the first time in a formal situation. **how many** what number. **how much** what amount or price.
– ORIGIN Old English.

Howard[1], E
Catherine (*c.*1521–42), fifth wife of Henry VIII. She married Henry after his divorce from Anne of Cleves in 1540. She was beheaded after being accused of infidelity.

Howard[2], E
John (Winston) (b.1939), Australian Liberal statesman, Prime Minister from 1996 with a Liberal–National Party coalition.

howdah /**how**-duh/ • **n.** a seat for riding on the back of an elephant.
– ORIGIN Urdu.

however • **adv. 1** used to introduce a statement that contrasts with something that has been said previously. **2** in whatever way or to whatever extent.

howitzer /**how**-it-ser/ • **n.** a short gun for firing shells at a high angle.
– ORIGIN Dutch *houwitser*.

howl • **n. 1** a long wailing cry made by an animal. **2** a loud cry of pain, amusement, etc. • **v.** make a howling sound.

howler • **n.** informal a stupid mistake.

howling ● adj. informal great: *the meal was a howling success.*

hoyden /hoy-duhn/ ● n. dated a girl who behaves in a high-spirited or wild way.
– ORIGIN prob. from Dutch *heiden* 'heathen'.

Hoyle, E
Sir Fred (1915–2001), English astrophysicist and writer. He was one of the proponents of the steady state theory of cosmology, and, mainly with the American physicist **William A. Fowler** (1911–95), described the processes by which heavy elements are built up inside stars.

h.p. (also **HP**) ● abbrev. **1** Brit. hire purchase. **2** horsepower.

HQ ● abbrev. headquarters.

hr ● abbrev. hour.

HRH ● abbrev. Brit. Her (or His) Royal Highness.

HRT ● abbrev. hormone replacement therapy.

Hsian E
var. of **Xian**.

HTML ● n. Computing Hypertext Mark-up Language.

HTTP ● abbrev. Computing Hypertext Transport (or Transfer) Protocol.

Huang Hai E
/hwang **hy**/ Chinese name for **Yellow Sea**.

Huang Ho E
/hwang **hoh**/ Chinese name for **Yellow River**.

hub ● n. **1** the central part of a wheel, rotating on or with the axle. **2** the centre of an activity or region.
– ORIGIN unknown.

Hubble, E
Edwin Powell (1889–1953), American astronomer, who showed that the more distant a galaxy was, the faster it was moving away. This demonstrated that the universe was uniformly expanding.

hubbub ● n. **1** a loud confused noise caused by a crowd. **2** a busy, noisy situation.
– ORIGIN perh. Irish.

hubby ● n. (pl. **hubbies**) informal a husband.

hubris /hyoo-briss/ ● n. excessive pride or self-confidence.
– DERIVATIVES **hubristic** adj.
– ORIGIN Greek.

huckster ● n. a person who sells small items, either door-to-door or from a stall.
– ORIGIN prob. German.

huddle ● v. (**huddles**, **huddling**, **huddled**) **1** crowd together. **2** curl one's body into a small space. ● n. a number of people or things crowded together.
– ORIGIN perh. German.

Hudson, E
Henry (*c.*1565–1611), English explorer, the first European to discover the North American bay, river, and strait which bear his name.

Hudson Bay E
a large inland sea in NE Canada, the largest such sea in the world.

Hudson River E
a river of eastern North America, which rises in the Adirondack Mountains and flows southwards to the Atlantic at New York.

hue ● n. **1** a colour or shade. **2** an aspect: *men of all political hues.*
– ORIGIN Old English.

hue and cry ● n. a strong public outcry.
– ORIGIN from Old French *hu e cri* 'outcry and cry'.

huff ● v. (in phr. **huff and puff**) **1** breathe out noisily. **2** show one's annoyance in an obvious way. ● n. a fit of annoyance.

huffy ● adj. easily offended.
– DERIVATIVES **huffily** adv.

hug ● v. (**hugs**, **hugging**, **hugged**) **1** hold tightly in one's arms. **2** keep close to: *a few craft hugged the shore.* ● n. an act of hugging.
– ORIGIN prob. Scandinavian.

huge ● adj. (**huger**, **hugest**) very large.
– DERIVATIVES **hugeness** n.
– ORIGIN Old French *ahuge.*

hugely ● adv. **1** very much. **2** very.

hugger-mugger ● n. **1** confusion. **2** secrecy.
– ORIGIN prob. from **huddle** and dialect *mucker* 'hoard money'.

Hughes[1], E
Ted (1930–98; full name *Edward James Hughes*), English poet, whose work reflects his view of the natural world as a place of violence, terror, and beauty. He was Poet Laureate 1984–98.

Hughes[2], E
Howard (Robard) (1905–76), American industrialist, film producer, and aviator. He broke many world aviation records (1935–8). For the last twenty-five years of his life he lived as a recluse.

Hugo E
Victor (1802–85; full name *Victor-Marie Hugo*), French poet, novelist, and dramatist, a leading figure of French romanticism. His works include the play *Hernani* and the novel *Les Misérables.*

Huguenot /hyoo-guh-noh/ ● n. a French Protestant of the 16th–17th centuries.
– ORIGIN French.

hula /hoo-luh/ ● n. a dance performed by Hawaiian women, in which the dancers sway their hips.
– ORIGIN Hawaiian.

hula hoop (also US trademark **Hula-Hoop**) ● n. a large hoop spun round the body by moving the hips in a circular way.

hulk ● n. **1** an old ship stripped of fittings and permanently moored. **2** a large or clumsy person or thing.
– ORIGIN Old English, 'fast ship'.

hulking ● adj. informal very large or clumsy.

Hull E
a city and port in NE England, at the junction of the Hull and Humber Rivers. Official name **Kingston-upon-Hull**.

hull[1] ● n. the main body of a ship.
– ORIGIN perh. the same as **hull**[2], or from **hold**[2].

hull[2] ● n. **1** the outer covering of a fruit or seed. **2** the cluster of leaves and stalk on a

strawberry or raspberry. ● **v.** remove the hulls from.
– ORIGIN Old English.

hullabaloo ● **n.** informal an uproar.
– ORIGIN from *hullo*.

hullo ● **exclam.** var. of **HELLO**.

hum ● **v.** (**hums**, **humming**, **hummed**) **1** make a low continuous sound like that of a bee. **2** sing with closed lips. **3** informal be in a state of great activity. **4** Brit. informal smell unpleasant. ● **n.** a low, steady continuous sound.
– DERIVATIVES **hummable** adj.

human ● **adj.** **1** having to do with human beings. **2** showing the better qualities of human beings, such as kindness. ● **n.** (also **human being**) a person.
– DERIVATIVES **humanly** adv. **humanness** n.
– ORIGIN Latin *humanus*.

humane /hyoo-mayn/ ● **adj.** showing concern and kindness towards others.
– DERIVATIVES **humanely** adv.

h

humanism ● **n.** **1** a system of thought that regards humans as capable of using their intelligence to live their lives, rather than relying on religious belief. **2** a Renaissance cultural movement which revived interest in ancient Greek and Roman thought.
– DERIVATIVES **humanist** n. & adj. **humanistic** adj.

humanitarian /hyoo-man-i-tair-i-uhn/ ● **adj.** concerned with human welfare. ● **n.** a humanitarian person.
– DERIVATIVES **humanitarianism** n.

humanity ● **n.** (pl. **humanities**) **1** human beings as a whole. **2** the condition of being human. **3** sympathy and kindness towards others. **4** (**humanities**) studies concerned with human culture, such as literature or history.

humanize (also **humanise**) ● **v.** (**humanizes**, **humanizing**, **humanized**) make more pleasant or suitable for people.

humankind ● **n.** human beings as a whole.

human nature ● **n.** the general characteristics and feelings shared by all people.

humanoid /hyoo-muh-noyd/ ● **adj.** having an appearance or character like that of a human. ● **n.** a humanoid being.

human rights ● **pl. n.** basic rights to which every person is entitled, such as freedom.

Humber E
an estuary in NE England, formed at the junction of the Rivers Ouse and Trent and flowing into the North Sea. It is spanned by a suspension bridge that, with a span of 1,410 m (4,626 ft), is the second longest in the world.

Humberside E
a former county of NE England, dissolved in 1996.

humble ● **adj.** (**humbler**, **humblest**) **1** having or showing a modest or low estimate of one's own importance. **2** of low rank. **3** not large, or elaborate: *humble brick bungalows.* ● **v.** (**humbles**, **humbling**, **humbled**) make (someone) seem less dignified or important.
– PHRASES **eat humble pie** make a humble apology. [ORIGIN from former *umbles* meaning 'offal'.]
– DERIVATIVES **humbly** adv.
– ORIGIN Latin *humilis* 'low, lowly'.

humbug ● **n.** **1** false or misleading talk or behaviour. **2** a person who is not sincere or honest. **3** Brit. a boiled peppermint sweet.
– ORIGIN unknown.

humdinger /hum-ding-er/ ● **n.** informal an outstanding person or thing.
– ORIGIN unknown.

humdrum ● **adj.** lacking excitement or variety; dull.
– ORIGIN prob. from **HUM**.

Hume E
/hyoom/, David (1711–76), Scottish philosopher, economist, and historian. He rejected the possibility of certainty in knowledge and claimed that the sole origin of knowledge is in experience.

humerus /hyoo-muh-ruhss/ ● **n.** (pl. **humeri** /hyoo-muh-ry/) the bone of the upper arm, between the shoulder and the elbow.
– DERIVATIVES **humeral** adj.
– ORIGIN Latin, 'shoulder'.

humid /hyoo-mid/ ● **adj.** (of the air or weather) damp and warm.
– ORIGIN Latin *humidus*.

humidify ● **v.** (**humidifies**, **humidifying**, **humidified**) increase the level of moisture in (air).
– DERIVATIVES **humidifier** n.

humidity ● **n.** **1** the state of being humid. **2** the amount of moisture in the air: *the humidity is in the low thirties.*

humiliate ● **v.** (**humiliates**, **humiliating**, **humiliated**) make (someone) feel ashamed or stupid in front of another.
– DERIVATIVES **humiliation** n.
– ORIGIN Latin *humiliare* 'make humble'.

humility ● **n.** the quality of being humble.

hummingbird ● **n.** a small, chiefly tropical American bird able to hover by beating its wings extremely fast.

hummock ● **n.** a small hill or mound.
– ORIGIN unknown.

hummus /huu-muhss/ (also **houmous**) ● **n.** a thick Middle Eastern dip made from ground chickpeas and sesame seeds.
– ORIGIN Arabic.

humor ● **n.** US = **HUMOUR**.

humorist ● **n.** a writer or speaker who is noted for being amusing.

humorous ● **adj.** **1** causing amusement. **2** showing a sense of humour.
– DERIVATIVES **humorously** adv.

humour (US **humor**) ● **n.** **1** the quality of being amusing. **2** a state of mind: *her good humour vanished.* **3** (also **cardinal humour**) each of four fluids of the body, formerly believed to determine a person's physical and mental qualities. ● **v.** agree with the wishes of (someone) so as to keep them happy.
– PHRASES **out of humour** in a bad mood.
– DERIVATIVES **humourless** (US **humorless**) adj.
– ORIGIN Latin *humor* 'moisture'.

hump ● **n.** **1** a rounded part projecting from the back of a camel or other animal or as an abnormality on a person's back. **2** a rounded raised mass projecting from the ground. ● **v.** **1** informal lift or carry with difficulty. **2** (**humped**) having a hump.
– PHRASES **get the hump** Brit. informal become annoyed or sulky.
– DERIVATIVES **humpy** adj.

– ORIGIN prob. from German *humpe*.
humpback ● n. = HUNCHBACK.
– DERIVATIVES **humpbacked** adj.
humpback bridge ● n. Brit. a small road bridge that slopes steeply on both sides.
humus /hyoo-muhss/ ● n. a substance found in soil, formed from dead or dying leaves and other plant material.
– ORIGIN Latin, 'soil'.
Hun ● n. **1** a member of a people from Asia who invaded Europe in the 4th–5th centuries. **2** informal, derog. a German (especially during the First and Second World Wars).
– ORIGIN Greek *Hounnoi*.

Hunan E
/hoo-**nan**/ a province of east central China; capital, Changsha.

hunch ● v. raise (one's shoulders) and bend the top of one's body forward. ● n. a belief that something is true, based on a feeling rather than evidence.
– ORIGIN unknown.
hunchback ● n. offens. a person with an abnormal hump on his or her back.
hundred ● cardinal number **1** ten more than ninety; 100. (Roman numeral: **c** or **C**.) **2** (**hundreds**) informal a large number.
– PHRASES **a** (or **one**) **hundred per cent** completely.
– DERIVATIVES **hundredfold** adj. & adv. **hundredth** ordinal number.
– ORIGIN Old English.
hundreds and thousands ● pl. n. Brit. tiny coloured sugar strands used for decorating cakes and desserts.
hundredweight ● n. (pl. **hundredweight** or **hundredweights**) **1** Brit. a unit of weight equal to 112 lb (about 50.8 kg). **2** US a unit of weight equal to 100 lb (about 45.4 kg).

Hundred Years War E
a war between France and England, usually dated 1337–1453, consisting of a series of conflicts in which successive English kings attempted to dominate France.

hung past and past part. of HANG. ● adj. **1** having no political party with an overall majority: *a hung parliament*. **2** (of a jury) unable to agree on a verdict. **3** (**hung up**) informal emotionally confused or disturbed.
Hungarian /hung-gair-i-uhn/ ● n. **1** a person from Hungary. **2** the language of Hungary. ● adj. relating to Hungary.

Hungary E
a country in central Europe; capital, Budapest.

hunger ● n. **1** a feeling of discomfort and a need to eat, caused by lack of food. **2** a strong desire: *her hunger for knowledge*. ● v. (**hungers, hungering, hungered**) (**hunger after/for**) have a strong desire for.
– ORIGIN Old English.
hunger strike ● n. a refusal to eat for a long period, carried out as a protest by a prisoner.
hung-over ● adj. suffering from a hangover.
hungry ● adj. (**hungrier, hungriest**) **1** feeling hunger. **2** having a strong desire: *a party hungry for power*.
– DERIVATIVES **hungrily** adv.
hunk ● n. **1** a large piece cut or broken from something larger. **2** informal a sexually attractive man.
– DERIVATIVES **hunky** adj.
– ORIGIN prob. Dutch or German.
hunker ● v. (**hunkers, hunkering, hunkered**) squat or crouch down low.
– ORIGIN prob. from German *hocken*.
hunkers ● pl. n. informal haunches.
hunky-dory ● adj. informal excellent.
– ORIGIN *hunky* from Dutch *honk* 'home'; the origin of *dory* is unknown.

Hunt, E
(William) Holman (1827–1910), English Pre-Raphaelite painter, known for his religious pictures such as *The Light of the World*.

hunt ● v. **1** chase and kill (a wild animal) for sport or food. **2** try to find by thorough searching. **3** (**hunt down**) chase and capture (someone). **4** (**hunted**) appearing alarmed or harassed. ● n. **1** an act of hunting. **2** a group of people who meet regularly to hunt animals as a sport.
– ORIGIN Old English.
hunter ● n. **1** a person or animal that hunts. **2** a watch with a hinged cover protecting the glass.
– DERIVATIVES **huntress** n.

Huntingdonshire E
a former county of SE England, which became part of Cambridgeshire in 1974.

huntsman ● n. **1** a person who hunts. **2** a person in charge of hounds during a fox hunt.
hurdle ● n. **1** one of a series of upright frames which athletes in a race must jump over. **2** an obstacle or difficulty. **3** a portable rectangular frame used as a temporary fence. ● v. (**hurdles, hurdling, hurdled**) jump over (a hurdle or other obstacle) while running.
– DERIVATIVES **hurdler** n.
– ORIGIN Old English.
hurdy-gurdy /her-di-ger-di/ ● n. (pl. **hurdy-gurdies**) a musical instrument with a droning sound played by turning a handle, with keys worked by the other hand.
hurl ● v. **1** throw with great force. **2** say (insulting words) fiercely.
hurling (also **hurley**) ● n. an Irish game resembling hockey.
hurly-burly ● n. busy and noisy activity.
– ORIGIN from HURL.

Huron, Lake E
/hyoo-ron/ the second-largest of the five Great Lakes of North America, on the border between Canada and the US.

hurrah (also **hooray, hurray**) ● exclam. used to express joy or approval.
– ORIGIN uncertain.
hurricane ● n. a severe storm with a violent wind, especially in the Caribbean.
– ORIGIN Spanish *huracán*.
hurricane lamp ● n. an oil lamp in which the flame is protected from the wind by a glass tube.
hurry ● v. (**hurries, hurrying, hurried**) **1** move or act quickly. **2** do (something) quickly or too quickly: *guided tours tend to be hurried*. ● n. great haste.
– DERIVATIVES **hurriedly** adv.
hurt ● v. (**hurts, hurting, hurt**) **1** cause pain or injury to. **2** feel pain. **3** cause distress to.

• n. injury or pain.
– ORIGIN Old French *hurter* 'to strike'.

hurtful • adj. causing mental pain or distress.

hurtle • v. (**hurtles, hurtling, hurtled**) move at great speed.
– ORIGIN from HURT.

Husain E
var. of **Hussein**[2], **Hussein**[3].

husband • n. a married man in relation to his wife. • v. use (resources) carefully and without waste.
– ORIGIN Old Norse, 'master of a house'.

husbandry • n. **1** farming. **2** careful use of resources.

hush • v. **1** make or become quiet. **2** (**hush up**) prevent from becoming generally known. • n. a silence.

hush-hush • adj. informal highly secret.

hush money • n. informal money paid to someone to prevent them from revealing information.

husk • n. the dry outer covering of some fruits or seeds.
– ORIGIN prob. from German *hūske* 'sheath'.

husky[1] • adj. (**huskier, huskiest**) **1** sounding low-pitched and slightly hoarse. **2** big and strong.
– DERIVATIVES **huskily** adv.

husky[2] • n. (pl. **huskies**) a powerful dog of a breed used in the Arctic for pulling sledges.
– ORIGIN North American dialect, 'Eskimo'.

Huss E
/*rhymes with* fuss/, John (*c.*1372–1415), Bohemian religious reformer. A rector of Prague University, he supported the views of Wyclif and was eventually burnt at the stake.

hussar /huu-zar/ • n. (now only in titles) a soldier in a light cavalry regiment.
– ORIGIN Hungarian *huszár*.

Hussein[1] E
/huu-sayn/, Abdullah ibn, see **Abdullah ibn Hussein**.

Hussein[2] E
/huu-sayn/ (also **Husain**), ibn Talal (1935–99), king of Jordan 1953–99. He sought to maintain good relations both with the West and with other Arab nations and in 1994 he signed a treaty normalizing relations with Israel.

Hussein[3] E
/huu-sayn/ (also **Husain**), Saddam (b.1937), Iraqi President, Prime Minister, and head of the armed forces since 1979. During his presidency Iraq fought a war with Iran (1980–8) and invaded Kuwait (1990).

hussy • n. (pl. **hussies**) dated or humorous a girl or woman who behaves in an immoral or cheeky way.
– ORIGIN from HOUSEWIFE.

hustings • n. (**the hustings**) the political meetings, speeches, and other campaigning that take place before an election.
– ORIGIN Old Norse, 'household assembly'.

hustle • v. (**hustles, hustling, hustled**) **1** push or move roughly. **2** (**hustle into**) make (someone) act quickly and without time for consideration. • n. busy movement and activity.
– DERIVATIVES **hustler** n.
– ORIGIN Dutch *hutselen* 'shake, toss'.

Huston E
/hyoo-stuhn/, John (1906–87), American-born Irish film director, whose films include *The Maltese Falcon* and *The African Queen*.

hut • n. a small simple house or shelter.
– ORIGIN German *hütte*.

hutch • n. a box with a wire mesh front, used for keeping small animals such as rabbits.
– ORIGIN Latin *hutica* 'storage chest'.

Huxley[1], E
Aldous (Leonard) (1894–1963), English novelist and essayist, best known for his novel *Brave New World*.

Huxley[2], E
Sir Julian (1887–1975), English biologist, who studied animal behaviour and was a notable interpreter of science to the public. He was the first director-general of UNESCO.

Huxley[3], E
Thomas Henry (1825–95), English biologist, a surgeon and leading supporter of Darwinism.

Huygens E
/hy-guhnz/, Christiaan (1629–95), Dutch physicist, mathematician, and astronomer. He proposed the wave theory of light, which enabled him to explain reflection and refraction. He also improved the lenses of his telescope, and recognized the nature of Saturn's rings.

hyacinth /hy-uh-sinth/ • n. a plant with sweet-smelling bell-shaped flowers.
– ORIGIN named after *Hyacinthus*, a youth loved by the god Apollo in Greek mythology.

hyaena • n. var. of HYENA.

hybrid /hy-brid/ • n. **1** the offspring of two plants or animals of different species or varieties, such as a mule. **2** a thing made by combining two different elements.
– ORIGIN Latin *hybrida*.

hybridize (also **hybridise**) • v. (**hybridizes, hybridizing, hybridized**) breed (individuals of two different species or varieties) to produce hybrids.
– DERIVATIVES **hybridization** (also **hybridisation**) n.

Hyderabad[1] E
/hy-duh-ruh-bad/ a city in central India, capital of the state of Andhra Pradesh.

Hyderabad[2] E
/hy-duh-ruh-bad/ a city in SE Pakistan, in the province of Sind.

Hydra E
/hy-druh/ Gk Myth. a many-headed snake whose heads grew again as they were cut off, killed by Hercules.

hydra • n. a minute freshwater invertebrate animal with a tubular body and tentacles around the mouth.
– ORIGIN named after the HYDRA.

hydrangea /hy-drayn-juh/ • n. a shrub with white, blue, or pink flowers growing in clusters.

– ORIGIN from Greek *hudro-* 'water' + *angeion* 'container'.

hydrant /hy-druhnt/ ● **n.** a water pipe with a nozzle to which a fire hose can be attached.

hydrate ● **n.** /hy-drayt/ a compound in which water molecules are chemically bound to another compound or an element. ● **v.** /hy-drayt/ (**hydrates**, **hydrating**, **hydrated**) cause to absorb or combine with water.
– DERIVATIVES **hydration** n.

hydraulic /hy-drol-ik/ ● **adj.** relating to or operated by a liquid moving in a confined space under pressure. ● **n.** (**hydraulics**) the branch of science concerned with the use of liquids moving under pressure to provide mechanical force.
– DERIVATIVES **hydraulically** adv.
– ORIGIN from Greek *hudro-* 'water' + *aulos* 'pipe'.

hydro ● **n.** (pl. **hydros**) Brit. a hotel or health farm providing hydropathic and other treatment.

hydro- (also **hydr-**) ● **comb. form 1** water; relating to water: *hydroelectric*. **2** combined with hydrogen: *hydrocarbon*.
– ORIGIN Greek *hudōr* 'water'.

hydrocarbon ● **n.** any of the many compounds of hydrogen and carbon.

hydrocephalus /hy-druh-sef-uh-luhss/ ● **n.** a condition in which fluid collects in the brain.
– ORIGIN from Greek *hudro-* 'water' + *kephalē* 'head'.

hydrochloric acid ● **n.** a corrosive acid containing hydrogen and chlorine.

hydrodynamics ● **n.** the branch of science concerned with the forces acting on or generated by liquids.
– DERIVATIVES **hydrodynamic** adj.

hydroelectric ● **adj.** having to do with the use of flowing water to generate electricity.
– DERIVATIVES **hydroelectricity** n.

hydrofoil ● **n. 1** a boat fitted with structures (known as foils) which lift the hull clear of the water at speed. **2** each of the foils of such a craft.

hydrogen /hy-druh-juhn/ ● **n.** a highly flammable gas which is the lightest of the chemical elements.

hydrogenated /hy-droj-uh-nay-tid/ ● **adj.** combined with hydrogen.
– DERIVATIVES **hydrogenation** n.

hydrogen bomb ● **n.** a nuclear bomb whose destructive power comes from the fusion of hydrogen nuclei.

hydrogen peroxide ● **n.** a liquid used in some disinfectants and bleaches.

hydrogen sulphide ● **n.** a poisonous gas with a smell of bad eggs.

hydrography /hy-drog-ruh-fi/ ● **n.** the science of charting seas, lakes, and rivers.
– DERIVATIVES **hydrographer** n. **hydrographic** adj.

hydrology /hy-drol-uh-ji/ ● **n.** the branch of science concerned with the properties and distribution of water on the earth's surface.
– DERIVATIVES **hydrological** adj. **hydrologist** n.

hydrolyse /hy-druh-lyz/ (also **hydrolyze**) ● **v.** (**hydrolyses**, **hydrolysing**, **hydrolysed**) break down (a compound) by chemical reaction with water.

hydrolysis /hy-drol-i-siss/ ● **n.** the chemical breakdown of a compound due to reaction with water.

hydrometer /hy-drom-i-ter/ ● **n.** an instrument for measuring the density of liquids.

hydropathy /hy-drop-uh-thi/ ● **n.** the treatment of illness through the use of water, either internally or by external means such as steam baths.
– DERIVATIVES **hydropathic** adj.

hydrophilic /hy-druh-fil-ik/ ● **adj.** having a tendency to mix with or dissolve in water.

hydrophobia ● **n. 1** extreme fear of water, especially as a symptom of rabies. **2** rabies.

hydrophobic ● **adj. 1** repelling or failing to mix with water. **2** having to do with hydrophobia.

hydroplane ● **n.** a light, fast motor boat designed to skim over the surface of water.

hydroponics /hy-druh-pon-iks/ ● **n.** the growing of plants in sand, gravel, or liquid, with added nutrients but without soil.
– DERIVATIVES **hydroponic** adj.
– ORIGIN from Greek *hudōr* 'water' + *ponos* 'labour'.

hydrosphere ● **n.** the seas, lakes, and other waters of the earth's surface.

hydrostatic /hy-druh-stat-ik/ ● **adj.** relating to the pressure and other characteristics of liquid at rest.

hydrotherapy ● **n.** the use of exercises in a pool to treat conditions such as arthritis.

hydrothermal ● **adj.** relating to the action of heated water in the earth's crust.

hydrous ● **adj.** containing water.

hydroxide ● **n.** a compound containing OH negative ions together with a metallic element.

hyena (also **hyaena**) ● **n.** a doglike African mammal.
– ORIGIN Greek *huaina* 'female pig'.

hygiene ● **n.** the practice of keeping oneself and one's surroundings clean in order to prevent illness or disease.
– ORIGIN Greek *hugieinē* 'of health'.

hygienic ● **adj.** clean and free of the organisms which spread disease.
– DERIVATIVES **hygienically** adv.

hygienist ● **n.** an expert in hygiene.

hygrometer /hy-grom-i-ter/ ● **n.** an instrument for measuring humidity.
– ORIGIN Greek *hugros* 'wet'.

hygroscopic ● **adj.** (of a substance) tending to absorb moisture from the air.

hymen /hy-muhn/ ● **n.** a membrane which partially closes the opening of the vagina and is usually broken when a woman or girl first has sexual intercourse.
– ORIGIN Greek *humēn* 'membrane'.

hymenopterous /hy-muh-nop-tuh-ruhss/ ● **adj.** (of an insect) belonging to a large group that includes the bees, wasps, and ants, having four transparent wings.
– ORIGIN Greek *humenopteros* 'membrane-winged'.

hymn ● **n.** a religious song of praise, especially a Christian one. ● **v.** praise or celebrate.
– ORIGIN Greek *humnos*.

hymnal /him-nuhl/ ● **n.** a book of hymns.

hymnody /him-nuh-di/ ● **n.** the singing or

composition of hymns.
– ORIGIN Greek *humnōidia*.

hype informal • n. publicity that is excessive or that exaggerates the quality of something. • v. (**hypes**, **hyping**, **hyped**) **1** publicize in an excessive way. **2** (**be hyped up**) be very excited or tense.
– ORIGIN unknown; sense 2 is from **HYPODERMIC**.

hyper • adj. informal full of nervous energy.

hyper- • prefix **1** over; above: *hypersonic*. **2** excessively: *hyperactive*.
– ORIGIN Greek *huper*.

hyperactive • adj. abnormally or extremely active.

hyperbola /hy-per-buh-luh/ • n. (pl. **hyperbolas** or **hyperbolae** /hy-per-buh-li/) a symmetrical curve formed when a cone is cut by a plane nearly parallel to the cone's axis.
– ORIGIN Greek *huperbolē* 'excess'.

hyperbole /hy-per-buh-li/ • n. exaggerated statements that are not meant to be taken in the strict sense of the words.
– ORIGIN Greek *huperbolē*.

hyperbolic /hy-per-bol-ik/ • adj. **1** (of language) deliberately exaggerated. **2** relating to a hyperbola.

hyperinflation • n. inflation of prices or wages occurring at a very high rate.

hyperlink • n. Computing a link from a hypertext document to another location.

hypermarket • n. esp. Brit. a very large supermarket.

hypermedia • n. Computing an extension to hypertext providing multimedia facilities, such as sound and video.

hypersensitive • adj. excessively sensitive.

hypersonic • adj. **1** relating to speeds of more than five times the speed of sound. **2** relating to sound frequencies above about a thousand million hertz.

hypertension • n. abnormally high blood pressure.
– DERIVATIVES **hypertensive** adj.

hypertext • n. Computing a software system allowing users to move quickly between related documents or sections of text.

hypertrophy /hy-per-truh-fi/ • n. abnormal enlargement of an organ or tissue resulting from an increase in size of its cells.
– DERIVATIVES **hypertrophied** adj.
– ORIGIN Greek *-trophia* 'nourishment'.

hyperventilate • v. (**hyperventilates**, **hyperventilating**, **hyperventilated**) breathe at an abnormally rapid rate.
– DERIVATIVES **hyperventilation** n.

hyphen /hy-fuhn/ • n. the sign (-) used to join words together or to divide a word into parts between one line and the next.
– ORIGIN Greek *huphen* 'together'.

hyphenate • v. (**hyphenates**, **hyphenating**, **hyphenated**) write or separate with a hyphen.
– DERIVATIVES **hyphenation** n.

hypnosis • n. the practice of causing a person to enter a state of consciousness in which they respond very readily to suggestions or commands.
– ORIGIN Greek *hupnos* 'sleep'.

hypnotherapy • n. the use of hypnosis to treat physical or mental problems.

hypnotic • adj. **1** having to do with hypnosis. **2** causing a very relaxed or drowsy state. **3** (of a drug) producing sleep.
– DERIVATIVES **hypnotically** adv.

hypnotism • n. the study or practice of hypnosis.
– DERIVATIVES **hypnotist** n.

hypnotize (also **hypnotise**) • v. (**hypnotizes**, **hypnotizing**, **hypnotized**) produce a state of hypnosis in.

hypo- (also **hyp-**) • prefix **1** under: *hypodermic*. **2** below normal: *hypothermia*.
– ORIGIN Greek *hupo*.

hypoallergenic • adj. unlikely to cause an allergic reaction.

hypochondria /hy-per-kon-dri-uh/ • n. constant and excessive anxiety about one's health.
– ORIGIN Greek *hupokhondria* 'abdomen below the ribs' (once thought to be the source of melancholy).

hypochondriac • n. a person who is excessively anxious about their health.

hypocrisy /hi-pok-ruh-si/ • n. behaviour in which a person pretends to have higher standards or beliefs than is the case.
– ORIGIN Greek *hupokrisis* 'acting of a theatrical part'.

hypocrite • n. a person who pretends to have higher standards or beliefs than is the case.
– DERIVATIVES **hypocritical** adj.

hypodermic • adj. (of a needle or syringe) used to inject a drug or other substance beneath the skin. • n. a hypodermic syringe or injection.
– ORIGIN Greek *derma* 'skin'.

hypotension • n. abnormally low blood pressure.
– DERIVATIVES **hypotensive** adj.

hypotenuse /hy-pot-uh-nyooz/ • n. the longest side of a right-angled triangle, opposite the right angle.
– ORIGIN from Greek *hupoteinousa grammē* 'subtending line'.

hypothermia /hy-puh-ther-mi-uh/ • n. the condition of having an abnormally low body temperature.
– ORIGIN Greek *thermē* 'heat'.

hypothesis /hy-poth-i-siss/ • n. (pl. **hypotheses** /hy-poth-i-seez/) a proposed explanation based on limited evidence, used as a starting point for further investigation.
– ORIGIN Greek *hupothesis* 'foundation'.

hypothesize (also **hypothesise**) • v. (**hypothesizes**, **hypothesizing**, **hypothesized**) put forward as a hypothesis.

hypothetical /hy-puh-thet-i-k'l/ • adj. based on an imagined or possible situation rather than fact.
– DERIVATIVES **hypothetically** adv.

hyrax /hy-raks/ • n. a small plant-eating mammal with a short tail, found in Africa and Arabia.
– ORIGIN Greek *hurax* 'shrew-mouse'.

hyssop /hiss-uhp/ • n. a bushy plant whose bitter minty leaves are used in cookery and herbal medicine.
– ORIGIN Greek *hyssōpos*.

hysterectomy /hiss-tuh-rek-tuh-mi/ • n. (pl. **hysterectomies**) a surgical operation to remove all or part of the womb.

– ORIGIN from Greek *hustera* 'womb'.

hysteria ● n. **1** a mental disorder whose symptoms include extreme and unpredictable emotions and attention-seeking behaviour. **2** extreme or uncontrollable emotion or excitement: *election hysteria*.
– ORIGIN from Greek *hustera* 'womb' (hysteria once being thought to be caused by a disorder of the womb).

hysteric ● n. **1** (**hysterics**) wildly emotional behaviour. **2** (**hysterics**) informal uncontrollable laughter. **3** a person suffering from hysteria.

hysterical ● adj. **1** having to do with hysteria. **2** wildly uncontrolled. **3** informal very funny.
– DERIVATIVES **hysterically** adv.

Hz ● abbrev. hertz.

I[1] (also **i**) ● n. (pl. **Is** or **I's**) **1** the ninth letter of the alphabet. **2** the Roman numeral for one.

I[2] ● pron. (first person sing.) used by a speaker to refer to himself or herself.
– ORIGIN Old English.

I.[3] ● abbrev. Island(s) or Isle(s).

iambic /I-am-bik/ ● adj. Poetry having one short or unstressed syllable followed by one long or stressed syllable.
– ORIGIN Greek *iambos*.

Ibadan E
/i-bad-uhn/ the second-largest city of Nigeria.

Iberian /I-beer-i-uhn/ ● adj. relating to Iberia (the peninsula that consists of modern Spain and Portugal). ● n. a person from Iberia.

ibex /I-beks/ ● n. (pl. **ibexes**) a wild mountain goat with long, curved horns.
– ORIGIN Latin.

ibid. /ib-id/ ● adv. in the same source (referring to a work previously mentioned).
– ORIGIN Latin *ibidem* 'in the same place'.

ibis /I-biss/ ● n. (pl. **ibises**) a large wading bird with a long curved bill.
– ORIGIN Greek.

Ibiza E
/i-bee-thuh/ the westernmost of the Balearic Islands; capital city, Ibiza.
– DERIVATIVES **Ibizan** adj. & n.

-ible ● suffix forming adjectives: **1** able to be: *defensible*. **2** suitable for being: *edible*. **3** causing: *horrible*.
– DERIVATIVES **-ibility** suffix **-ibly** suffix.
– ORIGIN Latin *-ibilis*.

Ibsen E
/ib-s'n/, Henrik (1828–1906), Norwegian dramatist, creator of realist prose tragedies dealing with ordinary people. His works include *The Master Builder*, *A Doll's House*, and *Ghosts*.

ibuprofen /I-byoo-proh-fen/ ● n. a synthetic compound used as a painkiller and to reduce inflammation.
– ORIGIN from the chemical name.

IC ● abbrev. integrated circuit.

-ic ● suffix **1** forming adjectives: *Islamic*. **2** forming nouns: *mechanic*. **3** Chem. referring to an element in a higher valency: *ferric*.
– ORIGIN Latin *-icus* or Greek *-ikos*.

-ical ● suffix forming adjectives: **1** from nouns or adjectives ending in *-ic* (such as *comical* from *comic*). **2** from nouns ending in *-y* (such as *pathological* from *pathology*).
– DERIVATIVES **-ically** suffix.

Icarus E
/ik-uh-ruhss/ Gk Myth. the son of Daedalus, who escaped from Crete using wings made by his father but was killed when he flew too near the sun and the wax attaching his wings melted.

ICBM ● abbrev. intercontinental ballistic missile.

ice ● n. **1** frozen water, a brittle transparent solid. **2** esp. Brit. an ice cream or water ice. ● v. (**ices**, **icing**, **iced**) **1** decorate with icing. **2** (**ice up/over**) become covered or blocked with ice.
– PHRASES **break the ice** start conversation when people meet for the first time. **on ice** (of a plan or proposal) waiting to be dealt with at a later time. **on thin ice** in a risky situation.
– ORIGIN Old English.

ice age ● n. a period when ice sheets covered much of the earth's surface, especially during the Pleistocene period.

iceberg ● n. a large mass of ice floating in the sea.
– PHRASES **the tip of the iceberg** the small visible part of a much larger problem that remains hidden.
– ORIGIN Dutch *ijsberg*.

iceberg lettuce ● n. a kind of lettuce having a closely packed round head of crisp leaves.

icebox ● n. **1** a chilled container for keeping food cold. **2** Brit. a compartment in a refrigerator for making and storing ice.

ice-breaker ● n. a ship designed for breaking a channel through ice.

ice cap ● n. a permanent covering of ice over a large area, especially at the North and South Poles.

ice cream ● n. a frozen dessert made with sweetened and flavoured milk fat.

iced ● adj. **1** cooled or mixed with ice: *iced water*. **2** decorated with icing.

ice field ● n. a large permanent expanse of ice at the North and South Poles.

ice hockey ● n. a form of hockey played on

an ice rink.

Iceland E
an island country in the North Atlantic; capital, Reykjavik.
– DERIVATIVES **Icelander** n.

Icelandic /Is-lan-dik/ ● **n.** the language of Iceland. ● **adj.** relating to Iceland.

ice lolly ● **n.** Brit. a piece of flavoured water ice or ice cream on a stick.

ice pack ● **n.** a bag filled with ice and put on part of the body to reduce swelling or lower temperature.

ice skate ● **n.** a boot with a blade attached to the sole, used for skating on ice. ● **v.** (**ice-skate**) (**ice-skates**, **ice-skating**, **ice-skated**) skate on ice as a sport or pastime.
– DERIVATIVES **ice skater** n.

ichneumon /ik-nyoo-muhn/ ● **n.** a small wasp which lays its eggs in or on the larvae of other insects.
– ORIGIN Greek *ikhneumōn* 'tracker'.

ichthyology /ik-thi-ol-uh-ji/ ● **n.** the branch of zoology concerned with fishes.
– DERIVATIVES **ichthyologist** n.
– ORIGIN Greek *ikhthus* 'fish'.

ichthyosaur /ik-thi-uh-sor/ (also **ichthyosaurus** /ik-thi-uh-sor-uhss/) ● **n.** a fossil reptile that lived in the sea, having a long pointed head, four flippers, and a vertical tail.

icicle ● **n.** a hanging, tapering piece of ice formed when dripping water freezes.
– ORIGIN Old English.

icing ● **n.** a mixture of sugar with liquid or fat, used to coat or fill cakes or biscuits.
– PHRASES **the icing on the cake** an additional thing which makes something good even better.

icing sugar ● **n.** esp. Brit. finely powdered sugar used to make icing.

icon /I-kon/ ● **n.** **1** (also **ikon**) (in the Orthodox Church) a painting of Christ or another holy figure, treated as holy and used as an aid to prayer. **2** a person or thing seen as a symbol of something: *he's an iron-jawed icon of American manhood.* **3** a symbol on a computer screen of a program or option.
– DERIVATIVES **iconic** adj.
– ORIGIN Greek *eikōn* 'image'.

iconify /I-kon-i-fy/ ● **v.** (**iconifies**, **iconifying**, **iconified**) reduce (a window on a computer screen) to an icon.

iconoclast /I-kon-uh-klast/ ● **n.** **1** a person who attacks popular beliefs or established values and practices. **2** hist. a person who destroyed images used in religious worship.
– DERIVATIVES **iconoclasm** n. **iconoclastic** adj.
– ORIGIN from Greek *eikōn* 'image' + *klan* 'to break'.

iconography /I-kuh-nog-ruh-fi/ ● **n.** **1** the use or study of pictures or symbols in visual arts. **2** the pictures or symbols associated with a person or movement.
– DERIVATIVES **iconographer** n. **iconographic** adj.

icosahedron /I-koss-uh-hee-druhn/ ● **n.** (pl. **icosahedra** /I-koss-uh-hee-druh/ or **icosahedrons**) a three-dimensional shape with twenty plane faces.
– ORIGIN Greek *eikosaedros* 'twenty-faced'.

-ics ● **suffix** (forming nouns) referring to a science, art, or activity: *politics.*
– ORIGIN Latin *-ica* or Greek *-ika.*

icy ● **adj.** (**icier**, **iciest**) **1** covered with ice. **2** very cold. **3** very unfriendly.
– DERIVATIVES **icily** adv. **iciness** n.

ID ● **abbrev.** identification or identity.

Id ● **n.** var. of **EID**.

I'd ● **contr.** **1** I had. **2** I should or I would.

id /id/ ● **n.** the part of the unconscious mind consisting of a person's basic inherited instincts, needs, and feelings. Compare with **EGO** and **SUPEREGO**.
– ORIGIN Latin, 'that'.

Idaho E
/I-duh-hoh/ a state of the north-western US, capital, Boise.
– DERIVATIVES **Idahoan** n. & adj.

idea ● **n.** **1** a thought or suggestion about a possible course of action. **2** a mental impression. **3** a belief. **4** (**the idea**) the aim or purpose.
– ORIGIN Greek, 'form, pattern'.

ideal ● **adj.** **1** most suitable; perfect. **2** desirable or perfect but existing only in the imagination: *in an ideal world, we might have made a different decision.* ● **n.** **1** a person or thing regarded as perfect. **2** a principle or standard that is worth trying to achieve: *tolerance and freedom, the liberal ideals.*
– DERIVATIVES **ideally** adv.

idealism ● **n.** **1** the belief that ideals can be achieved, even when this is unrealistic. **2** (in art or literature) the presenting of things as perfect or better than in reality.
– DERIVATIVES **idealist** n. **idealistic** adj.

idealize (also **idealise**) ● **v.** (**idealizes**, **idealizing**, **idealized**) regard or present as perfect or better than in reality.
– DERIVATIVES **idealization** (also **idealisation**) n.

idée fixe /ee-day feeks/ ● **n.** (pl. **idées fixes** /ee-day **feeks**/) an idea that dominates the mind; an obsession.
– ORIGIN French, 'fixed idea'.

identical ● **adj.** **1** exactly alike. **2** the same. **3** (of twins) developed from a single fertilized ovum, and therefore of the same sex and very similar in appearance.
– DERIVATIVES **identically** adv.
– ORIGIN Latin *identicus.*

identification ● **n.** **1** the action of identifying or the fact of being identified. **2** an official document or other proof of one's identity.

identify ● **v.** (**identifies**, **identifying**, **identified**) **1** prove or recognize as being a specified person or thing: *he couldn't identify his attackers.* **2** recognize as being worthy of attention. **3** (**identify with**) feel that one understands or feels the same as (someone else). **4** (**identify with**) associate (someone or something) closely with.
– DERIVATIVES **identifiable** adj. **identifier** n.

identikit ● **n.** trademark a picture of a person wanted by the police, put together according to witnesses' descriptions from a set of typical facial features.

identity ● **n.** (pl. **identities**) **1** the fact of being who or what a person or thing is: *she knew the identity of the bomber.* **2** a close similarity or feeling of understanding.
– ORIGIN Latin *identitas.*

identity parade ● n. Brit. a group of people assembled so that an eyewitness may identify a suspect for a crime from among them.

ideogram /id-i-uh-gram/ (also **ideograph**) ● n. a symbol used in a writing system to represent the idea of a thing rather than the sounds used to say it (e.g. a number).

ideologue /I-di-uh-log/ ● n. a person who follows an ideology in a strict and inflexible way.

ideology /I-di-**ol**-uh-ji/ ● n. (pl. **ideologies**) **1** a system of ideas and principles forming the basis of an economic or political theory. **2** the set of beliefs held by a particular group: *bourgeois ideology*.
– DERIVATIVES **ideological** adj.
– ORIGIN Greek *idea* 'form'.

idiocy /**id**-i-uh-si/ ● n. (pl. **idiocies**) extremely stupid behaviour.

idiom /**id**-i-uhm/ ● n. **1** a group of words whose meaning is different from the meanings of the individual words (e.g. *over the moon*). **2** a form of language and grammar used by particular people at a particular time or place. **3** a style of expression in music or art that is characteristic of a particular group or place: *an Impressionist idiom*.
– ORIGIN Greek *idiōma* 'private property'.

idiomatic ● adj. using or relating to expressions that are natural to a native speaker.

idiosyncrasy /id-i-oh-**sing**-kruh-si/ ● n. (pl. **idiosyncrasies**) **1** a person's particular way of behaving or thinking. **2** a distinctive or peculiar feature of a thing: *the architectural idiosyncrasies that all old houses have*.
– ORIGIN Greek *idiosunkrasia*.

idiosyncratic /id-i-oh-sing-**krat**-ik/ ● adj. individual or peculiar.

idiot ● n. informal a stupid person.
– ORIGIN Greek *idiōtēs* 'layman, ignorant person'.

idiotic ● adj. very stupid.
– DERIVATIVES **idiotically** adv.

idle ● adj. (**idler**, **idlest**) **1** avoiding work; lazy. **2** not working or in use. **3** having no purpose or effect: *she did not make idle threats*. ● v. (**idles**, **idling**, **idled**) **1** spend time doing nothing. **2** (of an engine) run slowly while out of gear.
– DERIVATIVES **idleness** n. **idler** n. **idly** adv.
– ORIGIN Old English, 'empty, useless'.

idol ● n. **1** a statue or picture of a god that is worshipped. **2** a person who is greatly admired: *a soccer idol*.
– ORIGIN Greek *eidōlon*.

idolatry /I-**dol**-uh-tri/ ● n. **1** worship of idols. **2** extreme admiration or devotion.
– DERIVATIVES **idolater** n. **idolatrous** adj.
– ORIGIN from Greek *eidōlon* 'idol' + *-latreia* 'worship'.

idolize (also **idolise**) ● v. (**idolizes**, **idolizing**, **idolized**) admire or love greatly or excessively.

idyll /i-dil/ ● n. **1** a very happy or peaceful period or situation. **2** a short poem or piece of writing describing a picturesque scene or incident in country life.
– ORIGIN Greek *eidullion* 'little form'.

idyllic ● adj. very happy, peaceful, or beautiful.

i.e. ● abbrev. that is to say.
– ORIGIN from Latin *id est* 'that is'.

if ● conj. **1** on the condition or in the event that: *if you have a complaint, write to the manager*. **2** despite the possibility that. **3** whether. **4** whenever. **5** expressing surprise, regret, or an opinion: *if you ask me, he's in love*.
– ORIGIN Old English.

> **USAGE** if
> Although **if** can mean 'whether', it is better to use the word **whether** rather than **if** in writing (*I'll see whether he left an address* rather than *I'll see if he left an address*).

iffy ● adj. informal **1** uncertain. **2** of doubtful quality or legality.

igloo ● n. a dome-shaped Eskimo house built from blocks of solid snow.
– ORIGIN Inuit, 'house'.

> **Ignatius Loyola, St** E
> /ig-nay-shuhss **loy**-uh-luh, loy-**oh**-luh/ (1491–1556), Spanish theologian and founder of the Jesuits. Feast day, 31 July.

igneous /ig-ni-uhss/ ● adj. (of rock) formed when molten rock has solidified.
– ORIGIN Latin *ignis* 'fire'.

ignite /ig-**nyt**/ ● v. (**ignites**, **igniting**, **ignited**) **1** catch fire or set on fire. **2** provoke or stir up: *the words ignited new fury in him*.
– DERIVATIVES **igniter** n.
– ORIGIN Latin *ignire*.

ignition ● n. **1** the action of igniting. **2** the mechanism providing the spark that ignites the fuel in an internal-combustion engine.

ignoble ● adj. not good or honest; dishonourable.
– ORIGIN from Latin *in-* 'not' + *gnobilis* 'noble'.

ignominious /ig-nuh-**min**-i-uhss/ ● adj. deserving or causing public disgrace: *they risked ignominious defeat*.
– DERIVATIVES **ignominiously** adv.
– ORIGIN Latin *ignominiosus*.

ignominy /ig-nuh-mi-ni/ ● n. public disgrace.

ignoramus /ig-nuh-**ray**-muhss/ ● n. (pl. **ignoramuses**) an ignorant or stupid person.
– ORIGIN Latin, 'we do not know'.

ignorance ● n. lack of knowledge or information.

ignorant ● adj. **1** lacking knowledge or awareness. **2** informal not polite; rude.
– ORIGIN Latin *ignorare* 'not know'.

ignore ● v. (**ignores**, **ignoring**, **ignored**) **1** deliberately take no notice of. **2** fail to consider (something important).
– ORIGIN Latin *ignorare* 'not know'.

iguana /i-**gwah**-nuh/ ● n. a large tropical American lizard with a spiny crest along the back.
– ORIGIN Spanish.

ikon ● n. var. of **ICON**.

ileum /**il**-i-uhm/ ● n. (pl. **ilea** /**il**-i-uh/) the third and lowest part of the small intestine.
– ORIGIN Latin.

iliac /**il**-i-ak/ ● adj. relating to the ilium or the nearby regions of the lower body.

> **Ilium** E
> /il-i-uhm/ = **TROY**.

ilium /**il**-i-uhm/ ● n. (pl. **ilia** /**il**-i-uh/) the large broad bone forming the upper part of each half of the pelvis.
– ORIGIN Latin.

ilk ● n. a type: *fascists, racists, and others of that ilk*.

– ORIGIN Old English, 'same'.

I'll • contr. I shall; I will.

ill • adj. **1** not in full health; unwell. **2** poor in quality. **3** harmful, hostile, or unfavourable. • adv. **1** badly or wrongly: *ill-chosen*. **2** only with difficulty: *she could ill afford the cost*. • n. **1** a problem or misfortune. **2** evil or harm.
– PHRASES **ill at ease** uncomfortable or embarrassed.
– ORIGIN Old Norse, 'evil, difficult'.

ill-advised • adj. unwise or badly thought out.

ill-bred • adj. badly brought up or rude.

ill-disposed • adj. unfriendly or unsympathetic.

illegal • adj. against the law.
– DERIVATIVES **illegality** n. **illegally** adv.

illegible /il-lej-i-b'l/ • adj. not clear enough to be read.
– DERIVATIVES **illegibility** n.

illegitimate /il-li-jit-i-muht/ • adj. **1** not allowed by law or rules. **2** (of a child) born of parents not lawfully married to each other.
– DERIVATIVES **illegitimacy** n.

ill-fated • adj. destined to fail or be unlucky.

ill-favoured (US **ill-favored**) • adj. unattractive.

ill-gotten • adj. obtained by illegal or unfair means.

illiberal • adj. restricting freedom of thought or behaviour.

illicit /il-li-sit/ • adj. forbidden by law, rules, or accepted standards.
– DERIVATIVES **illicitly** adv.
– ORIGIN Latin *illicitus*.

Illinois E
/il-li-**noy**/ a state in the Middle West of the US; capital, Springfield.
– DERIVATIVES **Illinoisan** n. & adj.

illiterate /il-lit-uh-ruht/ • adj. **1** unable to read or write. **2** not knowledgeable about a particular subject: *politically illiterate*.
– DERIVATIVES **illiteracy** n.

illness • n. a disease or period of sickness.

illogical • adj. not sensible or based on sound reasoning: *an illogical fear of the dark*.
– DERIVATIVES **illogicality** n. (pl. **illogicalities**) **illogically** adv.

ill-starred • adj. unlucky.

ill-tempered • adj. irritable or surly.

ill-treat • v. treat cruelly.

illuminate /il-lyoo-mi-nayt/ • v. (**illuminates**, **illuminating**, **illuminated**) **1** light up. **2** help to explain or make clear: *he illuminates science for the interested reader*. **3** decorate (a manuscript) with gold, silver, or coloured designs.
– DERIVATIVES **illuminator** n.
– ORIGIN Latin *illuminare*.

illumination • n. **1** lighting or light. **2** (**illuminations**) lights used in decorating a building or other structure. **3** understanding.

illumine • v. (**illumines**, **illumining**, **illumined**) literary illuminate.

illusion /il-lyoo-*zh*'n/ • n. **1** a false idea or belief: *he had no illusions about his playing*. **2** a thing that seems to be something that it is not or seems to exist but does not.
– ORIGIN Latin *illudere* 'to mock'.

illusionist • n. a magician or conjuror.

illusory /il-lyoo-suh-ri/ (also **illusive**) • adj. not real, although seeming to be.

illustrate • v. (**illustrates**, **illustrating**, **illustrated**) **1** provide (a book or magazine) with pictures. **2** make clear by using examples, charts, etc. **3** act as an example of.
– DERIVATIVES **illustrator** n.
– ORIGIN Latin *illustrare* 'light up'.

illustration • n. **1** a picture in a book or magazine. **2** the action of illustrating. **3** an example that proves something or helps to explain it.

illustrative • adj. acting as an example or explanation.

illustrious /il-luss-tri-uhss/ • adj. famous and admired for past achievements.
– ORIGIN Latin *illustris* 'clear, bright'.

ill will • n. hostility towards someone.

I'm • contr. I am.

image • n. **1** a likeness of someone or something in the form of a picture or statue. **2** a picture of someone or something seen on a television or computer screen, through a lens, or reflected in something. **3** a picture in the mind. **4** the impression that a person or thing presents to the public: *she tries to project an image of youth*. **5** a person or thing that looks very similar to another: *he's the image of his father*. **6** a word or phrase describing something in an imaginative way; a simile or metaphor. • v. (**images**, **imaging**, **imaged**) make or form an image of.
– ORIGIN Latin *imago*.

imager • n. an electronic or other device which records images.

imagery • n. **1** language using similes and metaphors that produces images in the mind. **2** images as a whole.

imaginable • adj. possible to be thought of or believed.

imaginary • adj. **1** existing only in the imagination. **2** Math. (of a number or quantity) expressed in terms of the square root of −1 (represented by *i* or *j*).

imagination • n. **1** the ability to form ideas or images in the mind. **2** the ability of the mind to be creative or solve problems.

imaginative • adj. using the imagination in a creative or inventive way.
– DERIVATIVES **imaginatively** adv.

imagine • v. (**imagines**, **imagining**, **imagined**) **1** form a mental picture of. **2** think that something is probable; assume. **3** believe (something unreal) to exist.
– ORIGIN from Latin *imaginare* 'form an image of' and *imaginari* 'imagine'.

imaginings • pl. n. thoughts or fantasies.

imago /i-may-goh/ • n. (pl. **imagos** or **imagines** /i-may-ji-neez/) the final and fully developed adult stage of an insect.
– ORIGIN Latin, 'image'.

imam /i-mahm/ • n. **1** the person who leads prayers in a mosque. **2** (**Imam**) a title of various Muslim religious leaders.
– ORIGIN Arabic, 'leader'.

imbalance • n. a lack of proportion or balance.

imbecile /im-bi-seel/ • n. informal a stupid person.
– DERIVATIVES **imbecilic** adj. **imbecility** n.
– ORIGIN Latin *imbecillus* 'weak'.

imbed • v. var. of EMBED.

imbibe /im-byb/ ● v. (**imbibes**, **imbibing**, **imbibed**) **1** formal drink (alcohol). **2** absorb (ideas or knowledge).
– ORIGIN Latin *imbibere.*

imbroglio /im-**broh**-li-oh/ ● n. (pl. **imbroglios**) a very confused or complicated situation.
– ORIGIN Italian.

imbue /im-byoo/ ● v. (**imbues**, **imbuing**, **imbued**) fill with a feeling or quality: *we were imbued with a sense of purpose.*
– ORIGIN Latin *imbuere* 'moisten'.

IMF ● abbrev. International Monetary Fund.

imitate ● v. (**imitates**, **imitating**, **imitated**) **1** follow as a model. **2** copy (a person's speech or behaviour) to amuse people. **3** make a copy of; simulate.
– DERIVATIVES **imitator** n.
– ORIGIN Latin *imitari.*

imitation ● n. **1** a copy. **2** the action of imitating.

imitative /**im**-i-tuh-tiv/ ● adj. following a model or example.

immaculate ● adj. **1** completely clean or tidy. **2** free from flaws or mistakes; perfect.
– DERIVATIVES **immaculately** adv.
– ORIGIN Latin *immaculatus.*

Immaculate Conception ● n. (in the Roman Catholic Church) the doctrine that the Virgin Mary was free from original sin from the moment she was conceived by her mother.

immanent /im-muh-nuhnt/ ● adj. present within or throughout; inherent: *love is a force immanent in the world.*
– DERIVATIVES **immanence** n.
– ORIGIN Latin *immanere* 'remain within'.

immaterial ● adj. **1** unimportant under the circumstances; irrelevant. **2** spiritual rather than physical.

immature ● adj. **1** not fully developed. **2** behaving in a way that is typical of someone younger; childish.
– DERIVATIVES **immaturity** n.

immeasurable ● adj. too large or extreme to measure.
– DERIVATIVES **immeasurably** adv.

immediate ● adj. **1** occurring or done at once. **2** nearest in time, space, or relationship. **3** most urgent; current. **4** direct: *a coronary was the immediate cause of death.*
– DERIVATIVES **immediacy** n.
– ORIGIN Latin *immediatus.*

immediately ● adv. **1** at once. **2** very close in time, space, or relationship. ● conj. esp. Brit. as soon as.

immemorial ● adj. existing from before what can be remembered or found in records: *they had lived there from time immemorial.*

immense ● adj. very large or great.
– DERIVATIVES **immensity** n.
– ORIGIN Latin *immensus* 'immeasurable'.

immensely ● adv. to a great extent; extremely.

immerse ● v. (**immerses**, **immersing**, **immersed**) **1** dip or cover completely in a liquid. **2** (**immerse oneself** or **be immersed**) involve oneself deeply in an activity or interest.
– ORIGIN Latin *immergere.*

immersion ● n. **1** the action of immersing someone or something in a liquid. **2** deep involvement.

immersion heater ● n. an electric device that is positioned in a domestic water tank to heat the water.

immigrant ● n. a person who comes to live permanently in a foreign country.

immigrate ● v. (**immigrates**, **immigrating**, **immigrated**) come to live permanently in a foreign country.
– DERIVATIVES **immigration** n.
– ORIGIN Latin *immigrare.*

imminent ● adj. about to happen.
– DERIVATIVES **imminence** n.
ORIGIN Latin *imminere* 'overhang'.

immiscible /im-**miss**-i-b'l/ ● adj. (of liquids) not able to be mixed together.

immobile ● adj. **1** not moving. **2** not able to move.
– DERIVATIVES **immobility** n.

immobilize (also **immobilise**) ● v. (**immobilizes**, **immobilizing**, **immobilized**) prevent from moving or operating as normal.
– DERIVATIVES **immobilization** (also **immobilisation**) n.

immoderate ● adj. not sensible or controlled; excessive.

immodest ● adj. not humble or decent.

immolate /im-muh-layt/ ● v. (**immolates**, **immolating**, **immolated**) kill or sacrifice by burning.
– DERIVATIVES **immolation** n.
– ORIGIN Latin *immolare* 'sprinkle with sacrificial meal'.

immoral ● adj. not following accepted standards of morality.
– DERIVATIVES **immorality** n.

immortal ● adj. **1** living forever. **2** deserving to be remembered forever. ● n. **1** an immortal god or other being. **2** a person who will be famous for a very long time.
– DERIVATIVES **immortality** n.

immortalize (also **immortalise**) ● v. (**immortalizes**, **immortalizing**, **immortalized**) make immortal.

immovable ● adj. **1** not able to be moved. **2** unable to be changed or persuaded: *an immovable truth.*
– DERIVATIVES **immovably** adv.

immune ● adj. **1** having a natural resistance to a particular infection. **2** not affected by something: *no one is immune to his charm.* **3** protected from something; exempt.
– ORIGIN Latin *immunis.*

immunity ● n. (pl. **immunities**) **1** the ability of an organism to resist a particular infection. **2** exemption from a duty or punishment.

immunize (also **immunise**) ● v. (**immunizes**, **immunizing**, **immunized**) make immune to infection.
– DERIVATIVES **immunization** (also **immunisation**) n.

immunodeficiency ● n. failure of the body's ability to resist infection.

immunology ● n. the branch of medicine and biology concerned with immunity to infection.
– DERIVATIVES **immunological** adj. **immunologist** n.

immunotherapy ● n. the prevention or treatment of disease with substances that stimulate the body's immune system.

immure /im-myoor/ • v. (**immures**, **immuring**, **immured**) confine or imprison.
– ORIGIN Latin *immurare*.

immutable /im-myoo-tuh-b'l/ • adj. unchanging or unchangeable.

imp • n. **1** a small, mischievous devil or sprite. **2** a mischievous child.
– ORIGIN Old English, 'young shoot'.

impact • n. /im-pakt/ **1** an act of one object hitting another. **2** a noticeable effect or influence: *man's impact on the environment.* • v. /im-pakt/ **1** hit another object. **2** have a strong effect: *the cuts impacted on the service the company provided.* **3** press firmly. **4** (**impacted**) (of a tooth) wedged between another tooth and the jaw.
– ORIGIN Latin *impingere* 'drive something in'.

impair • v. weaken or damage.
– DERIVATIVES **impairment** n.
– ORIGIN Old French *empeirier*.

impala /im-pah-luh/ • n. (pl. **impala**) an antelope of southern and East Africa, with lyre-shaped horns.
– ORIGIN Zulu.

impale • v. (**impales**, **impaling**, **impaled**) pierce with a sharp object.
– DERIVATIVES **impalement** n.
– ORIGIN Latin *impalare*.

impalpable • adj. **1** unable to be felt by touch. **2** not easily understood.

impart • v. **1** communicate (information). **2** give (a quality).
– ORIGIN Latin *impartire* 'give a share of'.

impartial • adj. treating all equally; not biased.
– DERIVATIVES **impartiality** n. **impartially** adv.

impassable • adj. impossible to travel along or over.

impasse /am-pahss/ • n. a situation in which no progress is possible; a deadlock.
– ORIGIN French.

impassioned • adj. filled with or showing great emotion.

impassive • adj. not feeling or showing emotion.
– DERIVATIVES **impassively** adv.

impasto /im-pass-toh/ • n. the technique of laying on paint thickly so that it stands out from the surface of a painting.
– ORIGIN Italian.

impatient • adj. **1** lacking patience or tolerance. **2** restlessly eager: *they are impatient for change.*
– DERIVATIVES **impatience** n. **impatiently** adv.

impeach • v. **1** question the worth of. **2** esp. US charge (the holder of a public office) with misconduct.
– DERIVATIVES **impeachment** n.
– ORIGIN Old French *empecher* 'impede'.

impeccable /im-pek-kuh-b'l/ • adj. without faults or mistakes; perfect.
– DERIVATIVES **impeccably** adv.
– ORIGIN Latin *impeccabilis* 'not liable to sin'.

impecunious /im-pi-kyoo-ni-uhss/ • adj. having little or no money.
– ORIGIN from IN-[1] + Latin *pecuniosus* 'wealthy'.

impedance /im-pee-duhnss/ • n. the total resistance of an electric circuit to the flow of alternating current.

impede /im-peed/ • v. (**impedes**, **impeding**, **impeded**) delay or block the progress or action of: *matters which would impede progress.*
– ORIGIN Latin *impedire* 'shackle the feet of'.

impediment /im-ped-i-muhnt/ • n. **1** a hindrance or obstruction. **2** (also **speech impediment**) a defect in a person's speech, such as a stammer.

impedimenta /im-ped-i-men-tuh/ • pl. n. equipment for an activity or expedition, seen as impeding progress.
– ORIGIN Latin.

impel /im-pel/ • v. (**impels**, **impelling**, **impelled**) drive or urge to do something.
– ORIGIN Latin *impellere*.

impending • adj. be about to happen.
– ORIGIN Latin *impendere* 'overhang'.

impenetrable /im-pen-i-truh-b'l/ • adj. **1** impossible to get through or into. **2** impossible to understand.

impenitent • adj. not feeling shame or regret.

imperative /im-pe-ruh-tiv/ • adj. **1** of vital importance. **2** giving a command. **3** Grammar (of a mood of a verb) expressing a command, as in *come here!* • n. an essential or urgent thing.
– ORIGIN Latin *imperativus* 'specially ordered'.

imperceptible • adj. too slight or gradual to be seen or felt.
– DERIVATIVES **imperceptibly** adv.

imperfect • adj. **1** faulty or incomplete. **2** Grammar (of a tense) referring to a past action in progress but not completed.
– DERIVATIVES **imperfection** n. **imperfectly** adv.

imperial • adj. **1** relating to an empire or an emperor. **2** (of weights and measures) conforming to a non-metric system formerly used in the UK.
– ORIGIN Latin *imperialis*.

imperialism • n. a policy of extending a country's power and influence through means such as establishing colonies or by military force.
– DERIVATIVES **imperialist** n. & adj.

imperil • v. (**imperils**, **imperilling**, **imperilled**; US **imperils**, **imperiling**, **imperiled**) put into danger.

imperious /im-peer-i-uhss/ • adj. expecting to be obeyed without question; domineering.
– ORIGIN Latin *imperiosus*.

impermanent • adj. not permanent.
– DERIVATIVES **impermanence** n.

impermeable /im-per-mi-uh-b'l/ • adj. not allowing fluid to pass through.

impersonal • adj. **1** not influenced by personal feelings. **2** lacking human feelings or atmosphere: *an impersonal tower block.* **3** Grammar (of a verb) used only with *it* as a subject (as in *it is snowing*).
– DERIVATIVES **impersonality** n. **impersonally** adv.

impersonal pronoun • n. the pronoun *it* when not referring to a thing, as in *it was snowing*.

impersonate • v. (**impersonates**, **impersonating**, **impersonated**) pretend to be (another person) to entertain or trick people.
– DERIVATIVES **impersonation** n. **impersonator** n.

impertinent • adj. not showing proper respect; cheeky.
– DERIVATIVES **impertinence** n.

imperturbable /im-per-**ter**-buh-b'l/ ● **adj.** unable to be upset or excited.

impervious /im-**per**-vi-uhss/ ● **adj. 1** not allowing fluid to pass through. **2 (impervious to)** unable to be affected by.

impetigo /im-pi-**ty**-goh/ ● **n.** a contagious skin infection forming spots and yellow crusty sores.
– ORIGIN Latin.

impetuous ● **adj.** acting or done quickly and without thought or care.
– ORIGIN Latin *impetuosus*.

impetus ● **n. 1** the force or energy with which a body moves. **2** a driving force: *the impetus for change*.
– ORIGIN Latin, 'assault, force'.

impinge ● **v. (impinges, impinging, impinged)** have an effect or impact: *parents impinge on our lives*.
– DERIVATIVES **impingement** n.
– ORIGIN Latin *impingere* 'drive something in or at'.

impious /**im**-pi-uhss/ ● **adj.** not showing respect or reverence.

implacable ● **adj. 1** unwilling to stop being hostile towards someone or something: *an implacable enemy*. **2** unstoppable.
– DERIVATIVES **implacably** adv.
– ORIGIN from IN-[1] + Latin *placabilis* 'easily calmed'.

implant ● **v.** /im-**plahnt**/ **1** insert (tissue or an artificial object) into the body. **2** establish (an idea) in the mind. ● **n.** /**im**-plahnt/ a thing implanted.
– DERIVATIVES **implantation** n.

implausible ● **adj.** not seeming reasonable or probable.
– DERIVATIVES **implausibility** n. **implausibly** adv.

implement ● **n.** /**im**-pli-muhnt/ a tool, utensil, or instrument that is used for a particular purpose. ● **v.** /**im**-pli-ment/ put into effect.
– DERIVATIVES **implementation** n.
– ORIGIN Latin *implere* 'fill up, employ'.

implicate ● **v.** /**im**-pli-kayt/ **(implicates, implicating, implicated) 1** show (someone) to be involved in a crime. **2 (be implicated in)** bear some of the responsibility for. **3** imply.
– ORIGIN Latin *implicare* 'involve, imply'.

implication ● **n. 1** the conclusion that can be drawn from something although it is not directly stated. **2** a likely consequence. **3** the state of being involved in something.

implicit /im-**pliss**-it/ ● **adj. 1** suggested though not directly expressed. **2 (implicit in)** found in (something), though not directly expressed. **3** with no doubt or question: *an implicit faith in God*.
– DERIVATIVES **implicitly** adv.
– ORIGIN Latin *implicare* 'involve, imply'.

implode /im-**plohd**/ ● **v. (implodes, imploding, imploded)** collapse violently inwards.
– DERIVATIVES **implosion** n.
– ORIGIN from IN-[2] + Latin *plodere, plaudere* 'to clap'.

implore ● **v. (implores, imploring, implored)** beg earnestly or desperately.
– ORIGIN Latin *implorare* 'invoke with tears'.

imply ● **v. (implies, implying, implied) 1** suggest rather than state directly. **2** suggest as a likely consequence: *the forecast traffic increase implied more pollution*.
– ORIGIN Latin *implicare* 'involve, imply'.

> **USAGE imply**
>
> Do not confuse the words **imply** and **infer**. They can describe the same situation, but from different points of view. If a speaker or writer **implies** something, as in *he implied that the General was a traitor*, it means that the person is suggesting something though not saying it directly. If you **infer** something from what has been said, as in *we inferred from his words that the General was a traitor*, this means that you come to the conclusion that this is what they really mean.

impolite ● **adj.** not having or showing good manners.

impolitic ● **adj.** unwise.

imponderable ● **adj.** difficult or impossible to assess.
– ORIGIN from PONDER.

import ● **v.** /im-**port**/ **1** bring (goods or services) into a country from abroad. **2** Computing transfer (data) into a file or document. ● **n.** /**im**-port/ **1** an imported article or service. **2** the action of importing. **3** the implied meaning of something. **4** importance.
– DERIVATIVES **importation** n. **importer** n.
– ORIGIN Latin *importare*.

important ● **adj. 1** having a great effect or of great value: *important meetings*. **2** (of a person) having great authority or influence.
– DERIVATIVES **importance** n. **importantly** adv.

importunate /im-**por**-tyuu-nuht/ ● **adj.** very persistent.
– ORIGIN Latin *importunus* 'inconvenient'.

importune /im-por-**tyoon**/ ● **v. (importunes, importuning, importuned)** bother with persistent requests.

impose ● **v. (imposes, imposing, imposed) 1** introduce (something) that must be obeyed or done: *they plan to impose a tax on fuel*. **2** force (something) to be accepted. **3 (impose on)** take unfair advantage of (someone).
– ORIGIN French *imposer*.

imposing ● **adj.** grand and impressive.

imposition ● **n. 1** the action of imposing something. **2** something imposed and felt to be unfair.

impossible ● **adj. 1** not able to occur, exist, or be done. **2** very difficult to deal with.
– DERIVATIVES **impossibility** n. (pl. **impossibilities**) **impossibly** adv.

impostor (also **imposter**) ● **n.** a person who pretends to be someone else in order to deceive or cheat others.
– ORIGIN Latin.

imposture ● **n.** an act of pretending to be someone else so as to deceive.

impotent /**im**-puh-tuhnt/ ● **adj. 1** helpless or powerless. **2** (of a man) unable to achieve an erection.
– DERIVATIVES **impotence** n.

impound ● **v. 1** seize and take legal possession of (something). **2** shut up (domestic animals) in an enclosure.

impoverish ● **v. 1** make poor. **2** make worse in quality.
– DERIVATIVES **impoverishment** n.
– ORIGIN Old French *empoverir*.

impracticable ● **adj.** not able to be done in practice: *it was impracticable to widen the road here*.

impractical ● **adj.** not adapted for use or action: *impractical high heels.*

imprecation ● **n.** formal a spoken curse.
– ORIGIN Latin.

imprecise ● **adj.** not exact.
– DERIVATIVES **imprecision** n.

impregnable ● **adj. 1** unable to be captured or broken into. **2** unable to be overcome: *an impregnable half-time lead.*
– ORIGIN Old French *imprenable.*

impregnate /im-preg-nayt/ ● **v.** (**impregnates, impregnating, impregnated**) **1** soak or saturate with a substance. **2** fill with a feeling or quality. **3** make pregnant.
– DERIVATIVES **impregnation** n.
– ORIGIN Latin *impregnare.*

impresario /im-pri-sah-ri-oh/ ● **n.** (pl. **impresarios**) a person who organizes theatrical or musical productions.
– ORIGIN Italian.

impress ● **v. 1** make (someone) feel admiration and respect. **2** make a mark or design on (something) using a stamp or seal. **3** (**impress on**) emphasize (an idea) in the mind of (someone). ● **n.** a mark or impression.
– ORIGIN Old French *empresser* 'press in'.

impression ● **n. 1** an idea, feeling, or opinion. **2** an effect produced on someone: *her courtesy made a good impression.* **3** an imitation of a person or thing, done to entertain. **4** a mark made by pressing on a surface.

impressionable ● **adj.** easily influenced.

Impressionism ● **n.** a style of painting concerned with showing the visual impression of a particular moment, especially the shifting effects of light.
– DERIVATIVES **Impressionist** n. & adj.

impressionist ● **n.** an entertainer who impersonates famous people.

impressionistic ● **adj.** based on personal impressions.

impressive ● **adj.** arousing admiration through size, quality, or skill.
– DERIVATIVES **impressively** adv. **impressiveness** n.

imprimatur/im-pri-mah-ter/ ● **n. 1** authority or approval. **2** an official licence issued by the Roman Catholic Church to print a religious book.
– ORIGIN Latin, 'let it be printed'.

imprint ● **v.** /im-**print**/ **1** make (a mark) on an object by pressure. **2** have an effect on. ● **n.** /**im**-print/ **1** a mark made by pressure. **2** a printer's or publisher's name and other details in a publication.
– ORIGIN Latin *imprimere.*

imprison ● **v.** put or keep in prison.
– DERIVATIVES **imprisonment** n.

improbable ● **adj.** not likely to be true or to happen.
– DERIVATIVES **improbability** n. **improbably** adv.

impromptu /im-promp-tyoo/ ● **adj. & adv.** done without being planned or rehearsed.
– ORIGIN from Latin *in promptu* 'in readiness'.

improper ● **adj. 1** not in accordance with accepted standards of behaviour. **2** not modest or decent.

improper fraction ● **n.** a fraction in which the numerator is greater than the denominator, such as ⁵⁄₄.

impropriety /im-pruh-pry-uh-ti/ ● **n.** (pl. **improprieties**) improper behaviour.

improve ● **v.** (**improves, improving, improved**) **1** make or become better. **2** (**improve on/upon**) produce something better than.
– DERIVATIVES **improver** n.
– ORIGIN Old French *emprower.*

improvement ● **n. 1** the action of improving or the state of being improved: *there's still room for improvement.* **2** a thing that makes something better or is better than something else.

improvident ● **adj.** not providing for future needs.

improvise ● **v.** (**improvises, improvising, improvised**) **1** invent and perform (music, drama, or poetry) on the spur of the moment. **2** make from whatever is available.
– DERIVATIVES **improvisation** n.
– ORIGIN Latin *improvisus* 'unforeseen'.

imprudent ● **adj.** not showing care for the results of an action; rash.

impudent /im-pyuu-duhnt/ ● **adj.** not showing proper respect for another person; cheeky.
– DERIVATIVES **impudence** n. **impudently** adv.
– ORIGIN Latin *impudens* 'shameless'.

impugn /im-pyoon/ ● **v.** express doubts about the truth or honesty of.
– ORIGIN Latin *impugnare* 'attack'.

impulse ● **n. 1** a sudden urge to act, without thought for the results. **2** a driving force: *the impulse for the book came from personal experience.* **3** a pulse of electrical energy.
– ORIGIN Latin *impulsus* 'a push'.

impulsion ● **n. 1** an urge to do something. **2** a driving force.

impulsive ● **adj.** acting or done without thinking ahead.
– DERIVATIVES **impulsively** adv.

impunity /im-pyoo-ni-ti/ ● **n.** freedom from punishment or harm: *rebels crossed the border with impunity.*
– ORIGIN Latin *impunitas.*

impure ● **adj. 1** mixed with unwanted substances: *impure coal.* **2** morally wrong.

impurity ● **n.** (pl. **impurities**) **1** the state of being impure. **2** a thing which spoils the purity of something.

impute /im-pyoot/ ● **v.** (**imputes, imputing, imputed**) believe that (something) has been done or caused by someone or something: *madness among the troops was imputed to shell shock.*
– DERIVATIVES **imputation** n.
– ORIGIN Latin *imputare* 'enter in the account'.

in ● **prep. 1** so as to be enclosed, surrounded, or inside. **2** expressing a period of time during which an event takes place. **3** expressing the length of time before an event is to take place. **4** expressing a state or quality: *he's in love.* **5** so as to be included or involved. **6** indicating the means of expression used: *put it in writing.* **7** expressing a value as a proportion of (a whole). ● **adv. 1** expressing the state of being enclosed, surrounded, or inside: *we were locked in.* **2** present at one's home or office. **3** expressing arrival. **4** (of the tide) rising or at its highest level. ● **adj.** informal fashionable.
– PHRASES **be in for** be going to experience. **in that** for the reason that. **the ins and outs** informal all the details.

– ORIGIN Old English.

in. ● abbrev. inch(es).

in-[1] ● prefix **1** not: *infertile.* **2** without; a lack of: *inappreciation.*
– ORIGIN Latin.

in-[2] ● prefix in; into; towards: *influx.*
– ORIGIN from **IN** or Latin *in.*

inability ● n. the state of being unable to do something.

in absentia /in ab-sen-ti-uh/ ● adv. while not present: *the suspects will be tried in absentia.*
– ORIGIN Latin, 'in absence'.

inaccessible ● adj. **1** unable to be reached or used. **2** difficult to understand or appreciate.

inaccurate ● adj. not accurate.
– DERIVATIVES **inaccuracy** n. **inaccurately** adv.

inaction ● n. lack of action where some is expected or appropriate.

inactive ● adj. not active or working.
– DERIVATIVES **inactivity** n.

inadequate ● adj. **1** not enough or not good enough. **2** unable to deal with a situation or with life.
– DERIVATIVES **inadequacy** n. (pl. **inadequacies**).

inadmissible ● adj. (of evidence in court) not accepted as valid.

inadvertent ● adj. not deliberate; unintentional.
– DERIVATIVES **inadvertently** adv.
– ORIGIN from **IN-**[1] + Latin *advertere* 'turn the mind to'.

inadvisable ● adj. likely to have unfortunate results; unwise.

inalienable ● adj. unable to be taken away or given away: *inalienable rights.*

inamorato /i-nam-uh-rah-toh/ ● n. (pl. **inamoratos**; fem. **inamorata**, pl. **inamoratas**) a person's lover.
– ORIGIN Italian.

inane ● adj. lacking sense; silly.
– DERIVATIVES **inanity** n. (pl **inanities**).
– ORIGIN Latin *inanis* 'empty, vain'.

inanimate ● adj. **1** not alive. **2** showing no sign of life.

inapplicable ● adj. not relevant or appropriate.

inappropriate ● adj. not suitable or appropriate.
– DERIVATIVES **inappropriately** adv.

inarticulate /in-ar-tik-yuu-luht/ ● adj. **1** unable to express one's ideas clearly. **2** not expressed in words: *inarticulate cries.*

inasmuch ● adv. (**inasmuch as**) **1** to the extent that. **2** considering that; since.

inattentive ● adj. not paying attention.
– DERIVATIVES **inattention** n.

inaudible ● adj. unable to be heard.

inaugural /in-aw-gyuu-ruhl/ ● adj. marking the beginning of an organization or period of office.

inaugurate /in-aw-gyuu-rayt/ ● v. (**inaugurates**, **inaugurating**, **inaugurated**) **1** begin or introduce (a system, project, etc.). **2** establish (someone) in office with a special ceremony. **3** mark the opening or introduction of (a building, service, etc) with a ceremony.
– DERIVATIVES **inauguration** n.
– ORIGIN Latin *inauguratus* 'consecrated after interpreting omens'.

inauspicious ● adj. not likely to lead to success.

inauthentic ● n. not genuine or sincere.

inboard ● adv. & adj. within or towards the centre of a ship, aircraft, or vehicle.

inborn ● adj. existing from birth.

inbound ● adj. & adv. travelling back to an original point of departure.

inbred ● adj. **1** produced by breeding from closely related individuals. **2** existing from birth; inborn.

inbreeding ● n. breeding from closely related people or animals.

inbuilt ● adj. present as an original or vital part.

Inc. ● abbrev. N. Amer. Incorporated.

Inca ● n. a member of a South American Indian people living in the central Andes before the Spanish conquest in the early 1530s.
– ORIGIN from an American Indian word meaning 'lord, royal person'.

incalculable ● adj. **1** too great to be calculated or estimated: *an archive of incalculable value.* **2** not able to be calculated or estimated.

in camera ● adv. see **CAMERA**.

incandescent /in-kan-dess-uhnt/ ● adj. **1** glowing as a result of being heated. **2** (of an electric light) containing a filament which glows white-hot when heated by an electric current.
– DERIVATIVES **incandescence** n.
– ORIGIN Latin *incandescere* 'glow'.

incantation ● n. words said as a magic spell or charm.
– DERIVATIVES **incantatory** adj.
– ORIGIN Latin *incantare* 'chant'.

incapable ● adj. **1** (**incapable of**) lacking the ability or required quality to do. **2** not in full possession of one's faculties.

incapacitate /in-kuh-pa-si-tayt/ ● v. (**incapacitates**, **incapacitating**, **incapacitated**) prevent from functioning in a normal way.
– DERIVATIVES **incapacitation** n.

incapacity ● n. (pl. **incapacities**) inability to do something.

incarcerate /in-kar-suh-rayt/ ● v. (**incarcerates**, **incarcerating**, **incarcerated**) imprison.
– DERIVATIVES **incarceration** n.
– ORIGIN Latin *incarcerare.*

incarnate ● adj. /in-kar-nuht/ **1** (of a god or spirit) in human form. **2** in physical form: *she was beauty incarnate.* ● v. /**in**-kar-nayt/ be the living embodiment of (a quality).
– ORIGIN Latin *incarnare* 'make flesh'.

incarnation ● n. **1** a living embodiment of a god, spirit, or quality. **2** (**the Incarnation**) (in Christian belief) the embodiment of God the Son in human flesh as Jesus Christ.

incautious ● adj. not concerned about possible problems.

incendiary /in-sen-di-uh-ri/ ● adj. **1** (of a bomb) designed to cause fires. **2** tending to stir up conflict. ● n. (pl. **incendiaries**) an incendiary bomb.
– ORIGIN Latin *incendiarius.*

incense[1] /in-senss/ ● n. a gum or other substance that is burned for the sweet smell it produces.
– ORIGIN Latin *incensum.*

incense² /in-senss/ ● v. (**incenses, incensing, incensed**) make very angry.
– ORIGIN Latin *incendere* 'set fire to'.

incentive ● n. a thing that influences or encourages someone to do something.
– ORIGIN Latin *incentivum* 'something that incites'.

inception ● n. the beginning of an organization or activity.
– ORIGIN Latin.

incessant ● adj. never stopping.
– DERIVATIVES **incessantly** adv.
– ORIGIN Latin.

incest ● n. sexual intercourse between people who are too closely related to marry each other.
– ORIGIN Latin *incestus*.

incestuous /in-sess-tyoo-uhss/ ● adj. **1** involving incest. **2** excessively close and wishing to keep out outside influence: *a small, incestuous legal community.*

inch ● n. **1** a unit of length equal to one twelfth of a foot (2.54 cm). **2** a quantity of rainfall that would cover a surface to a depth of one inch. **3** a very small amount or distance: *don't move an inch.* ● v. move along slowly and carefully.
– ORIGIN Latin *uncia* 'twelfth part'.

inchoate /in-koh-uht/ ● adj. just begun and so not fully formed or developed.
– ORIGIN Latin *inchoatus*.

incidence ● n. **1** the occurrence, rate, or frequency of something: *an increased incidence of cancer.* **2** Physics the meeting of a line or ray with a surface.

incident ● n. **1** an event. **2** a violent event, such as an attack. **3** the occurrence of dangerous or exciting events: *the plane landed without incident.* ● adj. **1** (**incident to**) resulting from. **2** (of light or other radiation) falling on a surface.
– ORIGIN Latin *incidere* 'happen to'.

incidental ● adj. **1** occurring in connection with or as a result of something else. **2** occurring as a minor result: *incidental expenses.*

incidentally ● adv. **1** by the way. **2** in an incidental way.

incidental music ● n. music used in a film or play as a background.

incinerate /in-sin-uh-rayt/ ● v. (**incinerates, incinerating, incinerated**) destroy by burning.
– DERIVATIVES **incineration** n.
– ORIGIN Latin *incinerare* 'burn to ashes'.

incinerator ● n. a device for incinerating rubbish.

incipient /in-sip-i-uhnt/ ● adj. beginning to happen or develop.
– ORIGIN Latin *incipere* 'begin'.

incise ● v. (**incises, incising, incised**) **1** make a cut or cuts in (a surface). **2** cut (a mark) into a surface.
– ORIGIN Latin *incidere*.

incision ● n. **1** a cut made as part of a surgical operation. **2** the action of cutting into something.

incisive ● adj. **1** showing clear thought and good understanding: *incisive criticism.* **2** quick and direct.

incisor ● n. a narrow-edged tooth at the front of the mouth.

incite ● v. (**incites, inciting, incited**) **1** stir up (violent or unlawful behaviour). **2** urge (someone) to act in a violent or unlawful way.
– DERIVATIVES **incitement** n.
– ORIGIN Latin *incitare*.

incivility ● n. rude speech or behaviour.

inclement /in-klem-uhnt/ ● adj. (of the weather) unpleasantly cold or wet.
– DERIVATIVES **inclemency** n.

inclination ● n. **1** a natural tendency to act or feel in a particular way: *John was a scientist by inclination.* **2** (**inclination for/to/towards**) an interest in or liking for. **3** a slope or slant. **4** the angle at which a straight line or plane slopes away from another.

incline ● v. /in-klyn/ (**inclines, inclining, inclined**) **1** (**be inclined to/to do**) tend or be willing to do or think. **2** (**be inclined**) have a particular tendency or talent: *Sam was mathematically inclined.* **3** lean or slope. **4** bend (one's head) forwards and downwards. ● n. /**in**-klyn/ a slope.
– ORIGIN Latin *inclinare*.

inclined plane ● n. a plane inclined at an angle to the horizontal, used as a means of reducing the force needed to raise a load.

include ● v. (**includes, including, included**) **1** have or contain as part of a whole: *the price includes bed and breakfast.* **2** make or treat as part of a whole.
– ORIGIN Latin *includere* 'shut in'.

including ● prep. containing as part of the whole in question.

inclusion ● n. **1** the action of including or the state of being included. **2** a person or thing that is included.

inclusive ● adj. **1** including everything expected or required. **2** (after a noun) between the limits stated: *the ages of 55 to 59 inclusive.*

incognito /in-kog-nee-toh/ ● adj. & adv. having one's true identity concealed.
– ORIGIN Italian, 'unknown'.

incoherent ● adj. **1** hard to understand; unclear. **2** not logical or well-organized.
– DERIVATIVES **incoherence** n. **incoherently** adv.

income ● n. money received during a certain period for work or from investments.

incomer ● n. esp. Brit. a person who has come to live in an area in which they have not grown up.

income support ● n. (in the UK and Canada) payment made by the state to people on a low income.

income tax ● n. tax that must be paid on personal income.

incoming ● adj. **1** coming in. **2** coming into office to replace another person.

incommensurable /in-kuh-men-shuh-ruh-b'l/ ● adj. not able to be judged or measured by the same standards.

incommensurate /in-kuh-men-shuh-ruht/ ● adj. (**incommensurate with**) not in keeping or in proportion with.

incommode ● v. (**incommodes, incommoding, incommoded**) formal cause inconvenience to.
– ORIGIN Latin *incommodare*.

incommunicado /in-kuh-myoo-ni-kah-doh/ ● adj. & adv. not allowed to communicate with other people.
– ORIGIN Spanish *incomunicado*.

incomparable /in-kom-puh-ruh-b'l/ ● adj. so

good that nothing can be compared to it: *the incomparable beauty of Venice.*

incompatible ● **adj.** **1** (of two things) not able to exist or be used together. **2** (of two people) unable to live or work together without disagreeing.
– DERIVATIVES **incompatibility** n.

incompetent ● **adj.** not skilful enough to do something successfully.
– DERIVATIVES **incompetence** n.

incomplete ● **adj.** not complete.

incomprehensible ● **adj.** not able to be understood.
– DERIVATIVES **incomprehension** n.

inconceivable ● **adj.** not able to be imagined or grasped mentally.
– DERIVATIVES **inconceivably** adv.

inconclusive ● **adj.** not leading to a firm conclusion.

incongruous /in-kong-groo-uhss/ ● **adj.** out of place.
– DERIVATIVES **incongruity** n. (pl. **incongruities**) **incongruously** adv.
– ORIGIN from **IN-**[1] + Latin *congruus* 'in agreement'.

inconsequential ● **adj.** not important.

inconsiderable ● **adj.** small in size, amount, etc.: *a not inconsiderable number.*

inconsiderate ● **adj.** thoughtlessly causing hurt or trouble to others.

inconsistent ● **adj.** **1** having contradictory elements. **2** (**inconsistent with**) not in keeping with.
– DERIVATIVES **inconsistency** n.

inconsolable ● **adj.** not able to be comforted.

inconspicuous ● **adj.** not noticeable.

inconstant ● **adj.** frequently changing.

incontestable ● **adj.** not able to be disputed.

incontinent ● **adj.** **1** unable to control the excretion of one's urine or faeces. **2** lacking self-restraint, uncontrolled.
– DERIVATIVES **incontinence** n.

incontrovertible ● **adj.** not able to be denied or disputed.

inconvenience ● **n.** slight trouble or difficulty. ● **v.** (**inconveniences**, **inconveniencing**, **inconvenienced**) cause inconvenience to.
– DERIVATIVES **inconvenient** adj.

incorporate ● **v.** (**incorporates**, **incorporating**, **incorporated**) include as part of a whole.
– DERIVATIVES **incorporation** n.
– ORIGIN Latin *incorporare* 'embody'.

incorporated ● **adj.** (of a company) formed into a legal corporation.

incorporeal /in-kor-por-i-uhl/ ● **adj.** without a physical body or form.

incorrect ● **adj.** not true, accurate, or following accepted standards; wrong.
– DERIVATIVES **incorrectly** adv. **incorrectness** n.

incorrigible ● **adj.** having bad habits that cannot be changed: *an incorrigible liar.*
– ORIGIN Latin *incorrigibilis.*

incorruptible ● **adj.** **1** too honest to be corrupted by taking bribes. **2** not prone to death or decay.

increase ● **v.** /in-kreess/ (**increases**, **increasing**, **increased**) make or become greater in size, amount, or intensity. ● **n.** /in-kreess/ a rise in amount, size, or intensity.
– ORIGIN Latin *increscere.*

increasingly ● **adv.** more and more.

incredible ● **adj.** **1** impossible or hard to believe. **2** informal extremely good.
– DERIVATIVES **incredibly** adv.

incredulity /in-kri-dyoo-li-ti/ ● **n.** the state of being unwilling or unable to believe something.

incredulous ● **adj.** unwilling or unable to believe something.

increment /ing-kri-muhnt/ ● **n.** an increase in a number or an amount: *salary increments.*
– DERIVATIVES **incremental** adj.
– ORIGIN Latin *incrementum.*

incriminate /in-krim-i-nayt/ ● **v.** (**incriminates**, **incriminating**, **incriminated**) make (someone) appear guilty of a crime or wrongdoing.
– DERIVATIVES **incrimination** n.
– ORIGIN Latin *incriminare* 'accuse'.

incubate /ing-kyuu-bayt/ ● **v.** (**incubates**, **incubating**, **incubated**) **1** (of a bird) sit on (eggs) to keep them warm and hatch them. **2** keep (bacteria, cells, etc.) at a suitable temperature so that they develop. **3** (of an infectious disease) develop slowly without obvious signs.
– DERIVATIVES **incubation** n.
– ORIGIN Latin *incubare* 'lie on'.

incubator ● **n.** **1** an apparatus used to hatch eggs or grow micro-organisms. **2** a heated enclosed apparatus in which premature babies can be cared for.

incubus /ing-kyuu-buhss/ ● **n.** (pl. **incubi** /ing-kyuu-by/) a male demon believed to have sexual intercourse with sleeping women.
– ORIGIN Latin *incubo* 'nightmare'.

inculcate /in-kul-kayt/ ● **v.** (**inculcates**, **inculcating**, **inculcated**) fix (an idea or habit) in someone's mind by repetition.
– DERIVATIVES **inculcation** n.
– ORIGIN Latin *inculcare* 'press in'.

incumbency ● **n.** (pl. **incumbencies**) the period during which a person is in office.

incumbent /in-kum-buhnt/ ● **adj.** **1** (**incumbent on/upon**) necessary for (someone) as a duty. **2** currently holding office: *the incumbent President.* ● **n.** the holder of an office or post.
– ORIGIN Latin *incumbere* 'lie or lean on'

incur /in-ker/ ● **v.** (**incurs**, **incurring**, **incurred**) bring (something unwelcome) upon oneself: *he incurred the crowd's anger.*
– ORIGIN Latin *incurrere* 'run into'.

incurable ● **adj.** not able to be cured.
– DERIVATIVES **incurably** adv.

incurious ● **adj.** not eager to know something.

incursion ● **n.** a sudden or brief invasion or attack.
– ORIGIN Latin.

indebted ● **adj.** **1** grateful. **2** owing money.

indecent ● **adj.** **1** causing offence, especially because involving sex. **2** not appropriate.
– DERIVATIVES **indecency** n. **indecently** adv.

indecent assault ● **n.** sexual assault that does not involve rape.

indecent exposure ● **n.** the crime of deliberately showing one's genitals in public.

indecipherable /in-di-sy-fuh-ruh-b'l/ ● **adj.** not able to be read or understood.

indecisive ● **adj. 1** not able to make decisions quickly. **2** not settling an issue: *an indecisive battle.*
– DERIVATIVES **indecision** n. **indecisively** adv. **indecisiveness** n.

indeed ● **adv. 1** used to emphasize a statement or answer: *this is praise indeed.* **2** used to introduce a further and stronger point.

indefatigable /in-di-fat-i-guh-b'l/ ● **adj.** never tiring or stopping.
– ORIGIN Latin *indefatigabilis.*

indefensible ● **adj.** not able to be justified or defended: *apartheid was morally indefensible.*

indefinable ● **adj.** not able to be defined or described exactly.

indefinite ● **adj. 1** not clearly expressed or defined; vague. **2** lasting for an unknown or unstated length of time.
– DERIVATIVES **indefinitely** adv.

indefinite article ● **n.** Grammar the word *a* or *an.*

indelible /in-del-i-b'l/ ● **adj. 1** (of ink or a mark) unable to be removed. **2** unable to be forgotten.
– DERIVATIVES **indelibly** adv.
– ORIGIN Latin *indelebilis.*

indelicate ● **adj. 1** lacking sensitive understanding. **2** slightly indecent.

indemnify /in-dem-ni-fy/ ● **v.** (**indemnifies, indemnifying, indemnified**) **1** pay money to (someone) for harm or loss. **2** protect or insure (someone) against legal responsibility for their actions.

indemnity /in-dem-ni-ti/ ● **n.** (pl. **indemnities**) **1** insurance against or protection from legal responsibility for one's actions. **2** a sum of money paid to compensate for damage or loss.
– ORIGIN Latin *indemnitas.*

indent ● **v.** /in-dent/ **1** form hollows, dents or notches in. **2** begin (a line of writing) further from the margin than the other lines. **3** make a written order for something. ● **n.** /in-dent/ Brit. an official order for goods.
– ORIGIN Latin *indentare.*

indentation ● **n. 1** the action of indenting. **2** a hollow or notch.

indenture /in-den-cher/ ● **n.** a formal agreement or contract, such as one formerly binding an apprentice to work for a master.

independence ● **n.** the state of being independent.

independent ● **adj. 1** free from outside control or influence: *you should take independent advice.* **2** (of a country) self-governing. **3** having or earning enough money to support oneself. **4** not connected with another; separate. **5** (of broadcasting, a school, etc.) not supported by public funds. ● **n.** an independent person or organization.
– DERIVATIVES **independently** adv.

in-depth ● **adj.** thorough and detailed.

indescribable ● **adj.** too extreme or vague to be described.
– DERIVATIVES **indescribably** adv.

indestructible ● **adj.** not able to be destroyed.

indeterminate /in-di-ter-mi-nuht/ ● **adj.** not exactly known or defined: *a woman of indeterminate age.*

index /in-deks/ ● **n.** (pl. **indexes** or in technical use **indices** /in-di-seez/) **1** an alphabetical list of names, subjects, etc., with references to the places in a book where they occur. **2** an alphabetical list or catalogue of books or documents. **3** a sign or measure of something. **4** a number indicating the relative level of prices, wages, etc. compared with that at a previous date: *a price index.* **5** Math. an exponent. ● **v.** record in or provide with an index.
– DERIVATIVES **indexation** n. **indexer** n.
– ORIGIN Latin, 'forefinger, sign'.

index finger ● **n.** the forefinger.

index-linked ● **adj.** Brit. (of wages, pensions, etc.) adjusted according to rises or falls in the retail price index.

India E
a country in southern Asia occupying the greater part of the Indian subcontinent; capital, New Delhi.

Indian ● **n. 1** a person from India. **2** an American Indian. ● **adj. 1** relating to India. **2** relating to American Indians.

USAGE Indian
Do not use **Indian** or **Red Indian** to talk about American native peoples, as these terms are now outdated; use **American Indian** instead.

Indiana E
/in-di-an-uh/ a state in the Middle West of the US; capital, Indianapolis.
– DERIVATIVES **Indianan** n. & adj.

Indianapolis E
/in-di-uh-nap-uh-liss/ the state capital of Indiana. It is the site of an annual motor race, known as the Indy 500.

Indian file ● **n.** single file.

Indian ink ● **n.** deep black ink used in drawing.

Indian Mutiny E
a revolt of Indians against British rule, 1857–8. It was followed by the establishment of direct rule by the British Crown in place of the East India Company administration.

Indian Ocean E
the ocean to the south of India, extending from the east coast of Africa to the East Indies and Australia.

Indian subcontinent E
the part of Asia south of the Himalayas which forms a peninsula extending into the Indian Ocean. The region is divided between India, Pakistan, and Bangladesh.

Indian summer ● **n.** a period of dry, warm weather in late autumn.

India rubber ● **n.** natural rubber.

indicate ● **v.** (**indicates, indicating, indicated**) **1** point out; show. **2** be a sign of. **3** give a reading of (a measurement). **4** state briefly. **5** (**be indicated**) be necessary or recommended: *in certain cases, surgery may be indicated.*
– DERIVATIVES **indication** n.
– ORIGIN Latin *indicare.*

indicative /in-dik-uh-tiv/ ● **adj. 1** acting as a sign: *he thought eyes highly indicative of char-*

acter. **2** Grammar (of a form of a verb) expressing a simple statement of fact (e.g. *she left*).

indicator ● **n. 1** a thing that indicates a state or level. **2** a device that gives particular information: *a speed indicator.* **3** a flashing light on a vehicle to show that it is about to change lanes or turn. **4** a chemical compound which changes colour at a specific pH value or in the presence of a particular substance.

indices pl. of **INDEX**.

indict /in-**dyt**/ ● **v.** formally accuse or charge (someone) with a serious crime.
– DERIVATIVES **indictable** adj.
– ORIGIN Latin *indicere* 'proclaim'.

indictment /in-**dyt**-muhnt/ ● **n. 1** a formal charge or accusation of a serious crime. **2** an indication that something is bad and deserves to be condemned: *rising crime is an indictment of our society.*

indifferent ● **adj. 1** having no interest or sympathy. **2** not very good.
– DERIVATIVES **indifference** n. **indifferently** adv.

indigenous /in-**dij**-i-nuhss/ ● **adj.** originating or occurring naturally in a place; native.
– ORIGIN Latin *indigena* 'a native'.

indigent /**in**-di-juhnt/ ● **adj.** very poor.
– ORIGIN Latin, 'lacking'.

indigestible ● **adj.** difficult or impossible to digest.

indigestion ● **n.** pain or discomfort in the stomach caused by difficulty in digesting food.

indignant ● **adj.** feeling or showing indignation.
– DERIVATIVES **indignantly** adv.
– ORIGIN Latin, 'regarding as unworthy'.

indignation ● **n.** annoyance caused by what is seen as unfair treatment.

indignity ● **n.** (pl. **indignities**) treatment that causes one to feel ashamed or embarrassed.

indigo /**in**-di-goh/ ● **n.** a dark blue colour or dye.
– ORIGIN Greek *indikos* 'Indian'.

indirect ● **adj. 1** not direct. **2** (of taxation) charged on goods and services rather than income or profits.
– DERIVATIVES **indirectly** adv.

indirect object ● **n.** a person or thing that is affected by the action of a transitive verb but is not the main object (e.g. *him* in *give him the book*).

indirect question ● **n.** Grammar a question in reported speech (e.g. *they asked who I was*).

indirect speech ● **n.** = **REPORTED SPEECH**.

indiscipline ● **n.** lack of discipline.

indiscreet ● **adj.** too ready to reveal things that should remain private.

indiscretion ● **n. 1** indiscreet behaviour. **2** an indiscreet act or remark.

indiscriminate /in-diss-**krim**-i-nuht/ ● **adj.** done or acting without careful judgement.
– DERIVATIVES **indiscriminately** adv.

indispensable ● **adj.** absolutely necessary.

indisposed ● **adj. 1** slightly unwell. **2** unwilling.

indisposition ● **n.** a slight illness.

indisputable ● **adj.** unable to be challenged or denied.
– DERIVATIVES **indisputably** adv.

indissoluble /in-dis-**sol**-yuu-b'l/ ● **adj.** unable to be destroyed; lasting.

indistinct ● **adj.** not clear or sharply defined.
– DERIVATIVES **indistinctly** adv.

indistinguishable ● **adj.** not able to be identified as different or distinct.

indium /**in**-di-uhm/ ● **n.** a soft, silvery-white metallic chemical element, used in some alloys and semiconductor devices.
– ORIGIN from **INDIGO**.

individual ● **adj. 1** single; separate. **2** having to do with one particular person: *the individual needs of the children.* **3** striking or unusual; original. ● **n. 1** a single person or item as distinct from a group. **2** a distinctive or original person.
– DERIVATIVES **individually** adv.
– ORIGIN from Latin *in-* 'not' + *dividere* 'to divide'.

individualism ● **n. 1** the quality of being independent and original. **2** the belief that individual people should have freedom of action rather than be controlled by the state.
– DERIVATIVES **individualist** n. & adj. **individualistic** adj.

individuality ● **n.** the quality or character of a person or thing that makes them different from others.

individualize (also **individualise**) ● **v.** (**individualizes**, **individualizing**, **individualized**) make (something) different to suit the needs of an individual person.

indivisible ● **adj. 1** unable to be divided or separated. **2** (of a number) unable to be divided by another number exactly without leaving a remainder.

Indo-China E
the peninsula of SE Asia containing Burma (Myanmar), Thailand, Malaya, Laos, Cambodia, and Vietnam.

indoctrinate /in-**dok**-tri-nayt/ ● **v.** (**indoctrinates**, **indoctrinating**, **indoctrinated**) make (someone) accept a set of beliefs without considering any alternatives.
– DERIVATIVES **indoctrination** n.
– ORIGIN from **DOCTRINE**.

Indo-European ● **adj.** relating to the family of languages spoken over most of Europe and Asia as far as northern India.

indolent /**in**-duh-luhnt/ ● **adj.** lazy.
– DERIVATIVES **indolence** n.
– ORIGIN Latin, 'not giving pain'.

indomitable /in-**dom**-i-tuh-b'l/ ● **adj.** impossible to defeat or subdue.
– ORIGIN Latin *indomitabilis* 'unable to be tamed'.

Indonesia E
/in-duh-**nee**-zi-uh, in-duh-**nee**-*zh*uh/ a SE Asian country consisting of many islands in the Malay Archipelago, of which the largest are Java, Sumatra, southern Borneo, western New Guinea, the Moluccas, and Sulawesi; capital, Djakarta (on Java). Former name (until 1949) **DUTCH EAST INDIES**.
– DERIVATIVES **Indonesian** adj. & n.

indoor ● **adj.** situated, done, or used inside a building or under cover. ● **adv.** (**indoors**) into or inside a building.

indubitable /in-**dyoo**-bi-tuh-b'l/ ● **adj.** impossible to doubt; unquestionable.
– DERIVATIVES **indubitably** adv.
– ORIGIN Latin *indubitabilis.*

induce /in-dyooss/ ● **v.** (**induces**, **inducing**, **induced**) **1** persuade or influence (someone) to do something. **2** bring about or cause: *herbs to induce sleep.* **3** bring on (labour in childbirth) by drugs or other artificial means.
– DERIVATIVES **inducer** n. **inducible** adj.
– ORIGIN Latin *inducere* 'lead in'.

inducement ● **n. 1** a thing that persuades someone to do something. **2** a bribe.

induct ● **v.** introduce (someone) formally to a post or organization.
– ORIGIN Latin *inducere* 'lead in'.

inductance ● **n.** Physics the property of an electric conductor or circuit that causes an electromotive force to be generated by a change in the current flowing.

induction ● **n. 1** the action of introducing someone to a post or organization. **2** the action of inducing something. **3** a method of reasoning in which a general rule or conclusion is drawn from particular facts or examples. **4** the production of an electric or magnetic state in an object by bringing an electrified or magnetized object close to but not touching it.

inductive ● **adj. 1** using induction to draw general conclusions from particular instances. **2** relating to electric or magnetic induction.

inductor ● **n.** a component of an electrical circuit which possesses inductance.

indulge ● **v.** (**indulges**, **indulging**, **indulged**) **1** (**indulge in**) allow oneself to enjoy the pleasure of. **2** satisfy (a desire or interest). **3** allow (someone) to do or have whatever they wish.
– ORIGIN Latin *indulgere.*

indulgence ● **n. 1** the action of indulging in something. **2** a thing that is indulged in; a luxury. **3** willingness to tolerate another's faults. **4** esp. hist. (in the Roman Catholic Church) the setting aside or cancellation by the Pope of the punishment still due for sins after formal forgiveness.

indulgent ● **adj.** readily allowing someone to do or have whatever they want or overlooking their faults.
– DERIVATIVES **indulgently** adv.

Indus E
/in-duhss/ a river of southern Asia, flowing from Tibet through Kashmir and Pakistan to the Arabian Sea.

industrial ● **adj.** having to do with industry.
– DERIVATIVES **industrially** adv.

industrial action ● **n.** Brit. a strike or other action taken by employees as a protest.

industrial estate ● **n.** esp. Brit. an area of land developed as a site for factories and other industrial use.

industrialism ● **n.** a social system in which industry forms the basis of the economy.

industrialist ● **n.** a person who owns or controls a manufacturing business.

industrialize (also **industrialise**) ● **v.** (**industrializes**, **industrializing**, **industrialized**) develop industries in (a country or region) on a wide scale.
– DERIVATIVES **industrialization** (also **industrialisation**) n.

industrial relations ● **pl. n.** the relations between management and workers.

Industrial Revolution E
the rapid development of industry that occurred in Britain in the late 18th and 19th centuries, brought about by the introduction of machinery.

industrious ● **adj.** hard-working.
– DERIVATIVES **industriously** adv.

industry ● **n.** (pl. **industries**) **1** the manufacture of goods in factories. **2** a branch of economic or commercial activity: *the tourist industry.* **3** hard work.
– ORIGIN Latin *industria.*

-ine ● **suffix 1** (forming adjectives) relating to; resembling: *canine* | *crystalline.* **2** forming feminine or abstract nouns: *heroine.* **3** Chem. forming names of alkaloids, amino acids, and other substances: *cocaine.*

inebriate /i-nee-bri-ayt/ ● **v.** (**inebriates**, **inebriating**, **inebriated**) make drunk.
– DERIVATIVES **inebriation** n.
– ORIGIN Latin *inebriare.*

inedible ● **adj.** not fit for eating.

ineducable /in-ed-yuu-kuh-b'l/ ● **adj.** considered incapable of being educated.

ineffable /in-ef-fuh-b'l/ ● **adj.** too great or extreme to be expressed in words: *the ineffable beauty of the Everglades.*
– ORIGIN Latin *ineffabilis.*

ineffective ● **adj.** not producing any or the desired effect.

ineffectual ● **adj. 1** ineffective. **2** lacking the required forcefulness to achieve something.
– DERIVATIVES **ineffectually** adv.

inefficient ● **adj.** failing to make the best use of time or resources.
– DERIVATIVES **inefficiency** n.

inelegant ● **adj.** not elegant or graceful.
– DERIVATIVES **inelegance** n.

ineligible ● **adj.** not eligible for a post or benefit.

ineluctable /in-i-luk-tuh-b'l/ ● **adj.** unable to be resisted or avoided.
– ORIGIN Latin *ineluctabilis.*

inept ● **adj.** lacking skill.
– DERIVATIVES **ineptitude** n.
– ORIGIN Latin *ineptus* 'unsuitable'.

inequality ● **n.** (pl. **inequalities**) lack of equality.

inequitable ● **adj.** unfair; unjust.

inequity ● **n.** (pl. **inequities**) lack of fairness or justice.

ineradicable /in-i-rad-i-kuh-b'l/ ● **adj.** unable to be destroyed or removed.

inert ● **adj. 1** lacking the ability or strength to move or act. **2** without active chemical properties: *an inert gas.*
– ORIGIN Latin *iners* 'unskilled, inactive'.

inertia /i-ner-shuh/ ● **n. 1** a tendency to do nothing or to remain unchanged. **2** Physics a property by which matter remains in a state of rest or continues moving in a straight line, unless changed by an external force.

inescapable ● **adj.** unable to be avoided or denied.

inessential ● **adj.** not absolutely necessary.

inestimable ● **adj.** too great to be measured.

inevitable ● **adj.** certain to happen; unavoidable.
– DERIVATIVES **inevitability** n. **inevitably** adv.
– ORIGIN Latin *inevitabilis.*

inexact ● **adj.** not quite accurate.

inexcusable ● adj. too bad to be justified or tolerated.

inexhaustible ● adj. (of a supply) never ending because available in unlimited quantities.

inexorable /in-ek-suh-ruh-b'l/ ● adj. impossible to stop or prevent.
– DERIVATIVES **inexorably** adv.
– ORIGIN Latin *inexorabilis.*

inexpensive ● adj. not costing a great deal; cheap.

inexperience ● n. lack of experience.
– DERIVATIVES **inexperienced** adj.

inexpert ● adj. lacking skill or knowledge in a particular field.

inexplicable /in-ik-splik-uh-b'l/ ● adj. unable to be explained.
– DERIVATIVES **inexplicably** adv.

inexpressive ● adj. showing no emotion.

in extremis /in ek-stree-miss/ ● adv. **1** in an extremely difficult situation. **2** at the point of death.
– ORIGIN Latin.

inextricable /in-ik-strik-uh-b'l/ ● adj. impossible to untangle or separate: *the past and the present are inextricable.*
– DERIVATIVES **inextricably** adv.

infallible /in-fal-li-b'l/ ● adj. incapable of making mistakes or being wrong.
– DERIVATIVES **infallibly** adv.

infamous /in-fuh-muhss/ ● adj. **1** well known for some bad quality or deed. **2** wicked.

infamy /in-fuh-mi/ ● n. (pl. **infamies**) **1** the state of being infamous. **2** a wicked act.

infancy ● n. **1** the state or period of being a baby or young child. **2** the early stage in the development of something.

infant ● n. **1** a very young child or baby. **2** Brit. a schoolchild between the ages of five and seven.
– ORIGIN Old French *enfant.*

infanta /in-fan-tuh/ ● n. hist. a daughter of the ruling monarch of Spain or Portugal.
– ORIGIN Spanish and Portuguese.

infanticide /in-fan-ti-syd/ ● n. the killing of an infant.

infantile /in-fuhn-tyl/ ● adj. **1** having to do with infants. **2** derog. childish.

infantry ● n. soldiers who fight on foot.
– DERIVATIVES **infantryman** n.
– ORIGIN Italian *infanteria.*

infatuate ● v. (**be infatuated with**) have an intense passion for.
– DERIVATIVES **infatuation** n.
– ORIGIN Latin *infatuare* 'make foolish'.

infect ● v. **1** affect with an organism that causes disease. **2** contaminate; affect badly.
– ORIGIN Latin *inficere* 'to taint'.

infection ● n. **1** the process of infecting or the state of being infected. **2** an infectious disease.

infectious ● adj. **1** (of a disease or disease-causing organism) able to be transmitted through the environment. **2** likely to spread infection. **3** likely to spread to or influence others.

infer ● v. (**infers, inferring, inferred**) work out from evidence rather than from direct statements.
– ORIGIN Latin *inferre* 'bring in'.

USAGE infer
For an explanation of the difference between **imply** and **infer**, see the note at **IMPLY**.

inference /in-fuh-ruhnss/ ● n. **1** a conclusion reached on the basis of evidence. **2** the process of reaching a conclusion in this way.

inferior ● adj. lower in rank, status, or quality. ● n. a person lower than another in rank, status, or ability.
– DERIVATIVES **inferiority** n.
– ORIGIN Latin.

infernal ● adj. **1** having to do with hell or the underworld. **2** informal very annoying: *an infernal nuisance.*
– ORIGIN Latin *infernus* 'below'.

inferno ● n. (pl. **infernos**) a large uncontrollable fire.
– ORIGIN Italian.

infertile ● adj. **1** unable to bear young. **2** (of land) unable to produce crops or vegetation.
– DERIVATIVES **infertility** n.

infest ● v. (of insects) be present in large numbers, so as to cause damage or disease.
– DERIVATIVES **infestation** n.
– ORIGIN Latin *infestare* 'to attack'.

infidel /in-fi-duhl/ ● n. archaic a person who has no religion or whose religion is not that of the majority.
– ORIGIN Latin *infidelis.*

infidelity ● n. (pl. **infidelities**) the action of being unfaithful to one's sexual partner.

infighting ● n. conflict within a group or organization.

infiltrate /in-fil-trayt/ ● v. (**infiltrates, infiltrating, infiltrated**) **1** secretly and gradually gain access to (an organization or place). **2** pass slowly into or through.
– DERIVATIVES **infiltration** n. **infiltrator** n.

infinite /in-fi-nit/ ● adj. **1** limitless in space or size. **2** very great in amount or degree: *with infinite care.*
– DERIVATIVES **infinitely** adv.
– ORIGIN Latin *infinitus.*

infinitesimal /in-fi-ni-tess-i-m'l/ ● adj. extremely small.
– DERIVATIVES **infinitesimally** adv.
– ORIGIN Latin *infinitesimus.*

infinitive /in-fin-i-tiv/ ● n. the basic form of a verb, normally occurring in English with the word *to,* as in *to see, to ask.*
– ORIGIN Latin *infinitus.*

infinity ● n. (pl. **infinities**) **1** the state of being infinite. **2** a very great number or amount. **3** Math. a number greater than any quantity or countable number (symbol ∞).

infirm ● adj. physically weak.
– ORIGIN Latin *infirmus.*

infirmary ● n. (pl. **infirmaries**) a hospital or place set aside for the care of the sick or injured.

infirmity ● n. (pl. **infirmities**) physical or mental weakness.

in flagrante delicto /in fluh-gran-tay di-lik-toh/ ● adv. in the very act of wrongdoing.
– ORIGIN Latin, 'in the heat of the crime'.

inflame ● v. (**inflames, inflaming, inflamed**) **1** make worse. **2** make very angry. **3** cause inflammation in.

inflammable ● adj. easily set on fire.

USAGE inflammable

The words **inflammable** and **flammable** both mean 'easily set on fire'. To avoid confusion it is better to say **flammable**, as the *in-* part of **inflammable** can give the impression that the word means 'not flammable'.

inflammation • n. a condition in which an area of the skin becomes reddened, swollen, hot, and often painful.

inflammatory • adj. **1** causing inflammation. **2** arousing angry feelings.

inflatable • adj. capable of being inflated. • n. a plastic or rubber object that is inflated before use.

inflate • v. (**inflates, inflating, inflated**) **1** expand by filling with air or gas. **2** make (something) seem more important than it actually is. **3** bring about inflation of (a currency) or in (an economy).
– ORIGIN Latin *inflare* 'blow into'.

inflation • n. **1** the action of inflating. **2** a general increase in prices.
– DERIVATIVES **inflationary** adj.

inflect • v. **1** Grammar (of a word) change by inflection. **2** vary the tone or pitch of (the voice).
– ORIGIN Latin *inflectere*.

inflection • n. **1** Grammar a change in the form of a word to show a grammatical function or a quality such as tense, person, or number. **2** a variation in tone or pitch of the voice. **3** esp. Math. a change of curvature from convex to concave.

inflexible • adj. **1** not able to be altered or adapted. **2** unwilling to change or compromise. **3** not able to be bent.

inflict • v. (**inflict on**) **1** cause (something unpleasant) to be suffered by. **2** impose (something unwelcome) on.
– DERIVATIVES **infliction** n.
– ORIGIN Latin *infligere* 'strike against'.

inflorescence /in-fluh-ress-uhnss/ • n. Bot. the complete flower head of a plant.
– ORIGIN Latin *inflorescere* 'come into flower'.

influence • n. **1** the power or ability to affect someone's beliefs or actions. **2** a person or thing with such ability or power. **3** the power arising out of status, or wealth. • v. (**influences, influencing, influenced**) have an influence on.
– ORIGIN Latin *influere* 'flow in'.

influential • adj. having great influence.

influenza • n. an infection of the respiratory passages, spread by a virus and causing fever, aching, and catarrh.
– ORIGIN Italian, 'influence'.

influx • n. the arrival or entry of large numbers of people or things.
– ORIGIN Latin *influxus*.

inform • v. **1** give facts or information to. **2** (**inform on**) give information about (someone's involvement in a crime) to the police.
– ORIGIN Latin *informare* 'describe'.

informal • adj. **1** relaxed, friendly, or unofficial. **2** (of clothes) suitable for everyday wear; casual. **3** referring to the language of everyday speech and writing, rather than that used in official situations.
– DERIVATIVES **informality** n. **informally** adv.

informant • n. a person who gives information to another.

information • n. **1** facts or knowledge provided or learned. **2** computer data.

information superhighway • n. an extensive electronic network such as the Internet, used for the rapid transfer of information.

information technology • n. the study or use of systems such as computers and telecommunications for storing, retrieving, and sending information.

informative • adj. providing useful information.

informed • adj. **1** having or showing knowledge. **2** (of a judgement) based on a sound understanding of the facts.

informer • n. a person who informs on another person to the police.

infra- • prefix below: *infrared*.
– ORIGIN Latin *infra*.

infraction • n. a breaking of a law or agreement.
– ORIGIN Latin.

infra dig /in-fruh **dig**/ • adj. informal beneath one's dignity.
– ORIGIN from Latin *infra dignitatem*.

infrared • n. electromagnetic radiation having a wavelength just greater than that of red light but less than that of microwaves. • adj. relating to such radiation.

infrastructure • n. the basic structures (e.g. buildings, roads, power supplies) needed for the operation of a society or organization.

infrequent • adj. not occurring often; rare.
– DERIVATIVES **infrequency** n. **infrequently** adv.

infringe • v. (**infringes, infringing, infringed**) **1** break (a law, agreement, etc.). **2** curb or limit (a right or privilege).
– DERIVATIVES **infringement** n.
– ORIGIN Latin *infringere*.

infuriate • v. /in-fyoor-i-ayt/ (**infuriates, infuriating, infuriated**) make angry.
– ORIGIN Latin *infuriare*.

infuse • v. (**infuses, infusing, infused**) **1** spread throughout; fill. **2** soak (tea, herbs, etc.) to extract the flavour or healing properties.
– DERIVATIVES **infuser** n.
– ORIGIN Latin *infundere* 'pour in'.

infusion • n. **1** a drink prepared by infusing. **2** the action of infusing.

-ing[1] • suffix **1** referring to a verbal action, activity, or result: *building*. **2** referring to material used for a process: *piping*. **3** forming the gerund of verbs (such as *painting* as in *I love painting*).
– ORIGIN Old English.

-ing[2] • suffix **1** forming the present participle of verbs: *calling*. **2** forming adjectives from nouns: *hulking*.
– ORIGIN Latin *-ent*.

ingenious /in-jee-ni-uhss/ • adj. clever, original, and inventive.
– DERIVATIVES **ingeniously** adv.
– ORIGIN Latin *ingeniosus*.

ingénue /an-*zh*uh-nyoo/ • n. an innocent or naive young woman.
– ORIGIN French.

ingenuity /in-ji-nyoo-i-ti/ • n. the quality of being ingenious.
– ORIGIN Latin *ingenuitas* 'ingenuousness'.

ingenuous /in-jen-yoo-uhss/ • adj. innocent

and unsuspecting.
– ORIGIN Latin *ingenuus* 'native, inborn'.
ingest • v. take (food or drink) into the body by swallowing or absorbing it.
– ORIGIN Latin *ingerere* 'bring in'.
inglenook • n. a space on either side of a large fireplace.
– ORIGIN from dialect *ingle* 'fire, fireplace' + **NOOK**.
inglorious • adj. causing shame; dishonourable.
ingoing • adj. going towards or into.
ingot /ing-guht/ • n. a rectangular block of steel, gold, or other metal.
– ORIGIN perh. from Old English, 'pour, cast'.
ingrained (also **engrained**) • adj. **1** (of a habit or attitude) firmly established and hard to change. **2** (of dirt) deeply embedded.
ingrate /in-grayt/ • n. literary an ungrateful person.
– ORIGIN Latin *ingratus*.
ingratiate /in-gray-shi-ayt/ • v. (**ingratiates, ingratiating, ingratiated**) (**ingratiate oneself**) gain favour with someone by flattering or trying to please them.
– ORIGIN from Latin *in gratiam* 'into favour'.
ingratitude • n. a lack of appropriate gratitude.
ingredient • n. **1** any of the substances that are combined to make a dish. **2** a part or element.
– ORIGIN Latin *ingredi* 'enter'.

Ingres E
/ang-gruh/, Jean Auguste Dominique (1780–1867), French neoclassicist painter, known for his historical and religious paintings.

ingress /in-gress/ • n. **1** the action of entering. **2** a place or means of access.
– ORIGIN Latin *ingressus*.
ingrown • adj. (of a toenail) having grown into the flesh.
– DERIVATIVES **ingrowing** adj.
inhabit • v. (**inhabits, inhabiting, inhabited**) live in or occupy.
– DERIVATIVES **inhabitable** adj.
– ORIGIN Latin *inhabitare*.
inhabitant • n. a person or animal that lives in or occupies a place.
inhalant • n. a medicine that is inhaled.
inhale /in-hayl/ • v. (**inhales, inhaling, inhaled**) breathe in (air, smoke, etc.).
– DERIVATIVES **inhalation** n.
– ORIGIN Latin *inhalare*.
inhaler • n. a portable device used for inhaling a drug.
inhere /in-hiuh/ • v. (**inhere, inhering, inhered**) (**inhere in/within**) formal exist in as an essential or permanent part.
– ORIGIN Latin *inhaerere* 'stick to'.
inherent /in-herr-uhnt/ • adj. existing in something as a permanent or essential quality: *the dog's inherent distrust of strangers.*
– DERIVATIVES **inherently** adv.
inherit • v. (**inherits, inheriting, inherited**) **1** receive (money, property, or a title) as an heir at the death of the previous holder. **2** derive (a quality or characteristic) from one's parents or ancestors. **3** receive or be left with (a situation, object, etc.) from a former owner.
– ORIGIN Latin *inhereditare* 'appoint as heir'.
inheritance • n. **1** a thing that is inherited. **2** the action of inheriting.
inheritance tax • n. (in the UK) tax on property and money that has been inherited.
inhibit • v. (**inhibits, inhibiting, inhibited**) **1** hinder or prevent (an action or process). **2** make (someone) unable to act in a relaxed and natural way.
– DERIVATIVES **inhibited** adj.
– ORIGIN Latin *inhibere*.
inhibition • n. **1** the action of inhibiting. **2** a feeling that makes one unable to act in a relaxed and natural way.
inhospitable • adj. **1** (of an environment) harsh and difficult to live in. **2** unwelcoming.
in-house • adj. & adv. within an organization.
inhuman • adj. **1** lacking good human qualities; cruel and barbaric. **2** not human.
inhumane • adj. without pity for misery or suffering; cruel.
inhumanity • n. (pl. **inhumanities**) cruel and brutal behaviour.
inimical /i-nim-i-k'l/ • adj. tending to obstruct or harm; hostile.
– ORIGIN Latin *inimicalis*.
inimitable /in-im-i-tuh-b'l/ • adj. impossible to imitate; unique.
– DERIVATIVES **inimitably** adv.
iniquity /i-ni-kwi-ti/ • n. (pl. **iniquities**) the quality of being unjust or wrong.
– DERIVATIVES **iniquitous** adj.
– ORIGIN Latin *iniquitas*.
initial • adj. existing or occurring at the beginning. • n. the first letter of a name or word. • v. (**initials, initialling, initialled**; US **initials, initialing, initialed**) mark with one's initials as a sign of approval or agreement.
– DERIVATIVES **initially** adv.
– ORIGIN Latin *initialis*.
initialism • n. an abbreviation consisting of initial letters pronounced separately (e.g. *BBC*).
initiate /i-ni-shi-ayt/ • v. (**initiates, initiating, initiated**) **1** cause (a process or action) to begin. **2** admit (someone) to a society or group with a formal ceremony. **3** (**initiate into**) introduce to (a new activity).
– DERIVATIVES **initiation** n. **initiator** n.
– ORIGIN Latin *initiare* 'begin'.
initiative • n. **1** the ability to act independently and with a fresh approach. **2** the power or opportunity to act before others do: *we have lost the initiative.* **3** a fresh approach to a problem.
inject • v. **1** introduce (a drug or other substance) into the body with a syringe. **2** give a drug to (a person or animal) with a syringe. **3** introduce (a different quality): *she tried to inject scorn into her tone.*
– ORIGIN Latin *inicere* 'throw in'.
injection • n. **1** an act of injecting. **2** a large sum of money used to help an organization.
in-joke • n. a joke that is shared only by a small group.
injudicious • adj. showing poor judgement; unwise.
injunction • n. **1** an order by a court of law stating that someone must or must not do something. **2** a strong warning.
– ORIGIN Latin.

injure ● v. (**injures**, **injuring**, **injured**) **1** do physical harm to. **2** damage: *their reputation could be injured by a libel.*

injured ● adj. **1** harmed. **2** offended.

injurious /in-joor-i-uhss/ ● adj. causing or likely to cause harm or damage.

injury ● n. (pl. **injuries**) **1** an instance of being injured. **2** the fact of being injured; harm or damage.
– ORIGIN Latin *injuria* 'a wrong'.

injury time ● n. Brit. (in soccer and other sports) extra playing time to make up for time lost as a result of injuries.

injustice ● n. **1** lack of justice. **2** an unjust act or occurrence.

ink ● n. **1** a coloured fluid used for writing, drawing, or printing. **2** a black liquid produced by a cuttlefish, octopus, or squid. ● v. cover (type or a stamp) with ink before printing.
– ORIGIN Old French *enque*.

inkling ● n. a slight suspicion; a hint.
– ORIGIN from archaic *inkle* 'say in an undertone'.

inkstand ● n. a stand for ink bottles, pens, and other stationery items.

inkwell ● n. a container for ink that fits into a hole in a desk.

inky ● adj. **1** as dark as ink. **2** stained with ink.

inlaid past and past part. of **INLAY**.

inland ● adj. & adv. in or into the interior of a country.

Inland Revenue ● n. (in the UK) the government department responsible for collecting income tax and some other taxes.

in-law ● n. a relative by marriage. ● comb. form related by marriage: *father-in-law.*

inlay ● v. (**inlays**, **inlaying**, **inlaid**) ornament by embedding pieces of a different material in a surface. ● n. **1** inlaid decoration. **2** a material used for inlaying.

inlet ● n. **1** a small arm of the sea, a lake, or a river. **2** a place or means of entry.

in-line skate ● n. a type of roller skate in which the wheels are fixed in a single line along the sole.

in loco parentis /in loh-koh puh-ren-tiss/ ● adv. & adj. (of an adult responsible for children) in the place of a parent.
– ORIGIN Latin.

inmate ● n. a person living in an institution such as a prison or hospital.
– ORIGIN prob. from **INN** + **MATE**[1].

in memoriam /in mi-mor-i-am/ ● prep. in memory of (a dead person).
– ORIGIN Latin.

inmost ● adj. innermost.

inn ● n. a public house.
– ORIGIN Old English.

innards ● pl. n. informal **1** internal organs. **2** the internal workings of a device or machine.
– ORIGIN from **INWARDS**.

innate /in-nayt/ ● adj. inborn; natural.
– DERIVATIVES **innately** adv.
– ORIGIN Latin *innatus*.

inner ● adj. **1** situated inside; close to the centre. **2** mental or spiritual: *inner strength.* **3** private; not expressed.

inner city ● n. an area in or near the centre of a city.

Inner Hebrides [E]
see **HEBRIDES**.

Inner Mongolia [E]
an autonomous region of northern China, on the border with Mongolia; capital, Hohhot.

innermost ● adj. **1** furthest in. **2** (of thoughts) most private.

inner tube ● n. a separate inflatable tube inside a tyre casing.

innings ● n. (pl. **innings**) (treated as sing.) Cricket each of the divisions of a game during which one side has a turn at batting.

innkeeper ● n. archaic a person who runs an inn.

innocent ● adj. **1** not guilty of a crime or offence. **2** without experience of evil or sexual matters. **3** not intended to cause offence: *an innocent mistake.* ● n. an innocent person.
– DERIVATIVES **innocence** n. **innocently** adv.
– ORIGIN Latin, 'not harming'.

innocuous /in-nok-yoo-uhss/ ● adj. not harmful or offensive.
– ORIGIN Latin *innocuus*.

innovate /in-nuh-vayt/ ● v. (**innovates**, **innovating**, **innovated**) introduce new methods, ideas, or products.
– DERIVATIVES **innovator** n.
– ORIGIN Latin *innovare* 'renew, alter'.

innovation ● n. **1** the action of innovating. **2** a new method, idea, or product.

innovative /in-nuh-vuh-tiv/ ● adj. **1** featuring new ideas or methods: *innovative designs.* **2** original and creative in thinking.

Innsbruck [E]
/inz-bruuk/ a city in western Austria, capital of Tyrol.

innuendo /in-yuu-en-doh/ ● n. (pl. **innuendoes** or **innuendos**) a remark which makes an indirect reference to something.
– ORIGIN Latin, 'by pointing to'.

innumerable ● adj. too many to be counted.
– ORIGIN Latin *innumerabilis*.

innumerate ● adj. without a basic knowledge of mathematics and arithmetic.

inoculate /i-nok-yuu-layt/ ● v. = **VACCINATE**.
– DERIVATIVES **inoculation** n.
– ORIGIN Latin *inoculare* 'graft a shoot of a plant'.

inoffensive ● adj. not objectionable or harmful.

inoperable ● adj. **1** (of an illness) not able to be cured by a medical operation. **2** not able to be used or operated.

inoperative ● adj. not working or taking effect.

inopportune ● adj. occurring at an inconvenient time.

inordinate /in-or-di-nuht/ ● adj. unusually large; excessive.
– DERIVATIVES **inordinately** adv.
– ORIGIN Latin *inordinatus* 'not arranged'.

inorganic ● adj. **1** not coming from a living organism. **2** referring to chemical compounds that do not contain carbon.

inpatient ● n. a patient who is staying day and night in a hospital while receiving treatment.

input ● n. **1** what is put or taken in by a system or process. **2** a person's contribution.

3 the action of putting data into a computer. **4** a place or device from which electricity or information enters a computer or other machine. • v. (**inputs**, **inputting**, **input**) put (data) into a computer.

inquest • n. **1** an official inquiry to gather the facts relating to an incident. **2** Brit. an inquiry by a coroner's court into the cause of a death.
– ORIGIN Old French *enqueste*.

inquire • v. = ENQUIRE.

inquiry • n. (pl. **inquiries**) = ENQUIRY.

inquisition • n. **1** a long period of intensive questioning or investigation. **2** the verdict of a coroner's jury.
– ORIGIN Latin.

inquisitive • adj. **1** eagerly seeking knowledge. **2** prying.

inquisitor /in-kwiz-i-ter/ • n. a person conducting an inquisition.

inroad • n. a gradual entry into or effect on a situation.

inrush • n. a sudden inward flow.

insalubrious /in-suh-loo-bri-uhss/ • adj. seedy; unwholesome.

insane • adj. **1** seriously mentally ill. **2** extremely foolish; irrational.
– DERIVATIVES **insanely** adv. **insanity** n.
– ORIGIN Latin *insanus*.

insanitary • adj. so dirty as to be a danger to health.

insatiable /in-say-shuh-b'l/ • adj. impossible to satisfy.
– DERIVATIVES **insatiably** adv.

inscribe • v. (**inscribes**, **inscribing**, **inscribed**) **1** write or carve (words or symbols) on a surface. **2** write a dedication to someone in (a book). **3** Geom. draw (a figure) within another so that their boundaries touch but do not intersect.
– ORIGIN Latin *inscribere*.

inscription • n. words or symbols inscribed on a monument, in a book, etc.

inscrutable /in-skroo-tuh-b'l/ • adj. impossible to understand or interpret.
– DERIVATIVES **inscrutably** adv.
– ORIGIN Latin *inscrutabilis*.

insect • n. a small invertebrate animal with six legs and a body divided into three segments (head, thorax, and abdomen).
– ORIGIN from Latin *animal insectum* 'segmented animal'.

insecticide • n. a substance used for killing insects.

insectivore /in-sek-ti-vor/ • n. an animal that feeds on insects.
– DERIVATIVES **insectivorous** adj.

insecure • adj. **1** not confident or assured. **2** not firm or firmly fixed. **3** (of a place) easily broken into.
– DERIVATIVES **insecurity** n.

inseminate /in-sem-i-nayt/ • v. (**inseminates**, **inseminating**, **inseminated**) introduce semen into (a woman or a female animal).
– DERIVATIVES **insemination** n.
– ORIGIN Latin *inseminare* 'sow'.

insensate • adj. **1** lacking physical sensation. **2** lacking sympathy; unfeeling.

insensible • adj. **1** unconscious. **2** numb; without feeling.
– DERIVATIVES **insensibility** n.

insensitive • adj. **1** having no concern for the feelings of others. **2** not able to feel physical sensation. **3** not aware of or able to respond to something.
– DERIVATIVES **insensitivity** n.

inseparable • adj. unable to be separated or treated separately.
– DERIVATIVES **inseparably** adv.

insert • v. /in-sert/ place, fit, or add into. • n. /in-sert/ a loose page or section in a magazine.
– ORIGIN Latin *inserere*.

insertion • n. **1** the action of inserting. **2** a change inserted in a text.

in-service • adj. (of training) intended to take place during the course of employment.

inset • n. /in-set/ **1** a thing inserted. **2** a small picture or map inserted within the border of a larger one. • v. /in-set/ (**insets**, **insetting**, **inset**) put in as an inset.

inshore • adj. at sea but close to the shore. • adv. towards or closer to the shore.

inside • n. **1** the inner side, part, or surface of something. **2** (**insides**) informal the stomach and bowels. **3** the side of a bend where the edge is shorter. • adj. situated on or in, or coming from, the inside. • prep. & adv. **1** situated or moving within. **2** informal in prison. **3** in less than (the period of time specified).

inside job • n. informal a crime committed by or with the help of a person associated with the place where it occurred.

inside leg • n. the length of a person's leg or trouser leg from crotch to ankle.

inside out • adv. with the inner surface turned outwards.
– PHRASES **know inside out** know very thoroughly.

insider • n. a person within an organization who has information not known to those outside it.

insidious /in-sid-i-uhss/ • adj. proceeding in a gradual and harmful way.
– DERIVATIVES **insidiously** adv.
– ORIGIN Latin *insidiosus* 'cunning'.

insight • n. **1** the ability to understand the truth about someone or something. **2** an understanding of this kind.
– DERIVATIVES **insightful** adj.

insignia /in-sig-ni-uh/ • n. (pl. **insignia**) a badge or symbol showing a person's rank, position, or membership of an organization.
– ORIGIN Latin.

insignificant • adj. having little or no importance or value.
– DERIVATIVES **insignificance** n.

insincere • adj. saying or doing things that one does not mean.
– DERIVATIVES **insincerely** adv. **insincerity** n.

insinuate /in-sin-yuu-ayt/ • v. (**insinuates**, **insinuating**, **insinuated**) **1** suggest (something bad) in an indirect and unpleasant way. **2** (**insinuate oneself into**) move oneself gradually into (a favourable position).
– ORIGIN Latin *insinuare*.

insinuation • n. an unpleasant hint or suggestion.

insipid /in-si-pid/ • adj. **1** lacking flavour. **2** lacking liveliness or interest.
– ORIGIN Latin *insipidus*.

insist • v. **1** demand or state something forcefully, without accepting refusal or

contradiction. **2** (**insist on**) persist in (doing).
– ORIGIN Latin *insistere* 'persist'.

insistent • **adj.** **1** insisting that something must be done. **2** repeated and demanding attention.
– DERIVATIVES **insistence** n. **insistently** adv.

in situ /in sit-yoo/ • **adv. & adj.** in the original or appropriate position.
– ORIGIN Latin.

insole • **n.** **1** a removable sole worn inside a shoe. **2** the fixed inner sole of a boot or shoe.

insolent • **adj.** rude and disrespectful.
– DERIVATIVES **insolence** n. **insolently** adv.
– ORIGIN Latin, 'arrogant'.

insoluble • **adj.** **1** impossible to solve. **2** (of a substance) unable to be dissolved.
– DERIVATIVES **insolubility** n.

insolvent • **adj.** not having enough money to pay one's debts.
– DERIVATIVES **insolvency** n.

insomnia • **n.** the condition of being unable to sleep.
– DERIVATIVES **insomniac** n. & adj.
– ORIGIN Latin.

insomuch • **adv.** (**insomuch that/as**) to the extent that.

insouciant /in-soo-si-uhnt/ • **adj.** casually unconcerned.
– DERIVATIVES **insouciance** n.
– ORIGIN French.

inspect • **v.** **1** look at closely. **2** visit (an organization) officially to check on standards.
– DERIVATIVES **inspection** n.
– ORIGIN Latin *inspicere.*

inspector • **n.** **1** an official who makes sure that regulations are obeyed. **2** a police officer ranking below a chief inspector.
– DERIVATIVES **inspectorate** n.

inspiration • **n.** **1** the process of being inspired. **2** a person or thing that inspires. **3** a sudden clever idea.
– DERIVATIVES **inspirational** adj.

inspire • **v.** (**inspires**, **inspiring**, **inspired**) **1** fill with the urge or ability to do or feel something. **2** create (a feeling) in a person. **3** give rise to: *the film was successful enough to inspire a sequel.*
– DERIVATIVES **inspiring** adj.
– ORIGIN Latin *inspirare* 'breathe into'.

inspired • **adj.** showing inspiration.

instability • **n.** (pl. **instabilities**) lack of stability.

install • **v.** (**installs**, **installing**, **installed**) **1** place or fix (equipment) in position ready for use. **2** establish in a new place or role.
– ORIGIN Latin *installare.*

installation • **n.** **1** the action of installing. **2** a large piece of equipment installed for use. **3** a military or industrial establishment. **4** an art exhibit constructed within a gallery.

instalment (US also **installment**) • **n.** **1** a sum of money due as one of several payments made over a period of time. **2** one of several parts of something published or broadcast at intervals.

instance • **n.** **1** an example or single occurrence of something. **2** a particular case. • **v.** (**instances**, **instancing**, **instanced**) give as an example.
– ORIGIN Latin *instantia* 'presence, urgency'.

instant • **adj.** **1** immediate. **2** (of food) processed to allow quick preparation. • **n.** **1** a precise moment of time. **2** a very short time.
– DERIVATIVES **instantly** adv.
– ORIGIN Latin.

instantaneous /in-stuhn-tay-ni-uhss/ • **adj.** happening or done immediately.
– DERIVATIVES **instantaneously** adv.

instead • **adv.** **1** as an alternative. **2** (**instead of**) in place of.

instep • **n.** the part of a person's foot between the ball and the ankle.
– ORIGIN unknown.

instigate /in-sti-gayt/ • **v.** (**instigates**, **instigating**, **instigated**) **1** cause to happen or begin. **2** (**instigate to/to do**) encourage (someone) to do.
– DERIVATIVES **instigation** n.
– ORIGIN Latin *instigare* 'urge'.

instil /in-stil/ (US **instill**) • **v.** (**instils**, **instilling**, **instilled**; US **instills**, **instilling**, **instilled**) gradually establish (an idea) in someone's mind.
– DERIVATIVES **instillation** n.
– ORIGIN Latin *instillare* 'put in by drops'.

instinct • **n.** **1** an inborn tendency to behave in a certain way. **2** a natural ability or skill.
– DERIVATIVES **instinctual** adj.
– ORIGIN Latin *instinctus* 'impulse'.

instinctive • **adj.** based on instinct rather than thought or training.
– DERIVATIVES **instinctively** adv.

institute • **n.** an organization for the promotion of science, education, etc. • **v.** (**institutes**, **instituting**, **instituted**) begin or establish.
– ORIGIN Latin *instituere* 'establish'.

institution • **n.** **1** an important organization or public body, such as a university or Church. **2** an organization providing residential care for people with special needs. **3** an established law or custom.

institutional • **adj.** having to do with or typical of an institution.
– DERIVATIVES **institutionally** adv.

institutionalize (also **institutionalise**) • **v.** (**institutionalizes**, **institutionalizing**, **institutionalized**) **1** establish as an accepted part of an organization or culture. **2** place in a residential institution. **3** (**be/become institutionalized**) suffer the ill effects of long-term residence in a residential institution.

instruct • **v.** **1** direct or command. **2** teach. **3** inform of a fact or situation.
– ORIGIN Latin *instruere* 'equip, teach'.

instruction • **n.** **1** a direction or order. **2** teaching or education.
– DERIVATIVES **instructional** adj.

instructive • **adj.** useful and informative.

instructor (or **instructress**) • **n.** a teacher.

instrument • **n.** **1** a tool or implement for precise work. **2** a measuring device. **3** (also **musical instrument**) a device for producing musical sounds.
– ORIGIN Latin *instrumentum.*

instrumental • **adj.** **1** acting as a means of achieving something. **2** (of music) performed on instruments. • **n.** a piece of music performed by instruments only.
– DERIVATIVES **instrumentally** adv.

instrumentalist • **n.** a player of a musical instrument.

instrumentation • **n.** **1** measuring instruments. **2** the arrangement of a piece of music for particular instruments.

insubordinate ● adj. disobedient.
– DERIVATIVES **insubordination** n.

insubstantial ● adj. lacking strength and solidity.

insufferable ● adj. **1** too extreme to bear; intolerable. **2** unbearably arrogant or conceited.
– DERIVATIVES **insufferably** adv.
– ORIGIN Latin *sufferre* 'suffer'.

insufficient ● adj. not enough.
– DERIVATIVES **insufficiency** n. **insufficiently** adv.

insular ● adj. **1** isolated from outside influences, and often narrow-minded as a result. **2** relating to an island.
– DERIVATIVES **insularity** n.
– ORIGIN Latin *insularis*.

insulate ● v. (**insulates**, **insulating**, **insulated**) **1** place material between one thing and another to prevent loss of heat or intrusion of sound. **2** cover with non-conducting material to prevent the passage of electricity. **3** protect from something unpleasant.
– DERIVATIVES **insulator** n.
– ORIGIN Latin *insula* 'island'.

insulation ● n. **1** the action of insulating or state of being insulated. **2** material used to insulate something.

insulin /in-syuu-lin/ ● n. a hormone produced in the pancreas, which regulates glucose levels in the blood, and the lack of which causes diabetes.
– ORIGIN Latin *insula* 'island' (with reference to the islets of Langerhans in the pancreas).

insult ● v. /in-**sult**/ speak to or treat with disrespect or abuse. ● n. /**in**-sult/ **1** an insulting remark or action. **2** a thing so worthless as to be offensive: *the pay offer is an absolute insult.*
– ORIGIN Latin *insultare* 'jump on'.

insuperable /in-syoo-puh-ruh-b'l/ ● adj. impossible to overcome.
– ORIGIN Latin *insuperabilis*.

insupportable ● adj. **1** unable to be supported or justified. **2** intolerable.

insurance ● n. **1** the action or business of insuring. **2** money paid to insure against something or by an insurance company in the event of damage, injury, etc. **3** a thing providing protection against a possible event.

insure ● v. (**insures**, **insuring**, **insured**) **1** arrange for compensation in the event of damage to or loss of (property, life, or a person), in exchange for regular payments to a company. **2** (**insure against**) protect (someone) against (a possible event). **3** = **ENSURE**.
– DERIVATIVES **insurer** n.
– ORIGIN from **ENSURE**.

insurgent /in-ser-juhnt/ ● n. a rebel or revolutionary.
– DERIVATIVES **insurgency** n. (pl. **insurgencies**).
– ORIGIN Latin *insurgere* 'rise up'.

insurmountable /in-ser-**mown**-tuh-b'l/ ● adj. too great to be overcome.

insurrection /in-suh-**rek**-sh'n/ ● n. a violent uprising against authority.
– DERIVATIVES **insurrectionary** adj.
– ORIGIN Latin.

intact ● adj. not damaged.
– ORIGIN Latin *intactus* 'untouched'.

intaglio /in-ta-li-oh/ ● n. (pl. **intaglios**) an incised or engraved design.
– ORIGIN Italian.

intake ● n. **1** an amount or quantity taken in. **2** an act of taking in.

intangible ● adj. **1** unable to be touched; not solid or real. **2** vague and abstract. ● n. an intangible thing.
– DERIVATIVES **intangibly** adv.

integer /in-ti-jer/ ● n. a whole number.
– ORIGIN Latin, 'whole'.

integral ● adj. /**in**-ti-gruhl, in-**teg**-ruhl/ **1** necessary to make a whole complete; fundamental. **2** included as part of a whole. ● n. /**in**-ti-gruhl/ Math. a function of which a given function is the derivative, and which may express the area under the curve of a graph of the function.
– DERIVATIVES **integrally** adv.

integral calculus ● n. Math. the part of calculus concerned with the integrals of functions.

integrate ● v. /**in**-ti-grayt/ (**integrates**, **integrating**, **integrated**) **1** combine or be combined to form a whole. **2** make (someone) accepted as part of a group.
– ORIGIN Latin *integrare* 'make whole'.

integrated circuit ● n. an electronic circuit on a small piece of semiconducting material, performing the same function as a larger circuit of separate components.

integration ● n. **1** the action of integrating. **2** the mixing of peoples or groups previously kept apart.

integrity /in-teg-ri-ti/ ● n. **1** the quality of being honest and morally upright. **2** the state of being whole or unified.
– ORIGIN Latin *integritas*.

integument /in-teg-yuu-muhnt/ ● n. a tough outer protective layer, especially of an animal or plant.
– ORIGIN Latin *integumentum*.

intellect ● n. **1** the power of reasoning and understanding objectively. **2** a person's mental powers.
– ORIGIN Latin *intellectus*.

intellectual /in-tuh-lek-chyuu-uhl/ ● adj. **1** relating or appealing to the intellect. **2** having a highly developed intellect. ● n. a person with a highly developed intellect.
– DERIVATIVES **intellectually** adv.

intellectualize (also **intellectualise**) ● v. (**intellectualizes**, **intellectualizing**, **intellectualized**) talk or write in an intellectual way.

intelligence ● n. **1** the ability to gain and apply knowledge and skills. **2** secret information collected about an enemy or competitor.
– ORIGIN Latin *intelligentia*.

intelligence quotient ● n. a number representing a person's reasoning ability, 100 being average.

intelligent ● adj. **1** having intelligence, especially of a high level. **2** (of a device) able to vary its state or action in response to varying situations and past experience.
– DERIVATIVES **intelligently** adv.

intelligentsia /in-tel-li-**jent**-si-uh/ ● n. intellectuals or highly educated people.

intelligible /in-tel-li-ji-b'l/ ● adj. able to be understood.
– DERIVATIVES **intelligibility** n. **intelligibly**

adv.
– ORIGIN Latin *intelligibilis*.

intemperate ● adj. lacking self-control.

intend ● v. **1** have as one's aim or plan. **2** plan that (something) should be, do, or mean something: *the book was intended as a satire*. **3** (**intend for/to do**) design or plan for a particular purpose.
– ORIGIN Latin *intendere* 'intend, extend'.

intended ● adj. planned or meant. ● n. (**one's intended**) informal one's fiancé(e).

intense ● adj. (**intenser**, **intensest**) **1** of extreme force, degree, or strength. **2** extremely earnest or serious.
– DERIVATIVES **intensely** adv.
– ORIGIN Latin *intensus* 'stretched tightly'.

intensify ● v. (**intensifies**, **intensifying**, **intensified**) make or become more intense.
– DERIVATIVES **intensification** n.

intensity ● n. (pl. **intensities**) the quality of being intense.

intensive ● adj. **1** very thorough or vigorous. **2** (of agriculture) aiming to achieve maximum production within a limited area. **3** (in combination) making much use of something: *labour-intensive methods*.
– DERIVATIVES **intensively** adv.

intensive care ● n. special medical treatment of a dangerously ill patient.

intent ● n. intention or purpose. ● adj. **1** (**intent on/upon**) determined to do. **2** (**intent on/upon**) attentively occupied with. **3** showing earnest and eager attention.
– DERIVATIVES **intently** adv.
– ORIGIN Old French *entent*.

intention ● n. **1** an aim or plan. **2** (**one's intentions**) a man's plans in respect to marriage.

intentional ● adj. deliberate.
– DERIVATIVES **intentionally** adv.

inter /in-ter/ ● v. (**inters**, **interring**, **interred**) place (a dead body) in a grave or tomb.
– ORIGIN Old French *enterrer*.

inter- ● prefix **1** between: *interbreed*. **2** so as to affect both: *interact*.
– ORIGIN Latin *inter*.

interact ● v. (of two people or things) act so as to affect each other.
– DERIVATIVES **interaction** n.

interactive ● adj. **1** influencing each other. **2** (of a computer or other electronic device) allowing a two-way flow of information between it and a user.

inter alia /in-ter ay-li-uh/ ● adv. among other things.
– ORIGIN Latin.

interbreed ● v. (**interbreeds**, **interbreeding**, **interbred**) breed with an animal of a different race or species.

intercede /in-ter-seed/ ● v. (**intercedes**, **interceding**, **interceded**) intervene on behalf of another.
– ORIGIN Latin *intercedere*.

intercept ● v. /in-ter-**sept**/ stop and prevent from continuing to a destination. ● n. /**in**-ter-sept/ **1** an act of intercepting. **2** Math. the point at which a line cuts the axis of a graph.
– DERIVATIVES **interception** n. **interceptor** n.
– ORIGIN Latin *intercipere* 'catch between'.

intercession /in-ter-sesh-uhn/ ● n. the action of interceding.
– ORIGIN Latin.

interchange ● v. /in-ter-**chaynj**/ (**interchanges**, **interchanging**, **interchanged**) **1** exchange (things) with each other. **2** put each of (two things) in the other's place. ● n. /**in**-ter-chaynj/ **1** the action of interchanging. **2** an exchange of words. **3** a road junction on several levels so that traffic streams do not intersect.
– DERIVATIVES **interchangeable** adj.

intercity ● adj. existing or travelling between cities.

intercom ● n. an electrical device allowing one-way or two-way communication.
– ORIGIN short for *intercommunication*.

intercommunication ● n. the process of communicating between people or groups.

interconnect ● v. connect with each other.

intercontinental ● adj. relating to or travelling between continents.

intercourse ● n. **1** communication or dealings between people. **2** sexual intercourse.
– ORIGIN Latin *intercursus*.

intercut ● v. (**intercuts**, **intercutting**, **intercut**) alternate (scenes) with contrasting scenes in a film.

interdenominational ● adj. relating to more than one religious denomination.

interdepartmental ● adj. relating to more than one department.

interdependent ● adj. dependent on each other.

interdict ● n. /**in**tərdikt/ an order forbidding something. ● v. /intər**dikt**/ esp. N. Amer. prohibit or forbid.
– ORIGIN Latin *interdictum*.

interdisciplinary ● adj. relating to more than one branch of knowledge.

interest ● n. **1** the state of wanting to know about something or someone. **2** the quality of arousing a person's curiosity or holding their attention. **3** a subject about which one is concerned or enthusiastic. **4** money paid for the use of money lent. **5** a person's advantage or benefit: *it is in his own interest*. **6** a share, right, or stake in property or a business. ● v. **1** arouse the curiosity or attention of. **2** (**interest in**) persuade (someone) to do or obtain. **3** (**interested**) not impartial: *interested parties*.
– ORIGIN Latin *interesse* 'be important'.

interesting ● adj. arousing curiosity or interest.

interface ● n. **1** a point where two things meet and interact. **2** a device or program enabling a user to communicate with a computer, or for connecting two items of hardware or software. ● v. (**interfaces**, **interfacing**, **interfaced**) (**interface with**) Computing connect with (something) by an interface.

interfere ● v. (**interferes**, **interfering**, **interfered**) **1** (**interfere with**) prevent from continuing or being carried out properly. **2** (**interfere with**) handle or adjust without permission. **3** become involved in something without being asked. **4** (**interfere with**) Brit. euphem. sexually molest.
– DERIVATIVES **interfering** adj.
– ORIGIN Old French *s'entreferir* 'strike each other'.

interference ● n. **1** the action of interfering.

2 disturbance to radio signals caused by unwanted signals from other sources. **3** Physics the combination of waves of the same wavelength from two or more sources, producing a new wave pattern.

interferon /in-ter-**feer**-on/ ● n. a protein released by animal cells which prevents a virus from reproducing itself.

intergalactic ● adj. relating to or situated between galaxies.

interim /**in**-tuh-rim/ ● n. (**the interim**) the time between two events. ● adj. lasting for a short time; provisional.
– ORIGIN Latin, 'meanwhile'.

interior ● adj. **1** situated within or inside; inner. **2** remote from the coast or frontier; inland. ● n. **1** the interior part. **2** the internal affairs of a country.
ORIGIN Latin 'inner'.

interior angle ● n. the angle between adjacent sides of a straight-sided figure.

interior design ● n. the design, decoration, and furnishings of the interior of a room or building.

interior monologue ● n. a piece of writing expressing a character's thoughts.

interject /in-ter-**jekt**/ ● v. say suddenly as an interruption.
– ORIGIN Latin *interjicere* 'interpose'.

interjection ● n. an exclamation (e.g. *ah!*).

interlace ● v. (**interlaces**, **interlacing**, **interlaced**) weave together.

interleave ● v. (**interleaves**, **interleaving**, **interleaved**) place something between the layers of.

interlink ● v. join or connect together.

interlock ● v. (of two parts) engage with each other by overlapping or fitting together. ● n. (also **interlock fabric**) a fabric with closely interlocking stitches allowing it to stretch.

interlocutor /in-ter-**lok**-yuu-ter/ ● n. formal a person who takes part in a conversation.
– ORIGIN Latin *interloqui* 'interrupt'.

interlocutory /in-ter-**lok**-yuu-tuh-ri/ ● adj. relating to dialogue.

interloper /**in**-ter-loh-per/ ● n. a person who interferes in another's affairs.
– ORIGIN from INTER- + archaic *landloper* 'vagabond'.

interlude ● n. **1** a period of time or activity that contrasts with what goes before or after: *a romantic interlude.* **2** a pause between the acts of a play. **3** a piece of music played between other pieces.
– ORIGIN Latin *interludium.*

intermarry ● v. (**intermarries**, **intermarrying**, **intermarried**) (of people of different races, castes, or religions) marry each other.
– DERIVATIVES **intermarriage** n.

intermediary /in-ter-**mee**-di-uh-ri/ ● n. (pl. **intermediaries**) a person who tries to settle a dispute.

intermediate /in-ter-**mee**-di-uht/ ● adj. **1** coming between two things in time, place, character, etc. **2** having more than basic knowledge or skills but not yet advanced. ● n. an intermediate person or thing.
– ORIGIN from Latin *inter-* 'between' + *medius* 'middle'.

interment /in-**ter**-muhnt/ ● n. the burial of a dead body.

intermezzo /in-ter-**met**-zoh/ ● n. (pl. **intermezzi** /in-ter-**met**-zi/ or **intermezzos**) a short connecting instrumental movement between parts of an opera or other musical work, or between the acts of a play.
– ORIGIN Italian.

interminable ● adj. endless: *interminable discussions.*
– DERIVATIVES **interminably** adv.
– ORIGIN Latin *interminabilis.*

intermingle ● v. (**intermingles**, **intermingling**, **intermingled**) mix together.

intermission ● n. **1** a pause or break. **2** an interval between parts of a play or film.
– ORIGIN Latin.

intermittent ● adj. happening at irregular intervals.
– DERIVATIVES **intermittently** adv.
– ORIGIN Latin.

intermix ● v. mix together.

intern ● n. /**in**-tern/ N. Amer. **1** a recent medical graduate receiving supervised training in a hospital. **2** a student or trainee who does a job to gain work experience. ● v. /in-**tern**/ confine as a prisoner.
– DERIVATIVES **internment** n.
– ORIGIN Latin *internus* 'internal'.

internal ● adj. **1** having to do with the inside. **2** inside the body. **3** relating to affairs and activities within a country. **4** existing or used within an organization. **5** in one's mind or soul.
– DERIVATIVES **internally** adv.
– ORIGIN Latin *internalis.*

internal-combustion engine ● n. an engine in which power is generated by the expansion of hot gases from the burning of fuel with air inside the engine.

internal exile ● n. banishment from a part of one's own country.

internalize (also **internalise**) ● v. (**internalizes**, **internalizing**, **internalized**) make (a belief or attitude) part of one's behaviour or thinking.

international ● adj. **1** existing or occurring between nations. **2** agreed on or used by all or many nations. ● n. **1** Brit. a game or contest between teams from different countries. **2** a player who has taken part in such a contest.
– DERIVATIVES **internationally** adv.

International Bank for Reconstruction and Development E
an agency of the United Nations which constitutes the main part of the World Bank.

International Court of Justice E
a judicial court of the United Nations which meets at The Hague.

International Date Line E
see DATE LINE.

internationalism ● n. belief in cooperation and understanding between nations.

internationalize (also **internationalise**) ● v. (**internationalizes**, **internationalizing**, **internationalized**) make international.
– DERIVATIVES **internationalization** (also **internationalisation**) n.

international law ● n. a body of rules recognized by nations as binding in their relations with one another.

International Monetary Fund E
an international organization which aims to promote international trade and monetary cooperation and the stabilization of exchange rates. It is affiliated to the UN, with headquarters in Washington DC.

internecine /in-ter-nee-syn/ ● adj. (of conflict) happening between members of a group: *internecine rivalries.*
– ORIGIN Latin *internecinus.*

internee ● n. a prisoner.

Internet ● n. an international information network linking computers.

interpersonal ● adj. relating to relationships between people.

interplanetary ● adj. situated or travelling between planets.

interplay ● n. the way in which things interact.

Interpol /in-ter-pol/ ● n. an international organization that coordinates investigations made by the police forces of member countries into international crimes.
– ORIGIN from *Inter(national) pol(ice).*

interpolate /in-ter-puh-layt/ ● v. (**interpolates, interpolating, interpolated**) **1** insert (something different or additional). **2** add (a remark) to a conversation. **3** Math. insert (an intermediate term) into a series by estimating it from surrounding known values.
– DERIVATIVES **interpolation** n.
– ORIGIN Latin *interpolare* 'refurbish'.

interpose ● v. (**interposes, interposing, interposed**) **1** place (something) between one thing and another. **2** intervene between parties.
– ORIGIN French *interposer.*

interpret ● v. (**interprets, interpreting, interpreted**) **1** explain the meaning of. **2** translate aloud the words of a person speaking a different language. **3** understand as having a particular meaning.
– DERIVATIVES **interpretable** adj. **interpretative** adj. **interpretive** adj.
– ORIGIN Latin *interpretari* 'explain'.

interpretation ● n. **1** the action of explaining the meaning of something. **2** an explanation. **3** the way in which a performer expresses a creative work.

interpreter ● n. a person who interprets foreign speech aloud.

interracial ● adj. existing between or involving different races.

interregnum /in-ter-reg-nuhm/ ● n. (pl. **interregnums** or **interregna** /in-ter-reg-nuh/) a period between regimes when normal government is suspended.
– ORIGIN Latin.

interrelate ● v. (**interrelates, interrelating, interrelated**) relate or connect to one other.
– DERIVATIVES **interrelation** n.

interrogate ● v. (**interrogates, interrogating, interrogated**) ask questions of (someone) thoroughly or aggressively.
– DERIVATIVES **interrogation** n. **interrogator** n.
– ORIGIN Latin *interrogare.*

interrogative /in-ter-rog-uh-tiv/ ● adj. in the form of a question or used in questions. ● n. a word used in questions, e.g. *how* or *what.*

interrogatory /in-ter-rog-uh-tuh-ri/ ● adj. questioning.

interrupt ● v. **1** stop the continuous progress of. **2** stop (a person who is speaking) by saying or doing something. **3** break the continuity of (a line, surface, or view).
– DERIVATIVES **interruption** n.
– ORIGIN Latin *interrumpere.*

intersect ● v. **1** divide (something) by passing or lying across it. **2** (of lines, roads, etc.) cross or cut each other.
– ORIGIN Latin *intersecare.*

intersection ● n. a place at which two roads, lines, etc. intersect.

intersperse ● v. (**intersperses, interspersing, interspersed**) (usu. **be interspersed**) scatter or place among or between other things.
– ORIGIN Latin *interspergere.*

interstate ● adj. existing or carried on between states. ● n. one of a system of motorways running between US states.

interstellar /in-ter-stel-ler/ ● adj. occurring or situated between stars.

interstice /in-ter-stiss/ ● n. a small space in something.
– ORIGIN Latin *interstitium.*

interstitial /in-ter-sti-sh'l/ ● adj. found in or relating to small spaces within something.

intertwine ● v. (**intertwines, intertwining, intertwined**) twist or twine together.

interval ● n. **1** a period of time between two events. **2** a pause. **3** Brit. a pause between parts of a performance or a sports match. **4** the difference in pitch between two sounds.
– ORIGIN Latin *intervallum* 'space between ramparts'.

intervene ● v. (**intervenes, intervening, intervened**) **1** come between (two people or things) so as to prevent or alter a situation. **2** (**intervening**) occurring between or among.
– ORIGIN Latin *intervenire.*

intervention ● n. the action of intervening to improve or control a situation.

interventionist ● adj. favouring intervention.

interview ● n. **1** an occasion on which a journalist or broadcaster puts a series of questions to a person. **2** a spoken examination of an applicant for a job or college place. **3** a session of formal questioning of a person by the police. ● v. hold an interview with.
– DERIVATIVES **interviewee** n. **interviewer** n.
– ORIGIN French *entrevue.*

interwar ● adj. existing in the period between the two world wars.

interweave ● v. (**interweaves, interweaving, interwove**; past part. **interwoven**) weave or become woven together.

intestate /in-tess-tayt/ ● adj. not having made a will before one dies.
– ORIGIN Latin *intestatus.*

intestine (also **intestines**) ● n. the long tubular organ leading from the end of the stomach to the anus.
– DERIVATIVES **intestinal** adj.
– ORIGIN Latin *intestinum.*

intimacy ● n. (pl. **intimacies**) **1** close familiarity or friendship. **2** an intimate act or remark.

intimate[1] ● adj. /in-ti-muht/ **1** close and friendly. **2** private and personal: *intimate de-*

tails. **3** euphem. having a sexual relationship. **4** involving very close connection. **5** (of knowledge) detailed. **6** having an informal friendly atmosphere. ● **n.** /**in**-ti-muht/ a very close friend.
– DERIVATIVES **intimately** adv.
– ORIGIN Latin *intimare* 'impress'.

intimate[2] /in-ti-mayt/ ● **v.** (**intimates, intimating, intimated**) state indirectly; hint.
– DERIVATIVES **intimation** n.
– ORIGIN Latin *intimare* (see INTIMATE[1]).

intimidate ● **v.** (**intimidates, intimidating, intimidated**) frighten into doing something.
– DERIVATIVES **intimidation** n.
– ORIGIN Latin *intimidare* 'make timid'.

into ● **prep.** **1** expressing movement or direction to a point on or within. **2** expressing a change of state or the result of an action. **3** in the direction of. **4** about or concerning. **5** expressing division: *three into twelve.*

intolerable ● **adj.** unable to be endured.
– DERIVATIVES **intolerably** adv.

intolerant ● **adj.** unwilling to tolerate ideas or behaviour that are different to one's own.
– DERIVATIVES **intolerance** n.

intonation ● **n.** **1** the rise and fall of the voice in speaking. **2** the action of intoning.

intone /in-tohn/ ● **v.** (**intones, intoning, intoned**) say or recite with little rise and fall of the pitch of the voice.
– ORIGIN Latin *intonare.*

in toto /in toh-toh/ ● **adv.** as a whole.
– ORIGIN Latin.

intoxicate ● **v.** (**intoxicates, intoxicating, intoxicated**) **1** (of alcoholic drink or a drug) cause (someone) to lose control of themselves. **2** excite or exhilarate: *he was intoxicated by cinema.*
– DERIVATIVES **intoxication** n.
– ORIGIN Latin *intoxicare.*

intra- /in-truh/ ● **prefix** (added to adjectives) on the inside; within: *intramural.*
– ORIGIN Latin.

intractable /in-trak-tuh-b'l/ ● **adj.** **1** hard to deal with. **2** stubborn.

intramural /in-truh-**myoor**-uhl/ ● **adj.** forming part of normal university or college studies.
– ORIGIN from INTRA- + Latin *murus* 'wall'.

intranet /in-truh-net/ ● **n.** Computing a private communications network created with Internet software.

intransigent /in-tran-zi-juhnt/ ● **adj.** refusing to change one's views or behaviour.
– DERIVATIVES **intransigence** n.
– ORIGIN from Spanish *los intransigentes* (a name adopted by extreme republicans).

intransitive /in-tran-zi-tiv/ ● **adj.** (of a verb) not taking a direct object, e.g. *look* in *look at the sky.* Opp. TRANSITIVE.

intrauterine /in-truh-**yoo**-tuh-ryn/ ● **adj.** within the womb.

intrauterine device ● **n.** a contraceptive device in the form of a coil, inserted into the womb.

intravenous /in-truh-**vee**-nuhss/ ● **adj.** within or into a vein or veins.
– DERIVATIVES **intravenously** adv.

intrepid ● **adj.** fearless; adventurous.
– DERIVATIVES **intrepidity** n.
– ORIGIN Latin *intrepidus* 'not alarmed'.

intricacy /in-tri-kuh-si/ ● **n.** (pl. **intricacies**) **1** the quality of being intricate. **2** (**intricacies**) details.

intricate ● **adj.** very complicated or detailed.
– DERIVATIVES **intricately** adv.
– ORIGIN Latin *intricare* 'entangle'.

intrigue ● **v.** /in-treeg/ (**intrigues, intriguing, intrigued**) **1** arouse the curiosity or interest of. **2** plot something illegal or harmful. ● **n.** /**in**-treeg/ **1** the plotting of something illegal or harmful. **2** a secret love affair.
– DERIVATIVES **intriguing** adj.
– ORIGIN French *intriguer* 'tangle, plot'.

intrinsic /in-trin-sik/ ● **adj.** belonging to the basic nature of someone or something; essential.
– ORIGIN Latin *intrinsecus* 'inwardly'.

intro- ● **prefix** into; inwards: *introvert.*
– ORIGIN Latin *intro* 'to the inside'.

introduce ● **v.** (**introduces, introducing, introduced**) **1** bring into use or operation for the first time. **2** present (someone) by name to another. **3** (**introduce to**) bring (a subject) to the attention of (someone) for the first time. **4** insert or bring into: *a device which introduces chlorine into the pool.* **5** occur at the start of. **6** provide an opening announcement for.
– ORIGIN Latin *introducere.*

introduction ● **n.** **1** the action of introducing. **2** an act of introducing one person to another. **3** a thing which introduces another, such as a section at the beginning of a book. **4** a thing newly brought in. **5** a book or course of study intended to introduce a subject. **6** a person's first experience of a subject or activity.

introductory ● **adj.** serving as an introduction; basic.

introspection ● **n.** the examination of one's own thoughts or feelings.
– DERIVATIVES **introspective** adj.
– ORIGIN Latin *introspicere* 'look into'.

introvert ● **n.** a shy, quiet person who is mainly concerned with their own thoughts and feelings. ● **adj.** (also **introverted**) having to do with an introvert.
– ORIGIN from Latin *intro-* 'to the inside' + *vertere* 'to turn'.

intrude ● **v.** (**intrudes, intruding, intruded**) come into a place or situation where one is unwelcome or uninvited.
– ORIGIN Latin *intrudere.*

intruder ● **n.** **1** a person who enters a place illegally. **2** a person who goes somewhere where they are not welcome.

intrusion ● **n.** **1** the action of intruding. **2** a thing that intrudes.

intrusive ● **adj.** **1** having an unwelcome effect. **2** (of igneous rock) that has been forced when molten into cracks in neighbouring strata.

intuit /in-tyoo-it/ ● **v.** understand or work out by intuition.
– ORIGIN Latin *intueri* 'contemplate'.

intuition ● **n.** the ability to understand or know something immediately, without conscious reasoning.

intuitive ● **adj.** having to do with intuition.
– DERIVATIVES **intuitively** adv.

Inuit /in-yuu-it/ ● **n.** **1** (pl. **Inuit** or **Inuits**) a member of a people of northern Canada and parts of Greenland and Alaska. **2** the lan-

guage of this people.
– ORIGIN Inuit, 'people'.

USAGE Inuit
For an explanation of the terms **Inuit** and **Eskimo**, see the note at **ESKIMO**.

inundate /in-uhn-dayt/ ● v. (**inundates, inundating, inundated**) (usu. **be inundated**) **1** flood. **2** overwhelm with things to be dealt with.
– DERIVATIVES **inundation** n.
– ORIGIN Latin *inundare* 'flood'.

inure /i-nyoor/ ● v. (**inures, inuring, inured**) (**be inured to**) become used to something unpleasant.
– ORIGIN Old French, 'in practice'.

invade ● v. (**invades, invading, invaded**) **1** enter (a country) so as to conquer or occupy it. **2** enter in large numbers. **3** (of a parasite or disease) spread into (an organism or bodily part). **4** intrude on: *his privacy was being invaded.*
– ORIGIN Latin *invadere.*

invalid[1] /in-vuh-lid/ ● n. a person made weak or disabled by illness or injury. ● v. (**invalids, invaliding, invalided**) (**be invalided**) be removed from service in the armed forces because of injury or illness.
– ORIGIN from **INVALID**[2].

invalid[2] /in-val-id/ ● adj. **1** not legally recognized. **2** not true because based on incorrect information or faulty reasoning.
– ORIGIN Latin *invalidus* 'not strong'.

invalidate ● v. (**invalidates, invalidating, invalidated**) make invalid.
– DERIVATIVES **invalidation** n.

invalidity ● n. **1** Brit. the condition of being an invalid. **2** the fact of being invalid.

invaluable ● adj. extremely useful.

invariable ● adj. **1** never changing. **2** Math. (of a quantity) constant.

invariably ● adv. always.

invasion ● n. **1** an act of invading a country. **2** the arrival of a large number of people or things. **3** an intrusion.

invasive ● adj. **1** tending to invade or intrude: *invasive grasses.* **2** (of medical procedures) involving the introduction of instruments or other objects into the body.

invective ● n. strongly abusive or critical language.
– ORIGIN Latin *invectivus* 'attacking'.

inveigh /in-vay/ ● v. (**inveigh against**) speak or write about with great hostility.
– ORIGIN Latin *invehere* 'carry in'.

inveigle /in-vay-g'l/ ● v. (**inveigles, inveigling, inveigled**) (**inveigle into**) persuade by trickery or flattery.
– ORIGIN Old French *aveugler* 'to blind'.

invent ● v. **1** create or design (a new device, process, etc.). **2** make up (a false story, name, etc.).
– DERIVATIVES **inventor** n.
– ORIGIN Latin *invenire* 'contrive'.

invention ● n. **1** the action of inventing. **2** something invented. **3** a false story. **4** creative ability.

inventive ● adj. having or showing creativity or original thought.
– DERIVATIVES **inventiveness** n.

inventory /in-vuhn-tuh-ri/ ● n. (pl. **inventories**) **1** a complete list of items. **2** a quantity of goods in stock.
– ORIGIN Latin *inventarium* 'a list of what is found'.

Invercargill E
/in-ver-kar-gil/ a city in New Zealand, capital of Southland region, South Island.

Inverness E
/in-ver-ness/ a city in Scotland, administrative centre of Highland region.

inverse /in-verss/ ● adj. opposite in position, direction, order, or effect. ● n. **1** a thing that is the opposite or reverse of another. **2** Math. a reciprocal quantity.
– ORIGIN Latin *inversus.*

inverse proportion (also **inverse ratio**) ● n. a relation between two quantities such that one increases in proportion as the other decreases.

inversion ● n. the action of inverting or the state of being inverted.

invert /in-vert/ ● v. put upside down or in the opposite position or order.
– ORIGIN Latin *invertere* 'turn inside out'.

invertebrate /in-ver-ti-bruht/ ● n. an animal having no backbone. ● adj. relating to such animals.

inverted comma ● n. esp. Brit. a quotation mark.

invest ● v. **1** put money into financial schemes, shares, or property with the expectation of making a profit. **2** devote (time or energy) to an undertaking with the expectation of a worthwhile result. **3** (**invest in**) informal buy (something) whose usefulness will repay the cost. **4** (**invest with**) provide with (a quality). **5** give (a rank or office) to.
– DERIVATIVES **investor** n.
– ORIGIN Latin *investire* 'clothe'.

investigate ● v. **1** carry out a systematic inquiry into (an incident or allegation) so as to establish the truth. **2** carry out research into (a subject).
– DERIVATIVES **investigation** n. **investigator** n.
– ORIGIN Latin *investigare* 'trace out'.

investigative /in-vess-ti-guh-tiv/ ● adj. **1** having to do with investigating. **2** (of journalism or a journalist) investigating and seeking to expose dishonesty or injustice.

investiture /in-vess-ti-cher/ ● n. **1** the action of formally investing a person with honours or rank. **2** a ceremony at which this takes place.

investment ● n. **1** the action of investing. **2** a thing worth buying because it may be profitable or useful in the future.

inveterate /in-vet-uh-ruht/ ● adj. **1** having a long-standing and firmly established habit: *an inveterate gambler.* **2** (of a feeling or habit) firmly established.
– ORIGIN Latin *inveteratus* 'made old'.

invidious /in-vid-i-uhss/ ● adj. unacceptable, unfair, and likely to arouse resentment or anger in others.
– ORIGIN Latin *invidiosus.*

invigilate /in-vij-i-layt/ ● v. (**invigilates, invigilating, invigilated**) Brit. supervise candidates during an examination.
– DERIVATIVES **invigilation** n. **invigilator** n.
– ORIGIN Latin *invigilare* 'watch over'.

invigorate /in-vig-uh-rayt/ ● v. (**invigorates,**

invigorating, **invigorated**) give strength or energy to.
– DERIVATIVES **invigorating** adj.
– ORIGIN Latin *invigorare* 'make strong'.

invincible /in-vin-si-b'l/ ● **adj.** too powerful to be defeated or overcome.
– DERIVATIVES **invincibility** n.
– ORIGIN Latin *invincibilis.*

inviolable /in-vy-uh-luh-b'l/ ● **adj.** never to be attacked or dishonoured.

inviolate /in-vy-uh-luht/ ● **adj.** free from injury or violation.
– ORIGIN Latin *inviolatus.*

invisible ● **adj. 1** unable to be seen, either by nature or because concealed. **2** relating to earnings which a country makes from the sale of services rather than commodities.
– DERIVATIVES **invisibility** n. **invisibly** adv.

invitation ● **n. 1** a request inviting someone to go somewhere or to do something. **2** the action of inviting. **3** a situation or action inviting a particular outcome or response: *his tactics were an invitation to disaster.*

invite ● **v.** (**invites**, **inviting**, **invited**) **1** ask in a friendly or formal way to go somewhere or to do something. **2** ask for (something) formally or politely. **3** tend to provoke (a particular outcome or response). ● **n.** informal an invitation.
– ORIGIN Latin *invitare.*

inviting ● **adj.** tempting or attractive.

in vitro /in vee-troh/ ● **adj. & adv.** (of biological processes) taking place in a test tube or elsewhere outside a living organism.
– ORIGIN Latin, 'in glass'.

invocation /in-vuh-kay-sh'n/ ● **n. 1** the action of invoking. **2** an appeal to a god or spirit.

invoice ● **n.** a list of goods or services provided, with a statement of the sum due. ● **v.** (**invoices**, **invoicing**, **invoiced**) send an invoice to.
– ORIGIN French *envoyer* 'send'.

invoke /in-vohk/ ● **v.** (**invokes**, **invoking**, **invoked**) **1** appeal to as an authority or in support of an argument. **2** call on (a god or spirit) in prayer or as a witness. **3** call earnestly for.
– ORIGIN Latin *invocare.*

involuntary ● **adj. 1** done without conscious control. **2** (especially of muscles or nerves) unable to be consciously controlled. **3** done against someone's will.
– DERIVATIVES **involuntarily** adv.

involve ● **v.** (**involves**, **involving**, **involved**) **1** (of a situation or event) include (something) as a necessary part or result. **2** cause to experience or participate in an activity or situation: *what organizations will be involved in these projects?*
– DERIVATIVES **involvement** n.
– ORIGIN Latin *involvere* 'entangle'.

involved ● **adj. 1** connected on an emotional or personal level: *she was involved with someone else.* **2** difficult to understand; complicated.

invulnerable ● **adj.** impossible to harm or damage.
– DERIVATIVES **invulnerability** n.

-in-waiting ● **comb. form** referring to a position as attendant to a royal person: *lady-in-waiting.*

inward ● **adj. 1** directed or proceeding towards the inside. **2** mental or spiritual. ● **adv.** var. of **INWARDS.**

inward-looking ● **adj.** self-absorbed.

inwards (also **inward**) ● **adv. 1** towards the inside. **2** towards the mind or spirit.

Io E
/I-oh/ Gk Myth. a priestess of Hera who was loved by Zeus, who turned her into a heifer to protect her from Hera's jealousy.

iodide /I-uh-dyd/ ● **n.** a compound of iodine with another element or group.

iodine /I-uh-deen/ ● **n. 1** a black, non-metallic chemical element of the halogen group. **2** an antiseptic solution of iodine in alcohol.
– ORIGIN Greek *iōdēs* 'violet-coloured'.

ion /I-uhn/ ● **n.** an atom or molecule with a net electric charge through loss or gain of electrons.
– DERIVATIVES **ionic** adj.
– ORIGIN Greek, 'going'.

Iona E
/I-oh-nuh/ a small island in the Inner Hebrides, site of a monastery founded by St Columba in about 563.

Ionesco E
/ee-uh-ness-koh/, Eugène (1912–94), Romanian-born French dramatist. His plays, such as *Rhinoceros,* are part of the movement known as the Theatre of the Absurd, drama which departs from conventional dramatic form to portray the futility of human struggle in a senseless world.

Ionian Islands E
a chain of about forty Greek islands off the western coast of mainland Greece, in the Ionian Sea, including Corfu, Cephalonia, Ithaca, and Zakinthos.

Ionian Sea E
the part of the Mediterranean Sea between western Greece and southern Italy.

ionize /I-uh-nyz/ (also **ionise**) ● **v.** (**ionizes**, **ionizing**, **ionized**) convert (an atom, molecule, or substance) into an ion or ions.
– DERIVATIVES **ionization** (also **ionisation**) n.

ionizer (also **ioniser**) ● **n.** a device which produces ions, used to improve the quality of the air in a room.

ionosphere /I-on-uh-sfeer/ ● **n.** the layer of the atmosphere above the mesosphere.

iota /I-oh-tuh/ ● **n.** an extremely small amount: *it won't make an iota of difference.*
– ORIGIN Greek; the letter *iota* is the smallest in the Greek alphabet.

IOU ● **n.** a signed document acknowledging a debt.
– ORIGIN from *I owe you.*

Iowa E
/I-uh-wuh/ a state in the Middle West of the US; capital, Des Moines.
– DERIVATIVES **Iowan** adj. & n.

ipso facto /ip-soh fak-toh/ ● **adv.** by that very fact or act.
– ORIGIN Latin.

Ipswich 
the county town of Suffolk.

IQ • **abbrev.** intelligence quotient.

Iqbal E
/**ik**-bal/, Sir Muhammad (1875–1938), Indian poet, philosopher, and political leader. As president of the Muslim League in 1930, he advocated the creation of a separate Muslim state in NW India, the beginning of the concept of Pakistan.

IRA • **abbrev.** Irish Republican Army.

Iran E
/i-**rahn**, i-**ran**/ a country in the Middle East, between the Caspian Sea and the Persian Gulf; capital, Tehran. Former name (until 1935) **PERSIA**.
– DERIVATIVES **Iranian** adj. & n.

Iran–Iraq War E
the war of 1980–8 between Iran and Iraq. It ended inconclusively after great loss of life.

Iraq E
/i-**rahk**, i-**rak**/ a country in the Middle East, on the Persian Gulf; capital, Baghdad.
– DERIVATIVES **Iraqi** adj. & n.

irascible /i-**rass**-i-b'l/ • **adj.** hot-tempered; irritable.
– DERIVATIVES **irascibility** n.
– ORIGIN Latin *irascibilis*.

irate /I-**rayt**/ • **adj.** extremely angry.
– ORIGIN Latin *iratus*.

ire /*rhymes with* fire/ • **n.** literary anger.
– ORIGIN Latin *ira*.

Ireland E
an island of the British Isles, lying west of Great Britain. It is divided into the Republic of Ireland and Northern Ireland.

Ireland, Republic of E
a country comprising approximately four fifths of Ireland; capital, Dublin. Also called **IRISH REPUBLIC**.

Irian Jaya E
/i-ri-uhn **jy**-uh/ a province of eastern Indonesia comprising the western half of the island of New Guinea together with the adjacent small islands; capital, Jayapura. Also called **WEST IRIAN**.

iridescent /i-ri-**dess**-uhnt/ • **adj.** showing bright colours that seem to change when seen from different angles.
– DERIVATIVES **iridescence** n.
– ORIGIN Latin *iris* 'rainbow'.

iridium /i-**rid**-i-uhm/ • **n.** a hard, dense silvery-white metallic element.
– ORIGIN Latin *iris* 'rainbow'.

iris • **n. 1** a coloured ring-shaped membrane behind the cornea of the eye, with the pupil in the centre. **2** a plant with sword-shaped leaves and purple or yellow flowers.
– ORIGIN Greek, 'rainbow, iris'.

Irish • **n.** (also **Irish Gaelic**) the Celtic language of Ireland. • **adj.** relating to Ireland or Irish.
– DERIVATIVES **Irishman** n. **Irishwoman** n.
– ORIGIN Old English.

Irish coffee • **n.** coffee mixed with a dash of Irish whisky.

Irish Free State E
the name for the Republic of Ireland 1921–37.

Irish National Liberation Army E
a small paramilitary organization seeking union between Northern Ireland and the Republic of Ireland.

Irish Republic E
see **IRELAND, REPUBLIC OF**.

Irish Republican Army E
the military arm of Sinn Fein, aiming for union between the Republic of Ireland and Northern Ireland.

Irish Sea E
the sea separating Ireland from England and Wales.

irk /erk/ • **v.** irritate; annoy.
– DERIVATIVES **irksome** adj.
– ORIGIN perh. from Old Norse, 'to work'.

Irkutsk E
/eer-**kuutsk**/ the chief city of Siberia.

iron • **n. 1** a strong magnetic silvery-grey metal. **2** a hand-held implement with a heated steel base, used to smooth clothes and linen. **3** a golf club used for hitting the ball at a high angle. **4** (**irons**) fetters or handcuffs. • **v. 1** smooth (clothes) with an iron. **2** (**iron out**) settle (a difficulty or problem).
– ORIGIN Old English.

Iron Age • **n.** the period that followed the Bronze Age, when weapons and tools came to be made of iron.

Iron Curtain • **n.** (**the Iron Curtain**) an imaginary barrier separating the former Soviet bloc and the West before the decline of communism in eastern Europe.

ironic /I-**ron**-ik/ • **adj. 1** using irony. **2** happening in the opposite way to what is expected.
– DERIVATIVES **ironical** adj. **ironically** adv.

ironing • **n.** clothes and linen that need to be or have just been ironed.

ironmonger • **n.** Brit. a person who sells tools and other hardware.
– DERIVATIVES **ironmongery** n.

ironworks • **n.** a place where iron is smelted or iron goods are made.

irony /**I**-ruh-ni/ • **n.** (pl. **ironies**) **1** the expression of meaning through the use of language which normally means the opposite. **2** a situation that appears opposite to what one expects.
– ORIGIN Greek *eirōneia* 'simulated ignorance'.

irradiate • **v.** (**irradiates**, **irradiating**, **irradiated**) **1** expose to radiation. **2** shine light on.
– DERIVATIVES **irradiation** n.
– ORIGIN Latin *irradiare*.

irrational • **adj.** not logical or reasonable.
– DERIVATIVES **irrationality** n. **irrationally** adv.

Irrawaddy E
/ir-ruh-**wod**-di/ the chief river of Burma (Myanmar), which rises in the north of the country and flows into the eastern part of the Bay of Bengal.

irreconcilable • **adj. 1** incompatible. **2** not able to be settled: *irreconcilable differences*.

irrecoverable • **adj.** not able to be recovered.

irredeemable ● adj. not able to be saved, improved, or corrected.
– DERIVATIVES **irredeemably** adv.

irredentist /ir-ri-den-tist/ ● n. a person who believes that territory formerly belonging to their country should be given back to it.
– ORIGIN Italian *irredentista*.

irreducible ● adj. not able to be reduced or simplified.

irrefutable /ir-ri-fyoo-tuh-b'l/ ● adj. impossible to deny or disprove.

irregular ● adj. **1** not regular in shape, arrangement, or occurrence. **2** not according to a rule or standard. **3** not belonging to regular army units. **4** Grammar (of a word) having inflections that are not formed in the usual way.
– DERIVATIVES **irregularity** n. (pl. **irregularities**).

irrelevant ● adj. not relevant.
– DERIVATIVES **irrelevance** n. **irrelevantly** adv.

irreligious ● adj. indifferent or hostile to religion.

irremediable /ir-ri-mee-di-uh-b'l/ ● adj. impossible to remedy.

irreparable /ir-rep-uh-ruh-b'l/ ● adj. impossible to put right or repair.
DERIVATIVES **irreparably** adv.

irreplaceable ● adj. impossible to replace if lost or damaged.

irrepressible ● adj. not able to be restrained.

irreproachable ● adj. very good and unable to be criticized.

irresistible ● adj. too tempting or powerful to be resisted.
– DERIVATIVES **irresistibly** adv.

irresolute ● adj. uncertain.

irrespective ● adj. (**irrespective of**) regardless of.

irresponsible ● adj. not showing a proper sense of responsibility.
– DERIVATIVES **irresponsibly** adv.

irretrievable ● adj. not able to be improved or set right.
– DERIVATIVES **irretrievably** adv.

irreverent ● adj. disrespectful.
– DERIVATIVES **irreverence** n. **irreverently** adv.

irreversible ● adj. impossible to be reversed or altered.
– DERIVATIVES **irreversibility** n. **irreversibly** adv.

irrevocable /ir-rev-uh-kuh-b'l/ ● adj. not able to be changed, reversed, or recovered.
– DERIVATIVES **irrevocably** adv.
– ORIGIN Latin *irrevocabilis*.

irrigate /ir-ri-gayt/ ● v. (**irrigates, irrigating, irrigated**) supply water to (land or crops) by means of channels.
– DERIVATIVES **irrigation** n.
– ORIGIN Latin *irrigare* 'moisten'.

irritable ● adj. easily annoyed or angered.
– DERIVATIVES **irritability** n. **irritably** adv.

irritant ● n. **1** a substance that irritates part of the body. **2** a source of continual annoyance.

irritate ● v. (**irritates, irritating, irritated**) **1** make annoyed. **2** cause inflammation in (a part of the body).
– DERIVATIVES **irritating** adj. **irritation** n.
– ORIGIN Latin *irritare*.

irruption /ir-rup-sh'n/ ● n. formal a sudden forcible entry.
– ORIGIN Latin *irrumpere* 'break into'.

Irving[1], E
Sir Henry (1838–1905; born *John Henry Brodribb*), English actor-manager, famous for his acting partnership with Ellen Terry.

Irving[2], E
Washington (1783–1859), American writer, best known for *The Sketch Book of Geoffrey Crayon, Gent*, which contains such stories as 'Rip Van Winkle'.

is 3rd person sing. present of **BE**.

ISA ● abbrev. individual savings account.

Isaac E
/I-zuhk/ (in the Bible) a Hebrew patriarch, son of Abraham and Sarah and father of Jacob and Esau.

Isabella I E
(1451–1504), queen of Castile 1474–1504 and of Aragon 1479–1504. Her marriage in 1469 to Ferdinand of Aragon marked the beginning of the unification of Spain.

Isabella of France E
(1292–1358), daughter of Philip IV of France and wife of Edward II of England (1308–27). She organized an invasion of England in 1326 with her lover Roger de Mortimer, murdering Edward and replacing him with her son, Edward III.

Isaiah E
/I-zy-uh/ a major Hebrew prophet of Judah in the 8th century BC.

-ise ● suffix var. of **-IZE**.

USAGE -ise
Most verbs ending in **-ise**, e.g. **realise, authorise**, can also be spelled **-ize**. However, there are some verbs which must always be spelled **-ise** and are not variants of the **-ize** spelling. The most common ones are: *advertise, compromise, devise, televise, surprise, exercise, improvise, surmise, chastise, despise, supervise*, and *enfranchise*.

-ish ● suffix forming adjectives: **1** having the qualities of: *girlish*. **2** of the nationality of: *Swedish*. **3** rather: *yellowish*.
– ORIGIN Old English.

Isherwood, E
Christopher (William Bradshaw) (1904–86), British-born American novelist, author of *Mr Norris Changes Trains* and *Goodbye to Berlin*.

Ishiguro E
/i-shi-goo-roh/, Kazuo (b.1954), Japanese-born British novelist, author of *The Remains of the Day*.

Ishmael E
/ish-mayl/ (in the Bible) a son of Abraham and Hagar, his wife Sarah's maid. Ishmael (or Ismail) is also important in Islamic belief as the traditional ancestor of Muhammad and of the Arab peoples.

Islam /iz-lahm/ ● n. **1** the religion of the Mus-

lims, based on belief in one God and revealed through Muhammad as the Prophet of Allah. **2** the Muslim world.
– ORIGIN Arabic, 'submission'.

Islamabad E
/iz-**lah**-muh-bad/ the capital of Pakistan.

Islamic /iz-**lam**-ik/ • **adj.** relating to Islam.
island • **n.** a piece of land surrounded by water.
– DERIVATIVES **islander** n.
– ORIGIN Old English.

Islay E
/I-lay/ the southernmost of the Inner Hebrides islands.

isle • **n.** literary (except in place names) an island.
– ORIGIN Old French *ile*.

Isle of Man E
an island in the Irish Sea which is a British Crown possession having home rule, with its own law-making body (the Tynwald) and judicial system; capital, Douglas.

Isle of Wight E
/*rhymes with* light/ an island and county off the south coast of England; administrative centre, Newport.

islet /I-lit/ • **n.** a small island.
islets of Langerhans /lang-er-hanz/ • **pl. n.** groups of cells in the pancreas that produce insulin.
– ORIGIN named after the German anatomist Paul *Langerhans* (1847–88).
-ism • **suffix** forming nouns referring to: **1** an action or its result: *baptism.* **2** a state or quality: *barbarism.* **3** a system, principle, or movement: *Anglicanism.* **4** a basis for prejudice: *racism.* **5** a medical condition: *alcoholism.*
– ORIGIN Greek *-ismos*.
isn't • **contr.** is not.
isobar /I-soh-bar/ • **n.** Meteorol. a line on a map connecting points having the same atmospheric pressure.
– ORIGIN Greek *isobaros* 'of equal weight'.
isohyet /I-soh-**hy**-it/ • **n.** Meteorol. a line on a map connecting points having the same amount of rainfall.
– ORIGIN from Greek *isos* 'equal' + *huetos* 'rain'.
isolate • **v.** (**isolates**, **isolating**, **isolated**) **1** place apart or alone; cut off. **2** Chem. & Biol. obtain or extract (a compound, microorganism, etc.) in a pure form.
– ORIGIN from **ISOLATED**.
isolated • **adj. 1** remote; lonely. **2** single; exceptional: *isolated incidents.*
– ORIGIN French *isolé*.
isolation • **n.** the action of isolating or the fact of being isolated.
isolationism • **n.** a policy of remaining apart from the political affairs of other countries.
– DERIVATIVES **isolationist** n.
isomer /I-suh-mer/ • **n.** Chem. each of two or more compounds with the same formula but a different arrangement of atoms and different properties.
– ORIGIN Greek *isomerēs* 'sharing equally'.
isometric • **adj.** having equal dimensions.
– ORIGIN Greek *isometria*.
isosceles /I-soss-i-leez/ • **adj.** (of a triangle) having two sides of equal length.
– ORIGIN Greek *isoskelēs*.
isotherm /I-soh-therm/ • **n.** a line on a map or diagram connecting points having the same temperature.
– DERIVATIVES **isothermal** adj. & n.
– ORIGIN from Greek *isos* 'equal' + *thermē* 'heat'.
isotope /I-suh-tohp/ • **n.** Chem. each of two or more forms of the same element that contain equal numbers of protons but different numbers of neutrons in their nuclei.
– ORIGIN from Greek *isos* 'equal' + *topos* 'place'.
ISP • **abbrev.** Internet service provider.

Israel[1] E
/iz-rayl/ (also **children of Israel**) the Hebrew nation or people, traditionally descended from the patriarch Jacob (also named Israel).

Israel[2] E
/iz-rayl/ a country in the Middle East, on the Mediterranean Sea; capital (not recognized as such by the UN), Jerusalem.

Israeli /iz-ray-li/ • **n.** (pl. **Israelis**) a person from Israel. • **adj.** relating to the modern country of Israel.
Israelite /iz-ruh-lyt/ • **n.** a member of the ancient Hebrew nation.

Issigonis E
/is-si-**goh**-niss/, Sir Alec (Arnold Constantine) (1906–88), Turkish-born British car designer, famous for the Morris Minor and the Mini.

issue • **n. 1** an important topic to be debated or settled. **2** the action of issuing. **3** each of a regular series of publications. • **v.** (**issues**, **issuing**, **issued**) **1** supply or give out. **2** formally send out or make known: *issue a statement.* **3** (**issue from**) come, go, or flow out from.
– PHRASES **at issue** under discussion. **take issue with** challenge.
– ORIGIN Old French.
-ist • **suffix** forming nouns and related adjectives referring to: **1** a person who believes something or is prejudiced: *sexist.* **2** a member of a profession: *dentist.* **3** a person who uses something: *flautist.*
– ORIGIN Greek *-istēs*.

Istanbul E
/i-stan-**buul**/ a port in Turkey on the Bosporus. It was formerly the Roman city of Constantinople (330–1453), and was the capital of Turkey 1453–1923.

isthmus /iss-muhss/ • **n.** (pl. **isthmuses**) a narrow strip of land with sea on either side, linking two larger areas of land.
– ORIGIN Greek *isthmos*.
IT • **abbrev.** information technology.
it • **pron.** (third person sing.) **1** used to refer to a thing previously mentioned or easily identified. **2** referring to an animal or child of unspecified sex. **3** used to identify a person: *it's me.* **4** used as a subject in statements about time, distance, or weather: *it is raining.* **5** used to refer to something specified later in the sentence: *it is impossible to get there today.* **6** used to refer to the situation or circumstances: *if it's convenient.*

– ORIGIN Old English.

Italian • n. **1** a person from Italy. **2** the language of Italy. • adj. relating to Italy or Italian.

italic /i-tal-ik/ • adj. referring to the sloping typeface used especially for emphasis and in foreign words. • n. (also **italics**) an italic typeface or letter.
– ORIGIN Greek *Italikos* 'Italian'.

italicize (also **italicise**) • v. (**italicizes, italicizing, italicized**) print (text) in italics.

Italy E
a country in southern Europe; capital, Rome.

itch • n. **1** an uncomfortable sensation that causes a desire to scratch the skin. **2** informal an impatient desire. • v. **1** have an itch. **2** informal feel an impatient desire to do something: *we itch to explore.*
– ORIGIN Old English.

itchy • adj. (**itchier, itchiest**) having or causing an itch.
– PHRASES **have itchy feet** informal have a strong urge to travel.
– DERIVATIVES **itchiness** n.

it'd • contr. **1** it had. **2** it would.

-ite • suffix **1** forming names of people from a certain country: *Israelite.* **2** usu. derog. referring to followers of a movement: *Luddite.* **3** forming names of minerals, rocks, fossils, or structures of anatomy: *ammonite.* **4** Chem. forming names of salts or esters of acids ending in *-ous*: *sulphite.*
– ORIGIN Greek *ītes.*

item • n. an individual article or unit.
– ORIGIN Latin, 'in like manner, also'.

itemize (also **itemise**) • v. (**itemizes, itemizing, itemized**) present as a list of individual items or parts.

iterate /it-uh-rayt/ • v. (**iterates, iterating, iterated**) do or say repeatedly.
– DERIVATIVES **iteration** n.
– ORIGIN Latin *iterare.*

Ithaca E
/ith-uh-kuh/ a Greek island in the Ionian Sea, the legendary home of Odysseus.

itinerant /I-tin-uh-ruhnt/ • adj. travelling from place to place. • n. an itinerant person.
– ORIGIN Latin *itinerari* 'travel'.

itinerary /I-tin-uh-ruh-ri/ • n. (pl. **itineraries**) a planned route or journey.

-itis • suffix forming names of diseases which cause inflammation: *cystitis.*
– ORIGIN Greek *-itēs.*

it'll • contr. **1** it shall. **2** it will.

its • possess. det. **1** belonging to or associated with a thing previously mentioned or easily identified. **2** belonging to or associated with a child or animal of unspecified sex.

USAGE its
Do not confuse the possessive **its** meaning 'belonging to it' (as in *turn the camera on its side*) with the form **it's** (short for either **it is** or **it has**, as in *it's my fault*).

it's • contr. **1** it is. **2** it has.

itself • pron. (third person sing.) **1** used to refer to something previously mentioned as the subject of the clause: *his horse hurt itself.* **2** used to emphasize a particular thing or animal mentioned: *she wanted him more than life itself.*

ITV • abbrev. Independent Television.

-ity • suffix forming nouns referring to a quality or condition: *humility.*
– ORIGIN Latin *-itas.*

IUD • abbrev. intrauterine device.

Ivan III E
/I-vuhn/ (1440–1505; known as **Ivan the Great**), grand duke of Muscovy 1462–1505. He consolidated and enlarged his territory and adopted the title 'Ruler of all Russia'.

Ivan IV E
/I-vuhn/ (1530–84; known as **Ivan the Terrible**), grand duke of Muscovy 1533–47 and first tsar of Russia 1547–84, who continued to expand Russian territory.

I've • contr. I have.

IVF • abbrev. in vitro fertilization.

Ivory, E
James (b.1928), American film director, who has made a number of films in partnership with the producer Ismail Merchant (b.1936), including *Heat and Dust* and *Howard's End.*

ivory • n. (pl. **ivories**) **1** a hard creamy-white substance which forms the tusks of an elephant or walrus. **2** the creamy-white colour of ivory.
– ORIGIN Old French *ivurie.*

Ivory Coast E
a country in West Africa, on the Gulf of Guinea; capital, Yamoussoukro.
– DERIVATIVES **Ivorian** adj. & n.

ivory tower • n. a situation in which someone leads a privileged life remote from normal difficulties.

ivy • n. an evergreen climbing plant, typically with five-pointed leaves.
– ORIGIN Old English.

Ivy League • n. a group of long-established universities in the eastern US.
– ORIGIN with reference to the ivy traditionally growing over their walls.

-ize (also **-ise**) • suffix forming verbs meaning: **1** make or become: *privatize.* **2** cause to resemble: *Americanize.* **3** treat in a specified way: *pasteurize.* **4** treat or cause to combine with a specified substance: *carbonize.*
– ORIGIN Greek *-izein.*

Izmir E
/iz-meer/ a seaport and naval base in western Turkey, on an inlet of the Aegean Sea. Former name SMYRNA.

J[1] (also **j**) ● n. (pl. **Js** or **J's**) the tenth letter of the alphabet.

J[2] ● abbrev. Physics joule(s).

jab ● v. (**jabs**, **jabbing**, **jabbed**) poke roughly or quickly with something sharp or pointed. ● n. **1** a quick, sharp poke or blow. **2** Brit. informal an injection, especially a vaccination.

jabber ● v. (**jabbers**, **jabbering**, **jabbered**) talk quickly and excitedly but with little sense.

jabot /*zha*-boh/ ● n. a ruffle on the front of a shirt or blouse.
– ORIGIN French.

jacaranda /ja-kuh-ran-duh/ ● n. a tropical American tree with blue flowers and sweet-smelling wood.
– ORIGIN from a South American Indian language.

jack ● n. **1** a device for lifting a motor vehicle off the ground. **2** a playing card ranking next below a queen. **3** (also **jack socket**) a socket designed to receive a jack plug. **4** the small white ball at which bowls players aim. **5** a small piece of metal used in tossing and catching games. ● v. (**jack up**) **1** raise with a jack. **2** informal increase by a large amount.
– ORIGIN from *Jack*, familiar form of the man's name *John*.

jackal /ja-k'l/ ● n. a wild dog that feeds on dead animals, found in Africa and Asia.
– ORIGIN Turkish *çakal*.

jackass ● n. **1** a stupid person. **2** a male ass or donkey.

jackboot ● n. a leather military boot reaching to the knee.

jackdaw ● n. a small grey-headed crow.
– ORIGIN from JACK + earlier *daw* (of Germanic origin).

jacket ● n. **1** an outer garment extending to the waist or hips, with sleeves. **2** a covering placed around something for protection or insulation. **3** the skin of a potato.
– ORIGIN Old French *jaquet*.

jacket potato ● n. Brit. a baked potato served with the skin on.

jack-in-the-box ● n. a toy consisting of a box containing a figure on a spring which pops up when the lid is opened.

jackknife ● n. (pl. **jackknives**) a large knife with a folding blade. ● v. (**jackknifes**, **jackknifing**, **jackknifed**) (of an articulated vehicle) bend into a V-shape in an uncontrolled skidding movement.

jack-o'-lantern ● n. a lantern made from a hollowed-out pumpkin or turnip in which holes are cut to resemble a face.

jack plug ● n. a plug consisting of a single shaft used to make a connection which transmits a signal.

jackpot ● n. a large cash prize in a game or lottery.
– ORIGIN first used in poker, where the pot grew until a player could open the bidding with two jacks or better.

jackrabbit ● n. a North American prairie hare.
– ORIGIN short for *jackass-rabbit*, because of its long ears.

Jack Russell (also **Jack Russell terrier**) ● n. a small breed of terrier with short legs.
– ORIGIN named after the English dog-breeder Revd John (*Jack*) *Russell* (1795–1883).

Jackson[1], E
Andrew (1767–1845; known as **Old Hickory**), American general and Democratic statesman, 7th President of the US 1829–37.

Jackson[2], E
Glenda (b.1936), English actress and Labour politician. After starring in films such as *Women in Love* and *A Touch of Class*, she became a Labour MP in 1992.

Jackson[3], E
Michael (Joe) (b.1958), American pop singer and songwriter, whose albums include *Thriller* and *Bad*.

Jackson[4], E
Thomas Jonathan (1824–63; known as **Stonewall Jackson**), American Confederate general. During the American Civil War he was a commander at the first battle of Bull Run (1861) and later became the deputy of Robert E. Lee.

Jack the Lad ● n. informal a cocky young man.
– ORIGIN nickname of *Jack* Sheppard, an 18th-century thief.

Jack the Ripper E
an unidentified 19th-century English murderer who brutally killed at least six prostitutes in the East End of London in 1888; the cases remain unsolved.

Jacob E
(in the Bible) a Hebrew patriarch, the younger of the twin sons of Isaac and Rebecca. His twelve sons became the founders of the twelve tribes of ancient Israel.

Jacobean /jak-uh-bee-uhn/ ● adj. having to do with the reign of James I of England (1603–1625).
– ORIGIN Latin *Jacobus* 'James'.

Jacobite /jak-uh-byt/ ● n. a supporter of the deposed James II and his descendants in their claim to the British throne.

jacquard /ja-kard/ ● n. a fabric with a woven pattern.
– ORIGIN named after the French weaver Joseph M. *Jacquard* (1787–1834).

jacuzzi /juh-koo-zi/ ● n. (pl. **jacuzzis**) trademark a large bath with jets of water to massage the body.

– ORIGIN named after the Italian-born American inventor Candido *Jacuzzi* (*c.*1903–86).

jade ● n. **1** a hard bluish green precious stone. **2** a light bluish green.
– ORIGIN from French *le jade*.

jaded ● adj. tired out or lacking enthusiasm after having had too much of something.
– ORIGIN from archaic *jade* 'a worn-out horse'.

Jaffa E
/jaf-fuh/ a city and port on the Mediterranean coast of Israel, united with Tel Aviv since 1949.

jag ● v. (**jags**, **jagging**, **jagged**) stab, pierce, or prick.

jagged /jag-gid/ ● adj. with rough, sharp points sticking out.

Jagger, F
Sir Mick (b.1943; full name *Michael Philip Jagger*), English rock singer and songwriter, who formed the Rolling Stones *c.*1962 with guitarist Keith Richards (b.1943).

jaguar /jag-yuu-er/ ● n. a large, heavily built cat that has a yellowish-brown coat with black spots, found in Central and South America.
– ORIGIN from a South American Indian language.

jail (Brit. also **gaol**) ● n. a place for holding people accused or convicted of a crime. ● v. put in jail.
– DERIVATIVES **jailer** (also **gaoler**) n.
– ORIGIN Old French *jaiole* and *gayole*.

jailbait ● n. informal a sexually attractive young woman who is too young to have sexual intercourse legally.

jailbird ● n. informal a person who is or has repeatedly been in prison.

jailbreak ● n. an escape from jail.

Jaipur E
/jy-poor/ a city in western India, the capital of Rajasthan.

Jakarta E
var. of **DJAKARTA**.

jalopy /juh-lop-i/ ● n. (pl. **jalopies**) informal an old car in a very poor condition.
– ORIGIN unknown.

jalousie /*zha*-loo-zee/ ● n. a blind or shutter made of a row of angled slats.
– ORIGIN French, 'jealousy'.

jam[1] ● v. (**jams**, **jamming**, **jammed**) **1** squeeze or pack tightly into a space. **2** push roughly and forcibly into position. **3** block (a road) through crowding. **4** become or make unable to operate due to a part becoming stuck. **5** (**jam on**) apply forcibly: *he jammed on the brakes.* **6** block a radio transmission by causing interference. **7** informal improvise with other musicians. ● n. **1** an instance of being blocked. **2** informal a difficult situation. **3** informal an improvised performance by a group of musicians.

jam[2] ● n. esp. Brit. a thick spread made from fruit and sugar.
– ORIGIN perh. from **JAM**[1].

Jamaica E
/juh-may-kuh/ an island country in the Caribbean Sea, south-east of Cuba; capital, Kingston.
– DERIVATIVES **Jamaican** adj. & n.

jamb /jam/ ● n. a side post of a doorway or window.
– ORIGIN Old French *jambe* 'leg'.

jamboree /jam-buh-ree/ ● n. a lavish or noisy celebration or party.
– ORIGIN unknown.

James[1], E
Henry (1843–1916), American-born British novelist and critic, author of *The Portrait of a Lady* and *What Maisie Knew*. He was the brother of William James.

James[2], E
Jesse (Woodson) (1847–82), American outlaw, who with his brother **Frank** and others specialized in bank and train robberies.

James[3], E
Dame P. D. (b.1920; full name *Phyllis Dorothy James*), English writer of detective fiction, whose novels feature the poet-detective Adam Dalgleish.

James[4], E
William (1842–1910), American philosopher and psychologist. He introduced the theory of the 'stream of consciousness', stating that consciousness is a constantly changing process or flow. He was the brother of Henry James.

James I E
(1566–1625), son of Mary, Queen of Scots, king of Scotland (as James VI) 1567–1625, and of England and Ireland 1603–25. His declaration of the divine right of kings (the doctrine that monarchs derive their authority from God) and his intended alliance with Spain made him unpopular with Parliament.

James II E
(1633–1701), son of Charles I, king of England, Ireland, and (as James VII) Scotland 1685–8. His Catholic beliefs led to the rebellion of the Duke of Monmouth in 1685 and to James' later deposition in favour of William of Orange and Mary II.

James, St[1] E
(known as **St James the Great**), an Apostle, brother of John. He was put to death by Herod Agrippa I (king of Judea AD 41–4). Feast day, 25 July.

James, St[2] E
(known as **St James the Less**), an Apostle. Feast day, 1 May or 9 October.

James, St[3] E
(known as **the Lord's brother**), leader of the early Christian Church at Jerusalem. Feast day, 1 May.

Jammu and Kashmir E
/jam-moo, kash-meer/ a mountainous state of NW India at the western end of the Himalayas, formerly part of Kashmir; capitals, Srinagar (in summer) and Jammu (in winter).

jammy ● adj. **1** covered or filled with jam.

2 Brit. informal lucky.

jam-packed • **adj.** informal extremely crowded or full to capacity.

Jan. • **abbrev.** January.

Janáček E
/yan-uh-chek/, Leoš (1854–1928), Czech composer. His works, much influenced by Moravian folk songs, include the opera *The Cunning Little Vixen* and the *Glagolitic Mass*.

jangle • **v.** (**jangles**, **jangling**, **jangled**) **1** make a ringing metallic sound. **2** (of one's nerves) be set on edge. • **n.** an instance of jangling.
– DERIVATIVES **jangly** adj.
– ORIGIN Old French *jangler*.

janitor /jan-i-ter/ • **n.** esp. N. Amer. a caretaker of a building.
– ORIGIN Latin.

Jansen E
/jan-s'n/, Cornelius Otto (1585–1638), Flemish Roman Catholic theologian and founder of Jansenism. He proposed a reform of Christianity through a return to the teachings of St Augustine.

January • **n.** (pl. **Januaries**) the first month of the year.
– ORIGIN from Latin *Januarius mensis* 'month of *Janus*'.

Janus E
/jay-nuhss/ the Roman god of doorways and gates and protector of the state in time of war.

Jap • **n. & adj.** informal, offens. = **JAPANESE**.

Japan E
a country in east Asia, occupying a string of islands in the Pacific roughly parallel with the Asiatic mainland; capital, Tokyo.

japan • **n.** a black glossy varnish originating in Japan. • **v.** (**japans**, **japanning**, **japanned**) cover with japan.

Japanese • **n.** (pl. same) **1** a person from Japan. **2** the language of Japan. • **adj.** relating to Japan.

Japan, Sea of E
the sea between Japan and the mainland of Asia.

jape • **n.** a practical joke.
– ORIGIN prob. from Old French *japer* 'to yelp, yap' and *gaber* 'to mock'.

japonica /juh-pon-i-kuh/ • **n.** an Asian shrub with bright red flowers and edible fruits.
– ORIGIN Latin, 'Japanese'.

jar[1] • **n.** a cylindrical container made of glass or pottery.
– ORIGIN French *jarre*.

jar[2] • **v.** (**jars**, **jarring**, **jarred**) **1** send a painful shock through (a part of the body). **2** strike against something with a jolt. **3** have an unpleasant effect. • **n.** an instance of jarring.

jardinière /*zh*ar-din-yair/ • **n.** an ornamental pot or stand for displaying plants.
– ORIGIN French, 'female gardener'.

jargon • **n.** words or expressions used by a particular group that are difficult for others to understand.
– ORIGIN Old French *jargoun*.

Jarrow E
a town in NE England, on the Tyne estuary. A series of hunger marches to London by the unemployed started from the town during the Depression of the 1930s.

Jaruzelski E
/ya-ruu-zel-ski/, Wojciech (b.1923), Polish general and statesman, Prime Minister 1981–5, head of state 1985–9, and President 1989–90. Following the victory of the trade union movement Solidarity in the 1989 elections he supervised Poland's transition to a democracy.

jasmine • **n.** a shrub or climbing plant with sweet-smelling flowers.
– ORIGIN French *jasmin*.

Jason E
Gk Myth. the leader of the Argonauts in the quest for the Golden Fleece.

jasper • **n.** a reddish-brown variety of chalcedony.
– ORIGIN Old French *jaspre*.

jaundice /jawn-diss/ • **n.** **1** Med. yellowing of the skin due to a bile disorder. **2** bitterness or resentment.
– DERIVATIVES **jaundiced** adj.
– ORIGIN Old French *jaunice* 'yellowness'.

jaunt • **n.** a short trip for pleasure.
– ORIGIN unknown.

jaunty • **adj.** lively and self-confident.
– DERIVATIVES **jauntily** adv.
– ORIGIN French *gentil* 'well-born'.

Java E
/jah-vuh/ a large island in the Malay Archipelago, forming part of Indonesia.
– DERIVATIVES **Javan** n. & adj.

javelin /jav-lin/ • **n.** a long spear thrown in a competitive sport or as a weapon.
– ORIGIN Old French *javeline*.

jaw • **n.** **1** each of the upper and lower bony structures forming the framework of the mouth and containing the teeth. **2** (**jaws**) the grasping, biting, or crushing mouthparts of an invertebrate animal. **3** (**jaws**) the gripping parts of a wrench, vice, etc. • **v.** informal talk or gossip at length.
– ORIGIN Old French *joe*.

jawbone • **n.** a bone forming the lower jaw.

jaw-dropping • **adj.** informal amazing.

jay • **n.** a noisy bird of the crow family with boldly patterned plumage.
– ORIGIN Latin *gaius, gaia*.

jaywalk • **v.** esp. N. Amer. walk along or across a road without regard for the traffic.
– DERIVATIVES **jaywalker** n.
– ORIGIN from **JAY** in the former sense 'silly person'.

jazz • **n.** a type of music of black American origin in which the players often improvise. • **v.** (**jazz up**) make more lively or attractive.
– ORIGIN unknown.

jazzy • **adj.** (**jazzier**, **jazziest**) **1** in the style of jazz. **2** bright, colourful, and showy.

jealous • **adj.** **1** envious of someone else's achievements or advantages. **2** resentful of someone regarded as a sexual rival. **3** very protective of one's rights or possessions: *they kept a jealous eye over their interests*.
– DERIVATIVES **jealously** adv. **jealousy** n.

– ORIGIN Old French *gelos*.

jeans • pl. n. hard-wearing trousers made of denim or another strong cotton fabric.
– ORIGIN Latin *Janua* 'Genoa'.

Jeddah E
/jed-duh/ var. of **JIDDAH**.

jeep • n. trademark a sturdy motor vehicle with four-wheel drive.
– ORIGIN from the initials *GP*, standing for *general purpose*.

jeer • v. (**jeers**, **jeering**, **jeered**) make rude and mocking remarks at someone. • n. a rude and mocking remark.
– ORIGIN unknown.

Jefferson, E
Thomas (1743–1826), American Democratic Republican statesman, 3rd President of the US 1801–9. He played a key role in the American leadership during the War of Independence and was the principal drafter of the Declaration of Independence (1776).

Jehovah /ji-hoh-vuh/ • n. a form of the Hebrew name of God used in some translations of the Bible.
– ORIGIN Hebrew.

Jehovah's Witness • n. a member of a Christian sect that denies many traditional Christian doctrines and preaches the Second Coming.

jejune /ji-joon/ • adj. **1** naive and simplistic. **2** (of ideas or writings) dull.
– ORIGIN Latin *jejunus* 'fasting, barren'.

jejunum /ji-joo-nuhm/ • n. the part of the small intestine between the duodenum and ileum.
– ORIGIN Latin, 'fasting'.

Jekyll /je-k'l/ • n. (in phr. **a Jekyll and Hyde**) a person displaying alternately good and evil personalities.
– ORIGIN after the central character in Robert Louis Stevenson's story *The Strange Case of Dr Jekyll and Mr Hyde*.

jell (also **gel**) • v. (**jells**, **jelling**, **jelled**) **1** (of jelly or a similar substance) set or become firmer. **2** take definite form or begin to work well.

jellied • adj. (of food) set in a jelly.

jelly • n. (pl. **jellies**) **1** Brit. a dessert consisting of a sweet, fruit-flavoured liquid set with gelatin to form a semi-solid mass. **2** a small sweet made with gelatin.
– ORIGIN Old French *gelee* 'frost, jelly'.

jellyfish • n. a sea animal with a soft body that has stinging tentacles around the edge.

jemmy (N. Amer. **jimmy**) • n. (pl. **jemmies**) a short crowbar.
– ORIGIN familiar form of the man's name *James*.

je ne sais quoi /*zh*uh nuh say **kwah**/ • n. a quality that is hard to describe.
– ORIGIN French, 'I do not know what'.

Jenner, E
Edward (1749–1823), English physician, the pioneer of vaccination. He deliberately infected people with small amounts of cowpox to protect them from catching smallpox.

jenny • n. (pl. **jennies**) a female donkey or ass.
– ORIGIN familiar form of the woman's name *Janet*.

jeopardize /jep-er-dyz/ (also **jeopardise**) • v. (**jeopardizes**, **jeopardizing**, **jeopardized**) put at risk of being harmed or lost.

jeopardy /jep-er-di/ • n. danger of loss or harm.
– ORIGIN from Old French *ieu parti* '(evenly) divided game'.

jerboa /jer-boh-uh/ • n. a rodent with very long hind legs that lives in the desert.
– ORIGIN Latin.

jeremiad /je-ri-my-ad/ • n. a list of one's troubles.
– ORIGIN with reference to the Lamentations of Jeremiah in the Old Testament.

Jeremiah E
/je-ri-my-uh/ (*c*.650–*c*.585 BC) a major Hebrew prophet who foresaw the fall of Assyria, the conquest of his country by Egypt and Babylon, and the destruction of Jerusalem.

Jericho E
/je-ri-koh/ a town in Palestine, in the West Bank north of the Dead Sea.

jerk • n. **1** a quick, sharp, sudden movement. **2** informal, esp. N. Amer. a stupid person. • v. move or raise with a jerk.

jerkin • n. a sleeveless jacket.
– ORIGIN unknown.

jerky • adj. moving in abrupt stops and starts.

Jerome E
/juh-rohm/, Jerome K. (1859–1927; full name *Jerome Klapka Jerome*), English novelist and dramatist, best known for his humorous novel *Three Men in a Boat*.

Jerome, St E
/juh-rohm/ (*c*.342–420), Christian scholar, who translated the Bible from Hebrew into Latin (the version known as the Vulgate). Feast day, 30 September.

Jerry • n. (pl. **Jerries**) Brit. informal, dated a German or Germans.
– ORIGIN prob. from **GERMAN**.

jerry-built • adj. badly or hastily built.
– ORIGIN uncertain.

jerrycan • n. a large flat-sided metal container for storing or carrying liquids.
– ORIGIN from **JERRY** + **CAN**[2], because first used in Germany.

Jersey E
the largest of the Channel Islands; capital, St Helier.

jersey • n. (pl. **jerseys**) **1** a knitted garment with long sleeves. **2** a distinctive shirt worn by a player of certain sports. **3** a soft knitted fabric. **4** (**Jersey**) an animal of a breed of light brown dairy cattle.
– ORIGIN from **JERSEY**.

Jerusalem E
/juh-roo-suh-luhm/ the holy city of the Jews, sacred also to Christians and Muslims, situated in Israel west of the River Jordan.

Jerusalem artichoke • n. a knobbly root vegetable with white flesh.
– ORIGIN Italian *girasole* 'sunflower'.

jest • n. a joke. • v. speak or act in a joking way.
– ORIGIN Old French *geste* 'exploit'.

jester ● n. hist. a professional joker or 'fool' at a medieval court.

Jesuit /jez-yuu-it/ ● n. a member of the Society of Jesus, a Roman Catholic order of priests founded by St Ignatius Loyola.
– DERIVATIVES **Jesuitical** adj.

Jesus[1] E
(also **Jesus Christ**) the central figure of the Christian religion, believed by Christians to be the Messiah and the Son of God. Jesus conducted a mission of preaching and healing in Palestine in about AD 28–30, which is described in the Gospels, as are his death by crucifixion and Resurrection from the dead.

Jesus[2] (also **Jesus Christ**) ● exclam. informal expressing irritation or surprise.

jet[1] ● n. **1** a rapid stream of liquid or gas forced out of a small opening. **2** an aircraft powered by jet engines. ● v. (**jets**, **jetting**, **jetted**) **1** spurt out in a jet. **2** travel by jet aircraft.
– ORIGIN French *jeter* 'to throw'.

jet[2] ● n. **1** a hard black semi-precious mineral. **2** (also **jet black**) a glossy black colour.
– ORIGIN Old French *jaiet*.

jeté /*zhe*-tay/ ● n. Ballet a spring from one foot to the other, with the following leg extended backwards while in the air.
– ORIGIN French.

jet engine ● n. an aircraft engine which provides force for forward movement by ejecting a high-speed jet of gas obtained by burning fuel in air.

jet lag ● n. extreme tiredness and other effects felt by a person after a long flight across different time zones.
– DERIVATIVES **jet-lagged** adj.

jetsam /jet-suhm/ ● n. unwanted material thrown overboard from a ship and washed ashore.
– ORIGIN from JETTISON.

jet set ● n. (**the jet set**) informal wealthy people who travel for pleasure often and widely.
– DERIVATIVES **jet-setter** n.

jet ski ● n. trademark a small jet-propelled vehicle which skims across the surface of water and is ridden in a similar way to a motorcycle.

jettison /jet-ti-suhn/ ● v. throw or drop from an aircraft or ship.
– ORIGIN Old French *getaison*.

jetty ● n. (pl. **jetties**) a landing stage or small pier.
– ORIGIN Old French *jetee*.

Jew ● n. a member of the people whose traditional religion is Judaism and who trace their origins to the ancient Hebrew people of Israel.
– ORIGIN Hebrew, 'Judah'.

jewel ● n. **1** a precious stone. **2** (**jewels**) pieces of jewellery. **3** a highly valued person or thing: *she was a jewel of a housekeeper.*
– DERIVATIVES **jewelled** (US **jeweled**) adj.
– PHRASES **the jewel in the crown** the most valuable part of something.
– ORIGIN Old French *joel*.

jeweller (US **jeweler**) ● n. a person who makes or sells jewellery.

jewellery (US **jewelry**) ● n. personal ornaments, such as necklaces, rings, or bracelets.

Jewess ● n. dated, usu. offens. a Jewish woman or girl.

Jewish ● adj. having to do with Jews or Judaism.
– DERIVATIVES **Jewishness** n.

Jewry /joo-ri/ ● n. (pl. **Jewries**) Jews as a group.

Jew's harp ● n. a small musical instrument like a U-shaped harp, held between the teeth and struck with a finger.

Jezebel /jez-uh-bel/ ● n. an immoral woman.
– ORIGIN the name of the wife of King Ahab in the Bible.

Jiang Jie Shi E
/jang jee **shee**/ var. of CHIANG KAI-SHEK.

jib[1] ● n. **1** Sailing a triangular sail in front of the mast. **2** the projecting arm of a crane.
– ORIGIN unknown.

jib[2] ● v. (**jibs**, **jibbing**, **jibbed**) **1** (**jib at**) be unwilling to do or accept (something). **2** (of a horse) refuse to go on.
– ORIGIN perh. from French *regimber* 'to buck'.

jibe[1] (also **gibe**) ● n. an insulting remark. ● v. (**jibes**, **jibing**, **jibed**) make jibes.
– ORIGIN perh. from Old French *giber* 'handle roughly'.

jibe[2] ● v. & n. US = GYBE.

Jibuti E
var. of DJIBOUTI.

Jiddah E
/jid-duh/ (also **Jeddah**) a seaport on the Red Sea coast of Saudi Arabia, near Mecca.

jiffy (also **jiff**) ● n. informal a moment.
– ORIGIN unknown.

jig ● n. **1** a lively leaping dance. **2** a device that holds a piece of work and guides the tools working on it. ● v. (**jigs**, **jigging**, **jigged**) **1** dance a jig. **2** move up and down with a quick jerky motion.
– ORIGIN unknown.

jigger ● n. **1** a machine or vehicle with a part that rocks or moves to and fro. **2** a measure of spirits or wine. ● v. (**jiggers**, **jiggering**, **jiggered**) Brit. informal **1** tamper with. **2** (**jiggered**) broken or exhausted.

jiggery-pokery ● n. informal, esp. Brit. dishonest behaviour.
– ORIGIN prob. from Scots *jouk* 'dodge, skulk'.

jiggle ● v. (**jiggles**, **jiggling**, **jiggled**) move lightly and quickly from side to side or up and down.
– DERIVATIVES **jiggly** adj.
– ORIGIN partly from JOGGLE.

jigsaw ● n. **1** a picture printed on cardboard or wood and cut into numerous interlocking shapes that have to be fitted together. **2** a machine saw with a fine blade allowing it to cut curved lines in a sheet of wood, metal, etc.

jihad /ji-hahd/ ● n. a holy war fought by Muslims against unbelievers.
– ORIGIN Arabic, 'effort'.

jilt ● v. abruptly break off a relationship with (a lover).
– ORIGIN unknown.

jimmy ● n. US = JEMMY.

jingle ● n. **1** a light ringing sound such as that made by metal objects being shaken together. **2** a short easily remembered slogan, verse, or tune. ● v. (**jingles**, **jingling**, **jingled**) make or cause to make a jingle.
– DERIVATIVES **jingly** adj.

jingoism ● n. esp. derog. excessive support for one's country.
– DERIVATIVES **jingoistic** adj.
– ORIGIN from *by jingo!* in a song adopted by those who supported the sending of a British fleet into Turkish waters to resist Russia in 1878.

jink ● v. change direction suddenly and nimbly.
– ORIGIN from **HIGH JINKS**, referring to antics at drinking parties.

Jinnah E
/jin-nah/, Muhammad Ali (1876–1948), Indian statesman and founder of Pakistan. He campaigned for India to be divided into separate Muslim and Hindu states, and in 1947 he became the first Governor General and President of Pakistan.

jinx ● n. a person or thing that brings bad luck. ● v. bring bad luck to.
– ORIGIN prob. from Latin *jynx* 'wryneck' (a bird).

jitterbug ● n. a fast dance performed to swing music, popular in the 1940s.

jitters ● pl. n. informal (**the jitters**) a feeling of extreme nervousness.
– DERIVATIVES **jittery** adj.
– ORIGIN unknown.

jiu-jitsu ● n. var. of **JU-JITSU**.

jive ● n. a lively dance popular in the 1940s and 1950s, performed to swing music or rock and roll. ● v. (**jives, jiving, jived**) dance the jive.
– ORIGIN unknown.

Joan of Arc, St E
(*c*.1412–31; known as **the Maid of Orleans**), French national heroine. She led the French armies to free Orleans from an English siege in the Hundred Years War. Captured by the Burgundians in 1430, she was handed over to the English and burnt at the stake as a heretic. Feast day, 30 May.

Job E
/johb/ (in the Bible) a wealthy man whose patience and piety were tried by undeserved misfortunes, but who kept his faith in God.

job ● n. **1** a paid position of regular employment. **2** a task. **3** informal a crime. **4** informal a procedure to improve the appearance of something: *a nose job*. ● v. (**jobs, jobbing, jobbed**) do casual or occasional work.
– PHRASES **a good job** informal, esp. Brit. a fortunate fact or circumstance. **just the job** Brit. informal exactly what is needed.
– ORIGIN unknown.

jobcentre ● n. (in the UK) a government office in a local area, which gives out benefits and information about available jobs to unemployed people.

jobless ● adj. without a paid job.
– DERIVATIVES **joblessness** n.

job lot ● n. a batch of articles sold or bought at one time.

job-share ● v. (**job-shares, job-sharing, job-shared**) (of two part-time employees) share a single full-time job. ● n. an arrangement of such a kind.

Jock ● n. informal, usu. offens. a Scotsman.
– ORIGIN Scottish form of the man's name *Jack*.

jockey ● n. (pl. **jockeys**) a professional rider in horse races. ● v. (**jockeys, jockeying, jockeyed**) struggle to gain or achieve something: *two men will be jockeying for the top job*.
– ORIGIN from **JOCK**.

jockstrap ● n. a support or protection for a man's genitals.
– ORIGIN from slang *jock* 'genitals'.

jocose /juh-kohss/ ● adj. formal playful or humorous.
– ORIGIN Latin *jocosus*.

jocular /jok-yuu-ler/ ● adj. humorous.
– DERIVATIVES **jocularity** n. **jocularly** adv.
– ORIGIN Latin *jocularis*.

jocund /jok-uhnd/ ● adj. formal cheerful and light-hearted.
– ORIGIN Latin *jocundus*.

jodhpurs /jod-perz/ ● pl. n. trousers worn for horse riding that are close-fitting below the knee.
– ORIGIN named after the Indian city of *Jodhpur*.

joey ● n. (pl. **joeys**) Austral. a young kangaroo, wallaby, or possum.
– ORIGIN Aboriginal.

jog ● v. (**jogs, jogging, jogged**) **1** run at a steady, gentle pace. **2** (**jog along/on**) continue in a steady, uneventful way. **3** knock slightly. **4** trigger (one's memory). ● n. **1** a spell of jogging. **2** a slight knock or nudge.
– ORIGIN from **JAG**.

jogger ● n. **1** a person who jogs as a form of exercise. **2** (**joggers**) tracksuit trousers worn for jogging.

joggle ● v. (**joggles, joggling, joggled**) move with repeated small jerks.
– ORIGIN from **JOG**.

Johannesburg E
/joh-han-nis-berg/ a city in South Africa, the country's largest city and the capital of the province of Gauteng.

John[1] E
(1165–1216; known as **John Lackland**), son of Henry II, king of England 1199–1216. Forced to sign Magna Carta by his barons (1215), he ignored its provisions and civil war broke out.

John[2], E
Augustus (Edwin) (1878–1961), Welsh painter, noted for his portraits of the wealthy and famous.

John[3], E
Sir Elton (Hercules) (b.1947; born *Reginald Kenneth Dwight*), English pop and rock singer, pianist, and songwriter, whose many hits include 'Candle in the Wind'.

john ● n. informal, esp. N. Amer. a toilet.
– ORIGIN from the man's name *John*.

John, St E
(known as **St John the Evangelist** or **St John the Divine**), an Apostle, brother of James, traditionally the author of the fourth Gospel, Revelation, and three epistles of the New Testament. Feast day, 27 December.

John Bull ● n. a character representing England or the typical Englishman.
– ORIGIN from a character in John Arbuthnot's satire *Law is a Bottomless Pit; or, the History*

of John Bull (1712).

johnny-come-lately • **n.** informal a newcomer or late starter.

John of Gaunt E
(1340–99), son of Edward III, the effective ruler of England during the final years of his father's reign and when Richard II was below the age of full legal responsibility.

John o'Groats E
/jon uh **grohts**/ a village at the extreme NE point of the Scottish mainland.

John Paul II E
(b.1920; born *Karol Jozef Wojtyla*), Polish cleric, pope since 1978.

Johns, E
Jasper (b.1930), American painter, sculptor, and printmaker, a key figure in the development of pop art.

Johnson[1], E
Amy (1903–41), English aviator, who in 1930 became the first woman to fly solo from London to Australia.

Johnson[2], E
Andrew (1808–75), American Democratic statesman, 17th President of the US 1865–9.

Johnson[3], E
Earvin (b.1959; known as **Magic Johnson**), American basketball player.

Johnson[4], E
Lyndon Baines (1908–73), American Democratic statesman, 36th President of the US 1963–9. His popularity was undermined by the increasing involvement of the US in the Vietnam War.

Johnson[5], E
Michael (b.1967), American sprinter, winner of five Olympic gold medals 1992–2000.

Johnson[6], E
Samuel (1709–84; known as **Dr Johnson**), English lexicographer, writer, and critic, known for his *Dictionary of the English Language*.

John the Baptist, St, E
Jewish preacher and prophet, who baptized Christ. He was beheaded by Herod Antipas. Feast day, 24 June.

John the Evangelist, St E
(also **John the Divine**) see **JOHN, ST**.

joie de vivre /*zh*wah duh vee-vruh/ • **n.** lively and cheerful enjoyment of life.
– ORIGIN French.

join • **v. 1** link or become linked to. **2** come together to form a whole. **3** become a member or employee of. **4** (**join up**) become a member of the armed forces. **5** take part in (an activity). **6** meet (someone) and do something together. • **n.** a place where things are joined.
– ORIGIN Old French *joindre*.

joiner • **n.** a person who makes the wooden parts of a building.

joinery • **n. 1** the wooden parts of a building. **2** the work of a joiner.

joint • **n. 1** a point at which parts are joined. **2** a structure in the body which joins two bones. **3** the part of a plant stem from which a leaf or branch grows. **4** Brit. a large piece of meat. **5** informal a place of a specified kind: *a burger joint*. **6** informal a cannabis cigarette. • **adj. 1** shared, held, or made by two or more people. **2** sharing in an achievement or activity: *a joint winner*. • **v. 1** (**jointed**) having joints. **2** cut (the body of an animal) into joints.
– PHRASES **out of joint 1** (of a joint of the body) out of position. **2** in a state of disorder.
– DERIVATIVES **jointly** adv.
– ORIGIN Old French *joindre* 'to join'.

joist /joysst/ • **n.** a length of timber or steel supporting part of the structure of a building.
– ORIGIN Old French *giste*.

jojoba /hoh-**hoh**-buh/ • **n.** an oil extracted from the seeds of a North American shrub, used in cosmetics.
– ORIGIN Mexican Spanish.

joke • **n. 1** a thing that someone says to cause amusement or laughter. **2** a trick played for fun. **3** informal a person or thing that is ridiculously inadequate: *public transport is a joke*. • **v.** (**jokes, joking, joked**) make jokes.
– DERIVATIVES **jokey** adj.
– ORIGIN perh. from Latin *jocus*.

joker • **n. 1** a person who is fond of joking. **2** a playing card with the figure of a jester, used as a wild card.

jollification • **n.** merrymaking.

jollity • **n. 1** lively and cheerful activity. **2** the quality of being jolly.

jolly • **adj.** (**jollier, jolliest**) **1** happy and cheerful. **2** lively and entertaining. • **v.** (**jollies, jollying, jollied**) informal encourage in a friendly way: *he jollied her along*. • **adv.** Brit. informal very.
– ORIGIN Old French *jolif* 'pretty'.

Jolly Roger • **n.** a pirate's flag with a white skull and crossbones on a black background.
– ORIGIN unknown.

Jolson E
/**johl**-s'n/, Al (1886–1950; born *Asa Yoelson*), Russian-born American singer, film actor, and comedian, who appeared in the first full-length film with sound, *The Jazz Singer*.

jolt • **v. 1** push or shake abruptly and roughly. **2** shock (someone) into taking action. • **n. 1** an act of jolting. **2** a shock.
– ORIGIN unknown.

Jonah E
/**joh**-nuh/ (in the Bible) a Hebrew prophet. He disobeyed God's call to preach and attempted to escape by sea, but was thrown overboard in a storm and swallowed by a great fish, before being saved.

Jones[1], E
Inigo (1573–1652), English architect and stage designer, who introduced the neoclassical Palladian style to England.

Jones[2], E
Tom (b.1940; born *Thomas Jones Woodward*), Welsh pop singer, whose hits include 'It's Not Unusual' and 'Delilah'.

Jonson, [E]
Ben (1572–1637; full name *Benjamin Jonson*), English dramatist and poet, known for the comedies *Volpone* and *The Alchemist*.

Joplin[1], [E]
Janis (1943–70), American singer. She died from a heroin overdose just before her most successful album, *Pearl*, and her number-one single 'Me and Bobby McGee' were released.

Joplin[2], [E]
Scott (1868–1917), American ragtime pianist and composer, whose compositions include 'Maple Leaf Rag' and 'The Entertainer'.

Jordan[1] [E]
a country in the Middle East east of the River Jordan; capital, Amman. Official name **HASHEMITE KINGDOM OF JORDAN**.
– DERIVATIVES **Jordanian** adj. & n.

Jordan[2] [E]
a river flowing southward from mountains in Syria and Lebanon through the Sea of Galilee into the Dead Sea. It is regarded as sacred by Christians, Jews, and Muslims.

Jordan[3], [E]
Michael (Jeffrey) (b.1963), American basketball player.

Jordan[4], [E]
Neil (b.1950), Irish film director and scriptwriter, whose films include *The Crying Game* and *Michael Collins*.

Joseph [E]
(in the Bible) a Hebrew patriarch, son of Jacob. He was given a coat of many colours by his father, but was then sold by his jealous brothers into captivity in Egypt.

Joseph, St, [E]
husband of the Virgin Mary. A carpenter of Nazareth, he was betrothed to Mary at the time of the Annunciation. Feast day, 19 March.

Joseph of Arimathea [E]
/a-ri-muh-**thee**-uh/ a member of the council at Jerusalem who obtained and buried Christ's body after the Crucifixion.

josh • v. informal tease playfully.
– ORIGIN unknown.

Joshua [E]
(*fl. c.*13th century BC), the Israelite leader who succeeded Moses and led his people into the Promised Land.

joss stick • n. a thin stick of a sweet-smelling substance, burnt as incense.
– ORIGIN from *joss*, referring to a Chinese religious statue.

jostle • v. (**jostles, jostling, jostled**) **1** push or bump against roughly. **2** (**jostle for**) struggle forcefully for.
– ORIGIN from **JOUST**.

jot • v. (**jots, jotting, jotted**) write quickly. • n. a very small amount: *it made not a jot of difference.*
– ORIGIN Greek *iōta*, the smallest letter of the Greek alphabet.

jotter • n. Brit. a small notebook.

jotting • n. a brief note.

Joule [E]
/jool/, James Prescott (1818–89), English physicist, who showed that the various forms of energy were basically the same and interchangeable.

joule /jool/ • n. the SI unit of work or energy.
– ORIGIN named after James P. **JOULE**.

journal • n. **1** a newspaper or magazine dealing with a particular subject. **2** a diary or daily record.
– ORIGIN Old French *jurnal*.

journalese • n. informal a poor writing style supposedly used by journalists, containing many clichés.

journalism • n. the activity or profession of being a journalist.

journalist • n. a person who writes for newspapers or magazines or prepares news or features to be broadcast on radio or television.
– DERIVATIVES **journalistic** adj.

journey • n. (pl. **journeys**) an act of travelling from one place to another. • v. (**journeys, journeying, journeyed**) travel.
– ORIGIN Old French *jornee* 'day'.

journeyman • n. **1** a skilled worker who is employed by another. **2** a worker who is reliable but not outstanding.
– ORIGIN from **JOURNEY** in the former sense 'day's work'.

joust /jowsst/ • v. (of medieval knights) fight on horseback with lances. • n. a jousting contest.
– DERIVATIVES **jouster** n.
– ORIGIN Old French *jouster* 'bring together'.

Jove /johv/ • n. (in phr. **by Jove**) dated used for emphasis or to indicate surprise.
– ORIGIN another name for **JUPITER**[1].

jovial /**joh**-vi-uhl/ • adj. cheerful and friendly.
– DERIVATIVES **joviality** n. **jovially** adv.
– ORIGIN Latin *jovialis* 'of Jupiter'.

jowl • n. **1** the lower part of a cheek when it is fleshy. **2** the loose skin at the throat of cattle.
– DERIVATIVES **jowly** adj.
– ORIGIN Old English.

joy • n. **1** great pleasure and happiness. **2** a cause of joy. **3** Brit. informal success or satisfaction: *you'll get no joy out of her.*
– DERIVATIVES **joyless** adj.
– ORIGIN Old French *joie*.

Joyce, [E]
James (Augustine Aloysius) (1882–1941), Irish novelist and poet, who revolutionized the form of the modern novel and developed the stream-of-consciousness technique. His works include *Ulysses* and *Finnegans Wake*.
– DERIVATIVES **Joycean** adj.

joyful • adj. feeling or causing joy.
– DERIVATIVES **joyfully** adv.

joyous • adj. esp. literary full of happiness and joy.
– DERIVATIVES **joyously** adv.

joypad • n. a device for a computer games console which uses buttons to control an image on the screen.

joyride • n. informal **1** a fast ride in a stolen vehicle. **2** a ride for enjoyment.
– DERIVATIVES **joyrider** n. **joyriding** n.

joystick • n. informal **1** the control column of an

aircraft. **2** a lever for controlling the movement of an image on a computer screen.

JP • abbrev. Justice of the Peace.

Juan Carlos E
/hwahn **kar**-loss/ (b.1938; full name *Juan Carlos Victor María de Borbón y Borbón*), king of Spain since 1975.

jubilant • adj. happy and triumphant.
– DERIVATIVES **jubilantly** adv.

jubilation /joo-bi-**lay**-sh'n/ • n. a feeling of great happiness and triumph.
– ORIGIN Latin *jubilare* 'shout for joy'.

jubilee • n. a special anniversary.
– ORIGIN from Latin *jubilaeus annus* 'year of jubilee'.

Judaea E
/joo-**dee**-uh/ the southern part of ancient Palestine, corresponding to the former kingdom of Judah.

Judah E
/**joo**-duh/ the southern part of ancient Palestine.

Judaic /joo-**day**-ik/ • adj. having to do with Judaism or the ancient Jews.

Judaism /**joo**-day-i-z'm/ • n. **1** the religion of the Jews, based on the Old Testament and the Talmud. **2** Jews as a group.
– ORIGIN Greek *Ioudaïsmos*.

Judas[1] E
/**joo**-duhss/ (full name **Judas Iscariot**) an Apostle. He betrayed Christ to the Jewish authorities in return for thirty pieces of silver.

Judas[2] /**joo**-duhss/ • n. a person who betrays a friend.
– ORIGIN from **Judas**[1].

judder • v. (**judders**, **juddering**, **juddered**) esp. Brit. shake rapidly and forcefully.
– DERIVATIVES **juddery** adj.

Jude, St E
/jood/ (also known as **Judas**) an Apostle, supposed brother of James. Feast day (with St Simon), 28 October.

judge • n. **1** a public officer who decides cases in a law court. **2** a person who decides the results of a competition. **3** a person with the necessary knowledge or skill to give an opinion. • v. (**judges**, **judging**, **judged**) **1** form an opinion about. **2** give a verdict on (a case or person) in a law court. **3** decide the results of (a competition).
– ORIGIN Old French *juge*.

judgement (also **judgment**) • n. **1** the ability to make sound decisions or form sensible opinions. **2** an opinion or conclusion. **3** a decision of a law court or judge.

judgemental (also **judgmental**) • adj. **1** having to do with the use of judgement. **2** excessively critical of others.

Judgement Day • n. the time of the Last Judgement.

judicature /**joo**-dik-uh-cher/ • n. **1** the organization and administration of justice. **2** (**the judicature**) judges as a group.
– ORIGIN Latin *judicare* 'to judge'.

judicial /joo-**di**-sh'l/ • adj. having to do with a law court or judge.
– DERIVATIVES **judicially** adv.
– ORIGIN Latin *judicium* 'judgement'.

judiciary /joo-**di**-shuh-ri/ • n. (pl. **judiciaries**) (**the judiciary**) judges as a group.

judicious /joo-**di**-shuhss/ • adj. having or done with good judgement.
– DERIVATIVES **judiciously** adv.

judo • n. a sport of unarmed combat, using holds and leverage to unbalance one's opponent.
– ORIGIN Japanese, 'gentle way'.

jug • n. **1** Brit. a cylindrical container with a handle and a lip, for holding and pouring liquids. **2** N. Amer. a large container for liquids, with a narrow mouth.
– ORIGIN perh. from *Jug*, informal form of the woman's names *Joan*, *Joanna*, and *Jenny*.

jugged • adj. (of a hare) stewed in a covered container.

juggernaut /**jug**-ger-nawt/ • n. Brit. a large heavy vehicle.
– ORIGIN Sanskrit 'Lord of the world', referring to an image of the Hindu god Krishna carried on a heavy chariot.

juggle • v. (**juggles**, **juggling**, **juggled**) **1** continuously toss and catch a number of objects so as to keep at least one in the air at any time. **2** manage to do (several activities) at the same time. • n. an act of juggling.
– DERIVATIVES **juggler** n.
– ORIGIN Old French *jogler*.

jugular /**jug**-yuu-ler/ • adj. having to do with the neck or throat. • n. (also **jugular vein**) any of several large veins in the neck, carrying blood from the head.
– ORIGIN Latin *jugulum* 'throat'.

juice • n. **1** the liquid present in fruit or vegetables, often made into a drink. **2** (**juices**) fluid produced by the stomach. **3** (**juices**) liquid coming from food during cooking. **4** informal electrical energy. **5** informal petrol. **6** (**juices**) informal one's creative abilities. • v. (**juices**, **juicing**, **juiced**) extract the juice from.
– ORIGIN Latin *jus* 'broth, juice'.

juicer • n. an appliance for extracting juice from fruit and vegetables.

juicy • adj. (**juicier**, **juiciest**) **1** full of juice. **2** informal interestingly scandalous: *bits of juicy gossip*.

ju-jitsu /joo **jit**-soo/ (also **jiu-jitsu**) • n. a Japanese system of unarmed combat and physical training.
– ORIGIN Japanese, 'gentle skill'.

jukebox • n. a machine that plays a selected musical recording when a coin is inserted.
– ORIGIN *juke* is from a word in a Creole language meaning 'disorderly'.

Jul. • abbrev. July.

julep /**joo**-lep/ • n. a sweet drink made from sugar syrup.
– ORIGIN Latin *julapium*.

julienne /joo-li-**en**/ • n. a portion of food cut into short, thin strips.
– ORIGIN French.

Julius Caesar, E
Gaius (100–44 BC), Roman general and statesman. He became consul in 59 BC and, after defeating Pompey in 48, became dictator of the Roman Empire. He was murdered on the Ides (15th) of March.

July • n. (pl. **Julys**) the seventh month of the year.

– ORIGIN from Latin *Julius mensis* 'month of July', named after **JULIUS CAESAR**.

jumble • n. **1** an untidy collection of things. **2** Brit. articles collected for a jumble sale. • v. (**jumbles**, **jumbling**, **jumbled**) mix up in a confused way.

jumble sale • n. Brit. a sale of various second-hand goods.

jumbo informal • n. (pl. **jumbos**) **1** a very large person or thing. **2** (also **jumbo jet**) a very large airliner. • adj. very large.

– ORIGIN prob. from **MUMBO-JUMBO**.

jump • v. **1** push oneself off the ground using the muscles in one's legs and feet. **2** move over, onto, or down from (a place) by jumping. **3** move suddenly and quickly. **4** (**jump at/on**) accept eagerly. **5** (**jump on**) informal attack suddenly. **6** pass abruptly from one subject or state to another. • n. **1** an act of jumping. **2** a large or sudden increase. **3** an obstacle to be jumped by a horse.

– PHRASES **jump the queue** move ahead of one's proper place in a queue. **jump ship** (of a sailor) leave a ship without permission. **one jump ahead** one stage ahead of a rival.

jumped-up • adj. informal considering oneself to be more important than one really is.

jumper[1] • n. **1** Brit. a pullover or sweater. **2** N. Amer. a pinafore dress.

– ORIGIN perh. from Old French *jupe* 'loose tunic'.

jumper[2] • n. a person or animal that jumps.

jump jet • n. a jet aircraft that can take off and land vertically.

jump lead • n. Brit. each of a pair of cables for recharging a battery in a motor vehicle by connecting it to the battery in another.

jump-start • v. start (a car with a flat battery) with jump leads or by a sudden release of the clutch while it is being pushed.

jumpsuit • n. a one-piece garment incorporating trousers and a sleeved top.

– ORIGIN first referring to a garment worn when parachuting.

jumpy • adj. (**jumpier**, **jumpiest**) informal **1** anxious and uneasy. **2** stopping and starting abruptly.

Jun. • abbrev. June.

junction • n. **1** a point where two or more things meet or are joined. **2** a place where two or more roads or railway lines meet.

– ORIGIN Latin.

juncture /jungk-cher/ • n. **1** a particular point in time. **2** a place where things join.

– ORIGIN Latin *junctura* 'joint'.

June • n. the sixth month of the year.

– ORIGIN from Latin *Junius mensis* 'month of June', named after **JUNO**.

Jung E

/yuung/, Carl (Gustav) (1875–1961), Swiss psychologist, who introduced the idea of introvert and extrovert personality and the 'collective unconscious'.

– DERIVATIVES **Jungian** adj. & n.

Jungfrau E

/yuung-frow/ a mountain in the Swiss Alps, 4,158 m (13,642 ft) high.

jungle • n. **1** an area of thick tropical forest and tangled vegetation. **2** a very bewildering or competitive situation: *a jungle of market forces*.

– ORIGIN Sanskrit, 'rough arid land'.

junior • adj. **1** having to do with young or younger people. **2** Brit. having to do with schoolchildren aged 7–11. **3** (after a name) referring to the younger of two people with the same name in a family. **4** low or lower in status. • n. **1** a person who is a specified number of years younger than someone else: *he's five years her junior.* **2** Brit. a child at a junior school. **3** (in sport) a young competitor. **4** a person with low status.

– ORIGIN Latin.

juniper /joo-ni-per/ • n. an evergreen shrub or small tree with sweet-smelling berry-like cones.

– ORIGIN Latin *juniperus*.

junk[1] informal • n. useless or worthless articles. • v. get rid of abruptly.

– ORIGIN unknown.

junk[2] • n. a flat-bottomed sailing boat used in China and the East Indies.

– ORIGIN Malay.

junket /jung-kit/ • n. **1** a dish of sweetened curds of milk. **2** informal an extravagant trip or party.

– ORIGIN first meaning a cream cheese made in a rush basket: from Old French *jonquette* 'rush basket'.

junk food • n. unhealthy food.

junkie (also **junky**) • n. informal a drug addict.

– ORIGIN from **JUNK**[1] in the sense 'heroin'.

junk mail • n. informal advertising material which has not been requested, sent by post.

junk shop • n. informal a shop selling second hand goods or cheap antiques.

Juno E

/joo-noh/ the most important Roman goddess, wife of Jupiter. Greek equivalent **HERA**.

junta /jun-tuh/ • n. military government that has taken power by force.

– ORIGIN Spanish and Portuguese, 'deliberative or administrative council'.

Jupiter[1] E

/joo-pi-ter/ the chief Roman god, originally a sky god associated with thunder and lightning. Greek equivalent **ZEUS**.

Jupiter[2] E

/joo-pi-ter/ the largest planet in the solar system, fifth in order from the sun and one of the brightest objects in the night sky.

Jura E

/joo-ruh/ an island of the Inner Hebrides.

Jurassic /juu-rass-ik/ • adj. Geol. having to do with the second period of the Mesozoic era (about 208 to 146 million years ago), a time when large reptiles flourished and the first birds appeared.

– ORIGIN French *jurassique*.

jurisdiction /joo-riz-**dik**-sh'n, joo-riss-**dik**-sh'n/ • n. **1** the official power to make legal decisions. **2** the area over which the legal authority of a court or other institution extends. **3** a system of law courts.

– DERIVATIVES **jurisdictional** adj.

– ORIGIN Latin.

jurisprudence /joo-riss-**proo**-duhnss/ • n. **1** the theory of law. **2** a legal system.

– ORIGIN Latin *jurisprudentia*.

jurist /joor-ist/ • n. an expert in law.

– ORIGIN Latin *jurista*.

juror ● n. a member of a jury.

jury ● n. (pl. **juries**) **1** a group of people who have to attend a legal case and give a verdict on the basis of evidence given in court. **2** a group of people judging a competition.
– PHRASES **the jury is out** a decision has not yet been reached.
– ORIGIN Old French *juree* 'oath'.

just ● adj. **1** right and fair. **2** deserved: *we all get our just deserts.* ● adv. **1** exactly. **2** exactly or nearly at this or that moment. **3** very recently. **4** by a small amount. **5** only.
– PHRASES **just in case** as a precaution. **just so** arranged or done very carefully.
– DERIVATIVES **justly** adv.
– ORIGIN Latin *justus*.

justice ● n. **1** just behaviour or treatment. **2** the quality of being fair and reasonable. **3** the administration of law in a fair and reasonable way. **4** a judge or magistrate.
– PHRASES **do oneself justice** perform as well as one is able. **do someone/thing justice** treat someone or something with due fairness.
– ORIGIN Old French *justise*.

Justice of the Peace ● n. (in the UK) a non-professional magistrate appointed to hear minor cases in a town or county.

justifiable ● adj. able to be shown to be right or reasonable.
– DERIVATIVES **justifiably** adv.

justify ● v. (**justifies**, **justifying**, **justified**) **1** prove to be right or reasonable. **2** be a good reason for. **3** Printing adjust (text) so that the lines of type form straight edges at both sides.
– DERIVATIVES **justification** n.
– ORIGIN Latin *justificare* 'do justice to'.

jut ● v. (**juts**, **jutting**, **jutted**) extend out, over, or beyond the main body or line of something.
– ORIGIN from JET[1].

jute /joot/ ● n. rough fibre made from the stems of a tropical plant, made into rope or sacking.
– ORIGIN Bengali.

Jutland E
/**jut**-luhnd/ a peninsula of NW Europe, forming the mainland of Denmark together with the north German state of Schleswig-Holstein.

Juvenal E
/**joo**-vuh-nuhl/ (*c.*60–*c.*140), Roman satirist, who savagely attacked the vice and folly of ancient Roman society in his poetry.

juvenile /**joo**-vuh-nyl/ ● adj. **1** having to do with young people or animals. **2** childish. ● n. **1** a young person or animal. **2** Law a person below the age at which they have adult status in law (18 in most countries).
– ORIGIN Latin *juvenilis*.

juvenile delinquency ● n. the regular committing of criminal acts by a young person.
– DERIVATIVES **juvenile deliquent** n.

juvenilia /joo-vuh-**nil**-i-uh/ ● pl. n. works produced by an author or artist when young.
– ORIGIN Latin.

juxtapose /juk-stuh-**pohz**/ ● v. (**juxtaposes**, **juxtaposing**, **juxtaposed**) place close together.
– DERIVATIVES **juxtaposition** n.
– ORIGIN French *juxtaposer*.

Kk

K[1] (also **k**) ● n. (pl. **Ks** or **K's**) the eleventh letter of the alphabet.

K[2] ● abbrev. **1** kelvin(s). **2** Computing kilobyte(s). **3** kilometre(s). **4** informal thousand. [ORIGIN from KILO-.] ● symb. the chemical element potassium. [ORIGIN Latin *kalium*.]

k ● abbrev. kilo-.

K2 E
the highest mountain in the Karakoram range, on the border between Pakistan and China. At a height of 8,611 m (28,250 ft), it is the second-highest peak in the world.

Kabbalah /kuh-**bah**-luh/ (also **Kabbala**) ● n. the ancient Jewish tradition of mystical interpretation of the Bible.
– DERIVATIVES **Kabbalist** n. **Kabbalistic** adj.
– ORIGIN Hebrew, 'tradition'.

Kabila E
/ka-**bee**-luh/, Laurent-Désiré (1939–2001), African statesman, President of the Democratic Republic of Congo (formerly Zaire) 1997–2001. He was assassinated by an army officer.

kabob ● n. US = KEBAB.

Kabul E
/**kah**-buul/ the capital of Afghanistan.

Kaffir /**kaf**-fer/ ● n. offens., esp. S. Afr. a black African.
– ORIGIN Arabic, 'infidel'.

USAGE Kaffir
The word **Kaffir** is a racially abusive and offensive term.

Kafka E
/**kaf**-kuh/, Franz (1883–1924), Czech novelist, who wrote in German. His works, such as *The Trial*, portray a nightmarish reality where the individual is isolated, perplexed, and threatened.
– DERIVATIVES **Kafkaesque** /kaf-kuh-**esk**/ adj.

kaftan /**kaf**-tan/ (also **caftan**) ● n. **1** a man's long belted tunic, worn in the Near East. **2** a woman's long loose dress.
– ORIGIN Persian.

kaiser /**ky**-zer/ ● **n.** hist. the German Emperor, the Emperor of Austria, or the head of the Holy Roman Empire.
– ORIGIN German.

Kalahari Desert E
/ka-luh-**hah**-ri/ a high, vast, arid plateau in southern Africa, mainly in Botswana.

Kalashnikov /kuh-**lash**-ni-kof/ ● **n.** a type of rifle or sub-machine gun made in Russia.
– ORIGIN named after the Russian designer Mikhail T. *Kalashnikov* (b.1919).

kale ● **n.** a type of cabbage with large leaves and a loosely packed head.
– ORIGIN Latin *caulis*.

kaleidoscope /kuh-**ly**-duh-skohp/ ● **n. 1** a tube containing mirrors and pieces of coloured glass or paper, whose reflections produce changing patterns when the tube is turned. **2** a constantly changing pattern.
– DERIVATIVES **kaleidoscopic** adj.
– ORIGIN from Greek *kalos* 'beautiful' + *eidos* 'form' + **-SCOPE**.

Kali E
/**kah**-li/ the most terrifying Hindu goddess, wife of Shiva.

Kama Sutra /kah-muh **soo**-truh/ ● **n.** an ancient text on the art of love and sexual technique.
– ORIGIN Sanskrit, 'love thread'.

kamikaze /ka-mi-**kah**-zi/ ● **n.** (in the Second World War) a Japanese aircraft loaded with explosives and making a deliberate suicidal crash on an enemy target. ● **adj.** having the potential to kill or harm oneself.
– ORIGIN Japanese, 'holy wind'.

Kampala E
/kam-**pah**-luh/ the capital of Uganda.

Kampuchea E
/kam-puu-**chee**-uh/ former name for **CAMBODIA**.
– DERIVATIVES **Kampuchean** n. & adj.

Kanchenjunga E
/kan-chen-**jung**-guh/ (also **Kangchenjunga** or **Kinchinjunga**) a mountain in the Himalayas. Rising to a height of 8,598 m (28,209 ft), it is the world's third-highest mountain.

Kandinsky E
/kan-**din**-ski/, Wassily (1866–1944), Russian painter and theorist. A pioneer of abstract art, he believed that painting should express inner feelings with colour and form.

kangaroo ● **n.** a large Australian marsupial with a long powerful tail and strong hind legs that enable it to travel by leaping.
– ORIGIN from an Aboriginal language.

kangaroo court ● **n.** an unofficial court formed by a group of people to try someone seen as guilty of an offence.

Kangchenjunga E
/kan-chen-**jung**-guh/ var. of **KANCHENJUNGA**.

Kansas E
/**kan**-zuhss/ a state in the central US; capital, Topeka.
– DERIVATIVES **Kansan** adj. & n.

Kant E
/*rhymes with* rant/, Immanuel (1724–1804), German philosopher, who attempted to establish the limitations of knowledge of the external world, and argued that there was an absolute moral law — the categorical imperative.
– DERIVATIVES **Kantian** adj. & n.

kaolin /**kay**-uh-lin/ ● **n.** a fine soft white clay, used for making china and in medicine.
– ORIGIN Chinese word, 'high hill'.

Kapil Dev E
/ka-pil **dev**/ (b.1959), Indian cricketer, who in 1994 set a record of 432 test match wickets.

kapok /**kay**-pok/ ● **n.** a substance resembling cotton wool which grows around the seeds of a tropical tree, used as padding.
– ORIGIN Malay.

Kapoor E
/ka-**poor**/, (Prithvi) Raj (1924–88), Indian actor and film-maker. His films include *Awara (The Vagabond)*, which he directed and in which he took the title role.

kaput /kuh-**puut**/ ● **adj.** informal broken and useless.
– ORIGIN German *kaputt*.

Karachi E
/kuh-**rah**-chi/ a major city and port in Pakistan, capital of Sind province.

Karajan E
/**ka**-ruh-yan/, Herbert von (1908–89), Austrian conductor, the principal conductor of the Berlin Philharmonic Orchestra (1955–89).

Karakoram E
/ka-ruh-**kor**-uhm/ a great mountain system of central Asia, which extends over 480 km (300 miles) south-eastwards from NE Afghanistan to Kashmir.

Karan E
/**ka**-ruhn/, Donna (b.1948), American fashion designer.

karaoke /ka-ri-**oh**-ki/ ● **n.** a form of entertainment in which people sing popular songs over pre-recorded backing tracks.
– ORIGIN Japanese, 'empty orchestra'.

karat ● **n.** US = **CARAT** (in sense 2).

karate /kuh-**rah**-ti/ ● **n.** an oriental system of unarmed combat using the hands and feet to deliver and block blows.
– ORIGIN Japanese, 'empty hand'.

Kariba Dam E
/kuh-**ree**-buh/ a dam on the Zambezi River. It was built in 1955–9, creating Lake Kariba, to provide hydroelectric power for Zimbabwe and Zambia.

karma /**kar**-muh/ ● **n.** (in Hinduism and Buddhism) the sum of a person's actions in this and previous lives, seen as affecting their future fate.
– DERIVATIVES **karmic** adj.
– ORIGIN Sanskrit, 'action, effect, fate'.

Karnak E
/**kar**-nak/ a village in Egypt on the Nile, now largely amalgamated with Luxor. It is the site of the northern part of ancient Thebes.

k

Karnataka E
/kuh-**nar**-tuh-kuh/ a state in SW India; capital, Bangalore. Former name (until 1973) **MYSORE**.

Karoo E
/kuh-**roo**/ (also **Karroo**) an elevated semi-desert plateau in South Africa.

karst /*rhymes with* cast/ ● **n.** Geol. a limestone region with underground streams and many cavities.
– ORIGIN from German *der Karst*, a limestone region in Slovenia.

kart ● **n.** a small unsprung racing-car with the engine at the back.
– DERIVATIVES **karting** n.
– ORIGIN from **GO-KART**.

kasbah /kaz-bah/ (also **casbah**) ● **n.** a North African citadel and the old, narrow streets that surround it.
– ORIGIN Arabic.

Kashmir E
/kash-**meer**/ a region on the northern border of India and NE Pakistan. The north-western part is controlled by Pakistan, most of it forming the state of Azad Kashmir, while the remainder is incorporated into the Indian state of Jammu and Kashmir.
– DERIVATIVES **Kashmiri** adj. & n.

k

Kasparov E
/kass-puh-roff/, Garry (b.1963; born *Garry Weinstein*), Azerbaijani chess player. In 1985 he became the youngest-ever world champion, at the age of 22.

Kathmandu E
/kat-man-**doo**/ the capital of Nepal.

Kauffmann E
/kowff-man/ (also **Kauffman**), (Maria Anna Catherina) Angelica (1740–1807), Swiss neoclassical painter, resident in London from 1766. She was a founder member of the Royal Academy (1768).

Kaunda E
/kah-**uun**-duh/, Kenneth (David) (b.1924), Zambian statesman, President 1964–91. He led Zambia to independence and served as its first President.

kayak /ky-ak/ ● **n.** a canoe made of a light frame with a watertight covering.
– ORIGIN Inuit.

Kaye, E
Danny (1913–87; born *David Daniel Kominski*), American actor and comedian. His films include *The Secret Life of Walter Mitty.*

Kazakhstan E
/ka-zuhk-**stahn**, ka-zuhk-**stan**/ a republic in central Asia, on the southern border of Russia; capital, Astana.

Kazan E
/kuh-**zan**/, Elia (1909–2003; born *Elia Kazanjoglous*), Turkish-born American film and theatre director, whose films include *A Streetcar Named Desire*, *On the Waterfront*, and *East of Eden*.

kazoo /kuh-**zoo**/ ● **n.** a simple musical instrument consisting of a pipe with a hole in it, over which is a membrane that vibrates and produces a buzzing sound when the player hums into it.

KB (also **Kb**) ● **abbrev.** kilobyte(s).

KBE ● **abbrev.** (in the UK) Knight Commander of the Order of the British Empire.

KC ● **abbrev.** King's Counsel.

kcal ● **abbrev.** kilocalorie(s).

KCB ● **abbrev.** (in the UK) Knight Commander of the Order of the Bath.

KCMG ● **abbrev.** (in the UK) Knight Commander of the Order of St Michael and St George.

Keating, E
Paul (John) (b.1944), Australian Labor statesman, Prime Minister 1991–6.

Keaton, E
Buster (1895–1966; born *Joseph Francis Keaton*), American actor and director, one of the biggest comedy stars of the silent-film era. His films include *The General*.

Keats, E
John (1795–1821), English poet, a leading figure of the romantic movement. His most famous poems include 'La Belle Dame sans Merci', 'Ode to a Nightingale', and 'Ode on a Grecian Urn'.

kebab /ki-**bab**/ (N. Amer. also **kabob**) ● **n.** a dish of pieces of meat, fish, or vegetables roasted or grilled on a skewer or spit.
– ORIGIN Arabic.

Keble E
/kee-b'l/, John (1792–1866), English churchman, co-founder of the Oxford Movement, which sought to restore Catholic teachings and ceremonial within the Church of England.

kecks ● **pl. n.** Brit. informal trousers.
– ORIGIN from former *kicks*.

kedgeree /kej-uh-ree/ ● **n.** a dish of smoked fish, rice, and hard-boiled eggs.
– ORIGIN Sanskrit.

Keegan E
/kee-g'n/, (Joseph) Kevin (b.1951), English footballer and manager. He played for England 1972–82 and was England coach 1999–2000.

keel ● **n.** a structure running along the bottom of a ship, often extended downwards to increase stability. ● **v.** (**keel over**) **1** (of a boat or ship) turn over on its side. **2** informal fall over.
– ORIGIN Old Norse.

keelhaul ● **v.** humorous punish severely.
– ORIGIN from a former punishment in which a person was dragged through the water under a boat.

Keeling Islands E
= **COCOS ISLANDS**.

keen[1] ● **adj. 1** eager and enthusiastic. **2** (**keen on**) interested in. **3** (of a blade) sharp. **4** quick to understand. **5** (of a sense) highly developed. **6** Brit. (of prices) very low.
– DERIVATIVES **keenly** adv. **keenness** n.
– ORIGIN Old English, 'wise, clever'.

keen[2] ● **v. 1** wail in grief for a dead person. **2** make an eerie wailing sound.

– ORIGIN Irish *caoinim* 'I wail'.

keep ● v. (**keeps**, **keeping**, **kept**) **1** have or stay in possession of. **2** retain for use in the future. **3** store in a regular place. **4** (of food) remain in good condition. **5** continue in a specified condition, position, or activity: *she kept quiet about it.* **6** honour or fulfil (a commitment or undertaking). **7** record or regularly make entries in (a note or diary). **8** cause to be late. **9** provide accommodation and food for. **10** (**kept**) dated supported financially in return for sexual favours. ● n. **1** food, clothes, and other essentials for living. **2** the strongest or central tower of a castle.
– PHRASES **for keeps** informal permanently. **keep from 1** cause (something) to remain a secret from. **2** avoid doing. **3** protect (someone) from. **keep on** continue to do, use, or employ. **keep to 1** avoid leaving (a path, road, or place). **2** stick to (a schedule or point). **3** honour (a promise). **keep up 1** move at the same rate as someone or something else. **2** continue (a course of action). **keep up with the Joneses** try hard not to be outdone by one's neighbours or peers.
– ORIGIN Old English.

keeper ● n. **1** a person who manages or looks after something or someone. **2** a goalkeeper or wicketkeeper.

keep-fit ● n. esp. Brit. regular exercises to improve personal fitness and health.

keeping ● n. (in phr. **in** (or **out of**) **keeping with**) in (or out of) harmony with.

keepsake ● n. a small item kept in memory of the person who gave it or originally owned it.

keg ● n. a small barrel.
– ORIGIN Old Norse.

Keller, E
Helen (Adams) (1880–1968), American writer, social reformer, and academic. Blind and deaf from the age of nineteen months, she championed the cause of blind and deaf people throughout the world.

Kelly[1], E
Gene (1912–96; full name *Eugene Curran Kelly*), American dancer and choreographer, known for his film musicals, including *An American in Paris* and *Singin' in the Rain*.

Kelly[2], E
Grace (Patricia) (1928–82; also called (from 1956) **Princess Grace of Monaco**), American film actress, whose films include *High Noon* and *Rear Window*. She married Prince Rainier III of Monaco in 1956. She died in a road accident.

Kelly[3], E
Ned (1855–80; full name *Edward Kelly*), Australian outlaw. Leader of a band of horse and cattle thieves and bank raiders, he was eventually captured and hanged.

kelp ● n. a very large brown seaweed.
– ORIGIN unknown.

Kelvin, E
William Thomson, 1st Baron (1824–1907), British physicist, who introduced the absolute scale of temperature and was the first to try to calculate the age of the earth scientifically.

kelvin ● n. the SI base unit of temperature, equal in to the degree Celsius.
– ORIGIN named after Lord **KELVIN**.

Kelvin scale ● n. the scale of temperature with absolute zero as zero and the freezing point of water as 273.15 kelvins.

Kempis, E
Thomas à, see **THOMAS À KEMPIS**.

ken ● n. (**one's ken**) one's range of knowledge or experience. ● v. (**kens**, **kenning**, **kenned** or **kent**) Sc. & N. Engl. **1** know. **2** recognize.
– ORIGIN Old English, 'tell, make known'.

kendo /ken-doh/ ● n. a Japanese form of fencing with two-handed bamboo swords.
– ORIGIN Japanese, 'sword way'.

Keneally E
/kuh-nal-li, kuh-nee-li/, Thomas (Michael) (b.1935), Australian novelist, author of *Schindler's Ark*.

Kennedy[1], E
John F. (1917–63; in full *John Fitzgerald Kennedy*), American statesman, 35th President of the US 1961–3. The youngest man ever to be elected US President (at 43), he was a popular advocate of civil rights. Kennedy was assassinated in Dallas, Texas.

Kennedy[2], E
Robert (1925–68; full name *Robert Francis Kennedy*), US Attorney General 1961–4. He was assassinated during his campaign as a prospective presidential candidate.

Kennedy, Cape E
former name for **CANAVERAL, CAPE**.

kennel ● n. **1** a small shelter for a dog. **2** (**kennels**) a boarding or breeding establishment for dogs.
– ORIGIN Old French *chenil*.

Kenneth I E
(d.858; known as **Kenneth MacAlpin**), king of Scotland *c.*844–58. He is traditionally considered to be the founder of the kingdom of Scotland, which was established following his defeat of the Picts in about 844.

Kensington E
a fashionable district in central London.

Kent C
a county on the SE coast of England; county town, Maidstone.

kent past and past part. of **KEN**.

Kentucky E
/ken-tuk-i/ a state in the south-eastern US; capital, Frankfort.
– DERIVATIVES **Kentuckian** adj. & n.

Kenya E
/ken-yuh/ an equatorial country in East Africa, on the Indian Ocean; capital, Nairobi.
– DERIVATIVES **Kenyan** adj. & n.

Kenya, Mount E
a mountain in central Kenya. Rising to a height of 5,200 m (17,058 ft), it is the second-highest mountain in Africa.

Kenyatta E
/ken-yat-tuh/, Jomo (*c.*1891–1978), Kenyan statesman, Prime Minister of Kenya 1963 and President 1964–78. He led Kenya to independence in 1963, subsequently serving as its first President.

kepi /kep-i/ ● **n.** (pl. **kepis**) a French military cap with a horizontal peak.
– ORIGIN French.

Kepler E
/kep-ler/, Johannes (1571–1630), German astronomer, who discovered the three laws governing the orbital motion of planets.

kept past and past part. of **KEEP**.

Kerala E
/ke-ruh-luh/ a state on the coast of SW India; capital, Thiruvananthapuram.

keratin /ke-ruh-tin/ ● **n.** a protein forming the basis of hair, feathers, hoofs, claws, and horns.
– ORIGIN Greek *keras* 'horn'.

kerb (US **curb**) ● **n.** a stone edging to a pavement.
– ORIGIN variant of **CURB**.

kerb-crawling ● **n.** Brit. driving slowly along the edge of the road in search of a prostitute.
– DERIVATIVES **kerb-crawler** n.

k

kerb drill ● **n.** Brit. a set of rules followed in order to cross a road safely, as taught to children.

kerbstone ● **n.** a long, narrow stone or concrete block, laid end to end with others to form a kerb.

kerchief /ker-chif/ ● **n. 1** a piece of fabric used to cover the head. **2** a handkerchief.
– ORIGIN Old French *cuevrechief*.

kerfuffle /ker-fuf-f'l/ ● **n.** informal, esp. Brit. a commotion or fuss.
– ORIGIN perh. from Scots *curfuffle*.

Kern, E
Jerome (David) (1885–1945), American composer. A major influence in the development of the musical, he is best known for *Showboat*.

kernel /ker-n'l/ ● **n. 1** a softer part of a nut, seed, or fruit stone contained within its hard shell. **2** the seed and hard husk of a cereal. **3** the central part of something.
– ORIGIN Old English, 'small corn'.

kerosene /ke-ruh-seen/ (also **kerosine**) ● **n.** a light fuel oil distilled from petroleum; paraffin oil.
– ORIGIN Greek *kēros* 'wax'.

Kerouac E
/ke-ruu-ak/, Jack (1922–69; born *Jean-Louis Lebris de Kérouac*), American novelist and poet. A leading figure of the 1950s movement known as the beat generation, he is best known for his semi-autobiographical novel *On the Road*.

Kerry E
a county on the SW coast of the Republic of Ireland; county town, Tralee.

Kesey E
/kee-zi/, Ken (Elton) (1935–2001), American novelist, author of *One Flew over the Cuckoo's Nest*.

kestrel ● **n.** a small falcon that hunts by hovering with rapidly beating wings.
– ORIGIN perh. from Old French *crecerelle*.

ketch ● **n.** a small sailing boat with two masts.
– ORIGIN prob. from **CATCH**.

ketchup (US also **catsup**) ● **n.** a spicy sauce made from tomatoes and vinegar.
– ORIGIN perh. from Chinese, 'tomato juice'.

ketone /kee-tohn/ ● **n.** Chem. any of a class of organic compounds including acetone.
– ORIGIN German *Aketon* 'acetone'.

kettle ● **n.** a metal or plastic container with a lid, spout, and handle, used for boiling water.
– PHRASES **a different kettle of fish** informal something completely different from the one just mentioned. **the pot calling the kettle black** used to suggest that a person is aiming at someone criticisms that could equally well apply to themselves.
– ORIGIN Latin *catillus* 'little pot'.

kettledrum ● **n.** a large drum shaped like a bowl, with adjustable pitch.

key[1] ● **n.** (pl. **keys**) **1** a small piece of shaped metal which is inserted into a lock and turned to open or close it. **2** an instrument for turning a screw, peg, or nut. **3** a lever pressed down by the finger in playing an instrument such as the piano or flute. **4** each of several buttons on a panel for operating a typewriter or computer. **5** a thing providing access or understanding: *a key to success.* **6** a list explaining the symbols used in a map or table. **7** a word or system for solving a code. **8** Music a group of notes based on a particular note and making up a scale. ● **adj.** of central importance: *a key figure.* ● **v.** (**keys**, **keying**, **keyed**) **1** enter (data) using a computer keyboard. **2** (**be keyed up**) be nervous, tense, or excited.
– ORIGIN Old English.

key[2] ● **n.** a low-lying island or reef in the Caribbean.
– ORIGIN Spanish *cayo* 'reef'.

keyboard ● **n. 1** a panel of keys for use with a computer or typewriter. **2** a set of keys on a musical instrument. **3** an electronic musical instrument with keys arranged as on a piano. ● **v.** enter (data) by means of a keyboard.
– DERIVATIVES **keyboarder** n.

keyhole ● **n.** a hole in a lock into which the key is inserted.

keyhole surgery ● **n.** surgery carried out through a very small cut made in the affected area.

Keynes E
/kaynz/, John Maynard, 1st Baron (1883–1946), English economist. He argued that full employment is determined by effective demand and requires government spending on public works to stimulate this.
– DERIVATIVES **Keynesian** adj. & n.

keynote ● **n. 1** a central theme. **2** Music the note on which a key is based. ● **adj.** (of a speech) setting out the central theme of a conference.

keypad ● **n.** a small keyboard or set of buttons for operating a portable electronic device or telephone.

key ring ● **n.** a metal ring for holding keys together in a bunch.

key signature ● **n.** Music a combination of

sharps or flats after the clef at the beginning of each stave, indicating the key of a composition.

keystone • n. **1** a central stone at the top of an arch, locking the whole together. **2** the central part of a policy or system.

keystroke • n. a single depression of a key on a keyboard.

keyword • n. **1** a word or concept of great importance. **2** a significant word mentioned in an index. **3** a word used in a computer system to indicate the content of a document.

KG • abbrev. (in the UK) Knight of the Order of the Garter.

kg • abbrev. kilogram(s).

KGB E
the state security police (1954–91) of the former USSR.

Khachaturian E
/ka-chuh-**choo**-ri-uhn/, Aram (Ilich) (1903–78), Georgian composer, who wrote the ballets *Gayane* and *Spartacus*.

khaki /kah-ki/ • n. (pl. **khakis**) **1** a cotton or wool fabric of a dull brownish-yellow colour. **2** a dull brownish yellow colour.
– ORIGIN Urdu, 'dust-coloured'.

Khama E
/**kah**-muh/, Sir Seretse (1921–80), Botswanan statesman, first President of Botswana 1966–80.

Khan[1] E
/*rhymes with* barn/, Imran (b.1952; full name *Imran Ahmad Khan Niazi*), Pakistani cricketer. After retiring from cricket in 1992, he entered politics in Pakistan.

Khan[2] E
/*rhymes with* barn/, Jahangir (b.1963), Pakistani squash player. He was world squash champion five consecutive times (1981–5), and again in 1988.

khan /*rhymes with* barn/ • n. a title given to rulers and officials in central Asia, Afghanistan, and certain other Muslim countries.
– ORIGIN Turkic, 'lord, prince'.

Khartoum E
/kar **toom**/ the capital of Sudan.

khazi /kah-zi/ • n. (pl. **khazies**) Brit. informal a toilet.
– ORIGIN Italian *casa* 'house'.

Khmer Republic E
former official name for **Cambodia**.

Khmer Rouge E
/kmair **roozh**/ a communist guerrilla organization in Cambodia which took power in 1975, after a civil war. Since the overthrow of the regime by the Vietnamese in 1979, Khmer Rouge forces have continued a programme of guerilla warfare from bases in Thailand.

Khomeini E
/kho-**may**-ni/, Ruhollah (1900–89; known as **Ayatollah Khomeini**), Iranian Shiite Muslim leader, who in 1979 established Iran as a fundamentalist Islamic republic after the overthrow of the shah.

Khrushchev E
/**kruus**-choff, kruus-**choff**/, Nikita (Sergeevich) (1894–1971), Soviet statesman, Premier of the USSR 1958–64. He came close to war with the US over the Cuban Missile Crisis in 1962 and also clashed with China.

Khufu E
/koo-foo/ see **Cheops**.

Khyber Pass E
/ky-ber/ a mountain pass in the Hindu Kush, on the border between Pakistan and Afghanistan. The pass was for long of great commercial and strategic importance.

kHz • abbrev. kilohertz.

kibble /kib-b'l/ • v. (**kibbles**, **kibbling**, **kibbled**) grind or chop (beans, grain, etc.) coarsely.
– ORIGIN unknown.

kibbutz /kib-buuts/ • n. (pl. **kibbutzim** /kib-buuts-im/) a farming settlement in Israel in which work is shared between its members.
– ORIGIN modern Hebrew, 'gathering'.

kibosh /ky-bosh/ • n. (in phr. **put the kibosh on**) informal firmly put an end to.
– ORIGIN unknown.

kick • v. **1** strike or propel forcibly with the foot. **2** strike out with the foot or feet. **3** informal succeed in giving up (a habit). **4** (of a gun) spring back when fired. • n. **1** an instance of kicking. **2** informal the strong effect of alcohol or a drug. **3** informal a thrill of excitement.
– PHRASES **kick against** disagree or be frustrated with. **kick the bucket** informal die. **kick in** come into effect. **a kick in the teeth** informal a serious setback. **kick off** (of a football match) start or restart with a kick from the centre spot. **kick oneself** be annoyed with oneself. **kick out** informal force to leave.
– DERIVATIVES **kicker** n.
– ORIGIN unknown.

kickback • n. **1** a sudden forceful springing back. **2** informal an underhand payment made to someone who has helped to arrange a business or political deal.

kick-boxing • n. a form of martial art which combines boxing with kicking with bare feet.

kick-off • n. the start of a football match.

kickstand • n. a rod attached to a bicycle or motorcycle that may be kicked upright to support the vehicle when it is not being ridden.

kick-start • v. **1** start (an engine on a motorcycle) with a downward thrust of a pedal. **2** stimulate: *the government should kick-start the economy.* • n. a device to kick-start an engine.

kid[1] • n. **1** informal a child or young person. **2** a young goat. • v. (**kids**, **kidding**, **kidded**) (of a goat) give birth.
– PHRASES **handle** (or **treat**) **with kid gloves** deal with very carefully.
– ORIGIN Old Norse.

kid[2] • v. (**kids**, **kidding**, **kidded**) informal fool into believing something.
– ORIGIN perh. from **kid[1]**, expressing the idea 'make a child or goat of'.

kid brother (or **kid sister**) • n. informal a younger brother or sister.

kiddie (also **kiddy**) • n. (pl. **kiddies**) informal a young child.

k

kidnap ● v. (**kidnaps**, **kidnapping**, **kidnapped**; US also **kidnaps**, **kidnaping**, **kidnaped**) take (someone) by force and hold them captive. ● n. an instance of kidnapping.
– DERIVATIVES **kidnapper** n.
– ORIGIN from **KID**[1] + slang *nap* 'seize'.

kidney ● n. (pl. **kidneys**) **1** each of a pair of organs that remove waste products from the blood and produce urine. **2** the kidney of a sheep, ox, or pig as food.
– ORIGIN uncertain.

kidney bean ● n. a dark red kidney-shaped bean.

kidney machine ● n. a machine that performs the functions of a kidney.

kidney stone ● n. a hard mass formed in the kidneys.

Kiel E
/keel/ a naval port in northern Germany, on the Baltic Sea.

Kierkegaard E
/**keer**-kuh-gard/, Søren (Aabye) (1813–55), Danish philosopher. A founder of existentialism, he believed in the importance of individual experience and choice.

Kiev E
/**kee**-eff/ the capital of Ukraine.

Kigali E
/ki-**gah**-li/ the capital of Rwanda.

Kildare E
/kil-**dair**/ a county in the east of the Republic of Ireland; county town, Naas.

kilim /ki-**leem**/ ● n. a carpet or rug woven without a pile, made in Turkey, Kurdistan, etc.
– ORIGIN Persian.

Kilimanjaro, Mount E
/ki-li-muhn-**jah**-roh/ an extinct volcano in northern Tanzania. Rising to 5,895 m (19,340 ft), it is the highest mountain in Africa.

Kilkenny E
/kil-**ken**-ni/ a county in the south-east of the Republic of Ireland; county town, Kilkenny.

kill ● v. **1** cause the death of. **2** put an end to. **3** informal overwhelm (someone) with an emotion: *the suspense is killing me.* **4** informal cause pain to. **5** pass (time). ● n. **1** an act of killing. **2** an animal or animals killed by a hunter or another animal.
– PHRASES **be in at the kill** be present at or benefit from the successful conclusion of an undertaking.
– ORIGIN prob. Germanic.

Killarney E
/kil-**lar**-ni/ a town in County Kerry, in the Republic of Ireland, famous for the beauty of the nearby lakes and mountains.

killer ● n. **1** a person or thing that kills. **2** informal something that is very difficult.

killer instinct ● n. a ruthless determination to succeed or win.

killer whale ● n. a large toothed whale with black-and-white markings and a prominent fin on its back.

killing ● n. an act of causing death. ● adj. informal exhausting.
– PHRASES **make a killing** make a great deal of money out of something.

killjoy ● n. a person who spoils the enjoyment of others by behaving very seriously.

kiln ● n. an oven for baking or drying clay, bricks, etc.
– ORIGIN Latin *culina* 'kitchen'.

kilo ● n. (pl. **kilos**) a kilogram.

kilo- /**ki**-loh, **kee**-loh/ ● comb. form referring to a factor of one thousand (10^3): *kilolitre.*
– ORIGIN Greek *khilioi* 'thousand'.

kilobyte ● n. Computing a unit of memory or data equal to 1,024 bytes.

kilocalorie ● n. a unit of energy of one thousand calories (equal to one large calorie).

kilogram (also **kilogramme**) ● n. the SI unit of mass, equal to 1,000 grams (approximately 2.205 lb).

kilohertz ● n. a measure of frequency equivalent to 1,000 cycles per second.

kilojoule ● n. 1,000 joules.

kilolitre (US **kiloliter**) ● n. 1,000 litres (equivalent to 220 imperial gallons).

kilometre /**kil**-uh-mee-ter, ki-**lom**-i-ter/ (US **kilometer**) ● n. a metric unit of measurement equal to 1,000 metres (approximately 0.62 miles).
– DERIVATIVES **kilometric** adj.

kiloton (also **kilotonne**) ● n. a unit of explosive power equivalent to 1,000 tons of TNT.

kilovolt ● n. 1,000 volts.

kilowatt ● n. 1,000 watts.

kilowatt-hour ● n. a measure of electrical energy equivalent to one kilowatt operating for one hour.

kilt ● n. a knee-length skirt of pleated tartan cloth, traditionally worn by men as part of Scottish Highland dress.
– DERIVATIVES **kilted** adj.
– ORIGIN Scandinavian.

kilter ● n. (in phr. **out of kilter**) out of balance.
– ORIGIN unknown.

Kimberley E
a city and diamond-mining centre in South Africa, in the province of Northern Cape.

Kim Il Sung E
/kim il **suung**/ (1912–94; born *Kim Song Ju*), Korean communist statesman, first Premier of North Korea 1948–72 and President 1972–94. He was committed to the reunification of his country, and in 1950 triggered the Korean War when he ordered his forces to invade South Korea.

kimono /ki-**moh**-noh/ ● n. (pl. **kimonos**) a long, loose Japanese robe having wide sleeves and tied with a sash.
– ORIGIN Japanese, 'wearing thing'.

kin ● n. (treated as pl.) one's family and relations.
– ORIGIN Old English.

-kin ● suffix forming nouns referring to things of small size, such as *catkin.*
– ORIGIN Dutch *-kijn*, *-ken*, German *-kīn*.

Kinchinjunga E
/kin-chin-**jung**-guh/ var. of **KANCHENJUNGA**.

kind[1] ● n. **1** a class or type of similar people or things. **2** character: *true to kind.* **3** each of the elements (bread and wine) of the Eucharist.
– PHRASES **in kind 1** in the same way. **2** (of pay-

ment) in goods or services instead of money. **kind of** informal rather. **one of a kind** unique. **two of a kind** the same or very similar.
– ORIGIN Old English.

> **USAGE kind**
> When using **kind** to refer to a plural noun, it is wrong to say *these kind* as in *these kind of questions are not relevant* (that is, to have *kind* in the singular): you should use *kinds* instead (*these kinds of questions are not relevant*).

kind[2] ● **adj.** considerate and generous.
– ORIGIN Old English, 'natural, native'.

kindergarten /kin-der-gar-tuhn/ ● **n.** a nursery school.
– ORIGIN German, 'children's garden'.

kindle /kin-d'l/ ● **v.** (**kindles**, **kindling**, **kindled**) **1** light (a flame). **2** arouse (an emotion).
– ORIGIN Old Norse, 'candle, torch'.

kindling ● **n.** small sticks used for lighting fires.

kindly ● **adv. 1** in a kind way. **2** please (used in a polite request). ● **adj.** (**kindlier**, **kindliest**) kind.
– PHRASES **not take kindly to** not be pleased by.
– DERIVATIVES **kindliness** n.

kindness ● **n. 1** the quality of being kind. **2** a kind act.

kindred /kin-drid/ ● **n. 1** (treated as pl.) one's family and relations. **2** relationship by blood. ● **adj.** similar in kind.
– ORIGIN Old English.

kindred spirit ● **n.** a person whose interests or attitudes are similar to one's own.

kinematics /kin-i-mat-iks/ ● **n.** the branch of mechanics concerned with the motion of objects without reference to the forces which cause the motion.
– DERIVATIVES **kinematic** adj.
– ORIGIN Greek *kinēma* 'motion'.

kinetic /ki-net-ik/ ● **adj.** relating to or resulting from motion.
– DERIVATIVES **kinetically** adv.
– ORIGIN Greek *kinētikos*.

kinetic energy ● **n.** Physics energy which a body possesses as a result of being in motion. Compare with **POTENTIAL ENERGY.**

kinetics /ki-net-iks/ ● **n. 1** the branch of chemistry concerned with the rates of chemical reactions. **2** Physics = **DYNAMICS** (in sense 1).

kinfolk ● **pl. n.** = **KINSFOLK.**

> **King**[1], E
> B. B. (b.1925; born *Riley B King*), American blues singer and guitarist.

> **King**[2], E
> Billie Jean (b.1943), American tennis player. She won a record twenty Wimbledon titles, including six singles titles.

> **King**[3], E
> Martin Luther (1929–68), American Baptist minister and civil rights leader. He opposed discrimination against blacks by organizing non-violent resistance and peaceful mass demonstrations. He was assassinated in Memphis.

> **King**[4], E
> William Lyon Mackenzie (1874–1950), Canadian Liberal statesman, Prime Minister 1921–6, 1926–30, and 1935–48.

king ● **n. 1** the male ruler of an independent state. **2** the best or most important person or thing in a field or group. **3** a playing card bearing a picture of a king, ranking next below an ace. **4** the most important chess piece, which the opponent has to checkmate in order to win.
– DERIVATIVES **kingly** adj. **kingship** n.
– ORIGIN Old English.

King Charles spaniel ● **n.** a small breed of spaniel with a white, black, and tan coat.
– ORIGIN named after King Charles II (see **CHARLES II**).

kingdom ● **n. 1** a country, state, or territory ruled by a king or queen. **2** an area in which a particular person or thing is dominant. **3** the spiritual reign of God. **4** each of the three divisions (animal, vegetable, and mineral) in which natural objects are classified.
– PHRASES **till** (or **until**) **kingdom come** informal forever. **to kingdom come** informal into the next world.

kingfisher ● **n.** a colourful bird with a long sharp beak, which dives to catch fish in streams and rivers.

kingmaker ● **n.** a person who brings leaders to power by using their political influence.
– ORIGIN first referring to the Earl of Warwick (see **WARWICK**).

king of beasts ● **n.** the lion.

King of Kings ● **n.** (in the Christian Church) God.

kingpin ● **n. 1** a large bolt in a central position. **2** a vertical bolt used as a pivot. **3** a person or thing that is essential to the success of an organization or operation.

king-sized (also **king-size**) ● **adj.** of a larger than normal size.

> **Kingsley**, E
> Charles (1819–75), English novelist and clergyman, author of the historical novel *Westward Ho!* and the children's story *The Water-Babies*.

> **Kingston** E
> the capital and chief port of Jamaica.

> **Kingston-upon-Hull** E
> official name for **HULL.**

> **Kingstown** E
> the capital and chief port of St Vincent in the Caribbean.

kink ● **n. 1** a sharp twist in something long and narrow. **2** a flaw or difficulty in a plan or operation. **3** a peculiar habit or characteristic. ● **v.** form a kink.
– ORIGIN German *kinke*.

kinky ● **adj.** (**kinkier**, **kinkiest**) **1** having kinks or twists. **2** informal having to do with unusual sexual behaviour.

> **Kinneret, Lake** E
> /kin-nuh-ret/ = Sea of Galilee (see **GALILEE, SEA OF**).

k

Kinsey E
/kin-zi/, Alfred Charles (1894–1956), American zoologist, who carried out pioneering studies into sexual behaviour by interviewing large numbers of people.

kinsfolk (also **kinfolk**) • pl. n. a person's blood relations.

Kinshasa E
/kin-**shah**-suh/ the capital of Zaire (Democratic Republic of Congo). Former name (until 1966) **LÉOPOLDVILLE**.

kinship • n. **1** blood relationship. **2** a sharing of characteristics or origins: *they felt a kinship with architects.*

kinsman (also **kinswoman**) • n. one of a person's blood relations.

kiosk /kee-ossk/ • n. **1** a small open-fronted hut from which newspapers, refreshments, tickets, etc. are sold. **2** Brit. a public telephone booth.
– ORIGIN Turkish *köşk* 'pavilion'.

kip Brit. informal • n. a sleep. • v. (**kips**, **kipping**, **kipped**) sleep.
– ORIGIN perh. from Danish *kippe* 'hovel'.

Kipling, E
(Joseph) Rudyard (1865–1936), British novelist, short-story writer, and poet, born in India. He is known for his poems, such as 'If', and for his children's books, including *The Jungle Book* and the *Just So Stories*.

kipper • n. a herring that has been split open, salted, and dried or smoked.
– ORIGIN Old English, referring to a male salmon in the spawning season.

kipper tie • n. a very wide tie.

kirby grip (also trademark **Kirbigrip**) • n. Brit. a hairgrip consisting of a thin folded and sprung metal strip.
– ORIGIN named after *Kirby*, Beard, & Co. Ltd, the original manufacturers.

Kirghizia E
/keer-giz-i-uh/ former name for **KYRGYZSTAN**.

Kiribati E
/ki-ri-**bas**, ki-ri-**bah**-ti/ a country in the SW Pacific including the Gilbert Islands, the Line islands, the Phoenix Islands, and Banaba (Ocean Island); capital, Bairiki (on Tarawa).

kirk • n. Sc. & N. Engl. **1** a church. **2** (**the Kirk** or **the Kirk of Scotland**) the Church of Scotland.
– ORIGIN related to **CHURCH**.

Kirk session • n. the lowest court in the Church of Scotland.

Kirkwall E
/kerk-wawl/ the chief town of the Orkney Islands, on Mainland.

kismet /kiz-met/ • n. fate.
– ORIGIN Arabic, 'division, lot'.

kiss • v. touch with the lips as a sign of love, affection, or greeting. • n. a touch with the lips.
– PHRASES **kiss of death** an action that ensures that an undertaking will fail. **kiss of life 1** mouth-to-mouth resuscitation. **2** something that revives a failing enterprise.
– DERIVATIVES **kissable** adj.
– ORIGIN Old English.

kiss curl • n. a small curl of hair on the forehead, at the nape of the neck, or in front of the ear.

kisser • n. **1** a person who kisses someone. **2** informal a person's mouth.

Kissinger E
/kiss-in-jer/, Henry (Alfred) (b.1923), German-born American statesman and diplomat, Secretary of State 1973–7. He helped negotiate the withdrawal of US troops from South Vietnam (1973).

kissogram • n. a novelty greeting delivered by a man or woman who accompanies it with a kiss.

kit[1] • n. **1** a set of articles or equipment for a specific purpose. **2** Brit. the clothing and items needed for an activity: *boys in football kit.* • v. (**kits**, **kitting**, **kitted**) (**kit out**) provide with appropriate clothing or equipment.
– ORIGIN Dutch *kitte* 'wooden container'.

kit[2] • n. the young of certain animals, e.g. the beaver, ferret, and mink.

kitbag • n. a long, cylindrical canvas bag for carrying a soldier's possessions.

kitchen • n. **1** a room where food is prepared and cooked. **2** a set of fittings and units installed in a kitchen.
– ORIGIN Old English.

Kitchener, E
(Horatio) Herbert, 1st Earl Kitchener of Khartoum (1850–1916), British soldier and statesman. In 1888 he defeated forces in the Sudan led by Muhammad Ahmad (1843–85; known as *the Mahdi*). He later served as Secretary of State for War (1914–16).

kitchenette • n. a small kitchen or part of a room equipped as a kitchen.

kitchen garden • n. a garden where vegetables and fruit are grown for household use.

kitchen-sink • adj. (of drama) realistic in dealing with drab or sordid subjects.

kitchenware • n. kitchen utensils.

kite • n. **1** a toy consisting of a light frame with thin material stretched over it, flown in the wind at the end of a long string. **2** a long-winged bird of prey with a forked tail. **3** Geom. a four-sided figure having two pairs of equal sides next to each other.
– ORIGIN Old English.

Kitemark • n. trademark (in the UK) an official kite-shaped mark on goods approved by the British Standards Institution.

kith /kith/ • n. (in phr. **kith and kin**) one's relations.
– ORIGIN Old English.

kitsch */rhymes with* rich/ • n. art, objects, or design considered to be unpleasantly bright or too sentimental.
– DERIVATIVES **kitschy** adj.
– ORIGIN German.

kitten • n. **1** a young cat. **2** the young of certain other animals, such as the rabbit and beaver.
– PHRASES **have kittens** Brit. informal be extremely nervous or upset.
– ORIGIN Old French *chitoun*.

kittenish • adj. playful, lively, or flirtatious.

kittiwake /kit-ti-wayk/ • n. a small gull that nests on sea cliffs and has a loud call that resembles its name.

kitty • n. (pl. **kitties**) **1** a fund of money for use by a number of people. **2** a pool of money in some card games.
– ORIGIN unknown.

kiwi • n. (pl. **kiwis**) **1** a flightless, tailless New Zealand bird with hair-like feathers and a long downcurved bill. **2** (**Kiwi**) informal a New Zealander.
– ORIGIN Maori.

kiwi fruit • n. (pl. **kiwi fruit**) the fruit of an Asian climbing plant, with a thin hairy skin, green flesh, and black seeds.

kJ • abbrev. kilojoule(s).

KKK • abbrev. Ku Klux Klan.

kl • abbrev. kilolitre(s).

klaxon /klak-suhn/ • n. trademark a vehicle horn or warning hooter.
– ORIGIN the name of the manufacturers.

Klee E
/*rhymes with* clay/, Paul (1879–1940), Swiss painter, resident in Germany from 1906. His work is characterized by his sense of colour and often has a childlike or fantasy quality.

Kleenex • n. (pl. **Kleenex** or **Kleenexes**) trademark a paper tissue.

Klein[1] E
/*rhymes with* fine/, Calvin (Richard) (b.1942), American fashion designer.

Klein[2] E
/*rhymes with* fine/, Melanie (1882–1960), Austrian-born psychoanalyst, the first to specialize in the psychoanalysis of small children.

Klemperer E
/klem-puh-ruh/, Otto (1885–1973), German-born conductor and composer.

kleptomania /klep-tuh-may-ni-uh/ • n. a recurring urge to steal.
– DERIVATIVES **kleptomaniac** n. & adj.
– ORIGIN Greek *kleptēs* 'thief'.

Klerk, E
F. W. de, see **DE KLERK**.

Klimt E
/klimt/, Gustav (1862–1918), Austrian painter and designer, known for his decorative and allegorical paintings and his portraits of women.

Klondike E
/klon-dyk/ a tributary of the Yukon River, in Yukon Territory, NW Canada. It gave its name to the surrounding region, which became famous when gold was found there in 1896.

Klosters E
/kloh-sterz/ an Alpine winter-sports resort in eastern Switzerland.

km • abbrev. kilometre(s).

knack • n. **1** a skill at performing a task. **2** a habit of doing something.
– ORIGIN prob. from former *knack* 'sharp blow or sound'.

knacker Brit. • n. a person who disposes of dead or unwanted animals. • v. (**knackers**, **knackering**, **knackered**) informal wear out.
– ORIGIN perh. from former *knack* 'trinket'.

knacker's yard • n. Brit. a place where old or injured animals are slaughtered.

knapsack • n. a small rucksack.
– ORIGIN Dutch *knapzack*.

knave • n. **1** archaic a dishonest man. **2** (in cards) a jack.
– DERIVATIVES **knavery** n. **knavish** adj.
– ORIGIN Old English, 'boy, servant'.

knead • v. **1** work (dough or clay) with the hands. **2** massage as if kneading.
– ORIGIN Old English.

knee • n. **1** the joint between the thigh and the lower leg. **2** the upper surface of a sitting person's thigh. • v. (**knees**, **kneeing**, **kneed**) hit with the knee.
– PHRASES **bring someone to their knees** reduce someone to a state of weakness or submissiveness.
– ORIGIN Old English.

kneecap • n. the outward-curving bone in front of the knee joint. • v. (**kneecaps**, **kneecapping**, **kneecapped**) shoot in the knee or leg as a punishment.

knee-jerk • n. an involuntary kick caused by a blow on the tendon just below the knee. • adj. automatic and unthinking: *a knee-jerk reaction*.

kneel • v. (**kneels**, **kneeling**, **knelt** or N. Amer. also **kneeled**) fall or rest on a knee or the knees.
– ORIGIN Old English.

kneeler • n. a cushion or bench for kneeling on.

knees-up • n. Brit. informal a lively party.

knell /nel/ • n. literary the sound of a bell rung solemnly.
– ORIGIN Old English.

knelt past and past part. of **KNEEL**.

Knesset E
/knes-set/ the parliament of modern Israel.

knew past of **KNOW**.

knickerbockers • pl. n. loose-fitting breeches gathered at the knee or calf.
– ORIGIN named after Diedrich *Knickerbocker*, the pretended author of Washington Irving's *History of New York* (1809).

knickers • pl. n. Brit. a woman's or girl's undergarment covering the body from the waist or hips to the top of the thighs and having two holes for the legs.
– PHRASES **get one's knickers in a twist** Brit. informal become upset or angry.
– ORIGIN from *knickerbockers*.

knick-knack • n. a cheap ornament.
– ORIGIN from **KNACK**.

knife • n. (pl. **knives**) **1** a cutting instrument consisting of a blade fixed into a handle. **2** a cutting blade on a machine. • v. (**knifes**, **knifing**, **knifed**) stab with a knife.
– PHRASES **at knifepoint** under threat of injury from a knife. **that one could cut with a knife** (of an accent or atmosphere) very obvious.
– ORIGIN Old Norse.

knife-edge • n. a very tense or dangerous situation.

knight • n. **1** (in the Middle Ages) a man of noble rank with a duty to fight for his king. **2** (in the UK) a man awarded a title by the monarch and entitled to use 'Sir' in front

k

of his name. **3** a chess piece that moves by jumping to the opposite corner of a rectangle two squares by three. ● **v.** give (a man) the title of knight.
– PHRASES **knight in shining armour** a gallant man who helps a woman in a difficult situation.
– DERIVATIVES **knighthood** n. **knightly** adj.
– ORIGIN Old English, 'boy, servant'.

knight errant ● **n.** a medieval knight who wandered in search of adventure.

Knightsbridge E
a district in London, to the south of Hyde Park, noted for its fashionable and expensive shops.

Knights Hospitallers E
a military and religious order founded in the 11th century to protect pilgrims, and later becoming a powerful military force.

Knights Templars E
(also **Knights Templar**) a religious and military order founded in 1118 for the protection of pilgrims to the Holy Land, and later becoming powerful and wealthy rivals to the Knights Hospitallers.

k

knit ● **v.** (**knits**, **knitting**, **knitted** or **knit**) **1** make (a garment) by looping yarn together with knitting needles or on a machine. **2** make (a plain stitch) in knitting. **3** join together. **4** tighten (one's eyebrows) in a frown. ● **n.** (**knits**) knitted garments.
– DERIVATIVES **knitter** n. **knitting** n.
– ORIGIN Old English.

knitting needle ● **n.** a long, thin, pointed rod used as part of a pair for hand knitting.

knitwear ● **n.** knitted garments.

knives pl. of **KNIFE**.

knob ● **n. 1** a rounded lump at the end or on the surface of something. **2** a ball-shaped handle. **3** a round control switch on a machine. **4** a small lump of something.
– DERIVATIVES **knobbed** adj. **knobby** adj.
– ORIGIN German *knobbe*.

knobble ● **n.** Brit. a small lump on something.
– DERIVATIVES **knobbly** adj.
– ORIGIN from **KNOB**.

knock ● **v. 1** strike a surface noisily to attract attention. **2** collide with. **3** force to move or fall with a blow. **4** make (a hole, dent, etc.) in something by striking it. **5** informal criticize. **6** (of a motor) make a rattling noise. ● **n. 1** a sudden short sound caused by a blow. **2** a blow or collision. **3** a setback.
– PHRASES **knock about** (or **around**) informal travel or spend time aimlessly. **knock back** informal consume (a drink) quickly. **knock down** informal reduce the price of (an article). **knock off** informal **1** stop work. **2** produce (a piece of work) quickly and easily. **3** Brit. steal. **be knocking on** informal be growing old. **knock on the head** Brit. informal put an end to (an idea, plan, etc.). **knock out 1** make unconscious. **2** informal astonish or greatly impress. **3** eliminate from a knockout competition. **4** informal produce (work) at a steady fast rate. **knock spots off** Brit. informal easily outdo. **the school of hard knocks** difficult but useful life experiences.
– ORIGIN Old English.

knockabout ● **adj.** (of comedy) rough and slapstick.

knock-back ● **n.** informal a refusal or setback.

knock-down ● **adj.** informal (of a price) very low.

knocker ● **n. 1** a hinged object fixed to a door and rapped by visitors to attract attention. **2** informal a person who continually finds fault. **3** (**knockers**) informal a woman's breasts.

knock-kneed ● **adj.** having legs that curve inwards at the knee.

knock-off ● **n.** informal a copy or imitation.

knock-on effect ● **n.** esp. Brit. an effect or result that affects others in a series.

knockout ● **n. 1** an act of knocking someone out. **2** Brit. a tournament in which the loser in each round is eliminated. **3** informal an extremely impressive person or thing.

knock-up ● **n.** Brit. (in racket sports) a period of practice play before a game.

knoll /nol/ ● **n.** a small hill or mound.
– ORIGIN Old English.

Knossos E
/**knoss**-uhss, **noss**-uhss/ the chief city of Minoan Crete, the remains of which are situated on the north coast of Crete.

knot[1] ● **n. 1** a fastening made by looping a piece of string, rope, etc. on itself and tightening it. **2** a tangled mass in hair, wool, etc. **3** a hard mass in wood at the point where the trunk and a branch join. **4** a hard lump of bodily tissue. **5** a small group of people. **6** a unit used to measure the speed of ships, aircraft, or winds, equivalent to one nautical mile per hour. ● **v.** (**knots**, **knotting**, **knotted**) **1** fasten with a knot. **2** tangle. **3** cause (a muscle) to become tense and hard. **4** (of the stomach) tighten as a result of tension.
– PHRASES **get knotted** Brit. informal go away. **tie the knot** informal get married.
– ORIGIN Old English; sense 6 comes from the former practice of measuring a ship's speed by using a float attached to a long knotted line.

knot garden ● **n.** a formal garden laid out in a complex design.

knothole ● **n.** a hole in a piece of wood where a knot has fallen out.

knotty ● **adj.** (**knottier**, **knottiest**) **1** full of knots. **2** extremely complex: *a knotty problem*.

know ● **v.** (**knows**, **knowing**, **knew**; past part. **known**) **1** be aware of as a result of observing, asking, or being informed. **2** be absolutely sure of something. **3** be familiar with. **4** have a good command of (a subject or language). **5** have personal experience of. **6** (**be known as**) be thought of as having a specified characteristic or title.
– PHRASES **be in the know** be aware of something known only to a few people. **know no bounds** have no limits. **know the ropes** have experience of the correct way of doing something.
– DERIVATIVES **knowable** adj.
– ORIGIN Old English, 'recognize'.

know-all (also **know-it-all**) ● **n.** informal a person who behaves as if they know everything.

know-how ● **n.** practical knowledge or skill.

knowing ● **adj.** suggesting that one has secret knowledge: *a knowing smile*.
– PHRASES **there is no knowing** it is not

possible to tell.
– DERIVATIVES **knowingly** adv. **knowingness** n.

knowledge • n. **1** information and skills gained through experience or education. **2** the sum of what is known. **3** awareness gained by experience of a fact or situation.
– PHRASES **to (the best of) my knowledge 1** so far as I know. **2** as I know for certain.

knowledgeable (also **knowledgable**) • adj. intelligent and well informed.
– DERIVATIVES **knowledgeably** adv.

known past part. of **KNOW**. • adj. **1** that is recognized, familiar, or can be known. **2** publicly acknowledged to be: *a known criminal*. **3** Math. (of a quantity or variable) having a value that can be stated.

Knox, E
John (c.1505–72), Scottish Protestant reformer, who played a central part in the establishment of the Church of Scotland and led opposition to the Catholic Mary, Queen of Scots.

knuckle • n. **1** a part of a finger at a joint where the bone is near the surface. **2** a knee-joint of a four-legged animal, or the part joining the leg to the foot, especially as a joint of meat. • v. **(knuckles, knuckling, knuckled)** rub or press with the knuckles.
– PHRASES **knuckle down 1** apply oneself seriously to a task. **2** (also **knuckle under**) submit. **near the knuckle** Brit. informal close to being indecent. **rap on** (or **over**) **the knuckles** reprimand or criticize.
– ORIGIN German or Dutch *knökel* 'little bone'.

knuckleduster • n. a metal guard worn over the knuckles in fighting to increase the effect of blows.

knucklehead • n. informal a stupid person.

knurl /*rhymes with* curl/ • n. a small projecting knob or ridge.
– DERIVATIVES **knurled** adj.
– ORIGIN prob. from German *knorre* 'knob'.

Knut E
var. of **CANUTE**.

KO[1] • abbrev. kick off.

KO[2] • n. a knockout in a boxing match. • v. **(KO's, KO'ing, KO'd)** knock (someone) out.

koala /koh-ah-luh/ • n. a bear-like tree-dwelling Australian marsupial that has thick grey fur and feeds on eucalyptus leaves.
– ORIGIN from an Aboriginal language.

Kobe E
/koh-bi/ a port in Japan, on the island of Honshu.

Koch E
/kokh/, Robert (1843–1910), German bacteriologist, who was the first to prove that specific diseases (anthrax, tuberculosis, and cholera) were caused by bacteria.

Kodály E
/koh-dy/, Zoltán (1882–1967), Hungarian composer, known for compositions such as the choral work *Psalmus Hungaricus* and the opera *Háry János*.

Kohl E
/*rhymes with* coal/, Helmut (b.1930), German statesman, Chancellor of the Federal Republic of Germany 1982–90, and of Germany 1990–8.

kohl /kohl/ • n. a black powder used as eye make-up.
– ORIGIN Arabic.

kohlrabi /kohl-rah-bi/ • n. (pl. **kohlrabies**) a variety of cabbage with an edible turnip-like stem.
– ORIGIN German.

koi /koy/ • n. (pl. **koi**) a large common Japanese carp.
– ORIGIN Japanese.

Kolkata /kol-kah-tuh/ official name for **CALCUTTA**. E

kook • n. N. Amer. informal a mad or unconventional person.
– DERIVATIVES **kooky** adj.
– ORIGIN prob. from **CUCKOO**.

kookaburra /kuu-kuh-bur-ruh/ • n. a very large, noisy, Australasian kingfisher that feeds on reptiles and birds.
– ORIGIN from an Aboriginal language.

Kooning, E
Willem de, see **DE KOONING**.

kopek /koh-pek/ (also **copeck** or **kopeck**) • n. a unit of money of Russia and some other countries of the former USSR, equal to one hundredth of a rouble.
– ORIGIN Russian *kopeĭka* 'small lance'.

Koran /ko-rahn/ (also **Quran** or **Qur'an** /kuu-rahn/) • n. the sacred book of Islam, believed to be the word of God as told to Muhammad and written down in Arabic.
– ORIGIN Arabic, 'recitation'.

Korbut E
/kor-buht/, Olga (b.1955), Soviet gymnast, winner of two gold medals at the 1972 Olympic Games.

Korda E
/kor-duh/, Sir Alexander (1893–1956; born *Sándor Kellner*), Hungarian-born British film producer and director, whose films include *The Third Man*.

Korea E
/kuh-ree-uh/ a region of east Asia forming a peninsula between the Sea of Japan and the Yellow Sea, divided since 1948 into the countries of North Korea and South Korea.

Korea, Democratic People's Republic of E
official name for **NORTH KOREA**.

Korea, Republic of E
official name for **SOUTH KOREA**.

Korean War E
the war of 1950–3 between North Korea and South Korea. North Korean forces invaded South Korea and were opposed by UN troops, dominated by US forces. China then entered the war on the side of North Korea. The war ended with the restoration of the previous boundaries.

korma /kor-muh/ • n. a mild Indian curry of meat or fish marinaded in yogurt or curds.
– ORIGIN Urdu.

Kos E
/*rhymes with* boss/ (also **Cos**) a Greek island in the SE Aegean, one of the Dodecanese group.

Kosciusko, Mount E
/kos-**chuuss**-koh/ a mountain in SE Australia, in the Great Dividing Range. Rising to 2,228 m (7,234 ft), it is the highest mountain in Australia.

kosher /**koh**-sher/ ● **adj. 1** (of food) prepared according to the requirements of Jewish law. **2** informal genuine and legitimate.
– ORIGIN Hebrew, 'proper'.

Kosovo E
/**koss**-uh-voh/ an autonomous province of Serbia; capital, Priština. The majority of the people are of Albanian descent.

Kosygin E
/ko-**see**-gin/, Aleksei (Nikolaevich) (1904–80), Soviet statesman, Premier of the USSR 1964–80.

Kowloon E
/kow-**loon**/ a peninsula on the SE coast of China, forming part of Hong Kong and separated from Hong Kong Island by Victoria Harbour.

kowtow /kow-**tow**/ ● **v. 1** hist. kneel and touch the ground with the forehead in submission as part of Chinese custom. **2** be excessively meek and obedient towards someone.
– ORIGIN Chinese.

kph ● **abbrev.** kilometres per hour.

kraal /krahl/ ● **n.** S. Afr. **1** a traditional African village of huts. **2** an enclosure for sheep and cattle.
– ORIGIN Dutch.

Krakatoa E
/kra-kuh-**toh**-uh/ a small volcanic island in Indonesia, lying between Java and Sumatra, scene of a great eruption in 1883 which destroyed most of the island.

Kraut /krowt/ ● **n.** informal, offens. a German.
– ORIGIN from SAUERKRAUT.

Kremlin /**krem**-lin/ ● **n.** (**the Kremlin**) the citadel in Moscow, housing the Russian government.
– ORIGIN Russian *kreml'*.

krill ● **pl. n.** small shrimp-like crustaceans which are the main food of baleen whales.
– ORIGIN Norwegian *kril* 'small fish fry'.

Krishna E
/**krish**-nuh/ one of the most popular Hindu gods, the eighth incarnation of Vishnu.

Krishnamurti E
/krish-nuh-**moor**-ti/, Jiddu (1895–1986), Indian spiritual leader. His spiritual philosophy is based on a rejection of organized religion and the attainment of self-realization by introspection.

krona /**kroh**-nuh/ ● **n. 1** (pl. **kronor** /**kroh**-nuh/) the basic unit of money of Sweden. **2** (pl. **kronur** /**kroh**-nuh/) the unit of money of Iceland.
– ORIGIN Swedish and Icelandic, 'crown'.

krone /**kroh**-nuh/ ● **n.** (pl. **kroner** /**kroh**-nuh/) the basic unit of money of Denmark and Norway.
– ORIGIN Danish and Norwegian, 'crown'.

Kronos E
var. of CRONUS.

Kruger E
/**kroo**-ger/, Stephanus Johannes Paulus (1825–1904), South African soldier and statesman, President of Transvaal (1883–99). His refusal to allow equal rights to non-Boer immigrants was one of the causes of the Second Boer War.

Kruger National Park E
a national park in South Africa, in eastern Transvaal.

krugerrand /**kroo**-ger-rand/ (also **Kruger**) ● **n.** a South African gold coin with a portrait of President Kruger on it.
– ORIGIN named after S. J. P. KRUGER.

krypton /**krip**-ton/ ● **n.** an inert, odourless, gaseous chemical element, present in small amounts in the air and used in some kinds of electric light.
– ORIGIN Greek *krupton* 'hidden'.

KStJ ● **abbrev.** Knight of the Order of St John.

KT ● **abbrev.** (in the UK) Knight of the Order of the Thistle.

kt ● **abbrev.** knot(s).

Kuala Lumpur E
/kwah-luh **luum**-poor/ the capital of Malaysia.

Kublai Khan E
/koo-bly **kahn**/ (1216–94), Mongol emperor of China, grandson of Genghis Khan. He completed the conquest of China begun by his grandfather and founded the Yuan dynasty.

Kubrick E
/**kyoo**-brik/, Stanley (1928–99), American film director, producer, and writer. His films include *2001: A Space Odyssey* and *A Clockwork Orange*.

kudos /**kyoo**-doss/ ● **n.** praise and honour.
– ORIGIN Greek.

USAGE kudos
Although it ends in *-s*, the word **kudos**, meaning 'praise' is not a plural word. This means that there is no singular form **kudo** and that use of it as if it were a plural, as in *he received many kudos for his work*, is wrong.

kudu /**koo**-doo/ ● **n.** (pl. **kudu** or **kudus**) a striped African antelope, the male of which has long spirally curved horns.
– ORIGIN Afrikaans.

Ku Klux Klan /koo kluks **klan**/ ● **n.** a secret organization of white people in the US who are violently opposed to black people.
– ORIGIN perh. from Greek *kuklos* 'circle' and CLAN.

kumquat /**kum**-kwot/ ● **n.** a small orange-like fruit.
– ORIGIN Chinese, 'little orange'.

Kundera E
/**kuun**-duh-ruh/, Milan (b.1929), Czech novelist, who emigrated to France in 1975 after his books were banned in Czechoslovakia. His works include *The Unbearable Lightness of Being*.

kung fu /kung foo/ ● **n.** a Chinese martial art resembling karate.
– ORIGIN Chinese, from words meaning 'merit' and 'master'.

Kuomintang E
/kwoh-min-**tang**/ (also **Guomindang**) a nationalist party founded in China in 1912. It was in power 1928–49 and subsequently formed the central administration of Taiwan.

Kurd /kerd/ ● **n.** a member of an Islamic people living in Kurdistan.
– ORIGIN the name in Kurdish (the language of the Kurds).

Kurdistan E
/ker-di-**stahn**, ker-di-**stan**/ a region in the Middle East south of the Caucasus, the traditional home of the Kurds. The area includes large parts of eastern Turkey, northern Iraq, western Iran, eastern Syria, Armenia, and Azerbaijan.

Kurosawa E
/kuu-ruh-**sah**-wuh/, Akira (1910–98), Japanese film director, known for such films as *Rashomon* and *Ran*.

Kuwait E
/kuu-**wayt**/ a country on the NW coast of the Persian Gulf; capital, Kuwait City.
– DERIVATIVES **Kuwaiti** adj. & n.

Kuwait City E
the capital city of Kuwait.

kV ● **abbrev.** kilovolt(s).

kW ● **abbrev.** kilowatt(s).

Kwangchow E
/kwang **chow**/ var. of **GUANGZHOU**.

Kwangtung E
/kwang-**tuung**/ var. of **GUANGDONG**.

KwaZulu/Natal E
/kwah-zoo-loo na-**tahl**/ a province of eastern South Africa; capital, Pietermaritzburg.

kWh ● **abbrev.** kilowatt-hour(s).

Kyd, E
Thomas (1558–94), English dramatist, who wrote *The Spanish Tragedy.*

Kyoto E
/ki-**oh**-toh/ an industrial city in Japan, on the island of Honshu. It was the imperial capital 794–1868.

Kyrgyzstan E
/keer-gi-**stahn**, keer-gi-**stan**/ a country in central Asia, on the north-western border of China; capital, Bishkek. Also called **KYRGYZ REPUBLIC**; former name (1936–91) **KIRGHIZIA**.

Kyushu E
/ki-**oo**-shoo/ the most southerly of the four main islands of Japan; capital, Fukuoka.

L[1] (also **l**) ● **n.** (pl. **Ls** or **L's**) **1** the twelfth letter of the alphabet. **2** the Roman numeral for 50.

L[2] ● **abbrev.** **1** (**L.**) Lake, Loch, or Lough. **2** large (as a clothes size). **3** Brit. learner driver. **4** lire.

l ● **abbrev.** **1** left. **2** (**l.**) line. **3** litre(s). ● **symb.** (in mathematical formulae) length.

£ ● **abbrev.** pound(s).
– ORIGIN from Latin *libra* 'pound, balance'.

LA ● **abbrev.** Los Angeles.

la ● **n.** Music var. of **LAH**.

Laayoune E
var. of **LA'YOUN**.

lab ● **n.** informal a laboratory.

label ● **n.** **1** a small piece of paper, fabric, etc. attached to an object and giving information about it. **2** the name or trademark of a fashion company. **3** a company that produces recorded music. **4** a classifying name given to a person or thing. ● **v.** (**labels, labelling, labelled**; US **labels, labeling, labeled**) **1** attach a label to. **2** put in a category.
– ORIGIN Old French, 'ribbon'.

labia /lay-bi-uh/ ● **pl. n.** (sing. **labium** /lay-bi-uhm/) Anat. the inner and outer folds of the vulva.
– ORIGIN Latin, 'lips'.

labial ● **adj.** esp. Anat. & Biol. relating to the lips or a labium.

labiate /lay-bi-uht/ ● **adj.** Bot. relating to plants of the mint family, having distinctive two-lobed flowers.
– ORIGIN Latin *labiatus*.

labor etc. ● **n.** US & Austral. = **LABOUR** etc.

laboratory /luh-bo-ruh-tuh-ri/ ● **n.** (pl. **laboratories**) a room or building for scientific experiments or teaching, or for the making of drugs or chemicals.
– ORIGIN Latin *laboratorium*.

laborious /luh-bor-i-uhss/ ● **adj.** **1** requiring much time and effort. **2** showing obvious signs of effort: *a slow, laborious speech.*
– DERIVATIVES **laboriously** adv.

labour (US & Austral. **labor**) ● **n.** **1** work. **2** workers as a group. **3** (**Labour**) the Labour Party. **4** the process of childbirth. ● **v.** **1** do hard physical work. **2** have difficulty despite working hard. **3** move with difficulty. **4** (**labour under**) be misled by (a mistaken belief).
– PHRASES **a labour of love** a task done for pleasure, not reward. **labour the point** talk

about something at excessive length.
– ORIGIN Latin *labor* 'toil, trouble'.

labour camp ● n. a prison camp where prisoners must undergo hard labour.

Labour Day ● n. a public holiday held in some countries in honour of working people.

laboured (US **labored**) ● adj. **1** done with great difficulty. **2** not natural or unprepared: *a laboured joke.*

labourer (US **laborer**) ● n. a person doing unskilled manual work.

labour exchange ● n. former term for **JOBCENTRE**.

labour force ● n. the members of a population who are able to work.

labour-intensive ● adj. needing a large workforce or a large amount of work in relation to what is produced.

Labour Party ● n. a British political party formed to represent the interests of ordinary working people.

labour-saving ● adj. designed to reduce the amount of work needed to do something.

Labrador[1] E
/lab-ruh-dor/ a coastal region of eastern Canada, forming the mainland part of the province of Newfoundland and Labrador.

Labrador[2] /lab-ruh-dor/ (also **Labrador retriever**) ● n. a breed of retriever with a black or yellow coat, also used as a guide dog.
– ORIGIN from **LABRADOR**[1].

laburnum /luh-ber-nuhm/ ● n. a small hardwood tree with hanging clusters of yellow flowers followed by pods of poisonous seeds.
– ORIGIN Latin.

labyrinth /lab-i-rinth/ ● n. **1** a complicated irregular network of passages. **2** a complex and confusing arrangement: *a labyrinth of laws and regulations.* **3** a complex structure in the inner ear which contains the organs of hearing and balance.
– DERIVATIVES **labyrinthine** /lab-i-rin-thyn/ adj.
– ORIGIN Greek *laburinthos.*

lac ● n. a substance secreted by an Asian insect (the **lac insect**), used to make varnish, shellac, etc.
– ORIGIN Hindi or Persian.

Lacan E
/la-kon/, Jacques (1901–81), French psychoanalyst, who reinterpreted Freudian psychoanalysis in the light of structural linguistics.
– DERIVATIVES **Lacanian** /la-kay-ni-uhn/ adj. & n.

lace ● n. **1** a fine open fabric of cotton or silk made by looping, twisting, or knitting thread in patterns. **2** a cord used to fasten a shoe or garment. ● v. (**laces**, **lacing**, **laced**) **1** fasten with a lace or laces. **2** twist or tangle together. **3** add an ingredient to (a drink or dish) to improve flavour or to make it stronger: *chefs laced their pastas with caviar.*
– ORIGIN Old French *laz.*

lacerate /lass-uh-rayt/ ● v. (**lacerates**, **lacerating**, **lacerated**) tear or deeply cut (the flesh or skin).
– DERIVATIVES **laceration** n.
– ORIGIN Latin *lacerare.*

lachrymal /lak-ri-muhl/ (also **lacrimal**) ● adj. tech. or literary connected with weeping or tears.
– ORIGIN Latin *lachrymalis.*

lachrymose /lak-ri-mohss/ ● adj. formal or literary **1** tearful. **2** sad: *a lachrymose children's classic.*

lacing ● n. a laced fastening of a shoe or garment.

lack ● n. the state of being without or not having enough of something. ● v. (also **lack for**) be without or without enough of.
– ORIGIN perh. partly from German *lak,* Dutch *laken.*

lackadaisical /lak-uh-day-zi-k'l/ ● adj. lacking enthusiasm and thoroughness.
– ORIGIN from archaic *lackaday,* expressing surprise or grief.

lackey ● n. (pl. **lackeys**) **1** a servant. **2** a person who is too willing to serve or obey others.
– ORIGIN French *laquais.*

lacking ● adj. missing or not having enough of.

lacklustre (US **lackluster**) ● adj. **1** lacking in energy or inspiration. **2** (of the hair or eyes) not shining.

laconic /luh-kon-ik/ ● adj. using very few words.
– DERIVATIVES **laconically** adv.
– ORIGIN Greek *Lakōnikos.*

lacquer /lak-ker/ ● n. **1** a varnish made of shellac, the sap of an Asian tree, or of synthetic substances. **2** decorative wooden goods coated with lacquer. **3** Brit. a chemical substance sprayed on hair to keep it in place. ● v. (**lacquers**, **lacquering**, **lacquered**) coat with lacquer.
– ORIGIN Hindi or Persian.

lacrimal ● adj. var. of **LACHRYMAL**.

lacrosse /luh-kross/ ● n. a team game in which a ball is thrown, carried, and caught with a long-handled stick bearing a net at one end.
– ORIGIN from French *le jeu de la crosse* 'the game of the hooked stick'.

lactate /lak-tayt/ ● v. (**lactates**, **lactating**, **lactated**) (of a female mammal) produce milk.
– ORIGIN Latin *lactare* 'suckle'.

lactation ● n. **1** the producing of milk by the mammary glands. **2** the suckling of a baby or young animal.

lacteal /lak-ti-uhl/ ● adj. conveying milk or milky fluid. ● n. (**lacteals**) Anat. vessels in the small intestine which absorb digested fats.
– ORIGIN Latin *lacteus.*

lactic /lak-tik/ ● adj. relating to or obtained from milk.

lactic acid ● n. an organic acid present in sour milk, and produced in the muscles during strenuous exercise.

lactose /lak-tohz/ ● n. Chem. a sugar present in milk.

lacto-vegetarian ● n. a person who eats only dairy products and vegetables.

lacuna /luh-kyoo-nuh/ ● n. (pl. **lacunae** /luh-kyoo-nee/ or **lacunas**) **1** a gap or missing portion. **2** a cavity or depression in bone.
– ORIGIN Latin, 'pool'.

lacy ● adj. (**lacier**, **laciest**) made of, resembling, or trimmed with lace.

lad ● n. informal **1** a boy or young man. **2** (**the lads**) esp. Brit. a group of men who have interests in common. **3** Brit. a very macho or high-

spirited man.
– DERIVATIVES **laddish** adj.
– ORIGIN unknown.

Ladakh E
/luh-**dahk**/ a high-altitude region of NW India, Pakistan, and China.

ladder ● n. **1** a structure consisting of a series of bars or steps between two uprights, used for climbing up or down. **2** a series of stages by which progress can be made: *the career ladder.* **3** Brit. a strip of unravelled fabric in tights or stockings. ● v. (**ladders, laddering, laddered**) Brit. make (a ladder) in tights or stockings.
– ORIGIN Old English.

laden ● adj. heavily loaded or weighed down.
– ORIGIN Old English.

la-di-da ● adj. informal affected or snobbish.
– ORIGIN imitating an affected way of speaking.

ladies pl. of **LADY**.

ladies' man ● n. informal a man who enjoys spending time and flirting with women.

ladle ● n. a large long-handled spoon with a cup-shaped bowl. ● v. (**ladles, ladling, ladled**) **1** serve or transfer with a ladle. **2** (**ladle out**) give out in large amounts.
– DERIVATIVES **ladleful** n.
– ORIGIN Old English.

Ladoga, Lake E
/**lah**-duh-guh/ a large lake in NW Russia, near the border with Finland. It is the largest lake in Europe, with an area of 17,700 sq. km (6,837 sq. miles).

lady ● n. (pl. **ladies**) **1** (in polite or formal use) a woman. **2** a woman of a high social position. **3** (**Lady**) a title used by peeresses, female relatives of peers, the wives and widows of knights, etc. **4** a well-mannered and sophisticated woman. **5** (**the Ladies**) Brit. a women's public toilet.
– PHRASES **My Lady** a polite form of address to female judges and certain noblewomen.
– ORIGIN Old English.

ladybird ● n. a small beetle with a red or yellow back with black spots.

Lady Day ● n. the Christian feast of the Annunciation, 25 March.

lady-in-waiting ● n. (pl. **ladies-in-waiting**) a woman who accompanies and looks after a queen or princess.

ladykiller ● n. informal a charming man who regularly seduces women.

ladylike ● adj. appropriate for or typical of a well-mannered woman or girl.

ladyship ● n. (**Her/Your Ladyship**) a respectful way of referring to or addressing a Lady.

lady's maid ● n. esp. hist. a maid who attended to the personal needs of her mistress.

lag[1] ● v. (**lags, lagging, lagged**) fall behind. ● n. (also **time lag**) a period of time between two events.
– ORIGIN perh. Scandinavian.

lag[2] ● v. (**lags, lagging, lagged**) cover (a water tank, pipes, etc.) with material designed to prevent heat loss.
– ORIGIN from earlier *lag* 'piece of insulating cover'.

lag[3] ● n. Brit. informal a person who has been frequently convicted and sent to prison.
– ORIGIN unknown.

lager ● n. a light fizzy beer.
– ORIGIN German *Lagerbier* 'beer brewed for keeping'.

laggard /lag-gerd/ ● n. a person who falls behind others.
– ORIGIN from **LAG**[1].

lagging ● n. material providing protection against heat loss for a water tank, pipes, etc.

lagoon ● n. a stretch of salt water separated from the sea by a low sandbank or coral reef.
– ORIGIN Italian and Spanish *laguna*.

Lagos E
/lay-goss/ the chief city of Nigeria, a port on the Gulf of Guinea. It was capital of Nigeria 1960–91.

lah (also **la**) ● n. Music the sixth note of a major scale, coming after 'soh' and before 'te'.
– ORIGIN from *labii*, taken from a Latin hymn.

Lahore E
/luh-**hor**/ the capital of Punjab province and the second-largest city of Pakistan.

laid past and past part. of **LAY**[1].

laid-back ● adj. informal relaxed and easygoing.

lain past part. of **LIE**[1].

Laing E
/lang/, R. D. (1927–89; full name *Ronald David Laing*), Scottish psychiatrist, who proposed that what society calls insanity is a defensive response to the tensions of the close-knit nuclear family.

lair ● n. **1** a wild animal's resting place. **2** a person's hiding place or den.
– ORIGIN Old English.

laird /*rhymes with* scared/ ● n. (in Scotland) a person who owns a large estate.
– ORIGIN Scots form of **LORD**.

laissez-faire /less-ay-fair/ ● n. a policy of leaving things to take their own course, without interfering.
ORIGIN French, 'allow to do'.

laity /lay-i-ti/ ● n. (**the laity**) people who do not belong to the clergy.
– ORIGIN from **LAY**[2].

lake[1] ● n. **1** a large area of water surrounded by land. **2** (**the Lakes**) the Lake District.
– ORIGIN Latin *lacus* 'pool, lake'.

lake[2] ● n. a purplish-red pigment originally made with lac.
– ORIGIN from **LAC**.

Lake Baikal, Lake Eyrie, etc. E
see **BAIKAL, LAKE; EYRIE, LAKE,** etc.

Lake District ● n. a region of lakes and mountains in Cumbria.

Lakshadweep E
/lak-**shad**-weep, luk-shuhd-**weep**/ a group of islands off the SW coast of India, forming a Union Territory in India.

Lakshmi E
/**luk**-shmi/ the Hindu goddess of prosperity, consort of Vishnu.

Lalique E
/la-leek/, René (1860–1945), French jeweller, famous for his art nouveau jewellery and decorative glassware.

lam • v. (**lams**, **lamming**, **lammed**) informal hit hard or repeatedly.
– ORIGIN perh. Scandinavian.

lama /lah-muh/ • n. **1** a title given as a mark of respect to a spiritual leader in Tibetan Buddhism. **2** a Tibetan or Mongolian Buddhist monk.
– ORIGIN Tibetan, 'superior one'.

Lamarck E
/la-**mark**/, Jean Baptiste de (1744–1829), French naturalist. He put forward an early theory of evolution (not now accepted) that organisms become transformed by their efforts to respond to their environment.
– DERIVATIVES **Lamarckian** n. & adj.

lamb • n. **1** a young sheep. **2** a mild-mannered, gentle, or innocent person. • v. (of a ewe) give birth to lambs.
– ORIGIN Old English.

lambada /lam-**bah**-duh/ • n. a fast Brazilian dance which couples perform in close physical contact.
– ORIGIN Portuguese, 'a beating'.

lambaste /lam-**baysst**/ (also **lambast** /lam-**bast**/) • v. (**lambastes** or **lambasts**, **lambasting**, **lambasted**) criticize harshly.
– ORIGIN from LAM + archaic *baste*, also meaning 'beat'.

lambent /lam-buhnt/ • adj. literary lit up or flickering with a soft glow.
– ORIGIN Latin *lambere* 'to lick'.

Lambeth Palace E
a palace in the London borough of Lambeth, the residence of the Archbishop of Canterbury.

Lamb of God • n. a title of Jesus Christ.

lame • adj. **1** walking with difficulty because of an injury or illness affecting the leg or foot. **2** (of an explanation or excuse) unconvincing and feeble. **3** (of something meant to be entertaining) dull and uninspiring.
– DERIVATIVES **lamely** adv. **lameness** n.
– ORIGIN Old English.

lamé /lah-may/ • n. fabric with interwoven gold or silver threads.
– ORIGIN French.

lame duck • n. **1** an unsuccessful person or thing. **2** N. Amer. an official in the final period of office, after the election of a successor.

lament /luh-**ment**/ • n. **1** a passionate expression of grief. **2** a song or poem expressing grief or regret. • v. **1** mourn (a person's death). **2** (**lamented** or **late lamented**) a way of referring to a dead person. **3** express regret or disappointment about.
– DERIVATIVES **lamentation** n.
– ORIGIN Latin *lamenta* 'weeping'.

lamentable /la-muhn-tuh-b'l/ • adj. very bad or regrettable.
– DERIVATIVES **lamentably** adv.

lamina /lam-i-nuh/ • n. (pl. **laminae** /lam-i-nee/) tech. a thin layer, plate, or scale of rock, tissue, or other material.
– DERIVATIVES **laminar** adj.
– ORIGIN Latin.

laminate • v. /lam-i-nayt/ (**laminates**, **laminating**, **laminated**) **1** cover (a flat surface) with a layer of protective material. **2** make by sticking layers together. **3** split into layers or leaves. **4** beat or roll (metal) into thin plates. • n. /**lam**-i-nuht/ a laminated structure or material.
– DERIVATIVES **lamination** n.

Lammas /lam-muhss/ (also **Lammas Day**) • n. the first day of August, formerly observed as harvest festival.
– ORIGIN Old English, 'loaf mass'.

lammergeier /**lam**-mer-gy-er/ (also **lammergeyer**) • n. a long-winged, long-tailed vulture, noted for dropping bones to break them and get at the marrow.
– ORIGIN German.

lamp • n. **1** an electric, oil, or gas device for giving light. **2** an electrical device producing radiation.
– ORIGIN Greek *lampas* 'torch'.

lampblack • n. a black pigment made from soot.

lampoon /lam-**poon**/ • v. publicly mock or ridicule. • n. a mocking attack.
– ORIGIN French *lampon*.

lamprey /**lam**-pri/ • n. (pl. **lampreys**) an eel-like jawless fish that has a sucker mouth with horny teeth.
– ORIGIN Latin *lampreda*.

LAN • abbrev. local area network.

Lanarkshire E
/lan-erk-sheer, **lan**-erk-sher/ a former county of SW central Scotland, now divided into the administrative regions of **North Lanarkshire** and **South Lanarkshire**.

Lancashire E
a county of NW England; administrative centre, Preston.

Lancaster[1] E
/**lang**-kass-ter/ the former county town of Lancashire.

Lancaster[2] E
/**lang**-kass-ter/, Burt (1913–94; full name *Burton Stephen Lancaster*), American actor, star of such films as *From Here to Eternity* and *Elmer Gantry*.

Lancaster, House of E
/**lang**-kass-ter/ the English royal house descended from John of Gaunt, Duke of Lancaster, that ruled England 1399–1461 and 1470–1. With the red rose as its emblem it fought the Wars of the Roses with the House of York.

Lancastrian /lang-**kass**-tri-uhn/ • n. **1** a person from Lancashire or Lancaster. **2** a follower of the House of Lancaster in the Wars of the Roses. • adj. relating to Lancashire or Lancaster, or the House of Lancaster.

lance • n. **1** a long weapon with a wooden shaft and a pointed steel head, formerly used by a horseman in charging. **2** a metal pipe supplying a jet of oxygen to a furnace or to make a very hot flame for cutting. • v. (**lances**, **lancing**, **lanced**) **1** Med. prick or cut open with a sharp instrument. **2** pierce.
– ORIGIN Latin *lancea*.

lance corporal • n. a rank of non-commissioned officer in the British army, above private and below corporal.

Lancelot E
/**lahn**-suh-lot/ (in Arthurian legend) the most famous of Arthur's knights, lover of Queen Guinevere and father of Galahad.

lanceolate /lahn-si-uh-luht/ • **adj.** tech. having a narrow oval shape tapering to a point at each end.
– ORIGIN Latin *lanceolatus*.

lancer • **n.** a soldier of a cavalry regiment armed or formerly armed with lances.

lancet /lahn-sit/ • **n.** a small, broad two-edged knife with a sharp point, used in surgery.
– ORIGIN Old French *lancette* 'small lance'.

Lancs. • **abbrev.** Lancashire.

land • **n. 1** the part of the earth's surface that is not covered by water. **2** an area of ground in terms of its ownership or use: *waste land.* **3** (**the land**) ground or soil used for farming. **4** a country or state. • **v. 1** put or go ashore. **2** come or bring down to the ground. **3** bring (a fish) to land with a net or rod. **4** informal succeed in obtaining or achieving (something desirable). **5** (**land up**) reach a place or destination. **6** (**land up with**) end up with (an unwelcome situation). **7** (**land in**) informal put in (a difficult situation). **8** informal inflict (a blow) on someone.
– PHRASES **how the land lies** what the situation is. **the land of Nod** humorous a state of sleep. [ORIGIN with biblical reference to the place name *Nod* (Book of Genesis, chapter 4).]
– DERIVATIVES **landless** adj.
– ORIGIN Old English.

land agent • **n.** Brit. **1** a person employed to manage an estate on behalf of its owners. **2** a person who deals with the sale of land.

landau /lan-dor/ • **n.** a four-wheeled enclosed horse-drawn carriage.
– ORIGIN named after *Landau* in Germany, where it was first made.

landed • **adj.** owning much land.

landfall • **n.** an arrival at land on a sea or air journey.

landfill • **n. 1** the disposal of waste material by burying it. **2** waste material buried in this way.

landform • **n.** a natural feature of the earth's surface.

landing • **n. 1** a place where people and goods can be landed from a boat. **2** a level area at the top of a staircase.

landing craft • **n.** a boat for putting troops and military equipment ashore on a beach.

landing gear • **n.** the undercarriage of an aircraft.

landing stage • **n.** a platform on to which passengers or cargo can be landed from a boat.

landlady • **n. 1** a woman who rents out land or property. **2** Brit. a woman who owns or runs lodgings or a public house.

landline • **n.** a conventional telecommunications connection by cable laid across land.

landlocked • **adj.** almost or entirely surrounded by land.

landlord • **n. 1** a man who rents out land or property. **2** Brit. a man who owns or runs lodgings or a public house.

landlubber • **n.** informal a person unfamiliar with the sea or sailing.
– ORIGIN from archaic *lubber* 'clumsy person'.

landmark • **n. 1** an object or feature of a landscape or town that is easily seen from a distance. **2** an event, discovery, or change marking an important stage: *a landmark of research.*

land mass • **n.** a continent or other large body of land.

landmine • **n.** an explosive mine laid on or just under the surface of the ground.

landowner • **n.** a person who owns land.

landscape • **n. 1** all the visible features of an area of land. **2** a picture of an area of countryside. • **v.** (**landscapes**, **landscaping**, **landscaped**) improve the appearance of (a piece of land) by changing its contours, planting trees and shrubs, etc.
– ORIGIN Dutch *lantscap*.

landscape gardening • **n.** the art and practice of laying out grounds.

Landseer E
/land-seer/, Sir Edwin Henry (1802–73), English painter and sculptor, best known for his animal subjects such as *The Monarch of the Glen* and the bronze lions in Trafalgar Square.

Land's End E
a rocky promontory in SW Cornwall, the westernmost point of England.

landslide • **n. 1** (Brit. also **landslip**) a mass of earth or rock that slides down from a mountain or cliff. **2** an overwhelming majority of votes for one party in an election.

landward • **adv.** (also **landwards**) towards land. • **adj.** facing towards land rather than the sea.

lane • **n. 1** a narrow road. **2** a division of a road for a single line of traffic. **3** each of a number of parallel strips of track or water for competitors in a race. **4** a course followed by ships or aircraft.
– ORIGIN Old English.

Lang, E
Fritz (1890–1976), Austrian-born film director resident in the US from 1933. His films include the futuristic *Metropolis* and the thriller *The Big Heat*.

Langland, E
William (*c.*1330–*c.*1400), English poet, author of the long allegorical poem *Piers Plowman*.

Langtry, E
Lillie (1853–1929; born *Emilie Charlotte le Breton*), British actress, who became the mistress of the Prince of Wales (later Edward VII).

language • **n. 1** the means of human communication, consisting of the use of spoken or written words in a structured way. **2** the system of communication used by a particular community or country. **3** a particular style of speaking or writing: *legal language.* **4** Computing a system of symbols and rules for writing programs.
– ORIGIN Old French *langage*.

language laboratory • **n.** a room with audio and visual equipment for learning a foreign language.

Languedoc-Roussillon E
/long-guh-dok roo-si-yon/ a region of southern France, on the Mediterranean coast.

languid /lang-gwid/ • **adj. 1** reluctant to exert oneself physically. **2** weak or faint from illness or fatigue.

– DERIVATIVES **languidly** adv.

languish • v. **1** grow weak or feeble. **2** be kept in an unpleasant place or situation: *he was languishing in jail.*
– ORIGIN Old French *languir.*

languor /lang-ger/ • n. tiredness or inactivity, especially when pleasurable.
– DERIVATIVES **languorous** adj.

lank • adj. (of hair) long, limp, and straight.
– ORIGIN Old English, 'thin'.

lanky • adj. awkwardly thin and tall.

lanolin • n. a fatty substance found naturally on sheep's wool and used to make ointments.
– ORIGIN from Latin *lana* 'wool' + *oleum* 'oil'.

lantern • n. **1** a lamp with a transparent case protecting the flame or electric bulb. **2** the light chamber at the top of a lighthouse.
– ORIGIN Latin *lanterna.*

lantern-jawed • adj. having long, thin jaws.

lanthanum /lan-thuh-nuhm/ • n. a silvery-white rare-earth metallic chemical element.
– ORIGIN Greek *lanthanein* 'escape notice'.

lanyard /lan-yerd/ • n. **1** a rope used to secure or raise and lower something such as a sail. **2** a cord around the neck or shoulder for holding a whistle or similar object.
– ORIGIN Old French *laniere.*

Lanzarote E
/lan-zuh-**rot**-i/ one of the Canary Islands; chief town, Arrecife.

Laois E
/leesh/ (also **Laoighis**, **Leix**) a county of the Republic of Ireland; county town, Portlaoise.

Laos E
/lowss, **lah**-oss/ a country in SE Asia; capital, Vientiane.
– DERIVATIVES **Laotian** adj. & n.

Lao-tzu E
/low-**tsoo**/ (also **Laoze** /**low**-tsay/) (*fl.* 6th century BC), Chinese philosopher. He is traditionally regarded as the founder of Taoism and author of the Tao-te-Ching, its most sacred scripture.

lap[1] • n. the flat area between the waist and knees of a seated person.
– PHRASES **in the lap of luxury** in conditions of great comfort and wealth.
– ORIGIN Old English, 'fold, flap'.

lap[2] • n. **1** one circuit of a track or racetrack. **2** a part of a journey. **3** an overlapping or projecting part. • v. (**laps**, **lapping**, **lapped**) overtake (a competitor in a race) to become one or more laps ahead.
– ORIGIN from LAP[1].

lap[3] • v. (**laps**, **lapping**, **lapped**) **1** (of an animal) take up (liquid) with the tongue. **2** (**lap up**) accept with obvious pleasure. **3** (of water) wash against with a gentle rippling sound.
– ORIGIN Old English.

La Palma E
/lah **pahl**-muh/ one of the Canary Islands.

La Paz E
/la **paz**, lah **pahz**/ the capital of Bolivia. Situated in the Andes at an altitude of 3,660 m (12,000 ft), La Paz is the highest capital city in the world.

lap dancing • n. erotic dancing in which the dancer performs a striptease near to or on the lap of a paying customer.

lapdog • n. **1** a small pampered pet dog. **2** a person who is completely under the influence of another.

lapel • n. the part on each side of a coat or jacket below the collar which is folded back against the front opening.
– ORIGIN from LAP[1].

lapidary /la-pi-duh-ri/ • adj. **1** relating to the engraving, cutting, or polishing of stones and gems. **2** (of language) elegant and concise.
– ORIGIN Latin *lapidarius.*

lapis lazuli /la-piss **laz**-yuu-li/ (also **lapis**) • n. a bright blue rock used in jewellery.
– ORIGIN Latin, 'stone of lapis lazuli'.

Lapland E
a region of northern Europe which lies mainly within the Arctic Circle and consists of the northern parts of Scandinavia, and the Kola Peninsula on the NW coast of Russia.
– DERIVATIVES **Laplander** n.

lap of honour • n. Brit. a celebratory circuit of a sports field, track, etc. by the victorious person or team.

Lapp • n. **1** a member of a people living in Lapland. **2** the language of this people.
– ORIGIN Swedish.

USAGE Lapp
Although the term **Lapp** is still very common, the people themselves prefer to be called **Sami**.

lappet /lap-pit/ • n. **1** a fold or hanging piece of flesh in some animals. **2** a loose or overlapping part of a garment.
– ORIGIN from LAP[1].

lapse • n. **1** a brief failure of concentration, memory, or judgement. **2** a decline from previously high standards. **3** a period of time between two events. • v. (**lapses**, **lapsing**, **lapsed**) **1** (of a right or agreement) become invalid because it is not used or renewed. **2** cease to follow the rules of a religion. **3** (**lapse into**) pass gradually into (a different state).
– ORIGIN Latin *lapsus.*

laptop • n. a portable microcomputer.

lapwing • n. a large crested plover with a dark green back and a black-and-white head.
– ORIGIN Old English.

Lara E
/**lah**-ruh/, Brian (Charles) (b.1969), West Indian cricketer. In 1994 he scored 375 against England, breaking the record test score, and 501 not out (for Warwickshire against Durham), a world record in first-class cricket.

larboard /lar-bord, lar-berd/ • n. Naut. archaic = PORT[3].
– ORIGIN from archaic *lade* 'load a ship', referring to the side on which cargo was loaded.

larceny /lar-suh-ni/ • n. (pl. **larcenies**) N. Amer. or dated theft of personal property.
– ORIGIN Old French *larcin.*

larch • n. a coniferous tree with bunches of deciduous bright green needles and hard wood.
– ORIGIN High German *larche.*

lard • n. fat from the abdomen of a pig, used in cooking. • v. **1** insert strips of fat or bacon in (meat) before cooking. **2** add excessively tech-

nical or obscure expressions to (talk or writing).
– ORIGIN Latin *lardum*.

larder • **n.** a room or large cupboard for storing food.
– ORIGIN Latin *lardarium*.

large • **adj. 1** relatively great in size, extent, or capacity. **2** of wide range or scope. • **v.** (**larges, larging, larged**) (**large it**) Brit. informal go out and have a good time.
– PHRASES **at large 1** escaped or not yet captured. **2** as a whole.
– ORIGIN Latin *larga* 'copious'.

large intestine • **n.** Anat. the caecum, colon, and rectum as a whole.

largely • **adv.** on the whole; mostly.

large-scale • **adj.** extensive.

largesse /lar-*zhess*/ (also **largess**) • **n. 1** generosity. **2** money or gifts given generously.
– ORIGIN Old French.

largo /lar-goh/ • **adv. & adj.** Music in a slow tempo and dignified style.
– ORIGIN Italian.

lariat /la-ri-uht/ • **n.** a rope used as a lasso or for tethering animals.
– ORIGIN from Spanish *la reata*.

lark[1] • **n.** a brown songbird that sings in flight.
– ORIGIN Old English.

lark[2] informal • **n. 1** an amusing adventure or escapade. **2** Brit. an activity regarded as foolish or a waste of time: *he's serious about this music lark.* • **v.** behave in a playful and mischievous way.
– ORIGIN perh. from dialect *lake* 'play'.

Larkin, E
Philip (Arthur) (1922–85), English poet, whose poetry is notable for its melancholy, bitterness, and stoic wit.

Larousse E
/la-rooss/, Pierre (1817–75), French lexicographer and editor of the *Grand dictionnaire universel du XIX*e *siècle*, which aimed to treat every area of human knowledge.

larva /lar-vuh/ • **n.** (pl. **larvae** /lar-vee/) an active immature form of an insect or other animal that undergoes metamorphosis, e.g. a caterpillar.
– ORIGIN Latin, 'ghost, mask'.

laryngitis /la-rin-jy-tiss/ • **n.** inflammation of the larynx.

larynx /la-ringks/ • **n.** (pl. **larynges** /luh-rin-jeez/) the hollow muscular organ forming an air passage to the lungs and containing the vocal cords.
– ORIGIN Greek *larunx*.

lasagne /luh-zan-yuh, luh-zahn-yuh/ • **n. 1** pasta in the form of wide strips. **2** an Italian dish consisting of this baked with meat or vegetables and a cheese sauce.
– ORIGIN Italian.

Lascaux E
/la-**skoh**/ the site of a cave in the Dordogne, France, with Palaeolithic wall paintings.

lascivious /luh-siv-i-uhss/ • **adj.** feeling or showing an open or offensive sexual desire.
– DERIVATIVES **lasciviously** adv.
– ORIGIN Latin *lascivia* 'lustfulness'.

laser • **n.** a device that produces an intense narrow beam of light.
– ORIGIN acronym from *light amplification by stimulated emission of radiation*.

laserdisc • **n.** a disc resembling a large compact disc, used for high-quality video and for interactive multimedia.

laser printer • **n.** a computer printer in which a laser is used to form a pattern on a light-sensitive drum, which attracts toner.

lash • **v. 1** beat with a whip or stick. **2** beat against: *waves lashed the coast.* **3** (**lash out**) launch a verbal or physical attack. **4** (of an animal) move (the tail) quickly and violently. **5** fasten securely with a cord or rope. • **n. 1** a sharp blow or stroke with a whip or stick. **2** the flexible part of a whip. **3** an eyelash.

lashings • **pl. n.** Brit. informal a large amount of food or drink.

Las Palmas E
/lahss **pahl**-muhss/ the capital of the Canary Islands, a port and resort on Gran Canaria.

lass (also **lassie**) • **n.** Sc. & N. Engl. a girl or young woman.
– ORIGIN Old Norse, 'unmarried'.

Lassa fever /lass-uh/ • **n.** an often fatal disease transmitted by a virus and occurring chiefly in West Africa.
– ORIGIN named after the village of *Lassa* in Nigeria.

lassitude /lass-i-tyood/ • **n.** physical or mental weariness; lack of energy.
– ORIGIN Latin *lassitudo*.

lasso /luh-soo/ • **n.** (pl. **lassos**) a rope with a noose at one end, used for catching cattle. • **v.** (**lassoes, lassoing, lassoed**) catch with a lasso.
– ORIGIN Spanish *lazo*.

last[1] • **adj. 1** coming after all others in time or order. **2** most recent. **3** lowest in importance or rank. **4** (**the last**) the least likely or suitable. **5** only remaining. • **adv.** on the last occasion before the present: *a woman last heard of in Cornwall.* • **n.** (pl. **last**) **1** the last person or thing. **2** (**the last of**) the only remaining part of.
– PHRASES **at last** (or **at long last**) in the end; eventually. **to the last** up to the last moment of a person's life.
– ORIGIN Old English.

last[2] • **v. 1** continue for a specified period of time. **2** remain operating or usable for a considerable or specified length of time. **3** (of provisions or resources) be enough for (someone) for a specified length of time: *enough food to last him for three months.*
– ORIGIN Old English.

last[3] • **n.** a shoemaker's model for shaping or repairing a shoe or boot.
– ORIGIN Old English.

last-ditch • **adj.** referring to a final desperate attempt to achieve something.

last-gasp • **adj.** informal at the last possible moment.

lasting • **adj.** enduring for a long time: *a lasting impression.*

Last Judgement • **n.** the judgement of humankind expected in some religions to take place at the end of the world.

lastly • **adv.** in the last place; last.

last minute (also **last moment**) • **n.** the latest possible time before an event.

last name • n. one's surname.

last post • n. (in the British armed forces) the second of two bugle calls giving notice of the hour of retiring at night, played also at military funerals and acts of remembrance.

last rites • pl. n. (in the Christian Church) rites administered to a person who is about to die.

last word • n. **1** a final statement. **2** the most modern or advanced example of something: *the room was the last word in luxury.*

Las Vegas E
/lass vay-guhss/ a city in southern Nevada, noted for its casinos and nightclubs.

lat. • abbrev. latitude.

latch • n. **1** a bar with a catch and lever used for fastening a door or gate. **2** a spring lock for an outer door, which can only be opened from the outside with a key. • v. **1** fasten with a latch. **2** (**latch on to**) associate oneself enthusiastically with.
– PHRASES **on the latch** (of a door or gate) closed but not locked.
– ORIGIN Old English, 'to grasp'.

late • adj. **1** acting, arriving, or happening after the proper or usual time. **2** belonging or taking place far on in a particular time or period. **3** far on in the day or night. **4** (**the/one's late**) (of a person) no longer alive: *her late husband.* **5** (**latest**) of most recent date or origin. • adv. **1** after the proper or usual time. **2** towards the end of a period. **3** far on in the day or night. **4** (**later**) at a time in the near future; afterwards. • n. (**the latest**) the most recent news or fashion.
– PHRASES **of late** recently.
– DERIVATIVES **lateness** n.
– ORIGIN Old English.

latecomer • n. a person who arrives late.

lateen sail /la-teen/ • n. a triangular sail set at an angle of 45° to the mast.
– ORIGIN from French *voile Latine* 'Latin sail'.

lately • adv. recently; not long ago.

latent • adj. existing but not yet developed, apparent, or active: *her latent talent.*
– DERIVATIVES **latency** n.
– ORIGIN Latin *latere* 'be hidden'.

lateral /lat-uh-ruhl/ • adj. having to do with, towards, or from the side or sides.
– DERIVATIVES **laterally** adv.
– ORIGIN Latin *lateralis.*

lateral thinking • n. esp. Brit. the solving of problems by an indirect and creative approach.

latex /lay-teks/ • n. **1** a milky fluid found in many plants, which thickens on exposure to the air. **2** a synthetic product resembling this, used to make paints, coatings, etc.
– ORIGIN Latin, 'liquid, fluid'.

lath /lath/ • n. (pl. **laths** /laths/) a thin, flat strip of wood.
– ORIGIN Old English.

lathe /*rhymes with* bathe/ • n. a machine for shaping wood or metal by means of a rotating drive which turns the piece being worked on against different cutting tools.
– ORIGIN prob. from Danish *lad* 'frame'.

lather /lah-*ther*, la-*ther*/ • n. **1** a frothy mass of bubbles produced by soap when mixed with water. **2** heavy sweat visible on a horse's coat as a white foam. • v. (**lathers**, **lathering**, **lathered**) **1** form a lather. **2** rub with soap until a lather is produced. **3** cover or spread liberally with (a substance).
– ORIGIN Old English.

Latimer E
/lat-i-mer/, Hugh (*c.*1485–1555), English Protestant bishop and martyr. One of Henry VIII's chief advisers when the king broke with the papacy, he was burnt at the stake as a heretic during the reign of Mary I.

Latin • n. the language of ancient Rome and its empire. • adj. relating to the Latin language.
– ORIGIN Latin *Latinus* 'of Latium' (an ancient region in central Italy).

Latin America E
the parts of the American continent where Spanish or Portuguese is the main national language (i.e. Mexico and the whole of Central and South America).
– DERIVATIVES **Latin American** n. & adj.

Latinate /lat-i-nayt/ • adj. (of language) having the character of Latin.

Latino /luh-tee-noh/ • n. (pl. **Latinos**; fem. **Latina**, pl. **Latinas**) N. Amer. a Latin American inhabitant of the United States.
– ORIGIN Latin American Spanish.

latitude /la-ti-tyood/ • n. **1** the distance of a place north or south of the equator. **2** (**latitudes**) regions with reference to their temperature and distance from the equator: *northern latitudes.* **3** scope for freedom of action or thought.
– ORIGIN Latin *latitudo* 'breadth'.

latrine /luh-treen/ • n. a communal toilet in a camp or barracks.
– ORIGIN Latin *latrina.*

latte /lat-tay/ • n. a drink of frothy steamed milk to which a shot of espresso coffee is added.
– ORIGIN Italian.

latter • adj. **1** nearer to the end than to the beginning. **2** recent: *in latter years.* **3** (**the latter**) referring to the second or second-mentioned of two people or things.
– ORIGIN Old English, 'slower'.

latter-day • adj. modern or contemporary: *a latter-day Noah.*

Latter-Day Saints • pl. n. the Mormons' name for themselves.

latterly • adv. **1** recently. **2** in the later stages of a period of time.

lattice • n. a structure or pattern consisting of strips crossing each other with square or diamond-shaped spaces left between.
– DERIVATIVES **latticed** adj. **latticework** n.
– ORIGIN Old French *lattis.*

Latvia E
/lat-vi-uh/ a country on the eastern shore of the Baltic Sea; capital, Riga.
– DERIVATIVES **Latvian** adj. & n.

laud /lawd/ • v. formal praise highly.
– ORIGIN Latin *laudare.*

Lauda E
/low-duh/, Niki (b.1949), Austrian motor-racing driver, three times World champion (1975; 1977; 1984).

laudable • adj. deserving praise and commendation.

laudanum /law-duh-nuhm/ • **n.** a solution prepared from opium and formerly used as a painkiller.
– ORIGIN Latin.

laudatory /law-duh-tuh-ri/ • **adj.** expressing praise and commendation.

laugh • **v. 1** make the sounds and movements that express great amusement. **2 (laugh at)** make fun of. **3 (laugh off)** dismiss (something) by treating it light-heartedly. • **n. 1** an act of laughing. **2 (a laugh)** informal a cause of laughter.
– PHRASES **have the last laugh** eventually be successful.
– ORIGIN Old English.

laughable • **adj.** so ridiculous as to be amusing.
– DERIVATIVES **laughably** adv.

laughing gas • **n.** non-technical term for **NITROUS OXIDE**.

laughing stock • **n.** a person who is ridiculed by everyone.

laughter • **n.** the action or sound of laughing.

launch[1] • **v. 1** move (a boat or ship) from land into the water. **2** send out or hurl (a rocket or other missile). **3** begin (an enterprise) or introduce (a new product). **4 (launch into)** begin energetically and enthusiastically. • **n.** an act of launching.
– ORIGIN Old French *launcher*.

launch[2] • **n.** a large motor boat.
– ORIGIN Spanish *lancha* 'pinnace'.

launcher • **n.** a structure that holds a rocket or missile during launching.

launder • **v.** (**launders**, **laundering**, **laundered**) **1** wash and iron (clothes or linen). **2** informal pass (illegally obtained money) through legitimate businesses or foreign banks to conceal its origins.
– ORIGIN Latin *lavanda* 'things to be washed'.

launderette (also **laundrette**) • **n.** a place with coin-operated washing machines and dryers for public use.

laundress • **n.** a woman employed to launder clothes and linen.

laundry • **n.** (pl. **laundries**) **1** clothes and linen that need to be washed or that have been newly washed. **2** a room or building where clothes and linen are washed and ironed.

laureate /lo-ri-uht/ • **n.** a person given an award for outstanding creative or intellectual achievement.
– ORIGIN Latin *laurea* 'laurel wreath'.

laurel • **n. 1** an evergreen shrub or small tree with dark green glossy leaves. **2 (laurels)** a crown woven from bay leaves and awarded as a sign of victory or mark of honour in classical times. **3 (laurels)** honour or praise.
– PHRASES **rest on one's laurels** be so satisfied with what one has already achieved that one makes no further effort.
– ORIGIN Latin *laurus*.

Laurel and Hardy E
an American comedy duo consisting of British-born **Stan Laurel** (1890–1965; born *Arthur Stanley Jefferson*) and **Oliver Hardy** (1892–1957). Famous for their brand of slapstick comedy, they starred in many films.

Lauren E
/lo-ruhn/, Ralph (b.1939), American fashion designer.

Laurier E
/lo-ri-ay/, Sir Wilfrid (1841–1919), Canadian Liberal statesman, Prime Minister 1896–1911. He was Canada's first French-Canadian and Roman Catholic Prime Minister.

lava • **n.** hot molten rock that erupts from a volcano or fissure, or solid rock formed when this cools.
– ORIGIN Italian.

lava lamp • **n.** a transparent electric lamp containing a thick liquid in which a suspended waxy substance rises and falls in constantly changing shapes.

lavatorial • **adj.** (of conversation or humour) referring to lavatories and excretion.

lavatory • **n.** (pl. **lavatories**) a toilet.
– ORIGIN Latin *lavatorium* 'place for washing'.

lavender • **n. 1** a small strong-smelling shrub with narrow leaves and bluish-purple flowers. **2** a pale bluish-mauve colour.
– ORIGIN Latin *lavandula*.

lavender water • **n.** a perfume made from distilled lavender.

Laver E
/lay-ver/, Rod (b.1938), Australian tennis player. In 1962 he became the second man (after Don Budge) to win the four major singles championships (British, American, French, and Australian) in one year; in 1969 he was the first to repeat this.

lavish • **adj. 1** very rich, elaborate, or luxurious. **2** giving or given in great amounts. • **v.** (**lavish on**) give or spend in large or extravagant quantities.
– DERIVATIVES **lavishly** adv.
– ORIGIN Old French *labasse* 'deluge of rain'.

Lavoisier E
/la-vwa-zi-ay/, Antoine Laurent (1743–94), French scientist, the father of modern chemistry. He was the first to recognize that combustion involved the combination of substances with the gas oxygen.

Law, E
(Andrew) Bonar (1858–1923), Canadian-born British Conservative statesman, Prime Minister 1922–3.

law • **n. 1** a rule or system of rules recognized by a country or community as governing the actions of its members. **2** such rules as a subject of study or as the basis of the legal profession. **3** a statement of fact to the effect that a particular phenomenon always occurs if certain conditions are present: *the second law of thermodynamics*. **4** a rule that controls correct behaviour in a sport.
– PHRASES **be a law unto oneself** behave in an unconventional or unpredictable manner. **lay down the law** issue instructions in an authoritative way. **take the law into one's own hands** illegally punish someone according to one's own ideas of justice.
– ORIGIN Old Norse, 'something fixed'.

law-abiding • **adj.** obedient to the laws of society.

lawbreaker • **n.** a person who breaks the law.

law court • n. a court of law.
lawful • adj. allowed by or obeying law or rules.
– DERIVATIVES **lawfully** adv.
lawless • adj. not governed by or obedient to laws.
– DERIVATIVES **lawlessness** n.
law lord • n. (in the UK) a member of the House of Lords qualified to perform its legal work.
lawmaker • n. a member of a government who makes laws.
lawn[1] • n. an area of mown grass in a garden or park.
– ORIGIN Old French *launde* 'wooded district, heath'.
lawn[2] • n. a fine linen or cotton fabric.
– ORIGIN prob. from *Laon*, a French city important for linen manufacture.
lawnmower • n. a machine for cutting the grass on a lawn.
lawn tennis • n. dated or formal tennis.
law of averages • n. the supposed principle that future events are likely to balance any past events.

Lawrence[1], E
D. H. (1885–1930; full name *David Herbert Lawrence*), English novelist, poet, and essayist. His novels, which include *Women in Love* and *Lady Chatterley's Lover*, are characterized by their condemnation of industrial society and their frank treatment of sexual relationships.

Lawrence[2], E
T. E. (1888–1935; full name *Thomas Edward Lawrence*; known as **Lawrence of Arabia**), British soldier and writer. From 1916 onwards he helped to organize the Arab revolt against the Turks in the Middle East, a period which he described in *The Seven Pillars of Wisdom*.

lawrencium /lo-ren-si-uhm/ • n. a very unstable chemical element made by high-energy collisions.
– ORIGIN named after the American physicist Ernest O. *Lawrence* (1901–58).

Law Society E
the professional body responsible for regulating solicitors in England and Wales.

lawsuit • n. a claim brought to a law court to be decided.
lawyer • n. a person who practises or studies law.
lax • adj. **1** not strict, severe, or careful enough. **2** (of limbs or muscles) relaxed.
– DERIVATIVES **laxity** n.
– ORIGIN Latin *laxus* 'loose, lax'.
laxative • n. a drug or medicine that causes a person to empty their bowels.
– ORIGIN Latin *laxare* 'loosen'.
lay[1] • v. (**lays, laying, laid**) **1** put down, especially gently or carefully. **2** put down and set in position for use: *have your carpet laid by a professional*. **3** assign or place: *lay the blame*. **4** (**lay before**) present (material) for consideration and action to. **5** (of a female bird, reptile, etc.) produce (an egg) from inside the body. **6** stake (an amount of money) in a bet. **7** vulgar have sexual intercourse with. • n. the general appearance of an area of land.
– PHRASES **lay off 1** discharge (a worker) because of a shortage of work. **2** informal give up. **lay out 1** construct or arrange (buildings or gardens) according to a plan. **2** arrange and present (material) for printing. **lay to rest** bury (a body) in a grave. **lay up** put out of action through illness or injury.
– ORIGIN Old English.

USAGE lay
Make sure that you use the words **lay** and **lie** correctly. **Lay** generally means 'put something down', as in *they are going to lay the carpet*, whereas **lie** means 'be in a horizontal position to rest', as in *why don't you lie down?* The past tense and past participle of **lay** is **laid**, as in *they laid the carpet*; the past tense of **lie** is **lay** (*he lay on the floor*) and the past participle is **lain** (*she had lain awake for hours*).

lay[2] • adj. **1** not belonging to the clergy. **2** not having professional qualifications or expert knowledge.
– ORIGIN Latin *laicus*.
lay[3] • n. a short lyric or narrative poem intended to be sung.
– ORIGIN Old French *lai*.
lay[4] past of LIE[1].
layabout • n. derog. a person who does little or no work.
lay-by • n. (pl. **lay-bys**) Brit. an area at the side of a road where vehicles may pull off the road and stop.
layer • n. **1** a sheet or thickness of material covering a surface. **2** (in combination) a person or thing that lays something: *a cable-layer*. • v. (**layers, layering, layered**) arrange or cut in a layer or layers.
– ORIGIN from LAY[1].
layette • n. a set of clothing and bedclothes for a newborn child.
– ORIGIN French.
layman (or **layperson**) • n. **1** a member of a Church who is not a priest or minister. **2** a person without professional or specialized knowledge.
lay-off • n. **1** a discharge of a worker or workers because of a shortage of work. **2** a temporary break from an activity.

La'youn E
/lah-yoon/ (also **Laayoune**) the capital of Western Sahara.

layout • n. **1** the way in which something, especially a page, is laid out. **2** a thing set out in a particular way.
lay reader • n. (in the Anglican Church) a layperson licensed to preach and to conduct some services.
laze • v. (**lazes, lazing, lazed**) spend time relaxing or doing very little.
lazy • adj. (**lazier, laziest**) **1** unwilling to work or use energy. **2** showing a lack of effort or care.
– DERIVATIVES **lazily** adv. **laziness** n.
– ORIGIN perh. from German *lasich* 'languid, idle'.
lazy eye • n. an eye with poor vision due to lack of use.
lb • abbrev. pound(s) (in weight).
– ORIGIN from Latin *libra*.
lbw • abbrev. Cricket leg before wicket.
LCD • abbrev. **1** Electron. & Computing liquid crystal display. **2** Math. lowest (or least) common de-

nominator.

LCM ● **abbrev.** Math. lowest (or least) common multiple.

LEA ● **abbrev.** (in the UK) Local Education Authority.

lea ● **n.** literary an open area of grassy land.
– ORIGIN Old English.

leach ● **v.** remove (a soluble substance) from soil or other material by the action of water passing through it.
– ORIGIN Old English, 'to water'.

Leacock, E
Stephen (Butler) (1869–1949), Canadian humorist and economist, known for his many humorous writings, including *Sunshine Sketches of a Little Town*.

lead[1] /leed/ ● **v.** (**leads**, **leading**, **led** /led/) **1** cause (a person or animal) to go with one. **2** be a route or means of access: *the street led into the square.* **3** (**lead to**) result in. **4** influence to do or believe something. **5** be in charge of. **6** have the advantage in a race or game. **7** be superior to (a competitor). **8** have (a particular way of life). **9** (**lead up to**) come before or result in. **10** (**lead on**) deceive (someone) into believing that one is attracted to them. ● **n. 1** the initiative in an action: *others followed our lead.* **2** (**the lead**) a position of advantage in a contest. **3** the chief part in a play or film. **4** a clue to be followed in solving a problem. **5** Brit. a strap or cord for restraining and guiding a dog. **6** a wire conveying electric current from a source to an appliance, or connecting two points of a circuit together. ● **adj.** playing the chief part in a musical group: *the lead singer.*
– PHRASES **lead astray** cause to act or think foolishly or wrongly.
– ORIGIN Old English.

lead[2] /led/ ● **n. 1** a heavy bluish-grey metallic element. **2** graphite used as the part of a pencil that makes a mark.
– ORIGIN Old English.

leaded ● **adj. 1** framed, covered, or weighted with lead. **2** (of petrol) containing lead.

leaden ● **adj. 1** dull, heavy, or slow. **2** dull grey: *a leaden sky.*

leader ● **n. 1** a person or thing that leads. **2** a person or thing that is the most successful or advanced in a particular area. **3** the main player in a music group. **4** Brit. a leading article in a newspaper.
– DERIVATIVES **leadership** n.

leading /lee-ding/ ● **adj.** most important or in first place: *leading politicians.*

leading article ● **n.** Brit. a newspaper article giving the editorial opinion.

leading light ● **n.** a person who is important in a particular field or organization.

leading question ● **n.** a question that prompts the answer wanted.

leaf ● **n.** (pl. **leaves**) **1** a flat green structure that grows from the stem or root of a plant. **2** the state of having leaves: *the trees were in leaf.* **3** a single sheet of paper. **4** gold, silver, or other metal in the form of very thin foil. **5** a hinged or detachable part of a table. ● **v. 1** (of a plant) put out new leaves. **2** (**leaf through**) turn over (pages), reading them quickly or casually.
– PHRASES **turn over a new leaf** start to act or behave in a better way.
– ORIGIN Old English.

leaflet ● **n. 1** a printed sheet of paper containing information or advertising. **2** a small leaf. ● **v.** (**leaflets**, **leafleted**, **leafleting**) distribute leaflets to.

leafy ● **adj.** (**leafier**, **leafiest**) **1** having many leaves. **2** full of trees and shrubs: *a leafy avenue.*

league[1] ● **n. 1** a collection of people, countries, or groups that combine to help or protect each other. **2** a group of sports clubs which play each other over a period for a championship. **3** a class of quality or excellence: *the two men were not in the same league.*
– PHRASES **in league** plotting with another or others.
– ORIGIN Italian *lega*.

league[2] ● **n.** a former measure of distance, usually about three miles.
– ORIGIN Latin *leuga*, *leuca*.

League of Nations E
an association of countries established in 1919 by the Treaty of Versailles to promote international cooperation and achieve international peace. It was replaced by the United Nations in 1945.

league table ● **n.** Brit. **1** a list of the competitors in a league ranked according to performance. **2** a list in order of merit or achievement.

leak ● **v. 1** accidentally allow contents to escape or enter through a hole or crack. **2** (of liquid, gas, etc.) escape or enter accidentally through a hole or crack. **3** deliberately give out (secret information). ● **n. 1** a hole or crack through which contents leak. **2** an instance of leaking.
– DERIVATIVES **leakage** n. **leaky** adj.
– ORIGIN prob. from German or Dutch.

Leakey E
Louis (Seymour Bazett) (1903–72), Kenyan archaeologist and anthropologist. He and his British-born wife **Mary (Douglas) Leakey** (1913–96) made important discoveries of early human-like remains in East Africa.

Lean, E
Sir David (1908–91), English film director. His films include *Lawrence of Arabia*, *Doctor Zhivago*, and *A Passage to India*.

lean[1] ● **v.** (**leans**, **leaning**, **leaned** or Brit. **leant**) **1** be in or move into a sloping position. **2** (**lean against/on**) slope and rest against. **3** (**lean on**) rely on for support. **4** (**lean to/towards**) favour (a view).
– ORIGIN Old English.

lean[2] ● **adj. 1** (of a person) having little fat; thin. **2** (of meat) containing little fat. **3** (of a period of time) difficult and unprofitable. **4** informal (of an industry or company) efficient. ● **n.** the lean part of meat.
– DERIVATIVES **leanness** n.
– ORIGIN Old English.

Leander E
/li-an-der/ Gk Myth. a young man, the lover of the priestess Hero. He was drowned swimming across the Hellespont to visit her.

leaning ● **n.** a tendency or preference: *communist leanings.*

lean-to ● n. (pl. **lean-tos**) a small building sharing a wall with a larger building and having a roof that leans against it.

leap ● v. (**leaps**, **leaping**, **leaped** or **leapt**) **1** jump high or a long way. **2** move quickly and suddenly: *Polly leapt to her feet.* **3** (**leap at**) accept eagerly. **4** increase dramatically. ● n. **1** an act of leaping. **2** a sudden abrupt change or increase.
– ORIGIN Old English.

leapfrog ● n. a game in which players in turn vault over others who are bending down. ● v. (**leapfrogs**, **leapfrogging**, **leapfrogged**) **1** perform such a vault. **2** reach a leading position by overtaking others.

leap year ● n. a year, occurring once every four years, which has 366 days.

Lear, E
Edward (1812–88), English writer of humorous verse and illustrator, known for such verses as 'The Owl and the Pussy-Cat' and 'The Jumblies'.

learn ● v. (**learns**, **learning**, **learned** or **learnt**) **1** gain knowledge of or skill in (something) through study or experience or by being taught. **2** become aware of by information or from observation. **3** memorize.
– ORIGIN Old English.

learned /ler-nid/ ● adj. having gained much knowledge by study.

learning ● n. knowledge or skills gained through study or by being taught.

learning curve ● n. the rate of a person's progress in gaining experience or new skills.

learning difficulties ● pl. n. difficulties in gaining knowledge and skills to the normal level expected of those of the same age.

lease ● n. a contract by which one party lets land, property, services, etc. to another for a specified time, in return for payment. ● v. (**leases**, **leasing**, **leased**) let or rent on lease.
– ORIGIN Old French *lesser.*

leasehold ● n. the holding of property by lease.

leash ● n. a dog's lead.
– ORIGIN Old French *laissier* 'let run on a slack lead'.

least ● det. & pron. (usu. **the least**) smallest in amount, extent, or significance. ● adv. to the smallest extent or degree.
– PHRASES **at least 1** not less than. **2** if nothing else. **3** anyway. **at the least** (or **very least**) **1** not less than. **2** taking the most unfavourable view. **not least** in particular.
– ORIGIN Old English.

leastways ● adv. dialect or informal at least.

leather ● n. **1** a material made from the skin of an animal by tanning or a similar process. **2** (**leathers**) leather clothes worn by a motorcyclist.
– ORIGIN Old English.

leatherjacket ● n. Brit. the tough-skinned larva of a large crane fly.

leathery ● adj. having a tough, hard texture like leather.

leave[1] ● v. (**leaves**, **leaving**, **left**) **1** go away from. **2** stop living at, attending, or working for: *he left home at 16.* **3** allow to remain; go away without taking. **4** (**be left**) remain to be used or dealt with. **5** cause to be in a particular state or position: *leave the door open.* **6** let (someone) do something without helping or interfering. **7** (**leave to**) entrust (a decision or action) to. **8** deposit (something) to be collected or attended to.
– PHRASES **leave be** informal avoid disturbing or interfering with (someone). **leave out** fail to include.
– ORIGIN Old English.

leave[2] ● n. **1** (also **leave of absence**) time when one has permission to be absent from work or duty. **2** formal permission: *seeking leave to appeal.*
– PHRASES **take one's leave** formal say goodbye.
– ORIGIN Old English.

leaven /lev-uhn/ ● n. a substance added to dough to make it ferment and rise. ● v. **1** (**leavened**) (of dough or bread) fermented by adding leaven. **2** improve: *the debate was leavened by humour.*
– ORIGIN Latin *levamen* 'relief'.

leaves pl. of LEAF.

leave-taking ● n. an act of saying goodbye.

leavings ● pl. n. things that have been left as worthless.

Leavis E
/lee-viss/, F. R. (1895–1978; full name *Frank Raymond Leavis*), English literary critic, who was concerned with establishing a critical approach that upheld strict intellectual standards.

Lebanon E
/leb-uh-nuhn/ a country in the Middle East with a coastline on the Mediterranean Sea; capital, Beirut.
– DERIVATIVES **Lebanese** adj. & n.

Le Carré E
/luh **ka**-ray/, John (b.1931; pen name of *David John Moore Cornwell*), English novelist. He is known for his spy novels, which often feature the British agent George Smiley and include *Tinker, Tailor, Soldier, Spy.*

lecher ● n. a lecherous man.
– DERIVATIVES **lechery** n.

lecherous ● adj. showing excessive or offensive sexual desire.
– ORIGIN Old French *lecheros.*

Le Corbusier E
/luh kor-**byoo**-zi-ay/ (1887–1965; born *Charles Édouard Jeanneret*), Swiss-born French architect and town planner. A highly influential modernist architect, he pioneered the use of new materials such as concrete and was particularly interested in prefabrication and the use of standardized building elements.

lectern /lek-tern/ ● n. a tall stand with a sloping top from which a speaker can read while standing up.
– ORIGIN Latin *lectrum.*

lecture ● n. **1** an educational talk to an audience. **2** a lengthy reprimand. ● v. (**lectures**, **lecturing**, **lectured**) **1** give an educational lecture or lectures. **2** criticize or reprimand.
– DERIVATIVES **lecturer** n.
– ORIGIN Latin *lectura.*

LED ● abbrev. light-emitting diode, a semiconductor diode which glows when a voltage is applied.

led past and past part. of **LEAD**[1].

Leda E
/lee-duh/ Gk Myth. the wife of the king of Sparta. She was loved by Zeus, who visited her in the form of a swan.

ledge • **n.** **1** a narrow horizontal surface sticking out from a wall, cliff, etc. **2** an underwater ridge.
– ORIGIN perh. from **LAY**[1].

ledger • **n.** a book or other collection of financial accounts.
– ORIGIN prob. from **LAY**[1] and **LIE**[1].

ledger line (also **leger line**) • **n.** Music a short line added for notes above or below the range of a stave.

Lee[1], E
Bruce (1941–73; born *Lee Yuen Kam*), American actor and kung-fu expert, who starred in films such as *Enter the Dragon*.

Lee[2], E
Laurie (1914–97), English writer, known for his autobiographical novel *Cider With Rosie*.

Lee[3], E
Robert E. (1807–70; full name *Robert Edward Lee*), American general, commander of the Confederate army of Northern Virginia for most of the American Civil War.

Lee[4], E
Spike (b.1957; born *Shelton Jackson Lee*), American film director. His films include *Do the Right Thing* and *Malcolm X*.

lee • **n.** **1** shelter from wind or weather given by an object. **2** (also **lee side**) the side sheltered from the wind. Contrasted with **WEATHER**.
– ORIGIN Old English, 'shelter'.

leech • **n.** **1** a worm that sucks the blood of animals or people. **2** a person who makes profit from or lives off others.
– ORIGIN Old English.

Leeds E
an industrial city in northern England, a unitary council formerly in Yorkshire.

leek • **n.** a vegetable related to the onion, with flat overlapping leaves forming a long cylindrical bulb.
– ORIGIN Old English.

leer • **v.** (**leers**, **leering**, **leered**) look or gaze in a lustful or unpleasant way. • **n.** a lustful or unpleasant look.
– ORIGIN perh. from Old English, 'cheek'.

leery • **adj.** (**leerier**, **leeriest**) cautious or wary.
– ORIGIN from **LEER**.

lees /leez/ • **pl. n.** the sediment of wine in the barrel; dregs.
– ORIGIN Latin *liae*.

Leeuwenhoek E
/lay-v'n-hook/, Antoni van (1632–1723), Dutch naturalist. He developed a lens for scientific purposes and was the first to accurately describe such objects as red blood cells, capillaries, spermatozoa, and bacteria.

leeward /lee-werd, loo-erd/ • **adj. & adv.** on or towards the side sheltered from the wind or towards which the wind is blowing. Contrasted with **WINDWARD**.

Leeward Islands E
/lee-werd/ a group of Caribbean islands forming the northern part of the Lesser Antilles, and including Guadeloupe, Antigua, St Kitts, and Montserrat.

leeway • **n.** the amount of freedom to move or act that is available: *we have a lot of leeway in how we do our jobs.*

left[1] • **adj.** **1** on or towards the side of a person or of a thing which is to the west when the person or thing is facing north. **2** relating to a left-wing person or group. • **adv.** on or to the left side. • **n.** **1** (**the left**) the left-hand side or direction. **2** a left turn. **3** a person's left fist, or a blow given with it. **4** (**the Left**) a left-wing group or party.
– PHRASES **have two left feet** be clumsy or awkward.
– DERIVATIVES **leftward** adj. & adv.
– ORIGIN Old English, 'weak'.

left[2] past and past part. of **LEAVE**[1].

Left Bank E
a district of the city of Paris, situated on the left bank of the River Seine and noted for its intellectual and artistic life.

left-field • **adj.** unconventional or experimental.

left hand • **n.** the region or direction on the left side. • **adj.** **1** on or towards the left side. **2** done with or using the left hand.

left-hand drive • **n.** a motor vehicle steering system with the steering wheel and other controls fitted on the left side.

left-handed • **adj.** **1** using or done with the left hand. **2** turning to the left.

left hander • **n.** **1** a left-handed person. **2** a blow struck with a person's left hand.

leftie • **n.** var. of **LEFTY**.

left luggage • **n.** Brit. travellers' luggage left in temporary storage at a railway station, bus station, or airport.

leftovers • **pl. n.** food remaining after the rest has been used.

left wing • **n.** **1** the radical, reforming, or socialist section of a political party. [ORIGIN with reference to the National Assembly in France (1789–91), where the nobles sat to the president's right and the commons to the left.] **2** the left side of a sports team on the field.
– DERIVATIVES **left-winger** n.

lefty (also **leftie**) • **n.** (pl. **lefties**) informal a left-wing person.

leg • **n.** **1** each of the limbs on which a person or animal moves and stands. **2** a long, thin support or prop, especially of a chair or table. **3** a section of a journey, process, or race. **4** (in sport) each of two or more games or stages that make up a round or match.
– PHRASES **leg before wicket** Cricket (of a batsman) judged to be out through obstructing the ball with the leg when the ball would otherwise have hit the wicket. **leg it** informal **1** travel by foot. **2** run away. **not have a leg to stand on** not be able to give reasons for one's arguments or actions. **on one's last legs** near the end of life or usefulness.

– ORIGIN Old Norse.

legacy • n. (pl. **legacies**) **1** an amount of money or property left to someone in a will. **2** something handed down by a predecessor.
– ORIGIN Old French *legacie.*

legal • adj. **1** having to do with or required by the law. **2** permitted by law.
– DERIVATIVES **legally** adv.
– ORIGIN Latin *legalis.*

legal aid • n. payment from public funds given to people who cannot afford to pay for legal advice.

legalese /lee-guh-leez/ • n. informal the formal and technical language of legal documents.

legality • n. (pl. **legalities**) **1** the state of being legal. **2** (**legalities**) obligations imposed by law.

legalize (also **legalise**) • v. (**legalizes**, **legalizing**, **legalized**) make legal.
– DERIVATIVES **legalization** (also **legalisation**) n.

legal tender • n. coins or banknotes that must be accepted if offered in payment of a debt.

legate /leg-uht/ • n. a member of the clergy who represents the Pope.
– ORIGIN Latin *legatus.*

legation /li-gay-sh'n/ • n. **1** a diplomatic minister and staff. **2** the official residence of a diplomat.

legato /li-gah-toh/ • adv. & adj. Music in a smooth, flowing manner.
– ORIGIN Italian, 'bound'.

legend • n. **1** a traditional story from the past which may or may not be true. **2** an extremely famous person: *a screen legend.* **3** an inscription, caption, or key.
– ORIGIN Latin *legenda* 'things to be read'.

legendary • adj. **1** having to do with legends. **2** remarkable enough to be famous.

legerdemain /lej-er-di-mayn/ • n. **1** skilful use of one's hands when performing conjuring tricks. **2** trickery.
– ORIGIN from French *léger de main* 'dexterous'

leggings • pl. n. **1** a woman's tight-fitting stretchy garment covering the legs, hips, and bottom. **2** strong protective coverings for the legs from knee to ankle.

leggy • adj. (**leggier**, **leggiest**) **1** long-legged. **2** (of a plant) having a long and straggly stem or stems.

legible • adj. (of handwriting or print) clear enough to read.
– DERIVATIVES **legibility** n. **legibly** adv.
– ORIGIN Latin *legibilis.*

legion • n. **1** a division of 3,000–6,000 men in the ancient Roman army. **2** (**a legion/legions of**) a vast number of people or things. • adj. great in number: *her fans are legion.*
– ORIGIN Latin.

legionnaire /lee-juh-nair/ • n. a member of the Foreign Legion, or of an association of former servicemen and servicewomen.

legionnaires' disease • n. a form of pneumonia spread chiefly in water droplets through air conditioning systems.
– ORIGIN because identified after an outbreak at an American Legion meeting.

leg iron • n. a metal band or chain placed around a prisoner's ankle as a restraint.

legislate /lej-iss-layt/ • v. (**legislates**, **legislating**, **legislated**) **1** make laws. **2** (**legislate for/against**) prepare for (a situation or event).

legislation • n. laws as a whole.
– ORIGIN Latin.

legislative /lej-iss-luh-tiv/ • adj. **1** having the power to make laws. **2** relating to laws or a legislature.

legislator • n. a person who makes laws.

legislature /lej-iss-luh-cher/ • n. the law-making body of a state.

legitimate • adj. /li-jit-i-muht/ **1** allowed by the law or rules. **2** able to be defended with reasoning: *a legitimate excuse.* **3** (of a child) born of parents lawfully married to each other. • v. /li-jit-i-mayt/ (**legitimates**, **legitimating**, **legitimated**) make legitimate.
– DERIVATIVES **legitimacy** n.
– ORIGIN Latin *legitimare.*

legitimize /li-jit-i-myz/ (also **legitimise**) • v. (**legitimizes**, **legitimizing**, **legitimized**) make (something) legitimate.

legless • adj. **1** having no legs. **2** Brit. informal extremely drunk.

legroom • n. space in which a seated person can put their legs.

legume /leg-yoom/ • n. a leguminous plant grown as a crop.
– ORIGIN Latin *legumen.*

leguminous /li-gyoo-mi-nuhss/ • adj. relating to plants that bear their seeds in pods, such as peas.

leg warmers • pl. n. a pair of knitted garments covering the legs from ankle to knee or thigh.

legwork • n. work that involves tiring or boring movement from place to place.

Lehár E
/lay-har/, Franz (Ferencz) (1870–1948), Hungarian composer, known for such operettas as *The Merry Widow.*

Le Havre E
/luh hah-vruh/ a port in northern France, on the English Channel at the mouth of the Seine.

lei /lay/ • n. a Polynesian garland of flowers.
– ORIGIN Hawaiian.

Leibniz E
/lyb-nits/, Gottfried Wilhelm (1646–1716), German philosopher and mathematician, who devised a method of calculus independently of Newton. In philosophy he proposed that the world is composed of single units (monads), all acting in harmony together.
– DERIVATIVES **Leibnizian** adj. & n.

Leicestershire E
/less-ter-sheer, less-ter-sher/ a county of central England; county town, Leicester.

Leics. • abbrev. Leicestershire.

Leigh E
/*rhymes with* Lee/, Vivien (1913–67; born *Vivian Mary Hartley*), British actress, born in India. Her films include *Gone with the Wind* and *A Streetcar Named Desire.*

Leighton, E
Frederic, 1st Baron Leighton of Stretton (1830–96), English painter and sculptor, famous for his neoclassical mythological scenes.

Leinster E
/len-ster/ a province in the south-east of the Republic of Ireland, centred on Dublin.

Leipzig E
/lyp-sig/ an industrial city in east central Germany.

leisure • n. time free for relaxation or enjoyment.
– PHRASES **at leisure 1** not occupied; free. **2** in an unhurried way.
– ORIGIN Old French *leisir.*

leisure centre • n. a public building offering facilities for sport and recreation.

leisurely • adj. relaxed and unhurried. • adv. without hurry.

leisurewear • n. casual clothes worn for leisure activities.

leitmotif /lyt-moh-teef/ (also **leitmotiv**) • n. a frequently repeated theme in a musical or literary composition.
– ORIGIN German *Leitmotiv.*

Leitrim E
/lee-trim/ a county of the Republic of Ireland, county town, Carrick-on-Shannon.

Leix E
var. of **Laois**.

Lely E
/lee-li/, Sir Peter (1618–80; Dutch name *Pieter van der Faes*), Dutch portrait painter, resident in England from 1641.

Le Mans E
/luh mon/ an industrial town in NW France. It is the site of a motor-racing circuit, on which an annual 24-hour endurance race is held.

lemming • n. a short-tailed Arctic rodent, noted for its periodic mass migrations.
– ORIGIN Norwegian and Danish.

Lemmon, E
Jack (1925–2001; born *John Uhler*), American actor, known for his roles in comedy films such as *Some Like It Hot.*

lemon • n. **1** a pale yellow citrus fruit with thick skin and acidic juice. **2** a drink made from or flavoured with lemon juice. **3** a pale yellow colour.
– ORIGIN Old French *limon.*

lemonade • n. a sweetened drink made from lemon juice or flavouring and water.

lemon balm • n. a bushy lemon-scented herb of the mint family.

lemon curd • n. a conserve made from lemons, butter, eggs, and sugar.

lemon grass • n. a tropical grass which yields an oil that smells of lemon, used in Asian cooking.

lemon sole • n. a common flatfish of the plaice family.
– ORIGIN French *limande.*

lemur /lee-mer/ • n. a primate with a pointed snout, that lives in trees in Madagascar.
– ORIGIN Latin *lemures* 'spirits of the dead'.

Lena E
/lay-nuh/ a river in Siberia, which rises near the western shore of Lake Baikal and flows generally north-east into the Laptev Sea, a part of the Arctic Ocean.

lend • v. (**lends**, **lending**, **lent**) **1** allow (someone) to use (something) on the understanding that it will be returned. **2** allow (someone) the use of (a sum of money) under an agreement to pay it back later. **3** contribute or add (a quality) to. **4** (**lend itself to**) (of a thing) be suitable for.
– DERIVATIVES **lender** n.
– ORIGIN Old English.

lending library • n. a public library from which books may be borrowed for a limited time.

Lendl E
/len-d'l/, Ivan (b.1960), Czech-born American tennis player. His many singles titles include the US, Australian, and the French Open championships.

length • n. **1** the measurement or extent of something from end to end. **2** the amount of time occupied by something. **3** the quality of being long. **4** the full distance that a thing extends for. **5** the extent of a garment in a vertical direction when worn. **6** the length of a horse, boat, etc., as a measure of the lead in a race. **7** a stretch or piece of something. **8** a degree to which a course of action is taken: *they go to great lengths to avoid the press.*
– PHRASES **at length 1** in detail; fully. **2** after a long time.
– ORIGIN Old English.

lengthen • v. make or become longer.

lengthways (also **lengthwise**) • adv. in a direction parallel with a thing's length.

lengthy • adj. (**lengthier**, **lengthiest**) very long.
– DERIVATIVES **lengthily** adv.

lenient /lee-ni-uhnt/ • adj. not strict; merciful.
– DERIVATIVES **leniency** n.
ORIGIN Latin *lenire* 'soothe'.

Lenin E
/len-in/, Vladimir Ilich (1870–1924; born *Vladimir Ilich Ulyanov*), the chief figure in the Russian Revolution and first Premier of the Soviet Union 1918–24. The leader of the Bolsheviks, in 1917 he established Bolshevik control after the overthrow of the tsar, becoming head of state the following year and introducing policies based on Marxist principles.

Leningrad E
/len-in-grad/ former name for **St Petersburg**.

Lennon, E
John (1940–80), English pop and rock singer, guitarist, and songwriter. A founder member of the Beatles, he wrote most of their songs in collaboration with Paul McCartney. He was assassinated in New York.

lens /lenz/ • n. **1** a piece of transparent curved material for concentrating or dispersing light rays. **2** the light-gathering device of a camera. **3** Anat. the transparent structure behind the iris by which light is focused on to the retina of the eye.

– ORIGIN Latin, 'lentil'.

Lent ● n. (in the Christian Church) the period immediately before Easter, which is devoted to fasting and penitence.
– ORIGIN short for **LENTEN**.

lent past and past part. of **LEND**.

Lenten ● adj. having to do with Lent.
– ORIGIN Old English, 'spring, Lent'.

lentil ● n. a pulse which is dried and then soaked and cooked before eating.
– ORIGIN Latin *lenticula*.

lento ● adv. & adj. Music slow or slowly.
– ORIGIN Italian.

Leo ● n. a constellation (the Lion) and sign of the zodiac, which the sun enters about 23 July.
– ORIGIN Latin.

Leo I, St E
(d.461; known as **Leo the Great**; canonized as **St Leo I**), pope 440–61. He defended orthodoxy and extended the power of the papacy to Africa, Spain, and Gaul. Feast day, 18 February or 11 April.

Leonard, E
Elmore (John) (b.1925), American novelist, author of *Freaky Deaky* and *Get Shorty*.

Leonardo da Vinci E
/lee-uh-nar-doh duh **vin**-chi/ (1452–1519), Italian painter, scientist, and engineer. His paintings include the *Mona Lisa* and *The Virgin of the Rocks*. His scientific interests were extremely wide-ranging and included studies of the human circulatory system and plans for a type of aircraft and a submarine.

leonine /lee-uh-nyn/ ● adj. having to do with or resembling a lion or lions.
– ORIGIN Latin *leoninus*.

leopard ● n. (fem. **leopardess**) a large solitary cat that has a fawn or brown coat with black spots, found in the forests of Africa and southern Asia.
– ORIGIN Greek *leopardos*.

Léopoldville E
/lee-uh-pohld-vil/ former name (until 1966) for **KINSHASA**.

leotard /lee-uh-tard/ ● n. a close-fitting, stretchy one-piece garment covering the body to the top of the thighs, worn for dance, gymnastics, and exercise.
– ORIGIN named after the French trapeze artist Jules *Léotard* (1839–70).

leper ● n. **1** a person suffering from leprosy. **2** a person who is shunned by others: *a social leper*.
– ORIGIN Old French *lepre*.

Lepidoptera /lep-i-**dop**-tuh-ruh/ ● pl. n. an order of insects comprising the butterflies and moths.
– ORIGIN from Greek *lepis* 'scale' + *pteron* 'wing'.

lepidopterist /lep-i-**dop**-tuh-rist/ ● n. a person who studies or collects butterflies or moths.

leprechaun /lep-ruh-kawn/ ● n. (in Irish folklore) a small, mischievous sprite.
– ORIGIN Old Irish *luchorpán*.

leprosy ● n. a contagious disease that causes discoloration and lumps on the skin and, in severe cases, disfigurement and deformities.

leprous ● adj. referring to or suffering from leprosy.

Lerner E
/ler-ner/, Alan J. (1918–1986; full name *Alan Jay Lerner*), American lyricist and dramatist, who wrote a number of musicals with composer Frederick Loewe (1904–88), including *My Fair Lady*.

Lerwick E
/ler-wik/ the capital of the Shetland Islands, on the island of Mainland.

lesbian ● n. a homosexual woman. ● adj. referring to lesbians or lesbianism.
– DERIVATIVES **lesbianism** n.
– ORIGIN from **LESBOS**, home of Sappho, who expressed affection for women in her poetry.

Lesbos E
/lez-boss/ a Greek island in the eastern Aegean.

lesion /lee-*zh*uhn/ ● n. a part of an organ or tissue which has been damaged.
– ORIGIN Latin *laedere* 'injure'.

Lesotho E
/luh-**soo**-too/ a landlocked country forming an enclave in South Africa; capital, Maseru.

less ● det. & pron. **1** a smaller amount of. **2** fewer in number. ● adv. to a smaller extent; not so much. ● prep. minus.
– ORIGIN Old English.

USAGE less
For an explanation of the difference between **less** and **fewer**, see the note at **FEW**.

-less ● suffix forming adjectives and adverbs: **1** (from nouns) without: *flavourless*. **2** (from verbs) not affected by: *tireless*.
– ORIGIN Old English, 'devoid of'.

lessee ● n. a person who holds the lease of a property.
– ORIGIN Old French *lesse*.

lessen ● v. make or become less.

lesser ● adj. not so great, large, or important as the other or the rest.

Lesser Antilles E
the part of the Antilles to the south-east, including the Virgin Islands, Leeward Islands, and Windward Islands.

Lesser Sunda Islands E
see **SUNDA ISLANDS**.

Lessing[1], E
Doris (May) (b.1919), British novelist and short-story writer, known for her feminist novel *The Golden Notebook* and a number of science-fiction works.

Lessing[2], E
Gotthold Ephraim (1729–81), German dramatist and critic, who founded the modern German dramatic tradition. His plays include the tragedy *Miss Sara Sampson*.

lesson ● n. **1** a period of learning or teaching. **2** a thing learned. **3** a thing that acts as a warning or encouragement. **4** a passage from the Bible read aloud during a church service.
– ORIGIN Old French *leçon*.

lessor ● n. a person who leases or lets a prop-

erty to another.
– ORIGIN Old French.

lest ● conj. formal **1** to avoid the risk of. **2** because of the possibility of.
– ORIGIN Old English.

let[1] ● v. (**lets**, **letting**, **let**) **1** allow. **2** used to express an intention, suggestion, or order: *let's have a drink.* **3** used to express an assumption upon which a theory or calculation is to be based: *let A stand for X.* **4** allow someone to have the use of (a room or property) in return for payment. ● n. Brit. a period during which a room or property is rented.
– PHRASES **let alone** not to mention. **let down** fail to support or help. **let go** allow to go free. **let oneself go 1** act in a relaxed way. **2** become careless in one's habits or appearance. **let off 1** cause (a gun, firework, or bomb) to fire or explode. **2** choose not to punish (someone). **3** excuse (someone) from a task. **let up** informal become less intense. **to let** available for rent.
– ORIGIN Old English, 'leave behind'.

let[2] ● n. (in racket sports) a situation under which a point is not counted and is played for again.
– ORIGIN Old English, 'hinder'.

let-down ● n. a disappointment.

lethal ● adj. **1** causing or able to cause death. **2** very harmful.
– DERIVATIVES **lethally** adv.
– ORIGIN Latin *lethalis.*

lethargic /li-thar-jik/ ● adj. lacking energy or enthusiasm.
– DERIVATIVES **lethargically** adv.

lethargy /leth-er-ji/ ● n. a lack of energy and enthusiasm.
– ORIGIN Greek *lēthargos* 'forgetful'.

Lethe E
/lee-thi/ Gk Myth. a river in Hades whose water when drunk made the souls of the dead forget their life on earth.

let-off ● n. informal an instance of unexpectedly avoiding something.

let's ● contr. let us.

letter ● n. **1** a sign representing one or more of the sounds used in speech; any of the symbols of an alphabet. **2** a written communication, sent by post or messenger. **3** the precise terms of something: *the letter of the law.* **4** (**letters**) knowledge of literature. ● v. (**letters**, **lettering**, **lettered**) write or provide with letters.
– DERIVATIVES **lettering** n.
– ORIGIN Latin *litera.*

letter bomb ● n. an explosive device hidden in a small package, which explodes when the package is opened.

letter box ● n. esp. Brit. a slot in a door through which mail is delivered.

letterhead ● n. a printed heading on stationery.

lettuce ● n. a cultivated plant with leaves that are eaten in salads.
– ORIGIN Old French *letues.*

let-up ● n. informal a brief time when something becomes less intense or difficult.

leucocyte /loo-koh-syt/ (also **leukocyte**) ● n. a white blood cell.
– ORIGIN from Greek *leukos* 'white' + *kutos* 'vessel'.

leukaemia /loo-kee-mi-uh/ (US **leukemia**) ● n. a serious disease in which increased numbers of immature or abnormal white cells are produced, stopping the production of normal blood cells.
– ORIGIN from Greek *leukos* 'white' + *haima* 'blood'.

levee[1] /lev-ay/ ● n. a formal reception of visitors or guests.
– ORIGIN French.

levee[2] /lev-i/ ● n. **1** an embankment built to prevent the overflow of a river. **2** a ridge of sediment deposited naturally alongside a river.
– ORIGIN French.

level ● n. **1** a horizontal plane or line. **2** a stage on a scale. **3** a height or distance from the ground or another base. **4** a floor within a multi-storey building. ● adj. **1** having a flat, horizontal surface. **2** at the same height as someone or something else. **3** equal in position. ● v. (**levels**, **levelling**, **levelled**; US **levels**, **leveling**, **leveled**) **1** make or become level. **2** aim or direct (a weapon, criticism, or accusation). **3** (**level with**) informal be honest with.
– DERIVATIVES **levelly** adv.
– ORIGIN Old French *livel.*

level crossing ● n. Brit. a place where a railway and a road cross at the same level.

level-headed ● adj. calm and sensible.

lever ● n. **1** a bar resting on a pivot, used to move a load with one end when pressure is applied to the other. **2** an arm or handle that is moved to operate a mechanism. ● v. (**levers**, **levering**, **levered**) **1** lift or move with a lever. **2** move with effort: *she levered herself up.*
– ORIGIN Old French *levier.*

leverage ● n. **1** the exertion of force by means of a lever. **2** the power to influence: *political leverage.*

leveret /lev-uh-rit/ ● n. a young hare in its first year.
– ORIGIN Old French.

Leverhulme E
/lee-ver-hyoom/, 1st Viscount (1851–1925, born *William Hesketh Lever*), English industrialist and philanthropist. His company, Lever Bros., came to form the basis of the international corporation Unilever. Leverhulme founded Port Sunlight on the Mersey for company workers.

Levi E
/lay-vi/, Primo (1919–87), Italian novelist and poet, of Jewish descent. His experiences as a survivor of Auschwitz are recounted in *If This is a Man.*

leviathan /li-vy-uh-thuhn/ ● n. **1** (in biblical use) a sea monster. **2** a very large or powerful thing.
– ORIGIN Hebrew.

Lévi-Strauss E
/lev-i strowss/, Claude (b.1908), French social anthropologist. He made pioneering structuralist studies of cultural systems such as myth and kinship.

levitate /lev-i-tayt/ ● v. (**levitates**, **levitating**, **levitated**) rise or cause to rise and hover

in the air.
– DERIVATIVES **levitation** n.
– ORIGIN Latin *levis* 'light'.

levity ● n. the treatment of a serious matter with humour or lack of respect.
– ORIGIN Latin *levitas*.

levy ● n. (pl. **levies**) **1** the imposing of a tax, fee, fine, etc. **2** a sum of money raised by a levy. ● v. (**levies**, **levying**, **levied**) impose or seize as a levy.
– ORIGIN Old French *lever* 'raise'.

lewd ● adj. crude and offensive in a sexual way.
– ORIGIN Old English.

Lewis[1], E
Cecil Day, see **DAY LEWIS**.

Lewis[2], E
C. S. (1898–1963; full name *Clive Staples Lewis*), British novelist, religious writer, and scholar, best known for his series of children's books, including *The Lion, the Witch, and the Wardrobe*.

Lewis[3], E
Carl (b.1961; full name *Frederick Carleton Lewis*), American track and field athlete. He won a number of Olympic gold medals 1984–96 for sprinting and the long jump.

Lewis[4], E
Jerry Lee (b.1935), American rock-and-roll singer and pianist. His hits include 'Great Balls of Fire'.

Lewis[5], E
Lennox (b.1965), English boxer, world heavyweight champion from 1999.

Lewis[6], E
Meriwether (1774–1809), American explorer. He led an expedition (with William Clark) across North America (1804–6).

Lewis[7], E
(Harry) Sinclair (1885–1951), American novelist, known for satirical works such as *Babbitt* and *Elmer Gantry*.

Lewis and Harris E
(also **Lewis with Harris**) the largest and northernmost island of the Outer Hebrides; chief town, Stornoway.

lexical ● adj. **1** relating to the words of a language. **2** relating to a dictionary.
– ORIGIN Greek *lexikos* 'of words'.

lexicography /leks-i-kog-ruh-fi/ ● n. the practice of writing dictionaries.
– DERIVATIVES **lexicographer** n.

lexicon ● n. **1** the vocabulary of a person, language, or branch of knowledge. **2** a dictionary.
– ORIGIN from Greek *lexikon biblion* 'book of words'.

ley[1] /*rhymes with* pay/ ● n. a piece of land where grass is grown temporarily.
– ORIGIN Old English, 'fallow'.

ley[2] /*rhymes with* pay *or* pea/ (also **ley line**) ● n. a supposed straight line connecting ancient sites, associated by some people with lines of energy.
– ORIGIN from **LEA**.

LF ● abbrev. low frequency.

Lhasa E
/lah-suh/ the capital of Tibet.

liability ● n. (pl. **liabilities**) **1** the state of being liable. **2** a sum of money that is owed. **3** a person or thing likely to cause one embarrassment or trouble.

liable ● adj. **1** responsible by law. **2** (**liable to**) subject by law to. **3** (**liable to do**) likely to do. **4** (**liable to**) likely to experience (something undesirable).
– ORIGIN perh. from French *lier* 'to bind'.

liaise /li-ayz/ ● v. (**liaises**, **liaising**, **liaised**) **1** cooperate on a matter of shared concern. **2** (**liaise between**) act as a link to assist communication between.
– ORIGIN from **LIAISON**.

liaison ● n. **1** communication or cooperation between people or organizations. **2** a sexual relationship.
– ORIGIN French.

liana /li-**ah**-nuh/ (also **liane** /li-**ahn**/) ● n. a woody climbing plant that hangs from trees in tropical forests.
– ORIGIN French *liane* 'clematis, liana'.

liar ● n. a person who tells lies.

lias /ly-uhss/ ● n. a blue-grey clayey limestone found chiefly in SW England.
– ORIGIN Old French *liais*.

libation /ly-**bay**-sh'n/ ● n. **1** a drink poured out as an offering to a god. **2** humorous an alcoholic drink.
– ORIGIN Latin.

libel ● n. the crime of publishing a false statement that harms a person's reputation. Compare with **SLANDER**. ● v. (**libels**, **libelling**, **libelled**; US **libels**, **libeling**, **libeled**) publish a false statement about.
– DERIVATIVES **libellous** (US also **libelous**) adj.
– ORIGIN Latin *libellus* 'little book'.

Liberace E
/li-buh-**rah**-chi/ (1919–87; full name *Wladziu Valentino Liberace*), American pianist, known for his romantic arrangements of piano works and for his flamboyant costumes.

liberal ● adj. **1** willing to respect and accept behaviour or opinions different from one's own. **2** (in politics) favouring individual liberty, free trade, and moderate reform. **3** (**Liberal**) (in the UK) relating to the Liberal Democrat party. **4** (of an interpretation) not strictly literal. **5** given, used, or giving in generous amounts. ● n. **1** a person of liberal views. **2** (**Liberal**) (in the UK) a Liberal Democrat.
– DERIVATIVES **liberalism** n. **liberality** n. **liberally** adv.
– ORIGIN Latin *liberalis*.

Liberal Democrat ● n. (in the UK) a member of the Liberal Democrat party.

liberalize (also **liberalise**) ● v. (**liberalizes**, **liberalizing**, **liberalized**) remove or loosen restrictions on (something).
– DERIVATIVES **liberalization** (also **liberalisation**) n.

liberate ● v. (**liberates**, **liberating**, **liberated**) **1** set free. **2** (**liberated**) free from conventional ideas about behaviour.
– DERIVATIVES **liberation** n. **liberator** n.
– ORIGIN Latin *liberare*.

Liberia E
/ly-**beer**-i-uh/ a country on the Atlantic coast of West Africa; capital, Monrovia.
– DERIVATIVES **Liberian** adj. & n.

libertarian ● n. a person who believes in very limited state intervention in people's lives.
– DERIVATIVES **libertarianism** n.

libertine /li-ber-teen/ ● n. a man who behaves immorally, especially in sexual matters.
– DERIVATIVES **libertinism** n.
– ORIGIN Latin *libertinus* 'freedman'.

liberty ● n. (pl. **liberties**) **1** the state of being free. **2** a right or privilege. **3** the ability to act as one pleases. **4** informal a disrespectful remark or action.
– PHRASES **take liberties 1** behave in an excessively familiar way towards a person. **2** treat something freely.
– ORIGIN Latin *libertas*.

Liberty, Statue of E
a statue at the entrance to New York harbour, a symbol of welcome to immigrants. Dedicated in 1886, it was designed by the French sculptor Frédéric-Auguste Bartholdi (1834–1904).

libidinous /li-bid-i-nuhss/ ● adj. having or showing excessive sexual drive.
ORIGIN Latin *libidinosus*.

libido /li-bee-doh/ ● n. (pl. **libidos**) sexual desire.
– ORIGIN Latin, 'desire, lust'.

Libra /lee-bruh/ ● n. a constellation (the Scales) and sign of the zodiac, which the sun enters about 23 September.
– ORIGIN Latin.

librarian ● n. a person in charge of or assisting in a library.

library ● n. (pl. **libraries**) **1** a building or room containing a collection of books and periodicals for use by the public or the members of an institution. **2** a private collection of books. **3** a collection of films, recorded music, etc., kept for research or borrowing.
– ORIGIN Latin *libraria* 'bookshop'.

libretto /li-bret-toh/ ● n. (pl. **libretti** /li-bret-ti/ or **librettos**) the words of an opera or other long vocal work.
– DERIVATIVES **librettist** n.
– ORIGIN Italian, 'small book'.

Libreville E
/lee-bruh-vil/ the capital of Gabon.

Libya E
/lib-i-uh/ a country in North Africa; capital, Tripoli.
– DERIVATIVES **Libyan** adj. & n.

lice pl. of LOUSE.

licence (US **license**) ● n. **1** a permit from an authority to own, use, or do something. **2** a writer's or artist's freedom to alter facts or ignore accepted rules. **3** freedom to behave without restraint.
– ORIGIN Latin *licentia* 'freedom'.

license (also **licence**) ● v. (**licenses**, **licensing**, **licensed**; also **licences**, **licencing**, **licenced**) **1** grant a licence to. **2** authorize.
– ORIGIN from LICENCE.

licensee ● n. the holder of a licence, especially to sell alcoholic drinks.

licentiate /ly-sen-shi-uht/ ● n. the holder of a certificate allowing them to practise a particular profession.
– ORIGIN Latin *licentiatus* 'having freedom'.

licentious /ly-sen-shuhss/ ● adj. sexually immoral.
– ORIGIN Latin *licentiosus*.

lichen /ly-kuhn, li-chuhn/ ● n. a simple plant consisting of a fungus living in close association with an alga, growing on rocks, walls, and trees.
– ORIGIN Greek *leikhēn*.

Lichtenstein E
/lik-tuhn-styn/, Roy (1923–97), American painter and sculptor. A leading figure of the pop art movement, he is best known for his paintings inspired by comic strips.

lick ● v. **1** pass the tongue over. **2** move lightly and quickly like a tongue: *the flames licked around the wood*. **3** informal totally defeat. ● n. **1** an act of licking. **2** informal a small amount or quick application of something: *a lick of paint*.
– ORIGIN Old English.

lickspittle ● n. a person who behaves with excessive obedience to those in power.

licorice ● n. US = LIQUORICE.

lid ● n. **1** a removable or hinged cover for the top of a container. **2** an eyelid.
– DERIVATIVES **lidded** adj.
– ORIGIN Old English.

lido /lee-doh/ ● n. (pl. **lidos**) a public open-air swimming pool.
– ORIGIN Italian, 'shore'.

lie[1] ● v. (**lies**, **lying**, **lay**; past part. **lain**) **1** be in or take up a horizontal position on a supporting surface. **2** be in a particular state: *the abbey lies in ruins*. **3** be found: *the solution lies in a return to traditional values*. **4** be situated in a specified position. ● n. the way, direction, or position in which something lies.
– PHRASES **lie low** avoid attention. **the lie** (N. Amer. **lay**) **of the land 1** the features of an area. **2** the current situation.
– ORIGIN Old English.

USAGE lie
For the correct use of **lay** and **lie**, see the note at LAY[1].

lie[2] ● n. **1** a deliberately false statement. **2** a situation involving deception. ● v. (**lies**, **lying**, **lied**) **1** tell a lie or lies. **2** (of a thing) present a false impression.
– ORIGIN Old English.

Liechtenstein E
/**likh**-tuhn-styn/ a small independent principality between Switzerland and Austria; capital, Vaduz.
– DERIVATIVES **Liechtensteiner** n.

lied /leed/ ● n. (pl. **lieder** /lee-der/) a type of German song for solo voice with piano accompaniment.
– ORIGIN German.

lie detector ● n. an instrument for determining whether a person is telling the truth.

lie-down ● n. esp. Brit. a short rest on a bed or sofa.

liege /leej/ ● n. hist. **1** (also **liege lord**) a feudal lord. **2** a vassal or subject.
– ORIGIN Old French.

lie-in ● n. esp. Brit. a prolonged stay in bed in the morning.

lieu /loo/ ● n. (in phr. **in lieu** or **in lieu of**) instead (of).
– ORIGIN French.

lieutenant /lef-ten-uhnt/ ● n. **1** a deputy or substitute acting for a person of higher rank. **2** a rank of officer in the British army or in the navy.
– ORIGIN Old French, 'place-holding'.

lieutenant colonel ● n. a rank of officer in the army and the US air force, above major and below colonel.

life ● n. (pl. **lives**) **1** the ability to grow, breathe, reproduce, etc., that distinguishes animals and plants from objects. **2** the existence of an individual human being or animal. **3** a particular type or aspect of people's existence: *school life.* **4** living things and their activity. **5** vitality or energy. **6** informal a sentence of imprisonment for life. **7** (in various games) each of a number of chances each player has before being put out.
– PHRASES **take one's life in one's hands** risk being killed.
– ORIGIN Old English.

life assurance ● n. esp. Brit. = **LIFE INSURANCE**.

lifebelt ● n. esp. Brit. a ring of buoyant material used to help a person who has fallen into water to stay afloat.

lifeblood ● n. a vital factor or force: *the cash is the lifeblood of our business.*

lifeboat ● n. **1** a boat launched from land to rescue people at sea. **2** a small boat kept on a ship for use in an emergency.

life cycle ● n. the series of changes in the life of an organism.

life expectancy ● n. the period that a person may expect to live.

life form ● n. any living thing.

lifeguard ● n. a person employed to rescue bathers who get into difficulty at a beach or swimming pool.

life insurance ● n. insurance that pays out a sum of money either on the death of the insured person or after a set period.

life jacket ● n. an inflatable jacket for keeping a person afloat in water.

lifeless ● adj. **1** dead or apparently dead. **2** not containing living things. **3** lacking energy or excitement.

lifelike ● adj. exactly like a living person or thing.

lifeline ● n. **1** a rope or line thrown to rescue someone in difficulties in water. **2** a thing which is essential for the continued existence of someone or something.

lifelong ● adj. lasting throughout a person's life.

life peer ● n. (in the UK) a peer whose title cannot be inherited.

life raft ● n. an inflatable raft for use in an emergency at sea.

lifesaver ● n. informal a thing that saves one from serious difficulty.

life sciences ● pl. n. the sciences concerned with the study of living organisms, including biology, botany, and zoology.

lifespan ● n. the length of time for which a person or animal lives or a thing functions.

lifestyle ● n. the way in which someone lives.

life-support ● adj. (of medical equipment) that keeps the body functioning after serious illness or injury.

life-threatening ● adj. potentially fatal.

lifetime ● n. the length of time that a person lives or a thing lasts.

Liffey E
/lif-fi/ a river of eastern Ireland, which flows from the Wicklow Mountains through Dublin and into the Irish Sea.

lift ● v. **1** raise or be raised to a higher position. **2** pick up and move to a different position. **3** formally end (a legal restriction). **4** (**lift off**) (of an aircraft, spacecraft, etc.) take off. ● n. **1** Brit. a platform or compartment housed in a shaft for raising and lowering people or things. **2** an act of lifting. **3** a free ride in another person's vehicle. **4** a device for carrying people up or down a mountain. **5** a feeling of increased cheerfulness. **6** upward force exerted by the air on an aerofoil or similar structure.
– PHRASES **not lift a finger** refuse to make the slightest effort.
– ORIGIN Old Norse.

lift-off ● n. the vertical take-off of a spacecraft, rocket, etc.

ligament /lig-uh-muhnt/ ● n. Anat. **1** a short band of tough, flexible tissue which connects two bones or cartilages or holds together a joint. **2** a structure that supports an organ and keeps it in position.
– ORIGIN Latin *ligamentum* 'bond'.

ligature /lig-uh-cher/ ● n. **1** a cord used to tie up a bleeding artery **2** Music a slur or tie.
– ORIGIN Latin *ligatura*.

Ligeti E
/lig-uh-ti/, György Sándor (b.1923), Hungarian composer. His orchestral works, such as *Apparitions*, dispense with the formal elements of melody, harmony, and rhythm.

light[1] ● n. **1** the natural form of energy that makes things visible. **2** a source of this. **3** a device producing a flame or spark. **4** an expression in someone's eyes. **5** understanding: *she saw light dawn on the woman's face.* **6** (**lights**) a person's opinions or standards. ● v. (**lights**, **lighting**, **lit**; past part. **lit** or **lighted**) **1** provide with light. **2** ignite or be ignited. ● adj. **1** having a considerable amount of light. **2** (of a colour or object) reflecting a lot of light; pale.
– PHRASES **bring** (or **come**) **to light** make (or become) widely known. **in (the) light of** taking (something) into consideration. **light at the end of the tunnel** an indication that a period of difficulty is ending. **light up 1** ignite a cigarette, pipe, or cigar before smoking it. **2** make or become lively or happy. **see the light** understand or realize something.
– ORIGIN Old English.

light[2] ● adj. **1** not heavy or heavy enough. **2** not strongly or heavily built. **3** relatively low in density, amount, or intensity. **4** carrying or suitable for small loads: *light commercial vehicles.* **5** gentle or delicate. **6** not serious. **7** (of sleep or a sleeper) easily disturbed.
– PHRASES **make light of** treat as unimportant.
– DERIVATIVES **lightly** adv. **lightness** n.
– ORIGIN Old English.

light[3] ● v. (**lights**, **lighting**, **lit** or **lighted**) (**light on/upon**) come upon or discover by chance.
– ORIGIN Old English, 'descend, alight'.

light bulb ● n. a glass bulb containing inert gas, which provides light when an electric current is passed through it.

lighten[1] ● v. **1** make or become lighter in weight. **2** make or become less serious.

lighten[2] ● v. make or become brighter.

lighter[1] ● n. a device producing a small flame, used to light cigarettes.

lighter[2] ● n. a flat-bottomed barge used to transfer goods to and from ships in harbour.
– ORIGIN German *luchter*.

light-fingered ● adj. prone to steal.

light-headed ● adj. dizzy and slightly faint.

light-hearted ● adj. amusing and entertaining.

light heavyweight ● n. a weight in boxing and other sports between middleweight and heavyweight.

lighthouse ● n. a tower or other structure containing a light to warn ships at sea.

light industry ● n. the manufacture of small or light articles.

lighting ● n. **1** equipment for producing light. **2** the arrangement or effect of lights.

lighting-up time ● n. Brit. the time at which motorists are required by law to switch their vehicles' lights on.

light meter ● n. an instrument measuring the intensity of light, used when taking photographs.

lightning ● n. the occurrence of a high-voltage electrical discharge between a cloud and the ground or within a cloud, accompanied by a bright flash. ● adj. very quick: *lightning speed.*
ORIGIN from LIGHTEN².

lightning conductor (also N. Amer. **lightning rod**) ● n. Brit. a metal rod or wire fixed in a high place to divert lightning into the ground.

light pen ● n. **1** Computing a hand-held pen-like device used for passing information to a computer. **2** a hand-held device for reading bar codes.

lights ● pl. n. the lungs of sheep, pigs, or bullocks as food for pets.
– ORIGIN from LIGHT² (because of their lightness).

lightweight ● n. **1** a weight in boxing and other sports between featherweight and welterweight. **2** informal a person of little importance: *a political lightweight.*

light year ● n. Astron. a unit of distance equivalent to the distance that light travels in one year, nearly 6 million million miles.

ligneous /lig-ni-uhss/ ● adj. consisting of or resembling wood.
– ORIGIN Latin *ligneus* 'relating to wood'.

lignin ● n. Bot. an organic substance deposited in the cell walls of many plants, making them rigid and woody.
– ORIGIN Latin *lignum* 'wood'.

lignite ● n. soft brownish coal.
– ORIGIN Latin *lignum* 'wood'.

likable ● adj. var. of LIKEABLE.

like[1] ● prep. **1** similar to. **2** in the manner of. **3** in a way appropriate to. **4** in this manner. **5** such as. ● conj. informal **1** in the same way that. **2** as if. ● n. (**the like**) things of the same kind. ● adj. having similar characteristics to another.
– PHRASES **and the like** et cetera.
– ORIGIN Old Norse.

USAGE like
When writing, do not use **like** to mean 'as if', as in *he's behaving like he owns the place*; you should use **as if** or **as though** instead.

like[2] ● v. (**likes**, **liking**, **liked**) **1** find agreeable or satisfactory. **2** wish for; want. ● n. (**likes**) the things one likes.
– ORIGIN Old English, 'be pleasing'.

likeable (also **likable**) ● adj. pleasant; easy to like.

likelihood ● n. the state of being likely.

likely ● adj. (**likelier**, **likeliest**) **1** probable. **2** promising: *a likely-looking spot.* ● adv. probably.

like-minded ● adj. having similar tastes or opinions.

liken ● v. (**liken to**) point out the resemblance of (someone or something) to.

likeness ● n. **1** resemblance. **2** outward appearance: *humans are made in God's likeness.* **3** a picture of a person.

likewise ● adv. **1** also; moreover. **2** similarly.

liking ● n. **1** a fondness for something. **2** one's taste: *just to his liking.*

lilac ● n. **1** a shrub or small tree with fragrant violet, pink, or white blossom. **2** a pale pinkish-violet colour.
– ORIGIN Persian, 'bluish'.

Lillee E
/*rhymes with* lily/, Dennis (Keith) (b.1949), Australian cricketer, who took 355 wickets in seventy test matches.

Lilliputian /lil-li-pyoo-sh'n/ ● adj. very small or unimportant.
– ORIGIN from the country of *Lilliput* in Jonathan Swift's *Gulliver's Travels*, inhabited by 6-inch high people.

lilo /ly-loh/ (also trademark **Li-lo**) ● n. (pl. **lilos**) an inflatable mattress used as a bed or for floating on water.
– ORIGIN from *lie low.*

Lilongwe E
/li-long-way/ the capital of Malawi.

lilt ● n. **1** a characteristic rising and falling of the voice when speaking. **2** a gentle rhythm in a tune. ● v. speak, sing, or sound with a lilt.
– ORIGIN unknown.

lily ● n. a plant with large trumpet-shaped flowers on a tall, slender stem.
– ORIGIN Greek *leirion*.

lily-livered ● adj. cowardly.

lily of the valley ● n. a plant of the lily family, with broad leaves and small white bell-shaped flowers.

lily pad ● n. a leaf of a water lily.

lily-white ● adj. **1** pure white. **2** totally innocent or pure.

Lima E
/lee-muh/ the capital of Peru.

limb ● n. **1** an arm, leg, or wing. **2** a large

branch of a tree. **3** a projecting part of a structure, object, or natural feature.
– PHRASES **out on a limb** isolated.
– DERIVATIVES **limbless** adj.
– ORIGIN Old English.

limber /*rhymes with* timber/ ● **adj.** supple; flexible. ● **v.** (**limbers**, **limbering**, **limbered**) (**limber up**) warm up in preparation for exercise or activity.
– ORIGIN perh. from *limber* in the dialect sense 'cart shaft'.

limbo[1] ● **n. 1** (in some Christian beliefs) the place between heaven and hell where the souls of people who have not been baptized go when they die. **2** an uncertain period of waiting.
– ORIGIN Latin *limbus* 'hem, limbo'.

limbo[2] ● **n.** (pl. **limbos**) a West Indian dance in which the dancer bends backwards to pass under a horizontal bar which is gradually lowered toward the ground.
– ORIGIN from LIMBER.

lime[1] ● **n.** quicklime, slaked lime, or any salt or alkali containing calcium.
– ORIGIN Old English.

lime[2] ● **n. 1** a rounded green citrus fruit similar to a lemon. **2** a bright light green colour.
– ORIGIN French.

lime[3] (also **lime tree**) ● **n.** a deciduous tree with heart-shaped leaves and yellowish blossom.
– ORIGIN Old English.

limekiln ● **n.** a kiln in which quicklime is produced.

limelight ● **n. 1** (**the limelight**) the focus of public attention. **2** a strong white light produced by heating lime, formerly used in theatres.

Limerick E
/**lim**-uh-rik/ a county in the west of the Republic of Ireland; county town, Limerick.

limerick ● **n.** a humorous five-line poem with a rhyme scheme *aabba*.
– ORIGIN said to be from the chorus 'will you come up to Limerick?', sung between verses at a party.

limestone ● **n.** a hard sedimentary rock composed mainly of calcium carbonate.

Limey ● **n.** (pl. **Limeys**) N. Amer. & Austral. informal, derog. a British person.
– ORIGIN from the former practice in the British navy of giving lime juice to sailors.

limit ● **n. 1** a point beyond which something does not or may not pass. **2** a restriction on the size or amount of something. **3** the furthest extent of one's endurance: *the horses were reaching their limit.* ● **v.** (**limits**, **limiting**, **limited**) put a limit on.
– PHRASES **off limits** out of bounds.
– DERIVATIVES **limitless** adj.
– ORIGIN Latin *limes* 'boundary'.

limitation ● **n. 1** a restriction. **2** a fault or failing.

limited ● **adj. 1** restricted in size, amount, or extent. **2** not great in ability.

limited company ● **n.** Brit. a private company whose owners have only a limited responsibility for its debts.

limn /lim/ ● **v.** literary depict or describe in painting or words.
– ORIGIN Latin *luminare* 'make light'.

Limoges E
/li-**mohzh**/ a city in west central France, noted for the production of porcelain.

limousine ● **n.** a large, luxurious car.
– ORIGIN French.

limp[1] ● **v. 1** walk with difficulty because of an injured leg or foot. **2** (of a damaged ship or aircraft) move with difficulty. ● **n.** a limping gait.
– ORIGIN from former *limphalt* 'lame'.

limp[2] ● **adj. 1** not stiff or firm. **2** without energy or will.
– DERIVATIVES **limply** adv.
– ORIGIN perh. from LIMP[1].

limpet ● **n.** a shellfish with a muscular foot for clinging tightly to rocks.
– ORIGIN Latin *lampreda*.

limpid ● **adj. 1** (of a liquid or the eyes) clear. **2** (of writing or music) clear or tuneful.
– ORIGIN Latin *limpidus*.

Limpopo E
/lim-**poh**-poh/ a river of SE Africa that rises near Johannesburg and flows in a curve to the north and east to meet the Indian Ocean in Mozambique.

linchpin (also **lynchpin**) ● **n. 1** a pin through the end of an axle keeping a wheel in position. **2** an extremely important person or thing.
– ORIGIN Old English.

Lincoln, E
Abraham (1809–65), American Republican statesman, 16th President of the US 1861–5. His election as President on an anti-slavery platform helped trigger the American Civil War; he was assassinated shortly after the war ended.

Lincolnshire E
/**ling**-k'n-sheer, **ling**-k'n-sher/ a county on the east coast of England; county town, Lincoln.

Lincs. ● **abbrev.** Lincolnshire.

linctus ● **n.** Brit. thick liquid cough medicine.
– ORIGIN Latin.

Lindbergh E
/**lind**-berg/, Charles (Augustus) (1902–74), American aviator, who in 1927 made the first solo transatlantic flight.

linden ● **n.** a lime tree.
– ORIGIN Old English.

Lindisfarne E
/**lin**-diss-farn/ a small island off the coast of Northumberland. It is the site of a church and monastery founded by St Aidan in 635. Also called **HOLY ISLAND**.

Lindsay, E
Sir Lionel (1874–1961), Australian art critic, watercolour painter, and graphic artist. His brother, **Norman** (1874–1969), was a graphic artist, painter, critic, and novelist.

line[1] ● **n. 1** a long, narrow mark or band. **2** a length of cord, wire, etc. **3** a row or series of people or things. **4** a row of written or printed words. **5** a direction, course, or channel: *lines of communication.* **6** a telephone connection. **7** a railway track or route. **8** an imaginary limit. **9** a series of military defences facing an enemy force. **10** a wrinkle in the skin. **11** the shape or outline of something. **12** a range of

commercial goods. **13** an area of activity: *their line of work.* **14** **(lines)** the words of an actor's part. **15** **(lines)** a number of repetitions of a sentence written out as a school punishment. ● v. **(lines, lining, lined) 1** stand or be positioned at intervals along. **2** **(line up)** arrange in a row. **3** **(line up)** have (someone or something) prepared. **4** **(lined)** marked or covered with lines.
– PHRASES **in line** under control. **in line for** likely to receive. **on the line** at serious risk. **out of line** informal behaving badly or wrongly.
– ORIGIN Old English.

line[2] ● v. **(lines, lining, lined)** cover the inner surface of (something) with a layer of different material.
– PHRASES **line one's pocket** make money by dishonest means.
– ORIGIN from former *line* 'flax'.

lineage /lin-i-ij/ ● n. ancestry or pedigree.

lineal /lin-i-uhl/ ● adj. **1** in a direct line of descent or ancestry. **2** linear.

lineaments /lin-i-uh-muhntz/ ● pl. n. literary the features of the face.
– ORIGIN Latin *lineamentum.*

linear /lin-i-er/ ● adj. **1** arranged in or extending along a straight line. **2** consisting of lines or outlines. **3** involving one dimension only. **4** progressing from one stage to another in a series of steps: *linear narrative.* **5** Math. able to be represented by a straight line on a graph.
– DERIVATIVES **linearity** n.

line dancing ● n. a type of country and western dancing in which a line of dancers follow a set pattern of steps.

line drawing ● n. a drawing based on the use of line rather than shading.

Lineker E
/lin-i-ker/, Gary (Winston) (b.1960), English footballer, who scored forty-eight goals for England, one short of Bobby Charlton's record.

linen ● n. **1** cloth woven from flax. **2** articles such as sheets or clothes made, or formerly made, of linen.
– ORIGIN Old English.

linen basket ● n. esp. Brit. a basket for dirty clothing.

liner[1] ● n. **1** a large passenger ship. [ORIGIN because such a ship travelled on a regular line or route.] **2** a cosmetic for outlining or emphasizing a facial feature.

liner[2] ● n. a lining of a garment, container, etc.

linesman ● n. **1** (in games played on a field or court) an official who assists the referee or umpire in deciding whether the ball is out of play. **2** Brit. a person who repairs telephone or electricity power lines.

line-up ● n. a group of people or things assembled for a particular purpose.

ling[1] ● n. a long-bodied edible sea fish of the cod family.
– ORIGIN prob. from Dutch.

ling[2] ● n. the common heather.
– ORIGIN Old Norse.

-ling ● suffix **1** forming nouns: *sapling.* **2** forming nouns indicating smallness: *gosling.*
– ORIGIN Old English.

linger ● v. **(lingers, lingering, lingered) 1** be slow or reluctant to leave. **2** **(linger over)** spend a long time over. **3** be slow to disappear or die.
– ORIGIN Germanic.

lingerie /lan-*zh*uh-ri/ ● n. women's underwear and nightclothes.
– ORIGIN French.

lingo ● n. (pl. **lingos** or **lingoes**) informal **1** a foreign language. **2** the jargon of a particular subject or group.
– ORIGIN prob. from Latin *lingua* 'tongue'.

lingua franca /ling-gwuh **frang**-kuh/ ● n. (pl. **lingua francas**) a language used as a common language between speakers whose native languages are different.
– ORIGIN Italian, 'Frankish tongue'.

linguine /ling-**gwee**-ni/ ● pl. n. small ribbons of pasta.
– ORIGIN Italian, 'little tongues'.

linguist ● n. **1** a person skilled in foreign languages. **2** a person who studies linguistics.
– ORIGIN Latin *lingua* 'language'.

linguistic ● adj. relating to language or linguistics. ● n. **(linguistics)** the scientific study of language.
– DERIVATIVES **linguistically** adv.

liniment ● n. an ointment rubbed on the body to relieve pain or bruising.
– ORIGIN Latin *linimentum.*

lining ● n. a layer of different material covering or attached to the inside of something.

link ● n. **1** a relationship or connection between people or things. **2** something that enables people to communicate. **3** a means of contact or transport between two places: *a satellite link.* **4** a loop in a chain. ● v. make or suggest a link with or between.
– ORIGIN Old Norse.

linkage ● n. **1** the action of linking. **2** a system of links.

links ● pl. n. a golf course, especially on grassland near the sea.
– ORIGIN Old English, 'rising ground'.

link-up ● n. **1** an instance of two or more people or things linking. **2** a connection enabling people or machines to communicate with each other.

Linnaeus E
/li-**nee**-uhss, li-**nay**-uhss/, Carolus (1707–78, Latinized name of *Carl von Linné*). Swedish botanist. His work in devising classification systems for flowering plants and animals formed the basis for modern systematic botany and zoology.
– DERIVATIVES **Linnaean** (also **Linnean**) adj. & n.

linnet ● n. a mainly brown and grey finch with a reddish breast and forehead.
– ORIGIN Old French *linette.*

lino ● n. (pl. **linos**) informal, esp. Brit. linoleum.

linocut ● n. a design carved in a block of linoleum, used for printing.

linoleum /li-**noh**-li-uhm/ ● n. a floor covering consisting of a canvas backing thickly coated with a preparation of linseed oil and powdered cork.
– ORIGIN from Latin *linum* 'flax' + *oleum* 'oil'.

linseed ● n. the seeds of the flax plant.
– ORIGIN Old English.

linseed oil ● n. oil extracted from linseed, used in paint and varnish.

lint • n. **1** short, fine fibres which separate from cloth or yarn during processing. **2** Brit. a fabric used for dressing wounds.
– ORIGIN perh. from Old French *linette* 'linseed'.

lintel • n. a horizontal support across the top of a door or window.
– ORIGIN Old French.

lion • n. (fem. **lioness**) **1** a large tawny-coloured cat of Africa and NW India, the male of which has a shaggy mane. **2** a brave, strong, or fierce person.
– PHRASES **the lion's share** the largest part.
– ORIGIN Old French *liun*.

lionize (also **lionise**) • v. (**lionizes**, **lionizing**, **lionized**) treat as a celebrity.

lip • n. **1** either of the two fleshy parts forming the edges of the mouth opening. **2** the edge of a hollow container or an opening. **3** informal cheeky talk.
– PHRASES **bite one's lip** stop oneself from laughing or saying something.
– ORIGIN Old English.

lipase /lip-ayz/ • n. an enzyme produced by the pancreas that promotes the breakdown of fats.
– ORIGIN Greek *lipos* 'fat'.

lip gloss • n. a glossy cosmetic applied to the lips.

lipid /lip-id/ • n. Chem. any of a class of fats that are insoluble in water.
– ORIGIN Greek *lipos* 'fat'.

liposuction /lip-oh-suk-sh'n/ • n. a technique in cosmetic surgery for removing excess fat from under the skin by suction.

lippy • adj. informal cheeky.

lip-read • v. understand speech from watching a speaker's lip movements.
– DERIVATIVES **lip-reader** n.

lip salve • n. Brit. a preparation to prevent or relieve sore or chapped lips.

lipstick • n. coloured cosmetic applied to the lips from a small solid stick.

lip-sync • v. (**lip-syncs**, **lip-syncing**, **lip-synced**) move one's lips in time to pre-recorded music or speech.

liquefy /lik-wi-fy/ • v. (**liquefies**, **liquefying**, **liquefied**) make or become liquid.
– DERIVATIVES **liquefaction** n.
– ORIGIN Latin *liquefacere*.

liqueur /li-kyoor/ • n. a strong, sweet flavoured alcoholic spirit.
– ORIGIN French.

liquid • n. a substance that flows freely but remains at a constant volume, such as water or oil. • adj. **1** relating to or being a liquid. **2** clear, like water: *looking into those liquid dark eyes.* **3** (of a sound) pure and flowing. **4** not fixed or stable. **5** (of assets) held in or easily converted into cash.
– ORIGIN Latin *liquidus*.

liquidate • v. (**liquidates**, **liquidating**, **liquidated**) **1** wind up the affairs of (a company) by determining what it owns and what it owes. **2** convert (assets) into cash. **3** pay off (a debt). **4** informal kill.
– ORIGIN Latin *liquidare* 'make clear'.

liquid crystal display • n. an electronic visual display in which the application of an electric current to a liquid crystal layer makes it no longer transparent.

liquidity /li-kwid-i-ti/ • n. the availability of liquid assets to a market or company.

liquidize (also **liquidise**) • v. (**liquidizes**, **liquidizing**, **liquidized**) Brit. convert (solid food) into a liquid or purée.

liquidizer (also **liquidiser**) • n. Brit. a machine for liquidizing.

liquid measure • n. a unit for measuring the volume of liquids.

liquor /lik-er/ • n. **1** alcoholic drink, especially spirits. **2** liquid that has been produced in or used for cooking.
– ORIGIN Latin.

liquorice /lik-uh-riss, lik-uh-rish/ (US **licorice**) • n. a sweet black substance made from the juice of a root and used as a sweet and in medicine.
– ORIGIN Old French *licoresse*.

lira /leer-uh/ • n. (pl. **lire** /leer-uh, leer-ay/) the basic unit of money of Turkey and formerly also of Italy.
– ORIGIN Italian.

Lisbon E
the capital of Portugal.

lisp • n. a speech defect in which *s* is pronounced like *th* in *thick* and *z* is pronounced like *th* in *this*. • v. speak with a lisp.
– ORIGIN Old English.

lissom (also **lissome**) • adj. slim, supple, and graceful.
– ORIGIN from LITHE + -SOME[1].

list[1] • n. a number of connected items or names written as a series. • v. **1** make a list of. **2** include in a list.
– ORIGIN French *liste*.

list[2] • v. (of a ship) lean over to one side. • n. an instance of listing.
– ORIGIN unknown.

listed • adj. (of a building in the UK) officially named as being of historical importance and so protected.

listen • v. **1** give one's attention to a sound. **2** make an effort to hear something. **3** (**listen in**) listen to a private conversation. **4** respond to advice or a request. • n. an act of listening.
– DERIVATIVES **listener** n.
– ORIGIN Old English, 'pay attention to'.

Lister, E
Joseph, 1st Baron (1827–1912), English surgeon, pioneer of antiseptic techniques in surgery.

listeria /li-steer-i-uh/ • n. a type of bacterium which infects humans and other animals through contaminated food.
– ORIGIN named after Joseph LISTER.

listing • n. **1** a list or catalogue. **2** an entry in a list.

listless • adj. lacking energy or enthusiasm.
– DERIVATIVES **listlessly** adv. **listlessness** n.
– ORIGIN from archaic *list* 'desire'.

list price • n. the price of an article as listed by the manufacturer.

Liszt E
/*rhymes with* list/, Franz (1811–86), Hungarian composer and pianist. A key figure in the romantic movement, his compositions include many piano works and twelve symphonic poems (a form which he invented).

lit past and past part. of LIGHT[1], LIGHT[3].

litany /lit-uh-ni/ ● n. (pl. **litanies**) **1** a series of prayers to God used in church services. **2** a boring recital.
– ORIGIN Greek *litaneia* 'prayer'.

liter ● n. US = **LITRE**.

literacy ● n. the ability to read and write.

literal ● adj. **1** being the usual or most basic sense of a word. **2** (of a translation) representing the exact words of the original text.
– ORIGIN Latin *litera* 'letter of the alphabet'.

literally ● adv. **1** in a literal way or sense. **2** informal used for emphasis (rather than to suggest literal truth).

literary ● adj. **1** having to do with literature. **2** (of language) typical of or suitable for literary works or formal writing.
– ORIGIN Latin *litera* 'letter of the alphabet'.

literate ● adj. **1** able to read and write **2** knowledgeable in a particular field: *computer literate*.

literati /li-tuh-rah-ti/ ● pl. n. educated people who are interested in literature.
– ORIGIN Latin.

literature ● n. **1** written works that are regarded as having artistic merit. **2** books and writings on a particular subject. **3** leaflets used to give information.

lithe /ly*th*/ ● adj. slim, supple, and graceful.
– ORIGIN Old English, 'gentle, meek'.

lithium /lith-i-uhm/ ● n. a silver-white metallic chemical element.
– ORIGIN Greek *lithos* 'stone'.

lithograph /li-thuh-grahf/ ● n. a print made by lithography.

lithography /li-thog-ruh-fi/ ● n. the process of printing from a flat metal surface treated so as to repel the ink except where it is required for printing.
– ORIGIN Greek *lithos* 'stone'.

Lithuania E
/lith-yoo-ay-ni-uh/ a country on the SE shore of the Baltic sea; capital, Vilnius.
– DERIVATIVES **Lithuanian** adj. & n.

litigant ● n. a person involved in a lawsuit.

litigate /lit-i-gayt/ ● v. (**litigates**, **litigating**, **litigated**) take a dispute or claim to a law court.
– DERIVATIVES **litigation** n.
– ORIGIN Latin *litigare*.

litigious /li-ti-juhss/ ● adj. having a tendency to go to law to settle disputes.

litmus /lit-muhss/ ● n. a dye that is red under acid conditions and blue under alkaline conditions.
– ORIGIN from Old Norse words meaning 'dye' and 'moss'.

litmus paper ● n. paper stained with litmus, used to test for acids or alkalis.

litmus test ● n. a reliable test of value or truth.

litotes /ly-toh-teez/ ● n. understatement in which something is expressed by the negative of its opposite (e.g. *I shan't be sorry* for *I shall be glad*).
– ORIGIN Greek.

litre (US **liter**) ● n. a metric unit of capacity equal to 1,000 cubic centimetres (about 1.75 pints).
– ORIGIN French.

litter ● n. **1** rubbish left in a public place. **2** an untidy collection of things. **3** a number of young born to an animal at one time. **4** (also **cat litter**) absorbent material lining a tray for a cat to urinate and defecate in indoors. **5** straw used as animal bedding. **6** (also **leaf litter**) decomposing leaves forming a layer on top of soil. **7** hist. a vehicle containing a bed or seat enclosed by curtains and carried by men or animals. ● v. (**litters**, **littering**, **littered**) make untidy with scattered articles.
– ORIGIN Old French *litiere*.

little ● adj. **1** small in size, amount, or degree. **2** (of a person) young or younger. **3** short in time or distance. ● det. & pron. **1** (**a little**) a small amount of. **2** (**a little**) a short time or distance. **3** not much. ● adv. (**less**, **least**) **1** (**a little**) to a small extent. **2** hardly or not at all.
– ORIGIN Old English.

Little Bear E
the constellation Ursa Minor.

little end ● n. the smaller end of the connecting rod in a piston engine, attached to the piston.

Little Englander ● n. informal a person opposed to an international role or policy for Britain.

little finger ● n. (in phr. **twist someone around one's little finger**) be able to make someone do whatever one wants.

little people ● pl. n. fairies or leprechauns.

littoral /lit-tuh-ruhl/ ● adj. relating to the shore of the sea or a lake.
– ORIGIN Latin *littoralis*.

Littré E
/lit-tray/, Émile (1801–81), French lexicographer and positivist philosopher. He was the author of the major *Dictionnaire de la langue française*.

liturgical /li-tur-ji-k'l/ ● adj. relating to liturgy.

liturgy /lit-er-ji/ ● n. (pl. **liturgies**) a set form of public worship used in the Christian Church.
– ORIGIN Greek *leitourgia*.

live[1] /liv/ ● v. (**lives**, **living**, **lived**) **1** remain alive. **2** be alive at a particular time. **3** spend one's life in a particular way: *they are living in fear*. **4** make one's home in a place or with a person. **5** (**live in/out**) reside at (or away from) the place where one works or studies. **6** supply oneself with the means of staying alive: *they live by hunting and fishing*.
– PHRASES **live down** succeed in making others forget (something embarrassing). **live off** (or **on**) **1** depend on as a source of income or support. **2** eat as a major part of one's diet. **live rough** live outdoors as a result of being homeless.
– ORIGIN Old English.

live[2] /lyv/ ● adj. **1** living. **2** (of a musical performance) played in front of an audience. **3** (of a broadcast) transmitted at the time of occurrence. **4** of interest and importance: *a live issue*. **5** (of a wire or device) connected to a source of electric current. **6** (of ammunition or explosive) able to explode. ● adv. as an actual event or performance: *the match will be televised live*.
– ORIGIN from **ALIVE**.

liveable (US also **livable**) ● adj. **1** fit to live in.

2 worth living.

lived-in ● adj. (of a room or building) showing comforting signs of wear and use.

live-in ● adj. **1** (of a domestic employee) living in an employer's house. **2** living with another in a sexual relationship: *his live-in girlfriend.*

livelihood ● n. a means of obtaining the necessities of life.
– ORIGIN Old English, 'way of life'.

livelong /liv-long/ ● adj. literary (of a period of time) entire.

lively ● adj. (**livelier**, **liveliest**) **1** full of life and energy. **2** (of a place) full of activity. **3** mentally quick or active.
– DERIVATIVES **liveliness** n.

liven ● v. (**liven up**) make or become more lively or interesting.

liver ● n. **1** a large organ in the abdomen that produces bile. **2** an animal's liver as food.
– ORIGIN Old English.

Liverpool[1] E
a city and seaport in NW England, at the mouth of the River Mersey.

Liverpool[2], E
Robert Banks Jenkinson, 2nd Earl of (1770–1828), British Tory statesman, Prime Minister 1812–27.

Liverpudlian /li-ver-**pud**-li-uhn/ ● n. a person from the city of Liverpool. ● adj. relating to Liverpool.
– ORIGIN from **LIVERPOOL**[1] + **PUDDLE**.

liver sausage ● n. a savoury meat paste in the form of a sausage containing cooked liver, or a mixture of liver and pork.

liver spot ● n. a small brown spot on the skin.

livery ● n. (pl. **liveries**) **1** a special uniform worn by a servant, an official, or a member of a City Company. **2** a distinctive design and colour scheme used on the vehicles or products of a company.
– DERIVATIVES **liveried** adj.
– ORIGIN first meaning 'the giving of food or clothing to servants': from Old French *livree* 'delivered'.

lives pl. of **LIFE**.

livestock ● n. farm animals.

live wire ● n. informal an energetic and lively person.

livid ● adj. **1** informal furiously angry. **2** having a dark inflamed appearance.
– ORIGIN Latin *lividus.*

living ● n. **1** a way or style of life. **2** an income which is enough to live on, or the means of earning it. ● adj. **1** alive. **2** (of a language) still used. **3** for daily life: *living quarters.*

living room ● n. a room in a house for general everyday use.

Livingstone, E
David (1813–73), Scottish missionary and explorer. He was the first European to discover the Zambezi River (1851) and the Victoria Falls (1855). In 1866 he went in search of the source of the Nile, and was found by Sir Henry Morton Stanley in 1871.

living wage ● n. a wage which is high enough to maintain a normal standard of living.

living will ● n. a written statement of a person's wishes regarding their medical treatment should they become too ill to give consent.

Livy E
/li-vi/ (59 BC–AD 17; Latin name *Titus Livius*), Roman historian, known for his history of Rome from its foundation to his own time.

Lizard E
a promontory in SW England, in Cornwall. Its southern tip is the southernmost point of the British mainland.

lizard ● n. a four-legged reptile with a long body and tail and a rough or spiny skin.
– ORIGIN Old French *lesard.*

Ljubljana E
/lyoo-bli-**ah**-nuh/ the capital of Slovenia.

'll ● contr. shall; will.

llama /**lah**-muh/ ● n. a domesticated animal of the camel family found in the Andes.
– ORIGIN Spanish.

Llandudno E
/lan-**did**-noh, hlan-**did**-noh/ a resort town in Conwy, northern Wales.

Llewelyn E
/loo-**el**-lin, hloo-**el**-lin/ (d.1282; also known as **Llywelyn ap Gruffydd**), prince of Gwynedd in North Wales. He proclaimed himself prince of all Wales in 1258 and was recognized as such by Henry III. However, his refusal to pay homage to Edward I led the latter to invade Wales (1277–84).

Llosa, E
Mario Vargas, see **VARGAS LLOSA**.

Lloyd George, E
David, 1st Earl Lloyd George of Dwyfor (1863–1945), British Liberal statesman, Prime Minister 1916–22. As Chancellor of the Exchequer (1908–15), he introduced old-age pensions (1908) and national insurance (1911).

Lloyd's Register E
(in full **Lloyd's Register of Shipping**) a classified list of merchant ships over a certain tonnage, published annually in London.

Lloyd Webber, E
Andrew, Baron Lloyd-Webber of Sydmonton (b.1948), English composer. His many musicals, several of them written in collaboration with the lyricist Sir Tim Rice, include *Jesus Christ Superstar, Cats,* and *The Phantom of the Opera.*

Llywelyn ap Gruffydd E
/hloo-el-lin ap **grif**-*fith*/ see **LLEWELYN**.

lo ● exclam. archaic used to draw attention to an interesting event.

loach /lohch/ ● n. a small freshwater fish with several long, thin growths near the mouth.
– ORIGIN Old French *loche.*

load ● n. **1** a heavy or bulky thing being or about to be carried. **2** a weight or source of pressure. **3** the total number or amount carried in a vehicle or container. **4** (**a load/loads of**) informal a lot of. **5** the amount of work to be done by a person or machine. ● v. **1** put a load on or in. **2** place (a load or large

quantity) on or in a vehicle or container. **3** insert (something) into a device so that it will operate. **4** put ammunition into (a firearm).
– ORIGIN Old English.

loaded ● adj. **1** carrying a load. **2** biased towards a particular outcome. **3** having an underlying meaning: *a loaded question.* **4** informal wealthy.

loaf[1] ● n. (pl. **loaves**) a quantity of bread that is shaped and baked in one piece.
– ORIGIN Old English.

loaf[2] ● v. idle one's time away.
– ORIGIN prob. from **LOAFER**.

loafer ● n. **1** a person who idles their time away. **2** trademark a flat casual leather shoe.
– ORIGIN perh. from German *Landläufer* 'tramp'.

loam ● n. a fertile soil of clay and sand containing humus.
– DERIVATIVES **loamy** adj.
– ORIGIN Old English, 'clay'.

loan ● n. **1** a sum of money that is lent to someone. **2** the action of lending something. ● v. give as a loan.
– ORIGIN Old Norse.

loan shark ● n. informal a moneylender who charges very high rates of interest.

loath /lohth/ (also **loth**) ● adj. reluctant; unwilling: *I was loath to leave.*
– ORIGIN Old English, 'hostile'.

loathe /loh*th*/ ● v. (**loathes**, **loathing**, **loathed**) feel hatred or disgust for.
– ORIGIN Old English.

loathsome ● adj. causing hatred or disgust.

loaves pl. of **LOAF**[1]

lob ● v. (**lobs**, **lobbing**, **lobbed**) throw or hit in a high arc. ● n. (in soccer or tennis) a ball lobbed over an opponent.
– ORIGIN prob. from German or Dutch.

lobby ● n. (pl. **lobbies**) **1** a meeting or waiting area inside the entrance of a public building. **2** (also **division lobby**) each of two corridors in the Houses of Parliament to which MPs go to vote. **3** a group of people who try to influence politicians on a particular issue. ● v. (**lobbies**, **lobbying**, **lobbied**) try to influence (a politician) on an issue.
– DERIVATIVES **lobbyist** n.
– ORIGIN Latin *lobia* 'covered walk'.

lobe ● n. **1** a roundish and flattish part that hangs down or projects from something. **2** each of the sections of the main part of the brain.
– DERIVATIVES **lobed** adj.
– ORIGIN Greek *lobos*.

lobelia /luh-bee-li-uh/ ● n. a garden plant with blue or scarlet flowers.
– ORIGIN named after the Flemish botanist Matthias de *Lobel* (1538–1616).

lobotomy /luh-bot-uh-mi/ ● n. (pl. **lobotomies**) a surgical operation involving cutting into part of the brain, formerly used to treat mental illness.

lobster ● n. a large edible shellfish with large pincers.
– ORIGIN Old English.

lobster pot ● n. a basket-like trap in which lobsters are caught.

local ● adj. **1** relating to a particular area or to the area in which one lives: *the local post office.* **2** affecting a particular part of the body: *a local anaesthetic.* **3** Computing (of a device) that can be accessed without the use of a network. ● n. **1** a person who lives in a particular area. **2** Brit. informal a pub near to a person's home.
– DERIVATIVES **locally** adv.
– ORIGIN Latin *locus* 'place'.

local area network ● n. a computer network that links devices within a building or group of buildings.

local authority ● n. Brit. a group of people responsible for local government.

locale /loh-kahl/ ● n. a place where something happens.
– ORIGIN French *local* 'locality'.

local government ● n. the administration of a particular county or district, with representatives elected by those who live there.

locality ● n. (pl. **localities**) **1** an area or neighbourhood. **2** the position or site of something.

localize (also **localise**) ● v. (**localizes**, **localizing**, **localized**) restrict to a particular place.
– DERIVATIVES **localization** (also **localisation**) n.

local time ● n. time as reckoned in a particular region or time zone.

locate ● v. (**locates**, **locating**, **located**) **1** discover the exact place or position of. **2** (**be located**) be situated in a particular place.
– ORIGIN Latin *locare* 'to place'.

location ● n. **1** a place where something is located. **2** the action of locating. **3** an actual place in which a film or broadcast is made, as distinct from in a studio.
– DERIVATIVES **locational** adj.

loc. cit. ● abbrev. in the passage already mentioned.
– ORIGIN Latin *loco citato*.

loch /lokh/ ● n. (in Scotland) a lake or a narrow strip of sea almost surrounded by land.
– ORIGIN Scottish Gaelic.

> **Loch Ness** E
> a deep lake in NW Scotland, which is 38 km (24 miles) long, with a maximum depth of 230 m (755 ft). It is said to be the home of a large creature, the **Loch Ness Monster**.

loci pl. of **LOCUS**.

lock[1] ● n. **1** a mechanism for keeping a door or container fastened, operated by a key. **2** a similar device used to prevent a vehicle or other machine from operating. **3** a short section of a canal or river with gates at each end which can be opened or closed to change the water level and so raise and lower boats. **4** (in wrestling and martial arts) a hold that prevents an opponent from moving a limb. ● v. **1** fasten with a lock. **2** shut in or keep safe by locking a door. **3** (**lock up/away**) imprison. **4** make or become fixed or immovable. **5** (**be locked in**) be deeply involved in: *they were locked in a legal battle.*
– PHRASES **lock, stock, and barrel** including everything.
– DERIVATIVES **lockable** adj.
– ORIGIN Old English.

lock[2] ● n. **1** a section of a person's hair that coils or hangs in a piece. **2** (**locks**) literary a person's hair.
– ORIGIN Old English.

l

Locke, John (1632–1704), English philosopher. He was an empiricist, arguing in *An Essay concerning Human Understanding* that all knowledge is based on human experience. A political liberal, he believed that the authority of rulers is limited.
– DERIVATIVES **Lockean** adj.

locker • n. a small lockable cupboard or compartment where belongings may be left.

locket • n. a small ornamental case worn round a person's neck on a chain, used to hold an item such as a tiny photograph.
– ORIGIN Old French *locquet* 'small lock'.

lockjaw • n. a form or sign of tetanus in which the jaws become stiff and tightly closed.

lockout • n. a situation in which an employer refuses to allow employees to enter their place of work until they agree to certain conditions.

locksmith • n. a person who makes and repairs locks.

lock-up • n. **1** a makeshift jail. **2** Brit. a garage or small shop separate from living quarters, that can be locked up.

loco[1] • n. (pl. **locos**) informal a locomotive.

loco[2] • adj. informal crazy.
– ORIGIN Spanish.

locomotion • n. movement or the ability to move from one place to another.
– ORIGIN from Latin *loco* 'from a place' + *motio* 'motion'.

locomotive • n. a powered railway vehicle used for pulling trains. • adj. relating to locomotion.

locum /loh-kuhm/ • n. a doctor or priest standing in for another who is temporarily away.
– ORIGIN from Latin *locum tenens* 'one holding a place'.

locus /loh-kuhss/ • n. (pl. **loci** /loh-sy/) **1** tech. a particular position, point, or place. **2** Math. a curve or other figure formed by all the points satisfying a particular condition.
– ORIGIN Latin.

locust • n. a large tropical grasshopper which migrates in vast swarms, destroying all the vegetation in an area.
– ORIGIN Latin *locusta*.

locution /luh-kyoo-sh'n/ • n. **1** a word or phrase. **2** a person's particular style of speech.
– ORIGIN Latin.

lode /*rhymes with* rode/ • n. a vein of metal ore in the earth.
– ORIGIN Old English, 'way, course'.

lodestar • n. the pole star.

lodestone • n. a piece of magnetic iron ore used as a magnet.

lodge • n. **1** a small house at the gates of a large house with grounds, occupied by an employee. **2** a porter's quarters at the entrance of a college or other large building. **3** a small country house where people stay while hunting, shooting, etc. **4** a branch of an organization such as the Freemasons. **5** a beaver's den. • v. (**lodges**, **lodging**, **lodged**) **1** formally present (a complaint, appeal, etc.). **2** fix or be fixed in a place. **3** rent accommodation in another person's house. **4** (**lodge in/with**) leave (something valuable) for safekeeping in (a place) or with (someone).
– ORIGIN Old French *loge* 'hut'.

lodger • n. a person who pays rent to live in a property with the owner.

lodging • n. **1** temporary accommodation. **2** (**lodgings**) a rented room or rooms in the same house as the owner.

lodging house • n. a private house providing rented accommodation.

loess /loh-iss/ • n. a loose, fine soil, originally deposited by the wind.
– ORIGIN Swiss German *lösch* 'loose'.

lo-fi (also **low-fi**) • adj. having to do with sound reproduction of a lower quality than hi-fi.
– ORIGIN from LOW[1] + *-fi* on the pattern of *hi-fi*.

loft • n. **1** a room or storage space directly under the roof of a house or other building. **2** a large, open living area in a converted warehouse or other large building. **3** a gallery in a church or hall. • v. kick, hit, or throw (a ball) high into the air.
– ORIGIN Old Norse, 'air, upper room'.

lofty • adj. (**loftier**, **loftiest**) **1** tall and impressive. **2** morally good; noble: *lofty ideals.* **3** haughty and aloof.
– DERIVATIVES **loftily** adv.

log[1] • n. **1** a part of the trunk or a large branch of a tree that has fallen or been cut off. **2** (also **logbook**) an official record of events during the voyage of a ship or aircraft. • v. (**logs**, **logging**, **logged**) **1** enter (facts) in a log. **2** achieve (a certain distance, speed, or time). **3** (**log in/on** or **out/off**) begin (or finish) using a computer system. **4** cut down (an area of forest) to use the wood commercially.
– DERIVATIVES **logger** n.
– ORIGIN unknown.

log[2] • n. a logarithm.

Logan, Mount a mountain in SW Yukon Territory, Canada. Rising to 6,054 m (19,850 ft), it is the highest peak in Canada and the second-highest peak in North America.

loganberry • n. an edible red soft fruit, similar to a large raspberry.
– ORIGIN named after the American horticulturalist John H. *Logan* (1841–1928).

logarithm /log-uh-ri-*th*uhm/ • n. one of a series of numbers, representing the power to which a fixed number (the base) must be raised to produce a given number, used to simplify calculations.
– DERIVATIVES **logarithmic** adj.
– ORIGIN from Greek *logos* 'reckoning, ratio' + *arithmos* 'number'.

logbook • n. **1** a log of a ship or aircraft. **2** Brit. an official document recording details about a vehicle and its owner.

loggerheads • pl. n. (in phr. **at loggerheads**) in strong disagreement.
– ORIGIN from dialect *logger* 'block of wood for hobbling a horse' + HEAD.

loggia /loh-ji-uh/ • n. a gallery with one or more open sides, especially one facing a garden.
– ORIGIN Italian, 'lodge'.

logic • n. **1** the science of reasoning. **2** good reasoning: *the strategy has a certain logic to it.* **3** an underlying system or set of principles

used in preparing a computer or electronic device to perform a specified task.
– DERIVATIVES **logician** n.
– ORIGIN from Greek *logikē tekhnē* 'art of reason'.

logical ● adj. **1** following the rules of logic. **2** showing clear, sound reasoning. **3** expected or reasonable under the circumstances: *a bridge is the logical choice.*
– DERIVATIVES **logically** adv.

-logical ● comb. form forming adjectives from nouns ending in *-logy* (such as *biological* from *biology*).
– DERIVATIVES **-logic** comb. form.

logistic /luh-jiss-tik/ ● adj. relating to logistics. ● n. (**logistics**) the detailed organization of a large and complex exercise.
– DERIVATIVES **logistical** adj.
– ORIGIN French *logistique* 'movement and supply of troops and equipment'.

logjam ● n. a situation that seems unable to be settled; a deadlock.

logo /loh-goh/ ● n. (pl. **logos**) a design or symbol chosen by an organization to identify its products.
– ORIGIN Greek *logos* 'word'.

-logy ● comb. form forming words referring to: **1** (also **-ology**) a subject of study or interest: *psychology.* **2** a type of writing or speech: *trilogy.*
– ORIGIN Greek *logos* 'word'.

loin ● n. **1** the part of the body on both sides of the spine between the lowest ribs and the hip bones. **2** a joint of meat from the back of this part of an animal. **3** (**loins**) literary a person's sexual organs.
– ORIGIN Old French *loigne.*

loincloth ● n. a piece of cloth wrapped round the hips, worn by men in some hot countries.

Loire E
/lwar/ a river of west central France, which rises in the Massif Central and flows 1,015 km (630 miles) north and west to the Bay of Biscay. It is France's longest river.

loiter ● v. (**loiters, loitering, loitered**) stand around without any obvious purpose.
– DERIVATIVES **loiterer** n.
– ORIGIN perh. from Dutch *loteren* 'wag about'.

loll ● v. **1** sit, lie, or stand in a lazy, relaxed way. **2** hang loosely: *he let his head loll back.*

lollipop ● n. a large, flat, rounded boiled sweet on the end of a stick.
– ORIGIN perh. from dialect *lolly* 'tongue' + **POP**[1].

lollipop lady (or **lollipop man**) ● n. Brit. informal a person employed to help children cross the road safely by holding up a circular sign on a pole to stop the traffic.

lollop ● v. (**lollops, lolloped, lolloping**) move in a series of clumsy bounding steps.
– ORIGIN prob. from **LOLL** and **TROLLOP**.

lolly ● n. (pl. **lollies**) Brit. informal **1** a lollipop. **2** money.

Lomé E
/loh-may/ the capital and chief port of Togo.

Lomond, Loch E
/loh-muhnd/ a lake in west central Scotland, the country's largest freshwater lake.

London E
the capital of the United Kingdom, situated on the River Thames.
– DERIVATIVES **Londoner** n.

Londonderry E
one of the Six Counties of Northern Ireland; chief town, Londonderry (also called **Derry**).

lone ● adj. **1** having no companions; solitary. **2** lacking the support of others: *I am certainly not a lone voice.*
– ORIGIN from **ALONE**.

lonely ● adj. (**lonelier, loneliest**) **1** sad because one has no friends or company. **2** spent alone: *lonely days.* **3** (of a place) remote.
– DERIVATIVES **loneliness** n.

lonely hearts ● pl. n. people looking for a lover or friend through the personal columns of a newspaper.

loner ● n. a person who prefers to be alone.

lonesome ● adj. esp. N. Amer. lonely.

long[1] ● adj. (**longer, longest**) **1** having a great length in space or time. **2** having or lasting a particular length, distance, or time: *the ship will be 150 metres long.* **3** (of a drink) large and refreshing. **4** (of odds in betting) reflecting a low level of probability. **5** (of a vowel) pronounced in a way that takes longer than a short vowel in the same position (e.g. in standard British English the vowel /oo/ in *food*). **6** (**long on**) informal well supplied with. ● n. a long time. ● adv. (**longer, longest**) **1** for a long time. **2** at a distant time: *long ago.* **3** throughout a specified period of time: *all day long.*
– PHRASES **as** (or **so**) **long as** provided that. **in the long run** (or **term**) eventually. **the long and the short of it** in brief; essentially. **long in the tooth** rather old.
– ORIGIN Old English.

long[2] ● v. (**long for/to do**) have a strong wish for or to do.
– ORIGIN Old English, 'grow long, yearn'.

long. ● abbrev. longitude.

Long Beach E
a port and resort in California, situated south of Los Angeles.

longboat ● n. **1** hist. the largest boat carried by a sailing ship. **2** = **LONGSHIP**.

longbow ● n. hist. a large bow drawn by hand.

long-distance ● adj. travelling or operating between distant places. ● adv. between distant places.

long division ● n. the process of dividing one number by another with all calculations written down.

longe ● n. var. of **LUNGE** (in sense 2).

longevity /lon-jev-i-ti/ ● n. long life.
– ORIGIN Latin *longaevitas.*

long face ● n. an unhappy or disappointed expression.

Longfellow, E
Henry Wadsworth (1807–82), American poet, known for 'The Wreck of the Hesperus' and *The Song of Hiawatha.*

Longford E
a county of the Republic of Ireland; county town, Longford.

l

longhand ● n. ordinary handwriting (as opposed to shorthand, typing, or printing).

long haul ● n. **1** a long distance over which goods or passengers are transported. **2** a long and difficult task.

longing ● n. a strong wish to do or have something.
– DERIVATIVES **longingly** adv.

Long Island E
an island on the coast of New York State. Its western tip, comprising the New York districts of Brooklyn and Queens, is linked to Manhattan by the Brooklyn Bridge.

longitude /long-i-tyood/ ● n. the distance of a place east or west of the Greenwich meridian, measured in degrees.
– ORIGIN Latin *longitudo*.

longitudinal /long-i-tyoo-di-n'l/ ● adj. **1** extending lengthwise. **2** relating to longitude.
– DERIVATIVES **longitudinally** adv.

long johns ● pl. n. informal underpants with closely fitted legs reaching to the ankles.

long jump ● n. an athletic event in which competitors jump as far as possible along the ground in one leap.

long-life ● adj. (of food or drink) treated so as to stay fresh for longer than usual.

long-playing ● adj. (of a record) 12 inches (about 30 cm) in diameter and designed to rotate at 33⅓ revolutions per minute.

long-range ● adj. **1** able to travel long distances. **2** relating to a period of time far into the future.

longship ● n. a long, narrow warship with oars and a sail, used by the Vikings.

longshore ● adj. relating to or moving along the seashore.
– ORIGIN from *along shore*.

long shot ● n. a scheme or guess that has only the slightest chance of succeeding or being accurate.

long-sighted ● adj. unable to see things clearly if they are close to the eyes.

long-standing ● adj. having existed for a long time.

long-suffering ● adj. bearing problems or annoying behaviour with patience.

long wave ● n. a radio wave of a wavelength above one kilometre (and a frequency below 300 kilohertz).

longways ● adv. lengthways.

long-winded ● adj. long and boring.

loo ● n. Brit. informal a toilet.
– ORIGIN uncertain.

loofah /loo-fuh/ ● n. a long rough object used like a bath sponge, consisting of the dried inner parts of a tropical fruit.
– ORIGIN Egyptian Arabic.

look ● v. **1** direct one's gaze in a particular direction. **2** give the impression of being: *her father looked unhappy.* **3** face in a particular direction: *the rooms look out over the harbour.* ● n. **1** an act of looking. **2** appearance. **3** (**looks**) a person's facial appearance. **4** a style or fashion.
– PHRASES **look after** take care of. **look at** think of in a specified way. **look down on** (also **look down one's nose at**) think that one is better than. **look for** try to find. **look in** make a short visit. **look into** investigate. **look on** watch without getting involved. **look out 1** be alert for possible trouble. **2** Brit. search for and produce (something). **look to** rely on (someone) to do something. **look up 1** improve. **2** search for and find (a piece of information) in a reference work. **3** informal visit or contact (a friend). **look up to** have a great deal of respect for.
– ORIGIN Old English.

lookalike ● n. a person who looks very similar to another.

looker ● n. informal a person with a specified appearance: *she's not a bad looker.*

look-in ● n. informal a chance to take part in something.

looking glass ● n. a mirror.

lookout ● n. **1** a place from which to keep watch. **2** a person keeping watch for danger or trouble. **3** (**one's lookout**) Brit. informal one's own concern.
– PHRASES **be on the lookout** (or **keep a lookout**) **for 1** be alert to. **2** keep searching for.

loom[1] ● n. a machine for weaving cloth.
– ORIGIN Old English, 'tool'.

loom[2] ● v. **1** appear as a vague and threatening shape: *vehicles loomed out of the darkness.* **2** (of an unfavourable event) seem about to happen.
– ORIGIN prob. from German or Dutch.

loony informal ● n. (pl. **loonies**) a mad or silly person. ● adj. (**loonier**, **looniest**) mad or silly.
– ORIGIN from LUNATIC.

loop ● n. **1** a shape produced by a curve that bends round and crosses itself. **2** an endless strip of tape or film allowing sounds or images to be continuously repeated. **3** a complete circuit for an electric current. **4** Computing a programmed sequence of instructions that is repeated until or while a particular condition is satisfied. ● v. **1** form into a loop or loops: *she looped her arms around his neck.* **2** follow a course that forms a loop or loops.
– PHRASES **loop the loop** (of an aircraft) fly in a vertical circle.
– ORIGIN unknown.

loophole ● n. an inexact wording or mistake in a law or contract that enables someone to avoid doing something.
– ORIGIN from former *loop* 'opening in a wall'.

loopy ● adj. (**loopier**, **loopiest**) informal mad or silly.

loose /looss/ ● adj. **1** not firmly or tightly fixed in place. **2** not fastened or packaged together. **3** not tied up or shut in: *the horses broke loose.* **4** (of a garment) not fitting tightly. **5** not dense or compact in structure. **6** not strict; inexact: *a loose interpretation.* **7** careless and indiscreet: *loose talk.* **8** dated immoral. ● v. (**looses**, **loosing**, **loosed**) **1** unfasten or set free. **2** (**loose off**) fire (a shot, bullet, etc.).
– PHRASES **on the loose** having escaped from being shut in or tied up.
– DERIVATIVES **loosely** adv. **looseness** n.
– ORIGIN Old Norse.

USAGE loose
Do not confuse the words **loose** and **lose**; **loose** means 'not fixed in place or tied up' (*a loose tooth*), while **lose** means 'no longer have' or 'become unable to find' (*I need to lose about a stone*).

loose box ● n. Brit. a stable or stall in which a

horse is kept without a tether.

loose cannon • n. a person who behaves in a way that is unexpected and that may cause harm.

loose end • n. a detail that is not yet settled or explained.
– PHRASES **be at a loose end** have nothing definite to do.

loose forward • n. Rugby a forward who plays at the back of the scrum.

loose-leaf • adj. (of a folder) allowing sheets of paper to be added or removed.

loosen • v. **1** make or become loose. **2** (**loosen up**) warm up in preparation for an activity.

loot • n. **1** private property taken from an enemy in war or stolen by thieves. **2** informal money. • v. **1** steal (goods) during a war or riot. **2** steal goods from (a place) during a war or riot.
– DERIVATIVES **looter** n.
– ORIGIN Sanskrit.

lop • v. (**lops, lopping, lopped**) **1** cut off (a branch or limb) from a tree or body. **2** informal make smaller or less by (a particular amount).
– DERIVATIVES **lopper** n.
– ORIGIN unknown.

lope • v. (**lopes, loping, loped**) run with a long bounding stride. • n. a long bounding stride.
– ORIGIN Old Norse, 'leap'.

lop-eared • adj. (of an animal) having drooping ears.
– ORIGIN from former *lop* 'hang loosely'.

lopsided • adj. with one side lower or smaller than the other.

loquacious /luh-kway-shuhss/ • adj. talkative.
– ORIGIN Latin *loqui* 'to talk'.

loquacity /luh-kwass-i-ti/ • n. the quality of being talkative.

Lorca E
/lor-kuh/, Federico García (1898–1936), Spanish poet and dramatist. His plays include the intense tragedies *Blood Wedding* and *The House of Bernada Alba*.

lord • n. **1** a nobleman. **2** (**Lord**) a title given to certain British peers or high officials: *Lord Derby*. **3** (**the Lords**) the House of Lords. **4** a master or ruler. **5** (**Lord**) a name for God or Christ.
– PHRASES **lord it over** act in an arrogant and bullying way towards. **the Lord's Prayer** the prayer taught by Christ to his disciples.
– ORIGIN Old English, 'bread-keeper'.

Lord Chamberlain • n. (in the UK) the official in charge of the royal household.

Lord Chancellor • n. the highest judge in the United Kingdom and Speaker of the House of Lords.

Lord Chief Justice • n. the second highest judge in the United Kingdom.

Lord Lieutenant • n. (in the UK) the representative of the Queen and head of magistrates in each county.

lordly • adj. (**lordlier, lordliest**) suitable for or like a lord.

Lord Mayor • n. the title of the mayor in London and some other large cities.

Lord Privy Seal • n. (in the UK) a senior cabinet minister without particular official duties.

Lord's E
a cricket ground in north London, headquarters of the MCC.

Lordship • n. (**His/Your** etc. **Lordship**) a form of address to a judge, bishop, or nobleman.

Lords spiritual • pl. n. the bishops in the House of Lords.

Lords temporal • pl. n. the members of the House of Lords other than the bishops.

lore • n. a body of traditions and knowledge on a subject: *farming lore*.
– ORIGIN Old English, 'instruction'.

Loren E
/luh-ren/, Sophia (b.1934; born *Sofia Scicolone*), Italian actress, known for such films as *The Millionairess* and *El Cid*.

Lorenzo de' Medici E
/luh-ren-zoh/ (1449–92), Italian statesman and scholar. A patron of the arts and humanist learning, he supported Botticelli, Leonardo da Vinci, and Michelangelo among others.

lorgnette /lor-nyet/ (also **lorgnettes**) • n. a pair of glasses or opera glasses held by a long handle at one side.
– ORIGIN French.

Lorraine, Claude E
see **CLAUDE LORRAINE**.

lorry • n. (pl. **lorries**) Brit. a large, heavy motor vehicle for transporting goods.
– ORIGIN perh. from the man's name *Laurie*.

Los Alamos E
/loss al-uh-moss/ a town in northern New Mexico. It has been a centre for nuclear research since the 1940s, when it was the site of the development of the first atomic and hydrogen bombs.

Los Angeles E
/los an-juh-leez/ a city on the Pacific coast of southern California, the second-largest city in the US.

lose /looz/ • v. (**loses, losing, lost**) **1** have (something or someone) taken away from one; no longer have or keep: *she lost her job in a hotel*. **2** become unable to find. **3** fail to win (a game or contest). **4** earn less (money) than one is spending. **5** waste (time or an opportunity). **6** (**be lost**) be destroyed or killed. **7** escape from. **8** (**lose oneself in/be lost in**) be or become deeply involved in. **9** (of a watch or clock) become slow by (a specified amount of time).
– PHRASES **lose heart** become discouraged. **lose out** not get a full chance or advantage.
– ORIGIN Old English.

USAGE lose
For an explanation on the difference between **lose** and **loose**, see the note at **LOOSE**.

loser • n. **1** a person or thing that loses or has lost. **2** informal a person who is generally unsuccessful in life.

losing battle • n. a struggle in which failure seems certain.

loss • n. **1** the fact or action of losing some-

thing or someone. **2** a person, thing, or amount lost. **3** the feeling of sadness after losing a valued person or thing. **4** a person or thing that is badly missed when lost.
– PHRASES **at a loss** uncertain or puzzled.
– ORIGIN Old English, 'destruction'.

loss-leader • **n.** a product sold at a loss to attract customers.

lost past and past part. of **LOSE**.
– PHRASES **be lost for words** be so surprised or upset that one cannot think what to say. **be lost on** fail to be understood by: *the irony is lost on him.*

lost cause • **n.** something that has no chance of success.

Lot [E]
(in the Bible) the nephew of Abraham, who was allowed to escape from the destruction of Sodom. His wife, who disobeyed orders and looked back, was turned into a pillar of salt.

lot • **pron. & adv.** informal (**a lot** or **lots**) a large number or amount. • **n. 1** an item or set of items for sale at an auction. **2** informal a group of people or things: *you lot think you're clever.* **3** a method of deciding something by chance, especially by choosing one from a number of pieces of paper. **4** a person's situation in life: *schemes to improve the lot of the poor.* **5** esp. N. Amer. a plot of land.
– PHRASES **draw** (or **cast**) **lots** decide by lot. **the lot** esp. Brit. the whole number or quantity. **throw in one's lot with** decide to share the fate of.
– ORIGIN Old English.

USAGE lot
Although **a lot of** and **lots of** are often used in speech, it is better not to use them when writing; use **many** or **a large number** instead.
The correct spelling is **a lot**; do not spell it as one word (**alot**).

loth • **adj.** var. of **LOATH**.

Lothario /luh-**thair**-i-oh/ • **n.** (pl. **Lotharios**) a man who behaves selfishly in his sexual relationships.
– ORIGIN from a character in Nicholas Rowe's play *The Fair Penitent* (1703).

lotion • **n.** a creamy liquid put on the skin as a medicine or cosmetic.
– ORIGIN Latin.

lottery • **n.** (pl. **lotteries**) **1** a means of raising money by selling numbered tickets and giving prizes to the holders of numbers drawn at random. **2** something whose success is controlled by luck.
– ORIGIN prob. from Dutch *loterij*.

lotus • **n. 1** a kind of large water lily. **2** (in Greek mythology) a fruit that causes dreamy forgetfulness.
– ORIGIN Greek *lōtos*.

lotus position • **n.** a cross-legged position for meditation, with the feet resting on the thighs.

louche /loosh/ • **adj.** having a bad reputation but still attractive: *his louche, creepy charm.*
– ORIGIN French, 'squinting'.

loud • **adj. 1** producing much noise. **2** expressed forcefully: *loud protests.* **3** very bright and lacking good taste: *a loud checked suit.* • **adv.** with much noise.
– PHRASES **out loud** aloud.
– DERIVATIVES **loudly** adv. **loudness** n.
– ORIGIN Old English.

loudhailer • **n.** esp. Brit. an electronic device for making the voice louder.

loudmouth • **n.** informal a person who talks too much or who makes offensive remarks.

loudspeaker • **n.** a device that converts electrical impulses into sound.

lough /lokh/ • **n.** (in Ireland) a loch.

Louis [E]
/*rhymes with* Lewis/, Joe (1914–81; born *Joseph Louis Barrow*; known as the **Brown Bomber**), American boxer, who was heavyweight champion of the world 1937–49.

Louis XIV [E]
/**loo**-i/ (1638–1715; known as **the Sun King**), king of France 1643–1715. His reign represented the high point of French power in Europe and the period also saw a flowering of French literature and art.

Louis XVI [E]
/**loo**-i/ (1754–93), king of France 1774–92. His minor concessions and reforms in the face of the emerging French Revolution proved disastrous. As the Revolution became more extreme, he was executed with his wife, Marie Antoinette.

Louisiana [E]
/loo-ee-zi-**an**-uh/ a state in the southern US, on the Gulf of Mexico; capital, Baton Rouge.
– DERIVATIVES **Louisianan** adj. & n.

Louisiana Purchase [E]
the territory sold by France to the US in 1803, comprising the western part of the Mississippi valley and including the modern state of Louisiana.

Louis Philippe [E]
/loo-i fi-**leep**/ (1773–1850), king of France 1830–48. His reign was undermined by radical discontent and he abdicated in 1848.

lounge • **v.** (**lounges**, **lounging**, **lounged**) lie, sit, or stand in a relaxed way. • **n. 1** Brit. a sitting room. **2** a room in a hotel, theatre, or airport in which to relax or wait.
– ORIGIN unknown.

lounge bar • **n.** Brit. a bar in a pub or hotel that is more comfortable or smarter than the public bar.

lounger • **n. 1** an outdoor chair that allows a person to lie back. **2** a person spending their time lazily.

lounge suit • **n.** Brit. a man's suit for ordinary day wear.

lour /*rhymes with* flour/ (also **lower**) • **v.** (of the sky) look dark and threatening.
– ORIGIN unknown.

Lourdes [E]
/**loo**-erd/ a town in SW France, at the foot of the Pyrenees. It has been a major place of Roman Catholic pilgrimage since 1858, when a peasant girl, Marie Bernarde Soubirous (St Bernadette), claimed to have seen visions of the Virgin Mary.

Lourenço Marques [E]
/luh-ren-soh **marks**/ former name for **MAPUTO**.

louse • n. **1** (pl. **lice**) a small insect which lives as a parasite on animals or plants. **2** (pl. **louses**) informal an unpleasant person. • v. (**louses**, **lousing**, **loused**) (**louse up**) informal spoil (something).
– ORIGIN Old English.

lousy • adj. (**lousier**, **lousiest**) **1** informal very poor or bad. **2** infested with lice.

lout • n. a rude or aggressive man or boy.
– DERIVATIVES **loutish** adj.
– ORIGIN perh. from Old English, 'bow down'.

Louth E
/*rhymes with* mouth/ a county on the east coast of the Republic of Ireland; county town, Dundalk.

Louvre E
/loo-vruh/ the principal museum and art gallery of France, in Paris.

louvre /loo-ver/ (US also **louver**) • n. each of a set of slanting slats fixed at intervals in a door, shutter, or cover to allow air or light through.
– ORIGIN Old French *lover* 'skylight'.

lovable (also **loveable**) • adj. giving rise to love or affection.

lovage /luv-ij/ • n. a herb with leaves that are used in cookery.
– ORIGIN Old French *luvesche*.

love • n. **1** a strong feeling of affection. **2** a strong feeling of affection linked with sexual attraction. **3** a great interest and pleasure in something. **4** a person or thing that one loves. **5** (in tennis, squash, etc.) a score of zero. • v. (**loves**, **loving**, **loved**) **1** feel love for. **2** like very much.
– PHRASES **make love** have sexual intercourse.
– DERIVATIVES **loveless** adj.
– ORIGIN Old English.

love affair • n. a romantic or sexual relationship between two people who are not married to each other.

love bite • n. a temporary red mark on the skin caused by biting or sucking during sexual play.

love child • n. a child born to parents who are not married to each other.

Lovelock, E
James (Ephraim) (b.1919), English scientist, best known for the **Gaia hypothesis**, first presented by him in 1972.

lovelorn • adj. unhappy because of loving someone who does not return one's love.
– ORIGIN from LOVE + a former word meaning 'lost'.

lovely • adj. (**lovelier**, **loveliest**) **1** very beautiful. **2** informal very pleasant.
– DERIVATIVES **loveliness** n.

love nest • n. informal a private place where two lovers spend time together.

lover • n. **1** a person having a sexual or romantic relationship with another. **2** a person who enjoys a specified thing: *a music lover.*

lovesick • adj. pining or feeling weak due to being in love.

low[1] • adj. **1** not high or tall or far above the ground. **2** below average in amount, extent, or strength: *cook over a low heat.* **3** lacking importance or quality; inferior. **4** (of a sound) deep or quiet. **5** depressed or lacking energy. **6** unfavourable. **7** lacking moral principles: *low cunning.* • n. **1** a low point, level or figure. **2** an area of low atmospheric pressure. • adv. **1** at or into a low position or state. **2** (of a sound) at a low pitch.
– ORIGIN Old Norse.

low[2] • v. (of a cow) moo.
– ORIGIN Old English.

lowbrow • adj. informal, derog. not intellectual or interested in culture.

Low Church • n. the part of the Church of England that places comparatively little emphasis on ritual and the authority of bishops and priests.

Low Countries E
the region of NW Europe comprising the Netherlands, Belgium, and Luxembourg.

low-down informal • adj. unfair or dishonest. • n. (**the low-down**) the important facts about something.

Lowell E
/loh-uhl/, Robert (Traill Spence) (1917–77), American poet. His work is notable for its intense confessional nature and for its complex imagery.

lower[1] • adj. **1** less high. **2** (of a geological period or formation) earlier: *the Lower Cretaceous.* **3** (in place names) situated to the south. • v. (**lowers**, **lowering**, **lowered**) **1** make or become lower. **2** move downwards. **3** (**lower oneself**) behave in a way that is humiliating.
– DERIVATIVES **lowermost** adj.

lower[3] • v. & n. var. of LOUR.

lower case • n. small letters as opposed to capitals.

lower class • n. the working class.

lower house (also **lower chamber**) • n. the larger body of a parliament with two chambers, usually with elected members.

lowest common denominator • n. Math. the lowest common multiple of the denominators of several fractions.

lowest common multiple • n. Math. the lowest quantity that is a multiple of two or more given quantities.

low-fi • adj. var. of LO-FI.

low frequency • n. (in radio) 30–300 kilohertz.

low gear • n. a gear that causes a vehicle to move slowly.

low-key • adj. not elaborate or showy; modest.

lowland /loh-luhnd/ • n. **1** (also **lowlands**) low-lying country. **2** (**the Lowlands**) the part of Scotland lying south and east of the Highlands.
– DERIVATIVES **lowlander** n.

low-level • adj. Computing (of a programming language) similar to machine code in form.

low life • n. dishonest or immoral people or activities.

lowly • adj. (**lowlier**, **lowliest**) low in status or importance: *a lowly admin assistant.*

low-lying • adj. (of land) not far above sea level.

low-rise • adj. (of a building) having few storeys.

Lowry E
/low-ri/, L. S. (1887–1976; full name *Laurence Stephen Lowry*), English painter, known for his paintings of small matchstick figures set against industrial urban landscapes.

low season • n. Brit. the least popular time of year for a holiday, when prices are lowest.

low tide (also **low water**) • n. the state of the tide when at its lowest level.

low-water mark • n. the level reached by the sea at low tide.

loyal • adj. firm and constant in one's support for a person, one's country, etc.
– DERIVATIVES **loyally** adv.
– ORIGIN Old French *loial*.

loyalist • n. **1** a person who remains loyal to the established ruler or government. **2** (**Loyalist**) a supporter of union between Great Britain and Northern Ireland.
– DERIVATIVES **loyalism** n.

loyalty • n. (pl. **loyalties**) **1** the state of being loyal. **2** a strong feeling of support.

lozenge /loz-inj/ • n. **1** a diamond-shaped figure. **2** a small tablet of medicine that is sucked to soothe a sore throat.
– ORIGIN Old French *losenge*.

LP • abbrev. long-playing (record).

L-plate • n. Brit. a sign with the letter L on it, attached to a vehicle to indicate that the driver is a learner.

LSD • n. lysergic acid diethylamide, a powerful drug that causes hallucinations.

Lt • abbrev. Lieutenant.

Ltd • abbrev. Brit. (after a company name) Limited.

Luanda E
/loo-an-duh/ the capital of Angola.

lubricant • n. a substance, e.g. oil or grease, for lubricating part of a machine.

lubricate /loo-bri-kayt/ • v. (**lubricates, lubricating, lubricated**) apply oil or grease to (machinery) so that it moves easily.
– DERIVATIVES **lubrication** n.
– ORIGIN Latin *lubricare* 'make slippery'.

lubricious /loo-bri-shuhss/ • adj. referring to sexual matters in a rude or offensive way; lewd.

Lucan E
/loo-k'n/ (AD 39–65; Latin name *Marcus Annaeus Lucanus*), Roman poet, author of the epic poem *Pharsalia*, dealing with the civil war between Julius Caesar and Pompey.

Lucas, E
George (Walton) (b.1944), American film director, producer, and screenwriter, who wrote and directed the science-fiction film *Star Wars* and its sequels.

lucent /loo-suhnt/ • adj. literary shining.
– ORIGIN Latin *lucere* 'shine'.

lucerne /loo-sern/ • n. = ALFALFA.
– ORIGIN Provençal *luzerno* 'glow-worm'.

Lucerne, Lake E
/loo-sern/ a lake in central Switzerland.

lucid /loo-sid/ • adj. **1** easy to understand; clear. **2** showing an ability to think clearly.
– DERIVATIVES **lucidity** n. **lucidly** adv.
– ORIGIN Latin *lucidus* 'bright'.

Lucifer /loo-si-fer/ • n. **1** the Devil. **2** (**lucifer**) archaic a match.
– ORIGIN Latin, 'light-bringing'.

luck • n. **1** good or bad things that happen by chance. **2** good fortune.
– PHRASES **try one's luck** attempt something risky. **worse luck** informal unfortunately.
– ORIGIN German *lucke*.

luckily • adv. it is fortunate that.

luckless • adj. unlucky; unfortunate.

Lucknow E
/luk-now/ a city in northern India, capital of the state of Uttar Pradesh.

lucky • adj. (**luckier, luckiest**) having, bringing, or resulting from good luck: *he had a lucky escape*.

lucky dip • n. Brit. a game in which small prizes are concealed in a container for people to pick out at random.

lucrative /loo-kruh-tiv/ • adj. making a large profit.
– ORIGIN Latin *lucrativus*.

lucre /loo-ker/ • n. literary money.
– ORIGIN Latin *lucrum*.

Lucretius E
/loo-kree-shuhss/ (*c.*94–*c.*55 BC), Roman poet and philosopher, known for his long poem *On the Nature of Things*.

Luddite /lud-dyt/ • n. a person opposed to new technology.
– ORIGIN perh. named after Ned *Lud*, one of the workers who in 1811–6 destroyed machinery which they thought was threatening their jobs.

ludicrous /loo-di-kruhss/ • adj. absurd; ridiculous.
– DERIVATIVES **ludicrously** adv.
– ORIGIN Latin *ludicrus*.

ludo • n. Brit. a board game in which players move counters according to throws of a dice.
– ORIGIN Latin, 'I play'.

luff • v. steer (a sailing ship) nearer the wind.
– ORIGIN Old French *lof*.

lug[1] • v. (**lugs, lugging, lugged**) carry or drag with great effort.
– ORIGIN prob. Scandinavian.

lug[2] • n. **1** Brit. informal an ear. **2** a projection on an object by which it may be carried or fixed in place.
– ORIGIN prob. Scandinavian.

luge /loozh/ • n. a light toboggan ridden in a sitting or lying position.
– ORIGIN Swiss French.

luggage • n. suitcases or other bags for a traveller's belongings.
– ORIGIN from LUG[1].

lugger • n. a small ship with two or three masts and a four-sided sail on each.

lugubrious /luu-goo-bri-uhss/ • adj. sad and dismal.
– ORIGIN Latin *lugubris*.

lugworm • n. a worm living in muddy sand by the sea, used as fishing bait.
– ORIGIN unknown.

Luke, St E
an evangelist, closely associated with St Paul and traditionally the author of the third Gospel and the Acts of the Apostles. Feast day, 18 October.

lukewarm • adj. **1** only slightly warm. **2** un-

enthusiastic.
– ORIGIN from dialect *luke* 'tepid'.

lull ● v. **1** calm or send to sleep with soothing sounds or movements. **2** cause (someone) to feel safe or confident, even if they are at risk of something bad. **3** calm (doubts, fears, etc.) by deception. ● n. a quiet period of between times of activity.

lullaby ● n. (pl. **lullabies**) a soothing song sung to send a child to sleep.

Lully E
/*rhymes with* fully/, Jean-Baptiste (1632–87), French composer, born in Italy. His operas, which include *Alceste* and *Armide*, mark the beginning of the French operatic tradition.

lumbago /lum-bay-goh/ ● n. pain in the lower back.
– ORIGIN Latin.

lumbar /lum-ber/ ● adj. relating to the lower back.
– ORIGIN Latin *lumbaris*.

lumber ● n. **1** esp. Brit. disused articles of furniture that take up space. **2** esp. N. Amer. timber sawn into rough planks. ● v. (**lumbers**, **lumbering**, **lumbered**) **1** Brit. informal give (someone) an unwanted responsibility. **2** move in a slow awkward way.

lumberjack (also **lumberman**) ● n. a person who fells trees, cuts them into logs, or transports them.

lumen /loo-muhn/ ● n. Physics the SI unit of flux of light.
– ORIGIN Latin, 'light'.

Lumière E
/loo-mi-air/, Auguste Marie Louis Nicholas (1862–1954) and Louis Jean (1864–1948), French pioneers of cinema, who patented a combined cine camera and projector in 1895.

luminary /loo-mi-nuh-ri/ ● n. (pl. **luminaries**) a person who inspires or influences others: *sporting luminaries.*

luminescence /loo-mi-ness-uhnss/ ● n. the production of light by a substance that has not been heated, as in fluorescence.
– DERIVATIVES **luminescent** adj.

luminosity ● n. the quality of being luminous.

luminous /loo-mi-nuhss/ ● adj. **1** bright or shining, especially in the dark. **2** Physics relating to visible light.
– ORIGIN Latin *luminosus*.

lump[1] ● n. **1** an irregularly shaped piece of something hard or solid. **2** a swelling under the skin. ● v. treat as alike, without regard for differences: *for analysis, all data were lumped together.*
– PHRASES **a lump in the throat** a feeling of tightness in the throat caused by strong emotion.
– ORIGIN perh. Germanic.

lump[2] ● v. (**lump it**) informal put up with something whether one likes it or not.

lumpectomy ● n. (pl. **lumpectomies**) a surgical operation in which a tumour or other lump is removed from the breast.

lumpen ● adj. **1** lumpy and misshapen. **2** stupid or loutish.
– ORIGIN German *Lumpen* 'rag, rogue'.

lumpish ● adj. stupid and slow.

lump sum ● n. a single payment made at one time, as opposed to a number of smaller payments on several occasions.

lumpy ● adj. (**lumpier**, **lumpiest**) full of or covered with lumps.

lunacy ● n. **1** insanity (not in technical use). **2** great stupidity.

lunar /loo-ner/ ● adj. having to do with or like the moon: *a lunar landscape.*
– ORIGIN Latin *luna* 'moon'.

lunar eclipse ● n. an eclipse in which the moon passes into the earth's shadow.

lunar month ● n. a month measured between one new moon and the next (roughly 29½ days).

lunatic ● n. **1** a person who is mentally ill (not in technical use). **2** a very foolish person.
– ORIGIN Latin *luna* 'moon' (from the former belief that changes of the moon caused insanity).

lunatic fringe ● n. a small section of a political group with extreme or eccentric views.

lunch ● n. a meal eaten in the middle of the day. ● v. eat lunch.
– DERIVATIVES **luncher** n.
– ORIGIN from **LUNCHEON**.

luncheon ● n. formal lunch.
– ORIGIN perh. from Spanish *lonja* 'slice'.

luncheon meat ● n. minced cooked pork mixed with cereal, sold in a tin.

luncheon voucher ● n. Brit. a voucher given to employees, that can be exchanged for food at restaurants and shops.

lung ● n. each of the pair of organs within the ribcage of humans and most vertebrates, into which air is drawn in breathing.
– DERIVATIVES **lungful** n.
– ORIGIN Old English.

lunge ● n. **1** a sudden forward movement of the body. **2** (also **longe**) a long rein on which a horse is made to move in a circle round its trainer. ● v. (**lunges**, **lunging** or **lungeing**, **lunged**) make a sudden forward movement of the body.
– ORIGIN French *allonger* 'lengthen'.

lupin /loo-pin/ (also **lupine** /loo-pin/) ● n. a plant with a tall stem bearing many small colourful flowers.
– ORIGIN Latin *lupinus*.

lupine /loo-pyn/ ● adj. having to do with a wolf or wolves.
– ORIGIN Latin *lupinus*.

lurch[1] ● n. a sudden unsteady movement. ● v. make a sudden unsteady movement.
– ORIGIN unknown.

lurch[2] ● n. (in phr. **leave in the lurch**) leave (someone) in a difficult situation without help or support.
– ORIGIN French *lourche*, a game resembling backgammon.

lurcher ● n. Brit. a dog that is a cross between a greyhound and a retriever, collie, or sheepdog.
– ORIGIN related to **LURK**.

lure /lyoor/ ● v. (**lures**, **luring**, **lured**) tempt to do something. ● n. **1** a type of bait used in fishing or hunting. **2** the attractive qualities of something: *the lure of the city.*
– ORIGIN Old French *luere*.

lurex /lyoo-reks/ ● n. trademark yarn or fabric containing a glittering metallic thread.
– ORIGIN unknown.

lurid /lyoor-id/ ● adj. **1** unpleasantly bright in

colour. **2** (of a description) deliberately containing vivid and shocking material.
– DERIVATIVES **luridly** adv.
– ORIGIN Latin *luridus* 'pale yellow'.

lurk ● v. wait in hiding so as to attack someone or something.
– DERIVATIVES **lurker** n.
– ORIGIN perh. from **LOUR**.

Lusaka E
/loo-**sah**-kuh/ the capital of Zambia.

luscious ● adj. **1** having a pleasingly rich, sweet taste. **2** (of a woman) sexually attractive.
– ORIGIN perh. from **DELICIOUS**.

lush[1] ● adj. **1** (of plants) growing thickly and strongly. **2** rich or luxurious: *lush bedlinen.*
– DERIVATIVES **lushly** adv. **lushness** n.
– ORIGIN perh. from Old French *lasche* 'lax'.

lush[2] ● N. Amer. informal a drunkard.
– ORIGIN perh. from **LUSH**[1].

lust ● n. **1** strong sexual desire. **2** a passionate desire for something. ● v. feel lust for someone or something.
– ORIGIN Old English.

lustful ● adj. filled with strong sexual desire.

lustre (US **luster**) ● n. **1** a soft glow or shine. **2** prestige or honour: *a celebrity player added lustre to the line-up.*
– ORIGIN French.

lustrous ● adj. having lustre; shining.

lusty ● adj. (**lustier**, **lustiest**) healthy and strong; vigorous.
– DERIVATIVES **lustily** adv.

lute ● n. a stringed instrument having a long neck and a rounded body with a flat front, played by plucking.
– ORIGIN Old French *lut.*

lutenist /loo-tuh-nist/ ● n. a lute player.

lutetium /loo-tee-shi-uhm/ ● n. a rare silvery-white metallic chemical element of the lanthanide series.
– ORIGIN Latin *Lutetia*, the ancient name of Paris.

Luther E
/**loo**-ther/, Martin (1483–1546), German Protestant theologian, the leading figure of the German Reformation. He preached the doctrine of justification by faith (the belief that people are freed from sin by their faith in God rather than by their good actions) and attacked papal authority. He was excommunicated in 1521.

Lutheran ● n. a member of the Lutheran Church, a Protestant Church based on the beliefs of Martin Luther. ● adj. relating to the teachings of Martin Luther or to the Lutheran Church.

Luthuli E
/loo-**too**-li/ (also **Lutuli**), Albert John (*c.*1898–1967), South African political leader. His presidency of the African National Congress (1952–60) was marked by a programme of civil disobedience.

Lutosławski E
/loo-tuh-**swahf**-ski/, Witold (1913–94), Polish composer, noted for his orchestral music.

Lutyens E
/**lut**-yuhnz/, Sir Edwin (Landseer) (1869–1944), English architect, known for his country houses in a romantic domestic style. He is also designed the layout of New Delhi and the Cenotaph in London.

lux /luks/ ● n. (pl. **lux**) the SI unit of illumination.
– ORIGIN Latin, 'light'.

Luxembourg E
/**luk**-suhm-berg/ a country in western Europe, an independent duchy situated between Belgium, Germany, and France; capital, Luxembourg.
– DERIVATIVES **Luxembourger** n.

Luxor E
/**luk**-sor/ a city in eastern Egypt, on the east bank of the Nile. It is the site of the southern part of ancient Thebes and contains many important ruins.

luxuriant /lug-*zh*oor-i-uhnt/ ● adj. (of vegetation or hair) growing thickly and strongly.
– DERIVATIVES **luxuriance** n. **luxuriantly** adv.
– ORIGIN Latin *luxuriare* 'grow very thickly'.

luxuriate /lug-*zh*oor-i-ayt/ ● v. (**luxuriates**, **luxuriating**, **luxuriated**) (**luxuriate in/over**) take pleasure in (something) enjoyable.

luxurious ● adj. **1** very comfortable, elegant, and expensive. **2** giving pleasure to the senses: *a luxurious scented bath.*
– DERIVATIVES **luxuriously** adv.

luxury ● n. (pl. **luxuries**) **1** comfortable and expensive living or surroundings: *a life of luxury.* **2** an item that is expensive and enjoyable but not essential.
– ORIGIN Latin *luxuria* 'lechery'.

Luzon E
/loo-**zon**/ the most northerly and the largest island in the Philippines.

LVO ● abbrev. Lieutenant of the Royal Victorian Order.

-ly ● suffix **1** having the qualities of: *brotherly.* **2** recurring at intervals of: *hourly.* **3** forming adverbs from adjectives: *greatly.*
– ORIGIN Old English.

Lyallpur E
/ly-uhl-**poor**/ former name for **FAISALABAD**.

lychee /ly-chee/ ● n. a small rounded fruit with sweet white flesh and thin rough skin.
– ORIGIN Chinese.

lychgate /**lich**-gayt/ ● n. a roofed gateway to a churchyard.
– ORIGIN Old English, 'body' (referring to the former practice of using such a gateway to shelter a coffin before burial).

Lycra /ly-kruh/ ● n. trademark a synthetic elastic fibre or fabric used for close-fitting clothing.
– ORIGIN unknown.

Lydia E
/**lid**-i-uh/ an ancient region of western Asia Minor.

lye ● n. a strongly alkaline solution used for washing or cleansing.

– ORIGIN Old English.

Lyell E
/ly-uhl/, Sir Charles (1797–1875), Scottish geologist. His view that the earth had been shaped over a long period of time by natural processes cleared the way for Darwin's theory of evolution.

lying[1] pres. part. of LIE[1].

lying[2] pres. part. of LIE[2].

lymph /limf/ ● n. a colourless fluid containing white blood cells, which bathes the tissues of the body.
– ORIGIN Latin *lympha*, *limpa* 'water'.

lymphatic /lim-fat-ik/ ● adj. relating to lymph or its production.

lymphatic system ● n. the network of vessels through which lymph drains from the tissues into the blood.

lymph node (also **lymph gland**) ● n. each of a number of small swellings in the lymphatic system where lymph is filtered and lymphocytes are formed.

lymphocyte /lim-fuh-syt/ ● n. a type of small white blood cell with a single round nucleus.

lymphoma /lim-foh-muh/ ● n. (pl. **lymphomas** or **lymphomata** /lim-foh-muh-tuh/) cancer of the lymph nodes.

Lynch, E
David (b.1946), American film and television director, known for films such as *Blue Velvet* and the television series *Twin Peaks*.

lynch ● v. (of a group) kill (someone) for an alleged crime without a legal trial, especially by hanging.
– ORIGIN named after Captain William *Lynch* of Virginia, who set up his own court of justice *c.*1780.

lynchpin ● n. var. of LINCHPIN.

Lynn, E
Dame Vera (b.1917; born *Vera Margaret Lewis*), English singer, known for her performances of such songs as 'We'll Meet Again' and 'White Cliffs of Dover' during the Second World War.

lynx ● n. a wild cat with a short tail and tufted ears.
– ORIGIN Greek *lunx*.

Lyons E
/lee-on/ an industrial city and river port in SE France, at the confluence of the Rhône and Saône Rivers.

lyre ● n. a stringed instrument like a small U-shaped harp with strings fixed to a crossbar, used in ancient Greece.
– ORIGIN Greek *lura*.

lyric ● n. **1** (also **lyrics**) the words of a song. **2** a lyric poem or verse. ● adj. (of poetry) expressing the writer's thoughts and emotions.
– ORIGIN Greek *lura* 'lyre'.

lyrical ● adj. **1** (of literature or music) expressing the writer's emotions in an imaginative and beautiful way. **2** relating to the words of a popular song.
– PHRASES **wax lyrical** talk in a very enthusiastic and unrestrained way.
– DERIVATIVES **lyrically** adv.

lyricism ● n. expression of emotion in writing or music in an imaginative and beautiful way.

lyricist ● n. a person who writes the words to popular songs.

M[1] (also **m**) ● n. (pl. **Ms** or **M's**) **1** the thirteenth letter of the alphabet. **2** the Roman numeral for 1,000. [ORIGIN from Latin *mille*.]

M[2] ● abbrev. **1** medium. **2** mega-. **3** Monsieur. **4** motorway.

m ● abbrev. **1** Physics mass. **2** metre(s). **3** mile(s). **4** milli-. **5** million(s).

MA ● abbrev. Master of Arts.

ma'am ● n. madam.

Maastricht Treaty E
/mah-strikht/ a treaty on European economic and monetary union, agreed by the twelve member states of the European Community at a summit meeting in the Dutch city of Maastricht in 1991.

mac ● n. Brit. informal a mackintosh.

macabre /muh-kah-bruh/ ● adj. disturbing and horrifying because concerned with death and injury.
– ORIGIN French.

macadam /muh-kad-uhm/ ● n. broken stone used with tar or bitumen for surfacing roads and paths.
– ORIGIN named after the British surveyor John L. *McAdam* (1756–1836).

macadamia /ma-kuh-day-mi-uh/ ● n. the edible nut of an Australian tree.
– ORIGIN named after the Australian chemist John *Macadam* (1827–65).

McAleese E
/mak-uh-leess/, Mary (Patricia) (b.1951), Irish stateswoman, President since 1997.

Macao E
/muh-kow/ a former Portuguese dependency on the SE coast of China, returned to China in 1999; capital, Macao City.
– DERIVATIVES **Macanese** adj. & n.

macaque /muh-kak/ ● n. a medium-sized monkey with a long face and cheek pouches for holding food.
– ORIGIN Bantu *makaku* 'some monkeys'.

macaroni /ma-kuh-roh-ni/ ● n. pasta in the form of narrow tubes.
– ORIGIN Italian *maccaroni*.

macaroon • n. a light biscuit made with egg white and ground almonds or coconut.
– ORIGIN French *macaron*.

MacArthur, E
Douglas (1880–1964), American general. Commander of US (later Allied) forces in the SW Pacific during the Second World War.

Macaulay E
/muh-**kaw**-li/, Thomas Babington, 1st Baron (1800–59), English historian and politican, best known for his *History of England*. As a civil servant in India, he helped to establish a new criminal code.

macaw /muh-**kaw**/ • n. a brightly coloured parrot with a long tail, native to Central and South America.
– ORIGIN Portuguese *macau*.

McCarthy, E
Joseph (Raymond) (1909–57), American Republican politician. Between 1950 and 1954 he was the instigator of widespread investigations into alleged communist infiltration in US public life.

McCarthyism • n. the practice of hunting out suspected communists in American public life, as carried out under Senator Joseph McCarthy in the 1950s.
– DERIVATIVES **McCarthyite** adj. & n.

McCartney, E
Sir (James) Paul (b.1942), English pop and rock singer, songwriter, and bass guitarist. A founder member of the Beatles, he wrote most of their songs in collaboration with John Lennon. After the group broke up in 1970 he formed the band Wings.

McCoy • n. (in phr. **the real McCoy**) informal the real thing.
– ORIGIN uncertain.

MacDiarmid E
/muhk-**der**-mid/, Hugh (1892–1978; pen name of *Christopher Murray Grieve*), Scottish poet and nationalist. The language of his poems drew on various Scottish dialects. He was a founder member of the National Party of Scotland (later the Scottish National Party).

MacDonald[1], E
Flora (1722–90), Scottish Jacobite heroine, who helped Charles Edward Stuart to escape from the English after his defeat at Culloden.

Macdonald[2], E
Sir John Alexander (1815–91), Scottish-born Canadian statesman, Prime Minister 1867–73 and 1878–91, the first Prime Minister of the Dominion of Canada.

MacDonald[3], E
(James) Ramsay (1866–1937), British Labour statesman, Prime Minister 1924, 1929–31, and 1931–5, Britain's first Labour Prime Minister.

mace[1] • n. **1** hist. a heavy club with a spiked metal head. **2** a ceremonial staff carried by an official such as a mayor. **3** (**Mace**) trademark a stinging chemical sprayed from an aerosol to disable attackers.
– ORIGIN Old French *masse* 'large hammer'.

mace[2] • n. a spice made from the dried outer covering of the nutmeg.
– ORIGIN Latin *macir*.

Macedonia[1] E
/ma-si-**doh**-ni-uh/ (also **Macedon** /ma-si-d'n/) an ancient country in SE Europe, at the northern end of the Greek peninsula. The region is now divided between Greece, Bulgaria, and the republic of Macedonia.

Macedonia[2] E
/ma-si-**doh**-ni-uh/ a region in the north-east of modern Greece.

Macedonia[3] E
/ma-si-**doh**-ni-uh/ a landlocked republic in the Balkans, formerly a constituent republic of Yugoslavia; capital, Skopje.

Macedonian • n. **1** a person from the republic of Macedonia. **2** a person from ancient Macedonia. • adj. having to do with Macedonia.

McEnroe E
/**mak**-in-roh/, John (Patrick) (b.1959), American tennis player. He won seven Wimbledon titles (three for the singles) and four US Open singles championships (1979–84).

macerate /mass-uh-rayt/ • v. (**macerates**, **macerating**, **macerated**) soften (food) by soaking it in a liquid.
– DERIVATIVES **maceration** n.
– ORIGIN Latin *macerare*.

McEwan E
/muh-**kyoo**-uhn/ Ian (Russell) (b.1948), English novelist. His works include *Enduring Love* and *Amsterdam*.

Mach /mak/ • n. used with a numeral (as **Mach 1**, **Mach 2**, etc.) to indicate the speed of sound, twice the speed of sound, etc.
– ORIGIN named after the Austrian physicist Ernst *Mach* (1838–1916).

machete /muh-**shet**-i/ • n. a broad, heavy knife used as a tool or weapon.
– ORIGIN Spanish.

Machiavelli E
/mak-i-uh-**vel**-li/, Niccolò di Bernardo dei (1469–1527), Italian statesman and political philosopher. He wrote *The Prince*, which advises rulers that to gain and retain power they may have to use deception, cruelty, and other unethical methods.

Machiavellian /mak-i-uh-**vel**-li-uhn/ • adj. trying to achieve what one wants in a cunning and underhand way.
– ORIGIN named after Niccolò **MACHIAVELLI**.

machinations /mash-i-**nay**-sh'nz/ • pl. n. plots and scheming.
– ORIGIN Latin *machinari* 'contrive'.

machine • n. **1** a device using mechanical power and having several parts, for performing a particular task. **2** an efficient group of influential people: *the council's publicity machine.* • v. (**machines**, **machining**, **machined**) make or work on (something) with a machine.
– ORIGIN Greek *mēkhanē*.

machine code (also **machine language**) • n. a computer programming language consisting of instructions which a computer can respond to directly.

machine gun • n. an automatic gun that fires bullets in rapid succession.

machine-readable • adj. in a form that a computer can process.

machinery • n. **1** machines as a whole, or the parts of a machine. **2** an organized system or structure: *the machinery of the state.*

machine tool • n. a fixed powered tool for cutting or shaping metal, wood, etc.

machinist • n. a person who operates a machine or who makes machinery.

machismo /muh-**kiz**-moh/ • n. strong or aggressive male pride.
– ORIGIN Mexican Spanish.

macho /**mach**-oh/ • adj. showing aggressive pride in being male.
– ORIGIN Mexican Spanish.

Machu Picchu E
/ma-choo **peek**-choo/ a fortified Inca town situated high in the Andes in Peru.

Mackenzie River E
the longest river in Canada, flowing 1,700 km (1,060 miles) north-westwards from the Great Slave Lake to the Arctic Ocean.

mackerel • n. an edible sea fish with a greenish blue back.
– ORIGIN Old French *maquerel.*

McKinley, E
William (1843–1901), American Republican statesman, 25th President of the US 1897–1901. He was assassinated by an anarchist.

McKinley, Mount E
a mountain in south central Alaska. Rising to 6,194 m (20,110 ft), it is the highest mountain in North America. Also called **Denali**.

Mackintosh, E
Charles Rennie (1868–1928), Scottish architect, designer, and painter. He was a leading exponent of art nouveau and pioneered functionalism in architecture and interior design.

mackintosh (also **macintosh**) • n. Brit. a full-length waterproof coat.
– ORIGIN named after the Scottish inventor Charles *Macintosh* (1766–1843).

Maclean[1] E
/muh-**klayn**/, Alistair (1922–87), Scottish novelist, writer of thrillers including *The Guns of Navarone* and *Where Eagles Dare.*

Maclean[2] E
/muh-**klayn**/, Donald (Duart) (1913–83), British Foreign Office official and Soviet spy, who fled to the USSR with Guy Burgess in 1951.

McLeish E
/muh-**kleesh**/, Henry (Baird) (b.1948), Scottish Labour statesman, First Minister of the Scottish Parliament 2000–1.

McLuhan E
/muh-**kloo**-uhn/, (Herbert) Marshall (1911–80), Canadian writer, known for his theories on the mass media.

Macmillan, E
(Maurice) Harold, 1st Earl of Stockton (1894–1986), British Conservative statesman, Prime Minister 1957–63.

MacNeice E
/muhk-**neess**/, (Frederick) Louis (1907–63), Northern Irish poet.

macramé /muh-**krah**-may/ • n. the craft of knotting cord or string in patterns to make decorative articles.
– ORIGIN French.

macro- • comb. form large or large-scale.
– ORIGIN Greek *makros.*

macrobiotic /mak-roh-by-**ot**-ik/ • adj. (of diet) consisting of organic unprocessed foods, based on Buddhist principles of the balance of yin and yang.
– ORIGIN from **macro-** + Greek *bios* 'life'.

macrocosm /**mak**-roh-ko-z'm/ • n. **1** the whole of a complex structure. **2** the universe.
– ORIGIN from Greek *makros kosmos* 'big world'.

macroeconomics • n. the branch of economics concerned with large-scale economic factors, such as interest rates.

macromolecule • n. Chem. a molecule containing a very large number of atoms, such as a protein.

macron • n. a written or printed mark (¯) used to indicate a long vowel in some languages, or a stressed vowel in verse.

macroscopic • adj. **1** large enough to be seen without a microscope. **2** relating to general analysis.

mad • adj. (**madder**, **maddest**) **1** insane. **2** very foolish. **3** done without thought or control: *a mad dash to get ready.* **4** informal very enthusiastic. **5** informal very angry.
– DERIVATIVES **madly** adv. **madness** n.
– ORIGIN Old English.

Madagascar E
/mad-uh-**gass**-ker/ an island country in the Indian Ocean, off the east coast of Africa; capital, Antananarivo. Former name (1960–75) **Malagasy Republic**.
– DERIVATIVES **Madagascan** adj. & n.

madam • n. **1** a polite form of address for a woman. **2** Brit. informal an arrogant or cheeky girl. **3** a woman who runs a brothel.
– ORIGIN from French *ma dame* 'my lady'.

Madame /muh-**dam**/ • n. (pl. **Mesdames** /may-**dam**/) a title or form of address for a French-speaking woman.

madcap • adj. acting without thought.

mad cow disease • n. informal = **BSE**

madden • v. make very annoyed.

madder • n. a red dye obtained from the roots of a plant.
– ORIGIN Old English.

made past and past part. of **make**.

Madeira[1] E
/muh-**deer**-uh/ an island in the Atlantic Ocean off NW Africa, the largest of the Madeiras, a group of islands which is an autonomous region of Portugal; capital, Funchal.
– DERIVATIVES **Madeiran** adj. & n.

Madeira[2] /muh-**deer**-uh/ • n. a strong sweet white wine from Madeira.

Madeira cake • n. Brit. a rich kind of sponge cake.

Mademoiselle /ma-duh-mwah-**zel**/ • n. (pl. **Mesdemoiselles** /may-duh-mwa-**zel**/) a title or form of address for an unmarried French-speaking woman.
– ORIGIN French.

made-up • adj. **1** wearing make-up. **2** invented; untrue.

madhouse • n. informal a scene of great confusion or uproar.

Madhya Pradesh E
/mud-yuh pruh-**desh**/ a large state in central India; capital, Bhopal.

Madison, E
James (1751–1836), American Democratic Republican statesman, 4th President of the US 1809–17. He played a leading part in drawing up the US Constitution (1787) and proposed the Bill of Rights (1791).

madman • n. **1** a man who is mentally ill. **2** a foolish or reckless person.

Madonna[1] • n. (**the Madonna**) the Virgin Mary.
– ORIGIN Italian.

Madonna[2] E
(b.1958; born *Madonna Louise Ciccone*), American pop singer and actress. Her albums include *Like a Virgin* and *Ray of Light*.

Madras[1] E
/muh-**drahss**, muh-**drass**/ a seaport on the east coast of India, capital of Tamil Nadu. Official name (since 1995) **CHENNAI**.

Madras[2] E
/muh-**drahss**, muh-**drass**/ former name for **TAMIL NADU**.

madras /muh-**drass**, muh-**drahss**/ • n. **1** a colourful striped or checked cotton fabric. **2** a hot spiced curry dish.
– ORIGIN named after **MADRAS**[1].

Madrid E
/muh-**drid**/ the capital of Spain.

madrigal • n. a 16th- or 17th-century song for several voices without instrumental accompaniment.
– ORIGIN Italian *madrigale*.

maelstrom /**mayl**-struhm/ • n. **1** a powerful whirlpool. **2** a situation of confusion or upheaval.
– ORIGIN Dutch.

maenad /**mee**-nad/ • n. (in ancient Greece) a female follower of the god Bacchus.
– ORIGIN Greek *Mainas*.

maestro /**my**-stroh/ • n. (pl. **maestri** /**my**-stri/ or **maestros**) **1** a notable male conductor or classical musician. **2** a notable man in any field of activity.
– ORIGIN Italian, 'master'.

Mafeking E
/**ma**-fi-king/ former name for **MAFIKENG**.

MAFF • abbrev. (in the UK) Ministry of Agriculture, Fisheries, and Food.

Mafia • n. **1** (**the Mafia**) an international criminal organization originating in Sicily. **2** (**mafia**) a powerful group who secretly influence matters: *the top tennis mafia*.
– ORIGIN Italian.

Mafikeng E
/**ma**-fi-keng/ a town in South Africa, in which a small British force was besieged for 215 days during the Second Boer War (1899–1900). Former name (until 1980) **MAFEKING**.

Mafioso /ma-fi-**oh**-soh/ • n. (pl. **Mafiosi** /ma-fi-**oh**-si/) a member of the Mafia.

magazine • n. **1** a periodical publication containing articles and pictures. **2** a chamber holding cartridges to be fed automatically to the breech of a gun. **3** a store for arms, ammunition, and explosives.
– ORIGIN Arabic, 'storehouse'.

Magellan E
/muh-**gel**-luhn/, Ferdinand (*c.*1480–1521; Portuguese name *Fernão Magalhães*), Portuguese explorer. In 1519 he sailed from Spain, rounding South America by the strait that now bears his name. He was killed by islanders in the Philippines, but his companions returned to Spain round Africa, completing the first circumnavigation of the world (1522).

Magellan, Strait of E
a passage separating Tierra del Fuego and other islands from mainland South America, connecting the Atlantic and Pacific Oceans.

magenta /muh-**jen**-tuh/ • n. a light mauvish crimson.
– ORIGIN named after *Magenta* in Italy.

Maggiore, Lake E
/maj-**jor**-ay/ a lake in northern Italy, extending into southern Switzerland.

maggot • n. a soft-bodied larva of a fly or other insect, found in decaying matter.
– ORIGIN perh. from Old Norse.

magi pl. of **MAGUS**.

magic • n. **1** the power of apparently influencing events by using mysterious or supernatural forces. **2** conjuring tricks. **3** a mysterious or wonderful quality: *the magic of the theatre*. • adj. **1** having supernatural powers. **2** informal very good. • v. (**magics**, **magicking**, **magicked**) move or do by or as if by magic.
– DERIVATIVES **magical** adj. **magically** adv.
– ORIGIN from Greek *magikē tekhnē* 'art of a magus'.

magician • n. **1** a person with magic powers. **2** a conjuror.

magic lantern • n. an early form of projector for showing photographic slides.

magisterial /ma-ji-**steer**-i-uhl/ • adj. **1** having or showing great authority: *a magisterial pronouncement*. **2** relating to a magistrate.
– ORIGIN Latin *magister* 'master'.

magistracy /**ma**-jiss-truh-si/ • n. (pl. **magistracies**) **1** the post of magistrate. **2** magistrates as a group.

magistrate • n. an official with authority to judge minor cases, and hold preliminary hearings.
– ORIGIN Latin *magistratus* 'administrator'.

magma /**mag**-muh/ • n. very hot fluid or semi-fluid material under the earth's crust, from which igneous rock is formed by cooling.
– ORIGIN Greek.

Magna Carta E
/mag-nuh **kar**-tuh/ a charter of liberty and political rights obtained from King John of England by his rebellious barons at Runnymede near Windsor in 1215. It was important because it recognized certain rights of landowners. nobles, the Church, and freemen.

magnanimous /mag-**nan**-i-muhss/ • adj. generous or forgiving towards a rival or

enemy.
– DERIVATIVES **magnanimity** n.
– ORIGIN from Latin *magnus* 'great' + *animus* 'soul'.

magnate /mag-nayt/ ● n. a wealthy and influential businessman or businesswoman.
– ORIGIN Latin *magnas* 'great man'.

magnesium /mag-nee-zi-uhm/ ● n. a silvery-white metallic element which burns with a brilliant white flame.
– ORIGIN Greek *Magnēsia*, relating to a mineral from Magnesia in Asia Minor.

magnet ● n. **1** a piece of iron or other material that can attract iron-containing objects and that points north and south when suspended. **2** a person or thing that has a powerful attraction: *the beach is a magnet for sun-worshippers.*
– ORIGIN from Greek *magnēs lithos* 'lodestone'.

magnetic ● adj. **1** having the property of magnetism. **2** very attractive.
– DERIVATIVES **magnetically** adv.

magnetic field ● n. a region around a magnet within which the force of magnetism acts.

magnetic north ● n. the direction in which the north end of a compass needle will point in response to the earth's magnetic field.

magnetic pole ● n. each of the points near the geographical North and South Poles, indicated by the needle of a magnetic compass.

magnetic storm ● n. a disturbance of the magnetic field of the earth.

magnetic tape ● n. tape used in recording sound, pictures, or computer data.

magnetism ● n. **1** the property displayed by magnets and produced by the movement of electric charges, which results in objects being attracted or pushed away. **2** the ability to attract and charm people.

magnetize (also **magnetise**) ● v. (**magnetizes**, **magnetizing**, **magnetized**) make magnetic.

magneto /mag-nee-toh/ ● n. (pl. **magnetos**) a small electric generator containing a permanent magnet and used to provide high-voltage pulses.

Magnificat /mag-nif-i-kat/ ● n. the hymn of the Virgin Mary, beginning 'my soul magnifies the Lord', sung as a regular part of a Christian service.
– ORIGIN Latin, 'magnifies'.

magnification ● n. **1** the action of magnifying. **2** the degree to which something can be magnified.

magnificent ● adj. **1** very attractive and impressive; splendid. **2** very good.
– DERIVATIVES **magnificence** n. **magnificently** adv.
– ORIGIN Latin, 'making great'.

magnify ● v. (**magnifies**, **magnifying**, **magnified**) **1** make (something) appear larger than it is with a lens or microscope. **2** make larger or stronger: *the tin roof magnified the tropical heat.* **3** archaic praise.
– DERIVATIVES **magnifier** n.
– ORIGIN Latin *magnificare.*

magnifying glass ● n. a lens that makes small things look larger than they are.

magnitude ● n. **1** great size or importance: *they were discouraged at the magnitude of the task.* **2** size. **3** the degree of brightness of a star.
– ORIGIN Latin *magnitudo.*

magnolia ● n. a tree or shrub with large white or pale pink flowers.
– ORIGIN named after the French botanist Pierre *Magnol* (1638–1715).

magnum ● n. (pl. **magnums**) a wine bottle of twice the standard size, normally 1½ litres.
– ORIGIN Latin, 'great thing'.

magnum opus /mag-nuhm **oh**-puhss, mag-nuhm **op**-uhss/ ● n. (pl. **magnum opuses** or **magna opera** /mag-nuh **op**-uh-ruh/) a work of art, music, or literature that is the most important that a person has produced.
– ORIGIN Latin, 'great work'.

magpie ● n. **1** a black and white bird with a long tail and a noisy cry. **2** a person who collects trivial objects.
– ORIGIN prob. from *Magot*, a former form of the woman's name *Marguerite*, + Latin *pica* 'magpie'.

Magritte E
/ma-**greet**/, René (François Ghislain) (1898–1967), Belgian surrealist painter. His works display startling or amusing juxtapositions of the ordinary, the strange, and the erotic.

magus /may-guhss/ ● n. (pl. **magi** /may-jy/) **1** a priest of ancient Persia. **2** a sorcerer. **3** (**the Magi**) the three wise men from the East who brought gifts to the infant Jesus.
ORIGIN Latin.

Magyar /mag-yar/ ● n. **1** a member of the predominant people in Hungary. **2** the Hungarian language.
– ORIGIN Hungarian.

Mahabharata E
/mah-huh-**bah**-ruh-tuh/ one of the two great Sanskrit epic poems of the Hindus, existing in its present form since about 400 AD.

maharaja /mah-huh-**rah**-juh/ (also **maharajah**) ● n. hist. an Indian prince.
– ORIGIN Hindi.

maharani /mah-huh-**rah**-ni/ ● n. hist. a maharaja's wife or widow.
– ORIGIN Hindi.

Maharashtra E
/mah-huh-**rass**-truh, mah-huh-**rah**-struh/ a large state in western India; capital, Bombay (Mumbai).

Maharishi /mah-huh-**ri**-shi/ ● n. a great Hindu wise man or spiritual leader.
– ORIGIN Sanskrit.

mahatma /muh-**hat**-muh/ ● n. a wise or holy Hindu leader.
– ORIGIN Sanskrit, 'great soul'.

mah-jong /mah-**jong**/ (also **mah-jongg**) ● n. a Chinese game played with rectangular pieces called tiles.
– ORIGIN Chinese dialect, 'sparrows'.

Mahler E
/**mah**-ler/, Gustav (1860–1911), Austrian composer and conductor. His music formed a link between romanticism and the experimentalism of Schoenberg. Compositions include nine symphonies and the symphonic song cycle *Das Lied von der Erde.*

mahogany ● n. **1** hard reddish-brown wood from a tropical tree, used for furniture. **2** a rich reddish-brown colour.

– ORIGIN unknown.

Mahore E
/muh-hor/ = MAYOTTE.

maid ● n. **1** a female servant. **2** archaic a girl or young woman.

maiden ● n. **1** archaic a girl or young woman, especially a virgin. **2** (also **maiden over**) Cricket an over in which no runs are scored. ● adj. **1** (of an older woman) unmarried. **2** first of its kind: *a maiden voyage.*
– ORIGIN Old English.

maidenhair fern ● n. a fern with fine stems and delicate foliage.

maidenhead ● n. archaic **1** a girl's or woman's virginity. **2** the hymen.

maiden name ● n. the surname of a married woman before her marriage.

maid of honour ● n. an unmarried noblewoman who waits on a queen or princess.

maidservant ● n. dated a female servant.

mail[1] ● n. **1** letters and parcels sent by post. **2** the postal system. **3** email. ● v. **1** send by post. **2** send post or email to.
– ORIGIN Old French *male* 'wallet'.

mail[2] ● n. hist. armour made of metal rings or plates.
– ORIGIN Old French *maille.*

Mailer, E
Norman (b.1923), American novelist and essayist. His novels include *The Naked and the Dead* and *The Presidential Papers.*

m

mailing ● n. an item of advertising posted to a large number of people.

mailing list ● n. a list of people to whom advertising matter or information may be mailed regularly.

mail order ● n. the buying or selling of goods by post.

mailshot ● n. Brit. a piece of advertising material sent to a large number of addresses.

maim ● v. injure (someone) so that part of the body is permanently damaged.
– ORIGIN Old French *mahaignier.*

Main E
/*rhymes with* mine/ a river of SW Germany which rises in northern Bavaria, flowing through Frankfurt and into the Rhine.

main ● adj. greatest or most important: *a main road.* ● n. **1** a chief water or gas pipe or electricity cable. **2** (**the mains**) Brit. public water, gas, or electricity supply through pipes or cables. **3** (**the main**) archaic the open ocean.
– PHRASES **in the main** on the whole.
– ORIGIN Old English, 'physical force'.

Maine E
a NE state of the US, on the Atlantic coast; capital, Augusta.

mainframe ● n. a large high-speed computer, especially one supporting a network of workstations.

Mainland[1] E
the largest island in Orkney.

Mainland[2] E
the largest island in Shetland.

mainland ● n. the main area of land of a country, not including islands and separate territories.

mainline ● v. (**mainlines, mainlining, mainlined**) informal inject (a drug) into a vein.

mainly ● adv. for the most part; chiefly.

mainmast ● n. the principal mast of a ship.

mainspring ● n. the most important or influential part: *faith was the mainspring of her life.*

mainstay ● n. a thing on which something else is based or depends: *cotton is the mainstay of the economy.*

mainstream ● n. the ideas, attitudes, or activities that are shared by most people.

maintain ● v. **1** cause to continue in the same state or at the same level: *he maintained close links with India.* **2** keep (a building, machine, etc.) in good condition by checking or repairing it regularly. **3** support financially. **4** state strongly to be the case.
– ORIGIN Old French *maintenir.*

maintenance ● n. **1** the action of maintaining something. **2** the provision of financial support for one's former husband or wife after divorce.

maisonette ● n. a flat on two storeys of a larger building.
– ORIGIN French *maisonnette* 'small house'.

maître d'hôtel /may-truh doh-**tel**/ ● n. (pl. **maîtres d'hôtel** /may-truh doh-**tel**/) the head waiter of a restaurant.
– ORIGIN French, 'master of the house'.

maize ● n. esp. Brit. a cereal plant bearing large grains set in rows on a cob.
– ORIGIN Spanish *maíz.*

majestic ● adj. beautiful or impressive; grand.
– DERIVATIVES **majestically** adv.

majesty ● n. (pl. **majesties**) **1** impressive beauty or grandeur: *the majesty of Ben Nevis.* **2** royal power. **3** (**His, Your,** etc. **Majesty**) a title given to a king or queen or their wife or widow.
– ORIGIN Latin *majestas.*

Major, E
John (b.1943), British Conservative statesman, Prime Minister 1990–7.

major ● adj. **1** important or serious. **2** greater or more important; main. **3** Music (of a scale) having intervals of semitone between the third and fourth, and seventh and eighth notes. Contrasted with MINOR. ● n. **1** a rank of army officer above captain. **2** Music a major key, interval, or scale. **3** N. Amer. a student specializing in a specified subject. ● v. (**major in**) N. Amer. & Austral./NZ specialize in (a particular subject) at college or university.
– ORIGIN Latin, 'greater'.

Majorca E
/muh-yor-kuh/ the largest of the Balearic Islands; capital, Palma.
– DERIVATIVES **Majorcan** adj. and n.

major-domo ● n. (pl. **major-domos**) the chief steward of a large household.
– ORIGIN Spanish and Italian.

major general ● n. a rank of army officer above brigadier.

majority ● n. (pl. **majorities**) **1** the greater number. **2** Brit. the number of votes by which one party or candidate in an election defeats the opposition. **3** the age when a person becomes an adult in law, usually 18 or 21.

USAGE majority
The main meaning of **majority** is 'the greater number' and it should be used with plural nouns: *the majority of cases.* Do not use **majority** with nouns that do not take a plural to mean 'the greatest part', as in *she ate the majority of the meal.*

majority rule • n. the principle that the greater number of people should exercise greater power.

Makarios III E
/muh-**kah**-ri-oss/ (1913–77; born *Mikhail Christodolou Mouskos*), Greek Cypriot archbishop and statesman, first President of the republic of Cyprus 1960–77.

make • v. (**makes**, **making**, **made**) **1** form by putting parts together or mixing substances. **2** cause: *the drips had made a pool on the floor.* **3** force to do something. **4** add up to. **5** be suitable as. **6** estimate as or decide on. **7** earn (money or profit). **8** arrive at or achieve. **9** (**make it**) become successful. **10** prepare to go in a particular direction or to do something: *he made towards the car.* • n. the manufacturer or trade name of a product.
– PHRASES **make do** manage with something that is not satisfactory. **make for 1** move towards. **2** tend to result in. **3** (**be made for**) be very suitable for. **make of 1** give (attention or importance) to. **2** understand the meaning of. **make off** leave hurriedly. **make off with** steal. **make or break** be the factor which decides whether (something) will succeed or fail. **make out 1** manage with difficulty to see, hear, or understand. **2** claim or pretend to be. **3** draw up (a list or document). **make over 1** transfer the ownership of. **2** give a new image to. **make sail** spread a sail or sails to begin a voyage. **make time** find time to do something. **make up 1** put together or prepare from parts or ingredients. **2** invent (a story). **3** (also **make up for**) do something to set right (a bad situation). **4** be friendly again after a quarrel. **5** apply cosmetics to. **make up one's mind** make a decision. **make way** allow room for someone or something else. **on the make** informal trying to make money or gain an advantage.
– ORIGIN Old English.

make-believe • n. a state of fantasy or pretence: *she's living in a world of make-believe.* • adj. imitating something real; pretend.

makeover • n. a complete change of a person's appearance with cosmetics, hairstyling, and clothes.

maker • n. **1** a person or thing that makes something. **2** (**our**, **the**, etc. **Maker**) God.
– PHRASES **meet one's Maker** die.

makeshift • adj. acting as a temporary substitute: *chairs formed a makeshift bed.*

make-up • n. **1** cosmetics. **2** the way in which something is formed or put together: *the make-up of the rock.*

makeweight • n. **1** something put on a scale to make up the required weight. **2** an extra person or thing needed to complete something.

making • n. **1** (in phr. **be the making of**) bring about the success of. **2** (**makings**) the necessary qualities.

mal- • comb. form **1** bad; badly: *malnourished.* **2** wrong or incorrectly: *malfunction.*
– ORIGIN Latin *male.*

Malabo E
/muh-**lah**-boh/ the capital of Equatorial Guinea, on the island of Bioko.

malachite /mal-uh-kyt/ • n. a bright green mineral that contains copper.
– ORIGIN Greek *molokhitis.*

maladjusted • adj. (of a person) failing to cope with normal social situations.

maladroit /mal-uh-**droyt**/ • adj. clumsy.

malady • n. (pl. **maladies**) a disease or illness.
– ORIGIN Old French *malade* 'ill'.

Malaga E
/**ma**-luh-guh/ a seaport on the coast of southern Spain.

Malagasy Republic E
former name for **MADAGASCAR**.

malaise /ma-**layz**/ • n. a general feeling of unease, illness, or low spirits.
– ORIGIN French.

malapropism /mal-uh-prop-i-z'm/ (US also **malaprop**) • n. the mistaken use of a word in place of a similar-sounding one (e.g. 'dance a *flamingo*' instead of *flamenco*).
– ORIGIN named after Mrs *Malaprop* in Richard Sheridan's play *The Rivals* (1775).

malaria • n. a disease that causes recurrent fever, caused by a parasite transmitted by mosquitoes.
– DERIVATIVES **malarial** adj.
– ORIGIN from Italian *mala aria* 'bad air' (once thought to cause the disease).

malarkey /muh-**lar**-ki/ • n. informal nonsense.
– ORIGIN unknown.

Malawi E
/muh-**lah**-wi/ a country of south central Africa; capital, Lilongwe. Former name (until 1966) **NYASALAND**.
– DERIVATIVES **Malawian** adj. & n.

Malawi, Lake E
= Lake Nyasa (see **NYASA, LAKE**).

Malay • n. **1** a member of a people inhabiting Malaysia and Indonesia. **2** the language of the Malays.

Malaya E
a former country in SE Asia, consisting of the southern part of the Malay Peninsula and some adjacent islands, now part of the federation of Malaysia and known as West Malaysia.

Malayan • n. = **MALAY**. • adj. relating to Malays or Malaya.

Malay Archipelago E
a very large group of islands, including Sumatra, Java, Borneo, the Philippines, and New Guinea, lying between SE Asia and Australia.

Malay Peninsula E
a peninsula in SE Asia separating the Indian Ocean from the South China Sea. It comprises the southern part of Thailand and the whole of Malaya (West Malaysia).

Malaysia E
a country in SE Asia; capital, Kuala Lumpur.
– DERIVATIVES **Malaysian** adj. & n.

Malcolm III E
(*c.*1031–93), king of Scotland 1058–93. He was responsible for helping to form Scotland into an organized kingdom.

Malcolm X E
(1925–65; born *Malcolm Little*), American political activist. He was a vigorous campaigner for black rights, initially advocating the use of violence. He converted to orthodox Islam in 1964 and was assassinated the following year.

malcontent • **n.** a person who is dissatisfied and rebellious.

Maldives E
/**mawl**-dyvz, **mawl**-deev/ a country consisting of a chain of coral islands in the Indian Ocean south-west of Sri Lanka; capital, Male.

Male E
/**mah**-lay/ the capital of the Maldives.

male • **adj.** **1** relating to the sex that can fertilize or inseminate the female. **2** having to do with men: *a deep male voice.* **3** (of a plant or flower) having stamens but not a pistil. **4** (of a fitting) manufactured to fit inside a corresponding female part. • **n.** a male person, animal, or plant.
– ORIGIN Old French *masle.*

malediction /mal-i-**dik**-sh'n/ • **n.** a curse.
– ORIGIN Latin *maledicere* 'speak evil of'.

malefactor /**mal**-i-fak-ter/ • **n.** formal a criminal or wrongdoer.
– ORIGIN Latin.

malevolent /muh-**lev**-uh-luhnt/ • **adj.** wishing evil to others.
– DERIVATIVES **malevolence** n.
– ORIGIN Latin.

malformation • **n.** the state of being abnormally shaped or formed.
– DERIVATIVES **malformed** adj.

malfunction • **v.** (of equipment or machinery) fail to function normally. • **n.** a failure to function normally.

Mali E
/**mah**-li/ a landlocked country in West Africa, south of Algeria; capital, Bamako. Former name (until 1958) **French Sudan**.
– DERIVATIVES **Malian** adj. & n.

Malibu E
/**ma**-li-boo/ a resort on the Pacific coast of southern California, west of Los Angeles.

malice • **n.** the desire to harm someone.
– ORIGIN Old French.

malicious • **adj.** meaning or meant to do harm.
– DERIVATIVES **maliciously** adv.

malign /muh-**lyn**/ • **adj.** harmful or evil. • **v.** say unpleasant things about.
– DERIVATIVES **malignity** /muh-**lig**-ni-ti/ n.
– ORIGIN Latin *malignus* 'tending to evil'.

malignancy • **n.** (pl. **malignancies**) **1** cancer. **2** a cancerous growth. **3** the quality of being harmful or evil.

malignant • **adj.** **1** harmful; malevolent. **2** (of a tumour) growing uncontrollably or likely to recur after removal; cancerous.
– ORIGIN Latin *malignare* 'plan maliciously'.

malinger • **v.** (**malingers, malingering, malingered**) pretend to be ill in order to avoid work.
– DERIVATIVES **malingerer** n.
– ORIGIN French *malingre* 'weak, sickly'.

Malinowski E
/ma-li-**noff**-ski/, Bronisław Kaspar (1884–1942), Polish anthropologist, who pioneered the use of intensive fieldwork in anthropology.

mall /mal, mawl/ • **n.** **1** a large enclosed pedestrian shopping area. **2** a sheltered walk.
– ORIGIN from *The Mall*, a walk in St James's Park, London.

mallard • **n.** a wild duck, the male of which has a dark green head.
– ORIGIN Old French, 'wild drake'.

Mallarmé E
/mal-lar-**may**/, Stéphane (1842–98), French symbolist poet, who experimented with rhythm and syntax by transposing words and omitting grammatical elements.

Malle E
/mal/, Louis (1932–95), French film director, known for such films as *Les Amants* and *Au Revoir les enfants.*

malleable /**mal**-li-uh-b'l/ • **adj.** **1** able to be hammered or pressed into shape without breaking or cracking. **2** easily influenced: *a malleable youth.*
– DERIVATIVES **malleability** n.
– ORIGIN Latin *malleus* 'a hammer'.

mallet • **n.** **1** a hammer with a large wooden head. **2** a long-handled wooden stick with a head like a hammer, for hitting a croquet or polo ball.
– ORIGIN Latin *malleus.*

mallow • **n.** a plant with pink or purple flowers.
– ORIGIN Latin *malva.*

malnourished • **adj.** suffering from malnutrition.

malnutrition • **n.** the state of not having enough food or not eating enough of the right foods.

malodorous • **adj.** smelling very unpleasant.

Malory E
/**mal**-uh-ri/, Sir Thomas (d.1471), English writer. His major work, *Le Morte d'Arthur*, is a prose translation of a collection of the legends of King Arthur, from French and other sources.

malpractice • **n.** illegal, corrupt, or careless professional behaviour.

malt • **n.** barley or other grain that has been soaked in water, allowed to sprout, and dried, used for brewing or distilling. • **v.** **1** make (grain) into malt. **2** (**malted**) mixed with malt or a malt extract.
– ORIGIN Old English.

Malta E
an island country in the central Mediterranean; capital, Valletta.

Malthus E
/**mal**-thuhss/, Thomas Robert (1766–1834), English economist and clergyman. He argued that, if unchecked, the population tends to increase at a greater rate than its food supplies, resulting in war, famine, and epidemic.
– DERIVATIVES **Malthusian** /mal-**thyoo**-zi-uhn/ adj. & n.

maltose /**mawl**-tohz/ ● n. a sugar produced by the breakdown of starch, for example by enzymes found in malt and saliva.

maltreat ● v. treat badly or cruelly.
– DERIVATIVES **maltreatment** n.

malt whisky ● n. whisky made only from malted barley.

Malvern Hills E
/**mawl**-vern/ a range of hills in western England, in Herefordshire and Worcestershire.

Malvinas, Islas E
/mal-**vee**-nass, iz-lass/ the name by which the Falkland Islands are known in Argentina.

mama (also **mamma**) ● n. dated or N. Amer. one's mother.

mamba ● n. a large, highly poisonous African snake.
– ORIGIN Zulu.

mambo ● n. (pl. **mambos**) a Latin American dance similar to the rumba.
– ORIGIN American Spanish.

Mamet E
/**ma**-mit/, David (b.1947), American dramatist, director, and screenwriter. His plays include *Glengarry Glen Ross* and *Oleanna*.

mammal ● n. a warm-blooded animal that has hair or fur, produces milk, and bears live young.
– DERIVATIVES **mammalian** adj.
– ORIGIN Latin *mamma* 'breast'.

mammary ● adj. relating to the breasts or the milk-producing organs of other mammals.
– ORIGIN Latin *mamma* 'breast'.

mammography /mam-**mog**-ruh-fi/ ● n. a technique using X-rays to examine the breasts for tumours.
– DERIVATIVES **mammogram** n.

Mammon ● n. wealth regarded as an evil influence or false object of worship.
– ORIGIN Aramaic, 'riches'; see Gospel of Matthew, chapter 6 and Gospel of Luke, chapter 16.

mammoth ● n. a large extinct form of elephant with a hairy coat and long curved tusks. ● adj. huge; enormous.
– ORIGIN Russian.

man ● n. (pl. **men**) **1** an adult human male. **2** a husband or lover. **3** a person. **4** human beings in general: *places untouched by man.* **5** a piece used in a board game. ● v. (**mans, manning, manned**) provide (a place or machine) with the people to operate or defend it.
– PHRASES **the man in the street** the average man. **man of the cloth** a clergyman. **to a man** with no exceptions.
– ORIGIN Old English.

USAGE man
Many people now think that the use of the word **man** to mean 'human beings in general' is outdated or sexist; you could use **the human race** or **humankind** instead.

-man ● comb. form forming nouns referring to: **1** a man of a particular nationality or origin: *Frenchman.* **2** a person belonging to a particular group or having a particular role: *chairman.* **3** a ship of a particular kind: *merchantman.*

USAGE -man
Using the suffix **-man** to create words referring to a job or role, as in **fireman** and **policeman**, is now often thought of as outdated and sexist. As a result, there has been a move away from **-man** words except where it is known that a man rather than a woman is being spoken about. Alternative non-specific terms which can be used include **firefighter** or **police officer**.

Man, Isle of E
see **ISLE OF MAN**.

manacle ● n. a metal band or chain fastened around a person's hands or ankles to restrict their movement. ● v. (**manacles, manacling, manacled**) restrict with a manacle or manacles.
– ORIGIN Old French *manicle* 'handcuff'.

manage ● v. (**manages, managing, managed**) **1** be in charge of (an organization or people). **2** succeed in doing: *she finally managed to call a cab.* **3** be able to cope despite difficulties. **4** control the use of (money or other resources). **5** be free to attend (an appointment).
– ORIGIN Italian *maneggiare* 'train a horse'.

manageable ● adj. able to be managed without difficulty.

management ● n. **1** the action of managing. **2** the managers of an organization.

manager ● n. **1** a person who manages staff, an organization, or a sports team. **2** a person in charge of the business affairs of a sports player, actor, etc.
DERIVATIVES **managerial** adj.

manageress ● n. a female manager.

Managua E
/muh-**nah**-gwuh/ the capital of Nicaragua.

Manama E
/muh-**nah**-muh/ the capital of Bahrain.

mañana /man-**yah**-nuh/ ● adv. tomorrow, or at some time in the future.
– ORIGIN Spanish.

man-at-arms ● n. archaic a soldier.

manatee /**man**-uh-tee/ ● n. a large plant-eating mammal that lives in the sea near tropical Atlantic coasts.
– ORIGIN Carib.

Manchester E
an industrial city in NW England.

Manchuria E
/man-**choo**-ri-uh/ a mountainous region forming the NE portion of China.

Mancunian ● n. a person from Manchester. ● adj. relating to Manchester.
– ORIGIN Latin *Mancunium* 'Manchester'.

mandala /**man**-duh-luh/ ● n. a circular design symbolizing the universe in Hinduism

and Buddhism.
– ORIGIN Sanskrit, 'disc'.

Mandalay E
/man-duh-**lay**/ a port on the Irrawaddy River in central Burma (Myanmar).

mandarin ● n. **1** (**Mandarin**) the official form of the Chinese language. **2** a high-ranking official in the former Chinese empire. **3** a powerful official. **4** a small citrus fruit with a loose yellow-orange skin.
– ORIGIN Hindi, 'counsellor'.

mandate ● n. /**man**-dayt/ **1** an official order or permission to do something. **2** the authority to carry out a policy, seen as given by a country's voters to the winner of an election: *a government with a popular mandate.* ● v. /man-**dayt**/ (**mandates**, **mandating**, **mandated**) give (someone) authority to do something.
– ORIGIN Latin *mandatum* 'something commanded'.

mandatory /**man**-duh-tuh-ri/ ● adj. required by law or rules; compulsory.

Mandela E
/man-**del**-uh/, Nelson (Rolihlahla) (b.1918), South African statesman, President 1994–9. He was sentenced to life imprisonment in 1964 as an activist for the African National Congress (ANC). He was released in 1990 and became the country's first democratically elected President in 1994.

mandible ● n. **1** the lower jawbone in mammals or fishes. **2** either of the upper and lower parts of a bird's beak. **3** either half of the crushing organ in an insect's mouthparts.
– ORIGIN Latin *mandibula*.

mandolin ● n. a musical instrument like a lute, having metal strings plucked with a plectrum.
– ORIGIN Italian *mandolino* 'little lute'.

mandrake ● n. a plant with a forked fleshy root that is used in herbal medicine and magic.
– ORIGIN Latin *mandragora*.

mandrel ● n. **1** a shaft or spindle in a lathe to which work is fixed while being turned. **2** a cylindrical rod round which metal or other material is forged or shaped.
– ORIGIN unknown.

mandrill ● n. a large West African baboon with a red and blue face.
– ORIGIN prob. from **MAN** + a local word.

mane ● n. **1** a growth of long hair on the neck of a horse, lion, or other mammal. **2** a person's long hair.
– ORIGIN Old English.

Manet E
/**man**-ay/, Édouard (1832–83), French painter. His realist approach greatly influenced the Impressionists. His works include *Déjeuner sur l'herbe* and *A Bar at the Folies-Bergère*.

maneuver ● n. & v. US = **MANOEUVRE**.

manful ● adj. brave or determined.
– DERIVATIVES **manfully** adv.

manga ● n. Japanese comic books and cartoon films with a science-fiction or fantasy theme.
– ORIGIN Japanese.

manganese /**mang**-guh-neez/ ● n. a hard grey metallic element used in special steels and magnetic alloys.
– ORIGIN Italian.

mange /maynj/ ● n. a skin disease in some animals caused by mites, resulting in severe itching and hair loss.
– ORIGIN Old French *mangeue*.

mangel-wurzel /**mang**-g'l wer-z'l/ ● n. = **MANGOLD**.

manger ● n. a long trough from which horses or cattle feed.
– ORIGIN Old French *mangeure*.

mangetout /**monzh**-too/ ● n. (pl. **mangetout** or **mangetouts** /**monzh**-too/) Brit. a variety of pea with an edible pod.
– ORIGIN French, 'eat all'.

mangle[1] ● n. esp. Brit. a machine with two or more cylinders turned by a handle, between which wet laundry is squeezed to remove water.
– ORIGIN Greek *manganon* 'axis, engine'.

mangle[2] ● v. (**mangles**, **mangling**, **mangled**) destroy or severely damage by tearing or crushing.
– ORIGIN Old French *mahaignier* 'maim'.

mango ● n. (pl. **mangoes** or **mangos**) an oval tropical fruit with yellow flesh.
– ORIGIN Portuguese *manga*.

mangold ● n. a variety of beet grown as feed for farm animals.
– ORIGIN German *Mangoldwurzel*.

mangrove ● n. a tropical tree or shrub found in coastal swamps, with tangled roots that grow above ground.
– ORIGIN prob. from an extinct Caribbean language.

mangy /**mayn**-ji/ ● adj. **1** having mange. **2** in poor condition; shabby.

manhandle ● v. (**manhandles**, **manhandling**, **manhandled**) **1** move (a heavy object) with effort. **2** push or drag (someone) roughly.

Manhattan E
/man-**hat**-t'n/ an island near the mouth of the Hudson River forming a borough of the city of New York.

manhole ● n. a covered opening through which a person can enter a sewer or other underground structure.

manhood ● n. **1** the state or period of being a man. **2** the men of a country. **3** the qualities associated with men, such as strength or courage.

mania /**may**-ni-uh/ ● n. **1** mental illness in which a person imagines things and has periods of wild excitement. **2** an extreme enthusiasm: *his mania for cars.*
– ORIGIN Greek, 'madness'.

-mania ● comb. form referring to a particular type of mental abnormality or obsession: *kleptomania*.
– DERIVATIVES **-maniac** comb. form.

maniac /**may**-ni-ak/ ● n. **1** a person who behaves in an extremely wild or violent way. **2** informal a person with an extreme enthusiasm for something.
– DERIVATIVES **maniacal** /muh-**ny**-uh-k'l/ adj.

manic ● adj. **1** having to do with mania. **2** showing wild excitement and energy.
– DERIVATIVES **manically** adv.

manic depression ● n. a mental disorder with alternating periods of happiness and depression.
– DERIVATIVES **manic-depressive** adj. & n.

manicure ● n. a cosmetic treatment of the hands and nails. ● v. (**manicures, manicuring, manicured**) give a manicure to.
– DERIVATIVES **manicurist** n.
– ORIGIN from Latin *manus* 'hand' + *cura* 'care'.

manifest[1] ● adj. clear and obvious. ● v. **1** show or display: *Liz manifested signs of depression.* **2** (of an illness or disorder) become noticeable.
– DERIVATIVES **manifestly** adv.
– ORIGIN Latin *manifestus* 'flagrant'.

manifest[2] ● n. a document listing the cargo, crew, or passengers of a ship or aircraft.
– ORIGIN Italian *manifesto* 'manifesto'.

manifestation ● n. **1** a sign or evidence of something. **2** an appearance of a god or spirit in physical form.

manifesto ● n. (pl. **manifestos**) a public declaration of the policy and aims of a group such as a political party.
– ORIGIN Italian.

manifold ● adj. many and various. ● n. a pipe with several openings that connect to other parts, especially one in an internal-combustion engine.
– ORIGIN Old English.

manikin (also **mannikin**) ● n. a very small person.
– ORIGIN Dutch *manneken* 'little man'.

Manila[1] E
/muh-**ni**-luh/ the capital and chief port of the Philippines, on the island of Luzon.

Manila[2] (also **Manilla**) ● n. strong brown paper made from a Philippine plant.
– ORIGIN from **MANILA[1]**.

manioc /man-i-ok/ ● n. = **CASSAVA**.
– ORIGIN from a South American Indian language.

manipulate ● v. (**manipulates, manipulating, manipulated**) **1** handle or control skilfully. **2** control or influence in a clever or underhand way.
– DERIVATIVES **manipulation** n. **manipulator** n.
– ORIGIN Latin *manipulus* 'handful'.

manipulative ● adj. manipulating others in a clever or underhand way.

Manipur E
/mu-ni-**poor**/ a small state in the far east of India, on the border with Burma (Myanmar); capital, Imphal.

Manitoba E
/man-i-**toh**-buh/ a province of central Canada, with a coastline on Hudson Bay; capital, Winnipeg.
– DERIVATIVES **Manitoban** adj. & n.

mankind ● n. human beings as whole.

manky ● adj. Brit. informal dirty.
– ORIGIN prob. from Latin *mancus* 'maimed'.

manly ● adj. (**manlier, manliest**) **1** having qualities associated with men, such as courage and strength. **2** suitable for a man.
– DERIVATIVES **manliness** n.

man-made ● adj. made or caused by human beings.

Mann, E
Thomas (1875–1955), German novelist. His works often deal with the role and character of the artist in relation to society, and include *Buddenbrooks*, *Death in Venice*, and *The Magic Mountain*.

manna ● n. **1** (in the Bible) the substance supplied by God as food to the Israelites in the wilderness (Book of Exodus, chapter 16). **2** something unexpected and beneficial.
– ORIGIN Hebrew.

manned ● adj. having a human crew.

mannequin /man-ni-kin/ ● n. a dummy used to display clothes in a shop.
– ORIGIN French.

manner ● n. **1** a way in which something is done or happens: *he was dancing in a peculiar manner.* **2** a person's outward behaviour or attitude towards others: *her shy manner.* **3** (**manners**) polite behaviour. **4** literary a kind or sort.
– PHRASES **all manner of** many different kinds of. **to the manner born** naturally at ease in a job or situation.
– ORIGIN Latin *manuarius* 'of the hand'.

mannered ● adj. **1** behaving in a specified way: *well-mannered.* **2** (of a style of writing, acting, etc.) artificial and affected.

mannerism ● n. **1** a distinctive personal gesture, habit, or way of speaking. **2** (**Mannerism**) a style of 16th-century Italian art in which people or objects were shown in an exaggerated or distorted way.
– DERIVATIVES **mannerist** n. & adj.

mannerly ● adj. well-mannered; polite.

mannikin ● n. var. of **MANIKIN**.

mannish ● adj. (of a woman) looking or behaving like a man.

manoeuvrable (US **maneuverable**) ● adj. (of a boat or aircraft) able to be manoeuvred easily.

manoeuvre /muh-**noo**-ver/ (US **maneuver**) ● n. **1** a movement or series of moves requiring skill and care. **2** a carefully planned scheme or action. **3** (**manoeuvres**) a large-scale military exercise. ● v. (**manoeuvres, manoeuvring, manoeuvred**; US **maneuvers, maneuvering, maneuvered**) **1** make a movement or series of moves skilfully and carefully. **2** guide skilfully or craftily.
– ORIGIN French *manœuvrer*.

man-of-war (also **man-o'-war**) ● n. hist. an armed sailing ship.

manometer /muh-**nom**-i-ter/ ● n. an instrument for measuring the pressure of fluids.
– ORIGIN Greek *manos* 'thin'.

manor ● n. **1** a large country house with lands. **2** (in medieval times) an area of land controlled by a lord.
– DERIVATIVES **manorial** adj.
– ORIGIN Old French *maner* 'dwelling'.

manpower ● n. the number of people working or available for work or service.

manqué /mong-kay/ ● adj. having never become what one might have been: *an actor manqué.*
– ORIGIN French.

Man Ray 
see **RAY[2]**

Mans, Le E
see **Le Mans**.

mansard /man-sard/ ● **n.** a roof with four sides, each of which becomes steeper halfway down.
– ORIGIN named after the French architect François *Mansart* (1598–1666).

manse /manss/ ● **n.** a house provided for the minister in the Presbyterian and some other churches.
– ORIGIN Latin *mansus*.

manservant ● **n.** a male servant.

Mansfield, E
Katherine (1888–1923; pen name of *Kathleen Mansfield Beauchamp*), New Zealand short-story writer.

mansion ● **n.** a large, impressive house.
– ORIGIN Latin, 'dwelling'.

manslaughter ● **n.** the crime of killing a person without meaning to do so.

Manson, E
Charles (b.1934), American cult leader. He founded a commune based on free love and complete subordination to him. In 1969 its members carried out a series of murders, including that of the American actress Sharon Tate.

Mantegna E
/man-**ten**-yuh/, Andrea (1431–1506), Italian painter and engraver, noted especially for his frescoes, which show his interest in classical antiquity.

mantel ● **n.** a mantelpiece or mantelshelf.
– ORIGIN from **mantle**.

mantelpiece ● **n. 1** a structure surrounding a fireplace. **2** a mantelshelf.

mantelshelf ● **n.** a shelf forming the top of a mantelpiece.

mantilla /man-**til**-luh/ ● **n.** (in Spain) a lace or silk scarf worn by women over the hair and shoulders.
– ORIGIN Spanish.

mantis (also **praying mantis**) ● **n.** (pl. **mantis** or **mantises**) an insect with a long body, that waits motionless for its prey with its forelegs folded.
– ORIGIN Greek, 'prophet'.

mantle ● **n. 1** a woman's loose sleeveless cloak. **2** a close covering, such as that of snow. **3** a mesh cover fixed round a gas jet, producing a glowing light when heated. **4** a role or responsibility that passes from one person to another. **5** the region of very hot, dense rock between the earth's crust and its core. ● **v.** (**mantles**, **mantling**, **mantled**) literary cover: *mists mantled the slopes*.
– ORIGIN Latin *mantellum*.

mantra /man-truh/ ● **n.** (originally in Hinduism and Buddhism) a word or sound repeated to aid concentration when meditating.
– ORIGIN Sanskrit, 'instrument of thought'.

manual ● **adj. 1** having to do with or operated by the hands. **2** working with the hands: *a manual worker*. ● **n.** a book giving instructions.
– DERIVATIVES **manually** adv.
– ORIGIN Latin *manualis*.

manufacture ● **v.** (**manufactures**, **manufacturing**, **manufactured**) **1** make (something) on a large scale using machinery. **2** invent (evidence or a story). ● **n.** the making of goods on a large scale using machinery.
– DERIVATIVES **manufacturer** n.
– ORIGIN French.

manure ● **n.** animal dung used for fertilizing land. ● **v.** (**manures**, **manuring**, **manured**) spread manure on.
– ORIGIN Old French *manouvrer* 'manoeuvre'.

manuscript ● **n. 1** a handwritten book, document, or piece of music. **2** an author's handwritten or typed text, before printing and publication.
– ORIGIN from Latin *manu* 'by hand' + *scriptus* 'written'.

Manx ● **adj.** relating to the Isle of Man.
– ORIGIN Old Norse.

Manx cat ● **n.** a breed of cat that has no tail.

many ● **det., pron., & adj.** (**more**, **most**) a large number of. ● **n.** (**the many**) the majority of people.
– ORIGIN Old English.

Maoism /mow-i-z'm/ ● **n.** the communist policies and theories of Mao Zedong as formerly practised in China.
– DERIVATIVES **Maoist** n. & adj.

Maori /mow-ri/ ● **n.** (pl. **Maori** or **Maoris**) **1** a member of the aboriginal people of New Zealand. **2** the language of this people.
– ORIGIN Maori.

Mao Zedong E
/mow dzi-**duung**/ (also **Mao Tse-tung** /mow tsay-**tuung**/) (1893–1976), Chinese statesman, chairman of the Communist Party of the Chinese People's Republic 1949–76 and head of state 1949–59. He defeated both the occupying Japanese and rival Kuomintang nationalist forces to create the People's Republic of China in 1949, becoming its first head of state. Although no longer head of state, he instigated the Cultural Revolution (1966–8).

map ● **n. 1** a diagram of an area showing physical features, cities, roads, etc. **2** a diagram or collection of data showing the way in which something is arranged or spread over an area. ● **v.** (**maps**, **mapping**, **mapped**) **1** show on a map. **2** (**map out**) plan in detail.
– PHRASES **put on the map** make famous.
– ORIGIN Latin *mappa* 'sheet, napkin'.

maple ● **n.** a tree with five-pointed leaves and a syrupy sap.
– ORIGIN Old English.

Maputo E
/muh-**poo**-toh, muh-**poo**-too/ the capital and chief port of Mozambique. Former name (until 1976) **Lourenço Marques**.

Maquis /ma-kee/ ● **n.** the French resistance movement during the German occupation of France in the Second World War.
– ORIGIN French, 'brushwood'.

Mar. ● **abbrev.** March.

mar ● **v.** (**mars**, **marring**, **marred**) spoil the appearance or quality of.
– ORIGIN Old English.

marabou /ma-ruh-boo/ ● **n. 1** an African stork with a large neck pouch. **2** down feathers from marabou used as trimming for hats or clothing.
– ORIGIN Arabic, 'holy man'.

maraca /muh-**rak**-uh/ ● n. a hollow club-shaped gourd or container filled with small beans, stones, etc., shaken as a musical instrument.
– ORIGIN Portuguese.

Maradona E
/ma-ruh-**don**-uh/, Diego (Armando) (b.1960), Argentinian footballer. He captained the Argentina team that won the World Cup in 1986, arousing controversy when his apparent handball scored a goal in the quarter-final match against England.

maraschino cherry ● n. a cherry preserved in maraschino, a liqueur made from cherries.
– ORIGIN Italian.

marathon ● n. **1** a long-distance running race, strictly one of 26 miles 385 yards (42.195 km). **2** a long and difficult task.
– ORIGIN from *Marathōn* in Greece, where the Greeks defeated the Persians in 490 BC; a messenger is said to have run from Marathon to Athens with the news.

maraud /muh-**rawd**/ ● v. make a raid in search of things to steal.
– DERIVATIVES **marauder** n.
– ORIGIN French, 'rogue'.

Marbella E
/mar-**bay**-uh/ a resort town on the Costa del Sol of southern Spain.

marble ● n. **1** a hard form of limestone, typically with coloured lines running through it, which is polished and used in sculpture and building. **2** a small ball of coloured glass used as a toy. **3** (**one's marbles**) informal one's mental powers.
– ORIGIN Greek *marmaros* 'shining stone'.

marbled ● adj. having coloured streaks like marble.

marbling ● n. colouring or marking that resembles marble.

marcasite /mar-kuh-syt, mar-kuh-zeet/ ● n. a semi-precious stone consisting of iron pyrites.
– ORIGIN Latin *marcasita*.

Marceau E
/mar-**soh**/, Marcel (b.1923), French mime artist, creator of the white-faced character Bip.

March ● n. the third month of the year.
– ORIGIN from Latin *Martius mensis* 'month of Mars'.

march ● v. **1** walk in time and with regular paces, like a soldier. **2** walk quickly and with determination. **3** force (someone) to walk quickly. **4** take part in an organized procession to make a protest. ● n. **1** an act of marching. **2** a procession organized as a protest. **3** a piece of music written to accompany marching.
– DERIVATIVES **marcher** n.
– ORIGIN French *marcher* 'to walk'.

Marches ● pl. n. land on the border between two countries or territories.
– ORIGIN Old French *marche*.

March hare ● n. informal a brown hare in the breeding season, noted for its wild behaviour.

marchioness /mar-shuh-**ness**/ ● n. **1** the wife or widow of a marquess. **2** a woman holding the rank of marquess in her own right.
– ORIGIN Latin *marchionissa*.

Marciano E
/mar-si-**ah**-noh/, Rocky (1923–69; born *Rocco Francis Marchegiano*), American boxer, who was world heavyweight champion 1952–6.

Marconi E
/mar-**koh**-ni/, Guglielmo (1874–1937), Italian electrical engineer, pioneer of radio communication. In 1895 he made a radio transmission over a distance of a mile, and in 1901 transmitted a signal across the Atlantic.

Marco Polo E
/mar-koh **poh**-loh/ (*c*.1254–*c*.1324), Italian traveller. With his father and uncle he travelled to China and the court of Kublai Khan via central Asia (1271–75).

Mardi Gras /mar-di **grah**/ ● n. a carnival held in some countries on Shrove Tuesday.
– ORIGIN French, 'fat Tuesday', the last day of feasting before the fast of Lent.

Mare, E
Walter de la, see **DE LA MARE**.

mare /mair/ ● n. the female of a horse or related animal.
– ORIGIN Old English.

mare's nest ● n. **1** a muddle. **2** a discovery that turns out to be worthless.

Margaret, Princess, E
Margaret Rose (1930–2002), only sister of Elizabeth II.

margarine ● n. a butter substitute made from vegetable oils or animal fats.
– ORIGIN French.

margin ● n. **1** an edge or border. **2** the blank border on each side of the print on a page. **3** an amount above or below a given level: *they won by a 17-point margin*. **4** the lower limit of possibility, success. etc.
– PHRASES **margin of error** a small amount allowed for in case of miscalculation.
– ORIGIN Latin *margo*.

marginal ● adj. **1** relating to a margin. **2** of minor importance. **3** Brit. (of a parliamentary seat) held by a small majority and so at risk in an election.
– DERIVATIVES **marginality** n.

marginalia /mar-ji-**nay**-li-uh/ ● pl. n. notes written or printed in the margin of a book or manuscript.

marginalize (also **marginalise**) ● v. (**marginalizes, marginalizing, marginalized**) make (a person or group) feel less important or powerful.
– DERIVATIVES **marginalization** (also **marginalisation**) n.

marginally ● adv. slightly.

Mariana Islands E
/ma-ri-**ah**-nuh/ a group of islands in the western Pacific, comprising Guam and the Northern Marianas.

Mariana Trench E
an ocean trench to the south-east of the Mariana Islands, with the greatest known ocean depth (11,034 m, 36,201 ft).

m

Marie Antoinette E
/ma-ri on-twuh-**net**/ (1755–93), French queen, wife of Louis XVI. Her extravagant lifestyle led to widespread unpopularity and, like her husband, she was executed during the French Revolution.

Marie Celeste E
var. of **MARY CELESTE**.

marigold • n. a plant of the daisy family with yellow or orange flowers.
– ORIGIN from the woman's name *Mary* + dialect *gold*, 'marigold'.

marijuana /ma-ri-**hwah**-nuh/ • n. cannabis.
– ORIGIN Latin American Spanish.

marina • n. a purpose-built harbour with moorings for yachts and small boats.
– ORIGIN Italian or Spanish.

marinade • n. /ma-ri-**nayd**/ a mixture of ingredients in which food is soaked before cooking in order to flavour or soften it. • v. /ma-ri-nayd/ (**marinades, marinading, marinaded**) = **MARINATE**.
– ORIGIN French.

marinate • v. (**marinates, marinating, marinated**) soak in a marinade.

marine • adj. **1** relating to the sea. **2** relating to shipping or a navy. • n. a member of a body of troops trained to serve on land or sea.
– ORIGIN Latin *marinus*.

mariner • n. formal or literary a sailor.

marionette • n. a puppet worked by strings.
– ORIGIN French.

marital • adj. relating to marriage or the relations between husband and wife.
– ORIGIN Latin *maritus* 'husband'.

maritime • adj. **1** relating to shipping or other activity taking place at sea. **2** living or found in or near the sea. **3** (of a climate) moist and mild due to the influence of the sea.
– ORIGIN Latin *maritimus*.

marjoram • n. a plant of the mint family, used as a herb in cooking.
– ORIGIN Latin *majorana*.

mark[1] • n. **1** a small area on a surface having a different colour from its surroundings. **2** something that acts as a pointer. **3** a sign or symbol that identifies something. **4** a sign of a quality or feeling: *a mark of respect*. **5** a characteristic feature. **6** a stage: *the runner had passed the ten mile mark*. **7** a point awarded for a correct answer or for a good performance in an examination. **8** a particular model of a vehicle or machine. • v. **1** make a mark on. **2** write a word or symbol on (an object) to identify it. **3** indicate the position of: *the pass marks the border between Alaska and the Yukon*. **4** (**mark out**) show to be different or special. **5** acknowledge (an important event). **6** (**mark up** or **down**) increase or reduce the price of (an item). **7** give a mark to (written work). **8** pay careful attention to. **9** Brit. (in team games) stay close to (an opponent) to prevent them getting or passing the ball.
– PHRASES **be quick off the mark** be fast in responding. **make a mark** have a notable effect. **mark time 1** (of troops) march on the spot. **2** pass time while waiting for something better. **on your marks** be ready to start (used to instruct competitors in a race). **up to the mark** up to the required standard.
– ORIGIN Old English.

m

mark[2] • n. the former basic unit of money of Germany, equal to 100 pfennig.
– ORIGIN Old Norse.

Mark, St E
an Apostle, the traditional author of the second Gospel. Feast day, 25 April.

Mark Antony E
see **ANTONY**.

marked • adj. **1** having an identifying mark. **2** clearly noticeable. **3** singled out as a target for attack: *a marked man*.
– DERIVATIVES **markedly** adv.

marker • n. **1** an object used to indicate a position, place, or route. **2** a felt-tip pen with a broad tip.

market • n. **1** a regular gathering for the buying and selling of food, livestock, or other goods. **2** an outdoor space or large hall where people offer goods for sale. **3** a particular area of trade or business. **4** demand for a particular product or service: *there's a market for ornamental daggers*. • v. (**markets, marketing, marketed**) advertise or promote.
– PHRASES **on the market** available for sale.
– DERIVATIVES **marketable** adj.
– ORIGIN Latin *mercatus*.

marketeer • n. a person who is in favour of a particular system of trade: *a free marketeer*.

market garden • n. a place where vegetables and fruit are grown for sale.

marketing • n. the promoting and selling of products or services.

marketplace • n. the world of trade: *the global marketplace*.

market research • n. the gathering of information about consumers' needs, likes, and dislikes.

market town • n. a medium-sized town where a regular market is held.

market value • n. the amount for which something can be sold in a competitive market.

marking • n. **1** an identifying mark. **2** (also **markings**) a pattern of marks on an animal.

Markova E
/mar-**koh**-vuh, **mar**-kuh-vuh/, Dame Alicia (b.1910; born *Lilian Alicia Marks*), English ballet dancer.

Marks, E
Simon, 1st Baron Marks of Broughton (1888–1964), English businessman. In 1926 he founded the retail chain Marks & Spencer, based on the Marks and Spencer Penny Bazaars set up by his father and Thomas Spencer.

marksman • n. a person skilled in shooting.
– DERIVATIVES **marksmanship** n.

mark-up • n. **1** an amount added to the cost of producing something, to cover the producer's costs and profit. **2** Computing a set of codes given to different parts of a text.

marl[1] • n. rock or soil consisting of clay and lime.
– ORIGIN Old French *marle*.

marl[2] • n. a type of fabric with differently coloured threads.
– ORIGIN from **MARBLED**.

Marlborough E
/mawl-bruh/, John Churchill, 1st Duke of (1650–1722), British general. He was commander of British and Dutch troops in the War of the Spanish Succession and won a series of victories over the French armies of Louis XIV.

Marley, E
Bob (1945–81; full name *Robert Nesta Marley*), Jamaican reggae singer, guitarist, and songwriter, who popularized reggae in the 1970s.

marlin • n. a large, edible fish of warm seas, with a pointed snout.
– ORIGIN from **MARLINSPIKE**.

marlinspike • n. a pointed metal tool used by sailors to separate strands of rope or wire.
– ORIGIN Dutch *marlen* 'keep binding'.

Marlowe, E
Christopher (1564–93), English dramatist and poet. His plays include the tragedies *Doctor Faustus* and *The Jew of Malta*.

marmalade • n. a preserve made from oranges.
– ORIGIN Portuguese *marmelada* 'quince jam'.

Marmara, Sea of E
/mar-muh-ruh/ a small sea in NW Turkey. Connected by the Bosporus to the Black Sea and by the Dardanelles to the Aegean, it separates European Turkey from Asian Turkey.

marmoreal /mar-mor-i-uhl/ • adj. literary made of or resembling marble.
– ORIGIN Latin *marmoreus*.

marmoset /mar-muh-zet/ • n. a small tropical American monkey with a silky coat and a long tail.
– ORIGIN Old French *marmouset* 'grotesque image'.

marmot /mar-muht/ • n. a heavily built burrowing rodent.
– ORIGIN French *marmotte*.

Marne E
/marn/ a river of east central France, which rises north of Dijon and flows north and west to join the Seine near Paris. Its valley was the scene of two important battles in the First World War (September 1914 and July 1918).

maroon[1] • n. a dark brownish-red colour.
– ORIGIN French *marron* 'chestnut'.

maroon[2] • v. (**be marooned**) be abandoned alone in a remote place.
– ORIGIN Spanish *cimarrón* 'runaway slave'.

marque • n. a make of car, as distinct from a specific model.
– ORIGIN French.

marquee • n. esp. Brit. a large tent used for social or business events.
– ORIGIN from **MARQUISE**.

Marquesas Islands E
/mar-kay-zuhss/ a group of volcanic islands in the South Pacific, forming part of French Polynesia.

marquess • n. a British nobleman ranking above an earl and below a duke.
– ORIGIN from **MARQUIS**.

marquetry /mar-ki-tri/ • n. inlaid work made from small pieces of coloured wood, used to decorate furniture.
– ORIGIN French *marqueter* 'become variegated'.

Márquez, E
Gabriel García, see **GARCÍA MÁRQUEZ**.

marquis /mar-kwiss/ • n. (in some European countries) a nobleman ranking above a count and below a duke.
– ORIGIN Old French *marchis*.

marquise /mar-keez/ • n. the wife or widow of a marquis, or a woman holding the rank of marquis in her own right.
– ORIGIN French, feminine of **MARQUIS**.

Marrakesh E
/ma-ruh-kesh/ (also **Marrakech**) a city in western Morocco, in the foothills of the High Atlas Mountains.

marram grass • n. a coarse grass that grows on sand dunes.
– ORIGIN Old Norse.

marriage • n. **1** the formal union of a man and a woman, by which they become husband and wife. **2** a combination of two or more elements.
– PHRASES **marriage of convenience** a marriage for practical reasons.
– ORIGIN Old French *mariage*.

marriageable • adj. suitable for marriage.

married • adj. joined in marriage.

marrow • n. **1** Brit. a long vegetable with a thin green skin and white flesh. **2** (also **bone marrow**) a soft fatty substance in the cavities of bones, in which blood cells are produced.
– PHRASES **to the marrow** to one's innermost being.
– ORIGIN Old English.

marrowbone • n. a bone containing edible marrow.

marry • v. (**marries**, **marrying**, **married**) **1** become the husband or wife of. **2** join (two people) in marriage. **3** (**marry into**) become a member of (a family) by marriage. **4** join together.
– ORIGIN Old French *marier*.

Mars[1] E
the Roman god of war. Greek equivalent **ARES**.

Mars[2] E
a small reddish planet which is the fourth in order from the sun.

Marseilles E
/mar-say/ a city and port on the Mediterranean coast of southern France.

Marsh, E
Dame Ngaio (Edith) (1899–1982), New Zealand writer of detective fiction.

marsh • n. an area of low-lying land which remains waterlogged.
– DERIVATIVES **marshy** adj.
– ORIGIN Old English.

marshal • n. **1** an officer of the highest rank in the armed forces of some countries. **2** (in the US) a type of law enforcement officer. **3** an official responsible for supervising public events. • v. (**marshals**, **marshalling**, **marshalled**; US **marshals**, **marshaling**, **marshaled**) **1** assemble (a group of people) in order. **2** bring together (facts, thoughts, etc.) in an organized way.
– ORIGIN Old French *mareschal* 'farrier,

commander'.

Marshall Islands E
a country consisting of two chains of islands in the NW Pacific; capital, Majuro.

Marshall Plan E
a US-sponsored programme of financial aid, initiated by Secretary of State George C. Marshall and passed by Congress in 1948, designed to boost the economies of western European countries after the Second World War.

marshmallow • n. a spongy sweet made from sugar, egg white, and gelatin.
– ORIGIN formerly made from the root of a plant growing in marshes.

marsh marigold • n. a plant with large yellow flowers which grows in damp ground and shallow water.

Marston Moor, Battle of E
a battle of the English Civil War, fought in 1644 on Marston Moor near York, in which the Royalist armies suffered a significant defeat.

marsupial /mar-syoo-pi-uhl/ • n. a mammal whose young are born incompletely developed and are carried and suckled in a pouch on the mother's belly.
– ORIGIN Greek *marsupion* 'little purse'.

mart • n. a trade centre or market.
– ORIGIN Dutch.

marten • n. a weasel-like forest animal.
– ORIGIN from Old French *peau martrine* 'marten fur'.

Martial E
/mar-sh'l/ (*c.*40–*c.*104 AD; Latin name *Marcus Valerius Martialis*), Roman poet. His fifteen books of epigrams reflect all facets of Roman life.

martial • adj. having to do with war.
– ORIGIN Latin *martialis*.

martial arts • pl. n. sports which originated as forms of self-defence or attack, such as judo and karate.

martial law • n. government by the military forces of a country, when ordinary laws do not apply.

Martian • n. a supposed inhabitant of the planet Mars.

Martin, E
Dean (1917–95; born *Dino Paul Crocetti*), American singer and actor, who joined with Frank Sinatra and Sammy Davis Jr in a number of films.

martin • n. a small short-tailed swallow.
– ORIGIN prob. from St *Martin* (see **MARTIN, ST**).

Martin, St E
(d.397), French bishop, a patron saint of France. Feast day, 11 November.

martinet • n. a person who enforces strict discipline.
– ORIGIN named after Jean *Martinet*, a 17th-century French drill master.

martingale • n. a strap or set of straps running from the noseband or reins to the girth of a horse, used to prevent the horse from raising its head too high.

– ORIGIN French.

Martinique E
/mar-ti-**neek**/ a French island in the Caribbean, in the Lesser Antilles; capital, Fort-de-France.
– DERIVATIVES **Martiniquan** n. & adj.

martyr • n. **1** a person who is killed because of their religious or other beliefs. **2** a person who exaggerates their difficulties in order to gain sympathy. • v. make a martyr of.
– DERIVATIVES **martyrdom** n.
– ORIGIN Greek *martur* 'witness'.

marvel • v. (**marvels**, **marvelling**, **marvelled**; US **marvels**, **marveling**, **marveled**) be filled with wonder. • n. a person or thing that causes a feeling of wonder.
– ORIGIN Old French *merveille*.

Marvell E
/mar-vel, **mar**-v'l/, Andrew (1621–78), English metaphysical poet, author of 'To his Coy Mistress' and 'Bermudas'. He also wrote verse satires attacking the corruption of Charles II and his ministers.

marvellous (US **marvelous**) • adj. **1** causing great wonder. **2** extremely good.
– DERIVATIVES **marvellously** (US **marvelously**) adv.

Marx, E
Karl (Heinrich) (1818–83), German political philosopher and economist, resident in England from 1849. The founder of modern communism with Friedrich Engels, he collaborated with him in the writing of the *Communist Manifesto*, and enlarged it in *Das Kapital*.

Marx Brothers E
a family of American comedians, consisting of the brothers **Chico** (Leonard, 1886–1961), **Harpo** (Adolph Arthur, 1888–1964), **Groucho** (Julius Henry, 1890–1977), and **Zeppo** (Herbert, 1901–79). Their films include *Duck Soup* and *A Night at the Opera*.

Marxism • n. the political and economic theories of Karl Marx and Friedrich Engels, which formed the basis for communism.
– DERIVATIVES **Marxist** n. & adj.

Mary, E
mother of Jesus; known as **the (Blessed) Virgin Mary** or **St Mary**. According to the Gospels she was a virgin betrothed to Joseph and conceived Jesus by the power of the Holy Spirit. Feast days, 1 January (Roman Catholic Church), 25 March (Annunciation), 15 August (Assumption), 8 September (Immaculate Conception).

Mary I E
(1516–58; known as **Bloody Mary**), daughter of Henry VIII, queen of England 1553–8. She restored Roman Catholicism as the state religion and instigated a series of religious persecutions against Protestants.

Mary II E
(1662–94), daughter of James II, queen of England 1689–94. Having been invited to replace her Catholic father on the throne after his deposition in 1689, she insisted that her husband, William of Orange, be crowned along with her.

Mary, Queen of Scots E
(1542–87; known as **Mary Stuart**), queen of Scotland 1542–67. A devout Catholic, she was unable to control her Protestant lords, and fled to England in 1567. She became the focus of several Catholic plots against Elizabeth I and was eventually beheaded.

Mary Celeste E
/si-lest/ (also **Marie Celeste**) an American brig that was found in the North Atlantic in 1872 in perfect condition but abandoned. The fate of the crew and the reason for the abandonment of the ship remain a mystery.

Maryland E
a state of the eastern US, on the Atlantic coast; capital, Annapolis.
– DERIVATIVES **Marylander** n.

Mary Magdalene, St E
/mag-duh-lin/ (also **Magdalen**) (in the New Testament) a follower of Jesus, who cured her of evil spirits; she is also traditionally identified with the 'sinner' mentioned in the Gospel of Luke, chapter 8. Feast day, 22 July.

marzipan • n. a sweet paste of ground almonds, sugar, and egg whites.
– ORIGIN Italian *marzapane*.

Masaccio E
/ma-**sach**-i-oh/, (1401–28); born *Tommaso Giovanni di Simone Guidi*), Italian painter, the first artist to apply the laws of perspective to painting.

Masaryk E
/**mass**-uh-rik/, Tomáš (Garrigue) (1850–1937), Czechoslovak statesman, first President of independent Czechoslovakia 1918–35.

mascara • n. a cosmetic for darkening and thickening the eyelashes.
– ORIGIN Italian, 'mask'.

Mascarene Islands E
/mass-kuh-**reen**/ a group of three islands in the western Indian Ocean, east of Madagascar, comprising Réunion, Mauritius, and Rodrigues.

mascot • n. a person, animal, or object that is supposed to bring good luck.
– ORIGIN French *mascotte*.

masculine • adj. **1** relating to men. **2** having qualities associated with men. **3** Grammar (of a gender of nouns and adjectives in certain languages) treated as male.
– DERIVATIVES **masculinity** n.
– ORIGIN Latin *masculus* 'male'.

Masefield E
/**mayss**-feeld/, John (Edward) (1878–1967), English poet and novelist, known for such collections of poems as *Salt-Water Ballads*. He was Poet Laureate 1930–67.

maser /**may**-zer/ • n. a form of laser generating a beam of microwaves.
– ORIGIN from *microwave amplification by the stimulated emission of radiation*.

Maseru E
/muh-**sair**-oo/ the capital of Lesotho.

mash • n. **1** a soft mass made by crushing a substance. **2** bran mixed with hot water, given as food to horses. **3** Brit. informal boiled and mashed potatoes. • v. crush or beat to a mash.
– ORIGIN Old English.

mask • n. **1** a covering for all or part of the face, worn as a disguise or for protection. **2** a device used to filter air breathed in or to supply gas for breathing. **3** a likeness of a person's face moulded in clay or wax. **4** a face pack. • v. **1** cover with a mask. **2** conceal or disguise. **3** cover (an area) so as to protect it during painting, etc.
– ORIGIN French *masque*.

masking tape • n. sticky tape used to cover areas on which paint is not wanted.

masochism /**mass**-uh-ki-z'm/ • n. the enjoyment of one's own pain or humiliation.
– DERIVATIVES **masochist** n. **masochistic** adj.
– ORIGIN named after the Austrian novelist Leopold von Sacher-*Masoch* (1835–95).

Mason, E
James (Neville) (1909–84), English actor. His many films include *A Star is Born*, *Lolita*, and *Georgy Girl*.

mason • n. **1** a builder and worker in stone. **2** (**Mason**) a Freemason.
– ORIGIN Old French *masson*.

Masonic • adj. relating to Freemasons.

masonry • n. stonework.

masque /mahsk/ • n. a form of dramatic entertainment popular in the 16th and 17th centuries, consisting of dancing and acting performed by masked players.
– ORIGIN prob. from former *masker* 'person wearing a mask'.

masquerade /mahss-kuh-**rayd**/ • n. **1** a pretence. **2** a ball at which those attending wear masks. • v. (**masquerades**, **masquerading**, **masqueraded**) pretend to be someone or something.
– ORIGIN French *mascarade*.

Mass • n. **1** the Christian service of the Eucharist or Holy Communion. **2** a musical setting of parts of this service.
– ORIGIN Latin *missa*.

mass • n. **1** a body of matter with no definite shape. **2** a large number of people or objects gathered together. **3** (**the masses**) the ordinary people. **4** (**the mass of**) the majority of. **5** (**a mass of**) a large amount of. **6** Physics the quantity of matter which a body contains. • adj done by or affecting large numbers: *a mass exodus*. • v. gather together in mass.
– ORIGIN Latin *massa*.

Massachusetts E
/mass-uh-**choo**-sits/ a state in the north-eastern US, on the Atlantic coast; capital, Boston.

massacre • n. **1** a brutal slaughter of a large number of people. **2** informal a very heavy defeat. • v. (**massacres**, **massacring**, **massacred**) **1** brutally kill (a large number of people). **2** informal defeat heavily.
– ORIGIN French.

massage • n. the rubbing and kneading of parts of the body with the hands to relieve tension or pain. • v. (**massages**, **massaging**, **massaged**) **1** give a massage to. **2** manipulate (figures) to give a more acceptable result.
– ORIGIN French.

massage parlour • n. **1** an establishment

m

in which massage is provided for payment. **2** euphem. a brothel.

masseur /ma-ser/ ● n. (fem. **masseuse** /ma-serz/) a person who provides massage professionally.
– ORIGIN French.

massif /ma-seef/ ● n. a compact group of mountains.
– ORIGIN French, 'massive'.

Massif Central E
/ma-seef son-**trahl**/ a mountainous plateau in south central France.

Massine E
/ma-**seen**/, Léonide Fédorovitch (1895–1979; born *Leonid Fyodorovich Myasin*), Russian-born French choreographer and ballet dancer. He invented the symphonic ballet, in which the choreography paralleled the structure of the music.

massive ● adj. **1** large and heavy or solid. **2** very large or severe.
– DERIVATIVES **massively** adv.
– ORIGIN French *massif*.

mass-market ● adj. (of goods) produced in large quantities and appealing to most people.

mass noun ● n. a noun referring to something which cannot be counted, usually without a plural and not used with *a* or *an*, e.g. *luggage, happiness*. Contrasted with **COUNT NOUN**.

mass number ● n. Physics the total number of protons and neutrons in a nucleus.

m

mass-produced ● adj. produced in large quantities using machinery.

mast ● n. **1** a tall upright post on a boat, carrying a sail or sails. **2** a tall upright post such as a radio transmitter.
– ORIGIN Old English.

mastectomy /ma-stek-tuh-mi/ ● n. (pl. **mastectomies**) an operation to remove a breast.
– ORIGIN Greek *mastos* 'breast'.

master ● n. **1** a man in a position of authority, control, or ownership. **2** a person skilled in a particular art or activity. **3** the head of a college or school. **4** esp. Brit. a male schoolteacher. **5** a person who holds a second or further degree. **6** an original film, recording, or document from which copies are made. **7** a title placed before the name of a boy. ● adj. **1** skilled in a particular trade: *a master builder*. **2** main: *the master bedroom*. ● v. (**masters**, **mastering**, **mastered**) **1** gain complete knowledge or skill in. **2** gain control of.
– ORIGIN Latin *magister*.

masterclass ● n. a class given to students by an expert musician.

masterful ● adj. **1** powerful and able to control others. **2** performed or performing very skilfully.
– DERIVATIVES **masterfully** adv.

master key ● n. a key that opens several locks, each of which also has its own key.

masterly ● adj. performed or performing very skilfully.

mastermind ● n. **1** a person who is very intelligent. **2** a person who plans and directs a complex scheme. ● v. plan and direct (a complex scheme).

master of ceremonies ● n. a person in charge of proceedings at a formal event, who introduces the speakers or performers.

masterpiece ● n. a work of outstanding skill.

mastery ● n. **1** complete knowledge or command of a subject or skill. **2** control or superiority: *man's mastery over nature*.

masthead ● n. **1** the highest part of a ship's mast. **2** the name of a newspaper or magazine printed at the top of the first page.

mastic /mass-tik/ ● n. **1** a gum from the bark of a Mediterranean tree, used in making varnish and chewing gum. **2** a putty-like waterproof substance used for filling and sealing in building.
– ORIGIN Greek *mastikhē*.

masticate ● v. (**masticates**, **masticating**, **masticated**) chew (food).
– DERIVATIVES **mastication** n.
– ORIGIN Latin *masticare*.

mastiff ● n. a dog of a large, strong breed with drooping ears and lips.
– ORIGIN Old French *mastin*.

mastodon /mass-tuh-don/ ● n. a large extinct elephant-like mammal.
– ORIGIN from Greek *mastos* 'breast' + *odous* 'tooth'.

mastoid /mass-toyd/ ● n. (also **mastoid process**) Anat. a part of the bone behind the ear, to which neck muscles are attached, and which has air spaces linked to the middle ear.

masturbate /mass-ter-bayt/ ● v. (**masturbates**, **masturbating**, **masturbated**) stimulate one's genitals with one's hand for sexual pleasure.
– DERIVATIVES **masturbation** n. **masturbatory** adj.
– ORIGIN Latin *masturbari*.

mat ● n. **1** a thick piece of decorative or protective material placed on the floor. **2** a piece of springy material for landing on in some sports. **3** a small piece of material placed on a surface to protect it. **4** a thick, untidy layer of hairy or woolly material.
– ORIGIN Old English.

matador /mat-uh-dor/ ● n. a bullfighter whose task is to kill the bull.
– ORIGIN Spanish, 'killer'.

Mata Hari E
/mah-tuh **hah**-ri/ (1876–1917; born *Margaretha Geertruida Zelle*), Dutch dancer and secret agent, who probably worked for both the French and German intelligence services before being executed by the French.

match[1] ● n. **1** a contest in which people or teams compete against each other. **2** a person or thing able to compete with another as an equal. **3** an exact equivalent. **4** a pair of things which correspond or are very similar. **5** a marriage or possible marriage partner. ● v. **1** correspond or cause to correspond. **2** be equal to. **3** place in competition with another.
– ORIGIN Old English, 'companion'.

match[2] ● n. a short, thin stick tipped with a mixture that is set alight when rubbed against a rough surface.
– ORIGIN Old French *meche*.

matchbox ● n. a small box in which matches are sold.

matchless ● adj. so good that nothing can

equal it.

matchmaker • n. a person who tries to arrange marriages or relationships between other people.

match point • n. (in tennis) a point which if won by one of the players will also win them the match.

mate[1] • n. **1** Brit. informal a friend. **2** (in combination) a fellow member or occupant: *his teammates.* **3** the sexual partner of an animal. **4** an assistant to a skilled worker. **5** an officer on a merchant ship below a master. • v. (**mates, mating, mated**) (of animals or birds) come together for breeding.
– ORIGIN German, 'comrade'.

mate[2] • n. & v. Chess = CHECKMATE.

mater /may-ter/ • n. Brit. informal, dated mother.
– ORIGIN Latin.

material • n. **1** the matter from which something is or can be made. **2** items needed for doing or creating something. **3** cloth. • adj. **1** having to do with physical objects rather than the mind or spirit. **2** essential or relevant: *evidence material to the case.*
– DERIVATIVES **materially** adv.
– ORIGIN Latin *materia* 'matter'.

materialism • n. the belief that material possessions and physical comfort are more important than spiritual values.
– DERIVATIVES **materialist** n. & adj. **materialistic** adj.

materialize (also **materialise**) • v. (**materializes, materializing, materialized**) **1** become fact; happen. **2** appear suddenly.

maternal • adj. **1** having to do with a mother. **2** related through the mother's side of the family.
– DERIVATIVES **maternally** adv.
– ORIGIN French *maternel.*

maternity • n. the state of being or becoming a mother.

matey • adj. Brit. informal familiar and friendly.

mathematics • n. the branch of science concerned with number, quantity, and space.
– DERIVATIVES **mathematical** adj. **mathematically** adv. **mathematician** n.
– ORIGIN Greek *mathēma* 'science'.

maths (N. Amer. **math**) • n. = MATHEMATICS.

Matilda E
(1102–67; known as **the Empress Maud**), English princess, daughter of Henry I and mother of Henry II. Although she was named Henry I's heir, her cousin Stephen seized the throne on Henry's death (1135). She waged an unsuccessful civil war against Stephen until 1148.

matinee /ma-ti-nay/ • n. an afternoon performance in a theatre or cinema.
– ORIGIN French, 'morning'.

matins /ma-tinz/ • n. a service of morning prayer.
– ORIGIN Old French *matines* 'mornings'.

Matisse E
/ma-teess/, Henri (Emile Benoît) (1869–1954), French painter and sculptor. His painting is characterized by a use of rich glowing colour; later paintings and sculptures show an increasing trend towards abstraction.

matriarch /may-tri-ark/ • n. **1** a woman who is the head of a family or tribe. **2** a powerful older woman.
– DERIVATIVES **matriarchal** adj. **matriarchy** n.
– ORIGIN Latin *mater* 'mother'.

matrices pl. of MATRIX.

matricide /ma-tri-syd/ • n. **1** the killing of one's mother. **2** a person who kills their mother.
– ORIGIN Latin *mater* 'mother'.

matriculate /muh-trik-yuu-layt/ • v. (**matriculates, matriculating, matriculated**) enrol or be enrolled at a college or university.
– DERIVATIVES **matriculation** n.
– ORIGIN Latin *matriculare.*

matrimony • n. marriage.
– DERIVATIVES **matrimonial** adj.
– ORIGIN Latin *matrimonium.*

matrix /may-triks/ • n. (pl. **matrices** /may-tri-seez/ or **matrixes**) **1** an environment or material in which something develops. **2** a mould in which something is cast or shaped. **3** Math. a rectangular arrangement of quantities in rows and columns that is manipulated according to particular rules. **4** a grid-like arrangement of elements.
– ORIGIN Latin, 'womb'.

matron • n. **1** a woman in charge of medical and living arrangements at a boarding school. **2** a dignified or sedate married woman. **3** Brit., dated a woman in charge of nursing in a hospital.
– DERIVATIVES **matronly** adj.
– ORIGIN Latin *matrona.*

matron of honour • n. a married woman attending the bride at a wedding.

matt (also **matte**) • adj. not shiny.
– ORIGIN French *mat.*

matted • adj. (of hair or fur) tangled into a thick mass.

matter • n. **1** physical substance or material; (in physics) that which occupies space and has mass. **2** a subject to be dealt with. **3** (**the matter**) the reason for a problem. **4** written or printed material. • v. (**matters, mattering, mattered**) be important.
– PHRASES **in the matter of** regarding. **a matter of** no more than (a specified period). **a matter of course** the natural or expected thing. **no matter** it is of no importance.
– ORIGIN Latin *materia.*

Matterhorn E
/mat-ter-horn/ a mountain in the Alps, on the border between Switzerland and Italy; it is 4,477 m (14,688 ft) high.

matter-of-fact • adj. unemotional and practical.

Matthau E
/mat-tow/, Walter (1920–2000; born *Walter Matuschanskayasky*), American actor, known for comedy films such as *The Odd Couple.*

Matthew, St E
an Apostle, the traditional author of the first Gospel. Feast day, 21 September.

Matthews, E
Sir Stanley (1915–2000), English footballer, who played for England fifty-four times and remained a professional player until he was 50.

Matthias, St E
/muh-thy-uhss/ an Apostle, chosen by lot to replace Judas. Feast day, 14 May or 9 August.

matting • n. material used for mats.

mattock • n. a farming tool similar to a pickaxe.
– ORIGIN Old English.

mattress • n. a fabric case filled with soft, firm, or springy material used for sleeping on.
– ORIGIN Arabic, 'carpet or cushion'.

maturation /mat-yuu-**ray**-sh'n/ • n. the action of maturing.

mature • adj. **1** fully grown. **2** sensible, like an adult. **3** (of certain foodstuffs or drinks) full-flavoured. • v. (**matures**, **maturing**, **matured**) **1** become mature. **2** (of an insurance policy) reach the end of its term and so become payable.
– DERIVATIVES **maturely** adv.
– ORIGIN Latin *maturus* 'timely, ripe'.

maturity • n. **1** the state or period of being mature. **2** the time when an insurance policy matures.

matutinal /ma-tyuu-**ty**-n'l/ • adj. formal having to do with the morning.
– ORIGIN Latin *matutinus* 'early'.

maudlin /**mawd**-lin/ • adj. sentimental and full of self-pity.
– ORIGIN from Mary *Magdalen* (see **MARY MAGDALENE, ST**), who was often depicted as weeping.

Maugham E
/mawm/, (William) Somerset (1874–1965), British novelist, short-story writer, and dramatist, born in France. His novels include *Of Human Bondage* and *The Moon and Sixpence*.

Maui E
/**mow**-i/ the second-largest of the Hawaiian islands, lying to the north-west of Hawaii.

maul • v. **1** wound by scratching and tearing. **2** treat savagely or roughly. • n. Rugby Union a loose scrum formed around a player with the ball off the ground.
– ORIGIN Latin *malleus* 'hammer'.

maunder • v. (**maunders**, **maundering**, **maundered**) talk in a rambling way.
– ORIGIN perh. from former *maunder* 'to beg'.

Maundy Thursday • n. the Thursday before Easter, when the British king or queen gives out specially minted coins (**Maundy money**) to a group of people at a public ceremony.
– ORIGIN from Latin *mandatum novum* 'new commandment'.

Maupassant E
/**moh**-pas-son/, (Henri René Albert) Guy de (1850–93), French novelist and short-story writer. His novels, written in a simple, direct narrative style, include *Une Vie* and *Bel-Ami*.

Mauriac E
/**mo**-ri-ak/, François (1885–1970), French novelist, dramatist, and critic. His novels, such as *Thérèse Desqueyroux*, reflect a religious but pessimistic view of life.

Mauritania E
/mo-ri-**tay**-ni-uh/ a country in West Africa with a coastline on the Atlantic Ocean; capital, Nouakchott.
– DERIVATIVES **Mauritanian** adj. & n.

Mauritius E
/muh-**ri**-shuhss/ an island country in the Indian Ocean, east of Madagascar; capital, Port Louis.
– DERIVATIVES **Mauritian** adj. & n.

mausoleum /maw-suh-**lee**-uhm/ • n. (pl. **mausolea** /maw-suh-**lee**-uh/ or **mausoleums**) a building housing a tomb or tombs.
– ORIGIN Greek *Mausōleion*.

mauve • n. a pale purple colour.
– ORIGIN French, 'mallow'.

maverick • n. an unconventional or independent-minded person.
– ORIGIN first meaning an unbranded calf: from Samuel A. *Maverick*, a 19th-century Texas rancher who did not brand his cattle.

maw • n. the jaws or throat.
– ORIGIN Old English.

mawkish • adj. sentimental in an excessive way.
– ORIGIN from former *mawk* 'maggot'.

max • abbrev. maximum.

maxi • n. (pl. **maxis**) a skirt or coat reaching to the ankle.

maxilla /mak-**sil**-luh/ • n. (pl. **maxillae** /mak-**sil**-lee/) **1** the bone of the upper jaw. **2** (in an insect or other arthropod) each of a pair of mouthparts.
– ORIGIN Latin, 'jaw'.

maxim • n. a short statement expressing a general truth or rule of behaviour.
– ORIGIN from Latin *propositio maxima* 'most important proposition'.

maximize (also **maximise**) • v. (**maximizes**, **maximizing**, **maximized**) **1** make as great as possible. **2** make the best use of.

maximum • n. (pl. **maxima** or **maximums**) the greatest amount, size, or strength possible or gained. • adj. greatest in amount, size, or strength.
– DERIVATIVES **maximal** adj.
– ORIGIN Latin, 'greatest thing'.

Maxwell[1], E
James Clerk (1831–79), Scottish physicist, who succeeded in unifying electricity and magnetism and identifying the electromagnetic nature of light.

Maxwell[2], E
(Ian) Robert (1923–91; born *Jan Ludvik Hoch*), Czech-born British publisher and media entrepreneur. He died in obscure circumstances while yachting off Tenerife; it later emerged that he had misappropriated company pension funds.

May • n. **1** the fifth month of the year. **2** (**may**) the hawthorn or its blossom.
– ORIGIN from Latin *Maius mensis* 'month of the goddess *Maia*'.

may • modal verb (3rd sing. present **may**; past **might**) **1** expressing possibility. **2** asking for or giving permission. **3** expressing a wish.
– PHRASES **be that as it may** in spite of that.
– ORIGIN Old English.

USAGE may
For an explanation of when to use **may** and **can**, see the note at **CAN**.

Maya /**my**-uh/ • n. (pl. **Maya** or **Mayas**) a member of a Central American people whose civilization died out *c.*900 AD.

m

– DERIVATIVES **Mayan** adj. & n.

maybe • adv. perhaps.

May Day • n. 1 May, celebrated as a spring festival or as a holiday in honour of workers.

Mayday • n. an international radio distress signal used by ships and aircraft.
– ORIGIN French *m'aidez* 'help me'.

Mayer E
/may-er/, Louis B. (1885–1957; full name *Louis Burt Mayer*; born *Eliezer Mayer*), Russian-born American film executive. In 1924 he formed Metro-Goldwyn-Mayer (MGM) with the Polish-born American film producer Samuel Goldwyn (1882–1974).

Mayfair E
a fashionable and wealthy district in the West End of London.

Mayflower E
the ship in which the Pilgrim Fathers sailed from England to America in 1620.

mayfly • n. an insect with transparent wings which lives for only a very short time.

mayhem • n. violent disorder.
ORIGIN Old French.

mayn't • contr. may not.

Mayo E
a county in the north-west of the Republic of Ireland; county town, Castlebar.

mayonnaise /may-uh-nayz/ • n. a thick creamy dressing made from egg yolks, oil, and vinegar.
ORIGIN French, 'from Port *Mahon*' (the capital of Minorca).

mayor • n. the elected head of a city or borough council.
– DERIVATIVES **mayoral** adj.
– ORIGIN Latin *major* 'greater'.

mayoralty /mair-uhl-ti/ • n. (pl. **mayoralties**) the time during which a mayor is in office.

mayoress • n. **1** the wife of a mayor. **2** a woman elected as mayor.

Mayotte E
/my-ot/ an island to the east of the Comoros in the Indian Ocean, an overseas territory of France; capital, Mamoutzu. Also called **MAHORE**.

maypole • n. a decorated pole with long ribbons attached to the top, traditionally used for dancing round on May Day.

maze • n. a complicated network of paths and walls or hedges through which one has to find a way.
– ORIGIN from **AMAZE**.

mazurka /muh-zer-kuh/ • n. a lively Polish dance.
– ORIGIN Polish, 'woman from the province of Mazovia'.

Mazzini E
/mat-see-ni/, Giuseppe (1805–72), Italian nationalist leader. He founded the patriotic movement Young Italy (1831) and was a leader of the movement for a united Italy.

MB • abbrev. **1** Bachelor of Medicine. [ORIGIN Latin *Medicinae Baccalaureus*.] **2** (also **Mb**) Computing megabyte(s).

MBA • abbrev. Master of Business Administration.

Mbabane E
/uhm-bah-bah-ni/ the capital of Swaziland.

MBE • abbrev. Member of the Order of the British Empire.

Mbeki E
/uhm-bee-ki/, Thabo (b.1942), South African statesman, President since 1999.

MC • abbrev. **1** Master of Ceremonies. **2** Military Cross.

MCC • abbrev. Marylebone Cricket Club.

MD • abbrev. **1** Doctor of Medicine. [ORIGIN Latin *Medicinae Doctor*.] **2** Brit. Managing Director.

Md • symb. the chemical element mendelevium.

MDF • abbrev. medium density fibreboard.

MDMA • abbrev. methylenedioxymethamphetamine, the drug Ecstasy.

ME • abbrev. myalgic encephalomyelitis, a medical condition with fever, aching, and severe tiredness.

me[1] • pron. (first person sing.) used as the object of a verb or preposition or after 'than', 'as', or the verb 'to be', to refer to the speaker himself or herself: *my grammor was atrocious, but Helen understood me.*
ORIGIN Old English.

USAGE me
For an explanation of when to use **me** and when to use **I**, see the note at **PERSONAL PRONOUN**.

me[2] (also **mi**) • n. Music the third note of a major scale, coming after 'ray' and before 'fah'.
– ORIGIN from *mira* in a Latin hymn.

mea culpa /may-uh kuul-puh/ • n. said to admit that something is one's fault.
– ORIGIN Latin, 'by my fault'.

Mead, E
Margaret (1901–78), American anthropologist and social psychologist. She worked in Samoa and the New Guinea area and wrote a number of studies of primitive cultures.

mead • n. an alcoholic drink made from honey and water.
– ORIGIN Old English.

meadow • n. an area of grassland.
– ORIGIN Old English.

meadowsweet • n. a tall plant with creamy-white sweet-smelling flowers.

meagre (US **meager**) • adj. small in quantity and poor in quality: *a meagre diet of bread and beans.*
– DERIVATIVES **meagreness** (US **meagerness**) n.
– ORIGIN Old French *maigre*.

meal[1] • n. **1** any of the regular daily occasions when food is eaten. **2** the food eaten on such an occasion.
– PHRASES **make a meal of** Brit. informal carry out (a task) with unnecessary care.
– ORIGIN Old English.

meal[2] • n. any grain or pulse that has been ground to a powder, used to make flour or feed animals.
– ORIGIN Old English.

meal ticket • n. a person or thing that is treated just as a source of money.

mealy • adj. having to do with meal: *a mealy flavour.*

mealy-mouthed • adj. unwilling to speak frankly.
– ORIGIN perh. from German *Mehl im Maule behalten* 'carry meal in the mouth'.

mean[1] • v. (**means, meaning, meant**) **1** intend to say or refer to. **2** (of a word) have as its explanation in the same language or its equivalent in another language. **3** intend to be or do: *it was meant to be a secret.* **4** have as a result or purpose. **5** be of specified importance: *animals mean more to him than people.*
– PHRASES **mean business** be serious.
– ORIGIN Old English.

mean[2] • adj. **1** unwilling to give or share. **2** unkind or unfair. **3** bad-tempered or aggressive. **4** poor in quality or appearance. **5** dated of a low social class. **6** informal excellent.
– DERIVATIVES **meanly** adv. **meanness** n.
– ORIGIN Old English.

mean[3] • n. **1** the average value of a set of quantities. **2** something in the middle of two extremes. • adj. **1** calculated as a mean. **2** equally far from two extremes.
– ORIGIN Latin *medianus* 'middle'.

meander /mi-an-der/ • v. (**meanders, meandering, meandered**) **1** follow a winding course. **2** wander in an aimless way. • n. a bend of a river that curves back on itself.
– ORIGIN from the river *Maeander* in Turkey.

m

meaning • n. **1** what is meant by a word, idea, or action. **2** a sense of purpose.

meaningful • adj. **1** having meaning. **2** worthwhile. **3** expressive: *meaningful glances.*
– DERIVATIVES **meaningfully** adv.

meaningless • adj. having no meaning or significance.
– DERIVATIVES **meaninglessly** adv. **meaninglessness** n.

means • n. **1** a thing or method for achieving a result. **2** money. **3** wealth: *a man of means.*
– PHRASES **by all means** of course. **by no means** certainly not. **a means to an end** a thing that is not valued in itself but is useful in achieving an aim.
– ORIGIN plural of **MEAN**[3].

means test • n. an official investigation of a person's finances to find out whether they qualify for welfare benefits from the state.

meant past and past part. of **MEAN**[1].

meantime • adv. (also **in the meantime**) meanwhile.

meanwhile • adv. **1** (also **in the meanwhile**) in the period of time between two events. **2** at the same time.

measles • n. an infectious disease causing fever and a red rash.
– ORIGIN prob. from Dutch *masel* 'spot'.

measly • adj. informal ridiculously small or few.

measure • v. (**measures, measuring, measured**) **1** find out the size, amount, or degree of (something) by comparing it with a standard. **2** be of (a specified size). **3** (**measure out**) take an exact quantity of. **4** (**measure up**) reach the required standard. • n. **1** a means of achieving a purpose. **2** a proposal for a law. **3** a standard unit used to express size, amount, or degree. **4** a measuring device marked with such units. **5** (**a measure of**) a certain amount of. **6** (**a measure of**) an indication of the extent or quality of. **7** a unit of metre in poetry.
– PHRASES **for good measure** as an amount or item that is more than what is strictly required. **have the measure of** understand the character or abilities of.
– DERIVATIVES **measurable** adj. **measurably** adv.
– ORIGIN Latin *mensura.*

measured • adj. **1** slow and regular in rhythm. **2** carefully considered: *measured prose.*

measureless • adj. literary having no limits.

measurement • n. **1** the action of measuring. **2** an amount, size, or extent found by measuring. **3** a standard unit used in measuring.

meat • n. **1** the flesh of an animal as food. **2** the chief part: *let's get to the meat of the matter.*
– ORIGIN Old English, 'food'.

meatball • n. a ball of minced or chopped meat.

Meath E
/rhymes with teeth/ a county in the east of the Republic of Ireland; county town, Navan.

meaty • adj. (**meatier, meatiest**) **1** resembling or full of meat. **2** fleshy or muscular. **3** substantial or satisfying: *the play offered meaty roles for actors.*

Mecca[1] E
a city in western Saudi Arabia, the birthplace of Muhammad and considered by Muslims to be the holiest city of Islam.

Mecca[2] • n. a place which attracts many people of a particular type.
– ORIGIN from **MECCA**[1].

mechanic • n. a skilled worker who repairs and maintains machinery.
– ORIGIN Greek.

mechanical • adj. **1** relating to or operated by a machine or machinery. **2** done without thought. **3** relating to physical forces or motion.
– DERIVATIVES **mechanically** adv.

mechanical engineering • n. the branch of engineering concerned with the design, building, and use of machines.

mechanics • n. **1** the branch of study concerned with motion and forces producing motion. **2** machinery or working parts. **3** the practical aspects of something: *the mechanics of cello playing.*

mechanism • n. **1** a piece of machinery. **2** the way in which something works or is brought about.

mechanize (also **mechanise**) • v. (**mechanizes, mechanizing, mechanized**) equip with machines or automatic devices.
– DERIVATIVES **mechanization** (also **mechanisation**) n.

medal • n. a metal disc with an inscription or design, awarded for achievement or to mark an event.
– ORIGIN Latin *medalia* 'half a denarius (an ancient Roman coin)'.

medallion • n. a piece of jewellery in the

shape of a medal, worn as a pendant.

medallist (US **medalist**) • n. a person awarded a medal.

meddle • v. (**meddles, meddling, meddled**) interfere in something that is not one's concern.
– DERIVATIVES **meddler** n.
– ORIGIN Old French.

meddlesome • adj. fond of interfering in others' affairs.

Medea E
/mi-dee-uh/ Gk Myth. a sorceress, who helped Jason to obtain the Golden Fleece and married him.

media • n. **1** television, radio, and newspapers as the means of mass communication. **2** pl. of MEDIUM.

USAGE media
The word **media** comes from the plural of the Latin word **medium**. In the normal sense 'television, radio, and newspapers', it often behaves as a collective noun (one referring to a group of people or things, such as **staff**), and can correctly be used with either a singular or a plural verb: *the media was informed* or *the media were informed*.

mediaeval • adj. var. of MEDIEVAL.

medial /mee-di-uhl/ • adj. situated in the middle.
– DERIVATIVES **medially** adv.
– ORIGIN Latin *medialis*.

median /mee-di-uhn/ • adj. **1** tech. situated in the middle. **2** having a value in the middle of a series of values. • n. **1** a median value. **2** Geom. a straight line drawn from one of the angles of a triangle to the middle of the opposite side.
– ORIGIN Latin *medianus*.

mediate /mee-di-ate/ • v. (**mediates, mediating, mediated**) try to settle a dispute between two other parties.
– DERIVATIVES **mediation** n. **mediator** n.
– ORIGIN Latin *mediare* 'place in the middle'.

medic • n. informal a doctor or medical student.

medical • adj. relating to the science or practice of medicine. • n. an examination to assess a person's physical health.
– DERIVATIVES **medically** adv.
– ORIGIN Latin *medicus* 'physician'.

medicament /muh-dik-uh-muhnt/ • n. a medicine.

medicate • v. (**medicates, medicating, medicated**) **1** give medicine or a drug to. **2** (**medicated**) containing a medicinal substance.
– ORIGIN Latin *medicari*.

medication • n. **1** a medicine or drug. **2** treatment with medicines.

medicinal • adj. **1** having healing properties. **2** relating to medicines.
– DERIVATIVES **medicinally** adv.

medicine • n. **1** the science or practice of the treatment and prevention of disease. **2** a substance taken by mouth in order to treat or prevent disease.
– PHRASES **give someone a dose of their own medicine** treat someone in the same unpleasant way that they treated others.
– ORIGIN Latin *medicus* 'physician'.

medicine man • n. (among North American Indians) a person believed to have magical powers of healing.

medieval /med-i-ee-v'l/ (also **mediaeval**) • adj. **1** relating to the Middle Ages. **2** informal very old-fashioned.
– ORIGIN from Latin *medium aevum* 'middle age'.

medievalist (also **mediaevalist**) • n. a scholar of medieval history or literature.

Medina E
/muh-dee-nuh/ a city in western Saudi Arabia. The site of Muhammad's burial place and the first Islamic mosque, it is the second most holy city of Islam.

medina /me-dee-nuh/ • n. the old quarter of a North African town.
– ORIGIN Arabic, 'town'.

mediocre /mee-di-oh-ker/ • adj. of only average or fairly low quality.
– ORIGIN Latin *mediocris* 'of middle height or degree'.

mediocrity /mee-di-ok-ri-ti/ • n. (pl. **mediocrities**) **1** the state of being mediocre. **2** a person of mediocre ability.

meditate • v. (**meditates, meditating, meditated**) **1** focus one's mind for a time for spiritual purposes or for relaxation. **2** (**meditate on/about**) think carefully about.
– ORIGIN Latin *meditari* 'contemplate'.

meditation • n. **1** the action of meditating. **2** a speech or piece of writing expressing considered thoughts on a subject.

meditative • adj. involving or absorbed in meditation.
– DERIVATIVES **meditatively** adv.

Mediterranean /med-i-tuh-ray-ni-uhn/ • adj. relating to the Mediterranean Sea or the countries around it.
– ORIGIN Latin *mediterraneus* 'inland'.

Mediterranean Sea E
an almost landlocked sea between southern Europe, the north coast of Africa, and SW Asia.

medium • n. (pl. **media** or **mediums**) **1** a means by which something is communicated or achieved. **2** a substance through which a force or other influence is transmitted. **3** a liquid with which pigments are mixed to make paint. **4** (pl. **mediums**) a person claiming to be able to communicate between the dead and the living. **5** the middle state between two extremes. • adj. between two extremes.
– ORIGIN Latin, 'middle'.

medium wave • n. esp. Brit. a radio wave of a frequency between 300 kilohertz and 3 megahertz.

medlar • n. a small brown apple-like fruit.
– ORIGIN Old French *medler*.

medley • n. (pl. **medleys**) **1** a varied mixture. **2** a collection of musical items performed as a continuous piece.
– ORIGIN Old French *medlee* 'melee'.

medulla /mi-dul-luh/ • n. **1** Anat. a separate inner region of an organ or tissue. **2** Bot. the soft internal tissue of a plant.
– ORIGIN Latin, 'pith or marrow'.

medulla oblongata /mi-dul-luh ob-long-gah-tuh/ • n. the part of the spinal cord extending into the brain.

Medusa E
/muh-**dyoo**-suh/ Gk Myth. the only mortal gorgon, killed by Perseus.

meek • **adj.** quiet, gentle, and obedient.
– DERIVATIVES **meekly** adv. **meekness** n.
– ORIGIN Old Norse, 'soft, gentle'.

meerkat • **n.** a small southern African mongoose.
– ORIGIN Dutch, 'sea cat'.

meerschaum /**meer**-shuhm, **meer**-shawm/ • **n. 1** a soft white clay-like material. **2** a tobacco pipe with a bowl made from meerschaum.
– ORIGIN German, 'sea foam'.

meet[1] • **v.** (**meets**, **meeting**, **met**) **1** come together with (someone) at the same place and time. **2** see or be introduced to (someone) for the first time. **3** touch or join. **4** experience (a situation). **5** (**meet with**) receive (a reaction). **6** satisfy (a requirement). • **n.** a meeting for races or foxhunting.
– ORIGIN Old English.

meet[2] • **adj.** archaic suitable or proper.
– ORIGIN from **METE**.

meeting • **n. 1** an organized gathering of people for a discussion or other purpose. **2** a situation in which people meet by chance or arrangement.

mega • **adj.** informal **1** very large. **2** excellent.

mega- • **comb. form 1** large. **2** referring to a factor of one million (10^6).
– ORIGIN Greek *megas* 'great'.

megabyte • **n.** Computing a unit of information equal to one million or (strictly) 1,048,576 bytes.

megahertz • **n.** (pl. **megahertz**) a unit of frequency equal to one million hertz.

megalith • **n.** a large stone that forms a prehistoric monument or part of one.
– DERIVATIVES **megalithic** adj.

megalomania /meg-uh-luh-**may**-ni-uh/ • **n. 1** obsession with having and using power. **2** the false belief that one has great power or importance.
– DERIVATIVES **megalomaniac** n. & adj.

megaphone • **n.** a large cone-shaped device for amplifying the voice.

megastar • **n.** informal a very famous entertainer or sports player.

megaton • **n.** a unit of explosive power equivalent to one million tons of TNT.

megawatt • **n.** a unit of power equal to one million watts.

Meghalaya E
/may-**gah**-luh-yuh/ a small state in the extreme north-east of India, on the northern border of Bangladesh; capital, Shillong.

meiosis /my-**oh**-siss/ • **n.** (pl. **meioses** /my-**oh**-seez/) Biol. a type of cell division that results in daughter cells each with half the number of chromosomes of the parent cell. Compare with **MITOSIS**.
– DERIVATIVES **meiotic** adj.
– ORIGIN Greek *meiōsis* 'lessening'.

Meir E
/may-**eer**/, Golda (1898–1978; born *Goldie Mabovich*), Israeli Labour stateswoman, Prime Minister 1969–74.

Meissen E
/**myss**-uhn/ a city in eastern Germany, famous for its porcelain.

meitnerium /myt-**neer**-i-uhm/ • **n.** a very unstable chemical element made by high-energy atomic collisions.
– ORIGIN named after the Swedish physicist Lise *Meitner* (1878–1968).

Mekong E
/mee-**kong**/ a river of SE Asia, which rises in Tibet and flows south-east and south through southern China, Laos, Cambodia, and Vietnam to its delta on the South China Sea.

melamine /**mel**-uh-meen/ • **n.** a hard plastic used for laminated coatings.
– ORIGIN German *Melamin*.

melancholia /me-luhn-**koh**-li-uh/ • **n.** severe depression.

melancholy • **n.** deep and long-lasting sadness. • **adj.** sad or depressed.
– DERIVATIVES **melancholic** adj.
– ORIGIN Greek *melankholia*.

Melanesia E
/mel-uh-**nee**-*zh*uh/ a region of the western Pacific to the south of Micronesia and west of Polynesia. It contains the Bismarck Archipelago, the Solomon Islands, Vanuatu, New Caledonia, Fiji, and the intervening islands.

melange /may-**lonzh**/ • **n.** a varied mixture.
– ORIGIN French.

melanin /**mel**-uh-nin/ • **n.** a dark pigment in the hair and skin, responsible for the tanning of skin exposed to sunlight.
– ORIGIN Greek *melas* 'black'.

melanoma /mel-uh-**noh**-muh/ • **n.** a form of skin cancer which develops in melanin-forming cells.

Melba, E
Dame Nellie (1861–1931; born *Helen Porter Mitchell*), Australian operatic soprano.

Melbourne[1] E
/**mel**-bern/ the capital of Victoria, SE Australia. It is the country's second-largest city.

Melbourne[2] E
/**mel**-bern, **mel**-born/, William Lamb, 2nd Viscount (1779–1848), British Whig statesman, Prime Minister 1834 and 1835–41.

meld • **v.** blend.
– ORIGIN perh. from **MELT** and **WELD**.

melee /**mel**-ay/ • **n. 1** a confused fight. **2** a disorderly mass of people.
– ORIGIN French.

mellifluous /mel-**lif**-luu-uhsss/ • **adj.** pleasingly smooth and musical to hear.
– ORIGIN from Latin *mel* 'honey' + *fluere* 'to flow'.

mellow • **adj. 1** pleasantly smooth or soft in sound, taste, or colour. **2** relaxed and good-humoured. • **v.** make or become mellow.
– ORIGIN perh. related to **MEAL**[2].

melodeon /mel-**oh**-di-ihn/ • **n. 1** a small accordion. **2** a small organ similar to the harmonium.

melodic /muh-**lod**-ik/ • **adj. 1** relating to melody. **2** pleasant-sounding.
– DERIVATIVES **melodically** adv.

melodious • **adj.** tuneful.

melodrama ● n. **1** a sensational play with exaggerated characters and exciting events. **2** exaggerated behaviour.
– ORIGIN from Greek *melos* 'music' + French *drame* 'drama'.

melodramatic ● adj. too dramatic or exaggerated.
– DERIVATIVES **melodramatically** adv.

melody ● n. (pl. **melodies**) **1** a tune. **2** the main part in harmonized music.
– ORIGIN Greek *melos* 'song'.

melon ● n. a large round fruit with sweet pulpy flesh and many seeds.
– ORIGIN Greek.

melt ● v. **1** make or become liquid by heating. **2** gradually disappear.
– ORIGIN Old English.

meltdown ● n. **1** an accident in a nuclear reactor in which the fuel overheats and melts the reactor core. **2** a disastrous collapse: *the 1987 stock-market meltdown.*

melting point ● n. the temperature at which a solid will melt.

melting pot ● n. a place where different peoples, styles, etc., are mixed together and influence each other.

Melville, E
Herman (1819–91), American novelist and short-story writer. His experiences on a whaling ship formed the basis of several novels, notably *Moby Dick*.

member ● n. **1** a person or organization belonging to a group or society. **2** a part of a complex structure. **3** archaic a part of the body.
– DERIVATIVES **membership** n.
– ORIGIN Latin *membrum* 'limb'.

membrane ● n. **1** a skin-like structure that lines, connects, or covers a cell or part of the body. **2** a thin skin-like sheet of material.
– DERIVATIVES **membranous** adj.
– ORIGIN Latin.

memento ● n. (pl. **mementos** or **mementoes**) an object kept as a reminder.
– ORIGIN Latin, 'remember!'

memento mori /mi-men-toh **mor**-i/ ● n. (pl. **memento mori**) an object kept as a reminder that death is inevitable.
– ORIGIN Latin, 'remember (that you have) to die'.

memo ● n. (pl. **memos**) informal a memorandum.

memoir /**mem**-war/ ● n. **1** a historical account or biography written from personal knowledge. **2** (**memoirs**) an account written by a public figure of their life and experiences.
– ORIGIN French *mémoire* 'memory'.

memorabilia /mem-uh-ruh-**bil**-i-uh/ ● pl. n. objects kept or collected because of their associations with memorable people or events.

memorable ● adj. worth remembering or easily remembered.
– DERIVATIVES **memorably** adv.

memorandum ● n. (pl. **memoranda** or **memorandums**) **1** a note sent from one person to another in an organization. **2** a note recording something for future use.
– ORIGIN Latin, 'something to be brought to mind'.

memorial ● n. an object or structure established in memory of a person or event. ● adj. in memory of someone.

memorize (also **memorise**) ● v. (**memorizes**, **memorizing**, **memorized**) learn by heart.

memory ● n. (pl. **memories**) **1** the faculty by which the mind stores and remembers information. **2** a person or thing remembered. **3** the length of time over which one can remember things. **4** a computer's equipment or capacity for storing information.
– PHRASES **in memory of** so as to commemorate.
– ORIGIN Old French *memorie*.

Memphis[1] E
/**mem**-fiss/ an ancient city of Egypt, whose ruins are situated on the Nile south of Cairo. It is the site of the pyramids of Saqqara and Giza and the Sphinx.

Memphis[2] E
/**mem**-fiss/ a river port on the Mississippi in Tennessee. It was the scene in 1968 of the assassination of Martin Luther King, and the childhood home and burial place of Elvis Presley.

memsahib /**mem**-sahb, **mem**-suh-heeb/ ● n. dated (in India) a respectful form of address for a married white woman.
– ORIGIN from an Indian pronunciation of *ma'am* + **SAHIB**.

men pl. of **MAN**.

menace ● n. **1** a dangerous or troublesome person or thing. **2** a threatening quality. ● v. (**menaces**, **menacing**, **menaced**) threaten.
– ORIGIN Latin *minax* 'threatening'.

ménage à trois /may-nah*zh* ah **trwah**/ ● n. an arrangement in which a married couple and the lover of one of them live together.
– ORIGIN French, 'household of three'.

menagerie /muh-**naj**-uh-ri/ ● n. a collection of wild animals kept in captivity for showing to the public.
– ORIGIN French.

Menai Strait E
/**men**-I/ a channel separating Anglesey from the mainland of NW Wales.

menaquinone /men-uh-**kwin**-ohn/ ● n. vitamin K, a compound produced by bacteria in the intestines, and essential for blood-clotting.
– ORIGIN from its chemical name.

mend ● v. **1** restore to the correct or working condition. **2** improve (an unpleasant situation).
– PHRASES **on the mend** improving in health or condition.
– ORIGIN shortening of **AMEND**.

mendacious /men-**day**-shuss/ ● adj. untruthful.
– DERIVATIVES **mendacity** n.
– ORIGIN Latin *mendax* 'lying'.

Mendel E
/**men**-d'l/, Gregor Johann (1822–84), Moravian monk, the founder of genetics. From systematically breeding peas he demonstrated the transmission of characteristics in a predictable way by factors (genes) which remain intact and independent between generations.

Mendeleev E
/men-duh-**lay**-eff/ (also **Mendeleyev**), Dmitri (Ivanovich) (1834–1907), Russian chemist, who developed the periodic table.

mendelevium /men-duh-**lee**-vi-uhm/ ● **n.** a very unstable chemical element made by high-energy collisions.
– ORIGIN named after Dmitri **MENDELEEV**.

Mendelssohn E
/**men**-d'l-s'n/, Felix (1809–47; full name *Jakob Ludwig Felix Mendelssohn-Bartholdy*), German composer and pianist. His works include the overture *Fingal's Cave*, the oratorio *Elijah*, and five symphonies.

mendicant /**men**-di-kuhnt/ ● **adj. 1** regularly engaged in begging. **2** (of a religious order) originally dependent on charitable donations. ● **n. 1** a beggar. **2** a member of a mendicant order.
– ORIGIN Latin *mendicus* 'beggar'.

Mendip Hills E
a range of limestone hills in SW England.

Menelaus E
/men-uh-**lay**-uhss/ Gk Myth. king of Sparta, husband of Helen and brother of Agamemnon. Helen was stolen from him by Paris, an event which provoked the Trojan War.

menfolk ● **pl. n.** the men of a family or community.

menhir /**men**-heer/ ● **n.** a tall stone set up as a monument in prehistoric times.
– ORIGIN Breton, 'long stone'.

menial /**mee**-ni-uhl/ ● **adj.** (of work) requiring little skill and lacking status. ● **n.** a person with a menial job.
– ORIGIN Old French.

meninges /mi-**nin**-jeez/ ● **pl. n.** (sing. **meninx**) the three membranes that enclose the brain and spinal cord.
– ORIGIN Greek *mēninx* 'membrane'.

meningitis /men-in-**jy**-tiss/ ● **n.** a disease in which the meninges become inflamed owing to infection.

meniscus /muh-**niss**-kuhss/ ● **n.** (pl. **menisci** /muh-**niss**-I/) **1** Physics the curved upper surface of a liquid in a tube. **2** a thin lens curving outwards on one side and inwards on the other.
– ORIGIN Greek *mēniskos* 'crescent'.

menopause ● **n.** the period in a woman's life (between about 45 and 50) when menstruation gradually stops.
– DERIVATIVES **menopausal** adj.
– ORIGIN from Greek *mēn* 'month' + **PAUSE**.

menorah /mi-**nor**-uh/ ● **n.** a large branched candlestick used in Jewish worship.
– ORIGIN Hebrew.

menses /**men**-seez/ ● **pl. n.** blood discharged from the womb during menstruation.
– ORIGIN Latin, 'months'.

menstrual ● **adj.** having to do with menstruation.
– ORIGIN Latin *menstrualis*.

menstruate ● **v.** (**menstruates**, **menstruating**, **menstruated**) (of a non-pregnant woman) discharge blood from the lining of the womb each month.
– DERIVATIVES **menstruation** n.

mensuration /men-syuu-**ray**-sh'n/ ● **n.** **1** measurement. **2** the part of geometry concerned with finding lengths, areas, and volumes.
– ORIGIN Latin.

-ment ● **suffix 1** forming nouns expressing the means or result of an action: *treatment*. **2** forming nouns from adjectives: *merriment*.
– ORIGIN French or Latin.

mental ● **adj. 1** having to do with the mind. **2** relating to disorders or illnesses of the mind. **3** informal mad.
– DERIVATIVES **mentally** adv.
– ORIGIN Latin *mens* 'mind'.

mental age ● **n.** a person's mental ability expressed as the age at which an average person reaches the same ability.

mental handicap ● **n.** a condition in which a person's intellectual ability is underdeveloped, preventing them from functioning normally in society.

mentality ● **n.** (pl. **mentalities**) a typical way of thinking.

menthol ● **n.** a substance found in peppermint oil, used as a flavouring and in decongestant medicines.
– DERIVATIVES **mentholated** adj.
– ORIGIN Latin *mentha* 'mint'.

mention ● **v. 1** refer to briefly. **2** refer to by name as being noteworthy. ● **n. 1** a reference to someone or something. **2** a formal acknowledgement of something noteworthy.
– ORIGIN Latin.

mentor ● **n.** an experienced person in an organization or institution who trains and advises new employees or students.
– ORIGIN named after *Mentor*, the adviser of Telemachus in Homer's *Odyssey*.

menu ● **n. 1** a list of dishes available in a restaurant. **2** the food to be served at a meal. **3** Computing a list of commands or facilities displayed on screen.
– ORIGIN French, 'detailed list'.

Menuhin E
/**men**-yuu-in/, Sir Yehudi (1916–99), American-born British violinist.

Menzies E
/**men**-ziz/, Sir Robert Gordon (1894–1978), Australian Liberal statesman, Prime Minister 1939–41 and 1949–66.

meow ● **n. & v.** var. of **MIAOW**.

MEP ● **abbrev.** Member of the European Parliament.

mercantile /**mer**-kuhn-tyl/ ● **adj.** relating to trade or commerce.
– ORIGIN Italian *mercante* 'merchant'.

mercenary ● **adj.** motivated chiefly by the desire to make money. ● **n.** (pl. **mercenaries**) a professional soldier hired to serve in a foreign army.
– ORIGIN Latin *mercenarius* 'hireling'.

mercer ● **n.** hist. a dealer in fabrics.
– ORIGIN Old French *mercier*.

merchandise ● **n.** /**mer**-chuhn-dyss/ goods for sale. ● **v.** /**mer**-chuhn-dyz/ (**merchandises**, **merchandising**, **merchandised**) promote the sale of.
– DERIVATIVES **merchandiser** n.
– ORIGIN Old French *marchand* 'merchant'.

merchant ● **n. 1** a trader who sells goods in large quantities. **2** informal, derog. a person fond

of a particular activity: *a speed merchant.* • **adj.** (of sailors or shipping) involved with commerce.
– ORIGIN Old French *marchant.*

merchantable • **adj.** suitable for sale.

merchant bank • **n.** esp. Brit. a bank dealing in commercial loans and investment.

merchantman • **n.** a ship carrying merchandise.

merchant navy (US **merchant marine**) • **n.** a country's commercial shipping.

Mercia E
/mer-si-uh/ a kingdom of central England during the Anglo-Saxon period.

merciful • **adj. 1** showing mercy. **2** giving relief from suffering: *a merciful release.*

mercifully • **adv. 1** in a merciful way. **2** to one's great relief.

merciless • **adj.** showing no mercy.
– DERIVATIVES **mercilessly** adv.

mercurial /mer-**kyoor**-i-uhl/ • **adj. 1** tending to change mood suddenly. **2** having to do with mercury.
– ORIGIN Latin *mercurialis* 'relating to the god Mercury'.

Mercury[1] E
the Roman god of eloquence, skill, trading, and thieving, herald and messenger of the gods. Greek equivalent **HERMES**.

Mercury[2] E
a small planet that is the closest to the sun in the solar system.

mercury • **n.** a heavy silvery-white liquid metallic element used in some thermometers and barometers.
– ORIGIN from **MERCURY[1]**.

mercy • **n.** (pl. **mercies**) **1** pity or forgiveness shown towards an enemy or offender in one's power. **2** something to be grateful for. • **adj.** motivated by pity: *a mercy killing.*
– PHRASES **at the mercy of** in the power of.
– ORIGIN Latin *merces* 'reward, pity'.

mere[1] • **adj. 1** that is nothing more than what is specified. **2** (**the merest**) the slightest.
– ORIGIN Latin *merus* 'pure, undiluted'.

mere[2] • **n.** literary a lake or pond.
– ORIGIN Old English.

Meredith E
/me-ruh-dith/, George (1828–1909), English novelist and poet. His verse includes the collection *Modern Love,* and his novels include *The Egoist.*

merely • **adv.** only.

meretricious /me-ri-**tri**-shuhss/ • **adj.** appearing attractive but in reality having no value.
– ORIGIN Latin *meretrix* 'prostitute'.

merganser /mer-gan-zer/ • **n.** a fish-eating diving duck with a long, thin jagged bill.
– ORIGIN from Latin *mergus* 'diver' + *anser* 'goose'.

merge • **v.** (**merges**, **merging**, **merged**) **1** combine or be combined into a whole: *the two building societies merged.* **2** blend gradually into something else.
– ORIGIN Latin *mergere* 'to dip'.

merger • **n.** a merging of two organizations into one.

meridian • **n.** a circle of constant longitude passing through a given place on the earth's surface and the poles.
– ORIGIN Latin *meridianum* 'noon' (because the sun crosses a meridian at noon).

meridional /muh-rid-i-uh-nuhl/ • **adj. 1** relating to southern Europe. **2** relating to a meridian.

meringue /muh-rang/ • **n.** beaten egg whites and sugar baked until crisp.
– ORIGIN French.

merino /muh-ree-noh/ • **n.** (pl. **merinos**) **1** a breed of sheep with long, fine wool. **2** a soft woollen material.
– ORIGIN Spanish.

meristem /me-ri-stem/ • **n.** a region of plant tissue consisting of actively dividing cells.
– ORIGIN Greek *meristos* 'divisible'.

merit • **n. 1** excellence. **2** a good point or quality. • **v.** (**merits**, **meriting**, **merited**) deserve.
– ORIGIN Latin *meritum* 'due reward'.

meritocracy • **n.** (pl. **meritocracies**) **1** government or leadership by people of great merit. **2** a society governed in such a way.
– DERIVATIVES **meritocratic** adj.

meritorious • **adj.** deserving reward or praise.

Merlin E
(in Arthurian legend) a magician who aided and supported King Arthur.

merlin • **n.** a small dark falcon.
– ORIGIN Old French *merilun.*

mermaid • **n.** a mythical sea creature with a woman's head and trunk and a fish's tail.
– ORIGIN from **MERE[2]** (in the former sense 'sea') + **MAID**.

merriment • **n.** cheerfulness and fun.

merry • **adj.** (**merrier**, **merriest**) **1** cheerful and lively. **2** Brit. informal slightly drunk.
– DERIVATIVES **merrily** adv. **merriness** n.
– ORIGIN Old English, 'pleasing'.

merry-go-round • **n. 1** a revolving machine with model horses or cars on which people ride for amusement. **2** a continuous cycle of activities or events.

merrymaking • **n.** cheerful celebration and fun.

Mersey E
a river of NW England, which rises in the Peak District of Derbyshire and flows to the Irish Sea near Liverpool.

Merseyside E
a metropolitan county of NW England.

mesa /**may**-suh/ • **n.** an isolated flat-topped hill with steep sides.
– ORIGIN Spanish, 'table'.

Mesdames pl. of **MADAME**.

Mesdemoiselles pl. of **MADEMOISELLE**.

mesh • **n. 1** material made of a network of wire or thread. **2** the spacing of the strands of a net. **3** a complex or restricting situation. • **v. 1** (**mesh with**) be in harmony with. **2** become entangled. **3** (of a gearwheel) lock together with another.
– ORIGIN prob. from Old English.

mesmeric /mez-me-rik/ • **adj.** hypnotic: *his*

m

mesmeric gaze.

mesmerism ● **n.** dated hypnotism.
– ORIGIN named after the Austrian physician Franz A. *Mesmer* (1734–1815).

mesmerize (also **mesmerise**) ● **v.** (**mesmerizes**, **mesmerizing**, **mesmerized**) completely capture the attention of.

meso- /me-zoh, mee-zoh/ ● **comb. form** middle: *mesosphere.*
– ORIGIN Greek *mesos.*

Mesolithic ● **adj.** relating to the middle part of the Stone Age.
– ORIGIN from Greek *mesos* 'middle' + *lithos* 'stone'.

Mesopotamia E
/mess-uh-puh-**tay**-mi-uh/ an ancient region of SW Asia in present-day Iraq, lying between the Rivers Tigris and Euphrates.

mesosphere ● **n.** the region of the earth's atmosphere above the stratosphere and below the thermosphere.

Mesozoic ● **adj.** Geol. relating to the era between the Palaeozoic and Cenozoic eras, about 245 to 65 million years ago, with evidence of the first mammals, birds, and flowering plants.
– ORIGIN from Greek *mesos* 'middle' + *zōion* 'animal'.

mess ● **n. 1** a dirty or untidy state. **2** a state of confusion or difficulty. **3** euphem. a household animal's excrement. **4** a place where members of the armed forces may eat and relax. ● **v. 1** make untidy or dirty. **2** (**mess about/around**) behave in a silly or playful way. **3** (**mess with**) informal meddle with.
– ORIGIN Old French *mes* 'portion of food'.

message ● **n. 1** a spoken or written communication. **2** an important point or central theme. ● **v.** (**messages**, **messaging**, **messaged**) send a message to.
– PHRASES **on** (or **off**) **message** (of a politician) following (or not following) the official party line.
– ORIGIN Old French.

messenger ● **n.** a person who carries a message.

Messerschmidt E
/mess-er-shmit/, Willy (1898–1978; full name *Wilhelm Emil Messerschmidt*), German aircraft designer and industrialist, designer of the Messerschmidt 109, the standard fighter of the German Air Force during the Second World War.

Messiaen E
/mess-i-an/, Olivier (Eugène Prosper Charles) (1908–92), French composer. His music was influenced by his Roman Catholic faith, birdsong, and Greek and Hindu rhythms.

messiah ● **n. 1** (**the Messiah**) the promised deliverer of the Jewish nation prophesied in the Hebrew Bible. **2** (**the Messiah**) Jesus regarded by Christians as the Messiah of these prophecies. **3** a leader or saviour.
– ORIGIN Hebrew, 'anointed'.

messianic /mess-i-an-ik/ ● **adj. 1** relating to the Messiah. **2** inspired by belief in a messiah.

Messieurs pl. of **MONSIEUR**.

Messina, Strait of E
/mess-ee-nuh/ a channel separating the island of Sicily from the 'toe' of Italy. The strait is noted for the strength of its currents.

Messrs pl. of **MR**.
– ORIGIN short for **MESSIEURS**.

messy ● **adj.** (**messier**, **messiest**) **1** untidy or dirty. **2** confused and difficult to deal with.
– DERIVATIVES **messily** adv. **messiness** n.

met past and past part. of **MEET**[1].

meta- (also **met-** before a vowel or h) ● **comb. form** forming words referring to: **1** a change of position or condition: *metamorphosis.* **2** position behind, after, or beyond: *metacarpus.*
– ORIGIN Greek *meta* 'with, across, after'.

metabolism /mi-**tab**-uh-li-z'm/ ● **n.** the chemical processes in a living thing by which food is used for tissue growth or energy production.
– DERIVATIVES **metabolic** adj.
– ORIGIN Greek *metabolē* 'change'.

metabolize (also **metabolise**) ● **v.** (**metabolizes**, **metabolizing**, **metabolized**) process or be processed by metabolism.

metacarpus /met-uh-**kar**-puhss/ ● **n.** (pl. **metacarpi** /met-uh-**kar**-pi/) the group of five bones of the hand between the wrist and the fingers.
– DERIVATIVES **metacarpal** adj. & n.
– ORIGIN Greek *metakarpion.*

metal ● **n.** a hard, shiny, solid material which is able to be shaped and can conduct electricity and heat.
– ORIGIN Greek *metallon.*

metal detector ● **n.** an electronic device that makes a noise when it is close to metal.

metallic ● **adj. 1** having to do with metal. **2** (of sound) sharp and ringing.

metallography /met-uh-**log**-ruh-fi/ ● **n.** the scientific study of the structure and properties of metals.

metallurgy /mi-**tal**-ler-ji, **met**-uh-ler-ji/ ● **n.** the scientific study of metals.
– DERIVATIVES **metallurgical** adj. **metallurgist** n.

metalwork ● **n. 1** the art of making things from metal. **2** metal objects as a group.

metamorphic ● **adj.** (of rock) having been changed by heat, pressure, or other natural agencies.

metamorphose /met-uh-**mor**-fohz/ ● **v.** (**metamorphoses**, **metamorphosing**, **metamorphosed**) **1** change completely in form or nature. **2** (of an insect or amphibian) undergo metamorphosis.

metamorphosis /met-uh-**mor**-fuh-siss/ ● **n.** (pl. **metamorphoses** /met-uh-**mor**-fuh-seez/) **1** the transformation of an insect or amphibian from an immature form or larva to an adult form. **2** a change in form or nature.
– ORIGIN Greek.

metaphor /**met**-uh-fer/ ● **n.** a figure of speech in which a word or phrase is used to represent or stand for something else (e.g. *food for thought*).
– ORIGIN Greek.

metaphorical /met-uh-fo-ri-k'l/ (also **metaphoric**) ● **adj.** having to do with metaphor.
– DERIVATIVES **metaphorically** adv.

metaphysical ● **adj. 1** relating to metaphys-

ics. **2** beyond physical matter: *the metaphysical battle of Good and Evil.*
– DERIVATIVES **metaphysically** adv.

metaphysical poets E
a group of 17th-century poets whose work is characterized by the use of complex and elaborate metaphors and the exploration of personal feeling. Members of the group include John Donne, George Herbert, Henry Vaughan, and Andrew Marvell.

metaphysics • n. philosophy concerned with abstract ideas such as the nature of existence, truth, and knowledge.
– ORIGIN from Greek *ta meta ta phusika* 'the things after the Physics', referring to the sequence of Aristotle's works.

metatarsus /met-uh-tar-suhss/ • n. (pl. **metatarsi** /met-uh-tar-si/) the bones of the foot, between the ankle and the toes.
– DERIVATIVES **metatarsal** adj. & n.

mete • v. (**metes**, **meting**, **meted**) (**mete out**) deal out (justice, punishment, etc.).
– ORIGIN Old English, 'measure'.

meteor • n. a small body of matter from outer space that glows as a result of friction with the earth's atmosphere and appears as a shooting star.
– ORIGIN Greek.

meteoric • adj. **1** relating to meteors or meteorites. **2** (of progress or development) very rapid.

meteorite • n. a piece of rock or metal that has fallen to the earth from space.

meteoroid • n. a small body that would become a meteor if it entered the earth's atmosphere.

meteorology /mee-ti-uh-rol-uh-ji/ • n. the study of conditions in the atmosphere, used for weather forecasting.
– DERIVATIVES **meteorological** adj. **meteorologist** n.

meter[1] • n. a device that measures and records the quantity, degree, or rate of something. • v. (**meters**, **metering**, **metered**) measure with a meter.
– ORIGIN from METE.

meter[2] • n. US = METRE[1], METRE[2].

-meter • comb. form **1** in names of measuring instruments: *thermometer.* **2** in nouns referring to lines of poetry with a specified number of measures: *hexameter.*
– ORIGIN Greek *metron* 'measure'.

methadone /meth-uh-dohn/ • n. a powerful painkiller, used as a substitute for morphine and heroin in the treatment of addiction.
– ORIGIN from its chemical name.

methane /mee-thayn/ • n. a flammable gas which is the main constituent of natural gas.
– ORIGIN from METHYL.

methanol • n. a poisonous flammable alcohol, used to make methylated spirit.

methinks • v. archaic or humorous it seems to me.
– ORIGIN Old English.

method • n. **1** a way of doing something. **2** orderliness of thought or behaviour.
– ORIGIN Greek *methodos* 'pursuit of knowledge'.

method acting • n. an acting technique in which an actor tries to identify completely with a character's emotions.

methodical (also **methodic**) • adj. orderly or systematic.
– DERIVATIVES **methodically** adv.

Methodist • n. a member of a Christian Protestant group originating in the 18th-century, based on the ideas of Charles and John Wesley. • adj. relating to Methodists or their beliefs.
– DERIVATIVES **Methodism** n.
– ORIGIN prob. from the idea of following a specified 'method' of Bible study.

methodology • n. (pl. **methodologies**) a system of methods used in a particular field.
DERIVATIVES **methodological** adj.

meths • n. Brit. informal methylated spirit.

Methuselah E
/mi-thyoo-zuh-luh/ (in the Bible) a patriarch, the grandfather of Noah, who is said to have lived for 909 years.

methyl /mee-thyl/ • n. Chem. the radical $-CH_3$, derived from methane.
– ORIGIN from Greek *methu* 'wine' + *hulē* 'wood'.

methyl alcohol • n. methanol.

methylated spirit (also **methylated spirits**) • n. alcohol for use as a solvent or fuel, made unfit for drinking by the addition of methanol and a violet dye.

meticulous /mi-tik-yuu-luhss/ • adj. very careful and precise.
– DERIVATIVES **meticulously** adv. **meticulousness** n.
– ORIGIN Latin *meticulosus* 'fearful'.

métier /may-ti-ay/ • n. **1** a trade, profession, or occupation. **2** a person's special ability.
– ORIGIN French.

metonym /met-uh-nim/ • n. a word or expression used as a substitute for something with which it is closely associated, e.g. *Washington* for the US government.
– DERIVATIVES **metonymic** adj. **metonymy** n.
– ORIGIN Greek *metōnumia* 'change of name'.

metre[1] (US **meter**) • n. the basic unit of length in the metric system, equal to 100 centimetres (approx. 39.37 inches).
– ORIGIN French.

metre[2] (US **meter**) • n. **1** the rhythm of a piece of poetry, determined by the number and length of feet in a line. **2** the basic rhythmic pattern of a piece of music.
– ORIGIN Greek *metron* 'measure'.

metric • adj. relating to or using the metric system.

metrical • adj. having to do with poetic metre.
– DERIVATIVES **metrically** adv.

metricate • v. (**metricates**, **metricating**, **metricated**) convert to a metric system of measurement.
– DERIVATIVES **metrication** n.

metric system • n. the decimal measuring system based on the metre, litre, and gram.

metric ton (also **metric tonne**) • n. a unit of weight equal to 1,000 kilograms (2,205 lb).

metro • n. (pl. **metros**) an underground railway system in a city.
– ORIGIN French.

metronome /met-ruh-nohm/ • n. a musicians' device that marks time at a selected rate by giving a regular tick.
– DERIVATIVES **metronomic** adj.

m

– ORIGIN from Greek *metron* 'measure' + *nomos* 'law'.

metropolis /mi-**trop**-uh-liss/ ● **n.** the main city of a country or region.
– ORIGIN Greek.

metropolitan /met-ruh-**pol**-i-t'n/ ● **adj.** relating to a metropolis.

metropolitan county ● **n.** (in England) each of six units of local government centred on a large urban area (established in 1974, although their councils were abolished in 1986).

mettle ● **n.** spirit and strength in the face of difficulty.
– ORIGIN from **METAL**.

Meuse E
/merz/ a river of western Europe, which rises in NE France and flows through Belgium and the Netherlands to the North Sea.

mew ● **v.** (of a cat or gull) make a high-pitched crying noise. ● **n.** a mewing noise.

mewl ● **v. 1** cry feebly. **2** mew.

mews ● **n.** (pl. **mews**) Brit. a row of houses or flats converted from stables in a small street or square.
– ORIGIN from *mew* 'place for keeping hawks' (first referring to stables on the site of hawk mews in London).

Mexican wave ● **n.** an effect like a moving wave produced by sections of a stadium crowd standing and sitting down again one after the other while raising and lowering their arms.
– ORIGIN first seen at the soccer World Cup in Mexico City in 1986.

m

Mexico E
a country in North America, with coastlines on the Gulf of Mexico and the Pacific Ocean; capital, Mexico City.
– DERIVATIVES **Mexican** adj. & n.

Mexico, Gulf of E
a large extension of the western Atlantic Ocean, bounded by the US to the north, by Mexico to the west and south, and by Cuba to the south-east.

Mexico City E
the capital of Mexico.

Meyerbeer E
/**my**-er-beer/, Giacomo (1791–1864; born *Jakob Liebmann Beer*), German composer. He settled in Paris, where he wrote a number of operas, notably *Les Huguenots*.

mezzanine /**mez**-zuh-neen, **mets**-uh-neen/ ● **n.** a floor extending over part of the area of a building, built between two full floors.
– ORIGIN Italian *mezzano* 'middle'.

mezzo /**met**-zoh/ (also **mezzo-soprano**) ● **n.** (pl. **mezzos**) a female singer with a voice pitched between soprano and contralto.
– ORIGIN Italian.

mg ● **abbrev.** milligram(s).

MHz ● **abbrev.** megahertz.

mi ● **n.** var. of **ME**[2].

mi. ● **abbrev.** mile(s).

MI5 ● **abbrev.** Military Intelligence section 5, the former name for the UK government agency responsible for internal security and the gathering of political and military information on British territory. Official name **SECURITY SERVICE**.

MI6 ● **abbrev.** Military Intelligence section 6, the former name for the UK government agency responsible for gathering political and military information overseas. Official name **SECRET INTELLIGENCE SERVICE**.

Miami E
/my-**am**-i/ a city, port, and resort on the coast of SE Florida.

miaow (also **meow**) ● **n.** the cry of a cat. ● **v.** make a miaow.

miasma /mi-**az**-muh, my-**az**-muh/ ● **n.** literary **1** an unpleasant or unhealthy vapour. **2** a heavy or unpleasant atmosphere.
– ORIGIN Greek, 'defilement'.

mica /**my**-kuh/ ● **n.** a mineral found as tiny shiny scales in rocks.
– ORIGIN Latin, 'crumb'.

mice pl. of **MOUSE**.

Michael, St E
one of the archangels. Feast day, 29 September.

Michaelmas /**mi**-k'l-muhss/ ● **n.** the day of the Christian festival of St Michael, 29 September.
– ORIGIN Old English, 'Saint Michael's Mass'.

Michelangelo E
/my-k'l-**an**-juh-loh/ (1475–1564; full name *Michelangelo Buonarroti*), Italian sculptor, painter, and architect. His many works include the frescos in the Sistine Chapel in Rome, sculptures such as *Pietà* and *David*, and the rebuilding of St Peter's in Rome.

Michelin E
/**mich**-uh-lin/, André (1853–1931) and Édouard (1859–1940), French industrialists, pioneers of the use of pneumatic tyres on motor vehicles.

Michelson E
/**my**-k'l-s'n/, Albert Abraham (1852–1931), American physicist, famous for showing experimentally (with Edward Morley) that the measured speed of light was unaffected by the motion of the observer, a result later explained by Einstein's theory of relativity.

Michigan E
/**mish**-i-g'n/ a state in the northern US; capital, Lansing.

Michigan, Lake E
one of the five Great Lakes of North America, the only one that is wholly within the US.

mickey ● **n.** (in phr. **take the mickey**) Brit. informal tease or ridicule someone.
– ORIGIN unknown.

micro- ● **comb. form 1** very small: *microchip*. **2** referring to a factor of one millionth (10^{-6}): *microgram*.
– ORIGIN Greek *mikros*.

microbe /**my**-krohb/ ● **n.** a micro-organism.
– DERIVATIVES **microbial** adj.
– ORIGIN from Greek *mikros* 'small' + *bios* 'life'.

microbiology ● **n.** the scientific study of micro-organisms.

microchip ● **n.** a tiny wafer of silicon or similar material used to make an integrated circuit.

microclimate ● **n.** the climate of a very

small or restricted area.

microcomputer • n. a small computer with a microprocessor as its central processor.

microcosm /my-kroh-ko-z'm/ • n. a thing that represents something much larger.
– DERIVATIVES **microcosmic** adj.
– ORIGIN from Greek *mikros kosmos* 'little world'.

microdot • n. a photograph reduced to a very small size.

microelectronics • n. the design, manufacture, and use of microchips and minute electric circuits.

microfiche /my-kroh-feesh/ • n. a piece of film containing greatly reduced photographs of the pages of a newspaper, book, etc.
– ORIGIN from Greek *mikros* 'small' + French *fiche* 'slip of paper'.

microfilm • n. a length of film containing greatly reduced photographs of a newspaper, book, etc.

microgram • n. one millionth of a gram.

microlight • n. esp. Brit. a very small, light aircraft for one or two people.

micrometer /my-krom-i-ter/ • n. an instrument which measures small distances or thicknesses.

micrometre (US **micrometer**) • n. one millionth of a metre.

micron • n. one millionth of a metre.

Micronesia[1] E
/my-kroh-**nee**-*zh*uh/ a region of the western Pacific, to the north of Melanesia and north and west of Polynesia. It includes the Mariana, Caroline, and Marshall island groups and Kiribati.

Micronesia[2] E
/my-kroh-**nee**-*zh*uh/ a group of associated Pacific island states comprising the Caroline Islands; capital, Kolonia (on Pohnpei). Full name **FEDERATED STATES OF MICRONESIA**.

micro-organism • n. an organism so small that it can only be seen with a microscope.

microphone • n. an instrument for changing sound waves into electrical energy which may then be amplified, transmitted, or recorded.

microprocessor • n. an integrated circuit which can perform the role of a central processing unit of a computer.

microscope • n. an instrument for magnifying very small objects.
– ORIGIN from Greek *mikros* 'small' + *skopein* 'look at'.

microscopic • adj. **1** so small as to be visible only with a microscope. **2** relating to a microscope.
– DERIVATIVES **microscopically** adv.

microscopy /my-kross-kuh-pi/ • n. the use of a microscope.

microsecond • n. one millionth of a second.

microsurgery • n. complex surgery performed using very small instruments and a microscope.

microwave • n. **1** an electromagnetic wave with a wavelength in the range 0.001–0.3 m. **2** (also **microwave oven**) an oven that uses microwaves to cook or heat food. • v. (**microwaves**, **microwaving**, **microwaved**) cook (food) in a microwave oven.

mid • adj. having to do with the middle point of a range. • prep. literary in the middle of.

mid- • comb. form in the middle of: *midway*.
– ORIGIN Old English.

Midas E
/**my**-duhss/ Gk Myth. a king of Phrygia in Asia Minor, who was given by Dionysus the power of turning everything he touched into gold.

Midas touch • n. the ability to make a lot of money out of anything one does.
– ORIGIN from King **MIDAS**.

midday • n. noon.

midden • n. a dunghill or rubbish heap.
– ORIGIN Scandinavian.

middle • adj. **1** at an equal distance from the edges or ends of something. **2** medium in rank, quality, or ability. • n. **1** a middle point or position. **2** informal a person's waist and stomach.

middle age • n. the period between youth and old age, about 45 to 60.
– DERIVATIVES **middle-aged** adj.

Middle Ages • pl. n. the period of European history from about 1000 to 1453.

Middle America • n. the conservative middle classes of the United States.

middlebrow • adj. informal, derog. only needing a moderate degree of thought to understand it: *a middlebrow magazine*.

middle C • n. Music the C near the middle of the piano keyboard, written on the first ledger line below the treble stave or the first ledger line above the bass stave.

middle class • n. the social group made up of business and professional people, between the upper and working classes.

middle ear • n. the air-filled central cavity of the ear, behind the eardrum.

Middle East • n. an area of SW Asia and northern Africa, stretching from the Mediterranean to Pakistan.
– DERIVATIVES **Middle Eastern** adj.

Middle England • n. the conservative middle classes in England.

Middle English • n. the English language from *c.*1150 to *c.*1470.

middle ground • n. an area of possible agreement between two opposing positions.

middleman • n. **1** a person who buys goods from producers and sells them to retailers or consumers. **2** a person who arranges business or political deals between other people.

middle of the road • adj. **1** (of views) not extreme. **2** (of music) bland and unadventurous.

Middlesex E
a former county of SE England, north-west of London. In 1965 it was divided between Hertfordshire, Surrey, and Greater London.

Middleton, E
Thomas (*c.*1570–1627), English dramatist, best known for the tragedies *Women Beware Women* and *The Changeling* (written with the dramatist William Rowley).

middleweight • n. a weight in boxing and other sports coming between welterweight and light heavyweight.

middling • adj. moderate or average in size,

amount, or rank.

Middx • **abbrev.** Middlesex.

midfield • **n.** **1** the central part of a sports field. **2** the players who play in a central position between attack and defence.
– DERIVATIVES **midfielder** n.

midge • **n.** a small two-winged fly that forms swarms near water, of which many kinds feed on blood.
– ORIGIN Old English.

midget • **n.** an extremely small person. • **adj.** extremely small: *a midget submarine.*

MIDI • **n.** a standard for interconnecting electronic musical instruments and computers.
– ORIGIN from *musical instrument digital interface.*

Midi E
/mi-di/ the south of France.

midi system • **n.** Brit. a set of compact pieces of stacking hi-fi equipment.

Midlands • **n.** (**the Midlands**) the inland counties of central England. • **adj.** (also **midland**) having to do with the Midlands.

midlife • **n.** the central period of a person's life, between around 45 and 60 years old.

Midlothian E
/mid-**loh**-*thi*-uhn/ an administrative region and former county of central Scotland; administrative centre, Dalkeith.

midnight • **n.** twelve o'clock at night.

midnight blue • **n.** a very dark blue.

midnight sun • **n.** the sun when seen at midnight during the summer within either the Arctic or Antarctic Circle.

midriff • **n.** the front of the body between the chest and the waist.
– ORIGIN Old English.

midshipman • **n.** a low-ranking officer in the Royal Navy.

midst archaic or literary • **prep.** in the middle of. • **n.** the middle point or part.
– PHRASES **in our** (or **your**, **their**, etc.) **midst** among us (or you or them).

midsummer • **n.** **1** the middle part of summer. **2** the summer solstice.

Midsummer Day (also **Midsummer's Day**) • **n.** 24 June.

midterm • **n.** the middle of a period of office, an academic term, or a pregnancy.

midway • **adv. & adj.** in or towards the middle.

midweek • **n.** the middle of the week. • **adj. & adv.** in the middle of the week.

midwife /**mid**-wyf/ • **n.** a nurse who is trained to assist women in childbirth.
– DERIVATIVES **midwifery** /mid-**wif**-uh-ri/ n.
– ORIGIN prob. from former *mid* 'with' + **WIFE**.

midwinter • **n.** **1** the middle part of winter. **2** the winter solstice.

mien /meen/ • **n.** a person's look or manner.
– ORIGIN prob. from French *mine* 'expression'.

Mies van der Rohe E
/meez van der **roh**-uh/, Ludwig (1886–1969), German-born American architect and furniture designer. A leading modernist, he designed such buildings as the Seagram Building (New York). He was also noted for his tubular steel furniture.

miffed • **adj.** informal offended or irritated.

might[1] • **modal verb** (3rd sing. present **might**) past of **MAY**[1]. **1** used to express possibility or make a suggestion. **2** used politely in questions and requests.

might[2] • **n.** great power or strength.
– ORIGIN Old English.

mightn't • **contr.** might not.

mighty • **adj.** (**mightier**, **mightiest**) **1** powerful or strong. **2** informal very large. • **adv.** informal, esp. N. Amer. extremely.
– DERIVATIVES **mightily** adv.

migraine /**mee**-grayn, **my**-grayn/ • **n.** a severe headache, often accompanied by nausea and disturbed vision.
– ORIGIN French.

migrant • **n.** **1** an animal that migrates. **2** a worker who moves from one place to another to find work. • **adj.** tending to migrate or having migrated.

migrate • **v.** (**migrates**, **migrating**, **migrated**) **1** (of an animal) move from one habitat to another according to the seasons. **2** move to settle in a new area in order to find work.
– DERIVATIVES **migration** n. **migratory** adj.
– ORIGIN Latin *migrare* 'move, shift'.

mike informal • **n.** a microphone.

mil[1] • **abbrev.** informal millions.

mil[2] • **n.** one thousandth of an inch.
– ORIGIN Latin *millesimum* 'thousandth'.

milady • **n.** hist. used to address or refer to an English noblewoman.

Milan E
/mi-**lan**/ a city in NW Italy, capital of Lombardy region and a leading financial and industrial centre.
– DERIVATIVES **Milanese** adj. & n.

milch /milsh, milch/ • **adj.** (of an animal) giving or kept for milk.
– ORIGIN Old English.

milch cow • **n.** a source of easy profit.

mild • **adj.** **1** gentle and calm. **2** not severe, harsh, or extreme. **3** not sharp or strong in flavour. **4** (of weather) fairly warm. • **n.** Brit. a kind of dark beer not strongly flavoured with hops.
– DERIVATIVES **mildly** adv. **mildness** n.
– ORIGIN Old English.

mildew • **n.** a coating of tiny fungi on plants or damp material such as paper or leather. • **v.** affect with mildew.
– ORIGIN Old English.

mild steel • **n.** strong steel containing a small percentage of carbon.

mile • **n.** **1** (also **statute mile**) a unit of length equal to 1,760 yards (approximately 1.609 kilometres). **2** (**miles**) informal a very long way. • **adv.** (**miles**) informal by a great amount or a long way.
– PHRASES **be miles away** informal be lost in thought. **stand** (or **stick**) **out a mile** informal be very obvious.
– ORIGIN Latin *milia* 'thousands'; a Roman 'mile' consisted of 1,000 paces.

mileage (also **milage**) • **n.** **1** a number of miles covered. **2** informal benefit or advantage: *he got a lot of mileage out of the mix-up.*

mileometer • **n.** var. of **MILOMETER**.

milestone • **n.** **1** a stone set up beside a road to mark the distance in miles to a particular place. **2** an event marking a significant new development or stage.

milieu /mee-lyer/ ● n. (pl. **milieux** or **milieus**) a person's social environment.
– ORIGIN French.

militant ● adj. prepared to take aggressive action in support of a political or social cause. ● n. a militant person.
– DERIVATIVES **militancy** n. **militantly** adv.

militarism ● n. the belief that a country should possess and readily use strong armed forces.
– DERIVATIVES **militarist** n. & adj. **militaristic** adj.

militarize (also **militarise**) ● v. (**militarizes**, **militarizing**, **militarized**) **1** supply with soldiers and military equipment. **2** make similar to an army.

military ● adj. having to do with soldiers or armed forces. ● n. (**the military**) the armed forces of a country.
DERIVATIVES **militarily** adv.
– ORIGIN Latin *militaris*.

military honours ● pl. n. ceremonies performed by troops as a mark of respect at the burial of a member of the armed forces.

military police ● n. a body responsible for police duties in the armed forces.

militate ● v. (**militates**, **militating**, **militated**) (**militate against**) be a powerful or decisive factor in preventing (something).
– ORIGIN Latin *militare* 'wage war'.

USAGE militate
For an explanation of the difference between **militate** and **mitigate**, see the note at **MITIGATE**.

militia /mi-li-shuh/ ● n. **1** a military force made up of civilians, used to supplement a regular army in an emergency. **2** a rebel force opposing a regular army.
– DERIVATIVES **militiaman** n.
– ORIGIN Latin, 'military service'.

milk ● n. **1** a white fluid produced by female mammals to feed their young. **2** the milk of cows as a food and drink for humans. ● v. **1** draw milk from (an animal). **2** exploit or defraud (someone) over a period of time. **3** take full advantage of (a situation).
– PHRASES **milk and honey** prosperity and abundance. **milk of human kindness** care and sympathy for others.
– ORIGIN Old English.

milk chocolate ● n. solid chocolate made with milk.

milk float ● n. Brit. an electrically powered van used for delivering milk to houses.

milkmaid ● n. archaic a girl or woman who works in a dairy.

milkman ● n. a man who delivers milk to houses.

milk round ● n. Brit. **1** a regular milk delivery along a fixed route. **2** a series of visits to universities and colleges by people from large companies looking to recruit students.

milk run ● n. a routine, uneventful journey.
– ORIGIN RAF slang for a sortie that was as simple as a milkman's round.

milkshake ● n. a cold drink made from milk whisked with ice cream.

milksop ● n. a timid and indecisive person.

milk tooth ● n. a temporary tooth in a child or young mammal.

milky ● adj. **1** containing milk. **2** having a soft white colour or clouded appearance.
– DERIVATIVES **milkily** adv. **milkiness** n.

Milky Way ● n. the galaxy of which our solar system is a part.

Mill, E
John Stuart (1806–73), English philosopher and economist. He was the author of *On Liberty*, which argued for the importance of individual liberty against interference by the state, and *Utilitarianism*.

mill ● n. **1** a building equipped with machinery for grinding grain into flour. **2** a device for grinding solid substances, such as peppercorns. **3** a building fitted with machinery for a manufacturing process. *a steel mill*. ● v. **1** grind in a mill. **2** cut or shape (metal) with a rotating tool. **3** (**milled**) (of a coin) having ribbed markings on the edge. **4** (**mill about/around**) move around in a confused mass.
– PHRASES **go** (or **put**) **through the mill** have (or cause to have) an unpleasant experience.
– ORIGIN Latin *mola* 'grindstone, mill'.

Millais E
/mil-lay/, Sir John Everett (1829–96), English Pre-Raphaelite painter. Although his early works depicted unidealized religious and moral subjects, he later produced sentimental paintings such as *Bubbles*.

millennial ● adj. relating to a millennium.

millennium /mil-len-i-uhm/ ● n. (pl. **millennia** or **millenniums**) **1** a period of a thousand years. **2** (**the millennium**) the point at which one period of a thousand years ends and another begins. **3** an anniversary of a thousand years.
– ORIGIN from Latin *mille* 'thousand' + *annus* 'year'.

USAGE millennium
The correct spelling is **millennium**, with two *ns*.

millennium bug ● n. an inability in older computing software to deal with dates of 1 January 2000 or later.

Miller[1], E
Arthur (b.1915), American dramatist. His plays include *Death of a Salesman* and *The Crucible*, which used the Salem witch trials of 1692 as an allegory for McCarthyism in America.

Miller[2], E
(Alton) Glenn (1904–44), American jazz trombonist and bandleader, known for the tune 'Moonlight Serenade'. He died when his aircraft disappeared over the English Channel.

Miller[3], E
Henry (Valentine) (1891–1980), American novelist. His novels *Tropic of Cancer* and *Tropic of Capricorn* were initially banned in the US due to their frank depiction of sex and use of obscenities.

miller ● n. a person who owns or works in a grain mill.

Millet E
/mee-yay/, Jean (François) (1814–75), French painter, famous for his paintings of peasants, such as *The Gleaners*.

millet ● n. a cereal which bears a large crop of small seeds, used to make flour or alcoholic

drinks.
– ORIGIN French.

Millett E
/mil-lit/, Kate (b.1934; full name *Katherine Millett*), American feminist, who advocated a radical feminism in *Sexual Politics*.

milli- • comb. form a thousand: *milligram*.
– ORIGIN Latin *mille* 'thousand'.

millibar • n. a unit for measuring atmospheric pressure.

Milligan, E
Spike (1918–2002; born *Terence Alan Milligan*), British comedian and writer, born in India, known for his appearances in the radio programme *The Goon Show*.

milligram (also **milligramme**) • n. one thousandth of a gram.

millilitre (US **milliliter**) • n. one thousandth of a litre.

millimetre (US **millimeter**) • n. one thousandth of a metre.

milliner • n. a person who makes or sells women's hats.
– DERIVATIVES **millinery** n.
– ORIGIN from **MILAN**.

million • cardinal number (pl. **millions** or (with numeral or quantifying word) **million**) **1** the number equivalent to a thousand multiplied by a thousand; 1,000,000 or 10^6. **2** (also **millions**) informal a very large number or amount.
– DERIVATIVES **millionth** ordinal number.

millionaire • n. (fem. **millionairess**) a person whose money and property are worth one million pounds or dollars or more.

millipede • n. a small invertebrate animal with a long body composed of many segments, most of which bear two pairs of legs.
– ORIGIN from Latin *mille* 'thousand' + *pes* 'foot'.

millisecond • n. one thousandth of a second.

millpond • n. a very still and calm stretch of water.

Mills, E
Sir John (Lewis Ernest Watts) (b.1908), English actor, star of such films as *Scott of the Antarctic* and *Ryan's Daughter*.

millstone • n. **1** each of a pair of circular stones used for grinding grain. **2** a burden of responsibility.

mill wheel • n. a wheel used to drive a watermill.

Milne, E
A. A. (1882–1956; full name *Alan Alexander Milne*), English writer of stories and poems for children, creator of the character Winnie-the-Pooh.

milometer /my-lom-i-ter/ (also **mileometer**) • n. Brit. an instrument on a vehicle for recording the number of miles travelled.

milord • n. hist. used to address or refer to an English nobleman.

Milosevic E
/mi-loss-uh-vich/, Slobodan (b.1941), Serbian statesman, President of Serbia 1989–97 and of Yugoslavia 1997–2000. His nationalist policies accelerated the break-up of Yugoslavia. He was deposed as Yugoslavian President after a popular uprising.

Milton, E
John (1608–74), English poet. His three major works, completed after he had gone blind, show his mastery of blank verse: they are the epic poems *Paradise Lost* and *Paradise Regained*, and the verse drama *Samson Agonistes*.

Milton Keynes E
/keenz/ a new town in south central England, the site of the headquarters of the Open University.

Milwaukee E
/mil-waw-ki/ an industrial port and city in SE Wisconsin, on the west shore of Lake Michigan.

mime • n. the use of gestures and facial expressions to tell a story or convey feelings, especially in the theatre. • v. (**mimes**, **miming**, **mimed**) **1** use mime to act out. **2** pretend to sing or play an instrument as a recording is being played.
– ORIGIN Greek *mimos*.

mimesis /mi-mee-siss/ • n. **1** imitative representation of the real world in art and literature. **2** Biol. mimicry of another animal or plant.
– ORIGIN Greek.

mimetic /mi-met-ik/ • adj. having to do with mimesis or mimicry.

mimic • v. (**mimics**, **mimicking**, **mimicked**) **1** imitate the voice or behaviour of. **2** (of an animal or plant) take on the appearance of (another) in order to hide or for protection. • n. **1** a person skilled in mimicking. **2** an animal or plant that mimics another.

mimicry • n. **1** imitation of someone or something. **2** Biol. the close external resemblance of an animal or plant to another.

mimosa /mi-moh-zuh/ • n. an acacia tree with delicate fern-like leaves and yellow flowers.
– ORIGIN prob. from Latin *mimus* 'mime'.

mimsy • adj. rather feeble and prim.
– ORIGIN coined by Lewis Carroll from **MISERABLE** and **FLIMSY**.

min. • abbrev. **1** minimum. **2** minute(s).

minaret /min-uh-ret/ • n. a slender tower of a mosque, with a balcony from which Muslims are called to prayer.
– ORIGIN Arabic.

minatory /min-uh-tuh-ri/ • adj. formal threatening.
– ORIGIN Latin *minari* 'threaten'.

mince • v. **1** cut up (meat) into very small pieces. **2** walk in an affected way with short, quick steps and swinging hips. • n. esp. Brit. minced meat.
– PHRASES **not mince (one's) words** voice one's disapproval directly.
– ORIGIN Old French *mincier*.

mincemeat • n. a mixture of dried fruit, candied peel, sugar, spices, and suet.
– PHRASES **make mincemeat of** informal defeat decisively.

mind • n. **1** the faculty of consciousness and thought. **2** a person's intellect or memory. **3** a

person's attention or will. ● v. **1** be distressed or annoyed by. **2** remember or take care to do. **3** watch out for. **4** take care of temporarily. **5** (**be minded**) be inclined to do.
– PHRASES **be in** (or **of**) **two minds** be unable to decide between alternatives. **give someone a piece of one's mind** rebuke someone. **have a** (or **a good** or **half a**) **mind to do** be inclined to do. **in one's mind's eye** in one's imagination. **mind one's Ps & Qs** be careful to be polite and avoid giving offence. **never mind 1** do not be concerned or distressed. **2** let alone. **out of one's mind** mad. **put one in mind of** remind one of.
– ORIGIN Old English.

Mindanao E
/min-duh-**now**/ the second-largest island in the Philippines.

mind-bending ● adj. informal altering one's state of mind.

mind-blowing ● adj. informal very impressive.

mind-boggling ● adj. informal overwhelming.

minded ● adj. inclined to think in a particular way: *liberal-minded.*

minder ● n. **1** a person employed to look after someone or something. **2** informal a bodyguard.

mindful ● adj. **1** (**mindful of/that**) aware of or recognizing that. **2** formal inclined to do something.

mindless ● adj. **1** acting or done without good reason and with no concern for the consequences. **2** (**mindless of**) not thinking of or concerned about. **3** (of an activity) simple and repetitive.
– DERIVATIVES **mindlessly** adv. **mindlessness** n.

mindset ● n. the established set of attitudes held by someone.

mine[1] ● possess. pron. referring to a thing or things belonging to or associated with the speaker.
– ORIGIN Old English.

mine[2] ● n. **1** a hole or passage dug in the earth for extracting coal or other minerals. **2** an abundant source: *the book is a mine of information.* **3** a type of bomb placed on or in the ground or water, which explodes on contact. ● v. (**mines, mining, mined**) **1** obtain from a mine. **2** dig for coal or other minerals. **3** lay a mine or mines on or in.
– ORIGIN Old French.

minefield ● n. **1** an area planted with explosive mines. **2** a subject or situation presenting hidden dangers.

miner ● n. a person who works in a mine.

mineral ● n. **1** a solid inorganic substance occurring naturally, such as copper. **2** an inorganic substance needed by the human body for good health, such as calcium. **3** a substance obtained by mining.
– ORIGIN Latin *minera* 'ore'.

mineralogy ● n. the scientific study of minerals.
– DERIVATIVES **mineralogical** adj. **mineralogist** n.

mineral water ● n. water containing dissolved salts.

Minerva E
/mi-**ner**-vuh/ the Roman goddess of war, wisdom, and handicrafts. Greek equivalent **ATHENE**.

mineshaft ● n. a deep, narrow shaft leading to a mine.

minestrone /mi-ni-**stroh**-ni/ ● n. an Italian soup containing vegetables and pasta.
– ORIGIN Italian *minestrare* 'serve at table'.

minesweeper ● n. a warship equipped for detecting and removing or destroying explosive mines.

Ming ● adj. (of Chinese porcelain) made during the Ming dynasty (1368–1644), having elaborate designs and vivid colours.
– ORIGIN Chinese, 'clear or bright'.

mingle ● v. (**mingles, mingling, mingled**) **1** mix together. **2** move around and chat at a social function.
– ORIGIN from former *meng* 'to mix'.

Mingus E
/**ming**-guhss/, Charles (1922–79), American jazz bassist and composer.

mingy /**min**-ji/ ● adj. informal not generous.
– ORIGIN perh. from **MEAN**[2] and **STINGY**.

mini ● adj. very small of its kind. ● n. (pl. **minis**) a very short skirt or dress.

mini- ● comb. form miniature: *minibus.*

miniature ● adj. of a much smaller size than normal. ● n. **1** a thing that is much smaller than normal. **2** a very small and minutely detailed portrait.
– ORIGIN Latin *minium* 'red lead' (formerly used to mark words in manuscripts).

miniaturist ● n. an artist who paints miniatures.

miniaturize (also **miniaturise**) ● v. (**miniaturizes, miniaturizing, miniaturized**) make on a smaller scale.

minibar ● n. a refrigerator in a hotel room containing a selection of drinks.

minibus ● n. a small bus for about ten to fifteen passengers.

minicab ● n. Brit. a car that is available for hire as a taxi but can only be ordered in advance.

minicomputer ● n. a computer of medium power.

minidisc ● n. a disc similar to a small CD but able to record sound or data as well as play it back.

minim ● n. Music, Brit. a note having the time value of two crotchets or half a semibreve, represented by a ring with a stem.
– ORIGIN Latin *minimus* 'smallest'.

minima pl. of **MINIMUM**.

minimal ● adj. **1** of a minimum amount, quantity, or degree. **2** Art using simple forms or structures. **3** Music characterized by the repetition and gradual alteration of short phrases.
– DERIVATIVES **minimally** adv.

minimalist ● n. a person who likes or produces minimal art or music. ● adj. relating to minimal art or music.
– DERIVATIVES **minimalism** n.

minimize (also **minimise**) ● v. (**minimizes, minimizing, minimized**) **1** reduce to the smallest possible amount or degree. **2** represent (something) as less important than it really is.

minimum ● n. (pl. **minima** or **minimums**) the smallest amount, extent, or strength possible or recorded. ● adj. smallest in amount, extent, or strength.
– ORIGIN Latin.

minimum wage ● n. the lowest wage permitted by law or by agreement.

minion ● n. an obedient or unimportant follower of a powerful person.
– ORIGIN French *mignon* 'pretty'.

miniskirt ● n. a very short skirt.

minister ● n. **1** a head of a government department. **2** a diplomat representing a state or monarch in a foreign country. **3** a member of the clergy. ● v. (**ministers**, **ministering**, **ministered**) (**minister to**) attend to the needs of.
– ORIGIN Latin, 'servant'.

ministerial ● adj. relating to a minister or ministers.

Minister of State ● n. (in the UK) a government minister ranking below a Secretary of State.

Minister of the Crown ● n. (in the UK and Canada) a member of the cabinet.

Minister without Portfolio ● n. a government minister with cabinet status but not in charge of a specific department of state.

ministrations ● pl. n. formal the providing of help or care.

ministry ● n. (pl. **ministries**) **1** a government department headed by a minister. **2** a period of government under one Prime Minister. **3** the work or office of a minister of religion.

m

mink ● n. a small stoat-like animal farmed for its fur.
– ORIGIN Swedish.

minke /**ming**-kuh/ ● n. a small whale with a dark grey back and white underparts.
– ORIGIN uncertain.

Minneapolis E
/min-ni-**ap**-puh-liss/ an industrial city and port on the Mississippi in SE Minnesota.

Minnesota E
/min-ni-**soh**-tuh/ a state in the north central US; capital, St Paul.
– DERIVATIVES **Minnesotan** n. & adj.

minnow ● n. **1** a small freshwater fish. **2** a small or unimportant person.
– ORIGIN prob. from Old English.

Minoan /mi-**noh**-uhn/ ● adj. relating to a Bronze Age civilization based on Crete (*c.*3000–1050 BC).
– ORIGIN named after king **MINOS**.

minor ● adj. **1** not important or serious. **2** Music (of a scale) having intervals of a semitone between the second and third, fifth and sixth, and the seventh and eighth notes. Contrasted with **MAJOR**. ● n. **1** a person under the age of full legal responsibility. **2** Music a minor key, interval, or scale.
– ORIGIN Latin, 'smaller, less'.

Minorca E
/mi-**nor**-kuh/ the second-largest of the Balearic Islands; capital, Mahón.
– DERIVATIVES **Minorcan** adj. & n.

minority ● n. (pl. **minorities**) **1** the smaller number or part. **2** a relatively small group of people differing from the majority in race, religion, etc.

Minos E
/**my**-noss/ Gk Myth. a legendary king of Crete, whose wife Pasiphaë gave birth to the Minotaur. Minos later demanded tribute from Athens in the form of young people to be eaten by the monster.

Minotaur E
/**mi**-nuh-tor, **my**-nuh-tor/ Gk Myth. a creature who was half-man and half-bull. Confined in Crete in a labyrinth and fed on human flesh, it was eventually killed by Theseus.

Minsk E
/minsk/ the capital of Belarus.

minster ● n. a large or important church.
– ORIGIN Greek *monastērion* 'monastery'.

minstrel ● n. a medieval singer or musician.
– ORIGIN Old French *menestral* 'entertainer, servant'.

mint[1] ● n. **1** a plant used as a herb in cookery. **2** the flavour of mint. **3** a peppermint sweet.
– DERIVATIVES **minty** adj.
– ORIGIN Greek *minthē*.

mint[2] ● n. **1** a place where money is coined. **2** (**a mint**) informal a large sum of money. ● adj. as new: *the car was in mint condition.* ● v. **1** make (a coin) by stamping metal. **2** produce for the first time.
– ORIGIN Latin *moneta* 'money'.

minuet ● n. a slow ballroom dance popular in the 18th century.
– ORIGIN French *menuet* 'fine, delicate'.

minus ● prep. **1** with the subtraction of. **2** (of temperature) falling below zero by (a specific number of degrees): *minus 40° centigrade.* **3** informal lacking: *he was minus a finger.* ● adj. **1** (before a number) below zero. **2** (after a grade) slightly below. **3** having a negative electric charge. ● n. **1** (also **minus sign**) the symbol –, indicating subtraction or a negative value. **2** informal a disadvantage.
– ORIGIN Latin, 'less'.

minuscule /**min**-uhss-kyool/ ● adj. extremely tiny.
– ORIGIN from Latin *minuscula littera* 'somewhat smaller letter'.

minute[1] /**min**-it/ ● n. **1** a period of time equal to sixty seconds or a sixtieth of an hour. **2** (**a minute**) informal a very short time. **3** (also **arc minute** or **minute of arc**) a measurement of an angle equal to one sixtieth of a degree.
– PHRASES **up to the minute** up to date.
– ORIGIN from Latin *pars minuta prima* 'first very small part'.

minute[2] /my-**nyoot**/ ● adj. **1** extremely small. **2** precise and careful: *a minute examination of the facts.*
– DERIVATIVES **minutely** adv.
– ORIGIN Latin *minutus* 'made small'.

minute[3] /**min**-it/ ● n. **1** (**minutes**) a written summary of the points discussed at a meeting. **2** an official written message. ● v. (**minutes**, **minuting**, **minuted**) **1** record (the points discussed at a meeting). **2** send a minute to.
– ORIGIN French.

minutiae /mi-**nyoo**-shi-ee/ ● pl. n. small or precise details.
– ORIGIN Latin.

minx ● n. a cheeky, cunning, or flirtatious girl or young woman.

– ORIGIN unknown.

Miocene /my-oh-seen/ • **adj.** Geol. relating to the fourth epoch of the Tertiary period (23.3 to 5.2 million years ago), a time when the first apes appeared.
– ORIGIN from Greek *meiōn* 'less' + *kainos* 'new'.

Mir E
/*rhymes with* near/ a Soviet space station, launched in 1986.

Mirabeau E
/mi-ruh-boh/, Honoré Gabriel Riqueti, Comte de (1749–91), French revolutionary politician. He supported a form of constitutional monarchy and was prominent in the early days of the French Revolution.

miracle • **n. 1** an extraordinary and welcome event believed to be the work of God, a saint, etc. **2** a remarkable and very welcome occurrence. **3** an outstanding example or achievement: *a miracle of modern design*.
– ORIGIN Latin *miraculum* 'object of wonder'.

miracle play • **n.** a medieval play based on biblical stories or the lives of the saints.

miraculous • **adj.** like a miracle; very surprising and welcome: *a miraculous escape*.
– DERIVATIVES **miraculously** adv.

mirage /mi-rahzh/ • **n. 1** an effect caused by hot air, in which a sheet of water seems to appear in a desert or on a hot road. **2** something that appears real or possible but is not in fact so.
– ORIGIN French.

mire • **n. 1** a stretch of swampy or boggy ground. **2** a difficult situation from which it is hard to escape. • **v.** (**mires**, **miring**, **mired**) (**be mired**) **1** become stuck in mud. **2** be in difficulties.
– ORIGIN Old Norse.

Miró E
/mi-roh/, Joan (1893–1983), Spanish surrealist painter. His work is characterized by spiky and amoeba-like forms on brightly coloured backgrounds.

mirror • **n. 1** a surface which reflects a clear image. **2** something accurately representing something else. • **v.** reflect.
– ORIGIN Old French *mirour*.

mirror image • **n.** an image which is identical in form to another but has the structure reversed, as if seen in a mirror.

mirth • **n.** laughter.
– DERIVATIVES **mirthful** adj.
– ORIGIN Old English.

miry • **adj.** very muddy or boggy.

mis- • **prefix 1** (added to verbs and their derivatives) wrongly, badly, or unsuitably: *mismanage*. **2** (added to some nouns) expressing a negative sense: *misadventure*.
– ORIGIN Old English.

misadventure • **n. 1** (also **death by misadventure**) Law death caused accidentally and not involving crime. **2** a mishap.

misalliance • **n.** an unsuitable or unhappy relationship or marriage.

misanthrope /miz-uhn-throhp/ • **n.** a person who dislikes and avoids other people.
– DERIVATIVES **misanthropic** adj. **misanthropy** n.
– ORIGIN from Greek *misein* 'to hate' + *anthrōpos* 'man'.

misapprehension • **n.** a mistaken belief.

misappropriate • **v.** (**misappropriates**, **misappropriating**, **misappropriated**) dishonestly or unfairly take for one's own use.
– DERIVATIVES **misappropriation** n.

misbegotten • **adj.** not carefully thought about or planned.

misbehave • **v.** (**misbehaves**, **misbehaving**, **misbehaved**) behave badly.
– DERIVATIVES **misbehaviour** n.

miscalculate • **v.** (**miscalculates**, **miscalculating**, **miscalculated**) calculate or assess wrongly.
– DERIVATIVES **miscalculation** n.

miscarriage • **n.** the birth of a fetus before it is able to survive independently.

miscarriage of justice • **n.** a failure of a court of law to achieve justice.

miscarry • **v.** (**miscarries**, **miscarrying**, **miscarried**) **1** (of a pregnant woman) have a miscarriage. **2** (of a plan) fail.

miscast • **v.** (**miscasts**, **miscasting**, **miscast**) (**be miscast**) (of an actor) be given an unsuitable role.

miscellaneous • **adj. 1** (of items or people) of various types. **2** (of a collection or group) made up of things of different kinds.
– ORIGIN Latin *miscellus* 'mixed'.

miscellany /mi-sel-luh-ni/ • **n.** (pl. **miscellanies**) a collection of different things.

mischance • **n.** bad luck.

mischief • **n. 1** playful misbehaviour. **2** harm or trouble caused by someone or something.
– ORIGIN Old French *meschief*.

mischievous /miss-chi-vuhss/ • **adj. 1** causing mischief. **2** intended to cause trouble.
– DERIVATIVES **mischievously** adv. **mischievousness** n.

miscible /miss-i-b'l/ • **adj.** (of liquids) capable of being mixed together.
– ORIGIN Latin *miscere* 'to mix'.

misconceive • **v.** (**misconceives**, **misconceiving**, **misconceived**) **1** fail to understand correctly. **2** (**be misconceived**) be badly judged or planned.

misconception • **n.** a false or mistaken idea or belief.

misconduct /miss-kon-dukt/ • **n.** unacceptable or improper behaviour.

misconstruction • **n.** the action of misunderstanding something.

misconstrue • **v.** (**misconstrues**, **misconstruing**, **misconstrued**) understand or interpret wrongly.

miscreant /miss-kri-uhnt/ • **n.** a person who behaves badly or unlawfully.
– ORIGIN Old French *mescreant* 'disbelieving'.

misdeed • **n.** a wrongful act.

misdemeanour (US **misdemeanor**) • **n. 1** a minor wrongdoing. **2** Law (in the US) an offence regarded as less serious than a felony.

misdiagnose • **v.** (**misdiagnoses**, **misdiagnosing**, **misdiagnosed**) diagnose incorrectly.
– DERIVATIVES **misdiagnosis** n.

misdial • **v.** (**misdials**, **misdialling**, **misdialled**; US **misdials**, **misdialing**, **misdialed**) dial a telephone number incorrectly.

misdirect • **v.** direct or instruct wrongly.
– DERIVATIVES **misdirection** n.

m

miser • n. a person who hoards wealth and spends as little as possible.
– ORIGIN Latin, 'wretched'.

miserable • adj. **1** very unhappy or depressed. **2** causing unhappiness or discomfort. **3** (of a person) gloomy and humourless. **4** too small; inadequate.
– DERIVATIVES **miserably** adv.

misericord /mi-ze-ri-kord/ • n. a ledge projecting from the underside of a hinged seat in the choir stall of a church, giving support to someone standing when the seat is folded up.
– ORIGIN Latin *misericors* 'compassionate'.

miserly • adj. **1** unwilling to spend money; ungenerous. **2** (of a quantity) too small.
– DERIVATIVES **miserliness** n.

misery • n. (pl. **miseries**) **1** great unhappiness. **2** a cause of this. **3** Brit. informal a person who is constantly miserable.

misfire • v. (**misfires**, **misfiring**, **misfired**) **1** (of a gun) fail to fire properly. **2** (of an internal-combustion engine) fail to ignite the fuel correctly. **3** fail to produce the intended result.

misfit • n. **1** a person whose behaviour or attitude sets them apart from others. **2** something that does not fit or fits badly.

misfortune • n. **1** bad luck. **2** an unfortunate event.

misgivings • pl. n. feelings of doubt or worry.

misgovern • v. govern unfairly or poorly.

misguided • adj. showing faulty judgement or reasoning.

mishandle • v. (**mishandles**, **mishandling**, **mishandled**) handle unwisely or wrongly.

mishap • n. an unlucky accident.

mishear • v. (**mishears**, **mishearing**, **misheard**) hear incorrectly.

mishit • v. (**mishits**, **mishitting**, **mishit**) hit or kick (a ball) badly.

mishmash • n. a confused mixture.
– ORIGIN from **MASH**.

misinform • v. give false or inaccurate information to.
– DERIVATIVES **misinformation** n.

misinterpret • v. (**misinterprets**, **misinterpreting**, **misinterpreted**) interpret wrongly.
– DERIVATIVES **misinterpretation** n.

misjudge • v. (**misjudges**, **misjudging**, **misjudged**) **1** form an incorrect opinion of. **2** estimate wrongly: *the horse misjudged the fence.*
– DERIVATIVES **misjudgement** (also **misjudgment**) n.

mislay • v. (**mislays**, **mislaying**, **mislaid**) lose (an object) by temporarily forgetting where one has left it.

mislead • v. (**misleads**, **misleading**, **misled**) give the wrong impression to.

mismanage • v. (**mismanages**, **mismanaging**, **mismanaged**) manage badly or wrongly.
– DERIVATIVES **mismanagement** n.

mismatch • n. a combination of people or things that do not match or suit each other. • v. match (people or things) unsuitably or incorrectly.

misnomer /miss-**noh**-mer/ • n. **1** an inaccurate name. **2** the wrong use of a name or term.
– ORIGIN Old French *mesnommer* 'misname'.

misogynist /mi-soj-uh-nist/ • n. a man who hates women.
– DERIVATIVES **misogynistic** adj.

misogyny /mi-soj-uh-ni/ • n. hatred of women.
– ORIGIN from Greek *misos* 'hatred' + *gunē* 'woman'.

misplace • v. (**misplaces**, **misplacing**, **misplaced**) **1** put in the wrong place. **2** (**misplaced**) unwise or inappropriate.

misprint • n. a mistake in printed text. • v. print wrongly.

mispronounce • v. (**mispronounces**, **mispronouncing**, **mispronounced**) pronounce wrongly.

misquote • v. (**misquotes**, **misquoting**, **misquoted**) quote inaccurately.

misread • v. (**misreads**, **misreading**, **misread**) read or interpret wrongly.

misrepresent • v. give a false or misleading account of.
– DERIVATIVES **misrepresentation** n.

misrule • n. **1** inefficient government. **2** disorder.

miss[1] • v. **1** fail to hit, reach, or come into contact with. **2** be too late for. **3** fail to notice, hear, or understand. **4** fail to be present at: *he missed the game with a leg injury.* **5** avoid. **6** (**miss out**) omit. **7** notice or feel the loss or absence of. • n. a failure to hit, catch, or reach something.
– ORIGIN Old English.

miss[2] • n. **1** (**Miss**) a title coming before the name of an unmarried woman or girl. **2** (**Miss**) used as a form of address to a teacher. **3** derog. or humorous a girl or young woman.
– ORIGIN short for *mistress*.

missal • n. a book of the texts used in the Catholic Mass.
– ORIGIN Latin *missa* 'Mass'.

misshapen • adj. not having the normal or natural shape.

missile • n. **1** an object which is thrown at a target. **2** a weapon carrying explosive, that is self-propelled or directed by remote control.
– ORIGIN Latin.

missing • adj. **1** absent and unable to be found. **2** not present when supposed to be.

missing link • n. a supposed fossil form believed to form a link between humans and apes.

mission • n. **1** an important assignment involving travel abroad. **2** an organization or institution involved in a long-term assignment abroad. **3** a military or scientific expedition. **4** the requirement of a religious organization to spread its faith. **5** a strongly felt aim or calling.
– ORIGIN Latin.

missionary • n. (pl. **missionaries**) a person sent on a religious mission. • adj. having to do with a missionary or religious mission: *missionary zeal.*

mission statement • n. a summary of the aims and values of an organization.

missis • n. var. of **MISSUS**.

Mississippi[1] E
/mis-sis-**sip**-pi/ a major river of North America, which rises in Minnesota and flows south to a delta on the Gulf of Mexico.

Mississippi[2] E
/mis-sis-**sip**-pi/ a state of the southern US, on the Gulf of Mexico; capital, Jackson.
– DERIVATIVES **Mississippian** adj. & n.

missive ● n. formal a letter.
– ORIGIN Latin *missivus*.

Missouri[1] E
/mi-**zuu**-uh-ri/ a major river of North America, which rises in the Rocky Mountains in Montana and meets the Mississippi just north of St Louis.

Missouri[2] E
/mi-**zuu**-uh-ri/ a state of the central US; capital, Jefferson City.
– DERIVATIVES **Missourian** n. & adj.

misspell ● v. (**misspells**, **misspelling**, **misspelt** or **misspelled**) spell wrongly.

misspend ● v. (**misspends**, **misspending**, **misspent**) spend foolishly.

missus (also **missis**) ● n. informal or humorous a person's wife.

missy ● n. (pl. **missies**) an affectionate or scornful form of address to a young girl.

mist ● n. **1** a cloud of tiny water droplets in the atmosphere, limiting the ability to see. **2** a condensed vapour settling on a surface. ● v. cover or become covered with mist.
– ORIGIN Old English.

mistake ● n. **1** a thing that is incorrect. **2** an error of judgement: *coming here was a mistake*. ● v. (**mistakes**, **mistaking**, **mistook**; past part. **mistaken**) **1** be wrong about. **2** (**mistake for**) confuse (someone or something) with.
– ORIGIN Old Norse, 'take in error'.

mistaken ● adj. **1** wrong in one's opinion or judgement. **2** based on a misunderstanding or faulty judgement.
– DERIVATIVES **mistakenly** adv.

mister ● n. **1** var. of MR. **2** informal a form of address to a man.

mistime ● v. (**mistimes**, **mistiming**, **mistimed**) choose an unsuitable moment to do or say.

mistle thrush ● n. a large thrush with a spotted breast.
– ORIGIN from the bird's fondness for mistletoe berries.

mistletoe ● n. an evergreen plant which grows on broadleaved trees and bears white berries in winter.
– ORIGIN Old English.

mistook past of MISTAKE.

mistral /miss-truhl/ ● n. a strong north-westerly wind that blows through southern France.
– ORIGIN French.

mistreat ● v. treat badly or unfairly.
– DERIVATIVES **mistreatment** n.

mistress ● n. **1** a woman in a position of authority or control. **2** a woman skilled in a particular subject or activity. **3** a woman having a sexual relationship with a man who is married to someone else. **4** esp. Brit. a female schoolteacher. **5** (**Mistress**) archaic Mrs.
– ORIGIN Old French *maistresse*.

mistrial ● n. a trial made invalid through a mistake in proceedings.

mistrust ● v. have no trust in. ● n. lack of trust.

misty ● adj. (**mistier**, **mistiest**) **1** full of or covered with mist. **2** indistinct or unclear.
– DERIVATIVES **mistiness** n.

misunderstand ● v. (**misunderstands**, **misunderstanding**, **misunderstood**) fail to understand correctly.

misunderstanding ● n. **1** a failure to understand. **2** a minor disagreement.

misuse ● v. (**misuses**, **misusing**, **misused**) **1** use wrongly. **2** treat badly or unfairly. ● n. the action of misusing something.

Mitchell[1], E
Joni (b.1943; born *Roberta Joan Anderson*), Canadian singer and songwriter.

Mitchell[2], E
Margaret (1900–49), American novelist, author of *Gone with the Wind*.

Mitchum, E
Robert (1917–97), American actor, known for such films as *Night of the Hunter* and *Farewell My Lovely*.

mite[1] ● n. a tiny creature like a spider, that lives on plants, animals, etc.
– ORIGIN Old English.

mite[2] ● n. **1** a small child or animal. **2** a very small amount. ● adv. (**a mite**) informal slightly.
– ORIGIN Dutch.

Mitford, E
Nancy (Freeman) (1904–73) and her sister Jessica (Lucy) (1917–96), English writers. Nancy is known for comic novels including *Love in a Cold Climate*. Jessica is best known for her works on American culture, notably *The American Way of Death*.

mitigate ● v. (**mitigates**, **mitigating**, **mitigated**) **1** make less severe, serious, or painful. **2** (**mitigating**) (of a fact or circumstance) lessening the seriousness of or blame attached to an action.
– DERIVATIVES **mitigation** n.
– ORIGIN Latin *mitigare* 'soften'.

USAGE mitigate
Take care not to confuse **mitigate** and **militate**: **mitigate** means 'make something bad less severe' (as in *drainage schemes helped to mitigate the problem*), while **militate** is used with **against** to mean 'be a powerful factor in preventing' (as in *laws that militate against personal freedom*).

mitochondrion /my-tuh-**kon**-dri-uhn/ ● n. (pl. **mitochondria** /my-tuh-**kon**-dri-uh/) Biol. a structure found in large numbers in most cells, in which respiration and energy production occur.
– DERIVATIVES **mitochondrial** adj.
– ORIGIN from Greek *mitos* 'thread' + *khondrion* 'small granule'.

mitosis /my-**toh**-siss/ ● n. (pl. **mitoses**) Biol. a type of cell division in which daughter cells have the same number and kind of chromosomes as the parent nucleus. Compare with MEIOSIS.
– ORIGIN Greek *mitos* 'thread'.

mitre (US **miter**) ● n. **1** a tall headdress that tapers to a point at front and back, worn by bishops. **2** a joint made between two pieces of wood cut at an angle so as to form a corner of 90°.
– ORIGIN Greek *mitra* 'belt or turban'.

mitt • n. **1** a mitten. **2** a fingerless glove.

mitten • n. a glove having a single section for all four fingers, with a separate section for the thumb.
– ORIGIN Old French *mitaine*.

Mitterrand E
/**mee**-tuh-ron/, François (Maurice Marie) (1916–96), French Socialist statesman, President 1981–95.

mix • v. **1** combine or be combined to form a whole. **2** make by mixing ingredients. **3** combine (different recordings) to produce a piece of music. **4** (**mix up**) spoil the arrangement of. **5** (**mix up**) confuse (a person or thing) with another. **6** meet people socially. • n. **1** a mixture. **2** the proportion of different people or things making up a mixture. **3** a version of a piece of music mixed in a different way from the original.
– PHRASES **be mixed up in** be involved in (underhand or dishonest activities).
– ORIGIN from **MIXED**.

mixed • adj. **1** consisting of different kinds, qualities, or elements. **2** having to do with both males and females.
– ORIGIN Latin *mixtus*.

mixed economy • n. an economic system combining private and state enterprise.

mixed farming • n. farming of both crops and livestock.

mixed marriage • n. a marriage between people of different races or religions.

mixed metaphor • n. a combination of metaphors that do not make sense when combined (e.g. *this tower of strength will forge ahead*).

mixer • n. **1** a device for mixing things. **2** a person considered in terms of their ability to mix socially. **3** a soft drink that can be mixed with alcohol.

mixer tap • n. a single tap through which both hot and cold water can be drawn at the same time.

mixture • n. **1** a substance made by mixing other substances together. **2** (**a mixture of**) a combination of different things in which each thing is distinct.

mix-up • n. informal a confusion or misunderstanding.

Mizoram E
/**miz**-oh-ram/ a state in the far north-east of India; capital, Aizawl.

mizzen • n. (also **mizzenmast**) the mast behind a ship's mainmast.
– ORIGIN Italian *mezzano* 'middle'.

ml • abbrev. **1** miles. **2** millilitres.

Mlle • abbrev. (pl. **Mlles**) Mademoiselle.

MM • abbrev. Military Medal.

mm • abbrev. millimetres.

Mme • abbrev. (pl. **Mmes**) Madame.

MMR • abbrev. measles, mumps, and rubella (a vaccination given to children).

mnemonic /ni-**mon**-ik/ • n. a pattern of letters or words used as an aid to memory. • adj. aiding the memory.
– ORIGIN Greek *mnēmōn* 'mindful'.

MO • abbrev. **1** Medical Officer. **2** modus operandi.

mo • n. informal, esp. Brit. a moment.

moa /**moh**-uh/ • n. a large extinct flightless bird resembling the emu, formerly found in New Zealand.
– ORIGIN Maori.

moan • n. **1** a low mournful sound, expressing suffering. **2** informal a trivial complaint. • v. **1** make a moan. **2** informal grumble.
– ORIGIN unknown.

moat • n. a wide ditch filled with water, surrounding and protecting a castle or town.
– ORIGIN Old French *mote* 'mound'.

mob • n. **1** a disorderly crowd of people. **2** Brit. informal a group of people. **3** (**the Mob**) N. Amer. the Mafia. **4** (**the mob**) informal, derog. the ordinary people. • v. (**mobs**, **mobbing**, **mobbed**) crowd round or into in an unruly way.
– ORIGIN from Latin *mobile vulgus* 'excitable crowd'.

mobile • adj. **1** able to move or be moved freely or easily. **2** (of a shop, library, etc.) set up inside a vehicle so as to travel around. **3** able or willing to move between occupations, homes, or social classes. **4** (of the features of the face) readily changing expression. • n. **1** a decorative structure hung so as to turn freely in the air. **2** a mobile phone.
– PHRASES **upwardly mobile** moving to a higher social class.
– ORIGIN Latin *mobilis*.

mobile home • n. a large caravan used as permanent living accommodation.

mobile phone • n. a portable telephone.

mobility • n. the quality of being mobile.

mobilize (also **mobilise**) • v. (**mobilizes**, **mobilizing**, **mobilized**) **1** prepare and organize (troops) for war. **2** organize (people or resources) for a task.
– DERIVATIVES **mobilization** (also **mobilisation**) n.

Möbius strip /**mer**-bi-uhss/ • n. a surface with one continuous side formed by joining the ends of a rectangle after twisting one end through 180°.
– ORIGIN named after the German mathematician August F. *Möbius* (1790–1868).

mobster • n. informal a gangster.

Mobutu E
/muh-**boo**-too/, Sese Seko (1930–97), Zairean statesman, President 1965–97. He seized power in a military coup and was finally forced to stand down in 1997.

moccasin • n. a soft leather shoe with the sole turned up and sewn to the upper, originally worn by North American Indians.
– ORIGIN from a North American Indian language.

mocha /**mok**-uh/ • n. **1** a fine-quality coffee. **2** a drink made with coffee and chocolate.
– ORIGIN named after *Mocha*, a port in Yemen.

mock • v. **1** tease scornfully; ridicule. **2** imitate in an unkind way. • adj. **1** not genuine or real. **2** (of an examination, battle, etc.) arranged for training or practice. • n. (**mocks**) Brit. informal examinations taken in school as training for public examinations.
– ORIGIN Old French *mocquer* 'deride'.

mockery • n. (pl. **mockeries**) **1** ridicule. **2** an action or situation that is an absurd or worthless version of something: *after a mockery of a trial, he was executed*.

mockingbird • n. a long-tailed American

songbird, noted for copying the calls of other birds.

mock-up ● n. a model or replica of a machine or structure for instructional or experimental purposes.

MOD ● abbrev. (in the UK) Ministry of Defence.

mod ● n. Brit. (especially in the 1960s) a young person of a group who wore smart fashionable clothes and rode motor scooters.

modal ● adj. **1** relating to the way something is done. **2** Grammar relating to the mood of a verb.
– DERIVATIVES **modality** n.

modal verb ● n. Grammar an auxiliary verb expressing necessity or possibility, e.g. *must, shall, will.*

mod cons ● pl. n. modern conveniences, that is the amenities and appliances characteristic of a well-equipped modern house.

mode ● n. **1** a way in which something occurs or is done. **2** a style in clothes, art, etc. **3** Music a set of notes forming a scale and from which melodies and harmonies are constructed.
– ORIGIN Latin *modus* 'measure, manner'.

model ● n. **1** a three-dimensional copy of a person or thing, typically on a smaller scale. **2** something used as an example. **3** a simplified mathematical description of a system or process. **4** an excellent example of a quality. **5** a person employed to display clothes by wearing them. **6** a person employed to pose for an artist. **7** a particular version of a product. ● v. (**models, modelling, modelled,** US **models, modeling, modeled**) **1** make or shape (a figure) in clay, wax, etc. **2** (in drawing, painting, etc.) cause to appear three-dimensional. **3** make a mathematical model of. **4** (**model on**) use as an example for something else. **5** work as a model.

modem /moh-dem/ ● n. a device for converting digital and analogue signals, especially to allow a computer to be connected to a telephone line.
– ORIGIN from *modulator* and *demodulator.*

moderate ● adj. /mod-uh-ruht/ **1** average in amount, intensity, or degree. **2** (of a political position) not extreme. ● n. /mod-uh-ruht/ a person with moderate views. ● v. /mod-uh-rayt/ (**moderates, moderating, moderated**) **1** make or become less extreme or intense. **2** review (examination papers or results) to ensure consistency of marking.
– DERIVATIVES **moderately** adv.
– ORIGIN Latin *moderare* 'reduce'.

moderation ● n. **1** the avoidance of extremes in one's actions or opinions. **2** the process of moderating.

moderator ● n. **1** a person who helps others to solve a dispute. **2** a chairman of a debate. **3** a person who moderates examination papers.

modern ● adj. **1** relating to the present or to recent times. **2** having or using the most up-to-date techniques or equipment. **3** (in art, architecture, etc.) marked by a significant break from traditional values.
– DERIVATIVES **modernity** n.
– ORIGIN Latin *modernus.*

modernism ● n. **1** modern ideas, methods, or styles. **2** a movement in the arts that aims to break with traditional styles or ideas.
– DERIVATIVES **modernist** n. & adj.

modernize (also **modernise**) ● v. (**modernizes, modernizing, modernized**) make modern.

modest ● adj. **1** having a humble view of one's abilities or achievements. **2** relatively moderate, limited, or small. **3** (especially of clothes) decent.
– DERIVATIVES **modestly** adv.
– ORIGIN Latin *modestus* 'keeping due measure'.

modesty ● n. the quality of being modest.

modicum /mod-i-kuhm/ ● n. a small quantity of something.
– ORIGIN Latin *modicus* 'moderate'.

modification ● n. **1** the action of modifying. **2** a change made.

modifier ● n. Grammar a word that qualifies the sense of a noun (e.g. *good* and *family* in *a good family house*).

modify ● v. (**modifies, modifying, modified**) make partial changes to.
– ORIGIN Latin *modificare.*

Modigliani E
/mo-di-lyah-ni/, Amedeo (1884–1920), Italian painter and sculptor, resident in France from 1906. His typical work consists of nudes with elongated forms and portraits.

modish /moh-dish/ ● adj. fashionable.

modular ● adj. made up of separate units.

modulate ● v. (**modulates, modulating, modulated**) **1** control or regulate. **2** vary the strength, tone, or pitch of (one's voice). **3** adjust the amplitude or frequency of (an oscillation or signal). **4** Music change from one key to another.
– ORIGIN Latin *modulari* 'measure'.

module ● n. **1** each of a set of parts or units that can be used to create a more complex structure. **2** each of a set of independent units of study or training forming part of a course. **3** an independent unit of a spacecraft.
– ORIGIN Latin *modulus.*

modulus /mod-yuu-luhss/ ● n. (pl. **moduli** /mod-yuu-li/) **1** Math. the magnitude of a number irrespective of whether it is positive or negative. **2** a constant factor relating a physical effect to the force producing it.

modus operandi /moh-duhss op-uh-ran-di/ ● n. (pl. **modi operandi** /moh-di op-uh-ran-di/) a way of operating or doing something.
ORIGIN Latin.

modus vivendi /moh-duhss vi-ven-di/ ● n. (pl. **modi vivendi** /moh-di vi-ven-di/) an arrangement allowing conflicting parties to exist peacefully together.
– ORIGIN Latin.

Mogadishu E
/mog-uh-di-shoo/ the capital of Somalia.

moggie (also **moggy**) ● n. (pl. **moggies**) Brit. informal a cat.
– ORIGIN from *Maggie,* familiar form of the woman's name *Margaret.*

Mogul /moh-guhl/ (also **Moghul** or **Mughal**) ● n. **1** a member of the Muslim dynasty of Mongol origin which ruled much of India in the 16th–19th centuries. **2** (**mogul**) informal an important or powerful person.
– ORIGIN Persian, 'Mongol'.

mohair ● n. a yarn or fabric made from the

m

hair of the angora goat.
– ORIGIN Arabic.

Mohave Desert E
var. of **MOJAVE DESERT**.

Mohican /moh-**hee**-kuhn/ ● **n.** a hairstyle in which the sides of the head are shaved and a central strip of hair is made to stand up.
– ORIGIN from the name of a North American Indian people.

moiety /**moy**-i-ti/ ● **n.** (pl. **moieties**) formal a half.
– ORIGIN Old French *moite.*

moire /mwar/ (also **moiré** /**mwah**-ray/) ● **n.** silk fabric treated to give it an appearance like that of rippled water.
– ORIGIN French, 'mohair' (the treatment first being used on mohair).

moist ● **adj.** slightly wet; damp.
– DERIVATIVES **moisten** v. **moistness** n.
– ORIGIN Old French *moiste.*

moisture ● **n.** tiny drops of water or other liquid in the air, in a substance, or condensed on a surface.

moisturize (also **moisturise**) ● **v.** (**moisturizes**, **moisturizing**, **moisturized**) make (something, especially skin) less dry.

moisturizer (also **moisturiser**) ● **n.** a cream for moisturizing the skin.

Mojave Desert E
/moh-**hah**-vi/ (also **Mohave**) a desert in southern California.

molar[1] /**moh**-ler/ ● **n.** a grinding tooth at the back of a mammal's mouth.
– ORIGIN Latin *mola* 'millstone'.

molar[2] ● **adj.** Chem. **1** relating to one mole of a substance. **2** (of a solution) containing one mole of solute per litre of solvent.

molasses /muh-**lass**-iz/ ● **n. 1** a thick, dark brown liquid obtained from raw sugar. **2** N. Amer. golden syrup.
– ORIGIN Latin *mellacium* 'must'.

mold ● **n. & v.** US = **MOULD**[1-3].

Moldavia E
/mol-**day**-vi-uh/ = **MOLDOVA**.

molder ● **v.** US = **MOULDER**.

molding ● **n.** US = **MOULDING**.

Moldova E
/mol-**doh**-vuh/ a country in SE Europe, between Romania and Ukraine; capital, Chişinău. Also called **MOLDAVIA**.
– DERIVATIVES **Moldovan** adj. & n.

moldy ● **adj.** US = **MOULDY**.

mole[1] ● **n. 1** a small burrowing mammal with dark fur, a long muzzle, and very small eyes. **2** a person within an organization who secretly passes confidential information to another organization or country.
– ORIGIN Germanic.

mole[2] ● **n.** a dark blemish on the skin where there is a high concentration of melanin.
– ORIGIN Old English.

mole[3] ● **n. 1** a large solid structure serving as a pier, breakwater, or causeway. **2** a harbour formed by a mole.
– ORIGIN Latin *moles* 'mass'.

mole[4] ● **n.** Chem. the SI unit of amount of substance, equal to the quantity containing as many elementary units as there are atoms in 0.012 kg of carbon-12.
– ORIGIN German *Molekul* 'molecule'.

molecular /muh-**lek**-yuu-ler/ ● **adj.** relating to or made up of molecules.

molecule /**mol**-i-kyool/ ● **n.** a group of atoms chemically bonded together, representing the smallest fundamental unit of a compound that can take part in a chemical reaction.
– ORIGIN French.

molehill ● **n.** a small mound of earth thrown up by a burrowing mole.
– PHRASES **make a mountain out of a molehill** exaggerate the importance of a small problem.

moleskin ● **n.** a thick cotton fabric with a shaved pile surface.

molest ● **v. 1** pester or harass in a hostile way. **2** assault sexually.
– DERIVATIVES **molestation** n. **molester** n.
– ORIGIN Latin *molestare* 'annoy'.

Molière E
/**mol**-i-air/(1622–73; pen name of *Jean-Baptiste Poquelin*), French dramatist. His comic plays about contemporary France include *Don Juan*, *Le Misanthrope*, and *Le Bourgeois gentilhomme.*

moll ● **n.** informal a gangster's female companion.
– ORIGIN from the woman's name *Mary.*

mollify ● **v.** (**mollifies**, **mollifying**, **mollified**) **1** lessen the anger or anxiety of. **2** reduce the severity of.
– ORIGIN Latin *mollis* 'soft'.

mollusc /**mol**-luhsk/ (US **mollusk**) ● **n.** an animal without a backbone belonging to a large group including snails, slugs, and mussels, with a soft body and often an external shell.
– ORIGIN Latin *mollis* 'soft'.

mollycoddle ● **v.** (**mollycoddles**, **mollycoddling**, **mollycoddled**) treat indulgently or too protectively.
– ORIGIN from *molly* 'girl' (see **MOLL**) + **CODDLE**.

Molotov cocktail /**mol**-uh-tof/ ● **n.** a crude bomb made up of a bottle of flammable liquid ignited by means of a wick.
– ORIGIN named after the Soviet statesman Vyacheslav *Molotov* (1890–1986).

molt ● **v. & n.** US = **MOULT**.

molten ● **adj.** (especially of metal and glass) made liquid by heat.
– ORIGIN former past participle of **MELT**.

molto /**mol**-toh/ ● **adv.** Music very.
– ORIGIN Italian.

Molucca Islands E
/muh-**luk**-kuh/ an island group in Indonesia, between Sulawesi and New Guinea; capital, Amboina. Former name **SPICE ISLANDS**.
– DERIVATIVES **Moluccan** n. & adj.

molybdenum /muh-**lib**-duh-nuhm/ ● **n.** a brittle silver-grey metallic element used in some steels and other alloys.
– ORIGIN Greek *molubdos* 'lead'.

mom ● **n.** N. Amer. = **MUM**[1].

Mombasa E
/mom-**ba**-suh/ a seaport and industrial city in SE Kenya.

moment ● **n. 1** a brief period of time. **2** an

exact point in time. **3** formal importance: *the issues were of little moment.*
– ORIGIN Latin *momentum*.

momentarily • **adv.** **1** for a very short time. **2** N. Amer. very soon.

momentary • **adj.** very brief or short-lived.

momentous • **adj.** very important.

momentum • **n.** (pl. **momenta**) **1** impetus gained by movement or progress. **2** Physics the quantity of motion of a moving body, equal to its mass multiplied by its velocity.
– ORIGIN Latin *movimentum*.

mommy • **n.** (pl. **mommies**) N. Amer. = **MUMMY**[1].

Mon. • **abbrev.** Monday.

Monaco E
/mon-uh-koh/ a principality forming an enclave within French territory on the Mediterranean coast near Italy.
DERIVATIVES **Monegasque** adj. & n.

Monaghan E
/mon-uh-huhn/ a county in the north of the Republic of Ireland; county town, Monaghan.

monarch • **n.** a king or queen as ruler of a country.
– DERIVATIVES **monarchical** adj.
– ORIGIN from Greek *monos* 'alone' + *arkhein* 'to rule'.

monarchism • **n.** support for the principle of monarchy.
– DERIVATIVES **monarchist** n. & adj.

monarchy • **n.** (pl. **monarchies**) **1** government by a monarch. **2** a state ruled by a monarch.

monastery • **n.** (pl. **monasteries**) a community of monks living under religious vows.
– ORIGIN Greek *monastērion*.

monastic • **adj.** **1** relating to monks or nuns or their communities. **2** resembling monks or their way of life.

Monday • **n.** the day of the week before Tuesday and following Sunday.
– ORIGIN Old English, 'day of the moon'.

Mondrian E
/mon-dri-ahn/, Piet (1872–1944), Dutch painter. He originated the abstract style he termed neo-plasticism, in which he limited himself to rectangular shapes and the colours blue, red, yellow, and black.

Monet E
/mon-ay/, Claude (1840–1926), French Impressionist painter, known for his series of paintings of single subjects painted at different times of day and under different weather conditions, such as the *Water-lilies* sequence.

monetarism • **n.** the theory that inflation is best controlled by limiting the supply of money circulating in an economy.
– DERIVATIVES **monetarist** n. & adj.

monetary • **adj.** having to do with money or currency.

money • **n.** **1** a means of payment in the form of coins and banknotes. **2** wealth. **3** payment or profit. **4** (**moneys** or **monies**) formal sums of money.
– PHRASES **put one's money where one's mouth is** informal take action to support one's statements.
– ORIGIN Latin *moneta* 'mint, money'.

moneyed • **adj.** having much money; rich.

money-grubbing • **adj.** informal greedily concerned with making money.

money order • **n.** a printed order for payment of a specified sum, issued by a bank or post office.

money spider • **n.** a very small black spider.

money-spinner • **n.** esp. Brit. a thing that brings in a large profit.

money supply • **n.** the total amount of money in circulation or in existence in a country.

-monger • **comb. form** **1** referring to a dealer or trader in a specified commodity: *fishmonger.* **2** esp. derog. referring to a person engaging in a particular activity: *rumour-monger.*
– ORIGIN Latin *mango* 'dealer'.

Mongol • **n.** **1** a person from Mongolia. **2** (**mongol**) offens. a person with Down's syndrome.
– DERIVATIVES **mongolism** n. (offens.).

Mongolia E
/mong-goh-li-uh/ a country of east Asia, bordered by Siberian Russia and China; capital, Ulan Bator.

mongoose • **n.** (pl. **mongooses**) a small meat-eating mammal with a long body and tail, native to Africa and Asia.
– ORIGIN from a central Indian language.

mongrel • **n.** a dog of no particular breed.
– ORIGIN prob. from **MINGLE** and **AMONG**.

monies pl. of **MONEY**.

moniker /mon-i-ker/ • **n.** informal a name.
– ORIGIN unknown.

monitor • **n.** **1** a person or device that monitors something. **2** a television used to view a picture from a particular camera or a display from a computer. **3** a school pupil with disciplinary or other special duties. **4** (also **monitor lizard**) a large tropical lizard. • **v.** observe so as to record, regulate, or control.
– ORIGIN Latin *monere* 'warn'.

Monk, E
Thelonious (Sphere) (1917–82), American jazz pianist and composer.

monk • **n.** a man belonging to a religious community and living under vows of poverty, chastity, and obedience.
– ORIGIN Greek *monakhos* 'solitary'.

monkey • **n.** (pl. **monkeys**) **1** a primate typically having a long tail and living in trees in tropical countries. **2** a mischievous child. • **v.** (**monkeys**, **monkeying**, **monkeyed**) **1** (**monkey about/around**) behave in a silly or playful way. **2** (**monkey with**) tamper with.
– ORIGIN unknown.

monkey business • **n.** informal mischievous or underhand behaviour.

monkey nut • **n.** Brit. a peanut.

monkey puzzle • **n.** a coniferous tree with branches covered in spirals of tough spiny leaves.

monkey wrench • **n.** a spanner with large adjustable jaws.

monkfish • **n.** an edible sea fish with a long

fleshy growth on the snout.

Monmouth, E
James Scott, Duke of (1649–85), illegitimate son of Charles II. A Protestant, in 1685 Monmouth led a rebellion against the Catholic James II, but was defeated at the Battle of Sedgemoor and executed.

Monmouthshire E
a county of SE Wales, on the border with England; administrative centre, Cwmbran.

mono • adj. monophonic. • n. monophonic reproduction.

mono- (also **mon-** before a vowel) • comb. form one; single: *monochrome.*
– ORIGIN Greek *monos.*

monochrome • adj. consisting of or displaying images in black and white or in varying tones of one colour.
– DERIVATIVES **monochromatic** adj.
– ORIGIN Greek *monokhrōmatos* 'of a single colour'.

monocle • n. a lens worn to improve sight in one eye.
– ORIGIN Latin *monoculus* 'one-eyed'.

monocotyledon /mon-oh-kot-i-**lee**-duhn/ • n. a flowering plant whose seeds have a single cotyledon (seed leaf).

monocular • adj. having to do with or using one eye.
– ORIGIN Latin *monoculus* 'having one eye'.

monogamy /muh-**nog**-uh-mi/ • n. the state of having only one husband, wife, or sexual partner at any one time.
– DERIVATIVES **monogamist** n. **monogamous** adj.
– ORIGIN from Greek *monos* 'single' + *gamos* 'marriage'.

monogram • n. a motif of two or more interwoven letters, typically a person's initials.
– DERIVATIVES **monogrammed** adj.

monograph /**mon**-uh-grahf/ • n. a scholarly written study of a single subject.

monolingual • adj. speaking or expressed in only one language.

monolith • n. a large single upright block of stone.
– ORIGIN from Greek *monos* 'single' + *lithos* 'stone'.

monolithic • adj. **1** formed of a single large block of stone. **2** massive and uniform: *a monolithic European superstate.*

monologue • n. **1** a long speech by one actor in a play or film. **2** a long, boring speech by one person during a conversation.
– ORIGIN Greek *monologos* 'speaking alone'.

monomania /mon-oh-**may**-ni-uh/ • n. an obsession with one thing.
– DERIVATIVES **monomaniac** n.

monomer /**mon**-uh-mer/ • n. Chem. a molecule that can be linked to other identical molecules to form a polymer.

monophonic • adj. (of sound reproduction) using only one transmission channel. Compare with STEREOPHONIC.

monoplane • n. an aircraft with one pair of wings.

monopolistic • adj. having to do with a monopoly.

monopolize (also **monopolise**) • v. (**monopolizes**, **monopolizing**, **monopolized**) dominate or take control of.

monopoly • n. (pl. **monopolies**) **1** the complete possession or control of the supply of a product or service by one person or organization. **2** an organization having a monopoly, or a product or service controlled by one.
– ORIGIN Greek *monopōlion.*

monorail • n. a railway in which the track consists of a single rail.

monosaccharide • n. a sugar that cannot be broken down to give a simpler sugar.

monosodium glutamate • n. a compound used to add flavour to food.

monosyllabic • adj. **1** consisting of one syllable. **2** using brief words because reluctant to have a conversation.

monosyllable • n. a word of one syllable.

monotheism /**mon**-oh-thee-i-z'm/ • n. the belief that there is a single god.
– DERIVATIVES **monotheist** n. **monotheistic** adj.

monotone • n. a continuing sound that is unchanging in pitch.

monotonous • adj. **1** boring because repetitive. **2** without variation of tone or pitch.
– DERIVATIVES **monotonously** adv. **monotony** n.

monoxide • n. Chem. an oxide containing one atom of oxygen.

Monroe[1], E
James (1758–1831), American Democratic Republican statesman, 5th President of the US 1817–25. He was the originator of the **Monroe doctrine**, which declared that any intervention by foreign powers in the politics of the Americas is a potentially hostile act against the US.

Monroe[2], E
Marilyn (1926–62; born *Norma Jean Mortenson*; later *Norma Jean Baker*), American actress. Her films include the comedies *Gentlemen Prefer Blondes*, *Some Like it Hot*, and *The Misfits*. She is thought to have died of an overdose of sleeping pills.

Monrovia E
/mon-**roh**-vi-uh/ the capital of Liberia.

Mons E
/monz/ a town in southern Belgium, the scene in 1914 of the first major battle of the First World War between British and German forces.

Monseigneur /mon-sen-**yer**/ • n. a title or form of address for a French-speaking prince, cardinal, archbishop, or bishop.
– ORIGIN French, 'my lord'.

Monsieur /muh-**syer**/ • n. (pl. **Messieurs** /mess-**yer**/) a title or form of address for a French-speaking man, corresponding to *Mr* or *sir.*
– ORIGIN French, 'my lord'.

Monsignor /mon-**seen**-yer/ • n. (pl. **Monsignori** /mon-seen-**yor**-i/) the title of various senior Roman Catholic priests and officials.
– ORIGIN Italian.

monsoon • n. **1** a seasonal wind in the Indian subcontinent and SE Asia, bringing rain when blowing from the south-west. **2** the

rainy season accompanying the monsoon.
– ORIGIN Arabic, 'season'.

monster • n. **1** a large and frightening imaginary creature. **2** a very cruel or wicked person. • adj. very large.
– ORIGIN Latin *monstrum*.

monstrosity • n. (pl. **monstrosities**) **1** a very large and ugly object. **2** a thing that is evil.

monstrous • adj. **1** very large and ugly or frightening. **2** very evil or wrong.

montage /mon-tah*zh*/ • n. **1** the technique of making a picture or film by putting together pieces from other pictures or films. **2** a picture or film resulting from this.
– ORIGIN French.

Montaigne E
/mon-**tayn**/, Michel (Eyquem) de (1533–92), French essayist, who wrote about prominent personalities and ideas of his age in his sceptical *Essays*.

Montana E
/mon-**tan**-uh/ a state in the western US, on the Canadian border; capital, Helena.
– DERIVATIVES **Montanan** adj. & n.

Mont Blanc E
/mon(t) **blong(k)**/ a peak in the Alps on the border between France and Italy. Rising to 4,807 m (15,771 ft), it is the highest peak in Western Europe.

Montcalm E
/mon-**kahm**/, Louis Joseph de Montcalm-Gozon, Marquis de (1712–59), French general. He defended Quebec against British forces, but was defeated and fatally wounded in the battle.

Monte Carlo E
a resort in Monaco, famous as a gambling resort and as the terminus of the annual Monte Carlo rally.

Montego Bay E
/mon-**tee**-goh/ a free port and tourist resort on the north coast of Jamaica.

Montenegro E
/mon-ti-**nee**-groh/ a republic in the Balkans, part of Yugoslavia; capital, Podgorica.
– DERIVATIVES **Montenegrin** adj. & n.

Montessori E
/mon-ti-**sor**-i/, Maria (1870–1952), Italian educationist, who advocated a child-centred approach to education.

Monteverdi E
/mon-ti-**vair**-di/, Claudio (1567–1643), Italian composer. His works include madrigals, the opera *Orfeo*, and his sacred *Vespers*.

Montevideo E
/mon-ti-vi-**day**-oh/ the capital of Uruguay.

Montezuma II E
/mon-ti-**zoo**-muh/ (1466–1520), ruler (1502–20) of the Aztec empire in Mexico. He was taken hostage and eventually killed when the Spanish invaded his country.

Montfort E
/**mont**-fert/, Simon de, Earl of Leicester (*c*.1208–65), English soldier, who led the baronial opposition to Henry III. He defeated Henry in 1264 and effectively ruled England until he was killed by forces led by Henry's son (the future Edward I).

Montgolfier E
/mon-**gol**-fi-ay/, Joseph Michel (1740–1810) and Jacques Étienne (1745–99), French pioneers in hot-air ballooning. In 1782 they successfully lifted a number of animals in a large balloon; the first ascent by humans followed in 1783.

Montgomery[1], E
Bernard Law, 1st Viscount Montgomery of Alamein (1887–1976; known as **Monty**), British Field Marshal. He won an important Allied victory at El Alamein (1942) and later commanded the Allied ground forces in Normandy in 1944.

Montgomery[2], E
L. M. (1874–1942), full name *Lucy Maud Montgomery*), Canadian novelist, author of *Anne of Green Gables*.

month • n. **1** each of the twelve named periods into which a year is divided. **2** a period of time between the same dates in successive calendar months, usually about 28 days.
– ORIGIN Old English.

monthly • adj. done or occurring once a month. • adv. once a month.

Montmartre E
/mon-**mar**-truh/ a district on a hill in northern Paris, formerly much frequented by artists.

Montparnasse E
/mon-par-**nass**/ a district of Paris, on the left bank of the River Seine, frequented by writers, artists, and intellectuals.

Montreal E
/mon-tri-**awl**/ a city and port on the St Lawrence in Quebec, SE Canada.

Mont St Michel E
/mon san mi-**shel**/ a rocky islet off the coast of NW France. An island only at high tide, it is linked to the mainland by a causeway and is crowned by a medieval Benedictine abbey-fortress.

Montserrat E
/**mon**-suh-rat/ an island in the Caribbean, one of the Leeward Islands and a British dependency; capital, Plymouth.
– DERIVATIVES **Montserratian** adj. & n. /mon-suh-**rash**-uhn/

monty • n. (in phr. **the full monty**) Brit. informal the full amount expected, desired, or possible.
– ORIGIN uncertain.

monument • n. **1** a statue or structure built to commemorate a person or event. **2** a structure or site of historical importance. **3** a notable or lasting example: *a monument to good taste*.

– ORIGIN Latin *monumentum*.

monumental • adj. **1** very large or impressive. **2** acting as a monument.

moo • v. (**moos**, **mooing**, **mooed**) (of a cow) make its typical deep vocal sound. • n. (pl. **moos**) such a sound.

mooch • v. Brit. informal stand or walk around in a bored or listless way.
– ORIGIN prob. from Old French *muscher* 'hide, skulk'.

mood • n. **1** a temporary state of mind. **2** a fit of bad temper or depression. **3** the atmosphere of a work of art. **4** Grammar a form of a verb expressing a fact, command, question, wish, or condition.
– ORIGIN Old English.

moody • adj. (**moodier**, **moodiest**) **1** having sudden fits of bad temper or depression. **2** giving a sad or mysterious impression.

moon • n. **1** (also **Moon**) the natural satellite of the earth. **2** a natural satellite of any planet. **3** literary a month. • v. **1** (**moon about/around**) behave or move in a listless or dreamy manner. **2** informal expose one's buttocks to someone as an insult or joke.
– PHRASES **over the moon** Brit. informal delighted.
– ORIGIN Old English.

moonlight • n. the light of the moon. • v. (**moonlights**, **moonlighting**, **moonlighted**) informal do a second job without declaring it for tax purposes.
– DERIVATIVES **moonlit** adj.

moonscape • n. a rocky and barren landscape like the moon's surface.

moonshine • n. informal **1** foolish talk or ideas. **2** N. Amer. secretly made or smuggled liquor.

moonstone • n. a white semi-precious form of feldspar.

moony • adj. dreamy because in love.

Moor • n. a member of a NW African Muslim people.
– DERIVATIVES **Moorish** adj.
– ORIGIN Greek *Mauros* 'inhabitant of Mauretania' (an ancient region of N. Africa).

moor[1] • n. a stretch of open uncultivated upland.
– ORIGIN Old English.

moor[2] • v. **1** make fast (a boat) by attaching it to the shore or to an anchor. **2** be secured in this way.
– ORIGIN prob. from Germanic.

Moore[1], E
Bobby (1941–93; full name *Robert Frederick Moore*), English footballer, who captained the English team that won the World Cup in 1966.

Moore[2], E
Henry (Spencer) (1898–1986), English sculptor and draughtsman. His sculptures consist mainly of semi-abstract reclining forms, large upright figures, and family groups.

moorhen • n. a black water bird with a red and yellow bill.

mooring (also **moorings**) • n. **1** a place where a boat is moored. **2** the ropes or cables by which a boat is moored.

moose • n. (pl. **moose**) N. Amer. = **ELK**.
– ORIGIN from an American Indian language.

moot • adj. subject to debate; uncertain: *a moot point*. • v. put forward for discussion.
– ORIGIN Old English, 'assembly'.

mop • n. **1** a bundle of thick strings or a sponge attached to a handle, used for wiping floors. **2** a thick mass of untidy hair. • v. (**mops**, **mopping**, **mopped**) **1** clean or soak up by wiping. **2** (**mop up**) clear up or put an end to.
– ORIGIN perh. from Latin *mappa* 'napkin'.

mope • v. (**mopes**, **moping**, **moped**) be listless and in low spirits.
– ORIGIN perh. Scandinavian.

moped /mow-ped/ • n. a light motorcycle with an engine capacity below 50 cc.
– ORIGIN from Swedish *trampcykel med motor och pedaler* 'pedal cycle with motor and pedals'.

moraine /muh-rayn/ • n. a mass of rocks and sediment carried down and deposited by a glacier.
– ORIGIN French dialect *morre* 'snout'.

moral • adj. **1** concerned with the principles of right and wrong behaviour. **2** following accepted standards of behaviour. **3** psychological rather than practical: *moral support*. • n. **1** a lesson about right or wrong that can be learned from a story or experience. **2** (**morals**) standards of good behaviour, or principles of right and wrong.
– DERIVATIVES **morally** adv.
– ORIGIN Latin *moralis*.

morale • n. the level of confidence and spirits of a person or group.
– ORIGIN French *moral*.

moralist • n. a person who teaches or promotes morality.
– DERIVATIVES **moralistic** adj.

morality • n. (pl. **moralities**) **1** principles concerning the difference between right and wrong. **2** moral behaviour. **3** the extent to which an action is right or wrong.

morality play • n. a play presenting a moral lesson and having personified qualities as the main characters, popular in the 15th and 16th centuries.

moralize (also **moralise**) • v. (**moralizes**, **moralizing**, **moralized**) comment on moral matters in a disapproving way.

moral victory • n. a defeat that can be interpreted as a victory because one has done the right thing.

morass /muh-rass/ • n. **1** an area of muddy or boggy ground. **2** a complicated situation: *a morass of lies*.
– ORIGIN Dutch *moeras*.

moratorium /mo-ruh-tor-i-uhm/ • n. (pl. **moratoriums** or **moratoria**) a temporary ban on an activity.
– ORIGIN Latin.

Moravia E
/muh-ray-vi-uh/ a region of the Czech Republic, situated between Bohemia and the Carpathian Mountains.

Moray E
/mu-ri/ (also **Morayshire**) an administrative region and former county of northern Scotland; administrative centre, Elgin.

moray /mo-ray/ (also **moray eel**) • n. an eel-like fish of warm seas.

– ORIGIN Portuguese *moréia*.

Moray Firth E
a deep inlet of the North Sea on the NE coast of Scotland.

morbid • adj. **1** having an unhealthy interest in death and disease. **2** Med. having to do with disease.
– DERIVATIVES **morbidity** n. **morbidly** adv.
– ORIGIN Latin *morbus* 'disease'.

mordant • adj. (of humour) sharply sarcastic. • n. a substance that combines with a dye and thereby fixes it in a material.
– ORIGIN Latin *mordere* 'to bite'.

Mordred E
/mor-drid/ (in Arthurian legend) the nephew of King Arthur, who rebelled against Arthur and caused his downfall.

More, E
Sir Thomas (1478–1535; canonized as **St Thomas More**), English scholar and statesman, Lord Chancellor 1529–32. A leading humanist, he wrote *Utopia*, describing an ideal city state. He was beheaded for refusing to acknowledge Henry VIII's supremacy over the English Church. Feast day, 22 June.

more • det. & pron. a greater or additional amount or degree. • adv. **1** forming the comparative of adjectives and adverbs. **2** to a greater extent. **3** again. **4** (**more than**) extremely: *more than happy to oblige.*
– PHRASES **more or less** to a certain extent. **no more 1** nothing or no further. **2** (**be no more**) no longer exist.
– ORIGIN Old English.

Morecambe, E
Eric (1926–84; born *John Eric Bartholomew*), English comedian. He was famous for his double act with comedian Ernie Wise (1925–99).

moreish • adj. Brit. informal so pleasant to eat that one wants more.

morel /muh-rel/ • n. an edible fungus with a brown oval or pointed cap.
– ORIGIN French *morille*.

morello /muh-rel-loh/ • n. (pl. **morellos**) a kind of sour dark cherry used in cooking.
– ORIGIN Italian, 'blackish'.

moreover • adv. as a further matter; besides.

mores /mor-ayz/ • pl. n. the customs and conventions of a community.
– ORIGIN Latin.

Morgan, E
(Hywel) Rhodri (b. 1939), Welsh Labour statesman, First Secretary of the Welsh Assembly from 2000.

morgue • n. a mortuary.
– ORIGIN French.

moribund /mo-ri-bund/ • adj. **1** at the point of death. **2** losing effectiveness and about to end.
– ORIGIN Latin *moribundus*.

Morisot E
/mo-ri-zoh/, Berthe (Marie Pauline) (1841–95), French Impressionist painter, known for her paintings of women and children and waterside scenes.

Morley, E
Edward Williams (1838–1923), American chemist, who collaborated with Albert Michelson in an experiment to determine the speed of light.

Mormon • n. a member of the Church of Jesus Christ of Latter-Day Saints.
– DERIVATIVES **Mormonism** n.
– ORIGIN *Mormon*, a prophet on whose book of supposed revelations the religion is based.

morn • n. literary morning.
– ORIGIN Old English.

morning • n. **1** the period of time between midnight and noon, especially from sunrise to noon. **2** sunrise. • adv. (**mornings**) informal every morning.
– ORIGIN from MORN.

morning-after pill • n. a contraceptive pill that is effective within about thirty-six hours after intercourse.

morning dress • n. a man's formal dress of a tailcoat and striped trousers.

morning glory • n. a climbing plant with trumpet-shaped flowers.

morning sickness • n. nausea occurring in the mornings during early pregnancy.

morning star • n. the planet Venus, when visible in the east before sunrise.

Morocco E
a country in NW Africa, with coastlines on the Mediterranean Sea and Atlantic Ocean; capital, Rabat.
– DERIVATIVES **Moroccan** adj. & n.

moron • n. informal a stupid person.
– DERIVATIVES **moronic** adj.
– ORIGIN Greek *mōros* 'foolish'.

Moroni E
/muh-roh-ni/ the capital of Comoros, on the island of Grande Comore.

morose • adj. sullen and ill-tempered.
– DERIVATIVES **morosely** adv.
– ORIGIN Latin *morosus* 'peevish'.

morph • v. (in computer animation) change smoothly and gradually from one image to another.
– ORIGIN from METAMORPHOSIS.

morpheme /mor-feem/ • n. the smallest unit of meaning that a word can be divided into (e.g. the units *like* and *-ly*, forming *likely*).

morphia • n. dated morphine.

morphine /mor-feen/ • n. a drug obtained from opium and used in medicine to relieve pain.
– ORIGIN named after the Roman god of sleep, *Morpheus*.

morphology • n. the scientific study of forms of living organisms or words.
– DERIVATIVES **morphological** adj.

Morris[1], E
William (1834–96), English designer, craftsman, and writer. He sought a revival of traditional craftsmanship, and founded the firm of Morris & Company to produce handcrafted goods for the home. His writings include *News from Nowhere*, which portrays a socialist Utopia.

Morris[2], E
William Richard, see NUFFIELD.

m

morris dancing • n. traditional English folk dancing performed by dancers wearing costumes with small bells attached and carrying handkerchiefs or sticks.
– ORIGIN from *Moorish* (see **MOOR**).

Morrison[1], E
Toni (b.1931; full name *Chloe Anthony Morrison*), American novelist. Her novels, such as *Beloved*, depict the black American experience.

Morrison[2], E
Van (b.1945; full name *George Ivan Morrison*), Northern Irish singer, instrumentalist, and songwriter. His albums include *Astral Weeks*.

morrow • n. (**the morrow**) archaic the following day.
– ORIGIN Old English.

Morse (also **Morse code**) • n. a code in which letters are represented by combinations of long and short light or sound signals.
– ORIGIN named after its American inventor Samuel F. B. *Morse* (1791–1872).

morsel • n. a small piece of food.
– ORIGIN Old French, 'little bite'.

mortal • adj. **1** subject to death. **2** causing death. **3** (of fear, pain, etc.) very strong. **4** (of conflict or an enemy) lasting until death. **5** (in Christian belief) referring to a sin that will deprive the soul of divine grace. Often contrasted with **VENIAL**. • n. a human being.
– DERIVATIVES **mortally** adv.
– ORIGIN Latin *mors* 'death'.

m

mortality • n. **1** the state of being mortal. **2** death. **3** (also **mortality rate**) the number of deaths in a particular area or period.

mortar • n. **1** a mixture of lime with cement, sand, and water, used to hold bricks or stones together. **2** a cup-shaped container in which substances are crushed with a pestle. **3** a short cannon for firing bombs at high angles.
– ORIGIN Latin *mortarium*.

mortar board • n. an academic cap with a flat square top and a tassel.

mortgage • n. **1** a legal agreement by which a person takes out a loan using their house or other property as a security. **2** an amount of money borrowed or lent under such an agreement. • v. (**mortgages**, **mortgaging**, **mortgaged**) transfer the legal right of ownership to (a property) to a creditor as security for the repayment of a loan.
– ORIGIN Old French, 'dead pledge'.

mortgagee • n. the lender in a mortgage.

mortgagor • n. the borrower in a mortgage.

mortician • n. esp. N. Amer. an undertaker.

mortify • v. (**mortifies**, **mortifying**, **mortified**) **1** cause to feel embarrassed or humiliated. **2** subdue (physical urges) by self-discipline.
– DERIVATIVES **mortification** n.
– ORIGIN Old French *mortifier*.

Mortimer, E
Roger de, 8th Baron of Wigmore and 1st Earl of March (*c.*1287–1330), English noble. In 1326 he invaded England with his lover Isabella of France, replacing her husband Edward II with her son, the future Edward III. When Edward III assumed power he had Mortimer executed.

mortise /**mor**-tiss/ (also **mortice**) • n. a hole or recess designed to receive a projection (a tenon) so that the two are held together.
– ORIGIN Old French *mortaise*.

mortise lock • n. a lock set into the framework of a door in a recess or mortise.

Morton, E
Jelly Roll (1885–1941; born *Ferdinand Joseph La Menthe Morton*), American jazz pianist, composer, and bandleader.

mortuary • n. (pl. **mortuaries**) a room or building in which dead bodies are kept until burial or cremation. • adj. relating to burial or tombs.
– ORIGIN Latin *mortuus* 'dead'.

Mosaic • adj. having to do with the biblical prophet Moses.

mosaic • n. a picture or pattern produced by arranging together small coloured pieces of stone, tile, or glass.
– ORIGIN French *mosaïque*.

Moscow E
the capital of Russia.

Mosel E
/**moh**-z'l/ (also **Moselle** /moh-**zel**/) a river of western Europe, which rises in the Vosges mountains of NE France and flows north-east through Luxembourg and Germany, where it meets the Rhine.

Moses[1] E
(*fl. c.*14th–13th centuries BC), Hebrew prophet and lawgiver. According to the Bible, he led the Israelites out of Egypt towards the Promised Land. During the journey he was inspired by God to write down the Ten Commandments.

Moses[2], E
Ed (b.1956; full name *Edwin Corley Moses*), American athlete, who set four successive world records for the 400-metres hurdles between 1976 and 1983.

Moses[3], E
Grandma (1860–1961; born *Anna Mary Robertson Moses*), American painter. She took up painting late in life, producing more than a thousand works in naive style.

mosey • v. (**moseys**, **moseying**, **moseyed**) informal walk or move in a leisurely manner.
– ORIGIN unknown.

Moslem • n. & adj. var. of **MUSLIM**.

Mosley E
/**mohz**-li/, Sir Oswald (Ernald), 6th Baronet (1896–1980), English Fascist leader and founder in 1932 of the British Union of Fascists (known as the Blackshirts).

mosque • n. a Muslim place of worship.
– ORIGIN French.

mosquito • n. (pl. **mosquitoes**) a small fly, some kinds of which transmit diseases through the bite of the female.
– ORIGIN Spanish and Portuguese, 'little fly'.

mosquito net • n. a fine net hung across a door or window or around a bed to keep mosquitoes away.

Moss, Sir Stirling (b.1929), English motor-racing driver. E

moss • n. a small green plant which grows in low carpets or rounded cushions in damp habitats.
– DERIVATIVES **mossy** adj.
– ORIGIN Old English.

Mossad /moss-**ad**/ the Supreme Institution for Intelligence and Special Assignments, the chief secret intelligence service of the state of Israel. E

most • det. & pron. **1** greatest in amount or degree. **2** the majority of. • adv. **1** to the greatest extent. **2** forming the superlative of adjectives and adverbs. **3** very.
– PHRASES **make the most of** use to the best advantage.
– ORIGIN Old English.

-most • suffix forming superlative adjectives and adverbs: *innermost*.
– ORIGIN Old English.

Mostar /moss-**tar**/ the chief town of Herzegovina. E

mostly • adv. **1** on the whole; mainly. **2** usually.

Most Reverend • n. the title of an Anglican archbishop or an Irish Roman Catholic bishop.

MOT • n. (in the UK) a compulsory annual test of motor vehicles of more than a specified age.
– ORIGIN from *Ministry of Transport*.

mote • n. a speck.
– ORIGIN Old English.

motel • n. a roadside hotel for motorists.
– ORIGIN from **MOTOR** and **HOTEL**.

motet /moh-tet/ • n. a short piece of sacred choral music.
– ORIGIN Old French, 'little word'.

moth • n. an insect like a butterfly which is mainly active at night.
– ORIGIN Old English.

mothball • n. a small ball made from a strong-smelling chemical, placed among stored clothes to deter clothes moths. • v. put (a plan or piece of equipment) into storage or on hold.

moth-eaten • adj. shabby or very worn.

mother • n. **1** a female parent. **2** (**Mother**) (especially as a title or form of address) the head of a convent. **3** informal an extreme or very large example of: *the mother of all traffic jams.* • v. (**mothers**, **mothering**, **mothered**) look after kindly and protectively.
– DERIVATIVES **motherhood** n.
– ORIGIN Old English.

motherboard • n. a printed circuit board containing the main components of a microcomputer.

mother country • n. a country in relation to its colonies.

Mothering Sunday • n. Brit. the fourth Sunday in Lent, traditionally a day for giving gifts to one's mother.

mother-in-law • n. (pl. **mothers-in-law**) the mother of one's husband or wife.

motherland • n. one's native country.

motherly • adj. like a mother; kind and protective.

mother-of-pearl • n. a smooth pearly substance lining the shells of oysters and some other molluscs.

Mother Superior • n. the head of a convent.

Mother Teresa see **TERESA, MOTHER**. E

mother tongue • n. a person's native language.

motif /moh-teef/ • n. **1** a single or repeated image forming a design. **2** a theme which frequently recurs in an artistic, musical, or literary work.
– ORIGIN French.

Motion, Andrew (b.1952), English poet and critic, Poet Laureate since 1999. E

motion • n. **1** the action of moving. **2** a movement or gesture. **3** a formal proposal put to a meeting. **4** Brit. an emptying of the bowels. • v. direct (someone) with a gesture.
– DERIVATIVES **motionless** adj.
– ORIGIN Latin *movere* 'to move'.

motion picture • n. esp. N. Amer. a cinema film.

motivate • v. (**motivates**, **motivating**, **motivated**) **1** provide with a motive for doing something. **2** stimulate the interest of.
– DERIVATIVES **motivator** n.

motivation • n. **1** the reason or reasons behind one's actions or behaviour. **2** enthusiasm.
– DERIVATIVES **motivational** adj.

motive • n. a factor influencing a person to act in a particular way. • adj. producing motion.
– ORIGIN Latin *motivus*.

motive power • n. the energy used to drive machinery.

mot juste /moh *zh*oost/ • n. (pl. **mots justes** /moh *zh*oost/) (**the mot juste**) the most appropriate word or expression.
– ORIGIN French.

motley • adj. made up of a variety of very different people or things.
– ORIGIN unknown.

motocross • n. cross-country racing on motorcycles.

motor • n. **1** a machine that supplies motive power for a vehicle or other device. **2** Brit. informal a car. • adj. **1** giving or producing motion. **2** relating to muscular movement or the nerves activating it. • v. Brit. informal travel in a car.
– ORIGIN Latin, 'mover'.

motorbike • n. a motorcycle.

motorboat • n. a boat powered by a motor.

motorcade • n. a procession of motor vehicles.

motor car • n. Brit. a car.

motorcycle • n. a two-wheeled vehicle that is powered by a motor.
– DERIVATIVES **motorcycling** n. **motorcyclist** n.

motorist • n. the driver of a car.

motor racing • n. the sport of racing in specially developed fast cars.

motor vehicle • n. a road vehicle powered by an internal-combustion engine.

motorway • n. Brit. a road designed for fast

traffic, with three lanes in each direction.

motte /mot/ ● **n.** hist. a mound forming the site of a castle or camp.
– ORIGIN French, 'mound'.

mottle ● **n.** a mottled marking.

mottled ● **adj.** marked with patches of a different colour.
– ORIGIN prob. from **MOTLEY**.

motto ● **n.** (pl. **mottoes** or **mottos**) a short sentence or phrase expressing the aims or beliefs of a person or group.
– ORIGIN Italian, 'word'.

moue /moo/ ● **n.** a pout.
– ORIGIN French.

mould[1] (US **mold**) ● **n. 1** a hollow container used to give shape to hot liquid material when it cools and hardens. **2** a jelly or mousse. **3** a distinctive type, style, or character: *he's a leader in the mould of Winston Churchill.* ● **v. 1** form (an object) out of a soft substance. **2** give a shape to (a soft substance). **3** influence the development of.
– ORIGIN prob. from Old French *modle*.

mould[2] (US **mold**) ● **n.** a furry growth of tiny fungi occurring in moist warm conditions.
– ORIGIN prob. from former *moul* 'grow mouldy'.

mould[3] (US **mold**) ● **n.** esp. Brit. soft loose earth.
– ORIGIN Old English.

moulder (US **molder**) ● **v.** (**moulders, mouldering, mouldered**; US **molders, moldering, moldered**) slowly decay.
– ORIGIN perh. from **MOULD**[3].

moulding (US **molding**) ● **n.** a moulded strip of wood, stone, or plaster as a decorative architectural feature.

mouldy (US **moldy**) ● **adj. 1** covered with or smelling of mould. **2** informal boring or worthless.

moult (US **molt**) ● **v.** shed old feathers, hair, or skin, to make way for a new growth. ● **n.** a period of moulting.
– ORIGIN Latin *mutare* 'to change'.

mound ● **n. 1** a raised mass of earth or other material. **2** a small hill. **3** a heap or pile. ● **v.** heap up into a mound.
– ORIGIN unknown.

mount[1] ● **v. 1** climb up or on to. **2** get up on (an animal or bicycle) to ride it. **3** (**be mounted**) be on horseback. **4** increase. **5** organize: *the company had successfully mounted takeover bids.* **6** put or fix in place or on a support. ● **n. 1** (also **mounting**) something on which an object is mounted for support or display. **2** a horse used for riding.
– ORIGIN Old French *munter*.

mount[2] ● **n.** archaic or in place names a mountain or hill.
– ORIGIN Old English.

mountain ● **n. 1** a very high, steep hill. **2** a large pile or quantity.
– ORIGIN Old French *montaigne*.

mountain ash ● **n.** a rowan tree.

mountain bike ● **n.** a sturdy bicycle with broad deep-treaded tyres.

mountaineering ● **n.** the sport or activity of climbing mountains.
– DERIVATIVES **mountaineer** n.

mountain lion ● **n.** N. Amer. a puma.

mountainous ● **adj. 1** having many mountains. **2** huge: *mountainous debts.*

Mount Ararat, Mount Cook, etc. E
see **ARARAT, MOUNT**; **COOK, MOUNT**, etc.

Mountbatten E
/mownt-**bat**-t'n/, Louis (Francis Albert Victor Nicholas), 1st Earl Mountbatten of Burma (1900–79), British admiral and administrator. He was supreme Allied commander in SE Asia (1943–5) and the last viceroy (1947) and first Governor General of India (1947–8). He was killed by an IRA bomb.

mountebank /mown-ti-bangk/ ● **n.** a swindler.
– ORIGIN from Italian *monta in banco!* 'climb on the bench!', referring to the raised platform used by people who sold patent medicines in public.

Mountie ● **n.** informal a member of the Royal Canadian Mounted Police.

mourn ● **v.** feel deep sorrow following the death or loss of.
– ORIGIN Old English.

Mourne Mountains E
/morn/ a range of hills in SE Northern Ireland, in County Down.

mourner ● **n.** a person who attends a funeral as a relative or friend of the dead person.

mournful ● **adj.** feeling, showing, or causing sadness or grief.
– DERIVATIVES **mournfully** adv.

mourning ● **n. 1** the expression of deep sorrow for someone who has died. **2** black clothes worn in a period of mourning.

mouse ● **n.** (pl. **mice**) **1** a small rodent with a pointed snout and a long thin tail. **2** a timid and quiet person. **3** (pl. also **mouses**) Computing a small hand-held device which controls cursor movements on a computer screen.
– ORIGIN Old English.

moussaka /moo-**sah**-kuh/ ● **n.** a Greek dish of minced lamb layered with aubergines and tomatoes and topped with a cheese sauce.
– ORIGIN Turkish, 'that which is fed liquid'.

mousse ● **n. 1** a light sweet or savoury dish made with cream or egg white and flavoured with fruit, fish, etc. **2** a light substance used to style the hair.
– ORIGIN French, 'moss or froth'.

Moussorgsky E
var. of **MUSSORGSKY**.

moustache (US also **mustache**) ● **n.** a strip of hair left to grow above a man's upper lip.
– DERIVATIVES **moustached** (US also **mustached**) adj.
– ORIGIN French.

mousy (also **mousey**) ● **adj. 1** (of hair) of a light brown colour. **2** timid.

mouth ● **n. 1** the opening in the body through which food is taken and sounds are made. **2** an opening or entrance. **3** the place where a river enters the sea. ● **v. 1** move the lips as if to form (words). **2** say in an insincere way.
– ORIGIN Old English.

mouthful ● **n. 1** a quantity of food or drink that fills or can be put in the mouth. **2** a long or complicated word or phrase.

mouth organ ● **n.** a harmonica.

mouthpart ● **n.** any of the projections surrounding the mouth of an insect and adapted for feeding.

mouthpiece • n. a part of a musical instrument, telephone, etc. that is designed to be put in or against the mouth.

mouth-to-mouth • adj. (of artificial respiration) in which a person breathes into someone's lungs through their mouth.

mouthwash • n. an antiseptic liquid for rinsing the mouth or gargling.

mouth-watering • adj. **1** smelling or looking delicious. **2** very attractive or tempting.

mouthy • adj. (**mouthier**, **mouthiest**) informal inclined to talk a lot.

movable (also **moveable**) • adj. **1** able to be moved. **2** (of a religious festival) occurring on a different date each year.

move • v. (**moves**, **moving**, **moved**) **1** go or cause to go in a specified direction or manner. **2** change position. **3** change the place where one lives. **4** change from one state or activity to another. **5** take or cause to take action. **6** make progress. **7** provoke sympathy, affection, or other feelings in. • n. **1** an instance of moving. **2** an action taken towards achieving a purpose. **3** a player's turn during a board game.
– PHRASES **make a move 1** take action. **2** Brit. set off. **move in** be socially active among (a particular group).
– ORIGIN Latin *movere*.

movement • n. **1** an act of moving. **2** the process of moving. **3** a group of people with a shared cause. **4** a trend or development. **5** (**movements**) a person's activities during a particular period of time. **6** Music a main division of a musical work.

movie • n. N. Amer. a cinema film.

moving • adj. **1** in motion. **2** arousing sadness or sympathy.

mow • v. (**mows**, **mowing**, **mowed**; past part. **mowed** or **mown**) **1** cut down or trim (grass or a cereal crop). **2** (**mow down**) kill by gunfire or by knocking down with a motor vehicle.
– DERIVATIVES **mower** n.
– ORIGIN Old English.

Mozambique E
/moh-zam-**beek**/ a country on the east coast of southern Africa; capital, Maputo.
– DERIVATIVES **Mozambican** adj. & n.

Mozart, E
(Johann Chrysostom) Wolfgang Amadeus (1756–91), Austrian composer. He was a child prodigy as a pianist and composer, and went on to write forty-one symphonies, twenty-seven piano concertos, twenty-six string quartets, and sixteen operas, including *Don Giovanni* and *The Magic Flute*.
– DERIVATIVES **Mozartian** adj. & n.

mozzarella /mot-suh-**rel**-luh/ • n. a firm white Italian cheese made from buffalo's or cow's milk.
– ORIGIN Italian.

MP • abbrev. Member of Parliament.

mpg • abbrev. miles per gallon.

mph • abbrev. miles per hour.

MPhil • abbrev. Master of Philosophy.

Mpumalanga E
/uhm-poo-muh-**lang**-uh/ a province of NE South Africa; capital, Nelspruit.

Mr • n. a title used before a man's surname or full name.
– ORIGIN from **MASTER**.

Mrs • n. a title used before a married woman's surname or full name.
– ORIGIN from **MISTRESS**.

MS • abbrev. **1** manuscript. **2** multiple sclerosis.

Ms • n. a title used before the surname or full name of a married or unmarried woman.

MSc • abbrev. Master of Science.

MS-DOS • abbrev. Computing, trademark Microsoft disk operating system.

MSP • abbrev. Member of the Scottish Parliament.

Mt • abbrev. (in place names) Mount.

Mubarak E
/moo-**ba**-rak/, (Muhammad) Hosni (Said) (b.1928), Egyptian statesman, President since 1981. He did much to establish closer links between Egypt and other Arab nations.

much • det. & pron. (**more**, **most**) **1** a large amount. **2** a poor example of something: *I'm not much of a gardener*. • adv. **1** to a great extent. **2** often.
– PHRASES **(as) much as** even though.
– ORIGIN Old English.

Mucha E
/moo-kuh/, Alphonse (1860–1939; born *Alfons Maria*), Czech painter and designer, a leading figure in the art nouveau movement.

muchness • n. (in phr. (**much**) **of a muchness**) very similar.

mucilage /myoo-si-lij/ • n. **1** a thick bodily fluid. **2** a thick or sticky solution extracted from plants, used in medicines and adhesives.
– DERIVATIVES **mucilaginous** /myoo-si-**laj**-i-nuhss/ adj.
– ORIGIN Latin *mucilago* 'musty juice'.

muck • n. **1** dirt or rubbish. **2** manure. • v. **1** (**muck up**) informal spoil. **2** (**muck about/around**) Brit. informal behave in a silly way. **3** (**muck about/around with**) Brit. informal interfere with. **4** (**muck in**) Brit. informal share tasks or accommodation. **5** (**muck out**) esp. Brit. remove manure and other dirt from (a stable).
– ORIGIN prob. Scandinavian.

muckraking • n. the action of searching out and publicizing scandal about famous people.
– ORIGIN coined by President Theodore Roosevelt in a speech referring to the man with the *muck rake* in Bunyan's *Pilgrim's Progress*.

mucky • adj. (**muckier**, **muckiest**) **1** dirty. **2** sordid or indecent.

mucous /myoo-kuhss/ • adj. relating to or covered with mucus.

mucous membrane • n. a tissue that produces mucus, lining many body cavities and organs.

mucus /myoo-kuhss/ • n. a slimy substance produced by the mucous membranes and glands of animals for lubrication, protection, etc.
– ORIGIN Latin.

mud • n. **1** soft, sticky matter consisting of mixed earth and water. **2** damaging informa-

tion or allegations.
– ORIGIN prob. from German *mudde*.

muddle ● v. (**muddles, muddling, muddled**) **1** bring into a disordered or confusing state. **2** confuse or puzzle (someone). **3** (**muddle up**) confuse (two or more things) with each other. **4** (**muddle along/through**) cope more or less satisfactorily. ● n. a muddled state.
– DERIVATIVES **muddled** adj.
– ORIGIN perh. from Dutch *modden* 'dabble in mud'.

muddy ● adj. (**muddier, muddiest**) **1** covered in or full of mud. **2** not bright or clear. ● v. (**muddies, muddying, muddied**) make muddy.

mudflap ● n. a flap hung behind the wheel of a vehicle to protect against mud and stones thrown up from the road.

mudflat ● n. a stretch of muddy land left uncovered at low tide.

mudguard ● n. a curved strip fitted over a wheel of a bicycle or motorcycle to protect against water and dirt thrown up from the road.

mud pack ● n. a paste applied to the face to improve the skin.

mud-slinging ● n. informal the casting of insults and accusations.

muesli /myooz-li/ ● n. (pl. **mueslis**) a mixture of oats, dried fruit, and nuts, eaten with milk at breakfast.
– ORIGIN Swiss German.

muezzin /moo-ez-zin/ ● n. a man who calls Muslims to prayer.
– ORIGIN Arabic, 'proclaim'.

m

muff[1] ● n. a short tube made of fur or other warm material into which the hands are placed for warmth.
– ORIGIN Dutch *mof*.

muff[2] ● v. informal handle clumsily; bungle.
– ORIGIN unknown.

muffin ● n. **1** (N. Amer. **English muffin**) a flattened bread roll eaten toasted with butter. **2** esp. N. Amer. a small cake with a rounded top.
– ORIGIN unknown.

muffle ● v. (**muffles, muffling, muffled**) **1** wrap or cover for warmth. **2** make (a sound) quieter or less distinct by covering its source.
– ORIGIN Old French *moufle* 'thick glove'.

muffler ● n. a scarf worn around the neck and face.

mufti[1] /muf-ti/ ● n. (pl. **muftis**) a Muslim legal expert who gives rulings on religious matters.
– ORIGIN Arabic, 'decide a point of law'.

mufti[2] /muf-ti/ ● n. civilian clothes when worn by military or police staff.
– ORIGIN perh. from MUFTI[1].

mug[1] ● n. **1** a large cylindrical cup with a handle. **2** informal a person's face. **3** Brit. informal a stupid or gullible person. ● v. (**mugs, mugging, mugged**) **1** attack and rob (someone) in a public place. **2** informal make faces before an audience or a camera.
– ORIGIN prob. Scandinavian.

mug[2] ● v. (**mugs, mugging, mugged**) (**mug up**) Brit. informal learn or study (a subject) quickly and intensively.
– ORIGIN unknown.

Mugabe E
/muu-gah-bi/, Robert (Gabriel) (b.1924), Zimbabwean statesman, first Prime Minister of independent Zimbabwe 1980–7 and President since 1987.

mugger ● n. a person who attacks and robs another in a public place.

muggins ● n. Brit. informal a foolish person.
– ORIGIN perh. a use of the surname *Muggins*, with reference to MUG[1].

muggy ● adj. (**muggier, muggiest**) (of the weather) unpleasantly warm and humid.
– ORIGIN from dialect *mug* 'mist, drizzle'.

Mughal ● n. var. of MOGUL.

mugshot ● n. informal a photograph of a person's face made for an official purpose.

Muhammad E
/muh-ham-mid/ (also **Mohammed**) (*c.*570–632), Arab prophet and founder of Islam. In Mecca he received a series of revelations which, as the Koran, became the basis of Islam. Opposition to his preaching forced him to flee to Medina in 622. Muhammad then led his followers into a series of battles and by the time of his death he had united most of Arabia under Islam.

Muhammad Ali[1] E
/ah-li, ah-lee/ (1769–1849), Ottoman viceroy and pasha of Egypt 1805–49. He modernized Egypt's infrastructure, making it the leading power in the eastern Mediterranean.

Muhammad Ali[2] E
/ah-li, ah-lee/ (b.1942; born *Cassius Marcellus Clay*), American boxer. He won the world heavyweight title in 1964, 1974, and 1978, the only boxer to be world champion three times.

mujahedin /muu-jah-hi-deen/ (also **mujaheddin, mujahideen**) ● pl. n. Islamic guerrilla fighters.
– ORIGIN Persian and Arabic, 'people who fight a holy war'.

Mujibur Rahman E
/muu-jee-boor ruh-mahn/ (1920–75), Bangladeshi statesman, first Prime Minister of independent Bangladesh 1972–5 and President 1975. He and his family were assassinated in a military coup.

mulatto /muu-lat-toh/ ● n. (pl. **mulattoes** or **mulattos**) a person with one white and one black parent.
– ORIGIN Spanish *mulato*.

mulberry ● n. **1** a dark red or white fruit resembling the loganberry. **2** a dark red or purple colour.
– ORIGIN Latin *morum* 'mulberry'.

mulch /mulch/ ● n. a mass of leaves, bark, or compost spread around a plant for protection or to enrich the soil. ● v. cover with mulch.
– ORIGIN prob. from dialect *mulch* 'soft'.

Muldoon, E
Sir Robert (David) (1921–92), New Zealand statesman, Prime Minister 1975–84.

mule[1] ● n. the offspring of a male donkey and a female horse.
– ORIGIN Latin *mulus, mula*.

mule[2] ● n. a slipper or light shoe without a back.

– ORIGIN French, 'slipper'.

muleteer /myoo-li-teer/ • n. a person who drives mules.

mulish • adj. stubborn.

Mull
an island of the Inner Hebrides; chief town, Tobermory.

mull[1] • v. (**mull over**) think about at length.
– ORIGIN uncertain.

mull[2] • v. warm (wine or beer) and add sugar and spices to it.
– ORIGIN unknown.

mullah /muul-luh/ • n. a Muslim learned in Islamic theology and sacred law.
– ORIGIN Arabic.

mullet • n. a sea fish that is caught for food.
– ORIGIN Greek *mullos*.

mulligatawny /mul-li-guh-taw-ni/ • n. a spicy meat soup originally made in India.
– ORIGIN Tamil, 'pepper water'.

mullion • n. a vertical bar between the panes of glass in a window.
– DERIVATIVES **mullioned** adj.
– ORIGIN prob. from Old French *moinel* 'middle'.

Mulroney
/muul-roo-ni/, (Martin) Brian (b.1939), Canadian Progressive Conservative statesman, Prime Minister 1984–93.

multi- • comb. form more than one; many: *multicultural*.
– ORIGIN Latin *multus*.

multicoloured (also **multicolour**; US **multicolored**, **multicolor**) • adj. having many colours.

multicultural • adj. relating to or made up of several cultural or ethnic groups.
– DERIVATIVES **multiculturalism** n.

multifaceted • adj. having many sides or aspects.

multifarious /mul-ti-fair-i-uhss/ • adj. having great variety.
– ORIGIN Latin *multifarius*.

multilateral • adj. involving three or more participants.

multilingual • adj. in or using several languages.

multimedia • adj. using more than one means of providing information. • n. Computing a system providing video and audio material as well as text.

multimillion • adj. consisting of several million.

multimillionaire • n. a person with assets worth several million pounds or dollars.

multinational • adj. involving several countries or nationalities. • n. a company operating in several countries.

multiparty • adj. involving several political parties.

multiple • adj. **1** having or involving several different people or things. **2** (of a disease or injury) affecting several parts of the body. • n. a number that may be divided by another a certain number of times without a remainder.
– ORIGIN Latin *multiplus*.

multiple-choice • adj. (of a question in an examination) giving several possible answers, from which the candidate must choose the correct one.

multiple sclerosis • n. see **SCLEROSIS**.

multiplex • adj. made up of many elements in a complex relationship. • n. a cinema with several separate screens.
– ORIGIN Latin.

multiplicand /mul-ti-pli-**kand**, **mul**-ti-pli-kand/ • n. a quantity which is to be multiplied by another (the multiplier).

multiplication • n. the process of multiplying.

multiplication sign • n. the sign ×, used to indicate that one quantity is to be multiplied by another.

multiplication table • n. a list of multiples of a particular number.

multiplicity • n. (pl. **multiplicities**) a large number or variety.

multiplier • n. **1** a quantity by which a given number (the multiplicand) is to be multiplied. **2** a device for increasing the intensity of an electric current, force, etc.

multiply[1] /mul-ti-ply/ • v. (**multiplies**, **multiplying**, **multiplied**) **1** Math. add (a number) to itself a specified number of times. **2** increase in number or quantity. **3** reproduce in large numbers.
– ORIGIN Latin *multiplicare*.

multiply[2] /mul-ti-pli/ • adv. in different ways or respects.

multi-purpose • adj. having several purposes.

multiracial • adj. having to do with people of many races.

multi-storey • adj. (of a building) having several storeys.

multitasking • n. Computing the carrying out of more than one program or task at the same time.

multitude • n. **1** a large number of people or things. **2** (**the multitude**) the mass of ordinary people.
– ORIGIN Latin *multitudo*.

multitudinous /mul-ti-tyoo-di-nuhss/ • adj. very numerous.

mum[1] • n. Brit. informal one's mother.

mum[2] • adj. (in phr. **keep mum**) informal remain silent so as not to reveal a secret.
– PHRASES **mum's the word** do not reveal a secret.

Mumbai
/muum-by/ official name for **BOMBAY**.

mumble • v. (**mumbles**, **mumbling**, **mumbled**) say something indistinctly and quietly. • n. a quiet and indistinct way of speaking.
– ORIGIN from **MUM**[2].

mumbo-jumbo • n. informal language that is complicated but has no real meaning.
– ORIGIN from *Mumbo Jumbo*, the supposed name of an African idol.

mummer • n. an actor in a traditional English folk play.
– ORIGIN Old French *momeur*.

mummify • v. (**mummifies**, **mummifying**, **mummified**) (especially in ancient Egypt) preserve (a body) as a mummy.
– DERIVATIVES **mummification** n.

mummy[1] • n. (pl. **mummies**) Brit. informal one's mother.
– ORIGIN uncertain.

mummy[2] • n. (pl. **mummies**) (especially in

ancient Egypt) a body that has been preserved for burial by embalming and wrapping in bandages.
– ORIGIN Arabic, 'embalmed body'.

mumps • pl. n. an infectious disease causing swelling of the glands at the sides of the face.
– ORIGIN from former *mump* 'grimace'.

Munch E
/muungk/, Edvard (1863–1944), Norwegian painter and engraver, famous for his use of vivid colour and distortion to express intense emotion, as in *The Scream*.

munch • v. eat steadily and in a way that can be heard by others.

munchies • pl. n. informal **1** snacks or small items of food. **2** (**the munchies**) a sudden strong desire for food.

mundane /mun-**dayn**/ • adj. **1** lacking interest or excitement. **2** relating to this earthly world rather than a heavenly or spiritual one.
– ORIGIN Latin *mundus* 'world'.

mung bean • n. a small round green bean grown in the tropics as a source of bean sprouts.
– ORIGIN Hindi.

Munich E
/myoo-nik/ a city in SE Germany, capital of Bavaria.

municipal • adj. relating to a municipality.
– ORIGIN Latin *municipalis*.

m

municipality /myoo-ni-si-**pal**-i-ti/ • n. (pl. **municipalities**) a town or district that has local government.

munificent /myoo-**nif**-i-suhnt/ • adj. very generous.
– DERIVATIVES **munificence** n.
– ORIGIN Latin *munificus*.

munitions • pl. n. military weapons, ammunition, equipment, and stores.
– ORIGIN Latin, 'fortification'.

Munster E
/**muun**-ster/ a province in the south-west of the Republic of Ireland.

mural • n. a painting done directly on a wall.
– ORIGIN Latin *murus* 'wall'.

murder • n. **1** the illegal deliberate killing of one person by another. **2** informal a very difficult or unpleasant situation. • v. (**murders, murdering, murdered**) **1** kill illegally and deliberately. **2** informal spoil by poor performance.
– DERIVATIVES **murderer** n. **murderess** n.
– ORIGIN Old English.

murderous • adj. **1** capable of or involving murder or extreme violence. **2** informal extremely difficult or unpleasant.

Murdoch[1] E
/**mer**-dok/, Dame (Jean) Iris (1919–99), British novelist and philosopher, born in Ireland. Her novels, which often explore spiritual life and complex sexual relationships, include *The Sea, The Sea*.

Murdoch[2] E
/**mer**-dok/, (Keith) Rupert (b.1931), Australian-born American publisher and media entrepreneur. The founder and head of News International Communications, he owns major newspaper, film, television, and publishing concerns in Australia, Britain, and the US.

murk • n. darkness or fog causing poor visibility.
– ORIGIN Old English.

murky • adj. (**murkier, murkiest**) **1** dark and gloomy. **2** (of water) dirty or cloudy. **3** suspicious because secret.

Murmansk E
/moor-**mansk**/ a port in NW Russia, on the Barents Sea. It is the largest city north of the Arctic Circle.

murmur • n. **1** something that is said quietly. **2** a low continuous background noise. **3** a quiet complaint. **4** Med. a recurring sound heard in the heart through a stethoscope and usually indicating disease or damage. • v. **1** say something in a murmur. **2** make a low continuous sound. **3** complain quietly.
– ORIGIN Latin.

Murnau E
/**moor**-now/, F. W. (1888–1931; born *Frederick Wilhelm Plumpe*), German film director. His films include *Nosferatu, Der letzte Mann*, and *Sunrise*.

Murphy's Law • n. a supposed law of nature, to the effect that anything that can go wrong will go wrong.

Murray E
Sir James (Augustus Henry) (1837–1915), Scottish lexicographer and chief editor of the first edition of the *Oxford English Dictionary*.

Murray River E
the chief river of Australia, which rises in the Great Dividing Range in New South Wales and flows 2,590 km (1,610 miles) before reaching the Indian Ocean south-east of Adelaide.

Murrumbidgee E
/mu-ruhm-**bi**-jee/ a river of SE Australia, which rises in the Great Dividing Range in New South Wales and flows westwards to join the Murray, of which it is a major tributary.

Muscat E
/**muus**-kat/ the capital of Oman.

Muscat and Oman E
former name for **OMAN**.

muscle • n. **1** a band of tissue in the body that can contract so as to move or hold the position of a part of the body. **2** power or strength. • v. (**muscles, muscling, muscled**) (**muscle in**) informal interfere forcibly in (another's affairs).
– DERIVATIVES **muscly** adj.
– ORIGIN Latin *musculus*.

muscle-bound • adj. having over-developed muscles.

Muscovite • n. a person from Moscow.

muscular • adj. **1** having to do with the muscles. **2** having well-developed muscles.
– DERIVATIVES **muscularity** n.

muscular dystrophy • n. an inherited condition in which the muscles gradually get weaker and waste away.

musculature ● n. the muscular system or arrangement of a body or an organ.

muse[1] ● n. **1** (**Muse**) (in Greek and Roman mythology) each of nine goddesses (Calliope, Clio, Euterpe, Terpsichore, Erato, Melpomene, Thalia, Polyhymnia, and Urania). who encouraged the arts and sciences. **2** a woman who is the inspiration for a creative artist.
– ORIGIN Greek *mousa*.

muse[2] ● v. (**muses, musing, mused**) **1** be absorbed in thought. **2** say to oneself in a thoughtful manner.
– ORIGIN Old French *muser*.

museum ● n. a building in which objects of interest or importance are stored and displayed.
– ORIGIN Greek *mouseion* 'seat of the Muses'.

museum piece ● n. Brit. an old-fashioned or useless person or object.

Museveni E
/muu-suh-vay-ni/, Yoweri (Kaguta) (b.1944), Ugandan statesman, President since 1986.

mush ● n. **1** a soft, wet mass. **2** excessive sentimentality.
– ORIGIN prob. from **MASH**.

mushroom ● n. a spore-producing body of a fungus, having a rounded head on a stalk and often edible. ● v. increase or develop rapidly.
– ORIGIN Old French *mousseron*.

mushroom cloud ● n. a mushroom-shaped cloud of dust and debris formed after a nuclear explosion.

mushy ● adj. (**mushier, mushiest**) **1** in the form of mush. **2** excessively sentimental.

music ● n. **1** the art of combining vocal or instrumental sounds in a pleasing way. **2** the sound so produced. **3** the signs in which music is written or printed.
– PHRASES **music to one's ears** something very pleasant to hear or learn.
– ORIGIN Old French *musique*.

musical ● adj. **1** relating to or accompanied by music. **2** fond of or skilled in music. **3** pleasant-sounding. ● n. a play or film in which singing and dancing play an essential part.
– DERIVATIVES **musicality** n. **musically** adv.

musical box ● n. Brit. a small box which plays a tune when the lid is opened.

musical chairs ● pl. n. **1** a party game in which players compete for a decreasing number of chairs when the accompanying music is stopped. **2** a situation in which people frequently exchange positions.

music centre ● n. Brit. a combined radio, cassette player, and record or compact disc player.

music hall ● n. **1** a form of variety entertainment popular in Britain in the 19th and early 20th centuries. **2** a theatre where such entertainment took place.

musician ● n. a person who plays a musical instrument or writes music.
– DERIVATIVES **musicianship** n.

musicology ● n. the study of music as an academic subject.
– DERIVATIVES **musicological** adj. **musicologist** n.

musk ● n. a strong-smelling substance produced by a type of male deer, used in making perfume.
– DERIVATIVES **musky** adj.
– ORIGIN Persian.

musket ● n. hist. a light gun with a long barrel.
– ORIGIN French *mousquet*.

musketeer ● n. hist. **1** a soldier armed with a musket. **2** a member of the household troops of the French king in the 17th and 18th centuries.

muskrat ● n. a large North American rodent with a musky smell, valued for its fur.

Muslim (also **Moslem**) ● n. a follower of Islam. ● adj. relating to Muslims or Islam.
– ORIGIN Arabic.

muslin ● n. lightweight cotton cloth in a plain weave.
– ORIGIN Italian *mussolina*.

musquash /muss-kwosh/ ● n. Brit. the fur of the muskrat.
– ORIGIN from an American Indian language.

mussel ● n. **1** a marine mollusc with a dark brown or purplish-black shell. **2** a freshwater mollusc, some kinds of which produce small pearls.
– ORIGIN Latin *musculus* 'muscle'.

Mussolini E
/muus-suh-lee-ni/, Benito (Amilcaro Andrea) (1883–1945; known as **Il Duce**, 'the leader'), Italian Fascist statesman, Prime Minister 1922–43. He entered the Second World War on Germany's side in 1940; forced to resign after the Allied invasion of Sicily, he was executed by Italian partisans.

Mussorgsky E
/muh-sorg-ski/ (also **Moussorgsky**), Modest (Petrovich) (1839–81), Russian composer, best known for the opera *Boris Godunov* and the piano suite *Pictures at an Exhibition*.

must[1] ● modal verb (past **had to** or in reported speech **must**) **1** be obliged to; should. **2** used to insist something. **3** expressing an opinion about something that is very likely: *you must be tired.* ● n. informal something that should not be missed.
– ORIGIN Old English.

must[2] ● n. grape juice before or during fermentation.
ORIGIN Latin *mustus* 'new'.

mustache ● n. US = **MOUSTACHE**.

mustachios /muh-stah-shi-ohz/ ● pl. n. a long or elaborate moustache.
– ORIGIN Italian *mostaccio*.

mustang ● n. a small wild horse of the southwestern US.
– ORIGIN from Spanish *mestengo* and *mostrenco*, both meaning 'wild cattle'.

mustard ● n. **1** a hot-tasting yellow or brown paste made from the crushed seeds of a plant, eaten with meat or used in cooking. **2** a brownish yellow colour.
– ORIGIN Old French *moustarde*.

mustard gas ● n. a liquid whose vapour causes severe irritation and blistering, used in chemical weapons.

muster ● v. (**musters, mustering, mustered**) **1** bring (troops) together. **2** (of people) gather together. **3** summon up (a feeling or attitude). ● n. an instance of mustering troops.
– PHRASES **pass muster** be accepted as adequate or satisfactory.

– ORIGIN Old French *moustrer*.

Mustique E
/mu-**steek**/ a small Caribbean island in the northern Grenadines.

mustn't • contr. must not.

musty • adj. having a stale or mouldy smell or taste.
– DERIVATIVES **mustiness** n.
– ORIGIN perh. from *moisty* 'moist'.

mutable /myoo-tuh-b'l/ • adj. liable to change.
– DERIVATIVES **mutability** n.
– ORIGIN Latin *mutabilis*.

mutant • adj. resulting from or showing the effect of mutation. • n. a mutant form.

mutate • v. (**mutates, mutating, mutated**) undergo mutation.

mutation • n. **1** the process or an instance of changing. **2** a change in genetic structure which results in a variant form and may be passed on to subsequent generations. **3** a form resulting from such a change.
– ORIGIN Latin.

mute • adj. **1** not speaking or temporarily speechless. **2** dated lacking the power of speech. **3** (of a letter) not pronounced. • n. **1** dated a person who is unable to speak. **2** a device used to dampen the sound of a musical instrument. • v. (**mutes, muting, muted**) **1** deaden or muffle the sound of. **2** reduce the strength of. **3** (**muted**) (of colour or lighting) not bright; subdued.
– ORIGIN Latin *mutus*.

mute swan • n. the commonest Eurasian swan, having an orange-red bill with a black knob at the base.

mutilate • v. (**mutilates, mutilating, mutilated**) **1** cause a severe injury to (someone). **2** cause serious damage to (something).
– DERIVATIVES **mutilation** n.
– ORIGIN Latin *mutilare* 'maim'.

mutineer • n. a person who mutinies.

mutinous • adj. rebellious.

mutiny • n. (pl. **mutinies**) an open rebellion against authority, especially by soldiers or sailors against their officers. • v. (**mutinies, mutinying, mutinied**) engage in mutiny; rebel.
– ORIGIN French *mutin* 'mutineer'.

mutt • n. informal, derog. a dog, especially a mongrel.
– ORIGIN from *muttonhead*, a dated term for a stupid person.

mutter • v. (**mutters, muttering, muttered**) **1** say in a voice which can barely be heard. **2** talk or grumble in secret or in private. • n. something said which can barely be heard.

mutton • n. the flesh of mature sheep used as food.
– ORIGIN Old French *moton*.

mutual • adj. **1** experienced or done by two or more people equally: *a partnership based on mutual respect.* **2** (of two or more people) having the same specified relationship to each other. **3** shared by two or more people: *a mutual friend.* **4** (of a building society or insurance company) owned by its members and dividing its profits between them.
– DERIVATIVES **mutuality** n. **mutually** adv.
– ORIGIN Old French *mutuel*.

muzak • n. trademark recorded light background music played in public places.
– ORIGIN from MUSIC.

muzzle • n. **1** the nose and mouth of an animal. **2** a guard fitted over an animal's muzzle to stop it biting or feeding. **3** the open end of the barrel of a firearm. • v. (**muzzles, muzzling, muzzled**) **1** put a muzzle on (an animal). **2** prevent (someone) expressing their opinions freely.
– ORIGIN Latin *musum*.

muzzy • adj. (**muzzier, muzziest**) **1** dazed or confused. **2** blurred or indistinct.
– ORIGIN unknown.

MW • abbrev. **1** medium wave. **2** megawatt(s).

my • possess. det. belonging to or associated with the speaker.
– ORIGIN Old English.

myalgia /my-**al**-juh/ • n. pain in a muscle or group of muscles.
– ORIGIN from Greek *mus* 'muscle' + *algos* 'pain'.

Myanmar E
/my-an-**mar**/ see BURMA.

mycelium /my-see-li-uhm/ • n. (pl. **mycelia**) Bot. a network of fine white threads making up the vegetative part of a fungus.
– ORIGIN Greek *mukēs* 'fungus'.

Mycenae E
/my-**see**-nee/ an ancient city in Greece, situated near the coast in the NE Peloponnese, the centre of an important late Bronze Age civilization.
– DERIVATIVES **Mycenaean** adj. & n.

mycology /my-**kol**-uh-ji/ • n. the scientific study of fungi.
– DERIVATIVES **mycologist** n.
– ORIGIN Greek *mukēs* 'fungus'.

myelin /**my**-uh-lin/ • n. a whitish fatty substance forming a sheath around nerve fibres.
– ORIGIN Greek *muelos* 'marrow'.

Mykonos E
/**mik**-uh-noss/ a Greek island in the Aegean, one of the Cyclades.

mynah (also **mynah bird**) • n. a southern Asian or Australasian starling with a loud call, some kinds of which can mimic human speech.
– ORIGIN Hindi.

myopia /my-**oh**-pi-uh/ • n. short-sightedness.
– ORIGIN from Greek *muein* 'shut' + *ōps* 'eye'.

myopic /my-**op**-ik/ • adj. (of a person) short-sighted.

myriad /**mi**-ri-uhd/ literary • n. (also **myriads**) a countless or very great number. • adj. countless.
– ORIGIN Greek *murias*.

myriapod /**mi**-ri-uh-pod/ • n. a centipede, millipede, or other insect having a long body with numerous leg-bearing segments.
– ORIGIN from Greek *murioi* '10,000' + *pous* 'foot'.

Myron E
/**my**-ruhn/ (*fl. c.*480–440 BC), Greek sculptor. None of his work is known to survive, but there are two certain copies, one being the *Discobolus*, a sculpture of a man throwing a discus.

myrrh /mer/ • n. a sweet-smelling gum resin obtained from certain trees and used in per-

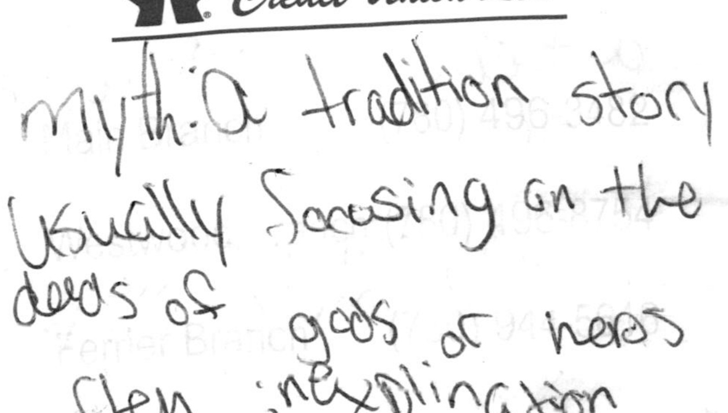
River City
Credit Union Ltd
myth: a tradition story
usually Focusing on the
deeds of
gods or heros
often inexplination
of some natural
phenomenon, as, the sun
the origin of

…rson'.
…ics or mysti-
…ficance that
…ig. **3** inspir-
…nd awe.
…nowledge of
…on. **2** vague
… belief.
…**ng**, **mysti-**
…ncertain or

…or mystery
…, making it

…ncerning the
…aining a nat-
…hold but false
… or thing.

… do with myths or
… not real.

… relating to or found in
…al.
… (pl. **mythologies**) **1** a collec-
…s. **2** a set of widely held but ex-
…ted or false stories or beliefs.
– DERIVATIVES **mythologist** n.

n…
i…
pla…
ing…
secret…
– ORIGIN G…

mystery pla…
based on biblica…
saints.

mystery tour ● n. Brit. a ple… to an unspecified destination.

mystic ● n. a person who seeks by contemplation to become closer to God and to reach truths beyond human understanding. ● adj. mystical.

myxomatosis /mik-suh-muh-**toh**-siss/ ● n. a highly infectious and usually fatal disease of rabbits, causing inflammation and discharge around the eyes.
– ORIGIN Greek *muxa* 'slime, mucus'.

m

n

Nn

N[1] (also **n**) ● n. (pl. **Ns** or **N's**) the fourteenth letter of the alphabet.

N[2] ● abbrev. North or Northern.

n ● symb. an unspecified or variable number.

'n (also **'n'**) ● contr. informal and: *rock 'n roll.*

Na ● symb. the chemical element sodium.
– ORIGIN Latin *natrium*.

n/a ● abbrev. not applicable.

NAAFI /na-fi/ ● abbrev. Brit. Navy, Army, and Air Force Institutes, an organization running shops or canteens for those in the armed forces.

naan ● n. var. of NAN[2].

nab ● v. (**nabs**, **nabbing**, **nabbed**) informal **1** catch (a wrongdoer). **2** take or grab suddenly.
– ORIGIN unknown.

> **Nabokov** E
> /**nab**-uh-koff, nuh-**boh**-koff/, Vladimir (Vladimorovich) (1899–1977), Russian-born American novelist and poet. He is best known for *Lolita*, about a middle-aged man's obsession with a twelve-year-old girl.

nacho /na-choh/ ● n. (pl. **nachos**) a small piece of tortilla topped with melted cheese, peppers, etc.
– ORIGIN perh. from Mexican Spanish *Nacho*, familiar form of *Ignacio*, first name of the chef credited with creating the dish.

nacre /nay-ker/ ● n. mother-of-pearl.
– ORIGIN French.

nadir /nay-deer/ ● n. **1** Astron. the point in the sky directly opposite the zenith and below an observer. **2** the lowest or worst point.
– ORIGIN Arabic, 'opposite to the zenith.'.

naevus /nee-vuhss/ (US **nevus**) ● n. (pl. **naevi** /nee-vy/) a birthmark or a mole on the skin.
– ORIGIN Latin.

naff Brit. informal ● v. (**naff off**) go away. ● adj. lacking taste or style.
– ORIGIN the verb is a euphemism for FUCK; the origin of the adjective is unknown.

nag[1] ● v. (**nags**, **nagging**, **nagged**) **1** harass (someone) constantly to do something they dislike. **2** be constantly worrying or painful to: *I was nagged by the feeling that something was wrong.*

– ORIGIN perh. Scandinavian or German.

nag[2] • **n.** informal, derog. a horse, especially one that is old or in poor condition.
– ORIGIN unknown.

Nagaland E
/nah-guh-land/ a state in the far north-east of India, on the border with Burma (Myanmar); capital, Kohima.

Nagasaki E
/nag-uh-sah-ki/ a city in Japan, on the island of Kyushu. It was the target of the second atom bomb, dropped by the United States in August 1945.

Nagorno-Karabakh E
/nuh-gor-noh ka-ruh-bakh/ a region of Azerbaijan in the southern foothills of the Caucasus; capital, Xankändi.

naiad /ny-ad/ • **n.** (pl. **naiads** or **naiades** /ny-uh-deez/) (in classical mythology) a water nymph.
– ORIGIN Greek *Naias*.

naif /ny-eef/ • **adj.** naive. • **n.** a naive person.
– ORIGIN French.

nail • **n. 1** a small metal spike with a flat head, used to join things together or as a hook. **2** a thin hard layer on the upper surface of the tip of the finger and toe in humans and other primates. • **v. 1** fasten with a nail or nails. **2** informal catch (a suspected criminal).
– PHRASES **a nail in the coffin** an action or event likely to cause something to fail or come to an end.
– ORIGIN Old English.

nail-biting • **adj.** causing great anxiety or tension.

n

nail file • **n.** a small file for shaping the fingernails and toenails.

nail polish (also **nail varnish**) • **n.** a glossy substance applied to the fingernails or toenails.

Naipaul E
/ny-pawl/, V. S. (b.1932; full name *Sir Vidiadhar Surajprasad Naipaul*), Trinidadian writer, resident in Britain since 1950. His novels include *A House for Mr Biswas* and *In a Free State*.

Nairobi E
/ny-roh-bi/ the capital of Kenya.

naive /ny-eev/ (also **naïve**) • **adj. 1** lacking experience, wisdom, or judgement. **2** lacking sophistication.
– DERIVATIVES **naively** (also **naïvely**) adv.
– ORIGIN French.

naivety /ny-eev-ti/ (also **naiveté** /ny-eev-tay/) • **n.** the state of being naive.

naked • **adj. 1** without clothes. **2** (of an object) without the usual covering. **3** not hidden; open: *naked aggression.* **4** exposed to harm.
– PHRASES **the naked eye** the normal power of the eyes, without the assistance of a microscope or other optical instrument.
– DERIVATIVES **nakedly** adv. **nakedness** n.
– ORIGIN Old English.

Namaqualand E
/nuh-mah-kwuh-land/ a region of SW Africa, the homeland of the Nama people. It is divided into **Little Namaqualand**, in the South African province of Northern Cape, and **Great Namaqualand**, in Namibia.

namby-pamby • **adj.** lacking courage or vigour; feeble.
– ORIGIN from the name of *Ambrose* Philips (d. 1749), an English poet ridiculed for his poor verse.

name • **n. 1** a word or words by which someone or something is known, addressed, or referred to. **2** a famous person: *the race will lure all the top names.* **3** a reputation: *he made a name for himself in the theatre.* • **v.** (**names, naming, named**) **1** give a name to. **2** identify or mention by name. **3** specify (a sum, time, or place). **4** appoint.
– PHRASES **in someone's name 1** registered as belonging to or reserved for someone. **2** on behalf of someone. **in the name of** for the sake of.
– ORIGIN Old English.

namecheck • **v.** publicly mention the name of.

name-dropping • **n.** the casual mention of famous people as if one knows them, so as to impress.

nameless • **adj. 1** having no name. **2** not identified by name; anonymous.

namely • **adv.** that is to say.

namesake • **n.** a person or thing with the same name as another.
– ORIGIN from *for the name's sake*.

Namibia E
/nuh-mib-i-uh/ a country in southern Africa, on the Atlantic Ocean; capital, Windhoek.
– DERIVATIVES **Namibian** adj. & n.

nan[1] /nan/ • **n.** Brit. informal one's grandmother.
– ORIGIN from NANNY.

nan[2] /nahn/ (also **naan**) • **n.** a type of soft flat Indian bread.
– ORIGIN Urdu and Persian.

Nanak E
/nah-nuuk/ (1469–1539; known as **Guru Nanak**), Indian religious leader and founder of Sikhism. Not seeking to create a new religion, he preached that spiritual liberation could be achieved through meditating on the name of God.

nancy boy (also **nancy**) • **n.** informal, derog. an effeminate or homosexual man.
– ORIGIN familiar form of the name *Ann*.

Nanjing E
/nan-jing/ (also **Nanking** /nan-king/) a city in eastern China, the capital of China 1368–1421, and again from 1928 to 1937.

nanny • **n.** (pl. **nannies**) **1** a woman employed to look after a child in its own home. **2** (also **nanny goat**) a female goat. • **adj.** interfering and overprotective: *the nanny state.*
– ORIGIN familiar form of the name *Ann*.

nano- /na-noh/ • **comb. form 1** referring to a factor of one thousand millionth (10^{-9}): *nanosecond.* **2** extremely small; submicroscopic: *nanotechnology.*
– ORIGIN Greek *nanos* 'dwarf'.

nanosecond • **n.** one thousand millionth of a second.

nanotechnology • **n.** technology on an atomic or molecular scale.

Nansen E
/**nan**-s'n/, Fridtjof (1861–1930), Norwegian Arctic explorer. He led a number of expeditions, including an unsuccessful attempt to reach the North Pole on board his ship *Fram* (1893–96).

Nantucket E
/nan-**tuk**-it/ an island off the coast of Massachusetts, south of Cape Cod.

nap[1] ● n. a short sleep during the day. ● v. (**naps**, **napping**, **napped**) have a nap.
– ORIGIN Old English.

nap[2] ● n. short raised fibres on the surface of fabrics such as velvet.
– ORIGIN Dutch or German *noppe*.

napalm /**nay**-pahm/ ● n. a highly flammable jelly-like form of petrol, used in firebombs and flame-throwers.
– ORIGIN from *naphthenic* and *palmitic acids* (compounds used in its manufacture).

nape ● n. the back of a person's neck.
– ORIGIN unknown.

naphtha /**naf**-thuh/ ● n. a flammable oil distilled from coal, shale, or petroleum.
– ORIGIN Greek.

naphthalene /**naf**-thuh-leen/ ● n. a crystalline substance distilled from coal tar, used in mothballs and for chemical manufacture.

Napier E
/**nay**-pi-er/, John (1550–1617), Scottish mathematician, the inventor of logarithms.

napkin ● n. a square piece of cloth or paper used at a meal to wipe the fingers or lips and to protect garments.
– ORIGIN Old French *nappe* 'tablecloth'.

Naples E
a city and port on the west coast of Italy.

Napoleon I E
(1769–1821; full name *Napoleon Bonaparte*), emperor of France 1804–14 and 1815. He seized power after the overthrow of the French revolutionary government in 1799. After defeats at Trafalgar (1805) and in Russia (1812), he abdicated and was exiled to Elba. He returned to power in 1815, but was defeated at Waterloo and exiled to St Helena.

Napoleon III E
(1808–73; full name *Charles Louis Napoleon Bonaparte*; known as **Louis-Napoleon**), emperor of France 1852–70. A nephew of Napoleon I, he was elected President of the Second Republic in 1848 and staged a coup in 1851, after which the empire was restored. He abdicated after defeat in the Franco-Prussian War.

Napoleonic Wars E
a series of French campaigns (1800–15) led by Napoleon Bonaparte against Austria, Russia, Great Britain, Portugal, Prussia, and other European powers. They ended with Napoleon's defeat at the Battle of Waterloo.

nappy ● n. (pl. **nappies**) Brit. a piece of material wrapped round a baby's bottom and between its legs to absorb and retain urine and faeces.
– ORIGIN short for **NAPKIN**.

Narayan E
/nuh-**ry**-uhn/, R. K. (1906–2001; full name *Rasipuram Krishnaswamy Narayan*), Indian novelist and short-story writer. His novels include *Swami and Friends*.

Narayanan E
/nuh-**rah**-yuh-nuhn/, K. R. (b.1920; full name *Kocheril Raman Narayanan*), Indian statesman, President since 1997.

narcissism /**nar**-siss-i-z'm/ ● n. excessive or sexual interest in oneself and one's physical appearance.
– DERIVATIVES **narcissist** n. **narcissistic** adj.
– ORIGIN from *Narcissus*, a youth in a Greek myth who fell in love with his reflection.

narcissus /nar-**siss**-uhss/ ● n. (pl. **narcissi** or **narcissuses**) a daffodil with a flower that has white or pale outer petals and an orange or yellow centre.
– ORIGIN Greek *narkissos*.

narcotic ● n. **1** an addictive drug which affects mood or behaviour. **2** a drug which causes drowsiness or unconsciousness, or relieves pain. ● adj. relating to narcotics.
– ORIGIN Greek *narkotikos*.

nark Brit. informal ● n. a police informer. ● v. annoy.
– ORIGIN Romany *nāk* 'nose'.

narrate ● v. (**narrates**, **narrating**, **narrated**) **1** give an account of. **2** provide a commentary for (a film, television programme, etc.).
– DERIVATIVES **narration** n. **narrator** n.
– ORIGIN Latin *narrare*.

narrative ● n. **1** a story. **2** the narrated part of a literary work, as distinct from dialogue. ● adj. having to do with narration.

narrow ● adj. (**narrower**, **narrowest**) **1** of small width in comparison to length. **2** limited in extent, amount, or scope. **3** only just achieved: *a narrow escape*. ● v. **1** become or make narrower. **2** (**narrow down**) reduce (the number of possibilities). ● n. (**narrows**) a narrow channel connecting two larger areas of water.
– DERIVATIVES **narrowly** adv.
– ORIGIN Old English.

narrowboat ● n. Brit. a canal boat less than 7 ft (2.1 metres) wide.

narrow-minded ● adj. unwilling to listen to or accept the views of others.

narwhal /**nar**-wuhl/ ● n. a small Arctic whale, the male of which has a long spirally twisted tusk.
– ORIGIN Danish *narhval*.

NASA /**na**-suh/ ● abbrev. (in the US) National Aeronautics and Space Administration.

nasal ● adj. relating to the nose.
– DERIVATIVES **nasally** adv.
– ORIGIN Latin *nasus* 'nose'.

nascent /**nay**-suhnt/ ● adj. just coming into existence and beginning to develop.
– ORIGIN Latin *nasci* 'be born'.

Naseby, Battle of E
/**nayz**-bi/ a major battle of the English Civil War, which took place in 1645 near Naseby in Northamptonshire, an important victory for the Parliamentarians over the Royalists.

Nash[1], E
(Frederic) Ogden (1902–71), American poet, famous for his light verse.

Nash², E
John (1752–1835), English town planner and neoclassical architect. He planned the layout of Regent's Park and Trafalgar Square, and many other parts of London.

Nash³, E
Paul (1889–1946), English painter and designer, a war artist in both World Wars.

Nash⁴, E
Richard (1674–1762; known as **Beau Nash**), Welsh dandy, an influential figure in matters of of fashion and etiquette.

Nashville E
the state capital of Tennessee, noted for its music industry.

Nassau E
/nass-aw/ the capital of the Bahamas, on the island of New Providence.

Nasser E
/nass-er/, Gamal Abdel (1918–70), Egyptian colonel and statesman, Prime Minister 1954–6 and President 1956–70. His nationalization of the Suez Canal brought war with Britain, France, and Israel in 1956.

nasturtium /nuh-ster-shuhm/ ● **n.** a garden plant with round leaves and orange, yellow, or red flowers.
– ORIGIN Latin.

nasty ● **adj.** **(nastier, nastiest) 1** unpleasant or disgusting. **2** spiteful, violent, or bad-tempered. **3** dangerous or serious: *a nasty bang on the head.*
– DERIVATIVES **nastily** adv. **nastiness** n.
– ORIGIN unknown.

natal /nay-t'l/ ● **adj.** relating to the place or time of one's birth.
– ORIGIN Latin *natalis.*

nation ● **n.** a large group of people sharing the same culture, language, or history, and inhabiting a particular state or area.
– ORIGIN Latin.

national ● **adj. 1** having to do with a nation. **2** owned, controlled, or financially supported by the state. ● **n.** a citizen of a particular country.
– DERIVATIVES **nationally** adv.

national curriculum ● **n.** a curriculum of study laid down to be taught in state schools.

national debt ● **n.** the total amount of money which a country's government has borrowed.

National Gallery E
an art gallery in Trafalgar Square, London, holding one of the chief national collections of pictures.

national grid ● **n.** Brit. the network of high-voltage power lines between major power stations.

National Health Service E
(in the UK) a system of national medical care paid for mainly by taxation.

National Insurance ● **n.** (in the UK) a system of payments by employees and employers to provide state assistance for people who are sick, unemployed, or retired.

nationalism ● **n. 1** patriotic feeling, often to an excessive degree. **2** belief in political independence for a particular country.
– DERIVATIVES **nationalist** n. & adj. **nationalistic** adj.

nationality ● **n.** (pl. **nationalities**) **1** the status of belonging to a particular nation. **2** an ethnic group forming a part of one or more political nations.

nationalize (also **nationalise**) ● **v.** **(nationalizes, nationalizing, nationalized)** transfer (an industry or business) from private to state ownership or control.
– DERIVATIVES **nationalization** (also **nationalisation**) n.

national park ● **n.** an area of environmental importance or natural beauty protected by the state and which the public may visit.

national service ● **n.** a period of compulsory service in the armed forces during peacetime.

National Trust E
(in the United Kingdom) a trust for the preservation of places of historic interest or natural beauty.

nationwide ● **adj. & adv.** throughout the whole nation.

native ● **n. 1** a person born in a specified place. **2** a local inhabitant. **3** an animal or plant that lives or grows naturally in a place. **4** dated, offens. a non-white original inhabitant of a country as regarded by Europeans. ● **adj. 1** associated with a person's place of birth. **2** (of a plant or animal) occurring naturally in a place. **3** relating to the original inhabitants of a place. **4** in a person's character: *native wit.*
– ORIGIN Latin *nativus.*

Native American ● **n.** a member of any of the original inhabitants of North and South America and the Caribbean Islands. ● **adj.** relating to these peoples.

native speaker ● **n.** a person who has spoken a particular language from earliest childhood.

Nativity ● **n.** **(the Nativity)** the birth of Jesus Christ.

NATO (also **Nato**) ● **abbrev.** North Atlantic Treaty Organization.

natter informal ● **v.** **(natters, nattering, nattered)** chat for a long time. ● **n.** a long chat.

natterjack toad ● **n.** a small toad with a bright yellow stripe down its back.
– ORIGIN perh. from NATTER + JACK.

natty ● **adj.** informal smart and fashionable.
– ORIGIN perh. from NEAT.

natural ● **adj. 1** existing in or obtained from nature; not made or caused by humans. **2** in accordance with nature; normal: *a natural death.* **3** born with a particular skill or quality: *a natural leader.* **4** relaxed and unaffected. **5** (of a parent or child) related by blood. **6** Music (of a note) not sharpened or flattened. ● **n. 1** a person with an inborn gift or talent. **2** an off-white colour. **3** Music a natural note or a sign (♮) indicating one.
– DERIVATIVES **naturalness** n.

natural gas ● **n.** gas consisting largely of methane, occurring underground and used as fuel.

natural history ● **n.** the scientific study of animals or plants.

naturalism • n. an artistic or literary style based on the highly detailed and realistic description of daily life.

naturalist • n. an expert in or student of natural history.

naturalistic • adj. **1** imitating real life or nature. **2** based on the theory of naturalism in art or literature.

naturalize (also **naturalise**) • v. (**naturalizes, naturalizing, naturalized**) **1** make (a foreigner) a citizen of a country. **2** introduce (a non-native plant or animal) into a region and establish it in the wild.
– DERIVATIVES **naturalization** (also **naturalisation**) n.

natural law • n. **1** a group of unchanging moral principles regarded as inborn in all human beings and forming a basis for behaviour. **2** an observable law relating to natural phenomena.

naturally • adv. **1** in a natural manner. **2** of course.

natural selection • n. the evolutionary process whereby organisms better adapted to their environment tend to survive and produce more offspring.

nature • n. **1** the physical world, including plants, animals, the landscape, and natural phenomena, as opposed to things made by people. **2** the inborn qualities or characteristics of a person or thing. **3** a kind, sort, or class: *topics of a religious nature*.
– ORIGIN Latin *natura* 'birth, nature'.

nature reserve • n. an area of land managed so as to preserve its plants, animals, and physical features.

nature trail • n. a signposted path through the countryside designed to draw attention to natural features.

naturism • n. nudism.
– DERIVATIVES **naturist** n. & adj.

naught • pron. archaic nothing.
– ORIGIN Old English.

naughty • adj. (**naughtier, naughtiest**) **1** (of a child) disobedient; badly behaved. **2** informal mildly indecent.
– DERIVATIVES **naughtiness** n.
– ORIGIN first meaning 'possessing nothing': from NAUGHT.

Nauru E
/nah-oo-roo/ an island republic in the SW Pacific, near the equator; no official capital.
– DERIVATIVES **Nauruan** adj. & n.

nausea /naw-zi-uh/ • n. **1** a feeling of sickness with the need to vomit. **2** disgust.
– ORIGIN Greek *nausia* 'seasickness'.

nauseate • v. (**nauseates, nauseating, nauseated**) cause to feel sick or disgusted.

nauseous • adj. **1** affected with nausea. **2** causing nausea.

nautical • adj. having to do with sailors or navigation; maritime.
– ORIGIN Greek *nautikos*.

nautical mile • n. a unit used in measuring distances at sea, equal to 1,852 metres (approximately 2,025 yards).

nautilus /naw-ti-luhss/ • n. (pl. **nautiluses** or **nautili** /naw-ti-ly/) a swimming mollusc with a spiral shell and short tentacles around the mouth.
– ORIGIN Greek *nautilos* 'sailor'.

naval • adj. having to do with a navy or navies.
– ORIGIN Latin *navalis*.

Navarre E
/nuh-var/ an autonomous region of northern Spain, on the border with France; capital, Pamplona.

nave • n. the central part of a church.
– ORIGIN Latin *navis* 'ship'.

navel • n. the small hollow in the centre of a person's stomach where the umbilical cord was cut at birth.
– ORIGIN Old English.

navel-gazing • n. absorption in oneself.

navigable • adj. wide and deep enough to be used by boats and ships.

navigate • v. (**navigates, navigating, navigated**) **1** plan and direct the route of a ship, aircraft, or other form of transport. **2** guide (a boat or vehicle) over a specified route. **3** sail or travel over.
– ORIGIN Latin *navigare* 'to sail'.

navigation • n. **1** the activity of navigating. **2** the movement of ships.
– DERIVATIVES **navigational** adj.

navigator • n. a person who navigates a ship, aircraft, etc.

Navratilova E
/na-vra-ti-**loh**-vuh/, Martina (b.1956), Czech-born American tennis player. Her successes include nine Wimbledon singles titles and eight successive grand slam doubles titles.

navvy • n. (pl. **navvies**) Brit. dated a labourer employed in building a road, canal, or railway.
– ORIGIN from NAVIGATOR in the former sense 'builder of a *navigation*' (a dialect word for a canal).

navy • n. (pl **navies**) **1** the branch of a country's armed services which fights at sea. **2** (also **navy blue**) a dark blue colour.
– ORIGIN Latin *navis* 'ship'.

Naxos E
/**nak**-soss/ a Greek island in the Aegean, the largest of the Cyclades.

nay • adv. **1** or rather: *it will take months, nay years*. **2** archaic or dialect no.
– ORIGIN Old Norse.

Nazareth E
/na-**zuh**-ruhth/ a historic town in northern Israel. Mentioned in the Gospels as the childhood home of Jesus, it is a centre of Christian pilgrimage.

Nazca Lines E
/naz-kuh/ a group of huge abstract designs on the coastal plain north of Nazca in Peru, which can only be seen clearly from the air. They belong to a pre-Inca culture, and their purpose is uncertain.

Nazi /naht-si/ • n. (pl. **Nazis**) hist. a member of the far-right National Socialist German Workers' Party.
– DERIVATIVES **Nazism** n.
– ORIGIN German, from the pronunciation of *Nati-* in *Nationalsozialist*.

NB • abbrev. note well.
– ORIGIN from Latin *nota bene*.

NCO • abbrev. non-commissioned officer.

n

N'Djamena E
/uhn-ja-**may**-nuh/ the capital of Chad. Former name (1900–1973) **Fort Lamy**.

NE ● **abbrev.** north-east or north-eastern.

Neagh, Lough E
/nay/ a shallow lake in Northern Ireland, the largest freshwater lake in the British Isles.

Neanderthal /ni-**an**-der-tahl/ ● **n. 1** (also **Neanderthal man**) an extinct human living in Europe between about 120,000–35,000 years ago. **2** informal a man who is rude, brutish, or who holds very old-fashioned views.
– ORIGIN named after a region in Germany where remains of Neanderthal man were found.

neap /neep/ (also **neap tide**) ● **n.** a tide just after the first or third quarters of the moon when there is least difference between high and low water.
– ORIGIN Old English.

Neapolitan /ni-uh-**pol**-i-tuhn/ ● **n.** a person from the city of Naples. ● **adj.** relating to Naples.

near ● **adv. 1** at or to a short distance in space or time. **2** almost: *a near perfect fit.* ● **prep.** (also **near to**) **1** at or to a short distance in space or time from. **2** close to: *she was near to death.* ● **adj. 1** at a short distance away in space or time. **2** close to being: *a near disaster.* **3** closely related. ● **v.** approach.
– DERIVATIVES **nearness** n.
– ORIGIN Old Norse.

nearby ● **adj. & adv.** not far away.

Near East ● **n.** the countries of SW Asia between the Mediterranean and India (including the Middle East).

nearly ● **adv.** very close to; almost.
– PHRASES **not nearly** nothing like.

near miss ● **n. 1** a narrowly avoided collision or accident. **2** a bomb or shot that just misses its target.

nearside ● **n.** esp. Brit. the side of a vehicle nearest the kerb.

near-sighted ● **adj.** short-sighted.

neat ● **adj. 1** tidy or carefully arranged. **2** clever but simple: *a neat solution to the labour shortage.* **3** (of a drink of spirits) not diluted. **4** N. Amer. informal excellent.
– DERIVATIVES **neatly** adv. **neatness** n.
– ORIGIN French *net* 'clean'.

neaten ● **v.** make neat.

neath ● **prep.** literary beneath.

Nebraska E
/ni-**brass**-kuh/ a state in the central US; capital, Lincoln.
– DERIVATIVES **Nebraskan** adj. & n.

Nebuchadnezzar II E
/neb-yuu-kuhd-**nez**-zer/ (*c.*630–562 BC), king of Babylon 605–562 BC. He extended his rule over neighbouring countries and in 586 BC he destroyed Jerusalem and deported many Israelites to Babylon.

nebula /**neb**-yuu-luh/ ● **n.** (pl. **nebulae** /**neb**-yuu-lee/ or **nebulas**) a cloud of gas or dust in outer space.
– DERIVATIVES **nebular** adj.
– ORIGIN Latin, 'mist'.

nebulizer /**neb**-yuu-ly-zer/ (also **nebuliser**) ● **n.** a device for producing a fine spray of liquid, used for inhaling a medicinal drug.

nebulous ● **adj.** not clearly defined; vague: *nebulous concepts.*

necessarily ● **adv.** as a necessary result; unavoidably.

necessary ● **adj. 1** needing to be done or present; essential: *major changes are necessary.* **2** that must be; unavoidable: *a necessary result.* ● **n.** (**necessaries**) the basic requirements of life, such as food.
– ORIGIN Latin *necessarius.*

necessitate ● **v.** (**necessitates**, **necessitating**, **necessitated**) **1** make necessary: *the cut necessitated eighteen stitches.* **2** force (someone) to do something.

necessitous ● **adj.** dated poor.

necessity ● **n.** (pl. **necessities**) **1** the state of being necessary. **2** something essential. **3** a situation that requires a particular course of action: *political necessity forced him to consider it.*

neck ● **n. 1** the part of the body connecting the head to the rest of the body. **2** a narrow connecting or end part, such as the part of a bottle near the mouth. **3** the length of a horse's head and neck as a measure of its lead in a race. ● **v.** informal kiss and caress passionately.
– PHRASES **get it in the neck** informal be severely criticized or punished. **neck and neck** level in a race or other competition. **neck of the woods** informal a particular place.
– ORIGIN Old English, 'nape of the neck'.

neckerchief ● **n.** a square of cloth worn round the neck.

necklace ● **n.** an ornamental chain or string of beads, jewels, or links worn round the neck.

necklet ● **n.** a close-fitting, rigid ornament worn around the neck.

neckline ● **n.** the edge of a woman's garment at or below the neck.

necktie ● **n.** N. Amer. or dated a tie worn around the neck.

necromancy /**nek**-ruh-man-si/ ● **n. 1** prediction of the future by supposedly communicating with dead people. **2** witchcraft or black magic.
– DERIVATIVES **necromancer** n. **necromantic** adj.
– ORIGIN from Greek *nekros* 'corpse' + *manteia* 'divination'.

necrophilia /nek-ruh-**fil**-i-uh/ ● **n.** sexual intercourse with or attraction towards corpses.
– DERIVATIVES **necrophiliac** n.

necropolis /ne-**krop**-uh-liss/ ● **n.** a cemetery.
– ORIGIN from Greek *nekros* 'corpse' + *polis* 'city'.

necrosis /ne-**kroh**-siss/ ● **n.** Med. the death of cells in the body due to disease, injury, or failure of the blood supply.
– DERIVATIVES **necrotic** adj.

nectar ● **n. 1** a sugary fluid produced by flowers and made into honey by bees. **2** (in Greek and Roman mythology) the drink of the gods. **3** a delicious drink.
– ORIGIN Greek *nektar.*

nectarine /**nek**-tuh-reen/ ● **n.** a variety of peach with smooth skin and rich firm flesh.
– ORIGIN from **nectar**.

née /nay/ ● **adj.** born (used in giving a married

woman's maiden name): *Mrs. Hargreaves, née Liddell.*
– ORIGIN French.

need ● v. **1** want (something) because it is essential or very important. **2** used to express what should or must be done: *need I say more?* ● n. **1** a situation in which something is necessary or must be done: *I was in need of a haircut.* **2** a thing that is needed. **3** a state of being poor or in great difficulty.
– ORIGIN Old English.

needful ● adj. necessary.

needle ● n. **1** a very thin pointed piece of metal with a hole or eye for thread at the blunter end, used in sewing. **2** a long thin piece of metal or plastic with a pointed end, used in knitting. **3** the pointed hollow end of a hypodermic syringe. **4** a stylus used to play records. **5** a thin pointer on a dial, compass, etc. **6** the thin, stiff leaf of a fir or pine tree. ● v. (**needles**, **needling**, **needled**) informal deliberately annoy (someone).
– ORIGIN Old English.

needlecord ● n. Brit. corduroy fabric with narrow ridges.

needlepoint ● n. closely stitched embroidery worked over canvas.

needless ● adj. unnecessary; avoidable.
– DERIVATIVES **needlessly** adv.

needlewoman ● n. a woman who has particular sewing skills.

needlework ● n. sewing or embroidery.

needn't ● contr. need not.

needy ● adj. (**needier**, **neediest**) very poor.

ne'er /nair/ ● contr. literary or dialect never.

ne'er-do-well ● n. a person who is lazy or useless.

nefarious /ni-fair-i-uhss/ ● adj. wicked or criminal.
– ORIGIN Latin *nefas* 'wrong'.

negate /ni-gayt/ ● v. (**negates**, **negating**, **negated**) **1** stop (something) from having an effect: *alcohol negates the effects of the drug.* **2** deny the existence of.
– ORIGIN Latin *negare*.

negation ● n. **1** the denial of something. **2** the absence or opposite of something actual or positive: *evil is not merely the negation of goodness.*

negative ● adj. **1** showing the absence rather than the presence of particular features: *a negative test result.* **2** expressing denial, disagreement, or refusal. **3** not hopeful or favourable. **4** (of a quantity) less than zero. **5** having to do with the kind of electric charge carried by electrons. **6** (of a photograph) showing light and shade or colours reversed from those of the original. **7** Grammar containing a word such as *not*, *no*, or *never*. ● n. **1** a negative word or statement. **2** a negative photograph, from which positive prints may be made.
– DERIVATIVES **negatively** adv. **negativity** n.

neglect ● v. **1** fail to give proper care or attention to. **2** fail to do something. ● n. the action of neglecting or the state of being neglected: *animals dying through neglect.*
– ORIGIN Latin *neglegere* 'disregard'.

neglectful ● adj. failing to give proper care or attention.

negligee /neg-li-*zhay*/ ● n. a woman's light, flimsy dressing gown.
– ORIGIN French, 'given little thought'.

negligence ● n. lack of proper care and attention.
– DERIVATIVES **negligent** adj.

negligible /neg-li-juh-b'l/ ● adj. so small or unimportant as to be not worth considering.
– ORIGIN French *négliger* 'to neglect'.

negotiable ● adj. able to be changed after discussion: *the price was not negotiable.*

negotiate ● v. (**negotiates**, **negotiating**, **negotiated**) **1** try to reach an agreement by discussion. **2** bring about by discussion. **3** find a way over or through (an obstacle or difficult path).
– DERIVATIVES **negotiator** n.
– ORIGIN Latin *negotiari* 'do in the course of business'.

negotiation (also **negotiations**) ● n. discussion aimed at reaching an agreement.

Negress /nee-gress/ ● n. dated, offens. a woman or girl of black African origin.

Negro ● n. (pl. **Negroes**) a member of a dark-skinned group of peoples that originated in Africa south of the Sahara.
– ORIGIN Latin *niger* 'black'.

USAGE Negro

Do not use the terms **Negro** and **Negress** to refer to black people, as they are now thought to be old-fashioned and offensive; use **black** instead.

Nehru E
/nair-oo/, Jawaharlal (1889–1964; known as **Pandit Nehru**), Indian statesman, Prime Minister 1947–64. The leader of the Indian National Congress, Nehru was imprisoned nine times by the British for his nationalist campaigns, but went on to become the first Prime Minister of independent India.

neigh ● n. a high-pitched cry made by a horse. ● v. make this cry.

neighbour (US **neighbor**) ● n. **1** a person living next door to or very near to another. **2** a person or place next to or near another. ● v. be next to or very near (something).
– DERIVATIVES **neighbourly** (US **neighborly**) adj.
– ORIGIN Old English.

neighbourhood (US **neighborhood**) ● n. **1** a district within a town or city. **2** the area surrounding a place, person, or object.
– PHRASES **in the neighbourhood of** about; approximately.

neighbourhood watch ● n. a scheme in which local groups of householders watch each other's homes to discourage burglary and other crimes.

neither /ny-*ther*, nee-*ther*/ ● det. & pron. not either. ● adv. **1** used to show that a negative statement is true of two things: *I am neither a liberal nor a conservative.* **2** used to show that a negative statement is also true of something else: *he didn't remember, and neither did I.*
– ORIGIN Old English.

Nelson, E
Horatio, Viscount Nelson, Duke of Bronte (1758–1805), British admiral. Nelson became a national hero as a result of his victories at sea in the Napoleonic Wars, especially the Battle of Trafalgar, in which he was mortally wounded.

nematode /nem-uh-tohd/ • **n.** a worm of a group with slender, cylindrical bodies.
– ORIGIN Greek *nēma* 'thread'.

nem. con. • **adv.** with no one disagreeing; unanimously.
– ORIGIN from Latin *nemine contradicente.*

nemesis /nem-i-siss/ • **n.** (pl. **nemeses** /nem-i-seez/) a means of deserved and unavoidable punishment or downfall.
– ORIGIN Greek, 'retribution'.

neo- /nee-oh/ • **comb. form 1** new: *neologism.* **2** a new or revived form of: *neoclassicism.*
– ORIGIN Greek *neos.*

neoclassical (also **neoclassic**) • **adj.** relating to the revival of a classical style in the arts.
– DERIVATIVES **neoclassicism** n.

neodymium /nee-oh-dim-i-uhm/ • **n.** a silvery-white metallic element.
– ORIGIN from **NEO-** + Greek *didumos* 'twin'.

Neolithic /nee-uh-lith-ik/ • **adj.** relating to the later part of the Stone Age.
– ORIGIN from **NEO-** + Greek *lithos* 'stone'.

neologism /ni-ol-uh-ji-z'm/ • **n.** a new word or expression.
– ORIGIN from **NEO-** + Greek *logos* 'word'.

neon • **n.** an inert gaseous element that glows orange when electricity is passed through it, used in fluorescent lighting.
– ORIGIN Greek, 'something new'.

neonatal • **adj.** relating to newborn children.

neophyte /nee-uh-fyt/ • **n. 1** a person who is new to a subject, skill, or belief. **2** a novice in a religious order, or a newly ordained priest.
– ORIGIN Greek *neophutos* 'newly planted'.

neoprene /nee-oh-preen/ • **n.** a synthetic substance resembling rubber.
– ORIGIN from **NEO-** + *prene* (perh. from **PROPYL**).

Nepal E
/ni-pawl/ a country in southern Asia, in the Himalayas; capital, Kathmandu.
– DERIVATIVES **Nepalese** adj. & n.

nephew • **n.** a son of one's brother or sister, or of one's brother-in-law or sister-in-law.
– ORIGIN Latin *nepos* 'grandson, nephew'.

nephritis /ni-fry-tiss/ • **n.** inflammation of the kidneys.
– ORIGIN Greek *nephros* 'kidney'.

ne plus ultra /nay pluus uul-trah/ • **n.** the highest form of something: *the ne plus ultra of editors.*
– ORIGIN Latin, 'not further beyond'.

nepotism /nep-uh-ti-z'm/ • **n.** favouritism shown to relatives or friends, especially by giving them jobs.
– ORIGIN Italian *nipote* 'nephew' (referring to privileges given to the 'nephews' of popes, often their illegitimate sons).

Neptune[1] E
the Roman god of water and of the sea. Greek equivalent **POSEIDON**.

Neptune[2] E
a distant planet of the solar system, eighth in order from the sun.

neptunium /nep-tyoo-ni-uhm/ • **n.** a rare radioactive metallic element.
– ORIGIN from **NEPTUNE**[2].

nerd • **n.** informal a person who is excessively interested in something and finds it difficult to get on with people.
– ORIGIN unknown.

Nereid /neer-i-id/ • **n.** Gk Myth. a sea nymph.

Nero E
/*rhymes with* hero/ (AD 37–68; full name *Nero Claudius Caesar Augustus Germanicus*), Roman emperor 54–68. He was infamous for his cruelty and his reign witnessed a fire which destroyed half of Rome.

Neruda E
/nuh-roo-duh/, Pablo (1904–73; born *Ricardo Eliezer Neftalí Reyes*), Chilean poet and diplomat. He is noted for his epic poem *Canto General*, covering the history of the Americas.

nerve • **n. 1** a fibre or bundle of fibres in the body that transmits impulses of sensation between the brain or spinal cord and other parts of the body. **2** (**nerves** or **one's nerve**) steadiness and courage in a demanding situation: *the journey tested her nerves to the full.* **3** (**nerves**) nervousness. **4** informal cheeky boldness. • **v.** (**nerves, nerving, nerved**) (**nerve oneself**) brace oneself for a demanding situation.
– PHRASES **get on someone's nerves** informal irritate someone. **touch** (or **hit**) **a** (**raw**) **nerve** refer to a sensitive subject.
– ORIGIN Latin *nervus.*

nerve cell • **n.** a neuron.

nerve centre • **n. 1** a group of connected nerve cells performing a particular function. **2** the control centre of an organization or operation.

nerve gas • **n.** a poisonous gas which affects the nervous system, causing death or disablement.

nerveless • **adj. 1** lacking strength or feeling. **2** confident.

nerve-racking (also **nerve-wracking**) • **adj.** stressful; frightening.

nervous • **adj. 1** easily frightened or worried. **2** anxious. **3** having to do with the nerves.
– DERIVATIVES **nervously** adv. **nervousness** n.

nervous breakdown • **n.** a period of mental illness resulting from severe depression or stress.

nervous system • **n.** the network of nerves which transmits nerve impulses between parts of the body.

nervy • **adj.** (**nervier, nerviest**) Brit. nervous or tense.

Nesbit, E
E. (1858–1924; full name *Edith Nesbit*), English novelist, known for her children's books, including *The Railway Children.*

ness • **n.** a headland.
– ORIGIN Old English.

-ness • **suffix** forming nouns referring to: **1** a state or condition: *liveliness.* **2** something in a certain state: *wilderness.*
– ORIGIN Old English.

Ness, Loch E
see **LOCH NESS**.

nest • **n. 1** a structure made by a bird for laying eggs and sheltering its young. **2** a place where an animal or insect breeds or shelters. **3** a set of similar objects that are designed to fit inside each other. • **v.** use or build a nest.

– ORIGIN Old English.

nest egg ● n. a sum of money saved for the future.

nestle ● v. (**nestles**, **nestling**, **nestled**) **1** settle comfortably within or against something: *the baby deer nestled in her arms.* **2** (of a place) lie in a sheltered position.
– ORIGIN Old English.

nestling ● n. a bird that is too young to leave the nest.

net[1] ● n. **1** a material made of twine or cord woven or tied together, with spaces in between. **2** a piece or structure of net for catching fish or insects, surrounding a goal, etc. **3** a light fabric with a very open weave. **4** a way of catching someone: *unregistered boats slipped through the net.* **5** (**the Net**) the Internet. ● v. (**nets**, **netting**, **netted**) catch or get with or as if with a net: *customs officials netted large hauls of drugs.*
– ORIGIN Old English.

net[2] (Brit. also **nett**) ● adj. **1** (of an amount) remaining after tax, discounts, or expenses have been deducted. **2** (of a weight) not including that of the packaging. **3** (of an effect or result) overall. ● v. (**nets**, **netting**, **netted**) acquire (a sum) as clear profit.
– ORIGIN French *net* 'neat'.

netball ● n. a team game in which goals are scored by throwing a ball through a net hanging from a hoop.

nether /ne*th*-er/ ● adj. lower in position.
– ORIGIN Old English.

Netherlands E
a country in western Europe, on the North Sea; capital, Amsterdam; seat of government, The Hague. Also called **HOLLAND**.
– DERIVATIVES **Netherlander** n. **Netherlandish** adj.

Netherlands Antilles E
two widely separated groups of Dutch islands in the Caribbean, in the Lesser Antilles; capital, Willemstad (on Curaçao).

nether regions ● pl. n. **1** (also **netherworld**) hell. **2** euphem. a person's genitals and bottom.

net profit ● n. the actual profit after working expenses have been paid.

nett ● adj. & v. Brit. = **NET**[2].

netting ● n. material made of net.

nettle ● n. a plant with leaves that are covered with stinging hairs. ● v. (**nettles**, **nettling**, **nettled**) annoy.
– PHRASES **grasp the nettle** Brit. tackle a difficulty boldly.
– ORIGIN Old English.

network ● n. **1** a system of railways, roads, lines, etc., that cross or connect with each other. **2** a group of broadcasting stations that connect to broadcast a programme at the same time. **3** a number of interconnected computers, operations, etc. **4** a group of people who keep in contact with each other to exchange information. ● v. keep in contact with others to exchange information.
– DERIVATIVES **networker** n.

neural /nyoor-uhl/ ● adj. relating to a nerve or the nervous system.

neuralgia /nyoo-ral-juh/ ● n. intense pain along a nerve in the head or face.
– DERIVATIVES **neuralgic** adj.

neuro- ● comb. form relating to nerves or the nervous system: *neurosurgery.*
– ORIGIN Greek *neuron* 'nerve, sinew'.

neurology ● n. the branch of medicine and biology concerned with the nervous system.
– DERIVATIVES **neurological** adj. **neurologist** n.

neuron (also **neurone**) ● n. a specialized cell that transmits nerve impulses.
– ORIGIN Greek, 'sinew, nerve'.

neurosis /nyoo-**roh**-siss/ ● n. (pl. **neuroses** /nyoo-**roh**-seez/) a mild mental illness involving symptoms such as depression, anxiety, or obsessive behaviour.

neurosurgery ● n. surgery performed on the nervous system.

neurotic ● adj. **1** having to do with neurosis. **2** informal excessively sensitive, anxious, or obsessive.

neurotransmitter ● n. a chemical substance released from a nerve fibre and bringing about the transfer of an impulse to another nerve, muscle, etc.

neuter ● adj. **1** Grammar (of a noun) not masculine or feminine. **2** (of an animal or plant) having no sexual or reproductive organs. ● v. (**neuters**, **neutering**, **neutered**) **1** castrate or spay (an animal). **2** take away the power of: *their only purpose is to neuter local democracy.*
– ORIGIN Latin, 'neither'.

neutral ● adj. **1** not supporting either side in a dispute or war. **2** lacking noticeable or strong qualities: *his tone was neutral, without sentiment.* **3** Chem. neither acid nor alkaline; having a pH of about 7. **4** electrically neither positive nor negative. ● n. **1** a state or person who remains neutral during a dispute or war. **2** a position of a gear mechanism in which the engine is disconnected from the driven parts.
– DERIVATIVES **neutrality** n. **neutrally** adv.
– ORIGIN Latin *neutralis* 'of neuter gender'.

neutralize (also **neutralise**) ● v. (**neutralizes**, **neutralizing**, **neutralized**) **1** stop (something) from having an effect. **2** make chemically neutral.
– DERIVATIVES **neutralization** (also **neutralisation**) n.

neutrino /nyoo-tree-noh/ ● n. (pl. **neutrinos**) a subatomic particle with a mass close to zero and no electric charge.
– ORIGIN Italian.

neutron ● n. a subatomic particle of about the same mass as a proton but without an electric charge.
– ORIGIN from **NEUTRAL**.

neutron bomb ● n. a nuclear weapon that produces large numbers of neutrons, killing people but doing little harm to property.

Nevada E
/ni-**vah**-duh/ a state of the western US; capital, Carson City.
– DERIVATIVES **Nevadan** adj. & n.

never ● adv. **1** not ever. **2** not at all.
– PHRASES **the never-never** Brit. informal hire purchase.
– ORIGIN Old English.

nevermore ● adv. literary never again.

nevertheless ● adv. in spite of that.

Nevis E
/**nee**-viss/ one of the Leeward Islands in the Caribbean, part of St Kitts and Nevis; capital, Charlestown.

Nevsky, E
Alexander, see **ALEXANDER NEVSKY**.

nevus • n. (pl. **nevi**) US = **NAEVUS**.

new • adj. **1** made, introduced, discovered, or experienced recently: *signing copies of his new book.* **2** not previously used or owned. **3** (**new to/at**) not used to or experienced at. **4** different from a recent previous one: *this would be her new home.* **5** better than before; renewed or reformed. • adv. newly.
– DERIVATIVES **newness** n.
– ORIGIN Old English.

New Age • n. a broad movement concerned with alternative approaches to traditional Western religion, culture, medicine, etc.

newborn • adj. recently born.

New Brunswick E
a province on the SE coast of Canada; capital, Fredericton.

New Caledonia E
an island in the South Pacific, a French overseas territory east of Australia; capital, Nouméa.

Newcastle[1] E
an industrial city and port in NE England, on the River Tyne. Full name **NEWCASTLE-UPON-TYNE**.

Newcastle[2], E
Thomas Pelham-Holles, 1st Duke of (1693–1768), British Whig statesman, Prime Minister 1754–6 and 1757–62.

Newcomen E
/**nyoo**-kum-uhn/, Thomas (1663–1729), English engineer, developer of the first practical steam engine (1712).

newcomer • n. **1** a person who has recently arrived. **2** a person who is new to an activity or situation.

New Deal E
the economic measures introduced by Franklin D. Roosevelt in 1933 to counteract the effects of the Depression of the 1930s.

New Delhi E
see **DELHI**.

newel /**nyoo**-uhl/ • n. **1** the central supporting pillar of a winding staircase. **2** (also **newel post**) the top or bottom supporting post of a stair rail.
– ORIGIN Old French *nouel* 'knob'.

New England E
an area on the NE coast of the US, comprising the states of Maine, New Hampshire, Vermont, Massachusetts, Rhode Island, and Connecticut.
– DERIVATIVES **New Englander** n.

newfangled • adj. derog. newly developed and unfamiliar.
– ORIGIN from dialect *newfangle* 'liking what is new'.

New Forest E
an area of heath and woodland in southern Hampshire.

Newfoundland[1] E
/**nyoo**-fuhnd-luhnd, **nyoo**-fuhnd-land/ a large island off the east coast of Canada, forming part of the province of Newfoundland and Labrador.
– DERIVATIVES **Newfoundlander** n.

Newfoundland[2] /**nyoo**-fuhnd-luhnd, **nyoo**-fuhnd-land/ • n. a dog of a very large breed with a thick coarse coat.
– ORIGIN from **NEWFOUNDLAND**[1].

Newfoundland and Labrador E
a province of eastern Canada, comprising the island of Newfoundland and the Labrador region; capital, St John's.

New Guinea E
an island in the western South Pacific, north of Australia, the second-largest island in the world. It is divided into two parts; the western half comprises part of Irian Jaya, the eastern half forms part of Papua New Guinea.
– DERIVATIVES **New Guinean** n. & adj.

New Hampshire E
a state in the north-eastern US, on the Atlantic coast; capital, Concord.

New Hebrides E
former name for **VANUATU**.

New Jersey E
a state in the north-eastern US, on the Atlantic coast; capital, Trenton.
– DERIVATIVES **New Jerseyan** n. & adj.

newly • adv. **1** recently. **2** again; afresh: *confidence for the newly single.*

newly-wed • n. a recently married person.

Newman[1], E
John Henry (1801–90), English clergyman and theologian. He was a leading member of the Oxford Movement, which sought to restore Catholic teachings and ceremonial within the Church of England. He later converted to Roman Catholicism and became a cardinal.

Newman[2], E
Paul (b.1925), American actor and film director, star of such films as *Butch Cassidy and the Sundance Kid*, *The Sting*, and *The Color of Money.*

new man • n. a man who rejects traditional male attitudes, often taking on childcare and housework.

Newmarket E
a town in Suffolk in eastern England, a noted horse-racing centre.

new maths • n. a system of teaching mathematics to children, with emphasis on investigation by them and on set theory.

New Mexico E
a state in the south-western US, on the border with Mexico; capital, Santa Fe.
– DERIVATIVES **New Mexican** adj. & n.

new moon • n. the phase of the moon when it first appears as a thin crescent.

New Orleans E
/or-leenz, or-**leenz**/ a city and port in SE Louisiana, on the Mississippi. It is noted for its annual Mardi Gras celebrations and for its association with blues and jazz.

news • n. **1** new information about recent events. **2** (**the news**) a broadcast or published news report. **3** (**news to**) informal information not previously known to (someone).

news agency • n. an organization that collects and distributes news items to newspapers or broadcasters.

newsagent • n. Brit. a shopkeeper who sells newspapers, magazines, etc.

newscast • n. a broadcast news report.
– DERIVATIVES **newscaster** n.

news conference • n. a press conference.

newsflash • n. a brief item of important news, interrupting other radio or television programmes.

newsgroup • n. a group of Internet users who exchange email on a subject of shared interest.

newsletter • n. a bulletin issued periodically to the members of a society or organization.

New South Wales E
a state of SE Australia; capital, Sydney.

newspaper • n. a daily or weekly publication containing news, articles, and advertisements.

newspeak • n. deliberately misleading and indirect language, used by politicians.
– ORIGIN from George Orwell's novel *Nineteen Eighty-Four.*

newsprint • n. cheap, low-quality printing paper used for newspapers.

newsreader • n. Brit. a person who reads the news on radio or television.

newsreel • n. a short cinema film of news and current affairs.

newsroom • n. the area in a newspaper or broadcasting office where news is processed.

newsworthy • adj. important enough to be mentioned as news.

newsy • adj. informal full of news.

newt • n. a small animal with a thin body and a long tail, that can live in water or on land.
– ORIGIN Old English.

New Territories E
part of Hong Kong on the south coast of mainland China, lying to the north of the Kowloon peninsula and including the islands of Lantau, Tsing Yi, and Lamma.

New Testament • n. the second part of the Christian Bible, recording the life and teachings of Christ and his earliest followers.

Newton, E
Sir Isaac (1642–1727), English mathematician and physicist, famous for his mathematical description of the laws of mechanics and gravitation. He also discovered that white light is made up of a mixture of colours, and in mathematics developed differential calculus.

newton • n. Physics the SI unit of force.
– ORIGIN named after Sir Isaac **NEWTON**.

new town • n. a town planned and built in an undeveloped or rural area.

New World • n. North and South America.

new year • n. the calendar year that has just begun or is about to begin, following 31 December.

New Year's Day • n. 1 January.

New Year's Eve • n. 31 December.

New York[1] E
a state in the north-eastern US; capital, Albany.
– DERIVATIVES **New Yorker** n.

New York[2] E
a major city and port in the south-east of New York State, on the Atlantic coast.
– DERIVATIVES **New Yorker** n.

New Zealand E
an island country in the South Pacific east of Australia; capital, Wellington.
– DERIVATIVES **New Zealander** n.

next • adj. **1** coming immediately after the present one in time, space, or order. **2** (of a day of the week) nearest (or the nearest but one) after the present. • adv. **1** immediately afterwards. **2** following in the specified order: *Joe was the next oldest after Martin.* • n. the next person or thing.
– PHRASES **next of kin** a person's closest living relative or relatives. **next to 1** beside. **2** following in order or importance. **3** almost. **the next world** (in some religious beliefs) the place where one goes after death.
– ORIGIN Old English.

next door • adv. & adj. in or to the next house or room.

nexus /nek-suhss/ • n. (pl. **nexus** or **nexuses**) a connection or series of connections: *the nexus between industry and political power.*
– ORIGIN Latin, 'a binding together'.

NGO • abbrev. non-governmental organization.

NHS • abbrev. (in the UK) National Health Service.

NI • abbrev. **1** (in the UK) National Insurance. **2** Northern Ireland.

niacin /ny-uh-sin/ • n. = NICOTINIC ACID.

Niagara Falls E
the waterfalls on the Niagara River, consisting of two main parts separated by Goat Island: the Horseshoe Falls adjoining the Canadian bank, which fall 47 m (158 ft), and the American Falls adjoining the American bank, which fall 50 m (167 ft).

Niagara River E
a river of North America, flowing northwards from Lake Erie to Lake Ontario.

Niamey E
/nyah-**may**/ the capital of Niger.

nib • n. the pointed end part of a pen.
– ORIGIN prob. from Dutch *nib* or German *nibbe* 'beak, nose'.

nibble • v. (**nibbles**, **nibbling**, **nibbled**) **1** take small bites out of. **2** bite gently. **3** gradually reduce: *the fringes of the region have been nibbled away by development.* • n. **1** a small bite of food. **2** (**nibbles**) informal small savoury snacks.
– ORIGIN prob. German or Dutch.

nibs • n. (**his nibs**) informal a mock title used to

refer to a man who thinks he is important.
– ORIGIN unknown.

Nicam /ny-kam/ ● n. a digital system used in British television to provide video signals with high-quality stereo sound.
– ORIGIN from *near instantaneously companded* (i.e. compressed and expanded) *audio multiplex*.

Nicaragua E
/ni-kuh-**rag**-yuu-uh, ni-kuh-**rag**-wuh/ a country in Central America, with a coastline on both the Atlantic and the Pacific Ocean; capital, Managua.
– DERIVATIVES **Nicaraguan** adj. & n.

Nice E
/*rhymes with* piece/ a resort city in south-east France, on the Mediterranean.

nice ● adj. **1** pleasant; satisfactory. **2** good-natured; kind. **3** involving a very fine detail or difference; subtle: *a nice distinction*.
– DERIVATIVES **nicely** adv. **niceness** n.
– ORIGIN Latin *nescius* 'ignorant'.

nicety ● n. (pl. **niceties**) **1** a fine detail or difference. **2** accuracy.

niche /neesh, nich/ ● n. **1** a shallow recess in a wall, in which an ornament may be displayed. **2** (**one's niche**) a position or role to which one is suited: *he found his niche as a writer.* **3** a particular group of people seen as a potential market for a product: *targeting the urban-youth niche*.
– ORIGIN French.

Nicholas II E
(1868–1918), tsar of Russia 1894–1917. Forced to abdicate after the Russian Revolution in 1917, he was later shot along with his family.

Nicholas, St E
(4th century), Christian bishop, patron saint of children, sailors, Greece, and Russia. The cult of Santa Claus (a corruption of his name) comes from the Dutch custom of giving gifts to children on his feast day (6 December).

Nicholson, E
Jack (b.1937), American actor. His films include *One Flew Over the Cuckoo's Nest*, *Terms of Endearment*, and *The Shining*.

nick ● n. **1** a small cut. **2** (**the nick**) Brit. informal prison or a police station. **3** Brit. informal condition: *the car's in good nick.* ● v. **1** make a nick or nicks in. **2** Brit. informal steal. **3** Brit. informal arrest.
– PHRASES **in the nick of time** only just in time.
– ORIGIN unknown.

nickel ● n. **1** a silvery-white metallic element used in alloys. **2** N. Amer. informal a five-cent coin.
– ORIGIN German *Kupfernickel*, the copper-coloured ore from which nickel was first obtained.

nicker ● n. (pl. **nicker**) Brit. informal a pound sterling.
– ORIGIN unknown.

Nicklaus E
/**nik**-lowss, **nik**-luhss/, Jack William (b.1940), American golfer, who has won over eighty tournaments.

nickname ● n. a familiar or amusing name for a person or thing. ● v. (**nicknames, nicknaming, nicknamed**) give a nickname to.
– ORIGIN from former *eke-name* 'additional name'.

Nicobar Islands E
see **ANDAMAN AND NICOBAR ISLANDS**.

Nicosia E
/ni-kuh-see-uh/ the capital of Cyprus. Since 1974 it has been divided into Greek and Turkish sectors.

nicotine ● n. a poisonous oily liquid found in tobacco.
– ORIGIN named after Jaques *Nicot*, a 16th-century diplomat who introduced tobacco to France.

nicotinic acid ● n. a vitamin of the B complex which occurs in foods such as milk and meat.

niece ● n. a daughter of one's brother or sister, or of one's brother-in-law or sister-in-law.
– ORIGIN Old French.

Nielsen E
/**neel**-s'n/, Carl August (1865–1931), Danish composer. He is best known for his six symphonies.

Niemeyer E
/**nee**-my-er/, Oscar (b.1907), Brazilian modernist architect, who designed the main public buildings of Brasilia.

Nietzsche E
/**nee**-chuh/, Friedrich Wilhelm (1844–1900), German philosopher. He rejected Christianity's compassion for the weak, and formulated the idea of the *Übermensch* (superman), who can rise above the restrictions of ordinary morality.
– DERIVATIVES **Nietzschean** adj. & n.

niff ● n. Brit. informal an unpleasant smell.
– ORIGIN perh. from **SNIFF**.

nifty ● adj. (**niftier, niftiest**) informal particularly good, fast, or useful.
– ORIGIN unknown.

Niger[1] E
/**ny**-jer/ a river of NW Africa, which rises on the NE border of Sierra Leone and flows through Mali, Niger, and Nigeria before reaching the Gulf of Guinea.

Niger[2] E
/**ny**-jer/ a landlocked country in West Africa, on the southern edge of the Sahara; capital, Niamey.

Nigeria E
/ny-**jeer**-i-uh/ a country on the coast of West Africa; capital, Abuja.
– DERIVATIVES **Nigerian** adj. & n.

niggardly ● adj. not generous; mean.
– ORIGIN Scandinavian.

nigger ● n. offens. a black person.
– ORIGIN Spanish *negro* 'black'.

USAGE nigger
The word **nigger** is very offensive, and should not be used; say **black** instead.

niggle ● v. (**niggles, niggling, niggled**) **1** worry or annoy slightly. **2** criticize in a petty way. ● n. a minor worry or criticism.

– DERIVATIVES **niggly** adj.
– ORIGIN prob. Scandinavian.

nigh • adv., prep., & adj. archaic near.
– ORIGIN Old English.

night • n. **1** the time from sunset to sunrise. **2** an evening until bedtime: *a great night out.*
– ORIGIN Old English.

nightcap • n. **1** hist. a cap worn in bed. **2** a hot or alcoholic drink taken at bedtime.

nightclub • n. a club that is open at night, usually having a bar and disco.

nightdress (also **nightgown**) • n. a light, loose garment worn by a woman or girl in bed.

nightfall • n. dusk.

nightie • n. informal a nightdress.

Nightingale, E
Florence (1820–1910), English nurse and medical reformer. She greatly improved sanitation and medical procedures at the army hospital at Scutari during the Crimean War.

nightingale • n. a small brownish thrush with a tuneful song, often heard at night.
– ORIGIN Old English.

nightlife • n. social activities or entertainment available at night.

night light • n. a lamp or candle providing a dim light during the night.

nightly • adj. & adv. happening every night.

nightmare • n. **1** a frightening or unpleasant dream. **2** a very unpleasant experience.
– DERIVATIVES **nightmarish** adj.
– ORIGIN Old English, 'male demon believed to have sexual intercourse with sleeping women'.

night owl • n. informal a person who enjoys staying up late at night.

night school • n. instruction provided in the evening for people who work during the day.

nightshirt • n. a long shirt worn in bed.

nightspot • n. informal a nightclub.

nightwatchman • n. a person who guards a building at night.

nihilism /ny-hi-li-z'm/ • n. the belief that nothing has any value, especially religious and moral principles.
– DERIVATIVES **nihilist** n. **nihilistic** adj.
– ORIGIN Latin *nihil* 'nothing'.

Nijinsky E
/ni-**jin**-ski/, Vaslav (Fomich) (1890–1950), Russian ballet dancer and choreographer. He was a leading dancer with Diaghilev's company, the Ballets Russes.

Nike E
/**ny**-ki/ the Greek goddess of victory.

Nikkei index E
/nik-**kay**/ a figure indicating the relative price of representative shares on the Tokyo Stock Exchange.

nil • n. nothing; zero.
– ORIGIN Latin *nihil.*

Nile E
a river in eastern Africa, the longest river in the world, which rises near Lake Victoria and flows 6,695 km (4,160 miles) generally northwards through Uganda, Sudan, and Egypt to reach the Mediterranean.

Nilsson E
/**nil**-suhn/, (Märta) Birgit (b.1918), Swedish operatic soprano.

nimble • adj. (**nimbler**, **nimblest**) quick and agile in movement or thought.
– DERIVATIVES **nimbly** adv.
– ORIGIN Old English.

nimbus /**nim**-buhss/ • n. (pl. **nimbi** /**nim**-by/ or **nimbuses**) **1** a large grey rain cloud. **2** a luminous cloud or a halo surrounding a supernatural being or saint.
– ORIGIN Latin.

Nimby /**nim**-bi/ • n. (pl. **Nimbys**) informal a person who objects to the siting of unpleasant developments in their neighbourhood.
– ORIGIN from *not in my back yard.*

nincompoop /**ning**-kuhm-poop/ • n. a stupid person.
– ORIGIN uncertain.

nine • cardinal number one less than ten; 9. (Roman numeral: **ix** or **IX**.)
– PHRASES (**up**) **to the nines** to a great or elaborate extent: *the women were dressed to the nines.*
– ORIGIN Old English.

ninepins • n. the traditional form of the game of skittles, using nine pins.

nineteen • cardinal number one more than eighteen; 19. (Roman numeral: **xix** or **XIX**.)
– DERIVATIVES **nineteenth** ordinal number.

ninety • cardinal number (pl. **nineties**) ten less than one hundred; 90. (Roman numeral: **xc** or **XC**.)
– DERIVATIVES **ninetieth** ordinal number.

Nineveh E
/**nin**-i-vuh/ an ancient city on the River Tigris, the capital of the ancient Assyrian empire.

ninny • n. (pl. **ninnies**) informal a foolish and weak person.
– ORIGIN perh. from **INNOCENT**.

ninth • ordinal number **1** that is number nine in a sequence; 9th. **2** (**a ninth**/**one ninth**) each of nine equal parts into which something is divided. **3** a musical interval spanning nine consecutive notes in a scale.

niobium /ny-**oh**-bi-uhm/ • n. a silver-grey metallic element.
– ORIGIN from *Niobe*, daughter of Tantalus in Greek mythology.

Nip • n. informal, offens. a Japanese person.
– ORIGIN Japanese *Nippon* 'Japan'.

nip[1] • v. (**nips**, **nipping**, **nipped**) **1** pinch, squeeze, or bite sharply. **2** Brit. informal go quickly. • n. **1** an act of nipping. **2** a sharp feeling of coldness.
– PHRASES **nip and tuck** neck and neck. **nip in the bud** stop at an early stage.
– ORIGIN prob. German or Dutch.

nip[2] • n. a small quantity or sip of spirits.
– ORIGIN prob. from former *nipperkin* 'small measure'.

nipper • n. informal a child.

nipple • n. **1** a small projection in the centre of each breast, containing (in females) the outlets of the milk-producing organs. **2** a small projection on a machine from which oil or other fluid is dispensed.
– ORIGIN perh. from Scots and northern English *neb* 'nose, beak'.

nippy • adj. (**nippier**, **nippiest**) informal **1** quick;

nimble. **2** chilly.

Niro, E
Robert De, see **De Niro**.

nirvana /neer-vah-nuh/ • **n.** (in Buddhism) a state of perfect happiness in which there is no suffering or desire, and no sense of self.
– ORIGIN Sanskrit.

Nissen hut /niss-uhn/ • **n.** Brit. a tunnel-shaped hut of corrugated iron with a cement floor.
– ORIGIN named after the British engineer Peter N. *Nissen* (1871–1930).

nit • **n.** informal **1** the egg of a human head louse. **2** Brit. a stupid person.
– ORIGIN Old English.

niterie /ny-tuh-ri/ • **n.** (pl. **niteries**) informal a nightclub.

nit-picking • **n.** informal petty criticism.

nitrate /ny-trayt/ • **n.** a salt or ester of nitric acid.

nitric acid • **n.** a very corrosive acid.

nitrify /ny-tri-fy/ • **v.** (**nitrifies, nitrifying, nitrified**) convert (ammonia or another nitrogen compound) into nitrites or nitrates.
– DERIVATIVES **nitrification** n.

nitrite /ny-tryt/ • **n.** a salt or ester of nitrous acid.

nitrogen /ny-truh-juhn/ • **n.** a gas forming about 78 per cent of the earth's atmosphere.
– ORIGIN Greek *nitron* 'nitre'.

nitrogenous /ny-troj-i-nuhss/ • **adj.** containing nitrogen in chemical combination.

nitroglycerine (also **nitroglycerin**) • **n.** an explosive liquid made from glycerol, used in dynamite.

nitrous /ny-truhss/ • **adj.** having to do with or containing nitrogen.

nitrous acid • **n.** a weak acid made by the action of acids on nitrites.

nitrous oxide • **n.** a gas used as an anaesthetic.

nitty-gritty • **n.** informal the most important details of a matter.
– ORIGIN unknown.

nitwit • **n.** informal a foolish person.

Niue E
/ni-oo-ay/ an island territory in the South Pacific to the east of Tonga; capital, Alofi. It is the world's largest coral island.

nix • **pron.** informal nothing.
– ORIGIN German.

Nixon, E
Richard (Milhous) (1913–94), American Republican statesman, 37th President of the US 1969–74. He was the first President to resign from office, owing to his involvement in the Watergate scandal.

Nizhni Novgorod E
/neezh-ni nov-guh-rod/ a river port in European Russia on the Volga. Former name (1932–91) **Gorky**[1].

NNE • **abbrev.** north-north-east.

NNW • **abbrev.** north-north-west.

No • **n.** var. of **Noh**.

no • **det.** **1** not any. **2** the opposite of: *she's no fool.* • **exclam.** used to refuse, deny, or disagree with something. • **adv.** not at all.
– PHRASES **no longer** not now as before. **no two ways about it** no possible doubt about something. **no way** informal not at all; certainly not. **or no** or not.
– ORIGIN Old English.

no. • **abbrev.** number.
– ORIGIN Latin *numero* 'by number'.

Noah E
/*rhymes with* mower/ (in the Bible) a Hebrew patriarch who made the ark which saved his family and specimens of every animal from the Flood.

nob • **n.** Brit. informal an upper-class person.
– ORIGIN unknown.

no-ball • **n.** a ball in cricket that is unlawfully bowled, counting as an extra run to the batting side.

nobble • **v.** (**nobbles, nobbling, nobbled**) Brit. informal **1** try to influence or thwart by underhand methods: *an attempt to nobble the jury.* **2** tamper with (a racehorse) to prevent it from winning a race. **3** stop (someone) so as to talk to them.
– ORIGIN prob. from dialect *knobble, knubble* 'knock'.

Nobel E
/noh-**bel**/, Alfred Bernhard (1833–96), Swedish chemist and engineer. He invented dynamite (1866), gelignite, and other high explosives, making a large fortune which enabled him to endow the Nobel prizes.

nobelium /noh-bee-li-uhm/ • **n.** a very unstable chemical element made by high-energy collisions.
– ORIGIN named after Alfred **Nobel**.

Nobel Prize • **n.** any of six international prizes awarded annually for outstanding work in various fields.
– ORIGIN named after Alfred **Nobel**.

nobility • **n.** **1** the quality of being noble. **2** the aristocracy.

noble • **adj.** (**nobler, noblest**) **1** belonging to the aristocracy. **2** having fine personal qualities or high moral principles. **3** magnificent; impressive. • **n.** a nobleman or noblewoman.
– DERIVATIVES **nobly** adv.
– ORIGIN Latin *nobilis* 'noted, high-born'.

noble gas • **n.** any of the gases helium, neon, argon, krypton, xenon, and radon, which seldom or never combine with other elements to form compounds.

nobleman (or **noblewoman**) • **n.** a man (or woman) who belongs to the aristocracy.

noblesse oblige /noh-bless oh-**bleezh**/ • **n.** noble or wealthy people should help those who are less fortunate.
– ORIGIN French.

nobody • **pron.** no person. • **n.** (pl. **nobodies**) an unimportant person.

no-claims bonus • **n.** Brit. a reduction in an insurance premium when no claim has been made during an agreed period.

nocturnal • **adj.** done or active at night.
– ORIGIN Latin *nocturnus* 'of the night'.

nocturne /nok-tern/ • **n.** a short piece of music of a dreamy, romantic nature.
– ORIGIN French.

nod • **v.** (**nods, nodding, nodded**) **1** lower and raise one's head briefly to show agreement or as a greeting or signal. **2** let one's head fall forward when drowsy or asleep. **3** (**nod off**) informal fall asleep. **4** make a mis-

take due to a brief lack of attention. ● n. an act of nodding.
– PHRASES **give someone/thing the nod** approve someone or something. **a nodding acquaintance** a slight acquaintance. **on the nod** Brit. informal by general agreement and without discussion.
– ORIGIN perh. German.

noddle ● n. informal a person's head.
– ORIGIN unknown.

node ● n. tech. **1** a point in a network at which lines cross or branch. **2** the part of a plant stem from which one or more leaves grows. **3** a small mass of distinct tissue in the body.
– DERIVATIVES **nodal** adj.
– ORIGIN Latin *nodus* 'knot'.

nodule /nod-yool/ ● n. a small swelling or lump.
– DERIVATIVES **nodular** adj.
– ORIGIN Latin *nodulus* 'little knot'.

Noel ● n. Christmas.
– ORIGIN French.

noggin ● n. informal **1** a person's head. **2** a small quantity of alcoholic drink.
– ORIGIN unknown.

no-go area ● n. Brit. an area which is dangerous or impossible to enter.

Noh /noh/ (also **No**) ● n. traditional Japanese drama with dance and song.
– ORIGIN Japanese.

no-hoper ● n. informal a person who is not expected to be successful.

noise ● n. **1** a sound or series of sounds that is loud or unpleasant. **2** disturbances that accompany and interfere with an electrical signal. ● v. **(noises, noising, noised)** dated make public.
– PHRASES **make —— noises** make remarks of the kind stated: *he made encouraging noises about the designs.*
– DERIVATIVES **noiseless** adj.
– ORIGIN Old French.

noisette /nwah-zet/ ● n. a small round piece of meat.
– ORIGIN French, 'little nut'.

noisome /noy-suhm/ ● adj. literary **1** having a very unpleasant smell. **2** very unpleasant.
– ORIGIN from **ANNOY**.

noisy ● adj. **(noisier, noisiest)** full of or making a lot of noise.
– DERIVATIVES **noisily** adv.

Nolan, E
Sir Sidney Robert (1917–93), Australian painter, known for his paintings of famous characters and events from Australian history.

nomad ● n. a member of a people that travels from place to place to find fresh pasture for its animals.
– ORIGIN Greek *nomas*.

nomadic ● adj. having the life of a nomad; wandering.

no-man's-land ● n. an area between two opposing armies that is not controlled by either.

nom de plume /nom duh **ploom**/ ● n. (pl. **noms de plume** /nom duh **ploom**/) a pen name.
– ORIGIN French.

nomenclature /noh-men-kluh-cher/ ● n. a system of names used in a particular subject: *chemical nomenclature.*
– ORIGIN Latin *nomenclatura*.

nominal ● adj. **1** in name but not in reality: *a purely nominal Arsenal fan.* **2** (of a sum of money) very small, but charged or paid as a sign that payment is necessary. **3** Grammar relating to or acting as a noun.
– DERIVATIVES **nominally** adv.
– ORIGIN Latin *nominalis*.

nominal value ● n. the face value of a coin, note, etc.

nominate ● v. **(nominates, nominating, nominated) 1** put forward as a candidate for a job, award, etc. **2** specify (a time, date, or place for an event) formally.
– DERIVATIVES **nomination** n.
– ORIGIN Latin *nominare* 'to name'.

nominative /nom-i-nuh-tiv/ ● adj. (of a grammatical case) expressing the subject of a verb.

nominee ● n. a person who is nominated for a job, award, etc.

non- ● prefix not: *non-specific.*
– ORIGIN Latin.

USAGE non
The prefixes **non-** and **un-** both mean 'not', but they tend to be used in slightly different ways. **Non-** is more neutral in meaning, while **un-** often suggests a particular bias or standpoint. For example, **unnatural** means that something is not natural in a bad way, whereas **non-natural** simply means 'not natural'.

nonagenarian /non-uh-juh-**nair**-i-uhn, noh-nuh-juh-**nair**-i-uhn/ ● n. a person between 90 and 99 years old.
– ORIGIN Latin *nonagenarius*.

nonagon /non-uh-guhn/ ● n. a plane figure with nine straight sides and angles.
– ORIGIN Latin *nonus* 'ninth'.

non-aligned ● adj. (of a country during the cold war) not allied to any of the major world powers.

nonce /nonss/ ● adj. (of a word or expression) coined for one occasion.
– PHRASES **for the nonce** for the present; temporarily.
– ORIGIN wrong division of former *then anes* 'the one (purpose)'.

nonchalant /non-shuh-luhnt/ ● adj. calm and relaxed.
– DERIVATIVES **nonchalance** n. **nonchalantly** adv.
– ORIGIN French, 'not being concerned'.

non-combatant ● n. a person who is not engaged in fighting during a war, especially a civilian, army chaplain, or army doctor.

non-commissioned ● adj. (of a military officer such as a corporal) appointed from the lower ranks rather than holding a commission.

non-committal ● adj. not showing what one thinks or which side one supports.

non compos mentis /non kom-poss **men**-tiss/ ● adj. not sane.
– ORIGIN Latin, 'not having control of one's mind'.

non-conductor ● n. a substance that does not conduct heat or electricity.

nonconformist ● n. **1** a person who does not follow accepted ideas or behaviour. **2 (Nonconformist)** a member of a Protestant

Church which does not follow the beliefs of the established Church of England.
– DERIVATIVES **nonconformity** n.

non-contributory • adj. (of a pension) funded by regular payments by the employer, not the employee.

nondescript /non-di-skript/ • adj. lacking special or interesting features: *a nondescript apartment building.*
– ORIGIN from **NON-** + former *descript* 'described'.

none • pron. **1** not any. **2** no one. • adv. (**none the**) not at all: *none the wiser.*
– ORIGIN Old English.

USAGE none
When you use **none of** with a plural noun or pronoun (such as *them*), or a singular noun that refers to a group of people or things, you can correctly use either a singular or plural verb: *none of them is coming tonight* or *none of them are coming tonight*; *none of the family was present* or *none of the family were present.* All these sentences are correct.

nonentity /non-en-ti-ti/ • n. (pl. **nonentities**) an unimportant person or thing.
– ORIGIN Latin *nonentitas* 'non-existence'.

nonetheless (also **none the less**) • adv. in spite of that; nevertheless.

non-event • n. an event which is not as interesting as it was expected to be.

non-existent • adj. not real or present.

non-ferrous • adj. (of metal) not iron or steel.

non-fiction • n. prose writing that deals with real people, facts, or events.

non-flammable • adj. not catching fire easily.

non-functional • adj. **1** not having a particular function. **2** not in working order.

non-intervention • n. the policy of not becoming involved in the affairs of other countries.

non-invasive • adj. (of medical procedures) not involving the introduction of instruments into the body.

non-member • n. a person who is not a member of a particular organization.

no-no • n. (pl. **no-nos**) informal a thing that is not possible or acceptable.

no-nonsense • adj. simple and straightforward; sensible.

nonpareil /non-puh-rayl/ • n. a person or thing having no match or equal.
– ORIGIN French.

nonplussed /non-plusst/ • adj. surprised and confused as to how to react.
– ORIGIN from Latin *non plus* 'not more'.

non-profit • adj. not intended to make a profit.

non-proliferation • n. the prevention of an increase in the number of nuclear weapons that are produced.

non-resident • adj. not living in a particular country or a place of work. • n. a person not living in a particular place.

nonsense • n. **1** words that make no sense. **2** foolish ideas or behaviour.

nonsensical • adj. ridiculous or foolish.

non sequitur /non sek-wi-ter/ • n. a conclusion that does not logically follow from the previous statement.
– ORIGIN Latin, 'it does not follow'.

non-specific • adj. not detailed or exact.

non-standard • adj. **1** not average or usual. **2** (of language) not of the form accepted as standard.

non-starter • n. informal something that has no chance of succeeding.

non-stick • adj. (of a pan or surface) covered with a substance that prevents food sticking to it during cooking.

non-stop • adj. **1** continuing without stopping. **2** having no stops on the way to a destination. • adv. without stopping.

non-verbal • adj. not using words or speech: *non-verbal communication.*

non-white • adj. (of a person) not white or not of European origin.

noodle • n. informal a silly person.
– ORIGIN unknown.

noodles • pl. n. long, thin strips of pasta.
– ORIGIN German *Nudel.*

nook • n. a corner or place that is sheltered or hidden from other people.
– PHRASES **every nook and cranny** every part of something.
– ORIGIN unknown.

nooky (also **nookie**) • n. informal sexual activity or intercourse.
– ORIGIN perh. from **NOOK**.

noon • n. twelve o'clock in the day; midday.
– ORIGIN from Latin *nona hora* 'ninth hour' (from sunrise).

noonday • n. the middle of the day.

no one • pron. no person.

noose • n. a loop with a knot which tightens as the rope or wire is pulled, used to hang people or trap animals.
– ORIGIN prob. from Old French *nous.*

nor • conj. & adv. and not; and not either.
– ORIGIN Old English.

nor' • abbrev. north: *nor'west.*

Nordic • adj. **1** relating to Scandinavia, Finland, and Iceland. **2** referring to a tall, blonde type of person typical of northern Europe.
– ORIGIN French *nordique.*

Norfolk E
/nor-fuhk/ a county on the east coast of England; county town, Norwich.

Norfolk Island E
an island in the South Pacific, an external territory of Australia.

Noriega E
/no-ri-ay-guh/, Manuel (Antonio Morena) (b.1940), Panamanian statesman and general, head of state 1983–9. Charged with drug trafficking by the US, he eventually surrendered to US troops sent into Panama and was convicted in 1992.

norm • n. **1** (**the norm**) the usual or standard thing: *strikes were the norm.* **2** a standard that is required or acceptable.
– ORIGIN Latin *norma* 'rule'.

normal • adj. **1** usual, typical, or expected. **2** tech. (of a line) intersecting a line or surface at right angles. • n. the normal state or condition: *her temperature was above normal.*
– DERIVATIVES **normality** (N. Amer. also **normalcy**) n. **normally** adv.

normalize (also **normalise**) ● v. (**normalizes, normalizing, normalized**) make or become normal.
– DERIVATIVES **normalization** (also **normalisation**) n.

Norman[1] ● n. a member of a people of Normandy in northern France who conquered England in 1066. ● adj. **1** relating to the Normans. **2** having to do with the style of Romanesque architecture used in Britain under the Normans.
– ORIGIN Old French *Normant*.

Norman[2], E
Greg (b.1955; full name *Gregory John Norman*), Australian golfer. He has won the British Open twice and the Australian Open five times.

Norman[3], E
Jessye (b.1945), American operatic soprano.

Norman Conquest E
the conquest of England by William of Normandy (William the Conqueror) after the Battle of Hastings in 1066.

Normandy E
a former province of NW France, on the English Channel, now divided into Lower Normandy and Upper Normandy; chief town, Rouen.

normative ● adj. formal relating to or setting a standard or norm.

Norse ● n. an ancient or medieval form of Norwegian or a related Scandinavian language. ● adj. relating to ancient or medieval Norway or Scandinavia.
– ORIGIN Dutch *noordsch*.

North, E
Frederick, Lord (1732–92), British Tory statesman, Prime Minister 1770–82. He was regarded as responsible for the loss of the American colonies.

north ● n. **1** the direction in which a compass needle normally points, towards the horizon on the left-hand side of a person facing east. **2** the northern part of a place. ● adj. **1** lying towards or facing the north. **2** (of a wind) blowing from the north. ● adv. to or towards the north.
– DERIVATIVES **northbound** adj. & adv.
– ORIGIN Old English.

North America E
a continent comprising the northern half of the American land mass and containing Canada, the United States, Mexico, and the countries of Central America.
– DERIVATIVES **North American** adj. & n.

Northamptonshire E
a county of central England; county town, Northampton.

Northants ● abbrev. Northamptonshire.

North Atlantic Drift E
a continuation of the Gulf Stream across the Atlantic Ocean and along the coast of NW Europe, where it has a warming effect on the climate.

North Atlantic Treaty Organization E
an association of European and North American states, formed in 1949 for the defence of Europe and the North Atlantic to counter Soviet power in Eastern Europe.

North Carolina E
a state of the east central US, on the Atlantic coast; capital, Raleigh.
– DERIVATIVES **North Carolinan** n. & adj.

Northcliffe, E
Alfred Charles William Harmsworth, 1st Viscount (1865–1922), British newspaper proprietor. His newspaper empire included *The Times*, the *Daily Mail*, and the *Daily Mirror*.

North Dakota E
a state in the north central US; capital, Bismarck.
– DERIVATIVES **North Dakotan** n. & adj.

north-east ● n. the direction or region halfway between north and east. ● adj. **1** lying towards or facing the north-east. **2** (of a wind) blowing from the north-east. ● adv. to or towards the north-east.
– DERIVATIVES **north-eastern** adj.

north-easterly ● adj. & adv. in a north-eastward position or direction.

North-East Passage E
a passage for ships along the northern coast of Europe and Asia, from the Atlantic to the Pacific via the Arctic Ocean. It was first navigated in 1878–9 by the Swedish explorer Baron Nordenskjöld (1832–1901).

north-eastward ● adv. (also **north-eastwards**) towards the north-east. ● adj. in, towards, or facing the north-east.

northerly ● adj. & adv. **1** towards or facing the north. **2** (of a wind) blowing from the north.

northern ● adj. **1** situated in or facing the north. **2** coming from or characteristic of the north.

Northern Cape E
a province of western South Africa; capital, Kimberley.

northerner ● n. a person from the north.

Northern Ireland E
a province of the United Kingdom occupying the NE part of Ireland; capital, Belfast.

Northern Lights ● pl. n. the aurora borealis.

Northern Province E
a province of northern South Africa; capital, Pietersburg.

Northern Rhodesia E
former name for **ZAMBIA**.

Northern Territory E
a state of north central Australia; capital, Darwin.

North Island E
the northernmost of the two main islands of New Zealand.

n

North Korea E
a country in the Far East, occupying the northern part of the peninsula of Korea; capital, Pyongyang. Official name **Democratic People's Republic of Korea**.
– DERIVATIVES **North Korean** adj. & n.

north-north-east • n. the direction halfway between north and north-east.

north-north-west • n. the direction halfway between north and north-west.

North Sea E
an arm of the Atlantic Ocean lying between the mainland of Europe and the coast of Britain.

North Star • n. the Pole Star.

North Uist E
see **Uist**.

Northumb. • abbrev. Northumberland.

Northumberland E
a county in NE England; county town, Morpeth.

Northumbria E
an area of NE England comprising Northumberland, Durham, and Tyne and Wear.
– DERIVATIVES **Northumbrian** adj. & n.

northward • adj. in a northerly direction. • adv. (also **northwards**) towards the north.

north-west • n. the direction or region halfway between north and west. • adj. **1** lying towards or facing the north-west. **2** (of a wind) blowing from the north-west. • adv. to or towards the north-west.
– DERIVATIVES **north-western** adj.

n

north-westerly • adj. & adv. in a northwestward position or direction.

North-West Frontier Province E
a province of NW Pakistan; capital, Peshawar.

North-West Passage E
a sea passage along the northern coast of the American continent, through the Canadian Arctic from the Atlantic to the Pacific. It was first navigated in 1903-6 by Roald Amundsen.

North-West Province E
a province of northern South Africa; capital, Mmabatho.

Northwest Territories E
a territory of northern Canada; capital, Yellowknife.

north-westward • adv. (also **north-westwards**) towards the north-west. • adj. in, towards, or facing the north-west.

North Yorkshire E
a county in NE England; administrative centre, Northallerton.

Norway E
a European country on the northern and western coastline of Scandinavia; capital, Oslo.

Norwegian /nor-wee-juhn/ • n. **1** a person from Norway. **2** the language spoken in Norway. • adj. relating to Norway.
– ORIGIN Latin *Norvegia* 'Norway'.

Norwich E
/no-rij, no-rich/ a city in eastern England, the county town of Norfolk.

nose • n. **1** the part of the face containing the nostrils and used in breathing and smelling. **2** the front end of an aircraft, car, or other vehicle. **3** the sense of smell. **4** a talent for finding something: *he had a nose for an opportunity.* **5** the characteristic smell of a wine. • v. (**noses**, **nosing**, **nosed**) **1** (of an animal) thrust its nose against or into something. **2** look around or pry into something. **3** make one's way slowly forward.
– PHRASES **cut off one's nose to spite one's face** do something which is supposed to harm someone else but which also harms oneself. **keep one's nose clean** informal stay out of trouble. **put someone's nose out of joint** informal offend someone.
– ORIGIN Old English.

nosebag • n. a bag containing fodder, hung from a horse's head.

nosebleed • n. an instance of bleeding from the nose.

nosedive • n. **1** a steep downward plunge by an aircraft. **2** a sudden marked decline: *his fortunes took a nosedive.* • v. (**nosedives**, **nosediving**, **nosedived**) make a nosedive.

nosegay • n. a small bunch of flowers.
– ORIGIN from **gay** in the former sense 'ornament'.

nosey • adj. var. of **nosy**.

nosh informal • n. food. • v. eat enthusiastically or greedily.
– ORIGIN Yiddish.

no-show • n. a person who has made a reservation or appointment but neither keeps nor cancels it.

nosh-up • n. Brit. informal a large meal.

nostalgia • n. longing for the happy times of the past.
– DERIVATIVES **nostalgic** adj.
– ORIGIN from Greek *nostos* 'return home' + *algos* 'pain'.

Nostradamus E
/noss-truh-dah-muhss/ (1503–66; Latinized name of *Michel de Nostredame*), French astrologer and physician, who made cryptic predictions about world events.

nostril • n. either of the two external openings of the nose through which air passes to the lungs.
– ORIGIN Old English, 'nose hole'.

nostrum • n. **1** a medicine that is prepared by an unqualified person and is not effective. **2** a favourite method for improving something: *right-wing nostrums such as cutting public spending.*
– ORIGIN Latin, 'something of our own making'.

nosy (also **nosey**) • adj. (**nosier**, **nosiest**) informal too inquisitive about other people's business.

nosy parker • n. a very inquisitive person.

not • adv. **1** used to form or express a negative: *she would not leave.* **2** less than: *not ten feet away.*
– ORIGIN from **nought**.

notable • adj. worthy of attention or notice. • n. a famous or important person.

notably • adv. **1** in particular. **2** in a notable

way.

notary (in full **notary public**) • n. (pl. **notaries**) a lawyer who is officially authorized to draw up and witness the signing of contracts and other documents.
– ORIGIN Latin *notarius* 'secretary'.

notation • n. a system of written symbols used to represent numbers, amounts, or elements in a subject such as music or mathematics.

notch • n. **1** a V-shaped cut or indentation on an edge or surface. **2** a point or level on a scale: *her opinion of him dropped a few notches.* • v. **1** make notches in. **2** (**notch up**) score or achieve.
– ORIGIN Old French *osche.*

note • n. **1** a brief written record, used as an aid to memory. **2** a short written message or document. **3** Brit. a banknote. **4** a single sound of a particular pitch and length made by a musical instrument or voice, or a symbol representing this. **5** a particular quality: *there was a note of scorn in his voice.* • v. (**notes, noting, noted**) **1** pay attention to. **2** record in writing.
– PHRASES **of note** important. **take note** pay attention.
– ORIGIN Latin *nota* 'a mark'.

notebook • n. **1** a small book for writing notes in. **2** a portable computer smaller than a laptop.

noted • adj. well known.

notepad • n. **1** a pad of paper for writing notes on. **2** a pocket-sized personal computer.

notepaper • n. paper for writing letters on.

noteworthy • adj. interesting or important.

nothing • pron. **1** not anything. **2** something that is not important or interesting. **3** nought. • adv. not at all.
– PHRASES **for nothing 1** without payment or charge. **2** to no purpose. **nothing but** only. **sweet nothings** words of affection between lovers.
– ORIGIN Old English.

nothingness • n. the state of not existing or a state where nothing exists.

notice • n. **1** the fact of being aware of or paying attention to something: *his silence did not escape my notice.* **2** information or warning that something is going to happen: *interest rates may change without notice.* **3** a formal statement that one is going to leave a job or end an agreement. **4** a sheet or placard put on display to give information. **5** a small announcement or advertisement published in a newspaper. **6** a short published review of a new film, play, or book. • v. (**notices, noticing, noticed**) become aware of.
– PHRASES **take notice** (**of**) pay attention (to).
– ORIGIN Latin *notitia.*

noticeable • adj. easily seen or noticed.
– DERIVATIVES **noticeably** adv.

notifiable • adj. (of an infectious disease) that must be reported to the health authorities.

notify • v. (**notifies, notifying, notified**) inform (someone) formally about something.
– DERIVATIVES **notification** n.
– ORIGIN Latin *notificare.*

notion • n. **1** an idea or belief. **2** an understanding: *I had no notion of what she meant.*
– ORIGIN Latin.

notional • adj. based on a guess or theory; hypothetical.
– DERIVATIVES **notionally** adv.

notoriety /noh-tuh-ry-i-ti/ • n. the state of being famous for something bad.

notorious • adj. famous for something bad.
– DERIVATIVES **notoriously** adv.
– ORIGIN Latin *notorius* 'generally known'.

Nottinghamshire E
a county in central England; county town, Nottingham.

Notting Hill E
a district of NW central London, the scene of an annual street carnival.

Notts. • abbrev. Nottinghamshire.

notwithstanding • prep. in spite of. • adv. nevertheless.

Nouakchott E
/nwak-**shot**/ the capital of Mauritania.

nougat /noo-gah, nug-uht/ • n. a sweet made from sugar or honey, nuts, and egg white.
– ORIGIN French.

nought • n. the figure 0. • pron. nothing.

noun • n. Grammar a word (other than a pronoun) that refers to a person, place, or thing.
– ORIGIN Latin *nomen* 'name'.

noun phrase • n. Grammar a word or group of words in a sentence that behave in the same way as a noun, that is as a subject, object, or object of a preposition.

nourish • v. **1** provide with the food or other substances necessary for growth and health. **2** keep (a feeling or belief) in one's mind for a long time.
– ORIGIN Latin *nutrire.*

nourishment • n. the food or other substances necessary for growth, health, and good condition.

nous /nowss/ • n. Brit. informal common sense.
– ORIGIN Greek, 'mind'.

nouveau riche /noo-voh **reesh**/ • n. people who have recently become rich and who like to display their wealth in an obvious or tasteless way.
– ORIGIN French, 'new rich'.

nouvelle cuisine /noo-vel kwi-**zeen**/ • n. a modern style of cookery that emphasizes fresh ingredients and the presentation of the dishes.
– ORIGIN French, 'new cookery'.

Nov. • abbrev. November.

nova /noh-vuh/ • n. (pl. **novae** /noh-vee/ or **novas**) a star that suddenly becomes very bright for a short period.
– ORIGIN Latin, 'new'.

Nova Scotia E
/noh-vuh **skoh**-shuh/ a province of eastern Canada; capital, Halifax.
– DERIVATIVES **Nova Scotian** adj. & n.

novel¹ • n. a prose story of book length about imaginary people and events.
– ORIGIN from Italian *novella storia* 'new story'.

novel² • adj. new in an interesting or unusual way.
– ORIGIN Latin *novus* 'new'.

novelette • n. esp. derog. a short novel.

novelist • n. a person who writes novels.

novella /nuh-vel-luh/ • n. a short novel or

long short story.
– ORIGIN Italian.

Novello E
/nuh-vel-loh/, Ivor (1893–1951; born *David Ivor Davies*), Welsh composer and songwriter, known for his musicals and for the song 'Keep the Home Fires Burning'.

novelty • n. (pl. **novelties**) **1** the quality of being new and unusual. **2** a new or unfamiliar thing: *in 1914 air travel was still a novelty.* **3** a small toy or ornament.

November • n. the eleventh month of the year.
– ORIGIN from Latin *novem* 'nine' (November being originally the ninth month of the Roman year).

novena /noh-vee-nuh/ • n. (in the Roman Catholic Church) a set of special prayers or services on nine successive days.
– ORIGIN Latin.

Novgorod E
/nov-guh-rod/ a city in NW Russia. The country's oldest city, it was settled in 862.

novice • n. **1** a person who is new to and lacks experience in a job or situation. **2** a person who has entered a religious order but has not yet taken their vows.
– ORIGIN Latin *novicius*.

novitiate /noh-vi-shi-uht/ • n. the period or state of being a novice in a religious order.

now • adv. **1** at the present time. **2** at or from this precise moment; immediately. • conj. as a result of the fact.
– PHRASES **now and again** (or **then**) from time to time.
– ORIGIN Old English.

nowadays • adv. at the present time, in contrast with the past.

nowhere • adv. not anywhere. • pron. no place.

nowt • pron. & adv. N. Engl. nothing.

noxious /nok-shuhss/ • adj. harmful or very unpleasant.
– ORIGIN Latin *noxius*.

nozzle • n. a spout used to control a stream of liquid or gas.
– ORIGIN from **NOSE**.

NSW • abbrev. New South Wales.

NT • abbrev. **1** National Trust. **2** New Testament.

-n't • contr. not, used with auxiliary verbs (e.g. *can't*).

nth /enth/ • adj. referring to the last or latest item in a long series.
– PHRASES **to the nth degree** to the utmost.

nuance /nyoo-ahnss/ • n. a very slight difference in meaning, expression, sound, etc.: *she was attuned to the nuances in his voice.*
– ORIGIN French.

nub • n. **1** (**the nub**) the central point of a matter. **2** a small lump.
– DERIVATIVES **nubby** adj.
– ORIGIN prob. from German *knubbe* 'knob'.

Nubia E
/nyoo-bi-uh/ an ancient region of southern Egypt and northern Sudan.

nubile /nyoo-byl/ • adj. (of a girl or young woman) sexually mature and attractive.
– ORIGIN Latin *nubilis* 'fit for marriage'.

nuclear • adj. **1** relating to the nucleus of an atom or cell. **2** using energy released in the fission or fusion of atomic nuclei. **3** possessing or involving nuclear weapons.

nuclear family • n. a couple and their children, as a basic unit of society.

nuclear fuel • n. a substance that will undergo nuclear fission and can be used as a source of nuclear energy.

nuclear physics • n. the science of atomic nuclei and the way they interact.

nuclear power • n. power generated by a nuclear reactor.

nuclear waste • n. radioactive waste material from the use or reprocessing of nuclear fuel.

nucleate /nyoo-kli-ayt/ • v. (**nucleates, nucleating, nucleated**) form a nucleus.

nuclei pl. of **NUCLEUS**.

nucleic acid /nyoo-klee-ik, nyoo-**klay**-ik/ • n. either of two complex organic substances, DNA and RNA, present in all living cells.

nucleus /nyoo-kli-uhss/ • n. (pl. **nuclei** /**nyoo**-kli-I/) **1** the central and most important part of an object or group. **2** Physics the positively charged central core of an atom. **3** Biol. a structure present in most cells, containing the genetic material.
– ORIGIN Latin, 'kernel'.

nude • adj. wearing no clothes. • n. a naked human figure as a subject in art.
– DERIVATIVES **nudity** n.
– ORIGIN Latin *nudus* 'plain, explicit'.

nudge • v. (**nudges, nudging, nudged**) **1** prod with one's elbow to attract attention. **2** touch or push gently. • n. a light prod or push.
– ORIGIN unknown.

nudist • n. a person who goes naked wherever possible.
– DERIVATIVES **nudism** n.

Nuffield E
/nuf-feeld/, William Richard Morris, 1st Viscount (1877–1963), British motor manufacturer and philanthropist, who opened the first Morris automobile factory in Oxford in 1912. He later founded the Nuffield Foundation for research.

nugatory /nyoo-guh-tuh-ri, **noo**-guh-tuh-ri/ • adj. having no purpose or value.
– ORIGIN Latin *nugatorius*.

nugget • n. **1** a small lump of gold or other precious metal found in the earth. **2** a small but valuable fact.
– ORIGIN unknown.

nuisance • n. a person or thing causing annoyance or difficulty.
– ORIGIN Old French, 'hurt'.

nuke informal • n. a nuclear weapon. • v. (**nukes, nuking, nuked**) attack with nuclear weapons.

null • adj. tech. having the value zero.
– PHRASES **null and void** having no legal force; invalid.
– ORIGIN Latin *nullus* 'none'.

Nullarbor Plain E
/**nul**-luh-bor/ a vast arid plain in SW Australia. It has no surface water and very sparse vegetation.

nullify • v. (**nullifies, nullifying, nullified**)

1 make legally invalid. **2** cancel out the effect of.
– DERIVATIVES **nullification** n.

nullity ● n. (pl. **nullities**) **1** the state of being legally invalid. **2** a thing of no importance or worth.

numb ● adj. lacking the power to feel, think, or react. ● v. make numb.
– DERIVATIVES **numbly** adv. **numbness** n.
– ORIGIN Germanic, 'taken'.

number ● n. **1** a quantity or value expressed by a word or symbol. **2** a quantity or amount. **3** (**a number of**) several. **4** a single issue of a magazine. **5** a song, dance, or other musical item. **6** a grammatical classification of words depending on whether one or more people or things are being referred to. ● v. (**numbers, numbering, numbered**) **1** amount to. **2** give a number to (each in a series). **3** count. **4** include as a member of a group: *he numbered Grieg among his friends.*
– PHRASES **someone's days are numbered** someone will not survive for much longer. **someone's number is up** informal someone is finished or about to die.
– DERIVATIVES **numberless** adj.
– ORIGIN Latin *numerus*.

number cruncher ● n. informal **1** a computer for performing complicated calculations. **2** usu. derog. a statistician or other person dealing with numerical data.

number one ● n. informal oneself. ● adj. most important; top.

number plate ● n. Brit. a sign on the front and rear of a vehicle showing its registration number.

numbskull (also **numskull**) ● n. informal a stupid person.

numeral ● n. a symbol or word representing a number.

numerate /nyoo-muh-ruht/ ● adj. having a good basic knowledge of arithmetic.
– DERIVATIVES **numeracy** n.
– ORIGIN Latin *numerus* 'a number'.

numeration ● n. the action of numbering or calculating.

numerator ● n. Math. the number above the line in a fraction.

numerical ● adj. having to do with a number or numbers.
– DERIVATIVES **numerically** adv.

numerology ● n. the branch of knowledge concerned with the supposed magical power of numbers.
– DERIVATIVES **numerologist** n.

numerous ● adj. **1** many. **2** consisting of many members.

Numidia E
/nyoo-**mid**-i-uh/ an ancient kingdom in North Africa, corresponding roughly to present-day Algeria.

numinous /nyoo-mi-nuhss/ ● adj. having a religious or spiritual quality.
– ORIGIN Latin *numen* 'divine will'.

numismatic ● adj. having to do with coins or medals. ● n. (**numismatics**) the study or collection of coins, banknotes, and medals.
– DERIVATIVES **numismatist** n.
– ORIGIN Greek *nomisma* 'current coin'.

numskull ● n. var. of **NUMBSKULL**.

nun ● n. a woman belonging to a female religious community and living under vows of poverty, chastity, and obedience.
– ORIGIN Latin *nonna*.

Nunavut E
/**nun**-uh-voot/ a province of northern Canada, created in 1999 as an Inuit territory; capital, Iqaluit.

nuncio /nun-si-oh/ ● n. (pl. **nuncios**) (in the Roman Catholic Church) a diplomatic representative of the pope.
– ORIGIN Latin *nuntius* 'messenger'.

nunnery ● n. (pl. **nunneries**) a religious house of nuns.

nuptial /nup-sh'l/ ● adj. having to do with marriage or weddings. ● n. (**nuptials**) a wedding.
– ORIGIN Latin *nuptiae* 'wedding'.

Nuremberg E
/**nyoo**-ruhm-berg/ a city in southern Germany, scene of the Nuremberg war trials (1945–6), in which Nazi war criminals were tried by international military tribunal.

Nureyev E
/nuh-**ray**-eff, **nyoo**-ri-eff/, Rudolf (1939–93), Russian-born ballet dancer and choreographer. He defected to the West and joined the Royal Ballet in London, where he began his partnership with Margot Fonteyn.

nurse ● n. **1** a person trained to care for sick, injured, or infirm people. **2** dated a person employed to look after young children. ● v. (**nurses, nursing, nursed**) **1** give medical and other care to (a sick person). **2** treat or hold carefully. **3** cling to (a belief or feeling) for a long time. **4** feed (a baby) at the breast.
– ORIGIN Old French *nourice*.

nursemaid ● n. dated a woman or girl employed to look after a young child or children.

nursery ● n. (pl. **nurseries**) **1** a room in a house set apart for young children. **2** (also **day nursery**) a nursery school. **3** a place where young plants and trees are grown for sale or for planting elsewhere.

nurseryman ● n. a worker in or owner of a plant or tree nursery.

nursery nurse ● n. Brit. a person trained to look after young children and babies in a nursery or crèche.

nursery rhyme ● n. a simple traditional song or poem for children.

nursery school ● n. a school for young children between three and five.

nursery slopes ● pl. n. gentle ski slopes suitable for beginners.

nursing home ● n. a private home providing accommodation and health care for elderly people.

nurture ● v. (**nurtures, nurturing, nurtured**) **1** encourage the growth or development of (a child, plant, etc.). **2** have (a hope, belief, or ambition) for a long time. ● n. the action of nurturing.
– ORIGIN Old French *noureture* 'nourishment'.

nut ● n. **1** a fruit consisting of a hard shell around an edible kernel. **2** the kernel of such a fruit. **3** a small flat piece of metal or other material with a hole through the centre for screwing on to a bolt. **4** informal a crazy person. **5** informal a person's head. ● v. (**nuts, nutting,**

nutted) informal butt with one's head.
– PHRASES **do one's nut** Brit. informal be extremely angry or agitated. **nuts and bolts** informal the basic practical details.
– DERIVATIVES **nutty** adj.
– ORIGIN Old English.

nutcase • n. informal a mad or foolish person.

nutcrackers • pl. n. a device for cracking nuts.

nutmeg • n. a spice obtained from the seed of a tropical tree.
– ORIGIN from Old French *nois muguede* 'musky nut'.

nutrient /nyoo-tri-uhnt/ • n. a substance that is essential for life and growth.
– ORIGIN Latin, 'nourishing'.

nutriment • n. nourishment.

nutrition • n. **1** the process of taking in and absorbing nutrients. **2** the branch of science concerned with this process.
– DERIVATIVES **nutritional** adj. **nutritionist** n.
– ORIGIN Latin.

nutritious • adj. full of nutrients; nourishing.

nutritive • adj. **1** having to do with nutrition. **2** nutritious.

nuts • adj. informal mad.

nutshell • n. (in phr. **in a nutshell**) in the fewest possible words.

nutter • n. Brit. informal a mad person.

Nuuk E
/nook/ the capital of Greenland. Former name (until 1979) **GODTHÅB**.

nuzzle • v. (**nuzzles, nuzzling, nuzzled**) rub or push against gently with the nose.
– ORIGIN from **NOSE**.

NVQ • abbrev. (in the UK) National Vocational Qualification, a qualification in a vocational subject set at various levels.

NW • abbrev. north-west or north-western.

NY • abbrev. New York.

Nyasa, Lake E
/ny-ass-uh/ a lake in east central Africa. At about 580 km (360 miles) long, it is the third-largest lake in Africa. Also called **LAKE MALAWI**.

Nyasaland E
/ny-ass-uh-land/ former name for **MALAWI**.

NYC • abbrev. New York City.

Nyerere E
/nye-rair-i/, Julius Kambarage (1922–99), Tanzanian statesman, President of Tanganyika 1962–4 and of Tanzania 1964–85. He led Tanganyika to independence in 1961 and in 1964 negotiated a union with Zanzibar, creating the new state of Tanzania.

nylon • n. **1** a strong, lightweight, synthetic material which can be made into sheets, fabric, or moulded objects. **2** (**nylons**) nylon stockings or tights.
– ORIGIN an invented word.

nymph • n. **1** (in Greek and Roman mythology) a spirit of nature in the form of a beautiful young woman. **2** an immature form of an insect such as a dragonfly.
– ORIGIN Greek *numphē* 'nymph, bride'.

nymphet • n. an attractive and sexually mature young girl.

nympho • n. (pl. **nymphos**) informal a nymphomaniac.

nymphomania • n. uncontrollable sexual desire in a woman.
– DERIVATIVES **nymphomaniac** n.

NZ • abbrev. New Zealand.

O[1] (also **o**) • n. (pl. **Os** or **O's**) **1** the fifteenth letter of the alphabet. **2** (also **oh**) zero.

O[2] • symb. the chemical element oxygen.

O[3] • exclam. used when addressing someone: *give us peace, O Lord.*

oaf • n. a stupid, rude, or clumsy man.
– DERIVATIVES **oafish** adj.
– ORIGIN Old Norse, 'elf'.

Oahu E
/oh-ah-hoo/ the third largest of the Hawaiian islands; chief town, Honolulu.

oak • n. a large tree which produces acorns and a hard wood used for building and furniture.
– ORIGIN Old English.

oak apple • n. a growth which forms on oak trees, caused by wasp larvae.

oaken • adj. literary made of oak.

oakum • n. hist. loose fibre obtained by untwisting old rope, used to fill cracks in wooden ships.
– ORIGIN Old English, 'off-combings'.

OAP • abbrev. Brit. old-age pensioner.

oar • n. a pole with a flat blade, used for rowing or steering a boat.
– PHRASES **put one's oar in** informal give an opinion without being asked.
– ORIGIN Old English.

oarsman (or **oarswoman**) • n. a rower.

oasis • n. (pl. **oases**) **1** a fertile place in a desert where water rises to ground level. **2** a pleasant area or period in the midst of a difficult situation.
– ORIGIN Greek.

oast house • n. a building containing a kiln for drying hops.
– ORIGIN Old English.

oat • n. **1** a cereal plant grown in cool climates. **2** (**oats**) the edible grain of this plant.
– PHRASES **get one's oats** Brit. informal have sex-

ual intercourse. **sow one's wild oats** have many sexual relationships while young.
– ORIGIN Old English.

oatcake • n. a savoury oatmeal biscuit.

oath • n. (pl. **oaths**) **1** a solemn promise to do something or that something is true. **2** a swear word.
– PHRASES **under** (or **on**) **oath** having sworn to tell the truth in a court of law.
– ORIGIN Old English.

oatmeal • n. meal made from ground oats, used in making porridge and oatcakes.

Ob E
/ob/ a river of Russia that rises in the Altai Mountains and flows generally north and west through Siberia for 5,410 km (3,481 miles) before entering the Gulf of Ob, an inlet of the Arctic Ocean.

ob- • prefix forming words meaning. **1** to, towards: *obverse.* **2** against: *obstruct.* **3** finality; completeness: *obsolete.*
– ORIGIN Latin.

Oban E
/oh-b'n/ a port and tourist resort on the west coast of Scotland, in Argyll and Bute.

obdurate /ob-dyuu ruht/ • adj. stubbornly refusing to change one's mind.
– DERIVATIVES **obduracy** n.
– ORIGIN Latin *obduratus* 'hardened'.

OBE • abbrev. Officer of the Order of the British Empire.

obedient • adj. willing to do what one is told.
– DERIVATIVES **obedience** n. **obediently** adv.
– ORIGIN Latin *oboedire* 'obey'.

obeisance /oh-bay-suhnss/ • n. **1** humble respect: *they paid obeisance to the Prince.* **2** a gesture expressing this, such as a bow.
– ORIGIN Old French *obeissance.*

obelisk • n. a four-sided stone pillar that tapers to a point, set up as a monument.
– ORIGIN Greek *obeliskos.*

Oberammergau E
/oh-ber-am-muh-gow/ a village in the Bavarian Alps of SW Germany, noted for its passion play, which is performed by the villagers every ten years.

obese • adj. very fat.
– DERIVATIVES **obesity** n.
ORIGIN Latin *obesus.*

obey • v. **1** do what is ordered by (a person, law, etc.). **2** behave in accordance with (a general principle or natural law).
– ORIGIN Latin *oboedire.*

obfuscate /ob-fuss-kayt/ • v. (**obfuscates**, **obfuscating**, **obfuscated**) make unclear or hard to understand.
– DERIVATIVES **obfuscation** n.
– ORIGIN Latin *obfuscare* 'darken'.

obituary /oh-bi-chuu-ri, oh-bi-tyuu-ri/ • n. (pl. **obituaries**) an announcement that someone has died, published in a newspaper in the form of a brief biography.
– ORIGIN Latin *obitus* 'death'.

object • n. /ob-jikt/ **1** a physical thing that can be seen and touched. **2** a person or thing to which an action or feeling is directed: *he was an object of ridicule among his staff.* **3** a purpose. **4** Grammar a noun or noun phrase acted on by a transitive verb or by a preposition. • v. /uhb-jekt/ express disapproval or opposition: *residents objected to the noise.*
– PHRASES **no object** not influencing or restricting choices: *money is no object.*
– DERIVATIVES **objector** n.
– ORIGIN Latin *objectum* 'thing presented to the mind'.

objectify • v. (**objectifies**, **objectifying**, **objectified**) **1** express (something abstract) in a physical form. **2** treat (someone) as an object rather than a person.
– DERIVATIVES **objectification** n.

objection • n. **1** an expression of disapproval or opposition. **2** the action of objecting: *a letter of objection.*

objectionable • adj. unpleasant or offensive.

objective • adj. **1** not influenced by personal feelings or opinions: *historians try to be objective.* **2** having actual existence outside the mind: *a matter of objective fact.* **3** Grammar relating to a case of nouns and pronouns used for the object of a transitive verb or a preposition. • n. a goal or aim.
– DERIVATIVES **objectively** adv. **objectivity** n.

object lesson • n. a clear practical example of a principle or ideal.

objet d'art /ob-*zhay* **dar**/ • n. (pl. **objets d'art** /ob-*zhay* **dar**/) a small decorative or artistic object.
– ORIGIN French, 'object of art'.

oblate /ob-layt/ • adj. Geom. (of a sphere) flattened at the poles.
– ORIGIN Latin *oblatus* 'carried inversely'.

oblation • n. a thing presented or offered to a god.
– ORIGIN Latin.

obligate • v. (**obligates**, **obligating**, **obligated**) (**be obligated**) be obliged to do something.
– ORIGIN Latin *obligare.*

obligation • n. **1** something one must do because of a law, agreement, promise, etc. **2** the state of being obliged to do something.
– PHRASES **under an obligation** owing gratitude to someone for something.

obligatory • adj. required by a law, rule, or custom; compulsory.

oblige • v. (**obliges**, **obliging**, **obliged**) **1** make (someone) do something by law, necessity, or because it is their duty: *he was obliged to do military service.* **2** perform a service or favour for. **3** (**be obliged**) be grateful.
– ORIGIN Latin *obligare.*

obliging • adj. helpful.
– DERIVATIVES **obligingly** adv.

oblique /uh-bleek/ • adj. **1** at an angle; slanting. **2** not done in a direct way: *an oblique attack on the President.* **3** Geom. (of a line, plane figure, or surface) inclined at other than a right angle.
– DERIVATIVES **obliquely** adv.
– ORIGIN Latin *obliquus.*

obliterate /uh-blit-uh-rayt/ • v. (**obliterates**, **obliterating**, **obliterated**) **1** destroy completely. **2** cover completely: *the clouds obliterated the moon.*
– DERIVATIVES **obliteration** n.
– ORIGIN Latin *obliterare* 'erase'.

oblivion • n. **1** the state of being unaware of what is happening around one. **2** the state of

being forgotten. **3** the state of being completely destroyed.
– ORIGIN Latin.

oblivious • adj. not aware of what is happening around one.

oblong • adj. rectangular in shape. • n. an oblong shape.
– ORIGIN Latin *oblongus* 'longish'.

obloquy /ob-luh-kwi/ • n. **1** strong public criticism. **2** disgrace brought about by strong public criticism.
– ORIGIN Latin *obloqui* 'speak against'.

obnoxious /uhb-nok-shuhss/ • adj. very unpleasant.
– ORIGIN Latin *obnoxius* 'exposed to harm'.

oboe /oh-boh/ • n. a woodwind instrument of treble pitch, played with a double reed.
– DERIVATIVES **oboist** n.
– ORIGIN Italian.

O'Brien[1], E
Edna (b.1932), Irish novelist and short-story writer, author of the novel *The Country Girls*.

O'Brien[2], E
Flann (1911–66; pen name of *Brian O'Nolan*), Irish novelist and journalist. His novels include *At Swim-Two-Birds*.

obscene • adj. **1** dealing with sexual matters in an offensive or disgusting way. **2** unacceptable because excessive: *obscene pay rises*.
– DERIVATIVES **obscenely** adv.
– ORIGIN Latin *obscaenus* 'hateful'.

obscenity • n. (pl. **obscenities**) **1** the state of being obscene. **2** an obscene action or word.

obscurantism /ob-skyuu-rant-i-z'm/ • n. the practice of deliberately preventing something from becoming understood.
– DERIVATIVES **obscurantist** n. & adj.

obscure • adj. **1** not discovered or known about. **2** not well known. **3** hard to understand or see: *obscure references to Proust*. • v. (**obscures**, **obscuring**, **obscured**) hide or make unclear.
– DERIVATIVES **obscurely** adv.
– ORIGIN Latin *obscurus* 'dark'.

obscurity • n. (pl. **obscurities**) **1** the state of being unknown or hard to understand. **2** something that is hard to understand.

obsequies /ob-si-kwiz/ • pl. n. funeral rites.
– ORIGIN Latin *obsequiae*.

obsequious /uhb-see-kwi-uhss/ • adj. obedient or respectful to an excessive degree.
– DERIVATIVES **obsequiously** adv. **obsequiousness** n.
– ORIGIN Latin *obsequium* 'compliance'.

observance • n. **1** behaving in accordance with a law, rule, or ritual. **2** (**observances**) acts performed for religious or ceremonial reasons.

observant • adj. quick to notice things.

observation • n. **1** the action of closely observing someone or something. **2** the ability to notice important details. **3** a comment based on something one has heard or noticed.
– DERIVATIVES **observational** adj.

observatory • n. (pl. **observatories**) a building housing an astronomical telescope or other scientific equipment for the study of natural phenomena.

observe • v. (**observes**, **observing**, **observed**) **1** notice. **2** watch carefully. **3** make a remark. **4** obey (a law or rule). **5** celebrate or take part in (a festival or ritual).
– DERIVATIVES **observable** adj. **observer** n.
– ORIGIN Latin *observare*.

obsess • v. (**be obsessed**) be thinking about someone or something continually and disturbingly.
– ORIGIN Latin *obsidere* 'besiege'.

obsession • n. **1** the state of being obsessed. **2** an idea or thought that dominates someone's thoughts.
– DERIVATIVES **obsessional** adj.

obsessive • adj. thinking continually about someone or something.
– DERIVATIVES **obsessively** adv.

obsidian /uhb-sid-i-uhn/ • n. a dark glass-like rock, formed when lava solidifies rapidly.
– ORIGIN Latin *obsidianus*.

obsolescent /ob-suh-less-uhnt/ • adj. becoming obsolete.
– DERIVATIVES **obsolescence** n.
– ORIGIN Latin *obsolescere* 'fall into disuse'.

obsolete • adj. no longer produced or used; out of date.
– ORIGIN Latin *obsoletus* 'grown old'.

obstacle • n. a thing that blocks one's way or hinders progress.
– ORIGIN Latin *obstaculum*.

obstetrician /ob-stuh-tri-sh'n/ • n. a doctor qualified to practise in obstetrics.

obstetrics • n. the branch of medicine and surgery concerned with childbirth.
– DERIVATIVES **obstetric** adj.
– ORIGIN Latin *obstetrix* 'midwife'.

obstinate • adj. **1** stubbornly refusing to change one's mind. **2** hard to deal with: *an obstinate problem*.
– DERIVATIVES **obstinacy** n. **obstinately** adv.
– ORIGIN Latin *obstinatus*.

obstreperous /uhb-strep-uh-ruhss/ • adj. noisy and difficult to control.
– ORIGIN Latin *obstrepere* 'shout at'.

obstruct • v. **1** be in the way of; block. **2** prevent or hinder.
– ORIGIN Latin *obstruere*.

obstruction • n. **1** the action of obstructing or the state of being obstructed. **2** an obstacle or blockage.

obstructive • adj. deliberately causing difficulties or delays.

obtain • v. **1** come into possession of; get. **2** formal be established or usual: *among themselves, a set of conventions obtains*.
– DERIVATIVES **obtainable** adj.
– ORIGIN Latin *obtinere*.

obtrude • v. (**obtrudes**, **obtruding**, **obtruded**) become noticeable in an unwelcome way.
– ORIGIN Latin *obtrudere*.

obtrusive • adj. noticeable in an unwelcome way.

obtuse /uhb-tyooss/ • adj. **1** annoyingly slow to understand. **2** (of an angle) more than 90° and less than 180°. **3** blunt.
– ORIGIN Latin *obtusus*.

obverse • n. **1** the side of a coin or medal bearing the head or main design. **2** the opposite of something.
– ORIGIN Latin *obversus* 'turned towards'.

obviate /ob-vi-ayt/ • v. (**obviates**, **obviating**, **obviated**) remove or prevent (a need or

difficulty).
– ORIGIN Latin *obviare*.

obvious • **adj.** easily seen or understood; clear.
– DERIVATIVES **obviously** adv.
– ORIGIN from Latin *ob viam* 'in the way'.

ocarina /ok-uh-ree-nuh/ • **n.** a small egg-shaped wind instrument with holes for the fingers.
– ORIGIN Italian.

O'Casey, E
Sean (1880–1964), Irish dramatist, best known for the tragi-comedy *Juno and the Paycock*.

occasion • **n. 1** a particular event, or the time at which it happens. **2** a special event or celebration. **3** a suitable time for something. **4** formal reason or cause: *we have occasion to rejoice.* • **v.** formal cause.
– PHRASES **on occasion** from time to time.
– ORIGIN Latin.

occasional • **adj.** happening or done from time to time.
– DERIVATIVES **occasionally** adv.

occidental • **adj.** relating to the countries of the West.
– ORIGIN Latin *occidentalis*.

occiput /ok-si-put/ • **n.** Anat. the back of the head.
– DERIVATIVES **occipital** /ok-**si**-pi-t'l/ adj.
– ORIGIN Latin.

occlude /uh-klood/ • **v.** (**occludes, occluding, occluded**) tech. close up or block (an opening or passage).
– ORIGIN Latin *occludere*.

occluded front • **n.** a weather front produced when a cold front catches up with a warm front, so that the warm air in between them is forced upwards.

occult /ok-kult, ok-kult/ • **n.** (**the occult**) supernatural beliefs, practices, or events. • **adj.** relating to the occult.
– DERIVATIVES **occultism** n. **occultist** n.
– ORIGIN Latin *occulere* 'conceal'.

occupancy • **n. 1** the action of occupying a place. **2** the proportion of accommodation occupied.

occupant • **n.** a person who occupies a place or job.

occupation • **n. 1** a job or profession. **2** the action of occupying or state of being occupied: *the Roman occupation of Britain.* **3** a way of spending time.

occupational • **adj.** having to do with a job or profession.

occupational therapy • **n.** the use of particular activities as an aid to recovery from illness.

occupy • **v.** (**occupies, occupying, occupied**) **1** live or work in. **2** enter and take control of (a place). **3** fill or take up (a space, time, or position). **4** keep busy: *he has occupied himself with research.*
– DERIVATIVES **occupier** n.
– ORIGIN Latin *occupare* 'seize'.

occur • **v.** (**occurs, occurring, occurred**) **1** happen. **2** be found or present: *radon occurs in rocks such as granite.* **3** (**occur to**) come into the mind of.
– ORIGIN Latin *occurrere* 'go to meet'.

occurrence /uh-ku-ruhnss/ • **n. 1** an incident or event. **2** the fact of something occurring.

ocean • **n.** a very large expanse of sea, especially each of the Atlantic, Pacific, Indian, Arctic, and Antarctic Oceans.
– ORIGIN Greek *ōkeanos* 'great stream encircling the earth'.

Oceania E
/oh-si-**ah**-ni-uh, oh-shi-**ah**-ni-uh/ the islands of the Pacific Ocean and adjacent seas.
– DERIVATIVES **Oceanian** adj. & n.

oceanic /oh-si-**an**-ik, oh-shi-**an**-ik/ • **adj.** relating to the ocean.

oceanography • **n.** the branch of science concerned with the study of the sea.
– DERIVATIVES **oceanographer** n.

ocelot /oss-i-lot/ • **n.** a striped and spotted wild cat, found in South and Central America.
– ORIGIN French.

ochre /**oh**-ker/ (US also **ocher**) • **n.** a type of earth varying from light yellow to brown or red, used as a pigment.
– ORIGIN Greek *ōkhra*.

o'clock • **adv.** used to specify the hour when telling the time.
– ORIGIN from *of the clock*.

O'Connell, E
Daniel (1775–1847; known as **the Liberator**), Irish nationalist leader. His election to Parliament in 1828 forced the British government to grant full political and civil liberties to Catholics in order to enable him to take his seat.

Oct. • **abbrev.** October.

octagon • **n.** a plane figure with eight straight sides and eight angles.
– DERIVATIVES **octagonal** adj.
– ORIGIN Greek *octagōnos* 'eight-angled'

octahedron /ok-tuh-**hee**-druhn/ • **n.** (pl. **octahedra** /ok-tuh-**hee**-druh/ or **octahedrons**) a three-dimensional shape with eight plane faces.
– ORIGIN Greek *oktaedron* 'eight-faced thing'.

octane • **n.** Chem. a liquid hydrocarbon present in petroleum spirit.

octave /ok-tiv/ • **n. 1** a series of eight musical notes occupying the interval between (and including) two notes. **2** the interval between two such notes.
– ORIGIN Latin *octavus* 'eighth'.

Octavian E
/ok-**tay**-vi-uhn/ see **AUGUSTUS**.

octavo /ok-**tah**-voh/ • **n.** (pl. **octavos**) a size of book page that results from folding each printed sheet into eight leaves (sixteen pages).
– ORIGIN from Latin *in octavo* 'in an eighth'.

octet • **n. 1** a group of eight musicians. **2** a musical composition for eight voices or instruments.

October • **n.** the tenth month of the year.
– ORIGIN from Latin *octo* 'eight' (October being originally the eighth month of the Roman year).

octogenarian /ok-tuh-ji-**nair**-i-uhn/ • **n.** a person who is between 80 and 89 years old.
– ORIGIN Latin *octoginta* 'eighty'.

octopus • **n.** (pl. **octopuses**) a sea animal

with a soft body and eight long tentacles.
– ORIGIN from Greek *oktō* 'eight' + *pous* 'foot'.

ocular /ok-yuu-ler/ ● **adj.** having to do with the eyes or vision.
– ORIGIN Latin *oculus* 'eye'.

oculist /ok-yuu-list/ ● **n.** a doctor who treats diseases or defects of the eye.
– ORIGIN Latin *oculus* 'eye'.

OD ● **v.** (**OD's**, **OD'ing**, **OD'd**) informal take an overdose of a drug.

odalisque /oh-duh-lisk/ ● **n.** hist. a female slave or concubine in a harem.
– ORIGIN French.

odd ● **adj.** **1** unusual or unexpected; strange. **2** (of whole numbers such as 3 and 5) having one left over as a remainder when divided by two. **3** occasional: *we have the odd drink together.* **4** spare; available: *an odd five minutes.* **5** separated from a pair or set. **6** in the region of: *fifty-odd years.*
– PHRASES **odd one out** a person or thing that differs from the other members of a group. **odds and ends** various articles or remnants.
– DERIVATIVES **oddly** adv. **oddness** n.
– ORIGIN Old Norse.

oddball ● **n.** informal a strange or eccentric person.

oddity ● **n.** (pl. **oddities**) **1** the quality of being strange. **2** a strange person or thing.

oddment ● **n.** an item or piece left over from a larger piece or set.

odds ● **pl. n.** **1** the ratio between the amount placed as a bet and the money which would be received if the bet was won: *odds of 8-1.* **2** (**the odds**) the chances of something happening. **3** (**the odds**) the advantage thought to be possessed by one person compared to another: *she won against all the odds.*
– PHRASES **at odds** in conflict or disagreement. **over the odds** Brit. (of a price) above what is thought acceptable.

odds-on ● **adj.** very likely to win, succeed, or happen.

ode ● **n.** a poem addressed to a person or thing or celebrating an event.
– ORIGIN Greek *ōidē* 'song'.

Oder E
/oh-der/ a river of central Europe which rises in the west of the Czech Republic and flows northwards through Poland before reaching the Baltic Sea.

Odessa E
/oh-dess-uh/ a city and port on the south coast of Ukraine, on the Black Sea.

Odin E
/oh-din/ (also **Woden** or **Wotan**) the supreme Scandinavian god and creator, god of victory and the dead.

odious ● **adj.** very unpleasant.
– ORIGIN Latin *odium* 'hatred'.

odium ● **n.** widespread hatred or disgust.
– ORIGIN Latin.

odoriferous /oh-duh-rif-uh-ruhss/ ● **adj.** having an odour.

odour (US **odor**) ● **n.** a smell.
– DERIVATIVES **odorous** adj. **odourless** (US **odorless**) adj.
– ORIGIN Latin *odor*.

Odysseus E
/oh-diss-i-uhss/ Gk Myth. the king of the Ionian island of Ithaca, whose wanderings and adventures after the fall of Troy were described in Homer's epic poem the *Odyssey.* Roman name **ULYSSES**.

odyssey /od-i-si/ ● **n.** (pl. **odysseys**) a long eventful journey.
– ORIGIN see **ODYSSEUS**.

OECD ● **abbrev.** Organization for Economic Co-operation and Development.

oedema /i-dee-muh/ (US **edema**) ● **n.** an excess of watery fluid in the cavities or tissues of the body.
– ORIGIN Greek *oidēma*.

Oedipus E
/ee-di-puhss/ Gk Myth. the son of Jocasta and of Laius, king of Thebes. He unwittingly killed his father and married his mother, and blinded himself when he discovered what he had done.

Oedipus complex /ee-di-puhss/ ● **n.** (in the theory of Sigmund Freud) the emotions aroused in a young child by an unconscious sexual desire for the parent of the opposite sex.
– DERIVATIVES **Oedipal** adj.
– ORIGIN from **OEDIPUS**.

o'er ● **adv. & prep.** archaic or literary = **OVER**.

oesophagus /ee-sof-fuh-guhss/ (US **esophagus**) ● **n.** (pl. **oesophagi** /ee-sof-fuh-jy/ or **oesophaguses**) the muscular tube which connects the throat to the stomach.
– ORIGIN Greek *oisophagos*.

oestrogen /ee-struh-juhn, ess-truh-juhn/ (US **estrogen**) ● **n.** any of a group of hormones which develop and maintain female characteristics of the body.
– ORIGIN from **OESTRUS**.

oestrus /ee-struhss, ess-truhss/ (US **estrus**) ● **n.** a recurring period of sexual readiness and fertility in many female mammals.
– ORIGIN Greek *oistros* 'gadfly, frenzy'.

oeuvre /er-vruh/ ● **n.** the body of work of an artist, composer, author, etc.
– ORIGIN French.

of ● **prep.** **1** expressing the relationship between a part and a whole. **2** belonging to; coming from. **3** used in expressions of measurement, value, or age. **4** made from. **5** used to show position: *north of Watford.* **6** used to show that something belongs to a category: *the city of Prague.*
– ORIGIN Old English.

USAGE **of**
It is wrong to write the word **of** instead of **have** or **'ve** in sentences such as *I could have told you that* (not *I could of told you that*).

off ● **adv.** **1** away from a place. **2** so as to be removed or separated: *he took off his coat.* **3** starting a journey or race. **4** so as to finish or be discontinued. **5** (of an electrical appliance or power supply) not working or connected. **6** having a particular level of wealth: *badly off.* ● **prep.** **1** away from. **2** situated or leading in a direction away from. **3** so as to be removed or separated from. **4** informal having a temporary dislike of. ● **adj.** **1** (of food) no longer fresh. **2** Brit. informal annoying or unfair. ● **n.** Brit. informal the start of a race or journey.

– PHRASES **off and on** now and then.
– ORIGIN Old English.

USAGE off
Say **off**, not **off of**, in a sentence such as *the cup fell off the table*; **off of** is not good English and should not be used in writing.

offal • n. the internal organs of an animal used as food.
– ORIGIN prob. from Dutch *afval*.

Offaly E
/off-uh-li/ a county in the central part of the Republic of Ireland; county town, Tullamore.

Offa's Dyke E
a series of earthworks between England and Wales, constructed by King Offa of Mercia in the second half of the 8th century.

offbeat • adj. informal unconventional; unusual.
off-colour • adj. Brit. slightly unwell.
offcut • n. a piece of wood, fabric, etc. that is left behind after cutting a larger piece.
off day • n. a day when a person is not at their best.

Offenbach E
/off-uhn-bahkh/, Jacques (1819–80; born *Jacob Offenbach*), German composer, resident in France from 1833. He is best known for the operetta *Orpheus in the Underworld* and the opera *The Tales of Hoffmann*.

offence (US **offense**) • n. **1** an act that breaks a law or rule. **2** a feeling of hurt or annoyance: *I didn't mean to give offence*.
offend • v. **1** make (someone) feel hurt or annoyed. **2** be displeasing to. **3** do something illegal.
– DERIVATIVES **offender** n.
– ORIGIN Latin *offendere* 'strike against'.
offensive • adj. **1** causing offence. **2** used in attack: *an offensive weapon*. • n. a campaign to attack or achieve something: *an offensive against crime*.
– PHRASES **be on the offensive** be ready to act aggressively.
– DERIVATIVES **offensively** adv.
offer • v. (**offers, offering, offered**) **1** present (something) so that it may be accepted, rejected, or considered. **2** express willingness to do something for someone. **3** provide: *the mall offers a variety of shops*. • n. **1** an expression of readiness to do or give something. **2** an amount of money that someone is willing to pay for something. **3** a specially reduced price.
– PHRASES **on offer 1** available. **2** for sale at a reduced price.
– ORIGIN Latin *offerre*.
offering • n. something that is offered; a gift or contribution.
offertory /off-er-tuh-ri/ • n. (pl. **offertories**) **1** (in the Christian Church) the offering of the bread and wine at Holy Communion. **2** a collection of money made at a Christian church service.
– ORIGIN Latin *offertorium*.
offhand • adj. rudely casual or abrupt. • adv. without previous thought.
office • n. **1** a room, set of rooms, or building used for business or clerical work. **2** a position of authority. **3** the holding of an official position. **4** (**offices**) service done for others: *the good offices of the rector*. **5** (also **Divine Office**) daily Christian services of prayers and psalms.
– ORIGIN Latin *officium* 'performance of a task'.
officer • n. **1** a person holding a position of authority in the armed services. **2** a person holding a position of authority in an organization or the government.
official • adj. **1** relating to an authority or public organization. **2** having the authorization of such a body. • n. a person holding public office or having official duties.
– DERIVATIVES **officialdom** n. **officially** adv.
officialese • n. formal and wordy language typical of official documents.
official secret • n. Brit. a piece of information that is important for national security and is officially classified as confidential.
officiate /uh-fi-shi-ayt/ • v. (**officiates, officiating, officiated**) **1** act as an official in charge of something: *two judges will officiate at the Grand Prix*. **2** perform a religious service or ceremony.
– ORIGIN Latin *officiare*.
officious • adj. asserting authority in an overbearing way.
offing • n. (in phr. **in the offing**) likely to happen soon.
off-key • adj. & adv. **1** Music not in the correct key or of the correct pitch. **2** inappropriate.
off-licence • n. Brit. a shop selling alcoholic drink to be drunk elsewhere.
off-limits • adj. out of bounds.
off-line • adj. not connected to a computer.
offload • v. **1** unload (a cargo). **2** get rid of (something) by passing it on to someone else.
off-peak • adj. & adv. at a time when demand is less.
off-putting • adj. unpleasant or unsettling.
off season • n. a time of year when people do not take part in a particular activity or a business is quiet.
offset • v. (**offsets, offsetting, offset**) **1** counteract (something) by having an equal and opposite force or effect. **2** place out of line.
offshoot • n. **1** a side shoot on a plant. **2** a thing that develops from something else: *the vehicle is an offshoot of a racing car*.
offshore • adj. & adv. **1** situated at sea some distance from the shore. **2** (of the wind) blowing towards the sea from the land. **3** made, situated, or registered abroad.
offside • adj. & adv. (in games such as football) occupying a position on the field where playing the ball is not allowed. • n. esp. Brit. the side of a vehicle furthest from the kerb.
offspring • n. (pl. **offspring**) a person's child or children, or the young of an animal.
offstage • adj. & adv. (in a theatre) not on the stage and so not visible to the audience.
off-white • n. a white colour with a grey or yellowish tinge.
oft • adv. archaic or literary often.
– ORIGIN Old English.
often (also archaic or N. Amer. **oftentimes**) • adv. **1** frequently. **2** in many cases.

ogle • v. (**ogles**, **ogling**, **ogled**) stare at in a lecherous way.
– ORIGIN prob. from German or Dutch.

ogre • n. (fem. **ogress**) **1** (in folklore) a man-eating giant. **2** a cruel or terrifying person.
– ORIGIN French.

oh • exclam. expressing surprise, disappointment, joy, acknowledgement, etc.

O'Higgins, E
Bernardo (*c.*1778–1842), Chilean revolutionary leader and statesman, head of state 1817–23. With the help of José de San Martín he defeated Spanish forces in 1817 and paved the way for Chilean independence the following year.

Ohio E
/oh-hy-oh/ a state in the north-eastern US; capital, Columbus.
– DERIVATIVES **Ohioan** adj. & n.

Ohm E
/*rhymes with* home/, Georg Simon (1789–1854), German physicist, famous for his law stating that electric current is proportional to voltage and inversely proportional to resistance.

ohm /ohm/ • n. the SI unit of electrical resistance. (Symbol: Ω)
– ORIGIN named after Georg S. **Ohm**.

OHMS • abbrev. on Her (or His) Majesty's Service.

-oid • suffix (forming adjectives and nouns) similar to: *asteroid*.
– ORIGIN Greek *-oeidēs*.

oik (also **oick**) • n. informal a rude or unpleasant person.
– ORIGIN unknown.

oil • n. **1** a thick, sticky liquid obtained from petroleum. **2** any of various thick liquids which cannot be dissolved in water and are obtained from animals or plants. **3** (also **oils**) oil paint. • v. treat or coat with oil.
– ORIGIN Latin *oleum*.

oilcan • n. a can with a long nozzle used for applying oil to machinery.

oilcloth • n. cotton fabric treated with oil to make it waterproof.

oilfield • n. an area where oil is found beneath the ground or the seabed.

oil-fired • adj. using oil as fuel.

oil paint • n. artist's paint made from ground pigment mixed with linseed or other oil.

oil rig (also **oil platform**) • n. a structure that stands on the seabed to provide a stable base above water for drilling oil wells.

oilskin • n. **1** heavy cotton cloth waterproofed with oil. **2** (**oilskins**) a set of garments made of oilskin.

oil slick • n. a layer of oil floating on an area of water.

oil well • n. a shaft made in rock so as to obtain oil.

oily • adj. (**oilier**, **oiliest**) **1** containing or covered with oil. **2** resembling oil. **3** (of a person) excessively polite and flattering.
– DERIVATIVES **oiliness** n.

oink • n. the grunting sound made by a pig. • v. make such a sound.

ointment • n. a smooth substance that is rubbed on the skin for medicinal purposes.
– ORIGIN Old French *oignement*.

Oireachtas E
/e-rek-tuhss/ the law-making body of the Republic of Ireland.

OK (also **okay**) informal • exclam. expressing agreement or acceptance. • adj. **1** satisfactory. **2** allowed. • adv. in a satisfactory way or to a satisfactory extent. • n. an authorization. • v. (**OK's**, **OK'ing**, **OK'd**) give approval to.
– ORIGIN prob. from *orl korrect*, humorous form of *all correct*.

okapi /oh-kah-pi/ • n. (pl. **okapi** or **okapis**) a large African mammal of the giraffe family, having a dark chestnut coat with stripes on the hindquarters and upper legs.
– ORIGIN a local word.

O'Keeffe, E
Georgia (1887–1986), American painter, known for her paintings depicting enlarged studies of flowers.

Oklahoma E
/oh-kluh-**hoh**-muh/ a state in the south central US; capital, Oklahoma City.
– DERIVATIVES **Oklahoman** n. & adj.

okra /ok-ruh, oh-kruh/ • n. a vegetable consisting of the long seed pods of a tropical plant.
– ORIGIN a West African word.

old • adj. (**older**, **oldest**) **1** having lived for a long time. **2** made or built long ago. **3** possessed or used for a long time. **4** dating from far back. **5** former. **6** of a specified age: *he was four years old*. **7** informal expressing affection or contempt: *good old Mum*.
– PHRASES **of old 1** in or belonging to the past. **2** for a long time. **the old days** a period in the past. **the old school** the traditional form or type: *a gentleman of the old school*.
– ORIGIN Old English.

old age • n. the later part of normal life.

old-age pensioner • n. an old person receiving a retirement pension.

Old Bailey E
the Central Criminal Court in London.

old boy (or **old girl**) • n. a former pupil of a school.

old boy network (also **old boys' network**) • n. an informal system through which men use their positions of influence to help others who went to the same school or university.

Old Delhi E
see **Delhi**.

olden • adj. of a former age.

Old English • n. the language of the Anglo-Saxons (up to about 1150).

Old English sheepdog • n. a large breed of sheepdog with a shaggy blue-grey and white coat.

old-fashioned • adj. no longer current or modern; dated.

Oldfield, E
Bruce (b.1950), English fashion designer.

Old French • n. the French language up to about 1400.

old gold • n. a dull brownish-gold colour.

old guard • n. the long-standing members of a group, who are often unwilling to accept change.

old hand • **n.** a person with a lot of experience.

old hat • **adj.** informal boringly familiar or out of date.

old lady • **n.** (**one's old lady**) informal one's mother, wife, or girlfriend.

old maid • **n. 1** derog. a single woman seen as too old for marriage. **2** a prim and fussy person.

old man • **n.** (**one's old man**) informal one's father, husband, or boyfriend.

old master • **n.** a great artist of former times.

Old Nick • **n.** informal the Devil.

Old Norse • **n.** the language of medieval Norway, Iceland, Denmark, and Sweden.

Old Pretender E
see **STUART**[2].

Old Testament • **n.** the first part of the Christian Bible, corresponding approximately to the Hebrew Bible.

old-time • **adj.** pleasingly traditional or old-fashioned.

old-timer • **n.** informal a person who has worked for an organization for a long time.

old wives' tale • **n.** a widely held traditional belief that is now thought to be unscientific or incorrect.

old woman • **n. 1** (**one's old woman**) informal one's mother, wife, or girlfriend. **2** derog. a fussy or timid person.

Old World • **n.** Europe, Asia, and Africa, seen as the part of the world known before the discovery of the Americas.

oleaginous /oh-li-**aj**-i-nuhss/ • **adj. 1** oily. **2** excessively flattering: *oleaginous speeches.*
– ORIGIN Latin *oleaginus* 'of the olive tree'.

oleander /oh-li-**an**-der/ • **n.** an evergreen shrub of warm countries with clusters of white, pink, or red flowers.
– ORIGIN Latin.

O level • **n.** hist. (in the UK except Scotland) the lower of the two main levels of the GCE examination.
– ORIGIN short for **ORDINARY LEVEL**.

olfactory /ol-**fak**-tuh-ri/ • **adj.** relating to the sense of smell.
– ORIGIN Latin *olfacere* 'to smell'.

oligarch /**ol**-i-gark/ • **n.** a ruler in an oligarchy.

oligarchy • **n.** (pl. **oligarchies**) **1** a small group of people having control of a state. **2** a state governed by such a group.
– DERIVATIVES **oligarchic** adj.
– ORIGIN from Greek *oligoi* 'few' + *arkhein* 'to rule'.

Oligocene /**ol**-i-goh-seen/ • **adj.** Geol. relating to the third epoch of the Tertiary period (35.4 to 23.3 million years ago), a time when the first primates appeared.
– ORIGIN from Greek *oligos* 'few' + *kainos* 'new'.

olive • **n. 1** a small oval fruit with a hard stone and bitter green or black flesh. **2** the small evergreen tree which produces this fruit. **3** (also **olive green**) a greyish-green colour. • **adj.** (of a person's complexion) yellowish brown.
– ORIGIN Latin *oliva.*

olive branch • **n.** an offer to restore friendly relations.
– ORIGIN with reference to Noah in the Book of Genesis, to whom a dove returned with an olive branch after the Flood.

olive oil • **n.** an oil obtained from olives, used in cookery and salad dressings.

Olivier E
/uh-**liv**-i-ay/, Laurence (Kerr), Baron Olivier of Brighton (1907–89), English actor and director. He performed all the major Shakespearean roles on stage and appeared in films such as *Henry V* and *Hamlet.*

Olympiad /uh-**lim**-pi-ad/ • **n.** a staging of the Olympic Games.

Olympian • **adj. 1** having to do with Mount Olympus in Greece. **2** superior and aloof like a god: *Olympian detachment.* • **n. 1** Gk Myth. any of the twelve gods living on Mount Olympus. **2** a person who is greatly admired. **3** a competitor in the Olympic Games.

Olympic • **adj.** relating to the Olympic Games. • **n.** (**the Olympics**) the Olympic Games.

Olympic Games • **pl. n. 1** a sports festival held every four years in different countries. **2** an ancient Greek festival with athletic and arts competitions, held every four years.

Olympus, Mount E
a mountain in northern Greece, believed by the ancient Greeks to be the home of the twelve greater gods.

OM • **abbrev.** (in the UK) Order of Merit.

Oman E
/oh-**mahn**/ a country at the eastern corner of Arabia; capital, Muscat.
– DERIVATIVES **Omani** adj. & n.

Oman, Gulf of E
an inlet of the Arabian Sea, connected by the Strait of Hormuz to the Persian Gulf.

Omar Khayyám E
/oh-mar ky-**am**/ (d.1123), Persian poet, mathematician, and astronomer, known for his poetic meditations on life and celebrations of worldly pleasures, translated in *The Rubáiyát of Omar Khayyám.*

ombudsman /**om**-buudz-muhn/ • **n.** an official appointed to investigate people's complaints against public organizations.
– ORIGIN Swedish, 'legal representative'.

omega /**oh**-mi-guh/ • **n.** the last letter of the Greek alphabet (Ω, ω).
– ORIGIN from Greek *ō mega* 'the great O'.

omelette (US also **omelet**) • **n.** a dish of beaten eggs cooked in a frying pan, usually with a savoury filling.
– ORIGIN French.

omen • **n. 1** an event seen as a sign of future good or bad luck. **2** future significance: *a bird of evil omen.*
– ORIGIN Latin.

ominous • **adj.** suggesting that something bad is going to happen.
– DERIVATIVES **ominously** adv.
– ORIGIN Latin *ominosus.*

omission • **n. 1** the action of leaving something out. **2** a failure to do something. **3** something that has been left out or not done.

omit • **v.** (**omits**, **omitting**, **omitted**) **1** leave out or exclude. **2** fail to do.

– ORIGIN Latin *omittere* 'let go'.

omni- ● comb. form **1** of all things: *omniscient.* **2** in all ways or places: *omnipresent.*
– ORIGIN Latin *omnis* 'all'.

omnibus ● n. **1** a book containing several works previously published separately. **2** a television or radio programme consisting of two or more programmes previously broadcast separately. **3** dated a bus.
– ORIGIN Latin, 'for all'.

omnipotent /om-ni-puh-tuhnt/ ● adj. having total power.
– DERIVATIVES **omnipotence** n.
– ORIGIN Latin *omnipotens.*

omnipresent ● adj. widespread: *the omnipresent threat of natural disasters.*
– DERIVATIVES **omnipresence** n.

omniscient /om-niss-i-uhnt/ ● adj. knowing everything.
– DERIVATIVES **omniscience** n.
– ORIGIN Latin *omnisciens.*

omnivore /om-ni-vor/ ● n. an omnivorous animal.

omnivorous /om-niv-uh-ruhss/ ● adj. eating both plants and meat.

Omsk E
/omsk/ a city in south central Russia.

on ● prep. **1** in contact with and supported by (a surface). **2** on to. **3** in the possession of. **4** forming part of the surface of: *a scratch on her arm.* **5** about: *a book on careers.* **6** as a member of (a committee, jury, etc.). **7** stored in or broadcast by. **8** in the course of (a journey) or while travelling in (a vehicle). **9** indicating the day or time of an event. **10** engaged in: *she's out on errands.* **11** regularly taking (a drug or medicine). **12** paid for by. **13** added to. ● adv. **1** in contact with and supported by a surface. **2** (of clothing) being worn. **3** with continued movement or action. **4** taking place or being presented: *there's a good film on today.* **5** (of an electrical appliance or power supply) functioning.
– PHRASES **be on about** Brit. informal talk about. **be on at** Brit. informal nag at. **be on to** informal **1** be close to discovering that (someone) has done something wrong. **2** (**be on to something**) have an idea that is likely to lead to an important discovery. **on to** moving to a place on the surface of or aboard.
– ORIGIN Old English.

onanism /oh-nuh-ni-z'm/ ● n. formal **1** masturbation. **2** sexual intercourse in which the penis is withdrawn before ejaculation.
– ORIGIN from *Onan* in the Bible (Book of Genesis, chapter 38).

Onassis[1] E
/oh-nass-iss/, Aristotle (Socrates) (1906–75), Greek shipping magnate and founder of the Greek national airline, Olympic Airways.

Onassis[2] E
/oh-nass-iss/, Jacqueline Lee Bouvier Kennedy (1929–94), American First Lady, the wife of John F. Kennedy. After Kennedy was assassinated she married Aristotle Onassis in 1968.

once ● adv. **1** on one occasion only. **2** on even one occasion: *he never once complained.* **3** formerly. **4** multiplied by one. ● conj. as soon as.
– PHRASES **all at once 1** suddenly. **2** all at the same time. **at once 1** immediately. **2** at the same time. **once upon a time** at some time in the past.

once-over ● n. informal a rapid inspection, search, or piece of work.

oncoming ● adj. moving towards one.

Ondaatje E
/on-**dah**-tyuh/, (Philip) Michael (b.1943), Sri Lankan-born Canadian writer, author of the novel *The English Patient.*

one ● cardinal number **1** the lowest cardinal number; 1. (Roman numeral: **i** or **I**.) **2** single, or a single person or thing. **3** (before a person's name) a certain. **4** the same. ● pron. **1** used to refer to a person or thing previously mentioned or easily identified. **2** a person of a specified kind: *her loved ones.* **3** (third person sing.) used to refer to the speaker or to represent people in general.
– PHRASES **at one** in agreement. **one and all** everyone. **one and only** unique. **one another** each other. **one day** at some time in the past or future.
– ORIGIN Old English.

one-armed bandit ● n. informal a fruit machine operated by pulling a long handle at the side.

one-dimensional ● adj. lacking depth; superficial.

O'Neill, E
Eugene (Gladstone) (1888–1953), American dramatist, best known for such tragedies as *Mourning Becomes Electra* and *The Iceman Cometh.*

one-liner ● n. informal a short joke or witty remark.

one-man band ● n. **1** a street entertainer who plays many instruments at the same time. **2** a person who runs a business alone.

oneness ● n. the state of being unified, whole, or in agreement.

one-night stand ● n. informal a sexual relationship lasting only one night.

one-off Brit. informal ● adj. made or happening only once. ● n. something made or happening only once.

onerous /oh-nuh-ruhss/ ● adj. involving much effort and difficulty.
– ORIGIN Latin *onerosus.*

oneself ● pron. (third person sing.) **1** used as the object of a verb or preposition when this is the same as the subject of the clause and the subject is 'one'. **2** used to emphasize that one does something individually or without help. **3** in one's normal state of body or mind.

one-sided ● adj. **1** unfairly biased. **2** (of a contest or conflict) very unequal.

one-time ● adj. former.

one-track mind ● n. informal a mind preoccupied with one subject.

one-upmanship ● n. informal the technique of gaining an advantage over someone else.

one-way ● adj. moving or allowing movement in one direction only.

ongoing ● adj. still in progress.

onion ● n. a vegetable consisting of a bulb with a strong taste and smell.
– PHRASES **know one's onions** informal be very

knowledgeable.
– ORIGIN Old French *oignon*.

online • adj. & adv. controlled by or connected to a computer.

onlooker • n. a spectator.

only • adv. **1** and no one or nothing more besides. **2** no longer ago than. **3** not until. **4** with the negative result that: *he turned, only to find his way blocked.* • adj. **1** single or solitary. **2** alone deserving consideration. • conj. informal except that.
– PHRASES **only just 1** by a very small margin. **2** very recently.
– ORIGIN Old English.

Ono E
/oh-noh/, Yoko (b.1933), American musician and artist, born in Japan. She married John Lennon in 1969 and collaborated with him on various experimental recordings.

o.n.o. • abbrev. Brit. or nearest offer.

onomatopoeia /on-uh-mat-uh-pee-uh/ • n. **1** the formation of a word from a sound similar to the noise described (e.g. *cuckoo, sizzle*). **2** the use of such words for effect.
– DERIVATIVES **onomatopoeic** adj.
– ORIGIN Greek *onomatopoiia* 'word-making'.

onrush • n. a surging rush forward.
– DERIVATIVES **onrushing** adj.

onset • n. the beginning of something.

onshore • adj. & adv. **1** situated on land. **2** (of the wind) blowing from the sea towards the land.

onside • adj. & adv. (in sport) not offside.

onslaught • n. **1** a fierce or destructive attack. **2** an overwhelmingly large quantity of people or things.
– ORIGIN Dutch *aenslag*.

onstage • adj. & adv. (in a theatre) on the stage and so visible to the audience.

Ontario E
/on-tair-i-oh/ a province of eastern Canada; capital, Toronto.
– DERIVATIVES **Ontarian** adj. & n.

Ontario, Lake E
the smallest and most easterly of the Great Lakes, on the US–Canadian border.

onto • prep. var. of *on to* (see **ON**).

USAGE onto
Be aware of the difference between the preposition **onto** or **on to** and the use of the adverb **on** followed by the preposition **to**: *she climbed on to* (or *onto*) *the roof* (in other words, so as to be on the surface of it) but *let's go on to* (continue to) *the next point.*

ontology /on-tol-uh-ji/ • n. philosophy concerned with the nature of being.
– DERIVATIVES **ontological** adj.

onus /oh-nuhss/ • n. a responsibility.
– ORIGIN Latin.

onward • adv. (also **onwards**) **1** in a continuing forward direction. **2** so as to make progress. • adj. moving forward.

onyx /on-iks/ • n. a semi-precious variety of agate with different colours in layers.
– ORIGIN Greek *onux* 'fingernail, onyx'.

oodles • pl. n. informal a very great number or amount.
– ORIGIN unknown.

oolite /oh-uh-lyt/ • n. limestone consisting of a mass of rounded grains.
– ORIGIN Latin *oolites* 'egg stone'.

oomph • n. informal excitement, energy, or sexual attractiveness.

oops • exclam. informal used to show awareness of a mistake or minor accident.

ooze • v. (**oozes**, **oozing**, **oozed**) **1** slowly seep out. **2** give a powerful impression of: *she oozes sex appeal.* • n. wet mud or slime.
– DERIVATIVES **oozy** adj.
– ORIGIN Old English, 'juice or sap'.

Op. (also **op.**) • abbrev. Music (before a number given to each work of a particular composer) opus.

op • n. informal a surgical operation.

opacity /oh-pa-si-ti/ • n. the condition of being opaque.

opal • n. a semi-transparent gemstone in which many small points of shifting colour can be seen.
– ORIGIN Latin *opalus*.

opalescent • adj. showing many small points of shifting colour.

opaque /oh-payk/ • adj. (**opaquer**, **opaquest**) **1** not able to be seen through. **2** difficult or impossible to understand.
– ORIGIN Latin *opacus* 'darkened'.

op. cit. • adv. in the work already mentioned.
– ORIGIN from Latin *opere citato*.

OPEC • abbrev. Organization of the Petroleum Exporting Countries.

open • adj. **1** not closed, fastened, or restricted. **2** not covered or protected. **3** (**open to**) likely to suffer from or be affected by. **4** spread out, expanded, or unfolded. **5** accessible or available. **6** frank and communicative. **7** undisguised: *open hostility.* **8** not finally settled. **9** (**open to**) making possible: *a message open to different interpretations.* • v. **1** make or become open. **2** formally begin or establish. **3** (**open on to/into**) give access to. **4** (**open out/up**) begin to talk frankly. • n. **1** (**the open**) fresh air or open countryside. **2** (**Open**) a championship or competition with no restrictions on who may compete.
– PHRASES **the open air** a free or unenclosed space outdoors. **in open court** in a court of law, before the judge and the public. **in** (or **into**) **the open** not secret. **open-and-shut** straightforward. **open up** (or **open fire**) begin shooting.
– DERIVATIVES **openness** n.
– ORIGIN Old English.

opencast (N. Amer. **open-pit**) • adj. Brit. (of mining) in which coal or ore is extracted from a level near the earth's surface, rather than from shafts.

open day • n. Brit. a day when the public may visit a place to which they do not usually have access.

open-ended • adj. having no limit decided in advance.

opener • n. **1** a device for opening something. **2** a person or thing that opens or begins something.

open-handed • adj. generous.

open-heart surgery • n. surgery in which the heart is exposed and the blood made to bypass it.

open house • n. a place or situation in which all visitors are welcome.

opening • n. **1** a gap. **2** a beginning. **3** a ceremony at which a building, show, etc. is declared to be open. **4** an opportunity. **5** an available job or position. • adj. coming at the beginning.

open letter • n. a letter addressed to a particular person but intended for publication in a newspaper or journal.

openly • adv. frankly or honestly.

open market • n. a situation in which companies can trade without restrictions.

open marriage • n. a marriage in which both partners agree that each may have sexual relations with others.

open mind • n. a mind willing to consider new ideas.
– DERIVATIVES **open-minded** adj.

open-plan • adj. having large rooms with few or no dividing walls.

open prison • n. Brit. a prison with the minimum of restrictions on prisoners' movements and activities.

open question • n. a matter that is not yet decided or cannot be decided.

open sandwich • n. a sandwich without a top slice of bread.

open season • n. the period of the year when restrictions on the killing of certain types of wildlife are lifted.

open secret • n. a supposed secret that is in fact known to many people.

Open University E
(in the UK) a university that teaches mainly by broadcasting, correspondence, and summer schools, and is open to those without formal academic qualifications.

O

open verdict • n. Law a verdict of a coroner's jury which states that a suspicious death has occurred but the cause is not known.

openwork • n. ornamental work in cloth, leather, etc. with regular patterns of openings and holes.

opera[1] • n. a dramatic work set to music for singers and musicians.
– ORIGIN Italian.

opera[2] pl. of **OPUS**.

operable • adj. **1** able to be used. **2** able to be treated by means of a surgical operation.

opera glasses • pl. n. small binoculars for use at the opera or theatre.

opera house • n. a theatre for the performance of opera.

operate • v. (**operates**, **operating**, **operated**) **1** function. **2** control the functioning of (a machine) or the activities of (an organization). **3** (of an armed force) carry out military activities. **4** be in effect: *a powerful law operates in politics.* **5** perform a surgical operation.
– ORIGIN Latin *operari*.

operatic • adj. having to do with opera.

operating system • n. the low-level software that supports a computer's basic functions.

operating theatre (N. Amer. **operating room**) • n. a room in which surgical operations are performed.

operation • n. **1** the action of operating. **2** an act of surgery performed on a patient. **3** an organized action involving a number of people. **4** a business organization. **5** Math. a process in which a number, quantity, etc., is altered according to set formal rules.

operational • adj. **1** in or ready for use. **2** relating to the functioning of an organization: *operational costs.*
– DERIVATIVES **operationally** adv.

operative • adj. **1** functioning. **2** (of a word) having the most importance in a phrase. **3** relating to surgery. • n. **1** a worker. **2** a secret agent.

operator • n. **1** a person who operates equipment or a machine. **2** a person who works at the switchboard of a telephone exchange. **3** a person or company that runs a business. **4** informal a person who acts in a specified way: *a smooth operator.* **5** Math. a symbol denoting an operation (e.g. ×, +).

operculum /oh-per-kyuu-luhm/ • n. (pl. **opercula** /oh-per-kyuu-luh/) **1** a flap of skin protecting a fish's gills. **2** a plate that closes the opening of a mollusc's shell.
– ORIGIN Latin, 'lid, covering'.

operetta • n. a short opera on a light or humorous theme.
– ORIGIN Italian, 'little opera'.

ophthalmia /off-thal-mi-uh/ • n. Med. inflammation of the eye.
– ORIGIN Greek.

ophthalmic • adj. relating to the eye and its diseases.

ophthalmic optician • n. Brit. an optician qualified to prescribe and supply glasses and contact lenses and to detect eye diseases.

ophthalmology /off-thal-**mol**-uh-ji/ • n. the study and treatment of disorders and diseases of the eye.
– DERIVATIVES **ophthalmologist** n.

opiate /**oh**-pi-uht/ • adj. relating to or containing opium. • n. **1** a drug obtained from or related to opium. **2** something that causes a false sense of contentment.

opine • v. (**opines**, **opining**, **opined**) formal state as one's opinion.
– ORIGIN Latin *opinari* 'think, believe'.

opinion • n. **1** a personal view not necessarily based on fact or knowledge. **2** the views of people in general: *public opinion.* **3** a formal statement of advice by an expert.
– PHRASES **a matter of opinion** something not able to be proven either way.
– ORIGIN Latin.

opinionated • adj. tending to put forward one's views forcefully.

opinion poll • n. the questioning of a small sample of people in order to assess wider public opinion.

opium • n. an addictive drug made from the juice of a poppy.
– ORIGIN Latin.

Oporto E
/oh-**por**-too/ the chief city and port of northern Portugal, famous for port wine.

opossum /uh-**poss**-uhm/ • n. **1** an American marsupial with a tail which it can use for grasping. **2** Austral./NZ a possum.
– ORIGIN Algonquian (an American Indian language), 'white dog'.

Oppenheimer E
/op-p'n-hy-mer/, Julius Robert (1904–67), American theoretical physicist. He was director of the laboratory at Los Alamos during the development of the first atom bomb, but opposed the development of the hydrogen bomb after the Second World War.

opponent ● **n. 1** a person who competes with or fights another in a contest or argument. **2** a person who disagrees with a proposal or practice.
– ORIGIN Latin *opponere* 'set against'.

opportune /op-per-tyoon, op-per-**tyoon**/ ● **adj.** done or occurring at an especially convenient or appropriate time.
– ORIGIN Latin *opportunus*.

opportunist ● **n.** a person who takes advantage of opportunities when they arise, regardless of whether or not they are right to do so. ● **adj.** opportunistic.
– DERIVATIVES **opportunism** n.

opportunistic ● **adj.** taking advantage of immediate opportunities.

opportunity ● **n.** (pl. **opportunities**) **1** a favourable time or situation for doing something. **2** a career opening: *job opportunities*.

opposable ● **adj.** Zool. (of the thumb of a primate) capable of facing and touching the other digits on the same hand.

oppose ● **v.** (**opposes**, **opposing**, **opposed**) **1** (also **be opposed to**) disagree with and try to prevent or resist. **2** compete with or fight. **3** (**opposed**) (of two or more things) conflicting. **4** (**opposing**) opposite.
– ORIGIN Old French *opposer*.

opposite ● **adj. 1** facing. **2** completely different. **3** being the other of a contrasted pair: *the opposite ends of the price range*. **4** (of angles) between opposite sides of the intersection of two lines. ● **n.** an opposite person or thing. ● **adv.** in an opposite position. ● **prep.** in a position opposite to.
– DERIVATIVES **oppositely** adv.
– ORIGIN Latin *oppositus*.

opposite number ● **n.** a person's counterpart in another organization.

opposite sex ● **n.** (**the opposite sex**) women in relation to men or vice versa.

opposition ● **n. 1** resistance or disagreement. **2** a group of opponents. **3** (**the Opposition**) Brit. the main party in parliament that is opposed to the one in the government. **4** a contrast or direct opposite.
– DERIVATIVES **oppositional** adj.

oppress ● **v. 1** treat in a very harsh and unfair way. **2** cause to feel distressed or anxious.
– DERIVATIVES **oppression** n. **oppressor** n.
– ORIGIN Old French *oppresser*.

oppressive ● **adj. 1** harsh and demanding strict obedience. **2** causing distress or anxiety. **3** (of weather) hot and airless.
– DERIVATIVES **oppressively** adv.

opprobrious /uh-proh-bri-uhss/ ● **adj.** highly critical.

opprobrium /uh-proh-bri-uhm/ ● **n. 1** harsh criticism. **2** public disgrace as a result of bad behaviour.
– ORIGIN Latin, 'infamy'.

opt ● **v.** make a choice.
– PHRASES **opt out 1** choose not to participate. **2** Brit. (of a school or hospital) decide to withdraw from local authority control.
– ORIGIN Latin *optare*.

optic ● **adj.** relating to the eye or vision. ● **n.** Brit. trademark a device fastened to the neck of an upside-down bottle for measuring out spirits.
– ORIGIN Greek *optikos*.

optical ● **adj.** relating to vision, light, or optics.
– DERIVATIVES **optically** adv.

optical fibre ● **n.** a thin glass fibre through which light can be transmitted.

optical illusion ● **n.** a thing that deceives the eye by appearing to be other than it is.

optician ● **n.** a person qualified to prescribe and supply glasses and contact lenses, and to detect eye diseases.

optic nerves ● **pl. n.** Anat. the pair of nerves transmitting impulses from the eyes to the brain.

optics ● **n.** the branch of science concerned with vision and the behaviour of light.

optimal ● **adj.** best or most favourable.
– DERIVATIVES **optimally** adv.

optimism ● **n.** hopefulness and confidence about the future or success of something.
– DERIVATIVES **optimist** n.
– ORIGIN French *optimisme*.

optimistic ● **adj.** hopeful and confident about the future.
– DERIVATIVES **optimistically** adv.

optimize (also **optimise**) ● **v.** (**optimizes**, **optimizing**, **optimized**) make the best use of (a situation or resource).
– DERIVATIVES **optimization** (also **optimisation**) n.

optimum ● **adj.** most likely to lead to a favourable outcome: *the optimum childbearing age*. ● **n.** (pl. **optima** or **optimums**) the most favourable conditions for growth or success.
– ORIGIN Latin, 'best thing'.

option ● **n. 1** a thing that is or may be chosen. **2** the freedom or right to choose. **3** a right to buy or sell something in the future.
– PHRASES **keep** (or **leave**) **one's options open** not commit oneself.

optional ● **adj.** available to be chosen but not compulsory.
– DERIVATIVES **optionally** adv.

optometry ● **n.** the occupation of measuring eyesight, prescribing lenses, and detecting eye disease.
– DERIVATIVES **optometrist** n.

opulent /op-yuu-luhnt/ ● **adj.** showily rich and luxurious.
– DERIVATIVES **opulence** n. **opulently** adv.
– ORIGIN Latin *opulens* 'wealthy'.

opus /oh-puhss, op-uhss/ ● **n.** (pl. **opuses** or **opera** /op-uh-ruh/) **1** Music a separate composition or set of compositions. **2** an artistic work.
– ORIGIN Latin, 'work'.

or ● **conj. 1** used to link alternatives. **2** introducing a word meaning the same as or explaining a preceding word or phrase. **3** otherwise.
– ORIGIN Old English.

-or ● **suffix 1** forming nouns referring to a person or thing that performs the action of a verb: *escalator*. **2** forming nouns referring to a state: *terror*.
– ORIGIN Latin.

oracle ● **n. 1** (in ancient Greece or Rome) a

priest or priestess who acted as a channel for advice or prophecy from the gods. **2** an authority which is always correct.
– ORIGIN Latin *oraculum*.

oracular /o-rak-yuu-ler/ ● **adj.** **1** having to do with an oracle. **2** hard to interpret.

oral ● **adj.** **1** spoken rather than written. **2** relating to or done by the mouth. ● **n.** a spoken examination.
– DERIVATIVES **orally** adv.
– ORIGIN Latin *oralis*.

orange ● **n.** **1** a large round citrus fruit with a tough bright reddish-yellow rind. **2** a drink made from or flavoured with orange juice. **3** a bright reddish-yellow colour. ● **adj.** reddish yellow.
– ORIGIN Old French *orenge*.

Orange, House of E
the Dutch royal house, originally a princely dynasty of the principality centred on the French town of Orange in the 16th century.

Orange, William of E
see **WILLIAM III**.

orangeade ● **n.** Brit. a fizzy soft drink flavoured with orange.

Orange Free State E
an area and former province in central South Africa. See also **FREE STATE**.

Orange Order ● **n.** a Protestant political society in Northern Ireland.
– DERIVATIVES **Orangeman** n.
– ORIGIN named after the Protestant king William of *Orange* (see **WILLIAM III**).

Orange River E
the longest river in South Africa, which rises in NE Lesotho and flows generally westward for 1,859 km (1,155 miles) to the Atlantic.

orangery ● **n.** (pl. **orangeries**) a type of large conservatory where orange trees are grown.

orang-utan /uh-rang-oo-tan/ (also **orang-utang** /uh-rang-oo-tang/) ● **n.** a large tree-dwelling ape with long red hair.
– ORIGIN Malay, 'forest person'.

orate ● **v.** (**orates**, **orating**, **orated**) make a long or pompous speech.

oration ● **n.** a formal speech.
– ORIGIN Latin.

orator ● **n.** a skilful public speaker.

oratorio /o-ruh-tor-i-oh/ ● **n.** (pl. **oratorios**) a large-scale musical work on a religious theme for orchestra and voices.
– ORIGIN Italian.

oratory[1] /o-ruh-tri/ ● **n.** (pl. **oratories**) a small chapel for private worship.

oratory[2] /o-ruh-tri/ ● **n.** powerful and persuasive public speaking.
– DERIVATIVES **oratorical** /o-ruh-to-ri-k'l/ adj.

orb ● **n.** **1** a spherical object or shape. **2** a golden globe with a cross on top, carried by a king or queen.
– ORIGIN Latin *orbis* 'ring'.

orbicular /or-bik-yuu-ler/ ● **adj.** tech. circular or spherical.

Orbison E
/or-bi-s'n/, Roy (1936–88), American singer and composer, known for such songs as 'Only the Lonely' and 'Oh, Pretty Woman'.

orbit ● **n.** **1** the regularly repeated elliptical course of a planet, moon, spacecraft, etc. around a star or planet. **2** an area of activity or influence. ● **v.** (**orbits**, **orbiting**, **orbited**) move in orbit round (a star or planet).
– ORIGIN Latin *orbita* 'course'.

orbital ● **adj.** **1** relating to an orbit or orbits. **2** Brit. (of a road) passing round the outside of a town.

orca /or-kuh/ ● **n.** = **KILLER WHALE**.
– ORIGIN French *orque* or Latin *orca*.

orchard ● **n.** a piece of enclosed land planted with fruit trees.
– ORIGIN Old English.

orchestra ● **n.** **1** a large group of musicians with string, woodwind, brass, and percussion sections. **2** (also **orchestra pit**) the part of a theatre where the orchestra plays.
– DERIVATIVES **orchestral** adj.
– ORIGIN Greek *orkhēstra*.

orchestrate ● **v.** (**orchestrates**, **orchestrating**, **orchestrated**) **1** arrange (music) for performance by an orchestra. **2** direct (a situation) to produce a desired effect.
– DERIVATIVES **orchestration** n. **orchestrator** n.

orchid ● **n.** a plant of a large family with complex showy flowers.
– ORIGIN Greek *orkhis* 'testicle'.

ordain ● **v.** **1** make (someone) a priest or minister. **2** order officially. **3** (of God or fate) decide in advance.
– ORIGIN Latin *ordinare*.

ordeal ● **n.** a prolonged painful or horrific experience.
– ORIGIN Old English.

order ● **n.** **1** the arrangement of people or things according to a particular sequence or method. **2** a state in which everything is in its correct place. **3** a state in which the laws regulating public behaviour are followed. **4** a command. **5** a request for something to be made, supplied, or served. **6** the set procedure followed in a meeting, law court, or religious service. **7** quality: *poetry of the highest order.* **8** a social class or system. **9** (**orders** or **holy orders**) the rank of an ordained minister in the Christian Church. **10** a society of monks, nuns, or friars living under the same rule. **11** an institution founded by a king or queen to honour good behaviour: *the Order of the Garter.* **12** Biol. a main classifying category of plants and animals that ranks below class and above family. ● **v.** (**orders**, **ordering**, **ordered**) **1** give a command. **2** request that (something) be made, supplied, or served. **3** arrange methodically.
– PHRASES **in order 1** in the correct condition for use. **2** suitable in the circumstances. **in order for** (or **that**) so that. **in order to** so as to. **of** (or **in**) **the order of** approximately. **on order** (of goods) requested but not yet received. **out of order 1** not working properly or at all. **2** Brit. informal unacceptable.
– ORIGIN Latin *ordo* 'row, series'.

orderly ● **adj.** **1** neatly and methodically arranged. **2** well behaved. ● **n.** (pl. **orderlies**) **1** a hospital attendant responsible for various non-medical tasks. **2** a soldier who carries orders or performs minor tasks for an officer.
– DERIVATIVES **orderliness** n.

order of magnitude ● **n.** **1** a level in a system of ordering things by size or amount, where each level is higher by a factor of ten. **2** size or quantity.

ordinal ● **adj.** relating to order in a series.
– ORIGIN Latin *ordinalis.*

ordinal number ● **n.** a number defining a thing's position in a series, such as 'first' or 'second'.

ordinance ● **n.** formal **1** an official order. **2** a religious rite.
– ORIGIN Old French *ordenance.*

ordinary ● **adj.** normal or usual.
– DERIVATIVES **ordinarily** adv. **ordinariness** n.
– ORIGIN Latin *ordinarius* 'orderly'.

ordinary grade ● **n.** (in Scotland) the lower of the two main levels of the Scottish Certificate of Education examination.

ordinary level ● **n.** = **O LEVEL.**

ordinate /or-di-nuht/ ● **n.** Math. a straight line from a point on a graph drawn parallel to the vertical axis and meeting the other; the *y*-coordinate.
– ORIGIN from Latin *linea ordinata applicata* 'line applied parallel'.

ordination ● **n.** the action of ordaining someone as a priest or minister.

ordnance /ord-nuhnss/ ● **n.** **1** large guns mounted on wheels. **2** US military equipment and stores.
– ORIGIN variant of **ORDINANCE.**

Ordnance Survey ● **n.** (in the UK) an official survey organization preparing detailed maps of the country.

Ordovician /or-duh-vish-i-uhn/ ● **adj.** Geol. relating to the second period of the Palaeozoic era, about 510 to 439 million years ago, when the first vertebrates appeared.
– ORIGIN Latin *Ordovices,* an ancient British tribe in North Wales.

ordure /or-dyuur/ ● **n.** dung.
– ORIGIN Old French.

ore ● **n.** a naturally occurring material from which a metal or valuable mineral can be extracted.
– ORIGIN Old English, 'unwrought metal'.

oregano /o-ri-gah-noh, uh-reg-uh-noh/ ● **n.** a plant with leaves used as a herb in cookery.
– ORIGIN Spanish.

Oregon E
/o-ri-g'n/ a state in the north-western US, on the Pacific coast; capital, Salem.
DERIVATIVES **Oregonian** adj. & n.

Orestes E
/o-ress-teez/ Gk Myth. the son of Agamemnon and Clytemnestra. He killed Clytemnestra and her lover to avenge the murder of Agamemnon.

Orff E
/orf/, Carl (1895–1982), German composer, best known for his secular cantata *Carmina Burana,* based on a collection of bawdy medieval Latin poems.

organ ● **n.** **1** a part of an animal or plant adapted for a particular function, for example the heart. **2** a large musical keyboard instrument with rows of pipes supplied with air from bellows. **3** a smaller keyboard instrument producing sounds electronically. **4** a newspaper or journal which puts forward the views of a political party or movement. **5** euphem. a man's penis.
– DERIVATIVES **organist** n.
– ORIGIN Greek *organon* 'tool, organ'.

organdie /or-guhn-di/ (US also **organdy**) ● **n.** a fine, semi-transparent, stiff cotton muslin.
– ORIGIN French *organdi.*

organelle /or-guh-nel/ ● **n.** Biol. a specialized structure within a cell.
– ORIGIN Latin *organella* 'little tool'.

organic ● **adj.** **1** having to do with living matter. **2** produced without artificial chemicals such as fertilizers. **3** Chem. having to do with compounds containing carbon and chiefly or ultimately of biological origin. **4** having to do with a bodily organ or organs. **5** (of the parts of a whole) fitting together harmoniously. **6** (of development or change) continuous or natural.
– DERIVATIVES **organically** adv.

organism ● **n.** **1** an individual animal, plant, or single-celled life form. **2** a whole made up of parts which are dependent on each other.

organization (also **organisation**) ● **n.** **1** the action of organizing. **2** a systematic arrangement or approach. **3** an organized group of people with a particular purpose, e.g. a business.
– DERIVATIVES **organizational** (also **organisational**) adj.

Organization of the Petroleum Exporting Countries E
an association of the thirteen major oil-producing countries, founded in 1960 to coordinate policies.

organize (also **organise**) ● **v.** (**organizes, organizing, organized**) **1** arrange in an orderly way. **2** Brit. make arrangements for.
– DERIVATIVES **organizer** (also **organiser**) n.
– ORIGIN Latin *organizare.*

organza /or-gan-zuh/ ● **n.** a thin, stiff, transparent fabric.
– ORIGIN prob. from *Lorganza,* a US trademark.

orgasm ● **n.** the climax of sexual excitement, experienced as intensely pleasurable sensations centred in the genitals. ● **v.** have an orgasm.
– DERIVATIVES **orgasmic** adj.
– ORIGIN Greek *orgasmos.*

orgiastic /or-ji-ass-tik/ ● **adj.** relating to or like an orgy.

orgy ● **n.** (pl. **orgies**) **1** a wild party with excessive drinking and much sexual activity. **2** excessive indulgence in a specified activity: *an orgy of killing.*
– ORIGIN Greek *orgia* 'secret rites'.

oriel window /or-i-uhl/ ● **n.** a window in a large bay built in the upper storey of a building.
– ORIGIN Old French *oriol* 'gallery'.

orient ● **n.** /or-i-uhnt/ (**the Orient**) literary the countries of the East. ● **v.** /or-i-ent/ **1** position in relation to the points of a compass or other specified positions. **2** (**orient oneself**) find one's position in relation to unfamiliar surroundings. **3** tailor to meet particular needs: *magazines oriented to students.*
– ORIGIN Latin *oriens* 'rising or east'.

oriental ● **adj.** having to do with the Far East. ● **n.** dated or offens. a person of Far Eastern descent.

orientate ● **v.** (**orientates, orientating, orientated**) = **ORIENT.**

orientation • n. **1** the action of orienting. **2** a position in relation to something else. **3** a person's attitude or natural tendency: *sexual orientation.*

orienteering • n. a competitive sport in which runners have to find their way across rough country with the aid of a map and compass.

orifice /o-ri-fiss/ • n. an opening in the body.
– ORIGIN French.

origami /o-ri-**gah**-mi/ • n. the Japanese art of folding paper into decorative shapes.
– ORIGIN Japanese.

origin • n. **1** the point where something begins. **2** a person's social background or ancestry. **3** Math. a fixed point from which coordinates are measured.
– ORIGIN Latin *origo.*

original • adj. **1** existing from the beginning. **2** produced by an artist, author, etc. rather than copied. **3** inventive or novel. • n. the earliest form of something, from which copies can be made.
– DERIVATIVES **originally** adv.

originality • n. **1** the ability to think independently or creatively. **2** the quality of being new or unusual.

original sin • n. (in Christian belief) the tendency of all human beings to be evil.

originate • v. (**originates**, **originating**, **originated**) **1** have a specified beginning. **2** create or initiate.
– DERIVATIVES **origination** n. **originator** n.

Orinoco E
/o-ri-**noh**-koh/ a river in northern South America, which rises in SE Venezuela and flows 2,060 km (1,280 miles) to the Atlantic Ocean.

oriole /or-i-ohl/ • n. a brightly coloured bird with a musical call.
– ORIGIN Latin *oriolus.*

orison /o-ri-zuhn/ • n. literary a prayer.
– ORIGIN Old French *oreison.*

Orissa E
/uh-**riss**-uh/ a state in eastern India, on the Bay of Bengal; capital, Bhubaneswar.

Orkney Islands E
a group of more than seventy islands off the NE tip of Scotland, forming an administrative region of Scotland; chief town, Kirkwall.

Orlando E
/or-**lan**-doh/ a resort city in central Florida.

Orleans E
/or-**lee**-uhnz/ a city in central France, on the Loire.

ormolu /or-muh-loo/ • n. a gold-coloured alloy of copper, zinc, and tin used in decoration.
– ORIGIN from French *or moulu* 'powdered gold'.

ornament • n. **1** an object designed to add beauty to something. **2** decorative items as a whole. **3** (**ornaments**) Music embellishments made to a melody.
– DERIVATIVES **ornamentation** n.
– ORIGIN Latin *ornamentum.*

ornamental • adj. used as an ornament; decorative.

ornate • adj. highly decorated.
– DERIVATIVES **ornately** adv.
– ORIGIN Latin *ornare* 'adorn'.

ornithology /or-ni-**thol**-uh-ji/ • n. the scientific study of birds.
– DERIVATIVES **ornithological** adj. **ornithologist** n.
– ORIGIN Greek *ornis* 'bird'.

orotund /o-roh-tund/ • adj. **1** (of a person's voice) deep and impressive. **2** (of writing or style) pompous.
– ORIGIN from Latin *ore rotundo* 'with rounded mouth'.

orphan • n. a child whose parents are dead. • v. (**be orphaned**) (of a child) be made an orphan.
– ORIGIN Greek *orphanos* 'bereaved'.

orphanage • n. a home which cares for orphans.

Orpheus E
/**or**-fi-uhss/ Gk Myth. a poet who went to the underworld to rescue his wife Eurydice after she died, but lost her because he failed to obey the condition that he must not look back at her.

Ortega E
/or-**tay**-guh/, Daniel (b.1945; full name *Daniel Ortega Saavedra*), Nicaraguan statesman, President 1985–90. The leader of the Sandinista National Liberation Front, he became President after the Sandinista election victory in 1984.

ortho- • comb. form **1** straight; rectangular; upright: *orthodontics.* **2** correct: *orthography.*
– ORIGIN Greek *orthos.*

orthodontics /or-thuh-**don**-tiks/ • n. the treatment of irregularities in the teeth and jaws.
– DERIVATIVES **orthodontic** adj. **orthodontist** n.
– ORIGIN Greek *odous* 'tooth'.

orthodox • adj. **1** in line with traditional or generally accepted beliefs. **2** conventional or normal. **3** (**Orthodox**) relating to Orthodox Judaism or the Orthodox Church.
– ORIGIN Greek *orthodoxos.*

Orthodox Church • n. a branch of the Christian Church in Greece and eastern Europe.

Orthodox Judaism • n. a branch of Judaism which teaches that the requirements of Jewish law and traditional custom must be strictly followed.

orthodoxy • n. (pl. **orthodoxies**) **1** orthodox beliefs or practice. **2** an idea which is generally accepted.

orthography /or-**thog**-ruh-fi/ • n. the conventional spelling system of a language.
– DERIVATIVES **orthographic** adj.

orthopaedics /or-thuh-**pee**-diks/ (US **orthopedics**) • n. the branch of medicine concerned with the correction of deformities of bones or muscles.
– DERIVATIVES **orthopaedic** (US **orthopedic**) adj.
– ORIGIN Greek *paideia* 'rearing of children'.

orthotics /or-**thot**-iks/ • n. the branch of medicine concerned with the provision and use of artificial supports or braces.
– DERIVATIVES **orthotic** adj. & n.

Orton, E
Joe (1933–67; born *John Kingsley Orton*), English dramatist, known for unconventional black comedies such as *Entertaining Mr Sloane* and *Loot*.

Orwell, E
George (1903–50; pen name of *Eric Arthur Blair*), British novelist and essayist, born in India. He wrote *Animal Farm*, a satire on Communism under Stalin, and *Nineteen Eighty-four*, about an oppressive future state in which total control is exercised by Big Brother.
– DERIVATIVES **Orwellian** adj.

-ory[1] • **suffix** forming nouns referring to a place for a particular function: *dormitory*.
– ORIGIN Latin *-oria*, *-orium*.

-ory[2] • **suffix** forming adjectives relating to a verbal action: *compulsory*.
– ORIGIN Latin *-orius*.

oryx /o-riks/ • **n.** a large antelope with long horns, found in arid regions of Africa and Arabia.
– ORIGIN Latin.

Osaka E
/oh-**sah**-kuh/ a port and commercial city in Japan, on the island of Honshu.

Osborne, E
John (James) (1929–94), English dramatist. His play *Look Back in Anger* ushered in a new era of kitchen-sink drama; its hero Jimmy Porter personified the so-called 'angry young man'.

Oscar • **n.** (trademark in the US) the nickname for a gold statuette given as an Academy award.
– ORIGIN uncertain.

oscillate /oss-i-layt/ • **v.** (**oscillates**, **oscillating**, **oscillated**) **1** move or swing back and forth at a regular rate. **2** waver between extremes of opinion or emotion.
– DERIVATIVES **oscillation** n. **oscillator** n.
– ORIGIN Latin *oscillare* 'to swing'.

oscilloscope • **n.** a device for showing changes in electrical current as a display on the screen of a cathode ray tube.

-ose[1] • **suffix** (forming adjectives) having a specified quality: *bellicose*.
– ORIGIN Latin *-osus*.

-ose[2] • **suffix** Chem. forming names of sugars and other carbohydrates: *cellulose*.
– ORIGIN from *glucose*.

osier /**oh**-zi-er/ • **n.** a small willow with long flexible shoots used in basketwork.
– ORIGIN Old French.

-osis • **suffix** (pl. **-oses**) referring to a process, condition, or diseased state: *metamorphosis*.
– ORIGIN Greek.

-osity • **suffix** forming nouns from adjectives ending in *-ose* or *-ous*: *verbosity*.
– ORIGIN French *-osité* or Latin *-ositas*.

Oslo E
/oz-loh/ the capital and chief port of Norway. Former name (until 1924) **CHRISTIANIA**.

Osman I E
/oz-muhn/ (also **Othman**) (1259–1326), Turkish conqueror, founder of the Ottoman (Osmanli) dynasty and empire.

osmium /oz-mi-uhm/ • **n.** a hard, dense silvery-white metallic element.
– ORIGIN Greek *osmē* 'smell'.

osmoregulation • **n.** Biol. the control of water content and salt concentration in the body of an organism.

osmosis /oz-**moh**-siss/ • **n.** **1** Biol. & Chem. a process by which molecules of a solvent pass through a membrane from a less concentrated solution into a more concentrated one. **2** the gradual absorbing of ideas.
– DERIVATIVES **osmotic** adj.
– ORIGIN Greek *ōsmos* 'a push'.

osprey • **n.** (pl. **ospreys**) a large fish-eating bird of prey with a white underside and crown.
– ORIGIN Old French *ospres*.

osseous /oss-i-uhss/ • **adj.** tech. consisting of or turned into bone.
– ORIGIN Latin *osseus* 'bony'.

ossicle /oss-i-k'l/ • **n.** a very small bone, especially in the ear.
– ORIGIN Latin *ossiculum*.

ossify /oss-i-fy/ • **v.** (**ossifies**, **ossifying**, **ossified**) **1** turn into bone or bony tissue. **2** cease developing.
– DERIVATIVES **ossification** n.
– ORIGIN Latin *os* 'bone'.

Ostend E
/o-**stend**/ a ferry port on the North Sea coast of NW Belgium.

ostensible • **adj.** apparently true, but not necessarily so.
– DERIVATIVES **ostensibly** adv.
– ORIGIN Latin *ostensibilis*.

ostentation • **n.** showy display which is intended to impress.
– ORIGIN Latin *ostendere* 'stretch out to view'.

ostentatious /oss-ten-**tay**-shuhss/ • **adj.** showy in a way which is intended to impress.

osteo- /oss-ti-oh/ • **comb. form** having to do with the bones: *osteoporosis*.
– ORIGIN Greek *osteon* 'bone'.

osteoarthritis • **n.** Med. a condition in which joint cartilage decays, causing pain and stiffness.

osteopathy /oss-ti-**op**-uh-thi/ • **n.** a system of complementary medicine involving the manipulation of the bones and muscles.
– DERIVATIVES **osteopath** n. **osteopathic** adj.

osteoporosis /oss-ti-oh-puh-**roh**-siss/ • **n.** a medical condition in which the bones become brittle and fragile.
– ORIGIN Greek *poros* 'passage, pore'.

ostinato /oss-ti-**nah**-toh/ • **n.** (pl. **ostinatos** or **ostinati** /oss-ti-**nah**-ti/) a continually repeated musical phrase or rhythm.
– ORIGIN Italian, 'obstinate'.

ostler /oss-ler/ • **n.** hist. a man employed at an inn to look after customers' horses.
– ORIGIN Old French *hostelier* 'innkeeper'.

ostracize /oss-truh-syz/ (also **ostracise**) • **v.** (**ostracizes**, **ostracizing**, **ostracized**) exclude from a society or group.
– DERIVATIVES **ostracism** n.
– ORIGIN Greek *ostrakizein*.

ostrich • **n.** **1** a large African bird with a long neck and long legs, that runs fast but cannot fly.
– ORIGIN Old French *ostriche*.

Oswald, E
Lee Harvey (1939–63), American alleged assassin of John F. Kennedy. He denied the charge of assassinating the president, but was murdered before he could be brought to trial.

OT • **abbrev.** Old Testament.

other • **adj. & pron.** **1** used to refer to a person or thing that is different from one already mentioned or known. **2** additional. **3** alternative of two. **4** those not already mentioned.
– ORIGIN Old English.

other half • **n.** Brit. informal one's wife, husband, or partner.

otherness • **n.** the quality or fact of being different.

otherwise • **adv.** **1** in different circumstances. **2** in other respects. **3** in a different way: *she was otherwise engaged.* **4** alternatively.

other woman • **n.** the mistress of a married man.

other-worldly • **adj.** **1** relating to an imaginary or spiritual world. **2** having little awareness of the realities of life.

Othman E
/oth-muhn/ var. of **OSMAN I.**

otiose /oh-ti-ohss, oh-shi-ohss/ • **adj.** serving no practical purpose.
– ORIGIN Latin *otiosus.*

O'Toole, E
Peter (Seamus) (b.1932), Irish-born British actor. His films include *Lawrence of Arabia* and *Goodbye Mr Chips.*

OTT • **abbrev.** Brit. informal over the top.

Ottawa E
/ot-tuh-wuh/ the federal capital of Canada.

otter • **n.** a fish-eating mammal with a long body, thick fur, and webbed feet, living partly in water and partly on land.
– ORIGIN Old English.

Otto, E
Nikolaus August (1832–91), German engineer. His name is given to the four-stroke cycle on which most internal-combustion engines work.

Ottoman • **adj.** hist. relating to the Turkish dynasty of Osman I or to the Ottoman Empire. • **n.** (pl. **Ottomans**) a Turk of the Ottoman period.
– ORIGIN Arabic.

ottoman • **n.** (pl. **ottomans**) a low padded seat without a back or arms.

Ottoman Empire E
the Turkish empire established by Osman I at the end of the 13th century and expanded by his successors to include all of Asia Minor and much of SE Europe. The empire finally collapsed after the First World War.

OU • **abbrev.** (in the UK) Open University.

Ouagadougou E
/wah-guh-doo-goo/ the capital of Burkina Faso.

oubliette /oo-bli-et/ • **n.** a secret dungeon with access only through a trapdoor in its ceiling.
– ORIGIN French.

ought • **modal verb** (3rd sing. present and past **ought**) **1** used to indicate duty or correctness. **2** used to indicate something that is probable. **3** used to indicate a desirable or expected state. **4** used to give or ask advice.
– ORIGIN Old English.

USAGE ought
The correct way of forming negative sentences with **ought** is *he ought not to have gone.* The sentences *he didn't ought to have gone* and *he hadn't ought to have gone* are found in dialect but should not be used in writing.

oughtn't • **contr.** ought not.

Ouija board /wee-juh/ • **n.** trademark a board with letters, numbers, and other signs around its edge, to which a pointer moves, supposedly in answer to questions at a seance.
– ORIGIN from French *oui* 'yes' + German *ja* 'yes'.

ounce • **n.** **1** a unit of weight of one sixteenth of a pound avoirdupois (approximately 28 grams). **2** a very small amount.
– ORIGIN Latin *uncia* 'twelfth part of a pound or foot'.

our • **possess. det.** **1** belonging to or having to do with the speaker and one or more others. **2** belonging to or having to do with people in general.
– ORIGIN Old English.

USAGE our
Do not confuse **our** and **are**. **Our** mainly means 'belonging to or having to do with us', as in *Jo and I had our hair cut*, whereas **are** is one of the forms of the present tense of the verb **to be**, as in *you are a bully.*

Our Father • **n.** God.

Our Lady • **n.** the Virgin Mary.

Our Lord • **n.** God or Jesus.

ours • **possess. pron.** used to refer to something belonging to or connected with the speaker and one or more others.

ourselves • **pron.** (first person pl.) **1** used as the object of a verb or preposition when this is the same as the subject of the clause and the subject is the speaker and one or more other people. **2** we or us personally.

-ous • **suffix** forming adjectives: **1** characterized by: *mountainous.* **2** Chem. referring to an element in a lower valency: *sulphurous.*
– ORIGIN Latin *-osus.*

Ouse[1] E
/ooz/ (also **Great Ouse**) a river of eastern England, which rises in Northamptonshire and flows through East Anglia to the Wash.

Ouse[2] E
/ooz/ a river of NE England, formed at the confluence of the rivers Ure and Swale in North Yorkshire and flowing through York to the Humber estuary.

oust /owsst/ • **v.** drive out from a position of power.
– ORIGIN Old French *ouster* 'take away'.

out • **adv.** **1** moving away from a place. **2** away from one's home or place of work. **3** outdoors. **4** so as to be revealed, heard, or known. **5** at or to an end: *the romance fizzled out.* **6** at a specified distance away from the target. **7** to sea, away from the land. **8** (of the tide) falling or at its lowest level. • **adj.** **1** not at home or one's place of work. **2** made public or available. **3** not possible or worth considering: *under-age drinking is out.* **4** no longer existing or current. **5** unconscious. **6** (of the ball in tennis, squash, etc.) not in the playing area. **7** Cricket & Baseball no longer batting. ● v. informal reveal the homosexuality of.

– PHRASES **out for** intent on having. **out of 1** from. **2** not having (something). **out to do** trying hard to do.

– ORIGIN Old English.

USAGE out

You should write **out of** rather than just **out** in sentences such as *he threw it out of the window.*

out- ● prefix **1** to the point of exceeding: *outperform.* **2** external; separate: *outbuildings.* **3** away from: *outpost.*

outage ● n. a period when a power supply or other service is not available.

out and out ● adj. absolute. ● adv. completely.

outback ● n. (**the outback**) the part of Australia that is remote and sparsely populated.

outbid ● v. (**outbids, outbidding, outbid**) bid more for something than.

outboard ● adj. & adv. **1** on, towards, or near the outside of a ship or aircraft. **2** (of a motor) portable and attachable to the outside of the stern of a boat.

outbound ● adj. & adv. outward bound.

outbreak ● n. a sudden or violent occurrence of war, disease, etc.

outbuilding ● n. a smaller building in the grounds of a main building.

outburst ● n. a sudden violent occurrence or release of something.

outcast ● n. a person rejected by their society or social group.

outclass ● v. be far better than.

outcome ● n. a consequence.

outcrop ● n. a part of a rock formation that is visible on the surface.

outcry ● n. (pl. **outcries**) a strong expression of public disapproval.

outdated ● adj. no longer used, valid, or fashionable.

outdistance ● v. (**outdistances, outdistancing, outdistanced**) leave (a competitor or pursuer) far behind.

outdo ● v. (**outdoes, outdoing, outdid**; past part. **outdone**) do better than (someone else).

outdoor ● adj. done, situated, or used outdoors.

outdoors ● adv. in or into the open air. ● n. any area outside buildings.

outer ● adj. **1** outside. **2** further from the centre or the inside.

– DERIVATIVES **outermost** adj.

Outer Hebrides E
see **Hebrides**.

outer space ● n. the universe beyond the earth's atmosphere.

outface ● v. (**outfaces, outfacing, outfaced**) defeat (someone) by confronting them boldly.

outfall ● n. the place where a river, drain, or sewer empties into the sea, a river, or a lake.

outfit ● n. **1** a set of clothes worn together. **2** informal a group of people undertaking a particular activity together. ● v. (**outfits, outfitting, outfitted**) (**be outfitted**) be provided with an outfit of clothes.

outfitter (also **outfitters**) ● n. Brit. dated a shop selling men's clothing.

outflank ● v. **1** move round the side of (an enemy) so as to attack them. **2** outwit.

outflow ● n. **1** the action of flowing or moving out. **2** something that flows or moves out.

outfox ● v. informal defeat (someone) by being more cunning than them.

outgoing ● adj. **1** friendly and confident. **2** leaving a job or position. **3** going out or away from a place. ● n. Brit. (**outgoings**) money that has to be spent regularly.

outgrow ● v. (**outgrows, outgrowing, outgrew**; past part. **outgrown**) **1** grow too big for. **2** leave behind as one matures. **3** grow faster or taller than.

outgrowth ● n. **1** something that grows out of something else. **2** a natural development or result.

outgun ● v. (**outguns, outgunning, outgunned**) have more or better weapons than.

outhouse ● n. a smaller building built on to or in the grounds of a house.

outing ● n. **1** a short trip taken for pleasure. **2** informal a public appearance in something: *an actress in her first screen outing.*

outlandish ● adj. strange or unfamiliar.

– ORIGIN Old English, 'not native'.

outlast ● v. last longer than.

outlaw ● n. a person who has broken the law and remains at large. ● v. make illegal.

outlay ● n. an amount of money spent.

outlet ● n. **1** a pipe or hole through which water or gas may escape. **2** a point from which goods are sold or distributed. **3** an output socket in an electrical device. **4** a means of expressing one's talents, energy, or emotions.

outlier /owt-ly-er/ ● n. a thing detached from a main body or system.

outline ● n. **1** a drawing or diagram showing the shape of an object. **2** the outer edges of an object. **3** a description of the main points of something. ● v. (**outlines, outlining, outlined**) **1** draw the outer edge or shape of. **2** give a summary of.

outlive ● v. (**outlives, outliving, outlived**) live or last longer than.

outlook ● n. **1** a person's attitude to life. **2** a view. **3** what is likely to happen in the future.

outlying ● adj. situated far from a centre.

outmanoeuvre ● v. (**outmanoeuvres, outmanoeuvring, outmanoeuvred**) **1** avoid (an opponent) by moving faster or more skilfully. **2** use skill and cunning to gain an advantage over.

outmoded ● adj. old-fashioned.

outnumber ● v. (**outnumbers, outnumbering, outnumbered**) be more numerous than.

out of date ● adj. **1** old-fashioned. **2** no longer valid.

outpace ● v. (**outpaces, outpacing, outpaced**) go faster than.

outpatient ● n. a patient attending a hospital for treatment without staying overnight.

outperform ● v. perform better than.

outplay ● v. play better than.

outpost ● n. **1** a small military camp at a distance from the main army. **2** a remote part of a country or empire.

outpouring ● n. **1** something that streams out rapidly. **2** an outburst of strong emotion.

output ● n. **1** the amount of something produced. **2** the process of producing something. **3** the power, energy, etc. supplied by a device or system. **4** Electron. a place where power or information leaves a system. ● v. (**outputs**, **outputting**, **output** or **outputted**) (of a computer) produce (data).

outrage ● n. **1** an extremely strong reaction of anger. **2** an extremely cruel, wicked, or shocking act. ● v. (**outrages**, **outraging**, **outraged**) cause to feel outrage.
– ORIGIN Old French.

outrageous ● adj. **1** shockingly bad or excessive. **2** very bold and unusual.
– DERIVATIVES **outrageously** adv.

outran past of OUTRUN.

outrank ● v. be of a higher rank or quality than.

outré /oo-tray/ ● adj. unusual and rather shocking.
– ORIGIN French, 'exceeded'.

outreach ● n. an organization's involvement with the community.

outrider ● n. a person in a vehicle or on horseback who escorts another vehicle.

outrigger ● n. a float fixed parallel to a canoe or small ship in order to help keep it stable.

outright ● adv. **1** altogether. **2** openly. **3** immediately. ● adj. **1** open and direct. **2** complete.

outrun ● v. (**outruns**, **outrunning**, **outran**; past part. **outrun**) run or travel faster or further than.

outsell ● v. (**outsells**, **outselling**, **outsold**) be sold in greater quantities than.

outset ● n. the beginning.

outshine ● v. (**outshines**, **outshining**, **outshone**) **1** shine more brightly than. **2** be much better than.

outside ● n. **1** the external side, part, or surface of something. **2** the side of a curve where the edge is longer. ● adj. **1** situated on or near the outside. **2** not belonging to a particular group. ● prep. & adv. **1** situated or moving beyond the boundaries of. **2** not being a member of.
– PHRASES **at the outside** at the most. **an outside chance** a remote possibility.

outsider ● n. **1** a person who does not belong to a particular group. **2** a competitor thought to have little chance of success.

outsize (also **outsized**) ● adj. very large.

outskirts ● pl. n. the outer parts of a town or city.

outsmart ● v. defeat (someone) by being cleverer than them.

outsold past and past part. of OUTSELL.

outsource ● v. arrange for (work) to be done outside a company.

outspoken ● adj. frank in stating one's opinions.

outspread ● adj. fully extended or expanded.

outstanding ● adj. **1** very good. **2** clearly noticeable. **3** not yet dealt with or paid.
– DERIVATIVES **outstandingly** adv.

outstay ● v. stay beyond the limit of (one's expected or permitted time).

outstretch ● v. stretch out.

outstrip ● v. (**outstrips**, **outstripping**, **outstripped**) **1** move faster than and overtake. **2** be better than.

out-take ● n. a sequence of a film or recording rejected during editing.

outvote ● v. (**outvotes**, **outvoting**, **outvoted**) defeat by gaining more votes.

outward ● adj. **1** on or from the outside. **2** going out or away from a place. ● adv. (also **outwards**) towards the outside.
– DERIVATIVES **outwardly** adv.

outweigh ● v. be greater or more important than.

outwit ● v. (**outwits**, **outwitting**, **outwitted**) deceive (someone) through being cleverer than them.

ouzo /oo-zoh/ ● n. a Greek aniseed-flavoured spirit.
– ORIGIN modern Greek.

ova pl. of OVUM.

oval ● adj. having a rounded and slightly elongated outline. ● n. an oval object or design.
– ORIGIN Latin *ovalis*.

Oval Office E
the office of the US President in the White House.

ovary ● n. (pl. **ovaries**) **1** a female reproductive organ in which eggs are produced. **2** the base of the reproductive organ of a flower.
– DERIVATIVES **ovarian** adj.
– ORIGIN Latin *ovarium*.

ovate /oh-vayt/ ● adj. tech. oval.
– ORIGIN Latin *ovatus*.

ovation ● n. a long, enthusiastic round of applause.
– ORIGIN Latin.

oven ● n. **1** an enclosed compartment in which food is cooked or heated. **2** a small furnace or kiln.
– ORIGIN Old English.

ovenproof ● adj. suitable for use in an oven.

over ● prep. **1** extending upwards from or above. **2** above so as to cover or protect. **3** expressing movement or a route across. **4** beyond and falling or hanging from: *the car toppled over the cliff.* **5** expressing length of time. **6** higher or more than. **7** expressing authority or control. **8** on the subject of. ● adv. **1** expressing movement or a route across an area. **2** beyond and falling or hanging from a point. **3** in or to the place indicated. **4** expressing action and result: *the car flipped over.* **5** finished. **6** expressing repetition of a process. ● n. Cricket a sequence of six balls bowled by a bowler from one end of the pitch.
– PHRASES **be over** be no longer affected by. **over and above** in addition to.
– ORIGIN Old English.

over- ● prefix **1** excessively: *overambitious.* **2** completely: *overjoyed.* **3** upper; outer: *overcoat.* **4** over; above: *overcast.*

overachieve ● v. (**overachieves**, **overachieving**, **overachieved**) do better than expected.
– DERIVATIVES **overachiever** n.

overact ● v. act a role in an exaggerated way.

overactive • **adj.** excessively active.

overall • **adj.** including everything. • **adv.** taken as a whole. • **n.** (also **overalls**) Brit. a loose-fitting garment worn over ordinary clothes for protection.

overambitious • **adj.** excessively ambitious.

overanxious • **adj.** excessively anxious.

overarching • **adj.** covering everything: *a single overarching principle.*

overarm • **adj. & adv.** (of an arm action) made with the hand brought forward and down from above shoulder level.

overate past of **OVEREAT**.

overawe • **v.** (**overawes**, **overawing**, **overawed**) impress (someone) so much that they are silent or nervous.

overbalance • **v.** (**overbalances**, **overbalancing**, **overbalanced**) fall due to loss of balance.

overbearing • **adj.** trying to control people in an unpleasant way.

overblown • **adj.** exaggerated or pretentious.

overboard • **adv.** from a ship into the water.
– PHRASES **go overboard** be very or too enthusiastic.

overbook • **v.** accept more reservations for (a flight or hotel) than there is room for.

overburden • **v.** give too much work to.

overcame past of **OVERCOME**.

overcast • **adj.** (of the sky or weather) cloudy.

overcautious • **adj.** excessively cautious.

overcharge • **v.** (**overcharges**, **overcharging**, **overcharged**) charge too high a price.

overcoat • **n.** **1** a long warm coat. **2** a top layer of paint or varnish.

overcome • **v.** (**overcomes**, **overcoming**, **overcame**; past part. **overcome**) **1** succeed in dealing with (a problem). **2** defeat. **3** (**be overcome**) be overwhelmed by an emotion.

overcompensate • **v.** (**overcompensates**, **overcompensating**, **overcompensated**) take excessive measures to make amends for something.

overconfident • **adj.** excessively confident.
– DERIVATIVES **overconfidence** n.

overcook • **v.** cook for too long.

overcrowd • **v.** fill beyond what is usual or comfortable.

overdevelop • **v.** (**overdevelops**, **overdeveloping**, **overdeveloped**) develop too much.

overdo • **v.** (**overdoes**, **overdoing**, **overdid**; past part. **overdone**) **1** do (something) excessively or in an exaggerated way. **2** use too much of: *don't overdo the garlic.* **3** (**overdone**) overcooked.

overdose • **n.** an excessive and dangerous dose of a drug. • **v.** (**overdoses**, **overdosing**, **overdosed**) take an overdose.

overdraft • **n.** an arrangement with a bank allowing one to draw more money than there is in one's account.

overdrawn • **adj.** (of a bank account) in a state in which the amount of money taken out is greater than the amount held.

overdress • **v.** dress too elaborately or formally.

overdrive • **n.** **1** a mechanism in a motor vehicle providing an extra gear above the usual top gear. **2** a state of great activity.

overdue • **adj.** not having arrived, happened, or been done at the expected or required time.

overeager • **adj.** excessively eager.

overeat • **v.** (**overeats**, **overeating**, **overate**; past part. **overeaten**) eat too much.

overemphasize (also **overemphasise**) • **v.** (**overemphasizes**, **overemphasizing**, **overemphasized**) place too much emphasis on.
– DERIVATIVES **overemphasis** n.

overenthusiasm • **n.** excessive enthusiasm.
– DERIVATIVES **overenthusiastic** adj.

overestimate • **v.** (**overestimates**, **overestimating**, **overestimated**) form too high an estimate of. • **n.** an estimate which is too high.

overexcite • **v.** (**overexcites**, **overexciting**, **overexcited**) excite too much.

overexert • **v.** (**overexert oneself**) make too great an effort.

overexpose • **v.** (**overexposes**, **overexposing**, **overexposed**) expose too much.

overfamiliar • **adj.** **1** too well known. **2** inappropriately informal.

overfill • **v.** fill to excess.

overflow • **v.** **1** flow over the brim of a container. **2** be too full or crowded. **3** (**overflow with**) be very full of (an emotion). • **n.** **1** the overflowing of a liquid. **2** the excess not able to be fitted into a space. **3** (also **overflow pipe**) an outlet for excess water.

overground • **adv. & adj.** on or above the ground.

overgrown • **adj.** **1** covered with plants that have been allowed to grow wild. **2** grown too large.

overgrowth • **n.** excessive growth.

overhang • **v.** (**overhangs**, **overhanging**, **overhung**) hang outwards over. • **n.** an overhanging part.

overhaul • **v.** **1** examine and repair. **2** Brit. overtake. • **n.** an act of examining and repairing.

overhead • **adv.** above one's head. • **adj.** situated above one's head. • **n.** (**overheads**) expenses incurred in running a business or organization.

overhead projector • **n.** a device that projects an enlarged image of a transparent photograph printed on plastic, by means of an overhead mirror.

overhear • **v.** (**overhears**, **overhearing**, **overheard**) hear accidentally.

overheat • **v.** make or become too hot.

overindulge • **v.** (**overindulges**, **overindulging**, **overindulged**) **1** have too much of something enjoyable. **2** give in to the wishes of (someone) too much: *his mother had overindulged him.*
– DERIVATIVES **overindulgence** n.

overjoyed • **adj.** extremely happy.

overkill • **n.** too much of something.

overlaid past and past part. of **OVERLAY**.

overlain past part. of **OVERLIE**.

overland • **adj. & adv.** by land.

overlap • **v.** (**overlaps**, **overlapping**, **overlapped**) **1** extend over so as to partly cover. **2** partly coincide in time. • **n.** an overlapping part or amount.

overlay • **v.** /oh-ver-lay/ (**overlays**, **overlay-**

ing, **overlaid**) **1** coat the surface of. **2** (of a quality or feeling) become more noticeable than (a previous one). ● **n.** /oh-ver-lay/ **1** a covering. **2** a transparent sheet over artwork or a map, giving additional detail.

overleaf ● **adv.** on the other side of the page.

overlie ● **v.** (**overlies**, **overlying**, **overlay**; past part. **overlain**) lie on top of.

overload ● **v.** /oh-ver-**lohd**/ **1** load too heavily. **2** put too great a demand on. ● **n.** /**oh**-ver-lohd/ an excessive amount.

overlook /oh-ver-**luuk**/ ● **v. 1** fail to notice. **2** ignore or disregard. **3** have a view of from above.

overlord ● **n.** a ruler.

overly ● **adv.** excessively.

overlying pres. part. of **OVERLIE**.

overmuch ● **adv., det., & pron.** too much.

overnight ● **adv. 1** for the duration of a night. **2** during a night. **3** suddenly. ● **adj. 1** for use overnight. **2** done or happening overnight. **3** sudden.

overpass ● **n.** a bridge by which a road or railway line passes over another.

overpay ● **v.** (**overpays**, **overpaying**, **overpaid**) pay too much.

overplay ● **v.** overemphasize.

overpower ● **v.** (**overpowers**, **overpowering**, **overpowered**) **1** defeat with greater strength. **2** overwhelm: *they were overpowered by the fumes.*

overpriced ● **adj.** too expensive.

overprotective ● **adj.** excessively protective.

overqualified ● **adj.** too highly qualified.

overran past of **OVERRUN**.

overrate ● **v.** (**overrates**, **overrating**, **overrated**) rate more highly than is deserved.

overreach ● **v.** (**overreach oneself**) fail through being too ambitious or trying too hard.

overreact ● **v.** react more strongly than is justified.
– DERIVATIVES **overreaction** n.

override ● **v.** (**overrides**, **overriding**, **overrode**; past part. **overridden**) **1** use one's authority to reject or cancel (a decision, order, etc.). **2** interrupt the action of (an automatic device). **3** be more important than. ● **n. 1** the action of overriding. **2** a device on a machine for overriding an automatic process.

overrule ● **v.** (**overrules**, **overruling**, **overruled**) reject or disallow by using one's higher authority.

overrun ● **v.** (**overruns**, **overrunning**, **overran**; past part. **overrun**) **1** spread over or occupy in large numbers. **2** be more than (a limit of time or cost).

overseas ● **adv.** in or to a foreign country. ● **adj.** relating to a foreign country.

oversee ● **v.** (**oversees**, **overseeing**, **oversaw**; past part. **overseen**) supervise.
– DERIVATIVES **overseer** n.

oversexed ● **adj.** having unusually strong sexual desires.

overshadow ● **v. 1** tower above and cast a shadow over. **2** cast a feeling of sadness over. **3** appear more important or successful than.

overshoe ● **n.** a protective shoe worn over a normal shoe.

overshoot ● **v.** (**overshoots**, **overshooting**, **overshot**) accidentally go further than (an intended place).

oversight ● **n.** an unintentional failure to notice or do something.

oversimplify ● **v.** (**oversimplifies**, **oversimplifying**, **oversimplified**) simplify (something) so much that an inaccurate impression of it is given.

oversized (also **oversize**) ● **adj.** bigger than the usual size.

oversleep ● **v.** (**oversleeps**, **oversleeping**, **overslept**) sleep longer or later than one has intended.

overspend ● **v.** (**overspends**, **overspending**, **overspent**) spend too much.

overspill ● **n.** Brit. part of the population of a city or town moving from an overcrowded area to live elsewhere.

overstate ● **v.** (**overstates**, **overstating**, **overstated**) state too strongly.
– DERIVATIVES **overstatement** n.

overstay ● **v.** stay longer than (an allowed time).

overstep ● **v.** (**oversteps**, **overstepping**, **overstepped**) go beyond (a limit).
– PHRASES **overstep the mark** go beyond what is acceptable.

overstretch ● **v.** make excessive demands on.

oversubscribed ● **adj. 1** (of something for sale) applied for in greater quantities than are available. **2** (of a course) having more applications than available places.

overt /oh-vert, **oh**-vert/ ● **adj.** done or shown openly.
– DERIVATIVES **overtly** adv.
– ORIGIN Old French, 'opened'.

overtake ● **v.** (**overtakes**, **overtaking**, **overtook**; past part. **overtaken**) **1** catch up with and pass while travelling in the same direction. **2** become greater or more successful than. **3** come unexpectedly upon: *the report was overtaken by events.*

overthrow ● **v.** (**overthrows**, **overthrowing**, **overthrew**; past part. **overthrown**) remove from power by force. ● **n.** a removal from power.

overtime ● **n.** time worked in addition to one's normal working hours.

overtone ● **n. 1** a musical tone which is a part of the harmonic series above a fundamental note, and may be heard with it. **2** a quality that accompanies something without being directly expressed: *the decision had political overtones.*

overture ● **n. 1** an orchestral piece at the beginning of a musical work. **2** an independent orchestral composition in one movement. **3** (**overtures**) approaches made with the aim of opening negotiations or establishing a relationship.
– ORIGIN Old French.

overturn ● **v. 1** turn over and come to rest upside down. **2** abolish or reverse (a decision, system, etc.).

overuse ● **v.** /oh-ver-**yooz**/ (**overuses**, **overusing**, **overused**) use too much. ● **n.** /oh-ver-yooss/ excessive use.

overview /**oh**-ver-vyoo/ ● **n.** a general review or summary.

overweening ● **adj.** showing too much con-

fidence or pride: *overweening ambition.*
– ORIGIN Old English, 'think'.

overweight ● **adj.** above a normal, desirable, or permitted weight.

overwhelm ● **v. 1** bury or drown beneath a huge mass. **2** overpower. **3** have a strong emotional effect on.
– ORIGIN Old English, 'engulf or submerge'.

overwinter ● **v.** (**overwinters, overwintering, overwintered**) **1** spend the winter in a specified place. **2** (of an insect, plant, etc.) survive through the winter.

overwork ● **v. 1** work too hard. **2** use (a word or idea) too much and so make it weaker in effect. ● **n.** excessive work.

overwrite ● **v.** (**overwrites, overwriting, overwrote**; past part. **overwritten**) Computing destroy (data) or the data in (a file) by entering new data in its place.

overwrought ● **adj. 1** very worried or nervously excited. **2** (of writing or a work of art) too elaborate.

Ovid E
/o-vid/ (43 BC–*c.*17 AD; full name *Publius Ovidius Naso*), Roman poet. He is best known for his love poems and for the *Metamorphoses*, a verse epic which retells Greek and Roman myths.

oviduct /**oh**-vi-dukt/ ● **n.** Anat. & Zool. the tube through which an ovum or egg passes from an ovary.

ovine /**oh**-vyn/ ● **adj.** relating to sheep.
– ORIGIN Latin *ovinus.*

oviparous /oh-**vip**-uh-ruhss/ ● **adj.** (of an animal such as a bird) producing young by means of eggs which are hatched after they have been laid by the parent. Compare with **VIVIPAROUS.**

ovoid /**oh**-voyd/ ● **adj. 1** egg-shaped. **2** oval. ● **n.** an ovoid shape.
– ORIGIN Latin *ovoides.*

ovulate /**ov**-yuu-layt/ ● **v.** (**ovulates, ovulating, ovulated**) discharge ova or ovules from the ovary.
– DERIVATIVES **ovulation** n.

ovule /**ov**-yool/ ● **n.** the part of the ovary of seed plants that after fertilization becomes the seed.
– ORIGIN Latin *ovulum* 'little egg'.

ovum /**oh**-vuhm/ ● **n.** (pl. **ova**) a mature female reproductive cell, which can divide to give rise to an embryo after fertilization by a male cell.
– ORIGIN Latin, 'egg'.

owe ● **v.** (**owes, owing, owed**) **1** be required to pay (money or goods) to (someone) in return for something received. **2** be obliged to do or give (something) to (someone): *I owe you an apology.* **3** (**owe something to**) have something because of.
– ORIGIN Old English.

Owen[1], E
Robert (1771–1858), Welsh social reformer and industrialist. A pioneer socialist, he founded a series of cooperative communities.

Owen[2], E
Wilfred (1893–1918), English poet. His experiences of fighting in the First World War inspired much of his poetry.

Owens, E
Jesse (1913–80; born *James Cleveland Owens*), American athlete, who won four gold medals at the Olympic Games in Berlin in 1936.

owing ● **adj.** yet to be paid or supplied.
– PHRASES **owing to** because of.

owl ● **n.** a bird of prey with large eyes and a hooked beak, active at night.
– ORIGIN Old English.

owlish ● **adj. 1** wise or solemn like an owl. **2** (of glasses or eyes) resembling the large round eyes of an owl.

own ● **adj. & pron. 1** belonging or relating to the person specified: *they can't handle their own children.* **2** done by the person specified. ● **v. 1** possess. **2** formal admit that something is the case. **3** (**own up**) admit that one has done something wrong.
– PHRASES **come into its** (or **one's**) **own** become fully effective. **hold one's own** remain in a position of strength in a difficult situation.
– ORIGIN Old English.

own brand ● **n.** Brit. a product made specially for a retailer and bearing the retailer's name.

owner ● **n.** a person who owns something.
– DERIVATIVES **ownership** n.

owner-occupier ● **n.** Brit. a person who owns the house or flat in which they live.

own goal ● **n.** (in soccer) a goal scored when a player accidentally hits the ball into their own team's goal.

ox ● **n.** (pl. **oxen**) **1** a cow or bull. **2** a castrated bull, used for pulling heavy loads.
– ORIGIN Old English.

oxbow ● **n.** a loop formed by a horseshoe bend in a river.

Oxbridge ● **n.** Oxford and Cambridge universities considered together.

Oxford E
a city in central England, the site of Oxford University.

Oxford Movement E
a Christian movement started in Oxford in 1833, seeking to restore traditional Catholic teachings and ceremonial within the Church of England. Also called **TRACTARIANISM.**

Oxfordshire E
a county of south central England; county town, Oxford.

oxidation ● **n.** Chem. the process of oxidizing or the result of being oxidized.

oxide /**ok**-syd/ ● **n.** Chem. a compound of oxygen with another element or group.

oxidize (also **oxidise**) ● **v.** (**oxidizes, oxidizing, oxidized**) **1** cause to combine with oxygen. **2** Chem. cause to undergo a reaction in which electrons are lost to another substance or molecule. Opp. **REDUCE.**
– DERIVATIVES **oxidization** (also **oxidisation**) n.

Oxon ● **abbrev. 1** Oxfordshire. **2** (in degree titles) of Oxford University.
– ORIGIN from *Oxonia*, Latinized form of **OXFORD.**

oxtail ● **n.** the tail of an ox (used in making soup).

Oxus E
/ok-suhss/ ancient name for **AMU DARYA**.

oxyacetylene /ok-si-uh-set-i-leen/ ● **adj.** (of welding or cutting techniques) using a very hot flame produced by mixing acetylene and oxygen.

oxygen ● **n.** a gas forming about 20 per cent of the earth's atmosphere and essential to life.
– ORIGIN from French *principe oxygène* 'acidifying constituent'.

oxygenate /ok-si-juh-nayt/ ● **v.** (**oxygenates**, **oxygenating**, **oxygenated**) supply with oxygen.

oxymoron /ok-si-mor-on/ ● **n.** a figure of speech in which apparently contradictory terms appear together (e.g. *a deafening silence*).
– ORIGIN Greek *oxumōros* 'pointedly foolish'.

oyez /oh-yez, oh-yay/ ● **exclam.** a call given by a town crier or court official to ask people to pay attention before an announcement.
– ORIGIN Old French, 'hear!'.

oyster ● **n.** **1** a shellfish with two hinged shells, several kinds of which are farmed for food or pearls. **2** a shade of greyish white.
– PHRASES **the world is one's oyster** one is able to enjoy a broad range of opportunities.
– ORIGIN Old French *oistre*.

oystercatcher ● **n.** a wading bird with black or black-and-white plumage and a strong orange-red bill.

Oz ● **n. & adj.** informal Australia or Australian.
– ORIGIN short for *Australia*.

oz ● **abbrev.** ounce(s).
– ORIGIN Italian *onza* 'ounce'.

Ozark Mountains E
/oh-zark/ a forested highland plateau dissected by valleys, lying within the states of Missouri, Arkansas, Oklahoma, Kansas, and Illinois.

ozone ● **n.** **1** a strong-smelling, poisonous form of oxygen, formed in electrical discharges or by ultraviolet light. **2** informal fresh invigorating air.
– ORIGIN German *Ozon*.

ozone-friendly ● **adj.** (of manufactured products) not containing chemicals that are destructive to the ozone layer.

ozone hole ● **n.** an area of the ozone layer where the ozone is greatly reduced, due to CFCs and other pollutants.

ozone layer ● **n.** a layer in the earth's stratosphere containing a high concentration of ozone, which absorbs most of the ultraviolet radiation reaching the earth from the sun.

Ozzie ● **n. & adj.** var. of **AUSSIE**.

Pp

P (also **p**) ● **n.** (pl. **Ps** or **P's**) the sixteenth letter of the alphabet.

p ● **abbrev.** **1** page. **2** Brit. penny or pence.

PA ● **abbrev.** **1** Brit. personal assistant. **2** public address.

Pa ● **abbrev.** pascal(s).

pa ● **n.** informal father.
– ORIGIN from **PAPA**.

p.a. ● **abbrev.** per annum.

pace[1] /payss/ ● **n.** **1** a single step taken when walking or running. **2** the way that a horse runs or walks. **3** rate of movement or change. ● **v.** (**paces**, **pacing**, **paced**) **1** walk up and down in a small area. **2** measure (a distance) by walking it and counting the number of steps taken. **3** set the speed at which (something) happens or develops. **4** (**pace oneself**) do something at a controlled and steady rate.
– PHRASES **keep pace with** progress at the same speed as. **put someone through their paces** make someone demonstrate their abilities.
– ORIGIN Latin *passus* 'stretch (of the leg)'.

pace[2] /pah-chay, pay-si/ ● **prep.** with due respect to (someone).
– ORIGIN Latin, 'in peace'.

pacemaker ● **n.** an artificial device for stimulating and regulating the heart muscle.

pacey ● **adj.** var. of **PACY**.

Pachelbel E
/pa-khuhl-bel/, Johann (1653–1706), German composer and organist. His works include the Canon and Gigue in D for three violins and continuo.

pachyderm /pak-i-derm/ ● **n.** a very large mammal with thick skin, e.g. an elephant.
– ORIGIN Greek *pakhudermos*.

pacific ● **adj.** **1** peaceful. **2** (**Pacific**) relating to the Pacific Ocean.
– ORIGIN Latin *pacificus* 'peacemaking'.

Pacific Ocean E
the largest of the world's oceans, lying between America to the east and Asia and Australasia to the west.

Pacific Rim E
the countries and regions of east Asia that border the Pacific Ocean.

pacifism ● **n.** the belief that disputes should be settled peacefully and that war and violence are always wrong.
– DERIVATIVES **pacifist** n. & adj.

pacify ● **v.** (**pacifies**, **pacifying**, **pacified**) **1** make less angry or upset. **2** bring peace to (a country or warring groups).
– DERIVATIVES **pacification** n. **pacifier** n.
– ORIGIN Latin *pacificare*.

Pacino E
/puh-chee-noh/, Al (b.1940; full name *Alfred Pacino*), American film actor. His films include *The Godfather* and *Scent of a Woman*.

pack[1] ● n. **1** a cardboard or paper container and the items inside it. **2** Brit. a set of playing cards. **3** a collection of related documents. **4** a group of animals that live and hunt together. **5** esp. derog. a group of similar things or people. **6** (**the pack**) the main body of competitors following the leader in a race. **7** Rugby a team's forwards. **8** (**Pack**) an organized group of Cub Scouts or Brownies. **9** a rucksack. **10** a pad of absorbent material, used for treating an injury. ● v. **1** fill (a bag) with items needed for travel. **2** place in a container for transport or storage. **3** cram a large number of things into. **4** (**packed**) crowded. **5** cover, surround, or fill. **6** informal carry (a gun).
– PHRASES **pack a punch** have a powerful effect. **pack in** informal give up (an activity or job). **pack off** informal send (someone) somewhere without much notice. **pack up** Brit. informal (of a machine) break down. **send packing** informal dismiss abruptly.
– ORIGIN German *pak*.

pack[2] ● v. fill (a jury or committee) with people likely to support a particular verdict or decision.
– ORIGIN prob. from former *pact* 'enter into an agreement with'.

package ● n. **1** an object or group of objects wrapped in paper or packed in a box. **2** N. Amer. a packet. **3** (also **package deal**) a set of proposals or terms offered or agreed as a whole. **4** Computing a collection of related programs or sets of instructions. ● v. (**packages, packaging, packaged**) **1** put (something) into a box or wrapping. **2** present in a favourable way.

package holiday (also **package tour**) ● n. a holiday organized by a travel agent, the price of which includes arrangements for transport and accommodation.

packaging ● n. materials used to wrap or protect goods.

packet ● n. **1** a paper or cardboard container. **2** (**a packet**) informal a large sum of money.
– ORIGIN from PACK[1].

packhorse ● n. a horse used to carry loads.

pack ice ● n. a large mass of ice floating in the sea.

packing ● n. material used to protect fragile goods while they are being transported.

packing case ● n. a large, strong box used for transporting or storing goods.

pact ● n. a formal agreement between people or groups.
– ORIGIN Latin *pactum* 'something agreed'.

pacy (also **pacey**) ● adj. (**pacier, paciest**) fast-moving.

pad[1] ● n. **1** a thick piece of soft or absorbent material. **2** the fleshy underpart of an animal's foot or of a human finger. **3** a protective guard worn over a part of the body by a sports player. **4** a number of sheets of blank paper fastened together at one edge. **5** a flat-topped structure or area used for helicopter take-off and landing or for rocket-launching. **6** informal a person's home. ● v. (**pads, padding, padded**) **1** fill or cover with a pad or padding. **2** (**pad out**) lengthen (a speech or piece of writing) with unnecessary material.
– ORIGIN uncertain.

pad[2] ● v. (**pads, padding, padded**) walk with soft, steady steps.
– ORIGIN German *padden*.

padding ● n. **1** soft material used to pad or stuff something. **2** unnecessary material added to lengthen a book, speech, etc.

paddle[1] ● n. **1** a short pole with a broad blade at one or both ends, used to propel a small boat. **2** a tool or part of a machine shaped like a paddle, used for stirring or mixing. ● v. (**paddles, paddling, paddled**) **1** propel (a boat) with a paddle or paddles. **2** (of a bird or other animal) swim with short fast strokes.
– ORIGIN unknown.

paddle[2] ● v. (**paddles, paddling, paddled**) walk with bare feet in shallow water. ● n. an act of paddling.
– ORIGIN uncertain.

paddle steamer (also **paddle boat**) ● n. a boat powered by steam and propelled by large wheels at the side or stern.

paddling pool ● n. a shallow artificial pool for children to paddle in.

paddock ● n. **1** a small field or enclosure for horses. **2** an enclosure next to a racecourse or track where horses or cars are displayed before a race.
– ORIGIN unknown.

Paddy ● n. (pl. **Paddies**) informal, offens. an Irishman.
– ORIGIN informal form of the Irish man's name *Padraig*.

paddy[1] ● n. (pl. **paddies**) a field where rice is grown.
– ORIGIN Malay.

paddy[2] ● n. Brit. informal a fit of temper.
– ORIGIN from PADDY.

Paderewski E
/pad uh ref ski/, Ignacy Jan (1860–1941), Polish pianist, composer, and statesman, Prime Minister 1919. He was the first Prime Minister of independent Poland, but resigned after only ten months in office.

padlock ● n. a detachable lock hanging by a hinged hook through a ring on the object fastened. ● v. secure with a padlock.
– ORIGIN unknown.

paean /pee-uhn/ ● n. a song of praise or triumph.
– ORIGIN Greek *paian* 'hymn of thanksgiving to Apollo'.

paediatrics /pee-di-at-riks/ (US **pediatrics**) ● n. the branch of medicine concerned with children and their diseases.
– DERIVATIVES **paediatric** (US **pediatric**) adj. **paediatrician** (US **pediatrician**) n.
– ORIGIN from Greek *pais* 'child' + *iatros* 'physician'.

paedophile /pee-duh-fyl/ (US **pedophile**) ● n. a person who is sexually attracted to children.
– DERIVATIVES **paedophilia** (US **pedophilia**) n.
– ORIGIN Greek *pais* 'child'.

paella /py-el-luh/ ● n. a Spanish dish of rice, saffron, chicken, seafood, and vegetables, cooked in a large shallow pan.
– ORIGIN Catalan.

pagan ● n. a person holding religious beliefs other than those of the main world religions. ● adj. relating to pagans or their beliefs.
– DERIVATIVES **paganism** n.
– ORIGIN Latin *paganus* 'rustic'.

Paganini E
/pag-uh-nee-ni/, Niccolò (1782–1840), Italian violinist and composer, famous for his virtuoso violin recitals.

page[1] • n. **1** one side of a leaf of a book, magazine, or newspaper. **2** both sides of such a leaf considered as a single unit. **3** Computing a section of data displayed on a screen at one time. • v. (**pages**, **paging**, **paged**) (**page through**) leaf through.
– ORIGIN Latin *pagina*.

page[2] • n. **1** a boy or young man employed in a hotel or club to run errands, open doors, etc. **2** a young boy attending a bride at a wedding. **3** hist. a boy in training for knighthood. • v. (**pages**, **paging**, **paged**) summon over a public address system or by means of a pager.
– ORIGIN Old French.

pageant /paj-uhnt/ • n. a public entertainment consisting of a procession of people in elaborate costumes, or an outdoor performance of a historical scene.
– ORIGIN unknown.

pageantry • n. elaborate display or ceremony.

pageboy • n. a page in a hotel or attending a bride at a wedding.

pager • n. a small radio device which bleeps or vibrates to inform the wearer that someone wishes to contact them or that it has received a message.

paginate /paj-i-nayt/ • n. (**paginates**, **paginating**, **paginated**) give numbers to the pages of a book, journal, etc.
– DERIVATIVES **pagination** n.

pagoda /puh-goh-duh/ • n. a Hindu or Buddhist temple or other sacred building.
– ORIGIN Portuguese *pagode*.

paid past and past part. of **PAY**.
– PHRASES **put paid to** informal stop abruptly.

paid-up • adj. **1** with all money due paid in full. **2** committed to a cause, group, etc.: *a fully paid-up socialist*.

pail • n. a bucket.
– ORIGIN uncertain.

pain • n. **1** a strongly unpleasant feeling caused by illness or injury. **2** mental suffering. **3** (also **pain in the neck**) informal an annoying or boring person or thing. **4** (**pains**) great care or trouble. • v. **1** cause pain to. **2** (**pained**) showing that one is annoyed or upset.
– PHRASES **on** (or **under**) **pain of** with the threat of the punishment of.
– ORIGIN Old French *peine*.

Paine, E
Thomas (1737–1809), English political writer. An influential radical thinker, he wrote *Common Sense*, which called for American independence, *The Rights of Man*, defending the French Revolution, and *The Age of Reason*, an attack on Christianity.

painful • adj. **1** affected with or causing pain. **2** informal very bad: *their attempts at reggae are painful*.
– DERIVATIVES **painfully** adv.

painkiller • n. a medicine for relieving pain.

painless • adj. **1** not causing pain. **2** involving little effort or stress.
– DERIVATIVES **painlessly** adv.

painstaking • adj. very careful and thorough: *painstaking attention to detail*.
– DERIVATIVES **painstakingly** adv.

paint • n. **1** a coloured substance which is spread over a surface to give a thin decorative or protective coating. **2** dated cosmetic make-up. • v. **1** apply paint to. **2** apply (a liquid) to a surface with a brush. **3** produce (a picture) with paint. **4** give a description of.
– PHRASES **paint the town red** informal go out and enjoy oneself in a lively way.
– ORIGIN Old French *peindre*.

paintball • n. a combat game in which participants shoot capsules of paint at each other with air guns.

paintbox • n. a box holding a palette of dry paints for painting pictures.

paintbrush • n. a brush for applying paint.

painter[1] • n. **1** an artist who paints pictures. **2** a person who paints buildings.

painter[2] • n. a rope attached to the bow of a boat for tying it to a quay.
– ORIGIN uncertain.

painterly • adj. like a painter; artistic: *she has a painterly eye*.

painting • n. a painted picture.

paintwork • n. esp. Brit. painted surfaces in a building or on a vehicle.

pair • n. **1** a set of two things used together or seen as a unit. **2** an article consisting of two joined or corresponding parts. **3** two people or animals that are related or considered together. • v. **1** join or connect to form a pair. **2** (**pair off/up**) form a couple.
– ORIGIN Old French *paire*.

Paisley E
/payz-li/, Ian (Richard Kyle) (b.1926), Northern Irish clergyman and politician. The co-founder of the Ulster Democratic Unionist Party (1972), he has been a vociferous defender of the Protestant Unionist position in Northern Ireland.

paisley /payz-li/ • n. an intricate pattern of curved shapes like feathers.
– ORIGIN named after the town of *Paisley* in Scotland.

pajamas • pl. n. US = **PYJAMAS**.

Paki • n. (pl. **Pakis**) Brit. informal, offens. a Pakistani.

Pakistan E
/pah-ki-stahn, pak-i-stan/ a country in the Indian subcontinent; capital, Islamabad.
– DERIVATIVES **Pakistani** adj. & n.

pal informal • n. a friend. • v. (**pals**, **palling**, **palled**) (**pal up**) form a friendship.
– ORIGIN Romany, 'brother, mate'.

palace • n. a large, impressive building forming the official residence of a king or queen, president, archbishop, etc.
– ORIGIN Old French *paleis*.

palace coup (also **palace revolution**) • n. the non-violent overthrow of a monarch or government by senior officials within the ruling group.

palaeo- /pa-li-oh, pay-li-oh/ (US **paleo-**) • comb. form older or ancient: *Palaeolithic*.
– ORIGIN Greek *palaios*.

Palaeocene /pa-li-oh-seen, pay-li-oh-seen/ (US **Paleocene**) • adj. Geol. relating to the earliest epoch of the Tertiary period (about 65 to 56.5 million years ago), a time of rapid de-

velopment of mammals.
– ORIGIN from Greek *palaios* 'ancient' + *kainos* 'new'.

palaeography /pa-li-og-ruh-fi, pay-li-og-ruh-fi/ (US **paleography**) ● **n.** the study of ancient writing systems and manuscripts.

Palaeolithic /pa-li-uh-**li**-thik, pay-li-uh-**li**-thik/ (US **Paleolithic**) ● **adj.** Archaeol. relating to the early phase of the Stone Age.
– ORIGIN from Greek *palaios* 'ancient' + *lithos* 'stone'.

palaeontology /pa-li-on-**tol**-uh-ji, pay-li-on-**tol**-uh-ji/ (US **paleontology**) ● **n.** the branch of science concerned with fossil animals and plants.
– DERIVATIVES **palaeontologist** (US **paleontologist**) n.
– ORIGIN from Greek *palaios* 'ancient' + *onta* 'beings'.

Palaeozoic /pa-li-uh-**zoh**-ik, pay-li-uh-**zoh**-ik/ (US **Paleozoic**) ● **adj.** Geol. relating to the era between the Precambrian aeon and the Mesozoic era (about 570 to 245 million years ago), which ended with the dominance of the reptiles.
– ORIGIN from Greek *palaios* 'ancient' + *zōē* 'life'.

palanquin /pa-luhn-**keen**/ ● **n.** (in India and the East) a covered litter for one passenger.
– ORIGIN Portuguese *palanquim*.

palatable /pa-luh-tuh-b'l/ ● **adj. 1** pleasant to taste. **2** acceptable.

palate ● **n. 1** the roof of the mouth. **2** a person's ability to distinguish between different flavours.
– ORIGIN Latin *palatum*.

palatial /puh-**lay**-sh'l/ ● **adj.** spacious or impressive, like a palace.

palatinate /puh-**lat**-i-nuht/ ● **n.** hist. a territory under the jurisdiction of a Count Palatine.

palatine /pa-luh-tyn/ ● **adj.** hist. **1** (of an official or feudal lord) having local authority that elsewhere belongs only to a sovereign. **2** (of a territory) subject to such authority.
– ORIGIN French.

Palau E
/puh-**low**/ (also **Belau**) an independent republic consisting of a group of islands in the western Pacific Ocean; capital, Koror.

palaver /puh-**lah**-ver/ ● **n.** informal lengthy and boring fuss or discussion.
– ORIGIN Portuguese *palavra* 'word'.

palazzo /puh-**lat**-soh/ ● **n.** (pl. **palazzos** or **palazzi** /puh-**lat**-si/) a large, grand building in Italy.
– ORIGIN Italian, 'palace'.

pale[1] ● **adj. 1** of a light shade or colour. **2** (of a person's face) having little colour, through shock, illness, etc. **3** not very good or impressive: *a pale imitation.* ● **v.** (**pales, paling, paled**) **1** become pale in one's face. **2** seem less important: *his version of the song pales in comparison to the original.*
– ORIGIN Old French.

pale[2] ● **n. 1** a wooden stake used with others to form a fence. **2** a boundary.
– PHRASES **beyond the pale** outside the boundaries of acceptable behaviour.
– ORIGIN Old French *pal*.

paleo- ● **comb. form** US = PALAEO-.

Palermo E
/puh-**lair**-moh/ the capital of the Italian island of Sicily.

Palestine E
/**pal**-i-styn/ a territory in the Middle East on the eastern coast of the Mediterranean Sea. In 1948 the state of Israel was established in what was traditionally Palestine, but the name continued to be used in the context of the struggle for territory and rights of displaced Palestinian Arabs. In 1993 an agreement between Israel and the Palestine Liberation Organization gave some autonomy to the Gaza Strip and the West Bank.

Palestine Liberation Organization E
a political and military organization formed in 1964 to unite various Palestinian Arab groups and ultimately to bring about an independent state of Palestine.

Palestrina E
/pal-uh-**stree**-nuh/, Giovanni Pierluigi da (*c.*1525–94), Italian composer, known for his sacred music, including 105 masses.

palette /**pa**-lit/ ● **n. 1** a thin board on which an artist lays and mixes paints. **2** the range of colours used by an artist.
– ORIGIN French, 'little shovel'.

palette knife ● **n. 1** a thin blade with a handle, for mixing, applying, or removing paint. **2** Brit. a kitchen knife with a long, blunt, round-ended blade.

palimpsest /**pal**-imp-sesst/ ● **n. 1** a parchment on which writing has been applied over earlier writing which has been erased. **2** something used again or altered but still bearing traces of its earlier form: *the house is a palimpsest of the taste of successive owners.*
– ORIGIN from Greek *palin* 'again' + *psēstos* 'rubbed smooth'.

palindrome /**pal**-in-drohm/ ● **n.** a word or phrase that reads the same backwards as forwards, e.g. *madam*.
– ORIGIN Greek *palindromos* 'running back again'.

paling /**pay**-ling/ ● **n. 1** a fence made from stakes. **2** a stake used in such a fence.

palisade /pa-li-**sayd**/ ● **n.** a fence of stakes or iron railings.
– ORIGIN French *palissade*.

pall[1] /pawl/ ● **n. 1** a cloth spread over a coffin, hearse, or tomb. **2** a dark cloud of smoke, dust, etc. **3** a general atmosphere of gloom or fear: *the murder has cast a pall of terror over the village.*
– ORIGIN Latin *pallium* 'covering, cloak'.

pall[2] /pawl/ ● **v.** become less appealing through familiarity.
– ORIGIN from APPAL.

Palladio E
/puh-**lah**-di-oh/, Andrea (1508–80), Italian architect. He led a revival of classical architecture, promoting the Roman ideals of symmetry and harmonic proportions.

palladium /puh-**lay**-di-uhm/ ● **n.** a rare silvery-white metallic element resembling platinum.
– ORIGIN from *Pallas*, an asteroid discovered just before the element.

p

Pallas E
/**pal**-luhss/ Gk Myth. (also **Pallas Athene**) one of the names of **ATHENE**.

pall-bearer ● n. a person helping to carry or escorting a coffin at a funeral.

pallet[1] ● n. a straw mattress or makeshift bed.
– ORIGIN Old French *paillete*.

pallet[2] ● n. a portable platform on which goods can be moved, stacked, and stored.
– ORIGIN French, 'little blade'.

palliasse /**pal**-li-ass/ ● n. a straw mattress.
– ORIGIN French *paillasse*.

palliate /**pal**-li-ayt/ ● v. (**palliates**, **palliating**, **palliated**) **1** make (the symptoms of a disease) less severe without curing it. **2** make (something bad) less severe.
– DERIVATIVES **palliation** n.
– ORIGIN Latin *palliare* 'to cloak'.

palliative /**pal**-li-uh-tiv/ ● n. **1** a medicine that relieves pain without curing it. **2** something that makes a problem less severe but does not solve it. ● adj. having to do with a palliative.

pallid ● adj. **1** pale, especially because of poor health. **2** feeble.
– ORIGIN Latin *pallidus*.

pallor ● n. an unhealthy pale appearance.
– ORIGIN Latin.

pally ● adj. informal having a close, friendly relationship.

palm[1] ● n. **1** (also **palm tree**) an evergreen tree of warm regions, with a crown of long feathered or fan-shaped leaves. **2** a prize or symbol of victory.
– ORIGIN Latin *palma* 'palm (of a hand)'.

palm[2] ● n. the inner surface of the hand between the wrist and fingers. ● v. **1** hide (a small object) in the hand. **2** (**palm off**) sell or dispose of (something) by fraud. **3** (**palm off**) informal persuade (someone) to accept something worthless by deception.
– ORIGIN Latin *palma*.

Palma E
/**pah**-muh, **pal**-muh/ the capital of the Balearic Islands, a port and resort on the island of Majorca. Full name **PALMA DE MALLORCA**.

palmate /**pal**-mayt/ ● adj. esp. Bot. & Zool. shaped like a hand with the fingers spread out.

Palm Beach E
a resort town in SE Florida, on an island just off the coast.

Palmer, E
Arnold (Daniel) (b.1929), American golfer. His many championships include four victories in the US Masters, the US Open, and the British Open.

Palmerston E
/**pah**-mer-st'n/, Henry John Temple, 3rd Viscount (1784–1865), British Whig statesman, Prime Minister 1855–8 and 1859–65. He oversaw the successful conclusion of the Crimean War in 1856 and the suppression of the Indian Mutiny in 1858.

palmistry ● n. the supposed interpretation of a person's character or prediction of their future by examining the hand.
– DERIVATIVES **palmist** n.

Palm Springs E
a resort city in southern California, east of Los Angeles, noted for its hot mineral springs.

Palm Sunday ● n. the Sunday before Easter.

palmtop ● n. a computer small and light enough to be held in one hand.

palmy ● adj. (**palmier**, **palmiest**) comfortable and prosperous: *the palmy days of the 1970s.*

palomino /pa-luh-**mee**-noh/ ● n. (pl. **palominos**) a pale golden or tan-coloured horse with a white mane and tail.
– ORIGIN Latin American Spanish.

palp /*rhymes with* scalp/ ● n. Zool. each of a pair of long segmented feelers near the mouth of some insects and crustaceans.
– ORIGIN Latin *palpus*.

palpable /**pal**-puh-b'l/ ● adj. **1** able to be touched or felt. **2** so powerful as to be almost touched or felt: *a palpable sense of loss.*
– DERIVATIVES **palpably** adv.
– ORIGIN Latin *palpabilis*.

palpate /pal-**payt**/ ● v. (**palpates**, **palpating**, **palpated**) medically examine (a part of the body) by touch.

palpitate /**pal**-pi-tayt/ ● v. (**palpitates**, **palpitating**, **palpitated**) **1** (of the heart) beat rapidly or irregularly. **2** shake; tremble.
– ORIGIN Latin *palpitare* 'tremble, throb'.

palpitation ● n. **1** throbbing or trembling. **2** (**palpitations**) a noticeably rapid, strong, or irregular heartbeat.

palsy /**pawl**-zi/ ● n. (pl. **palsies**) dated paralysis. ● v. (**palsies**, **palsying**, **palsied**) (**be palsied**) be affected with paralysis.
– ORIGIN Old French *paralisie*.

paltry ● adj. (**paltrier**, **paltriest**) **1** (of an amount) very small. **2** petty; trivial.
– ORIGIN prob. from dialect *pelt* 'rubbish'.

Pamir Mountains E
/puh-**meer**/ a mountain system of central Asia, centred in Tajikistan and extending into Kyrgyzstan, Afghanistan, Pakistan, and western China.

pampas /**pam**-puhss/ ● n. large treeless plains in South America.
– ORIGIN from an American Indian language.

pamper ● v. (**pampers**, **pampering**, **pampered**) give (someone) a great deal of attention and comfort.
– ORIGIN first meaning 'cram with food': prob. from German or Dutch.

pamphlet /**pam**-flit/ ● n. a small leaflet containing information about a single subject. ● v. (**pamphlets**, **pamphleting**, **pamphleted**) distribute pamphlets to.
– ORIGIN from the name of a 12th-century Latin love poem *Pamphilus, seu de Amore.*

pamphleteer ● n. a writer of pamphlets.

Pamplona E
/pam-**ploh**-nuh/ a city in northern Spain, noted for the fiesta of San Fermin in July, which is celebrated with the running of bulls through the streets.

Pan E
a Greek god of flocks and herds, represented with the horns, ears, and legs of a goat on a man's body.

pan[1] ● n. **1** a metal container for cooking food in. **2** a bowl fitted at either end of a pair of scales. **3** Brit. the bowl of a toilet. **4** a hollow in the ground in which water collects. ● v. (**pans**, **panning**, **panned**) **1** informal criticize severely. **2** (**pan out**) informal end up or conclude. **3** wash gravel in a shallow bowl to separate out (gold).
– ORIGIN Old English.

pan[2] ● v. (**pans**, **panning**, **panned**) swing (a video or film camera) to give a panoramic effect or follow a subject.
– ORIGIN short for **PANORAMA**.

pan- ● comb. form including everything or everyone: *pan-African*.
– ORIGIN Greek.

panacea /pan-uh-see-uh/ ● n. a solution or remedy for all difficulties or diseases.
– ORIGIN Greek *panakeia*.

panache /puh-**nash**/ ● n. impressive confidence of style or manner.
– ORIGIN French, 'plume'.

Panama E
/**pan**-uh-mah/ a country in Central America, on the isthmus connecting North and South America; capital, Panama City.
DERIVATIVES **Panamanian** adj. & n.

panama ● n. a man's wide-brimmed hat of straw-like material.
– ORIGIN named after **PANAMA**.

Panama Canal E
a canal across the Isthmus of Panama, connecting the Atlantic and Pacific Oceans.

Panama City E
the capital of Panama.

panatella /pa-nuh-**tel**-luh/ ● n. a long thin cigar.
– ORIGIN Latin American Spanish *panatela* 'long thin biscuit'.

pancake ● n. **1** a thin, flat cake of batter, fried and turned in a pan. **2** theatrical make-up consisting of a flat solid layer of compressed powder.

Pancake Day ● n. Shrove Tuesday, when pancakes are traditionally eaten.

panchromatic ● adj. (of black-and-white photographic film) sensitive to all visible colours of the spectrum.

pancreas /**pang**-kri-uhss/ ● n. (pl. **pancreases**) a large gland behind the stomach which produces digestive enzymes and releases them into the duodenum.
– DERIVATIVES **pancreatic** adj.
– ORIGIN from Greek *pan* 'all' + *kreas* 'flesh'.

panda ● n. **1** (also **giant panda**) a large black-and-white bear-like mammal native to bamboo forests in China. **2** (also **red panda**) a raccoon-like Himalayan mammal with thick reddish-brown fur and a bushy tail.
– ORIGIN Nepali, the language of Nepal.

pandemic /pan-**dem**-ik/ ● adj. (of a disease) widespread over a whole country or large part of the world. ● n. an outbreak of such a disease.
– ORIGIN from Greek *pan* 'all' + *dēmos* 'people'.

pandemonium /pan-di-**moh**-ni-uhm/ ● n. uproar or confusion.
– ORIGIN first meaning 'the place of all demons', in Milton's *Paradise Lost*.

pander ● v. (**panders**, **pandering**, **pandered**) (**pander to**) indulge (an immoral or distasteful desire or habit).
– ORIGIN from *Pandare*, a character in Chaucer's *Troilus and Criseyde* who acts as a lovers' go-between.

Pandit E
/**pun**-dit/, Vijaya (Lakshmi) (1900–90), Indian politician and diplomat, sister of Jawaharlal Nehru. Having been imprisoned by the British for nationalist activities, after India's independence she became the first woman to serve as president of the United Nations General Assembly (1953–4).

Pandora E
Gk Myth. the first mortal woman, who was sent to earth by Zeus with a box or jar of evils. She opened the box, letting out the evils and leaving only hope inside.

Pandora's box ● n. a process that once begun creates many problems.

p. & p. ● abbrev. Brit. postage and packing.

pane ● n. a single sheet of glass in a window or door.
– ORIGIN Latin *pannus* 'piece of cloth'.

panegyric /pa-ni-**ji**-rik/ ● n. a speech or text in praise of someone or something.
– ORIGIN Greek *panēgurikos* 'of public assembly'.

panel ● n. **1** a section of a door, vehicle, garment, etc. **2** a flat board on which instruments or controls are fixed. **3** a small group of people brought together to investigate or decide on a matter.
– DERIVATIVES **panelled** (US **paneled**) adj.
– ORIGIN Latin *pannus* 'piece of cloth'.

panel beater ● n. Brit. a person whose job is to beat out the bodywork of motor vehicles.

panel game ● n. Brit. a broadcast quiz played by a team of people.

panelling (US **paneling**) ● n. wooden panels as a decorative wall covering.

panellist (US **panelist**) ● n. a member of a panel taking part in a broadcast game or discussion.

pang ● n. a sudden sharp pain or painful emotion.
– ORIGIN perh. from **PRONG**.

pangolin /pang-**guh**-lin/ ● n. an insect-eating mammal whose body is covered with horny overlapping scales.
– ORIGIN Malay, 'roller'.

panic ● n. **1** sudden uncontrollable fear or anxiety. **2** informal frenzied hurry to do something. ● v. (**panics**, **panicking**, **panicked**) feel or cause to feel panic.
– DERIVATIVES **panicky** adj.
– ORIGIN from **PAN**, noted for causing terror.

panic button ● n. a button for summoning help in an emergency.

panicle /**pan**-i-k'l/ ● n. Bot. a loose branching cluster of flowers.
– ORIGIN Latin *panicula*.

Panjabi ● n. (pl. **Panjabis**) var. of **PUNJABI**.

panjandrum /pan-**jan**-druhm/ ● n. a self-important person in a position of authority.
– ORIGIN from an invented word in a nonsense verse (1755) by Samuel Foote.

p

Pankhurst, E
Mrs Emmeline (1858–1928), English suffragette. In 1903 Emmeline and her daughters founded the Women's Social and Political Union, starting an increasingly militant campaign for the right for women to vote. This was eventually granted in 1918.

pannier • **n.** **1** a bag or box fitted on either side of the rear wheel of a bicycle or motorcycle. **2** each of a pair of baskets carried by a donkey etc.
– ORIGIN Old French *panier*.

panoply /**pan**-uh-pli/ • **n.** a complete or impressive collection or display.
– ORIGIN from Greek *pan* 'all' + *hopla* 'arms'.

panorama • **n.** **1** a clear view of a wide area. **2** a complete survey of a subject or sequence of events.
– DERIVATIVES **panoramic** adj.
– ORIGIN from Greek *pan* 'all' + *horama* 'view'.

pan pipes • **pl. n.** a musical instrument made from a row of short pipes fixed together.
– ORIGIN from the god **PAN**.

pansy • **n.** **1** a plant of the viola family, with brightly coloured flowers. **2** informal, derog. an effeminate or homosexual man.
– ORIGIN French *pensée* 'thought, pansy'.

pant • **v.** **1** breathe with short, quick breaths. **2** (**pant for**) long for. • **n.** a short, quick breath.
– ORIGIN Old French *pantaisier* 'be agitated, gasp'.

pantaloons • **pl. n.** **1** women's baggy trousers gathered at the ankles. **2** hist. men's close-fitting breeches fastened below the calf or at the foot.
– ORIGIN from *Pantalone*, a character in Italian comic theatre represented as a foolish old man wearing pantaloons.

pantechnicon /pan-**tek**-ni-kuhn/ • **n.** Brit. a large van for transporting furniture.
– ORIGIN from Greek *pan* 'all' + *tekhnikon* 'piece of art'.

pantheism /**pan**-thee-i-z'm/ • **n.** **1** the belief that God is present in all things. **2** belief in many or all gods.

pantheon /**pan**-thi-uhn/ • **n.** **1** all the gods of a people or religion. **2** an ancient temple dedicated to all the gods. **3** a collection of particularly famous or important people.
– ORIGIN from Greek *pan* 'all' + *theion* 'holy'.

panther • **n.** **1** a black leopard. **2** N. Amer. a puma or a jaguar.
– ORIGIN Greek *panthēr*.

panties • **pl. n.** informal knickers.

pantile /**pan**-tyl/ • **n.** a curved roof tile.
– ORIGIN from **PAN¹** + **TILE**.

pantomime • **n.** Brit. a theatrical entertainment involving music, topical jokes, and slapstick comedy.
– ORIGIN Greek *pantomimos* 'imitator of all'.

pantothenic acid /pan-tuh-**then**-ik/ • **n.** a vitamin of the B complex, found in rice, bran, etc., and essential for the oxidation of fats and carbohydrates.
– ORIGIN Greek *pantothen* 'from every side'.

pantry • **n.** (pl. **pantries**) a small room or cupboard in which food, crockery, and cutlery are kept.
– ORIGIN Old French *paneter* 'baker'.

pants • **pl. n.** **1** Brit. underpants or knickers. **2** esp. N. Amer. trousers.
– ORIGIN short for **PANTALOONS**.

pantyhose • **pl. n.** N. Amer. women's nylon tights.

pap¹ • **n.** **1** bland soft or semi-liquid food suitable for babies or invalids. **2** worthless or trivial reading matter or entertainment.
– ORIGIN prob. from Latin *pappare* 'eat'.

pap² • **n.** archaic or dialect a woman's breast or nipple.
– ORIGIN prob. Scandinavian.

papa /puh-**pah**, **pop**-puh/ • **n.** N. Amer. or dated one's father.
– ORIGIN French.

papacy /**pay**-puh-si/ • **n.** (pl. **papacies**) the position or period of office of the pope.
– ORIGIN Latin *papa* 'pope'.

papal /**pay**-p'l/ • **adj.** relating to the pope or the papacy.

paparazzo /pa-puh-**rat**-zoh/ • **n.** (pl. **paparazzi** /pa-puh-**rat**-zi/) a freelance photographer who pursues celebrities to take photographs of them.
– ORIGIN Italian, the name of a character in Fellini's film *La Dolce Vita*.

papaya /puh-**py**-uh/ • **n.** a tropical fruit with orange flesh and small black seeds.
– ORIGIN Spanish and Portuguese.

paper • **n.** **1** material manufactured in thin sheets from the pulp of wood, used for writing or printing on or as wrapping material. **2** (**papers**) documents. **3** a newspaper. **4** a government report or policy document. **5** an essay or dissertation read at a conference or published in a journal. **6** a set of examination questions. • **v.** (**papers**, **papering**, **papered**) **1** cover with wallpaper. **2** (**paper over**) disguise (an awkward problem) instead of resolving it. • **adj.** officially recorded but having no real existence or use: *a paper profit*.
– PHRASES **on paper 1** in writing. **2** in theory rather than in reality.
– ORIGIN Old French *papir*.

paperback • **n.** a book bound in stiff paper or flexible card.

paper boy (or **paper girl**) • **n.** a boy (or girl) who delivers newspapers to people's homes.

paper clip • **n.** a piece of bent wire or plastic used for holding several sheets of paper together.

paperknife • **n.** a blunt knife used for opening envelopes.

paper round • **n.** a job of regularly delivering newspapers.

paper-thin • **adj.** very thin or insubstantial.

paper tiger • **n.** a person or thing that appears threatening but is actually weak.

paperweight • **n.** a small, heavy object for keeping loose papers in place.

paperwork • **n.** routine work involving written documents.

papier mâché /pa-pi-ay **mash**-ay/ • **n.** a mixture of paper and glue that is easily moulded but becomes hard when dry.
– ORIGIN French, 'chewed paper'.

papilla /puh-**pil**-luh/ • **n.** (pl. **papillae** /puh-**pil**-lee/) a small projection on a part of the body or on a plant.
– ORIGIN Latin, 'nipple'.

papilloma /pa-pil-**loh**-muh/ • **n.** (pl. **papillomas** or **papillomata** /pa-pil-**loh**-muh-tuh/) Med. a small wart-like growth.

papist /**pay**-pist/ derog. • **n.** a Roman Catholic.

● **adj.** Roman Catholic.

paprika /pap-ri-kuh, puh-pree-kuh/ ● **n.** an orange-red powdered spice made from certain varieties of sweet pepper.
– ORIGIN Hungarian.

Papua E
/pap-wuh, pap-yuu-uh/ the SE part of the island of New Guinea, now part of the independent state of Papua New Guinea.

Papua New Guinea E
a country in the western Pacific comprising the eastern half of the island of New Guinea together with some neighbouring islands; capital, Port Moresby.
– DERIVATIVES **Papua New Guinean** adj. & n.

papyrus /puh-py-ruhss/ ● **n.** (pl. **papyri** /puh-py-ry/ or **papyruses**) a material made in ancient Egypt from the stem of a water plant, used for writing or painting on.
– ORIGIN Greek *papuros.*

par ● **n.** Golf the number of strokes a first-class player should normally require for a particular hole or course.
– PHRASES **above** (or **below** or **under**) **par** above (or below) the usual or expected level or amount. **on a par with** equal to.
– ORIGIN Latin, 'equal'.

para- (also **par-**) ● **prefix 1** beside; adjacent to: *parallel.* **2** distinct from, but similar to: *paramilitary.*
– ORIGIN Greek *para.*

parable ● **n.** a simple story used to illustrate a moral or spiritual lesson.
– ORIGIN Latin *parabola* 'comparison'.

parabola /puh-rab-uh-luh/ ● **n.** (pl. **parabolas** or **parabolae** /puh-rab-uh-lee/) an open plane curve of the kind formed by the intersection of a cone with a plane parallel to its side.
– ORIGIN Latin.

parabolic /pa-ruh-bol-ik/ ● **adj.** having to do with or like a parabola.

Paracelsus E
/pa-ruh-sel-suhss/ (*c.*1493–1541: born *Theophrastus Phillipus Aureolus Bombastus von Hohenheim*), Swiss physician. He developed a new approach to medicine based on observation and experience, and regarded illness as having a specific external cause (rather than resulting from an imbalance of the bodily humours).

paracetamol /pa-ruh-see-tuh-mol, pa-ruh-set-uh-mol/ ● **n.** (pl. **paracetamol** or **paracetamols**) Brit. a drug used to reduce pain and fever.
– ORIGIN from its chemical name.

parachute ● **n.** a cloth canopy which allows a person or heavy object attached to it to descend slowly when dropped from a high position. ● **v.** (**parachutes**, **parachuting**, **parachuted**) drop by parachute.
– DERIVATIVES **parachutist** n.
– ORIGIN from French *para-* 'protection against' + *chute* 'fall'.

parade ● **n. 1** a public procession. **2** a formal march or gathering of troops for inspection or display. **3** a series of people or things. **4** a boastful display. **5** Brit. a row of shops. ● **v.** (**parades**, **parading**, **paraded**) **1** walk, march, or display in a parade. **2** display (something) publicly in order to impress others. **3** (**parade as**) appear falsely to be.
– ORIGIN French, 'a showing'.

parade ground ● **n.** a place where troops gather for parade.

paradigm /pa-ruh-dym/ ● **n. 1** a typical example, pattern, or model of something. **2** a model underlying the theories and practice of a scientific subject.
– DERIVATIVES **paradigmatic** /pa-ruh-dig-mat-ik/ adj.
– ORIGIN Greek *paradeigma.*

paradise ● **n. 1** (in some religions) heaven. **2** the Garden of Eden. **3** a very pleasant or beautiful place or state.
– ORIGIN Old French *paradis.*

paradox ● **n. 1** a statement that sounds absurd or seems to contradict itself, but may in fact be true. **2** a person or thing that combines contradictory qualities.
– DERIVATIVES **paradoxical** adj. **paradoxically** adv.
– ORIGIN Greek *paradoxon* 'contrary opinion'.

paraffin ● **n. 1** (Brit. **paraffin wax**) a flammable waxy solid obtained from petroleum or shale and used for sealing and waterproofing and in candles. **2** (also **paraffin oil**) Brit. a liquid fuel made in a similar way.
– ORIGIN German.

paragliding ● **n.** a sport in which a person glides through the air by means of a wide parachute after jumping from or being hauled to a height.

paragon ● **n.** a person who is excellent, or who is a perfect example of a particular quality.
– ORIGIN Italian *paragone* 'touchstone'.

paragraph ● **n.** a distinct section of a piece of writing, beginning on a new line.
– ORIGIN French *paragraphe.*

Paraguay E
/pa-ruh-gwy/ a country in central South America; capital, Asunción.
– DERIVATIVES **Paraguayan** adj. & n.

parakeet /pa-ruh-keet/ (also **parrakeet**) ● **n.** a small green parrot with a long tail.
– ORIGIN Old French *paroquet.*

parallax /pa-ruhl-laks/ ● **n.** the apparent difference in the position of an object when viewed from different positions.
– ORIGIN Greek *parallaxis* 'a change'.

parallel ● **adj. 1** (of lines, planes, or surfaces) side by side and having the same distance continuously between them. **2** occurring or existing at the same time or in a similar way: *a parallel universe.* ● **n. 1** a person or thing that is similar to or can be compared to to another. **2** a similarity or comparison. **3** (also **parallel of latitude**) each of the imaginary parallel circles of latitude on the earth's surface. ● **v.** (**parallels**, **paralleling**, **paralleled**) **1** run or lie parallel to. **2** be similar or corresponding to.
– PHRASES **in parallel** at the same time.
– ORIGIN Greek *parallēlos.*

parallel bars ● **pl. n.** a pair of parallel rails used in gymnastics.

parallelogram /pa-ruh-lel-luh-gram/ ● **n.** a plane figure with four straight sides and opposite sides parallel.

Paralympics ● **pl. n.** an international athletic competition for disabled athletes.

– DERIVATIVES **Paralympic** adj.
– ORIGIN from *paraplegic* and *Olympics*.

paralyse (esp. US also **paralyze**) ● v. (**paralyses, paralysing, paralysed**) **1** cause (a person or part of the body) to become unable to move. **2** prevent from functioning.

paralysis /puh-ral-i-siss/ ● n. (pl. **paralyses** /puh-ral-i-seez/) **1** the loss of the ability to move part or most of the body. **2** inability to act or function.
– ORIGIN Greek *paralusis*.

paralytic ● adj. **1** relating to paralysis. **2** Brit. informal extremely drunk.

Paramaribo E
/pa-ruh-ma-ri-boh/ the capital of Suriname.

paramedic ● n. a person who is trained to do medical work but is not a fully qualified doctor.

parameter /puh-ram-i-ter/ ● n. **1** something that decides or limits the way in which something is done: *they set the parameters of the debate.* **2** Math. a quantity which is fixed for the case in question but may vary in other cases.
– ORIGIN from Greek *para-* 'beside' + *metron* 'measure'.

paramilitary ● adj. organized on similar lines to a military force. ● n. (pl. **paramilitaries**) a member of a paramilitary organization.

paramount ● adj. **1** more important than anything else. **2** having supreme power.
– ORIGIN from Old French *par* 'by' + *amont* 'above'.

paramour ● n. archaic a lover.
– ORIGIN from Old French *par amour* 'by love'.

paranoia /pa-ruh-noy-uh/ ● n. **1** a mental condition in which one mistakenly believes that one is being persecuted, or that one is very important. **2** unjustified suspicion and mistrust of others.
– ORIGIN Latin.

p

paranoid ● adj. relating to or suffering from paranoia.

paranormal ● adj. beyond the scope of normal scientific understanding.

parapet /pa-ruh-pit/ ● n. a low protective wall along the edge of a roof, bridge, or balcony.
– ORIGIN French.

paraphernalia /pa-ruh-fer-nay-li-uh/ ● n. miscellaneous equipment needed for a particular activity.
– ORIGIN Latin, 'property owned by a married woman'.

paraphrase ● v. (**paraphrases, paraphrasing, paraphrased**) express the meaning of (something) using different words. ● n. a rewording of a passage.

paraplegia /pa-ruh-plee-juh/ ● n. paralysis of the legs and lower body.
– DERIVATIVES **paraplegic** adj. & n.
– ORIGIN Greek.

parapsychology ● n. the study of mental phenomena which are outside the area of orthodox psychology.

paraquat /pa-ruh-kwot, pa-ruh-kwat/ ● n. a poisonous weedkiller.
– ORIGIN from **PARA-** + **QUATERNARY**.

parasailing ● n. the sport of gliding through the air wearing an open parachute while being towed by a motor boat.

parasite ● n. **1** an organism which lives in or on another organism and gets its food from it. **2** derog. a person who lives off others.
– DERIVATIVES **parasitism** n.
– ORIGIN Greek *parasitos* 'person eating at another's table'.

parasitic ● adj. (of an organism) living as a parasite.

parasitize /pa-ruh-sy-tyz, pa-ruh-si-tyz/ (also **parasitise**) ● v. (**parasitizes, parasitizing, parasitized**) live in or on as a parasite.

parasol ● n. a light umbrella used to give shade from the sun.
– ORIGIN Italian *parasole*.

paratroops ● pl. n. troops equipped to be dropped by parachute from aircraft.
– DERIVATIVES **paratrooper** n.

parboil ● v. partly cook by boiling.
– ORIGIN Latin *perbullire* 'boil thoroughly'.

parcel ● n. **1** an object or objects wrapped in paper in order to be carried or sent by post. **2** a quantity or amount of something. ● v. (**parcels, parcelling, parcelled**; US **parcels, parceling, parceled**) **1** make (something) into a parcel by wrapping it. **2** (**parcel out**) divide (something) into portions and then share it out.
– ORIGIN Old French *parcelle*.

parch ● v. **1** make dry through strong heat. **2** (**parched**) informal extremely thirsty.
– ORIGIN unknown.

parchment ● n. **1** a stiff material made from the skin of a sheep or goat, formerly used for writing on. **2** paper treated to resemble parchment.
– ORIGIN Old French *parchemin*.

pardon ● n. **1** the action of forgiving someone for an error or offence. **2** an official cancellation of the punishment for an offence. ● v. **1** forgive (a person, mistake, or offence). **2** give (an offender) a pardon. ● exclam. used to ask a speaker to repeat something because one did not hear or understand it.
– DERIVATIVES **pardonable** adj.
– ORIGIN Latin *perdonare* 'concede'.

pare ● v. (**pares, paring, pared**) **1** trim by cutting away the outer edges of. **2** (**pare away/down**) gradually reduce (something).
– ORIGIN Old French *parer*.

parent ● n. **1** a father or mother. **2** an animal or plant from which younger ones are derived. **3** an organization which owns or controls a number of smaller organizations. ● v. be or act as a parent to.
– DERIVATIVES **parental** adj. **parenthood** n.
– ORIGIN Latin *parere* 'bring forth'.

parentage ● n. the identity and origins of one's parents.

parenthesis /puh-ren-thi-siss/ ● n. (pl. **parentheses** /puh-ren-thi-seez/) **1** a word or phrase added as an explanation or afterthought, in writing marked off by brackets, dashes, or commas. **2** (**parentheses**) a pair of round brackets ().
– ORIGIN Greek.

parenthetic /pa-ruhn-thet-ik/ ● adj. relating to or added as a parenthesis.
– DERIVATIVES **parenthetical** adj.

par excellence /par ek-suh-lonss/ ● adj. (after a noun) better or more than all others of the same kind: *a designer par excellence.*

– ORIGIN French, 'by excellence'.

pariah /puh-ry-uh/ ● **n.** an outcast.
– ORIGIN Tamil, 'hereditary drummers' (drummers in southern India were of low caste and were not allowed to join in with religious processions).

parietal /puh-ry-i-tuhl/ ● **adj.** Anat. relating to the wall of the body or of a body cavity.
– ORIGIN Latin *paries* 'wall'.

parings ● **pl. n.** thin strips pared off from something.

Paris[1] E
the capital of France.

Paris[2] E
Gk Myth, a Trojan prince, the son of Priam. His abduction of Helen, wife of Menelaus king of Sparta, brought about the Trojan War, in which he killed Achilles but was later himself killed.

parish ● **n. 1** (in the Christian Church) a district with its own church and clergy. **2** (also **civil parish**) Brit. the smallest unit of local government in rural areas.
– ORIGIN Old French *paroche.*

parish council ● **n.** the administrative body in a civil parish.

parishioner ● **n.** a person who lives in a particular Church parish.

parish register ● **n.** a book recording christenings, marriages, and burials at a parish church.

Parisian /puh-ri-zi-uhn/ ● **adj.** relating to Paris. ● **n.** a person from Paris.

parity /pa-ri-ti/ ● **n.** the state of being equal or equivalent: *the euro's slide to parity with the dollar.*
– ORIGIN Latin *paritas.*

Park, E
Mungo (1771–1806), Scottish explorer. He undertook a series of explorations in West Africa (1795–7), among them the navigation of the Niger.

park ● **n. 1** a large public garden in a town. **2** a large area of woodland and pasture attached to a country house. **3** an area devoted to a specified purpose: *a wildlife park.* **4** an area in which vehicles may be parked. ● **v.** stop and leave (a vehicle) temporarily.
– ORIGIN Old French *parc.*

parka ● **n.** a large windproof hooded jacket.
– ORIGIN Russian.

Parker[1], E
Charlie (1920–55; known as **Bird** or **Yardbird**), American jazz saxophonist.

Parker[2], E
Dorothy (Rothschild) (1893–1967), American humorist, literary critic, and writer, famous for her cutting wit.

parking meter ● **n.** a machine next to a parking space in a street, into which coins are inserted to pay for parking a vehicle.

parking ticket ● **n.** a notice informing a driver of a fine for parking illegally.

Parkinson's disease ● **n.** a progressive disease of the brain and nervous system marked by trembling, muscular rigidity, and slow, imprecise movement.
– ORIGIN named after the English surgeon James *Parkinson* (1755–1824).

parkland (also **parklands**) ● **n.** open land consisting of fields and scattered groups of trees.

parky ● **adj.** Brit. informal chilly.
– ORIGIN unknown.

parlance /par-luhnss/ ● **n.** a way of using words associated with a particular subject: *medical parlance.*
– ORIGIN Old French.

parley /par-li/ ● **n.** (pl. **parleys**) a meeting between opponents or enemies to discuss terms for a truce. ● **v.** (**parleys**, **parleying**, **parleyed**) hold a parley.
– ORIGIN perh. from Old French *parlee* 'spoken'.

parliament /par-luh-muhnt/ ● **n. 1** (**Parliament**) (in the UK) the highest law-making body, consisting of the Sovereign, the House of Lords, and the House of Commons. **2** a similar body in other countries.
– ORIGIN Old French *parlement* 'speaking'.

parliamentarian ● **n.** a member of a parliament who is experienced in parliamentary procedures.

parliamentary /par-luh-men-tri/ ● **adj.** having to do with a parliament.

parliamentary private secretary ● **n.** (in the UK) a Member of Parliament assisting a government minister.

parlour (US **parlor**) ● **n. 1** dated a sitting room. **2** a shop or business providing specified goods or services: *an ice-cream parlour.* **3** a room or building equipped for milking cows.
– ORIGIN Old French *parlur* 'place for speaking'.

parlous /par-luhss/ ● **adj.** archaic dangerously uncertain; precarious.
– ORIGIN from **PERILOUS**.

Parmesan /par-mi-zan/ ● **n.** a hard, dry Italian cheese used chiefly in grated form.
– ORIGIN Italian *Parmigiano* 'of *Parma*' (an Italian city).

Parmigianino E
/par-mi-ja-**nee**-noh/ (also **Parmigiano** /par-mi-**jah**-noh/) (1503–40; born *Girolano Francesco Maria Mazzola*), Italian painter, who made an important contribution to early mannerism.

Parnassus, Mount E
/par-**nass**-uhss/ a mountain in central Greece, just north of Delphi. Believed to be sacred by the ancient Greeks, it was associated with Apollo and the Muses.

Parnell E
/par-**nel**/, Charles Stewart (1846–91), Irish nationalist leader. As leader of the Irish Home Rule faction in Parliament he raised the profile of Irish affairs. He was forced to retire from public life in 1890 after his involvement in a divorce case.

parochial /puh-**roh**-ki-uhl/ ● **adj. 1** relating to a parish. **2** having a narrow outlook or range.
– DERIVATIVES **parochialism** n.
– ORIGIN Latin *parochialis.*

parody /pa-ruh-di/ ● **n.** (pl. **parodies**) a piece of writing, music, etc. that deliberately copies

p

the style of another, so as to be amusing. ● **v.** (**parodies**, **parodying**, **parodied**) produce a parody of.
– DERIVATIVES **parodic** adj.
– ORIGIN Greek *parōidia* 'burlesque poem'.

parole ● **n.** the temporary or permanent release of a prisoner before the end of a sentence, on the promise of good behaviour. ● **v.** (**paroles**, **paroling**, **paroled**) release (a prisoner) on parole.
– ORIGIN Old French, 'word'.

paroxysm /pa-ruhk-si-z'm/ ● **n.** a sudden attack or outburst: *a paroxysm of coughing overcame him.*
– DERIVATIVES **paroxysmal** adj.
– ORIGIN Greek *paroxusmos.*

parquet /par-ki, par-kay/ ● **n.** flooring composed of wooden blocks arranged in a geometric pattern.
– DERIVATIVES **parquetry** n.
– ORIGIN French.

Parr, E
Katherine (1512–48), sixth and last wife of Henry VIII, whom she married in 1543.

parr ● **n.** (pl. **parr**) a young salmon or trout.
– ORIGIN unknown.

parrakeet ● **n.** var. of PARAKEET.

parricide /pa-ri-syd/ ● **n. 1** the killing of a parent or other near relative. **2** a person who commits parricide.
– ORIGIN Latin *parricidium.*

parrot ● **n.** a tropical bird with brightly coloured plumage and a hooked bill, some kinds of which are able to mimic human speech. ● **v.** (**parrots**, **parroting**, **parroted**) repeat mechanically.
– ORIGIN prob. from French dialect *perrot.*

parrot-fashion ● **adv.** repeated without thought or understanding.

Parry, E
Sir (Charles) Hubert (Hastings) (1848–1918), English composer, best known for his setting of William Blake's poem 'Jerusalem'.

parry ● **v.** (**parries**, **parrying**, **parried**) **1** ward off (a weapon or attack) with a countermove. **2** avoid answering (a question) directly. ● **n.** (pl. **parries**) an act of parrying.
– ORIGIN prob. from French *parer.*

parse /parz/ ● **v.** (**parses**, **parsing**, **parsed**) analyse (a sentence) into the parts it is made up of and describe their roles.
– ORIGIN perh. from Old French *pars* 'parts'.

parsec ● **n.** a unit of distance in astronomy, equal to about 3.25 light years.
– ORIGIN from PARALLAX and SECOND[2].

parsimony /par-si-muh-ni/ ● **n.** extreme unwillingness to spend money.
– DERIVATIVES **parsimonious** adj.
– ORIGIN Latin *parsimonia.*

parsley ● **n.** a herb with crinkly or flat leaves, used for seasoning or garnishing food.
– ORIGIN Greek *petroselinon.*

parsnip ● **n.** a long tapering cream-coloured root vegetable.
– ORIGIN Old French *pasnaie.*

parson ● **n.** (in the Church of England) a parish priest.
– ORIGIN Latin *persona* 'person'.

parsonage ● **n.** a church house provided for a parson.

Parsons, E
Sir Charles (Algernon) (1854–1931), British engineer, scientist, and manufacturer, who built the first practical steam turbine in 1884, designed to drive electricity generators.

parson's nose ● **n.** informal the piece of fatty flesh at the rump of a cooked fowl.

part ● **n. 1** a piece or section which is combined with others to make up a whole. **2** some but not all of something. **3** a specified fraction of a whole: *a twentieth part.* **4** a measure allowing comparison between the amounts of different ingredients used in a mixture: *a mix of one part cement to five parts ballast.* **5** a role played by an actor or actress. **6** a person's contribution to a situation. **7** (**parts**) informal a region. ● **v. 1** move apart or divide to leave a central space. **2** leave someone's company. **3** (**part with**) give up possession of. ● **adv.** partly: *part jazz, part blues.*
– PHRASES **part company** go in different directions. **take the part of** give support to.
– ORIGIN Latin *pars.*

partake ● **v.** (**partakes**, **partaking**, **partook**; past part. **partaken**) formal **1** (**partake in**) participate in (an activity). **2** (**partake of**) be characterized by. **3** (**partake of**) eat or drink.
– ORIGIN from earlier *partaker* 'person who takes a part'.

parterre /par-tair/ ● **n.** a group of flower beds laid out in a formal pattern.
– ORIGIN French.

part exchange ● **n.** Brit. a way of buying something in which an article that one owns is given as part of the payment for a more expensive one, with the balance in money.

parthenogenesis /par-thi-noh-**jen**-i-siss/ ● **n.** Biol. reproduction from an ovum without fertilization.
– ORIGIN from Greek *parthenos* 'virgin' + *genesis* 'creation'.

Parthenon E
/par-thi-nuhn/ the temple of Athene Parthenos, built on the Acropolis in Athens in 447–432 BC.

partial ● **adj. 1** not complete or whole. **2** favouring one side in a dispute above the other. **3** (**partial to**) having a liking for: *I'm very partial to bacon and eggs.*
– DERIVATIVES **partiality** n. **partially** adv.

participate ● **v.** (**participates**, **participating**, **participated**) take part.
– DERIVATIVES **participant** n. **participatory** adj.
– ORIGIN Latin *participare* 'share in'.

participation ● **n.** the action of taking part in an activity or event.

participle /par-tiss-i-p'l/ ● **n.** Grammar a word formed from a verb (e.g. *going*, *gone*, *being*, *been*) and used as an adjective or noun (as in *burnt toast*) or used to make compound verb forms (*is going*, *has been*).
– ORIGIN Latin *participium* 'sharing'.

particle ● **n. 1** a tiny portion of matter. **2** Physics a component of the physical world smaller than an atom, e.g. an electron. **3** Grammar an adverb or preposition that has little meaning, e.g. *in*, *up*, *off*, or *over*, used with verbs to make phrasal verbs.
– ORIGIN Latin *particula* 'little part'.

particular ● adj. **1** relating to an individual member of a group or class. **2** more than is usual: *particular care.* **3** very careful or concerned about something. ● n. a detail.
– PHRASES **in particular** especially.
– ORIGIN Latin *particularis.*

particularity ● n. (pl. **particularities**) **1** the quality of being individual. **2** (**particularities**) small details.

particularize (also **particularise**) ● v. (**particularizes**, **particularizing**, **particularized**) formal treat individually or in detail.

particularly ● adv. **1** more than is usual; especially. **2** in particular.

particulate /par-**tik**-yuu-luht, par-**tik**-yuu-layt/ ● adj. relating to or in the form of minute particles. ● n. (**particulates**) matter in such a form.
– ORIGIN Latin *particula* 'particle'.

parting ● n. Brit. a line of scalp revealed by combing the hair away in opposite directions on either side.

parting shot ● n. a cutting remark made by someone as they leave.

partisan /par-ti-zan, par-ti-**zan**/ ● n. **1** a strong supporter of a party, cause, or person. **2** a member of an armed group fighting secretly against an occupying force. ● adj. prejudiced.
– ORIGIN French.

partition ● n. **1** a light wall or other structure dividing a space into parts. **2** division into parts. ● v. **1** divide into parts. **2** divide (a room) with a partition.
– ORIGIN Latin.

partitive /**par**-ti-tiv/ ● adj. (of a grammatical construction) indicating that only a part of a whole is referred to (e.g. *a slice of bacon, some of the children*).

partly ● adv. to some extent; not completely.

partner ● n. **1** a person who takes part in a business or other undertaking with another or others. **2** either of two people doing something as a pair. **3** either member of a married couple or of an established unmarried couple. ● v. (**partners**, **partnering**, **partnered**) be the partner of.
– ORIGIN Old French *parcener.*

partnership ● n. **1** the state of being a partner or partners. **2** an association of two or more people as partners.

part of speech ● n. a category in which a word is placed in accordance with its grammatical function, e.g. noun, pronoun, adjective, verb.

Parton, E
Dolly (Rebecca) (b.1946), American country music singer and songwriter, known for such hits as 'Jolene'.

partook past of PARTAKE.

partridge ● n. (pl. **partridge** or **partridges**) a short-tailed game bird with mainly brown plumage.
– ORIGIN Old French *perdriz.*

part song ● n. a song with three or more voice parts without musical accompaniment.

part-time ● adj. & adv. for only part of the usual working day or week.

parturient /par-**tyoor**-i-uhnt/ ● adj. tech. about to give birth; in labour.

parturition /par-tyuu-ri-sh'n/ ● n. tech. the action of giving birth.
– ORIGIN Latin.

party ● n. (pl. **parties**) **1** a social gathering of invited guests. **2** an organized political group that puts forward candidates to be elected for government. **3** a group of people taking part in an activity or trip. **4** a person or group forming one side in an agreement or dispute. ● v. (**parties**, **partying**, **partied**) informal enjoy oneself with others by drinking, dancing, etc.
– PHRASES **be party** (or **a party**) **to** be involved in.
– ORIGIN Old French *partie.*

party line ● n. a policy or policies officially adopted by a political party.

party politics ● pl. n. politics that relate to political parties rather than to the public good.

party-pooper ● n. informal a person who spoils other people's fun.

party wall ● n. a wall shared by two adjoining buildings or rooms.

Parvati E
/**par**-vuh-ti/ a benevolent Hindu goddess, wife of Shiva.

parvenu /**par**-vuh-nyoo/ ● n. derog. a person from a humble background who has recently become wealthy or famous.
– ORIGIN French, 'arrived'.

Pasadena E
/pa-suh-**dee**-nuh/ a city in California, northeast of Los Angeles.

Pascal E
/pass-**kahl**/, Blaise (1623–62), French mathematician, physicist, and philosopher. He showed that air has weight, that air pressure is lower at high altitudes, and that the pressure of a fluid is transmitted equally in all directions. He also made a mechanical calculator and a syringe, and founded the theory of probability.

pascal /pass-kuhl/ ● n. the SI unit of pressure.
– ORIGIN named after PASCAL.

paschal /pass-kuhl, pahss-kuhl/ ● adj. **1** relating to Easter. **2** relating to the Jewish Passover.
– ORIGIN Latin *pascha* 'feast of Passover'.

pas de deux /pah di **der**/ ● n. (pl. **pas de deux**) Ballet a dance for a couple.
– ORIGIN French, 'step of two'.

pasha /*rhymes with* rasher/ ● n. hist. the title of a Turkish officer of high rank.
– ORIGIN Turkish.

pashmina /pash-**mee**-nuh/ ● n. a shawl of a fine-quality material made from goat's wool.
– ORIGIN Persian, 'wool, down'.

paso doble /pa-soh **doh**-blay/ ● n. (pl. **paso dobles**) a fast-paced Latin American ballroom dance.
– ORIGIN Spanish, 'double step'.

Pasolini E
/pa-suh-**lee**-ni/, Pier Paolo (1922–75), Italian film director. His films include *The Gospel According to St Matthew* and *The Decameron.*

pass[1] ● v. **1** move or go onward, past, through,

or across. **2** change from one state or condition to another. **3** transfer (something) to someone. **4** kick, hit, or throw (the ball) to a teammate. **5** (of time) go by. **6** occupy or spend (time). **7** be done or said: *not another word passed between them.* **8** come to an end. **9** be successful in (an examination, test, or course). **10** declare to be satisfactory. **11** approve (a proposal or law) by voting. **12** express (a judgement or opinion). ● **n. 1** an act of passing. **2** a success in an examination. **3** an official document allowing the holder to go somewhere or use something. **4** informal a sexual advance. **5** a particular state of affairs: *this is a sad pass.*
– PHRASES **pass away** euphem. die. **pass off** happen in a specified way. **pass off as** pretend that (something) is something else. **pass out** become unconscious. **pass up** refrain from taking up (an opportunity).
– ORIGIN Old French *passer.*

pass[2] ● **n.** a route over or through mountains.
– ORIGIN from **PACE**[1].

passable ● **adj. 1** acceptable, but not outstanding. **2** able to be travelled along or on.
– DERIVATIVES **passably** adv.

passage ● **n. 1** the action of passing. **2** a way through something. **3** a journey by sea or air. **4** the right to pass through somewhere: *a permit for safe passage.* **5** a short section from a text or musical work.

passageway ● **n.** a corridor or other narrow passage between buildings or rooms.

passbook ● **n.** a book issued by a bank or building society to an account holder, recording what has been put into or taken out of the account.

Passchendaele, Battle of E
/**pash**-uhn-dayl/ a prolonged episode of trench warfare involving appalling loss of life during the First World War in 1917, near the village of Passchendaele in western Belgium.

passé /pass-ay/ ● **adj.** no longer fashionable.
– ORIGIN French, 'gone by'.

passenger ● **n.** a person travelling in a vehicle, ship, or aircraft other than the driver, pilot, or crew.
– ORIGIN Old French *passager* 'passing'.

passer-by ● **n.** (pl. **passers-by**) a person who happens to be walking past something or someone.

passerine /pass-uh-ryn, pass-uh-reen/ ● **adj.** referring to birds of a large group having feet adapted for perching and including all songbirds.
– ORIGIN Latin *passer* 'sparrow'.

passim /pass-im/ ● **adv.** (of references) at various places throughout the text.
– ORIGIN Latin, 'everywhere'.

passing ● **adj. 1** done quickly and casually. **2** (of a similarity) slight. ● **n. 1** the ending of something. **2** euphem. a person's death.
– PHRASES **in passing** briefly and casually.

passion ● **n. 1** very strong emotion. **2** intense sexual love. **3** an intense enthusiasm for something. **4** (**the Passion**) the suffering and death of Jesus.
– DERIVATIVES **passionless** adj.
– ORIGIN Latin.

passionate ● **adj.** showing or caused by passion: *he's passionate about football.*
– DERIVATIVES **passionately** adv.

passion flower ● **n.** a climbing plant with a flower whose parts are said to suggest objects associated with Christ's Crucifixion.

passion fruit ● **n.** the edible purple fruit of some species of passion flower.

passive ● **adj. 1** accepting or allowing what happens or what others do, without resistance. **2** Grammar (of verbs) in which the subject undergoes the action of the verb (e.g. *they were killed* as opposed to the active form *he killed them*). ● **n.** a passive form of a verb.
– DERIVATIVES **passively** adv. **passivity** n.
– ORIGIN Latin *passivus.*

passive resistance ● **n.** non-violent opposition to authority.

passive smoking ● **n.** breathing in smoke from other people's cigarettes, cigars, or pipes.

pass key ● **n. 1** a key given only to those who are officially allowed access. **2** a master key.

Passover ● **n.** the major Jewish spring festival, commemorating the liberation of the Israelites from slavery in Egypt.
– ORIGIN from *pass over,* with reference to the exemption of the Israelites from the death of their firstborn (Book of Exodus).

passport ● **n. 1** an official government document certifying the holder's identity and citizenship and entitling them to travel abroad. **2** a thing that enables someone to achieve something: *qualifications are a passport to success.*

password ● **n.** a secret word or phrase used to enter a place or use a computer.

past ● **adj. 1** gone by in time and no longer existing. **2** (of time) that has gone by. **3** Grammar (of a tense) expressing a past action or state. ● **n. 1** a past period or the events in it. **2** a person's earlier life. **3** Grammar a past tense or form of a verb. ● **prep. 1** beyond in time or space. **2** in front of or from one side to the other of. **3** beyond the scope or power of. ● **adv. 1** so as to pass from one side to the other. **2** used to indicate the passage of time.
– ORIGIN from **PASS**[1].

pasta ● **n.** dough formed into various shapes (e.g. spaghetti, lasagne), cooked as part of a dish or in boiling water.
– ORIGIN Italian, 'paste'.

paste ● **n. 1** a soft, moist substance. **2** a glue made from water and starch. **3** a hard glassy substance used in making imitation gems. ● **v.** (**pastes**, **pasting**, **pasted**) **1** coat or stick with paste. **2** Computing insert (a section of text) into a document.
– ORIGIN Latin *pasta.*

pasteboard ● **n.** thin board made by pasting together sheets of paper.

pastel ● **n. 1** a crayon made of powdered pigments bound with gum or resin. **2** a picture drawn with pastels. **3** a pale shade of a colour.
– ORIGIN Italian *pastello.*

Pasternak E
/pass-ter-nak/, Boris (Leonidovich) (1890–1960), Russian poet and novelist. He is best known as the author of *Doctor Zhivago,* describing the experience of the Russian intelligentsia during the Revolution.

Pasteur E
/pa-**ster**/, Louis (1822–95), French chemist and bacteriologist, who introduced pasteurization and made pioneering studies in vaccination techniques.

pasteurize /pahss-tyuu-ryz, pahss-chuu-ryz/ (also **pasteurise**) ● v. (**pasteurizes, pasteurizing, pasteurized**) make (milk) safe to eat by heating it to destroy most of the micro-organisms in it.
– DERIVATIVES **pasteurization** (also **pasteurisation**) n.
– ORIGIN named after **PASTEUR**.

pastiche /pa-**steesh**/ ● n. an artistic work in a style that imitates that of another work, artist, or period.
– ORIGIN Italian *pasticcio*.

pastille /**pass**-tuhl/ ● n. a small sweet or lozenge.
– ORIGIN Latin *pastillus*.

pastime ● n. an activity done regularly for enjoyment.
– ORIGIN from **PASS**[1] + **TIME**.

past master ● n. a person who is experienced or expert in an activity.

pastor /**pah**-ster/ ● n. a minister in charge of a Christian church or congregation.
– ORIGIN Latin, 'shepherd'.

pastoral /**pahss**-tuh-ruhl/ ● adj. **1** relating to the farming or grazing of sheep or cattle. **2** (of a creative work) portraying country life. **3** relating to the giving of spiritual guidance by a Christian minister. **4** relating to a teacher's responsibility for the general well-being of pupils or students.

past participle ● n. Grammar the form of a verb which is used in forming perfect and passive tenses and sometimes as an adjective, e.g. *looked* in *have you looked?*, *lost* in *lost property*.

pastrami /pass-**trah**-mi/ ● n. highly seasoned smoked beef.
– ORIGIN Yiddish.

pastry ● n. (pl. **pastries**) **1** a dough of flour, fat, and water, used in baked dishes such as pies. **2** a cake consisting of sweet pastry with a filling.
– ORIGIN from **PASTE**.

pasturage ● n. land used for pasture.

pasture ● n. land covered with grass, suitable for grazing cattle or sheep. ● v. (**pastures, pasturing, pastured**) put (animals) to graze in a pasture.
– ORIGIN Latin *pastura* 'grazing'.

pasty[1] /**pass**-ti/ (also **pastie**) ● n. (pl. **pasties**) Brit. a folded pastry case filled with meat and vegetables.
– ORIGIN Old French *pastee*.

pasty[2] /**pay**-sti/ ● adj. (of a person's skin) unhealthily pale.

pat[1] ● v. (**patted, patting**) tap quickly and gently with the flat of the hand. ● n. **1** an act of patting. **2** a compact mass of a soft substance.
– PHRASES **a pat on the back** an expression of praise or encouragement.

pat[2] ● adj. too quick or easy and not convincing: *a pat answer*.
– PHRASES **have off** (or **down**) **pat** have (something) memorized perfectly.
– ORIGIN prob. from **PAT**[1].

Patagonia E
/pa-tuh-**goh**-ni-uh/ a region of South America, in southern Argentina and Chile.
– DERIVATIVES **Patagonian** adj. & n.

patch ● n. **1** a piece of material used to mend a hole or strengthen a weak point. **2** a small area differing from its surroundings. **3** a small plot of land: *a cabbage patch*. **4** Brit. informal a brief period of time: *a bad patch*. **5** Brit. informal an area for which someone is responsible or in which they operate. **6** a shield worn over a sightless or injured eye. ● v. **1** mend, strengthen, or protect with a patch. **2** (**patch up**) informal treat (injuries) or repair (something) quickly or temporarily. **3** (**patch up**) informal settle (a dispute).
– PHRASES **not a patch on** Brit. informal much less good than.
– ORIGIN perh. from Old French dialect *pieche* 'piece'.

patchwork ● n. **1** needlework in which small pieces of cloth in different designs are sewn edge to edge. **2** a thing composed of many different parts: *a patchwork of educational courses*.

patchy ● adj. **1** existing or happening in small, isolated areas: *patchy fog*. **2** uneven in quality; inconsistent.

pate /*rhymes with* gate/ ● n. archaic a person's head.
– ORIGIN unknown.

pâté /**pa**-tay/ ● n. a rich savoury paste made from finely minced or mashed meat, fish, or other ingredients.
– ORIGIN French.

pâté de foie gras /pa-tay duh fwah **grah**/ ● n. a pâté made from goose liver.

patella /puh-**tel**-luh/ ● n. (pl. **patellae** /puh-**tel**-lee/) Anat. the kneecap.
– ORIGIN Latin, 'small dish'.

patent /**pay**-t'nt, **pa**-t'nt/ ● n. a government licence giving someone the sole right to make, use, or sell an invention for a set period. ● adj. /**pay**-t'nt/ **1** easily recognizable; obvious: *she smiled with patent insincerity*. **2** made and sold under a patent. ● v. obtain a patent for.
– ORIGIN Latin *patere* 'lie open'.

patent leather ● n. glossy varnished leather.

patent medicine ● n. a medicine made and sold under a patent and available without prescription.

pater /**pay**-ter/ ● n. Brit. informal, dated father.
– ORIGIN Latin.

paterfamilias /pay-ter-fuh-**mi**-li-ass/ ● n. (pl. **patresfamilias** /pay-treez-fuh-**mi**-li-ass/) the male head of a family.
– ORIGIN Latin, 'father of the family'.

paternal ● adj. **1** like a father. **2** related through the father.
– DERIVATIVES **paternally** adv.

paternalism ● n. the policy of protecting the people one has control over, but also of restricting their freedom or responsibilities.
– DERIVATIVES **paternalist** n. & adj. **paternalistic** adj.

paternity ● n. **1** the state of being a father. **2** descent from a father.

paternity suit ● n. esp. N. Amer. a court case held to establish the identity of a child's father.

paternoster /pa-ter-**noss**-ter/ ● n. (in the

Roman Catholic Church) the Lord's Prayer.
– ORIGIN from Latin *pater noster* 'our father', the first words of the Lord's Prayer.

path • n. **1** a way or track laid down for walking or made by continual treading. **2** the direction in which a person or thing moves. **3** a course of action.
– ORIGIN Old English.

path-breaking • adj. pioneering; original.

Pathé E
/pa-thay/, Charles (1863–1957), French film pioneer. In 1896 he and his brothers founded a film production and distribution company which became internationally known for its newsreels.

pathetic • adj. **1** arousing pity. **2** informal completely inadequate.
– DERIVATIVES **pathetically** adv.
– ORIGIN Greek *pathētikos* 'sensitive'.

patho- • comb. form relating to disease: *pathology.*
– ORIGIN Greek *pathos* 'suffering'.

pathogen /pa-thuh-juhn/ • n. a micro-organism that can cause disease.
– DERIVATIVES **pathogenic** adj.

pathological (US **pathologic**) • adj. **1** relating to or caused by a disease. **2** informal compulsive: *a pathological liar.*
– DERIVATIVES **pathologically** adv.

pathology • n. **1** the branch of medicine concerned with the causes and effects of diseases. **2** the typical behaviour of a disease.
– DERIVATIVES **pathologist** n.

pathos /pay-thoss/ • n. a quality that arouses pity or sadness.
– ORIGIN Greek, 'suffering'.

pathway • n. a path or its course.

-pathy • comb. form **1** referring to feelings: *telepathy.* **2** referring to medical treatment: *homeopathy.*
– ORIGIN Greek *patheia* 'feeling'.

patience • n. **1** the ability to accept delay, trouble, or suffering without becoming angry or upset. **2** Brit. a card game for one player.
– ORIGIN Latin *patientia.*

patient • adj. having or showing patience. • n. a person receiving or registered to receive medical treatment.
– DERIVATIVES **patiently** adv.

patina /pa-ti-nuh/ • n. **1** a green or brown film on the surface of old bronze. **2** a soft glow on wooden furniture produced by age and polishing.
– ORIGIN Latin, 'shallow dish'.

patio • n. (pl. **patios**) a paved outdoor area next to a house.
– ORIGIN Spanish.

patio door • n. a large glass sliding door leading to a patio, garden, etc.

patisserie /puh-tiss-uh-ri, puh-tee-suh-ri/ • n. a shop where pastries and cakes are sold.
– ORIGIN French.

Patna E
/pat-nuh/ a city in NE India, on the Ganges, capital of the state of Bihar.

patois /pat-wah/ • n. (pl. **patois** /pat-wahz/) the local dialect of a region.
– ORIGIN French, 'rough speech'.

Paton E
/pay-t'n/, Alan (Stewart) (1903–88), South African writer and politician, known for his novel *Cry, the Beloved Country,* a passionate condemnation of apartheid.

patresfamilias pl. of **PATERFAMILIAS**.

patriarch /pay-tri-ark/ • n. **1** the male head of a family or tribe. **2** a biblical figure regarded as a father of the human race, e.g. Abraham. **3** a powerful or respected older man. **4** a high-ranking bishop in the Catholic Church. **5** the head of an independent Orthodox Church.
– DERIVATIVES **patriarchal** adj.
– ORIGIN Greek *patriarkhēs.*

patriarchy • n. (pl. **patriarchies**) **1** a form of social organization in which the father or eldest male is the head of the family. **2** a society in which men hold most or all of the power.

patrician /puh-tri-sh'n/ • n. an aristocrat. • adj. typical of aristocrats.
– ORIGIN Latin *patricius* 'having a noble father'.

patricide /pa-tri-syd/ • n. **1** the killing of one's father. **2** a person who kills their father.
– ORIGIN Latin *patricidium.*

Patrick, St E
(5th century), patron saint of Ireland, who played a leading part in the conversion of the country to Christianity. Feast day, 17 March.

patrimony /pa-tri-muh-ni/ • n. (pl. **patrimonies**) property inherited from one's father or male ancestor.
– ORIGIN Latin *patrimonium.*

patriot /pa-tri-uht, pay-tri-uht/ • n. a person who strongly supports their country and is prepared to defend it.
– DERIVATIVES **patriotic** adj. **patriotism** n.
– ORIGIN Latin *patriota* 'fellow countryman'.

patrol • n. **1** a person or group sent to keep watch over an area. **2** the action of patrolling an area. • v. (**patrols, patrolling, patrolled**) keep watch over (an area) by regularly walking or travelling around it.
– ORIGIN French *patrouiller* 'paddle in mud'.

patron • n. **1** a person who gives financial or other support to a person, organization, or cause. **2** a regular customer of a restaurant, hotel, etc.
– ORIGIN Latin *patronus* 'protector'.

patronage /pa-truh-nij, pay-truh-nij/ • n. **1** support given by a patron. **2** the giving of help or a job to someone in return for their support. **3** the regular custom attracted by a restaurant, hotel, etc.

patronize (also **patronise**) • v. (**patronizes, patronizing, patronized**) **1** treat (someone) in a way that suggests they are inferior. **2** be a regular customer of.

patron saint • n. the protecting or guiding saint of a person or place.

patronymic /pa-truh-nim-ik/ • n. a name derived from the name of a father or ancestor, e.g. *O'Brien.*
– ORIGIN Greek *patrōnumikos.*

patter[1] • v. (**patters, pattering, pattered**) **1** make a repeated light tapping sound. **2** run with quick light steps. • n. a repeated light tapping sound.

– ORIGIN from **PAT**[1].

patter[2] ● **n.** **1** fast continuous talk, such as that used by a comedian. **2** the jargon of a profession or social group.
– ORIGIN from **PATERNOSTER** (from the fast and mechanical way in which the prayer was often said).

pattern ● **n.** **1** a repeated decorative design. **2** a regular form or order in which a series of things occur: *working patterns.* **3** a model, design, or set of instructions for making something. **4** an example for others to follow. **5** a sample of cloth or wallpaper. ● **v.** **1** decorate with a pattern. **2** give a regular form to.
– ORIGIN from **PATRON** in the former sense 'something serving as a model'.

patty ● **n.** (pl. **patties**) **1** N. Amer. a small flat cake of minced food, especially meat. **2** a small pie or pasty.
– ORIGIN French *pâté*.

paucity /paw-si-ti/ ● **n.** smallness or lack of something: *a paucity of information.*
– ORIGIN Latin *paucus* 'few'.

Paul, St E
(died *c.*64; known as **Paul the Apostle** or **Saul of Tarsus**), Christian missionary. A Pharisee, he was at first opposed to Christianity, but was converted to it after a vision on the way to Damascus and became one of the first major Christian missionaries and theologians. Feast day, 29 June.

Pauli E
/pow-li/, Wolfgang (1900–58), Austrian-born American physicist. He predicted the discovery of the neutrino and originated the **exclusion principle**, according to which no two electrons in an atom can have the same set of quantum numbers.

Pauling E
/paw-ling/, Linus Carl (1901–94), American chemist, noted for his study of molecular structure and chemical bonding. His suggestion of a helical structure for proteins formed the basis for the explanation of the structure of DNA.

paunch ● **n.** a stomach that is large or sticks out.
– DERIVATIVES **paunchy** adj.
– ORIGIN Old French *paunche*.

pauper ● **n.** a very poor person.
– ORIGIN Latin, 'poor'.

pause ● **n.** **1** a temporary stop in action or speech. **2** Music a mark (𝄐) over a note or rest that is to be lengthened by an unspecified amount. ● **v.** (**pauses**, **pausing**, **paused**) stop temporarily.
– ORIGIN Greek *pausis*.

Pavarotti E
/pav-uh-rot-ti/, Luciano (b.1935), Italian operatic tenor.

pave ● **v.** (**paves**, **paving**, **paved**) cover (a piece of ground) with flat stones or bricks.
– DERIVATIVES **paving** n.
– ORIGIN Old French *paver*.

pavement ● **n.** **1** Brit. a raised path for pedestrians at the side of a road. **2** N. Amer. the hard surface of a road or street. **3** Geol. a horizontal expanse of bare rock with cracks or joints.
– ORIGIN Latin *pavimentum* 'trodden down floor'.

pavilion ● **n.** **1** Brit. a building at a sports ground used for changing and taking refreshments. **2** a decorative shelter in a park or large garden. **3** a marquee used at a show or fair. **4** a temporary display stand at a trade exhibition.
– ORIGIN Old French *pavillon*.

Pavlov E
/pav-loff/, Ivan (Petrovich) (1849–1936), Russian physiologist. He is best known for his studies on conditioned reflexes in dogs, showing how the secretion of saliva can be stimulated not only by food but also by the sound of a bell associated with the presentation of food.

Pavlova E
/pav-**loh**-vuh, **pav**-luh-vuh/, Anna (Pavlovna) (1881–1931), Russian ballet dancer, resident in Britain from 1912. She was famous for her solo dance *The Dying Swan*.

paw ● **n.** an animal's foot having claws and pads. ● **v.** **1** feel or scrape with a paw or hoof. **2** informal touch in a way that is clumsy or unwanted.
– ORIGIN Old French *poue*.

pawl /pawl/ ● **n.** a pivoted bar or lever whose free end engages with the teeth of a cogwheel or ratchet, allowing it to move or turn in one direction only.
– ORIGIN perh. from German and Dutch *pal*.

pawn[1] ● **n.** **1** a chess piece of the smallest size and value. **2** a person used by others for their own purposes.
– ORIGIN Old French *poun*.

pawn[2] ● **v.** leave (an object) with a pawnbroker as security for money lent. ● **n.** the state of being pawned: *everything was in pawn.*
– ORIGIN Old French *pan* 'pledge'.

pawnbroker ● **n.** a person licensed to lend money at interest in exchange for an article left with them, which they can sell if one does not repay the loan.

pawnshop ● **n.** a pawnbroker's shop.

pawpaw /paw-paw/ (also **papaw** /puh-paw/) ● **n.** a papaya.
– ORIGIN Spanish and Portuguese *papaya*.

pay ● **v.** (**pays**, **paying**, **paid**) **1** give (someone) money due for work, goods, or a debt. **2** give (a sum of money) thus owed. **3** result in a profit or advantage: *crime doesn't pay.* **4** suffer as a result of an action: *someone's got to pay for all that grief.* **5** give (attention, respect, or a compliment) to. **6** make (a visit or a call) to. ● **n.** money paid for work.
– PHRASES **pay back** take revenge on. **pay off** **1** dismiss with a final payment. **2** informal yield good results.
– ORIGIN Old French *payer* 'appease'.

payable ● **adj.** **1** that must be paid. **2** able to be paid.

PAYE ● **abbrev.** (in the UK) pay as you earn, a system whereby an employer deducts income tax from an employee's wages.

payee ● **n.** a person to whom money is paid.

paying guest ● **n.** a lodger.

payload ● **n.** **1** passengers and cargo as the part of a vehicle's load which money. **2** an explosive warhead carried by an aircraft or missile.

paymaster • n. **1** a person who pays another and therefore controls them. **2** an official who pays troops or workers.

payment • n. **1** the action of paying or the process of being paid. **2** an amount paid.

pay-off • n. informal **1** a bribe. **2** the return on investment or on a bet. **3** a final outcome.

payola /pay-**oh**-luh/ • n. N. Amer. bribery in return for the unofficial promotion of a product in the media.

payphone • n. a public telephone operated by coins or by a credit or prepaid card.

payroll • n. a list of a company's employees and the amount of money they are to be paid.

Pb • symb. the chemical element lead.
– ORIGIN Latin *plumbum*.

PC • abbrev. **1** personal computer. **2** police constable. **3** (also **pc**) politically correct; political correctness.

p.c. • abbrev. per cent.

PCB • abbrev. **1** Electron. printed circuit board. **2** Chem. polychlorinated biphenyl, a poisonous compound formed as waste in some industrial processes.

PE • abbrev. physical education.

pea • n. a round green seed within a pod, eaten as a vegetable.
– ORIGIN Old English.

peace • n. **1** freedom from noise or anxiety. **2** freedom from or the ending of war.
– PHRASES **hold one's peace** remain silent.
– ORIGIN Old French *pais*.

peaceable • adj. **1** inclined to avoid war. **2** free from conflict; peaceful.
– DERIVATIVES **peaceably** adv.

peaceful • adj. **1** free from noise or anxiety. **2** not involving war or violence. **3** inclined to avoid conflict.
– DERIVATIVES **peacefully** adv. **peacefulness** n.

p

peacekeeping • n. the use of an international military force to maintain a truce.
– DERIVATIVES **peacekeeper** n.

peace offering • n. a gift given in an attempt to make peace in a conflict.

peacetime • n. a period when a country is not at war.

peach • n. **1** a round fruit with juicy yellow flesh, red and yellow skin, and a stone inside. **2** a pinkish-orange colour. **3** informal an exceptionally good or attractive person or thing.
– ORIGIN Old French *pesche*.

peacock • n. a large male bird with very long tail feathers with eye-like markings that can be fanned out in display.
– ORIGIN Old English.

peahen • n. a large, mainly brown bird, the female of the peacock.

peak • n. **1** the pointed top of a mountain. **2** a mountain with a pointed top. **3** a stiff brim at the front of a cap. **4** the point of highest activity, achievement or intensity. • v. reach a highest point or maximum. • adj. maximum.
– ORIGIN prob. from a dialect word meaning 'pointed'.

Peak District E
a limestone plateau in Derbyshire, at the southern end of the Pennines.

Peake, E
Mervyn (Laurence) (1911–68), British novelist, poet, and artist, born in China. He is best known for the surreal trilogy comprising *Titus Groan*, *Gormenghast*, and *Titus Alone*.

peaked • adj. (of a cap) having a peak.

peaky • adj. (**peakier**, **peakiest**) pale from illness or tiredness.
– ORIGIN from former *peak* 'decline in health'.

peal • n. **1** a loud or long-lasting ringing of a bell or bells. **2** a loud repeated or echoing sound of thunder or laughter. **3** a set of bells. • v. ring or resound in a peal.
– ORIGIN from **APPEAL**.

peanut • n. **1** the oval edible seed of a plant native to South America, whose seeds develop in underground pods. **2** (**peanuts**) informal a very small sum of money.

peanut butter • n. a spread made from ground roasted peanuts.

pear • n. a yellowish-green or brownish-green edible fruit, narrow at the stalk and wider towards the tip.
– PHRASES **go pear-shaped** Brit. informal go wrong.
– ORIGIN Old English.

pearl • n. **1** a small, hard, shiny white ball formed within the shell of an oyster and having great value as a gem. **2** a thing of great worth.
– ORIGIN Old French *perle*.

pearl barley • n. barley reduced to small round grains by grinding.

pearlescent • adj. having a soft glow resembling that of mother-of-pearl.

Pearl Harbor E
a harbour on the Hawaiian island of Oahu, the site of a major American naval base, where a surprise attack on 7 December 1941 by Japanese aircraft brought the US into the Second World War.

pearly • adj. like a pearl in lustre or colour.

Pearly Gates • pl. n. informal the gates of heaven.
– ORIGIN from a reference in the Book of Revelation.

Pearson, E
Lester Bowles (1897–1972), Canadian diplomat and Liberal statesman, Prime Minister 1963–8. As Secretary of State for External Affairs (1948–57) he acted as a mediator in the resolution of the Suez crisis (1956).

Peary E
/*rhymes with* weary/, Robert Edwin (1856–1920), American explorer, the first person to reach the North Pole, on 6 April 1909.

peasant • n. **1** a poor smallholder or farm labourer of low social status. **2** informal a rude or uneducated person.
– DERIVATIVES **peasantry** n.
– ORIGIN Old French *paisent*.

Peasants' Revolt E
an uprising in 1381 among peasants and artisans from south-east England. The rebels occupied London and secured Richard II's concession to their demands, which included the lifting of the poll tax, but after the death of Wat Tyler they were persuaded to disperse by the king.

pea-shooter • n. a toy weapon consisting of a small tube out of which dried peas are blown.

pea-souper • n. Brit. a very thick yellowish fog.

peat • n. partly decomposed vegetable matter formed in boggy ground, dried for use in gardening and as fuel.
– DERIVATIVES **peaty** adj.
– ORIGIN Latin *peta*.

pebble • n. a small stone made smooth and round by the action of water or sand.
– DERIVATIVES **pebbly** adj.
– ORIGIN Old English.

pebble-dash • n. mortar with pebbles in it, used as a coating for the outside walls of buildings.

pecan /pee-k'n, pi-**kan**/ • n. a smooth pinkish brown nut obtained from a tree of the southern US.
– ORIGIN from an American Indian language.

peccadillo /pek-kuh-**dil**-loh/ • n. (pl. **peccadilloes** or **peccadillos**) a minor fault.
– ORIGIN Spanish.

peccary /**pek**-kuh-ri/ • n. (pl. **peccaries**) a piglike mammal found from the south-western US to Paraguay.
– ORIGIN Carib.

Peck, (Eldred) Gregory (1916–2003), American actor, star of such films as *To Kill a Mockingbird* and *The Big Country*.

peck[1] • v. **1** (of a bird) strike or bite with its beak. **2** kiss lightly and quickly. • n. **1** an act of pecking. **2** a light, quick kiss.
– ORIGIN unknown.

peck[2] • n. a measure of capacity for dry goods, equal to a quarter of a bushel.
– ORIGIN Old French *pek*.

pecker • n. (in phr. **keep your pecker up**) Brit. informal remain cheerful.
– ORIGIN *pecker* prob. in the sense 'beak'.

pecking order • n. a strict order of importance among members of a group.

peckish • adj. informal hungry.

pectin • n. a jelly-like substance present in ripe fruits, used to set jams and jellies.
– ORIGIN Greek *pektos* 'congealed'.

pectoral /**pek**-tuh-ruhl/ • adj. having to do with the breast or chest. • n. a pectoral muscle.
– ORIGIN Latin *pectoralis*.

pectoral muscle • n. each of four large paired muscles which cover the front of the ribcage.

peculiar • adj. **1** strange or odd. **2** (**peculiar to**) belonging only to.
– DERIVATIVES **peculiarly** adv.
– ORIGIN Latin *peculiaris* 'of private property'.

peculiarity • n. (pl. **pecularities**) **1** an unusual or distinctive feature or habit. **2** the state of being peculiar.

pecuniary /pi-**kyoo**-ni-uh-ri/ • adj. formal having to do with money.
– ORIGIN Latin *pecuniarius*.

pedagogue /**ped**-uh-gog/ • n. formal a teacher.
– ORIGIN Greek *paidagōgos*, referring to a slave who accompanied a child to school.

pedagogy /**ped**-uh-gog-i/ • n. the profession or theory of teaching.

pedal /**ped**-uhl/ • n. **1** each of a pair of foot-operated levers for powering a bicycle or other vehicle. **2** a foot-operated throttle, brake, or clutch control. **3** a foot-operated lever on a piano, organ, etc. for sustaining or softening the tone. • v. (**pedals**, **pedalling**, **pedalled**; US **pedals**, **pedaling**, **pedaled**) work the pedals of a bicycle to move along.
– ORIGIN French *pédale*.

USAGE pedal

Do not confuse the words **pedal** and **peddle**. **Pedal** is a noun referring to a foot-operated lever, as on a bicycle; as a verb it means 'work the pedals of a bicycle'. **Peddle** is a verb meaning 'sell goods'.

pedalo /**ped**-uh-loh/ • n. (pl. **pedalos** or **pedaloes**) Brit. a small pedal-operated pleasure boat.

pedal-pushers • pl. n. women's calf-length trousers.

pedant /**ped**-uhnt/ • n. a person excessively concerned with minor detail or with displaying technical knowledge.
– DERIVATIVES **pedantic** adj. **pedantry** n.
– ORIGIN French *pédant*.

peddle • v. (**peddles**, **peddling**, **peddled**) **1** sell (goods) by going from place to place. **2** sell (an illegal drug or stolen item). **3** derog. promote (an idea) persistently or widely.
– ORIGIN from **PEDLAR**.

USAGE peddle

For an explanation of the difference between **pedal** and **peddle**, see the note at **PEDAL**.

peddler • n. var. of **PEDLAR**.

pederasty /**ped**-uh-rass-ti/ • n. sexual intercourse between a man and a boy.
– DERIVATIVES **pederast** n.
– ORIGIN Greek *paiderastia*.

pedestal • n. **1** the base or support on which a statue or column is mounted. **2** each of the two supports of a desk or table which has a space for the knees. **3** the supporting column of a washbasin or toilet pan.
– ORIGIN Italian *piedestallo*.

pedestrian • n. a person walking rather than travelling in a vehicle. • adj. dull and boring.
– ORIGIN Latin *pedester* 'going on foot'.

pedestrianize (also **pedestrianise**) • v. (**pedestrianizes**, **pedestrianizing**, **pedestrianized**) make (a street or area) accessible only to pedestrians.

pediatrics • n. US = **PAEDIATRICS**.

pedicure • n. a cosmetic treatment of the feet and toenails.
– ORIGIN French.

pedigree • n. **1** the record of descent of an animal, showing it to be pure-bred. **2** a person's family background or ancestry. **3** the history of a thing.
– ORIGIN from Old French *pé de grue* 'crane's foot', a mark used to represent succession in pedigrees.

pediment • n. the triangular upper part above the entrance of a classical building.
– ORIGIN perh. from **PYRAMID**.

pedlar (also **peddler**) • n. **1** a travelling trader who sells small goods. **2** a person who sells illegal drugs or stolen goods.

– ORIGIN perh. from dialect *ped* 'pannier'.

pedometer /pi-**dom**-i-ter/ ● **n.** an instrument for estimating the distance travelled on foot by recording the number of steps taken.
– ORIGIN Latin *pes* 'foot'.

pee informal ● **v.** (**pees**, **peeing**, **peed**) urinate. ● **n. 1** an act of urinating. **2** urine.
– ORIGIN from the first letter of PISS.

peek ● **v. 1** look quickly or secretly. **2** stick out slightly so as to be just visible: *the bus peeked over the top of the hill.* ● **n.** a quick or secret look.
– ORIGIN unknown.

Peel, E
Sir Robert (1788–1850), British Conservative statesman, Prime Minister 1834–5 and 1841–6. As Home Secretary (1828–30) he established the Metropolitan Police. He resigned as Prime Minister after his repeal of the Corn Laws split the Conservatives.

peel ● **v. 1** remove the skin from (a fruit or vegetable). **2** (of a surface or object) lose parts of its outer layer or covering in small pieces. ● **n.** the outer skin of a fruit or vegetable.
– DERIVATIVES **peelings** pl. n.
– PHRASES **peel off** remove (an article of clothing).
– ORIGIN Latin *pilare* 'strip hair from'.

peeler ● **n.** a type of knife for peeling fruit and vegetables.

peen (also **pein**) ● **n.** the rounded or wedge-shaped end of a hammer head opposite the face.
– ORIGIN prob. Scandinavian.

peep[1] ● **v. 1** look quickly and secretly. **2** (**peep out**) come slowly or partially into view. ● **n. 1** a quick or secret look. **2** a glimpse of something.

peep[2] ● **n.** a weak or brief high-pitched sound. ● **v.** make a peep.
– PHRASES **not a peep** not the slightest sound or complaint.

peephole ● **n.** a small hole in a door through which callers can be seen.

peeping Tom ● **n.** a person who gains sexual pleasure from secretly watching people undress or engage in sexual activity.
– ORIGIN the name of the tailor said to have watched Lady Godiva ride naked through Coventry.

peep show ● **n.** a form of entertainment in which pictures are viewed through a lens or hole set into a box.

peer[1] ● **v.** (**peers**, **peering**, **peered**) look with difficulty or concentration.
– ORIGIN uncertain.

peer[2] ● **n. 1** a member of the nobility in Britain or Ireland. **2** a person of the same age, status, or ability as another specified person.
– ORIGIN Old French.

peerage ● **n. 1** the title and rank of peer or peeress. **2** (**the peerage**) peers as a whole.

peeress ● **n. 1** a woman holding the rank of a peer in her own right. **2** the wife or widow of a peer.

peer group ● **n.** a group of people of approximately the same age and status.

peerless ● **adj.** better than all others; unrivalled.

peeved ● **adj.** informal annoyed or irritated.
– ORIGIN from PEEVISH.

peevish ● **adj.** irritable.
– ORIGIN unknown.

peewit ● **n.** Brit. a lapwing.

peg ● **n. 1** a projecting pin or bolt used for hanging things on, securing something in place, or marking a position. **2** a clip for hanging up washing on a line. ● **v.** (**pegs**, **pegging**, **pegged**) **1** fix, attach, or mark with a peg or pegs. **2** fix (a price, rate, etc.) at a particular level. **3** (**peg out**) informal die.
– PHRASES **off the peg** esp. Brit. (of clothes) ready-made.
– ORIGIN prob. German.

Pegasus E
/peg-uh-suhss/ Gk Myth. a winged horse which sprang from the blood of Medusa when Perseus cut off her head.

peg leg ● **n.** informal a wooden leg.

Pei E
/pay/, I. M. (b.1917; full name *Ieoh Ming Pei*), American architect, born in China. His buildings include the glass and steel pyramid in the forecourt of the Louvre in Paris.

pein ● **n.** var. of PEEN.

pejorative /pi-**jo**-ruh-tiv/ ● **adj.** expressing contempt or disapproval.
– DERIVATIVES **pejoratively** adv.
– ORIGIN French *péjoratif*.

Pekinese ● **n.** (pl. **Pekinese**) a small dog with long hair, short legs, and a snub nose.

Peking E
/pee-**king**/ var. of BEIJING.

pelargonium /pe-luh-**goh**-ni-uhm/ ● **n.** a garden plant with red, pink, or white flowers.
– ORIGIN Latin.

Pelé E
/pel-ay/ (b.1940; born *Edson Arantes do Nascimento*), Brazilian footballer, who appeared 111 times for Brazil and scored over 1,200 goals in first-class soccer.

pelf ● **n.** archaic money.
– ORIGIN Old French *pelfre* 'spoils'.

Pelham E
/pel-uhm/, Henry (1696–1754), British Whig statesman, Prime Minister 1743–54.

pelican ● **n.** a large waterbird with a long bill and a throat pouch.
– ORIGIN Greek *pelekan*.

pelican crossing ● **n.** (in the UK) a pedestrian crossing with traffic lights operated by pedestrians.

pelisse /pi-**leess**/ ● **n.** hist. a woman's long cloak with armholes or sleeves.
– ORIGIN French.

pellagra /pel-**lag**-ruh, pel-**lay**-gruh/ ● **n.** a disease caused by an inadequate diet, in which a person has inflamed skin, diarrhoea, and mental disturbance.
– ORIGIN Italian.

pellet ● **n. 1** a small compressed mass of a substance. **2** a piece of small shot or other lightweight bullet.
– ORIGIN Old French *pelote* 'metal ball'.

pell-mell ● **adj. & adv.** in a confused or rushed way.

– ORIGIN French *pêle-mêle.*

pellucid /pel-lyoo-sid/ ● **adj. 1** transparent or semi-transparent; clear. **2** easily understood.
– ORIGIN Latin *pellucidus.*

pelmet ● **n.** a narrow border fitted across the top of a window to conceal the curtain fittings.
– ORIGIN prob. from French *palmette* 'small palm leaf'.

Peloponnese E
/pel-uh-puhn-**neez**/ the mountainous southern peninsula of Greece.

Peloponnesian War E
/pel-uh-puh-**nee**-*zh*'n/ the war of 431–404 BC fought between Athens and Sparta with their respective allies, and ending with the total defeat of Athens.

pelt[1] ● **v. 1** hurl missiles at. **2** (**pelt down**) (chiefly of rain) fall very heavily.
– PHRASES (**at**) **full pelt** as fast as possible.
– ORIGIN unknown.

pelt[2] ● **n.** the skin of an animal with the fur, wool, or hair still on it.
– ORIGIN Latin *pellis* 'skin'.

pelvic girdle ● **n.** (in vertebrates) the enclosing structure formed by the pelvis.

pelvis /pel-viss/ ● **n.** (pl. **pelvises** or **pelves** /pel-veez/) the large bony frame at the base of the spine to which the lower limbs are attached.
– DERIVATIVES **pelvic** adj.
– ORIGIN Latin, 'basin'.

Pembrokeshire E
a county of SW Wales; administrative centre, Haverfordwest.

Pembs. ● **abbrev.** Pembrokeshire.

pen[1] ● **n. 1** an instrument for writing or drawing with ink. **2** an electronic device used to enter commands into a computer. ● **v.** (**pens, penning, penned**) write or compose.
– ORIGIN Latin *penna* 'feather' (pens were originally made from a quill feather).

pen[2] ● **n.** a small enclosure for farm animals. ● **v.** (**pens, penning, penned**) **1** put or keep in a pen. **2** (**pen up/in**) confine (someone) in a restricted space.
– ORIGIN Old English.

penal ● **adj. 1** relating to the punishment of offenders under the legal system. **2** very severe: *penal rates of interest.*
– ORIGIN Old French.

penalize (also **penalise**) ● **v.** (**penalizes, penalizing, penalized**) **1** give (someone) a penalty or punishment. **2** put in an unfavourable position.

penalty ● **n.** (pl. **penalties**) **1** a punishment for breaking a law, rule, or contract. **2** something unpleasant suffered as a result of an action or circumstance: *feeling cold is one of the penalties of old age.* **3** a penalty kick.

penalty kick ● **n.** Soccer a free shot at the goal awarded to the attacking team after a foul within an area around the goal.

penance ● **n. 1** an act that one does, or that is given to one by a priest, as a punishment for having done wrong. **2** a sacrament in which a member of the Church confesses sins to a priest and is given a penance or formal forgiveness.

– ORIGIN Old French.

Penang E
/pi-**nang**/ (also **Pinang**) an island of Malaysia, situated off the west coast of the Malay Peninsula.

pence pl. of **PENNY** (used for sums of money).

penchant /pon-shon/ ● **n.** a strong liking: *a penchant for champagne.*
– ORIGIN French, 'leaning'.

pencil ● **n.** an instrument for writing or drawing, consisting of a thin stick of graphite enclosed in a wooden case. ● **v.** (**pencils, pencilling, pencilled**; US **pencils, penciling, penciled**) **1** write, draw, or colour with a pencil. **2** (**pencil in**) arrange or note down provisionally.
– ORIGIN Old French *pincel* 'paintbrush'.

pendant ● **n. 1** a piece of jewellery that hangs from a necklace chain. **2** a light designed to hang from the ceiling. ● **adj.** hanging downwards.
– ORIGIN Old French, 'hanging'.

pendent ● **adj.** hanging down.

Penderecki E
/pen-duh-**ret**-ski/, Krzysztof (b.1933), Polish composer. His music frequently uses unorthodox effects, as in his *Threnody for the Victims of Hiroshima* for fifty-two strings.

pending ● **adj. 1** awaiting decision or settlement. **2** about to happen. ● **prep.** until.
– ORIGIN from **PENDANT.**

pendulous ● **adj.** hanging down, drooping.

pendulum ● **n.** a weight hung from a fixed point so that it can swing freely, used to regulate the mechanism of a clock.
– ORIGIN Latin, 'thing hanging down'.

Penelope E
Gk Myth. the wife of Odysseus. When her husband did not return from Troy, she put off her suitors by saying that she would marry only when she had finished a piece of weaving, and every night unravelled her previous work.

peneplain /pee-ni-playn/ ● **n.** a level land surface produced by erosion over a long period.
– ORIGIN Latin *paene* 'almost'.

penetrate ● **v.** (**penetrates, penetrating, penetrated**) **1** force a way into or through. **2** gain access to (an enemy organization or a competitor's market). **3** understand. **4** (**penetrating**) (of a sound) clearly heard through or above other sounds. **5** (of a man) insert the penis into the vagina or anus of (a sexual partner).
– DERIVATIVES **penetration** n. **penetrative** adj.
– ORIGIN Latin *penetrare* 'go into'.

penfriend ● **n.** a person with whom one becomes friendly by exchanging letters.

penguin ● **n.** a flightless black and white seabird of the southern hemisphere.
– ORIGIN unknown.

penicillin ● **n.** an antibiotic.
– ORIGIN Latin *penicillum* 'paintbrush'.

peninsula ● **n.** a long, narrow piece of land projecting out into a sea or lake.
– DERIVATIVES **peninsular** adj.
– ORIGIN Latin.

Peninsular War E
a campaign waged on the Iberian peninsula between the French and the British, the latter assisted by Spanish and Portuguese forces, from 1808 to 1814 during the Napoleonic Wars. The French were finally driven back over the Pyrenees.

penis /pee-niss/ ● n. (pl. **penises** or **penes** /pee-neez/) the male organ that is used for sexual intercourse and urinating.
– DERIVATIVES **penile** adj.
– ORIGIN Latin, 'tail'.

penitent ● adj. feeling sorrow and regret for having done wrong. ● n. a person who repents or does penance.
– DERIVATIVES **penitence** n. **penitential** adj.
– ORIGIN Latin *paenitere* 'repent'.

penitentiary /pen-i-ten-shuh-ri/ ● n. (pl. **penitentiaries**) (in North America) a prison for people convicted of serious crimes.

penknife ● n. a small knife with a blade which folds into the handle.

Penn, E
William (1644–1718), English Quaker, who in 1682 founded the colony of Pennsylvania as a sanctuary for Quakers and other Nonconformists.

pen name ● n. a name used by a writer instead of their real name.

pennant ● n. a long, narrow, pointed flag flown on a ship.
– ORIGIN from **PENDANT** and **PENNON**.

penne /pen-nay/ ● pl. n. pasta in the form of short wide tubes.
– ORIGIN Italian, 'quills'.

penniless ● adj. without money.

Pennine Hills E
a range of hills in northern England, extending from the Scottish border southwards to the Peak District in Derbyshire.

pennon ● n. = **PENNANT**.
– ORIGIN Old French.

Pennsylvania E
/pen-sil-vay-ni-uh/ a state of the northeastern US; capital, Harrisburg.
– DERIVATIVES **Pennsylvanian** adj. & n.

penny ● n. (pl. **pennies** (for separate coins); **pence** (for a sum of money)) **1** a British bronze coin worth one hundredth of a pound. **2** a former British coin worth one twelfth of a shilling.
– PHRASES **in for a penny, in for a pound** willing to see an undertaking through, whatever it involves. **the penny dropped** informal someone has finally realized something.
– ORIGIN Old English.

penny-farthing ● n. Brit. an early type of bicycle with a very large front wheel and a small rear wheel.

penny-pinching ● adj. miserly.

pennyworth ● n. **1** an amount of something worth a penny. **2** (**one's pennyworth**) Brit. one's contribution to a discussion.

pen pal ● n. informal a penfriend.

pen-pusher ● n. informal, derog. a clerical worker.

pension¹ /pen-sh'n/ ● n. a regular payment made by the state or a company to retired people and to some widows and disabled people. ● v. (**pension off**) dismiss (someone) from employment and pay them a pension.
– DERIVATIVES **pensionable** adj. **pensioner** n.
– ORIGIN Latin, 'payment'.

pension² /pon-syon/ ● n. a small hotel in France and other European countries.
– ORIGIN French.

pensive ● adj. engaged in deep thought.
– DERIVATIVES **pensively** adv.
– ORIGIN Old French *pensif*.

penta- ● comb. form five; having five: *pentagon*.
– ORIGIN Greek *pente*.

pentacle /pen-tuh-k'l/ ● n. a pentagram.
– ORIGIN Latin *pentaculum*.

pentagon ● n. **1** a plane figure with five straight sides and five angles. **2** (**the Pentagon**) the headquarters of the US Department of Defense.

pentagram ● n. a five-pointed star drawn using a continuous line, used as a mystic and magical symbol.

pentameter /pen-tam-i-ter/ ● n. a line of verse consisting of five metrical feet.

Pentateuch /pen-tuh-tyook/ ● n. the first five books of the Old Testament and Hebrew Scriptures.
– ORIGIN Greek.

pentathlon ● n. an athletic event comprising five different events for each competitor.
– DERIVATIVES **pentathlete** n.
– ORIGIN Greek.

pentatonic /pen-tuh-ton-ik/ ● adj. Music consisting of a scale of five notes.

Pentecost /pen-ti-kost/ ● n. **1** the Christian festival celebrating the descent of the Holy Spirit on the disciples of Jesus, held on Whit Sunday. **2** a Jewish festival that takes place fifty days after the second day of Passover.
– ORIGIN from Greek *pentēkostē hēmera* 'fiftieth day'.

Pentecostal ● adj. **1** relating to Pentecost. **2** relating to a group of Christian Churches that emphasizes baptism in the Holy Spirit, evidence of which includes 'speaking in tongues' and healing.
– DERIVATIVES **Pentecostalism** n.

penthouse ● n. a flat on the top floor of a tall building.
– ORIGIN Old French *apentis*.

penultimate ● adj. last but one.
– ORIGIN from Latin *paene* 'almost' + *ultimus* 'last'.

penumbra /pi-num-bruh/ ● n. (pl. **penumbrae** /pi-num-bree/ or **penumbras**) the partially shaded outer region of the shadow cast by an object.
– ORIGIN from Latin *paene* 'almost' + *umbra* 'shadow'.

penurious /pi-nyoor-i-uhss/ ● adj. formal extremely poor.

penury /pen-yuu-ri/ ● n. extreme poverty.
– ORIGIN Latin *penuria*.

peon /pee-uhn, pay-on/ ● n. an unskilled Spanish-American worker.
– ORIGIN Portuguese *peão* and Spanish *peón*.

peony /pee-uh-ni/ ● n. a herbaceous or shrubby plant grown for its large flowers.
– ORIGIN Greek *paiōnia*.

people ● pl. n. **1** human beings in general or considered as a whole. **2** (**the people**) the ordinary citizens of a country. **3** (**one's people**)

one's relatives, or one's employees or supporters. **4** (pl. **peoples**) the members of a particular nation, community, or ethnic group. ● v. **(peoples, peopling, peopled)** **(be peopled)** (of a place) have particular people living in it.
– ORIGIN Old French *poeple*.

people carrier ● n. a large motor vehicle with three rows of seats.

People's Republic of China E
official name for **CHINA**.

pep informal ● n. liveliness. ● v. **(peps, pepping, pepped)** **(pep up)** make more lively.
– ORIGIN from **PEPPER**.

pepper ● n. **1** a hot-tasting powder made from peppercorns, used to flavour food. **2** the fruit of a tropical American plant, of which sweet peppers and chilli peppers are varieties. ● v. **(peppers, peppering, peppered)** **1** season with pepper. **2** **(pepper with)** scatter in large amounts over or through. **3** hit repeatedly with small missiles or gunshot.
– DERIVATIVES **peppery** adj.
– ORIGIN Sanskrit.

peppercorn ● n. the dried berry of a climbing vine, used whole as a spice or ground to make pepper.

peppercorn rent ● n. Brit. a very low or nominal rent.

peppermint ● n. **1** a plant of the mint family which produces an oil which is used as a flavouring in food. **2** a sweet flavoured with peppermint oil.

pepperoni /pep-puh-roh-ni/ ● n. beef and pork sausage seasoned with pepper.
– ORIGIN Italian *peperone* 'chilli'.

pepper spray ● n. an aerosol spray containing oils made from cayenne pepper, used as a disabling weapon.

pep pill ● n. informal a pill containing a stimulant drug.

pepsin ● n. the chief digestive enzyme in the stomach.
– ORIGIN Greek *pepsis* 'digestion'.

pep talk ● n. informal a talk intended to make someone feel more courageous or enthusiastic.

peptic ● adj. relating to digestion.
– ORIGIN Greek *peptikos* 'able to digest'.

peptic ulcer ● n. an ulcer in the lining of the stomach or small intestine.

peptide ● n. Biochem. a compound consisting of two or more linked amino acids.
– ORIGIN German *Peptid*.

Pepys E
/peeps/, Samuel (1633–1703), English diarist and naval administrator, remembered for his *Diary*, which describes events such as the Great Plague and the Fire of London.

per ● prep. **1** for each. **2** by means of. **3** **(as per)** in accordance with.
– ORIGIN Latin.

per- ● prefix **1** through; all over: *pervade*. **2** completely; very: *perfect*.

peradventure ● adv. archaic perhaps.
– ORIGIN from Old French *per* (or *par*) *auenture* 'by chance'.

perambulate /puh-ram-byuu-layt/ ● v. **(perambulates, perambulating, perambulated)** formal walk or travel from place to place.
– DERIVATIVES **perambulation** n.
– ORIGIN Latin *perambulare*.

perambulator ● n. formal a pram.

per annum ● adv. for each year.
– ORIGIN Latin.

percale /per-kayl/ ● n. a closely woven fine cotton fabric.
– ORIGIN French.

per capita /per ka-pi-tuh/ (also **per caput** /per ka-puut/) ● adv. & adj. for each person.
– ORIGIN Latin, 'by heads'.

perceive ● v. **(perceives, perceived, perceiving)** **1** become aware of through the senses. **2** regard as.
– DERIVATIVES **perceivable** adj.
– ORIGIN Old French *perçoivre*.

per cent ● adv. by a specified amount in or for every hundred. ● n. one part in every hundred.

percentage ● n. **1** a rate, number, or amount in each hundred. **2** a proportion or share, especially a share in the profits of something.

percentile /per-sen-tyl/ ● n. Stat. each of 100 equal groups into which a large group of people can be divided.

perceptible ● adj. able to be perceived.
– DERIVATIVES **perceptibly** adv.

perception ● n. **1** the ability to see, hear, or become aware of something through the senses. **2** a way of understanding or regarding something. **3** the ability to understand the true nature of something; insight.
– ORIGIN Latin.

perceptive ● adj. having or showing insight.
– DERIVATIVES **perceptively** adv. **perceptiveness** n.

perceptual ● adj. relating to the ability to perceive.

Perceval E
/per-si-v'l/, Spencer (1762–1812), British Tory statesman, Prime Minister 1809–12. He was shot dead in the House of Commons by a bankrupt merchant who blamed the government for his insolvency.

perch[1] ● n. **1** a branch, bar, etc. on which a bird rests or roosts. **2** a high or narrow seat. ● v. **1** sit, rest, or place somewhere. **2** **(be perched)** (of a building) be above or on the edge of something.
– ORIGIN Old French *perche*.

perch[2] ● n. (pl. **perch** or **perches**) a freshwater fish with a spiny fin on its back.
– ORIGIN Old French *perche*.

perchance ● adv. archaic by some chance; perhaps.
– ORIGIN from Old French *par cheance*.

percipient /per-sip-i-uhnt/ ● adj. having insight or understanding.

percolate /per-kuh-layt/ ● v. **(percolates, percolating, percolated)** **1** filter through a porous surface or substance. **2** (of information or ideas) spread gradually through a group of people. **3** prepare (coffee) in a percolator.
– DERIVATIVES **percolation** n.
– ORIGIN Latin *percolare* 'strain through'.

percolator ● n. a machine for making coffee, consisting of a pot in which boiling water is circulated through a small chamber that holds the ground beans.

percussion • **n. 1** musical instruments that are played by being struck or shaken. **2** percussion instruments forming a band or section of an orchestra.
– DERIVATIVES **percussionist** n.
– ORIGIN Latin.

perdition /per-**di**-sh'n/ • **n.** (in Christian belief) a state of eternal damnation into which a sinful person who has not repented passes after death.
– ORIGIN Latin.

peregrinations /pe-ri-gri-**nay**-sh'nz/ • **pl. n.** archaic travel or wandering from place to place.
– ORIGIN Latin *peregrinari* 'travel abroad'.

peregrine /**pe**-ri-grin/ • **n.** a falcon with a bluish-grey back and wings and pale underparts.
– ORIGIN Latin, 'pilgrim falcon'.

peremptory /puh-**remp**-tuh-ri/ • **adj.** insisting on immediate attention or obedience: *she dreaded his peremptory orders.*
– DERIVATIVES **peremptorily** adv.
– ORIGIN Latin *peremptorius* 'deadly'.

perennial • **adj. 1** lasting a year or several years. **2** (of a plant) living for several years. **3** lasting or doing something for a very long time.
– DERIVATIVES **perennially** adv.
– ORIGIN Latin *perennis* 'lasting the year through'.

Peres E
/pe-rez/, Shimon (b.1923), Polish-born Israeli Labour statesman, Prime Minister 1984–6 and 1995–6. As Foreign Minister he played a major role in negotiating the PLO–Israeli peace accord (1993).

perestroika /pe-ri-**stroy**-kuh/ • **n.** the economic and political reforms introduced in the former Soviet Union during the 1980s.
– ORIGIN Russian, 'restructuring'.

perfect • **adj.** /**per**-fikt/ **1** having all the required elements or qualities. **2** free from any flaw. **3** complete: *it made perfect sense.* **4** Grammar (of a tense) describing a completed action or a state or habitual action which began in the past (e.g. *they have eaten*). **5** Math. (of a number) equal to the sum of its positive divisors, e.g. the number 6, whose divisors (1, 2, 3) also add up to 6. • **v.** /per-**fekt**/ make perfect or complete.
– ORIGIN Latin *perfectus* 'completed'.

perfection • **n. 1** the process of perfecting something. **2** the state of being perfect.

perfectionism • **n.** refusal to accept any standard short of perfection.
– DERIVATIVES **perfectionist** n. & adj.

perfectly • **adv. 1** in a perfect way. **2** absolutely; completely: *you know perfectly well who it is.*

perfect pitch • **n.** the ability to recognize the pitch of a note or produce any given note.

perfidious /per-**fid**-i-uhss/ • **adj.** literary deceitful and disloyal: *a perfidious lover.*

perfidy /**per**-fi-di/ • **n.** literary deceit; disloyalty.
– ORIGIN Latin *perfidia.*

perforate /**per**-fuh-rayt/ • **v.** (**perforates**, **perforating**, **perforated**) pierce and make a hole or holes in.
– DERIVATIVES **perforation** n.
– ORIGIN Latin *perforare.*

perforce • **adv.** formal necessarily; unavoidably.
– ORIGIN from Old French *par force* 'by force'.

perform • **v. 1** carry out or complete (an action or function). **2** function or do something to a specified standard: *the car performs well at low speeds.* **3** present entertainment to an audience.
– DERIVATIVES **performer** n.
– ORIGIN Old French *parfournir.*

performance • **n. 1** the action of performing. **2** an act of performing a play, concert, song, etc. **3** informal a fuss. **4** the capabilities of a machine or product.

performing arts • **pl. n.** creative activities that are performed in front of an audience, such as drama, music, and dance.

perfume • **n.** /**per**-fyoom/ **1** a sweet-smelling liquid used to give a pleasant smell to one's body. **2** a pleasant smell. • **v.** /per-**fyoom**/ (**perfumes**, **perfuming**, **perfumed**) **1** give a pleasant smell to. **2** put perfume on or in.
– ORIGIN French *parfum.*

perfumery • **n.** (pl. **perfumeries**) **1** the making and selling of perfumes. **2** a shop that sells perfumes.
– DERIVATIVES **perfumer** n.

perfunctory /per-**fungk**-tuh-ri/ • **adj.** carried out with a minimum of effort or thought.
– DERIVATIVES **perfunctorily** adv.
– ORIGIN Latin *perfunctorius* 'careless'.

Pergamum E
/per-guh-muhm/ an ancient city in western Asia Minor, in present-day Turkey. One of the greatest of the Hellenistic cities, it was especially famed for its library.

pergola /**per**-guh-luh/ • **n.** an arched structure forming a framework for climbing or trailing plants.
– ORIGIN Latin *pergula* 'projecting roof'.

perhaps • **adv. 1** expressing uncertainty or possibility. **2** used when making a polite request or suggestion.
– ORIGIN from **PER** + former *hap* 'luck'.

peri- • **prefix** round; about: *pericardium.*
– ORIGIN Greek *peri.*

perianth /**pe**-ri-anth/ • **n.** the outer part of a flower, consisting of the sepals and petals.
– ORIGIN from Greek *peri* 'around' + *anthos* 'flower'.

pericardium /pe-ri-**kar**-di-uhm/ • **n.** (pl. **pericardia** /pe-ri-**kar**-di-uh/) Anat. the membrane enclosing the heart.
– ORIGIN Latin.

pericarp • **n.** the part of a fruit formed from the wall of the ripened ovary.
– ORIGIN from Greek *peri-* 'around' + *karpos* 'fruit'.

Pericles E
/pe-ri-kleez/ (*c.*495–429 BC), Athenian statesman and general. He extended the Athenian empire and masterminded strategy in the Peloponnesian War. He also promoted culture, including the building of the Parthenon.

peridot /**pe**-ri-dot/ • **n.** a green semi-precious stone.
– ORIGIN French.

peridotite /**pe**-ri-do-tyt/ • **n.** a dense rock that is rich in magnesium and iron, thought to be the main constituent of the earth's mantle.

perigee /**pe**-ri-jee/ • **n.** Astron. the point in the

orbit of the moon or a satellite at which it is nearest to the earth.
– ORIGIN from Greek *peri-* 'around' + *gē* 'earth'.

perihelion /pe-ri-hee-li-uhn/ ● **n.** (pl. **perihelia** /pe-ri-hee-li-uh/) Astron. the point in a planet's orbit at which it is closest to the sun. Opp. APHELION.
– ORIGIN from Greek *peri-* 'around' + *hēlios* 'sun'.

peril ● **n.** a situation of serious and immediate danger.
– ORIGIN Old French.

perilous ● **adj.** full of danger or risk.
– DERIVATIVES **perilously** adv.

perimeter ● **n. 1** the continuous line forming the boundary of a closed figure. **2** the outermost parts or boundary of an area or object.
– ORIGIN from Greek *peri-* 'around' + *metron* 'measure'.

period ● **n. 1** a length or portion of time. **2** a major division of geological time, forming part of an era. **3** a lesson in a school. **4** (also **menstrual period**) a monthly flow of blood from the lining of the womb, occurring in women of child-bearing age when not pregnant. **5** esp. N. Amer. a full stop. ● **adj.** belonging to or typical of a past historical time: *period furniture.*
– ORIGIN Greek *periodos* 'course'.

periodic /peer-i-od-ik/ ● **adj.** appearing or occurring at intervals.

periodical ● **adj.** occurring or appearing at intervals. ● **n.** a magazine or newspaper that is published at regular intervals.
– DERIVATIVES **periodically** adv.

periodic table ● **n.** a table of the chemical elements arranged in order of atomic number.

period piece ● **n.** an object or work that is typical of or set in an earlier historical period.

peripatetic /pe-ri-puh-tet-ik/ ● **adj. 1** travelling from place to place. **2** working or based in a succession of places.
– ORIGIN Greek *peripatētikos* 'walking up and down'.

peripheral /puh-rif-uh-ruhl/ ● **adj. 1** relating to or situated on the outer limits of something. **2** of secondary importance. **3** (of a device) able to be attached to and used with a computer, though not a built-in part of it.
– DERIVATIVES **peripherally** adv.

peripheral nervous system ● **n.** the nervous system outside the brain and spinal cord.

periphery /puh-rif-uh-ri/ ● **n.** (pl. **peripheries**) **1** the outer limits or edge of an area or object. **2** the less important part of a subject or group.
– ORIGIN Greek *periphereia* 'circumference'.

periphrasis /puh-rif-ruh-siss/ ● **n.** (pl. **periphrases** /puh-rif-ruh-seez/) the use of indirect language.
– ORIGIN from Greek *peri-* 'around' + *phrazein* 'declare'.

periscope ● **n.** a tube attached to a set of mirrors or prisms, by which one can see things that are above or behind something else.

perish ● **v. 1** die. **2** suffer complete ruin or destruction. **3** rot. **4** (**be perished**) Brit. be very cold.
– ORIGIN Latin *perire* 'pass away'.

perishable ● **adj.** (of food) likely to rot quickly.

perishing ● **adj.** Brit. informal very cold.

peristalsis /pe-ri-stal-siss/ ● **n.** the contraction and relaxation of the muscles of the intestines, creating movements which push the contents of the intestines forward.
– ORIGIN Greek *peristallein* 'wrap around'.

peritoneum /pe-ri-tuh-nee-uhm/ ● **n.** (pl. **peritoneums** or **peritonea** /pe-ri-tuh-nee-uh/) the membrane lining the cavity of the abdomen and covering the abdominal organs.
– DERIVATIVES **peritoneal** adj.
– ORIGIN Latin.

peritonitis /pe-ri-tuh-ny-tiss/ ● **n.** inflammation of the peritoneum.

periwig ● **n.** hist. a man's wig.
– ORIGIN French *perruque*.

periwinkle[1] ● **n.** a plant with flat five-petalled flowers.
– ORIGIN Latin *pervinca*.

periwinkle[2] ● **n.** = WINKLE.
– ORIGIN unknown.

perjure ● **v.** (**perjures**, **perjuring**, **perjured**) (**perjure oneself**) commit perjury.
– ORIGIN Latin *perjurare* 'swear falsely'.

perjury /per-juh-ri/ ● **n.** the offence of deliberately telling a lie in court when under oath.

perk[1] ● **v.** (**perk up**) make or become more cheerful or lively.
– ORIGIN perh. from Old French *percher* 'to perch'.

perk[2] ● **n.** informal a benefit to which an employee is entitled.
– ORIGIN from PERQUISITE.

perky ● **adj.** (**perkier**, **perkiest**) cheerful and lively.

perm ● **n.** a method of setting the hair in curls and treating it with chemicals so that the style lasts for several months. ● **v.** treat (the hair) in such a way.

permafrost ● **n.** a thick layer of soil beneath the surface that remains frozen throughout the year.

permanent ● **adj.** lasting or intended to last for a long time or forever.
– DERIVATIVES **permanence** n. **permanently** adv.
– ORIGIN Latin *permanere* 'remain to the end'.

permeable ● **adj.** allowing liquids or gases to pass through.
– DERIVATIVES **permeability** n.

permeate ● **v.** (**permeates**, **permeating**, **permeated**) spread throughout.
– ORIGIN Latin *permeare* 'pass through'.

Permian /per-mi-uhn/ ● **adj.** Geol. relating to the last period of the Palaeozoic era, about 290 to 245 million years ago, when reptiles increased rapidly in number.
– ORIGIN from *Perm*, a Russian province with deposits from this period.

permissible ● **adj.** allowable.

permission ● **n.** the action of allowing someone to do something.

permissive ● **adj.** allowing or showing freedom of behaviour, especially in sexual matters.
– DERIVATIVES **permissiveness** n.

permit ● **v.** /per-mit/ (**permits**, **permitting**,

P

permitted) **1** give permission to (someone) or for (something). **2** make possible: *the weather did not permit play.* ● **n.** /**per**-mit/ an official document giving permission to do something.
– ORIGIN Latin *permittere.*

permutation ● **n. 1** each of several possible ways in which a number of things can be ordered or arranged. **2** Math. the action of changing the arrangement of a set of items.
– ORIGIN Latin.

pernicious /per-**nish**-uhss/ ● **adj.** having a harmful effect.
– ORIGIN Latin *perniciosus* 'destructive'.

pernickety ● **adj.** informal, esp. Brit. fussy.
– ORIGIN unknown.

Perón[1] E
/pe-**ron**/, Eva (1919–52; full name *María Eva Duarte de Perón*; known as **Evita**), Argentinian politician. A former actress, after her marriage to Juan Perón she became de facto Minister of Health and of Labour and championed social reforms and women's rights.

Perón[2] E
/pe-**ron**/, Juan Domingo (1895–1974), Argentinian soldier and statesman, President 1946–55 and 1973–4. During his first term of office he won support for his social reforms but became increasingly dictatorial and was deposed.

peroration ● **n.** the concluding part of a speech.
– ORIGIN Latin *perorare* 'speak at length'.

peroxide ● **n. 1** Chem. a compound containing two oxygen atoms bonded together. **2** hydrogen peroxide. ● **v.** (**peroxides, peroxiding, peroxided**) bleach (hair) with peroxide.

perpendicular /per-puhn-**dik**-yuu-ler/ ● **adj.** at an angle of 90° to a line, plane, or surface, or to the ground. ● **n.** a perpendicular line.
– ORIGIN Latin *perpendicularis.*

p

perpetrate /per-pi-trayt/ ● **v.** (**perpetrates, perpetrating, perpetrated**) carry out (a bad or illegal action).
– DERIVATIVES **perpetration** n. **perpetrator** n.
– ORIGIN Latin *perpetrare* 'perform'.

perpetual /per-**pet**-yoo-uhl/ ● **adj. 1** never ending or changing. **2** so frequent as to seem continual: *their perpetual money worries.*
– DERIVATIVES **perpetually** adv.
– ORIGIN Latin *perpetualis.*

perpetuate ● **v.** (**perpetuates, perpetuating, perpetuated**) cause to continue for a long time.
– DERIVATIVES **perpetuation** n.
– ORIGIN Latin *perpetuare.*

perpetuity ● **n.** the state of lasting forever.

perplex ● **v.** puzzle greatly.
– ORIGIN Latin *perplexus* 'entangled'.

perplexity ● **n.** (pl. **perplexities**) **1** the state of being puzzled. **2** a puzzling thing.

perquisite /per-kwi-zit/ ● **n.** formal a special right or privilege enjoyed as a result of one's position.
– ORIGIN Latin *perquisitum* 'acquisition'.

Perrault E
/pe-**roh**/, Charles (1628–1703), French writer, known for such fairy tales as 'Sleeping Beauty' and 'Cinderella'.

Perrin E
/pe-**ran**/, Jean Baptiste (1870–1942), French physical chemist, who provided the definitive proof of the existence of atoms.

Perry E
Fred (1909–95; full name *Frederick John Perry*), British-born American tennis player. His record of winning three consecutive singles titles at Wimbledon (1934–6) was unequalled until 1978.

per se /per **say**/ ● **adv.** by or in itself or themselves.
– ORIGIN Latin.

persecute ● **v.** (**persecutes, persecuting, persecuted**) **1** treat in a cruel or unfair way over a long period. **2** persistently harass.
– DERIVATIVES **persecution** n. **persecutor** n.
– ORIGIN Old French *persecuter.*

Persephone E
/per-**sef**-fuh-ni/ a Greek goddess, the daughter of Zeus and Demeter. She was carried off by Hades and made queen of the underworld, but allowed to return to earth for part of each year. Roman name **PROSERPINA.**

Perseus E
/**per**-si-uhss/ Gk Myth. the son of Zeus and Danae. He cut off the head of the gorgon Medusa. Riding the winged horse Pegasus, he also rescued Andromeda.

persevere ● **v.** (**perseveres, persevering, persevered**) continue in a course of action in spite of difficulty or lack of success.
– DERIVATIVES **perseverance** n.
– ORIGIN Latin *perseverare* 'abide by strictly'.

Persia E
/**per**-shuh/ former name for **IRAN.**

Persian ● **n. 1** a person from Persia (now Iran). **2** the language of ancient Persia or modern Iran. **3** a long-haired breed of domestic cat. ● **adj.** relating to Persia or Iran.

Persian Gulf E
an arm of the Arabian Sea. It extends northwestwards between Arabia and the coast of SW Iran.

persiflage /**per**-si-flahzh/ ● **n.** formal light mockery or banter.
– ORIGIN French *persifler* 'to banter'.

persimmon /per-**sim**-muhn/ ● **n.** an edible fruit resembling a large tomato, with very sweet flesh.
– ORIGIN from an American Indian language.

persist ● **v. 1** continue doing something in spite of difficulty or opposition. **2** continue to exist.
– ORIGIN Latin *persistere* 'continue steadfastly'.

persistent ● **adj. 1** continuing to do something in spite of difficulty or opposition. **2** continuing or recurring for a long time.
– DERIVATIVES **persistence** n. **persistently** adv.

person ● **n.** (pl. **people** or **persons**) **1** an individual human being. **2** an individual's body: *concealed on his person.* **3** Grammar a category used in the classification of pronouns or verb forms according to whether they indicate the speaker (**first person**), the person spoken to (**second person**), or a third party (**third person**).

– PHRASES **in person** actually present.
– ORIGIN Latin *persona* 'mask, character in a play'.

-person ● **comb. form** used as a neutral alternative to *-man* in nouns referring to status, authority, etc.: *salesperson.*

persona /per-**soh**-nuh/ ● **n.** (pl. **personas** or **personae** /per-**soh**-nee/) the aspect of a person's character that is presented to others: *her public persona.*
– ORIGIN Latin, 'mask, character in a play'.

personable ● **adj.** having a pleasant appearance and manner.

personage ● **n.** an important or famous person.
– ORIGIN Old French.

personal ● **adj. 1** having to do with or belonging to a particular person. **2** done by a particular person rather than someone else: *a personal appearance.* **3** concerning a person's private life. **4** making offensive reference to a person's character or appearance. **5** relating to a person's body.

personal assistant ● **n.** a secretary or administrative assistant working for one particular person.

personal column ● **n.** a section of a newspaper containing private advertisements or messages.

personal computer ● **n.** a microcomputer designed for use by one person.

personal identification number ● **n.** a number used with an individual's bank card to validate electronic transactions.

personality ● **n.** (pl. **personalities**) **1** the qualities that form a person's character. **2** qualities that make someone interesting or popular. **3** a celebrity.

personalize (also **personalise**) ● **v.** (**personalizes**, **personalizing**, **personalized**) **1** design or produce (something) to meet someone's individual requirements. **2** make (something) identifiable as belonging to a particular person. **3** cause (a subject) to become concerned with personalities or feelings.

personally ● **adv. 1** in person. **2** from one's own viewpoint.
– PHRASES **take personally** interpret (a remark) as directed against oneself and be upset by it.

personal organizer ● **n.** a loose-leaf notebook with a diary and address book.

personal pronoun ● **n.** each of the pronouns (*I, you, he, she, it, we, they, me, him, her, us,* and *them*) that show person, gender, number, and case.

USAGE personal pronoun

I, **we**, **they**, **he**, and **she** are **subjective** personal pronouns, which means they are used as the subject of the sentence, often coming before the verb (*she lives in Paris*). **Me**, **us**, **them**, **him**, and **her**, on the other hand, are **objective** personal pronouns, which means that they are used as the object of a verb or preposition (*John hates me*). This explains why it is wrong to use *me* in *John and me went to the shops*: the personal pronoun is in subject position, so it must be **I**.

Where a personal pronoun is used alone, the situation is more difficult. Some people say that statements such as *she's younger than me* are wrong and that the correct form is *she's younger than I*. This is based on the fact that **than** is a conjunction and so the personal pronoun is still in the subject position even though there is no verb (in full it would be *she's younger than I am*). Yet for most people the supposed 'correct' form does not sound natural and it is mainly found in very formal writing; it is usually perfectly acceptable to say *she's younger than me.*

personal stereo ● **n.** a small portable cassette or compact disc player, used with headphones.

persona non grata /per-soh-nuh nohn **grah**-tuh/ ● **n.** (pl. **personae non gratae** /per-soh-nee nohn **grah**-tee/) a person who is not welcome somewhere because they have done something unacceptable.
– ORIGIN Latin.

personify /per-**son**-i-fy/ ● **v.** (**personifies**, **personifying**, **personified**) **1** represent (a quality or concept) by a figure in human form. **2** give human characteristics to (something non-human). **3** embody (a quality) in a physical form.
– DERIVATIVES **personification** n.

personnel /per-suh-**nel**/ ● **pl. n.** people who work for an organization or the armed forces.
– ORIGIN French, 'personal'.

perspective ● **n. 1** the art of representing solid objects on a flat surface so as to convey the impression of height, width, depth, and relative distance. **2** a view. **3** a particular way of seeing something. **4** understanding of how important things are in relation to others.
– ORIGIN from Latin *perspectiva ars* 'science of optics'.

perspex ● **n.** trademark a tough transparent plastic used instead of glass.
– ORIGIN Latin *perspicere* 'look through'.

perspicacious /per-spi-**kay**-shuhss/ ● **adj.** quickly achieving an insight into and understanding of things.
– DERIVATIVES **perspicacity** n.
– ORIGIN Latin *perspicax* 'seeing clearly'.

perspicuous /per-**spik**-yuu-uhss/ ● **adj.** clearly expressed and easily understood.
– ORIGIN Latin *perspicuus* 'clear'.

perspiration ● **n. 1** sweat. **2** the process of sweating.

perspire ● **v.** (**perspires**, **perspiring**, **perspired**) give out sweat through the pores of the skin.
– ORIGIN Latin *perspirare.*

persuade ● **v.** (**persuades**, **persuading**, **persuaded**) cause (someone) to do or believe something through reasoning or argument.
– ORIGIN Latin *persuadere.*

persuasion ● **n. 1** the action of persuading. **2** a belief or set of beliefs: *writers of all political persuasions.*

persuasive ● **adj. 1** good at persuading someone to do or believe something. **2** providing sound reasoning or argument.
– DERIVATIVES **persuasively** adv. **persuasiveness** n.

pert ● **adj. 1** attractively lively or cheeky. **2** (of a part of the body) attractive because neat and jaunty.
– ORIGIN Latin *apertus* 'opened'.

pertain ● **v.** be appropriate, related, or relevant: *matters pertaining to the government.*
– ORIGIN Latin *pertinere* 'extend to'.

p

Perth[1] E
the capital of the state of Western Australia.

Perth[2] E
a town in eastern Scotland, the administrative centre of Perth and Kinross region.

Perth and Kinross E
an administrative region of central Scotland; administrative centre, Perth.

pertinacious /per-ti-**nay**-shuhss/ ● **adj.** formal persistent.
– ORIGIN Latin *pertinax* 'holding fast'.

pertinent ● **adj.** relevant or appropriate.
– DERIVATIVES **pertinence** n. **pertinently** adv.
– ORIGIN Latin *pertinere* 'extend to'.

perturb ● **v.** make anxious or unsettled.
– ORIGIN Latin *perturbare.*

perturbation /per-ter-**bay**-sh'n/ ● **n. 1** anxiety; uneasiness. **2** an alteration in the normal state or path of a system or moving object.

Peru E
a country in South America on the Pacific coast; capital, Lima.
– DERIVATIVES **Peruvian** adj. & n.

peruse /puh-**rooz**/ ● **v.** (**peruses, perusing, perused**) formal read or examine thoroughly or carefully.
– DERIVATIVES **perusal** n.
– ORIGIN perh. from **PER-** + **USE**.

pervade ● **v.** (**pervades, pervading, pervaded**) spread or be present throughout.
– ORIGIN Latin *pervadere* 'go or come through'.

pervasive ● **adj.** spreading widely through or present everywhere in something.
– DERIVATIVES **pervasively** adv. **pervasiveness** n.

perverse ● **adj. 1** showing a deliberate and stubborn desire to behave unacceptably. **2** contrary to that which is accepted or expected.
– DERIVATIVES **perversely** adv. **perversity** n.

perversion ● **n. 1** the action of perverting. **2** abnormal or unacceptable sexual behaviour.

pervert ● **v.** /per-**vert**/ **1** alter from an original meaning or state to a distortion of what was first intended. **2** lead away from what is right, natural, or acceptable. ● **n.** /**per**-vert/ a person with abnormal or unacceptable sexual behaviour.
– ORIGIN Latin *pervertere* 'turn about'.

perverted ● **adj.** sexually abnormal and unacceptable.

pervious /**per**-vi-uhss/ ● **adj.** allowing water to pass through.
– ORIGIN Latin *pervius* 'having a passage through'.

peseta /puh-**say**-tuh/ ● **n.** the former basic unit of money of Spain.
– ORIGIN Spanish, 'little weight'.

Peshawar E
/per-**shah**-wuh/ the capital of North-West Frontier Province, in Pakistan. Situated near the Khyber Pass, it is of strategic and military importance.

pesky ● **adj.** informal annoying.
– ORIGIN perh. from **PEST**.

pessary /**pess**-uh-ri/ ● **n.** (pl. **pessaries**) a small soluble block inserted into the vagina to treat infection or as a contraceptive.
– ORIGIN Latin *pessarium.*

pessimism ● **n.** lack of hope or confidence in the future.
– DERIVATIVES **pessimist** n. **pessimistic** adj.
– ORIGIN Latin *pessimus* 'worst'.

pest ● **n. 1** a destructive animal that attacks crops, food, or livestock. **2** informal an annoying person or thing.
– ORIGIN French *peste* or Latin *pestis* 'plague'.

pester ● **v.** (**pesters, pestering, pestered**) trouble with persistent requests or interruptions.
– ORIGIN French *empestrer* 'encumber'.

pesticide ● **n.** a substance for destroying insects or other pests.

pestilence ● **n.** archaic a deadly epidemic disease.
– ORIGIN Latin *pestilentia.*

pestilent ● **adj. 1** deadly. **2** informal, dated annoying.

pestilential ● **adj. 1** relating to or causing infectious diseases. **2** informal annoying.

pestle /**pess**-uhl/ ● **n.** a heavy tool with a rounded end, used for crushing and grinding substances in a mortar.
– ORIGIN Latin *pistillum.*

pesto /**pess**-toh/ ● **n.** a sauce of crushed basil leaves, pine nuts, garlic, Parmesan cheese, and olive oil, served with pasta.
– ORIGIN Italian.

pet[1] ● **n. 1** an animal or bird kept for companionship or pleasure. **2** a person treated with special favour. ● **adj. 1** relating to or kept as a pet. **2** favourite or particular: *my pet hate.* ● **v.** (**pets, petting, petted**) **1** stroke or pat (an animal). **2** caress sexually.
– ORIGIN unknown.

pet[2] ● **n.** a fit of sulking or bad temper.
– ORIGIN unknown.

Pétain E
/**pay**-tan/, (Henri) Philippe (Omer) (1856–1951), French general, head of state 1940–2. He agreed an armistice with Nazi Germany in 1940 and established the French government at Vichy (effectively a puppet regime for the Third Reich) until the German occupation in 1942.

petal ● **n.** each of the segments forming the outer part of a flower.
– ORIGIN Greek *petalon* 'leaf'.

petard /pi-**tard**/ ● **n.** (in phr. **be hoist with one's own petard**) have problems when one's schemes against others backfire on one.
– ORIGIN French, 'small bomb made of a box filled with powder'.

peter ● **v.** (**peters, petering, petered**) (**peter out**) come to an end gradually.
– ORIGIN unknown.

Peter I E
(1672–1725; known as **Peter the Great**), tsar of Russia 1682–1725. He expanded his territory in the Baltic and his administrative reforms transformed Russia into a significant European power.

P

Peter, St E
an Apostle; born *Simon*. He is regarded by Roman Catholics as the first bishop of the Church at Rome, where he is said to have been martyred in about AD 67. Feast day, 29 June.

Peterloo massacre E
an attack by cavalry forces on 16 August 1819 against a large but peaceable crowd of supporters of political reform. Eleven civilians were killed and more than 500 were injured.

petersham ● **n.** a corded tape used for stiffening in dresses and hats.
– ORIGIN named after the English army officer Lord *Petersham* (1790–1851).

Peterson, E
Oscar (Emmanuel) (b.1925), Canadian jazz pianist and composer.

petiole /pee-ti-ohl/ ● **n.** Bot. the stalk that joins a leaf to a stem.
– ORIGIN Latin *petiolus* 'little foot, stalk'.

petit bourgeois /puh-ti **boor**-*zh*wah/ ● **adj.** having to do with the lower middle class, especially in being conventional and conservative.
– ORIGIN French, 'little citizen'.

petite ● **adj.** (of a woman) attractively small and dainty.
– ORIGIN French, 'small'.

petit four /puh-ti **for**/ ● **n.** (pl. **petits fours** /puh-ti **forz**/) a very small fancy cake, biscuit, or sweet.
– ORIGIN French, 'little oven'.

petition ● **n. 1** a formal written request signed by many people and appealing to authority about a particular cause. **2** an appeal or request. ● **v.** make or present a petition to.
– ORIGIN Latin.

petit mal /puh-ti **mal**/ ● **n.** a mild form of epilepsy with only brief spells of unconsciousness. Compare with **GRAND MAL**.
– ORIGIN French, 'little sickness'.

petit point /puh-ti **poynt**, puh-ti **pwan**/ ● **n.** embroidery on canvas, using small diagonal stitches.
– ORIGIN French, 'little stitch'.

pet name ● **n.** a name used to express fondness or familiarity.

Petra E
an ancient city of SW Asia, in present-day Jordan. Its ruins include temples and tombs carved from the red sandstone cliffs.

Petrarch E
/pet-rark/ (1304–74), Italian poet, known for the *Canzoniere*, a sonnet sequence in praise of a woman called Laura.

petrel /pet-ruhl/ ● **n.** a black and white seabird that flies far from land.
– ORIGIN from St *Peter*, because of the bird's habit of flying low with legs dangling, and so appearing to walk on the water.

Petri dish /pet-ri, pee-tri/ ● **n.** a shallow transparent dish with a flat lid, used in laboratories.
– ORIGIN named after the German bacteriologist Julius R. *Petri* (1852–1922).

petrify ● **v.** (**petrifies**, **petrifying**, **petrified**) **1** change (organic matter) into stone by encrusting or replacing its original substance with a mineral deposit. **2** paralyse with fear.
– ORIGIN Latin *petrificare*.

petrochemical ● **adj.** relating to the chemical properties and processing of petroleum and natural gas. ● **n.** a chemical obtained from petroleum and natural gas.
– ORIGIN from **PETROLEUM**.

Petrograd E
/pet-roh-grad/ former name for **ST PETERSBURG**.

petrol ● **n.** Brit. refined petroleum used as fuel in motor vehicles.

petrol bomb ● **n.** Brit. a simple bomb consisting of a bottle containing petrol and a cloth wick.

petroleum ● **n.** an oil found in layers of rock and refined to produce petrol, paraffin, and diesel oil.
– ORIGIN Latin.

petroleum jelly ● **n.** a semi-transparent substance obtained from petroleum, used as a lubricant or ointment.

petticoat ● **n.** a woman's light, loose undergarment in the form of a skirt or dress.
– ORIGIN from former *petty coat* 'small coat'.

pettifogging ● **adj.** petty; trivial.
– ORIGIN from **PETTY** + former *fogger* 'underhand dealer'.

pettish ● **adj.** childishly sulky.
– DERIVATIVES **pettishly** adv.

petty ● **adj.** (**pettier**, **pettiest**) **1** of little importance. **2** (of a person's behaviour) small-minded. **3** minor: *a petty official*.
– DERIVATIVES **pettiness** n.
– ORIGIN French *petit* 'small'.

petty cash ● **n.** a small amount of money kept in an office for minor payments.

petty officer ● **n.** a rank of non-commissioned officer in the navy.

petulant /pet-yuu-luhnt/ ● **adj** childishly sulky or bad-tempered.
– DERIVATIVES **petulance** n. **petulantly** adv.
– ORIGIN Latin *petulans* 'impudent'.

petunia /pi-tyoo-ni-uh/ ● **n.** a South American plant with white, purple, or red funnel-shaped flowers.
– ORIGIN from an American Indian word meaning 'tobacco'.

pew ● **n. 1** (in a church) a long bench with a back. **2** Brit. informal a seat.
– ORIGIN Old French *puye* 'balcony'.

pewter ● **n.** a grey alloy of tin with copper and antimony.
– ORIGIN Old French *peutre*.

pfennig /fen-nig/ ● **n.** a former unit of money of Germany, equal to one hundredth of a mark.
– ORIGIN German.

PG ● **abbrev.** (in film classification) parental guidance, indicating that some scenes may be unsuitable for children.

pH ● **n.** Chem. a figure expressing how acid or alkaline a substance is (7 is neutral, lower values are more acid and higher values more alkaline).
– ORIGIN from *p* representing German *Potenz* 'power' + *H*, the symbol for hydrogen.

phaeton /fay-tuhn/ ● **n.** hist. a light, open four-wheeled horse-drawn carriage.
– ORIGIN from *Phaethōn* in Greek mythology, who was allowed to drive the chariot of the

sun for a day.

phagocyte /fag-uh-syt/ ● **n.** a type of body cell which surrounds and absorbs bacteria and other small particles.
– DERIVATIVES **phagocytic** adj.
– ORIGIN from Greek *phago-* 'eating' + *kutos* 'vessel'.

phalanger /fuh-lan-jer/ ● **n.** a tree-dwelling marsupial native to Australia and New Guinea.
– ORIGIN Greek *phalangion* 'spider's web' (because of its webbed toes).

phalanx /fa-langks/ ● **n.** (pl. **phalanxes**) **1** a group of similar people or things. **2** a body of troops or police officers in close formation.
– ORIGIN Greek.

phallic ● **adj.** relating to or resembling a penis.

phallus /fal-luhss/ ● **n.** (pl. **phalli** /fal-lee/ or **phalluses**) a penis.
– ORIGIN Greek *phallos*.

phantasm /fan-ta-z'm/ ● **n.** literary a figment of the imagination.
– ORIGIN Greek *phantasma*.

phantasmagoria /fan-taz-muh-gor-i-uh/ ● **n.** a sequence of real or imaginary images like that seen in a dream.
– DERIVATIVES **phantasmagoric** adj. **phantasmagorical** adj.
– ORIGIN prob. from French *fantasmagorie*.

phantom ● **n. 1** a ghost. **2** a figment of the imagination. ● **adj.** not really existing.
– ORIGIN Greek *phantasma*.

pharaoh /fair-oh/ ● **n.** a ruler in ancient Egypt.
– DERIVATIVES **pharaonic** /fair-ay-on-ik/ adj.
– ORIGIN Greek *Pharaō*.

Pharisee /fa-ri-see/ ● **n.** a member of an ancient Jewish sect who followed traditional Jewish law very strictly.
– ORIGIN Greek *Pharisaios*.

pharmaceutical /far-muh-syoo-ti-k'l/ ● **adj.** relating to medicinal drugs. ● **n.** a manufactured medicinal drug.
– ORIGIN Greek *pharmakeutikos*.

pharmacist ● **n.** a person qualified to prepare and dispense medicinal drugs.

pharmacology ● **n.** the branch of medicine concerned with the uses, effects, and action of drugs.
– DERIVATIVES **pharmacological** adj. **pharmacologist** n.

pharmacy ● **n.** (pl. **pharmacies**) **1** a place where medicinal drugs are prepared or sold. **2** the science or practice of preparing and dispensing medicinal drugs.

pharynx /fa-ringks/ ● **n.** (pl. **pharynges** /fa-rin-jeez/) the cavity behind the nose and mouth, connecting them to the oesophagus.
– ORIGIN Greek *pharunx*.

phase ● **n. 1** a distinct stage in a process of change or development. **2** each of the forms in which the moon or a planet appears, according to the amount that it is lit up. **3** Physics the stage that a regularly varying quantity (e.g. an alternating electric current) has reached in relation to zero or another chosen value. ● **v.** (**phases**, **phasing**, **phased**) **1** carry out in gradual stages. **2** (**phase in/out**) gradually introduce or withdraw (something).
– ORIGIN French.

PhD ● **abbrev.** Doctor of Philosophy.
– ORIGIN from Latin *philosophiae doctor*.

pheasant ● **n.** a large long-tailed game bird.
– ORIGIN Greek *phasianos* 'bird of Phasis', a river in the Caucasus.

phenol /fee-nol/ ● **n.** Chem. a poisonous white solid obtained from coal tar. Also called **CARBOLIC ACID**.
– ORIGIN French *phène* 'benzene'.

phenomenal ● **adj.** excellent.
– DERIVATIVES **phenomenally** adv.

phenomenon /fi-nom-i-nuhn/ ● **n.** (pl. **phenomena**) **1** a fact or situation that is observed to exist or happen. **2** a remarkable person or thing.
– ORIGIN Greek *phainomenon* 'thing appearing to view'.

USAGE phenomenon

The word **phenomenon** comes from Greek, and its plural form is **phenomena**. It is wrong to use **phenomena** as if it were a singular form; say *this is a strange phenomenon*, not *this is a strange phenomena*.

phenotype /fee-noh-typ/ ● **n.** Biol. the observable characteristics of an individual, determined by its genetic make-up and the environment.
– ORIGIN Greek *phainein* 'to show'.

pheromone /fe-ruh-mohn/ ● **n.** a chemical substance released by an animal and causing a response in others of its species.
– ORIGIN from Greek *pherein* 'convey' + **HORMONE**.

phial /fy-uhl/ ● **n.** a small cylindrical glass bottle.
– ORIGIN Greek *phialē* 'broad flat container'.

Phidias E
/fid-i-uhss/ (5th century BC), Athenian sculptor, noted for the Elgin marbles and his vast statue of Zeus.

Philadelphia E
/fil-uh-del-fi-uh/ the chief city of Pennsylvania, the site of the signing of the Declaration of Independence (1776).

philander /fi-lan-der/ ● **v.** (**philanders**, **philandering**, **philandered**) (of a man) have casual sexual relationships with women.
– DERIVATIVES **philanderer** n.
– ORIGIN Greek *philandros* 'fond of men'.

philanthropist ● **n.** a person who donates money to good causes or otherwise helps others.

philanthropy ● **n.** the practice of donating money to help people in need.
– DERIVATIVES **philanthropic** adj.
– ORIGIN Greek *philanthrōpia*.

philately /fi-lat-uh-li/ ● **n.** the collection and study of postage stamps.
– DERIVATIVES **philatelist** n.
– ORIGIN from Greek *philo-* 'loving' + *ateleia* 'exemption from payment'.

Philby E
/fil-bi/, Kim (1912–88; born *Harold Adrian Russell Philby*), British Foreign Office official and spy. A Soviet agent from the 1930s, he defected to the USSR in 1963.

-phile ● **comb. form** referring to a person or thing having a liking for a specified thing: *bibliophile*.
– ORIGIN Greek *philos* 'loving'.

philharmonic ● adj. (in the names of orchestras) devoted to music.

-philia ● comb. form referring to a liking for something: *paedophilia.*
– ORIGIN Greek *philia* 'fondness'.

Philip, Prince, E
Duke of Edinburgh (b.1921), husband of Elizabeth II. The son of Prince Andrew of Greece and Denmark, he married Princess Elizabeth in 1947.

Philip, St[1], E
an Apostle. Feast day, 1 May.

Philip, St[2], E
deacon of the early Christian Church; known as **St Philip the Evangelist**. Feast day, 6 June.

philippic /fi **lip** pik/ ● n. a bittor vorbal attack.
– ORIGIN Greek *philippikos,* the name given to Demosthenes' speeches against Philip II of Macedon.

Philippines E
/fil-li-peenz/ a country in SE Asia consisting of an archipelago of over 7,000 islands; capital, Manila.

Philistine /fil-i-styn/ ● n. **1** a member of a people of ancient Palestine who came into conflict with the Israelites. **2** (**philistine**) a person who is hostile to or not interested in culture and the arts.
– DERIVATIVES **philistinism** /fil-i-stin-i-z'm/ n.
– ORIGIN Greek *Philistinos.*

philo- ● comb. form referring to a liking for a specified thing: *philology.*
– ORIGIN Greek *philos* 'loving'.

philology ● n. the study of the structure, historical development, and relationships of a language or languages.
– DERIVATIVES **philological** adj. **philologist** n.
– ORIGIN Greek *philologia.*

philosopher ● n. a person who studies or engages in philosophy.

philosopher's stone ● n. (in alchemy) a supposed substance believed to change any metal into gold or silver.

philosophical ● adj. **1** relating to the study of philosophy. **2** calm in difficult circumstances.
– DERIVATIVES **philosophically** adv.

philosophize (also **philosophise**) ● v. (**philosophizes, philosophizing, philosophized**) theorize about serious issues.

philosophy ● n. (pl. **philosophies**) **1** the study of the fundamental nature of knowledge, reality, and existence. **2** the theories of a particular philosopher. **3** an attitude that guides one's behaviour.
– ORIGIN Greek *philosophia* 'love of wisdom'.

philtre /fil-ter/ (US **philter**) ● n. a love potion.
– ORIGIN Greek *philtron.*

phlebitis /fli-by-tiss/ ● n. Med. inflammation of the walls of a vein.
– ORIGIN Greek *phleps* 'vein'.

phlegm /flem/ ● n. **1** thick mucus which forms in the nose and throat, especially when one has a cold. **2** calmness of temperament.
– ORIGIN Greek *phlegma* 'inflammation'.

phlegmatic /fleg-mat-ik/ ● adj. calm and unemotional.

phloem /floh-em/ ● n. Bot. the tissue in plants which conducts food materials downwards from the leaves.
– ORIGIN Greek *phloos* 'bark'.

phlox /floks/ ● n. a garden plant with clusters of colourful scented flowers.
– ORIGIN Greek, 'flame'.

Phnom Penh E
/nom **pen**/ the capital of Cambodia.

-phobe ● comb. form referring to a person having a fear or dislike of a specified thing: *homophobe.*
– ORIGIN Greek *phobos* 'fear'.

phobia ● n. an extreme or irrational fear of something.
– DERIVATIVES **phobic** adj. & n.

-phobia ● comb. form extreme or irrational fear or dislike of a specified thing: *arachnophobia.*

Phoenicia E
/fuh-nee-shuh/ an ancient country in the eastern Mediterranean, corresponding to present-day Lebanon and the coastal plains of Syria. It was a centre of trade during the early part of the 1st millennium BC.
– DERIVATIVES **Phoenician** n. & adj.

Phoenix E
/fee-niks/ the state capital of Arizona.

phoenix /fee-niks/ ● n. (in classical mythology) a bird that burned itself on a funeral pyre and was born again from the ashes.
– ORIGIN Greek *phoinix.*

phone ● n. a telephone. ● v. (**phones, phoning, phoned**) telephone.

-phone ● comb. form referring to an instrument connected with sound: *megaphone.*
– ORIGIN Greek *phōnē* 'sound, voice'.

phone book ● n. a telephone directory.

phonecard ● n. a prepaid card allowing the user to make calls on a public telephone.

phone-in ● n. a radio or television programme during which listeners or viewers join in by telephone.

phoneme /foh-neem/ ● n. any of the distinct units of sound that distinguish one word from another, e.g. *p, b, d,* and *t* in *pad, pat, bad,* and *bat.*
– ORIGIN Greek *phōnēma* 'sound, speech'.

phonetic ● adj. **1** having to do with speech sounds. **2** (of a system of spelling) that closely matches the sounds represented. ● n. (**phonetics**) the study of speech sounds.
– DERIVATIVES **phonetically** adv.
– ORIGIN Greek *phōnētikos.*

phoney (also **phony**) informal ● adj. (**phonier, phoniest**) not genuine. ● n. (pl. **phoneys** or **phonies**) a person or thing that is not genuine.
– ORIGIN unknown.

phonic /fon-ik, foh-nik/ ● adj. relating to speech sounds.

phono- ● comb. form relating to sound: *phonograph.*
– ORIGIN Greek *phōnē* 'sound, voice'.

phonograph ● n. Brit. an early form of gramophone.

phonology /fuh-nol-uh-ji/ ● n. the system of relationships between the basic speech sounds of a language.

P

phony ● **adj. & n.** var. of **PHONEY.**

phosphate /foss-fayt/ ● **n.** Chem. a salt or ester of phosphoric acid.

phosphine /foss-feen/ ● **n.** a foul-smelling gas formed from phosphorus and hydrogen.

phosphor /foss-fer/ ● **n.** a synthetic fluorescent or phosphorescent substance.

phosphorescence ● **n.** light that is given out by a substance without burning or heat.
– DERIVATIVES **phosphorescent** adj.

phosphoric /foss-fo-rik/ ● **adj.** relating to or containing phosphorus.

phosphoric acid ● **n.** Chem. an acid obtained by treating phosphates with sulphuric acid.

phosphorus /foss-fuh-ruhss/ ● **n.** a chemical element in the form of a yellowish wax-like substance which glows in the dark and ignites in the air.
– DERIVATIVES **phosphorous** adj.
– ORIGIN Greek *phōsphoros.*

photo ● **n.** (pl. **photos**) a photograph.

photo- ● **comb. form 1** relating to light. **2** relating to photography.
– ORIGIN sense 1 from Greek *phōs* 'light'.

photocall ● **n.** Brit. an occasion on which famous people pose for photographers by arrangement.

photocell ● **n.** = **PHOTOELECTRIC CELL.**

photochemistry ● **n.** the branch of chemistry concerned with the chemical effects of light.
– DERIVATIVES **photochemical** adj.

photocopy ● **n.** (pl. **photocopies**) a photographic copy of a document or picture. ● **v.** (**photocopies**, **photocopying**, **photocopied**) make a photocopy of.
– DERIVATIVES **photocopier** n.

photoelectric ● **adj.** involving the emission of electrons from a surface by the action of light.

photoelectric cell ● **n.** a device using a photoelectric effect to generate current.

photo finish ● **n.** a close finish of a race in which the winner is identifiable only from a photograph of competitors crossing the line.

photofit ● **n.** Brit. a picture of a person made from various photographs of facial features.

photogenic /foh-tuh-jen-ik/ ● **adj. 1** looking attractive in photographs. **2** Biol. giving out light.

photograph ● **n.** a picture made with a camera, in which an image is focused on to film and then made visible by chemical treatment. ● **v.** take a photograph of.
– DERIVATIVES **photographer** n. **photographic** adj.

photography ● **n.** the taking and processing of photographs.

photojournalism ● **n.** the use of photographs to give news.

photometer /foh-tom-i-ter/ ● **n.** an instrument for measuring the strength of light.
– DERIVATIVES **photometric** adj. **photometry** n.

photomontage /foh-toh-mon-tahzh/ ● **n.** a picture consisting of photographs placed together or overlapping.

photon /foh-ton/ ● **n.** Physics a particle representing a quantum of light or other electromagnetic radiation.

photo opportunity ● **n.** a photocall.

photosensitive ● **adj.** responding to light.

photostat ● **n.** trademark **1** a type of machine for making photocopies on special paper. **2** a copy made by a photostat.

photosynthesis ● **n.** the process by which green plants use sunlight to form nutrients from carbon dioxide and water.
– DERIVATIVES **photosynthetic** adj.

phototropism /foh-toh-troh-pi-z'm/ ● **n.** Biol. the moving of a plant or other organism either towards or away from a source of light.

phrasal verb ● **n.** a verb combined with an adverb or preposition to give a new meaning that cannot be deduced from the individual parts, e.g. *give out.*

phrase ● **n. 1** a small group of words forming a unit within a clause. **2** Music a group of notes forming a distinct unit within a longer passage. ● **v.** (**phrases**, **phrasing**, **phrased**) put into a particular form of words.
– DERIVATIVES **phrasal** adj.
– ORIGIN Greek *phrasis.*

phrase book ● **n.** a book listing and translating useful expressions in a foreign language.

phraseology /fray-zi-ol-uh-ji/ ● **n.** (pl. **phraseologies**) a particular way in which words are used: *legal phraseology.*

phrasing ● **n.** division of music into phrases.

phrenology /fri-nol-uh-ji/ ● **n.** esp. hist. the study of the shape and size of a person's skull as a supposed indication of their character.
– ORIGIN Greek *phrēn* 'mind'.

Phrygia E
/fri-ji-uh/ an ancient region of west central Asia Minor. It reached the peak of its power in the 8th century BC under King Midas.

Phuket E
/poo-ket/ a major resort and port of Thailand, on Phuket island.

phyllo ● **n.** var. of **FILO.**

phylloquinone /fi-loh-kwi-nohn/ ● **n.** vitamin K_1, a compound found in leafy green vegetables and essential for blood-clotting.
– ORIGIN from Greek *phullon* 'leaf' + **QUINONE.**

phylum /fy-luhm/ ● **n.** (pl. **phyla** /fy-luh/) Zool. a classifying category that ranks above class and below kingdom.
– ORIGIN Greek *phulon* 'race'.

physic ● **n.** archaic medicinal drugs or medical treatment.
– ORIGIN Latin *physica.*

physical ● **adj. 1** relating to the body as opposed to the mind. **2** relating to things that can be seen, heard, or touched. **3** involving bodily contact or activity. **4** relating to physics or the operation of natural forces. ● **n.** a medical examination to find out a person's bodily fitness.
– DERIVATIVES **physicality** n. **physically** adv.

physical chemistry ● **n.** the branch of chemistry concerned with applying the techniques and theories of physics to the study of chemical systems.

physical education ● **n.** instruction in physical exercise and games.

physical geography ● **n.** the branch of geography concerned with natural features.

physical sciences ● **pl. n.** the sciences concerned with the study of inanimate natural objects, including physics, chemistry, and astronomy.

physician • n. a person qualified to practise medicine.

physics • n. **1** the branch of science concerned with the nature and properties of matter and energy. **2** the physical properties and nature of something.
– DERIVATIVES **physicist** n.
– ORIGIN Latin *physica* 'natural things'.

physiognomy /fi-zi-**og**-nuh-mi, fi-zi-**on**-uh-mi/ • n. (pl. **physiognomies**) a person's facial features or expression.
– ORIGIN Greek *phusiognōmonia*.

physiology • n. **1** the branch of biology concerned with the normal functions of living organisms and their parts. **2** the way in which a living organism or bodily part functions.
– DERIVATIVES **physiological** adj. **physiologist** n.

physiotherapy • n. the treatment of disease or injury by massage and exercise.
– DERIVATIVES **physiotherapist** n.

physique • n. the form, size, and development of a person's body.
– ORIGIN French, 'physical'.

phytoplankton /fy-toh-plangk-tuhn/ • n. Biol. plankton consisting of microscopic plants.
– ORIGIN Greek *phuton* 'a plant'.

pi /py/ • n. the numerical value of the ratio of the circumference of a circle to its diameter (approximately 3.14159).
– ORIGIN from the initial letter of Greek *periphereia* 'circumference'.

Piaf E
/**pee**-af/, Edith (1915–63; born *Edith Giovanna Gassion*), French singer, known for such songs as 'Je ne regrette rien'.

Piaget E
/pi-a-*zhay*/, Jean (1896–1980), Swiss psychologist. His work on the intellectual and logical abilities of children was central to the study of the development of human thought processes.

pianissimo /pi-uh-**niss**-i-moh/ • adv. & adj. Music very soft or softly.
– ORIGIN Italian, 'softest'.

piano[1] /pi-**an**-oh/ • n. (pl. **pianos**) a large keyboard musical instrument with metal strings, which are struck by hammers when the keys are pressed.
– DERIVATIVES **pianist** n.
– ORIGIN from PIANOFORTE.

piano[2] /pi-**ah**-noh/ • adv. & adj. Music soft or softly.
– ORIGIN Italian.

piano accordion • n. an accordion with the melody played on a small vertical keyboard like that of a piano.

pianoforte /pi-an-oh-**for**-tay/ • n. formal = PIANO[1].
– ORIGIN from Italian *piano e forte* 'soft and loud'.

pianola /pi-uh-**noh**-luh/ • n. trademark a piano equipped to be played automatically with a roll of perforated paper which controls the movement of the keys to produce a tune.

piazza /pi-**at**-zuh/ • n. a public square or marketplace, especially in Italy.
– ORIGIN Italian.

picador /**pik**-uh-dor/ • n. (in bullfighting) a person on horseback who goads the bull with a lance.
– ORIGIN Spanish.

picaresque /pi-kuh-**resk**/ • adj. relating to fiction dealing with the adventures of a dishonest but appealing hero.
– ORIGIN Spanish *picaresco*.

Picasso, E
Pablo (1881–1973), Spanish painter, sculptor, and graphic artist, resident in France from 1904. A prolific and versatile artist, he developed cubism together with Braque, and later adopted a neoclassical figurative style. Notable works include *Les Demoiselles d'Avignon* and *Guernica*.

piccalilli /pik-kuh-lil-li/ • n. (pl. **piccalillies** or **piccalillis**) a pickle of chopped vegetables, mustard, and hot spices.
– ORIGIN prob. from PICKLE and CHILLI.

piccaninny /**pik**-kuh-nin-ni/ (US **pickaninny**) • n. (pl. **piccaninnies**) offens. a small black child.
– ORIGIN Spanish *pequeño* or Portuguese *pequeno* 'little'.

piccolo • n. (pl. **piccolos**) a small flute sounding an octave higher than the ordinary one.
– ORIGIN Italian, 'small flute'.

pick[1] • v. **1** (also **pick up**) take hold of and move. **2** remove (a flower or fruit) from where it is growing. **3** choose from a number of alternatives. • n. **1** an act of selecting something. **2** (**the pick of**) informal the best person or thing in a group.
– PHRASES **pick and choose** select only the best from a number of alternatives. **pick at 1** repeatedly pull at (something) with one's fingers. **2** eat in small amounts. **pick someone's brains** informal obtain information by questioning someone with expertise. **pick a fight** provoke an argument or fight. **pick holes in** find fault with. **pick a lock** open a lock with an instrument other than the proper key. **pick off** shoot (one of a group). **pick on** single out for unfair treatment. **pick over** (or **pick through**) sort through (a number of items) carefully. **pick someone's pockets** steal something from a person's pocket. **pick up 1** go to collect. **2** improve or increase. **3** informal casually strike up a relationship with (someone) as a sexual approach. **4** learn or become aware of. **5** receive (a signal or sound). **pick one's way** walk slowly and carefully.
– DERIVATIVES **picker** n.
– ORIGIN unknown.

pick[2] • n. **1** (also **pickaxe**) a tool consisting of a curved iron bar with pointed ends, fixed at right angles to its handle, used for breaking up hard ground or rock. **2** a plectrum.
– ORIGIN from PIKE[2].

picket • n. **1** a person or group of people standing outside a workplace trying to persuade others not to enter during a strike. **2** a pointed wooden stake driven into the ground. • v. (**pickets**, **picketing**, **picketed**) act as a picket outside (a workplace).
– ORIGIN French *piquet*.

pickings • pl. n. profits or gains.

pickle • n. **1** a relish consisting of vegetables or fruit preserved in vinegar, brine, or mustard. **2** (**a pickle**) informal a difficult situation. • v. (**pickles**, **pickling**, **pickled**) **1** preserve

p

(food) in pickle. **2** (**pickled**) informal drunk.
– ORIGIN Dutch or German *pekel*.

pick-me-up ● n. informal a thing that makes one feel more lively or cheerful.

pickpocket ● n. a person who steals from people's pockets.

pickup ● n. **1** (also **pickup truck**) a small truck with low sides. **2** an act of picking up a person or goods. **3** an improvement.

picky ● adj. (**pickier**, **pickiest**) informal fussy.

picnic ● n. a packed meal eaten outdoors, or an occasion when such a meal is eaten. ● v. (**picnics**, **picnicking**, **picnicked**) have or take part in a picnic.
– PHRASES **be no picnic** informal be difficult or unpleasant.
– DERIVATIVES **picnicker** n.
– ORIGIN French *pique-nique*.

Pict ● n. a member of an ancient people inhabiting northern Scotland in Roman times.
– ORIGIN Latin *Picti*.

pictograph (also **pictogram**) ● n. **1** a picture representing a word or phrase. **2** a picture representing statistics on a chart, graph, or computer screen.
– ORIGIN Latin *pingere* 'to paint'.

pictorial ● adj. having to do with or using pictures.
– DERIVATIVES **pictorially** adv.
– ORIGIN Latin *pictorius*.

picture ● n. **1** a painting, drawing, or photograph. **2** an image on a television screen. **3** a cinema film. **4** (**the pictures**) the cinema. **5** an impression formed from a description of something. **6** informal a state of being fully informed: *in the picture*. ● v. (**pictures**, **picturing**, **pictured**) **1** show in a picture. **2** form a mental image of.
– ORIGIN Latin *pictura*.

picture-postcard ● adj. charmingly attractive: *picture-postcard villages*.

picturesque ● adj. attractive in a quaint or charming way.

picture window ● n. a large window consisting of one pane of glass.

piddle ● v. (**piddles**, **piddling**, **piddled**) informal **1** urinate. **2** (**piddling**) very unimportant or trivial.
– ORIGIN prob. from **PISS** and **PUDDLE**.

pidgin ● n. a simple form of a language with elements taken from local languages, used for communication between people not sharing a common language.
– ORIGIN Chinese alteration of English *business*.

pie ● n. a baked dish of ingredients encased in or topped with pastry.
– PHRASES **pie in the sky** informal a pleasant idea that is very unlikely to happen.
– ORIGIN prob. the same word as former *pie* 'magpie'.

piebald ● adj. (of a horse) having irregular patches of two colours.
– ORIGIN from *pie* in *magpie* + *bald* in the former sense 'streaked with white'.

piece ● n. **1** a portion separated from the whole. **2** an item used in building something or forming part of a set. **3** a musical or written work. **4** a token used to make moves in a board game. **5** a coin of specified value. ● v. (**pieces**, **piecing**, **pieced**) (**piece together**) assemble from individual parts.
– PHRASES **go to pieces** become so upset that one cannot function normally. **in one piece** unharmed or undamaged. (**all**) **of a piece** all the same. **say one's piece** give one's opinion.
– ORIGIN Old French.

pièce de résistance /pyess duh ray-zisstonss/ ● n. the most important or impressive feature of a creative work.
– ORIGIN French, 'piece (i.e. means) of resistance'.

piecemeal ● adj. & adv. done in a gradual and inconsistent way.
– ORIGIN from **PIECE** + an Old English word meaning 'measure'.

piecework ● n. work paid for according to the amount produced.

pie chart ● n. a diagram in which a circle is divided into sections that each represent a proportion of the whole.

pied /*rhymes with* ride/ ● adj. having two or more different colours.
– ORIGIN first meaning 'black and white like a magpie'.

pied-à-terre /pyay-dah-**tair**/ ● n. (pl. **pieds-à-terre** /pyay-dah-**tair**/) a small flat or house kept for occasional use, one's permanent home being elsewhere.
– ORIGIN French, 'foot to earth'.

Piedmont E
/**peed**-mont/ a region of NW Italy; capital, Turin. It was the centre of the movement for a united Italy in the 19th century.

pie-eyed ● adj. informal very drunk.

pier ● n. **1** a structure leading out to sea and used as a landing stage for boats or as a place of entertainment. **2** a pillar supporting an arch or bridge.
– ORIGIN Latin *pera*.

Pierce, E
Franklin (1804–69), American Democratic statesman, 14th President of the US 1853–7.

pierce ● v. (**pierces**, **piercing**, **pierced**) **1** make a hole in or through with a sharp object. **2** force or cut a way through. **3** (**piercing**) very sharp, cold, or high-pitched.
– ORIGIN Old French *percer*.

Piero della Francesca E
/pyair-oh del-luh fran-**chess**-kuh/ (1416–92), Italian painter. He is known for his frescoes, in which he used perspective and proportion to create harmonious compositions.

piety /py-uh-ti/ ● n. (pl. **pieties**) **1** the quality of being deeply religious. **2** a conventional belief accepted without thinking: *the accepted pieties of our time*.
– ORIGIN Latin *pietas*.

piffle ● n. informal nonsense.

piffling ● adj. informal unimportant.

pig ● n. **1** a domestic or wild mammal with sparse bristly hair and a flat snout. **2** informal a greedy or dirty person. **3** informal, derog. a police officer. **4** an oblong mass of iron or lead from a smelting furnace. ● v. (**pigs**, **pigging**, **pigged**) informal gorge oneself with food.
– PHRASES **make a pig's ear of** Brit. informal handle unskilfully. **a pig in a poke** something that is bought without first being seen.
– DERIVATIVES **piggish** adj. **piglet** n.

– ORIGIN prob. from an Old English word meaning 'acorn' or 'pig bread'.

pigeon • n. a fat bird with a small head and a cooing voice.
– ORIGIN Old French *pijon* 'young bird'.

pigeonhole • n. **1** each of a set of small compartments where letters or messages may be left for people. **2** a category to which someone or something is assigned. • v. (**pigeonholes**, **pigeonholing**, **pigeonholed**) place in a particular category.

pigeon-toed • adj. having the toes or feet turned inwards.

piggery • n. (pl. **piggeries**) a farm or enclosure where pigs are kept.

Piggott, E
Lester (Keith) (b.1935), English jockey. He was champion jockey eleven times and won the Derby a record nine times.

piggy • adj. like a pig: *little piggy eyes.*

piggyback • n. a ride on someone's back and shoulders.

piggy bank • n. a money box shaped like a pig.

pig-headed • adj. stupidly stubborn.

pig iron • n. crude iron as first obtained from a smelting furnace.

pigment /pig-muhnt/ • n. **1** a natural substance that gives a plant or animal its colour. **2** a substance used for colouring or painting.
– DERIVATIVES **pigmentation** n.
– ORIGIN Latin *pigmentum.*

pigmented • adj. having a natural colour.

pigmy • n. var. of PYGMY.

Pigs, Bay of E
a bay on the SW coast of Cuba, scene of an unsuccessful attempt in 1961 by US-backed Cuban exiles to overthrow Fidel Castro.

pigskin • n. leather made from the hide of a pig.

pigsty • n. (pl. **pigsties**) **1** an enclosure for pigs. **2** a very dirty or untidy place.

pigswill • n. kitchen scraps fed to pigs.

pigtail • n. a plaited length of hair worn at the back or on each side of the head.

pike[1] • n. (pl. **pike**) a freshwater fish with a long body and sharp teeth.
– ORIGIN from PIKE[2].

pike[2] • n. hist. a weapon with a pointed metal head on a long wooden shaft.
– ORIGIN French *pique.*

pike[3] • n. a jackknife position in diving or gymnastics.
– ORIGIN unknown.

pikestaff • n. (in phr. **as plain as a pikestaff**) very obvious.
– ORIGIN alteration of *as plain as a packstaff*, the staff being that of a pedlar, on which he rested his pack of wares.

pilaf /pi-laf/ (also **pilau** /pi-low/) • n. a Middle Eastern or Indian dish of spiced rice and often meat and vegetables.
– ORIGIN Turkish.

pilaster /pi-lass-ter/ • n. a flat rectangular column that sticks out from a wall.
– ORIGIN Latin *pilastrum.*

Pilate E
/py-luht/, Pontius (died *c.*36 AD), Roman governor of Judaea *c.*26–*c.*36, who presided at the trial of Jesus Christ and authorized his crucifixion.

pilchard • n. a small edible fish of the herring family.
– ORIGIN unknown.

pile[1] • n. **1** a heap of things lying one on top of another. **2** informal a large amount. **3** a large imposing building. • v. (**piles**, **piling**, **piled**) **1** place (things) one on top of the other. **2** (**pile up**) form a pile or very large quantity. **3** (**pile on**) informal exaggerate for effect. **4** (**pile into**/**out of**) get into or out of (a vehicle) in a disorganized way.
– ORIGIN Latin *pila* 'pillar, pier'.

pile[2] • n. a heavy post driven into the ground to support foundations.
– ORIGIN Old English, 'dart, stake'.

pile[3] • n. the soft projecting surface of a carpet or a fabric, consisting of many small threads.
– ORIGIN Latin *pilus* 'hair'.

piledriver • n. **1** a machine for driving piles into the ground. **2** Brit. informal a forceful act, blow, or shot.

piles • pl. n. haemorrhoids.
– ORIGIN prob. from Latin *pila* 'ball'.

pile-up • n. informal a crash involving several vehicles.

pilfer • v. (**pilfers**, **pilfering**, **pilfered**) steal (things of little value).
– ORIGIN Old French *pelfrer* 'to pillage'.

pilgrim • n. a person who journeys to a holy place for religious reasons.
– ORIGIN Provençal *pelegrin.*

pilgrimage • n. a pilgrim's journey.

Pilgrim Fathers • pl. n. the group of 102 people led by English Puritans who sailed in the *Mayflower* from Plymouth to New England in 1620.

pill • n. **1** a small round mass of solid medicine for swallowing whole. **2** (**the Pill**) a contraceptive pill.
– ORIGIN Latin *pilula* 'little ball'.

pillage • v. (**pillages**, **pillaging**, **pillaged**) (in wartime) rob or steal with violence. • n. the action of pillaging.
– ORIGIN Old French.

pillar • n. **1** a tall upright structure used as a support for a building. **2** a source of reliable support: *he's a pillar of the community.*
– PHRASES **from pillar to post** from one place to another in an unsatisfactory way.
– DERIVATIVES **pillared** adj.
– ORIGIN Latin *pila* 'pillar'.

pillar box • n. (in the UK) a large red cylindrical public postbox.

pillbox • n. **1** a small round hat. **2** a small, partly underground, concrete fort.

pillion • n. a seat for a passenger behind a motorcyclist.
– ORIGIN Irish *pillín* 'small cushion'.

pillock • n. Brit. informal a stupid person.
– ORIGIN from former *pillicock* 'penis'.

pillory • n. (pl. **pillories**) a wooden framework with holes for the head and hands, in which offenders were formerly imprisoned and exposed to public abuse. • v. (**pillories**, **pillorying**, **pilloried**) attack or ridicule publicly.
– ORIGIN Old French *pilori.*

pillow • n. a rectangular cloth bag stuffed with soft materials, used to support the head

when lying down.
– DERIVATIVES **pillowy** adj.
– ORIGIN Latin *pulvinus* 'cushion'.

pillowcase ● n. a removable cloth cover for a pillow.

pillow talk ● n. intimate conversation between lovers in bed.

pilot ● n. **1** a person who operates the flying controls of an aircraft. **2** a person with local knowledge who is qualified to take charge of a ship entering or leaving a harbour. **3** something done or produced as a test before introducing it more widely. ● v. (**pilots**, **piloting**, **piloted**) **1** act as a pilot of (an aircraft or ship). **2** test (a scheme, project, etc.) before introducing it more widely.
– ORIGIN Latin *pilotus*.

pilot light ● n. a small gas burner kept alight permanently to light a larger burner when needed.

pimiento /pi-**myen**-toh/ (also **pimento**) ● n. (pl. **pimientos**) a red sweet pepper.
– ORIGIN Spanish.

pimp ● n. a man who controls prostitutes and arranges clients for them, taking a percentage of their earnings in return. ● v. act as a pimp.
– ORIGIN unknown.

pimpernel ● n. a low-growing plant with bright five-petalled flowers.
– ORIGIN Old French *pimpernelle*.

pimple ● n. a small, hard inflamed spot on the skin.
– DERIVATIVES **pimply** adj.
– ORIGIN Old English, 'break out in pustules'.

PIN (also **PIN number**) ● abbrev. personal identification number.

pin ● n. **1** a thin piece of metal with a sharp point at one end and a round head at the other, used as a fastener. **2** a metal projection from an electric plug or an integrated circuit. **3** a small brooch. **4** Med. a steel rod used to join the ends of broken bones while they heal. **5** a metal peg in a hand grenade that prevents it exploding. **6** a skittle. **7** (**pins**) informal legs. ● v. (**pins**, **pinning**, **pinned**) **1** attach or fasten with a pin or pins. **2** hold someone firmly so they are unable to move. **3** (**pin down**) force (someone) to be specific. **4** (**pin down**) restrict the actions of (an enemy) by firing at them. **5** (**pin on**) fix (blame or responsibility) on.
– ORIGIN Latin *pinna* 'point, edge'.

pina colada /pee-nuh kuh-**lah**-duh/ ● n. a cocktail made with rum, pineapple juice, and coconut.
– ORIGIN Spanish, 'strained pineapple'.

pinafore ● n. **1** (also **pinafore dress**) a collarless, sleeveless dress worn over a blouse or jumper. **2** Brit. a woman's loose sleeveless garment worn over clothes to keep them clean.
– ORIGIN from PIN + AFORE.

Pinang [E]
var. of PENANG.

pinball ● n. a game in which small metal balls are shot across a sloping board and score points by striking targets.

pince-nez /panss-**nay**/ ● n. a pair of glasses with a nose clip instead of earpieces.
– ORIGIN French, 'that pinches the nose'.

pincer ● n. **1** (**pincers**) a tool made of two pieces of metal with blunt inward-curving jaws, used for gripping and pulling things. **2** a front claw of a lobster or similar type of shellfish.
– ORIGIN Old French *pincier* 'to pinch'.

pinch ● v. **1** grip (flesh) tightly between finger and thumb. **2** (of a shoe) hurt (a foot) by being too tight. **3** Brit. informal steal. ● n. **1** an act of pinching. **2** an amount of an ingredient that can be held between fingers and thumb.
– PHRASES **at a pinch** if absolutely necessary. **feel the pinch** experience financial hardship.
– ORIGIN Old French *pincier* 'to pinch'.

pincushion ● n. a small pad for holding pins.

Pindar [E]
/**pin**-der/ (*c.*518–*c.*438 BC), Greek lyric poet, famous for his odes, which celebrate victories in athletic contests.

pine[1] ● n. (also **pine tree**) an evergreen coniferous tree having clusters of long needle-shaped leaves.
– ORIGIN Latin *pinus*.

pine[2] ● v. (**pines**, **pining**, **pined**) **1** become very weak because one misses someone so much. **2** (**pine for**) miss and long for the return of.
– ORIGIN Old English.

pineal gland /py-nee-uhl, **pin**-i-uhl/ ● n. a small gland at the back of the skull within the brain, secreting a hormone-like substance in some mammals.
– ORIGIN Latin *pinea* 'pine cone'.

pineapple ● n. a large juicy tropical fruit with yellow flesh surrounded by a tough skin.
– ORIGIN from PINE[1] + APPLE.

pine marten ● n. a dark brown weasel-like mammal that lives in trees.

pine nut ● n. the edible seed of various pine trees.

ping ● n. a short high-pitched ringing sound. ● v. make or cause to make such a sound.

ping-pong ● n. informal table tennis.

pinhole ● n. a very small hole.

pinion[1] /**pin**-yuhn/ ● n. the outer part of a bird's wing including the flight feathers. ● v. **1** tie or hold the arms or legs of. **2** cut off the pinion of (a bird) to prevent flight.
– ORIGIN Old French *pignon*.

pinion[2] /**pin**-yuhn/ ● n. a small cogwheel or spindle that engages with a large cogwheel.
– ORIGIN French *pignon*.

pink[1] ● adj. **1** of a colour between red and white. **2** having to do with homosexuals: *the pink economy.* ● n. **1** pink colour or material. **2** (**the pink**) informal the best condition: *in the pink of health.*
– ORIGIN from PINK[2].

pink[2] ● n. a plant with sweet-smelling pink or white flowers and grey-green leaves.
– ORIGIN perh. short for *pink eye*, 'small or half-shut eye'.

pink[3] ● v. cut a zigzag edge on.
– ORIGIN perh. from German *pinken* 'strike'.

Pinkerton, [E]
Allan (1819–84), Scottish-born American detective, who established the first American private detective agency (1850).

pinkie ● n. informal the little finger.

– ORIGIN partly from Dutch *pink*.

pinking shears • **pl. n.** shears with a serrated blade, used to cut a zigzag edge in fabric.

pin money • **n.** a small sum of money for spending on inessentials.
– ORIGIN first referring to an allowance to a woman from her husband.

pinna /**pin**-nuh/ • **n.** (pl. **pinnae** /**pin**-nee/) Anat. the external part of the ear.
– ORIGIN Latin.

pinnace /**pin**-nis/ • **n.** esp. hist. a small boat forming part of the equipment of a larger vessel.
– ORIGIN French *pinace*.

pinnacle • **n. 1** a high pointed piece of rock. **2** a small pointed turret on a roof. **3** the most successful point.
– ORIGIN Latin *pinnaculum*.

pinnate /**pin**-nayt/ • **adj.** Bot. & Zool. having leaflets or other parts arranged on either side of a stem or axis.
– ORIGIN Latin *pinnatus* 'feathered'.

PIN number • **n.** see **PIN**.

pinny • **n.** (pl. **pinnies**) informal a pinafore.

Pinochet E
/pin-uh-shay, pin-uh-**chay**/, Augusto (b.1915; full name *Augusto Pinochet Ugarte*), Chilean general and statesman, President 1974–90. After his overthrow of President Allende he imposed a military dictatorship until forced to give way to a democratically elected President.

pinpoint • **n.** a tiny dot. • **adj.** absolutely precise. • **v.** find the exact position of.

pinprick • **n.** a very small dot.

pins and needles • **n.** a tingling feeling in a limb recovering from numbness.

pinstripe • **n.** a very narrow pale stripe in dark cloth.
– DERIVATIVES **pinstriped** adj.

pint • **n. 1** a unit of liquid or dry capacity equal to one eighth of a gallon, in Britain equal to 0.568 litre and in the US equal to 0.473 litre (for liquid measure) or 0.551 litre (for dry measure). **2** Brit. informal a pint of beer.
– ORIGIN Old French *pinte*.

pintail • **n.** a duck with a long pointed tail.

Pinter E
/**pin**-ter/, Harold (b.1930), English dramatist and actor. His plays are noted for their use of realistic dialogue broken up by significant pauses; they include *The Birthday Party*, *The Caretaker*, and *The Homecoming*.

pintle • **n.** a pin or bolt on which a rudder turns.
– ORIGIN Old English, 'penis'.

pint-sized • **adj.** informal very small.

pin-tuck • **n.** a very narrow ornamental tuck in a garment.

pin-up • **n.** a poster featuring a sexually attractive person.

pinwheel • **n.** a small cogwheel in which the teeth are formed by pins set into the rim.

pioneer • **n. 1** a person who explores or settles in a new region. **2** a person who develops new ideas or techniques. • **v.** (**pioneers**, **pioneering**, **pioneered**) be a pioneer of.
– ORIGIN French *pionnier* 'foot soldier'.

pious • **adj. 1** deeply religious. **2** pretending to be good or religious so as to impress. **3** (of a hope) sincere but unlikely to be fulfilled.
– DERIVATIVES **piously** adv.
– ORIGIN Latin *pius* 'dutiful'.

pip[1] • **n.** a small hard seed in a fruit.
– ORIGIN Old French *pepin*.

pip[2] • **n. 1** (**the pips**) Brit. a series of short high-pitched sounds used as a signal on the radio. **2** Brit. a star on the shoulder of an army officer's uniform, showing rank. **3** any of the spots on a playing card, domino, or dice.

pip[3] • **v.** (**pips**, **pipping**, **pipped**) Brit. informal (**be pipped**) be defeated by a small margin or at the last moment.
– ORIGIN from PIP[1] or PIP[2].

pipe • **n. 1** a tube used to carry water, gas, oil, etc. **2** a device for smoking tobacco, consisting of a narrow tube that opens into a small bowl in which the tobacco is burned. **3** a wind instrument consisting of a single tube with holes along its length that are covered by the fingers to produce different notes. **4** one of the tubes by which notes are produced in an organ. **5** (**pipes**) bagpipes. • **v.** (**pipes**, **piping**, **piped**) **1** send through a pipe. **2** transmit (music, a programme, a signal, etc.) by wire or cable. **3** play (a tune) on a pipe. **4** sing or say in a high voice. **5** decorate with piping.
– PHRASES **pipe down** informal be less noisy. **pipe up** say something suddenly.
– ORIGIN Latin *pipare* 'to peep, chirp'.

piped music • **n.** pre-recorded background music played through loudspeakers.

pipe dream • **n.** a hope or scheme that will never be realized.
– ORIGIN referring to a dream experienced when smoking an opium pipe.

pipeline • **n.** a long pipe for carrying oil, gas, etc. over a distance.
– PHRASES **in the pipeline** in the process of being developed.

pipe organ • **n.** an organ using pipes instead of or as well as reeds.

Piper, E
John (1903–92), English painter and decorative designer, known for his watercolours and for his stained glass.

piper • **n.** a person who plays a pipe or bagpipes.

pipette /pi-**pet**/ • **n.** a thin tube used in a laboratory for handling small quantities of liquid, the liquid being drawn into the tube by suction.
– ORIGIN French, 'little pipe'.

piping • **n. 1** lengths of pipe. **2** lines of icing or cream, used to decorate cakes and desserts. **3** thin cord covered in fabric and inserted along a seam or hem for decoration.
– PHRASES **piping hot** (of food or water) very hot. [ORIGIN with reference to the whistling sound made by very hot liquid or food.]

pipistrelle /pi-pi-**strel**, **pip**-i-strel/ • **n.** a small insect-eating bat.
– ORIGIN French.

pipit /**pi**-pit/ • **n.** a brown songbird of open country.

pipsqueak • **n.** informal an unimportant person.

piquant /**pee**-kuhnt, **pee**-kont/ • **adj. 1** having a pleasantly sharp or spicy taste. **2** stimulating to the mind.
– DERIVATIVES **piquancy** n. **piquantly** adv.

– ORIGIN French, 'stinging, pricking'.

pique /peek/ ● **n.** resentment arising from hurt pride. ● **v.** (**piques, piquing, piqued**) **1** stimulate (interest). **2** (**be piqued**) feel hurt or resentful.
– ORIGIN French *piquer* 'prick, irritate'.

piracy ● **n. 1** the practice of attacking and robbing ships at sea. **2** the use or reproduction of another's work without permission.

Piraeus E
/py-ree-uhss, pi-ray-uhss/ the chief port of Athens.

Pirandello E
/pi-ruhn-del-loh/, Luigi (1867–1936), Italian dramatist and novelist. His plays, such as *Six Characters in Search of an Author*, challenged the conventions of naturalism and made an important contibution to modern drama.

piranha /pi-rah-nuh/ ● **n.** a freshwater fish with very sharp teeth that it uses to tear flesh from prey.
– ORIGIN Portuguese.

pirate ● **n.** a person who attacks and robs ships at sea. ● **adj. 1** (of a film, recording, etc.) that has been reproduced and used for profit without permission: *pirate videos*. **2** (of an organization) broadcasting without official permission: *a pirate radio station*. ● **v.** (**pirates, pirating, pirated**) reproduce (a film, recording, etc.) for profit without permission.
– ORIGIN Greek *peiratēs*.

pirouette /pi-ruu-et/ ● **n.** (in ballet) an act of spinning on one foot. ● **v.** (**pirouettes, pirouetting, pirouetted**) perform a pirouette.
– ORIGIN French, 'spinning top'.

Pisa E
/pee-zuh/ a city in northern Italy, in Tuscany. It is noted for the 'Leaning Tower of Pisa', which leans about 5 m (17 ft) from the perpendicular over its height of 55 m (181 ft).

piscatorial /piss-kuh-tor-i-uhl/ ● **adj.** formal relating to fishing.
– ORIGIN Latin *piscator* 'fisherman'.

Pisces /py-seez/ ● **n.** a constellation (the Fish or Fishes) and sign of the zodiac, which the sun enters about 20 February.
– ORIGIN Latin.

piscina /pi-see-nuh/ ● **n.** (pl. **piscinas** or **piscinae** /pi-see-nee/) a stone basin near the altar in some churches, for draining water used in the Mass.
– ORIGIN Latin, 'fish pond'.

piscine /pi-syn/ ● **adj.** relating to fish.

piss vulgar ● **v.** urinate. ● **n. 1** urine. **2** an act of urinating.
– PHRASES **piss about/around** Brit. mess around. **piss off** go away. **piss someone off** annoy someone. **take the piss** Brit. mock.
– ORIGIN Old French *pisser*.

Pissarro E
/pi-sah-roh/, Camille (1830–1903), French Impressionist painter, known for his landscapes and cityscapes.

pissed ● **adj.** vulgar **1** Brit. drunk. **2** (**pissed off**) very annoyed.

piss-up ● **n.** Brit. vulgar a heavy drinking session.

pistachio /pi-sta-shi-oh/ ● **n.** (pl. **pistachios**) a small nut with an edible pale green kernel, the seed of an Asian tree.
– ORIGIN Greek *pistakion*.

piste /peesst/ ● **n.** a course or run for skiing.
– ORIGIN French, 'racetrack'.

pistil /piss-til/ ● **n.** Bot. the female organs of a flower, comprising the stigma, style, and ovary.
– ORIGIN Latin *pistillum* 'pestle'.

pistol ● **n.** a small gun that is held in one hand.
– ORIGIN French *pistole*.

piston ● **n.** a sliding disc or cylinder fitting closely inside a tube in which it moves up and down as part of an engine or pump.
– ORIGIN Italian *pistone* 'large pestle'.

pit[1] ● **n. 1** a large hole in the ground. **2** a mine for coal, chalk, etc. **3** a hollow in a surface. **4** a sunken area in a workshop floor allowing access to the underside of a motor vehicle. **5** an area at the side of a track where racing cars are serviced and refuelled. **6** a part of a theatre where an orchestra plays. **7** hist. an enclosure in which animals were made to fight. **8** (**the pits**) informal a very bad place or situation. ● **v.** (**pits, pitting, pitted**) **1** (**pit against**) set in competition with. **2** make a hollow in the surface of.
– PHRASES **the pit of the stomach** the lower part of the stomach.
– ORIGIN Old English.

pit[2] esp. N. Amer. ● **n.** the stone of a fruit. ● **v.** (**pits, pitting, pitted**) remove the pit from (fruit).
– ORIGIN prob. from Dutch.

pit bull terrier ● **n.** a fierce American type of bull terrier.

Pitcairn Islands E
/pit-kairn/ a British dependency comprising a group of islands in the South Pacific. The only settlement is Adamstown, on Pitcairn Island, the chief island of the group.

pitch[1] ● **n. 1** Brit. an area of ground where outdoor team games are played. **2** the extent to which a sound or tone is high or low. **3** the steepness of a roof. **4** a particular level of intensity: *the crowd were at the right pitch of excitement*. **5** a form of words used to persuade: *a sales pitch*. **6** Brit. a place where a street seller or performer is situated. ● **v. 1** throw or fall heavily or roughly. **2** set at a particular musical pitch. **3** set or aim at a particular level, target, or audience. **4** set up (a tent or camp). **5** (**pitch in**) informal join in enthusiastically with an activity. **6** (**pitch up**) informal arrive. **7** (of a moving ship, aircraft, or vehicle) rock from side to side or from front to back. **8** (**pitched**) (of a roof) sloping.
– ORIGIN perh. from Old English, 'stigmata'.

pitch[2] ● **n.** a sticky black substance which hardens on cooling, made from tar or turpentine and used for waterproofing.
– ORIGIN Old English.

pitch-black (also **pitch-dark**) ● **adj.** completely dark.

pitchblende /pich-blend/ ● **n.** a mineral found in dark pitch-like masses and containing radium.
– ORIGIN German *Pechblende*.

pitched battle ● **n.** a fierce fight involving a large number of people.

pitcher ● **n.** a large jug.
– ORIGIN Old French *pichier* 'pot'.

pitchfork • n. a farm tool with a long handle and two sharp metal prongs, used for lifting hay.
– ORIGIN from former *pickfork*.

piteous • adj. deserving or arousing pity.
– DERIVATIVES **piteously** adv.
– ORIGIN Old French *piteus*.

pitfall • n. a hidden danger or difficulty.

pith • n. **1** spongy white tissue lining the rind of citrus fruits. **2** spongy tissue in the stems and branches of many plants. **3** the most important part of something.
– ORIGIN Old English.

pithead • n. the top of a mineshaft and the area around it.

pith helmet • n. a head covering made from the dried pith of a plant, used for protection from the sun.

pithy • adj. **1** (of a fruit or plant) containing much pith. **2** (of language or style) concise and expressing a point clearly.

pitiable • adj. **1** deserving or arousing pity. **2** deserving contempt: *the article shows a pitiable lack of understanding.*

pitiful • adj. **1** deserving or arousing pity. **2** very small or poor.
– DERIVATIVES **pitifully** adv.

pitiless • adj. showing no pity.

Pitman, E
Sir Isaac (1813–97), English inventor of a shorthand system.

piton /pee-ton/ • n. a peg or spike driven into a crack to support a climber or a rope.
– ORIGIN French, 'eye bolt'.

Pitt¹, E
William, 1st Earl of Chatham (1708–78; known as **Pitt the Elder**), British statesman. As Secretary of State (effectively Prime Minister) 1756–61 and 1766–8, he masterminded British strategy in the Seven Years War, culminating in a successful conclusion for Britain in 1763.

Pitt², E
William (1759–1806; known as **Pitt the Younger**), British statesman, Prime Minister 1783–1801 and 1804–6, the son of Pitt the Elder. The youngest-ever Prime Minister, he introduced financial reforms to reduce the national debt.

pitta /pit-tuh/ • n. a type of flat bread which can be split open to hold a filling.
– ORIGIN modern Greek, 'cake or pie'.

pittance • n. a very small or inadequate amount of money.
– ORIGIN Old French *pitance* 'pity'.

Pittsburgh E
/pits-berg/ an industrial city in SW Pennsylvania.

pituitary gland /pi-tyoo-i-tuh-ri/ • n. a pea-sized gland attached to the base of the brain, which controls growth and development.
– ORIGIN Latin *pituitarius* 'secreting phlegm'.

pity • n. (pl. **pities**) **1** a feeling of sorrow and sympathy caused by the sufferings of others. **2** a cause for regret or disappointment. • v. (**pities, pitying, pitied**) feel pity for.
– ORIGIN Old French *pite* 'compassion'.

pivot • n. **1** the central point, pin, or shaft on which a mechanism turns or is balanced. **2** a person or thing playing a central part in an activity or organization. • v. (**pivots, pivoting, pivoted**) **1** turn or balance on a central point. **2** (**pivot on**) depend on.
– ORIGIN French.

pivotal • adj. **1** fixed or turning on a pivot. **2** of central importance: *a pivotal role.*

pixel • n. any of the tiny areas of light on a display screen which make up an an image.
– ORIGIN from *picture element*.

pixie (also **pixy**) • n. (pl. **pixies**) an imaginary fairy-like being portrayed as a tiny man with pointed ears and a pointed hat.
– ORIGIN unknown.

Pizarro E
/pi-zah-roh/, Francisco (*c.*1478–1541), Spanish conquistador, who defeated the Inca empire and built his own capital at Lima (1535).

pizza • n. a flat, round base of dough baked with a topping of tomatoes, cheese, and other ingredients.
– ORIGIN Italian, 'pie'.

pizzazz • n. informal liveliness and style.
– ORIGIN prob. invented by Diana Vreeland, fashion editor of *Harper's Bazaar.*

pizzeria /peet-zuh-ree-uh/ • n. a restaurant serving pizzas.
– ORIGIN Italian.

pizzicato /pit-zi-kah-toh/ • adv. & adj. Music plucking the strings of an instrument with one's finger.
– ORIGIN Italian, 'pinched'.

pl. • abbrev. **1** (also **Pl.**) place. **2** plural.

placard /pla-kard/ • n. a sign for public display, either fixed to a wall or carried during a demonstration.
– ORIGIN Old French *placquart*.

placate /pluh-kayt/ • v. (**placates, placating, placated**) make less angry or hostile.
– DERIVATIVES **placatory** adj.
– ORIGIN Latin *placare*.

place • n. **1** a particular position or area. **2** a portion of space occupied by or set aside for someone or something: *they hurried to their places at the table.* **3** an opportunity to study on a course or be a member of a team. **4** a position in a sequence: *she finished in second place.* **5** the position of a figure in a decimal number. **6** (in place names) a square or short street. • v. (**places, placing, placed**) **1** put in a particular position or situation. **2** find an appropriate place or role for. **3** give a specified position in a sequence: *the survey placed the company 13th for achievement.* **4** remember where one has seen (someone or something). **5** arrange for (something) to be done: *they placed a contract for three boats.*
– PHRASES **in place of** instead of. **put someone in his** (or **her**) **place** make someone feel less proud or confident. **take place** occur.
– ORIGIN Old French.

placebo /pluh-see-boh/ • n. (pl. **placebos**) a medicine prescribed for the mental benefit of the patient rather than for any physical effect.
– ORIGIN Latin, 'I shall be acceptable'.

placement • n. **1** the action of placing. **2** a temporary job undertaken to gain work experience.

place name • n. the name of a geographical location, such as a town, lake, or mountain.

placenta /pluh-sen-tuh/ • n. (pl. **placentae**

/pluh-**sen**-tee/ or **placentas**) an organ in the womb of a pregnant mammal, which supplies blood and nourishment to the fetus through the umbilical cord.
– ORIGIN Latin.

placid ● **adj.** not easily upset or excited.
– DERIVATIVES **placidity** n. **placidly** adv.
– ORIGIN Latin *placidus*.

placing ● **n.** a ranking in a competition.

placket ● **n.** **1** an opening in a garment, covering fastenings or for access to a pocket. **2** a flap of material used to strengthen such an opening.
– ORIGIN from **PLACARD** in a former sense 'garment worn under an open coat'.

plagiarize /**play**-juh-ryz/ (also **plagiarise**) ● **v.** (**plagiarizes**, **plagiarizing**, **plagiarized**) take (the work or idea of someone else) and pretend it is one's own.
– DERIVATIVES **plagiarism** n. **plagiarist** n.
– ORIGIN Latin *plagiarius* 'kidnapper'.

plague ● **n.** **1** an infectious disease spread by bacteria and causing fever and delirium. **2** a very large number of destructive insects or animals. ● **v.** (**plagues**, **plaguing**, **plagued**) **1** cause continual trouble to. **2** pester continually.
– ORIGIN Latin *plaga* 'stroke, wound'.

plaice ● **n.** (pl. **plaice**) an edible brown flatfish with orange spots.
– ORIGIN Old French *plaiz*.

plaid /plad/ ● **n.** fabric woven in a chequered or tartan design.
– ORIGIN Scottish Gaelic, 'blanket'.

plain ● **adj.** **1** simple or ordinary. **2** without a pattern. **3** unmarked: *a plain envelope*. **4** easy to see or understand; clear. **5** (of language) direct. **6** (of a woman or girl) not attractive. **7** sheer; simple: *plain stupidity*. **8** (of a knitting stitch) made by putting the needle through the front of the stitch from left to right. ● **adv.** informal used for emphasis: *that's plain stupid*. ● **n.** a large area of flat land with few trees.
– DERIVATIVES **plainly** adv. **plainness** n.
– ORIGIN Latin *planus* 'flat, plain'.

plain chocolate ● **n.** Brit. dark, slightly bitter chocolate without added milk.

plain clothes ● **pl. n.** ordinary clothes rather than uniform.

plain flour ● **n.** Brit. flour that does not contain a raising agent.

plain sailing ● **n.** smooth and easy progress.

> **Plains of Abraham** E
> a plateau beside the city of Quebec, the scene in 1759 of a British victory over the French, resulting in British control over Canada.

plainsong (also **plainchant**) ● **n.** unaccompanied medieval church music sung by a number of voices together.

plaintiff ● **n.** a person who brings a case against another in a court of law. Compare with **DEFENDANT**.
– ORIGIN Old French *plaintif* 'plaintive'.

plaintive ● **adj.** sounding sad and mournful.
– DERIVATIVES **plaintively** adv.
– ORIGIN Old French.

plait ● **n.** Brit. a single length of hair, rope, or other material made up of three or more intertwined strands. ● **v.** form into a plait or plaits.
– ORIGIN Old French *pleit* 'a fold'.

plan ● **n.** **1** a detailed proposal for doing or achieving something. **2** an intention. **3** a scheme for making regular payments towards a pension, insurance policy, etc. **4** a map or diagram. ● **v.** (**plans**, **planning**, **planned**) **1** decide on and arrange in advance. **2** (**plan for**) make preparations for. **3** make a plan of (something to be made or built).
– DERIVATIVES **planner** n.
– ORIGIN French.

planar /**play**-ner/ ● **adj.** Math. relating to or in the form of a plane.

> **Planck** E
> /*rhymes with* plank/, Max (Karl Ernst Ludwig) (1858–1947), German theoretical physicist. He was the founder of quantum theory, proposing that electromagnetic radiation from heated bodies is not given out as a continuous flow but is made up of separate units or quanta of energy.

plane[1] ● **n.** **1** a completely flat surface. **2** a level of existence or thought: *the spiritual plane*. ● **adj.** **1** completely flat. **2** relating to two-dimensional surfaces or sizes. ● **v.** (**planes**, **planing**, **planed**) **1** (of a bird) soar without moving the wings. **2** (of a boat) skim over the surface of water.
– ORIGIN Latin *planum*.

plane[2] ● **n.** an aeroplane.

plane[3] (also **planer**) ● **n.** a tool used to smooth a wooden surface by cutting shavings from it. ● **v.** (**planes**, **planing**, **planed**) smooth with a plane.
– ORIGIN Latin *plana*.

plane[4] (also **plane tree**) ● **n.** a tall tree with maple-like leaves and a peeling bark.
– ORIGIN Old French.

planet ● **n.** **1** a large round object in space that orbits round a star. **2** (**the planet**) the earth.
– DERIVATIVES **planetary** adj.
– ORIGIN Greek *planētēs*.

planetarium /plan-i-**tair**-i-uhm/ ● **n.** (pl. **planetariums** or **planetaria** /plan-i-**tair**-i-uh/) a building in which images of stars, planets, and constellations are projected onto a curved ceiling.
– ORIGIN Latin.

plangent /**plan**-juhnt/ ● **adj.** literary (of a sound) loud and mournful.
– ORIGIN Latin *plangere* 'to lament'.

plank ● **n.** **1** a long, flat piece of timber, used in flooring. **2** a basic part of a political or other programme: *crime reduction is a central plank of the manifesto*.
– ORIGIN Latin *planca* 'board'.

planking ● **n.** planks used as a building material.

plankton ● **n.** tiny organisms living in the sea or fresh water.
– DERIVATIVES **planktonic** adj.
– ORIGIN Greek *planktos* 'wandering'.

planning ● **n.** **1** the process of making plans for something. **2** the control by local government of building and development in towns and cities.

planning permission ● **n.** Brit. formal permission from local government for building work.

plant ● **n.** **1** a living thing that grows in the ground, having roots with which it absorbs

substances and leaves in which it makes nutrients by photosynthesis. **2** a place where an industrial or manufacturing process takes place. **3** machinery used in an industrial or manufacturing process. **4** a person placed in a group as a spy. **5** a thing put among someone's belongings to make them appear guilty of something. ● **v. 1** place (a seed, bulb, or plant) in the ground so that it can grow. **2** place in a specified position. **3** secretly place (a bomb). **4** put (something) among someone's belongings as a plant. **5** send (someone) to join a group to act as a spy. **6** fix (an idea) in someone's mind.
– ORIGIN Latin *planta* 'sprout' and *plantare* 'fix in place'.

Plantagenet /plan-**taj**-uh-nuht/ ● **adj.** relating to the English royal dynasty which held the throne from the accession of Henry II in 1154 until the death of Richard III in 1485.

plantain[1] /**plan**-tin, **plan**-tayn/ ● **n.** a low-growing plant, with a rosette of leaves and green flowers.
– ORIGIN Old French.

plantain[2] /**plan**-tin, **plan**-tayn/ ● **n.** a type of banana eaten as a vegetable.
– ORIGIN Spanish *plá(n)tano*.

plantation ● **n. 1** a large estate on which crops such as coffee, sugar, and tobacco are grown. **2** an area in which trees have been planted.

planter ● **n. 1** a manager or owner of a plantation. **2** a decorative container in which plants are grown.

plaque /plak, plahk/ ● **n. 1** an ornamental tablet fixed to a wall to commemorate a person or event. **2** a sticky deposit on teeth, which encourages the growth of bacteria.
– ORIGIN French.

plasma /**plaz**-muh/ ● **n. 1** the colourless fluid part of blood, lymph, or milk, in which cells or fat globules are suspended. **2** Physics a gas of positive ions and free electrons with little or no overall electric charge.
– ORIGIN Greek.

Plassey, Battle of E
/*rhymes with* gassy/ a battle at Plassey in West Bengal in 1757, in which the British led by Robert Clive defeated the nawab (governor) of Bengal, establishing British supremacy in that region.

plaster ● **n. 1** a soft mixture of lime with sand or cement and water for spreading on walls and ceilings to form a smooth hard surface when dried. **2** (also **plaster of Paris**) a hard white substance made by adding water to powdered gypsum, used for setting broken bones and making sculptures and casts. **3** (also **sticking plaster**) an sticky strip of material for covering cuts and wounds. ● **v.** (**plasters**, **plastering**, **plastered**) **1** apply plaster to. **2** coat thickly. **3** make (hair) lie flat by applying liquid to it.
– DERIVATIVES **plasterer** n.
– ORIGIN Latin *plastrum*.

plasterboard ● **n.** board made of plaster set between two sheets of paper, used to line interior walls and ceilings.

plastered ● **adj.** informal very drunk.

plastic ● **n. 1** a chemically produced material that can be moulded into shape while soft and then set into a hard or slightly flexible form. **2** informal credit cards or other plastic cards that can be used as money. ● **adj. 1** made of plastic. **2** easily shaped. **3** not sincere: *a plastic smile.*
– DERIVATIVES **plasticity** n.
– ORIGIN Greek *plastikos*.

plasticine (also **Plasticine**) ● **n.** trademark a soft modelling material.

plasticky ● **adj. 1** resembling plastic. **2** artificial or of low quality.

plastic surgery ● **n.** surgery performed to repair or reconstruct parts of the body damaged as a result of injury or for cosmetic reasons.

plate ● **n. 1** a flat dish for holding food. **2** bowls, cups, and other utensils made of gold or silver. **3** a thin, flat piece of metal used to join or strengthen something or forming part of a machine. **4** a small, flat piece of metal with writing on it fixed to a wall or door. **5** a sheet of metal or other material with an image of type or illustrations on it, from which copies are printed. **6** a printed photograph or illustration in a book. **7** a thin, flat structure in a plant or animal body. **8** Geol. each of the several rigid pieces which together make up the earth's surface. ● **v.** (**plates**, **plating**, **plated**) cover (a metal object) with a thin coating of a different metal.
– PHRASES **on one's plate** esp. Brit. occupying one's time or energy.
– ORIGIN Old French *plat* 'platter' or *plate* 'sheet of metal'.

plateau /**plat**-oh/ ● **n.** (pl. **plateaux** /**plat**-ohz/ or **plateaus**) **1** an area of fairly level high ground. **2** a state of little or no change following a period of activity or progress.
– ORIGIN French.

plate glass ● **n.** thick fine-quality glass used for shop windows and doors.

platelet ● **n.** Physiol. a small disc-shaped cell fragment without a nucleus, found in large numbers in blood and involved in clotting.

platen /**plat**-uhn/ ● **n.** a cylindrical roller in a typewriter against which the paper is held.
– ORIGIN French *platine* 'flat piece'.

platform ● **n. 1** a raised level surface on which people or things can stand. **2** a raised structure along the side of a railway track where passengers get on and off trains. **3** a raised structure standing in the sea from which oil or gas wells are drilled. **4** the stated policy of a political party: *seeking election on a platform of low taxes.* **5** an opportunity for the expression or exchange of views. **6** a very thick sole on a shoe.
– ORIGIN French *plateforme* 'ground plan'.

Plath E
/plath/, Sylvia (1932–63), American poet. Her work, much of which was published after she committed suicide, is notable for its treatment of extreme and painful states of mind. She was the wife of Ted Hughes.

platinum /**plat**-i-nuhm/ ● **n.** a precious silvery-white metal. ● **adj.** greyish-white or silvery like platinum.
– ORIGIN Spanish *platina*.

platinum disc ● **n.** a platinum disc awarded to a recording artist or group for sales above a specified figure.

platitude ● **n.** a remark that has been used too often to be interesting or thoughtful.

– DERIVATIVES **platitudinous** adj.
– ORIGIN French.

Plato E
/**play**-toh/(*c.*429–*c.*347 BC), Greek philosopher, a disciple of Socrates. A highly influential figure in Western thought, he put forward the theory of 'ideas' or 'forms', in which abstract entities or **universals** are contrasted with their objects or **particulars** in the material world.

Platonic /pluh-**ton**-ik/ ● **adj. 1** having to do with the philosopher Plato or his ideas. **2** (**platonic**) (of love or friendship) intimate and affectionate but not sexual.

platoon ● **n.** a subdivision of a company of soldiers.
– ORIGIN French *peloton*.

platter ● **n.** a large flat serving dish.
– ORIGIN Old French *plater*.

platypus /**plat**-i-puhss/ (also **duck-billed platypus**) ● **n.** (pl. **platypuses**) an egg-laying Australian mammal with a duck-like bill and webbed feet, living partly on land and partly in water.
– ORIGIN Greek *platupous* 'flat-footed'.

plaudits ● **pl. n.** praise.
– ORIGIN Latin *plaudite* 'applaud!'.

plausible ● **adj. 1** seeming reasonable or probable. **2** skilled at producing persuasive arguments: *a plausible liar.*
– DERIVATIVES **plausibility** n. **plausibly** adv.
– ORIGIN Latin *plaudere* 'applaud'.

Plautus E
/**plaw**-tuhss/, Titus Maccius (*c.*250–184 BC), Roman comic dramatist.

play ● **v. 1** take part in games for enjoyment. **2** take part in (a sport or contest). **3** compete against (another player or team). **4** take a specified position in a sports team. **5** act the role of (a character) in a play or film. **6** perform (a piece of music) or perform on (a musical instrument). **7** move (a piece) or display (a playing card) in one's turn in a game. **8** make (a CD, tape, etc.) produce sounds. **9** be cooperative: *he needs financial backing, but the banks won't play.* ● **n. 1** games that are taken part in for enjoyment. **2** the performing of a sporting match: *rain wrecked the second day's play.* **3** a move in a sport or game. **4** the state of being active or effective: *luck came into play.* **5** a piece of writing performed by actors in a theatre or on the television or radio. **6** freedom of movement: *bolts should have half an inch of play.* **7** constantly changing movement: *the play of light across the surface.*
– PHRASES **be played out** be drained of energy. **make great play of** draw attention to (something) in an exaggerated way. **make a play for** informal attempt to attract or gain. **play about** (or **around**) behave in a casual or irresponsible way. **play along** pretend to cooperate. **play by ear 1** perform (music) without having to read from a score. **2** (**play it by ear**) informal proceed without having formed a plan. **play down** disguise the importance of. **play fast and loose** behave irresponsibly or immorally. **play for time** use excuses or unnecessary acts to gain time. **play into someone's hands** give someone an advantage without meaning to do so. **play someone off against another** bring one person into conflict with another for one's own advantage. **play on** take advantage of (someone's weak point). **play up 1** emphasize the importance of. **2** Brit. informal cause problems. **play with fire** take foolish risks.
– DERIVATIVES **playable** adj.
– ORIGIN Old English, 'to exercise'.

playback ● **n.** the replaying of previously recorded sound or moving images.

playboy ● **n.** a wealthy man who spends his time enjoying himself.

Player, E
Gary (b.1936), South African golfer. His many championships include three victories in the British Open and three in the US Masters (1961, 1974, and 1978).

player ● **n. 1** a person taking part in a sport or game. **2** a person who is influential in a particular area: *a major player in political circles.* **3** a person who plays a musical instrument. **4** a device for playing compact discs, tapes, etc. **5** an actor.

playful ● **adj. 1** fond of games and amusement. **2** light-hearted.
– DERIVATIVES **playfully** adv. **playfulness** n.

playground ● **n.** an outdoor area provided for children to play on.

playgroup (also **playschool**) ● **n.** Brit. a regular play session for pre-school children, organized by parents.

playhouse ● **n.** a theatre.

playing card ● **n.** each of a set of rectangular pieces of card with numbers and symbols on one side, used to play various games.

playing field ● **n.** a field used for outdoor team games.

playlist ● **n.** a list of songs or pieces of music chosen to be broadcast on a radio station.

playmate ● **n.** a friend with whom a child plays.

play-off ● **n.** an extra match played to decide the outcome of a contest.

playpen ● **n.** a small portable enclosure in which a baby or small child can play safely.

plaything ● **n. 1** a toy. **2** a person who is treated as amusing but unimportant.

playwright ● **n.** a person who writes plays.

plaza ● **n. 1** an open public space in a town or city. **2** N. Amer. a shopping centre.
– ORIGIN Spanish, 'place'.

plc (also **PLC**) ● **abbrev.** Brit. public limited company.

plea ● **n. 1** a request made in an urgent and emotional way. **2** a formal statement made by or on behalf of a person charged with an offence in a law court.
– ORIGIN Old French *plait, plaid* 'agreement'.

plead ● **v.** (**pleads**, **pleading**, **pleaded** or N. Amer. or Sc. **pled**) **1** make an urgent and emotional request. **2** argue in support of: *he visited the country to plead his cause.* **3** Law state formally in court whether one is guilty or not guilty of the offence with which one is charged. **4** present as an excuse for doing or not doing something.
– ORIGIN Old French *plaidier* 'go to law'.

pleading ● **adj.** earnestly appealing: *a pleading look.*
– DERIVATIVES **pleadingly** adv.

pleasant ● **adj. 1** satisfactory and enjoyable. **2** friendly and likeable.

– DERIVATIVES **pleasantly** adv. **pleasantness** n.
– ORIGIN Old French *plaisant.*

pleasantry • n. (pl. **pleasantries**) **1** an unimportant remark made as part of a polite conversation. **2** a mildly amusing joke.

please • v. (**pleases**, **pleasing**, **pleased**) **1** cause to feel happy and satisfied. **2** wish: *do as you please.* **3** (**please oneself**) consider only one's own wishes. • adv. used in polite requests or questions, or to accept an offer.
– ORIGIN Old French *plaisir.*

pleased • adj. **1** feeling or showing pleasure and satisfaction. **2** (**pleased to do**) willing or glad to do.

pleasing • adj. giving pleasure or satisfaction.
– DERIVATIVES **pleasingly** adv.

pleasurable • adj. enjoyable.
– DERIVATIVES **pleasurably** adv.

pleasure • n. **1** a feeling of happy satisfaction and enjoyment. **2** an event or activity which one enjoys. **3** a pleasant physical feeling. • adj. intended for enjoyment rather than business: *pleasure boats.* • v. (**pleasures**, **pleasuring**, **pleasured**) give pleasure to.
– PHRASES **at one's pleasure** formal as and when someone wishes.
– ORIGIN Old French *plaisir* 'to please'.

pleat • n. a fold in fabric or a garment, held by stitching the top or side. • v. fold or form into pleats.
– ORIGIN from **PLAIT**.

pleb • n. informal, derog. a member of the lower social classes.
– ORIGIN from **PLEBEIAN**.

plebeian /pli-bee-uhn/ • n. **1** (in ancient Rome) a commoner. **2** a member of the lower social classes. • adj. lower-class or unsophisticated.
– ORIGIN Latin *plebs* 'the common people'.

plebiscite /pleb-i-syt/ • n. a vote by everyone entitled to do so on an important public issue.
– ORIGIN French *plébiscite.*

plectrum • n. (pl. **plectrums** or **plectra**) a thin flat piece of plastic or tortoiseshell used to pluck the strings of a guitar or similar musical instrument.
– ORIGIN Greek *plēktron* 'something with which to strike'.

pled North American or Scottish past part. of **PLEAD**.

pledge • n. **1** a solemn promise or undertaking. **2** something valuable given as a guarantee that a debt will be paid or a promise kept. **3** (**the pledge**) a solemn promise to stop drinking alcohol. **4** a thing given as a token of love, favour, or loyalty. • v. (**pledges**, **pledging**, **pledged**) **1** solemnly promise to do or give something. **2** give (something valuable) as a guarantee on a loan.
– ORIGIN Old French *plege* 'person acting as surety for another'.

Pleistocene /ply-stuh-seen/ • adj. Geol. relating to the first epoch of the Quaternary period (from 1.64 million to about 10,000 years ago), a time which included the ice ages and the appearance of humans.
– ORIGIN from Greek *pleistos* 'most' + *kainos* 'new'.

plenary /plee-nuh-ri/ • adj. **1** full; complete: *plenary powers.* **2** (of a meeting at a conference or assembly) to be attended by all participants. • n. a plenary meeting.
– ORIGIN Latin *plenus* 'full'.

plenipotentiary /plen-i-puh-ten-shuh-ri/ • n. (pl. **plenipotentiaries**) a person given full power by a government to act on its behalf. • adj. (of power) complete.
– ORIGIN from Latin *plenus* 'full' + *potentia* 'power'.

plenitude • n. formal a large amount of something.
– ORIGIN Old French.

plenteous • adj. literary plentiful.

plentiful • adj. existing in great quantities.
– DERIVATIVES **plentifully** adv.

plenty • pron. a large amount or quantity, or as much as is needed. • n. a situation in which food and other necessities are available in sufficiently large quantities. • adv. informal fully; enough.
– ORIGIN Old French *plente.*

plenum /plee-nuhm/ • n. **1** an assembly of all the members of a group or committee. **2** Physics a space completely filled with matter, or the whole of space seen in such a way.
– ORIGIN Latin, 'full space'.

pleonasm /plee-oh-na-z'm/ • n. the use of more words than are necessary to express meaning (e.g. *see with one's eyes*).
– ORIGIN Greek *pleonasmos.*

plethora /pleth-uh-ruh/ • n. an excessive amount: *a plethora of complaints.*
– ORIGIN Latin.

pleura /ploor-uh/ • n. (pl. **pleurae** /ploor-ee/) Anat. each of a pair of membranes lining the thorax and covering the lungs.
– DERIVATIVES **pleural** adj.
– ORIGIN Greek, 'side of the body, rib'.

pleurisy /ploor-i-si/ • n. inflammation of the pleurae, causing pain during breathing.

plexus • n. (pl. **plexus** or **plexuses**) **1** Anat. a network of nerves or vessels in the body. **2** a complex network or web-like structure.
– ORIGIN Latin, 'plaited formation'.

pliable /ply-uh-b'l/ • adj. **1** easily bent. **2** easily influenced or persuaded.
– DERIVATIVES **pliability** n.
– ORIGIN French.

pliant • adj. pliable.

plié /plee-ay/ • n. Ballet a movement in which a dancer bends the knees and straightens them again, having the feet turned out and heels on the ground.
– ORIGIN French, 'bent'.

pliers /ply-erz/ • pl. n. pincers having jaws with flat surfaces, used for gripping small objects or bending wire.
– ORIGIN French *plier* 'to bend'.

plight[1] • n. a dangerous or difficult situation.
– ORIGIN Old French *plit* 'fold'.

plight[2] • v. archaic **1** solemnly promise (faith or loyalty). **2** (**be plighted to**) be engaged to be married to.
– ORIGIN Old English.

plimsoll (also **plimsole**) • n. Brit. a light rubber-soled canvas sports shoe.
– ORIGIN prob. from the resemblance of the side of the sole to a **PLIMSOLL LINE**.

Plimsoll line • n. a marking on a ship's side showing the limit to which the ship may be legally submerged in the water when loaded

with cargo.
– ORIGIN named after the English politician Samuel *Plimsoll* (1824–98).

plinth • n. a heavy block or slab supporting a statue or forming the base of a column.
– ORIGIN Greek *plinthos* 'tile, brick'.

Pliny[1] E
/pli-ni/ (23–79; known as **Pliny the Elder**; Latin name *Gaius Plinius Secundus*), Roman scholar. His *Natural History* is a vast collection of ancient scientific knowledge.

Pliny[2] E
/pli-ni/ (*c.*61–*c.*112; known as **Pliny the Younger**; Latin name *Gaius Plinius Caecilius Secundus*), Roman senator and writer. The nephew of Pliny the Elder, he is noted for his letters describing Roman life.

Pliocene /ply-uh-seen/ • adj. Geol. relating to the last epoch of the Tertiary period (5.2 to 1.64 million years ago), a time when the first hominids appeared.
– ORIGIN from Greek *pleiōn* 'more' + *kainos* 'new'.

PLO • abbrev. Palestine Liberation Organization.

plod • v. (**plods**, **plodding**, **plodded**) **1** walk slowly with heavy steps. **2** work slowly and steadily at a dull task. • n. a slow, heavy walk.

plonk[1] informal • v. set down heavily or carelessly. • n. a sound like that of something being set down heavily.

plonk[2] • n. Brit. informal cheap wine.
– ORIGIN prob. from *blanc* in French *vin blanc* 'white wine'.

plonker • n. Brit. informal a foolish or incompetent person.
– ORIGIN from PLONK[1].

plop • n. a sound like that of a small, solid object dropping into water. • v. (**plops**, **plopping**, **plopped**) fall or drop with such a sound.

plosive • adj. referring to a consonant (e.g. *d* and *t*) that is produced by stopping the airflow coming out of the mouth and then suddenly releasing it.
– ORIGIN from EXPLOSIVE.

plot • n. **1** a secret plan to do something illegal or wrong. **2** the main sequence of events in a play, novel, or film. **3** a small piece of ground marked out for building, gardening, etc. • v. (**plots**, **plotting**, **plotted**) **1** secretly make plans to carry out (something illegal or wrong). **2** invent the plot of (a play, novel, or film). **3** mark (a route or position) on a chart or graph.
– DERIVATIVES **plotter** n.
– ORIGIN Old English; sense 1 is from Old French *complot* 'dense crowd, secret project'.

plough (US **plow**) • n. **1** a large farming implement with one or more blades fixed in a frame, used to turn over and cut furrows in soil. **2** (**the Plough**) a formation of seven stars in the constellation Ursa Major (the Great Bear). • v. **1** turn up (earth) with a plough. **2** (**plough through/into**) (of a vehicle) move in a fast or uncontrolled way through or into. **3** move forward with difficulty or force. **4** (**plough in**) invest (money) in a business.
– ORIGIN Old English.

ploughman's lunch • n. Brit. a meal of bread and cheese with pickle and salad.

ploughshare • n. the main cutting blade of a plough.

plover /*rhymes with* lover/ • n. a wading bird with a short bill.
– ORIGIN Old French.

plow • n. & v. US = PLOUGH.

ploy • n. a cunning act performed to gain an advantage.
– ORIGIN unknown.

pluck • v. **1** take hold of (something) and quickly remove it from its place. **2** pull out (a hair, feather, etc.) **3** pull the feathers from (a bird's carcass) to prepare it for cooking. **4** sound (a stringed musical instrument) with one's finger or a plectrum. **5** (**pluck up**) summon up (courage) in order to do something frightening. • n. courage.
– ORIGIN Old English.

plucky • adj. (**pluckier**, **pluckiest**) determined and brave.
– DERIVATIVES **pluckily** adv.

plug • n. **1** a piece of solid material tightly blocking a hole. **2** a device with metal pins that fit into holes in a socket to make an electrical connection. **3** informal an electrical socket. **4** informal a piece of publicity promoting a product or event. **5** a piece of tobacco for chewing. • v. (**plugs**, **plugging**, **plugged**) **1** block (a hole). **2** (**plug in**) connect (an electrical appliance) to the mains by means of a socket. **3** (**plug into**) gain access to (an information system or area of activity). **4** informal promote (a product or event) by mentioning it publicly. **5** informal shoot or hit. **6** (**plug away**) informal proceed steadily with a task.
– ORIGIN Dutch and German *plugge*.

plughole • n. Brit. a hole at the lowest point of a bath or sink, through which the water drains away.

plug-in • n. Computing a module or piece of software which can be added to an existing system to give extra features.

plum • n. **1** a soft oval fruit with purple, reddish, or yellow skin, containing a flattish pointed stone. **2** a reddish-purple colour. • adj. informal highly desirable: *a plum job*.
– ORIGIN Latin *prunum*.

plumage /ploo-mij/ • n. a bird's feathers.
– ORIGIN Old French.

plumb[1] • v. **1** measure (the depth of water). **2** explore or experience fully: *she plumbed the depths of despair.* **3** test (an upright surface) to find out if it is vertical. • n. a heavy object attached to a line for finding the depth of water or whether an upright surface is vertical. • adv. informal exactly: *plumb in the centre.* • adj. vertical.
– ORIGIN Latin *plumbum* 'lead'.

plumb[2] • v. (**plumb in**) install (a bath, washing machine, etc.) and connect it to water and drainage pipes.
– ORIGIN from PLUMBER.

plumber • n. a person who fits and repairs the pipes and fittings of water supply, sanitation, or heating systems.
– ORIGIN Old French *plommier* 'person working with lead'.

plumbing • n. the system of pipes, tanks, and fittings required for the water supply, heating, and sanitation in a building.

plumb line ● n. a line with a heavy weight attached to it, used to find the depth of water or to check that something is vertical.

plume ● n. **1** a long, soft feather or set of feathers. **2** a long spreading cloud of smoke or vapour. ● v. (**plumes**, **pluming**, **plumed**) **1** (**plumed**) decorated with feathers. **2** (of smoke or vapour) spread out in a plume.
– ORIGIN Latin *pluma* 'down'.

plummet ● v. (**plummets**, **plummeting**, **plummeted**) **1** fall straight down at high speed. **2** decrease rapidly in value or amount. ● n. **1** a steep and rapid fall or drop. **2** a plumb line or weight.
– ORIGIN Old French *plommet* 'small sounding lead'.

plummy ● adj. (**plummier, plummiest**) **1** like a plum. **2** Brit. informal (of a person's voice) typical of the English upper classes.

plump[1] ● adj. **1** rather fat. **2** full and rounded in shape. ● v. (**plump up**) make or become full and round.
– ORIGIN Dutch *plomp* or German *plump* 'blunt, obtuse'.

plump[2] ● v. **1** set or sit down heavily. **2** (**plump for**) decide in favour of (one of two or more possibilities).

plum pudding ● n. a rich suet pudding containing raisins, currants, and spices.

plumy ● adj. resembling or decorated with feathers.

plunder ● v. (**plunders**, **plundering**, **plundered**) enter (a place) by force and steal goods from it. ● n. **1** the action of plundering. **2** goods obtained by plundering.
– ORIGIN German *plündern* 'rob of household goods'.

plunge ● v. (**plunges**, **plunging**, **plunged**) **1** fall or move suddenly and uncontrollably. **2** jump or dive quickly and energetically. **3** (**plunge in**) begin (a course of action) without thought or care. **4** (**be plunged into**) be suddenly brought into: *the area was plunged into darkness.* **5** push or thrust quickly. ● n. an act of plunging.
– PHRASES **take the plunge** informal decide to do something important or difficult after consideration.
– ORIGIN Old French *plungier* 'thrust down'.

plunge pool ● n. **1** a deep basin at the foot of a waterfall formed by the action of the falling water. **2** a small, deep swimming pool.

plunger ● n. **1** a part of a device that can be pushed down. **2** a rubber cup on a long handle, used to clear blocked pipes by means of suction.

pluperfect ● adj. Grammar (of a tense) referring to an action completed earlier than a past point of time, formed by *had* and the past participle (as in *he had gone by then*).
– ORIGIN from Latin *plus quam perfectum* 'more than perfect'.

plural ● adj. **1** more than one in number. **2** Grammar (of a word or form) referring to more than one. ● n. Grammar a plural word or form.
– ORIGIN Latin *pluralis*.

pluralism ● n. **1** a political system of power-sharing among a number of political parties. **2** the existence or toleration in society of a number of groups that belong to different races or have different political or religious beliefs. **3** the holding of more than one ecclesiastical position at the same time by one person.
– DERIVATIVES **pluralist** n. & adj. **pluralistic** adj.

plurality ● n. (pl. **pluralities**) **1** the state of being plural. **2** a large number of people or things.

pluralize (also **pluralise**) ● v. (**pluralizes**, **pluralizing**, **pluralized**) **1** make more numerous. **2** give a plural form to (a word).

plus ● prep. **1** with the addition of. **2** informal together with. ● adj. **1** (after a number or amount) at least: *$500,000 plus.* **2** (after a grade) rather better than: *B plus.* **3** (before a number) above zero: *plus 60 degrees centigrade.* **4** having a positive electric charge. ● n. **1** (also **plus sign**) the symbol +, indicating addition or a positive value. **2** informal an advantage. ● conj. informal also.
– ORIGIN Latin, 'more'.

plus fours ● pl. n. men's baggy trousers that are cut short to fit closely below the knee, formerly worn for hunting and golf.
– ORIGIN so named because the overhang at the knee required an extra four inches of material.

plush ● n. a fabric of silk, cotton, or wool, with a long, soft nap. ● adj. informal expensively luxurious.
– ORIGIN from former French *pluche*.

Plutarch E
/ploo-tark/(*c.*46–*c.*120), Greek biographer and philosopher, known for *Parallel Lives*, a collection of biographies of prominent Greeks and Romans.

Pluto[1] E
the Greek god of the underworld. Also called **HADES**.

Pluto[2] E
the most remote known planet of the solar system, ninth in order from the sun.

plutocracy /ploo-tok-ruh si/ ● n. (pl. **plutocracies**) **1** government by the wealthy. **2** a society governed by the wealthy.
– ORIGIN from Greek *ploutos* 'wealth' + *kratos* 'strength'.

plutocrat ● n. usu. derog. a person who is powerful because they are rich.

plutonium /ploo-toh-ni-uhm/ ● n. a radioactive metallic element used as a fuel in nuclear reactors and as an explosive in atomic weapons.
– ORIGIN from **PLUTO**[2].

ply[1] ● n. (pl. **plies**) **1** a thickness or layer of a material. **2** each of a number of layers or strands of which something is made.
– ORIGIN French *pli* 'a fold'.

ply[2] ● v. (**plies, plying, plied**) **1** work steadily with (a tool) or at (one's job). **2** (of a ship or vehicle) travel regularly over a route. **3** (**ply with**) keep presenting (someone) with (food, drink, or questions).
– ORIGIN from **APPLY**.

Plymouth[1] E
a port and naval base in SW England, on the Devon coast. In 1620 it was the scene of the Pilgrim Fathers' departure to North America in the *Mayflower*.

Plymouth² E
a town in SE Massachusetts, the site in 1620 of the landing of the Pilgrim Fathers and the earliest permanent European settlement in New England.

plywood ● n. thin strong board consisting of layers of wood glued together.

PM ● abbrev. Prime Minister.

p.m. ● abbrev. after noon.
– ORIGIN from Latin *post meridiem.*

PMS ● abbrev. premenstrual syndrome.

PMT ● abbrev. Brit. premenstrual tension.

pneumatic /nyoo-**mat**-ik/ ● adj. containing or operated by air or gas under pressure: *a pneumatic drill.*
– DERIVATIVES **pneumatically** adv.
– ORIGIN Greek *pneumatikos.*

pneumococcus /nyoo-muh-**kok**-kuhss/ ● n. (pl. **pneumococci** /nyoo-muh-**kok**-ky/) a bacterium associated with pneumonia and some forms of meningitis.

pneumonia /nyoo-**moh**-ni-uh/ ● n. an infection causing inflammation of one or both lungs.
– ORIGIN Greek *pneumōn* 'lung'.

PO ● abbrev. **1** postal order. **2** Post Office.

Po E
/*rhymes with* go/ a river in northern Italy. Italy's longest river, it rises in the Alps and flows 668 km (415 miles) eastwards to the Adriatic.

poach¹ ● v. cook by simmering in a small amount of liquid.
– ORIGIN Old French *pochier.*

poach² ● v. **1** take (game or fish) illegally from private or protected areas. **2** take or get in an unfair or secret way: *they tried to poach passengers by offering better seats.*
– DERIVATIVES **poacher** n.
– ORIGIN prob. from **POKE**.

Pocahontas E
/pok-uh-**hon**-tuhss/ (*c.*1595–1617), American Indian princess. She rescued Captain John Smith, an English colonist, from death at the hands of her father. She later married another colonist, John Rolfe.

pock ● n. a pockmark.
– DERIVATIVES **pocked** adj.
– ORIGIN Old English.

pocket ● n. **1** a small bag sewn into or on clothing, used for carrying small articles. **2** a small group or area that is set apart or different from its surroundings: *the city's parks provide pockets of natural beauty.* **3** informal the money one has available: *gifts to suit every pocket.* **4** an opening at the corner or on the side of a billiard table into which balls are struck. ● v. (**pockets**, **pocketing**, **pocketed**) **1** put into one's pocket. **2** take (something belonging to someone else). **3** earn or win (money).
– PHRASES **in someone's pocket** dependent on and influenced by someone. **line one's pocket** make money dishonestly.
– DERIVATIVES **pocketable** adj.
– ORIGIN Old French *pokete* 'little bag'.

pocketbook ● n. **1** Brit. a notebook. **2** US a wallet, purse, or handbag.

pocket money ● n. Brit. **1** a small regular allowance given to a child by their parents. **2** a small amount of money for minor expenses.

pockmark ● n. **1** a hollow scar or mark on the skin left by a spot. **2** a mark or hollow area disfiguring a surface. ● v. cover with pockmarks.

pod¹ ● n. a long seed-case of a pea, bean, or similar plant. ● v. (**pods**, **podding**, **podded**) remove (peas or beans) from their pods before cooking.
– ORIGIN unknown.

pod² ● n. a small herd of whales or similar sea mammals.
– ORIGIN unknown.

Podgorica E
/pod-**gor**-it-suh/ the capital of Montenegro. Former name (1946–93) **TITOGRAD**.

podgy ● adj. Brit. informal chubby.
– ORIGIN unknown.

podium /**poh**-di-uhm/ ● n. (pl. **podiums** or **podia** /**poh**-di-uh/) a small platform on which a person stands when conducting an orchestra or giving a speech.
– ORIGIN Greek *podion* 'little foot'.

Poe E
/*rhymes with* go/, Edgar Allan (1809–49), American short-story writer, poet, and critic. His work includes the horror story 'The Fall of the House of Usher', the detective story 'The Murders in the Rue Morgue', and the poem 'The Raven'.

poem ● n. a piece of imaginative writing in verse, expressing the writer's feelings or describing a place or event.
– ORIGIN Greek *poiēma* 'fiction, poem'.

poesy /**poh**-i-zi/ ● n. archaic poetry.

poet ● n. a person who writes poems.
– DERIVATIVES **poetess** n.

poetic ● adj. (also **poetical**) having to do with poetry. ● n. (**poetics**) the study of linguistic techniques in poetry and literature.
– DERIVATIVES **poetically** adv.

poetic justice ● n. suitable or deserved punishment or reward.

poetic licence ● n. freedom to depart from the accepted rules of a language or facts of a matter for artistic effect.

Poet Laureate ● n. (pl. **Poets Laureate**) a poet appointed by the British monarch to write poems for important occasions.

poetry ● n. **1** poems as a whole or as a form of literature. **2** a quality of beauty or emotional power: *poetry and fire are balanced in the music.*

po-faced ● adj. Brit. serious and disapproving.
– ORIGIN perh. from *po* 'chamber pot'.

pogo stick ● n. a toy for bouncing around on, consisting of a pole with a bar to stand on and a spring near the bottom and a handle at the top.

pogrom /**pog**-rom/ ● n. an organized massacre of an ethnic group, originally that of Jews in Russia or eastern Europe.
– ORIGIN Russian, 'devastation'.

poignant /**poy**-nyuhnt/ ● adj. arousing a painful sense of sadness or regret.
– DERIVATIVES **poignancy** n.
– ORIGIN Old French, 'pricking'.

poinsettia /poyn-**set**-ti-uh/ ● n. a small shrub with large showy scarlet bracts, which resemble petals.

– ORIGIN named after the American diplomat and botanist Joel R. *Poinsett* (1779–1851).

point ● n. **1** the tapered, sharp end of a tool, weapon, or other object. **2** a particular place or moment. **3** an item, detail, or idea. **4** (**the point**) the most important part of what is being discussed. **5** the advantage or purpose of something: *what's the point of it all?* **6** a particular feature or quality: *the building has its good points.* **7** a unit of scoring, value, or measurement. **8** a very small dot or mark. **9** (in geometry) something having position but not magnitude. **10** each of thirty-two directions marked at equal distances round a compass. **11** a narrow piece of land jutting out into the sea. **12** (**points**) Brit. a junction of two railway lines, with a pair of rails that can be moved sideways to allow a train to pass from one line to the other. **13** Brit. an electrical socket. **14** (**points**) a set of electrical contacts in the distributor of a motor vehicle. ● v. **1** direct someone's attention in a particular direction by extending one's finger. **2** aim (something). **3** face in or indicate a particular direction: *a sign pointing left.* **4** (**point out**) make someone aware of. **5** (**point to**) indicate that (something) is likely to happen. **6** fill in the joints of (brickwork or tiling) with mortar or cement.

– PHRASES **a case in point** an example that illustrates what is being discussed. **make a point of** make a special effort to do something. **on the point of** on the verge of. **point of order** a query in a formal meeting as to whether the rules of behaviour are being followed correctly. **point of view** a particular attitude or opinion.

– ORIGIN Old French *pointe* or *point.*

point-blank ● adj. (of a shot or missile) fired from very close to its target. ● adv. in a blunt and very direct way: *they refused point blank to pay the tax.*

point duty ● n. Brit. the duties of a police officer who is stationed at a junction to control traffic.

pointed ● adj. **1** having a sharpened or tapered tip or end. **2** (of a remark or look) directed towards a particular person and expressing a clear message.

pointer ● n. **1** a long, thin piece of metal on a scale or dial which moves to give a reading. **2** a rod used for pointing to features on a map or chart. **3** a hint or tip. **4** a breed of dog that on scenting game stands rigid looking towards it.

pointillism /pwan-til-li-z'm/ ● n. a way of painting using tiny dots of various pure colours, which become blended in the viewer's eye.

– DERIVATIVES **pointillist** n. & adj.

– ORIGIN French *pointiller* 'mark with dots'.

pointing ● n. mortar or cement used to fill the joints of brickwork or tiling.

pointless ● adj. having little or no sense or purpose.

point-to-point ● n. (pl. **point-to-points**) an amateur cross-country steeplechase for horses used in hunting.

poise ● n. **1** a graceful way of holding the body. **2** a calm and confident manner. ● v. **1** be or cause to be balanced or suspended. **2** (**poised**) calm and confident. **3** (**be poised to do**) be ready to do.

– ORIGIN Old French *pois.*

poison ● n. **1** a substance that causes death or injury when swallowed or absorbed by a living organism. **2** a harmful influence: *gossip is a spreading poison.* ● v. **1** harm or kill with poison. **2** put poison on or in. **3** have a harmful effect on.

– DERIVATIVES **poisoner** n.

– ORIGIN Old French, 'magic potion'.

poisoned chalice ● n. something offered which seems attractive but which is likely to cause problems to the person receiving it.

poisonous ● adj. **1** producing or having the effect of poison. **2** extremely unpleasant or spiteful.

poison pen letter ● n. an anonymous letter that is spiteful or abusive.

poke ● v. (**pokes, poking, poked**) **1** prod with a finger or a sharp object. **2** (**poke about/around**) look or search around. **3** push or stick out in a particular direction: *she poked her tongue out.* ● n. an act of poking.

– PHRASES **poke fun at** make fun of.

– ORIGIN uncertain.

poker[1] ● n. a metal rod used for prodding and stirring an open fire.

poker[2] ● n. a card game in which the players bet on the value of the hands dealt to them, sometimes using bluff.

– ORIGIN perh. from German *pochen* 'to brag'.

poker face ● n. a blank expression that hides one's true feelings.

poky (also **pokey**) ● adj. (**pokier, pokiest**) (of a room or building) uncomfortably small and cramped.

– ORIGIN from **POKE**.

Poland E
a country in central Europe with a coastline on the Baltic Sea; capital, Warsaw.

polar ● adj. **1** relating to the North or South Poles or the regions around them. **2** having an electrical or magnetic field. **3** completely opposite.

polar bear ● n. a large white arctic bear.

Polaris E
/puh-**lah**-riss/ the Pole Star.

polarity ● n. (pl. **polarities**) **1** the state of having poles or opposites. **2** the direction of a magnetic or electric field.

polarize (also **polarise**) ● v. (**polarizes, polarizing, polarized**) **1** divide into two sharply contrasting groups with different opinions: *the nation's media are polarized in the controversy.* **2** Physics restrict the vibrations of (a transverse wave, especially light) to one direction. **3** give magnetic or electric polarity to.

– DERIVATIVES **polarization** (also **polarisation**) n.

Polaroid ● n. trademark **1** a material that polarizes the light passing through it, used in sunglasses. **2** a type of camera that produces a finished print rapidly after each exposure.

polder /**pohl**-der/ ● n. (in the Netherlands) a piece of land reclaimed from the sea or a river.

– ORIGIN Dutch.

Pole ● n. a person from Poland.

pole[1] ● n. a long, thin rounded piece of wood or metal, used as a support. ● v. (**poles, poling, poled**) push (a boat) along with a pole.

– ORIGIN Old English.

pole[2] ● n. **1** either of the two points (**North Pole** or **South Pole**) at opposite ends of the earth's axis. **2** each of the two opposite points of a magnet at which magnetic forces are strongest. **3** the positive or negative terminal of an electric cell or battery. **4** either of two contrasting opinions.
– PHRASES **be poles apart** have nothing in common.
– ORIGIN Greek *polos* 'axis, sky'.

poleaxe (US also **poleax**) ● n. **1** a battleaxe. **2** a butcher's axe used to slaughter animals. ● v. (**poleaxes, poleaxing, poleaxed**) **1** knock down or stun with a heavy blow. **2** shock greatly.
– ORIGIN from **POLL** + **AXE**.

polecat ● n. **1** a dark brown weasel-like animal with an unpleasant smell. **2** N. Amer. a skunk.
– ORIGIN perh. from Old French *pole* 'chicken' + **CAT**.

polemic /puh-lem-ik/ ● n. **1** a strong verbal or written attack. **2** (also **polemics**) the practice of engaging in fierce discussion. ● adj. (also **polemical**) having to do with fierce discussion.
– DERIVATIVES **polemicist** n.
– ORIGIN Greek *polemos* 'war'.

polenta /puh-len-tuh/ ● n. (in Italian cookery) maize flour or a dough made from this, which is boiled and then fried or baked.
– ORIGIN Latin, 'pearl barley'.

pole position ● n. the most favourable position at the start of a motor race.
– ORIGIN from *pole* in horse racing to mean the starting position next to the inside boundary fence.

Pole Star ● n. a star located in the part of the sky above the North Pole. Also called **POLARIS**.

pole vault ● n. an athletic event in which competitors attempt to vault over a high bar with the aid of a long pole.

police ● n. an official group of people employed by a state to prevent and solve crime and keep public order. ● v. (**polices, policing, policed**) **1** keep law and order in (an area). **2** ensure that (rules) are obeyed.
– ORIGIN Latin *politia* 'policy'.

policeman (or **policewoman**) ● n. a member of a police force.

police officer ● n. a policeman or policewoman.

police state ● n. a state in which political police secretly watch and control citizens' activities.

police station ● n. the building that houses a local police force.

policy[1] ● n. (pl. **policies**) a course of action adopted or proposed by an organization or person.
– ORIGIN Greek *politeia* 'citizenship'.

policy[2] ● n. (pl. **policies**) a contract of insurance.
– ORIGIN French *police*.

polio ● n. = **POLIOMYELITIS**.

poliomyelitis /poh-li-oh-my-uh-ly-tiss/ ● n. an infectious disease that can cause temporary or permanent paralysis.
– ORIGIN from Greek *polios* 'grey' + *muelos* 'marrow'.

Polish /poh-lish/ ● n. the language of Poland. ● adj. relating to Poland.

polish /pol-ish/ ● v. **1** make smooth and shiny by rubbing. **2** improve: *he's got to polish up his French.* **3** (**polish off**) finish quickly. ● n. **1** a substance used to polish something. **2** an act of polishing. **3** shiny appearance produced by polishing. **4** refinement or elegance.
– DERIVATIVES **polisher** n.
– ORIGIN Latin *polire*.

politburo /pol-it-byuu-roh/ ● n. (pl. **politburos**) the chief policy-making committee of a communist party, especially that of the former USSR.
– ORIGIN from Russian *politicheskoe byuro* 'political bureau'.

polite ● adj. (**politer, politest**) **1** respectful and considerate towards others; courteous. **2** civilized or well bred: *polite society.*
– DERIVATIVES **politely** adv. **politeness** n.
– ORIGIN Latin *politus* 'polished'.

politic ● adj. (of an action) sensible and wise in the circumstances.
– ORIGIN Greek *politikos*.

political ● adj. **1** relating to the government or public affairs of a country. **2** related to or interested in politics.
– DERIVATIVES **politically** adv.

political correctness ● n. the avoidance of language or behaviour seen as discriminating against or offensive to certain groups of people.

politically correct (or **incorrect**) ● adj. showing (or failing to show) political correctness.

political prisoner ● n. a person imprisoned for their political beliefs or actions.

political science ● n. the study of political activity and behaviour.

politician ● n. a person who is involved in politics as a job, either as a holder of or a candidate for an elected office.

politicize (also **politicise**) ● v. (**politicizes, politicizing, politicized**) **1** cause (someone) to become involved in politics. **2** cause (an issue) to become political.
– DERIVATIVES **politicization** (also **politicisation**) n.

politicking ● n. esp. derog. political activity.

politics ● n. **1** the activities associated with governing a country or area, and with the political relations between states. **2** a particular set of political beliefs. **3** activities concerned with gaining or using power within an organization or group: *office politics.*

polity ● n. (pl. **polities**) **1** a form of government. **2** a society as a politically organized state.
– ORIGIN Greek *politeia* 'citizenship'.

> **Polk** E
> /*rhymes with* poke/, James Knox (1795–1849), American Democratic statesman, 11th President of the US 1845–9.

polka /pol-kuh/ ● n. a lively dance for couples.
– ORIGIN Czech *půlka* 'half-step'.

polka dot ● n. each of a number of round dots that are evenly spaced to form a pattern.

poll /*rhymes with* pole *or* doll/ ● n. **1** the process of voting in an election. **2** a record of the number of votes cast. ● v. **1** record the opin-

ion or vote of. **2** (of a candidate in an election) receive a specified number of votes.
– ORIGIN perh. from German.

pollack /pol-luhk/ (also **pollock**) ● **n.** an edible greenish-brown fish of the cod family.
– ORIGIN perh. from Celtic.

pollard /pol-lerd/ ● **v.** cut off the top and branches of (a tree) to encourage new growth.
– ORIGIN from **POLL**.

pollen ● **n.** a powdery substance produced by the male part of a flower, containing the fertilizing agent.
– ORIGIN Latin, 'fine powder'.

pollen count ● **n.** a measure of the amount of pollen in the air.

pollinate ● **v.** (**pollinates, pollinating, pollinated**) carry pollen to and fertilize (a flower or plant).
– DERIVATIVES **pollination** n. **pollinator** n.

Pollock, E
(Paul) Jackson (1912–56), American painter. He invented the style of abstract art known as action painting, whereby he poured, splashed, or dripped paint on to the canvas.

pollock ● **n.** var. of **POLLACK**.

pollster /pohl-ster/ ● **n.** a person who carries out opinion polls.

poll tax ● **n.** a tax paid at the same rate by every adult.
– ORIGIN from **POLL** in the former sense 'head'.

pollutant ● **n.** a substance that causes pollution.

pollute ● **v.** (**pollutes, polluting, polluted**) make dirty with harmful or poisonous substances.
– DERIVATIVES **polluter** n. **pollution** n.
– ORIGIN Latin *polluere*.

Pollux E
/pol luhks/ Gk Myth. see **CASTOR AND POLLUX**

Polo, E
Marco, see **MARCO POLO**.

polo ● **n.** a game similar to hockey, played on horseback with a long-handled mallet.
– ORIGIN from a word in a Tibetan language meaning 'ball'.

polonaise /pol-uh-nayz/ ● **n.** a slow stately dance of Polish origin.
– ORIGIN French, 'Polish'.

polo neck ● **n.** Brit. a high, close-fitting, turned-over collar on a sweater.

polonium /puh-loh-ni-uhm/ ● **n.** a rare radioactive metallic element.
– ORIGIN Latin *Polonia* 'Poland'.

polo shirt ● **n.** a casual short-sleeved shirt with a collar and two or three buttons at the neck.

Pol Pot E
/pol pot/ (*c.*1925–98; born *Saloth Sar*), Cambodian leader of the Khmer Rouge, Prime Minister 1976–9. During his regime millions of Cambodians were killed in a brutal 'reconstruction' of the country. Overthrown in 1979, Pol Pot led the Khmer Rouge in a guerrilla war against the new government until 1985.

poltergeist /pol-ter-gyst/ ● **n.** a supernatural being supposedly responsible for throwing objects about.
– ORIGIN from German *poltern* 'make a disturbance' + *Geist* 'ghost'.

poltroon /pol-troon/ ● **n.** archaic a complete coward.
– ORIGIN Italian *poltrone*.

poly- ● **comb. form** many; much: *polygon*.
– ORIGIN Greek *polus* 'much', *polloi* 'many'.

polyandry /po-li-an-dri/ ● **n.** the practice of having more than one husband at the same time.
– ORIGIN from Greek *anēr* 'male'.

polyanthus /po-li-an-thuhss/ ● **n.** (pl. **polyanthus**) a flowering garden plant that is a hybrid from the wild primrose.
– ORIGIN Greek *anthos* 'flower'.

polychromatic ● **adj.** multicoloured.

polychrome ● **adj.** painted, printed, or decorated in several colours.
– ORIGIN Greek *khrōma* 'colour'.

polyester ● **n.** a synthetic fibre or resin used to make fabric for clothes.

polyethylene /po-li-eth-i-leen/ ● **n.** = **POLYTHENE**.

polygamy /puh-lig-uh-mi/ ● **n.** the practice of having more than one wife or husband at the same time.
– DERIVATIVES **polygamist** n. **polygamous** adj.
– ORIGIN Greek *polugamos* 'often marrying'.

polyglot /po-li-glot/ ● **adj.** knowing or using several languages.
– ORIGIN Greek *poluglōttos* 'many-tongued'.

polygon /po-li-guhn/ ● **n.** a plane figure with three or more straight sides and angles.
– DERIVATIVES **polygonal** /puh-li-guh-n'l/ adj.

polygraph ● **n.** a lie detector.

polygyny /puh-li-ji-ni/ ● **n.** the practice of having more than one wife at the same time.
– ORIGIN Greek *gunē* 'woman'.

polyhedron /po-li-hee-druhn/ ● **n.** (pl. **polyhedra** /po-li-hee-druh/ or **polyhedrons**) a solid figure with many plane faces.
– DERIVATIVES **polyhedral** adj.

polymath /po-li-math/ ● **n.** a person with a wide knowledge of many subjects.
– DERIVATIVES **polymathic** adj.
– ORIGIN Greek *polumathēs* 'having learned much'.

polymer /po-li-mer/ ● **n.** Chem. a substance with a molecular structure formed from many identical small molecules bonded together.
– ORIGIN Greek *polumeros* 'having many parts'.

polymerize (also **polymerise**) ● **v.** (**polymerizes, polymerizing, polymerized**) combine or cause to combine to form a polymer.

polymorphic (also **polymorphous**) ● **adj.** having several different forms.

Polynesia E
/pol-i-nee-*zh*uh/ a region of the central Pacific, to the east of Micronesia and Melanesia. It includes Hawaii, Samoa, and French Polynesia.

polyp /pol-ip/ ● **n.** **1** a simple sea creature which remains fixed in the same place, such as coral. **2** Med. a small lump that sticks out from a mucous membrane.
– ORIGIN Greek *polupous*.

polyphonic ● **adj.** (especially of vocal music) in two or more parts, each having a melody of its own.

– ORIGIN Greek *phōnē* 'voice, sound'.

polyphony /puh-li-fuh-ni/ ● n. the combination of a number of musical parts, each forming an individual melody and harmonizing with each other.

polysaccharide /po-li-sak-kuh-ryd/ ● n. a carbohydrate (e.g. starch or cellulose) whose molecules consist of chains of sugar molecules.

polystyrene /po-li-sty-reen/ ● n. a synthetic resin which is a polymer of styrene.

polysyllabic ● adj. having more than one syllable.

polytechnic ● n. (formerly, in Britain) a college offering courses at degree level or below (now called a 'university').

polytheism /po-li-thee-i-z'm/ ● n. the belief in more than one god.

– DERIVATIVES **polytheistic** adj.

– ORIGIN Greek *polutheos* 'of many gods'.

polythene ● n. esp. Brit. a tough, light, flexible plastic, used for packaging.

– ORIGIN from *polyethylene.*

polyunsaturated ● adj. (of a fat) having a chemical structure that is thought not to lead to the formation of cholesterol in the blood.

polyurethane /po-li-yoor-i-thayn/ ● n. a synthetic resin used in paints and varnishes.

polyvinyl acetate ● n. a synthetic resin used in paints and adhesives.

Pom ● n. = POMMY.

pomade /puh-mayd, puh-mahd/ ● n. a scented oil or cream for making the hair glossy and smooth.

– ORIGIN French *pommade.*

pomander /puh-man-der, pom-uhn-der/ ● n. a ball or perforated container of sweet-smelling substances used to perfume a room or cupboard.

– ORIGIN from Latin *pomum de ambra* 'apple of ambergris'.

pomegranate /pom-i-gran-it/ ● n. a round tropical fruit with a tough orange skin and red flesh containing many seeds.

– ORIGIN from Latin *pomum granatum* 'apple having many seeds'.

pomelo /pom-uh-loh/ ● n. (pl. **pomelos**) a large citrus fruit similar to a grapefruit.

– ORIGIN unknown.

Pomeranian ● n. a small dog of a breed with long silky hair.

– ORIGIN from *Pomerania*, a region of central Europe.

pommel /pum-m'l/ ● n. **1** the upward curving or projecting front part of a saddle. **2** a rounded knob on the end of the handle of a sword.

– ORIGIN Old French *pomel.*

Pommy ● n. (pl. **Pommies**) Austral./NZ informal, derog. a British person.

– ORIGIN uncertain.

pomp ● n. the special clothes, music, and customs that form a grand public ceremony.

– ORIGIN Greek *pompē* 'procession'.

Pompadour E
/pom-puh-door/, Jeanne Antoinette Poisson, Marquise de (1721–64), French noblewoman and mistress of Louis XV. She gained considerable influence at court, but later became unpopular as a result of her interference in political affairs.

Pompeii E
/pom-pay/ an ancient city in Italy, south-east of Naples. It was buried by an eruption of Mount Vesuvius in AD 79; excavations of the site have revealed well-preserved remains.

Pompey E
/pom-pi/ (106–48 BC; known as **Pompey the Great**; Latin name *Gnaeus Pompeius Magnus*), Roman general and statesman. He shared power with Caesar and Crassus (the first Triumvirate), but later quarrelled with Caesar, who defeated him at Pharsalus.

Pompidou E
/pom-pi-doo/, Georges (Jean Raymond) (1911–74), French statesman, Prime Minister 1962–8 and President 1969–74.

Pompidou Centre E
a modern art gallery, exhibition centre, and concert hall in Paris, designed by Sir Richard Rogers and the Italian architect Renzo Piano (b.1937) and opened in 1977.

pompom (also **pompon**) ● n. a small woollen ball attached to a garment for decoration.

– ORIGIN French *pompon* 'tuft, topknot'.

pompous ● adj. solemn or self-important in an affected or foolish way.

– DERIVATIVES **pomposity** n. **pompously** adv.

ponce Brit. informal ● n. **1** a man who lives off a prostitute's earnings. **2** derog. an effeminate man. ● v. (**ponces, poncing, ponced**) (**ponce about/around**) behave in a way that wastes time or looks foolish.

– DERIVATIVES **poncey** (also **poncy**) adj.

– ORIGIN perh. from POUNCE.

Ponce de León E
/pon-say day lay-on/, Juan (*c.*1460–1521), Spanish explorer, who landed on the coast of Florida in 1513, claiming the area for Spain.

poncho ● n. (pl. **ponchos**) a garment made of a thick piece of woollen cloth with a slit in the middle for the head.

– ORIGIN Latin American Spanish.

pond ● n. a small area of still water.

– ORIGIN from POUND[3].

ponder ● v. (**ponders, pondering, pondered**) consider carefully.

– ORIGIN Latin *ponderare* 'weigh'.

ponderous ● adj. **1** slow and clumsy because very heavy. **2** boringly solemn or long-winded: *ponderous newspaper editorials.*

– DERIVATIVES **ponderously** adv.

– ORIGIN Latin *ponderosus.*

Pondicherry E
/pon-di-che-ri/ a Union Territory of SE India; capital, Pondicherry.

pondweed ● n. a plant that grows in still or running water.

pong Brit. informal ● n. a strong, unpleasant smell. ● v. smell strongly and unpleasantly.

– DERIVATIVES **pongy** adj.

– ORIGIN unknown.

poniard /pon-yerd/ ● n. hist. a small, thin dagger.

– ORIGIN French *poignard.*

pontiff ● n. the Pope.

– ORIGIN Latin *pontifex* 'high priest'.

pontifical /pon-ti-fi-k'l/ ● adj. having to do with a pope; papal.

pontificate ● v. /pon-ti-fi-kayt/ (**pontificates, pontificating, pontificated**) express one's opinions in a pompous and overbearing way. ● n. /pon-ti-fi-kuht/ (also **Pontificate**) (in the Roman Catholic Church) the office or term of office of pope or bishop.

pontoon[1] /pon-toon/ ● n. Brit. a card game in which players try to obtain cards with a value totalling twenty-one.
– ORIGIN prob. from French *vingt-et-un* 'twenty-one'.

pontoon[2] /pon-toon/ ● n. **1** a flat-bottomed boat or hollow metal cylinder used with others to support a temporary bridge or floating landing stage. **2** a bridge or landing stage supported by pontoons.
– ORIGIN French *ponton*.

pony ● n. (pl. **ponies**) a horse of a small breed, especially one below 15 hands.
– ORIGIN prob. from French *poulenet* 'small foal'.

ponytail ● n. a hairstyle in which the hair is drawn back and tied at the back of the head.

pony-trekking ● n. Brit. the leisure activity of riding across country on a pony or horse.

poo ● exclam., n., & v. var. of **POOH**.

pooch ● n. informal a dog.
– ORIGIN unknown.

poodle ● n. **1** a breed of dog with a curly coat that is usually clipped. **2** Brit. a person who is excessively willing to do as they are told.
– ORIGIN German *Pudelhund*.

poof /puuf/ (also **pouf, poofter**) ● n. Brit. informal, derog. an effeminate or homosexual man.
– ORIGIN perh. from *puff* in the former sense 'braggart'.

pooh (also **poo**) informal ● exclam. expressing disgust at an unpleasant smell. ● n. **1** excrement. **2** an act of defecating. ● v. defecate.

pooh-pooh ● v. informal dismiss (an idea) as being foolish or impractical.

pool[1] ● n. **1** a small area of still water. **2** (also **swimming pool**) an artificial pool for swimming in. **3** a small, shallow patch of liquid lying on a surface.
– ORIGIN Old English.

pool[2] ● n. **1** a supply of vehicles, people, goods, or funds that is shared between a number of people and available for use when needed. **2** (**the pools** or **football pools**) a form of gambling on the results of football matches. **3** a game played on a billiard table using 16 balls. ● v. put into a common fund to be used by a number of people: *they pooled their wages and bought food.*
– ORIGIN French *poule* 'stake, kitty'.

Poona E
/poo-nuh/ (also **Pune**) an industrial city in Maharashtra, western India.

poop (also **poop deck**) ● n. a raised deck at the back of a ship.
– ORIGIN Latin *puppis* 'stern'.

poor ● adj. **1** having very little money. **2** of a low standard or quality. **3** (**poor in**) lacking in. **4** deserving pity or sympathy.
– PHRASES **poor relation** a person or thing that is less good than others of the same type.
– ORIGIN Old French *poure*.

poorhouse ● n. Brit. a workhouse.

poorly ● adv. in a poor way. ● adj. esp. Brit. unwell.

pootle ● v. (**pootles, pootling, pootled**) Brit. informal move or travel in a leisurely manner.
– ORIGIN from **TOOTLE** and *poodle* in the same sense.

pop[1] ● v. (**pops, popping, popped**) **1** make a sudden short explosive sound. **2** go or come quickly or unexpectedly. **3** put or place quickly. **4** (of a person's eyes) open wide and appear to bulge. ● n. **1** a popping sound. **2** informal, dated a sweet fizzy drink.
– PHRASES **have** (or **take**) **a pop at** informal attack. **pop the question** informal propose marriage.

pop[2] ● n. (also **pop music**) popular modern commercial music, with a strong melody and beat. ● adj. **1** relating to pop music. **2** usu. derog. (of a scientific or academic subject) made easy to understand by the general public.

pop[3] ● n. informal, esp. US father.
– ORIGIN from **PAPA**.

pop art ● n. art based on modern popular culture that uses material from advertisements, films, etc.

popcorn ● n. maize kernels which are heated until they burst open and are then eaten as a snack.

Pope, E
Alexander (1688–1744), English poet, famous for his biting wit and metrical skill. His satirical poetry includes the mock epic *The Rape of the Lock* and *The Dunciad*.

pope ● n. (often **the Pope**) the Bishop of Rome as head of the Roman Catholic Church.
– ORIGIN Greek *papas* 'bishop, patriarch'.

popery ● n. derog. Roman Catholicism.

pop-eyed ● adj. informal having bulging eyes.

popgun ● n. a child's toy gun which shoots a harmless pellet or cork.

popinjay /pop-in-jay/ ● n. dated a vain person who dresses in a showy way.
– ORIGIN Old French *papingay* 'parrot'.

popish ● adj. derog. Roman Catholic.

Popish Plot E
a fictitious Jesuit plot concocted in 1678 by Titus Oates, an Anglican priest (1649–1705), involving a plan to kill Charles II and put the Catholic Duke of York on the English throne. The 'discovery' of the plot led to the execution of about thirty-five Catholics.

poplar ● n. a tall, thin tree with soft wood.
– ORIGIN Latin *populus*.

poplin ● n. a cotton fabric with a finely ribbed surface.
– ORIGIN from former French *papeline*.

Popocatépetl E
/po-puh-kat-uh-pet-uhl/ an active volcano in Mexico, south-east of Mexico City.

poppadom /pop-puh-duhm/ ● n. (in Indian cookery) a thin circular piece of spiced bread that is fried until crisp.
– ORIGIN Tamil.

Popper, E
Sir Karl Raimund (1902–94), Austrian-born British philosopher, who argued that scientific hypotheses can never be finally confirmed as true, but are tested by attempts to falsify them.

popper ● n. Brit. informal a press stud.

poppet ● n. Brit. informal a pretty or charming child.
– ORIGIN Latin *puppa* 'girl, doll'.

poppy ● n. a plant with red, pink, or yellow flowers and small black seeds.
– ORIGIN Latin *papaver*.

poppycock ● n. informal nonsense.
– ORIGIN from Dutch dialect *pap* 'soft' + *kak* 'dung'.

popster ● n. informal a pop musician.

populace /pop-yuu-luhss/ ● n. the general public.
– ORIGIN Italian *popolaccio* 'common people'.

popular ● adj. **1** liked or admired by many people. **2** intended for or suited to the taste of the general public: *the popular press*. **3** (of a belief or attitude) widely held among the general public. **4** (of political activity) carried on by the people as a whole: *a popular revolt*.
– DERIVATIVES **popularly** adv.
– ORIGIN Latin *populus* 'people'.

popularity ● n. the state of being liked or supported by many people.

popularize (also **popularise**) ● v. (**popularizes**, **popularizing**, **popularized**) **1** make popular. **2** make (something scientific or academic) understandable or interesting to the general public.
– DERIVATIVES **popularization** (also **popularisation**) n.

populate ● v. (**populates**, **populating**, **populated**) **1** form the population of: *the island is populated by 8,000 people*. **2** cause people to settle in (a place).
– ORIGIN Latin *populare* 'supply with people'.

population ● n. **1** all the inhabitants of a place. **2** a particular group within this: *the country's immigrant population*.

populist ● n. a politician who wants to appeal to or represent the interests and views of ordinary people. ● adj. relating to populists.
– DERIVATIVES **populism** n.

populous ● adj. having a large population.

pop-up ● n. **1** (of a book or greetings card) containing folded pictures that rise up to form a three-dimensional scene when opened. **2** Computing (of a menu or other feature) that can be quickly brought to the screen on top of what is being worked on.

porcelain /por-suh-lin/ ● n. **1** a type of fine semi-transparent china. **2** articles made of porcelain.
– ORIGIN Italian *porcellana* 'cowrie shell, china'.

porch ● n. a covered shelter over the entrance of a building.
– ORIGIN Old French *porche*.

porcine /por-syn/ ● adj. relating to or like a pig or pigs.
– ORIGIN Latin *porcinus*.

porcupine /por-kyuu-pyn/ ● n. a large rodent with protective spines on the body and tail.
– ORIGIN from Latin *porcus* 'pig' + *spina* 'thorn'.

pore¹ ● n. a tiny opening in the skin or other surface through which gases, liquids, or microscopic particles may pass.
– ORIGIN Greek *poros*.

pore² ● v. (**pores**, **poring**, **pored**) (**pore over/through**) study or read with close attention.
– ORIGIN perh. from **PEER¹**.

pork ● n. the flesh of a pig used as food.
– ORIGIN Latin *porcus* 'pig'.

porker ● n. a young pig raised and fattened for food.

porky informal ● adj. fat. ● n. (pl. **porkies**) (also **porky-pie**) Brit. a lie.

porn (also **porno**) informal ● n. pornography. ● adj. pornographic.

pornography ● n. pictures, writing, or films that are intended to arouse sexual excitement.
– DERIVATIVES **pornographer** n. **pornographic** adj.
– ORIGIN Greek *pornographos* 'writing about prostitutes'.

porous ● adj. (of a rock or other material) having tiny spaces through which liquid or air may pass.
– DERIVATIVES **porosity** n.
– ORIGIN Latin *porus* 'pore'.

porphyry /por-fi-ri/ ● n. (pl. **porphyries**) a hard, reddish igneous rock containing crystals of feldspar.
– ORIGIN Greek *porphuritēs*.

porpoise /por-puhss, por-poyz/ ● n. a small toothed whale with a blunt rounded snout.
– ORIGIN Old French *porpois*.

porridge ● n. **1** a dish consisting of oatmeal boiled with water or milk. **2** Brit. informal time spent in prison.
– ORIGIN from **POTTAGE**.

> **Porsche** [E]
> /porsh/, Ferdinand (1875–1952), Austrian car designer. His designs include the Volkswagen and various sports and racing cars.

port¹ ● n. **1** a town or city with a harbour. **2** a harbour.
– PHRASES **port of call** a place where a ship or person stops on a journey.
– ORIGIN Latin *portus*.

port² ● n. a strong sweet dark red wine from Portugal.
– ORIGIN from **OPORTO**.

port³ ● n. the side of a ship or aircraft that is on the left when one is facing forward. Opp. **STARBOARD**.
– ORIGIN prob. originally the side turned towards the port.

port⁴ ● n. **1** an opening in the side of a ship for boarding or loading. **2** an opening in the body of an aircraft or armoured vehicle through which a gun is fired. **3** a socket in a computer network into which a device is plugged.
– ORIGIN Latin *porta* 'gate'.

portable ● adj. able to be easily carried or moved.
– DERIVATIVES **portability** n.

portage /por-tij/ ● n. **1** the carrying of a boat or its cargo overland between two waterways. **2** a place at which this is necessary.
– ORIGIN French.

portal ● n. **1** a large and impressive doorway or gate. **2** an Internet site providing a directory of links to other sites.
– ORIGIN Latin *porta*.

> **Port-au-Prince** [E]
> /port-oh-**prinss**/ the capital of Haiti.

portcullis ● n. a strong, heavy grating that is

lowered to block a gateway to a castle.
– ORIGIN from Old French *porte coleice* 'sliding door'.

Port Elizabeth E
a port and resort in South Africa, on the coast of the province of Eastern Cape.

portend /por-**tend**/ ● v. be a sign or warning that (something important or unpleasant) is likely to happen.
– ORIGIN Latin *portendere.*

portent /**por**-tent, **por**-tuhnt/ ● n. a sign or warning that something important or unpleasant is likely to happen.
– ORIGIN Latin *portentum* 'omen, token'.

portentous ● adj. **1** being a sign that something important is likely to happen. **2** excessively solemn.

Porter, E
Cole (1892–1964), American songwriter. He is known for such songs as 'Let's Do It' and 'Begin the Beguine', and the musical *Kiss me, Kate.*

porter[1] ● n. **1** a person employed to carry luggage and other loads. **2** a hospital employee who moves equipment or patients. **3** dark brown bitter beer.
– ORIGIN Old French *porteour.*

porter[2] ● n. Brit. an employee in charge of the entrance of a large building.
– ORIGIN Old French *portier.*

portfolio ● n. (pl. **portfolios**) **1** a thin, flat case for carrying drawings, maps, etc. **2** a set of pieces of creative work intended to demonstrate a person's ability. **3** a range of investments held by a person or organization. **4** the area of responsibility of a government minister.
– ORIGIN Italian *portafogli.*

porthole ● n. a small window on the outside of a ship or aircraft.

portico /**por**-ti-koh/ ● n. (pl. **porticoes** or **porticos**) a roof supported by columns at regular intervals, often forming a porch.
– ORIGIN Latin *porticus* 'porch'.

portion ● n. **1** a part or a share. **2** an amount of food suitable for or served to one person. ● v. divide into portions and share out.
– ORIGIN Latin.

Port Louis E
/loo-iss, **loo**-i/ the capital of Mauritius.

portly ● adj. rather fat.
– ORIGIN Old French *port* 'bearing, gait'.

portmanteau /port-**man**-toh/ ● n. (pl. **portmanteaus** or **portmanteaux** /port-**man**-tohz/) a large travelling bag that opens into two equal parts.
– ORIGIN French *portemanteau.*

portmanteau word ● n. a word made by joining the first part of one word to the end of another, e.g. *brunch* from *breakfast* and *lunch.*

Port Moresby E
/**morz**-bi/ the capital of Papua New Guinea, on the island of New Guinea.

Port-of-Spain E
the capital of Trinidad and Tobago, on the island of Trinidad.

Porto Novo E
/por-toh **noh**-voh/ the capital of Benin.

portrait ● n. **1** a painting, drawing, or photograph of a person. **2** a written or filmed description.
– DERIVATIVES **portraitist** n.
– ORIGIN Old French *portraire* 'portray'.

portraiture ● n. **1** the art of making portraits. **2** portraits as a form of art.

portray ● v. **1** show or describe in a work of art or literature. **2** describe in a particular way: *he is portrayed as having relentless energy.*
– DERIVATIVES **portrayal** n.
– ORIGIN Old French *portraire.*

Port Said E
/*rhymes with* side/ a port in Egypt, on the Mediterranean coast at the north end of the Suez Canal.

Portsmouth E
a port and naval base on the south coast of England, a unitary council formerly in Hampshire.

Port Stanley E
= STANLEY[1].

Portugal E
a country in SW Europe, with a coastline on the Atlantic Ocean; capital, Lisbon.

Portuguese /port-yuu-**geez**, por-chuu-**geez**/ ● n. (pl. **Portuguese**) **1** a person from Portugal. **2** the language of Portugal and Brazil. ● adj. relating to Portugal.

Port Vila E
– VILA.

pose ● v. (**poses, posing, posed**) **1** present or be (a problem, question, etc.). **2** sit or stand in a particular position in order to be photographed, painted, or drawn. **3** (**pose as**) pretend to be. **4** behave in a way that is meant to impress people. ● n. **1** a position adopted in order to be painted, drawn, or photographed. **2** a way of behaving intended to impress or mislead.
– ORIGIN Old French *poser.*

Poseidon E
/puh-**sy**-d'n/ the Greek god of the sea, water, and earthquakes. Roman equivalent NEPTUNE[1].

poser ● n. **1** a person who behaves in a way that is meant to impress. **2** a puzzling question or problem.

poseur /poh-**zer**/ ● n. a person who poses in order to impress; a poser.
– ORIGIN French.

posh ● adj. informal **1** very elegant or luxurious. **2** esp. Brit. upper-class.
– ORIGIN perh. from former slang *posh* 'a dandy'.

posit /**poz**-it/ ● v. (**posits, positing, posited**) put forward as fact or as a basis for argument.
– ORIGIN Latin, 'placed'.

position ● n. **1** a place where someone or something is or should be. **2** a way in which someone or something is placed or arranged: *he raised himself to a sitting position.* **3** a situation. **4** a job. **5** a person's place or import-

ance in relation to others: *she finished in second position.* **6** a point of view. ● **v.** put or arrange in a particular position.
– DERIVATIVES **positional** adj.
– ORIGIN Latin.

positive ● **adj. 1** showing the presence rather than the absence of particular features: *a positive test result.* **2** expressing agreement, confirmation, or permission. **3** hopeful, favourable, or confident. **4** with no possibility of doubt; certain. **5** (of a quantity) greater than zero. **6** having to do with the kind of electric charge opposite to that carried by electrons. **7** (of a photograph) showing light and shade or colours true to the original. **8** (of an adjective or adverb) expressing the basic degree of a quality (e.g. *brave*). Contrasted with COMPARATIVE and SUPERLATIVE. ● **n.** a positive quality or photograph.
– DERIVATIVES **positively** adv. **positivity** n.
– ORIGIN Latin *positivus.*

positive discrimination ● **n.** Brit. the policy of providing jobs or other opportunities to people who belong to groups which suffer discrimination.

positivism ● **n.** a system of philosophy that recognizes only things that can be scientifically or logically proved.
– DERIVATIVES **positivist** n. & adj.

positron /poz-i-tron/ ● **n.** Physics a subatomic particle with the same mass as an electron and an equal but positive charge.

posse /poss-i/ ● **n. 1** N. Amer. hist. a body of men summoned by a sheriff to enforce the law. **2** informal a group of people who are the same in some way: *a posse of students.*
– ORIGIN Latin, 'be able, power'.

possess ● **v. 1** have as property; own. **2** (also **be possessed of**) have (an ability or quality): *he did not possess a sense of humour.* **3** (of a demon or spirit) have complete power over. **4** (of an emotion, idea, etc.) dominate the mind of.
– DERIVATIVES **possessor** n.
– ORIGIN Latin *possidere* 'occupy, hold'.

possession ● **n. 1** the state of possessing something. **2** a thing owned. **3** (in sport) temporary control of the ball by a player or team.

possessive ● **adj. 1** demanding someone's total attention and love. **2** unwilling to share one's possessions. **3** Grammar expressing possession (e.g. *theirs, John's*).

possessive determiner ● **n.** Grammar a determiner showing possession (e.g. *my*).

possessive pronoun ● **n.** Grammar a pronoun showing possession (e.g. *mine*).

possibility ● **n.** (pl. **possibilities**) **1** a thing that is possible. **2** the state of being possible. **3** (**possibilities**) general qualities of a promising nature: *the house had possibilities.*

possible ● **adj. 1** capable of existing, happening, or being done. **2** that may be so, but that is not certain: *the possible cause of the plane crash.* ● **n.** a possible candidate for a job or member of a team.
– ORIGIN Latin *possibilis.*

possibly ● **adv. 1** perhaps. **2** in accordance with what is possible: *be as noisy as you possibly can.*

possum ● **n. 1** an Australasian marsupial that lives in trees. **2** N. Amer. informal an opossum.
– PHRASES **play possum** pretend to be unconscious, dead, or unaware of something.
– ORIGIN from OPOSSUM.

post[1] ● **n. 1** a long, strong, upright piece of timber or metal used as a support or a marker. **2** (**the post**) the starting post or winning post in a race. ● **v. 1** display (a notice) in a public place. **2** announce.
– ORIGIN Latin *postis* 'doorpost'.

post[2] esp. Brit. ● **n. 1** the official service or system that delivers letters and parcels. **2** letters and parcels delivered. **3** a single collection or delivery of post. ● **v.** send via the postal system.
– PHRASES **keep posted** keep (someone) informed of the latest news.
– ORIGIN French *poste* 'station, stand'.

post[3] ● **n. 1** a place where someone is on duty or where an activity is carried out. **2** a job. ● **v. 1** put (a soldier, police officer, etc.) in a particular place. **2** send (someone) to a place to take up a job.
– ORIGIN Italian *posto.*

post- ● **prefix** after: *postgraduate.*
– ORIGIN Latin.

postage ● **n. 1** the sending of letters and parcels by post. **2** the charge for sending something by post.

postage stamp ● **n.** an adhesive stamp that is stuck on a letter or parcel to show the amount of postage paid.

postal ● **adj.** relating to or sent by post.

postal order ● **n.** Brit. a document that can be bought from the Post Office and sent to someone who exchanges it for money.

postbox ● **n.** a large public box into which letters are posted for collection by the post office.

postcard ● **n.** a card for sending a message by post without an envelope.

postcode ● **n.** Brit. a group of letters and numbers added to a postal address to assist the sorting of mail.

post-coital ● **adj.** occurring or done after sexual intercourse.

post-date ● **v.** (**post-dates**, **post-dating**, **post-dated**) **1** put a date later than the actual one on (a cheque or document). **2** occur at a later date than: *Stonehenge was believed to post-date these structures.*

postdoctoral ● **adj.** (of research) done after the completion of a doctorate.

poster ● **n.** a large printed picture or notice used for decoration or advertisement.

poste restante /pohst ress-tuhnt/ ● **n.** Brit. a department in a post office that keeps letters until they are collected by the person they are addressed to.
– ORIGIN French, 'mail remaining'.

posterior ● **adj.** tech. at or nearer the rear. Opp. ANTERIOR. ● **n.** humorous a person's bottom.
– ORIGIN Latin.

posterity ● **n.** all future generations of people.
– ORIGIN Old French *posterite.*

postern /poss-tern/ ● **n.** archaic a back or side entrance.
– ORIGIN Old French *posterne.*

postgraduate ● **adj.** relating to study done after completing a first degree. ● **n.** a person taking a postgraduate course.

post-haste ● **adv.** with great speed.

posthumous /poss-tyuu-muhss/ • **adj.** happening or appearing after the person involved has died: *he was awarded a posthumous Military Cross.*
– DERIVATIVES **posthumously** adv.
– ORIGIN Latin *postumus* 'last'.

post-Impressionism • **n.** a former style of art in which emphasis was placed on the artist's emotions, as expressed by colour, line, and shape.

post-industrial • **adj.** (of an economy or society) no longer relying on heavy industry.

posting • **n.** esp. Brit. an appointment to a job abroad.

postman (or **postwoman**) • **n.** Brit. a person who is employed to deliver or collect post.

postmark • **n.** an official mark stamped on a letter or parcel, giving the date of posting and cancelling the postage stamp. • **v.** stamp with a postmark.

postmaster (or **postmistress**) • **n.** a person in charge of a post office.

postmodernism • **n.** a style and movement in the arts that features a deliberate mixing of different styles and draws attention to artistic traditions.
– DERIVATIVES **postmodern** adj. **postmodernist** n. & adj.

post-mortem • **n. 1** an examination of a dead body to find out the cause of death. **2** a detailed discussion of an event after it has occurred.
– ORIGIN Latin.

post-natal • **adj.** having to do with the period after childbirth.

post office • **n. 1** the public department or organization responsible for postal services. **2** a building where postal business is carried on.

post office box • **n.** a numbered box in a post office where letters are kept until called for.

postpone • **v.** (**postpones**, **postponing**, **postponed**) arrange for (something) to take place at a time later than that first planned.
– DERIVATIVES **postponement** n.
– ORIGIN Latin *postponere.*

postprandial • **adj.** formal having to do with the period after a meal.
– ORIGIN from Latin *prandium* 'a meal'.

postscript • **n.** an additional remark at the end of a letter, following the signature.
– ORIGIN Latin *postscriptum* 'thing written under'.

postulant /poss-tyuu-luhnt/ • **n.** a candidate who wishes to enter a religious order.

postulate /poss-tyuu-layt/ • **v.** (**postulates**, **postulating**, **postulated**) suggest or accept that (something) is true, as a basis for a theory or discussion.
– DERIVATIVES **postulation** n.
– ORIGIN Latin *postulare* 'ask'.

posture • **n. 1** a particular position of the body. **2** the usual way in which a person holds their body: *abdominal exercises aid good posture.* **3** an approach or attitude towards something. • **v.** (**postures**, **posturing**, **postured**) behave in a way that is meant to impress or mislead others.
– DERIVATIVES **postural** adj.
– ORIGIN Latin *positura.*

posy • **n.** (pl. **posies**) a small bunch of flowers.
– ORIGIN first meaning 'motto or line of verse written inside a ring': from **POESY**.

pot[1] • **n.** a rounded container used for storage or cooking. • **v.** (**pots**, **potting**, **potted**) **1** plant in a pot. **2** preserve (food) in a sealed pot or jar. **3** informal hit or kill by shooting. **4** Billiards & Snooker strike (a ball) into a pocket.
– PHRASES **go to pot** informal be ruined through neglect.
– ORIGIN Old English.

pot[2] • **n.** informal cannabis.
– ORIGIN prob. from Mexican Spanish *potiguaya* 'cannabis leaves'.

potable /poh-tuh-b'l/ • **adj.** formal (of water) safe to drink.
– ORIGIN French.

potash • **n.** an alkaline compound of potassium, used in making soap and fertilizers.
– ORIGIN from *pot* + *ash*, because first obtained from a solution made from ashes that was evaporated in a pot.

potassium /puh-tass-i-uhm/ • **n.** a soft silvery-white reactive metallic element.
– ORIGIN from **POTASH**.

potassium nitrate • **n.** a white salt which occurs naturally in nitre, used to make gunpowder and preserve meat.

potato • **n.** (pl. **potatoes**) a starchy plant tuber which is cooked and eaten as a vegetable.
– ORIGIN Spanish *patata* 'sweet potato'.

pot belly • **n.** a large stomach that sticks out.

potboiler • **n.** informal a book, film, etc. produced purely to make the writer or artist a living by appealing to popular taste.

poteen /po-teen/ • **n.** (in Ireland) whisky that is made illegally.
– ORIGIN from Irish *fuisce poitín* 'little pot of whisky'.

potent • **adj. 1** having great power, influence, or effect: *a potent antibiotic.* **2** (of a man) able to achieve an erection or to reach an orgasm.
– DERIVATIVES **potency** n.
– ORIGIN Latin, 'being powerful'.

potentate • **n.** a monarch or ruler.
– ORIGIN Latin *potentatus* 'power'.

potential • **adj.** capable of becoming or developing into something: *a campaign to woo potential customers.* • **n. 1** qualities or abilities that may be developed and lead to success: *a young broadcaster with great potential.* **2** (often **potential for/to do**) the possibility of something happening. **3** Physics the difference in voltage between two points in an electric field or circuit.
– DERIVATIVES **potentiality** n. **potentially** adv.
– ORIGIN Latin *potentia* 'power'.

potential energy • **n.** Physics energy which a body possesses as a result of its position or state. Compare with **KINETIC ENERGY**.

potentiometer /poh-ten-shi-om-i-ter/ • **n.** an instrument for measuring or adjusting an electromotive force.

pothole • **n. 1** a deep underground cave formed by water eroding the rock. **2** a hole in a road surface.
– DERIVATIVES **potholed** adj.
– ORIGIN from dialect *pot* 'pit'.

p

potholing • n. exploring potholes as a sport or pastime.

potion • n. a drink with healing, magical, or poisonous powers.
– ORIGIN Latin.

pot luck • n. a situation in which one must take a chance that whatever is available will be acceptable.

Potomac E
/puh-**toh**-mak/ a river of the eastern US, which rises in the Appalachian Mountains and flows through Washington DC into Chesapeake Bay on the Atlantic coast.

pot-pourri /poh-**poor**-i, poh-puh-**ree**/ • n. (pl. **pot-pourris**) **1** a mixture of dried petals and spices placed in a bowl to perfume a room. **2** a mixture of things.
– ORIGIN French, 'rotten pot'.

potshot • n. a shot aimed unexpectedly or at random.

pottage • n. archaic soup or stew.
– ORIGIN Old French *potage* 'that which is put into a pot'.

potted • adj. **1** grown or preserved in a pot. **2** put into a short, understandable form: *a potted history of Australia.*

Potter[1], E
Dennis (Christopher George) (1935–94), English television dramatist. His series include *Pennies from Heaven* and *The Singing Detective.*

Potter[2], E
(Helen) Beatrix (1866–1943), English writer and illustrator of stories for children, such as *The Tale of Peter Rabbit.*

potter[1] • v. (**potters**, **pottering**, **pottered**) **1** do minor pleasant tasks in a relaxed way. **2** move or go in an unhurried way.
– ORIGIN unknown.

potter[2] • n. a person who makes pottery.

potter's wheel • n. a flat revolving disc on which wet clay is shaped into pots.

pottery • n. (pl. **potteries**) **1** articles made of baked clay. **2** the craft of making such articles.

potting shed • n. a shed used for potting plants and storing garden tools and supplies.

potty[1] • adj. Brit. informal **1** foolish; crazy. **2** extremely enthusiastic about someone or something.
– ORIGIN unknown.

potty[2] • n. (pl. **potties**) informal a bowl for a child to use as a toilet.

pouch • n. **1** a small flexible bag, carried in a pocket or attached to a belt. **2** a pocket of skin in which animals such as kangaroos carry their young.
– ORIGIN Old French *poche.*

pouf • n. var. of **POOF** or **POUFFE**.

pouffe /poof/ (also **pouf**) • n. a large firm cushion used as a seat or stool.
– ORIGIN French.

Poulenc E
/**poo**-langk/, Francis (Jean Marcel) (1899–1963), French composer. His work includes choral pieces, many songs, and the ballet *Les Biches.*

poulterer • n. Brit. a person who sells poultry.

poultice /**pohl**-tiss/ • n. a soft moist mass of flour, plant material, etc., put on the skin to reduce inflammation.
– ORIGIN Latin *puls* 'pottage, pap'.

poultry /**pohl**-tri/ • n. chickens, turkeys, ducks, and geese.
– ORIGIN Old French *pouletrie.*

pounce • v. (**pounces**, **pouncing**, **pounced**) **1** move suddenly so as to seize or attack. **2** (**pounce on**) take swift advantage of (a mistake). • n. an act of pouncing.
– ORIGIN uncertain.

Pound, E
Ezra (Weston Loomis) (1885–1972), American poet and critic. He is best known for his unfinished series of poems, the *Cantos*, which draw on a vast range of classical and other references and which had a significant influence on modern poetry.

pound[1] • n. **1** a unit of weight equal to 16 oz avoirdupois (0.4536 kg), or 12 oz troy (0.3732 kg). **2** (also **pound sterling**) (pl. **pounds sterling**) the basic unit of money of the UK, equal to 100 pence.
– PHRASES **one's pound of flesh** something which one is owed, but, if given, would cause suffering or trouble to the person who owes it.
– ORIGIN from Latin *libra pondo.*

pound[2] • v. **1** hit heavily again and again. **2** walk or run with heavy steps. **3** throb with a strong regular rhythm. **4** crush or grind into a powder or paste.
– ORIGIN Old English.

pound[3] • n. a place where stray dogs or illegally parked vehicles may officially be taken and kept until claimed.
– ORIGIN uncertain.

poundage • n. Brit. **1** a charge made for every pound in weight of something, or for every pound sterling in value. **2** weight.

-pounder • comb. form **1** a person or thing weighing a specified number of pounds: *the shark was a 184-pounder.* **2** a gun designed to fire a shell weighing a specified number of pounds.

pour • v. **1** flow or cause to flow in a steady stream. **2** (of rain) fall heavily. **3** prepare and serve (a drink). **4** come or go in large numbers: *letters poured in.* **5** (**pour out**) express (one's feelings) freely.
– PHRASES **pour oil on troubled waters** try to calm a dispute.
– ORIGIN unknown.

Poussin E
/**poo**-san/, Nicolas (1594–1665), French painter. A leading painter in the classical tradition, his subjects included biblical scenes, classical mythology, and historical landscapes.

pout • v. push one's lips forward as a sign of sulking or to look sexually attractive. • n. a pouting expression.
– DERIVATIVES **pouty** adj.
– ORIGIN perh. from Swedish dialect *puta* 'be inflated'.

poverty • n. **1** the state of being very poor. **2** the state of being lacking in quality or amount: *the poverty of her imagination.*
– ORIGIN Old French *poverte.*

poverty trap • n. Brit. a situation in which an

increase in someone's income results in a loss of state benefits, leaving them no better off.

POW ● abbrev. prisoner of war.

powder ● n. **1** a mass of fine dry particles. **2** a cosmetic in this form that is put on a person's face. ● v. (**powders, powdering, powdered**) **1** sprinkle or cover with powder. **2** make into a powder.
– DERIVATIVES **powdery** adj.
– ORIGIN Old French *poudre*.

powder blue ● n. a soft, pale blue.

powder keg ● n. a situation which is likely to suddenly become dangerous or violent.
– ORIGIN from *powder* in the sense 'gunpowder'.

powder puff ● n. a soft pad for putting powder on the face.

powder room ● n. euphem. a women's toilet in a public building.

> **Powell** E
> /**poh**-uhl/, Anthony (Dymoke) (1905–2000), English novelist, best known for his sequence of novels *A Dance to the Music of Time*, a satirical portrayal of the English upper middle classes.

power ● n. **1** the ability to do something: *the power of speech*. **2** the ability to influence people or events. **3** the right or authority to do something. **4** political authority or control. **5** a country seen as having international influence and military strength: *a world power*. **6** strength, force, or energy. **7** capacity or performance of an engine or other device. **8** energy that is produced by mechanical, electrical, or other means. **9** Physics the rate of doing work, measured in watts or horse power. **10** Math. the product obtained when a number is multiplied by itself a certain number of times. ● v. (**powers, powering, powered**) **1** supply with power. **2** move with speed or force.
– PHRASES **power of attorney** the authority to act for another person in particular legal or financial matters. **the powers that be** the authorities.
– ORIGIN Old French *poeir*.

powerboat ● n. a fast motor boat.

power cut ● n. a temporary interruption in an electricity supply.

powerful ● adj. having power.
– DERIVATIVES **powerfully** adv.

powerhouse ● n. a person or thing having great energy or power.

powerless ● adj. without the power to take action.

power plant ● n. a power station.

power station ● n. a building where electrical power is generated.

power steering ● n. steering aided by power from the vehicle's engine.

powwow ● n. **1** informal a meeting for discussion. **2** a North American Indian ceremony involving feasting and dancing.
– ORIGIN from a word in a North American Indian langauge meaning 'magician'.

> **Powys** E
> /**poh**-iss, **pow**-iss/ a county of east central Wales; administrative centre, Llandrindod Wells.

pox ● n. **1** any disease caused by a virus and producing a rash of pus-filled pimples that leave pockmarks on healing. **2** (**the pox**) informal syphilis.
– ORIGIN from *pocks*, plural of **POCK**.

poxy ● adj. Brit. informal of poor quality.

pp ● abbrev. **1** (**pp.**) pages. **2** (also **p.p.**) per procurationem (used when signing a letter on someone else's behalf). [ORIGIN Latin, 'through the agency of'.]

PPE ● abbrev. philosophy, politics, and economics.

ppm ● abbrev. part(s) per million.

PPS ● abbrev. **1** post (additional) postscript. **2** Brit. Parliamentary Private Secretary.

PPV ● abbrev. pay-per-view.

PR ● abbrev. **1** proportional representation. **2** public relations.

practicable ● adj. able to be done successfully.
– DERIVATIVES **practicability** n.

practical ● adj. **1** having to do with the actual doing or use of something rather than theory: *the candidate should have practical experience of agriculture*. **2** likely to be successful or useful: *practical solutions to common transport problems*. **3** skilled at making or doing things. **4** almost complete; virtual: *it was a practical certainty*. ● n. Brit. an examination or lesson in which students have to do or make things.
– DERIVATIVES **practically** adv.
– ORIGIN Greek *praktikos* 'concerned with action'.

practicality ● n. (pl. **practicalities**) **1** the state of being practical. **2** (**practicalities**) the real facts or aspects of a situation rather than theories.

practical joke ● n. a trick played on someone in order to make them look foolish.

practice ● n. **1** the action of doing something rather than the theories about it: *putting policy into practice*. **2** the usual way of doing something. **3** the work, business, or place of work of a doctor, dentist, or lawyer. **4** the doing of something repeatedly to improve one's skill: *maths improves with practice*. ● v. US = **PRACTISE**.
– ORIGIN from **PRACTISE**.

practise (US **practice**) ● v. (**practises, practising, practised**; US **practices, practicing, practiced**) **1** do (something) repeatedly so as to become skilful. **2** do (something) regularly as part of one's normal behaviour: *irrigation has been practised in the area for many years*. **3** be working in (a particular profession). **4** (**practised**) expert as a result of much experience. **5** follow the teaching and rules of (a religion).
– ORIGIN Latin *practicare*.

> **USAGE** practise
> Do not confuse **practice** and **practise**. **Practice** is a noun meaning 'the action of doing something rather than the theories about it', as in *putting policy into practice*. **Practice** is also the spelling for the verb in American English. In British English, the verb is spelt **practise**, as in *I need to practise my French*.

practitioner ● n. a person who practises a profession or activity.

pragmatic ● adj. dealing with things in a practical and sensible way.
– DERIVATIVES **pragmatically** adv.

p

– ORIGIN Greek *pragmatikos* 'relating to fact'.

pragmatism ● n. the attitude or policy of approaching matters in a practical way.
– DERIVATIVES **pragmatist** n.

Prague E
/prahg/ the capital of the Czech Republic.

Praia E
/pry-uh/ the capital of the Cape Verde Islands, on the island of São Tiago.

prairie ● n. (in North America) a large open area of grassland.
– ORIGIN French.

prairie dog ● n. a type of rodent that lives in burrows in the grasslands of North America.

praise ● v. (**praises**, **praising**, **praised**) **1** express approval of or admiration for. **2** express thanks to or respect for (one's God). ● n. the expression of approval or admiration: *the audience was full of praise for the production.*
– ORIGIN Old French *preisier.*

praiseworthy ● adj. deserving praise.

praline /prah-leen, pray-leen/ ● n. a smooth substance made from nuts boiled in sugar, used as a filling for chocolates.
– ORIGIN named after Marshal de Plessis-*Praslin* (1598–1675), the French soldier whose cook invented it.

pram ● n. Brit. a four-wheeled vehicle for a baby, pushed by a person on foot.
– ORIGIN from **PERAMBULATOR**.

prance ● v. (**prances**, **prancing**, **pranced**) **1** walk with exaggerated movements. **2** (of a horse) move with high steps.
– ORIGIN unknown.

prang ● v. Brit. informal crash (a motor vehicle or aircraft).

prank ● n. a practical joke or mischievous act.
– ORIGIN unknown.

prankster ● n. a person fond of playing pranks.

praseodymium /pray-zi-oh-di-mi-uhm/ ● n. a silvery-white metallic element.
– ORIGIN German *Praseodym.*

prat ● n. Brit. informal a stupid person.
– ORIGIN unknown.

prate ● v. (**prates**, **prating**, **prated**) talk too much in a foolish or boring way.
– ORIGIN Dutch or German *praten.*

pratfall ● n. informal a fall on to one's bottom.

prattle ● v. (**prattles**, **prattling**, **prattled**) talk too much in a foolish or trivial way. ● n. foolish or trivial talk.
– ORIGIN German *pratelen.*

prawn ● n. an edible shellfish like a large shrimp.
– ORIGIN unknown.

praxis /prak-siss/ ● n. practice as opposed to theory.
– ORIGIN Greek, 'doing'.

Praxiteles E
/prak-sit-uh-leez/ (mid 4th century BC), Athenian sculptor. He is noted for a statue of Aphrodite, of which there are only Roman copies.

pray ● v. **1** say a prayer. **2** wish or hope strongly for something: *after days of rain, we were praying for sun.* ● adv. formal or archaic please: *pray continue.*
– ORIGIN Old French *preier.*

prayer ● n. **1** a request for help or expression of thanks made to God or a god. **2** (**prayers**) a religious service at which people gather to pray together. **3** an earnest hope or wish.

prayerful ● adj. **1** having to do with praying or prayers. **2** liking to pray; devout.

praying mantis ● n. see **MANTIS**.

pre- ● prefix before: *pre-arrange.*
– ORIGIN Latin *prae-.*

preach ● v. **1** give a religious talk to a group of people. **2** recommend (a course of action) to someone: *my parents have always preached moderation.* **3** (**preach at**) give moral advice to (someone) in an annoying or boring way.
– DERIVATIVES **preacher** n.
– ORIGIN Old French *prechier.*

preachy ● adj. giving moral advice in a boring or overbearing way.

preamble /pree-am-b'l, pree-am-b'l/ ● n. an introduction; an opening statement.
– ORIGIN Latin *praeambulus* 'going before'.

pre-arrange ● v. (**pre-arranges**, **pre-arranging**, **pre-arranged**) arrange beforehand.

prebendary /pre-buhn-duh-ri/ ● n. (pl. **prebendaries**) (in the Christian Church) an honorary canon.
– ORIGIN Latin *praebenda* 'pension'.

Precambrian /pree-kam-bri-uhn/ ● adj. Geol. relating to the earliest period of the earth's history, ending about 570 million years ago, a time when living organisms first appeared.

precarious ● adj. **1** likely to fall or to cause someone to fall: *a precarious pile of books.* **2** uncertain.
– DERIVATIVES **precariously** adv.
– ORIGIN Latin *precarius* 'obtained by begging'.

precast ● adj. (of concrete) made into a form that is ready for use in building.

precaution ● n. **1** something done in advance to avoid problems or danger. **2** (**precautions**) informal contraception.
– DERIVATIVES **precautionary** adj.
– ORIGIN Latin.

precede ● v. (**precedes**, **preceding**, **preceded**) **1** happen before in time or order: *a gun battle had preceded the explosions.* **2** go in front of (someone).
– ORIGIN Latin *praecedere.*

precedence /press-i-duhnss, pree-si-duhnss/ ● n. the state of coming before others in order or importance: *his desire for power took precedence over everything else.*

precedent /press-i-d'nt/ ● n. an earlier event, action, or legal case that is taken as an example to be followed in a similar situation.

precentor /pri-sen-ter/ ● n. a person who leads the singing or (in a synagogue) the prayers in a religious service.
– ORIGIN Latin *praecinere* 'sing before'.

precept /pree-sept/ ● n. a general rule about how to behave or what to think.
– ORIGIN Latin *praeceptum* 'something advised'.

precession ● n. **1** the slow movement of the axis of a spinning body around another axis. **2** Astron. the earlier occurrence of equinoxes each year.
– ORIGIN Latin *praecedere* 'go before'.

precinct /pree-singkt/ ● n. **1** Brit. an area in a

p

town that is closed to traffic. **2** the area around a place or building, often enclosed by a wall. **3** N. Amer. one of the districts into which a city or town is divided for elections or policing purposes.
– ORIGIN Latin *praecinctum*.

precious • adj. **1** having great value. **2** greatly loved or valued. **3** sophisticated in a way that is artificial and exaggerated.
– PHRASES **precious little** (or **few**) informal very little (or few).
– DERIVATIVES **preciousness** n.
– ORIGIN Latin *pretiosus*.

precious metal • n. a valuable metal such as gold, silver, or platinum.

precious stone • n. a very attractive and valuable piece of mineral, used in jewellery.

precipice • n. a tall and very steep rock face or cliff.
– ORIGIN Latin *praecipitium* 'abrupt descent'.

precipitate • v. /pri-sip-i-tayt/ (**precipitates**, **precipitating**, **precipitated**) **1** cause (something bad) to happen suddenly or too soon. **2** cause to move suddenly and with force. **3** Chem. cause (a substance) to be deposited in solid form from a solution. **4** cause (moisture in the atmosphere) to condense and fall as rain, snow, etc. • adj. /pri-sip-i-tuht/ done or occurring suddenly or without thought. • n. /pri-sip-i-tayt, pri-sip-i-tuht/ Chem. a substance precipitated from a solution.
– ORIGIN Latin *praecipitare* 'throw headlong'.

precipitation • n. **1** rain, snow, sleet, or hail. **2** Chem. the action of precipitating a substance from a solution.

precipitous /pri-sip-i-tuhss/ • adj. **1** dangerously high or steep. **2** sudden and considerable: *a precipitous decline in exports*.

precis /pray-si/ • n. (pl. **precis** /pray-si, pray-seez/) a summary. • v. (**precises** /pray-seez/, **precising** /pray-see-ing/, **precised** /pray-seed/) make a precis of.
– ORIGIN French, 'precise'.

precise • adj. **1** expressed very clearly and with great detail: *precise directions*. **2** careful about details and accuracy. **3** particular: *at that precise moment the car stopped*.
– DERIVATIVES **precisely** adv.
– ORIGIN Old French *prescis*.

precision • n. the state of being precise. • adj. very accurate: *a precision instrument*.

preclude • v. (**precludes**, **precluding**, **precluded**) prevent (something) from happening or (someone) from doing something.
– ORIGIN Latin *praecludere* 'shut off'.

precocious /pri-koh-shuhss/ • adj. (of a child) having developed certain abilities or tendencies at an earlier age than usual.
– ORIGIN Latin *praecoquere* 'ripen fully'.

precocity /pri-koss-i-ti/ • n. the state of being precocious.

precognition /pree-kog-ni-sh'n/ • n. knowledge of an event before it happens, gained by paranormal means.

preconceived • adj. (of an idea or opinion) formed before full knowledge or evidence is available.

preconception • n. a preconceived idea or opinion.

precondition • n. something that must exist or happen before other things can happen or be done.

precursor • n. a person or thing that comes before another of the same kind.
– ORIGIN Latin *praecursor*.

pre-date • v. (**pre-dates**, **pre-dating**, **pre-dated**) exist or occur at a date earlier than.

predator /pred-uh-ter/ • n. an animal that hunts and kills others for food.
– ORIGIN Latin *praedator* 'plunderer'.

predatory • adj. **1** (of an animal) killing others for food. **2** taking advantage of others.

predecease • v. (**predeceases**, **predeceasing**, **predeceased**) formal die before (another person).

predecessor • n. **1** a person who held a job or office before the current holder. **2** a thing that has been followed or replaced by another: *the chapel was built on the site of its predecessor*.
– ORIGIN Latin *praedecessor*.

predestination • n. the Christian belief that everything has been decided or planned in advance by God.

predestine • v. (**predestines**, **predestining**, **predestined**) (of God or fate) decide in advance that (something) will happen or that (someone) will have a particular fate.

predetermine • v. (**predetermines**, **predetermining**, **predetermined**) establish or decide in advance.

predeterminer • n. Grammar a word or phrase that occurs before a determiner, e.g. *both*.

predicament • n. a difficult situation.
– ORIGIN Latin *praedicamentum* 'something declared'.

predicate • n. /pred-i-kuht/ Grammar the part of a sentence or clause containing a verb and stating something about the subject (e.g. *went home* in *John went home*). • v. /pred-i-kayt/ (**predicates**, **predicating**, **predicated**) (**predicate on/upon**) base (something) on.
– ORIGIN Latin *praedicare* 'declare'.

predicative /pri-dik-uh-tiv/ • adj. Grammar (of an adjective or noun) forming part or the whole of the predicate, as *old* in *the dog is old* (but not in *the old dog*).

predict • v. state that (an event) will happen in the future.
– DERIVATIVES **predictive** adj. **predictor** n.
– ORIGIN Latin *praedicere*.

predictable • adj. **1** able to be predicted. **2** always behaving or occurring in the way expected and therefore boring.
DERIVATIVES **predictability** n. **predictably** adv.

prediction • n. **1** a thing predicted; a forecast. **2** the action of predicting.

predilection /pree-di-lek-sh'n/ • n. a preference or special liking for something.
– ORIGIN Latin *praediligere* 'prefer'.

predispose • v. (**predisposes**, **predisposing**, **predisposed**) make (someone) likely to be, do, or think something: *certain people are predisposed to become drug abusers*.
– DERIVATIVES **predisposition** n.

predominant • adj. **1** present as the main element: *the bird's predominant colour was white*. **2** having the greatest control or power.
– DERIVATIVES **predominance** n. **predominantly** adv.

predominate • v. (**predominates**, **predominating**, **predominated**) **1** be the main element. **2** have control or power.

pre-eminent ● adj. better than all others; outstanding.
– DERIVATIVES **pre-eminence** n.

pre-empt ● v. **1** take action so as to prevent (something) happening. **2** prevent (someone) from saying something by speaking first.
– DERIVATIVES **pre-emption** n.
– ORIGIN Latin *praeemere* 'buy in advance'.

pre-emptive ● adj. done to prevent someone from doing something: *a pre-emptive attack.*

preen ● v. **1** (of a bird) tidy and clean its feathers with its beak. **2** make oneself look attractive and then admire one's appearance. **3** (**preen oneself**) feel very pleased with oneself.
– ORIGIN prob. from Latin *ungere* 'anoint'.

pre-existing ● adj. existing from an earlier time.

prefabricated ● adj. (of a building) made in sections that can be easily put together on site.

preface /pref-uhss/ ● n. an introduction to a book, stating its subject or aims. ● v. (**prefaces**, **prefacing**, **prefaced**) (**preface with/by**) say or do something to introduce (a book, speech, or event).
– ORIGIN Old French.

prefect ● n. **1** Brit. a senior pupil who is appointed to enforce discipline in a school. **2** a chief officer, magistrate, or regional governor in certain countries.
– ORIGIN Latin *praeficere* 'put in authority over'.

prefecture ● n. a district administered by a prefect.

prefer ● v. (**prefers**, **preferring**, **preferred**) **1** like (someone or something) better than another or others. **2** put forward (a formal accusation) for consideration by a court of law.
– ORIGIN Latin *praeferre* 'carry before'.

preferable ● adj. more desirable or suitable.
– DERIVATIVES **preferably** adv.

P

preference ● n. **1** a greater liking for one alternative over another or others. **2** a thing preferred. **3** favour shown to one person over another or others: *preference is given to those who make a donation.*

preferential ● adj. favouring a particular person or group: *minority businesses were given preferential treatment.*
– DERIVATIVES **preferentially** adv.

preferment ● n. formal promotion to a job or position.

prefigure ● v. (**prefigures**, **prefiguring**, **prefigured**) be an early sign or version of: *the violence of this passage prefigures her mature writing.*

prefix ● n. **1** a word, letter, or number placed before another. **2** a letter or group of letters placed at the beginning of a word to alter its meaning (e.g. *non*). ● v. **1** add as a prefix. **2** add a prefix to.

pregnancy ● n. (pl. **pregnancies**) the state or period of being pregnant.

pregnant ● adj. **1** (of a woman or female animal) having a child or young developing in the womb. **2** full of meaning: *a pregnant pause.*
– ORIGIN Latin *praegnans.*

prehensile /pri-hen-syl/ ● adj. (of an animal's limb or tail) capable of grasping things.
– ORIGIN Latin *prehendere* 'to grasp'.

prehistoric ● adj. relating to the period before written records.

prehistory ● n. **1** the period of time before written records. **2** the early stages of the development of something: *the prehistory of capitalism.*

pre-industrial ● adj. before the development of industries on a wide scale.

prejudge ● v. (**prejudges**, **prejudging**, **prejudged**) make a judgement about (someone or something) before having all the necessary information.

prejudice ● n. **1** an opinion about someone or something that is not based on reason or experience: *English prejudice against foreigners.* **2** dislike or unfair behaviour based on such opinions. ● v. (**prejudices**, **prejudicing**, **prejudiced**) **1** give rise to prejudice in (someone). **2** cause harm to: *delay is likely to prejudice the child's welfare.*
– ORIGIN Latin *praejudicium.*

prejudicial ● adj. harmful to someone or something.

prelate /prel-uht/ ● n. a bishop or other high-ranking Christian priest.
– ORIGIN Latin *praelatus* 'civil dignitary'.

preliminary ● adj. happening before or preparing for a main action or event: *preliminary talks.* ● n. (pl. **preliminaries**) a preliminary action or event.
– ORIGIN from Latin *prae* 'before' + *limen* 'threshold'.

prelude ● n. **1** an action or event acting as an introduction to something more important. **2** a piece of music acting as an introduction to a longer piece.
– ORIGIN Latin *praeludere* 'play beforehand'.

premarital ● adj. occurring before marriage.

premature ● adj. **1** occurring or done before the proper time: *the sun can cause premature ageing.* **2** (of a baby) born before the normal length of pregnancy is completed.
– DERIVATIVES **prematurely** adv.
– ORIGIN Latin *praematurus* 'very early'.

premeditated ● adj. (of an action, especially a crime) planned in advance.

premenstrual ● adj. occurring or experienced before menstruation.

premenstrual syndrome ● n. a range of symptoms (including emotional tension) experienced by some women before menstruation.

premier ● adj. first in importance, order, or position. ● n. a Prime Minister or other head of government.
– DERIVATIVES **premiership** n.
– ORIGIN Old French.

premiere /prem-i-air/ ● n. the first performance or showing of a play, film, ballet, etc. ● v. (**premieres**, **premiering**, **premiered**) give the premiere of.
– ORIGIN French.

premise /prem-iss/ (Brit. also **premiss**) ● n. a statement or idea that forms the basis for a theory, argument, or line of reasoning.
– ORIGIN Old French *premisse.*

premises ● pl. n. the building and land occupied by a business.

premium ● n. (pl. **premiums**) **1** an amount paid for an insurance policy. **2** an extra sum

added to a basic price or other payment. ● **adj.** (of a product) of high quality and more expensive.
– PHRASES **at a premium 1** scarce and in demand. **2** above the usual price. **put** (or **place**) **a premium on** treat as particularly valuable.
– ORIGIN Latin *praemium* 'reward'.

Premium Bond ● **n.** (in the UK) a government certificate that pays no interest but is entered in regular draws for cash prizes.

premolar ● **n.** a tooth between the canines and molar teeth.

premonition /prem-uh-**ni**-sh'n, pree-muh-**ni**-sh'n/ ● **n.** a strong feeling that something is about to happen.
– DERIVATIVES **premonitory** adj.
– ORIGIN Latin *praemonere* 'forewarn'.

prenatal ● **adj.** before birth.

preoccupation ● **n. 1** the state of being preoccupied. **2** a matter that preoccupies someone.

preoccupy ● **v.** (**preoccupies, preoccupying, preoccupied**) fill the mind of (someone) completely: *she was preoccupied with paying the bills.*

preordained ● **adj.** decided or determined beforehand.

prep ● **n.** Brit. informal (especially in a private school) school work done outside lessons.
– ORIGIN from **PREPARATION.**

prepaid past and past part. of **PREPAY.**

preparation ● **n. 1** the action of preparing. **2** something done to prepare for something. **3** a substance that has been prepared for use as a medicine, cosmetic, etc.

preparatory ● **adj.** done in order to prepare for something.

preparatory school ● **n. 1** Brit. a private school for pupils aged seven to thirteen. **2** N. Amer. a private school that prepares pupils for college or university.

prepare ● **v.** (**prepares, preparing, prepared**) **1** make ready for use. **2** make or get ready to do or deal with something: *she took time off to prepare for her exams.* **3** (**be prepared to do**) be willing to do.
– ORIGIN Latin *praeparare.*

preparedness ● **n.** readiness.

prepay ● **v.** (**prepays, prepaying, prepaid**) pay for in advance.
– DERIVATIVES **prepayment** n.

preponderance ● **n.** the state of being greater in number: *the preponderance of women among older people.*

preponderant ● **adj.** greater in number or importance.

preponderate ● **v.** (**preponderates, preponderating, preponderated**) be greater in number or importance.
– ORIGIN Latin *praeponderare* 'weigh more'.

preposition /prep-uh-**zi**-sh'n/ ● **n.** Grammar a word used with a noun or pronoun to show place, position, time, or method.
– DERIVATIVES **prepositional** adj.

USAGE preposition

A preposition (a word such as *from, to, on, after,* etc.) usually comes before a noun or pronoun and gives information about how, when, or where something has happened (*she arrived after dinner*). Some people believe that a preposition should never come at the end of a sentence, as in *where do you come from?*, and that you should say *from where do you come?* instead. However, this can result in English that sounds very awkward and unnatural, and is not a rule that has to be followed as long as the meaning of what you are saying is clear.

A preposition such as **between** should be followed by an object pronoun such as **me, him,** or **us** rather than a subject pronoun such as **I, he,** and **we.** It is therefore correct to say *between you and me* and wrong to say *between you and I.*

prepossessing ● **adj.** attractive or appealing in appearance.

preposterous ● **adj.** completely ridiculous or outrageous.
– DERIVATIVES **preposterously** adv.
– ORIGIN Latin *praeposterus* 'reversed, absurd'.

prep school ● **n.** a preparatory school.

pre-pubescent ● **adj.** having to do with the period before puberty.

prepuce /pree-pyooss/ ● **n.** Anat. = **FORESKIN.**
– ORIGIN French.

prequel ● **n.** a story or film about events which happen before those of an existing work.
– ORIGIN from **PRE-** + **SEQUEL.**

Pre-Raphaelite /pree-raf-fuh-lyt/ ● **n.** a member of a group of English 19th-century artists who painted in the style of Italian artists from before the time of Raphael. ● **adj.** relating to or typical of the Pre-Raphaelites.

prerequisite /pree-rek-wi-zit/ ● **n.** a thing that must exist or happen before something else can happen or exist: *our solar system is a prerequisite for our existence.* ● **adj.** required before something else can happen or exist.

prerogative /pri-rog-uh-tiv/ ● **n.** a right or privilege belonging to a particular person or group: *owning a car used to be the prerogative of the rich.*
– ORIGIN Latin *praerogativa* 'verdict of the people voting first in the assembly'.

presage /press-ij/ ● **v.** /also pri-sayj/ (**presages, presaging, presaged**) be a sign or warning of: *the clouds above the moor presaged rain.* ● **n.** an omen.
– ORIGIN Latin *praesagire* 'forebode'.

Presbyterian /prez-bi-teer-i-uhn/ ● **adj.** relating to a Protestant Church governed by elders who are all of equal rank. ● **n.** a member of a Presbyterian Church.
– DERIVATIVES **Presbyterianism** n.
– ORIGIN Greek *presbuteros* 'elder'.

presbytery /prez-bi-tuh-ri/ ● **n.** (pl. **presbyteries**) **1** an administrative body in a Presbyterian Church. **2** the house of a Roman Catholic parish priest. **3** the eastern part of a church near the altar.

prescient /press-i-uhnt/ ● **adj.** having knowledge of events before they happen.
– DERIVATIVES **prescience** n.
– ORIGIN Latin *praescire* 'know beforehand'.

prescribe ● **v.** (**prescribes, prescribing, prescribed**) **1** recommend and permit the use of (a medicine or treatment). **2** state officially that (something) should be done.
– ORIGIN Latin *praescribere* 'direct in writing'.

prescription ● **n. 1** a doctor's written instruction stating that a patient may be issued with a medicine or treatment. **2** the action of prescribing.

prescriptive • adj. stating what should be done; prescribing.

presence • n. **1** the state of being present: *my presence in the flat made her happy.* **2** a person's impressive manner or appearance. **3** a person or thing that seems to be present but is not seen. **4** a group of soldiers or police stationed in a particular place: *the USA would maintain a presence in the region.*
– PHRASES **presence of mind** the ability to remain calm and take quick, sensible action in a difficult situation.

present[1] /pre-z'nt/ • adj. **1** being or occurring in a particular place. **2** existing or occurring now. **3** Grammar (of a tense) expressing an action or state now happening or existing. • n. (**the present**) the period of time now occurring.
– PHRASES **at present** now. **for the present** for now; temporarily.
– ORIGIN Latin *praesens* 'being at hand'.

present[2] • v. /pri-zent/ **1** give formally at a ceremony. **2** offer (something) for consideration or payment. **3** formally introduce (someone) to someone else. **4** put (a show or exhibition) before the public. **5** introduce and appear in (a television or radio show). **6** be the cause of (a problem). **7** give (a particular impression) to others: *the EC presented a united front over the crisis.* **8** (**present oneself**) appear or attend on a formal occasion. • n. /pre-z'nt/ a thing given to someone as a gift.
– ORIGIN Latin *praesentare* 'place before'.

presentable • adj. looking clean or smart enough to be seen in public.

presentation • n. the action of presenting something or the way in which it is presented.
– DERIVATIVES **presentational** adj.

presenter • n. a person who presents a television or radio programme.

presentiment /pri-zen-ti-muhnt/ • n. a feeling that something unpleasant is going to happen.
– ORIGIN from former French *présentiment*.

presently • adv. **1** soon. **2** now.

present participle • n. Grammar the form of a verb, ending in *-ing*, which is used in forming tenses describing continuous action (e.g. *I'm thinking*), as a noun (e.g. *good thinking*), and as an adjective (e.g. *running water*).

preservation • n. the action of preserving or the state of being preserved.

preservative • n. a substance used to prevent food or wood from decaying.

preserve • v. (**preserves**, **preserving**, **preserved**) **1** keep in its original or existing state: *all records of the past were carefully preserved.* **2** keep safe from harm. **3** treat (food) to prevent it from decaying. • n. **1** a type of jam made with fruit boiled with sugar. **2** something seen as reserved for a particular person or group: *jobs that used to be the preserve of men.* **3** a place where game is protected and kept for private hunting.
– DERIVATIVES **preserver** n.
– ORIGIN Latin *praeservare*.

preset • v. (**presets**, **presetting**, **preset**) set (the controls of an electrical device) before it is used.

preside • v. (**presides**, **presiding**, **presided**) **1** be in charge of a meeting, court, etc. **2** (**preside over**) be in charge of (a situation).
– ORIGIN Latin *praesidere*.

presidency • n. (pl. **presidencies**) the job of president or the period of time this is held.

president • n. **1** the elected head of a republic. **2** the head of an organization.
– DERIVATIVES **presidential** adj.

Presley, E
Elvis (Aaron) (1935–77), American rock-and-roll and pop singer. He dominated early rock and roll with songs such as 'Heartbreak Hotel' and 'Blue Suede Shoes', and also starred in a number of films.

press[1] • v. **1** move into contact with something by using steady force: *the dog pressed against her leg.* **2** push (something) to operate a device. **3** apply pressure to (something) to flatten or shape it. **4** move in a particular direction by pushing. **5** (**press on/ahead**) continue in one's action. **6** forcefully put forward (an opinion or claim). **7** make strong efforts to persuade (someone) to do something. **8** (of time) be short. **9** (**be pressed for**) have too little of: *I'm really pressed for time.* • n. **1** a device for crushing, flattening, or shaping something. **2** a printing press. **3** (**the press**) newspapers or journalists as a whole. **4** a closely packed mass of people or things.
– ORIGIN Latin *pressare* 'keep pressing'.

press[2] • v. hist. force to serve in the army or navy.
– PHRASES **press into service** (or **use**) put to a particular use as a makeshift measure.
– ORIGIN Latin *praestare* 'provide'.

press conference • n. a meeting with journalists in order to make an announcement or answer questions.

press gang • n. hist. a body of men employed to force men to serve in the army or navy. • v. (**press-gang**) force into doing something.

pressing • adj. **1** needing urgent action. **2** (of an invitation) strongly expressed. • n. an object made by moulding under pressure.

press release • n. an official statement issued to journalists.

press stud • n. Brit. a small fastener with two parts that fit together when pressed.

press-up • n. Brit. an exercise in which a person lies facing the floor and raises their body by pressing down on their hands.

pressure • n. **1** the steady force brought to bear on an object by something in contact with it. **2** the use of persuasion or threats to make someone do something. **3** a feeling of stress caused by the need to do something: *pressure of work.* **4** the force per unit area applied by a fluid against a surface. • v. (**pressures**, **pressuring**, **pressured**) persuade or force into doing something.
– ORIGIN Latin *pressura*.

pressure cooker • n. an airtight pot in which food can be cooked quickly under steam pressure.

pressure group • n. a group that tries to influence government policy or public opinion in the interest of a particular cause.

pressurize (also **pressurise**) • v. (**pressurizes**, **pressurizing**, **pressurized**) **1** persuade or force into doing something. **2** keep the air pressure in (an aircraft cabin) the same as it is at ground level.

prestidigitation /press-ti-di-ji-tay-sh'n/ ● **n.** formal magic tricks performed as entertainment.
– ORIGIN French.

prestige /pre-steez*h*/ ● **n.** respect and admiration resulting from achievements, high quality, etc.: *her prestige in the United States was tremendous.*
– ORIGIN French, 'illusion, glamour'.

prestigious /press-ti-juhss/ ● **adj.** having or bringing prestige.

presto ● **adv. & adj.** Music in a quick tempo.
– ORIGIN Italian.

prestressed ● **adj.** (of concrete) strengthened by means of rods or wires inserted under tension before setting.

presumably ● **adv.** as may be presumed; probably.

presume ● **v.** (**presumes**, **presuming**, **presumed**) **1** suppose that something is probably true. **2** be bold enough to do something that one should not do: *don't presume to give me orders in my own house.* **3** (**presume on/upon**) take advantage of one's good relationship with someone.
– ORIGIN Latin *praesumere* 'anticipate'.

presumption ● **n. 1** an act of presuming something to be true. **2** an idea that is presumed to be true. **3** arrogant or disrespectful behaviour.

presumptuous ● **adj.** behaving with disrespectful boldness.

presuppose ● **v.** (**presupposes**, **presupposing**, **presupposed**) **1** depend on (something) in order to exist or be true. **2** assume to be the case.
– DERIVATIVES **presupposition** n.

pretence (US **pretense**) ● **n. 1** an act or the action of pretending. **2** a claim to have or be something: *he disclaimed any pretence to superiority.*

pretend ● **v. 1** make it seem that something is the case when in fact it is not. **2** give the appearance of feeling or having (an emotion or quality). **3** (**pretend to**) claim to have (a quality or title).
– ORIGIN Latin *praetendere* 'stretch forth, claim'.

pretender ● **n.** a person who claims a right to a title or position.

pretension ● **n. 1** (also **pretensions**) a claim to have or be something: *a pub with no pretensions to be a restaurant.* **2** the quality of being pretentious.

pretentious ● **adj.** trying to impress by pretending to be more important or better than one actually is.

preternatural /pree-ter-**nach**-uh-ruhl/ ● **adj.** beyond what is normal or natural.
– DERIVATIVES **preternaturally** adv.
– ORIGIN Latin *praeter* 'beyond'.

pretext ● **n.** a false reason used to justify an action.
– ORIGIN Latin *praetextus* 'outward display'.

Pretoria E
/pri-tor-i-uh/ the administrative capital of South Africa.

Pretoria-Witwatersrand-Vereeniging E
/fuh-ree-ni-king/ former name for **GAUTENG**.

prettify ● **v.** (**prettifies**, **prettifying**, **prettified**) make (something) seem pretty.

pretty ● **adj.** (**prettier**, **prettiest**) having an attractive or pleasant appearance. ● **adv.** informal to a certain extent; fairly.
– PHRASES **be sitting pretty** informal be in a favourable position. **a pretty penny** informal a large sum of money.
– DERIVATIVES **prettily** adv. **prettiness** n.
– ORIGIN Old English, 'cunning, crafty'.

pretzel /pret-z'l/ ● **n.** a crisp biscuit in the shape of a knot or stick and flavoured with salt.
– ORIGIN German.

prevail ● **v. 1** prove more powerful than: *it is hard for logic to prevail over emotion.* **2** (**prevail on/upon**) persuade to do something. **3** be widespread or current.
– ORIGIN Latin *praevalere.*

prevailing wind ● **n.** a wind from the direction that is most usual at a particular place or time.

prevalent /prev-uh-luhnt/ ● **adj.** widespread in a particular area.
– DERIVATIVES **prevalence** n.
– ORIGIN Latin *praevalere* 'prevail'.

prevaricate /pri-va-ri-kayt/ ● **v.** (**prevaricates**, **prevaricating**, **prevaricated**) avoid giving a direct answer to a question.
– DERIVATIVES **prevarication** n.
– ORIGIN Latin *praevaricari* 'walk crookedly'.

prevent ● **v. 1** stop (something) from happening. **2** stop (someone) from doing something.
– DERIVATIVES **preventable** adj. **preventer** n. **prevention** n.
– ORIGIN Latin *praevenire* 'precede'.

preventive (also **preventative**) ● **adj.** designed to prevent something from occurring.

preview ● **n. 1** a viewing or showing of something before it becomes generally available. **2** a review of a forthcoming film, book, etc. ● **v.** give or have a preview of.

Previn E
/prev-in/, André (George) (b.1929), German-born American conductor, pianist, and composer, conductor of the Royal Philharmonic Orchestra (1987–91).

previous ● **adj. 1** coming before in time or order: *the events of the previous day.* **2** (**previous to**) before.
– DERIVATIVES **previously** adv.
– ORIGIN Latin *praevius.*

prey ● **n. 1** an animal hunted and killed by another for food. **2** a person likely to be harmed or deceived by someone or something: *she fell prey to Will's charms.* ● **v.** (**prey on/upon**) **1** hunt and kill for food. **2** take advantage of or cause distress to.
– ORIGIN Old French *preie.*

Priam E
/**pry**-uhm/ Gk Myth. the king of Troy at the time of its destruction by the Greeks. The father of Paris and Hector, he was killed by the son of Achilles.

priapic /pry-ap-ik/ ● **adj.** (of a man) having a strong sexual appetite.
– ORIGIN Greek *Priapos*, a god of fertility.

price ● n. **1** the amount of money for which something is bought or sold. **2** something unwelcome that must be done or given in order to achieve something: *the price of their success was a day spent in discussion.* **3** the odds in betting. ● v. (**prices, pricing, priced**) decide the price of.
– PHRASES **at any price** no matter what is involved. **at a price** at a high cost. **a price on someone's head** a reward offered for someone's capture or death.
– ORIGIN Old French *pris.*

priceless ● adj. **1** very valuable. **2** informal very amusing.

pricey ● adj. (**pricier, priciest**) informal expensive.

prick ● v. **1** make a small hole in (something) with a sharp point. **2** cause (someone) to have a slight prickling feeling: *tears were pricking her eyelids.* ● n. **1** a mark, hole, or pain caused by pricking someone or something. **2** vulgar a man's penis. **3** vulgar a stupid or unpleasant man.
– PHRASES **prick up one's ears 1** (of a horse or dog) make the ears stand erect when alert. **2** (of a person) suddenly begin to pay attention.
– DERIVATIVES **pricker** n.
– ORIGIN Old English.

prickle ● n. **1** a small thorn on a plant or a pointed spine on an animal. **2** a tingling feeling on the skin. ● v. (**prickles, prickling, prickled**) have a tingling feeling on the skin.
– ORIGIN Old English.

prickly ● adj. **1** having prickles. **2** causing a tingling feeling. **3** easily offended or annoyed.

prickly pear ● n. a cactus which produces prickly, pear-shaped fruits.

pride ● n. **1** deep pleasure or satisfaction gained from achievements, qualities, or possessions. **2** a cause or source of this: *the swimming pool is the pride of the village.* **3** self-respect: *he swallowed his pride and asked for help.* **4** an excessively high opinion of oneself. **5** a group of lions. ● v. (**prides, priding, prided**) (**pride oneself on/upon**) be especially proud of (a quality or skill).
– PHRASES **pride of place** the most noticeable or important position.
– ORIGIN Old English.

priest ● n. **1** a person who is qualified to perform certain religious ceremonies in the Catholic, Orthodox, or Anglican Church. **2** a person who performs ceremonies in a non-Christian religion.
– DERIVATIVES **priesthood** n. **priestly** adj.
– ORIGIN Old English.

priestess ● n. a female priest of a non-Christian religion.

Priestley[1], E
J. B. (1894–1984; full name *John Boynton Priestley*), English novelist, dramatist, and critic. His works include the novel *The Good Companions* and the mystery drama *An Inspector Calls.*

Priestley[2], E
Joseph (1733–1804), English scientist and theologian, who discovered 'dephlogisticated air' (oxygen) in 1774.

prig ● n. a person who behaves as if they are superior to others in moral matters.
– DERIVATIVES **priggish** adj.
– ORIGIN unknown.

prim ● adj. very formal and correct and disapproving of anything rude.
– DERIVATIVES **primly** adv.
– ORIGIN prob. from Old French *prin* 'excellent'.

prima ballerina /pree-muh bal-luh-ree-nuh/ ● n. the chief female dancer in a ballet or ballet company.
– ORIGIN Italian.

primacy /pry-muh-si/ ● n. the fact of being most important.
– ORIGIN Latin *primatia.*

prima donna ● n. **1** the chief female singer in an opera or opera company. **2** a very temperamental and self-important person.
– ORIGIN Italian, 'first lady'.

primaeval ● adj. var. of **PRIMEVAL**.

prima facie /pry-muh fay-shi-ee/ ● adj. & adv. Law accepted as correct until proved otherwise.
– ORIGIN Latin.

primal ● adj. having to do with early human life; primeval.
– ORIGIN Latin *primalis.*

primary ● adj. **1** of chief importance: *the government's primary aim is to reduce unemployment.* **2** earliest in time or order. **3** relating to education for children between the ages of about five and eleven. ● n. (pl. **primaries**) (in the US) a preliminary election to appoint delegates to a party conference or to select candidates for an election.
– DERIVATIVES **primarily** adv.
– ORIGIN Latin *primarius.*

primary care ● n. health care provided in the community by doctors and specialist clinics.

primary colour ● n. any of a group of colours from which all others can be obtained by mixing.

primate /pry-mayt/ ● n. **1** a mammal of an order including monkeys, apes, and humans. **2** (in the Christian Church) an archbishop.
– ORIGIN Latin *primas* 'of the first rank'.

prime[1] ● adj. **1** of chief importance. **2** of the highest quality; excellent. **3** (of a number) that can be divided only by itself and one (e.g. 2, 3, 5). ● n. **1** a time of greatest vigour or success in a person's life. **2** a prime number.
– ORIGIN Latin *primus* 'first'.

prime[2] ● v. (**primes, priming, primed**) **1** make (something, especially a firearm or bomb) ready for use or action. **2** prepare (someone) for a situation by giving them information. **3** cover (a surface) with primer.
– ORIGIN prob. from Latin *primus* 'first'.

prime minister ● n. the head of a government.

primer[1] ● n. a substance painted on a surface as a base coat.

primer[2] ● n. a book for teaching children to read or giving a basic introduction to a subject.
– ORIGIN from Latin *primarius liber* 'primary book'.

prime time ● n. the time at which a radio or television audience is expected to be greatest.

primeval /pry-mee-v'l/ (also **primaeval**) • **adj.** relating to the earliest times in history.
– ORIGIN Latin *primaevus*.

primitive • **adj. 1** relating to the earliest times in history or stages in development: *primitive mammals.* **2** referring to a simple form of society that has not yet developed industry or writing. **3** offering a very basic level of comfort. **4** (of behaviour or emotion) not based on reason; instinctive.
– DERIVATIVES **primitively** adv.
– ORIGIN Latin *primitivus* 'first of its kind'.

primogeniture /pry-moh-jen-i-cher/ • **n. 1** the state of being the firstborn child. **2** the system by which the eldest son inherits all his parents' property.
– ORIGIN Latin *primogenitura*.

primordial /pry-mor-di-uhl/ • **adj.** existing at or from the beginning of time.
– ORIGIN Latin *primordialis* 'first of all'.

primp • **v.** make small adjustments to (one's hair, clothes, or make-up).
– ORIGIN from **PRIM**.

primrose • **n.** a plant of woods and hedges with pale yellow flowers.
– ORIGIN prob. from Latin *prima rosa* 'first rose'.

primula /prim-yuu-luh/ • **n.** a plant of a genus that includes primroses and cowslips.
– ORIGIN from Latin *primula veris* 'little first thing'.

Primus /pry-muhss/ • **n.** trademark a portable cooking stove that burns oil.

prince • **n. 1** a son or other close male relative of a monarch. **2** a male monarch of a small state. **3** (in some European countries) a nobleman.
– ORIGIN Latin *princeps* 'first, chief'.

Prince Albert, Prince Charles, etc. E
see **ALBERT, PRINCE**; **CHARLES, PRINCE**, etc.

prince consort • **n.** the husband of a reigning queen who is himself a prince.

Prince Edward Island E
an island and province in the Gulf of St Lawrence, in eastern Canada; capital, Charlottetown.

princeling • **n. 1** the ruler of a small or unimportant country. **2** a young prince.

princely • **adj. 1** relating to or suitable for a prince. **2** (of a sum of money) generous.

Princes in the Tower E
the sons of Edward IV, namely **Edward, Prince of Wales** (b.1470) and **Richard, Duke of York** (b.1472). They were taken to the Tower of London by their uncle (the future Richard III) and probably murdered there in about 1483.

princess • **n. 1** a daughter or other close female relative of a monarch. **2** the wife or widow of a prince.

Princess Anne, Princess Margaret, etc. E
see **ANNE, PRINCESS**; **MARGARET, PRINCESS**, etc.

Princess Royal • **n.** a title that may be given to the eldest daughter of a reigning British monarch.

Princeton University E
a university at Princeton in New Jersey, founded in 1746.

principal • **adj.** most important; main. • **n. 1** the most important person in an organization or group. **2** the head of a school or college. **3** a sum of money lent or invested, on which interest is paid. **4** a person for whom another acts as a representative.
– DERIVATIVES **principally** adv.
– ORIGIN Latin *principalis* 'first, original'.

USAGE principal

Do not confuse **principal** and **principle**. **Principal** is usually an adjective meaning 'main or most important' (*the country's principal cities*), whereas **principle** is a noun that usually means 'a truth or general law used as the basis for something' (*the general principles of law*).

principal boy • **n.** Brit. a woman who takes the leading male role in a pantomime.

principality • **n.** (pl. **principalities**) **1** a state ruled by a prince. **2** (**the Principality**) Brit. Wales.

principle • **n. 1** a truth or general law that is used as a basis for a theory or system of belief: *a country run on Islamic principles.* **2** (**principles**) rules or beliefs governing one's personal behaviour. **3** a general scientific theorem or natural law: *the principle that gas under pressure heats up.* **4** Chem. an active or characteristic element of a substance.
– PHRASES **in principle** in theory. **on principle** because of one's beliefs about what is right and wrong.
– ORIGIN Latin *principium* 'source'.

principled • **adj.** based on one's beliefs about what is right and wrong.

print • **v. 1** produce (a book, newspaper, etc.) by a process involving the transfer of words or pictures to paper. **2** produce (words or pictures) in this way. **3** produce (a photographic print) from a negative. **4** write (words) clearly without joining the letters. **5** mark with a coloured design: *a fabric printed with roses.* • **n. 1** printed words in a book, newspaper, etc. **2** a mark where something has pressed or touched a surface: *paw prints.* **3** a printed picture or design. **4** a photograph printed on paper from a negative or transparency. **5** a piece of fabric with a coloured design.
– PHRASES **in** (or **out of**) **print** (of a book) available (or no longer available) from the publisher.
– DERIVATIVES **printable** adj.
– ORIGIN Old French *preinte* 'pressed'.

printed circuit • **n.** an electronic circuit based on thin strips of a conducting material on an insulating board.

printer • **n. 1** a person or business involved in printing. **2** a machine for printing.

printing • **n. 1** the production of books, newspapers, etc. **2** all the copies of a book printed at one time. **3** handwriting in which the letters are written separately.

printing press • **n.** a machine for printing from type or plates.

printout • **n.** a page of printed material from a computer's printer.

prion /pree-on/ • **n.** a protein particle believed to be the cause of certain brain diseases such as BSE and CJD.

– ORIGIN from *pro(teinaceous) in(fectious particle).*

prior[1] ● **adj. 1** coming before in time, order, or importance. **2** (**prior to**) before.
– ORIGIN Latin, 'former, elder'.

prior[2] ● **n.** (fem. **prioress**) **1** (in an abbey) the person next in rank below an abbot (or abbess). **2** the head of a priory.
– ORIGIN Latin 'former, elder'.

prioritize (also **prioritise**) ● **v.** (**prioritizes, prioritizing, prioritized**) **1** treat as most important. **2** decide the order of importance of (items or tasks).

priority ● **n.** (pl. **priorities**) **1** the state of being more important: *safety should take priority over any other matter.* **2** a thing seen as more important than others. **3** the right to go before other traffic.

priory ● **n.** (pl. **priories**) a monastery or nunnery governed by a prior or prioress.

prise (US **prize**) ● **v.** (**prises, prising, prised**; US **prizes, prizing, prized**) force open or apart.
– ORIGIN Old French, 'a grasp'.

prism ● **n. 1** a transparent object with triangular ends, that breaks up light into the colours of the rainbow. **2** a solid geometric figure whose two ends are parallel and of the same size and shape, and whose sides are parallelograms.
– ORIGIN Greek *prisma* 'thing sawn'.

prismatic ● **adj. 1** relating to or shaped like a prism. **2** (of colours) formed or distributed by a prism.

prison ● **n.** a building where criminals or people awaiting trial are confined.
– ORIGIN Old French *prisun.*

prison camp ● **n.** a camp where prisoners of war or political prisoners are kept.

prisoner ● **n. 1** a person found guilty of a crime and sent to prison. **2** a person captured and kept confined. **3** a person trapped by a situation: *I was a prisoner of my own fame.*

prisoner of conscience ● **n.** a person imprisoned for their political or religious views.

prisoner of war ● **n.** a person captured and imprisoned by the enemy in war.

prissy ● **adj.** too concerned with behaving in a correct and respectable way.
– ORIGIN perh. from **PRIM** and **SISSY**.

Priština E
/**preesh**-ti-nuh/ the capital of the autonomous province of Kosovo.

pristine /**priss**-teen/ ● **adj. 1** in its original condition: *pristine copies of an early magazine.* **2** clean and fresh as if new.
– ORIGIN Latin *pristinus* 'former'.

privacy /**pri**-vuh-si, **pry**-vuh-si/ ● **n.** a state in which one is not watched or disturbed by others.

private ● **adj. 1** for or belonging to a particular person or group only: *his private plane.* **2** (of thoughts, feelings, etc.) not to be made known. **3** not sharing thoughts and feelings with others. **4** (of a service or industry) provided by an individual or commercial company rather than the state. **5** (of a person) working for oneself rather than for the state or an organization. **6** not connected with a person's work or official role: *rumours about his private life.* **7** where one will not be disturbed; secluded. ● **n.** (also **private soldier**) a soldier of the lowest rank in the army.
– DERIVATIVES **privately** adv.
– ORIGIN Latin *privatus* 'withdrawn from public life'.

private company ● **n.** Brit. a company whose shares may not be offered to the public for sale.

private detective (also **private investigator**) ● **n.** a detective who is not a police officer and who carries out investigations for private clients.

private enterprise ● **n.** business or industry managed by independent companies rather than the state.

privateer /pry-vuh-**teer**/ ● **n.** hist. a privately owned armed ship, authorized by a government for use in war.

private eye ● **n.** informal a private detective.

private means ● **pl. n.** Brit. income from investments, property, etc., rather than from employment.

private member ● **n.** (in the UK, Canada, Australia, and New Zealand) a member of a parliament who does not hold a government office.

private parts ● **pl. n.** euphem. a person's genitals.

private school ● **n.** Brit. an independent school supported mainly by the payment of fees by pupils.

private secretary ● **n. 1** a secretary who deals with the personal matters of their employer. **2** a civil servant acting as an aide to a senior government official.

private sector ● **n.** the part of the economy not under direct state control.

privation /pry-**vay**-sh'n/ ● **n.** a state in which one lacks essentials such as food and warmth.
– ORIGIN Latin.

privatize (also **privatise**) ● **v.** (**privatizes, privatizing, privatized**) transfer (a business or industry) from public to private ownership.
– DERIVATIVES **privatization** (also **privatisation**) n.

privet /**pri**-vit/ ● **n.** a shrub with small dark green leaves.
– ORIGIN unknown.

privilege ● **n. 1** a special right or advantage for a particular person or group. **2** an opportunity to do something regarded as a special honour: *she had the privilege of giving the opening lecture.* **3** the rights and advantages of rich and powerful people: *a young man of wealth and privilege.*
– ORIGIN Latin *privilegium* 'law affecting an individual'.

privileged ● **adj. 1** having a privilege or privileges. **2** (of information) legally protected from being made public.

privy /**pri**-vi/ ● **adj.** (**privy to**) sharing in the knowledge of (something secret). ● **n.** (pl. **privies**) a toilet in a small shed outside a house.
– ORIGIN Old French *prive* 'private'.

Privy Council ● **n.** a body of advisers appointed by a sovereign or a Governor General.

prize[1] ● **n. 1** a thing given as a reward to a winner or to mark an outstanding achieve-

ment. **2** something of great value that is worth struggling to achieve. ● **adj. 1** having been or likely to be awarded a prize. **2** outstanding of its kind. ● **v.** (**prizes, prizing, prized**) value highly.
– ORIGIN Old French *preisier* 'praise'.

prize² ● **v.** US = **PRISE.**

prizefight ● **n.** a boxing match for prize money.
– DERIVATIVES **prizefighter** n.

pro¹ ● **n.** (pl. **pros**) informal a professional.

pro² ● **n.** (pl. **pros**) (usu. in phr. **pros and cons**) an advantage or argument in favour of something. ● **prep. & adv.** in favour of.
– ORIGIN Latin, 'for, on behalf of'.

pro-¹ ● **prefix 1** supporting: *pro-choice*. **2** referring to motion forwards, out, or away: *propel*.
– ORIGIN Latin *pro* 'in front of, instead of'.

pro-² ● **prefix** before: *proactive*.
– ORIGIN Greek *pro*.

proactive ● **adj.** creating or controlling a situation rather than just responding to it.
– DERIVATIVES **proactively** adv.

probability ● **n.** (pl. **probabilities**) **1** the extent to which something is probable. **2** an event that is likely to happen: *revolution was a strong probability.*

probable ● **adj.** likely to happen or be the case.
– ORIGIN Latin *probabilis*.

probably ● **adv.** almost certainly.

probate ● **n.** the official process of proving that a will is valid.
– ORIGIN Latin *probatum* 'something proved'.

probation ● **n. 1** the release of an offender from prison, subject to a period of good behaviour under supervision. **2** a period of training and testing a person who has started a new job.
– DERIVATIVES **probationary** adj.

probationer ● **n. 1** a person serving a probationary period in a job. **2** an offender on probation.

probation officer ● **n.** a person who supervises offenders on probation.

probe ● **n. 1** a blunt-ended surgical instrument for exploring a wound or part of the body. **2** a small measuring or testing device. **3** an investigation. **4** (also **space probe**) an unmanned exploratory spacecraft. ● **v.** (**probes, probing, probed**) **1** physically explore or examine. **2** investigate closely.
– ORIGIN Latin *proba* 'proof'.

probity /proh-bi-ti/ ● **n.** honesty and decency.
– ORIGIN Latin *probitas*.

problem ● **n.** something that is difficult to deal with or understand.
– ORIGIN Greek *problēma*.

problematic ● **adj.** presenting a problem.
– DERIVATIVES **problematical** adj.

proboscis /pruh-boss-iss/ ● **n.** (pl. **proboscces** /pruh-boss-eez/, **proboscides** /pruh-boss-i-deez/, or **proboscises**) **1** the long, flexible nose of a mammal, e.g. an elephant's trunk. **2** an elongated sucking organ or mouthpart of an insect or worm.
– ORIGIN Greek *proboskis* 'means of obtaining food'.

proboscis monkey ● **n.** a monkey native to the forests of Borneo, the male of which has a large dangling nose.

procedure ● **n. 1** an established or official way of doing something. **2** a series of actions done in a certain way.
– DERIVATIVES **procedural** adj.
– ORIGIN French *procédure*.

proceed ● **v. 1** begin a course of action. **2** go on to do something. **3** (of an action) continue. **4** move forward.
– ORIGIN Latin *procedere*.

proceedings ● **pl. n. 1** an event or a series of activities. **2** action taken in a court of law to settle a dispute.

proceeds ● **pl. n.** money obtained from an event or activity.

process¹ /proh-sess/ ● **n. 1** a series of actions taken towards achieving a particular end. **2** a natural series of changes: *the ageing process*. **3** a summons to appear in a court of law. **4** a natural projection on part of the body or in an organism. ● **v. 1** perform a series of operations to change or preserve (something). **2** Computing operate on (data) by means of a program. **3** deal with, using an established procedure.
– ORIGIN Latin *processus* 'progression'.

process² /pruh-sess/ ● **v.** walk in procession.
– ORIGIN from **PROCESSION.**

procession ● **n. 1** a number of people or vehicles moving forward in an orderly way. **2** a large number of people or things coming one after the other.
– ORIGIN Latin.

processor ● **n. 1** a machine that processes something. **2** Computing a central processing unit.

pro-choice ● **adj.** supporting the right of a woman to choose to have an abortion.

proclaim ● **v. 1** announce officially or publicly. **2** declare (someone) officially or publicly to be. **3** show clearly.
– DERIVATIVES **proclamation** n.
– ORIGIN Latin *proclamare* 'cry out'.

proclivity /pruh-kliv-i-ti/ ● **n.** (pl. **proclivities**) a tendency to do something regularly; an inclination.
– ORIGIN Latin *proclivitas*.

procrastinate /proh-krass-ti-nayt/ ● **v.** (**procrastinates, procrastinating, procrastinated**) delay or postpone action.
– DERIVATIVES **procrastination** n.
– ORIGIN Latin *procrastinare* 'defer till the morning'.

procreate ● **v.** (**procreates, procreating, procreated**) produce young.
– DERIVATIVES **procreation** n. **procreative** adj.
– ORIGIN Latin *procreare* 'generate'.

proctor ● **n.** Brit. an officer in charge of discipline at certain universities.
– ORIGIN Latin *procurator* 'administrator'.

procurator fiscal ● **n.** (pl. **procurators fiscal** or **procurator fiscals**) (in Scotland) a local coroner and public prosecutor.

procure ● **v.** (**procures, procuring, procured**) obtain.
– DERIVATIVES **procurement** n.
– ORIGIN Latin *procurare* 'manage'.

procurer ● **n.** (fem. **procuress**) a person who obtains a woman as a prostitute for another person.

Procyon E
/proh-si-uhn/ the eighth-brightest star in the sky, and the brightest in the constellation Canis Minor.

prod ● v. (**prods**, **prodding**, **prodded**) **1** poke with a finger or pointed object. **2** stimulate or persuade to do something. ● n. **1** a poke. **2** a stimulus or reminder. **3** a pointed implement.
– ORIGIN perh. from **POKE** and dialect *brod* 'to goad, prod'.

prodigal ● adj. **1** using money or resources in a wasteful way. **2** lavish. ● n. (also **prodigal son**) a person who leaves home and wastes their money on pleasure but returns repentant. [ORIGIN referring to the story in the Gospel of Luke.]
– ORIGIN Latin *prodigalis*.

prodigious /pruh-dij-uhss/ ● adj. impressively large.
– DERIVATIVES **prodigiously** adv.
– ORIGIN Latin *prodigiosus*.

prodigy ● n. (pl. **prodigies**) **1** a young person with exceptional abilities. **2** an amazing or unusual thing.
– ORIGIN Latin *prodigium* 'portent'.

produce ● v. /pruh-dyooss/ (**produces**, **producing**, **produced**) **1** make, manufacture, or create. **2** cause to happen or exist. **3** show or provide for inspection or use. **4** administer the financial aspects of (a film or broadcast) or the staging of (a play). **5** supervise the making of (a musical recording). ● n. /prod-yooss/ things that have been produced or grown: *dairy produce*.
– DERIVATIVES **producer** n.
– ORIGIN Latin *producere* 'bring forth'.

product ● n. **1** an article or substance manufactured for sale. **2** a result: *her suntan was the product of a sunbed*. **3** a substance produced during a natural, chemical, or manufacturing process. **4** Math. a quantity obtained by multiplying quantities together.
– ORIGIN Latin *productum* 'something produced'.

production ● n. **1** the action of producing. **2** the amount of something produced. **3** a film, record, or play, viewed in terms of its making or staging.

production line ● n. an assembly line.

productive ● adj. **1** producing or able to produce large amounts of goods or crops. **2** achieving or producing a significant amount or result.
– DERIVATIVES **productively** adv.

productivity ● n. **1** the state of being productive. **2** the efficiency with which things are produced.

profane ● adj. **1** not holy or religious: *topics both sacred and profane*. **2** not showing respect for God or holy things. ● v. (**profanes**, **profaning**, **profaned**) treat (something holy) with a lack of respect.
– ORIGIN Latin *profanus* 'outside the temple'.

profanity ● n. (pl. **profanities**) **1** profane behaviour. **2** a swear word.

profess ● v. **1** claim that one has (a quality or feeling). **2** declare one's faith in (a religion).
– ORIGIN Latin *profiteri* 'declare publicly'.

professed ● adj. **1** (of a quality or feeling) claimed openly but often falsely. **2** openly declared.

profession ● n. **1** a job that needs training and a formal qualification. **2** a body of people engaged in a profession. **3** a claim. **4** a declaration of belief in a religion.

professional ● adj. **1** relating to or belonging to a profession. **2** engaged in an activity as a paid job rather than as an amateur. **3** competent. ● n. **1** a professional person. **2** a person who is very skilled in a particular activity.
– DERIVATIVES **professionally** adv.

professionalism ● n. the ability or skill expected of a professional.

professor ● n. **1** a university academic of the highest rank. **2** N. Amer. a university teacher.
– DERIVATIVES **professorial** adj. **professorship** n.
– ORIGIN Latin.

proffer ● v. (**proffers**, **proffering**, **proffered**) offer for acceptance.
– ORIGIN Old French *proffrir*.

proficient ● adj. competent; skilled.
– DERIVATIVES **proficiency** n.
– ORIGIN Latin *proficere* 'to advance'.

profile ● n. **1** an outline of a person's face as seen from one side. **2** a short descriptive article about someone. **3** the extent to which a person or organization attracts public notice: *her high profile as an opera star*. ● v. (**profiles**, **profiling**, **profiled**) **1** describe in a short article. **2** (**be profiled**) appear in outline.
– PHRASES **keep a low profile** try not to attract attention.
– ORIGIN from former Italian *profilo* 'a drawing or border'.

profit ● n. **1** a financial gain. **2** advantage; benefit. ● v. (**profits**, **profiting**, **profited**) benefit, especially financially.
– ORIGIN Latin *profectus* 'progress'.

profitable ● adj. **1** (of a business or activity) yielding financial gain. **2** useful: *he'd had a profitable day*.
– DERIVATIVES **profitability** n. **profitably** adv.

profit and loss account ● n. an account to which incomes and gains are added and expenses and losses taken away, so as to show the resulting profit or loss.

profiteering ● n. the making of a large profit in an unfair way.

profiterole ● n. a small ball of choux pastry filled with cream and covered with chocolate sauce.
– ORIGIN French, 'small profit'.

profit margin ● n. the difference between the cost of producing something and the price for which it is sold.

profit-sharing ● n. a system in which the people who work for a company receive a direct share of its profits.

profligate /prof-li-guht/ ● adj. **1** recklessly extravagant or wasteful. **2** indulging excessively in physical pleasures. ● n. a profligate person.
– DERIVATIVES **profligacy** n.
– ORIGIN Latin *profligatus* 'dissolute'.

pro forma /proh for-muh/ ● adv. & adj. as a matter of form or politeness. ● n. a standard document or form.
– ORIGIN Latin.

profound ● adj. (**profounder**, **profoundest**) **1** very great: *profound social change*. **2** showing great knowledge or insight. **3** demanding

deep study or thought.
– DERIVATIVES **profoundly** adv. **profundity** n.
– ORIGIN Latin *profundus* 'deep'.

Profumo E
/pruh-**fyoo**-moh/, John (Dennis) (b.1915), British Conservative politician. He was Secretary of State for War under Harold Macmillan, but resigned in 1963 following news of his relationship with the model Christine Keeler, also the mistress of a Soviet diplomat.

profuse ● **adj.** done or appearing in large quantities; abundant: *profuse apologies.*
– DERIVATIVES **profusely** adv.
– ORIGIN Latin *profusus* 'lavish'.

profusion /pruh-**fyoo**-*zh*'n/ ● **n.** an abundance or large quantity.

progenitor /proh-**jen**-i-ter/ ● **n. 1** an ancestor or parent. **2** the originator of an artistic, political, or intellectual movement.
– ORIGIN Latin.

progeny /**proj**-uh-ni/ ● **n.** offspring.
– ORIGIN Old French *progenie.*

progesterone /pruh-**jess**-tuh-rohn/ ● **n.** a hormone that stimulates the womb to prepare for pregnancy.

progestogen /proh-**jess**-tuh-juhn/ ● **n.** a hormone that maintains pregnancy and prevents further ovulation.

prognosis /prog-**noh**-siss/ ● **n.** (pl. **prognoses** /prog-**noh**-seez/) a forecast, especially of the likely course of an illness.
– ORIGIN Greek.

prognostic /prog-**noss**-tik/ ● **adj.** predicting the likely course of an illness.

prognosticate ● **v.** (**prognosticates, prognosticating, prognosticated**) make a forecast about.
– DERIVATIVES **prognostication** n. **prognosticator** n.

programmatic ● **adj.** having to do with a programme or method.

programme (US **program**) ● **n. 1** a planned series of events. **2** a radio or television broadcast. **3** a set of related measures or activities with a long-term aim. **4** a sheet or booklet giving details about a play, concert, etc. **5** (**program**) a series of software instructions to control the operation of a computer. ● **v.** (**programmes, programming, programmed**; US **programs, programing, programed**) **1** (**program**) provide (a computer) with a program. **2** cause to behave in a particular way. **3** arrange according to a plan.
– DERIVATIVES **programmable** adj. **programmer** n.
– ORIGIN Greek *programma.*

progress ● **n.** /**proh**-gress/ **1** forward movement towards a destination. **2** development towards a better or more modern state. ● **v.** /pruh-**gress**/ move or develop towards a destination or a more advanced state.
– ORIGIN Latin *progressus* 'an advance'.

progression ● **n. 1** a gradual movement or development towards a destination or a more advanced state. **2** a number of things coming one after the other.

progressive ● **adj. 1** happening gradually or in stages. **2** favouring new ideas or social reform. ● **n.** a person who supports social reform.
– DERIVATIVES **progressively** adv.

prohibit ● **v.** (**prohibits, prohibiting, prohibited**) **1** formally forbid by law or a rule. **2** make impossible; prevent.
– ORIGIN Latin *prohibere* 'keep in check'.

prohibition /proh-hi-**bi**-sh'n, proh-i-**bi**-sh'n/ ● **n. 1** the action of prohibiting. **2** an order that forbids something. **3** (**Prohibition**) the prevention by law of the manufacture and sale of alcohol in the US from 1920 to 1933.

prohibitive ● **adj. 1** forbidding or restricting something. **2** (of a price) excessively high.
– DERIVATIVES **prohibitively** adv.

project ● **n.** /**pro**-jekt/ **1** an enterprise carefully planned to achieve a particular aim. **2** a piece of research work by a student. ● **v.** /pruh-**jekt**/ **1** forecast on the basis of present trends. **2** plan. **3** stick out beyond something else. **4** send forward or outward. **5** cause (light, shadow, or an image) to fall on a surface. **6** present (a particular image) to others.
– ORIGIN Latin *projectum* 'something prominent'.

projectile ● **n.** a missile fired or thrown at a target.

projection ● **n. 1** a forecast based on present trends. **2** the projecting of an image, sound, etc. **3** a thing that sticks out.
– DERIVATIVES **projectionist** n.

projector ● **n.** a device for projecting slides or film on to a screen.

Prokofiev E
/pruh-**kof**-i-ef/, Sergei (Sergeevich) (1891–1953), Russian composer. His works include seven symphonies, the ballet *Romeo and Juliet*, and the opera *The Love for Three Oranges.*

prolapse /**proh**-laps/ ● **n.** a condition in which a part or organ of the body has slipped from its normal position.
– ORIGIN Latin *prolabi* 'slip forward'.

prolate /**proh**-layt/ ● **adj.** Geom. (of a sphere) lengthened in the direction of a polar diameter.
– ORIGIN Latin *prolatus* 'carried forward'.

prole informal, derog. ● **n.** a member of the working class.
– ORIGIN from **PROLETARIAT**.

proletarian /proh-li-**tair**-i-uhn/ ● **adj.** relating to the proletariat. ● **n.** a member of the proletariat.
– ORIGIN Latin *proletarius.*

proletariat ● **n.** workers or working-class people.

pro-life ● **adj.** seeking to ban abortion and euthanasia.
– DERIVATIVES **pro-lifer** n.

proliferate /pruh-**lif**-uh-rayt/ ● **v.** (**proliferates, proliferating, proliferated**) **1** reproduce rapidly. **2** increase rapidly in number.
– DERIVATIVES **proliferation** n.
– ORIGIN Latin *prolificus.*

prolific ● **adj. 1** producing much fruit or foliage or many offspring. **2** (of an artist, author, etc.) producing many works.
– DERIVATIVES **prolifically** adv.
– ORIGIN Latin *prolificus.*

prolix /**proh**-liks, pruh-**liks**/ ● **adj.** (of speech or writing) long and boring.
– DERIVATIVES **prolixity** n.
– ORIGIN Latin *prolixus* 'poured forth'.

prologue (US **prolog**) ● **n. 1** an introductory

p

section or scene in a book, play, or musical work. **2** an event or action leading to another.
– ORIGIN Greek *prologos*.

prolong ● v. cause to last longer.
– DERIVATIVES **prolongation** n.
– ORIGIN Latin *prolongare*.

prolonged ● adj. continuing for a long time.

prom ● n. informal **1** Brit. = **PROMENADE** (in sense 1). **2** Brit. a promenade concert. **3** N. Amer. a formal dance at a high school or college.

promenade /prom-uh-**nahd**, prom-uh-**nayd**, **prom**-uh-nahd, **prom**-uh-nayd/ ● n. **1** a paved public walk along a seafront. **2** a leisurely walk, ride, or drive. ● v. (**promenades, promenading, promenaded**) go for a leisurely walk, ride, or drive.
– ORIGIN French.

promenade concert ● n. Brit. a concert of classical music at which part of the audience stands up rather than sits.

Prometheus E
/pruh-**mee**-thi-uhss/ Gk Myth. a Titan, who returned fire to earth after Zeus had hidden it from man. As a punishment Zeus chained him to a rock and an eagle fed each day on his liver; he was rescued by Hercules.
– DERIVATIVES **Promethean** adj.

promethium /pruh-**mee**-thi-uhm/ ● n. an unstable radioactive metallic chemical element.
– ORIGIN from **PROMETHEUS**.

prominence ● n. the state of being prominent.

prominent ● adj. **1** important; famous. **2** sticking out: *a man with big, prominent eyes.* **3** particularly noticeable.
– DERIVATIVES **prominently** adv.
– ORIGIN Latin *prominere* 'jut out'.

promiscuous /pruh-**miss**-kyuu-uhss/ ● adj. having many brief sexual relationships.
– DERIVATIVES **promiscuity** n.
– ORIGIN Latin *promiscuus* 'indiscriminate'.

promise ● n. **1** an assurance that one will do something or that something will happen. **2** potential excellence: *he showed great promise as a junior officer.* ● v. (**promises, promising, promised**) **1** make a promise. **2** give good grounds for expecting.
– ORIGIN Latin *promissum*.

Promised Land ● n. (**the Promised Land**) (in the Bible) the land of Canaan, promised to Abraham and his descendants in the Book of Genesis.

promising ● adj. showing signs of future success.

promissory note ● n. a signed document containing a written promise to pay a stated sum.

promo /**proh**-moh/ ● n. (pl. **promos**) informal a promotional film, video, etc.

promontory /**prom**-uhn-tuh-ri/ ● n. (pl. **promontories**) a point of high land jutting out into the sea or a lake.
– ORIGIN Latin *promontorium*.

promote ● v. (**promotes, promoting, promoted**) **1** aid the progress of (a cause, venture, or aim). **2** publicize (a product or celebrity). **3** raise to a higher position or rank.
– ORIGIN Latin *promovere* 'move forward'.

promoter ● n. **1** the organizer of a sporting event or theatrical production. **2** a supporter of a cause or aim.

promotion ● n. **1** activity that supports or encourages. **2** the publicizing of a product or celebrity. **3** movement to a higher position or rank.
– DERIVATIVES **promotional** adj.

prompt ● v. **1** cause to happen. **2** (**prompt to/to do**) cause (someone) to do (something). **3** help or encourage (a hesitating speaker). **4** supply a forgotten word or line to (an actor). ● n. **1** a word or phrase used to prompt an actor. **2** Computing a word or symbol on a VDU screen to show that input is required. ● adj. done or acting without delay. ● adv. Brit. exactly or punctually: *12 o'clock prompt.*
– DERIVATIVES **promptly** adv.
– ORIGIN Latin *promptus* 'brought to light'.

prompter ● n. a person who prompts the actors during a play.

promulgate /**prom**-uhl-gayt/ ● v. (**promulgates, promulgating, promulgated**) **1** promote or make widely known. **2** officially declare the introduction of (a law).
– DERIVATIVES **promulgation** n.
– ORIGIN Latin *promulgare* 'expose to public view'.

prone ● adj. **1** (**prone to/to do**) likely to suffer from, do, or experience (something unfortunate). **2** lying flat and face downwards.
– ORIGIN Latin *pronus* 'leaning forward'.

prong ● n. **1** each of two or more projecting pointed parts on a fork. **2** each of the separate parts of an attack, argument, etc.
– ORIGIN perh. from German *prange* 'pinching instrument'.

pronominal /proh-**nom**-i-n'l/ ● adj. having to do with a pronoun.

pronoun ● n. a word used instead of a noun to indicate someone or something already mentioned or known, e.g. *I, this.*

pronounce ● v. (**pronounces, pronouncing, pronounced**) **1** make the sound of (a word or part of a word). **2** declare or announce. **3** (**pronounce on**) pass judgement or make a decision on.
– ORIGIN Latin *pronuntiare*.

pronounced ● adj. very noticeable: *a pronounced squint.*

pronouncement ● n. a formal public statement.

pronto ● adv. informal promptly.
– ORIGIN Spanish.

pronunciation /pruh-nun-si-**ay**-sh'n/ ● n. the way in which a word is pronounced.

proof ● n. **1** evidence proving that something is true. **2** the process of proving that something is true. **3** a series of stages in the solving of a mathematical or philosophical problem. **4** a copy of printed material used for making corrections before final printing. **5** a standard used to measure the strength of distilled alcoholic liquor. ● adj. (in combination) able to resist: *bulletproof.*
– ORIGIN Old French *proeve*.

proof positive ● n. final or absolute proof of something.

proof-read ● v. read (printed proofs) and mark any errors.
– DERIVATIVES **proof-reader** n.

prop[1] ● n. **1** a pole or beam used as a temporary support. **2** a source of support or assist-

ance. **3** (also **prop forward**) Rugby a forward at either end of the front row of a scrum. ● v. (**props**, **propped**, **propping**) **1** support with a prop. **2** lean (something) against something else. **3** (**prop up**) support (someone experiencing difficulties).
– ORIGIN prob. from Dutch *proppe* 'support for vines'.

prop[2] ● n. a portable object used on the set of a play or film.
– ORIGIN from **PROPERTY**.

propaganda ● n. information that is often biased or misleading, used to promote a political cause or point of view.
– ORIGIN Latin *congregatio de propaganda fide* 'congregation for propagation of the faith'.

propagandist ● n. esp. derog. a person who spreads propaganda.

propagate ● v. (**propagates**, **propagating**, **propagated**) **1** produce (a new plant) from a parent plant. **2** promote (an idea, knowledge, etc.) widely.
– DERIVATIVES **propagation** n. **propagator** n.
– ORIGIN Latin *propagare*.

propane /proh-payn/ ● n. a flammable gas present in natural gas and used as bottled fuel.

propel ● v. (**propels**, **propelling**, **propelled**) drive or push forwards.
– ORIGIN Latin *propellere*.

propellant ● n. **1** a compressed gas that forces out the contents of an aerosol. **2** a substance used to provide thrust in a rocket engine.

propeller ● n. a revolving shaft with two or more angled blades, for propelling a ship or aircraft.

propelling pencil ● n. a pencil with a thin lead that is extended as the point is worn away.

propensity ● n. (pl. **propensities**) a tendency to behave in a certain way.
– ORIGIN Latin *propensus* 'inclined'.

proper ● adj. **1** truly what something is said to be; genuine. **2** (after a noun) according to the precise meaning of the word: *the World Cup proper.* **3** suitable or correct. **4** excessively respectable. **5** (**proper to**) belonging exclusively to.
– ORIGIN Old French *propre*.

proper fraction ● n. a fraction that is less than one, with the numerator less than the denominator.

properly ● adv. **1** in a proper way. **2** in the precise sense.

proper noun (also **proper name**) ● n. a name for a person, place, or organization, having an initial capital letter.

property ● n. (pl. **properties**) **1** a thing or things belonging to someone. **2** a building and the land belonging to it. **3** Law the right to the possession, use, or disposal of something. **4** a quality or characteristic: *a perfumed oil with calming properties.*
– ORIGIN Latin *proprietas*.

prophecy /prof-fi-si/ ● n. (pl. **prophecies**) **1** a prediction about what will happen. **2** the power of prophesying.
– ORIGIN Greek *prophēteia*.

prophesy /prof-fi-sy/ ● v. (**prophesies**, **prophesying**, **prophesied**) predict.

prophet ● n. (fem. **prophetess**) **1** a person sent by God to teach people about his intentions. **2** a person who predicts the future.
– ORIGIN Greek *prophētēs* 'spokesman'.

prophetic /pruh-fet-ik/ ● adj. **1** accurately predicting the future. **2** having to do with a prophet or prophecy.

prophylactic /prof-fi-lak-tik/ ● adj. intended to prevent disease. ● n. a preventive medicine or course of action.
– ORIGIN Greek *prophulaktikos*.

propinquity /pruh-ping-kwi-ti/ ● n. nearness in time or space.
– ORIGIN Latin *propinquitas*.

propitiate /pruh-pish-i-ayt/ ● v. (**propitiates**, **propitiating**, **propitiated**) win or regain the favour of.
– DERIVATIVES **propitiation** n. **propitiatory** adj.
– ORIGIN Latin *propitiare* 'make favourable'.

propitious /pruh-pish-uhss/ ● adj. favourable.

proponent /pruh-poh-nuhnt/ ● n. a person who proposes a theory, plan, or project.
– ORIGIN Latin *proponere* 'put forward'.

proportion ● n. **1** a part, share, or number considered in relation to a whole. **2** the relationship of one thing to another in terms of size or quantity. **3** the correct relation between things. **4** (**proportions**) dimensions; size.
– PHRASES **in** (or **out of**) **proportion** regarded without (or with) exaggeration. **sense of proportion** the ability to judge the relative importance of things.
– ORIGIN Latin.

proportional ● adj. corresponding in size or amount to something else.
– DERIVATIVES **proportionality** n. **proportionally** adv.

proportional representation ● n. a system in which parties in an election gain seats in proportion to the number of votes cast for them.

proportionate ● adj. = **PROPORTIONAL**.

proportioned ● adj. having parts that relate in size in a particular way to other parts: *a tall, perfectly proportioned woman.*

proposal ● n. **1** a plan or suggestion. **2** the action of proposing something. **3** an offer of marriage.

propose ● v. (**proposes**, **proposing**, **proposed**) **1** put forward (an idea or plan) for consideration. **2** put forward for an official post. **3** put forward (a motion) to a lawmaking body or committee. **4** plan or intend. **5** make an offer of marriage to someone.
– ORIGIN Latin *proponere*.

proposition ● n. **1** a statement expressing a judgement or opinion. **2** a proposed scheme. **3** a matter or person to be dealt with: *it's a tough proposition.* ● v. informal ask (someone) to have sexual intercourse with one.

propound /pruh-pownd/ ● v. put forward (an idea, theory, etc.) for consideration.
– ORIGIN Latin *proponere* 'put forward'.

proprietary ● adj. **1** having to do with an owner or ownership. **2** (of a product) marketed under a registered trade name.
– ORIGIN Latin *proprietarius* 'proprietor'.

proprietary name ● n. a name of a product or service registered as a trademark.

proprietor ● n. (fem. **proprietress**) **1** the

owner of a business. **2** a holder of property.

proprietorial /pruh-pry-uh-tor-i-uhl/ ● **adj.** **1** relating to an owner. **2** possessive.

propriety ● **n.** (pl. **proprieties**) **1** correctness of behaviour or morals. **2** the quality of being appropriate. **3** (**proprieties**) the rules of generally accepted behaviour.
– ORIGIN Latin *proprietas* 'property'.

propulsion ● **n.** the action of propelling or driving forward.
– DERIVATIVES **propulsive** adj.

pro rata /proh rah-tuh, proh ray-tuh/ ● **adj.** proportional. ● **adv.** proportionally.
– ORIGIN Latin, 'according to the rate'.

prosaic /proh-zay-ik/ ● **adj.** **1** (of language) ordinary or unimaginative. **2** dull; mundane: *prosaic day-to-day concerns.*
– DERIVATIVES **prosaically** adv.

proscenium /pruh-see-ni-uhm/ ● **n.** (pl. **prosceniums** or **proscenia** /pruh-see-ni-uh/) **1** the part of a stage in front of the curtain. **2** (also **proscenium arch**) an arch framing the opening between the stage and the part of the theatre in which the audience sits.
– ORIGIN Greek *proskēnion.*

proscribe ● **v.** (**proscribes, proscribing, proscribed**) **1** officially forbid. **2** criticize or condemn.
– ORIGIN Latin *proscribere* 'publish by writing'.

prose ● **n.** ordinary written or spoken language.
– ORIGIN from Latin *prosa oratio* 'straightforward discourse'.

prosecute ● **v.** (**prosecutes, prosecuting, prosecuted**) **1** take legal proceedings against (someone) or with reference to (a crime). **2** continue (a course of action) with the intention to complete it.
– ORIGIN Latin *prosequi* 'pursue'.

prosecution ● **n.** **1** the prosecuting of someone in respect of a criminal charge. **2** (**the prosecution**) the party prosecuting someone in a lawsuit.

prosecutor ● **n.** **1** a person who prosecutes someone. **2** a lawyer who conducts the case against a person accused of a crime.

proselyte /pross-i-lyt/ ● **n.** a convert from one opinion, religion, or party to another.
– ORIGIN Greek *prosēluthos.*

proselytize /pross-i-li-tyz/ (also **proselytise**) ● **v.** (**proselytizes, proselytizing, proselytized**) convert from one religion or opinion to another.
– DERIVATIVES **proselytizer** n.

Proserpina E
/pruh-ser-pi-nuh/ Rom. Myth. Roman name for **PERSEPHONE**.

prosody /pross-uh-di/ ● **n.** **1** the patterns of rhythm and sound used in poetry. **2** the study of these patterns or the rules governing them.
– DERIVATIVES **prosodic** adj.
– ORIGIN Greek *prosōidia* 'song sung to music'.

prospect ● **n.** **1** the possibility of something occurring. **2** a mental picture of a future event. **3** (**prospects**) chances for success. **4** a person who is likely to be successful. ● **v.** (**prospect for**) search for (mineral deposits).
– DERIVATIVES **prospector** n.
– ORIGIN Latin *prospectus* 'view'.

prospective ● **adj.** likely to happen or be in the future.
– DERIVATIVES **prospectively** adv.

prospectus ● **n.** (pl. **prospectuses**) a printed booklet advertising a school or university or giving details of a share offer.
– ORIGIN Latin, 'view, prospect'.

prosper ● **v.** (**prospers, prospering, prospered**) succeed or flourish.
– ORIGIN Latin *prosperare.*

prosperous ● **adj.** rich and successful.
– DERIVATIVES **prosperity** n.

Prost E
/*rhymes with* frost/, Alain (b.1955), French motor-racing driver, who won the Formula One world championship four times between 1985 and 1993.

prostate /pross-tayt/ ● **n.** a gland surrounding the neck of the bladder in male mammals that produces a component of semen.
– ORIGIN Greek *prostatēs* 'one that stands before'.

prosthesis /pross-thee-siss/ ● **n.** (pl. **prostheses** /pross-thee-seez/) an artificial body part.
– DERIVATIVES **prosthetic** /pross-thet-ik/ adj.
– ORIGIN Greek.

prosthetics /pross-thet-iks/ ● **pl. n.** artificial body parts.

prostitute ● **n.** a person who has sexual intercourse for payment. ● **v.** (**prostitutes, prostituting, prostituted**) **1** offer (someone or oneself) as a prostitute. **2** put (one's abilities) to an unworthy use for money.
– DERIVATIVES **prostitution** n.
– ORIGIN Latin *prostituere* 'offer for sale'.

prostrate ● **adj.** /pross-trayt/ **1** lying stretched out on the ground with one's face downwards. **2** completely overcome with distress or exhaustion. ● **v.** /pross-trayt/ (**prostrates, prostrating, prostrated**) **1** (**prostrate oneself**) throw oneself flat on the ground. **2** (**be prostrated**) be completely overcome with stress or exhaustion.
– DERIVATIVES **prostration** n.
– ORIGIN Latin *prosternere.*

protactinium /proh-tak-tin-i-uhm/ ● **n.** a rare radioactive metallic chemical element.

protagonist ● **n.** **1** the leading character in a drama, film, or novel. **2** an important person in a real situation. **3** a person who actively supports a cause or idea.
– ORIGIN Greek *prōtagōnistēs.*

protean /proh-ti-uhn, proh-tee-uhn/ ● **adj.** able to change or adapt.
– ORIGIN from the Greek sea god *Proteus,* who was able to change shape at will.

protect ● **v.** **1** keep safe from harm or injury. **2** (**protected**) (of a threatened plant or animal species) safeguarded through laws against collecting or hunting.
– ORIGIN Latin *protegere* 'cover in front'.

protection ● **n.** **1** the action of protecting or the state of being protected. **2** a thing that protects. **3** the payment of money to criminals to prevent them from attacking oneself or one's property.

protectionism ● **n.** the theory or practice of shielding a country's own industries from foreign competition by taxing imports.
– DERIVATIVES **protectionist** n. & adj.

protective ● **adj.** **1** able or intended to pro-

tect. **2** having a strong wish to keep someone safe from harm.
– DERIVATIVES **protectively** adv.

protector • n. **1** a person or thing that protects. **2** (**Protector**) hist. a person who ruled a kingdom instead of or on behalf of a sovereign.

protectorate • n. a state that is controlled and protected by another.

protégé /prot-i-*zhay*, **proh**-ti-*zhay*/ • n. (fem. **protégée**) a person who is guided and supported by an older and more experienced person.
– ORIGIN French, 'protected'.

protein • n. any of a group of organic compounds forming part of body tissues and making up an important part of the diet.
– ORIGIN Greek *prōteios* 'primary'.

pro tem /proh **tem**/ • adv. & adj. for the time being.
– ORIGIN Latin *pro tempore*.

protest • n. **1** a statement or action expressing disapproval or objection. **2** an organized public demonstration objecting to an official policy. • v. **1** express an objection to what someone has said or done. **2** state strongly in response to an accusation or criticism: *she protested her innocence*.
– DERIVATIVES **protester** (also **protestor**) n.
– ORIGIN Latin *protestari* 'assert formally'.

Protestant /prot-iss-tuhnt/ • n. a member or follower of any of the Western Christian Churches that are separate from the Roman Catholic Church. • adj. relating to or belonging to any of the Protestant Churches.
– DERIVATIVES **Protestantism** n.
– ORIGIN from PROTEST.

protestation /prot-i-**stay**-sh'n/ • n. **1** a firm declaration that something is or is not the case. **2** an objection or protest.

proto- • comb. form **1** original; primitive: *prototype*. **2** first: *protozoan*.
– ORIGIN Greek *prōtos*.

protocol • n. **1** the official system of rules governing affairs of state or diplomatic occasions. **2** the accepted code of behaviour in a particular situation.
– ORIGIN first meaning 'original note of an agreement': from Greek *prōtokollon* 'first page'.

proton /**proh**-ton/ • n. Physics a subatomic particle with a positive electric charge, occurring in all atomic nuclei.
– ORIGIN Greek, 'first thing'.

protoplasm /**proh**-tuh-pla-z'm/ • n. Biol. the material comprising the living part of a cell.
– ORIGIN Greek *prōtoplasma*.

prototype • n. a first or earlier form from which other forms are developed or copied.
– DERIVATIVES **prototypical** adj.

protozoan /proh-tuh-**zoh**-uhn/ • n. a single-celled microscopic animal such as an amoeba.
– ORIGIN from Greek *protos* 'first' + *zōion* 'animal'.

protracted • adj. lasting longer than usual or expected.
– ORIGIN Latin *protrahere* 'prolong'.

protractor • n. an instrument for measuring angles, in the form of a flat semicircle marked with degrees.

protrude • v. (**protrudes**, **protruding**, **protruded**) stick out beyond or above a surface.
– DERIVATIVES **protrusion** n.
– ORIGIN Latin *protrudere* 'thrust forward'.

protuberance /pruh-tyoo-buh-ruhnss/ • n. a thing that protrudes.

protuberant • adj. bulging.
– ORIGIN Latin *protuberare* 'swell out'.

proud • adj. **1** feeling pride or satisfaction in one's own or another's achievements. **2** having an excessively high opinion of oneself. **3** having self-respect. **4** (often **proud of**) slightly projecting from a surface.
– PHRASES **do proud** informal **1** cause to feel pleased. **2** treat very well.
– DERIVATIVES **proudly** adv.
– ORIGIN Old French *prud* 'valiant'.

Proudhon E
/**proo**-don/, Pierre Joseph (1809–65), French social theorist. His pamphlet *What is Property?* argues that property, in the sense of the exploitation of one person's labour by another, is theft.

Proust E
/*rhymes with* roost/, Marcel (1871–1922), French novelist, author of the long novel *À la recherche du temps perdu*; its central theme is the releasing of the creative energies of past experience from the unconscious.
– DERIVATIVES **Proustian** adj.

prove /proov/ • v. (**proves**, **proving**, **proved**; past part. **proved** or **proven** /**proo**-v'n or **proh**-v'n/) **1** show by evidence or argument that (something) is true or exists. **2** show or be seen to be: *the scheme has proved a great success*. **3** (**prove oneself**) show one's abilities or courage.
– DERIVATIVES **provable** adj.
– ORIGIN Old French *prover*.

USAGE prove
Prove has two past participles, **proved** and **proven**. You can correctly use either in sentences such as *this hasn't been proved yet* or *this hasn't been proven yet*. However, you should always use **proven** when the word is an adjective coming before the noun: *a proven talent*, not *a proved talent*.

provenance /**prov**-uh-nuhnss/ • n. **1** the origin or earliest known history of something. **2** a record of ownership of a work of art or an antique.
– ORIGIN French.

Provençal /prov-on-**sahl**/ • n. **1** a person from Provence in southern France. **2** the language of Provence. • adj. relating to Provence.

Provence–Alpes–Côte d'Azur E
/pro-vonss-alp-koht-da-**zyoor**/ a region of SE France.

provender /**prov**-in-der/ • n. animal fodder.
– ORIGIN Old French *provendre*.

proverb • n. a short saying stating a general truth or piece of advice.
– ORIGIN Latin *proverbium*.

proverbial • adj. **1** referred to in a proverb or saying. **2** well known.

provide • v. (**provides**, **providing**, **provided**) **1** make available for use; supply. **2** (**provide with**) equip or supply (someone) with. **3** (**provide for**) make enough preparation or ar-

p

rangements for.
– DERIVATIVES **provider** n.
– ORIGIN Latin *providere* 'attend to'.

provided • **conj.** on the condition that.

providence • **n.** the protective care of God or of nature as a spiritual power.

provident • **adj.** careful in planning for the future.

providential • **adj.** happening by chance and at a favourable time.
– DERIVATIVES **providentially** adv.

providing • **conj.** on the condition that.

province • **n.** **1** a main administrative division of a country or empire. **2** (**the provinces**) the whole of a country outside the capital. **3** (**one's province**) one's particular area of knowledge, interest, or responsibility.
– ORIGIN Latin *provincia*.

provincial • **adj.** **1** relating to a province or the provinces. **2** unsophisticated or narrow-minded. • **n.** a person who lives in the regions outside the capital city of a country.
– DERIVATIVES **provincialism** n. **provinciality** n. **provincially** adv.

provision • **n.** **1** the action of providing. **2** something provided. **3** (**provision for/against**) arrangements for possible future events or requirements. **4** (**provisions**) supplies of food, drink, or equipment. **5** a condition in a legal document. • **v.** supply with provisions.

provisional • **adj.** arranged for the present, possibly to be changed later.
– DERIVATIVES **provisionally** adv.

proviso /pruh-vy-zoh/ • **n.** (pl. **provisos**) a condition attached to an agreement.
– ORIGIN from Latin *proviso quod* 'it being provided that'.

provocation • **n.** **1** the action of provoking. **2** action or speech that provokes.

provocative • **adj.** **1** deliberately causing annoyance or anger. **2** intended to arouse sexual desire or interest.
– DERIVATIVES **provocatively** adv.

provoke • **v.** (**provokes, provoking, provoked**) **1** cause (a strong reaction or emotion) in someone. **2** deliberately annoy or anger. **3** stir up to do something.
– ORIGIN Latin *provocare* 'to challenge'.

provost /prov-uhst/ • **n.** **1** Brit. a person in charge of certain university colleges and public schools. **2** Sc. a mayor.
– ORIGIN Old English.

prow /prow/ • **n.** the pointed front part of a ship.
– ORIGIN Old French *proue*.

prowess • **n.** skill or expertise in a particular activity.
– ORIGIN Old French *proesce*.

prowl • **v.** move about in a stealthy or restless way.
– PHRASES **on the prowl** moving around in a stealthy way.
– DERIVATIVES **prowler** n.
– ORIGIN unknown.

proximate • **adj.** closest in space, time, or relationship.
– ORIGIN Latin *proximatus* 'drawn near'.

proximity • **n.** nearness in space, time, or relationship.

proxy • **n.** (pl. **proxies**) **1** the authority to represent someone else, especially in voting. **2** a person authorized to act on behalf of another.
– ORIGIN from former *procuracy* 'the position of a procurator'.

Prozac /proh-zak/ • **n.** trademark a drug which is taken to treat depression.
– ORIGIN an invented name.

prude • **n.** a person who is easily shocked by matters relating to sex.
– DERIVATIVES **prudery** n. **prudish** adj.
– ORIGIN French *prudefemme* 'good woman and true'.

prudent • **adj.** acting with or showing care and thought for the future.
– DERIVATIVES **prudence** n. **prudently** adv.
– ORIGIN Latin *prudens*.

prudential • **adj.** prudent.

prune[1] • **n.** a dried plum with a black, wrinkled appearance.
– ORIGIN Greek *prounon* 'plum'.

prune[2] • **v.** (**prunes, pruning, pruned**) **1** trim (a tree or bush) by cutting away dead or unwanted branches or stems. **2** remove unwanted parts from.
– ORIGIN Old French *proignier*.

prurient /proor-i-uhnt/ • **adj.** having an excessive interest in sexual matters.
– DERIVATIVES **prurience** n.
– ORIGIN Latin *prurire* 'itch, be wanton'.

Prussia E
a former kingdom of Germany, which became a major European power under Frederick the Great. It formed the centre of Bismarck's new German Empire after 1871, but following Germany's defeat in the First World War the Prussian monarchy was abolished.
– DERIVATIVES **Prussian** adj. & n.

pry[1] • **v.** (**pries, prying, pried**) enquire too intrusively into a person's private affairs.
– ORIGIN unknown.

pry[2] • **v.** (**pries, prying, pried**) esp. N. Amer. = **PRISE.**
– ORIGIN from **PRISE.**

PS • **abbrev.** postscript.

psalm /sahm/ • **n.** a song or poem in praise of God and contained in the biblical Book of Psalms.
– DERIVATIVES **psalmist** n.
– ORIGIN Greek *psalmos* 'song sung to harp music'.

psalter /sawl-ter/ • **n.** a book containing the biblical Psalms.
– ORIGIN Greek *psaltērion* 'stringed instrument'.

psephology /se-fol-uh-ji/ • **n.** the statistical study of elections and trends in voting.
– DERIVATIVES **psephologist** n.
– ORIGIN Greek *psēphos* 'pebble, vote'.

pseud /syood/ • **n.** informal a person who tries to impress others by pretending to have knowledge or expertise they do not really possess.

pseudo /syoo-doh/ • **adj.** not genuine; fake or insincere.

pseudo- • **comb. form** false; not genuine: *pseudonym*.
– ORIGIN Greek *pseudēs* 'false'.

pseudonym /syoo-duh-nim/ • **n.** a false name, especially one used by an author.
– ORIGIN from Greek *pseudēs* 'false' + *onoma* 'name'.

pseudonymous /syoo-don-i-muhss/ • **adj.**

writing or written under a false name.

p.s.i. • abbrev. pounds per square inch.

psoriasis /suh-ry-uh-siss/ • n. a skin disease marked by red, itchy, scaly patches.
– ORIGIN Greek.

psych /syk/ • v. **1** (**psych up**) informal mentally prepare (someone) for a testing task. **2** (**psych out**) intimidate (an opponent) by appearing very confident or aggressive.

psyche /sy-ki/ • n. the human soul, mind, or spirit.
– ORIGIN Greek *psukhē* 'breath, soul'.

psychedelia /sy-kuh-**dee**-li-uh/ • n. music or art based on the experiences produced by psychedelic drugs.

psychedelic /sy-kuh-**del**-ik, sy-kuh-**dee**-lik/ • adj. **1** (of drugs) producing hallucinations. **2** having bright colours or a swirling pattern.
– ORIGIN from Greek *psukhē* 'soul' + *dēlos* 'clear, manifest'.

psychiatrist • n. a doctor specializing in the treatment of mental illness.

psychiatry /sy-**ky**-uh-tri/ • n. the branch of medicine concerned with mental illness.
– DERIVATIVES **psychiatric** /sy-ki-**a**-trik/ adj.
– ORIGIN from Greek *psukhē* 'soul, mind' + *iatreia* 'healing'.

psychic /sy-kik/ • adj. **1** relating to abilities or events that cannot be explained by natural laws, especially those involving telepathy or clairvoyance. **2** (of a person) appearing to be telepathic or clairvoyant. • n. a person claiming to have psychic powers.
– DERIVATIVES **psychical** adj. **psychically** adv.

psycho • n. (pl. **psychos**) informal a psychopath.

psycho- • comb. form relating to the mind or psychology: *psychotherapy*.
– ORIGIN Greek *psukhē* 'soul, mind'.

psychoanalyse (US **psychoanalyze**) • v. (**psychoanalyses**, **psychoanalysing**, **psychoanalysed**; US **psychoanalyzes**, **psychoanalyzing**, **psychoanalyzed**) treat using psychoanalysis.

psychoanalysis • n. a method of treating mental disorders by investigating the conscious and unconscious elements in the mind.
– DERIVATIVES **psychoanalyst** n. **psychoanalytic** adj.

psychological • adj. **1** having to do with the mind. **2** relating to psychology.
– DERIVATIVES **psychologically** adv.

psychological warfare • n. actions intended to reduce an opponent's confidence.

psychology • n. **1** the scientific study of the human mind and its functions. **2** the mental characteristics or attitude of a person.
– DERIVATIVES **psychologist** n.

psychometrics • n. the science of measuring mental abilities and processes.
– DERIVATIVES **psychometric** adj.

psychopath • n. a person having a serious mental illness that causes them to behave violently.
– DERIVATIVES **psychopathic** adj.

psychosis /sy-**koh**-siss/ • n. (pl. **psychoses** /sy-**koh**-seez/) a severe mental illness in which a person loses contact with reality.

psychosomatic /sy-koh-suh-**mat**-ik/ • adj. **1** (of a physical illness) caused or made worse by a mental factor such as stress. **2** relating to the relationship between mind and body.

psychotherapy • n. the treatment of mental disorder by psychological rather than medical means.
– DERIVATIVES **psychotherapist** n.

psychotic /sy-**kot**-ik/ • adj. relating to or having a psychosis. • n. a person with a psychosis.

PT • abbrev. physical training.

Pt • abbrev. **1** Part. **2** (**pt**) pint. **3** (**Pt.**) Point (on maps).

PTA • abbrev. parent–teacher association.

ptarmigan /**tar**-mi-guhn/ • n. a grouse of northern mountains and the Arctic, having grey and black plumage which changes to white in winter.
– ORIGIN Scottish Gaelic.

Pte • abbrev. Private (in the army).

pterodactyl /te-ruh-**dak**-til/ • n. a pterosaur of the late Jurassic period, with a long thin head and neck.
– ORIGIN from Greek *pteron* 'wing' + *daktulos* 'finger'.

pterosaur /te-ruh-sor/ • n. a fossil flying reptile of the Jurassic and Cretaceous periods.
– ORIGIN from Greek *pteron* 'wing' + *sauros* 'lizard'.

PTO • abbrev. please turn over.

Ptolemaic system (also **Ptolemaic theory**) • n. the former theory that the earth is the centre of the universe. Compare with **COPERNICAN SYSTEM**.

Ptolemy[1] E
/**tol**-uh-mi/ the name of all the Macedonian rulers of Egypt, a dynasty founded by Ptolemy, the general of Alexander the Great, who declared himself king of Egypt (as Ptolemy I) after Alexander's death. The dynasty ended with the death of Cleopatra in 30 BC.

Ptolemy[2] E
/**tol**-uh-mi/ (2nd century) Greek astronomer and geographer. His theory that the earth is the centre of the universe was adopted as Christian doctrine until the late Renaissance. His *Geography* was also a standard work for centuries.

pub • n. Brit. a building in which beer and other drinks are served.
– ORIGIN from **PUBLIC HOUSE**.

pub crawl • n. Brit. informal a tour of several pubs, with drinks at each.

puberty • n. the period during which adolescents reach sexual maturity and become able to have children.
– ORIGIN Latin *pubertas*.

pubes /pyoo-beez/ • n. **1** (pl. **pubes**) the lower part of the abdomen at the front of the pelvis, covered with hair from puberty. **2** pl. of **PUBIS**.
– ORIGIN Latin, 'pubic hair, genitals'.

pubescence /pyuu-**bess**-uhnss/ • n. the time when puberty begins.
– DERIVATIVES **pubescent** adj. & n.
– ORIGIN Latin *pubescere* 'reach puberty'.

pubic • adj. relating to the pubes or pubis.

pubis /**pyoo**-biss/ • n. (pl. **pubes** /**pyoo**-beez/) either of a pair of bones forming the two sides of the pelvis.
– ORIGIN from Latin *os pubis* 'bone of the

pubes'.

public • adj. **1** having to do with or available to the people as a whole. **2** involved in the affairs of the community: *a public figure.* **3** intended to be seen or heard by people in general: *a public apology.* **4** provided by the state rather than an independent, commercial company. • n. (**the public**) **1** ordinary people in general. **2** a group of people with a particular interest: *the reading public.*
– DERIVATIVES **publicly** adv.
– ORIGIN Latin *publicus.*

public address system • n. a system of microphones and loudspeakers used to amplify speech or music.

publican • n. Brit. a person who owns or manages a pub.
– ORIGIN Latin *publicanus.*

publication • n. **1** the action of publishing something. **2** a book or journal that is published.

public bar • n. Brit. the more plainly furnished bar in a pub.

public company • n. a company whose shares are traded freely on a stock exchange.

public enemy • n. a well-known wanted criminal.

public house • n. formal = **PUB**.

publicist • n. a person responsible for publicizing a product or celebrity.

publicity • n. **1** attention given to someone or something by the media. **2** information used for advertising or promotional purposes.

publicize (also **publicise**) • v. (**publicizes**, **publicizing**, **publicized**) **1** make widely known. **2** advertise or promote.

public limited company • n. (in the UK) a company with shares offered to the public subject to conditions of limited legal responsibility for any company debts.

public relations • pl. n. the business of creating a good public image for an organization or famous person.

public school • n. **1** (in the UK) a private fee-paying secondary school. **2** (chiefly in North America) a school supported by public funds.

public sector • n. the part of an economy that is controlled by the state.

public servant • n. a person who works for the state or for local government.

public transport • n. buses, trains, and other forms of transport that are available to the public and run on fixed routes.

public utility • n. an organization supplying the community with electricity, gas, water, or sewerage.

publish • v. **1** produce (a book, newspaper, piece of music, etc.) for public sale. **2** print in a book, newspaper, or journal so as to make generally known.
– DERIVATIVES **publishing** n.
– ORIGIN Latin *publicare* 'make public'.

publisher • n. a company or person that publishes books, newspapers, journals, or music.

Puccini E
/puu-chee-ni/, Giacomo (1858–1924), Italian composer, known for such operas as *La Bohème*, *Tosca*, and *Madama Butterfly.*

puce /pyooss/ • n. a dark red or purple-brown colour.
– ORIGIN French, 'flea, flea-colour'.

puck • n. a black disc made of hard rubber, used in ice hockey.
– ORIGIN unknown.

pucker • v. (**puckers**, **puckering**, **puckered**) tightly gather into wrinkles or small folds. • n. a wrinkle or small fold.
– ORIGIN prob. from **POCKET**.

pudding • n. **1** a cooked dessert. **2** esp. Brit. the dessert course of a meal. **3** a baked or steamed savoury dish made with suet and flour: *steak and kidney pudding.* **4** the intestines of a pig or sheep stuffed with oatmeal, spices, and meat and boiled.
– ORIGIN prob. from Old French *boudin* 'black pudding'.

pudding basin • n. a deep round bowl used for cooking steamed puddings.

puddle • n. a small pool of rainwater or other liquid on the ground.
– ORIGIN Old English, 'small ditch'.

pudendum /pyoo-den-duhm/ • n. (pl. **pudenda** /pyoo-den-duh/) a person's external genitals, especially a woman's.
– ORIGIN from Latin *pudenda membra* 'parts to be ashamed of'.

pudgy • adj. informal fat or flabby.
– ORIGIN unknown.

puerile /pyoor-yl/ • adj. childishly silly.
– ORIGIN Latin *puerilis.*

puerility /pyoor-il-i-ti/ • n. (pl. **puerilities**) childish behaviour.

puerperal fever • n. fever caused by infection of the womb after childbirth.
– ORIGIN from Latin *puer* 'child, boy' + *parus* 'bearing'.

Puerto Rico E
/pwair-toh ree-koh/ an island of the Greater Antilles in the Caribbean; capital, San Juan. It is an autonomous commonwealth in voluntary association with the US.
– DERIVATIVES **Puerto Rican** adj. & n.

puff • n. **1** a short amount of air or smoke. **2** an act of drawing quickly on a pipe, cigarette, or cigar. **3** a light pastry case. **4** informal breath: *out of puff.* • v. **1** breathe in repeated short gasps. **2** move with short, noisy puffs of air or steam. **3** smoke a pipe, cigarette, or cigar. **4** (**be puffed/puffed out**) be out of breath. **5** (**puff out/up**) swell or cause to swell.

puff adder • n. a large African viper which inflates the upper part of its body and hisses loudly when under threat.

puffa jacket • n. Brit. a type of thick padded jacket.

puffball • n. a fungus with a large round head which bursts when ripe to release a cloud of spores.

puffery • n. exaggerated praise.

puffin • n. a seabird of the North Atlantic, with a large brightly coloured triangular bill.
– ORIGIN prob. from **PUFF**.

puff pastry • n. light flaky pastry.

puffy • adj. (**puffier**, **puffiest**) **1** softly rounded: *puffy clouds.* **2** (of a part of the body) swollen and soft.
– DERIVATIVES **puffiness** n.

pug • n. a small dog with a broad flat nose and deeply wrinkled face.

– ORIGIN perh. from German.

pugilist /pyoo-ji-list/ ● n. dated a boxer.
– DERIVATIVES **pugilistic** adj.
– ORIGIN Latin *pugil* 'boxer'.

Pugin E
/pyoo-jin/, Augustus Welby Northmore (1812–52), English architect and theorist. A leader of the Gothic revival, he is known for his work on the external detail and internal fittings for the Houses of Parliament.

pugnacious /pug-nay-shuhss/ ● adj. eager or quick to argue or fight.
– DERIVATIVES **pugnacity** n.
– ORIGIN Latin *pugnare* 'to fight'.

pug nose ● n. a short nose with an upturned tip.

puke informal ● v. (**pukes**, **puking**, **puked**) vomit. ● n. vomit.

pukka /puk-kuh/ ● adj. **1** genuine. **2** socially acceptable. **3** informal excellent.
– ORIGIN Hindi, 'cooked, ripe, substantial'.

pulchritude /pul-kri-tyood/ ● n. literary beauty.
– ORIGIN Latin *pulcher* 'beautiful'.

pule /pyool/ ● v. (**pules**, **puling**, **puled**) literary cry in a complaining or weak way.

Pulitzer E
/puu-lit-ser/, Joseph (1847–1911), Hungarian-born American newspaper proprietor and editor, who established the annual Pulitzer Prizes, awarded for achievement in American journalism, literature, or music.

pull ● v. **1** apply force to (something) so as to move it towards oneself or the origin of the force. **2** remove by pulling. **3** move steadily: *the bus pulled away.* **4** move oneself with effort: *she pulled away from him.* **5** strain (a muscle, ligament, etc.). **6** attract as a customer. **7** (**pull at/on**) take deep breaths from (a cigarette). **8** informal cancel (an event). **9** informal succeed in attracting sexually. **10** informal bring out (a weapon) for use. ● n. **1** an act of pulling. **2** a deep drink of something or a breath of smoke from a cigarette, pipe, etc. **3** a force, influence, or attraction.
– PHRASES **pull back** retreat. **pull someone's leg** deceive someone for a joke. **pull off** informal succeed in achieving or winning (something difficult). **pull out** withdraw. **pull strings** make use of one's influence to gain an advantage. **pull oneself together** regain one's self-control. **pull one's weight** do one's fair share of work.
– ORIGIN Old English, 'pluck, snatch'.

pullet ● n. a young hen.
– ORIGIN Old French *poulet*.

pulley ● n. (pl. **pulleys**) a wheel with a grooved rim around which a rope, chain, or belt passes, used to raise heavy weights.
– ORIGIN Old French *polie*.

pullover ● n. a knitted garment put on over the head and covering the top half of the body.

pullulate /pul-yuu-layt/ ● v. (**pullulates**, **pullulating**, **pullulated**) **1** reproduce or spread so as to become very widespread. **2** be full of activity.
– ORIGIN Latin *pullulare* 'to sprout'.

pulmonary /pul-muh-nuh-ri/ ● adj. relating to the lungs.
– ORIGIN Latin *pulmo* 'lung'.

pulp ● n. **1** a soft, wet mass of crushed material. **2** the soft fleshy part of a fruit. **3** a soft, wet mass of fibres made from rags or wood, used in papermaking. ● v. crush into a pulp. ● adj. (of writing) popular and badly written: *pulp fiction*.
– DERIVATIVES **pulpy** adj.
– ORIGIN Latin *pulpa*.

pulpit ● n. a raised platform in a church or chapel from which the preacher delivers a sermon.
– ORIGIN Latin *pulpitum* 'platform'.

pulsar /pul-sar/ ● n. a type of star that gives off regular rapid pulses of radio waves.
– ORIGIN from *pulsating star*.

pulsate /pul-sayt/ ● v. (**pulsates**, **pulsating**, **pulsated**) **1** expand and contract with strong regular movements. **2** produce a regular throbbing feeling or sound. **3** (**pulsating**) very exciting.
– DERIVATIVES **pulsation** n.
– ORIGIN Latin *pulsare*.

pulse[1] ● n. **1** the regular throbbing of the arteries as blood is sent through them. **2** a single vibration or short burst of sound, electric current, light, etc. **3** a musical beat or other regular rhythm. ● v. (**pulses**, **pulsing**, **pulsed**) pulsate.
– ORIGIN Latin *pulsus* 'beating'.

pulse[2] ● n. the edible seeds of some plants of the pea family, such as lentils.
– ORIGIN Latin *puls* 'porridge of meal or pulse'.

pulverize (also **pulverise**) ● v. (**pulverizes**, **pulverizing**, **pulverized**) **1** crush to fine particles. **2** informal defeat utterly.
– ORIGIN Latin *pulverizare*.

puma ● n. a large American wild cat with a tawny or greyish coat.
– ORIGIN from a South American Indian language.

pumice /pum-iss/ ● n. a light form of solidified lava, used to remove hard skin.
– ORIGIN Old French *pomis*.

pummel ● v. (**pummels**, **pummelling**, **pummelled**; US **pummels**, **pummeling**, **pummeled**) strike repeatedly with the fists.
– ORIGIN from **POMMEL**.

pump[1] ● n. a mechanical device using suction or pressure to raise or move liquids, compress gases, or force air into inflatable objects. ● v. **1** move by or as if by a pump. **2** fill (something) with (liquid, gas, etc.). **3** move vigorously up and down.
– PHRASES **pump iron** informal exercise with weights.
– ORIGIN Dutch *pomp* 'ship's pump'.

pump[2] ● n. **1** esp. N. Engl. a plimsoll. **2** a light shoe for dancing.
– ORIGIN unknown.

pumpernickel /pum-per-ni-k'l/ ● n. dark, heavy German bread made from wholemeal rye.
– ORIGIN German.

pumpkin ● n. **1** a large rounded orange-yellow fruit with a thick rind and edible flesh. **2** Brit. = **SQUASH**[2].
– ORIGIN from former French *pompon*.

pun ● n. a joke that uses the different meanings of a word or the fact that there are words of the same sound and different meanings. ● v. (**puns**, **punning**, **punned**) make a pun.

p

– ORIGIN uncertain.

punch[1] • v. **1** strike with the fist. **2** press (a button or key on a machine). • n. **1** a blow with the fist. **2** informal effectiveness: *photos give their argument extra punch.*

– ORIGIN from **POUNCE**.

punch[2] • n. **1** a device or machine for making holes in paper, metal, etc. **2** a tool or machine for impressing a design or stamping a die on a material. • v. **1** pierce a hole in (a material). **2** pierce (a hole).

– ORIGIN perh. from *puncheon*, in the same sense, or from **PUNCH**[1].

punch[3] • n. a drink made from wine or spirits mixed with water, fruit juices, spices, etc.

– ORIGIN prob. from a Sanskrit word meaning 'five' (because the drink had five ingredients).

punchbag • n. Brit. a stuffed bag suspended from a rope, used for punching as exercise or training.

punchball • n. Brit. a stuffed ball mounted on a stand, used for punching as exercise or training.

punchbowl • n. **1** a deep bowl for mixing and serving punch. **2** esp. Brit. a deep round hollow in a hilly area.

punch-drunk • adj. confused or numb as a result of being punched many times.

punchline • n. the final part of a joke or story, providing the humour or climax.

punch-up • n. informal, esp. Brit. a brawl.

punchy • adj. (**punchier**, **punchiest**) effective; forceful.

punctilio /pungk-ti-li-oh/ • n. (pl. **punctilios**) a fine or petty point of behaviour or procedure.

– ORIGIN Italian *puntiglio* and Spanish *puntillo* 'small point'.

punctilious /pungk-**ti**-li-uhss/ • adj. showing great attention to detail or correct behaviour.

punctual • adj. happening or keeping to the appointed time.

– DERIVATIVES **punctuality** n. **punctually** adv.

– ORIGIN Latin *punctualis*.

punctuate /**pungk**-chuu-ayt, **pungk**-tyuu-ayt/ • v. (**punctuates**, **punctuating**, **punctuated**) **1** interrupt at intervals throughout. **2** put punctuation marks in.

– ORIGIN Latin *punctuare* 'bring to a point'.

punctuation • n. the marks, such as full stop, comma, and brackets, used in writing to separate sentences and to make meaning clear.

puncture • n. a small hole caused by a sharp object. • v. (**punctures**, **puncturing**, **punctured**) **1** make a puncture in. **2** cause (a person's mood, feeling, etc.) to suddenly collapse.

– ORIGIN Latin *punctura*.

pundit /**pun**-dit/ • n. an expert who frequently gives opinions about a subject in public.

– DERIVATIVES **punditry** n.

– ORIGIN Sanskrit, 'learned'.

Pune E
var. of **POONA**.

pungent /**pun**-juhnt/ • adj. **1** having a sharply strong taste or smell. **2** (of remarks or humour) sharp.

– DERIVATIVES **pungency** n.

– ORIGIN Latin *pungere* 'to prick'.

Punic Wars E
/**pyoo**-nik/ three wars between Rome and Carthage in the period 264 to 146 BC, which ended in the total destruction of Carthage and the unquestioned dominance of Rome in the western Mediterranean.

punish • v. **1** impose a penalty on (someone) for an offence. **2** impose a penalty on someone for (an offence). **3** treat harshly or unfairly.

– DERIVATIVES **punishable** adj.

– ORIGIN Latin *punire*.

punishment • n. **1** the action of punishing. **2** the penalty imposed for an offence. **3** informal rough treatment.

punitive /**pyoo**-ni-tiv/ • adj. intended as punishment.

Punjab[1] E
/puhn-**jahb**/ a state of NW India; capital, Chandigarh.

Punjab[2] E
/puhn-**jahb**/ a province of Pakistan; capital, Lahore.

Punjabi /pun-**jah**-bi, puun-**jah**-bi/ (also **Panjabi** /pan-**jah**-bi/) • n. (pl. **Punjabis**) **1** a person from Punjab. **2** the language of Punjab.

punk • n. **1** (also **punk rock**) a loud, fast form of rock music with aggressive lyrics and behaviour. **2** (also **punk rocker**) an admirer or player of punk music. **3** informal, esp. N. Amer. a worthless person or a criminal. • adj. relating to punk rock.

– ORIGIN perh. from archaic *punk* 'prostitute' or from **SPUNK**.

punnet • n. Brit. a small light container for fruit.

– ORIGIN perh. from dialect *pun* 'a pound'.

punt[1] /punt/ • n. a long, narrow, flat-bottomed boat that is moved forward with a long pole. • v. travel in a punt.

– ORIGIN Latin *ponto*.

punt[2] /punt/ Brit. informal • v. bet on or make a risky investment in. • n. a bet.

– ORIGIN French *ponte* 'player against the bank'.

punt[3] /puunt/ • n. the former basic unit of money of the Republic of Ireland.

– ORIGIN Irish, 'a pound'.

punter • n. **1** informal a person who places a bet. **2** Brit. informal a customer or client.

puny /**pyoo**-ni/ • adj. (**punier**, **puniest**) **1** small and weak. **2** not very good.

– DERIVATIVES **punily** adv.

– ORIGIN Old French *puisne* 'junior or inferior person'.

pup • n. **1** a puppy. **2** a young wolf, seal, rat, or other mammal. • v. (**pups**, **pupping**, **pupped**) give birth to a pup or pups.

– ORIGIN from **PUPPY**.

pupa /**pyoo**-puh/ • n. (pl. **pupae** /**pyoo**-pee/) an insect in the form between larva and adult.

– DERIVATIVES **pupal** adj.

– ORIGIN Latin, 'girl, doll'.

pupate • v. (**pupates**, **pupating**, **pupated**) become a pupa.

pupil[1] • n. a person who is taught by another.

– ORIGIN Latin *pupillus* 'little boy' and *pupilla* 'little girl'.

pupil[2] • n. the dark circular opening in the

centre of the iris of the eye, which alters the amount of light reaching the retina.
– ORIGIN Latin *pupilla* 'little doll' (from the tiny reflected images visible in the eye).

puppet • n. **1** a model of a person or animal which can be moved either by strings or by a hand inside it. **2** a person under the control of another.
– DERIVATIVES **puppeteer** n. **puppetry** n.
– ORIGIN from **POPPET**.

puppy • n. (pl. **puppies**) a young dog.
– ORIGIN perh. from Old French *poupee* 'doll, toy'.

puppy fat • n. fat on a child's body which disappears as they grow up.

puppy love • n. strong but short-lived love felt by a young person.

purblind /per-blynd/ • adj. **1** partially sighted. **2** lacking awareness or understanding.
– ORIGIN from **PURE** 'utterly' + **BLIND**.

Purcell E
/per-s'l, per-sel/, Henry (1659–95), English composer. His works include choral odes and songs for royal occasions, as well as the first English opera, *Dido and Aeneas*.

purchase • v. (**purchases**, **purchasing**, **purchased**) get by payment; buy. • n. **1** the action of buying. **2** a thing bought. **3** firm contact or grip.
– DERIVATIVES **purchaser** n.
– ORIGIN Old French *pourchacier* 'seek to obtain or bring about'.

purdah /per-duh/ • n. the practice in certain Muslim and Hindu societies of screening women from men or strangers.
– ORIGIN Urdu and Persian, 'veil'.

pure • adj. **1** not mixed with any other substance or material. **2** free of impurities. **3** innocent or good. **4** complete; nothing but: *a shout of pure anger.* **5** theoretical rather than practical: *pure mathematics.* **6** (of a sound) perfectly in tune and with a clear tone.
– DERIVATIVES **purely** adv.
– ORIGIN Latin *purus*.

pure-bred • adj. (of an animal) bred from parents of the same breed.

purée /pyoor-ay/ • n. a soft, wet mass of crushed or sieved fruit or vegetables. • v. (**purées**, **puréeing**, **puréed**) make a purée of.
– ORIGIN French, 'purified'.

purgation /per-gay-sh'n/ • n. purification.
– ORIGIN Latin.

purgative /per-guh-tiv/ • adj. have a strong laxative effect. • n. a laxative.

purgatory /per-guh-tuh-ri/ • n. (pl. **purgatories**) (in Catholic belief) a place to which the souls of sinners who are making up for their sins go before going to heaven.
– ORIGIN Latin *purgatorium*.

purge • v. (**purges**, **purging**, **purged**) **1** rid (someone or something) of people or undesirable or harmful things. **2** empty one's bowels as a result of taking a laxative. • n. an act of purging.
– ORIGIN Latin *purgare* 'purify'.

purify • v. (**purifies**, **purified**) make pure.
– DERIVATIVES **purification** n.

puritan • n. **1** (**Puritan**) a member of a group of English Protestants in the 16th and 17th centuries who sought to simplify forms of worship. **2** a person with strong moral beliefs who is critical of the behaviour of others.
– DERIVATIVES **puritanical** adj.

purity • n. the state of being pure.

purl • adj. (of a knitting stitch) made by putting the needle through the front of the stitch from right to left.
– ORIGIN uncertain.

purler • n. Brit. informal a headlong fall.
– ORIGIN from dialect *purl* 'upset'.

purlieus /per-lyooz/ • pl. n. the area near or surrounding a place.
– ORIGIN prob. from Old French *puralee* 'a walk round to settle boundaries'.

purloin /per-loyn/ • v. formal steal.
– ORIGIN Old French *purloigner* 'put away'.

purple • n. a colour between red and blue. • adj. of a colour between red and blue.
– DERIVATIVES **purplish** adj. **purply** adj.
– ORIGIN Greek *porphura*, referring to molluscs that yielded a crimson dye.

purple patch • n. informal a run of success or good luck.

purple prose • n. prose that is too elaborate.

purport • v. /per-port/ appear to be or do, especially falsely. • n. /per-port/ the meaning of something.
– ORIGIN Latin *proportare*.

purpose • n. **1** the reason for which something is done or for which something exists. **2** strong determination. • v. (**purposes**, **purposing**, **purposed**) formal have as one's aim.
– PHRASES **on purpose** deliberately.
– ORIGIN Old French *porpos*.

purposeful • adj. having or showing determination.
– DERIVATIVES **purposefully** adv.

purposeless • adj. having no purpose.

purposely • adv. deliberately.

purposive • adj. having a clear purpose.

purr • v. **1** (of a cat) make a low continuous sound expressing contentment. **2** (of a vehicle or engine) move or run smoothly while making a similar sound. • n. a purring sound.

purse • n. **1** a small pouch for carrying money. **2** N. Amer. a handbag. **3** money for spending. **4** a sum of money given as a prize in a sporting contest. • v. (**purses**, **pursing**, **pursed**) form (one's lips) into a tight round shape.
– ORIGIN Latin *bursa*.

purser • n. a ship's officer who keeps the accounts.

pursuance • n. formal the carrying out of a plan or action.

pursuant /per-syoo-uhnt/ • adv. (**pursuant to**) formal in accordance with.
– ORIGIN Old French.

pursue • v. (**pursues**, **pursuing**, **pursued**) **1** follow in order to catch or attack. **2** try to achieve (a goal). **3** engage in or continue with (an activity). **4** continue to investigate or discuss.
– ORIGIN Old French *pursuer*.

pursuit • n. **1** the action of pursuing. **2** a leisure or sporting activity.

purulent /pyoor-uu-luhnt/ • adj. containing or giving out pus.
– ORIGIN Latin *purulentus*.

purvey • v. provide or supply (food or drink)

as one's business.
– DERIVATIVES **purveyor** n.
– ORIGIN Old French *purveier* 'foresee'.

purview ● n. the range of the influence or concerns of something: *the case may be within the purview of the legislation.*
– ORIGIN Old French *purveu* 'foreseen'.

pus ● n. a thick yellowish or greenish liquid produced in infected tissue.
– ORIGIN Latin.

Pusey E
/pyoo-zi/, Edward Bouverie (1800–82), English theologian. He founded the Oxford Movement and became its leader after the withdrawal of John Henry Newman (1841).

push ● v. **1** apply force to (someone or something) so as to move them away from oneself or from the source of the force. **2** move (one's body or a part of it) into a specified position. **3** move forward by using force. **4** urge (someone) to greater effort. **5** (**push for**) demand persistently. **6** informal promote the use or acceptance of. **7** informal sell (an illegal drug). ● n. **1** an act of pushing. **2** a great effort: *one last push.*
– PHRASES **at a push** Brit. informal only if necessary or with difficulty. **when push comes to shove** informal when one must commit oneself to action.
– DERIVATIVES **pusher** n.
– ORIGIN Old French *pousser.*

pushbike ● n. Brit. informal a bicycle.

pushchair ● n. Brit. a folding chair on wheels, in which a young child can be pushed along.

Pushkin E
/puush-kin/, Aleksandr (Sergeevich) (1799–1837), Russian poet, novelist, and dramatist. His works include the verse novel *Eugene Onegin* and the blank-verse historical drama *Boris Godunov.*

pushover ● n. informal **1** a person who is easy to influence or defeat. **2** a thing that is easily done.

pushy ● adj. (**pushier**, **pushiest**) excessively self-assertive or ambitious.

pusillanimous /pyoo-si-lan-i-muhss/ ● adj. lacking courage.
– DERIVATIVES **pusillanimity** /pyoo-si-luh-nim-i-ti/ n.
– ORIGIN from Latin *pusillus* 'very small' + *animus* 'mind'.

puss ● n. informal a cat.
– ORIGIN prob. from German *pūs* or Dutch *poes.*

pussy ● n. (pl. **pussies**) **1** (also **pussy cat**) informal a cat. **2** vulgar a woman's genitals.

pussyfoot ● v. (**pussyfoots**, **pussyfooting**, **pussyfooted**) act very cautiously.

pussy willow ● n. a willow with soft fluffy catkins that appear before the leaves.

pustule /pus-tyool/ ● n. a small blister or pimple containing pus.
– DERIVATIVES **pustular** adj.
– ORIGIN Latin *pustula.*

put ● v. (**puts**, **putting**, **put**) **1** move to or place in a particular position. **2** bring into a particular state: *she tried to put me at ease.* **3** (**put on/on to**) make subject to: *the decision to put VAT on domestic fuel.* **4** give a value, figure, or limit to. **5** express in a particular way. **6** (of a ship) go in a particular direction: *the boat put out to sea.* **7** throw (a shot or weight) as an athletic sport.
– PHRASES **put down 1** suppress (an uprising or riot) by force. **2** kill (a sick, old, or injured animal). **3** pay (a sum) as a deposit. **4** informal humiliate by criticizing in the presence of others. **put off 1** cancel or postpone an appointment with. **2** cause to feel dislike or lose enthusiasm. **3** distract. **put on 1** present or provide (a play, service, etc.). **2** become heavier by (a specified amount). **3** assume (an expression, accent, etc.). **put out** inconvenience, upset, or annoy. **put up 1** present, provide, or offer. **2** accommodate for a short time. **3** propose for election or adoption. **put up to** informal encourage to do (something wrong or unwise). **put up with** tolerate.
– ORIGIN Old English.

putative /pyoo-tuh-tiv/ ● adj. generally considered to be.
– ORIGIN Latin *putativus.*

put-down ● n. informal a humiliating or critical remark.

Putin E
/poo-teen/, Vladimir (b.1952), Russian statesman, Prime Minister of the Russian Federation 1999–2000, and President since 2000.

putrefy /pyoo-tri-fy/ ● v. (**putrefies**, **putrefying**, **putrefied**) decay or rot and produce a very unpleasant smell.
– DERIVATIVES **putrefaction** n.
– ORIGIN Latin *putrefacere.*

putrescent /pyoo-tress-uhnt/ ● adj. becoming putrid; rotting.

putrid ● adj. **1** decaying or rotting and producing a very unpleasant smell. **2** informal very unpleasant.
– ORIGIN Latin *putridus.*

putsch /puuch/ ● n. a violent attempt to overthrow a government.
– ORIGIN Swiss German, 'thrust, blow'.

putt /put/ ● v. (**putts**, **putting**, **putted**) strike a golf ball gently so that it rolls into or near a hole. ● n. a stroke of this kind.
– ORIGIN Scots form of **PUT**.

puttee /put-tee/ ● n. a long strip of cloth wound round the leg from ankle to knee for protection and support.
– ORIGIN Hindi, 'band, bandage'.

putter/put-ter/ ● n. the rapid irregular sound of a small petrol engine. ● v. (**putters**, **puttering**, **puttered**) move with or make such a sound.

putting green ● n. a smooth area of short grass surrounding a hole on a golf course.

Puttnam E
/put-nuhm/, Sir David (Terence) (b.1941), English film producer, known for such films as *Chariots of Fire* and *The Killing Fields.*

putty ● n. a paste that is easily pressed into shape and hardens as it sets, used for sealing glass in window frames, filling holes in wood, etc.
– ORIGIN French *potée* 'potful'.

puzzle ● v. (**puzzles**, **puzzling**, **puzzled**) **1** confuse because difficult to understand. **2** think hard about something difficult to understand. ● n. **1** a game, toy, or problem designed to test mental skills or knowledge. **2** a person or thing that is difficult to understand.

– DERIVATIVES **puzzlement** n. **puzzler** n.
– ORIGIN unknown.

PVA • abbrev. polyvinyl acetate, a synthetic resin used in paints and glues.

PVC • abbrev. polyvinyl chloride, a synthetic resin used in pipes, flooring, and other products.

> **Pygmalion** E
> /pig-**may**-li-uhn/ Gk Myth. a king of Cyprus who made an ivory statue of a beautiful woman and loved it so much that in answer to his prayer Aphrodite gave it life.

pygmy (also **pigmy**) • n. (pl. **pygmies**) **1** a member of a people of very short stature in equatorial Africa. **2** a person who is lacking in a particular respect: *intellectual pygmies.* • adj. very small; dwarf.
– ORIGIN Greek *pugmaios* 'dwarf'.

pyjamas (US **pajamas**) • pl. n. a suit of loose trousers and jacket for sleeping in.
– ORIGIN from the Persian words for 'leg' + 'clothing'.

pylon • n. (also **electricity pylon**) a tall metal structure for carrying electricity cables.
– ORIGIN Greek *pulōn* 'gateway'.

pylorus /py-**lor**-uhss/ • n. (pl. **pylori** /py-**lor**-I/) the opening from the stomach into the small intestine.
– ORIGIN Greek *pulouros* 'gatekeeper'.

> **Pyongyang** E
> /pyong-**yang**/ the capital of North Korea.

pyramid • n. **1** a very large stone structure with a square or triangular base and sloping sides that meet in a point at the top. **2** Geom. a polyhedron of which one face is a polygon and the other faces are triangles with a common vertex.
– DERIVATIVES **pyramidal** adj.
– ORIGIN Greek *puramis*.

pyramid selling • n. a system of selling goods in which agency rights are sold to an increasing number of distributors at successively lower levels.

pyre • n. a large heap of wood on which a dead body is ritually burnt.
– ORIGIN Greek *pur* 'fire'.

> **Pyrenees** E
> /pi-ruh-**neez**/ a range of mountains between France and Spain, extending from the Atlantic coast to the Mediterranean.
> – DERIVATIVES **Pyrenean** adj.

Pyrex • n. trademark a hard heat-resistant type of glass.

pyridoxine /pi-ri-**dok**-sin, pi-ri-**dok**-seen/ • n. vitamin B_6, a compound present in cereals, liver oils, and yeast, and important in the metabolism of fats.
– ORIGIN from *pyrid(ine)* (a liquid chemical) + *oxy(gen)*.

pyrites /py-ry-teez/ (also **iron pyrites** or **pyrite**) • n. a shiny yellow mineral that is a compound of iron and sulphur.
– ORIGIN Greek *puritēs* 'of fire'.

pyro- • comb. form relating to fire: *pyromania.*
– ORIGIN Greek *pur* 'fire'.

pyromania • n. a very strong desire to set fire to things.
– DERIVATIVES **pyromaniac** n.

pyrotechnic /py-ruh-**tek**-nik/ • adj. **1** relating to fireworks. **2** brilliant or spectacular.

pyrotechnics • pl. n. **1** a firework display. **2** the art of making fireworks or staging firework displays. **3** a spectacular performance or display: *vocal pyrotechnics.*

pyrrhic /**pir**-rik/ • adj. (of a victory) won at too great a cost to have been worthwhile for the victor.
– ORIGIN named after *Pyrrhus*, a king of ancient Epirus whose victory over the Romans incurred heavy losses.

> **Pythagoras** E
> /py-**thag**-uh-ruhss/ *c.*580–500 BC, Greek philosopher, best known for his theorem of the right-angled triangle. His analysis of the courses of the sun, moon, and stars into circular motions was not set aside until the 17th century.
> – DERIVATIVES **Pythagorean** /py-thag-uh-**ree**-uhn/ adj. & n.

Pythagoras' theorem • n. the theorem that the square on the hypotenuse of a right-angled triangle is equal in area to the sum of the squares on the other two sides.

python • n. a large snake which crushes its prey.
– ORIGIN Greek *Puthōn*, a huge serpent killed by Apollo.

pyx /piks/ • n. (in the Christian Church) the container in which the blessed bread of the Eucharist is kept.
– ORIGIN Greek *puxis* 'box'.

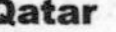

Qq

Q[1] (also **q**) • n. (pl. **Qs** or **Q's**) the seventeenth letter of the alphabet.

Q[2] • abbrev. question.

> **Qaddafi** E
> var. of **Gaddafi**.

> **Qatar** E
> /ka-**tar**/ a sheikhdom occupying a peninsula on the west coast of the Persian Gulf; capital, Doha.
> – DERIVATIVES **Qatari** adj. & n.

QC • abbrev. Law Queen's Counsel.

QED • abbrev. quod erat demonstrandum, used to convey that something proves the truth of one's claim.
– ORIGIN Latin, 'which was to be demonstrated'.

qt • abbrev. quart(s).

qua /kway, kwah/ • conj. formal in the capacity of.
– ORIGIN Latin.

quack[1] • n. the harsh sound made by a duck. • v. make this sound.

quack[2] • n. **1** an unqualified person who falsely claims to have medical knowledge. **2** Brit. informal a doctor.
– DERIVATIVES **quackery** n.
– ORIGIN Dutch *quacksalver.*

quad • n. **1** a quadrangle. **2** a quadruplet.

quad bike • n. a motorcycle with four large tyres, for off-road use.

quadrangle • n. **1** a four-sided geometrical figure. **2** a square or rectangular courtyard enclosed by buildings.
– DERIVATIVES **quadrangular** adj.
– ORIGIN from Latin *quadri-* 'four' + *angulus* 'corner, angle'.

quadrant • n. **1** each of four parts of a circle, plane, etc. divided by two lines or planes at right angles. **2** hist. an instrument for measuring altitude in astronomy and navigation.
– ORIGIN Latin *quadrans* 'quarter'.

quadraphonic /kwod-ruh-fon-ik/ • adj. (of sound reproduction) transmitted through four channels.

quadrate /kwod-ruht/ • adj. roughly square or rectangular.
– ORIGIN Latin *quadrare* 'make square'.

quadratic /kwod-rat-ik/ • adj. Math. involving the second and no higher power of an unknown quantity or variable.

quadrennial /kwod-ren-ni-uhl/ • adj. lasting for or recurring every four years.
– ORIGIN from Latin *quadri-* 'four' + *annus* 'year'.

quadri- • comb. form four; having four: *quadriplegia.*
– ORIGIN Latin.

quadriceps /kwod-ri-seps/ • n. (pl. **quadriceps**) a large muscle at the front of the thigh.
– ORIGIN Latin, 'four-headed'.

quadrilateral • n. a four-sided figure. • adj. having four straight sides.

quadrille /kwod-ril/ • n. a square dance performed by four couples.
– ORIGIN French.

quadrillion /kwod-ril-lyuhn/ • cardinal number a thousand million million.

quadriplegia /kwod-ri-plee-juh/ • n. Med. paralysis of all four limbs.
– DERIVATIVES **quadriplegic** adj. & n.

quadruped /kwod-ruu-ped/ • n. an animal which has four feet.
– ORIGIN from Latin *quadru-* 'four' + *pes* 'foot'.

quadruple • adj. **1** consisting of four parts or elements. **2** four times as much or as many. • v. (**quadruples**, **quadrupling**, **quadrupled**) multiply by four.
– ORIGIN Latin *quadruplus.*

quadruplet • n. each of four children born at one birth.

quaff /kwoff/ • v. drink heartily.
– DERIVATIVES **quaffable** adj.

quagmire /kwag-myr, kwog-myr/ • n. **1** a soft boggy area of land that gives way underfoot. **2** a complicated or difficult situation.
– ORIGIN from former *quag* 'a marshy place' + MIRE.

quail[1] • n. (pl. **quail** or **quails**) a small short-tailed game bird.
– ORIGIN Old French *quaille.*

quail[2] • v. feel or show fear or worry.
– ORIGIN unknown.

quaint • adj. attractively unusual or old-fashioned.
– ORIGIN Old French *cointe* 'wise'.

quake • v. (**quakes**, **quaking**, **quaked**) **1** (of the earth) shake or tremble. **2** shudder with fear. • n. informal an earthquake.
– ORIGIN Old English.

Quaker • n. a member of the Religious Society of Friends, a Christian movement devoted to peaceful principles and rejecting all set forms of worship.
– DERIVATIVES **Quakerism** n.
– ORIGIN from QUAKE.

qualification • n. **1** the action of qualifying. **2** a pass of an examination or a successful completion of a course. **3** a quality that makes someone suitable for a job or activity. **4** a statement that restricts the meaning of another statement.

qualifier • n. **1** a person or team that qualifies for a competition. **2** a match or contest to decide which individuals or teams qualify for a competition. **3** Grammar a word or phrase used to qualify another word.

qualify • v. (**qualifies, qualifying, qualified**) **1** meet the necessary standard or conditions to be able to do or receive something. **2** become officially recognized as able to work in a particular profession: *the training needed to qualify as a solicitor.* **3** add restrictions to (a statement) to limit its meaning. **4** Grammar (of a word or phrase) describe (another word) in a particular way (e.g. in *the open door, open* is an adjective qualifying *door*).
– ORIGIN Latin *qualificare.*

qualitative /kwol-i-tuh-tiv/ • adj. having to do with or measured by quality.
– DERIVATIVES **qualitatively** adv.

quality • n. (pl. **qualities**) **1** the standard of how good something is as measured against other similar things. **2** general excellence. **3** a distinctive feature.
– ORIGIN Latin *qualitas.*

quality control • n. a system of maintaining standards in manufactured products by testing a sample to see if it meets the required standard.

qualm /kwahm/ • n. a feeling of doubt or unease about one's behaviour.
– ORIGIN perh. from an Old English word meaning 'pain'.

quandary /kwon-duh-ri/ • n. (pl. **quandaries**) a state of uncertainty.
– ORIGIN perh. from Latin *quando* 'when'.

quango /kwang-goh/ • n. (pl. **quangos**) Brit. derog. a semi-public organization with financial support from and senior appointments made by the government.
– ORIGIN acronym from *quasi non-governmental organization.*

Quant E
/kwont/, Mary (b.1934), English fashion designer. She was a principal creator of the '1960s look', popularizing the miniskirt and promoting bold colours and geometric designs.

quanta pl. of **QUANTUM**.

quantify ● v. (**quantifies**, **quantifying**, **quantified**) express or measure the quantity of.
– DERIVATIVES **quantifiable** adj. **quantification** n.

quantitative /kwon-ti-tuh-tiv/ ● adj. relating to or measured by quantity.
– DERIVATIVES **quantitatively** adv.

quantity ● n. (pl. **quantities**) **1** a certain amount or number. **2** the aspect of something that can be measured in number, amount, size, or weight: *wages depended on quantity of output*. **3** a considerable number or amount.
– ORIGIN Latin *quantitas*.

quantity surveyor ● n. Brit. a person who calculates the amount and cost of materials needed for building work.

quantum /kwon-tuhm/ ● n. (pl. **quanta**) Physics a distinct quantity of energy corresponding to that involved in the absorption or emission of energy by an atom.
– ORIGIN Latin.

quantum leap ● n. a sudden large increase or advance.

quantum mechanics ● n. the branch of physics concerned with describing the behaviour of subatomic particles in terms of quanta.

quantum theory ● n. a theory of matter and energy based on the idea of quanta.

quarantine ● n. a period of isolation for people or animals that have or may have a disease. ● v. (**quarantines**, **quarantining**, **quarantined**) put in quarantine.
– ORIGIN Italian *quarantina* 'forty days'.

quark /kwark/ ● n. Physics any of a group of subatomic particles which carry a fractional electric charge and are believed to be building blocks of protons, neutrons, and other particles.
– ORIGIN invented by Murray **GELL-MANN**.

quarrel ● n. **1** an angry argument or disagreement. **2** a reason for disagreement. ● v. (**quarrels**, **quarrelling**, **quarrelled**; US **quarrels**, **quarreling**, **quarreled**) **1** have a quarrel. **2** (**quarrel with**) disagree with.
– ORIGIN Latin *querella* 'complaint'.

quarrelsome ● adj. likely to quarrel.

quarry[1] ● n. (pl. **quarries**) an area of the earth's surface which has been dug open so that stone or other materials can be obtained. ● v. (**quarries**, **quarrying**, **quarried**) take (stone or other materials) from a quarry.
– ORIGIN Old French *quarriere*.

quarry[2] ● n. (pl. **quarries**) **1** an animal being hunted. **2** a person or thing that is chased or sought.
– ORIGIN Old French *couree* 'parts of a deer given to the hounds'.

quarry tile ● n. an unglazed floor tile.
– ORIGIN Old French *quarrel* 'lattice windowpane'.

quart ● n. a unit of liquid capacity equal to a quarter of a gallon, equivalent in Britain to approximately 1.13 litres and in the US to approximately 0.94 litre.
– ORIGIN from Latin *quarta pars* 'fourth part'.

quarter ● n. **1** each of four equal parts into which something is or can be divided. **2** a period of three months. **3** a quarter-hour. **4** one fourth of a pound weight, equal to 4 ounces avoirdupois. **5** a part of a town or city with a specific character or use: *the business quarter*. **6** a US or Canadian coin worth 25 cents. **7** one fourth of a hundredweight (Brit. 28 lb or US 25 lb). **8** (**quarters**) rooms or lodgings. **9** a person, area, etc. regarded as the source of something: *help came from an unexpected quarter*. **10** mercy shown to an opponent: *they gave the enemy no quarter*. ● v. (**quarters**, **quartering**, **quartered**) **1** divide into quarters. **2** (**be quartered**) be lodged. **3** hist. cut the body of (an executed person) into four parts.
– ORIGIN Latin *quartarius*.

quarterback ● n. Amer. Football a player stationed behind the centre who directs a team's attacking play.

quarter day ● n. Brit. each of four days in the year on which some tenancies begin and end and quarterly payments fall due.

quarterdeck ● n. the part of a ship's upper deck near the stern.

quarter-final ● n. a match of a knockout competition coming before the semi-final.

quarter-hour (also **quarter of an hour**) ● n. a period of fifteen minutes.

quarter-light ● n. Brit. a window in the side of a motor vehicle other than a main door window.

quarterly ● adj. & adv. produced or occurring once every quarter of a year. ● n. (pl. **quarterlies**) a publication produced four times a year.

quartermaster ● n. a regimental officer in charge of providing accommodation and supplies.

quarter sessions ● pl. n. hist. (in England, Wales, and Northern Ireland) a court of limited powers, held quarterly.

quarterstaff ● n. a heavy pole 6–8 feet long, formerly used as a weapon.

quarter tone ● n. Music half a semitone.

quartet ● n. **1** a group of four people playing music or singing together. **2** a composition for a quartet. **3** a set of four.
– ORIGIN Italian *quartetto*.

quartile /kwor-tyl/ ● n. Stat. each of four equal groups into which a population can be divided.
– ORIGIN Latin *quartilis*.

quarto /kwor-toh/ ● n. (pl. **quartos**) a size of book page resulting from folding a sheet into four leaves.
– ORIGIN from Latin *in quarto* 'in the fourth'.

quartz ● n. a hard mineral consisting of silica, typically occurring as colourless or white hexagonal prisms.
– ORIGIN German *Quarz*.

quartz clock (or **watch**) ● n. a clock (or watch) regulated by vibrations of an electrically driven quartz crystal.

quartzite ● n. compact, hard, granular rock consisting mainly of quartz.

quasar /kway-zar/ ● n. Astron. a kind of galaxy which gives off enormous amounts of energy.
– ORIGIN from *quasi-stellar radio source*.

quash ● v. **1** officially reject (a legal decision) as invalid. **2** put an end to.
– ORIGIN Old French *quasser* 'annul'.

quasi- /kway-zy/ ● comb. form seemingly: *quasi-scientific.*
– ORIGIN Latin, 'as if, almost'.

quaternary /kwuh-ter-nuh-ri/ ● adj. **1** fourth in order or rank. **2** (**Quaternary**) Geol. relating to the most recent period in the Cenozoic era, from about 1.64 million years ago to the present.
– ORIGIN Latin *quaternarius.*

quatrain /kwot-rayn/ ● n. a verse of four lines, typically with alternate rhymes.
– ORIGIN French.

quatrefoil /kat-ruh-foyl/ ● n. an ornamental design of four leaves, resembling a flower or clover leaf.
– ORIGIN from Old French *quatre* 'four' + *foil* 'leaf'.

quaver ● v. (**quavers**, **quavering**, **quavered**) (of a voice) tremble. ● n. **1** a tremble in a voice. **2** Brit. a musical note having the value of half a crotchet, shown by a large dot with a hooked stem.
– DERIVATIVES **quavery** adj.
– ORIGIN from dialect *quave* 'quake, tremble'.

quay /kee/ ● n. a platform lying alongside or projecting into water for loading and unloading ships.
– ORIGIN Old French *kay.*

quayside ● n. a quay and the area around it.

queasy ● adj. (**queasier**, **queasiest**) feeling sick.
– DERIVATIVES **queasiness** n.
– ORIGIN perh. from Old French *coisier* 'to hurt'.

Quebec [E]
/kwi-**bek**/ a province in eastern Canada; capital, Quebec (also called Quebec City). The province is a focal point of the French-Canadian nationalist movement.

queen ● n. **1** the female ruler of an independent state. **2** (also **queen consort**) a king's wife. **3** the best or most important woman or thing in a field or group. **4** a playing card bearing a picture of a queen, ranking next below a king. **5** the most powerful chess piece, able to move in any direction. **6** a reproductive female in a colony of ants, bees, wasps, or termites. **7** informal a very feminine homosexual man. ● v. (**queen it**) (of a woman) act in an unpleasantly superior way.
– DERIVATIVES **queenly** adj.
– ORIGIN Old English.

Queen Charlotte Islands [E]
a group of more than 150 islands off the west coast of Canada, in British Columbia.

queen mother ● n. the widow of a king and mother of the sovereign.

Queensberry Rules ● pl. n. the standard rules of boxing.
– ORIGIN named after the 9th Marquess of *Queensberry* (1844–1900).

Queen's Counsel ● n. a senior barrister appointed on the recommendation of the Lord Chancellor.

Queen's English ● n. the English language as correctly written and spoken in Britain.

Queen's evidence ● n. Engl. Law evidence for the prosecution given by someone involved in the crime being tried.

Queen's Guide (or **Queen's Scout**) ● n. (in the UK) a Guide (or Scout) who has reached the highest rank of proficiency.

Queen's highway ● n. Brit. the public road network.

queen-sized (also **queen-size**) ● adj. of a larger size than the standard but smaller than king-sized.

Queensland [E]
a state of NE Australia; capital, Brisbane.
– DERIVATIVES **Queenslander** n.

queer ● adj. **1** strange; odd. **2** informal, derog. (of a man) homosexual. ● n. informal, derog. a homosexual man.
– PHRASES **queer someone's pitch** Brit. informal spoil someone's plans or chances of doing something.
– ORIGIN perh. from German *quer* 'oblique, perverse'.

quell ● v. **1** put an end to (a rebellion or other disorder) by force. **2** suppress (an unpleasant feeling).
– ORIGIN Old English, 'kill'.

quench ● v. **1** satisfy (thirst) by drinking. **2** put out (a fire).
– ORIGIN Old English.

quern /kwern/ ● n. a simple hand mill for grinding grain.
– ORIGIN Old English.

querulous /kwe-ruu-luhss, kwe-ryuu-luhss/ ● adj. complaining in an irritable way.
– DERIVATIVES **querulously** adv.
– ORIGIN Latin *querulus.*

query ● n. (pl. **queries**) a question expressing doubt or asking for information. ● v. (**queries**, **querying**, **queried**) ask a query.
– ORIGIN Latin *quaerere* 'ask, seek'.

quest ● n. **1** a long or difficult search. **2** (in medieval romance) an expedition by a knight to carry out a specific task. ● v. search for something.
– ORIGIN Old French *queste.*

question ● n. **1** a sentence worded or expressed so as to obtain information. **2** a doubt or problem. **3** the raising of a doubt or objection: *he obeyed without question.* **4** a matter depending on conditions: *it's only a question of time.* ● v. **1** ask questions of. **2** express doubt about.
– PHRASES **in question 1** being discussed. **2** in doubt. **out of the question** not possible.
– DERIVATIVES **questioner** n.
– ORIGIN Old French.

questionable ● adj. **1** open to doubt. **2** likely to be dishonest or morally wrong.

question mark ● n. a punctuation mark (?) indicating a question.

questionnaire /kwess-chuh-**nair**/ ● n. a set of printed questions written for a survey.
– ORIGIN French.

quetzal /ket-suhl, kwet-suhl/ ● n. a long-tailed tropical American bird with iridescent green plumage.
– ORIGIN Aztec, 'bright tail feather'.

queue ● n. **1** a line of people or vehicles waiting their turn for something. **2** Computing a list of data items, commands, etc., stored so as to be retrievable in a definite order. ● v. (**queues**, **queuing** or **queueing**, **queued**) wait in a queue.

– ORIGIN French, 'tail'.

queue-jump • v. Brit. move forward out of turn in a queue.

quibble • n. a slight objection or criticism. • v. (**quibbles**, **quibbling**, **quibbled**) argue about a trivial matter.
– ORIGIN from former *quib* 'a petty objection'.

quiche /keesh/ • n. a baked flan with a savoury filling thickened with eggs.
– ORIGIN French.

quick • adj. **1** moving fast. **2** lasting or taking a short time: *a quick worker.* **3** with little or no delay. **4** intelligent or alert. • n. **1** (**the quick**) the tender flesh below the growing part of a fingernail or toenail. **2** the most sensitive part: *his laughter cut us to the quick.*
– DERIVATIVES **quickly** adv. **quickness** n.
– ORIGIN Old English, 'alive'.

quicken • v. make or become quicker.

quick-fire • adj. **1** fast and unhesitating. **2** (of a gun) firing shots in rapid succession.

quickie informal • n. **1** a rapidly consumed alcoholic drink. **2** a brief act of sexual intercourse.

quicklime • n. a white caustic alkaline substance consisting of calcium oxide, obtained by heating limestone.

quicksand • n. (also **quicksands**) loose wet sand that sucks in anything resting on it.

quicksilver • n. liquid mercury. • adj. moving or changing rapidly.

quickstep • n. a fast foxtrot.

quick-tempered • adj. easily angered.

quick-witted • adj. able to think or respond quickly.

quid[1] • n. (pl. **quid**) Brit. informal one pound sterling.
– ORIGIN uncertain.

quid[2] • n. a lump of chewing tobacco.
– ORIGIN from **CUD**.

quiddity /kwid-i-ti/ • n. the essential nature of a person or thing.
– ORIGIN Latin *quidditas*.

quid pro quo /kwid proh **kwoh**/ • n. (pl. **quid pro quos**) a favour given in return for something.
– ORIGIN Latin, 'something for something'.

quiescent /kwi-ess-uhnt/ • adj. in a state or period of inactivity.
– DERIVATIVES **quiescence** n.
– ORIGIN Latin *quiescere* 'be still'.

quiet • adj. (**quieter**, **quietest**) **1** making little or no noise. **2** free from activity or excitement. **3** without being disturbed: *a quiet drink.* **4** discreet: *I'll have a quiet word with him.* **5** (of a person) calm and shy. • n. absence of noise or disturbance.
– PHRASES **on the quiet** informal secretly or without drawing attention.
– DERIVATIVES **quietly** adv. **quietness** n.
– ORIGIN Latin *quies* 'rest, quiet'.

> **USAGE** quiet
> Do not confuse **quiet** and **quite**. **Quiet** means 'making little or no noise', as in *he spoke in a quiet voice*, whereas **quite** means 'fairly' or 'completely', as in *it's quite warm* or *I quite agree.*

quieten • v. esp. Brit. make or become quiet and calm.

quietism • n. calm acceptance of things as they are.

quietude • n. a state of calmness and quiet.

quietus /kwy-ee-tuhss/ • n. (pl. **quietuses**) literary death or a cause of death.
– ORIGIN from Latin *quietus est* 'he is quit'.

quiff • n. esp. Brit. a tuft of hair, brushed upwards and backwards from a man's forehead.
– ORIGIN unknown.

quill • n. **1** a main wing or tail feather of a bird. **2** the hollow shaft of a feather. **3** a pen made from a quill. **4** a spine of a porcupine, hedgehog, etc.
– ORIGIN prob. from German *quiele*.

quilt • n. **1** a warm bed covering made of padding enclosed between layers of fabric. **2** a bedspread with decorative stitching.
– ORIGIN Old French *cuilte*.

quilted • adj. (of clothes or bedspreads) made of two layers of fabric with padding between them.

quin • n. informal, esp. Brit. a quintuplet.

quince • n. the hard, acid, pear-shaped fruit of an Asian tree.
– ORIGIN Old French *cooin*.

> **Quincey** E
> Thomas De, see **DE QUINCEY**.

quincunx /kwin-kungks/ • n. (pl. **quincunxes**) an arrangement of five objects with four at the corners of a square or rectangle and the fifth at its centre.
– ORIGIN Latin, 'five twelfths'.

quinine /**kwi**-neen, kwi-**neen**/ • n. a bitter compound present in cinchona bark, formerly used to treat malaria.
– ORIGIN from a South American Indian word meaning 'bark'.

quinone /**kwi**-nohn/ • n. Chem. any of a group of organic compounds related to benzene but having two hydrogen atoms replaced by oxygen.
– ORIGIN Spanish *quina* 'cinchona bark'.

quinquennial /kwing-**kwen**-ni-uhl/ • adj. lasting for or happening every five years.
– ORIGIN from Latin *quinque* 'five' + *annus* 'year'.

quintessence /kwin-tess-uhnss/ • n. **1** the perfect or most typical example: *her reply was the quintessence of wit.* **2** a refined essence or extract of a substance.
– ORIGIN from Latin *quinta essentia* 'fifth essence'.

quintessential /kwin-ti-sen-sh'l/ • adj. representing the perfect or most typical example.
– DERIVATIVES **quintessentially** adv.

quintet • n. **1** a group of five people playing music or singing together. **2** a composition for a quintet. **3** a set of five.
– ORIGIN Italian *quintetto*.

quintuple /**kwin**-tyuu-p'l, kwin-**tyoo**-p'l/ • adj. **1** consisting of five parts or elements. **2** five times as much or as many.
– ORIGIN Latin *quintuplus*.

quintuplet /**kwin**-tyuu-plit, kwin-**tyoo**-plit/ • n. each of five children born at one birth.

quip • n. a witty remark. • v. (**quips**, **quipping**, **quipped**) make a quip.
– ORIGIN perh. from Latin *quippe* 'indeed'.

quire /*rhymes with* squire/ • n. **1** four sheets of paper folded to form eight leaves. **2** 25 sheets of paper; one twentieth of a ream.

q

– ORIGIN Old French *quaier*.

quirk • n. **1** a peculiar habit in a person's behaviour. **2** a strange thing that happens by chance: *a quirk of fate*.
– DERIVATIVES **quirky** adj. (**quirkier**, **quirkiest**).
– ORIGIN unknown.

quisling /kwiz-ling/ • n. a traitor collaborating with an occupying enemy force.
– ORIGIN from Major Vidkun *Quisling* (1887–1945), who ruled Norway during the Second World War on behalf of the German occupying forces.

quit • v. (**quits**, **quitting**, **quitted** or **quit**) **1** leave (a place). **2** resign from (a job). **3** informal, esp. N. Amer. stop (doing something). • adj. (**quit of**) rid of.
– ORIGIN Old French *quiter*.

quite • adv. **1** to the greatest degree; completely. **2** to a certain extent; moderately. • exclam. (also **quite so**) expressing agreement.
– PHRASES **quite a lot** (or **a bit**) a considerable number or amount.
– ORIGIN from **QUIT**.

USAGE quite
For an explanation of the difference between **quite** and **quiet**, see the note at **QUIET**.

Quito E
/kee-toh/ the capital of Ecuador.

quits • adj. on equal terms because a debt or score has been settled.
– PHRASES **call it quits** decide to stop doing something.
– ORIGIN perh. from Latin *quietus est* 'he is quit', used as a receipt.

quitter • n. informal a person who gives up easily.

quiver[1] • v. (**quivers**, **quivering**, **quivered**) shake or vibrate with a slight rapid motion. • n. a quivering movement or sound.
– ORIGIN Old English, 'nimble, quick'.

quiver[2] • n. a case for carrying arrows.
– ORIGIN Old French *quiveir*.

quixotic /kwik-sot-ik/ • adj. high-minded and unselfish to an impractical extent: *the quixotic desire to do good*.
– ORIGIN from Don *Quixote*, hero of a book by **CERVANTES**.

quiz • n. (pl. **quizzes**) a game or competition involving a set of questions as a test of knowledge. • v. (**quizzes**, **quizzing**, **quizzed**) question (someone).
– ORIGIN uncertain.

quizzical • adj. showing mild or amused puzzlement.
– DERIVATIVES **quizzically** adv.

quoin /koyn, kwoyn/ • n. **1** an external angle of a wall or building. **2** a cornerstone.
– ORIGIN from **COIN**, in the former senses 'cornerstone' and 'wedge'.

quoit /koyt, kwoyt/ • n. a ring thrown in a game to land over or as near as possible to an upright peg.
– ORIGIN prob. French.

quondam /kwon-dam/ • adj. formal former.
– ORIGIN Latin, 'formerly'.

quorate /kwor-uht/ • adj. Brit. (of a meeting) having a quorum.

quorum /kwor-uhm/ • n. (pl. **quorums**) the minimum number of members that must be present at a meeting to make its business valid.
– ORIGIN Latin, 'of whom'.

quota • n. **1** a limited quantity of a product which may be produced, exported, or imported. **2** a share that one is entitled to receive or has to contribute. **3** a fixed number of a group allowed to do something.
– ORIGIN from Latin *quota pars* 'how great a part'.

quotable • adj. suitable for or worth quoting.

quotation • n. **1** a passage or remark repeated by someone other than the person who originally said or wrote it. **2** the action of quoting. **3** a formal statement of the estimated cost of a job. **4** a registration granted to a company enabling their shares to be officially listed and traded on a stock exchange.

quotation mark • n. each of a set of punctuation marks, single (' ') or double (" "), used either to mark the beginning and end of a title or quotation, or to indicate slang words.

quote • v. (**quotes**, **quoting**, **quoted**) **1** repeat or copy out (a passage or remark by another person). **2** (**quote as**) put forward or describe as: *the noise level is quoted as being low*. **3** give someone (an estimated price). **4** give (a company) a listing on a stock exchange. • n. **1** a quotation. **2** (**quotes**) quotation marks.
– ORIGIN Latin *quotare* 'mark with numbers'.

quoth /*rhymes with* oath/ • v. archaic said.
– ORIGIN from former *quethe* 'say'.

quotidian /kwuh-tid-i-uhn/ • adj. **1** daily. **2** ordinary or everyday.
– ORIGIN Latin *quotidianus*.

quotient /kwoh-shuhnt/ • n. **1** Math. a result obtained by dividing one quantity by another. **2** a degree of a quality: *my coolness quotient evaporated on the spot*.
– ORIGIN Latin *quotiens* 'how many times'.

Qur'an /kuh-rahn/ (also **Quran**) • n. = **KORAN**.

q.v. • abbrev. used to direct a reader to another part of a book for further information.
– ORIGIN from Latin *quod vide* 'which see'.

R¹ (also **r**) ● n. (pl. **Rs** or **R's**) the eighteenth letter of the alphabet.
– PHRASES **the three Rs** reading, writing, and arithmetic.

R² ● abbrev. **1** rand. **2** Regina or Rex. **3** (**R.**) River.

r ● abbrev. **1** radius. **2** right.

RA ● abbrev. **1** (in the UK) Royal Academician or Royal Academy. **2** (in the UK) Royal Artillery.

Rabat E
/ruh-**bat**/ the capital of Morocco.

rabbi /rab-by/ ● n. (pl. **rabbis**) a Jewish religious leader or teacher of Jewish law.
ORIGIN Hebrew, 'my master'.

rabbinic /ruh-**bin**-ik/ (also **rabbinical**) ● adj. relating to rabbis or to Jewish law or teachings.

rabbit ● n. **1** a burrowing mammal with long ears and a short tail. **2** the fur of the rabbit. ● v. (**rabbits, rabbiting, rabbited**) **1** (**rabbiting**) hunting for rabbits. **2** Brit. informal chatter. [ORIGIN from *rabbit and pork*, rhyming slang for 'talk'.]
– DERIVATIVES **rabbity** adj.
– ORIGIN prob. from Old French.

rabbit punch ● n. a sharp chop with the edge of the hand to the back of the neck.

rabble ● n. **1** a disorderly crowd. **2** (**the rabble**) ordinary people seen as common or uncouth.
– ORIGIN perh. from dialect, 'to gabble'.

rabble-rouser ● n. a person who stirs up popular opinion for political reasons.

Rabelais E
/**rab**-uh-lay/, François (*c.*1494–1553), French satirist. His writings are noted for their earthy humour and imaginative use of language; they include *Pantagruel* and *Gargantua*.
– DERIVATIVES **Rabelaisian** /rab-uh-**lay**-zi-uhn/ adj.

rabid /rab-id, ray-bid/ ● adj. **1** extreme; fanatical: *a rabid anti-Communist.* **2** affected with rabies.
– DERIVATIVES **rabidly** adv.

rabies /**ray**-beez, **ray**-biz/ ● n. a dangerous disease of dogs and other mammals, caused by a virus that can be transmitted through the saliva to humans, causing madness and convulsions.
– ORIGIN Latin.

Rabin E
/ruh-**been**/, Yitzhak (1922–95), Israeli statesman and military leader, Prime Minister 1974–7 and 1992–5. In 1993 he negotiated a PLO–Israeli peace accord with Yasser Arafat. He was assassinated by a Jewish extremist.

RAC ● abbrev. (in the UK) Royal Automobile Club.

raccoon /ruh-**koon**/ (also **racoon**) ● n. a greyish-brown American mammal with a black face and striped tail.
– ORIGIN from an American Indian word.

race¹ ● n. **1** a competition between runners, horses, vehicles, etc. to see which is fastest over a set course. **2** a situation in which people compete to achieve something: *the race for mayor.* **3** a strong current flowing through a narrow channel. ● v. (**races, racing, raced**) **1** compete in a race. **2** have a race with. **3** move or progress rapidly. **4** (of an engine) operate at excessive speed.
– DERIVATIVES **racer** n.
– ORIGIN Old Norse.

race² ● n. **1** each of the major divisions of humankind, based on particular physical characteristics. **2** racial origin or the qualities associated with this: *rights based on race.* **3** a group of people sharing the same culture, language, etc.: *we Scots were a bloodthirsty race.* **4** a group of people or things with a common feature. **5** a subdivision of a species.
– ORIGIN French.

racecourse ● n. a ground or track for horse or dog racing.

racehorse ● n. a horse bred and trained for racing.

raceme /ra-seem, ruh-**seem**/ ● n. a flower cluster with the separate flowers along a central stem, the lower flowers developing first. Compare with CYME.
– ORIGIN Latin *racemus* 'bunch of grapes'.

race meeting ● n. Brit. a sporting event consisting of a series of horse races held at one course.

race relations ● pl. n. relations between members of different races within a country.

racetrack ● n. **1** a racecourse. **2** a track for motor racing.

Rachmaninov E
/rak-**man**-in-off/, Sergei (Vasilevich) (1873–1943), Russian composer and pianist, resident in the US from 1917. He is known for his compositions for piano, including concertos and the Prelude in C sharp minor.

racial ● adj. **1** having to do with race. **2** relating to relations or differences between races: *racial discrimination.*
– DERIVATIVES **racially** adv.

racialism ● n. racism.
– DERIVATIVES **racialist** n. & adj.

Racine E
/ra-**seen**/, Jean (1639–99), French dramatist, the leading tragedian of the French classical period. His plays include *Andromaque* and *Phèdre.*

racing ● n. a sport that involves competing in races. ● adj. **1** moving swiftly. **2** (of a person) following horse racing.

racing car ● n. a car built for racing.

racism • n. **1** the belief that each race has certain qualities or abilities, giving rise to the belief that certain races are better than others. **2** discrimination against or hostility towards other races.
– DERIVATIVES **racist** n. & adj.

rack[1] • n. **1** a framework for holding or storing things. **2** (**the rack**) hist. a frame on which a person was tortured by being stretched. • v. **1** (also **wrack**) cause great pain to. **2** place in or on a rack. **3** (**rack up**) achieve (a score or amount).
– PHRASES **rack** (or **wrack**) **one's brains** think very hard.
– ORIGIN Dutch *rec* or German *rek*.

rack[2] • n. a joint of meat that includes the front ribs.
– ORIGIN unknown.

rack[3] (also **wrack**) • n. (in phr. **go to rack and ruin**) fall into a bad condition.
– ORIGIN Old English, 'vengeance'.

rack[4] • n. var. of WRACK[3].

rack-and-pinion • adj. (of a mechanism) using a fixed bar with cogs or teeth that engage with a smaller cog.

racket[1] (also **racquet**) • n. **1** a bat with a stringed round or oval frame, used in tennis, badminton, and squash. **2** (**rackets**) a ball game for two or four people played with rackets in a four-walled court.
– ORIGIN French *raquette*.

racket[2] • n. **1** a loud unpleasant noise. **2** informal a dishonest scheme for obtaining money. • v. (**rackets**, **racketing**, **racketed**) make a loud unpleasant noise.
– DERIVATIVES **rackety** adj.

racketeer • n. a person who makes money through dishonest activities.
– DERIVATIVES **racketeering** n.

raconteur /ra-kon-ter/ • n. (fem. **raconteuse** /ra-kon-**terz**/) a person who tells stories in an interesting way.
– ORIGIN French.

racoon • n. var. of RACCOON.

racquet • n. var. of RACKET[1].

racy • adj. (**racier**, **raciest**) lively and exciting, especially in a sexual way.

RADA /rah-duh/ • abbrev. (in the UK) Royal Academy of Dramatic Art.

radar • n. a system for finding the position and speed of aircraft, ships, etc., by sending out pulses of radio waves which are reflected back off the object.
– ORIGIN from *radio detection and ranging*.

radar trap • n. an area of road in which radar is used by the police to detect speeding vehicles.

raddled • adj. showing signs of age or tiredness.
– ORIGIN from RUDDY.

radial • adj. **1** arranged in lines coming out from a central point to the edge of a circle: *radial markings resembling spokes.* **2** (also **radial-ply**) (of a tyre) in which the layers of fabric have their cords running at right angles to the circumference of the tyre.
– DERIVATIVES **radially** adv.
– ORIGIN Latin *radialis*.

radian /ray-di-uhn/ • n. an angle of 57.3 degrees, equal to that at the centre of a circle formed by an arc equal in length to the radius.

radiant • adj. **1** shining or glowing brightly. **2** showing great joy, love, or health. **3** (of heat) transmitted by radiation.
– DERIVATIVES **radiance** n. **radiantly** adv.

radiate • v. (**radiates**, **radiating**, **radiated**) **1** (with reference to light, heat, or other energy) send out or be sent out in rays or waves. **2** show (a strong feeling or quality). **3** spread out from a central point: *rows of cells radiated from a central hall.*
– ORIGIN Latin *radiare*.

radiation • n. **1** the action of radiating. **2** energy sent out as electromagnetic waves or subatomic particles.

radiation sickness • n. illness caused when a person is exposed to X-rays, gamma rays, or other radiation.

radiator • n. **1** a device that radiates heat, consisting of a metal case through which hot water circulates, or one heated by electricity or oil. **2** a cooling device in a vehicle or aircraft engine.

radical • adj. **1** having to do with the basic nature of something; fundamental: *a radical overhaul of the regulations.* **2** supporting complete political or social reform. **3** departing from tradition; new. **4** Math. relating to the root of a number or quantity. **5** relating to the root or stem base of a plant. • n. **1** a supporter of radical political or social reform. **2** Chem. a group of atoms behaving as a unit in certain compounds.
– DERIVATIVES **radicalism** n. **radically** adv.
– ORIGIN Latin *radix* 'root'.

radical sign • n. Math. the sign $\surd$ which indicates the square root of the number following (or a higher root indicated by a raised numeral before the symbol).

radicchio /ra-dee-ki-oh/ • n. (pl. **radicchios**) a variety of chicory with dark red leaves.
– ORIGIN Italian.

radices pl. of RADIX.

radicle /ra-di-k'l/ • n. the part of a plant embryo that develops into the primary root.
– ORIGIN Latin *radicula* 'little root'.

radii pl. of RADIUS.

radio • n. (pl. **radios**) **1** the sending and receiving of electromagnetic waves carrying sound messages. **2** broadcasting in sound. **3** a device for receiving radio programmes, or for sending and receiving radio messages. • v. (**radioes**, **radioing**, **radioed**) send a message by radio.
– ORIGIN Latin *radius* 'ray'.

radio- • comb. form **1** referring to radio waves or broadcasting: *radiogram.* **2** connected with rays, radiation, or radioactivity: *radiography.*

radioactive • adj. giving out harmful radiation or particles.

radioactivity • n. **1** the sending out of harmful radiation or particles, caused when atomic nuclei break up spontaneously. **2** radioactive particles.

radiocarbon • n. a radioactive isotope of carbon used in carbon dating.

radiogram • n. Brit. dated a combined radio and record player.

radiography • n. the production of images by X-rays or other radiation.
– DERIVATIVES **radiographer** n.

radioisotope • n. a radioactive isotope.

r

radiology • n. the study and use of X-rays and similar radiation in medicine.
– DERIVATIVES **radiological** adj. **radiologist** n.

radiophonic • adj. having to do with sound produced electronically.

radiotelephone • n. a telephone using radio transmission.

radio telescope • n. an instrument used to detect radio waves from space.

radiotherapy • n. the treatment of cancer or other disease using X-rays or similar radiation.

radio wave • n. an electromagnetic wave having a frequency in the range 10^4 to 10^{11} or 10^{12} hertz.

radish • n. the crisp, hot-tasting, red root of a plant that is eaten raw.
– ORIGIN Latin *radix* 'root'.

radium /ray-di-uhm/ • n. a reactive, radioactive metallic element.
– ORIGIN Latin *radius* 'ray'.

radius /ray-di-uhss/ • n. (pl. **radii** /ray-di-I/ or **radiuses**) **1** a straight line from the centre to the circumference of a circle or sphere. **2** a specified distance from a centre in all directions: *pubs within a two mile radius.* **3** the thicker and shorter of the two bones in the human forearm.
– ORIGIN Latin, 'spoke, ray'.

radix /ray-diks/ • n. (pl. **radices** /ray-di-seez/) Math. the base of a system of calculation.
– ORIGIN Latin, 'root'.

radon /ray-don/ • n. a rare radioactive gaseous element.
– ORIGIN from **RADIUM**.

Raeburn E
/ray-bern/, Sir Henry (1756–1823), Scottish portrait painter.

RAF • abbrev. (in the UK) Royal Air Force.

raffia • n. fibre from the leaves of a tropical palm tree, used for making hats, baskets, etc.
– ORIGIN Malagasy (the language of Madagascar).

raffish • adj. slightly disreputable, but in an attractive way.
– ORIGIN from **RIFF-RAFF**.

raffle • n. a lottery with goods as prizes. • v. (**raffles**, **raffling**, **raffled**) offer as a prize in a raffle.
– ORIGIN Old French.

Raffles, E
Sir (Thomas) Stamford (1781–1826), British colonial administrator. As Lieutenant General of Sumatra he persuaded the East India Company to buy the undeveloped island of Singapore (1819), helping to develop it into an important trading centre.

Rafsanjani E
/raf-san-**jah**-ni/, Ali Akbar Hashemi (b.1934), Iranian statesman and religious leader, President 1989–97, who sought to improve Iran's relations with the West.

raft¹ • n. **1** a flat structure of pieces of timber fastened together, used as a boat or floating platform. **2** a small inflatable boat.
– ORIGIN Old Norse.

raft² • n. a large amount.
– ORIGIN perh. Scandinavian.

rafter • n. a beam forming part of the internal framework of a roof.
– ORIGIN Old English.

rag¹ • n. **1** a piece of old cloth. **2** (**rags**) old or tattered clothes. **3** informal a low-quality newspaper.
– PHRASES **lose one's rag** informal lose one's temper.
– ORIGIN prob. from **RAGGED**.

rag² • n. Brit. a programme of entertainments organized by students to raise money for charity. • v. (**rags**, **ragging**, **ragged**) tease or play tricks on.
– ORIGIN unknown.

rag³ • n. a piece of ragtime music.

raga /rah-guh/ • n. (in Indian music) a traditional pattern of notes used as a basis for improvising a piece of music.
– ORIGIN Sanskrit, 'colour, musical tone'.

ragamuffin • n. a person in ragged, dirty clothes.
– ORIGIN prob. from **RAG¹**.

rag-and-bone man • n. Brit. a person who goes from door to door, collecting second-hand items to sell.

ragbag • n. a collection of widely different things.

rage • n. violent uncontrollable anger. • v. (**rages**, **raging**, **raged**) **1** feel or express rage. **2** continue with great force: *the argument raged for days.*
– PHRASES **all the rage** very popular or fashionable for a short time.
– ORIGIN Old French.

ragged /rag-gid/ • adj. **1** (of clothes) old and torn. **2** rough or irregular. **3** not smooth or steady: *he endured our ragged singing.*
– PHRASES **run someone ragged** exhaust someone.
– ORIGIN Scandinavian.

raglan • adj. (of a sleeve) continuing in one piece up to the neck of a garment.
– ORIGIN named after Lord *Raglan*, a British commander in the Crimean War (1788–1855).

ragout /ra-goo/ • n. a spicy stew of meat and vegetables.
– ORIGIN French.

ragtag • adj. disorganized and very varied: *a ragtag force of men.*
– ORIGIN from **RAG¹** + **TAG¹**.

ragtime • n. an early form of jazz music played especially on the piano.
– ORIGIN prob. from the idea of the 'ragged' rhythm.

rag trade • n. informal the clothing or fashion industry.

ragwort • n. a plant with yellow flowers and ragged leaves.

Rahman E
see **ABDUL RAHMAN**, **MUJIBUR RAHMAN**.

raid • n. **1** a sudden attack on an enemy or on a building to commit a crime. **2** a surprise visit by police to arrest suspects or seize illegal goods. • v. make a raid on.
– DERIVATIVES **raider** n.
– ORIGIN Scots, from **ROAD**.

rail¹ • n. **1** a bar or series of bars fixed on supports or attached to a wall or ceiling, forming part of a fence or used to hang things on. **2** each of the two metal bars laid on the ground to form a railway track. **3** railways as a means of transport. • v. provide or enclose with a rail or rails.

– PHRASES **go off the rails** informal begin behaving in an uncontrolled way.
– ORIGIN Old French *reille* 'iron rod'.

rail[2] • v. **(rail against/at)** complain strongly about.
– ORIGIN French *railler*.

railcard • n. Brit. a pass entitling the holder to reduced rail fares.

railhead • n. the point at which a railway ends.

railing • n. a fence made of rails.

raillery /rayl-luh-ri/ • n. good-humoured teasing.
– ORIGIN from **RAIL**[2].

railroad • n. N. Amer. a railway. • v. informal rush or force into doing something.

railway • n. Brit. **1** a track made of rails along which trains run. **2** a system of such tracks with the trains, organization, and staff required to run it.

raiment /ray-muhnt/ • n. archaic clothing.
– ORIGIN from **ARRAY**.

rain • n. **1** the condensed moisture of the atmosphere falling in separate drops. **2 (rains)** falls of rain. **3** a large quantity of things falling together: *a rain of stones thundered down.* • v. **1 (it rains, it is raining, it rained)** rain falls. **2 (be rained off)** (of an event) be prevented by rain from continuing or taking place. **3** fall or cause to fall in large quantities.
– PHRASES **rain cats and dogs** rain heavily.
– ORIGIN Old English.

rainbow • n. an arch of colours in the sky, caused by the refraction and dispersion of the sun's light by water droplets in the atmosphere.

rainbow trout • n. a large trout with reddish sides, native to western North America and introduced elsewhere.

rain check • n. (in phr. **take a rain check**) refuse an offer but imply that one may take it up later.
– ORIGIN referring to a ticket given for later use when an outdoor event is rained off.

raincoat • n. a coat made from waterproofed or water-resistant fabric.

rainfall • n. the amount of rain falling within an area in a particular time.

rainforest • n. a dense forest found in tropical areas with consistently heavy rainfall.

rainy • adj. **(rainier, rainiest)** having a lot of rain.
– PHRASES **a rainy day** a time in the future when money may be needed.

raise • v. **(raises, raising, raised) 1** lift or move upwards or into an upright position. **2** increase the amount, level, or strength of. **3** cause to be heard, felt, or considered: *doubts have been raised.* **4** collect or bring together (money or people). **5** bring up (a child). **6** breed or grow (animals or plants). **7** abandon (a blockade, ban, etc.). **8** Brit. informal establish contact with (someone) by telephone or radio. **9 (raise something to)** Math. multiply a quantity to (a specified power). • n. esp. N. Amer. an increase in salary.
– PHRASES **raise hell** informal make a noisy disturbance. **raise the roof** make a lot of noise, especially by cheering.
– DERIVATIVES **raiser** n.
– ORIGIN Old Norse.

raisin • n. a partially dried grape.
– ORIGIN Old French, 'grape'.

raison d'être /ray-zon de-truh/ • n. (pl. **raisons d'être** /ray-zon de-truh/) the most important reason for someone or something's existence.
– ORIGIN French, 'reason for being'.

Raj /rahj/ • n. **(the Raj)** hist. the period of British rule in India.
– ORIGIN Hindi, 'reign'.

raja /rah-juh/ (also **rajah**) • n. hist. an Indian king or prince.
– ORIGIN Hindi or Sanskrit.

Rajasthan E
/rah-juh-**stahn**/ a state in western India, on the Pakistani border; capital, Jaipur.
– DERIVATIVES **Rajasthani** n. & adj.

Rajneesh E
/ruj-**neesh**/, Bhagwan Shree (1931–90; born *Chandra Mohan Jain*), Indian guru. He founded an ashram in Poona, India, and a commune in Oregon, becoming notorious for his doctrine of communal therapy and salvation through free love.

rake[1] • n. a tool consisting of a pole with metal prongs at the end, used for drawing together leaves or cut grass or smoothing soil. • v. **(rakes, raking, raked) 1** draw together or smooth with a rake. **2** scratch with a sweeping movement. **3** sweep with gunfire, a look, or a beam of light. **4** search through.
– PHRASES **rake it in** informal make a lot of money. **rake up** (or **over**) revive the memory of (something best forgotten).
– ORIGIN Old English or Old Norse.

rake[2] • n. a fashionable and rich man who lives an immoral life.
– ORIGIN from former *rakehell* in the same sense.

rake[3] • v. **(rakes, raking, raked)** set at a sloping angle. • n. the angle at which something slopes.
– ORIGIN prob. from German *ragen* 'to project'.

rake-off • n. informal a share of the profits from an illegal or underhand deal.

rakish • adj. having a dashing, jaunty, or slightly disreputable appearance.

Raleigh E
/rah-li, raw-li/ (also **Ralegh**), Sir Walter (*c.*1552–1618), English explorer and writer. He organized several voyages of exploration and colonization to the Americas, and introduced potato and tobacco plants to England. He was executed by James I on a charge of conspiracy.

rally • v. **(rallies, rallying, rallied) 1** (with reference to troops) bring or come together again so as to continue fighting. **2** bring or come together as support or for united action: *his family rallied round.* **3** recover in health or strength. **4** (of share, currency, or commodity prices) increase after a fall. • n. (pl. **rallies**) **1** a mass meeting held as a protest or in support of a cause. **2** a long-distance competition for motor vehicles over roads or rough country. **3** a quick or strong recovery. **4** (in tennis and other racket sports) a long exchange of strokes between players.
– ORIGIN French *rallier*.

rallying • n. the sport of taking part in a

motor rally. • **adj.** having the effect of calling people to action: *a rallying cry.*

RAM • **abbrev.** Computing random-access memory.

ram • **n. 1** an adult male sheep. **2** a battering ram. **3** a striking or plunging device in a machine. • **v.** (**rams**, **ramming**, **rammed**) **1** roughly force (something) into place. **2** hit or be hit with force.
– ORIGIN Old English.

Ramadan /ram-uh-dan/ (also **Ramadhan** /**ram**-uh-zan/) • **n.** the ninth month of the Muslim year, during which Muslims fast from sunrise to sunset.
– ORIGIN Arabic.

Ramakrishna E
/rah-muh-**krish**-nuh/ (1836–86; born *Gadadhar Chatterjee*), Indian Hindu religious leader. He condemned lust, money, and the caste system, and preached that all religions leading to the attainment of mystical experience are equally good.

Raman E
/**rah**-muhn/, Sir Chandrasekhara Venkata (1888–1970), Indian physicist, who discovered the Raman effect, one of the most important proofs of the quantum theory of light.

Ramayana E
/rah-**mah**-juh-nuh/ one of the two great Sanskrit epic poems of the Hindus, composed *c.*300 BC.

Rambert E
/**rom**-bair/, Dame Marie (1888–1982; born *Cyvia Rambam*), Polish-born British ballet dancer and teacher. She formed and directed the Ballet Club, which became known as the Ballet Rambert in 1935.

ramble • **v.** (**rambles**, **rambling**, **rambled**) **1** walk for pleasure in the countryside. **2** talk or write in a confused way and for a long time: *he rambled on about Norman archways.* • **n.** a walk taken for pleasure in the countryside.
– DERIVATIVES **rambler** n.
– ORIGIN prob. from Dutch *rammelen* 'wander about on heat' (referring to an animal).

rambutan /ram-**byoo**-tuhn/ • **n.** the red fruit of a tropical tree, with soft spines and a slightly sour taste.
– ORIGIN Malay.

Rameau E
/**ram**-oh/, Jean-Philippe (1683–1764), French composer, best known for his four volumes of harpsichord pieces.

ramekin /**ram**-i-kin/ • **n.** a small dish for baking and serving an individual portion of food.
– ORIGIN French *ramequin.*

Rameses E
/**ram**-i-seez/ var. of **Ramses**.

ramifications • **pl. n.** complex results of an action or event: *any change is bound to have legal ramifications.*

ramify /**ra**-mi-fy/ • **v.** (**ramifies**, **ramifying**, **ramified**) form parts that branch out.
– ORIGIN Latin *ramificare.*

ramp • **n. 1** a sloping surface joining two different levels. **2** a movable set of steps for entering or leaving an aircraft.
– ORIGIN Old French *ramper* 'creep'.

rampage • **v.** /ram-**payj**/ (**rampages**, **rampaging**, **rampaged**) rush around in a wild and violent way. • **n.** /**ram**-payj/ a period of wild and violent behaviour: *thugs went on the rampage through the city.*
– ORIGIN perh. from **ramp** and **rage**.

rampant • **adj. 1** flourishing or spreading in an uncontrolled way: *rampant inflation.* **2** Heraldry (of an animal) shown standing on its left hind foot with its forefeet in the air: *two lions rampant.*
– ORIGIN Old French, 'crawling'.

rampart • **n.** a wall built to defend a castle or town, having a broad top with a walkway.
– ORIGIN French *rempart.*

ram raid • **n.** a robbery in which a shop window is rammed with a vehicle.

ramrod • **n.** a rod formerly used to ram down the charge of a firearm.

Ramsay E
/**ram**-zi/, Sir William (1852–1916), Scottish chemist. He discovered the noble gases, determining their atomic weights and places in the periodic table.

Ramses II E
/**ram**-seez/ (also **Rameses**) (died *c.*1225 BC; known as **Ramses the Great**), Egyptian pharaoh *c.*1292–*c.*1225 BC. He built vast monuments and statues, including the two rock temples at Abu Simbel.

Ramsey E
/**ram**-zi/, Sir Alf (1920–99; full name *Alfred Ernest Ramsey*), English footballer and manager. As manager of England 1963–74 he was in charge of the team that won the World Cup in 1966.

ramshackle • **adj.** in a very bad condition.
– ORIGIN from **ransack**.

ran past of **run**.

ranch • **n.** a large farm in America or Australia, where cattle or other animals are bred. • **v.** run a ranch.
– DERIVATIVES **rancher** n.
– ORIGIN Spanish *rancho* 'group of people eating together'.

rancid • **adj.** (of foods containing fat or oil) smelling or tasting unpleasant as a result of being stale.
– ORIGIN Latin *rancidus* 'stinking'.

rancour (US **rancor**) • **n.** bitter feeling or resentment.
– DERIVATIVES **rancorous** adj.
– ORIGIN Latin *rancor* 'rankness'.

Rand E
/rand, rahnt/ (**the Rand**) = **Witwatersrand**.

rand /rand/ • **n.** the basic unit of money of South Africa.
– ORIGIN from *the Rand* (see **Rand**).

R & B • **abbrev.** rhythm and blues.

random • **adj.** done or happening without a deliberate order, purpose, or choice: *winning cards will be drawn at random.*
– DERIVATIVES **randomly** adv. **randomness** n.
– ORIGIN Old French *randon* 'great speed'.

random access • **n.** the process of storing or finding information on a computer without having to read through items in a particular sequence.

randy ● adj. (**randier**, **randiest**) informal sexually aroused or excited.
– ORIGIN perh. from former Dutch *randen* 'to rant'.

rang past of RING².

range ● n. **1** the limits between which something varies: *a population in the range of 250,000 to 1 million.* **2** a set of different things of the same general type: *a wide range of activities.* **3** the distance over which a sound, missile, etc. can travel: *he sat down within range of the rifles.* **4** a line of mountains or hills. **5** a large area of open land for grazing or hunting. **6** an area used as a testing ground for military equipment or for shooting practice. **7** a large cooking stove with several burners or hotplates. ● v. (**ranges**, **ranging**, **ranged**) **1** vary between particular limits. **2** arrange in a row or rows or in a particular way. **3** (**range against**) be in opposition to. **4** travel over or cover a wide area.
– ORIGIN Old French, 'row, rank'.

rangefinder ● n. an instrument for estimating the distance of an object.

ranger ● n. **1** a keeper of a park, forest, or area of countryside. **2** (**Ranger** or **Ranger Guide**) Brit. a senior Guide.

Rangoon E
/rang-**goon**/ the capital of Burma (Myanmar).

rangy /rayn-ji/ ● adj. (of a person) tall and slim with long limbs.

Ranjit Singh E
/run-jit sing/ (1780–1839; known as the **Lion of the Punjab**), Indian maharaja, founder of the Sikh state of Punjab. He proclaimed himself maharaja of Punjab in 1801, and made it the most powerful state in India.

Rank, E
J. Arthur, 1st Baron (1888–1972; full name *Joseph Arthur Rank*), English industrialist and film executive, who founded the Rank Organization (1941), a film production and distribution company.

rank¹ ● n. **1** a position within the armed forces or an organization. **2** a line or row of people or things. **3** high social position. **4** (**the ranks**) (in the armed forces) those who are not commissioned officers. **5** (**ranks**) the members of a group: *the ranks of the unemployed.* ● v. **1** give (someone or something) a rank within a system. **2** hold a specified rank. **3** arrange in a row or rows.
– PHRASES **break rank** (or **ranks**) fail to support a group to which one belongs. **close ranks** unite so as to defend shared interests. **pull rank** use one's higher rank to take advantage of someone. **rank and file** the ordinary members of an organization.
– ORIGIN Old French *ranc*.

rank² ● adj. **1** having a very unpleasant smell. **2** (of vegetation) growing too thickly. **3** complete: *a rank amateur.*
– ORIGIN Old English, 'proud, sturdy'.

ranking ● n. a position on a scale of achievement or importance. ● adj. having a specified rank: *high-ranking officers.*

rankle ● v. (**rankles**, **rankling**, **rankled**) (of a comment or fact) cause continuing annoyance or resentment.
– ORIGIN Old French *rancler* 'fester'.

ransack ● v. **1** go hurriedly through (a place) stealing things and causing damage. **2** search carelessly.
– ORIGIN Old Norse.

ransom ● n. a sum of money demanded or paid for the release of someone who is held captive. ● v. obtain the release of (someone) by paying a ransom.
– PHRASES **hold to ransom** force (someone) to do something by threatening damaging action. **a king's ransom** a huge amount of money.
– ORIGIN Old French *ransoun*.

Ransome, E
Arthur (Michell) (1884–1967), English novelist and journalist, author of the children's classic *Swallows and Amazons*.

rant ● v. speak in a loud, angry, and forceful way.
– ORIGIN Dutch *ranten* 'talk nonsense'.

Rao E
/*rhymes with* cow/, P. V. Narasimha (b.1921; full name *Pamulaparti Venkata Narasimha Rao*), Indian statesman, Prime Minister 1991–6.

rap ● v. (**raps**, **rapping**, **rapped**) **1** hit (a hard surface) several times. **2** strike sharply. **3** informal criticize sharply. **4** say sharply: *he rapped out an order.* ● n. **1** a quick, sharp knock or blow. **2** informal a criticism. **3** a type of popular music in which words are spoken rapidly and rhythmically over an instrumental backing. **4** N. Amer. informal a criminal charge: *a murder rap.*
– PHRASES **take the rap** informal be punished or blamed for something.
– DERIVATIVES **rapper** n.
– ORIGIN prob. Scandinavian.

rapacious /ruh-pay-shuhss/ ● adj. very greedy.
– ORIGIN Latin *rapere* 'to snatch'.

rapacity /ruh-pa-si-ti/ ● n. greed.

rape¹ ● v. (**rapes**, **raping**, **raped**) **1** (of a man) force (someone) to have sexual intercourse with him against their will. **2** spoil or destroy (a place). ● n. an act of raping someone.
– ORIGIN Latin *rapere* 'seize'.

rape² ● n. a plant with yellow flowers, grown for its oil-rich seed.
– ORIGIN Latin *rapum*, *rapa* 'turnip'.

Raphael E
/raf-fay-uhl/ (1483–1520; Italian name *Raffaello Sanzio*), Italian painter and architect. His many works include the altarpiece the *Sistine Madonna* and a series of frescoes in the Vatican; as an architect he took charge of the work on St Peter's in Rome.

rapid ● adj. happening in a short time or at great speed. ● pl. n. (**rapids**) a part of a river where the water flows very fast, often over rocks.
– DERIVATIVES **rapidity** n. **rapidly** adv.
– ORIGIN Latin *rapidus*.

rapier ● n. a thin, light sword.
– ORIGIN French *rapière*.

rapine /ra-pyn, ra-pin/ ● n. literary the violent seizure of property.

– ORIGIN Old French.

rapist • n. a man who commits rape.

rapport /rap-por/ • n. a close relationship in which people understand each other and communicate well.
– ORIGIN French.

rapprochement /ra-prosh-mon/ • n. a renewal of friendly relations between two countries or groups.
– ORIGIN French.

rapscallion /rap-skal-li-uhn/ • n. archaic a mischievous person.
– ORIGIN perh. from **RASCAL**.

rapt • adj. completely interested or absorbed in someone or something.
– ORIGIN Latin *raptus* 'seized'.

rapture • n. **1** great pleasure or joy. **2** (**raptures**) the expression of great pleasure or enthusiasm.

rapturous • adj. feeling or expressing great pleasure or enthusiasm.
– DERIVATIVES **rapturously** adv.

rare¹ • adj. (**rarer**, **rarest**) **1** not occurring or found very often. **2** unusually good: *a player of rare skill.*
– ORIGIN Latin *rarus.*

rare² • adj. (**rarer**, **rarest**) (of red meat) lightly cooked, so that the inside is still red.
– ORIGIN Old English, 'half-cooked'.

rarebit (also **Welsh rarebit**) • n. a dish of melted cheese on toast.
– ORIGIN unknown.

rarefied /rair-i-fyd/ • adj. **1** (of air) of lower pressure than usual; thin. **2** understood by a limited group of people with particular knowledge: *his rarefied books are not for undergrads.*

rarely • adv. not often.

raring • adj. informal very eager: *she was raring to go.*
– ORIGIN from **ROAR** or **REAR²**.

rarity • n. (pl. **rarities**) **1** the state of being rare. **2** a rare thing.

Rarotonga E
/ra-ruh-tong-guh/ an island in the South Pacific, the chief island of the Cook Islands; chief town, Avarua (also the capital of the Cook Islands).

Ras al Khaimah E
/rahss al ky-mer/ one of the seven member states of the United Arab Emirates; capital, Ras al Khaimah.

rascal • n. **1** a mischievous or cheeky person. **2** dated a dishonest man.
– DERIVATIVES **rascally** adj.
– ORIGIN Old French *rascaille* 'rabble'.

rash¹ • adj. acting or done without considering the possible results.
– DERIVATIVES **rashly** adv.
– ORIGIN Germanic.

rash² • n. **1** an area of red spots or patches on a person's skin. **2** a series of unpleasant things happening within a short time: *a rash of strikes.*
– ORIGIN prob. from Old French *rasche* 'sores, scurf'.

rasher • n. a thin slice of bacon.
– ORIGIN unknown.

rasp • n. **1** a coarse file for use on metal, wood, or other hard material. **2** a harsh, grating noise. • v. **1** (of a rough surface or object) scrape (something). **2** make a harsh, grating noise.
– ORIGIN Old French *rasper.*

raspberry • n. **1** an edible reddish-pink soft fruit. **2** informal a sound made with the tongue and lips, expressing mockery or contempt. [ORIGIN from *raspberry tart*, rhyming slang for 'fart'.]
– ORIGIN unknown.

Rasputin E
/ra-spyoo-tin/, Grigori (Efimovich) (1871–1916), Russian monk, who exerted great influence over Tsar Nicholas II and his family during the First World War. He was assassinated by a group loyal to the tsar.

Rasta /rass-tuh/ • n. informal = **RASTAFARIAN**.

Rastafarian /rass-tuh-fair-i-uhn, rass-tuh-fah-ri-uhn/ • n. a member of a Jamaican religious movement which believes that Haile Selassie (the former Emperor of Ethiopia) was the Messiah and that blacks are the chosen people.
– DERIVATIVES **Rastafarianism** n.
– ORIGIN from *Ras Tafari*, the name by which Haile Selassie was known.

rat • n. **1** a rodent resembling a large mouse, considered a serious pest. **2** informal an unpleasant person. • v. (**rats**, **ratting**, **ratted**) (**rat on**) informal **1** inform on. **2** break (an agreement or promise).
– ORIGIN Old English.

ratable • adj. var. of **RATEABLE**.

ratafia /ra-tuh-fee-uh/ • n. an almond-flavoured biscuit like a small macaroon.
– ORIGIN French.

ratatouille /ra-tuh-too-i, ra-tuh-twee/ • n. a dish of stewed onions, courgettes, tomatoes, aubergines, and peppers.
– ORIGIN French.

ratbag • n. Brit. informal an unpleasant person.

ratchet • n. a device consisting of a bar or wheel with a set of angled teeth in which a cog, tooth, or pivoted bar fits, allowing movement in one direction only. • v. (**ratchets**, **ratcheting**, **ratcheted**) (**ratchet up/down**) cause to rise (or fall) as a step in a process.
– ORIGIN French *rochet.*

rate¹ • n. **1** a measure, quantity, or frequency measured against another: *companies joined the scheme at the rate of ten a month.* **2** the speed with which something moves or happens. **3** a fixed price paid or charged: *a basic rate of pay.* **4** (**rates**) (in the UK) a tax on land and buildings paid to a local authority by a business. • v. (**rates**, **rating**, **rated**) **1** give a standard or value to (something) according to a particular scale. **2** consider to be of a certain quality or standard: *Atkinson rates him as our top defender.* **3** be worthy of; merit. **4** informal have a high opinion of.
– PHRASES **at any rate** whatever happens or may have happened.
– ORIGIN Latin *rata.*

rate² • v. (**rates**, **rating**, **rated**) archaic scold angrily.
– ORIGIN unknown.

rateable (also **ratable**) • adj. able to be rated or estimated.

rateable value • n. (in the UK) a value given to a business property based on its size, location, etc., used to calculate the rates payable by its owner.

rather ● adv. **1** (**would rather**) would prefer. **2** to some extent; fairly. **3** used to correct something one has said or to be more precise: *I walked, or rather, limped, home.* **4** instead of.
– ORIGIN Old English, 'earlier, sooner'.

ratify ● v. (**ratifies**, **ratifying**, **ratified**) give formal consent to.
– DERIVATIVES **ratification** n.
– ORIGIN Latin *ratificare*.

rating ● n. **1** a classification or ranking based on quality, standard, or performance. **2** (**ratings**) the estimated audience size of a television or radio programme. **3** Brit. a sailor in the navy who does not hold a commission.

ratio ● n. (pl. **ratios**) the relationship between two amounts, showing the number of times one value contains or is contained within the other.
– ORIGIN Latin, 'reckoning'.

ratiocination /ra-ti-oss-i-**nay**-sh'n, ra-shi-oss-i-**nay**-sh'n/ ● n. formal thinking in a logical way; reasoning.
– ORIGIN Latin *ratiocinari* 'calculate'.

ration ● n. **1** a fixed amount of food, fuel, etc., officially allowed to each person during a shortage. **2** (**rations**) a regular allowance of food supplied to members of the armed forces. ● v. limit the supply of (food, fuel, etc.).
– ORIGIN Latin, 'reckoning, ratio'.

rational ● adj. **1** based on reason or logic: *a rational explanation.* **2** able to think sensibly or logically.
– DERIVATIVES **rationality** n. **rationally** adv.

rationale /ra-shuh-**nahl**/ ● n. a set of reasons for a course of action or a belief.

rationalism ● n. the belief that opinions and actions should be based on reason and knowledge rather than on religious belief or emotions.
– DERIVATIVES **rationalist** n.

rationalize (also **rationalise**) ● v. (**rationalizes**, **rationalizing**, **rationalized**) **1** try to find a logical reason for (an action or attitude). **2** reorganize (a process or system) so as to make it more logical. **3** make (a company) more efficient by disposing of unwanted staff or equipment.
– DERIVATIVES **rationalization** (also **rationalisation**) n.

rat race ● n. informal a way of life which is a fiercely competitive struggle for wealth or power.

rattan /ruh-**tan**/ ● n. the thin, pliable stems of a tropical climbing palm, used to make furniture.
– ORIGIN Malay.

Rattigan E
/**rat**-ti-g'n/, Sir Terence (Mervyn) (1911–77), English dramatist. His plays include *The Winslow Boy* and *The Browning Version*.

Rattle, E
Sir Simon (Denis) (b.1955), English conductor, known for his work with the City of Birmingham Symphony Orchestra as principal conductor and music director.

rattle ● v. (**rattles**, **rattling**, **rattled**) **1** make or move with a rapid series of short, sharp sounds. **2** informal make (someone) nervous or irritated. **3** (**rattle off**) say or do quickly and easily. **4** (**rattle on/away**) talk rapidly and at length. ● n. **1** a rattling sound. **2** a device or toy that makes a rattling sound.
– ORIGIN Dutch and German *ratelen*.

rattlesnake ● n. an American viper with horny rings on the tail that produce a rattling sound.

rattletrap ● n. informal an old or rickety vehicle.

rattling ● adj. informal, dated very: *a rattling good story.*

ratty ● adj. **1** resembling a rat. **2** informal in bad condition. **3** Brit. informal irritable.

raucous /raw-kuhss/ ● adj. sounding loud and harsh.
– DERIVATIVES **raucously** adv.
– ORIGIN Latin *raucus* 'hoarse'.

raunchy ● adj. (**raunchier**, **raunchiest**) informal sexually exciting or direct.
– ORIGIN unknown.

ravage ● v. (**ravages**, **ravaging**, **ravaged**) cause great damage to. ● n. (**ravages**) the destruction caused by something.
– ORIGIN French *ravager*.

rave ● v. (**raves**, **raving**, **raved**) **1** talk angrily or without making sense. **2** speak or write about someone or something with great enthusiasm. ● n. Brit. a very large event with dancing to loud, fast electronic music.
– ORIGIN prob. from Old French *raver*.

Ravel E
/ra-**vel**/, Maurice (Joseph) (1875–1937), French composer, known for the orchestral work *Boléro* and the ballet *Daphnis and Chloë*.

ravel ● v. (**ravels**, **ravelling**, **ravelled**; US **ravels**, **raveling**, **raveled**) (**ravel out**) untangle.
– ORIGIN prob. from Dutch *ravelen* 'fray out'.

raven ● n. a large black crow. ● adj. (of hair) of a glossy black colour.
– ORIGIN Old English.

ravening ● adj. very hungry.

ravenous ● adj. very hungry.
– DERIVATIVES **ravenously** adv.
– ORIGIN Old French *ravineus*.

raver ● n. informal a person who has an exciting or wild social life.

rave review ● n. a very enthusiastic review of a film play, book, etc.

rave-up ● n. Brit. informal a lively party.

ravine /ruh-**veen**/ ● n. a deep, narrow gorge with steep sides.
– ORIGIN French, 'violent rush'.

raving ● n. (**ravings**) wild talk that makes no sense. ● adj. & adv. informal used for emphasis: *she'd never been a raving beauty.*

ravioli /rav-i-**oh**-li/ ● pl. n. small pasta cases containing minced meat, cheese, or vegetables.
– ORIGIN Italian.

ravish ● v. **1** dated rape. **2** (**be ravished**) be filled with great pleasure. **3** (**ravishing**) very beautiful.
– ORIGIN Old French *ravir*.

raw ● adj. **1** (of food) not cooked. **2** (of a material or substance) in its natural state; not processed. **3** new to an activity or job and therefore lacking experience. **4** (of the skin) red and painful from being rubbed or scraped. **5** (of an emotion or quality) strong

and undisguised. **6** (of the weather) cold and damp.
– PHRASES **in the raw** informal naked.
– DERIVATIVES **rawness** n.
– ORIGIN Old English.

Rawalpindi E
/rawl-**pin**-di/ a city in Punjab province, northern Pakistan.

raw-boned ● adj. bony or gaunt.

Ray[1] E
/ray/, John (1627–1705), English naturalist, who developed early systematic classifications of plants.

Ray[2] E
/ray/, Man (1890–1976; born *Emmanuel Rudnitsky*), American photographer and painter. A leading surrealist, he is known for his photographs in which images were manipulated and superimposed on one another.

Ray[3] E
/ry/, Satyajit (1921–92), Indian film director. His films, such as *Pather Panchali*, were the first Indian films to come to the attention of Western audiences.

ray[1] ● n. **1** a line of light or other radiation coming from a point. **2** a trace of a good quality: *a ray of hope.*
– ORIGIN Old French *rai.*

ray[2] ● n. a broad flat fish with a long thin tail.
– ORIGIN Latin *raia.*

ray[3] (also **re**) ● n. Music the second note of a major scale, coming after 'doh' and before 'me'.
– ORIGIN the first syllable of *resonare*, taken from a Latin hymn.

Rayleigh E
/ray-li/, John William Strutt, 3rd Baron (1842–1919), English physicist. He described the scattering of light by molecules, responsible for the blue colour of the sky, and (with William Ramsay) discovered argon and other inert gases.

rayon ● n. a synthetic fibre or fabric made from viscose.
– ORIGIN invented name.

raze ● v. (**razes**, **razing**, **razed**) completely destroy (a building, town, etc.).
– ORIGIN Old French *raser* 'shave closely'.

razor ● n. an instrument with a sharp blade, used to shave unwanted hair from the face or body.
– ORIGIN Old French *rasor.*

razor wire ● n. metal wire with sharp edges or studded with small sharp blades, used as a barrier.

razzle ● n. (in phr. **on the razzle**) informal out celebrating or enjoying oneself.
– ORIGIN from RAZZLE-DAZZLE.

razzle-dazzle ● n. = RAZZMATAZZ.
– ORIGIN from DAZZLE.

razzmatazz (also **razzamatazz**) ● n. informal noisy and exciting activity, intended to attract attention.
– ORIGIN prob. from RAZZLE-DAZZLE.

RC ● abbrev. **1** Red Cross. **2** Roman Catholic.

Rd ● abbrev. Road (used in street names).

RE ● abbrev. religious education.

re[1] /ree, ray/ ● prep. with regard to; about.
– ORIGIN Latin *res* 'thing'.

re[2] ● n. var. of RAY[3].

re- ● prefix **1** once more; anew: *reactivate.* **2** with return to a previous state: *restore.*
– ORIGIN Latin.

USAGE re-
Words formed with the prefix **re-** are usually spelt without a hyphen (*react*). However, if the word to which **re-** is attached begins with **e**, then a hyphen is used to make it clear (*re-examine, re-enter*). You should also use a hyphen when the word formed with **re-** would be exactly the same as a word that already exists; so you should use **re-cover** to mean 'cover again' and **recover** to mean 'get well again'.

're ● abbrev. informal are (usually after the pronouns you, we, and they).

reach ● v. **1** stretch out an arm so as to touch or grasp something. **2** be able to touch (something) with an outstretched arm or leg. **3** arrive at; get as far as: *we reached the bridge in good time.* **4** achieve or come to (a particular point or state). **5** make contact with. ● n. **1** the distance to which someone can stretch out their arm or arms to touch something: *the ball landed just beyond his reach.* **2** the extent to which someone or something has power, influence, or the ability to do something: *university was out of her reach.* **3** a continuous stretch of river between two bends.
– DERIVATIVES **reachable** adj.
– ORIGIN Old English.

react ● v. **1** respond to something in a particular way. **2** interact and undergo a chemical or physical change.

reactant ● n. Chem. a substance that takes part in and undergoes change during a reaction.

reaction ● n. **1** something done or experienced as a result of an event or situation: *her immediate reaction was one of relief.* **2** (**reactions**) a person's ability to respond to an event. **3** a response by the body to a drug or substance to which someone is allergic. **4** a way of thinking or behaving that is deliberately different from that of the past. **5** a process in which substances interact causing chemical or physical change.

reactionary ● adj. opposing political or social progress or reform. ● n. (pl. **reactionaries**) a person holding reactionary views.

reactivate ● v. (**reactivates**, **reactivating**, **reactivated**) bring (something) back into action.
– DERIVATIVES **reactivation** n.

reactive ● adj. **1** showing a reaction. **2** tending to react chemically.

reactor ● n. an apparatus or structure in which nuclear energy is produced in a controlled way.

read /reed/ ● v. (**reads**, **reading** /ree-ding/, **read** /red/) **1** understand the meaning of (written or printed words or symbols). **2** speak (written or printed words) aloud. **3** have a particular wording. **4** discover by reading. **5** interpret in a particular way. **6** (**read into**) think that (something) has a meaning that it may not possess. **7** esp. Brit. study (a subject) at a university. **8** (of a meas-

uring instrument) show (a measurement or figure). **9** (of a computer) copy or transfer (data). ● **n. 1** esp. Brit. an act of reading. **2** informal a book considered in terms of how interesting it is to read.
– PHRASES **read between the lines** look for or discover a meaning that is not openly stated. **take as read** accept without the need for discussion. **well read** very knowledgeable as a result of reading widely.
– DERIVATIVES **readable** adj.
– ORIGIN Old English, 'advise'.

reader ● **n. 1** a person who reads. **2** a book containing extracts of a text or texts for teaching purposes. **3** a device that produces on a screen a readable image from a microfiche or microfilm.

readership ● **n.** the readers of a publication as a group.

readily ● **adv. 1** willingly. **2** easily.

reading ● **n. 1** an instance of something being read to an audience. **2** a way of interpreting something. **3** a figure recorded on a measuring instrument. **4** a stage of debate in parliament through which a bill must pass before it can become law.

reading age ● **n.** a child's ability to read, measured by comparing it with the average ability of children of a particular age.

readjust ● **v. 1** adjust again. **2** adapt to a changed situation.
– DERIVATIVES **readjustment** n.

read-only memory ● **n.** Computing memory read at high speed but not capable of being changed by program instructions.

read-write ● **adj.** Computing capable of reading existing data and accepting alterations or further input.

ready ● **adj.** (**readier**, **readiest**) **1** prepared for an activity or situation. **2** made suitable and available for immediate use: *dinner's ready.* **3** easily available or obtained. **4** (**ready to do**) willing or eager to do. **5** quick: *a ready wit.* ● **n.** (**readies** or **the ready**) Brit. informal available money; cash. ● **v.** (**readies**, **readying**, **readied**) prepare.
– PHRASES **at the ready** available for immediate use. **make ready** prepare.
– DERIVATIVES **readiness** n.
– ORIGIN Old English.

ready-made ● **adj.** prepared in advance for immediate use.

ready money ● **n.** money in the form of cash that is immediately available.

ready-to-wear ● **adj.** (of clothes) sold through shops rather than made to order for an individual customer.

> **Reagan** E
> /ray-g'n/, Ronald (Wilson) (b.1911), American Republican statesman, 40th President of the US 1981–9. He was a Hollywood actor before entering politics. His presidency saw the launch of the Strategic Defense Initiative as well as the Irangate scandal, involving the covert sale by the US of arms to Iran.

reagent /ri-ay-juhnt/ ● **n.** a substance that produces a chemical reaction, used in tests and experiments.

real ● **adj. 1** actually existing or occurring. **2** not artificial; genuine: *the earring was real gold.* **3** worthy of the description; proper: *he's my only real friend.* **4** adjusted for changes in the power of money to buy things: *real incomes had fallen by 30 per cent.* **5** Math. (of a number or quantity) having no imaginary part. ● **adv.** informal, esp. N. Amer. really; very.
– DERIVATIVES **realness** n.
– ORIGIN Latin *realis.*

real ale ● **n.** Brit. beer that is fermented in the cask and served without additional gas pressure.

realign ● **v.** change to a different position or state.
– DERIVATIVES **realignment** n.

realism ● **n. 1** the acceptance of a situation as it is and acting accordingly. **2** (in art or literature) the presentation of things in a way that is accurate and true to life.
– DERIVATIVES **realist** n.

realistic ● **adj. 1** having a sensible and practical idea of what can be achieved. **2** showing things in a way that is accurate and true to life.
– DERIVATIVES **realistically** adv.

reality ● **n.** (pl. **realities**) **1** the state of things as they actually exist: *he refuses to face reality.* **2** a thing that is real. **3** the state of being real.

realize (also **realise**) ● **v.** (**realizes**, **realizing**, **realized**) **1** become fully aware of as a fact. **2** achieve (a wish or plan). **3** be sold for (a particular amount). **4** convert (property, shares, etc.) into money by selling.
– DERIVATIVES **realizable** (also **realisable**) adj. **realization** (also **realisation**) n.

really ● **adv. 1** in actual fact. **2** very; thoroughly. ● **exclam.** expressing interest, surprise, doubt, or protest.

realm ● **n. 1** esp. literary a kingdom. **2** a field of activity or interest: *the realms of history.*
– ORIGIN Old French *reaume.*

real property ● **n.** Law property consisting of land or buildings.

real tennis ● **n.** the original form of tennis, played with a solid ball on an enclosed court.

real-time ● **adj.** (of a computer system) in which input data is processed almost immediately.

ream ● **n. 1** 500 sheets of paper. **2** (**reams**) a large quantity.
– ORIGIN Old French *raime.*

reap ● **v. 1** cut or gather (a crop or harvest). **2** receive (a reward or benefit) as a result of one's actions.
– ORIGIN Old English.

reaper ● **n. 1** a person or machine that harvests a crop. **2** (**the Reaper** or **the Grim Reaper**) death, shown as a cloaked skeleton holding a scythe.

reappear ● **v.** appear again.
– DERIVATIVES **reappearance** n.

reappraisal ● **n.** a new or different appraisal.

rear[1] ● **n. 1** the back part of something. **2** (also **rear end**) informal a person's bottom. ● **adj.** at the back.
– PHRASES **bring up the rear** be or come last.
– ORIGIN Old French *rere.*

rear[2] ● **v. 1** bring up and care for (offspring). **2** breed (animals). **3** (of an animal) raise itself upright on its hind legs. **4** (of a building, mountain, etc.) extend to a great height.
– ORIGIN Old English, 'set upright'.

rear admiral • n. a naval rank above commodore and below vice admiral.

rearguard • n. a body of troops protecting the rear of the main force.

rearm • v. provide with or obtain a new supply of weapons.
– DERIVATIVES **rearmament** n.

rearmost • adj. furthest back.

rearrange • v. (**rearranges**, **rearranging**, **rearranged**) arrange again in a different way.
– DERIVATIVES **rearrangement** n.

rearward • adj. directed towards the back. • adv. (also **rearwards**) towards the back.

reason • n. **1** a cause or explanation. **2** good cause to do something: *we have reason to celebrate.* **3** the power to think, understand, and draw conclusions logically. **4** (**one's reason**) one's sanity. **5** what is right or possible: *I'll answer anything, within reason.* • v. **1** think, understand, and draw conclusions logically. **2** (**reason with**) persuade (someone) by giving reasons.
– PHRASES **it stands to reason** it is obvious or logical.
– ORIGIN Old French *reisun.*

reasonable • adj. **1** fair and sensible. **2** appropriate in a particular situation: *they had a reasonable time to reply.* **3** fairly good. **4** not too expensive.
– DERIVATIVES **reasonableness** n. **reasonably** adv.

reassemble • v. (**reassembles**, **reassembling**, **reassembled**) put back together.

reassert • v. assert again.

reassess • v. assess again; reconsider.
– DERIVATIVES **reassessment** n.

reassign • v. assign again or differently.
– DERIVATIVES **reassignment** n.

reassure • v. (**reassures**, **reassuring**, **reassured**) cause to feel less worried or afraid.
– DERIVATIVES **reassurance** n.

rebarbative /ri-bar-buh-tiv/ • adj. formal unattractive and objectionable.
– ORIGIN French *rébarbatif.*

rebate /ree-bayt/ • n. **1** a partial refund to someone who has paid too much for tax, rent, etc. **2** a discount on an amount of money due.
– ORIGIN Old French *rebatre* 'beat back'.

rebel • n. /reb-uhl/ a person who rebels. • v. /ri-bel/ (**rebels**, **rebelling**, **rebelled**) **1** fight against or refuse to obey an established government or ruler. **2** resist authority, control, or accepted behaviour.
– ORIGIN Old French *rebelle.*

rebellion • n. **1** an act of rebelling against a government or ruler. **2** opposition to authority or control.

rebellious • adj. rebelling or wanting to rebel.
– DERIVATIVES **rebelliously** adv. **rebelliousness** n.

rebirth • n. **1** a return to life or activity: *a rebirth of faith in the old values.* **2** the process of being born again.

reborn • adj. brought back to life or activity.

rebound • v. /ri-**bownd**/ **1** bounce back after hitting a hard surface. **2** (**rebound on/upon**) have an unexpected and unpleasant effect on: *his tricks are rebounding on him.* • n. /ree-bownd/ a ball or shot that rebounds.
– PHRASES **on the rebound** while still upset after the ending of a romantic relationship.
– ORIGIN Old French *rebondir.*

rebuff • v. reject in an abrupt or unkind way. • n. an abrupt or unkind rejection.
– ORIGIN from former French *rebuffer.*

rebuild • v. (**rebuilds**, **rebuilding**, **rebuilt**) build again.

rebuke • v. (**rebukes**, **rebuking**, **rebuked**) criticize or reprimand sharply. • n. a sharp criticism.
– ORIGIN Old French *rebuker* 'beat down'.

rebut /ri-but/ • v. (**rebuts**, **rebutting**, **rebutted**) claim or prove to be false.
– ORIGIN Old French *rebuter* 'rebuke'.

rebuttal • n. a claim or proof that something is false.

recalcitrant /ri-kal-si-truhnt/ • adj. unwilling to cooperate; disobedient.
– DERIVATIVES **recalcitrance** n.
– ORIGIN Latin *recalcitrare* 'kick out with the heels'.

recall /ri-kawl/ • v. **1** remember. **2** cause one to think of. **3** officially order (someone) to return. **4** (of a manufacturer) request the return of (faulty products). • n. /also ree-kawl/ **1** the action or ability of remembering. **2** an act of officially recalling someone or something.

recant /ri-kant/ • v. withdraw a former opinion or belief.
– ORIGIN Latin *recantare* 'revoke'.

recap informal • v. (**recaps**, **recapping**, **recapped**) recapitulate. • n. a recapitulation.

recapitulate /ree-kuh-pit-yuu-layt/ • v. (**recapitulates**, **recapitulating**, **recapitulated**) give a summary of what has just been said.
– DERIVATIVES **recapitulation** n.
– ORIGIN Latin *recapitulare* 'go through heading by heading'.

recapture • v. (**recaptures**, **recapturing**, **recaptured**) **1** capture (a person or animal that has escaped). **2** recover (something taken or lost). **3** bring back or experience again (a past time, event, or feeling). • n. an act of recapturing.

recast • v. (**recasts**, **recasting**, **recast**) **1** cast (metal) again or differently. **2** present in a different form.

recce /rek-ki/ • n. Brit. informal reconnaissance.

recede • v. (**recedes**, **receding**, **receded**) **1** move back or further away. **2** gradually become weaker or smaller: *her panic receded.* **3** (**receding**) (of part of the face) sloping backwards.
– ORIGIN Latin *recedere.*

receipt • n. **1** the action of receiving something. **2** a written statement confirming that something has been paid for or received. **3** (**receipts**) an amount of money received over a period by a business.
– ORIGIN Old French *receite.*

receive • v. (**receives**, **receiving**, **received**) **1** be given or paid. **2** accept or take in (something sent or offered). **3** form (an idea) from an experience. **4** experience or meet with: *the event received wide press coverage.* **5** entertain as a guest. **6** admit as a member. **7** detect or pick up (broadcast signals). **8** (**received**) widely accepted as true.

– DERIVATIVES **receivable** adj.
– ORIGIN Old French *receivre*.

received pronunciation ● n. the standard form of British English pronunciation, based on educated speech in southern England.

receiver ● n. **1** a radio or television apparatus that converts broadcast signals into sound or images. **2** the part of a telephone that converts electrical signals into sounds. **3** (Brit. also **official receiver**) a person appointed to manage the financial affairs of a bankrupt business.

receivership ● n. the state of being managed by an official receiver.

recent ● adj. having happened or been done only a short time ago.
– DERIVATIVES **recently** adv.
– ORIGIN Latin *recens*.

receptacle /ri-sep-tuh-k'l/ ● n. a container.
– ORIGIN Latin *receptaculum*.

reception ● n. **1** the action of receiving. **2** the way in which something is received: *an enthusiastic reception*. **3** a formal social occasion held to welcome someone or celebrate an event. **4** the area in a hotel, office, etc. where visitors are greeted. **5** the quality with which broadcast signals are received.
– ORIGIN Latin.

receptionist ● n. a person who greets and deals with clients and visitors to an office, hotel, etc.

receptive ● adj. **1** able or willing to receive something. **2** willing to consider new ideas.
– DERIVATIVES **receptivity** n.

receptor /ri-sep-ter/ ● n. an organ or cell in the body that responds to a stimulus such as light and transmits a signal to a sensory nerve.

recess /ri-sess, ree-sess/ ● n. **1** a small space set back in a wall or set into a surface. **2** (**recesses**) remote or hidden places. **3** a break between sessions of a parliament, law court, etc. ● v. set (a fitment) back into a wall or surface.
– ORIGIN Latin *recessus*.

recession ● n. a temporary economic decline during which trade and industrial activity are reduced.
– DERIVATIVES **recessionary** adj.

recessive ● adj. (of a gene) appearing in offspring only if a contrary gene is not also inherited. Compare with **DOMINANT**.

recharge ● v. (**recharges**, **recharging**, **recharged**) charge (a battery or battery-operated device) again.
– DERIVATIVES **rechargeable** adj.

recherché /ruh-shair-shay/ ● adj. unusual or little known and therefore not easily understood.
– ORIGIN French, 'carefully sought out'.

recidivist /ri-sid-i-vist/ ● n. a person who constantly commits crimes and is not discouraged by being punished.
– DERIVATIVES **recidivism** n.
– ORIGIN French *récivider* 'fall back'.

recipe ● n. **1** a list of ingredients and instructions for preparing a dish. **2** something likely to lead to a particular outcome: *high interest rates are a recipe for disaster*.
– ORIGIN Latin, 'receive!'.

recipient /ri-sip-i-uhnt/ ● n. a person who receives something.

reciprocal /ri-sip-ruh-k'l/ ● adj. **1** given or done in return: *he showed no reciprocal interest in me*. **2** (of an agreement or arrangement) affecting two parties equally. ● n. Math. the quantity obtained by dividing the number one by a given quantity.
– DERIVATIVES **reciprocally** adv.

reciprocate ● v. (**reciprocates**, **reciprocating**, **reciprocated**) respond to (an action or emotion) with a similar one.
– ORIGIN Latin *reciprocare* 'move backwards and forwards'.

reciprocity /re-si-pross-i-ti/ ● n. a situation in which two parties provide the same help or advantages to each other.

recital ● n. **1** the performance of a programme of music by a soloist or small group. **2** a long account of a series of things: *a recital of Adam's failures*.

recitation /re-si-tay-sh'n/ ● n. **1** the action of reciting. **2** something that is recited.

recitative /re-si-tuh-teev/ ● n. a passage in an opera or oratorio used for conversation or to tell the story, sung in a rhythm like that of ordinary speech.

recite ● v. (**recites**, **reciting**, **recited**) **1** repeat (a passage) aloud from memory in front of an audience. **2** state (facts, events, etc.) in order.
– ORIGIN Latin *recitare*.

reckless ● adj. without thought or care for the results of an action.
– DERIVATIVES **recklessly** adv. **recklessness** n.
– ORIGIN Old English.

reckon ● v. **1** calculate. **2** have an opinion about; think. **3** (**reckon on**) rely on or expect: *they had reckoned on one more day of privacy*. **4** (**reckon with** or **without**) take (or fail to take) into account.
– PHRASES **to be reckoned with** to be treated as important.
– ORIGIN Old English, 'recount, tell'.

reckoning ● n. **1** the action of calculating something. **2** a person's opinion. **3** punishment for one's actions.
– PHRASES **into** (or **out of**) **the reckoning** among (or not among) those who are likely to be successful.

reclaim ● v. **1** recover possession of. **2** make (waste land or land formerly under water) usable.
– DERIVATIVES **reclamation** n.

recline ● v. (**reclines**, **reclining**, **reclined**) lean or lie back in a relaxed position.
– DERIVATIVES **recliner** n.
– ORIGIN Latin *reclinare*.

recluse /ri-klooss/ ● n. a person who avoids others and lives alone.
– ORIGIN Old French *reclus* 'shut up'.

reclusive ● adj. avoiding the company of other people.

recognition ● n. **1** the action of recognizing or the state of being recognized. **2** appreciation or acknowledgement.

recognize (also **recognise**) ● v. (**recognizes**, **recognizing**, **recognized**) **1** know (someone or something) from having come across them before. **2** accept as genuine, legal, or valid: *the qualifications are recognized by the Department of Education*. **3** show official appreciation of.

– DERIVATIVES **recognizable** (also **recognisable**) adj.
– ORIGIN Latin *recognoscere*.

recoil ● v. **1** suddenly move back in fear, horror, or disgust. **2** (of a gun) suddenly move backwards as a reaction on firing a bullet, shell, etc. **3** (**recoil on/upon**) have an unpleasant effect on. ● n. the action of recoiling.
– ORIGIN Old French *reculer* 'move back'.

recollect /rek-uh-lekt/ ● v. remember.

recollection ● n. **1** the action of remembering. **2** a memory.

recommence ● v. (**recommences, recommencing, recommenced**) begin again.

recommend ● v. **1** put forward as being suitable for a purpose or role. **2** make appealing or desirable: *the house had much to recommend it.*
– DERIVATIVES **recommendation** n.

recompense /rek-uhm-penss/ ● v. (**recompenses, recompensing, recompensed**) **1** make amends to (someone) for loss or harm suffered; compensate. **2** pay or reward for work. ● n. compensation or reward.
– ORIGIN Latin *recompensare*.

reconcile /rek-uhn-syl/ ● v. (**reconciles, reconciling, reconciled**) **1** restore friendly relations between. **2** find a satisfactory way of dealing with (opposing facts, ideas, etc.): *an attempt to reconcile freedom with commitment.* **3** (**reconcile to**) make (someone) accept (something unwelcome).
– DERIVATIVES **reconcilable** adj.
– ORIGIN Latin *reconciliare*.

reconciliation /rek-uhn-si-li-ay-sh'n/ ● n. **1** the end of a disagreement and the return to friendly relations. **2** the action of reconciling opposing ideas, facts, etc.

recondite /rek-uhn-dyt, ri-kon-dyt/ ● adj. (of a subject or knowledge) little known.
– ORIGIN Latin *reconditus* 'hidden'.

recondition ● v. Brit. bring back to a good condition; renovate.

reconnaissance /ri-kon-ni-suhnss/ ● n. military observation of an area to gain information.
– ORIGIN French.

reconnoitre /rek-uh-noy-ter/ (US **reconnoiter**) ● v. (**reconnoitres, reconnoitring, reconnoitred**; US **reconnoiters, reconnoitering, reconnoitered**) make a military observation of (an area).
– ORIGIN former French.

reconsider ● v. (**reconsiders, reconsidering, reconsidered**) consider again, with the possibility of changing a decision.
– DERIVATIVES **reconsideration** n.

reconstitute ● v. (**reconstitutes, reconstituting, reconstituted**) **1** change the form of (an organization). **2** restore (dried food) to its original state by adding water.
– DERIVATIVES **reconstitution** n.

reconstruct ● v. **1** construct again. **2** create or act out (a past event) from evidence.
– DERIVATIVES **reconstruction** n. **reconstructive** adj.

reconvene ● v. (**reconvenes, reconvening, reconvened**) meet again after a break.

record ● n. /rek-ord/ **1** a permanent account of something that is kept for evidence or information. **2** the previous behaviour or performance of a person or thing: *the team preserved their unbeaten home record.* **3** (also **criminal record**) a list of a person's previous criminal convictions. **4** the best performance or most remarkable event of its kind that has been officially recognized. **5** a thin plastic disc carrying recorded sound in grooves on each surface. ● v. /ri-kord/ **1** make a record of. **2** convert (sound, a broadcast, etc.) into permanent form in order to be reproduced later.
– PHRASES **for the record** so that the true facts are recorded. **on** (or **off**) **the record** made (or not made) as an official statement.
– DERIVATIVES **recordable** adj. **recordist** n.
– ORIGIN Latin *recordari* 'remember'.

recorded delivery ● n. Brit. a service in which a person receiving an item through the post has to sign a form as a record that it has been delivered.

recorder ● n. **1** a device for recording sound, pictures, etc. **2** a person who keeps records. **3** (**Recorder**) (in England and Wales) a barrister appointed to serve as a part-time judge. **4** a simple woodwind instrument with holes along it for the fingers.

recording ● n. **1** a piece of music, film, etc. that has been recorded. **2** the process of recording.

record player ● n. a device for playing records, with a turntable and a stylus that picks up sound from the groove.

recount[1] /ri-kownt/ ● v. tell someone about something.
– ORIGIN Old French *reconter* 'tell again'.

recount[2] ● v. /ree-kownt/ count again. ● n. /ree-kownt/ an act of counting something again.

recoup ● v. recover (a loss).
– ORIGIN French *recouper* 'cut back'.

recourse ● n. **1** a source of help in a difficult situation. **2** (**recourse to**) the use of someone or something as a source of help.
– ORIGIN Latin *recursus*.

recover ● v. (**recovers, recovering, recovered**) **1** return to a normal state of health, mind, or strength. **2** find or regain possession or control of: *he recovered his balance.* **3** regain (an amount of money spent or owed).
– DERIVATIVES **recoverable** adj.
– ORIGIN Old French *recoverer*.

re-cover ● v. (**re-covers, re-covering, re-covered**) put a new cover on.

recovery ● n. (pl. **recoveries**) the action or an act of recovering.

recreate ● v. (**recreates, recreating, recreated**) make or do again.

recreation[1] /rek-ri-ay-sh'n/ ● n. enjoyable leisure activity.
– DERIVATIVES **recreational** adj.
– ORIGIN Latin.

recreation[2] /ree-kri-ay-sh'n/ ● n. the action of recreating something.

recreation ground ● n. Brit. a piece of public land used for sports and games.

recrimination ● n. an accusation in response to one from someone else.
– ORIGIN Latin *recriminari*.

recruit ● v. **1** take on (someone) to serve in the armed forces or work for an organization. **2** informal persuade. ● n. a newly recruited

person.
– DERIVATIVES **recruiter** n. **recruitment** n.
– ORIGIN from former French *recrute*.

recta pl. of **RECTUM**.

rectangle • n. a plane figure with four straight sides and four right angles, and with unequal adjacent sides.
– DERIVATIVES **rectangular** adj.
– ORIGIN Latin *rectangulum*.

rectify • v. (**rectifies**, **rectifying**, **rectified**) **1** put right; correct. **2** convert (alternating current) to direct current.
– DERIVATIVES **rectification** n.
– ORIGIN Latin *rectificare*.

rectilinear /rek-ti-lin-i-er/ • adj. within or moving in a straight line or lines.
– ORIGIN Latin *rectilineus*.

rectitude • n. morally correct behaviour.
– ORIGIN Old French.

recto • n. (pl. **rectos**) a right-hand page of an open book. Contrasted with **VERSO**.
– ORIGIN Latin, 'on the right'.

rector • n. **1** (in the Church of England) a priest in charge of a parish. **2** (in the Roman Catholic Church) a priest in charge of a church or a religious institution. **3** the head of certain universities, colleges, and schools. **4** (in Scotland) a person elected to represent students on a university's governing body.
– ORIGIN Latin, 'ruler'.

rectory • n. (pl. **rectories**) the house of a rector.

rectum /rek-tuhm/ • n. (pl. **rectums** or **recta** /rek-tuh/) the final section of the large intestine, ending at the anus.
– DERIVATIVES **rectal** adj.
– ORIGIN from Latin *rectum intestinum* 'straight intestine'.

recumbent /ri-kum-buhnt/ • adj. lying down.
– ORIGIN Latin *recumbere*.

recuperate /ri-koo-puh-rayt/ • v. (**recuperates**, **recuperating**, **recuperated**) **1** recover from illness or tiredness. **2** regain (something lost).
– DERIVATIVES **recuperation** n. **recuperative** adj.
– ORIGIN Latin *recuperare*.

recur • v. (**recurs**, **recurring**, **recurred**) happen again or repeatedly.
– DERIVATIVES **recurrence** n.
– ORIGIN Latin *recurrere*.

recurrent • adj. happening often or repeatedly.

recurring decimal • n. a decimal fraction in which a figure or group of figures is repeated indefinitely, as in *0.666 …*

recusant /rek-yuu-zuhnt/ • n. a person who refuses to obey an authority or a regulation.
– ORIGIN Latin *recusare* 'refuse'.

recycle • v. (**recycles**, **recycling**, **recycled**) **1** convert (waste) into a form in which it can be reused. **2** use again.
– DERIVATIVES **recyclable** adj. **recycler** n.

red • adj. (**redder**, **reddest**) **1** of the colour of blood or fire. **2** (of hair or fur) reddish-brown. **3** informal, esp. derog. communist or socialist. • n. **1** red colour or material. **2** informal, esp. derog. a communist or socialist.
– PHRASES **in the red** having spent more than is in one's bank account. **see red** informal suddenly become very angry.
– DERIVATIVES **reddish** adj. **redness** n.
– ORIGIN Old English.

red admiral • n. a butterfly having dark wings with red bands and white spots.

Red Army Faction E
a left-wing terrorist group in former West Germany, active from 1968 onwards. It was originally led by Andreas Baader (1943–77) and Ulrike Meinhof (1934–76). Also called **BAADER-MEINHOF GROUP**.

red-blooded • adj. (of a man) full of energy, especially sexual energy.

red-brick • adj. (of a British university) founded in the late 19th or early 20th century and with buildings of red brick, as distinct from the older universities.

Red Brigades E
a left-wing terrorist organization based in Italy and active from the early 1970s.

red card • n. (in soccer) a red card shown by the referee to a player being sent off.

red carpet • n. a strip of red carpet for an important visitor to walk along.

redcoat • n. hist. a British soldier.

Red Crescent • n. the equivalent of the Red Cross in Muslim countries.

Red Cross • n. the International Movement of the Red Cross and the Red Crescent, an organization that helps victims of war or natural disaster.

redcurrant • n. a small edible red berry.

redden • v. make or become red.

redecorate • v. (**redecorates**, **redecorating**, **redecorated**) decorate again or differently.
– DERIVATIVES **redecoration** n.

redeem • v. **1** make up for the faults or bad aspects of: *a poor debate redeemed by an outstanding speech.* **2** save from sin or evil. **3** fulfil (a promise). **4** regain possession of (something) in exchange for payment. **5** exchange (a coupon) for goods or money. **6** repay (a debt).
– DERIVATIVES **redeemable** adj.
– ORIGIN Latin *redimere* 'buy back'.

Redeemer • n. (**the Redeemer**) Jesus Christ.

redemption • n. the action of redeeming or the state of being redeemed.
– DERIVATIVES **redemptive** adj.

redeploy • v. move (troops, employees, or resources) to a new place or task.
– DERIVATIVES **redeployment** n.

redevelop • v. (**redevelops**, **redeveloping**, **redeveloped**) develop again or differently.
– DERIVATIVES **redevelopment** n.

red flag • n. a warning of danger.

Redford, E
(Charles) Robert (b.1936), American film actor and director, known for his roles in films such as *Butch Cassidy and the Sundance Kid* and *The Sting*, and as the director of *Ordinary People*.

Redgrave[1], E
Sir Michael (Scudamore) (1908–85), English actor, who played many Shakespearean stage roles and also starred in films such as *The Browning Version*.

Redgrave², E
Sir Steve (b.1962; full name *Steven Geoffrey Redgrave*), English rower, who won five consecutive Olympic gold medals 1984–2000.

Redgrave³, E
Vanessa (b.1937), English actress, daughter of Sir Michael Redgrave. Her films include *Julia* and *Howard's End*.

red-handed • adj. in or just after the act of doing something wrong.

redhead • n. a person with red hair.

red herring • n. a thing that draws attention away from something important.
– ORIGIN from the use of the scent of a smoked herring in training hounds.

red-hot • adj. **1** so hot as to glow red. **2** very exciting or recent.

redid past of **REDO**.

Red Indian • n. dated = **AMERICAN INDIAN**.

redirect • v. direct to a different place or purpose.

rediscover • v. (**rediscovers**, **rediscovering**, **rediscovered**) discover (something forgotten or ignored) again.
– DERIVATIVES **rediscovery** n.

redistribute • v. (**redistributes**, **redistributing**, **redistributed**) distribute again or differently.
– DERIVATIVES **redistribution** n.

red lead • n. a red form of lead oxide used as a pigment.

red-letter day • n. an important or memorable day.
– ORIGIN from the practice of highlighting a festival in red on a calendar.

red light • n. a red light instructing moving vehicles to stop.

red-light district • n. an area with many brothels, strip clubs, etc.
– ORIGIN from the use of a red light as the sign of a brothel.

red meat • n. meat that is red when raw, e.g. beef.

redneck • n. informal, derog. a rural working-class white person from the southern US, with conservative views.

redo • v. (**redoes**, **redoing**, **redid**; past part. **redone**) do again or differently.

redolent /red-uh-luhnt/ • adj. (**redolent of/with**) **1** strongly suggestive of: *names redolent of horse racing*. **2** literary strongly smelling of.
– DERIVATIVES **redolence** n.
– ORIGIN Latin *redolere* 'give out a strong smell'.

Redon E
/re-don/, Odilon (1840–1916), French symbolist painter and graphic artist.

redouble • v. (**redoubles**, **redoubling**, **redoubled**) make or become greater or more intense.

redoubt • n. a temporary or additional fortification without defences flanking it.
– ORIGIN French *redoute*.

redoubtable • adj. worthy of respect or fear: *he was a redoubtable debater*.
– ORIGIN Old French *redouter* 'to fear'.

redound /ri-downd/ • v. (**redound to**) formal contribute greatly to (a person's credit).
– ORIGIN Latin *redundare* 'surge'.

red pepper • n. the ripe red fruit of a sweet pepper.

redress • v. /ree-**dress**/ set right (something unfair or wrong). • n. /ri-**dress**/ payment or action to make amends for a wrong.
– ORIGIN Old French *redresser*.

Red Sea E
a long, narrow landlocked sea separating Africa from Arabia. It is linked to the Indian Ocean by the Gulf of Aden and to the Mediterranean by the Suez Canal.

redskin • n. dated or offens. an American Indian.

red tape • n. complicated official rules which hinder progress.
– ORIGIN from the red or pink tape used to bind official documents.

reduce • v. (**reduces**, **reducing**, **reduced**) **1** make or become less. **2** (**reduce to**) change (something) to (a different or simpler form). **3** (**reduce to**) bring to (a particular state): *she was reduced to stunned silence*. **4** boil (a sauce or other liquid) so that it becomes thicker. **5** Chem. cause to combine chemically with hydrogen. **6** Chem. cause to undergo a reaction in which electrons are gained from another substance or molecule. Opp. **OXIDIZE**.
– PHRASES **reduced circumstances** poverty after being more wealthy.
– DERIVATIVES **reducer** n. **reducible** adj.
– ORIGIN Latin *reducere* 'bring back'.

reduction • n. **1** the action of reducing something. **2** the amount by which something is reduced. **3** a smaller copy of a picture or photograph.

reductive • adj. presenting a subject or problem in an over-simplified form.

redundant • adj. **1** no longer needed or useful: *the old skills had become redundant*. **2** Brit. made unemployed because one's job is no longer needed.
– DERIVATIVES **redundancy** n. (pl. **redundancies**).
– ORIGIN Latin *redundare* 'surge'.

redwood • n. a giant coniferous tree with reddish wood, found in California and Oregon.

Reed¹, E
Sir Carol (1906–76), English film director. His films include *The Third Man* and the musical *Oliver!*

Reed², E
(Robert) Oliver (1938–1999), English film actor, known for such films as *Women In Love* and *The Four Musketeers*.

reed • n. **1** a tall plant with a hollow stem, growing in water or on marshy ground. **2** a piece of thin cane or metal which vibrates in a current of air to produce the sound of certain musical instruments, such as a clarinet.
– ORIGIN Old English.

reed organ • n. a keyboard instrument similar to a harmonium, in which air is drawn upwards past metal reeds.

re-educate • v. (**re-educates**, **re-educating**, **re-educated**) educate or train to behave or think differently.

reedy • adj. **1** (of a sound or voice) high and thin in tone. **2** full of reeds. **3** (of a person) tall

r

and thin.

reef • n. **1** a ridge of jagged rock or coral just above or below the surface of the sea. **2** a vein of gold or other ore. **3** each of several strips across a sail that can be drawn in so as to reduce the area exposed to the wind. • v. take in a reef or reefs of (a sail).
– ORIGIN Old Norse, 'rib'.

reefer • n. informal a cannabis cigarette.
– ORIGIN perh. from Mexican Spanish *grifo* 'smoker of cannabis'.

reefer jacket • n. a thick close-fitting double-breasted jacket.

reef knot • n. a type of double knot that is very secure.

reek • v. have a very unpleasant smell. • n. a very unpleasant smell.
– ORIGIN Old English, 'give out smoke'.

reel • n. **1** a cylinder on which film, wire, thread, etc. can be wound. **2** a lively Scottish or Irish folk dance. • v. **1** (**reel in**) bring towards one by turning a reel. **2** (**reel off**) say rapidly and with ease. **3** stagger. **4** feel shocked or bewildered.
– ORIGIN Old English.

re-elect • v. elect again.
– DERIVATIVES **re-election** n.

re-emerge • v. (**re-emerges**, **re-emerging**, **re-emerged**) emerge again.
– DERIVATIVES **re-emergence** n.

re-enact • v. act out (a past event).
– DERIVATIVES **re-enactment** n.

re-enter • v. (**re-enters**, **re-entering**, **re-entered**) enter again.
– DERIVATIVES **re-entry** n.

reeve • n. the chief magistrate of a town or district in Anglo-Saxon England.
– ORIGIN Old English.

re-examine • v. (**re-examines**, **re-examining**, **re-examined**) examine again or further.
– DERIVATIVES **re-examination** n.

ref • n. informal (in sports) a referee.

refectory • n. (pl. **refectories**) a room used for meals in an educational or religious institution.
– ORIGIN Latin *refectorium*.

refer • v. (**refers**, **referring**, **referred**) **1** (**refer to**) write or say about; mention. **2** (**refer to**) (of a word or phrase) describe. **3** (**refer to**) turn to (something) for information; consult. **4** (**refer to**) pass (a person or matter) to (an authority or specialist) for a decision. **5** fail (a candidate in an examination).
– DERIVATIVES **referable** adj.
– ORIGIN Latin *referre* 'carry back'.

referee • n. **1** an official who supervises a game to ensure that players keep to the rules. **2** a person who provides a reference for a person applying for a job. **3** a person appointed to assess an academic work for publication. • v. (**referees**, **refereeing**, **refereed**) be a referee of.

reference • n. **1** the action of referring to something. **2** a mention of a source of information in a book or article. **3** a letter from a previous employer giving information about someone's ability, used when applying for a new job.
– PHRASES **terms of reference** the scope of an activity or area of knowledge. **with** (or **in**) **reference to** in relation to.

reference library • n. a library in which the books are to be consulted rather than borrowed.

referendum /re-fuh-ren-duhm/ • n. (pl. **referendums** or **referenda** /re-fuh-ren-duh/) a direct vote by the electorate of a country on a single political issue.
– ORIGIN Latin, 'something to be referred'.

referral • n. the action of referring someone or something to a specialist or higher authority.

refill • v. /ree-fil/ fill again. • n. /ree-fil/ an act of refilling something.
– DERIVATIVES **refillable** adj.

refine • v. (**refines**, **refining**, **refined**) **1** remove unwanted substances from. **2** improve by making minor changes: *computer applications that have been refined for years.* **3** (**refined**) well educated, elegant, and having good taste.

refinement • n. **1** the process of refining. **2** an improvement. **3** the quality of being well educated, elegant, and having good taste.

refinery • n. (pl. **refineries**) a factory where a substance is refined.

refit • v. /ree-fit/ (**refits**, **refitting**, **refitted**) replace or repair equipment and fittings in (a ship, building, etc.). • n. /ree-fit/ an act of refitting.

reflect • v. **1** throw back (heat, light, or sound) from a surface. **2** (of a mirror or shiny surface) show an image of. **3** show in a realistic or appropriate way: *schools should reflect cultural differences.* **4** (**reflect well/badly on**) bring about a good or bad impression of. **5** (**reflect on/upon**) think seriously about.
– ORIGIN Latin *reflectere* 'bend back'.

reflecting telescope • n. a telescope in which a mirror is used to collect and focus light.

reflection • n. **1** the process of light, heat, or sound being reflected. **2** an image formed by reflection. **3** a sign. **4** a source of shame or blame. **5** serious thought.

reflective • adj. **1** providing a reflection. **2** thoughtful.
– DERIVATIVES **reflectivity** n.

reflector • n. **1** a piece of glass, plastic, etc. on the back of a vehicle for reflecting light. **2** an object or device which reflects radio waves, sound, or other waves.

reflex • n. an action done without conscious thought as a response to something. • adj. **1** done as a reflex. **2** (of an angle) more than 180°.
– ORIGIN Latin *reflexus* 'a bending back'.

reflex camera • n. a camera in which the image given by the lens is reflected by an angled mirror to the viewfinder.

reflexive • adj. **1** Grammar (of a pronoun) that refers back to the subject of a clause, e.g. *myself* in the clause *I hurt myself.* **2** Grammar (of a verb or clause) having a reflexive pronoun as its object (e.g. *wash oneself*). **3** done without conscious thought; reflex.
– DERIVATIVES **reflexively** adv.

reflexology • n. a system of massage used to relieve tension and treat illness, based on the theory that there are points on the feet, hands, and head linked to every part of the body.
– DERIVATIVES **reflexologist** n.

refocus • v. (**refocuses**, **refocusing**, **refocused** or **refocusses**, **refocussing**, **refocussed**) **1** adjust the focus of (a lens or one's eyes). **2** focus (attention) on something new or different.

reform • v. **1** make changes in (something) so as to improve it. **2** make (someone) improve their behaviour. • n. the action or an act of reforming.
– DERIVATIVES **reformer** n.
– ORIGIN Latin *reformare* 'form again'.

re-form • v. form again.

reformation • n. **1** the action of reforming. **2** (**the Reformation**) a 16th-century movement for the reform of the Roman Catholic Church, that ended in the establishment of the Protestant Churches.

reformist • adj. supporting gradual political or social reform. • n. a supporter of such a policy.
– DERIVATIVES **reformism** n.

refract • v. (of water, air, or glass) make (a ray of light) change direction when it enters at an angle.
– DERIVATIVES **refraction** n.
ORIGIN Latin *refringere* 'break up'

refracting telescope • n. a telescope which uses a lens to collect and focus the light.

refractive • adj. having to do with refraction.

refractor • n. a lens or other object which causes refraction.

refractory • adj. **1** stubborn or difficult to control. **2** Med. (of a disease or medical condition) not responding to treatment. **3** tech. heat-resistant.
– ORIGIN Latin *refractarius*.

refrain[1] • v. (**refrain from**) stop oneself from (doing something).
– ORIGIN Latin *refrenare*.

refrain[2] • n. the part of a song that is repeated at the end of each verse.
– ORIGIN Latin *refringere* 'break up'.

refresh • v. **1** give new strength or energy to. **2** prompt (someone's memory) by going over previous information.

refresher course • n. a course intended to improve or update one's skills or knowledge.

refreshing • adj. **1** giving new energy or strength. **2** pleasantly new or different.

refreshment • n. **1** a light snack or drink. **2** the giving of fresh strength or energy.

refrigerant • n. a substance used for keeping things cold.

refrigerate • v. (**refrigerates**, **refrigerating**, **refrigerated**) make (food or drink) cold so as to chill or preserve it.
– DERIVATIVES **refrigeration** n.
– ORIGIN Latin *refrigerare*.

refrigerator • n. an appliance or compartment in which food and drink is stored at a low temperature.

refuel • v. (**refuels**, **refuelling**, **refuelled**; US **refuels**, **refueling**, **refueled**) supply with more fuel.

refuge • n. a place or state of safety from danger or trouble: *he took refuge in the French embassy.*
– ORIGIN Latin *refugium*.

refugee • n. a person who has been forced to leave their country because of a war or because they are being persecuted for their beliefs.

refulgent /ri-ful-juhnt/ • adj. literary shining very brightly.
– ORIGIN Latin *refulgere* 'shine out'.

refund • v. /ri-fund/ pay back (money) to. • n. /ree-fund/ a repayment of a sum of money.
– DERIVATIVES **refundable** adj.
– ORIGIN Latin *refundere* 'pour back'.

refurbish • v. redecorate and improve (a building or room).
– DERIVATIVES **refurbishment** n.

refuse[1] /ri-fyooz/ • v. (**refuses**, **refusing**, **refused**) **1** state that one is unwilling to do something. **2** state that one is unwilling to give or accept (something offered or requested).
– DERIVATIVES **refusal** n.
– ORIGIN Old French *refuser*.

refuse[2] /ref-yooss/ • n. matter thrown away as worthless.
– ORIGIN perh. from Old French *refusé* 'refused'.

refute /ri-fyoot/ • v. (**refutes**, **refuting**, **refuted**) prove (a statement or person) to be wrong.
– DERIVATIVES **refutation** n.
– ORIGIN Latin *refutare* 'repel, rebut'.

regain • v. **1** get back (something) after losing possession or control of it. **2** get back to (a place).

regal • adj. having to do with or fit for a monarch, especially in being magnificent or dignified.
– DERIVATIVES **regality** n. **regally** adv.
– ORIGIN Latin *regalis*.

regale • v. (**regales**, **regaling**, **regaled**) **1** entertain (someone) with conversation. **2** supply (someone) generously with food or drink.
– ORIGIN French *régaler*.

regalia /ri-gay-li-uh/ • n. **1** objects such as the crown and sceptre, symbolizing royalty and used at coronations or other state occasions. **2** the distinctive clothing and objects of an order, rank, or office, worn at formal occasions.
– ORIGIN Latin, 'royal privileges'.

regard • v. **1** think of in a particular way. **2** look steadily at. • n. **1** concern or care: *she rescued him without regard for herself.* **2** high opinion; respect. **3** a steady look. **4** (**regards**) best wishes.
– PHRASES **as regards** concerning. **with** (or **in**) **regard to** as concerns.
– ORIGIN Old French *regarder* 'to watch'.

regarding • prep. about; concerning.

regardless • adv. **1** (**regardless of**) without concern for. **2** despite what is happening: *they were determined to carry on regardless.*

regatta • n. a sporting event consisting of a series of boat or yacht races.
– ORIGIN Italian, 'a fight or contest'.

regency /ree-juhn-si/ • n. (pl. **regencies**) **1** a period of government by a regent. **2** (**the Regency**) the period when George, Prince of Wales, acted as regent in Britain (1811–20). • adj. (**Regency**) in the classical style of British architecture, furniture, etc. popular during the late 18th and early 19th centuries.

regenerate /ri-jen-uh-rayt/ • v. (**regenerates**, **regenerating**, **regenerated**) **1** bring

new life or strength to. **2** grow (new tissue).
– DERIVATIVES **regeneration** n. **regenerative** adj.

regent • n. a person appointed to rule a state because the monarch is too young or unfit to rule, or is absent. • adj. (after a noun) acting as regent: *Prince Regent*.
– ORIGIN Latin, 'ruling'.

reggae /reg-gay/ • n. a style of popular music with a strong beat, originating in Jamaica.
– ORIGIN perh. from Jamaican English *rege-rege* 'quarrel'.

regicide /rej-i-syd/ • n. **1** the killing of a king. **2** a person who kills a king.
– ORIGIN Latin *rex* 'king'.

regime /ray-*zheem*/ • n. **1** a government, especially one that strictly controls a state. **2** an ordered way of doing something; a system.
– ORIGIN French.

regimen /rej-i-muhn/ • n. a course of medical treatment, diet, or exercise, followed to improve one's health.
– ORIGIN Latin *regere* 'to rule'.

regiment • n. /rej-i-muhnt/ **1** a permanent unit of an army. **2** a large number of people or things. • v. /rej-i-ment/ organize according to a strict system.
– DERIVATIVES **regimental** adj. **regimentation** n.
– ORIGIN Latin *regimentum* 'rule'.

Regina /ri-jy-nuh/ • n. the reigning queen (used following a name or in the titles of lawsuits, e.g. *Regina v. Jones*, the Crown versus Jones).
– ORIGIN Latin.

region • n. **1** an area of a country or the world having particular characteristics: *the equatorial regions*. **2** an administrative district of a city or country. **3** (**the regions**) the parts of a country outside the capital or centre of government. **4** a part of the body.
– PHRASES **in the region of** approximately.
– DERIVATIVES **regional** adj. **regionally** adv.
– ORIGIN Latin, 'direction, district'.

regionalism • n. loyalty to one's own region in cultural and political terms, rather than to central government.
– DERIVATIVES **regionalist** n. & adj.

register • n. **1** an official list or record. **2** a particular part of the range of a person's voice or a musical instrument. **3** the level and style of a piece of writing or speech, varying according to the situation in which it is used and indicated by the kinds of words used (e.g. informal, formal). **4** a sliding device controlling a set of organ pipes, or a set of organ pipes controlled by such a device. **5** (in electronic devices) a location in a store of data. • v. (**registers**, **registering**, **registered**) **1** enter in a register. **2** put one's name on a register. **3** express (an opinion or emotion). **4** become aware of: *he had not even registered her presence*. **5** (of a measuring instrument) record or show (a reading) automatically.
– ORIGIN Latin *registrum*.

registered post • n. Brit. a postal service in which the sender can claim compensation if the item sent is damaged, late, or lost.

register office • n. (in the UK) a local government building where civil marriages are performed and births, marriages, and deaths are recorded.

registrar /rej-i-strar, rej-i-**strar**/ • n. **1** an official responsible for keeping official records. **2** the chief administrative officer in a university. **3** Brit. a hospital doctor who is training to be a specialist.

registration • n. **1** the action of registering. **2** (also **registration number**) Brit. the series of letters and figures identifying a motor vehicle and shown on a number plate.

registry • n. (pl. **registries**) a place where official records are kept.

registry office • n. (in non-official use) a register office.

Regius professor /ree-ji-uhss/ • n. (in the UK) the holder of a university chair founded by a sovereign or appointed by the Crown.
– ORIGIN Latin *regius* 'royal'.

regress /ri-gress/ • v. return to an earlier or less advanced state.
– DERIVATIVES **regression** n.
– ORIGIN Latin *regredi*.

regressive • adj. **1** returning to an earlier or less advanced state. **2** (of a tax) taking a proportionally greater amount from those on lower incomes.

regret • v. (**regrets**, **regretting**, **regretted**) feel or express sorrow or disappointment about (something one has done or which one should have done). • n. a feeling of such sorrow or disappointment.
– ORIGIN Old French *regreter* 'lament the dead'.

regretful • adj. feeling or showing regret.

regretfully • adv. **1** in a regretful way. **2** it is regrettable that.

regrettable • adj. giving rise to regret; undesirable.
– DERIVATIVES **regrettably** adv.

regroup • v. form into organized groups again after being attacked or defeated.

regular • adj. **1** following or arranged in a pattern, especially with the same space between one thing and the next: *the association holds regular meetings*. **2** done or happening frequently. **3** doing the same thing often: *regular worshippers*. **4** following or controlled by an accepted standard. **5** usual. **6** Grammar (of a word) following the normal pattern of inflection. **7** belonging to the permanent professional armed forces of a country. **8** (of a geometrical figure) having all sides and all angles equal. **9** informal, dated absolute; complete: *this place is a regular fisherman's paradise*. • n. a regular customer, soldier, etc.
– DERIVATIVES **regularity** n. (pl. **regularities**) **regularly** adv.
– ORIGIN Latin *regula* 'rule'.

regularize (also **regularise**) • v. (**regularizes**, **regularizing**, **regularized**) **1** make regular. **2** make (a temporary situation) legal or official.

regulate • v. (**regulates**, **regulating**, **regulated**) **1** control the rate or speed of (a machine or process). **2** control by means of rules.
– DERIVATIVES **regulator** n.

regulation • n. **1** a rule made by an authority. **2** the action of regulating. • adj. informal of a familiar or expected type: *regulation blonde hair*.

regulatory /reg-yuh-luh-tri, reg-yuh-**lay**-tuh-ri/ • adj. acting to regulate something: *a regulatory authority*.

regulo /reg-yuu-loh/ ● n. Brit. trademark used before a number to indicate a temperature setting in a gas oven.

regurgitate /ri-ger-ji-tayt/ ● v. (**regurgitates**, **regurgitating**, **regurgitated**) **1** bring (swallowed food) up again to the mouth. **2** repeat (information) without understanding it.
– DERIVATIVES **regurgitation** n.
– ORIGIN Latin *regurgitare*.

rehabilitate ● v. (**rehabilitates**, **rehabilitating**, **rehabilitated**) **1** restore (someone who has been ill or in prison) to normal life by training and therapy. **2** restore the reputation of (someone previously out of favour).
– DERIVATIVES **rehabilitation** n.
– ORIGIN Latin *rehabilitare*.

rehash ● v. reuse (old ideas or material) with no great change or improvement. ● n. a reuse of old ideas or material.

rehearsal ● n. **1** a trial performance of a play or other work for later public performance. **2** the action of rehearsing.

rehearse ● v. (**rehearses**, **rehearsing**, **rehearsed**) **1** practise (a play, piece of music, etc.) for later public performance. **2** state (points that have been made many times before).
– ORIGIN Old French *rehercier*.

reheat ● v. heat again.

rehouse ● v. (**rehouses**, **rehousing**, **rehoused**) provide with new housing.

rehydrate ● v. (**rehydrates**, **rehydrating**, **rehydrated**) cause to absorb moisture after dehydration.
– DERIVATIVES **rehydration** n.

Reich E
/rykh/, Steve (b.1936; full name *Stephen Michael Reich*), American minimalist composer. His work is influenced by Balinese and West African music and includes *The Desert Music* for chorus and orchestra.

reign ● v. **1** rule as monarch. **2** be the dominant quality or aspect: *confusion reigned in the city.* **3** (**reigning**) currently holding a particular title in sport. ● n. **1** the period of rule of a monarch. **2** the period during which someone or something is best or most important.
– ORIGIN Old French *reignier*.

reimburse /ree-im-berss/ ● v. (**reimburses**, **reimbursing**, **reimbursed**) repay (money) to (a person who has spent or lost it).
– DERIVATIVES **reimbursement** n.
– ORIGIN Latin *imbursare* 'put in a purse'.

Reims E
/reemz/ (also **Rheims**) a city of northern France, chief town of Champagne-Ardenne region. It was the traditional coronation place of most French kings.

rein ● n. (**reins**) **1** long, narrow straps attached to a horse's bit, used to control a horse. **2** the power to direct and control: *a new chairperson is taking over the reins.* ● v. **1** control (a horse) by pulling on its reins. **2** (**rein in/back**) restrain.
– PHRASES (**a**) **free rein** freedom of action.
– ORIGIN Old French *rene*.

reincarnate /ree-in-kar-nayt/ ● v. (**be reincarnated**) be born again in another body.

reincarnation ● n. **1** the rebirth of a soul in a new body. **2** a person in whom a soul is believed to have been born again.

reindeer ● n. (pl. **reindeer** or **reindeers**) a deer with large branching antlers, found in the northern tundra and subarctic regions.
– ORIGIN Old Norse.

reinforce ● v. (**reinforces**, **reinforcing**, **reinforced**) **1** make stronger. **2** strengthen (a military force) with additional personnel or equipment.
– ORIGIN French *renforcer*.

reinforced concrete ● n. concrete in which metal bars or wire are embedded to strengthen it.

reinforcement ● n. **1** the action of reinforcing. **2** (**reinforcements**) extra personnel sent to strengthen an army or similar force.

Reinhardt E
/ryn-hart/, Django (1910–53; born *Jean Baptiste Reinhardt*), Belgian jazz guitarist, famous for his improvisational style.

reinstate ● v. (**reinstates**, **reinstating**, **reinstated**) restore to a former position or state.
– DERIVATIVES **reinstatement** n.

reinterpret ● v. (**reinterprets**, **reinterpreting**, **reinterpreted**) interpret in a new or different light.
– DERIVATIVES **reinterpretation** n.

reintroduce ● v. (**reintroduces**, **reintroducing**, **reintroduced**) **1** bring into effect again. **2** put (a species of animal or plant) back into a place where it once lived.
– DERIVATIVES **reintroduction** n.

reinvigorate ● v. (**reinvigorates**, **reinvigorating**, **reinvigorated**) give new energy or strength to.

reissue ● v. (**reissues**, **reissuing**, **reissued**) produce or publish a new supply or different form of (a book, record, or other product). ● n. a new issue of a product.

reiterate ● v. (**reiterates**, **reiterating**, **reiterated**) say again or repeatedly.
– DERIVATIVES **reiteration** n.
– ORIGIN Latin *reiterare* 'go over again'.

Reith E
/*rhymes with* teeth/, John (Charles Walsham), 1st Baron (1889–1971), Scottish administrator and politician, first director general (1927–38) of the BBC. He championed the moral and intellectual role of public broadcasting.

reject ● v. /ri-jekt/ **1** refuse to accept (something faulty or unsatisfactory). **2** refuse to agree to. **3** fail to show proper affection or care for. **4** (of the body) react against (a transplanted organ). ● n. /ree-jekt/ a rejected person or thing.
– DERIVATIVES **rejection** n.
– ORIGIN Latin *reicere* 'throw back'.

rejig ● v. (**rejigs**, **rejigging**, **rejigged**) Brit. rearrange.

rejoice ● v. (**rejoices**, **rejoicing**, **rejoiced**) feel or show great joy.
– ORIGIN Old French *rejoir*.

rejoin[1] ● v. join again.

rejoin[2] ● v. say in reply; retort.
– ORIGIN Old French *rejoindre*.

rejoinder ● n. a quick or witty reply.

rejuvenate /ri-joo-vuh-nayt/ ● v. (**rejuvenates**, **rejuvenating**, **rejuvenated**) make (someone or something) look younger or

more lively.
– DERIVATIVES **rejuvenation** n.
– ORIGIN Latin *juvenis* 'young'.

rekindle • v. (**rekindles**, **rekindling**, **rekindled**) **1** relight (a fire). **2** revive a past feeling, hope, etc.

relapse • v. /ri-laps/ (**relapses**, **relapsing**, **relapsed**) **1** (of a sick or injured person) become ill again after a period of improvement. **2** (**relapse into**) return to (a worse state). • n. /ree-laps/ a return to ill health after a temporary improvement.
– ORIGIN Latin *relabi* 'slip back'.

relate • v. (**relates**, **relating**, **related**) **1** give an account of. **2** (**be related**) be connected by blood or marriage. **3** have a connection or link with: *many drowning accidents are related to alcohol use.* **4** (**relate to**) have to do with. **5** (**relate to**) feel sympathy with.
– ORIGIN Latin *referre* 'bring back'.

related • adj. belonging to the same family, group, or type; connected.

relation • n. **1** the way in which two or more people or things are related. **2** (**relations**) the way in which two or more people or groups feel about and behave towards each other. **3** a relative. **4** (**relations**) formal sexual intercourse.
– PHRASES **in relation to** in connection with.

relationship • n. **1** the way in which two or more people or things are connected. **2** the way in which two or more people or groups behave towards each other. **3** a loving and sexual association between two people.

relative /rel-uh-tiv/ • adj. **1** considered in relation or in proportion to something else. **2** existing only in comparison to something else: *months of relative calm ended in April.* **3** Grammar (of a pronoun, determiner, or adverb) referring to an earlier noun, sentence, or clause (e.g. *which* in *a conference in Paris which ended on Friday*). **4** Grammar (of a clause) connected to a main clause by a relative pronoun, determiner, or adverb. • n. a person connected by blood or marriage.
– PHRASES **relative to 1** compared with or in relation to. **2** concerning.

relative atomic mass • n. the ratio of the average mass of one atom of an element to one twelfth of the mass of an atom of carbon-12.

relatively • adv. in comparison or proportion to something else.

relative molecular mass • n. the ratio of the average mass of one molecule of an element or compound to one twelfth of the mass of an atom of carbon-12.

relativism • n. the idea that knowledge, truth, and morality exist in relation to culture, society, or historical context, and are not always the same.
– DERIVATIVES **relativist** n.

relativity • n. **1** the state of being relative to something else. **2** Physics a description of matter, energy, space, and time according to Einstein's theories.

relaunch • v. launch again or in a different form. • n. an instance of relaunching.

relax • v. **1** make or become less tense, anxious, or rigid. **2** rest from work or engage in a recreational activity. **3** make (a rule or restriction) less strict.
– ORIGIN Latin *relaxare*.

relaxant • n. a drug that promotes relaxation or reduces tension.

relaxation • n. the action of relaxing or the state of being relaxed.

relay /ree-lay/ • n. **1** a group of people or animals engaged in a task for a time and then replaced by a similar group. **2** a race between teams of runners, each team member in turn covering part of the total distance. **3** an electrical device which opens or closes a circuit in response to a current in another circuit. **4** a device to receive, strengthen, and transmit a signal again. • v. /also ri-lay/ **1** receive and pass on (information). **2** broadcast by means of a relay.
– ORIGIN Old French *relayer*.

release • v. (**releases**, **releasing**, **released**) **1** set free from imprisonment etc. **2** free from a duty. **3** allow to move freely. **4** allow (information) to be generally available. **5** make (a film or recording) available to the public. • n. **1** the action of releasing. **2** a film or recording released to the public.
– ORIGIN Old French *relesser*.

relegate • v. (**relegates**, **relegating**, **relegated**) place in a lower rank or position.
– DERIVATIVES **relegation** n.
– ORIGIN Latin *relegare* 'send away'.

relent • v. **1** finally agree to something after refusing it. **2** become less strong or severe.
– ORIGIN from Latin *re-* 'back' + *lentare* 'to bend'.

relentless • adj. **1** never stopping or weakening. **2** harsh or inflexible.
– DERIVATIVES **relentlessly** adv.

relevant • adj. closely connected or appropriate to the current matter.
– DERIVATIVES **relevance** n.
– ORIGIN Latin *relevare* 'raise up'.

reliable • adj. able to be relied on.
– DERIVATIVES **reliability** n. **reliably** adv.

reliance • n. dependence on or trust in someone or something.
– DERIVATIVES **reliant** adj.

relic • n. **1** an object, custom, or belief surviving from an earlier time. **2** a part of a holy person's body or belongings kept and treated as holy after their death.
– ORIGIN Latin *reliquiae* 'remains'.

relict /rel-ikt/ • n. a thing which has survived from an earlier period.
– ORIGIN Latin *relictus* 'left behind'.

relief • n. **1** a feeling of reassurance and relaxation after anxiety or distress have been removed. **2** a cause of relief. **3** the action of relieving. **4** (also **light relief**) a break in a tense or boring situation. **5** assistance given to people in need or difficulty. **6** a person or group replacing others who have been on duty. **7** a way of cutting a design into wood, stone, etc. so that parts of it stand out from the surface.
– ORIGIN Latin *relevare* 'raise again'.

relief map • n. a map that shows hills and valleys by shading.

relieve • v. (**relieves**, **relieving**, **relieved**) **1** lessen or remove (pain, distress, or difficulty). **2** (**be relieved**) stop feeling distressed or anxious. **3** release (someone) from duty by taking their place. **4** (**relieve of**) take (a re-

sponsibility) from. **5** bring military support for (a place which is under siege). **6** make less boring. **7** (**relieve oneself**) euphem. urinate or defecate.
– ORIGIN Old French *relever*.

religion ● n. **1** the belief in and worship of a God or gods. **2** a particular system of faith and worship.
– ORIGIN Latin, 'obligation, reverence'.

religiosity /ri-lij-i-oss-i-ti/ ● n. the state of being excessively religious.

religious ● adj. **1** having to do with or believing in a religion. **2** very careful or regular.
– DERIVATIVES **religiously** adv.

Religious Society of Friends E
official name for the Quakers (see **QUAKER**).

relinquish ● v. give up, especially unwillingly.
– DERIVATIVES **relinquishment** n.
– ORIGIN Latin *relinquere*.

reliquary /rel-i-kwuh-ri/ ● n. (pl. **reliquaries**) a container for holy relics.

relish ● n. **1** great enjoyment. **2** pleasurable anticipation. **3** a highly flavoured sauce or pickle eaten with plain food to add flavour. ● v. **1** enjoy greatly. **2** look forward to.
– ORIGIN Old French *reles* 'remainder'.

relive ● v. (**relives**, **reliving**, **relived**) live through (an experience or feeling) again in one's imagination.

reload ● v. load again.

relocate ● v. (**relocates**, **relocating**, **relocated**) move to a new place and establish one's home or business there.
– DERIVATIVES **relocation** n.

reluctance ● n. unwillingness to do something.

reluctant ● adj. unwilling and hesitant.
– DERIVATIVES **reluctantly** adv.
– ORIGIN Latin *reluctari* 'struggle against'.

rely ● v. (**relies**, **relying**, **relied**) (**rely on/upon**) **1** trust or have faith in. **2** be dependent on.
– ORIGIN Old French *relier* 'bind together'.

remade past and past part. of **REMAKE**.

remain ● v. **1** stay in the same place or condition. **2** continue to be: *he remained alert*. **3** be left over.
– ORIGIN Latin *remanere*.

remainder ● n. **1** a part, number, or amount that is left over. **2** the number which is left over when one quantity does not exactly divide into another.

remains ● pl. n. **1** things remaining. **2** historical or archaeological relics. **3** a person's body after death.

remake ● v. (**remakes**, **remaking**, **remade**) make again or differently. ● n. a film or piece of music that has been filmed or recorded again and re-released.

remand Law ● v. place (a person charged with a crime) on bail or in jail. ● n. the state of being remanded.
– ORIGIN Latin *remandare* 'commit again'.

remark ● v. **1** say as a comment. **2** notice. ● n. **1** a comment. **2** the quality of being noticeable.
– ORIGIN French *remarquer* 'note again'.

remarkable ● adj. extraordinary or striking.
– DERIVATIVES **remarkably** adv.

rematch ● n. a second match or game between two sports teams or players.

Rembrandt E
/rem-brant/ (1606–69; full name *Rembrandt Harmensz van Rijn*), Dutch painter, famous for the group portrait the *Night Watch* and more than sixty self-portraits.

remedial ● adj. **1** intended as a remedy. **2** provided for children with learning difficulties.

remedy ● n. (pl. **remedies**) **1** a medicine or treatment for a disease or injury. **2** a means of dealing with or improving an undesirable situation. ● v. (**remedies**, **remedying**, **remedied**) put right (an undesirable situation).
– ORIGIN Latin *remedium*.

remember ● v. (**remembers**, **remembering**, **remembered**) **1** have in or bring to one's mind (someone or something from the past). **2** keep something necessary in mind: *remember to post the letters*. **3** bear (someone) in mind by making them a gift or by mentioning them in prayer. **4** (**remember to**) convey greetings from (one person) to (another).
– ORIGIN Latin *rememorari*.

remembrance ● n. **1** the action of remembering. **2** a memory. **3** a thing kept or given as a reminder of someone.

Remembrance Sunday (also **Remembrance Day**) ● n. (in the UK) the Sunday nearest 11 November, when those who were killed in war are remembered.

remind ● v. **1** cause (someone) to remember to do something. **2** (**remind of**) cause (someone) to think of (something) because of a resemblance.

reminder ● n. **1** a thing that makes someone remember something. **2** a letter sent to remind someone to pay a bill.

reminisce /re-mi-niss/ ● v. (**reminisces**, **reminiscing**, **reminisced**) think or talk about the past for enjoyment.

reminiscence ● n. **1** a story told about an event that one remembers. **2** the enjoyable remembering of past events.
– ORIGIN Latin *reminiscentia*.

reminiscent ● adj. **1** (**reminiscent of**) tending to remind one of. **2** absorbed in memories.

remiss /ri-miss/ ● adj. lacking care or attention to duty.
– ORIGIN Latin *remittere* 'slacken'.

remission ● n. **1** the cancellation of a debt or charge. **2** Brit. the reduction of a prison sentence as a reward for good behaviour. **3** a temporary period during which a serious illness becomes less severe. **4** formal forgiveness of sins.

remit ● v. /ri-mit/ (**remits**, **remitting**, **remitted**) **1** cancel (a debt or punishment). **2** send (money) in payment. **3** refer (a matter for decision) to an authority. ● n. /ree-mit/ the task officially given to an individual or organization.
– ORIGIN Latin *remittere* 'send back'.

remittance ● n. **1** a sum of money sent in payment. **2** the action of remitting money.

remix ● v. produce a different version of (a musical recording) by altering the balance of the separate tracks. ● n. a remixed musical recording.

remnant ● n. **1** a small remaining quantity. **2** a piece of cloth left when the greater part has been used or sold.
– ORIGIN Old French *remenant.*

remonstrate /rem-uhn-strayt/ ● v. (**remonstrates**, **remonstrating**, **remonstrated**) make a strongly critical protest.
– DERIVATIVES **remonstration** n.
– ORIGIN Latin *remonstrare* 'demonstrate'.

remorse ● n. deep regret or guilt for something wrong one has done.
– ORIGIN Latin *remorsus.*

remorseful ● adj. filled with remorse or repentance.
– DERIVATIVES **remorsefully** adv.

remorseless ● adj. **1** without remorse. **2** (of something unpleasant) relentless.
– DERIVATIVES **remorselessly** adv.

remortgage ● v. (**remortgages**, **remortgaging**, **remortgaged**) take out another or a different mortgage on.

remote ● adj. (**remoter**, **remotest**) **1** far away in space or time. **2** situated far from the main cities or towns: *a remote Welsh valley.* **3** distantly related. **4** having very little connection. **5** (of a chance or possibility) unlikely to occur. **6** unfriendly and distant. **7** (of an electronic device) operating or operated by means of radio or infrared signals.
– DERIVATIVES **remotely** adv. **remoteness** n.
– ORIGIN Latin *remotus* 'removed'.

remote control ● n. **1** control of a machine from a distance by means of signals transmitted from a radio or electronic device. **2** a device that controls a machine in this way.
– DERIVATIVES **remote-controlled** adj.

removal ● n. **1** the action of removing. **2** Brit. the transfer of furniture and other contents when moving house.

remove ● v. (**removes**, **removing**, **removed**) **1** take off or away from the position occupied. **2** abolish or get rid of. **3** dismiss from a post. **4** (**be removed**) be very different from. **5** (**removed**) separated by a particular number of steps of descent: *his second cousin once removed.* ● n. the extent to which two things are separated: *the chairman was at one remove from what was going on.*
– DERIVATIVES **removable** adj. **remover** n.
– ORIGIN Latin *removere.*

remunerate /ri-myoo-nuh-rayt/ ● v. (**remunerates**, **remunerating**, **remunerated**) pay (someone) for work done.
– DERIVATIVES **remunerative** adj.
– ORIGIN Latin *remunerari* 'reward'.

remuneration ● n. money paid for work.

Renaissance /ri-nay-suhnss, ri-nay-sonss/ ● n. **1** the revival of art and literature under the influence of classical styles in the 14th–16th centuries. **2** (**renaissance**) a revival of interest in something.
– ORIGIN French, 'rebirth'.

Renaissance man ● n. a person with a wide range of talents or interests.

renal /ree-n'l/ ● adj. tech. having to do with the kidneys.
– ORIGIN Latin *renalis.*

rename ● v. (**renames**, **renaming**, **renamed**) give a new name to.

renascent ● adj. becoming active again.
– DERIVATIVES **renascence** n.
– ORIGIN Latin.

rend ● v. (**rends**, **rending**, **rent**) literary **1** tear to pieces. **2** cause great emotional pain to.
– ORIGIN Old English.

Rendell E
/ren-d'l/, Ruth (Barbara) (b.1930), English writer of detective fiction and psychological crime novels. She also writes under the pen name of Barbara Vine.

render ● v. (**renders**, **rendering**, **rendered**) **1** provide (a service, help, etc.). **2** present for inspection, consideration, or payment. **3** cause to be or become: *she was rendered speechless.* **4** interpret or perform artistically. **5** melt down (fat) so as to separate out its impurities. **6** cover (a wall) with a coat of plaster.
– ORIGIN Old French *rendre.*

rendering ● n. **1** a performance of a piece of music or drama. **2** a coat of plaster.

rendezvous /ron-day-voo/ ● n. (pl. **rendezvous** /ron-day-voo, ron-day-vooz/) **1** a meeting at an agreed time and place. **2** a meeting place. ● v. (**rendezvouses** /ron-day-vooz/, **rendezvousing** /ron-day-voo-ing/, **rendezvoused** /ron-day-vood/) meet at an agreed time and place.
– ORIGIN French *rendez-vous!* 'present yourselves!'.

rendition ● n. a performance or version of a dramatic or musical work.

renegade /ren-i-gayd/ ● n. a person who deserts and betrays an organization, country, or set of principles.
– ORIGIN Spanish *renegado.*

renege /ri-nayg, ri-neeg/ ● v. (**reneges**, **reneging**, **reneged**) go back on a promise or contract.
– ORIGIN Latin *renegare.*

renegotiate ● v. (**renegotiates**, **renegotiating**, **renegotiated**) negotiate again in order to change the original agreed terms.

renew ● v. **1** begin again after an interruption. **2** give fresh life or strength to. **3** extend the period of validity of (a licence, subscription, or contract). **4** replace (something broken or worn out).
– DERIVATIVES **renewal** n.

renewable ● adj. **1** capable of being renewed. **2** (of energy or its source) not exhausted when used.

Renfrewshire E
/ren-froo-sheer, ren-froo-sher/ an administrative region and former county of west central Scotland, divided into **Renfrewshire** and **East Renfrewshire**.

rennet /ren-nit/ ● n. curdled milk from the stomach of a calf, used in curdling milk for cheese.
– ORIGIN prob. from **RUN**.

Reno E
/ree-noh/ a city in western Nevada, known as a gambling resort and for its liberal laws enabling quick marriages and divorces.

Renoir[1] E
/ruh-nwar, ren-wahr/, Jean (1894–1979), French film director, son of Auguste Renoir. His films include *La Grande illusion* and *La Règle du jeu*.

Renoir[2] /ruh-nwar, ren-wahr/, (Pierre) Auguste (1841–1919), French Impressionist painter. His style is marked by light, fresh colours and indistinct outlines; works include *Le Moulin de la galette.*

renounce • v. (**renounces**, **renouncing**, **renounced**) **1** formally give up (a right or possession). **2** declare that one no longer has (a particular belief). **3** abandon (a cause, bad habit, etc.).
– ORIGIN Old French *renoncer.*

renovate /ren-uh-vayt/ • v. (**renovates**, **renovating**, **renovated**) restore (something old) to a good state of repair.
– DERIVATIVES **renovation** n.
– ORIGIN Latin *renovare* 'renew'.

renown • n. the state of being famous.
– DERIVATIVES **renowned** adj.
– ORIGIN Old French *renomer* 'make famous'.

rent[1] • n. a regular payment made to a landlord for the use of property or land. • v. **1** pay someone for the use of. **2** let someone use (something) in return for payment.
– ORIGIN Old French *rente.*

rent[2] • n. a large tear in a piece of fabric.
– ORIGIN from **REND**.

rent[3] past and past part. of **REND**.

rental • n. **1** an amount paid as rent. **2** the action of renting. • adj. relating to or available for rent.

rent boy • n. Brit. informal a young male prostitute.

renunciation • n. the action or an act of renouncing.

reoccur • v. (**reoccurs**, **reoccurring**, **reoccurred**) occur again or repeatedly.
– DERIVATIVES **reoccurrence** n.

reopen • v. open again.

reorder • v. (**reorders**, **reordering**, **reordered**) **1** order again. **2** arrange again. • n. a repeated order for goods.

reorganize (also **reorganise**) • v. (**reorganizes**, **reorganizing**, **reorganized**) change the organization of.
– DERIVATIVES **reorganization** (also **reorganisation**) n.

reorient /ree-or-i-ent, ree-o-ri-ent/ • v. **1** change the focus or direction of. **2** (**reorient oneself**) find one's bearings again.

rep • n. informal a representative.

repaid past and past part. of **REPAY**.

repair[1] • v. **1** restore (something damaged, worn, or faulty) to a good condition. **2** set right (a break in relations). • n. **1** the action of repairing. **2** a result of this. **3** the condition of an object: *the cottages were in good repair.*
– DERIVATIVES **repairable** adj. **repairer** n.
– ORIGIN Latin *reparare.*

repair[2] • v. (**repair to**) formal go to (a place).
– ORIGIN Old French *repairer.*

reparable /rep-uh-ruh-b'l/ • adj. able to be repaired or put right.

reparation /rep-uh-ray-sh'n/ • n. **1** the making of amends for a wrong. **2** (**reparations**) compensation for war damage paid by a defeated state.
– ORIGIN Latin.

repartee /rep-ar-tee/ • n. quick, witty comments or replies.
– ORIGIN French *repartie* 'replied promptly'.

repast /ri-pahst/ • n. formal a meal.
– ORIGIN Old French.

repatriate /ree-pat-ri-ayt, ree-pay-tri-ayt/ • v. (**repatriates**, **repatriating**, **repatriated**) send (someone) back to their own country.
– DERIVATIVES **repatriation** n.
– ORIGIN Latin *repatriare* 'return to one's country'.

repay • v. (**repays**, **repaying**, **repaid**) **1** pay back (a loan). **2** pay back money owed to. **3** do or give something as a reward for (a favour or kindness). **4** be worthy of: *these sites would repay detailed investigation.*
– DERIVATIVES **repayment** n.

repayment mortgage • n. a mortgage in which the borrower repays the money borrowed and interest together in fixed instalments over a fixed period.

repeal • v. officially cancel (a law or act of parliament). • n. the action of repealing.
– ORIGIN Old French *repeler.*

repeat • v. **1** say or do again. **2** (**repeat itself**) occur again in the same way or form. **3** (of food) be tasted again after being swallowed, as a result of indigestion. • n. **1** an instance of repeating. **2** a repeated broadcast of a television or radio programme.
– ORIGIN Latin *repetere.*

repel • v. (**repels**, **repelling**, **repelled**) **1** drive or force back or away. **2** be disgusting to. **3** (of a magnetic pole or electric field) force (something similarly magnetized or charged) away. **4** (of a substance) able to keep something out: *leather uppers to repel moisture.*
– ORIGIN Latin *repellere.*

repellent (also **repellant**) • adj. **1** able to repel a particular thing: *water-repellent nylon.* **2** causing disgust or distaste. • n. **1** a substance that deters insects. **2** a substance used to treat something to make it repel water.

repent • v. **1** feel or express regret or remorse. **2** feel regret or remorse about.
– DERIVATIVES **repentance** n. **repentant** adj.
– ORIGIN Old French *repentir.*

repercussions • pl. n. the consequences of an event or action.
– ORIGIN Latin *repercutere* 'push back'.

repertoire /rep-er-twar/ • n. the works known or regularly performed by a performer or company.
– ORIGIN French.

repertory /rep-er-tuh-ri/ • n. (pl. **repertories**) **1** the performance by a company of the plays, operas, or ballets in its repertoire at regular short intervals. **2** = **REPERTOIRE**.
– ORIGIN Latin *repertorium* 'catalogue, storehouse'.

repetition • n. **1** the action or an instance of repeating. **2** a thing that repeats another.

repetitious • adj. having too much repetition; repetitive.

repetitive • adj. repeated many times or too much.
– DERIVATIVES **repetitively** adv.

repetitive strain injury • n. a condition in which prolonged repetitive action causes pain or weakening in the tendons and muscles involved.

rephrase • v. (**rephrases**, **rephrasing**, **rephrased**) express differently.

repine • v. (**repines**, **repining**, **repined**)

r

literary be unhappy; fret.

replace ● v. (**replaces**, **replacing**, **replaced**) **1** take the place of. **2** provide a substitute for. **3** put back in a previous position.
– DERIVATIVES **replaceable** adj.

replacement ● n. **1** the action of replacing someone or something. **2** a person or thing that takes the place of another.

replay ● v. **1** play back (a recording). **2** play (a match) again. ● n. **1** an instance of replaying. **2** a replayed match.

replenish ● v. fill up (a stock or supply) again after some has been used.
– DERIVATIVES **replenishment** n.
– ORIGIN Old French *replenir.*

replete /ri-pleet/ ● adj. **1** (**replete with**) filled or well-supplied with. **2** very full with food.
– DERIVATIVES **repletion** n.
– ORIGIN Latin *replere* 'fill up'.

replica /rep-li-kuh/ ● n. an exact copy or model of something.
– ORIGIN Italian.

replicate /rep-li-kayt/ ● v. (**replicates**, **replicating**, **replicated**) make an exact copy of.
– DERIVATIVES **replication** n. **replicator** n.
– ORIGIN Latin *replicare.*

reply ● v. (**replies**, **replying**, **replied**) **1** say or write something as an answer. **2** respond with a similar action: *they replied to the shelling with a mortar attack.* ● n. (pl. **replies**) **1** the action of replying. **2** a spoken or written answer.
– ORIGIN Old French *replier.*

report ● v. **1** give a spoken or written account of something. **2** cover an event or situation as a journalist. **3** (**be reported**) be said or rumoured. **4** make a formal complaint about. **5** present oneself as having arrived or as ready to do something. **6** (**report to**) be responsible to (a manager). ● n. **1** an account given of a matter after investigation. **2** an account of an event or situation. **3** Brit. a teacher's written assessment of a pupil's progress. **4** a sudden loud noise of an explosion or gunfire.
– ORIGIN Latin *reportare* 'bring back'.

reportage /rep-or-**tahzh**, ri-por-tij/ ● n. the reporting of news by the media.

r

reported speech ● n. a speaker's words reported with the required changes of person and tense (e.g. *he said that he would go*, based on *I will go*). Contrasted with DIRECT SPEECH.

reporter ● n. a person who reports news for a newspaper or broadcasting company.

repose[1] ● n. a state of calm or peace. ● v. (**reposes**, **reposing**, **reposed**) **1** rest. **2** be placed or kept in a particular place.
– ORIGIN Old French *reposer.*

repose[2] ● v. (**reposes**, **reposing**, **reposed**) (**repose in**) place (one's confidence or trust) in.
– ORIGIN from POSE.

repository /ri-poz-i-tuh-ri/ ● n. (pl. **repositories**) **1** a place or container for storage. **2** a place where something is found in large quantities.
– ORIGIN Latin *repositorium.*

repossess ● v. retake possession of (something) when a buyer fails to make the required payments.
– DERIVATIVES **repossession** n.

reprehensible ● adj. wrong or bad and deserving condemnation.
– ORIGIN Latin *reprehendere* 'rebuke'.

represent ● v. **1** be entitled or appointed to act and speak on behalf of. **2** be a specimen or example of. **3** (**be represented**) be present to a particular degree: *abstraction is well represented in this exhibition.* **4** show or describe in a particular way. **5** depict in a work of art. **6** be a symbol of.
– ORIGIN Latin *repraesentare.*

representation ● n. **1** the action or an instance of representing. **2** an image, model, or other depiction of something. **3** (**representations**) statements made to an authority to pass on an opinion or make a protest.

representational ● adj. **1** relating to representation. **2** relating to art which shows the physical appearance of things.

representative ● adj. **1** typical of a class or group. **2** containing typical examples of all types: *a representative sample.* **3** (of a law-making assembly) consisting of people chosen to act and speak on behalf of a wider group. ● n. **1** a person chosen to act and speak for another or others. **2** an agent of a firm who visits potential clients to sell its products. **3** an example of a class or group.

repress ● v. **1** overcome or bring under control by force. **2** try not to have or show (a thought or feeling).
– DERIVATIVES **repression** n.
– ORIGIN Latin *reprimere* 'press back'.

repressed ● adj. **1** (of a thought or feeling) not expressed openly and kept in one's mind. **2** having feelings and desires that one does not let oneself express.

repressive ● adj. restricting personal freedom.

reprieve ● v. (**reprieves**, **reprieving**, **reprieved**) **1** cancel the punishment of. **2** abandon or postpone plans to close: *the threatened pits could be reprieved.* ● n. **1** the cancellation of a punishment. **2** a short rest from difficulty or danger.
– ORIGIN Old French *reprendre.*

reprimand /rep-ri-mahnd/ ● n. a formal expression of disapproval. ● v. give a reprimand to.
– ORIGIN French *réprimande.*

reprint ● v. /ree-**print**/ print again with few or no changes. ● n. /ree-print/ **1** an act of reprinting. **2** a copy of a book that has been reprinted.

reprisal /ri-pry-z'l/ ● n. an act of retaliation.
– ORIGIN Old French *reprisaille.*

reprise /ri-preez/ ● n. **1** a repeated passage in music. **2** a further performance of something. ● v. (**reprises**, **reprising**, **reprised**) repeat (a piece of music or a performance).
– ORIGIN French, 'taken up again'.

reproach ● v. **1** express one's disapproval of or disappointment with. **2** (**reproach with**) accuse of: *his wife reproached him with cowardice.* ● n. an expression of disapproval or disappointment.
– PHRASES **above** (or **beyond**) **reproach** perfect.
– ORIGIN Old French *reprochier.*

reproachful ● adj. expressing disapproval or disappointment.

– DERIVATIVES **reproachfully** adv.

reprobate /rep-ruh-bayt/ ● n. a person who behaves in an immoral way.
– ORIGIN Latin *reprobare* 'disapprove'.

reproduce ● v. (**reproduces**, **reproducing**, **reproduced**) **1** produce a copy of. **2** produce again in a different situation: *the problems are difficult to reproduce in a laboratory.* **3** produce offspring.
– DERIVATIVES **reproducible** adj.

reproduction ● n. **1** the action of reproducing. **2** a copy of a work of art. ● adj. made to imitate the style of an earlier period or particular craftsman: *reproduction furniture.*
– DERIVATIVES **reproductive** adj.

reproof /ri-proof/ ● n. a criticism or reprimand.
– ORIGIN Old French *reprover* 'reprove'.

reprove ● v. (**reproves**, **reproving**, **reproved**) criticize or reprimand.
– ORIGIN Old French *reprover.*

reptile ● n. a cold-blooded vertebrate animal, of a class that includes snakes, lizards, crocodiles, turtles, and tortoises.
– DERIVATIVES **reptilian** adj. & n.
– ORIGIN Latin *reptilis* 'crawling'.

republic ● n. a state in which power is held by the people and their elected representatives, and which has a president rather than a monarch.
– ORIGIN Latin *respublica.*

republican ● adj. **1** having to do with or like a republic. **2** supporting the principles of a republic. **3** (**Republican**) (in the US) supporting the Republican Party. ● n. **1** a person in favour of republican government. **2** (**Republican**) (in the US) a member of the Republican Party. **3** (**Republican**) a supporter of a united Ireland.
– DERIVATIVES **republicanism** n.

Republican Party F
one of the two main US political parties (the other being the Democratic Party), favouring a right-wing stance.

repudiate /ri-pyoo-di-ayt/ ● v. (**repudiates**, **repudiating**, **repudiated**) **1** refuse to accept or be associated with. **2** deny the truth or validity of.
– DERIVATIVES **repudiation** n.
– ORIGIN Latin *repudiatus* 'cast off'.

repugnance /ri-pug-nuhnss/ ● n. great disgust.
– ORIGIN Latin *repugnare* 'oppose'.

repugnant ● adj. disgusting or very unpleasant.

repulse ● v. (**repulses**, **repulsing**, **repulsed**) **1** drive back (an attacking enemy) by force. **2** reject or refuse to accept. **3** cause to feel intense dislike or disgust.
– ORIGIN Latin *repellere.*

repulsion ● n. **1** a feeling of intense dislike or disgust. **2** Physics a force under the influence of which objects tend to move away from each other.

repulsive ● adj. **1** arousing strong distaste or disgust. **2** Physics relating to repulsion between objects.

reputable /rep-yuu-tuh-b'l/ ● adj. having a good reputation.

reputation ● n. the beliefs or opinions that are generally held about someone or something.

repute ● n. **1** the opinion generally held of someone or something. **2** good reputation. ● v. (**reputes**, **reputing**, **reputed**) **1** (**be reputed**) have a particular reputation. **2** (**reputed**) generally believed to be so: *the reputed flatness of the country.*
– DERIVATIVES **reputedly** adv.
– ORIGIN Latin *reputare* 'think over'.

request ● n. **1** an act of asking politely or formally for something. **2** a thing that is asked for in such a way. ● v. politely or formally ask for (something) or ask (someone) to do something.
– ORIGIN Latin *requirere* 'require'.

requiem /rek-wi-uhm, rek-wi-em/ ● n. **1** (especially in the Roman Catholic Church) a Mass for the souls of the dead. **2** a musical composition based on such a Mass.
– ORIGIN Latin.

require ● v. (**requires**, **requiring**, **required**) **1** need for a purpose. **2** instruct or expect (someone) to do something. **3** make compulsory: *the minimum required by law.*
– ORIGIN Latin *requirere.*

requirement ● n. **1** something needed. **2** something compulsory.

requisite /rek-wi-zit/ ● adj. made necessary by circumstances or regulations. ● n. a thing that is necessary for a purpose.
– ORIGIN Latin *requisitus* 'deemed necessary'.

requisition /rek-wi-zi-sh'n/ ● n. **1** an official order allowing property or materials to be taken and used. **2** the taking of goods for military or public use. ● v. officially take or use during a war or emergency.

reran past of RERUN.

reredos /reer-doss/ ● n. (pl. **reredos**) an ornamental screen at the back of an altar in a church.
– ORIGIN Old French *areredos.*

re-release ● v. (**re-releases**, **re-releasing**, **re-released**) release (a recording or film) again. ● n. a re-released recording or film.

rerun ● v. (**reruns**, **rerunning**, **reran**; past part. **rerun**) show, stage, or perform again. ● n. a rerun event or programme.

resat past and past part. of RESIT.

reschedule ● v. (**reschedules**, **rescheduling**, **rescheduled**) **1** change the time of (a planned event). **2** arrange a new scheme of repayments of (a debt).

rescind /ri-sind/ ● v. cancel (a law, order, or agreement).
– ORIGIN Latin *rescindere.*

rescue ● v. (**rescues**, **rescuing**, **rescued**) save from a dangerous or distressing situation. ● n. an act of rescuing or a time when someone is rescued.
– DERIVATIVES **rescuer** n.
– ORIGIN Old French *rescoure.*

research ● n. /ri-serch, ree-serch/ the study of materials and sources in order to establish facts and reach new conclusions. ● v. /ri-serch/ carry out research into (a subject) or for (a book, programme, etc.).
– DERIVATIVES **researcher** n.
– ORIGIN from former French *recercher.*

research and development ● n. (in industry) work directed towards new ideas and improvement of products and processes.

resemblance ● n. **1** the fact of resembling

someone or something. **2** a way in which things resemble each other.

resemble • v. (**resembles**, **resembling**, **resembled**) look like or be similar to: *the fruit resembles a pear.*
– ORIGIN Old French *resembler.*

resent • v. feel bitter or angry about.
– ORIGIN from former French *resentir* 'feel'.

resentful • adj. feeling bitter about something one thinks is unfair.
– DERIVATIVES **resentfully** adv.

resentment • n. bitterness or anger about something one thinks is unfair.

reservation • n. **1** the action of reserving. **2** an arrangement whereby something is reserved. **3** an area of land set aside for occupation by North American Indians or Australian Aboriginals. **4** an expression of doubt about a statement or claim.

reserve • v. (**reserves**, **reserving**, **reserved**) **1** keep for future use. **2** arrange for (a seat, ticket, etc.) to be kept for the use of a particular person. **3** retain or hold (a right or power). • n. **1** a supply of something available for use if required. **2** money kept available by a bank, company, or government. **3** a military force kept to reinforce or protect others, or for use in an emergency. **4** an extra player in a team, serving as a possible substitute. **5** (**the reserves**) the second-choice team. **6** an area of land set aside for wildlife or for a native people. **7** a lack of warmth or openness.
– ORIGIN Latin *reservare* 'keep back'.

reserved • adj. slow to reveal emotion or opinions.

reserve price • n. the price named as the lowest acceptable by the seller for an item sold at auction.

reservist • n. a member of a military reserve force.

reservoir • n. **1** a large lake used as a source of water supply. **2** a container or part of a machine designed to hold fluid. **3** a supply or source of something: *a fine reservoir of comic talent.*
– ORIGIN French.

reset • v. (**resets**, **resetting**, **reset**) **1** set again or differently. **2** set (a counter, clock, etc.) to zero.

resettle • v. (**resettles**, **resettling**, **resettled**) settle in a different place.
– DERIVATIVES **resettlement** n.

reshuffle • v. (**reshuffles**, **reshuffling**, **reshuffled**) change around the positions of (members of a team, especially government ministers). • n. an act of reshuffling.

reside • v. (**resides**, **residing**, **resided**) **1** live in a particular place. **2** (of a right or legal power) belong to a person or group. **3** (of a quality) be present in: *intelligence and judgement reside in old men.*

residence • n. **1** the fact of residing somewhere. **2** a person's home. **3** the official house of a government minister or other official.

residency • n. (pl. **residencies**) **1** the fact of living in a place. **2** the time that an artist, writer, etc. spends working for a particular institution.

resident • n. **1** a person who lives somewhere on a long-term basis. **2** Brit. a guest in a hotel. • adj. **1** living somewhere on a long-term basis. **2** attached to and working regularly for a particular institution.
– ORIGIN Latin *residere* 'remain'.

residential • adj. **1** suitable for living in. **2** (of a job, course, etc.) requiring someone to live at a particular place.

residual • adj. remaining after the greater part or quantity has gone or been taken away.
– DERIVATIVES **residually** adv.

residue /rez-i-dyoo/ • n. **1** a small amount of something that remains after the main part has gone or been taken. **2** a substance that remains after a process such as combustion.
– ORIGIN Latin *residuum.*

residuum /ri-zi-dyoo-uhm/ • n. (pl. **residua** /ri-zi-dyoo-uh/) tech. a chemical residue.
– ORIGIN Latin.

resign • v. **1** voluntarily leave a job. **2** (**be resigned**) accept that something undesirable cannot be avoided.
– ORIGIN Latin *resignare* 'cancel'.

resignation • n. **1** an act of resigning. **2** a letter stating an intention to resign. **3** acceptance of something undesirable but inevitable.

resilient • adj. **1** able to recoil or spring back into shape after bending, stretching, or being compressed. **2** able to recover quickly from difficult conditions.
– DERIVATIVES **resilience** n.
– ORIGIN Latin *resilire* 'leap back'.

resin /rez-in/ • n. **1** a sticky substance produced by some trees. **2** a synthetic polymer used as the basis of plastics, adhesives, varnishes, etc.
– DERIVATIVES **resinous** adj.
– ORIGIN Latin *resina.*

resist • v. **1** withstand the action or effect of. **2** try to prevent or fight against. **3** refrain from (something tempting).
– ORIGIN Latin *resistere.*

resistance • n. **1** the action of resisting. **2** (also **resistance movement**) a secret organization that fights against an enemy or authority. **3** the impeding effect exerted by one thing on another. **4** the ability not to be affected by something. **5** the degree to which a material or device opposes the passage of an electric current.
– DERIVATIVES **resistant** adj.

resistor • n. Physics a device that resists the passage of an electric current.

resit Brit. • v. (**resits**, **resitting**, **resat**) take (an examination) again after failing. • n. an examination held for this purpose.

Resnais E
/ruh-**nay**/, Alain (b.1922), French film director. His films include *Hiroshima mon amour* and *L'Année dernière à Marienbad.*

resolute /rez-uh-loot/ • adj. determined.
– DERIVATIVES **resolutely** adv.
– ORIGIN Latin *resolutus* 'loosened, paid'.

resolution • n. **1** a firm decision. **2** a formal expression of opinion or intention by a law-making body. **3** the quality of being resolute. **4** the resolving of a problem or dispute. **5** the process of separating something into its individual parts. **6** the degree to which detail is visible in a photograph or on a television screen.

resolve • v. (**resolves**, **resolving**, **resolved**) **1** find a solution to. **2** decide firmly on a course of action. **3** (of a law-making body) take a decision by a formal vote. **4** (**resolve into**) separate into (individual parts). • n. firm determination.
– DERIVATIVES **resolvable** adj.
– ORIGIN Latin *resolvere.*

resonance • n. the quality of being resonant.

resonant • adj. **1** (of sound) deep, clear, and ringing. **2** (of a room, musical instrument, or hollow body) tending to prolong sounds. **3** (**resonant with**) filled with. **4** suggesting images, memories, or emotions.
– ORIGIN Latin *resonare* 'resound'.

resonate • v. (**resonates**, **resonating**, **resonated**) make a deep, clear, ringing sound.
– DERIVATIVES **resonator** n.

resort • v. (**resort to**) adopt (a strategy or course of action) so as to resolve a difficult situation. • n. **1** a place visited for holidays or recreation. **2** the action of resorting to something. **3** a strategy or course of action.
– ORIGIN Old French *resortir* 'come or go out again'.

resound /ri-zownd/ • v. **1** fill or be filled with a ringing, booming, or echoing sound. **2** (**resounding**) definite; unmistakable: *a resounding success.*

resource /ri-sorss, ri-zorss/ • n. **1** (**resources**) a stock or supply of materials or assets that can be drawn on when needed. **2** (**resources**) a country's means of supporting itself, as represented by its minerals, land, and other assets. **3** (**resources**) personal qualities that allow one to cope with difficult circumstances. • v. (**resources**, **resourcing**, **resourced**) provide with resources.
– ORIGIN Old French dialect *resourdre* 'rise again'.

resourceful • adj. able to find quick and clever ways to overcome difficulties.
– DERIVATIVES **resourcefully** adv. **resourcefulness** n.

respect • n. **1** a feeling of admiration for someone because of their qualities or achievements. **2** consideration for the feelings or rights of others. **3** (**respects**) polite greetings. **4** a particular aspect or point: *the government's record in this respect is a mixed one.* • v. **1** have respect for. **2** avoid harming or interfering with. **3** agree to recognize and observe (a law, rule, etc).
– ORIGIN Latin *respectus.*

respectable • adj. **1** regarded by society as being proper, correct, and good. **2** adequate or acceptable; fairly good.
– DERIVATIVES **respectability** n. **respectably** adv.

respectful • adj. feeling or showing respect.
– DERIVATIVES **respectfully** adv.

respecting • prep. with reference to.

respective • adj. belonging or relating separately to each of two or more people or things: *they chatted about their respective lives.*

respectively • adv. separately and in the order already mentioned.

respell • v. (**respells**, **respelling**, **respelled** or esp. Brit. **respelt**) spell (a word) differently so as to show its pronunciation.

> **Respighi** [E]
> /re-spee-gi/, Ottorino (1879–1936), Italian composer. He is best known for his suites the *Fountains of Rome* and the *Pines of Rome.*

respiration • n. **1** the action of breathing. **2** a single breath. **3** a process in living organisms involving the production of energy, typically with the intake of oxygen and the release of carbon dioxide.

respirator • n. **1** an apparatus worn over the face to prevent the breathing in of dust, smoke, or other harmful substances. **2** an apparatus used to provide artificial respiration.

respiratory /ri-spi-ruh-tuh-ri, ress-puh-ruh-tuh-ri, ri-spy-ruh-tuh-ri/ • adj. relating to respiration.

respiratory tract • n. the passage formed by the mouth, nose, throat, and lungs, through which air passes during breathing.

respire • v. (**respires**, **respiring**, **respired**) **1** breathe. **2** (of a plant) carry out respiration.
– ORIGIN Latin *respirare* 'breathe out'.

respite /ress-pyt, ress-pit/ • n. a short period of rest or relief from something difficult or unpleasant.
– ORIGIN Old French *respit.*

respite care • n. temporary care of a sick, elderly, or disabled person, providing relief for the person who usually looks after them.

resplendent /ri-splen-duhnt/ • adj. bright and colourful in an impressive way.
– ORIGIN Latin.

respond • v. say or do something in reply or as a reaction.
– ORIGIN Latin *respondere.*

respondent • n. **1** an accused person in a lawsuit. **2** a person who responds to a questionnaire or an advertisement.

response • n. an answer or reaction.

responsibility • n. (pl. **responsibilities**) **1** the state of being responsible. **2** the opportunity or ability to act independently. **3** a thing which one is required to do as part of a job or legal obligation.

responsible • adj. **1** having an obligation to do something, or having control over or care for someone. **2** being the cause of something and so able to be blamed or credited for it. **3** capable of being trusted; reliable. **4** (of a job) involving important duties or control over others. **5** (**responsible to**) having to report to (a senior person).
– DERIVATIVES **responsibly** adv.
– ORIGIN Latin *respondere* 'answer'.

responsive • adj. responding readily and with enthusiasm.

rest[1] • v. **1** stop work or movement in order to relax or recover one's strength. **2** place or be placed so as to stay in a specified position: *his feet rested on the table.* **3** (**rest on**) depend or be based on. **4** (**rest in/on**) place (trust, hope, or confidence) in or on. **5** (**rest with**) (of power, responsibility, etc.) belong to. **6** (of a matter) be left without further action. • n. **1** the action or a period of resting. **2** a motionless state. **3** Music an interval of silence of a specified length. **4** an object that is used to hold or support something.
– ORIGIN Old English.

rest[2] • n. **1** the remaining part of something.

2 the remaining people or things. ● **v.** remain or be left in a specified condition: *rest assured we will do all we can.*
– ORIGIN Latin *restare* 'remain'.

restaurant /ress-tuh-ront, ress-tront/ ● **n.** a place where people pay to sit and eat meals that are cooked on the premises.
– ORIGIN French.

restaurateur /ress-tuh-ruh-**ter**/ ● **n.** a person who owns and manages a restaurant.
– ORIGIN French.

restful ● **adj.** having a quiet and soothing quality.

rest home ● **n.** an institution where old or frail people live and are cared for.

restitution ● **n.** **1** the restoration of something lost or stolen to its proper owner. **2** payment for injury or loss.
– ORIGIN Latin.

restive ● **adj.** unable to keep still or silent; restless.
– ORIGIN Old French.

restless ● **adj.** **1** unable to rest or relax as a result of anxiety or boredom. **2** offering no rest: *a restless night.*
– DERIVATIVES **restlessly** adv. **restlessness** n.

restoration ● **n.** **1** the returning of something to a former condition, place, or owner. **2** the repairing or renovating of a building, work of art, etc. **3** the restoring of a previous practice, right, or situation. **4** (**the Restoration**) the re-establishment of Charles II as King of England in 1660, or the period following this.

restorative ● **adj.** having the ability to restore health or strength. ● **n.** a medicine or drink that restores health or strength.

restore ● **v.** (**restores**, **restoring**, **restored**) **1** return to a previous condition, place, or owner. **2** repair or renovate (a building, work of art, etc.). **3** bring back (a previous practice, situation, etc.).
– DERIVATIVES **restorer** n.
– ORIGIN Latin *restaurare.*

restrain ● **v.** **1** keep under control or within limits. **2** stop (someone) moving or acting as they wish.
– ORIGIN Latin *restringere* 'tie back'.

restrained ● **adj.** **1** reserved or unemotional. **2** not richly decorated or brightly coloured.

restraint ● **n.** **1** the action of restraining. **2** a measure or condition that restrains: *the financial restraints of a budget.* **3** a device which limits or prevents freedom of movement. **4** unemotional or controlled behaviour.

restrict ● **v.** **1** put a limit on. **2** stop (someone) moving or acting as they wish.
– ORIGIN Latin *restringere* 'tie back'.

restricted ● **adj.** **1** limited in size or amount. **2** not made public for reasons of national security.

restriction ● **n.** **1** a limiting condition or measure. **2** the action of restricting.

restrictive ● **adj.** preventing freedom of action or movement.

restrictive practice ● **n.** Brit. **1** an arrangement by a group of workers to limit output or restrict the entry of new workers in order to protect their jobs. **2** an arrangement that restricts or controls competition between companies.

restroom ● **n.** N. Amer. a toilet in a public building.

restructure ● **v.** (**restructures**, **restructuring**, **restructured**) **1** organize differently. **2** convert (a debt) into another debt that is repayable at a later time.

result ● **n.** **1** a thing that is caused or produced by something else; an outcome. **2** an item of information obtained by experiment or calculation. **3** a final score or mark in a sporting event or examination. **4** a successful outcome: *determination and persistence guarantee results.* ● **v.** **1** happen because of something else. **2** (**result in**) have (a specified outcome).
– ORIGIN Latin *resultare* 'spring back'.

resultant ● **adj.** occurring as a result.

resume ● **v.** (**resumes**, **resuming**, **resumed**) **1** begin again or continue after an interruption. **2** return (a seat or place).
– ORIGIN Latin *resumere* 'take back'.

résumé /rez-yuu-may/ ● **n.** **1** a summary. **2** N. Amer. a curriculum vitae.
– ORIGIN French, 'resumed'.

resumption ● **n.** the action of beginning something again after an interruption.

resurface ● **v.** (**resurfaces**, **resurfacing**, **resurfaced**) **1** put a new coating on (a surface). **2** come back up to the surface of deep water. **3** arise again.

resurgent ● **adj.** becoming stronger or more popular again.
– DERIVATIVES **resurgence** n.
– ORIGIN Latin *resurgere* 'rise again'.

resurrect ● **v.** **1** restore to life. **2** revive (a practice, belief, etc).

resurrection ● **n.** **1** the action of resurrecting. **2** (**the Resurrection**) (in Christian belief) the time when Jesus Christ rose from the dead.
– ORIGIN Latin.

resuscitate /ri-suss-i-tayt/ ● **v.** (**resuscitates**, **resuscitating**, **resuscitated**) revive from unconsciousness.
– DERIVATIVES **resuscitation** n.
– ORIGIN Latin *resuscitare* 'raise again'.

retail ● **n.** the sale of goods to the general public. ● **v.** **1** sell (goods) to the public. **2** (**retail at/for**) be sold for (a specified price).
– DERIVATIVES **retailer** n.
– ORIGIN Old French *retaillier.*

retain ● **v.** **1** continue to have; keep possession of. **2** absorb and continue to hold (a substance). **3** keep in place. **4** obtain the services of (a barrister) with a preliminary payment.
– ORIGIN Latin *retinere* 'hold back'.

retainer ● **n.** **1** a thing that holds something in place. **2** a fee paid in advance to a barrister to secure their services. **3** dated a servant who has worked for a family for a long time.

retake ● **v.** (**retakes**, **retaking**, **retook**; past part. **retaken**) **1** take (a test or examination) again. **2** regain possession of. ● **n.** a test or examination that is retaken.

retaliate /ri-tal-i-ayt/ ● **v.** (**retaliates**, **retaliating**, **retaliated**) make an attack in return for a similar attack.
– DERIVATIVES **retaliation** n. **retaliatory** adj.
– ORIGIN Latin *retaliare* 'return in kind'.

retard ● **v.** /ri-tard/ hold back the development or progress of. ● **n.** /ree-tard/ offens. a mentally handicapped person.

– DERIVATIVES **retardation** n.
– ORIGIN Latin *retardare.*

retardant ● adj. preventing or inhibiting: *fire-retardant polymers.*

retarded ● adj. offens. less developed mentally than is usual for one's age.

retch ● v. make the sound and movement of vomiting.
– ORIGIN Germanic, 'spittle'.

retention ● n. **1** the action of retaining. **2** failure to remove a substance from the body; *fluid retention.*

retentive ● adj. (of a person's memory) able to retain facts and impressions easily.

rethink ● v. (**rethinks**, **rethinking**, **rethought**) consider (a course of action) again. ● n. an instance of rethinking.

reticent /ret-i-suhnt/ ● adj. not revealing one's thoughts or feelings readily.
– DERIVATIVES **reticence** n.
– ORIGIN Latin *reticere* 'remain silent'.

reticulated ● adj. arranged or marked like a net or network.
– ORIGIN Latin *reticulatus.*

retina /ret-i-nuh/ ● n. (pl. **retinas** or **retinae** /ret-i-nee/) a layer at the back of the eyeball containing cells that are sensitive to light and from which impulses are sent to the brain.
– DERIVATIVES **retinal** adj.
– ORIGIN Latin.

retinol /ret-i-nol/ ● n. vitamin A.

retinue /ret-i-nyoo/ ● n. a group of advisers or assistants accompanying an important person.
– ORIGIN Old French *retenir* 'retain'.

retire ● v. (**retires**, **retiring**, **retired**) **1** leave one's job and stop working, especially because one has reached a particular age. **2** withdraw from a race or match because of injury. **3** leave a place. **4** (of a jury) leave the courtroom to decide the verdict of a trial. **5** go to bed.
– DERIVATIVES **retired** adj.
– ORIGIN French *retirer* 'draw back'.

retirement ● n. **1** the action of retiring. **2** the period of one's life after retiring from work.

retiring ● adj. avoiding others; shy.

retook past of **RETAKE**.

retort[1] ● v. say something sharp or witty in answer to a remark. ● n. a sharp or witty reply.
– ORIGIN Latin *retorquere* 'twist back'.

retort[2] ● n. **1** a container or furnace for carrying out a chemical process on a large scale. **2** dated a glass container with a long neck, used in distilling liquids and other chemical operations.
– ORIGIN Latin *retorta.*

retouch ● v. improve (a painting or photograph) by making slight additions or alterations.

retrace ● v. (**retraces**, **retracing**, **retraced**) **1** go back over (the same route that one has just taken). **2** discover and follow (a route taken by someone else).

retract ● v. **1** draw or be drawn back. **2** withdraw (a statement) because it is not correct or true. **3** go back on (an agreement).
– DERIVATIVES **retractable** adj. **retraction** n.
– ORIGIN Latin *retrahere* 'draw back'.

retractile /ri-trak-tyl/ ● adj. capable of being retracted: *retractile claws.*

retrain ● v. teach or learn new skills.

retreat ● v. **1** (of an army) withdraw from attacking enemy forces. **2** move back from a difficult situation. **3** go to a quiet or secluded place. ● n. **1** an act of retreating. **2** a quiet or secluded place. **3** a place where a person goes to be alone and pray for a time.
– ORIGIN Latin *retrahere* 'draw back'.

retrench ● v. reduce costs or spending in response to economic difficulty.
– DERIVATIVES **retrenchment** n.
– ORIGIN French *retrancher* 'cut out'.

retrial ● n. a second or further trial.

retribution /ret-ri-byoo-sh'n/ ● n. severe punishment in revenge for something.
– DERIVATIVES **retributive** /ri-trib-yuu-tiv/ adj.
– ORIGIN Latin.

retrieve ● v. (**retrieves**, **retrieves**, **retrieving**) **1** get or bring back. **2** find or extract (information stored in a computer). **3** rescue from a state of difficulty or collapse.
– DERIVATIVES **retrievable** adj. **retrieval** n.
– ORIGIN Old French *retrover* 'find again'.

retriever ● n. a dog of a breed used for finding and bringing back game that has been shot.

retro ● adj. imitative of a style from the recent past.
– ORIGIN French.

retro- ● comb. form **1** back or backwards: *retrogress.* **2** behind: *retrorocket.*
– ORIGIN Latin *retro.*

retroactive ● adj. (especially of a law) taking effect from a date in the past.

retrograde ● adj. **1** moving backwards. **2** making a situation worse.
– ORIGIN Latin *retrogradus.*

retrogressive ● adj. returning to an earlier and worse state.
– DERIVATIVES **retrogression** n.

retrorocket ● n. a small rocket on a spacecraft or missile, fired in the direction of travel to slow it down.

retrospect ● n. (in phr. **in retrospect**) when looking back on a past event.

retrospective ● adj. **1** looking back on or dealing with past events. **2** (of an exhibition) showing the development of an artist's work over a period of time. ● n. a retrospective exhibition.
– DERIVATIVES **retrospectively** adv.

retroussé /ruh-troo-say/ ● adj. (of a person's nose) turned up at the tip.
– ORIGIN French, 'tucked up'.

retrovirus /ret-roh-vy-ruhss/ ● n. any of a group of RNA viruses which insert a DNA copy of their genetic material into the host cell in order to replicate, e.g. HIV.
– ORIGIN from the initials of *reverse transcriptase* + **VIRUS**.

retsina /ret-see-nuh/ ● n. a Greek white wine flavoured with resin.
– ORIGIN modern Greek.

return ● v. **1** come or go back to a place. **2** (**return to**) go back to (a particular state or activity). **3** give, send, or put back. **4** feel, say, or do (the same feeling, action, etc.) in response: *she returned his kiss.* **5** (of a judge or jury) give (a verdict). **6** yield (a profit). **7** elect (a person or party) to office. ● n. **1** an act or the action of returning. **2** a profit from an investment. **3** esp. Brit. a ticket allowing travel to a place and back again. **4** a ticket for an event

that has been returned because no longer wanted.
– DERIVATIVES **returnable** adj. **returner** n.
– ORIGIN Old French *returner.*

returnee • n. a person returning to work after a long absence.

reunify • v. (**reunifies**, **reunifying**, **reunified**) restore political unity to.
– DERIVATIVES **reunification** n.

Réunion E
/ree-yoo-nyuhn/ a volcanically active island in the Indian Ocean east of Madagascar; capital, Saint-Denis. The island is an administrative region of France.

reunion • n. **1** the action or an instance of reuniting. **2** a social gathering of people who have not seen each other for some time.

reunite • v. (**reunites**, **reuniting**, **reunited**) bring or come together again after a period of separation.

reuse /ree-yooz/ • v. (**reuses**, **reusing**, **reused**) use again or more than once.
– DERIVATIVES **reusable** adj.

Rev. • abbrev. Reverend.

rev informal • n. (**revs**) the number of revolutions of an engine per minute. • v. (**revs**, **revving**, **revved**) increase the running speed of (an engine) by pressing the accelerator.

revamp • v. /ree-vamp/ alter (something) so as to improve its appearance. • n. /ree-vamp/ an improved version.

Revd • abbrev. Reverend.

reveal • v. **1** make (previously unknown or secret information) known. **2** cause (something hidden) to be seen.
– ORIGIN Latin *revelare.*

revealing • adj. **1** giving out interesting information. **2** (of a garment) allowing much of the wearer's body to be seen.

reveille /ri-val-li/ • n. a signal sounded on a bugle or drum to wake up soldiers.
– ORIGIN French *réveillez!* 'wake up!'.

revel • v. (**revels**, **revelling**, **revelled**; US **revels**, **reveling**, **reveled**) **1** enjoy oneself in a lively and noisy way. **2** (**revel in**) gain great pleasure from. • n. (**revels**) lively and noisy celebrations.
– DERIVATIVES **reveller** (US **reveler**) n. **revelry** n. (pl. **revelries**).
– ORIGIN Old French *reveler* 'rise up in rebellion'.

revelation • n. **1** the revealing of something previously unknown. **2** a surprising thing.

revelatory /rev-uh-lay-tuh-ri, rev-uh-luh-tuh-ri/ • adj. revealing something previously unknown.

revenge • n. something harmful done in return for an injury or wrong. • v. (**revenges**, **revenging**, **revenged**) **1** (**revenge oneself** or **be revenged**) take revenge for a wrong done to oneself. **2** take revenge on behalf of (someone else) or for (a wrong).
– ORIGIN Old French *revencher.*

revengeful • adj. eager for revenge.

revenue • n. **1** the income received by an organization. **2** a state's annual income, received from taxes.
– ORIGIN Latin *revenire* 'return'.

reverberate • v. (**reverberates**, **reverberating**, **reverberated**) **1** (of a loud noise) be repeated as an echo. **2** have continuing serious effects.
– DERIVATIVES **reverberation** n.
– ORIGIN Latin *reverberare* 'strike again'.

Revere E
/ri-veer/, Paul (1735–1818), American patriot. In 1775 he rode from Boston to Lexington to warn fellow American revolutionaries of the approach of British troops.

revere /ri-veer/ • v. (**reveres**, **revering**, **revered**) respect or admire deeply.
– ORIGIN Latin *revereri.*

reverence • n. deep respect.

reverend • adj. a title or form of address to members of the Christian clergy.

reverent • adj. showing reverence.
– DERIVATIVES **reverential** adj. **reverently** adv.

reverie /rev-uh-ri/ • n. a daydream.
– ORIGIN Old French.

revers /ri-veer/ • n. (pl. **revers** /ri-veer, ri-veerz/) the turned-back edge of a garment revealing the underside.
– ORIGIN French, 'reverse'.

reversal • n. **1** a change to an opposite direction, position, or course of action. **2** a harmful change of fortune.

reverse • v. (**reverses**, **reversing**, **reversed**) **1** move backwards. **2** make (something) the opposite of what it was. **3** turn the other way round or inside out. **4** cancel (a judgement by a lower court or authority). • adj. **1** going in or turned towards the opposite direction. **2** operating or behaving in a way opposite to that which is usual. • n. **1** a complete change of direction or action. **2** (**the reverse**) the opposite. **3** a setback or defeat. **4** the opposite side or face to the observer.
– DERIVATIVES **reversible** adj.
– ORIGIN Latin *revertere* 'turn back'.

reversion • n. a return to a previous state.

revert • v. (**revert to**) return to (a previous state).
– ORIGIN Latin *revertere* 'turn back'.

review • n. **1** a formal examination of something so as to make changes if necessary. **2** a critical assessment of a book, play, or other work. **3** a report of an event that has already happened. **4** a ceremonial display and formal inspection of military or naval forces. • v. **1** carry out or write a review of. **2** view or inspect again.
– DERIVATIVES **reviewer** n.
– ORIGIN from former French *reveue.*

revile • v. (**reviles**, **reviling**, **reviled**) criticize in a rude or scornful way.
– ORIGIN Old French *reviler.*

revise • v. (**revises**, **revising**, **revised**) **1** examine and alter (text). **2** reconsider and change (an opinion). **3** Brit. reread previous work in order to prepare for an examination.
– ORIGIN Latin *revisere* 'look at again'.

revision • n. **1** the action of revising. **2** a revised edition or form of something.

revitalize (also **revitalise**) • v. (**revitalizes**, **revitalizing**, **revitalized**) give new life and vitality to.
– DERIVATIVES **revitalization** (also **revitalisation**) n.

revival • n. **1** an improvement in the condition, strength, or popularity of something. **2** a new production of an old play.

revivalism • n. the promotion of a revival of religious faith.
– DERIVATIVES **revivalist** n. & adj.

revive • v. (**revives**, **reviving**, **revived**) **1** restore to consciousness, health, or strength. **2** start doing or using again.
– ORIGIN Latin *revivere.*

revivify /ree-viv-i-fy/ • v. (**revivifies**, **revivifying**, **revivified**) give new life or strength to.

revoke • v. (**revokes**, **revoking**, **revoked**) end the validity of (a law, decree, decision, etc.).
– DERIVATIVES **revocation** n.
– ORIGIN Latin *revocare* 'call back'.

revolt • v. **1** rebel against an authority. **2** cause to feel disgust. • n. an act of rebellion.
– ORIGIN French *révolter.*

revolting • adj. extremely unpleasant; disgusting.

revolution • n. **1** the overthrow of a government or social order by force, in favour of a new system. **2** a great and far-reaching change. **3** motion in orbit or in a circular course around a central point. **4** a single movement around a central point.
– ORIGIN Latin.

revolutionary • adj. **1** involving or causing great change. **2** engaged in or relating to political revolution. • n. (pl. **revolutionaries**) a person who starts or supports a political revolution.

revolutionize (also **revolutionise**) • v. (**revolutionizes**, **revolutionizing**, **revolutionized**) change completely or fundamentally.

revolve • v. (**revolves**, **revolving**, **revolved**) **1** move in a circle around a central point. **2** (**revolve about/around**) move in a circular orbit around. **3** (**revolve around**) treat as the most important point or element.
– ORIGIN Latin *revolvere* 'roll back'.

revolver • n. a pistol with revolving chambers enabling several shots to be fired without reloading.

revue • n. a light theatrical show with short sketches, songs, and dances.
– ORIGIN French, 'review'.

revulsion • n. a feeling of disgust and horror.
– ORIGIN Latin.

reward • n. **1** a thing given in recognition of service, effort, or achievement. **2** a fair return for good or bad behaviour. • v. **1** give a reward to. **2** show one's appreciation of (an action) with a reward. **3** (**be rewarded**) receive what one deserves.
– ORIGIN Old French *reguard* 'regard'.

rewarding • adj. providing satisfaction.

rewind • v. (**rewinds**, **rewinding**, **rewound**) wind (a film or tape) back to the beginning.

rewire • v. (**rewires**, **rewiring**, **rewired**) provide with new electric wiring.

rewrite • v. (**rewrites**, **rewriting**, **rewrote**; past part. **rewritten**) write again in an altered or improved form. • n. an instance of rewriting.

Reykjavik E
/rayk-yuh-vik/ the capital of Iceland.

Reynolds[1], E
Albert (b.1933), Irish Fianna Fáil statesman, Taoiseach (Prime Minister) 1992–4.

Reynolds[2], E
Sir Joshua (1723–92), English painter, known for his portraits. He was the first president of the Royal Academy (1768).

RFC • abbrev. Rugby Football Club.

rhapsodize (also **rhapsodise**) • v. (**rhapsodizes**, **rhapsodizing**, **rhapsodized**) express great enthusiasm about someone or something.

rhapsody • n. (pl. **rhapsodies**) **1** an expression of great enthusiasm or joy. **2** an emotional piece of music in one extended movement.
– DERIVATIVES **rhapsodic** adj.
– ORIGIN Greek *rhapsōidia.*

Rhea E
/ree-uh/ Gk Myth. one of the Titans, wife of Cronus and mother of Zeus, Demeter, Poseidon, Hera, and Hades. Rhea rescued Zeus from being eaten by his father by hiding him and giving Cronus a stone wrapped in blankets instead.

rhea /ree-uh/ • n. a large flightless bird of South American grasslands, resembling a small ostrich with greyish-brown plumage.
– ORIGIN from **RHEA**.

Rheims E
var. of **REIMS**.

rhenium /ree-ni-uhm/ • n. a rare silvery-white metallic element.
– ORIGIN Latin *Rhenus* 'Rhine'.

rheology /ri-ol-uh-ji/ • n. the branch of physics concerned with the deformation and flow of matter.
– DERIVATIVES **rheological** adj. **rheologist** n.
– ORIGIN Greek *rheos* 'stream'.

rheostat /ree-uh-stat/ • n. an instrument used to control the current in an electrical circuit by varying the amount of resistance in it.
– ORIGIN Greek *rheos* 'stream'.

rhesus factor /ree-suhss/ • n. a substance on red blood cells which can cause disease in a newborn baby whose blood contains the factor while the mother's blood does not.
– ORIGIN from **RHESUS MONKEY**, in which the substance was first observed.

rhesus monkey /ree-suhss/ • n. a small brown macaque with red skin on the face and rump, native to southern Asia.
– ORIGIN Latin *Rhesus.*

rhetoric /ret-uh-rik/ • n. **1** the art of effective or persuasive speaking or writing. **2** persuasive language that is empty or insincere.
– ORIGIN from Greek *rhētorikē tekhnē* 'art of rhetoric'.

rhetorical /ri-to-ri-k'l/ • adj. **1** relating to rhetoric. **2** intended to persuade or impress. **3** (of a question) asked for effect or to make a statement rather than to obtain an answer.
– DERIVATIVES **rhetorically** adv.

rheumatic /roo-mat-ik/ • adj. relating to or suffering from rheumatism.
– ORIGIN Greek *rheuma* 'stream'.

rheumatic fever • n. an acute fever marked by inflammation and pain in the joints, caused by an infection.

rheumatism • n. any disease marked by inflammation and pain in the joints and muscles.
– ORIGIN Greek *rheumatismos.*

rheumatoid /roo-muh-toyd/ • adj. relating to or resembling rheumatism.

rheumatoid arthritis • n. a disease causing inflammation in the joints, that gradually becomes more severe.

rheumy /*rhymes with* gloomy/ • adj. (of the eyes) full of a watery fluid.
– ORIGIN Greek *rheuma* 'stream'.

Rhine E
a river in western Europe which rises in the Swiss Alps and flows through Germany and the Netherlands to the North Sea.

rhinestone • n. an imitation diamond.
– ORIGIN from French *caillou du Rhin* 'pebble of the Rhine'.

rhino • n. (pl. **rhino** or **rhinos**) informal a rhinoceros.

rhinoceros /ry-noss-uh-ruhss/ • n. (pl. **rhinoceros** or **rhinoceroses**) a large plant-eating mammal with one or two horns on the nose and thick folded skin, found in Africa and South Asia.
– ORIGIN from Greek *rhis* 'nose' + *keras* 'horn'.

rhinoplasty /ry-noh-plass-ti/ • n. (pl. **rhinoplasties**) plastic surgery performed on the nose.

rhizome /ry-zohm/ • n. a horizontal underground plant stem bearing both roots and shoots.
– ORIGIN Greek *rhizōma.*

Rhode Island E
a state in the north-eastern US, on the Atlantic coast; capital, Providence.
– DERIVATIVES **Rhode Islander** n.

Rhodes[1] E
a Greek island in the SE Aegean, the largest of the Dodecanese group.

Rhodes[2], E
Cecil (John) (1853–1902), British-born South African statesman, Prime Minister of Cape Colony 1890–6. He expanded British territory in southern Africa, developing Rhodesia from 1889.

Rhodes[3], E
Wilfred (1877–1973), English cricketer, who played for Yorkshire and England, scoring almost 40,000 runs and taking a record 4,187 first-class wickets.

Rhodesia E
/roh-dee-*zh*uh/ former name for **ZIMBABWE**.
– DERIVATIVES **Rhodesian** adj. & n.

rhodium /roh-di-uhm/ • n. a hard, dense silvery-white metallic element.
– ORIGIN Greek *rhodon* 'rose'.

rhododendron /roh-duh-den-druhn/ • n. a shrub with large clusters of bright trumpet-shaped flowers.
– ORIGIN from Greek *rhodon* 'rose' + *dendron* 'tree'.

rhomboid /rom-boyd/ • adj. having or resembling the shape of a rhombus. • n. a quadrilateral of which only the opposite sides and angles are equal.

rhombus /rom-buhss/ • n. (pl. **rhombuses** or **rhombi** /rom-by/) Geom. a parallelogram with four straight equal sides forming two opposite acute angles and two opposite obtuse angles.
– ORIGIN Greek *rhombos.*

Rhône E
/*rhymes with* moan/ a river in SW Europe which rises in the Swiss Alps and flows westwards into France to Lyons and then southwards to reach the Mediterranean west of Marseilles.

rhubarb • n. the thick red stems of a plant, which are cooked and eaten as a fruit.
– ORIGIN Latin *rheubarbarum* 'foreign rhubarb'.

rhumba • n. var. of **RUMBA**.

rhyme • n. **1** a word that has or ends with the same sound as another. **2** similarity of sound between words or the endings of words. **3** a short poem with rhyming lines. • v. (**rhymes**, **rhyming**, **rhymed**) **1** (of a word or line) have or end with the same sound as another. **2** (**rhyme with**) put (a word) together with (another word with a similar sound).
– PHRASES **rhyme or reason** logical explanation.
– ORIGIN Old French *rime.*

rhyming slang • n. a type of slang that replaces words with rhyming words, often with the rhyming element omitted (e.g. *butcher's*, short for *butcher's hook*, meaning 'look').

rhyolite /ry-uh-lyt/ • n. a pale volcanic rock of granitic composition.
– ORIGIN German *Rhyolit.*

rhythm /ri-*th*uhm/ • n. **1** a strong, regular repeated pattern of music, sound, or movement. **2** a particular pattern of this kind: *a slow waltz rhythm.* **3** the measured flow of words and phrases in verse or prose, as determined by length of and stress on syllables. **4** a regularly recurring sequence of events: *the daily rhythms of the tides.*
– ORIGIN French *rhythme.*

rhythm and blues • n. popular music of US black origin, arising from a combination of blues and jazz.

rhythmic • adj. **1** having or relating to rhythm. **2** happening regularly.
– DERIVATIVES **rhythmical** adj. **rhythmically** adv.

rhythm section • n. the part of a pop or jazz group supplying the rhythm, in particular the bass and drums.

rib • n. **1** each of a series of thin curved bones attached in pairs to the spine and curving round to protect the chest. **2** a curved structure that supports a vault. **3** a curved strut forming part of the framework of a boat's hull. • v. (**ribs, ribbing, ribbed**) informal tease good-naturedly.
– ORIGIN Old English.

ribald /ri-buhld, ry-bawld/ • adj. humorous in a coarse way.
– ORIGIN Old French *riber* 'be licentious'.

ribaldry • n. ribald talk or behaviour.

riband /ri-buhnd/ • n. archaic a ribbon.
– ORIGIN Old French *riban.*

ribbed • adj. having a pattern of raised bands.

r

ribbon • n. **1** a long, narrow strip of fabric, used for tying something or for decoration. **2** a long, narrow strip. **3** a narrow band of inked material used to produce the characters in some typewriters and computer printers.
– ORIGIN from **RIBAND**.

ribcage • n. the bony frame formed by the ribs.

riboflavin /ry-boh-**flay**-vin/ • n. vitamin B_2.
– ORIGIN from *ribose* (a sugar found in DNA) + Latin *flavus* 'yellow'.

ribonucleic acid /ry-boh-nyoo-**klay**-ik, ry-boh-nyoo-**klee**-ik/ • n. see **RNA**.
– ORIGIN from *ribose* (a sugar found in DNA) + **NUCLEIC ACID**.

Rice, E
Sir Tim (b.1944; full name *Timothy Miles Bindon Rice*), English lyricist, co-writer (with Sir Andrew Lloyd Webber) of such musicals as *Joseph and the Amazing Technicolor Dreamcoat*, *Jesus Christ Superstar*, and *Evita*.

rice • n. the grains of a cereal plant which is grown for food on wet land in warm countries.
– ORIGIN Old French *ris*.

ricepaper • n. thin edible paper made from the pith of a shrub, used in oriental painting and in baking biscuits and cakes.

Rich, E
Buddy (1917–87; born *Bernard Rich*), American jazz drummer and bandleader.

rich • adj. **1** having a great deal of money or property. **2** (of a country) having valuable natural resources or a successful economy. **3** of expensive materials or workmanship. **4** plentiful. **5** having something in large amounts: *fruits rich in vitamins*. **6** (of food) containing much fat, sugar, etc: *rich sauces*. **7** (of a colour, sound, or smell) pleasantly deep and strong. **8** (of soil or land) fertile.
– ORIGIN Old English.

Richard, E
Sir Cliff (b.1940, born *Harry Roger Webb*), British pop singer, known for songs such as 'Living Doll' and 'Devil Woman'.

Richard I E
(1157–99; known as **Richard Coeur de Lion** or **Richard the Lionheart**), son of Henry II, king of England 1189–99. He led the Third Crusade, defeating Saladin, but failing to capture Jerusalem. Returning home, he was held hostage by the Holy Roman emperor until a large ransom was paid.

Richard II E
(1367–1400), son of the Black Prince, king of England 1377–99. His early reign (when he was below the age of full legal responsibility) was dominated by John of Gaunt and he was eventually overthrown by Gaunt's son Henry, who became Henry IV.

Richard III E
(1452–85), brother of Edward IV, king of England 1483–5. He served as Protector to his nephew Edward V, who, after two months, was declared illegitimate and subsequently disappeared. Richard was killed by Henry Tudor at Bosworth Field.

Richards[1], E
Sir Gordon (1904–86), English jockey. He was champion jockey twenty-six times between 1925 and 1953.

Richards[2], E
Viv (b.1952; full name *Isaac Vivian Alexander Richards*), West Indian cricketer. He captained the West Indian team 1985–91, and scored over 6,000 runs during his test career.

Richardson[1], E
Sir Ralph (David) (1902–83), English actor, known as a Shakespearean stage actor and for films such as *Oh! What a Lovely War*.

Richardson[2], E
Samuel (1689–1761), English novelist, author of *Pamela*, written in the form of letters and journals.

Richard the Lionheart E
see **RICHARD I**.

Richelieu E
/**reesh**-lyer/, Armand Jean du Plessis, duc de (1585–1642), French cardinal and statesman, who dominated French government during his time as chief minister of Louis XIII (1624–42).

riches • pl. n. **1** wealth. **2** valuable natural resources.

richly • adv. **1** in a rich way. **2** fully.

Richter scale /**rik**-ter/ • n. a scale for expressing the severity of an earthquake.
– ORIGIN named after the American geologist Charles F. *Richter* (1900–85).

Richthofen E
/**rikht**-hoh-v'n/, Manfred, Freiherr von (1882–1918; known as **the Red Baron**), German fighter pilot in the First World War. He was eventually shot down after destroying eighty enemy planes.

rick[1] • n. a stack of hay, corn, or straw.
– ORIGIN Old English.

rick[2] • n. a slight sprain or strain, especially in the neck or back. • v. strain (one's neck or back) slightly.
– ORIGIN dialect.

rickets /**ri**-kits/ • n. a disease of children caused by lack of vitamin D, in which the bones become soft and distorted.
– ORIGIN perh. from Greek *rhakhitis* 'rickets'.

rickety • adj. poorly made and likely to collapse.

rickshaw • n. a light two-wheeled vehicle pulled by one or more people, used in Asian countries.
– ORIGIN Japanese, 'person-strength-vehicle'.

ricochet • v. (**ricochets** /**ri**-kuh-shayz/, **ricocheting** /**ri**-kuh-shay-ing/, **ricocheted** /**ri**-kuh-shayd/) (of a bullet or fast-moving object) rebound off a surface. • n. /**ri**-kuh-shay/ **1** a shot or hit that ricochets. **2** the action of ricocheting.
– ORIGIN French.

ricotta /ri-**kot**-tuh/ • n. a soft white Italian cheese.
– ORIGIN Italian, 'cooked twice'.

rictus /**rik**-tuhss/ • n. a fixed grimace or grin.
– ORIGIN Latin, 'open mouth'.

rid ● v. (**rids**, **ridding**, **rid**) **1** (**rid of**) make (someone or something) free of (an unwanted person or thing). **2** (**be** (or **get**) **rid of**) be freed or relieved of.
– ORIGIN Old Norse.

riddance ● n. (in phr. **good riddance**) said to express relief at being rid of someone or something.

ridden past part. of RIDE. ● adj. (in combination) full of a particular thing: *guilt-ridden.*

riddle[1] ● n. **1** a cleverly worded question that is asked as a game. **2** a puzzling person or thing.
– ORIGIN Old English.

riddle[2] ● v. (**be riddled**) **1** have many holes. **2** be filled with something undesirable: *a policy riddled with inadequacies.* ● n. a large coarse sieve.
– ORIGIN Old English.

ride ● v. (**rides**, **riding**, **rode**; past part. **ridden**) **1** sit on and control the movement of (a horse, bicycle, or motorcycle). **2** travel in a vehicle. **3** travel over on horseback or on a bicycle or motorcycle: *ride the scenic trail.* **4** be carried or supported by: *surfers rode the waves.* **5** sail or float: *a ship rode at anchor in the dock.* **6** (**ride up**) (of a piece of clothing) gradually move upwards. **7** (**ride on**) depend on. ● n. **1** an act of riding. **2** a roller coaster, roundabout, etc. ridden at a fair or amusement park. **3** a path for horse riding.
– PHRASES **ride high** be successful. **a rough** (or **easy**) **ride** a difficult (or easy) time. **take someone for a ride** informal deceive someone.
– ORIGIN Old English.

rider ● n. **1** a person who rides a horse, bicycle, motorcycle, etc. **2** a condition added to an agreement or document.

ridge ● n. **1** a long narrow hilltop or mountain range. **2** a narrow raised band on a surface. **3** Meteorol. a long region of high pressure. **4** the edge formed where the two sloping sides of a roof meet at the top.
– ORIGIN Old English, 'spine, crest'.

ridged ● adj. having raised lines on the surface.

ridicule ● n. mockery or derision. ● v. (**ridicules**, **ridiculing**, **ridiculed**) make fun of.

ridiculous ● adj. causing mockery or derision; absurd.
– DERIVATIVES **ridiculously** adv.
– ORIGIN Latin *ridiculus* 'laughable'.

riding[1] ● n. the sport or activity of riding horses.

riding[2] ● n. (**the East/North/West Riding**) each of three former administrative divisions of Yorkshire.
– ORIGIN Old Norse, 'third part'.

riding crop ● n. a short flexible whip with a loop for the hand, used when riding.

> **Ridley**, E
> Nicholas (*c.*1500–55), English Protestant bishop and martyr. He opposed the Catholic policies of Mary I, for which he was burnt at the stake in Oxford.

rife ● adj. **1** (of something undesirable) widespread. **2** (**rife with**) full of.
– ORIGIN Old English.

riff ● n. a short repeated phrase in popular music or jazz.
– ORIGIN from RIFFLE.

riffle ● v. (**riffles**, **riffling**, **riffled**) **1** turn over pages quickly and casually. **2** (**riffle through**) search quickly through.
– ORIGIN perh. from RUFFLE.

riff-raff ● n. people who are considered to be socially unacceptable.
– ORIGIN from Old French *rif et raf* 'one and all'.

rifle[1] ● n. a gun with a long spirally grooved barrel to make a bullet spin and thereby increase accuracy over a long distance. ● v. (**rifles**, **rifling**, **rifled**) hit or kick (a ball) hard and straight.
– ORIGIN French *rifler* 'graze, scratch'.

rifle[2] ● v. (**rifles**, **rifling**, **rifled**) search through something hurriedly to find or steal something.
– ORIGIN Old French *rifler* 'plunder'.

rifleman ● n. a soldier armed with a rifle.

rifle range ● n. a place for practising rifle shooting.

rift ● n. **1** a crack, split, or break. **2** a serious break in friendly relations.
– ORIGIN Scandinavian.

rift valley ● n. a steep-sided valley formed by subsidence of the earth's surface between nearly parallel faults.

rig[1] ● v. (**rigs**, **rigging**, **rigged**) **1** provide (a boat) with sails and rigging. **2** assemble and adjust (the equipment of a sailing boat) to make it ready for operation. **3** (often **rig up**) set up (a device or structure). **4** (**rig out**) provide with clothes of a particular type. ● n. **1** the arrangement of a boat's sails and rigging. **2** an apparatus for a particular purpose: *a lighting rig.* **3** an oil rig.
– ORIGIN perh. Scandinavian.

rig[2] ● v. (**rigs**, **rigging**, **rigged**) arrange in a dishonest way so as to gain an advantage: *the elections had been rigged.*
– ORIGIN unknown.

> **Riga** E
> /ree-guh/ the capital of Latvia.

> **Rigel** 
> /ry-juhl, **ry**-guhl/ the seventh-brightest star in the sky, and the brightest in the constellation Orion.

rigger ● n. (in combination) a ship rigged in a particular way: *a square-rigger.*

rigging ● n. **1** the system of ropes or chains supporting a ship's masts. **2** the ropes and wires supporting the structure of a hang-glider or parachute.

right ● adj. **1** on or towards the side of a person or of a thing which is to the east when the person or thing is facing north. **2** morally good or justified. **3** factually correct. **4** most appropriate: *the right man for the job.* **5** in a satisfactory, sound, or normal condition. **6** relating to a right-wing person or group. **7** Brit. informal complete: *I felt a right idiot.* ● adv. **1** on or to the right side. **2** to the furthest extent; completely *the car spun right off the track.* **3** exactly; directly. **4** correctly or satisfactorily. **5** informal immediately. ● n. **1** that which is morally right. **2** an entitlement to have or do something. **3** (**rights**) the authority to perform, publish, or film a particular work or event. **4** (**the right**) the right-hand side or direction. **5** a right turn. **6** (**the Right**) a right-wing group or political party. ● v. **1** restore to

a normal or upright position. **2** restore to a normal or correct condition. **3** make amends for (a wrong).
– PHRASES **by rights** if things were fair or correct. **in one's own right** as a result of one's own qualifications or efforts. **right** (or **straight**) **away** immediately.
– DERIVATIVES **rightward** adj. & adv.
– ORIGIN Old English.

right angle ● n. an angle of 90°, as in a corner of a square.
– PHRASES **at right angles to** forming an angle of 90° with.
– DERIVATIVES **right-angled** adj.

righteous /ry-chuhss/ ● adj. morally right or justifiable.
– DERIVATIVES **righteously** adv. **righteousness** n.

rightful ● adj. **1** having a clear right to something. **2** correct; fitting.
– DERIVATIVES **rightfully** adv.

right hand ● n. **1** the region or direction on the right side. **2** the most important position next to someone. ● adj. **1** on or towards the right side. **2** done with or using the right hand.

right-hand drive ● n. a motor-vehicle steering system with the steering wheel and other controls fitted on the right side.

right-handed ● adj. **1** using or done with the right hand. **2** turning to the right.

right-hander ● n. a right-handed person.

right-hand man ● n. a chief assistant.

rightly ● adv. **1** in accordance with what is true or just. **2** with good reason.

right-minded ● adj. having sound views and principles.

right of way ● n. **1** the legal right to pass along a specific route through another person's property. **2** a public path through another's property. **3** the right to proceed before another vehicle.

right side ● n. the side of something intended to be uppermost or foremost.

right wing ● n. **1** the conservative or reactionary section of a political party. [ORIGIN see **LEFT WING**.] **2** the right side of a sports team on the field.
– DERIVATIVES **right-winger** n.

rigid ● adj. **1** unable to bend or be forced out of shape. **2** not able to be changed or adapted: *rigid rules.*
– DERIVATIVES **rigidity** n. **rigidly** adv.
– ORIGIN Latin *rigidus.*

rigmarole /rig-muh-rohl/ ● n. **1** a lengthy and complicated process. **2** a long, rambling story.
– ORIGIN prob. from former *ragman roll,* referring to a legal document recording a list of offences.

rigor mortis /ri-ger **mor**-tiss, ry-ger **mor**-tiss/ ● n. stiffening of the joints and muscles a few hours after death, lasting from one to four days.
– ORIGIN Latin, 'stiffness of death'.

rigorous ● adj. **1** extremely thorough or accurate. **2** (of a rule, system, etc.) strictly applied or followed. **3** harsh or severe: *rigorous military training.*
– DERIVATIVES **rigorously** adv.

rigour (US **rigor**) ● n. **1** the quality of being rigorous. **2** (**rigours**) demanding or extreme conditions.
– ORIGIN Latin *rigor* 'stiffness'.

rile ● v. (**riles**, **riling**, **riled**) informal annoy or irritate.
– ORIGIN from **ROIL**.

Riley[1] ● n. (in phr. **the life of Riley**) informal a luxurious or carefree existence.
– ORIGIN unknown.

Riley[2], E
Bridget (Louise) (b.1931), English painter, known for her abstract paintings which create optical illusions of light and movement.

Rilke E
/ril-kuh/, Rainer Maria (1875–1926; pen name of *René Karl Wilhelm Josef Maria Rilke*), Austrian poet, born in Prague. He believed that art was a quasi-religious vocation; works include the *Duino Elegies* and *Sonnets to Orpheus.*

rill ● n. a small stream.
– ORIGIN prob. German.

rim ● n. **1** the upper or outer edge of something circular. **2** a limit or boundary. ● v. (**rims**, **rimming**, **rimmed**) (**be rimmed**) be provided or marked with a rim.
– ORIGIN Old English, 'a border, coast'.

Rimbaud E
/ram-boh/, (Jean Nicholas) Arthur (1854–91), French poet, known for his collections of symbolist prose poems *Les Illuminations* and *Une Saison en enfer.*

rime /rym/ ● n. tech. & literary hoar frost.
– ORIGIN Old English.

Rimini E
/rim-i-ni/ a port and resort on the Adriatic coast of NE Italy.

Rimsky-Korsakov E
/rim-ski **kor**-suh-kof/, Nikolai (Andreevich) (1844–1908), Russian composer, known for his orchestral suite *Scheherazade* and his operas drawing on Russian and Slavic folk tales.

rind ● n. a tough outer layer or covering of fruit, cheese, or bacon.
– ORIGIN Old English.

ring[1] ● n. **1** a small circular band of precious metal, worn on a finger. **2** a circular band, object, or mark. **3** an enclosed space in which a sport, performance, or show takes place. **4** a group of people or things arranged in a circle. **5** a group of people working together illegally or secretly: *a drug ring.* ● v. **1** surround. **2** draw a circle round.
– ORIGIN Old English.

ring[2] ● v. (**rings**, **ringing**, **rang**; past part. **rung**) **1** make or cause to make a clear resonating sound. **2** (**ring with**) echo with (a sound). **3** esp. Brit. call by telephone. **4** (**ring off**) Brit. end a telephone call by replacing the receiver. **5** call for attention by sounding a bell. **6** sound (the hour, a peal, etc.) on a bell or bells. **7** (of the ears) be filled with a buzzing or humming sound. **8** (**ring up**) record (an amount) on a cash register. ● n. **1** an act of ringing. **2** a loud clear sound or tone. **3** Brit. informal a telephone call. **4** a quality communicated by something heard: *the tale had a ring of truth.*
– ORIGIN Old English.

ring binder ● n. a binder with ring-shaped

clasps that can be opened to pass through holes in paper.

ringdove ● n. Brit. a wood pigeon.

ringer ● n. **1** a person or device that rings. **2** informal the double of a person or thing.

ring fence ● n. a fence completely enclosing a piece of land. ● v. (**ring-fences**, **ring-fencing**, **ring-fenced**) (**ring-fence**) guarantee that (funds for a particular purpose) will not be spent on anything else.

ring finger ● n. the finger next to the little finger of the left hand, on which the wedding ring is worn.

ringing ● adj. **1** having a clear resonant sound. **2** (of a statement) forceful and clear: *a ringing declaration of support.*

ringleader ● n. a person who leads others in crime or causing trouble.

ringlet ● n. a corkscrew-shaped curl of hair.

ringmaster ● n. the person directing a circus performance.

ring pull ● n. a ring on a can that is pulled to open it.

ring road ● n. a road encircling a town.

ringside ● n. the area beside a boxing ring or circus ring.

ringside seat ● n. a very good position from which to observe something.

ringworm ● n. a skin disease occurring in small circular itchy patches, caused by various fungi.

rink ● n. **1** (also **ice rink**) an enclosed area of ice for skating, ice hockey, or curling. **2** (also **roller rink**) a smooth enclosed floor for roller skating.
– ORIGIN perh. from Old French *renc* 'rank'.

rinse ● v. (**rinses**, **rinsing**, **rinsed**) **1** wash with clean water to remove soap or dirt. **2** remove (soap or dirt) by rinsing. ● n. **1** an act of rinsing. **2** an antiseptic liquid for cleansing the mouth. **3** a liquid for conditioning or colouring the hair.
– ORIGIN Old French *rincer.*

Rio de Janeiro E
/ree-oh duh juh-**neer**-oh/ (also **Rio**) the chief port and former capital of Brazil.

Rio Grande E
/ree-oh **grand**, ree-oh **gran**-di/ a river of North America which rises in the Rocky Mountains of SW Colorado and flows generally south-eastwards to the Gulf of Mexico.

riot ● n. **1** a violent disturbance of the peace by a crowd. **2** a confused or lavish combination or display: *a riot of colour.* **3** (**a riot**) informal a highly entertaining person or thing. ● v. take part in a riot.
– PHRASES **run riot** behave in a violent and uncontrolled way.
– DERIVATIVES **rioter** n.
– ORIGIN Old French *riote* 'debate'.

riotous ● adj. **1** involving public disorder. **2** involving wild and uncontrolled behaviour.

RIP ● abbrev. rest in peace (used on graves).
– ORIGIN from Latin *requiescat in pace.*

rip[1] ● v. (**rips**, **ripping**, **ripped**) **1** tear. **2** pull forcibly away. **3** move rapidly: *fire ripped through the house.* **4** (**rip off**) informal cheat (someone). **5** (**rip off**) informal steal. ● n. a long tear.
– PHRASES **let rip** informal move or act without restraint.
– ORIGIN unknown.

rip[2] (also **rip tide**) ● n. a stretch of fast-flowing rough water caused by the meeting of currents.
– ORIGIN perh. from RIP[1].

riparian /ri-**pair**-i-uhn, ry-**pair**-i-uhn/ ● adj. relating to or situated on the banks of a river.
– ORIGIN Latin *riparius.*

ripcord ● n. a cord that is pulled to open a parachute.

ripe ● adj. **1** (of fruit or grain) ready for harvesting and eating. **2** (of a cheese or wine) fully matured. **3** (**ripe for**) having reached a fitting time for. **4** (of a person's age) advanced.
– DERIVATIVES **ripeness** n.
– ORIGIN Old English.

ripen ● v. become or make ripe.

rip-off ● n. informal **1** an article that is greatly overpriced. **2** a poor-quality copy.

riposte /ri-**posst**/ ● n. a quick clever reply.
– ORIGIN French.

ripping ● adj. Brit. informal, dated excellent.

ripple ● n. **1** a small wave or series of waves. **2** a rising and falling sound that spreads through a group of people. **3** a feeling or effect that spreads through someone or something: *the news will create a ripple of concern in boardrooms.* ● v. (**ripples**, **rippling**, **rippled**) **1** form or cause to form ripples. **2** (of a sound or feeling) spread through a person or place.
– ORIGIN unknown.

rip-roaring ● adj. full of energy and vigour.

rise ● v. (**rises**, **rising**, **rose**; past part. **risen**) **1** come or go up. **2** get up from lying, sitting, or kneeling. **3** increase in number, size, strength, or quality. **4** (of land) slope upwards. **5** (of the sun, moon, or stars) appear above the horizon. **6** reach a higher social or professional position. **7** (**rise above**) succeed in not being restricted by: *he struggled to rise above his humble background.* **8** (**rise to**) respond well to (a difficult situation). **9** (often **rise up**) rebel. **10** (of a river) have its source. ● n. **1** an act of rising. **2** an upward slope or hill. **3** Brit. a pay increase.
– ORIGIN Old English.

riser ● n. **1** a person who usually gets out of bed at a particular time of the morning: *an early riser.* **2** a vertical section between the treads of a staircase.

risible /ri-zi-b'l/ ● adj. causing laughter.
– DERIVATIVES **risibly** adv.
– ORIGIN Latin *risibilis.*

rising ● adj. approaching a specified age. ● n. a revolt.

rising damp ● n. Brit. moisture absorbed from the ground into a wall.

risk ● n. **1** a situation that could be dangerous or have a bad outcome. **2** the possibility that something unpleasant will happen. **3** a person or thing causing a risk: *gloss paint can pose a fire risk.* ● v. **1** expose to danger or loss. **2** act in such a way that something bad could happen. **3** take a risk by doing (something).
– PHRASES **at one's own risk** taking responsibility for one's own safety or possessions.
– ORIGIN Italian *risco* 'danger'.

risky ● adj. (**riskier**, **riskiest**) involving risk.
– DERIVATIVES **riskily** adv.

Risorgimento E
/ri-sor-ji-**men**-toh/ a movement for the unification and independence of Italy in the 19th century. With French aid, the Austrians were driven out of northern Italy by 1859, and the south was won over by Garibaldi. Voting resulted in Victor Emmanuel II becoming the first king of a united Italy in 1861.

risotto /ri-zot-toh/ • **n.** (pl. **risottos**) an Italian dish of rice cooked in stock with ingredients such as meat or seafood.
– ORIGIN Italian.

risqué /riss-kay, riss-kay, ree-skay/ • **adj.** slightly indecent or rude.
– ORIGIN French.

rissole • **n.** a small cake or ball of meat and spices, coated in breadcrumbs and fried.
– ORIGIN French.

rite • **n.** a religious or other solemn ceremony.
– PHRASES **rite of passage** a ceremony or event, e.g. marriage, marking an important stage in someone's life.
– ORIGIN Latin *ritus* '(religious) usage'.

ritual • **n.** **1** a religious or solemn ceremony involving a series of actions performed according to a set order. **2** a series of actions always followed by someone without variation: *her visits became a ritual.* • **adj.** relating to or done as a ritual.
– DERIVATIVES **ritually** adv.

ritualistic • **adj.** having to do with or done as a ritual.

ritzy • **adj.** (**ritzier**, **ritziest**) informal expensively stylish.
– ORIGIN from César *Ritz* (1850–1918), a Swiss hotel owner whose name became associated with luxury hotels.

rival • **n.** **1** a person or thing competing with another for the same thing. **2** a person or thing equal to another in quality: *she has no rivals as a female rock singer.* • **v.** (**rivals**, **rivalling**, **rivalled**; US **rivals**, **rivaling**, **rivaled**) be comparable to.
– DERIVATIVES **rivalrous** adj.
– ORIGIN Latin *rivalis.*

rivalry • **n.** (pl **rivalries**) a situation in which two people or groups are competing for the same thing.

riven /ri-vuhn/ • **adj.** torn apart; split.
– ORIGIN Old Norse.

river • **n.** **1** a large natural flow of water travelling along a channel to the sea, a lake, or another river. **2** a large quantity of a flowing liquid.
– ORIGIN Old French.

Rivera E
/ri-**vair**-uh/, Diego (1886–1957), Mexican painter, known for his murals.

rivet /ri-vit/ • **n.** a short metal pin or bolt for holding together two metal plates. • **v.** (**rivets**, **riveting**, **riveted**) **1** fasten with a rivet or rivets. **2** (**be riveted**) be completely involved or absorbed.
– ORIGIN Old French.

riviera /ri-vi-air-uh/ • **n.** a coastal region with a subtropical climate and vegetation, especially that of southern France and northern Italy.
– ORIGIN Italian, 'seashore'.

rivulet /riv-yuu-lit/ • **n.** a very small stream.
– ORIGIN from former French *riveret* 'small river'.

Riyadh E
/ree-**ahd**/ the capital of Saudi Arabia.

RM • **abbrev.** (in the UK) Royal Marines.

RN • **abbrev.** (in the UK) Royal Navy.

RNA • **n.** ribonucleic acid, a substance in living cells which carries instructions from DNA for controlling the synthesis of proteins.

RNLI • **abbrev.** (in the UK) Royal National Lifeboat Institution.

roach[1] • **n.** (pl. **roach**) a common freshwater fish of the carp family.
– ORIGIN Old French *roche.*

roach[2] • **n.** N. Amer. informal a cockroach.

road • **n.** **1** a wide way between places, with a hard surface for vehicles to travel on. **2** a way to achieving a particular outcome: *on the road to recovery.*
– ORIGIN Old English, 'journey on horseback'.

roadblock • **n.** a barrier put across a road by the police or army to stop and examine traffic.

road fund licence • **n.** Brit. a disc displayed on a vehicle certifying payment of road tax.

road hog • **n.** informal a reckless or inconsiderate motorist.

roadholding • **n.** the ability of a moving vehicle to remain stable.

roadie • **n.** informal a person employed by a touring pop or rock group to set up and maintain equipment.

road rage • **n.** violent anger arising from conflict with the driver of another motor vehicle.

roadshow • **n.** **1** each of a series of radio or television programmes broadcast from different places. **2** a touring political or promotional campaign.

roadster • **n.** an open-top car with two seats.

road tax • **n.** Brit. a tax to be paid on motor vehicles using public roads.

road test • **n.** **1** a test of the performance of a vehicle on the road. **2** a test of equipment carried out in working conditions.

roadway • **n.** **1** a road. **2** the part of a road intended for vehicles.

roadworks • **pl. n.** Brit. repairs to roads or to pipes or cables under roads.

roadworthy • **adj.** (of a vehicle) fit to be used on the road.

roam • **v.** **1** travel aimlessly over a wide area. **2** wander over, through, or about (a place).
– ORIGIN unknown.

roan • **adj.** (of a horse) having a bay, chestnut, or black coat with hairs of another colour. • **n.** a roan animal.
– ORIGIN Old French.

roar • **n.** **1** a long, deep, sound as made by a lion, natural force, or engine. **2** a loud, deep sound made by a person, as an expression of pain, anger, or great amusement. • **v.** **1** make a roar. **2** laugh loudly. **3** move, act, or happen very fast.
– ORIGIN Old English.

roaring • **adj.** informal complete: *a roaring success.*
– PHRASES **do a roaring trade** informal do very good business. **the roaring forties** stormy ocean areas between latitudes 40° and 50°

r

south.

roast ● v. **1** (of meat or vegetables) cook or be cooked in an oven or over a fire. **2** process (coffee beans, nuts, etc.) with intense heat. **3** make or become very warm. ● adj. (of food) having been roasted. ● n. a joint of meat that has been roasted.
– ORIGIN Old French *rostir*.

roasting informal ● adj. very hot and dry. ● n. a severe criticism or reprimand.

rob ● v. (**robs**, **robbing**, **robbed**) **1** take property unlawfully from (a person or place) by force or threat of force. **2** deprive of something needed or important: *poor health has robbed her of a normal social life.*
– DERIVATIVES **robber** n.
– ORIGIN Old French *rober*.

robbery ● n. (pl. **robberies**) the action of robbing a person or place.

Robbins[1], E
Harold (1916–97), American novelist, author of *The Carpetbaggers* and *The Betsy.*

Robbins[2], E
Jerome (1918 98), American ballet dancer and choreographer, who choreographed the musicals *The King and I, West Side Story,* and *Fiddler on the Roof.*

robe ● n. **1** a loose outer garment reaching to the ankles, worn on formal or ceremonial occasions. **2** a bathrobe or dressing gown. ● v. (**robes**, **robing**, **robed**) clothe in a robe or robes.
– ORIGIN Old French, 'garment, booty'.

Robert I E
(1274–1329; known as **Robert the Bruce**), king of Scotland 1306–29. He defeated Edward II at Bannockburn (1314) and re-established Scotland as a separate kingdom.

Robeson E
/rohb-s'n/, Paul (Bustill) (1898–1976), American singer and actor, known for his rich bass voice.

Robespierre E
/rohbz-pyair/, Maximilien François Marie Isidore de (1758–94), French revolutionary leader. As leader of the radical Jacobins he backed the execution of Louis XVI and initiated the Terror (mid 1793–July 1794, when the Jacobins executed anyone considered a threat to their regime), but he then fell from favour and was guillotined.

robin ● n. a small songbird of the thrush family, with a red breast and brown back and wings.
– ORIGIN Old French.

Robin Hood E
a semi-legendary English medieval outlaw, associated with Sherwood Forest in Nottinghamshire, and said to have robbed the rich and helped the poor.

Robinson[1], E
Mary (Terese Winifred) (b.1944), Irish Labour stateswoman, President 1990–7, Ireland's first woman President.

Robinson[2], E
Smokey (b.1940; born *William Robinson*), American soul singer and songwriter.

Robinson[3], E
Sugar Ray (1920–89; born *Walker Smith*), American boxer. He was world welterweight champion (1946–51) and seven times middleweight champion.

robot /roh-bot/ ● n. a machine capable of carrying out a complex series of actions automatically.
– ORIGIN Czech *robota* 'forced labour'.

robotic /roh-bot-ik/ ● adj. **1** relating to robots. **2** mechanical, stiff, or unemotional. ● n. (**robotics**) the branch of technology concerned with the design, construction, and use of robots.

Robson E
/rob-s'n/, Dame Flora (1902–84), English actress.

robust ● adj. **1** sturdy or able to withstand difficult conditions. **2** strong and healthy. **3** determined and forceful: *a robust defence.*
– ORIGIN Latin *robustus* 'firm and hard'.

rock[1] ● n. **1** the hard mineral material of the earth's crust. **2** a mass of rock projecting out of the ground or water. **3** a boulder. **4** Geol. any natural material with a particular make-up of minerals. **5** Brit. a kind of hard sweet in the form of a cylindrical stick. **6** informal a diamond or other precious stone.
– PHRASES **on the rocks** informal **1** in difficulties and likely to fail. **2** (of a drink) served undiluted and with ice cubes.
– ORIGIN Latin *rocca*.

rock[2] ● v. **1** move gently to and fro or from side to side. **2** shake violently. **3** shock or distress greatly. **4** informal dance to or play rock music. ● n. **1** (also **rock music**) a form of popular music with a strong beat, played on electric guitars, drums, etc. **2** a rocking movement.
– ORIGIN Old English.

rockabilly ● n. a type of popular music combining rock and roll and country music.
– ORIGIN from **ROCK AND ROLL** and **HILLBILLY**.

Rockall E
a rocky islet in the North Atlantic, about 400 km (250 miles) north-west of Ireland. It was formally annexed by Britain in 1955 but has since become the subject of territorial dispute between Britain, Denmark, Iceland, and Ireland.

rock and roll (also **rock 'n' roll**) ● n. a type of popular dance music originating in the 1950s, having a heavy beat and simple melodies.

rock-bottom ● adj. at the lowest possible level.

rock cake ● n. esp. Brit. a small currant cake with a hard rough surface.

rock climbing ● n. the sport or pastime of climbing rock faces.

rock crystal ● n. transparent quartz.

Rockefeller E
/rok-uh-fel-ler/, John D. (1839–1937; full name *John Davison Rockefeller*), American industrialist and philanthropist. Both he and his son, **John D. Rockefeller Jr** (1874–1960), established many philanthropic institutions.

rocker ● n. **1** a person who performs or enjoys rock music. **2** a curved piece of wood on the bottom of a rocking chair.

– PHRASES **off one's rocker** informal mad.

rockery ● n. (pl. **rockeries**) a heaped arrangement of rocks with soil between them, planted with rock plants.

rocket[1] ● n. **1** a cylinder-shaped missile or spacecraft propelled by a stream of burning gases. **2** a firework that shoots into the air and then explodes. **3** Brit. informal a severe reprimand. ● v. (**rockets**, **rocketing**, **rocketed**) move or increase very rapidly and suddenly: *sales of milk are rocketing.*
– ORIGIN Italian *rocchetto* 'small spindle (for spinning)'.

rocket[2] ● n. an edible Mediterranean plant, eaten in salads.
– ORIGIN French *roquette.*

rocketry ● n. the branch of science and technology concerned with rockets.

rock garden ● n. a rockery.

Rockies E
= **ROCKY MOUNTAINS.**

rocking chair ● n. a chair mounted on a curved bar or springs.

rocking horse ● n. a model of a horse mounted on curved bars or springs for a child to ride on.

rock plant ● n. a plant that grows on or among rocks.

rock pool ● n. a pool of water among rocks along a shoreline.

rock salt ● n. common salt occurring naturally as a mineral.

rock solid ● adj. completely firm or stable.

rocky[1] ● adj. (**rockier**, **rockiest**) **1** made of rock. **2** full of rocks.

rocky[2] ● adj. (**rockier**, **rockiest**) unsteady or unstable.

Rocky Mountains E
(also **the Rockies**) the chief mountain system of North America, which extends from the US–Mexico border to the Yukon Territory of northern Canada.

rococo /ruh-**koh**-koh/ ● adj. relating to an elaborately ornate style of European furniture or architecture of the 18th century, with decorative motifs and asymmetrical curves.
– ORIGIN French.

rod ● n. **1** a thin straight bar, especially of wood or metal. **2** a fishing rod. **3** a type of light-sensitive cell in the eye, responsible mainly for black-and-white vision in poor light. Compare with **CONE.**
– ORIGIN Old English.

Roddick, E
Anita (Lucia) (b.1943), English businesswoman and founder of the Body Shop chain, selling cosmetics made from natural ingredients and not tested on animals.

rode past of **RIDE.**

rodent ● n. a mammal of a large group including rats, mice, and squirrels, having strong constantly growing incisors.
– ORIGIN Latin *rodere* 'gnaw'.

rodeo /**roh**-di-oh, roh-**day**-oh/ ● n. (pl. **rodeos**) a contest or entertainment in which cowboys show their skills.
– ORIGIN Spanish.

Rodgers, E
Richard (Charles) (1902–79), American composer. He collaborated with Oscar Hammerstein II on a succession of musicals, including *The Sound of Music.*

Rodin E
/**roh**-dan/, Auguste (1840–1917), French sculptor, known for such works as *The Thinker* and *The Kiss.*

rodomontade /ro-doh-mon-**tayd**/ ● n. boastful talk or behaviour.
– ORIGIN Italian *rodomonte* 'boaster'.

roe[1] ● n. **1** (also **hard roe**) the mass of eggs contained in the ovaries of a female fish or shellfish, used as food. **2** (**soft roe**) the ripe testes of a male fish, used as food.
– ORIGIN German or Dutch *roge.*

roe[2] (also **roe deer**) ● n. (pl. **roe** or **roes**) a small deer with a reddish summer coat that turns greyish in winter.
– ORIGIN Old English.

roebuck ● n. a male roe deer.

roentgen /**runt**-yuhn, **rernt**-yuhn, **ront**-yuhn/ ● n. a unit of quantity of ionizing radiation.
– ORIGIN named after Wilhelm **RÖNTGEN.**

roger ● exclam. your message has been received and understood (used in radio communication). ● v. (**rogers**, **rogering**, **rogered**) Brit. vulgar (of a man) have sexual intercourse with.
– ORIGIN from the man's name *Roger.*

Rogers[1], E
Ginger (1911–95; born *Virginia Katherine McMath*), American actress and dancer. She is famous for her dancing partnership with Fred Astaire.

Rogers[2], E
Sir Richard (George) (b.1933), British architect, born in Italy. He is famous for glass and steel buildings with pipes on the outside, such as the Pompidou Centre, designed with the Italian architect Renzo Piano (b.1937), and the Lloyd's Building in London.

rogue ● n. **1** a dishonest or immoral man. **2** a mischievous but likeable person. **3** an elephant living apart from the herd.
– ORIGIN prob. from Latin *rogare* 'beg, ask'.

rogues' gallery ● n. informal a collection of photographs of known criminals.

roguish ● adj. playfully mischievous.

roil /royl/ ● v. **1** make (a liquid) muddy by disturbing the sediment. **2** (of a liquid) move in a turbulent manner.
– ORIGIN perh. from Old French *ruiler* 'mix mortar'.

roister /**roy**-ster/ ● v. (**roisters**, **roistering**, **roistered**) enjoy oneself or celebrate in a noisy way.
– DERIVATIVES **roisterer** n.
– ORIGIN French *rustre* 'ruffian'.

role ● n. **1** an actor's part in a play or film. **2** a person's or thing's function in a particular situation: *religion plays a vital role in society.*
– ORIGIN from former French *roule* 'roll', referring to the roll of paper on which an actor's part was written.

role model ● n. a person who others look to

as an example to be imitated.

role playing (also **role play**) ● **n.** the acting out of a particular role.

roll ● **v. 1** move by turning over and over. **2** move forward on wheels or with a smooth, wave-like motion. **3** (of a moving ship, aircraft, or vehicle) sway from side to side. **4** (of a machine or device) begin operating. **5** (often **roll up**) turn (something flexible) over and over on itself to form a cylindrical or round shape. **6** (**roll up**) curl up tightly. **7** flatten (something) by passing a roller over it or by passing it between rollers. **8** (of a loud, deep sound) reverberate. **9** pronounce (an *r*) with a trill. ● **n. 1** a cylinder formed by rolling flexible material. **2** a rolling movement. **3** a gymnastic exercise in which the body is rolled into a tucked position and turned in a forward or backward circle. **4** a long, deep, reverberating sound. **5** a very small loaf of bread. **6** an official list or register of names.
– PHRASES **on a roll** informal experiencing a long spell of success or good luck. **roll up** informal arrive. **roll up one's sleeves** prepare to fight or work.
– ORIGIN Old French *roller*.

roll-call ● **n.** the reading aloud of a list of names to discover who is present.

roller ● **n. 1** a rotating cylinder used to move, flatten, or spread something. **2** a small cylinder on which hair is rolled to produce curls. **3** a long swelling wave that appears to roll steadily towards the shore.

Rollerblade ● **n.** trademark an in-line skate.
– DERIVATIVES **rollerblader** n.

roller blind ● **n.** a window blind fitted on a roller.

roller coaster ● **n.** a fairground attraction consisting of a light railway track with many tight turns and steep slopes, on which people ride in small open carriages.

roller skate ● **n.** each of a pair of boots having four small wheels and used for gliding across a hard surface.

roller towel ● **n.** a long towel with the ends joined and hung on a roller.

rollicking[1] ● **adj.** cheerfully lively and amusing.
– ORIGIN perh. from **ROMP** and **FROLIC**.

rollicking[2] ● **n.** Brit. informal a severe reprimand.
– ORIGIN from **BOLLOCKING**.

rolling pin ● **n.** a cylinder for rolling out dough.

rolling stock ● **n.** locomotives, carriages, or other vehicles used on a railway.

rollmop ● **n.** a rolled uncooked pickled herring fillet.
– ORIGIN German *Rollmops*.

roll neck ● **n.** a loosely turned-over collar.

roll-on ● **adj.** (of a deodorant or cosmetic) applied by means of a rotating ball in the neck of the container.

roll-on roll-off ● **adj.** (of a ferry) in which vehicles are driven directly on at the start of the voyage and driven off at the end of it.

Rolls, E
Charles Stewart (1877–1910), English motoring and aviation pioneer, founder with Henry Royce of the company Rolls-Royce Ltd in 1906.

roll-up ● **n.** Brit. informal a hand-rolled cigarette.

roly-poly ● **n.** Brit. a pudding made of a sheet of suet pastry covered with jam or fruit, formed into a roll, and steamed or baked. ● **adj.** informal round and plump.
– ORIGIN from **ROLL**.

ROM ● **abbrev.** Computing read-only memory.

Roman ● **adj. 1** relating to ancient Rome or its empire or people. **2** relating to modern Rome. **3** referring to the alphabet used for writing Latin, English, and most European languages. **4** (**roman**) (of type) of a plain upright kind used in ordinary print. ● **n. 1** a person who lives in Rome. **2** (**roman**) roman type.

Roman Catholic ● **adj.** relating to the Roman Catholic Church. ● **n.** a member of this Church.
– DERIVATIVES **Roman Catholicism** n.

Roman Catholic Church ● **n.** the part of the Christian Church which has the Pope as its head.

Romance /roh-**manss**, **roh**-manss/ ● **n.** the group of languages descended from Latin, such as French, Spanish, Portuguese, and Italian.
– ORIGIN Latin *Romanicus* 'Roman'.

romance /roh-**manss**, **roh**-manss/ ● **n. 1** a pleasurable feeling of excitement and wonder associated with love. **2** a love affair. **3** a book or film dealing with love in a sentimental or idealized way. **4** a feeling of mystery, excitement, and remoteness from everyday life: *the romance of the past*. **5** a medieval story dealing with adventures of knights. ● **v.** (**romances**, **romancing**, **romanced**) try to gain the love of.
– ORIGIN from **ROMANCE**.

Roman Empire E
the empire under Roman rule established in 27 BC and divided into two parts in AD 395. At its greatest extent Roman rule or influence extended from Armenia and Mesopotamia in the east to the Iberian peninsula in the west, and from the Rhine and Danube in the north to Egypt and provinces on the Mediterranean coast of North Africa.

Romanesque /roh-muh-**nesk**/ ● **adj.** relating to a style of architecture common in Europe *c.*900–1200, with massive vaulting and round arches.
– ORIGIN French.

Romania E
/roo-**may**-ni-uh/ (also **Rumania**) a country in SE Europe with a coastline on the Black Sea; capital, Bucharest.
– DERIVATIVES **Romanian** (also **Rumanian**) adj. & n.

Roman nose ● **n.** a nose with a high bridge.

Roman numeral ● **n.** any of the letters used as numbers in the ancient Roman system: I = 1, V = 5, X = 10, L = 50, C = 100, D = 500, M = 1,000.

romantic ● **adj. 1** having to do with love or romance. **2** showing or regarding life in an unrealistic and idealized way. **3** (**Romantic**) relating to the artistic and literary movement of romanticism. ● **n. 1** a person with romantic beliefs or attitudes. **2** (**Romantic**) a writer or artist of the Romantic movement.
– DERIVATIVES **romantically** adv.

romanticism ● **n.** a literary and artistic

movement which began in the late 18th century and emphasized creative inspiration and individual feeling.

romanticize (also **romanticise**) • v. (**romanticizes, romanticizing, romanticized**) make (something) seem better or more appealing than it really is.

Romany /rom-uh-ni, roh-muh-ni/ • n. (pl. **Romanies**) **1** the language of the gypsies. **2** a gypsy.
– ORIGIN Romany *Rom* 'man, husband'.

Rome E
the capital of Italy, and the former capital of the Roman Empire.

Rome, Treaty of E
a treaty setting up and defining the aims of the European Economic Community. It was signed at Rome in March 1957 by France, West Germany, Italy, Belgium, the Netherlands, and Luxembourg.

Romeo /roh-mi-oh/ • n. (pl. **Romeos**) an attractive, passionate male lover.
– ORIGIN the hero of Shakespeare's *Romeo and Juliet*.

Rommel E
/rom-m'l/, Erwin (1891–1944; known as **the Desert Fox**), German Field Marshal. As commander of the German army force sent to North Africa in 1941, he captured Tobruk but was defeated by Montgomery at El Alamein.

romp • v. **1** play about roughly and energetically. **2** (**romp through**) informal achieve (something) easily. **3** (**romp home/in**) informal finish as the easy winner of a contest. • n. **1** a spell of romping. **2** a light-hearted film or other work.
– ORIGIN perh. from **RAMP**.

rompers (also **romper suit**) • pl. n. a young child's one-piece outer garment.

Romulus E
/rom-yuu-luhss/ Rom. Myth. one of the twin sons of Mars, he and his brother Remus were abandoned at birth but were found and suckled by a she-wolf and later brought up by a shepherd family. Remus was killed and Romulus went on to found the city of Rome.

rondeau • n. (pl. **rondeaux** /ron-doh, ron-dohz/) a poem of ten or thirteen lines with only two rhymes throughout and with the opening words used twice as a refrain.
– ORIGIN French.

rondo /ron-doh/ • n. (pl. **rondos**) a musical form with a recurring leading theme.
– ORIGIN Italian.

Röntgen E
/runt-yuhn, rernt-guhn/, Wilhelm Conrad (1845–1923), German physicist, the discoverer of X-rays.

röntgen • n. var. of **ROENTGEN**.

rood /rood/ • n. a crucifix.
– ORIGIN Old English.

rood screen • n. a screen of wood or stone separating the nave from the chancel of a church.

roof • n. (pl. **roofs**) **1** the upper covering of a building or vehicle. **2** the top inner surface of a covered space: *the roof of the cave fell in.* **3** the upper limit of prices or wages. • v. (usu. **be roofed**) cover with a roof.
– PHRASES **go through the roof** informal (of prices or figures) reach extremely high levels. **hit** (or **go through**) **the roof** informal suddenly become very angry.
– ORIGIN Old English.

roofer • n. a person who builds or repairs roofs.

roofing • n. material for constructing a building's roof.

roof of the mouth • n. the palate.

roof rack • n. a framework for carrying luggage on the roof of a vehicle.

rook[1] • n. a crow with black plumage and a bare face, nesting in colonies in treetops.
– ORIGIN Old English.

rook[2] • n. a chess piece that can move in any direction along a rank or file on which it stands.
– ORIGIN Arabic.

rookery • n. (pl. **rookeries**) a collection of rooks' nests high in a clump of trees.

rookie • n. informal a new recruit or member.
– ORIGIN perh. from **RECRUIT**.

room /room, ruum/ • n. **1** a part of a building enclosed by walls, floor, and ceiling. **2** (**rooms**) a set of rooms rented out to lodgers. **3** space viewed in terms of its capacity to do or hold things: *there was no room to move.* **4** scope: *room for improvement.* • v. N. Amer. share lodgings.
– ORIGIN Old English.

room service • n. the providing of food and drink to hotel guests in their rooms.

roomy • adj. (**roomier, roomiest**) having plenty of room.

Roosevelt[1] E
/roh-zuh-velt/, Franklin D. (1882–1945; full name *Franklin Delano Roosevelt*), American Democratic statesman, 32nd President of the US 1933–45. His New Deal of 1933 helped to lift the US out of the Depression. He served four terms in office.

Roosevelt[2] E
/roh-zuh-velt/, Theodore (1858–1919; known as **Teddy Roosevelt**), American Republican statesman, 26th President of the US 1901–9. He won the Nobel Peace Prize in 1906 for negotiating the end of the Russo-Japanese War.

roost • n. a place where birds or bats regularly settle to rest. • v. (of a bird or bat) settle or gather for rest.
– ORIGIN Old English.

rooster • n. esp. N. Amer. a male domestic fowl.

root[1] • n. **1** the part of a plant normally below ground, which acts as a support and collects water and nourishment. **2** the part of a bodily structure such as a hair or tooth that is embedded in tissue. **3** the basic cause or origin: *money is the root of all evil.* **4** (**roots**) family, ethnic, or cultural origins. **5** a form from which words have been made by adding prefixes or suffixes or by other modification. **6** Math. a number that when multiplied by itself one or more times gives a specified number. • v. **1** cause (a plant) to establish roots. **2** (**be rooted**) be firmly established. **3** (**be rooted**) stand still through fear or amazement. **4** (**root out/up**) find and get rid of.
– PHRASES **put down roots** (of a person) begin to have a settled life in a place. **take root**

become established.
– DERIVATIVES **rootless** adj.
– ORIGIN Old English.

root² ● v. **1** (of an animal) turn up the ground with its snout in search of food. **2** rummage. **3** (**root for**) informal support enthusiastically.
– ORIGIN Old English.

root mean square ● n. Math. the square root of the arithmetic mean of the squares of a set of values.

root sign ● n. Math. the radical sign.

rootstock ● n. **1** a rhizome. **2** a plant on to which another variety is grafted.

root vegetable ● n. a vegetable which grows as the root of a plant.

rope ● n. **1** a length of thick cord made by twisting together strands of hemp, nylon, etc. **2** a number of objects strung together: *a rope of pearls.* **3** (**the ropes**) the ropes enclosing a boxing or wrestling ring. **4** (**the ropes**) informal the established way of doing something: *I showed her the ropes.* ● v. (**ropes**, **roping**, **roped**) **1** catch or tie with rope. **2** (**rope in/into**) persuade (someone) to take part in something.
– PHRASES **on the ropes** in a state of near collapse.
– ORIGIN Old English.

ropy (also **ropey**) ● adj. (**ropier**, **ropiest**) Brit. informal poor in quality or health.

rorqual /ror-kwuhl/ ● n. a whale of a small group with pleated skin on the underside, e.g the blue whale.
– ORIGIN Norwegian *røyrkval* 'fin whale'.

rosary /roh-zuh-ri/ ● n. (pl. **rosaries**) **1** (in the Roman Catholic Church) a form of worship in which sets of prayers are repeated. **2** a string of beads for keeping count of prayers said.
– ORIGIN Latin *rosarium* 'rose garden'.

Roscommon E
/ross-**kom**-muhn/ a county in the north central part of the Republic of Ireland; county town, Roscommon.

rose¹ ● n. **1** a sweet-smelling flower that grows on a prickly bush. **2** a cap with holes in it attached to a shower, the spout of a watering can, or the end of a hose to produce a spray. **3** a warm pink colour.
– PHRASES **be coming up roses** be developing successfully. **rose-coloured spectacles** referring to a viewpoint that is naively optimistic.
– ORIGIN Latin *rosa*.

rose² past of RISE.

rosé /roh-zay/ ● n. light pink wine.
– ORIGIN French, 'pink'.

roseate /roh-zi-uht/ ● adj. literary rose-coloured.

Rosebery E
/rohz-buh-ri/, Archibald Philip Primrose, 5th Earl of (1847–1929), British Liberal statesman, Prime Minister 1894–5.

rose hip ● n. fuller form of HIP².

rosemary ● n. an evergreen shrub with leaves which are used as a herb in cooking.
– ORIGIN from Latin *ros marinus* 'dew of the sea'.

Roses, Wars of the E
see **WARS OF THE ROSES**.

Rosetta Stone E
/roh-zet-tuh/ an inscribed stone found near Rosetta on the mouth of the Nile in 1799, which provided the key to the deciphering of Egyptian hieroglyphs. Its text is written in three scripts: hieroglyphic, Egyptian demotic, and Greek; by comparing these, the French Egyptologist Jean-François Champollion (1790–1832) deciphered the hieroglyphs in 1822.

rosette ● n. **1** a rose-shaped decoration made of ribbon, worn by supporters of a sports team or political party or awarded as a prize. **2** a design or object resembling a rose.
– ORIGIN French, 'little rose'.

rose water ● n. scented water made with rose petals.

rose window ● n. a circular window in a church with a branching rose-like pattern.

rosewood ● n. a close-grained timber of a tropical tree used for making furniture and musical instruments.

Rosh Hashana /rosh huh-**shah**-nuh/ (also **Rosh Hashanah**) ● n. the Jewish New Year festival.
– ORIGIN Hebrew, 'head of the year'.

rosin /roz-in/ ● n. a kind of resin, rubbed on the bows of stringed instruments.
– ORIGIN Latin *rosina*.

Ross¹, E
Diana (b.1944), American pop and soul singer. Originally the lead singer of the Supremes, she went on to become a solo artist.

Ross², E
Sir James Clark (1800–62), British explorer, who discovered the north magnetic pole in 1831, and headed an expedition to the Antarctic 1839–43.

Rossetti¹ E
/ruh-zet-ti/, Christina (Georgina) (1830–94), English poet, who wrote religious poetry, love poetry, and children's verse. She was the sister of Dante Gabriel Rossetti.

Rossetti² E
/ruh-**zet**-ti/, Dante Gabriel (1828–82), English Pre-Raphaelite painter and poet. He is best known for his idealized paintings of women, such as *Beata Beatrix*. He was the brother of Christina Rossetti.

Rossini E
/ros-see-ni/, Gioacchino Antonio (1792–1868), Italian composer, who wrote over thirty operas, including *The Barber of Seville* and *William Tell*.

roster /ross-ter, **rohss**-ter/ ● n. **1** a list of people's names and the jobs they have to do at a particular time. **2** a list of sports players available for team selection. ● v. (**rosters**, **rostering**, **rostered**) put (a person's name) on a roster.
– ORIGIN Dutch *rooster* 'list'.

rostrum /ross-truhm/ ● n. (pl. **rostra** /ross-truh/ or **rostrums**) a platform on which a person stands to make a public speech, receive a prize, or conduct an orchestra.
– ORIGIN Latin, 'beak'; the word first referred to an orator's platform in ancient Rome, which was decorated with beak-like projections

from captured warships.

Roswell E
a town in New Mexico, the scene of a mysterious crash in July 1947. Some investigators have claimed that the crashed object was a UFO.

rosy ● adj. (**rosier**, **rosiest**) **1** pink. **2** promising: *critics saw a rosy future for the novel.*

rot ● v. (**rots**, **rotting**, **rotted**) decay. ● n. **1** the process or state of decaying. **2** (**the rot**) Brit. a decline in standards: *there's enough talent in the team to stop the rot.* **3** a disease that causes tissue decay in plants. **4** informal rubbish: *don't talk rot.*
– ORIGIN Old English.

rota ● n. esp. Brit. a list showing times and names for people to take their turn to perform duties.
– ORIGIN Latin, 'wheel'.

Rotarian ● n. a member of Rotary.

rotary ● adj. **1** revolving around a central point. **2** having a rotating part or parts: *a rotary mower.* ● n. (**Rotary**) a worldwide charitable society of business and professional people organized into local Rotary clubs.

rotate ● v. (**rotates**, **rotating**, **rotated**) **1** move in a circle round a central point. **2** (of a job) pass to each member of a group in a regularly recurring order. **3** grow (different crops) one after the other on the same area of land.
– DERIVATIVES **rotator** n. **rotatory** /roh-tay-tuh-ri/ adj.
– ORIGIN Latin *rotare* 'turn in a circle'.

rotation ● n. the action of rotating.
– DERIVATIVES **rotational** adj.

rote ● n. the learning of something by regular repetition: *a poem learnt by rote.*
– ORIGIN unknown.

Roth E
/roth/, Philip (Milton) (b.1933), American novelist and short-story writer, author of the novel *Portnoy's Complaint.*

Rothko E
/roth-koh/, Mark (1903–70; born *Marcus Rothkovich*), American painter, born in Latvia. He is known for his abstract paintings featuring hazy rectangles of colour.

Rothschild E
/roths-chyld/, Meyer Amschel (1743–1812), German financier, who founded the Rothschild banking house in Frankfurt at the end of the 18th century.

rotisserie /roh-tiss-uh-ri/ ● n. a rotating spit for roasting and barbecuing meat.
– ORIGIN French.

rotor ● n. **1** the rotating part of a turbine, electric motor, or other device. **2** a hub with a number of blades spreading out from it that is rotated to provide the lift for a helicopter.

Rotorua E
/roh-tuh-roo-uh/ a city and health resort on North Island, New Zealand. It lies at the centre of a region of thermal springs and geysers.

rotten ● adj. **1** suffering from decay. **2** corrupt. **3** informal very bad. ● adv. informal very much: *your mother spoiled you rotten.*
– ORIGIN Old Norse.

rotten borough ● n. Brit. hist. (before the Reform Act of 1832) a borough that was able to elect an MP though having very few voters.

rotter ● n. informal, dated a cruel or unpleasant person.

Rotterdam E
/rot-ter-dam/ a city in the Netherlands, at the mouth of the River Meuse. It is one of the world's largest ports and a major oil refinery.

Rottweiler /rot-vy-ler, rot-wy-ler/ ● n. a large powerful black-and-tan breed of dog.
– ORIGIN from *Rottweil*, a town in SW Germany.

rotund /roh-tund/ ● adj. rounded and plump.
– DERIVATIVES **rotundity** n.
– ORIGIN Latin *rotundus.*

rotunda /roh-tun-duh/ ● n. a round building or room.
– ORIGIN from Italian *rotonda camera* 'round chamber'.

rouble /roo-b'l/ (also **ruble**) ● n. the basic unit of money of Russia and some other former republics of the USSR.
– ORIGIN Russian.

roué /roo-ay/ ● n. a man who leads an immoral life.
– ORIGIN French, 'broken on a wheel', referring to the torture thought to be deserved by such a person.

rouge /roo*zh*/ ● n. a red powder or cream used for colouring the cheeks.
– ORIGIN French, 'red'.

rough ● adj. **1** not smooth or level. **2** not gentle: *rough treatment.* **3** (of weather or the sea) wild and stormy. **4** plain and basic: *rough wooden tables.* **5** harsh in sound or taste. **6** not worked out in every detail: *a rough guess.* **7** informal difficult and unpleasant. ● n. **1** a basic version or state: *jot things down in rough first.* **2** esp. Brit. a violent person. **3** (on a golf course) the area of longer grass around the fairway and the green. ● v. **1** (**rough out**) make a rough version of. **2** (**rough it**) informal live with only very basic necessities. **3** (**rough up**) informal beat (someone) up.
– PHRASES **rough and ready** basic but effective. **rough edges** small flaws in something that is otherwise satisfactory. **rough justice** treatment that is not fair or in accordance with the law. **sleep rough** Brit. sleep outside in uncomfortable conditions. **take the rough with the smooth** accept the difficult aspects of life as well as the good.
– DERIVATIVES **roughness** n.
– ORIGIN Old English.

roughage ● n. material in cereals, vegetables, and fruit that cannot be digested and which helps food to pass through the gut.

rough and tumble ● n. a competitive situation without rules.

roughcast ● n. plaster of lime, cement, and gravel, used on outside walls.

rough diamond ● n. a person who is of good character but lacks manners or education.

roughen ● v. make or become rough.

rough-hewn ● adj. (of a person) not educated or polite.

roughly ● adv. **1** in a rough way. **2** approximately: *a walk of roughly 13 miles.*

roughneck ● **n.** **1** informal a rough, impolite person. **2** an oil-rig worker.

roughshod ● **adj.** (in phr. **ride roughshod over**) fail to consider the wishes or feelings of.

roulade /roo-lahd/ ● **n.** a piece of meat, sponge cake, or other food, spread with a filling and rolled up.
– ORIGIN French.

roulette ● **n.** a gambling game in which a ball is dropped on to a revolving wheel with numbered compartments, the players betting on the number at which the ball comes to rest.
– ORIGIN French, 'small wheel'.

round ● **adj.** **1** shaped like a circle, cylinder, or sphere. **2** having a curved shape. **3** (of a voice or musical tone) rich and smooth. **4** (of a number) expressed in convenient units rather than exactly, for example to the nearest whole number. ● **n.** **1** a circular shape or piece. **2** a route by which a number of people or places are visited in turn: *a newspaper round.* **3** a regular sequence of activities: *the daily round.* **4** each of a sequence of stages in a sports contest. **5** a single division of a boxing or wrestling match. **6** a song for three or more unaccompanied voices or parts, each singing the same theme but starting one after another. **7** the amount of ammunition needed to fire one shot. **8** a set of drinks bought for all the members of a group. **9** Brit. a slice of bread. **10** Brit. the quantity of sandwiches made from two slices of bread. ● **adv.** esp. Brit. **1** so as to move in a circle. **2** so as to cover the whole area surrounding a particular centre. **3** so as to turn and face in the opposite direction. **4** used in describing the position of something: *it's the wrong way round.* **5** so as to surround or give support: *the family rallied round to help her.* **6** so as to reach a new place or position. ● **prep.** esp. Brit. **1** on every side of (a central point). **2** so as to encircle. **3** from or on the other side of. **4** so as to cover the whole area of: *she went round the house to check its condition.* ● **v.** **1** pass and go round. **2** make (a figure) less exact but more convenient for calculations: *we'll round the weight up to the nearest kilo.* **3** make or become round in shape.
– PHRASES **round off** **1** smooth the edges of. **2** complete in a suitable or satisfying way. **round on** make a sudden attack on. **round up** collect (people or animals) together.
– DERIVATIVES **roundness** n.
– ORIGIN Old French.

roundabout ● **n.** Brit. **1** a road junction at which traffic moves in one direction round a central island to reach one of the roads opening on to it. **2** a large revolving device in a playground, for children to ride on. **3** a merry-go-round. ● **adj.** not following a direct route.

rounded ● **adj.** **1** round or curved. **2** complete and balanced: *a rounded human being.*

roundel /rown-d'l/ ● **n.** **1** a small disc. **2** a circular identifying mark painted on military aircraft.
– ORIGIN Old French *rondel.*

rounders ● **n.** a ball game in which players run round a circuit of bases after hitting the ball with a cylindrical wooden bat.

Roundhead ● **n.** hist. a member or supporter of the Parliamentary party in the English Civil War.
– ORIGIN with reference to their short-cropped hair.

roundly ● **adv.** **1** in a firm or thorough way. **2** in a circular shape.

round robin ● **n.** **1** a tournament in which each competitor plays in turn against every other. **2** a petition.

round-table ● **adj.** (of talks or a meeting) at which parties meet on equal terms for discussion.

round trip ● **n.** a journey to a place and back again.

round-up ● **n.** **1** a gathering together of people or things. **2** a summary.

roundworm ● **n.** a parasitic worm with a rounded body, found in the intestines of some mammals.

rouse /rowz/ ● **v.** (**rouses**, **rousing**, **roused**) **1** bring or come out of sleep. **2** stir up; arouse: *his evasiveness roused my curiosity.*
– ORIGIN prob. from Old French.

rousing ● **adj.** stirring: *a rousing speech.*

Rousseau[1] E
/roo-soh/, Henri (Julien) (1844–1910), French painter, known for his colourful paintings of fantastic dreams and exotic jungle landscapes, such as *Tropical Storm with Tiger.*

Rousseau[2] E
/roo-soh/, Jean-Jacques (1712–78), French philosopher and writer, born in Switzerland. He believed that civilization warps the fundamental goodness of human nature, but that the ill effects can be moderated by active participation in democratic politics.

roustabout /rowsst-uh-bowt/ ● **n.** an unskilled or casual labourer.
– ORIGIN perh. from **ROUSE**.

rout[1] /rowt/ ● **n.** **1** a disorderly retreat of defeated troops. **2** a decisive defeat. ● **v.** defeat decisively.
– ORIGIN Old French *rute.*

rout[2] /rowt/ ● **v.** **1** cut a groove in (a surface). **2** rummage.
– ORIGIN from **ROOT**[2].

route /root/ ● **n.** a way taken in getting from a starting point to a destination. ● **v.** (**routes**, **routeing** or **routing**, **routed**) send along a particular course.
– ORIGIN Old French *rute* 'road'.

routine ● **n.** **1** a sequence of actions that is regularly followed. **2** a set sequence in a dance or comedy act. ● **adj.** **1** performed as part of a regular procedure: *a routine inspection.* **2** without variety; dull.
– DERIVATIVES **routinely** adv.
– ORIGIN French.

roux /roo/ ● **n.** (pl. **roux**) a mixture of butter and flour used in making sauces.
– ORIGIN from French *beurre roux* 'browned butter'.

rove ● **v.** (**roves**, **roving**, **roved**) **1** travel constantly without a fixed destination. **2** (of eyes) look in all directions.
– DERIVATIVES **rover** n.
– ORIGIN perh. from dialect *rave* 'to stray'.

row[1] /roh/ ● **n.** a number of people or things in a line.
– PHRASES **in a row** informal one after the other.

– ORIGIN Old English.

row² /roh/ ● v. **1** propel (a boat) with oars. **2** row a boat as a sport. ● n. a spell of rowing.
– DERIVATIVES **rower** n.
– ORIGIN Old English.

row³ /row/ informal, esp. Brit. ● n. **1** an angry quarrel. **2** a loud noise. ● v. have an angry quarrel.
– ORIGIN unknown.

rowan /roh-uhn, row-uhn/ ● n. a small tree with white flowers and red berries.
– ORIGIN Scandinavian.

rowdy ● adj. (**rowdier**, **rowdiest**) noisy and disorderly. ● n. (pl. **rowdies**) a rowdy person.
– DERIVATIVES **rowdily** adv. **rowdiness** n.
– ORIGIN unknown.

rowing machine ● n. an exercise machine with oars and a sliding seat.

Rowlandson E
/roh-luhnd-s'n/, Thomas (1756–1827), English painter and caricaturist, famous for his satirical depictions of English society.

Rowling E
/roh-ling/, J. K. (b.1965; full name *Joanne Kathleen Rowling*), Welsh novelist, creator of the *Harry Potter* series of children's books.

rowlock /rol-luhk, rul-uhk/ ● n. a fitting on the side of a boat for holding an oar.

Rowntree E
/rown-tree/, Henry Isaac (1838–83), English entrepreneur and philanthropist. He founded the family cocoa and chocolate manufacturing firm in York, while his brother **Joseph** (1836–1925) founded three Rowntree trusts (1904) to support research into social welfare.

royal ● adj. **1** relating to or having the status of a king or queen. **2** of a quality or size suitable for a king or queen: *a royal fortune*. ● n. informal a member of the royal family.
– DERIVATIVES **royally** adv.
– ORIGIN Old French *roial*.

Royal Academy of Arts E
(also **Royal Academy**) an institution established in London in 1768, to cultivate painting, sculpture, and architecture in Britain.

royal blue ● n. a deep, vivid blue.

Royal Commission ● n. (in the UK) a commission of inquiry appointed by the Crown on the recommendation of the government.

royal icing ● n. esp. Brit. hard white icing.

Royal Institution E
a British society founded in 1799 for the diffusion of scientific knowledge.

royalist ● n. **1** a person who supports the principle of having a king or queen. **2** (**Royalist**) hist. a supporter of the King against Parliament in the English Civil War.

royal jelly ● n. a substance produced by worker bees and fed by them to larvae which are being raised as potential queen bees.

Royal Society E
(in full **Royal Society of London**) the oldest and most prestigious scientific society in Britain, founded in 1662.

Royal Society of Arts E
an institution established in London in 1754. Its original purpose was to forge a link between art and commerce; it now holds examinations for a wide range of vocational and professional qualifications.

royalty ● n. (pl. **royalties**) **1** people of royal blood or status. **2** the status or power of a king or queen. **3** a sum paid for the use of a patent or to an author or composer for each copy of a work sold or for each time it is performed.

royal warrant ● n. a warrant issued by the king or queen indicating that goods or services are supplied to the royal family.

Royce, E
Sir (Frederick) Henry (1863–1933), English engine designer. He founded Rolls-Royce Ltd with Charles Stewart Rolls in 1906 and was the designer of the Rolls-Royce Silver Ghost car.

RP ● abbrev. received pronunciation.

rpm ● abbrev. revolutions per minute.

RSA ● abbrev. **1** Republic of South Africa. **2** Royal Society of Arts.

RSPB ● abbrev. (in the UK) Royal Society for the Protection of Birds.

RSPCA ● abbrev. (in the UK) Royal Society for the Prevention of Cruelty to Animals.

RSVP ● abbrev. répondez s'il vous plaît; please reply (used at the end of invitations).
– ORIGIN French.

Rt Hon. ● abbrev. Brit. Right Honourable, a title given to certain government ministers.

Rt Revd (also **Rt Rev.**) ● abbrev. Right Reverend, a title given to a bishop.

rub ● v. (**rubs**, **rubbing**, **rubbed**) **1** move back and forth over (a surface) while pressing against it. **2** apply (a substance) with a rubbing action. **3** (**rub down**) dry, smooth, or clean by rubbing. **4** (**rub in/into**) work (fat) into (a mixture) by breaking and blending it with the fingertips. ● n. **1** an act of rubbing. **2** an ointment for rubbing on the skin. **3** (**the rub**) the central difficulty. [ORIGIN from Shakespeare's *Hamlet* (III. i. 65).]
– PHRASES **rub it in** informal firmly draw someone's attention to an embarrassing fact. **rub off** be transferred by contact. **rub out** erase (pencil marks) with a rubber. **rub shoulders** come into contact. **rub (up) the wrong way** irritate.
– ORIGIN perh. from German *rubben*.

Rub' al Khali E
/ruub al kah-li/ a vast desert in Arabia, extending from central Saudi Arabia southwards to Yemen and eastwards to the United Arab Emirates and Oman.

rubato /ruu-bah-toh/ (also **tempo rubato**) ● n. (pl. **rubatos** or **rubati** /ruu-bah-ti/) Music temporary disregard for strict tempo to allow an expressive quickening or slackening.
– ORIGIN Italian, 'robbed'.

rubber¹ ● n. **1** a tough elastic substance made from a tropical plant or from chemicals. **2** Brit. a piece of such material used for erasing pencil marks.
– DERIVATIVES **rubbery** adj.

rubber² ● n. **1** a series of matches between the same sides in cricket, tennis, etc. **2** a unit of play in the card game bridge.

– ORIGIN unknown.

rubber band • n. a loop of rubber for holding things together.

rubberneck informal • n. a person who turns their head to stare at something in a foolish way. • v. stare in such a way.

rubber plant • n. an evergreen tree of SE Asia with large dark green shiny leaves.

rubber stamp • n. a hand-held device for imprinting dates, addresses, etc. • v. (**rubber-stamp**) approve automatically without proper consideration.

rubbing • n. an impression of a design on brass or stone, made by placing a sheet of paper over it and rubbing it with chalk or a pencil.

rubbish • n. esp. Brit. **1** waste material. **2** nonsense. • v. Brit. informal criticize and reject as worthless. • adj. Brit. informal very bad.
– DERIVATIVES **rubbishy** adj.
– ORIGIN Old French *rubbous*.

rubble • n. rough fragments of stone, brick, concrete, etc.
– ORIGIN perh. from Old French *robe* 'spoils'.

rubella /roo-**bel**-luh/ • n. a disease transmitted by a virus and with symptoms like mild measles.
– ORIGIN Latin, 'reddish things'.

Rubens E
/**roo**-buhnz/, Sir Peter Paul (1577–1640), Flemish Baroque painter. He is best known for his portraits and mythological paintings featuring voluptuous female nudes.

Rubicon /**roo**-bi-k'n, **roo**-bi-kon/ • n. a point of no return.
– ORIGIN a stream marking a boundary between Italy and Gaul; by leading his army across it, Julius Caesar caused a civil war.

rubicund /**roo**-bi-kuhnd/ • adj. having a reddish complexion.
– ORIGIN Latin *rubicundus*.

rubidium /ruu-**bid**-i-uhm/ • n. a rare soft silvery reactive metallic element.
– ORIGIN Latin *rubidus* 'red'.

Rubinstein[1] E
/**roo**-bin-styn/, Anton (Grigorevich) (1829–94), Russian composer and pianist. Best known as a pianist, he also composed piano music, operas, and symphonies.

Rubinstein[2] E
/**roo**-bin-styn/, Artur (1888–1982), Polish-born American pianist.

Rubinstein[3] E
/**roo**-bin-styn/, Helena (1882–1965), Polish-born American beautician who established an international cosmetics company.

ruble • n. var. of **ROUBLE**.

rubric /**roo**-brik/ • n. **1** a heading on a document. **2** a set of instructions or rules. **3** a direction as to how a church service should be conducted.
– ORIGIN first referring to text written in red for emphasis: from Latin *rubrica terra* 'ochre as writing material'.

ruby • n. (pl. **rubies**) **1** a precious stone of a deep red colour. **2** a deep red colour.
– ORIGIN Latin *rubinus*.

ruby wedding • n. the fortieth anniversary of a wedding.

RUC • abbrev. Royal Ulster Constabulary.

ruche /roosh/ • n. a frill or pleat of fabric.
– DERIVATIVES **ruched** adj.
– ORIGIN French.

ruck[1] • n. **1** Rugby a loose scrum formed around a player with the ball on the ground. **2** a tightly packed crowd of people.
– ORIGIN prob. Scandinavian.

ruck[2] • v. (**ruck up**) make or form creases or folds.
– ORIGIN Old Norse.

ruck[3] • n. Brit. informal a brawl.
– ORIGIN perh. from **RUCTION** or **RUCKUS**.

rucksack /**ruk**-sak, **ruuk**-sak/ • n. a bag with two shoulder straps which allow it to be carried on the back.
– ORIGIN German.

ruckus /**ruk**-uhss/ • n. a row or commotion.
– ORIGIN perh. from **RUCTION** and **RUMPUS**.

ructions • pl. n. informal angry protests or trouble.
– ORIGIN perh. from **INSURRECTION**.

rudder • n. a hinged upright piece of wood or metal near the back of a boat or an aeroplane, used for steering.
– ORIGIN Old English, 'paddle, oar'.

rudderless • adj. lacking direction; not knowing what to do.

ruddy • adj. (**ruddier**, **ruddiest**) **1** reddish. **2** (of a person's face) having a healthy red colour. **3** Brit. informal, dated used as a euphemism for 'bloody'.
– ORIGIN Old English.

rude • adj. **1** offensively impolite or bad-mannered. **2** referring to sex in an offensive way. **3** very abrupt: *a rude awakening.* **4** esp. Brit. hearty: *rude health.* **5** dated roughly made.
– DERIVATIVES **rudely** adv. **rudeness** n.
– ORIGIN Latin *rudis* 'not wrought'.

rudiment /**roo**-di-muhnt/ • n. **1** (**rudiments**) the basic facts of a subject. **2** Biol. an undeveloped part or organ.
– ORIGIN Latin *rudimentum*.

rudimentary /roo-di-**men**-tuh-ri/ • adj. **1** involving only the basic facts or elements: *a rudimentary education.* **2** not highly or fully developed: *a rudimentary stage of evolution.*

rue • v. (**rues**, **rueing** or **ruing**, **rued**) bitterly regret (a past event or action).
– ORIGIN Old English.

rueful • adj. expressing regret: *a rueful grin.*
– DERIVATIVES **ruefully** adv.

ruff • n. **1** a starched frill worn round the neck. **2** a ring of feathers or hair round the neck of a bird or mammal.
– ORIGIN prob. from **ROUGH**.

ruffian • n. a violent person.
– ORIGIN Old French.

ruffle • v. (**ruffles**, **ruffling**, **ruffled**) **1** disturb the smooth surface of. **2** upset the composure of: *he had been ruffled by her questions.* **3** (**ruffled**) gathered into a frill. • n. a gathered frill on a garment.
– ORIGIN unknown.

rufous /**roo**-fuhss/ • adj. reddish brown in colour.
– ORIGIN Latin *rufus* 'red, reddish'.

rug • n. **1** a small carpet. **2** esp. Brit. a thick woollen blanket.
– ORIGIN prob. Scandinavian.

Rugby E
a town in central England, in Warwickshire. Rugby School was founded there in 1567.

rugby (also **rugby football**) • n. a team game played with an oval ball that may be kicked, carried, and passed by hand.
– ORIGIN named after *Rugby* School (see **RUGBY**).

rugby league • n. a form of rugby played in teams of thirteen.

rugby union • n. a form of rugby played in teams of fifteen.

rugged /rug-gid/ • adj. **1** having a rocky surface. **2** having or requiring toughness and determination. **3** (of a man) having attractively masculine features.
– DERIVATIVES **ruggedly** adv. **ruggedness** n.
– ORIGIN prob. Scandinavian.

rugger • n. Brit. informal rugby.

Ruhr E
/ruu-er/ a region of coal mining and heavy industry in the state of North Rhine-Westphalia, western Germany.

ruin • n. **1** the destruction or collapse of something. **2** (also **ruins**) a building (or the remains of a building) that has suffered much damage. **3** the complete loss of a person's money and property. • v. **1** completely destroy. **2** have a very damaging effect on: *the motorway has ruined village life.* **3** make very poor or bankrupt.
– ORIGIN Latin *ruina*.

ruination • n. the action of ruining or the state of being ruined.

ruinous • adj. **1** disastrous or destructive. **2** in ruins.

rule • n. **1** a statement of what must be done or not done. **2** control of a country or group: *British rule.* **3** a code of practice and discipline for a religious community. **4** (**the rule**) the normal state of things. **5** a ruler. • v. (**rules, ruling, ruled**) **1** have power over (a people or country). **2** have a powerful and restricting influence on: *her whole life was ruled by fear.* **3** state with legal authority that (something) is the case. **4** make lines on (paper).
– PHRASES **as a rule** usually, but not always. **rule of thumb** a fairly accurate guide based on practice rather than theory. **rule out/in** exclude (or include) as a possibility.
– ORIGIN Old French *reule*.

ruler • n. **1** a person who rules a people or country. **2** a straight rigid strip of plastic, wood, or metal, marked at regular intervals and used to draw straight lines or measure distances.

ruling • n. a decision or statement made by an authority. • adj. having control: *the ruling party.*

rum[1] • n. an alcoholic spirit made from sugar cane or molasses.
– ORIGIN perh. from former *rumbullion*.

rum[2] • adj. Brit. informal, dated peculiar.
– ORIGIN unknown.

Rumania E
/roo-may-ni-uh/ var. of **ROMANIA**.

rumba /rum-buh/ (also **rhumba**) • n. **1** a rhythmic dance with Spanish and African elements. **2** a ballroom dance based on this.
– ORIGIN Latin American Spanish.

rumble • v. (**rumbles, rumbling, rumbled**) **1** make or move with a continuous deep sound, like thunder. **2** (**rumble on**) (of a dispute) continue in a low-key way. **3** Brit. informal find out the truth about (someone or something). • n. a continuous deep sound like distant thunder.
– ORIGIN prob. from Dutch *rommelen*.

rumble strip • n. one of a series of raised strips set in a road to warn drivers to slow down.

rumbustious /rum-buss-chuhss, rum-buss-ti-uhss/ • adj. informal, esp. Brit. high-spirited or difficult to control.
– ORIGIN prob. from archaic *robustious* 'boisterous'.

ruminant • n. a mammal that chews the cud, such as cattle, sheep, or deer.
– ORIGIN Latin *ruminari* 'chew over again'.

ruminate /roo-mi-nayt/ • v. (**ruminates, ruminating, ruminated**) **1** think deeply about something. **2** (of a cow, sheep, etc.) chew the cud.
– DERIVATIVES **rumination** n.

ruminative • adj. thinking deeply about things.

rummage • v. (**rummages, rummaging, rummaged**) search for something in a careless way. • n. an act of rummaging.
– ORIGIN Old French *arrumer* 'stow in a hold'.

rummy • n. a card game in which the players try to form sets and sequences of cards.
– ORIGIN unknown.

rumour (US **rumor**) • n. a story spread among a number of people which is unconfirmed or likely to be false. • v. (**be rumoured**) be spread as a rumour.
– ORIGIN Latin *rumor* 'noise'.

rump • n. **1** the hind part of the body of a mammal or the lower back of a bird. **2** a small piece left over from something larger.
– ORIGIN prob. Scandinavian.

rumple • v. (**rumples, rumpling, rumpled**) make untidy.
– ORIGIN Dutch *rompel* 'wrinkle'.

rumpus • n. (pl. **rumpuses**) a noisy disturbance.
– ORIGIN uncertain.

run • v. (**runs, running, ran**; past part. **run**) **1** move fast using one's legs. **2** move forcefully or quickly: *the tanker ran aground.* **3** pass: *Helen ran her fingers through her hair.* **4** (of a bus, train, etc.) make a regular journey on a particular route. **5** be in charge of. **6** continue or proceed. **7** function or cause to function. **8** pass into or reach a specified state or level: *inflation is running at 11 per cent.* **9** (**run in**) (of a quality) be common in (members of a family). **10** (of a liquid) flow. **11** (of dye or colour) dissolve and spread when wet. **12** stand as a candidate in an election. **13** enter or be entered in a race. **14** publish (a story) in a newspaper or magazine. **15** transport in a car. **16** smuggle (goods). • n. **1** an act or spell of running. **2** a journey or route. **3** a course that is regularly used: *a ski run.* **4** a continuous period or sequence: *a run of bad luck.* **5** an enclosed area in which animals or birds may run freely in the open. **6** a rapid series of musical notes. **7** (**the run**) the average type: *she stood out from the general run of women.* **8** (**the run of**) unrestricted use of or

access to somewhere. **9** a point scored in cricket or baseball. **10** a ladder in stockings or tights. **11** (**the runs**) informal diarrhoea.
– PHRASES **be run off one's feet** be extremely busy. **on the run** escaping from arrest. **run across** meet or find by chance. **run away with** win (a competition or prize) easily. **run by** (or **past**) tell (someone) about (something) to find out their opinion. **run down 1** knock down with a vehicle. **2** criticize. **3** reduce in size or resources. **4** gradually lose power or become worse. **run into 1** collide with. **2** meet by chance. **run off 1** produce (a copy) on a machine. **2** write or recite with little effort. **run on** continue without stopping. **run out 1** use up or be used up. **2** become no longer valid. **3** Cricket dismiss (a batsman) by hitting the bails with the ball while the batsman is still running. **run over 1** knock down with a vehicle. **2** overflow. **run through 1** stab so as to kill. **2** (also **run over**) go over as a quick rehearsal or reminder. **run up 1** allow (a bill, score, etc.) to build up. **2** make quickly. **run up against** experience (a difficulty or problem).
– ORIGIN Old English.

runabout ● n. a small car.

runaround ● n. (in phr. **give someone the runaround**) informal treat someone badly by giving them misleading information.

runaway ● n. a person who has run away from their home or an institution. ● adj. **1** (of an animal or vehicle) running out of control. **2** happening quickly or uncontrollably: *runaway success.*

rundown ● n. a brief summary. ● adj. (**rundown**) **1** in a poor, or neglected state. **2** tired and rather unwell.

rune /roon/ ● n. **1** a letter of an ancient Germanic alphabet. **2** a symbol with mysterious or magical significance.
– DERIVATIVES **runic** adj.
– ORIGIN Old English, 'secret, mystery'.

rung[1] ● n. **1** a horizontal bar on a ladder for a person's foot. **2** a level or rank.
– ORIGIN Old English.

rung[2] past part. of RING[2].

run-in ● n. **1** the approach to an action or event. **2** informal a disagreement or fight.

runnel ● n. **1** a gutter. **2** a stream.
– ORIGIN from dialect *rindle.*

runner ● n. **1** a person or animal that runs. **2** a messenger or agent for a bank, bookmaker, etc. **3** a rod, groove, blade, or roller on which something slides. **4** a shoot of a plant which grows along the ground and can take root at points along its length. **5** a long, narrow rug.
– PHRASES **do a runner** Brit. informal leave hastily to escape something.

runner bean ● n. esp. Brit. a climbing bean plant with scarlet flowers and long green edible pods.

runner-up ● n. (pl. **runners-up**) a competitor or team coming second in a contest.

running ● adj. **1** (of water) flowing naturally or supplied through pipes and taps. **2** producing liquid or pus: *a running sore.* **3** continuous or recurring: *a running joke.* **4** (after a noun) in succession: *the third week running.*
– PHRASES **in** (or **out of**) **the running** in (or no longer in) with a chance of success. **make** (or **take up**) **the running** set the pace.

running battle ● n. a battle which does not occur at a fixed place.

running board ● n. a footboard extending along the side of a vehicle.

running commentary ● n. a verbal description of events, given as they happen.

running mate ● n. esp. US an election candidate for the lesser of two linked political positions.

running repairs ● pl. n. minor or temporary repairs carried out on machinery while it is in use.

running total ● n. a total that is continually adjusted to take account of further items.

runny ● adj. (**runnier, runniest**) **1** more liquid in consistency than is usual or expected. **2** (of a person's nose) producing mucus.

run-off ● n. a further contest after a clear winner has not emerged in a previous one.

run-of-the-mill ● adj. ordinary.

runt ● n. the smallest animal in a litter.
– ORIGIN unknown.

run-through ● n. **1** a rehearsal. **2** a brief summary.

run-up ● n. the period before an important event during which preparations are made.

runway ● n. a strip of hard ground where aircraft take off and land.

Runyon E
/run-yuhn/, (Alfred) Damon (1884–1946), American journalist and short-story writer, noted for his stories about New York's underworld.

rupee /roo-pee, ruu-pee/ ● n. the basic unit of money of India, Pakistan, and some other countries.
– ORIGIN Sanskrit, 'wrought silver'.

Rupert, Prince E
(1619–82), English Royalist general, nephew of Charles I. He initially won a series of victories, but was defeated by Parliamentarian forces at Marston Moor (1644) and Naseby (1645).

rupture ● v. (**ruptures, rupturing, ruptured**) **1** break or burst suddenly. **2** (**be ruptured** or **rupture oneself**) suffer a hernia in the abdomen. **3** disturb (good relations). ● n. **1** an instance of rupturing. **2** a hernia in the abdomen.
– ORIGIN Latin *ruptura.*

rural ● adj. having to do with the countryside rather than the town.
– DERIVATIVES **rurality** n. **rurally** adv.
– ORIGIN Latin *ruralis.*

ruse /rooz/ ● n. an action intended to deceive or trick someone.
– ORIGIN Old French *ruser* 'use trickery'.

rush[1] ● v. **1** move or act with urgent haste. **2** transport with urgent haste. **3** deal with too quickly. **4** (of air or a liquid) flow strongly. **5** try to attack or capture (a person or place) suddenly. ● n. **1** a sudden quick movement towards something. **2** a sudden spell of hasty activity: *the pre-Christmas rush.* **3** a sudden strong demand for a product. **4** a sudden strong feeling. **5** a sudden thrill experienced after taking certain drugs. **6** (**rushes**) the first prints made of a film after a period of shooting.
– ORIGIN Old French *ruser* 'drive back'.

rush² • n. a marsh or waterside plant, some kinds of which are used for matting, baskets, etc.
– ORIGIN Old English.

Rushdie
/**rush**-di, **ruush**-di/, (Ahmed) Salman (b.1947), Indian-born British novelist. His novels include *Midnight's Children* and *The Satanic Verses*. The latter was regarded by Muslims as blasphemous and in 1989 a fatwa was issued by Ayatollah Khomeini condemning Rushdie to death; the Iranian government dissociated itself from the fatwa in 1998.

rush hour • n. a time at the start and end of the working day when traffic is at its heaviest.

Rushmore, Mount
a mountain in the Black Hills of South Dakota, with giant busts of four US Presidents—George Washington, Thomas Jefferson, Abraham Lincoln, and Theodore Roosevelt—carved into it.

rusk • n. a dry biscuit eaten by babies.
– ORIGIN Spanish or Portuguese *rosca* 'twist, roll of bread'.

Ruskin,
John (1819–1900), English art and social critic. He was a champion of Gothic architecture and the Pre-Raphaelite painters. His political writings attacked capitalism and utilitarianism.

Russell¹,
Bertrand (Arthur William), 3rd Earl Russell (1872–1970), British philosopher and mathematician. As a philosopher, he was a proponent of neutral monism (the belief that both physical and mental phenomena can be explained in terms of a single common substance). His work on mathematical logic was very influential on set theory.

Russell²,
George William (1867–1935), Irish poet and journalist. A leading figure in the Irish literary revival, his works include the poetic drama *Deirdre*.

Russell³,
John, 1st Earl Russell (1792–1878), British Whig statesman, Prime Minister 1846–52 and 1865–6. He was responsible for introducing the Reform Bill of 1832 into Parliament.

Russell⁴,
Ken (b. 1927; born Henry Kenneth Alfred Russell), English film director. His films include *Women in Love* and *The Rainbow*.

russet • adj. reddish brown. • n. **1** a reddish-brown colour. **2** a variety of dessert apple with a slightly rough greenish-brown skin.
– ORIGIN Old French *rousset*.

Russia
a country in northern Asia and eastern Europe; capital, Moscow. Official name **RUSSIAN FEDERATION**.

Russian • n. **1** a person from Russia. **2** the language of Russia. • adj. relating to Russia.

Russian Orthodox Church • n. the national Church of Russia.

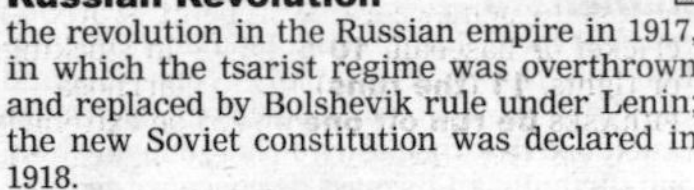

Russian Revolution
the revolution in the Russian empire in 1917, in which the tsarist regime was overthrown and replaced by Bolshevik rule under Lenin; the new Soviet constitution was declared in 1918.

Russian roulette • n. a dangerous game of chance in which a single bullet is loaded into the chamber of a revolver, one player takes the gun, spins the cylinder, holds it to their head and fires it, then (if still alive) passes it to the next person, who does the same, and so on.

Russo-Japanese War
a war between the Russian empire and Japan 1904–5, caused by territorial disputes in Manchuria and Korea. Russia suffered a series of defeats and the peace settlement resulted in Japanese dominance in the disputed region.

rust • n. **1** a reddish-brown flaky coating formed on iron or steel by the effect of moisture, and gradually wearing it away. **2** a disease of plants caused by a fungus, which results in rust-coloured patches. **3** a reddish-brown colour. • v. be affected with rust.
– ORIGIN Old English.

rustic • adj. **1** having to do with life in the country. **2** simple and charming in a way seen as typical of the countryside. • n. an unsophisticated country person.
– DERIVATIVES **rusticity** n.
– ORIGIN Latin *rusticus*.

rusticate /russ-ti-kayt/ • v. (**rusticates**, **rusticating**, **rusticated**) **1** Brit. suspend (a student) from a university as a punishment. **2** (**rusticated**) (of stonework) shaped in large blocks with sunken joints and a roughened surface.
– ORIGIN Latin *rusticus* 'rustic'.

rustle • v. **1** make or move with a soft crackling sound. **2** round up and steal (cattle, horses, or sheep). **3** (**rustle up**) informal produce (food or a drink) quickly. • n. a rustling sound.
– DERIVATIVES **rustler** n.

rustproof • adj. not able to be worn away by rust.

rusty • adj. (**rustier**, **rustiest**) **1** affected by rust. **2** (of knowledge or a skill) weakened by lack of recent practice.

rut¹ • n. **1** a long deep track made by the repeated passing of the wheels of vehicles. **2** a pattern of behaviour that has become dull but is hard to change.
– ORIGIN prob. from Old French *rute* 'road'.

rut² • n. an annual period of sexual activity in some animals, during which the males fight each other for access to the females. • v. (**ruts**, **rutting**, **rutted**) engage in such activity.
– ORIGIN Old French.

Ruth,
Babe (1895–1948; born *George Herman Ruth*), American baseball player. He set a record of 714 home runs which remained unbroken until 1974.

ruthenium /ruu-thee-ni-uhm/ • n. a hard silvery-white metallic chemical element.
– ORIGIN from *Ruthenia*, a region of central Europe.

Rutherford E
/ru*th*-er-ferd/, Sir Ernest, 1st Baron Rutherford of Nelson (1871–1937), New Zealand physicist, the founder of nuclear physics. He concluded that the positive charge in an atom, and virtually all its mass, is concentrated in a central nucleus, and was the first to change one element (nitrogen) into another (oxygen) by bombardment with alpha particles.

rutherfordium /ru*th*-er-for-di-uhm/ • **n.** a very unstable chemical element made by high-energy atomic collisions.
– ORIGIN named after Ernest **RUTHERFORD**.

ruthless • **adj.** having no sympathy or pity.
– DERIVATIVES **ruthlessly** adv. **ruthlessness** n.
– ORIGIN from archaic *ruth* 'pity'.

Rutland E
a unitary authority in the east Midlands, formerly the smallest county in England; administrative centre, Oakham.

Rwanda E
/roo-an-duh/ a country in central Africa, north of Burundi; capital, Kigali. Official name **RWANDESE REPUBLIC**.
– DERIVATIVES **Rwandan** (also **Rwandese**) adj. & n.

Ryder E
/ry-der/, Sue, Baroness Ryder of Warsaw and Cavendish (1923–2000), English philanthropist. She co-founded an organization to care for former inmates of concentration camps, which expanded to provide homes for disabled people.

Ryder Cup E
a golf tournament held every two years and played between teams of male professionals from the US and Europe.

rye • **n. 1** a cereal plant similar to wheat, which grows in poor soils. **2** whisky in which much of the grain used in producing it is fermented rye.
– ORIGIN Old English.

ryegrass • **n.** a grass used for fodder and lawns.
– ORIGIN unknown.

Ryukyu Islands E
/ri-oo-kyoo/ a chain of islands in the western Pacific, belonging to Japan and stretching about 960 km (600 miles) from the southern tip of the Japanese island of Kyushu to Taiwan.

Ss

S[1] (also **s**) • **n.** (pl. **Ss** or **S's**) the nineteenth letter of the alphabet.

S[2] • **abbrev. 1** Saint. **2** siemens. **3** small. **4** South or Southern.

s • **abbrev.** second or seconds.

's • **contr.** informal **1** is. **2** has. **3** us. **4** does.

-'s • **suffix 1** showing possession in singular nouns, and also in plural nouns not having a final *-s*: *John's car* | *the children's teacher.* **2** forming the plural of a letter or symbol: *9's.*

SA • **abbrev. 1** South Africa. **2** South America. **3** South Australia.

sabbath • **n.** (often **the Sabbath**) a day intended for rest and religious worship, kept by Jews from Friday evening to Saturday evening, and by most Christians on Sunday.
– ORIGIN Hebrew, 'to rest'.

sabbatical /suh-bat-i-k'l/ • **n.** a period of paid leave granted to a university teacher for study or travel.
– ORIGIN Greek *sabbatikos* 'of the sabbath'.

saber • **n.** US = **SABRE**.

sable /*rhymes with* table/ • **n. 1** a marten with a short tail and dark brown fur, native to Japan and Siberia. **2** the fur of the sable.
– ORIGIN Old French.

sabotage /sab-uh-tah*zh*/ • **v.** (**sabotages**, **sabotaging**, **sabotaged**) deliberately destroy or damage. • **n.** the action of sabotaging.
– ORIGIN French.

saboteur /sab-uh-ter/ • **n.** a person who sabotages something.
– ORIGIN French.

sabre /say-ber/ (US **saber**) • **n. 1** a heavy sword with a curved blade and a single cutting edge. **2** a light fencing sword with a tapering curved blade.
– ORIGIN French.

sabretooth (also **sabre-toothed tiger**) • **n.** a large extinct member of the cat family with massive curved upper canine teeth.

sac • **n.** a hollow, flexible structure in the body or a plant resembling a bag or pouch, and containing liquid or air.
– ORIGIN Latin *saccus* 'sack, bag'.

saccharin /sak-kuh-rin/ • **n.** a sweet-tasting synthetic substance used as a low-calorie substitute for sugar.
– ORIGIN Greek *sakkharon* 'sugar'.

saccharine /sak-kuh-rin, sak-kuh-reen/ • **adj. 1** sweet or sentimental. **2** relating to or containing sugar.

sacerdotal /sass-er-**doh**-t'l, sak-er-**doh**-t'l/ • **adj.** relating to priests.
– ORIGIN Latin *sacerdotalis*.

sachet /sa-shay/ • **n.** esp. Brit. a small sealed bag or packet containing a small quantity of something.
– ORIGIN French, 'little bag'.

sack[1] • **n. 1** a large bag made of strong fabric, paper, or plastic, used for storing and carrying goods. **2** (**the sack**) informal dismissal from employment. **3** (**the sack**) informal bed. • **v.** informal dismiss from employment.

– DERIVATIVES **sackable** adj.
– ORIGIN Greek *sakkos* 'sack, sackcloth'.

sack² • v. (in the past) enter by force, rob, and destroy (a place). • n. the sacking of a town or city.
– ORIGIN French *sac*.

sackcloth • n. a coarse fabric woven from flax or hemp.
– PHRASES **sackcloth and ashes** an expression of extreme sorrow or remorse. [ORIGIN with reference to the wearing of sackcloth and having ashes sprinkled on the head as a sign of penitence (Gospel of Matthew, chapter 11).]

sacking • n. coarse material for making sacks.

Sackville-West, E
Vita (1892–1962; full name *Victoria Mary Sackville-West*), English novelist and poet, author of the novel *All Passion Spent*. She is also known for the garden which she created at Sissinghurst in Kent.

sacra pl. of **SACRUM**.

sacral /say-kruhl, sak-ruhl/ • adj. Anat. relating to the sacrum.

sacrament /sak-ruh-muhnt/ • n. **1** (in the Christian Church) a religious ceremony in which the participants receive the grace of God, such as baptism and the Eucharist. **2** (also **the Blessed Sacrament** or **the Holy Sacrament**) (in Catholic use) bread and wine used in the Eucharist.
– DERIVATIVES **sacramental** adj.
– ORIGIN Latin *sacramentum* 'solemn oath'.

sacred /say-krid/ • adj. **1** connected with a god or goddess and treated as holy. **2** (of a text) having to do with the teachings of a religion. **3** religious: *sacred music*.
– ORIGIN Latin *sacrare* 'consecrate'.

sacred cow • n. a long-standing idea, custom, or institution that is thought to be above criticism (with reference to the respect of Hindus for the cow as a sacred animal).

sacrifice • n. **1** the killing of an animal or person or the giving up of a possession as an offering to a god or goddess. **2** an animal, person, or object offered in this way. **3** an act of giving up something one values for the sake of something that is more important. • v. (**sacrifices**, **sacrificing**, **sacrificed**) give as a sacrifice.
– DERIVATIVES **sacrificial** adj.
– ORIGIN Latin *sacrificium*.

sacrilege /sak-ri-lij/ • n. the treating of something sacred or highly valued with great disrespect.
– DERIVATIVES **sacrilegious** adj.
– ORIGIN Latin *sacrilegium*.

sacristan /sak-ri-stuhn/ • n. a person in charge of a sacristy.

sacristy /sak-ri-sti/ • n. (pl. **sacristies**) a room in a church where a priest prepares for a service, and where things used in worship are kept.
– ORIGIN Latin *sacristia*.

sacrosanct /sak-ruh-sangkt/ • adj. seen as too important or valuable to be changed or questioned.
– ORIGIN Latin *sacrosanctus*.

sacrum /say-kruhm/ • n. (pl. **sacra** /say-kruh/ or **sacrums**) a triangular bone in the lower back between the two hip bones of the pelvis.
– ORIGIN from Latin *os sacrum* 'sacred bone'.

sad • adj. (**sadder**, **saddest**) **1** unhappy. **2** causing sorrow: *a sad story*. **3** informal very inadequate or unfashionable: *sad people singing boating songs*.
– DERIVATIVES **sadness** n.
– ORIGIN Old English 'sated, weary'.

Sadat E
/sa-**dat**/, (Muhammad) Anwar al- (1918–81), Egyptian statesman, President 1970–81. He worked to achieve peace in the Middle East, attending talks with Menachim Begin at Camp David in 1978. He was assassinated by members of the Islamic Jihad.

Saddam Hussein E
/sad-**dam**/ see **HUSSEIN³**.

sadden • v. make unhappy.

saddle • n. **1** a seat with a raised ridge at the front and back, fastened on the back of a horse for riding. **2** a seat on a bicycle or motorcycle. **3** a low part of a hill or mountain ridge between two higher points. **4** a joint of meat consisting of the two loins. • v. (**saddles**, **saddling**, **saddled**) **1** put a saddle on (a horse). **2** (**be saddled with**) be burdened with (a responsibility or task).
– ORIGIN Old English.

saddleback • n. **1** a hill with a ridge along the top that dips in the middle. **2** a pig of a black breed with a white stripe across the back.

saddlebag • n. a bag attached to a saddle.

saddler • n. a person who makes, repairs, or deals in equipment for horses.

saddlery • n. (pl. **saddleries**) **1** saddles and other equipment for horses. **2** a saddler's business or premises.

Sade E
/sahd/, Donatien Alphonse François, Comte de (1740–1814; known as **the Marquis de Sade**), French writer and soldier. He wrote a number of sexually explicit books, including *Les 120 Journées de Sodome*.

sadhu /sah-doo/ • n. a Hindu holy man.
– ORIGIN Sanskrit.

sadism /say-di-z'm/ • n. sexual or other pleasure that is gained from hurting or humiliating other people.
– DERIVATIVES **sadist** n. **sadistic** adj.
– ORIGIN named after the Marquis de **SADE**.

sadly • adv. **1** in a sad way. **2** it is sad that.

sadomasochism /say-doh-**mass**-uh-ki-z'm/ • n. a sexual practice which is a combination of sadism and masochism.
– DERIVATIVES **sadomasochist** n. **sadomasochistic** adj.

sae • abbrev. Brit. stamped addressed envelope.

safari • n. (pl. **safaris**) an expedition to observe or hunt animals in their natural environment.
– ORIGIN Arabic, 'to travel'.

safari park • n. an area of parkland where wild animals can move freely and may be observed by visitors driving through.

safe • adj. **1** protected from danger or risk. **2** not leading to harm or injury. **3** (of a place) giving security or protection. **4** based on good reasons and not likely to be wrong: *it's a safe bet that they won't sell*. • n. a strong fireproof

S

cabinet with a complex lock, used for storing valuables.
– PHRASES **safe and sound** uninjured. **to be on the safe side** so as to be sure of avoiding risks.
– DERIVATIVES **safely** adv.
– ORIGIN Old French *sauf*.

safe deposit box (also **safety deposit box**) ● n. a metal box for valuables in a bank or hotel.

safeguard ● n. a measure taken to protect or prevent something. ● v. protect with a safeguard.

safe house ● n. a house in a secret location, used by people in hiding.

safekeeping ● n. the keeping of something in a safe place.

safe seat ● n. a parliamentary seat that is certain to be held by the same party in an election.

safe sex ● n. sexual activity in which people protect themselves against sexually transmitted diseases.

safety ● n. the condition of being safe. ● adj. designed to prevent injury or damage: *a safety barrier.*

safety belt ● n. a belt securing a person to their seat in a vehicle or aircraft.

safety catch ● n. a device that prevents a gun being fired or a machine being operated accidentally.

safety deposit box ● n. a safe deposit box.

safety match ● n. a match that can be lit only by striking it on a specially prepared surface.

safety net ● n. **1** a net placed to catch an acrobat in case of a fall. **2** a safeguard against possible hardship.

safety pin ● n. a pin with a point that is bent back to the head and is held in a guard when closed.

safety razor ● n. a razor with a guard to reduce the risk of cutting the skin.

safety valve ● n. a valve that opens automatically to relieve excessive pressure.

saffron ● n. an orange-yellow spice used in cooking, made from the dried stigmas of a crocus.
– ORIGIN Arabic.

sag ● v. (**sags**, **sagging**, **sagged**) **1** sink downwards gradually under weight or pressure. **2** hang down loosely or unevenly. ● n. an instance of sagging.
– DERIVATIVES **saggy** adj.
– ORIGIN from German *sacken*, Dutch *zakken* 'subside'.

saga ● n. **1** a long traditional story describing heroic adventures. **2** a long, involved account or series of incidents.
– ORIGIN Old Norse, 'narrative'.

sagacious /suh-gay-shuhss/ ● adj. having good judgement; wise.
– DERIVATIVES **sagacity** n. /suh-ga-si-ti/
– ORIGIN Latin *sagax* 'wise'.

Sagan[1] E
/say-g'n/, Carl (Edward) (1934-96), American astronomer. He showed that amino acids and other organic molecules were formed when mixtures of simple compounds were irradiated with ultraviolet light - a possible step towards the origin of life.

Sagan[2] E
/sa-gon/, Françoise (b.1935; pen name of *Françoise Quoirez*), French novelist, dramatist, and short-story writer, known for her novel *Bonjour Tristesse*.

sage[1] ● n. a Mediterranean plant with greyish-green leaves that are used as a herb in cookery.
– ORIGIN Old French *sauge*.

sage[2] ● n. a very wise man. ● adj. wise: *sage remarks.*
– DERIVATIVES **sagely** adv.
– ORIGIN Old French.

Sagittarius /saj-i-tair-i-uhss/ ● n. a constellation (the Archer) and sign of the zodiac, which the sun enters about 22 November.
– ORIGIN Latin, 'archer'.

sago /say-goh/ ● n. flour or starchy granules obtained from a palm, often cooked with milk to make a pudding.
– ORIGIN Malay.

Sahara Desert E
(also **the Sahara**) a vast desert in North Africa, extending from the Atlantic in the west to the Red Sea in the east, and from the Mediterranean in the north to the Sahel in the south. The largest desert in the world, it covers an area of about 9,065,000 sq. km (3,500,000 sq. miles).
– DERIVATIVES **Saharan** adj.

Sahel E
/suh-hel/ a vast semi-arid region of North Africa, to the south of the Sahara, which comprises the northern part of the region known as Sudan.
– DERIVATIVES **Sahelian** /suh-hee-li-uhn/ adj. & n.

sahib /sahb, suh-heeb/ ● n. Ind. a polite form of address for a man.
– ORIGIN Arabic, 'friend, lord'.

said past and past part. of SAY. ● adj. referring to someone or something already mentioned: *the said agreement.*

Saigon E
/sy-gon/ a city and port on the south coast of Vietnam. Official name (since 1975) **Ho Chi Minh City**.

sail ● n. **1** a piece of material spread on a mast to catch the wind and propel a boat or ship. **2** a trip in a sailing boat or ship. **3** a flat structure attached to the arm of a windmill to catch the wind. ● v. **1** travel in a sailing boat as a sport or pastime. **2** travel in a ship or boat using sails or engine power. **3** begin a voyage. **4** direct or control (a boat or ship). **5** move smoothly or confidently. **6** (**sail through**) informal succeed easily at.
– PHRASES **sail close to the wind** behave in a risky way.
– ORIGIN Old English.

sailboard ● n. a board with a mast and a sail, used in windsurfing.

sailcloth ● n. **1** strong fabric used for making sails. **2** a similar fabric used for making hard-wearing clothes.

sailing boat (or **sailing ship**) ● n. a boat (or ship) with sails.

sailor ● n. **1** a person who works as a member of the crew of a ship or boat. **2** a person who sails as a sport or pastime. **3** (**a good/bad**

sailor) a person who rarely (or often) becomes seasick.

sailplane • n. a glider designed to be able to fly for a long time.

Sainsbury, E
John James (1844–1928), English grocer. He opened his first grocery store in London in 1875, and the business was later developed by members of his family into the large Sainsbury supermarket chain.

saint /saynt/, before a name /suhnt/ • n. **1** a holy or good person whom Christians believe will go to heaven after death. **2** a person of great goodness who is declared to be a saint by the Church after death. **3** informal a very good or kind person.
– DERIVATIVES **sainthood** n.
ORIGIN Old French *saint*.

St Agnes, St Barnabas, E
etc. see **Agnes, St**; **Barnabas, St**; etc.

St Andrews E
a town in east Scotland, in Fife. It is noted for its university and its championship golf courses.

St Andrew's cross • n. a diagonal or X-shaped cross, especially white on a blue background (as a national emblem of Scotland). Also called **saltire**.

St Bernard • n. a breed of very large dog originally kept to rescue travellers by monks of a hospice on the Great St Bernard, a pass across the Alps.

St Christopher and Nevis, Federation of E
official name for **St Kitts and Nevis**.

St Croix E
/kroy/ an island in the Caribbean, the largest of the US Virgin Islands; chief town, Christiansted.

sainted • adj. dated very good or kind, like a saint.

St Elmo's fire /suhnt el-mohz/ • n. a luminous electrical discharge sometimes seen on a ship or aircraft during a storm.
– ORIGIN seen as a sign of protection given by *St Elmo*, the patron saint of sailors.

St George's E
the capital of Grenada in the Caribbean.

St George's cross • n. a +-shaped cross, red on a white background.

St Helena E
/hi-lee-nuh/ an island in the South Atlantic, a British dependency; capital, Jamestown. It is famous as the place of Napoleon's exile (1815–21) and death.
– DERIVATIVES **St Helenian** adj. & n.

St Helens, Mount E
an active volcano in SW Washington state. An eruption in May 1980 spread volcanic ash and debris over a large area.

St Helier E
/hel-i-er/ the capital of Jersey.

St John E
an island in the Caribbean, one of the three chief islands of the US Virgin Islands; chief town, Cruz Bay.

St John's E
the capital of Newfoundland.

St Kilda E
a small uninhabited island group of the Outer Hebrides.

St Kitts and Nevis E
a country in the Caribbean consisting of two adjoining islands of the Leeward Islands; capital, Basseterre (on St Kitts). Official name **Federation of St Christopher and Nevis**.

Saint Laurent F
/san lor-on/, Yves (Mathieu) (b.1936), French fashion designer.

St Lawrence River E
a river of North America, which flows from Lake Ontario along the border between Canada and the US to the Gulf of St Lawrence on the Atlantic coast.

St Lawrence Seaway E
a waterway for ocean-going ships in North America, which flows for 3,768 km (2,342 miles) through the Great Lakes and along the course of the St Lawrence River to the Atlantic.

St Louis E
a city and port in eastern Missouri, on the Mississippi.

St Lucia E
/loo-shuh/ a country in the Caribbean, one of the Windward Islands; capital, Castries.
– DERIVATIVES **St Lucian** adj. & n.

saintly • adj. very holy or good.
– DERIVATIVES **saintliness** n.

St Moritz E
/san muh-rits, san mo-rits/ a resort and winter-sports centre in SE Switzerland.

St Petersburg E
/pee-terz-berg/ a city and seaport in NW Russia. Former names **Petrograd** (1914-24) and **Leningrad** (1924-91).

St Pierre and Miquelon E
/san pyair, mee-klon/ a group of eight small islands off the south coast of Newfoundland. An overseas territory of France, the islands form the last remaining French possession in North America.

Saint-Saëns E
/san-son/, (Charles) Camille (1835–1921), French composer, known for his symphonic poem *Danse macabre* and the *Carnaval des animaux*.

saint's day • n. (in the Christian Church) a day on which a saint is particularly honoured.

St Swithin's day • n. 15 July, a Church festival honouring St Swithin and believed to be a day on which, if it rains, it will continue raining for the next forty days.

St Thomas E
an island in the Caribbean, the second-largest of the US Virgin Islands, chief town, Charlotte Amalie.

St-Tropez E
/san-truh-**pay**/ a port and resort on the Mediterranean coast of southern France.

St Vincent and the Grenadines E
/**vin**-s'nt, **gren**-uh-deenz/ an island state in the Windward Islands in the Caribbean, consisting of the island of St Vincent and some of the Grenadines; capital, Kingstown.

saith /seth/ archaic 3rd person sing. present of SAY.

saithe /sayth/ ● n. an edible North Atlantic fish of the cod family.
– ORIGIN Old Norse.

sake[1] /sayk/ ● n. (**for the sake of**) **1** so as to achieve or keep. **2** out of consideration for (someone).
– ORIGIN Old English, 'contention'.

sake[2] /**sah**-ki, sa-**kay**/ ● n. a Japanese alcoholic drink made from rice.
– ORIGIN Japanese.

Sakharov E
/**sak**-uh-roff/, Andrei (Dmitrievich) (1921–89), Russian nuclear physicist and civil rights campaigner. Having helped to develop the Soviet hydrogen bomb, he campaigned against nuclear proliferation. He was also a prominent campaigner for human rights in the USSR.

Saki E
/**sah**-ki/ (1870–1916; pen name of *Hector Hugh Munro*), British short-story writer, born in Burma. His stories often deal with the supernatural and the macabre, depicting animals as agents seeking revenge on humankind.

salaam /suh-**lahm**/ ● n. a gesture of greeting or respect in Arabic-speaking and Muslim countries, consisting of a low bow with the hand touching the forehead. ● v. make a salaam.
– ORIGIN from Arabic, 'peace be upon you'.

salable ● adj. var. of SALEABLE.

salacious /suh-**lay**-shuhss/ ● adj. having too much interest in sexual matters.
– ORIGIN Latin *salax*.

salad ● n. a cold dish of raw vegetables.
– ORIGIN Old French *salade*.

salad cream ● n. Brit. a creamy dressing resembling mayonnaise.

salad days ● pl. n. (**one's salad days**) the period when one is young and inexperienced.
– ORIGIN from Shakespeare's *Antony and Cleopatra* (I. v. 72).

Saladin E
/**sal**-uh-din/ (1137–93; Arabic name *Salah-ad-Din Yusuf ibn-Ayyub*), sultan of Egypt and Syria 1174–93. He regained Jerusalem from the Christians in 1187, but was defeated by Richard the Lionheart in 1191.

salamander /**sal**-uh-man-der/ ● n. **1** an animal with bright markings resembling a newt, that can live in water and on land. **2** a mythical lizard-like creature said to live in fire.
– ORIGIN Greek *salamandra*.

salami /suh-**lah**-mi/ ● n. (pl. **salami** or **salamis**) a type of spicy preserved sausage.
– ORIGIN Italian.

Salamis E
/**sal**-uh-miss/ a Greek island in the Saronic Gulf, to the west of Athens.

salaried ● adj. earning or offering a salary: *a salaried job.*

salary ● n. (pl. **salaries**) a fixed regular payment made by an employer to an employee.
– ORIGIN Latin *salarium* 'allowance to buy salt'.

Salazar E
/sal-uh-**zar**/, Antonio de Oliveira (1889–1970), Portuguese statesman, Prime Minister 1932–68. He ruled the country as a virtual dictator, enacting a new authoritarian constitution along Fascist lines.

sale ● n. **1** the exchange of something for money. **2** (**sales**) the activity or profession of selling. **3** a period in which goods are sold at reduced prices. **4** a public event at which goods are sold or auctioned.
– PHRASES **sale or return** Brit. an arrangement by which goods may be taken by a retailer with the right to return unsold items without payment.
– ORIGIN Old English.

saleable (also **salable**) ● adj. good enough to be sold.

Salem E
/**say**-luhm/ a city and port in NE Massachusetts, on the Atlantic coast. It was the scene in 1692 of a notorious series of witchcraft trials.

saleroom ● n. esp. Brit. a room in which auctions are held.

salesman (or **saleswoman**) ● n. a person whose job is to sell or promote goods.
– DERIVATIVES **salesmanship** n.

salesperson ● n. a salesman or saleswoman.

salient /**say**-li-uhnt/ ● adj. **1** most important: *the salient points of the case.* **2** (of an angle) pointing outwards. ● n. a piece of land or a fortified building that juts out to form an angle.
– DERIVATIVES **salience** n.
– ORIGIN Latin *salire* 'to leap'.

Salieri E
/sal-i-**air**-i/, Antonio (1750–1825), Italian composer. He was hostile to Mozart, but the story that he poisoned him is without foundation.

saline /**say**-lyn/ ● adj. containing salt.
– DERIVATIVES **salinity** n.
– ORIGIN Latin *sal* 'salt'.

Salinger E
/**sal**-in-jer/, J. D. (b.1919; full name *Jerome David Salinger*), American novelist and short-story writer, best known for his novel *The Catcher in the Rye.*

Salisbury[1] E
/**sawlz**-buh-ri/ a city in southern England, in Wiltshire. It is noted for its 13th-century cathedral, whose spire, at 123 m (404 ft), is the highest in England.

Salisbury[2]
/sawlz-buh-ri/ former name for **HARARE**.

Salisbury[3]
/sawlz-buh-ri/, Robert Arthur Talbot Gascoigne-Cecil, 3rd Marquess of (1830–1903), British Conservative statesman, Prime Minister 1885–6, 1886–92, and 1895–1902.

saliva /suh-ly-vuh/ ● n. a watery liquid produced by glands in the mouth, helping chewing, swallowing, and digestion.
– DERIVATIVES **salivary** /suh-ly-vuh-ri/ adj.
– ORIGIN Latin.

salivate /sal-i-vayt/ ● v. (**salivates, salivating, salivated**) **1** produce saliva. **2** show great excitement at the prospect of something.
– DERIVATIVES **salivation** n.
– ORIGIN Latin *salivare*.

Salk
/sawlk/, Jonas Edward (1914–95), American microbiologist, who developed the standard **Salk vaccine** against polio in the early 1950s.

sallow ● adj. (of a person's complexion) yellowish in colour.
– ORIGIN Old English, 'dusky'.

Sallust
/sal-luhst/ (86–35 BC; Latin name *Gaius Sallustius Crispus*), Roman historian and politician.

sally ● n. (pl. **sallies**) **1** a sudden charge out of a place surrounded by an enemy. **2** a witty or lively reply. ● v. (**sallies, sallying, sallied**) (**sally forth/out**) set out.
– ORIGIN French *saillie*.

salmon /*rhymes with* gammon/ ● n. (pl. **salmon** or **salmons**) a large fish with edible pink flesh, that matures in the sea and moves to freshwater streams to spawn.
– ORIGIN Latin *salmo*.

salmonella /sal-muh-nel-luh/ ● n. (pl. **salmonellae** /sal-muh-nel-lee/) a bacterium that occurs mainly in the gut and can cause food poisoning.
– ORIGIN named after the American veterinary surgeon Daniel E. *Salmon* (1850–1914).

Salome
/suh-loh-mi/ (in the New Testament) the daughter of Herodias, who danced before her stepfather Herod Antipas. Given a choice of reward for her dancing, she asked for the head of St John the Baptist, and thus caused him to be beheaded.

salon ● n. **1** a place where a hairdresser, beautician, or clothes designer carries out their work. **2** a reception room in a large house. **3** hist. a regular gathering of writers, artists, etc., held in a fashionable household.
– ORIGIN French.

Salonica
/suh-lon-i-kuh/ = **THESSALONIKI**.

saloon ● n. **1** Brit. a lounge bar in a pub. **2** a large public lounge on a ship. **3** N. Amer. dated a bar. **4** Brit. a car having a closed body and separate boot.
– ORIGIN French *salon*.

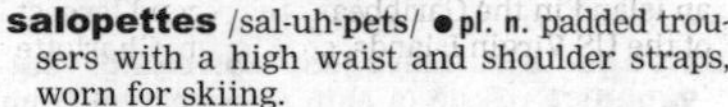
Salop
/sal-uhp/ = **SHROPSHIRE**.

salopettes /sal-uh-pets/ ● pl. n. padded trousers with a high waist and shoulder straps, worn for skiing.
– ORIGIN French *salopette*.

salsa /sal-suh/ ● n. **1** a type of Latin American dance music containing elements of jazz and rock. **2** a dance performed to this music. **3** a spicy tomato sauce.
– ORIGIN Spanish, 'sauce'.

salsify /sal-si-fy/ ● n. a plant with a long edible root like that of a parsnip.
– ORIGIN French *salsifis*.

salt ● n. **1** (also **common salt**) sodium chloride, a white substance in the form of crystals used for flavouring or preserving food. **2** Chem. any compound formed by the reaction of an acid with a base. ● adj. containing or treated with salt. ● v. **1** season or preserve with salt. **2** sprinkle (a road or path) with salt in order to melt snow or ice.
– PHRASES **rub salt into the wound** make a painful experience even more upsetting. **the salt of the earth** a person of great goodness and strength of character. [ORIGIN with reference to the Gospel of Matthew, chapter 5.] **take with a pinch** (or **grain**) **of salt** be aware that (something) may be untrue or exaggerated. **worth one's salt** good at one's job.
– ORIGIN Old English.

salt cellar ● n. a container for salt.
– ORIGIN *cellar* is from Old French *salier* 'salt-box'.

saltire /sawl-tyr, sol-tyr/ ● n. Heraldry an X-shaped cross.
– ORIGIN Old French *saultoir*.

Salt Lake City
the capital of Utah. Founded in 1847 by Brigham Young, the city is the world headquarters of the Church of Latter-Day Saints (Mormons).

salt marsh ● n. an area of coastal grassland that is regularly flooded by seawater.

salt pan ● n. a hollow in the ground in which salt water evaporates to leave a deposit of salt.

saltpetre /sawlt-pee-ter, solt-pee-ter/ (US **saltpeter**) ● n. potassium nitrate.
– ORIGIN Latin *salpetra*.

saltwater ● adj. having to do with or found in the sea.

salty ● adj. (**saltier, saltiest**) **1** tasting of or containing salt. **2** (of language or humour) coarse.
– DERIVATIVES **saltiness** n.

salubrious /suh-loo-bri-uhss/ ● adj. good for one's health: *a salubrious district.*
– ORIGIN Latin *salubris*.

salutary /sal-yuu-tuh-ri/ ● adj. (of something unpleasant) beneficial because allowing one to learn from experience.
– ORIGIN Latin *salutaris*.

salutation ● n. a greeting.

salute ● n. **1** a gesture of respect or acknowledgement. **2** a raising of a hand to the head, made as a formal military gesture of respect. **3** the shooting of a gun or guns as a formal

sign of respect or celebration. ● v. (**salutes**, **saluting**, **saluted**) **1** make a formal salute to. **2** express admiration and respect for.
– ORIGIN Latin *salutare* 'greet'.

salvage ● v. (**salvages**, **salvaging**, **salvaged**) **1** rescue (a ship or its cargo) from loss at sea. **2** save from being lost or destroyed: *she tried hard to salvage her dignity.* ● n. **1** the action of salvaging. **2** cargo rescued from a wrecked ship.
– ORIGIN Latin *salvagium*.

salvage yard ● n. a place where disused machinery and vehicles are broken up and parts salvaged.

salvation ● n. **1** (in Christian belief) the state of being saved from sin, believed to be brought about by faith in Christ. **2** a means of protecting someone from harm or loss: *his only salvation was to outwit the enemy.*
– ORIGIN Latin.

Salvation Army E
a worldwide Christian evangelical organization on quasi-military lines, founded by William Booth in 1865 to help the poor.

salve ● n. **1** an ointment used to soothe or heal the skin. **2** something that reduces guilty feelings: *the idea provided a salve for his guilt.* ● v. (**salves**, **salving**, **salved**) (**salve one's conscience**) do something to feel less guilty.
– ORIGIN Old English.

salver ● n. a tray.
– ORIGIN French *salve*.

salvia ● n. a plant grown for its bright scarlet flowers.
– ORIGIN Latin, 'sage'.

salvo ● n. (pl. **salvos** or **salvoes**) **1** a shooting of a number of guns at the same time in a battle. **2** a sudden series of aggressive statements or acts.
– ORIGIN Italian *salva* 'salutation'.

sal volatile /sal vuh-**lat**-i-li/ ● n. a scented solution used as smelling salts.
– ORIGIN Latin, 'volatile salt'.

Salzburg E
/**salts**-berg/ a city in western Austria, noted for its annual music festivals.

Samaria E
/suh-**mair**-i-uh/ a region of ancient Palestine, between Galilee in the north and Judaea in the south. The chief city of the region was also called Samaria.

Samaritan ● n. **1** (**good Samaritan**) a kind or helpful person. [ORIGIN with reference to the story of the man from ancient Samaria who helped a man in need whom others had passed by (Gospel of Luke).] **2** (**the Samaritans**) (in the UK) an organization which counsels those in distress by telephone.

samarium /suh-**mair**-i-uhm/ ● n. a hard silvery-white metallic chemical element.
– ORIGIN named after a 19th-century Russian official called *Samarsky*.

Samarkand E
/sam-ar-**kand**, **sam**-er-kand/ (also **Samarqand**) a city in eastern Uzbekistan. One of the oldest cities of Asia (3rd or 4th millennium BC), in the 14th century it became the capital of Tamerlane's Mongol empire.

samba ● n. /**sam**-buh/ a Brazilian dance of African origin. ● v. (**sambas**, **sambaing** /**sam**-buh-(r)ing/, **sambaed** /**sam**-buhd/) dance the samba.
– ORIGIN Portuguese.

same ● adj. **1** (**the same**) exactly alike. **2** (**this/that same**) referring to a person or thing just mentioned. ● pron. **1** (**the same**) the same thing as previously mentioned. **2** (**the same**) identical people or things. ● adv. in the same way.
– PHRASES **all** (or **just**) **the same** in spite of this.
– DERIVATIVES **sameness** n.
– ORIGIN Old Norse.

samey ● adj. Brit. informal lacking in variety.

samizdat /**sam**-iz-dat/ ● n. (in the former Soviet Union) the secret copying and distribution of literature banned by the state.
– ORIGIN Russian, 'self-publishing house'.

Samoa[1] E
/suh-**moh**-uh/ a group of islands in Polynesia, divided between American Samoa and the state of Samoa.

Samoa[2] E
/suh-**moh**-uh/ a country consisting of the western islands of Samoa; capital, Apia. Former name (until 1997) **WESTERN SAMOA**.

Samos E
/**say**-moss/ a Greek island in the Aegean, close to the coast of western Turkey.

samosa /suh-**moh**-suh/ ● n. a triangular fried Indian pastry containing spiced vegetables or meat.
– ORIGIN Persian and Urdu.

samovar /**sam**-uh-var/ ● n. a decorated Russian tea urn.
– ORIGIN Russian, 'self-boiler'.

sampan /**sam**-pan/ ● n. a small boat propelled with an oar at the stern, used in the Far East.
– ORIGIN from Chinese words meaning 'three' and 'board'.

sample ● n. **1** a small part or quantity intended to show what the whole is like. **2** a specimen taken for scientific testing. ● v. (**samples**, **sampling**, **sampled**) **1** take a sample or samples of. **2** get a taste of: *sample some entertaining nights out in Liverpool.* **3** (**sampling**) the process of copying and recording parts of a piece of music in electronic form, to be used in a different piece of music.
– ORIGIN Old French *essample* 'example'.

sampler ● n. **1** a piece of embroidery done to demonstrate a person's skill at various stitches. **2** a device for sampling music.

Sampras E
/**sam**-pruhss/, Peter (b.1971), American tennis player. In 1990 he became the youngest man to win the US Open, and in 2000 won his seventh Wimbledon singles title, a record 13th grand slam title.

Samson E
(in the Bible) an Israelite leader famous for his strength. He was betrayed by his lover Delilah to the Philistines, who cut off his hair, the source of his strength.

Samuel E
(in the Bible) a Hebrew prophet and ruler of the Israelites after their defeat by the Philistines.

samurai /sam-uh-ry/ ● n. (pl. **samurai**) hist. a member of a powerful Japanese military class.
– ORIGIN Japanese.

Sana'a E
/sa-**nah**, sah-nuh/ (also **Sanaa**) the capital of Yemen.

San Andreas fault E
/san an-**dray**-uhss/ a fault line extending for some 965 km (600 miles) through the length of coastal California. Seismic activity is common along its course.

sanatorium /san-uh-**tor**-i-uhm/ ● n. (pl. **sanatoriums** or **sanatoria** /san-uh-**tor**-i-uh/) **1** a place for the care of people with a long illness or recovering from illness. **2** Brit. a place in a boarding school for sick children.
– ORIGIN Latin.

sanctify /sangk-ti-fy/ ● v. (**sanctifies**, **sanctifying**, **sanctified**) **1** make or declare holy **2** give religious or official approval to: *love sanctified by the sacrament of marriage.*
– DERIVATIVES **sanctification** n.
– ORIGIN Latin *sanctificare.*

sanctimonious /sangk-ti-**moh**-ni-uhss/ ● adj. making a show of being morally better than other people.
– ORIGIN Latin *sanctimonia* 'sanctity'.

sanction ● n. **1** a threatened penalty for disobeying a law or rule. **2** (**sanctions**) measures taken by a state to try to force another to do something. **3** official permission or approval. ● v. give official permission for.
– ORIGIN Latin.

sanctity ● n. (pl. **sanctities**) **1** holiness. **2** the state of being very important and worthy of great respect: *the sanctity of human life.*
– ORIGIN Old French *saintcite.*

sanctuary ● n. (pl. **sanctuaries**) **1** a place of safety. **2** a nature reserve. **3** a place where injured or unwanted animals are cared for. **4** a holy place. **5** the part of the chancel of a church containing the high altar.
– ORIGIN Latin *sanctuarium.*

sanctum /sangk-tuhm/ ● n. (pl. **sanctums**) **1** a sacred place. **2** a private place.
– ORIGIN Latin.

Sand E
/son/, George (1804–76; pen name of *Amandine-Aurore Lucille Dupin, Baronne Dudevant*), French novelist. Her early novels depict women's struggle against conventional morals.

sand ● n. **1** a substance formed of very fine particles resulting from the erosion of rocks, found in beaches, river beds, the seabed, and deserts. **2** (**sands**) a wide area of sand. ● v. **1** smooth with sandpaper or a sander. **2** sprinkle with sand.
– ORIGIN Old English.

sandal ● n. a shoe with a partly open upper part or straps attaching the sole to the foot.
– ORIGIN Greek *sandalon* 'wooden shoe'.

sandalwood ● n. the sweet-smelling wood of an Indian or SE Asian tree.
– ORIGIN *sandal* from Latin *sandalum.*

sandbag ● n. a bag of sand, used for protection against floods or explosions. ● v. (**sandbags**, **sandbagging**, **sandbagged**) protect with sandbags.

sandbank ● n. a build-up of sand forming a raised bank in the sea or a river.

sandbar ● n. a long, narrow sandbank.

sandblast ● v. roughen or clean with a jet of sand driven by compressed air or steam.

sandboy ● n. (in phr. **as happy as a sandboy**) extremely happy or carefree.
– ORIGIN prob. first referring to a boy going around selling sand.

sandcastle ● n. a model of a castle built out of sand.

sander ● n. a power tool used for smoothing a surface.

sandman ● n. (**the sandman**) an imaginary man supposed to make children sleep by sprinkling sand in their eyes.

sandpaper ● n. paper with sand or another rough substance stuck to it, used for smoothing surfaces. ● v. (**sandpapers**, **sandpapering**, **sandpapered**) smooth with sandpaper.

sandpiper ● n. a wading bird with a long bill and long legs, found in coastal areas.

sandpit ● n. Brit. a shallow box or hollow containing sand, for children to play in.

Sandringham House E
/san-dring-uhm/ a country residence of the British royal family, in Norfolk.

sandstone ● n. rock formed of sand or quartz grains tightly pressed together.

sandstorm ● n. a strong wind in a desert carrying clouds of sand.

sandwich ● n. **1** two pieces of bread with a filling between them. **2** Brit. a sponge cake of two or more layers with jam or cream between them. ● v. **1** (**sandwich between**) insert between (two people or things). **2** (**sandwich together**) join (two things) by putting something between them.
– ORIGIN named after the 4th Earl of *Sandwich* (1718–92).

sandwich board ● n. a pair of advertisement boards connected by straps by which they are hung over a person's shoulders.

sandwich course ● n. Brit. a training course with alternate periods of study and work in business or industry.

Sandwich Islands E
former name for **HAWAII**.

sandy ● adj. (**sandier**, **sandiest**) **1** covered in or consisting of sand. **2** light yellowish brown.

sane ● adj. **1** having a normal mind; not mad. **2** sensible: *sane advice.*
– ORIGIN Latin *sanus* 'healthy'.

San Francisco E
/san fran-**siss**-koh/ a city and seaport on the coast of California.

sang past of **SING**.

sangfroid /song-**frwah**/ ● n. the ability to stay calm in difficult circumstances.
– ORIGIN French, 'cold blood'.

sangria /sang-**gree**-uh/ ● n. a Spanish drink of red wine, lemonade, fruit, and spices.
– ORIGIN Spanish, 'bleeding'.

sanguinary /**sang**-gwi-nuh-ri/ ● adj. esp. archaic

S

involving much bloodshed.

sanguine /sang-gwin/ ● **adj.** cheerfully confident about the future.
– ORIGIN Old French, 'blood red'.

Sanhedrin /san-**hed**-rin, san-**hee**-drin/ (also **Sanhedrim** /san-**hed**-rim, san-**hee**-drim/) ● **n.** the highest court of justice and the supreme council in ancient Jerusalem.
– ORIGIN Hebrew.

sanitarium /san-i-**tair**-i-uhm/ ● **n.** (pl. **sanitariums** or **sanitaria** /san-i-**tair**-i-uh/) N. Amer. = **SANATORIUM**.

sanitary ● **adj. 1** relating to sanitation. **2** hygienic.
– ORIGIN Latin *sanitas* 'health'.

sanitary towel (N. Amer. **sanitary napkin**) ● **n.** a pad worn by women to absorb menstrual blood.

sanitation ● **n.** arrangements to protect public health, such as the provision of clean drinking water and the disposal of sewage.

sanitize (also **sanitise**) ● **v.** (**sanitizes**, **sanitizing**, **sanitized**) **1** make hygienic. **2** make (something unpleasant) seem more acceptable.

sanity ● **n. 1** the condition of being sane. **2** reasonable behaviour.

San José E
/san ho-**zay**/ the capital of Costa Rica.

San Juan E
/san **hwahn**/ the capital of Puerto Rico.

sank past of **SINK**.

San Marino E
/san muh-**ree**-noh/ a republic forming a small enclave in Italy; capital, the town of San Marino.

San Martín E
/san mar-**teen**/, José de (1778–1850), Argentinian soldier and statesman. Having assisted in the liberation of his country from Spanish rule (1812–13), he went on to aid in the liberation of Chile (1817–18) and Peru (1820–4).

sans /sanz/ ● **prep.** literary without: *she plays her role sans accent*.
– ORIGIN Old French *sanz*.

San Salvador E
/san **sal**-vuh-dor/ the capital of El Salvador.

Sanskrit /**san**-skrit/ ● **n.** an ancient language of India, still in use as a language of religion and scholarship.
– ORIGIN Sanskrit, 'composed'.

Sansovino E
/san-suh-**vee**-noh/, Jacopo Tatti (1486–1570), Italian sculptor and architect. He is famous for his buildings in Venice, including St Mark's Library.

Santa Claus (also informal **Santa**) ● **n.** Father Christmas.
– ORIGIN Dutch *Sante Klaas* 'St Nicholas'.

Santa Fé de Bogotá E
/san-tuh fay day bog-uh-**tah**/ official name for **BOGOTÁ**.

Santiago E
/san-ti-**ah**-goh/ the capital of Chile.

Santo Domingo E
/san-toh duh-**ming**-goh/ the capital of the Dominican Republic.

Santorini E
/san-to-**ree**-ni/ = **THERA**.

São Paulo E
/san **pow**-loo/ a city in southern Brazil, the largest city in Brazil and the capital of São Paulo state.

São Tomé and Príncipe E
/san to-**may**, **prin**-si-pay/ a country consisting of two main islands and several smaller ones in the Gulf of Guinea; capital, São Tomé.

sap ● **n.** the liquid that circulates in plants, carrying food to all parts. ● **v.** (**saps**, **sapping**, **sapped**) gradually weaken (a person's strength).
– ORIGIN Old English.

sapient /**say**-pi-uhnt/ ● **adj.** formal wise or intelligent.
– ORIGIN Latin *sapere* 'be wise'.

sapling ● **n.** a young, slender tree.

saponify /suh-**pon**-i-fy/ ● **v.** (**saponifies**, **saponifying**, **saponified**) turn (fat or oil) into soap by reaction with an alkali.
– ORIGIN Latin *sapo* 'soap'.

sapper ● **n.** a military engineer who lays or finds and defuses mines.
– ORIGIN French *saper* 'dig a trench to approach an enemy position'.

sapphic /**saf**-fik/ ● **adj. 1** (**Sapphic**) relating to Sappho or her poetry. **2** formal relating to lesbians.

sapphire /**saf**-fyr/ ● **n. 1** a transparent blue precious stone. **2** a bright blue colour.
– ORIGIN Greek *sappheiros*, prob. referring to lapis lazuli.

Sappho E
/**saf**-foh/ (early 7th century BC), Greek lyric poet, who lived on Lesbos. Many of her poems express her affection and love for women, and have given rise to her association with lesbianism.

Sapporo E
/suh-**por**-oh/ a city in northern Japan, capital of the island of Hokkaido.

sappy ● **adj.** (**sappier**, **sappiest**) N. Amer. informal over-sentimental.

saprophyte /**sap**-ruh-fyt/ ● **n.** Biol. a plant, fungus, or micro-organism that lives on decaying matter.
– DERIVATIVES **saprophytic** adj.
– ORIGIN from Greek *sapros* 'putrid' + *phuton* 'plant'.

saraband /**sa**-ruh-band/ (also **sarabande**) ● **n.** a slow, dignified Spanish dance.
– ORIGIN Spanish and Italian *zarabanda*.

Saracen /**sa**-ruh-suhn/ ● **n.** an Arab or Muslim at the time of the Crusades.
– ORIGIN Greek *Sarakēnos*.

Sarajevo E
/sa-ruh-**yay**-voh/ the capital of Bosnia-Herzegovina.

sarcasm ● **n.** a way of using words that implies the opposite of what they mean, so as to upset or mock someone.
– ORIGIN Greek *sarkasmos*.

S

sarcastic • **adj.** using sarcasm.
– DERIVATIVES **sarcastically** adv.

sarcoma /sar-**koh**-muh/ • **n.** (pl. **sarcomas** or **sarcomata** /sar-**koh**-muh-tuh/) Med. a cancerous tumour of a kind found chiefly in connective tissue.
– ORIGIN Greek *sarkōma.*

sarcophagus /sar-**kof**-fuh-guhss/ • **n.** (pl. **sarcophagi** /sar-**kof**-fuh-gy/) a stone coffin.
– ORIGIN Latin.

sardine • **n.** a young pilchard or other small herring-like fish.
– ORIGIN Latin *sardina.*

Sardinia E
/sar-**din**-i-uh/ a large Italian island in the Mediterranean Sea to the west of Italy; capital, Cagliari.

sardonic /sar-**don**-ik/ • **adj.** mocking: *a sardonic smile.*
– DERIVATIVES **sardonically** adv.
– ORIGIN French *sardonique.*

sardonyx /sar-duh-niks, sar-**don**-iks/ • **n.** onyx in which white layers alternate with yellow or reddish ones.
– ORIGIN Greek *sardonux.*

sargasso /sar-**gass**-oh/ • **n.** a brown seaweed which floats in large masses.
– ORIGIN Portuguese *sargaço.*

Sargasso Sea E
a region of the western Atlantic Ocean between the Azores and the Caribbean, where sargasso seaweed proliferates. It is the breeding place of freshwater eels from Europe and eastern North America, and is known for its usually calm conditions.

sarge • **n.** informal sergeant.

Sargent, E
John Singer (1856–1925), American painter, resident in London from 1885. He is best known for his portraits.

sari /**sah**-ri/ (also **saree**) • **n.** (pl. **saris** or **sarees**) a length of cotton or silk draped around the body, worn by women from the Indian subcontinent.
– ORIGIN Hindi.

Sark E
one of the Channel Islands, a small island to the east of Guernsey.

sarky • **adj.** Brit. informal sarcastic.
– DERIVATIVES **sarkily** adv.

sarnie • **n.** Brit. informal a sandwich.

sarong /suh-**rong**/ • **n.** a long piece of cloth wrapped round the body and tucked at the waist or under the armpits.
– ORIGIN Malay, 'sheath'.

Saronic Gulf E
/suh-**ron**-ik/ an inlet of the Aegean Sea on the coast of SE Greece.

sarsaparilla /sar-suh-puh-**ril**-luh/ • **n.** **1** the dried roots of various plants, used as a flavouring. **2** a sweet drink flavoured with this.
– ORIGIN Spanish *zarzaparilla.*

sarsen /**sar**-suhn/ • **n.** a sandstone boulder of a kind used at Stonehenge in England.
– ORIGIN prob. from **SARACEN**.

sartorial /sah-**tor**-i-uhl/ • **adj.** having to do with a person's style of dress.
– DERIVATIVES **sartorially** adv.
– ORIGIN Latin *sartor* 'tailor'.

Sartre E
/**sar**-truh/, Jean-Paul (1905–80), French philosopher, novelist, and dramatist. A leading existentialist, he dealt in his work with the nature of human life and the structures of consciousness. His works include the novel *Nausée* and the treatise *Being and Nothingness.*

SAS • **abbrev.** Special Air Service.

sash[1] • **n.** a long strip of cloth worn over one shoulder or round the waist.
– ORIGIN Arabic 'muslin, turban'.

sash[2] • **n.** a frame holding the glass in a window.
– ORIGIN from **CHASSIS**.

sashay /sa-**shay**/ • **v.** informal swing the hips from side to side when walking.
– ORIGIN French *chassé* 'chased'.

sash window • **n.** a window with one or two sashes which can be slid up and down to open it.

Saskatchewan E
/suh-**skach**-uh-wuhn/ a province of central Canada; capital, Regina.

sassafras /**sass**-uh-frass/ • **n.** an extract made from the sweet-smelling leaves or bark of a North American tree, used in medicines and perfumes.
– ORIGIN Spanish *sasafrás.*

Sassenach /**sass**-uh-nakh, **sass**-uh-nak/ Sc. & Ir. derog. • **n.** an English person. • **adj.** English.
– ORIGIN Scottish Gaelic or Irish.

Sassoon E
/suh-**soon**/, Siegfried (Lorraine) (1886–1967), English poet and novelist, known for his poems written while he was serving in the First World War.

sassy • **adj.** (**sassier**, **sassiest**) informal confident or cheeky.

SAT • **abbrev.** standard assessment task.

sat past and past part. of **SIT**.

Satan • **n.** the Devil.
– ORIGIN Hebrew, 'adversary'.

satanic • **adj.** having to do with Satan.

satanism • **n.** the worship of Satan.
– DERIVATIVES **satanist** n. & adj.

satchel • **n.** a shoulder bag with a long strap, used to carry school books.
– ORIGIN Old French *sachel.*

sated • **adj.** having had as much as one wants, or so much that one does not want any more.
– ORIGIN Old English, 'become sated or weary'.

sateen /sa-**teen**/ • **n.** a cotton fabric with a glossy surface.
– ORIGIN from **SATIN**.

satellite • **n.** **1** an artificial object placed in orbit round the earth or another planet to collect information or for communication. **2** a natural object that orbits a planet. • **adj.** (of a country, community, or organization) dependent on or controlled by a larger or more powerful one.
– ORIGIN Latin *satelles* 'attendant'.

satellite dish • **n.** a bowl-shaped aerial which transmits signals to or receives them from a communications satellite.

satellite television ● n. television in which the signals are broadcast via satellite.

satiate /say-shi-ayt/ ● v. (**satiates**, **satiating**, **satiated**) give (someone) as much or more than they want.
– DERIVATIVES **satiation** n.
– ORIGIN Latin *satiare*.

Satie E
/sa-ti, sah-ti/, Erik (Alfred Leslie) (1866–1925), French avant-garde composer.

satiety /suh-ty-i-ti/ ● n. the feeling or state of being fully satisfied.

satin ● n. a smooth, glossy fabric. ● adj. having a smooth, glossy surface or finish.
– DERIVATIVES **satiny** adj.
– ORIGIN Arabic, 'of *Tsinkiang*', a town in China.

satinwood ● n. the glossy yellowish wood of a tropical tree, used in making furniture.

satire /sat-yr/ ● n. **1** the use of humour, irony, exaggeration, or ridicule to reveal and criticize people's bad points. **2** a play, novel, etc. using satire.
– DERIVATIVES **satirist** n.
– ORIGIN Latin *satira* 'poetic medley'.

satirical (also **satiric**) ● adj. containing or using satire.
– DERIVATIVES **satirically** adv.

satirize /sat-i-ryz/ (also **satirise**) ● v. (**satirizes**, **satirizing**, **satirized**) mock and criticize using satire.

satisfaction ● n. **1** the state of being satisfied. **2** Law the payment of a debt or fulfilment of a duty or claim. **3** something that makes up for an injustice: *the work will stop if they don't get satisfaction.*

satisfactory ● adj. acceptable.
– DERIVATIVES **satisfactorily** adv.

satisfy ● v. (**satisfies**, **satisfying**, **satisfied**) **1** please (someone) by doing or giving them what they want or need. **2** meet (a demand, desire, or need).
– ORIGIN Latin *satisfacere* 'to content'.

satrap /sat-rap/ ● n. **1** a governor of a province in the ancient Persian empire. **2** a subordinate or local ruler.
– ORIGIN Latin *satrapa*.

satsuma /sat-soo-muh/ ● n. a variety of tangerine with a loose skin.
– ORIGIN named after the former Japanese province of *Satsuma*.

S

saturate /sach-uh-rayt/ ● v. (**saturates**, **saturating**, **saturated**) **1** soak thoroughly with a liquid. **2** cause (a substance) to combine with, dissolve, or hold the greatest possible quantity of another substance. **3** supply (a market) beyond the point at which there is demand for a product.
– ORIGIN Latin *saturare* 'fill, glut'.

saturated ● adj. Chem. (of fats) having only single bonds between carbon atoms in their molecules and as a consequence being less easily processed by the body.

saturation ● n. the action of saturating or the state of being saturated. ● adj. to the fullest extent: *saturation bombing.*

saturation point ● n. the stage beyond which no more can be absorbed or accepted.

Saturday ● n. the day of the week before Sunday and following Friday.
– ORIGIN from Latin *Saturni dies* 'day of Saturn'.

Saturn[1] E
the Roman god of agriculture. Greek equivalent **CRONUS**.

Saturn[2] E
the sixth planet from the sun in the solar system, circled by a system of broad flat rings.

saturnine /sat-er-nyn/ ● adj. **1** (of a person) serious or gloomy. **2** (of looks) dark and brooding.
– ORIGIN Latin *Saturninus* 'of Saturn' (associated with slowness and gloom by astrologers).

satyr /sat-er/ ● n. **1** (in Greek mythology) a lustful, drunken woodland god, with a man's head and a horse's ears and tail or (in Roman mythology) with a goat's ears, tail, legs, and horns. **2** a man with strong sexual desires.
– ORIGIN Greek *saturos*.

sauce ● n. **1** thick liquid served with food to add moistness and flavour. **2** informal, esp. Brit. cheek.
– ORIGIN Old French.

sauce boat ● n. a long, narrow jug for serving sauce.

saucepan ● n. a deep cooking pan, with a long handle and a lid.

saucer ● n. a small shallow dish on which a cup stands.
– ORIGIN Old French *saussier* 'sauce boat'.

saucy ● adj. (**saucier**, **sauciest**) informal sexually suggestive in a light-hearted way: *saucy bedroom secrets.*
– DERIVATIVES **saucily** adv.

Saudi Arabia E
/sow-di/ a country in SW Asia occupying most of Arabia; capital, Riyadh.
– DERIVATIVES **Saudi Arabian** adj. & n.

sauerkraut /sow-er-krowt/ ● n. a German dish of chopped pickled cabbage.
– ORIGIN German.

Saul E
(in the Bible) the first king of Israel (11th century BC).

Saul of Tarsus E
see **PAUL, ST**.

sauna /saw-nuh/ ● n. **1** a small room used as a hot-air or steam bath for cleaning and refreshing the body. **2** a session in a sauna.
– ORIGIN Finnish.

saunter ● v. (**saunters**, **sauntering**, **sauntered**) walk in a slow, relaxed way. ● n. a leisurely stroll.
– ORIGIN unknown.

saurian /saw-ri-uhn/ ● adj. having to do with or like a lizard.
– ORIGIN Greek *sauros* 'lizard'.

sausage ● n. **1** a short tube of raw minced meat in a skin, that is grilled or fried before eating. **2** a tube of cooked or preserved minced meat eaten cold in slices.
– PHRASES **not a sausage** Brit. informal nothing at all.
– ORIGIN Old French *saussiche*.

sausage dog ● n. Brit. informal a dachshund.

sausage meat ● n. minced meat with spices and cereal, used in sausages or as a stuffing.

sausage roll ● n. a piece of sausage meat baked in a roll of pastry.

Saussure E
/soh-**syoor**/, Ferdinand de (1857–1913), Swiss linguistics scholar. He was a founder of modern linguistics and his work is fundamental to the development of structuralism.

sauté /**soh**-tay/ ● adj. fried quickly in a little hot fat. ● n. a dish cooked in such a way. ● v. (**sautés**, **sautéing**, **sautéed** or **sautéd**) cook in such a way.
– ORIGIN French, 'jumped'.

Savage, E
Michael Joseph (1872–1940), New Zealand Labour statesman, Prime Minister 1935–40. New Zealand's first Labour Prime Minister, he introduced social security legislation and other reforms.

savage ● adj. **1** fierce and violent. **2** cruel and vicious: *a savage attack.* **3** uncivilized or primitive. ● n. a member of a people seen as primitive and uncivilized. ● v. (**savages**, **savaging**, **savaged**) **1** attack ferociously. **2** criticize harshly.
– DERIVATIVES **savagely** adv. **savagery** n.
– ORIGIN Old French *sauvage* 'wild'.

savannah (also **savanna**) ● n. a grassy plain in tropical regions, with few trees.
– ORIGIN Spanish *sabana*.

savant /**sav**-uhnt/ ● n. a very knowledgeable person.
– ORIGIN French, 'knowing'.

save[1] ● v. (**saves**, **saving**, **saved**) **1** keep safe or rescue from harm, death, or danger. **2** (in Christian use) prevent (a soul) from being damned. **3** store up for future use. **4** Computing store (data). **5** avoid the need to use up: *computers save time.* **6** guard against: *dust jackets save wear and tear on books.* **7** prevent an opponent from scoring (a goal or point). ● n. esp. Soccer an act of preventing a goal.
– PHRASES **save one's breath** not bother to say something pointless.
– ORIGIN Latiin *salvare*.

save[2] ● prep. & conj. formal except.
– ORIGIN Latin *salvus* 'safe'.

saveloy /**sav**-uh-loy/ ● n. Brit. a spicy dried pork sausage.
– ORIGIN Italian *cervellata*.

saver ● n. **1** a person who regularly saves money through a bank or scheme. **2** something that prevents a resource from being used up: *a space-saver.*

saving ● n. **1** a reduction in money, time, or other resource used. **2** (**savings**) money saved. ● adj. (in combination) preventing a resource from being wasted: *energy-saving.* ● prep. except.

saving grace ● n. a good quality which makes up for the faults of something.

saviour (US **savior**) ● n. **1** a person who saves someone or something from danger or harm. **2** (**the/our Saviour**) (in Christianity) God or Jesus Christ.
– ORIGIN Old French *sauveour*.

savoir faire /sav-war **fair**/ ● n. the ability to act appropriately in social situations.
– ORIGIN French, 'know how to do'.

Savonarola E
/sav-on-uh-**roh**-luh/, Girolamo (1452–98), Italian preacher and religious reformer. His passionate preaching against immorality and corruption gained him great popularity and he became virtual ruler of Florence (1494–5). He was executed after refusing to obey the pope's order forbidding him to preach.

savory[1] ● n. a plant used as a herb in cookery.
– ORIGIN Latin *satureia*.

savory[2] ● adj. & n. US = SAVOURY.

savour (US **savor**) ● v. **1** fully appreciate the taste of (food or drink). **2** enjoy or appreciate to the full. ● n. a characteristic taste or smell.
– ORIGIN Old French.

savoury (US **savory**) ● adj. **1** (of food) salty or spicy rather than sweet. **2** morally acceptable or respectable: *the less savoury aspects of the story.* ● n. (pl. **savouries**) esp. Brit. a savoury snack.

Savoy E
an area of SE France bordering on NW Italy.
DERIVATIVES **Savoyard** adj. & n.

savoy ● n. a cabbage of a variety with wrinkled leaves.
– ORIGIN from SAVOY.

savvy informal ● n. practical knowledge or understanding. ● adj. (**savvier**, **savviest**) having common sense.
– ORIGIN black and pidgin English imitating Spanish *sabe usted* 'you know'.

saw[1] ● n. **1** a hand tool for cutting hard materials, having a long, thin jagged blade. **2** a power-driven cutting tool with a toothed rotating disc or moving band. ● v. (**saws**, **sawing**, **sawed**; past part. Brit. **sawn** or N. Amer. **sawed**) **1** cut with a saw. **2** move something back and forward as if cutting with a saw.
– ORIGIN Old English.

saw[2] past of SEE[1].

saw[3] ● n. a proverb or wise saying.
– ORIGIN Old English.

sawdust ● n. powdery particles of wood produced by sawing.

sawmill ● n. a factory in which logs are sawn by machine.

sawn Brit. past part. of SAW[1].

sawn-off (N. Amer. **sawed-off**) ● adj. (of a gun) having had the barrel shortened in order to be easier to handle and to have a wider field of fire.

sawtooth (also **sawtoothed**) ● adj. shaped like the teeth of a saw.

sawyer ● n. a person who saws timber.

sax ● n. informal a saxophone.

Saxe-Coburg-Gotha E
/saks koh-berg-**goh**-tuh, **goh**-thuh/ the name of the British royal house 1901–17. The name dates from the accession of Edward VII, whose father Prince Albert was a prince of the German duchy of Saxe-Coburg and Gotha.

saxifrage /**saks**-i-frayj/ ● n. a low-growing plant of rocky or stony ground, with small red, white, or yellow flowers.
– ORIGIN Latin *saxifraga*.

Saxon ● n. **1** a member of a Germanic people that conquered and settled in southern Eng-

land in the 5th–6th centuries. **2** a person from modern Saxony in Germany. ● **adj. 1** relating to the Saxons who settled in England. **2** relating to modern Saxony.
– ORIGIN Greek *Saxones*.

Saxony E
/sak-**suh**-ni/ a large region and former kingdom of Germany, including the modern states of Saxony, Saxony-Anhalt, and Lower Saxony.

saxophone /saks-uh-fohn/ ● **n.** a metal wind instrument with a reed like a clarinet.
– DERIVATIVES **saxophonist** /saks-**off**-uh-nist/ n.
– ORIGIN named after the Belgian instrument-maker Adolphe *Sax* (1814–94).

say ● **v.** (**says, saying, said**) **1** speak words so as to communicate something. **2** (of a text or symbol) convey information or instructions. **3** (of a clock or watch) indicate (a time). **4** (**be said**) be claimed or reported. **5** (**say for**) present (a consideration) in favour of: *he had nothing to say for himself.* **6** suggest (something) as an example or theory. ● **n.** an opportunity to state one's opinion or to influence events.
– PHRASES **go without saying** be obvious. **say the word** give permission or instructions. **when all is said and done** when everything is taken into account.
– ORIGIN Old English.

Sayers, E
Dorothy L. (1893–1957; full name *Dorothy Leigh Sayers*), English novelist, known for her detective fiction featuring the amateur detective Lord Peter Wimsey.

saying ● **n.** a well-known expression containing advice or wisdom.

say-so ● **n.** (usu. **on someone's say-so**) informal the power to decide or allow something.

scab ● **n. 1** a crust that forms over a cut or wound as it heals. **2** a skin disease in animals causing itching and hair loss. **3** a plant disease caused by a fungus. **4** derog. a person who refuses to take part in a strike.
– DERIVATIVES **scabby** adj.
– ORIGIN Old Norse.

scabbard /**skab**-berd/ ● **n. 1** a cover for the blade of a sword or dagger. **2** a cover for a gun or tool.
– ORIGIN Old French *escalberc*.

scabies /**skay**-beez/ ● **n.** a skin disease with itching and small raised red spots, caused by a mite.
– ORIGIN Latin.

scabious /**skay**-bi-uhss/ ● **n.** a plant with blue, pink, or white pincushion-shaped flowers.
– ORIGIN from Latin *scabiosa herba* 'rough, scabby plant'.

scabrous /**skay**-bruhss, **skab**-ruhss/ ● **adj. 1** rough and covered with scabs. **2** indecent or sordid: *scabrous and obscene publications.*
– ORIGIN Latin *scabrosus*.

Scafell Pike E
/skaw-**fel**/ a mountain in the Lake District of NW England. Rising to a height of 978 m (3,210 ft), it is the highest peak in England.

scaffold ● **n. 1** a raised wooden platform used formerly for public executions. **2** a structure made using scaffolding.
– ORIGIN Old French *eschaffaut*.

scaffolding ● **n.** a temporary structure made of wooden planks and metal poles, used while building, repairing, or cleaning a building.

scalable ● **adj. 1** able to be climbed. **2** able to be changed in size or scale.

scalar /**skay**-ler/ Math. & Physics ● **adj.** having only magnitude, not direction. ● **n.** a scalar quantity.
– ORIGIN Latin *scalaris*.

scalawag ● **n.** US = **SCALLYWAG**.

scald ● **v. 1** burn with very hot liquid or steam. **2** heat (a liquid) to near boiling point. **3** dip briefly in boiling water. ● **n.** a burn caused by hot liquid or steam.
– ORIGIN Latin *excaldare*.

scale[1] ● **n. 1** each of the small overlapping plates protecting the skin of fish and reptiles. **2** a dry flake of skin. **3** a white deposit formed in a kettle, boiler, etc. in which water containing lime is used. **4** tartar formed on teeth. ● **v.** (**scales, scaling, scaled**) remove scale or scales from.
– ORIGIN Old French *escale*.

scale[2] ● **n. 1** an ordered range of values forming a system for measuring or grading something: *a pay scale.* **2** a measuring instrument based on such a system. **3** relative size or extent: *he operated on a grand scale.* **4** a ratio of size in a map, model, drawing, or plan. **5** an arrangement of the notes in a system of music in ascending or descending order of pitch. ● **v.** (**scales, scaling, scaled**) **1** climb up or over (something high and steep). **2** represent (something) in measurements in proportion to the size of the original. **3** (**scale back/down** or **up**) reduce (or increase) in size, number, or extent.
– PHRASES **to scale** reduced or enlarged in proportion to something.
– ORIGIN Latin *scala* 'ladder'.

scalene /**skay**-leen/ ● **adj.** (of a triangle) having sides unequal in length.
– ORIGIN Greek *skalēnos* 'unequal'.

scales ● **pl. n.** an instrument for weighing.
– PHRASES **tip** (or **turn**) **the scales** be the deciding factor.
– ORIGIN Old Norse, 'bowl'.

scallion /**skal**-li-uhn/ ● **n.** N. Amer. a spring onion.
– ORIGIN Old French *scaloun*.

scallop /**skol**-luhp, **skal**-luhp/ ● **n. 1** an edible shellfish with two hinged fan-shaped shells. **2** each of a series of small curves like the edge of a scallop shell, forming a decorative edging. ● **v.** (**scallops, scalloping, scalloped**) decorate with scallops.
– ORIGIN Old French *escalope*.

scallywag (US also **scalawag**) ● **n.** informal a mischievous person.
– ORIGIN unknown.

scalp ● **n. 1** the skin covering the top and back of the head. **2** (formerly, among American Indians) the scalp and the hair belonging to it cut away from an enemy's head as a battle trophy. ● **v.** take the scalp of (an enemy).
– ORIGIN prob. Scandinavian.

scalpel ● **n.** a knife with a small sharp blade, used by a surgeon.
– ORIGIN Latin *scalpellum* 'small chisel'.

scaly ● **adj. 1** covered in scales. **2** (of skin) dry and flaking.

S

scam • n. informal a dishonest scheme.
– ORIGIN unknown.

scamp • n. informal a mischievous person.
– ORIGIN from former *scamp* 'rob on the highway'.

scamper • v. (**scampers, scampering, scampered**) run with quick light steps. • n. an act of scampering.
– ORIGIN prob. from **SCAMP**.

scampi • pl. n. small lobsters that are fried in breadcrumbs before eating.
– ORIGIN Italian.

scan • v. (**scans, scanning, scanned**) **1** look at quickly in order to find relevant features or information. **2** move a detector or beam across (something). **3** convert (a document or picture) into digital form for storing or processing on a computer. **4** analyse the metre of a line of verse. **5** (of verse) follow metrical rules. • n. **1** an act of scanning. **2** a medical examination using a scanner. **3** an image obtained by scanning.
– ORIGIN Latin *scandere* 'climb'.

scandal • n. **1** an action or event seen as wrong or unacceptable and causing general outrage. **2** outrage or gossip arising from this.
– ORIGIN Latin *scandalum* 'cause of offence'.

scandalize (also **scandalise**) • v. (**scandalizes, scandalizing, scandalized**) shock by acting in a way which does not conform to accepted or moral behaviour.

scandalous • adj. **1** causing general outrage by being wrong or illegal. **2** (of a state of affairs) shockingly bad.
– DERIVATIVES **scandalously** adv.

Scandinavia E
a large peninsula in NW Europe, occupied by Norway and Sweden. It is also a cultural region consisting of the countries of Norway, Sweden, and Denmark and sometimes also of Iceland, Finland, and the Faroe Islands.

Scandinavian • adj. relating to Scandinavia. • n. **1** a person from Scandinavia. **2** the northern branch of the Germanic languages, made up of Danish, Norwegian, Swedish, Icelandic, and Faroese.

scandium /skan-di-uhm/ • n. a soft silvery-white metallic chemical element.
– ORIGIN Latin.

scanner • n. **1** a machine that examines the body through the use of radiation, ultrasound etc. **2** a device that scans documents and converts them into digital data.

scansion /skan-sh'n/ • n. **1** the action of scanning a line of verse to determine its rhythm. **2** the rhythm of a line of verse.

scant • adj. hardly any; not enough: *she gave it scant attention.*
– ORIGIN Old Norse, 'short'.

scanty • adj. (**scantier, scantiest**) too little in quantity or amount.
– DERIVATIVES **scantily** adv.

scapegoat • n. a person who is blamed for the wrongdoings or mistakes of others. • v. make a scapegoat of.
– ORIGIN from former *scape* 'escape' + **GOAT**.

scapula /skap-yuu-luh/ • n. (pl. **scapulae** /skap-yuu-lee/ or **scapulas**) Anat. = **SHOULDER BLADE**.
– ORIGIN Latin.

scapular /skap-yuu-ler/ • adj. Anat. & Zool. relating to the shoulder or shoulder blade. • n. a short cloak worn by monks, covering the shoulders.

scar[1] • n. **1** a mark left on the skin or within body tissue after the healing of a wound or burn. **2** a mark left at the point where a leaf or other part separates from a plant. **3** a lasting effect left after an unpleasant experience. • v. (**scars, scarring, scarred**) mark or be marked with a scar or scars.
– ORIGIN Greek *eskhara* 'scab'.

scar[2] • n. a steep high cliff or rock outcrop.
– ORIGIN Old Norse, 'low reef'.

scarab /ska-ruhb/ • n. **1** a large dung beetle, treated as sacred in ancient Egypt. **2** an ancient Egyptian gem in the form of a scarab.
– ORIGIN Greek *skarabeios*.

scarce • adj. **1** (of a resource) available in quantities that are too small to meet the demand for it. **2** rarely found.
– PHRASES **make oneself scarce** informal leave a place to avoid trouble.
– DERIVATIVES **scarcity** n.
– ORIGIN Old French *escars*.

scarcely • adv. **1** only just. **2** only a very short time before. **3** used to suggest that something is unlikely: *they could scarcely all be wrong.*

scare • v. (**scares, scaring, scared**) **1** frighten or become frightened. **2** (**scare away/off**) drive or keep (someone) away by fear. • n. **1** a sudden attack of fright. **2** a period of general alarm: *she stopped eating meat because of a health scare.*
– ORIGIN Old Norse.

scarecrow • n. an object made to look like a person, set up to scare birds away from a field where crops are growing.

scarf[1] • n. (pl. **scarves** or **scarfs**) a length or square of fabric worn around the neck or head.
– ORIGIN prob. from Old French *escharpe* 'pilgrim's pouch'.

scarf[2] • v. join the ends of (two pieces of timber or metal) by cutting them so that they fit together by overlapping. • n. a joint made by scarfing.
– ORIGIN Old Norse.

scarify /ska-ri-fy/ • v. (**scarifies, scarifying, scarified**) **1** make shallow cuts in (the skin). **2** cut and remove unwanted material from (a lawn).
– DERIVATIVES **scarification** n.
– ORIGIN Old French *scarifier*.

scarlatina /skar-luh-tee-nuh/ • n. = **SCARLET FEVER**.
– ORIGIN Latin.

Scarlatti E
/skar-lat-ti/, (Pietro) Alessandro (Gaspare) (1660–1725), Italian composer, an important early composer of operas. His son **(Giuseppe) Domenico Scarlatti** (1685–1757) wrote over 550 sonatas for the harpsichord.

scarlet • n. a bright red colour.
– ORIGIN Latin *scarlata* 'brightly coloured cloth'.

scarlet fever • n. an infectious disease that particularly affects children, causing fever and a scarlet rash.

scarlet woman • n. a woman known for having many sexual relationships.

S

scarp ● n. a very steep bank or slope.
– ORIGIN Italian *scarpa*.
scarper ● v. (**scarpers**, **scarpering**, **scarpered**) Brit. informal run away.
– ORIGIN prob. from Italian *scappare* 'to escape'.
scarves pl. of **SCARF**[1].
scary ● adj. (**scarier**, **scariest**) informal frightening.
– DERIVATIVES **scarily** adv.
scat ● v. (**scats**, **scatting**, **scatted**) informal go away.
– ORIGIN perh. from **SCATTER**.
scathing /skay-*th*ing/ ● adj. harshly critical.
– ORIGIN Old Norse, 'harm, injure'.
scatological ● adj. obsessed with excrement and excretion.
– DERIVATIVES **scatology** n.
– ORIGIN Greek *skōr* 'dung'.
scatter ● v. (**scatters**, **scattering**, **scattered**) **1** throw in various random directions. **2** separate and move off in different directions. **3** (**be scattered**) occur or be found at various places.
– ORIGIN prob. from **SHATTER**.
scatterbrained ● adj. disorganized and lacking in concentration.
scatty ● adj. informal absent-minded and disorganized.
– ORIGIN from *scatterbrained*.
scavenge /ska-vinj/ ● v. (**scavenges**, **scavenging**, **scavenged**) **1** search for and collect (anything usable) from waste. **2** (of an animal or bird) search for (dead animals) as food.
scavenger ● n. a person or animal that scavenges.
– ORIGIN Old French *escauwer* 'inspect'.
SCE ● abbrev. Scottish Certificate of Education.
scenario /si-nah-ri-oh/ ● n. (pl. **scenarios**) **1** a written outline of a film, novel, or stage work. **2** a possible sequence of future events.
– ORIGIN Italian.
scene ● n. **1** the place where an incident occurs or occurred. **2** a view or landscape as seen by a spectator. **3** an incident: *scenes of violence*. **4** a sequence of continuous action in a play, film, opera, etc. **5** a public display of emotion or anger. **6** a specified area of activity or interest: *the literary scene*.
– PHRASES **behind the scenes** out of public view.
– ORIGIN Latin *scena*.
scenery ● n. **1** the natural features of a landscape considered in terms of their appearance. **2** the painted background used to represent a place on a stage or film set.
scenic ● adj. (of natural scenery) impressive or beautiful.
scent ● n. **1** a pleasant smell. **2** perfume. **3** a trail indicated by the smell of an animal. ● v. **1** give a pleasant scent to. **2** recognize by the sense of smell. **3** sense the approach of: *the Premier scented victory*.
– DERIVATIVES **scented** adj.
– ORIGIN Latin *sentire* 'perceive, smell'.
sceptic /skep-tik/ (US **skeptic**) ● n. a person who questions accepted beliefs or statements.
– DERIVATIVES **scepticism** (US **skepticism**) n.
– ORIGIN Greek *skeptikos*.
sceptical (US **skeptical**) ● adj. not easily convinced; having doubts.
sceptre /sep-ter/ (US **scepter**) ● n. a staff carried by a monarch on ceremonial occasions.
– ORIGIN Greek *skēptron*.
Schadenfreude /shah-d'n-froy-duh/ ● n. pleasure felt at the misfortune of another.
– ORIGIN German.
schedule /shed-yool, sked-yool/ ● n. **1** a plan for carrying out something, giving lists of intended events and times. **2** a timetable. ● v. (**schedules**, **scheduling**, **scheduled**) plan for (something) to happen or for (someone) to do something.
– DERIVATIVES **scheduler** n.
– ORIGIN Latin *schedula* 'slip of paper'.
scheduled ● adj. **1** forming part of a schedule. **2** (of an airline or flight) forming part of a regular service rather than specially chartered.
schema /skee-muh/ ● n. (pl. **schemata** /skee-muh-tuh/ or **schemas**) tech. an outline of a plan or theory.
– ORIGIN Greek *skhēma* 'form, figure'.
schematic ● adj. **1** (of a diagram) outlining the main features; simplified. **2** (of thought, ideas, etc.) formulaic.
schematize (also **schematise**) ● v. (**schematizes**, **schematizing**, **schematized**) arrange or show in a schematic form.
scheme ● n. **1** a systematic plan for achieving a particular aim. **2** a secret or underhand plan; a plot. **3** an ordered system or pattern: *a classical rhyme scheme*. ● v. (**schemes**, **scheming**, **schemed**) make secret plans.
– DERIVATIVES **schemer** n.
– ORIGIN Greek *skhēma* 'form'.
scherzo /skair-tsoh/ ● n. (pl. **scherzos** or **scherzi** /skair-tsi/) Music a short lively movement in a symphony or sonata.
– ORIGIN Italian, 'jest'.

Schiaparelli E
/skyap-uh-rel-li/, Elsa (1896–1973), Italian-born French fashion designer.

Schiele E
/shee-luh/, Egon (1890–1918), Austrian painter and draughtsman, known for his explicit nude studies.

Schiller E
/shil-ler/, (Johann Christoph) Friedrich von (1759–1805), German dramatist, poet, and historian. His plays include the trilogy *Wallenstein* and *William Tell*. Among his poems is 'Ode to Joy', which Beethoven set to music in his Ninth Symphony.

Schindler E
/shind-ler/, Oskar (1908–74), German industrialist. He saved more than 1,200 Jews from concentration camps by employing them in his factories in Cracow and Czechoslovakia.

schism /si-z'm, ski-z'm/ ● n. **1** a deep disagreement between two groups. **2** the formal separation of a Church into two Churches owing to differences in belief.
– ORIGIN Greek *skhisma* 'cleft'.
schismatic ● adj. having to do with schism.
schist /shist/ ● n. a metamorphic rock which consists of layers of different minerals.
– ORIGIN Greek *skhistos* 'split'.
schizoid /skit-soyd/ ● adj. having a mental

condition similar to schizophrenia.

schizophrenia /skit-suh-free-ni-uh/ ● **n.** a long-term mental disorder whose symptoms include inappropriate actions and feelings and withdrawal from reality into fantasy.
– ORIGIN Latin.

schizophrenic /skits-uh-fren-ik/ ● **adj.** **1** suffering from schizophrenia. **2** informal having contradictory elements. ● **n.** a schizophrenic person.

Schliemann E
/**shlee**-man/, Heinrich (1822–90), German archaeologist. He excavated the mound of Hissarlik, Turkey, the traditional site of Troy, and later undertook excavations at Mycenae.

schlock /shlok/ ● **n.** informal, esp. N. Amer. cheap or poor quality goods.
– ORIGIN prob. from Yiddish, 'an apoplectic stroke'.

schmaltz /shmawlts/ ● **n.** informal excessive sentimentality.
– DERIVATIVES **schmaltzy** adj.
– ORIGIN Yiddish.

schmuck /shmuk/ ● **n.** N. Amer. informal a stupid person.
– ORIGIN Yiddish, 'penis'.

schnapps /shnaps/ ● **n.** a strong alcoholic drink resembling gin.
– ORIGIN German *Schnaps* 'dram of liquor'.

schnitzel /**shnit**-z'l/ ● **n.** a thin slice of veal, coated in breadcrumbs and fried.
– ORIGIN German, 'slice'.

Schoenberg E
/**shern**-berg/, Arnold (1874–1951), Austrian-born American composer. He wrote the first atonal pieces and also introduced the technique of serialism in his work *Serenade*.

scholar ● **n.** **1** a person who studies a particular subject in detail. **2** a student who holds a scholarship.
– ORIGIN Latin *scholaris*.

scholarly ● **adj.** **1** relating to serious academic study **2** having knowledge or learning.

scholarship ● **n.** **1** serious academic study. **2** a grant made to support a student's education, awarded on the basis of achievement.

scholastic ● **adj.** having to do with schools and education.

scholasticism ● **n.** the system of theology and philosophy taught in medieval universities.

school[1] ● **n.** **1** an institution for educating children. **2** a day's work at school. **3** any institution at which instruction is given in a particular subject. **4** a department of a university. **5** a group of artists, philosophers, etc. sharing similar ideas. ● **v.** **1** formal or N. Amer. send to school; educate. **2** train to do something: *his instincts had schooled him to avoid them.*
– PHRASES **school of thought** a particular way of thinking.
– ORIGIN Greek *skholē* 'philosophy'.

school[2] ● **n.** a large group of fish or sea mammals.
– ORIGIN German or Dutch *schōle*.

schooling ● **n.** education received at school.

schoolmarm ● **n.** esp. N. Amer. a schoolmistress, especially one who is prim and strict.

schoolmaster (or **schoolmistress**) ● **n.** a teacher in a school.

schoolteacher ● **n.** a person who teaches in a school.

schooner /**skoo**-ner/ ● **n.** **1** a sailing ship with two or more masts. **2** Brit. a large glass for sherry.
– ORIGIN perh. from dialect *scun* 'skim along'.

Schopenhauer E
/**shop**-uhn-how-er/, Arthur (1788–1860), German philosopher. In *The World as Will and Idea*, he argues that the will (self-consciousness) is the only reality; happiness can only be achieved by renouncing it.

Schröder E
/**shrer**-der/, Gerhard (b.1944), German Social Democratic Party statesman, Chancellor of Germany since 1998.

Schrödinger E
/**shrer**-ding-er/, Erwin (1887–1961), Austrian theoretical physicist, pioneer of the use of wave mechanics to describe the structure of atoms.

schtum /shtuum/ ● **adj.** var. of **SHTUM**.

Schubert E
/**shoo**-bert/, Franz (1797–1828), Austrian composer. His works include more than 600 songs, the 'Trout' piano quintet, and nine symphonies.

Schulz E
/shuults/, Charles (1922–2000), American cartoonist, who created the 'Peanuts' comic strip.

Schumacher E
/**shoo**-mak-er/, Michael (b.1969), German racing driver, winner of Formula One world championships in 1994, 1995, 2000, and 2001.

Schumann E
/**shoo**-muhn/, Robert (Alexander) (1810–56), German romantic composer. He was particularly noted for his songs and piano music.

Schwarzenegger E
/**shworts**-uh-neg-ger/, Arnold (b.1947), Austrian-born American actor, noted for his action roles in such films as *The Terminator*.

Schwarzkopf E
/**shvarts**-kopf/, Dame (Olga Maria) Elisabeth (Friederike) (b.1915), German operatic soprano.

Schweitzer E
/**shwyt**-ser/, Albert (1875–1965), German theologian, musician, and medical missionary, born in Alsace. From 1913 he worked as a missionary in Gabon, where he established a hospital.

sciatic /sy-**at**-ik/ ● **adj.** **1** having to do with the hip. **2** affecting the sciatic nerve.
– ORIGIN French *sciatique*.

sciatica ● **n.** pain affecting the back, hip, and outer side of the leg, caused by pressure on the sciatic nerve.

sciatic nerve ● **n.** a major nerve extending from the lower end of the spinal cord down the back of the thigh.

science • n. **1** the systematic study of the structure and behaviour of the physical and natural world through observation and experiment. **2** an organized body of knowledge on any subject.
– ORIGIN Latin *scientia*.

science fiction • n. fiction based on imagined future worlds and showing scientific or technological changes.

science park • n. an area devoted to scientific research or the development of science-based industries.

scientific • adj. **1** relating to or based on science. **2** systematic; methodical.
– DERIVATIVES **scientifically** adv.

scientist • n. a person who has expert knowledge of one or more of the natural or physical sciences.

Scientology • n. trademark a religious system based on the seeking of self-knowledge and spiritual fulfilment through courses of study and training.
– DERIVATIVES **Scientologist** n.
– ORIGIN Latin *scientia* 'knowledge'.

sci-fi • n. informal = SCIENCE FICTION.

Scilly Isles E
/**sil**-li/ a group of about 140 small islands off the south-western tip of England; capital, Hugh Town (on St Mary's).
– DERIVATIVES **Scillonian** adj. & n.

scimitar /**sim**-i-ter/ • n. a short sword with a curved blade, used in Eastern countries.
– ORIGIN French *cimeterre* or Italian *scimitarra*.

scintilla /sin-**til**-luh/ • n. a tiny trace or amount: *not a scintilla of doubt*.
– ORIGIN Latin, 'spark'.

scintillate /**sin**-ti-layt/ • v. (**scintillates**, **scintillating**, **scintillated**) give off flashes of light; sparkle.
– ORIGIN Latin *scintillare* 'to sparkle'.

scintillating • adj. **1** sparkling. **2** brilliant and exciting.

scion /**sy**-uhn/ • n. **1** a young shoot or twig of a plant that is cut off to create a new plant. **2** a descendant of a notable family.
– ORIGIN Old French *ciun*.

scissors • pl. n. (also **a pair of scissors**) a tool for cutting cloth and paper, consisting of two crossing blades pivoted in the middle. • adj. (**scissor**) (of an action) in which two things move like a pair of scissors: *a scissor kick*.
– ORIGIN Old French *cisoires*.

S

sclerosis /skleer-**oh**-siss, skluh-**roh**-siss/ • n. Med. **1** abnormal hardening of body tissue. **2** (in full **multiple sclerosis**) a disease involving damage to the sheaths of nerve cells and leading to partial or complete paralysis.
– ORIGIN Greek *sklērōsis*.

scoff[1] • v. speak about something in a scornful way.
– ORIGIN perh. Scandinavian.

scoff[2] • v. Brit. informal eat quickly and greedily.
– ORIGIN Dutch *schoft* 'quarter of a day, meal'.

scold • v. angrily rebuke or criticize.
– ORIGIN prob. from Old Norse, 'person who writes and recites epic poems'.

sconce • n. a candle holder attached to a wall with an ornamental bracket.
– ORIGIN Old French *esconse* 'lantern'.

scone /skon, skohn/ • n. a small plain cake made from flour, fat, and milk.
– ORIGIN perh. from Dutch *schoonbroot* 'fine bread'.

scoop • n. **1** a utensil resembling a spoon, having a short handle and a deep bowl. **2** the bowl-shaped part of a digging machine or dredger. **3** informal a piece of news published or broadcast before other newspapers or broadcast stations know about it. • v. **1** pick up with a scoop. **2** create (a hollow). **3** pick up in a quick, smooth movement.
– ORIGIN German *schōpe* 'waterwheel bucket'.

scoot • v. informal go or leave somewhere quickly.
– ORIGIN unknown.

scooter • n. **1** (also **motor scooter**) a light two-wheeled motorcycle. **2** a child's toy consisting of a footboard mounted on two wheels and a long steering handle, moved by pushing one foot against the ground.

scope • n. **1** the extent of the area or subject matter that something deals with or to which it is relevant: *such questions go beyond the scope of this book*. **2** the opportunity or possibility for doing something.
– ORIGIN Greek *skopos* 'target'.

-scope • comb. form referring to an instrument for observing or examining: *telescope*.
– ORIGIN Greek *skopein* 'look at'.

scorbutic /skor-**byoo**-tik/ • adj. relating to or affected with scurvy.
– ORIGIN Latin *scorbutus* 'scurvy'.

scorch • v. **1** burn or become burnt on the surface or edges. **2** (**scorched**) dried out and withered as a result of extreme heat. **3** informal move very fast.
– ORIGIN perh. from Old Norse, 'be shrivelled'.

scorcher • n. informal a very hot day.

score • n. **1** the number of points, goals, runs, etc. achieved by an individual or side in a game. **2** (pl. **score**) a group or set of twenty. **3** (**scores of**) a large amount or number of. **4** a written representation of a musical composition showing all the vocal and instrumental parts. • v. (**scores**, **scoring**, **scored**) **1** gain (a point, goal, run, etc.) in a game. **2** be worth (a number of points). **3** record the score during a game. **4** cut a mark on (a surface). **5** (**score out/through**) delete (text) by drawing a line through it. **6** orchestrate or arrange (a piece of music).
– PHRASES **settle a score** take revenge on someone.
– DERIVATIVES **scorer** n.
– ORIGIN Old Norse, 'notch, tally, twenty'.

scoreline • n. the number of points or goals scored in a match.

scorn • n. the feeling that someone or something is worthless; contempt. • v. **1** express scorn for. **2** reject in a contemptuous way.
– DERIVATIVES **scornful** adj. **scornfully** adv.
– ORIGIN Old French *escarn*.

Scorpio • n. Astrol. the eighth sign of the zodiac (the Scorpion), which the sun enters about 23 October.
– ORIGIN Latin.

scorpion • n. a creature related to the spiders, with pincers and a poisonous sting at the end of its tail.
– ORIGIN Greek *skorpios* 'scorpion'.

Scorsese E
/skor-say-zi/, Martin (b.1942), American film director, known for such films as *Mean Streets*, *Taxi Driver*, and *Raging Bull*.

Scot • n. a person from Scotland.
– ORIGIN Latin *Scottus*.

Scotch • adj. dated = **SCOTTISH**. • n. (also **Scotch whisky**) whisky made in Scotland.
– ORIGIN from **SCOTTISH**.

scotch • v. put an end to.
– ORIGIN perh. related to **SKATE**[1].

Scotch egg • n. a hard-boiled egg coated in sausage meat, rolled in breadcrumbs, and fried.

scot-free • adv. without suffering any punishment or injury.
– ORIGIN from the former word *scot* 'a tax'.

Scotland F
a country forming the northernmost part of Great Britain and of the United Kingdom; capital, Edinburgh.

Scotland Yard E
the headquarters of the London Metropolitan Police, situated in New Scotland Yard, Westminster.

Scots • adj. = **SCOTTISH**. • n. the form of English used in Scotland.

Scots pine • n. a pine tree grown for timber and other products.

Scott[1], E
Sir George Gilbert (1811–78), English Gothic revival architect, who designed the Albert Memorial in London. His grandson **Sir Giles Gilbert Scott** (1880–1960) designed the Gothic Anglican cathedral in Liverpool.

Scott[2], E
Sir Peter (Markham) (1909–89), English naturalist and artist, son of Sir Robert Scott. He founded the Wildfowl Trust at Slimbridge in Gloucestershire.

Scott[3], E
Ridley (b.1939), English film director. His films include *Alien*, *Blade Runner*, and *Thelma and Louise*.

Scott[4], E
Sir Robert (Falcon) (1868–1912), English explorer and naval officer. In 1910–12 Scott and four companions made a journey to the South Pole, arriving there in 1912 to discover that Roald Amundsen had beaten them by a month. Scott and his companions died on the return journey.

Scott[5], E
Sir Walter (1771–1832), Scottish novelist and poet, known for historical novels such as *Waverley* and *Ivanhoe*.

Scottish • adj. relating to Scotland or its people.

Scottish Borders E
an administrative region of southern Scotland; administrative centre, Melrose.

Scottish terrier • n. a small rough-haired breed of terrier.

scoundrel • n. a dishonest person.
– ORIGIN unknown.

scour[1] • v. clean or brighten by rubbing with something rough or a detergent.
– ORIGIN Old French *escurer*.

scour[2] • v. subject to a thorough search.
– ORIGIN unknown.

scourge • n. **1** hist. a whip used for punishment. **2** a person or thing causing great trouble or suffering: *the scourge of mass unemployment*. • v. (**scourges**, **scourging**, **scourged**) **1** hist. whip with a scourge. **2** cause great suffering to.
– ORIGIN Old French *escorge*.

Scouse /skowss/ Brit. informal • n. **1** the dialect or accent of people from Liverpool. **2** (also **Scouser**) a person from Liverpool. • adj. relating to Liverpool.
– ORIGIN from *lobscouse*, a stew formerly eaten by sailors.

scout • n. **1** a person sent ahead of a main force to gather information about the enemy. **2** (also **Scout**) a member of the Scout Association, a boys' organization founded by Lord Baden-Powell. **3** a talent scout. **4** an instance of scouting. • v. **1** make a detailed search in order to find or discover something. **2** act as a scout.
– ORIGIN Old French *escouter* 'listen'.

scow /skow/ • n. a flat-bottomed sailing dinghy.
– ORIGIN Dutch *schouw* 'ferry boat'.

scowl • n. an angry or bad-tempered expression. • v. frown in an angry or bad-tempered way.
– ORIGIN prob. Scandinavian.

scrabble • v. (**scrabbles**, **scrabbling**, **scrabbled**) **1** grope around with one's fingers to find or hold on to something. **2** move quickly and awkwardly; scramble.
– ORIGIN Dutch *schrabbelen*.

scrag • v. (**scrags**, **scragging**, **scragged**) informal, esp. Brit. handle roughly; beat up.
– ORIGIN perh. from Scots and northern English *crag* 'neck'.

scraggy • adj. thin and bony.

scram • v. (**scrams**, **scramming**, **scrammed**) informal go away quickly.
– ORIGIN prob. from **SCRAMBLE**.

scramble • v. (**scrambles**, **scrambling**, **scrambled**) **1** move or make one's way quickly and awkwardly, using one's hands as well as one's feet. **2** make confused. **3** put (a broadcast transmission or telephone conversation) into a form that can only be understood if received by a decoding device. **4** cook (beaten eggs with a little liquid) in a pan. **5** (of fighter aircraft) take off immediately in an emergency. **6** informal act in a hurried way: *firms scrambled to win contracts*. • n. **1** an act of scrambling. **2** Brit. a motorcycle race over rough and hilly ground.

scrambler • n. a device for scrambling a broadcast transmission or telephone conversation.

scrap[1] • n. **1** a small piece or amount of something. **2** (**scraps**) bits of uneaten food left after a meal. **3** waste metal or other material that has been discarded for reprocessing. • v. (**scraps**, **scrapping**, **scrapped**) **1** remove from use. **2** abolish or cancel (a plan or law).
– ORIGIN Old Norse.

scrap[2] informal • n. a short fight or quarrel. • v. (**scraps**, **scrapping**, **scrapped**) have a short

S

fight or quarrel.
– ORIGIN perh. from **SCRAPE**.

scrapbook ● n. a book of blank pages for sticking cuttings, drawings, or pictures in.

scrape ● v. (**scrapes**, **scraping**, **scraped**) **1** drag or pull a hard or sharp implement across (a surface or object) to remove dirt or waste matter. **2** use a sharp or hard implement to remove (dirt or unwanted matter). **3** rub against a rough or hard surface. **4** just manage to achieve or pass. ● n. **1** an act or sound of scraping. **2** an injury or mark caused by scraping. **3** informal an embarrassing or difficult situation.
– ORIGIN Old English, 'scratch with the fingernails'.

scrappy ● adj. (**scrappier**, **scrappiest**) disorganized, untidy, or incomplete.

scrapyard ● n. Brit. a place where scrap is collected.

scratch ● v. **1** make a long mark or wound on (a surface) with something sharp or pointed. **2** rub (a part of one's body) with one's fingernails to relieve itching. **3** (of a bird or mammal) rake the ground with the beak or claws in search of food. **4** cross out (writing). **5** withdraw from a competition. **6** cancel or abandon (a plan or project). ● n. **1** a mark or wound made by scratching. **2** an act of scratching. **3** informal a slight injury. ● adj. put together from whatever is available: *a scratch squad.*
– PHRASES **from scratch** from the very beginning. **up to scratch** up to the required standard; satisfactory.
– ORIGIN uncertain.

scratch card ● n. a card with a section or sections coated in a waxy substance which may be scraped away to reveal whether a prize has been won.

scratchy ● adj. (**scratchier**, **scratchiest**) **1** causing scratching. **2** (of a voice or sound) rough.

scrawl ● v. write in a hurried, careless way. ● n. hurried, careless handwriting.
– ORIGIN prob. from **CRAWL**.

scrawny ● adj. (**scrawnier**, **scrawniest**) unattractively thin and bony.
– ORIGIN from dialect *scranny.*

scream ● v. **1** make a loud, piercing cry or sound expressing great emotion or pain. **2** move very rapidly. ● n. **1** a screaming cry or sound. **2** (**a scream**) informal an extremely funny person or thing.
– ORIGIN perh. Dutch.

scree ● n. a mass of small loose stones that form or cover a slope on a mountain.
– ORIGIN prob. from Old Norse, 'landslip'.

screech ● n. a loud, harsh cry or sound. ● v. make or move with a screech.
– DERIVATIVES **screechy** adj.

screech owl ● n. Brit. = **BARN OWL**.

screed ● n. **1** a long speech or piece of writing. **2** a layer of material applied to level a floor.
– ORIGIN prob. from **SHRED**.

screen ● n. **1** an upright partition used to divide a room, give shelter, or conceal something. **2** something that provides shelter or concealment. **3** the flat front surface of a television, VDU, or monitor, on which images and data are displayed. **4** a blank surface on which films are projected. **5** (**the screen**) films or television. ● v. **1** conceal, protect, or shelter with a screen. **2** show (a film or video) or broadcast (a television programme). **3** protect from something dangerous or unpleasant. **4** test for the presence or absence of a disease.
– ORIGIN Old French *escren.*

screenplay ● n. the script of a film, including acting instructions and scene directions.

screen-print ● v. force ink on to (a surface) through a screen of fine material so as to create a picture or pattern. ● n. (**screen print**) a picture or design produced by screen-printing.

screen saver ● n. Computing a program which replaces an unchanging screen display with a moving image to prevent damage to the phosphor.

screen test ● n. a filmed test to discover whether an actor is suitable for a film role.

screenwriter ● n. a person who writes a screenplay.

screw ● n. **1** a metal pin with a spiral thread running around it, used to join things together by being turned and pressed in. **2** a cylinder with a spiral ridge running round the outside that can be turned to seal an opening, apply pressure, adjust position, etc. **3** (also **screw propeller**) a ship's or aircraft's propeller. **4** vulgar an act of sexual intercourse. **5** informal, derog. a prison warder. ● v. **1** fasten or tighten with a screw or screws. **2** rotate (something) so as to attach or remove it by means of a spiral thread. **3** informal cheat or swindle. **4** vulgar have sexual intercourse with.
– PHRASES **screw up 1** crush into a tight mass. **2** informal cause to fail or go wrong. **3** informal make emotionally disturbed.
– ORIGIN Old French *escroue* 'female screw, nut'.

screwball informal, esp. N. Amer. ● n. a crazy or eccentric person. ● adj. crazy; absurd.

screwdriver ● n. a tool with a shaped tip that fits into the head of a screw to turn it.

screwy ● adj. informal, esp. N. Amer. rather odd or eccentric.

Scriabin E
/skri-**ah**-bin/ (also **Skryabin**), Aleksandr (Nikolaevich) (1872–1915), Russian composer and pianist. Much of his later music reflects his interest in mysticism, especially *The Divine Poem* (his third symphony).

scribble ● v. (**scribbles**, **scribbling**, **scribbled**) **1** write or draw carelessly or hurriedly. **2** informal write for a living or as a hobby. ● n. a piece of writing or a picture produced carelessly or hurriedly.
– DERIVATIVES **scribbler** n.
– ORIGIN Latin *scribillare.*

scribe ● n. hist. a person who copied out documents.
– DERIVATIVES **scribal** adj.
– ORIGIN Latin *scriba.*

scrim ● n. strong, coarse fabric used for heavy-duty lining or upholstery.
– ORIGIN unknown.

scrimmage ● n. a confused struggle or fight.
– ORIGIN from **SKIRMISH**.

scrimp ● v. be very careful with money;

economize.
– ORIGIN Scots, 'meagre'.

scrip • n. a provisional certificate of money subscribed to a bank or company, entitling the holder to dividends.
– ORIGIN short for *subscription receipt*.

script • n. **1** the written text of a play, film, or broadcast. **2** handwriting as distinct from print. **3** Brit. a candidate's written answers in an examination. • v. write a script for.
– ORIGIN Latin *scriptum*.

scriptural • adj. having to do with the Bible.

scripture (also **scriptures**) • n. **1** the sacred writings of Christianity contained in the Bible. **2** the sacred writings of another religion.
– ORIGIN Latin *scriptura* 'writings'.

scriptwriter • n. a person who writes a script.

scrivener /skriv-uh-ner/ • n. hist. a clerk or scribe.
– ORIGIN Old French *escrivein*.

scrofula /skrof-yuu-luh/ • n. hist. a disease with glandular swellings.
– DERIVATIVES **scrofulous** adj.
– ORIGIN Latin *scrofa* 'breeding sow' (said to be subject to the disease).

scroll • n. **1** a roll of parchment or paper for writing or painting on. **2** an ornamental design or carving resembling a partly unrolled scroll. • v. move displayed text or graphics on a computer screen in order to view different parts of them.
– ORIGIN from former *scrow* 'roll'.

scroll bar • n. a long thin section at the edge of a computer display by which material can be scrolled using a mouse.

Scrooge • n. a person who is mean with money.
– ORIGIN from Ebenezer *Scrooge*, a miser in Charles Dickens's story *A Christmas Carol*.

scrotum /skroh-tuhm/ • n. (pl. **scrota** /skroh-tuh/ or **scrotums**) the pouch of skin containing the testicles.
– DERIVATIVES **scrotal** adj.
– ORIGIN Latin.

scrounge • v. (**scrounges**, **scrounging**, **scrounged**) informal try to get (something) from others without having to pay or work for it.
– PHRASES **on the scrounge** engaged in scrounging.
– DERIVATIVES **scrounger** n.
– ORIGIN from dialect *scrunge* 'steal'.

scrub[1] • v. (**scrubs**, **scrubbing**, **scrubbed**) **1** rub hard so as to clean. **2** informal cancel or abandon. • n. an act of scrubbing.
– ORIGIN prob. from German or Dutch *schrobben*, *schrubben*.

scrub[2] • n. **1** vegetation consisting mainly of brushwood or stunted trees. **2** land covered with such vegetation.
– DERIVATIVES **scrubby** adj.
– ORIGIN from **SHRUB**.

scrubber • n. **1** a brush for scrubbing. **2** Brit. informal, derog. a woman who has many brief sexual relationships.

scruff[1] • n. the back of a person's or animal's neck.
– ORIGIN from dialect *scuff*.

scruff[2] • n. Brit. informal a scruffy person.
– ORIGIN from **SCURF**.

scruffy • adj. (**scruffier**, **scruffiest**) shabby and untidy or dirty.

scrum • n. **1** Rugby a formation of players in which the forwards of each team push against each other with heads down and the ball is thrown in. **2** Brit. informal a disorderly crowd.
– ORIGIN from **SCRUMMAGE**.

scrummage • n. = **SCRUM**.
– ORIGIN from **SCRIMMAGE**.

scrummy • adj. informal delicious.
– ORIGIN from **SCRUMPTIOUS**.

scrump • v. Brit. informal steal (fruit) from an orchard or garden.
– ORIGIN from dialect, 'withered apple'.

scrumptious • adj. informal extremely delicious or attractive.
– ORIGIN unknown.

scrumpy • n. Brit. rough strong cider, as made in the West Country of England.

scrunch • v. **1** make a loud crunching noise. **2** crush or squeeze into a tight mass. • n. a loud crunching noise.

scruple • n. a feeling of doubt as to whether an action is morally right. • v. (**scruples**, **scrupling**, **scrupled**) (**not scruple to do**) not hesitate to do (something), even if it may be wrong.
– ORIGIN Latin *scrupus* 'anxiety'.

scrupulous • adj. **1** very careful and thorough. **2** very concerned to avoid doing wrong.
– DERIVATIVES **scrupulously** adv.

scrutineer • n. Brit. a person who ensures that an election is organized correctly.

scrutinize (also **scrutinise**) • v. (**scrutinizes**, **scrutinizing**, **scrutinized**) examine closely and thoroughly.

scrutiny • n. (pl. **scrutinies**) close and critical examination.
– ORIGIN Latin *scrutinium*.

scuba /skoo-buh/ • n. an aqualung.
– ORIGIN acronym from *self-contained underwater breathing apparatus*.

scuba-diving • n. the sport or pastime of swimming underwater using a scuba.

scud • v. (**scuds**, **scudding**, **scudded**) move fast because driven by the wind
– ORIGIN uncertain.

scuff • v. **1** scrape (a shoe or other object) against something. **2** mark by scuffing. **3** drag (one's feet) when walking. • n. a mark made by scuffing.

scuffle • n. a short, confused fight or struggle. • v. (**scuffles**, **scuffling**, **scuffled**) engage in a scuffle.
– ORIGIN prob. Scandinavian.

scull • n. **1** each of a pair of small oars used by a single rower. **2** an oar placed over the back of a boat to propel it with a side to side motion. **3** a light, narrow boat propelled with a scull or a pair of sculls. • v. propel a boat with sculls.
– DERIVATIVES **sculler** n.
– ORIGIN unknown.

scullery • n. (pl. **sculleries**) a small room at the back of a house, used for washing dishes and other dirty household work.
– ORIGIN Old French *escuelerie*.

scullion /skul-li-uhn/ • n. hist. a servant who did the most menial kitchen tasks.
– ORIGIN perh. from **SCULLERY**.

sculpt • v. make by carving stone or wood.

S

sculptor ● n. (fem. **sculptress**) an artist who makes sculptures.

sculpture ● n. **1** the art of making three-dimensional figures and shapes, by carving stone or wood or casting metal. **2** a work of such a kind. ● v. (**sculptures**, **sculpturing**, **sculptured**) **1** make by sculpting. **2** (**sculptured**) having strong, smooth curves.
– DERIVATIVES **sculptural** adj.
– ORIGIN Latin *sculpere* 'carve'.

scum ● n. **1** a layer of dirt or froth on the surface of a liquid. **2** informal a worthless person or group of people.
– DERIVATIVES **scummy** adj.
– ORIGIN German or Dutch *schūm*.

scumbag ● n. informal an unpleasant person.

scupper[1] ● n. a hole in a ship's side to allow water to run away from the deck.
– ORIGIN perh. from Old French *escopir* 'to spit'.

scupper[2] ● v. (**scuppers**, **scuppering**, **scuppered**) esp. Brit. **1** sink (a ship) deliberately. **2** informal prevent from working or succeeding.
– ORIGIN unknown.

scurf ● n. flakes on the surface of the skin, occurring as dandruff.
– ORIGIN Old English, 'cut to shreds'.

scurrility ● n. (pl. **scurrilities**) the quality of being insulting and abusive.

scurrilous /skur-ri-luhss/ ● adj. insulting and abusive and likely to damage a person's reputation.
– ORIGIN Latin *scurrilus*.

scurry ● v. (**scurries**, **scurrying**, **scurried**) move hurriedly with short quick steps. ● n. a situation of hurried and confused movement.
– ORIGIN from HURRY.

scurvy ● n. a disease caused by a lack of vitamin C, characterized by bleeding gums and the opening of previously healed wounds.
– ORIGIN from SCURF.

scut ● n. the short tail of a hare, rabbit, or deer.
– ORIGIN unknown.

scutter ● v. (**scutters**, **scuttering**, **scuttered**) esp. Brit. move hurriedly with short steps.
– ORIGIN perh. from SCUTTLE[2].

S

scuttle[1] ● n. a metal container with a lid and a handle, used to store coal for a domestic fire.
– ORIGIN Latin *scutella* 'dish'.

scuttle[2] ● v. (**scuttles**, **scuttling**, **scuttled**) run hurriedly or secretively with short quick steps.
– ORIGIN prob. from SCUD.

scuttle[3] ● v. (**scuttles**, **scuttling**, **scuttled**) **1** sink (one's own ship) deliberately. **2** deliberately cause (a scheme) to fail.
– ORIGIN perh. from Spanish *escotilla* 'hatchway'.

scuzzy ● adj. informal, esp. N. Amer. dirty and unpleasant.
– ORIGIN prob. from *disgusting*.

Scylla E
/sil-luh/ Gk Myth. a female sea monster who devoured sailors when they tried to navigate the narrow channel between her cave and the whirlpool Charybdis.

scythe ● n. a tool used for cutting crops such as grass or corn, with a long curved blade at the end of a long pole. ● v. (**scythes**, **scything**, **scythed**) **1** cut with a scythe. **2** move through rapidly and forcefully.
– ORIGIN Old English.

Scythia E
/*sith*-i-uh/ an ancient region of SE Europe and Asia. The Scythian empire, which existed between the 8th and 2nd centuries BC, was centred on the northern shores of the Black Sea.
– DERIVATIVES **Scythian** adj. & n.

SDLP ● abbrev. (in Northern Ireland) Social Democratic and Labour Party.

SE ● abbrev. **1** south-east. **2** south-eastern.

sea ● n. **1** the large continuous area of salt water that surrounds the land masses of the earth. **2** a particular area of this. **3** a vast expanse or quantity: *a sea of faces*.
– PHRASES **at sea 1** sailing on the sea. **2** confused; uncertain.
– ORIGIN Old English.

sea anemone ● n. a sea creature with a tube-shaped body which bears a ring of stinging tentacles around the mouth.

sea bass ● n. a sea fish resembling the freshwater perch.

seabed ● n. the ground under the sea.

seabird ● n. a bird that lives near the sea.

seaboard ● n. a region bordering the sea.

Seaborg E
/see-borg/, Glenn (Theodore) (1912–99), American nuclear chemist. During 1940–58 Seaborg and his colleagues discovered nine of the transuranic elements (plutonium to nobelium).

seaborgium /see-borg-i-uhm/ ● n. a very unstable chemical element made by high-energy atomic collisions.
– ORIGIN named after Glenn SEABORG.

sea change ● n. a great or remarkable transformation.
– ORIGIN from Shakespeare's *Tempest*.

sea cow ● n. a manatee.

sea dog ● n. informal an old or experienced sailor.

seafaring ● adj. travelling by sea. ● n. travel by sea.
– DERIVATIVES **seafarer** n.

seafood ● n. shellfish and sea fish as food.

seafront ● n. the part of a coastal town next to and facing the sea.

seagoing ● adj. **1** (of a ship) suitable for voyages on the sea. **2** relating to sea travel.

seagull ● n. a gull.

sea horse ● n. a small sea fish with an upright posture and a head and neck suggestive of a horse.

seal[1] ● n. **1** a device or substance used to join two things together or to prevent fluid passing through something. **2** a piece of wax with a design stamped into it, attached to a document as a guarantee that it is genuine. **3** a confirmation or guarantee: *the scheme has the government's seal of approval*. ● v. **1** fasten or close securely. **2** (**seal off**) isolate (an area) by preventing entrance to and exit from it. **3** apply a coating to (a surface) to prevent fluid passing through it. **4** make definite;

conclude.
– ORIGIN Old French *seel*.

seal[2] ● n. a water-dwelling mammal with flippers and a streamlined body.
– ORIGIN Old English.

sealant ● n. material used to make something airtight or watertight.

sea level ● n. the level of the sea's surface, used in calculating the height of geographical features.

sealing wax ● n. a mixture of shellac and rosin with turpentine, used to make seals.

sea lion ● n. a large seal of the Pacific Ocean, the male of which has a mane on the neck and shoulders.

seam ● n. **1** a line where two pieces of fabric are sewn together. **2** a line where the edges of two pieces of wood or other material touch each other. **3** an underground layer of a mineral such as coal or gold.
– ORIGIN Old English.

seaman ● n. a sailor, especially one below the rank of officer.

seamed ● adj. having a seam or seams: *seamed stockings*.

sea mile ● n. a nautical mile.

seamless ● adj. smooth and without seams or obvious joins.
– DERIVATIVES **seamlessly** adv.

seamstress ● n. a woman who sews, especially as a job.

seamy ● adj. (**seamier**, **seamiest**) immoral and unpleasant; sordid.

Seanad E
/shan-uhd/ the upper House of Parliament in the Republic of Ireland.

seance /say-onss/ ● n. a meeting at which people attempt to make contact with the dead.
– ORIGIN French.

Sea of Azov, Sea of Galilee, etc. E
see **AZOV, SEA OF**; **GALILEE, SEA OF**, etc.

seaplane ● n. an aircraft with floats or skis instead of wheels, designed to land on and take off from water.

seaport ● n. a town or city with a harbour for seagoing ships.

sear ● v. **1** burn or scorch with a sudden intense heat. **2** (of pain) be experienced as a sudden burning sensation.
– ORIGIN Old English.

search ● v. **1** try to find something by looking carefully and thoroughly. **2** examine (something) thoroughly in order to find something or someone. **3** (**searching**) investigating very deeply: *searching questions*. ● n. an act of searching.
– PHRASES **search me!** informal I do not know.
– DERIVATIVES **searchable** adj. **searcher** n.
– ORIGIN Old French *cerchier*.

search engine ● n. Computing a program for finding data, files, or documents on a database or network.

searchlight ● n. a powerful outdoor electric light with a movable beam.

search party ● n. a group of people organized to look for someone or something.

search warrant ● n. a legal document authorizing a police officer or other official to enter and search premises.

sea salt ● n. salt produced by the evaporation of seawater.

seascape ● n. a view or picture of an expanse of sea.

seashell ● n. the shell of a marine mollusc.

seashore ● n. an area of sandy or rocky land next to the sea.

seasick ● adj. suffering from nausea caused by the motion of a ship at sea.
– DERIVATIVES **seasickness** n.

seaside ● n. a beach area or holiday resort.

season ● n. **1** each of the four divisions of the year (spring, summer, autumn, and winter) marked by particular weather and daylight hours. **2** a period of the year with particular weather, or when a particular activity is done: *the cricket season*. ● v. **1** add salt, herbs, or spices to (food). **2** make more interesting. **3** keep (wood) so as to dry it for use as timber. **4** (**seasoned**) experienced: *a seasoned traveller*.
– PHRASES **in season 1** (of fruit, vegetable, etc.) plentiful and ready to eat. **2** (of a female mammal) ready to mate.
– ORIGIN Old French *seson*.

seasonable ● adj. usual for or appropriate to a particular season.

seasonal ● adj. **1** relating to or typical of a particular season of the year. **2** changing according to the season: *seasonal rainfall*.
– DERIVATIVES **seasonally** adv.

seasoning ● n. salt, herbs, or spices added to food to improve the flavour.

season ticket ● n. a ticket allowing travel within a particular period or admission to a series of events.

seat ● n. **1** a thing made or used for sitting on. **2** the part of a chair for sitting on. **3** a sitting place for a passenger in a vehicle or for a member of an audience. **4** a person's buttocks. **5** esp. Brit. a place in an elected parliament or council. **6** Brit. a parliamentary constituency. **7** a site or location. **8** a large country house belonging to an aristocratic family. ● v. **1** arrange for (someone) to sit somewhere. **2** (**seat oneself** or **be seated**) sit down. **3** (of a place) have enough seats for.
– ORIGIN Old Norse.

seat belt ● n. a belt used to secure someone in the seat of a motor vehicle or aircraft.

Seattle E
/see-at-t'l/ a port and industrial city in the state of Washington.

sea urchin ● n. a sea animal which has a shell covered in spines.

sea wall ● n. a wall built to prevent the sea advancing on to an area of land.

seaweed ● n. large algae growing in the sea or on rocks at the edge of the sea.

seaworthy ● adj. (of a boat) in a good enough condition to sail on the sea.

sebaceous /si-bay-shuhss/ ● adj. tech. relating to or producing oil or fat.
– ORIGIN Latin *sebaceus*.

Sebastian, St E
(late 3rd century), Roman martyr. According to legend he was shot by archers, recovered, and was then clubbed to death. Feast day, 20 January.

Sebastopol E
/si-**bass**-tuh-pol/ a fortress and naval base in Ukraine, near the southern tip of the Crimea. It was subjected to a year-long siege during the Crimean War, eventually falling to Anglo-French forces in September 1855.

sec[1] ● **abbrev.** secant.

sec[2] ● **n.** informal a very short time.

secant /**see**-kuhnt, **sek**-uhnt/ ● **n.** **1** Math. (in a right-angled triangle) the ratio of the hypotenuse to the shorter side adjacent to an acute angle. **2** Geom. a straight line that cuts a curve in two or more parts.
– ORIGIN Latin *secare* 'to cut'.

secateurs /sek-uh-**terz**, **sek**-uh-terz/ ● **pl. n.** Brit. a pair of pruning clippers for use with one hand.
– ORIGIN French, 'cutters'.

secede /si-**seed**/ ● **v.** (**secedes, seceding, seceded**) withdraw formally from a federation of states or a political or religious organization.
– ORIGIN Latin *secedere* 'withdraw'.

secession /si-**sesh**-uhn/ ● **n.** the action of seceding.

secluded ● **adj.** **1** (of a place) sheltered and private. **2** not having much contact with other people.
– ORIGIN Latin *secludere* 'keep away from others'.

seclusion ● **n.** the state of being private and away from other people.

second[1] /**sek**-uhnd/ ● **ordinal number** **1** that is number two in a sequence; 2nd. **2** lower in position, rank, or importance. **3** (**seconds**) goods of less than perfect quality. **4** (**seconds**) informal a second helping of food at a meal. **5** secondly. **6** a person assisting a person fighting in a duel or boxing match. **7** Brit. a place in the second highest grade in an examination for a degree. ● **v.** **1** formally support (a nomination or resolution) before adoption or further discussion. **2** express agreement with.
– ORIGIN Latin *secundus*.

second[2] /**sek**-uhnd/ ● **n.** **1** the unit of time in the SI system, equal to one-sixtieth of a minute. **2** informal a very short time. **3** (also **arc second** or **second of arc**) a measurement of an angle equal to one sixtieth of a minute.
– ORIGIN from Latin *secunda minuta* 'second minute'.

second[3] /si-**kond**/ ● **v.** Brit. temporarily move (a worker) to another position or role.
– DERIVATIVES **secondment** n.
– ORIGIN from French *en second* 'in the second rank (of officers)'.

secondary ● **adj.** **1** coming after or less important than something primary. **2** relating to education for children from the age of eleven to sixteen or eighteen.
– DERIVATIVES **secondarily** adv.

secondary sexual characteristics ● **pl. n.** physical characteristics developed at puberty which distinguish between the sexes but are not involved in reproduction.

second best ● **adj.** next after the best. ● **n.** a less good alternative.

second class ● **n.** **1** a set of people or things grouped together as the second best. **2** the second-best accommodation in an aircraft, train, or ship. **3** Brit. the second-highest division in the results of the examinations for a university degree. ● **adj. & adv.** relating to the second class.

Second Coming ● **n.** (in Christian belief) the expected return of Christ to Earth at the Last Judgement.

second-degree ● **adj.** Med. (of burns) that cause blistering but not permanent scars.

second-guess ● **v.** predict (someone's actions or thoughts) by guesswork.

second-hand ● **adj. & adv.** **1** (of goods) having had a previous owner. **2** learned from others rather than from one's own experience.

secondly ● **adv.** in the second place; second.

second name ● **n.** Brit. a surname.

second nature ● **n.** a habit that has become instinctive.

second person ● **n.** see **PERSON** (sense 3).

second-rate ● **adj.** of poor quality.

second sight ● **n.** the supposed ability to sense future or distant events.

second string ● **n.** an alternative resource or course of action in case another one fails.

second thoughts ● **pl. n.** a change of opinion or decision reached after reconsideration.

second wind ● **n.** fresh energy enabling one to continue with an activity after being tired.

Second World War E
a war (1939–45) in which the Axis Powers (Germany, Italy, and Japan) were defeated by an alliance eventually including the United Kingdom and its dominions, the Soviet Union, and the United States.

secret ● **adj.** **1** kept from or not known by others. **2** fond of having or keeping secrets. ● **n.** **1** something secret. **2** a method of achieving something that is not generally known: *the secret of a happy marriage is compromise.* **3** something not properly understood: *the secrets of the universe.*
– DERIVATIVES **secrecy** n. **secretly** adv.
– ORIGIN Latin *secretus* 'separate'.

secret agent ● **n.** a spy acting for a country.

secretariat /sek-ri-**tair**-i-uht/ ● **n.** a governmental administrative department.

secretary ● **n.** (pl. **secretaries**) **1** a person employed to type letters, keep records, etc. **2** an administrative official of a society or other organization. **3** the chief assistant of a UK government minister.
– DERIVATIVES **secretarial** adj.
– ORIGIN Latin *secretarius* 'confidential officer'.

secretary bird ● **n.** a long-legged African bird of prey, with a crest resembling a quill pen stuck behind the ear.

Secretary General ● **n.** (pl. **Secretaries General**) the principal administrator of some organizations.

Secretary of State ● **n.** **1** (in the UK) the head of a major government department. **2** (in the US) the head of the State Department, responsible for foreign affairs.

secrete[1] /si-**kreet**/ ● **v.** (**secretes, secreting, secreted**) (of a cell, gland, or organ) produce and discharge (a substance).
– DERIVATIVES **secretory** adj.

secrete[2] /si-**kreet**/ ● **v.** (**secretes, secret-**

S

ing, **secreted**) hide.
– ORIGIN from **SECRET**.

Secret Intelligence Service E
official name for **MI6**.

secretion • n. **1** a process by which substances are produced and discharged from a cell, gland, or organ. **2** a substance discharged in such a way.
– ORIGIN Latin, 'separation'.

secretive • adj. inclined to hide one's feelings and intentions or to withhold information.
– DERIVATIVES **secretively** adv.

secret police • n. a police force working in secret against a government's political opponents.

secret service • n. a government department concerned with spying.

secret society • n. an organization whose members are sworn to secrecy about its activities.

sect • n. a group of people with different religious beliefs from those of a larger group to which they belong.
– ORIGIN Latin *secta* 'following, faction'.

sectarian • adj. having to do with a sect or sects.
– DERIVATIVES **sectarianism** n.

section • n. **1** any of the parts into which something is divided or from which it is made up. **2** a distinct group within a larger body of people or things. **3** the shape resulting from cutting a solid by or along a plane. **4** a representation of the internal structure of something as if it has been cut through. • v. divide into sections.
– DERIVATIVES **sectional** adj.
– ORIGIN Latin.

sector • n. **1** an area or part that is distinct from others. **2** a distinct part of an economy, society, or field of activity. **3** a part of a circle between two lines drawn from its centre to its circumference.
– ORIGIN Latin, 'cutter'.

secular /sek-yuu-ler/ • adj. **1** not religious or spiritual. **2** (of clergy) not subject to or bound by religious rule.
– DERIVATIVES **secularism** n.
– ORIGIN Latin *saecularis* 'relating to an age or period'.

secure • adj. **1** certain to remain safe. **2** fixed or fastened so as not to give way, become loose, or be lost. **3** feeling free from fear or anxiety. • v. (**secures**, **securing**, **secured**) **1** protect against danger or threat. **2** fix or fasten in a secure way. **3** succeed in obtaining.
– DERIVATIVES **securely** adv.
– ORIGIN Latin *securus*.

security • n. (pl. **securities**) **1** the state of being or feeling secure. **2** the safety of a state or organization. **3** a valuable item given as a guarantee that one will repay a loan. **4** a certificate proving that one owns stocks or bonds.

Security Council E
a permanent body of the United Nations seeking to maintain peace and security. It consists of fifteen members, of which five (China, France, the UK, the US, and Russia) are permanent and have the power of veto.

Security Service E
official name for **MI5**.

sedan /si-dan/ • n. **1** hist. an enclosed chair carried between two horizontal poles. **2** N. Amer. a car for four or more people.
– ORIGIN perh. from Latin *sella* 'saddle'.

sedate[1] • adj. **1** calm and unhurried. **2** respectable and rather dull.
– DERIVATIVES **sedately** adv.
– ORIGIN Latin *sedare* 'settle'.

sedate[2] • v. (**sedates**, **sedating**, **sedated**) put (someone) under sedation.

sedation • n. the administering of a sedative drug to calm someone or to make them sleep.
– ORIGIN Latin.

sedative • adj. making someone calm or sleepy. • n. a sedative drug.

sedentary /sed-uhn-tri/ • adj. **1** sitting, seated. **2** tending to sit down a lot; taking little exercise. **3** tending to stay in the same place for much of the time.
– ORIGIN Latin *sedentarius*.

sedge • n. a grass-like plant with triangular stems and small flowers, growing in wet ground.
– ORIGIN Old English.

Sedgemoor, Battle of E
a battle fought in 1685 at Sedgemoor in Somerset, at which the forces of the rebel Duke of Monmouth were decisively defeated by James II's troops.

sediment • n. **1** matter that settles to the bottom of a liquid. **2** Geol. material carried in particles by water or wind and deposited on land or the seabed.
– ORIGIN Latin *sedimentum* 'settling'.

sedimentary • adj. (of rock) that has formed from sediment.

sedition • n. actions or speech urging rebellion against the authority of a state or ruler.
– DERIVATIVES **seditious** adj.
– ORIGIN Latin.

seduce • v. (**seduces**, **seducing**, **seduced**) **1** persuade to do something unwise. **2** tempt into sexual activity.
– DERIVATIVES **seducer** n. **seduction** n. **seductress** n.
– ORIGIN Latin *seducere* 'lead aside'.

seductive • adj. tempting and attractive.
– DERIVATIVES **seductively** adv.

sedulous /sed-yuu-luhss/ • adj. showing dedication and great care.
– DERIVATIVES **sedulously** adv.
– ORIGIN Latin *sedulus* 'zealous'.

sedum /see-duhm/ • n. a plant of a large group having fleshy leaves.
– ORIGIN Latin.

see[1] • v. (**sees**, **seeing**, **saw**; past part. **seen**) **1** become aware of with the eyes. **2** experience or witness. **3** work out after thinking or from information: *I saw that he was right.* **4** think of in a particular way. **5** meet (someone one knows) socially or by chance. **6** meet regularly as a boyfriend or girlfriend. **7** consult (a specialist or professional). **8** give an interview or consultation to. **9** guide or lead to a place: *don't bother seeing me out.*
– PHRASES **see off** go with (a person who is leaving) to their point of departure. **see through** **1** carry on with (an undertaking)

S

until it is completed. **2** realize the true nature of. **see to 1** deal with. **2** ensure that.
– ORIGIN Old English.

see² ● **n.** the district or position of a bishop or archbishop.
– ORIGIN Latin *sedes* 'seat'.

seed ● **n. 1** a small object produced by a flowering plant that is capable of developing into another such plant. **2** the beginning of a feeling, process, or condition. **3** archaic a man's semen. **4** any of the stronger competitors in a sports tournament who have been kept apart from playing each other in the early rounds. ● **v. 1** sow (land) with seeds. **2** remove the seeds from. **3** (**be seeded**) make (a competitor) a seed in a tournament.
– ORIGIN Old English.

seedbed ● **n.** a bed of fine soil in which seeds are grown.

seed leaf ● **n.** a cotyledon.

seedling ● **n.** a young plant raised from seed.

seed money ● **n.** money provided to start up a project.

seedy ● **adj.** (**seedier**, **seediest**) unpleasant because dirty or immoral.
– DERIVATIVES **seediness** n.

Seeger E
/see-ger/, Pete (b.1919), American folk musician and songwriter, a major figure in the American folk revival. His songs include 'Where Have All the Flowers Gone?'.

seeing ● **conj.** because; since.

seek ● **v.** (**seeks**, **seeking**, **sought**) **1** try to find or obtain. **2** (**seek out**) search for and find. **3** (**seek to do**) try or want to do. **4** ask for.
– DERIVATIVES **seeker** n.
– ORIGIN Old English.

seem ● **v. 1** give the impression of being. **2** (**cannot seem to do**) be unable to do, despite having tried.
– ORIGIN Old Norse, 'appropriate'.

seeming ● **adj.** appearing to be real or true; apparent.

seemly ● **adj.** respectable or in good taste.
– ORIGIN Old Norse, 'fitting'.

seen past part. of **SEE¹**.

seep ● **v.** (of a liquid) flow or leak slowly through a substance.
– ORIGIN perh. from Old English, 'to soak'.

S

seepage /see-pij/ ● **n.** the slow escape of a liquid or gas through a material.

seer /*rhymes with* beer/ ● **n.** a person supposedly able to see visions of the future.

seersucker ● **n.** a fabric with a puckered surface.
– ORIGIN from Persian, 'milk and sugar' (with reference to the stripes of the fabric).

see-saw ● **n.** a long plank balanced on a fixed support, on each end of which children sit and move up and down by pushing the ground with their feet. ● **v.** repeatedly change between two states or positions.
– ORIGIN from **SAW¹**.

seethe ● **v.** (**seethes**, **seething**, **seethed**) **1** (of a liquid) boil or churn as if boiling. **2** be filled with great but unexpressed anger. **3** be crowded with people or things.
– ORIGIN Old English.

see-through ● **adj.** transparent or semi-transparent.

segment ● **n.** /seg-muhnt/ **1** each of the parts into which something is divided. **2** Geom. a part of a circle cut off by a chord, or a part of a sphere cut off by a plane. ● **v.** /seg-**ment**/ divide into segments.
– DERIVATIVES **segmental** adj. **segmentation** n.
– ORIGIN Latin *segmentum*.

Segovia E
/si-**goh**-vi-uh/, Andrés (1893–1987), Spanish guitarist and composer, the leading figure in the revival of the guitar as a classical instrument.

segregate /seg-ri-gayt/ ● **v.** (**segregates**, **segregating**, **segregated**) **1** set apart from the rest or from each other. **2** separate along racial, sexual, or religious lines.
– ORIGIN Latin *segregare* 'separate from the flock'.

segregation ● **n. 1** the action of segregating. **2** the enforced separation of different racial groups in a place.

segue /seg-way/ ● **v.** (**segues**, **seguing**, **segued**) (in music and film) move without interruption from one song or scene to another. ● **n.** an instance of this.
– ORIGIN Italian, 'follows'.

Seine E
/sayn/ a river of northern France. Rising north of Dijon, it flows north-westwards through Paris to the English Channel.

seine /*rhymes with* rain/ ● **n.** a fishing net which hangs vertically in the water with floats at the top and weights at the bottom.
– ORIGIN Greek *sagēnē*.

seismic /syz-mik/ ● **adj. 1** having to do with earthquakes. **2** very great in size or effect: *seismic pressures affecting American society.*
– DERIVATIVES **seismically** adv.
– ORIGIN Greek *seismos* 'earthquake'.

seismograph /syz-muh-grahf/ ● **n.** an instrument that measures and records details of earthquakes.

seismology /syz-**mol**-uh-ji/ ● **n.** the branch of science concerned with earthquakes.
– DERIVATIVES **seismologist** n.

seize ● **v.** (**seized**, **seizing**, **seized**) **1** take hold of suddenly and forcibly. **2** take possession of by force. **3** (of the police or another authority) officially take possession of. **4** take (an opportunity) eagerly and decisively. **5** (**seize on/upon**) take eager advantage of. **6** (often **seize up**) (of a machine or part) become jammed.
– ORIGIN from Latin *ad proprium sacire* 'claim as one's own'.

seizure ● **n. 1** the action of seizing. **2** a stroke or an epileptic fit.

seldom ● **adv.** not often.
– ORIGIN Old English.

select ● **v.** carefully choose as being the best or most suitable. ● **adj. 1** carefully chosen as being among the best. **2** used by or made up of wealthy or sophisticated people.
– DERIVATIVES **selectable** adj.
– ORIGIN Latin *seligere* 'choose'.

select committee ● **n.** a small parliamentary committee appointed for a special purpose.

selection ● **n. 1** the action of selecting. **2** a

number of selected things. **3** a range of things from which a choice may be made.

selective • adj. **1** having to do with selection. **2** tending to choose carefully. **3** (of a process or agent) affecting some things and not others.
– DERIVATIVES **selectively** adv. **selectivity** n.

selector • n. **1** a person appointed to select a team in a sport. **2** a device for selecting a particular function of a machine.

selenium /si-lee-ni-uhm/ • n. a grey crystalline non-metallic chemical element with semiconducting properties.
– DERIVATIVES **selenide** n.
– ORIGIN Greek *selēnē* 'moon'.

Seles E
/sel-ess/, Monica (b.1973), American tennis player, born in Yugoslavia. In 1990 she became the youngest woman to win a grand slam singles title, the French Open. She was stabbed by a fan of Steffi Graf in 1993, but later resumed her career.

self • n. (pl. **selves**) **1** a person's essential being that distinguishes them from others. **2** a person's particular nature or personality: *he was back to his old self.* • pron. (pl. **selves**) oneself.
– ORIGIN Old English.

self- • comb. form having to do with, to, or by oneself or itself: *self-adhesive.*

self-absorption • n. obsession with one's own emotions, interests, or situation.
– DERIVATIVES **self-absorbed** adj.

self-abuse • n. **1** behaviour which causes damage or harm to oneself. **2** euphem. masturbation.

self-addressed • adj. (of an envelope) bearing one's own address.

self-adhesive • adj. sticking without requiring moistening.

self-appointed • adj. having taken up a job or title without the approval of others.

self-assembly • n. the construction of a piece of furniture from materials sold in kit form.

self-assertion • n. confidence in expressing one's views.

self-assessment • n. **1** assessment of oneself or one's performance in relation to a set standard. **2** one's own calculation of how much tax one owes.

self-assurance • n. confidence in one's own abilities or character.
– DERIVATIVES **self-assured** adj.

self-awareness • n. conscious knowledge of one's own character, feelings, etc.
– DERIVATIVES **self-aware** adj.

self-catering • adj. Brit. (of a holiday or accommodation) offering facilities for people to cook their own meals.

self-centred • adj. obsessed with oneself and one's affairs.

self-confessed • adj. openly admitting to having certain qualities: *a self-confessed chocoholic.*

self-confidence • n. trust in one's abilities, qualities, and judgement.
– DERIVATIVES **self-confident** adj.

self-congratulation • n. excessive pride in one's achievements or qualities.
– DERIVATIVES **self-congratulatory** adj.

self-conscious • adj. nervous or awkward because very aware of oneself or one's actions.
– DERIVATIVES **self-consciously** adv.

self-contained • adj. **1** complete in itself. **2** esp. Brit. (of accommodation) having its own kitchen and bathroom and its own private entrance. **3** not depending on or influenced by others.

self-control • n. the ability to control one's emotions or behaviour in difficult situations.

self-deception • n. the action or practice of deceiving oneself into believing that something false is true.

self-defeating • adj. (of an action or policy) unable to achieve the goal it is designed to bring about.

self-defence • n. the defence of oneself through physical force.

self-denial • n. the denial of one's own interests and needs.

self-deprecating • adj. modest about or critical of oneself.
– DERIVATIVES **self-deprecation** n.

self-destruct • v. explode or disintegrate automatically, having been preset.

self-destructive • adj. causing harm to oneself.

self-determination • n. **1** the process by which a country gains independence and runs its own affairs. **2** the right of a person to control their own life.

self-discipline • n. the ability to control one's feelings and overcome one's weaknesses.

self-effacing • adj. not wanting to attract attention to oneself.

self-employed • adj. working for oneself as a freelance or the owner of a business rather than for an employer.
– DERIVATIVES **self-employment** n.

self-esteem • n. confidence in one's own worth or abilities.

self-evident • adj. obvious.

self-explanatory • adj. not needing explanation; clearly understood.

self-expression • n. the expression of one's feelings or thoughts, especially in an art form.

self-fertilization (also **self-fertilisation**) • n. the fertilization of plants and some invertebrate animals by their own pollen or sperm.

self-fulfilling • adj. (of an opinion or prediction) bound to come true because people expect it to, and behave accordingly.

self-help • n. the use of one's own efforts and resources to achieve things.

self-image • n. the idea one has of one's abilities, appearance, and personality.

self-importance • n. an exaggerated sense of one's own importance.
– DERIVATIVES **self-important** adj.

self-improvement • n. the improvement of one's knowledge, status, or character by one's own efforts.

self-induced • adj. brought about by oneself.

self-indulgent • adj. indulging one's desires excessively.
– DERIVATIVES **self-indulgence** n.

self-inflicted • adj. (of a wound or other harm) inflicted on oneself by one's own actions.

self-interest • n. one's personal interest or advantage.

selfish • adj. concerned mainly with one's own needs or wishes.
– DERIVATIVES **selfishly** adv. **selfishness** n.

selfless • adj. concerned more with the needs and wishes of others than with one's own.

self-made • adj. having become successful or rich by one's own efforts.

self-opinionated • adj. having an excessively high regard for one's own opinions.

self-perpetuating • adj. able to make itself continue indefinitely without outside intervention.

self-pity • n. excessive concern with and unhappiness over one's own troubles.
– DERIVATIVES **self-pitying** adj.

self-pollination • n. the pollination of a flower by pollen from the same plant.

self-portrait • n. a portrait by an artist of himself or herself.

self-possessed • adj. calm, confident, and in control of one's feelings.
– DERIVATIVES **self-possession** n.

self-preservation • n. the protection of oneself from harm or death.

self-proclaimed • adj. proclaimed to be such by oneself, without the agreement of others: *self-proclaimed experts.*

self-raising flour • n. Brit. flour that has baking powder already added.

self-regard • n. **1** consideration for oneself. **2** vanity.
– DERIVATIVES **self-regarding** adj.

self-regulating • adj. regulating itself without intervention from outside bodies.
– DERIVATIVES **self-regulation** n. **self-regulatory** adj.

self-reliance • n. reliance on one's own powers and resources.
– DERIVATIVES **self-reliant** adj.

self-respect • n. pride and confidence in oneself.

self-restraint • n. self-control.

self-righteous • adj. certain that one is totally correct or morally superior.

self-sacrifice • n. the giving up of one's own interests or wishes in order to help others.
– DERIVATIVES **self-sacrificing** adj.

selfsame • adj. (**the selfsame**) the very same.

self-satisfied • adj. smugly pleased with oneself.
– DERIVATIVES **self-satisfaction** n.

self-seeking • adj. concerned only with one's own welfare and interests.

self-service • adj. (of a shop or restaurant) in which customers select goods and pay at a checkout.

self-serving • adj. = **SELF-SEEKING**.

self-starter • n. an ambitious person who acts on their own initiative.

self-styled • adj. using a description or title that one has given oneself: *self-styled experts.*

self-sufficient • adj. able to do or produce what one needs without outside help.
– DERIVATIVES **self-sufficiency** n.

self-taught • adj. having gained knowledge or skill by reading or experience rather than through teaching.

self-worth • n. = **SELF-ESTEEM**.

sell • v. (**sells, selling, sold**) **1** hand over in exchange for money. **2** deal in (goods or property). **3** (of goods) achieve sales. **4** (**sell out**) sell all of one's stock of something. **5** (**sell up**) sell all of one's property or assets. **6** persuade someone of the merits of. **7** (**sell out**) abandon one's principles for reasons of convenience.
– ORIGIN Old English.

Sellafield E
the site of a nuclear power station and reprocessing plant on the coast of Cumbria in NW England. In 1957 a fire there caused a serious escape of radioactive material. Former name (1947–81) **WINDSCALE**.

sell-by date • n. esp. Brit. a date marked on a product giving the date by which it should be sold.

seller • n. **1** a person who sells. **2** a product that sells in a specified way: *the book became a million-seller.*

Sellers, E
Peter (1925–80), English comic actor, best known for his role as Inspector Clouseau in the 'Pink Panther' series of films.

selling point • n. a feature of a product for sale that makes it attractive to customers.

Sellotape • n. Brit. trademark transparent adhesive tape.
– ORIGIN from **CELLULOSE** + **TAPE**.

sell-out • n. **1** the selling of an entire stock of something. **2** an event for which all tickets are sold. **3** a sale of a company. **4** a betrayal.

selvedge /sel-vij/ • n. an edge produced on woven fabric during manufacture that prevents it from unravelling.
– ORIGIN from **SELF** + **EDGE**.

selves pl. of **SELF**.

Selznick E
/selz-nik/, David O. (1902–65; full name *David Oliver Selznick*), American film producer, known for such films as *King Kong* and *Gone with the Wind.*

semantic /si-man-tik/ • adj. having to do with meaning. • (**semantics**) n. **1** the branch of linguistics concerned with the meaning or words. **2** the meaning of a word, phrase, etc.
– DERIVATIVES **semantically** adv.
– ORIGIN Greek *sēmantikos* 'significant'.

semaphore • n. a system of sending messages by holding the arms or two flags in certain positions according to an alphabetic code.
– ORIGIN French *sémaphore.*

semblance • n. the way something looks or seems.
– ORIGIN Old French *sembler* 'seem'.

semen /see-muhn/ • n. the liquid containing sperm that is produced by males.
– ORIGIN Latin, 'seed'.

semester /si-mess-ter/ • n. a half-year term in a school or university, especially in North America.
– ORIGIN Latin *semestris* 'six-monthly'.

semi • n. (pl. **semis**) informal **1** Brit. a semi-detached house. **2** a semi-final.

semi- • prefix **1** half: *semicircular.* **2** partly:

semi-conscious.
– ORIGIN Latin.

semiaquatic • **adj. 1** (of an animal) living partly on land and partly in water. **2** (of a plant) growing in very wet ground.

semi-automatic • **adj.** (of a firearm) having a mechanism for automatic loading but not for continuous firing.

semibreve /sem-i-breev/ • **n.** Brit. a musical note having the time value of four crotchets, represented by a ring with no stem.

semicircle • **n.** a half of a circle or of its circumference.
– DERIVATIVES **semicircular** adj.

semicolon /sem-i-**koh**-luhn/ • **n.** a punctuation mark (;) indicating a more noticeable pause than that indicated by a comma.

semiconductor • **n.** a solid that conducts electricity in certain conditions, but not as well as most metals do.

semi-conscious • **adj.** partially conscious.

semi-detached • **adj.** (of a house) joined to another house on one side by a common wall.

semi-final • **n.** (in sport) a match or round coming immediately before the final.
– DERIVATIVES **semi-finalist** n.

seminal • **adj. 1** (of a work, event, or idea) strongly influencing later developments. **2** referring to semen.
– ORIGIN Latin *seminalis.*

seminar /sem-i-nar/ • **n. 1** a meeting for discussion or training. **2** a small group of students at university, meeting to discuss topics with a teacher.
– ORIGIN German.

seminary /sem-i-nuh-ri/ • **n.** (pl. **seminaries**) a training college for priests or rabbis.
– ORIGIN Latin *seminarium.*

semiotics /sem-i-ot-iks/ • **n.** the study of signs and symbols.
– DERIVATIVES **semiotic** adj. **semiotician** n.
– ORIGIN Greek *sēmeiotikos* 'of signs'.

semipermeable • **adj.** (of a membrane) allowing small molecules to pass through it but not large ones.

semi-precious • **adj.** referring to minerals which can be used as gems but are less valuable than precious stones.

semiquaver • **n.** Brit. a musical note having the time value of half a quaver, represented by a large dot with a two-hooked stem.

semi-retired • **adj.** having retired from employment but continuing to work part-time.

semi-skilled • **adj.** (of work or a worker) having or needing some, but not full, training.

semi-skimmed • **adj.** Brit. (of milk) having had some of the cream removed.

Semite /see-myt/ • **n.** a member of a people speaking a Semitic language, in particular the Jews and Arabs.
– ORIGIN Greek *Sēm* 'Shem', son of Noah in the Bible, from whom these people are traditionally descended.

Semitic /si-mit-ik/ • **n.** a family of languages that includes Hebrew and Arabic. • **adj.** relating to these languages or their speakers.

semitone • **n.** the smallest interval used in classical Western music, equal to half a tone.

semolina • **n.** the hard grains left after the milling of flour, used in puddings and in pasta.
– ORIGIN Italian *semolino.*

Semtex • **n.** a plastic explosive that is easily moulded.
– ORIGIN prob. from *Semtin* (a village in the Czech Republic near the place of production) and EXPLOSIVE.

senate • **n. 1** the smaller but higher law-making body in the US, US states, France, and other countries. **2** the governing body of a university or college. **3** the state council of the ancient Roman republic and empire.
– ORIGIN Latin *senatus.*

senator • **n.** a member of a senate.
– DERIVATIVES **senatorial** adj.

send • **v.** (**sends, sending, sent**) **1** cause to go or be taken to a destination. **2** cause to move sharply or quickly. **3** cause to be in a specified state: *it nearly sent me crazy.*
– PHRASES **send down** Brit. **1** expel (a student) from a university. **2** informal sentence to imprisonment. **send for 1** order (someone) to come. **2** order by post. **send up** informal ridicule (someone) by imitating them.
– ORIGIN Old English.

send-off • **n.** a gathering of people to express good wishes to someone who is leaving.

send-up • **n.** informal an imitation of someone or something.

Seneca[1] E
/sen-i-kuh/, Lucius Annaeus (*c.*4 BC–AD 65; known as **Seneca the Younger**), Roman statesman, philosopher, and dramatist. Son of Seneca the Elder, he is known for his letters and philosophical essays.

Seneca[2] E
/sen-i-kuh/, Marcus (or Lucius) Annaeus (*c.*55 BC–*c.*39 AD; known as **Seneca the Elder**), Roman writer. He is best known for his works on rhetoric.

Senegal E
/sen-i-gawl/ a country on the coast of West Africa; capital, Dakar.
– DERIVATIVES **Senegalese** /sen-i-guh-**leez**/ adj. & n.

senescence /si-ness-uhnss/ • **n.** the deterioration of an organism with age.
– DERIVATIVES **senescent** adj.
– ORIGIN Latin *senescere* 'grow old'.

senile /see-nyl/ • **adj.** having a loss of mental abilities because of old age.
– DERIVATIVES **senility** n.
– ORIGIN Latin *senilis.*

senile dementia • **n.** severe mental deterioration in old age, with loss of memory and lack of control of bodily functions.

senior • **adj. 1** having to do with older people. **2** Brit. having to do with schoolchildren above the age of about eleven. **3** US of the final year at a university or high school. **4** (after a name) referring to the elder of two with the same name in a family: *Henry James senior.* **5** high or higher in rank or status. • **n. 1** a person who is a specified number of years older than someone else: *she was two years his senior.* **2** (in sport) a competitor of above a certain age or of the highest status.
– DERIVATIVES **seniority** n.
– ORIGIN Latin.

senior citizen • **n.** an elderly person.

Senna, Ayrton (1960–94), Brazilian motor-racing driver, who won the Formula One world championship in 1988, 1990, and 1991. He died after a crash during the San Marino Grand Prix in 1994. E

senna ● n. a laxative prepared from the dried pods of a tree of warm climates.
– ORIGIN Arabic.

Sennacherib /si-**nak**-uh-rib/ (d.681 BC) king of Assyria 705–681 BC. In 701 he put down a Jewish rebellion, besieging Jerusalem but sparing it from destruction. He also rebuilt the city of Nineveh and made it his capital. E

señor /sen-yor/ ● n. (pl. **señores** /sen-yor-ayz/) (in Spanish-speaking countries) a form of address for a man, corresponding to *Mr* or *sir*.
– ORIGIN Spanish.

señora /sen-yor-uh/ ● n. (in Spanish-speaking countries) a form of address for a woman, corresponding to *Mrs* or *madam*.

señorita /sen-yuh-ree-tuh/ ● n. (in Spanish-speaking countries) a form of address for an unmarried woman, corresponding to *Miss*.

sensation ● n. **1** a feeling resulting from something that happens to or comes into contact with the body. **2** the ability to have such feelings: *gradual loss of sensation.* **3** a vague impression: *the eerie sensation that she was being watched.* **4** a widespread reaction of interest and excitement, or a person or thing causing it.

sensational ● adj. **1** causing or trying to cause great public interest and excitement. **2** informal very impressive or attractive.
– DERIVATIVES **sensationally** adv.

sensationalism ● n. (in the media) the use of exciting or shocking stories or language at the expense of accuracy.
– DERIVATIVES **sensationalist** adj.

sensationalize (also **sensationalise**) ● v. (**sensationalizes**, **sensationalizing**, **sensationalized**) present (information) in an exaggerated way, so as to make it seem more interesting or exciting.

sense ● n. **1** one of the five faculties of sight, smell, hearing, taste, and touch, by which the body perceives things. **2** a feeling that something is the case. **3** (**sense of**) awareness of or sensitivity to: *a sense of direction.* **4** a sensible and practical attitude. **5** reason or purpose: *there's no sense in standing in the rain.* **6** a meaning or interpretation of a word or expression. ● v. (**senses**, **sensing**, **sensed**) **1** perceive by a sense. **2** be vaguely aware of.
– PHRASES **make sense** be understandable or sensible.
– ORIGIN Latin *sensus* 'faculty of feeling, thought, meaning'.

senseless ● adj. **1** unconscious: *beaten senseless.* **2** lacking meaning, purpose, or common sense.

sense organ ● n. an organ of the body which responds to external stimuli by sending impulses to the sensory nervous system.

sensibility ● n. (pl. **sensibilities**) **1** the ability to appreciate and respond to emotion or art. **2** (**sensibilities**) a person's feelings which might be easily offended or shocked.

sensible ● adj. **1** having common sense. **2** practical rather than decorative.
– DERIVATIVES **sensibly** adv.

sensitive ● adj. **1** quick to detect or be affected by slight changes. **2** appreciating the feelings of others. **3** easily offended or upset. **4** needing careful handling because controversial: *sensitive information.*
– DERIVATIVES **sensitively** adv.
– ORIGIN Latin *sensitivus.*

sensitivity ● n. (pl. **sensitivities**) **1** the state of being sensitive. **2** (**sensitivities**) a person's feelings which might be easily offended or hurt.

sensitize (also **sensitise**) ● v. (**sensitizes**, **sensitizing**, **sensitized**) make sensitive or aware.

sensor ● n. a device which detects or measures a physical property.

sensory ● adj. relating to sensation or the senses.

sensual /sen-syuu-uhl, sen-shuu-uhl/ ● adj. relating to the senses as a source of pleasure.
– DERIVATIVES **sensuality** n. **sensually** adv.

sensuous /sen-syuu-uhss, sen-shuu-uhss/ ● adj. **1** relating to the senses rather than the intellect. **2** attractive or pleasing physically.
– ORIGIN Latin *sensus* 'sense'.

sent past and past part. of **SEND**.

sentence ● n. **1** a set of words that is complete in itself, conveying a statement, question, exclamation, or command. **2** the punishment given to someone found guilty by a court. ● v. (**sentences**, **sentencing**, **sentenced**) declare the punishment decided for (an offender).
– ORIGIN Latin *sententia* 'opinion'.

sententious /sen-ten-shuhss/ ● adj. given to making pompous comments on moral issues.
– DERIVATIVES **sententiously** adv.
– ORIGIN Latin *sententia* 'opinion'.

sentient /sen-shuhnt/ ● adj. able to perceive or feel things.
– DERIVATIVES **sentience** n.
– ORIGIN Latin *sentire* 'to feel'.

sentiment ● n. **1** an opinion or feeling. **2** excessive feelings of tenderness, sadness, or nostalgia.
– ORIGIN Latin *sentimentum.*

sentimental ● adj. prone to or causing excessive feelings of tenderness, sadness, or nostalgia.
– DERIVATIVES **sentimentality** n. **sentimentally** adv.

sentimentalize (also **sentimentalise**) ● v. (**sentimentalizes**, **sentimentalizing**, **sentimentalized**) present in a sentimental way.

sentinel /sen-ti-nuhl/ ● n. a soldier or guard whose job is to stand and keep watch.
– ORIGIN Italian *sentinella.*

sentry ● n. (pl. **sentries**) a soldier stationed to keep guard or to control access to a place.
– ORIGIN perh. from **SENTINEL**.

Seoul /*rhymes with* soul/ the capital of South Korea. E

sepal /sep-uhl, see-puhl/ ● n. Bot. each of the leaf-like parts of a flower that surround the petals.
– ORIGIN Greek *skepē* 'covering'.

S

separable ● adj. able to be separated or treated separately.

separate ● adj. /sep-uh-ruht/ **1** forming a unit by itself. **2** different; distinct. ● v. /sep-uh-rayt/ (**separates**, **separating**, **separated**) **1** move or come apart. **2** stop living together as a couple. **3** divide into distinct parts. **4** remove for use or rejection. **5** form a distinction or boundary between: *six years separated the brothers.*
– DERIVATIVES **separately** adv.
– ORIGIN Latin *separare.*

separation ● n. **1** the action of separating. **2** the state in which a husband and wife remain married but live apart.

separatist ● n. a member of a group within a country who want to separate from the rest of the country to form an independent state.
– DERIVATIVES **separatism** n.

Sephardi /si-far-di/ ● n. (pl. **Sephardim** /si-far-dim/) a Jew of Spanish or Portuguese descent.
– DERIVATIVES **Sephardic** adj.
– ORIGIN Hebrew.

sepia /see-pi-uh/ ● n. **1** a reddish-brown colour, associated with early photographs. **2** a brown pigment prepared from cuttlefish ink.
– ORIGIN Greek, 'cuttlefish'.

sepoy /see-poy, si-poy/ ● n. hist. an Indian soldier serving under British or other European orders.
– ORIGIN Urdu and Persian.

seppuku /sep-poo-koo/ ● n. = HARA-KIRI.
– ORIGIN Japanese.

sepsis /sep-siss/ ● n. Med. the presence in tissues of harmful bacteria, through infection of a wound.
– ORIGIN Greek.

Sept. ● abbrev. September.

septa pl. of SEPTUM.

September ● n. the ninth month of the year.
– ORIGIN Latin *septem* 'seven' (being originally the seventh month of the Roman year).

septet /sep-tet/ ● n. a group of seven people playing music or singing together.
– ORIGIN Latin *septem* 'seven'.

septic /sep-tik/ ● adj. (of a wound or a part of the body) infected with bacteria.
– ORIGIN Greek *sēptikos.*

septicaemia /sep-ti-see-mi-uh/ (US **septicemia**) ● n. blood poisoning caused by bacteria.

septic tank ● n. a underground tank in which sewage is allowed to decompose through bacterial activity before being drained.

septuagenarian /sep-tyuu-uh-ji-nair-i-uhn/ ● n. a person who is between 70 and 79 years old.
– ORIGIN Latin *septuagenarius.*

Septuagint /sep-tyuu-uh-jint/ ● n. a Greek version of the Hebrew Bible (or Old Testament).
– ORIGIN Latin *septuaginta* 'seventy', because of the tradition that it was produced by seventy-two translators.

septum /sep-tuhm/ ● n. (pl. **septa** /sep-tuh/) a partition separating two cavities in the body, such as that between the nostrils.
– ORIGIN Latin.

septuple /sep-tyuu-p'l, sep-tyoo-p'l/ ● adj. consisting of seven parts.
– ORIGIN Latin *septem* 'seven'.

septuplet /sep-tyuu-plit, sep-tyoo-plit/ ● n. each of seven children born at one birth.

sepulchral /si-pul-kruhl/ ● adj. **1** having to do with a tomb or burial. **2** gloomy.
– DERIVATIVES **sepulchrally** adv.

sepulchre /sep-uhl-ker/ (US **sepulcher**) ● n. a stone tomb.
– ORIGIN Latin *sepulcrum* 'burial place'.

sequel ● n. **1** a book, film, or programme that continues the story of an earlier one. **2** something that takes place after or as a result of an earlier event.
– ORIGIN Latin *sequella.*

sequence ● n. **1** a particular order in which related things follow each other. **2** a set of related things that follow each other in a particular order. ● v. (**sequences**, **sequencing**, **sequenced**) arrange in a sequence.
– ORIGIN Latin *sequentia.*

sequential ● adj. following in a logical order or sequence.
– DERIVATIVES **sequentially** adv.

sequester /si-kwess-ter/ ● v. (**sequesters**, **sequestering**, **sequestered**) **1** isolate or hide away. **2** = SEQUESTRATE.
– ORIGIN Latin *sequestrare* 'commit for safekeeping'.

sequestrate /si-kwess-trayt, see-kwi-strayt/ ● v. (**sequestrates**, **sequestrating**, **sequestrated**) take legal possession of (assets) until a debt has been paid.
– DERIVATIVES **sequestration** n.

sequin ● n. a small, shiny disc sewn on to clothing for decoration.
– DERIVATIVES **sequinned** (also **sequined**) adj.
– ORIGIN first referring to a Venetian gold coin: from Italian *zecchino.*

sequoia /si-kwoy-uh/ ● n. a redwood tree.
– ORIGIN named after *Sequoya*, a Cherokee Indian scholar.

sera pl. of SERUM.

seraglio /si-rah-li-oh/ ● n. (pl. **seraglios**) **1** the women's apartments in a Muslim house or palace. **2** a harem.
– ORIGIN Italian *serraglio.*

seraph /se-ruhf/ ● n. (pl. **seraphim** /se-ruh-fim/ or **seraphs**) a type of angel associated with light and purity.
– DERIVATIVES **seraphic** adj.
– ORIGIN Hebrew.

Serbia E
a republic in the Balkans, part of Yugoslavia; capital, Belgrade.
– DERIVATIVES **Serbian** adj. & n.

serenade ● n. a piece of music sung or played in the open air at night, especially by a man under the window of his lover. ● v. (**serenades**, **serenading**, **serenaded**) entertain with a serenade.
– ORIGIN Italian *serenata.*

serendipity /se-ruhn-dip-i-ti/ ● n. the occurrence of events by chance in a fortunate way.
– DERIVATIVES **serendipitous** adj.
– ORIGIN coined by Horace Walpole in 1754, from *Serendip* (a former name for Sri Lanka).

serene ● adj. calm and peaceful.
– DERIVATIVES **serenely** adv. **serenity** n.
– ORIGIN Latin *serenus.*

S

Serengeti E
/se-ruhn-get-i/ a vast plain in Tanzania, site of the Serengeti National Park.

serf • n. (in the feudal system) an agricultural labourer who was tied to working on a particular estate.
– ORIGIN Latin *servus* 'slave'.

serge /*rhymes with* urge/ • n. a hard-wearing woollen or worsted fabric.
– ORIGIN Old French *sarge*.

sergeant /sar-juhnt/ • n. **1** a rank of non-commissioned officer in the army or air force above corporal. **2** Brit. a police officer ranking below an inspector.
– ORIGIN Old French *sergent*.

sergeant major • n. a warrant officer in the British army who assists with administrative duties.

serial • adj. **1** consisting of or taking place in a series. **2** repeatedly committing the same offence: *a serial killer.* • n. a story or play published or broadcast in regular instalments.
– DERIVATIVES **serially** adv.

serialism • n. Music a compositional technique using a fixed series of notes which is subject to change only in specific ways.
– DERIVATIVES **serialist** adj. & n.

serialize (also **serialise**) • v. (**serializes, serializing, serialized**) publish or broadcast (a story or play) in regular instalments.
– DERIVATIVES **serialization** (also **serialisation**) n.

serial number • n. an identification number showing the position of a manufactured item in a series.

series • n. (pl. **series**) **1** a number of similar or related things coming one after another. **2** a sequence of related television or radio programmes.
– ORIGIN Latin, 'row, chain'.

serious • adj. **1** needing careful consideration or action. **2** solemn or thoughtful. **3** sincere and in earnest. **4** dangerous or severe: *serious injury.*
– DERIVATIVES **seriousness** n.
– ORIGIN Latin *serius*.

seriously • adv. in a serious way or to a serious extent.

sermon • n. a talk on a religious or moral subject, especially one given during a church service.
– ORIGIN Latin, 'discourse, talk'.

sermonize (also **sermonise**) • v. (**sermonizes, sermonizing, sermonized**) give moral advice to someone.

serotonin /se-ruh-toh-nin/ • n. a compound present in blood which constricts the blood vessels and acts as a neurotransmitter.
– ORIGIN from SERUM + TONIC.

serpent • n. literary a large snake.
– ORIGIN Latin *serpere* 'to creep'.

serpentine /ser-puhn-tyn/ • adj. winding or twisting.

serrated • adj. having a jagged edge like the teeth of a saw.
– ORIGIN Latin *serratus*.

serration • n. a tooth or point of a serrated edge.

serried • adj. (of rows of people or things) standing close together.
– ORIGIN prob. from French *serré* 'close together'.

serum /seer-uhm/ • n. (pl. **sera** /seer-uh/ or **serums**) the thin liquid which separates out when blood clots.
– ORIGIN Latin, 'whey'.

servant • n. a person employed to perform domestic duties in a household or for a person.
– ORIGIN Old French.

serve • v. (**serves, serving, served**) **1** perform duties or services for. **2** be employed as a member of the armed forces. **3** spend (a period) in a job or in prison. **4** present food or drink to. **5** attend to (a customer in a shop). **6** fulfil (a purpose). **7** treat in a specified way. **8** (of food or drink) be enough for. **9** (in tennis, badminton, etc.) hit the ball or shuttlecock to begin play for each point of a game. • n. an act of serving in tennis, badminton, etc.
– PHRASES **serve someone right** be someone's deserved misfortune.
– ORIGIN Latin *servire*.

server • n. **1** a person or thing that serves. **2** a computer or computer program which manages access to a centralized resource or service in a network.

servery • n. (pl. **serveries**) Brit. a counter, hatch, or room from which meals are served.

service • n. **1** the action of serving. **2** a period of employment with an organization. **3** an act of assistance. **4** a ceremony of religious worship according to a set form. **5** a system supplying a public need such as transport, or utilities such as water. **6** a department or organization run by the state: *the probation service.* **7** (**the services**) the armed forces. **8** a set of matching crockery used for serving a particular meal: *a dinner service.* **9** (in tennis, badminton, etc.) a serve. **10** a periodic inspection and maintenance of a vehicle or other machine. • v. (**services, servicing, serviced**) **1** perform maintenance or repair work on. **2** provide a service or services for. **3** pay interest on (a debt).
– ORIGIN Latin *servitium* 'slavery'.

serviceable • adj. **1** usable or in working order. **2** useful and hard-wearing rather than attractive.

service area (also **services**) • n. esp. Brit. a roadside area where services are available to motorists.

service charge • n. a charge added to a bill for service in a restaurant.

service industry • n. a business that provides a service for a customer, but is not involved in manufacturing.

serviceman (or **servicewoman**) • n. a person serving in the armed forces.

service provider • n. Computing a company which provides access to the Internet.

service road • n. a road running parallel to a main road and giving access to houses, shops, or businesses.

service station • n. a garage selling petrol and oil and sometimes offering vehicle maintenance.

serviette • n. Brit. a table napkin.
– ORIGIN Old French.

servile • adj. **1** excessively willing to serve or please others. **2** having to do with a slave or slaves.

– DERIVATIVES **servility** n.
– ORIGIN Latin *servilis*.

serving • n. a quantity of food suitable for or served to one person.

servitude /ser-vi-tyood/ • n. **1** the state of being a slave. **2** the state of being completely controlled by someone more powerful.
– ORIGIN Latin *servitudo*.

servomechanism • n. a powered mechanism producing motion or forces at a higher level of energy than the input level, e.g. in the brakes and steering of large motor vehicles.

sesame /sess-uh-mi/ • n. a tall plant of tropical and subtropical areas, grown for its oil-rich seeds.
– ORIGIN Greek *sēsamon, sēsamē*.

session • n. **1** a period devoted to a particular activity: *a training session.* **2** a meeting of a council, court, or law-making body to conduct its business. **3** a period during which such meetings are regularly held.
– ORIGIN Latin.

session musician • n. a freelance musician hired to play on recording sessions.

set[1] • v. (**sets, setting, set**) **1** put, lay, or stand in a specified place or position. **2** bring into a specified state. **3** give someone (a task). **4** decide on or fix (a time, value, or limit). **5** establish as (an example or record). **6** adjust (a device) as required: *be careful not to set the volume too loud.* **7** prepare (a table) for a meal. **8** harden into a solid, semi-solid, or fixed state. **9** arrange (damp hair) into the required style. **10** put (a broken or dislocated bone or limb) into the correct position for healing. **11** (of the sun or moon) appear to move towards and below the earth's horizon.
– PHRASES **set about** start doing something with energy or determination. **set apart** give (someone) an air of unusual superiority. **set aside 1** temporarily stop using (land) for growing crops. **2** annul (a legal decision). **set forth 1** begin a journey. **2** describe in writing or speech. **set off 1** begin a journey. **2** cause (a bomb or alarm) to go off. **set on** (or **upon**) attack violently. **set out 1** begin a journey. **2** intend to do something. **3** arrange or display in a particular order. **set up 1** place or erect in position. **2** establish (a business, institution, etc.).
– ORIGIN Old English.

set[2] • n. **1** a number of things or people grouped together. **2** a group of people with common interests or occupations: *the literary set.* **3** the way in which something is set or positioned: *that cold set of his jaw.* **4** a radio or television receiver. **5** (in tennis and other games) a group of games counting as a unit towards a match. **6** a collection of scenery, stage furniture, etc., used for a scene in a play or film. **7** (in jazz or popular music) a sequence of songs or pieces forming part or all of a live show or recording. **8** Math. a collection of distinct entities satisfying specified conditions and regarded as a unit.
– ORIGIN partly from Old French *sette*, partly from SET[1].

set[3] • adj. **1** fixed or arranged in advance. **2** firmly fixed and unchanging. **3** having a fixed wording. **4** ready or likely to do something.

setback • n. a problem that halts progress.

set piece • n. **1** part of a novel, film, etc. that is arranged for maximum effect. **2** a carefully organized move in a team game.

set square • n. a right-angled triangular plate for drawing lines, especially at 90°, 45°, 60°, or 30°.

sett • n. the earth or burrow of a badger.
– ORIGIN from SET[2].

settee • n. a long padded seat for more than one person.
– ORIGIN perh. from SETTLE[2].

setter • n. a dog of a large long-haired breed trained to stand rigid when scenting game.

setting • n. **1** the way or place in which something is set. **2** a piece of metal in which a precious stone is fixed to form a piece of jewellery. **3** a piece of music composed for particular words. **4** (also **place setting**) a set of crockery and cutlery for one person at a meal.

settle[1] • v. (**settles, settling, settled**) **1** reach an agreement about (an argument or problem). **2** (often **settle down**) adopt a more steady or secure life. **3** make one's home in a new place. **4** become or make calmer or quieter. **5** (often **settle in**) begin to feel comfortable in a new situation. **6** sit or rest comfortably or securely. **7** pay (a debt). **8** (**settle for**) accept (something less than satisfactory). **9** sink slowly downwards.
– ORIGIN Old English, 'to seat, place'.

settle[2] • n. a wooden bench with a high back and arms.
– ORIGIN Old English.

settlement • n. **1** the action of settling. **2** an official agreement intended to settle a dispute. **3** a place where people establish a community.

Settlement, Act of E
an act of 1701 that stipulated that the British Crown should go to Sophia of Hanover (granddaughter of James I) or to her Protestant heirs, so excluding Roman Catholics, including the Stuarts, from the succession.

settler • n. a person who settles in an area.

set-to • n. (pl. **set-tos**) informal a fight or argument.

set-up • n. informal **1** the way in which something is organized. **2** an organization.

Seurat E
/ser-rah/, Georges Pierre (1859–91), French painter, who developed the technique of pointillism. His first major painting using this technique was *Sunday Afternoon on the Island of La Grande Jatte.*

seven • cardinal number one more than six; 7. (Roman numeral: **vii** or **VII**.)
– ORIGIN Old English.

Seven Hills of Rome E
the seven hills on which the ancient city of Rome was built: Aventine, Caelian, Capitoline, Esquiline, Quirinal, Viminal, and Palatine.

seventeen • cardinal number one more than sixteen; 17. (Roman numeral: **xvii** or **XVII**.)
– DERIVATIVES **seventeenth** ordinal number.

seventh • ordinal number **1** that is number seven in a sequence; 7th. **2** (**a seventh/one seventh**) each of seven equal parts into which something is divided. **3** a musical interval spanning seven consecutive notes in a scale.

Seventh-Day Adventist ● n. a member of a strict Protestant sect which preaches the imminent return of Christ to Earth and observes Saturday as the sabbath.

seventy ● cardinal number (pl. **seventies**) ten less than eighty; 70. (Roman numeral: **lxx** or **LXX**.)
– DERIVATIVES **seventieth** ordinal number.

Seven Wonders of the World E
the seven most spectacular man-made structures of the ancient world. They comprise the pyramids of Egypt; the Hanging Gardens of Babylon; the Mausoleum of Halicarnassus in present-day Turkey; the Colossus of Rhodes; the temple of Artemis at Ephesus in present-day Turkey; the statue of Zeus at Olympia in the Peloponnese; and the Pharos (lighthouse) of Alexandria.

Seven Years War E
a war (1756–63) in which Britain, Prussia, and Hanover fought against Austria, France, Russia, Saxony, Sweden, and Spain. By the end of the war Britain had become the supreme European naval and colonial power and Prussia had considerably strengthened its position in central Europe.

sever ● v. (**severs, severing, severed**) **1** cut off or divide by cutting. **2** put an end to (a connection or relationship).
– ORIGIN Old French *severer*.

several ● det. & pron. more than two but not many. ● adj. separate or respective.
– DERIVATIVES **severally** adv.
– ORIGIN Old French.

severance ● n. **1** the action of ending a connection or relationship. **2** the state of being separated or cut off.

severance pay ● n. money paid to an employee on the early ending of a contract.

severe ● adj. **1** (of something bad or difficult) very great. **2** strict or harsh. **3** very plain in style or appearance.
– DERIVATIVES **severely** adv. **severity** n.
– ORIGIN Latin *severus*.

Severn E
a river of SW Britain. Rising in central Wales, it flows north-east then south to the Bristol Channel.

S

Seville E
/suh-**vil**/ a city in southern Spain, the capital of Andalusia.

sew ● v. (**sews, sewing, sewed**; past part. **sewn** or **sewed**) join, fasten, or repair by making stitches with a needle and thread or a sewing machine.
– ORIGIN Old English.

sewage /soo-ij/ ● n. waste water and excrement conveyed in sewers.
– ORIGIN from **SEWER**.

sewer /soo-er/ ● n. an underground pipe for carrying off drainage water and waste matter.
– ORIGIN Old French *seuwiere*.

sewerage ● n. **1** the provision of drainage by sewers. **2** US = **SEWAGE**.

sewing machine ● n. a machine with a mechanically driven needle for sewing.

sewn past part. of **SEW**.

sex ● n. **1** either of the two main categories (male and female) into which humans and most other living things are divided on the basis of their reproductive functions. **2** the fact of being male or female. **3** the group of all members of either sex. **4** sexual intercourse.
– ORIGIN Latin *sexus*.

sexagenarian /seks-uh-ji-**nair**-i-uhn/ ● n. a person between 60 and 69 years old.
– ORIGIN Latin *sexaginta* 'sixty'.

sex appeal ● n. the quality of being attractive in a sexual way.

sex chromosome ● n. a chromosome concerned in determining the sex of an organism (in mammals the X and Y chromosomes).

sexism ● n. prejudice or discrimination on the basis of sex.
– DERIVATIVES **sexist** adj. & n.

sexless ● adj. **1** not sexually attractive or active. **2** neither male nor female.

sex life ● n. a person's sexual activity and relationships.

sex object ● n. a person regarded solely in terms of their sexual attractiveness or availability.

sex symbol ● n. a person famous for their sexual attractiveness.

sextant /seks-tuhnt/ ● n. an instrument used for measuring the angular distances between objects, used in navigation and surveying.
– ORIGIN first referring to the sixth part of a circle: from Latin *sextans* 'sixth part'.

sextet ● n. **1** a group of six people playing music or singing together. **2** a composition for a sextet. **3** a set of six.
– ORIGIN from Latin *sex* 'six'.

sexton ● n. a person who looks after a church and churchyard.
– ORIGIN Old French *segrestein*.

sextuple /seks-tyuu-p'l, seks-**tyoo**-p'l/ ● adj. **1** made up of six parts. **2** six times as much or as many.
– ORIGIN Latin *sextuplus*.

sextuplet /seks-tyuu-plit, seks-**tyoo**-plit/ ● n. each of six children born at one birth.

sexual ● adj. **1** relating to sexual intercourse, or to physical attraction or contact between individuals. **2** relating to the sexes. **3** (of reproduction) involving the fusion of male and female cells.
– DERIVATIVES **sexually** adv.

sexual harassment ● n. the making of unwanted sexual advances or remarks to a person, especially at work.

sexual intercourse ● n. sexual contact in which a man puts his erect penis into a woman's vagina.

sexuality ● n. (pl. **sexualities**) **1** capacity for sexual feelings. **2** a person's sexual preference.

sexual politics ● n. relations between the sexes regarded in terms of power.

sexy ● adj. (**sexier, sexiest**) **1** sexually attractive or exciting. **2** sexually aroused.
– DERIVATIVES **sexily** adv. **sexiness** n.

Seychelles E
/say-shelz/ (also **the Seychelles**) a country consisting of a group of about ninety islands in the Indian Ocean; capital, Victoria.
– DERIVATIVES **Seychellois** /say-shel-**wah**/ adj. & n.

Seymour[1], E
Jane (*c.*1509–37), third wife of Henry VIII and mother of Edward VI.

Seymour[2], E
Lynn (b.1939; born *Lynn Springbett*), Canadian ballet dancer.

SGML • abbrev. Computing Standard Generalized Mark-up Language.

Shaanxi E
/shahn-**shee**/ (also **Shensi**) a province of central China; capital, Xian. It is the site of the earliest settlements of the ancient Chinese civilizations.

shabby • adj. (**shabbier**, **shabbiest**) **1** worn out or scruffy. **2** dressed in old or worn clothes. **3** mean and unfair: *a shabby trick.*
– DERIVATIVES **shabbily** adv.
– ORIGIN Germanic.

shack • n. a roughly built hut or cabin. • v. (**shack up**) informal live with someone as a lover.
– ORIGIN perh. from a Central American Indian word.

shackle • n. **1** (**shackles**) a pair of rings connected by a chain, used to fasten a prisoner's wrists or ankles together. **2** (**shackles**) restraints: *the shackles of racism and colonialism.* **3** a metal link or loop, closed by a bolt and used to secure a chain or rope to something. • v. (**shackles**, **shackling**, **shackled**) **1** chain with shackles. **2** restrain; limit.
– ORIGIN Old English.

Shackleton, E
Sir Ernest Henry (1874–1922), British Antarctic explorer. During his second expedition Shackleton abandoned his ship when it was crushed in the ice. He and five of his crew eventually reached South Georgia after a 1,300-km (800-mile) voyage in an open boat.

shad • n. (pl. **shad** or **shads**) an edible herring-like sea fish that enters rivers to spawn.
– ORIGIN Old English.

shade • n. **1** darkness and coolness caused by shelter from direct sunlight. **2** a form of a colour, with regard to how light or dark it is. **3** a position of relative inferiority: *your bravery puts me in the shade.* **4** a variety. **5** a slight amount: *she felt a shade anxious.* **6** a lampshade. **7** (**shades**) informal sunglasses. **8** literary a ghost. • v. (**shades**, **shading**, **shaded**) **1** screen from direct light. **2** cover or reduce the light of. **3** darken or colour with parallel pencil lines or a block of colour. **4** change gradually: *outrage began to shade into dismay.*
– ORIGIN Old English.

shading • n. **1** the representation of light and shade on a drawing or map. **2** a very slight variation.

shadow • n. **1** a dark shape produced by an object coming between light rays and a surface. **2** partial or complete darkness. **3** a position of less importance: *he lived in the shadow of his father.* **4** sadness or gloom. **5** the slightest trace: *without a shadow of a doubt.* **6** a weak or less good version: *a shadow of her former self.* **7** a person secretly following and observing another. • v. **1** cast a shadow over. **2** follow and observe secretly.
– ORIGIN Old English.

shadow-boxing • n. boxing against an imaginary opponent as a form of training.

shadowy • adj. **1** full of shadows. **2** mysterious

shady • adj. (**shadier**, **shadiest**) **1** situated in shade. **2** giving shade. **3** informal of doubtful honesty or legality.

shaft • n. **1** a long, narrow part forming the handle of a tool or club, the body of a spear or arrow, etc. **2** a ray of light or bolt of lightning. **3** a long, narrow hole giving access to a mine, accommodating a lift, etc. **4** each of the pair of poles between which a horse is harnessed to a vehicle. **5** a long cylindrical rotating rod for the transmission of mechanical power in a machine. • v. informal treat harshly or unfairly.
– ORIGIN Old English.

Shaftesbury E
Anthony Ashley Cooper, 7th Earl of (1801–85), English Tory politician and social reformer. He campaigned for much of the legislation designed to improve conditions for the working class.

shag[1] • n. coarse tobacco. • adj. (of pile on a carpet) long and rough.
– ORIGIN Old English.

shag[2] • n. a greenish-black cormorant.
– ORIGIN perh. from SHAG[1].

shag[3] Brit. vulgar • v. (**shags**, **shagging**, **shagged**) have sexual intercourse with. • n. an act of sexual intercourse.
– ORIGIN unknown.

shaggy • adj. (**shaggier**, **shaggiest**) **1** (of hair or fur) long, thick, and untidy. **2** having shaggy hair or fur.

shah /*rhymes with* lah/ • n. hist. a title of the former monarch of Iran.
– ORIGIN Persian, 'king'.

shake • v. (**shakes**, **shaking**, **shook**; past part. **shaken**) **1** move quickly and jerkily up and down or to and fro. **2** remove by shaking: *they shook the sand out of their shoes.* **3** tremble with strong emotion. **4** shock or disturb. **5** get rid of or put an end to. **6** make a threatening gesture with: *he shook his fist.* • n. **1** an act of shaking. **2** informal a milkshake.
– PHRASES **in two shakes (of a lamb's tail)** informal very quickly. **no great shakes** informal not very good. **shake down** settle down. **shake hands (with someone)** clasp someone's right hand in one's own when meeting or leaving them, to congratulate them, or as a sign of agreement. **shake up** **1** stir into action. **2** make major changes to.
– ORIGIN Old English.

shaker • n. **1** a container used for mixing ingredients by shaking. **2** a container with a pierced top from which a powder is poured by shaking.

Shakespeare, E
William (1564–1616), English dramatist and poet. His plays include comedies, such as *A Midsummer Night's Dream*; historical plays, including *Henry V*; the Greek and Roman plays, such as *Julius Caesar*; tragedies, such as *Hamlet* and *King Lear*; and the group of late tragicomedies, such as *The Tempest*. He also wrote over 150 sonnets.
– DERIVATIVES **Shakespearean** (also **Shakespearian**) n. & adj.

S

shake-up ● **n.** informal a major reorganization.

shako /shay-koh, sha-koh/ ● **n.** (pl. **shakos**) a cylindrical military hat with a peak and a plume or pompom.
– ORIGIN from Hungarian *csákó süveg* 'peaked cap'.

shaky ● **adj.** (**shakier**, **shakiest**) **1** shaking; unsteady. **2** not safe or certain: *they got off to a shaky start.*
– DERIVATIVES **shakily** adv.

shale ● **n.** soft rock formed from compressed mud or clay, that can be split into thin layers.
– ORIGIN prob. from German *Schale.*

shall ● **modal verb** (3rd sing. present **shall**) **1** used with *I* and *we* to express the future tense. **2** expressing a strong statement, intention, or order. **3** used in questions to make offers or suggestions.
– ORIGIN Old English.

USAGE shall

There are traditional rules as to when to use **shall** and when to use **will**. These state that when forming the future tense, **shall** should be used with **I** and **we** (*I shall be late*), while **will** should be used with **you, he, she, it,** and **they** (*he will not be there*). However, when you want to tell someone what to do or show that you are determined, this rule is reversed: **will** is used with **I** and **we** (*I will not tolerate this*), and **shall** is used with **you, he, she, it,** and **they** (*you shall go to school*). Nowadays, people do not follow these rules so strictly and are more likely to use the shortened forms **I'll, she'll**, etc., especially when speaking.

shallot /shuh-**lot**/ ● **n.** a small vegetable of the onion family.
– ORIGIN French *eschalotte.*

shallow ● **adj. 1** having a short distance between the top and the bottom; not deep. **2** not thinking or thought out seriously: *a shallow analysis of society.* ● **n.** (**shallows**) a shallow area of water.
– DERIVATIVES **shallowly** adv. **shallowness** n.
– ORIGIN from SHOAL[2]

shalom /shuh-**lom**/ ● **exclam.** said by Jews at meeting or parting.
– ORIGIN Hebrew, 'peace'.

shalt archaic 2nd person sing. of SHALL.

sham ● **n. 1** a thing that is not as good or genuine as it seems to be: *our current free health service is a sham.* **2** a person who pretends to be something they are not. ● **adj.** not genuine; false. ● **v.** (**shams**, **shamming**, **shammed**) pretend or pretend to be: *was he ill or was he shamming?*
– ORIGIN perh. from SHAME.

shaman /shay-muhn, sha-muhn/ ● **n.** (pl. **shamans**) (among some peoples of northern Asia and North America) a person believed to be able to contact good and evil spirits.
– DERIVATIVES **shamanic** /shuh-**man**-ik/ adj. **shamanism** n.
– ORIGIN Russian.

shamble ● **v.** (**shambles**, **shambling**, **shambled**) walk in a slow, shuffling, awkward way.
– ORIGIN prob. from dialect *shamble* 'ungainly'.

shambles ● **n.** informal a state of complete disorder.
– ORIGIN first meaning 'meat market': from Latin *scamellum* 'little bench'.

shambolic ● **adj.** Brit. informal very disorganized.
– ORIGIN from SHAMBLES.

shame ● **n. 1** a feeling of embarrassment or distress arising from one's awareness that one has done something wrong or foolish. **2** loss of respect; dishonour: *the incident brought shame on his family.* **3** a cause of shame. **4** a cause for regret or disappointment: *it's a shame that he is not better known.* ● **v.** (**shames**, **shaming**, **shamed**) cause to feel ashamed.
– PHRASES **put to shame** be much better than.
– ORIGIN Old English.

shamefaced ● **adj.** showing shame.

shameful ● **adj.** causing shame.
– DERIVATIVES **shamefully** adv.

shameless ● **adj.** showing no shame: *his shameless hypocrisy.*
– DERIVATIVES **shamelessly** adv. **shamelessness** n.

Shamir E
/sha-**meer**/, Yitzhak (b.1915), Polish-born Israeli Likud statesman, Prime Minister 1983–4 and 1986–92.

shammy ● **n.** (pl. **shammies**) informal chamois leather.

shampoo ● **n. 1** a liquid soap for washing the hair. **2** a similar substance for cleaning a carpet, car, etc. **3** an act of washing with shampoo. ● **v.** (**shampoos**, **shampooing**, **shampooed**) wash or clean with shampoo.
– ORIGIN Hindi, 'to press'.

shamrock ● **n.** a clover-like plant with three leaves on each stem, the national emblem of Ireland.
– ORIGIN Irish *seamróg.*

shandy ● **n.** (pl. **shandies**) beer mixed with lemonade or ginger beer.
– ORIGIN unknown.

Shanghai E
/shang-**hy**/ a city and port on the east coast of China. It is China's most populous city.

shanghai /shang-**hy**/ ● **v.** (**shanghais**, **shanghaiing**, **shanghaied**) informal force or trick (someone) into doing something.
– ORIGIN first meaning 'force to join a ship's crew': from SHANGHAI.

shank ● **n. 1** the lower part of a person's leg. **2** the lower part of an animal's foreleg, especially as a cut of meat. **3** the shaft of a tool.
– PHRASES **Shanks's pony** (also **Shanks's mare**) one's own legs as a means of transport.
– ORIGIN Old English.

Shankar E
/**shang**-kuh/, Ravi (b.1920), Indian sitar player and composer. His recitals in the US and Europe did much to stimulate Western interest in Indian music.

Shannon E
the longest river of Ireland. It rises in County Leitrim and flows 390 km (240 miles) south and west to the Atlantic.

S

shan't • contr. shall not.
shantung /shan-tung/ • n. a type of soft silk with a coarse surface.
– ORIGIN from *Shantung* in China.
shanty[1] • n. (pl. **shanties**) a small roughly built hut.
– ORIGIN perh. from Canadian French *chantier* 'lumberjack's cabin'.
shanty[2] • n. (pl. **shanties**) a song with alternating solo and chorus, sung by sailors when working.
– ORIGIN prob. from French *chantez!* 'sing!'.
shanty town • n. a settlement in or near a town where poor people live in shanties.
shape • n. **1** the outward form of someone or something as produced by their outline. **2** a piece of material, paper, etc., made or cut in a particular form. **3** a particular condition: *the house was in poor shape.* **4** orderly or definite arrangement. • v. (**shapes**, **shaping**, **shaped**) **1** give a shape to. **2** have a great influence on: *spiritual teachings shaped by feminism.* **3** (also **shape up**) develop in a particular way.
– PHRASES **in (good) shape** in good physical condition. **out of shape 1** not having its usual or original shape. **2** in poor physical condition. **shape up** improve one's fitness, behaviour, etc. **take shape** take on a distinct form.
– DERIVATIVES **shaper** n.
– ORIGIN Old English.
shapeless • adj. lacking a definite or attractive shape.
shapely • adj. (**shapelier**, **shapeliest**) having an attractive shape.
shard • n. a sharp piece of broken pottery, glass, etc.
– ORIGIN Old English.
share • n. **1** a part of a larger amount which is divided among or contributed by a number of people. **2** any of the equal parts into which a company's wealth is divided, entitling the holder to a proportion of the profits. **3** an amount thought to be normal or acceptable: *the theory has had its share of critics.* • v. (**shares**, **sharing**, **shared**) **1** have or give a share of. **2** have or use jointly with others: *they shared a flat.* **3** (**share in**) participate in. **4** tell someone about.
– DERIVATIVES **sharer** n.
– ORIGIN Old English.
shareholder • n. an owner of shares in a company.
sharia /shuh-ree-uh/ • n. Islamic law, based on the teachings of the Koran and the traditions of Muhammad.
– ORIGIN Arabic.

Sharjah E
/shar-juh/ one of the seven member states of the United Arab Emirates; capital, Sharjah.

shark[1] • n. a large sea fish with a triangular fin on its back, many kinds of which prey on other animals.
– ORIGIN unknown.
shark[2] • n. informal a person who dishonestly obtains money from others.
– ORIGIN perh. from German *Schurke* 'worthless rogue'.
sharkskin • n. a stiff, slightly shiny synthetic fabric.

Sharma E
/shar-muh/, Shankar Dayal (b.1918), Indian statesman, President 1992–7.

Sharon E
/shuh-ron/, Ariel (b. 1928), Israeli Likud statesman, Prime Minister since 2001.

sharp • adj. **1** having a cutting or piercing edge or point. **2** tapering to a point or edge. **3** sudden and noticeable: *a sharp increase.* **4** clear and definite. **5** producing a sudden, piercing feeling. **6** quick to understand, notice, or respond. **7** quick to take advantage. **8** (of a food, taste, or smell) strong and slightly bitter. **9** (of musical sound) above true or normal pitch. **10** (of a note or key) higher by a semitone than a specified note or key: *F sharp.* • adv. **1** precisely: *at 7.30 sharp.* **2** suddenly or abruptly. • n. a musical note raised a semitone above natural pitch, shown by the sign ♯.
– DERIVATIVES **sharply** adv. **sharpness** n.
– ORIGIN Old English.
sharpen • v. make or become sharp.
– DERIVATIVES **sharpener** n.

Sharpeville massacre E
the killing of sixty-seven anti-apartheid demonstrators by security forces at Sharpeville, a black township south of Johannesburg, on 21 March 1960.

sharpish • Brit. informal quickly.
sharp practice • n. dishonest business dealings.
sharpshooter • n. a person skilled in shooting.
sharp-tongued • adj. using harsh or critical language.
sharp-witted • adj. intelligent and shrewd.
shat past and past part. of SHIT.

Shatt al-Arab E
/shat al a-ruhb/ a river of SW Asia, formed by the confluence of the Tigris and Euphrates Rivers and flowing through SE Iraq to the Persian Gulf.

shatter • v. (**shatters**, **shattering**, **shattered**) **1** break suddenly and violently into pieces. **2** damage or destroy: *the crisis will shatter their confidence.* **3** upset greatly. **4** (**shattered**) informal completely exhausted.
shave • v. (**shaves**, **shaving**, **shaved**) **1** cut the hair off one's face with a razor. **2** remove hair from (part of the body) with a razor. **3** cut (a thin slice or slices) from something. **4** reduce by a small amount. **5** pass very close to. • n. an act of shaving.
– DERIVATIVES **shaver** n.
– ORIGIN Old English.
shaven • adj. shaved.
shaving • n. a thin strip cut off a surface.

Shaw, E
(George) Bernard (1856–1950), Irish dramatist and writer. His best-known plays combine comedy with a questioning of conventional morality and thought; they include *Man and Superman*, *Pygmalion*, and *St Joan*.

shawl • n. a large piece of fabric worn by women over the shoulders or head or wrapped round a baby.
– ORIGIN Urdu and Persian.
shaykh • n. var. of SHEIKH.

she ● **pron.** (third person sing.) **1** used to refer to a woman, girl, or female animal previously mentioned or easily identified. **2** used to refer to a ship, country, or other thing thought of as female.
– ORIGIN Old English.

sheaf ● **n.** (pl. **sheaves**) **1** a bundle of grain stalks tied together after reaping. **2** a bundle of papers.
– ORIGIN Old English.

shear ● **v.** (**shears**, **shearing**, **sheared**; past part. **shorn** or **sheared**) **1** cut the wool off (a sheep). **2** cut off with scissors or shears. **3** (**be shorn of**) have (something) taken away from one. **4** break off because of a strain in the structure of something. ● **n.** a strain produced by pressure in the structure of a substance, so that each layer slides over the next.
– DERIVATIVES **shearer** n.
– ORIGIN Old English.

shears (also **a pair of shears**) ● **pl. n.** a cutting implement like very large scissors.

sheath /sheeth/ ● **n.** (pl. **sheaths** /shee*thz*, sheeths/) **1** a cover for the blade of a knife or sword. **2** a condom. **3** a close-fitting covering. **4** (also **sheath dress**) a close-fitting dress.
– ORIGIN Old English

sheathe /shee*th*/ ● **v.** (**sheathes**, **sheathing**, **sheathed**) **1** put (a knife or sword) into a sheath. **2** cover in a close-fitting or protective covering: *her legs were sheathed in black stockings.*

sheath knife ● **n.** a short knife similar to a dagger, carried in a sheath.

sheaves pl. of **SHEAF**.

shebang /shi-bang/ ● **n.** (in phr. **the whole shebang**) informal the whole thing; everything.
– ORIGIN unknown.

shebeen /shi-been/ ● **n.** a place where alcoholic drink is sold illegally.
– ORIGIN Anglo-Irish *síbín*.

shed[1] ● **n.** **1** a simple building used for storage or to shelter animals. **2** a large building, often with one or more sides open, for storing vehicles or machinery.
– ORIGIN prob. from **SHADE**.

shed[2] ● **v.** (**sheds**, **shedding**, **shed**) **1** allow (leaves, hair, skin, etc.) to fall off naturally. **2** get rid of. **3** take off (clothes). **4** give off (light). **5** accidentally drop or spill. **6** allow (something) to pour out.
– PHRASES **shed tears** cry.
– ORIGIN Old English, 'divide, scatter'.

she'd ● **contr.** she had; she would.

sheen ● **n.** a soft shine on a surface.
– ORIGIN prob. from **SHINE**.

sheep ● **n.** (pl. **sheep**) a grass-eating mammal with a thick woolly coat, kept in flocks for its wool or meat.
– PHRASES **like sheep** (of people) easily led or influenced.
– ORIGIN Old English.

sheep dip ● **n.** a liquid for cleansing sheep of parasites or preserving their wool.

sheepdog ● **n.** a breed of dog trained to guard and herd sheep.

sheepish ● **adj.** embarrassed from shame or shyness.
– DERIVATIVES **sheepishly** adv.

sheepshank ● **n.** a knot used to shorten a rope temporarily.

sheepskin ● **n.** a sheep's skin with the wool on, made into a garment or rug.

sheer[1] ● **adj.** **1** nothing but; absolute: *sheer hard work.* **2** (of a cliff, wall, etc.) vertical or almost vertical. **3** (of a fabric) very thin. ● **adv.** vertically.
– ORIGIN prob. from **SHINE**.

sheer[2] ● **v.** (**sheers**, **sheering**, **sheered**) **1** change course quickly. **2** move away from an unpleasant topic.
– ORIGIN perh. from German *scheren* 'to shear'.

sheet[1] ● **n.** **1** a large rectangular piece of cotton or other fabric, used on a bed to lie on or under. **2** a broad flat piece of metal or glass. **3** a rectangular piece of paper. **4** a wide expanse or moving mass of water, flames, etc.
– ORIGIN Old English.

sheet[2] ● **n.** a rope attached to the lower corner of a sail, to hold and adjust it.
– ORIGIN Old English, 'lower corner of a sail'.

sheeting ● **n.** material formed into or used as a sheet.

sheet music ● **n.** music published on loose sheets of paper and not bound into a book.

Sheffield E
an industrial city in northern England, a unitary council formerly in Yorkshire.

sheikh /shayk, sheek/ (also **shaykh** or **sheik**) ● **n.** **1** the leader of an Arab tribe, family, or village. **2** a leader in a Muslim community or organization.
– ORIGIN Arabic, 'old man, leader'.

sheila ● **n.** Austral./NZ informal a girl or woman.
– ORIGIN unknown.

shekel /*rhymes with* heckle/ ● **n.** the basic unit of money of modern Israel.
– ORIGIN Hebrew.

shelf ● **n.** (pl. **shelves**) **1** a flat length of wood or other rigid material, attached to a wall or forming part of a piece of furniture and used to display or store things. **2** a ledge of rock.
– PHRASES **off the shelf** taken from existing supplies, not made to order. **on the shelf** (of a woman) past an age when she might expect to be married.
– ORIGIN German *schelf*.

shelf life ● **n.** the length of time for which an item remains able to be eaten, used, or sold.

shell ● **n.** **1** the hard protective outer case of an animal such as a shellfish or turtle. **2** the outer covering of an egg, nut kernel, or seed. **3** a metal case filled with explosive, to be fired from a large gun. **4** a hollow case. **5** an outer structure or framework. **6** a light rowing boat for racing. ● **v.** **1** fire explosive shells at. **2** remove the shell or pod from. **3** (**shell out**) informal pay (an amount of money).
– ORIGIN Old English.

she'll ● **contr.** she shall; she will.

shellac /shuh-lak/ ● **n.** lac resin melted into thin flakes, used for making varnish.
– ORIGIN from **SHELL** + **LAC**.

Shelley[1], E
Mary (Wollstonecraft) (1797–1851), English writer, author of the Gothic novel *Frankenstein, or the Modern Prometheus.* She eloped with Percy Bysshe Shelley and later married him.

Shelley[2], E
Percy Bysshe (1792–1822), English poet, a leading figure of the romantic movement. His works include *Adonais*, an elegy on the death of Keats, and the lyrical drama *Prometheus Unbound*.

shellfish ● n. a water animal that has a shell and that can be eaten, such as a crab or oyster.

shell shock ● n. a mental illness that can affect soldiers who have been in battle for a long time.

shell suit ● n. a casual outfit consisting of a loose jacket and trousers with a soft lining and a shiny outer layer.

shelter ● n. **1** a place giving protection from bad weather or danger. **2** a place providing food and accommodation for the homeless. **3** protection from danger or bad weather: *he waited in the shelter of a rock.* ● v. (**shelters, sheltering, sheltered**) **1** provide with shelter. **2** find protection or take cover. **3** (**sheltered**) protected from the more unpleasant aspects of life.
– ORIGIN uncertain.

sheltered housing (also **sheltered accommodation**) ● n. Brit. accommodation for elderly or handicapped people consisting of private units with some shared facilities and a warden.

shelve ● v. (**shelves, shelving, shelved**) **1** place on a shelf. **2** decide not to continue with (a plan), either temporarily or permanently. **3** (of ground) slope downwards.

shelves pl. of SHELF.

shelving ● n. shelves.

shenanigans /shi-nan-i-guhnz/ ● pl. n. informal **1** secret or dishonest activity. **2** high spirited behaviour.
– ORIGIN unknown.

Shensi E
/shen-**shee**/ var. of SHAANXI.

shepherd ● n. a person who looks after sheep. ● v. guide or direct: *she shepherded them through the door.*
DERIVATIVES **shepherdess** n.
– ORIGIN Old English.

shepherd's pie ● n. a dish of minced meat under a layer of mashed potato.

sherbet ● n. **1** Brit. a flavoured sweet fizzing powder eaten alone or made into a drink. **2** (in Arab countries) a drink of sweet diluted fruit juices.
– ORIGIN Arabic, 'drink'.

Sheridan, E
Richard Brinsley (1751–1816), Irish dramatist and Whig politician, known for witty comedies such as *The Rivals* and *The School for Scandal*.

sheriff ● n. **1** (also **high sheriff**) (in England and Wales) the chief executive officer of the Crown in a county. **2** (in Scotland) a judge. **3** US an elected officer in a county, responsible for keeping the peace.
– ORIGIN Old English, 'shire reeve'.

Sherman, E
William Tecumseh (1820–91), American general. As chief Union commander in the west during the American Civil War, he marched his army through Georgia, crushing Confederate forces and inflicting widespread destruction.

Sherpa /sher-puh/ ● n. (pl. **Sherpa** or **Sherpas**) a member of a Himalayan people living on the borders of Nepal and Tibet.
– ORIGIN Tibetan, 'inhabitant of an Eastern country'.

sherry ● n. (pl. **sherries**) a strong wine originally from southern Spain.
– ORIGIN from Spanish *vino de Xeres* 'Xeres wine' (Xeres being the former name of the city of *Jerez de la Frontera*).

she's ● contr. she is; she has.

Shetland Islands E
a group of about 100 islands off the north coast of Scotland, forming the administrative region of Shetland; chief town, Lerwick.
– DERIVATIVES **Shetlander** n.

Shetland pony ● n. a small breed of pony with a rough coat.

Shevardnadze E
/shev-ard-**nahd**-zi/, Eduard (Amvrosievich) (b.1928), Soviet statesman and head of state of Georgia 1992–2003.

shew ● v. archaic = SHOW.

Shia /shi-uh/ ● n. (pl. **Shia** or **Shias**) **1** one of the two main branches of Islam. **2** a Muslim who follows this branch of Islam.
– ORIGIN Arabic, 'party (of Ali)'.

shiatsu /shi-at-soo/ ● n. a Japanese therapy in which pressure is applied with the hands to points on the body.
– ORIGIN Japanese, 'finger pressure'.

shibboleth /shib-buh-leth/ ● n. a long-standing belief or principle held by a group of people, often thought of as outdated: *the conflict challenged a series of military shibboleths.*
– ORIGIN Hebrew, 'ear of corn'; first meaning in English 'a word which a foreigner is unable to pronounce' (according to the Book of Judges, the word was used as a test of nationality).

shied past and past part. of SHY[2].

shield ● n. **1** a broad piece of armour held for protection against blows or missiles. **2** a sporting trophy consisting of an engraved metal plate mounted on a piece of wood. **3** a drawing or model of a shield used for displaying a coat of arms. **4** a person or thing that acts as a barrier or screen. ● v. protect or hide: *the runners were shielded from view by the tunnel.*
– ORIGIN Old English.

shift ● v. **1** move or change from one position to another. **2** transfer (blame, responsibility, etc.) to someone else. **3** Brit. informal move quickly. ● n. **1** a slight change in position or direction. **2** a period of time worked by a group of workers who start work as another group finishes. **3** a straight dress without a waist. **4** a key used to switch between two sets of characters or functions on a keyboard. **5** archaic a clever or underhand plan.
– PHRASES **shift for oneself** manage alone as best one can.
– DERIVATIVES **shifter** n.
– ORIGIN Old English, 'arrange, divide'.

shiftless ● adj. lazy and lacking ambition.

shifty ● adj. (**shiftier, shiftiest**) informal seem-

S

ing dishonest or untrustworthy.

Shiite /shee-yt/ • n. a follower of the Shia branch of Islam.

Shikoku E
/shi-**koh**-koo/ the smallest of the four main islands of Japan; capital, Matsuyama.

shillelagh /shi-**lay**-luh, shi-**lay**-li/ • n. (In Ireland) a wooden cudgel.
– ORIGIN named after the Irish town of *Shillelagh*.

shilling • n. **1** a former British coin worth one twentieth of a pound or twelve pence. **2** the basic unit of money of Kenya, Tanzania, and Uganda.
– ORIGIN Old English.

shilly-shally • v. (**shilly-shallies, shilly-shallying, shilly-shallied**) be unable to make up one's mind.
– ORIGIN from *shill I, shall I?*

Shilton, E
Peter (b.1949), English footballer. A goalkeeper, he won a record 125 England caps.

shim • n. a thin strip of material used in machinery to fill up a space between parts or reduce wear.
– ORIGIN unknown.

shimmer • v. (**shimmers, shimmering, shimmered**) shine with a soft wavering light. • n. a soft wavering light or shine.
– DERIVATIVES **shimmery** adj.
– ORIGIN Old English.

shimmy • v. (**shimmies, shimmying, shimmied**) move swiftly and smoothly.
– ORIGIN unknown.

shin • n. **1** the front of the leg below the knee. **2** a cut of beef from the lower part of a cow's leg. • v. (**shins, shinning, shinned**) (**shin up/down**) climb quickly up or down by gripping with one's arms and legs.
– ORIGIN Old English.

shindig • n. informal a large, lively party.
– ORIGIN prob. from SHIN and DIG.

shine • v. (**shines, shining, shone** or **shined**) **1** give out or reflect light. **2** direct (a torch or other light) somewhere. **3** (of a person's eyes) be bright with an emotion. **4** be very good at something. **5** (past and past part. **shined**) polish. • n. a quality of brightness.
– PHRASES **take the shine off** cause (something) to seem less good. **take a shine to** informal develop a liking for.
– ORIGIN Old English.

shiner • n. informal a black eye.

shingle[1] • n. a mass of small rounded pebbles, especially on a seashore.
– ORIGIN unknown.

shingle[2] • n. **1** a rectangular wooden tile used on walls or roofs. **2** dated a woman's short haircut, tapering from the back of the head to the nape of the neck.
– DERIVATIVES **shingled** adj.
– ORIGIN prob. from Latin *scindula* 'a split piece of wood'.

shingles • n. a disease with painful blisters forming along the path of a nerve or nerves.
– ORIGIN Latin *cingulum* 'girdle'.

Shinto /**shin**-toh/ • n. a Japanese religion involving the worship of ancestors and nature spirits.
– ORIGIN Chinese, 'way of the gods'.

shinty • n. a Scottish game resembling hockey, played with curved sticks and taller goalposts.
– ORIGIN unknown.

shiny • adj. (**shinier, shiniest**) reflecting light.

ship • n. a large boat for transporting people or goods by sea. • v. (**ships, shipping, shipped**) **1** transport on a ship or by other means. **2** (of a boat) take in (water) over the side.
– PHRASES **a sinking ship** a failing organization or project. **when one's ship comes in** when one's fortune is made.
– DERIVATIVES **shipload** n. **shipper** n.
– ORIGIN Old English.

-ship • suffix forming nouns referring to: **1** a quality or condition: *companionship*. **2** status or office: *citizenship*. **3** a skill: *workmanship*. **4** the members of a group: *membership*.
– ORIGIN Old English.

shipboard • adj. used or occurring on board a ship.

shipbuilder • n. a person or company that designs and builds ships.
– DERIVATIVES **shipbuilding** n.

Shipley, E
Jenny (b.1952; full name *Jennifer Mary Shipley*), New Zealand National Party stateswoman, Prime Minister 1997–9.

shipmate • n. a fellow member of a ship's crew.

shipment • n. **1** the action of transporting goods. **2** an amount of goods shipped.

shipping • n. **1** ships as a whole. **2** the transport of goods.

shipshape • adj. orderly and neat.

shipwreck • n. **1** the destruction of a ship at sea by sinking or breaking up. **2** a ship so destroyed. • v. (**be shipwrecked**) suffer a shipwreck.

shipwright • n. a shipbuilder.

shipyard • n. a place where ships are built and repaired.

shire /*rhymes with* fire/ • n. **1** Brit. a county in England. **2** (**the Shires**) the country areas of the English Midlands regarded as strongholds of traditional country life.
– ORIGIN Old English.

shire horse • n. a heavy powerful breed of horse, used for pulling loads.

shirk • v. avoid (work or a duty).
– DERIVATIVES **shirker** n.
– ORIGIN perh. from German *Schurke* 'scoundrel'.

shirred /*rhymes with* bird/ • adj. (of fabric) gathered by means of threads in parallel rows.
– ORIGIN unknown.

shirt • n. a garment for the upper body, with a collar and sleeves and buttons down the front.
– PHRASES **keep your shirt on** informal stay calm. **put one's shirt on** Brit. informal bet all one has on.
– ORIGIN Old English.

shirtsleeves • pl. n. (in phr. **in one's shirtsleeves**) wearing a shirt without a jacket over it.

shirtwaister • n. a dress with the bodice shaped like a shirt and a seam at the waist.

shirty • adj. (**shirtier, shirtiest**) Brit. informal

bad-tempered or annoyed.

shish kebab /shish ki-bab/ ● n. a dish of pieces of meat and vegetables cooked and served on skewers.
– ORIGIN Turkish *şiş kebap*.

shit vulgar ● v. (**shits, shitting, shitted** or **shit** or **shat**) **1** pass faeces from the body. **2** (**shit oneself**) be very frightened. ● n. **1** faeces. **2** rubbish; nonsense. **3** an unpleasant person. ● exclam. expressing disgust or annoyance.
– PHRASES **not give a shit** not care at all. **when the shit hits the fan** when the disastrous effects of something become known.
– ORIGIN Old English, 'diarrhoea'.

shite ● n. & exclam. vulgar = SHIT.

shitty ● adj. (**shittier, shittiest**) vulgar unpleasant or very bad.

Shiva E
/shee-vuh, shi-vuh/ (also **Siva**) a Hindu god associated with the powers of reproduction and dissolution.

shiver[1] ● v. (**shivers, shivering, shivered**) shake slightly from fear, cold, or excitement. ● n. a trembling movement.
– DERIVATIVES **shivery** adj.
– ORIGIN perh. from Old English, 'jaw'.

shiver[2] ● n. a splinter or fragment. ● v. (**shivers, shivering, shivered**) break into shivers.
– ORIGIN Germanic, 'to split'.

shoal[1] ● n. a large number of fish swimming together. ● v. (of fish) form shoals.
– ORIGIN prob. from Dutch *schōle* 'troop'.

shoal[2] ● n. **1** an area of shallow water. **2** a submerged sandbank that can be seen at low tide.
– ORIGIN Old English.

shock[1] ● n. **1** a sudden event or experience that causes a feeling of surprise or distress. **2** a serious medical condition associated with a fall in blood pressure, caused by loss of blood, severe injury, etc. **3** a violent shaking movement caused by an impact, explosion, or earthquake. **4** an electric shock. ● v. **1** cause (someone) to feel surprised and upset. **2** cause (someone) to feel outraged or disgusted.
– DERIVATIVES **shockproof** adj.
– ORIGIN French *choc*.

shock[2] ● n. an untidy or thick mass of hair.
– ORIGIN uncertain.

shock[3] ● n. a group of twelve sheaves of grain placed upright against each other to allow the grain to dry and ripen.
– ORIGIN perh. from Dutch or German *schok*.

shock absorber ● n. a device for absorbing jolts and vibrations on a vehicle.

shocker ● n. informal a shocking person or thing.

shock-headed ● adj. having thick, shaggy, and unkempt hair.

shocking ● adj. **1** causing shock or disgust. **2** Brit. informal very bad.
– DERIVATIVES **shockingly** adv.

shocking pink ● n. a very bright shade of pink.

Shockley, E
William (Bradford) (1910–89), American physicist. He led the group that developed the transistor in 1948.

shock therapy (also **shock treatment**) ● n. treatment of certain mental illnesses by giving electric shocks to the brain.

shock troops ● pl. n. troops trained to carry out sudden attacks.

shock wave ● n. a moving wave of very high pressure caused by explosion or by a body travelling faster than sound.

shod past and past part. of SHOE.

shoddy ● adj. (**shoddier, shoddiest**) **1** badly made or done. **2** dishonest or immoral.
– ORIGIN unknown.

shoe ● n. **1** a covering for the foot with a stiff sole, ending just below the ankle. **2** a horseshoe. **3** a socket on a camera for fitting a flash unit. ● v. (**shoes, shoeing, shod**) **1** fit (a horse) with a shoe or shoes. **2** (**be shod**) be wearing shoes of a particular kind.
– PHRASES **be** (or **put oneself**) **in another person's shoes** imagine oneself in another person's situation.
– ORIGIN Old English.

shoehorn ● n. a curved piece of metal or plastic, used for easing one's heel into a shoe. ● v. force into a space that is too small.

shoelace ● n. a cord or leather strip passed through holes or hooks on opposite sides of a shoe and pulled tight and fastened.

shoemaker ● n. a person who makes footwear as a profession.

shoestring ● n. informal (in phr. **on a shoestring**) with only a very small amount of money.

shoe tree ● n. a shaped block put into a shoe when it is not being worn to keep it in shape.

shogun /shoh-guhn/ ● n. (formerly, in Japan) a hereditary leader of the army.
– ORIGIN Japanese.

shone past and past part. of SHINE.

shook past of SHAKE.

shoot ● v. (**shoots, shooting, shot**) **1** kill or wound with a bullet or arrow. **2** fire a gun or other weapon. **3** move suddenly and rapidly. **4** direct (a glance, question, or remark) at someone. **5** (in sport) kick, hit, or throw the ball or puck in an attempt to score a goal. **6** film or photograph (a scene, film, etc.). **7** (**shooting**) (of a pain) sudden and piercing. **8** (of a boat) sweep swiftly down (rapids). **9** move (a bolt) to fasten or unfasten a door. **10** send out buds or shoots. ● n. **1** a new part growing from a tree or other plant. **2** an occasion of taking photographs professionally or making a film or video: *a fashion shoot*. **3** an occasion when a group of people hunt and shoot game for sport.
– PHRASES **shoot a line** Brit. informal describe something in an exaggerated or untruthful way. **shoot one's mouth off** informal talk boastfully or too freely. **the whole shooting match** informal everything. **shoot up** informal inject oneself with a narcotic drug.
– ORIGIN Old English.

shooter ● n. **1** a person who uses a gun. **2** informal a gun.

shooting gallery ● n. a room or fairground booth for shooting at targets.

shooting star ● n. a small, rapidly moving meteor that burns up on entering the earth's atmosphere.

shooting stick ● n. a walking stick with a handle that unfolds to form a seat and a

S

pointed end which can be stuck in the ground.

shoot-out ● n. **1** informal a gun battle that continues until one side is killed or defeated. **2** Soccer a tie-breaker decided by each side taking a specified number of penalty kicks.

shop ● n. **1** a building or part of a building where goods or services are sold. **2** a place where things are manufactured or repaired; a workshop. ● v. (**shops**, **shopping**, **shopped**) **1** go to a shop or shops to buy goods. **2** (**shop around**) look for the best available price or rate for something. **3** Brit. informal inform on.
– PHRASES **talk shop** discuss matters concerning one's work outside working hours.
– ORIGIN Old French *eschoppe* 'lean-to booth'.

shopaholic ● n. informal a person with an uncontrollable urge to go shopping.

shop floor ● n. Brit. the part of a factory where production is carried out.

shopkeeper ● n. the owner and manager of a shop.

shoplifting ● n. the stealing of goods from a shop by someone pretending to be a customer.
– DERIVATIVES **shoplifter** n.

shopper ● n. **1** a person who is shopping. **2** Brit. a bag for holding shopping.

shopping ● n. **1** the buying of goods from shops. **2** goods bought from shops.

shopping centre ● n. a group of shops situated together.

shop-soiled ● adj. Brit. (of an article) dirty or damaged from being displayed or handled in a shop.

shop steward ● n. a person elected by workers in a factory to represent them in dealings with management.

shore[1] ● n. **1** the land along the edge of a sea, lake, etc. **2** (**shores**) literary a country with a coast: *distant shores.*
– PHRASES **on shore** on land.
– DERIVATIVES **shoreward** adj. & adv. **shorewards** adv.
– ORIGIN Dutch or German *schōre.*

shore[2] ● v. (**shores**, **shoring**, **shored**) (**shore up**) **1** support or hold up with a prop or beam. **2** support or strengthen: *raising interest rates to shore up the dollar.* ● n. a prop or beam set up to support something weak or unstable.
– ORIGIN Dutch or German *schore.*

shoreline ● n. the line along which a sea, lake, etc. meets the land.

shorn past part. of **SHEAR**.

short ● adj. **1** of a small length in space or time. **2** small in height. **3** smaller than is usual or expected: *a short speech.* **4** (**short of/on**) not having enough of. **5** in scarce supply: *food is short.* **6** rude and abrupt. **7** (of odds in betting) reflecting a high level of probability. **8** (of a vowel) pronounced in a way that takes a shorter time than a long vowel in the same position (e.g. in standard British English the vowel sound in *good*). **9** (of pastry) containing a high proportion of fat to flour and therefore crumbly. ● adv. not as far as expected or required: *he pitched the ball short.* ● n. Brit. informal a drink of spirits, served in small measures. ● v. short-circuit.
– PHRASES **be caught short 1** be put at a disadvantage. **2** Brit. informal urgently need to go to the lavatory. **for short** as an abbreviation or nickname. **go short** not have enough of something. **in short** to sum up; briefly. **in the short run** (or **term**) in the near future. **make short work of** do, eat, or drink quickly. **short for** an abbreviation or nickname for. **short of 1** less than or not reaching as far as. **2** without going so far as (some extreme action). **stop short** stop suddenly.
– DERIVATIVES **shortness** n.
– ORIGIN Old English.

shortage ● n. a situation in which there is not enough of something needed.

shortbread (also **shortcake**) ● n. a rich, crumbly type of biscuit made with butter, flour, and sugar.

short-change ● v. (**short-changes**, **short-changing**, **short-changed**) **1** cheat (someone) by giving them less than the correct change. **2** treat (someone) unfairly by not giving them what they deserve.

short circuit ● n. a faulty connection in an electrical circuit in which the current flows along a shorter route than it should do. ● v. (**short-circuit**) **1** cause or suffer a short circuit. **2** shorten (a process) by using a more direct but irregular method.

shortcoming ● n. a failure to meet a certain standard; a fault.

shortcrust pastry ● n. Brit. crumbly pastry made with flour, fat, and a little water.

short cut ● n. **1** a route that is shorter than the usual one. **2** a way of doing something which is quicker than usual.

short division ● n. the process of dividing one number by another without writing down one's calculations.

shorten ● v. make or become shorter.

shortening ● n. fat used for making pastry.

shortfall ● n. an amount by which something falls short of what is required.

short fuse ● n. informal a quick temper.

shorthand ● n. a method of rapid writing by means of abbreviations and symbols, used for recording what is said.

short-handed ● adj. & adv. without enough or the usual number of staff.

shortlist ● n. a list of selected candidates from which a final choice is made. ● v. put on a shortlist.

short-lived ● adj. lasting only a short time.

shortly ● adv. **1** in a short time; soon. **2** abruptly or sharply.

short-range ● adj. **1** able to travel only over short distances. **2** relating to a period of time in the near future.

shorts ● pl. n. short trousers that reach to the knees or thighs.

short shrift ● n. abrupt and unsympathetic treatment.
– ORIGIN first meaning 'little time allowed for making confession': from **SHRIVE**.

short-sighted ● adj. **1** unable to see things clearly unless they are close to the eyes. **2** lacking foresight.

short-staffed ● adj. short-handed.

short-tempered ● adj. tending to lose one's temper quickly.

short wave ● n. a radio wave of a wavelength between about 10 and 100 metres (and a frequency of about 3 to 30 megahertz).

Shostakovich E
/shoss-tuh-**koh**-vich/, Dmitri (Dmitrievich) (1906–75), Russian composer, best known for his fifteen symphonies.

shot[1] ● n. **1** the firing of a gun or cannon. **2** (in sport) a hit, stroke, or kick of the ball as an attempt to score. **3** informal an attempt. **4** a photograph. **5** a film sequence photographed continuously by one camera. **6** a person with a particular level of ability in shooting: *he was an excellent shot.* **7** (pl. **shot**) a ball of stone or metal fired from a large gun or cannon. **8** (also **lead shot**) tiny lead pellets used in a shotgun. **9** a heavy ball thrown by a shot-putter. **10** the launch of a rocket: *a moon shot.* **11** informal a small drink of spirits. **12** informal an injection of a drug or vaccine.
– PHRASES **like a shot** informal without hesitation. **a shot in the arm** informal a source of encouragement.
– ORIGIN Old English.

shot[2] past and past part. of **SHOOT**. ● adj. **1** (of coloured cloth) woven with different colours, giving a contrasting effect when looked at from different angles. **2** informal ruined or worn out.
– PHRASES **get** (or **be**) **shot of** Brit. informal get (or be) rid of. **shot through with** filled with (a quality).

shotgun ● n. a gun for firing small shot at short range.

shotgun marriage (also **shotgun wedding**) ● n. informal a wedding that has to take place quickly because the bride is pregnant.

shot put ● n. an athletic contest in which a very heavy round ball is thrown as far as possible.
– DERIVATIVES **shot-putter** n.

should ● modal verb (3rd sing. **should**) **1** used to indicate what is right or ought to be done. **2** used to indicate what is probable. **3** formal used to state what would happen if something else was the case: *if you should change your mind, I'll be at the hotel.* **4** used with *I* and *we* to express a polite request, opinion, or hope.
– ORIGIN past of **SHALL**.

USAGE **should**
As with **shall** and **will**, there are traditional rules as to when to use **should** and when to use **would**. These say that **should** is used with **I** and **we** (*I said I should be late*), while **would** is used with **you**, **he**, **she**, **it**, and **they** (*you didn't say you would be late*). Nowadays, these rules are no longer strictly followed and it is usually acceptable to use **would** instead. Also, the shortened forms **I'd**, **we'd**, etc., are now normally used, especially when speaking, so that the question does not arise.

shoulder ● n. **1** the joint between the upper arm or forelimb and the main part of the body. **2** a joint of meat from the upper foreleg and shoulder blade of an animal. **3** a steep sloping side of a mountain. ● v. (**shoulders**, **shouldering**, **shouldered**) **1** put (something heavy) over one's shoulder or shoulders to carry. **2** take on (a responsibility). **3** push aside with one's shoulder.
– PHRASES **shoulder arms** hold a rifle against the right side of the body, barrel upwards. **shoulder to shoulder** side by side or acting together.
– ORIGIN Old English.

shoulder bag ● n. a bag with a long strap that is hung over the shoulder.

shoulder blade ● n. either of the large, flat, triangular bones at the top of the back; the scapula.

shoulder strap ● n. **1** a narrow strip of material going over the shoulder from front to back of a garment. **2** a long strap attached to a bag for carrying it over the shoulder.

shouldn't ● contr. should not.

shout ● v. **1** speak or call out very loudly. **2** (**shout down**) prevent (someone) from speaking or being heard by shouting. ● n. **1** a loud cry or call. **2** (**one's shout**) Brit. informal one's turn to buy a round of drinks.
– PHRASES **give someone a shout** informal call on or get in touch with someone. **in with a shout** informal having a good chance.
– ORIGIN perh. from **SHOOT**.

shove ● v. (**shoves**, **shoving**, **shoved**) **1** push roughly. **2** put (something) somewhere carelessly or roughly. **3** (**shove off**) informal go away. ● n. a strong push.
– ORIGIN Old English.

shovel ● n. a tool resembling a spade with a broad blade and upturned sides, used for moving earth, snow, etc. ● v. (**shovels**, **shovelling**, **shovelled**; US **shovels**, **shoveling**, **shoveled**) **1** move with a shovel. **2** (**shovel down/in**) informal eat (food) quickly and in large quantities.
– ORIGIN Old English.

show ● v. (**shows**, **showing**, **showed**; past part. **shown** or **showed**) **1** be or make visible: *wrinkles were starting to show on her face.* **2** offer for inspection or viewing. **3** present an image of: *a postcard showing Mount Etna.* **4** lead or guide. **5** treat (someone) in a particular way. **6** be evidence of; prove. **7** cause (someone) to understand something by explaining it or doing it oneself. **8** (also **show up**) informal arrive for an appointment. ● n. **1** a theatrical performance, especially a musical. **2** a light entertainment programme on television or radio. **3** an event or competition involving the public display of animals, plants, or products. **4** an impressive or pleasing sight. **5** a display of a quality or feeling. **6** an outward display intended to give a false impression: *he smoked for show he didn't enjoy it.*
– PHRASES **get the show on the road** informal begin an undertaking. **good** (or **bad**) **show!** informal, dated used to express approval (or disapproval). **show someone the door** tell someone to leave or make them leave. **show one's hand** reveal one's plans. **show off** **1** boastfully display one's abilities or possessions. **2** display (something) that is a source of pride. **show of hands** a vote by the raising of hands. **show round** point out interesting features in a place to (someone). **show up** **1** reveal as being bad or faulty. **2** informal embarrass or humiliate.
– ORIGIN Old English, 'look at, inspect'.

showbiz ● n. informal show business.

show business ● n. the theatre, films, television, and pop music as a profession or industry.

showcase ● n. **1** a glass case used for displaying articles in a shop or museum. **2** an occasion for presenting something favourably.

● v. (**showcases**, **showcasing**, **showcased**) put on display.
showdown ● n. a final meeting or test intended to settle a dispute.
shower /*rhymes with* flower/ ● n. **1** a short period of rain or snow. **2** a large number of things that fall or arrive together: *a shower of crumbs.* **3** a cubicle or bath in which a person stands under a spray of water to wash. **4** an act of washing oneself in a shower. **5** Brit. informal a worthless group of people. ● v. (**showers**, **showering**, **showered**) **1** fall or throw in a shower. **2** (**shower on/with**) give (a great number of things) to. **3** wash oneself in a shower.
– ORIGIN Old English.
showery ● adj. with frequent showers of rain.
showgirl ● n. an actress who sings and dances in musicals, variety shows, etc.
show house (also **show home**) ● n. Brit. a house on a newly built estate which is furnished and decorated to be shown to possible buyers.
showing ● n. **1** a presentation of a cinema film or television programme. **2** a performance of a particular quality: *poor opinion poll showings.*
showjumping ● n. the sport of riding horses over a course of obstacles in an arena.
showman ● n. **1** the manager or presenter of a circus, fair, etc. **2** a person who is skilled at entertaining people or getting their attention.
– DERIVATIVES **showmanship** n.
shown past part. of **SHOW**.
show-off ● n. informal a person who boastfully displays their abilities or possessions.
showpiece ● n. an outstanding example of its type: *the factory is a showpiece of British industry.*
showplace ● n. a place of beauty or interest that attracts many visitors.
showroom ● n. a room used to display cars, furniture, or other goods for sale.
show-stopper ● n. informal a very impressive performance that receives prolonged applause.
– DERIVATIVES **show-stopping** adj.
show trial ● n. a public trial that is held to influence or satisfy public opinion, rather than to ensure that justice is done.
showy ● adj. (**showier**, **showiest**) very bright or colourful and attracting much attention.
shrank past of **SHRINK**.
shrapnel /shrap-n'l/ ● n. small metal fragments thrown out by the explosion of a shell or bomb.
– ORIGIN named after General Henry *Shrapnel*, the British inventor (1761–1842).
shred ● n. **1** a strip of material that has been torn, cut, or scraped from something. **2** a very small amount: *not a shred of evidence.* ● v. (**shreds**, **shredding**, **shredded**) tear or cut into shreds.
– DERIVATIVES **shredder** n.
– ORIGIN Old English.
shrew ● n. **1** a small mammal resembling a mouse, with a long pointed snout. **2** a bad-tempered woman.
– ORIGIN Old English.
shrewd ● adj. having or showing good judgement.
– DERIVATIVES **shrewdly** adv. **shrewdness** n.
– ORIGIN from **SHREW** in the former sense 'evil person or thing'.
shrewish ● adj. (of a woman) bad-tempered or nagging.
shriek ● v. make a high-pitched piercing sound or cry. ● n. a high-pitched piercing cry or sound.
shrike ● n. a songbird with a hooked bill, that impales its prey on thorns.
shrill ● adj. (of a voice or sound) high-pitched and piercing. ● v. make a shrill noise.
– DERIVATIVES **shrillness** n. **shrilly** adv.
– ORIGIN Germanic.
shrimp ● n. **1** (pl. **shrimp** or **shrimps**) a small edible shellfish. **2** informal, derog. a small, weak person.
– ORIGIN prob. from German *schrempen* 'to wrinkle'.
shrine ● n. **1** a place believed to be holy because it is connected to a holy person or event. **2** a niche containing a religious statue or object.
– ORIGIN Old English, 'container for holy relics'.
shrink ● v. (**shrinks**, **shrinking**, **shrank**; past part. **shrunk** or (especially as adj.) **shrunken**) **1** become or make smaller. **2** (of clothes) become smaller as a result of being washed in water that is too hot. **3** move back or away in fear or disgust. **4** (**shrink from**) be unwilling to do. ● n. informal a psychiatrist.
– ORIGIN Old English; the noun is from *headshrinker*, an American term for a psychiatrist.
shrinkage ● n. the process of shrinking or the amount by which something has shrunk.
shrinking violet ● n. informal a very shy person.
shrink-wrap ● v. (**shrink-wraps**, **shrink-wrapping**, **shrink-wrapped**) enclose in clinging plastic film.
shrive /*rhymes with* drive/ ● v. (**shrives**, **shriving**, **shrove**; past part. **shriven**) archaic (of a priest) hear the confession of, give a religious duty to, and declare (someone) free from sin.
– ORIGIN Old English.
shrivel ● v. (**shrivels**, **shrivelling**, **shrivelled**; US **shrivels**, **shriveling**, **shriveled**) wrinkle and shrink through loss of moisture.
– ORIGIN perh. Scandinavian.

Shropshire E
a county of England, on the border with Wales; county town, Shrewsbury.

shroud ● n. **1** a length of cloth in which a dead person is wrapped for burial. **2** a thing that surrounds or hides something. **3** (**shrouds**) a set of ropes supporting the mast of a sailing boat. ● v. cover or hide: *the hills were shrouded by mist.*
– ORIGIN Old English, 'garment'.
Shrove Tuesday ● n. the day before Ash Wednesday.
shrub ● n. a woody plant which is smaller than a tree and divided into separate stems from near the ground.
– DERIVATIVES **shrubby** adj.
– ORIGIN Old English.
shrubbery ● n. (pl. **shrubberies**) an area in a

garden planted with shrubs.

shrug ● v. (**shrugs**, **shrugging**, **shrugged**) **1** raise (one's shoulders) slightly and briefly as a sign that one does not know or care about something. **2** (**shrug off**) treat as unimportant. ● n. **1** an act of shrugging one's shoulders. **2** a woman's close-fitting jacket cut short at the front and back so that only the arms and shoulders are covered.
– ORIGIN unknown.

shrunk (also **shrunken**) past part. of **SHRINK**.

shtum /shtuum/ (also **schtum**) ● adj. informal (in phr. **keep shtum**) stay silent.
– ORIGIN Yiddish.

shudder ● v. (**shudders**, **shuddering**, **shuddered**) tremble or shake violently, especially from fear or disgust. ● n. an act of shuddering.
– ORIGIN Dutch *schüderen*.

shuffle ● v. (**shuffles**, **shuffling**, **shuffled**) **1** walk without lifting one's feet completely from the ground. **2** restlessly shift one's position. **3** rearrange (a pack of cards) by sliding them over each other quickly. **4** rearrange (people or things). **5** (**shuffle off**) avoid (a responsibility). ● n. an act of shuffling.
– DERIVATIVES **shuffler** n.
– ORIGIN perh. from German *schuffeln*.

shufti /shuuf-ti/ ● n. (pl. **shuftis**) Brit. informal a quick look.
– ORIGIN Arabic, 'try to see'.

shun ● v. (**shuns**, **shunning**, **shunned**) avoid or reject.
– ORIGIN Old English, 'hate, shrink back'.

shunt ● v. **1** push or pull (a railway vehicle or vehicles) from one set of tracks to another. **2** move to a different position, especially a less important one.
– ORIGIN perh. from **SHUN**.

shut ● v. (**shuts**, **shutting**, **shut**) **1** move into position to block an opening. **2** (**shut in/out**) keep in or out by closing something such as a door. **3** prevent access to. **4** esp. Brit. (with reference to a shop or other business) stop operating for business. **5** close (a book, curtains, etc.)
– PHRASES **shut down** cease business or operation. **shut off** stop flowing or working. **shut up** informal stop talking.
– ORIGIN Old English, 'put a bolt in position to hold fast'.

shutdown ● n. an act of closing a factory or of turning off a machine.

Shute, E
Nevil (1899–1960; pen name of *Nevil Shute Norway*), English novelist, resident in Australia after 1945. His novels include *A Town Like Alice* and *On the Beach*.

shut-eye ● n. informal sleep.

shutter ● n. **1** each of a pair of hinged panels inside or outside a window that can be closed for security or to keep out the light. **2** a device that opens and closes to expose the film in a camera. ● v. (**shutters**, **shuttering**, **shuttered**) close the shutters of (a window or building).

shuttle ● n. **1** a form of transport that travels regularly between two places. **2** (in weaving) a bobbin for carrying the weft thread across the cloth, between the warp threads. **3** a bobbin carrying the lower thread in a sewing machine. ● v. (**shuttles**, **shuttling**, **shuttled**) **1** travel regularly between places. **2** transport in a shuttle.
– ORIGIN Old English, 'dart, missile'.

shuttlecock ● n. a light cone-shaped object consisting of a rounded piece of cork or plastic with feathers attached, struck with rackets in badminton.

shy[1] ● adj. (**shyer**, **shyest**) **1** nervous or timid in the company of other people. **2** (**shy of/about**) unwilling or reluctant to do. **3** (in combination) having a specified dislike: *camera-shy*. **4** (**shy of**) informal short of. ● v. (**shies**, **shying**, **shied**) **1** (of a horse) suddenly turn aside in fright. **2** (**shy from**) avoid through nervousness or lack of confidence.
– DERIVATIVES **shyly** adv. **shyness** n.
– ORIGIN Old English.

shy[2] ● v. (**shies**, **shying**, **shied**) throw at a target.
– ORIGIN unknown.

shyster ● n. informal a dishonest person, especially a lawyer.
– ORIGIN perh. from *Scheuster*, a 19th-century lawyer.

SI ● abbrev. Système International, the International system of units of measurement.

Siam E
/sy-am/ former name for **THAILAND**.

Siamese (also **Siamese cat**) ● n. a breed of cat that has short pale fur with darker face, ears, feet, and tail.

Siamese twins ● pl. n. twins whose bodies are joined at birth.

Sian E
var. of **XIAN**.

Sibelius E
/si-bay-li-uhss/, Jean (1865–1957; born *Johan Julius Christian Sibelius*), Finnish composer. His works include seven symphonies and the symphonic poems *The Swan of Tuonela* and *Finlandia*.

Siberia E
/sy-beer-i-uh/ a vast region of Russia, extending from the Urals to the Pacific and from the Arctic coast to the northern borders of Kazakhstan, Mongolia, and China.
– DERIVATIVES **Siberian** adj. & n.

S

sibilant ● adj. literary making a hissing sound. ● n. a speech sound made with a hissing effect, e.g. *s*, *sh*.
– ORIGIN Latin *sibilare* 'hiss'.

sibling ● n. a brother or sister.
– ORIGIN Old English, 'relative'.

sibyl ● n. (in ancient Greece and Rome) a woman supposedly able to pass on the oracles and prophecies of a god.
– DERIVATIVES **sibylline** adj.
– ORIGIN Greek *Sibulla*.

sic /sik/ ● adv. (after a copied or quoted word that appears odd or wrong) written exactly as it stands in the original.
– ORIGIN Latin, 'thus'.

Sichuan E
/si-chwahn/ (also **Szechuan** or **Szechwan**) a province of west central China; capital, Chengdu.

Sicily E
a large Italian island in the Mediterranean, off the south-western tip of Italy; capital, Palermo.
– DERIVATIVES **Sicilian** /si-sil-i-uhn/ adj. & n.

sick ● adj. **1** physically or mentally ill. **2** wanting to vomit. **3** (**sick of**) bored by or annoyed about. **4** informal behaving in an abnormal or cruel way. **5** informal (of humour) dealing with unpleasant subjects in a cruel or upsetting way. ● n. Brit. informal vomit.
– PHRASES **be sick 1** be ill. **2** Brit. vomit.
– ORIGIN Old English.

sickbay ● n. a room or building in a school or on a ship that is set aside for sick people.

sickbed ● n. the bed of a person who is ill.

sicken ● v. **1** make (someone) disgusted or shocked. **2** (**be sickening for**) showing the first symptoms of (an illness). **3** (**sickening**) informal very annoying.

Sickert E
/sik-ert/, Walter Richard (1860–1942), British painter, known for his paintings of theatre and music-hall scenes and drab domestic interiors.

sickie ● n. Brit. informal a period of sick leave taken when one is not really ill.

sickle ● n. a short-handled farming tool with a semicircular blade, used for cutting corn.
– ORIGIN Latin *secula*.

sick leave ● n. permission to be away from work because of illness.

sickly ● adj. (**sicklier**, **sickliest**) **1** often ill. **2** looking unhealthy. **3** (of flavour, colour, etc.) so bright or sweet as to cause sickness. **4** excessively sentimental.

sickness ● n. **1** the state of being ill. **2** a particular type of illness or disease. **3** nausea or vomiting.

sicko ● n. (pl. **sickos**) informal a perverted person.

Siddhartha Gautama E
/sid-dar-tuh gow-tuh-muh/ see **BUDDHA**.

side ● n. **1** a position to the left or right of an object, place, or central point. **2** either of the two halves into which something can be divided. **3** an upright or sloping surface of something that is not the top, bottom, front, or back. **4** each of the flat surfaces of a solid object, or either of the two surfaces of something flat and thin, e.g. paper. **5** each of the lines forming the boundary of a plane figure. **6** either of the two faces of a record or of the two separate tracks on a cassette tape. **7** a part near the edge of something. **8** a person or group opposing another or others in a dispute or contest. **9** a sports team. **10** a particular aspect: *he had a disagreeable side.* **11** a person's line of descent as traced through either their father or mother. **12** Brit. informal a television channel. ● adj. additional or less important: *a side dish.* ● v. (**sides**, **siding**, **sided**) (**side with/against**) support or oppose in a conflict or dispute.
– PHRASES **on the side** informal **1** in addition to one's regular job. **2** as a secret additional sexual relationship. **3** (**on the —— side**) rather ——: *he's a little on the large side.* **side by side** close together and facing the same way. **take sides** support one person or cause against another or others.
– DERIVATIVES **sideward** adj. & adv. **sidewards** adv.
– ORIGIN Old English.

sidebar ● n. a short piece of additional information placed alongside a main article in a newspaper or magazine.

sideboard ● n. **1** a flat-topped piece of furniture with cupboards and drawers, used for storing crockery, glasses, etc. **2** (**sideboards**) Brit. sideburns.

sideburns ● pl. n. a strip of hair growing down each side of a man's face in front of his ears.
– ORIGIN reversal of the name of the American General Ambrose *Burnside* (1824–81), who had sideburns.

sidecar ● n. a small, low vehicle attached to the side of a motorcycle for carrying passengers.

side effect ● n. a secondary, usually bad effect of a drug.

sidekick ● n. informal a person's assistant.

sidelight ● n. Brit. a small additional light on either side of a motor vehicle's headlights.

sideline ● n. **1** an activity done in addition to one's main job. **2** either of the two lines along the longer sides of a football field, basketball court, etc. **3** (**the sidelines**) a position of watching a situation rather than being directly involved in it. ● v. (**sidelines**, **sidelining**, **sidelined**) remove from a team, game, or influential position.

sidelong ● adj. & adv. to or from one side; sideways.

side-on ● adj. & adv. on, from, or towards a side.

sidereal /sy-deer-i-uhl/ ● adj. relating to the distant stars or their apparent positions in the sky.
– ORIGIN Latin *sidus* 'star'.

side road ● n. a minor road joining or branching from a main road.

side-saddle ● adv. (of a woman rider) sitting with both feet on the same side of the horse.

sideshow ● n. **1** a small show or stall at an exhibition, fair, or circus. **2** a minor incident or issue that diverts attention from the main subject.

side-splitting ● adj. informal very amusing.

sidestep ● v. (**sidesteps**, **sidestepping**, **sidestepped**) **1** avoid by stepping sideways. **2** avoid dealing with or discussing.

side street ● n. a minor street.

sideswipe ● n. a critical remark made while discussing another matter.

sidetrack ● v. distract from the main issue.

sidewalk ● n. N. Amer. a pavement.

sideways ● adv. & adj. **1** to, towards, or from the side. **2** unconventional: *a sideways look at life.*

siding ● n. a short track at the side of and joining a railway line, where trains are left.

sidle ● v. (**sidles**, **sidling**, **sidled**) walk in a stealthy or timid way.
– ORIGIN from **SIDELONG**.

Sidney, E
Sir Philip (1554–86), English poet, courtier, and soldier, author of *Arcadia*, a prose romance that includes poems.

Sidon E
/sy-d'n/ a city in Lebanon, on the Mediterranean coast. Founded in the 3rd millennium BC, it was a Phoenician seaport and city state.

siege • n. **1** a military operation in which enemy forces try to capture a town or building by surrounding it and cutting off its supplies. **2** a similar operation by a police team to force an armed person to surrender.
– PHRASES **lay siege to** begin a siege of.
– ORIGIN Old French *sege* 'a seat'.

Siemens E
/see-muhnz/, Ernst Werner von (1816–92), German electrical engineer. He developed the process of electroplating and devised an electric generator which used an electromagnet. His brother **Sir Charles William Siemens** (1823–83; born *Karl Wilhelm Siemens*) moved to England, where he developed the open-hearth steel furnace.

siemens /see-muhnz/ • n. Physics the SI unit of conductance.
– ORIGIN named after Sir Charles **SIEMENS**.

Siena E
/see-en-nuh/ a city in west central Italy, in Tuscany. In the 13th and 14th centuries it was the centre of a flourishing school of art.
– DERIVATIVES **Sienese** /si-uh-**neez**/ adj. & n.

sienna • n. a kind of earth used as a pigment in painting, normally yellowish-brown (**raw sienna**) or deep reddish-brown when roasted (**burnt sienna**).
– ORIGIN from Italian *terra di Sienna* 'earth of Siena'.

Sierra Leone E
/si-err-uh li-**ohn**/ a country on the coast of West Africa; capital, Freetown.
– DERIVATIVES **Sierra Leonean** adj. & n.

siesta /si-ess-tuh/ • n. an afternoon rest or nap, especially in hot countries.
– ORIGIN Spanish.

sieve /siv/ • n. a utensil consisting of a mesh held in a frame, used for straining solids from liquids or separating coarser from finer particles. • v. (**sieves**, **sieving**, **sieved**) put through a sieve.
– ORIGIN Old English.

sift • v. **1** put (a substance) through a sieve. **2** examine thoroughly to sort out what is important or useful.
– DERIVATIVES **sifter** n.
– ORIGIN Old English.

sigh • v. **1** let out a long, deep, breath expressing sadness, relief, etc. **2** (**sigh for**) literary long for. • n. an act of sighing.
– ORIGIN Old English.

sight • n. **1** the ability to see. **2** the action of seeing: *he hates the sight of blood.* **3** the area or distance within which someone can see or something can be seen. **4** a thing that one sees. **5** (**sights**) places of interest to tourists. **6** (**a sight**) informal a person or thing that looks ridiculous or unattractive. **7** (also **sights**) a device that someone looks through to aim a gun or see with a telescope or similar instrument. • v. **1** manage to see or glimpse. **2** take aim by looking through the sights of a gun.
– PHRASES **at first sight** on the first impression. **catch sight of** glimpse. **in** (or **within**) **sight of** close to gaining. **lose sight of** fail to consider or be aware of. **on** (or **at**) **sight** as soon as someone or something has been seen. **raise** (or **lower**) **one's sights** increase (or lower) one's expectations. **set one's sights on** hope strongly to achieve. **a sight —** informal considerably: *she is a sight cleverer than Sarah.* **a sight for sore eyes** informal a person or thing that one is very pleased to see.
– ORIGIN Old English.

USAGE sight
For an explanation of the difference between **sight** and **site**, see the note at **SITE**.

sighted • adj. **1** having the ability to see; not blind. **2** having a particular kind of sight: *keen-sighted.*

sightless • adj. blind.

sight-read • v. read and perform (music) at sight, without preparation.

sightseeing • n. the activity of visiting places of interest.
– DERIVATIVES **sightseer** n.

sign • n. **1** a thing that indicates that something else exists, is happening, or may happen. *I dared not show any sign of weakness.* **2** a signal, gesture, or notice giving information or an instruction. **3** a symbol or word used to represent something in algebra, music, or other subjects. **4** each of the twelve divisions of the zodiac. • v. **1** write one's name on (something) to authorize it. **2** recruit (a sports player, musician, etc.) by signing a contract. **3** use gestures to give instructions.
– PHRASES **sign off** end a letter, broadcast, or other message. **sign on 1** commit oneself to a job. **2** Brit. register as unemployed. **3** employ (someone). **sign out** sign to indicate that one has borrowed or hired (something). **sign up** commit oneself to a course, job, etc.
– DERIVATIVES **signer** n.
– ORIGIN Latin *signum* 'mark, token'.

Signac E
/seen-yak/, Paul (1863–1935), French pointillist painter. His technique was characterized by the use of small dashes and patches of pure colour rather than dots.

signal[1] • n. **1** a gesture, action, or sound giving information or an instruction. **2** a sign of a situation. **3** a device that uses lights or a movable arm, used to tell drivers to stop or beware on a road or railway. **4** an electrical impulse or radio wave sent or received. • v. (**signals**, **signalling**, **signalled**; US **signals**, **signaling**, **signaled**) **1** give a signal. **2** indicate by means of a signal.
– DERIVATIVES **signaller** n.
– ORIGIN Latin *signum* 'mark, token'.

signal[2] • adj. noteworthy; striking.
– ORIGIN Italian *segnalato* 'distinguished'.

signal box • n. Brit. a building beside a railway track from which signals, points, and other equipment are controlled.

signalman • n. a railway worker responsible for operating signals and points.

signatory /sig-nuh-tuh-ri/ • n. (pl. **signatories**) a party that has signed an agreement.
– ORIGIN Latin *signare* 'to sign, mark'.

signature • n. **1** a person's name written in a distinctive way, used in signing something. **2** the action of signing a document. **3** a distinctive product or quality by which someone

or something can be recognized: *the chef produced the pâté that was his signature.*
– ORIGIN Latin *signare* 'to sign'.

signature tune ● n. esp. Brit. a special tune used to announce a particular television or radio programme.

signboard ● n. a board displaying the name or logo of a business or product.

signet ● n. hist. a small seal used to authorize an official document.
– ORIGIN Latin *signetum*.

signet ring ● n. a ring with letters or a design set into it.

significance ● n. **1** importance. **2** the meaning of something.
– ORIGIN Latin *significantia*.

significant ● adj. **1** important or large enough to have an effect or be noticed. **2** having a meaning that is not directly stated: *a significant look.*
– DERIVATIVES **significantly** adv.

significant figure ● n. Math. each of the digits of a number that are used to express it to the required degree of accuracy.

signify ● v. (**signifies**, **signifying**, **signified**) **1** be a sign of; mean. **2** make known (a feeling or intention).
– DERIVATIVES **signification** n.
– ORIGIN Latin *significare*.

signing ● n. **1** Brit. a person who has recently been recruited to a sports team, record company, etc. **2** an event at which an author signs copies of their book to gain publicity and sales.

sign language ● n. a system of communication used among and with deaf people, consisting of signs made by the hands and face.

signor /see-nyor/ ● n. (pl. **signori** /see-**nyor**-ee/) a title or form of address for an Italian-speaking man, corresponding to *Mr* or *sir*.
– ORIGIN Italian.

signora /see-**nyor**-uh/ ● n. a title or form of address for an Italian-speaking married woman, corresponding to *Mrs* or *madam*.
– ORIGIN Italian.

signorina /see-nyuh-**ree**-nuh/ ● n. a title or form of address for an Italian-speaking unmarried woman, corresponding to *Miss*.
– ORIGIN Italian.

signpost ● n. a sign on a post, giving the direction and distance to a nearby place. ● v. esp. Brit. mark (a place or road) with a signpost or signposts.

Sihanouk E
/si-uh-**nuuk**/, Norodom (b.1922), Cambodian king 1941–55 and since 1993, Prime Minister 1955–60, and head of state 1960–70 and 1975–6.

Sikh /seek/ ● n. a member of a religion that developed from Hinduism, based on the belief that there is only one God. ● adj. relating to Sikhs or Sikhism.
– DERIVATIVES **Sikhism** n.
– ORIGIN Punjabi, 'disciple'

Sikkim E
/sik-kim/ a state of NE India, in the eastern Himalayas; capital, Gangtok.
– DERIVATIVES **Sikkimese** adj. & n.

Sikorsky E
/si-**kor**-ski/, Igor (Ivanovich) (1889–1972), Russian-born American aircraft designer, who built the first large four-engined aircraft (1913) and developed the first mass-produced helicopter (1939).

silage /sy-lij/ ● n. grass or other green crops that are stored in a silo without being dried, used as animal feed in the winter.
– ORIGIN Spanish *ensilar* 'put into a silo'.

silence ● n. **1** complete lack of sound. **2** a situation in which someone is unwilling to speak or discuss something: *he withdrew into sullen silence.* ● v. (**silences**, **silencing**, **silenced**) make silent.
– ORIGIN Latin *silentium*.

silencer ● n. a device for reducing the noise made by a gun or exhaust system.

silent ● adj. **1** where there is no sound. **2** not speaking or not spoken aloud: *a silent prayer.* **3** not prone to speak much. **4** (of a film) without an accompanying soundtrack. **5** (of a letter) written but not pronounced, e.g. *b* in *doubt*.
– DERIVATIVES **silently** adv.

Silesia E
/sy-**lee**-*zh*uh/ a region of central Europe, now largely in SW Poland.

silhouette /si-luu-**et**/ ● n. **1** the dark shape and outline of someone or something seen against a lighter background. **2** a picture that shows someone or something as a black shape on a light background. ● v. (**silhouettes**, **silhouetting**, **silhouetted**) show as a silhouette: *the castle was silhouetted against the sky.*
– ORIGIN named after the French author and politician Étienne de *Silhouette* (1709–67).

silica /si-li-kuh/ ● n. a compound of silicon and oxygen that occurs as quartz and is found in sandstone and many other rocks.
– ORIGIN Latin *silex* 'flint'.

silicate /si-li-kayt, si-li-kuht/ ● n. a compound of silica combined with a metal oxide.

silicon /si-li-k'n/ ● n. a non-metallic chemical element that is a semiconductor, used in making electronic circuits.
– ORIGIN Latin *silex* 'flint'.

silicon chip ● n. a microchip.

silicone /si-li-kohn/ ● n. a synthetic substance made from silicon, used to make plastics, rubber, paints, etc.

Silicon Valley E
an area in California south of San Francisco, noted for its computing and electronics industries.

silicosis /si-li-**koh**-siss/ ● n. a lung disease caused by breathing in dust that contains silica.

silk ● n. **1** a fine, soft shiny fibre produced by silkworms, made into thread or fabric. **2** (**silks**) garments made from silk, worn by a jockey. **3** Brit. informal a Queen's Counsel. [ORIGIN because entitled to wear a silk gown.]
– PHRASES **take silk** Brit. become a Queen's Counsel.
– ORIGIN Latin *sericus*.

silken ● adj. **1** smooth and shiny like silk. **2** made of silk.

silkworm ● n. a caterpillar that spins a silk cocoon from which silk fibre is produced.

silky ● adj. (**silkier**, **silkiest**) **1** smooth and shiny like silk. **2** (of a person's voice) smooth.

sill • **n. 1** a piece of stone, wood, or metal at the foot of a window or doorway. **2** Geol. a sheet of igneous rock intruded between and parallel with existing strata.
– ORIGIN Old English.

Sillitoe E
/sil-li-toh/, Alan (b.1928), English writer, noted for his novels about working-class life, including *Saturday Night and Sunday Morning*.

silly • **adj.** (**sillier**, **silliest**) **1** lacking in common sense or judgement; foolish. **2** Cricket (of a fielding position) very close to the batsman: *silly mid-on*.
– DERIVATIVES **silliness** n.
– ORIGIN Germanic, 'luck, happiness'.

silo /sy-loh/ • **n.** (pl. **silos**) **1** a tower on a farm, used to store grain. **2** a pit or airtight structure in which green crops are stored as silage. **3** an underground chamber in which a guided missile is kept ready for firing.
– ORIGIN Spanish.

silt • **n.** fine sand or clay carried by running water and deposited as a sediment. • **v.** (**silt up**) fill or block with silt.
– DERIVATIVES **silty** adj.
– ORIGIN prob. Scandinavian.

Silurian /sy-lyoor-i-uhn/ • **adj.** Geol. relating to the third period of the Palaeozoic era, about 439 to 409 million years ago, a time when the first fish and land plants appeared.
– ORIGIN from *Silures*, the Latin name of a people of ancient Wales.

silver • **n. 1** a precious shiny greyish-white metallic element. **2** a shiny grey-white colour. **3** coins made from silver or from a metal that resembles silver. **4** silver dishes, containers, or cutlery. • **v.** (**silvers**, **silvering**, **silvered**) **1** cover or plate with silver. **2** literary give a silvery appearance to: *the moon silvered the turf*.
– PHRASES **be born with a silver spoon in one's mouth** be born into a rich upper-class family. **the silver screen** the cinema industry.
– DERIVATIVES **silvery** adj.
– ORIGIN Old English.

silver birch • **n.** a birch tree with silver-grey bark.

silverfish • **n.** a small silvery wingless insect that lives in buildings.

silver jubilee • **n.** the twenty-fifth anniversary of an important event.

silver medal • **n.** a medal made of or coloured silver, awarded for second place in a race or competition.

silver plate • **n. 1** a thin layer of silver applied as a coating to another metal. **2** plates, dishes, etc. made of or plated with silver.

silverside • **n.** Brit. the upper side of a round of beef from the outside of the leg.

silversmith • **n.** a person who makes silver articles.

silver-tongued • **adj.** persuasive in speaking; eloquent.

silver wedding • **n.** the twenty-fifth anniversary of a wedding.

silviculture /sil-vi-kul-cher/ • **n.** the growing and cultivation of trees.
– DERIVATIVES **silvicultural** adj.
– ORIGIN Latin *silva* 'wood'.

Simenon E
/see-muh-non/, Georges (Joseph Christian) (1903–89), Belgian-born French novelist, author of detective novels featuring Commissaire Maigret.

simian /sim-i-uhn/ • **adj.** relating to or like apes or monkeys. • **n.** an ape or monkey.
– ORIGIN Latin *simia* 'ape'.

similar • **adj. 1** like something but not exactly the same: *the nuts are similar to almonds*. **2** (of geometrical figures) the same in shape but not in size.
– DERIVATIVES **similarity** n. **similarly** adv.
– ORIGIN Latin *similis* 'like'.

simile /sim-i-li/ • **n.** a figure of speech in which one thing is compared to another of a different kind, using the words *as* or *like* (e.g. *the family was as solid as a rock*).
– ORIGIN Latin.

similitude /si-mil-i-tyood/ • **n.** the quality of being similar.

simmer • **v.** (**simmers**, **simmering**, **simmered**) **1** stay or cause to stay just below boiling point. **2** be in a state of anger or excitement which is only just kept under control. **3** (**simmer down**) become calmer and quieter. • **n.** a state just below boiling point.
– ORIGIN from dialect *simper*.

Simnel E
/sim-n'l/, Lambert (*c.*1475–1525), English pretender and rebel. He was trained by Yorkists to impersonate firstly one of the Princes in the Tower and later the Earl of Warwick in an attempt to overthrow Henry VII.

Simon[1], E
(Marvin) Neil (b.1927), American dramatist, known for such comedies as *Barefoot in the Park* and *The Odd Couple*.

Simon[2], E
Paul (b.1942), American singer and songwriter. He achieved fame with **Art Garfunkel** (b.1941) for such albums as *Bridge Over Troubled Water* and later pursued a solo career.

Simon, St E
an Apostle; known as **Simon the Zealot**. Feast day, 28 October.

simony /sy-muh-ni, sim-uh-ni/ • **n.** esp. hist. the buying or selling of Church privileges such as pardons.
– ORIGIN from *Simon* Magus in the Bible, who offered money to the Apostles.

simper • **v.** (**simpers**, **simpering**, **simpered**) smile in a coy and silly way. • **n.** a coy and silly smile.
– ORIGIN unknown.

simple • **adj.** (**simpler**, **simplest**) **1** easily understood or done. **2** plain and basic: *a simple white blouse*. **3** composed of a single element; not compound. **4** of very low intelligence. **5** of low status; humble. **6** (of interest) payable on the sum loaned only. Compare with **COMPOUND**[1].
– ORIGIN Latin *simplus*.

simple fracture • **n.** a fracture of a bone only, without breaking of the skin.

simpleton • **n.** a person who is foolish or eas-

S

ily deceived.

simplicity ● n. the quality of being simple.

simplify ● v. (**simplifies**, **simplifying**, **simplified**) make easier to do or understand.
– DERIVATIVES **simplification** n.

simplistic ● adj. treating complex issues and problems as more simple than they really are.
– DERIVATIVES **simplistically** adv.

simply ● adv. **1** in a simple way. **2** just; merely. **3** absolutely: *it made him simply furious.*

Simpson[1], E
O. J. (b.1947; full name *Orenthal James Simpson*), American football player and actor. In 1994 he was arrested for the murder of his wife and her male companion, but was acquitted after a lengthy trial.

Simpson[2], E
Wallis (1896–1986; born *Wallis Warfield*), American wife of Edward, Duke of Windsor (Edward VIII). Her relationship with the king caused a scandal and forced the king's abdication.

simulacrum /sim-yuu-lay-kruhm/ ● n. (pl. **simulacra** /sim-yuu-lay-kruh/ or **simulacrums**) something that looks like or is similar to something else: *he was a simulacrum of his brother.*
– ORIGIN Latin.

simulate ● v. (**simulates**, **simulating**, **simulated**) **1** imitate the appearance or nature of. **2** produce a computer model of. **3** pretend to feel (an emotion).
– DERIVATIVES **simulation** n.
– ORIGIN Latin *simulare* 'copy, represent'.

simulator ● n. a machine that imitates the controls and conditions of a real vehicle, process, etc., used for training or testing.

simulcast /sim-uhl-kahst/ ● n. a broadcast of the same programme on radio and television at the same time.
– ORIGIN from **SIMULTANEOUS** and **BROADCAST**.

simultaneity /sim-uhl-tuh-nay-i-ti/ ● n. the quality of being simultaneous.

simultaneous /sim-uhl-tay-ni-uhss/ ● adj. occurring or done at the same time.
– DERIVATIVES **simultaneously** adv.
– ORIGIN Latin *simul* 'at the same time'.

simultaneous equations ● pl. n. equations involving two or more unknowns that are to have the same values in each equation.

sin[1] /*rhymes with* tin/ ● n. **1** an act that breaks a religious or moral law. **2** an act that causes strong disapproval. ● v. (**sins**, **sinning**, **sinned**) commit a sin.
– ORIGIN Old English.

sin[2] /*rhymes with* line/ ● abbrev. sine.

Sinai E
/sy-ny, sy-ni-I/ an arid mountainous peninsula in NE Egypt. It was occupied by Israel between 1967 and 1982.

Sinatra E
/si-nah-truh/, Frank (1915–98; full name *Francis Albert Sinatra*), American singer and film actor. His many hits include 'My Way'.

sin bin ● n. informal (in sport) a place to which offending players can be sent as a penalty during a game.

since ● prep. in the period between (a time in the past) and the present: *what's happened since Monday?* ● conj. **1** during or in the time after. **2** because. ● adv. **1** from the time mentioned until the present. **2** ago.
– ORIGIN Old English.

sincere ● adj. (**sincerer**, **sincerest**) free from pretence or deceit in behaviour or feelings; genuine and honest.
– DERIVATIVES **sincerely** adv.
– ORIGIN Latin *sincerus* 'clean, pure'.

sincerity ● n. the quality of being sincere.

Sind E
/sind/ a province of SE Pakistan; capital, Karachi.

sine /*rhymes with* line/ ● n. (in a right-angled triangle) the ratio of the side opposite a particular acute angle to the hypotenuse.
– ORIGIN Latin *sinus* 'curve'.

sinecure /syn-i-kyoor, sin-i-kyoor/ ● n. a job for which the holder is paid but which requires little or no work.
– ORIGIN from Latin *sine cura* 'without care'.

sine die /see-nay dee-ay/ ● adv. (with reference to proceedings that have been adjourned) with no date set for being restarted.
– ORIGIN Latin, 'without a day'.

sine qua non /see-nay kwah nohn/ ● n. a thing that is absolutely necessary.
– ORIGIN Latin, 'without which not'.

sinew /sin-yoo/ ● n. **1** a piece of tough fibrous tissue that joins muscle to bone. **2** (**sinews**) the parts of a system that give it strength or bind it together.
– DERIVATIVES **sinewy** adj.
– ORIGIN Old English.

sinful ● adj. **1** wicked. **2** disgraceful: *a sinful waste.*
– DERIVATIVES **sinfully** adv. **sinfulness** n.

sing ● v. (**sings**, **singing**, **sang**; past part. **sung**) **1** make musical sounds with the voice, especially words with a set tune. **2** perform (a song) in this way. **3** make a whistling sound.
– PHRASES **sing someone's praises** praise someone highly.
– DERIVATIVES **singer** n.
– ORIGIN Old English.

singalong ● n. an informal occasion when people sing together in a group.

Singapore E
/sing-uh-por/ a country in SE Asia consisting of the island of Singapore and some fifty-four smaller islands; capital, Singapore City.
– DERIVATIVES **Singaporean** adj. & n.

singe ● v. (**singes**, **singeing**, **singed**) burn the surface of (something) slightly. ● n. a slight burn.
– ORIGIN Old English.

Singer[1], E
Isaac Bashevis (1904–91), Polish-born American novelist and short-story writer. His novels, written in Yiddish, include *The Slave.*

Singer[2], E
Isaac Merrit (1811–75), American inventor, who made the first commercially successful sewing machine (1851).

Singhalese /sing-guh-leez/ ● n. & adj. var. of **SINHALESE**.

S

single ● adj. **1** one only. **2** designed or suitable for one person. **3** consisting of one part. **4** taken separately from others in a group (used for emphasis): *he wrote down every single word.* **5** not involved in an established romantic or sexual relationship. **6** Brit. (of a ticket) valid for an outward journey only. ● n. **1** a single person or thing. **2** a short record or CD with one song on each side. **3** (**singles**) a game or competition for individual players. ● v. (**singles**, **singling**, **singled**) (**single out**) choose (someone or something) from a group for special treatment.
– DERIVATIVES **singly** adv.
– ORIGIN Latin *singulus*.

single-breasted ● adj. (of a jacket or coat) fastened by one row of buttons at the centre of the front.

single cream ● n. Brit. thin cream with a low fat content.

single file ● n. a line of people or things arranged one behind another.

single-handed ● adv. & adj. done without help from others.
– DERIVATIVES **single-handedly** adv.

single market ● n. an association of countries that have few or no restrictions on the movement of goods, money, or people within the group.

single-minded ● adj. concentrating on one particular aim.

single parent ● n. a person bringing up a child or children without a partner.

singlet ● n. esp. Brit. a vest or similar sleeveless garment.
– ORIGIN from SINGLE.

singleton ● n. **1** a single person or thing of its kind. **2** informal a person who is not in a long-term relationship.

sing-song ● adj. (of a person's voice) having a repeated rising and falling rhythm. ● n. Brit. informal an informal gathering for singing.

singular ● adj. **1** very good or great; remarkable. **2** Grammar (of a word or form) referring to just one person or thing. **3** strange or eccentric. ● n. Grammar the singular form of a word.
– DERIVATIVES **singularity** n. **singularly** adv.
– ORIGIN Latin *singularis*.

Sinhalese /sin-huh-leez, sin-uh-leez/ (also **Singhalese**) ● n. (pl. **Sinhalese**, **Singhalese**) **1** a member of an Indian people forming the majority of the population of Sri Lanka. **2** the language spoken by this people. ● adj. relating to the Sinhalese.
– ORIGIN Sanskrit, 'Sri Lanka'.

sinister ● adj. seeming evil or dangerous.
– ORIGIN Latin, 'left'.

sink ● v. (**sinks**, **sinking**, **sank**; past part. **sunk**) **1** go down below the surface of liquid. **2** (with reference to a ship) go or cause to go to the bottom of the sea. **3** move slowly downwards. **4** gradually decrease in amount or strength. **5** (**sink into**) cause (something sharp) to go through (a surface). **6** (**sink in**) become fully understood. **7** pass into a particular state: *she sank into sleep.* **8** (**sink in/into**) put (money or resources) into. ● n. a fixed basin with a water supply and outflow pipe.
– PHRASES **a sinking feeling** an unpleasant feeling caused by worry or dismay. **sink or swim** fail or succeed by one's own efforts.
– ORIGIN Old English.

sinker ● n. a weight used to keep a fishing line beneath the water.

sinkhole ● n. a hole in the ground caused by water erosion and providing a route for surface water to disappear underground.

sinner ● n. a person who sins.

Sinn Fein E
/shin fayn/ a political movement and party seeking a united republican Ireland.

Sino- /sy-noh/ ● comb. form Chinese; Chinese and ...: *Sino-American.*
– ORIGIN Latin *Sinae*.

sinology /sy-nol-uh-ji, si-nol-uh-ji/ ● n. the study of Chinese language, history, and culture.
– DERIVATIVES **sinologist** n.

sinuous /sin-yuu-uhss/ ● adj. **1** having many curves and turns. **2** moving in a graceful, swaying way.
– ORIGIN Latin *sinuosus*.

sinus /sy-nuhss/ ● n. a hollow space within the bones of the face that connects with the nostrils.
– ORIGIN Latin, 'a bend'.

sinusitis /si-nuh-sy-tiss/ ● n. inflammation of a sinus.

Sioux /soo/ ● n. (pl. **Sioux**) a member of a North American Indian people living in the northern Mississippi valley area.
– ORIGIN Ojibwa (an American Indian language).

sip ● v. (**sips**, **sipping**, **sipped**) drink in small mouthfuls. ● n. a small mouthful of liquid.
– ORIGIN perh. from SUP[1].

siphon (also **syphon**) ● n. a tube used to convey liquid from one container to another, using air pressure to maintain the flow. ● v. **1** draw off or convey (liquid) by means of a siphon. **2** (**siphon off**) take (small amounts of money) from a source over time.
– ORIGIN Greek, 'pipe'.

sir (also **Sir**) ● n. **1** a polite form of address to a man. **2** used as a title before the forename of a knight or baronet.
– ORIGIN from SIRE.

sire /*rhymes with* fire/ ● n. **1** the male parent of an animal. **2** literary a father or other male ancestor. **3** archaic a respectful form of address to a king. ● v. (**sires**, **siring**, **sired**) be the male parent of.
– ORIGIN Old French.

siren ● n. **1** a device that makes a long loud warning sound. **2** Gk Myth. each of a group of creatures who were part woman, part bird, whose singing lured sailors on to rocks. **3** a woman who is attractive but also dangerous.
– ORIGIN Greek *Seirēn*.

Sirius E
/si-ri-uhss/ the brightest star in the sky, in the constellation Canis Major.

sirloin ● n. the best part of a loin of beef.
– ORIGIN Old French, 'above the loin'.

sirocco /si-rok-koh/ ● n. (pl. **siroccos**) a hot wind blowing from North Africa to southern Europe.
– ORIGIN Arabic, 'east wind'.

sirup ● n. US = SYRUP.

SIS ● abbrev. (in the UK) Secret Intelligence Service.

sisal /sy-z'l/ • **n.** fibre made from the leaves of a tropical Mexican plant, used for ropes or matting.
– ORIGIN named after the Mexican port of *Sisal*.

Sisley E
/siz-li/, Alfred (1839–99), French Impressionist painter, noted for his landscapes.

sissy • **n.** (pl. **sissies**) informal an effeminate or weak person.
– ORIGIN from **SISTER**.

sister • **n. 1** a woman or girl in relation to other children of her parents. **2** a female friend or colleague. **3** a member of a religious order of women. **4** Brit. a senior female nurse. • **adj.** belonging to the same group or type as something else: *a sister organization.*
– DERIVATIVES **sisterly** adj.
– ORIGIN Old English.

sisterhood • **n. 1** a feeling of closeness and understanding between women. **2** a group of women linked by a shared interest or belief.

sister-in-law • **n.** (pl. **sisters-in-law**) **1** the sister of one's wife or husband. **2** the wife of one's brother or brother-in-law.

Sistine Chapel E
/siss-teen/ a chapel in the Vatican, built in the late 15th century, containing frescoes by Michelangelo, Botticelli, and other artists.

Sisyphean /siss-i-fee-uhn/ • **adj.** (of a task) unending.
– ORIGIN from *Sisyphus* in Greek mythology whose punishment was to endlessly roll a large stone to the top of a hill, only for it to roll down again.

sit • **v.** (**sits**, **sitting**, **sat**) **1** be or put in a position in which one's weight is supported by one's buttocks and one's back is upright. **2** be in a particular position or state. **3** serve as a member of a council, jury, or other official body. **4** (of a parliament, court of law, etc.) be carrying on its business. **5** Brit. take (an examination). **6** (of a table or room) have enough seats for. **7** (**sit for**) pose for (an artist or photographer).
– PHRASES **sit in for** temporarily carry out the duties of. **sit out** not take part in. **sit tight** informal hold back from taking action. **sit up** go to bed later than usual.
– ORIGIN Old English.

USAGE sit
It is good English to use the present participle **sitting** rather than the past participle **sat** with the verb 'to be': say *we were sitting there for hours* rather than *we were sat there for hours.*

sitar /si-tar/ • **n.** a large, long-necked Indian lute.
– ORIGIN Persian.

sitcom • **n.** informal a situation comedy.

sit-down • **adj.** (of a protest) in which demonstrators occupy their workplace or sit on the ground in a public place.

site • **n. 1** a place where something is or will be located. **2** a place where an event or activity is occurring or has occurred. • **v.** (**sites**, **siting**, **sited**) establish or build in a particular place.
– ORIGIN Latin *situs* 'position'.

USAGE site
Do not confuse **site** and **sight**. **Site** means 'a place where something is located or happens' (as in *the site of a famous temple*), while **sight** means 'the ability to see' (as in *he lost his sight in an accident*).

Sitka /sit-kuh/ • **n.** a fast-growing North American spruce tree, grown for its strong lightweight wood.
– ORIGIN from the town of *Sitka* in Alaska.

sitter • **n. 1** a person who sits, especially for a portrait. **2** a person who looks after children, pets, or a house while the parents or owners are away.

sitting • **n. 1** a period of posing for a portrait. **2** a period when a group of people are served a meal. **3** a period of time during which a court of law, committee, or parliament is carrying on business. • **adj.** (of an elected representative) currently present or in office.

Sitting Bull E
(*c.*1831–90; Sioux name *Tatanka Iyotake*), Sioux chief. He led the Sioux in the fight to retain their lands, and defeated General Custer's forces at the Battle of Little Bighorn (1876).

sitting duck • **n.** informal a person or thing that is easy to attack.

sitting room • **n.** esp. Brit. a room for sitting and relaxing in.

sitting tenant • **n.** Brit. a tenant who is living in rented accommodation.

situate • **v.** (**situates**, **situating**, **situated**) **1** put in a particular place. **2** (**be situated**) be in particular circumstances.
– ORIGIN Latin *situare* 'place'.

situation • **n. 1** a set of circumstances in which one finds oneself. **2** the location and surroundings of a place. **3** a job.
– DERIVATIVES **situational** adj.

situation comedy • **n.** a comedy series in which the characters are involved in amusing situations.

sit-up • **n.** an exercise designed to strengthen the abdominal muscles, in which a person sits up from a horizontal position without using the arms.

Siva E
/shee-vuh/ var. of **SHIVA**.

six • **cardinal number 1** one more than five; 6. (Roman numeral: **vi** or **VI**.) **2** Cricket a hit that reaches the boundary without first bouncing, scoring six runs.
– PHRASES **at sixes and sevens** in a state of confusion or disorder. **knock for six** Brit. informal completely surprise.
– DERIVATIVES **sixfold** adj. & adv.
– ORIGIN Old English.

Six Counties E
the counties of Northern Ireland.

Six Day War E
a war, 5–10 June 1967, in which Israel occupied Sinai, the Old City of Jerusalem, the West Bank, and the Golan Heights and defeated an Egyptian, Jordanian, and Syrian alliance.

six-pack • **n. 1** a pack of six cans of beer. **2** informal a set of well-developed stomach muscles.

S

sixpence ● n. Brit. a former coin worth six old pence (2½ p).

six-shooter ● n. a revolver with six chambers.

sixteen ● cardinal number one more than fifteen; 16. (Roman numeral: **xvi** or **XVI**.)
– DERIVATIVES **sixteenth** ordinal number.

sixth ● ordinal number **1** that is number six in a sequence; 6th. **2** (**a sixth/one sixth**) each of six equal parts into which something is divided. **3** a musical interval spanning six consecutive notes in a scale.

sixth-form college ● n. Brit. a college for pupils aged 16–18.

sixth sense ● n. a supposed extra sense giving awareness of things by intuition rather than normal perception.

sixty ● cardinal number (pl. **sixties**) ten more than fifty; 60. (Roman numeral: **lx** or **LX**.)
– DERIVATIVES **sixtieth** ordinal number.

size[1] ● n. **1** the overall measurements or extent of something. **2** each of the series of standard measurements in which articles are made or sold: *the dress was several sizes too big.* ● v. (**sizes, sizing, sized**) **1** group according to size. **2** (**size up**) form a judgement of. **3** alter the size of.
– ORIGIN Old French *sise*.

size[2] ● n. a sticky solution used to glaze paper, stiffen textiles, and prepare plastered walls for decoration. ● v. (**sizes, sizing, sized**) treat with size.
– ORIGIN perh. the same as **SIZE**[1].

sizeable (also **sizable**) ● adj. fairly large.

sizzle ● v. (**sizzles, sizzling, sizzled**) **1** (of food) make a hissing sound when being fried. **2** (**sizzling**) informal very hot or exciting.

sjambok /sham-bok/ ● n. (in South Africa) a long, stiff whip.
– ORIGIN South African Dutch.

ska /skah/ ● n. a style of fast popular music originating in Jamaica.
– ORIGIN unknown.

> **Skanda** E
> /skan-duh/ the Hindu war god, first son of Shiva and Parvati and brother of Ganesha.

skate[1] ● n. an ice skate or roller skate. ● v. (**skates, skating, skated**) **1** move on skates. **2** (**skate over/round/around**) pass over or refer only briefly to (a subject or problem).
– PHRASES **get one's skates on** Brit. informal hurry up.
– DERIVATIVES **skater** n. **skating** n.
– ORIGIN Dutch *schaats*.

skate[2] ● n. (pl. **skate** or **skates**) an edible sea fish with a flattened diamond-shaped body.
– ORIGIN Old Norse.

skateboard ● n. a short narrow board with two small wheels fixed to the bottom of either end, on which a person can ride. ● v. ride on a skateboard.
– DERIVATIVES **skateboarder** n.

skedaddle ● v. (**skedaddles, skedaddling, skedaddled**) informal leave quickly.
– ORIGIN unknown.

skein /skayn/ ● n. a length of thread or yarn, loosely coiled and knotted.
– ORIGIN Old French *escaigne*.

skeletal /skel-i-t'l, skuh-lee-t'l/ ● adj. **1** having to do with a skeleton. **2** very thin. **3** existing only in outline.
– DERIVATIVES **skeletally** adv.

skeleton ● n. **1** a framework of bone or cartilage supporting or containing the body of an animal. **2** a supporting framework or structure. **3** a basic outline of a plan, written work, etc. ● adj. referring to an essential or minimum number of people: *a skeleton staff.*
– PHRASES **skeleton in the cupboard** a shocking or embarrassing fact that someone wishes to keep secret.
– ORIGIN Greek, 'dried up thing'.

skeleton key ● n. a key designed to fit many locks.

skeptic ● n. US = **SCEPTIC**.

sketch ● n. **1** a rough drawing or painting. **2** a short humorous scene in a comedy show. **3** a brief written or spoken account. ● v. **1** make a sketch of. **2** give a brief account or outline of.
– ORIGIN Italian *schizzo*.

sketchbook (also **sketch pad**) ● n. a pad of drawing paper for sketching on.

sketchy ● adj. (**sketchier, sketchiest**) not thorough or detailed; rough.
– DERIVATIVES **sketchily** adv.

skew ● n. a bias towards one particular group or subject: *the paper had a working-class skew.* ● v. **1** suddenly change direction or move at an angle. **2** make biased or distorted.
– ORIGIN Old French *eschiver* 'eschew'.

skewbald ● adj. (of a horse) with patches of white and another colour.
– ORIGIN uncertain.

skewer ● n. a long piece of wood or metal used for holding pieces of food together during cooking. ● v. (**skewers, skewering, skewered**) hold in place or pierce with a pin or skewer.
– ORIGIN unknown.

skew-whiff ● adv. & adj. Brit. informal not straight; askew.

ski ● n. (pl. **skis**) each of a pair of long, narrow pieces of wood, metal, or plastic, attached to boots for travelling over snow. ● v. (**skis, skiing, skied**) travel on skis.
– DERIVATIVES **skier** n.
– ORIGIN Norwegian.

> **Skiathos** E
> /skee-a-thoss/ a Greek island in the Aegean Sea, part of the Northern Sporades group.

skid ● v. (**skids, skidding, skidded**) **1** (of a vehicle) slide sideways in an uncontrolled way. **2** slip; slide. ● n. **1** an act of skidding. **2** a runner attached to the underside of an aircraft for use when landing on snow or grass.
– PHRASES **on the skids** informal in a bad state. **put the skids under** informal stop (someone) from being successful.
– ORIGIN perh. from **SKI**.

skid row ● n. informal, esp. N. Amer. a run-down part of a town where homeless people and alcoholics live.

skiff ● n. a light rowing boat, usually for one person.
– ORIGIN Italian *schifo*.

ski jump ● n. a steep slope levelling off before a sharp drop to allow a skier to leap through the air.

skilful (US **skillful**) ● adj. having or showing skill.

S

– DERIVATIVES **skilfully** (US **skillfully**) adv.

ski lift • n. a set of moving seats attached to an overhead cable, used to transport skiers to the top of a run.

skill • n. **1** the ability to do something well. **2** a particular ability.
– ORIGIN Old Norse, 'knowledge'.

skilled • adj. **1** having or showing skill. **2** (of work) requiring special abilities or training.

skillet • n. a frying pan.
– ORIGIN perh. from Old French *escuelete* 'little dish'.

skim • v. (**skims**, **skimming**, **skimmed**) **1** remove (a substance) from the surface of a liquid. **2** move quickly and lightly over or on a surface or through the air. **3** read through (something) quickly, noting only the main points. **4** (**skim over**) deal with (a subject) briefly.
– ORIGIN Old French *escumer*.

skimmed milk (N. Amer. also **skim milk**) • n. milk from which the cream has been removed.

skimp • v. spend less money, time, etc. than is really needed in an attempt to economize: *don't skimp on holiday insurance*.
– ORIGIN unknown.

skimpy • adj. (**skimpier**, **skimpiest**) **1** less than is necessary; meagre. **2** (of clothes) short and revealing.

skin • n. **1** the thin layer of tissue forming the outer covering of the body of a person or animal. **2** the skin of a dead animal used for clothing or other items. **3** the peel or outer layer of a fruit or vegetable. **4** an outer layer. • v. (**skins**, **skinning**, **skinned**) **1** remove the skin from. **2** graze (a part of one's body).
– PHRASES **by the skin of one's teeth** only just. **get under someone's skin** informal annoy someone greatly. **have a thick skin** be unaffected by criticism. **it's no skin off my** (or **his** etc.) **nose** informal one is not upset by something.
– DERIVATIVES **skinless** adj.
– ORIGIN Old English.

skin-deep • adj. not deep or lasting; superficial.

skin diving • n. the activity of swimming under water without a diving suit, using an aqualung and flippers.
– DERIVATIVES **skin-diver** n.

skinflint • n. informal a very mean person.

skinful • n. Brit. informal enough alcohol to make one drunk.

skinhead • n. a young person of a group with very short hair, especially one who is aggressive and racist.

skink • n. a smooth-bodied lizard with short or absent limbs.
– ORIGIN Greek *skinkos*.

skinny • adj. (**skinnier**, **skinniest**) **1** very thin. **2** (of a garment) tight-fitting.

skint • adj. Brit. informal having little or no money.
– ORIGIN from *skinned*, in the same sense.

skintight • adj. (of a garment) very close-fitting.

skip[1] • v. (**skips**, **skipping**, **skipped**) **1** move along lightly, stepping from one foot to the other with a little jump. **2** jump repeatedly over a rope which is held at both ends and turned over the head and under the feet. **3** omit or move quickly over (part of something being read or watched). **4** fail to attend or deal with: *try not to skip breakfast*. • n. a skipping movement.
– ORIGIN prob. Scandinavian.

skip[2] • n. Brit. a large open-topped container for holding and carrying away bulky refuse.
– ORIGIN Old Norse, 'basket, bushel'.

skipper informal • n. **1** the captain of a ship, boat, or aircraft. **2** the captain of a sports team. • v. (**skippers**, **skippering**, **skippered**) be captain of.
– ORIGIN Dutch or German *schipper*.

skirl • n. a shrill sound made by bagpipes.
– ORIGIN prob. Scandinavian.

skirmish • n. a spell of unplanned fighting between small groups of troops. • v. take part in a skirmish.
– DERIVATIVES **skirmisher** n.
– ORIGIN Old French *eskirmir*.

skirt • n. **1** a woman's garment that hangs from the waist. **2** the part of a coat or dress that hangs below the waist. • v. **1** go round or past the edge of. **2** (also **skirt around**) avoid dealing with.
– ORIGIN Old Norse, 'shirt'.

skirting (also **skirting board**) • n. Brit. a wooden board running along the base of the wall of a room.

skit • n. a short comedy sketch or piece of humorous writing that makes fun of something by imitating it.
– ORIGIN perh. from Old Norse.

skitter • v. (**skitters**, **skittering**, **skittered**) move lightly and quickly.
– ORIGIN uncertain.

skittish • adj. **1** (of a horse) nervous; inclined to shy. **2** lively or changeable.
– DERIVATIVES **skittishly** adv. **skittishness** n.
– ORIGIN perh. from **SKIT**.

skittle • n. **1** (**skittles**) a game played with wooden pins set up to be bowled down with a wooden ball. **2** a pin used in the game of skittles.
– ORIGIN unknown.

skive /*rhymes with* dive/ • v. (**skives**, **skiving**, **skived**) Brit. informal avoid work or a duty by staying away or leaving early.
– DERIVATIVES **skiver** n.
– ORIGIN perh. from French *esquiver* 'slink away'.

skivvy • n. (pl. **skivvies**) Brit. informal a low-ranking female domestic servant.
– ORIGIN unknown.

Skopje E
/skop-yay/ the capital of Macedonia.

Skryabin E
var. of **SCRIABIN**.

skua /skyoo-uh/ • n. a large seabird like a gull.
– ORIGIN Old Norse.

skulduggery (also **skullduggery**) • n. underhand or dishonest behaviour.
– ORIGIN Scots *sculduddery*.

skulk • v. hide or move around in a stealthy way.
– ORIGIN Scandinavian.

skull • n. **1** the bony framework that surrounds and protects the brain. **2** informal a person's head or brain.
– PHRASES **skull and crossbones** a picture of

a skull with two thigh bones crossed below it, formerly used by pirates and now as a warning symbol.
– ORIGIN unknown.

skullcap • n. a small close-fitting cap without a peak.

skunk • n. a black-and-white striped American mammal able to spray foul-smelling liquid at attackers.
– ORIGIN from an American Indian language.

sky • n. (pl. **skies**) the region of the upper atmosphere seen from the earth. • v. (**skies**, **skying**, **skied**) informal hit (a ball) high into the air.
– PHRASES **the sky is the limit** there is no limit.
– DERIVATIVES **skyward** adj. & adv. **skywards** adv.
– ORIGIN Old Norse, 'cloud'.

sky blue • n. a bright clear blue.

skydiving • n. the sport of jumping from an aircraft and performing acrobatic movements before landing by parachute.
– DERIVATIVES **skydiver** n.

Skye E
the largest island of the Inner Hebrides; chief town, Portree.

sky-high • adv. & adj. very high.

skylark • n. a lark that sings while in flight. • v. play about light-heartedly.

skylight • n. a window set in a roof or ceiling.

skyline • n. an outline of land and buildings seen against the sky.

skyrocket • v. (**skyrockets**, **skyrocketing**, **skyrocketed**) informal (of a price or amount) increase very rapidly.

skyscraper • n. a very tall building.

slab • n. **1** a large, thick, flat piece of stone or concrete. **2** a thick slice or piece of cake, bread, etc.
– ORIGIN unknown.

slack[1] • adj. **1** not taut or held tightly in position; loose. **2** (of business or trade) not busy. **3** careless or lazy. **4** (of a tide) between the ebb and the flow. • n. **1** the part of a rope or line which is not held taut. **2** (**slacks**) casual trousers. • v. **1** (**slack off/up**) decrease in intensity or speed. **2** Brit. informal work slowly.
– DERIVATIVES **slacker** n. **slackly** adv. **slackness** n.
– ORIGIN Old English.

slack[2] • n. coal dust or small pieces of coal.
– ORIGIN prob. German or Dutch.

slacken • v. **1** make or become less active or intense. **2** make or become less tight.

slag • n. **1** stony waste matter that is left when metal has been separated from ore by smelting or refining. **2** Brit. informal, derog. a woman who has many sexual partners. • v. (**slags**, **slagging**, **slagged**) (**slag off**) Brit. informal criticize in a rude or harsh way.
– ORIGIN German *slagge*.

slag heap • n. a mound of waste material from a mine or industrial site.

slain past part. of SLAY.

slake • v. (**slakes**, **slaking**, **slaked**) satisfy (a desire, thirst, etc.).
– ORIGIN Old English, 'become less eager'.

slaked lime • n. calcium hydroxide, a soluble substance produced by combining quicklime with water.

slalom /slah-luhm/ • n. a skiing or canoeing race following a winding course marked out by poles.
– ORIGIN Norwegian, 'sloping track'.

slam • v. (**slams**, **slamming**, **slammed**) **1** shut forcefully and loudly. **2** push, put, or hit with great force: *she slammed down the phone.* **3** informal criticize severely. • n. a loud bang caused when a door is slammed.
– ORIGIN prob. Scandinavian.

slammer • n. informal prison.

slander • n. the crime of saying something untrue that harms a person's reputation. Compare with LIBEL. • v. (**slanders**, **slandering**, **slandered**) make false and harmful statements about.
– DERIVATIVES **slanderous** adj.
– ORIGIN Old French *esclandre*.

slang • n. very informal words and phrases that are more common in speech than in writing and are used by a particular group of people.
– DERIVATIVES **slangy** adj.
– ORIGIN unknown.

slanging match • n. esp. Brit. a long exchange of insults.

slant • v. **1** slope or lean. **2** present (information) from a particular point of view. • n. **1** a sloping position. **2** a point of view: *a new slant on science.*
– DERIVATIVES **slantwise** adj. & adv.
– ORIGIN Scandinavian.

slap • v. (**slaps**, **slapping**, **slapped**) **1** hit with the palm of one's hand or a flat object. **2** hit against something with a slapping sound. **3** (**slap down**) informal reprimand forcefully. **4** (**slap on**) put (something) on a surface quickly or carelessly. • n. **1** an act of slapping. **2** informal make-up. • adv. (also **slap bang**) informal suddenly and forcefully.
– PHRASES **slap in the face** an unexpected rejection.

slapdash • adj. done too hurriedly and carelessly.

slapper • n. Brit. informal, derog. a woman who has many sexual partners.

slapstick • n. comedy based on deliberately clumsy actions and humorously embarrassing events.
– ORIGIN first referring to a device consisting of two pieces of wood joined at one end, used by clowns to make a loud slapping sound.

slap-up • adj. informal, esp. Brit. (of a meal) large and extravagant.

slash • v. **1** cut with a violent sweeping movement. **2** informal reduce (a price, quantity, etc.) greatly. • n. **1** a cut made with a wide, sweeping stroke. **2** a slanting stroke (/) used between alternatives, in fractions and ratios, or between separate elements of a text.
– DERIVATIVES **slasher** n.
– ORIGIN Old French *esclachier* 'break in pieces'.

slat • n. each of a series of thin, narrow pieces of wood or other material, arranged so as to overlap or fit into each other.
– DERIVATIVES **slatted** adj.
– ORIGIN Old French *esclat* 'splinter'.

slate • n. **1** a grey, green, or bluish-purple rock easily split into smooth, flat plates, used as roofing material and formerly for writing

S

on. **2** a list of candidates for election to a post. ● **v.** (**slates**, **slating**, **slated**) **1** Brit. informal criticize severely. **2** schedule.
– ORIGIN Old French *esclate* 'splinter'.

slather /sla-*th*er/ ● **v.** (**slathers**, **slathering**, **slathered**) informal spread or smear thickly.
– ORIGIN unknown.

slattern /slat-tern/ ● **n.** dated a dirty, untidy woman.
– DERIVATIVES **slatternly** adj.
– ORIGIN unknown.

slaughter /slaw-ter/ ● **n. 1** the killing of farm animals for food. **2** the killing of a large number of people in a cruel or violent way. ● **v.** (**slaughters**, **slaughtering**, **slaughtered**) **1** kill (animals) for food. **2** kill (people) in a cruel or violent way. **3** informal defeat thoroughly.
– DERIVATIVES **slaughterer** n.
– ORIGIN Old Norse, 'butcher's meat'.

slaughterhouse ● **n.** a place where animals are killed for food.

Slav /slahv/ ● **n.** a member of a group of peoples in central and eastern Europe who speak Slavic languages.
– ORIGIN Greek *Sklabos*.

slave ● **n. 1** hist. a person who is the legal property of another and is forced to obey them. **2** a person who is strongly influenced or controlled by something: *a slave to fashion*. ● **v.** (**slaves**, **slaving**, **slaved**) work very hard.
– ORIGIN Latin *sclava* 'Slavonic captive'.

slave-driver ● **n.** informal a person who makes others work very hard.

slave labour ● **n.** work that is very demanding and very poorly paid.

slaver[1] /slay-ver/ ● **n.** hist. a person dealing in or owning slaves.

slaver[2] /sla-ver, slay-ver/ ● **v.** (**slavers**, **slavering**, **slavered**) let saliva run from the mouth. ● **n.** saliva running from the mouth.
– ORIGIN prob. from German.

slavery ● **n. 1** the state of being a slave. **2** the practice of owning slaves.

slave trade ● **n.** hist. the buying and selling of people as slaves.

Slavic /slah-vik/ ● **n.** the group of languages that includes Russian, Polish, and Czech. ● **adj.** relating to these languages or their speakers.

slavish ● **adj.** following or copying something without trying to be original: *a slavish addiction to fashion*.
– DERIVATIVES **slavishly** adv.

S

Slavonic /sluh-von-ik/ ● **n. & adj.** = **SLAVIC**.

slay ● **v.** (**slays**, **slaying**, **slew**; past part. **slain**) archaic kill in a violent way.
– DERIVATIVES **slayer** n.
– ORIGIN Old English.

sleaze ● **n.** informal immoral or dishonest behaviour, especially in politics.

sleazy ● **adj.** (**sleazier**, **sleaziest**) **1** immoral or dishonest. **2** (of a place) dirty and seedy.
– ORIGIN unknown.

sled ● **n. & v.** (**sleds**, **sledding**, **sledded**) N. Amer. = **SLEDGE**.
– ORIGIN German *sledde*.

sledge ● **n. 1** a vehicle on runners for travelling over snow or ice, either pushed, pulled, or allowed to slide downhill. **2** Brit. a toboggan. ● **v.** (**sledges**, **sledging**, **sledged**) ride on a sledge.
– ORIGIN Dutch *sleedse*.

sledgehammer ● **n.** a large, heavy hammer.
– ORIGIN Old English.

sleek ● **adj. 1** (of hair or fur) smooth and glossy. **2** having a wealthy and smart appearance. **3** elegant and streamlined.
– DERIVATIVES **sleekly** adv.
– ORIGIN from **SLICK**.

sleep ● **n.** a state of rest in which the nervous system is inactive, the eyes are closed, the muscles are relaxed, and the mind is unconscious. ● **v.** (**sleeps**, **sleeping**, **slept**) **1** be asleep. **2** (**sleep in**) remain asleep or in bed later than usual. **3** provide (a specified number of people) with beds or bedrooms. **4** (**sleep with**) have sexual intercourse or a sexual relationship with. **5** (**sleep around**) have many sexual partners.
– PHRASES **put to sleep** kill (an animal) painlessly. **sleep on it** informal leave a decision until the next day, so as to have more time to consider it.
– DERIVATIVES **sleepless** adj.
– ORIGIN Old English.

sleeper ● **n. 1** Brit. each of the beams on which a railway track rests. **2** Brit. a ring or bar worn in a pierced ear to keep the hole from closing. **3** a sleeping car or a train carrying sleeping cars. **4** a film, book, etc. that suddenly achieves success after first attracting little attention.

sleeping bag ● **n.** a warm padded bag to sleep in, especially when camping.

sleeping car ● **n.** a railway carriage with beds or berths.

sleeping partner ● **n.** Brit. a partner who is not involved in the work of a firm.

sleeping pill ● **n.** a tablet used to help one sleep.

sleeping policeman ● **n.** Brit. a road hump.

sleeping sickness ● **n.** a tropical disease marked by extreme tiredness.

sleepover ● **n.** esp. N. Amer. an occasion of spending the night away from home.

sleepwalk ● **v.** walk around while asleep.

sleepy ● **adj.** (**sleepier**, **sleepiest**) **1** needing or ready for sleep. **2** (of a place) without much activity.
– DERIVATIVES **sleepily** adv. **sleepiness** n.

sleet ● **n.** rain containing some ice, or snow melting as it falls. ● **v.** (**it sleets**, **it is sleeting**, **it sleeted**) sleet falls.
– DERIVATIVES **sleety** adj.
– ORIGIN Germanic.

sleeve ● **n. 1** the part of a garment covering a person's arm. **2** a protective cover for a record. **3** a tube fitting over a rod, spindle, or smaller tube.
– PHRASES **up one's sleeve** kept secret and ready for use when needed.
– DERIVATIVES **sleeved** adj. **sleeveless** adj.
– ORIGIN Old English.

sleigh ● **n.** a sledge drawn by horses or reindeer.
– ORIGIN Dutch *slee*.

sleight /*rhymes with* slight/ ● **n.** (in phr. **sleight of hand**) skilful use of the hands, especially when performing magic tricks.
– ORIGIN Old Norse, 'sly'.

slender ● **adj.** (**slenderer**, **slenderest**) **1** gracefully thin. **2** barely enough: *the party*

has kept a slender majority.
– ORIGIN unknown.

slept past and past part. of **SLEEP**.

sleuth /*rhymes with* truth/ informal ● n. a detective. ● v. investigate.
– ORIGIN Old Norse 'track'.

S level ● n. (in the UK except Scotland) an examination taken together with an A level in the same subject but covering more advanced topics.
– ORIGIN short for *Special level.*

slew[1] ● v. turn or slide violently or uncontrollably. ● n. a slewing movement.
ORIGIN unknown.

slew[2] past of **SLAY**.

slice ● n. **1** a thin, broad piece of food cut from a larger portion. **2** a portion or share. **3** a utensil with a broad, flat blade for lifting foods such as fish. **4** (in sports) a sliced stroke or shot. ● v. (**slices**, **slicing**, **sliced**) **1** cut into slices. **2** cut with a sharp implement. **3** (often **slice through**) move easily and quickly. **4** (in sport) hit (the ball) at a slight angle so that it spins and curves as it travels.
– ORIGIN Old French *esclice* 'splinter'.

slick ● adj. **1** done or operating in an impressively smooth and efficient way. **2** self-confident but insincere. **3** (of skin or hair) smooth and glossy. **4** (of a surface) smooth, wet, and slippery. ● n. a smooth patch of oil. ● v. make (hair) flat and slick with water, oil, or cream.
– ORIGIN prob. from Old Norse, 'smooth'.

slide ● v. (**slides**, **sliding**, **slid**) **1** move along a smooth surface while remaining in contact with it. **2** move smoothly, quickly, or without being noticed. **2** gradually become lower or worse. ● n. **1** a structure with a smooth sloping surface for children to slide down. **2** a smooth stretch of ice for sliding on. **3** an act of sliding. **4** a rectangular piece of glass on which an object is placed to be viewed under a microscope. **5** a small piece of photographic film held in a frame and viewed with a projector. **6** Brit. a hairslide.
– ORIGIN Old English.

slide rule ● n. a ruler with a sliding central strip, marked with logarithmic scales and used for making calculations.

sliding scale ● n. a scale of fees, wages, etc., that varies according to particular conditions.

slight ● adj. **1** small in degree. **2** lacking depth: *the novel had a rather slight plot.* **3** not sturdy and strongly built. ● v. insult (someone) by treating them without proper respect. ● n. an insult.
– ORIGIN Old Norse, 'smooth'.

slightly ● adv. **1** to a small degree. **2** (of a person's build) in a slender way.

> **Sligo** E
> /sly-goh/ a county in the west of the Republic of Ireland; county town, Sligo.

slim ● adj. (**slimmer**, **slimmest**) **1** gracefully thin. **2** small in width and long and narrow in shape. **3** very small: *a slim chance.* ● v. (**slims**, **slimming**, **slimmed**) make or become thinner.
– DERIVATIVES **slimmer** n.
– ORIGIN German or Dutch.

slime ● n. an unpleasantly moist, soft, and slippery substance.
– ORIGIN Old English.

slimline ● adj. **1** slender in design. **2** (of food or drink) low in calories.

slimy ● adj. (**slimier**, **slimiest**) **1** like or covered by slime. **2** informal pleasant or flattering in an insincere way.

sling ● n. **1** a flexible loop of fabric used to support or raise a hanging weight. **2** a weapon in the form of a strap or loop, used to hurl small missiles. ● v. (**slings**, **slinging**, **slung**) **1** hang or carry loosely: *he slung the hammock between two trees.* **2** informal throw carelessly.
– ORIGIN prob. from German.

slingback ● n. a shoe held in place by a strap around the ankle above the heel.

slingshot ● n. a hand-held catapult.

slink ● v. (**slinks**, **slinking**, **slunk**) move quietly in a secretive way.
– ORIGIN Old English, 'crawl, creep'.

slinky ● adj. (**slinkier**, **slinkiest**) informal graceful and curvy.

slip[1] ● v. (**slips**, **slipping**, **slipped**) **1** lose one's balance and slide for a short distance. **2** accidentally slide out of position or from someone's grasp. **3** fail to grip a surface. **4** pass gradually to a worse condition. **5** (usu. **slip up**) make a careless error. **6** move or place quietly, quickly, or secretly. **7** get free from: *the balloon slipped its moorings.* **8** fail to be remembered by. ● n. **1** an act of slipping. **2** a minor or careless mistake. **3** a loose-fitting short petticoat. **4** Cricket a fielding position close behind and to one side of the batsman.
– PHRASES **give someone the slip** informal escape from someone. **let slip** reveal accidentally in conversation. **slip of the pen** (or **the tongue**) a minor mistake in writing (or speech).
– DERIVATIVES **slippage** n.
– ORIGIN prob. from German *slippen.*

slip[2] ● n. **1** a small piece of paper for writing on or that gives printed information. **2** a cutting taken from a plant for grafting or planting.
– PHRASES **a slip of a boy/girl/thing** a small, slim young person.
– ORIGIN prob. from Dutch or German *slippe* 'cut, strip'.

slip[3] ● n. a creamy mixture of clay and water used for decorating pottery.
– ORIGIN uncertain.

slip knot ● n. a knot that can be undone by a pull, or that can slide along the rope on which it is tied.

slip-on ● adj. (of shoes or clothes) having no fastenings and therefore able to be put on and taken off quickly.

slipped disc ● n. a disc between vertebrae in the spine that is displaced, pressing on nearby nerves and causing pain.

slipper ● n. a comfortable slip-on shoe that is worn indoors.

slippery ● adj. **1** difficult to hold firmly or stand on through being smooth or wet. **2** (of a person) difficult to trust.

slippery slope ● n. a course of action likely to lead to something bad.

slippy ● adj. (**slippier**, **slippiest**) informal slippery.

slip road ● n. Brit. a road entering or leaving a

motorway.

slipshod • adj. careless, thoughtless, or disorganized.

slipstream • n. **1** a current of air or water driven back by a revolving propeller or jet engine. **2** the partial vacuum created behind a moving vehicle.

slip-up • n. informal a mistake.

slipway • n. a slope leading into water, used for launching and landing boats and ships or for building and repairing them.

slit • n. a long, narrow cut or opening. • v. (**slits**, **slitting**, **slit**) make a slit in.
– ORIGIN Old English.

slither • v. (**slithers**, **slithering**, **slithered**) **1** move smoothly over a surface with a twisting motion. **2** slide unsteadily on a loose or slippery surface.
– DERIVATIVES **slithery** adj.
– ORIGIN from dialect *slidder*.

slitty • adj. esp. derog. (of the eyes) long and narrow.

sliver /*rhymes with* river *or* diver/ • n. a small, narrow, sharp piece cut or split off a larger piece.
– ORIGIN from dialect *slive* 'cleave'.

Sloane[1], E
Sir Hans (1660–1753), Irish physician and naturalist. His books and specimens formed the basis of the British Museum Library and the Natural History Museum in London.

Sloane[2] (also **Sloane Ranger**) • n. Brit. informal a fashionable upper-class young woman.
– DERIVATIVES **Sloaney** adj.
– ORIGIN from *Sloane* Square, London + Lone *Ranger*, a fictional cowboy hero.

slob informal • n. a lazy and untidy person. • v. (**slobs**, **slobbing**, **slobbed**) behave in a lazy, untidy way.
– ORIGIN Irish *slab* 'mud'.

slobber • v. (**slobbers**, **slobbering**, **slobbered**) **1** have much saliva dripping from the mouth. **2** (**slobber over**) show excessive enthusiasm for.
– DERIVATIVES **slobbery** adj.
– ORIGIN prob. from Dutch *slobberen* 'walk through mud'.

sloe /*rhymes with* slow/ • n. the small bluish-black fruit of the blackthorn, with a sharp sour taste.
– ORIGIN Old English.

slog • v. (**slogs**, **slogging**, **slogged**) **1** work hard over a period of time. **2** move with difficulty or effort. **3** strike forcefully. **4** (**slog it out**) fight or compete fiercely. • n. a spell of difficult, tiring work or travelling.
– ORIGIN unknown.

slogan • n. a short, memorable phrase used in advertising or associated with a political group.
– ORIGIN from Scottish Gaelic *sluagh* 'army' + *gairm* 'shout'.

sloop • n. a type of sailing boat with one mast.
– ORIGIN Dutch *sloep*.

slop • v. (**slops**, **slopping**, **slopped**) **1** (of a liquid) spill over the edge of a container. **2** apply (something) carelessly. **3** (**slop out**) empty the contents of a chamber pot. **4** (**slop about/around**) esp. Brit. dress in an untidy or casual way. • n. **1** (**slops**) waste liquid. **2** (**slops**) unappetizing semi-liquid food.
– ORIGIN prob. from SLIP[3].

slope • n. **1** a surface with one end or side at a higher level than another. **2** a part of the side of a hill or mountain. • v. (**slopes**, **sloping**, **sloped**) **1** slant up or down. **2** informal move in an aimless way. **3** (**slope off**) informal leave without attracting attention.
– ORIGIN uncertain.

sloppy • adj. (**sloppier**, **sloppiest**) **1** (of a substance) containing too much liquid. **2** careless and disorganized. **3** (of a garment) casual and loose-fitting.
– DERIVATIVES **sloppily** adv. **sloppiness** n.

slosh • v. **1** (of liquid in a container) move around with a splashing sound. **2** move through liquid with a splashing sound. **3** pour (liquid) clumsily. • n. an act or sound of splashing.
– ORIGIN from SLUSH.

sloshed • adj. informal drunk.

slot • n. **1** a long, narrow opening into which something may be inserted. **2** a place given to someone or something in an arrangement or scheme. • v. (**slots**, **slotting**, **slotted**) **1** place or be placed into a slot. **2** (**slot in/into**) fit easily into (a new role or situation).
– ORIGIN Old French *esclot*.

sloth /slohth/ • n. **1** laziness. **2** a slow-moving tropical American mammal that hangs upside down from branches.
– DERIVATIVES **slothful** adj.
– ORIGIN Old English.

slot machine • n. a fruit machine or (Brit.) vending machine.

slouch • v. stand, move, or sit in a lazy, drooping way. • n. **1** a lazy, drooping way of standing or sitting. **2** informal an incompetent person: *he was no slouch at making a buck*.
– DERIVATIVES **slouchy** adj.
– ORIGIN unknown.

slouch hat • n. a hat with a wide flexible brim.

slough[1] /*rhymes with* plough/ • n. **1** a swamp. **2** a situation without progress or activity.
– ORIGIN Old English.

slough[2] /*rhymes with* rough/ • v. (of an animal) cast off (an old skin).
– ORIGIN perh. from German *sluwe* 'peel'.

Slovakia E
/sluh-vak-i-uh/ a country in central Europe; capital, Bratislava.
– DERIVATIVES **Slovakian** adj. & n.

Slovenia E
/sluh-vee-ni-uh/ a country in SE Europe, formerly a republic of Yugoslavia; capital, Ljubljana.
– DERIVATIVES **Slovenian** adj. & n.

slovenly • adj. **1** untidy and dirty. **2** careless: *slovenly speech*.
– DERIVATIVES **slovenliness** n.
– ORIGIN perh. from Flemish *sloef* 'dirty' or Dutch *slof* 'careless'.

slow • adj. **1** moving or capable of moving only at a low speed. **2** taking a long time. **3** (of a clock or watch) showing a time earlier than the correct time. **4** not quick to understand, think, or learn. **5** with little activity: *sales were slow*. **6** (of an oven) giving off heat gently. • v. (often **slow down/up**) **1** reduce speed. **2** live or work less actively.

– DERIVATIVES **slowly** n. **slowness** n.
– ORIGIN Old English.

slowcoach • n. Brit. informal a person who acts or moves slowly.

slow cooker • n. a large electric pot used for cooking food very slowly.

slow motion • n. the showing of film or video more slowly than it was made or recorded, so that the action appears much slower than in real life.

slow-worm • n. a small lizard without legs.
– ORIGIN Old English.

slub • n. **1** a lump in yarn or thread. **2** fabric woven from yarn with such a texture.
– ORIGIN unknown.

sludge • n. **1** thick, soft, wet mud or a similar substance. **2** dirty oil or industrial waste.
– DERIVATIVES **sludgy** adj.
– ORIGIN uncertain.

slug[1] • n. **1** a small mollusc like a snail without a shell. **2** informal a small amount of an alcoholic drink. **3** informal a bullet.
– ORIGIN prob. Scandinavian.

slug[2] • v. (**slugs, slugging, slugged**) informal, esp. N. Amer. **1** strike with a hard blow. **2** (**slug it out**) settle a dispute or contest by fighting or competing fiercely.
– ORIGIN unknown.

sluggard • n. a lazy, inactive person.
– ORIGIN from former *slug* 'be lazy'.

sluggish • adj. **1** slow-moving or inactive. **2** not lively or alert.
– DERIVATIVES **sluggishly** adv. **sluggishness** n.

sluice /slooss/ • n. **1** (also **sluice gate**) a sliding device for controlling the flow of water. **2** an artificial channel for carrying off surplus water. **3** an act of rinsing. • v. (**sluices, sluicing, sluiced**) wash or rinse with water.
– ORIGIN Old French *escluse*.

slum • n. **1** a dirty and overcrowded area of a city or town inhabited by very poor people. **2** a house or building unfit to be lived in. • v. (**slums, slumming, slummed**) (often **slum it**) informal willingly spend time in uncomfortable conditions or at a lower social level.
– ORIGIN unknown.

slumber literary • v. (**slumbers, slumbering, slumbered**) sleep. • n. a sleep.
ORIGIN from Scots and northern English *sloom*.

slump • v. **1** sit, lean, or fall heavily and limply. **2** decline greatly or over a lengthy period. • n. a sudden fall in prices or a long period of low economic activity.
– ORIGIN prob. from Norwegian *slumpe* 'to fall'.

slung past and past part. of SLING.

slunk past and past part. of SLINK.

slur • v. (**slurs, slurring, slurred**) **1** speak in an unclear way. **2** Music perform (a group of two or more notes) in a smooth, flowing way. • n. **1** an insulting remark or accusation intended to damage someone's reputation. **2** Music a curved line indicating that notes are to be slurred.
– ORIGIN unknown.

slurp • v. eat or drink with a loud sucking sound. • n. a sound of slurping.
– ORIGIN Dutch *slurpen*.

slurry /*rhymes with* hurry/ • n. a semi-liquid mixture of manure, cement, or coal and water.
– ORIGIN unknown.

slush • n. **1** partially melted snow or ice. **2** informal excessively romantic or emotional talk or writing.
– DERIVATIVES **slushy** adj.

slush fund • n. a reserve of money used for illegal purposes.
– ORIGIN nautical slang referring to money collected to buy luxuries, from the sale of watery food known as *slush*.

slut • n. a woman who is slovenly or who has many sexual partners.
– DERIVATIVES **sluttish** adj.
– ORIGIN unknown.

sly • adj. (**slyer, slyest**) **1** having a cunning and deceitful nature. **2** (of a remark, glance, or expression) suggesting secret knowledge. **3** (of an action) done secretly: *a sly sip of water.*
– PHRASES **on the sly** in a secret way.
– DERIVATIVES **slyly** adv. **slyness** n.
– ORIGIN Old Norse, 'cunning'.

smack[1] • n. **1** a sharp blow given with the palm of the hand. **2** a loud, sharp sound. **3** a loud kiss. • v. **1** hit with a smack. **2** hit or smash into. **3** part (one's lips) noisily. • adv. **1** in a sudden and violent way. **2** exactly.
– ORIGIN Dutch *smacken*.

smack[2] • v. (**smack of**) **1** have a flavour or smell of. **2** suggest the presence or effects of (something wrong or unpleasant). • n. (**a smack of**) a flavour, smell, or suggestion of.
– ORIGIN Old English.

smack[3] • n. a sailing boat with one mast, used for coasting or fishing.
– ORIGIN Dutch *smak*.

smack[4] • n. informal heroin.
– ORIGIN prob. from Yiddish, 'a sniff'.

smacker (also **smackeroo**) • n. informal **1** a loud kiss. **2** Brit. one pound sterling. **3** N. Amer. one dollar.

small • adj. **1** of less than normal size. **2** not great in amount, number, strength, or power. **3** young. **4** unimportant. **5** (of a business or its owner) operating on a modest scale: *a small farmer.* • n. (**smalls**) Brit. informal underwear. • adv. **1** into small pieces. **2** in a small size: *you shouldn't write so small.*
– PHRASES **feel** (or **look**) **small** feel (or look) foolish. **small beer** esp. Brit. something unimportant. **the small of the back** the part of a person's back where the spine curves in at the waist. **the small screen** television.
– DERIVATIVES **smallness** n.
– ORIGIN Old English.

small arms • pl. n. portable firearms.

small change • n. **1** coins of low value. **2** something unimportant.

small claims court • n. a local court in which claims for small sums of money can be decided quickly and cheaply, without legal representation.

small fry • pl. n. **1** young or small fish. **2** unimportant people or things.

smallholding • n. Brit. a piece of agricultural land that is smaller than a farm.
– DERIVATIVES **smallholder** n.

small hours • pl. n. (**the small hours**) the early hours of the morning after midnight.

small intestine • n. the part of the intestine that runs between the stomach and the large intestine.

small-minded • adj. having a narrow outlook.

smallpox • n. a disease spread by a virus, with fever and pustules that leave permanent scars.

small print • n. details printed so that they are not easily noticed in an agreement or contract.

small-scale • adj. of limited size or extent.

small talk • n. polite conversation about unimportant matters.

small-time • adj. informal unimportant.

smarmy • adj. Brit. informal polite and friendly in an insincere and excessive way.
– ORIGIN unknown.

smart • adj. **1** clean, tidy, and stylish. **2** bright and fresh in appearance: *a smart green van.* **3** (of a place) fashionable and upmarket. **4** esp. N. Amer. intelligent. **5** quick: *I gave him a smart salute.* • v. **1** give a sharp, stinging pain. **2** feel upset and annoyed.
– PHRASES **look smart** esp. Brit. be quick.
– DERIVATIVES **smartly** adv. **smartness** n.
– ORIGIN Old English.

smart alec (also **smart aleck**) • n. informal a person who irritates others by always having a clever answer to a question.

smart card • n. a plastic card on which information is stored in electronic form.

smarten • v. (**smarten up**) make or become smarter.

smartish • adv. informal, esp. Brit. quickly.

smash • v. **1** break violently into pieces. **2** hit or collide with forcefully. **3** (in sport) strike (the ball) hard. **4** completely defeat, destroy, or foil. • n. **1** an act or sound of smashing. **2** (also **smash hit**) informal a very successful song, film, or show.

smash-and-grab • adj. (of a robbery) in which the thief smashes a shop window and seizes goods.

smasher • n. Brit. informal a very attractive or impressive person or thing.

smashing • adj. Brit. informal excellent.

smattering (also **smatter**) • n. **1** a small amount. **2** a slight knowledge of a language or subject.
– ORIGIN unknown.

smear • v. **1** coat or mark with a greasy or sticky substance. **2** blur or smudge. **3** damage the reputation of (someone) by false accusations. • n. **1** a greasy or sticky mark. **2** a false accusation. **3** a sample thinly spread on a slide for examination under a microscope.
– DERIVATIVES **smeary** adj.
– ORIGIN Old English.

smear test • n. a test to detect signs of cervical cancer.

smell • n. **1** the faculty of perceiving odours by means of the organs in the nose. **2** a quality that is sensed by this; an odour. **3** an act of smelling. • v. (**smells**, **smelling**, **smelt** or **smelled**) **1** perceive the odour of. **2** sniff at (something) in order to find out its odour. **3** send out an odour. **4** have a strong or unpleasant odour. **5** detect or sense: *I can smell trouble.*
– PHRASES **smell a rat** informal suspect a trick.
– ORIGIN unknown.

smelling salts • pl. n. esp. hist. a chemical mixed with perfume, sniffed by someone who feels faint.

smelly • adj. (**smellier**, **smelliest**) having a strong or unpleasant smell.

smelt[1] • v. extract (metal) from its ore by a process involving heating and melting.
– DERIVATIVES **smelter** n.
– ORIGIN Dutch or German *smelten*.

smelt[2] past and past part. of SMELL.

smelt[3] • n. (pl. **smelt** or **smelts**) a small silvery fish.
– ORIGIN Old English.

Smetana E
/smet-uh-nuh/, Bedřich (1824–84), Czech composer, the founder of Czech music. His works include the opera *The Bartered Bride* and the cycle of symphonic poems *Ma Vlast ('My Country')*.

smidgen (also **smidgeon** or **smidgin**) • n. informal a tiny amount.
– ORIGIN perh. from Scots *smitch* in the same sense.

smile • v. (**smiles**, **smiling**, **smiled**) **1** form one's features into a pleased, friendly, or amused expression, with the corners of the mouth turned up. **2** (**smile at/on/upon**) favour: *fortune smiled on him.* • n. an act of smiling.
– ORIGIN perh. Scandinavian.

smiley • adj. informal smiling and cheerful.

smirch /smerch/ • v. **1** make dirty. **2** discredit (a person or their reputation).

smirk • v. smile in an irritatingly smug or silly way. • n. a smug or silly smile.
– ORIGIN Old English.

smite • v. (**smites**, **smiting**, **smote**; past part. **smitten**) **1** archaic strike with a firm blow. **2** archaic defeat or conquer. **3** (**be smitten**) be affected severely by a disease. **4** (**be smitten**) be strongly attracted to someone.
– ORIGIN Old English, 'to smear'.

Smith[1], E
Adam (1723–90), Scottish economist and philosopher. He advocated minimal state interference in economic matters, and his theories formed the basis of modern economics.

Smith[2], E
Bessie (1894–1937), American blues singer.

Smith[3], E
Ian (Douglas) (b.1919), Rhodesian statesman, Prime Minister 1964–79. As Prime Minister he led a white minority government. In 1965 he issued a unilateral declaration of independence from Britain (UDI) because he would not agree to black majority rule. He resigned in 1979.

Smith[4], E
Joseph (1805–44), American religious leader and founder of the Church of Jesus Christ of Latter-Day Saints (the Mormons).

Smith[5], E
Stevie (1902–71; pen name of *Florence Margaret Smith*), English poet and novelist. Her witty verse includes the collection *Not Waving But Drowning*.

smith • n. **1** a worker in metal. **2** a blacksmith. • v. treat (metal) by heating, hammering, and forging it.
– ORIGIN Old English.

S

smithereens /smi-*th*uh-**reenz**/ • **pl. n.** informal small pieces.
– ORIGIN prob. from Irish *smidirín.*

Smithsonian Institution E
/smith-**soh**-ni-uhn/ a US foundation for education and scientific research in Washington DC, opened in 1846.

smithy /smi-*th*i/ • **n.** (pl. **smithies**) a blacksmith's workshop.
– ORIGIN Old Norse.

smitten past part. of **SMITE**.

smock • **n. 1** a loose dress or blouse having the upper part closely gathered in smocking. **2** a loose overall worn to protect one's clothes.
– ORIGIN Old English.

smocking • **n.** decoration on a garment created by gathering a section of the material into tight pleats and holding them together with decorative parallel stitches.

smog • **n.** fog or haze made worse by other pollutants in the atmosphere such as smoke.
– ORIGIN from **SMOKE** and **FOG**.

smoke • **n. 1** a visible vapour in the air produced by a burning substance. **2** an act of smoking tobacco. **3** informal a cigarette or cigar. **4** (**the Smoke** or **the Big Smoke**) Brit. a big city. • **v.** (**smokes, smoking, smoked**) **1** give out smoke. **2** breathe the smoke of tobacco or a drug in and out. **3** preserve (meat or fish) by exposing it to smoke. **4** treat (glass) so as to darken it. **5** (**smoke out**) drive out of a place by using smoke.
– PHRASES **go up in smoke** informal (of a plan) come to nothing. **there is no smoke without fire** rumours usually have some basis in fact.
– DERIVATIVES **smokeless** adj.
– ORIGIN Old English.

smoke alarm • **n.** a device that detects and gives a warning of the presence of smoke.

smokeless zone • **n.** Brit. a district in which it is illegal to create smoke.

smoker • **n.** a person who smokes tobacco regularly.

smokescreen • **n. 1** a cloud of smoke created to conceal military operations. **2** a thing designed to disguise someone's real intentions or activities.

smokestack • **n.** a chimney or funnel for discharging smoke from a locomotive, ship, factory, etc.

smoking gun • **n.** a piece of evidence that proves without doubt that someone is guilty of wrongdoing.

smoking jacket • **n.** a man's comfortable jacket, formerly worn while smoking after dinner.

smoky • **adj.** (**smokier, smokiest**) **1** producing or filled with smoke. **2** having the taste or smell of smoked food.

smolder • **v.** US = **SMOULDER**.

smolt /smohlt/ • **n.** a young salmon or trout after the parr stage, when it migrates to the sea for the first time.
– ORIGIN unknown.

smooch • **v.** informal **1** kiss and cuddle. **2** Brit. dance slowly in a close embrace.
– DERIVATIVES **smoochy** adj.

smooth • **adj. 1** having an even and regular surface. **2** (of a liquid) without lumps. **3** (of movement) without jerks. **4** happening without difficulties. **5** charming in a very confident or flattering way. **6** (of a flavour) not harsh or bitter. • **v.** (also **smoothe**) (**smooths** or **smoothes, smoothing, smoothed**) **1** make smooth. **2** (**smooth over**) deal successfully with (a problem).
– DERIVATIVES **smoothly** adv. **smoothness** n.
– ORIGIN Old English.

smoothie • **n. 1** informal a man with a smooth, confident manner. **2** a thick, smooth drink of fresh fruit puréed with milk, yogurt, or ice cream.

smooth snake • **n.** a harmless grey or reddish snake found in heathy country.

smooth-talking • **adj.** informal using very persuasive or flattering language.

smooth-tongued • **adj.** insincerely flattering.

smorgasbord /smor-guhz-bord/ • **n.** a meal consisting of a range of open sandwiches and savoury items.
– ORIGIN Swedish.

smote past of **SMITE**.

smother • **v.** (**smothers, smothering, smothered**) **1** suffocate by covering the nose and mouth. **2** put out (a fire) by covering it. **3** (**smother in/with**) cover entirely with. **4** cause (someone) to feel overwhelmed by being too protective of them. **5** stifle: *she smothered a sigh.*
– ORIGIN Old English.

smoulder (US **smolder**) • **v.** (**smoulders, smouldering, smouldered**; US **smolders, smoldering, smoldered**) **1** burn slowly with smoke but no flame. **2** feel strong and barely hidden anger, hatred, lust, etc.
– ORIGIN Dutch *smeulen.*

smudge • **v.** (**smudges, smudging, smudged**) make or become blurred or smeared. • **n.** a smudged mark.
– DERIVATIVES **smudgy** adj.
– ORIGIN unknown.

smug • **adj.** (**smugger, smuggest**) irritatingly pleased with oneself.
– DERIVATIVES **smugly** adv. **smugness** n.
– ORIGIN German *smuk* 'pretty'.

smuggle • **v.** (**smuggles, smuggling, smuggled**) **1** move (goods) illegally into or out of a country. **2** convey (someone or something) somewhere secretly.
– DERIVATIVES **smuggler** n.
– ORIGIN German *smuggelen.*

smut • **n. 1** a small flake of soot or dirt. **2** indecent talk, writing, or pictures.
– ORIGIN German *schmutzen.*

Smuts E
/smuts/, Jan (Christiaan) (1870–1950), South African statesman and soldier, Prime Minister 1919–24 and 1939–48. He led Boer forces in the Boer War, but afterwards supported co-operation with Britain. He later played a leading role in the formation of the United Nations.

smutty • **adj. 1** indecent. **2** dirty or sooty.

Smyrna E
/smer-nuh/ an ancient city on the site of modern Izmir in Turkey.

Sn • **symb.** the chemical element tin.
– ORIGIN Latin *stannum* 'tin'.

snack • **n.** a small quantity of food eaten be-

S

tween meals or in place of a meal. ● **v.** eat a snack.
– ORIGIN Dutch.

snaffle ● **n.** a simple bit on a horse's bridle, used with a single set of reins. ● **v.** (**snaffles, snaffling, snaffled**) informal secretly take for oneself.
– ORIGIN prob. German or Dutch.

snag ● **n. 1** an unexpected difficulty. **2** a sharp or jagged projection. **3** a small tear. ● **v.** (**snags, snagging, snagged**) catch or tear on a sharp projection.
– ORIGIN prob. Scandinavian.

snaggle ● **v.** (**snaggles, snaggling, snaggled**) become knotted or tangled.
– ORIGIN from SNAG.

snaggle-toothed ● **adj.** having irregular or projecting teeth.

snail ● **n.** a slow-moving mollusc with a spiral shell into which it can withdraw its whole body.
– ORIGIN Old English.

snake ● **n. 1** a reptile with a long slender limbless body, many kinds of which have a poisonous bite. **2** (also **snake in the grass**) a person who pretends to be someone's friend but is secretly working against them. ● **v.** (**snakes, snaking, snaked**) move with the twisting motion of a snake.
– ORIGIN Old English.

snake charmer ● **n.** an entertainer who appears to make snakes move by playing music.

snaky ● **adj.** (**snakier, snakiest**) **1** long and curvy. **2** cold and cunning.

snap ● **v.** (**snaps, snapping, snapped**) **1** break with a sharp cracking sound. **2** (of an animal) make a sudden bite. **3** open or close with a brisk movement or sharp sound. **4** (**snap up**) quickly buy (something that is in short supply). **5** suddenly lose one's self-control. **6** say something quickly and irritably. **7** (**snap out of**) informal get out of (a bad mood) by a sudden effort. **8** take a snapshot of. ● **n. 1** an act or sound of snapping. **2** a brief spell of particular weather: *a cold snap.* **3** a snapshot. **4** Brit. a card game in which players compete to call 'snap' as soon as two cards of the same type are exposed. ● **adj.** done on the spur of the moment: *a snap decision.*
– ORIGIN prob. from Dutch or German *snappen* 'seize'.

snapdragon ● **n.** a plant with brightly coloured flowers which have a mouth-like opening.

snapper ● **n.** a marine fish noted for snapping its toothed jaws.

snappish ● **adj.** irritable.

snappy ● **adj.** (**snappier, snappiest**) informal **1** irritable and sharp. **2** cleverly brief and to the point: *snappy dialogue.* **3** neat and stylish: *a snappy dresser.*
– PHRASES **make it snappy** do it quickly.

snapshot ● **n.** an informal photograph, taken quickly.

snare ● **n. 1** a trap for catching small animals, consisting of a loop of wire that pulls tight. **2** a situation that is likely to lure someone into trouble. **3** (also **snare drum**) a drum with a length of wire stretched across the head to produce a rattling sound. ● **v.** (**snares, snaring, snared**) catch in a snare or trap.
– ORIGIN Old Norse; sense 3 is probably from German or Dutch, 'harp string'.

snarl ● **v. 1** growl with bared teeth. **2** say something aggressively. ● **n.** an act or sound of snarling.
– DERIVATIVES **snarly** adj.
– ORIGIN Germanic.

snarl-up ● **n.** informal a traffic jam. ● **v.** (**snarl up**) entangle.
– ORIGIN from SNARE.

snatch ● **v. 1** seize quickly in a rude or eager way. **2** informal steal or kidnap suddenly. **3** quickly take when the chance presents itself: *he snatched a few hours' sleep.* ● **n. 1** an act of snatching. **2** a fragment of music or talk.
– ORIGIN perh. from SNACK.

snazzy ● **adj.** (**snazzier, snazziest**) informal smart and stylish.
– ORIGIN unknown.

sneak ● **v.** (**sneaks, sneaking, sneaked** or N. Amer. informal **snuck**) **1** go or do in a secretive way. **2** Brit. informal inform someone in authority of a person's wrongdoings. ● **n.** Brit. informal a telltale. ● **adj.** acting or done secretly or unofficially: *a sneak preview.*
– ORIGIN perh. from former *snike* 'to creep'.

sneaker ● **n.** esp. N. Amer. a soft shoe worn for sports or casual occasions.

sneaking ● **adj.** (of a feeling) remaining persistently in one's mind.

sneaky ● **adj.** guiltily secretive or sly.
– DERIVATIVES **sneakily** adv.

sneer ● **n.** a scornful or mocking smile, remark, or tone. ● **v.** (**sneers, sneering, sneered**) smile or speak in a scornful or mocking way.

sneeze ● **v.** (**sneezes, sneezing, sneezed**) suddenly expel air from the nose and mouth due to irritation of one's nostrils. ● **n.** an act of sneezing.
– PHRASES **not to be sneezed at** informal not to be rejected without careful consideration.
– DERIVATIVES **sneezy** adj.
– ORIGIN Old English.

snick ● **v. 1** cut a small notch in. **2** make a clicking sound. ● **n. 1** a small notch or cut. **2** a sharp click.
– ORIGIN prob. from former *snick or snee* 'fight with knives'.

snicker ● **v.** (**snickers, snickering, snickered**) **1** snigger. **2** (of a horse) make a gentle high-pitched neigh. ● **n.** an act or sound of snickering.

snide ● **adj.** disrespectful or mocking in an indirect way.
– ORIGIN unknown.

sniff ● **v. 1** draw in air audibly through the nose. **2** (**sniff at**) show contempt or dislike for: *the price is not to be sniffed at.* **3** (**sniff around/round**) informal investigate something secretly. **4** (**sniff out**) informal discover by hidden investigation. ● **n. 1** an act of sniffing. **2** informal a hint. **3** informal a slight chance.
– DERIVATIVES **sniffer** n.

sniffer dog ● **n.** informal a dog trained to find drugs or explosives by smell.

sniffle ● **v.** (**sniffles, sniffling, sniffled**) sniff slightly or repeatedly. ● **n. 1** an act of sniffling. **2** a slight head cold.
– DERIVATIVES **sniffly** adj.

S

sniffy • adj. informal scornful.
– DERIVATIVES **sniffily** adv.

snifter • n. informal a small quantity of an alcoholic drink.

snigger • n. a half-suppressed laugh. • v. (**sniggers**, **sniggering**, **sniggered**) give such a laugh.
– ORIGIN from **SNICKER**.

snip • v. (**snips**, **snipping**, **snipped**) cut with scissors using small, quick strokes. • n. **1** an act of snipping. **2** a small piece that has been cut off. **3** Brit. informal a bargain.
– ORIGIN German, 'small piece'.

snipe /*rhymes with* pipe/ • n. (pl. **snipe** or **snipes**) a brown wading bird with a long straight bill. • v. (**snipes**, **sniping**, **sniped**) **1** shoot at someone from a hiding place at long range. **2** criticize in a sly or petty way.
ORIGIN prob. Scandinavian.

sniper • n. a hidden gunman who shoots at someone at long range.

snippet • n. a small piece or brief extract.

snitch informal • v. **1** steal. **2** inform on someone. • n. an informer.
– ORIGIN unknown.

snivel • v. (**snivels**, **snivelling**, **snivelled**; US **snivels**, **sniveling**, **sniveled**) **1** cry and sniffle. **2** complain in a whining or tearful way.
– ORIGIN Old English, 'mucus'.

snob • n. **1** a person who greatly respects social status or wealth and who looks down on people of a lower class. **2** a person who believes that their tastes in a particular area are superior to others: *a wine snob*.
– DERIVATIVES **snobbery** n. (pl. **snobberies**) **snobby** adj.
– ORIGIN from dialect, 'cobbler'.

snobbish • adj. typical of a snob.
– DERIVATIVES **snobbishly** adv.

snog Brit. informal • v. (**snogs**, **snogging**, **snogged**) kiss and caress. • n. an act or spell of kissing and caressing.
– ORIGIN unknown.

snood /snood/ • n. **1** a hairnet or pouch worn over the hair at the back of a woman's head. **2** a wide ring of knitted material worn as a hood or scarf.
– ORIGIN Old English.

snook /snook/ • n. (in phr. **cock a snook**) informal, esp. Brit. openly show contempt or a lack of respect for someone or something.
– ORIGIN unknown.

snooker • n. **1** a game played with cues on a billiard table, in which the players use a white cue ball to pocket the other balls in a set order. **2** a position in a game of snooker or pool in which a player cannot make a direct shot at any permitted ball. • v. (**snookers**, **snookering**, **snookered**) **1** subject to a snooker. **2** (**be snookered**) informal be placed in an impossible position.
– ORIGIN unknown.

snoop informal • v. investigate secretly. • n. **1** an act of snooping. **2** a person who snoops.
– DERIVATIVES **snooper** n.
– ORIGIN Dutch *snœpen* 'eat on the sly'.

snooty • adj. (**snootier**, **snootiest**) informal treating people as if they are inferior.
– DERIVATIVES **snootily** adv.
– ORIGIN from **SNOUT**.

snooze informal • n. a short, light sleep. • v. (**snoozes**, **snoozing**, **snoozed**) have a short, light sleep.
– ORIGIN unknown.

snore • n. a snorting sound in a person's breathing while they are asleep. • v. (**snores**, **snoring**, **snored**) make such a sound while asleep.
– DERIVATIVES **snorer** n.

snorkel /snor-k'l/ • n. a tube for a swimmer to breathe through while under water. • v. (**snorkels**, **snorkelling**, **snorkelled**; US **snorkels**, **snorkeling**, **snorkeled**) swim using a snorkel.
– ORIGIN German *Schnorchel*.

snort • n. **1** an explosive sound made by the sudden forcing of breath through the nose. **2** informal an inhaled dose of cocaine. **3** informal a measure of an alcoholic drink. • v. **1** make a snort. **2** informal inhale (cocaine).

snot • n. informal mucus in the nose.
– ORIGIN prob. from Dutch or German.

snotty • adj. (**snottier**, **snottiest**) informal **1** full of or covered with mucus from the nose. **2** having a superior or arrogant attitude.

snout • n. **1** the projecting nose and mouth of an animal. **2** the projecting front or end of something such as a pistol. **3** Brit. informal a police informer.
– ORIGIN Dutch or German *snūt*.

Snow, [E]
C. P., 1st Baron Snow of Leicester (1905–80; full name *Charles Percy Snow*), English novelist and scientist. He is best known for his sequence of eleven novels *Strangers and Brothers*.

snow • n. **1** frozen water vapour in the atmosphere that falls in light white flakes or settles on the ground as a white layer. **2** (**snows**) falls of snow. • v. **1** (**it snows**, **it is snowing**, **it snowed**) snow falls. **2** (**be snowed in/up**) be unable to leave a place due to a large quantity of snow. **3** (**be snowed under**) be overwhelmed with a large quantity of something.
– ORIGIN Old English.

snowball • n. a ball of packed snow. • v. **1** throw snowballs at. **2** increase rapidly in size, strength, or importance.

snowboard • n. a board resembling a short, broad ski, used for sliding downhill on snow.
– DERIVATIVES **snowboarder** n. **snowboarding** n.

snowbound • adj. **1** prevented from travelling or going out by snow. **2** (of a place) cut off because of snow.

Snowdon [E]
a mountain in NW Wales. Rising to 1,085 m (3,560 ft), it is the highest mountain in Wales. Welsh name **Yr Wyddfa**.

snowdrift • n. a bank of deep snow heaped up by the wind.

snowdrop • n. a plant which bears drooping white flowers during the late winter.

snowfall • n. **1** a fall of snow. **2** the quantity of snow falling within a particular area in a given time.

snowflake • n. each of the many feathery ice crystals that fall as snow.

snowline • n. the altitude above which some snow remains on the ground throughout the year.

snowman • n. a model of a human figure made with compressed snow.

snowmobile • n. a motor vehicle for travelling over snow.

snowplough (US **snowplow**) • n. a device or vehicle for clearing roads of snow.

snowshoe • n. a flat device resembling a racket, which is attached to the sole of a boot and used for walking on snow.

snowstorm • n. a heavy fall of snow accompanied by a high wind.

snowy • adj. (**snowier**, **snowiest**) **1** covered with snow. **2** (of weather or a period of time) having snow falling. **3** having to do with or like snow.

snowy owl • n. a large northern owl, the male being entirely white.

snub • v. (**snubs**, **snubbing**, **snubbed**) ignore or reject scornfully. • n. an act of snubbing. • adj. (of a person's nose) short and turned up at the end.
– ORIGIN Old Norse, 'chide'.

snuck N. Amer. informal past and past part. of **SNEAK**.

snuff[1] • v. **1** put out (a candle). **2** (**snuff out**) abruptly put an end to. **3** (**snuff it**) Brit. informal die.
– ORIGIN unknown.

snuff[2] • n. powdered tobacco that is sniffed up the nostril. • v. sniff at.
– ORIGIN prob. from Dutch *snuftabak*; the verb is from Dutch *snuffen* 'to snuffle'.

snuffer • n. a small metal cone on the end of a handle, used to snuff a candle.

snuffle • v. (**snuffles**, **snuffling**, **snuffled**) **1** breathe noisily through a partially blocked nose. **2** (of an animal) make repeated sniffing sounds. • n. **1** a snuffling sound. **2** (**the snuffles**) informal a cold.
– DERIVATIVES **snuffly** adj.
– ORIGIN prob. from German and Dutch *snuffelen*.

snug • adj. (**snugger**, **snuggest**) **1** warm and cosy. **2** close-fitting. • n. Brit. a small, cosy public room in a pub or small hotel.
– DERIVATIVES **snugly** adv.
– ORIGIN prob. from German or Dutch.

snuggery • n. (pl. **snuggeries**) a cosy place.

snuggle • v. (**snuggles**, **snuggling**, **snuggled**) settle into a warm, comfortable position.
– ORIGIN from **SNUG**.

so[1] • adv. **1** to such a great extent. **2** extremely; very much. **3** to the same extent: *he isn't so bad as you'd think*. **4** referring back to something previously mentioned. **5** similarly: *times have changed and so have I*. **6** thus. • conj. **1** therefore. **2** (**so that**) with the result or aim that. **3** and then. **4** in the same way.
– PHRASES **and so on** (or **forth**) and similar things. **or so** approximately. **so long!** informal goodbye. **so much as** even: *without so much as a word*. **so to speak** (or **say**) indicating that one is not talking literally.
– ORIGIN Old English.

so[2] • n. var. of **SOH**.

soak • v. **1** make or become thoroughly wet by leaving or remaining in liquid. **2** (of a liquid) spread completely throughout. **3** (**soak up**) absorb (a liquid). **4** (**soak up**) expose oneself to: *soak up the Mediterranean sun*. • n. **1** an act or spell of soaking. **2** informal a heavy drinker.
– ORIGIN Old English.

so-and-so • n. (pl. **so-and-sos**) informal **1** a person or thing whose name the speaker does not know. **2** euphem. a person who is disliked: *a nosy so-and-so*.

Soane, E
Sir John (1753–1837), English neoclassical architect. His designs include his house in London, now a museum.

soap • n. **1** a substance used with water for washing and cleaning, made of natural oils or fats combined with an alkali. **2** informal a soap opera. • v. wash with soap.
– ORIGIN Old English.

soapbox • n. **1** a box used as a makeshift stand for public speaking. **2** an opportunity for someone to air their views publicly.

soap opera • n. a television or radio serial dealing with daily events in the lives of a group of characters.
– ORIGIN so named because such serials were originally sponsored by soap manufacturers.

soapstone • n. a soft rock consisting largely of talc.

soapy • adj. (**soapier**, **soapiest**) **1** containing or covered with soap. **2** like soap.

soar • v. **1** fly or rise high into the air. **2** maintain height in the air by gliding. **3** increase rapidly above the usual level.
– ORIGIN Old French *essorer*.

sob • v. (**sobs**, **sobbing**, **sobbed**) **1** cry making loud gasps. **2** say while sobbing. • n. an act or sound of sobbing.
– ORIGIN perh. Dutch or German.

sober • adj. (**soberer**, **soberest**) **1** not drunk. **2** serious. **3** (of a colour or clothes) not bright or likely to attract attention. • v. (**sobers**, **sobering**, **sobered**) **1** (**sober up**) make or become sober after drinking alcohol. **2** make or become serious.
– DERIVATIVES **soberly** adv.
– ORIGIN Latin *sobrius*.

Sobers, E
Gary (b.1936; full name *Sir Garfield St Aubrun Sobers*), West Indian cricketer. During his test career he scored more than 8,000 runs and took 235 wickets.

sobriety /suh-**bry**-uh-ti/ • n. the state of being sober.

sobriquet /soh-bri-kay/ (also **soubriquet**) • n. a person's nickname.
– ORIGIN French.

sob story • n. informal a story intended to arouse sympathy.

so-called • adj. called by the name or term specified.

soccer • n. a form of football played with a round ball which may not be handled during play except by the goalkeepers, the object being to score goals.
– ORIGIN shortening of *Assoc* from **ASSOCIATION FOOTBALL**.

sociable • adj. **1** willing to talk and take part in activities with others. **2** friendly and welcoming: *a very sociable little village*.
– DERIVATIVES **sociability** n. **sociably** adv.
– ORIGIN Latin *sociabilis*.

social • adj. **1** having to do with society and its organization. **2** needing the company of others: *we are social beings as well as individuals*. **3** (of an activity) in which people meet each other for pleasure. **4** (of birds, in-

sects, or mammals) breeding or living in organized communities. • n. an informal social gathering.
– DERIVATIVES **socially** adv.
– ORIGIN Latin *socialis* 'allied'.

social climber • n. derog. a person who is anxious to improve their social status.

social contract • n. an unspoken agreement among the members of a society to cooperate for the benefit of all, for example by giving up some individual freedom in return for protection from the state.

socialism • n. a political and economic theory which holds that a country's land, transport, natural resources, and chief industries should be owned or controlled by the community as a whole.
– DERIVATIVES **socialist** n. & adj.

socialite • n. a person who mixes in fashionable society.

socialize (also **socialise**) • v. (**socializes**, **socializing**, **socialized**) **1** mix socially with others. **2** make (someone) behave in a way that is acceptable to society.

social science • n. **1** the scientific study of human society and social relationships. **2** a subject within this field, such as economics.

social security • n. (in the UK) money provided by the state for people with an inadequate or no income.

social services • n. services provided by the state for the community, such as education and medical care.

social studies • n. the study of human society.

social work • n. work carried out by people trained to help improve the conditions of people who are poor, old, etc.
– DERIVATIVES **social worker** n.

society • n. (pl. **societies**) **1** people living together in an ordered community. **2** a community of people living in a country or region, and having shared customs, laws, and organizations. **3** (also **high society**) people who are fashionable, wealthy, and influential. **4** an organization formed for a particular purpose. **5** the situation of being in the company of other people: *she shunned the society of others.*
– DERIVATIVES **societal** adj.
– ORIGIN Latin *societas*.

Society Islands E
a group of islands in the South Pacific, forming part of French Polynesia.

Society of Jesus E
official name for the Jesuits (see **JESUIT**).

socio-economic • adj. relating to the interaction of social and economic factors.

sociology • n. the study of the development, structure, and functioning of human society.
– DERIVATIVES **sociological** adj. **sociologist** n.

sociopath /**soh**-si-oh-path/ • n. a person with a mental disorder showing itself in extreme antisocial attitudes and behaviour.

sock • n. **1** a knitted garment for the foot and lower part of the leg. **2** informal a hard blow. • v. informal hit forcefully.
– PHRASES **pull one's socks up** informal make an effort to improve. **put a sock in it** Brit. informal stop talking. **sock it to** informal make a strong impression on.
– ORIGIN Greek *sukkhos* 'comic actor's shoe'.

socket • n. **1** a hollow in which something fits or revolves. **2** an electrical device into which a plug or light bulb is fitted.
– ORIGIN Old French *soket* 'small ploughshare'.

Socrates E
/**sok**-ruh-teez/(469–399 BC), Greek philosopher. He was concerned with questions of ethics and engaged in dialogue with others in an attempt to reach understanding. He was sentenced to death for impiety and corrupting the young, and died by drinking hemlock.
– DERIVATIVES **Socratic** adj.

sod[1] • n. **1** grass-covered ground. **2** a piece of turf.
– ORIGIN Dutch or German *sode*.

sod[2] Brit. vulgar • n. **1** an unpleasant person. **2** a person of a specified kind: *a lucky sod.* **3** a difficult or problematic thing. • v. (**sods**, **sodding**, **sodded**) **1** used to express anger or annoyance. **2** (**sod off**) go away.
– PHRASES **sod all** absolutely nothing.
– ORIGIN short for **SODOMITE**.

soda • n. **1** (also **soda water**) carbonated water. **2** N. Amer. a sweet fizzy drink.
– ORIGIN Latin.

sodden • adj. **1** soaked through. **2** (in combination) having drunk an excessive amount of an alcoholic drink: *whisky-sodden.*
– ORIGIN first meaning 'boiled': from **SEETHE**.

sodium • n. a soft silver-white metallic chemical element of which common salt and soda are compounds.
– ORIGIN from **SODA**.

sodium bicarbonate • n. a soluble white powder used in fizzy drinks and as a raising agent in baking.

sodium chloride • n. the chemical name for common salt.

sodium hydroxide • n. a strongly alkaline white compound used in many industrial processes; caustic soda.

Sodom E
/**sod**-uhm/ a town in ancient Palestine. According to the Bible God destroyed it by fire, together with Gomorrah, for the wickedness of its inhabitants.

sodomite /**sod**-uh-myt/ • n. a person who engages in sodomy.

sodomy • n. anal intercourse.
– ORIGIN from Latin *peccatum Sodomiticum* 'sin of Sodom' (from the Book of Genesis chapter 19).

Sod's Law • n. = **MURPHY'S LAW**.

sofa • n. a long padded seat with a back and arms, for two or more people.
– ORIGIN French.

sofa bed • n. a sofa that can be converted into a bed.

Sofia E
/**soh**-fi-uh, suh-**fee**-uh/ the capital of Bulgaria.

soft • adj. **1** easy to mould, cut, compress, or fold. **2** not rough in texture. **3** quiet and gentle. **4** (of light or colour) not harsh. **5** not strict or strict enough. **6** informal (of a job or way of life) requiring little effort. **7** informal foolish. **8** (**soft on**) informal have romantic feelings for. **9** (of a drink) not alcoholic. **10** (of a

drug) not likely to cause addiction. **11** (of water) free from mineral salts.
– PHRASES **have a soft spot for** be fond of. **a soft** (or **easy**) **touch** informal a person who is easily persuaded.
– DERIVATIVES **softly** adv. **softness** n.
– ORIGIN Old English.

softback • n. = PAPERBACK.

softball • n. a form of baseball played on a smaller field with a larger, softer ball.

soft-boiled • adj. (of an egg) lightly boiled, leaving the yolk soft.

soften • v. **1** make or become soft or softer. **2** (**soften up**) make (someone) more likely to do something.
– DERIVATIVES **softener** n.

soft focus • n. deliberate slight blurring in a photograph or film.

soft fruit • n. Brit. a small fruit without a stone, e.g. a strawberry.

soft furnishings • pl. n. Brit. curtains, chair coverings, and other cloth items used to decorate a room.

soft-hearted • adj. kind and compassionate.

softie (also **softy**) • n. (pl. **softies**) informal a weak or soft-hearted person.

softly-softly • adj. cautious and patient.

soft palate • n. the fleshy, flexible part towards the back of the roof of the mouth.

soft sell • n. the selling of something in a gently persuasive way.

soft-soap • v. informal use flattery to persuade.

soft target • n. a person or thing that is unprotected or vulnerable.

soft-top • n. a motor vehicle with a roof that can be folded back.

software • n. programs and other operating information used by a computer.

softwood • n. the wood from a conifer as opposed to that of broadleaved trees.

softy • n. var. of SOFTIE.

soggy • adj. (**soggier**, **soggiest**) very wet and soft.
– ORIGIN from dialect *sog* 'a swamp'.

soh /soh/ (also **so** or **sol**) • n. Music the fifth note of a major scale, coming after 'fah' and before 'lah'.
– ORIGIN the first syllable of *solve*, taken from a Latin hymn.

soi-disant /swah-dee-zon/ • adj. self-styled: *soi-disant journalists.*
– ORIGIN French.

soigné /swun-yay/ • adj. (fem. **soignée** /swun-yay/) elegant and well groomed.
– ORIGIN French.

soil[1] • n. **1** the upper layer of earth in which plants grow. **2** the territory of a particular nation.
– ORIGIN Old French.

soil[2] • v. **1** make dirty. **2** bring discredit to: *the scandal soiled the reputations of all involved.* • n. sewage.
– ORIGIN Old French *soiller.*

soirée /swah-ray/ • n. an evening social gathering for conversation or music.
– ORIGIN French.

sojourn /so-juhn, so-jern/ literary • n. a temporary stay. • v. stay temporarily.
– ORIGIN Old French *sojourner.*

sol • n. var. of SOH.

solace /sol-iss/ • n. comfort in time of distress. • v. (**solaces**, **solacing**, **solaced**) give solace to.
– ORIGIN Old French *solas.*

solar /soh-ler/ • adj. having to do with the sun or its rays.
– ORIGIN Latin *sol* 'sun'.

solar battery (also **solar cell**) • n. a device that converts the sun's radiation into electricity.

solar eclipse • n. an eclipse in which the sun is hidden by the moon.

solarium /suh-lair-i-uhm/ • n. (pl. **solariums** or **solaria** /suh-lair-i-uh/) **1** a room equipped with sunlamps or sunbeds. **2** a room with large areas of glass to let in sunlight.
– ORIGIN Latin.

solar panel • n. a panel designed to absorb the sun's rays as a source of energy for generating electricity or heating.

solar plexus • n. a network of nerves at the pit of the stomach.

solar power • n. power obtained by harnessing the energy of the sun's rays.

solar system • n. the sun together with the planets, asteroids, comets, etc. in orbit around it.

solar year • n. the time between one spring or autumn equinox and the next, or between one winter or summer solstice and the next (365 days, 5 hours, 48 minutes, and 46 seconds).

sold past and past part. of SELL.

solder /sohl-der/ • n. a soft alloy used for joining metals. • v. (**solders**, **soldering**, **soldered**) join with solder.
– ORIGIN Old French *soudure.*

soldering iron • n. an electrical tool for melting and applying solder.

soldier • n. **1** a person who serves in an army. **2** a private in an army. **3** Brit. informal a strip of bread or toast, dipped into a soft-boiled egg. • v. (**soldiers**, **soldiering**, **soldiered**) **1** serve as a soldier. **2** (**soldier on**) informal keep trying or working.
– PHRASES **soldier of fortune** a professional soldier hired to serve in a foreign army.
– DERIVATIVES **soldierly** adj.
– ORIGIN Old French.

soldiery • n. **1** soldiers as a group. **2** military training or knowledge.

sole[1] • n. **1** the underside of a person's foot. **2** the section forming the underside of a piece of footwear. • v. (**soles**, **soling**, **soled**) (**be soled**) (of a shoe) have the sole replaced.
– ORIGIN Latin *solea* 'sandal, sill'.

sole[2] • n. (pl. **sole**) an edible marine flatfish.
– ORIGIN Latin *solea* 'sandal, sill', from its shape.

sole[3] • adj. **1** one and only. **2** belonging or restricted to one person or group.
– DERIVATIVES **solely** adv.
– ORIGIN Latin *sola* 'alone'.

solecism /sol-i-si-z'm/ • n. **1** a grammatical mistake. **2** an instance of bad manners or incorrect behaviour.
– ORIGIN Greek *soloikismos.*

solemn • adj. **1** formal and dignified: *a solemn procession.* **2** serious. **3** deeply sincere.
– DERIVATIVES **solemnly** adv.
– ORIGIN Latin *sollemnis* 'customary'.

solemnity /suh-lem-ni-ti/ • **n.** (pl. **solemnities**) **1** the state of being solemn. **2** (**solemnities**) solemn ceremonies or rites.

solemnize /sol-uhm-nyz/ (also **solemnise**) • **v.** (**solemnizes**, **solemnizing**, **solemnized**) duly perform (a religious ceremony).

solenoid /sol-uh-noyd, soh-luh-noyd/ • **n.** a coil of wire which becomes magnetic when an electric current is passed through it.
– ORIGIN Greek *sōlēn* 'channel, pipe'.

Solent E
/soh-luhnt/ (**the Solent**) a channel between the NW coast of the Isle of Wight and the mainland of southern England.

soli pl. of **SOLO**.

solicit • **v.** (**solicits**, **soliciting**, **solicited**) **1** ask for or try to obtain (something) from someone. **2** ask for something from (someone). **3** approach someone and offer one's services as a prostitute.
– DERIVATIVES **solicitation** n.
– ORIGIN Latin *sollicitare* 'agitate'.

solicitor • **n.** Brit. a lawyer qualified to deal with property and wills, to advise clients and instruct barristers, and to represent clients in lower courts. Compare with **BARRISTER**.

solicitous • **adj.** showing interest or concern about a person's well-being.
– DERIVATIVES **solicitously** adv.

solicitude • **n.** care or concern.

solid • **adj.** (**solider**, **solidest**) **1** firm and stable in shape. **2** strongly built or made. **3** not hollow or having spaces or gaps. **4** consisting of the same substance throughout. **5** (of time) uninterrupted: *two solid hours of entertainment.* **6** able to be relied on: *solid evidence.* **7** Geom. three-dimensional. • **n. 1** a solid substance or object. **2** (**solids**) food that is not liquid. **3** a three-dimensional body or shape.
– DERIVATIVES **solidity** n. **solidly** adv.
– ORIGIN Latin *solidus*.

solidarity • **n.** agreement and support resulting from shared interests, feelings, or opinions.

solidify • **v.** (**solidifies**, **solidifying**, **solidified**) make or become hard or solid.
– DERIVATIVES **solidification** n.

solid-state • **adj.** (of an electronic device) using solid semiconductors, e.g. transistors, as opposed to valves.

soliloquy /suh-lil-uh-kwi/ • **n.** (pl. **soliloquies**) a speech in a play when a character speaks their thoughts aloud when alone or regardless of hearers.
– ORIGIN Latin *solus* 'alone' + *loqui* 'speak'.

Soliman E
/sol-i-muhn/ var. of **SULEIMAN I**.

solipsism /sol-ip-siz-uhm/ • **n.** the view that the self is all that can be known to exist.
– ORIGIN from Latin *solus* 'alone' + *ipse* 'self'.

solitaire /sol-i-tair, sol-i-tair/ • **n. 1** a game for one player played by removing pegs from a board one at a time by moving others over them. **2** the card game patience. **3** a single gem in a piece of jewellery.
– ORIGIN French.

solitary • **adj. 1** done or existing alone. **2** (of a place) secluded or isolated. **3** single: *not a solitary shred of evidence.* • **n.** (pl. **solitaries**) **1** a person living in solitude for personal or religious reasons. **2** informal solitary confinement.
– ORIGIN Latin *solitarius*.

solitary confinement • **n.** the isolating of a prisoner in a separate cell as a punishment.

solitude • **n.** the state of being alone.

solmization /sol-mi-zay-sh'n/ (also **solmisation**) • **n.** Music a system of associating each note of a scale with a particular syllable (typically the sequence doh, ray, me, fah, so, la, te), especially to teach singing.
– ORIGIN French.

solo • **n.** (pl. **solos**) **1** (pl. **solos** or **soli**) a piece of music, song, or dance for one performer. **2** a flight undertaken by a single pilot. • **adj. & adv.** for or done by one person. • **v.** (**soloes**, **soloing**, **soloed**) **1** perform a solo. **2** fly an aircraft alone.
– ORIGIN Latin *solus* 'alone'.

soloist • **n.** a musician or singer who performs a solo.

Solomon E
/sol-uh-muhn/, king of ancient Israel *c.*970–*c.*930 BC, son of David. He extended his kingdom and became famous for his wisdom.

Solomon Islands E
a country consisting of a group of islands in the SW Pacific, to the east of New Guinea; capital, Honiara.
– DERIVATIVES **Solomon Islander** n.

Solon E
/soh-lon/ (*c.*630–*c.*560 BC), Athenian statesman and lawgiver. His division of the citizens into four classes based on wealth rather than birth laid the foundations of Athenian democracy.

solstice /sol-stiss/ • **n.** each of the two times in the year, at midsummer and midwinter, when the sun reaches its highest or lowest point in the sky at noon, marked by the longest and shortest days.
– ORIGIN Latin *solstitium*.

Solti E
/shol-ti/, Sir Georg (1912–97), Hungarian-born British conductor. He was conductor of the Chicago Symphony Orchestra (1969–91) and of the London Philharmonic Orchestra (1979–83).

soluble • **adj. 1** (of a substance) able to be dissolved. **2** (of a problem) able to be solved.
– DERIVATIVES **solubility** n.
– ORIGIN Latin *solubilis*.

solute /sol-yoot/ • **n.** a substance that is dissolved in another substance.

solution • **n. 1** a means of solving a problem. **2** the correct answer to a puzzle. **3** a mixture formed when a substance is dissolved in a liquid. **4** the action of dissolving.
– ORIGIN Latin.

solve • **v.** (**solves**, **solving**, **solved**) find an answer to or way of dealing with (a problem or mystery).
– ORIGIN Latin *solvere* 'loosen, unfasten'.

solvency • **n.** the state of having more money than one owes.

solvent • **adj. 1** having more money than one owes. **2** able to dissolve other substances. • **n.** the liquid in which another substance is dissolved to form a solution.

solvent abuse • **n.** the deliberate inhaling

S

of the intoxicating fumes of certain solvents, e.g. glue.

Solway Firth E
an inlet of the Irish Sea, separating Cumbria (in England) from Dumfries and Galloway (in Scotland).

Solyman E
var. of **SULEIMAN I**.

Solzhenitsyn E
/sol-*zh*uh-**nit**-sin/, Alexander (b.1918), Russian novelist. He spent eight years in a labour camp for criticizing Stalin. He was exiled in 1974, eventually returning to Russia in 1994. His novels include *One Day in the Life of Ivan Denisovich* and *The Gulag Archipelago*.

Som. ● abbrev. Somerset.

Somalia E
/suh-**mah**-li-uh/ a country in NE Africa; capital, Mogadishu.
– DERIVATIVES **Somali** adj. & n.

somatic /suh-**mat**-ik/ ● **adj.** having to do with the body rather than the mind.
– ORIGIN Greek *sōmatikos*.

sombre (US also **somber**) ● **adj. 1** dark or dull. **2** very solemn or serious.
– DERIVATIVES **sombrely** adv.
– ORIGIN French.

sombrero /som-**brair**-oh/ ● **n.** (pl. **sombreros**) a broad-brimmed Mexican hat.
– ORIGIN Spanish.

some ● **det. 1** an unspecified amount or number of. **2** referring to an unknown or unspecified person or thing. **3** (used with a number) approximately. **4** a considerable amount or number of: *she went to some trouble over this.* **5** a certain small amount or number of: *he liked some music but generally wasn't musical.* **6** expressing admiration: *that was some goal.* ● **pron. 1** an unspecified number or amount of people or things. **2** a certain small number or amount.
– ORIGIN Old English.

-some ● **suffix 1** producing: *loathsome.* **2** characterized by being: *wholesome.* **3** apt to: *tiresome.* **4** referring to a group of a specified number: *foursome.*
– ORIGIN Old English.

somebody ● **pron.** someone.

some day (also **someday**) ● **adv.** at some time in the future.

somehow ● **adv. 1** by one means or another. **2** for an unknown or unspecified reason.

someone ● **pron. 1** an unknown or unspecified person. **2** a person of importance or authority.

someplace ● **adv. & pron.** informal, esp. N. Amer. somewhere.

somersault ● **n.** a movement in which a person turns head over heels in the air or on the ground and finishes on their feet. ● **v.** perform a somersault.
– ORIGIN Old French *sombresault*.

Somerset E
a county of SW England; county town, Taunton.

something ● **pron. 1** an unspecified or unknown thing. **2** an unspecified or unknown amount or degree. ● **adv.** informal used for emphasis: *my back hurts something terrible.*
– PHRASES **quite** (or **really**) **something** informal something impressive or notable. **something else** informal an exceptional person or thing. **thirty-something** (**forty-something**, etc.) informal an unspecified age between thirty and forty (forty and fifty, etc.).

sometime ● **adv.** at some unspecified or unknown time. ● **adj.** former: *the sometime editor of the paper.*

sometimes ● **adv.** occasionally.

somewhat ● **adv.** to some extent.

somewhere ● **adv. 1** in or to an unspecified or unknown place. **2** used to indicate an approximate amount. ● **pron.** some unspecified place.
– PHRASES **get somewhere** informal make progress.

Somme, Battle of the E
a major battle of the First World War between the British and the Germans, in the upper valley of the river Somme in northern France during July–November 1916.

somnambulism /som-**nam**-byuu-li-z'm/ ● **n.** sleepwalking.
– DERIVATIVES **somnambulist** n.
– ORIGIN Latin *somnus* 'sleep' + *ambulare* 'to walk'.

somnolent /**som**-nuh-luhnt/ ● **adj. 1** sleepy. **2** causing sleepiness: *a somnolent summer day.*
– DERIVATIVES **somnolence** n.
– ORIGIN Latin *somnolentus*.

Somoza E
/suh-**moh**-zuh/, Anastasio (1925–80; full name *Anastasio Somoza Debayle*), Nicaraguan statesman, President 1967–79. His dictatorial regime was overthrown by the Sandinistas and he was assassinated while in exile in Paraguay.

son ● **n. 1** a boy or man in relation to his parents. **2** a male descendant. **3** (**the Son**) (in Christian belief) Jesus Christ. **4** (also **my son**) used as a form of address for a boy or younger man.
– PHRASES **Son of Man** Jesus Christ.
– ORIGIN Old English.

sonar /**soh**-nar/ ● **n. 1** a system for detecting objects under water by giving out sound pulses and measuring their return after being reflected. **2** an apparatus used for this.
– ORIGIN from *sound navigation and ranging*.

sonata /suh-**nah**-tuh/ ● **n.** a classical composition for an instrumental soloist often with a piano accompaniment.
– ORIGIN Italian, 'sounded'.

Sondheim E
/**sond**-hym/, Stephen (Joshua) (b.1930), American composer and lyricist. He wrote the lyrics for *West Side Story* and also wrote the musicals *A Little Night Music* and *Sweeney Todd*.

son et lumière /son ay **loo**-mi-air/ ● **n.** an entertainment held by night at a historic building, telling its history by the use of lighting effects and recorded sound.
– ORIGIN French, 'sound and light'.

song ● **n. 1** a set of words set to music. **2** singing: *they broke into song.* **3** the musical phrases uttered by some birds, whales, and

insects. **4** a poem.
– PHRASES **for a song** informal very cheaply. **on song** Brit. informal performing well. **a song and dance** informal a fuss.
– ORIGIN Old English.

songbird • n. a bird with a musical song.

song cycle • n. a set of linked songs.

songster • n. (fem. **songstress**) a person who sings.

song thrush • n. a thrush with a song in which phrases are repeated.

songwriter • n. a writer of songs or the music for them.

sonic • adj. relating to or using sound waves.
– DERIVATIVES **sonically** adv.
– ORIGIN Latin *sonus* 'sound'.

sonic boom • n. an explosive noise caused by the shock wave from an object travelling faster than the speed of sound.

son-in-law • n. (pl. **sons-in-law**) the husband of one's daughter.

sonnet • n. a poem of fourteen lines using a fixed rhyme scheme.
– ORIGIN Italian *sonetto* 'little sound'.

sonny • n. informal **1** an informal form of address to a young boy. **2** (also **Sonny Jim**) a humorous or scornful way of addressing a man.

sonogram • n. **1** a graph showing the distribution of energy at different frequencies in a sound. **2** a visual image produced from an ultrasound examination.
– ORIGIN Latin *sonus* 'sound'.

sonorous /son-uh-ruhss/ • adj. (of a sound) deep and full.
– ORIGIN Latin *sonor* 'sound'.

Sontag E
/son-tag/, Susan (b.1933), American writer and critic. She is known for her writings on modern culture, such as the collection of essays *Against Interpretation*.

soon • adv. **1** in or after a short time. **2** early. **3** used to indicate a preference: *I'd just as soon Tim did it.*
– PHRASES **no sooner than** at the very moment that. **sooner or later** eventually.
– DERIVATIVES **soonish** adv.
– ORIGIN Old English.

soot • n. a black powdery substance produced when coal, wood, etc. is burnt.
– ORIGIN Old English.

sooth /*rhymes with* truth/ • n. archaic truth.
– ORIGIN Old English.

soothe • v. (**soothes**, **soothing**, **soothed**) **1** gently calm. **2** relieve (pain or discomfort).
– ORIGIN Old English, 'verify'.

soothsayer • n. a person supposed to be able to foresee the future.

sooty • adj. (**sootier**, **sootiest**) covered with or coloured like soot.

sop • n. a thing given or done to calm or please someone who is angry or upset. • v. (**sops**, **sopping**, **sopped**) (**sop up**) soak up (liquid).
– ORIGIN Old English.

sophism /soff-i-z'm/ • n. a false argument.
– ORIGIN Greek *sophisma* 'clever device'.

sophist /soff-ist/ • n. a person who uses clever but false arguments.

sophisticate • n. a sophisticated person.

sophisticated • adj. **1** (of a machine or system) highly developed and complex. **2** having worldly experience and taste in matters of culture or fashion.
– DERIVATIVES **sophistication** n.
– ORIGIN Latin *sophisticare* 'tamper with'.

sophistry /soff-iss-tri/ • n. (pl. **sophistries**) **1** the use of false arguments. **2** a false argument.

Sophocles E
/soff-uh-kleez/ (*c.*496–406 BC), Greek dramatist, noted for such tragedies as *Antigone* and *Oedipus Rex* (also called *Oedipus Tyrannus*).

sophomore /soff-uh-mor/ • n. N. Amer. a second-year university or high-school student.
– ORIGIN prob. from SOPHISM.

soporific /sop-uh-ri-fik/ • adj. causing drowsiness or sleep.
– ORIGIN Latin *sopor* 'sleep'.

sopping • adj. wet through.

soppy • adj. (**soppier**, **soppiest**) Brit. informal **1** sentimental in an excessive or silly way. **2** feeble: *she was too soppy for our adventurous games.*
– DERIVATIVES **soppily** adv.
– ORIGIN from SOP.

soprano /suh-prah-noh/ • n. (pl. **sopranos**) the highest singing voice. • adj (of an instrument) of a high or the highest pitch in its family: *a soprano saxophone.*
– ORIGIN Italian.

sorbet /sor-bay, sor-bit/ • n. a water ice.
– ORIGIN French.

Sorbonne E
/sor-bon/ part of the University of Paris, containing the faculties of science and literature.

sorcerer • n. (fem. **sorceress**) a person believed to practise magic.
– DERIVATIVES **sorcery** n.
– ORIGIN Old French *sorcier.*

sordid • adj. **1** involving dishonest or immoral actions and motives. **2** extremely dirty and unpleasant.
– DERIVATIVES **sordidly** adv.
– ORIGIN Latin *sordidus.*

sore • adj. **1** painful or aching. **2** suffering pain in a part of one's body. **3** urgent: *in sore need.* **4** informal, esp. N. Amer. upset and angry. • n. a raw or painful place on the body. • adv. archaic extremely: *sore afraid.*
– PHRASES **sore point** an issue about which someone feels distressed or annoyed. **stand** (or **stick**) **out like a sore thumb** be obviously different.
– DERIVATIVES **soreness** n.
– ORIGIN Old English.

sorely • adv. extremely; badly.

sorghum /sor-guhm/ • n. a cereal found in warm regions, grown for grain and animal feed.
– ORIGIN Italian *sorgo.*

sorority /suh-ro-ri-ti/ • n. (pl. **sororities**) N. Amer. a society for female students in a university or college.
– ORIGIN Latin *soror* 'sister'.

sorrel[1] /*rhymes with* quarrel/ • n. an edible plant with arrow-shaped leaves and a bitter flavour.
– ORIGIN Old French *sorele.*

sorrel[2] /*rhymes with* quarrel/ • n. **1** a light

S

reddish-brown colour. **2** a horse with a sorrel coat.
– ORIGIN Old French *sorel.*

Sorrento E
/suh-ren-toh/ a town on the west coast of central Italy.

sorrow ● n. **1** deep distress caused by loss or disappointment. **2** a cause of sorrow.
– ORIGIN Old English.

sorrowful ● adj. **1** feeling or showing sorrow. **2** causing sorrow.
– DERIVATIVES **sorrowfully** adv.

sorry ● adj. (**sorrier, sorriest**) **1** feeling sympathy for someone else's misfortune. **2** feeling or expressing regret. **3** in a poor or pitiful state. **4** unpleasant and regrettable: *a sorry business.*
– ORIGIN Old English, 'distressed'.

sort ● n. **1** a category of people or things with a common feature or features. **2** informal a person with a specified nature: *a friendly sort.* ● v. **1** arrange systematically in groups. **2** (often **sort out**) separate from a mixed group. **3** (**sort out**) resolve (a problem). **4** (**sort out**) informal deal with (a troublesome person).
– PHRASES **of a sort** (or **of sorts**) of a rather poor kind. **out of sorts** slightly unwell or unhappy. **sort of** informal to some extent.
– ORIGIN Old French *sorte.*

sorted ● adj. Brit. informal **1** organized; arranged. **2** emotionally well balanced.

sortie ● n. **1** an attack by troops coming out from a position of defence. **2** a flight by a single aircraft on a military operation. **3** a short trip. ● v. (**sorties, sortieing, sortied**) make a sortie.
– ORIGIN French.

SOS ● n. **1** an international signal of extreme distress. **2** an urgent appeal for help.
– ORIGIN letters chosen as being easily transmitted and recognized in Morse code.

so-so ● adj. neither very good nor very bad.

sot ● n. a person who is regularly drunk.
– ORIGIN Latin *sottus* 'foolish person'.

sotto voce /sot-toh voh-chay/ ● adv. & adj. in a quiet voice.
– ORIGIN Italian *sotto* 'under' + *voce* 'voice'.

soubriquet /soo-bri-kay/ ● n. var. of **SOBRIQUET**.

soufflé ● n. a light, spongy baked dish made by mixing egg yolks and another ingredient such as cheese or fruit with stiffly beaten egg whites.
– ORIGIN French, 'blown'.

sought past and past part. of **SEEK**.

sought after ● adj. much in demand.

souk /sook/ (also **suq**) ● n. an Arab market.
– ORIGIN Arabic.

soul ● n. **1** the spiritual element of a person, believed to be immortal. **2** a person's inner character. **3** emotional or intellectual energy or power: *their performance lacked soul.* **4** a perfect example of a particular quality: *she's the soul of discretion.* **5** an individual: *poor soul.* **6** (also **soul music**) a kind of music using elements of gospel music and rhythm and blues, popularized by American blacks.
– ORIGIN Old English.

soul-destroying ● adj. unbearably dull and repetitive.

soulful ● adj. expressing deep sadness or love: *a soulful glance.*
– DERIVATIVES **soulfully** adv.

soulless ● adj. **1** lacking character or interest. **2** lacking human feelings: *soulless dark eyes.*

soulmate ● n. a person ideally suited to another.

soul-searching ● n. close examination of one's emotions and motives.

sound[1] ● n. **1** vibrations which travel through air or water and are sensed by the ear. **2** a thing that can be heard. **3** music, speech, and sound effects accompanying a film or broadcast. **4** an impression given by words. ● v. **1** make a sound. **2** utter: *sound a warning.* **3** give a specified impression: *the job sounds great.* **4** (**sound off**) express one's opinions forcefully.
– DERIVATIVES **soundless** adj.
– ORIGIN Latin *sonus.*

sound[2] ● adj. **1** in good condition. **2** based on solid judgement. **3** financially secure. **4** competent or reliable. **5** (of sleep) deep and unbroken. **6** severe or thorough: *a sound thrashing.* ● adv. in a sound way.
– DERIVATIVES **soundly** adv.
– ORIGIN Old English.

sound[3] ● v. **1** find out the depth of water in (the sea, a lake, etc.) using a line, pole, or sound echoes. **2** (**sound out**) question (someone) as to their opinions.
– ORIGIN Old French *sonder.*

sound[4] ● n. a narrow stretch of water forming an inlet or connecting two larger bodies of water.
– ORIGIN Old Norse, 'swimming, strait'.

sound barrier ● n. the point at which an aircraft reaches the speed of sound.

sound bite ● n. a short memorable extract from a speech or interview.

soundcheck ● n. a test of sound equipment before a musical performance or recording.

sound effect ● n. a sound other than speech or music made artificially for use in a play, film, etc.

sounding ● n. **1** a measurement of the depth of water, taken by sounding. **2** (**soundings**) information found out before taking action.

sounding board ● n. a person or group whose reactions to ideas or opinions are used to find out if they are valid or likely to succeed.

soundproof ● adj. preventing sound getting in or out. ● v. make soundproof.

sound system ● n. a set of equipment for reproducing and amplifying sound.

soundtrack ● n. the sound accompaniment to a film.

sound wave ● n. a wave of alternate compression and reduction in density by which sound travels through air or water.

soup ● n. a savoury liquid dish made by boiling meat, fish, or vegetables in stock or water. ● v. (**soup up**) informal increase the power and efficiency of (an engine or other machine).
– ORIGIN Old French *soupe* 'sop, broth'.

soupçon /soop-son/ ● n. a very small quantity.
– ORIGIN French.

soup kitchen ● n. a place where free food is served to homeless or very poor people.

sour • adj. **1** having a sharp taste like lemon or vinegar. **2** tasting or smelling unpleasant due to staleness. **3** resentful or angry. • v. make or become sour.
– PHRASES **go** (or **turn**) **sour** become less pleasant. **sour grapes** an attitude in which someone pretends to hate something because they cannot have it themselves. [ORIGIN with reference to Aesop's fable *The Fox and the Grapes*.]
– DERIVATIVES **sourly** adv. **sourness** n.
– ORIGIN Old English.

source • n. **1** a place, person, or thing from which something originates. **2** a place where a river or stream begins. **3** a person, book, or document that provides information or evidence. • v. (**sources, sourcing, sourced**) obtain from a particular source.
– ORIGIN Old French *sourse*.

sour cream • n. cream that has been made sour by adding bacteria.

sourdough • n. bread made from fermenting dough.

sourpuss • n. informal a bad-tempered or sulky person.

Sousa E
/soo-zuh/, John Philip (1854–1932), American composer and conductor, who composed more than a hundred marches, including *The Stars and Stripes*.

souse /sowss/ • v. (**souses, sousing, soused**) **1** soak in liquid. **2** (**soused**) pickled or marinaded: *soused herring*.
– ORIGIN Old French *sous* 'pickle'.

soutane /soo-**tahn**/ • n. a type of cassock worn by Roman Catholic priests.
– ORIGIN Italian *sottana*.

south • n. **1** the direction which is 90° clockwise from east. **2** the southern part of a country, region, or town. • adj. **1** lying towards, near, or facing the south. **2** (of a wind) blowing from the south. • adv. to or towards the south.
– ORIGIN Old English.

South Africa E
a country occupying the southernmost part of Africa; administrative capital, Pretoria; legislative capital, Cape Town.
– DERIVATIVES **South African** adj. & n.

South America E
a continent comprising the southern half of the American land mass; it includes the Falkland Islands, the Galapagos Islands, and Tierra del Fuego.
– DERIVATIVES **South American** adj. & n.

Southampton E
a port on the south coast of England, a unitary council formerly in Hampshire.

South Australia E
a state comprising the central southern part of Australia; capital, Adelaide.

South Carolina E
a state of the US on the Atlantic coast; capital, Columbia.
– DERIVATIVES **South Carolinian** n. & adj.

South Dakota E
a state in the north central US; capital, Pierre.
– DERIVATIVES **South Dakotan** n. & adj.

south-east • n. the direction or region halfway between south and east. • adj. **1** lying towards or facing the south-east. **2** (of a wind) blowing from the south-east. • adv. to or towards the south-east.
– DERIVATIVES **south-eastern** adj.

south-easterly • adj. & adv. in a south-eastward position or direction.

south-eastward • adv. (also **south-eastwards**) towards the south-east. • adj. in, towards, or facing the south-east.

southerly • adj. & adv. **1** towards or facing the south. **2** (of a wind) blowing from the south.

southern • adj. **1** situated in or facing the south. **2** coming from or characteristic of the south.

Southern Alps E
a mountain range in South Island, New Zealand.

southerner • n. a person from the south of a region.

Southern Lights • pl. n. the aurora australis.

Southern Ocean E
the expanse of ocean surrounding Antarctica.

Southern Rhodesia E
former name for **ZIMBABWE**.

Southey E
/*suth*-i/, Robert (1774–1843), English poet, best known for poems such as the 'Battle of Blenheim'. He was Poet Laureate 1813–43.

South Georgia E
a barren island in the South Atlantic, a dependency of the Falkland Islands.

South Island E
the more southerly and larger of the two main islands of New Zealand.

South Korea E
a country in the Far East, occupying the southern part of the peninsula of Korea; capital, Seoul. Official name **REPUBLIC OF KOREA**.
– DERIVATIVES **South Korean** adj. & n.

south-south-east • n. the direction halfway between south and south-east.

south-south-west • n. the direction halfway between south and south-west.

South Uist E
see **UIST**.

southward /sowth-werd/ Naut. /su-*th*erd/ • adj. in a southerly direction. • adv. (also **southwards**) towards the south.

south-west • n. the direction or region halfway between south and west. • adj. **1** lying towards or facing the south-west. **2** (of a wind) blowing from the south-west. • adv. to or towards the south-west.
– DERIVATIVES **south-western** adj.

south-westerly • adj. & adv. in a south-westward position or direction.

south-westward • adv. (also **south-westwards**) towards the south-west. • adj.

in, towards, or facing the south-west.

South Yorkshire E
a metropolitan county of northern England.

souvenir /soo-vuh-neer/ ● n. a thing that is kept as a reminder of a person, place, or event.
– ORIGIN French.

sou'wester /sow-wess-ter/ ● n. a waterproof hat with a broad brim or flap covering the back of the neck.

sovereign ● n. **1** a king or queen who is the supreme ruler of a country. **2** a former British gold coin worth one pound sterling. ● adj. **1** possessing supreme power. **2** (of a nation or its affairs) completely independent.
– ORIGIN Old French *soverain*.

sovereignty ● n. complete power or authority.

soviet /soh-vi-uht, sov-i-uht/ ● n. **1** (**Soviet**) a citizen of the former Soviet Union. **2** an elected council in the former Soviet Union. ● adj. (**Soviet**) having to do with the former Soviet Union.
– ORIGIN Russian *sovet* 'council'.

Soviet Union E
a former federation of Communist republics occupying the northern half of Asia and part of eastern Europe. It was dissolved in 1991. Full name **Union of Soviet Socialist Republics**.

sow[1] /soh/ ● v. (**sows, sowing, sowed**; past part. **sown** or **sowed**) **1** plant (seed) by scattering it on or in the earth. **2** plant (an area) with seed. **3** spread (something unwelcome).
– DERIVATIVES **sower** n.
– ORIGIN Old English.

sow[2] /sow/ ● n. an adult female pig.
– ORIGIN Old English.

Soweto E
/suh-wet-oh/ a large urban area, consisting of several townships, in South Africa. In 1976 violent police action against demonstrations opposing the compulsory use of Afrikaans in schools resulted in the deaths of hundreds of people.

sown past part. of **sow**[1].

soy ● n. **1** (also **soy sauce**) a sauce made with fermented soya beans, used in Chinese and Japanese cooking. **2** = **soya**.
– ORIGIN Chinese.

soya ● n. a plant which produces an edible bean that is high in protein.
– ORIGIN Malay.

Soyinka E
/shoy-ing-kuh/, Wole (b.1934), Nigerian dramatist, novelist, and critic. His works include the play *The Lion and the Jewel* and the novel *The Interpreters*.

sozzled ● adj. informal very drunk.
– ORIGIN from dialect *sozzle* 'mix sloppily'.

spa ● n. **1** a mineral spring considered to have health-giving properties. **2** a place with a mineral spring.
– ORIGIN from *Spa*, a small town in Belgium noted for its mineral springs.

space ● n. **1** unoccupied ground or area. **2** an unoccupied area. **3** the dimensions of height, depth, and width within which all things exist and move. **4** (also **outer space**) the physical universe beyond the earth's atmosphere. **5** an interval of time: *forty men died in the space of two days.* **6** the freedom to live and develop as one wishes. ● v. (**spaces, spacing, spaced**) **1** position (two or more items) at a distance from one another. **2** (**be spaced out**) informal be in a state of great happiness or confusion, especially from taking drugs.
– ORIGIN Old French *espace*.

space age ● n. (**the space age**) the era that started when the exploration of space became possible. ● adj. (**space-age**) having advanced technology: *a space-age control room.*

space capsule ● n. a small spacecraft or the part of a larger one that contains the instruments or crew, designed to be returned to earth.

spacecraft ● n. (pl. **spacecraft** or **spacecrafts**) a vehicle used for travelling in space.

spaceman ● n. a male astronaut.

space probe ● n. an unmanned exploratory spacecraft.

spaceship ● n. a manned spacecraft.

space shuttle ● n. a rocket-launched spacecraft, used for journeys between earth and craft orbiting the earth.

space station ● n. a large artificial satellite used as a long-term base for manned operations in space.

spacesuit ● n. a sealed and pressurized suit designed to allow an astronaut to survive in space.

space–time ● n. Physics the concepts of time and three-dimensional space seen as joined in a four-dimensional continuum.

spacious ● adj. (of a room or building) having plenty of space.
– DERIVATIVES **spaciousness** n.

spade ● n. a tool with a rectangular metal blade and a long handle, used for digging.
– PHRASES **call a spade a spade** speak plainly and frankly.
– ORIGIN Old English.

spades ● n. one of the four suits in a pack of playing cards, represented by an upside-down black heart-shaped figure with a small stalk.
– PHRASES **in spades** informal in large amounts or to a high degree.
– ORIGIN Italian *spade* 'swords'.

spadework ● n. hard or routine work done to prepare for something.

spaghetti /spuh-get-ti/ ● pl. n. pasta in long strands.
– ORIGIN Italian, 'little strings'.

spaghetti western ● n. informal a western film made in Europe by an Italian director.

Spain E
a country in SW Europe, occupying the greater part of the Iberian peninsula; capital, Madrid.

spake archaic past of **speak**.

spam ● n. trademark a canned meat product made mainly from ham.
– ORIGIN prob. from the first two and last two letters of *spiced ham*.

span ● n. **1** the full extent of something from side to side. **2** the length of time for which something lasts. **3** a wingspan. **4** a part of a bridge between the uprights supporting it. **5** the maximum distance between the tips of

the thumb and little finger. • **v.** (**spans**, **spanning**, **spanned**) extend across or over.
– ORIGIN Old English.

spandex • **n.** trademark a type of stretchy polyurethane fabric.
– ORIGIN from **EXPAND**.

spangle • **n. 1** a small thin piece of glittering material, used to decorate a garment. **2** a spot of bright colour or light.
– DERIVATIVES **spangled** adj. **spangly** adj.
– ORIGIN Dutch *spange* 'buckle'.

Spaniard /span-yerd/ • **n.** a person from Spain.

spaniel • **n.** a breed of dog with a long silky coat and drooping ears.
– ORIGIN Old French *espaigneul* 'Spanish (dog)'.

Spanish • **n.** the main language of Spain and of much of Central and South America. • **adj.** relating to Spain or Spanish.

Spanish Armada E
see **ARMADA**.

Spanish Civil War E
the conflict (1936–9) between Nationalist forces and Republicans in Spain. The Nationalists, led by General Franco, were victorious and Franco established a Fascist dictatorship.

Spanish Inquisition E
an ecclesiastical court established in 1478 and directed originally against converts from Judaism and Islam but later also against Protestants. It operated with great severity and was not suppressed until the early 19th century.

Spanish Sahara E
former name for **WESTERN SAHARA**.

Spanish Succession, War of the E
a European war (1701–14), provoked by the death of the Spanish king Charles II without an heir. An alliance of Britain, the Netherlands, and the Holy Roman emperor threw back a French invasion of the Low Countries and prevented Spain and France from being united under one crown.

spank • **v.** slap on the buttocks with one's open hand or a flat object. • **n.** a slap or series of slaps of this type.

spanking • **adj. 1** brisk: *a spanking pace.* **2** informal impressive or pleasing: *a spanking white Rolls Royce.* • **n.** a series of spanks.

spanner • **n.** Brit. a tool for gripping and turning a nut or bolt.
– PHRASES **spanner in the works** a thing that prevents a plan from being successfully accomplished.
– ORIGIN German *spannen* 'draw tight'.

spar[1] • **n.** a thick, strong pole used for a mast or yard on a ship.
– ORIGIN Old French *esparre.*

spar[2] • **v.** (**spars**, **sparring**, **sparred**) **1** make the motions of boxing without landing heavy blows, as a form of training. **2** argue without hostility. • **n.** a period of sparring.
– ORIGIN Old English, 'strike out'.

spare • **adj. 1** additional to what is required. **2** not currently in use or occupied. **3** thin. **4** elegantly simple: *her clothes are spare in style.* • **n.** an item kept in case another is lost, broken, or worn out. • **v.** (**spares**, **sparing**, **spared**) **1** give (something of which one has enough) to (someone). **2** refrain from killing or harming. **3** protect from something unpleasant.
– PHRASES **go spare** Brit. informal become extremely angry. **spare no expense** (or **no expense spared**) be prepared to pay any amount. **to spare** left over.
– ORIGIN Old English, 'meagre'.

spare ribs • **pl. n.** trimmed ribs of pork.
– ORIGIN prob. from German *ribbesper.*

spare tyre • **n. 1** an extra tyre carried in a motor vehicle. **2** informal a roll of fat round a person's waist.

sparing • **adj.** not wasteful; economical.
– DERIVATIVES **sparingly** adv.

Spark, E
Dame Muriel (b.1918), Scottish novelist, author of *The Prime of Miss Jean Brodie.*

spark • **n. 1** a small fiery particle produced by burning or caused by friction. **2** a flash of light produced by an electrical discharge. **3** an electrical discharge which ignites the explosive mixture in an internal-combustion engine. **4** a small but concentrated amount: *a tiny spark of anger.* **5** a sense of liveliness and excitement. • **v. 1** produce sparks. **2** ignite. **3** (also **spark off**) trigger: *the announcement sparked off protests.*
– PHRASES **bright spark** a lively person.
– DERIVATIVES **sparky** adj.
– ORIGIN Old English.

sparkle • **v.** (**sparkles**, **sparkling**, **sparkled**) **1** shine brightly with flashes of light. **2** be lively and witty. **3** (**sparkling**) (of drink) fizzy. • **n. 1** a glittering flash of light. **2** liveliness and wit.
– DERIVATIVES **sparkly** adj.

sparkler • **n.** a hand-held firework that gives out sparks.

spark plug (also **sparking plug**) • **n.** a device for firing the explosive mixture in an internal-combustion engine.

sparrow • **n.** a small bird with brown and grey plumage.
– ORIGIN Old English.

sparrowhawk • **n.** a small hawk that preys on small birds.

sparse • **adj.** thinly scattered.
– DERIVATIVES **sparsely** adv. **sparsity** n.
– ORIGIN Latin *sparsus.*

Sparta E
/spar-tuh/ a city in the southern Peloponnese in Greece. It was a powerful city state in the 5th century BC.

Spartacus E
/spar-tuh-kuhss/ (died *c.*71 BC), Thracian slave and gladiator. He led a revolt against Rome in 73, but was eventually defeated and killed in battle.

Spartan • **adj. 1** having to do with Sparta. **2** (**spartan**) lacking in comfort or luxury. • **n.** a citizen of Sparta.

spasm • **n. 1** a sudden involuntary contraction of a muscle. **2** a sudden brief spell: *a spasm of coughing.*

S

– ORIGIN Greek *spasmos*.

spasmodic ● adj. **1** occurring or done in brief, irregular bursts. **2** caused by a spasm or spasms.

– DERIVATIVES **spasmodically** adv.

spastic ● adj. **1** relating to or affected by muscle spasm. **2** having to do with cerebral palsy. ● n. **1** offens. a person with cerebral palsy. **2** informal, offens. a stupid person.

– DERIVATIVES **spasticity** n.

– ORIGIN Greek *spastikos* 'pulling'.

> **USAGE** spastic
> You should not use the word **spastic** because many people think it is offensive; say *person with cerebral palsy* instead.

spat[1] past and past part. of **SPIT**[1].

spat[2] ● n. a short cloth covering for the instep and ankle.

– ORIGIN from *spatterdash*, a long legging formerly worn when riding.

spat[3] ● n. informal a petty quarrel.

spate ● n. **1** a large number of similar things coming quickly one after another. **2** esp. Brit. a sudden flood in a river.

– ORIGIN unknown.

spathe /spay*th*/ ● n. Bot. a large bract enclosing the flower cluster of certain plants.

– ORIGIN Greek, 'broad blade'.

spatial /spay-sh'l/ ● adj. having to do with space.

– DERIVATIVES **spatially** adv.

– ORIGIN Latin *spatium* 'space'.

spatter ● v. (**spatters**, **spattering**, **spattered**) **1** cover with drops or spots. **2** splash over a surface. ● n. a spray or splash.

– ORIGIN from Dutch or German *spatten* 'burst, spout'.

spatula /spat-yuu-luh/ ● n. an implement with a broad, flat, blunt blade, used for mixing or spreading.

– ORIGIN Latin.

spatulate /spat-yuu-luht/ ● adj. having a broad, rounded end.

spawn ● v. **1** (of a fish, frog, etc.) release or deposit eggs. **2** give rise to: *the affair spawned a rash of publications.* ● n. the eggs of fish, frogs, etc.

– ORIGIN Old French *espaundre*.

spay ● v. sterilize (a female animal) by removing the ovaries.

– ORIGIN Old French *espeer* 'cut with a sword'.

speak ● v. (**speaks**, **speaking**, **spoke**; past part. **spoken**) **1** say something. **2** (**speak to**) talk to. **3** communicate in or be able to communicate in (a specified language). **4** (**speak for**) express the views or position of. **5** (**speak out/up**) express one's opinions frankly and publicly. **6** (**speak up**) speak more loudly. **7** be evidence of: *her behaviour around him spoke strongly of a crush.* **8** (**speak to**) appeal or relate to. **9** make a speech.

– PHRASES **speak in tongues** speak in an unknown language during religious worship, one of the gifts of the Holy Spirit (Acts 2). **speak volumes** convey a great deal without using words.

– ORIGIN Old English.

speakeasy ● n. (pl. **speakeasies**) informal (in the US during Prohibition) a secret illegal liquor shop or drinking club.

speaker ● n. **1** a person who speaks. **2** a person who speaks a specified language. **3** a person who makes a speech at a formal occasion. **4** (**Speaker**) the officer who is in charge of proceedings in a law-making assembly. **5** a loudspeaker.

speaking ● adj. **1** used for or engaged in speech: *a clear speaking voice.* **2** able to communicate in a specified language.

– PHRASES **on speaking terms** slightly acquainted.

spear ● n. **1** a weapon with a pointed metal tip and a long shaft. **2** a pointed stem of asparagus or broccoli. ● v. pierce or strike with a pointed object.

– ORIGIN Old English.

spearhead ● n. an individual or group leading an attack or movement. ● v. lead (an attack or movement).

spearmint ● n. common garden mint, which is used in cooking as a herb.

spec[1] ● n. (in phr. **on spec**) informal in the hope of success but without any specific preparation or plan.

– ORIGIN short for *speculation*.

spec[2] ● n. informal a detailed working description.

special ● adj. **1** better, greater, or otherwise different from what is usual. **2** organized or intended for a particular purpose. **3** used by or intended for a particular person or group. ● n. **1** something designed or organized for a particular occasion or purpose. **2** a dish not on the regular menu but served on a particular day.

– ORIGIN Latin *specialis*.

> **Special Air Service** E
> (in the UK) a specialist army regiment trained in commando techniques, used in clandestine operations.

> **Special Branch** E
> (in the UK) the police department dealing with political security.

special constable ● n. (in the UK) a person who is trained to act as a police officer on particular occasions.

special effects ● pl. n. illusions created for films and television by props, camerawork, computer graphics, etc.

specialist ● n. a person who is highly skilled or knowledgeable in a particular field. ● adj. involving detailed knowledge within a field.

– DERIVATIVES **specialism** n.

speciality /spesh-i-al-i-ti/ (N. Amer. & Med. also **specialty**) ● n. (pl. **specialities**) **1** a pursuit, area of study, or skill to which someone has devoted themselves and in which they are expert. **2** a product for which a person or region is famous. **3** (usu. **specialty**) a branch of medicine or surgery.

specialize (also **specialise**) ● v. (**specializes**, **specializing**, **specialized**) **1** concentrate on and become expert in a particular skill or area. **2** (**be specialized**) (of an organ or part) be adapted or set apart to serve a special function.

– DERIVATIVES **specialization** (also **specialisation**) n.

specially ● adv. **1** for a special purpose. **2** particularly.

USAGE specially
For an explanation of the difference between **specially** and **especially**, see the note at **ESPECIALLY**.

special needs • **pl. n.** particular educational requirements of children with learning difficulties, physical disability, or emotional and behavioural difficulties.

special pleading • **n.** argument in which the speaker deliberately ignores aspects that are unfavourable to their point of view.

specialty /spesh-uhl-ti/ • **n.** (pl. **specialties**) N. Amer. & Med. = **SPECIALITY**.

specie /spee-shee, spee-shi/ • **n.** money in the form of coins rather than notes.
– ORIGIN Latin *species* 'form, kind'.

species /spee-shiz, spee-sheez/ • **n.** (pl. **species**) **1** Biol. a group of animals or plants consisting of similar individuals capable of breeding with each other. **2** a kind: *a species of criticism*.
– ORIGIN Latin, 'appearance, form'.

specific /spuh-si-fik/ • **adj. 1** clearly defined or identified. **2** precise and clear: *when ordering goods be specific*. **3** (**specific to**) belonging or relating only to. • **n.** (**specifics**) precise details.
– DERIVATIVES **specifically** adv.
– ORIGIN Latin *specificus*.

specification • **n. 1** the action of specifying. **2** (also **specifications**) a detailed description of the design and materials used to make something. **3** a standard of workmanship and materials required to be met in a piece of work.

specify • **v.** (**specifies**, **specifying**, **specified**) state or identify clearly and definitely.

specimen • **n. 1** an individual animal, plant, object, etc. used as an example of its species or type for study or display. **2** a sample for medical testing. **3** a typical example of something. **4** informal a person or animal of a specific type: *a sorry specimen*.
– ORIGIN Latin, 'pattern, model'.

specious /spee-shuhss/ • **adj. 1** seeming reasonable, but actually wrong. **2** misleading in appearance.
– ORIGIN Latin *speciosus* 'fair, plausible'.

speck • **n.** a tiny spot or particle. • **v.** mark with small spots.
– ORIGIN Old English.

speckle • **n.** a small spot or patch of colour. • **v.** (**speckles**, **speckling**, **speckled**) mark with speckles.
– ORIGIN Dutch *spekkel*.

specs • **pl. n.** informal a pair of spectacles.

spectacle • **n.** a visually striking performance or display.
– PHRASES **make a spectacle of oneself** draw attention to oneself by behaving in a ridiculous way in public.
– ORIGIN Latin *spectaculum* 'public show'.

spectacles • **pl. n.** Brit. a pair of glasses.

spectacular • **adj.** very impressive, striking, or dramatic. • **n.** a performance or event produced on a large scale and with striking effects.
– DERIVATIVES **spectacularly** adv.

spectate • **v.** (**spectates**, **spectating**, **spectated**) be a spectator.

spectator • **n.** a person who watches at a show, game, or other event.
– ORIGIN Latin.

specter • **n.** US = **SPECTRE**.

spectra pl. of **SPECTRUM**.

spectral • **adj. 1** having to do with or like a spectre. **2** having to do with spectra or the spectrum.

spectre (US **specter**) • **n. 1** a ghost. **2** a possible unpleasant or dangerous occurrence: *the spectre of nuclear holocaust*.
– ORIGIN French.

spectrometer • **n.** an apparatus used for recording and measuring spectra.

spectroscope • **n.** an apparatus for producing and recording spectra for examination.

spectroscopy /spek-tross-kuh-pi/ • **n.** the branch of science concerned with the investigation and measurement of spectra produced when matter interacts with or gives out electromagnetic radiation.

spectrum /spek-truhm/ • **n.** (pl. **spectra** /spek-truh/) **1** a band of colours produced by separating light into elements with different wavelengths, e.g. in a rainbow. **2** the entire range of wavelengths of light. **3** the components of a sound or other phenomenon arranged according to frequency, energy, etc. **4** a range of beliefs, qualities, etc.: *he's towards the other end of the political spectrum*.
– ORIGIN Latin, 'image, apparition'.

speculate /spek-yuu-layt/ • **v.** (**speculates**, **speculating**, **speculated**) **1** form a theory without firm evidence. **2** invest in stocks, property, or other ventures in the hope of financial gain but with the risk of loss.
– DERIVATIVES **speculation** n. **speculator** n.
– ORIGIN Latin *speculari* 'observe'.

speculative • **adj. 1** based on theory or guesswork rather than knowledge. **2** (of an investment) involving a high risk of loss.
– DERIVATIVES **speculatively** adv.

speculum /spek-yuu-luhm/ • **n.** (pl. **specula** /spek-yuu-luh/) Med. a metal instrument that is used to make an opening or canal in the body wider to allow inspection.
– ORIGIN Latin, 'mirror'.

sped past and past part. of **SPEED**.

speech • **n. 1** the expression of thoughts and feelings using spoken language. **2** a formal talk delivered to an audience. **3** a sequence of lines written for one character in a play.
– ORIGIN Old English.

speechify • **v.** (**speechifies**, **speechifying**, **speechified**) deliver a speech in a boring or pompous way.

speechless • **adj.** unable to speak due to shock or strong emotion.

speech therapy • **n.** treatment to help people with speech and language problems.
– DERIVATIVES **speech therapist** n.

speed • **n. 1** the rate at which someone or something moves or operates. **2** rapidity of movement or action. **3** each of the possible gear ratios of a bicycle. **4** the light-gathering power of a camera lens. **5** the sensitivity of photographic film to light. **6** informal an amphetamine drug. • **v.** (**speeds**, **speeding**, **speeded** or **sped**) **1** move quickly. **2** (**speed up**) move or work more quickly. **3** (of a motorist) travel at a speed greater than the legal limit. **4** archaic make prosperous or successful: *may God speed you*.

– PHRASES **at speed** quickly. **up to speed** fully informed or up to date.
– ORIGIN Old English.

speedboat • n. a motor boat designed for high speed.

speed bump (Brit. also **speed hump**) • n. a ridge set in a road to control the speed of vehicles.

speed camera • n. a roadside camera designed to catch speeding vehicles.

speed limit • n. the maximum speed at which a vehicle may legally travel on a particular stretch of road.

speedometer /spee-**dom**-i-ter/ • n. an instrument on a vehicle's dashboard indicating its speed.

speedway • n. a form of motorcycle racing in which the riders race laps around an oval dirt track.

speedy • adj. (**speedier**, **speediest**) done, occurring, or moving quickly.
– DERIVATIVES **speedily** adv.

Speke E
/speek/, John Hanning (1827–64), English explorer, who with Sir Richard Burton was the first European to discover Lake Tanganyika (1858). Speke later reached and named Lake Victoria.

speleology /spee-li-**ol**-uh-ji/ • n. the study or exploration of caves.
– ORIGIN Greek *spēlaion* 'cave'.

spell[1] • v. (**spells**, **spelling**, **spelled** or esp. Brit. **spelt**) **1** write or name the letters that form (a word) in correct order. **2** (of letters) form (a word). **3** lead to: *the plans would spell disaster.* **4** (**spell out**) explain clearly.
– DERIVATIVES **speller** n.
– ORIGIN Old French *espeller.*

spell[2] • n. **1** a form of words thought to have magical power. **2** a state of enchantment brought on by a spell.
– ORIGIN Old English, 'narration'.

spell[3] • n. a short period of time.
– ORIGIN unknown.

spellbind • v. (**spellbinds**, **spellbinding**, **spellbound**) hold the complete attention of, as if by a spell: *the singer held the audience spellbound.*

spellchecker (also **spelling checker**) • n. a computer program which checks the spelling of words in text by comparing them with a stored list of words.

spelling • n. the way in which a word is spelled.

spelt past and past part. of SPELL[1].

Spencer, E
Sir Stanley (1891–1959), English painter, known for his religious and visionary works set in his native village of Cookham in Berkshire.

spend • v. (**spends**, **spending**, **spent**) **1** pay out (money) to buy or hire goods or services. **2** use or use up (energy or resources). **3** pass (time) in a specified way. • n. informal an amount of money paid out.
– PHRASES **spend a penny** Brit. informal, euphem. urinate. [ORIGIN with reference to the coin-operated locks of public toilets.]
– DERIVATIVES **spender** n.
– ORIGIN Latin *expendere* 'pay out'.

Spender, E
Sir Stephen (1909–95), English poet and critic. He was one of a group of left-wing poets of the 1930s who used industrial imagery in their work.

spendthrift • n. a person who spends money in an extravagant, irresponsible way.

Spenser, E
Edmund (*c.*1552–99), English poet. He is best known for the allegorical romance the *Faerie Queene*, celebrating Queen Elizabeth I.

spent past and past part. of SPEND. • adj. used up.

sperm • n. (pl. **sperm** or **sperms**) **1** semen. **2** a spermatozoon.
– ORIGIN Greek *sperma* 'seed'.

spermatozoon /sper-muh-tuh-**zoh**-on/ • n. (pl. **spermatozoa** /sper-muh-tuh-**zoh**-uh/) the male sex cell of an animal, by which the ovum is fertilized.
– ORIGIN from Greek *sperma* 'seed' + *zōion* 'animal'.

sperm count • n. the number of spermatozoa in a measured amount of semen, used as an indication of a man's fertility.

spermicide • n. a substance that kills spermatozoa, used as a contraceptive.

sperm whale • n. a toothed whale with a massive head, feeding largely on squid.

spew • v. **1** pour out in large quantities rapidly and forcibly. **2** informal vomit.
– ORIGIN Old English.

SPF • abbrev. sun protection factor.

sphagnum /sfag-nuhm/ • n. a kind of moss that grows on bogs.
– ORIGIN Latin.

sphere • n. **1** a round solid figure in which every point on the surface is at an equal distance from the centre. **2** an area of activity, interest, or expertise: *the sphere of foreign affairs.*
– ORIGIN Greek *sphaira* 'ball'.

spherical • adj. shaped like a sphere.
– DERIVATIVES **spherically** adv.

spheroid /sfeer-oyd/ • n. an object that is roughly the same shape as a sphere.

sphincter /**sfingk**-ter/ • n. Anat. a ring of muscle that surrounds an opening such as the anus, and can be tightened to close it.
– ORIGIN Greek *sphinktēr.*

sphinx • n. an ancient Egyptian stone figure having a lion's body and a human or animal head.
– ORIGIN Greek, first referring to a mythical winged monster with a woman's head and a lion's body, who set a riddle and killed those who failed to solve it.

spic • n. US informal, offens. a Spanish-speaking person from Central or South America or the Caribbean.
– ORIGIN perh. from *speak the* in 'no speak the English'.

spice • n. **1** a strong-tasting vegetable substance used to flavour food. **2** an element providing interest and excitement. • v. (**spices**, **spicing**, **spiced**) **1** flavour with spice. **2** (**spice up**) make more exciting or interesting.
– ORIGIN Old French *espice.*

Spice Islands E
former name for **MOLUCCA ISLANDS**.

spick and span • adj. neat, clean, and well looked after.
– ORIGIN from Old Norse words meaning 'chip' + 'new'.

spicy • adj. (**spicier**, **spiciest**) **1** strongly flavoured with spice. **2** mildly indecent: *spicy jokes.*
– DERIVATIVES **spiciness** n.

spider • n. an eight-legged arachnid (insect-like creature), most kinds of which spin webs in which to capture insects.
– ORIGIN Old English.

spider plant • n. a plant having long narrow leaves with a central yellow stripe.

spidery • adj. long and thin, like a spider's legs: *spidery handwriting.*

spiel /shpeel, speel/ • n. informal an elaborate and insincere speech, made to persuade someone to believe or buy something.
– ORIGIN German, 'a game'.

Spielberg, E
Steven (b.1947), American film director and producer, known for such films as *ET, Jurassic Park*, and *Schindler's List.*

spiffing • adj. Brit. informal, dated excellent.
– ORIGIN unknown.

spigot /spi-guht/ • n. **1** a small peg or plug. **2** US a tap. **3** the plain end of a section of a pipe fitting into the socket of the next one.
– ORIGIN perh. from Provençal *espigou.*

spike[1] • n. **1** a thin, pointed piece of metal or wood. **2** each of several metal points set into the sole of a sports shoe to prevent slipping. • v. (**spikes**, **spiking**, **spiked**) **1** impale on or pierce with something sharp. **2** form into or cover with sharp points. **3** informal secretly add alcohol or a drug to (drink or food). **4** put an end to (a plan or undertaking).
– ORIGIN perh. from German or Dutch *spiker.*

spike[2] • n. Bot. a flower cluster formed of many flower heads attached directly to a long stem.
– ORIGIN Latin *spica* 'ear of corn'.

spikenard /spyk-nard/ • n. a perfumed ointment made from the rhizome of a Himalayan plant.
– ORIGIN from Latin *spica* 'spike' + Greek *nardos* 'spikenard'.

spiky • adj. (**spikier**, **spikiest**) **1** like a spike or having many spikes. **2** informal easily annoyed.

spill[1] • v. (**spills**, **spilling**, **spilt** or **spilled**) **1** flow or cause to flow over the edge of a container. **2** move or empty out from a place. • n. **1** an instance of a liquid spilling or the quantity spilt. **2** a fall from a horse or bicycle.
– PHRASES **spill the beans** informal reveal secret information. **spill blood** kill or wound people.
– DERIVATIVES **spillage** n.
– ORIGIN Old English, 'kill, shed blood'.

spill[2] • n. a thin strip of wood or paper used for lighting a fire.
– ORIGIN Dutch or German.

spilt past and past part. of **SPILL**[1].

spin • v. (**spins**, **spinning**, **spun**) **1** turn round quickly. **2** (of a person's head) have a sensation of dizziness. **3** (of a ball) move through the air with a revolving motion. **4** draw out and twist (the fibres of wool, cotton, etc.) to convert them into yarn. **5** (of a spider or a silkworm or other insect) produce (gossamer or silk) or construct (a web or cocoon) by forcing out a fine thread from a special gland. **6** (**spin out**) make (something) last as long as possible. • n. **1** a spinning motion. **2** informal a brief trip in a vehicle for pleasure. **3** a favourable slant given to a news story.
– PHRASES **flat spin** Brit. informal a state of agitation. **spin a yarn** tell a far-fetched story.
– DERIVATIVES **spinner** adj.
– ORIGIN Old English.

spina bifida /spy-nuh bi-fi-duh/ • n. a defect present from birth in which part of the spinal cord is exposed through a gap in the backbone, and which can cause paralysis and other problems.
– ORIGIN Latin.

spinach • n. a vegetable with large dark green leaves.
– ORIGIN prob. from Old French *espinache.*

spinal • adj. relating to the spine.

spinal column • n. the spine.

spinal cord • n. the bundle of nerve fibres in the spine that connects all parts of the body to the brain.

spindle • n. **1** a slender rounded rod with tapered ends, used in spinning wool, flax, etc. by hand. **2** a rod serving as an axis that revolves or on which something revolves. **3** a turned piece of wood used as a banister or chair leg.
– ORIGIN Old English.

spindly • adj. long or tall and thin.

spin doctor • n. informal a spokesperson for a political party or politician employed to give a favourable interpretation of events to the media.

spindrift • n. **1** spray blown from the crests of waves by the wind. **2** driving snow.
– ORIGIN from former *spoon* 'run before wind or sea' + **DRIFT**.

spin dryer • n. a machine for removing water from wet clothes by spinning them in a revolving drum.

spine • n. **1** a series of vertebrae extending from the skull to the small of the back, enclosing the spinal cord. **2** the part of a book that encloses the inner edges of the pages. **3** a hard pointed projection found on certain plants (e.g. cacti) and animals (e.g. hedgehogs).
– ORIGIN Latin *spina* 'thorn, backbone'.

spine-chiller • n. a story or film that causes terror and excitement.
– DERIVATIVES **spine-chilling** adj.

spineless • adj. **1** (of an animal) having no spine. **2** lacking courage and determination.

spinet /spi-net, spin-it/ • n. a type of small harpsichord.
– ORIGIN Italian *spinetta.*

spine-tingling • adj. informal thrilling or pleasurably frightening.

spinnaker /spin-nuh-ker/ • n. a large three-cornered sail set forward of the mainsail of a racing yacht when the wind is coming from behind.
– ORIGIN prob. from *Sphinx*, the yacht first using such a sail.

spinneret • n. an organ through which the silk, gossamer, or thread of spiders, silkworms, and certain other insects is produced.

spinney • n. (pl. **spinneys**) Brit. a small area of trees and bushes.
– ORIGIN Old French *espinei*.

spinning top • n. see TOP².

spinning wheel • n. a machine for spinning yarn or thread with a spindle driven by a wheel attached to a crank or treadle.

spin-off • n. a product or benefit produced during or after the main activity.

Spinoza E
/spi-**noh**-zuh/, Baruch (or Benedict) de (1632–77), Dutch philosopher. He believed in the absolute unity of the universe and God (pantheism).

spinster • n. esp. derog. a single woman beyond the usual age for marriage.
– DERIVATIVES **spinsterhood** n.
– ORIGIN first meaning 'woman who spins'.

spiny • adj. (**spinier**, **spiniest**) full of or covered with prickles.

spiracle /spy-ruh-k'l/ • n. Zool. an external opening used for breathing in certain insects, fish, and other animals.
– ORIGIN Latin *spiraculum*.

spiral • adj. winding in a continuous curve around a central point or axis. • n. **1** a spiral curve, shape, or pattern. **2** a rise or fall of prices, wages, etc., occurring in stages, each of which occurs as a response to a previous rise or fall. • v. (**spirals**, **spiralling**, **spiralled**; US **spirals**, **spiraling**, **spiraled**) **1** follow a spiral course. **2** show a continuous and dramatic increase or decrease.
– DERIVATIVES **spirally** adv.
– ORIGIN Latin *spiralis*.

spire • n. a tall pointed structure on the top of a building, especially a church tower.
– ORIGIN Old English, 'tall plant stem'.

spirit • n. **1** the part of a person that consists of their character and feelings rather than their body, often believed to survive after their body is dead. **2** a supernatural being. **3** typical character, quality, or mood: *the spirit of the times*. **4** (**spirits**) a person's mood. **5** courage, energy, and determination. **6** the real meaning of something as opposed to its strict interpretation: *the rule had been broken in spirit if not in letter*. **7** esp. Brit. strong distilled alcohol for drinking, such as rum. **8** purified distilled alcohol, such as methylated spirits. • v. (**spirits**, **spiriting**, **spirited**) (**spirit away**) take away rapidly and secretly.
– PHRASES **when the spirit moves someone** when someone feels inclined to do something.
– ORIGIN Latin *spiritus*.

spirited • adj. **1** full of energy, enthusiasm, and determination. **2** having a specified character: *a generous-spirited man*.

spiritless • adj. lacking courage, energy, or determination.

spirit level • n. a sealed glass tube partially filled with a liquid, containing an air bubble whose position reveals whether a surface is perfectly level.

spiritual • adj. **1** having to do with the human spirit as opposed to physical things. **2** having to do with religion or religious belief. • n. a religious song of a kind associated with black Christians of the southern US.
– DERIVATIVES **spirituality** n. **spiritually** adv.

spiritualism • n. the belief that it is possible to communicate with the spirits of the dead.

spirituous /spi-ri-tyoo-uhss/ • adj. archaic containing much alcohol.

spirogyra /spy-ruh-jy-ruh/ • n. a type of algae consisting of long green threads.
– ORIGIN from Greek *speira* 'coil' + *guros* 'round'.

spit¹ • v. (**spits**, **spitting**, **spat** or **spit**) **1** eject saliva forcibly from one's mouth. **2** forcibly eject (food or liquid) from one's mouth. **3** say in a hostile way. **4** (of a fire or something being cooked) give out small bursts of sparks or hot fat. **5** (**it spits**, **it is spitting**) Brit. light rain falls. • n. **1** saliva. **2** an act of spitting.
– PHRASES **be the spitting image of** (or **be the spit of**) informal look exactly like. **spit and polish** thorough cleaning and polishing. **spit-and-sawdust** Brit. informal (of a pub) dirty or run-down. **spit blood** feel or express strong anger. **spit in the eye** (or **face**) **of** show contempt for. **spit it out** informal say it quickly.
– ORIGIN Old English.

spit² • n. **1** a long, thin metal rod pushed through meat in order to hold and turn it while it is roasted. **2** a narrow point of land projecting into the sea.
– ORIGIN Old English.

spite • n. a desire to hurt, annoy, or offend. • v. (**spites**, **spiting**, **spited**) deliberately hurt, annoy, or offend.
– PHRASES **in spite of** without being affected by. **in spite of oneself** although one did not want or expect to do so.
– ORIGIN Old French *despit* 'contempt'.

spiteful • adj. deliberately hurtful.
– DERIVATIVES **spitefully** adv. **spitefulness** n.

spitfire • n. a person with a fierce temper.

spit-roasted • adj. cooked on a spit.

spittle • n. saliva.
– ORIGIN from dialect *spattle*.

spittoon /spit-toon/ • n. a container for spitting into.

Spitz, E
Mark (Andrew) (b.1950), American swimmer, who won seven gold medals in the 1972 Olympic Games.

spiv • n. Brit. informal a flashily dressed man who makes a living by dishonest business dealings.
– ORIGIN unknown.

splash • v. **1** (of a liquid) fall or cause to fall in scattered drops. **2** cover with scattered drops. **3** strike or move around in water, causing it to fly about. **4** (**splash down**) (of a spacecraft) land on water. **5** display (a story or photograph) in a prominent place in a newspaper or magazine. **6** (**splash out**) Brit. informal spend money freely. • n. **1** an instance of splashing. **2** a small quantity of liquid that has splashed on to a surface. **3** a small quantity of liquid added to a drink. **4** a bright patch of colour. **5** informal a prominent news story.
– PHRASES **make a splash** informal attract a great deal of attention.
– DERIVATIVES **splashy** adj.

splat • n. informal a sound of something soft and wet or heavy striking a surface.
– ORIGIN from SPLATTER.

splatter • v. (**splatters**, **splattering**, **splat-**

tered) splash with a sticky or thick liquid.

splay • v. spread out or further apart.
– ORIGIN from **DISPLAY**.

spleen • n. **1** an organ in the abdomen involved in the production and removal of blood cells and forming part of the immune system. **2** bad temper.
– ORIGIN Greek *splēn*; sense 2 comes from the former belief that the spleen was the seat of bad temper.

splendid • adj. **1** magnificent; very impressive. **2** informal excellent.
– DERIVATIVES **splendidly** adv.
– ORIGIN Latin *splendidus*.

splendour (US **splendor**) • n. magnificent and impressive appearance.

splenetic /spli-net-ik/ • adj. bad-tempered or spiteful.
– ORIGIN Latin *spleneticus*.

splice • v. (**splices**, **splicing**, **spliced**) **1** join (a rope or ropes) by interweaving the strands at the ends. **2** join (pieces of timber, film, or tape) at the ends. • n. a spliced join.
– ORIGIN prob. from Dutch *splissen*.

spliff • n. informal a cannabis cigarette.
– ORIGIN unknown.

splint • n. a strip of rigid material for supporting a broken bone when it has been set.
– ORIGIN Dutch or German *splinte* 'metal plate or pin'.

splinter • n. a small, thin, sharp piece of wood, glass, etc. broken off from a larger piece. • v. (**splinters**, **splintering**, **splintered**) break into splinters.
– DERIVATIVES **splintery** adj.
– ORIGIN Dutch.

splinter group • n. a small organization that has broken away from a larger one.

split • v. (**splits**, **splitting**, **split**) **1** break into parts by force. **2** divide into parts or groups. **3** (also **split up**) end a marriage or other relationship. **4** (**be splitting**) informal (of one's head) be suffering great pain from a headache. • n. **1** a tear or crack. **2** an instance of splitting or being split. **3** (**the splits**) (in gymnastics and dance) an act of leaping in the air or sitting down with the legs straight and at right angles to the body.
– ORIGIN Dutch *splitten* '(of a storm or rock) break up a ship'.

split end • n. a tip of a person's hair which has split from dryness.

split infinitive • n. a construction consisting of an infinitive with an adverb or other word placed between *to* and the verb.

USAGE split infinitive

Many people still think that splitting infinitives (putting a word between *to* and the verb) is wrong. They think that you should say *she used secretly to admire him* rather than *she used to secretly admire him*, although this sometimes sounds awkward or gives a different emphasis to what is being said. For this reason, the rule about not splitting infinitives is not followed so strictly today, although it is best not to split them if you are writing.

split-level • adj. **1** (of a room or building) having the floor at different levels. **2** (of a cooker) having the oven and hob in separate units.

split pea • n. a pea dried and split in half for cooking.

split screen • n. a cinema, television, or computer screen on which two or more separate images are displayed.

split second • n. a very brief moment of time. • adj. (**split-second**) very rapid or accurate: *split-second timing*.

splodge • n. Brit. a spot or smear.

splosh informal • v. move with a soft splashing sound. • n. a splash.

splotch informal • n. a spot or smear.
– DERIVATIVES **splotchy** adj.
– ORIGIN perh. from **SPOT** and former *plotch* 'blotch'.

splurge informal • n. a sudden burst of extravagance. • v. (**splurges**, **splurging**, **splurged**) spend extravagantly.

splutter • v. (**splutters**, **spluttering**, **spluttered**) **1** make a series of short explosive spitting or choking sounds. **2** say in a rapid and unclear way. • n. a spluttering sound.

Spock, E
Benjamin McLane (1903–98; known as **Dr Spock**), American paediatrician and writer, author of the influential manual *The Common Sense Book of Baby and Child Care* which promoted a liberal approach to child-rearing.

spoil • v. (**spoils**, **spoiling**, **spoilt** (esp. Brit.) or **spoiled**) **1** make something less good or enjoyable. **2** (of food) become unfit for eating. **3** harm the character of (a child) by being not being strict enough. **4** treat with great or excessive kindness. **5** (**be spoiling for**) be extremely eager for. • n. (**spoils**) stolen goods.
– ORIGIN Latin *spoliare*.

spoilage • n. the decay of food and other perishable goods.

spoiler • n. **1** a flap on an aircraft wing which can be raised to create drag and so reduce speed. **2** a similar device on a motor vehicle intended to improve road-holding at high speeds.

spoilsport • n. a person who spoils the pleasure of others.

spoke[1] • n. **1** each of the bars or wire rods connecting the centre of a wheel to its rim. **2** each of the metal rods in an umbrella to which the material is attached.
– ORIGIN Old English.

spoke[2] past of **SPEAK**.

spoken past part. of **SPEAK**. • adj. (in combination) speaking in a specified way: *a soft-spoken man*.
– PHRASES **be spoken for 1** be already claimed. **2** already have a romantic commitment.

spokesman (or **spokeswoman**) • n. a person who makes statements on behalf of a group.

spokesperson • n. (pl. **spokespersons** or **spokespeople**) a spokesman or spokeswoman.

spondee /spon-dee/ • n. Poetry a foot consisting of two long (or stressed) syllables.
– ORIGIN from Greek *spondeios pous* 'foot of a ritual offering of drink'.

sponge • n. **1** a water-dwelling invertebrate animal with a soft porous body. **2** a piece of a light, absorbent substance used for washing, as padding, etc. **3** a very light cake made with eggs, sugar, and flour but little or no fat. • v.

S

(**sponges**, **sponging** or **spongeing**, **sponged**) **1** wipe or clean with a wet sponge or cloth. **2** informal obtain money or food from others without giving anything in return.
– ORIGIN Greek *spongos*.

sponge bag • n. Brit. a toilet bag.

sponge pudding • n. Brit. a steamed or baked pudding of fat, flour, and eggs.

sponger • n. informal a person who lives at others' expense.

spongy • adj. (**spongier**, **spongiest**) like a sponge.

sponsor • n. **1** a person or organization that pays for or contributes to the costs of an event or programme in return for advertising. **2** a person who pledges an amount of money to a charity after another person has participated in a fund-raising event. **3** a person who introduces and supports a proposal for a new law. • v. be a sponsor for.
– DERIVATIVES **sponsorship** n.
– ORIGIN Latin.

spontaneous /spon-tay-ni-uhss/ • adj. **1** performed or occurring as a result of an unplanned impulse. **2** open, natural, and relaxed. **3** (of a process or event) happening naturally, without being made to do so.
– DERIVATIVES **spontaneity** n. **spontaneously** adv.
– ORIGIN Latin *spontaneus*.

spoof • n. informal an imitation of something in which its characteristic features are exaggerated for comic effect.
– ORIGIN coined by the English comedian Arthur Roberts (1852–1933).

spook informal • n. **1** a ghost. **2** esp. N. Amer. a spy. • v. frighten.
– ORIGIN Dutch.

spooky • adj. (**spookier**, **spookiest**) informal sinister or ghostly.
– DERIVATIVES **spookily** adv.

spool • n. a cylindrical device on which thread, film, fishing line, etc. can be wound. • v. wind on to a spool.
– ORIGIN Old French *espole* or German *spōle*.

spoon • n. an implement consisting of a small, shallow bowl on a long handle, used for eating, stirring, and serving food. • v. transfer with a spoon.
– DERIVATIVES **spoonful** n.
– ORIGIN Old English, 'chip of wood'.

S

spoonbill • n. a tall wading bird having a long bill with a very broad flat tip.

spoonerism • n. a mistake in speech in which the initial sounds or letters of two or more words are accidentally swapped around, as in *you have hissed the mystery lectures*.
– ORIGIN named after the English scholar Revd W. A. *Spooner* (1844–1930), who is supposed to have made such errors.

spoon-feed • v. (**spoon-feeds**, **spoon-feeding**, **spoon-fed**) provide (someone) with so much help or information that they do not need to think for themselves.

spoor • n. the track or scent of an animal.
– ORIGIN Dutch *spor*.

Sporades E
/spo-ruh-deez/ two groups of Greek islands in the Aegean Sea. The **Northern Sporades** lie close to the east coast of mainland Greece, while the **Southern Sporades** are situated off the west coast of Turkey.

sporadic /spuh-rad-ik/ • adj. occurring at irregular intervals or only in a few places.
– DERIVATIVES **sporadically** adv.
– ORIGIN Greek *sporadikos*.

spore • n. Biol. a tiny reproductive cell produced by lower plants, fungi, and protozoans.
– ORIGIN Greek *spora* 'sowing, seed'.

sporran /spo-ruhn/ • n. a small pouch worn around the waist so as to hang in front of the kilt as part of men's Scottish Highland dress.
– ORIGIN Scottish Gaelic *sporan*.

sport • n. **1** an activity involving physical effort and skill in which a person or team competes against another or others. **2** informal a person who behaves in a good or specified way in response to teasing, defeat, etc: *be a sport!* **3** pleasure gained from an activity such a hunting. • v. **1** wear (a distinctive item). **2** amuse oneself or play in a lively way.
– ORIGIN from DISPORT.

sporting • adj. **1** connected with or interested in sport. **2** fair and generous.

sportive • adj. playful; light-hearted.

sports car • n. a low-built fast car.

sports jacket • n. a man's informal jacket resembling a suit jacket.

sportsman (or **sportswoman**) • n. **1** a person who takes part in a sport. **2** a person who behaves in a sporting way.

sportswear • n. clothes worn for sport or for casual outdoor use.

sporty • adj. (**sportier**, **sportiest**) informal **1** fond of or good at sport. **2** (of clothing) suitable for wearing for sport or for casual use. **3** (of a car) compact and with fast acceleration.

spot • n. **1** a small round mark on a surface. **2** a pimple. **3** a particular place, point, or position. • v. (**spots**, **spotting**, **spotted**) **1** notice or recognize (someone or something) that is difficult to detect or that one is searching for. **2** mark with spots. **3** (**it spots**, **it is spotting**) rain slightly.
– PHRASES **on the spot 1** immediately. **2** at the scene of an action or event.
– DERIVATIVES **spotted** adj. **spotter** n.
– ORIGIN perh. from Dutch *spotte*.

spot check • n. a test made without warning on a randomly selected subject. • v. (**spot-check**) make a spot check on.

spotless • adj. absolutely clean or pure.

spotlight • n. **1** a lamp projecting a narrow, strong beam of light directly on to a place or person. **2** (**the spotlight**) intense public attention. • v. (**spotlights**, **spotlighting**, **spotlighted** or **spotlit**) light up with a spotlight.

spot on • adj. & adv. Brit. informal completely accurate or accurately.

spotty • adj. (**spottier**, **spottiest**) marked with or having spots.

spot-weld • v. join by welding at a number of separate points.

spouse • n. a husband or wife.
– ORIGIN Latin *sponsus*.

spout • n. **1** a projecting tube or lip through or over which liquid can be poured from a container. **2** a stream of liquid flowing out with great force. **3** a pipe, trough, or chute for conveying liquid, grain, etc. • v. **1** send out or

flow forcibly in a stream. **2** express (one's views) in a lengthy or emphatic way.
– PHRASES **up the spout** Brit. informal useless or ruined.
– ORIGIN from Old Norse, 'to spit'.

sprain • v. wrench the ligaments of (a joint) so as to cause pain and swelling. • n. the result of such a wrench.
– ORIGIN unknown.

sprang past of **SPRING**.

sprat • n. a small edible sea fish of the herring family.
– ORIGIN Old English.

sprawl • v. **1** sit, lie, or fall with one's limbs spread out in an awkward way. **2** spread out irregularly over a large area. • n. **1** a sprawling movement. **2** the disorganized expansion of an urban or industrial area into the nearby countryside.
– ORIGIN Old English, 'move the limbs convulsively'.

spray[1] • n. **1** liquid sent through the air in tiny drops. **2** a liquid which can be forced out of an aerosol or other container in a spray. • v. **1** apply (liquid) in a spray. **2** cover or treat with a spray. **3** (of liquid) be sent through the air in a spray. **4** scatter over an area.
– ORIGIN from Dutch *spraeyen* 'sprinkle'.

spray[2] • n. **1** a stem or small branch of a tree or plant, bearing flowers and leaves. **2** a bunch of cut flowers arranged in an attractive way.
– ORIGIN Old English.

spray gun • n. a device resembling a gun which is used to spray a liquid such as paint under pressure.

spread • v. (**spreads, spreading, spread**) **1** open out so as to increase in surface area, width, or length. **2** stretch out (limbs, hands, fingers, or wings) so that they are far apart. **3** extend over a wide area or a specified period of time. **4** reach or cause to reach more and more people: *panic spread among the crowd.* **5** apply (a substance) in an even layer. • n. **1** the action of spreading. **2** the extent, width, or area covered by something. **3** the range of something. **4** a soft paste that can be spread on bread. **5** an article or advertisement covering several pages of a newspaper or magazine. **6** informal a large meal.
– ORIGIN Old English.

spreadeagle • v. (**spreadeagles, spreadeagling, spreadeagled**) (**be spreadeagled**) be stretched out with the arms and legs extended.

spreadsheet • n. a computer program in which figures arranged in a grid can be manipulated and used in calculations.

spree • n. a spell of unrestrained activity: *a shopping spree.*
– ORIGIN unknown.

sprig • n. a small stem bearing leaves or flowers, taken from a bush or plant.
– ORIGIN German *sprick*.

sprightly • adj. (**sprightlier, sprightliest**) (especially of an old person) lively; energetic.
– ORIGIN from **SPRITE**.

spring • v. (**springs, springing, sprang** or N. Amer. **sprung**; past part. **sprung**) **1** move suddenly or quickly upwards or forwards. **2** move or do suddenly: *the drawer sprang open.* **3** (**spring from**) come or appear from. **4** (**spring up**) suddenly develop or appear. **5** (**sprung**) (of a vehicle or item of furniture) provided with springs. • n. **1** the season after winter and before summer. **2** a spiral metal coil that can be pressed or pulled but returns to its former shape when released. **3** a sudden jump upwards or forwards. **4** a place where water wells up from an underground source. **5** elastic quality.
– PHRASES **spring a leak** (of a boat or container) develop a leak.
– ORIGIN Old English.

spring balance • n. a balance that measures weight by the tension of a spring.

springboard • n. **1** a strong, flexible board from which a diver or gymnast may jump in order to push off more powerfully. **2** a thing providing driving force to an action or enterprise.

springbok • n. a southern African gazelle that leaps when disturbed.
– ORIGIN Afrikaans.

spring chicken • n. informal a young person: *I'm no spring chicken.*

spring clean • n. Brit. a thorough cleaning of a house or room. • v. (**spring-clean**) clean thoroughly.

springer (also **springer spaniel**) • n. a small spaniel of a breed originally used to flush game birds out of cover.

spring greens • pl. n. the leaves of young cabbage plants of a variety that does not develop a heart.

spring-loaded • adj. containing a compressed or stretched spring pressing one part against another.

spring onion • n. Brit. a small onion with a long green stem, eaten raw in salads.

> **Springsteen**, **E**
> Bruce (b.1949), American rock singer, songwriter, and guitarist, known for such albums as *Born in the USA*.

spring tide • n. a tide just after a new or full moon, when there is the greatest difference between high and low water.

springy • adj. (**springier, springiest**) **1** springing back quickly when squeezed or stretched. **2** (of movements) light and confident.

sprinkle • v. (**sprinkles, sprinkling, sprinkled**) **1** scatter or pour small drops or particles over. **2** scatter or pour (small drops or particles) over an object or surface. **3** distribute something randomly throughout. • n. a small amount that is sprinkled.
– ORIGIN perh. from Dutch *sprenkelen*.

sprinkler • n. **1** a device for watering lawns. **2** an automatic fire extinguisher installed in a ceiling.

sprinkling • n. a small, thinly distributed amount.

sprint • v. run at full speed over a short distance. • n. **1** an act of sprinting. **2** a short, fast race.
– ORIGIN from Swedish *spritta*.

sprit • n. Sailing a small pole reaching diagonally from a mast to the upper outer corner of a sail.
– ORIGIN Old English, 'punting pole'.

sprite • n. an elf or fairy.

– ORIGIN a contraction of **SPIRIT**.

sprocket • n. each of several projections on the rim of a wheel that engage with the links of a chain or with holes in film, tape, or paper.
– ORIGIN unknown.

sprout • v. **1** produce shoots. **2** grow (plant shoots or hair). • n. **1** a shoot of a plant. **2** a Brussels sprout.
– ORIGIN Germanic.

spruce[1] • adj. neat and smart. • v. (**spruces**, **sprucing**, **spruced**) (**spruce up**) make smarter.
– ORIGIN perh. from **SPRUCE**[2] in the former sense 'Prussian'.

spruce[2] • n. a widespread coniferous tree with a conical shape and hanging cones.
– ORIGIN from former *Pruce* 'Prussia'.

sprung past part. and N. Amer. past of **SPRING**.

spry • adj. (of an old person) lively.
– ORIGIN unknown.

spud • n. informal a potato.
– ORIGIN unknown.

spume /spyoom/ • n. literary froth or foam that is found on waves.
– ORIGIN Latin *spuma*.

spun past and past part. of **SPIN**.

spunk • n. **1** informal courage and determination. **2** Brit. vulgar semen.
– DERIVATIVES **spunky** adj. (**spunkier**, **spunkiest**).
– ORIGIN perh. from **SPARK** and the former word *funk* 'spark'.

spur • n. **1** a device with a small spike or a spiked wheel, worn on a rider's heel for urging a horse forward. **2** an encouragement: *wars act as a spur to invention.* **3** a projection from a mountain or mountain range. **4** Bot. a slender projection from the base of a flower. **5** a short branch road or railway line. • v. (**spurs**, **spurring**, **spurred**) **1** urge (a horse) forward with spurs. **2** encourage.
– PHRASES **on the spur of the moment** on a momentary impulse.
– ORIGIN Old English.

spurge • n. a plant or shrub with milky latex and small greenish flowers.
– ORIGIN Old French *espurge*.

spurious /*rhymes with* curious/ • adj. **1** false or fake. **2** (of a line of reasoning) apparently but not actually correct.
– ORIGIN Latin *spurius* 'false'.

spurn • v. reject with contempt.
– ORIGIN Old English.

spurt • v. **1** gush out in a sudden stream. **2** move with a sudden burst of speed. • n. **1** a sudden gushing stream. **2** a sudden burst of activity or speed.
– ORIGIN unknown.

sputter • v. (**sputters**, **sputtering**, **sputtered**) **1** make a series of soft explosive sounds. **2** speak in a series of bursts that are hard to understand.
– ORIGIN Dutch *sputteren*.

sputum • n. a mixture of saliva and mucus coughed up from the throat or lungs.
– ORIGIN Latin.

spy • n. (pl. **spies**) **1** a person employed to collect and report secret information on an enemy or competitor. **2** a device that observes others secretly. • v. (**spies**, **spying**, **spied**) **1** be a spy. **2** (**spy on**) watch secretly. **3** see or notice: *he could spy a figure in the distance.*
– ORIGIN Old French *espier* 'espy'.

spyglass • n. a small telescope.

sq • abbrev. square.

squab /skwob/ • n. a young pigeon that is yet to leave the nest.
– ORIGIN unknown.

squabble • n. a noisy quarrel about an unimportant matter. • v. (**squabbles**, **squabbling**, **squabbled**) have a squabble.

squad • n. **1** a small number of soldiers assembled for drill or working together. **2** a group of sports players from which a team is chosen. **3** a division of a police force dealing with a particular type of crime.
– ORIGIN Italian *squadra* 'square'.

squad car • n. a police patrol car.

squaddie • n. (pl. **squaddies**) Brit. informal a private soldier.

squadron • n. **1** an operational unit in an air force. **2** a main division of an armoured or cavalry regiment. **3** a group of warships on a particular duty.
– ORIGIN Italian *squadrone* 'soldiers in a square formation'.

squalid • adj. **1** extremely dirty and unpleasant. **2** very immoral or dishonest: *a squalid attempt to buy votes.*
– ORIGIN Latin *squalidus*.

squall • n. a sudden violent gust of wind or localized storm. • v. (of a baby) cry noisily and continuously.
– ORIGIN prob. from **SQUEAL**.

squalor /*rhymes with* collar/ • n. the state of being squalid.

squander • v. (**squanders**, **squandering**, **squandered**) waste (money, time, etc.) in a reckless or foolish way.
– ORIGIN unknown.

square • n. **1** a plane figure with four equal straight sides and four right angles. **2** an open four-sided area surrounded by buildings. **3** the product of a number multiplied by itself. **4** an area within a military barracks or camp used for drill. **5** an L-shaped or T-shaped instrument used for obtaining or testing right angles. **6** informal an old-fashioned or boring person. • adj. **1** having the shape of a square. **2** having or forming a right angle. **3** (of a unit of measurement) equal to the area of a square whose side is of the unit specified. **4** (after a noun) referring to the length of each side of a square shape or object: *the room was ten metres square.* **5** at right angles. **6** level or parallel. **7** broad and solid in shape. **8** informal old-fashioned or boringly conventional. • adv. directly; straight. • v. (**squares**, **squaring**, **squared**) **1** make square or rectangular. **2** (**squared**) marked out in squares. **3** multiply (a number) by itself. **4** (**square with**) agree or be consistent: *do those claims square with the facts?* **5** settle (a bill or debt). **6** make the score of (a match or game) even. **7** bring (one's shoulders) into a position in which they appear square and broad.
– PHRASES **back to square one** informal back to where one started. **square up** take up the position of a person about to fight.
– DERIVATIVES **squarish** adj.
– ORIGIN Old French *esquare*.

square-bashing • n. Brit. informal military drill performed repeatedly on a barrack square.

square dance ● n. a country dance that starts with four couples facing one another in a square.

squarely ● adv. in a straightforward way; directly.

square meal ● n. a large and balanced meal.

square measure ● n. a unit of measurement relating to area.

square number ● n. the product of a number multiplied by itself, e.g. 1, 4, 9.

square-rigged ● adj. (of a sailing ship) having the main sails at right angles to the length of the ship.

square root ● n. a number which produces a specified quantity when multiplied by itself.

squash[1] ● v. **1** crush or squeeze (something) so that it becomes flat, soft, or out of shape. **2** force into a restricted space. **3** suppress or reject: *the revolt was squashed.* ● n. **1** a state of being squashed. **2** Brit. a concentrated liquid made from fruit juice and sugar, diluted to make a drink. **3** (also **squash rackets**) a game in which two players use rackets to hit a small rubber ball against the walls of a closed court.
– DERIVATIVES **squashy** adj.
– ORIGIN from **QUASH**.

squash[2] ● n. (pl. **squash** or **squashes**) a gourd with flesh that can be cooked and eaten as a vegetable.
– ORIGIN from a North American Indian language.

squat ● v. (**squats**, **squatting**, **squatted**) **1** crouch or sit with the knees bent and the heels close to the bottom or thighs. **2** unlawfully occupy an uninhabited building or area of land. ● adj. (**squatter**, **squattest**) short or low, and wide. ● n. **1** a squatting position. **2** a building occupied unlawfully.
– DERIVATIVES **squatter** n.
– ORIGIN Old French *esquatir* 'flatten'.

squat thrust ● n. an exercise in which the legs are thrust backwards to their full extent from a squatting position with the hands on the floor.

squaw /skwaw/ ● n. offens. an American Indian woman or wife.
– ORIGIN from a North American Indian language.

squawk ● v. **1** (of a bird) make a loud, harsh noise. **2** say something in a loud, ugly tone. ● n. an act of squawking.

squeak ● n. **1** a short, high-pitched sound or cry. **2** a single remark or sound: *I didn't hear a squeak from him.* ● v. **1** make a squeak. **2** say something in a high-pitched tone. **3** informal only just manage to achieve something.
– DERIVATIVES **squeaky** adj.

squeaky clean ● adj. informal **1** completely clean. **2** morally good.

squeal ● n. a long, high-pitched cry or noise. ● v. **1** make a squeal. **2** say something in a high-pitched tone. **3** (often **squeal on**) informal inform on someone.

squeamish ● adj. **1** easily disgusted or made to feel sick. **2** having very strong moral views.
– ORIGIN Old French *escoymos*.

squeegee /skwee-jee/ ● n. a scraping implement with a rubber-edged blade, used for cleaning windows.
– ORIGIN from **SQUEEZE**.

squeeze ● v. (**squeezes**, **squeezing**, **squeezed**) **1** firmly press from opposite or all sides. **2** extract (liquid or a soft substance) from something by squeezing. **3** (**squeeze in/into/through**) manage to get into or through (a restricted space). **4** (**squeeze in**) manage to find time for. ● n. **1** an act of squeezing or the state of being squeezed. **2** a hug. **3** a small amount of liquid produced by squeezing.
– PHRASES **put the squeeze on** informal pressurize into doing something.
– DERIVATIVES **squeezable** adj. **squeezer** n.
– ORIGIN unknown.

squelch ● v. make a soft sucking sound such as that of treading in thick mud. ● n. a squelching sound.
– DERIVATIVES **squelchy** adj.

squib ● n. a small firework that hisses before exploding.
– ORIGIN unknown.

squid ● n. (pl. **squid** or **squids**) a mollusc with a long body, eight arms, and two long tentacles.
– ORIGIN unknown.

squidgy ● adj. (**squidgier**, **squidgiest**) informal, esp. Brit. soft and moist.

squiffy ● adj. informal esp. Brit. slightly drunk.
– ORIGIN unknown.

squiggle ● n. a short line that curls and loops irregularly.
– DERIVATIVES **squiggly** adj.
– ORIGIN perh. from **SQUIRM** and **WIGGLE** or **WRIGGLE**.

squillion ● cardinal number informal an indefinite very large number.
– ORIGIN humorous formation on the pattern of *billion*.

squint ● v. **1** look at someone or something with partly closed eyes. **2** partly close (one's eyes). **3** have a squint affecting one eye. ● n. **1** a permanent condition in which one eye does not look in the same direction as the other. **2** informal a quick or casual look.
– ORIGIN perh. from Dutch *schuinte* 'slant'.

squire ● n. **1** a country gentleman. **2** Brit. informal used as a friendly form of address by one man to another. **3** hist. a young nobleman acting as an attendant to a knight before becoming a knight himself.
– ORIGIN Old French *esquier* 'esquire'.

squirm ● v. **1** wriggle or twist the body from side to side. **2** be embarrassed or ashamed. ● n. a wriggling movement.
– ORIGIN prob. from **WORM**.

squirrel ● n. a rodent with a bushy tail that lives in trees. ● v. (**squirrels**, **squirrelling**, **squirrelled**; US also **squirrels**, **squirreling**, **squirreled**) (**squirrel away**) hide (money or valuables) in a safe place.
– ORIGIN Old French *esquireul*.

squirt ● v. **1** (of a liquid) be or cause to be forced out in a thin jet from a small opening. **2** wet with a jet of liquid. ● n. **1** a thin jet of liquid. **2** informal a weak or insignificant person.

squish ● v. **1** make a soft squelching sound. **2** informal squash. ● n. a soft squelching sound.
– DERIVATIVES **squishy** adj.

Sri Lanka E
/sri **lang**-kuh, shri **lang**-kuh/ an island country off the SE coast of India; capital, Colombo. Former name (until 1972) **Ceylon**.
– DERIVATIVES **Sri Lankan** adj. & n.

SS[1] • **abbrev.** **1** Saints. **2** steamship.

SS[2] • **n.** the Nazi special police force.
– ORIGIN short for German *Schutzstaffel* 'defence squadron'.

SSE • **abbrev.** south-south-east.

SSW • **abbrev.** south-south-west.

St • **abbrev.** **1** Saint. **2** Street.

st • **abbrev.** stone (in weight).

stab • **v.** (**stabs**, **stabbing**, **stabbed**) **1** thrust a knife or other pointed weapon into. **2** thrust a pointed object at. **3** (of a pain) cause a sudden sharp feeling. • **n.** **1** an act of stabbing. **2** a sudden sharp feeling or pain. **3** (**a stab at**) informal an attempt to do.
– ORIGIN unknown.

stability • **n.** the state of being stable.

stabilize (also **stabilise**) • **v.** (**stabilizes**, **stabilizing**, **stabilized**) make or become stable.
– DERIVATIVES **stabilization** (also **stabilisation**) n.

stabilizer (also **stabiliser**) • **n.** **1** the horizontal tailplane of an aircraft. **2** a device used to reduce the rolling of a ship. **3** (**stabilizers**) Brit. a pair of small supporting wheels fitted on a child's bicycle. **4** a substance preventing the breakdown of emulsions in food or paint.

stable[1] • **adj.** (**stabler**, **stablest**) **1** not likely to give way or overturn; firmly fixed. **2** not worsening in health after an injury or operation. **3** emotionally well-balanced. **4** not likely to change or fail. **5** not liable to undergo chemical decomposition or radioactive decay.
– DERIVATIVES **stably** adv.
– ORIGIN Latin *stabilis*.

stable[2] • **n.** **1** a building for housing horses. **2** an establishment where racehorses are kept and trained. • **v.** (**stables**, **stabling**, **stabled**) put or keep (a horse) in a stable.
– ORIGIN Old French *estable* 'stable, pigsty'.

stable lad • **n.** Brit. a person employed in a stable.

stablemate • **n.** a horse from the same stable as another.

stabling • **n.** accommodation for horses.

staccato /stuh-kah-toh/ • **adv. & adj.** Music with each sound or note sharply separated from the others. • **n.** (pl. **staccatos**) **1** Music a staccato passage or performance. **2** a series of short, detached sounds or words.
– ORIGIN Italian, 'detached'.

stack • **n.** **1** a neat pile of objects. **2** a rectangular or cylindrical pile of hay, straw, etc. **3** informal a large quantity. **4** a chimney. • **v.** **1** arrange in a stack. **2** fill or cover with stacks of things. **3** cause (aircraft) to fly at different altitudes while waiting to land. **4** arrange (a pack of cards) dishonestly. **5** (**be stacked against/in favour of**) (of a situation) be very likely to produce an unfavourable or favourable outcome for.
– ORIGIN Old Norse, 'haystack'.

stadium /stay-di-uhm/ • **n.** (pl. **stadiums** or **stadia** /stay-di-uh/) an athletic or sports ground with rows of seats for spectators.
– ORIGIN Greek *stadion* 'racing track'.

staff • **n.** **1** the employees of an organization. **2** a group of army officers assisting a commanding officer. **3** a long stick used as a support or weapon. **4** a rod or sceptre held as a sign of office or authority. **5** Music = **stave** (in sense 3). • **v.** provide with staff.
– ORIGIN Old English.

staff nurse • **n.** Brit. an experienced hospital nurse.

Staffordshire E
a county of central England; county town, Stafford.

staffroom • **n.** esp. Brit. a common room for teachers in a school or college.

Staffs. • **abbrev.** Staffordshire.

stag • **n.** a fully adult male deer.
– ORIGIN from an Old Norse word meaning 'male bird'.

stag beetle • **n.** a large dark beetle, the male of which has large jaws resembling antlers.

stage • **n.** **1** a point, period, or step in a process. **2** a raised floor or platform on which actors, entertainers, or speakers perform. **3** (**the stage**) the acting profession. **4** a scene of action or place of debate. **5** each of two or more sections of a rocket or spacecraft that are discarded in turn when their fuel is exhausted. • **v.** (**stages**, **staging**, **staged**) **1** present a performance of (a play or other show). **2** organize (a public event). **3** cause (something) to happen: *she's going to stage a comeback*.
– ORIGIN Old French *estage* 'dwelling'.

stagecoach • **n.** a large closed horse-drawn vehicle formerly used to carry passengers along a regular route.

stage direction • **n.** an instruction in a play script indicating the position or tone of an actor, or specifying sound effects, lighting, etc.

stage door • **n.** an actors' entrance from the street to the backstage area of a theatre.

stage fright • **n.** nervousness before or during a performance.

stagehand • **n.** a person dealing with scenery or props during a play.

stage-manage • **v.** (**stage-manages**, **stage-managing**, **stage-managed**) **1** be the stage manager of. **2** arrange carefully to create a certain effect.

stage manager • **n.** the person responsible for lighting and other technical arrangements for a stage play.

stage name • **n.** a name taken for professional purposes by an actor.

stage whisper • **n.** a loud whisper by an actor on stage, intended to be heard by the audience.

stagey • **adj.** var. of **stagy**.

stagger • **v.** (**staggers**, **staggering**, **staggered**) **1** walk or move unsteadily, as if about to fall. **2** astonish. **3** spread over a period of time. **4** arrange (objects or parts) so that they are not in line. • **n.** an act of staggering.
– ORIGIN Old Norse.

staging • **n.** **1** a way of staging a play. **2** a temporary platform for working on.

staging post • **n.** a place at which people or vehicles regularly stop during a journey.

stagnant • **adj.** **1** (of water or air) not moving and often having an unpleasant smell.

2 showing little activity.
– ORIGIN Latin *stagnare* 'form a pool of standing water'.

stagnate • v. (**stagnates**, **stagnating**, **stagnated**) become stagnant.
– DERIVATIVES **stagnation** n.

stag night • n. an all-male celebration, especially one held for a man about to be married.

stagy (also **stagey**) • adj. excessively theatrical or exaggerated.

staid • adj. respectable and unadventurous.
– ORIGIN from **STAY**[1].

stain • v. **1** mark or discolour with something that is not easily removed. **2** damage (someone's reputation). **3** colour with a dye or chemical. • n. **1** a discoloured patch or dirty mark that is difficult to move. **2** a thing that damages a person's reputation. **3** a dye or chemical used to colour materials.
– ORIGIN Old French *desteindre*.

stained glass • n. coloured glass used to form pictures or decorative designs, used for church windows.

stainless • adj. unmarked by or resistant to stains.

stainless steel • n. a form of steel containing chromium, resistant to tarnishing and rust.

stair • n. **1** each of a set of fixed steps. **2** (**stairs**) a set of such steps leading from one floor of a building to another.
– ORIGIN Germanic, 'climb'.

staircase • n. a set of stairs and its surrounding structure.

stairway • n. a staircase.

stairwell • n. a shaft in which a staircase is built.

stake[1] • n. **1** a strong post with a point at one end, driven into the ground to support a tree, form part of a fence, etc. **2** (**the stake**) hist. a wooden post to which a person was tied before being burned alive. • v. (**stakes**, **staking**, **staked**) **1** support (a plant) with a stake. **2** (**stake out**) mark (an area) with stakes so as to claim ownership. **3** (**stake out**) informal keep (a place or person) under secret observation.
– ORIGIN Old English.

stake[2] • n. **1** a sum of money gambled. **2** a share or interest in a business or situation. **3** (**stakes**) prize money. **4** (**stakes**) a competitive situation: *one step ahead in the fashion stakes*. • v. (**stakes**, **staking**, **staked**) gamble (money or something of value).
– PHRASES **at stake 1** at risk. **2** in question.
– ORIGIN perh. from **STAKE**[1], from the idea of an object being placed as a wager on a stake.

stake-out • n. informal a period of secret observation.

stalactite /sta-luhk-tyt/ • n. a tapering structure hanging from the roof of a cave, formed of calcium salts deposited by dripping water.
– ORIGIN Greek *stalaktos* 'dripping'.

stalagmite /sta-luhg-myt/ • n. a tapering column rising from the floor of a cave, formed of calcium salts deposited by dripping water.
– ORIGIN Greek *stalagma* 'a drop'.

stale • adj. (**staler**, **stalest**) **1** (of food) no longer fresh or pleasant to eat. **2** no longer new and interesting. **3** no longer performing well because no longer interested. • v. (**stales**, **staling**, **staled**) make or become stale.
– ORIGIN prob. from Old French *estaler* 'to halt'.

stalemate • n. **1** Chess a position counting as a draw, in which a player is not in check but can only move into check. **2** a situation in which further progress by opposing parties seems impossible.

Stalin E
/stah-lin/, Joseph (1879–1953; born *Iosif Vissarionovich Dzhugashvili*), Soviet statesman, General Secretary of the Communist Party of the USSR 1922–53. His regime was marked by rapid industrialization, the organization of agriculture on a collective basis, and the ruthless suppression of his opponents.

Stalinabad E
/stah-lin-uh-bad/ former name for **DUSHANBE**.

Stalinism • n. the policies adopted by Joseph Stalin, based on dictatorial state control and the pursuit of communism.
– DERIVATIVES **Stalinist** n. & adj.

stalk[1] • n. **1** the main stem of a plant. **2** the attachment or support of a leaf, flower, or fruit. **3** a slender support or stem.
– ORIGIN prob. from an Old English word meaning 'rung of a ladder'.

stalk[2] • v. **1** follow or approach stealthily. **2** harass with unwanted and obsessive attention. **3** walk in a proud, stiff, or angry manner.
– DERIVATIVES **stalker** n.
– ORIGIN Old English.

stalking horse • n. a person or thing that is used to disguise the real purpose of something.

stall • n. **1** a stand, booth, or compartment for the sale of goods in a market. **2** an individual compartment for an animal in a stable or cowshed. **3** a stable or cowshed. **4** (also **starting stall**) a compartment in which a horse is held prior to the start of a race. **5** a compartment for one person in a set of toilets, shower cubicles, etc. **6** (**stalls**) Brit. the ground-floor seats in a theatre. **7** a seat in the choir or chancel of a church. • v. **1** (of a motor vehicle or its engine) stop running. **2** (of an aircraft) be moving at a speed too low to allow effective operation of the controls. **3** stop making progress. **4** delay by putting something off till a later date: *she was stalling for time*.
– ORIGIN Old English.

stallion • n. an adult male horse that has not been castrated.
– ORIGIN Old French *estalon*.

stalwart /stawl-wert, stol-wert/ • adj. **1** loyal, reliable, and hard-working. **2** dated sturdy. • n. a stalwart supporter or member of an organization.
– ORIGIN Scots.

stamen /stay-muhn/ • n. Bot. a male fertilizing organ of a flower.
– ORIGIN Latin, 'thread'.

stamina • n. the ability to keep up physical or mental effort over a long period.
– ORIGIN Latin, plural of **STAMEN** in the sense 'threads spun by the Fates'.

stammer • v. (**stammers**, **stammering**,

S

stammered) **1** speak with sudden unwanted pauses and a tendency to repeat the first letters of words. **2** say in such a way. • **n.** a tendency to stammer.
– ORIGIN Old English.

stamp • **v. 1** bring down (one's foot) heavily on the ground or an object. **2** walk with heavy, forceful steps. **3** (**stamp out**) put an end to by taking decisive action: *measures to stamp out BSE.* **4** press against with a device that leaves a mark or pattern. **5** impress (a pattern or mark). **6** (**stamp on**) fix in the mind: *the date was stamped on his memory.* • **n. 1** a small piece of paper stuck to a posted item to record payment of postage. **2** an instrument for stamping a pattern or mark. **3** a mark or pattern made by a stamp. **4** a distinctive impression or quality. **5** a particular class or type: *men of his own stamp.* **6** an act of stamping the foot.
– ORIGIN Germanic.

stamp duty • **n.** a duty which must be paid for the legal recognition of certain documents.

stampede • **n. 1** a sudden panicked rush of a number of horses, cattle, etc. **2** a sudden rapid movement or reaction of a large group of people due to interest or panic. • **v.** (**stampedes**, **stampeding**, **stampeded**) take part in or cause a stampede.
– ORIGIN Spanish *estampida* 'crash'.

stamping ground • **n.** a place one regularly visits or spends time at.

stance /stahnss, stanss/ • **n. 1** the way in which someone stands. **2** an attitude or standpoint.
– ORIGIN French.

stanch /stawnch/ • **v.** US = **STAUNCH**[2].

stanchion /stan-shuhn/ • **n.** an upright bar, post, or frame forming a support or barrier.
– ORIGIN Old French *stanchon*.

stand • **v.** (**stands**, **standing**, **stood**) **1** be in or rise to an upright position, supported by one's feet. **2** place or be situated in a particular position. **3** move to a specified place: *stand aside.* **4** remain stationary or unchanged. **5** be in a specified state or condition. **6** adopt a particular attitude towards an issue. **7** be likely to do something: *investors stood to lose heavily.* **8** act in a specified capacity. **9** tolerate or like: *I can't stand it.* **10** Brit. be a candidate in an election. • **n. 1** an attitude towards a particular issue. **2** a determined effort to hold one's ground or resist something. **3** a stopping of motion or progress. **4** a large structure for spectators to sit or stand in at different levels. **5** a raised platform for a band, orchestra, or speaker. **6** a rack, base, or item of furniture for holding or displaying something. **7** a small temporary stall or booth from which goods are sold or displayed. **8** (**the stand**) a witness box.
– PHRASES **stand by 1** look on without becoming involved. **2** remain loyal to or abide by. **3** be ready to take action if needed. **stand down** (also **stand aside**) resign from or leave a job. **stand for 1** be an abbreviation of or symbol for. **2** put up with. **stand in** deputize. **stand out 1** stick out or be easily noticeable. **2** be clearly better. **stand up** informal fail to keep a date with (someone). **stand up for** speak or act in support of.
– ORIGIN Old English.

> **USAGE** stand
>
> It is good English to use the present participle **standing** rather than the past participle **stood** with the verb 'to be': say *we were standing there for hours* rather than *we were stood there for hours.*

standard • **n. 1** a level of quality or achievement. **2** a required or agreed level of quality or achievement. **3** something used as a measure in order to make comparisons. **4** (**standards**) principles of good behaviour. **5** a military or ceremonial flag. • **adj. 1** used or accepted as normal or average. **2** (of a size, measure, etc.) regularly used or produced. **3** (of a work, writer, etc.) viewed as authoritative and so widely read.
– ORIGIN Old French *estendart*.

standard assessment task • **n.** (in the UK) a standard test given to schoolchildren to assess their progress.

standard-bearer • **n. 1** a soldier carrying the standard of a unit, regiment, or army. **2** a leading figure in a cause or movement.

Standard Grade • **n.** (in Scotland) an examination equivalent to the GCSE.

standardize (also **standardise**) • **v.** (**standardizes**, **standardizing**, **standardized**) cause to conform to a standard.
– DERIVATIVES **standardization** (also **standardisation**) n.

standard lamp • **n.** esp. Brit. a lamp with a tall stem whose base stands on the floor.

standard of living • **n.** the amount of money and level of comfort available to a person or community.

standby • **n.** (pl. **standbys**) **1** readiness for duty or immediate action. **2** a person or thing ready to be used in an emergency. • **adj.** (of tickets for a journey or performance) unreserved and sold only at the last minute if still available.

stand-in • **n.** a substitute.

standing • **n. 1** status or reputation. **2** duration: *a problem of long standing.* • **adj. 1** (of a jump or start of a race) performed from rest or an upright position. **2** existing permanently; remaining in force or use.

standing joke • **n.** something regularly causing amusement.

standing order • **n.** Brit. **1** an instruction to a bank to make regular fixed payments to someone. **2** an order placed on a regular basis with a retailer.

standing ovation • **n.** a long period of applause during which the audience rise to their feet.

stand-off • **n.** a deadlock between two equally matched opponents.

stand-offish • **adj.** informal distant and cold in manner.

standpipe • **n.** a vertical pipe extending from a water supply, connecting to a temporary tap to the mains.

standpoint • **n.** an attitude towards a particular issue.

standstill • **n.** a situation without movement or activity.

stand-up • **adj.** (of comedy or a comedian) performed or performing by standing in front of an audience and telling jokes.

Stanislaus, St E
/stan-is-lawss/ (1030–79; known as **St Stanislaus of Cracow**), patron saint of Poland. Feast day, 11 April.

Stanislavsky E
/stan-is-**laf**-ski/, Konstantin (Sergeevich) (1863–1938; born *Konstantin Sergeevich Alekseev*), Russian theatre director and actor. His theories on training actors led to the development of method acting.

stank past of STINK.

Stanley[1] E
(also **Port Stanley**) the chief port and town of the Falkland Islands, situated on the island of East Falkland.

Stanley[2], E
Sir Henry Morton (1841 1904; born *John Rowlands*), Welsh explorer. As a newspaper correspondent he was sent to Africa to find David Livingstone; he found him in 1871 at Lake Tanganyika. Stanley later made further explorations in central Africa.

stanza /stan-zuh/ • n. a group of lines forming the basic unit in a poem; a verse.
– ORIGIN Italian, 'standing place, stanza'.

staphylococcus /staf-fi-luh-**kok**-kuhss/ • n. (pl. **staphylococci** /staf-fi-luh-**kok**-ky/) a bacterium of a group including many kinds that cause pus to be formed.
– ORIGIN from Greek *staphulē* 'bunch of grapes' + *kokkos* 'berry'.

staple[1] • n. **1** a small U-shaped piece of wire used to fasten papers together. **2** a small U-shaped metal bar that is driven into wood to hold things in place. • v. (**staples**, **stapling**, **stapled**) secure with a staple or staples.
– ORIGIN Old English, 'pillar'.

staple[2] • n. **1** a main item of trade or production. **2** a main or important element of something. • adj. main or important: *a staple food*.
– ORIGIN German or Dutch *stapel* 'pillar, emporium'.

stapler • n. a device for fastening papers together with staples.

star • n. **1** a huge mass of burning gas which is visible as a glowing point in the night sky. **2** a simplified representation of a star, often used to indicate a category of excellence. **3** a famous or talented entertainer or sports player. **4** an outstanding person or thing. • v. (**stars**, **starring**, **starred**) **1** (of a film, play, etc.) have (someone) as a leading performer. **2** (of a performer) have a leading role in a film, play, etc.
– ORIGIN Old English.

star anise • n. a small star-shaped fruit with an aniseed flavour, used in Asian cookery.

starboard /**star**-bord, **star**-berd/ • n. the side of a ship or aircraft on the right when one is facing forward. Opp. PORT[3]. • v. turn (a ship or its helm) to starboard.
– ORIGIN Old English, 'rudder side'.

starch • n. **1** a carbohydrate which is obtained from cereals and potatoes and is an important part of the human diet. **2** powder or spray made from this substance, used to stiffen fabric. • v. stiffen with starch.
– ORIGIN Old English, 'stiffened'.

starchy • adj. **1** (of food) containing a lot of starch. **2** stiff and formal in manner.

Starck, E
Philippe (b.1949), French designer, noted for his stylish household objects and furniture.

stardom • n. the state of being a famous entertainer or sports player.

stardust • n. magical quality or feeling.

stare • v. (**stares**, **staring**, **stared**) look at someone or something with great concentration and the eyes wide open. • n. an act of staring.
– ORIGIN Old English.

starfish • n. a sea creature having a flattened body with five or more arms extending from a central point.

stargazer • n. informal an astronomer or astrologer.

stark • adj. **1** severe or bare in appearance. **2** unpleasantly or sharply clear. **3** complete; sheer: *stark terror*.
– PHRASES **stark naked** completely naked.
– DERIVATIVES **starkly** adv.
– ORIGIN Old English.

starkers • adj. informal, esp. Brit. completely naked.

starlet • n. informal a promising young actress or performer.

starlight • n. light coming from the stars.

starling • n. a songbird with dark shiny plumage.
– ORIGIN Old English.

starlit • adj. lit by stars.

Star of David • n. a six-pointed figure made up of two equilateral triangles, used as a Jewish and Israeli symbol.

Starr, E
Ringo (b.1940; born *Richard Starkey*), English drummer in the Beatles.

starry • adj. (**starrier**, **starriest**) **1** full of or lit by stars. **2** informal relating to stars in entertainment.

starry-eyed • adj. naively enthusiastic or idealistic.

Stars and Stripes • pl. n. the national flag of the US.

starship • n. (in science fiction) a large spaceship for travel between stars.

star sign • n. a sign of the zodiac.

star-struck • adj. fascinated and greatly impressed by famous people.

star-studded • adj. informal featuring a number of famous people.

start • v. **1** begin to do, be, or happen. **2** begin to operate. **3** cause to happen or operate. **4** begin to move or travel. **5** jump or jerk from surprise. • n. **1** an act of beginning or the point at which something begins. **2** an advantage given at the beginning of a race. **3** a jerk of surprise.
– PHRASES **for a start** in the first place. **start out** (or **up**) begin a project or business. **to start with** as the first thing to be taken into account.
– ORIGIN Old English, 'to caper, leap'.

starter • n. **1** a person or thing that starts. **2** esp. Brit. the first course of a meal. **3** an automatic device for starting a machine.

starting block • n. a block for bracing the

S

feet of a runner at the start of a race.

starting price • n. the final odds at the start of a horse race.

startle • v. (**startles**, **startling**, **startled**) cause to feel sudden shock or alarm.
– DERIVATIVES **startled** adj.
– ORIGIN Old English, 'kick, struggle'.

startling • adj. **1** alarming. **2** very surprising or remarkable.

starve • v. (**starves**, **starving**, **starved**) **1** suffer or die from hunger. **2** cause to starve. **3** (**be starving** or **starved**) informal feel very hungry. **4** (**be starved of**) be deprived of.
– DERIVATIVES **starvation** n.
– ORIGIN Old English, 'to die'.

stash informal • v. store safely in a secret place. • n. a secret store of something.
– ORIGIN unknown.

stasis /stay-siss/ • n. formal or tech. a period or state when there is no change or development.
– ORIGIN Greek, 'standing, stoppage'.

state • n. **1** the condition of someone or something at a particular time. **2** a nation or territory considered as an organized political unit under one government. **3** an area forming part of a federal republic. **4** (**the States**) the United States of America. **5** the government of a country. **6** ceremony associated with monarchy or government: *he was buried in state*. **7** (**a state**) informal an agitated, untidy, or dirty condition. • v. (**states**, **stating**, **stated**) express definitely in speech or writing.
– PHRASES **state-of-the-art** using the newest ideas and most up-to-date features.
– DERIVATIVES **statehood** n.
– ORIGIN partly from ESTATE, partly from Latin *status* 'standing'.

stateless • adj. not recognized as a citizen of any country.

stately • adj. (**statelier**, **stateliest**) dignified or grand.

stately home • n. Brit. a large and fine house occupied or formerly occupied by an aristocratic family.

statement • n. **1** a clear expression of something in speech or writing. **2** a formal account of facts or events given to the police or in court. **3** a document setting out what has been paid into and out of a bank account.

S

state school • n. Brit. a school funded and controlled by the state.

statesman (or **stateswoman**) • n. an experienced and respected political leader or figure.

static /sta-tik/ • adj. **1** lacking movement, action, or change. **2** Physics concerned with bodies at rest or forces in equilibrium. Often contrasted with DYNAMIC. **3** (of an electric charge) acquired by objects that cannot conduct a current. • n. **1** static electricity. **2** crackling on a telephone, radio, etc.
– DERIVATIVES **statically** adv.
– ORIGIN Greek *statikos* 'causing to stand'.

station • n. **1** a place where passenger trains stop on a railway line. **2** a place where a specified activity or service is based: *a radar station*. **3** a broadcasting company. **4** the place where someone or something stands or is placed. **5** a person's social rank or position. **6** Austral/NZ a large sheep or cattle farm. • v. assign to a station.
– ORIGIN Latin.

stationary • adj. not moving or changing.

USAGE stationary

Do not confuse **stationary** and **stationery**: **stationary** is an adjective meaning 'not moving or changing', while **stationery** is a noun meaning 'paper and other writing materials'.

stationer • n. a seller of stationery.
– ORIGIN Latin *stationarius* 'tradesman at a fixed location'.

stationery • n. paper and other materials needed for writing.

stationmaster • n. an official in charge of a railway station.

station wagon • n. N. Amer. & Austral./NZ an estate car.

statistic • n. a fact or piece of data obtained from a study of a large quantity of numerical data.
– ORIGIN German *Statistik*.

statistical • adj. having to do with statistics.
– DERIVATIVES **statistically** adv.

statistics • n. the collection and analysis of numerical data in large quantities.
– DERIVATIVES **statistician** n.

statuary /stat-yoo-uh-ri/ • n. statues as a whole.

statue • n. a carved or cast figure of a person or animal.
– ORIGIN Latin *statua*.

Statue of Liberty E
see LIBERTY, STATUE OF.

statuesque /sta-tyuu-esk, sta-chuu-esk/ • adj. (of a woman) attractively tall, graceful, and dignified.

statuette • n. a small statue.
– ORIGIN French.

stature • n. **1** a person's natural height when standing. **2** importance or reputation.
– ORIGIN Latin *statura*.

status • n. **1** a person's social or professional position in relation to others. **2** high rank or social standing. **3** the situation at a particular time. **4** official classification.
– ORIGIN Latin, 'standing'.

status quo /stay-tuhss kwoh/ • n. the existing state of affairs.
– ORIGIN Latin, 'the state in which'.

status symbol • n. a possession intended to show a person's wealth or high status.

statute • n. **1** a written law. **2** a rule of an organization.
– ORIGIN Latin *statutum* 'thing set up'.

statute book • n. (**the statute book**) the body of a nation's laws.

statute law • n. the body of principles and rules of law laid down in statutes.

statutory • adj. required or permitted by law.

staunch[1] /stawnch/ • adj. very loyal and committed.
– ORIGIN Old French *estanche* 'watertight'.

staunch[2] /stawnch, stahnch/ (US **stanch**) • v. stop or slow down (a flow of blood from a wound).
– ORIGIN Old French *estanchier*.

Stavanger E
/stuh-vang-er/ a seaport in SW Norway, an important centre servicing oilfields in the North Sea.

stave • n. **1** any of the lengths of wood fixed side by side to make a barrel, bucket, etc. **2** a strong post or pole. **3** (also **staff**) Music a set of five parallel lines on or between which a note is written to indicate its pitch. • v. **1** (**staves, staving, staved** or **stove**) (**stave in**) break (something) by forcing it inwards. **2** (past and past part. **staved**) (**stave off**) stop or delay (something bad).
– ORIGIN from *staves*, variant plural of **STAFF**.

stay[1] • v. **1** remain in the same place. **2** remain in a specified state or position: *inflation will stay down.* **3** live somewhere temporarily as a visitor or guest. **4** stop, delay, or prevent. • n. **1** a period of staying somewhere. **2** a suspension or postponement of the proceedings of a law court: *a stay of execution.* **3** (**stays**) hist. a corset made of two pieces laced together and stiffened by strips of whalebone.
– PHRASES **stay on** continue to study, work, or be somewhere after others have left. **stay put** remain somewhere without moving.
– ORIGIN Old French *ester.*

stay[2] • n. **1** a large rope, wire, or rod used to support a ship's mast. **2** a supporting wire or cable on an aircraft.
– ORIGIN Old English.

staying power • n. informal endurance or stamina.

STD • abbrev. **1** sexually transmitted disease. **2** Brit. subscriber trunk dialling.

stead • n. the place or role that someone or something should have or fill: *she was appointed in his stead.*
– PHRASES **stand in good stead** be useful to (someone) in the future.
– ORIGIN Old English.

steadfast • adj. determined and firm.
– ORIGIN Old English, 'standing firm'.

steady • adj. (**steadier, steadiest**) **1** firmly fixed, supported, or balanced. **2** not faltering or wavering. **3** sensible and reliable. **4** regular, even, and continuous in development, frequency, or strength. • v. (**steadies, steadying, steadied**) make or become steady.
– DERIVATIVES **steadily** adv. **steadiness** n.

steak • n. **1** high-quality beef from the hindquarters of the animal, cut into thick slices for grilling or frying. **2** a thick slice of other meat or fish. **3** poorer-quality beef for stewing.
– ORIGIN Old Norse.

steal • v. (**steals, stealing, stole**; past part. **stolen**) **1** take (something) without permission and without intending to return it. **2** do secretly: *I stole a look at my watch.* **3** move quietly or secretively. • n. informal a bargain.
– PHRASES **steal the show** attract the most attention and praise.
– ORIGIN Old English.

stealth • n. cautious and secretive action or movement.
– ORIGIN prob. from **STEAL**.

stealthy • adj. (**stealthier, stealthiest**) cautious and secretive.
– DERIVATIVES **stealthily** adv.

steam • n. **1** the hot vapour into which water is converted when heated, which condenses in the air into a mist of tiny water droplets. **2** power derived from steam under pressure. **3** momentum: *the dispute gathered steam.* • v. **1** give off or produce steam. **2** (**steam up**) mist over with steam. **3** cook (food) by heating it in steam from boiling water. **4** clean or treat with steam. **5** (of a ship or train) travel somewhere under steam power. **6** informal move quickly or forcefully.
– PHRASES **let off steam** informal get rid of suppressed energy or strong emotion. **run out of steam** informal lose momentum or enthusiasm.
– ORIGIN Old English.

steamboat • n. a boat propelled by a steam engine.

steam engine • n. **1** an engine that uses the expansion or rapid condensation of steam to generate power. **2** a steam locomotive.

steamer • n. **1** a ship or boat powered by steam. **2** a type of saucepan in which food can be steamed.

steam hammer • n. a large steam-powered hammer used in forging.

steam iron • n. an electric iron that gives off steam from holes in its flat surface.

steamroller • n. a heavy, slow-moving vehicle with a roller, used to flatten the surfaces of roads during construction. • v. (**steamrollers, steamrollering, steamrollered**) (also **steamroll**) **1** forcibly pass (a law) by restricting debate. **2** force into doing something.

steamy • adj. (**steamier, steamiest**) **1** producing or filled with steam. **2** hot and humid. **3** informal involving passionate sexual activity.

steed • n. archaic a horse.
– ORIGIN Old English.

steel • n. **1** a hard, strong grey or bluish-grey alloy of iron with carbon, used as a structural material and in manufacturing. **2** strength and determination: *nerves of steel.* • v. mentally prepare (oneself) to do something difficult.
– ORIGIN Old English.

steel band • n. a band that plays music on steel drums.

steel drum • n. a percussion instrument made out of an oil drum with one end beaten down and divided into sections to give different notes.

steel wool • n. fine strands of steel matted together into a mass, used to clean or smooth things.

steelworks • n. a factory where steel is produced.

steely • adj. (**steelier, steeliest**) **1** like steel in colour, brightness, or strength. **2** coldly determined.

steep[1] • adj. **1** rising or falling sharply. **2** (of a rise or fall in an amount) very large or rapid. **3** informal (of a price or demand) excessive.
– DERIVATIVES **steeply** adv. **steepness** n.
– ORIGIN Old English, 'extending to a great height'.

steep[2] • v. **1** soak in water or other liquid. **2** (**be steeped in**) have a great deal of a particular quality: *a city steeped in history.*
– ORIGIN Germanic.

steepen • v. become or make steeper.

steeple • n. a church tower and spire.

S

– ORIGIN Old English.

steeplechase ● n. **1** a horse race run on a racecourse with ditches and hedges as jumps. **2** a running race in which runners must clear hurdles and water jumps.
– DERIVATIVES **steeplechaser** n.
– ORIGIN so named because originally the race was run across country, with a steeple marking the finishing point.

steeplejack ● n. a person who climbs tall structures such as chimneys and steeples in order to carry out repairs.

steer[1] ● v. **1** guide or control the movement of (a vehicle, ship, etc.). **2** direct or guide in a particular direction.
– PHRASES **steer clear of** take care to avoid.
– ORIGIN Old English.

steer[2] ● n. a bullock.
– ORIGIN Old English.

steerage ● n. hist. the cheapest accommodation in a ship.

steering ● n. the mechanism in a vehicle, ship, or aircraft which allows it to be steered.

steering column ● n. a shaft that connects the steering wheel of a vehicle to the rest of the steering mechanism.

steering committee (also **steering group**) ● n. a committee that decides on the priorities or order of business of an organization.

steering wheel ● n. a wheel that a driver turns in order to steer a vehicle.

steersman ● n. a person who steers a boat or ship.

Stein E
/styn/, Gertrude (1874–1946), American writer, who developed an experimental stream-of-consciousness style, notably in *The Autobiography of Alice B. Toklas*. Her home in Paris was a focus for the avant-garde.

Steinbeck E
/styn-bek/, John (Ernst) (1902–68), American novelist, famous for *Of Mice and Men* and *The Grapes of Wrath*, both realistically depicting the lives of migrant agricultural workers of California.

Steiner E
/sty-ner/, Rudolf (1861–1925), Austrian philosopher, founder of the Anthroposophical Society in 1912, which set up Steiner Schools and influenced the development of child-centred education.

stellar /stel-ler/ ● adj. having to do with a star or stars.
– ORIGIN Latin *stellaris*.

stem[1] ● n. **1** the main long thin part of a plant or shrub. **2** the stalk supporting a fruit, flower, or leaf. **3** a long, thin supporting part of something, such as that of a wine glass or tobacco pipe. **4** a vertical stroke in a letter or musical note. **5** Grammar the root or main part of a word, to which other elements are added. ● v. (**stems**, **stemming**, **stemmed**) (**stem from**) be caused by.
– ORIGIN Old English.

stem[2] ● v. (**stems**, **stemming**, **stemmed**) stop or slow down (the flow or progress of something).
– ORIGIN Old Norse.

stench ● n. a strong and very unpleasant smell.
– ORIGIN Old English.

stencil ● n. a thin sheet of card, plastic, or metal with a pattern or letters cut out of it, used to produce a design on the surface below by applying ink or paint through the holes. ● v. (**stencils**, **stencilling**, **stencilled**; US **stencils**, **stenciled**, **stenciling**) decorate with a stencil.
– ORIGIN Old French *estancler* 'decorate brightly'.

Stendhal E
/ston-dahl/ (1783–1842; pen name of *Marie Henri Beyle*), French novelist, author of *Le Rouge et le noir* and *La Chartreuse de Parme*.

Steno E
/stee-noh/, Nicolaus (1638–86; Danish name *Niels Steensen*), Danish anatomist and geologist. He stated that fossils are the petrified remains of living organisms, that many rocks arise from consolidation of sediments, and that such rocks occur in layers in the order in which they were laid down.

stenography /sti-nog-ruh-fi/ ● n. N. Amer. the action of writing in shorthand and transcribing the shorthand on a typewriter.
– DERIVATIVES **stenographer** n.
– ORIGIN Greek *stenos* 'narrow'.

stentorian /sten-tor-i-uhn/ ● adj. (of a person's voice) loud and powerful.
– ORIGIN from *Stentor*, a herald in the Trojan War.

step ● n. **1** an act of lifting and putting down the foot or feet, as in walking. **2** the distance covered by a step. **3** a flat surface on which to place one's foot when moving from one level to another. **4** a position or grade in a scale or ranking. **5** a measure or action taken to achieve something: *a major step forward*. **6** (**steps** or **a pair of steps**) Brit. a stepladder. ● v. (**steps**, **stepping**, **stepped**) lift and put down one's foot or feet.
– PHRASES **step down** withdraw or resign from a job. **step in 1** become involved in a difficult situation. **2** act as a substitute for someone. **step out of line** behave inappropriately or disobediently. **step up** increase the amount, speed, or strength of.
– ORIGIN Old English.

step- ● comb. form referring to a relationship resulting from a remarriage: *stepmother*.
– ORIGIN Old English.

step aerobics ● pl. n. a type of aerobics that involves stepping up on to and down from a block.

stepbrother ● n. a son of one's stepmother or stepfather.

stepchild ● n. a child of one's husband or wife by a previous marriage.

stepdaughter ● n. a daughter of one's husband or wife by a previous marriage.

stepfather ● n. a man who is married to one's mother after the divorce of one's parents or the death of one's father.

stephanotis /stef-fuh-noh-tiss/ ● n. a climbing plant with waxy white flowers.
– ORIGIN Greek, 'fit for a wreath'.

S

Stephen E
(*c.*1097–1154), grandson of William the Conqueror, king of England 1135–54. He seized the throne from Matilda soon after the death of Henry I. Civil war followed until Matilda was forced to leave England in 1148.

Stephen, St[1] E
(died *c.*35), one of the original seven deacons in Jerusalem. He was charged with blasphemy and stoned, thus becoming the first Christian martyr. Feast day, 26 or 27 December.

Stephen, St[2] E
(*c.*977–1038), first king and patron saint of Hungary, reigned 1000–38. Feast day, 2 September or 20 August.

Stephenson, E
George (1781–1848), British engineer, a pioneer of steam locomotives and railways. He built his first locomotive in 1814, and with his son **Robert** (1803–59), built the *Rocket* (1829), the prototype for all future steam locomotives.

stepladder • n. a short folding ladder with flat steps and a small platform.

stepmother • n. a woman who is married to one's father after the divorce of one's parents or the death of one's mother.

steppe /step/ • n. a large area of flat grassland without trees in SE Europe or Siberia.
– ORIGIN Russian *step'*.

stepping stone • n. **1** a raised stone on which to step when crossing a stream or muddy area. **2** an action that helps one to make progress towards a goal.

stepsister • n. a daughter of one's stepmother or stepfather.

stepson • n. a son of one's husband or wife by a previous marriage.

-ster • suffix **1** referring to a person engaged in or associated with a particular activity: *gangster*. **2** referring to a person having a particular quality: *youngster*.
– ORIGIN Old English.

stereo /ste-ri-oh/ • n. (pl. **stereos**) **1** stereophonic sound. **2** a stereophonic CD player, record player, etc. • adj. stereophonic.

stereophonic • adj. (of sound reproduction) using two or more channels so that the sound seems to come from more than one source. Compare with **MONOPHONIC**.
– ORIGIN Greek *stereos* 'solid'.

stereoscope • n. a device by which two photographs of the same object taken at slightly different angles are viewed together, creating an impression of depth and solidity.
– DERIVATIVES **stereoscopic** adj.

stereotype • n. an over-simplified idea of the typical characteristics of a person or thing. • v. (**stereotypes**, **stereotyping**, **stereotyped**) view as a stereotype.

stereotypical • adj. relating to a stereotype.
– DERIVATIVES **stereotypically** adv.

sterile • adj. **1** not able to produce children, young, crops, or fruit. **2** lacking in imagination, creativity, or excitement. **3** free from bacteria or other living micro-organisms.
– DERIVATIVES **sterilely** adv. **sterility** n.
– ORIGIN Latin *sterilis*.

sterilize (also **sterilise**) • v. (**sterilizes**, **sterilizing**, **sterilized**) **1** make sterile. **2** make unable to produce offspring by removing or blocking the sex organs.
– DERIVATIVES **sterilization** (also **sterilisation**) n.

sterling • n. British money. • adj. excellent: *she does sterling work*.
– ORIGIN prob. from Old English *steorra* 'star' (because some early Norman pennies bore a small star).

sterling silver • n. silver of at least 92¼ per cent purity.

stern[1] • adj. **1** grimly serious or strict, especially in the exercise of discipline. **2** severe.
– DERIVATIVES **sternly** adv. **sternness** n.
– ORIGIN Old English.

stern[2] • n. the rear of a ship or boat.
– ORIGIN prob. from Old Norse, 'steering'.

Sterne, E
Laurence (1713–68), Irish novelist, author of the nine-volume novel *The Life and Opinions of Tristram Shandy*.

sternum /ster-nuhm/ • n. (pl. **sternums** or **sterna** /ster-nuh/) the breastbone.
– ORIGIN Greek *sternon* 'chest'.

steroid /ste-royd, steer-oyd/ • n. **1** any of a large class of organic compounds that includes certain hormones and vitamins. **2** an anabolic steroid.
– ORIGIN from **STEROL**.

sterol /steer-ol, ste-rol/ • n. Biochem. any of a group of naturally occurring unsaturated steroid alcohols.
– ORIGIN from the ending of words such as **CHOLESTEROL**.

stertorous /ster-tuh-ruhss/ • adj. (of breathing) noisy and laboured.
– ORIGIN Latin *stertere* 'to snore'.

stethoscope /steth-uh-skohp/ • n. a medical instrument for listening to the action of someone's heart or breathing, having a disc that is placed against the chest and two tubes connected to earpieces.
– ORIGIN from Greek *stēthos* 'breast' + *skopein* 'look at'.

Stetson /stet-suhn/ • n. (trademark in the US) a hat with a high crown and a very wide brim, traditionally worn by cowboys.
– ORIGIN named after the American hat manufacturer John B. *Stetson* (1830–1906).

stevedore /stee-vuh-dor/ • n. a person employed at a dock to load and unload ships.
– ORIGIN Spanish *estivador*.

Stevenson, E
Robert Louis (Balfour) (1850–94), Scottish novelist, poet, and travel writer. His works include *Treasure Island*, *The Strange Case of Dr Jekyll and Mr Hyde*, and *Kidnapped*.

stew • n. **1** a dish of meat and vegetables cooked slowly in liquid in a closed dish. **2** informal a state of anxiety or agitation. • v. **1** cook slowly in liquid in a closed dish. **2** Brit. (of tea) become strong and bitter with prolonged brewing. **3** informal be in a stuffy atmosphere. **4** informal be in an agitated state.
– ORIGIN Old French *estuve*.

steward • n. **1** a person who looks after the passengers on a ship or aircraft. **2** a person

responsible for supplies of food to a college, club, etc. **3** an official who supervises arrangements at a large public event. **4** a person employed to manage a large house or estate.
– DERIVATIVES **stewardship** n.
– ORIGIN Old English.

stewardess ● n. a woman who looks after the passengers on a ship or aircraft.

Stewart[1], E
Sir Jackie (b.1939; born *John Young Stewart*), Scottish motor-racing driver. He was three times world champion (1969; 1971; 1973).

Stewart[2], E
James (Maitland) (1908–97), American actor, famous for such films as *The Philadelphia Story, It's a Wonderful Life*, and *Vertigo*.

Stewart Island E
an island of New Zealand, situated off the south coast of South Island.

stick[1] ● n. **1** a thin piece of wood that has fallen or been cut off a tree. **2** a piece of trimmed wood used for support in walking or as a weapon. **3** (in hockey, polo, etc.) a long, thin implement used to hit or direct the ball or puck. **4** a long, thin object: *a stick of dynamite.* **6** the threat of punishment as a means of persuasion. **7** Brit. informal severe criticism.
– ORIGIN Old English.

stick[2] ● v. (**sticks**, **sticking**, **stuck**) **1** push (something pointed) into or through something. **2** (**stick in/into/through**) be fixed with its point embedded in. **3** stab or pierce with a sharp object. **4** protrude or extend in a certain direction. **5** informal put somewhere in a quick or careless way. **6** adhere or cause to adhere. **7** (**be stuck**) be fixed in a particular position or unable to move. **8** (**be stuck**) be unable to continue with a task or find the solution.
– PHRASES **be stuck with** informal be unable to get rid of or escape from. **get stuck in** (or **into**) Brit. informal start doing something with determination. **stick it out** informal put up with or carry on with something difficult. **stick out** be very noticeable. **stick to** continue doing or using. **stick up for** support.
– ORIGIN Old English.

sticker ● n. a sticky label or notice.

stick insect ● n. a long, slender insect that resembles a twig.

stick-in-the-mud ● n. informal a person who resists change.

stickleback ● n. a small freshwater or coastal fish with sharp spines along its back.
– ORIGIN from Old English words meaning 'thorn' + 'back'.

stickler ● n. a person who insists on a certain type of behaviour.
– ORIGIN Old English, 'set in order'.

sticky ● adj. (**stickier**, **stickiest**) **1** tending or designed to stick. **2** like glue in texture. **3** (of the weather) hot and humid.

stiff ● adj. **1** not easily bent. **2** difficult to turn or operate. **3** unable to move easily and without pain. **4** not relaxed or friendly. **5** severe or strong: *stiff fines.* ● n. informal a dead body.
– DERIVATIVES **stiffly** adv. **stiffness** n.
– ORIGIN Old English.

stiffen ● v. **1** make or become stiff. **2** make or become stronger.

stiff upper lip ● n. the tendency to endure difficulties without complaining.

stifle ● v. (**stifles**, **stifling**, **stifled**) **1** prevent from breathing freely; suffocate. **2** smother or suppress.
– ORIGIN perh. from Old French *estouffer*.

stifling ● adj. unpleasantly hot and stuffy.

stigma /stig-muh/ ● n. (pl. **stigmas** or in sense 2 **stigmata** /stig-**mah**-tuh, **stig**-muh-tuh/) **1** a mark or sign of disgrace. **2** (**stigmata**) (in Christian tradition) marks on a person's body corresponding to those left on Christ's body by the Crucifixion. **3** Bot. the part of a pistil that receives the pollen during pollination.
– ORIGIN Greek, 'mark made by a pointed instrument'.

stigmatize (also **stigmatise**) ● v. (**stigmatizes**, **stigmatizing**, **stigmatized**) regard or treat as shameful.

stile ● n. an arrangement of steps set into a fence or wall that allows people to climb over.
– ORIGIN Old English.

stiletto ● n. (pl. **stilettos**) **1** esp. Brit. a thin, high heel on a woman's shoe. **2** a short dagger with a tapering blade.
– ORIGIN Italian, 'little dagger'.

still[1] ● adj. **1** not moving. **2** (of a drink) not fizzy. ● n. **1** a state of deep and quiet calm. **2** a photograph or a single shot from a cinema film. ● adv. **1** even now or at a particular time. **2** nevertheless. **3** even: *better still.* ● v. make or become still.
– DERIVATIVES **stillness** n.
– ORIGIN Old English.

still[2] ● n. an apparatus for distilling alcoholic drinks such as whisky.
– ORIGIN from DISTIL.

stillbirth ● n. the birth of an infant that has died in the womb.

stillborn ● adj. (of an infant) born dead.

still life ● n. a painting or drawing of an arrangement of objects such as flowers or fruit.

stilt ● n. **1** either of a pair of upright poles with supports for the feet, enabling the user to walk above the ground. **2** each of a set of posts supporting a building.
– ORIGIN Germanic.

stilted ● adj. (of speech or writing) stiff and unnatural.

Stilton ● n. trademark a kind of strong, rich blue cheese.
– ORIGIN so named because it was formerly sold at an inn in *Stilton*, Cambridgeshire.

stimulant ● n. **1** a substance that acts to stimulate activity in the body. **2** something that stimulates activity, interest, or enthusiasm.

stimulate ● v. (**stimulates**, **stimulating**, **stimulated**) **1** Biol. cause a reaction in an organ or tissue. **2** make more active, interested, or enthusiastic.
– DERIVATIVES **stimulation** n.
– ORIGIN Latin *stimulare* 'urge, goad'.

stimulus /stim-yuu-luhss/ ● n. (pl. **stimuli** /stim-yuu-ly, **stim**-yuu-lee/) something that causes a reaction or that promotes activity, interest, etc.

– ORIGIN Latin, 'goad, spur, incentive'.

sting ● n. **1** a sharp-pointed organ of an insect, capable of inflicting a wound by injecting poison. **2** any of a number of tiny hairs on certain plants, causing inflammation if touched. **3** a wound from a sting. **4** a sharp tingling sensation or hurtful effect. ● v. (**stings**, **stinging**, **stung**) **1** wound with a sting. **2** produce a stinging sensation. **3** hurt; upset. **4** (**sting into**) provoke (someone) to do (something).
– DERIVATIVES **stinger** n.
– ORIGIN Old English.

stinging nettle ● n. a nettle covered in stinging hairs.

stingray ● n. a ray (flat sea fish) with a long poisonous spine at the base of the tail.

stingy /stin-ji/ ● adj. (**stingier**, **stingiest**) informal mean.
– ORIGIN perh. from STING.

stink ● v. (**stinks**, **stinking**, **stank** or **stunk**; past part. **stunk**) **1** have a strong unpleasant smell. **2** informal be sordid or immoral. ● n. **1** a strong, unpleasant smell. **2** informal a row or fuss.
– ORIGIN Old English.

stinker ● n. informal a very unpleasant person or thing.

stinking ● adj. **1** foul-smelling. **2** informal very unpleasant. ● adv. informal extremely: *stinking rich.*

stinky ● adj. (**stinkier**, **stinkiest**) informal having a strong unpleasant smell.

stint ● v. (also **stint on**) restrict how much someone can have of (something). ● n. an allotted period of work.
– ORIGIN Old English, 'make blunt'.

stipend /sty-pend/ ● n. a fixed regular sum paid as a salary to a priest, teacher, or public official.
– ORIGIN Latin *stipendium.*

stipendiary /sty-pen-di-uh-ri/ ● adj. receiving a stipend; working for pay rather than voluntarily.

stipple ● v. (**stipples**, **stippling**, **stippled**) **1** mark (a surface) with many small dots. **2** produce a decorative effect on (paint or other material) by roughening its surface when wet.
– ORIGIN Dutch *stippelen* 'to prick'.

stipulate /stip-yuu-layt/ ● v. (**stipulates**, **stipulating**, **stipulated**) demand or specify as part of an agreement.
– DERIVATIVES **stipulation** n.
– ORIGIN Latin *stipulari.*

stir[1] ● v. (**stirs**, **stirring**, **stirred**) **1** move an implement round and round in (a liquid or soft substance) to mix it. **2** move slightly or begin to be active. **3** wake or rise from sleep. **4** (also **stir up**) arouse (a strong feeling) in someone. **5** Brit. informal deliberately cause trouble by spreading rumours. ● n. **1** an act of stirring. **2** a disturbance or commotion.
– DERIVATIVES **stirrer** n.
– ORIGIN Old English.

stir[2] ● n. informal prison.
– ORIGIN perh. from Romany *sturbin* 'jail'.

stir-crazy ● adj. informal mentally disturbed as a result of being confined or imprisoned.

stir-fry ● v. (**stir-fries**, **stir-frying**, **stir-fried**) fry quickly over a high heat while stirring briskly.

Stirling[1] E
a city in central Scotland, administrative centre of Stirling region.

Stirling[2], E
Sir James Fraser (1926–92), Scottish architect, known for his use of geometric shapes and coloured decoration in public buildings such as the Neuestaatsgalerie in Stuttgart.

stirring ● adj. causing great excitement or strong emotion. ● n. a first sign of activity, movement, or emotion.

stirrup ● n. each of a pair of loops attached at either side of a horse's saddle to support the rider's foot.
– ORIGIN Old English.

stirrup pump ● n. a hand-operated water pump with a footrest resembling a stirrup.

stitch ● n. **1** a loop of thread or yarn resulting from a single pass of the needle in sewing, knitting, or crocheting. **2** a method of sewing, knitting, or crocheting that produces a particular pattern. **3** informal the smallest item of clothing: *swimming with not a stitch on.* **4** a sudden sharp pain in the side of the body, caused by hard exercise. ● v. make or mend with stitches.
– PHRASES **in stitches** informal laughing uncontrollably. **stitch up** Brit. informal make (someone) appear guilty of something they did not do.
– DERIVATIVES **stitching** n.
– ORIGIN Old English.

stoat ● n. a small brown mammal of the weasel family.
– ORIGIN unknown.

stock ● n. **1** a supply of goods or materials available for sale or use. **2** farm animals bred and kept for their meat or milk. **3** the capital of a company raised through the selling of shares in it. **4** (**stocks**) shares in a company. **5** securities issued by the government in fixed units with a fixed rate of interest. **6** water in which bones, meat, fish, or vegetables have been slowly simmered. **7** a person's ancestry. **8** a breed, variety, or population of an animal or plant. **9** the trunk or woody stem of a tree or shrub. **10** a plant with sweet-smelling white, pink, or lilac flowers. **11** (**the stocks**) hist. a wooden structure with holes for a person's feet and hands, in which criminals were locked as a public punishment. ● adj. **1** usually kept in stock and thus regularly available for sale. **2** constantly recurring or conventional: *stock characters.* ● v. **1** have or keep a stock of. **2** provide or fill with a stock of something. **3** (**stock up**) collect stocks of something.
– PHRASES **take stock** make an overall assessment of a particular situation.
– ORIGIN Old English, 'trunk, post'.

stockade ● n. **1** a barrier or enclosure formed from upright wooden posts. **2** esp. N. Amer. a military prison.
– ORIGIN from former French *estocade.*

stockbreeder ● n. a farmer who breeds livestock.

stockbroker ● n. a broker who buys and sells stocks and shares on behalf of clients.

stock car ● n. an ordinary car that has been strengthened for use in a race in which cars collide with each other.

stock cube ● n. a cube of dried meat, vegetable, or fish stock for use in cooking.

stock exchange • n. a market in which stocks and shares are bought and sold.

Stockhausen E
/stok-how-z'n/, Karlheinz (b.1928), German composer. He is known for his use of electronic music and for serialist works such as *Gruppen*, for three orchestras.

Stockholm E
/stok-hohm/ the capital of Sweden.

stocking • n. **1** either of a pair of separate close-fitting nylon garments covering the foot and leg, worn especially by women. **2** US or archaic a long sock worn by men.
– DERIVATIVES **stockinged** adj.
– ORIGIN from *stock* in the dialect sense 'stocking'.

stock-in-trade • n. the typical subject or commodity a person, company, or profession uses or deals in.

stockist • n. Brit. a retailer that stocks goods of a particular type for sale.

stockman • n. a person who looks after livestock.

stock market • n. a stock exchange.

stockpile • n. a large stock of goods or materials that has been gathered together. • v. (**stockpiles**, **stockpiling**, **stockpiled**) gather together a large stock of.

stockpot • n. a pot in which stock is prepared by long, slow cooking.

stock-still • adv. completely still.

stocktaking • n. the action of recording the amount of stock held by a business.

stocky • adj. (**stockier**, **stockiest**) (of a person) short and sturdy.

stodge • n. informal, esp. Brit. food that is heavy and filling.
– DERIVATIVES **stodgy** adj.
– ORIGIN prob. from **STUFF** and *podge* 'fat'.

stoic /stoh-ik/ • n. a stoical person. • adj. stoical
– DERIVATIVES **stoicism** n.
– ORIGIN Greek *stōikos*.

stoical • adj. enduring pain and hardship without showing one's feelings or complaining.
– DERIVATIVES **stoically** adv.

stoke • v. (**stokes**, **stoking**, **stoked**) **1** add coal to (a fire, furnace, etc.). **2** encourage (a strong emotion). **3** (**stoke up**) informal eat a large quantity of food to give one energy.

Stoker, E
Bram (1847–1912; full name *Abraham Stoker*), Irish novelist, author of the vampire story *Dracula*.

stoker • n. a person who tends the furnace on a steamship or steam train.
– ORIGIN Dutch.

stole[1] • n. a woman's long scarf or shawl, worn loosely over the shoulders.
– ORIGIN Greek, 'clothing'.

stole[2] past of **STEAL**.

stolen past part. of **STEAL**.

stolid • adj. calm, dependable, and showing little emotion.
– ORIGIN Latin *stolidus*.

stoma /stoh-muh/ • n. (pl. **stomas** or **stomata** /stoh-muh-tuh/) **1** a tiny pore in a leaf or stem of a plant, allowing movement of gases in and out. **2** a small mouth-like opening in some lower animals.
– ORIGIN Greek, 'mouth'.

stomach • n. **1** the internal organ in which the first part of digestion occurs. **2** the belly. **3** an appetite or desire for something: *they had no stomach for a fight.* • v. **1** consume (food or drink) without feeling sick. **2** accept or approve of.
– ORIGIN Greek *stomakhos* 'gullet'.

stomach pump • n. a syringe attached to a long tube, used for removing the contents of a person's stomach.

stomata pl. of **STOMA**.

stomp • v. tread heavily and noisily.
– ORIGIN from **STAMP**.

Stone, E
Oliver (b.1946), American film director, screenwriter, and producer, known for films such as *Born on the Fourth of July* and *Wall Street*.

stone • n. **1** the hard non-metallic mineral matter of which rock is made. **2** a small piece of stone on the ground. **3** a piece of stone shaped as a memorial or to mark out a boundary. **4** a gem. **5** a hard seed in certain fruits. **6** (pl. **stone**) Brit. a unit of weight equal to 14 lb (6.35 kg). • v. (**stones**, **stoning**, **stoned**) **1** throw stones at in order to injure or kill. **2** remove the stone from (a fruit). • adv. completely: *stone cold.*
– PHRASES **leave no stone unturned** try every possible course of action in order to achieve something. **a stone's throw** a short distance.
– ORIGIN Old English.

Stone Age • n. a period that came before the Bronze Age, when weapons and tools were made of stone.

stone circle • n. a prehistoric monument consisting of stones arranged in a circle.

stoned • adj. informal strongly affected by drugs or alcohol.

stoneground • adj. (of flour) ground with millstones.

Stonehenge E
a prehistoric stone monument on Salisbury Plain in Wiltshire, built in several phases from *c.*2950 BC. It is believed to have been used for ritual and astronomical purposes.

stonemason • n. a person who prepares and builds with stone.

stonewall • v. delay or block by refusing to answer questions or by giving evasive replies, especially in politics.

stonewashed • adj. (of a garment or fabric) washed with small stones to produce a worn or faded appearance.

stonework • n. the parts of a building that are made of stone.

stony • adj. (**stonier**, **stoniest**) **1** full of stones. **2** like stone. **3** cold and unfeeling.
– DERIVATIVES **stonily** adv.

stood past and past part. of **STAND**.

stooge • n. **1** derog. a less important person used by another to do routine or unpleasant work. **2** a performer who is the butt of a comedian's jokes.
– ORIGIN unknown.

stool • n. **1** a seat without a back or arms.

S

2 Med. a piece of faeces.
– PHRASES **fall between two stools** Brit. fail to be either of two satisfactory alternatives.
– ORIGIN Old English.

stool pigeon ● n. a police informer.
– ORIGIN so named from the original use of a pigeon fixed to a stool as a decoy.

stoop ● v. **1** bend one's head or body forwards and downwards. **2** have the head and shoulders permanently bent forwards. **3** lower one's standards so far as to do something morally wrong. ● n. a stooping posture.
– ORIGIN Old English.

stop ● v. (**stops, stopping, stopped**) **1** come or bring to an end. **2** prevent from happening or from doing something. **3** cease moving or operating. **4** (of a bus or train) call at a place to pick up or set down passengers. **5** Brit. informal stay somewhere for a short time. **6** block or close up (a hole or leak). **7** withhold. **8** (in full **stop payment of** or **on**) instruct a bank to withhold payment on (a cheque). ● n. **1** an act of stopping. **2** a place chosen for a bus or train to stop. **3** an object or part of a mechanism which prevents movement. **4** a set of organ pipes of a particular tone and range of pitch.
– PHRASES **pull out all the stops** make a very great effort to achieve something. [ORIGIN with reference to the stops of an organ.]
– ORIGIN Old English.

stopcock ● n. an externally operated valve regulating the flow of a liquid or gas through a pipe.

Stopes E
/stohps/, Marie (Charlotte Carmichael) (1880–1958), Scottish birth-control campaigner. In 1921 she founded the pioneering Mothers' Clinic for Birth Control in London.

stopgap ● n. a temporary solution or substitute.

stoppage ● n. **1** an instance of stopping. **2** an instance of industrial action. **3** a blockage. **4** (**stoppages**) Brit. deductions from wages by an employer for the payment of tax, National Insurance, etc.

stoppage time ● n. = INJURY TIME.

Stoppard E
/stop-pard/, Sir Tom (b.1937; born *Thomas Straussler*), British dramatist, born in Czechoslovakia. He is best known for clever comedies, such as *Rosencrantz and Guildenstern are Dead* and *Jumpers*.

stopper ● n. a plug for sealing a hole. ● v. (**stoppers, stoppering, stoppered**) seal with a stopper.

stop press ● n. Brit. late news added to a newspaper either just before printing or after printing has begun.

stopwatch ● n. a special watch with buttons that start and stop the display, used to time races.

storage ● n. **1** the action of storing. **2** space available for storing.

storage heater ● n. Brit. an electric heater that stores up heat during the night and releases it during the day.

store ● n. **1** an amount or supply kept for use as needed. **2** (**stores**) supplies of equipment and food kept for use by members of an army, navy, or other institution. **3** a place where things are kept for future use or sale. **4** N. Amer. a shop. **5** Brit. a large shop selling different types of goods. ● v. (**stores, storing, stored**) **1** keep for future use. **2** enter (information) in the memory of a computer.
– PHRASES **in store** about to happen. **set store by** consider to be of a particular degree of importance.
– ORIGIN Old French *estore*.

storehouse ● n. a building used for storing goods.

storey (N. Amer. also **story**) ● n. (pl. **storeys** or **stories**) a part of a building made up of all the rooms that are on the same level.
ORIGIN Latin *historia* 'history'.

stork ● n. a tall long-legged bird with a long heavy bill and white and black plumage.
– ORIGIN Old English.

storm ● n. **1** a violent disturbance of the atmosphere with strong winds and rain, thunder, lightning, or snow. **2** an uproar or controversy: *the book caused a storm in America*. ● v. **1** move angrily or forcefully. **2** (of troops) suddenly attack and capture (a place). **3** shout angrily.
– PHRASES **a storm in a teacup** Brit. great anger or excitement about a trivial matter.
– ORIGIN Old English.

storm cloud ● n. a heavy, dark rain cloud.

storm drain ● n. a drain built to carry away excess water in times of heavy rain.

Stormont Castle E
/stor-mont/ a castle in Belfast which is the headquarters of the Northern Ireland Assembly.

storm petrel ● n. a small petrel with blackish plumage.

storm troops ● pl. n. shock troops.

stormy ● adj. (**stormier, stormiest**) **1** affected by a storm. **2** full of angry or violent outbursts of feeling.

Stornoway E
/storn-uh-way/ a port on Lewis, in the Outer Hebrides, the administrative centre of the Western Isles.

story[1] ● n. (pl. **stories**) **1** an account of imaginary or real people and events told for entertainment. **2** an item of news. **3** informal a lie.
– ORIGIN Old French *estorie*.

story[2] ● n. N. Amer. = STOREY.

storyline ● n. the plot of a novel, play, film, etc.

stoup /stoop/ ● n. a basin for holy water in a church.
– ORIGIN Old Norse.

stout ● adj. **1** rather fat or heavily built. **2** (of an object) sturdy and thick. **3** brave and determined: *he put up a stout defence*. ● n. a kind of strong, dark beer brewed with roasted malt or barley.
– ORIGIN Old French.

stove[1] ● n. an apparatus for cooking or heating that operates by burning fuel or using electricity.
– ORIGIN Dutch or German.

stove[2] past and past part. of STAVE.

stow ● v. **1** pack or store (an object) tidily. **2** (**stow away**) hide oneself on a ship, aircraft, etc. so as to travel secretly or without

S

paying.
– ORIGIN from BESTOW.

stowaway • n. a person who stows away.

Stowe, Harriet (Elizabeth) Beecher (1811–96), American novelist, author of the anti-slavery novel *Uncle Tom's Cabin*. E

strabismus /struh-**biz**-muhss/ • n. the condition of having a squint.
– ORIGIN Greek *strabismos*.

Strachey /**stray**-chi/, (Giles) Lytton (1880–1932), English biographer. A member of the Bloomsbury Group, he is best known for his collection of witty biographies *Eminent Victorians*. E

straddle • v. (**straddles**, **straddling**, **straddled**) **1** sit or stand with one leg on either side of. **2** extend across both sides of.
– ORIGIN from dialect *striddling* 'astride'.

Stradivari /strad-i-**vah**-ri/, Antonio (*c.*1644–1737), Italian violin-maker, who devised the proportions of the modern violin. E

strafe /strahf, strayf/ • v. (**strafes**, **strafing**, **strafed**) attack with machine-gun fire or bombs from low-flying aircraft.
– ORIGIN from the German First World War catchphrase *Gott strafe England* 'may God punish England'.

straggle • v. (**straggles**, **straggling**, **straggled**) **1** trail slowly behind the person or people in front. **2** grow or spread out in an untidy way.
– DERIVATIVES **straggler** n. **straggly** adj.
– ORIGIN perh. from dialect *strake* 'go'.

straight • adj. **1** extending in one direction only; without a curve or bend. **2** properly positioned so as to be level, upright, or symmetrical. **3** in proper order or condition. **4** honest and direct. **5** (of thinking) clear and logical. **6** in continuous succession: *his fourth straight win*. **7** (of an alcoholic drink) undiluted. **8** (of drama) serious. **9** informal conventional or respectable. **10** informal heterosexual. • adv. **1** in a straight line or in a straight way. **2** without delay. • n. the straight part of something.
– PHRASES **straight away** immediately. **straight up** informal Brit. honestly.
– ORIGIN from STRETCH.

S

straight angle • n. Math. an angle of 180°.

straight edge • n. a bar with one edge accurately straight, used for testing straightness.

straighten • v. **1** make or become straight. **2** stand or sit erect after bending.

straightforward • adj. **1** easy to do or understand. **2** honest and open.
– DERIVATIVES **straightforwardly** adv.

straightjacket • n. var. of STRAITJACKET.

straight-laced • adj. var. of STRAIT-LACED.

straight man • n. a comedian's stooge.

strain[1] • v. **1** force (a part of one's body or oneself) to make an unusually great effort. **2** injure (a limb, muscle, or organ) by making it work too hard. **3** make great or excessive demands on. **4** pull or push forcibly at something. **5** pour (a mainly liquid substance) through a sieve to separate out any solid matter. • n. **1** a force tending to strain something to an extreme degree. **2** an injury caused by straining a muscle, limb, etc. **3** a severe demand on strength or resources. **4** a state of tension or exhaustion caused by severe pressures. **5** the sound of a piece of music as it is played.
– ORIGIN Old French *estreindre*.

strain[2] • n. **1** a distinct breed or variety of an animal, plant, or other organism. **2** a tendency in a person's character.
– ORIGIN Old English, 'acquisition, gain'.

strained • adj. **1** not relaxed or comfortable. **2** produced by deliberate effort; not graceful or spontaneous.

strainer • n. a device for straining liquids, having holes punched in it or made of crossed wire.

strait • n. **1** (also **straits**) a narrow passage of water connecting two seas or other large areas of water. **2** (**straits**) a situation having a specified degree of trouble or difficulty: *the economy is in dire straits*.
– ORIGIN Old French *estreit* 'narrow'.

straitened • adj. characterized by poverty: *straitened circumstances*.

straitjacket (also **straightjacket**) • n. **1** a strong garment with long sleeves which can be tied together to confine the arms of a violent prisoner or mental patient. **2** a severe restriction.

strait-laced (also **straight-laced**) • adj. having very strict moral attitudes.

strand[1] • v. **1** drive or leave aground on a shore. **2** leave without the means to move from a place: *the lorries are stranded in France*. • n. literary a beach or shore.
– ORIGIN Old English.

strand[2] • n. **1** a single thin length of thread, wire, etc. **2** an element that forms part of a complex whole.
– ORIGIN unknown.

strange • adj. **1** unusual or surprising. **2** not previously visited, seen, or encountered: *she found herself in bed in a strange place*.
– DERIVATIVES **strangely** adv.
– ORIGIN Old French *estrange*.

stranger • n. **1** a person whom one does not know. **2** a person who does not know, or is not known in, a particular place.

strangle • v. (**strangles**, **strangling**, **strangled**) **1** squeeze the neck of, especially so as to cause death. **2** suppress or hinder (an impulse, action, or sound).
– DERIVATIVES **strangler** n.
– ORIGIN Old French *estrangler*.

stranglehold • n. **1** a grip around the neck of a person that can kill by depriving them of oxygen. **2** complete or overwhelming control.

strangulation • n. the action of strangling or the state of being strangled.

strap • n. **1** a strip of flexible material used for fastening, securing, carrying, or holding on to. **2** a strip of metal, often hinged, used for fastening or securing. **3** (**the strap**) punishment by beating with a leather strap. • v. (**straps**, **strapping**, **strapped**) **1** fasten or secure with a strap. **2** Brit. bind (an injured part of the body) with adhesive plaster.
– DERIVATIVES **strapless** adj. **strappy** adj.
– ORIGIN dialect form of STROP[1].

strapping • adj. (of a person) big and strong.

Strasbourg E
/straz-berg/ a city in NE France, in Alsace. It is the headquarters of the Council of Europe and of the European Parliament.

strata pl. of STRATUM.

stratagem /stra-tuh-juhm/ • n. a plan or scheme intended to outwit an opponent.
– ORIGIN Greek *stratēgēma*.

strategic /struh-tee-jik/ • adj. **1** forming part of a long-term plan to achieve a specific purpose. **2** relating to the gaining of long-term military advantage. **3** (of bombing or weapons) done or for use against industrial areas and communication centres in enemy territory. Often contrasted with TACTICAL.
– DERIVATIVES **strategically** adv.

Strategic Defense Initiative E
a projected US system of defence, using satellites armed with lasers to intercept and destroy intercontinental ballistic missiles.

strategy /stra-ti-ji/ • n. (pl. **strategies**) **1** a plan designed to achieve a particular long-term aim. **2** the art of planning and directing military activity in a war or battle. Often contrasted with *tactics* (see TACTIC).
– DERIVATIVES **strategist** n.
– ORIGIN Greek *stratēgia* 'generalship'.

Stratford-upon-Avon E
a town in Warwickshire, famous as the birth and burial place of William Shakespeare.

stratify /stra-ti-fy/ • v. (**stratifies**, **stratifying**, **stratified**) **1** form or arrange into strata. **2** arrange or classify.
– DERIVATIVES **stratification** n.

stratosphere /stra-tuh-sfeer/ • n. **1** the layer of the earth's atmosphere above the troposphere and below the mesosphere. **2** informal the very highest levels of something.
– DERIVATIVES **stratospheric** /stra-tuhss-fe-rik/ adj.

stratum /strah-tuhm, stray-tuhm/ • n. (pl. **strata** /strah-tuh, stray-tuh/) **1** a layer or a series of layers of rock. **2** a thin layer within any structure. **3** a level or class of society.
– ORIGIN Latin, 'something laid down'.

stratus /strah-tuhss, stray-tuhss/ • n. cloud forming a continuous horizontal grey sheet.
– ORIGIN Latin, 'strewn'.

Strauss[1] E
/strowss/, Johann (1804–49; known as **Strauss the Elder**), Austrian composer. A leading composer of waltzes, he is best known for the *Radetzky March*.

Strauss[2] E
/strowss/, Johann (1825–99; known as **Strauss the Younger**), Austrian composer, son of Strauss the Elder. He composed many famous waltzes, such as *The Blue Danube*, and is also noted for the operetta *Die Fledermaus*.

Strauss[3] E
/strowss/, Richard (1864–1949), German composer. He is noted for operas such as *Der Rosenkavalier* and symphonic poems such as *Also Sprach Zarathustra*.

Stravinsky E
/struh-vin-ski/, Igor (Fyodorovich) (1882–1971), Russian-born American composer. He is known for the ballets *The Firebird* and *The Rite of Spring*, marked by their irregular rhythms and dissonances, and for later neoclassical works such as the opera *The Rake's Progress*.

straw • n. **1** dried stalks of grain, used as fodder or for thatching, packing, etc. **2** a single dried stalk of grain. **3** a thin hollow tube of paper or plastic for sucking drink from a container. **4** a pale yellow colour.
– PHRASES **clutch at straws** resort in desperation to something which is unlikely to be helpful. [ORIGIN from the proverb *a drowning man will clutch at a straw*.] **draw the short straw** be chosen to perform an unpleasant task. **the last** (or **final**) **straw** a further difficulty that comes after a series of difficulties and makes a situation unbearable. [ORIGIN from the proverb *the last straw breaks the laden camel's back*.]
– ORIGIN Old English.

strawberry • n. a sweet red fruit with a seed-studded surface.

strawberry blonde • adj. (of hair) having a light reddish-blonde colour.

straw poll • n. an unofficial test of opinion.

stray • v. **1** move away aimlessly from a group or from the right course or place. **2** (of the eyes or a hand) move idly in a specified direction. • adj. **1** not in the right place; separated from a group. **2** (of a domestic animal) having no home or having wandered away from home. • n. a stray person or thing.
– ORIGIN Old French *estrayer*.

streak • n. **1** a long, thin mark. **2** an element of a specified kind in someone's character: *a ruthless streak*. **3** a spell of specified success or luck: *a winning streak*. • v. **1** mark with streaks. **2** move very fast in a specified direction. **3** informal run naked in a public place so as to shock or amuse.
– DERIVATIVES **streaker** n. **streaking** n.
– ORIGIN Old English.

streaky • adj. (**streakier**, **streakiest**) **1** having streaks. **2** Brit. (of bacon) from the belly, so having alternate strips of fat and lean.

stream • n. **1** a small, narrow river. **2** a continuous flow of liquid, air, gas, people, etc. **3** Brit. a group in which schoolchildren of the same age and ability are taught. • v. **1** run or move in a continuous flow. **2** (usu. **be streaming**) run with tears, sweat, or other liquid. **3** float at full extent in the wind. **4** Brit. put (schoolchildren) in streams.
– PHRASES **on stream** in or into operation or existence.
– ORIGIN Old English.

streamer • n. a long, narrow strip of material used as a decoration or flag.

streaming • adj. (of a cold) accompanied by running of the nose and eyes.

streamline • v. (**streamlines**, **streamlining**, **streamlined**) **1** design or form in a way that presents very little resistance to a flow of air or water. **2** make (an organization or system) more efficient by employing faster or simpler working methods.

Streep, E
Meryl (b.1949; born *Mary Louise Streep*), American actress, known for such films as *Kramer vs Kramer* and *Sophie's Choice*.

street ● n. a public road in a city, town, or village. ● adj. **1** relating to fashionable urban youth: *street style*. **2** homeless: *street children*.
– PHRASES **on the streets 1** homeless. **2** working as a prostitute.
– ORIGIN from Latin *strāta via* 'paved way'.

streetcar ● n. N. Amer. a tram.

street value ● n. the price a commodity would fetch if sold illegally.

streetwalker ● n. a prostitute who seeks clients in the street.

streetwise ● adj. informal having the skills and knowledge necessary for dealing with modern urban life.

Streisand E
/stry-sand, stry-s'nd/, Barbra (Joan) (b.1942), American singer, actress, and film director, who starred in *Funny Girl* and *A Star is Born*

strength /strength, strengkth/ ● n. **1** the quality of being strong. **2** a good or useful quality. **3** the number of people comprising a group. **4** a full complement of people: *100 staff below strength*.
– PHRASES **go from strength to strength** progress with increasing success. **on the strength of** on the basis of.
– ORIGIN Old English.

strengthen ● v. make or become stronger.

strenuous /stren-yuu-uhss/ ● adj. requiring or using great exertion.
– ORIGIN Latin *strenuus* 'brisk'.

streptococcus /strep-tuh-**kok**-kuhss/ ● n. (pl. **streptococci** /strep-tuh-**kok**-ky/) a bacterium of a large genus including those causing various serious infections.
– DERIVATIVES **streptococcal** adj.
– ORIGIN Greek *streptos* 'twisted'.

streptomycin /strep-toh-**my**-sin/ ● n. Med. an antibiotic used against tuberculosis.
– ORIGIN from Greek *streptos* 'twisted' + *mukēs* 'fungus'.

stress ● n. **1** pressure or tension exerted on an object. **2** a state of mental or emotional strain. **3** particular emphasis. **4** emphasis given to a syllable or word in speech. ● v. **1** emphasize. **2** give emphasis to (a syllable or word) when pronouncing it. **3** subject to pressure, tension, or strain.
– ORIGIN from DISTRESS, or partly from Old French *estresse* 'narrowness'.

stressful ● adj. causing mental or emotional stress.

stretch ● v. **1** (of something soft or elastic) be able to be made longer or wider without tearing or breaking. **2** pull (something) tightly from one point to another. **3** extend one's body or a part of one's body to its full length. **4** extend over an area or period of time. **5** (of finances or resources) be enough for a particular purpose. **6** make demands on. ● n. **1** an act of stretching. **2** the fact of being stretched. **3** the capacity to stretch or be stretched; elasticity. **4** a continuous expanse or period: *a treacherous stretch of road*.
– PHRASES **at full stretch** using the maximum amount of one's resources or energy. **stretch one's legs** go for a short walk.
– DERIVATIVES **stretchy** adj.
– ORIGIN Old English.

stretcher ● n. a framework of two poles with a long piece of canvas slung between them, used for carrying sick, injured, or dead people. ● v. (**stretchers**, **stretchering**, **stretchered**) carry on a stretcher.

stretch marks ● pl. n. marks on the skin, especially on the abdomen, caused by stretching of the skin from obesity or during pregnancy.

strew ● v. (**strews**, **strewing**, **strewed**; past part. **strewn** or **strewed**) **1** (**be strewn**) be scattered untidily over a surface or area. **2** (**be strewn with**) be covered with untidily scattered things.
– ORIGIN Old English.

stria /stree-uh/ ● n. (pl. **striae** /stree-ee/) tech. a linear mark, ridge, or groove.
– ORIGIN Latin, 'furrow'.

striated /stry-ayt-id/ ● adj. tech. marked with a series of ridges or grooves.
– DERIVATIVES **striation** n.

stricken North American or archaic past part. of STRIKE. ● adj. **1** seriously affected by something unpleasant. **2** (of a face or look) showing great distress.

strict ● adj. **1** demanding that rules concerning behaviour are obeyed. **2** (of a rule) rigidly enforced. **3** following rules or beliefs exactly: *a strict vegetarian*.
– DERIVATIVES **strictly** adv. **strictness** n.
– ORIGIN Latin *strictus* 'tightened'.

stricture /strik-cher/ ● n. **1** a rule restricting behaviour or action. **2** a sternly critical remark.

stride ● v. (**strides**, **striding**, **strode**) **1** walk with long, decisive steps. **2** (**stride across/over**) cross (an obstacle) with one long step. ● n. **1** a long, decisive step. **2** the length of a step in running or walking. **3** a step towards an aim. **4** (**one's stride**) a good or regular rate of progress.
– PHRASES **take something in one's stride** deal with something difficult in a calm way.
– ORIGIN Old English.

strident ● adj. **1** loud and harsh. **2** presenting a point of view in an excessively forceful way.
– DERIVATIVES **stridency** n.
– ORIGIN Latin *stridere* 'creak'.

strife ● n. angry or bitter disagreement.
– ORIGIN Old French *estrif*.

strike ● v. (**strikes**, **striking**, **struck**) **1** deliver a blow to. **2** come into forcible contact with. **3** (in sport) hit or kick (a ball) so as to score a run, point, or goal. **4** ignite (a match) by rubbing it against a rough surface. **5** (of a disaster, disease, etc.) occur suddenly and have harmful effects on. **6** attack suddenly. **7** (**strike into**) cause (a strong emotion) in. **8** cause to become suddenly: *he was struck dumb*. **9** suddenly come into the mind of: *a thought struck Melissa*. **10** (of employees) refuse to work as a form of organized protest. **11** (**strike on/upon**) discover unexpectedly. **12** (**strike off**) officially remove (someone) from membership of a professional group. **13** (**strike out**) start out on a new or independent course. **14** reach (an agreement or compromise). **15** (of a clock) show the time by

sounding a chime or stroke. ● n. **1** an act of striking by employees. **2** a refusal to do something as an organized protest: *a rent strike.* **3** a sudden attack. **4** (in sport) an act of striking a ball.
– PHRASES **strike up 1** begin to play a piece of music. **2** begin (a friendship or conversation) with someone.
– ORIGIN Old English, 'go, flow'.

striker ● n. **1** an employee on strike. **2** the player who is to strike the ball in a game. **3** (chiefly in soccer) a forward or attacker.

striking ● adj. **1** noticeable. **2** very good-looking or beautiful.

Strindberg E
/**strind**-berg/, (Johan) August (1849–1912), Swedish dramatist and novelist. His early plays, such as *Miss Julie*, were naturalistic in style, while later dramas, such as *A Dream Play*, introduced expressionist techniques.

string ● n. **1** material consisting of threads twisted together to form a thin length. **2** a piece of such material. **3** a length of catgut or wire on a musical instrument, producing a note by vibration. **4** (**strings**) the stringed instruments in an orchestra. **5** a piece of catgut, nylon, etc., interwoven with others to form the head of a sports racket. **6** a set of things tied or threaded together on a thin cord. **7** a sequence of similar items or events: *a string of blockbusters.* ● v. (**strings**, **stringing**, **strung**) **1** arrange on a string. **2** (**be strung** or **be strung out**) be arranged in a long line. **3** fit a string or strings to (a musical instrument, a racket, or a bow).
– PHRASES **no strings attached** informal there are no special conditions or restrictions. **string up** kill by hanging.
– DERIVATIVES **stringed** adj.
– ORIGIN Old English.

string bean ● n. any of various beans eaten in their pods.

stringent /**strin**-juhnt/ ● adj. (of regulations or requirements) strict, precise, and demanding.
– DERIVATIVES **stringency** n.
– ORIGIN Latin *stringere* 'draw tight'.

string quartet ● n. a chamber music group made up of first and second violins, viola, and cello.

stringy ● adj. (**stringier**, **stringiest**) **1** resembling string. **2** tall, wiry, and thin. **3** (of food) tough and fibrous.

strip[1] ● v. (**strips**, **stripping**, **stripped**) **1** remove all coverings or clothes from. **2** take off one's clothes. **3** leave bare of accessories or fittings. **4** remove (paint) from a surface. **5** (**strip of**) deprive (someone) of (rank, power, or property). ● n. **1** an act of undressing. **2** Brit. the identifying outfit worn by the members of a sports team while playing.
– ORIGIN Germanic.

strip[2] ● n. **1** a long, narrow piece of cloth, paper, etc. **2** a long, narrow area of land.
– ORIGIN German *strippe* 'strap, thong'.

stripe ● n. **1** a long narrow band or strip of a different colour or texture from its surroundings. **2** a V-shaped stripe sewn on to a uniform to show military rank. ● v. (**stripes**, **striping**, **striped**) (usu. **be striped**) mark with stripes.
– DERIVATIVES **striped** adj. **stripy** (also **stripey**) adj.
– ORIGIN perh. from Dutch or German.

strip light ● n. Brit. a fluorescent lamp in the shape of a tube.

stripling ● n. archaic a young man.
– ORIGIN prob. from STRIP[2] (from the idea of 'narrowness', i.e. slimness).

stripper ● n. **1** a device or substance for stripping. **2** a striptease performer.

strip-search ● v. search (someone) for concealed drugs, weapons, or other items, by stripping off their clothes.

striptease ● n. a form of entertainment in which a performer gradually undresses to music in a sexually exciting way.

strive ● v. (**strives**, **striving**, **strove** or **strived**; past part. **striven** or **strived**) **1** make great efforts. **2** (**strive against**) fight vigorously against.
– ORIGIN Old French *estriver.*

strobe informal ● n. a stroboscope. ● v. (**strobes**, **strobing**, **strobed**) flash at rapid intervals.

stroboscope /**stroh**-buh-skohp/ ● n. an instrument which shines a bright light at rapid intervals so that a moving object appears stationary.
– DERIVATIVES **stroboscopic** adj.
– ORIGIN Greek *strobos* 'whirling'.

strode past of STRIDE.

stroke ● n. **1** an act of hitting. **2** Golf an act of hitting the ball with a club, as a unit of scoring. **3** a sound made by a striking clock. **4** an act of stroking with the hand. **5** a mark made by drawing a pen, pencil, or paintbrush once across paper or canvas. **6** a line forming part of a written or printed character. **7** a short diagonal line separating characters or figures. **8** one of a series of repeated movements. **9** a style of swimming. **10** the action of moving the oar in rowing. **11** a sudden disabling attack or loss of consciousness caused by an interruption in the flow of blood to the brain. ● v. (**strokes**, **stroking**, **stroked**) move one's hand with gentle pressure over.
– PHRASES **at a stroke** by a single action having immediate effect. **stroke of luck** a fortunate unexpected occurrence.
– ORIGIN Old English.

stroke play ● n. play in golf in which the score is reckoned by counting the number of strokes taken overall.

stroll ● v. walk in a leisurely way. ● n. a short leisurely walk.
– ORIGIN prob. from German *strollen.*

Stromboli E
/**strom**-buh-li, strom-**boh**-li/ a volcanic island in the Mediterranean, off the north-east coast of Sicily.

strong ● adj. (**stronger**, **strongest**) **1** physically powerful. **2** done with or exerting great force. **3** able to withstand great force or pressure. **4** secure, stable, or firmly established. **5** great in power, influence, or ability. **6** (of something seen, heard, or smelt) very intense: *a strong smell.* **7** (of language) forceful and using swear words. **8** full-flavoured. **9** (of a solution or drink) containing a large proportion of a substance. **10** used after a number to indicate the size of a group: *a crowd several thousands strong.* **11** Grammar (of verbs)

forming the past tense and past participle by a change of vowel within the stem rather than by addition of a suffix (e.g. *swim*, *swam*, *swum*).
– PHRASES **going strong** informal continuing to be healthy, vigorous, or successful.
– DERIVATIVES **strongly** adv.
– ORIGIN Old English.

strong-arm • **adj.** using force or violence.

strongbox • **n.** a small lockable metal box in which valuables may be kept.

stronghold • **n. 1** a place that has been strengthened against attack. **2** a place of strong support for a cause or political party.

strongroom • **n.** a room, typically one in a bank, designed to protect valuable items against fire and theft.

strontium /stron-ti-uhm/ • **n.** a soft silver-white metallic chemical element.

strop[1] • **n.** a strip of leather for sharpening razors.
– ORIGIN prob. from Latin *stroppus* 'thong'.

strop[2] • **n.** Brit. informal a temper.

stroppy • **adj.** Brit. informal bad-tempered.
– ORIGIN perh. from **OBSTREPEROUS**.

strove past of **STRIVE**.

struck past and past part. of **STRIKE**.

structural • **adj.** relating to or forming part of a structure.
– DERIVATIVES **structurally** adv.

structuralism • **n.** a theory that texts, languages, and social systems should be regarded as a structure whose various parts have meaning only when considered in relation to each other.
– DERIVATIVES **structuralist** n. & adj.

structure • **n. 1** the arrangement of and relations between the parts of something complex. **2** a building or other object constructed from several parts. **3** the quality of being well organized. • **v.** (**structures**, **structuring**, **structured**) give structure to.
– ORIGIN Latin *structura*.

strudel /stroo-d'l/ • **n.** a dessert of thin pastry rolled up round a fruit filling and baked.
– ORIGIN German, 'whirlpool'.

struggle • **v.** (**struggles**, **struggling**, **struggled**) **1** make great efforts to get free. **2** try hard under difficult circumstances to do something. **3** make one's way with difficulty. • **n. 1** an act of struggling. **2** a very difficult task.

strum • **v.** (**strums**, **strumming**, **strummed**) play (a guitar or similar instrument) by sweeping the thumb or a plectrum up or down the strings.

strumpet • **n.** archaic a woman who has many sexual partners.
– ORIGIN unknown.

strung past and past part. of **STRING**.

strut • **n. 1** a bar used to support or strengthen a structure. **2** a strutting walk. • **v.** (**struts**, **strutting**, **strutted**) walk in a proud way, with one's back straight and head up.
– ORIGIN Old English, 'stick out stiffly'.

strychnine /strik-neen/ • **n.** a bitter and highly poisonous substance obtained from the fruit of an Asian tree.
– ORIGIN Greek *strukhnos*, referring to a kind of nightshade.

Stuart[1], E
Charles Edward (1720–88; known as **the Young Pretender** or **Bonnie Prince Charlie**), pretender to the British throne. The son of James Stuart, he led the Jacobite uprising of 1745–6, but was defeated at the Battle of Culloden (1746).

Stuart[2], E
James (Francis Edward) (1688–1766; known as **the Old Pretender**), pretender to the British throne. The son of James II (James VII of Scotland), he arrived in Scotland too late to alter the outcome of the 1715 Jacobite uprising and left the leadership of the 1745–6 rebellion to his son Charles Stuart.

Stuart[3], E
Mary, see **MARY, QUEEN OF SCOTS**.

Stuart[4] • **adj.** relating to the royal family ruling Scotland 1371–1714 and Britain 1603–1649 and 1660–1714.

stub • **n. 1** the remaining part of a pencil, cigarette, or similar-shaped object after use. **2** a shortened or unusually short thing. **3** the counterfoil of a cheque, ticket, or other document. • **v.** (**stubs**, **stubbing**, **stubbed**) **1** accidentally strike (one's toe) against something. **2** (also **stub out**) extinguish (a cigarette) by pressing the lighted end against something.
– ORIGIN Old English, 'stump of a tree'.

stubble • **n. 1** the cut stalks of cereal plants left in the ground after harvesting. **2** short, stiff hairs growing on a man's face when he has not shaved for a while.
– DERIVATIVES **stubbly** adj.
– ORIGIN Old French *stuble*.

stubborn • **adj. 1** determined not to change one's attitude or position. **2** difficult to move, remove, or cure: *a stubborn stain*.
– DERIVATIVES **stubbornly** adv. **stubbornness** n.
– ORIGIN unknown.

Stubbs, E
George (1724–1806), English painter and engraver, noted for his sporting scenes and paintings of horses and lions.

stubby • **adj.** (**stubbier**, **stubbiest**) short and thick.

stucco • **n.** fine plaster used for coating wall surfaces or moulding into architectural decorations.
– DERIVATIVES **stuccoed** adj.
– ORIGIN Italian.

stuck past part. of **STICK**[2].

stuck-up • **adj.** informal snobbishly aloof.

stud[1] • **n. 1** a piece of metal with a large head, that pierces and projects from a surface. **2** a small projection fixed to the base of a shoe or boot to provide better grip. **3** a small piece of jewellery which is pushed through a pierced ear or nostril. **4** a device for fastening a collar to a shirt, consisting of two buttons joined with a bar. • **v.** (**studs**, **studding**, **studded**) (usu. **be studded**) **1** decorate with studs or similar small objects. **2** strew or scatter: *the sky was studded with stars*.
– ORIGIN Old English, 'post'.

stud[2] • **n. 1** an establishment where horses are kept for breeding. **2** (also **stud horse**) a stallion. **3** informal man who has many sexual

partners or is considered sexually desirable.
– ORIGIN Old English.

student ● n. **1** a person studying at a university or college. **2** esp. N. Amer. a school pupil. **3** a person who takes a particular interest in a subject. ● adj. referring to someone who is studying to enter a profession: *a student nurse.*
– ORIGIN Latin *studere* 'apply oneself to'.

studio ● n. (pl. **studios**) **1** a room where an artist works or where dancers practise. **2** a room from which television or radio programmes are broadcast, or in which they are recorded. **3** a place where film or sound recordings are made.
– ORIGIN Italian.

studio flat ● n. Brit. a flat containing one main room.

studious ● adj. **1** spending a lot of time studying or reading. **2** done deliberately or with great care.

study ● n. (pl. **studies**) **1** the devotion of time and attention to gaining knowledge. **2** a detailed investigation and analysis of a subject or situation. **3** a room for reading, writing, or academic work. **4** a piece of work done for practice or as an experiment. ● v. (**studies**, **studying**, **studied**) **1** make a study of; learn about. **2** look at closely in order to observe or read. **3** (**studied**) done with deliberate and careful effort: *studied politeness.*
– ORIGIN Latin *studium* 'zeal'.

stuff ● n. **1** matter, material, articles, or activities of a particular or unspecified kind. **2** basic characteristics: *Helen was made of sterner stuff.* **3** (**one's stuff**) informal an area in which one is expert: *he knows his stuff.* ● v. **1** fill tightly with something. **2** force tightly or hastily into a container or space. **3** fill out the skin of (a dead animal or bird) with material to restore the original shape and appearance.
– PHRASES **get stuffed** Brit. informal said to express dismissal or contempt.
– ORIGIN Old French *estoffe* 'material'.

stuffed shirt ● n. informal a conservative, pompous person.

stuffing ● n. **1** a mixture used to stuff poultry or meat before cooking. **2** padding used to stuff cushions, furniture, or soft toys.

stuffy ● adj. (**stuffier**, **stuffiest**) **1** lacking fresh air or ventilation. **2** conventional and narrow-minded. **3** (of a person's nose) blocked up.

stultify /stul-ti-fy/ ● v. (**stultifies**, **stultifying**, **stultified**) (usu. as adj. **stultifying**) cause to feel bored or drained of energy.
– ORIGIN Latin *stultificare.*

stumble ● v. (**stumbles**, **stumbling**, **stumbled**) **1** trip and lose one's balance. **2** walk unsteadily. **3** make a mistake in speaking. **4** (**stumble across/on/upon**) find by chance. ● n. an act of stumbling.
– ORIGIN Old Norse.

stumbling block ● n. an obstacle.

stump ● n. **1** the part of a tree trunk that sticks up from the ground after the rest has fallen or been cut down. **2** a remaining piece of something. **3** Cricket each of the three upright pieces of wood which form a wicket. ● v. **1** baffle. **2** Cricket dismiss (a batsman) by dislodging the bails with the ball while the batsman is out of the crease but not running. **3** (**stump up**) Brit. informal pay (a sum or money).
– ORIGIN German *stumpe* or Dutch *stomp.*

stumpy ● adj. short and thick; squat.

stun ● v. (**stuns**, **stunning**, **stunned**) **1** knock unconscious or into a semi-conscious state. **2** astonish or shock (someone) so that they are temporarily unable to react.
– ORIGIN Old French *estoner* 'astonish'.

stung past and past part. of **STING**.

stunk past and past part. of **STINK**.

stunner ● n. informal a strikingly beautiful or impressive person or thing.

stunning ● adj. extremely impressive or attractive.

stunt[1] ● v. slow down the growth or development of.
– ORIGIN Germanic.

stunt[2] ● n. **1** an action displaying spectacular skill and daring. **2** something unusual done to attract attention: *a publicity stunt.*
– ORIGIN unknown.

stuntman (or **stuntwoman**) ● n. a person taking an actor's place in performing dangerous stunts.

stupefy /styoo-pi-fy/ ● v. (**stupefies**, **stupefying**, **stupefied**) **1** make (someone) unable to think or feel properly. **2** astonish and shock.
– DERIVATIVES **stupefaction** n.
– ORIGIN Latin *stupefacere.*

stupendous /styoo-pen-duhss/ ● adj. extremely impressive.
– ORIGIN Latin *stupendus* 'to be wondered at'.

stupid ● adj. (**stupider**, **stupidest**) **1** lacking intelligence or common sense. **2** informal used to express exasperation or boredom: *your stupid paintings!* **3** dazed and unable to think clearly.
– DERIVATIVES **stupidity** n. **stupidly** adv.
– ORIGIN Latin *stupidus.*

stupor /styoo-per/ ● n. a state of near-unconsciousness.
– ORIGIN Latin.

sturdy ● adj. (**sturdier**, **sturdiest**) **1** strongly and solidly built or made. **2** confident and determined: *a sturdy independence.*
– DERIVATIVES **sturdily** adv. **sturdiness** n.
– ORIGIN Old French *esturdi* 'dazed'.

sturgeon /ster-juhn/ ● n. a very large fish with bony plates on the body, found in seas and rivers and caught for its caviar and flesh.
– ORIGIN Old French.

Sturt E
/stert/, Charles (1795–1869), English explorer. He led three expeditions in Australia, becoming the first European to discover the Darling River (1828) and the source of the Murray (1830)

stutter ● v. (**stutters**, **stuttering**, **stuttered**) **1** have difficulty talking because one is unable to stop repeating the first sound of a word. **2** (of a machine or gun) produce a series of short, sharp sounds. ● n. a tendency to stutter while speaking.
– DERIVATIVES **stutterer** n.
– ORIGIN Germanic.

Stuttgart E
/shtuut-gart/ an industrial city in western Germany.

sty[1] ● n. (pl. **sties**) a pigsty.
– ORIGIN Old English.

sty[2] (also **stye**) ● n. (pl. **sties** or **styes**) an inflamed swelling on the edge of an eyelid.
– ORIGIN dialect *styany*.

Stygian /sti-ji-uhn/ ● adj. literary very dark.
– ORIGIN from the river STYX.

style ● n. **1** a way of doing something. **2** a distinctive appearance, design, or arrangement. **3** a way of painting, writing, etc., characteristic of a particular period, person, etc. **4** elegance and sophistication. **5** Bot. a narrow extension of the ovary, bearing the stigma. ● v. (**styles**, **styling**, **styled**) **1** design, make, or arrange in a particular form. **2** give a particular name, description, or title to.
– ORIGIN Latin *stilus* 'stylus, style'.

styli pl. of STYLUS.

stylish ● adj. **1** having or displaying a good sense of style. **2** fashionably elegant.
– DERIVATIVES **stylishly** adv. **stylishness** n.

stylist ● n. a person who designs fashionable clothes or cuts hair.

stylistic ● adj. having to do with style, especially literary style.
– DERIVATIVES **stylistically** adv.

stylized (also **stylised**) ● adj. done or treated in an artificial style.

stylus /sty-luhss/ ● n. (pl. **styli** /sty-ly/) **1** a pointed implement used for scratching or tracing letters or engraving. **2** a pen-like device used to input handwriting directly into a computer. **3** a hard point following a groove in a gramophone record and transmitting the recorded sound for reproduction.
– ORIGIN Latin *stilus*.

stymie /sty-mi/ ● v. (**stymies**, **stymying** or **stymieing**, **stymied**) informal prevent or slow down the progress of.
– ORIGIN a golfing term.

styptic /stip-tik/ ● adj. Med. able to make bleeding stop.
– ORIGIN Greek *stuptikos*.

styrene /sty-reen/ ● n. Chem. an unsaturated liquid hydrocarbon obtained from petroleum and used to make plastics and resins.
– ORIGIN from *styrax*, a gum resin.

styrofoam ● n. (trademark in the US) a kind of expanded polystyrene, used for making food containers.
– ORIGIN from POLYSTYRENE + FOAM.

S

Styx E
/*rhymes with* sticks/ Gk Myth. one of the nine rivers in the underworld, over which Charon ferried the souls of the dead.

suave /swahv/ ● adj. (**suaver**, **suavest**) (of a man) charming, confident, and elegant.
– DERIVATIVES **suavely** adv. **suavity** n.
– ORIGIN Latin *suavis* 'agreeable'.

sub informal ● n. **1** a submarine. **2** a substitute. ● v. (**subs**, **subbing**, **subbed**) act as a substitute.

sub- ● prefix **1** under: *submarine*. **2** lower in rank or importance: *subaltern*. **3** below; less than: *sub-zero*. **4** secondary or subsequent: *subdivision*.
– ORIGIN Latin *sub* 'under, close to'.

subaltern /sub-uhl-tern/ ● n. an officer in the British army below the rank of captain.
– ORIGIN from Latin *sub-* 'next below' + *alternus* 'every other'.

sub-aqua ● adj. relating to swimming or exploring under water, especially with an aqualung.

subatomic ● adj. smaller than or occurring within an atom.

subcategory ● n. (pl. **subcategories**) a secondary category.

subconscious ● adj. having to do with the part of the mind of which one is not fully aware but which influences one's actions and feelings. ● n. (**one's/the subconscious**) this part of the mind.
– DERIVATIVES **subconsciously** adv.

subcontinent ● n. a large part of a continent considered as a particular area, such as North America.

subcontract /sub-kuhn-trakt/ ● v. employ a firm or person outside one's company to do (work).

subcontractor ● n. a firm or person that carries out work for a company as part of a larger project.

subculture ● n. a cultural group within a larger culture, having beliefs or interests that are different from those of the larger culture.

subcutaneous ● adj. Anat. & Med. under the skin.

subdivide ● v. (**subdivides**, **subdividing**, **subdivided**) divide (something) into smaller parts.

subdivision ● n. **1** the action of subdividing. **2** a secondary division.

subdue ● v. (**subdues**, **subduing**, **subdued**) **1** overcome, quieten, or bring under control. **2** bring (a country) under control by force.
– ORIGIN Latin *subducere* 'draw from below'.

subdued ● adj. **1** quiet and rather thoughtful or depressed. **2** (of colour or lighting) soft; muted.

subedit ● v. (**subedits**, **subediting**, **subedited**) Brit. check and correct (text) before printing.
– DERIVATIVES **subeditor** n.

subgroup ● n. a small group that is part of a larger group.

sub-heading ● n. a heading given to a subsection of a piece of writing.

subhuman ● adj. not behaving like a human being or not fit for human beings.

subject ● n. /sub-jikt/ **1** a person or thing that is being discussed, studied, or dealt with. **2** a branch of knowledge studied or taught. **3** Grammar the word or words in a sentence that name who or what performs the action of the verb. **4** a member of a state that is ruled by a king or queen. ● adj. /sub-jikt/ **1** (**subject to**) likely or able to be affected by (something bad). **2** (**subject to**) dependent on (something) in order to happen. **3** under the control or authority of. ● adv. /sub-jikt/ (**subject to**) conditionally upon. ● v. /suhb-jekt/ (**subject to**) **1** cause to undergo (something bad). **2** bring under one's control or authority.
– DERIVATIVES **subjection** n.
– ORIGIN Latin *subicere* 'bring under'.

subjective ● adj. **1** based on or influenced by personal opinions. **2** Grammar relating to a case of nouns and pronouns used for the subject of a sentence.
– DERIVATIVES **subjectively** adv. **subjectivity** n.

subject matter ● n. the ideas, information, or theme of a book, work of art, speech, etc.

sub judice /sub **joo**-di-si/ ● adj. Law being considered by a court of law and therefore forbidden to be publicly discussed elsewhere.
– ORIGIN Latin, 'under a judge'.

subjugate /sub-juu-gayt/ ● v. (**subjugates, subjugating, subjugated**) conquer and bring under control.
– DERIVATIVES **subjugation** n.
– ORIGIN Latin *subjugare* 'bring under a yoke'.

subjunctive /suhb-**jungk**-tiv/ ● adj. Grammar (of a form of a verb) expressing what is imagined or wished or possible.
– ORIGIN Latin *subjunctivus*.

USAGE subjunctive

The **subjunctive** form of a verb is used to express what is imagined, wished, or possible. It is usually the same as the ordinary (**indicative**) form of the verb except in the third person singular (*he, she,* or *it*), where the normal **-s** ending is omitted. For example, you should say *face* rather than *faces* in the sentence *the report recommends that he face the tribunal*. The subjunctive is also different from the indicative when using the verb 'to be'; for example, you should say *I were* rather than *I was* in the sentence *I wouldn't try it if I were you*.

sublet /sub-let/ ● v. (**sublets, subletting, sublet**) lease (a property one is already leasing oneself) to a third party.

sublimate /sub-li-mayt/ ● v. (**sublimates, sublimating, sublimated**) **1** transform into a purer or idealized form. **2** Chem. – SUBLIME.
– DERIVATIVES **sublimation** n.
– ORIGIN Latin *sublimare* 'raise up'.

sublime ● adj. (**sublimer, sublimest**) **1** of very high quality and causing great admiration. **2** extreme: *the sublime confidence of youth*. ● v. Chem. (**sublimes, subliming, sublimed**) (of a solid substance) change directly into vapour when heated, forming a solid deposit again on cooling.
– DERIVATIVES **sublimely** adv.
– ORIGIN Latin *sublimis*.

subliminal /suhb-**lim**-i-n'l/ ● adj. (of a stimulus or mental process) affecting someone's mind without their being aware of it.
– DERIVATIVES **subliminally** adv.
– ORIGIN from SUB- + Latin *limen* 'threshold'.

sub-machine gun ● n. a hand-held lightweight machine gun.

submarine ● n. a streamlined warship designed to operate under the sea for long periods. ● adj. existing or done under the surface of the sea.
– DERIVATIVES **submariner** n.

submerge ● v. (**submerges, submerging, submerged**) **1** push or hold under water. **2** go below the surface of water. **3** completely cover or hide.
– ORIGIN Latin *submergere*.

submerse ● v. (**submerses, submersing, submersed**) tech. submerge.

submersible ● adj. designed to operate under water. ● n. a small boat or craft that is submersible.

submersion ● n. the action of submerging.

submicroscopic ● adj. too small to be seen by an ordinary microscope.

submission ● n. **1** the action of submitting. **2** a proposal or application submitted for consideration.

submissive ● adj. very obedient or passive.

submit ● v. (**submits, submitting, submitted**) **1** accept or give in to a superior force or stronger person. **2** present (a proposal or application) for consideration or judgement.
– ORIGIN Latin *submittere*.

subnormal ● adj. lower or less than normal, especially with respect to intelligence.

subordinate ● adj. /suh-**bor**-di-nuht/ **1** lower in rank or position. **2** less important. ● n. /suh-**bor**-di-nuht/ a person under the authority of another. ● v. (**subordinates, subordinating, subordinated**) /suh-**bor**-di-nayt/ treat as less important.
– DERIVATIVES **subordination** n.
– ORIGIN Latin *subordinatus* 'placed in an inferior rank'.

subordinate clause ● n. a clause that forms part of and is dependent on a main clause (e.g. 'when it rang' in *she answered the phone when it rang*).

suborn /suh-**born**/ ● v. pay or persuade (someone) to commit an unlawful act such as perjury.
– ORIGIN Latin *subornare* 'incite secretly'.

sub-plot ● n. a plot in a play, novel, etc. that is secondary to the main plot.

subpoena /suhb-**pee**-nuh/ Law ● n. a writ ordering a person to attend a court. ● v. (**subpoenas, subpoenaing, subpoenaed** or **subpoena'd**) summon with a subpoena.
– ORIGIN from Latin *sub poena* 'under penalty'.

subroutine ● n. Computing a set of instructions designed to perform a frequently used operation within a program.

sub-Saharan ● adj. from or forming part of the African regions south of the Sahara.

subscribe ● v. (**subscribes, subscribing, subscribed**) **1** (often **subscribe to**) arrange to receive something regularly by paying in advance. **2** (**subscribe to**) contribute (a sum of money) to a project or cause. **3** apply to take part in. **4** (**subscribe to**) express agreement with (an idea or proposal).
– DERIVATIVES **subscriber** n.
– ORIGIN Latin *subscribere* 'write below'.

subscript ● adj. (of a letter, figure, or symbol) written or printed below the line.

subscription ● n. **1** the action of subscribing. **2** a payment to subscribe to something.

subsection ● n. a division of a section.

subsequent ● adj. coming after something in time.
– DERIVATIVES **subsequently** adv.
– ORIGIN Latin *subsequi* 'follow after'.

subservient ● adj. **1** excessively willing to obey others. **2** less important.
– DERIVATIVES **subservience** n.

subset ● n. **1** a part of a larger group of related things. **2** Math. a set of which all the elements are contained in another set.

subside ● v. (**subsides, subsiding, subsided**) **1** become less strong, violent, or severe. **2** (of water) go down to a lower or the normal level. **3** (of a building) sink lower into the ground. **4** (of the ground) cave in; sink. **5** (**subside into**) give way to (a strong feeling).
– ORIGIN Latin *subsidere*.

S

subsidence /suhb-sy-duhnss, sub-si-duhnss/ ● **n.** the gradual caving in or sinking of an area of land.

subsidiary ● **adj. 1** related but less important. **2** (of a company) controlled by another company. ● **n.** (pl. **subsidiaries**) a subsidiary company.
– ORIGIN Latin *subsidiarius.*

subsidize (also **subsidise**) ● **v.** (**subsidizes, subsidizing, subsidized**) **1** support (an organization or activity) financially. **2** pay part of the cost of producing (something) to reduce its price.
– DERIVATIVES **subsidization** (also **subsidisation**) n.

subsidy ● **n.** (pl. **subsidies**) **1** a sum of money granted from public funds to help an industry or business keep the price of a product or service low. **2** a sum of money granted to support an undertaking that is in the public interest.
– ORIGIN Latin *subsidium* 'assistance'.

subsist ● **v.** maintain or support oneself at a basic level.
– ORIGIN Latin *subsistere* 'stand firm'.

subsistence ● **n. 1** the action of subsisting. **2** the means of doing this. ● **adj.** (of production) at a level which is enough only for one's own use, without any surplus for trade: *subsistence agriculture.*

subsistence level (also **subsistence wage**) ● **n.** a standard of living (or wage) that provides only the basic necessities of life.

subsoil ● **n.** the soil lying immediately under the surface soil.

subsonic ● **adj.** relating to or flying at a speed or speeds less than that of sound.

substance ● **n. 1** a particular kind of matter with the same properties. **2** the physical matter of which a person or thing consists. **3** solid basis in reality or fact: *the claim has no substance.* **4** the quality of being important: *a man of substance.* **5** the most important or essential part or meaning. **6** the subject matter of a text or work of art. **7** an intoxicating or narcotic drug.
– PHRASES **in substance** essentially.
– ORIGIN Latin *substantia* 'being'.

substandard ● **adj.** below the usual or required standard.

substantial ● **adj. 1** of considerable importance, size, or worth. **2** strongly built or made.

substantially ● **adv. 1** considerably. **2** for the most part; mainly: *things will remain substantially the same.*

substantiate /suhb-stan-shi-ayt/ ● **v.** (**substantiates, substantiating, substantiated**) provide evidence to prove the truth of.
– ORIGIN Latin *substantiare* 'give substance'.

substantive /sub-stuhn-tiv, suhb-stan-tiv/ ● **adj.** dealing with real or important matters.
– DERIVATIVES **substantively** adv.

substation ● **n.** a set of equipment reducing the high voltage of electrical power transmission to that suitable for supply to consumers.

substitute ● **n. 1** a person or thing acting or used in place of another. **2** a sports player who is allowed to replace another after a match has begun. ● **v.** (**substitutes, substituting, substituted**) take the place of; use instead of: *frozen peas can be substituted for fresh.*
– DERIVATIVES **substitution** n.
– ORIGIN Latin *substituere.*

substratum ● **n.** (pl. **substrata**) a layer of rock or soil beneath the surface of the ground.

subsume ● **v.** (**subsumes, subsuming, subsumed**) include or absorb in something else.
– ORIGIN Latin *subsumere.*

subtenant ● **n.** a person who leases property from a tenant.

subtend ● **v.** (of a line, arc, etc.) form (an angle) at a particular point when straight lines from its extremities meet.
– ORIGIN Latin *subtendere.*

subterfuge /sub-ter-fyooj/ ● **n.** a trick or deception used in order to achieve one's goal.
– ORIGIN Latin *subterfugere* 'escape secretly'.

subterranean /sub-tuh-ray-ni-uhn/ ● **adj.** existing or happening under the earth's surface.
– ORIGIN Latin *subterraneus.*

subtext ● **n.** an underlying theme in a piece of writing or speech.

subtitle ● **n. 1** (**subtitles**) captions displayed at the bottom of a cinema or television screen that translate or transcribe the dialogue. **2** a secondary title of a published work. ● **v.** (**subtitles, subtitling, subtitled**) provide with a subtitle or subtitles.

subtle ● **adj.** (**subtler, subtlest**) **1** so delicate or precise as to be difficult to describe. **2** good at noticing and understanding things. **3** done in a clever but understated way: *subtle lighting.* **4** using clever and indirect methods to achieve something.
– DERIVATIVES **subtlety** n. **subtly** adv.
– ORIGIN Latin *subtilis.*

subtotal ● **n.** the total of one set of a larger group of figures to be added.

subtract ● **v.** take away (a number or amount) from another to calculate the difference.
– DERIVATIVES **subtraction** n. **subtractive** adj.
– ORIGIN Latin *subtrahere* 'draw away'.

subtropical ● **adj.** having to do with the regions next to or bordering on the tropics.

suburb ● **n.** an outlying residential district of a city.
– DERIVATIVES **suburban** adj. **suburbanite** n.
– ORIGIN from Latin *sub-* 'near to' + *urbs* 'city'.

suburbia ● **n.** suburbs and suburban life.

subversive ● **adj.** trying to undermine an established system or institution. ● **n.** a subversive person.
– DERIVATIVES **subversively** adv.

subvert ● **v.** undermine the power and authority of (an established system or institution).
– DERIVATIVES **subversion** n.
– ORIGIN Latin *subvertere.*

subway ● **n. 1** Brit. a tunnel under a road for use by pedestrians. **2** N. Amer. an underground railway.

sub-zero ● **adj.** (of temperature) below freezing.

succeed ● **v. 1** achieve an aim or purpose. **2** gain fame, wealth, or social status. **3** take over a role, title, etc., from (someone). **4** become the new rightful holder of a position, title, etc. **5** come after and take the place of.
– ORIGIN Latin *succedere* 'come close after'.

success ● n. **1** the accomplishment of an aim or purpose. **2** the gaining of fame, wealth, or social status. **3** a person or thing that achieves success.
– ORIGIN Latin *successus*.

successful ● adj. **1** accomplishing an aim or purpose. **2** having achieved fame, wealth, or social status.
– DERIVATIVES **successfully** adv.

succession ● n. **1** a number of people or things following one after the other. **2** the action or right of inheriting a position, title, etc.
– PHRASES **in quick succession** following one another at short intervals. **in succession** following one after the other without interruption.

successive ● adj. following one another or following others.
– DERIVATIVES **successively** adv.

successor ● n. a person or thing that succeeds another.

succinct /suhk-singkt/ ● adj. briefly and clearly expressed.
– DERIVATIVES **succinctly** adv.
– ORIGIN Latin *succingere* 'tuck up'.

succour /suk-ker/ (US **succor**) ● n. help and support in times of hardship and distress. ● v. give help to.
– ORIGIN Latin *succursus*.

succubus /suk-kyuu-buhss/ ● n. (pl. **succubi** /suk-kyuu-by/) a female demon believed to have sexual intercourse with sleeping men.
– ORIGIN Latin, 'prostitute'.

succulent ● adj. **1** (of food) tender, juicy, and tasty. **2** (of a plant) having thick fleshy leaves or stems adapted to storing water. ● n. a succulent plant.
– DERIVATIVES **succulence** n.
– ORIGIN Latin *succulentus*.

succumb ● v. **1** give in to (pressure, temptation, etc.). **2** die from the effect of a disease or injury.
– ORIGIN Latin *succumbere*.

such ● det., predet., & pron. **1** of the type previously mentioned. **2** (**such —— as/that**) of the type about to be mentioned. **3** to so high a degree, so great: *autumn's such a beautiful season*.
– PHRASES **as such** in the exact sense of the word. **such as 1** for example. **2** of a kind that; like.
– ORIGIN Old English.

suchlike ● pron. things of the type mentioned: *old chairs, tables, and suchlike*. ● det. of the type mentioned.

suck ● v. **1** draw into the mouth by tightening the lip muscles and breathing in. **2** hold (something) in the mouth and draw at it by tightening the lip and cheek muscles. **3** pull forcefully in a specified direction: *he was sucked under the surface of the river*. **4** (**suck in/into**) involve (someone) in something that they would not choose to do. **5** (**suck up to**) informal try to please someone in authority to gain advantage for oneself. **6** N. Amer. informal be very bad. ● n. an act of sucking.
– ORIGIN Old English.

sucker ● n. **1** a rubber cup that sticks to a surface by suction. **2** an organ that allows an animal to cling to a surface by suction. **3** informal a person who is easily fooled. **4** (**a sucker for**) informal a person especially influenced by or fond of (a specified thing): *I was a sucker for flattery*. **5** a shoot springing from the base of a tree or other plant.

suckle ● v. (**suckles**, **suckling**, **suckled**) (with reference to a baby or young animal) feed from the breast or teat.

suckling ● n. a young child or animal that is still feeding on its mother's milk.

Sucre[1] E
/soo-kray/ the judicial capital of Bolivia.

Sucre[2] E
/soo-kray/, Antonio José de (1795–1830), Venezuelan revolutionary and statesman, first President of Bolivia 1826–8. As Bolívar's Chief of Staff he assisted in the liberation of Ecuador, Peru, and Bolivia from the Spanish.

sucrose /syoo krohz/ ● n. a compound which is the chief component of cane or beet sugar.
– ORIGIN French *sucre* 'sugar'.

suction ● n. the process of removing air or liquid from a space or container, creating a partial vacuum that causes something else to be sucked in or surfaces to stick together.
– ORIGIN Latin.

Sudan[1] E
/soo-dahn, soo-dan/ (also **the Sudan**) a country in NE Africa, with a coastline on the Red Sea; capital, Khartoum.
– DERIVATIVES **Sudanese** /soo-duh-neez/ adj. & n.

Sudan[2] E
/soo-dahn, soo-dan/ (also **the Sudan**) a vast region of North Africa, extending across the continent from the southern edge of the Sahara to the tropical equatorial zone in the south.

sudden ● adj. occurring or done quickly and unexpectedly.
– DERIVATIVES **suddenness** n.
– ORIGIN Old French *sudein*.

sudden death ● n. a means of deciding the winner in a tied match, in which play continues and the winner is the first side or player to score.

sudden infant death syndrome ● n. tech. = **COT DEATH**.

suddenly ● adv. quickly and unexpectedly.

suds ● pl. n. froth made from soap and water.
– ORIGIN prob. from **SEETHE**.

sue ● v. (**sues**, **suing**, **sued**) **1** take legal action against (a person or institution). **2** (**sue for**) formal appeal formally to a person for: *sue for peace*.
– ORIGIN Old French *suer*.

suede ● n. leather with the flesh side rubbed to make a velvety nap.
– ORIGIN from French *gants de Suède* 'gloves of Sweden'.

suet ● n. the hard white fat on the kidneys and loins of cattle, sheep, and other animals, used in making puddings, pastry, etc.
– ORIGIN Old French.

Suetonius E
/swee-toh-ni-uhss/ (*c.*69–*c.*150 AD; full name *Gaius Suetonius Tranquillus*), Roman biographer and historian, best known for *Lives of the Caesars*.

S

Suez Canal E
a shipping canal connecting the Mediterranean at Port Said with the Red Sea, completed in 1869. In 1875 it came under British control; its nationalization by Egypt in 1956 prompted the Suez crisis.

Suez crisis E
a short conflict following the nationalization of the Suez Canal by Egypt in 1956. Britain and France made a military alliance with Israel to regain control of the canal, but international criticism forced the withdrawal of forces.

suffer • v. (**suffers**, **suffering**, **suffered**) **1** experience (something bad or unpleasant). **2** (**suffer from**) be affected by (an illness or ailment). **3** become or appear worse in quality: *his relationship with Anne did suffer.* **4** archaic tolerate.
– DERIVATIVES **sufferer** n.
– ORIGIN Latin *sufferre.*

sufferance • n. lack of objection rather than actual approval; toleration.

suffice /suh-fyss/ • v. (**suffices**, **sufficing**, **sufficed**) **1** be enough or adequate. **2** meet the needs of.
– ORIGIN Latin *sufficere.*

sufficiency • n. (pl. **sufficiencies**) **1** the quality of being sufficient. **2** an adequate amount.

sufficient • adj. & det. enough; adequate.
– DERIVATIVES **sufficiently** adv.

suffix /suf-fiks/ • n. a letter or group of letters added at the end of a word to form a derivative (e.g. *-ation*).

suffocate • v. (**suffocates**, **suffocating**, **suffocated**) **1** die or kill from lack of air or inability to breathe. **2** feel trapped.
– DERIVATIVES **suffocation** n.
– ORIGIN Latin *suffocare* 'stifle'.

Suffolk E
/suf-fuhk/ a county of eastern England; county town, Ipswich.

suffrage /suf-frij/ • n. the right to vote in political elections.
– ORIGIN Latin *suffragium.*

suffragette /suf-fruh-jet/ • n. hist. a woman who campaigned for the right to vote in an election.

suffuse /suh-fyooz/ • v. (**suffuses**, **suffusing**, **suffused**) gradually spread through or over.
– DERIVATIVES **suffusion** n.
– ORIGIN Latin *suffundere* 'pour into'.

Sufi /soo-fi/ • n. (pl. **Sufis**) a member of a Muslim group leading a very religious, strict, and simple life.
– DERIVATIVES **Sufism** n.
– ORIGIN Arabic.

sugar • n. **1** a sweet crystalline substance obtained from sugar cane and sugar beet. **2** Biochem. any of the class of soluble crystalline sweet-tasting carbohydrates, including sucrose and glucose. • v. **1** sweeten, sprinkle, or coat with sugar. **2** make more pleasant.
– ORIGIN Old French *sukere.*

sugar beet • n. beet of a variety from which sugar is extracted.

sugar cane • n. a tropical grass with tall thick stems from which sugar is extracted.

sugar daddy • n. informal a rich older man who gives many gifts to a young woman.

sugar snap • n. a type of mangetout with thick pods.

sugar soap • n. Brit. an alkaline preparation containing washing soda and soap, used for cleaning or removing paint.

sugary • adj. **1** coated in or containing much sugar. **2** excessively sentimental.

suggest • v. **1** put forward for consideration. **2** cause one to think that (something) exists or is the case. **3** say or express indirectly. **4** (**suggest itself**) (of an idea) come into one's mind.
– ORIGIN Latin *suggerere.*

suggestible • adj. open to suggestion; easily influenced.

suggestion • n. **1** an idea or plan put forward for consideration. **2** the action of suggesting. **3** something that suggests or indicates a certain fact or situation. **4** a slight trace or indication: *a suggestion of a smile.*

suggestive • adj. **1** making one think about something. **2** bringing to mind sexual matters.
– DERIVATIVES **suggestively** adv.

suicide • n. **1** the action of killing oneself deliberately. **2** a person who does this. **3** a course of action which is extremely damaging to one's own interests. • adj. referring to a military operation carried out by people who do not expect to survive it: *a suicide bomber.*
– DERIVATIVES **suicidal** adj. **suicidally** adv.
– ORIGIN from Latin *sui* 'of oneself' + *caedere* 'kill'.

sui generis /soo-i jen-uh-riss/ • adj. unique.
– ORIGIN Latin, 'of its own kind'.

suit • n. **1** a set of clothes made of the same fabric, consisting of a jacket and trousers or a skirt. **2** a set of clothes for a particular activity. **3** any of the sets into which a pack of playing cards is divided (spades, hearts, diamonds, and clubs). **4** a lawsuit. **5** the process of trying to win a woman's affection with a view to marriage. • v. **1** be convenient for or acceptable to. **2** go well with the features, figure, or character of. **3** (**suit oneself**) do exactly what one wants.
– ORIGIN Old French *siwte.*

suitable • adj. right or appropriate for a particular person, purpose, or situation.
– DERIVATIVES **suitability** n. **suitably** adv.

suitcase • n. a case with a handle and a hinged lid, used for carrying clothes and other personal possessions.

suite /sweet/ • n. **1** a set of rooms for one person's or family's use. **2** a set of furniture of the same design. **3** Music a set of instrumental compositions to be played in succession. **4** a set of pieces from an opera or musical arranged as one instrumental work.
– ORIGIN French.

suitor /syoo-ter/ • n. a man who wants to marry a woman.

Sulawesi E
/suul-uh-way-si/ an island in Indonesia, to the east of Borneo; chief town, Ujung Pandang. Former name **CELEBES**.

Suleiman I E
/soo-li-muhn, soo-lay-**man**/ (also **Soliman** or **Solyman**) (*c.*1494–1566; known as **Suleiman the Magnificent**), sultan of the Ottoman Empire 1520–66. The Ottoman Empire reached its fullest extent under his rule.

sulfur etc. • n. US = SULPHUR etc.

sulk • v. be silent, miserable, and bad-tempered through annoyance or disappointment. • n. a period of sulking.

sulky • adj. (**sulkier**, **sulkiest**) miserable, bad-tempered, and resentful.
– DERIVATIVES **sulkily** adv.
– ORIGIN perh. from former *sulke* 'hard to dispose of'.

Sulla E
/**sul**-luh/ (138–78 BC; full name *Lucius Cornelius Sulla Felix*), Roman general and politician. He was elected dictator in 82 and implemented constitutional reforms in favour of the Senate.

sullen • adj. bad-tempered and sulky.
– DERIVATIVES **sullenly** adv.
– ORIGIN Old French *sulein*.

Sullivan, E
Sir Arthur (Seymour) (1842–1900), English composer. He wrote light operas in collaboration with Sir W. S. Gilbert, including *HMS Pinafore* and *The Mikado*.

sully • v. (**sullies**, **sullying**, **sullied**) spoil the purity or cleanliness of: *he never sullied his lips with swear words.*
– ORIGIN perh. from French *souiller* 'to soil'.

sulphate (US **sulfate**) • n. Chem. a salt or ester of sulphuric acid.

sulphide /**sul**-fyd/ (US **sulfide**) • n. Chem. a compound of sulphur with another element or group.

sulphur (US & Chem. **sulfur**) • n. a combustible non-metallic chemical element which typically occurs as yellow crystals.
– ORIGIN Latin *sulfur*, *sulphur*.

sulphur dioxide • n. a colourless poisonous gas formed by burning sulphur.

sulphuric /sul-**fyoor**-ik/ (US **sulfuric**) • adj. containing sulphur or sulphuric acid.

sulphuric acid • n. a strong corrosive acid.

sulphurous (US **sulfurous**) • adj. containing or derived from sulphur.

sultan • n. a Muslim ruler.
– DERIVATIVES **sultanate** n.
– ORIGIN Arabic, 'power, ruler'.

sultana • n. **1** a seedless raisin. **2** a wife or concubine of a sultan.
– ORIGIN Italian.

sultry • adj. (**sultrier**, **sultriest**) **1** (of the weather) hot and humid. **2** suggesting sexual passion.
– ORIGIN from former *sulter* 'swelter'.

sum • n. **1** a particular amount of money. **2** the total amount resulting from the addition of two or more numbers or amounts. **3** an arithmetical problem. • v. (**sums**, **summing**, **summed**) (**sum up**) **1** concisely describe the character of: *selfish—that summed her up.* **2** summarize briefly.
– ORIGIN Latin *summa* 'main part'.

Sumatra E
/suu-**mah**-truh/ a large island of Indonesia, to the south-west of the Malay Peninsula; chief city, Medan.

Sumer E
/**soo**-mer/ an ancient region of SW Asia in present-day Iraq.

summarize (also **summarise**) • v. (**summarizes**, **summarizing**, **summarized**) give a brief account of.

summary • n. (pl. **summaries**) a brief statement of the main points of something. • adj. **1** done immediately, without attention to details. **2** Law (of a judicial process) conducted without the usual legal formalities.
– DERIVATIVES **summarily** adv.
– ORIGIN Latin *summarius*.

summation /sum-**may**-sh'n/ • n. **1** the process of adding things together. **2** the action of summing up. **3** a summary.

summer • n. the season after spring and before autumn.
– DERIVATIVES **summery** adj.
– ORIGIN Old English.

summer house • n. a small building in a garden, used for relaxation during fine weather.

summer school • n. a course of lectures held during school and university summer vacations.

summer time • n. Brit. time as advanced one hour ahead of standard time to achieve longer evening daylight in summer.

summing-up • n. **1** a summary. **2** Law a judge's review of evidence at the end of a case.

summit • n. **1** the highest point of a hill or mountain. **2** the highest possible level of achievement. **3** a meeting between heads of government.
– ORIGIN Old French *somete*.

summon • v. **1** officially ask (someone) to be present. **2** urgently demand (help). **3** call people to attend (a meeting). **4** cause (a quality or reaction) to emerge from within oneself: *she managed to summon up a smile.*
– ORIGIN Latin *summonere* 'give a hint'.

summons • n. (pl. **summonses**) **1** an order to appear in a law court. **2** an act of summoning.

sumo /**soo**-moh/ • n. (pl. **sumos**) Japanese wrestling in which a wrestler must not go outside a circle or touch the ground with any part of his body except the soles of his feet.
– ORIGIN Japanese.

sump • n. the base of an internal-combustion engine, which serves as a reservoir of oil for the lubrication system.
– ORIGIN Dutch or German *sump* 'marsh'.

sumptuous • adj. splendid and expensive-looking.
– ORIGIN Latin *sumptuosus*.

sum total • n. = SUM (in sense 2).

sun • n. **1** (also **Sun**) the star round which the earth orbits. **2** any similar star. **3** the light or warmth received from the sun. • v. (**suns**, **sunning**, **sunned**) (**sun oneself**) sit or lie in the sun.
– PHRASES **under the sun** in existence.
– ORIGIN Old English.

sun-baked • adj. exposed to the sun's heat.

S

sunbathe ● v. (**sunbathes**, **sunbathing**, **sunbathed**) sit or lie in the sun to get a suntan.
– DERIVATIVES **sunbather** n.

sunbeam ● n. a ray of sunlight.

sunbed ● n. Brit. **1** a lounger for sunbathing. **2** an apparatus for getting a tan, consisting of two banks of sunlamps between which one lies or stands.

sunblock ● n. a cream for protecting the skin from sunburn.

sunburn ● n. inflammation of the skin caused by too much exposure to the ultraviolet rays of the sun. ● v. (**sunburns**, **sunburning**, **sunburned** or **sunburnt**) (**be sunburned**) suffer from sunburn.

suncream ● n. a cream used for protecting the skin from sunburn.

sundae ● n. a dish of ice cream with fruit, nuts, syrup, etc.
– ORIGIN perh. from **SUNDAY**, either because the dish was made with ice cream left over from Sunday, or because it was sold only on Sundays.

Sunda Islands E
/sun-duh/ a chain of islands in the south-west of the Malay Archipelago, consisting of two groups: the **Greater Sunda Islands** and the **Lesser Sunda Islands**.

Sunday ● n. the day of the week before Monday and following Saturday, observed by Christians as a day of religious worship.
– ORIGIN Old English, 'day of the sun'.

Sunday best ● n. a person's best clothes.

Sunday school ● n. a class held on Sundays to teach children about Christianity.

sunder ● v. (**sunders**, **sundering**, **sundered**) literary split apart.
– ORIGIN Old English.

sundew ● n. a flesh-eating plant of boggy places, with leaves bearing sticky hairs for trapping insects.

sundial ● n. an instrument showing the time by the shadow cast by a pointer.

sundown ● n. esp. N. Amer. sunset.

sundress ● n. a light, loose sleeveless dress.

sun-dried ● adj. dried in the sun, as opposed to by artificial heat.

sundry ● adj. of various kinds. ● n. (**sundries**) various items not important enough be mentioned individually.
– ORIGIN Old English, 'distinct, separate'.

sunflower ● n. a tall plant with very large golden flowers, grown for its edible seeds which produce oil.

sung past part. of **SING**.

sunglasses ● pl. n. glasses tinted to protect the eyes from sunlight or glare.

sunk past and past part. of **SINK**.

sunken ● adj. **1** having sunk. **2** at a lower level than the surrounding area.
– ORIGIN former past part. of **SINK**.

sun-kissed ● adj. made warm or brown by the sun.

sunlamp ● n. a lamp giving off ultraviolet rays, used to produce an artificial suntan.

sunlight ● n. light from the sun.
– DERIVATIVES **sunlit** adj.

Sunni /suu-ni, sun-ni/ ● n. (pl. **Sunni** or **Sunnis**) **1** one of the two main branches of Islam. **2** a Muslim who follows this branch of Islam.
– ORIGIN Arabic, 'custom, standard rule'.

sunny ● adj. (**sunnier**, **sunniest**) **1** bright with or receiving much sunlight. **2** cheerful.

sunrise ● n. **1** the time in the morning when the sun rises. **2** the colours and light visible in the sky at sunrise.

sunroof ● n. a panel in the roof of a car that can be opened for extra ventilation.

sunscreen ● n. a cream or lotion rubbed on to the skin to protect it from the sun.

sunset ● n. **1** the time in the evening when the sun sets. **2** the colours and light visible in the sky at sunset.

sunshade ● n. a device giving protection from the sun.

sunshine ● n. **1** sunlight unbroken by cloud. **2** cheerfulness or happiness.

sunspot ● n. Astron. a temporary darker and cooler patch on the sun's surface.

sunstroke ● n. heatstroke brought about by excessive exposure to the sun.

suntan ● n. a golden-brown colouring of the skin caused by exposure to the sun.
– DERIVATIVES **suntanned** adj.

sunup ● n. esp. N. Amer. sunrise.

Sun Yat-sen E
/suun yat-sen/ (also **Sun Yixian** /suun jee-shee-an/) (1866–1925), Chinese Kuomintang statesman, provisional President of the Republic of China 1911–12 and President of the Southern Chinese Republic 1923–5. He played a leading part in the revolution of 1911 which overthrew the ruling Manchu dynasty.

sup[1] ● v. (**sups**, **supping**, **supped**) dated or N. Engl. take (drink or liquid food) by sips or spoonfuls. ● n. a sip.
– ORIGIN Old English.

sup[2] ● v. (**sups**, **supping**, **supped**) dated eat supper.
– ORIGIN Old French *super*.

super ● adj. informal excellent. ● n. informal a superintendent.

super- ● comb. form **1** above; over; beyond: *superstructure*. **2** to a great or extreme degree: *supercool*. **3** extra large of its kind: *superpower*.
– ORIGIN Latin *super*.

superannuate ● v. (**superannuates**, **superannuating**, **superannuated**) **1** retire (someone) with a pension. **2** (**superannuated**) belonging to a superannuation scheme. **3** (**superannuated**) too old to be effective or useful.
– ORIGIN from Latin *super-* 'over' + *annus* 'year'.

superannuation ● n. regular payment made into a fund by an employee towards a future pension.

superb ● adj. **1** excellent. **2** magnificent or splendid.
– DERIVATIVES **superbly** adv.
– ORIGIN Latin *superbus*.

superbug ● n. informal a bacterium, insect, etc. which has developed resistance to antibiotics or pesticides.

supercharge ● v. (**supercharges**, **supercharging**, **supercharged**) **1** provide with a supercharger. **2** (**supercharged**) having powerful emotional associations.

S

supercharger ● n. a device that increases the pressure of the fuel-air mixture in an internal-combustion engine, thereby giving greater efficiency.

supercilious ● adj. behaving in a way that shows one thinks one is better than others.
– ORIGIN Latin *superciliosus* 'haughty'.

supercomputer ● n. a particularly powerful mainframe computer.

superconductivity ● n. Physics the property of zero electrical resistance in some substances at very low temperatures.

superconductor ● n. a substance which has the property of superconductivity.

supercool ● v. Chem. cool (a liquid) below its freezing point without solidification or crystallization.

superego ● n. (pl. **superegos**) the part of the mind that acts as a conscience, reflecting social standards that have been learned. Compare with **EGO** and **ID**.

superficial ● adj. **1** existing or happening at or on the surface. **2** apparent rather than real: *the resemblance is superficial.* **3** not thorough: *a superficial reading of the document.* **4** lacking the ability to think deeply about things.
– DERIVATIVES **superficiality** n. (pl. **superficialities**) **superficially** adv.
– ORIGIN Latin *superficialis.*

superfluous ● adj. unnecessary because more than is needed.
– ORIGIN Latin *superfluus.*

superglue ● n. a very strong quick-setting glue.

supergrass ● n. Brit. informal a police informer who gives information about the criminal activities of a large number of people.

superhero ● n. (pl. **superheroes**) a fictional hero with superhuman powers.

superhuman ● adj. having or showing exceptional ability or powers.

superimpose ● v. (**superimposes, superimposing, superimposed**) place or lay (one thing) over another.
– DERIVATIVES **superimposition** n.

superintend ● v. manage or oversee.

superintendent ● n. **1** a person in charge of an organization, department, etc. **2** (in the UK) a police officer ranking above chief inspector. **3** (in the US) the chief of a police department.
– ORIGIN Latin *superintendere.*

superior ● adj. **1** higher in status, quality, or power. **2** of high standard or quality. **3** thinking one is better than others; conceited. ● n. a person of superior rank.
– ORIGIN Latin, 'higher'.

Superior, Lake E
the largest of the five Great Lakes of North America, on the border between Canada and the US. With an area of 82,350 sq. km (31,800 sq. miles), it is the largest freshwater lake in the world.

superiority ● n. the state of being superior.

superlative /soo-per-luh-tiv/ ● adj. **1** of the highest quality or degree. **2** Grammar (of an adjective or adverb) expressing the highest degree of a quality (e.g. *bravest*). Contrasted with **POSITIVE** and **COMPARATIVE**. ● n. an exaggerated expression of praise.
– ORIGIN Latin *superlativus.*

superman ● n. informal a man with exceptional physical or mental ability.

supermarket ● n. a large self-service shop selling foods and household goods.

supermodel ● n. a very successful and famous fashion model.

supernatural ● adj. regarded as caused by some force beyond the laws of nature. ● n. (**the supernatural**) supernatural events.
– DERIVATIVES **supernaturally** adv.

supernova /soo-per-noh-vuh/ ● n. (pl. **supernovae** /soo-per-noh-vee/ or **supernovas**) Astron. a star that undergoes a catastrophic explosion, becoming suddenly very much brighter.

supernumerary /soo-puh-nyoo-muh-ruh-ri/ ● adj. **1** present in excess of the normal or required number. **2** not belonging to a regular staff but engaged for extra work. ● n. (pl. **supernumeraries**) a supernumerary person or thing.
– ORIGIN Latin *supernumerarius* 'soldier added to a legion after it is complete'.

superpower ● n. any of the few most powerful nations of the world.

superscript ● adj. (of a letter, figure, or symbol) written or printed above the line.

supersede /soo-per-seed/ ● v. (**supersedes, superseding, superseded**) take the place of.
– ORIGIN Latin *supersedere* 'be superior to'.

supersonic ● adj. having to do with a speed greater than that of sound.

superstar ● n. an extremely famous and successful performer or sports player.

superstition ● n. **1** excessive willingness to believe in the supernatural. **2** a widely held but irrational belief in supernatural influences.
– ORIGIN Latin.

superstitious ● adj. influenced by superstition.

superstore ● n. a very large out-of-town supermarket.

superstructure ● n. **1** a structure built on top of something else. **2** the part of a building above its foundations. **3** the parts of a ship, other than masts and rigging, above its hull and main deck.

supertanker ● n. a very large oil tanker.

supertax ● n. an additional tax on something already taxed.

supervene /soo-per-veen/ ● v. (**supervenes, supervening, supervened**) occur as an interruption or change to an existing situation.
– ORIGIN Latin *supervenire* 'come in addition'.

supervise ● v. watch and direct the performance of (a task or activity) or the work of (a person).
– DERIVATIVES **supervision** n. **supervisor** n. **supervisory** adj.
– ORIGIN Latin *supervidere* 'survey, supervise'.

superwoman ● n. informal a woman with exceptional physical or mental ability.

supine /syoo-pyn/ ● adj. **1** lying face upwards. **2** failing to act as a result of laziness or lack of courage.
– ORIGIN Latin *supinus* 'bent backwards'.

supper ● n. a light or informal evening meal.
– ORIGIN Old French *super* 'to sup'.

supplant ● v. take the place of.

– ORIGIN Latin *supplantare* 'trip up'.
supple ● adj. (**suppler**, **supplest**) flexible.
– ORIGIN Latin *supplex* 'submissive'.
supplement ● n. **1** a thing added to something else to improve or complete it. **2** a separate section added to a newspaper or periodical. **3** an additional charge payable for an extra service or facility. ● v. provide a supplement for.
– DERIVATIVES **supplemental** adj.
– ORIGIN Latin *supplementum*.
supplementary ● adj. completing or improving something.
suppliant /sup-pli-uhnt/ ● n. a person who makes a humble request.
supplicate /sup-pli-kayt/ ● v. (**supplicates**, **supplicating**, **supplicated**) humbly ask or beg for something.
– DERIVATIVES **supplicant** n. **supplication** n.
– ORIGIN Latin *supplicare* 'implore'.
supply ● v. (**supplies**, **supplying**, **supplied**) **1** make (something needed) available to someone. **2** provide with something needed. ● n. (pl. **supplies**) **1** a stock or amount of something supplied or available. **2** the action of supplying. **3** (**supplies**) provisions and equipment necessary for an army or expedition.
– PHRASES **supply and demand** the amount of goods or services available and the desire of buyers for them, considered as factors deciding its price.
– DERIVATIVES **supplier** n.
– ORIGIN Latin *supplere* 'fill up'.
support ● v. **1** bear all or part of the weight of. **2** give help, encouragement, or approval to. **3** be actively interested in (a sports team). **4** provide with a home and the necessities of life. **5** be capable of sustaining (life). **6** confirm or back up: *the studies support our findings.* ● n. **1** a person or thing that supports. **2** the action of supporting. **3** help, encouragement, or approval.
– ORIGIN Latin *supportare*.
supporter ● n. a person who supports a sports team, policy, etc.
supportive ● adj. providing encouragement or emotional help.
suppose ● v. (**supposes**, **supposing**, **supposed**) **1** think that something is true or likely, but without proof. **2** (of a theory or argument) think or require that something is the case as a necessary condition. **3** (**be supposed to do**) be required or expected to do.
– ORIGIN Latin *supponere*.
supposedly ● adv. according to what is generally believed or supposed.
supposition ● n. an assumption.
suppository ● n. (pl. **suppositories**) a small piece of a medical substance that is placed in the rectum or vagina and left to dissolve.
– ORIGIN Latin *suppositorium* 'thing placed underneath'.
suppress ● v. **1** forcibly put an end to. **2** prevent from being expressed or published.
– DERIVATIVES **suppression** n.
– ORIGIN Latin *supprimere* 'press down'.
suppressant ● n. a drug which acts to prevent one of the body's functions from working.
suppurate /sup-pyuh-rayt/ ● v. (**suppurates**, **suppurating**, **suppurated**) form or give off pus.
– DERIVATIVES **suppuration** n.
– ORIGIN from Latin *sub-* 'below' + *pus* 'pus'.
supranational ● adj. having power or influence that goes beyond national boundaries or governments.
supremacist ● n. a person who believes that a particular group is superior to all others.
– DERIVATIVES **supremacism** n.
supremacy /soo-prem-uh-si/ ● n. the state of being superior to all others in authority, power, or status.
supreme ● adj. **1** highest in authority or rank. **2** very great or greatest.
– ORIGIN Latin *supremus* 'highest'.
supreme court ● n. the highest law court in a country or state.
supremo /soo-pree-moh/ ● n. (pl. **supremos**) Brit. informal a person with most power or authority in a particular area.
– ORIGIN Spanish, 'supreme'.
suq ● n. var. of **SOUK**.
sur- ● prefix = **SUPER-**.
– ORIGIN French.
surcharge ● n. an extra charge or payment. ● v. (**surcharges**, **surcharging**, **surcharged**) make (someone) pay a surcharge.
surd /*rhymes with* curd/ ● n. Math. a number which cannot be expressed as a ratio of two whole numbers.
– ORIGIN Latin *surdus* 'deaf, mute'.
sure /shoor, shor/ ● adj. **1** completely confident that one is right. **2** (**sure of/to do**) certain to receive, get, or do. **3** undoubtedly true. **4** steady and confident. ● adv. informal certainly.
– DERIVATIVES **sureness** n.
– ORIGIN Old French *sur*.
sure-fire ● adj. informal certain to succeed.
sure-footed ● adj. **1** unlikely to stumble or slip. **2** confident and competent.
surely ● adv. **1** it must be true that. **2** certainly.
surety /shoor-i-ti, shoor-ti/ ● n. (pl. **sureties**) **1** a person who accepts responsibility if another person fails to pay a debt, appear in court, etc. **2** money given as a guarantee that someone will do something.
surf ● n. the mass or line of foam formed by waves breaking on a seashore or reef. ● v. **1** stand or lie on a surfboard and ride on the crest of a wave towards the shore. **2** occupy oneself by moving from site to site on (the Internet).
– DERIVATIVES **surfer** n. **surfing** n.
– ORIGIN unknown.
surface ● n. **1** the outside part or uppermost layer of something. **2** the upper limit of a body of liquid. **3** outward appearance as distinct from less obvious aspects. ● adj. **1** relating to or occurring on the surface. **2** outward or superficial: *surface politeness.* ● v. (**surfaces**, **surfacing**, **surfaced**) **1** rise or come up to the surface. **2** become apparent. **3** provide with a particular surface.
– ORIGIN French.
surface tension ● n. the tension of the surface film of a liquid, which tends to minimize surface area.
surfboard ● n. a long, narrow board used in surfing.
surfeit ● n. an excess.
– ORIGIN Old French.

surge ● n. **1** a sudden powerful forward or upward movement. **2** a sudden large temporary increase. **3** a powerful rush of an emotion. ● v. (**surges**, **surging**, **surged**) **1** move in a surge. **2** increase suddenly and powerfully.
– ORIGIN Latin *surgere* 'to rise'.

surgeon ● n. **1** a medical practitioner qualified to practise surgery. **2** a doctor in the navy.
– ORIGIN Old French *serurgien*.

surgery ● n. (pl. **surgeries**) **1** the medical treatment of bodily injuries or disorders by cutting open the body and removing or repairing parts. **2** Brit. a place where a doctor or nurse treats or advises patients. **3** Brit. an occasion on which an MP, lawyer, or other professional person gives advice.

surgical ● adj. **1** relating to or used in surgery. **2** worn to correct or relieve an injury, illness, or deformity: *surgical stockings*. **3** done with great precision: *surgical bombing*.
– DERIVATIVES **surgically** adv.

surgical spirit ● n. Brit. methylated spirit used for cleansing the skin before injections or surgery.

Suriname E
/soo-ri-**nam**/ (also **Surinam**) a country on the NE coast of South America; capital, Paramaribo. Former name (until 1948) **Dutch Guiana**.
– DERIVATIVES **Surinamese** /soo-ri-nuh-**meez**/ adj. & n.

surly ● adj. (**surlier**, **surliest**) bad-tempered and unfriendly.
– ORIGIN from former *sirly* 'haughty'.

surmise /ser-myz/ ● v. (**surmises**, **surmising**, **surmised**) suppose without having evidence. ● n. a guess.
– ORIGIN Old French, 'accused'.

surmount ● v. **1** overcome (a difficulty). **2** stand or be placed on top of.

surname ● n. an inherited name common to all members of a family.

surpass ● v. **1** be greater or better than. **2** (**surpassing**) archaic outstanding.

surplice /ser-pliss/ ● n. a white robe worn over a cassock by clergy and choristers at Christian church services.
– ORIGIN Old French *sourpelis*.

surplus ● n. **1** an amount left over when requirements have been met. **2** the amount by which the amount of money received is greater than the amount of money spent over a given period. ● adj. more than what is needed or used.
– ORIGIN from Latin *super-* 'in addition' + *plus* 'more'.

surprise ● n. **1** a feeling of mild astonishment or shock caused by something unexpected. **2** an unexpected or astonishing thing. ● v. (**surprises**, **surprising**, **surprised**) **1** cause to feel surprise. **2** capture, attack, or discover suddenly and unexpectedly.
– ORIGIN Old French.

surreal ● adj. having the qualities of a dream; very strange.
– DERIVATIVES **surreally** adv.

surrealism ● n. a 20th-century movement in art and literature which sought to release the creativity of the unconscious mind, often by combining unrelated images in a strange way.
– DERIVATIVES **surrealist** n. & adj.

surrender ● v. (**surrenders**, **surrendering**, **surrendered**) **1** give in to an opponent and submit to their authority. **2** give up (a person, right, or possession) on demand. **3** (**surrender to**) abandon oneself entirely to (a powerful emotion or influence). ● n. an act of surrendering.
– ORIGIN Old French *surrendre*.

surreptitious /sur-ruhp-**ti**-shuhss/ ● adj. done secretly.
– ORIGIN Latin *surreptitius* 'obtained secretly'.

Surrey E
a county of SE England; county town, Kingston-upon-Thames.

surrogate /sur-ruh-guht/ ● n. **1** a person who stands in for another in a role or office. **2** (in the Christian Church) a bishop's deputy who grants marriage licences.
– DERIVATIVES **surrogacy** n.
– ORIGIN Latin *surrogare* 'elect as a substitute'.

surrogate mother ● n. a woman who bears a child on behalf of another woman.

surround ● v. **1** be all round; encircle. **2** be associated with: *the incident was surrounded by controversy*. ● n. a border or edging.
– ORIGIN Latin *superundare* 'overflow'.

surroundings ● pl. n. the conditions or area around a person or thing: *a school in rural surroundings*.

surtax ● n. an extra tax on something already taxed.

surtitle ● n. a caption projected on a screen above the stage in an opera, translating the text being sung.

surveillance /ser-vay-luhnss/ ● n. close observation of a suspected spy or criminal.
– ORIGIN French.

survey ● v. /ser-vay/ (**surveys**, **surveying**, **surveyed**) **1** look carefully and thoroughly at. **2** examine and record the features of (an area of land) to produce a map or description. **3** Brit. examine and report on the condition of (a building). **4** conduct a survey among (a group of people). ● n. /ser-vay/ **1** a general view, examination, or description. **2** an investigation of the opinions or experience of a group of people, based on a series of questions. **3** an act of surveying. **4** a map or report obtained by surveying.
– ORIGIN Old French *surveier*.

S

surveyor ● n. a person who surveys land, buildings, etc. as a profession.

survival ● n. **1** the state of surviving. **2** an object or practice that has survived from an earlier time.

survive ● v. (**survives**, **surviving**, **survived**) **1** continue to live or exist. **2** continue to live or exist in spite of (an accident or ordeal). **3** remain alive after the death of: *he was survived by his wife*.
– DERIVATIVES **survivable** adj.
– ORIGIN Old French *sourvivre*.

survivor ● n. a person who has survived.

susceptibility ● n. (pl. **susceptibilities**) **1** the state of being susceptible. **2** (**susceptibilities**) a person's feelings, regarded as being easily hurt.

susceptible /suh-sep-ti-b'l/ ● adj. **1** (often

susceptible to) likely to be influenced or harmed by a particular thing. **2** easily influenced by emotions.
– ORIGIN Latin *susceptibilis*.

sushi /soo-shi/ ● **n.** a Japanese dish consisting of small balls or rolls of cold rice with vegetables, egg, or raw seafood.
– ORIGIN Japanese.

suspect ● **v.** /suh-spekt/ **1** believe (something) to be likely or possible. **2** believe (someone) to be guilty of a crime or offence, without certain proof. **3** doubt the genuineness or truth of. ● **n.** /suss-pekt/ a person suspected of a crime or offence. ● **adj.** /suss-pekt/ possibly dangerous or false: *a suspect package*.
– ORIGIN Latin *suspicere* 'mistrust'.

suspend ● **v. 1** halt temporarily. **2** temporarily remove (someone) from a post as a punishment or during investigation. **3** postpone or delay (an action, event, or judgement). **4** (**suspended**) Law (of a sentence) not enforced as long as no further offence is committed within a specified period. **5** hang from somewhere.
– ORIGIN Latin *suspendere*.

suspended animation ● **n.** temporary stopping of most vital functions, without death.

suspender ● **n. 1** Brit. an elastic strap attached to a belt or garter, fastened to the top of a stocking to hold it up. **2** (**suspenders**) N. Amer. braces for holding up trousers.

suspender belt ● **n.** Brit. a woman's undergarment made up of a decorative belt and suspenders.

suspense ● **n.** a state of excited or anxious uncertainty about what may happen.
– DERIVATIVES **suspenseful** adj.
– ORIGIN Old French *suspens* 'abeyance'.

suspension ● **n. 1** the action of suspending or the state of being suspended. **2** the system of springs and shock absorbers by which a vehicle is supported on its wheels. **3** a mixture in which particles are dispersed throughout a fluid.

suspension bridge ● **n.** a bridge in which the deck is suspended from cables running between towers.

suspicion ● **n. 1** a feeling that something is possible or that someone is guilty of a crime or offence. **2** cautious distrust. **3** a very slight trace: *a suspicion of a smile*.
– ORIGIN Old French *suspeciun*.

suspicious ● **adj. 1** feeling suspicion. **2** giving an impression of being dishonest or dangerous. **3** (**suspicious of**) not able to trust (someone or something).
– DERIVATIVES **suspiciously** adv.

suss ● **v.** (**susses**, **sussing**, **sussed**) (often **suss out**) Brit. informal realize or understand the true character or nature of.
– ORIGIN from SUSPECT.

Sussex E
a former county of southern England, divided in 1974 into the counties of East Sussex and West Sussex.

sustain ● **v. 1** strengthen or support (someone) physically or mentally. **2** bear (the weight of an object). **3** suffer (something unpleasant). **4** keep (something) going over time or continuously.
– ORIGIN Latin *sustinere*.

sustainable ● **adj. 1** able to be sustained. **2** (of industry, development, or agriculture) avoiding using up natural resources.
– DERIVATIVES **sustainability** n. **sustainably** adv.

sustenance ● **n. 1** food and drink as needed to stay alive. **2** the process of sustaining something.

Sutherland[1], E
Graham (Vivian) (1903–80), English painter, known for his portraits, landscapes, and religious paintings.

Sutherland[2], E
Dame Joan (b.1926), Australian operatic soprano.

suture /soo-cher/ ● **n. 1** a stitch or row of stitches holding together the edges of a wound or surgical incision. **2** a thread used for this. ● **v.** (**sutures**, **suturing**, **sutured**) stitch up with a suture.
– ORIGIN Latin *sutura*.

Suva E
/soo-vuh/ the capital of Fiji, on the island of Viti Levu.

suzerainty /soo-zuh-rayn-ti/ ● **n.** the right of one country to rule over another country that has its own ruler but is not fully independent.
– DERIVATIVES **suzerain** n.
– ORIGIN French.

Suzman E
/suuz-muhn/, Helen (b.1917), South African politician, of Lithuanian-Jewish descent. From 1961 to 1974 she was the sole MP opposed to apartheid.

svelte ● **adj.** slender and elegant.
– ORIGIN Italian *svelto*.

Sven E
/sven/ var. of **SWEYN I**.

Svengali /sven-gah-li/ ● **n.** a person who exercises a controlling influence on another.
– ORIGIN from *Svengali*, a character in George du Maurier's novel *Trilby*.

SW ● **abbrev. 1** south-west. **2** south-western.

swab ● **n. 1** a pad used for cleaning wounds or applying medication. **2** a specimen of something produced from the body, taken with a swab. ● **v.** (**swabs**, **swabbing**, **swabbed**) clean or absorb with a swab.
– ORIGIN Dutch *zwabber*.

swaddle ● **v.** (**swaddles**, **swaddling**, **swaddled**) wrap in garments or cloth.
– ORIGIN from SWATHE[2].

swaddling clothes ● **pl. n.** strips of cloth formerly wrapped round a newborn child to calm it.

swag ● **n. 1** an ornamental garland of flowers, fruit, and greenery. **2** a curtain or drape fastened to hang in a drooping curve. **3** informal money or goods taken by a thief or burglar.
– ORIGIN prob. from Scandinavian.

swagger ● **v.** (**swaggers**, **swaggering**, **swaggered**) walk or behave in a very confident or arrogant manner. ● **n.** a swaggering walk.
– ORIGIN prob. from SWAG.

Swahili /swuh-hee-li, swah-hee-li/ ● **n.** (pl. **Swahili**) a Bantu language widely spoken in

East Africa.
– ORIGIN Arabic, 'coasts'.

swain • n. **1** archaic a country youth. **2** literary a young lover.
– ORIGIN Old Norse, 'lad'.

swallow[1] • v. **1** cause (food, drink, etc.) to pass down the throat. **2** move the throat muscles as if doing this, especially through fear. **3** take in and cause to disappear: *the dark mist swallowed her up.* **4** believe (an untrue or unlikely statement) without question. **5** put up with (unfair treatment). **6** resist expressing: *he swallowed his pride.* • n. an act of swallowing.
– ORIGIN Old English.

swallow[2] • n. a swift-flying songbird with a forked tail.
– ORIGIN Old English.

swallow dive • n. Brit. a dive performed with one's arms outspread until close to the water.

swallowtail • n. **1** a deeply forked tail. **2** a large brightly coloured butterfly with tail-like projections on the hindwings.

swam past of **SWIM**.

swami /swah-mi/ • n. (pl. **swamis**) a male Hindu religious teacher.
– ORIGIN Hindi, 'master, prince'.

swamp • n. a bog or marsh. • v. **1** flood with water. **2** overwhelm with too much of something: *the country was swamped with goods from abroad.*
– DERIVATIVES **swampy** adj.
– ORIGIN prob. from a Germanic word meaning 'sponge' or 'fungus'.

swan • n. a large white waterbird with a long flexible neck, short legs, and webbed feet. • v. (**swans**, **swanning**, **swanned**) Brit. informal go around in a casual or carefree way.
– ORIGIN Old English.

swank informal • v. display one's wealth, knowledge, or achievements in an attempt to impress others. • n. behaviour or talk intended to impress others.
– ORIGIN unknown.

swanky • adj. (**swankier**, **swankiest**) informal **1** stylishly luxurious and expensive. **2** inclined to show off.

Swansea E
a city in South Wales. Welsh name **ABERTAWE**.

swansong • n. the final performance or activity of a person's career.
– ORIGIN suggested by German *Schwanengesang*, referring to a mythical song sung by a dying swan.

swap (also **swop**) • v. (**swaps**, **swapping**, **swapped**) exchange or substitute. • n. an act of exchanging one thing for another.

sward /sword/ • n. an expanse of short grass.
– ORIGIN Old English, 'skin'.

swarf /swahf/ • n. fine chips or filings produced by machining.
– ORIGIN Old English or Old Norse.

swarm • n. **1** a large or dense group of flying insects. **2** a large number of honeybees that leave a hive with a queen in order to establish a new colony. **3** a large group of people or things. • v. **1** move in or form a swarm. **2** (**swarm with**) be crowded or overrun with. **3** (**swarm up**) climb rapidly by gripping with one's hands and feet.
– ORIGIN Old English.

swarthy • adj. (**swarthier**, **swarthiest**) having a dark skin.
– ORIGIN Old English.

swashbuckling • adj. engaging in or full of daring and romantic adventures.
– DERIVATIVES **swashbuckler** n.

swastika /swoss-ti-kuh/ • n. an ancient symbol in the form of an equal-armed cross with each arm continued at a right angle, used (in clockwise form) as the emblem of the German Nazi party.
– ORIGIN Sanskrit, 'well-being'.

swat /*rhymes with* swot/ • v. (**swats**, **swatting**, **swatted**) hit or crush with a sharp blow from a flat object.
– ORIGIN northern English and US form of **SQUAT**.

swatch • n. **1** a piece of fabric used as a sample. **2** a number of fabric samples bound together.
– ORIGIN unknown.

swathe[1] /sway*th*/ (N. Amer. also **swath** /swawth/) • n. (pl. **swathes** or **swaths** /sway*thz*, swawths/) **1** a row or line of grass, corn, etc. as it falls when cut down. **2** a broad strip or area: *vast swathes of countryside.*
– ORIGIN Old English, 'track, trace'.

swathe[2] /sway*th*/ • v. (**swathes**, **swathing**, **swathed**) wrap in several layers of fabric.
– ORIGIN Old English.

sway • v. **1** move slowly and rhythmically backwards and forwards or from side to side. **2** cause (someone) to change their opinion: *he's easily swayed.* • n. **1** a swaying movement. **2** power or influence.
– PHRASES **hold sway** have great power or influence.
– ORIGIN perh. from German *swājen* 'be blown to and fro' or Dutch *zwaaien* 'swing'.

Swaziland E
/swah-zi-land/ a small kingdom in southern Africa, bounded by South Africa and Mozambique; capital, Mbabane.

swear • v. (**swears**, **swearing**, **swore**; past part. **sworn**) **1** promise solemnly or on oath. **2** force to follow a certain course of action: *I am sworn to secrecy.* **3** use offensive or obscene language.
– PHRASES **swear by** informal have great confidence in. **swear in** admit (someone) to a position or job by directing them to take a formal oath.
– ORIGIN Old English.

swear word • n. an offensive or obscene word.

sweat • n. moisture given out through the pores of the skin, especially as a reaction to heat, physical effort, or anxiety. • v. (**sweats**, **sweating**, **sweated** or N. Amer. **sweat**) **1** give off sweat. **2** make a great deal of effort: *I've sweated over this for six months.* **3** be in a state of extreme anxiety: *I let her sweat for a while.* **4** (of a substance) give off moisture. **5** cook (chopped vegetables) slowly in a pan with a small amount of fat.
– PHRASES **break sweat** informal work hard physically. **no sweat** informal no problem.
– ORIGIN Old English.

sweatband • n. a band of absorbent material worn to soak up sweat.

S

sweated labour ● n. hard work done under poor conditions for very low wages.

sweater ● n. a pullover with long sleeves.

sweatpants ● pl. n. loose, warm trousers with an elasticated or drawstring waist.

sweatshirt ● n. a loose knitted cotton sweater.

sweatshop ● n. a factory or workshop employing workers for long hours in poor conditions.

sweaty ● adj. (**sweatier**, **sweatiest**) soaked in or causing sweat.

swede ● n. **1** (**Swede**) a person from Sweden. **2** Brit. a round yellow root vegetable.

Sweden E
a country occupying the eastern part of the Scandinavian peninsula; capital, Stockholm.

Swedish ● n. the Scandinavian language of Sweden. ● adj. relating to Sweden.

sweep ● v. (**sweeps**, **sweeping**, **swept**) **1** clean (an area) by brushing away dirt or litter. **2** move or push with great force. **3** (**sweep away/aside**) remove or abolish swiftly and suddenly. **4** search (an area). **5** affect swiftly and widely: *violence swept the country*. ● n. **1** an act of sweeping. **2** a long, swift, curving movement. **3** a long curved stretch of road, river, etc. **4** the range of something. **5** (also **chimney sweep**) a person whose job is cleaning out the soot from chimneys.
– ORIGIN Old English.

sweeper ● n. **1** a person or device that cleans by sweeping. **2** Soccer a player stationed behind the other defenders, free to defend at any point across the field.

sweeping ● adj. **1** extending or performed in a long, continuous curve. **2** wide in range or effect. **3** (of a statement) too general. ● n. (**sweepings**) dirt or refuse collected by sweeping.

sweepstake ● n. (also **sweepstakes**) a form of gambling in which all the stakes are divided among the winners.

sweet ● adj. **1** having the pleasant taste of sugar or honey. **2** having a pleasant smell. **3** (of air, water, etc.) fresh and pure. **4** working, moving, or done smoothly or easily. **5** delightful: *the sweet life*. **6** pleasant and kind. **7** charming and endearing: *a sweet little cat*. ● n. Brit. **1** a small piece of confectionery made with sugar. **2** a sweet dish forming a course of a meal.
– DERIVATIVES **sweetly** adv.
– ORIGIN Old English.

sweet-and-sour ● adj. cooked with both sugar and a sour substance.

sweetbread ● n. the thymus gland or pancreas of an animal, used for food.

sweetcorn ● n. a variety of maize with kernels that have a high sugar content, eaten as a vegetable.

sweeten ● v. **1** make or become sweet or sweeter. **2** make more agreeable or acceptable.

sweetener ● n. **1** a substance used to sweeten food or drink. **2** informal a bribe.

sweetheart ● n. a person that one is in a romantic relationship with.

sweetie ● n. informal **1** Brit. a sweet. **2** used as a term of affection.

sweetmeat ● n. archaic an item of confectionery or sweet food.

sweetness ● n. the quality of being sweet.
– PHRASES **sweetness and light** good-natured benevolence or harmony.

sweet pea ● n. a climbing plant of the pea family with colourful sweet-smelling flowers.

sweet pepper ● n. a large variety of pepper with a mild or sweet flavour.

sweet potato ● n. the edible tuber of a tropical climbing plant, with pinkish-orange flesh.

sweet-talk ● v. informal persuade to do something by flattery or kind words.

sweet tooth ● n. a great liking for sweet foods.

sweet william ● n. a sweet-smelling plant with clusters of vivid red, pink, or white flowers.

swell ● v. (**swells**, **swelling**, **swelled**, past part. **swollen** or **swelled**) **1** become larger or rounder in size. **2** increase in strength, amount, or volume. ● n. **1** a full or gently rounded form. **2** a gradual increase in sound, amount, or strength. **3** a slow, regular movement of the sea in rolling waves that do not break. ● adj. N. Amer. informal, dated excellent.
– ORIGIN Old English.

swelling ● n. a place on the body that has swollen as a result of illness or an injury.

swelter ● v. (**swelters**, **sweltering**, **sweltered**) be uncomfortably hot.
– ORIGIN Germanic.

swept past and past part. of SWEEP.

swerve ● v. (**swerves**, **swerving**, **swerved**) abruptly go off from a straight course. ● n. an abrupt change of course.
– ORIGIN Old English, 'leave, turn aside'.

Sweyn I E
/swayn/ (also **Sven**) (d.1014; known as **Sweyn Forkbeard**), king of Denmark *c.*985–1014. He invaded England, driving out Ethelred the Unready in 1013. Sweyn then became king of England but died five weeks later.

Swift, E
Jonathan (1667–1745), Irish satirist, poet, and Anglican cleric, author of the satire *Gulliver's Travels*.

swift ● adj. **1** happening quickly or promptly. **2** moving or capable of moving at high speed. ● n. a fast-flying bird with long, slender wings.
– DERIVATIVES **swiftly** adv. **swiftness** n.
– ORIGIN Old English.

swig informal ● v. (**swigs**, **swigging**, **swigged**) drink quickly. ● n. a swift drink.
– ORIGIN unknown.

swill ● v. Brit. **1** rinse out with large amounts of water. **2** (of liquid) swirl round in a container or cavity. ● n. kitchen refuse and waste food mixed with water for feeding to pigs.
– ORIGIN Old English.

swim ● v. (**swims**, **swimming**, **swam**; past part. **swum**) **1** propel oneself through water by moving one's arms and legs. **2** be immersed in or covered with liquid. **3** experience a dizzily confusing feeling. ● n. a period of swimming.
– PHRASES **in the swim** involved in current events.
– DERIVATIVES **swimmer** n.

– ORIGIN Old English.

swimming costume • n. Brit. a woman's one-piece swimsuit.

swimmingly • adv. informal smoothly and satisfactorily.

swimming trunks • pl. n. shorts worn by men for swimming.

swimsuit • n. a woman's one-piece swimming costume.

swimwear • n. clothing worn for swimming.

Swinburne, E
Algernon Charles (1837–1909), English poet and critic. His poetry shows great metrical skill and variety.

swindle • v. (**swindles**, **swindling**, **swindled**) use deception to obtain (money) or deprive (someone) of money or possessions. • n. a scheme designed to obtain money dishonestly.
– DERIVATIVES **swindler** n.
– ORIGIN German *schwindeln* 'tell lies'.

Swindon E
an industrial town in central England, a unitary council formerly in Wiltshire.

swine • n. **1** (pl. **swine**) formal or N. Amer. a pig. **2** (pl. **swine** or **swines**) informal an unpleasant person.
– DERIVATIVES **swinish** adj.
– ORIGIN Old English.

swing • v. (**swings**, **swinging**, **swung**) **1** move back and forth or from side to side while hanging. **2** move by grasping a support and leaping. **3** move in a smooth, curving line. **4** (**swing at**) attempt to hit. **5** change from one opinion, mood, or state of affairs to another. **6** have a decisive influence on (a vote, judgement, etc.). **7** informal succeed in bringing about: *we might be able to swing something*. • n. **1** a seat hanging from ropes or chains, on which someone can sit and swing. **2** an act of swinging. **3** a clear change in public opinion. **4** a style of jazz or dance music with an easy flowing but vigorous rhythm.
– PHRASES **get into the swing of things** informal become used to an activity. **in full swing** at the height of activity.
– ORIGIN Old English, 'to beat, whip'.

swing door • n. a door that can be opened in either direction and swings back when released.

swingeing • adj. esp. Brit. severe or otherwise extreme: *swingeing cuts in public expenditure*.
– ORIGIN Old English, 'shatter'.

swinging • adj. informal lively, exciting, and fashionable.

swipe informal • v. (**swipes**, **swiping**, **swiped**) **1** hit or try to hit with a swinging blow. **2** steal. **3** pass (a swipe card) through an electronic reader. • n. **1** a sweeping blow. **2** a verbal attack.
– ORIGIN perh. from SWEEP.

swipe card • n. a plastic card carrying coded information which is read when the card is slid through an electronic device.

swirl • v. move in a twisting or spiralling pattern. • n. a swirling movement or pattern.
– DERIVATIVES **swirly** adj.
– ORIGIN perh. German or Dutch.

swish • v. move with a hissing or rushing sound. • n. a swishing sound or movement. • adj. Brit. informal impressively smart.

Swiss • adj. relating to Switzerland or its people. • n. (pl. **Swiss**) a person from Switzerland.

Swiss roll • n. Brit. a flat rectangular sponge cake spread with jam or cream and rolled up.

switch • n. **1** a device for making and breaking an electrical connection. **2** a change or exchange. **3** a flexible shoot cut from a tree. • v. **1** change in position, direction, or focus. **2** exchange. **3** (**switch off/on**) turn an electrical device off (or on). **4** (**switch off**) informal cease to pay attention.
– ORIGIN prob. from German.

switchback • n. **1** Brit. a road, railway, etc. with alternate sharp ascents and descents. **2** a roller coaster.

switchblade • n. N. Amer. a flick knife.

switchboard • n. an installation for the manual control of telephone connections.

switched-on • adj. Brit. informal aware of what is going on or what is up to date.

Swithin, St E
(also **Swithun**) (d.862), English bishop of Winchester. Feast day, 15 July. According to tradition, if it rains on St Swithin's Day it will do so for the next forty days.

Switzerland E
a country in central Europe; capital, Berne.

swivel • n. a connecting device between two parts enabling one to revolve without turning the other. • v. (**swivels**, **swivelling**, **swivelled**; US **swivels**, **swiveling**, **swiveled**) turn round, or around a central point.
– ORIGIN Old English, 'move, sweep'.

swizz • n. Brit. informal an instance of being mildly cheated or disappointed.
– ORIGIN prob. from SWINDLE.

swizzle stick • n. a stick used for frothing up or taking the fizz out of drinks.

swollen past part. of SWELL.

swoon • v. faint from extreme emotion. • n. an instance of swooning.
– ORIGIN Old English, 'overcome'.

swoop • v. **1** move rapidly downwards through the air. **2** carry out a sudden raid. • n. an act of swooping.
– PHRASES **at** (or **in**) **one fell swoop** see FELL[4].
– ORIGIN perh. from SWEEP.

swop • v. & n. var. of SWAP.

sword • n. **1** a weapon with a long metal blade and a hilt with a handguard, used for thrusting or striking. **2** (**the sword**) literary military power; violence.
– PHRASES **put to the sword** kill in war.
– ORIGIN Old English.

swordfish • n. a large sea fish with a streamlined body and a sword-like snout.

swordplay • n. fencing with swords or foils.

swordsman • n. a man who fights with a sword.

swordstick • n. a hollow walking stick containing a blade that can be used as a sword.

swore past of SWEAR.

sworn past part. of SWEAR. • adj. **1** given under oath. **2** determined to remain the specified thing: *sworn enemies*.

swot Brit. informal, derog. ● **v.** (**swots**, **swotting**, **swotted**) (also **swot up**) study hard. ● **n.** a person who spends a lot of time studying.
– DERIVATIVES **swotty** adj.
– ORIGIN from **SWEAT**.

swum past part. of **SWIM**.

swung past and past part. of **SWING**.

sybarite /si-buh-ryt/ ● **n.** a person who is very fond of luxury and pleasure.
– DERIVATIVES **sybaritic** adj.
– ORIGIN first referring to a person from Sybaris, an ancient Greek city in Italy.

sycamore ● **n. 1** a European tree of the maple family. **2** N. Amer. a plane tree.
– ORIGIN Greek *sukomoros*.

sycophant /si-kuh-fant/ ● **n.** a person who flatters someone important to try to gain favour with them.
– DERIVATIVES **sycophancy** n. **sycophantic** adj.
– ORIGIN Greek *sukophantēs*.

Sydney E
the capital of New South Wales in SE Australia. It is the country's largest city and chief port.

syllabic /sil-lab-ik/ ● **adj.** relating to or based on syllables.

syllable /sil-luh-b'l/ ● **n.** a unit of pronunciation having one vowel sound and forming all or part of a word (e.g. *butter* has two syllables).
– ORIGIN Greek *sullabē*.

syllabus /sil-luh-buhss/ ● **n.** (pl. **syllabuses** or **syllabi** /sil-luh-by/) the topics in a course of study or teaching.
– ORIGIN Latin.

syllogism /sil-luh-ji-z'm/ ● **n.** a form of reasoning in which a conclusion is drawn from two propositions (e.g. *all dogs are animals; all animals have four legs; therefore all dogs have four legs*).
– ORIGIN Greek *sullogismos*.

sylph /silf/ ● **n. 1** an imaginary spirit of the air. **2** a slender woman or girl.
– ORIGIN Latin *sylphes* (plural).

sylvan ● **adj.** literary having to do with woods; wooded: *a sylvan setting*.
– ORIGIN Latin *silva* 'a wood'.

symbiosis /sim-bi-oh-siss, sim-by-oh-siss/ ● **n.** (pl. **symbioses** /sim-bi-oh-seez, sim-by-oh-seez/) Biol. a situation in which two different organisms live with and are dependent on each other, to the advantage of both.
– DERIVATIVES **symbiotic** /sim-bi-ot-ik, sim-by-ot-ik/ adj.
– ORIGIN Greek *sumbiōsis*.

symbol ● **n. 1** a thing that represents something else: *the limousine was a symbol of his wealth*. **2** a mark or character used as a standard representation of something, e.g. a letter standing for a chemical element.
– ORIGIN Greek *sumbolon* 'mark, token'.

symbolic ● **adj. 1** serving as a symbol. **2** involving the use of symbols or symbolism.
– DERIVATIVES **symbolically** adv.

symbolism ● **n. 1** the use of symbols to represent ideas or qualities. **2** symbolic meaning attached to objects.
– DERIVATIVES **symbolist** n. & adj.

symbolize (also **symbolise**) ● **v.** (**symbolizes**, **symbolizing**, **symbolized**) **1** be a symbol of. **2** represent by means of symbols.

symmetrical ● **adj.** made up of exactly similar parts facing each other or around an axis; showing symmetry.
– DERIVATIVES **symmetric** adj. **symmetrically** adv.

symmetry /sim-mi-tri/ ● **n.** (pl. **symmetries**) **1** the quality of being made up of exactly similar parts facing each other or around an axis. **2** the quality of being similar or equal.
– ORIGIN Latin *symmetria*.

sympathetic ● **adj. 1** feeling or showing sympathy. **2** showing approval of an idea or action. **3** pleasing or likeable. **4** referring to the part of the nervous system supplying the internal organs, blood vessels, and glands.
– DERIVATIVES **sympathetically** adv.

sympathize (also **sympathise**) ● **v.** (**sympathizes**, **sympathizing**, **sympathized**) **1** feel or express sympathy. **2** agree with an opinion.

sympathy ● **n.** (pl. **sympathies**) **1** the feeling of being sorry for someone. **2** understanding between people. **3** support for or approval of something. **4** (**in sympathy**) in keeping: *the extension is in sympathy with the original structure*.
– ORIGIN Greek *sumpatheia*.

symphonic ● **adj.** relating to or having the form or character of a symphony.

symphony ● **n.** (pl. **symphonies**) an elaborate musical composition for full orchestra.
– ORIGIN Greek *sumphōnia*.

symphony orchestra ● **n.** a large classical orchestra, including string, woodwind, brass, and percussion instruments.

symposium /sim-poh-zi-uhm/ ● **n.** (pl. **symposia** /sim-poh-zi-uh/ or **symposiums**) a conference or meeting to discuss a particular academic subject.
– ORIGIN Greek *sumposion*.

symptom ● **n. 1** Med. a change in the body or mind which is the sign of a disease. **2** a sign of an undesirable situation.
– ORIGIN Greek *sumptōma*.

symptomatic ● **adj.** acting as a symptom of something.

syn- ● **prefix** united; acting together: *syndrome*.
– ORIGIN Greek *sun* 'with'.

synagogue /sin-uh-gog/ ● **n.** a building where a Jewish assembly meets for religious worship and instruction.
– ORIGIN Greek *sunagōgē* 'meeting'.

synapse /sy-naps, si-naps/ ● **n.** a gap between two nerve cells, across which impulses are conducted.
– DERIVATIVES **synaptic** adj.
– ORIGIN Greek *sunapsis*.

sync (also **synch**) informal ● **n.** synchronization.
– PHRASES **in** (or **out of**) **sync** working well (or badly) together.

synchromesh ● **n.** a system of gear changing in which the driving and driven gearwheels are made to revolve at the same speed during engagement.
– ORIGIN from *synchronized mesh*.

synchronicity ● **n.** the occurrence of events at the same time, which appear to be related but have no obvious connection.

synchronize (also **synchronise**) ● **v.** (**synchronizes**, **synchronizing**, **synchronized**) cause to happen or operate at the same time or rate.

synchronized swimming ● n. a sport in which teams of swimmers perform coordinated movements in time to music.

synchronous /sing-kruh-nuhss/ ● adj. existing or occurring at the same time.
– ORIGIN Greek *sunkhronos*.

syncline ● n. a land formation in which strata are folded so as to slope up on opposite sides of a ridge.
– ORIGIN from Greek *klinein* 'to lean'.

syncopated /sing-kuh-payt-id/ ● adj. (of music or a rhythm) having the beats or accents altered so that strong beats become weak and vice versa.
– DERIVATIVES **syncopation** n.
– ORIGIN from **SYNCOPE**.

syncope /sing-kuh-pi/ ● n. Med. fainting caused by low blood pressure.
– ORIGIN Greek *sunkopē*.

syncretism /sing-kri-ti-z'm/ ● n. the combining of different religions, cultures, or schools of thought.
– DERIVATIVES **syncretic** adj.
– ORIGIN Greek *sunkretizein* 'unite against a third party'.

syndicate ● n. /sin-di-kuht/ a group of individuals or organizations combined to promote a common interest. ● v. /sin-di-kayt/ (**syndicates**, **syndicating**, **syndicated**) **1** control or manage by a syndicate. **2** publish or broadcast in a number of media at the same time.
– DERIVATIVES **syndication** n.

syndrome ● n. **1** a group of symptoms which consistently occur together. **2** a combination of opinions, emotions, or behaviour that is typical of a particular group of people.
– ORIGIN Greek *sundromē*.

synecdoche /si-nek-duh-ki/ ● n. a figure of speech in which a part is made to represent the whole or vice versa, as in *England lost by six wickets* (meaning 'the English cricket team').
– ORIGIN Greek *sunekdokhē*.

synergy /sin-er-ji/ (also **synergism**) ● n. cooperation of two or more things to produce a combined effect greater than the sum of their separate effects.
– ORIGIN Greek *sunergos* 'working together'.

Synge E
/sing/, J. M. (1871–1909; full name *Edmund John Millington Synge*), Irish dramatist, best known for the comedy *The Playboy of the Western World*.

synod /si-nod/ ● n. an official meeting of the ministers and other members of a Christian Church.
– ORIGIN Greek *sunodos* 'meeting'.

synonym /sin-uh-nim/ ● n. a word or phrase that means the same as another word or phrase in the same language.
– ORIGIN Greek *sunōnumon*.

synonymous /si-non-i-muhss/ ● adj. **1** (of a word or phrase) having the same meaning as another word or phrase in the same language. **2** closely associated with something: *his name was synonymous with victory*.

synopsis /si-nop-siss/ ● n. (pl. **synopses** /si-nop-seez/) a brief summary or general survey.
– ORIGIN Greek.

synoptic ● adj. **1** having to do with a synopsis. **2** (**Synoptic**) referring to the Gospels of Matthew, Mark, and Luke, which describe events from a similar point of view.

synovial /sy-noh-vi-uhl/ ● adj. relating to joints of the body enclosed in a flexible membrane containing a lubricating fluid.
– ORIGIN Latin *synovia*.

syntax ● n. **1** the arrangement of words and phrases to create sentences. **2** a set of rules for the formation of sentences.
– DERIVATIVES **syntactic** adj. **syntactical** adj.
– ORIGIN Greek *suntaxis*.

synthesis /sin-thuh-siss/ ● n. (pl. **syntheses** /sin-thuh-seez/) **1** the combination of parts to form a connected whole. **2** the production of chemical compounds by reaction from simpler materials.
– ORIGIN Greek *sunthesis*.

synthesize /sin-thuh-syz/ (also **synthesise**) ● v. (**synthesizes**, **synthesizing**, **synthesized**) **1** make by chemical synthesis. **2** combine into an organized whole. **3** produce (sound) electronically.

synthesizer ● n. an electronic musical instrument producing sounds by generating and combining signals of different frequencies.

synthetic /sin-thet-ik/ ● adj. **1** made by chemical synthesis, especially to imitate a natural product: *synthetic rubber*. **2** not genuine. ● n. a synthetic textile.
– DERIVATIVES **synthetically** adv.

syphilis /sif-fi-liss/ ● n. a serious sexually transmitted disease spread by bacteria.
– DERIVATIVES **syphilitic** adj. & n.
– ORIGIN Latin.

syphon ● n. & v. var. of **SIPHON**.

Syracuse E
/sy-ruh-kyooz/ a port in Sicily, a flourishing centre of Greek culture in the 5th and 4th centuries BC.

Syria E
/si-ri-uh/ a country in the Middle East, on the Mediterranean Sea; capital, Damascus.
– DERIVATIVES **Syrian** adj. & n.

syringe /si-rinj/ ● n. a tube with a nozzle and piston for sucking in and forcing out liquid in a thin stream, often one fitted with a hollow needle for injecting drugs or withdrawing bodily fluids. ● v. (**syringes**, **syringing**, **syringed**) spray liquid into or over with a syringe.
– ORIGIN Latin *syringa*.

syrup (US also **sirup**) ● n. **1** a thick sweet liquid made by dissolving sugar in boiling water. **2** a thick sweet liquid containing medicine or used as a drink: *cough syrup*.
– ORIGIN Arabic, 'beverage'.

syrupy (US also **sirupy**) ● adj. **1** thick or sweet, like syrup. **2** excessively sentimental.

system ● n. **1** a set of things working together as a mechanism or network. **2** a person's body. **3** Computing a group of related hardware units or programs or both. **4** an organized scheme or method. **5** orderliness. **6** the existing political or social order.
– ORIGIN Greek *sustēma*.

systematic ● adj. done or acting according to a system.

– DERIVATIVES **systematically** adv.

systematize (also **systematise**) ● v. (**systematizes**, **systematizing**, **systematized**) arrange according to an organized system.

systemic /si-stem-ik, si-steem-ik/ ● adj. relating to a system as a whole.

systems analyst ● n. a person who studies a complex process or operation in order to improve its efficiency.

systole /siss-tuh-li/ ● n. the phase of the heartbeat when the heart muscle contracts and pumps blood into the arteries. Often contrasted with **DIASTOLE**.
– DERIVATIVES **systolic** /si-stol-lik/ adj.
– ORIGIN Greek *sustolē*.

Szechuan E
/sech-wahn/ (also **Szechwan**) var. of **SICHUAN**.

T (also **t**) ● n. (pl. **Ts** or **T's**) the twentieth letter of the alphabet.
– PHRASES **to a T** informal to perfection.

t ● abbrev. ton(s).

TA ● abbrev. (in the UK) Territorial Army.

ta ● exclam. Brit. informal thank you.

tab[1] ● n. **1** a small flap or strip of material attached to something. **2** Brit. Mil. a collar marking showing an officer of high rank. **3** informal, esp. N. Amer. a restaurant bill. **4** N. Amer. a ring pull.
– PHRASES **keep tabs on** informal monitor the activities of.
– ORIGIN perh. from **TAG**[1].

tab[2] ● n. = **TABULATOR**. ● v. (**tabs**, **tabbing**, **tabbed**) = **TABULATE**.

tab[3] ● n. informal a tablet, especially one containing an illicit drug.

tabard /tab-erd, tab-ard/ ● n. a sleeveless jacket consisting only of front and back pieces with a hole for the head.
– ORIGIN Old French *tabart*.

tabby ● n. (pl. **tabbies**) a grey or brownish cat with dark stripes.
– ORIGIN French *tabis* 'striped silk taffeta'.

tabernacle /tab-er-na-k'l/ ● n. **1** (in the Bible) a tent used by the Israelites to house the Ark of the Covenant during the Exodus. **2** a meeting place for Mormon or Nonconformist worship.
– ORIGIN Latin *tabernaculum* 'tent'.

table ● n. **1** a piece of furniture with a flat top supported by legs, for eating, writing, or working at. **2** a set of facts or figures displayed in rows or columns. **3** (**tables**) multiplication tables. ● v. (**tables**, **tabling**, **tabled**) Brit. present formally for discussion at a meeting.
– PHRASES **on the table** available for discussion. **turn the tables** reverse a situation to one's own advantage.
– ORIGIN Latin *tabula* 'tablet, list'.

tableau /tab-loh/ ● n. (pl. **tableaux** /tab-lohz/) a group of models or motionless figures representing a scene.
– ORIGIN French, 'picture'.

tablecloth ● n. a cloth spread over a table.

table d'hôte /tah-bluh **doht**/ ● n. a restaurant menu or meal offered at a fixed price and with limited choices.
– ORIGIN French, 'host's table'.

tableland ● n. a broad, high, level region; a plateau.

table manners ● pl. n. behaviour that is conventionally required while eating at a table.

Table Mountain E
a flat-topped mountain near the south-west tip of South Africa, overlooking Cape Town.

tablespoon ● n. **1** a large spoon for serving food. **2** the amount held by such a spoon, in the UK considered to be 15 millilitres.

tablet ● n. **1** a slab of stone, clay, or wood on which an inscription is written. **2** a pill in the shape of a disc or cylinder.
– ORIGIN Old French *tablete*.

table tennis ● n. a game played with small bats and a small, hollow ball hit across a table divided by a net.

tableware ● n. crockery, cutlery, and glassware used for serving and eating meals at a table.

table wine ● n. wine of moderate quality considered suitable for drinking with a meal.

tabloid ● n. a newspaper having pages half the size of those of a broadsheet, written in a popular style.
– ORIGIN first referring to a tablet of medicine: the current sense reflects the idea of information being presented in a form that is easily digested.

taboo ● n. (pl. **taboos**) a social or religious custom placing a ban or restriction on a particular thing or person. ● adj. banned or restricted by social custom: *sex was a taboo subject*.
– ORIGIN Tongan (the language of Tonga), 'forbidden'.

tabular /tab-yuu-ler/ ● adj. (of data) made up of or presented in columns or tables.
– ORIGIN Latin *tabularis*.

tabulate /tab-yuu-layt/ ● v. (**tabulates**, **tabulating**, **tabulated**) arrange (data) in the form of columns or tables.
– DERIVATIVES **tabulation** n.

tabulator ● n. a facility in a word-processing program, or a device on a typewriter, for advancing to set positions in order to produce columns or tables.

tachograph ● n. a tachometer used in commercial road vehicles to provide a record of

s
t

engine speeds.
– ORIGIN Greek *takhos* 'speed'.

tachometer /ta-kom-i-ter/ ● **n.** an instrument which measures the working speed of an engine.

tachycardia /ta-ki-kar-di-uh/ ● **n.** an abnormally rapid heart rate.
– ORIGIN from Greek *takhus* 'swift' + *kardia* 'heart'.

tacit /ta-sit/ ● **adj.** understood or meant without being stated: *tacit agreement.*
– DERIVATIVES **tacitly** adv.
– ORIGIN Latin *tacitus* 'silent'.

taciturn /ta-si-tern/ ● **adj.** saying little.
– DERIVATIVES **taciturnity** n.
– ORIGIN Latin *taciturnus.*

Tacitus E
/ta-si-tuhss/ (*c.*56–*c.*120 AD; full name *Publius Cornelius Tacitus*), Roman historian, author of major works on the history of the Roman Empire.

tack[1] ● **n. 1** a small broad-headed nail. **2** N. Amer. a drawing pin. **3** a long stitch used to fasten fabrics together temporarily. **4** a course of action. **5** Sailing an act of tacking. ● **v. 1** fasten or fix with tacks. **2 (tack on)** add (something) to something already existing. **3** change the direction of a sailing boat so that the wind blows into the sails from the opposite side.
– ORIGIN prob. from Old French *tache* 'clasp, large nail'.

tack[2] ● **n.** equipment used in horse riding.
– ORIGIN from **TACKLE**.

tack[3] ● **n.** informal cheap, shoddy, or tasteless material.
– ORIGIN from **TACKY**[2].

tackle ● **n. 1** the equipment needed for a task or sport. **2** a mechanism consisting of ropes, pulley blocks, and hooks for lifting heavy objects. **3** (in sport) an act of tackling an opponent. **4** Brit. vulgar a man's genitals. ● **v. (tackles, tackling, tackled) 1** make determined efforts to deal with (a difficult task). **2** begin to talk to (someone) about a difficult issue. **3** (in soccer, hockey, rugby, etc.) prevent (an opponent in possession of the ball) from moving past with the ball.
– DERIVATIVES **tackler** n.
– ORIGIN prob. from German *takel*.

tacky[1] ● **adj. (tackier, tackiest)** (of glue, paint, etc.) slightly sticky because not fully dry.

tacky[2] ● **adj. (tackier, tackiest)** informal showing poor taste and quality.
– ORIGIN unknown.

taco /tak-oh/ ● **n.** (pl. **tacos**) a Mexican dish consisting of a folded tortilla filled with spicy meat or beans.
– ORIGIN Spanish, 'plug, wad'.

tact ● **n.** sensitivity and skill in dealing with others or with difficult issues.
– ORIGIN Latin *tactus* 'touch, sense of touch'.

tactful ● **adj.** having or showing tact.
– DERIVATIVES **tactfully** adv.

tactic ● **n. 1** an action or plan that is intended to achieve something. **2 (tactics)** the art of directing and organizing the movement of armed forces and equipment during a war. Often contrasted with **STRATEGY**.
– DERIVATIVES **tactician** n.
– ORIGIN from Greek *taktikē tekhnē* 'art of tactics'.

tactical ● **adj. 1** done or planned to gain a specific end. **2** (of bombing or weapons) done or for use in immediate support of military or naval operations. Often contrasted with **STRATEGIC**. **3** (of voting) aimed at preventing the strongest candidate from winning by supporting the next strongest, without regard to one's true political preference.
– DERIVATIVES **tactically** adv.

tactile ● **adj. 1** having to do with the sense of touch. **2** liking to touch others in a friendly way.
– ORIGIN Latin *tactilis.*

tactless ● **adj.** thoughtless and insensitive.
– DERIVATIVES **tactlessly** adv. **tactlessness** n.

tad informal ● **adv. (a tad)** to a small extent. ● **n.** a small amount.
– ORIGIN perh. from **TADPOLE**.

tadpole ● **n.** the larva of an amphibian such as a frog or toad, at the stage when it lives in water and has gills and a tail.
– ORIGIN from an Old English word meaning 'toad' + **POLL**.

Tadzhikistan E
var. of **TAJIKISTAN**.

tae kwon do /ty kwon **doh**/ ● **n.** a modern Korean martial art similar to karate.
– ORIGIN Korean (the language of Korea), 'art of hand and foot fighting'.

taffeta /taf-fi-tuh/ ● **n.** a fine shiny silk or similar synthetic fabric.
– ORIGIN Latin.

taffrail ● **n.** a rail round a ship's stern.
– ORIGIN Dutch *tafereel.*

Taffy (also **Taff**) ● **n.** (pl. **Taffies**) Brit. informal, usu. offens. a Welshman.
– ORIGIN representing a supposed Welsh pronunciation of the man's name *Davy* or *David* (Welsh *Dafydd*).

Taft E
/taft/, William Howard (1857–1930), American Republican statesman, 27th President of the US 1909–13.

tag[1] ● **n. 1** a label identifying something or giving information about it. **2** an electronic device attached to someone to monitor their movements. **3** a nickname or description by which someone or something is widely known. **4** a frequently repeated quotation or phrase. **5** a metal or plastic point at the end of a shoelace. ● **v. (tags, tagging, tagged) 1** attach a tag to. **2 (tag on/to)** add to as an afterthought. **3 (tag along/on)** accompany someone without being invited.
– ORIGIN unknown.

tag[2] ● **n.** a children's game in which one chases the rest, and anyone who is caught then becomes the person doing the chasing.
– ORIGIN perh. from **TIG**.

tagliatelle /tal-yuh-tel-li/ ● **pl. n.** pasta in narrow ribbons.
– ORIGIN Italian.

Tagore E
/tuh-gor/, Rabindranath (1861–1941), Indian writer and philosopher. He wrote poetry, plays, novels, and short stories, and pioneered the use of colloquial Bengali in literature.

Tagus E
/tay-guhss/ a river in SW Europe, the longest river of the Iberian peninsula, which rises in eastern Spain and flows over 1,000 km (625 miles) into Portugal, reaching the Atlantic near Lisbon.

tag wrestling • n. a form of wrestling involving pairs of wrestlers who fight as a team, each taking turns in the ring.

Tahiti E
/tuh-**hee**-ti/ an island in the South Pacific, one of the Society Islands; capital, Papeete.

t'ai chi ch'uan /ty chee **chwahn**/ (also **t'ai chi**) • n. a Chinese martial art and system of callisthenics, consisting of sequences of very slow controlled movements.
– ORIGIN Chinese, 'great ultimate boxing'.

tail • n. **1** the part at the rear of an animal, that sticks out from the rest of the body. **2** something resembling an animal's tail. **3** the rear part of an aircraft, with the tailplane and rudder. **4** the final, more distant, or weaker part: *the tail of a hurricane.* **5** (**tails**) the side of a coin without the image of a head on it. **6** (**tails**) informal a tailcoat. **7** informal a person secretly following another to observe their movements. • v. **1** informal secretly follow and observe. **2** (**tail off/away**) gradually become smaller or weaker. **3** (**tail back**) Brit. (of traffic) become congested and form a tailback.
– PHRASES **on someone's tail** informal following someone closely. **with one's tail between one's legs** informal dejected or humiliated.
– ORIGIN Old English.

tailback • n. Brit. a long queue of traffic extending back from a busy junction or other obstruction.

tailcoat • n. Brit. a man's formal morning or evening coat, with a long skirt divided at the back into tails and cut away in front.

tail end • n. the last part of something.

tail fin • n. **1** Zool. a fin at the rear of a fish's body. **2** a projecting vertical surface on the tail of an aircraft, providing stability.

tailgate • n. **1** a hinged flap giving access to the back of a truck. **2** the door at the back of an estate or hatchback car.

tailor • n. a person whose occupation is making men's clothing for individual customers. • v. **1** make (clothes) to fit individual customers. **2** make or adapt for a particular purpose or person.
– ORIGIN Old French *taillour* 'cutter'.

tailored • adj. (of clothes) smart, fitted, and well cut.

tailoring • n. **1** the activity or trade of a tailor. **2** the style or cut of a garment or garments.

tailor-made • adj. made or adapted for a particular purpose or person.

tailpiece • n. a part added to the end of a piece of writing.

tailplane • n. Brit. a horizontal aerofoil at the tail of an aircraft.

tailspin • n. a spin by an aircraft.

tailwind • n. a wind blowing in the direction of travel of a vehicle or aircraft.

Tainan E
/ty-**nahn**/ a city on the SW coast of Taiwan. It was the capital of Taiwan 1684–1885.

taint • n. a trace of an undesirable quality or substance. • v. **1** make impure. **2** affect with an undesirable quality: *his reputation was tainted by scandal.*
– ORIGIN Old French *teint* 'tinged'.

Taipei E
/ty-**pay**/ the capital of Taiwan.

Taiwan E
/ty-**wahn**/ an island country off the SE coast of China; capital, Taipei. Official name **Republic of China**. Former name **Formosa**.
– DERIVATIVES **Taiwanese** /ty-wuh-**neez**/ adj. & n.

Tajikistan E
/tuh-jee-ki-**stahn**, tuh-jee-ki-**stan**/ (also **Tadzhikistan**) a republic in central Asia, north of Afghanistan; capital, Dushanbe.

Taj Mahal E
/tahj muh-**hahl**/ a marble mausoleum at Agra in northern India, built by the emperor Shah Jahan (1592–1666) in memory of his favourite wife, completed *c.*1649.

take • v. (**takes, taking, took**; past part. **taken**) **1** reach for and hold. **2** occupy (a place or position). **3** gain possession of by force. **4** carry or bring with one. **5** remove from a place. **6** subtract. **7** consume as food, drink, medicine, or drugs. **8** bring into a specified state: *the invasion took Europe to the brink of war.* **9** experience or be affected by: *the lad took a savage beating.* **10** use as a route or a means of transport. **11** accept or receive. **12** require or use up. **13** hold: *the hotel takes just 20 guests.* **14** act on (an opportunity). **15** see or deal with in a specified way: *he took it as an insult.* **16** tolerate: *I can't take it any more.* **17** undertake or perform (an action or task). **18** be taught or examined in (a subject). • n. **1** a sequence of sound or vision photographed or recorded continuously. **2** a particular version of or approach to something: *his whimsical take on life.* **3** an amount gained from one source or in one session.
– PHRASES **take after** resemble (a parent or ancestor). **take as read** Brit. assume. **take back** retract (a statement). **take in 1** cheat or deceive. **2** make (a garment) tighter by altering its seams. **3** cover, understand, or absorb. **take in hand 1** undertake to control or reform (someone). **2** start dealing with (a task). **take it on one** (or **oneself**) **to do** decide to do without asking for permission or advice. **take it out of** exhaust the strength of. **take off 1** become airborne. **2** remove (clothing). **3** mimic (someone). **4** depart hastily. **take on 1** engage (an employee). **2** undertake (a task). **3** acquire (a particular meaning or quality). **take something out on** relieve frustration or anger by mistreating (someone). **take over** assume control of or responsibility for. **take one's time** not hurry. **take to 1** fall into the habit of. **2** form a liking or develop an ability for. **3** go to (a place) to escape danger. **take up 1** become interested in (a pursuit). **2** occupy (time, space, or attention). **3** pursue (a matter) further. **take up on** accept an offer or challenge from. **take up with** begin to associate with.
– ORIGIN Old Norse.

takeaway • n. Brit. **1** a restaurant or shop sell-

t

ing cooked food to be eaten elsewhere. **2** a meal of such food.

take-home pay • **n.** the pay received by an employee after the tax and insurance have been taken out.

take-off • **n. 1** the action of becoming airborne. **2** an act of mimicking someone or something.

takeout • **n.** N. Amer. a takeaway.

takeover • **n.** an act of taking control of something such as a company from someone else.

taking • **n.** (**takings**) the amount of money earned by a business from the sale of goods or services.
– PHRASES **for the taking** available to take advantage of.

Talbot E
/tawl-buht/, (William Henry) Fox (1800–77), English pioneer of photography. He produced the first photograph on paper in 1835 and five years later invented a process for producing a negative from which multiple positive prints could be made.

talc • **n. 1** talcum powder. **2** a soft mineral that is a form of magnesium silicate.

talcum powder • **n.** the mineral talc in powdered form used on the skin to make it feel smooth and dry.
– ORIGIN Latin.

tale • **n. 1** a story. **2** a lie.
– ORIGIN Old English.

talent • **n. 1** natural ability or skill. **2** people possessing such ability or skill. **3** informal people seen in terms of their sexual attractiveness or availability. **4** an ancient weight and unit of currency.
– DERIVATIVES **talented** adj. **talentless** adj.
– ORIGIN Greek *talanton* 'weight, sum of money': sense 1 derives from the parable of the talents (Gospel of Matthew, chapter 25).

talent scout • **n.** a person whose job is searching for talented performers.

Taliban E
/tal-i-ban/ a fundamentalist Muslim movement whose militia took control of much of Afghanistan from early 1995, and in 1996 set up an Islamic state.

talisman /tal-iz-muhn/ • **n.** (pl. **talismans**) an object thought to have magic powers and to bring good luck.
– ORIGIN Arabic.

talk • **v. 1** speak in order to give information or express ideas or feelings. **2** have the power of speech. **3** (**talk over/through**) discuss (something) thoroughly. **4** (**talk back**) reply disrespectfully. **5** (**talk down to**) speak to (someone) in a way that suggests one feels superior to them. **6** (**talk round**) convince (someone) to adopt a particular point of view. **7** (**talk into/out of**) persuade or dissuade (someone) to or from. **8** reveal secret information. • **n. 1** conversation. **2** an address or lecture. **3** (**talks**) formal discussions. **4** rumour or speculation.
– PHRASES **now you're talking** informal expressing enthusiastic agreement or approval.
– ORIGIN from TALE or TELL[1].

talkative • **adj.** fond of talking.

talking point • **n.** a topic that provokes discussion or argument.

talking-to • **n.** informal a sharp reprimand.

talk show • **n.** a chat show.

tall • **adj. 1** of great or more than average height. **2** measuring a specified distance from top to bottom. **3** difficult to believe and unlikely to be true: *a tall story.*
– PHRASES **a tall order** an unreasonable or difficult demand.
– ORIGIN prob. from Old English, 'swift, prompt'.

tallboy • **n.** Brit. a tall chest of drawers in two sections, one standing on the other.

Talleyrand E
/tal-li-rand/, Charles Maurice de (1754–1838; full surname *Talleyrand-Périgord*), French statesman. He became head of the new government after the fall of Napoleon (1814) and recalled Louis XVIII to the throne.

Tallinn E
/tal-lin/ the capital of Estonia.

Tallis E
/tal-liss/, Thomas (*c.*1505–85), English composer, noted for his church music.

tallow /tal-loh/ • **n.** a hard substance made from animal fat, used in making candles and soap.
– ORIGIN perh. from German.

tall ship • **n.** a sailing ship with a high mast or masts.

tally • **n.** (pl. **tallies**) **1** a current score or amount. **2** a record of a score or amount. **3** (also **tally stick**) hist. a piece of wood scored across with notches for the items of an account. • **v.** (**tallies, tallying, tallied**) **1** agree or correspond. **2** calculate the total number of.
– ORIGIN Old French *tallie.*

tally-ho • **exclam.** a huntsman's cry to the hounds on sighting a fox.
– ORIGIN prob. from French *taïaut.*

Talmud /tal-muud/ • **n.** a collection of ancient writings on Jewish civil and ceremonial law and legend.
– DERIVATIVES **Talmudic** adj.
– ORIGIN Hebrew, 'instruction'.

talon • **n.** a claw of a bird of prey.
– ORIGIN Old French, 'heel'.

talus /tay-luhss/ • **n.** (pl. **tali** /tay-ly/) the bone in the ankle that forms a movable joint with the shin bone.
– ORIGIN Latin, 'ankle, heel'.

tamarind /tam-uh-rind/ • **n.** sticky brown acidic pulp from the pod of a tropical African tree, used in Asian cookery.
– ORIGIN Arabic, 'Indian date'.

tamarisk /tam-uh-risk/ • **n.** a shrub or small tree with tiny scale-like leaves on slender branches.
– ORIGIN Latin *tamariscus.*

Tambo E
/tam-boh/, Oliver (1917–93), South African politician. He was president of the African National Congress 1977–91, when he resigned in favour of Nelson Mandela who had recently been released from prison.

tambour /tam-boor/ • **n.** hist. a small drum.
– ORIGIN French, 'drum'.

tambourine /tam-buh-reen/ • **n.** a percussion instrument like a shallow drum with metal discs around the edge, played by being

shaken or hit with the hand.
– ORIGIN French *tambourin* 'small tambour'.

tame ● adj. **1** (of an animal) not dangerous or frightened of people. **2** not exciting, adventurous, or controversial. **3** informal (of a person) willing to cooperate. ● v. (**tames**, **taming**, **tamed**) **1** make (an animal) tame. **2** make less powerful and easier to control.
– DERIVATIVES **tamely** adv. **tamer** n.
– ORIGIN Old English.

Tamerlane E
/tam-er-layn/ (also **Tamburlaine** /tam-ber-layn/) (1336–1405), Mongol ruler of Samarkand 1369–1405. He conquered Persia, northern India, and Syria and was the ancestor of the Mogul dynasty in India.

Tamil /tam-il/ ● n. **1** a member of a people living in parts of South India and Sri Lanka. **2** the language of the Tamils.
– ORIGIN Tamil.

Tamil Nadu E
/tam-il nah-doo/ a state in the extreme south-east of India; capital, Madras (Chennai). Former name (until 1968) **MADRAS**.

Tamil Tigers E
a Sri Lankan guerrilla organization that seeks the establishment of an independent state (Eelam) in the north-east of the country for the Tamil community.

tam-o'-shanter /tam-uh-shan-ter/ ● n. a round Scottish cap with a bobble in the centre.
– ORIGIN named after the hero of Robert Burns's poem *Tam o' Shanter*.

tamp ● v. firmly ram or pack (a substance) down or into something.
– ORIGIN prob. from French *tampon* 'tampon, plug'.

tamper ● v. (**tampers**, **tampering**, **tampered**) (**tamper with**) interfere with (something) without permission or so as to cause damage.
– ORIGIN from **TEMPER**.

tampon ● n. a plug of soft material put into the vagina to absorb menstrual blood.
– ORIGIN French.

tan[1] ● n. **1** a yellowish-brown colour. **2** a golden-brown shade of skin developed by pale-skinned people after being in the sun. ● v. (**tans**, **tanning**, **tanned**) **1** become golden-brown from being in the sun. **2** convert (animal skin) into leather.
– ORIGIN Old English.

tan[2] ● abbrev. tangent.

tandem ● n. a bicycle with seats and pedals for two riders, one behind the other.
– PHRASES **in tandem 1** alongside each other. **2** one behind another.
– ORIGIN Latin, 'at length'.

tandoor /tan-door, tan-door/ ● n. a clay oven of a type used originally in northern India and Pakistan.
– ORIGIN Arabic.

tandoori /tan-door-i/ ● adj. (of Indian food) cooked in a tandoor.

tang ● n. **1** a strong taste, flavour, or smell. **2** the projection on the blade of a tool by which the blade is held firmly in the handle.
– ORIGIN Old Norse.

Tanganyika E
/tang-guh-nyee-kuh/ see **TANZANIA**.

Tanganyika, Lake E
/tang-guh-nyee-kuh/ a lake in East Africa, in the Great Rift Valley and forming most of the border of Zaire (Democratic Republic of Congo) with Tanzania and Burundi. It is the longest freshwater lake in the world.

tangent /tan-juhnt/ ● n. **1** a straight line or plane that touches a curve or curved surface at a point, but if extended does not cross it at that point. **2** Math. the ratio of the sides (other than the hypotenuse) opposite and adjacent to an angle in a right-angled triangle. **3** a completely different line of thought or action: *her mind went off at a tangent*.
– ORIGIN Latin *tangere* 'to touch'.

tangential /tan-jen-sh'l/ ● adj. **1** relating to or along a tangent. **2** only slightly connected or relevant.
– DERIVATIVES **tangentially** adv.

tangerine ● n. **1** a small citrus fruit with a loose skin. **2** a deep orange-red colour.
– ORIGIN from *Tanger*, the former name of **TANGIER**.

tangible /tan-ji-b'l/ ● adj. **1** able to be perceived by touch. **2** definite or real: *we need tangible results*.
– DERIVATIVES **tangibility** n. **tangibly** adv.
– ORIGIN Latin *tangibilis*.

Tangier E
/tan-jeer/ a seaport on the northern coast of Morocco, on the Strait of Gibraltar.

tangle ● v. (**tangles**, **tangling**, **tangled**) **1** twist (strands) together into a confused mass. **2** (**tangle with**) informal become involved in a conflict with. ● n. **1** a confused mass of something twisted together. **2** a muddle.
– ORIGIN prob. Scandinavian.

tango ● n. (pl. **tangos**) a Latin American ballroom dance with marked rhythms and postures and abrupt pauses. ● v. (**tangoes**, **tangoing**, **tangoed**) dance the tango.
– ORIGIN Latin American Spanish.

tangy ● adj. (**tangier**, **tangiest**) having a strong, sharp flavour or smell.

tank ● n. **1** a large container or storage chamber for liquid or gas. **2** the container holding the fuel supply in a motor vehicle. **3** a container with clear sides in which to keep fish. **4** a heavy armoured fighting vehicle carrying guns and moving on a continuous metal track. ● v. (**be/get tanked up**) informal drink heavily or become drunk.
– ORIGIN perh. from a word in an Indian language meaning 'underground cistern'.

tankard ● n. a tall beer mug with a handle and sometimes a hinged lid.
– ORIGIN perh. from Dutch *tanckaert*.

tank engine ● n. a steam locomotive carrying fuel and water holders in its own frame, not in a separate wagon.

tanker ● n. a ship, road vehicle, or aircraft for carrying liquids in bulk.

tank top ● n. a close-fitting sleeveless top worn over a shirt or blouse.

tannery ● n. (pl. **tanneries**) a place where animal hides are tanned.

tannic acid • n. = TANNIN.

tannin • n. a bitter-tasting substance present in tea, some barks, grapes, etc.
– DERIVATIVES **tannic** adj.
– ORIGIN French *tanin*.

tannoy • n. Brit. trademark a type of public address system.
– ORIGIN from *tantalum alloy*, a substance used in the system.

tantalize (also **tantalise**) • v. (**tantalizes, tantalizing, tantalized**) tease (someone) with the sight or promise of something that they cannot have.
– ORIGIN from *Tantalus* in Greek mythology, who was punished by being provided with fruit and water which moved away when he reached for them.

tantalum /tan-tuh-luhm/ • n. a hard silver-grey metallic chemical element.
– ORIGIN from *Tantalus* (see TANTALIZE).

tantamount • adj. (**tantamount to**) equivalent in seriousness to.
– ORIGIN from Italian *tanto montare* 'amount to as much'.

tantra /tan-truh/ • n. a Hindu or Buddhist text dealing with mystical or magical practices.
– DERIVATIVES **tantric** adj.
– ORIGIN Sanskrit, 'loom, doctrine'.

tantrum • n. an uncontrolled outburst of anger and frustration.
– ORIGIN unknown.

Tanzania E
/tan-zuh-neer/ a country in East Africa consisting of a mainland area (the former state of Tanganyika) and the island of Zanzibar; capital, Dodoma.
– DERIVATIVES **Tanzanian** adj. & n.

Taoiseach /tee-shuhkh/ • n. the Prime Minister of the Irish Republic.
– ORIGIN Irish, 'chief, leader'.

Taoism /tow-i-z'm/ • n. a Chinese philosophy based on the Tao, or fundamental principle underlying the universe, incorporating the principles of yin and yang and emphasizing humility and religious piety.
– DERIVATIVES **Taoist** n. & adj.
– ORIGIN Chinese, 'the right way'.

tap[1] • n. **1** a device by which a flow of liquid or gas from a pipe or container can be controlled. **2** a device connected to a telephone for listening secretly to conversations. **3** an instrument for cutting a threaded hole in a material. • v. (**taps, tapping, tapped**) **1** draw liquid through the tap or spout of (a cask, barrel, etc.). **2** draw sap from (a tree) by cutting into it. **3** take some of (a supply). **4** connect a device to (a telephone) so that conversations can be listened to secretly. **5** cut a thread in (something) to accept a screw.
– PHRASES **on tap** informal freely available whenever needed.
– ORIGIN Old English, 'stopper for a cask'.

tap[2] • v. (**taps, tapping, tapped**) **1** strike with a quick light blow or blows. **2** strike lightly and repeatedly against something else. • n. **1** a quick light blow. **2** a piece of metal attached to the toe and heel of a tap dancer's shoe.
– ORIGIN Old French *taper*.

tapas /tap-uhss/ • pl. n. small Spanish savoury dishes served with drinks at a bar.
– ORIGIN Spanish, 'lid' (because the dishes were served on a dish balanced on the glass of a drink).

tap dance • n. a dance performed wearing shoes fitted with metal taps, characterized by rhythmical tapping of the toes and heels.
– DERIVATIVES **tap dancer** n. **tap-dancing** n.

tape • n. **1** light, flexible material in a narrow strip, used to hold, fasten, or mark off something. **2** (also **adhesive tape**) a strip of paper or plastic coated with a sticky substance, used to stick things together. **3** long, narrow material with magnetic properties, used for recording sound, pictures, or computer data. **4** a cassette or reel containing magnetic tape. • v. (**tapes, taping, taped**) **1** record (sound or pictures) on tape. **2** fasten, attach, or mark off with tape.
– ORIGIN Old English.

tape deck • n. a piece of equipment for playing audio tapes, as part of a stereo system.

tape measure • n. a strip of tape marked for measuring the length of something.

taper • v. (**tapers, tapering, tapered**) **1** reduce in thickness towards one end. **2** (**taper off**) gradually lessen. • n. a slender candle.
– ORIGIN Old English.

tape recorder • n. a device for recording sounds on magnetic tape and then reproducing them.
– DERIVATIVES **tape recording** n.

tapestry • n. (pl. **tapestries**) a piece of thick fabric with designs woven or embroidered on it.
– ORIGIN Old French *tapisserie*.

tapeworm • n. a flatworm with a long ribbon-like body, the adult of which lives as a parasite in the intestines.

tapioca /ta-pi-oh-kuh/ • n. a starchy substance in the form of hard white grains used for puddings and other dishes.
– ORIGIN Tupi-Guarani (an American Indian language), 'squeezed-out dregs'.

tapir /tay-peer, tay-per/ • n. a pig-like animal with a long flexible snout.
– ORIGIN Tupi (an American Indian language).

tappet • n. a moving part in a machine which transmits motion in a straight line between a cam and another part.
– ORIGIN from TAP[2].

taproom • n. a room in which beer is available on tap.

taproot • n. a tapering root growing straight downwards and forming the centre from which other roots spring.

tar[1] • n. **1** a dark, thick flammable liquid distilled from wood or coal, used in road-making and for preserving timber. **2** a similar substance formed by burning tobacco. • v. (**tars, tarring, tarred**) cover with tar.
– PHRASES **tar and feather** smear with tar and then cover with feathers as a punishment. **tar with the same brush** consider to have the same faults.
– ORIGIN Old English.

tar[2] • n. informal, dated a sailor.
– ORIGIN perh. short for TARPAULIN, formerly used as a nickname for a sailor.

taramasalata /ta-ruh-muh-suh-lah-tuh/ • n. a Greek dip made from the roe of cod or other fish.
– ORIGIN from modern Greek *taramas* 'roe' +

salata 'salad'.

Taranaki E
/ta-ruh-na-ki/ Maori name for Mount Egmont (see **EGMONT, MOUNT**).

Tarantino E
/ta-ruhn-tee-noh/, Quentin (Jerome) (b.1963), American film director, screenwriter, and actor, who directed the films *Reservoir Dogs* and *Pulp Fiction*.

tarantula /tuh-ran-tyuu-luh/ ● **n.** **1** a very large hairy spider found chiefly in tropical and subtropical America. **2** a large black spider of southern Europe.
– ORIGIN Italian *tarantola*.

tardy ● **adj.** (**tardier**, **tardiest**) **1** late. **2** slow to act or respond.
– DERIVATIVES **tardily** adv. **tardiness** n.
– ORIGIN Latin *tardus*.

tare /tair/ ● **n.** **1** the common vetch. **2** (in the Bible) a weed.
– ORIGIN unknown.

target ● **n.** **1** a person, object, or place selected as the aim of an attack. **2** a board marked with a series of circles sharing the same centre, aimed at in archery or shooting. **3** a result which one aims to achieve: *a sales target*. ● **v.** (**targets**, **targeting**, **targeted**) **1** select as an object of attention or attack. **2** aim or direct.
– PHRASES **on** (or **off**) **target** succeeding (or not succeeding) in hitting or achieving the thing aimed at.
– ORIGIN Old English, 'small round shield'.

tariff ● **n.** **1** a tax to be paid on a particular class of imports or exports. **2** a table of the fixed charges made by a business such as a hotel or restaurant.
– ORIGIN Italian *tariffa*.

tarmac ● **n.** **1** (trademark in the UK) material used for surfacing roads or other outdoor areas, consisting of broken stone mixed with tar. **2** (**the tarmac**) a runway surfaced with such material. ● **v.** (**tarmacs**, **tarmacking**, **tarmacked**) surface with tarmac.
– ORIGIN from **TAR**[1] + **MACADAM**.

tarn ● **n.** a small mountain lake.
– ORIGIN Old Norse.

tarnish ● **v.** **1** cause (metal) to lose its shine by exposure to air or damp. **2** make less respected: *tarnish one's reputation*. ● **n.** a film or stain formed on an exposed surface of a mineral or metal.
– ORIGIN French *ternir*.

tarot /ta-roh/ ● **n.** a set of special playing cards used for fortune telling.
– ORIGIN French.

tarpaulin /tar-por-lin/ ● **n.** **1** heavy-duty waterproof cloth. **2** a covering of this.
– ORIGIN prob. from **TAR**[1] + **PALL**[1].

tarragon /ta-ruh-guhn/ ● **n.** a plant with narrow leaves, used as a herb in cooking.
– ORIGIN Latin *tragonia* and *tarchon*.

tarry[1] /*rhymes with* starry/ ● **adj.** having to do with or covered with tar.

tarry[2] /*rhymes with* marry/ ● **v.** (**tarries**, **tarrying**, **tarried**) archaic stay longer than intended.
– ORIGIN unknown.

tarsal /tar-s'l/ Anat. & Zool. ● **adj.** relating to the tarsus. ● **n.** a bone of the tarsus.

tarsier /tar-si-er/ ● **n.** a small tree-dwelling primate with very large eyes, native to the islands of SE Asia.
– ORIGIN French.

tarsus /tar-suhss/ ● **n.** (pl. **tarsi** /tar-sy/) the group of small bones in the ankle and upper foot.
– ORIGIN Greek *tarsos* 'flat of the foot, the eyelid'.

tart[1] ● **n.** an open pastry case containing a sweet or savoury filling.
– DERIVATIVES **tartlet** n.
– ORIGIN Old French *tarte*.

tart[2] ● **n.** informal **1** derog. a woman who has many sexual partners. **2** a prostitute. ● **v.** informal **1** (**tart oneself up**) Brit. make oneself look attractive with clothes or make-up. **2** (**tart up**) improve the appearance of.
– DERIVATIVES **tarty** adj.
– ORIGIN prob. from **SWEETHEART**.

tart[3] ● **adj.** **1** sharp or acid in taste. **2** (of a remark or tone of voice) sharp or hurtful.
– DERIVATIVES **tartly** adv. **tartness** n.
– ORIGIN Old English, 'harsh, severe'.

tartan ● **n.** a woollen cloth woven in a pattern of coloured checks and intersecting lines.
– ORIGIN perh. from Old French *tertaine*, referring to a kind of cloth.

Tartar /tar-ter/ ● **n.** **1** hist. a member of a combined group of central Asian peoples who conquered much of Asia and eastern Europe in the early 13th century. **2** (**tartar**) a person who is fierce or difficult to deal with.
– ORIGIN *Tatar*, the name of a tribe formerly living in parts of Russia and Ukraine.

tartar /tar-ter/ ● **n.** **1** a hard deposit that forms on the teeth and contributes to their decay. **2** a deposit formed during the fermentation of wine.
– ORIGIN Greek *tartaron*.

tartare /tar-tar/ ● **adj.** (of fish or meat) served raw, seasoned, and shaped into small cakes: *steak tartare*.
– ORIGIN French, 'Tartar'.

tartare sauce (also **tartar sauce**) ● **n.** a cold sauce consisting of mayonnaise mixed with chopped onions, gherkins, and capers.

tartaric acid ● **n.** Chem. an organic acid found in unripe grapes and used in baking powders and as a food additive.
– ORIGIN from **TARTAR**.

Tartarus E
/tar-tuh-ruhss/ Gk Myth. a part of the underworld where the wicked were punished.

tartrazine /tar-truh-zeen/ ● **n.** Chem. a brilliant yellow synthetic dye made from tartaric acid and used to colour food, drugs, and cosmetics.

Tashkent E
/tash-**kent**/ the capital of Uzbekistan.

task ● **n.** a piece of work to be done. ● **v.** (**task with**) give (a task) to.
– PHRASES **take to task** reprimand or criticize.
– ORIGIN Old French *tasche*.

task force ● **n.** **1** an armed force organized for a special operation. **2** a group of people specially organized for a task.

taskmaster ● **n.** a person who imposes a demanding workload on someone.

Tasman E
/taz-muhn/, Abel (Janszoon) (1603–*c.*1659), Dutch navigator. During an expedition (1642–3) he became the first European to reach Tasmania, New Zealand, Tonga, and Fiji.

Tasmania E
/taz-may-ni-uh/ a state of Australia consisting of the island of Tasmania and several smaller islands; capital, Hobart. Former name (until 1855) **Van Diemen's Land**.
– DERIVATIVES **Tasmanian** adj. & n.

Tasmanian devil • n. a heavily built aggressive marsupial with a large head, powerful jaws, and mainly black fur, found only in Tasmania.

Tasman Sea E
the part of the South Pacific between Australia and New Zealand.

tassel • n. **1** a tuft of hanging threads, knotted together at one end and used for decoration in soft furnishing and clothing. **2** the tufted head of some plants.
– ORIGIN Old French, 'clasp'.

taste • n. **1** the sensation of flavour perceived in the mouth on contact with a substance. **2** the ability to perceive this. **3** a small portion of food or drink taken as a sample. **4** a brief experience of something. **5** a liking for something. **6** the ability to pick out what is of good quality or appropriate: *I liked his taste in clothes.* • v. (**tastes**, **tasting**, **tasted**) **1** perceive the flavour of. **2** have a particular flavour. **3** test the flavour of (something) by eating or drinking a small portion of it. **4** have a brief experience of.
– PHRASES **to taste** according to personal liking.
– ORIGIN Old French *taster* 'try, taste'.

taste bud • n. any of the clusters of nerve endings on the tongue and in the lining of the mouth which provide the sense of taste.

tasteful • adj. showing good judgement as to quality, appearance, or appropriate behaviour: *a tasteful lounge bar.*
– DERIVATIVES **tastefully** adv.

tasteless • adj. **1** lacking flavour. **2** lacking in good judgement as to quality, appearance, or appropriate behaviour.
– DERIVATIVES **tastelessly** adv.

taster • n. **1** a person who tests food or drink by tasting it. **2** a sample of something.

tasty • adj. (**tastier**, **tastiest**) **1** (of food) having a pleasant flavour. **2** Brit. informal attractive; appealing.

tat • n. Brit. informal tasteless or badly made articles.
– ORIGIN prob. from **tatty**.

Tate Gallery E
a national museum of art in London, founded by the sugar manufacturer Sir Henry Tate (1819–99). In 2000 it split into two establishments; Tate Britain (the original Tate Gallery, at Millbank) and Tate Modern (on Bankside).

Tati E
/ta-ti/, Jacques (1908–82; born *Jacques Tatischeff*), French film director and actor. His films include *Monsieur Hulot's Holiday* and *Mon Oncle*.

Tatra Mountains E
/ta-truh, **tah**-truh/ a range of mountains in eastern Europe on the Polish–Slovak border, part of the Carpathian system.

tattered • adj. **1** old and torn. **2** ruined; in tatters.

tatters • pl. n. irregularly torn pieces of cloth, paper, etc.
– PHRASES **in tatters** informal **1** torn in many places. **2** destroyed; ruined.
– ORIGIN Old Norse, 'rags'.

tatting • n. **1** a kind of knotted lace made by hand with a small shuttle. **2** the process of making such lace.
– ORIGIN unknown.

tattle • n. gossip. • v. (**tattles**, **tattling**, **tattled**) engage in gossip.
– ORIGIN Flemish *tatelen*, *tateren*.

tattoo[1] • n. (pl. **tattoos**) **1** a military display consisting of music, marching, and exercises. **2** a rhythmic tapping or drumming. **3** an evening drum or bugle signal calling soldiers back to their quarters.
– ORIGIN Dutch *taptoe!* 'close the tap of the cask!'.

tattoo[2] • n. (pl. **tattoos**) a permanent design made by inserting pigment into punctures in the skin. • v. (**tattoos**, **tattooing**, **tattooed**) mark in this way.
– DERIVATIVES **tattooist** n.
– ORIGIN from a language of Polynesia.

tatty • adj. (**tattier**, **tattiest**) informal worn and shabby.
– ORIGIN Old English, 'rag'.

Tatum E
/tay-tuhm/, Art (1910–56; full name *Arthur Tatum*), American jazz pianist.

taught past and past part. of **teach**.

taunt • n. a remark made in order to anger, upset, or provoke someone. • v. provoke or hurt with taunts.
– ORIGIN from French *tant pour tant* 'tit for tat'.

taupe /*rhymes with* rope/ • n. a grey tinged with brown.
– ORIGIN French, 'mole, moleskin'.

Taupo, Lake E
/tow-poh/ the largest lake of New Zealand, in the centre of North Island. Maori name **Taupomoana**.

Taurus /taw-ruhss/ • n. Astron. a constellation (the Bull) and sign of the zodiac, which the sun enters about 21 April.
– ORIGIN Latin.

Taurus Mountains E
a range of mountains in southern Turkey, parallel to the Mediterranean coast.

taut • adj. **1** stretched or pulled tight. **2** (of muscles or nerves) tense.
– DERIVATIVES **tauten** v. **tautly** adv.
– ORIGIN perh. from **tough**.

tautology /taw-tol-uh-ji/ • n. (pl. **tautologies**) the saying of the same thing over again in different words, seen as a fault of style (e.g. *they arrived one after the other in succession*).
– DERIVATIVES **tautological** adj. **tautologous** adj.

– ORIGIN from Greek *tauto-* 'same' + *logos* 'word'.

Tavener, E
Sir John (Kenneth) (b.1944), English composer. His music is primarily religious and has been influenced by his conversion to the Russian Orthodox Church.

tavern • n. archaic or N. Amer. an inn or public house.
– ORIGIN Old French *taverne.*

taverna /tuh-ver-nuh/ • n. a small Greek restaurant.
– ORIGIN modern Greek.

tawdry • adj. (**tawdrier**, **tawdriest**) **1** showy but cheap and of poor quality. **2** sleazy or unpleasant: *the tawdry business of politics.*
– DERIVATIVES **tawdriness** n.
– ORIGIN short for *tawdry lace*, from *St Audrey's lace*, a fine silk lace or ribbon.

tawny • adj. (**tawnier**, **tawniest**) of an orange-brown or yellowish-brown colour.
– ORIGIN Old French *tane.*

tawny owl • n. a common owl with either reddish-brown or grey plumage, and a quavering hoot.

tax • n. money that must be paid to the state, charged as a proportion of personal income and business profits or added to the cost of some goods and services. • v. **1** impose a tax on. **2** pay tax on (a vehicle). **3** make heavy demands on: *the ordeal would severely tax her strength.* **4** accuse (someone) of a wrongdoing.
– DERIVATIVES **taxable** adj.
– ORIGIN Latin *taxare* 'to censure, charge'.

taxation • n. **1** the imposing of tax. **2** money paid as tax.

tax avoidance • n. Brit. the arrangement of one's financial affairs so as to pay only the minimum of tax that is legally required.

tax break • n. informal a tax reduction or advantage allowed by government.

tax-deductible • adj. permitted to be deducted from income before the amount of tax to be paid is calculated.

tax disc • n. Brit. a circular label displayed on the windscreen of a vehicle, certifying payment of road tax.

tax evasion • n. the illegal non-payment or underpayment of tax.

tax exile • n. a wealthy person who chooses to live in a country with low taxes.

tax haven • n. a country or independent area where taxes are low.

taxi • n. (pl. **taxis**) a motor vehicle licensed to transport passengers in return for payment of a fare. • v. (**taxies**, **taxiing**, **taxied**) (of an aircraft) move slowly along the ground before take-off or after landing.
– ORIGIN short for *taxicab* or *taximeter cab.*

taxicab • n. a taxi.

taxidermy /tak-si-der-mi/ • n. the art of preparing, stuffing, and mounting the skins of dead animals so that they look like living ones.
– DERIVATIVES **taxidermist** n.
– ORIGIN from Greek *taxis* 'arrangement' + *derma* 'skin'.

taximeter • n. a device used in taxis that automatically records the distance travelled and the fare to be paid.
– ORIGIN French *taximètre.*

taxing • adj. physically or mentally demanding.

taxi rank (N. Amer. **taxi stand**) • n. a place where taxis park while waiting to be hired.

taxman • n. informal an inspector or collector of taxes.

taxonomy /taks-on-uh-mi/ • n. **1** the branch of science concerned with classification. **2** a system of classifying things.
– DERIVATIVES **taxonomic** adj. **taxonomist** n.
– ORIGIN from Greek *taxis* 'arrangement' + *-nomia* 'distribution'.

tax return • n. a form on which a taxpayer makes a statement of their income and personal circumstances, used to assess how much tax that person should pay.

tax year • n. a year as reckoned for the purposes of taxation (in Britain from 6 April).

Tay E
the longest river in Scotland, which flows 192 km (120 miles) eastwards through Loch Tay in central Scotland to the Firth of Tay.

Tay, Firth of E
the estuary of the River Tay, on the North Sea coast of Scotland. It is spanned by the longest railway bridge in Britain (3,553 m; 11,653 feet).

tayberry • n. (pl. **tayberries**) a dark red soft fruit produced by crossing a blackberry and a raspberry.
– ORIGIN named after the River **TAY**.

Taylor[1], E
Dame Elizabeth (b.1932), American actress, born in England. Her films include *National Velvet*, *Cleopatra*, and *Who's Afraid of Virginia Woolf?* She has been married eight times, including twice to the actor Richard Burton.

Taylor[2], E
Zachary (1784–1850), American Whig statesman, 12th President of the US 1849–50.

TB • abbrev. tubercle bacillus; tuberculosis.

t.b.a. • abbrev. to be announced.

Tbilisi E
/tuh-bi-lee-si/ the capital of Georgia. Former name (1845–1936) **TIFLIS**.

T-bone • n. a large piece of loin steak containing a T-shaped bone.

tbsp (also **tbs**) (pl. **tbsp** or **tbsps**) • abbrev. tablespoonful.

Tchaikovsky E
/chy-koff-ski/, Pyotr (Ilich) (1840–93), Russian composer. His works include the ballets *Swan Lake* and *The Nutcracker*, the overture *1812*, and his sixth symphony, the 'Pathétique'.

te (N. Amer. **ti**) • n. Music the seventh note of a major scale, coming after 'lah'.
– ORIGIN alteration of former *si*, adopted to avoid having two notes (*soh* and *si*) beginning with the same letter.

tea • n. **1** a hot drink made by soaking the dried leaves of the tea plant in boiling water. **2** the dried leaves of an evergreen Asian shrub or small tree, used to make tea. **3** a drink made from the leaves, fruits, or flowers

of other plants. **4** Brit. a light afternoon meal consisting of sandwiches, cakes, etc., with tea to drink. **5** Brit. a cooked evening meal.
– ORIGIN Chinese.

tea bag • n. a small sachet containing tea leaves, on to which boiling water is poured to make tea.

tea break • n. Brit. a short rest period during the working day.

teacake • n. Brit. a light sweet bun containing dried fruit.

teach • v. (**teaches**, **teaching**, **taught**) **1** give information to (a class or pupil) so as to help them to learn something. **2** show (someone) how to do something. **3** make (someone) realize, understand, or be less likely to do something: *the experience taught me the real value of money.*
– DERIVATIVES **teaching** n.
– ORIGIN Old English, 'show'.

teacher • n. a person who teaches in a school.

tea chest • n. a light metal-lined wooden box in which tea is transported.

tea cloth • n. a tea towel.

tea cosy • n. a thick or padded cover placed over a teapot to keep the tea hot.

teacup • n. a cup from which tea is drunk.

tea dance • n. an afternoon tea with dancing.

teak • n. hard wood used in shipbuilding and for making furniture, obtained from a tree native to India and SE Asia.
– ORIGIN Portuguese *teca*.

teal • n. (pl. **teal** or **teals**) **1** a small freshwater duck. **2** (also **teal blue**) a dark greenish-blue colour.
– ORIGIN unknown.

team • n. **1** a group of players forming one side in a competitive game or sport. **2** two or more people working together. **3** two or more horses in harness together to pull a vehicle. • v. **1** (**team up**) come together as a team to achieve a common goal. **2** (**team with**) match with: *a pinstripe suit teamed with a white shirt.*
– ORIGIN Old English.

teammate • n. a fellow member of a team.

team player • n. a person who plays or works well as a member of a team.

team spirit • n. trust and cooperation among the members of a team.

teamwork • n. organized effort as a group.

teapot • n. a pot with a handle, spout, and lid, in which tea is prepared.

tear[1] /*rhymes with* rare/ • v. (**tears**, **tearing**, **tore**; past part. **torn**) **1** rip a hole or split in. **2** (usu. **tear up**) pull apart or to pieces. **3** damage (a muscle or ligament) by overstretching it. **4** (usu. **tear down**) energetically demolish or destroy. **5** (**tear apart**) disrupt and force apart. **6** (**be torn**) be unsure of which of two options or parties to choose or support. **7** informal move very quickly. **8** (**tear into**) attack verbally. • n. a hole or split caused by tearing.
– PHRASES **tear one's hair out** informal feel extreme desperation. **tear someone off a strip** Brit. informal rebuke someone angrily. **that's torn it** Brit. informal expressing dismay when something has happened to disrupt someone's plans.
– ORIGIN Old English.

tear[2] /*rhymes with* rear/ • n. a drop of clear salty liquid produced by glands in a person's eye when they are crying or when the eye is irritated.
– PHRASES **in tears** crying.
– DERIVATIVES **teary** adj.
– ORIGIN Old English.

tearaway • n. Brit. a person who behaves in a wild or reckless way.

teardrop • n. a single tear. • adj. shaped like a tear.

tear duct • n. a passage through which tears pass from the glands which produce them to the eye or from the eye to the nose.

tearful • adj. **1** crying or inclined to cry. **2** causing tears: *a tearful farewell.*
– DERIVATIVES **tearfully** adv.

tear gas • n. gas that causes severe irritation to the eyes, used in warfare and riot control.

tear-jerker • n. informal a very sad story, film, or song.

tea room • n. a small restaurant or cafe where tea and other light refreshments are served.

tea rose • n. a garden rose having flowers that are pale yellow tinged with pink, and a delicate scent like that of tea.

tease • v. (**teases**, **teasing**, **teased**) **1** playfully make fun of or attempt to provoke. **2** tempt sexually. **3** (**tease out**) find out by searching through a mass of information. **4** gently pull (tangled wool, hair, etc.) into separate strands. • n. informal a person who teases.
– ORIGIN Old English.

teasel (also **teazle**) • n. a tall prickly plant with spiny purple flower heads.
– ORIGIN Old English.

teaser • n. informal a tricky question or task.

tea set • n. a set of crockery for serving tea.

teaspoon • n. **1** a small spoon used for adding sugar to and stirring hot drinks. **2** the amount held by such a spoon, in the UK considered to be 5 millilitres.

teat • n. **1** a nipple on a woman's breast or an animal's udder. **2** Brit. a plastic nipple-shaped device by which a baby or young animal can suck milk from a bottle.
– ORIGIN Old French *tete*.

tea towel • n. esp. Brit. a cloth for drying washed crockery, cutlery, and glasses.

teazle • n. var. of TEASEL.

technetium /tek-nee-shi-uhm/ • n. an unstable radioactive metallic element made by high-energy collisions.
– ORIGIN Greek *tekhnētos* 'artificial'.

technical • adj. **1** having to do with the practical skills of a particular subject, art, or craft. **2** having to do with the practical use of machinery and methods in science and industry. **3** requiring specialized knowledge in order to be understood. **4** according to the law or rules when applied strictly: *a technical violation of the treaty.*
– DERIVATIVES **technically** adv.
– ORIGIN Greek *tekhnē* 'art'.

technical college • n. a college of further education providing courses in applied sciences and other practical subjects.

technicality • n. (pl. **technicalities**) **1** a small formal detail in a set of rules. **2** (**tech-**

nicalities) details of theory or practice within a particular field. **3** the use of technical terms or methods.

technical knockout ● **n.** Boxing the ending of a fight by the referee because a contestant is unable to continue, the opponent being declared the winner.

technician ● **n. 1** a person employed to look after technical equipment or do practical work in a laboratory. **2** an expert in the techniques of a particular science or craft.

Technicolor ● **n.** trademark **1** a process of producing cinema films in colour. **2** (**technicolor** or Brit. also **technicolour**) informal vivid colour.

technique ● **n. 1** a particular way of doing something, especially something requiring special skills. **2** a person's level of practical skill.
– ORIGIN French.

techno ● **n.** a style of fast electronic dance music, with a strong beat and few or no vocals.
– ORIGIN short for *technological* (see **TECHNOLOGY**).

technocracy /tek-nok-ruh-si/ ● **n.** (pl. **technocracies**) a social or political system in which scientific or technical experts hold a great deal of power.
– DERIVATIVES **technocrat** n.

technology ● **n.** (pl. **technologies**) **1** the application of scientific knowledge for practical purposes. **2** the branch of knowledge concerned with applied sciences.
– DERIVATIVES **technological** adj. **technologically** adv. **technologist** n.
– ORIGIN Greek *tekhnologia* 'systematic treatment'.

technophobe ● **n.** a person who dislikes or fears new technology.
– DERIVATIVES **technophobia** n. **technophobic** adj.

tectonic /tek-ton-ik/ Geol. ● **adj.** having to do with the structure of the earth's crust and the large-scale processes which take place within it. ● **n.** (**tectonics**) large-scale processes affecting the structure of the earth's crust.
– ORIGIN Greek *tektonikos*.

teddy ● **n.** (pl. **teddies**) **1** (also **teddy bear**) a soft toy bear. **2** a woman's all-in-one undergarment.
– ORIGIN from *Teddy*, informal form of the man's name *Theodore*, with reference to President *Theodore* Roosevelt (see **ROOSEVELT²**), an enthusiastic bear-hunter.

Teddy boy ● **n.** Brit. (in the 1950s) a young man of a group who wore clothes based on Edwardian fashion, had their hair slicked up in a quiff, and liked rock-and-roll music.
– ORIGIN from *Teddy*, informal form of the man's name *Edward*.

tedious ● **adj.** too long, slow, or dull.
– DERIVATIVES **tediously** adv.
– ORIGIN Latin *taedium* 'tedium'.

tedium ● **n.** the state of being tedious.

tee ● **n. 1** a cleared space on a golf course, from which the ball is struck at the beginning of play for each hole. **2** a small peg placed in the ground to support a golf ball before it is struck from a tee. ● **v.** (**tees, teeing, teed**) Golf **1** (**tee up**) place the ball on a tee ready to make the first stroke of the round or hole. **2** (**tee off**) begin a round or hole by playing the ball from a tee.
– ORIGIN unknown.

teem¹ ● **v.** (**teem with**) be full of or swarming with.
– ORIGIN Old English, 'give birth to'.

teem² ● **v.** (of rain) fall heavily.
– ORIGIN Old Norse, 'to empty'.

teen informal ● **adj.** relating to teenagers. ● **n.** a teenager.

-teen ● **suffix** forming the names of numerals from 13 to 19.
– ORIGIN Old English.

teenage ● **adj.** having to do with a teenager or teenagers.
– DERIVATIVES **teenaged** adj.

teenager ● **n.** a person aged between 13 and 19 years.

teens ● **pl. n.** the years of a person's age from 13 to 19.

teensy ● **adj.** (**teensier, teensiest**) informal very tiny.
– ORIGIN prob. from **TEENY**.

teeny ● **adj.** (**teenier, teeniest**) informal tiny.
– ORIGIN from **TINY**.

teeny-bopper ● **n.** informal a young teenager who follows the latest fashions in clothes and pop music.

teeny-weeny (also **teensy-weensy**) ● **adj.** informal very tiny.

teepee ● **n.** var. of **TEPEE**.

Tees E
a river of NE England which rises in Cumbria and flows generally south-eastwards to the North Sea at Middlesbrough.

tee shirt ● **n.** var. of **T-SHIRT**.

teeter ● **v.** (**teeters, teetering, teetered**) **1** move or balance unsteadily. **2** be unable to decide between different options.
– ORIGIN Old Norse, 'shake, shiver'.

teeth pl. of **TOOTH**.

teethe ● **v.** (**teethes, teething, teethed**) cut one's milk teeth.

teething troubles (also **teething problems**) ● **pl. n.** short-term problems that occur in the early stages of a new project.

teetotal ● **adj.** choosing not to drink alcohol.
– DERIVATIVES **teetotalism** n. **teetotaller** n.
– ORIGIN emphatic repetition from **TOTAL** (total abstinence from all alcohol).

TEFL /tef-uhl/ ● **abbrev.** teaching of English as a foreign language.

Teflon /tef-lon/ ● **n.** trademark a tough synthetic resin used to make seals and bearings and to coat non-stick cooking utensils.

Tegucigalpa E
/te-goo-si-gal-puh/ the capital of Honduras.

Tehran E
/tair-ahn/ (also **Teheran**) the capital of Iran.

Te Kanawa E
/tay **kah**-nuh-wuh/, Dame Kiri (Janette) (b.1944), New Zealand operatic soprano, resident in Britain since 1966.

Tel Aviv E
/tel uh-veev/ (also **Tel Aviv-Jaffa**) a city on the Mediterranean coast of Israel.

tele- /tel-i/ ● comb. form **1** to or at a distance: *telecommunication*. **2** relating to television: *telethon*. **3** done by means of the telephone: *telesales*.
– ORIGIN Greek, 'far off'.

telecast ● n. a television broadcast. ● v. transmit by television.

telecommunication ● n. **1** communication over a distance by cable, telegraph, telephone, or broadcasting. **2** (**telecommunications**) the branch of technology concerned with this.

telecoms (also **telecomms**) ● n. telecommunications.

tele-evangelist ● n. var. of **TELEVANGELIST**.

telegenic /te-li-jen-ik/ ● adj. having an appearance or manner that is attractive on television.

telegram ● n. a message sent by telegraph and delivered in written or printed form, now used in the UK only for international messages.

telegraph ● n. a system or device for transmitting messages from a distance along a wire, especially one creating signals by making and breaking an electrical connection. ● v. **1** dated send (a message) by telegraph. **2** convey (a message), especially by body language.
– DERIVATIVES **telegraphy** n.

telegraphese ● n. informal the abrupt, abbreviated style of language used in telegrams.

telegraphic ● adj. having to do with telegraphs or telegrams.

telegraph pole ● n. a tall pole used to carry telegraph or telephone wires above the ground.

telekinesis /te-li-ki-nee-siss/ ● n. the supposed ability to move objects at a distance by mental power or other non-physical means.
– DERIVATIVES **telekinetic** adj.
– ORIGIN Greek *kinēsis* 'motion'.

Telemann E
/tay-luh-man/, Georg Philipp (1681–1767), German composer and organist. His prolific output includes six hundred overtures, forty-four Passions, and forty operas.

telemarketing ● n. the marketing of goods or services by telephone calls to potential customers.

telemessage ● n. a message sent by telephone or telex and delivered in written form.

teleology /tee-li-ol-uh-ji/ ● n. the philosophical theory that all things in nature have a purpose and happen because of that.
– DERIVATIVES **teleological** adj.
– ORIGIN from Greek *telos* 'end' + *logos* 'reason'.

telepathy ● n. the supposed communication of thoughts or ideas by means other than the known senses.
– DERIVATIVES **telepathic** adj.

telephone ● n. **1** a system for transmitting voices over a distance using wire or radio, by converting sound vibrations to electrical signals. **2** an instrument used as part of such a system, having a handset with a transmitting microphone and a set of numbered buttons by which a connection can be made to another such instrument. ● v. (**telephones**, **telephoning**, **telephoned**) call or speak to using the telephone.
– DERIVATIVES **telephonic** adj. **telephonically** adv.

telephone box ● n. esp. Brit. a public booth or enclosure housing a payphone.

telephone directory ● n. a book listing the names, addresses, and telephone numbers of the people in a particular area.

telephone exchange ● n. a set of equipment that connects telephone lines during a call.

telephone number ● n. a number given to a particular telephone and used in making connections to it.

telephonist ● n. Brit. an operator of a telephone switchboard.

telephony /ti-lef-fuh-ni/ ● n. the working or use of telephones.

telephoto lens ● n. a lens that produces a magnified image of a distant object.

teleprinter ● n. Brit. a device for transmitting telegraph messages as they are keyed, and for printing messages received.

telesales ● pl n. the selling of goods or services over the telephone.

telescope ● n. an optical instrument designed to make distant objects appear nearer, containing an arrangement of lenses, or of curved mirrors and lenses, by which rays of light are collected and focused and the resulting image magnified. ● v. (**telescopes**, **telescoping**, **telescoped**) **1** (of an object made up of several tubes fitting into each other) slide into itself so as to become smaller. **2** condense or combine so as to occupy less space or time: *at sea the years are telescoped into hours*.
– DERIVATIVES **telescopic** adj.

teletext ● n. a news and information service transmitted to televisions with appropriate receivers.

telethon ● n. a long television programme broadcast to raise money for a charity.
– ORIGIN from **TELE-** + *marathon*.

televangelist (also **tele-evangelist**) ● n. esp. N. Amer. an evangelical preacher who appears regularly on television.

televise ● v. (**televises**, **televising**, **televised**) broadcast on television.

television ● n. **1** a system for converting visual images with sound into electrical signals, transmitting them, and displaying them electronically on a screen. **2** the activity or medium of broadcasting on television. **3** (also **television set**) a device with a screen for receiving television signals.
– DERIVATIVES **televisual** adj.

telex ● n. **1** an international system in which printed messages are transmitted and received by teleprinters using the public telecommunications network. **2** a device used for this. **3** a message sent by this system. ● v. **1** communicate with (someone) by telex. **2** send (a message) by telex.
– ORIGIN from **TELEPRINTER** and **EXCHANGE**.

Telford, E
Thomas (1757–1834), Scottish civil engineer. He built hundreds of miles of roads, more than a thousand bridges, and a number of canals.

Tell, E
William, a legendary 14th-century hero of the liberation of Switzerland from Austrian oppression. He was required to hit with an arrow an apple placed on the head of his son, which he did successfully.

tell ● v. (**tells**, **telling**, **told**) **1** communicate information to. **2** instruct to do something. **3** express in words: *he tried to make them laugh by telling jokes.* **4** (**tell on**) informal inform on. **5** (**tell off**) informal reprimand. **6** determine correctly: *you can tell they're in love.* **7** be able to recognize (a difference). **8** (of an experience) have a noticeable effect on someone.
– PHRASES **tell tales** gossip about another person's secrets or faults. **tell the time** be able to find out the time from reading the face of a clock or watch. **there is no telling** it is not possible to know what has happened or will happen.
– ORIGIN Old English, 'relate, count'.

Teller E
/tel-ler/, Edward (b.1908), Hungarian-born American physicist, who worked on the first atom bombs and contributed to the development of the first hydrogen bomb (1952).

teller ● n. **1** a person who deals with customers' transactions in a bank. **2** a person appointed to count votes. **3** a person who tells something.

telling ● adj. having an important or revealing effect.
– DERIVATIVES **tellingly** adv.

telling-off ● n. (pl. **tellings-off**) informal a reprimand.

telltale ● adj. revealing something: *the telltale signs of a woman in love.* ● n. a person who reports others' wrongdoings.

tellurium /tel-lyoor-i-uhm/ ● n. a silvery-white crystalline non-metallic element with semiconducting properties.
– ORIGIN Latin *tellus* 'earth'.

telly ● n. (pl. **tellies**) Brit. informal = TELEVISION.

temazepam /tuh-maz-i-pam, tuh-may-zi-pam/ ● n. Med. a tranquillizing drug.

temerity /ti-me-ri-ti/ ● n. excessive confidence or boldness.
– ORIGIN Latin *temeritas.*

temp informal ● n. an employee who is employed on a temporary basis. ● v. work as a temp.

temper ● n. **1** a person's state of mind: *she regained her good temper.* **2** a tendency to become angry easily. **3** an angry state of mind. **4** the degree of hardness of a metal. ● v. (**tempers**, **tempering**, **tempered**) **1** harden (a metal) by reheating and then cooling it. **2** make (something) less extreme by adding something that balances or modifies it: *their idealism is tempered with realism.*
– PHRASES **keep** (or **lose**) **one's temper** manage (or fail to manage) to control one's anger.
– ORIGIN Latin *temperare* 'mingle'.

tempera /tem-puh-ruh/ ● n. a method of painting with powdered colours mixed with egg yolk.
– ORIGIN from Italian *pingere a tempera* 'paint in distemper'.

temperament ● n. a person's nature in terms of the effect it has on their behaviour.
– ORIGIN Latin *temperamentum* 'correct mixture'.

temperamental ● adj. **1** relating to or caused by temperament. **2** tending to change mood in an unreasonable way.
– DERIVATIVES **temperamentally** adv.

temperance ● n. complete avoidance of drinking alcohol.
– ORIGIN Old French *temperaunce.*

temperate ● adj. **1** (of a region or climate) having mild temperatures. **2** showing self-control.
– ORIGIN Latin *temperatus.*

temperature ● n. **1** the degree of heat present in a substance, object, or place. **2** informal a body temperature above the normal. **3** the degree of excitement or tension in a situation: *the temperature of the debate lowered.*
– ORIGIN Latin *temperatura* 'the state of being mixed'.

tempest ● n. a violent windy storm.
– ORIGIN Latin *tempestas* 'weather, storm'.

tempestuous /tem-pess-tyoo-uhss/ ● adj. **1** very stormy. **2** full of strong and changeable emotion: *a tempestuous relationship.*

tempi pl. of TEMPO.

template /tem-playt/ ● n. **1** a shaped piece of rigid material used as a pattern for cutting out, shaping, or drilling. **2** something serving as a model for others to copy.
– ORIGIN prob. from *temple* 'device in a loom for keeping the cloth stretched'.

Temple, E
Shirley (b.1928; latterly *Shirley Temple Black*), American child star, star of such films as *Rebecca of Sunnybrook Farm.* She later represented the US at the United Nations and as an ambassador.

temple[1] ● n. a building devoted to the worship of a god or gods.
– ORIGIN Latin *templum* 'open or consecrated space'.

temple[2] ● n. the flat part either side of the head between the forehead and the ear.
– ORIGIN Old French.

tempo /tem-poh/ ● n. (pl. **tempos** or **tempi** /tem-pi/) **1** Music the speed at which a passage of music is played. **2** the pace of an activity or process.
– ORIGIN Italian.

temporal[1] /tem-puh-ruhl/ ● adj. **1** relating to time. **2** relating to worldly affairs.
– DERIVATIVES **temporally** adv.
– ORIGIN Latin *temporalis.*

temporal[2] /tem-puh-ruhl/ ● adj. Anat. having to do with or situated in the temples of the head.

temporary ● adj. lasting for only a short time.
– DERIVATIVES **temporarily** adv.
– ORIGIN Latin *temporarius.*

temporize (also **temporise**) ● v. (**temporizes**, **temporizing**, **temporized**) act so as to gain time before making a decision.
– ORIGIN French *temporiser* 'bide one's time'.

tempo rubato ● n. see RUBATO.

tempt ● v. **1** try to persuade (someone) to do something, even if they know it is wrong. **2** (**be tempted to do**) have an urge or inclination to do. **3** attract; charm.
– PHRASES **tempt fate** (or **providence**) do

something risky or dangerous.
– DERIVATIVES **tempter** n. **tempting** adj.
– ORIGIN Latin *temptare* 'handle, test'.

temptation ● n. **1** the action of tempting or the state of being tempted. **2** a tempting thing.

temptress ● n. a sexually attractive woman.

ten ● cardinal number one more than nine; 10. (Roman numeral: **x** or **X**.)
– PHRASES **ten out of ten** referring to an excellent performance. **ten to one** very probably.
– DERIVATIVES **tenfold** adj. & adv.
– ORIGIN Old English.

tenable ● adj. **1** able to be defended against attack or objection. **2** (of a post, grant, etc.) able to be held or used for a specified period: *a scholarship tenable for three years.*
– ORIGIN French.

tenacious /ti-nay-shuhss/ ● adj. **1** holding firmly to something. **2** continuing to exist for longer than might be expected: *a tenacious belief.*
– DERIVATIVES **tenaciously** adv. **tenacity** /ti-nass-i-ti/ n.
– ORIGIN Latin *tenere* 'to hold'.

tenancy ● n. (pl. **tenancies**) possession of land or property as a tenant.

tenant ● n. **1** a person who rents land or property from a landlord. **2** Law a person privately owning land or property. ● v. (usu. **be tenanted**) occupy (property) as a tenant.
– ORIGIN Old French, 'holding'.

tenant farmer ● n. a person who farms rented land.

tench ● n. (pl. **tench**) a freshwater fish of the carp family.
– ORIGIN Old French *tenche.*

Ten Commandments ● pl. n. (in the Bible) the rules of conduct given by God to Moses on Mount Sinai.

tend[1] ● v. **1** frequently behave in a particular way or have a certain characteristic. **2** go or move in a particular direction.
– ORIGIN Latin *tendere* 'stretch, tend'.

tend[2] ● v. care for or look after.
– ORIGIN from ATTEND.

tendency ● n. (pl. **tendencies**) **1** an inclination to behave in a particular way. **2** a group within a larger political party or movement.

tendentious /ten-den-shuhss/ ● adj. expressing a strong opinion: *a tendentious reading of history.*
– ORIGIN German *tendenziös.*

tender[1] ● adj. (**tenderer, tenderest**) **1** gentle and kind. **2** (of food) easy to cut or chew. **3** (of a part of the body) painful to the touch. **4** young and vulnerable. **5** easily damaged.
– DERIVATIVES **tenderly** adv. **tenderness** n.
– ORIGIN Old French *tendre.*

tender[2] ● v. (**tenders, tendering, tendered**) **1** offer or present formally. **2** make a formal written offer to carry out work, supply goods, etc. for a stated fixed price. **3** offer (money) as payment. ● n. a tendered offer.
– ORIGIN Latin *tendere* 'stretch, hold out'.

tender[3] ● n. **1** a vehicle used by a fire service for carrying equipment. **2** a wagon attached to a steam locomotive to carry fuel and water. **3** a boat used to ferry people and supplies to and from a ship.
– ORIGIN TEND[2] or ATTEND.

tender-hearted ● adj. having a kind, gentle, or sentimental nature.

tenderize (also **tenderise**) ● v. (**tenderizes, tenderizing, tenderized**) make (meat) more tender by beating or slow cooking.

tenderloin ● n. the tenderest part of a loin of beef, pork, etc., taken from under the short ribs in the hindquarters.

tendinitis /ten-di-ny-tiss/ (also **tendonitis** /ten-duh-ny-tiss/) ● n. inflammation of a tendon.

tendon /ten-duhn/ ● n. a strong band or cord of tissue attaching a muscle to a bone.
– ORIGIN Greek *tenōn* 'sinew'.

tendril ● n. **1** a thread-like part of a climbing plant, which stretches out and twines round any suitable support. **2** a slender ringlet of hair.
– ORIGIN prob. from Old French *tendron* 'young shoot'.

tenebrous /ten-i-bruhss/ ● adj. literary dark; shadowy.
– ORIGIN Latin *tenebrosus.*

tenement /ten-uh-muhnt/ ● n. **1** a separate residence within a house or block of flats. **2** (also **tenement house**) a house divided into several separate residences.
– ORIGIN Latin *tenementum.*

Tenerife E
/ten-uh-reef/ the largest of the Canary Islands; capital, Santa Cruz.

tenet /ten-it/ ● n. a central principle or belief.
– ORIGIN Latin, 'he holds'.

ten-gallon hat ● n. a large, broad-brimmed hat, traditionally worn by cowboys.

Teng Hsiao-p'ing E
/teng show-ping/ var. of DENG XIAOPING.

tenner ● n. Brit. informal a ten-pound note.

Tennessee E
/ten-nuh-see/ a state in the central south-eastern US; capital, Nashville.
– DERIVATIVES **Tennesseean** n. & adj.

Tenniel E
/ten-ni-uhl/, Sir John (1820–1914), English illustrator and cartoonist, who illustrated Lewis Carroll's *Alice's Adventures in Wonderland* and *Through the Looking Glass.*

tennis ● n. a game for two or four players, who use rackets to strike a ball over a net stretched across a grass or clay court.
– ORIGIN prob. from Old French *tenez* 'take, receive' (called by the server in real tennis).

tennis elbow ● n. inflammation of the tendons of the elbow caused by overuse of the forearm muscles.

tennis shoe ● n. a light canvas or leather soft-soled shoe suitable for tennis or casual wear.

Tennyson E
/ten-ni-s'n/, Alfred, 1st Baron Tennyson of Aldworth and Freshwater (1809–92), English poet, Poet Laureate 1850–92. His works include *In Memoriam*, 'The Charge of the Light Brigade', and *Idylls of the King.*

tenon /ten-uhn/ ● n. a projecting piece of wood made to be inserted into a mortise in another piece of wood.
– ORIGIN French.

t

tenor[1] ● n. a singing voice between baritone and alto or countertenor, the highest of the ordinary adult male range. ● adj. referring to an instrument of the second or third lowest pitch in its family: *a tenor sax.*
– ORIGIN Latin *tenere* 'to hold' (because the tenor part 'held' the melody).

tenor[2] ● n. the general meaning or nature of something: *the even tenor of her marriage.*
– ORIGIN Latin, 'course'.

tenpin ● n. a skittle used in tenpin bowling.

tenpin bowling ● n. a game in which ten skittles are set up at the end of a track and bowled down with hard balls.

tense[1] ● adj. **1** stretched tight or rigid. **2** feeling or causing anxiety and nervousness. ● v. (**tenses**, **tensing**, **tensed**) make or become tense.
– DERIVATIVES **tensely** adv. **tenseness** n.
– ORIGIN Latin *tensus.*

tense[2] ● n. Grammar a set of forms of a verb that indicate the time or completeness of the action expressed by the verb.
– ORIGIN Latin *tempus* 'time'.

tensile /ten-syl/ ● adj. **1** relating to tension. **2** capable of being drawn out or stretched.

tensile strength ● n. the resistance of a material to breaking under tension.

tension ● n. **1** the state of being stretched tight. **2** mental or emotional strain. **3** a situation in which there is strain because of differing views or aims: *months of tension between the military and the government.* **4** the degree of stitch tightness in knitting and machine sewing. **5** voltage of specified magnitude: *high tension.*
– DERIVATIVES **tensional** adj.

tent ● n. a portable shelter made of cloth, supported by one or more poles and stretched tight by cords attached to pegs driven into the ground.
– ORIGIN Old French *tente.*

tentacle ● n. a long thin flexible part extending from the body of an animal, used for feeling or holding things, or for moving about.
– DERIVATIVES **tentacled** adj.
– ORIGIN Latin *tentaculum.*

tentative ● adj. **1** done without confidence; hesitant: *a few tentative steps.* **2** not certain or fixed: *a tentative conclusion.*
– DERIVATIVES **tentatively** adv. **tentativeness** n.
– ORIGIN Latin *tentativus.*

tenterhook ● n. (in phr. **on tenterhooks**) in a state of nervous suspense.
– ORIGIN first meaning a hook used to fasten cloth on a *tenter*, a framework on which fabric was held during manufacture.

tenth ● ordinal number **1** that is number ten in a sequence; 10th. **2** (**a tenth/one tenth**) each of ten equal parts into which something is divided. **3** a musical interval spanning an octave and a third in a scale.

tenuous ● adj. **1** very slight or weak: *a tenuous distinction.* **2** very slender or fine.
– DERIVATIVES **tenuously** adv.
– ORIGIN Latin *tenuis* 'thin'.

tenure /ten-yer/ ● n. **1** the conditions under which land or buildings are held or occupied. **2** the holding of a job.
– ORIGIN Old French.

tenured ● adj. having a permanent post.

Tenzing Norgay E
/ten-sing **nor**-gay/ (1914–86), Sherpa mountaineer. In 1953 he and Sir Edmund Hillary were the first to reach the summit of Mount Everest.

tepee /tee-pee/ (also **teepee** or **tipi**) ● n. a cone-shaped tent made of skins or cloth on a frame of poles, used by American Indians.
– ORIGIN Sioux, 'dwelling'.

tepid ● adj. **1** lukewarm. **2** not enthusiastic: *a tepid response.*
– ORIGIN Latin *tepidus.*

tequila /tuh-kee-luh/ ● n. a Mexican liquor made from an American plant.
– ORIGIN named after the town of *Tequila* in Mexico.

terabyte ● n. Computing a unit of information equal to one million million (10^{12}) or (strictly) 2^{40} bytes.
– ORIGIN Greek *teras* 'monster'.

terbium /ter-bi-uhm/ ● n. a silvery-white metallic chemical element.
– ORIGIN from *Ytterby*, a Swedish quarry where it was first found.

tercel /ter-suhl/ ● n. Falconry a male hawk.
– ORIGIN Old French.

tercentenary ● n. (pl. **tercentenaries**) a three-hundredth anniversary.
– ORIGIN Latin *ter* 'thrice'.

Terence E
(*c.*190–159 BC; Latin name *Publius Terentius Afer*), Roman comic dramatist.

Teresa, Mother E
(also **Theresa**) (1910–97; born *Agnes Gonxha Bojaxhiu*), Roman Catholic nun and missionary, born in what is now Macedonia of Albanian parentage. She emigrated to India and founded the Order of Missionaries of Charity, which became noted for its work among the poor in Calcutta (Kolkata).

Teresa of Ávila, St E
/av-i-luh/ (1515–82), Spanish Carmelite nun and mystic. She introduced a number of reforms to her order. Feast day, 15 October.

Tereshkova E
/te-rish-**koh**-vuh/, Valentina (Vladimirovna) (b.1937), Russian cosmonaut, who in June 1963 became the first woman in space.

tergiversation /ter-ji-ver-say-shun/ ● n. the use of evasive or ambiguous language.
– ORIGIN Latin *tergiversari* 'turn one's back'.

term ● n. **1** a word or phrase used to describe a thing or to express an idea. **2** (**terms**) language used on a particular occasion: *a protest in the strongest possible terms.* **3** (**terms**) requirements or conditions laid down or agreed. **4** (**terms**) relations: *we're on good terms.* **5** a period for which something lasts or is intended to last. **6** each of the periods in the year during which teaching is given in a school or college or during which a law court holds sessions. **7** (also **full term**) the completion of a normal length of pregnancy. **8** Math. each of the quantities in a ratio, series, or mathematical expression. ● v. call by a specified term.
– PHRASES **come to terms with** become able to accept or deal with. **the —— term** a period that is a specified way into the future: *in the*

long term. **on terms 1** friendly or equal. **2** (in sport) level in score. **terms of reference** Brit. the scope of an inquiry or discussion.
– DERIVATIVES **termly** adj. & adv.
– ORIGIN Latin *terminus* 'end, limit'.

termagant /ter-muh-guhnt/ ● **n.** a bad-tempered or overbearing woman.
– ORIGIN Italian *Trivagante* 'thrice-wandering', referring to a violent imaginary god or goddess in medieval morality plays.

terminable ● **adj. 1** able to be terminated. **2** coming to an end after a certain time.

terminal ● **adj. 1** having to do with or situated at the end. **2** (of a disease) predicted to lead to death. ● **n. 1** the station at the end of a railway or bus route. **2** a departure and arrival building for passengers at an airport. **3** a point of connection for closing an electric circuit. **4** a keyboard and screen connected to a central computer system.
– DERIVATIVES **terminally** adv.
– ORIGIN Latin *terminalis*.

terminal velocity ● **n.** Physics the constant speed that a freely falling object reaches when the resistance of the medium through which it is falling prevents it from moving any faster.

terminate ● **v.** (**terminates**, **terminating**, **terminated**) **1** bring to an end. **2** (**terminate in**) have an end at or in. **3** (of a train or bus service) end its journey. **4** end (a pregnancy) early by artificial means.
– DERIVATIVES **termination** n. **terminator** n.

terminology ● **n.** (pl. **terminologies**) the set of terms used in a subject of study, profession, etc.
– DERIVATIVES **terminological** adj.

terminus ● **n.** (pl. **termini** or **terminuses**) a railway or bus terminal.
– ORIGIN Latin, 'end, limit'.

termite /ter-myt/ ● **n.** a small, soft-bodied insect which feeds on wood and lives in colonies in large nests of earth.
– ORIGIN Latin *termes* 'woodworm'.

tern /*rhymes with* fern/ ● **n.** a white seabird with long pointed wings and a forked tail.
– ORIGIN Scandinavian.

ternary /ter-nuh-ri/ ● **adj. 1** composed of three parts. **2** Math. using three as a base.
– ORIGIN Latin *ternarius*.

terpsichorean /terp-si-kuh-ree-uhn/ formal ● **adj.** relating to dancing. ● **n.** a dancer.
– ORIGIN from *Terpsichore*, the ancient Greek and Roman Muse of dance.

terrace ● **n. 1** each of a series of flat areas on a slope, used for growing plants and crops. **2** a patio. **3** Brit. a row of houses in the same style built in one block. **4** Brit. a flight of wide, shallow steps providing standing room for spectators in a stadium. ● **v.** (**terraces**, **terracing**, **terraced**) make (sloping land) into terraces.
– DERIVATIVES **terracing** n.
– ORIGIN Old French, 'rubble, platform'.

terraced ● **adj.** (of a house) forming part of a terrace.

terracotta /te-ruh-kot-tuh/ ● **n. 1** unglazed, brownish-red earthenware, used as a decorative building material and in modelling. **2** a strong brownish-red colour.
– ORIGIN from Italian *terra cotta* 'baked earth'.

terra firma /te-ruh fer-muh/ ● **n.** dry land; the ground.
– ORIGIN Latin, 'firm land'.

terrain /te-rayn/ ● **n.** a stretch of land with regard to its physical features: *rough terrain*.
– ORIGIN French.

terra incognita /te-ruh in-kog-ni-tuh/ ● **n.** unknown territory.
– ORIGIN Latin, 'unknown land'.

terrapin ● **n.** a small freshwater turtle.
– ORIGIN from an American Indian language.

terrarium /tuh-rair-i-uhm/ ● **n.** (pl. **terrariums** or **terraria** /tuh-rair-i-uh/) **1** a glass-fronted case for keeping small reptiles, amphibians, etc. **2** a sealed transparent container in which plants are grown.
– ORIGIN Latin *terra* 'earth'.

terrazzo /te-rat-zoh/ ● **n.** flooring material consisting of chips of marble or granite set in concrete and polished smooth.
– ORIGIN Italian, 'terrace'.

terrestrial /tuh-ress-tri-uhl/ ● **adj. 1** having to do with the earth or dry land. **2** (of an animal or plant) living on or in the ground. **3** (of television broadcasting) using ground-based equipment rather than a satellite.
– ORIGIN Latin *terrestris*.

terrible ● **adj. 1** extremely bad, serious, or unpleasant. **2** unhappy or guilty: *I felt terrible about forgetting her name*. **3** causing terror.
– ORIGIN Latin *terribilis*.

terribly ● **adv. 1** extremely. **2** very badly.

terrier ● **n.** a small breed of dog originally used to hunt animals that live underground.
– ORIGIN from Old French *chien terrier* 'earth dog'.

terrific ● **adj. 1** of great size, amount, or strength. **2** informal excellent.
– DERIVATIVES **terrifically** adv.
– ORIGIN Latin *terrificus*.

terrify ● **v.** (**terrifies**, **terrifying**, **terrified**) cause to feel terror.

terrine /tuh-reen/ ● **n.** a mixture of chopped meat, fish, or vegetables that is pressed into a container and served cold.
– ORIGIN French, 'large earthenware pot'.

territorial ● **adj. 1** relating to an area of land or sea that is owned by a particular country. **2** (of an animal) having and defending a territory. ● **n.** (**Territorial**) (in the UK) a member of the Territorial Army.
– DERIVATIVES **territoriality** n. **territorially** adv.

Territorial Army ● **n.** (in the UK) a military reserve force of people who volunteer to train as soldiers in their spare time.

territorial waters ● **pl. n.** the waters under the control of a state, especially those within a stated distance from its coast.

territory ● **n.** (pl. **territories**) **1** an area under the control of a ruler or state. **2** (**Territory**) an organized division of a country not having the full rights of a state. **3** an area defended by an animal against others of the same sex or species. **4** an area in which one has rights, responsibilities, or knowledge.
– ORIGIN Latin *territorium*.

terror ● **n. 1** extreme fear. **2** a cause of terror. **3** the use of terror to intimidate people: *weapons of terror*. **4** informal a person that causes trouble or annoyance.
– ORIGIN Latin.

terrorist ● **n.** a person who uses violence and

t

intimidation in an attempt to achieve political aims.
– DERIVATIVES **terrorism** n.

terrorize (also **terrorise**) • v. (**terrorizes**, **terrorizing**, **terrorized**) threaten and frighten (someone) over a period of time.

Terry, E
Dame (Alice) Ellen (1847–1928), English actress. George Bernard Shaw created a number of roles for her.

terry • n. fabric with raised loops of thread on both sides.
– ORIGIN unknown.

terse • adj. (**terser**, **tersest**) using few words; abrupt.
– DERIVATIVES **tersely** adv. **terseness** n.
– ORIGIN Latin *tersus* 'wiped, polished'.

tertiary /ter-shuh-ri/ • adj. **1** third in order or level. **2** Brit. (of education) at a level beyond that provided by schools. **3** (of medical treatment) provided at a specialist institution. **4** (**Tertiary**) Geol. relating to the first period of the Cenozoic era, about 65 to 1.64 million years ago.
– ORIGIN Latin *tertiarius*.

terylene • n. Brit. trademark a polyester fibre used to make clothing, bed linen, etc.

TESL • abbrev. teaching of English as a second language.

Tesla E
/tess-luh/, Nikola (1856–1943), American electrical engineer, born in what is now Croatia. He developed the first alternating-current induction motor, as well as a coil for producing high-frequency alternating currents, and a wireless guidance system for ships.

tesla /tess-luh/ • n. Physics the SI unit of magnetic flux density.
– ORIGIN named after Nikola **Tesla**.

TESOL /tess-ol/ • abbrev. teaching of English to speakers of other languages.

TESSA • n. (formerly in the UK) a special savings account allowing savers to invest a certain amount without paying tax on the interest.

tessellated /tess-uh-lay-tid/ • adj. (of a floor) decorated with mosaics.
– DERIVATIVES **tessellation** n.
– ORIGIN Latin *tessellare* 'decorate with mosaics'.

tessera /tess-uh-ruh/ • n. (pl. **tesserae** /tess-uh-ree, tess-uh-ray/) a small block of stone, tile, etc. used in a mosaic.
– ORIGIN Greek.

tessitura /tess-i-tyoor-uh/ • n. Music the range within which most notes of a vocal part fall.
– ORIGIN Italian, 'texture'.

test[1] • n. **1** a procedure intended to establish the quality, performance, or reliability of something. **2** a short examination of skill or knowledge. **3** a means of testing something. **4** a difficult situation that reveals the strength or quality of someone or something. **5** an examination of part of the body or a body fluid for medical purposes. **6** Chem. a procedure for identifying a substance or revealing whether it is present. **7** a test match. • v. **1** subject to a test. **2** touch or taste before proceeding further. **3** severely try (a person's endurance or patience).
– PHRASES **test the water** find out feelings or opinions before proceeding further.
– ORIGIN Latin *testum* 'earthen pot'.

test[2] • n. Zool. the shell of some invertebrates and protozoans.
– ORIGIN Latin *testa* 'tile, jug, shell'.

testa /tess-tuh/ • n. (pl. **testae** /tess-tee/) Bot. the protective outer covering of a seed.
– ORIGIN Latin, 'tile, shell'.

testament • n. **1** a person's will. **2** evidence or proof of a fact, event, or quality: *the show's success is a testament to her talent.*
– ORIGIN Latin *testamentum* 'a will'.

testamentary • adj. having to do with a will.

testate /tess-tayt/ • adj. having made a valid will before one dies.
– ORIGIN Latin *testatus* 'testified'.

testator /tess-tay-ter/ • n. (fem. **testatrix** /tess-tay-triks/) Law a person who has made a will or given a legacy.
– ORIGIN Latin.

test card • n. Brit. a still television picture transmitted outside normal programme hours to help judge the quality of the image.

test case • n. Law a case setting an example for future cases.

test-drive • v. (**test-drives**, **test-driving**, **test-drove**; past part. **test-driven**) drive (a motor vehicle) to judge its performance and quality.

tester • n. **1** a person or device that tests. **2** a sample of a product allowing customers to try it before buying.

testicle • n. either of the two oval organs that produce sperm in male mammals, enclosed in the scrotum behind the penis.
– DERIVATIVES **testicular** adj.
– ORIGIN Latin *testiculus*.

testify • v. (**testifies**, **testifying**, **testified**) **1** give evidence as a witness in a law court. **2** serve as evidence or proof: *luxurious villas testify to the wealth here.*
– ORIGIN Latin *testificari*.

testimonial /tess-ti-moh-ni-uhl/ • n. **1** a formal statement of a person's good character and qualifications. **2** a public tribute to someone and to their achievements.

testimony • n. (pl. **testimonies**) **1** a formal statement, especially one given in a court of law. **2** evidence or proof of something.
– ORIGIN Latin *testimonium*.

testis /tess-tiss/ • n. (pl. **testes** /tess-teez/) Anat. & Zool. an organ which produces sperm.
– ORIGIN Latin, 'witness'.

test match • n. an international cricket or rugby match played between teams representing two different countries.

testosterone /tess-toss-tuh-rohn/ • n. a steroid hormone that stimulates the development of male secondary sexual characteristics.
– ORIGIN from **testis**.

test pilot • n. a pilot who flies new or modified aircraft to test their performance.

test tube • n. a thin glass tube closed at one end, used to hold material for laboratory testing or experiments.

test-tube baby • n. informal a baby conceived by in vitro fertilization.

testy • adj. easily irritated.
– DERIVATIVES **testily** adv. **testiness** n.
– ORIGIN first meaning 'headstrong': from Old

French *teste* 'head'.

tetanus /tet-uh-nuhss/ ● **n.** a disease causing the muscles to stiffen and go into spasms, spread by bacteria.
– ORIGIN Latin.

tetchy ● **adj.** bad-tempered and irritable.
– DERIVATIVES **tetchily** adv. **tetchiness** n.
– ORIGIN prob. from Old French *teche* 'blotch, fault'.

tête-à-tête /tayt-ah-tayt/ ● **n.** (pl. **tête-à-tête** or **tête-à-têtes** /tayt-ah-tayt/) a private conversation between two people.
– ORIGIN French, 'head-to-head'.

tether ● **n.** a rope or chain used to tie an animal to a post, fence, etc. ● **v.** (**tethers**, **tethering**, **tethered**) tie with a tether.
– ORIGIN Old Norse.

tetra- (also **tetr-** before a vowel) ● **comb. form** four; having four: *tetrahedron.*
– ORIGIN Greek *tettares* 'four'.

tetrahedron /tet-ruh-hee-druhn/ ● **n.** (pl. **tetrahedra** /tet-ruh-hee-druh/ or **tetrahedrons**) a solid having four plane triangular faces.

tetralogy /ti-tral-uh-ji/ ● **n.** (pl. **tetralogies**) a group of four related literary or operatic works.

tetrameter /ti-tram-i-ter/ ● **n.** Poetry a verse of four metrical feet.

tetrapod /te-truh-pod/ ● **n.** Zool. an animal of a group which includes all vertebrates apart from fishes.
– ORIGIN Greek *tetrapous* 'four-footed'.

Teuton /tyoo-tuhn/ ● **n.** a member of an ancient Germanic people who lived in Jutland.
– ORIGIN Latin *Teutones* (plural).

Teutonic /tyoo-ton-ik/ ● **adj.** **1** relating to the Teutons. **2** informal, usu. derog. displaying qualities thought to belong to Germans.

Texas E
a state in the southern US, on the border with Mexico; capital, Austin.
– DERIVATIVES **Texan** adj. & n.

text ● **n.** **1** a written or printed work seen in terms of its content rather than its form. **2** the main body of a written work as distinct from appendices, illustrations, etc. **3** written or printed words or computer data. **4** a written work chosen as a subject of study. **5** a passage from the Bible as the subject of a sermon.
– ORIGIN Latin *textus* 'tissue, literary style'.

textbook ● **n.** a book used as a standard work for the study of a subject. ● **adj.** done in exactly the recommended way: *a textbook example of damage control.*

textile ● **n.** a type of cloth or woven fabric. ● **adj.** relating to fabric or weaving.
– ORIGIN Latin *textilis.*

textual ● **adj.** relating to a text or texts.
– DERIVATIVES **textually** adv.

texture ● **n.** the feel, appearance, or consistency of a surface, substance, or fabric. ● **v.** (**textures**, **texturing**, **textured**) give a rough or raised texture to.
– DERIVATIVES **textural** adj.
– ORIGIN Latin *textura* 'weaving'.

TGV ● **n.** a French high-speed passenger train.
– ORIGIN abbreviation of French *train à grande vitesse.*

-th (also **-eth**) ● **suffix** forming ordinal and fractional numbers from *fourth* onwards.
– ORIGIN Old English.

Thackeray E
/thak-uh-ri/, William Makepeace (1811–63), British novelist, best known as the author of the satire *Vanity Fair.*

Thailand E
a kingdom in SE Asia; capital, Bangkok. Former name (until 1939) **Siam**.
– DERIVATIVES **Thai** adj. & n.

thalidomide /thuh-lid-uh-myd/ ● **n.** a drug formerly used as a sedative, but found to cause malformation of the fetus when taken in early pregnancy.

thallium /thal-li-uhm/ ● **n.** a soft silvery-white metallic chemical element whose compounds are very poisonous.
– ORIGIN Greek *thallos* 'green shoot'.

Thames E
a river of southern England, flowing 338 km (210 miles) eastwards from the Cotswolds through London to the North Sea.

than ● **conj. & prep.** **1** used to introduce the second part of a comparison. **2** used to introduce an exception or contrast. **3** used in expressions indicating one thing happening immediately after another.
– ORIGIN Old English.

USAGE than
For an explanation of whether to use **I** and **we** or **me** and **us** after **than**, see the note at **PERSONAL PRONOUN**.

thane /thayn/ ● **n.** **1** (in Anglo-Saxon England) a lesser nobleman granted land by the king or a higher-ranking nobleman. **2** (in Scotland) a nobleman who held land from a king.
– ORIGIN Old English, 'servant, soldier'.

thank ● **v.** **1** express gratitude to. **2** ironic blame or hold responsible: *you have only yourself to thank.*
– PHRASES **thank you** a polite expression of gratitude.
– ORIGIN Old English.

thankful ● **adj.** **1** pleased and relieved. **2** expressing gratitude.
– DERIVATIVES **thankfulness** n.

thankfully ● **adv.** **1** in a thankful way. **2** fortunately.

thankless ● **adj.** **1** (of a job or task) unpleasant and unlikely to be appreciated by others. **2** not showing or feeling gratitude.

thanks ● **pl. n.** **1** an expression of gratitude. **2** thank you.
– PHRASES **no thanks to** despite the unhelpfulness of. **thanks to** due to.
– ORIGIN Old English.

thanksgiving ● **n.** **1** the expression of gratitude to God. **2** (**Thanksgiving**) (in North America) a national holiday commemorating a harvest festival celebrated by the Pilgrim Fathers, held in the US on the fourth Thursday in November and in Canada on the second Monday in October.

that ● **pron. & det.** **1** (pl. **those**) used to refer to a person or thing seen or heard by the speaker or already mentioned or known. **2** (pl. **those**) referring to the more distant of two things near to the speaker. **3** (as pronoun) (pl. **that**) used

instead of which, who, when, etc. to introduce a clause that defines or identifies something: *the woman that owns the place.* ● **adv.** **1** to such a degree; so. **2** informal very: *he wasn't that far away.* ● **conj.** introducing a statement or suggestion: *she said that she'd be late.*
– ORIGIN Old English.

USAGE that

When is it right to use **that** and when should you use **which**? The general rule is that, when introducing clauses that define or identify something, it is acceptable to use **that** or **which**: *a book which aims to simplify scientific language* or *a book that aims to simplify scientific language.* You should use **which**, but never **that**, to introduce a clause giving additional information: *the book, which costs £15, has sold over a million copies* not *the book, that costs £15, has sold over a million copies.*

thatch ● **n.** **1** a roof covering of straw, reeds, or similar material. **2** informal the hair on a person's head. ● **v.** cover with thatch.
– DERIVATIVES **thatcher** n.
– ORIGIN Old English, 'cover'.

Thatcher, E
Margaret (Hilda), Baroness Thatcher of Kesteven (b.1925), British Conservative stateswoman, Prime Minister 1979–90. She was the country's first woman Prime Minister. Her term of office was marked by monetarist policies, privatization, and trade union legislation.
– DERIVATIVES **Thatcherism** n.

thaw ● **v.** **1** become or make liquid or soft after being frozen. **2** (**it thaws**, **it is thawing**, **it thawed**) the weather becomes warmer and causes snow and ice to melt. **3** make or become friendlier. ● **n.** **1** a period of warmer weather that thaws ice and snow. **2** an increase in friendliness.
– ORIGIN Old English.

the ● **det.** **1** used to refer to one or more people or things already mentioned or easily understood; the definite article. **2** used to refer to someone or something that is the only one of its kind: *the sun.* **3** used to refer to something in a general rather than specific way: *the computer has changed our way of life.*
– ORIGIN Old English.

theatre (US **theater**) ● **n.** **1** a building in which plays and other dramatic performances are given. **2** the writing and production of plays. **3** the dramatic quality of a play: *this is intense, moving theatre.* **4** (also **lecture theatre**) a room for lectures with seats in tiers. **5** the area in which something happens: *a new theatre of war has opened up.*
– ORIGIN Greek *theatron*.

theatrical ● **adj.** **1** having to do with acting, actors, or the theatre. **2** exaggerated and excessively dramatic. ● **n.** (**theatricals**) theatrical performances or behaviour.
– DERIVATIVES **theatricality** n. **theatrically** adv.

theatrics /thi-a-triks/ ● **n.** theatricals.

Thebes[1] E
/theebz/ the Greek name for a city of ancient Egypt, whose ruins are situated at present-day Luxor and Karnak. It was the capital of Egypt under the 18th dynasty (*c.*1550–1290 BC) and is the site of major temples.

Thebes[2] E
/theebz/ a city in ancient Greece, north-west of Athens. It became a major military power in Greece in the 4th century BC.

thee ● **pron.** archaic or dialect you (as the singular object of a verb or preposition).
– ORIGIN Old English.

theft ● **n.** the action or crime of stealing.
– ORIGIN Old English.

their ● **possess. det.** **1** belonging to or associated with the people or things previously mentioned or easily identified. **2** belonging to or associated with a person whose sex is not specified (used in place of either 'his' or 'his or her'). **3** (**Their**) used in titles.
– ORIGIN Old Norse.

USAGE their

Do not confuse **their** and **there**. **Their** means 'belonging to them' (as in *I went round to their house*) while **there** means 'in, at, or to that place' (as in *it will take an hour to get there*).

For an explanation of the use of **their** in the singular to mean 'his or her', see the note at **THEY**.

theirs ● **possess. pron.** used to refer to something belonging to or associated with two or more people or things previously mentioned.

theism /thee-i-z'm/ ● **n.** belief in the existence of a creator who intervenes in the universe. Compare with **DEISM**.
– DERIVATIVES **theist** n. **theistic** adj.
– ORIGIN Greek *theos* 'god'.

them ● **pron.** (third person pl.) **1** used as the object of a verb or preposition to refer to two or more people or things previously mentioned or easily identified. **2** referring to a person whose sex is not specified (used in place of either 'him' or 'him or her').
– ORIGIN Old Norse.

USAGE them

For an explanation of the use of **them** in the singular to mean 'his or her', see the note at **THEY**.

thematic ● **adj.** arranged according to subject or having to do with a subject.
– DERIVATIVES **thematically** adv.

theme ● **n.** **1** a subject on which a person speaks, writes, or thinks. **2** Music a prominent or frequently recurring melody or group of notes in a composition. **3** an idea that is often repeated in a work of art or literature. ● **adj.** **1** (of music) accompanying the beginning and end of a film or programme. **2** (of a restaurant or pub) designed in the style of a particular country, historical period, etc.
– ORIGIN Greek *thema* 'proposition'.

theme park ● **n.** an amusement park designed in accordance with a particular setting or idea.

themself ● **pron.** (third person sing.) informal used instead of 'himself' or 'herself' to refer to a person whose sex is not specified.

USAGE themself

The standard reflexive pronoun (a word such as 'myself' or 'herself') corresponding to **they** and **them** is **themselves**, as in *they can do it themselves.* The singular form **themself** has been used recently to correspond to the singular use of **they** when referring to a person whose sex is not specified, as in *helping someone to help themself.* However, **themself** is not good English, and you should use **themselves** instead.

themselves • **pron.** (third person pl.) **1** used as the object of a verb or preposition to refer to a group of people or things previously mentioned as the subject of the clause. **2** they or them personally. **3** used instead of 'himself' or 'herself' to refer to a person of unspecified sex.

then • **adv. 1** at that time. **2** after that. **3** also. **4** therefore.
– PHRASES **but then (again)** on the other hand. **then and there** immediately.
– ORIGIN Old English.

thence (also **from thence**) • **adv.** formal **1** from a place or source previously mentioned. **2** as a consequence.

thenceforth (also **from thenceforth**) • **adv.** archaic or formal from that time, place, or point onward.

thenceforward • **adv.** thenceforth.

theocracy /thi-ok-ruh-si/ • **n.** (pl. **theocracies**) a system of government in which priests rule in the name of God or a god.
– DERIVATIVES **theocratic** adj.
– ORIGIN Greek *theos* 'god'.

theodolite /thi-od-uh-lyt/ • **n.** an instrument with a rotating telescope used in surveying for measuring horizontal and vertical angles.
– ORIGIN Latin *theodelitus.*

Theodosius I E
/thi-uh-**doh**-si-uhss/ (*c.*346–95; full name *Flavius Theodosius*; known as **Theodosius the Great**), Roman emperor 379–95. A pious Christian, in 391 he banned all forms of pagan worship.

theologian /thi-uh-**loh**-juhn/ • **n.** a person expert in or studying theology.

theology • **n.** (pl. **theologies**) **1** the study of God and religious belief. **2** a system of religious beliefs and theory: *Christian theology.*
– DERIVATIVES **theological** adj. **theologist** n.

Theophrastus E
/thi-uh-**frass**-tuhss/ (*c.*370–*c.*287 BC), Greek philosopher and scientist, the pupil of Aristotle. He is known for *Characters*, a collection of sketches of psychological types.

theorem /**theer**-uhm/ • **n. 1** Physics & Math. a general proposition or rule that can be proved by reasoning. **2** Math. a rule expressed by symbols or formulae.
– ORIGIN Greek *theōrēma* 'proposition'.

theoretical (also **theoretic**) • **adj. 1** concerned with the theory of a subject rather than its practical application. **2** based on theory rather than experience or practice: *British players have a theoretical advantage.*
– DERIVATIVES **theoretically** adv.

theoretician /theer-uh-**ti**-sh'hn/ • **n.** a person who develops or studies the theory of a subject.

theorist • **n.** a theoretician.

theorize (also **theorise**) • **v.** (**theorizes, theorizing, theorized**) form a theory or theories about something.

theory • **n.** (pl. **theories**) **1** an idea or set of ideas that is intended to explain something. **2** a set of principles on which an activity is based: *a theory of education.*
– PHRASES **in theory** in an ideal situation, but probably not in reality.
– ORIGIN Greek *theōria* 'speculation'.

theosophy /thi-**oss**-uh-fi/ • **n.** a philosophy which believes that a knowledge of God may be achieved through such things as intuition, meditation, and prayer.
– DERIVATIVES **theosophical** adj.
– ORIGIN Greek *theosophos* 'wise concerning God'.

Thera E
/**theer**-uh/ a Greek island in the southern Cyclades. The island suffered a volcanic eruption in about 1500 BC; remains of an ancient Minoan civilization have been preserved beneath the volcanic debris. Also called **SANTORINI**.

therapeutic /the-ruh-**pyoo**-tik/ • **adj. 1** relating to the healing of disease. **2** having a good effect on the body or mind.
– DERIVATIVES **therapeutically** adv.

therapy • **n.** (pl. **therapies**) **1** treatment intended to relieve or heal a physical disorder or illness. **2** the treatment of mental disorders or problems using psychological methods.
– DERIVATIVES **therapist** n.
– ORIGIN Greek *therapeia* 'healing'.

there • **adv. 1** in, at, or to that place or position. **2** on that issue. **3** used in attracting attention to someone or something. **4** (**there is/are**) used to indicate the fact or existence of something. • **exclam.** used to comfort someone.
– PHRASES **here and there** in various places. **there and then** immediately.
– ORIGIN Old English.

USAGE there
For an explanation of the difference between **there** and **their**, see the note at **THEIR**.

thereabouts (also **thereabout**) • **adv.** near that place, time, or figure.

thereafter • **adv.** formal after that time.

thereat • **adv.** archaic or formal **1** at that place. **2** on account of or after that.

thereby • **adv.** by that means; as a result of that.

therefore • **adv.** for that reason.

therein • **adv.** archaic or formal in that place, document, or respect.

thereof • **adv.** formal of the thing just mentioned.

thereon • **adv.** formal on or following from the thing just mentioned.

there's • **contr. 1** there is. **2** there has.

Theresa, Mother E
see **TERESA, MOTHER**.

thereto • **adv.** archaic or formal to that or that place.

thereupon • **adv.** formal immediately or shortly after that.

therewith • **adv.** archaic or formal **1** with or in the thing mentioned. **2** soon or immediately after that.

thermal • **adj. 1** relating to heat. **2** (of a garment) made of a fabric that provides good insulation to keep the body warm. • **n. 1** an

upward current of warm air, used by birds, gliders, and balloonists to gain height. **2** (**thermals**) thermal underwear.
– DERIVATIVES **thermally** adv.
– ORIGIN Greek *thermē* 'heat'.

thermal spring • n. a spring of naturally hot water.

thermionic /ther-mi-**on**-ik/ • adj. relating to the emission of electrons from substances heated to very high temperatures.

thermocouple • n. a device for measuring or sensing a temperature difference, consisting of two wires of different metals connected at two points, between which a voltage is developed in proportion to any temperature difference.

thermodynamics • n. the branch of science concerned with the relations between heat and other forms of energy involved in physical and chemical processes.
– DERIVATIVES **thermodynamic** adj.

thermoelectric • adj. producing electricity by a difference of temperatures.

thermometer • n. an instrument for measuring temperature, typically consisting of a graduated glass tube containing mercury or alcohol which expands when heated.

thermonuclear • adj. relating to or using nuclear fusion reactions that occur at very high temperatures.

thermopile /ther-moh-pyl/ • n. a set of thermocouples arranged for measuring small quantities of heat transmitted by radiation.

thermoplastic • adj. (of a substance) becoming plastic when heated.

Thermopylae E
/ther-**mop**-i-li/ a pass between the mountains and the sea in Greece, north-west of Athens. In 480 BC it was the scene of a defensive action by an outnumbered Greek force against the invading Persians under Xerxes I. The defenders included 300 Spartans who fought to the death to delay the Persian advance.

thermoregulation • n. Physiol. the regulation of bodily temperature.

Thermos • n. trademark a vacuum flask.
– ORIGIN Greek, 'hot'.

thermosetting • adj. (of a substance) setting permanently when heated.

thermosphere • n. the upper region of the atmosphere above the mesosphere.

thermostat /ther-muh-stat/ • n. a device that automatically regulates temperature or activates a device at a set temperature.
– DERIVATIVES **thermostatic** adj. **thermostatically** adv.

thesaurus /thi-saw-ruhss/ • n. (pl. **thesauri** /thi-saw-ry/ or **thesauruses**) a book containing lists of words which have the same, similar, or a related meaning.
– ORIGIN Greek *thēsauros* 'storehouse, treasure'.

these pl. of **THIS**.

Theseus E
/**thee**-si-uhss/ Gk Myth. the son of Poseidon (or, in another account, of Aegeus, king of Athens). His many exploits included the killing of the Minotaur.

thesis /thee-siss/ • n. (pl. **theses** /thee-seez/) **1** a statement or theory put forward to be supported or proved. **2** a long piece of written work involving personal research, written as part of a university degree.
– ORIGIN Greek, 'placing, a proposition'.

thespian /thess-pi-uhn/ • adj. relating to drama and the theatre. • n. an actor or actress.
– ORIGIN from the ancient Greek dramatic poet *Thespis* (6th century BC).

Thessaloníki E
/thess-uh-luh-**nee**-ki/ a seaport in Macedonia in NE Greece. Also called **SALONICA**.

Thessaly E
/**thess**-uh-li/ a region of NE Greece.

they • pron. (third person pl.) **1** used to refer to two or more people or things previously mentioned or easily identified. **2** people in general. **3** used to refer to a person whose sex is not specified (in place of either 'he' or 'he or she').
– ORIGIN Old Norse.

USAGE they
Many people now think that the traditional use of **he** to refer to a person of either sex is outdated and sexist; the alternative, **he or she**, is rather clumsy. For this reason, **they** (with its counterparts **them** or **their**) have become acceptable instead, as in *anyone can join if they are a resident* and *each to their own*.

they'd • contr. **1** they had. **2** they would.

they'll • contr. **1** they shall. **2** they will.

they're • contr. they are.

they've • contr. they have.

thiamine /thy-uh-meen/ (also **thiamin** /thy-uh-min/) • n. vitamin B_1, a compound found in unrefined cereals, beans, and liver.
– ORIGIN Greek *theion* 'sulphur'.

thick • adj. **1** with opposite sides or surfaces relatively far apart. **2** (of a garment or fabric) made of heavy material. **3** made up of a large number of things or people close together: *thick forest*. **4** (**thick with**) densely filled or covered with. **5** (of the air or atmosphere) heavy, dense, or difficult to see through. **6** (of a liquid or a semi-liquid substance) relatively firm in consistency. **7** informal stupid. **8** (of a voice) hoarse or husky. **9** (of an accent) very marked and difficult to understand. **10** informal very close and friendly. • n. (**the thick**) the middle or the busiest part: *in the thick of battle*.
– PHRASES **thick and fast** rapidly and in great numbers. **(as) thick as thieves** informal very close or friendly. **through thick and thin** under all circumstances, no matter how difficult.
– DERIVATIVES **thickly** adv.
– ORIGIN Old English.

thicken • v. make or become thick or thicker.
– PHRASES **the plot thickens** the situation is becoming more complicated and puzzling.

thickening • n. **1** a thicker area or part. **2** a substance added to a liquid to make it thicker.

thicket • n. a dense group of bushes or trees.
– ORIGIN Old English.

thickness • n. **1** the distance through an object, as distinct from width or height. **2** the state or quality of being thick. **3** a layer of material. **4** a thicker part of something: *beams set into the thickness of the wall.*

thickset ● adj. heavily or solidly built.

thief ● n. (pl. **thieves**) a person who steals another person's property.
– ORIGIN Old English.

thieve ● v. (**thieves**, **thieving**, **thieved**) steal things.
– DERIVATIVES **thievery** n.

thigh ● n. the part of the leg between the hip and the knee.
– ORIGIN Old English.

thimble ● n. a metal or plastic cap with a closed end, worn to protect the finger and push the needle in sewing.
– ORIGIN Old English.

thimbleful ● n. a small quantity of something.

Thimphu E
/tim-poo, thim-poo/ (also **Thimbu** /tim-boo, thim-boo/) the capital of Bhutan.

thin ● adj. (**thinner**, **thinnest**) **1** having opposite surfaces or sides close together. **2** (of a garment or fabric) made of light material. **3** having little flesh or fat on the body. **4** having few parts or members in relation to to the area covered or filled: *a thin crowd.* **5** not dense or heavy. **6** containing much liquid and not much solid substance. **7** (of a sound) faint and high-pitched. **8** weak and inadequate: *the evidence is rather thin.* ● v. (**thins**, **thinning**, **thinned**) **1** make or become less thick. **2** (often **thin out**) remove some plants from (an area) to allow the others more room to grow.
– PHRASES **into thin air** so as to become invisible or non-existent.
– DERIVATIVES **thinly** adv. **thinness** n.
– ORIGIN Old English.

thine ● possess. pron. & possess. det. archaic your or yours.
– ORIGIN Old English.

thing ● n. **1** an inanimate object. **2** an unspecified object. **3** (**things**) personal belongings or clothing. **4** an action, activity, or thought. **5** (**things**) unspecified matters: *how are things?* **6** (**the thing**) informal what is needed, acceptable, or fashionable. **7** (**one's thing**) informal one's special interest.
– ORIGIN Old English.

thingamajig /thing-uh-muh-jig/ ● n. = **THINGUMMY**.

thingummy /thing-uh-mi/ (also **thingamy**) ● n. (pl. **thingummies**) informal a person or thing whose name one has forgotten, does not know, or does not wish to mention.

thingy ● n. (pl. **thingies**) = **THINGUMMY**.

think ● v. (**thinks**, **thinking**, **thought**) **1** have a particular opinion, belief, or idea about someone or something. **2** direct one's mind towards someone or something. **3** (**think of/about**) take into account or consideration. **4** (**think of/about**) consider the possibility or advantages of. **5** call something to mind. ● n. an act of thinking.
– PHRASES **think better of** reconsider and decide not to do. **think nothing** (or **little**) **of** consider (an activity others see as odd, wrong, or difficult) as easy or normal. **think over** consider carefully. **think twice** consider a course of action carefully before embarking on it. **think up** informal invent.
– DERIVATIVES **thinker** n.
– ORIGIN Old English.

thinking ● adj. intelligent: *MacLean is the thinking man's player.* ● n. a person's ideas or opinions.
– PHRASES **put on one's thinking cap** informal think hard about a problem.

think tank ● n. a body of experts providing advice and ideas on specific political or economic problems.

thinner ● n. a solvent used to thin paint or other solutions.

third ● ordinal number **1** that is number three in a sequence; 3rd. **2** (**a third/one third**) each of three equal parts into which something is divided. **3** Music an interval spanning three consecutive notes in a scale. **4** Brit. a place in the third grade in the examinations for a university degree.
– DERIVATIVES **thirdly** adv.
– ORIGIN Old English.

third class ● n. **1** a set of people or things considered together as the third best. **2** Brit. the third-highest division in the results of the examinations for a university degree. **3** hist. the cheapest and least comfortable accommodation in a train or ship. ● adj. & adv. relating to the third class.

third-degree ● adj. (of burns) being of the most severe kind, affecting tissue below the skin. ● n. (**the third degree**) long and harsh questioning to obtain information or a confession.

third party ● n. a person or group besides the two main ones involved in a situation or dispute. ● adj. Brit. (of insurance) covering damage or injury suffered by a person other than the insured.

third person ● n. **1** a third party. **2** see **PERSON** (sense 3).

third-rate ● adj. of very poor quality.

Third Reich /rykh, ryk/ ● n. the Nazi regime in Germany, 1933–45.
– ORIGIN German *Reich* 'empire'.

third way ● n. a political agenda which is moderate and based on general agreement rather than left- or right-wing.

Third World ● n. the developing countries of Asia, Africa, and Latin America.
– ORIGIN first used to distinguish the developing countries from the capitalist and Communist blocs.

thirst ● n. **1** a feeling of needing or wanting to drink. **2** the state of not having enough water to stay alive. **3** (**thirst for**) a strong desire for. ● v. **1** (**thirst for/after**) have a strong desire for. **2** archaic feel a need to drink.
– ORIGIN Old English.

thirsty ● adj. (**thirstier**, **thirstiest**) **1** feeling or causing thirst: *modelling is thirsty work.* **2** (of an engine or plant) consuming a lot of fuel or water. **3** (**thirsty for**) having or showing a strong desire for.
– DERIVATIVES **thirstily** adv. **thirstiness** n.

thirteen ● cardinal number one more than twelve; 13. (Roman numeral: **xiii** or **XIII**.)
– DERIVATIVES **thirteenth** ordinal number.
– ORIGIN Old English.

thirty ● cardinal number (pl. **thirties**) ten less than forty; 30. (Roman numeral: **xxx** or **XXX**.)

– DERIVATIVES **thirtieth** ordinal number.
– ORIGIN Old English.

Thirty Years War E
a European war of 1618–48 between the Catholic Holy Roman emperor and some of his German Protestant states. It developed into a struggle that also involved France, Sweden, and Spain.

this ● pron. & det. (pl. **these**) **1** used to identify a specific person or thing close at hand, just mentioned, or being indicated or experienced. **2** referring to the nearer of two things close to the speaker. **3** (as determiner) used with periods of time related to the present: *how are you this morning?* ● adv. to the degree or extent indicated.
– ORIGIN Old English.

thistle ● n. a plant with a prickly stem and leaves and rounded heads of purple flowers.
– ORIGIN Old English.

thistledown ● n. the light fluffy down of thistle seeds, which enable them to be blown about in the wind.

thither ● adv. archaic or literary to or towards that place.
– ORIGIN Old English.

tho' (also **tho**) ● conj. & adv. informal spelling of **THOUGH**.

thole /thohl/ (also **thole pin**) ● n. a pin fitted to the gunwale of a rowing boat, forming the point on which an oar turns.
– ORIGIN Old English.

Thomas[1], E
Dylan (Marlais) (1914–53), Welsh poet. His work includes *Under Milk Wood*, a portrait of a Welsh town that combines poetic prose with songs and ballads.

Thomas[2], E
(Philip) Edward (1878–1917), English poet. His work offers a sympathetic but unidealized depiction of rural life.

Thomas, St E
an Apostle; known as **Doubting Thomas**. He earned his nickname by saying that he would not believe that Christ had risen again until he had seen and touched his wounds. Feast day, 21 December.

Thomas à Kempis E
/uh kem-piss/ (*c.*1380–1471; born *Thomas Hemerken*), German theologian. He is the probable author of *On the Imitation of Christ*, a manual of spiritual devotion.

Thomas Aquinas, St, E
see **AQUINAS, ST THOMAS**.

Thomas More, St E
see **MORE**.

Thompson[1], E
Daley (b.1958), English athlete. His decathlon titles include gold medals in the Olympics of 1980 and 1984.

Thompson[2], E
Emma (b.1959), English actress and screenwriter, known for such films as *Howard's End* and *Sense and Sensibility*.

Thompson[3], E
Flora (Jane) (1876–1947), English writer, author of the semi-autobiographical trilogy *Lark Rise to Candleford*.

Thomson[1], E
Sir Joseph John (1856–1940), English atomic physicist, who discovered the electron and researched into the electrical conductivity of gases.

Thomson[2], E
Sir William, see **KELVIN**.

thong ● n. **1** a narrow strip of leather or other material, used as a fastening or as the lash of a whip. **2** a skimpy bathing garment or pair of knickers like a G-string.
– ORIGIN Old English.

Thor E
/thor/ the Scandinavian god of thunder and the weather.

thorax /thor-aks/ ● n. (pl. **thoraces** /thor-uh-seez/ or **thoraxes**) **1** the part of the body between the neck and the abdomen. **2** the middle section of the body of an insect, bearing the legs and wings.
– DERIVATIVES **thoracic** adj.
– ORIGIN Greek.

Thoreau E
/thor-oh/, Henry David (1817–62), American essayist and poet, a key figure of the idealistic social and philosophical movement known as Transcendentalism. He is best known for *Walden, or Life in the Woods*, an account of a two-year experiment in self-sufficiency.

thorium /thor-i-uhm/ ● n. a white radioactive metallic chemical element.
– ORIGIN named after **THOR**.

thorn ● n. **1** a stiff, sharp-pointed woody projection on a plant. **2** a thorny bush, shrub, or tree.
– PHRASES **a thorn in someone's side** (or **flesh**) a source of continual annoyance or trouble.
– ORIGIN Old English.

Thorndike, E
Dame (Agnes) Sybil (1882–1976), English actress, noted for her Shakespearean roles.

thorny ● adj. (**thornier**, **thorniest**) **1** having many thorns or thorn bushes. **2** causing distress or difficulty.

thorough ● adj. **1** complete with regard to every detail. **2** performed with or showing great care and completeness. **3** absolute; utter: *he is a thorough nuisance.*
– DERIVATIVES **thoroughly** adv. **thoroughness** n.
– ORIGIN Old English, 'through'.

thoroughbred ● adj. **1** of pure breed. **2** informal of outstanding quality. ● n. a thoroughbred animal.

thoroughfare ● n. a road or path forming a route between two places.

thoroughgoing ● adj. **1** involving or dealing with every detail or aspect. **2** complete; absolute.

those pl. of **THAT**.

thou[1] ● pron. archaic or dialect you (as the singular subject of a verb).
– ORIGIN Old English.

thou[2] ● n. (pl. **thou** or **thous**) **1** informal a thousand. **2** one thousandth of an inch.

though ● conj. **1** despite the fact that; although. **2** however; but. ● adv. however: *he was able to write, though.*
– ORIGIN Old English.

thought[1] ● n. **1** an idea or opinion produced by thinking or that occurs suddenly in the mind. **2** the action of thinking. **3** (**one's thoughts**) one's mind. **4** careful consideration: *I haven't given it much thought.* **5** (**thought of**) an intention, hope, or idea of: *they had no thought of surrender.* **6** the forming of opinions or the opinions so formed: *traditions of Western thought.*
– PHRASES **not give a second thought** fail to give more than the slightest consideration to.
– ORIGIN Old English.

thought[2] past and past part. of **THINK**.

thoughtful ● adj. **1** deep in thought. **2** showing careful consideration. **3** showing regard for other people.
– DERIVATIVES **thoughtfully** adv. **thoughtfulness** n.

thoughtless ● adj. **1** not showing consideration for other people. **2** without consideration of the consequences.
– DERIVATIVES **thoughtlessly** adv. **thoughtlessness** n.

thousand ● cardinal number **1** (**a/one thousand**) the number equivalent to the product of a hundred and ten; 1,000. (Roman numeral: **m** or **M.**) **2** (**thousands**) informal an unspecified large number.
– DERIVATIVES **thousandth** ordinal number.
– ORIGIN Old English.

Thrace E
/thrayss/ an ancient country lying west of the Black Sea and north of the Aegean, now divided between Turkey, Bulgaria, and Greece.
– DERIVATIVES **Thracian** /thray-sh'n/ adj. & n.

thrall /thrawl/ ● n. the state of being in another's power: *she was in thrall to her husband.*
– ORIGIN Old Norse, 'slave'.

thrash ● v. **1** beat repeatedly and violently with a stick or whip. **2** move in a violent or uncontrolled way. **3** informal defeat heavily. **4** (**thrash out**) discuss frankly and thoroughly so as to reach a decision.
– ORIGIN Old English.

thread ● n. **1** a long, thin strand of cotton, nylon, or other fibres used in sewing or weaving. **2** a long thin line or piece of something. **3** (also **screw thread**) a spiral ridge on the outside of a screw or bolt or on the inside of a cylindrical hole, to allow two parts to be screwed together. **4** a theme running throughout a situation or piece of writing. ● v. **1** pass a thread through. **2** move or weave in and out of obstacles. **3** (**threaded**) (of a hole, screw, etc) having a screw thread.
– ORIGIN Old English.

threadbare ● adj. thin and tattered with age.

threadworm ● n. a thin, thread-like worm, living as a parasite.

threat ● n. **1** a stated intention to harm someone. **2** a person or thing likely to cause harm or danger. **3** the possibility of trouble or danger: *many jobs came under threat.*
– ORIGIN Old English, 'oppression'.

threaten ● v. **1** make a threat to (someone) or to do (something). **2** put at risk: *a broken finger threatened his career.* **3** (of a situation or the weather) seem likely to produce (an unwelcome result).

three ● cardinal number one more than two; 3. (Roman numeral: **iii** or **III.**)
– DERIVATIVES **threefold** adj. & adv.
– ORIGIN Old English.

three-dimensional ● adj. having or appearing to have length, breadth, and depth.

three-legged race ● n. a race run by pairs of people, one member of each pair having their left leg tied to the right leg of the other.

three-line whip ● n. (in the UK) a written notice, underlined three times to stress its urgency, to members of a political party to attend a vote in parliament.

threepence /threp-uhnss, thruu-puhnss/ ● n. Brit. the sum of three pence, especially before decimalization (1971).

threepenny bit /thri-puh-ni, thruu-puh-ni/ ● n. Brit. a former coin worth three old pence (1¼ p).

three-piece ● adj. **1** (of a set of furniture) consisting of a sofa and two armchairs. **2** (of a set of clothes) consisting of trousers or a skirt with a waistcoat and jacket.

three-point turn ● n. a method of turning a vehicle round in a narrow space by moving forwards, backwards, and forwards again in a sequence of arcs.

three-quarter ● adj. consisting of three quarters of something in terms of length, angle, time, etc. ● n. Rugby each of four players in a team positioned across the field behind the halfbacks.

threescore ● cardinal number literary sixty.

threesome ● n. a group of three people.

Three Wise Men E
another name for the Magi (see **MAGUS**).

threnody /thren-uh-di/ ● n. (pl. **threnodies**) a song, piece of music, or poem expressing grief or regret.
– ORIGIN Greek *thrēnōidia.*

thresh ● v. separate grain from (corn or other crops).
– DERIVATIVES **thresher** n.

threshold /thresh-ohld, thresh-hohld/ ● n. **1** a strip of wood or stone forming the bottom of a doorway. **2** a level or point at which something is about to begin: *she was on the threshold of a dazzling career.*
– ORIGIN Old English.

threw past of **THROW**.

thrice /thryss/ ● adv. archaic or literary **1** three times. **2** extremely; very: *I was thrice blessed.*
– ORIGIN Old English.

thrift ● n. **1** carefulness and economy in the use of money and other resources. **2** a plant with low-growing tufts of slender leaves and rounded pink flower heads, found on sea cliffs and mountains.
– ORIGIN Old Norse, 'grasp'.

thriftless ● adj. spending money in an extravagant and wasteful way.

thrifty ● adj. (**thriftier**, **thriftiest**) careful and economical with money.

thrill ● n. **1** a sudden feeling of excitement and

pleasure. **2** an exciting or pleasurable experience. **3** a nervous tremor of emotion or sensation. ● v. **1** have or cause to have a thrill. **2** (**thrill to**) feel very excited at.
– ORIGIN from dialect *thirl* 'pierce, bore'.

thriller ● n. a novel, play, or film with an exciting plot, typically involving crime or spying.

thrips /thrips/ (also **thrip**) ● n. (pl. **thrips**) a tiny black insect which sucks plant sap, noted for swarming on warm still summer days.
– ORIGIN Greek, 'woodworm'.

thrive ● v. (**thrives**, **thriving**, **thrived** or **throve**; past part. **thrived** or **thriven**) **1** grow or develop well or vigorously. **2** prosper; flourish.
– ORIGIN Old Norse, 'grasp'.

thro' ● prep., adv., & adj. literary or informal = THROUGH.

throat ● n. **1** the passage which leads from the back of the mouth, through which food passes to the oesophagus and air passes to the lungs. **2** the front part of the neck.
– PHRASES **be at each other's throats** fight persistently. **force something down someone's throat** force something on a person's attention. **stick in one's throat** be unwelcome or unacceptable.
– ORIGIN Old English.

throaty ● adj. (**throatier**, **throatiest**) (of a voice or other sound) deep and husky.
– DERIVATIVES **throatily** adv.

throb ● v. (**throbs**, **throbbing**, **throbbed**) **1** beat or sound with a strong, regular rhythm. **2** feel pain in a series of pulsations. ● n. a strong, regular beat or sound.

throes /throhz/ ● pl. n. severe or violent pain and struggle.
– PHRASES **in the throes of** struggling in the midst of.
– ORIGIN perh. from Old English, 'calamity'.

thrombosis /throm-**boh**-siss/ ● n. (pl. **thromboses** /throm-**boh**-seez/) the formation of a blood clot in a part of the circulatory system.
– ORIGIN Greek, 'curdling'.

throne ● n. **1** a chair for a king, queen, or bishop, used during ceremonies. **2** (**the throne**) the power or rank of a king or queen.
– ORIGIN Greek *thronos* 'elevated seat'.

throng ● n. a large, densely packed crowd. ● v. gather in large numbers in (a place).
– ORIGIN Old English.

throttle ● n. a device controlling the flow of fuel or power to an engine. ● v. (**throttles**, **throttling**, **throttled**) **1** attack or kill by choking or strangling. **2** control (an engine or vehicle) with a throttle.
– ORIGIN perh. from THROAT.

through ● prep. & adv. **1** moving in one side and out of the other side of (an opening or place). **2** (prep.) expressing the location of something beyond (an opening or an obstacle): *the approach to the church is through a gate.* **3** continuing in time towards: *she struggled through until pay day.* **4** from beginning to end: *we sat through some very boring speeches.* **5** by means of. **6** (adv.) so as to be connected by telephone. ● adj. **1** (of public transport or a ticket) continuing or valid to the final destination. **2** (of traffic, roads, etc.) passing straight through a place. **3** having successfully passed to the next stage of a competition. **4** informal having finished an activity, relationship, etc.
– ORIGIN Old English.

throughout ● prep. & adv. all the way through.

throughput ● n. the amount of material or items passing through a system or process.

throve past of THRIVE.

throw ● v. (**throws**, **throwing**, **threw**; past part. **thrown**) **1** send (something) from one's hand through the air by a rapid movement of the arm and hand. **2** move or place hurriedly or roughly. **3** direct or cast (light, an expression, etc.) in a particular direction. **4** send suddenly into a particular state: *the country was thrown into chaos.* **5** confuse or put off. **6** have (a fit or tantrum). **7** informal hold (a party). **8** form (ceramic ware) on a potter's wheel. ● n. **1** an act of throwing. **2** a small rug or light cover for furniture. **3** (**a throw**) informal a single turn, round, or item.
– PHRASES **throw away 1** get rid of (something useless or unwanted). **2** fail to make use of (an opportunity). **throw out** get rid of; force to leave. **throw up** vomit.
– ORIGIN Old English, 'to twist, turn'.

throwaway ● adj. **1** intended to be thrown away after being used once or a few times. **2** (of a remark) expressed in a casual way.

throwback ● n. a return to an earlier ancestral type or characteristic.

throw-in ● n. Soccer & Rugby the act of throwing the ball from the sideline to restart the game after the ball has gone out of play.

thru ● prep., adv., & adj. informal = THROUGH.

thrum ● v. (**thrums**, **thrumming**, **thrummed**) make a continuous rhythmic humming sound. ● n. a continuous rhythmic humming sound.

thrush[1] ● n. a songbird with a brown back and spotted breast.
– ORIGIN Old English.

thrush[2] ● n. infection of the mouth and throat or the genitals by a yeast-like fungus.
– ORIGIN uncertain.

thrust ● v. (**thrusts**, **thrusting**, **thrust**) **1** push suddenly or violently. **2** make one's way forcibly. **3** (**thrust on/upon**) force (something) unwelcome on. ● n. **1** a sudden or violent lunge or attack. **2** the main point of an argument. **3** the force produced by an engine to propel a jet or rocket.
– ORIGIN Old Norse.

thrusting ● adj. aggressively ambitious.

Thucydides E
/thyoo-**sid**-i-deez/ (*c.*455–*c.*400 BC), Greek historian, noted for his *History of the Peloponnesian War.*

thud ● n. a dull, heavy sound. ● v. (**thuds**, **thudding**, **thudded**) move, fall, or strike something with a thud.
– ORIGIN prob. from Old English, 'to thrust, push'.

thug ● n. a violent man.
– DERIVATIVES **thuggery** n. **thuggish** adj.
– ORIGIN Hindi, 'swindler, thief'.

thulium /**thyoo**-li-uhm/ ● n. a soft silvery-white metallic chemical element.
– ORIGIN from *Thule*, a country said in ancient times to be the northernmost part of the

world.

thumb • n. the short, thick first digit of the hand. • v. **1** press or indicate with one's thumb. **2** turn over (pages) with one's thumb. **3** (**thumbed**) (of a book's pages) worn or dirty from repeated handling. **4** request (a free ride in a passing vehicle) by signalling with one's thumb.
– PHRASES **thumbs up** (or **down**) informal an indication of satisfaction or approval (or of rejection or failure). [ORIGIN referring to the sign of approval or disapproval used by spectators at a Roman amphitheatre (although they used the gestures in reverse).] **under someone's thumb** completely under someone's control.
– ORIGIN Old English.

thumb index • n. a set of lettered notches cut down the side of a book for easy reference.

thumbnail • adj. brief or concise: *a thumbnail sketch.*

thumbscrew • n. an instrument of torture that crushes the thumbs.

thumbtack • n. N. Amer. a drawing pin.

thump • v. **1** hit heavily with the fist or a blunt object. **2** put down forcefully or noisily. **3** (of a person's heart or pulse) beat strongly. • n. a heavy dull blow or noise.

thumping • adj. **1** pounding; throbbing. **2** informal impressively large: *a thumping 64 per cent majority.*

thunder • n. **1** a loud rumbling or crashing noise heard after a lightning flash due to the expansion of rapidly heated air. **2** a resounding loud deep noise. • v. **1** (**it thunders, it is thundering, it thundered**) thunder sounds. **2** move heavily and forcefully. **3** speak loudly and angrily.
– ORIGIN Old English.

Thunder Bay E
a city and port on Lake Superior in SW Ontario.

thunderbolt • n. a flash of lightning with a crash of thunder at the same time.

thunderclap • n. a crash of thunder.

thundercloud • n. a cloud with a towering or spreading top, charged with electricity and producing thunder and lightning.

thundering • adj. making a resounding, loud, deep noise.

thunderous • adj. **1** very loud. **2** (of a person's expression) very angry or threatening.

thunderstorm • n. a storm with thunder and lightning.

thunderstruck • adj. extremely surprised or shocked.

Thurber E
/ther-ber/, James (Grover) (1894–1961), American humorist and cartoonist, author of the story 'The Secret Life of Walter Mitty'.

thurible /thyoo-ri-b'l/ • n. a container in which incense is burnt; a censer.
– ORIGIN Latin *thuribulum.*

Thursday • n. the day of the week before Friday and following Wednesday.
– ORIGIN Old English, 'day of thunder' (named after the god **THOR**).

thus • adv. formal **1** as a result of this; therefore. **2** in this way. **3** to this point; so.
– ORIGIN Old English.

thwack • v. strike forcefully with a sharp blow. • n. a sharp blow.

thwart /thwort/ • v. prevent from succeeding in or accomplishing something.
– ORIGIN Old Norse, 'transverse'.

thy (also **thine** before a vowel) • **possess. det.** archaic or dialect your.
– ORIGIN Old English.

thyme /*rhymes with* time/ • n. a low-growing plant of the mint family, used as a herb in cooking.
– ORIGIN Greek *thumon.*

thymus /thy-muhss/ • n. (pl. **thymi** /thy-my/) a gland in the neck which produces white blood cells for the immune system.
– ORIGIN Greek *thumos.*

thyroid /thy-royd/ • n. (also **thyroid gland**) a large gland in the neck which produces hormones regulating growth and development.
– ORIGIN from Greek *khondros thureoeidēs* 'shield-shaped cartilage'.

thyself • pron. (second person sing.) archaic or dialect yourself.

Tiananmen Square E
/tyen-uhn-muhn/ a square in the centre of Beijing, the largest public open space in the world. In spring 1989 government troops opened fire there on unarmed pro-democracy protesters, killing over 2,000.

Tianjin E
/tyen-jin/ (also **Tientsin**) a port in NE China.

Tian Shan E
var. of **TIEN SHAN**.

tiara • n. a jewelled ornamental band worn on the front of a woman's hair.
– ORIGIN Greek.

Tiber E
/ty-ber/ a river of central Italy, which rises in Tuscany and flows generally south-westwards through Rome to the Tyrrhenian Sea.

Tiberias, Lake E
/ty-beer-i-uhss/ = Sea of Galilee (see **GALILEE, SEA OF**).

Tiberius E
/ty-beer-i-uhss/ (42 BC–AD 37; full name *Tiberius Julius Caesar Augustus*), Roman emperor AD 14–37, the son-in-law and stepson of Augustus. His reign was marked by many treason trials and executions.

Tibet E
/ti-bet/ a country in Asia on the northern side of the Himalayas, since 1965 forming an autonomous region of China; capital, Lhasa.
– DERIVATIVES **Tibetan** adj. & n.

tibia /ti-bi-uh/ • n. (pl. **tibiae** /ti-bi-ee/) the inner of the two bones between the knee and the ankle, parallel with the fibula.
– ORIGIN Latin, 'shin bone'.

tic • n. a recurring spasm in the muscles of the face.
– ORIGIN Italian *ticchio.*

tick[1] • n. **1** a mark (✓) used to show that something is correct or has been chosen or checked. **2** a regular short, sharp sound. **3** Brit. informal a moment. • v. **1** mark with a tick. **2** make regular ticking sounds. **3** (**tick away**/

by/past) (of time) pass inevitably. **4** (**tick over**) (of an engine) run slowly in neutral. **5** (**tick off**) Brit. informal reprimand.
– ORIGIN prob. Germanic.

tick[2] ● n. a tiny creature related to the spiders, which attaches itself to the skin and sucks blood.
– ORIGIN Old English.

tick[3] ● n. (in phr. **on tick**) on credit.
– ORIGIN prob. from the phrase *on the ticket*, referring to a promise to pay.

tick[4] ● n. **1** a fabric case stuffed to form a mattress or pillow. **2** = TICKING.
– ORIGIN prob. from Greek *thēkē* 'case'.

ticker ● n. informal **1** a watch. **2** a person's heart.

ticker tape ● n. a paper strip on which information is recorded in a machine.

ticket ● n. **1** a piece of paper or card giving the holder a right to admission to a place or event or to travel on public transport. **2** an official notice of a traffic offence. **3** a label attached to an item in a shop, giving its price, size, etc.
– ORIGIN Old French *estiquet*.

ticking ● n. a hard-wearing material used to cover mattresses.
– ORIGIN from TICK[4].

tickle ● v. (**tickles**, **tickling**, **tickled**) **1** lightly touch in a way that causes itching or twitching and often laughter. **2** be appealing or amusing to. ● n. an act of tickling or feeling of being tickled.
– DERIVATIVES **tickly** adj.
– ORIGIN perh. from TICK[1], or from Scots and dialect *kittle* 'to tickle'.

ticklish ● adj. **1** sensitive to being tickled. **2** (of a cough) causing constant irritation in the throat.

tidal ● adj. relating to or affected by tides.
– DERIVATIVES **tidally** adv.

tidal wave ● n. an exceptionally large ocean wave, caused by an earthquake, storm, etc.

tidbit ● n. US = TITBIT.

tiddler ● n. Brit. informal **1** a small fish. **2** a young or unusually small person or thing.
– ORIGIN perh. from TIDDLY[2] or *tittlebat*, a child's word for *stickleback*.

tiddly[1] ● adj. (**tiddlier**, **tiddliest**) informal, esp. Brit. slightly drunk.
– ORIGIN perh. from former slang *tiddlywink*, referring to an unlicensed pub.

tiddly[2] ● adj. (**tiddlier**, **tiddliest**) Brit. informal little; tiny.
– ORIGIN unknown.

tiddlywinks ● pl. n. a game in which small plastic counters are flicked into a central container, using a larger counter.
– ORIGIN unknown.

tide ● n. **1** the alternate rising and falling of the sea due to the attraction of the moon and sun. **2** a powerful surge of feeling or trend of events: *the tide of racism sweeping Europe.* ● v. (**tides**, **tiding**, **tided**) (**tide over**) help (someone) through a difficult period.
– ORIGIN Old English, 'time, period, era'.

tideline ● n. a line made by the sea on a beach at the highest point of a tide.

tidemark ● n. Brit. a dirty mark left around the inside of a bath at the level reached by the water.

tidewater ● n. water brought or affected by tides.

tidings ● pl. n. literary news; information.
– ORIGIN Old English.

tidy ● adj. (**tidier**, **tidiest**) **1** arranged neatly and in order. **2** liking to keep oneself and one's possessions neat and in order. **3** informal (of an amount) considerable. ● n. (pl. **tidies**) **1** (also **tidy-up**) an act of tidying. **2** a container for holding small objects. ● v. (**tidies**, **tidying**, **tidied**) **1** (often **tidy up**) make tidy. **2** (**tidy away**) put away for the sake of tidiness.
– DERIVATIVES **tidily** adv. **tidiness** n.
– ORIGIN first meaning 'timely': from TIDE.

tie ● v. (**ties**, **tying**, **tied**) **1** attach or fasten with string, cord, etc. **2** form into a knot or bow. **3** restrict to a particular situation or place. **4** connect. **5** achieve the same score or ranking as another competitor. ● n. (pl. **ties**) **1** a thing that ties. **2** a strip of material worn beneath a collar, tied in a knot at the front. **3** a result in a game or match in which two or more competitors are equal. **4** Brit. a sports match in which the winners proceed to the next round of the competition. **5** Music a curved line above or below two notes of the same pitch indicating that they are to be played as one note. **6** a rod or beam holding parts of a structure together.
– PHRASES **tie in** link or agree with something. **tie up 1** restrict the movement of (someone) by binding their limbs. **2** bring to a satisfactory conclusion. **3** informal occupy (someone) so that they have no time for any other activity.
– ORIGIN Old English.

tie-break (also **tie-breaker**) ● n. a means of deciding a winner from competitors who have tied.

tied ● adj. **1** Brit. (of accommodation) rented by someone on condition that they work for its owner. **2** (of a public house) owned and controlled by a brewery.

tie-dye ● n. a method of producing textile patterns by tying parts of the fabric to shield it from the dye.

tie-in ● n. **1** a connection or association. **2** a product produced to take commercial advantage of a related film, book, etc.

Tien Shan E
/tyen **shan**/ (also **Tian Shan**) a range of mountains in the Xinjiang autonomous region of China and eastern Kyrgyzstan.

Tientsin E
/tyen-**tsin**/ var. of TIANJIN.

tiepin ● n. an ornamental pin for holding a tie in place.

Tiepolo E
/ti-ep-uh-loh/, Giovanni Battista (1696–1770), Italian painter, known for his rococo frescoes and altarpieces.

tier ● n. one of a series of rows or levels placed one above and behind the other.
– DERIVATIVES **tiered** adj.
– ORIGIN French *tire* 'sequence, order'.

Tierra del Fuego E
/ti-air-uh del **fway**-goh/ an island at the southern tip of South America, separated from the mainland by the Strait of Magellan. It is divided between Argentina and Chile.

tie-up • n. a link or connection.

tiff • n. informal a trivial quarrel.
– ORIGIN prob. dialect.

Tiffany E
/tif-fuh-ni/, Louis Comfort (1848–1933), American glass-maker and interior decorator, famous for his art nouveau stained glass, vases, and lamps.

Tiflis E
/tif-leess/ former name for **TBILISI**.

tig • n. Brit. = **TAG**[2].
– ORIGIN perh. from **TICK**[1].

tiger • n. **1** a large member of the cat family, with a yellow-brown coat striped with black, native to the forests of Asia. **2** (also **tiger economy**) a fast-growing economy of one of the smaller East Asian countries.
– DERIVATIVES **tigerish** adj.
– ORIGIN Greek *tigris*.

tiger lily • n. a tall Asian lily which has orange flowers spotted with black or purple.

tiger moth • n. a moth with boldly spotted and streaked wings.

tiger prawn (also **tiger shrimp**) • n. a large edible prawn marked with dark bands.

tight • adj. **1** fixed, closed, or fastened firmly. **2** (of clothes) close-fitting. **3** well sealed against something such as water or air. **4** (of a rope, fabric, or surface) stretched so as to leave no slack. **5** (of an area or space) allowing little room for movement: *it was a tight squeeze in the tiny room.* **6** (of people or things) closely packed together. **7** (of a form of control) strictly imposed: *security was tight.* **8** (of money or time) limited. • adv. very firmly, closely, or tensely.
– DERIVATIVES **tightly** adv. **tightness** n.
– ORIGIN prob. from Germanic.

tighten • v. make or become tight or tighter.

tight-fisted • adj. informal not willing to spend or give much money.

tight-knit (also **tightly knit**) • adj. (of a group of people) bound together by strong relationships and common interests.

tight-lipped • adj. unwilling to give away information or express emotion.

tightrope • n. a rope or wire stretched high above the ground, on which acrobats balance.

tights • pl. n. a close-fitting garment made of stretchy material, covering the legs, hips, and bottom.

Tigray E
/tee-gray/ (also **Tigre**) a province of northern Ethiopia; capital, Mekele.
– DERIVATIVES **Tigrayan** (also **Tigrean**) adj. & n.

tigress • n. a female tiger.

Tigris E
/ty-griss/ a river of SW Asia which rises in the mountains of eastern Turkey and flows south-eastwards through Iraq to join the Euphrates, forming the Shatt al-Arab.

tilde /til-duh/ • n. an accent (˜) placed over Spanish *n* or Portuguese *a* or *o* to change the way they are pronounced.
– ORIGIN Spanish.

tile • n. a thin square or rectangular piece of baked clay, concrete, cork, etc., used for covering roofs, floors, or walls. • v. (**tiles, tiling, tiled**) cover with tiles.
– PHRASES **on the tiles** informal, esp. Brit. having a lively night out.
– DERIVATIVES **tiler** n.
– ORIGIN Latin *tegula*.

tiling • n. a surface covered by tiles.

till[1] • prep. & conj. less formal way of saying **UNTIL**.
– ORIGIN Old English (not a shortened form of *until*).

till[2] • n. a cash register or drawer for money in a shop, bank, or restaurant.
– ORIGIN unknown.

till[3] • v. prepare (land) for growing crops.
– ORIGIN Old English, 'strive for'.

tiller • n. a horizontal bar fitted to the head of a boat's rudder post and used for steering.
– ORIGIN Old French *telier* 'weaver's beam, stock of a crossbow'.

tilt • v. **1** move into a sloping position. **2** begin to adopt a particular opinion: *he is tilting towards a new economic course.* **3** (**tilt at**) hist. (in jousting) thrust at with a lance or other weapon. • n. **1** a tilting position or movement. **2** a bias. **3** hist. a joust. **4** (**tilt at**) an attempt at (winning something).
– PHRASES **(at) full tilt** with maximum speed or force.
– ORIGIN perh. from Old English, 'unsteady'.

tilth • n. **1** cultivation of land. **2** the condition of tilled soil.
– ORIGIN Old English.

timber • n. wood prepared for use in building and carpentry. • exclam. used to warn that a tree is about to fall after being cut.
– DERIVATIVES **timbered** adj.
– ORIGIN Old English, 'a building'.

timber wolf • n. a large wolf found mainly in northern North America, with grey streaked fur.

timbre /tam-ber/ • n. the character of a musical sound or voice as distinct from its pitch and strength.
– ORIGIN French.

Timbuktu E
/tim-buk-too/ (also **Timbuctoo**) a town in northern Mali, formerly a major trading centre on the trans-Saharan trade routes.

time • n. **1** the unlimited continued progress of existence and events in the past, present, and future, regarded as a whole. **2** a point of time as measured in hours and minutes past midnight or noon: *the time is 9.30.* **3** the right or agreed moment to do something: *the departure time.* **4** (**a time**) an indefinite period. **5** (also **times**) a point or period of time: *Victorian times.* **6** the length of time taken to complete an activity. **7** time as available or used: *a waste of time.* **8** an instance of something happening or being done: *this is the first time I have got into debt.* **9** (**times**) (following a number) expressing multiplication. **10** the rhythmic pattern or tempo of a piece of music. **11** the normal rate of pay for time spent working. **12** Brit. the moment at which the opening hours of a public house end. **13** informal a prison sentence. • v. (**times, timing, timed**) **1** arrange a time for. **2** do at a

particular time. **3** measure the time taken by. **4** (**time out**) Computing (of a computer or a program) cancel (an operation) automatically because a set interval of time has passed. **5** (**times**) informal multiply (a number).
– PHRASES **behind the times** not aware of or using the latest ideas or techniques. **for the time being** until some other arrangement is made. **in time 1** not late. **2** eventually. **on time** punctual; punctually. **time will tell** the truth about something will be established in the future.
– ORIGIN Old English.

time-and-motion study ● n. a study of the efficiency of a company's working methods.

time bomb ● n. a bomb designed to explode at a set time.

time capsule ● n. a container in which a selection of objects typical of the present time is buried for discovery in the future.

time frame ● n. a specified period of time.

time-honoured ● adj. (of a custom or tradition) respected or valued because it has existed for a long time.

timekeeper ● n. **1** a person who records the amount of time taken by a process or activity. **2** a person regarded in terms of their punctuality.
– DERIVATIVES **timekeeping** n.

time-lapse ● adj. (of a photographic technique) taking a sequence of frames at set intervals to record changes that take place slowly over time.

timeless ● adj. not affected by the passage of time or changes in fashion.

timely ● adj. done or occurring at a good or appropriate time.

time off ● n. time spent away from one's usual work or studies.

timepiece ● n. an instrument for measuring time; a clock or watch.

timer ● n. **1** an automatic mechanism for operating a device at a preset time. **2** a person or device that records the amount of time taken by a process or activity.

timescale ● n. the time allowed for or taken by a process or sequence of events.

time-server ● n. a person who makes very little effort at work because they are waiting to leave or retire.

timeshare ● n. an arrangement in which joint owners use a property as a holiday home at different specified times.

time sheet ● n. a piece of paper for recording the number of hours worked.

time signature ● n. Music an indication of rhythm following a clef.

timetable ● n. a list or plan of times at which events are scheduled to take place. ● v. (**timetables**, **timetabling**, **timetabled**) schedule to take place at a particular time.

time trial ● n. (in various sports) a test of a competitor's individual speed over a set distance.

timid ● adj. (**timider**, **timidest**) lacking in courage or confidence.
– DERIVATIVES **timidity** n. **timidly** adv.
– ORIGIN Latin *timidus*.

timing ● n. **1** the choice, judgement, or control of when something should be done. **2** a particular time when something happens.

Timor E
/tee-mor/ the largest of the Lesser Sunda Islands, in the southern Malay Archipelago.
– DERIVATIVES **Timorese** adj. & n.

timorous /tim-uh-ruhss/ ● adj. lacking in courage or confidence; nervous.
– ORIGIN Latin *timorosus*.

Timor Sea E
an arm of the Indian Ocean between Timor and NW Australia.

Timothy, St E
(1st century AD), Christian martyr and disciple of St Paul, traditionally the first bishop of Ephesus. Feast day, January 22 or 26.

timpani /tim-puh-ni/ (also **tympani**) ● pl. n. kettledrums.
– ORIGIN Italian.

tin ● n. **1** a silvery-white metallic chemical element. **2** an airtight container with a lid, made of tinplate or aluminium. **3** Brit. a sealed tinplate or aluminium container for preserving food; a can. **4** an open metal container for baking food. ● v. (**tins**, **tinning**, **tinned**) **1** cover with a thin layer of tin. **2** (**tinned**) Brit. preserved in a tin.
– ORIGIN Old English.

tincture /tingk-cher/ ● n. **1** a medicine made by dissolving a drug in alcohol. **2** a slight trace.
– ORIGIN Latin *tinctura* 'dyeing'.

tinder ● n. dry material which burns easily, used for lighting a fire.
– ORIGIN Old English.

tinderbox ● n. hist. a box containing tinder, flint, a steel, and other items for lighting fires.

tine /*rhymes with* line/ ● n. a prong or sharp point, especially of a fork.
– DERIVATIVES **tined** adj.
– ORIGIN Old English.

tinfoil ● n. metal foil used for covering or wrapping food.

ting ● n. a sharp, clear ringing sound. ● v. produce a ting.

tinge ● v. (**tinges**, **tinging** or **tingeing**, **tinged**) (often **be tinged**) **1** colour slightly. **2** give a small amount of a quality to: *a visit tinged with sadness.* ● n. a slight trace of a colour or quality.
– ORIGIN Latin *tingere* 'to dip or colour'.

tingle ● n. a slight prickling or stinging sensation. ● v. (**tingles**, **tingling**, **tingled**) experience or cause to experience a tingle.
– DERIVATIVES **tingly** adj.
– ORIGIN perh. from **TINKLE**.

tinker ● n. **1** a travelling mender of pots, kettles, etc. **2** Brit. derog. a gypsy or other person living in a travelling community. **3** an act of tinkering with something. ● v. (**tinkers**, **tinkering**, **tinkered**) (**tinker with**) try to repair or improve by making many small changes.
– ORIGIN unknown.

tinkle ● v. (**tinkles**, **tinkling**, **tinkled**) make a light, clear ringing sound. ● n. a tinkling sound.

tinnitus /tin-ni-tuhss, ti-ny-tuhss/ ● n. Med. ringing or buzzing in the ears.
– ORIGIN Latin.

tinny ● adj. **1** having a thin, metallic sound. **2** made of thin or poor-quality metal.

tin-opener ● **n.** esp. Brit. a tool for opening tins of food.

tinplate ● **n.** sheet steel or iron coated with tin.

tinpot ● **adj.** informal of poor quality; worthless.

tinsel ● **n.** a form of decoration made up of thin strips of shiny metal foil attached to a length of thread.
– ORIGIN Old French *estincele* 'spark'.

Tinseltown ● **n.** derog. the glamorous but artificial world of Hollywood and its film industry.

tint ● **n. 1** a shade of colour. **2** a dye for colouring the hair. ● **v. 1** colour slightly. **2** dye (hair) with a tint.
– ORIGIN Latin *tinctus* 'dyeing'.

tintinnabulation /tin-tin-nab-yuu-**lay**-sh'n/ ● **n.** a ringing or tinkling sound.
– ORIGIN Latin *tintinnabulum* 'tinkling bell'.

Tintoretto E
/tin-tuh-**ret**-toh/ (1518–940; born *Jacopo Robusti*), Italian mannerist painter, known for his religious paintings.

tin whistle ● **n.** a small flute-like instrument made from a thin metal tube.

tiny ● **adj.** (**tinier**, **tiniest**) very small.
– DERIVATIVES **tinily** adv. **tininess** n.
– ORIGIN unknown.

tip[1] ● **n. 1** the pointed or rounded end of something thin or tapering. **2** a small part fitted to the end of an object. ● **v.** (**tips**, **tipping**, **tipped**) attach to or cover the tip of.
– PHRASES **on the tip of one's tongue** almost but not quite spoken or coming to mind.
– DERIVATIVES **tipped** adj.
– ORIGIN Old Norse.

tip[2] ● **v.** (**tips**, **tipping**, **tipped**) **1** overbalance so as to fall or turn over. **2** be or put in a sloping position. **3** empty out (the contents of a container) by holding it at an angle. ● **n. 1** Brit. a place where rubbish is left. **2** informal a dirty or untidy place.
– ORIGIN perh. Scandinavian.

tip[3] ● **n. 1** a small sum of money given as a reward for services provided. **2** a piece of practical advice. **3** a prediction about the likely winner of a race or contest. ● **v.** (**tips**, **tipping**, **tipped**) **1** give a tip to. **2** Brit. predict as likely to win or achieve something. **3** (**tip off**) informal give (someone) secret information.
– ORIGIN prob. from TIP[1].

tipi ● **n.** var. of TEPEE.

tip-off ● **n.** informal a piece of secret information.

Tipperary E
/tip-puh-**rair**-i/ a county in the centre of the Republic of Ireland; county town, Clonmel.

Tippett E
/**tip**-pit/, Sir Michael (Kemp) (1905–98), English composer. His work includes five operas, four symphonies, and the oratorio *A Child of Our Time*.

tipple ● **v.** (**tipples**, **tippling**, **tippled**) drink alcohol regularly. ● **n.** informal an alcoholic drink.
– DERIVATIVES **tippler** n.

tipster ● **n.** a person who gives tips as to the likely winner of a race or contest.

tipsy ● **adj.** (**tipsier**, **tipsiest**) slightly drunk.
– DERIVATIVES **tipsily** adv.
– ORIGIN from TIP[2].

tiptoe ● **v.** (**tiptoes**, **tiptoeing**, **tiptoed**) walk quietly and carefully with one's heels raised.
– PHRASES **on tiptoe** (or **tiptoes**) with one's heels raised.

tip-top ● **adj.** of the very best quality.

tirade /ty-**rayd**, ti-**rayd**/ ● **n.** a long speech of angry criticism.
– ORIGIN French.

Tirana E
/ti-**rah**-nuh/ (also **Tiranë**) the capital of Albania.

tire[1] ● **v.** (**tires**, **tiring**, **tired**) **1** make or become in need of rest or sleep. **2** exhaust the patience or interest of. **3** (**tire of**) become impatient or bored with.
– ORIGIN Old English.

tire[2] ● **n.** US = TYRE.

tired ● **adj. 1** in need of sleep or rest. **2** (**tired of**) bored with. **3** (of a statement or idea) uninteresting because too familiar.
– DERIVATIVES **tiredly** adv. **tiredness** n.

Tiree E
/ty-**ree**/ an island in the Inner Hebrides.

tireless ● **adj.** having or showing great effort or energy.
– DERIVATIVES **tirelessly** adv.

tiresome ● **adj.** causing one to feel bored or impatient.
– DERIVATIVES **tiresomely** adv.

Tirich Mir E
/ti-rich **meer**/ the highest peak in the Hindu Kush, in NW Pakistan, rising to 7,690 m (25,230 ft).

'tis ● **contr.** literary it is.

tissue /**ti**-shoo, **tiss**-yoo/ ● **n. 1** any of the distinct types of material of which animals or plants are made, consisting of specialized cells and their products. **2** a piece of absorbent paper used as a disposable handkerchief.
– PHRASES **a tissue of lies** a story that is full of lies.
– ORIGIN Old French *tissu* 'woven'.

tissue paper ● **n.** very thin, soft paper.

tit[1] ● **n.** a titmouse.
ORIGIN prob. Scandinavian.

tit[2] ● **n.** vulgar a woman's breast.
– ORIGIN Old English, 'teat, nipple'.

tit[3] ● **n.** (in phr. **tit for tat**) a situation in which one insults or hurts someone to retaliate for something they have done.
– ORIGIN from former *tip for tap*, from TIP[2].

Titan /**ty**-tuhn/ ● **n. 1** Gk Myth. any of the older gods before the Olympians; they were the children of Uranus (Heaven) and Gaia (Earth). **2** (**titan**) a person who is very strong, clever, or important.

Titanic E
a British passenger liner which struck an iceberg and sank on her maiden voyage across the Atlantic in April 1912, with the loss of 1,490 lives.

titanic ● **adj.** of very great strength, size, or power.

titanium /ti-**tay**-ni-uhm, ty-**tay**-ni-uhm/ ● **n.** a silver-grey metal used in strong, corrosion-resistant alloys.

– ORIGIN from **TITAN**.

titbit (US **tidbit**) ● n. **1** a small piece of tasty food. **2** a small and particularly interesting item of information.

– ORIGIN from dialect *tid* 'tender' + **BIT**[1].

titch (also **tich**) ● n. Brit. informal a small person.

– ORIGIN from *Little Tich*, stage name of Harry Relph, an English music-hall comedian (1868–1928).

titchy ● adj. Brit. informal very small.

tithe /ty*th*/ ● n. one tenth of what people produced or earned in a year, formerly taken as a tax to support the Church and clergy.

– ORIGIN Old English, 'tenth'.

Titian E
/**ti**-sh'n/ (*c.*1488–1576; Italian name *Tiziano Vecellio*), Italian painter. He is known for his many mythological works, including *Bacchus and Ariadne*.

Titicaca, Lake E
/ti-ti-**kah**-kah/ a lake in the Andes, on the border between Peru and Bolivia. At an altitude of 3,809 m (12,497 ft), it is the highest large lake in the world.

titillate /ti-til-layt/ ● v. (**titillates**, **titillating**, **titillated**) make (someone) feel mildly interested or sexually excited.

– DERIVATIVES **titillation** n.

– ORIGIN Latin *titillare* 'tickle'.

titivate /ti-ti-vayt/ ● v. (**titivates**, **titivating**, **titivated**) informal make smarter or more attractive.

– DERIVATIVES **titivation** n.

– ORIGIN perh. from **TIDY**.

title ● n. **1** the name of a book, musical composition, or other artistic work. **2** a name that describes someone's position or job. **3** a word, such as *Dr*, *Mrs*, or *Lord*, used before or instead of someone's name to indicate their rank or profession. **4** the position of being the champion of a major sports competition. **5** a caption or credit in a film or broadcast. ● v. (**titles**, **titling**, **titled**) give a title to.

– ORIGIN Latin *titulus*.

titled ● adj. having a title indicating nobility or rank.

title deed ● n. a legal document giving evidence of a person's right to own a property.

title music ● n. music played during the credits at the beginning or end of a television programme or film.

title role ● n. the role in a play or film from which the work's title is taken.

titmouse ● n. (pl. **titmice**) a small songbird that searches for food among foliage and branches.

– ORIGIN from **TIT**[1] + the former word *mose* 'titmouse'.

Tito E
/**tee**-toh/ (1892–1980; born *Josip Broz*), Yugoslav Marshal and statesman, Prime Minister 1945–53 and President 1953–80. He led the Communist resistance movement against the German invasion of Yugoslavia (1941), and became head of the new government at the end of the war.

Titograd E
/**tee**-toh-grad/ former name for **PODGORICA**.

titrate /ty-**trayt**/ ● v. (**titrates**, **titrating**, **titrated**) Chem. calculate the amount of a substance in (a solution) by measuring the volume of a standard reagent required to react with it.

– DERIVATIVES **titration** n.

– ORIGIN French *titre* 'fineness of alloyed gold or silver'.

titter ● n. a short, quiet laugh. ● v. (**titters**, **tittering**, **tittered**) give a titter.

tittle ● n. a tiny amount or part of something.

– ORIGIN Latin *titulus* 'title'.

tittle-tattle ● n. gossip. ● v. (**tittle-tattles**, **tittle-tattling**, **tittle-tattled**) engage in gossip.

– ORIGIN from **TATTLE**.

titular /tit-yuu-ler/ ● adj. **1** relating to a title. **2** holding a formal position or title without any real authority.

– DERIVATIVES **titularly** adv.

Titus E
/ty-tuhss/ (AD 39–81; full name *Titus Vespasianus Augustus*), Roman emperor 79–81, son of Vespasian.

tizzy (also **tizz**) ● n. (pl. **tizzies** or **tizzes**) informal a state of nervous excitement or worry.

– ORIGIN unknown.

T-junction ● n. a road junction at which one road joins another at right angles without crossing it.

TLC ● abbrev. informal tender loving care.

TNT ● abbrev. trinitrotoluene, a high explosive.

to ● prep. **1** in the direction of. **2** situated in the direction mentioned from: *there are mountains to the north*. **3** so as to reach (a particular state). **4** identifying the person or thing affected or a relationship between one person or thing and another: *you were unkind to her.* **5** esp. Brit. (in telling the time) before (the hour specified). **6** indicating a rate of return: *ten miles to the gallon*. **7** indicating that two things are attached. **8** used to introduce the second part of a comparison: *it's nothing to what it once was*. ● infinitive marker used with the base form of a verb to indicate that the verb is in the infinitive. ● adv. so as to be closed or nearly closed: *he pulled the door to.*

– ORIGIN Old English.

USAGE **to**
Do not confuse **to** with **too** or **two**. **To** mainly means 'in the direction of' (as in *the next train to London*), while **too** means 'more than is desired, allowed, or possible' (as in *she was driving too fast*). **Two** is a number meaning 'one less than three' (as in *we met two years ago*).

toad ● n. a tailless amphibian with a short stout body and short legs.

– ORIGIN Old English.

toadstool ● n. a fungus, typically in the form of a rounded cap on a stalk.

– ORIGIN a fanciful name.

toady ● n. (pl. **toadies**) a person who behaves in an excessively respectful way towards others. ● v. (**toadies**, **toadying**, **toadied**) act in an excessively respectful way.

– ORIGIN said to be from *toad-eater*, a charlatan's assistant who ate toads (regarded as poisonous) to demonstrate the power of the charlatan's remedy.

to and fro ● adv. in a constant movement backwards and forwards or from side to side.

toast ● n. **1** sliced bread that has been put near a fire or heated element until it is brown. **2** an act of raising glasses at a gathering and drinking together in honour of a person or thing. **3** a person who is respected or admired: *he was the toast of Oxford.* ● v. **1** brown (bread) by putting it near a fire or heated element. **2** drink a toast to.
– ORIGIN Old French *toster* 'roast'; sense 2 came from the idea that the name of the lady whose health was being drunk flavoured the drink like the pieces of spiced toast formerly placed in wine.

toaster ● n. an electrical device for making toast.

toastie ● n. Brit. informal a toasted sandwich or snack.

toasting fork ● n. a long-handled fork for making toast in front of a fire.

toastmaster (or **toastmistress**) ● n. an official responsible for proposing toasts and making other formal announcements at a large social event.

tobacco ● n. (pl. **tobaccos**) the dried nicotine-rich leaves of an American plant, used for smoking or chewing.
– ORIGIN Spanish *tabaco*.

tobacconist ● n. esp. Brit. a shopkeeper who sells cigarettes and tobacco.

Tobago E
see **TRINIDAD AND TOBAGO**.

toboggan ● n. a light, narrow vehicle on runners, used for sliding downhill over snow or ice.
– DERIVATIVES **tobogganist** n.
– ORIGIN from a North American Indian language.

Tobruk E
/tuh-**bruuk**/ a port on the Mediterranean coast of NE Libya. It was the scene of fierce fighting during the Second World War.

toby jug ● n. a beer jug or mug in the form of a seated old man wearing a three-cornered hat.
– ORIGIN said to come from an 18th-century poem about *Toby Philpot*, a soldier who liked to drink.

toccata /tuh-**kah**-tuh/ ● n. a musical composition for a keyboard instrument designed to show the performer's touch and technique.
– ORIGIN Italian, 'touched'.

tocopherol /to-**kof**-fuh-rol/ ● n. vitamin E.
– ORIGIN from Greek *tokos* 'offspring' + *pherein* 'to bear'.

tocsin /**tok**-sin/ ● n. archaic an alarm bell or signal.
– ORIGIN Provençal *tocasenh*.

tod ● n. (in phr. **on one's tod**) Brit. informal on one's own.
– ORIGIN from rhyming slang *Tod Sloan*, an American jockey (1873–1933).

today ● adv. **1** on or during this present day. **2** at the present period of time. ● n. **1** this present day. **2** the present period of time.
– ORIGIN Old English, 'on this day'.

toddle ● v. (**toddles, toddling, toddled**) **1** (of a young child) move with short unsteady steps while learning to walk. **2** informal walk in a casual or leisurely way. ● n. an act of toddling.
– ORIGIN unknown.

toddler ● n. a young child who is just beginning to walk.

toddy ● n. (pl. **toddies**) a drink made of spirits with hot water and sugar.
– ORIGIN Sanskrit.

to-do ● n. informal a commotion or fuss.
– ORIGIN from *much to do*, 'much needing to be done'.

toe ● n. **1** any of the five digits at the end of the foot. **2** the lower end, tip, or point of something. ● v. (**toes, toeing, toed**) push or touch with one's toes.
– PHRASES **on one's toes** ready and alert. **toe the line** obey authority.
– ORIGIN Old English.

toecap ● n. a piece of steel or leather on the front part of a boot or shoe.

toehold ● n. a small foothold.

toenail ● n. a nail on the upper surface of the tip of each toe.

toerag ● n. Brit. informal an unpleasant person.
– ORIGIN first referring to a rag wrapped round the foot as a sock, such as might be worn by a homeless person.

toff ● n. Brit. informal, derog. a rich, upper-class person.
– ORIGIN perh. from **TUFT**, used to refer to a gold cap tassel worn by titled undergraduates at Oxford and Cambridge.

toffee ● n. a kind of firm sweet which softens when sucked or chewed, made by boiling together sugar and butter.
– ORIGIN alteration of **TAFFY**.

toffee apple ● n. Brit. an apple coated with a layer of toffee and fixed on a stick.

toffee-nosed ● adj. Brit. informal snobbish.

tofu /**toh**-foo/ ● n. curd made from mashed soya beans, used in Asian and vegetarian cookery.
– ORIGIN Chinese, 'rotten beans'.

tog[1] informal ● n. (**togs**) clothes. ● v. (**togs, togging, togged**) (**be togged up/out**) be fully dressed for a particular occasion or activity.
– ORIGIN prob. from former criminals' slang *togeman* 'light cloak'.

tog[2] ● n. Brit. a unit of thermal resistance used to express the insulating properties of clothes and quilts.
– ORIGIN from **TOG**[1], on the pattern of an earlier unit called the *clo* (first part of *clothes*).

toga /**toh**-guh/ ● n. a loose outer garment made of a single piece of cloth, worn by the citizens of ancient Rome.
– ORIGIN Latin.

together ● adv. **1** with or near to another person or people. **2** so as to touch, combine, or be united. **3** regarded as a whole. **4** (of two people) married or in a sexual relationship. **5** at the same time: *they both spoke together.* **6** without interruption. ● adj. informal level-headed and well organized.
– PHRASES **together with** as well as.
– DERIVATIVES **togetherness** n.
– ORIGIN Old English.

toggle ● n. a narrow piece of wood or plastic attached to a garment, pushed through a loop to act as a fastener.
– ORIGIN unknown.

toggle switch ● n. an electric switch operated by means of a projecting lever that is moved up and down.

Togo E
/**toh**-goh/ a country in West Africa; capital, Lomé. Official name **TOGOLESE REPUBLIC**.
– DERIVATIVES **Togolese** /toh-guh-**leez**/ adj. & n.

toil • v. **1** work extremely hard or without a rest. **2** move somewhere slowly and with difficulty. • n. exhausting work.
– DERIVATIVES **toiler** n.
– ORIGIN Old French *toiler* 'strive'.

toilet • n. **1** a large bowl for urinating or defecating into. **2** dated the process of washing oneself, dressing, and attending to one's appearance.
– ORIGIN first referring to a cloth cover for a dressing table: from French *toilette* 'cloth'.

toilet bag • n. Brit. a waterproof bag for holding toothpaste, soap, etc. when travelling.

toiletries • pl. n. articles used in washing and taking care of one's body, such as soap and shampoo.

toilette /twah-**let**/ • n. = **TOILET** (in sense 2).
– ORIGIN French (see **TOILET**).

toilet-train • v. teach (a young child) to use the toilet.

toilet water • n. a diluted form of perfume.

toilsome • adj. archaic involving hard work.

Tojo E
/**toh**-joh/, Hideki (1884–1948), Japanese military leader and statesman, Prime Minister 1941–4. He initiated the Japanese attack on Pearl Harbor.

Tokelau E
/toh-kuh-**lah**-oo/ a group of three islands in the western Pacific, between Kiribati and Samoa, forming an overseas territory of New Zealand.

token • n. **1** a thing that represents a fact, quality, or feeling. **2** a voucher that can be exchanged for goods or services. **3** a disc used to operate a machine. • adj. done just for the sake of appearances: *cases like this often bring token fines.*
– ORIGIN Old English.

tokenism • n. the fact of doing something in an insincere way, so as to be seen to be obeying the law or satisfying a particular group of people.
– DERIVATIVES **tokenistic** adj.

Tokyo E
/**toh**-ki-oh/ the capital of Japan.

told past and past part. of **TELL**.

Toledo E
/tuh-**lay**-doh/ a city in central Spain, noted for the manufacture of steel and sword blades since the first century BC.

tolerable • adj. **1** able to be tolerated. **2** fairly good.
– DERIVATIVES **tolerably** adv.

tolerance • n. **1** the ability to accept things one dislikes or disagrees with. **2** the amount by which the measurement of a value can vary without causing problems.

tolerant • adj. **1** showing tolerance. **2** able to endure specified conditions or treatment: *rye is tolerant of drought.*

tolerate • v. (**tolerates**, **tolerating**, **tolerated**) **1** allow (something that one dislikes or disagrees with) to exist or happen. **2** patiently accept (something unpleasant). **3** able to be exposed to (a drug, etc.) without being harmed.
– DERIVATIVES **toleration** n.
– ORIGIN Latin *tolerare* 'endure'.

Tolkien E
/**tol**-keen/, J. R. R. (1892–1973; full name *John Ronald Reuel Tolkien*), British novelist and literary scholar, born in South Africa. He is famous for the fantasy adventures *The Hobbit* and *The Lord of the Rings*.

toll[1] /tohl/ • n. **1** a charge payable to use a bridge or road or (N. Amer.) for a long-distance telephone call. **2** the number of deaths or casualties arising from an accident, disaster, etc. **3** the cost or damage resulting from something.
– ORIGIN Greek *telōnion* 'toll house'.

toll[2] /tohl/ • v. **1** (of a bell) sound with a slow, even series of strokes. **2** announce (the time, a service, or a person's death) in this way. • n. a single ring of a bell.
– ORIGIN prob. from dialect *toll* 'drag, pull'.

tollbooth • n. a roadside kiosk where tolls are paid.

toll gate • n. a barrier across a road where a toll must be paid to go through.

Tolpuddle martyrs E
/**tol**-pud-d'l/ six farm labourers from the village of Tolpuddle in Dorset who, in 1834, were transported to Australia after attempting to form a trade union. Two years later, after widespread protests, they were pardoned and repatriated.

Tolstoy E
/**tol**-stoy/, Count Leo (1828–1910; Russian name *Lev Nikolaevich Tolstoi*), Russian writer, best known for the novels *War and Peace* and *Anna Karenina*.

tom • n. the male of various animals, especially a domestic cat.
– ORIGIN first meaning an ordinary man: from the man's name *Thomas*.

tomahawk /**tom**-uh-hawk/ • n. a light axe formerly used as a tool or weapon by American Indians.
– ORIGIN from a North American Indian language.

tomato • n. (pl. **tomatoes**) a glossy red fruit, eaten as a vegetable or in salads.
– ORIGIN from a Central American Indian language.

tomb • n. **1** a burial place consisting of a stone structure above ground or a large underground vault. **2** a monument to a dead person, built over their burial place. **3** (**the tomb**) literary death.
– ORIGIN Greek *tumbos*.

Tombaugh E
/**tom**-baw/, Clyde William (1906–97), American astronomer, who in 1930 discovered the planet Pluto.

tombola /tom-**boh**-luh/ • n. Brit. a game in which tickets are drawn from a revolving drum to win prizes.
– ORIGIN Italian.

tomboy • n. a girl who enjoys rough, noisy activities traditionally associated with boys.
– DERIVATIVES **tomboyish** adj.

tombstone • n. a flat inscribed stone standing or laid over a grave.

tomcat • n. a male domestic cat.

Tom, Dick, and Harry • n. ordinary people in general.

tome • n. humorous a large, serious book.
– ORIGIN Greek *tomos* 'roll of papyrus, volume'.

tomfoolery • n. silly behaviour.

Tommy • n. (pl. **Tommies**) informal a British private soldier.
– ORIGIN from a use of the name *Thomas Atkins* in examples of completed official forms in the British army.

tomography /tuh-mog-ruh-fi/ • n. a technique for displaying a cross section through a human body or other solid object using X-rays or ultrasound.
– DERIVATIVES **tomographic** adj.
– ORIGIN Greek *tomos* 'slice'.

tomorrow • adv. **1** on the day after today. **2** in the near future. • n. **1** the day after today. **2** the near future.

tomtit • n. a small titmouse or similar bird.

tom-tom • n. a drum beaten with the hands, associated with North American Indian, African, or Eastern cultures.
– ORIGIN Hindi.

-tomy • comb. form cutting as part of a surgical process: *hysterectomy.*
– ORIGIN Greek *-tomia.*

ton /tun/ • n. **1** (also **long ton**) a unit of weight equal to 2,240 lb avoirdupois (1016.05 kg). **2** (also **short ton**) esp. N. Amer. a unit of weight equal to 2,000 lb avoirdupois (907.19 kg). **3** a metric ton. **4** (also **displacement ton**) a unit of measurement of a ship's weight equal to 2,240 lb or 35 cu. ft (0.99 cubic metres). **5** informal a large number or amount. **6** Brit. informal a hundred miles an hour. • adv. (**tons**) Brit. informal much; a lot.
– ORIGIN from **TUN**.

tonal /toh-n'l/ • adj. **1** relating to tone. **2** (of music) written using traditional keys and harmony.
– DERIVATIVES **tonally** adv.

tonality • n. (pl. **tonalities**) the character of a piece of music as determined by the key in which it is played.

tone • n. **1** a musical sound with reference to its pitch, quality, and strength. **2** the sound of a person's voice, expressing a feeling or mood. **3** general character: *trust her to lower the tone of the conversation.* **4** a basic interval in classical Western music, equal to two semitones. **5** a particular brightness, deepness, or shade in a colour. **6** the normal level of firmness in a resting muscle. • v. (**tones, toning, toned**) **1** (often **tone up**) give greater strength or firmness to (the body or a muscle). **2** (**tone down**) make less harsh, extreme, or strong.
– ORIGIN Greek *tonos* 'tension, tone'.

tone-deaf • adj. unable to notice differences of musical pitch accurately.

tone poem • n. a piece of orchestral music on a descriptive or poetic theme.

toner • n. **1** a liquid applied to the skin to reduce oiliness and improve its condition. **2** a powder used in photocopiers.

Tonga E
/tong-uh, tong-guh/ a country in the South Pacific consisting of an island group southeast of Fiji; capital, Nuku'alofa. Also called the **FRIENDLY ISLANDS**.
– DERIVATIVES **Tongan** n. & adj.

Tongariro, Mount E
/tong-uh-reer-oh/ a mountain in North Island, New Zealand, held sacred by the Maoris.

tongs • pl. n. a tool with two movable arms that are joined at one end, used for picking up and holding things.
– ORIGIN Old English.

tongue • n. **1** the fleshy organ in the mouth, used for tasting, licking, swallowing, and (in humans) producing speech. **2** the tongue of an ox or lamb as food. **3** a person's manner of speaking: *I have a sharp tongue.* **4** a language. **5** a strip of leather or fabric under the laces in a shoe. **6** the clapper of a bell. • v. (**tongues, tonguing, tongued**) **1** Music sound (a note) distinctly on a wind instrument by interrupting the air flow with the tongue. **2** lick with the tongue.
– PHRASES **lose one's tongue** be unable to express oneself after a shock. **the gift of tongues** the power of speaking in unknown languages, believed to be one of the gifts of the Holy Spirit. **hold one's tongue** informal remain silent. (**with**) **tongue in cheek** not seriously meaning what one is saying.
– ORIGIN Old English.

tongue and groove • n. wooden boards which are placed next to each other and joined by means of interlocking ridges and hollows down their sides.

tongue-lashing • n. a loud or severe scolding.

tongue-tied • adj. too shy or embarrassed to speak.

tongue-twister • n. a sequence of words that are difficult to pronounce quickly.

tonic • n. **1** a drink taken as a medicine, to give a feeling of energy or well-being. **2** something that makes one feel happier or healthier. **3** tonic water.
– ORIGIN Greek *tonikos* 'for stretching'.

tonic sol-fa • n. a system of naming the notes of the scale used to teach singing, with doh as the keynote of all major keys and lah as the keynote of all minor keys.

tonic water • n. a fizzy soft drink with a bitter flavour, used as a mixer with spirits.

tonight • adv. on the present or approaching evening or night. • n. the evening or night of the present day.

tonnage • n. **1** weight in tons. **2** the size or carrying capacity of a ship measured in tons.

tonne /tun/ • n. = **METRIC TON**.
– ORIGIN French.

tonsil • n. either of two small masses of tissue in the throat, one on each side of the root of the tongue.
– ORIGIN Latin *tonsillae* (plural).

tonsillectomy /ton-sil-lek-tuh-mi/ • n. (pl. **tonsillectomies**) a surgical operation to remove the tonsils.

tonsillitis • n. inflammation of the tonsils.

tonsorial /ton-sor-i-uhl/ ● **adj.** formal having to do with hairdressing.

tonsure /ton-syer, ton-sher/ ● **n.** a part of a monk's or priest's head left bare on top by shaving off the hair.
– ORIGIN Latin *tonsura*.

too ● **adv. 1** more than is desirable, allowed, or possible. **2** in addition. **3** informal very: *you're too kind.*
– ORIGIN Old English.

USAGE too
For an explanation of the difference between **too**, **to**, and **two**, see the note at **TO**.

took past of **TAKE**.

tool ● **n. 1** a device or implement used to carry out a particular function. **2** a thing used to help perform a job. **3** a person used by another. ● **v. 1** (usu. **be tooled**) impress a design on (a leather book cover) with a heated tool. **2** equip with tools for industrial production.
– ORIGIN Old English.

toolbar ● **n.** Computing a strip of icons used to perform certain functions.

toolmaker ● **n.** a person who makes and repairs tools for use in a manufacturing process.

toot ● **n.** a short, sharp sound made by a horn, trumpet, or similar instrument. ● **v.** make or cause to make a toot.
– ORIGIN perh. from German *tūten*.

tooth ● **n.** (pl. **teeth**) **1** each of a set of hard enamel-coated structures in the jaws, used for biting and chewing. **2** a cog on a gearwheel or a point on a saw or comb. **3** (**teeth**) genuine force or effectiveness: *the law would be fine if it had teeth.*
– PHRASES **fight tooth and nail** fight very fiercely.
– DERIVATIVES **toothed** adj.
– ORIGIN Old English.

toothache ● **n.** pain in a tooth or teeth.

toothbrush ● **n.** a small brush with a long handle, used for cleaning the teeth.

toothcomb ● **n.** Brit. (in phr. **with a fine toothcomb**) with a very thorough search.
– ORIGIN from a misreading of *fine-tooth comb*, i.e. a comb with narrow, closely-spaced teeth.

toothed whale ● **n.** any of the large group of whales with teeth, including sperm whales, killer whales, dolphins, etc.

tooth fairy ● **n.** a fairy said to take children's milk teeth after they fall out and leave a coin under their pillow.

toothless ● **adj. 1** having no teeth. **2** lacking real force or effectiveness.

toothpaste ● **n.** a paste used for cleaning the teeth.

toothpick ● **n.** a thin, pointed piece of wood or plastic used for removing bits of food stuck between the teeth.

toothsome ● **adj. 1** (of food) temptingly tasty. **2** informal attractive.

toothy ● **adj.** (**toothier**, **toothiest**) having or showing large noticeable teeth: *he gave a toothy grin.*
– DERIVATIVES **toothily** adv.

tootle ● **v.** (**tootles**, **tootling**, **tootled**) casually make a series of sounds on a horn, trumpet, etc.
– ORIGIN from **TOOT**.

tootsie /tuut-si/ (also **tootsy**) ● **n.** (pl. **tootsies**) informal **1** a person's foot. **2** a young woman.
– ORIGIN from **FOOT**.

top[1] ● **n. 1** the highest or uppermost point, part, or surface. **2** a thing placed on, fitted to, or covering the upper part of something. **3** (**the top**) the highest or most important rank, level, or position. **4** the utmost degree: *she shouted at the top of her voice.* **5** esp. Brit. the end that is furthest away: *the bus stop at the top of the road.* **6** a garment covering the upper part of the body. ● **adj.** highest in position, rank, or degree: *my office is on the top floor.* ● **v.** (**tops**, **topping**, **topped**) **1** be more, better, or taller than. **2** be at the highest place or rank in. **3** reach the top of (a hill or rise). **4** (usu. **be topped**) provide with a top or topping. **5** informal kill.
– PHRASES **on top** in addition. **on top of 1** so as to cover. **2** very near to. **3** in control of. **4** in addition to. **on top of the world** feeling very happy. **over the top** informal, esp. Brit. in an excessive or exaggerated way. **top up 1** add to (a number or amount) to bring it up to a certain level. **2** fill up (a partly full container).
– DERIVATIVES **topmost** adj.
– ORIGIN Old English.

top[2] ● **n.** a toy with a rounded top and pointed base, that can be set to spin.
– ORIGIN Old English.

topaz ● **n.** a colourless, yellow, or pale blue precious stone.
– ORIGIN Greek *topazos*.

top brass ● **n.** see **BRASS** (sense 5).

topcoat ● **n. 1** an overcoat. **2** an outer coat of paint.

top dog ● **n.** informal a person who is successful or dominant in their field.

top-drawer ● **adj.** informal of the highest quality or social class.

tope ● **v.** (**topes**, **toping**, **toped**) archaic frequently drink too much alcohol.
– DERIVATIVES **toper** n.
– ORIGIN perh. from former *top* 'overbalance'.

top flight ● **n.** the highest rank or level.

topgallant /top-gal-luhnt, tuh-gal-luhnt/ ● **n. 1** the section of a square-rigged sailing ship's mast immediately above the topmast. **2** a sail set on such a mast.

top hat ● **n.** a man's formal black hat with a high cylindrical crown.

top-heavy ● **adj. 1** too heavy at the top and likely to be unstable. **2** (of an organization) having too large a number of senior executives.

topiary /toh-pi-uh-ri/ ● **n.** (pl. **topiaries**) **1** the art of clipping shrubs or trees into attractive shapes. **2** shrubs or trees clipped in such a way.
– ORIGIN Latin *topiarius* 'ornamental gardener'.

topic ● **n.** a subject of a text, speech, conversation, etc.
– ORIGIN from Greek *ta topika*, 'matters concerning commonplaces'.

topical ● **adj. 1** relating to or dealing with current affairs. **2** relating to a particular subject.
– DERIVATIVES **topicality** n. **topically** adv.

topknot ● **n. 1** a knot of hair arranged on the top of the head. **2** a decorative knot or bow of ribbon worn on the top of the head. **3** a tuft or crest of hair or feathers on the head of an animal or bird.

topless ● **adj.** having the breasts uncovered.

topmast /**top**-mahst, **top**-muhst/ ● **n.** the second section of a square-rigged sailing ship's mast, immediately above the lower mast.

top-notch ● **adj.** informal of the highest quality.

topography /tuh-**pog**-ruh-fi/ ● **n. 1** the arrangement of the physical features of an area. **2** a detailed description or representation on a map of such features.
– DERIVATIVES **topographic** adj. **topographical** adj.
– ORIGIN Greek *topos* 'place'.

topology /tuh-**pol**-uh-ji/ ● **n.** Math. the study of geometrical properties and spatial relations which remain unaffected by certain changes in shape or size of figures.

topper ● **n.** informal a top hat.

topping ● **n.** a layer of food poured or spread over another food. ● **adj.** Brit. informal, dated excellent.

topple ● **v.** (**topples**, **toppling**, **toppled**) overbalance or cause to overbalance and fall.
– ORIGIN from TOP[1].

topsail /**top**-sayl, **top**-s'l/ ● **n. 1** a sail set on a ship's topmast. **2** a sail set lengthwise, above the gaff.

top secret ● **adj.** of the highest secrecy.

topside ● **n.** Brit. the outer side of a round of beef.

topsoil ● **n.** the top layer of soil.

topspin ● **n.** a fast forward spin given to a moving ball, resulting in a curved path or a strong forward motion on rebounding.

topsy-turvy ● **adj. & adv. 1** upside down. **2** in a state of confusion.
– ORIGIN prob. from TOP[1] and former *terve* 'overturn'.

tor ● **n.** a steep hill or rocky peak.
– ORIGIN perh. Celtic.

Torah /**tor**-uh, tor-**ah**/ ● **n.** (in Judaism) the law of God as revealed to Moses and recorded in the Pentateuch.
– ORIGIN Hebrew, 'instruction, law'.

torch ● **n. 1** Brit. a portable battery-powered electric lamp. **2** esp. hist. a piece of wood or cloth soaked in tallow and ignited. ● **v.** informal set fire to.
– PHRASES **carry a torch for** be in love with (someone) who is not in love with one.
– ORIGIN Latin *torqua, torques* 'necklace'.

tore past of TEAR[1].

toreador /**to**-ri-uh-dor/ ● **n.** a bullfighter, especially one on horseback.
– ORIGIN Spanish.

torment ● **n.** /**tor**-ment/ **1** great physical or mental suffering. **2** a cause of torment. ● **v.** /tor-**ment**/ **1** make (someone) suffer greatly. **2** annoy or tease unkindly.
– DERIVATIVES **tormentor** n.
– ORIGIN Latin *tormentum* 'instrument of torture'.

torn past part. of TEAR[1].

tornado /tor-**nay**-doh/ ● **n.** (pl. **tornadoes** or **tornados**) a violently rotating wind storm having the appearance of a funnel-shaped cloud.
– ORIGIN perh. from Spanish *tronada* 'thunderstorm'.

Toronto E
the capital of Ontario and the largest city in Canada.

torpedo ● **n.** (pl. **torpedoes**) a long narrow self-propelled underwater missile fired from a ship, submarine, or an aircraft. ● **v.** (**torpedoes**, **torpedoing**, **torpedoed**) **1** attack with a torpedo or torpedoes. **2** ruin (a plan or project).
– ORIGIN first meaning an electric ray: from Latin, 'numbness'.

torpid ● **adj.** inactive and lacking energy.
– DERIVATIVES **torpidity** n. **torpidly** adv.
– ORIGIN Latin *torpidus*.

torpor /**tor**-per/ ● **n.** the state of being inactive and lacking in energy.
– ORIGIN Latin.

torque /tork/ ● **n.** a force that tends to cause rotation.
– ORIGIN Latin *torquere* 'to twist'.

Torquemada E
/tor-ki-**mah**-duh/ , Tomás de (*c.*1420–98), Spanish monk and Grand Inquisitor. He persuaded Ferdinand and Isabella to establish the Spanish Inquisition in 1478, and also instigated the expulsion of the Jews from Spain in and after 1492.

torrent ● **n. 1** a strong and fast-moving stream of water or other liquid. **2** an overwhelmingly large outpouring: *a torrent of abuse*.
– ORIGIN French.

torrential ● **adj.** (of rain) falling rapidly and heavily.

Torres Strait E
/**to**-riss/ a channel separating the northern tip of Queensland, Australia, from the island of New Guinea.

Torricelli E
/to-ri-**chel**-li/, Evangelista (1608–47), Italian mathematician and physicist, inventor of the mercury barometer.

torrid ● **adj. 1** very hot and dry. **2** full of sexual passion. **3** full of difficulty.
– ORIGIN Latin *torridus*.

torsion /**tor**-sh'n/ ● **n.** the action of twisting or the state of being twisted.
– DERIVATIVES **torsional** adj.
– ORIGIN Latin.

torso ● **n.** (pl. **torsos**) the trunk of the human body.
– ORIGIN Italian, 'stalk, stump'.

tort ● **n.** Law a wrongful act or a violation of a right (other than under contract) leading to legal liability.
– ORIGIN Latin *tortum* 'wrong, injustice'.

torte /**tor**-tuh, tort/ ● **n.** (pl. **torten** /**tor**-tuhn/ or **tortes**) a sweet cake or tart.
– ORIGIN German.

Tortelier E
/tor-**tel**-li-ay/, Paul (1914–90), French cellist.

tortellini /tor-tuhl-**lee**-ni/ ● **n.** stuffed pasta parcels rolled and formed into small rings.
– ORIGIN Italian.

tortilla /tor-**tee**-yuh/ ● **n. 1** (in Mexican cookery) a thin, flat maize pancake. **2** (in Spanish cookery) a thick omelette containing potato.

– ORIGIN Spanish, 'little cake'.

tortoise /tor-tuhss, tor-toyz/ ● **n.** a slow-moving land reptile with a domed shell into which it can draw its head and legs.

– ORIGIN Latin *tortuca*.

tortoiseshell ● **n. 1** the semi-transparent mottled yellow and brown shell of certain turtles, used to make jewellery or ornaments. **2** a domestic cat with markings resembling tortoiseshell. **3** a butterfly with mottled orange, yellow, and black markings.

Tortola E
/tor-**toh**-luh/ the main island of the British Virgin Islands in the Caribbean; chief town, Road Town (also the capital of the British Virgin Islands).

tortuous /tor-chuu-uhss, tor-tyuu-uhss/ ● **adj. 1** full of twists and turns. **2** excessively lengthy and complex.

– DERIVATIVES **tortuosity** n. **tortuously** adv.

– ORIGIN Latin *tortuosus*.

torture ● **n. 1** the act of causing severe pain as a punishment or to make someone do something. **2** great suffering or anxiety. ● **v.** (**tortures, torturing, tortured**) inflict torture on.

– DERIVATIVES **torturer** n.

– ORIGIN Latin *tortura* 'torment'.

torturous ● **adj.** characterized by pain or suffering.

Tory ● **n.** (pl. **Tories**) a member or supporter of the British Conservative Party.

– ORIGIN first referring to Irish peasants dispossessed by English settlers and living as robbers: prob. from Irish *toraidhe* 'outlaw'.

Toscanini E
/toss-kuh-**nee**-ni/, Arturo (1867–1957), Italian conductor.

tosh ● **n.** Brit. informal nonsense.

– ORIGIN unknown.

toss ● **v. 1** throw lightly or casually. **2** move from side to side or back and forth. **3** jerk (one's head or hair) sharply backwards. **4** throw (a coin) into the air so as to make a choice, based on which side of the coin faces uppermost when it lands. **5** shake or turn (food) in a liquid to coat it lightly. ● **n.** an act of tossing.

– PHRASES **not give** (or **care**) **a toss** Brit. informal not care at all.

– ORIGIN unknown.

tosser ● **noun** Brit. vulgar a stupid person.

toss-up ● **n.** informal **1** the tossing of a coin to make a choice. **2** a situation in which any of two or more outcomes is equally possible.

tot[1] ● **n. 1** a very young child. **2** esp. Brit. a small drink of spirits.

– ORIGIN unknown.

tot[2] ● **v.** (**tots, totting, totted**) (**tot up**) esp. Brit. **1** add up (numbers or amounts). **2** collect up over time.

– ORIGIN from TOTAL or Latin *totum* 'the whole'.

total ● **adj. 1** comprising the whole number or amount. **2** complete. ● **n.** a total number or amount. ● **v.** (**totals, totalling, totalled**; US **totals, totaling, totaled**) **1** amount to (a total number). **2** find the total of. **3** N. Amer. informal destroy or kill.

– DERIVATIVES **totally** adv.

– ORIGIN Latin *totalis*.

total eclipse ● **n.** an eclipse in which the whole of the disc of the sun or moon is covered.

totalitarian /toh-tal-i-**tair**-i-uhn/ ● **adj.** (of government) consisting of only one leader or party and having complete power and control. ● **n.** a person in favour of such a system.

– DERIVATIVES **totalitarianism** n.

totality ● **n. 1** the whole of something. **2** Astron. the time during which the sun or moon is totally covered during an eclipse.

totalizator (also **totalisator**) ● **n. 1** a device showing the number and amount of bets staked on a race. **2** = TOTE[1].

tote[1] ● **n.** (**the tote**) informal a system of betting based on the use of the totalizator, in which winnings are calculated according to the amount staked rather than odds offered.

tote[2] ● **v.** (**totes, toting, toted**) informal, esp. N. Amer. carry.

– ORIGIN prob. dialect.

tote bag ● **n.** a large bag for carrying a number of items.

totem /toh-tuhm/ ● **n.** a natural object or animal believed by a particular society to have spiritual meaning and adopted by it as an emblem.

– DERIVATIVES **totemic** /toh-**tem**-ik/ adj.

– ORIGIN from a North American Indian language.

totem pole ● **n.** a pole on which totems are hung or on which the images of totems are carved.

totter ● **v.** (**totters, tottering, tottered**) **1** move in an unsteady way. **2** shake or rock as if about to collapse. **3** be insecure or on the point of failure. ● **n.** a tottering walk.

– ORIGIN Dutch *touteren* 'to swing'.

totty ● **n.** Brit. informal girls or women regarded as sexually desirable.

– ORIGIN from TOT[1].

toucan /too-kuhn/ ● **n.** a tropical American bird with a massive bill and brightly coloured plumage.

– ORIGIN from a South American Indian language.

touch ● **v. 1** come into or be in physical contact with. **2** bring one's hand or another part of one's body into contact with. **3** harm or interfere with. **4** use or consume: *I haven't touched a cent of the money.* **5** have an effect on. **6** (**be touched**) feel moved with gratitude or sympathy. ● **n. 1** an act or manner of touching. **2** the ability to be aware of something through physical contact, especially with the fingers. **3** a small amount. **4** a distinctive detail or feature. **5** a distinctive or skilful way of dealing with something: *a sure political touch.*

– PHRASES **in touch 1** in or into communication. **2** possessing up-to-date knowledge. **lose touch** no longer be in communication. **out of touch** lacking up-to-date knowledge. **touch down** (of an aircraft or spacecraft) land. **touch on** (or **upon**) deal briefly with (a subject). **touch up** make small improvements to.

– ORIGIN Old French *tochier*.

touch-and-go ● **adj.** (of an outcome) possible but very uncertain.

touchdown ● **n. 1** the moment at which an

aircraft touches down. **2** Rugby & Amer. Football an act of scoring by touching the ball down behind the opponents' goal line.

touché /too-**shay**/ ● **exclam.** **1** (in fencing) used to acknowledge a hit by one's opponent. **2** used to acknowledge a good point made at one's expense.
– ORIGIN French, 'touched'.

touching ● **adj.** arousing gratitude or sympathy; moving. ● **prep.** concerning.

touchline ● **n.** Rugby & Soccer the boundary line on each side of the field.

touchpaper ● **n.** a strip of paper treated with nitre, for setting light to fireworks or gunpowder.

touch screen ● **n.** a display device which allows the user to interact with a computer by touching areas on the screen.

touchstone ● **n.** **1** a piece of stone formerly used for testing alloys of gold by observing the colour of the mark which they made on it. **2** a standard.

touch-tone ● **adj.** (of a telephone) generating tones to dial rather than pulses.

touch-type ● **v.** (**touch-types**, **touch-typing**, **touch-typed**) type using all of one's fingers and without looking at the keys.

touchy ● **adj.** (**touchier**, **touchiest**) **1** quick to take offence. **2** (of a situation or issue) requiring careful handling.
– ORIGIN perh. from TETCHY, influenced by TOUCH.

touchy-feely ● **adj.** informal, usu. derog. openly expressing affection or other emotions.

tough ● **adj.** **1** strong enough to withstand wear and tear. **2** able to endure difficulty or pain. **3** strict. **4** involving considerable difficulty or hardship. **5** (of a person) rough or violent. ● **n.** informal a rough and violent man.
– DERIVATIVES **toughness** n.
– ORIGIN Old English.

toughen ● **v.** make or become tough.

Toulouse E
/too-**looz**/ a city in SW France, chief city of the Midi-Pyrénées region.

Toulouse-Lautrec E
/too-looz loh-**trek**/, Henri (Marie Raymond) de (1864–1901), French painter and lithographer, noted for his lithographs depicting actors, music-hall singers, and others in Montmartre.

toupee /too-pay/ ● **n.** a small wig or hairpiece worn to cover a bald spot.
– ORIGIN French.

tour ● **n.** **1** a journey for pleasure in which several different places are visited. **2** a short trip to view or inspect something. **3** a series of performances or matches in several different places by performers or sports players. ● **v.** make a tour of.
– ORIGIN Old French, 'turn'.

tour de force /toor duh **forss**/ ● **n.** (pl. **tours de force** /toor duh **forss**/) a performance or achievement accomplished with great skill.
– ORIGIN French, 'feat of strength'.

Tour de France E
/toor duh **fronss**/ a French long-distance race for professional cyclists held annually since 1903.

tourer ● **n.** a car, caravan, or bicycle designed for touring.

tourism ● **n.** the commercial organization and operation of holidays and visits to places of interest.

tourist ● **n.** **1** a person who travels for pleasure. **2** a member of a touring sports team.

tourist class ● **n.** the cheapest accommodation or seating in a ship, aircraft, or hotel.

touristy ● **adj.** informal, usu. derog. appealing to or visited by many tourists.

tourmaline /**toor**-muh-lin, **toor**-muh-leen/ ● **n.** a brittle grey or black mineral used as a gemstone and in electrical devices.
– ORIGIN Sinhalese, 'carnelian'.

tournament ● **n.** **1** a series of contests between a number of competitors. **2** a medieval sporting event in which knights jousted with blunted weapons for a prize.
– ORIGIN Old French *torneiement*.

tourney /**toor**-ni, **ter**-ni/ ● **n.** (pl. **tourneys**) a medieval joust.
– ORIGIN Old French *tornei*.

tourniquet /**toor**-ni-kay, **tor**-ni-kay/ ● **n.** a cord or tight bandage which is tied around a limb to stop the flow of blood through an artery.
– ORIGIN French.

tour operator ● **n.** a travel agent specializing in package holidays.

tousle /**tow**-z'l/ ● **v.** (**tousles**, **tousling**, **tousled**) make (a person's hair) untidy.
– ORIGIN Germanic.

tout /towt/ ● **v.** **1** attempt to sell (something). **2** attempt to persuade people of the worth of. **3** Brit. resell (a ticket) for a popular event at a price higher than the official one. ● **n.** (also **ticket tout**) Brit. a person who buys up tickets for an event to resell them at a profit.
– ORIGIN Germanic.

tow[1] ● **v.** use a vehicle or boat to pull (another vehicle or boat) along. ● **n.** an act of towing.
– PHRASES **in tow** **1** (also **on tow**) being towed. **2** accompanying or following someone.
– ORIGIN Old English.

tow[2] ● **n.** short coarse fibres of flax or hemp, used for making yarn etc.
– ORIGIN Old English.

towards (esp. N. Amer. also **toward**) ● **prep.** **1** in the direction of. **2** getting nearer to (a time or aim). **3** in relation to. **4** contributing to the cost of.
– ORIGIN Old English.

towel ● **n.** a piece of absorbent cloth or paper used for drying. ● **v.** (**towels**, **towelling**, **towelled**; US **towels**, **toweling**, **toweled**) dry with a towel.
– ORIGIN Old French *toaille*.

towelling (US **toweling**) ● **n.** absorbent cloth used for towels and bathrobes.

tower ● **n.** **1** a tall, narrow building or part of a building. **2** a tall structure that houses machinery, operators, etc. **3** a tall structure used as a container or for storage. ● **v.** (**towers**, **towering**, **towered**) **1** rise to or reach a great height. **2** (**towering**) very important or influential. **3** (**towering**) very great: *a towering rage*.
– ORIGIN Old English.

tower block ● **n.** Brit. a tall modern building containing many floors of offices or flats.

Tower Bridge E
a bridge across the Thames in London, famous for its twin towers and for the sections of roadway which are able to be lifted to allow the passage of large ships.

Tower of Babel E
/**bay**-b'l/ (in the Bible) a tower built in an attempt to reach heaven, which God frustrated by confusing the languages of its builders so that they could not understand one another.

Tower of London E
(also **the Tower**) a fortress by the Thames in London. Begun in 1078, it was later used as a state prison, and is now a museum containing the Crown jewels.

town • n. **1** a settlement larger than a village and generally smaller than a city. **2** the central part of a town or city, with its business or shopping area. **3** densely populated areas, as contrasted with the country or suburbs.
– PHRASES **go to town** informal do something thoroughly or enthusiastically. **on the town** informal enjoying the nightlife of a city or town.
– ORIGIN Old English, 'homestead, village'.

town clerk • n. (in the UK, until 1974) the secretary and legal adviser of a town corporation.

town council • n. (especially in the UK) a town's elected governing body.
– DERIVATIVES **town councillor** n.

town crier • n. hist. a person employed to make public announcements in the streets.

town hall • n. a building housing local government offices.

town house • n. **1** a tall, narrow terrace house, generally having three or more floors. **2** an urban residence of a person owning another property in the country.

townie • n. informal a person who lives in a town.

town planning • n. the planning and control of the construction, growth, and development of a town or other urban area.
– DERIVATIVES **town planner** n.

township • n. (in South Africa) a suburb or city where mainly black people live, formerly selected for black occupation by apartheid legislation.
– ORIGIN Old English.

townspeople (also **townsfolk**) • pl. n. the people living in a town or city.

towpath • n. a path beside a river or canal, originally used as a pathway for horses towing barges.

tow rope • n. a rope, cable, etc. used in towing.

toxic • adj. **1** poisonous. **2** relating to or caused by poison.
– DERIVATIVES **toxicity** n.
– ORIGIN Latin *toxicum* 'poison'.

toxicology /toks-i-**kol**-uh-ji/ • n. the branch of science concerned with the nature, effects, and detection of poisons.
– DERIVATIVES **toxicological** adj. **toxicologist** n.

toxic shock syndrome • n. acute septicaemia in women, often caused by infection from a tampon or IUD that has been kept in the body for too long.

toxin • n. a poison produced by a micro-organism or other organism, to which the body reacts by producing antibodies.

toy • n. **1** an object for a child to play with. **2** a gadget or machine that provides amusement for an adult. • v. (**toy with**) **1** consider casually. **2** move or touch absent-mindedly or nervously. **3** eat or drink in an unenthusiastic way. • adj. (of a breed of dog) much smaller than is normal for the breed.
– ORIGIN unknown.

toy boy • n. Brit. informal a male lover who is much younger than his partner.

Toynbee[1] E
/**toyn**-bee/, Arnold (1852–83), English economist and social reformer, known for his pioneering work *The Industrial Revolution*.

Toynbee[2] E
/**toyn**-bee/, Arnold (Joseph) (1889–1975), English historian, known for his twelve-volume *Study of History*.

trace[1] • v. (**traces**, **tracing**, **traced**) **1** find by careful investigation. **2** find or describe the origin or development of. **3** follow the course or position of with one's eye, mind, or finger. **4** copy (a drawing or map) by drawing over its lines on a piece of transparent paper placed on top of it. **5** draw (a pattern or outline). • n. **1** a mark or other sign of the existence or passing of something. **2** a very small amount. **3** a barely noticeable indication: *a trace of a smile*. **4** a line or pattern on paper or a screen, showing something that a machine is recording.
– DERIVATIVES **traceable** adj.
– ORIGIN Old French *tracier*.

trace[2] • n. each of the two side straps, chains, or ropes by which a horse is attached to a vehicle that it is pulling.
– ORIGIN Old French *trais*.

trace element • n. a chemical element present or required only in tiny amounts.

tracer • n. a bullet or shell whose course is made visible by a trail of flames or smoke, used to assist in aiming.

tracery • n. (pl. **traceries**) **1** Archit. a decorative design of holes and outlines in stone. **2** a delicate branching pattern.

trachea /truh-**kee**-uh, **tray**-ki-uh/ • n. (pl. **tracheae** /truh-**kee**-ee, **tray**-ki-ee/ or **tracheas**) Anat. the tube carrying air between the larynx and the bronchial tubes; the windpipe.
– ORIGIN from Greek *trakheia artēria* 'rough artery'.

tracheotomy /tra-ki-**ot**-uh-mi/ (also **tracheostomy** /tra-ki-**oss**-tuh-mi/) • n. (pl. **tracheotomies**) a surgical incision in the windpipe, made to enable someone to breathe when the windpipe is blocked.

tracing • n. **1** a copy of a drawing or map made by tracing. **2** a faint or delicate mark or pattern.

track • n. **1** a rough path or small road. **2** a prepared course or circuit for racing. **3** a mark or line of marks left by a person, animal, or vehicle in passing. **4** a continuous line of rails on a railway. **5** a section of a record, compact disc, or cassette tape containing one song or piece of music. **6** a strip or rail along which something such as a curtain may be

moved. **7** a jointed metal band around the wheels of a heavy vehicle. • **v. 1** follow the trail or movements of. **2** (**track down**) find after a thorough search. **3** follow a particular course. **4** (of a film or television camera) move along with the subject being filmed. [ORIGIN with reference to early filming when a camera was moved along a track.]
– PHRASES **keep** (or **lose**) **track of** keep (or fail to keep) fully aware of or informed about. **on the right** (or **wrong**) **track** following a course likely to result in success (or failure).
ORIGIN Old French *trac*.

trackball • **n.** a small ball set in a holder that can be rotated by hand to move a cursor on a computer screen.

tracker • **n.** a person who tracks.

track events • **pl. n.** athletic events that take place on a running track.

tracking • **n.** Electron. the maintenance of a constant difference in frequency between connected circuits or parts.

track record • **n.** the past achievements or performance of a person, organization, or product.

tracksuit • **n.** a warm outfit consisting of a sweatshirt and trousers.

tract[1] • **n. 1** a large area of land. **2** a major passage in the body: *the digestive tract*.
– ORIGIN Latin *tractus* 'drawing'.

tract[2] • **n.** a short piece of writing in pamphlet form, on a religious or political subject.
– ORIGIN prob. from Latin *tractatus* 'treatise'.

tractable • **adj. 1** easy to control or influence. **2** (of a problem) easy to deal with.
– DERIVATIVES **tractability** n.
– ORIGIN Latin *tractabilis*.

Tractarianism • **n.** = **OXFORD MOVEMENT**.
– ORIGIN from *Tracts for the Times*, a series of theological pamphlets started by J. H. Newman.

traction • **n. 1** the action of pulling a thing along a surface. **2** the power used for pulling. **3** Med. the application of a sustained pull on a limb or muscle, to maintain the position of a fractured bone. **4** the grip of a tyre on a road or a wheel on a rail.
– ORIGIN Latin.

traction engine • **n.** a steam or diesel-powered road vehicle used for pulling very heavy loads.

tractor • **n.** a powerful motor vehicle with large rear wheels, used on farms for moving equipment.
– ORIGIN Latin.

Tracy, E
Spencer (1900–67), American actor, known for such films as *Captain Courageous* and *Guess Who's Coming to Dinner?*

trad • **adj.** informal traditional.

trade • **n. 1** the buying and selling of goods and services. **2** a commercial activity of a particular kind: *the tourist trade*. **3** a job requiring manual skills and special training. **4** (**the trade**) the people engaged in a particular area of business. • **v.** (**trades**, **trading**, **traded**) **1** buy and sell goods and services. **2** buy or sell (a particular item). **3** exchange. **4** (**trade in**) exchange (a used article) as part of a payment for another. **5** (**trade on**) take advantage of. **6** (**trade off**) exchange (something of value) as part of a compromise.
– DERIVATIVES **tradable** (or **tradeable**) adj.
– ORIGIN German, 'track'.

trademark • **n. 1** a symbol, word, or words chosen to represent a company or product. **2** a distinctive characteristic.

trade name • **n. 1** a name that has the status of a trademark. **2** a name by which something is known in a particular trade or profession.

trade-off • **n.** a compromise.

trader • **n. 1** a person who trades goods, currency, or shares. **2** a merchant ship.

Tradescant E
/trad-i-skant/, John (1570–1638), English botanist and horticulturalist, the earliest known collector of plants and other natural history specimens.

tradescantia /trad-i-skan-ti-uh/ • **n.** an American plant with triangular three-petalled flowers.
– ORIGIN named after John **TRADESCANT**.

tradesman • **n.** a person engaged in trading or a trade.

Trades Union Congress E
(in the UK) the official representative body of British trade unions, founded in 1868.

trade surplus • **n.** the amount by which the value of a country's exports is more than the cost of its imports.

trade union (Brit. also **trades union**) • **n.** an organized association of workers formed to work for their rights and interests.
– DERIVATIVES **trade unionist** (also **trades unionist**) n.

trade wind • **n.** a wind blowing steadily towards the equator from the north-east in the northern hemisphere or the south-east in the southern hemisphere.
– ORIGIN from former *blow trade* 'blow steadily'.

trading estate • **n.** Brit. a specially designed industrial and commercial area.

trading post • **n.** a store or small settlement established for trading in a remote place.

tradition • **n. 1** the passing on of customs or beliefs from generation to generation. **2** a long-established custom or belief passed on in this way. **3** a method or style established by an artist, writer, or movement, and followed by others.
– ORIGIN Latin.

traditional • **adj. 1** having to do with or following tradition. **2** (of jazz) in the style of the early 20th century.
– DERIVATIVES **traditionally** adv.

traditionalism • **n.** the belief that traditions should be kept and change should be limited.
– DERIVATIVES **traditionalist** n. & adj.

traduce /truh-dyooss/ • **v.** (**traduces**, **traducing**, **traduced**) say unpleasant or untrue things about.
– ORIGIN Latin *traducere* 'expose to ridicule'.

Trafalgar, Battle of E
/truh-fal-ger/ a decisive naval battle fought on 21 October 1805 off the cape of Trafalgar on the south coast of Spain during the Napoleonic Wars. The British fleet under Nelson defeated the fleets of France and Spain.

traffic • **n. 1** vehicles moving on public roads. **2** the movement of ships or aircraft. **3** the carrying of goods or passengers as a business.

4 the messages or signals sent through a communications system. **5** the action of trading in something illegal. • v. (**trafficks**, **trafficking**, **trafficked**) deal or trade in something illegal.
– DERIVATIVES **trafficker** n.
– ORIGIN French *traffique*.

traffic calming • n. the deliberate slowing of traffic in residential areas, by building road humps or other obstructions.
– ORIGIN German *Verkehrsberuhigung*.

traffic island • n. a raised area in the middle of a road which provides a safe place for pedestrians to stand.

traffic jam • n. a line or lines of traffic at or almost at a standstill.

traffic lights • pl. n. a set of automatically operated coloured lights for controlling traffic.

traffic warden • n. Brit. an official who locates and reports on vehicles breaking parking regulations.

tragedian /truh-jee-di-uhn/ • n. **1** (fem. **tragedienne** /truh-jee-di-en/) an actor or actress who plays tragic roles. **2** a writer of tragedies.

tragedy • n. (pl. **tragedies**) **1** an event causing great sadness or suffering. **2** a serious play with an unhappy ending.
– ORIGIN Greek *tragōidia*.

tragic • adj. **1** extremely sad. **2** suffering great sadness. **3** relating to tragedy in a literary work.
– DERIVATIVES **tragically** adv.

tragicomedy • n. (pl. **tragicomedies**) a play or novel containing elements of both comedy and tragedy.
– DERIVATIVES **tragicomic** adj.

trail • n. **1** a mark or a series of signs left behind by the passage of someone or something. **2** a track or scent used in following someone or hunting an animal. **3** a long thin part stretching behind or hanging down from something: *trails of ivy.* **4** a beaten path through rough country. **5** a route planned or followed for a particular purpose: *the tourist trail.* • v. **1** draw or be drawn along behind. **2** follow the trail of. **3** walk or move slowly or wearily. **4** (**trail away/off**) (of the voice or a speaker) fade gradually before stopping. **5** be losing to an opponent in a contest. **6** (of a plant) grow along the ground or so as to hang down.
– ORIGIN Old French *traillier* 'to tow' or German *treilen* 'haul (a boat)'.

trailblazer • n. **1** a person who makes a new track through wild country. **2** a person who is the first to do something new.
– DERIVATIVES **trailblazing** n. & adj.

trailer • n. **1** an unpowered vehicle pulled by another. **2** the rear section of an articulated truck. **3** N. Amer. a caravan. **4** an extract from a film or programme used to advertise it.

trailer park • n. N. Amer. a caravan site.

trailer truck • n. US an articulated truck.

trailing edge • n. the rear edge of an aircraft wing or propeller blade.

train • v. **1** teach (a person or animal) a particular skill or type of behaviour. **2** be taught a particular skill or type of behaviour. **3** make or become physically fit through a course of exercise and diet. **4** (**train on**) point (something) at. **5** make (a plant) grow in a particular direction or into a required shape. • n. **1** a series of railway carriages or wagons moved by a locomotive. **2** a number of vehicles or pack animals moving in a line. **3** a series of connected events or thoughts. **4** a long piece of trailing material attached to the back of a formal dress or robe.
– PHRASES **in train** in progress.
– DERIVATIVES **training** n.
– ORIGIN Old French *trahiner*.

trainee • n. a person undergoing training for a particular job or profession.

trainer • n. **1** a person who trains people or animals. **2** Brit. a soft shoe for sports or casual wear.

training college • n. (in the UK) a college where future teachers are trained.

trainspotter • n. Brit. **1** a person who collects locomotive numbers as a hobby. **2** derog. a person who obsessively studies every detail of any minority interest.
– DERIVATIVES **trainspotting** n.

traipse • v. (**traipses**, **traipsing**, **traipsed**) walk or move wearily, reluctantly, or aimlessly. • n. a boring or tiring walk.
– ORIGIN unknown.

trait /tray, trayt/ • n. **1** a distinguishing quality or characteristic. **2** a genetically determined characteristic.
– ORIGIN French.

traitor • n. a person who betrays their country or a cause.
– DERIVATIVES **traitorous** adj.
– ORIGIN Old French *traitour*.

Trajan E
/tray-j'n/ (*c.*53–117 AD; Latin name *Marcus Ulpius Traianus*), Roman emperor 98–117.

trajectory /truh-jek-tuh-ri/ • n. (pl. **trajectories**) the path followed by a moving object.
– ORIGIN Latin *trajectoria*.

tram (also **tramcar**) • n. Brit. a passenger vehicle powered by electricity and running on rails laid in a public road.
– ORIGIN German and Dutch *trame* 'beam, barrow shaft'.

tramlines • pl. n. Brit. **1** rails for a tram. **2** informal a pair of parallel lines at the sides of a tennis court or at the side or back of a badminton court.

trammel • n. (**trammels**) literary restrictions to freedom of action. • v. (**trammels**, **trammelling**, **trammelled**; US **trammels**, **trammeling**, **trammeled**) restrict or block the freedom or progress of.
– ORIGIN Old French *tramail*.

tramp • v. **1** walk heavily or noisily. **2** walk wearily over a long distance. • n. **1** a homeless person who travels around and lives by begging or doing casual work. **2** the sound of heavy steps. **3** a long walk. **4** a cargo ship running between many different ports rather than sailing a fixed route. **5** N. Amer. informal a woman who has many sexual partners.
– ORIGIN prob. German.

trample • v. (**tramples**, **trampling**, **trampled**) **1** tread on and crush. **2** (**trample on/upon/over**) treat with contempt.
– ORIGIN from TRAMP.

trampoline • n. a strong fabric sheet connected by springs to a frame, used as a springboard and landing area in doing acrobatic or

gymnastic exercises.
– DERIVATIVES **trampolining** n.
– ORIGIN Italian *trampolino.*

tramway • n. **1** Brit. a set of rails for a tram. **2** a tram system.

trance /*rhymes with* dance/ • n. **1** a half-conscious state in which someone does not respond to things that happen to them. **2** a state of inattention. **3** (also **trance music**) a type of electronic dance music with hypnotic rhythms.
– ORIGIN Old French *transir* 'depart, fall into a trance'.

tranche /*rhymes with* branch/ • n. any of the parts into which an amount of money or a number of shares in a company is divided.
– ORIGIN Old French, 'slice'.

tranquil • adj. free from disturbance; calm.
– DERIVATIVES **tranquillity** (also **tranquility**) n. **tranquilly** adv.
– ORIGIN Latin *tranquillus.*

tranquillize (also **tranquillise**; US **tranquilize**) • v. (**tranquillizes, tranquillizing, tranquillized**; US **tranquilizes, tranquilizing, tranquilized**) give a calming or sedative drug to.

tranquillizer (also **tranquilliser**; US **tranquilizer**) • n. a medicinal drug taken to reduce tension or anxiety.

trans- • prefix **1** across; beyond: *transcontinental.* **2** on or to the other side of: *transatlantic.* **3** into another state or place: *translate.*
– ORIGIN from Latin *trans* 'across'.

transact • v. conduct or carry out (business).

transaction • n. **1** an instance of buying or selling. **2** the action of conducting business.
– ORIGIN Latin.

transatlantic • adj. **1** crossing the Atlantic. **2** concerning countries on both sides of the Atlantic, especially Britain and the US. **3** relating to or situated on the other side of the Atlantic.

> **Transcaucasia** E
> /tranz-kaw-**kay**-*zh*uh/ a region to the south of the Caucasus mountains, between the Black Sea and the Caspian, and comprising the present-day republics of Georgia, Armenia, and Azerbaijan.

transceiver • n. a combined radio transmitter and receiver.

transcend • v. **1** be or go beyond the range or limits of. **2** be better than.
– ORIGIN Latin *transcendere.*

transcendent • adj. **1** going beyond normal or physical human experience. **2** (of God) existing apart from and not subject to the limitations of the material universe.
– DERIVATIVES **transcendence** n.

transcendental • adj. going beyond human knowledge and into a spiritual area.

Transcendental Meditation • n. (trademark in the US) a technique for making oneself calm and promoting harmony by meditation and repetition of a mantra.

transcontinental • adj. crossing or extending across a continent or continents.

transcribe • v. (**transcribes, transcribing, transcribed**) **1** put (thoughts, speech, or data) into written or printed form. **2** make a copy of (something) in another alphabet or language. **3** arrange (a piece of music) for a different instrument or voice.
– ORIGIN Latin *transcribere.*

transcript • n. a written or printed version of material that was originally spoken or presented in another form.
– ORIGIN Latin *transcriptum.*

transcription • n. **1** a transcript. **2** the action of transcribing. **3** a piece of music transcribed for a different instrument or voice.

transducer /tranz-**dyoo**-ser, trahnz-**dyoo**-ser/ • n. a device that converts variations in a physical quantity (such as pressure or brightness) into an electrical signal, or vice versa.
– DERIVATIVES **transduction** n.
– ORIGIN Latin *transducere* 'lead across'.

transect • v. tech. cut across or make a transverse section in.
– ORIGIN from TRANS- + Latin *secare* 'divide by cutting'.

transept /tran-sept, trahn-sept/ • n. (in a cross-shaped church) either of the two parts forming the arms of the cross shape, at right angles from the nave.
– ORIGIN Latin *transeptum.*

transfer • v. (**transfers, transferring, transferred**) **1** move (someone or something) from one place to another. **2** move to another department, job, etc. **3** change to another place, route, or means of transport during a journey. **4** pass (property, or a right or responsibility) to another. • n. **1** an act or the action of transferring. **2** Brit. a small coloured picture or design on paper, which can be transferred to another surface by being pressed or heated.
– DERIVATIVES **transferable** adj.
– ORIGIN Latin *transferre.*

transference • n. the action of transferring something from one place to another.

transfer fee • n. Brit. a fee paid by one soccer or rugby club to another for the transfer of a player.

transfigure • v. (**transfigures, transfiguring, transfigured**) (**be transfigured**) be transformed into something more beautiful or spiritual.
– DERIVATIVES **transfiguration** n.
– ORIGIN Latin *transfigurare.*

transfix • v. **1** make motionless with horror, wonder, or astonishment. **2** pierce with a sharp object.
– ORIGIN Latin *transfigere.*

transform • v. **1** change or be changed in appearance, form, or nature. **2** change the voltage of (an electric current).

transformation • n. a marked change in nature, form, or appearance.
– DERIVATIVES **transformational** adj.

transformer • n. a device for changing the voltage of an alternating current by electromagnetic induction.

transfusion • n. a medical process in which blood is transferred from one person or animal to another.
– ORIGIN Latin *transfundere* 'pour from one container to another'.

transgenic /tranz-**jen**-ik, trahnz-**jen**-ik/ • adj. Biol. containing genetic material into which DNA from a different organism has been artificially added.

transgress • v. go beyond the limits set by (a

moral principle, standard or law).
– DERIVATIVES **transgression** n. **transgressive** adj. **transgressor** n.
– ORIGIN Latin *transgredi* 'step across'.

transient /tran-zi-uhnt, **trahn**-zi-uhnt/ ● **adj.** **1** lasting only for a short time. **2** staying or working in a place for a short time only. ● **n.** a transient person.
– DERIVATIVES **transience** n. **transiently** adv.
– ORIGIN Latin *transire* 'go across'.

transistor ● **n. 1** a semiconductor device with three connections, able to amplify or rectify an electric current. **2** (also **transistor radio**) a portable radio using circuits containing transistors.
– ORIGIN from **TRANSFER** + **RESISTOR**.

transit ● **n. 1** the carrying of people or things from one place to another. **2** an act of passing through or across a place.
– ORIGIN Latin *transitus*.

transition ● **n. 1** the process of changing from one state or condition to another. **2** a period of such change.
– DERIVATIVES **transitional** adj.

transition metal ● **n.** Chem. any of the set of metallic elements occupying the central block in the periodic table, e.g. iron, manganese, chromium, and copper.

transitive /tran-zi-tiv, **trahn**-zi-tiv/ ● **adj.** Grammar (of a verb) able to take a direct object, e.g. *saw* in *he saw the donkey*. Opp. **INTRANSITIVE**.
– DERIVATIVES **transitivity** n.
– ORIGIN Latin *transitivus*.

transitory /tran-zi-tuh-ri, **trahn**-zi-tuh-ri/ ● **adj.** short-lived.
– ORIGIN Latin *transitorius*.

Transjordan E
former name (until 1949) of the region east of the River Jordan that now forms the main part of the kingdom of Jordan.

translate ● **v.** (**translates**, **translating**, **translated**) **1** express the sense of (words or text) in another language. **2** be expressed in another language. **3** (**translate into**) convert or be converted into another form or medium.
– DERIVATIVES **translatable** adj.
– ORIGIN Latin *translatus* 'carried across'.

translation ● **n. 1** the action or process of translating. **2** a text or word that is translated.

translator ● **n.** a person who translates from one language into another.

t

transliterate ● **v.** (**transliterates**, **transliterating**, **transliterated**) write or print (a letter or word) using the corresponding letters of a different alphabet or language.
– DERIVATIVES **transliteration** n.
– ORIGIN from **TRANS-** + Latin *littera* 'letter'.

translucent /tranz-**loo**-suhnt, trahnz-**loo**-suhnt/ ● **adj.** allowing light to pass through partially; semi-transparent.
– DERIVATIVES **translucence** (also **translucency**) n.
– ORIGIN Latin *translucere* 'shine through'.

transmigration ● **n.** the passing of a person's soul after their death into another body.

transmission ● **n. 1** the action of transmitting or the state of being transmitted. **2** a programme or signal that is transmitted. **3** the mechanism by which power is transmitted from an engine to the axle in a motor vehicle.

transmit ● **v.** (**transmits**, **transmitting**, **transmitted**) **1** cause to pass on from one place or person to another. **2** broadcast or send out (an electrical signal or a radio or television programme). **3** allow (heat, light, etc.) to pass through a medium.
– DERIVATIVES **transmissible** adj.
– ORIGIN Latin *transmittere*.

transmitter ● **n.** a device used to produce and transmit electromagnetic waves carrying messages or signals, especially those of radio or television.

transmogrify /tranz-**mog**-ri-fy, trahnz-**mog**-ri-fy/ ● **v.** (**transmogrifies**, **transmogrifying**, **transmogrified**) esp. humorous change into something else in a surprising or magical manner.
– ORIGIN unknown.

transmute /tranz-**myoot**, trahnz-**myoot**/ ● **v.** (**transmutes**, **transmuting**, **transmuted**) change in form, nature, or substance.
– DERIVATIVES **transmutation** n.
– ORIGIN Latin *transmutare*.

transnational ● **adj.** extending or operating across national boundaries.

transom /tran-suhm/ ● **n. 1** the flat surface forming the stern of a boat. **2** a strengthening crossbar above a door or window.
– ORIGIN Old French *traversin*.

transparency ● **n.** (pl. **transparencies**) **1** the condition of being transparent. **2** a positive transparent photograph printed on plastic or glass, and viewed using a slide projector.

transparent /tranz-**pa**-ruhnt, trahnz-**pa**-ruhnt, tranz-**pair**-uhnt, trahnz-**pair**-uhnt/ ● **adj. 1** allowing light to pass through so that objects behind can be distinctly seen. **2** obvious or evident.
– DERIVATIVES **transparently** adv.
– ORIGIN Latin *transparere* 'shine through'.

transpire ● **v.** (**transpires**, **transpiring**, **transpired**) **1** come to be the case. **2** happen. **3** (of a plant or leaf) give off water vapour through the stomata (tiny pores in the surface).
– DERIVATIVES **transpiration** n.
– ORIGIN Latin *transpirare*.

transplant ● **v.** /tranz-**plahnt**, trahnz-**plahnt**/ **1** transfer to another place or situation. **2** take (living tissue or an organ) and put it in another part of the body or in another body. ● **n.** /**tranz**-plahnt, **trahnz**-plahnt/ **1** an operation in which an organ or tissue is transplanted. **2** a person or thing that has been transplanted.
– DERIVATIVES **transplantation** n.
– ORIGIN Latin *transplantare*.

transponder /tran-**spon**-der, trahn-**spon**-der/ ● **n.** a device for receiving a radio signal and automatically transmitting a different signal.
– ORIGIN from **TRANSMIT** and **RESPOND**.

transport ● **v.** /tran-**sport**, trahn-**sport**/ **1** carry (people or goods) from one place to another by means of a vehicle, aircraft, or ship. **2** (**be transported**) be overwhelmed with a strong emotion. **3** hist. send (a convict) to a penal colony. ● **n.** /**tran**-sport, **trahn**-sport/ **1** a system or means of transporting.

2 the action of transporting. **3** a large vehicle, ship, or aircraft for carrying troops or stores. **4** (**transports**) overwhelmingly strong emotions.
– DERIVATIVES **transportation** n.
– ORIGIN Latin *transportare* 'carry across'.

transportable • adj. able to be carried or moved.
– DERIVATIVES **transportability** n.

transport cafe • n. Brit. a roadside cafe for drivers of haulage vehicles.

transporter • n. a large vehicle used to carry heavy objects.

transpose • v. (**transposes**, **transposing**, **transposed**) **1** cause (two or more things) to change places with each other. **2** move to a different place or situation. **3** write or play (music) in a different key from the original.
– DERIVATIVES **transposable** adj. **transposition** n.
– ORIGIN Old French *transposer*.

transsexual (also **transexual**) • n. a person born with the physical characteristics of one sex who emotionally and psychologically feels that they belong to the opposite sex.

trans-ship • v. (**trans-ships**, **trans-shipping**, **trans-shipped**) transfer (cargo) from one ship or other form of transport to another.
– DERIVATIVES **trans-shipment** n.

transubstantiation • n. (in Christian belief) the doctrine that when the bread and wine of the Eucharist have been consecrated they become the body and blood of Christ.
– ORIGIN Latin *transubstantiare* 'change in substance'.

transuranic /tranz-yuu-**ran**-ik, trahnz-yuu-**ran**-ik/ • adj. Chem. (of an element) having a higher atomic number than uranium (92).

Transvaal E
/tranz-**vahl**/ (also **the Transvaal**) a former province in NE South Africa. In 1994 it was divided into the provinces of Northern Transvaal, Pretoria-Witwatersrand-Vereeniging, Eastern Transvaal, and the eastern part of North-West Province.

transverse • adj. placed or extending across something.
– DERIVATIVES **transversely** adv.
– ORIGIN Latin *transvertere* 'turn across'.

transvestite • n. a person who derives pleasure from dressing in clothes usually worn by the opposite sex.
– DERIVATIVES **transvestism** n.
– ORIGIN German *Transvestit*.

Transylvania E
/tran-sil-**vay**-ni-uh/ a region of NW Romania.

trap • n. **1** a device, pit, or enclosure designed to catch and hold animals. **2** an unpleasant situation from which it is hard to escape. **3** a trick causing someone to do something that they do not intend or that will affect them badly. **4** a container or device used to collect a specified thing. **5** a curve in the waste pipe from a bath, basin, or toilet that is always full of liquid to prevent the upward passage of gases. **6** the compartment from which a greyhound is released at the start of a race. **7** a device for hurling a clay pigeon into the air. **8** esp. hist. a light, two-wheeled carriage pulled by a horse or pony. **9** informal a person's mouth. • v. (**traps**, **trapping**, **trapped**) **1** catch or hold in a trap. **2** trick into doing something.
– ORIGIN Old English.

trapdoor • n. a hinged or removable panel in a floor, ceiling, or roof.

trapeze • n. (also **flying trapeze**) a horizontal bar hanging by two ropes high above the ground, used by acrobats in a circus.
– ORIGIN French.

trapezium /truh-**pee**-zi-uhm/ • n. (pl. **trapezia** /truh-**pee**-zi-uh/ or **trapeziums**) Geom. **1** Brit. a quadrilateral with one pair of sides parallel. **2** N. Amer. a quadrilateral with no sides parallel.
– ORIGIN Latin.

trapezoid /**tra**-pi-zoyd, truh-**pee**-zoyd/ • n. Geom. **1** Brit. a quadrilateral with no sides parallel. **2** N. Amer. a quadrilateral with one pair of sides parallel.

trapper • n. a person who traps wild animals.

trappings • pl. n. **1** the signs or objects associated with a particular situation or role: *the trappings of success*. **2** a horse's ornamental harness.
– ORIGIN Old French *drap* 'drape'.

Trappist • n. a monk belonging to a branch of the Cistercian order of monks who have taken a vow of silence.
– ORIGIN French *trappiste*.

trash • n. **1** N. Amer. waste material. **2** poor-quality writing, art, etc. **3** N. Amer. a person or people of very low social status. • v. informal wreck or destroy.
– DERIVATIVES **trashy** adj.
– ORIGIN unknown.

trash can • n. N. Amer. a dustbin.

trattoria /trat-tuh-**ree**-uh/ • n. an Italian restaurant.
– ORIGIN Italian.

trauma /**traw**-muh, **trow**-muh/ • n. (pl. **traumas**) **1** a deeply distressing experience. **2** Med. physical injury. **3** emotional shock following a stressful event.
– DERIVATIVES **traumatic** adj.
– ORIGIN Greek, 'wound'.

traumatize (also **traumatise**) • v. (**traumatizes**, **traumatizing**, **traumatized**) cause (someone) to experience lasting shock as a result of a disturbing experience or injury.

travail /**tra**-vayl/ (also **travails**) • n. archaic painful or laborious effort.
– ORIGIN Old French.

travel • v. (**travels**, **travelling**, **travelled**; US also **travels**, **traveling**, **traveled**) **1** make a journey. **2** journey along (a road) or through (a region). **3** move or go from one place to another: *light travels faster than sound*. • n. **1** the action of travelling. **2** (**travels**) journeys, especially abroad. • adj. (of a device) sufficiently compact for use when travelling: *a travel iron*.
– ORIGIN from TRAVAIL.

travel agency • n. an agency that makes the necessary arrangements for travellers.
– DERIVATIVES **travel agent** n.

travelled • adj. **1** having travelled to many places. **2** used by people travelling: *a well-travelled route*.

traveller (US also **traveler**) • n. **1** a person who is travelling or who often travels. **2** a gypsy. **3** (also **New Age traveller**) a person who holds New Age values and leads a travelling and unconventional lifestyle.

traveller's cheque • **n.** a cheque for a fixed amount that may be cashed or used in payment abroad after endorsement by the holder's signature.

travelling salesman • **n.** a representative of a firm who visits businesses to show samples and gain orders.

travelogue • **n.** a film, book, or illustrated lecture about a person's travels.

travel-sick • **adj.** suffering from nausea caused by the motion of a moving vehicle, boat, or aircraft.

– DERIVATIVES **travel-sickness** n.

traverse /tra-verss, truh-verss/ • **v.** (**traverses**, **traversing**, **traversed**) travel or extend across or through.

– DERIVATIVES **traversal** n.

– ORIGIN Latin *traversare*.

travesty /tra-vi-sti/ • **n.** (pl. **travesties**) an absurd or shocking misrepresentation: *the trial was a travesty of justice.* • **v.** (**travesties**, **travestying**, **travestied**) represent in such a way.

– ORIGIN French *travestir* 'to disguise'.

trawl • **v.** **1** catch fish with a trawl net or seine. **2** search through thoroughly. • **n.** **1** an act of trawling. **2** (also **trawl net**) a large wide-mouthed fishing net dragged by a boat along the bottom of the sea or a lake.

– ORIGIN prob. from Dutch *traghelen* 'to drag'.

trawler • **n.** a fishing boat used for trawling.

tray • **n.** a flat container with a raised rim, used for carrying things.

– ORIGIN Old English.

treacherous • **adj.** **1** unable to be trusted; disloyal. **2** having hidden or unpredictable dangers: *treacherous currents.*

– DERIVATIVES **treacherously** adv.

– ORIGIN Old French *trecherous*.

treachery • **n.** behaviour that involves betraying a person's trust in one.

treacle • **n.** esp. Brit. **1** molasses. **2** golden syrup.

– DERIVATIVES **treacly** adj.

– ORIGIN Greek *thēriakē* 'antidote against venom'.

tread • **v.** (**treads**, **treading**, **trod**; past part. **trodden** or **trod**) **1** walk in a specified way. **2** press down or crush with the feet. **3** walk on or along. • **n.** **1** a way or the sound of walking. **2** the top surface of a step or stair. **3** the part of a vehicle tyre that grips the road. **4** the part of the sole of a shoe that rests on the ground.

– PHRASES **tread water** stay in an upright position in deep water by moving the feet with a walking movement.

– ORIGIN Old English.

treadle • **n.** a lever worked by the foot to operate a machine.

– ORIGIN Old English, 'stair, step'.

treadmill • **n.** **1** a large wheel turned by the weight of people or animals treading on steps fitted into it, formerly used to drive machinery. **2** a device used for exercise consisting of a continuous moving belt on which to walk or run. **3** a job or situation that is tiring, boring, or unpleasant.

treason (also **high treason**) • **n.** the crime of betraying one's country.

– DERIVATIVES **treasonable** adj. **treasonous** adj.

– ORIGIN Old French *treisoun*.

treasure • **n.** **1** a quantity of precious metals, gems, or other valuable objects. **2** a very valuable object. **3** informal a much loved or highly valued person. • **v.** (**treasures**, **treasuring**, **treasured**) **1** keep carefully (a valuable or valued item). **2** value highly.

– ORIGIN Old French *tresor*.

treasure hunt • **n.** a game in which players search for hidden objects by following a trail of clues.

treasurer • **n.** a person appointed to manage the finances of a society, company, etc.

treasure trove • **n.** **1** Engl. Law (abolished in 1996) valuables of unknown ownership that are found hidden and declared the property of the Crown. **2** a store of valuable or pleasant things.

– ORIGIN from Old French *tresor trové* 'found treasure'.

treasury • **n.** (pl. **treasuries**) **1** the funds or revenue of a state, institution, or society. **2** (**Treasury**) (in some countries) the government department responsible for the overall management of the economy.

treat • **v.** **1** behave towards or deal with in a certain way. **2** give medical care or attention to. **3** apply a process or a substance to. **4** present or discuss (a subject). **5** (**treat to**) provide (someone) with (food, drink, or entertainment) at one's expense. **6** (**treat oneself**) do or have something very pleasurable. • **n.** **1** a surprise gift, event, etc. that gives great pleasure. **2** (**one's treat**) an act of treating someone to something.

– DERIVATIVES **treatable** adj.

– ORIGIN Old French *traitier*.

treatise /tree-tiss, tree-tiz/ • **n.** a written work dealing formally and systematically with a subject.

– ORIGIN Old French *tretis*.

treatment • **n.** **1** a way of behaving towards someone or dealing with something. **2** medical care for an illness or injury. **3** the use of a substance or process to preserve or give particular properties to something: *treatment of hazardous waste.* **4** the presentation or discussion of a subject.

treaty • **n.** (pl. **treaties**) a formal agreement between states.

– ORIGIN Old French *traite*.

Treaty of Rome, Treaty of Versailles, etc. E
see **ROME, TREATY OF**; **VERSAILLES, TREATY OF**, etc.

treble[1] • **adj.** **1** consisting of three parts. **2** multiplied or occurring three times. • **predet.** three times as much or as many. • **pron.** an amount which is three times as large as usual. • **v.** (**trebles**, **trebling**, **trebled**) make or become treble.

– ORIGIN Latin *triplus* 'triple'.

treble[2] • **n.** **1** a high-pitched voice, especially a boy's singing voice. **2** the high-frequency output of a radio or audio system.

– ORIGIN from **TREBLE**[1].

treble clef • **n.** Music a clef placing G above middle C on the second-lowest line of the stave.

Treblinka E
/tre-**bling**-kuh/ a Nazi concentration camp in Poland in the Second World War.

tree • **n. 1** a woody perennial plant consisting of a trunk and branches growing to a considerable height. **2** (also **tree diagram**) a diagram with a structure of branching connecting lines.
– ORIGIN Old English.

tree fern • **n.** a large palm-like fern with a trunk-like stem.

tree house • **n.** a structure built in a tree for children to play in.

treeline • **n.** the height above which no trees grow on a mountain.

tree ring • **n.** each of a number of rings in the cross section of a tree trunk, representing a single year's growth.

tree surgeon • **n.** a person who treats old or damaged trees in order to preserve them.

trefoil /tre-foyl, tree-foyl/ • **n. 1** a small plant with yellow flowers and clover-like leaves. **2** architectural stonework in the form of three rounded lobes like a clover leaf.
– ORIGIN Latin *trifolium*.

trek • **n.** a long difficult journey, especially one made on foot. • **v.** (**treks**, **trekking**, **trekked**) go on a trek.
– DERIVATIVES **trekker** n.
– ORIGIN South African Dutch *trekken* 'to pull, travel'.

trellis • **n.** a framework of bars used as a support for climbing plants.
– ORIGIN Old French *trelis*.

tremble • **v.** (**trembles**, **trembling**, **trembled**) **1** shake uncontrollably as a result of anxiety, excitement, or weakness. **2** be in a state of great worry or fear. **3** (of a thing) shake slightly. • **n.** a trembling feeling, movement, or sound.
– DERIVATIVES **trembly** adj. (informal).
– ORIGIN Old French *trembler*.

trembler • **n.** Brit. an automatic vibrator for making and breaking an electric circuit.

tremendous • **adj. 1** very great in amount, scale, or intensity. **2** informal extremely good or impressive.
– DERIVATIVES **tremendously** adv.
– ORIGIN Latin *tremendus*.

tremolo • **n.** (pl. **tremolos**) a wavering effect in singing or playing some musical instruments.
– ORIGIN Italian.

tremor • **n. 1** a quivering movement that one cannot control. **2** (also **earth tremor**) a slight earthquake. **3** a sudden feeling of fear or excitement.
– ORIGIN Latin.

tremulous • **adj. 1** shaking or quivering slightly. **2** nervous.
– ORIGIN Latin *tremulus*.

trench • **n. 1** a long, narrow ditch. **2** a ditch dug by troops to provide shelter from enemy fire. **3** (also **ocean trench**) a long, deep depression in the ocean bed.
– ORIGIN Old French *trenche*.

trenchant /tren-chuhnt/ • **adj.** (of speech or writing) expressed strongly and clearly.
– DERIVATIVES **trenchantly** adv.
– ORIGIN Old French, 'cutting'.

trench coat • **n.** a belted double-breasted raincoat.

trencher • **n.** hist. a wooden plate or platter.
– ORIGIN Old French *trenchour*.

trench warfare • **n.** warfare in which opposing troops fight from trenches facing each other.

trend • **n. 1** a general direction in which something is developing or changing. **2** a fashion.
– ORIGIN Old English, 'revolve, rotate'.

trendsetter • **n.** a person who leads the way in fashion or ideas.

trendy • **adj.** (**trendier**, **trendiest**) informal very fashionable or up to date.
– DERIVATIVES **trendily** adv. **trendiness** n.

Trent E
the chief river of central England, which rises in Staffordshire and flows generally north-eastwards, joining with the River Ouse to form the Humber estuary

trepan /tri-pan/ • **n.** esp. hist. a saw used by surgeons for making holes in the skull. • **v.** (**trepans**, **trepanning**, **trepanned**) make holes in (a person's skull) with a trepan.
– ORIGIN Greek *trupan* 'to bore'.

trepidation • **n.** a feeling of fear or nervousness about something that may happen.
– ORIGIN Latin.

trespass • **v. 1** enter someone's land or property without their permission. **2** (**trespass on**) make unfair claims on or take advantage of (something). **3** (**trespass against**) archaic do wrong or harm to. • **n. 1** Law entry to a person's land or property without their permission. **2** archaic a wrongdoing.
– DERIVATIVES **trespasser** n.
– ORIGIN Old French *trespasser* 'pass over, trespass'.

tress • **n.** a long lock of a woman's hair.
– ORIGIN Old French *tresse*.

trestle • **n.** a framework made of a horizontal beam supported by two pairs of sloping legs, used in pairs to support a flat surface such as a table top.
– ORIGIN Old French *trestel*.

trestle table • **n.** a table consisting of a board or boards laid on trestles.

Trevino E
/truh-vee-noh/, Lee (Buck) (b.1939), American golfer, the first to win all three Open championships (Canadian, US, and British) in the same year (1971).

Trevithick E
/truh-**vith**-ik/, Richard (1771–1833), English engineer. A pioneer in the use of steam power, he built the world's first steam railway locomotive (1804).

trews /trooz/ • **pl. n.** esp. Brit. trousers.
– ORIGIN Irish or Scottish Gaelic.

tri- /try/ • **comb. form** three; having three: *triathlon*.
– ORIGIN Latin *tres*, Greek *treis* 'three'.

triad /try-ad/ • **n. 1** a group or set of three connected people or things. **2** (also **Triad**) a Chinese secret society involved in organized crime.
– DERIVATIVES **triadic** adj.
– ORIGIN Greek *trias*.

triage /tree-ah*zh*, try-ij/ • **n.** (in a hospital or in war) the assessment of the seriousness of wounds or illnesses to decide the order in

which a large number of patients should be treated.
– ORIGIN French.

trial • n. **1** a formal examination of evidence in a court of law in order to decide if a person is guilty of a crime. **2** a test of performance, qualities, or suitability. **3** (**trials**) an event in which horses or dogs compete or perform. **4** something that tests a person's endurance or patience. • v. (**trials**, **trialling**, **trialled**; US **trials**, **trialing**, **trialed**) test (something) to assess its suitability or performance.
– PHRASES **on trial 1** being tried in a court of law. **2** undergoing tests. **trial and error** the process of experimenting with various methods until one finds the most successful.
– ORIGIN Latin *triallum*.

trial run • n. the first use of a new system or product.

triangle • n. **1** a plane figure with three straight sides and three angles. **2** a musical instrument consisting of a steel rod bent into a triangle, sounded with a rod. **3** an emotional relationship involving a couple and a third person with whom one of them is involved.
– ORIGIN Latin *triangulum*.

triangular • adj. **1** shaped like a triangle. **2** involving three people.

triangulate • v. /try-ang-gyuu-layt/ (**triangulates**, **triangulating**, **triangulated**) divide (an area) into triangles for surveying purposes.
– DERIVATIVES **triangulation** n.

Triassic /try-ass-ik/ • adj. Geol. referring to the earliest period of the Mesozoic era (about 245 to 208 million years ago), a time when the first dinosaurs, ammonites, and primitive mammals appeared.
– ORIGIN Latin *trias* 'set of three', because the strata are divisible into three groups.

triathlon /try-ath-lon/ • n. an athletic contest involving three different events, typically swimming, cycling, and long-distance running.
– DERIVATIVES **triathlete** n.
– ORIGIN from **TRI-**, on the pattern of *decathlon*.

tribal • adj. having to do with a tribe or tribes.
– DERIVATIVES **tribally** adv.

tribalism • n. behaviour and attitudes that are based on one's loyalty to a tribe or other social group.

tribe • n. **1** a social group in a traditional society consisting of linked families or communities sharing customs and beliefs. **2** a category in scientific classification that ranks above genus and below family. **3** informal a large number of people.
– ORIGIN Latin *tribus*.

> **USAGE tribe**
> The word **tribe** can cause offence when used to refer to a community living within a traditional society today, and it is better in such cases to use alternative terms such as **community** or **people**. However, when talking about such communities in the past, it is perfectly acceptable to say **tribe**: *the area was inhabited by Slavic tribes*.

tribesman (or **tribeswoman**) • n. a member of a tribe in a traditional society.

tribulation /trib-yuu-lay-sh'n/ • n. **1** great trouble or suffering. **2** a cause of this.
– ORIGIN Latin.

tribunal /try-byoo-nuhl, tri-byoo-nuhl/ • n. **1** Brit. a group of people established to settle certain types of dispute. **2** a court of justice.
– ORIGIN Latin, 'raised platform provided for a magistrate's seat'.

tribune • n. (in ancient Rome) an official chosen by the ordinary people to protect their interests.
– ORIGIN Latin *tribunus* 'head of a tribe'.

tributary /trib-yuu-tuh-ri/ • n. (pl. **tributaries**) **1** a river or stream flowing into a larger river or lake. **2** hist. a person or state that pays money to another more powerful state or ruler.
– ORIGIN Latin *tributarius*.

tribute • n. **1** an act, statement, or gift that is intended to show gratitude, respect, or admiration. **2** something resulting from and indicating the worth of something else: *his victory was a tribute to his persistence*. **3** hist. payment made periodically by a state to a more powerful one.
– ORIGIN Latin *tributum*.

trice /*rhymes with* nice/ • n. (in phr. **in a trice**) in a moment.
– ORIGIN first meaning 'a tug': from Dutch *trīsen* 'pull sharply'.

triceps /try-seps/ • n. (pl. **triceps**) the large muscle at the back of the upper arm.
– ORIGIN Latin, 'three-headed'.

triceratops /try-se-ruh-tops/ • n. a large plant-eating dinosaur having a huge head with two large horns, a smaller horn on the snout, and a bony frill above the neck.
– ORIGIN from Greek *trikeratos* 'three-horned' + *ōps* 'face'.

trichology /tri-kol-uh-ji/ • n. the branch of medicine concerned with the hair and scalp.
– DERIVATIVES **trichologist** n.
– ORIGIN Greek *thrix* 'hair'.

trick • n. **1** an act or scheme intended to deceive or outwit someone. **2** a skilful act performed for entertainment. **3** an illusion: *a trick of the light*. **4** a habit or mannerism. **5** (in bridge, whist, etc.) a sequence of cards forming a single round of play. • adj. intended to trick: *a trick question*. • v. **1** deceive or outwit with cunning or skill. **2** (**trick into**/**out of**) deceive (someone) into doing or parting with.
– PHRASES **do the trick** informal achieve the required result. **trick or treat** a children's custom of calling at houses at Halloween with the threat of pranks if they are not given a small gift. **turn a trick** informal (of a prostitute) have a session with a client.
– DERIVATIVES **trickery** n.
– ORIGIN Old French *triche*.

trickle • v. (**trickles**, **trickling**, **trickled**) **1** (of a liquid) flow in a small stream. **2** come or go slowly or gradually: *details began to trickle out*. • n. **1** a small flow of liquid. **2** a small number of people or things moving slowly.

trickster • n. a person who cheats or deceives people.

tricksy • adj. **1** clever in an inventive or deceptive way. **2** playful or mischievous.

tricky • adj. (**trickier**, **trickiest**) **1** requiring care and skill because difficult or awkward. **2** deceitful or crafty.

tricolour /tri-kuh-ler, try-kul-er/ (US **tricolor**) ● n. a flag with three bands of different colours, especially the French national flag.

tricorne /try-korn/ (also **tricorn**) ● n. a hat with a brim turned up on three sides.
– ORIGIN Latin *tricornis*.

tricuspid /try-kuss-pid/ ● n. a tooth with three cusps or points.
– ORIGIN from Latin *tri-* 'three' + *cuspis* 'sharp point'.

tricycle ● n. a vehicle similar to a bicycle, but having three wheels, two at the back and one at the front.

trident ● n. a three-pronged spear.
– ORIGIN Latin.

tried past and past part. of **TRY**.

triennial /try-en-ni-uhl/ ● adj. lasting for or recurring every three years.

trier ● n. a person who always makes an effort, however unsuccessful they may be.

Trieste E
/tree-esst/ a city in NE Italy, the largest port on the Adriatic.

trifle ● n. 1 a thing of little value or importance. 2 a small amount. 3 Brit. a cold dessert of sponge cake and fruit covered with layers of custard, jelly, and cream. ● v. (**trifles**, **trifling**, **trifled**) (**trifle with**) treat without seriousness or respect.
– ORIGIN Old French *truffler* 'mock'.

trifling ● adj. unimportant or trivial.

trigger ● n. 1 a device that releases a spring or catch and so sets off a gun or mechanism. 2 an event that causes something to happen. ● v. (**triggers**, **triggering**, **triggered**) 1 cause (a device) to function. 2 cause to happen.
– ORIGIN Dutch *trekker*.

trigger-happy ● adj. excessively willing to fire a gun or take other violent action.

trigonometry /tri-guh-nom-i-tri/ ● n. the branch of mathematics concerned with the relationships between the sides and angles of triangles and with the functions of angles.
– DERIVATIVES **trigonometric** adj.
– ORIGIN Greek *trigōnos* 'three-cornered'.

trike ● n. informal a tricycle.

trilateral ● adj. 1 shared by or involving three parties: *trilateral talks*. 2 Geom. on or with three sides.

trilby ● n. (pl. **trilbies**) esp. Brit. a soft felt hat with a narrow brim and indented crown.
– ORIGIN from the heroine of George du Maurier's novel *Trilby*, in the stage version of which such a hat was worn.

trilingual ● adj. 1 speaking three languages fluently. 2 written or carried out in three languages.

trill ● n. a quavering or vibrating sound. ● v. produce a quavering or warbling sound.
– ORIGIN Italian *trillo*.

trillion ● cardinal number 1 a million million (1,000,000,000,000 or 10^{12}). 2 Brit. dated a million million million (1,000,000,000,000,000,000 or 10^{18}).
– DERIVATIVES **trillionth** ordinal number.

trilobite /try-luh-byt/ ● n. a fossil marine arthropod with a rear part divided into three segments.
– ORIGIN from Greek *tri-* 'three' + *lobos* 'lobe'.

trilogy ● n. (pl. **trilogies**) a group of three related novels, plays, or films.

trim ● v. (**trims**, **trimming**, **trimmed**) 1 make (something) neat by cutting away unwanted parts: *trim the lawn*. 2 cut off (unwanted parts): *trim the fat off the meat*. 3 reduce the size, amount, or number of. 4 decorate (something) along its edges. 5 adjust (a sail) to take advantage of the wind. ● n. 1 decoration along the edges of something. 2 the upholstery or interior lining of a car. 3 an act of trimming. 4 the state of being in good order. ● adj. (**trimmer**, **trimmest**) neat and smart.
– PHRASES **in trim** slim and fit.
– DERIVATIVES **trimmer** n.
– ORIGIN Old English, 'arrange'.

trimaran /try-muh-ran/ ● n. a yacht with three hulls side by side.
– ORIGIN from **TRI-** + **CATAMARAN**.

Trimble, C
(William) David, (b.1944), Ulster Unionist statesman, first First Minister of the Northern Ireland Assembly from 1999.

trimester /try-mess-ter/ ● n. 1 a period of three months, as a division of the duration of pregnancy. 2 N. Amer. each of the three terms in an academic year.
– ORIGIN Latin *trimestris*.

trimming ● n. 1 (**trimmings**) small pieces trimmed off. 2 decoration for clothing or furniture. 3 (**the trimmings**) informal the traditional accompaniments to something: *roast turkey with all the trimmings*.

Trincomalee E
/tring-kuhm-uh-lee/ the chief port of Sri Lanka, on the east coast.

Trinidad and Tobago E
/tri-ni-dad, tuh-bay-goh/ a country in the Caribbean consisting of two islands off the NE coast of Venezuela; capital, Port-of-Spain (on Trinidad).
– DERIVATIVES **Trinidadian** /tri-ni-day-di-uhn/ adj. & n. **Tobagan** adj. & n. **Tobagonian** adj. & n.

trinity ● n. (pl. **trinities**) 1 (**the Trinity** or **the Holy Trinity**) (in Christian belief) the three persons (Father, Son, and Holy Spirit) that together make up God. 2 a group of three people or things.
– ORIGIN Latin *trinitas*.

trinket ● n. a small ornament or item of jewellery that is of little value.
– ORIGIN unknown.

trio ● n. (pl. **trios**) 1 a set or group of three. 2 a group of three musicians.
– ORIGIN Italian.

triode /try-ohd/ ● n. a semiconductor device with three connections, typically allowing the flow of current in one direction only.
– ORIGIN from **TRI-** + **ELECTRODE**.

trip ● v. (**trips**, **tripping**, **tripped**) 1 catch one's foot on something and stumble or fall. 2 (**trip up**) make a mistake. 3 walk, run, or dance with quick light steps. 4 activate (a mechanism). 5 (of part of an electric circuit) disconnect automatically as a safety measure. 6 informal experience hallucinations as a result of taking a drug such as LSD. ● n. 1 a journey or excursion. 2 an instance of tripping or falling. 3 informal a hallucinatory experience caused by taking a drug. 4 informal a self-

indulgent attitude or activity: *a power trip.* **5** a device that trips a mechanism or circuit.
– PHRASES **trip the light fantastic** humorous dance. [ORIGIN from 'Trip it as you go On the light fantastic toe' (Milton's *L'Allegro*).]
– ORIGIN Dutch *trippen* 'to skip, hop'.

tripartite /try-**par**-tyt/ ● adj. **1** consisting of three parts. **2** shared by or involving three parties.

tripe ● n. **1** the stomach of a cow or sheep used as food. **2** informal nonsense; rubbish.
– ORIGIN Old French, 'entrails of an animal'.

triple ● adj. **1** consisting of or involving three parts, things, or people. **2** having three times the usual size, quality, or strength. ● predet. three times as much or as many. ● n. a thing that is three times as large as usual or is made up of three parts. ● v. (**triples**, **tripling**, **tripled**) make or become three times as much or as many.
– DERIVATIVES **triply** adv.
– ORIGIN Old French.

triple jump ● n. an athletic event in which competitors attempt to jump as far as possible by performing a hop, a step, and a jump from a running start.

triplet ● n. **1** each of three children or animals born at the same birth. **2** Music a group of three equal notes to be performed in the time of two or four. **3** a set of three rhyming lines of verse.

triple time ● n. musical time with three beats to the bar.

triplicate ● adj. /**trip**-li-kuht/ existing in three copies or examples. ● v. /**trip**-li-kayt/ (**triplicates**, **triplicating**, **triplicated**) **1** make three copies of. **2** multiply by three.
– ORIGIN Latin *triplicare* 'make three'.

tripod /**try**-pod/ ● n. a three-legged stand for supporting a camera or other apparatus.
– ORIGIN Greek.

Tripoli[1] E
/**trip**-uh-li/ the capital and chief port of Libya.

Tripoli[2] E
/**trip**-uh-li/ a port in NW Lebanon.

tripos /**try**-poss/ ● n. the final honours examination for a BA degree at Cambridge University.
– ORIGIN Latin *tripus* 'tripod', with reference to the stool on which a graduate sat to deliver a satirical speech at the degree ceremony.

tripper ● n. Brit. informal a person who goes on a pleasure trip.

triptych /**trip**-tik/ ● n. **1** a picture or carving on three panels, hinged together vertically and used as an altarpiece. **2** a set of three related artistic works.

Tripura E
/**tri**-puu-ruh/ a small state in the far north-east of India; capital, Agartala.

tripwire ● n. a wire that is stretched close to the ground and sets off a trap, explosion, or alarm when disturbed.

trireme /**try**-reem/ ● n. an ancient Greek or Roman war ship with three banks of oars.
– ORIGIN Latin *triremis*.

trisect /try-**sekt**/ ● v. divide into three parts.
– ORIGIN from TRI- + Latin *secare* 'cut'.

Tristan da Cunha E
/tri-stuhn duh **koo**-nuh/ the largest of a small group of islands in the South Atlantic, a dependency of the British colony of St Helena.

trite ● adj. (of a remark or idea) unoriginal and dull because of overuse.
– ORIGIN Latin *tritus* 'rubbed'.

triumph ● n. **1** a great victory or achievement. **2** the state of being victorious or successful. **3** joy or satisfaction resulting from a success or victory. **4** a highly successful example: *their marriage was a triumph of togetherness.* ● v. achieve a triumph.
– DERIVATIVES **triumphal** adj.
– ORIGIN Latin *triumphus*.

triumphalism ● n. excessive rejoicing over one's success or achievements.
– DERIVATIVES **triumphalist** adj. & n.

triumphant ● adj. **1** having won a battle or contest. **2** joyful after a victory or achievement.
– DERIVATIVES **triumphantly** adv.

triumvirate /try-**um**-vi-ruht/ ● n. **1** a group of three powerful or important people or things. **2** (in ancient Rome) a group of three men holding power.
– ORIGIN from Latin *trium virorum* 'of three men'.

trivet ● n. **1** a metal stand on which hot dishes are placed. **2** an iron tripod placed over a fire for a cooking pot or kettle to stand on.
– ORIGIN prob. from Latin *tripes* 'three-legged'.

trivia /**tri**-vi-uh/ ● pl. n. unimportant details or pieces of information.
– ORIGIN Latin.

trivial ● adj. of little value or importance.
– DERIVATIVES **triviality** n. (pl. **trivialities**) **trivially** adv.
– ORIGIN first meaning 'belonging to the trivium' (an introductory course at a medieval university involving the study of grammar, rhetoric, and logic): from Latin *trivium*, literally 'place where three roads meet'.

trivialize (also **trivialise**) ● v. (**trivializes**, **trivializing**, **trivialized**) make (something) seem less important or complex than it really is.
– DERIVATIVES **trivialization** (also **trivialisation**) n.

Trobriand Islands E
/**troh**-bri-uhnd/ a group of islands in the SW Pacific, in Papua New Guinea, situated off the south-eastern tip of New Guinea.

trochee /**troh**-kee/ ● n. Poetry a foot consisting of one long or stressed syllable followed by one short or unstressed syllable.
– DERIVATIVES **trochaic** adj.
– ORIGIN from Greek *trokhaios pous* 'running foot'.

trod past and past part. of TREAD.

trodden past part. of TREAD.

troglodyte /**trog**-luh-dyt/ ● n. a person who lives in a cave.
– ORIGIN Greek *trōglodutēs*.

troika /**troy**-kuh/ ● n. **1** a Russian vehicle pulled by a team of three horses side by side. **2** a group of three people working together.
– ORIGIN Russian.

Trojan /**troh**-juhn/ ● n. an inhabitant of ancient Troy.
– PHRASES **work like a Trojan** work extremely

hard.

Trojan Horse • n. something intended to weaken or defeat an enemy secretly.
– ORIGIN from the hollow wooden statue of a horse in which the ancient Greeks hid themselves in order to enter Troy.

Trojan War E
the legendary ten-year siege of Troy by the Greeks, who were attempting to recover Helen, wife of Menelaus, who had been abducted by Paris. The war ended with the capture of Troy by the Greeks, who concealed a group of men inside a hollow wooden horse so large that the city walls had to be breached for it to be taken inside.

troll[1] /*rhymes with* doll *or* dole/ • n. (in folklore) an ugly giant or dwarf that lives in a cave.
– ORIGIN Old Norse and Swedish, 'witch'.

troll[2] /*rhymes with* dole *or* doll/ • v. fish by trailing a baited line along behind a boat.
– DERIVATIVES **troller** n.
– ORIGIN uncertain.

trolley • n. (pl. **trolleys**) **1** Brit. a large metal basket on wheels, for transporting heavy or bulky items such as shopping. **2** a small table on wheels used to convey food and drink. **3** (also **trolley wheel**) a wheel attached to a pole, used for collecting current from an overhead electric wire to drive a tram.
– PHRASES **off one's trolley** Brit. informal mad.
– ORIGIN perh. from TROLL[2].

trolleybus • n. a bus powered by electricity obtained from overhead wires by means of a trolley wheel.

trollop • n. dated or humorous a woman who has many sexual partners.
– ORIGIN perh. from former *trull* 'prostitute'.

Trollope E
/**trol**-luhp/, Anthony (1815–82), English novelist, author of the six 'Barsetshire' novels and the six 'Palliser' novels.

trombone • n. a large brass wind instrument with a sliding tube which is moved to produce different notes.
– DERIVATIVES **trombonist** n.
– ORIGIN French or Italian.

trompe l'œil /tromp loy/ • n. (pl. **trompe l'œils** /tromp loy/) a method of painting that creates the illusion of a three-dimensional object or space.
– ORIGIN French, 'deceives the eye'.

Tromsø E
/**trom**-ser/ the chief city of Arctic Norway.

troop • n. **1** (**troops**) soldiers or armed forces. **2** a unit of an armoured or cavalry division. **3** a group of people or animals of a particular kind: *a troop of musicians.* • v. come or go as a group.
– PHRASES **troop the colour** Brit. perform the ceremony of parading a regiment's flag along ranks of soldiers.
– ORIGIN French *troupe.*

troop carrier • n. a large aircraft or armoured vehicle designed for transporting troops.

trooper • n. **1** a private soldier in a cavalry or armoured unit. **2** Austral./NZ & US a mounted police officer. **3** US a state police officer.

trope /*rhymes with* rope/ • n. a figurative or metaphorical use of a word or expression.
– ORIGIN Greek *tropos* 'turn, trope'.

trophy • n. (pl. **trophies**) **1** a cup or other decorative object awarded as a prize. **2** a souvenir of an achievement, e.g. a head of an animal killed when hunting.
– ORIGIN French *trophée.*

tropic /*rhymes with* topic/ • n. **1** the line of latitude 23°26′ north (**tropic of Cancer**) or south (**tropic of Capricorn**) of the equator. **2** (**the tropics**) the region between the tropics of Cancer and Capricorn.
– ORIGIN Greek *tropikos.*

tropical • adj. **1** having to do with the tropics. **2** very hot and humid.
– DERIVATIVES **tropically** adv.

tropism /**troh**-pi-z'm, **trop**-i-z'm/ • n. Biol. the turning of all or part of an organism in a particular direction in response to an external stimulus.
– ORIGIN Greek *tropos* 'turning'.

troposphere /**tro**-puh-sfeer, **troh**-puh-sfeer/ • n. the lowest region of the atmosphere, extending from the earth's surface to the lower boundary of the stratosphere.
– ORIGIN Greek *tropos* 'turning'.

Trossachs E
/**tross**-uhks/ (**the Trossachs**) a picturesque wooded valley in central Scotland.

trot • v. (**trots**, **trotting**, **trotted**) **1** (of a horse) move at a pace faster than a walk. **2** (of a person) run at a moderate pace with short steps. **3** (**trot out**) informal produce (an account that has been produced many times before). • n. **1** a trotting pace. **2** an act of trotting. **3** (**the trots**) informal diarrhoea.
– PHRASES **on the trot** informal Brit. one after another.
– ORIGIN Latin *trottare.*

troth /trohth, troth/ • n. (in phr. **pledge** (or **plight**) **one's troth**) archaic make a solemn promise to marry.
– ORIGIN from TRUTH.

Trotsky E
/**trot**-ski/, Leon (1879–1940; born *Lev Davidovich Bronshtein*), Russian revolutionary. He helped to organize the Revolution of October 1917 and built up the Red Army. Exiled in 1929, he then settled in Mexico where he was later murdered by a Stalinist assassin.

Trotskyism • n. the political or economic principles of Leon Trotsky, especially the theory that socialism should be established throughout the world by continuing revolution.
– DERIVATIVES **Trotskyist** n. & adj. **Trotskyite** n. & adj. (derog.).

trotter • n. a pig's foot.

troubadour /**troo**-buh-dor/ • n. (in medieval France) a travelling poet who composed and sang in Provençal.
– ORIGIN French.

trouble • n. **1** difficulty or problems. **2** effort made to do something. **3** a cause of worry or inconvenience. **4** (**in trouble**) in a situation in which one is likely to be punished or blamed. **5** public disorder. • v. (**troubles**, **troubling**, **troubled**) **1** cause distress or in-

convenience to. **2** (**troubled**) experiencing problems or anxiety. **3** (**trouble about**/**over**/**with**) be anxious about. **4** (**trouble to do**) make the effort to do.
– ORIGIN Old French *truble*.

troublemaker • n. a person who regularly causes trouble.

troubleshooter • n. a person who investigates and solves problems in an organization.
– DERIVATIVES **troubleshooting** n.

troublesome • adj. causing difficulty or annoyance.

trouble spot • n. a place where difficulties or conflict regularly occur.

troublous • adj. archaic full of troubles: *troublous times.*

trough • n. **1** a long, narrow open container for animals to eat or drink out of. **2** a channel used to convey a liquid. **3** Meteorol. a long region of low pressure. **4** a point of low activity or achievement.
– ORIGIN Old English.

trounce • v. (**trounces**, **trouncing**, **trounced**) defeat heavily in a contest.
– ORIGIN unknown.

troupe • n. a group of entertainers who tour to different venues.
– ORIGIN French.

trouper • n. **1** an entertainer with long experience. **2** a reliable and uncomplaining person.

trouser • v. (**trousers**, **trousering**, **trousered**) Brit. informal receive or take for oneself.

trousers • pl. n. an outer garment covering the body from the waist to the ankles, with a separate part for each leg.
– PHRASES **wear the trousers** informal be the dominant partner in a relationship.
– ORIGIN Irish and Scottish Gaelic.

trousseau /troo-soh/ • n. (pl. **trousseaux** or **trousseaus** /troo-sohz/) the clothes, linen, and other belongings collected by a bride for her marriage.
– ORIGIN French, 'small bundle'.

trout • n. (pl. **trout** or **trouts**) an edible fish of the salmon family, found chiefly in fresh water.
– ORIGIN Old English.

trove • n. a store of valuable or delightful things.
– ORIGIN from **TREASURE TROVE**.

trowel • n. **1** a small hand-held tool with a curved scoop for lifting plants or earth. **2** a small hand-held tool with a flat, pointed blade, used to apply and spread mortar or plaster.
– ORIGIN Latin *truella*.

Troy E
the city of King Priam, which (according to Homer) was captured by the Greeks after a ten-year siege. It was regarded as having been a purely legendary city until Heinrich Schliemann identified the mound of Hissarlik in Turkey as the site of Troy. Also called **ILIUM**.

troy (also **troy weight**) • n. a system of weights used for precious metals and gems, with a pound of 12 ounces or 5,760 grains. Compare with **AVOIRDUPOIS**.
– ORIGIN from a weight used at the fair of *Troyes* in France.

truant • n. a pupil who stays away from school without permission or explanation. • adj. wandering; straying: *her truant husband.* • v. (also **play truant**) (of a pupil) stay away from school without permission or explanation.
– DERIVATIVES **truancy** n.
– ORIGIN first referring to a person begging through choice: from Old French.

truce • n. an agreement between enemies to stop fighting for a certain time.
– ORIGIN Old English, 'belief, trust'.

Trucial States E
/troo-sh'l/ former name for **UNITED ARAB EMIRATES**.

truck[1] • n. **1** a large road vehicle, used for carrying goods, materials, or troops. **2** Brit. an open railway vehicle for carrying goods in bulk.
– ORIGIN perh. from former *truckle* 'wheel, pulley'.

truck[2] • n. (in phr. **have no truck with**) refuse to deal with or consider.
– ORIGIN prob. from Old French.

trucker • n. a long-distance truck driver.

truculent /truk-yuu-luhnt/ • adj. quick to argue or fight.
– DERIVATIVES **truculence** n. **truculently** adv.
– ORIGIN Latin *truculentus*.

Trudeau E
/troo-doh/, Pierre (Elliott) (b.1919), Canadian Liberal statesman, Prime Minister of Canada 1968–79 and 1980–4. He secured the complete national sovereignty of Canada in 1982.

trudge • v. (**trudges**, **trudging**, **trudged**) walk slowly and with heavy steps. • n. a long and tiring walk.
– ORIGIN unknown.

true • adj. (**truer**, **truest**) **1** in accordance with fact or reality. **2** rightly so called: *true love.* **3** real or actual: *my true intentions.* **4** accurate and exact. **5** upright or level. **6** loyal or faithful. **7** (**true to**) in keeping with (a standard or expectation).
– PHRASES **come true** actually happen or become the case. **out of true** not in the correct or exact shape or alignment.
– ORIGIN Old English, 'steadfast, loyal'.

Trueman, E
Fred (b.1931; full name *Frederick Sewards Trueman*), English cricketer, the first bowler to take 300 test wickets (1964).

true north • n. north according to the earth's axis, not magnetic north.

Truffaut E
/troo-foh/, François (1932–84), French film director. His films include *Les Quatre cents coups*, *Jules et Jim*, and *The Last Metro*.

truffle • n. **1** an underground fungus that resembles a rough-skinned potato, eaten as a delicacy. **2** a soft chocolate sweet.
– ORIGIN a former French word.

trug • n. Brit. a shallow oblong wooden basket, used for carrying garden flowers, fruit, and vegetables.
– ORIGIN perh. a dialect form of **TROUGH**.

truism • n. a statement that is obviously true and says nothing new or interesting.

t

Truk Islands E
/*rhymes with* truck/ a group of fourteen islands and numerous atolls in the western Pacific, in the Caroline Islands group.

truly ● adv. **1** in a truthful way. **2** absolutely or completely. **3** genuinely or properly. **4** in actual fact; really.
– PHRASES **yours truly 1** used as a formula for ending a letter. **2** humorous used to refer to oneself.

Truman, E
Harry S. (1884–1972), American Democratic statesman, 33rd President of the US 1945–53. He authorized the use of the atom bomb against Japan (1945), helped to establish NATO, and involved the US in the Korean War.

trump ● n. **1** (in bridge, whist, etc.) a playing card of the suit chosen to rank above the others, which can win a trick where a card of a different suit has been led. **2** a valuable resource that may be used as a surprise to gain an advantage. ● v. **1** play a trump on (a card of another suit). **2** beat by saying or doing something better. **3** (**trump up**) invent (a false accusation or excuse).
– PHRASES **come** (or **turn**) **up trumps** informal, esp. Brit. **1** have a better outcome than expected. **2** be especially generous or helpful.
– ORIGIN from **TRIUMPH**.

trumpery ● n. (pl. **trumperies**) archaic articles, practices, or beliefs with superficial appeal but little real worth.
– ORIGIN Old French *tromperie*.

trumpet ● n. **1** a brass musical instrument with a flared end. **2** something shaped like a trumpet, such as a flower head. **3** the loud cry of an elephant. ● v. (**trumpets**, **trumpeting**, **trumpeted**) **1** play a trumpet. **2** (of an elephant) make its typical loud cry. **3** proclaim widely or loudly.
– PHRASES **blow one's own trumpet** talk openly and boastfully about one's achievements.
– DERIVATIVES **trumpeter** n.
– ORIGIN Old French *trompette*.

truncate /trung-kayt/ ● v. (**truncates**, **truncating**, **truncated**) shorten by cutting off the top or the end.
– DERIVATIVES **truncation** n.
– ORIGIN Latin *truncare* 'maim'.

truncheon /trun-chuhn/ ● n. esp. Brit. a short thick stick carried as a weapon by a police officer.
– ORIGIN Old French *tronchon* 'stump'.

trundle ● v. (**trundles**, **trundling**, **trundled**) move or roll slowly and unevenly.
– ORIGIN from dialect *trendle* 'revolve'.

trunk ● n. **1** the main woody stem of a tree. **2** a person's or animal's body apart from the limbs and head. **3** the long nose of an elephant. **4** a large box with a hinged lid for storing or transporting clothes and other articles. **5** N. Amer. the boot of a car. ● adj. having to do with the main routes of a transport or communication network: *a trunk road.*
– ORIGIN Latin *truncus*.

trunk call ● n. Brit. dated a long-distance telephone call made within a country.

trunks ● pl. n. men's shorts worn for swimming or boxing.

truss ● n. **1** a framework of rafters, posts, and bars which supports a roof, bridge, or other structure. **2** a padded belt worn to support a hernia. **3** a compact cluster of flowers or fruit growing on one stalk. ● v. **1** support with a truss or trusses. **2** bind or tie up tightly. **3** tie up the wings and legs of (a bird) before cooking.
– ORIGIN Old French *trusser* 'bind in'.

trust ● n. **1** firm belief in the reliability, truth, ability, or strength of someone or something. **2** acceptance of the truth of a statement without proof. **3** the state of being responsible for someone or something. **4** an arrangement whereby a person (a trustee) holds or uses property for the benefit of one or more others. **5** an organization or company managed by trustees. ● v. **1** have trust in. **2** (**trust with**) have the confidence to allow (someone) to have, use, or look after. **3** (**trust to**) give (someone or something) to (another) for safekeeping. **4** (**trust to**) rely on (luck, fate, etc.). **5** hope: *I trust that you have enjoyed this book.*
– DERIVATIVES **trusted** adj.
– ORIGIN Old Norse, 'strong'.

trustee ● n. a person given legal powers to hold and manage property for the benefit of one or more others.
– DERIVATIVES **trusteeship** n.

trustful ● adj. having total trust in someone.
– DERIVATIVES **trustfully** adv.

trust fund ● n. a fund consisting of money or property that is held and managed for another person by a trust.

trusting ● adj. tending to trust others; not suspicious.
– DERIVATIVES **trustingly** adv.

trustworthy ● adj. honest, truthful, and reliable.
– DERIVATIVES **trustworthiness** n.

trusty ● adj. archaic or humorous reliable or faithful.

truth /trooth/ ● n. (pl. **truths** /troo*thz*, trooths/) **1** the state of being true. **2** (also **the truth**) that which is true. **3** a fact or belief that is accepted as true.
– ORIGIN Old English.

truthful ● adj. **1** telling or expressing the truth. **2** lifelike.
– DERIVATIVES **truthfully** adv. **truthfulness** n.

try ● v. (**tries**, **trying**, **tried**) **1** make an attempt to do something. **2** (also **try out**) test (something new or different) in order to see if it is suitable, effective, or pleasant. **3** attempt to open (a door). **4** (**try on**) put on (an item of clothing) to see if it fits or suits one. **5** make severe demands on: *try one's patience.* **6** put (someone) on trial. **7** investigate and decide (a case or issue) in a formal trial. ● n. (pl. **tries**) **1** an attempt. **2** an act of testing something new or different. **3** Rugby an act of touching the ball down behind the opposing goal line, scoring points and entitling the scoring side to a kick at goal.
– PHRASES **tried and tested** (or **true**) having proved effective or reliable before. **try one's hand at** attempt to do for the first time. **try it on** Brit. informal deliberately test someone's patience or attempt to deceive someone.
– ORIGIN Old French *trier* 'sift'.

t

USAGE **try**
Try to and **try and** both mean the same thing, but it is better to use **try to** in writing (*we should try to help them* rather than *we should try and help them*).

trying • **adj.** difficult or annoying.

try square • **n.** an implement used to check and mark right angles in building work.

tryst /trist/ • **n.** literary a private, romantic meeting between lovers.
– ORIGIN Latin *trista* 'an appointed place in hunting'.

tsar /zar, tsar/ (also **czar** or **tzar**) • **n.** an emperor of Russia before 1917.
– DERIVATIVES **tsarist** n. & adj.
– ORIGIN Russian.

tsarina /zah-ree-nuh, tsah-ree-nuh/ (also **czarina** or **tzarina**) • **n.** an empress of Russia before 1917.

tsetse /tet-si, tset-si/ (also **tsetse fly**) • **n.** an African bloodsucking fly which transmits sleeping sickness and other diseases.
– ORIGIN from a southern African language.

T-shirt (also **tee shirt**) • **n.** a short-sleeved casual top, having the shape of a T when spread out flat.

tsp • **abbrev.** (pl. **tsp** or **tsps**) teaspoonful.

T-square • **n.** a T-shaped instrument for drawing or testing right angles.

tsunami /tsoo-nah-mi/ • **n.** (pl. **tsunami** or **tsunamis**) a tidal wave caused by an earthquake or other disturbance.
– ORIGIN Japanese, 'harbour wave'.

Tuamotu Archipelago E
/too-uh-**moh**-too/ a group of about eighty coral islands in the South Pacific, in French Polynesia. It is the largest group of coral atolls in the world.

tub • **n.** **1** a low, wide, open container with a flat bottom. **2** a small plastic or cardboard container for food. **3** informal a bath. **4** informal, derog. a short, broad boat that handles awkwardly.
– ORIGIN prob. German or Dutch.

tuba • **n.** a large low-pitched brass wind instrument.
– ORIGIN Latin, 'trumpet'.

tubby • **adj.** (**tubbier**, **tubbiest**) informal (of a person) short and rather fat.

tube • **n.** **1** a long, hollow cylinder for conveying or holding something. **2** a flexible metal or plastic container sealed at one end and having a cap at the other: *a toothpaste tube*. **3** a hollow cylindrical organ or structure in an animal or plant. **4** Brit. trademark (**The Tube**) the underground railway system in London.
– ORIGIN Latin *tubus*.

tuber • **n.** **1** a thickened underground part of a stem or rhizome, e.g. that of the potato, bearing buds from which new plants grow. **2** a thickened fleshy root, e.g. of the dahlia.
– ORIGIN Latin, 'hump, swelling'.

tubercle /tyoo-ber-k'l/ • **n.** **1** a small lump on a bone or on the surface of an animal or plant. **2** a small rounded swelling in the lungs or other tissues, characteristic of tuberculosis.
– ORIGIN Latin *tuberculum* 'small lump or swelling'.

tubercle bacillus • **n.** the bacterium that causes tuberculosis.

tubercular /tyuu-ber-kyuu-ler/ • **adj.** **1** relating to or affected with tuberculosis. **2** having or covered with tubercles.

tuberculosis /tyuu-ber-kyuu-**loh**-siss/ • **n.** an infectious disease transmitted by a bacterium, in which tubercles (small swellings) appear in the tissues, especially the lungs.

tuberculous /tyuu-**ber**-kyuu-luhss/ • **adj.** = TUBERCULAR.

tuberose /tyoo-buh-rohz/ • **n.** a Mexican plant with heavily scented white waxy flowers and a bulb-like base.

tuberous /tyoo-buh-ruhss/ • **adj.** (of a plant) having or forming a tuber or tubers.

tubing • **n.** a length or lengths of material in the form of tubes.

tub-thumping • **n.** informal, derog. the expression of opinions in a loud and aggressive way.

tubular • **adj.** **1** long, round, and hollow like a tube. **2** made from a tube or tubes.

tubular bells • **pl. n.** an orchestral instrument consisting of a row of hanging metal tubes struck with a mallet.

tubule /tyoo-byool/ • **n.** a tiny tube.
– ORIGIN Latin *tubulus*.

TUC • **abbrev.** (in the UK) Trades Union Congress.

tuck • **v.** **1** push, fold, or turn under or between two surfaces. **2** draw (part of one's body) together into a small space. **3** (often **tuck away**) store in a safe or secret place. **4** (**tuck in/up**) settle (someone) in bed by pulling the edges of the bedclothes firmly under the mattress. **5** (**tuck in/into**) informal eat food heartily. **6** make a flattened, stitched fold in (a garment or material). • **n.** **1** a flattened, stitched fold in a garment or material. **2** Brit. informal food eaten by children at school as a snack.
– ORIGIN Old English, 'punish, ill-treat'.

tucker • **n.** Austral./NZ informal food.

-tude • **suffix** forming abstract nouns such as *solitude*.
– ORIGIN Latin *-tudo*.

Tudor • **adj.** relating to the English royal dynasty which held the throne from the accession of Henry VII in 1485 until the death of Elizabeth I in 1603.

Tuesday • **n.** the day of the week before Wednesday and following Monday.
– ORIGIN named after the Germanic god *Tīw*.

tufa /tyoo-fuh/ • **n.** **1** a rock composed of calcium carbonate and formed as a deposit from mineral springs. **2** = TUFF.
– ORIGIN Italian.

tuff /*rhymes with* tough/ • **n.** rock formed from volcanic ash.
– ORIGIN Latin *tofus*.

tuffet • **n.** **1** a tuft or clump. **2** a footstool or low seat.
– ORIGIN from TUFT.

tuft • **n.** a bunch of threads, grass, or hair, held or growing together at the base.
– DERIVATIVES **tufted** adj. **tufty** adj.
– ORIGIN prob. from Old French *tofe*.

tug • **v.** (**tugs**, **tugging**, **tugged**) pull hard or suddenly. • **n.** **1** a hard or sudden pull. **2** (also **tugboat**) a small, powerful boat for towing larger boats and ships.
– ORIGIN from TOW[1].

tug of war • n. a contest in which two teams pull at opposite ends of a rope until one drags the other over a central line.

tuition • n. teaching or instruction.
– ORIGIN Latin.

tulip • n. a spring-flowering plant with boldly coloured cup-shaped flowers.
– ORIGIN French *tulipe*.

Tull E
/*rhymes with* dull/, Jethro (1674–1741), English agriculturalist, inventor of the seed drill (1701).

tulle /tyool/ • n. a soft, fine net material, used for making veils and dresses.
– ORIGIN from *Tulle*, a town in SW France.

tumble • v. (**tumbles**, **tumbling**, **tumbled**) **1** fall suddenly, clumsily, or headlong. **2** move in a headlong way: *they tumbled from the vehicle.* **3** decrease rapidly in amount or value. **4** (**tumble to**) informal suddenly realize. • n. **1** an instance of tumbling. **2** an untidy or confused arrangement or state: *a tumble of untamed curls.* **3** a handspring or other acrobatic feat.
– ORIGIN German *tummeln*.

tumbledown • adj. (of a building) falling or fallen into ruin.

tumble-dryer • n. a machine that dries washed clothes by spinning them in hot air inside a rotating drum.

tumbler • n. **1** a drinking glass with straight sides and no handle or stem. [ORIGIN formerly having a rounded bottom so as not to stand upright.] **2** an acrobat. **3** a part of a lock that holds the bolt until lifted by a key.

tumbleweed • n. N. Amer. & Austral./NZ a plant of dry regions which breaks off near the ground in late summer, forming light masses blown about by the wind.

tumbril /tum-bril/ (also **tumbrel**) • n. hist. an open cart that tilted backwards to empty out its load, used to take prisoners to the guillotine during the French Revolution.
– ORIGIN Old French *tomberel*.

tumescent /tyuu-mess-uhnt/ • adj. swollen or becoming swollen.
– DERIVATIVES **tumescence** n.

tumid /tyoo-mid/ • adj. (of a part of the body) swollen.
– ORIGIN Latin *tumidus*.

tummy • n. (pl. **tummies**) informal a person's stomach or abdomen.
– ORIGIN a child's pronunciation of STOMACH.

tummy button • n. informal a person's navel.

tumour (US **tumor**) • n. a swelling of a part of the body caused by an abnormal growth of tissue.
– ORIGIN Latin *tumor*.

tumult • n. **1** a loud, confused noise, as caused by a large mass of people. **2** confusion or disorder.
– ORIGIN Latin *tumultus*.

tumultuous /tyuu-**mul**-tyuu-uhss/ • adj. **1** very loud or uproarious. **2** excited, confused, or disorderly.

tumulus /tyoo-myuu-luhss/ • n. (pl. **tumuli** /tyoo-myuu-ly/) an ancient burial mound.
– ORIGIN Latin.

tun • n. a large beer or wine cask.
– ORIGIN Latin *tunna*.

tuna • n. (pl. **tuna** or **tunas**) a large edible fish of warm seas.
– ORIGIN Spanish *atún*.

tundra /tun-druh/ • n. a vast, flat, treeless Arctic region of Europe, Asia, and North America in which the subsoil is permanently frozen.
– ORIGIN Lappish (the language of Lapland).

tune • n. a melody or melodious piece of music. • v. (**tunes**, **tuning**, **tuned**) **1** adjust (a musical instrument) to the correct pitch. **2** adjust (a radio or television) to the frequency of the required signal. **3** adjust (an engine) or balance (mechanical parts) so that they run smoothly and efficiently. **4** adjust or adapt to a purpose or situation: *the animals are finely tuned to life in the desert.*
– PHRASES **in** (or **out of**) **tune** in (or not in) the correct musical pitch. **to the tune of** informal amounting to or involving (a sum of money).
– DERIVATIVES **tunable** (also **tuneable**) adj.
– ORIGIN from TONE.

tuneful • adj. having a pleasing tune.
– DERIVATIVES **tunefully** adv.

tuneless • adj. not having a pleasing tune.
– DERIVATIVES **tunelessly** adv.

tuner • n. **1** a person who tunes musical instruments, especially pianos. **2** a part of a stereo system that receives radio signals.

tungsten /tung-stuhn/ • n. a hard grey metallic element with a very high melting point, used to make electric light filaments.
– ORIGIN Swedish.

tunic • n. **1** a loose sleeveless garment reaching to the thigh or knees. **2** a close-fitting short coat worn as part of a uniform.
– ORIGIN Latin *tunica*.

tuning fork • n. a two-pronged steel device used for tuning instruments, which vibrates when struck to give a note of specific pitch.

Tunis E
/tyoo-niss/ the capital of Tunisia.

Tunisia E
/tyoo-**niz**-i-uh/ a country in North Africa; capital, Tunis.
– DERIVATIVES **Tunisian** adj. & n.

tunnel • n. a passage that is built underground, e.g. for a road or railway, or by a burrowing animal. • v. (**tunnels**, **tunnelling**, **tunnelled**; US **tunnels**, **tunneling**, **tunneled**) dig or force a passage underground or through something.
– ORIGIN Old French *tonel* 'small cask'.

tunnel vision • n. **1** a condition in which things cannot be seen properly if they are not close to the centre of the field of view. **2** informal the tendency to focus only on a single or limited aim or view.

tunny • n. (pl. **tunny** or **tunnies**) a tuna.
– ORIGIN Greek *thunnos*.

tup /tup/ esp. Brit. • n. a ram. • v. (**tups**, **tupping**, **tupped**) (of a ram) mate with (a ewe).
– ORIGIN unknown.

tuppence • n. Brit. = TWOPENCE.

tuppenny • adj. Brit. = TWOPENNY.

turban • n. a long length of material wound round a cap or the head, worn by Muslim and Sikh men.
– DERIVATIVES **turbaned** (also **turbanned**) adj.
– ORIGIN Persian.

t

turbid /ter-bid/ ● adj. (of a liquid) cloudy or muddy; not clear.
– DERIVATIVES **turbidity** n.
– ORIGIN Latin *turbidus*.

turbine /ter-byn, ter-bin/ ● n. a machine for producing power in which a wheel or rotor is made to revolve by a fast-moving flow of water, steam, gas, or air.
– ORIGIN Latin *turbo* 'spinning top, whirl'.

turbo /ter-boh/ ● n. (pl. **turbos**) = TURBOCHARGER.

turbocharger ● n. a supercharger driven by a turbine powered by the engine's exhaust gases.
– DERIVATIVES **turbocharged** adj.

turbofan ● n. a jet engine in which a turbine-driven fan provides additional thrust.

turbojet ● n. a jet engine in which the jet gases also operate a turbine-driven device for compressing the air drawn into the engine.

turboprop ● n. a jet engine in which a turbine is used to drive a propeller.

turbot ● n. (pl. **turbot** or **turbots**) an edible flatfish which has large bony swellings on the body.
– ORIGIN Scandinavian.

turbulence ● n. **1** violent or unsteady movement of air or water, or of some other fluid. **2** conflict or confusion: *political turbulence*.

turbulent /ter-byuu-luhnt/ ● adj. **1** involving much conflict, disorder, or confusion. **2** (of air or water) moving unsteadily or violently.
– DERIVATIVES **turbulently** adv.
– ORIGIN Latin *turbulentus* 'full of commotion'.

turd ● n. vulgar **1** a lump of excrement. **2** an unpleasant person.
– ORIGIN Old English.

tureen /tyuu-**reen**, tuh-**reen**/ ● n. a deep covered dish from which soup is served.
– ORIGIN French *terrine* 'large earthenware pot'.

turf ● n. (pl. **turfs** or **turves**) **1** grass and the surface layer of earth held together by its roots. **2** a piece of such grass and earth cut from the ground. **3** (**the turf**) horse racing or racecourses generally. **4** (**one's turf**) informal one's territory. ● v. **1** (**turf off/out**) informal, esp. Brit. force to leave somewhere. **2** cover with turf.
– ORIGIN Old English.

Turgenev E
/ter-**gen**-yef/, Ivan (Sergeevich) (1818–83), Russian novelist, dramatist, and short-story writer, author of the novel *Fathers and Sons*.

turgid /ter-jid/ ● adj. **1** swollen or full: *a turgid river*. **2** (of language or style) pompous and boring.
– DERIVATIVES **turgidity** n.
– ORIGIN Latin *turgidus*.

Turin E
/tyuu-**rin**/ a city in NW Italy, the first capital of a unified Italy (1861–4).

Turing E
/**tyuu**-ring/, Alan Mathison (1912–54), English mathematician, who developed the concept of a theoretical computing machine (a key step in the development of the first computer) and devised a test for machine intelligence.

Turin Shroud E
a relic preserved at Turin Cathedral, venerated as the shroud in which Christ's body was wrapped for burial. Scientific tests have dated the shroud to the 13th–14th centuries.

Turk ● n. a person from Turkey.

Turkestan E
/ter-ki-**stahn**, ter-ki-**stan**/ (also **Turkistan**) a region of central Asia between the Caspian Sea and the Gobi Desert. It is divided into eastern Turkestan, now the Xinjiang autonomous region of China, and western Turkestan, which comprises the present-day countries of Turkmenistan, Kazakhstan, Uzbekistan, Tajikistan, and Kyrgyzstan.

Turkey E
a country in western Asia, with a small enclave in SE Europe; capital, Ankara.

turkey ● n. (pl. **turkeys**) **1** a large game bird native to North America, that is bred for food. **2** informal, esp. N. Amer. an extremely unsuccessful play or film.
– PHRASES **talk turkey** N. Amer. informal talk frankly and openly.
– ORIGIN short for TURKEYCOCK, first referring to the guineafowl (which was imported through Turkey), and then wrongly to the American bird.

turkeycock ● n. a male turkey.

Turkish ● n. the language of Turkey. ● adj. relating to Turkey or its language.

Turkish bath ● n. **1** a cleansing treatment that involves sitting in a room filled with very hot air or steam, followed by washing and massage. **2** a building or room where such a treatment is available.

Turkish delight ● n. a sweet consisting of flavoured gelatin coated in icing sugar.

Turkistan E
var. of TURKESTAN.

Turkmenistan E
/terk-men-i-**stahn**, terk-men-i-**stan**/ a republic in central Asia; capital, Ashgabat. Also called TURKMENIA /terk-**mee**-ni-uh/.

Turks and Caicos Islands E
/**kay**-koss/ a British dependency in the Caribbean, comprising two island groups between Haiti and the Bahamas; capital, Cockburn Town (on the island of Grand Turk).

turmeric /ter-muh-rik/ ● n. a bright yellow powder obtained from a plant of the ginger family, used as a spice in Asian cookery.
– ORIGIN perh. from French *terre mérite* 'deserving earth'.

turmoil ● n. a state of great disturbance, confusion, or uncertainty.
– ORIGIN unknown.

turn ● v. **1** move around a central point. **2** move so as to face or go in a different direction. **3** make or become: *Emma turned pale*. **4** shape (something) on a lathe. **5** give an elegant form to: *he can turn a fine phrase*. **6** (of the tide) change from coming in to going out or vice versa. **7** twist or sprain (an ankle). ● n. **1** an act of turning. **2** a bend in a road, river, etc. **3** a place where a road meets or branches off another. **4** the time when a member of a group must or is allowed to do something: *it*

was his turn to speak. **5** a time when one period of time ends and another begins: *the turn of the century.* **6** a change in circumstances. **7** a short walk or ride. **8** a brief feeling of illness: *a funny turn.* **9** a short performance: *a comic turn.* **10** one round in a coil of rope or other material.
– PHRASES **at every turn** on every occasion. **do someone a good** (or **bad**) **turn** do something that is helpful (or unhelpful) for someone. **in turn** one after the other. **out of turn** at a time when it is inappropriate or not one's turn. **take turns** (or **take it in turns**) (of two or more people) do something alternately or one after the other. **to a turn** to exactly the right degree. **turn against** become or make hostile towards. **turn away** refuse entry to. **turn down** reject an offer of something or from someone. **turn in 1** hand over to the authorities. **2** informal go to bed in the evening. **turn off 1** switch off. **2** informal cause to feel bored or disgusted. **turn of mind** a particular way of thinking. **turn on 1** switch on. **2** suddenly attack. **3** informal excite sexually. **turn out 1** switch off (an electric light). **2** produce (something). **3** empty (one's pockets). **4** prove to be the case. **5** be present at an event. **6** (**be turned out**) be dressed in a particular way. **turn over 1** (of an engine) start or continue to run properly. **2** hand (someone) over to the control of someone else. **turn tail** informal turn round and run away. **turn to 1** start doing or becoming involved with. **2** go to for help or information. **turn up 1** increase the volume or strength of (a device). **2** be found, especially by chance. **3** put in an appearance. **4** reveal or discover.
– ORIGIN Latin *tornare.*

turnaround (also **turnround**) ● n. **1** a sudden or unexpected change. **2** the process of completing or the time needed to complete a task.

turncoat ● n. a person who deserts one party or cause in order to join an opposing one.

Turner, E
J. M. W. (1775–1851; full name *Joseph Mallord William Turner*), English painter. He is noted for his landscapes and seascapes, such as *Rain, Steam, Speed* and *The Fighting Téméraire.*

turning ● n. **1** a place where a road branches off another. **2** the action of using a lathe. **3** (**turnings**) shavings of wood resulting from turning wood on a lathe.

turnip ● n. a round root vegetable with white or cream flesh.
– ORIGIN from a unknown first element + Latin *napus* 'turnip'.

turnkey ● n. (pl. **turnkeys**) archaic a jailer.

turn-off ● n. **1** a junction at which a road branches off. **2** informal a person or thing that causes one to feel bored or disgusted.

turn-on ● n. informal a person or thing that causes one to feel sexually excited.

turnout ● n. the number of people attending or taking part in an event.

turnover ● n. **1** the amount of money taken by a business in a particular period. **2** the rate at which employees leave a workforce and are replaced. **3** the rate at which goods are sold and replaced in a shop. **4** a small pie made by folding a piece of pastry over on itself to enclose a filling.

turnpike ● n. **1** hist. a toll gate. **2** hist. a road on which a toll was collected. **3** US a motorway on which a toll is charged.
– ORIGIN first meaning a spiked barrier fixed across a road as a defence: from **PIKE²**.

turnstile ● n. a mechanical gate with revolving horizontal arms that allow only one person at a time to pass through.

turntable ● n. a circular revolving platform or support, e.g. for the record in a record-player.

turn-up ● n. Brit. **1** the end of a trouser leg folded upwards on the outside. **2** informal an unusual or unexpected event.

turpentine /ter-puhn-tyn/ ● n. **1** (also **crude** or **gum turpentine**) a substance produced by certain trees and distilled to make rosin and oil of turpentine. **2** (also **oil of turpentine**) a strong-smelling oil distilled from this, used in mixing paints and varnishes.
– ORIGIN Old French *terebentine.*

Turpin, E
Dick (1706–39), English highwayman.

turpitude /ter-pi-tyood/ ● n. formal wickedness.
– ORIGIN Latin *turpitudo.*

turps ● n. informal turpentine.

turquoise /ter-kwoyz, ter-kwahz/ ● n. **1** a greenish-blue or sky-blue semi-precious stone. **2** a greenish-blue colour.
– ORIGIN Old French *turqueise* 'Turkish stone'.

turret ● n. **1** a small tower at the corner of a building or wall. **2** an armoured, usually revolving tower for a gun and gunners in a ship, aircraft, fort, or tank.
– DERIVATIVES **turreted** adj.
– ORIGIN Old French *tourete* 'small tower'.

turtle ● n. a sea or freshwater reptile with a bony or leathery shell and flippers or webbed toes.
– PHRASES **turn turtle** (of a boat) turn upside down.
– ORIGIN prob. from French *tortue* 'tortoise'.

turtle dove ● n. a small dove with a soft purring call.
– ORIGIN Latin *turtur.*

turtleneck ● n. **1** Brit. a high, round, close-fitting neck on a knitted garment. **2** N. Amer. = **POLO NECK**.

turves pl. of **TURF**.

Tuscany E
a region of west central Italy; capital, Florence.
– DERIVATIVES **Tuscan** adj.

tusk ● n. a long, pointed tooth which protrudes from a closed mouth, as in the elephant, walrus, or wild boar.
– DERIVATIVES **tusked** adj.
– ORIGIN Old English.

Tussaud E
/tuh-sawd/, Madame (1761–1850; née *Marie Grosholtz*), French founder of Madame Tussaud's, a permanent waxworks exhibition in London.

tussle ● n. a vigorous struggle or scuffle. ● v. (**tussles, tussling, tussled**) engage in a tussle.
– ORIGIN perh. from dialect *touse* 'handle roughly'.

tussock /tus-suhk/ ● **n.** a dense clump or tuft of grass.
– DERIVATIVES **tussocky** adj.
– ORIGIN perh. from dialect *tusk* 'tuft'.

Tutankhamen E
/too-t'n-**kah**-m'n/ (also **Tutankhamun** /too-t'n-kah-**moon**/) (died *c.*1352 BC), Egyptian pharaoh of the 18th dynasty, reigned *c.*1361–*c.*1352 BC. His tomb, containing a wealth of contents, was discovered by Howard Carter in 1922.

tutee /tyoo-**tee**/ ● **n.** a student or pupil of a tutor.

tutelage /**tyoo**-ti-lij/ ● **n.** **1** protection of or authority over someone or something. **2** instruction; tuition.
– ORIGIN Latin *tutela* 'keeping'.

tutelary /**tyoo**-ti-luh-ri/ ● **adj.** serving as a protector, guardian, or patron.

tutor ● **n.** **1** a private teacher who teaches a single pupil or a very small group. **2** esp. Brit. a university or college teacher responsible for students assigned to them. **3** Brit. a book of instruction in a particular subject. ● **v.** act as a tutor to.
– ORIGIN Latin.

tutorial ● **n.** **1** a period of tuition given by a university or college tutor. **2** a written account or explanation of a subject, intended for private study. ● **adj.** relating to a tutor or a tutor's tuition.

tutti /**tuut**-ti/ ● **adv. & adj.** Music with all voices or instruments together.
– ORIGIN Italian.

tutti-frutti /toot-ti-**froot**-ti/ ● **n.** (pl. **tutti-fruttis**) a type of ice cream containing mixed fruits.
– ORIGIN Italian, 'all fruits'.

Tutu E
/**too**-too/, Desmond (Mpilo) (b.1931), South African clergyman. As General Secretary of the South African Council of Churches (1979–84) he became a leading voice in the struggle against apartheid.

tutu /**too**-too/ ● **n.** a female ballet dancer's costume consisting of a bodice and a very short, stiff attached skirt made of many layers of fabric and projecting horizontally from the waist.
– ORIGIN French.

Tuvalu E
/too-**vah**-loo/ a country in the SW Pacific consisting of a group of nine main islands; capital, Funafuti. Former name **ELLICE ISLANDS**.
– DERIVATIVES **Tuvaluan** /too-vuh-**loo**-uhn, too-**vah**-loo-uhn/ adj. & n.

tux ● **n.** informal, esp. N. Amer. a tuxedo.

tuxedo /tuk-**see**-doh/ ● **n.** (pl. **tuxedos** or **tuxedoes**) esp. N. Amer. **1** a man's dinner jacket. **2** a formal evening suit including such a jacket.
– DERIVATIVES **tuxedoed** adj.
– ORIGIN from *Tuxedo* Park, the site of a country club in New York.

TV ● **abbrev.** television.

twaddle ● **n.** informal trivial or foolish speech or writing.
– ORIGIN unknown.

Twain, E
Mark (1835–1910; pen name of *Samuel Langhorne Clemens*), American novelist and humorist, author of *The Adventures of Tom Sawyer* and *The Adventures of Huckleberry Finn*.

twain ● **cardinal number** archaic = **TWO**.
– PHRASES **never the twain shall meet** the two things in question are too different to exist alongside each other. [ORIGIN from a poem by Rudyard Kipling.]
– ORIGIN Old English.

twang ● **n.** **1** a strong ringing sound such as that made by the plucked string of a musical instrument. **2** a distinctive nasal way of speaking. ● **v.** make or cause to make a twang.
– DERIVATIVES **twangy** adj.

'twas ● **contr.** archaic or literary it was.

twat /twat, twot/ ● **n.** vulgar **1** a woman's genitals. **2** a stupid or unpleasant person.
– ORIGIN unknown.

tweak ● **v.** **1** twist or pull with a small but sharp movement. **2** informal improve by making fine adjustments. ● **n.** an act of tweaking.
– ORIGIN prob. from dialect *twick* 'pull sharply'.

twee ● **adj.** Brit. excessively quaint, pretty, or sentimental.
– ORIGIN from a child's pronunciation of **SWEET**.

tweed ● **n.** **1** a rough woollen cloth flecked with mixed colours. **2** (**tweeds**) clothes made of tweed.
– DERIVATIVES **tweedy** adj.
– ORIGIN from a Scots form of **TWILL**.

tweet ● **n.** the chirp of a small or young bird. ● **v.** make a chirping noise.

tweeter ● **n.** a loudspeaker designed to reproduce high frequencies.

tweeze ● **v.** (**tweezes**, **tweezing**, **tweezed**) pluck or pull with or as if with tweezers.

tweezers ● **pl. n.** (also **pair of tweezers**) a small instrument like a pair of pincers for plucking out hairs and picking up small objects.
– ORIGIN from former *tweeze* 'case of surgical instruments'.

twelfth /twelfth/ ● **ordinal number** **1** that is number twelve in a sequence; 12th. **2** (**a twelfth/one twelfth**) each of twelve equal parts into which something is divided. **3** a musical interval spanning an octave and a fifth in a scale. **4** (**the (Glorious) Twelfth**) (in the UK) 12 August, the day on which the grouse-shooting season begins.

Twelfth Night ● **n.** **1** 6 January, the feast of the Epiphany. **2** the evening of 5 January, formerly the twelfth and last day of Christmas festivities.

twelve ● **cardinal number** two more than ten; 12. (Roman numeral: **xii** or **XII**.)
– ORIGIN Old English.

twelvemonth ● **n.** archaic a year.

twenty ● **cardinal number** (pl. **twenties**) ten less than thirty; 20. (Roman numeral: **xx** or **XX**.)
– DERIVATIVES **twentieth** ordinal number.
– ORIGIN Old English.

24-7 (also **24/7**) ● **adv.** informal, esp. N. Amer. twenty-four hours a day, seven days a week; all the time.

twenty-twenty (also **20/20**) ● **adj.** (of vision) of normal sharpness.

'twere • contr. archaic or literary it were.

twerp • n. informal a silly or annoying person.
– ORIGIN unknown.

twice • adv. **1** two times. **2** double in degree or quantity.
– ORIGIN Old English.

twiddle • v. (**twiddles, twiddling, twiddled**) play or fiddle with (something) in an aimless or nervous way. • n. an act of twiddling.
– PHRASES **twiddle one's thumbs** have nothing to do.
– DERIVATIVES **twiddly** adj.

twig[1] • n. a slender woody shoot growing from a branch or stem of a tree or shrub.
– DERIVATIVES **twiggy** adj.
– ORIGIN Old English.

twig[2] • v. (**twigs, twigging, twigged**) Brit. informal come to understand or realize something.
– ORIGIN unknown.

twilight • n. **1** the soft glowing light from the sky when the sun is below the horizon. **2** a period or state of gradual decline: *the twilight of his career.*
– ORIGIN from Old English, 'two' + LIGHT[1].

twilight zone • n. a state or area which does not have clear limits or meaning.

twilit • adj. dimly lit by twilight.

twill • n. a fabric woven so as to have a surface of diagonal parallel ridges.
– DERIVATIVES **twilled** adj.
– ORIGIN Old English, 'two'.

twin • n. **1** one of two children or animals born at the same birth. **2** something containing or consisting of two matching parts. • adj. forming or being one of a pair of twins or matching things. • v. (**twins, twinning, twinned**) **1** link or combine as a pair. **2** Brit. link (a town) with another in a different country, for the purposes of cultural exchange.
– ORIGIN Old English.

twine • n. strong string consisting of strands of hemp or cotton twisted together. • v. (**twines, twining, twined**) wind round something.
– ORIGIN Old English, 'thread, linen'.

twinge • n. **1** a sudden, sharp pain in a part of the body. **2** a brief, sharp pang of emotion.
– ORIGIN Old English, 'pinch, wring'.

twinkle • v. (**twinkles, twinkling, twinkled**) **1** (of a star or light) shine with a gleam that changes constantly from bright to faint. **2** (of a person's eyes) sparkle with amusement or liveliness. • n. a twinkling sparkle or gleam.
– PHRASES **in a twinkling (of an eye)** in an instant.
– DERIVATIVES **twinkly** adj.
– ORIGIN Old English.

twinkle-toed • adj. informal nimble and quick on one's feet.

twinset • n. esp. Brit. a woman's matching cardigan and jumper.

twin-tub • n. a type of washing machine having two top-loading drums, one for washing and the other for spin-drying.

twirl • v. spin quickly and lightly round. • n. **1** an act of twirling. **2** a spiral shape.
– DERIVATIVES **twirly** adj.
– ORIGIN prob. from archaic *trill* 'twiddle, spin'.

twist • v. **1** bend, curl, or distort. **2** force out of the natural position: *she twisted her ankle.* **3** turn or bend round or into a different direction. **4** take or have a winding course. **5** deliberately change the meaning of. **6** (**twisted**) unpleasantly or unhealthily abnormal. • n. **1** an act of twisting. **2** a thing with a spiral shape. **3** force producing twisting; torque. **4** a new or unexpected development: *the plot includes a clever twist.* **5** (**the twist**) a dance with a twisting movement of the body, popular in the 1960s.
– PHRASES **round the twist** Brit. informal crazy. **twist someone's arm** informal forcefully persuade someone to do something that they are reluctant to do.
– DERIVATIVES **twisty** adj.
– ORIGIN Old English.

twister • n. **1** Brit. informal a swindler or dishonest person. **2** N. Amer. a tornado.

twit[1] • n. informal, esp. Brit. a silly person.
– ORIGIN perh. from TWIT[2].

twit[2] • v. (**twits, twitting, twitted**) informal tease good-humouredly.
– ORIGIN Old English, 'reproach with'.

twitch • v. make a short, sudden jerking movement. • n. **1** a twitching movement. **2** a pang: *he felt a twitch of annoyance.*
– ORIGIN Germanic.

twitcher • n. Brit. informal a birdwatcher devoted to spotting rare birds.

twitchy • adj. (**twitchier, twitchiest**) informal nervous.

twitter • v. (**twitters, twittering, twittered**) **1** (of a bird) make a series of short high sounds. **2** talk rapidly in a nervous or trivial way. • n. **1** a twittering sound. **2** informal an agitated or excited state.

'twixt • contr. betwixt.

two • cardinal number one less than three; 2. (Roman numeral: **ii** or **II**.)
– PHRASES **put two and two together** draw an obvious conclusion from what is known or evident. **two by two** side by side in pairs.
– DERIVATIVES **twofold** adj. & adv.
– ORIGIN Old English.

> **USAGE** two
> For an explanation of the difference between **two**, **to**, and **too**, see the note at TO.

two-bit • adj. N. Amer. informal insignificant, cheap, or worthless.

two-dimensional • adj. having or appearing to have length and breadth but no depth.

two-faced • adj. insincere and deceitful.

twopence /tup-puhnss/ (also **tuppence**) • n. Brit. **1** the sum of two pence before decimalization (1971). **2** informal anything at all: *he didn't care twopence.*

twopenn'orth /too-pen-nuhth/ • n. an amount that is worth or costs twopence.
– PHRASES **add (or put in) one's twopenn'orth** informal give one's opinion.

twopenny /tup-puh-ni/ (also **tuppeny**) • adj. Brit. costing two pence before decimalization (1971).

twopenny-halfpenny • adj. Brit. informal insignificant or worthless.

two-piece • adj. consisting of two matching items.

twosome • n. a set of two people or things.

two-step • n. a round dance with a sliding step in march or polka time.

two-time • v. (**two-times**, **two-timing**, **two-timed**) informal be unfaithful to (a lover or husband or wife).

two-way • adj. **1** involving movement or communication in opposite directions. **2** (of a switch) permitting a current to be switched on or off from either of two points.
– PHRASES **two-way street** a shared obligation: *trust is a two-way street.*

two-way mirror • n. a panel of glass that can be seen through from one side and is a mirror on the other.

-ty[1] • suffix forming nouns referring to quality or condition: *beauty.*
– ORIGIN Latin *-tas.*

-ty[2] • suffix referring to specified groups of ten: *forty.*
– ORIGIN Old English.

tycoon • n. a wealthy, powerful person in business or industry.
– ORIGIN Japanese, 'great lord'.

tying pres. part. of **TIE**.

tyke • n. informal a small mischievous child.
– ORIGIN Old Norse, 'bitch'.

Tyler[1], E
John (1790–1862), American Whig statesman, 10th President of the US 1841–5.

Tyler[2], E
Wat (d.1381), English leader of the Peasants' Revolt of 1381. He led his followers to London and secured Richard II's concession to the rebels' demands, but was killed by royal supporters.

tympani • pl. n. var. of **TIMPANI**.

tympanum /tim-puh-nuhm/ • n. (pl. **tympanums** or **tympana** /tim-puh-nuh/) the eardrum.
– ORIGIN Greek *tumpanon* 'drum'.

Tyndale E
/tin-d'l/, William (*c*.1494–1536), English translator and Protestant martyr. His translations of the Bible into English formed the basis of the Authorized Version. Opposition to his work forced him to leave England and he was executed as a heretic in Antwerp.

Tyndall E
/tin-d'l/, John (1820–93), Irish physicist. He is known for his work on heat and the scattering of light by suspended particles, so becoming the first person to explain the blue colour of the sky.

t

Tyne E
a river that rises in NE England and flows generally eastwards to the North Sea.

Tyne and Wear E
/weer/ a metropolitan county of NE England.

Tyneside E
an industrial conurbation on the banks of the River Tyne, stretching from Newcastle-upon-Tyne to the coast.

Tynwald /tin-wuhld/ • n. the parliament of the Isle of Man.
– ORIGIN Old Norse, 'place of assembly'.

type • n. **1** a category of people or things that share particular qualities or features: *a new type of battery.* **2** informal a person of a specified nature: *a sporty type.* **3** printed characters or letters. • v. (**types**, **typing**, **typed**) write using a typewriter or computer.
– DERIVATIVES **typing** n.
– ORIGIN Greek *tupos* 'impression, type'.

typecast • v. (**be typecast**) (of an actor) be repeatedly cast in the same type of role because their appearance is appropriate or they are known for such roles.

typeface • n. Printing a particular design of type.

typescript • n. a typed copy of a text.

typeset • v. (**typeset**, **typesetting**, **typeset**) arrange or generate the type for (text to be printed).
– DERIVATIVES **typesetter** n.

typewriter • n. an electric, electronic, or manual machine with keys for producing print-like characters.
– DERIVATIVES **typewriting** n. **typewritten** adj.

typhoid (also **typhoid fever**) • n. an infectious fever caused by bacteria, resulting in red spots on the chest and abdomen and severe irritation of the intestines.
– ORIGIN from **TYPHUS**.

typhoon /ty-foon/ • n. a tropical storm in the region of the Indian or western Pacific oceans.
– ORIGIN partly from Arabic, partly from a Chinese dialect word meaning 'big wind'.

typhus /ty-fuhss/ • n. an infectious disease caused by bacteria, resulting in a purple rash, headaches, fever, and usually delirium.
– ORIGIN Greek *tuphos* 'smoke, stupor'.

typical • adj. **1** having the distinctive qualities of a particular type of person or thing: *it's a typical example of a small American town.* **2** characteristic of a particular person or thing.
– DERIVATIVES **typically** adv.

typify • v. (**typifies**, **typifying**, **typified**) be typical of.

typist • n. a person skilled in typing and employed for this purpose.

typo /ty-poh/ • n. (pl. **typos**) informal a small mistake in typed or printed text.

typography /ty-pog-ruh-fi/ • n. **1** the process of setting and arranging types and printing from them. **2** the style and appearance of printed material.
– DERIVATIVES **typographer** n. **typographic** adj. **typographical** adj.

tyrannical • adj. using power over others in a cruel and unfair way.
– DERIVATIVES **tyrannically** adv.

tyrannize /ti-ruh-nyz/ (also **tyrannise**) • v. (**tyrannizes**, **tyrannizing**, **tyrannized**) dominate or treat cruelly.

tyrannosaurus rex /ti-ran-nuh-sor-uhss recks/ • n. a very large meat-eating dinosaur with powerful jaws and small claw-like front legs.
– ORIGIN from Greek *turannos* 'tyrant' + *sauros* 'lizard'.

tyranny • n. (pl. **tyrannies**) **1** cruel and oppressive government or rule. **2** a state under such rule.
– DERIVATIVES **tyrannous** adj.

tyrant • n. a cruel and oppressive person, especially a ruler.
– ORIGIN Greek *turannos.*

Tyre E
/ty-er/ a port in Lebanon, on the Mediterranean. Founded in the 2nd millennium BC, it was a major Phoenician port and trading centre.

tyre (US **tire**) • **n.** a rubber covering that is inflated or that surrounds an inflated inner tube, that fits around a wheel to form a soft contact with the road.
– ORIGIN prob. from **ATTIRE**.

tyro /ty-roh/ • **n.** (pl. **tyros**) a beginner or novice.
– ORIGIN Latin, 'recruit'.

Tyrol E
/ti-**ruhl**/ an Alpine state of Austria; capital, Innsbruck.
– DERIVATIVES **Tyrolean** /ti-ruh-lee-uhn/ adj. & n

Tyrone E
/ty-**rohn**/ one of the Six Counties of Northern Ireland; chief town, Omagh.

Tyrrhenian Sea E
/ti-ree-ni-uhn/ a part of the Mediterranean Sea between mainland Italy and the islands of Sicily and Sardinia.

Tyson, E
Mike (b.1966; full name *Michael Gerald Tyson*), American boxer, who became undisputed world heavyweight champion in 1987. He was imprisoned 1992–5 for rape; after his release he reclaimed the WBC and WBA titles in 1996.

tzar • **n.** var. of **TSAR**.

tzarina • **n.** var. of **TSARINA**.

U[1] (also **u**) • **n.** (pl. **Us** or **U's**) the twenty-first letter of the alphabet.

U[2] • **abbrev. 1** (in names of sports clubs) United. **2** Brit. universal (referring to films classified as suitable for everyone to see).

Ubanghi Shari E
/yoo-bang-gi shah-ri/ former name for **CENTRAL AFRICAN REPUBLIC**.

U-bend • **n.** a section of a waste pipe shaped like a U.

ubiquitous /yoo-bi-kwi-tuhss/ • **adj.** present, appearing, or found everywhere.
– DERIVATIVES **ubiquitously** adv. **ubiquity** n.
– ORIGIN Latin *ubique* 'everywhere'.

U-boat • **n.** a German submarine of the First or Second World War.
– ORIGIN German *U-boot*, short for *Unterseeboot* 'undersea boat'.

UCAS /yoo-kass/ • **abbrev.** (in the UK) Universities and Colleges Admissions Service.

Uccello E
/oo-**chel**-loh/, Paolo (*c.*1397–1475; born *Paolo di Dono*), Italian painter. His paintings, such as *The Rout of San Romano*, are early examples of the use of perspective.

UDA • **abbrev.** Ulster Defence Association.

udder • **n.** the milk-producing gland of female cattle, sheep, goats, horses, etc., hanging near the hind legs as a bag-like organ with two or more teats.
– ORIGIN Old English.

UDR • **abbrev.** Ulster Defence Regiment.

UEFA /yoo-ee-fuh, yoo-ay-fuh/ • **abbrev.** Union of European Football Associations.

Uffizi E
/uuf-**feet**-si/ an important art gallery and museum in Florence.

UFO • **n.** (pl. **UFOs**) a mysterious object seen in the sky for which it is claimed no scientific explanation can be found, believed by some to be a vehicle carrying beings from outer space.
– ORIGIN short for *unidentified flying object*.

Uganda E
/yoo-**gan**-duh/ a country in East Africa; capital, Kampala.
– DERIVATIVES **Ugandan** adj. & n.

Ugli fruit /ug-li/ • **n.** (pl. **Ugli fruit**) trademark a mottled green and yellow citrus fruit which is a hybrid of a grapefruit and tangerine.
– ORIGIN from **UGLY**.

ugly • **adj.** (**uglier**, **ugliest**) **1** unpleasant or unattractive in appearance. **2** hostile or threatening: *the mood in the room turned ugly*.
– DERIVATIVES **ugliness** n.
– ORIGIN Old Norse, 'to be dreaded'.

ugly duckling • **n.** a person who turns out to be beautiful or talented against all expectations.
– ORIGIN from one of Hans Christian Andersen's fairy tales, in which the 'ugly duckling' becomes a swan.

UHF • **abbrev.** ultra-high frequency.

UHT • **abbrev.** ultra heat treated (a process used to extend the shelf life of milk).

Uist E
/yoo-ist/ two islands in the Outer Hebrides, **North Uist** and **South Uist**.

UK • **abbrev.** United Kingdom.

Ukraine E
/yoo-**krayn**/ (also **the Ukraine**) a country in eastern Europe, to the north of the Black Sea; capital, Kiev.
– DERIVATIVES **Ukrainian** adj. & n.

ukulele /yoo-kuh-lay-li/ • **n.** a small four-stringed guitar of Hawaiian origin.
– ORIGIN Hawaiian, 'jumping flea'.

Ulan Bator E
/oo-lahn **bah**-ter/ (also **Ulaanbaatar**) the capital of Mongolia. Former name (until 1924) **Urga**.

Ulanova E
/oo-**lah**-nuh-vuh/, Galina (Sergeevna) (1910–98), Russian ballet dancer.

ulcer • n. an open sore on the body or on a bodily organ.
– DERIVATIVES **ulcerous** adj.
– ORIGIN Latin *ulcus*.

ulcerate • v. (**ulcerates, ulcerating, ulcerated**) develop into or become affected by an ulcer.
– DERIVATIVES **ulceration** n.

-ule • suffix forming nouns conveying smallness: *capsule*.
– ORIGIN Latin *-ulus, -ula, -ulum*.

ullage /ul-lij/ • n. **1** the amount by which a container falls short of being full. **2** loss of liquid by evaporation or leakage.
– ORIGIN Old French *euillier* 'fill up'.

ulna /ul-nuh/ • n. (pl. **ulnae** /ul-nee/ or **ulnas**) the thinner and longer of the two bones in the human forearm.
– DERIVATIVES **ulnar** adj.
– ORIGIN Latin.

Ulster[1] E
a former province of Ireland, in the north of the island. The nine counties of Ulster are now divided between Northern Ireland and the Republic of Ireland.

Ulster[2] E
(in general use) Northern Ireland.

ulster • n. a man's long, loose overcoat of rough cloth.
– ORIGIN from **Ulster**[1], where it was originally sold.

Ulsterman (or **Ulsterwoman**) • n. a person from Northern Ireland or Ulster.

ulterior • adj. other than what is obvious or admitted: *she had some ulterior motive in coming.*
– ORIGIN Latin, 'further, more distant'.

ultimate • adj. **1** being or happening at the end of a process; final. **2** being the best or most extreme example of its kind: *the ride gained the ultimate accolade of three stars.* **3** basic or fundamental: *atoms are the ultimate constituents of anything that exists.* • n. (**the ultimate**) the best imaginable of its kind: *the ultimate in decorative luxury.*
– DERIVATIVES **ultimately** adv.
– ORIGIN Latin *ultimatus*.

ultimatum /ul-ti-**may**-tuhm/ • n. (pl. **ultimatums** or **ultimata** /ul-ti-**may**-tuh/) a final warning issued by a person or country to another party that action will be taken unless that party agrees to meet their demands.
– ORIGIN Latin, 'thing that has come to an end'.

ultra informal • adv. very: *ultra modern furniture.*

ultra- • prefix **1** beyond; on the other side of: *ultramarine.* **2** extreme; extremely: *ultramicroscopic.*
– ORIGIN Latin *ultra*.

ultra-high frequency • n. a radio frequency in the range 300 to 3,000 megahertz.

ultramarine • n. a brilliant deep blue pigment and colour.
– ORIGIN Latin *ultramarinus* 'beyond the sea' (because the pigment was obtained from lapis lazuli, which was imported).

ultramicroscope • n. a microscope used to detect very small particles by observing light scattered from them.
– DERIVATIVES **ultramicroscopic** adj.

ultrasonic • adj. involving sound waves with a frequency above the upper limit of human hearing. • n. (**ultrasonics**) **1** the science and application of ultrasonic waves. **2** ultrasound.
– DERIVATIVES **ultrasonically** adv.

ultrasound • n. sound or other vibrations having an ultrasonic frequency, used in medical scans.

ultraviolet • n. electromagnetic radiation having a wavelength just shorter than that of violet light but longer than that of X-rays. • adj. referring to such radiation.

ultra vires /ul-truh **vy**-reez, uul-trah **veer**-ayz/ • adj. & adv. beyond one's legal power or authority.
– ORIGIN Latin, 'beyond the powers'.

ululate /yoo-lyuu-layt, **ul**-yuu-layt/ • v. (**ululates, ululating, ululated**) howl or wail.
– DERIVATIVES **ululation** n.
– ORIGIN Latin *ululare*.

Uluru E
/uu-**loo**-uh-roo/ Aboriginal name for **Ayers Rock**.

Ulysses E
/yoo-li-seez/ Rom. Myth. Roman name for **Odysseus**.

umbel /um-buhl/ • n. Bot. a flower cluster in which stalks spring from a common centre and form a flat or curved surface.
– ORIGIN Latin *umbella* 'sunshade'.

umber /*rhymes with* number/ • n. a natural pigment, normally dark yellowish-brown in colour (**raw umber**) or dark brown when roasted (**burnt umber**).
– ORIGIN from French *terre d'ombre*, 'earth of shadow'.

umbilical /um-**bil**-i-k'l, um-bi-**ly**-k'l/ • adj. having to do with the navel or umbilical cord.
– DERIVATIVES **umbilically** adv.

umbilical cord • n. a flexible cord-like structure containing blood vessels, attaching a fetus to the placenta and nourishing it while it is in the womb.

umbilicus /um-**bil**-li-kuhss, um-bi-**ly**-kuhss/ • n. (pl. **umbilici** /um-**bil**-li-sy, um-bi-**ly**-sy/ or **umbilicuses**) Anat. the navel.
– ORIGIN Latin.

umbra /um-bruh/ • n. (pl. **umbras** or **umbrae** /um-bree/) the dark central part of the shadow cast by the earth or the moon in an eclipse, or of a sunspot.
– ORIGIN Latin, 'shade'.

umbrage /um-brij/ • n. (in phr. **take umbrage**) take offence or become annoyed.
– ORIGIN first meaning 'shade, ground for suspicion': from Latin *umbra*.

umbrella • n. a device consisting of a circular fabric canopy on a folding metal frame supported by a central rod, used as protection against rain. • adj. including or containing

many different parts: *an umbrella organization.*
– ORIGIN Italian *ombrella.*

Umbria E
/**um**-bri-uh/ a region of central Italy; capital, Perugia.

umlaut /**uum**-lowt/ ● **n.** a mark (¨) used over a vowel in some languages to indicate how it should be pronounced.
– ORIGIN German.

Umm al Qaiwain E
/uum al ky-**wyn**/ one of the seven member states of the United Arab Emirates.

umpire ● **n.** (in certain sports) an official who enforces the rules of a game and settles disputes arising from the play. ● **v.** (**umpires, umpiring, umpired**) act as an umpire.
– ORIGIN Old French *nonper* 'not equal'.

umpteen ● **cardinal number** informal very many.
– DERIVATIVES **umpteenth** ordinal number.

UN ● **abbrev.** United Nations.

un-[1] ● **prefix 1** (added to adjectives, participles, and their derivatives) not: *unacademic.* **2** (added to nouns) a lack of: *untruth.*
– ORIGIN Old English.

USAGE **un-**
For an explanation of the difference between the prefixes **un-** and **non-**, see the note at **NON-**.

un-[2] ● **prefix** added to verbs: **1** referring to the reversal or cancellation of an action or state: *unsettle.* **2** referring to deprivation, separation, or change to a lesser state: *unmask.*
– ORIGIN Old English.

unabashed ● **adj.** not embarrassed or ashamed.

unabated ● **adj.** without any reduction in intensity or strength.

unable ● **adj.** not having the skill, means, strength, or opportunity to do something.

unabridged ● **adj.** (of a text) not cut or shortened.

unacceptable ● **adj.** not satisfactory or allowable.
– DERIVATIVES **unacceptability** n. **unacceptably** adv.

unaccompanied ● **adj. 1** having no companion or escort. **2** without instrumental accompaniment. **3** without something specified occurring at the same time.

unaccountable ● **adj. 1** unable to be explained. **2** not responsible for or required to explain the outcome of something.
– DERIVATIVES **unaccountably** adv.

unaccounted ● **adj.** (**unaccounted for**) not taken into consideration or explained.

unaccustomed ● **adj. 1** not usual or customary. **2** (**unaccustomed to**) not familiar with or used to.

unacknowledged ● **adj. 1** existing or having taken place but not accepted or admitted to. **2** (of a person or their work) deserving but not receiving recognition.

unacquainted ● **adj. 1** (**unacquainted with**) having no experience of or familiarity with. **2** not having met before.

unadulterated ● **adj. 1** not mixed with any different or inferior substances. **2** complete; total: *pure, unadulterated jealousy.*

unadventurous ● **adj.** not offering, involving, or eager for new or exciting things.

unadvisedly ● **adv.** in an unwise or rash way.

unaffected ● **adj. 1** feeling or showing no effects. **2** (of a person) sincere and genuine.

unaffiliated ● **adj.** not officially attached to or connected with an organization.

unaffordable ● **adj.** too expensive to be afforded by the average person.

unafraid ● **adj.** feeling no fear.

unaided ● **adj.** needing or having no help.

unalike ● **adj.** differing from each other.

unalloyed ● **adj. 1** (of metal) not alloyed. **2** complete; total: *unalloyed delight.*

unaltered ● **adj.** remaining the same.

unambiguous ● **adj.** not open to more than one interpretation; clear in meaning.
– DERIVATIVES **unambiguously** adv.

unambitious ● **adj. 1** not motivated by a strong desire to succeed. **2** (of a plan or piece of work) not involving anything new, exciting, or demanding.

un-American ● **adj. 1** not American in nature. **2** US, esp. hist. against the interests of the US and therefore treasonable.

unanimous /yoo-**nan**-i-muhss/ ● **adj. 1** fully in agreement. **2** (of an opinion, decision, or vote) held or carried by everyone involved.
– DERIVATIVES **unanimity** /yoo-nuh-**nim**-i-ti/ n. **unanimously** adv.
– ORIGIN Latin *unanimus.*

unannounced ● **adj.** without warning or notice: *he arrived unannounced.*

unanswerable ● **adj. 1** unable to be answered. **2** unable to be proved wrong.

unanswered ● **adj.** not answered.

unapologetic ● **adj.** not sorry for one's actions.
– DERIVATIVES **unapologetically** adv.

unappealing ● **adj.** not inviting or attractive.

unappetizing (also **unappetising**) ● **adj.** not inviting or attractive.

unappreciated ● **adj.** not fully understood, recognized, or valued.

unappreciative ● **adj.** not fully understanding or recognizing something.

unapproachable ● **adj.** not welcoming or friendly.

unarguable ● **adj.** not able to be disagreed with.
– DERIVATIVES **unarguably** adv.

unarmed ● **adj.** not equipped with or carrying weapons.

unashamed ● **adj.** feeling or showing no guilt or embarrassment.
– DERIVATIVES **unashamedly** adv.

unasked ● **adj. 1** (of a question) not asked. **2** without being asked or invited.

unassailable ● **adj.** unable to be attacked, questioned, or defeated.

unassertive ● **adj.** not having or showing a confident and forceful personality.

unassisted ● **adj.** not helped by anyone or anything.

unassuming ● **adj.** not wanting to draw attention to oneself or one's abilities.

unattached ● **adj.** without a husband or wife or established lover.

unattainable ● **adj.** not able to be reached or

achieved.

unattended • adj. without the owner or a responsible person present; not being watched or looked after.

unattractive • adj. not pleasing, appealing, or inviting.
– DERIVATIVES **unattractively** adv. **unattractiveness** n.

unattributed • adj. (of a quotation, story, or work of art) of unknown or unpublished origin.
– DERIVATIVES **unattributable** adj.

unauthorized (also **unauthorised**) • adj. not having official permission or approval.

unavailable • adj. **1** not able to be used or obtained. **2** (of a person) not free to do something.
– DERIVATIVES **unavailability** n.

unavailing • adj. achieving little or nothing.

unavoidable • adj. not able to be avoided or prevented.
– DERIVATIVES **unavoidably** adv.

unaware • adj. having no knowledge of a situation or fact. • adv. (**unawares**) so as to surprise; unexpectedly.

unbalance • v. (**unbalances**, **unbalancing**, **unbalanced**) **1** upset the balance of. **2** (**unbalanced**) emotionally or mentally disturbed. **3** (**unbalanced**) not giving equal coverage or treatment to all aspects.

unbearable • adj. not able to be endured.
– DERIVATIVES **unbearably** adv.

unbeatable • adj. not able to be bettered or beaten.

unbeaten • adj. not defeated or bettered.

unbecoming • adj. **1** not flattering: *an unbecoming red dress.* **2** (of behaviour) improper; unseemly.

unbeknown (also **unbeknownst**) • adj. (**unbeknown to**) without the knowledge of.

unbelievable • adj. **1** unlikely to be true. **2** extraordinary.
– DERIVATIVES **unbelievably** adv.

unbeliever • n. a person without religious belief.

unbend • v. (**unbends**, **unbending**, **unbent**) **1** straighten. **2** become less formal or strict.

unbending • adj. unwilling to change one's mind; inflexible.

unbiased (also **unbiassed**) • adj. showing no prejudice.

unbidden • adj. without having been invited.

unbleached • adj. not bleached.

unblock • v. remove an obstruction from.

unblushing • adj. not feeling or showing embarrassment or shame.
– DERIVATIVES **unblushingly** adv.

unborn • adj. (of a baby) not yet born.

unbound • adj. not bound or tied up.

unbounded • adj. having no limits.

unbowed • adj. not having been defeated.

unbreakable • adj. not able to be broken.

unbridgeable • adj. (of a gap or difference between two people) not able to be closed or made less significant.

unbridled • adj. uncontrolled: *unbridled lust.*

unbroken • adj. **1** not broken or interrupted. **2** (of a record in sport) not beaten. **3** (of a horse) not broken in.

unbuckle • v. (**unbuckles**, **unbuckling**, **unbuckled**) unfasten the buckle of.

unburden • v. (**unburden oneself**) confide in someone about a worry or problem.

unbutton • v. unfasten the buttons of.

uncalled • adj. (**uncalled for**) undesirable and unnecessary.

uncanny • adj. strange or mysterious.
– DERIVATIVES **uncannily** adv.

uncared • adj. (**uncared for**) not looked after properly.

uncaring • adj. not sympathetic to or concerned for others.

unceasing • adj. not ceasing; continuous.
– DERIVATIVES **unceasingly** adv.

unceremonious • adj. impolite or abrupt.
– DERIVATIVES **unceremoniously** adv.

uncertain • adj. **1** not known, reliable, or definite. **2** not completely confident or sure.
– PHRASES **in no uncertain terms** clearly and forcefully.
– DERIVATIVES **uncertainly** adv.

uncertainty • n. (pl. **uncertainties**) **1** the state of being uncertain. **2** something that is uncertain or causes one to feel uncertain.

unchallengeable • adj. not able to be questioned or opposed.

unchallenged • adj. not questioned or opposed.

unchanged • adj. not changed.

unchanging • adj. remaining the same.

uncharacteristic • adj. not typical of a particular person or thing.
– DERIVATIVES **uncharacteristically** adv.

uncharismatic • adj. lacking attractiveness and charm.

uncharitable • adj. unkind or unsympathetic to others.
– DERIVATIVES **uncharitably** adv.

uncharted • adj. (of an area of land or sea) not mapped or surveyed.

unchecked • adj. (of something undesirable) not controlled or restrained.

unchristian • adj. **1** not in line with the teachings of Christianity. **2** ungenerous or unfair.

uncircumcised • adj. (of a boy or man) not circumcised.

uncivil • adj. not polite.

uncivilized (also **uncivilised**) • adj. **1** (of a place or people) not having developed a modern culture or way of life. **2** not behaving in accordance with accepted moral standards.

unclaimed • adj. not having been claimed.

unclasp • v. unfasten (a clasp or similar device).

unclassified • adj. not classified.

uncle • n. the brother of one's father or mother or the husband of one's aunt.
– ORIGIN Latin *avunculus* 'maternal uncle'.

unclean • adj. **1** dirty. **2** immoral. **3** (of food) considered impure and forbidden by a particular religion.

unclear • adj. not easy to see, hear, or understand.

unclench • v. release (a clenched part of the body).

Uncle Sam • n. the United States or its government, often shown as a tall man with a tall hat and white beard.

unclog • v. (**unclogs**, **unclogging**, **un-**

clogged) remove a blockage from.
unclothed • adj. naked.
unclouded • adj. **1** (of the sky) not dark or overcast. **2** not spoiled by anything: *unclouded happiness.*
uncluttered • adj. not cluttered by too many objects or unnecessary items.
uncoil • v. straighten from a coiled position.
uncoloured (US **uncolored**) • adj. **1** having no colour. **2** not influenced: *her views were uncoloured by her husband's.*
uncomfortable • adj. **1** not physically comfortable. **2** uneasy or awkward.
– DERIVATIVES **uncomfortably** adv.
uncommercial • adj. not making or intended to make a profit.
uncommon • adj. **1** out of the ordinary; unusual. **2** remarkably great.
– DERIVATIVES **uncommonly** adv.
uncommunicative • adj. unwilling to talk or give out information.
uncompetitive • adj. not cheaper or better than others and therefore not able to compete commercially.
uncomplaining • adj. not complaining.
– DERIVATIVES **uncomplainingly** adv.
uncomplicated • adj. simple or straightforward.
uncomplimentary • adj. rude or insulting.
uncomprehending • adj. unable to understand something.
– DERIVATIVES **uncomprehendingly** adv.
uncompromising • adj. **1** unwilling to change one's mind or behaviour. **2** harsh or relentless.
– DERIVATIVES **uncompromisingly** adv.
unconcealed • adj. not concealed; obvious.
unconcern • n. a lack of worry or interest.
– DERIVATIVES **unconcerned** adj.
unconditional • adj. not subject to any conditions.
– DERIVATIVES **unconditionally** adv.
unconfined • adj. **1** not confined to a limited space. **2** (of joy or excitement) very great.
unconfirmed • adj. not yet proved to be true.
uncongenial • adj. **1** not friendly or pleasant to be with. **2** not suitable: *the atmosphere was uncongenial to good conversation.*
unconnected • adj. **1** not joined together or to something else. **2** not associated or linked in a sequence.
unconscionable /un-**kon**-shuh-nuh-b'l/ • adj. not right or reasonable.
– DERIVATIVES **unconscionably** adv.
– ORIGIN from former *conscionable* 'conscientious'.
unconscious • adj. **1** not awake and aware of and responding to one's surroundings. **2** done or existing without one realizing. **3** (**unconscious of**) unaware of. • n. (**the unconscious**) the part of the mind which cannot be accessed by the conscious mind but which affects behaviour and emotions.
– DERIVATIVES **unconsciously** adv. **unconsciousness** n.
unconstitutional • adj. not in accordance with the constitution or a country or the rules of an organization.
unconstrained • adj. not restricted or limited.
unconsummated • adj. (of a marriage) not having been consummated.
uncontaminated • adj. not contaminated.
uncontentious • adj. not causing or likely to cause disagreement or controversy.
uncontested • adj. not contested.
uncontrollable • adj. not controllable.
– DERIVATIVES **uncontrollably** adv.
uncontrolled • adj. not controlled.
uncontroversial • adj. not controversial.
unconventional • adj. not following what is generally done or believed.
– DERIVATIVES **unconventionality** n. **unconventionally** adv.
unconvinced • adj. not certain that something is true or can be relied on.
unconvincing • adj. failing to convince or impress.
– DERIVATIVES **unconvincingly** adv.
uncooked • adj. not cooked; raw.
uncool • adj. informal not fashionable or impressive.
uncooperative • adj. unwilling to help others or do what they ask.
uncoordinated • adj. **1** badly organized. **2** clumsy.
uncorroborated • adj. not supported or confirmed by evidence.
uncountable • adj. too many to be counted.
uncouth • adj. lacking good manners.
– ORIGIN Old English, 'unknown'.
uncover • v. (**uncovers**, **uncovering**, **uncovered**) **1** remove a cover or covering from. **2** discover (something previously secret or unknown).
uncritical • adj. not willing to criticize or judge something.
– DERIVATIVES **uncritically** adv.
uncross • v. **1** move (something) back from a crossed position. **2** (**uncrossed**) Brit. (of a cheque) not crossed.
uncrowned • adj. not formally crowned as a king or queen.
unction /ungk-sh'n/ • n. **1** formal the smearing of someone with oil or ointment as a religious ceremony. **2** excessive politeness or flattery.
– ORIGIN Latin.
unctuous /ungk-tyuu-uhss/ • adj. excessively flattering or friendly.
– DERIVATIVES **unctuously** adv.
uncultivated • adj. **1** (of land) not used for growing crops. **2** not highly educated.
uncultured • adj. not having good taste, manners, or education.
uncut • adj. not cut.
undamaged • adj. not damaged.
undated • adj. not provided or marked with a date.
undaunted • adj. not discouraged by difficulty, danger, or disappointment.
undeceive • v. (**undeceives**, **undeceiving**, **undeceived**) tell (someone) that an idea or belief is mistaken.
undecided • adj. **1** (of a person) not having made a decision. **2** not settled or resolved.
undefeated • adj. not defeated.
undefined • adj. not clear or defined.
– DERIVATIVES **undefinable** adj.
undemanding • adj. not demanding.
undemocratic • adj. not according to the

principles of democracy.
– DERIVATIVES **undemocratically** adv.
undemonstrative • adj. not tending to express feelings openly.
undeniable • adj. unable to be denied or questioned.
– DERIVATIVES **undeniably** adv.
under • prep. **1** extending or directly below: *stores of gas under the North Sea.* **2** at a lower level, layer, or grade than. **3** expressing control by (another): *I was under his spell.* **4** according to the rules of. **5** used to express grouping or classification. **6** undergoing (a process): *the hotel is still under construction.* • adv. extending or directly below something.
– PHRASES **under way 1** (of a boat) moving through the water. **2** having started and making progress.
– ORIGIN Old English.
under- • prefix **1** below; beneath: *undercover.* **2** lower in status: *undersecretary.* **3** insufficiently; incompletely: *undernourished.*
underachieve • v. (**underachieves, underachieving, underachieved**) do less well than is expected.
– DERIVATIVES **underachievement** n. **underachiever** n.
under age • adj. too young to take part legally in a particular activity.
underarm • adj. & adv. (of a throw or stroke in sport) made with the arm or hand below shoulder level. • n. a person's armpit.
underbelly • n. (pl. **underbellies**) **1** the soft underside of an animal. **2** a hidden unpleasant or criminal part of society.
undercarriage • n. **1** a wheeled structure beneath an aircraft which supports the aircraft on the ground. **2** the supporting frame under the body of a vehicle.
undercharge • v. (**undercharges, undercharging, undercharged**) charge (someone) a price or amount that is too low.
underclass • n. the lowest social class in a country or community, consisting of the poor and unemployed.
underclothes • pl. n. clothes worn under others next to the skin.
– DERIVATIVES **underclothing** n.
undercoat • n. a layer of paint applied after the primer and before the topcoat.
undercover • adj. & adv. involving secret work for investigation or spying.
undercurrent • n. **1** a current of water below the surface and moving in a different direction from any surface current. **2** an underlying feeling or influence.
undercut • v. (**undercuts, undercutting, undercut**) **1** offer goods or services at a lower price than (a competitor). **2** cut or wear away the part under. **3** weaken; undermine: *the chairman's authority was being undercut.*
underdeveloped • adj. **1** not fully developed. **2** (of a country or region) not advanced economically.
underdog • n. a competitor thought to have little chance of winning a fight or contest.
underdone • adj. (of food) not cooked enough.
underdress • v. (**be underdressed**) be dressed too plainly or informally for a particular occasion.
underemployed • adj. not having enough work.
– DERIVATIVES **underemployment** n.
underestimate • v. (**underestimates, underestimating, underestimated**) **1** estimate (something) to be smaller or less important than it really is. **2** think of (someone) as less capable than they really are. • n. an estimate that is too low.
– DERIVATIVES **underestimation** n.
underfed • adj. not fed or nourished enough.
underfelt • n. Brit. felt laid under a carpet for protection or support.
underfoot • adv. **1** under one's feet; on the ground. **2** constantly present and in one's way.
underfund • v. fail to provide with enough funding.
– DERIVATIVES **underfunding** n.
undergarment • n. an article of underclothing.
undergo • v. (**undergoes, undergoing, underwent**; past part. **undergone**) experience (something unpleasant or difficult).
– ORIGIN Old English, 'undermine'.
undergraduate • n. a student at a university who has not yet taken a first degree.
underground • adj. & adv. **1** beneath the surface of the ground. **2** in secrecy or hiding. • n. **1** Brit. an underground railway. **2** a secret group or movement working against an existing government.
undergrowth • n. a dense growth of shrubs and other plants.
underhand • adj. acting or done in a secret or dishonest way.
underlay[1] • v. (**underlays, underlaying, underlaid**) place something under (something else) to support or raise it. • n. material laid under a carpet for protection or support.
underlay[2] past tense of **UNDERLIE**.
underlie • v. (**underlies, underlying, underlay**; past part. **underlain**) lie or be situated under.
– DERIVATIVES **underlying** adj.
underline • v. (**underlines, underlining, underlined**) **1** draw a line under (a word or phrase) for emphasis. **2** emphasize.
underling • n. esp. derog. a person of lower status.
underlying pres. part. of **UNDERLIE**.
underman • v. (**undermans, undermanning, undermanned**) fail to provide with enough workers.
undermine • v. (**undermines, undermining, undermined**) **1** damage or weaken: *this could undermine years of hard work.* **2** wear away the base or foundation of (a rock formation). **3** dig beneath (a building) so as to make it collapse.
underneath • prep. & adv. **1** situated directly below. **2** so as to be hidden by. • n. the part or side facing towards the ground.
– ORIGIN Old English.
undernourished • adj. not having enough food or the right type of food for good health.
– DERIVATIVES **undernourishment** n.
underpaid past and past part. of **UNDERPAY**.
underpants • pl. n. an undergarment covering the lower part of the body and having two holes for the legs.
underpart • n. a lower part or portion.

underpass ● n. a road or tunnel passing under another road or a railway.

underpay ● v. (**underpays**, **underpaying**, **underpaid**) pay too little to (someone) or for (something).

underperform ● v. perform less well than expected.
– DERIVATIVES **underperformance** n.

underpin ● v. (**underpins**, **underpinning**, **underpinned**) **1** support (a structure) from below by laying a solid foundation or replacing weak materials with stronger ones. **2** support or form the basis for (an argument, claim, etc.).

underplay ● v. try to make (something) seem less important than it really is.

underprivileged ● adj. not enjoying the same rights or standard of living as the majority of the population.

underrate ● v. (**underrates**, **underrating**, **underrated**) fail to recognize the real extent, value, or importance of.

underscore ● v. (**underscores**, **underscoring**, **underscored**) = **UNDERLINE**.

undersea ● adj. relating to or situated below the sea or the surface of the sea.

undersecretary ● n. (pl. **undersecretaries**) (in the UK) a junior minister or senior civil servant.

undersell ● v. (**undersells**, **underselling**, **undersold**) sell something at a lower price than (a competitor).

undershirt ● n. N. Amer. an undergarment worn under a shirt; a vest.

undershoot ● v. (**undershoots**, **undershooting**, **undershot**) fall short of (a point or target).

underside ● n. the bottom or lower side or surface of something.

undersigned ● n. (**the undersigned**) formal the person or people who have signed the document in question.

undersized (also **undersize**) ● adj. of less than the usual size.

underskirt ● n. a petticoat.

undersold past and past part. of **UNDERSELL**.

underspend ● v. (**underspends**, **underspending**, **underspent**) spend too little or less than has been planned.

understaffed ● adj. (of an organization) having too few members of staff to operate effectively.

understand ● v. (**understands**, **understanding**, **understood**) **1** know or realize the intended meaning of (words or a speaker). **2** know or be aware of the importance or cause of. **3** know how (someone) feels or why they behave in a particular way. **4** believe to be the case from information received: *I understand you're at university.* **5** supply (a missing word or phrase) in one's mind.

understandable ● adj. **1** able to be understood. **2** to be expected; normal or reasonable.
– DERIVATIVES **understandably** adv.

understanding ● n. **1** the ability to understand something. **2** intellect: *a child of sufficient intelligence and understanding.* **3** a person's judgement of a situation. **4** sympathetic awareness or tolerance. **5** an informal or unspoken agreement. ● adj. sympathetically aware of other people's feelings.
– DERIVATIVES **understandingly** adv.

understate ● v. (**understates**, **understating**, **understated**) describe or represent (something) as being smaller or less important than it really is.
– DERIVATIVES **understatement** n.

understated ● adj. presented or expressed in a subtle and effective way.

understood past and past part. of **UNDERSTAND**.

understudy ● n. (pl. **understudies**) an actor who learns another's role in order to be able to act in their absence. ● v. (**understudies**, **understudying**, **understudied**) be an understudy for.

undersubscribed ● adj. (of a course or event) having more places available than applications.

undertake ● v. (**undertake**, **undertaking**, **undertook**; past part. **undertaken**) **1** make oneself responsible for and begin (an activity). **2** formally guarantee or promise.

undertaker ● n. a person whose business is preparing dead bodies for burial or cremation and making arrangements for funerals.

undertaking ● n. **1** a formal promise to do something. **2** a task that is taken on. **3** the management of funerals as a profession.

undertone ● n. **1** a subdued or muted tone of sound or colour. **2** an underlying quality or feeling.

undertow ● n. = **UNDERCURRENT**.

underuse ● v. /un-der-yooz/ (**underuses**, **underusing**, **underused**) fail to use (something) enough. ● n. /un-der-yooss/ insufficient use.

undervalue ● v. (**undervalues**, **undervaluing**, **undervalued**) **1** fail to rate highly enough. **2** underestimate how much (something) is worth.

underwater ● adj. & adv. situated or occurring beneath the surface of the water.

underwear ● n. clothing worn under other clothes next to the skin.

underweight ● adj. below a weight considered normal or desirable.

underwent past of **UNDERGO**.

underwhelm ● v. humorous fail to impress or make a good impact on.
– ORIGIN from **OVERWHELM**.

underwired ● adj. (of a bra) having a semicircular wire support stitched under each cup.

underworld ● n. **1** the world of criminals or of organized crime. **2** (in myths and legends) the home of the dead, imagined as being under the earth.

underwrite ● v. (**underwrites**, **underwriting**, **underwrote**; past part. **underwritten**) **1** sign and accept legal responsibility for (an insurance policy). **2** finance or otherwise support or guarantee.
– DERIVATIVES **underwriter** n.

undeserved ● adj. not deserved or earned.
– DERIVATIVES **undeservedly** adv.

undeserving ● adj. not deserving or worthy of something good.

undesirable ● adj. harmful, offensive, or unpleasant. ● n. an unpleasant or offensive person.

undesired ● adj. not wanted or desired.

undetectable • adj. not able to be detected.

undetected • adj. not detected or discovered.

undetermined • adj. not firmly decided or settled.

undeterred • adj. persevering despite setbacks.

undeveloped • adj. not having developed or been developed.

undeviating • adj. constant and steady.

undid past of UNDO.

undies • pl. n. informal articles of underwear.

undifferentiated • adj. not different or recognized as different.

undigested • adj. **1** (of food) not digested. **2** (of information) not having been properly understood or absorbed.

undignified • adj. appearing foolish.

undiluted • adj. **1** (of a liquid) not diluted. **2** not moderated or weakened in any way: *pure, undiluted happiness.*

undiminished • adj. not reduced or lessened.

undiplomatic • adj. insensitive and tactless.

undisciplined • adj. uncontrolled in behaviour or manner.

undisclosed • adj. not revealed or made known.

undiscovered • adj. not discovered.

undiscriminating • adj. lacking good judgement or taste.

undisguised • adj. (of a feeling) not disguised or concealed.

undismayed • adj. not dismayed or discouraged by a setback.

undisputed • adj. not disputed or called in question.

undistinguished • adj. not very good or impressive.

undisturbed • adj. not disturbed.

undivided • adj. **1** not divided, separated, or broken into parts. **2** devoted completely to one object: *you have my undivided attention.*

undo • v. (**undoes**, **undoing**, **undid**; past part. **undone**) **1** unfasten or loosen. **2** cancel or reverse the effects of (a previous action). **3** formal cause the downfall of: *Iago's hatred of women undoes him.*

undocumented • adj. not recorded in or proved by documents.

undoing • n. a person's ruin or downfall.

undone • adj. **1** not tied or fastened. **2** not done or finished. **3** archaic or humorous ruined by a disastrous setback.

undoubted • adj. not questioned or doubted by anyone.
– DERIVATIVES **undoubtedly** adv.

undreamed /un-**dreemd**, un-**dremt**/ (Brit. also **undreamt** /un-**dremt**/) • adj. (**undreamed of**) not previously thought to be possible.

undress • v. **1** (also **get undressed**) take off one's clothes. **2** take the clothes off (someone else). • n. the state of being naked or only partially clothed.

undressed • adj. **1** wearing no clothes. **2** not treated, processed, or prepared for use. **3** (of food) not having a dressing.

undrinkable • adj. not fit to be drunk because of impurity or poor quality.

undue • adj. more than is reasonable or necessary; excessive.
– DERIVATIVES **unduly** adv.

undulate /un-dyuu-layt/ • v. (**undulates**, **undulating**, **undulated**) **1** move with a smooth wave-like motion. **2** have a wavy form or outline.
– DERIVATIVES **undulation** n.
– ORIGIN Latin *undulatus.*

undyed • adj. (of fabric) not dyed; of its natural colour.

undying • adj. lasting forever.

unearned • adj. not earned or deserved.

unearned income • n. income from investments rather than from work.

unearth • v. **1** find in the ground by digging. **2** discover by investigation or searching.

unearthly • adj. **1** unnatural or mysterious. **2** informal unreasonably early or inconvenient: *she couldn't call the doctor at such an unearthly hour.*

unease • n. anxiety or discontent.

uneasy • adj. (**uneasier**, **uneasiest**) troubled or uncomfortable.
– DERIVATIVES **uneasily** adv. **uneasiness** n.

uneatable • adj. not fit to be eaten.

uneaten • adj. not eaten.

uneconomic • adj. not profitable or making efficient use of resources.

uneconomical • adj. wasteful of money or other resources.

unedifying • adj. distasteful or unpleasant.

uneducated • adj. poorly educated.

unelectable • adj. very likely to be defeated at an election.

unelected • adj. (of an official) not elected.

unembarrassed • adj. not feeling or showing embarrassment.

unemotional • adj. not having or showing strong feelings.

unemployable • adj. not able to get paid employment because of a lack of skills or qualifications.

unemployed • adj. **1** without a paid job but available to work. **2** (of a thing) not in use.

unemployment • n. **1** the state of being unemployed. **2** the number or proportion of unemployed people.

unemployment benefit • n. payment made by the state or a trade union to an unemployed person.

unencumbered • adj. not having any burden or obstacle to one's progress.

unending • adj. seeming to last or continue for ever.

unendurable • adj. not able to be tolerated or endured.

unenlightened • adj. not reasonable and tolerant in outlook.

unenterprising • adj. lacking initiative or resourcefulness.

unenthusiastic • adj. not having or showing enthusiasm.
– DERIVATIVES **unenthusiastically** adv.

unenviable • adj. difficult, undesirable, or unpleasant.

unequal • adj. **1** not equal in quantity, size, or value. **2** not fair or evenly balanced. **3** (**unequal to**) not having the ability or resources to meet (a challenge).

– DERIVATIVES **unequally** adv.
unequalled (US **unequaled**) • **adj.** better or greater than all others.
unequivocal • **adj.** leaving no doubt; clear in meaning: *an unequivocal answer.*
– DERIVATIVES **unequivocally** adv.
unerring • **adj.** always right or accurate.
– DERIVATIVES **unerringly** adv.
UNESCO /yoo-ness-koh/ • **abbrev.** United Nations Educational, Scientific, and Cultural Organization.
unethical • **adj.** not morally correct.
– DERIVATIVES **unethically** adv.
uneven • **adj.** **1** not level or smooth. **2** not regular, consistent, or equal.
– DERIVATIVES **unevenly** adv. **unevenness** n.
uneventful • **adj.** not marked by interesting or exciting events.
– DERIVATIVES **uneventfully** adv.
unexceptionable • **adj.** not able to be objected to, but not particularly new or exciting.
unexceptional • **adj.** not out of the ordinary; usual.
– DERIVATIVES **unexceptionally** adv.
unexciting • **adj.** not exciting; dull.
unexpected • **adj.** not expected or thought likely to happen.
– DERIVATIVES **unexpectedly** adv. **unexpectedness** n.
unexplained • **adj.** not made clear or accounted for.
– DERIVATIVES **unexplainable** adj.
unexplored • **adj.** not explored, investigated, or evaluated.
unexposed • **adj.** **1** not exposed. **2** (**unexposed to**) not introduced to or knowing about.
unexpressed • **adj.** (of a thought or feeling) not communicated or made known.
unexpurgated • **adj.** (of a text) complete and containing all the original material.
unfailing • **adj.** **1** without error. **2** reliable or constant.
– DERIVATIVES **unfailingly** adv.
unfair • **adj.** not based on or showing fairness.
– DERIVATIVES **unfairly** adv. **unfairness** n.
unfaithful • **adj.** **1** not faithful; disloyal. **2** having sexual relations with a person other than one's husband, wife, or lover.
unfamiliar • **adj.** **1** not known or recognized. **2** (**unfamiliar with**) not having knowledge or experience of.
– DERIVATIVES **unfamiliarity** n.
unfashionable • **adj.** not fashionable or popular.
– DERIVATIVES **unfashionably** adv.
unfasten • **v.** open the fastening of.
unfathomable • **adj.** **1** too strange or difficult to be understood. **2** impossible to measure the depth or extent of.
unfavourable (US **unfavorable**) • **adj.** **1** expressing lack of approval. **2** unlikely to lead to success: *unfavourable circumstances.*
– DERIVATIVES **unfavourably** (US **unfavorably**) adv.
unfazed • **adj.** informal not surprised or worried by something unexpected.
unfeasible • **adj.** inconvenient or impractical.
– DERIVATIVES **unfeasibly** adv.
unfeeling • **adj.** unsympathetic, harsh, or cruel.
unfeigned • **adj.** genuine; sincere.
unfertilized (also **unfertilised**) • **adj.** not fertilized.
unfettered • **adj.** unrestrained or uninhibited.
unfilled • **adj.** vacant or empty.
unfinished • **adj.** not finished.
unfit • **adj.** **1** unsuitable or inadequate for something. **2** not in good physical condition.
unfitted • **adj.** unfit for something.
unfitting • **adj.** unsuitable or unbecoming.
unfixed • **adj.** **1** unfastened; loose. **2** uncertain or variable.
unflagging • **adj.** tireless or persistent.
unflappable • **adj.** informal calm in a crisis.
unflattering • **adj.** not flattering.
– DERIVATIVES **unflatteringly** adv.
unflinching • **adj.** not afraid or hesitant.
– DERIVATIVES **unflinchingly** adv.
unfocused (also **unfocussed**) • **adj.** **1** not focused; out of focus. **2** without a specific aim or direction.
unfold • **v.** **1** open or spread out from a folded position. **2** reveal or be revealed.
unforced • **adj.** produced naturally and without effort.
unforeseen • **adj.** not anticipated or predicted.
– DERIVATIVES **unforeseeable** adj.
unforgettable • **adj.** highly memorable.
– DERIVATIVES **unforgettably** adv.
unforgivable • **adj.** so bad as to be unable to be forgiven or excused.
– DERIVATIVES **unforgivably** adv.
unforgiven • **adj.** not forgiven.
unforgiving • **adj.** **1** not willing to forgive or excuse faults. **2** (of conditions) harsh; hostile.
unformed • **adj.** **1** without a definite form. **2** not fully developed.
unforthcoming • **adj.** **1** not willing to give out information. **2** not available when needed.
unfortunate • **adj.** **1** unlucky. **2** regrettable or inappropriate. • **n.** a person who suffers bad fortune.
– DERIVATIVES **unfortunately** adv.
unfounded • **adj.** having no basis in fact: *unfounded rumours.*
unfreeze • **v.** (**unfreezes**, **unfreezing**, **unfroze**; past part. **unfrozen**) **1** thaw. **2** remove restrictions placed on the use of (an asset).
unfrequented • **adj.** visited only rarely.
unfriendly • **adj.** (**unfriendlier**, **unfriendliest**) not friendly.
– DERIVATIVES **unfriendliness** n.
unfroze past of **UNFREEZE**.
unfrozen past part. of **UNFREEZE**.
unfulfilled • **adj.** not fulfilled.
– DERIVATIVES **unfulfilling** adj.
unfunny • **adj.** not amusing.
unfurl • **v.** spread out (something that is rolled or folded).
unfurnished • **adj.** **1** without furniture. **2** archaic not supplied.
ungainly • **adj.** clumsy; awkward.
– DERIVATIVES **ungainliness** n.

– ORIGIN from former *gainly* 'graceful', from Old Norse.

ungenerous • adj. not generous; mean.

ungentlemanly • adj. (of a man's behaviour) not well-mannered or pleasant.

ungodly • adj. **1** disrespectful to God; wicked. **2** informal inconveniently early or late: *calls at ungodly hours.*

ungovernable • adj. impossible to control or govern.

ungraceful • adj. lacking in grace; clumsy.
– DERIVATIVES **ungracefully** adv.

ungracious • adj. not polite, kind, or pleasant.
– DERIVATIVES **ungraciously** adv.

ungrammatical • adj. not following grammatical rules.
– DERIVATIVES **ungrammatically** adv.

ungrateful • adj. not feeling or showing gratitude.
– DERIVATIVES **ungratefully** adv. **ungratefulness** n.

unguarded • adj. **1** without protection or a guard. **2** not well considered; careless: *an unguarded remark.*

unguent /ung-gwuhnt/ • n. a soft greasy or thick substance used as ointment or for lubrication.
– ORIGIN Latin *unguentum.*

ungulate /ung-gyuu-luht, ung-gyuu-layt/ • n. Zool. a mammal with hoofs.
– ORIGIN Latin *ungulatus.*

unhand • v. archaic release from one's grasp.

unhappy • adj. (**unhappier**, **unhappiest**) **1** not happy. **2** unfortunate.
– DERIVATIVES **unhappily** adv. **unhappiness** n.

unharmed • adj. not harmed.

UNHCR • abbrev. United Nations High Commission for Refugees.

unhealthy • adj. (**unhealthier**, **unhealthiest**) **1** in poor health. **2** not good for health.
– DERIVATIVES **unhealthily** adv.

unheard • adj. **1** not heard or listened to. **2** (**unheard of**) previously unknown.

unheeded • adj. heard or noticed but ignored.

unheeding • adj. not paying attention.

unhelpful • adj. not helpful.
– DERIVATIVES **unhelpfully** adv.

unheralded • adj. not previously announced; without warning.

unhesitating • adj. without doubt or hesitation.
– DERIVATIVES **unhesitatingly** adv.

unhinge • v. (**unhinges**, **unhinging**, **unhinged**) make mentally unbalanced.

unhistorical • adj. not in accordance with history or historical study.

unholy • adj. **1** wicked. **2** (of an alliance) unnatural and likely to be harmful. **3** informal dreadful: *an unholy row.*

unhoped • adj. (**unhoped for**) beyond one's hopes or expectations.

unhorse • v. (**unhorses**, **unhorsing**, **unhorsed**) drag or cause to fall from a horse.

unhurried • adj. moving or acting without urgency.
– DERIVATIVES **unhurriedly** adv.

unhurt • adj. not hurt or harmed.

unhygienic • adj. not hygienic.

uni • n. (pl. **unis**) informal university.

uni- • comb. form one; having or made up of one: *unicycle.*
– ORIGIN Latin *unus.*

unicameral /yoo-ni-kam-uh-ruhl/ • adj. (of a law-making body) having a single chamber.
– ORIGIN Latin *camera* 'chamber'.

UNICEF /yoo-ni-sef/ • abbrev. United Nations Children's (originally International Children's Emergency) Fund.

unicellular • adj. Biol. consisting of a single cell.

unicorn • n. a mythical animal represented as a horse with a single horn projecting from its forehead.
– ORIGIN Latin *unicornis.*

unicycle • n. a cycle with a single wheel.
– DERIVATIVES **unicyclist** n.

unidentifiable • adj. unable to be identified.

unidentified • adj. not recognized or identified.

unification • n. the process of being unified.

uniform • adj. not varying; the same in all cases and at all times. • n. the distinctive clothing worn by members of the same organization or school.
– DERIVATIVES **uniformed** adj. **uniformity** n. **uniformly** adv.
– ORIGIN Latin *uniformis.*

unify /yoo-ni-fy/ • v. (**unifies**, **unifying**, **unified**) make or become united or uniform.
– ORIGIN Latin *unificare.*

unilateral • adj. performed by or affecting only one person, group, etc.
– DERIVATIVES **unilaterally** adv.

unimaginable • adj. impossible to imagine or understand.
– DERIVATIVES **unimaginably** adv.

unimaginative • adj. not using or showing imagination; dull.
– DERIVATIVES **unimaginatively** adv.

unimpaired • adj. not weakened or damaged.

unimpeachable • adj. beyond doubt or criticism: *an unimpeachable witness.*

unimpeded • adj. not obstructed or hindered.

unimportant • adj. lacking in importance.
– DERIVATIVES **unimportance** n.

unimpressed • adj. not impressed.

unimpressive • adj. not impressive.

uninformed • adj. lacking awareness or understanding of the facts.

uninhabitable • adj. not suitable for living in.

uninhabited • adj. without inhabitants.

uninhibited • adj. expressing oneself or acting freely.
– DERIVATIVES **uninhibitedly** adv.

uninitiated • adj. without the necessary special knowledge or experience.

uninjured • adj. not harmed or damaged.

uninspired • adj. **1** dull. **2** not filled with excitement.

uninspiring • adj. not producing excitement or interest.

unintelligent • adj. lacking intelligence.

unintelligible • adj. impossible to understand.
– DERIVATIVES **unintelligibility** n. **unintelligibly** adv.

unintended • adj. not planned or meant.

unintentional • adj. not done on purpose.
– DERIVATIVES **unintentionally** adv.

uninterested • adj. not interested or concerned.

USAGE uninterested
For an explanation of the difference between **uninterested** and **disinterested**, see the note at **DISINTERESTED**.

uninteresting • adj. not interesting.

uninterrupted • adj. **1** continuous. **2** not obstructed: *a location with uninterrupted views.*

uninvited • adj. arriving or acting without invitation.

uninviting • adj. not attractive; unpleasant.

uninvolved • adj. not involved.

union • n. **1** the action of uniting or the fact of being united: *he supported closer economic union with Europe.* **2** a state of harmony or agreement. **3** a marriage. **4** a club, society, or association formed by people with a common interest or purpose. **5** a trade union. **6** (also **Union**) a political unit consisting of a number of states or provinces with the same central government.
– ORIGIN Latin, 'unity'.

Union, Act of E
(in British history) either of the parliamentary acts by which the countries of the United Kingdom were brought together as a political whole. By the first Act of Union (1707) Scotland was joined with England to form Great Britain. The second Act of Union (1801) established the United Kingdom of Great Britain and Ireland.

unionist • n. **1** a member of a trade union. **2** (**Unionist**) a person in Northern Ireland in favour of union with Great Britain.
– DERIVATIVES **unionism** n.

unionize (also **unionise**) • v. (**unionizes, unionizing, unionized**) become or cause to become members of a trade union.
– DERIVATIVES **unionization** (also **unionisation**) n.

Union Jack (also **Union flag**) • n. the national flag of the United Kingdom.

Union of Myanmar E
official name for **BURMA**.

Union of Soviet Socialist Republics E
full name of **SOVIET UNION**.

Union Territory E
any of several territories of India which are administered by the central government.

unipolar • adj. having or relating to a single pole.

unique • adj. **1** being the only one of its kind. **2** (**unique to**) belonging or connected to (one particular person, group, or place). **3** very special or unusual.
– DERIVATIVES **uniquely** adv. **uniqueness** n.
– ORIGIN French.

unisex • adj. suitable for both sexes.

unison • n. **1** the fact of two or more things being said or happening at the same time. **2** Music a coincidence in pitch of sounds or notes.
– ORIGIN Latin *unisonus.*

unit • n. **1** an individual thing, group, or person that is complete in itself but that can also form part of something larger. **2** a device, part, or item of furniture with a specified function: *a sink unit.* **3** a self-contained section of a building or group of buildings. **4** a subdivision of a larger military grouping. **5** a fixed quantity that is used as a standard measurement. **6** one as a number or quantity.
– ORIGIN Latin *unus.*

Unitarian /yoo-ni-tair-i-uhn/ • n. a member of a Christian Church that believes in the unity of God and rejects the idea of the Trinity.
– DERIVATIVES **Unitarianism** n.
– ORIGIN Latin *unitarius.*

unitary • adj. **1** single; uniform. **2** relating to a unit or units.

unitary authority (also **unitary council**) • n. (chiefly in the UK) a division of local government established in place of a two-tier system of local councils.

unite • v. (**unites, uniting, united**) come or bring together for a common purpose or to form a whole.
– DERIVATIVES **united** adj.
– ORIGIN Latin *unire* 'join together'.

United Arab Emirates E
an independent state on the south coast of the Persian Gulf; capital, Abu Dhabi. It was formed in 1971 by the federation of the independent sheikhdoms formerly called the Trucial States: Abu Dhabi, Ajman, Dubai, Fujairah, Ras al Khaimah (joined early 1972), Sharjah, and Umm al Qaiwain.

United Kingdom E
a country of western Europe consisting of England, Wales, Scotland, and Northern Ireland; capital, London. Full name **UNITED KINGDOM OF GREAT BRITAIN AND NORTHERN IRELAND**.

United Nations E
an international organization of over 150 countries set up in 1945, in succession to the League of Nations, to promote international peace, security, and cooperation.

United States E
a country occupying most of the southern half of North America and including also Alaska and the Hawaiian Islands; capital, Washington DC. The US is a federal republic comprising fifty states and the Federal District of Columbia. Full name **UNITED STATES OF AMERICA**.

unit trust • n. Brit. a company that invests money in a range of businesses on behalf of individuals, who can buy small units of investment.

unity • n. (pl. **unities**) **1** the state of being united or forming a whole. **2** a thing forming a complex whole. **3** Math. the number one.

universal • adj. **1** involving or done by all people or things in the world or in a particular group. **2** true or applicable in all cases.
– DERIVATIVES **universality** n. **universally** adv.

universalize (also **universalise**) • v. (**universalizes, universalizing, universalized**) make universal.
– DERIVATIVES **universalization** (also **universalisation**) n.

universal joint • n. a joint which can transmit rotary power by a shaft at any selected angle.

universal suffrage • n. the right of all adults (with minor exceptions) to vote in political elections.

universe • n. all existing matter and space considered as a whole.
– ORIGIN Latin *universus* 'combined into one, whole'.

university • n. (pl. **universities**) a high-level educational institution in which students study for degrees and academic research is done.
– ORIGIN Latin *universitas* 'the whole'.

unjust • adj. unfair.
– DERIVATIVES **unjustly** adv.

unjustifiable • adj. impossible to justify.
– DERIVATIVES **unjustifiably** adv.

unjustified • adj. not justified.

unkempt • adj. having an untidy appearance.
– ORIGIN from Old English, 'combed'.

unkind • adj. not caring or kind; rather cruel.
– DERIVATIVES **unkindly** adv. **unkindness** n.

unknowable • adj. not able to be known.

unknowing • adj. not knowing or aware.
– DERIVATIVES **unknowingly** adv.

unknown • adj. not known or familiar. • n. an unknown person or thing.
– PHRASES **unknown to** without the knowledge of.

unknown quantity • n. a person or thing whose ability or value is not yet known.

Unknown Soldier • n. an unidentified member of a country's armed forces killed in war, buried in a national memorial to represent all those killed but unidentified.

unlabelled (US **unlabeled**) • adj. without a label.

unlace • v. (**unlaces**, **unlacing**, **unlaced**) undo the laces of.

unladen • adj. not carrying a load.

unladylike • adj. (of a woman) not well-mannered or modest.

unlaid • adj. not laid.

unlamented • adj. not mourned or regretted.

unlatch • v. unfasten the latch of.

unlawful • adj. not obeying or allowed by law or rules.
– DERIVATIVES **unlawfully** adv.

unleaded • adj. (of petrol) without added lead.

unlearn • v. (**unlearns**, **unlearning**, **unlearned** or **unlearnt**) try to forget (something learned).

unlearned[1] /un-ler-nid/ • adj. not well educated.

unlearned[2] /un-lernd/ (also **unlearnt** /un-lernt/) • adj. not having been learned.

unleash • v. set free.

unleavened • adj. (of bread) made without yeast or other raising agent.

unless • conj. except when; if not.
– ORIGIN from ON or IN + LESS.

unlettered • adj. poorly educated or unable to read and write.

unlicensed • adj. not having a licence for the sale of alcoholic drinks.

unlike • prep. **1** different from; not like. **2** in contrast to: *unlike Tim, she was not superstitious.* **3** uncharacteristic of. • adj. different from each other.

> **USAGE** unlike
>
> It is not good English to use **unlike** as a conjunction (a word connecting words or clauses of a sentence together), as in *she was behaving unlike she'd ever behaved before.* You should use **as** with a negative instead: *she was behaving as she'd never behaved before.*

unlikely • adj. (**unlikelier**, **unlikeliest**) not likely to happen, be done, or be true.
– DERIVATIVES **unlikelihood** n.

unlimited • adj. not limited; infinite.

unlined[1] • adj. not marked with lines or wrinkles.

unlined[2] • adj. without a lining.

unlisted • adj. not included on a list of stock exchange prices or telephone numbers.

unlit • adj. **1** not provided with lighting. **2** not having been lit.

unlived-in • adj. not appearing to be inhabited.

unload • v. **1** remove (goods) from a vehicle, ship, etc. **2** informal get rid of.

unlock • v. undo the lock of (something) using a key.

unlooked • adj. (**unlooked for**) unexpected.

unloose • v. (**unlooses**, **unloosing**, **unloosed**) undo; let free.

unloosen • v. = UNLOOSE.

unloved • adj. loved by no one.

unlovely • adj. not attractive; ugly.

unlucky • adj. (**unluckier**, **unluckiest**) having, bringing, or resulting from bad luck.
– DERIVATIVES **unluckily** adv.

unmade • adj. **1** (of a bed) not arranged tidily. **2** Brit. (of a road) without a hard, smooth surface.

unman • v. (**unmans**, **unmanning**, **unmanned**) literary deprive of manly qualities such as self-control or courage.

unmanageable • adj. difficult or impossible to manage or control.
– DERIVATIVES **unmanageably** adv.

unmanned • adj. not having or needing a crew or staff.

unmannerly • adj. not well mannered.

unmarked • adj. **1** not marked. **2** not noticed.

unmarried • adj. not married.

unmask • v. reveal the true character of.

unmatched • adj. not matched or equalled.

unmentionable • adj. too embarrassing or offensive to be spoken about.

unmerciful • adj. showing no mercy.
– DERIVATIVES **unmercifully** adv.

unmerited • adj. not deserved.

unmetalled • adj. Brit. (of a road) not having a hard surface.

unmindful • adj. (**unmindful of**) not conscious or aware of.

unmissable • adj. that should not or cannot be missed.

unmistakable (also **unmistakeable**) • adj. not able to be mistaken for anything else.
– DERIVATIVES **unmistakably** (also **unmistakeably**) adv.

u

unmitigated • adj. absolute: *an unmitigated disaster.*
unmotivated • adj. **1** not motivated or enthusiastic. **2** without apparent motive: *an unmotivated attack.*
unmoved • adj. **1** not affected by emotion or excitement. **2** not changed in purpose or position.
unmoving • adj. not moving; still.
unmusical • adj. **1** not pleasing to the ear. **2** (of a person) unable to play or enjoy music.
unnameable • adj. unmentionable.
unnatural • adj. **1** different to what is found in nature. **2** different to what is normal or expected.
– DERIVATIVES **unnaturally** adv.
unnavigable • adj. not able to be sailed on by ships or boats.
unnecessary • adj. not necessary; more than is necessary.
– DERIVATIVES **unnecessarily** adv.
unnerve • v. (**unnerves**, **unnerving**, **unnerved**) make (someone) feel nervous or frightened.
– DERIVATIVES **unnerving** adj.
unnoticeable • adj. not easily seen or noticed.
unnoticed • adj. not noticed.
unnumbered • adj. **1** not given a number. **2** not counted; countless.
unobserved • adj. not seen.
unobstructed • adj. not obstructed.
unobtainable • adj. not able to be obtained.
unobtrusive • adj. not conspicuous or attracting attention.
– DERIVATIVES **unobtrusively** adv.
unoccupied • adj. not occupied.
unofficial • adj. not officially authorized or confirmed.
– DERIVATIVES **unofficially** adv.
unopened • adj. not opened.
unopposed • adj. not opposed; unchallenged.
unorganized (also **unorganised**) • adj. not organized.
unoriginal • adj. lacking originality.
– DERIVATIVES **unoriginality** n. **unoriginally** adv.
unorthodox • adj. different from what is usual, traditional, or accepted.
– DERIVATIVES **unorthodoxy** n.
unostentatious • adj. not ostentatious; simple.
unpack • v. **1** open and remove the contents of (a suitcase or container). **2** remove from a packed container.
unpaid • adj. **1** (of a debt) not yet paid. **2** (of work or leave) done without payment. **3** not receiving payment for work done.
unpalatable • adj. **1** not pleasant to taste. **2** difficult to accept.
unparalleled • adj. having no equal; exceptional.
unpardonable • adj. (of a fault or offence) unforgivable.
– DERIVATIVES **unpardonably** adv.
unparliamentary • adj. (of language) against the rules of behaviour of a parliament.
unpasteurized (also **unpasteurised**) • adj. not pasteurized.
unpatriotic • adj. not patriotic.
unpaved • adj. lacking a metalled or paved surface.
unperson • n. (pl. **unpersons**) a person whose name or existence is officially denied or ignored.
unperturbed • adj. not concerned or worried.
unpick • v. **1** undo the sewing of (stitches or a garment). **2** carefully analyse the different elements of.
unpin • v. (**unpins**, **unpinning**, **unpinned**) unfasten or detach by removing a pin or pins.
unpitying • adj. not feeling or showing pity.
unplanned • adj. not planned.
unplayable • adj. **1** not able to be played or played on: *the pitch was unplayable.* **2** (of music) too difficult to perform.
unpleasant • adj. **1** not pleasant. **2** not friendly or kind.
– DERIVATIVES **unpleasantly** adv.
unpleasantness • n. **1** the state of being unpleasant. **2** bad feeling or quarrelling between people.
unplug • v. (**unplugs**, **unplugging**, **unplugged**) **1** disconnect (an electrical device) by removing its plug from a socket. **2** remove a blockage from. **3** (**unplugged**) trademark (of pop or rock music) performed or recorded with acoustic rather than electrically amplified instruments.
unplumbed • adj. **1** not provided with plumbing. **2** not fully explored or understood.
– DERIVATIVES **unplumbable** adj.
unpolished • adj. **1** not having a polished surface. **2** (of a work) not polished; unrefined.
unpopular • adj. not liked or popular.
– DERIVATIVES **unpopularity** n.
unpopulated • adj. without inhabitants.
unpractised (US **unpracticed**) • adj. not trained or experienced.
unprecedented • adj. never done or known before.
– DERIVATIVES **unprecedentedly** adv.
unpredictable • adj. not able to be predicted; changeable.
– DERIVATIVES **unpredictability** n. **unpredictably** adv.
unprejudiced • adj. without prejudice; unbiased.
unpremeditated • adj. not planned beforehand.
unprepared • adj. **1** not ready or able to deal with something. **2** not made ready for use.
unprepossessing • adj. not attractive or impressive.
unpretentious • adj. not pretentious; modest.
unprincipled • adj. not acting in accordance with moral principles.
unprintable • adj. (of words, comments, or thoughts) too offensive to be published.
unproblematic • adj. not presenting a problem or difficulty.
– DERIVATIVES **unproblematically** adv.
unproductive • adj. **1** not producing or able to produce large amounts of goods, crops, etc.

2 not achieving much; not very useful.

unprofessional • adj. not in accordance with professional standards or behaviour.
– DERIVATIVES **unprofessionally** adv.

unprofitable • adj. **1** not yielding a profit. **2** not helpful or useful.

unpromising • adj. not giving hope of future success or good results.

unprompted • adj. without being prompted.

unpronounceable • adj. too difficult to pronounce.

unprotected • adj. **1** not protected or kept safe from harm. **2** (of sexual intercourse) done without using a condom.

unproven /un-**proo**-vuhn, un-**proh**-vuhn/ (also **unproved**) • adj. **1** not shown by evidence or argument as true. **2** not tried and tested.

unprovoked • adj. (of an attack, crime, etc.) not directly provoked.

unpublished • adj. **1** (of a work) not published. **2** (of an author) having no writings published.

unpunished • adj. (of an offence or offender) not receiving any punishment or penalty.

unputdownable • adj. informal (of a book) so absorbing that one cannot stop reading it.

unqualified • adj. **1** not having the necessary qualifications or requirements. **2** complete: *an unqualified success.*

unquantifiable • adj. impossible to express or measure.

unquenchable • adj. not able to be quenched or satisfied.

unquestionable • adj. not able to be denied or doubted.
– DERIVATIVES **unquestionably** adv.

unquestioned • adj. **1** not denied or doubted. **2** accepted without question.

unquiet • adj. **1** unable to be still; restless. **2** anxious.

unravel • v. (**unravels, unravelling, unravelled**; US **unravels, unraveling, unraveled**) **1** undo (twisted, knitted, or woven threads). **2** become undone. **3** solve (a mystery or puzzle). **4** begin to fail or collapse: *the country, hardly created, had begun to unravel.*

unreachable • adj. unable to be reached or contacted.

unreactive • adj. having little tendency to react chemically.

unread • adj. not having been read.

unreadable • adj. **1** not clear enough to read. **2** too dull or difficult to be worth reading.
– DERIVATIVES **unreadably** adv.

unready • adj. not ready or prepared.

unreal • adj. **1** strange and not seeming real. **2** not related to reality; unrealistic.
– DERIVATIVES **unreality** n. **unreally** adv.

unrealistic • adj. **1** not showing things in a realistic way. **2** not having a sensible understanding of what can be achieved.
– DERIVATIVES **unrealistically** adv.

unrealized (also **unrealised**) • adj. **1** not achieved or created. **2** not converted into money: *unrealized property assets.*

unreason • n. lack of reasonable thought.

unreasonable • adj. **1** not based on good sense. **2** beyond the limits of what is acceptable or achievable.
– DERIVATIVES **unreasonableness** n. **unreasonably** adv.

unreasoning • adj. not guided by or based on reason.

unrecognizable (also **unrecognisable**) • adj. not able to be recognized.
– DERIVATIVES **unrecognizably** (also **unrecognisably**) adv.

unrecognized (also **unrecognised**) • adj. **1** not identified from previous encounters or knowledge. **2** not accepted as valid.

unreconstructed • adj. not converted to the current political theory or movement.

unrecorded • adj. not recorded.

unrefined • adj. **1** not processed to remove impurities. **2** not elegant or cultured.

unregenerate /un-ri-**jen**-uh-ruht/ • adj. not reforming; stubbornly wrong or bad.

unregistered • adj. not officially recognized and recorded.

unregulated • adj. not controlled by regulations or laws.

unrehearsed • adj. not rehearsed.

unrelated • adj. not related.

unreleased • adj. (especially of a film or recording) not released.

unrelenting • adj. **1** not stopping or becoming less severe. **2** not giving in to other people's requests.
– DERIVATIVES **unrelentingly** adv.

unreliable • adj. not able to be relied upon.
– DERIVATIVES **unreliability** n. **unreliably** adv.

unrelieved • adj. lacking variation or change; boring.

unremarkable • adj. not particularly interesting or surprising.

unremarked • adj. not noticed or remarked upon.

unremitting • adj. never relaxing or slackening.

unremunerative • adj. bringing little or no profit or income.

unrepeatable • adj. **1** not able to be repeated. **2** too offensive or shocking to be said again.

unrepentant • adj. showing no regret for one's wrongdoings.
– DERIVATIVES **unrepentantly** adv.

unrepresentative • adj. not typical of a class, group, or body of opinion.

unrequited • adj. (of love) not returned.
– ORIGIN from *requite* 'make a suitable return for'.

unreserved • adj. **1** without doubts or reservations; complete. **2** honest and open. **3** not set apart or booked in advance.
– DERIVATIVES **unreservedly** adv.

unresolved • adj. (of a problem, dispute, etc.) not resolved.

unresponsive • adj. not responsive.

unrest • n. **1** a state of rebellious discontent in a group of people. **2** a state of uneasiness.

unrestrained • adj. not restrained or restricted.
– DERIVATIVES **unrestrainedly** adv.

unrestricted • adj. not limited or restricted.

unrewarding • adj. not rewarding or satisfying.

unripe • adj. not ripe.

unrivalled (US **unrivaled**) • adj. greater or

better than all others.

unroll • v. open out (something that is rolled up).

unromantic • adj. not romantic.

unruffled • adj. (of a person) calm and unconcerned.

unruly • adj. (**unrulier**, **unruliest**) disorderly and disruptive.
– DERIVATIVES **unruliness** n.
– ORIGIN from archaic *ruly* 'orderly', from **RULE**.

unsafe • adj. **1** not safe; dangerous. **2** Law (of a verdict or conviction) not based on trustworthy evidence and likely to be unjust. **3** (of sexual activity) in which precautions are not taken against the spread of sexually transmitted diseases.

unsaid past and past part. of **UNSAY**. • adj. not said.

unsaleable (also **unsalable**) • adj. not able to be sold.

unsalted • adj. not salted.

unsanitary • adj. not hygienic.

unsatisfactory • adj. unacceptable because not good enough.
– DERIVATIVES **unsatisfactorily** adv.

unsatisfied • adj. not satisfied.

unsatisfying • adj. not satisfying.

unsaturated • adj. Chem. (of fats) having double and triple bonds between carbon atoms in their molecules and as a consequence being more easily processed by the body.

unsavoury (US **unsavory**) • adj. **1** unpleasant to taste, smell, or look at. **2** not morally respectable: *an unsavoury reputation.*

unsay • v. (**unsays**, **unsaying**, **unsaid**) withdraw (a statement).

unscarred • adj. not scarred or damaged.

unscathed • adj. without suffering any injury, damage, or harm.

unscented • adj. not scented.

unscheduled • adj. not scheduled.

unschooled • adj. **1** lacking schooling or training. **2** natural and spontaneous.

unscientific • adj. not in accordance with scientific principles or methods.
– DERIVATIVES **unscientifically** adv.

unscrew • v. unfasten by twisting.

unscripted • adj. said without a prepared script; unplanned.

unscrupulous • adj. without moral principles; dishonest or unfair.
– DERIVATIVES **unscrupulously** adv.

unsealed • adj. not sealed.

unseasonable • adj. (of weather) unusual for the time of year.
– DERIVATIVES **unseasonably** adv.

unseasonal • adj. unusual or inappropriate for the time of year.

unseasoned • adj. **1** (of food) not flavoured with salt, pepper, or other spices. **2** (of timber) not treated or matured. **3** (of a person) inexperienced.

unseat • v. **1** cause to fall from a saddle or seat. **2** remove from a position of power.

unsecured • adj. (of a loan) made without an asset given as security.

unseeded • adj. (of a competitor in a sports tournament) not seeded.

unseeing • adj. with one's eyes open but without noticing or seeing anything.

unseemly • adj. (of behaviour or actions) not proper or appropriate.

unseen • adj. **1** not seen or noticed. **2** esp. Brit. (of a passage for translation in an examination) not previously read or prepared.

unselfconscious • adj. not shy or embarrassed.
– DERIVATIVES **unselfconsciously** adv.

unselfish • adj. not selfish.
– DERIVATIVES **unselfishly** adv.

unsentimental • adj. not showing or influenced by sentimental feelings.

unserviceable • adj. not in working order; unfit for use.

unsettle • v. (**unsettles**, **unsettling**, **unsettled**) make anxious; disturb.
– DERIVATIVES **unsettling** adj.

unsettled • adj. **1** changeable or likely to change: *unsettled weather.* **2** agitated; uneasy. **3** not yet resolved.

unshackle • v. (**unshackles**, **unshackling**, **unshackled**) release from restraints; set free.

unshakeable (also **unshakable**) • adj. (of a belief, feeling, etc.) firm and unable to be changed or disputed.

unshaken • adj. strong and unwavering.

unshaven • adj. not having shaved or been shaved.

unsheathe • v. (**unsheathes**, **unsheathing**, **unsheathed**) draw or pull out (a knife or similar weapon) from a sheath.

unshockable • adj. impossible to shock.

unsightly • adj. unpleasant to look at; ugly.

unsigned • adj. not bearing a person's signature.

unsinkable • adj. unable to be sunk.

unskilful (US **unskillful**) • adj. not having or showing skill.
– DERIVATIVES **unskilfully** (US **unskillfully**) adv.

unskilled • adj. not having or needing special skill or training.

unsmiling • adj. not smiling; serious or unfriendly.

unsociable • adj. **1** not enjoying the company of others. **2** not likely to produce friendly relations: *watching TV is an unsociable activity.*

unsocial • adj. **1** (of hours of work) falling outside the normal working day and so socially inconvenient. **2** antisocial.

unsold • adj. (of an item) not sold.

unsolicited • adj. not asked for.

unsolved • adj. not solved.

unsophisticated • adj. **1** lacking experience of cultured society. **2** not complicated or highly developed; basic.

unsound • adj. **1** not safe or strong; in poor condition. **2** not based on reliable evidence or reasoning.

unsparing • adj. merciless; severe.

unspeakable • adj. **1** not able to be expressed in words. **2** too bad or horrific to be expressed in words.
– DERIVATIVES **unspeakably** adv.

unspecific • adj. not specific; vague.

unspecified • adj. not stated clearly.

unspectacular • adj. not spectacular; unremarkable.

unspoilt (also **unspoiled**) • adj. (of a place) largely unaffected by building or development.

unspoken • adj. understood without being expressed in speech: *an unspoken rule.*

unsporting • adj. not fair or sportsmanlike.

unsportsmanlike • adj. not behaving according to the spirit of fair play in a particular sport.

unsprung • adj. not provided with springs.

unstable • adj. (**unstabler**, **unstablest**) **1** likely to change or collapse. **2** prone to mental problems or sudden changes of mood.

unstated • adj. not stated.

unsteady • adj. (**unsteadier**, **unsteadiest**) **1** liable to fall or shake; not firm. **2** not uniform or regular.
– DERIVATIVES **unsteadily** adv. **unsteadiness** n.

unstick • v. (**unsticks**, **unsticking**, **unstuck**) separate (a thing stuck to another).
– PHRASES **come unstuck** informal fail.

unstinting • adj. given or giving freely.

unstoppable • adj. impossible to stop or prevent.
– DERIVATIVES **unstoppably** adv.

unstressed • adj. (of a syllable) not pronounced with stress.

unstructured • adj. without formal organization or structure.

unstuck past and past part. of **UNSTICK**.

unstudied • adj. natural and unaffected.

unsubstantial • adj. having little or no solidity or reality.

unsubstantiated • adj. not supported or proven by evidence.

unsubtle • adj. obvious; clumsy.

unsuccessful • adj. not successful.
– DERIVATIVES **unsuccessfully** adv.

unsuitable • adj. not right or suitable for a particular purpose or occasion.
– DERIVATIVES **unsuitability** n. **unsuitably** adv.

unsuited • adj. not right or appropriate.

unsullied • adj. not spoiled.

unsung • adj. not celebrated or praised: *unsung heroes.*

unsupervised • adj. not done or acting under supervision.

unsupported • adj. **1** not supported. **2** not proved to be true by evidence.

unsure • adj. **1** lacking confidence. **2** not fixed or certain.

unsurfaced • adj. (of a road or path) not provided with a hard upper layer.

unsurpassed • adj. better or greater than any other.

unsurprising • adj. expected and so not causing surprise.
– DERIVATIVES **unsurprisingly** adv.

unsuspected • adj. **1** not known or thought to exist. **2** not regarded with suspicion.

unsuspecting • adj. not aware of the presence of danger; feeling no suspicion.

unsustainable • adj. **1** not able to be maintained at the current level. **2** upsetting the ecological balance by using up natural resources.

unswayed • adj. not influenced or affected.

unsweetened • adj. (of food or drink) without added sugar or sweetener.

unswerving • adj. not changing or becoming weaker.

unsymmetrical • adj. not symmetrical.

unsympathetic • adj. **1** not sympathetic. **2** not supporting an idea or action. **3** not likeable: *an unsympathetic character.*
– DERIVATIVES **unsympathetically** adv.

unsystematic • adj. not done or acting according to a fixed plan.

untainted • adj. not tainted.

untameable (also **untamable**) • adj. not able to be tamed or controlled.

untangle • v. (**untangles**, **untangling**, **untangled**) **1** free from tangles. **2** free from complications or confusion.

untapped • adj. (of a resource) not yet exploited or used.

untarnished • adj. **1** (of metal) not tarnished. **2** not spoiled.

untasted • adj. (of food or drink) not sampled.

untaught • adj. **1** not having been taught or educated. **2** natural or spontaneous.

untenable • adj. not able to be defended against criticism or attack.

untended • adj. not cared for or looked after.

untested • adj. not subjected to testing; unproven.

unthinkable • adj. too unlikely or unpleasant to be considered a possibility.
– DERIVATIVES **unthinkably** adv.

unthinking • adj. without proper consideration.
– DERIVATIVES **unthinkingly** adv.

unthreatening • adj. not threatening.

untidy • adj. (**untidier**, **untidiest**) **1** not arranged tidily. **2** not inclined to be neat.
– DERIVATIVES **untidily** adv. **untidiness** n.

untie • v. (**unties**, **untying**, **untied**) undo or unfasten (something tied).

until • prep. & conj. up to (the point in time or the event mentioned).
– ORIGIN from Old Norse *und* 'as far as' + **TILL**[1].

untimely • adj. **1** happening or done at an unsuitable time. **2** (of a death or end) happening too soon or sooner than normal.

untiring • adj. continuing at the same rate without loss of energy.

untitled • adj. **1** (of a book or other work) having no title. **2** not having a title indicating high rank.

unto • prep. **1** archaic = **TO**. **2** archaic = **UNTIL**.
– ORIGIN from **UNTIL**.

untold • adj. **1** too much or too many to be counted. **2** not narrated or recounted.

untouchable • adj. **1** not able to be touched or affected. **2** unable to be rivalled. • n. hist. a member of the lowest caste in Hindu society.
– DERIVATIVES **untouchability** n.

> **USAGE** untouchable
> The use of the term **untouchable** to refer to a member of the lowest Hindu social class is now illegal in India and Pakistan. The official term today is **scheduled caste**.

untouched • adj. **1** not handled, used, or tasted. **2** (of a subject) not treated or discussed. **3** not affected, changed, or damaged in any way.

untoward • adj. unexpected and usually unwanted.

untraceable • adj. unable to be found or traced.

untrained • adj. not having been trained in a particular skill.

untrammelled (US also **untrammeled**) • adj. not restricted or hampered.

untranslatable • adj. not able to be translated.

untreatable • adj. for whom or which no medical care is available or possible.

untreated • adj. **1** not given medical care. **2** not treated by the use of a chemical, physical, or biological agent.

untried • adj. not yet tested; inexperienced.

untrodden • adj. not having been walked on.

untroubled • adj. not troubled.

untrue • adj. **1** false. **2** not faithful or loyal.

untrustworthy • adj. unable to be trusted.

untruth • n. (pl. **untruths**) **1** a lie. **2** the quality of being false.

untruthful • adj. not truthful.
– DERIVATIVES **untruthfully** adv.

untutored • adj. not formally taught.

untying pres. part. of **UNTIE**.

untypical • adj. unusual or uncharacteristic.
– DERIVATIVES **untypically** adv.

unusable • adj. not fit to be used.

unused • adj. **1** not used. **2** (**unused to**) not accustomed to.

unusual • adj. **1** not often done or occurring. **2** remarkable or interesting because different.
– DERIVATIVES **unusually** adv.

unutterable • adj. too great or awful to describe.
– DERIVATIVES **unutterably** adv.

unuttered • adj. not spoken or expressed.

unvalued • adj. not valued.

unvaried • adj. not varied.

unvarnished • adj. **1** not varnished. **2** plain and straightforward: *the unvarnished truth.*

unvarying • adj. not varying.
– DERIVATIVES **unvaryingly** adv.

unveil • v. **1** remove a veil or covering from. **2** show or announce publicly for the first time.

unverifiable • adj. unable to be verified.

unverified • adj. not verified.

unversed • adj. (**unversed in**) not experienced or skilled in.

unviable • adj. not capable of working successfully.

unvoiced • adj. **1** not expressed in words. **2** (of a speech sound) produced without vibration of the vocal cords.

unwaged • adj. esp. Brit. **1** unemployed or doing unpaid work. **2** (of work) unpaid.

unwanted • adj. not wanted.

unwarrantable • adj. unjustifiable.
– DERIVATIVES **unwarrantably** adv.

unwarranted • adj. not warranted.

unwary • adj. not cautious.

unwashed • adj. not washed.
– PHRASES **the (great) unwashed** derog. ordinary people; the masses.

unwatchable • adj. disturbing or boring to watch.

unwatched • adj. not watched.

unwavering • adj. not wavering.

unweaned • adj. not weaned.

unwearied • adj. not wearied.

unwearying • adj. never tiring or slackening.

unwed • adj. not married.

unwelcome • adj. not welcome.

unwelcoming • adj. unfriendly or inhospitable.

unwell • adj. ill.

unwholesome • adj. not wholesome.

unwieldy • adj. hard to move or manage because of its size, shape, or weight.
– ORIGIN from **WIELD**.

unwilling • adj. not willing.
– DERIVATIVES **unwillingly** adv. **unwillingness** n.

unwind • v. (**unwinds**, **unwinding**, **unwound**) **1** undo after winding. **2** relax after a period of work or tension.

unwinking • adj. (of a stare or light) unwavering.

unwise • adj. foolish.
– DERIVATIVES **unwisely** adv.

unwitting • adj. **1** not aware of the full facts. **2** unintentional.
– DERIVATIVES **unwittingly** adv.
– ORIGIN Old English, 'not knowing or realizing'.

unwonted /un-wohn-tid/ • adj. unaccustomed or unusual.

unworkable • adj. impractical.

unworldly • adj. **1** having little awareness of the realities of life. **2** not seeming to belong to this world.
– DERIVATIVES **unworldliness** n.

unworried • adj. not worried.

unworthy • adj. (**unworthier**, **unworthiest**) not deserving attention, effort, or respect.
– DERIVATIVES **unworthiness** n.

unwound past and past part. of **UNWIND**.

unwrap • v. (**unwraps**, **unwrapping**, **unwrapped**) remove the wrapping from.

unwritten • adj. not written.

unyielding • adj. not yielding.

unzip • v. (**unzips**, **unzipping**, **unzipped**) **1** unfasten the zip of. **2** Computing decompress (a compressed file).

up • adv. **1** towards a higher place or position. **2** to the place where someone is: *she didn't hear him creeping up behind her.* **3** at or to a higher level or value. **4** into the desired or a proper condition: *the government set up an inquiry.* **5** out of bed. **6** in a publicly visible place: *sticking up posters.* **7** (of the sun) visible in the sky. **8** towards the north. **9** Brit. towards or in the capital or a major city. **10** into a happy mood. • prep. **1** from a lower to a higher point of. **2** from one end to another of (a street or other area). • adj. **1** directed or moving towards a higher place or position. **2** at an end. **3** (of the road) being repaired. **4** cheerful. **5** (of a computer system) working properly. • v. (**ups**, **upping**, **upped**) increase (a level or amount).
– PHRASES **something is up** informal something unusual is happening. **up against** close to or touching. **up and down** in various places

throughout. **up before** appearing for a hearing in the presence of (a judge, magistrate, etc.). **up for 1** available for. **2** being considered for. **3** informal ready to take part in. **up to 1** as far as. **2** (also **up until**) until. **what's up?** informal **1** what is going on? **2** what is the matter?
– ORIGIN Old English.

up- • prefix **1** (added to verbs and their derivatives) upwards: *upturned*. **2** (added to verbs and their derivatives) to a more recent time: *update*. **3** (added to nouns) referring to motion up: *uphill*. **4** (added to nouns) higher: *upland*.

up-and-coming • adj. likely to become successful.

upbeat • n. (in music) an unaccented beat coming before an accented beat. • adj. informal cheerful.

upbraid • v. scold or criticize.
– ORIGIN Old English, 'allege as a basis for censure'.

upbringing • n. the way in which a person is taught and looked after as a child.

upcoming • adj. forthcoming.

upcountry • adv. & adj. inland.

update • v. /up-dayt/ (**updates**, **updating**, **updated**) **1** make more modern. **2** give the latest information to. • n. /**up**-dayt/ an act of updating or an updated version.

Updike, E
John (Hoyer) (b.1932), American novelist, poet, and short-story writer, known for his quartet of novels *Rabbit, Run*, *Rabbit Redux*, *Rabbit is Rich*, and *Rabbit at Rest*.

upend • v. set or turn on its end or upside down.

upfield • adv. (in sport) in or to a position nearer to the opponents' end of a field.

upfront informal • adv. (usu. **up front**) **1** at the front; in front. **2** (of a payment) in advance. • adj. **1** bold and frank. **2** (of a payment) made in advance.

upgrade • v. (**upgrades**, **upgrading**, **upgraded**) raise to a higher standard or rank. • n. an act of upgrading or an upgraded version.
– DERIVATIVES **upgradeable** (also **upgradable**) adj.

upheaval • n. a violent or sudden change or disruption.

uphill • adv. towards the top of a slope. • adj. **1** sloping upwards. **2** difficult: *an uphill struggle*.

uphold • v. (**upholds**, **upholding**, **upheld**) **1** confirm or support. **2** maintain (a custom or practice).

upholster /up-hohl-ster, up-hol-ster/ • v. (**upholsters**, **upholstering**, **upholstered**) provide (furniture) with a soft, padded covering.
– DERIVATIVES **upholsterer** n.

upholstery • n. **1** the soft, padded covering used to upholster furniture. **2** the art or practice of upholstering furniture.

upkeep • n. **1** the process of keeping something in good condition. **2** the cost of this or of supporting a person.

upland • n. (also **uplands**) an area of high or hilly land.

uplift • v. **1** raise. **2** (**be uplifted**) (of an island, mountain, etc.) be created by an upward movement of the earth's surface. **3** make more hopeful or happy. • n. **1** an act of uplifting. **2** support from a garment for a woman's bust. **3** a feeling of fresh hope or happiness.

uplighter • n. a lamp designed to throw light upwards.

upmarket • adj. & adv. esp. Brit. expensive and of high quality.

upon • prep. formal = **ON**.

upper • adj. **1** situated above another part. **2** higher in position or status. **3** situated on higher ground. • n. **1** the part of a boot or shoe above the sole. **2** informal a stimulating drug.
– PHRASES **have the upper hand** have an advantage or control. **the upper crust** informal the upper classes.

upper case • n. capital letters.

upper class • n. the social group with the highest status. • adj. relating to the upper class.

uppercut • n. a punch delivered with an upwards motion and the arm bent.

upper house (also **upper chamber**) • n. the higher house in a parliament with two chambers.

uppermost • adj. highest in place, rank, or importance. • adv. at or to the uppermost position.

upper school • n. a secondary school for children aged from about fourteen upwards.

Upper Volta E
former name for **BURKINA FASO**.

uppish • adj. informal self-assertive and arrogant.

uppity • adj. informal self-important.
– ORIGIN from **UP**.

upright • adj. **1** vertical; erect. **2** greater in height than breadth. **3** strictly honest or respectable. **4** (of a piano) having vertical strings. • adv. in or into an upright position. • n. a vertical post, structure, or line.

uprising • n. an act of rebellion.

upriver • adv. & adj. towards or situated at a point nearer the source of a river.

uproar • n. **1** a loud and emotional noise or disturbance. **2** a public expression of outrage.
– ORIGIN Dutch *uproer*.

uproarious • adj. **1** very noisy; causing uproar. **2** very funny.
– DERIVATIVES **uproariously** adv.

uproot • v. **1** pull (a plant, tree, etc.) out of the ground. **2** move (someone) from their home or a familiar location.

upscale • adj. & adv. N. Amer. upmarket.

upset • v. /up-set/ (**upsets**, **upsetting**, **upset**) **1** make unhappy, disappointed, or worried. **2** knock over. **3** disrupt or disturb. • n. /**up**-set/ **1** a state of being upset. **2** an unexpected result or situation. • adj. **1** /up-**set**/ unhappy, disappointed, or worried. **2** /**up**-set/ (of a person's stomach) having disturbed digestion.
– DERIVATIVES **upsetting** adj.

upshot • n. the eventual outcome or conclusion.

upside • n. the positive aspect of something.

upside down • adv. & adj. **1** with the upper

u

part where the lower part should be. **2** in or into total disorder.
– ORIGIN from *up so down*, perh. meaning 'up as if down'.

upstage ● adv. & adj. at or towards the back of a stage. ● v. (**upstages**, **upstaging**, **upstaged**) divert attention from (someone) towards oneself.

upstairs ● adv. on or to an upper floor. ● adj. situated on an upper floor. ● n. an upper floor.

upstanding ● adj. honest and respectable.

upstart ● n. derog. a person who has suddenly become important and behaves arrogantly.

upstate ● adj. & adv. US in or to a part of a state remote from its large cities.

upstream ● adv. & adj. situated or moving in the direction opposite to that in which a stream or river flows.

upstroke ● n. an upwards stroke.

upsurge ● n. an increase.

upswing ● n. an upward trend.

uptake ● n. the action of taking up or making use of something.
PHRASES **be quick** (or **slow**) **on the uptake** informal be quick (or slow) to understand something.

uptempo ● adj. & adv. Music played with a fast or increased tempo.

upthrust ● n. **1** Physics the upward force that a fluid exerts on a body floating in it. **2** Geol. the upward movement of part of the earth's surface.

uptight ● adj. informal **1** nervously tense or angry. **2** unable to express one's feelings and desires.

up to date ● adj. using or aware of the latest developments and trends.

uptown ● adj. & adv. esp. N. Amer. in or into the residential area of a town or city.

upturn ● n. an improvement or upward trend.

upturned ● adj. turned upwards or upside down.

upward ● adv. (also **upwards**) towards a higher level. ● adj. moving or leading towards a higher level.
– PHRASES **upwards of** more than.
– DERIVATIVES **upwardly** adv.

upwind ● adv. & adj. into the wind.

Ur E
/er/ an ancient Sumerian city in present-day Iraq. It reached its peak in the late 3rd millennium BC.

Ural Mountains E
/*rhymes with* mural/ a mountain range in northern Russia, extending 1,600 km (1,000 miles) southwards from the Arctic Ocean to the Aral Sea in Kazakhstan.

uranium /yuu-ray-ni-uhm/ ● n. a radioactive metallic chemical element used as a fuel in nuclear reactors.
– ORIGIN from **URANUS**[2].

Uranus[1] E
/yoo-ruh-nuhss, yuu-**ray**-nuhss/ the most ancient of the Greek gods and first ruler of the universe. He was overthrown and castrated by his son Cronus.

Uranus[2] E
/yoo-ruh-nuhss, yuu-**ray**-nuhss/ a distant planet of the solar system, seventh in order from the sun.

urban ● adj. having to do with a town or city.
– ORIGIN Latin *urbanus*.

urbane /er-bayn/ ● adj. (of a man) confident, polite, and refined.
– ORIGIN first meaning 'urban': from Latin *urbanus*.

urbanite ● n. informal a town or city dweller.

urbanity ● n. an urbane quality or manner.

urbanize (also **urbanise**) ● v. (**urbanizes**, **urbanizing**, **urbanized**) make or become urban.
– DERIVATIVES **urbanization** (also **urbanisation**) n.

urban myth (also esp. N. Amer. **urban legend**) ● n. an entertaining story or piece of information of uncertain origin that is circulated as though true.

urchin ● n. a poor child dressed in rags.
– ORIGIN Old French *herichon* 'hedgehog'.

Urdu /oor-doo, er-doo/ ● n. a language of Pakistan and India, closely related to Hindi.
– ORIGIN Persian, 'language of the camp'.

urea /yuu-ree-uh/ ● n. a colourless compound found in urine.
– ORIGIN Latin.

ureter /yuu-ree-ter/ ● n. the duct by which urine passes from the kidney to the bladder.
– ORIGIN Greek *ourētēr*.

urethra /yuu-ree-thruh/ ● n. the duct by which urine is conveyed out of the body, and which in males also carries semen.
– DERIVATIVES **urethral** adj.
– ORIGIN Greek *ourēthra*.

Urga F
/oor-guh/ former name for **ULAN BATOR**.

urge ● v. (**urges**, **urging**, **urged**) **1** encourage or ask earnestly to do something. **2** strongly recommend. ● n. a strong desire or impulse.
– ORIGIN Latin *urgere* 'press, drive'.

urgent ● adj. **1** requiring immediate action or attention. **2** earnest and insistent.
– DERIVATIVES **urgency** n. **urgently** adv.

urinal /yuu-ry-nuhl, yoor-i-nuhl/ ● n. a container into which men urinate, that is attached to the wall in a public toilet.

urinary ● adj. **1** relating to urine. **2** referring to the organs, structures, and ducts in which urine is produced and discharged.

urinate ● v. (**urinates**, **urinating**, **urinated**) discharge urine.
– DERIVATIVES **urination** n.
– ORIGIN Latin *urinare*.

urine /yoo-rin, yoo-ryn/ ● n. a yellowish fluid stored in the bladder and discharged through the urethra, made up of water and waste substances removed from the blood by the kidneys.
– ORIGIN Latin *urina*.

URL ● abbrev. uniform (or universal) resource locator, the address of a World Wide Web page.

urn ● n. **1** a tall vase with a stem and base, especially one for storing a cremated person's ashes. **2** a large metal container with a tap, in which tea or coffee is made and kept hot.
– ORIGIN Latin *urna*.

urology /yuu-rol-uh-ji/ ● n. the branch of

medicine concerned with the urinary system.
– DERIVATIVES **urological** adj. **urologist** n.

Ursa Major E
/er-suh **may**-jer/ one of the largest and most prominent northern constellations (the Great Bear). The seven brightest stars form a formation called the Plough or Big Dipper.

Ursa Minor E
/er-suh **my**-ner/ a northern constellation (the Little Bear), which contains the Pole Star.

ursine /er-syn/ ● **adj.** having to do with bears.
– ORIGIN Latin *ursinus.*

Uruguay E
/**yoor**-uh-gwy/ a country on the Atlantic coast of South America; capital, Montevideo.
– DERIVATIVES **Uruguayan** adj. & n.

US ● **abbrev.** United States.

us ● **pron.** (first person pl.) **1** used by a speaker to refer to himself or herself and one or more others as the object of a verb or preposition. **2** used after the verb 'to be' and after 'than' or 'as'.
– ORIGIN Old English.

USAGE us
For an explanation of whether to use **us** or **we** following **than**, see the note at **PERSONAL PRONOUN**.

USA ● **abbrev.** United States of America.

usable (also **useable**) ● **adj.** able to be used.
– DERIVATIVES **usability** (also **useability**) n.

usage ● **n. 1** the action of using something or the fact of being used: *a survey of water usage.* **2** the way in which words are used in a language.

USB ● **abbrev.** Computing universal serial bus, a connector which enables any of a variety of devices to be plugged in to a computer.

use ● **v.** /yooz/ (**uses**, **using**, **used**) **1** do something with a device or object, or adopt a method, as a means of achieving a purpose: *the table can also be used as a desk.* **2** (**use up**) consume the whole of. **3** treat in a particular way. **4** exploit unfairly. **5** /yooss/ (**used to**) did repeatedly or existed in the past. **6** /yoosst/ (**be/get used to**) be or become familiar with through experience. ● **n.** /yooss/ **1** the action of using something or the state of being used: *the software is ideal for use in schools and colleges.* **2** the ability or power to exercise something: *he lost the use of his legs.* **3** a purpose for something or a way in which something can be used: *the herb has various uses in cookery.* **4** value: *what's the use of crying?*
– PHRASES **make use of** use.
– ORIGIN Old French *user.*

useable ● **adj.** var. of **USABLE**.

used ● **adj. 1** having already been used. **2** second-hand.

useful ● **adj. 1** able to be used for a practical purpose or in several ways. **2** informal skilful.
– DERIVATIVES **usefully** adv. **usefulness** n.

useless ● **adj. 1** serving no purpose. **2** informal having little ability or skill.

user ● **n.** a person who uses or operates something.

user-friendly ● **adj.** easy to use or understand.

usher ● **n. 1** a person who shows people to their seats in a theatre or cinema or in church. **2** an official in a law court who swears in jurors and witnesses and keeps order. ● **v.** (**ushers**, **ushering**, **ushered**) show or guide somewhere: *she ushered Susan out of the room.*
– ORIGIN Old French *usser* 'doorkeeper'.

usherette ● **n.** a woman who shows people to their seats in a cinema or theatre.

USS ● **abbrev.** United States Ship.

USSR ● **abbrev.** hist. Union of Soviet Socialist Republics.

Ustinov E
/**yoo**-sti-noff/ , Sir Peter (Alexander) (b.1921), British actor, director, and dramatist, of Russian descent. His films include *Spartacus* and *Death on the Nile.*

usual ● **adj.** happening or done regularly or often: *he carried out his usual evening routine.* ● **n.** informal (**the usual**) the drink someone regularly prefers.
– DERIVATIVES **usually** adv.
– ORIGIN Latin *usualis.*

Usumbura E
/oo-zuhm-**boo**-uh-ruh/ former name for **BUJUMBURA**.

usurious /yoo-*zh*oor-i-uhss, yoo-**zyoor**-i-uhss/ ● **adj.** relating to usury.

usurp /yuu-**zerp**/ ● **v. 1** take (a position of power) illegally or by force. **2** take the place of (someone in power) illegally.
– DERIVATIVES **usurpation** n. **usurper** n.
– ORIGIN Latin *usurpare* 'seize for use'.

usury /**yoo**-*zh*uh-ri/ ● **n.** the practice of lending money at unreasonably high rates of interest.
– DERIVATIVES **usurer** n.
– ORIGIN Latin *usura.*

Utah E
/**yoo**-tah/ a state in the western US; capital, Salt Lake City.
– DERIVATIVES **Utahan** /yoo-**tah**-uhn/ adj. & n.

Utamaro E
/oo-tuh-**mah**-roh/, Kitagawa (1753–1806); born *Kitagawa Nebsuyoshi*), Japanese painter and printmaker, noted for his sensual depictions of women.

utensil ● **n.** a tool or container, especially for household use.
– ORIGIN Latin *utensilis* 'usable'.

uterine /yoo-tuh-ryn/ ● **adj.** having to do with the uterus.

uterus /yoo-tuh-ruhss/ ● **n.** (pl. **uteri** /**yoo**-tuh-ry/) the womb.
– ORIGIN Latin.

utilitarian /yuu-ti-li-**tair**-i-uhn/ ● **adj. 1** useful or practical rather than attractive. **2** relating to utilitarianism.

utilitarianism ● **n.** the belief that the greatest happiness of the greatest number should be the guiding principle of right behaviour.

utility ● **n.** (pl. **utilities**) **1** the state of being useful or profitable. **2** a public utility. ● **adj.** having several functions or uses.
– ORIGIN Latin *utilitas.*

utility room ● **n.** a room where a washing machine and other domestic equipment is kept.

utility vehicle ● n. a truck having low sides and used for small loads.

utilize (also **utilise**) ● v. (**utilizes, utilizing, utilized**) make practical and effective use of.
– DERIVATIVES **utilization** (also **utilisation**) n.
– ORIGIN French *utiliser.*

utmost ● adj. most extreme; greatest. ● n. (**the utmost**) the greatest or most extreme extent or amount.
– ORIGIN Old English, 'outermost'.

Utopia /yoo-**toh**-pi-uh/ ● n. an imagined perfect place.
– ORIGIN the title of a book by Sir Thomas More, from Greek *ou* 'not' + *topos* 'place'.

utopian ● adj. idealistic. ● n. an idealistic reformer.
– DERIVATIVES **utopianism** n.

Utrecht E
/yoo-**trekht**/ a city in the central Netherlands, capital of a province of the same name.

Uttar Pradesh E
/uut-tar pruh-**desh**/ a large state in northern India; capital, Lucknow.

utter[1] ● adj. complete; absolute.
– DERIVATIVES **utterly** adv.
– ORIGIN Old English, 'outer'.

utter[2] ● v. (**utters, uttering, uttered**) make (a sound) or say (something).
– ORIGIN Dutch *ūteren* 'speak, make known'.

utterance ● n. **1** a word, statement, or sound uttered. **2** the action of uttering.

uttermost ● adj. & n. utmost.

U-turn ● n. **1** the turning of a vehicle in a U-shaped course so as to face the opposite way. **2** a reversal of policy.

UV ● abbrev. ultraviolet.

uvula /yoo-vyuu-luh/ ● n. (pl. **uvulae** /yoo-vyuu-lee/) a fleshy part of the soft palate which hangs above the throat.
– ORIGIN Latin, 'little grape'.

uxorious /uk-sor-i-uhss/ ● adj. (of a man) very or excessively fond of his wife.
– ORIGIN Latin *uxorious.*

Uzbekistan E
/uuz-bek-i-**stahn**, uuz-bek-i-**stan**/ an independent republic in central Asia; capital, Tashkent.

Uzi /oo-zi/ ● n. a type of sub-machine gun.
– ORIGIN from the name of *Uziel* Gal, the 20th-century Israeli army officer who designed it.

V[1] (also **v**) ● n. (pl. **Vs** or **V's**) **1** the twenty-second letter of the alphabet. **2** the Roman numeral for five.

V[2] ● abbrev. volt(s).

v ● abbrev. **1** Grammar verb. **2** versus. **3** very.

VA ● abbrev. (in the UK) Order of Victoria and Albert.

vacancy ● n. (pl. **vacancies**) **1** an unoccupied position or job. **2** an available room in a hotel, guest house, etc. **3** empty space.

vacant ● adj. **1** empty. **2** (of a position) not filled. **3** showing no intelligence or interest.
– DERIVATIVES **vacantly** adv.

vacate /vay-kayt, vuh-kayt/ ● v. (**vacates, vacating, vacated**) **1** leave (a place). **2** give up (a position or job).
– ORIGIN Latin *vacare* 'leave empty'.

vacation ● n. **1** a holiday period between terms in universities and law courts. **2** N. Amer. a holiday. **3** the action of leaving a place. ● v. N. Amer. take a holiday.
– DERIVATIVES **vacationer** n.

vaccinate /vak-si-nayt/ ● v. (**vaccinates, vaccinating, vaccinated**) treat with a vaccine to produce immunity against a disease.
– DERIVATIVES **vaccination** n.

vaccine /vak-seen/ ● n. a substance injected into the body to cause it to produce antibodies and so provide immunity against a disease.
– ORIGIN Latin *vaccinus.*

vacillate /va-si-layt/ ● v. (**vacillates, vacillating, vacillated**) waver between different opinions or actions.
– DERIVATIVES **vacillation** n.
– ORIGIN Latin *vacillare* 'sway'.

vacuole /vak-yuu-ohl/ ● n. Biol. a space inside a cell, enclosed by a membrane and containing fluid.
– ORIGIN Latin *vacuus* 'empty'.

vacuous /vak-yuu-uhss/ ● adj. showing a lack of thought or intelligence.
– DERIVATIVES **vacuity** /vuh-**kyoo**-i-ti/ n.
– ORIGIN Latin *vacuus* 'empty'.

vacuum /vak-yuu-uhm/ ● n. (pl. **vacuums** or **vacua** /vak-yuu-uh/) **1** a space entirely empty of matter. **2** a space from which the air has been completely or partly removed. **3** a gap left by the loss of someone or something important. **4** (pl. **vacuums**) informal a vacuum cleaner. ● v. informal clean with a vacuum cleaner.
– ORIGIN Latin.

vacuum cleaner ● n. an electrical device that collects dust by means of suction.

vacuum flask ● n. esp. Brit. a container that keeps a substance hot or cold by means of a double wall enclosing a vacuum.

vacuum-pack ● v. seal (a product) in a pack or wrapping with the air removed.

vacuum tube ● n. a sealed glass tube containing a near vacuum which allows the free passage of electric current.

vade mecum /vah-di **may**-kuhm, vay-di **mee**-kuhm/ ● n. a handbook or guide kept constantly at hand.
– ORIGIN Latin, 'go with me'.

Vaduz E
/va-**duuts**/ the capital of Liechtenstein.

vagabond /vag-uh-bond/ ● **n. 1** a vagrant. **2** informal, dated a rogue.
– ORIGIN Latin *vagabundus*.

vagary /vay-guh-ri/ ● **n.** (pl. **vagaries**) an unexpected and mysterious change.
– ORIGIN Latin *vagari* 'wander'.

vagina /vuh-jy-nuh/ ● **n.** (pl. **vaginas**) the muscular tube leading from the vulva to the cervix in women and most female mammals.
– DERIVATIVES **vaginal** adj.
– ORIGIN Latin, 'sheath, scabbard'.

vagrant /vay-gruhnt/ ● **n.** a person without a home or job. ● **adj.** living like a vagrant.
– DERIVATIVES **vagrancy** n.
– ORIGIN Old French *vagarant* 'wandering about'.

vague ● **adj. 1** not certain or definite. **2** thinking or expressing oneself in an imprecise way.
– DERIVATIVES **vaguely** adv. **vagueness** n.
– ORIGIN Latin *vagus* 'wandering, uncertain'.

vain ● **adj. 1** having an excessively high opinion of oneself. **2** useless or meaningless: *a vain boast*.
– PHRASES **in vain** without success. **take someone's name in vain** use someone's name in a way that shows a lack of respect.
– DERIVATIVES **vainly** adv.
– ORIGIN Latin *vanus* 'empty'.

vainglory ● **n.** literary excessive vanity.
– DERIVATIVES **vainglorious** adj.

valance /va-luhnss/ ● **n.** a length of fabric attached to the base of a bed beneath the mattress to cover the space below.
– DERIVATIVES **valanced** adj.
– ORIGIN perh. from Old French *avaler* 'descend'.

vale ● **n.** literary a valley.
– ORIGIN Latin *vallis*.

valediction /va-li-**dik**-sh'n/ ● **n. 1** the action of saying farewell. **2** a farewell speech.
– ORIGIN from Latin *vale* 'goodbye' + *dicere* 'to say'.

valedictory /va-li-**dik**-tuh-ri/ ● **adj.** serving as a farewell.

valence /vay-luhnss/ ● **n.** Chem. = **VALENCY**.

Valencia E
/vuh-**len**-si-uh/ an autonomous region of eastern Spain; capital, the city of Valencia.

valency /vay-luhn-si/ ● **n.** (pl. **valencies**) Chem. the combining power of an element, as measured by the number of hydrogen atoms it can displace or combine with.
– ORIGIN Latin *valentia* 'power'.

valentine ● **n. 1** a card sent on St Valentine's Day (14 February) to a person one loves or is attracted to. **2** a person to whom one sends such a card.

Valentine, St E
either of two early Italian martyrs commemorated on 14 February—a Roman priest and a bishop of Terni. St Valentine was regarded as the patron of lovers.

Valentino E
/va-luhn-**tee**-noh/ , Rudolph (1895–1926; born *Rodolfo Guglielmi di Valentina d'Antonguolla*), Italian-born American actor, the romantic hero of silent films such as *The Sheikh*.

Valera, E
Eamon de, see **DE VALERA**.

Valerian E
/vuh-**leer**-i-uhn/ (d.260; Latin name *Publius Licinius Valerianus*), Roman emperor 253–60.

valerian /vuh-leer-i-uhn/ ● **n. 1** a plant with clusters of small pink, red, or white flowers. **2** a sedative drug obtained from a valerian root.
– ORIGIN Latin *valeriana*.

valet /va-lay, va-lit/ ● **n. 1** a man's personal male attendant, responsible for his clothes and appearance. **2** a hotel employee performing such duties for guests. **3** a person employed to clean or park cars. ● **v.** (**valets**, **valeting**, **valeted**) **1** act as a valet to. **2** clean (a car).
– ORIGIN French.

valetudinarian /va-li-tyoo-di-**nair**-i-uhn/ ● **n.** a person in poor health or who worries too much about their health.
– ORIGIN Latin *valetudinarius* 'in ill health'.

Valhalla E
/val-**hal**-luh/ Scand. Myth. a palace in which heroes killed in battle were believed to feast with Odin for ever.

valiant ● **adj.** showing courage or determination.
– DERIVATIVES **valiantly** adv.
– ORIGIN Old French *vailant*.

valid ● **adj. 1** (of a reason, argument, etc.) sound or logical. **2** legally binding or officially acceptable.
– DERIVATIVES **validity** n. **validly** adv.
– ORIGIN Latin *validus* 'strong'.

validate ● **v.** (**validates**, **validating**, **validated**) **1** check or prove the validity of. **2** make or declare legally valid.
– DERIVATIVES **validation** n.

valise /vuh-leez/ ● **n.** a small travelling bag or suitcase.
– ORIGIN French.

Valium /va-li-uhm/ ● **n.** trademark a tranquillizing drug used to relieve anxiety.
– ORIGIN unknown.

Valletta E
/vuh-**let**-tuh/ the capital and chief port of Malta.

valley ● **n.** (pl. **valleys**) a low area between hills or mountains.
– ORIGIN Latin *vallis*.

Valley of the Kings E
a valley near ancient Thebes in Egypt where the pharaohs of the New Kingdom (*c*.1550–1070 BC) were buried.

Valois, E
Dame Ninette de, see **DE VALOIS**.

valor ● **n.** US = **VALOUR**.

valorize /va-luh-ryz/ (also **valorise**) ● **v.** (**valorizes**, **valorizing**, **valorized**) give value or validity to.
– ORIGIN French *valorisation*.

valour (US **valor**) ● **n.** courage in the face of danger.

– DERIVATIVES **valorous** adj.
– ORIGIN Latin *valor*.

Valparaíso E
/val-puh-ry-zoh/ the principal port of Chile.

valuable ● adj. **1** worth a great deal of money. **2** extremely useful or important. ● n. (**valuables**) valuable items.
– DERIVATIVES **valuably** adv.

valuation ● n. an estimate of how much something is worth.

value ● n. **1** the amount of money that something is worth. **2** the importance or usefulness of something. **3** (**values**) standards of behaviour. **4** Math. the amount represented by a letter, symbol, or number. **5** Music the relative length of the sound represented by a note. ● v. (**values, valuing, valued**) **1** estimate the value of. **2** consider to be important or beneficial.
– DERIVATIVES **valueless** adj. **valuer** n.
– ORIGIN Old French.

value added tax ● n. a tax on the amount by which goods or services rise in value at each stage of production.

valve ● n. **1** a device for controlling the passage of fluid through a pipe or duct. **2** a cylindrical mechanism used to vary the length of the tube in a brass musical instrument. **3** a structure in the heart or in a blood vessel that allows blood to flow in one direction only. **4** each of the halves of the hinged shell of a bivalve mollusc.
– ORIGIN Latin *valva* 'leaf of a folding or double door'.

valvular ● adj. relating to or having a valve or valves.

vamoose /vuh-mooss/ ● v. (**vamooses, vamoosing, vamoosed**) informal leave hurriedly.
– ORIGIN Spanish *vamos* 'let us go'.

vamp[1] ● n. the upper front part of a boot or shoe. ● v. (**vamp up**) informal improve (something) by adding something more interesting.
– ORIGIN first referring to the foot of a stocking: from Old French *avant* 'before' + *pie* 'foot'.

vamp[2] ● n. informal a woman who uses her sexual attraction to control men.
– DERIVATIVES **vampish** adj.
– ORIGIN short for **VAMPIRE**.

vampire /vam-pyr/ ● n. **1** (in folklore) a corpse supposed to leave its grave at night to drink the blood of the living. **2** (also **vampire bat**) a small bat that feeds on blood by piercing the skin with its teeth, found mainly in tropical America.
– DERIVATIVES **vampiric** /vam-pi-rik/ adj. **vampirism** n.
– ORIGIN Hungarian *vampir*.

van[1] ● n. **1** a covered motor vehicle used for moving goods or people. **2** Brit. a railway carriage for conveying luggage, mail, etc.
– ORIGIN shortening of **CARAVAN**.

van[2] ● n. (**the van**) the leading part of an advancing group.
– ORIGIN short for **VANGUARD**.

vanadium /vuh-nay-di-uhm/ ● n. a hard grey metallic chemical element, used to make alloy steels.
– ORIGIN from an Old Norse name of the Scandinavian goddess Freyja.

Van Allen, E
James Alfred (b.1914), American physicist, whose experiments led to the discovery of the Van Allen belts, two regions of high radiation surrounding the earth at heights of several thousand kilometres.

Vanbrugh E
/van-bruh/, Sir John (1664–1726), English architect and dramatist. Among his architectural works are Castle Howard (Yorkshire) and Blenheim Palace (Oxfordshire), both in collaboration with Nicholas Hawksmoor. His comedies include *The Relapse*.

Van Buren E
/van **byuu**-ruhn/, Martin (1782–1862), American Democratic statesman, 8th President of the US 1837–41.

Vancouver[1] E
/van-**koo**-ver/ a city and port in British Columbia, SW Canada.

Vancouver[2] E
/van-**koo**-ver/, George (1757–98), English navigator, who charted much of the west coast of North America.

Vancouver Island E
a large island off the Pacific coast of Canada, in SW British Columbia.

vandal ● n. a person who deliberately destroys or damages property.
– DERIVATIVES **vandalism** n.
– ORIGIN Latin *Vandalus*, referring to a Germanic people that plundered parts of Europe in the 4th and 5th centuries.

vandalize (also **vandalise**) ● v. (**vandalizes, vandalizing, vandalized**) deliberately destroy or damage (property).

Vanderbilt E
/van-der-bilt/, Cornelius (1794–1877), American businessman and philanthropist, who made a fortune from shipping and railroads.

Van der Post F
/van der **posst**/, Sir Laurens (Jan) (1906–96), South African explorer and writer, author of *The Lost World of the Kalahari*.

van de Velde[1] E
/van duh **vel**-duh/, Henri (Clemens) (1863–1957), Belgian architect, designer, and teacher, a pioneer of art nouveau design and architecture in Europe.

van de Velde[2] E
/van duh **vel**-duh/, Willem (1611–93;; known as **Willem van de Velde the Elder**), Dutch painter of marine subjects.

Van Diemen's Land E
/van **dee**-muhnz/ former name for **TASMANIA**.

Van Dyck E
/van **dyk**/ (also **Vandyke**), Sir Anthony (1599–1641), Flemish painter, known for his portraits of English courtiers, which greatly influenced portraiture in England.

vane ● n. **1** a broad blade attached to a rotating axis or wheel which is moved by wind or water, forming part of a windmill, propeller, or turbine. **2** a weathervane.
– ORIGIN Germanic.

Van Eyck E
/van **yk**/, Jan (*c.*1370–1441), Flemish painter, noted for his innovative use of oils. His works include *The Adoration of the Lamb* (known as the Ghent Altarpiece) and *The Arnolfini Marriage.*

Van Gogh E
/van **gokh**, van **goff**/, Vincent (Willem) (1853–90), Dutch post-Impressionist painter, famous for his studies of sunflowers. Suffering from severe depression, he cut off part of his own ear and eventually committed suicide.

vanguard ● n. **1** the leading part of an advancing army. **2** a group of people leading the way in new developments or ideas.
– ORIGIN Old French *avantgarde.*

vanilla ● n. a substance obtained from the pods of a tropical orchid or produced artificially, used as a flavouring.
– ORIGIN Spanish *vainilla* 'pod'.

vanish ● v. **1** disappear suddenly and completely: *the smile vanished from her lips.* **2** gradually stop existing.
– ORIGIN Old French *esvanir.*

vanishing point ● n. the point in the distance at which receding parallel lines appear to meet.

vanity ● n. (pl. **vanities**) **1** excessive pride in one's appearance or achievements. **2** the quality of being pointless or futile: *the vanity of human wishes.*
– ORIGIN Latin *vanitas.*

vanity case ● n. a small case fitted with a mirror and compartments for make-up.

vanity unit ● n. a unit made up of a washbasin set into a flat top with cupboards beneath.

vanquish /vang-kwish/ ● v. defeat thoroughly.
– ORIGIN Old French *vainquir.*

vantage /vahn-tij/ (also **vantage point**) ● n. a place or position giving a good view.
– ORIGIN Old French *avantage* 'advantage'.

Vanuatu E
/van-oo-**ah**-too/ a country consisting of a group of islands in the SW Pacific; capital, Vila.
– DERIVATIVES **Vanuatuan** adj. & n.

vapid /vap-id/ ● adj. offering nothing that is stimulating or challenging.
– DERIVATIVES **vapidity** n.
– ORIGIN Latin *vapidus.*

vaporize (also **vaporise**) ● v. (**vaporizes, vaporizing, vaporized**) convert into vapour.
– DERIVATIVES **vaporization** (also **vaporisation**) n.

vaporizer (also **vaporiser**) ● n. a device that is used to breathe in medicine in the form of a vapour.

vapour (US **vapor**) ● n. **1** moisture or another substance that is diffused or suspended in the air: *a cloud of water vapour.* **2** Physics a gaseous substance that can be made into liquid by pressure alone.
– DERIVATIVES **vaporous** adj.
– ORIGIN Latin *vapor* 'steam, heat'.

vapour trail ● n. a trail of condensed water from an aircraft or rocket at high altitude, seen as a white streak against the sky.

Varah E
/**vah**-ruh/, (Edward) Chad (b.1911), English clergyman, founder of the Samaritans (1953).

Varanasi E
/vuh-**rah**-nuh-si/ a city on the Ganges, in Uttar Pradesh, northern India. It is a holy city and a place of pilgrimage for Hindus, who undergo ritual purification in the Ganges.

Vargas Llosa E
/var-guhss **yoh**-suh/, (Jorge) Mario (Pedro) (b.1936), Peruvian novelist, dramatist, and essayist, author of the novels *Aunt Julia and the Scriptwriter* and *The War of the End of the World.*

variable ● adj. **1** often changing or likely to change; not consistent: *the photos are of variable quality.* **2** able to be changed. **3** Math. (of a quantity) able to take on different numerical values. ● n. a variable situation, feature, or quantity.
– DERIVATIVES **variability** n. **variably** adv.

variance ● n. the amount by which something changes or is different from something else.
– PHRASES **at variance (with)** disagreeing or opposing.

variant ● n. a form or version that varies from other forms of the same thing.

variation ● n. **1** a change or slight difference in condition, amount, or level. **2** a different or distinct form or version. **3** Music a new but still recognizable version of a theme.
– DERIVATIVES **variational** adj.

varicoloured /vair-i-kul-erd/ (US **varicolored**) ● adj. consisting of several different colours.

varicose /va-ri-kohss, va-ri-kuhss/ ● adj. (of a vein) swollen, twisted, and lengthened, as a result of poor circulation.
– ORIGIN Latin *varicosus.*

varied ● adj. involving a number of different types or elements: *a long and varied career.*

variegated /vair-i-gay-tid/ ● adj. having irregular patches or streaks of different colours.
– DERIVATIVES **variegation** /vair-i-**gay**-sh'n/ n.
– ORIGIN Latin *variegare* 'make varied'.

variety ● n. (pl. **varieties**) **1** the quality of being different or varied: *it's the variety that makes my job so enjoyable.* **2** (**a variety of**) a number of things of the same type that have different features. **3** a thing which has some differences from others of the same general class: *fifty varieties of pasta.* **4** a form of entertainment made up of a series of different acts, such as singing, dancing, and comedy. **5** Biol. a subdivision of a species.
– ORIGIN Latin *varietas.*

various ● adj. different from one another; of different kinds or sorts. ● det. & pron. more than one; individual and separate.

– DERIVATIVES **variously** adv.
– ORIGIN Latin *varius* 'changing, diverse'.

varlet /var-lit/ • **n. 1** archaic a rogue or rascal. **2** hist. a male servant.
– ORIGIN Old French, from *valet* (see **VALET**).

varnish • **n.** resin dissolved in a liquid, applied to wood or metal to give a hard, clear, shiny surface when dry. • **v.** apply varnish to.
– ORIGIN Old French *vernis*.

varsity • **n.** (pl. **varsities**) **1** Brit. dated or S. Afr. university. **2** N. Amer. a sports team representing a university or college.
ORIGIN shortening of **UNIVERSITY**.

vary • **v.** (**varies**, **varying**, **varied**) **1** differ in size, degree, or nature from something else of the same general class: *the houses vary in price*. **2** change from one form or state to another. **3** alter (something) to make it less uniform.
– ORIGIN Latin *variare*.

Vasarely E
/va-suh-rel-i/, Viktor (1908–97), Hungarian-born French painter, best known for his geometric abstract paintings.

Vasari E
/vuh-sah-ri/, Giorgio (1511–74), Italian painter, architect, and biographer. His *Lives of the Most Excellent Painters, Sculptors, and Architects* laid the basis for the study of art history in the West.

Vasco da Gama E
/vass-koh/ see **DA GAMA**.

vascular /vass-kyuu-ler/ • **adj.** referring to the system of vessels for carrying blood or (in plants) sap, water, and nutrients.
– ORIGIN Latin *vascularis*.

vas deferens /vass def-uh-renz/ • **n.** (pl. **vasa deferentia** /vay-suh def-uh-ren-shuh/) Anat. either of the ducts which convey sperm from the testicles to the urethra.
– ORIGIN from Latin *vas* 'vessel, duct' + *deferens* 'carrying away'.

vase • **n.** a decorative container used as an ornament or for displaying cut flowers.
– ORIGIN French.

vasectomy /vuh-sek-tuh-mi/ • **n.** (pl. **vasectomies**) the surgical cutting and sealing of part of each vas deferens as a means of sterilization.

vaseline /vass-uh-leen/ • **n.** trademark a type of petroleum jelly used as an ointment and lubricant.
– ORIGIN from German *Wasser* 'water' + Greek *elaion* 'oil'.

vassal /vass-uhl/ • **n. 1** hist. a man who promised to fight for a monarch or lord in return for holding a piece of land. **2** a country that is controlled by or dependent on another.
– ORIGIN Latin *vassallus* 'retainer'.

vast • **adj.** of very great extent or quantity; huge.
– DERIVATIVES **vastly** adv. **vastness** n.
– ORIGIN Latin *vastus* 'void, immense'.

VAT • **abbrev.** value added tax.

vat • **n.** a large tank or tub used to hold liquid.
– ORIGIN Germanic.

Vatican • **n.** the official residence of the Pope in Rome.

Vatican City E
an independent papal state in the city of Rome, the seat of government of the Roman Catholic Church.

vaudeville /vaw-duh-vil, voh-duh-vil/ • **n.** a type of entertainment featuring a mixture of musical and comedy acts.
– DERIVATIVES **vaudevillian** adj. & n.
– ORIGIN French.

Vaughan[1] E
/vawn/, Henry (1621–95), Welsh religious writer and metaphysical poet.

Vaughan[2] E
/vawn/, Sarah (Lois) (1924–90), American jazz singer and pianist.

Vaughan Williams, E
Ralph (1872–1958), English composer. His works, frequently reflecting his interest in Tudor composers and English folk songs, include *Fantasia on a Theme by Thomas Tallis* and *A London Symphony*.

vault[1] • **n. 1** a roof in the form of an arch or a series of arches. **2** a large room used for storage, especially in a bank. **3** a chamber beneath a church or in a graveyard used for burials.
– DERIVATIVES **vaulted** adj.
– ORIGIN Old French *voute*.

vault[2] • **v.** jump over in a single movement, using one's hands or a pole to push oneself. • **n.** an act of vaulting.
– ORIGIN Old French *volter* 'turn a horse'.

vaulting • **n.** the arrangement of vaults in a roof or ceiling.

vaulting horse • **n.** a padded wooden block used for vaulting over by gymnasts and athletes.

vaunted /*rhymes with* haunted/ • **adj.** much praised or boasted about.
– ORIGIN Latin *vantare*.

VC • **abbrev.** Victoria Cross.

VCR • **abbrev.** video cassette recorder.

VD • **abbrev.** venereal disease.

VDU • **abbrev.** visual display unit.

've • **abbrev.** informal have.

veal • **n.** meat from a young calf.
– ORIGIN Old French *veel*.

vector /vek-ter/ • **n. 1** Math. & Physics a quantity having direction as well as magnitude, especially as determining the position of one point in space relative to another. **2** the carrier of a disease or infection.
– DERIVATIVES **vectorial** adj.
– ORIGIN Latin, 'carrier'.

VE day • **n.** the day (8 May) marking the Allied victory in Europe in 1945.
– ORIGIN short for *Victory in Europe*.

veer • **v.** (**veers**, **veering**, **veered**) **1** change direction suddenly. **2** (of the wind) change direction clockwise around the points of the compass. • **n.** a sudden change of direction.
– ORIGIN French *virer*.

veg[1] /vej/ • **n.** (pl. **veg**) Brit. informal a vegetable or vegetables.

veg[2] /vej/ • **v.** (**vegges**, **vegging**, **vegged**) (**veg out**) informal relax completely.
– ORIGIN from **VEGETATE**.

V

Vega[1] E
/vay-guh/, Lope de (1562–1635; full name *Lope Felix de Vega Carpio*), Spanish dramatist and poet, the founder of Spanish drama.

Vega[2] E
/vee-guh/ the fifth-brightest star in the sky, and the brightest in the constellation Lyra.

vegan /vee-guhn/ • **n.** a person who does not eat or use any animal products.
– ORIGIN from **VEGETARIAN**.

vegetable /vej-tuh-b'l, vej-i-tuh-b'l/ • **n. 1** a plant used as food. **2** informal, offens. a person who is incapable of normal mental or physical activity as a result of brain damage.
– ORIGIN Latin *vegetabilis* 'animating'.

vegetable oil • **n.** an oil derived from plants, e.g. olive oil or sunflower oil.

vegetal /vej-i-tuhl/ • **adj.** formal relating to plants.
– ORIGIN Latin *vegetalis*.

vegetarian • **n.** a person who does not eat meat for moral, religious, or health reasons. • **adj.** eating or including no meat.
– DERIVATIVES **vegetarianism** n.

vegetate • **v.** (**vegetates**, **vegetating**, **vegetated**) spend time in a dull, inactive, unchallenging way.
– ORIGIN Latin *vegetare* 'enliven'.

vegetation • **n.** plants in general.

vegetative /vej-i-tuh-tiv/ • **adj. 1** relating to vegetation or the growth of plants. **2** Biol. relating to reproduction or breeding by asexual means. **3** Med. alive but in a coma and without apparent brain activity.

veggie burger • **n.** a savoury cake resembling a hamburger but made with vegetables or soya instead of meat.

vehement /vee-uh-muhnt/ • **adj.** showing strong feeling.
– DERIVATIVES **vehemence** n. **vehemently** adv.
– ORIGIN Latin, 'impetuous, violent'.

vehicle /vee-i-k'l/ • **n. 1** a thing used for transporting people or goods on land, such as a car or truck. **2** a means of expressing something: *she used paint as a vehicle for her ideas.* **3** a film, programme, song, etc., intended to display the leading performer to the best advantage.
– DERIVATIVES **vehicular** /vi-**hik**-yuu-ler/ adj.
– ORIGIN Latin *vehiculum*.

veil • **n. 1** a piece of fine material worn to protect or hide the face. **2** a piece of fabric forming part of a nun's headdress, resting on the head and shoulders. **3** a thing that hides or disguises. • **v. 1** cover with a veil. **2** (**veiled**) partially hidden or disguised.
– ORIGIN Latin *velum* 'sail, veil'.

vein • **n. 1** any of the tubes forming part of the circulation system by which blood is carried from all parts of the body towards the heart. **2** (in general use) a blood vessel. **3** a very thin rib running through a leaf. **4** (in insects) a hollow rib forming part of the supporting framework of a wing. **5** a streak of a different colour in wood, marble, cheese, etc. **6** a fracture in rock containing a deposit of minerals or ore. **7** a source of a quality: *a rich vein of satire.*
– DERIVATIVES **veined** adj.
– ORIGIN Old French *veine*.

Velázquez E
/vuh-lass-kwez/, Diego Rodríguez de Silva y (1599–1660), Spanish painter. He is famous for portraits such as *Pope Innocent X* and *Las Meninas*.

Velcro • **n.** trademark a fastener made up of two strips of fabric which stick together when pressed.
– ORIGIN from French *velours croché* 'hooked velvet'.

veld /velt/ (also **veldt**) • **n.** open, uncultivated country or grassland in southern Africa.
– ORIGIN Afrikaans, 'field'.

Velde, van de[1], E
Henri, see **VAN DE VELDE[1]**.

Velde, van de[2], E
Willem, see **VAN DE VELDE[2]**.

vellum /vel-luhm/ • **n.** fine parchment made from animal skin.
– ORIGIN Old French *velin*.

velociraptor /vi-loss-i-rap-ter/ • **n.** a small meat-eating dinosaur with a large slashing claw on each foot.
– ORIGIN Latin.

velocity /vi-loss-i-ti/ • **n.** (pl. **velocities**) **1** the speed of something in a given direction. **2** (in general use) speed.
– ORIGIN Latin *velocitas*.

velodrome /vel-uh-drohm/ • **n.** a cycle-racing track with steeply banked curves.
– ORIGIN French.

velour /vuh-loor/ • **n.** a plush woven fabric resembling velvet.
– ORIGIN French *velours* 'velvet'.

velvet • **n.** a fabric of silk, cotton, or nylon with a thick short pile on one side.
– DERIVATIVES **velvety** adj.
– ORIGIN Old French *veluotte*.

velveteen • **n.** a cotton fabric with a pile resembling velvet.

venal /vee-n'l/ • **adj.** open to bribery.
– DERIVATIVES **venality** n.
– ORIGIN Latin *venum* 'thing for sale'.

vend • **v.** offer (small items) for sale.
– ORIGIN Latin *vendere* 'sell'.

vendetta /ven-det-tuh/ • **n. 1** a prolonged feud between families in which people are murdered in return for previous murders. **2** a prolonged bitter quarrel with someone.
– ORIGIN Italian.

vending machine • **n.** a machine that dispenses small articles when a coin or token is inserted.

vendor (US also **vender**) • **n. 1** a person or company offering something for sale. **2** Law a person who is selling a property.

veneer /vi-neer/ • **n. 1** a thin decorative covering of fine wood applied to a coarser wood or other material. **2** an attractive appearance that disguises true nature or feelings.
– DERIVATIVES **veneered** adj.
– ORIGIN German *furnieren*.

venerable • **adj. 1** greatly respected because of age, wisdom, or character. **2** (in the Anglican Church) a title given to an archdeacon.

venerate /ven-uh-rayt/ • **v.** (**venerates**, **venerating**, **venerated**) regard with great respect.
– DERIVATIVES **veneration** n.

– ORIGIN Latin *venerari* 'revere'.

venereal /vi-neer-i-uhl/ • **adj.** **1** relating to venereal disease. **2** formal relating to sexual desire or sexual intercourse.
– ORIGIN Latin *venereus.*

venereal disease • **n.** a disease caught by sexual intercourse with a person already infected.

Venetian /vuh-nee-sh'n/ • **adj.** relating to Venice. • **n.** a person from Venice.

venetian blind • **n.** a window blind consisting of horizontal slats which can be turned to control the amount of light that passes through.

Venezuela E
/ven-iz-way-luh/ a republic in northern South America, with a coastline on the Caribbean; capital, Caracas. Official name (from 1999) **Bolivarian Republic of Venezuela**.
– DERIVATIVES **Venezuelan** adj. & n.

vengeance /ven-juhnss/ • **n.** the action of punishing or harming someone in return for an injury or wrong.
– PHRASES **with a vengeance** with great intensity.
– ORIGIN Old French.

vengeful • **adj.** wanting to harm someone in return for an injury or wrong.

venial /vee-ni-uhl/ • **adj.** **1** (in Christian belief) referring to a sin that will not deprive the soul of divine grace. Often contrasted with **mortal**. **2** (of a fault or offence) slight and pardonable.
– ORIGIN Latin *venialis.*

Venice E
a city in NE Italy, built on numerous islands that are separated by canals and linked by bridges.

venison /ven-i-s'n/ • **n.** meat from a deer.
– ORIGIN Old French *venesoun.*

Venn diagram • **n.** a diagram representing mathematical sets as circles, common elements of the sets being represented by overlapping sections of the circles.
– ORIGIN named after the English logician John *Venn* (1834–1923).

venom • **n.** **1** poisonous fluid produced by animals such as snakes and scorpions and injected by biting or stinging. **2** extreme hatred or bitterness.
– ORIGIN Old French *venim.*

venomous • **adj.** **1** producing venom. **2** full of hatred or bitterness.
– DERIVATIVES **venomously** adv.

venous /vee-nuhss/ • **adj.** relating to a vein or the veins.

vent[1] • **n.** an opening that allows air, gas, or liquid to pass out of or into a confined space. • **v.** **1** give free expression to (a strong emotion). **2** discharge (air, gas, or liquid) through an outlet.
– ORIGIN French *vent* 'wind' or *éventer* 'expose to air'.

vent[2] • **n.** a slit in a garment.
– ORIGIN Old French *fente* 'slit'.

ventilate • **v.** (**ventilates, ventilating, ventilated**) **1** cause air to enter and circulate freely in (a room or building). **2** discuss (an opinion or issue) in public.
– DERIVATIVES **ventilation** n.
– ORIGIN Latin *ventilare* 'blow'.

ventilator • **n.** **1** a machine or opening for ventilating a room or building. **2** a machine that pumps air in and out of a person's lungs to help them to breathe.

ventral • **adj.** tech. having to do with the underside or abdomen. Compare with **dorsal**.
– ORIGIN Latin *venter* 'belly'.

ventricle /ven-tri-k'l/ • **n.** each of the two larger and lower cavities of the heart.
– ORIGIN Latin *ventriculus.*

ventriloquist /ven-tril-uh-kwist/ • **n.** an entertainer who makes their voice seem to come from a dummy of a person or animal.
– DERIVATIVES **ventriloquism** n.
– ORIGIN from Latin *venter* 'belly' + *loqui* 'speak'.

venture • **n.** **1** a risky or daring journey or undertaking. **2** a business enterprise involving considerable risk. • **v.** (**ventures, venturing, ventured**) **1** dare to do something dangerous or risky. **2** dare to say something bold.
– DERIVATIVES **venturer** n.
– ORIGIN shortening of **adventure**.

venture capital • **n.** capital invested in a project in which there is a large element of risk.

venturesome • **adj.** willing to do something difficult or risky.

Venturi E
/ven-tyuu-ri/, Robert (Charles) (b.1925), American postmodernist architect. Among his buildings are the Sainsbury Wing of the National Gallery in London.

venue /ven-yoo/ • **n.** the place where an event or meeting is held.
– ORIGIN Old French, 'a coming'.

Venus[1] E
the Roman goddess of love. Greek equivalent **Aphrodite**.

Venus[2] E
the second planet from the sun in the solar system, the brightest object in the sky after the sun and moon.

Venus flytrap • **n.** a plant with hinged leaves that spring shut on and digest insects which land on them.

veracious /vuh-ray-shuhss/ • **adj.** formal speaking or representing the truth.
– ORIGIN Latin *verus* 'true'.

veracity /vuh-rass-i-ti/ • **n.** the quality of being true or accurate.

veranda /vuh-ran-duh/ (also **verandah**) • **n.** a roofed platform along the outside of a house, level with the ground floor.
– ORIGIN Portuguese *varanda* 'railing'.

verb • **n.** Grammar a word used to describe an action, state, or occurrence, such as *hear, become,* or *happen.*
– ORIGIN Latin *verbum* 'word, verb'.

verbal • **adj.** **1** relating to or in the form of words. **2** spoken rather than written. **3** relating to a verb.
– DERIVATIVES **verbally** adv.

verbalize (also **verbalise**) • **v.** (**verbalizes, verbalizing, verbalized**) express in words.
– DERIVATIVES **verbalization** (also **verbalisation**) n.

verbal noun • n. Grammar a noun formed as an inflection of a verb, such as *smoking* in *smoking is forbidden*.

verbatim /ver-**bay**-tim/ • adv. & adj. in exactly the same words as were used originally.
– ORIGIN Latin.

verbena /ver-**bee**-nuh/ • n. an ornamental plant with heads of bright showy flowers.
– ORIGIN Latin, 'sacred bough'.

verbiage /ver-bi-ij/ • n. excessively long or technical speech or writing.
– ORIGIN French.

verbose /ver-**bohss**/ • adj. using more words than are needed.
– DERIVATIVES **verbosity** n.
– ORIGIN Latin *verbosus*.

verdant /ver-duhnt/ • adj. green with grass or other lush vegetation.
– ORIGIN perh. from Old French *verdeant*.

Verdi E
/**vair**-di/, Giuseppe (Fortunino Francesco) (1813–1901), Italian composer, famous for his many operas, including *La Traviata* and *Aida*, as well as for his *Requiem*.

verdict • n. **1** a formal decision made by a jury in a court of law as to whether a person is innocent or guilty. **2** an opinion or judgement made after testing or trying something.
– ORIGIN Old French *verdit*.

verdigris /ver-di-gree, ver-di-greess/ • n. a bright bluish-green substance formed on copper or brass by oxidation.
– ORIGIN from Old French *vert de Grece* 'green of Greece'.

Verdun, Battle of E
/ver-**dun**/ a long and severe battle of the First World War, fought in 1916 at the town of Verdun in NE France.

verdure /ver-dyer/ • n. lush green vegetation.
– ORIGIN Old French *verd* 'green'.

verge • n. **1** an edge or border. **2** Brit. a grass edging by the side of a road or path. **3** a limit beyond which something will happen: *she was on the verge of tears*. • v. (**verges**, **verging**, **verged**) (**verge on**) be very close or similar to.
– ORIGIN Old French.

verger • n. an official in a church who acts as a caretaker and attendant.
– ORIGIN Old French.

Vergil E
var. of **VIRGIL**.

verify /ve-ri-fy/ • v. (**verifies**, **verifying**, **verified**) make sure or show that (something) is true, accurate, or justified.
– DERIVATIVES **verifiable** adj. **verification** n.
– ORIGIN Latin *verificare*.

V

verily • adv. archaic truly; certainly.
– ORIGIN from **VERY**.

verisimilitude /ve-ri-si-**mil**-i-tyood/ • n. the appearance of being true or real.
– ORIGIN Latin *verisimilitudo*.

veritable • adj. rightly so called (used for emphasis): *a veritable price explosion*.
– DERIVATIVES **veritably** adv.

verity • n. (pl. **verities**) **1** a true principle or belief. **2** truth.
– ORIGIN Latin *veritas*.

Verlaine E
/vair-**len**/, Paul (1844–96), French symbolist poet, known for such collections of poetry as *Poèmes saturniens* and *Romances sans paroles*.

Vermeer E
/ver-**meer**/, Jan (1632–75), Dutch painter, known for his paintings of domestic interior scenes, for example *The Kitchen-Maid*.

vermicelli /ver-mi-**chel**-li, ver-mi-**sel**-li/ • pl. n. **1** pasta made in long slender threads. **2** Brit. shreds of chocolate used to decorate cakes.
– ORIGIN Italian, 'little worms'.

vermiform • adj. tech. resembling or having the form of a worm.

vermilion /ver-**mil**-yuhn/ (also **vermillion**) • n. a brilliant red pigment or colour.
– ORIGIN Old French *vermeillon*.

vermin • n. **1** wild mammals and birds which harm crops, farm animals, or game, or which carry disease. **2** worms or insects that live on the bodies of people or animals. **3** very unpleasant and destructive people.
– DERIVATIVES **verminous** adj.
– ORIGIN Old French.

Vermont E
/ver-**mont**/ a state in the north-eastern US; capital, Montpelier.
– DERIVATIVES **Vermonter** n.

vermouth /ver-muhth, ver-**mooth**/ • n. a red or white wine flavoured with herbs.
– ORIGIN French *vermout*.

vernacular /ver-**nak**-yuu-ler/ • n. the language or dialect spoken by the ordinary people of a country or region.
– ORIGIN Latin *vernaculus* 'native'.

vernal /ver-n'l/ • adj. having to do with the season of spring.
– ORIGIN Latin *vernalis*.

vernal equinox • n. the spring equinox.

Verne E
/vern/, Jules (1828–1905), French novelist, one of the first writers of science fiction. His best-known works include *Twenty Thousand Leagues under the Sea* and *Around the World in Eighty Days*.

vernier /ver-ni-er/ • n. a small movable graduated scale for indicating fractions of the main scale on a measuring device.
– ORIGIN named after the French mathematician Pierre *Vernier* (1580–1637).

Veronese E
/ve-ruh-**nay**-zi/, Paolo (*c*.1528–88; born *Paolo Caliari*), Italian painter, known for his richly coloured feast scenes, such as *The Marriage at Cana*.

verruca /vuh-**roo**-kuh/ • n. (pl. **verrucae** /vuh-**roo**-kee/ or **verrucas**) a contagious wart on the sole of the foot.
– ORIGIN Latin.

Versace E
/vair-**sah**-chay/, Gianni (1946–97), Italian fashion designer. He was shot dead outside his home in Miami.

Versailles E
/vair-**sy**/ a palace built for Louis XIV near the town of Versailles, south-west of Paris.

Versailles, Treaty of E
the name of two treaties: firstly, a treaty which ended the War of American Independence in 1783; secondly, a treaty signed in 1919 which formally ended the First World War.

versatile • adj. able to adapt or be adapted to many different functions or activities.
– DERIVATIVES **versatility** n.
– ORIGIN Latin *versatilis*.

verse • n. **1** writing arranged with a regular rhythm, and often having a rhyme. **2** a group of lines that form a unit in a poem or song. **3** each of the short numbered divisions of a chapter in the Bible or other scripture.
– ORIGIN Latin *versus* 'furrow, line of writing'.

versed • adj. (**versed in**) experienced or skilled in; knowledgeable about.
– ORIGIN Latin *versatus*.

versify • v. (**versifies**, **versifying**, **versified**) write verse or turn (writing) into verse.
– DERIVATIVES **versification** n.

version • n. **1** a form of something that differs in some way from other forms of the same type of thing: *the car comes in two-door and four-door versions*. **2** an account of a matter from a particular person's point of view.
– ORIGIN Latin.

verso /ver-soh/ • n. (pl. **versos**) a left-hand page of an open book. Contrasted with **RECTO**.
– ORIGIN from Latin *verso folio* 'on the turned leaf'.

versus • prep. **1** against. **2** as opposed to.
– ORIGIN Latin, 'towards'.

vertebra /ver-ti-bruh/ • n. (pl. **vertebrae** /ver-ti-bray, ver-ti-bree/) each of the series of small bones forming the backbone.
– DERIVATIVES **vertebral** adj.
– ORIGIN Latin.

vertebrate /ver-ti-bruht/ • n. an animal having a backbone, including mammals, birds, reptiles, amphibians, and fishes.

vertex /ver-teks/ • n. (pl. **vertices** /ver-ti-seez/ or **vertexes**) **1** the highest point. **2** Geom. each angular point of a polygon, triangle, or other figure. **3** a meeting point of two lines that form an angle.
– ORIGIN Latin, 'whirlpool, vertex'.

vertical • adj. at right angles to a horizontal plane; having the top directly above the bottom. • n. **1** (**the vertical**) a vertical line or plane. **2** an upright structure.
– DERIVATIVES **verticality** n. **vertically** adv.
– ORIGIN Latin *verticalis*.

vertiginous /ver-tij-i-nuhss/ • adj. extremely high or steep and causing vertigo.
– DERIVATIVES **vertiginously** adv.

vertigo /ver-ti-goh/ • n. a feeling of giddiness caused by looking down from a great height.
– ORIGIN Latin, 'whirling'.

vervain /ver-vayn/ • n. a plant with small blue, white, or purple flowers, used in herbal medicine.
– ORIGIN Old French *verveine*.

verve • n. vigour, spirit, and style.
– ORIGIN French.

Verwoerd E
/fer-voo-ert/, Hendrik (Frensch) (1901–66), South African statesman, Prime Minister 1958–66. As Minister of Bantu Affairs (1950–8) he developed the policy of apartheid. As Premier he banned the ANC (1960) and withdrew South Africa from the Commonwealth, declaring it a republic in 1961.

very • adv. in a high degree. • adj. **1** actual; precise. **2** emphasizing an extreme point in time or space. **3** mere: *the very thought of drink made him feel sick*.
– ORIGIN Latin *verus* 'true'.

Very Reverend • adj. a title given to a dean in the Anglican Church.

Vesalius E
/vi-say-li-uhss/, Andreas (1514–64), Flemish anatomist. His major work, *De Humani Corporis Fabrica*, was based on actual dissection and examination, and became the foundation of modern anatomy.

vesicle /ves-si-k'l, vee-si-k'l/ • n. **1** a small fluid-filled sac or cyst in an animal or plant. **2** a blister full of clear fluid.
– ORIGIN Latin *vesicula* 'small bladder'.

Vespasian E
/ve-spay-*zh*'n/ (AD 9–79; Latin name *Titus Flavius Vespasianus*), Roman emperor 69–79. His reign saw the restoration of financial and military order.

vespers • n. a service of evening prayer.
– ORIGIN Latin *vesperas* 'evensong'.

Vespucci E
/ve-spoo-chi/, Amerigo (1451–1512), Italian explorer. He reached the coast of Venezuela on his first voyage (1499–1500) and later explored the Brazilian coastline. The Latin form of his first name is believed to have given rise to the name of America.

vessel • n. **1** a ship or large boat. **2** a hollow container used to hold liquid. **3** a tube or duct carrying a fluid within an animal body or plant structure.
– ORIGIN Old French *vessele*.

vest • n. **1** Brit. a sleeveless undergarment worn on the upper part of the body. **2** a sleeveless garment worn for a particular purpose: *a bulletproof vest*. **3** N. Amer. & Austral. a waistcoat or sleeveless jacket. • v. **1** (**vest in**) give (power, property, etc.) to. **2** give (someone) the legal right to power, property, etc.
– ORIGIN Latin *vestis* 'garment'.

Vesta E
the Roman goddess of the hearth and household. The fire in her temple in Rome was kept constantly burning, tended by the vestal virgins.

vestal virgin • n. (in ancient Rome) a virgin dedicated to the goddess Vesta and vowed to chastity.

vested interest • n. a personal reason for wanting something to happen.

vestibule /vess-ti-byool/ • n. a room or hall just inside the outer door of a building.
– ORIGIN Latin *vestibulum* 'entrance court'.

vestige /vess-tij/ • n. **1** a remaining trace of something that once existed: *the last vestiges of colonialism*. **2** the smallest amount.
– ORIGIN Latin *vestigium* 'footprint'.

vestigial /ve-sti-ji-uhl, ve-sti-juhl/ • adj. forming a very small remaining part.

vestment • n. a robe worn by the clergy or members of a choir during services.
– ORIGIN Latin *vestimentum*.

vestry ● **n.** (pl. **vestries**) a room in a church, used as an office and for changing into ceremonial robes.
– ORIGIN Latin *vestiarium*.

Vesuvius E
/vi-soo-vi-uhss/ an active volcano near Naples, in southern Italy. A violent eruption in AD 79 buried the towns of Pompeii and Herculaneum.

vet[1] ● **n.** a veterinary surgeon. ● **v.** (**vets, vetting, vetted**) investigate (a person's background) before employing them.

vet[2] ● **n.** N. Amer. informal a veteran.

vetch ● **n.** a plant with purple, pink, or yellow flowers, grown for silage or fodder.
– ORIGIN Old French *veche*.

veteran ● **n.** **1** a person who has had long experience in a particular field. **2** an ex-member of the armed forces.
– ORIGIN Latin *veteranus*.

veteran car ● **n.** Brit. an old car, specifically one made before 1919.

veterinarian ● **n.** N. Amer. = **VETERINARY SURGEON**.

veterinary /vet-ri-nuh-ri, vet-uhn-ri/ ● **adj.** relating to the treatment of injuries and diseases in animals.
– ORIGIN Latin *veterinarius*.

veterinary surgeon ● **n.** Brit. a person qualified to treat diseased or injured animals.

veto /vee-toh/ ● **n.** (pl. **vetoes**) **1** a right to reject a decision or proposal made by a lawmaking body. **2** any refusal to allow something. ● **v.** (**vetoes, vetoing, vetoed**) use a veto against.
– ORIGIN Latin, 'I forbid'.

vex ● **v.** make annoyed or worried.
– DERIVATIVES **vexation** n.
– ORIGIN Latin *vexare* 'shake'.

vexatious ● **adj.** causing annoyance or worry.

vexed ● **adj.** **1** difficult to resolve and much debated: *the vexed question of Europe.* **2** annoyed or worried.

VHF ● **abbrev.** very high frequency.

VHS ● **abbrev.** trademark video home system (as used by domestic video recorders).

via ● **prep.** **1** travelling through (a place) on the way to a destination. **2** by way of; through. **3** by means of.
– ORIGIN Latin, 'way, road'.

viable /vy-uh-b'l/ ● **adj.** **1** capable of working successfully; feasible. **2** (of a plant, animal, or cell) capable of surviving or living successfully.
– DERIVATIVES **viability** n.
– ORIGIN French.

viaduct ● **n.** a long bridge-like structure carrying a road or railway across a valley or other low ground.
– ORIGIN from Latin *via* 'way' + *ducere* 'to lead'.

Viagra /vy-ag-ruh/ ● **n.** trademark a synthetic compound used to help a man achieve an erection.
– ORIGIN prob. from *virility* and the name *Niagara*.

vial /vy-uhl/ ● **n.** a small container used for holding liquid medicines.
– ORIGIN from **PHIAL**.

viands /vy-uhndz/ ● **pl. n.** archaic food.
– ORIGIN Old French *viande*.

viaticum /vy-at-i-kuhm/ ● **n.** (pl. **viatica** /vy-at-i-kuh/) the Eucharist as given to a person near or in danger of death.
– ORIGIN Latin.

vibe (also **vibes**) ● **n.** informal the atmosphere produced by a place or a mood passing between people.

vibrant ● **adj.** **1** full of energy and enthusiasm. **2** (of sound) strong or resonant. **3** (of colour) bright.
– DERIVATIVES **vibrancy** n. **vibrantly** adv.
– ORIGIN Latin *vibrare* 'vibrate'.

vibraphone /vy-bruh-fohn/ ● **n.** an electrical percussion instrument giving a vibrato effect.

vibrate ● **v.** (**vibrates, vibrating, vibrated**) **1** move with small movements rapidly to and fro. **2** (of a sound) resonate.
– ORIGIN Latin *vibrare*.

vibration ● **n.** an instance or the state of vibrating.
– DERIVATIVES **vibrational** adj.

vibrato /vi-brah-toh/ ● **n.** Music a rapid, slight variation in pitch in singing or playing some musical instruments.
– ORIGIN Italian.

vibrator ● **n.** a vibrating device used for massage or sexual stimulation.

viburnum /vy-ber-nuhm/ ● **n.** a shrub or small tree with clusters of small white flowers.
– ORIGIN Latin, 'wayfaring tree'.

vicar ● **n.** (in the Church of England) a priest in charge of a parish.
– ORIGIN Old French *vicaire*.

vicarage ● **n.** the house of a vicar.

vicarious /vi-kair-i-uhss, vy-kair-i-uhss/ ● **adj.** experienced in one's imagination after watching or reading about another person's actions or feelings: *the vicarious thrill of watching other children being bad.*
– DERIVATIVES **vicariously** adv.
– ORIGIN Latin *vicarius* 'substitute'.

vice[1] ● **n.** **1** immoral or wicked behaviour. **2** criminal activities involving prostitution, pornography, or drugs. **3** an immoral or wicked quality in a person's character. **4** a bad habit.
– ORIGIN Old French.

vice[2] (US **vise**) ● **n.** a metal tool with movable jaws which are used to hold an object firmly in place while work is done on it.
– ORIGIN Old French *vis*.

vice- ● **comb. form** next in rank to and able to deputize for: *vice-president*.
– ORIGIN Latin *vice* 'in place of'.

vice admiral ● **n.** a high rank of naval officer, above rear admiral and below admiral.

vice chancellor ● **n.** a deputy chancellor of a British university who is in charge of its administration.

Vicente E
/vi-sen-ti/, Gil (*c.*1465–*c.*1536), Portuguese dramatist and poet, Portugal's most important dramatist. His works include religious dramas, farces, pastoral plays, and satirical comedies.

vice-president ● **n.** an official or executive serving as a deputy to a president.

viceregal ● adj. relating to a viceroy.

viceroy ● n. a person sent by a monarch to govern a colony.
– ORIGIN from archaic French.

vice versa /vyss ver-suh, vy-suh ver-suh/ ● adv. reversing the order of the items just mentioned.
– ORIGIN Latin, 'in-turned position'.

Vichy E
/vee-shi/ a spa town in south central France. During the Second World War it was the headquarters of the regime set up after the German occupation of northern France to administer unoccupied France; the regime functioned as a puppet government for the Nazis.

vicinity ● n. (pl. **vicinities**) the area near or surrounding a place.
– ORIGIN Latin *vicinitas*.

vicious ● adj. **1** cruel or violent. **2** (of an animal) wild and dangerous.
– DERIVATIVES **viciously** adv. **viciousness** n.
– ORIGIN Latin *vitiosus*.

vicious circle ● n. a situation in which one problem leads to another, which then makes the first one worse.

vicissitudes /vi-siss-i-tyoodz/ ● pl. n. changes of circumstances or fortune.
– ORIGIN Latin *vicissitudo*.

Vicksburg E
/**viks**-berg/ a city on the Mississippi River, in western Mississippi. During the American Civil War it was the last remaining obstacle to Union control of the Mississippi and it fell to Union forces after a six-week siege in 1863.

Vico E
/**vee**-koh/, Giambattista (1668–1744), Italian philosopher. He believed that civilizations are subject to recurring cycles of barbarism, heroism, and reason. His approach influenced later philosophers such as Marx.

victim ● n. **1** a person harmed or killed as a result of a crime or accident. **2** a person who is tricked: *the victim of a hoax*.
– PHRASES **fall victim to** be hurt, killed, or destroyed by.
– ORIGIN Latin *victima*.

victimize (also **victimise**) ● v. (**victimizes, victimizing, victimized**) single out for cruel or unfair treatment.
– DERIVATIVES **victimization** (also **victimisation**) n.

victor ● n. a person who defeats an opponent in a battle, game, or competition.
– ORIGIN Latin.

Victor Emmanuel II E
(1820–78), ruler of Sardinia 1849–61 and first king of united Italy 1861–78. After being crowned king of Italy he added Venetia to the kingdom in 1866 and Rome in 1870.

Victor Emmanuel III E
(1869–1947), last king of Italy 1900–46. He invited Mussolini to form a government in 1922 and lost all political power. After the loss of Sicily to the Allies (1943), he dismissed Mussolini and concluded an armistice.

Victoria[1] E
a state of SE Australia; capital, Melbourne.

Victoria[2] E
the capital of the Seychelles, on the island of Mahé.

Victoria[3] E
the capital of Hong Kong.

Victoria[4] E
(1819–1901), queen of Great Britain and Ireland 1837–1901 and empress of India 1876–1901. She came to the throne on the death of her uncle, William IV; her reign was the longest in British history. Victoria largely retired from public life after Prince Albert's death in 1861.

Victoria, Lake E
the largest lake in Africa, with shores in Uganda, Tanzania, and Kenya, and drained by the Nile. Also called **VICTORIA NYANZA**.

Victoria and Albert Museum E
a national museum in South Kensington, London, containing collections of pictures, textiles, ceramics, and furniture.

Victoria Falls E
a waterfall 109 m (355 ft) high, on the River Zambezi, on the Zimbabwe–Zambia border.

Victorian ● adj. relating to the reign of Queen Victoria, or to the attitudes associated with that period.

Victoriana ● pl. n. articles from the Victorian period.

Victoria Nyanza E
/ni-**an**-zuh/ another name for Lake Victoria (see **VICTORIA, LAKE**).

Victoria plum ● n. Brit. a large red dessert plum.

victorious ● adj. having won a victory.
– DERIVATIVES **victoriously** adv.

Victory E
the flagship of Lord Nelson at the Battle of Trafalgar, now on display at Portsmouth.

victory ● n. (pl. **victories**) an act of defeating an opponent in a battle or competition.
– ORIGIN Latin *victoria*.

victual /vi-t'l/ dated ● n. (**victuals**) food or provisions. ● v. (**victuals, victualling, victualled**; US **victuals, victualing, victualed**) provide with food or other stores.
– ORIGIN Latin *victualis*.

victualler /vi-t'l-er/ (US **victualer**) ● n. **1** Brit. a person who is licensed to sell alcoholic liquor. **2** dated a person providing or selling food or other provisions.

vicuña /vi-**koo**-nyuh, vy-**kyoo**-nuh/ ● n. **1** a wild relative of the llama, having fine silky wool. **2** cloth made from this wool.
– ORIGIN from a South American Indian language.

Vidal E
/vi-**dahl**/, Gore (b.1925; born *Eugene Luther Vidal*), American novelist, dramatist, and essayist. His novels, many of them satirical comedies, include *Williwaw* and *Myra Breckenridge*.

V

video • n. (pl. **videos**) **1** a system of recording and reproducing moving visual images using magnetic tape. **2** a film or other recording on magnetic tape. **3** a cassette of videotape. **4** Brit. a video recorder. • v. (**videoes**, **videoing**, **videoed**) film or make a video recording of.
– ORIGIN Latin *videre* 'to see'.

videoconference • n. an arrangement in which television sets linked to telephone lines are used to allow a group of people to communicate with and see each other.
– DERIVATIVES **videoconferencing** n.

videodisc • n. a CD-ROM or other disc used to store visual images.

video game • n. a computer game played on a VDU screen.

videophone • n. a telephone device transmitting and receiving a visual image as well as sound.

video recorder • n. a device which, when linked to a television set, can be used for recording on and playing videotapes.

videotape • n. **1** magnetic tape for recording and reproducing visual images and sound. **2** a cassette on which this tape is held. • v. (**videotapes**, **videotaping**, **videotaped**) record on video.

vie • v. (**vies**, **vying**, **vied**) compete eagerly with others in order to do or achieve something.
– ORIGIN prob. from the former word *envy*, from Latin *invitare* 'challenge'.

Vienna E
the capital of Austria.
– DERIVATIVES **Viennese** adj. & n.

Vientiane E
/vyen-**tyahn**/ the capital of Laos.

Vietnam E
/vyet-**nam**/ a country in SE Asia; capital, Hanoi.
– DERIVATIVES **Vietnamese** adj. & n.

Vietnam War E
a war between Communist North Vietnam and US-backed South Vietnam. Following the partition of Vietnam in 1954, the North had attempted to unite the country as a Communist state. The US army was sent to Vietnam in 1964 in support of the South, finally withdrawing in 1973. The war ended in 1975 with victory for the North and the reunification of the country under a Communist regime the next year.

view • n. **1** the ability to see something or to be seen from a particular position: *the mountains came into view.* **2** a sight from a particular position of beautiful natural scenery. **3** an attitude or opinion. • v. **1** look at or inspect. **2** regard in a particular way: *she views beggars as potential thieves.* **3** inspect (a house or other property) with the prospect of buying or renting. **4** watch on television.
– PHRASES **in view 1** visible. **2** in one's mind or as one's aim. **in view of** because or as a result of. **with a view to** with the hope or intention of.
– DERIVATIVES **viewable** adj.
– ORIGIN Old French *vieue.*

viewer • n. **1** a person who views something. **2** a device for looking at film transparencies or similar photographic images.

viewership • n. the audience for a particular television programme or channel.

viewfinder • n. a device on a camera showing the field of view of the lens, used in framing and focusing the picture.

viewpoint • n. **1** a position giving a good view. **2** an opinion.

Vigée-Lebrun E
/vee-*zh*ay-luh-**bruhn**/, (Marie Louise) Élisabeth (1755–1842), French painter, known for her portraits of women and children.

vigil /vi-jil/ • n. a period of staying awake during the night to keep watch or pray.
– ORIGIN Latin, 'awake'.

vigilant • adj. keeping careful watch for possible danger or difficulties.
– DERIVATIVES **vigilance** n. **vigilantly** adv.
– ORIGIN Latin *vigilare* 'keep awake'.

vigilante /vi-ji-**lan**-ti/ • n. a member of a self-appointed group of people who undertake law enforcement in their community without legal authority.
– DERIVATIVES **vigilantism** n.
– ORIGIN Spanish, 'vigilant'.

vignette /vee-**nyet**/ • n. **1** a brief vivid description, account, or episode. **2** a small illustration or portrait photograph which fades into its background without a definite border.
– ORIGIN French.

vigor • n. US = VIGOUR.

vigorous • adj. **1** strong, healthy, and full of energy. **2** involving physical strength, effort, or energy.
– DERIVATIVES **vigorously** adv. **vigorousness** n.

vigour (US **vigor**) • n. **1** physical strength and good health. **2** effort, energy, and enthusiasm.
– ORIGIN Latin *vigor.*

Viking • n. a member of the Scandinavian seafaring people who settled in parts of Britain and NW Europe between the 8th and 11th centuries.
– ORIGIN Old Norse.

Vila E
/vee-luh/ (also **Port Vila**) the capital of Vanuatu.

vile • adj. **1** extremely unpleasant. **2** wicked.
– DERIVATIVES **vilely** adv.
– ORIGIN Latin *vilis* 'cheap, base'.

vilify /vil-i-fy/ • v. (**vilifies**, **vilifying**, **vilified**) speak or write about in a very abusive way.
– DERIVATIVES **vilification** n.
– ORIGIN Latin *vilificare.*

Villa E
/vee-yuh, **veel**-yuh/, Pancho (1878–1923; born *Doroteo Arango*), Mexican revolutionary. He played a leading role in the revolution of 1910–11. In 1914, together with Venustiano Carranza, he overthrew the dictatorial regime of General Victoriano Huerta.

villa • n. **1** (especially in continental Europe) a large country house in its own grounds. **2** Brit. a detached or semi-detached house in a residential district. **3** a rented holiday home abroad.
– ORIGIN Latin.

village • n. **1** a small settlement in a country

area. **2** a self-contained district within a town or city.
– DERIVATIVES **villager** n.
– ORIGIN Old French.

villain ● n. **1** a wicked person. **2** a bad character in a novel or play whose evil actions or motives are important to the plot.
– DERIVATIVES **villainous** adj. **villainy** n.
– ORIGIN first meaning 'an unsophisticated country person': from Old French *vilein*.

Villa-Lobos E
/vil-luh-**loh**-boss/, Heitor (1887–1959), Brazilian composer, who used folk music in many of his instrumental compositions.

villein /vil-luhn, vil-layn/ ● n. (in medieval England) a poor man who had to work for a lord in return for a small piece of land on which to grow food.
– ORIGIN from VILLAIN.

villus /vil-luhss/ ● n. (pl. **villi** /vil-ly/) Anat. any of many short narrow finger-like growths of tissue on some membranes of the body, especially the small intestine.
– ORIGIN Latin, 'shaggy hair'.

Vilnius E
/vil-ni-uhss/ the capital of Lithuania.

vim ● n. informal energy; enthusiasm.
– ORIGIN perh. from Latin *vis* 'energy'.

vinaigrette /vi-ni-**gret**, vi-nay-**gret**/ ● n. salad dressing of oil, wine vinegar, and seasoning.
– ORIGIN French.

Vinci, E
Leonardo da, see **LEONARDO DA VINCI**.

vindaloo /vin-duh-**loo**/ ● n. a very hot Indian curry made with meat or fish.
– ORIGIN prob. from Portuguese *vin d'alho* 'wine and garlic sauce'.

vindicate /vin-di-kayt/ ● v. (**vindicates**, **vindicating**, **vindicated**) **1** clear of blame or suspicion. **2** show to be right or justified.
– DERIVATIVES **vindication** n.
– ORIGIN Latin *vindicare* 'claim, avenge'.

vindictive ● adj. having a strong or unreasoning desire for revenge.
– DERIVATIVES **vindictiveness** n.
– ORIGIN Latin *vindicta* 'vengeance'.

vine ● n. **1** a climbing plant, especially one that produces grapes. **2** the thin stem of a climbing plant.
– ORIGIN Latin *vinea* 'vineyard, vine'.

vinegar ● n. a sour-tasting liquid containing acetic acid, used as a seasoning or for pickling.
– DERIVATIVES **vinegary** adj.
– ORIGIN from Old French *vyn egre* 'sour wine'.

vineyard ● n. a plantation of grapevines, producing grapes used in winemaking.

vino ● n. (pl. **vinos**) informal wine.
– ORIGIN Spanish and Italian, 'wine'.

vinous /vy-nuhss/ ● adj. having to do with or like wine.

Vinson Massif E
/vin-s'n ma-**seef**/ the highest mountain range in Antarctica, rising to 5,140 m (16,863 ft).

vintage ● n. **1** the year or place in which wine was produced. **2** a wine of high quality made from the crop of a single specified district in a good year. **3** the harvesting of grapes for winemaking. **4** the wine of a particular season. **5** the time that something was produced. ● adj. **1** referring to vintage wine. **2** referring to something from the past of high quality.
– ORIGIN Old French *vendange*.

vintage car ● n. Brit. an old car, specifically one made between 1919 and 1930.

vintner /**vint**-ner/ ● n. a wine merchant.
– ORIGIN Old French *vinetier*.

vinyl /vy-n'l/ ● n. a type of strong plastic, used in making floor coverings, paint, and, especially formerly, gramophone records.
– ORIGIN Latin *vinum* 'wine'.

viol /vy-uhl/ ● n. a musical instrument of the Renaissance and baroque periods, resembling a violin but with six strings.
– ORIGIN Provençal *viola*.

viola[1] /vi-**oh**-luh/ ● n. an instrument of the violin family, larger than the violin and tuned a fifth lower.
– ORIGIN Italian and Spanish.

viola[2] /vy-uh-luh/ ● n. a plant of a group that includes the pansies and violets.
– ORIGIN Latin, 'violet'.

violate ● v. (**violates**, **violating**, **violated**) **1** break (a rule or formal agreement). **2** treat with disrespect. **3** rape or sexually assault.
– DERIVATIVES **violation** n. **violator** n.
– ORIGIN Latin *violare* 'treat violently'.

violence ● n. **1** behaviour involving physical force intended to hurt, damage, or kill. **2** physical or emotional force or energy.

violent ● adj. **1** using or involving violence. **2** very forceful or powerful: *violent dislike.*
– DERIVATIVES **violently** adv.
– ORIGIN Latin, 'vehement, violent'.

violet ● n. **1** a small plant with purple, blue, or white five-petalled flowers. **2** a bluish-purple colour.
– ORIGIN Old French *violette*.

violin ● n. a musical instrument having four strings, played with a bow.
– DERIVATIVES **violinist** n.
– ORIGIN Italian *violino* 'small viola'.

violist /vi-**oh**-list/ ● n. a viola player.

violoncello /vy-uh-luhn-**chel**-loh/ ● n. formal = **CELLO**.
– ORIGIN Italian.

VIP ● abbrev. very important person.

viper ● n. **1** a poisonous snake with large fangs and a patterned body. **2** a spiteful or treacherous person.
– ORIGIN Latin *vipera*.

virago /vi-**rah**-goh/ ● n. (pl. **viragos** or **viragoes**) a domineering, violent, or bad-tempered woman.
– ORIGIN Latin, 'heroic woman, female warrior'.

viral ● adj. having to do with or caused by a virus or viruses.
– DERIVATIVES **virally** adv.

Virchow E
/ver-koh/, Rudolf Karl (1821–1902), German physician and pathologist. The founder of the branch of pathology based on the examination of cells, he argued that the cell was the basis of life and that diseases were reflected in specific cellular abnormalities.

Virgil E
/ver-jil/ (also **Vergil**) (70–19 BC; Latin name *Publius Vergilius Maro*), Roman poet, author of the *Aeneid*, an epic poem which describes the travels of Aeneas after the fall of Troy. He also wrote the *Eclogues*, ten pastoral poems, and the *Georgics*, a didactic poem on farming.
– DERIVATIVES **Virgilian** adj.

virgin • n. **1** a person who has never had sexual intercourse. **2** (**the Virgin**) the Virgin Mary. **3** a person who is inexperienced in a particular activity: *a political virgin.* • adj. **1** having had no sexual experience. **2** not yet used or spoilt: *virgin forest.* **3** (of olive oil) obtained from the first pressing of olives.
– DERIVATIVES **virginal** adj.
– ORIGIN Latin *virgo*.

Virgin Birth • n. the doctrine that Christ was born from a mother, Mary, who was a virgin.

Virginia E
a state of the eastern US, on the Atlantic coast; capital, Richmond.
– DERIVATIVES **Virginian** n. & adj.

Virgin Islands E
a group of Caribbean islands in the Greater Antilles. The **British Virgin Islands** consists of about forty islands in the north-east of the group; capital, Road Town (on Tortola). The remaining islands (about fifty) make up the **Virgin Islands of the United States**, admininstered by the US as an unincorporated territory; capital, Charlotte Amalie (on St Thomas).

virginity • n. the state of being a virgin.

Virgin Mary E
the mother of Jesus (see **MARY**).

Virgo • n. a constellation (the Virgin) and sign of the zodiac, which the sun enters about 23 August.
– ORIGIN Latin.

viridian /vi-rid-i-uhn/ • n. a bluish-green pigment or colour.
– ORIGIN Latin *viridis* 'green'.

virile • adj. (of a man) strong, energetic, and having a strong sex drive.
– DERIVATIVES **virility** n.
– ORIGIN Latin *virilis*.

virology /vy-rol-uh-ji/ • n. the branch of science concerned with the study of viruses.
– DERIVATIVES **virologist** n.

virtual • adj. **1** almost or nearly the thing described, but not completely: *poaching could lead to the virtual extinction of the tiger.* **2** Computing not existing in reality but made by software to appear to do so.
– DERIVATIVES **virtuality** n. **virtually** adv.
– ORIGIN Latin *virtualis*.

virtual reality • n. Computing a system in which images that look like real objects are created by computer and can be interacted with by using special electronic equipment.

virtue /ver-tyoo/ • n. **1** behaviour showing high moral standards. **2** a good or desirable personal quality. **3** archaic virginity or chastity.
– PHRASES **by virtue of** as a result of.
– ORIGIN Latin *virtus* 'valour, merit'.

virtuoso /ver-tyoo-oh-soh/ • n. (pl. **virtuosi** /ver-tyoo-oh-si/ or **virtuosos**) a person highly skilled in music or another art.
– DERIVATIVES **virtuosic** adj. **virtuosity** n.
– ORIGIN Italian, 'learned, skilful'.

virtuous • adj. **1** having high moral standards. **2** archaic chaste.

virulent /vi-ruu-luhnt, vir-yuu-luhnt/ • adj. **1** (of a disease or poison) extremely harmful. **2** (of a virus) spreading very quickly. **3** bitterly hostile: *a virulent attack.*
– DERIVATIVES **virulence** n. **virulently** adv.
– ORIGIN Latin *virulentus* 'poisonous'.

virus /vy-ruhss/ • n. **1** a very simple submicroscopic organism which can cause disease and is only able to reproduce inside the living cells of a host. **2** informal an infection or disease caused by a virus. **3** (also **computer virus**) a piece of code introduced secretly into a system in order to damage or destroy data.
– ORIGIN Latin, 'slimy liquid, poison'.

visa /vee-zuh/ • n. a note on a passport indicating that the holder is allowed to enter, leave, or stay for a specified period of time in a country.
– ORIGIN Latin.

visage /vi-zij/ • n. literary a person's facial features or expression.
– ORIGIN Old French.

vis-à-vis /veez-ah-vee/ • prep. in relation to.
– ORIGIN French, 'face to face'.

viscera /viss-uh-ruh/ • pl. n. (sing. **viscus**) the internal organs of the body, especially those in the abdomen.
– ORIGIN Latin.

visceral • adj. **1** relating to the viscera. **2** relating to deep inward feelings rather than to the intellect.
– DERIVATIVES **viscerally** adv.

viscid /viss-id/ • adj. sticky.
– ORIGIN Latin *viscidus*.

Visconti E
/viss-kon-ti/, Luchino (1906–76; full name *Don Luchino Visconti, Conte di Modrone*), Italian film and theatre director. His films include *The Leopard* and *Death in Venice*.

viscose /viss-kohz, viss-kohss/ • n. **1** a thick orange-brown solution obtained by treating cellulose with certain chemicals. **2** rayon fabric made from this.
– ORIGIN Latin *viscus* 'birdlime'.

viscosity /viss-koss-i-ti/ • n. (pl. **viscosities**) the state of being viscous.

viscount /vy-kownt/ • n. a British nobleman ranking above a baron and below an earl.
– ORIGIN Latin *vicecomes*.

viscountess /vy-kown-tiss/ • n. the wife or widow of a viscount, or a woman holding the rank of viscount in her own right.

viscous /viss-kuhss/ • adj. having a thick, sticky consistency between solid and liquid.
– ORIGIN Latin *viscosus*.

viscus /viss-kuhss/ sing. form of **VISCERA**.
– ORIGIN Latin.

vise • n. US = **VICE**[2].

Vishnu E
/vish-noo/ a Hindu god regarded by his worshippers as the supreme deity and saviour, and by others as the preserver of the cosmos in a triad with Brahma and Shiva.

visibility • n. **1** the state of being able to see

or be seen. **2** the distance one can see depending on light and weather conditions.

visible • **adj.** able to be seen or noticed.
– DERIVATIVES **visibly** adv.
– ORIGIN Latin *visibilis*.

vision • **n. 1** the faculty of being able to see: *he kept rubbing his eyes, which blurred his vision.* **2** the ability to think about the future with imagination or wisdom. **3** an experience of seeing something in the mind, or in a dream or trance. **4** the images seen on a television screen. **5** a person or sight of great beauty.
ORIGIN Latin.

visionary • **adj. 1** thinking about the future with imagination or wisdom. **2** relating to supernatural or dreamlike visions. • **n.** (pl. **visionaries**) a visionary person.

visit • **v.** (**visits**, **visiting**, **visited**) **1** go to see and spend time with (someone) socially. **2** go to see and spend time in (a place). **3** inflict (something harmful or unpleasant) on someone. • **n. 1** an act of visiting. **2** a temporary stay at a place.
– ORIGIN Latin *visitare*.

visitant • **n. 1** literary a supernatural being; a ghost. **2** archaic a visitor.

visitation • **n. 1** an official or formal visit. **2** the appearance of a god or goddess, or other supernatural being. **3** a disaster or difficulty seen as a punishment from God: *a visitation of the plague.* **4** (**the Visitation**) the visit of the Virgin Mary to Elizabeth related in the Gospel of Luke, chapter 1.

visitor • **n. 1** a person visiting a person or place. **2** a bird present in a particular area for only part of the year.

visor /vy-zer/ (also **vizor**) • **n. 1** a movable part of a helmet that can be pulled down to cover the face. **2** a screen for protecting the eyes from unwanted light. **3** N. Amer. a stiff peak at the front of a cap.
– ORIGIN Old French *viser*.

vista • **n.** a pleasing view.
– ORIGIN Italian, 'view'.

visual • **adj.** relating to seeing or sight: *her work has a visual appeal.* • **n.** a picture, piece of film, or display used to illustrate or accompany something.
– DERIVATIVES **visually** adv.
– ORIGIN Latin *visualis*.

visual display unit • **n.** Brit. a device for displaying information from a computer on a screen.

visualize (also **visualise**) • **v.** (**visualizes**, **visualizing**, **visualized**) form an image of (something) in the mind.
– DERIVATIVES **visualization** (also **visualisation**) n.

vital • **adj. 1** absolutely necessary. **2** essential for life: *the vital organs.* **3** full of energy. • **n.** (**vitals**) the body's important internal organs.
– DERIVATIVES **vitally** adv.
– ORIGIN Latin *vitalis*.

vitality • **n.** the state of being strong and active.

vitalize (also **vitalise**) • **v.** (**vitalizes**, **vitalizing**, **vitalized**) give strength and energy to: *yoga calms and vitalizes the body and mind.*

vital signs • **pl. n.** measurements, specifically pulse rate, temperature, rate of breathing, and blood pressure, that indicate the state of a patient's essential body functions.

vital statistics • **pl. n.** informal the measurements of a woman's bust, waist, and hips.

vitamin /vi-tuh-min, vy-tuh-min/ • **n.** any of a group of organic compounds which are present in many foods and are essential for normal nutrition.
– ORIGIN from Latin *vita* 'life' + *amine*, because vitamins were originally thought to contain an amino acid.

vitamin A • **n.** retinol, a compound which is essential for growth and vision in dim light and is found in vegetables, egg yolk, and fish liver oil.

vitamin B • **n.** any of a group of substances essential for the working of certain enzymes in the body.

vitamin C • **n.** ascorbic acid, a compound found in citrus fruits and green vegetables, essential in maintaining healthy connective tissue.

vitamin D • **n.** any of a group of compounds found in liver and fish oils, essential for the absorption of calcium.

vitamin E • **n.** tocopherol, a compound found in wheatgerm oil, egg yolk, and leafy vegetables and important in stabilizing cell membranes.

vitamin K • **n.** any of a group of compounds found mainly in green leaves and essential for the blood-clotting process.

vitiate /vi-shi-ayt/ • **v.** (**vitiates**, **vitiating**, **vitiated**) formal make less good or effective: *personal secrets vitiate the whole meaning of marriage.*
– ORIGIN Latin *vitiare* 'impair'.

viticulture /vi-ti-kul-cher/ • **n. 1** the cultivation of grapevines. **2** the study of grape cultivation.
– DERIVATIVES **viticultural** adj. **viticulturist** n.
– ORIGIN from Latin *vitis* 'vine'.

Viti Levu E
/vee-tee lev-oo/ the largest of the Fiji islands; chief settlement, Suva.

vitreous /vi-tri-uhss/ • **adj.** resembling or containing glass.
– ORIGIN Latin *vitreus*.

vitreous humour • **n.** the transparent jelly-like tissue filling the eyeball behind the lens.

vitrify /vi-tri-fy/ • **v.** (**vitrifies**, **vitrifying**, **vitrified**) convert into glass or a glass-like substance by exposure to heat.
– DERIVATIVES **vitrification** n.
– ORIGIN Latin *vitrum* 'glass'.

vitriol /vi-tri-uhl/ • **n. 1** archaic sulphuric acid. **2** extreme bitterness or malice.
– DERIVATIVES **vitriolic** adj.
– ORIGIN Latin *vitriolum*.

Vitruvius E
/vi-troo-vi-uhss/ (*fl.* 1st century BC; full name *Marcus Vitruvius Pollio*), Roman architect, who wrote a ten-volume treatise on architecture and related matters.

vituperation • **n.** bitter and abusive language.
– ORIGIN Latin.

vituperative /vi-tyoo-puh-ruh-tiv, vy-tyoo-puh-ruh-tiv/ • **adj.** bitter and abusive.

Vitus, St E
/vy-tuhss/ (died *c.*300), Christian martyr. He was the patron of those who suffered from epilepsy and certain nervous disorders, including St Vitus's dance (Sydenham's chorea). Feast day, 15 June.

viva[1] /vy-vuh/ • **n.** Brit. an oral examination for an academic qualification.
– ORIGIN short for **VIVA VOCE**.

viva[2] /vee-vuh/ • **exclam.** long live! (used to express acclaim or support).
– ORIGIN Italian.

vivace /vi-vah-chay/ • **adv. & adj.** Music in a lively and brisk manner.
– ORIGIN Italian.

vivacious /vi-vay-shuhss, vy-vay-shuhss/ • **adj.** attractively lively.
– DERIVATIVES **vivaciously** adv. **vivacity** n.
– ORIGIN Latin *vivax* 'lively, vigorous'.

Vivaldi E
/vi-val-di/ , Antonio (Lucio) (1678–1741), Italian baroque composer, best known for the concerto *The Four Seasons*.

vivarium /vi-vair-i-uhm, vy-vair-i-uhm/ • **n.** (pl. **vivaria** /vi-vair-i-uh, vy-vair-i-uh/) a place prepared for keeping animals in conditions similar to their natural environment for the purposes of study or as pets.
– ORIGIN Latin, 'warren, fish pond'.

viva voce /vy-vuh voh-chay, vy-vuh voh-chi/ • **n.** Brit. = **VIVA[1]**.
– ORIGIN Latin, 'with the living voice'.

vivid • **adj. 1** producing powerful feelings or strong, clear images in the mind. **2** (of a colour) very deep or bright.
– DERIVATIVES **vividly** adv. **vividness** n.
– ORIGIN Latin *vividus* 'lively, vigorous'.

vivify /vi-vi-fy/ • **v.** (**vivifies, vivifying, vivified**) make more lively or interesting.
– ORIGIN Latin *vivificare.*

viviparous /vi-vip-uh-ruhss/ • **adj.** (of an animal) bringing forth live young which have developed inside the body of the parent. Compare with **OVIPAROUS**.
– ORIGIN Latin *viviparus.*

vivisection • **n.** the practice of performing operations on live animals for scientific research (used by people opposed to such work).
– ORIGIN Latin *vivus* 'living'.

vixen • **n. 1** a female fox. **2** a spiteful or quarrelsome woman.
– ORIGIN perh. from Old English, 'of a fox'.

Viyella /vy-el-luh/ • **n.** trademark a fabric made from a mixture of cotton and wool.
– ORIGIN from *Via Gellia*, a valley in Derbyshire.

viz. • **adv.** namely; in other words.
– ORIGIN short for Latin *videlicet.*

vizier /vi-zeer/ • **n.** hist. an important official in some Muslim countries.
– ORIGIN Arabic.

vizor • **n.** var. of **VISOR**.

Vladimir I E
/vlad-i-meer/ (956–1015; canonized as **St Vladimir**), grand prince of Kiev 980–1015. He became a Christian after his marriage to a sister of the Byzantine emperor, resulting in Christianity in Russia developing in close association with the Orthodox Church. Feast day, 15 July.

Vladivostok E
/vlad-i-voss-tok/ a city and port in the extreme south-east of Russia, on the Sea of Japan.

VLF • **abbrev.** very low frequency (referring to radio waves of frequency 3–30 kilohertz and wavelength 10–100 kilometres).

V-neck • **n.** a neckline having straight sides meeting at a point to form a V-shape.

VO • **abbrev.** (in the UK) Royal Victorian Order.

vocabulary • **n.** (pl. **vocabularies**) **1** the body of words used in a particular language or in a particular activity. **2** the body of words known to a person. **3** a list of words and their meanings, accompanying a text.
– ORIGIN Latin *vocabularius.*

vocal • **adj. 1** relating to the human voice. **2** expressing opinions or feelings freely or loudly. **3** (of music) consisting of or including singing. • **n. 1** (also **vocals**) a musical performance involving singing. **2** a part of a piece of music that is sung.
– DERIVATIVES **vocally** adv.
– ORIGIN Latin *vocalis.*

vocal cords • **pl. n.** folds of the lining of the larynx whose edges vibrate in the airstream to produce the voice.

vocalist • **n.** a singer.

vocalize /voh-kuh-lyz/ (also **vocalise**) • **v.** (**vocalizes, vocalizing, vocalized**) **1** produce (a sound or word). **2** express (something) with words. **3** Music sing with several notes to one vowel.
– DERIVATIVES **vocalization** (also **vocalisation**) n.

vocation • **n. 1** a strong feeling that one ought to pursue a particular career or occupation. **2** a person's career or occupation.
– ORIGIN Latin.

vocational • **adj.** relating to or directed towards an occupation or employment.
– DERIVATIVES **vocationally** adv.

vocative /vok-uh-tiv/ • **adj.** Grammar (of a case) used in addressing a person or thing.
– ORIGIN Latin *vocativus.*

vociferous /vuh-sif-uh-ruhss/ • **adj.** vehement or loud: *he was a vociferous opponent of the takeover.*
– DERIVATIVES **vociferously** adv.
– ORIGIN Latin *vociferari* 'exclaim'.

vodka • **n.** a clear Russian alcoholic spirit made from rye, wheat, or potatoes.
– ORIGIN Russian, 'little water'.

vogue • **n.** the fashion or style current at a particular time.
– DERIVATIVES **voguish** adj.
– ORIGIN French.

voice • **n. 1** the sound produced in a person's larynx and uttered through the mouth, as speech or song. **2** the ability to speak or sing. **3** Music the range of pitch or type of tone with which a person sings. **4** Music a vocal part in a composition. **5** an opinion or the right to express an opinion. **6** Grammar a form of a verb showing the relation of the subject to the action. • **v.** (**voices, voicing, voiced**) **1** express in words. **2** (**voiced**) (of a speech sound) produced with vibration of the vocal cords.
– ORIGIN Old French *vois.*

voice box • **n.** the larynx.

voiceless ● adj. (of a speech sound) produced without vibration of the vocal cords.

voicemail ● n. a centralized electronic system which can store messages from telephone callers.

voice-over ● n. a piece of narration in a film or broadcast not accompanied by an image of the speaker.

void ● adj. **1** not valid or legally binding. **2** completely empty. **3** (**void of**) free from; lacking. ● n. a completely empty space. ● v. **1** declare to be no longer valid. **2** discharge or empty (water, gases, or waste matter).
– ORIGIN Old French *vuide*.

voile /voyl, vwahl/ ● n. a thin, semi-transparent fabric of cotton, wool, or silk.
– ORIGIN French, 'veil'.

volatile /vol-uh-tyl/ ● adj. **1** (of a substance) easily evaporated at normal temperatures. **2** liable to change rapidly and unpredictably. ● n. a volatile substance.
– DERIVATIVES **volatility** n.
– ORIGIN Latin *volare* 'to fly'.

vol-au-vent /vol-oh-von/ ● n. a small round case of puff pastry filled with a savoury mixture.
– ORIGIN French, 'flight in the wind'.

volcanic ● adj. relating to or produced by a volcano or volcanoes.
– DERIVATIVES **volcanically** adv.

volcanism (also **vulcanism**) ● n. Geol. volcanic activity or phenomena.

volcano ● n. (pl. **volcanoes** or **volcanos**) a mountain or hill having a crater through which lava, rock fragments, hot vapour, and gas are or have been erupted from the earth's crust.
– ORIGIN Latin *Volcanus* 'Vulcan' (see **VULCAN**).

vole ● n. a small mouse-like rodent with a rounded muzzle.
– ORIGIN Norwegian *vollmus* 'field mouse'.

Volga E
/vol-guh/ the longest river in Europe, which rises in NW Russia and flows 3,688 km (2,292 miles) to the Caspian Sea.

volition /vuh-li-sh'n/ ● n. the power of choosing freely and making one's own decisions.
– DERIVATIVES **volitional** adj.
– ORIGIN Latin.

volley ● n. (pl. **volleys**) **1** a number of bullets, arrows, or other missiles fired at one time. **2** a series of questions, insults, etc. directed rapidly at someone. **3** (in sport) a strike of the ball made before it touches the ground. ● v. (**volleys**, **volleying**, **volleyed**) strike (the ball) before it touches the ground.
– ORIGIN French *volée*.

volleyball ● n. a game for two teams in which a ball is hit by hand over a net and points are scored if the ball touches the ground on the opponent's side of the court.

volt ● n. the SI unit of electromotive force, the difference of potential that would carry one ampere of current against a resistance of one ohm.
– ORIGIN named after A. *Volta* (see **VOLTA²**).

Volta¹ E
/vol-tuh/ a river of West Africa, which is formed in central Ghana by the junction of its headwaters, the Black Volta, the White Volta, and the Red Volta, and flows generally southwards into the Gulf of Guinea.

Volta² E
/vol-tuh/, Alessandro Giuseppe Antonio Anastasio, Count (1745–1827), Italian physicist. He invented the voltaic pile or electrochemical battery (1800), the first device to produce a continuous electric current.

voltage ● n. an electromotive force or potential difference expressed in volts.

voltaic /vol-tay-ik/ ● adj. referring to electricity produced by chemical action in a primary battery.

Voltaire E
/vol-tair/ (1694–1778; pen name of *François-Marie Arouet*), French writer, dramatist, and poet. He frequently came into conflict with the Establishment as a result of his radical views. His works include *Lettres philosophiques* and the satire *Candide*.

volte-face /volt-fass/ ● n. an abrupt and complete reversal of attitude or policy.
– ORIGIN French.

voltmeter ● n. an instrument for measuring electric potential in volts.

voluble /vol-yuu-b'l/ ● adj. speaking easily and at length.
– DERIVATIVES **volubility** n. **volubly** adv.
– ORIGIN Latin *volvere* 'to roll'.

volume ● n. **1** a book, especially one forming part of a larger work or series. **2** the amount of space occupied by a substance or object or enclosed within a container. **3** the amount or quantity of something. **4** degree of loudness. **5** fullness of the hair.
– ORIGIN first referring to a roll of parchment with writing on: from Latin *volumen* 'a roll'.

volumetric /vol-yuu-met-rik/ ● adj. relating to the measurement of volume.
– DERIVATIVES **volumetrically** adv.

voluminous /vuh-lyoo-mi-nuhss/ ● adj. **1** (of clothing) loose and full. **2** (of writing) very lengthy.
– ORIGIN Latin *voluminosus* 'having many coils' or *volumen* 'a roll'.

volumize (also **volumise**) ● v. (**volumizes**, **volumizing**, **volumized**) give volume or body to (hair).

voluntary ● adj. **1** done or acting of one's own free will. **2** working or done without payment. **3** under the conscious control of the brain. ● n. (pl. **voluntaries**) an organ solo played before, during, or after a church service.
– DERIVATIVES **voluntarily** adv.
– ORIGIN Latin *voluntarius*.

volunteer ● n. **1** a person who freely offers to do something. **2** a person who works for an organization without being paid. **3** a person who freely enrols for military service rather than being ordered to do so. ● v. (**volunteers**, **volunteering**, **volunteered**) **1** freely offer to do something. **2** say or suggest something without being asked. **3** freely enrol for military service.
– ORIGIN French *volontaire* 'voluntary'.

voluptuary /vuh-lup-tyuu-uh-ri, vuh-lup-chuu-uh-ri/ ● n. (pl. **voluptuaries**) a person devoted to luxury and sensual pleasure.
– ORIGIN Latin *voluptuarius*.

voluptuous /vuh-**lup**-tyuu-uhss, vuh-**lup**-chuu-uhss/ ● **adj. 1** giving sensual pleasure. **2** (of a woman) curvaceous and sexually attractive.
– DERIVATIVES **voluptuously** adv. **voluptuousness** n.
– ORIGIN Latin *voluptuosus*.

vomit ● **v.** (**vomits**, **vomiting**, **vomited**) **1** bring up matter from the stomach through the mouth. **2** give out (something) in an uncontrolled stream. ● **n.** matter vomited from the stomach.
– ORIGIN Latin *vomere* 'to vomit'.

von Braun E
see **BRAUN**.

Vonnegut E
/von-ni-guht/, Kurt (b.1922), American novelist and short-story writer, author of *Slaughterhouse-Five*.

voodoo ● **n.** a black religious cult practised in the Caribbean and the southern US, combining elements of Roman Catholic ritual with traditional African rites, and involving sorcery and possession by spirits.
– ORIGIN from an African language.

voracious /vuh-**ray**-shuhss/ ● **adj. 1** wanting or eating great quantities of food. **2** eagerly consuming something: *his voracious reading of literature.*
– DERIVATIVES **voraciously** adv. **voracity** n.
– ORIGIN Latin *vorax*.

vortex /**vor**-teks/ ● **n.** (pl. **vortexes** or **vortices** /**vor**-ti-seez/) a whirling mass of water or air.
– ORIGIN Latin, 'eddy'.

Vosges E
/vohzh/ a mountain system of eastern France, in Alsace.

votary /**voh**-tuh-ri/ ● **n.** (pl. **votaries**) a person who has taken vows to dedicate their life to God or religious service.
– ORIGIN Latin *vovere* 'vow'.

vote ● **n. 1** a formal indication of a choice between two or more candidates or courses of action. **2** (**the vote**) the right to participate in an election. **3** (**the vote**) a particular group of voters or the votes cast by them: *the green vote.* ● **v.** (**votes**, **voting**, **voted**) give or register a vote.
– PHRASES **vote of (no) confidence** a vote showing that a majority continues to support (or no longer supports) the policy of a leader or governing body.
– DERIVATIVES **voter** n.
– ORIGIN Latin *votum* 'a vow, wish'.

votive ● **adj.** offered to a god as a sign of gratitude.
– ORIGIN Latin *votivus*.

V

vouch ● **v.** (**vouch for**) **1** state or confirm the truth or accuracy of. **2** say that (someone) is reliable, honest, etc.
– ORIGIN Old French *voucher* 'summon'.

voucher ● **n.** a piece of paper that entitles the holder to a discount, or that may be exchanged for goods or services.

vouchsafe ● **v.** (**vouchsafes**, **vouchsafing**, **vouchsafed**) give or say in a gracious or superior way.
– ORIGIN first as *vouch* something *safe* on someone, i.e. 'warrant the secure conferment of'.

vow ● **n.** a solemn promise. ● **v.** solemnly promise to do something.
– ORIGIN Old French *vou*.

vowel ● **n. 1** a speech sound in which the mouth is open and the tongue is not touching the top of the mouth, the teeth, or the lips. **2** a letter representing such a sound, such as *a, e, i, o, u*.
– ORIGIN Old French *vouel*.

vox pop ● **n.** Brit. informal popular opinion as represented by informal comments from members of the public.
– ORIGIN short for Latin *vox populi* 'the people's voice'.

voyage ● **n.** a long journey by sea or in space. ● **v.** (**voyages**, **voyaging**, **voyaged**) go on a voyage.
– DERIVATIVES **voyager** n.
– ORIGIN Old French *voiage*.

voyeur /vwa-**yer**, voy-**er**/ ● **n. 1** a person who gains sexual pleasure from watching others when they are naked or taking part in sexual activity. **2** a person who enjoys seeing the pain or distress of others.
– DERIVATIVES **voyeurism** n. **voyeuristic** adj.
– ORIGIN French.

vs ● **abbrev.** versus.

V-sign ● **n.** Brit. a gesture of abuse or contempt made by holding up the hand with the back facing outwards and making a V shape with the first two fingers.

VSO ● **abbrev.** Voluntary Service Overseas.

Vulcan E
the Roman god of fire. Greek equivalent **HEPHAESTUS**.

vulcanism ● **n.** var. of **VOLCANISM**.

vulcanite /**vul**-kuh-nyt/ ● **n.** hard black vulcanized rubber.
– ORIGIN from **VULCAN**.

vulcanize (also **vulcanise**) ● **v.** (**vulcanizes**, **vulcanizing**, **vulcanized**) harden (rubber or rubber-like material) by treating it with sulphur at a high temperature.

vulgar ● **adj. 1** lacking sophistication or good taste. **2** referring to sex or bodily functions in a rude way. **3** dated having to do with ordinary people.
– DERIVATIVES **vulgarity** n. (pl. **vulgarities**) **vulgarly** adv.
– ORIGIN Latin *vulgaris*.

vulgar fraction ● **n.** Brit. a fraction expressed by numerator and denominator, not decimally.

vulgarian /vul-**gair**-i-uhn/ ● **n.** a person who lacks good taste and sophistication.

vulgarism ● **n.** a vulgar word or expression.

vulgarize (also **vulgarise**) ● **v.** (**vulgarizes**, **vulgarizing**, **vulgarized**) spoil (something) by making it ordinary or less refined.
– DERIVATIVES **vulgarization** (also **vulgarisation**) n.

vulgar tongue ● **n.** the language spoken by the ordinary people of a country.

Vulgate /**vul**-gayt/ ● **n.** the main Latin version of the Bible, prepared in the 4th century and later revised and adopted as the official text for the Roman Catholic Church.
– ORIGIN from Latin *vulgata editio* 'edition prepared for the public'.

vulnerable /**vul**-nuh-ruh-b'l/ ● **adj.** exposed

to being attacked or harmed.
– DERIVATIVES **vulnerability** n. (pl. **vulnerabilities**) **vulnerably** adv.
– ORIGIN Latin *vulnerabilis.*
vulpine /vul-pyn/ ● **adj.** having to do with or like a fox or foxes.
– ORIGIN Latin *vulpinus.*
vulture /vul-cher/ ● **n. 1** a large bird of prey with the head and neck bare of feathers, that feeds on dead animals. **2** a person who tries to benefit from the difficulties of others.
– ORIGIN Latin *vulturius.*
vulva /vul-vuh/ ● **n.** the female external genitals.
– ORIGIN Latin, 'womb'.
vying pres. part. of **VIE**.

W[1] (also **w**) ● **n.** (pl. **Ws** or **W's**) the twenty-third letter of the alphabet.
W[2] ● **abbrev. 1** watt(s). **2** West or Western.
w ● **abbrev.** with.
WA ● **abbrev.** Western Australia.
wacko (also **whacko**) informal, esp. N. Amer. ● **adj.** mad; insane. ● **n.** (pl. **wackos** or **wackoes**) a crazy person.
wacky (also **whacky**) ● **adj.** (**wackier, wackiest**) informal funny or amusing in a slightly odd way.
– ORIGIN from **WHACK**.
wad /wod/ ● **n. 1** a lump or bundle of a soft material, as used for padding, stuffing, or wiping. **2** a bundle of paper, banknotes, or documents. **3** informal a large amount of something: *wads of money.* ● **v.** (**wads, wadding, wadded**) **1** compress (a soft material) into a wad. **2** line or fill with soft material.
– DERIVATIVES **wadding** n.
– ORIGIN perh. from Dutch *watten* or French *ouate* 'padding'.
waddle ● **v.** (**waddles, waddling, waddled**) walk with short steps and a clumsy swaying motion. ● **n.** a waddling way of walking.
– ORIGIN perh. from **WADE**.

Wade, E
(Sarah) Virginia (b.1945), English tennis player. Her singles titles include the US Open (1968), the Australian Open (1972), and Wimbledon (1977).

wade ● **v.** (**wades, wading, waded**) **1** walk through water or mud. **2** (**wade through**) read through (a long piece of writing) with effort. **3** (**wade in/into**) informal attack or intervene in a forceful way.
– ORIGIN Old English, 'move onward'.
wader ● **n. 1** a sandpiper, plover, or other wading bird. **2** (**waders**) high waterproof boots, used by anglers.
wadi /wah-di, wod-i/ ● **n.** (pl. **wadis**) (in Arabic-speaking countries) a valley, ravine, or channel that is dry except in the rainy season.
– ORIGIN Arabic.
wafer ● **n. 1** a very thin light, crisp sweet biscuit. **2** a thin disc of unleavened bread used in the Eucharist. **3** Electron. a very thin slice of a semiconductor crystal used in solid-state electric circuits.
– ORIGIN Old French *gaufre* 'honeycomb'.
wafer-thin ● **adj.** very thin or thinly.
waffle[1] informal ● **v.** (**waffles, waffling, waffled**) speak or write at length in a vague or trivial way. ● **n.** lengthy but vague or trivial talk or writing.
– DERIVATIVES **waffler** n. **waffly** adj.
– ORIGIN from dialect *waff* 'yelp'.
waffle[2] ● **n.** a small crisp batter cake, eaten hot with butter or syrup.
– ORIGIN Dutch *wafel.*
waft /woft/ ● **v.** pass easily or gently through the air. ● **n. 1** a gentle movement of air. **2** a scent carried in the air.
– ORIGIN German or Dutch *wachten* 'to guard'.
wag[1] ● **v.** (**wags, wagging, wagged**) move rapidly to and fro. ● **n.** a wagging movement.
– ORIGIN Old English, 'to sway'.
wag[2] ● **n.** informal a person fond of making jokes.
– ORIGIN prob. from former *waghalter* 'person likely to be hanged'.
wage ● **n.** (also **wages**) **1** a fixed regular payment for work. **2** the result or effect of doing something wrong: *the wages of sin.* ● **v.** (**wages, waging, wages**) carry on (a war or campaign).
– ORIGIN Old French.
wager ● **n. & v.** = **BET**.
– ORIGIN Old French, 'to wage'.
waggish ● **adj.** informal humorous or playful.
waggle ● **v.** (**waggles, waggling, waggled**) move with short quick movements from side to side or up and down. ● **n.** an act of waggling.
– DERIVATIVES **waggly** adj.
– ORIGIN from **WAG**[1].

Wagner E
/vahg-ner/, (Wilhelm) Richard (1813–83), German composer. He developed a type of opera which he called music drama, combining music, drama, legend, and spectacle; works include *The Flying Dutchman* and the four-opera cycle *Der Ring des Nibelungen.*
– DERIVATIVES **Wagnerian** adj. & n.

wagon (Brit. also **waggon**) ● **n. 1** a vehicle, especially a horse-drawn one, for transporting goods. **2** Brit. a railway vehicle for carrying goods in bulk.
– PHRASES **on the wagon** informal not drinking any alcohol.
– ORIGIN Dutch *wagen.*
wagon-lit /va-gon-lee/ ● **n.** (pl. **wagons-lits** /va-gon-lee/) a sleeping car on a train in con-

tinental Europe.
– ORIGIN French.

wagtail • n. a slender songbird with a long tail that is frequently wagged up and down.

waif • n. a poor and homeless child.
– ORIGIN Old French *gaif*, originally referring to an unclaimed piece of property.

Waikato E
/wy-**kah**-toh/ the longest river of New Zealand, which flows 434 km (270 miles) generally north-westwards from Lake Taupo to the Tasman Sea.

Waikiki E
/wy-ki-kee/ a Hawaiian beach resort, a suburb of Honolulu, on the island of Oahu.

wail • n. **1** a long high-pitched cry of pain, grief, or anger. **2** a sound resembling this. • v. give or utter a wail.
– ORIGIN Old Norse.

wain • n. archaic a wagon or cart.
– ORIGIN Old English.

wainscot /wayn-skot, wayn-skuht/ • n. an area of wooden panelling on the lower part of the walls of a room.
– DERIVATIVES **wainscoting** (also **wainscotting**) n.
– ORIGIN German *wagenschot*.

wainwright • n. hist. a wagon-builder.

waist • n. **1** the part of the human body below the ribs and above the hips. **2** a narrow part in the middle of something such as a violin.
– ORIGIN prob. from an Old English word related to **WAX²**.

waistband • n. a strip of cloth encircling the waist, attached to a skirt or a pair of trousers.

waistcoat /wayst-koht, wess-kit/ • n. Brit. a close-fitting waist-length garment with buttons down the front and no sleeves or collar.

waistline • n. **1** the measurement around a person's body at the waist. **2** the part of a garment that is shaped to fit at or near the waist.

wait • v. **1** stay where one is or delay action until a particular time or event. **2** be delayed or deferred. **3** (**wait on/upon**) act as an attendant to. **4** act as a waiter or waitress. • n. a period of waiting.
– PHRASES **in wait** watching for someone and preparing to attack them.
– ORIGIN Old French *waitier*.

Waitangi, Treaty of E
/wy-**tang**-i/ a treaty signed in 1840 by Maori leaders and the British government at Waitangi in New Zealand, which formed the basis of the British annexation of New Zealand.

waiter • n. a man whose job is to serve customers at their tables in a restaurant.

waiting list (N. Amer. **wait list**) • n. a list of people waiting for something not immediately available.

waitress • n. a woman whose job is to serve customers at their tables in a restaurant.
– DERIVATIVES **waitressing** n.

waive • v. (**waives**, **waiving**, **waived**) refrain from insisting on or applying (a right or claim).
– ORIGIN Old French *gaiver* 'allow to become a waif, abandon'.

waiver • n. **1** an act of waiving a right or claim. **2** a document recording this.

Wajda E
/vy-der/, Andrzej (b.1929), Polish film director, known for such films as *Ashes and Diamonds* and *Man of Iron*.

wake¹ • v. (**wakes**, **waking**, **woke**; past part. **woken**) **1** (often **wake up**) emerge or cause to emerge from sleep. **2** cause to stir or come to life. **3** (**wake up to**) become alert to or aware of. • n. **1** a watch held beside the body of someone who has died. **2** a party held after a funeral.
– ORIGIN Old English.

wake² • n. a trail of disturbed water or air left by the passage of a ship or aircraft.
– PHRASES **in the wake of** following as a result of.
– ORIGIN prob. from Old Norse, 'hole or opening in ice' (as made by a ship).

wakeful • adj. **1** unable or not needing to sleep. **2** alert and aware of possible dangers.
– DERIVATIVES **wakefulness** n.

waken • v. wake from sleep.
– ORIGIN Old English, 'be aroused'.

Waldheim E
/**vald**-hym/, Kurt (b.1918), Austrian diplomat and statesman, President 1986–92; Secretary General of the United Nations 1972–81. He denied allegations that as an army intelligence officer he had had direct knowledge of Nazi atrocities during the Second World War.

wale • n. **1** a ridge on a textured woven fabric such as corduroy. **2** a horizontal wooden strip fitted to strengthen a boat's side.
– ORIGIN Old English, 'stripe, weal'.

Wales E
a principality of Great Britain and the United Kingdom, to the west of central England; capital, Cardiff. Welsh name **CYMRU**.

Wałęsa E
/va-**wen**-suh/, Lech (b.1943), Polish trade unionist and statesman, President 1990–5. He founded the trade union movement Solidarity (1980) and became President after Solidarity's landslide victory in the 1989 elections.

walk • v. **1** move at a fairly slow pace using one's legs. **2** travel over (a route or area) on foot. **3** guide or accompany (someone) on foot. **4** take (a dog) out for exercise. • n. **1** a journey on foot. **2** an unhurried rate of movement on foot. **3** a person's way of walking. **4** a path for walking.
– PHRASES **walk (all) over** informal **1** treat unfairly or thoughtlessly. **2** defeat easily. **walk off with** (or **away with**) informal **1** steal. **2** win. **walk of life** the position within society that someone holds.
– ORIGIN Old English, 'roll, wander'.

walkabout • n. **1** esp. Brit. an informal stroll among a crowd conducted by an important visitor. **2** Austral. a traditional journey on foot undertaken by an Australian Aboriginal.

Walker[1], E
Alice (Malsenior) (b.1944), American writer and critic, author of *The Color Purple*.

Walker[2], E
John (b.1952), New Zealand athlete. He was the first athlete to run a mile in less than 3 minutes 50 seconds (1975).

walker • n. **1** a person who walks. **2** a harness set into a frame on wheels, used for helping a baby learn to walk.

Walker Cup E
a golf tournament held every two years and played between teams of male amateurs from the US and from Great Britain and Ireland.

walkie-talkie • n. a portable two-way radio.

walk-in • adj. (of a storage area) large enough to walk into.

walking stick • n. a stick with a curved handle used for support when walking.

Walkman • n. (pl. **Walkmans** or **Walkmen**) trademark a type of personal stereo.

walk-on • adj. (of a part in a play or film) small and not involving any speaking.

walkout • n. a sudden angry departure as a protest or strike.

walkover • n. an easy victory.

walkway • n. a raised passageway in a building, or a wide path in a park or garden.

wall • n. **1** a continuous upright structure forming a side of a building or room, or enclosing or dividing an area of land. **2** a protective barrier: *a wall of silence.* **3** Soccer a line of defenders forming a barrier against a free kick taken near the penalty area. **4** the outer layer or lining of a bodily organ or cavity. • v. enclose or block by building a wall.
– PHRASES **drive up the wall** informal make very irritated. **go to the wall** informal (of a business) fail. **wall-to-wall 1** (of a carpet) fitted to cover an entire floor. **2** informal very numerous or plentiful.
– DERIVATIVES **walling** n.
– ORIGIN Latin *vallum* 'rampart'.

wallaby • n. (pl. **wallabies**) an Australasian marsupial similar to but smaller than a kangaroo.
– ORIGIN Dharuk (an Aboriginal language).

Wallace[1], E
Alfred Russel (1823–1913), English naturalist. His theory of the origin of species was very similar to that of Charles Darwin.

Wallace[2], E
(Richard Horatio) Edgar (1875–1932), English crime novelist.

Wallace[3], E
Sir William (*c.*1270–1305), a leader of Scottish resistance to English rule. He defeated the army of Edward I at Stirling in 1297, but after Edward's second invasion of Scotland in 1298 Wallace was defeated and later executed.

wallah /wol-luh/ • n. Ind. or informal a person of a specified kind or having a specified role: *an office wallah.*
– ORIGIN from Hindi, 'doer, fellow'.

wall bars • pl. n. Brit. parallel horizontal bars attached to the wall of a gymnasium, on which exercises are performed.

Wallenberg E
/vah-luhn-berg/, Raoul (1912–?), Swedish diplomat. In 1944 in Budapest he helped many thousands of Jews to escape death by issuing them with Swedish passports. In 1945 he was arrested by Soviet forces and imprisoned; his fate remains uncertain.

Waller E
/wol-ler/, Fats (1904–43; born *Thomas Wright Waller*), American jazz pianist, songwriter, bandleader, and singer.

wallet • n. a pocket-sized, flat, folding holder for money and plastic cards.
– ORIGIN prob. from Germanic.

wall-eyed • adj. having eyes that show an abnormal amount of white, as caused by a squint.
– ORIGIN Old Norse.

wallflower • n. **1** a plant with fragrant flowers that bloom in early spring. **2** informal a girl who has no one to dance with at a dance or party.

Wallis, E
Sir Barnes Neville (1887–1979), English inventor, who devised the bouncing bomb used against dams in Germany in the Second World War.

Wallis and Futuna Islands E
/fuh-tyoo-nuh/ an overseas territory of France comprising two groups of islands in the central Pacific; capital, Mata-Utu.

Walloon /wol-loon/ • n. **1** a member of a people who speak a French dialect and live in southern and eastern Belgium and neighbouring parts of France. **2** the French dialect spoken by this people.
– ORIGIN French *Wallon*.

wallop informal • v. (**wallops**, **walloping**, **walloped**) **1** hit very hard. **2** heavily defeat (an opponent). • n. a heavy blow.
– ORIGIN Old French *waloper* 'to gallop'.

wallow • v. **1** roll about or lie in mud or water. **2** (of a boat or aircraft) roll from side to side. **3** (**wallow in**) indulge without restraint in (something pleasurable). • n. **1** an act of wallowing. **2** an area of mud or shallow water where mammals go to wallow.
– ORIGIN Old English.

wallpaper • n. **1** paper pasted in strips over the walls of a room to provide a decorative or textured surface. **2** Computing an optional background pattern or picture on a screen. • v. (**wallpapers**, **wallpapering**, **wallpapered**) apply wallpaper to (a wall or room).

Wall Street E
a street in Manhattan, where the New York Stock Exchange and other leading American financial institutions are located.

Wall Street Crash E
the collapse of prices on the New York Stock Exchange in October 1929, a major factor in the early stages of the Depression.

wally • n. (pl. **wallies**) Brit. informal a silly or inept person.
– ORIGIN perh. a shortened form of the man's name *Walter*.

walnut • n. **1** an edible wrinkled nut enclosed by a hard round shell. **2** the tree which pro-

W

duces this nut, a source of valuable ornamental wood.
– ORIGIN Old English.

Walpole[1] E
/wawl-pohl/, Horace, 4th Earl of Orford (1717–97), English writer and Whig politician, son of Sir Robert Walpole. He wrote *The Castle of Otranto*, one of the first Gothic novels.

Walpole[2] E
/wawl-pohl/, Sir Robert, 1st Earl of Orford (1676–1745), British Whig statesman, First Lord of the Treasury and Chancellor of the Exchequer 1715–17 and 1721–42. Walpole is regarded as the first British Prime Minister, having presided over the cabinet for George I and George II.

walrus • **n.** a large marine mammal having two large downward-pointing tusks, found in the Arctic Ocean.
– ORIGIN prob. Dutch.

walrus moustache • **n.** a long, thick, drooping moustache.

Walsh, E
Courtney (Andrew) (b.1962), West Indian cricketer. In 2001 he set a new record of 500 test match wickets.

Walsingham E
/wawl-sing-uhm/, Sir Francis (*c.*1530–90), English politician. As Secretary of State to Queen Elizabeth I he developed a spy network that gathered information about Catholic plots to overthrow the queen.

Walton[1], E
Ernest Thomas Sinton (1903–95), Irish physicist. In 1932, with Sir John Cockcroft, he succeeded in splitting the atom.

Walton[2], E
Izaak (1593–1683), English writer, author of *The Compleat Angler*, which combines practical information on fishing with folklore, verse, and ballads.

Walton[3], E
Sir William (Turner) (1902–83), English composer. His works include two symphonies, a viola concerto, and the oratorio *Belshazzar's Feast*.

waltz /wawlts, wolts/ • **n.** a dance in triple time performed by a couple, who turn rhythmically round and round as they progress around the dance floor. • **v. 1** dance a waltz. **2** move or act in a casual or inconsiderate way: *she waltzed in and took all the credit.*
– ORIGIN German *Walzer.*

waltzer • **n.** a fairground ride in which cars spin round as they are carried round a track that moves up and down.

wan /won/ • **adj. 1** (of a person) pale and appearing ill or exhausted. **2** (of light) pale; weak. **3** (of a smile) weak; strained.
– DERIVATIVES **wanly** adv.
– ORIGIN Old English, 'dark'.

wand • **n. 1** a rod used in casting magic spells or performing tricks. **2** a slender rod held as a symbol of office. **3** a hand-held electronic device passed over a bar code to read the data.
– ORIGIN Old Norse.

wander • **v.** (**wanders**, **wandering**, **wandered**) **1** walk or move in a leisurely, casual, or aimless way. **2** move slowly away from a fixed point or place: *please don't wander off again.* • **n.** an act or spell of wandering.
– DERIVATIVES **wanderer** n.
– ORIGIN Old English.

wanderlust • **n.** a strong desire to travel.
– ORIGIN German.

wane • **v.** (**wanes**, **waning**, **waned**) **1** (of the moon) have a progressively smaller part of its visible surface lit up, so that it appears to decrease in size. **2** become weaker.
– PHRASES **on the wane** becoming weaker.
– ORIGIN Old English, 'lessen'.

wangle • **v.** (**wangles**, **wangling**, **wangled**) informal obtain (something desired) by trickery or persuasion.
– ORIGIN unknown.

wank Brit. vulgar • **v.** (also **wank off**) masturbate. • **n.** an act of masturbating.
– ORIGIN unknown.

wanker • **n.** Brit. vulgar a stupid or unpleasant person.

wannabe /won-nuh-bee/ • **n.** informal, derog. a person who tries to be like someone else or to fit in with a particular group of people.

want • **v. 1** have a desire to possess or do. **2** desire sexually. **3** (**be wanted**) (of a suspected criminal) be sought by the police. **4** (often **want for**) lack or be short of something desirable or essential. **5** informal, esp. Brit. ought to, should, or need to do something: *you don't want to believe all you hear.* **6** informal, esp. Brit. (of a thing) require: *the wheel wants greasing.* • **n. 1** a desire for something. **2** lack or shortage. **3** poverty.
– ORIGIN Old Norse, 'be lacking'.

wanting • **adj. 1** lacking in something required, necessary, or usual. **2** absent; not provided.

wanton /won-t'n/ • **adj. 1** (of a cruel or violent action) deliberate and unprovoked. **2** having many sexual partners.
– DERIVATIVES **wantonly** adv. **wantonness** n.
– ORIGIN from former *wan-* 'badly' + Old English *togen* 'trained'.

WAP • **abbrev.** Wireless Application Protocol, a means of enabling a mobile phone to browse the Internet and display data.

wapiti /wop-i-ti/ • **n.** (pl. **wapitis**) a large North American red deer.
– ORIGIN Shawnee (an American Indian language), 'white rump'.

War. • **abbrev.** Warwickshire.

war • **n. 1** a state of armed conflict between different nations, states, or armed groups. **2** a sustained contest between rivals or campaign against something undesirable: *a war on drugs.* • **v.** (**wars**, **warring**, **warred**) engage in a war.
– PHRASES **be on the warpath** be very angry with someone. [ORIGIN with reference to American Indians heading towards a battle with an enemy.]
– ORIGIN Old French *guerre.*

Warbeck E
/wor-bek/, Perkin (1474–99), Flemish claimant to the English throne. Encouraged by Yorkists, he claimed to be one of the Princes in the Tower in a bid to overthrow Henry VII. After attempting to begin a revolt he was imprisoned and later executed.

warble ● v. (**warbles, warbling, warbled**) **1** (of a bird) sing softly and with constantly changing notes. **2** (of a person) sing in a trilling or quavering voice. ● n. a warbling sound or utterance.
– ORIGIN Old French *werbler.*

warbler ● n. a small songbird typically living in trees and bushes and having a warbling song.

Warburg E
/wor-berg/, Otto Heinrich (1883–1970), German biochemist, who pioneered the use of the techniques of chemistry for biochemical investigations.

war chest ● n. a reserve of funds used for fighting a war.

war crime ● n. an action carried out during a war that violates accepted international rules of war.

ward ● n. **1** a room or division in a hospital for one or more patients. **2** a division of a city or borough that is represented by a councillor or councillors. **3** a young person under the care and control of a guardian appointed by their parents or a court. **4** any of the internal ridges or bars in a lock which prevent the turning of any key without corresponding grooves. ● v. (**ward off**) prevent from harming or affecting one.
– ORIGIN Old English, 'keep safe, guard'.

-ward (also **-wards**) ● suffix **1** (usu. **-wards**) (forming adverbs) towards the specified place or direction: *homewards.* **2** (usu. **-ward**) (forming adjectives) turned or tending towards: *upward.*
– ORIGIN Old English.

war dance ● n. a dance performed before a battle or to celebrate victory.

warden ● n. **1** a person responsible for the supervision of a particular place or procedure. **2** Brit. the head of certain schools, colleges, or other institutions. **3** esp. N. Amer. a prison governor.
– ORIGIN Old French *wardein, guarden* 'guardian'.

warder ● n. (fem. **wardress**) esp. Brit. a prison guard.
– ORIGIN Old French *warder* 'to guard'.

wardrobe ● n. **1** a large, tall cupboard in which clothes may be hung or stored. **2** a person's entire collection of clothes. **3** the costume department or costumes of a theatre or film company.
– ORIGIN Old French *warderobe, garderobe* 'private chamber'.

wardroom ● n. a commissioned officers' mess on board a warship.

-wards ● suffix var. of **-WARD**.

ware ● n. **1** pottery of a specified type: *porcelain ware.* **2** manufactured articles of a specified type. **3** (**wares**) articles offered for sale.
– ORIGIN Old English, 'commodities'.

warehouse /wair-howss/ ● n. **1** a large building where raw materials or manufactured goods may be stored. **2** a large wholesale or retail store.

warfare ● n. the state of or activities involved in war.

war game ● n. **1** a military exercise carried out to test or improve tactics. **2** a mock military conflict carried out as a game or sport.

warhead ● n. the explosive head of a missile, torpedo, or similar weapon.

Warhol E
/wor-hohl/, Andy (*c.*1928–87; born *Andrew Warhola*), American painter, graphic artist, and film-maker. A leading pop artist, he is famous for his prints and paintings of familiar objects (such as Campbell's soup tins) and celebrities (such as Marilyn Monroe).

warhorse ● n. informal a soldier, politician, sports player, etc. who has fought many campaigns or contests.

warlike ● adj. **1** hostile: *a warlike clan.* **2** directed towards or prepared for war.

warlock ● n. a man who practises witchcraft.
– ORIGIN Old English, 'traitor, monster', also 'the Devil'.

warlord ● n. a military commander, especially one controlling a region.

warm ● adj. **1** at a fairly or comfortably high temperature. **2** (of clothes or coverings) made of a material that helps the body to retain heat. **3** enthusiastic, affectionate, or kind. **4** (of a colour) containing red, yellow, or orange tones. **5** (of a scent or trail) fresh; strong. **6** close to finding or guessing what is sought. ● v. **1** make or become warm. **2** (**warm to/towards**) become more interested in or enthusiastic about. ● n. **1** (**the warm**) a warm place or area. **2** an act of warming.
– PHRASES **warm up 1** prepare for exercise by doing gentle stretches and exercises. **2** (of an engine or electrical appliance) reach a temperature high enough to allow it to operate efficiently. **3** entertain (an audience or crowd) to make them more enthusiastic before the arrival of the main act.
– DERIVATIVES **warmly** adv. **warmness** n.
– ORIGIN Old English.

warm-blooded ● adj. **1** (of animals, chiefly mammals and birds) maintaining a constant body temperature by their body's chemical processes. **2** passionate.

warm-hearted ● adj. sympathetic and kind.

warmonger /wor-mung-ger/ ● n. a person who seeks to bring about or promote war.

warmth ● n. **1** the quality, state, or sensation of being warm. **2** enthusiasm, affection, or kindness. **3** strength of emotion: *he denied the charge with a warmth he regretted.*

warn ● v. **1** inform of a possible danger or problem. **2** give (someone) advice against wrong or foolish actions or conduct. **3** (**warn off**) order (someone) to keep away or to refrain from doing something.
– ORIGIN Old English.

Warne, E
Shane (Keith) (b.1969), Australian cricketer.

warning ● n. **1** a statement or event that indicates a danger or problem that may or is about to happen. **2** advice against wrong or foolish actions. **3** advance notice.

War of American Independence E
see **AMERICAN INDEPENDENCE, WAR OF.**

warp ● v. **1** make or become bent or twisted as a result of heat or damp. **2** make abnormal or strange: *his hatred has warped his judgement.* ● n. **1** a distortion or twist in shape. **2** the

lengthwise threads on a loom over and under which the weft threads are passed to make cloth.
– ORIGIN Old English.

warpaint • n. **1** paint traditionally used to decorate the face and body before battle. **2** informal elaborate or excessive make-up.

warplane • n. an aircraft designed and equipped to engage in air combat or to drop bombs.

warrant • n. **1** an official authorization giving the police or some other body the power to make an arrest, search premises, etc. **2** a document entitling the holder to receive goods, money, or services. **3** justification or authority: *there is no warrant for this assumption.* • v. **1** justify or necessitate. **2** officially state or guarantee.
– ORIGIN first meaning 'protector', 'protect from danger': from Old French *guarant.*

warrant officer • n. a rank of officer in the army, RAF, or US navy, below the commissioned officers and above the non-commissioned officers.

warranty • n. (pl. **warranties**) **1** a written guarantee promising to repair or replace an article if necessary within a specified period. **2** a guarantee made by a person insured that certain statements are true or that certain conditions shall be fulfilled.

Warren, E
Robert Penn (1905–89), American poet, novelist, and critic. In 1986 he was made the first American Poet Laureate.

warren • n. **1** a network of interconnecting rabbit burrows. **2** a complex network of paths or passages.
– ORIGIN Old French *garenne* 'game park'.

warrior • n. a brave or experienced soldier or fighter.
– ORIGIN Old French *werreior, guerreior.*

Warsaw E
/wor-saw/ the capital of Poland.

Warsaw Pact E
a treaty of mutual defence and military aid signed at Warsaw in 1955 by Communist states of Europe under Soviet influence. The Pact was dissolved in 1991.

warship • n. a ship equipped with weapons and designed to take part in warfare at sea.

Wars of the Roses E
the 15th-century English civil wars between the Houses of York and Lancaster, represented by white and red roses respectively. The struggle was largely ended in 1485 by the death of the Yorkist king Richard III at the Battle of Bosworth and the accession of the Lancastrian Henry Tudor (Henry VII).

wart • n. **1** a small, hard growth on the skin, caused by a virus. **2** any rounded growth on the skin of an animal or the surface of a plant.
– PHRASES **warts and all** informal including faults or unattractive qualities.
– DERIVATIVES **warty** adj.
– ORIGIN Old English.

warthog • n. an African wild pig with a large head, warty lumps on the face, and curved tusks.

wartime • n. a period during which a war is taking place.

Warwick E
/wo-rik/, Richard Neville, Earl of (1428–71; known as **Warwick the Kingmaker**), English statesman. During the Wars of the Roses he fought first on the Yorkist side, helping Edward IV to gain the throne (1461), and then on the Lancastrian side, briefly restoring Henry VI to the throne (1470).

Warwickshire E
a county of central England; county town, Warwick.

wary • adj. (**warier, wariest**) (often **wary of**) cautious about possible dangers or problems.
– DERIVATIVES **warily** adv. **wariness** n.
– ORIGIN from *ware,* 'beware'.

was 1st and 3rd person sing. past of **BE**.

wash • v. **1** clean with water and, typically, soap or detergent. **2** (of flowing water) carry or move in a particular direction. **3** be carried by flowing water. **4** (**wash over**) occur all around without greatly affecting (someone). **5** informal seem convincing or genuine: *excuses just don't wash with us.* • n. **1** an act of washing or of being washed. **2** a quantity of clothes needing to be or just having been washed. **3** the water or air disturbed by a moving boat or aircraft. **4** a medicinal or cleansing solution: *antiseptic skin wash.* **5** a thin coating of paint or metal. **6** silt or gravel carried by water and deposited as sediment.
– PHRASES **be washed out** be postponed or cancelled because of rain. **wash one's dirty linen** (or **laundry**) **in public** informal discuss one's personal affairs in public. **wash one's hands of** take no further responsibility for. [ORIGIN with reference to Pontius Pilate washing his hands after the condemnation of Christ (Gospel of Matthew, chapter 27).] **wash up** esp. Brit. clean crockery and cutlery after use.
– DERIVATIVES **washable** adj.
– ORIGIN Old English.

washbasin • n. a basin used for washing one's hands and face.

washboard • n. **1** a ridged or corrugated wooden or metal board, against which clothes are scrubbed during washing. **2** a similar board played as a percussion instrument by scraping. • adj. (of a man's stomach) lean and with well-defined muscles.

washed out • adj. **1** faded by or as if by repeated washing. **2** pale and tired.

washed-up • adj. informal no longer effective or successful.

washer • n. **1** a person or device that washes. **2** a small flat ring fixed between a nut and bolt to spread the pressure or between two joining surfaces to prevent leakage.

washerwoman • n. a woman whose occupation is washing clothes.

washing • n. a quantity of clothes, bedlinen, etc. that is to be washed or has just been washed.

washing machine • n. a machine for washing clothes, bedlinen, etc.

washing powder • n. esp. Brit. powdered detergent for washing laundry.

washing soda • n. sodium carbonate, used dissolved in water for washing and cleaning.

Washington[1] E
a state of the north-western US, on the Pacific coast; capital, Olympia.
– DERIVATIVES **Washingtonian** n, & adj.

Washington[2] E
the capital of the US. It extends over the same area as the District of Columbia. Full name **WASHINGTON DC**.
– DERIVATIVES **Washingtonian** n. & adj.

Washington[3], E
George (1732–99), American general and statesman, 1st President of the US 1789–97. Washington helped win the War of Independence, chaired the convention (1787) that drew up the American Constitution, and served two terms as President.

washing-up ● n. Brit. crockery, cutlery, and other kitchen utensils that are to be washed.

washout ● n. informal a disappointing failure.

washroom ● n. N. Amer. a room with washing and toilet facilities.

washstand ● n. esp. hist. a piece of furniture designed to hold a jug, bowl, or basin for washing one's hands and face.

wasn't ● contr. was not.

Wasp ● n. N. Amer. an upper- or middle-class American white Protestant, thought to be a member of the most powerful social group.
– ORIGIN from *white Anglo-Saxon Protestant*.

wasp ● n. a stinging winged insect which nests in complex colonies and has a black and yellow-striped body.
– ORIGIN Old English.

waspish ● adj. sharply irritable.
– DERIVATIVES **waspishly** adv.

wassail /wos-sayl, wos-s'l/ archaic ● n. **1** spiced ale or mulled wine drunk during celebrations for Twelfth Night and Christmas Eve. **2** lively festivities involving the drinking of much alcohol. ● v. **1** make merry with much alcohol. **2** go from house to house at Christmas singing carols.
– ORIGIN Old Norse, 'be in good health!'.

wastage ● n. **1** the action or process of wasting. **2** an amount wasted. **3** (also **natural wastage**) the reduction in the size of a workforce through people willingly resigning or retiring rather than being made redundant.

waste ● v. (**wastes, wasting, wasted**) **1** use carelessly, extravagantly, or to no purpose. **2** fail to make full or good use of. **3** (**be wasted on**) be unappreciated by. **4** (often **waste away**) gradually become weaker and thinner. **5** literary destroy or ruin (a place). **6** N. Amer. informal kill or severely injure. **7** (**wasted**) informal under the influence of alcohol or illegal drugs. ● adj. **1** discarded as no longer useful or required. **2** (of an area of land) not used, cultivated, or built on. ● n. **1** an act or instance of wasting. **2** material that is not wanted or cannot be used. **3** a large area of barren, uninhabited land.
– PHRASES **go to waste** be wasted. **lay waste (to)** completely destroy.
– ORIGIN Old French.

waste-disposal unit ● n. an electrically operated device fitted to the waste pipe of a kitchen sink for grinding up food waste.

wasteful ● adj. using or using up something carelessly, extravagantly, or to no purpose.
– DERIVATIVES **wastefully** adv. **wastefulness** n.

wasteland ● n. a barren or empty area of land.

waster ● n. **1** a wasteful person or thing. **2** informal a person who does little or nothing of value.

wastrel /way-struhl/ ● n. literary a wasteful or worthless person.
– ORIGIN from **WASTE**, first referring to a strip of waste land.

watch ● v. **1** look at attentively. **2** keep under careful observation. **3** exercise care, caution, or restraint about. **4** (**watch for**) look out for. **5** (**watch out**) be careful. **6** keep up an interest in. ● n. **1** a small timepiece usually worn on a strap on one's wrist. **2** an act or instance of watching. **3** a period of keeping watch during the night. **4** a fixed period of duty on a ship, usually lasting four hours. **5** a shift worked by firefighters or police officers.
– PHRASES **keep watch** stay on the lookout for danger or trouble. **watch one's back** protect oneself against unexpected danger.
– DERIVATIVES **watcher** n.
– ORIGIN Old English.

watchable ● adj. (of a film or television programme) moderately enjoyable to watch.

watchdog ● n. **1** a dog kept to guard private property. **2** a person or group that monitors the practices of companies providing a particular service.

watchful ● adj. alert to possible difficulty or danger.
– DERIVATIVES **watchfully** adv. **watchfulness** n.

watching brief ● n. **1** Brit. Law instructions held by a barrister to follow a case on behalf of a client who is not directly involved. **2** an interest in a proceeding in which one is not directly concerned.

watchman ● n. a man employed to look after an empty building.

watchtower ● n. a tower built to create a high observation point.

watchword ● n. a word or phrase expressing a central aim or belief.

water ● n. **1** the liquid which forms the seas, lakes, rivers, and rain and is the basis of the fluids of living things. **2** (**waters**) an area of sea under the legal authority of a particular country. **3** (**the waters**) the water of a mineral spring used for medicinal purposes. **4** (**waters**) amniotic fluid, especially as discharged shortly before birth. ● v. (**waters, watering, watered**) **1** pour water over (a plant or an area of ground). **2** give a drink of water to (an animal). **3** (of the eyes or mouth) produce tears or saliva. **4** dilute (a drink) with water. **5** (**water down**) make less forceful or controversial by changing or leaving out things. **6** (of a river) flow through (an area).
– PHRASES **hold water** (of a theory) appear sound. **make water** (of a ship or boat) take in water through a leak. **water on the brain** informal hydrocephalus. **water under the bridge** past events that are over and done with.
– DERIVATIVES **waterless** adj.
– ORIGIN Old English.

water-based ● adj. (of a substance or solution) using or having water as a main ingre-

W

dient.

waterbed • n. a bed with a water-filled rubber or plastic mattress.

water biscuit • n. a thin, crisp unsweetened biscuit made from flour and water.

water buffalo • n. a large black buffalo with heavy swept-back horns, used for carrying heavy loads.

water cannon • n. a device that ejects a powerful jet of water, used to disperse a crowd.

water chestnut • n. the crisp, white-fleshed tuber of a tropical plant, used in oriental cookery.

water closet • n. dated a flush toilet.

watercolour (US **watercolor**) • n. **1** artists' paint made with a water-soluble binder, and thinned with water rather than oil. **2** a picture painted with watercolours. **3** the art of painting with watercolours.
– DERIVATIVES **watercolourist** (US **watercolorist**) n.

watercourse • n. a brook, stream, or artificially constructed water channel.

watercress • n. a cress which grows in running water and whose strong-tasting leaves are used in salad.

water diviner • n. Brit. a person who searches for underground water by using a dowsing rod.

waterfall • n. a stream of water falling from a height, formed when a river or stream flows over a precipice or steep slope.

Waterford E
a county in the south-east of the Republic of Ireland; county town, Waterford; main administrative centre, Dungarvan.

waterfowl • pl. n. ducks, geese, or other large birds living in water.

waterfront • n. a part of a town or city alongside a body of water.

Watergate E
a US political scandal in which an attempt to bug the Democratic Party headquarters (in the Watergate building, Washington DC) by the Republican organization working to re-elect President Nixon led to Nixon's resignation (1974).

waterhole • n. a hollow in which water collects, typically one at which animals drink.

water ice • n. a frozen dessert consisting of fruit juice or purée in a sugar syrup.

watering can • n. a portable water container with a long spout and a removable cap with tiny holes in it, used for watering plants.

watering hole • n. **1** a waterhole from which animals regularly drink. **2** informal a pub or bar.

watering place • n. **1** a watering hole. **2** a spa or seaside resort.

water level • n. **1** the height reached by a body of water. **2** a water table.

water lily • n. a plant that grows in water, with large round floating leaves and large cup-shaped flowers.

waterline • n. **1** the level normally reached by the water on the side of a ship. **2** a line on a shore, riverbank, etc. marking the level reached by the sea or a river.

waterlogged • adj. saturated with or full of water.
– ORIGIN from archaic *waterlog* 'make a ship unmanageable by flooding'.

Waterloo, Battle of E
a battle fought in 1815 near the village of Waterloo (in present-day Belgium), in which Napoleon's army was defeated by the British (under the Duke of Wellington) and Prussians.

water main • n. the main pipe in a water supply system.

watermark • n. a faint design made in some paper that can be seen when held against the light, identifying the maker.

water meadow • n. a meadow that is periodically flooded by a stream or river.

watermelon • n. a large melon-like fruit with smooth green skin, red pulp, and watery juice.

watermill • n. a mill worked by a waterwheel.

water pistol • n. a toy pistol that shoots a jet of water.

water polo • n. a seven-a-side game played by swimmers in a pool, with a ball like a football that is thrown into the opponents' net.

waterproof • adj. unable to be penetrated by water. • n. Brit. a waterproof garment. • v. make waterproof.

water rat • n. **1** a large rat-like rodent living both on land and in water. **2** Brit. a water vole.

water-resistant • adj. partially able to resist the penetration of water.

Waters, E
Muddy (1915–83; born *McKinley Morganfield*), American blues singer and guitarist.

watershed • n. **1** an area of land that separates waters flowing to different rivers, basins, or seas. **2** a turning point in a state of affairs. **3** Brit. the time after which programmes that are unsuitable for children are broadcast on television.
– ORIGIN from WATER + *shed* in the sense 'ridge of high ground'.

waterside • n. the area next to a sea, lake, or river.

waterski • n. (pl. **waterskis**) each of a pair of skis enabling the wearer to skim the surface of the water when towed by a motor boat. • v. (**waterskis**, **waterskiing**, **waterskied**) travel on waterskis.
– DERIVATIVES **waterskier** n.

waterspout • n. a funnel-shaped column of water and spray formed by a whirlwind occurring over the sea.

water table • n. the level below which the ground is saturated with water.

watertight • adj. **1** closely sealed, fastened, or fitted so as to prevent water passing through. **2** (of an argument or account) unable to be called into question.

water tower • n. a tower that supports a water tank at a height to create the pressure required to distribute the water through a piped system.

water vole • n. a large vole living both on land and in water, which digs burrows in the banks of rivers.

waterway • n. a river, canal, or other route for travel by water.

waterwheel • n. a large wheel driven by flowing water, used to work machinery or to raise water to a higher level.

water wings • pl. n. inflated floats fixed to the arms of someone learning to swim to help them stay afloat.

waterworks • pl. n. **1** an establishment for managing a water supply. **2** informal the shedding of tears.

watery • adj. **1** consisting of, containing, or resembling water. **2** (of food or drink) thin or tasteless as a result of containing too much water. **3** weak or pale.

Watson[1], E
James Dewey (b.1928), American biologist who, with Francis Crick, proposed the double helix structure of the DNA molecule.

Watson[2], E
John Broadus (1878–1958), American psychologist, founder of behaviourism (the theory that behaviour can be explained by conditioning, and that psychological disorders are best treated by altering behaviour patterns).

Watson-Watt, E
Sir Robert Alexander (1892–1973), Scottish physicist, who pioneered the development of radar into a practical system for locating aircraft.

Watt, E
James (1736–1819), Scottish engineer, who greatly improved the efficiency of the steam engine.

watt • n. the SI unit of power, equivalent to one joule per second and corresponding to the rate of energy in an electric circuit where the potential difference is one volt and the current one ampere.
– ORIGIN named after James **WATT**.

wattage • n. an amount of electrical power expressed in watts.

Watteau E
/wot-toh/, Jean Antoine (1684–1721), French painter. An initiator of the rococo style, he is best known for his idealized paintings of young people in rural settings.

watt-hour • n. a measure of electrical energy equivalent to a power consumption of one watt for one hour.

wattle[1] /wot-t'l/ • n. a material for making fences, walls, etc., consisting of rods interlaced with twigs or branches.
– ORIGIN Old English.

wattle[2] /wot-t'l/ • n. a fleshy lobe hanging from the head or neck of the turkey and some other birds.
– ORIGIN unknown.

wattle and daub • n. a material formerly used in building walls, consisting of wattle covered with mud or clay.

Watts, E
George Frederick (1817–1904), English painter and sculptor, known for his portraits of public figures, including Gladstone and Tennyson.

Waugh[1] E
/*rhymes with* war/, Evelyn (Arthur St John) (1903–66), English novelist, author of *Decline and Fall* and *Brideshead Revisited*.

Waugh[2] E
/*rhymes with* war/, Steve (Rodger) (b.1965), Australian cricketer, captain of Australia since 1999.

wave • v. (**waves**, **waving**, **waved**) **1** move one's hand to and fro in greeting or as a signal. **2** move (one's hand or arm, or something held in one's hand) to and fro. **3** move to and fro with a swaying motion while remaining fixed to one point. **4** style (hair) so that it curls slightly. • n. **1** a ridge of water moving along the surface of the sea or arching and breaking on the shore. **2** a sudden occurrence of or increase in a phenomenon or emotion. **3** a gesture made by waving one's hand. **4** a slightly curling lock of hair. **5** Physics a periodic disturbance of the particles of a substance without overall movement of the particles, as in the transmission of sound, light, heat, etc.
– PHRASES **make waves** informal **1** create a significant impression. **2** cause trouble.
– ORIGIN Old English.

waveband • n. a range of wavelengths between two given limits, used in radio transmission.

waveform • n. Physics a curve showing the shape of a wave at a given time.

wavelength • n. **1** Physics the distance between successive crests of a wave, especially as a distinctive feature of sound, light, radio waves, etc. **2** a person's way of thinking when communicated to another: *we weren't on the same wavelength.*

wavelet • n. a small wave.

waver • v. (**wavers**, **wavering**, **wavered**) **1** move quiveringly; flicker. **2** begin to weaken; falter. **3** be indecisive.
– ORIGIN Old Norse, 'flicker'.

wavy • adj. (**wavier**, **waviest**) having or consisting of a series of wave-like curves.

wax[1] • n. **1** beeswax. **2** a soft solid oily substance that melts easily, used for making candles or polishes. • v. **1** polish or treat with wax. **2** remove hair from (a part of the body) by applying wax and then peeling it off with the hairs.
– ORIGIN Old English.

wax[2] • v. **1** (of the moon) gradually have a larger part of its visible surface lit up, so that it appears to increase in size. **2** literary become larger or stronger. **3** speak or write in the specified way: *they waxed lyrical about the old days.*
– ORIGIN Old English.

waxen • adj. **1** having a smooth, pale, semi-transparent surface like that of wax. **2** archaic or literary made of wax.

waxwing • n. a crested songbird, mainly pinkish-brown and with bright red tips to some wing feathers.

waxwork • n. **1** a lifelike dummy modelled in wax. **2** (**waxworks**) an exhibition of waxworks.

waxy • adj. (**waxier**, **waxiest**) resembling wax in consistency or appearance.
– DERIVATIVES **waxiness** n.

way • n. **1** a method, style, or manner of doing something. **2** the typical manner in which someone behaves or in which something happens. **3** a road, track, path, or street. **4** a route or means taken in order to reach, enter, or leave a place. **5** the route along which someone or something is travelling or would travel if unobstructed. **6** a specified direction. **7** the distance in space or time between two points: *September was a long way off.* **8** informal a particular area: *they live over Maidenhead way.* **9** a particular aspect: *I've changed in every way.* **10** a specified condition or state: *the family was in a poor way.* **11** (**ways**) parts into which something divides or is divided. **12** forward motion of a ship or boat through water. • **adv.** informal at or to a considerable distance or extent.
– PHRASES **by the way** incidentally. **by way of 1** via. **2** as a form of. **3** by means of. **come one's way** happen or become available to one. **get** (or **have**) **one's** (**own**) **way** get or do what one wants in spite of opposition. **give way 1** yield. **2** collapse or break under pressure. **3** allow another to be or go first. **4** (**give way to**) be replaced or superseded by. **go one's own way** act as one wishes. **go one's way** (of events, circumstances, etc.) be favourable to one. **have a way with** have a particular talent for dealing with or ability in. **have one's way with** humorous have sexual intercourse with. **lead the way** go first along a route or be the first to do something. **one way and another** (or **one way or the other**) **1** taking most considerations into account. **2** by some means. **3** whichever of two given alternatives is the case. **on the** (or **its**) **way** about to arrive or happen. **on the** (or **one's**) **way out** informal **1** going out of fashion or favour. **2** dying. **the other way round** (or **around**; Brit. also **about**) **1** in the opposite position or direction. **2** the opposite of what is expected or supposed. **out of the way 1** (of a place) remote. **2** dealt with or finished. **3** no longer an obstacle to someone's plans. **4** unusual or exceptional. **ways and means** the methods and resources for achieving something.
– ORIGIN Old English.

waybill • n. a list of passengers or goods being carried on a vehicle.

wayfarer • n. literary a person who travels on foot.
– DERIVATIVES **wayfaring** n.

waylay • v. (**waylays, waylaying, waylaid**) **1** intercept (someone) in order to attack them. **2** stop (someone) and detain them with questions, conversation, etc.

waymark • n. (also **waymarker**) a sign forming one of a series used to mark out a footpath or similar route.

> **Wayne,** [E]
> John (1907–79; born *Marion Michael Morrison*), American actor, star of westerns such as *The Searchers* and *True Grit.*

W

way-out • adj. informal unconventional or experimental.

-ways • suffix forming adjectives and adverbs of direction or manner: *lengthways.*

wayside • n. the edge of a road.
– PHRASES **fall by the wayside** fail to persist in an undertaking. [ORIGIN with biblical allusion to the Gospel of Luke, chapter 8.]

way station • n. N. Amer. a stopping place on a journey.

wayward • adj. self-willed and unpredictable.
– ORIGIN shortening of former *awayward* 'turned away'.

wazzock /waz-zuhk/ • n. Brit. informal a stupid or annoying person.
– ORIGIN unknown.

Wb • abbrev. weber(s).

WBA • abbrev. World Boxing Association.

WBC • abbrev. World Boxing Council.

WC • abbrev. Brit. water closet.

we • pron. (first person pl.) **1** used by a speaker to refer to himself or herself and one or more other people considered together. **2** people in general. **3** used in formal contexts for or by a royal person, or by a writer, to refer to himself or herself. **4** you (used in a superior way): *how are we today?*
– ORIGIN Old English.

> **USAGE** we
> For an explanation of whether to use **we** or **us** following **than**, see the note at **PERSONAL PRONOUN.**

weak • adj. **1** lacking physical strength and energy. **2** likely to break or give way under pressure. **3** not secure, stable, or firmly established. **4** lacking power, influence, or ability. **5** lacking intensity: *a weak light from a single street lamp.* **6** (of a liquid or solution) heavily diluted. **7** not convincing or forceful. **8** Grammar (of verbs) forming the past tense and past participle by addition of a suffix (in English, typically *-ed*).
– PHRASES **the weaker sex** dated women seen as a group. **weak at the knees** helpless with emotion.
– ORIGIN Old English.

weaken • v. make or become weak.

weak-kneed • adj. **1** weak and shaky from fear or excitement. **2** lacking in determination or courage.

weakling • n. a weak person or animal.

weakly • adv. in a weak way. • adj. (**weaklier, weakliest**) weak or sickly.

weakness • n. **1** the state or condition of being weak. **2** a disadvantage or fault. **3** a person or thing that one is unable to resist. **4** (**weakness for**) a self-indulgent liking for.

weal[1] /*rhymes with* feel/ (also esp. Med. **wheal**) • n. a red, swollen mark left on flesh by a blow or pressure.
– ORIGIN variant of **WALE.**

weal[2] /*rhymes with* feel/ • n. formal that which is best for someone or something: *guardians of the public weal.*
– ORIGIN Old English, 'wealth, well-being'.

wealth • n. **1** a large amount of money, property, or possessions. **2** the state of being rich. **3** a large amount of something desirable.
– ORIGIN from **WELL**[1] or **WEAL**[2].

wealthy • adj. (**wealthier, wealthiest**) rich.

wean[1] • v. **1** make (a young mammal) used to food other than its mother's milk. **2** (often **wean off**) make (someone) give up a habit or addiction. **3** (**be weaned on**) be strongly influenced by (something) from an early age.
– ORIGIN Old English.

wean[2] • n. Sc. & N. Engl. a young child.

– ORIGIN from *wee ane* 'little one'.

weapon ● n. **1** a thing designed or used to inflict bodily harm or physical damage. **2** a means of gaining an advantage or defending oneself.
– DERIVATIVES **weaponry** n.
– ORIGIN Old English.

wear ● v. (**wears**, **wearing**, **wore**; past part. **worn**) **1** have on one's body as clothing, decoration, or protection. **2** display or present (a particular facial expression or appearance). **3** damage or destroy or suffer damage or destruction by friction or use. **4** withstand continued use to a specified degree: *the fabric wears well wash after wash.* **5** (**wear off**) lose effectiveness or strength. **6** (**wear down**) overcome by persistence. **7** (**wear out**) exhaust. **8** (**wearing**) mentally or physically tiring. **9** (**wear on**) (of time) pass slowly or tediously. ● n. **1** the action of wearing or the state of being worn. **2** clothing suitable for a particular purpose or of a particular type. **3** damage sustained from continuous use. **4** the capacity for withstanding such damage.
– PHRASES **wear thin** gradually dwindle or be used up.
– DERIVATIVES **wearable** adj. **wearer** n.
– ORIGIN Old English.

wearisome ● adj. causing one to feel tired or bored.

weary ● adj. (**wearier**, **weariest**) **1** tired. **2** causing tiredness. **3** (often **weary of**) reluctant to experience any more of. ● v. (**wearies**, **wearying**, **wearied**) **1** make weary. **2** (**weary of**) grow tired of.
– DERIVATIVES **wearily** adv. **weariness** n.
– ORIGIN Old English.

weasel ● n. **1** a small slender meat-eating mammal related to the stoat, with reddish-brown fur. **2** informal a deceitful or treacherous person.
– DERIVATIVES **weaselly** adj.
– ORIGIN Old English.

weather ● n. the state of the atmosphere at a place and time in terms of temperature, wind, rain, etc. ● adj. referring to the side from which the wind is blowing. Contrasted with LEE. ● v. (**weathers**, **weathering**, **weathered**) **1** wear away or change in form or appearance by being exposed to the weather for a long time. **2** come safely through.
– PHRASES **keep a weather eye on** be watchful for developments. **make heavy weather of** informal have unnecessary difficulty in dealing with (a task or problem). [ORIGIN from the nautical phrase *make good* or *bad weather of it*, referring to a ship in a storm.] **under the weather** informal slightly unwell or depressed.
– ORIGIN Old English.

weather-beaten ● adj. damaged, worn, or tanned through being exposed to the weather.

weatherboard esp. Brit. ● n. **1** a sloping board attached to the bottom of an outside door to keep out the rain. **2** each of a series of horizontal boards nailed to outside walls with edges overlapping to keep out the rain.

weathercock ● n. a weathervane in the form of a cockerel.

weatherman (or **weatherwoman**) ● n. a person who broadcasts a description and forecast of weather conditions.

weather station ● n. an observation post where weather and atmospheric conditions are observed and recorded.

weathervane ● n. a revolving pointer to show the direction of the wind.

weave[1] ● v. (**weaves**, **weaving**, **wove**; past part. **woven** or **wove**) **1** form (fabric) by interlacing long threads passing in one direction with others at a right angle to them. **2** make fabric in this way. **3** make (basketwork or a wreath) by interlacing rods or flowers. **4** (**weave into**) make (facts, events, or other elements) into (a story). ● n. a particular way in which fabric is woven: *cloth of a very fine weave.*
– ORIGIN Old English.

weave[2] ● v. (**weaves**, **weaving**, **weaved**) move from side to side to get around obstructions.
– ORIGIN prob. from Old Norse, 'to wave, brandish'.

weaver ● n. **1** a person who weaves fabric. **2** (also **weaver bird**) a songbird of tropical Africa and Asia, which builds elaborately woven nests.

web ● n. **1** a network of fine threads constructed by a spider, used to catch its prey. **2** a complex system of interconnected elements: *a web of lies.* **3** (**the Web**) = WORLD WIDE WEB. **4** a membrane between the toes of a swimming bird or other animal living in water.
– ORIGIN Old English.

Webb, E
(Martha) Beatrice (1858–1943) and Sidney (James), Baron Passfield (1859–1947), English socialists, economists, and historians. They helped to establish the London School of Economics (1895).

webbed ● adj. (of an animal's feet) having the toes connected by a web.

webbing ● n. strong fabric used for making straps and belts and for supporting the seats of upholstered chairs.

webcam (also **Webcam**) ● n. (trademark in the US) a video camera connected to a computer, so that the film produced may be viewed on the Internet.

webcast ● n. a live video broadcast of an event transmitted across the Internet.

Weber[1] E
/vay-ber/, Carl Maria (Friedrich Ernst) von (1786–1826), German composer, known for his opera *Der Freischütz*.

Weber[2] E
/vay-ber/, Max (1864–1920), German economist and sociologist. His work on the relationship between economy and society established him as one of the founders of modern sociology.

weber /vay-ber/ ● n. the SI unit of magnetic flux, sufficient to cause an electromotive force of one volt in a circuit of one turn when generated or removed in one second.
– ORIGIN named after the German physicist Wilhelm Eduard *Weber* (1804–91).

Webern E
/vay-bern/, Anton (Friedrich Ernst) von (1883–1945), Austrian serialist composer.

webmaster ● n. Computing a person who is responsible for a particular server on the Internet.

web page ● n. Computing a hypertext document able to be accessed via the Internet.

website ● n. Computing a location connected to the Internet that maintains one or more web pages.

Webster[1], E
John (*c.*1580–*c.*1625), English dramatist, best known for the tragedies *The White Devil* and *The Duchess of Malfi*.

Webster[2], E
Noah (1758–1843), American lexicographer. His *American Dictionary of the English Language* (1828) was the first dictionary to give comprehensive coverage of American usage.

wed ● v. (**weds**, **wedding**, **wedded** or **wed**) **1** formal or literary marry. **2** formal or literary give or join in marriage. **3** (**wedded**) having to do with marriage: *wedded bliss.* **4** combine (two desirable factors or qualities). **5** (**be wedded to**) be entirely devoted to (an activity, belief, etc.).
– ORIGIN Old English.

we'd ● contr. **1** we had. **2** we should or we would.

wedding ● n. a marriage ceremony.

wedding breakfast ● n. Brit. a celebratory meal eaten just after a wedding (at any time of day) by the couple and their guests.

wedding march ● n. a piece of march music played at the entrance of the bride or the exit of the couple at a wedding.

wedding ring ● n. a ring worn by a married person, given to them by their husband or wife at their wedding.

Wedekind E
/vay-duh-kind/, Frank (1864–1918), German expressionist dramatist, best known for *The Awakening of Spring*, an explicit portrayal of sexual awakening.

wedge ● n. **1** a piece of wood, metal, etc. with a thick end that tapers to a thin edge, that is driven between two objects or parts of an object to secure or separate them. **2** a wedge-shaped thing or piece. **3** a golf club with a low, angled face for hitting the ball as high as possible into the air. **4** a shoe with a fairly high heel forming a solid block with the sole. ● v. (**wedges**, **wedging**, **wedged**) **1** fix in position using a wedge. **2** force into a narrow space.
– PHRASES **drive a wedge between** cause a disagreement or hostility between. **the thin end of the wedge** informal an action unimportant in itself but likely to lead to more serious developments.
– ORIGIN Old English.

Wedgwood /wej-wuud/ ● n. trademark ceramic ware made by the English potter Josiah Wedgwood (1730–95) and his successors.

wedlock ● n. the state of being married.
– PHRASES **born in** (or **out of**) **wedlock** born of married (or unmarried) parents.
– ORIGIN Old English, 'marriage vow'.

Wednesday ● n. the day of the week before Thursday and following Tuesday.
– ORIGIN Old English, named after the god **ODIN**.

wee[1] ● adj. (**weer**, **weest**) esp. Sc. little.
– ORIGIN Old English.

wee[2] informal, esp. Brit. ● n. **1** an act of urinating. **2** urine. ● v. (**wees**, **weeing**, **weed**) urinate.

weed ● n. **1** a wild plant growing where it is not wanted and in competition with plants which have been deliberately grown. **2** informal cannabis. **3** (**the weed**) informal tobacco. **4** informal a weak or skinny person. ● v. **1** remove weeds from. **2** (**weed out**) remove (inferior or unwanted items or members) from something.
– ORIGIN Old English.

weedkiller ● n. a substance used to destroy weeds.

weedy ● adj. (**weedier**, **weediest**) **1** containing or covered with many weeds. **2** informal thin and weak.

week ● n. **1** a period of seven days. **2** the period of seven days generally reckoned from and to midnight on Saturday night. **3** esp. Brit. (preceded by a specified day) a week after (that day): *I've got to go to the church social on Saturday week.* **4** the five days from Monday to Friday, or the time spent working during this period.
– ORIGIN Old English.

weekday ● n. a day of the week other than Sunday or Saturday.

weekend ● n. Saturday and Sunday. ● v. informal spend a weekend somewhere.

weekender ● n. a person who spends weekends away from their main home.

weekly ● adj. **1** done, produced, or occurring once a week. **2** calculated in terms of a week: *weekly income.* ● adv. once a week. ● n. (pl. **weeklies**) a newspaper or other publication issued every week.

weeny ● adj. (**weenier**, **weeniest**) informal tiny.

weep ● v. (**weeps**, **weeping**, **wept**) **1** shed tears. **2** discharge liquid: *the sores began to weep.* **3** (**weeping**) used in names of trees and shrubs with drooping branches, e.g. **weeping willow**. ● n. a fit or spell of shedding tears.
– ORIGIN Old English.

weepie (also **weepy**) ● n. (pl. **weepies**) informal a sentimental or emotional film, novel, or song.

weepy ● adj. (**weepier**, **weepiest**) informal **1** tearful. **2** sentimental.
– DERIVATIVES **weepily** adv. **weepiness** n.

weevil /wee-v'l/ ● n. a small beetle with a long snout, several kinds of which are pests of crops or stored foodstuffs.
– ORIGIN Old English.

wee-wee ● n. informal, esp. Brit. a child's word for urine.

weft ● n. (in weaving) the crosswise threads that are passed over and under the warp threads on a loom to make cloth.
– ORIGIN Old English.

Wegener E
/vay-guh-ner/, Alfred Lothar (1880–1930), German meteorologist and geologist. He was the first serious proponent of the theory of continental drift.

weigh ● v. **1** find out how heavy (someone or something) is. **2** have a specified weight. **3** (**weigh out**) measure and take out (a portion of a particular weight). **4** (**weigh down**)

W

be heavy and troublesome to. **5** (**weigh on**) be depressing or worrying to. **6** (**weigh in**) (of a boxer or jockey) be officially weighed before or after a contest. **7** (often **weigh up**) assess the nature or importance of. **8** (often **weigh against**) influence a decision or action: *the evidence weighed heavily against him.* **9** (**weigh in**) informal forcefully contribute to a competition or argument. **10** (**weigh into**) join in or attack forcefully or enthusiastically.
– PHRASES **weigh anchor** (of a boat) take up the anchor when ready to sail.
– ORIGIN Old English.

weighbridge • n. a machine for weighing vehicles, set into the ground to be driven on to.

weigh-in • n. an official weighing, e.g. of boxers before a fight.

weight • n. **1** the heaviness of a person or thing. **2** Physics the force exerted on the mass of a body by a gravitational field. **3** the quality of being heavy. **4** a unit or system of units used for expressing how much something weighs. **5** a piece of metal known to weigh a definite amount and used on scales to determine how heavy something is. **6** a heavy object. **7** (**weights**) heavy blocks or discs used in weightlifting or weight training. **8** ability to influence decisions or actions: *their recommendation will carry great weight.* **9** the importance attached to something. **10** a feeling of pressure or worry: *a weight on one's mind.* • v. **1** make heavier or keep in place with a weight. **2** attach importance or value to. **3** (**be weighted**) be planned or arranged so as to give someone or something an advantage.
– PHRASES **be worth one's weight in gold** be exceedingly useful or helpful. **throw one's weight about** (or **around**) informal assert oneself in an unpleasant way.
– ORIGIN Old English.

weighting • n. **1** adjustment made to take account of special circumstances or compensate for a distorting factor. **2** Brit. additional wages or salary paid to allow for a higher cost of living in a particular area.

weightless • adj. (of a body) not apparently acted on by gravity.
– DERIVATIVES **weightlessness** n.

weightlifting • n. the sport or activity of lifting barbells or other heavy weights.
– DERIVATIVES **weightlifter** n.

weight training • n. physical training that involves lifting weights.

weighty • adj. (**weightier**, **weightiest**) **1** heavy. **2** very serious and important. **3** very influential.

Weill E
/*rhymes with* vile/, Kurt (1900–50), German composer, resident in the US from 1935. He is best known for his collaboration with Bertolt Brecht on the opera *The Threepenny Opera.*

Weimar Republic E
/vy-mar/ the German republic of 1919–33, so called because its constitution was drawn up at the city of Weimar in central Germany. It was eventually overthrown by the Nazi Party of Adolf Hitler.

weir • n. **1** a low dam built across a river to raise the level of water upstream or regulate its flow. **2** an enclosure of stakes set in a stream as a trap for fish.
– ORIGIN Old English.

weird • adj. **1** suggesting something supernatural. **2** informal very strange.
– DERIVATIVES **weirdly** adv. **weirdness** n.
– ORIGIN Old English, 'destiny, fate'.

weirdo • n. (pl. **weirdos**) informal a strange or eccentric person.

Weismann E
/vyss-muhn/, August Friedrich Leopold (1834–1914), German biologist, one of the founders of modern genetics. He proposed a theory of heredity which ruled out the transmission of acquired characteristics.

Weissmuller E
/wyss-muul-ler/, Johnny (1904–84; full name *John Peter Weissmuller*), American swimmer and actor. He won three Olympic gold medals in 1924 and two in 1928, and later starred in the Tarzan films.

Weizmann E
/vyts-muhn/, Chaim (Azriel) (1874–1952), Russian-born Israeli statesman, President 1949–52. He played an important role in persuading the US government to recognize the new state of Israel (1948) and became its first President.

welch /welch/ • v. var. of WELSH.

welcome • n. **1** an instance or way of greeting someone. **2** a pleased or approving reaction. • exclam. used to greet someone in a friendly way. • v. (**welcomes**, **welcoming**, **welcomed**) **1** greet (someone arriving) in a polite or friendly way. **2** be glad to receive or hear of. • adj. **1** (of a guest or new arrival) gladly received. **2** very pleasing because much needed or desired. **3** allowed or invited to do a specified thing. **4** (**welcome to**) used to indicate relief at giving up something to another: *you're welcome to it!*
– ORIGIN Old English, 'a person whose coming is pleasing'.

weld • v. **1** join together (metal parts) by heating the surfaces to the point of melting and pressing or hammering them together. **2** make or shape (an article) in such a way. **3** cause to combine and form a whole. • n. a welded joint.
– DERIVATIVES **welder** n.
– ORIGIN from WELL² in the former sense 'melt or weld (heated metal)'.

welfare • n. **1** the health, happiness, and fortunes of a person or group. **2** organized efforts designed to promote the basic well-being of people in need. **3** esp. N. Amer. financial support given for this purpose.
– ORIGIN from WELL¹ + FARE.

welfare state • n. a system under which the state undertakes to protect the health and well-being of its citizens by means of grants, pensions, and other benefits.

well¹ • adv. (**better**, **best**) **1** in a good way. **2** in prosperity or comfort: *they lived well.* **3** in a favourable or approving way. **4** thoroughly: *add the lemon juice and mix well.* **5** to a great extent or degree: *everything was planned well in advance.* **6** Brit. informal very; extremely: *he was well out of order.* **7** very probably; in all likelihood. **8** without difficulty: *she could well afford to pay for it herself.* **9** with good reason.

10 archaic luckily; opportunely: *hail fellow, well met*. ● **adj.** (**better**, **best**) **1** in good health. **2** in a satisfactory state or position. **3** sensible; advisable. ● **exclam.** used to express surprise, anger, resignation, etc., or when pausing in speech.
– PHRASES **as well** in addition. **as well** (or **just as well**) **1** with equal reason or an equally good result. **2** sensible, appropriate, or desirable. **be well out of** Brit. informal be fortunate to be no longer involved in. **be well up on** know a great deal about. **leave** (or **let**) **well alone** refrain from interfering with or trying to improve something. **well and truly** completely.
– ORIGIN Old English.

USAGE well
The adverb **well** is often used with a past participle (such as *known*) to form compound adjectives: **well known**, **well dressed**, and so on. Such adjectives should be written without a hyphen when they are used alone after a verb (*she is well known as a writer*) but with a hyphen when they come before a noun (*a well-known writer*).

well[2] ● **n.** **1** a shaft sunk into the ground to obtain water, oil, or gas. **2** a hollow made to hold liquid. **3** a plentiful source or supply. **4** an enclosed space in the middle of a building, giving room for stairs or a lift or allowing in light or air. ● **v.** (often **well up**) **1** (of a liquid) rise up to the surface and spill or be about to spill. **2** (of an emotion) arise and become stronger.
– ORIGIN Old English.

we'll ● **contr.** we shall; we will.

well advised ● **adj.** sensible; wise.

well appointed ● **adj.** (of a building or room) having a high standard of equipment or furnishing.

well-being ● **n.** the state of being comfortable, healthy, or happy.

well disposed ● **adj.** having a positive, sympathetic, or friendly attitude.

well done ● **adj.** **1** carried out successfully or satisfactorily. **2** (of food) thoroughly cooked. ● **exclam.** used to express congratulation or approval.

well endowed ● **adj.** **1** having plentiful supplies of a resource. **2** informal, humorous (of a man) having large genitals. **3** informal, humorous (of a woman) large-breasted.

Welles E
/welz/, (George) Orson (1915–85), American film director and actor. He is best known as the director of *Citizen Kane*, in which he also starred.

well-heeled ● **adj.** informal wealthy.

well hung ● **adj.** informal, humorous (of a man) having large genitals.

wellie ● **n.** var. of **WELLY**.

Wellington[1] E
the capital of New Zealand, on North Island.

Wellington[2], E
Arthur Wellesley, 1st Duke of (1769–1852; known as **the Iron Duke**). British soldier and Tory statesman, Prime Minister 1828–30 and 1834. He was commander of British forces in the Peninsular War, and in 1815 defeated Napoleon at Waterloo.

wellington (also **wellington boot**) ● **n.** esp. Brit. a knee-length waterproof rubber or plastic boot.
– ORIGIN named after the 1st Duke of *Wellington* (see **WELLINGTON**[2]).

well known ● **adj.** known widely or thoroughly.

well meaning (also **well meant**) ● **adj.** having good intentions but not necessarily the desired effect.

well-nigh ● **adv.** esp. literary almost.

well off ● **adj.** **1** wealthy. **2** in a favourable situation or circumstances.

well preserved ● **adj.** (of an old person) showing little sign of ageing.

well rounded ● **adj.** **1** having a pleasing curved shape. **2** (of a person) plump. **3** (of a person) having a personality that is fully developed in all aspects.

Wells, E
H. G. (1866–1946; full name *Herbert George Wells*), English novelist, famous for his science-fiction novels, such as *The War of the Worlds* and *The Time Machine*.

well spoken ● **adj.** speaking in an educated and refined way.

wellspring ● **n.** literary **1** the place where a spring comes out of the ground. **2** an abundant source of something: *a wellspring of creativity*.

well thumbed ● **adj.** (of a book) having been read often and bearing marks of frequent handling.

well-to-do ● **adj.** wealthy; prosperous.

well travelled ● **adj.** **1** (of a person) having travelled widely. **2** (of a route) much frequented by travellers.

well trodden ● **adj.** much frequented by travellers.

well turned ● **adj.** **1** (of a phrase or compliment) elegantly expressed. **2** (of a woman's ankle or leg) attractively shaped.

well-wisher ● **n.** a person who desires happiness or success for another, or who expresses such a desire.

well worn ● **adj.** **1** showing signs of extensive use or wear. **2** (of a phrase or idea) used or repeated so often that it no longer has interest or significance.

welly (also **wellie**) ● **n.** (pl. **wellies**) Brit. informal **1** = **WELLINGTON**. **2** power or vigour.

Welsh ● **n.** the language of Wales. ● **adj.** relating to Wales.
– DERIVATIVES **Welshness** n.
– ORIGIN Old English.

welsh (also **welch**) ● **v.** (**welsh on**) fail to honour (a debt or obligation).
– ORIGIN unknown.

Welsh rarebit (also **Welsh rabbit**) ● **n.** = **RAREBIT**.

welt ● **n.** **1** a leather rim round the edge of the upper of a shoe, to which the sole is attached. **2** a ribbed, reinforced, or decorative border on a garment. **3** a weal.
– ORIGIN unknown.

welter ● **n.** a large number of items in no order.
– ORIGIN Dutch or German *welteren* 'writhe, wallow'.

welterweight ● **n.** a weight in boxing and other sports intermediate between light-

weight and middleweight.
– ORIGIN unknown.

wen • n. a boil or other swelling or growth on the skin.
– ORIGIN Old English.

Wenceslas, St E
/wen-suhss-lass/ (also **Wenceslaus**) (*c.*907–29; known as **Good King Wenceslas**), Duke of Bohemia and patron saint of the Czech Republic. Feast day, 28 September.

wench /wench/ • n. archaic or humorous a girl or young woman.
– ORIGIN shortening of former *wenchel* 'child, servant, prostitute'.

wend • v. (**wend one's way**) go slowly or by an indirect route.
– ORIGIN Old English, 'to turn, depart'.

Wendy house • n. Brit. a toy house large enough for children to play in.
– ORIGIN named after the house built around *Wendy* in J. M. Barrie's play *Peter Pan*.

went past of **GO**[1].

wept past and past part. of **WEEP**.

were 2nd person sing. past, pl. past, and past subjunctive of **BE**.

we're • contr. we are.

weren't • contr. were not.

werewolf /wair-wuulf, weer-wuulf/ • n. (pl. **werewolves**) (in folklore) a person who periodically changes into a wolf, typically when there is a full moon.
– ORIGIN Old English.

Weser E
/vay-zer/ a river of NW Germany, which is formed at the junction of the Werra and Fulda Rivers in Lower Saxony and flows northwards to the North Sea.

Wesker E
/wess-ker/, Arnold (b.1932), English dramatist. His plays are associated with the British kitchen-sink drama of the 1950s.

Wesley E
/wez-li/, John (1703–91), English preacher and co-founder of Methodism (1791). His brother **Charles** (1707–88) was also a founding Methodist, and both wrote many hymns.

Wesleyan • adj. having to do with the teachings of John Wesley or the main branch of the Methodist Church which he founded. • n. a follower of Wesley or of the main Methodist tradition.

Wessex E
the kingdom of the West Saxons, established in Hampshire in the early 6th century and gradually extended by conquest to include much of southern England.

West[1], E
Mae (1892–1980), American actress and dramatist. She became famous on Broadway, acting in her own comedies, before embarking on her Hollywood career.

West[2], E
Dame Rebecca (1892–1983; born *Cicily Isabel Fairfield*), Irish-born British writer and feminist.

west • n. **1** the direction in which the sun sets at the equinoxes. **2** the western part of a country, region, or town. **3** (**the West**) Europe and North America seen in contrast to other civilizations. **4** (**the West**) hist. the non-Communist states of Europe and North America. • adj. **1** lying towards or facing the west. **2** (of a wind) blowing from the west. • adv. to or towards the west.
– ORIGIN Old English.

West Bank E
a region west of the River Jordan and northwest of the Dead Sea; 97 per cent of its inhabitants are Palestinian Arabs. It became part of Jordan in 1948 and was occupied by Israel from 1967. The Palestinians were granted limited autonomy under an agreement of 1993.

West Bengal E
a state in eastern India; capital, Calcutta (Kolkata).

West Country E
the south-western counties of England.

West End E
the entertainment and shopping area of London to the west of the City.

westerly • adj. & adv. **1** towards or facing the west. **2** (of a wind) blowing from the west.

western • adj. **1** situated in or facing the west. **2** (usu. **Western**) coming from, or characteristic of the west, in particular Europe and North America. • n. a film or novel about cowboys in western North America.

Western Australia E
a state comprising the western part of Australia; capital, Perth.

Western Cape E
a province of south-western South Africa; capital, Cape Town.

Western Church • n. the part of the Christian Church originating in the Western Roman Empire, including the Roman Catholic, Anglican, Lutheran, and Reformed Churches.

westerner • n. a person from the west of a region.

Western Front E
the zone of fighting in western Europe in the First World War, in which the German army engaged the armies to its west, i.e. France, the UK (and its dominions), and, from 1917, the US.

Western Isles[1] E
= **HEBRIDES**.

Western Isles[2] E
an administrative region of Scotland, consisting of the Outer Hebrides; administrative centre, Stornoway.

westernize (also **westernise**) • v. (**westernizes, westernizing, westernized**) bring under the cultural, political, or economic influence of Europe and North America.
– DERIVATIVES **westernization** (also **westernisation**) n.

Western Sahara E
a region of NW Africa, on the Atlantic coast between Morocco and Mauritania; capital, La'youn.

Western Samoa E
former name for **SAMOA²**.

West Indian • n. a person from the West Indies, or a person of West Indian descent. • adj. relating to the West Indies.

West Indies E
a chain of islands extending from the Florida peninsula to the coast of Venezuela, between the Caribbean and the Atlantic. They consist of three main island groups, the Greater and Lesser Antilles and the Bahamas, with Bermuda lying further to the north.

Westinghouse, E
George (1846–1914), American engineer, who developed vacuum-operated safety brakes and electrically controlled signals for railways.

West Irian E
= **IRIAN JAYA**.

West Lothian E
an administrative region and former county of east central Scotland.

Westmeath E
/west-**meeth**/ a county of the Republic of Ireland; county town, Mullingar.

West Midlands E
a metropolitan county of central England.

Westminster E
an inner London borough which contains the Houses of Parliament. Full name **CITY OF WESTMINSTER**.

Westminster, Palace of E
the Houses of Parliament.

Westminster Abbey E
the church of St Peter in Westminster, where most of England's monarchs have been crowned and where some of the nation's leading figures have been buried.

west-north-west • n. the direction halfway between west and north-west.

west-south-west • n. the direction halfway between west and south-west.

West Sussex E
a county of SE England; county town, Chichester.

West Virginia E
a state of the eastern US; capital, Charleston.
– DERIVATIVES **West Virginian** n. & adj.

westward • adj. towards the west. • adv. (also **westwards**) in a westerly direction.

West Yorkshire E
a metropolitan county of northern England.

wet • adj. (**wetter, wettest**) **1** covered or saturated with liquid. **2** (of the weather) rainy. **3** involving the use of water or liquid. **4** (of paint, ink, etc.) not yet having dried or hardened. **5** Brit. informal lacking forcefulness or strength of character. • v. (**wets, wetting, wet** or **wetted**) **1** cover or touch with liquid. **2** urinate in or on. **3** (**wet oneself**) urinate involuntarily. • n. **1** liquid that makes something damp. **2** (**the wet**) rainy weather. **3** Brit. informal a feeble person.
– PHRASES **wet the baby's head** Brit. informal celebrate a baby's birth with a drink. **wet behind the ears** informal lacking experience. **wet one's whistle** informal have a drink.
– DERIVATIVES **wetly** adv. **wetness** n.
– ORIGIN Old English.

wet blanket • n. informal a person who spoils other people's enjoyment with their disapproving or unenthusiastic manner.

wet dream • n. an erotic dream that causes involuntary ejaculation of semen.

wether /*rhymes with* weather/ • n. a castrated ram.
– ORIGIN Old English.

wetland • n. (also **wetlands**) swampy or marshy land.

wet nurse • n. esp. hist. a woman employed to breastfeed another woman's child.

wet rot • n. a brown fungus causing decay in moist timber.

wetsuit • n. a close-fitting rubber garment covering the entire body, worn for warmth in water sports or diving.

we've • contr. we have.

Wexford E
a county in the south-east of the Republic of Ireland; county town, Wexford.

Weyden E
/**vay**-d'n/, Rogier van der (*c.*1400–64), Flemish painter, known for his portraits and religious paintings.

whack informal • v. **1** strike forcefully with a sharp blow. **2** defeat heavily. **3** place or insert roughly or carelessly. • n. **1** a sharp blow. **2** a try or attempt. **3** Brit. a specified share of or contribution to something: *he paid a fair whack of the bill.*
– PHRASES **top** (or **full**) **whack** esp. Brit. the maximum price or rate.

whacked (also **whacked out**) • adj. informal **1** esp. Brit. completely exhausted. **2** esp. N. Amer. under the influence of drugs.

whacking • adj. Brit. informal very large.

whacko • adj. & n. (pl. **whackos**) var. of **WACKO**.

whacky • adj. var. of **WACKY**.

whale • n. (pl. **whale** or **whales**) a very large marine mammal with a horizontal tail fin and a blowhole on top of the head for breathing.
– PHRASES **have a whale of a time** informal enjoy oneself very much.
– ORIGIN Old English.

whalebone • n. an elastic horny substance which grows in thin parallel plates in the upper jaw of some whales and is used by them to strain plankton from the seawater.

whaler • n. **1** a whaling ship. **2** a seaman engaged in whaling.

whaling • n. the practice or industry of hunting and killing whales for their oil, meat, or whalebone.

wham informal • exclam. used to express the sound of a hard impact or the idea of a sudden occurrence. • v. (**whams, whamming, whammed**) strike something forcefully.

whammy ● **n.** (pl. **whammies**) informal an event with a powerful and unpleasant effect; a blow.

whap ● **v.** (**whaps**, **whapping**, **whapped**) & **n.** esp. N. Amer. var. of **WHOP**.

wharf /worf/ ● **n.** (pl. **wharves** or **wharfs**) a level quayside area to which a ship may be moored to load and unload.
– ORIGIN Old English.

Wharton E
/wor-t'n/, Edith (Newbold) (1862–1937), American novelist and short-story writer, resident in France from 1907. Her novels include *The Age of Innocence*.

what ● **pron. & det.** **1** asking for information specifying something. **2** (as pronoun) asking for repetition of something not heard or confirmation of something not understood. **3** (as pronoun) the thing or things that. **4** whatever. **5** used to emphasize something surprising or remarkable. ● **adv.** **1** to what extent? **2** informal, dated used for emphasis or to invite agreement.
– PHRASES **give someone what for** informal, esp. Brit. punish or scold someone severely. **what for?** informal for what reason? **what's what** informal what is useful or important. **what with** because of.
– ORIGIN Old English.

whatever ● **pron. & det.** everything or anything that; no matter what. ● **pron.** used for emphasis instead of 'what' in questions. ● **adv.** **1** at all; of any kind. **2** informal no matter what happens.

whatnot ● **n.** informal used to refer to an unidentified item or items having something in common with items already named.

whatsit ● **n.** informal a person or thing whose name one cannot recall, does not know, or does not wish to specify.

whatsoever ● **adv.** at all. ● **det. & pron.** archaic whatever.

wheal ● **n.** var. of **WEAL**[1].

wheat ● **n.** a cereal widely grown in temperate countries, the grain of which is ground to make flour.
– ORIGIN Old English.

wheatear ● **n.** a songbird with black and grey, buff, or white plumage and a white rump.
– ORIGIN prob. from **WHITE** + **ARSE**.

wheaten ● **adj.** made of wheat.

wheatgerm ● **n.** a nutritious foodstuff consisting of the extracted embryos of grains of wheat.

wheatmeal ● **n.** flour made from wheat from which some of the bran and germ has been removed.

Wheatstone, E
Sir Charles (1802–75), English physicist and inventor, known for his electrical inventions which included the rheostat, and with Sir W. F. Cooke (1806–79), the electric telegraph.

wheedle ● **v.** (**wheedles**, **wheedling**, **wheedled**) use endearments or flattery to persuade someone to do something.
– ORIGIN perh. from German *wedeln* 'cringe, fawn'.

wheel ● **n.** **1** a circular object that revolves on an axle, fixed below a vehicle to enable it to move along or forming part of a machine. **2** something resembling a wheel or having a wheel as its essential part. **3** (**wheels**) informal a car. **4** a turn or rotation. ● **v.** **1** push or pull (a vehicle with wheels). **2** carry in or on a vehicle with wheels. **3** fly or turn in a wide circle or curve. **4** turn round quickly to face another way. **5** (**wheel in/on/out**) informal produce (something that is unimpressive because it has been frequently seen or heard before).
– PHRASES **wheel and deal** take part in commercial or political scheming.
– ORIGIN Old English.

wheelbarrow ● **n.** a small cart with a single wheel at the front and two supporting legs and two handles at the rear, used for carrying loads in building or gardening.

wheelbase ● **n.** the distance between the front and rear axles of a vehicle.

wheelchair ● **n.** a chair on wheels for an invalid or disabled person.

wheel clamp ● **n.** a device placed around the wheel of an unlawfully parked car to prevent it being driven away.

wheeler ● **n.** (in combination) a vehicle having a specified number of wheels: *a three-wheeler.*

wheeler dealer (also **wheeler and dealer**) ● **n.** a person who takes part in commercial or political scheming.

wheelhouse ● **n.** a shelter for the person at the wheel of a boat or ship.

wheelie ● **n.** informal a manoeuvre whereby a bicycle or motorcycle is ridden for a short distance with the front wheel raised off the ground.

wheelie bin (also **wheely bin**) ● **n.** Brit. informal a large refuse bin set on wheels.

wheelspin ● **n.** rotation of a vehicle's wheels without movement of the vehicle forwards or backwards.

wheelwright ● **n.** esp. hist. a person who makes or repairs wooden wheels.

wheeze ● **v.** (**wheezes**, **wheezing**, **wheezed**) **1** breathe with a whistling or rattling sound in the chest, as a result of a blockage in the air passages. **2** (of a device) make an irregular rattling or spluttering sound. ● **n.** **1** a sound of a person wheezing. **2** Brit. informal a clever or amusing scheme or trick.
– DERIVATIVES **wheezily** adv. **wheeziness** n. **wheezy** adj.
– ORIGIN prob. from Old Norse, 'to hiss'.

whelk ● **n.** a shellfish with a heavy pointed spiral shell, some kinds of which are eaten as food.
– ORIGIN Old English.

whelp ● **n.** esp. archaic **1** a puppy. **2** derog. a boy or young man. ● **v.** give birth to (a puppy).
– ORIGIN Old English.

when ● **adv.** **1** at what time? **2** how soon? **3** in what circumstances? **4** at which time or in which situation. ● **conj.** **1** at or during the time that. **2** at any time that; whenever. **3** after which; and just then. **4** in view of the fact that: *why buy when you can borrow?* **5** although; whereas.
– ORIGIN Old English.

whence (also **from whence**) ● **adv.** formal or archaic **1** from what place or source? **2** from which; from where. **3** to the place from which. **4** as a consequence of which.

whenever ● **conj.** **1** at whatever time; on whatever occasion. **2** every time that. ● **adv.**

W

used for emphasis instead of 'when' in questions.

whensoever • conj. & adv. formal word for WHENEVER.

where • adv. **1** in or to what place or position? **2** in what direction or respect? **3** at, in, or to which. **4** the place or situation in which. **5** in or to a place or situation in which.
– ORIGIN Old English.

whereabouts • adv. where or approximately where? • n. the place where someone or something is.

whereas • conj. **1** in contrast or comparison with the fact that. **2** taking into consideration the fact that.

whereat • adv. & conj. archaic or formal at which.

whereby • adv. by which.

wherefore archaic • adv. for what reason? • adv. & conj. as a result of which.

wherein • adv. formal **1** in which. **2** in what place or respect?

whereof • adv. formal of what or which.

wheresoever • adv. & conj. formal word for WHEREVER.

whereupon • conj. immediately after which.

wherever • adv. **1** in or to whatever place. **2** used for emphasis instead of 'where' in questions. • conj. in every case when.

wherewithal • n. the money or other resources needed for a particular purpose.

wherry /*rhymes with* sherry/ • n. (pl. **wherries**) **1** a light rowing boat used chiefly for carrying passengers. **2** Brit. a large light barge.
– ORIGIN unknown.

whet /wet/ • v. (**whets, whetting, whetted**) **1** sharpen the blade of (a tool or weapon). **2** excite or stimulate (someone's desire, interest, or appetite).
– ORIGIN Old English.

whether • conj. **1** expressing a doubt or choice between alternatives. **2** expressing an enquiry or investigation. **3** indicating that a statement applies whichever of the alternatives mentioned is the case.
– ORIGIN Old English.

USAGE whether

For an explanation on whether to use **whether** or **if**, see the note at IF.

whetstone • n. a fine-grained stone used for sharpening cutting tools.

whey /way/ • n. the watery part of milk that remains after curds have formed.
– ORIGIN Old English.

which • pron. & det. **1** asking for information specifying one or more people or things from a definite set. **2** used to refer to something previously mentioned when introducing a clause giving further information.
– ORIGIN Old English.

W

whichever • det. & pron. **1** any which; that or those which. **2** regardless of which.

whiff • n. **1** a smell that is smelt only briefly or faintly. **2** Brit. informal an unpleasant smell. **3** a trace or hint of something bad or exciting. **4** a puff or breath of air or smoke.

whiffy • adj. (**whiffier, whiffiest**) Brit. informal having an unpleasant smell.

Whig • n. hist. a member of the British reforming party that sought the supremacy of Parliament, succeeded in the 19th century by the Liberal Party.
– ORIGIN prob. a shortening of Scots *whiggamore*, the nickname of 17th-century Scottish rebels.

while • n. **1** (**a while**) a period of time. **2** (**a while**) for some time. **3** (**the while**) at the same time; meanwhile. **4** (**the while**) literary during the time that. • conj. **1** at the same time as. **2** whereas (indicating a contrast). **3** although. • adv. during which. • v. (**whiles, whiling, whiled**) (**while away**) pass (time) in a leisurely way.
– PHRASES **worth while** (or **worth one's while**) worth the time or effort spent.
– ORIGIN Old English.

whilst • conj. & adv. esp. Brit. while.

whim • n. a sudden desire or change of mind.
– ORIGIN unknown.

whimper • v. (**whimpers, whimpering, whimpered**) make a series of low, feeble sounds expressing fear, pain, or discontent. • n. a whimpering sound.

whimsical • adj. **1** playfully old-fashioned or fanciful. **2** showing sudden changes of direction or behaviour.
– DERIVATIVES **whimsicality** n. **whimsically** adv.

whimsy (also **whimsey**) • n. (pl. **whimsies** or **whimseys**) **1** playfully old-fashioned or fanciful behaviour or humour. **2** a fanciful or odd thing. **3** a whim.
– ORIGIN prob. from archaic *whim-wham* 'trinket, whim'.

whin • n. esp. N. Engl. gorse.
– ORIGIN prob. Scandinavian.

whinchat /win-chat/ • n. a small songbird with a brown back and orange-buff underparts.

whine • n. **1** a long, high-pitched complaining cry. **2** a long, high-pitched unpleasant sound. **3** a feeble or petty complaint. • v. (**whines, whining, whined**) **1** give or make a whine. **2** complain in a feeble or petty way.
– DERIVATIVES **whiny** adj.
– ORIGIN Old English, 'whistle through the air'.

whinge Brit. informal • v. (**whinges, whingeing, whinged**) complain persistently and irritably. • n. an act of whingeing.
– DERIVATIVES **whinger** n.
– ORIGIN Old English.

whinny • n. (pl. **whinnies**) a gentle, high-pitched neigh. • v. (**whinnies, whinnying, whinnied**) (of a horse) make such a sound.

whip • n. **1** a length of leather or cord fastened to a handle, used for beating a person or urging on an animal. **2** an official of a political party appointed to maintain parliamentary discipline among its members. **3** Brit. a written notice from such an official requesting attendance for voting. **4** a dessert made from cream or eggs beaten into a light fluffy mass. **5** a violent striking or beating movement. • v. (**whips, whipping, whipped**) **1** strike with a whip. **2** (of a flexible object or rain or wind) strike or beat violently. **3** move or take out fast or suddenly. **4** beat (cream, eggs, etc.) into a froth. **5** Brit. informal steal.
– PHRASES **whip up 1** make or prepare very quickly. **2** deliberately excite or provoke. **3** stimulate (a particular feeling) in someone.

– ORIGIN prob. from German and Dutch *wippen* 'swing, leap, dance'.

whipcord • n. **1** thin, tough, tightly twisted cord used for making the flexible end part of whips. **2** a closely woven ribbed worsted fabric.

whiplash • n. **1** the lashing action of a whip. **2** the flexible part of a whip. **3** injury caused by a severe jerk to the head.

whippersnapper • n. informal a young and inexperienced person who is bold and overconfident.
– ORIGIN perh. representing *whipsnapper*, expressing noise and unimportance.

whippet • n. a dog of a small slender breed, bred for racing.
– ORIGIN partly from former *whippet* 'move briskly'.

whipping boy • n. a person who is blamed or punished for the faults or incompetence of others.
– ORIGIN first referring to a boy educated with a young prince and punished instead of him.

whippoorwill /wip-per-wil/ • n. a North and Central American nightjar with a distinctive call.

whippy • adj. flexible; springy.

whip-round • n. Brit. informal a collection of contributions of money for a particular purpose.

whipsaw • n. a saw with a narrow blade and a handle at both ends.

whirl • v. **1** move rapidly round and round. **2** (of the head or mind) seem to spin round. • n. **1** a rapid movement round and round. **2** frantic activity: *the mad social whirl*. **3** a sweet or biscuit with a spiral shape.
– PHRASES **give something a whirl** informal give something a try. **in a whirl** in a state of confusion.
– ORIGIN prob. from Old Norse.

whirligig • n. **1** a toy that spins round, e.g. a top or windmill. **2** = ROUNDABOUT (in sense 2).
– ORIGIN from WHIRL + former *gig* 'toy for whipping'.

whirlpool • n. **1** a current of water whirling in a circle, often drawing floating objects towards its centre. **2** (also **whirlpool bath**) a heated pool in which hot bubbling water is continuously circulated.

whirlwind • n. **1** a column of air moving rapidly round and round in a funnel shape. **2** a very energetic or disorderly person or process. • adj. very rapid and unexpected: *a whirlwind romance*.

whirr (also **whir**) • v. (**whirs** or **whirrs**, **whirring**, **whirred**) (of something rapidly rotating or moving to and fro) make a low, continuous, regular sound. • n. a whirring sound.
– ORIGIN prob. Scandinavian.

whisk • v. **1** move or take suddenly, quickly, and lightly. **2** beat (a substance) with a light, rapid movement. • n. **1** a utensil for whisking eggs or cream. **2** a bunch of grass, twigs, or bristles for flicking away dust or flies. **3** a brief, rapid action or movement.
– ORIGIN Scandinavian.

whisker • n. **1** a long hair or bristle growing from the face or snout of an animal. **2** (**whiskers**) the hair growing on a man's face. **3** (**a whisker**) informal a very small amount.
– ORIGIN from WHISK.

whisky (also Ir. & US **whiskey**) • n. (pl. **whiskies**) a spirit distilled from malted grain, especially barley or rye.
– ORIGIN from Irish and Scottish Gaelic *uisge beatha* 'water of life'.

whisper • v. (**whispers**, **whispering**, **whispered**) **1** speak very softly using one's breath rather than one's throat. **2** literary rustle or murmur softly. • n. **1** a whispered utterance, or a whispering tone of voice. **2** literary a soft rustling or murmuring sound. **3** a rumour or piece of gossip. **4** a slight trace.
– DERIVATIVES **whisperer** n. **whispery** adj.
– ORIGIN Old English.

whist /wist/ • n. a card game in which points are scored according to the number of tricks won.
– ORIGIN earlier as *whisk*: perh. from WHISK (with reference to whisking away the tricks).

whistle • n. **1** a clear, high-pitched sound made by forcing breath through pursed lips, or between one's teeth. **2** any similar sound. **3** an instrument used to produce such a sound. • v. (**whistles**, **whistling**, **whistled**) **1** give out a whistle. **2** produce (a tune) in such a way. **3** move rapidly through the air or a narrow opening with a whistling sound. **4** blow a whistle. **5** (**whistle for**) wish for or expect (something) which will not happen.
– PHRASES **blow the whistle on** informal bring (a secret activity) to an end by informing on the person responsible. (**as**) **clean as a whistle** extremely clean or clear.
– DERIVATIVES **whistler** n.
– ORIGIN Old English.

whistle-blower • n. informal a person who informs on someone engaged in a secret or illegal activity.

Whistler, E
James (Abbott) McNeill (1834–1903), American painter and etcher. He is best known for his portraits, such as *Arrangement in Grey and Black: The Artist's Mother*, and views of the Thames.

whistle-stop • adj. very fast and with only brief pauses.

whit /wit/ • n. a very small part or amount.
– PHRASES **not a whit** not at all.
– ORIGIN prob. from WIGHT in the former sense 'small amount'.

White[1], E
Patrick (Victor Martindale) (1912–90), Australian novelist, born in Britain. His novels include *The Tree of Man* and *Voss*.

White[2], E
T. H. (1906–64; full name *Terence Hanbury White*), British novelist, born in India. He is best known for his series of four books entitled *The Once and Future King*, a reworking of the story of King Arthur.

white • adj. **1** having the colour of milk or fresh snow, due to the reflection of all visible rays of light. **2** very pale. **3** relating to a human group having light-coloured skin. **4** innocent and pure: *white as the driven snow*. **5** Brit. (of coffee or tea) served with milk or cream. **6** (of food such as bread or rice) light in colour through having been refined. **7** (of wine) made from white grapes, or dark grapes

with the skins removed, and having a yellowish colour. ● n. **1** white colour. **2** (also **whites**) white clothes or material. **3** the visible pale part of the eyeball around the iris. **4** the outer part which surrounds the yolk of an egg; the albumen. **5** a member of a light-skinned people.
– DERIVATIVES **whitely** adv. **whiteness** n. **whitish** adj.
– ORIGIN Old English.

white admiral ● n. a butterfly with dark brown wings bearing a broad white band.

white ant ● n. = TERMITE.

whitebait ● n. the small silvery-white young of herrings, sprats, and similar marine fish as food.

white belt ● n. a white belt worn by a beginner in judo or karate.

whiteboard ● n. a wipeable board with a white surface used for teaching or presentations.

white-collar ● adj. relating to the work done or people who work in an office or other professional environment.

white elephant ● n. a possession that is useless or troublesome.
– ORIGIN from the story that the kings of Siam gave such animals to courtiers they disliked, in order to ruin them financially by the great cost of looking after the animals.

white feather ● n. a white feather given to someone as a sign that they are considered a coward.
– ORIGIN with reference to a white feather in the tail of a game bird, being a mark of bad breeding.

whitefish ● n. a mainly freshwater fish of the salmon family, widely used as food.

white flag ● n. a white flag or cloth used as a symbol of surrender, truce, or a desire to negotiate.

whitefly ● n. a minute winged bug covered with powdery white wax, damaging plants by feeding on sap and coating them with honeydew.

white gold ● n. a silver-coloured alloy of gold with another metal.

whitehead ● n. informal a pale or white-topped pimple on the skin.

white heat ● n. the temperature or state of something that is so hot that it gives out white light.

white hope (also **great white hope**) ● n. a person expected to bring much success to a team or organization.

white-hot ● adj. so hot as to glow white.

White House E
(**the White house**) the official residence of the US president in Washington DC.

white-knuckle ● adj. causing fear or nervous excitement.
– ORIGIN with reference to the effect caused by gripping tightly to steady oneself on a fairground ride.

white lie ● n. a harmless lie told to avoid hurting someone's feelings.

white light ● n. apparently colourless light containing all the wavelengths of the visible spectrum at equal intensity (such as ordinary daylight).

white magic ● n. magic used only for good purposes.

white meat ● n. pale meat such as poultry, veal, and rabbit.

whiten ● v. make or become white.
– DERIVATIVES **whitener** n.

White Nile E
the main, western branch of the Nile between the Ugandan–Sudanese border and its confluence with the Blue Nile at Khartoum.

white noise ● n. Physics noise containing many frequencies with equal intensities.

white-out ● n. a dense blizzard.

White Paper ● n. (in the UK) a government report giving information or proposals on an issue.

white sauce ● n. a sauce consisting of flour blended and cooked with butter and milk or stock.

white spirit ● n. Brit. a colourless liquid distilled from petroleum, used as a paint thinner and solvent.

white tie ● n. **1** a white bow tie worn by men as part of full evening dress. **2** full evening dress.

white trash ● n. N. Amer. derog. poor white people.

white-van man ● n. Brit. informal an aggressive male driver of a delivery or workman's van (typically white in colour).

whitewash ● n. **1** a solution of lime and water or of whiting, size, and water, used for painting walls white. **2** a deliberate concealment of someone's mistakes or faults. **3** a victory by the same side in every game of a series. ● v. **1** paint with whitewash. **2** conceal (mistakes or faults). **3** defeat with a whitewash.

white water ● n. a fast shallow stretch of water in a river.

white witch ● n. a person who uses witchcraft to help others.

whither archaic or literary ● adv. **1** to what place or state? **2** what is the likely future of? **3** to which (with reference to a place). **4** to whatever place.
– ORIGIN Old English.

whiting[1] ● n. (pl. **whiting**) a slender-bodied sea fish with edible white flesh.
– ORIGIN Dutch *wijting*.

whiting[2] ● n. ground chalk used for purposes such as whitewashing and cleaning metal plate.

Whitlam E
/wit-luhm/, (Edward) Gough (b.1916), Australian Labor statesman, Prime Minister 1972–5. He refused to call a general election after the opposition blocked finance bills in the Senate and became the first elected Prime Minister to be dismissed by the British Crown.

Whitman, E
Walt (1819–92), American poet, best known for such poems as 'I Sing the Body Electric' and 'Song of Myself'.

Whitney, Mount E
a mountain in the Sierra Nevada range in eastern California. Rising to 4,418 m (14,495 ft), it is the highest peak in the continental US outside Alaska.

Whitsun /wit-suhn/ ● n. Whitsuntide.

Whit Sunday • **n.** the seventh Sunday after Easter, a Christian festival commemorating the descent of the Holy Spirit at Pentecost (Acts, chapter 2).
– ORIGIN Old English, 'white Sunday'.

Whitsuntide /wit-suhn-tyd/ • **n.** the weekend or week including Whit Sunday.

Whittington, E
Dick (d.1423; full name *Sir Richard Whittington*), English merchant, who was Lord Mayor of London three times.

Whittle, E
Sir Frank (1907–90), English aeronautical engineer, inventor of the jet aircraft engine. He took out the first patent for a turbojet engine in 1930; the first flight using his jet engine took place in 1941.

whittle • **v.** (**whittles**, **whittling**, **whittled**) **1** carve (wood) by repeatedly cutting small slices from it. **2** make by whittling. **3** (**whittle away/down**) reduce by a gradual series of steps.
– ORIGIN from dialect *whittle* 'knife'.

whizz (also **whiz**) • **v.** (**whizzes**, **whizzing**, **whizzed**) **1** move quickly through the air with a whistling or whooshing sound. **2** move or go fast. **3** (**whizz through**) do or deal with quickly. • **n. 1** a whizzing sound. **2** informal a fast movement or brief journey. **3** (also **wiz**) informal a person who is extremely clever at something. [ORIGIN influenced by **WIZARD**.] **4** Brit. informal amphetamines.
– DERIVATIVES **whizzy** adj.

whizz-kid (also **whiz-kid**) • **n.** informal a young person who is very successful or highly skilled.

WHO • **abbrev.** World Health Organization.

who • **pron. 1** what or which person or people? **2** introducing a clause giving further information about a person or people previously mentioned.
– ORIGIN Old English.

USAGE who
When writing, **who** should be used as the subject of a verb (*who decided this?*) and **whom** should be used as the object of a verb or preposition (*whom do you think we should support?*). When speaking, however, most people think it is acceptable to use **who** instead of **whom**, as in *who do you think we should support?*

whoa /woh/ • **exclam.** used as a command to a horse to stop or slow down.

who'd • **contr. 1** who had. **2** who would.

whodunnit (US **whodunit**) • **n.** informal a story or play about a murder in which the identity of the murderer is not revealed until the end.

whoever • **pron. 1** the person or people who; any person who. **2** regardless of who. **3** used for emphasis instead of 'who' in questions.

whole • **adj. 1** complete; entire. **2** emphasizing a large extent or number: *a whole range of issues*. **3** in one piece. • **n. 1** a thing that is complete in itself. **2** (**the whole**) all of something. • **adv.** informal entirely; wholly: *a whole new meaning*.
– PHRASES **as a whole** in general. **on the whole** taking everything into account; in general. **the whole nine yards** informal, esp. N. Amer. everything possible or available.
– DERIVATIVES **wholeness** n.
– ORIGIN Old English.

wholefood • **n.** (also **wholefoods**) Brit. food that has been processed as little as possible and is free from additives.

wholehearted • **adj.** completely sincere and committed.
– DERIVATIVES **wholeheartedly** adv.

wholemeal • **adj.** Brit. referring to flour or bread made from wholewheat, including the husk.

whole number • **n.** a number without fractions; an integer.

wholesale • **n.** the selling of goods in large quantities to be sold to the public by others. • **adv. 1** being sold in such a way. **2** on a large scale. • **adj.** done on a large scale. • **v.** (**wholesales**, **wholesaling**, **wholesaled**) sell (goods) wholesale.
– DERIVATIVES **wholesaler** n.

wholesome • **adj.** helping towards good health and physical or moral well-being.

wholewheat • **n.** whole grains of wheat including the husk.

wholly /hohl-li, hoh-li/ • **adv.** entirely; fully.

whom • **pron.** used instead of 'who' as the object of a verb or preposition.

whomever • **pron.** esp. formal used instead of 'whoever' as the object of a verb or preposition.

whomp /womp/ informal • **v.** strike heavily. • **n.** a thump.

whomsoever • **relative pronoun** formal used instead of 'whosoever' as the object of a verb or preposition.

whoop /hoop, woop/ • **n. 1** a loud cry of joy or excitement. **2** a long rasping indrawn breath. • **v.** give or make a whoop.

whoopee informal • **exclam.** /wuu-**pee**/ expressing wild excitement or joy. • **n.** /**wuu**-pee/ wild celebrations and merrymaking.
– PHRASES **make whoopee 1** celebrate wildly. **2** have sexual intercourse.

whoopee cushion • **n.** a rubber cushion that makes a sound like the breaking of wind when someone sits on it.

whooping cough /hoo-ping/ • **n.** a contagious disease chiefly affecting children, caused by bacteria and characterized by coughs followed by a rasping indrawn breath.

whoops (also **whoops-a-daisy**) • **exclam.** informal expressing mild dismay.
– ORIGIN prob. from **UPSY-DAISY**.

whoosh /wuush, woosh/ (also **woosh**) • **v.** move quickly or suddenly and with a rushing sound. • **n.** a whooshing movement.

whop /wop/ (esp. N. Amer. also **whap**) informal • **v.** (**whops**, **whopping**, **whopped**) hit hard. • **n.** a heavy blow or its sound.
– ORIGIN from dialect *wap* 'strike'.

whopper • **n.** informal **1** a thing that is extremely large. **2** a complete or blatant lie.

whopping • **adj.** informal extremely large.

whore /*rhymes with* door/ • **n. 1** a prostitute. **2** derog. a woman who has many sexual partners.
– ORIGIN Old English.

whorehouse • **n.** informal a brothel.

whorl /worl, werl/ • **n. 1** Zool. each of the turns

in the spiral shell of a mollusc. **2** Bot. a coil of leaves, flowers, or branches encircling a stem. **3** a complete circle in a fingerprint.
– ORIGIN prob. from **WHIRL**.

who's ● contr. **1** who is. **2** who has.

> **USAGE** who's
> Do not confuse **who's** with **whose**. **Who's** is short for either **who is** or **who has**, as in *he has a son who's a doctor* or *who's done the reading?*, whereas **whose** means 'belonging to or associated with which person' or 'of whom or which', as in *whose is this?* or *he's a man whose opinion I respect.*

whose ● possess. det. & pron. **1** belonging to or associated with which person. **2** (as possess. det.) of whom or which.
– ORIGIN Old English.

whosesoever ● relative pronoun & det. formal whoever's.

whosever ● relative pronoun & det. belonging to or associated with whichever person; whoever's.

whosoever ● pron. formal term for **WHOEVER**.

whup /wup/ ● v. (**whups, whupping, whupped**) informal, esp. N. Amer. beat; thrash.
– ORIGIN variant of **WHIP**.

why ● adv. **1** for what reason or purpose? **2** (with reference to a reason) on account of which; for which. **3** the reason that: *that's why they are still friends.* ● exclam. **1** expressing surprise or annoyance. **2** used to add emphasis to a response. ● n. (pl. **whys**) a reason or explanation.
– ORIGIN Old English.

WI ● abbrev. **1** West Indies. **2** Brit. Women's Institute.

Wicca /wik-kuh/ ● n. the religious cult of modern witchcraft.
– DERIVATIVES **Wiccan** adj. & n.
– ORIGIN Old English, 'witch'.

wick ● n. a length of thread up which liquid fuel is drawn to the flame in a candle, lamp, or lighter.
– PHRASES **get on someone's wick** Brit. informal annoy someone.
– ORIGIN Old English.

wicked ● adj. **1** evil. **2** playfully mischievous. **3** informal excellent; wonderful.
– DERIVATIVES **wickedly** adv. **wickedness** n.
– ORIGIN prob. from **WICCA**.

wicker ● n. easily bent twigs plaited or woven to make items such as furniture and baskets.
– DERIVATIVES **wickerwork** n.
– ORIGIN Scandinavian.

wicket ● n. **1** Cricket each of the sets of three stumps with two bails across the top at either end of the pitch, defended by a batsman. **2** a small door or gate.
– ORIGIN Old French *wiket*.

wicketkeeper ● n. Cricket a fielder positioned close behind a batsman's wicket.

> **Wicklow** E
> a county in the east of the Republic of Ireland; county town, Wicklow.

widdle informal ● v. (**widdles, widdling, widdled**) urinate. ● n. an act of urinating.
– ORIGIN from **PIDDLE**.

wide ● adj. (**wider, widest**) **1** of great or more than average width. **2** (after a measurement and in questions) from side to side. **3** open to the full extent. **4** including a great variety of people or things. **5** spread among a large number or over a large area. **6** (in combination) extending over the whole of: *industry-wide*. **7** at a distance from a point or mark. **8** (especially in football) at or near the side of the field. ● adv. **1** to the full extent. **2** far from a particular point or mark. **3** (especially in football) at or near the side of the field.
– PHRASES **wide awake** fully awake. **wide of the mark 1** a long way from an intended target. **2** inaccurate.
– DERIVATIVES **widely** adv.
– ORIGIN Old English.

wide-angle ● adj. (of a lens) having a shorter distance between its centre and its focus than is standard and hence a field covering a wide angle.

wide boy ● n. Brit. informal a man involved in petty criminal activities.

wide-eyed ● adj. **1** having one's eyes wide open in amazement. **2** inexperienced; innocent.

widen ● v. make or become wider.

widescreen ● adj. referring to a cinema or television screen presenting a wide field of vision in relation to height.

widespread ● adj. spread among a large number or over a large area.

widgeon ● n. var. of **WIGEON**.

widget /wij-it/ ● n. informal a small gadget or mechanical device.
– ORIGIN perh. from **GADGET**.

widow ● n. **1** a woman whose husband has died and who has not married again. **2** humorous a woman whose husband is often away taking part in a specified activity: *a golf widow.* ● v. (**be widowed**) become a widow or widower.
– ORIGIN Old English.

widower ● n. a man whose wife has died and who has not married again.

widowhood ● n. the state or period of being a widow or widower.

widow's peak ● n. a V-shaped growth of hair towards the centre of the forehead.

widow's weeds ● pl. n. black clothes worn by a widow in mourning.
– ORIGIN *weeds* is used in the former sense 'garments' and is from Old English.

width /witth, width/ ● n. **1** the measurement or extent of something from side to side; the lesser or least of two or more dimensions of a body. **2** a piece of something at its full extent from side to side. **3** wide range or extent.

widthways (also **widthwise**) ● adv. in a direction parallel with a thing's width.

wield ● v. **1** hold and use (a weapon or tool). **2** have and be able to use (power or influence).
– ORIGIN Old English, 'govern, subdue, direct'.

> **Wiesenthal** E
> /vee-z'n-tahl/, Simon (b.1908), Austrian Jewish investigator of Nazi war crimes. A survivor of the concentration camps, he has since campaigned to bring Nazi war criminals to justice.

wife ● n. (pl. **wives**) a married woman considered in relation to her husband.
– DERIVATIVES **wifely** adj.

– ORIGIN Old English, 'woman'.

wig ● n. a covering for the head made of real or artificial hair.
– ORIGIN shortening of *periwig*, a kind of wig worn in the 17th and 18th centuries.

wigeon /*rhymes with* pigeon/ (also **widgeon**) ● n. a duck with mainly reddish-brown and grey plumage, the male having a whistling call.
– ORIGIN perh. suggested by **PIGEON**.

wiggle ● v. (**wiggles, wiggling, wiggled**) move with short movements up and down or from side to side. ● n. a wiggling movement.
– DERIVATIVES **wiggly** adj.
– ORIGIN German and Dutch *wiggelen*.

Wight, Isle of E
see **ISLE OF WIGHT**.

wigwam ● n. a dome-shaped or conical dwelling made by fastening mats, skins, or bark over a framework of poles (as used formerly by some North American Indian peoples).
– ORIGIN from a word meaning 'their house' in a North American Indian language.

Wilberforce, E
William (1759–1833), English politician and social reformer. His campaigning led to the abolition of the slave trade (1807) and the ending of slavery within the British Empire (1833).

wild ● adj. **1** (of animals or plants) living or growing in the natural environment. **2** (of people) not civilized. **3** (of scenery or a region) barren or uninhabited. **4** uncontrolled. **5** not based on reason or evidence: *a wild guess*. **6** informal very enthusiastic or excited. **7** informal very angry. **8** (of looks, appearance, etc.) indicating distraction. ● n. **1** (**the wild**) a natural state. **2** (also **the wilds**) a remote uninhabited area.
– DERIVATIVES **wildly** adv. **wildness** n.
– ORIGIN Old English.

wild card ● n. **1** a playing card that can have any value, suit, colour, or other property in a game according to the choice of the player holding it. **2** a person or thing whose qualities are uncertain. **3** Computing a character that will match any character or sequence of characters in a search.

wildcat ● n. a small Eurasian and African cat, typically grey with black markings and a bushy tail, believed to be the ancestor of the domestic cat. ● adj. (of a strike) sudden and unofficial.

wild duck ● n. a mallard.

Wilde, E
Oscar (Fingal O'Flahertie Wills) (1854–1900), Irish dramatist, novelist, and poet. His works include the comedies *Lady Windermere's Fan* and *The Importance of Being Earnest* and the novel *The Picture of Dorian Gray*. Wilde was imprisoned (1895–7) for homosexual offences and died in exile in Paris.

wildebeest /wil-duh-beest, vil-duh-beest/ ● n. (pl. **wildebeest** or **wildebeests**) = **GNU**.
– ORIGIN Afrikaans, 'wild beast'.

Wilder[1], E
Billy (1906–2002; born *Samuel Wilder*), Austrian-born American film director and screenwriter. His films include *Double Indemnity* and *Some Like It Hot*.

Wilder[2], E
Thornton (Niven) (1897–1975), American novelist and dramatist. His works include the novel *The Bridge of San Luis Rey* and the play *Our Town*.

wilderness ● n. **1** an uncultivated, uninhabited, and inhospitable region. **2** a position of disfavour.
– ORIGIN Old English, 'land inhabited only by wild animals'.

wildfire ● n. hist. a highly flammable liquid used in warfare.
– PHRASES **spread like wildfire** spread with great speed.

wildfowl ● pl. n. game birds.

wild goose chase ● n. a foolish and hopeless search for or pursuit of something unattainable.

wildlife ● n. the native animals of a region.

wild rice ● n. a tall American grass with edible grains, related to rice.

wiles ● pl. n. devious or cunning plans.
– ORIGIN perh. from Old Norse, 'craft'.

wilful (US also **willful**) ● adj. **1** deliberate. **2** stubborn and determined.
– DERIVATIVES **wilfully** (US **willfully**) adv. **wilfulness** (US **willfulness**) n.

Wilhelm I E
/vil-helm/ (1797–1888), king of Prussia 1861–88 and emperor of Germany 1871–88. He became the first emperor of Germany after Prussia's victory against France in 1871.

Wilhelm II E
/vil-helm/ (1859–1941; known as **Kaiser Wilhelm**), emperor of Germany 1888–1918, grandson of Wilhelm I and also of Queen Victoria. After Germany's defeat in the First World War he abdicated and went into exile.

Wilkins, E
Maurice Hugh Frederick (b.1916), New Zealand-born British biochemist and molecular biologist. Together with Rosalind Franklin (1920–58) he confirmed the double helix structure of DNA proposed by Francis Crick and James Watson.

will[1] ● modal verb (3rd sing. present **will**; past **would**) **1** expressing the future tense. **2** expressing a strong intention or claim about the future. **3** expressing inevitable events: *accidents will happen*. **4** expressing a request: *will you stop here, please?* **5** expressing desire, consent, or willingness: *will you have a cognac?* **6** expressing facts about ability or capacity: *a rock so light that it will float on water*.
– ORIGIN Old English.

USAGE will
For an explanation of the difference between **will** and **shall**, see the note at **SHALL**.

will[2] ● n. **1** the faculty by which a person decides on and takes action. **2** (also **will power**) control or restraint deliberately exerted. **3** a desire or intention. **4** a legal document containing instructions for what will be done with one's money and property after one's death. ● v. **1** intend or desire to happen. **2** bring about by the exercise of mental powers. **3** leave in one's will.
– PHRASES **at will** at whatever time or in what-

ever way one pleases.
– ORIGIN Old English.

willful ● adj. US var. of **WILFUL**.

William I
(*c.*1027–87; known as **William the Conqueror**), king of England 1066–87, the first Norman king of England. He invaded England and defeated Harold II at the Battle of Hastings (1066).

William II
(*c.*1060–1100; known as **William Rufus**), son of William I, king of England 1087–1100. He was killed by an arrow while out hunting.

William III
(1650–1702; known as **William of Orange**), grandson of Charles I, king of Great Britain and Ireland 1689–1702. In 1688 he deposed James II at the invitation of disaffected politicians and, having accepted the Declaration of Rights, was crowned along with his wife Mary.

William IV
(1765–1837), son of George III, king of Great Britain and Ireland 1830–7. He came to the throne after the death of his brother George IV.

Williams[1],
Hank (1923–53; born *Hiram King Williams*), American country singer and songwriter.

Williams[2],
John (Christopher) (b.1941), Australian guitarist and composer.

Williams[3],
Tennessee (1911–83; born *Thomas Lanier Williams*), American dramatist. His plays include *The Glass Menagerie, A Streetcar Named Desire,* and *Cat on a Hot Tin Roof.*

Williams[4],
William Carlos (1883–1963), American poet, essayist, novelist, and short-story writer. His collections of poetry include *Spring and All.*

William the Conqueror,
William I of England (see **WILLIAM I**).

willie ● n. var. of **WILLY**.

willies ● pl. n. (**the willies**) informal a strong feeling of nervous discomfort.
– ORIGIN unknown.

willing ● adj. **1** ready, eager, or prepared to do something. **2** given or done readily.
– DERIVATIVES **willingly** adv. **willingness** n.

will-o'-the-wisp ● n. **1** a dim, flickering light seen hovering at night on marshy ground, thought to result from the combustion of natural gases. **2** a person or thing that is difficult or impossible to reach or catch.
– ORIGIN first as *Will with the wisp*, the sense of *wisp* being 'handful of lighted hay'.

willow ● n. a tree or shrub which typically grows near water, has narrow leaves, and bears catkins.
– ORIGIN Old English.

willowherb ● n. a plant with long narrow leaves and pink or pale purple flowers.

willow pattern ● n. a conventional design in pottery featuring a Chinese scene depicted in blue on white, typically including figures on a bridge, a willow tree, and birds.

willowy ● adj. **1** bordered, shaded, or covered by willows. **2** (of a person) tall and slim.

willy (also **willie**) ● n. (pl. **willies**) Brit. informal a penis.
– ORIGIN informal form of the man's name *William.*

willy-nilly ● adv. **1** whether one likes it or not. **2** without direction or planning.
– ORIGIN later spelling of *will I, nill I* 'I am willing, I am unwilling'.

Wilson[1],
Sir Angus (Frank Johnstone) (1913–91), English novelist and short-story writer. His novels include *The Old Men at the Zoo.*

Wilson[2],
(James) Harold, Baron Wilson of Rievaulx (1916–95), British Labour statesman, Prime Minister 1964–70 and 1974–6. He faced severe economic problems in both terms of office. His government introduced a number of social reforms, including comprehensive schooling.

Wilson[3],
(Thomas) Woodrow (1856–1924), American Democratic statesman, 28th President of the US 1913–21. He took America into the First World War in 1917 and later played a leading role in the formation of the League of Nations.

wilt[1] ● v. **1** (of a plant) become limp through loss of water, heat, or disease; droop. **2** (of a person) lose one's energy.
– ORIGIN perh. from dialect *welk* 'lose freshness', of German origin.

wilt[2] archaic 2nd person sing. of **WILL**[1].

Wilts. ● abbrev. Wiltshire.

Wiltshire
a county of southern England; county town, Trowbridge.

wily /*rhymes with* highly/ ● adj. (**wilier**, **wiliest**) skilled at gaining an advantage, especially deceitfully.

Wimbledon
a major annual international tennis championship, held at the headquarters of the All England Lawn Tennis and Croquet Club in the London suburb of Wimbledon.

wimp informal ● n. a weak and cowardly person. ● v. (**wimp out**) withdraw from something in a cowardly way.
– DERIVATIVES **wimpy** adj.
– ORIGIN uncertain, perh. from **WHIMPER**.

wimple ● n. a cloth headdress covering the head, neck, and sides of the face, formerly worn by women and still by some nuns.
– ORIGIN Old English.

win ● v. (**wins**, **winning**, **won**) **1** be successful or victorious in (a contest or conflict). **2** gain as a result of success in a contest, conflict, etc. **3** gain (someone's attention, support, or love). **4** (**win over**) gain the support or favour of. **5** (**win out/through**) manage to succeed or achieve something by effort. ● n. a victory in

a game or contest.
– ORIGIN Old English, 'strive, contend', also 'subdue and take possession of, acquire'.

wince • v. (**winces**, **wincing**, **winced**) give a slight unintentional grimace or flinch due to pain or distress. • n. an instance of wincing.
– ORIGIN Old French *guenchir* 'turn aside'.

winceyette /win-si-et/ • n. Brit. a lightweight brushed cotton fabric, used especially for nightclothes.
– ORIGIN from *wincey*, a lightweight wool and cotton fabric.

winch • n. **1** a hauling or lifting device consisting of a rope or chain winding around a horizontal rotating drum, turned by a crank or by motor. **2** the crank of a wheel or axle. • v. hoist or haul with a winch.
– ORIGIN Old English, 'reel, pulley'.

Winckelmann E
/ving-k'l-man/, Johann (Joachim) (1717–68), German archaeologist and art historian. He was influential in developing art history as an intellectual discipline and in popularizing the art and culture of ancient Greece.

wind[1] /wind/ • n. **1** the perceptible natural movement of the air. **2** breath as needed in physical exertion, speech, playing an instrument, etc. **3** Brit. air swallowed while eating or gas generated in the stomach and intestines by digestion. **4** meaningless talk. **5** wind or woodwind instruments forming a band or section of an orchestra. • v. **1** cause to have difficulty breathing because of exertion or a blow to the stomach. **2** Brit. make (a baby) bring up wind after feeding by patting its back.
– PHRASES **get wind of** informal hear a rumour of. **put the wind up** Brit. informal alarm or frighten.
– ORIGIN Old English.

wind[2] /wynd/ • v. (**winds**, **winding**, **wound** /wownd/) **1** move in or take a twisting or spiral course. **2** pass (something) around a thing or person so as to encircle or enfold them. **3** (with reference to a length of something) twist or be twisted around itself or a core. **4** make (a clockwork device) work by turning a key or handle. **5** turn (a key or handle) repeatedly. **6** move (an audio or video tape or a film) back or forwards to a desired point. • n. **1** a twist or turn in a course. **2** a single turn made when winding.
– PHRASES **wind down 1** (of a clockwork mechanism) gradually lose power. **2** draw or bring gradually to a close. **3** informal relax. **wind up 1** gradually bring to an end. **2** informal end up in a specified state, situation, or place. **3** Brit. informal tease or irritate.
– ORIGIN Old English, 'go rapidly', 'twine'.

windbag • n. informal a person who talks a lot but says little of any value.

windbreak • n. a row of trees, or a wall or screen providing shelter from the wind.

windcheater • n. esp. Brit. a wind-resistant jacket with a close-fitting neck, waistband, and cuffs.

wind chill • n. the cooling effect of wind on a surface.

wind chimes • pl. n. pieces of glass, metal rods, or similar items, hung near a door or window so as to chime in the draught.

winder /*rhymes with* minder/ • n. a device for winding something.

Windermere E
/win-der-meer/ a lake in Cumbria, in the south-eastern part of the Lake District. At about 17 km (10 miles) in length, it is the largest lake in England.

windfall • n. **1** an apple or other fruit blown from a tree by the wind. **2** a piece of unexpected good fortune.

wind farm • n. an area containing a group of energy-producing windmills or wind turbines.

Windhoek E
/wint-huuk, vint-huuk/ the capital of Namibia.

winding /*rhymes with* finding/ • n. **1** a twisting movement or course. **2** a thing that winds or is wound round something. • adj. having a twisting or spiral course.

winding sheet • n. a shroud.

wind instrument • n. **1** a musical instrument in which sound is produced by the vibration of air, typically by the player blowing into the instrument. **2** a woodwind instrument as distinct from a brass instrument.

windlass • n. a winch, especially one on a ship or in a harbour.
– ORIGIN prob. from Old Norse, 'winding pole'.

windmill • n. a building with sails or vanes that turn in the wind and generate power to grind corn, generate electricity, or draw water.

window • n. **1** an opening in a wall or roof, fitted with glass in a frame to let in light or air and allow people to see out. **2** an opening through which customers are served in a bank, ticket office, etc. **3** a transparent panel in an envelope to show an address. **4** Computing a framed area on a display screen for viewing information. **5** (**window on/into/to**) a means of observing and learning about (something). **6** an interval or opportunity for action.
– ORIGIN Old Norse.

window box • n. a long narrow box in which flowers and other plants are grown on an outside window sill.

window dressing • n. **1** the arrangement of a display in a shop window. **2** the presentation of something in a superficially attractive way to give a favourable impression.

window frame • n. a frame holding the glass of a window.

window ledge • n. a window sill.

windowpane • n. a pane of glass in a window.

window seat • n. **1** a seat below a window, especially one in a bay or alcove. **2** a seat next to a window in an aircraft or train.

window-shop • v. look at the goods displayed in shop windows, especially without intending to buy.

window sill • n. a ledge or sill forming the bottom part of a window.

windpipe • n. the trachea.

Windscale E
former name for **SELLAFIELD**.

windscreen • n. Brit. a glass screen at the front of a motor vehicle.

windscreen wiper • n. Brit. a device for keeping a windscreen clear of rain, having a rubber blade on an arm that moves in an arc.

windshield • n. N. Amer. a windscreen.

windsock • n. a light, flexible cylinder or cone mounted on a mast to show the direction and strength of the wind.

Windsor[1] E
a town in southern England, on the River Thames.

Windsor[2] E
the name of the British royal family since 1917. Previously Saxe-Coburg-Gotha, it was changed in response to anti-German feeling in the First World War.

Windsor, Duke of E
the title conferred on Edward VIII on his abdication in 1936.

Windsor Castle E
a residence of the British royal family at Windsor.

windsurfing • n. the sport of riding on water on a sailboard.
– DERIVATIVES **windsurf** v. **windsurfer** n.

windswept • adj. **1** exposed to strong winds. **2** (of a person's hair or appearance) untidy after being exposed to the wind.

wind tunnel • n. a tunnel-like apparatus for producing an airstream, in order to investigate flow or the effect of wind on the full-size object.

wind-up • n. Brit. informal an attempt to tease or irritate someone.

windward • adj. & adv. facing the wind or on the side facing the wind. Contrasted with **LEEWARD**. • n. the side from which the wind is blowing.

Windward Islands E
a group of Caribbean islands forming the southern part of the Lesser Antilles, and including Martinique, Dominica, St Lucia, Barbados, St Vincent and the Grenadines, and Grenada.

windy[1] /win-di/ • adj. (**windier**, **windiest**) marked by or exposed to strong winds.

windy[2] /wyn-di/ • adj. following a winding course.

wine • n. **1** an alcoholic drink made from fermented grape juice. **2** a fermented alcoholic drink made from other fruits or plants.
– ORIGIN Old English.

wine bar • n. a bar or small restaurant that specializes in serving wine.

wine bottle • n. a glass bottle for wine.

wine cellar • n. **1** a cellar for storing wine. **2** a stock of wine.

wine glass • n. a glass with a stem and foot, used for drinking wine.

wine list • n. a list of the wines available in a restaurant.

winemaker • n. a producer of wine.

winery • n. (pl. **wineries**) an establishment where wine is made.

wine vinegar • n. vinegar made from wine rather than malt.

Winfrey, E
Oprah (b.1954), American chat-show host and film actress, famous for *The Oprah Winfrey Show.*

wing • n. **1** a modified forelimb or other appendage enabling a bird, bat, insect, or other creature to fly. **2** a rigid horizontal structure projecting from both sides of an aircraft and supporting it in the air. **3** a part of a large building. **4** a group within an organization having particular views or a particular function. **5** (**the wings**) the sides of a theatre stage out of view of the audience. **6** the part of a soccer, rugby, or hockey field close to the sidelines. **7** an attacking player positioned near the sidelines. **8** Brit. a raised part of the body of a vehicle above the wheel. • v. **1** fly, or move quickly as if flying. **2** shoot so as to wound in the wing or arm. **3** (**wing it**) informal speak or act without preparation.
– PHRASES **in the wings** ready for use or action at the appropriate time. **under one's wing** in or into one's protective care.
– DERIVATIVES **winged** adj.
– ORIGIN Old Norse; sense 3 of the verb was originally theatrical slang referring to the playing of a role without proper knowledge of the text (by relying on a prompter in the wings or by studying in the wings between scenes).

wingbeat (also **wingstroke**) • n. one complete set of motions of a wing in flying.

wing chair • n. an armchair with side pieces projecting forwards from a high back.

wing collar • n. a high stiff shirt collar with turned-down corners.

winger • n. **1** an attacking player on the wing in soccer, hockey, etc. **2** (in combination) a member of a specified political wing: *a Tory right-winger.*

wing mirror • n. a rear-view mirror projecting from the side of a vehicle.

wing nut • n. a nut with a pair of projections for the fingers to turn it on a screw.

wingspan • n. the maximum extent across the wings of an aircraft, bird, etc., measured from tip to tip.

wink • v. **1** close and open one eye quickly as a signal of affection or greeting or to convey a message. **2** shine or flash intermittently. • n. an act of winking.
– ORIGIN Old English.

winkle • n. a small edible shore-dwelling mollusc with a spiral shell. • v. (**winkles**, **winkling**, **winkled**) (**winkle out**) esp. Brit. take out or obtain with difficulty.
– ORIGIN shortening of **PERIWINKLE[2]**.

winner • n. **1** a person or thing that wins. **2** informal a successful or highly promising thing.

winning • adj. **1** gaining, resulting in, or relating to victory. **2** attractive. • n. (**winnings**) money won, especially by gambling.
– DERIVATIVES **winningly** adv.

winning post • n. a post marking the end of a race.

Winnipeg E
/win-ni-peg/ the capital of the province of Manitoba in Canada.

Winnipeg, Lake E
a large lake in the province of Manitoba in Canada.

winnow • v. **1** blow air through (grain) in

order to remove the chaff. **2** remove (chaff) from grain. **3** reduce the number in a set of (people or things) gradually until only the best ones are left.
– ORIGIN Old English.

wino ● n. (pl. **winos**) informal a person who drinks excessive amounts of cheap wine or other alcohol.

winsome ● adj. attractive or appealing.
– ORIGIN Old English, 'joy'.

winter ● n. the coldest season of the year, after autumn and before spring. ● adj. **1** (of fruit) ripening late in the year. **2** (of crops) sown in autumn for harvesting the following year. ● v. (**winters**, **wintering**, **wintered**) spend the winter in a particular place.
– ORIGIN Old English.

wintergreen ● n. **1** a low-growing plant with spikes of white bell-shaped flowers. **2** an American shrub whose leaves produce oil. **3** (also **oil of wintergreen**) a pungent oil obtained from these plants or from birch bark, used medicinally and as a flavouring.

Winter Olympics ● pl. n. an international contest of winter sports held every four years at a two-year interval from the Olympic games.

winter sports ● pl. n. sports performed on snow or ice.

wintertime ● n. the season or period of winter.

wintry ● adj. (**wintrier**, **wintriest**) characteristic of winter, especially in being very cold or bleak.

wipe ● v. (**wipes**, **wiping**, **wiped**) **1** clean or dry by rubbing with a cloth or one's hand. **2** remove (dirt or moisture) in this way. **3** erase (data) from a magnetic medium. ● n. **1** an act of wiping. **2** an absorbent disposable cleaning cloth.
PHRASES **wipe out 1** remove or eliminate. **2** kill (a large number of people).
– DERIVATIVES **wipeable** adj. **wiper** n.
– ORIGIN Old English.

wire ● n. **1** metal drawn out into a thin flexible thread or rod. **2** a length or quantity of wire used for fencing, to carry an electric current, etc. **3** a concealed electronic listening device. **4** informal a telegram. ● v. (**wires**, **wiring**, **wired**) **1** install electric circuits or wires in. **2** provide, fasten, or reinforce with wire. **3** informal, esp. N. Amer. send a telegram to.
– PHRASES **down to the wire** informal until the very last minute.
– ORIGIN Old English.

wire brush ● n. a brush with tough wire bristles for cleaning hard surfaces.

wired ● adj. informal **1** making use of computers and information technology to transfer or receive information. **2** nervous or tense. **3** intoxicated by drugs or alcohol.

wireless ● n. dated, esp. Brit. **1** a radio receiving set. **2** broadcasting using radio signals. ● adj. lacking or not needing wires.

wiretapping ● n. the practice of tapping a telephone line to monitor conversations secretly.

wire wool ● n. Brit. = STEEL WOOL.

wireworm ● n. the worm-like larva of a kind of beetle, which feeds on roots and can cause damage to crops.

wiring ● n. a system of wires providing electric circuits for a device or building.

Wirral E
/wir-ruhl/ a peninsula on the coast of NW England, between the estuaries of the Rivers Dee and Mersey. Full name THE WIRRAL PENINSULA.

wiry ● adj. (**wirier**, **wiriest**) **1** resembling wire in form and texture. **2** lean, tough, and sinewy.

Wisconsin E
/wiss-**kon**-sin/ a state in the northern US, bordering on Lakes Superior and Michigan; capital, Madison.
– DERIVATIVES **Wisconsinite** n.

Wisdom, E
Sir Norman (b.1915), English film actor and comedian, star of such films as *The Bulldog Breed*.

wisdom ● n. **1** the quality of being wise. **2** the body of knowledge and experience that develops within a specified society or period: *oriental wisdom*.

wisdom tooth ● n. each of the four hindmost molars in humans, which usually appear at about the age of twenty.

wise[1] ● adj. **1** having or showing experience, knowledge, and good judgement. **2** (**wise to**) informal aware of. ● v. (**wises**, **wising**, **wised**) (**wise up**) informal become alert or aware.
– DERIVATIVES **wisely** adv.
– ORIGIN Old English.

wise[2] ● n. archaic manner, way, or extent.
– ORIGIN Old English.

-wise ● suffix **1** forming adjectives and adverbs of manner or respect: *clockwise*. **2** informal with respect to: *weather-wise*.

wiseacre /wyz-ay-ker/ ● n. a person who pretends to be wise or knowledgeable.
ORIGIN Dutch *wijsseggher* 'soothsayer'.

wisecrack informal ● n. a witty remark or joke. ● v. make a wisecrack.

wise guy ● n. informal a person who makes sarcastic or rude remarks so as to demonstrate their cleverness.

wish ● v. **1** desire something that cannot or probably will not happen. **2** want to do something. **3** ask (someone) to do something or that (something) be done. **4** express a hope that (someone) has (happiness, success, etc.). **5** (**wish on**) hope that (something unpleasant) will happen to. ● n. **1** a desire or hope. **2** (**wishes**) an expression of a hope for someone's happiness, success, or welfare. **3** a thing wished for.
– ORIGIN Old English.

wishbone ● n. a forked bone between the neck and breast of a bird.

wishful ● adj. **1** having or expressing a wish for something to happen. **2** based on impractical wishes rather than facts.
– DERIVATIVES **wishfully** adv.

wish-fulfilment ● n. the satisfying of wishes in dreams or fantasies.

wishing well ● n. a well into which one drops a coin and makes a wish.

wishy-washy ● adj. **1** (of a drink or soup) weak or thin. **2** feeble or bland.

wisp ● n. a small thin bunch, strand, or amount of something.
– DERIVATIVES **wispy** adj.

– ORIGIN uncertain.

wisteria /wi-steer-i-uh/ (also **wistaria** /wi-stair-i-uh/) ● n. a climbing shrub with hanging clusters of pale bluish-lilac flowers.
– ORIGIN named after the American anatomist Caspar *Wistar* (or *Wister*) (1761–1818).

wistful ● adj. having or showing a feeling of vague or regretful longing.
– DERIVATIVES **wistfully** adv.
– ORIGIN prob. from former *wistly* 'intently', influenced by **WISHFUL**.

wit ● n. **1** (also **wits**) the capacity for inventive thought and quick understanding; keen intelligence. **2** a natural aptitude for using words and ideas in a quick and inventive way to create humour. **3** a person with this aptitude.
– ORIGIN Old English.

witch ● n. **1** a woman thought to have evil magic powers. **2** a follower or practitioner of modern witchcraft. **3** informal an ugly or unpleasant old woman.
– DERIVATIVES **witchy** adj.
– ORIGIN Old English.

witchcraft ● n. the practice of magic, especially the use of spells and the calling up of evil spirits. See also **WICCA**.

witch doctor ● n. a tribal magician credited with powers of healing, seeing the future, and protection against the magic of others.

witchery ● n. the practice of magic.

witches' sabbath ● n. see **SABBATH** (sense 2).

witch hazel ● n. **1** a shrub with fragrant yellow or orange flowers. **2** a lotion made from the bark and leaves of this plant.
– ORIGIN for *wych*, see **WYCH ELM**.

witch-hunt ● n. a campaign directed against a person or group seen as abnormal or a threat to society.

witching hour ● n. midnight, regarded as the time when witches are supposedly active.
– ORIGIN with reference to *the witching time of night* from Shakespeare's *Hamlet* (III. ii. 377).

with ● prep. **1** accompanied by. **2** in the same direction as. **3** possessing; having. **4** indicating the instrument used to perform an action or the material used for a purpose: *cut it with a knife.* **5** in opposition to or competition with. **6** indicating the manner or attitude in which a person does something. **7** indicating responsibility: *leave it with me.* **8** in relation to. **9** employed by. **10** using the services of. **11** affected by (a particular fact or condition). **12** indicating separation or removal from something.
– PHRASES **with it** informal **1** up to date or fashionable. **2** alert and able to understand.
– ORIGIN Old English.

withal /wi-*th*awl/ archaic ● adv. in addition.

withdraw ● v. (**withdraws**, **withdrawing**, **withdrew**; past part. **withdrawn**) **1** remove or take away. **2** take (money) out of an account. **3** discontinue or retract. **4** leave or cause to leave a place. **5** stop taking part in an activity or being a member of a team or organization. **6** depart to another place in search of quiet or privacy. **7** cease to take an addictive drug.

withdrawal ● n. **1** the action or an act of withdrawing. **2** the process of ceasing to take an addictive drug.

withdrawn past part. of **WITHDRAW**. ● adj. unusually shy or reserved.

wither ● v. (**withers**, **withering**, **withered**) **1** (of a plant) become dry and shrivelled. **2** become shrunken or wrinkled from age or disease. **3** fall into decay or decline. **4** (**withering**) scornful: *a withering look.*
– ORIGIN prob. a variant of **WEATHER**.

withers ● pl. n. the highest part of a horse's back, lying at the base of the neck above the shoulders.
– ORIGIN prob. from former *widersome.*

withhold ● v. (**withholds**, **withholding**, **withheld**) **1** refuse to give (something due to or wanted by another). **2** suppress or restrain (an emotion or reaction).

within ● prep. **1** inside. **2** inside the range or bounds of. **3** occurring inside (a period of time): *the concert sold out within two hours.* **4** not further off than (used with distances). ● adv. **1** inside. **2** internally.

without ● prep. **1** not accompanied by or having the use of. **2** in which the action mentioned does not happen. **3** archaic or literary outside. ● adv. archaic or literary outside.

withstand ● v. (**withstands**, **withstanding**, **withstood**) **1** remain undamaged or unaffected by. **2** offer strong resistance or opposition to.

withy /wi-*th*i/ ● n. (pl. **withies**) a tough flexible branch of a willow, used for making baskets or tying.
– ORIGIN Old English.

witless ● adj. foolish; stupid.

witness ● n. **1** a person who sees an event take place. **2** a person giving sworn testimony to a court of law or the police. **3** a person who is present at the signing of a document and signs it themselves to confirm this. ● v. **1** be a witness to. **2** be the place, period, etc. in which (an event) takes place.
– ORIGIN Old English.

witness box (N. Amer. **witness stand**) ● n. Law the place in a court where a witness stands to give evidence.

witter ● v. (**witters**, **wittering**, **wittered**) (usu. **witter on**) Brit. informal speak at length about trivial things.

Wittgenstein E
/vit-guhn-styn/, Ludwig (Josef Johann) (1889–1951), British philosopher, born in Austria. His two major works, *Tractatus Logico-Philosophicus* and *Philosophical Investigations*, examine language and its relationship to the world.

witticism ● n. a witty remark.

witting ● adj. aware of what one is doing.
– DERIVATIVES **wittingly** adv.
– ORIGIN Old English, 'to know'.

witty ● adj. (**wittier**, **wittiest**) showing or characterized by quick and inventive verbal humour.
– DERIVATIVES **wittily** adv.

Witwatersrand E
/wit-waw-terz-rand/ (**the Witwatersrand**) a region of South Africa, around the city of Johannesburg. The region contains rich gold deposits. Also called **THE RAND**.

wives pl. of **WIFE**.

wiz ● n. var. of **WHIZZ** (in sense 3).

wizard ● n. **1** a man who has magical powers. **2** a person who is very skilled in a particular field or activity. ● adj. Brit. informal, dated very

W

good; excellent.
– ORIGIN first meaning 'philosopher, wise man': from **WISE**[1]

wizardry ● n. **1** the art or practice of magic. **2** great skill in a particular field or activity.

wizened /wi-zuhnd/ ● adj. shrivelled or wrinkled with age.
– ORIGIN from archaic *wizen* 'shrivel', from Old English.

WNW ● abbrev. west-north-west.

woad /*rhymes with* road/ ● n. a yellow-flowered plant whose leaves were formerly used to make blue dye.
– ORIGIN Old English.

wobble ● v. (**wobbles**, **wobbling**, **wobbled**) **1** move unsteadily from side to side. **2** (of the voice) tremble. ● n. a wobbling movement or sound.
– ORIGIN Germanic.

wobbler ● n. **1** a person or thing that wobbles. **2** = **WOBBLY**.

wobbly ● adj. (**wobblier**, **wobbliest**) **1** tending to wobble. **2** weak and unsteady from illness, tiredness, or anxiety. ● n. Brit. informal a fit of temper or panic.

Wodehouse E
/wuud-howss/, Sir P. G. (1881–1975; full name *Pelham Grenville Wodehouse*), English writer, known for his humorous stories of the upper-class world of Bertie Wooster and his valet Jeeves.

Woden E
/woh-d'n/ = **ODIN**.

wodge ● n. Brit. informal a large piece or amount.
– ORIGIN from **WEDGE**.

woe ● n. literary **1** great sorrow or distress. **2** (**woes**) troubles.
– PHRASES **woe betide someone** a person will be in trouble if they do a specified thing.
– ORIGIN Old English.

woebegone /woh-bi-gon/ ● adj. sad or miserable in appearance.
– ORIGIN from **WOE** + former *begone* 'surrounded'.

woeful ● adj. **1** full of sorrow. **2** very bad.
– DERIVATIVES **woefully** adv.

wog ● n. Brit. informal, offens. a person who is not white.
– ORIGIN unknown.

woggle ● n. a loop or ring through which the ends of a Scout's neckerchief are threaded.
– ORIGIN unknown.

wok ● n. a bowl-shaped frying pan used in Chinese cookery.
– ORIGIN Chinese.

woke past of **WAKE**[1].

woken past part. of **WAKE**[1].

wold /*rhymes with* cold/ ● n. (especially in British place names) a piece of high, open, uncultivated land or moor.
– ORIGIN Old English.

Wolf E
/volf/, Hugo (Philipp Jakob) (1860–1903), Austrian composer, known for his songs.

wolf ● n. (pl. **wolves**) a meat-eating mammal that lives and hunts in packs and is the largest member of the dog family. ● v. (**wolfs**, **wolfing**, **wolfed**) (usu. **wolf down**) devour (food) greedily.
– PHRASES **cry wolf** raise repeated false alarms, so that a real cry for help is ignored. [ORIGIN with reference to the fable of the shepherd boy who deluded people with false cries of 'Wolf!'] **keep the wolf from the door** have enough money to be able to buy food.
– DERIVATIVES **wolfish** adj.
– ORIGIN Old English.

Wolfe[1], E
James (1727–59), British general. One of the leaders of the expedition sent to seize French Canada, he was fatally wounded while leading his troops to victory on the Plains of Abraham, near Quebec.

Wolfe[2], E
Tom (b.1931; born *Thomas Kennerley Wolfe Jr*), American novelist and journalist, best known for his novel *The Bonfire of the Vanities*.

wolfhound ● n. a dog of a large breed originally used to hunt wolves.

wolfram /wuul-fruhm/ ● n. tungsten or its ore.
– ORIGIN German.

Wolfson E
/wuulf-s'n/, Sir Isaac (1897–1991), Scottish businessman and philanthropist. He established the Wolfson Foundation for promoting and funding medical research and education.

wolf whistle ● n. a whistle with a rising and falling pitch, used to express sexual attraction or admiration. ● v. (**wolf-whistles**, **wolf-whistling**, **wolf-whistled**) (**wolf-whistle**) whistle in such a way at.

Wollongong E
/wuul-uhng-gong/ a city on the coast of New South Wales, SE Australia.

Wollstonecraft E
/wuul-stuhn-krahft/, Mary (1759–97), English writer and feminist. In *A Vindication of the Rights of Woman* she defied assumptions about male supremacy and championed educational equality for women. She was the mother of Mary Shelley.

Wolsey E
/wuul-zi/, Thomas (*c.*1474–1530; known as **Cardinal Wolsey**), English cardinal and statesman. He dominated policy in the early part of Henry VIII's reign, but his failure to gain papal permission for Henry's divorce from Catherine of Aragon resulted in his arrest for treason. He died on his way to trial.

wolverine /wuul-vuh-reen/ ● n. a heavily built meat-eating mammal with a long brown coat and a bushy tail, native to northern tundra and forests.
– ORIGIN formed from *wolv-*, plural stem of **WOLF**.

wolves pl. of **WOLF**.

woman ● n. (pl. **women**) **1** an adult human female. **2** a female worker or employee. **3** a wife or lover.
– DERIVATIVES **womanliness** n. **womanly** adj.
– ORIGIN from the Old English words for **WIFE** and **MAN**.

womanhood ● n. **1** the state or condition of

being a woman. **2** women considered as a group. **3** the qualities traditionally associated with women.

womanish ● **adj.** derog. suitable for or characteristic of a woman.

womanize (also **womanise**) ● **v.** (**womanizes**, **womanizing**, **womanized**) (of a man) enter into many casual sexual relationships with women.
– DERIVATIVES **womanizer** (also **womaniser**) n.

womankind ● **n.** women considered as a group.

womb ● **n.** the organ in the lower body of a woman or female mammal where offspring are conceived and in which they develop before birth.
– ORIGIN Old English.

wombat /wom-bat/ ● **n.** a burrowing plant-eating Australian marsupial which resembles a small bear with short legs.
– ORIGIN from an extinct Aboriginal language.

women pl. of **WOMAN**.

womenfolk ● **pl. n.** the women of a family or community considered as a group.

women's lib ● **n.** informal = **WOMEN'S LIBERATION**.
– DERIVATIVES **women's libber** n.

women's liberation ● **n.** the liberation of women from inequalities and lower status in relation to men (now generally replaced by the term *feminism*).

won past and past part. of **WIN**.

Wonder, E
Stevie (b.1950; born *Steveland Judkins Morris*), American singer, songwriter, and musician, known for albums such as *Innervisions*. He has been blind since birth.

wonder ● **n. 1** a feeling of surprise and admiration, caused by something beautiful, unexpected, or unfamiliar. **2** a person or thing that causes such a feeling. ● **v.** (**wonders**, **wondering**, **wondered**) **1** desire to know. **2** feel doubt. **3** feel amazement and admiration. ● **adj.** having remarkable qualities or abilities: *a wonder drug.*
– PHRASES **no wonder** it is not surprising.
– ORIGIN Old English.

wonderful ● **adj.** extremely good, pleasant, or remarkable.
– DERIVATIVES **wonderfully** adv.

wonderland ● **n.** a place full of wonderful things.

wonderment ● **n.** a state of awed admiration or respect.

wondrous ● **adj.** literary inspiring wonder.

wonk ● **n.** N. Amer. informal, derog. a studious or hard-working person.
– ORIGIN unknown.

wonky ● **adj.** (**wonkier**, **wonkiest**) informal **1** crooked. **2** unsteady or faulty.
– ORIGIN fanciful formation.

W

wont /wohnt/ ● **adj.** archaic or literary accustomed. ● **n.** (**one's wont**) formal or humorous one's normal behaviour.
– ORIGIN Old English.

won't ● **contr.** will not.

wonted /wohn-tid/ ● **adj.** archaic or literary usual.

woo ● **v.** (**woos**, **wooing**, **wooed**) **1** try to gain the love of (a woman). **2** seek the support or custom of.
– ORIGIN Old English.

Wood, E
Sir Henry (Joseph) (1869–1944), English conductor, who instituted the first of the Promenade Concerts (1895) which he conducted every year until he died.

wood ● **n. 1** the hard fibrous material forming the main substance of the trunk or branches of a tree or shrub, used for fuel or timber. **2** (also **woods**) a small forest. **3** (**the wood**) wooden barrels used for storing alcoholic drinks. **4** a golf club with a wooden or other head that is relatively broad from face to back. **5** = **BOWL**².
– PHRASES **be unable to see the wood for the trees** fail to grasp the main issue because of over-attention to details. **out of the woods** out of danger or difficulty. **touch wood** touch something wooden to ward off bad luck.
– ORIGIN Old English.

wood anemone ● **n.** a spring-flowering anemone with pink-tinged white flowers, growing in woodland and shady places.

woodbine ● **n.** Brit. the common honeysuckle.

woodblock ● **n. 1** a block of wood from which woodcut prints are made. **2** a hollow wooden block used as a percussion instrument.

woodchip ● **n.** esp. Brit. wallpaper with small chips of wood embedded in it to give a grainy surface texture.

woodchuck ● **n.** a North American marmot with a heavy body and short legs.
– ORIGIN an alteration (by association with **WOOD**) of an American Indian name.

woodcock ● **n.** (pl. **woodcock**) a long-billed woodland bird of the sandpiper family, with brown plumage.

woodcut ● **n.** a print of a type made from a design cut in relief in a block of wood.

woodcutter ● **n.** a person who cuts down wood.

wooded ● **adj.** (of land) covered with woods.

wooden ● **adj. 1** made of wood. **2** resembling or characteristic of wood. **3** stiff and awkward.
– DERIVATIVES **woodenly** adv.

wooden spoon ● **n.** esp. Brit. the last place in a race or competition.
– ORIGIN from the former practice of giving a spoon to the candidate coming last in the Cambridge mathematical tripos.

woodland ● **n.** (also **woodlands**) land covered with trees.

woodlouse ● **n.** (pl. **woodlice**) a small land crustacean with a greyish segmented body which it is able to roll into a ball.

woodpecker ● **n.** a bird with a strong bill and a stiff tail, typically pecking at tree trunks to find insects and drumming on dead wood to mark territory.

wood pigeon ● **n.** a common large pigeon, mainly grey with white patches forming a ring round its neck.

wood pulp ● **n.** wood fibre reduced chemically or mechanically to pulp and used in the manufacture of paper.

woodruff (also **sweet woodruff**) ● **n.** a white-flowered plant with sweet-scented

leaves used to flavour drinks and in perfumery.
– ORIGIN Old English.

Woods, Ⓔ
Tiger (b.1975; born *Eldrick Woods*), American golfer. In 2000 he became the youngest player to win all four of golf's grand slam events.

woodshed ● n. a shed where firewood is stored.

woodsman ● n. a forester, hunter, or woodcutter.

Woodstock Ⓔ
a small town in New York State. It gave its name in the summer of 1969 to a huge rock festival held some 96 km (60 miles) to the south-west.

woodturning ● n. the activity of shaping wood with a lathe.
– DERIVATIVES **woodturner** n.

woodwind ● n. wind instruments other than brass instruments forming a section of an orchestra.

woodwork ● n. **1** the wooden parts of a room, building, or other structure. **2** Brit. the activity or skill of making things from wood.
– PHRASES **come out of the woodwork** (of an unpleasant person or thing) emerge from obscurity.
– DERIVATIVES **woodworker** n. **woodworking** n.

woodworm ● n. **1** the wood-boring larva of a kind of small brown beetle. **2** the damaged condition of wood resulting from infestation with this larva.

woody ● adj. (**woodier**, **woodiest**) **1** covered with trees. **2** made of, resembling, or suggestive of wood.

woodyard ● n. a yard where wood is chopped or stored.

woof[1] /woof/ ● n. the barking sound made by a dog. ● v. bark.

woof[2] /woof/ ● n. = WEFT.
– ORIGIN Old English.

woofer /woo-fer, wuu-fer/ ● n. a loudspeaker designed to reproduce low frequencies.

wool ● n. **1** the fine soft hair forming the coat of a sheep, goat, or similar animal. **2** a metal or mineral made into a mass of fine fibres.
– PHRASES **pull the wool over someone's eyes** deceive someone.
– ORIGIN Old English.

Woolf Ⓔ
/wuulf/, (Adeline) Virginia (1882–1941; born *Adeline Virginia Stephen*), English novelist, essayist, and critic, a member of the Bloomsbury Group. Her best-known novels include *Mrs Dalloway* and *To the Lighthouse*.

woollen (US **woolen**) ● adj. **1** made of wool. **2** relating to the production of wool. ● n. (**woollens**) woollen garments.

woolly ● adj. (**woollier**, **woolliest**) **1** made of wool. **2** (of an animal or plant) covered with wool or hair resembling wool. **3** resembling wool in texture or appearance. **4** confused or unclear: *woolly thinking*. ● n. (pl. **woollies**) informal, esp. Brit. a woollen garment, especially a pullover.

Woolsack ● n. (in the UK) the Lord Chancellor's wool-stuffed seat in the House of Lords.

Woomera Ⓔ
/woo-muh-ruh/ a town in central South Australia, the site of a vast area used in the 1950s for nuclear tests and since the 1960s for tracking space satellites.

woosh ● v. & n. var. of WHOOSH.

woozy ● adj. (**woozier**, **wooziest**) informal unsteady, dizzy, or dazed.
– DERIVATIVES **woozily** adv.
– ORIGIN unknown.

wop ● n. informal, offens. an Italian or other southern European.
– ORIGIN perh. from Italian *guappo* 'bold, showy'.

Worcester sauce (also **Worcestershire sauce**) ● n. a tangy sauce containing soy sauce and vinegar.

Worcestershire Ⓔ
a county of west central England; administrative centre, Worcester.

Worcs. ● abbrev. Worcestershire.

word ● n. **1** a separate meaningful element of speech or writing, used with others to form sentences. **2** a remark or statement. **3** (**a word**) even the smallest amount of something spoken or written: *don't believe a word*. **4** (**words**) angry talk. **5** (**the word**) a command, slogan, or signal. **6** (**one's word**) a person's account of the truth. **7** (**one's word**) a promise. **8** news. ● v. express in particular words.
– PHRASES **have a word** speak briefly to someone. **in so many words** precisely in the way mentioned. **in a word** briefly. **take someone's word** (**for it**) believe what someone says or writes without checking for oneself. **word of mouth** spoken communication as a means of conveying information.
– DERIVATIVES **wordless** adj.
– ORIGIN Old English.

wording ● n. the way in which something is worded.

word-perfect ● adj. (of an actor or speaker) knowing one's part or speech by heart.

wordplay ● n. the witty exploitation of the meanings of words.

word processor ● n. a computer or program for creating, editing, storing, and printing a document or piece of text.

wordsmith ● n. a skilled user of words.

Wordsworth, Ⓔ
William (1770–1850), English poet. His *Lyrical Ballads*, written with Coleridge, was a landmark in romanticism. His other poems include 'I Wandered Lonely as a Cloud'. He was Poet Laureate 1843–50.

wordy ● adj. using or expressed in too many words.

wore past of WEAR.

work ● n. **1** activity involving mental or physical effort done in order to achieve a result. **2** such activity as a means of earning money. **3** a task or tasks to be done. **4** a thing or things done or made. **5** (**works**) esp. Brit. a place where industrial or manufacturing processes are carried out. **6** (**works**) esp. Brit. activities involving building or repair. **7** (**works**) the mechanism of a machine. **8** Mil. a defensive structure. ● v. (**works**, **working**, **worked** or archaic **wrought**) **1** do work as

W

one's job. **2** make (someone) do work. **3** (of a machine or system) function properly. **4** (of a machine) be in operation. **5** have the desired result: *her plan worked admirably.* **6** bring (a material or mixture) to a desired shape or consistency. **7** produce (an article or design) using a specified material or sewing stitch. **8** cultivate (land) or extract materials from (a mine or quarry). **9** move gradually or with difficulty into another position.
– PHRASES **get worked up** gradually come into a state of great excitement, anger, or anxiety. **have one's work cut out** be faced with a hard or lengthy task. **work out 1** solve or be capable of being solved. **2** develop in a good or specified way. **3** plan in detail. **4** understand the character of. **5** engage in vigorous physical exercise. **work to rule** esp. Brit. follow official working rules and hours exactly in order to reduce output and efficiency, as a form of industrial action. **work up to** proceed gradually towards (something more advanced).
– ORIGIN Old English.

workable • **adj. 1** able to be shaped, dug, etc. **2** capable of producing the desired result.

workaday • **adj.** ordinary.

workaholic • **n.** informal a person who works very hard and finds it difficult to stop working.

workbench • **n.** a bench at which carpentry or other mechanical or practical work is done.

worker • **n. 1** a person who works. **2** a person who achieves a specified thing: *a miracle-worker.* **3** a neuter or undeveloped female bee, wasp, ant, etc., large numbers of which perform the basic work of a colony.

work experience • **n.** short-term experience of employment, arranged for older pupils by schools.

workforce • **n.** the people engaged in or available for work in a particular area, firm, or industry.

workhorse • **n.** a person or machine that works hard and reliably over a long period.

workhouse • **n.** hist. (in the UK) a public institution in which poor people received board and lodging in return for work.

working • **adj. 1** having paid employment. **2** doing manual work. **3** functioning or able to function. **4** good enough as the basis for work or argument and likely to be changed later: *a working title.* • **n. 1** the parts of a mine or quarry from which minerals are being extracted. **2** (**workings**) the way in which a machine, organization, or system operates. **3** (**workings**) a record of the calculations made in solving a mathematical problem.

working capital • **n.** the capital of a business which is used in its day-to-day trading operations.

working class • **n.** the social group made up of people who are employed for wages, especially in manual or industrial work.

working girl • **n.** informal, euphem. a prostitute.

working party (also **working group**) • **n.** Brit. a group appointed to study and report on a particular question and make recommendations.

workload • **n.** the amount of work to be done by someone or something.

workman • **n. 1** a man employed to do manual labour. **2** a person who works in a specified way.

workmanlike • **adj.** showing efficient skill.

workmanship • **n.** the degree of skill with which a product is made or a job done.

workmate • **n.** esp. Brit. a person with whom one works.

work of art • **n.** a creative product with strong imaginative or artistic appeal.

workout • **n.** a session of vigorous physical exercise.

work permit • **n.** an official document giving a foreigner permission to take a job in a country.

workpiece • **n.** an object being worked on with a tool or machine.

worksheet • **n. 1** a paper listing questions or tasks for students. **2** a paper recording work done or in progress.

workshop • **n. 1** a room or building in which goods are made or repaired. **2** a meeting at which a group engages in intensive discussion and activity on a particular subject or project.

work-shy • **adj.** not inclined to work.

workspace • **n. 1** an area rented or sold for commercial purposes. **2** Computing a memory storage facility for temporary use.

workstation • **n.** a desktop computer terminal, typically networked and more powerful than a personal computer.

worktop • **n.** Brit. a flat surface for working on.

world • **n. 1** (**the world**) the earth with all its countries and peoples. **2** a region or group of countries: *the English-speaking world.* **3** all that belongs to a particular period or area of activity: *the theatre world.* **4** (**one's world**) a person's life and activities. **5** (**the world**) secular or material matters as opposed to spiritual ones. **6** a planet. **7** (**a/the world**) a very large amount of: *that makes a world of difference.*
– PHRASES **the best of both** (or **all possible**) **worlds** the benefits of widely differing situations, enjoyed at the same time. **out of this world** informal extremely enjoyable or impressive.
– ORIGIN Old English.

World Bank E
an international banking organization established to control the distribution of economic aid between member nations, and to make loans to them in times of financial crisis. See also **INTERNATIONAL BANK FOR RECONSTRUCTION AND DEVELOPMENT**.

world-beater • **n.** a person or thing that is better than all others in its field.

world-class • **adj.** of or among the best in the world.

World Cup • **n.** a competition between teams from many countries in a sport.

world English • **n.** the English language including all of its regional varieties around the world.

World Health Organization E
an agency of the United Nations, established to promote health and control communicable diseases.

W

worldly ● adj. (**worldlier**, **worldliest**) **1** of or concerned with material things rather than spiritual ones. **2** experienced and sophisticated.
– PHRASES **worldly goods** everything that someone owns.

worldly-wise ● adj. having enough experience not to be easily shocked or deceived.

world music ● n. music from the developing world incorporating traditional and/or popular elements.

world order ● n. a set of arrangements established internationally for preserving global political stability.

world power ● n. a country that has great influence in international affairs.

world-ranking ● adj. among the best in the world.

World Series E
the professional championship for major league baseball, played at the end of the season between the champions of the American League and the National League.

World Trade Organization E
an international body founded to promote international trade and economic development by reducing tariffs and other restrictions.

world war ● n. a war involving many large nations in different parts of the world, especially the wars of 1914–18 and 1939–45.

World War I E
= **FIRST WORLD WAR**.

World War II E
= **SECOND WORLD WAR**.

world-weary ● adj. bored with or cynical about life.

worldwide ● adj. extending or applicable throughout the world. ● adv. throughout the world.

World Wide Web ● n. Computing an extensive information system on the Internet providing facilities for documents to be connected to other documents by hypertext links.

worm ● n. **1** an earthworm or other creeping or burrowing invertebrate animal having a long slender soft body and no limbs. **2** (**worms**) intestinal or other internal parasites. **3** a maggot regarded as eating dead bodies buried in the ground: *food for worms.* **4** informal a weak or despicable person. ● v. **1** move by crawling or wriggling. **2** (**worm one's way into**) gradually move one's way into. **3** (**worm out of**) obtain (information) from (someone) by cunning persistence.
– ORIGIN Old English.

worm cast ● n. a convoluted mass of soil, mud, or sand thrown up at the surface by a burrowing worm.

wormhole ● n. **1** a hole made by a burrowing insect larva or worm in wood, fruit, etc. **2** Physics a hypothetical connection between widely separated regions of space-time.

wormwood ● n. **1** a woody shrub with a bitter taste, used as an ingredient of vermouth and absinthe and in medicine. **2** bitterness or grief, or a source of this.
– ORIGIN Old English.

wormy ● adj. (**wormier**, **wormiest**) worm-eaten or full of worms.

worn past part. of **WEAR**. ● adj. **1** suffering from wear. **2** very tired.

worn out ● adj. **1** exhausted. **2** worn to the point of being no longer usable.

worried ● adj. feeling, showing, or expressing anxiety.

worrisome ● adj. causing anxiety or concern.

worry ● v. (**worries**, **worrying**, **worried**) **1** feel or cause to feel troubled over actual or potential difficulties. **2** annoy or disturb. **3** (of a dog) tear at or pull about with the teeth. **4** (of a dog) chase and attack (livestock). ● n. (pl. **worries**) **1** the state of being worried. **2** a source of anxiety.
– DERIVATIVES **worrier** n.
– ORIGIN Old English, 'strangle'.

worry beads ● pl. n. a string of beads that one fingers so as to calm oneself.

worse ● adj. **1** less good, satisfactory, or pleasing. **2** more serious or severe. **3** more ill or unhappy. ● adv. **1** less well. **2** more seriously or severely. ● n. a worse event or circumstance.
– PHRASES **worse off** less fortunate or wealthy.
– ORIGIN Old English.

worsen ● v. make or become worse.

worship ● n. **1** the feeling or expression of deep respect and adoration for a god or goddess. **2** religious rites and ceremonies. **3** great admiration or devotion. **4** (**His/Your Worship**) esp. Brit. a title of respect for a magistrate or mayor. ● v. (**worships**, **worshipping**, **worshipped**; US also **worships**, **worshiping**, **worshiped**) **1** show great respect and adoration for (a deity). **2** feel great admiration or devotion for.
– DERIVATIVES **worshipper** n.
– ORIGIN Old English, 'worthiness, acknowledgement of worth'.

worshipful ● adj. **1** feeling or showing great respect and admiration. **2** (**Worshipful**) Brit. a title given to justices of the peace.

worst ● adj. most bad, severe, or serious. ● adv. **1** most severely or seriously. **2** least well. ● n. the worst part, event, or circumstance. ● v. get the better of.
– PHRASES **do one's worst** do as much damage as one can.
– ORIGIN Old English.

worsted /wuus-tid/ ● n. **1** a fine smooth yarn spun from long strands of combed wool. **2** fabric made from such yarn.
– ORIGIN from *Worstead*, a parish in Norfolk, England.

Worth, E
Charles Frederick (1825–95), English fashion designer, resident in France from 1845. He founded Parisian *haute couture* and introduced the bustle.

worth ● adj. **1** equivalent in value to the sum or item specified. **2** deserving to be treated or regarded in the way specified: *the museums are worth a visit.* **3** having income or property amounting to a specified sum. ● n. **1** the value or merit of someone or something. **2** an amount of a commodity equivalent to a specified sum of money: *hundreds of pounds worth of clothes.*
– PHRASES **for all one is worth** informal as ener-

getically or enthusiastically as one can.
– ORIGIN Old English.

worthless • adj. **1** having no real value or use. **2** having no good qualities.

worthwhile • adj. worth the time, money, or effort spent.

worthy • adj. (**worthier**, **worthiest**) **1** (often **worthy of**) deserving or good enough. **2** deserving effort, attention, or respect. **3** showing good intent but lacking in humour or imagination. • n. (pl. **worthies**) usu. humorous a person important in a particular sphere: *local worthies*.
– DERIVATIVES **worthily** adv.

-worthy • comb. form **1** deserving of a specified thing: *newsworthy*. **2** suitable for a specified thing: *roadworthy*.

Wotan E
/woh-tan/ = ODIN.

would • modal verb (3rd sing. present **would**) **1** past of WILL[1], in various senses. **2** (expressing the conditional mood) indicating the consequence of an imagined event. **3** expressing a desire or inclination. **4** expressing a polite request. **5** expressing a conjecture or opinion: *I would have to agree*. **6** literary expressing a wish or regret: *would that he had lived to finish it*.

USAGE **would**
For an explanation of the difference between **would** and **should**, see the note at SHOULD.

would-be • adj. usu. derog. desiring or hoping to be a specified type of person: *a would-be actress*.

wouldn't • contr. would not.

wouldst archaic 2nd person sing. of WOULD.

wound[1] /woond/ • n. **1** a bodily injury caused by a cut, blow, or other impact. **2** an injury to a person's feelings or reputation. • v. **1** inflict a wound on. **2** injure (a person's feelings).
– ORIGIN Old English.

wound[2] past and past part. of WIND[2].

Wounded Knee, Battle of E
the last major confrontation (1890) between the US Army and American Indians, at the village of Wounded Knee in South Dakota. More than 300 largely unarmed Sioux men, women, and children were massacred.

wove past of WEAVE[1].

woven past part. of WEAVE[1].

wow informal • exclam. expressing astonishment or admiration. • n. a sensational success. • v. impress and excite greatly.

WP • abbrev. word processing or word processor.

WPC • abbrev. (in the UK) woman police constable.

wpm • abbrev. words per minute (used after a number to indicate typing speed).

W

wrack[1] • v. var. of RACK[1], RACK[3].

wrack[2] • n. a coarse brown seaweed which grows on the shoreline.
– ORIGIN prob. from archaic and dialect *wrack* 'shipwreck', from Dutch *wrak*.

WRAF • abbrev. (in the UK, until 1994) Women's Royal Air Force.

wraith /rayth/ • n. a ghost or ghostly image of someone, especially one seen shortly before or after their death.
– ORIGIN unknown.

wrangle • n. a long and complicated dispute or argument. • v. (**wrangles**, **wrangling**, **wrangled**) engage in a wrangle.
– ORIGIN perh. from German *wrangen* 'to struggle'.

wrap • v. (**wraps**, **wrapping**, **wrapped**) **1** cover or enclose in paper or soft material. **2** arrange (paper or soft material) round something. **3** encircle or wind round: *he wrapped an arm around her waist*. **4** Computing cause (a word or unit of text) to be carried over to a new line automatically. **5** informal finish filming or recording. • n. **1** a loose outer garment or piece of material. **2** paper or material used for wrapping. **3** informal the end of a session of filming or recording.
– PHRASES **under wraps** kept secret. **wrap up** **1** put on or dress in warm clothes. **2** complete (a meeting or deal). **3** (**wrapped up**) engrossed or involved to the exclusion of other things.
– DERIVATIVES **wrapping** n.
– ORIGIN unknown.

wrapped • adj. Austral. informal delighted.
– ORIGIN blend of *wrapped up* 'engrossed' and RAPT.

wrapper • n. a piece of paper or other material used for wrapping something.

wrasse /rass/ • n. (pl. **wrasse** or **wrasses**) a brightly coloured marine fish with thick lips and strong teeth.
– ORIGIN Cornish *wrah*.

wrath /roth, rawth/ • n. extreme anger.
– ORIGIN Old English.

wrathful • adj. literary full of or characterized by great anger.
– DERIVATIVES **wrathfully** adv.

wreak • v. **1** cause (a large amount of damage or harm). **2** inflict (vengeance).
– ORIGIN Old English, 'drive (out), avenge'.

wreath /reeth/ • n. (pl. **wreaths** /reeths, ree*thz*/) **1** an arrangement of flowers or leaves fastened in a ring and used for decoration or for laying on a grave. **2** a curl or ring of smoke or cloud.
– ORIGIN Old English.

wreathe /ree*th*/ • v. (**wreathes**, **wreathing**, **wreathed**) **1** (usu. **be wreathed**) surround or encircle. **2** (of smoke) move with a curling motion.
– ORIGIN from WRITHE.

wreck • n. **1** the destruction of a ship at sea. **2** a ship destroyed at sea. **3** a building, vehicle, etc. that has been destroyed or badly damaged. **4** a person in a very bad physical or mental state. • v. **1** cause the destruction of (a ship) by sinking or breaking up. **2** destroy or badly damage. **3** spoil completely.
– DERIVATIVES **wrecker** n.
– ORIGIN Old French *wrec*.

wreckage • n. the remains of something that has been badly damaged or destroyed.

wrecked • adj. informal **1** exhausted. **2** drunk.

Wren[1], E
Sir Christopher (1632–1723), English architect, who designed St Paul's Cathedral in London, the Greenwich Observatory, and many of London's churches.

Wren[2] • n. (in the UK) a member of the former Women's Royal Naval Service.
– ORIGIN from the acronym *WRNS*.

wren • n. a very small songbird with a cocked tail.
– ORIGIN Old English.

wrench • v. **1** pull or twist suddenly and violently. **2** injure (a part of the body) as a result of a sudden twisting movement. • n. **1** a sudden violent twist or pull. **2** a feeling of sudden pain and distress caused by one's own or another's departure. **3** an adjustable tool like a spanner, used for gripping and turning nuts or bolts.
– ORIGIN Old English.

wrest /rest/ • v. **1** forcibly pull from a person's grasp. **2** take (power or control) after effort or resistance.
– ORIGIN Old English.

wrestle • v. (**wrestles**, **wrestling**, **wrestled**) **1** take part in a fight or contest that involves close grappling with one's opponent. **2** struggle with a difficulty or problem. **3** take out or move (an object) with difficulty and some physical effort. • n. **1** a wrestling bout or contest. **2** a hard struggle.
– DERIVATIVES **wrestler** n. **wrestling** n.

wretch • n. **1** an unfortunate person. **2** informal a contemptible person.
– ORIGIN Old English.

wretched • adj. (**wretcheder**, **wretchedest**) **1** in a very unhappy or unfortunate state. **2** of poor quality. **3** used to express anger or annoyance: *she disliked the wretched man intensely.*
– DERIVATIVES **wretchedly** adv.

wriggle • v. (**wriggles**, **wriggling**, **wriggled**) **1** twist and turn with quick writhing movements. **2** (**wriggle out of**) avoid by devious means. • n. a wriggling movement.
– DERIVATIVES **wriggly** adj.
– ORIGIN German *wriggelen.*

Wright[1], E
Frank Lloyd (1869–1959), American architect. His 'prairie-style' houses (with long low horizontal lines) revolutionized American domestic architecture. Among his best-known public buildings is the Guggenheim Museum of Art in New York.

Wright[2], E
Orville (1871–1948) and Wilbur (1867–1912), American aviation pioneers. In 1903 the Wright brothers were the first to make powered sustained and controlled flights in an aeroplane, which they had designed and built themselves.

wright • n. a maker or builder: *playwright.*
– ORIGIN Old English.

wring • v. (**wrings**, **wringing**, **wrung**) **1** squeeze and twist to force liquid from. **2** break (an animal's neck) by twisting forcibly. **3** squeeze (someone's hand) tightly. **4** (**wring from/out of**) obtain with difficulty or effort. • n. an act of wringing.
– ORIGIN Old English.

wringer • n. a device for wringing water from wet clothes or other objects.

wringing • adj. extremely wet.

wrinkle • n. a slight line or fold, especially in fabric or the skin of the face. • v. (**wrinkles**, **wrinkling**, **wrinkled**) make or become wrinkled.
– DERIVATIVES **wrinkled** adj.
– ORIGIN perh. from Old English, 'sinuous'.

wrinkly • adj. (**wrinklier**, **wrinkliest**) having many wrinkles. • n. (pl. **wrinklies**) Brit. informal, derog. an old person.

wrist • n. the joint connecting the hand with the forearm.
– ORIGIN Old English.

wristband • n. a band worn round the wrist.

wristwatch • n. a watch worn on a strap round the wrist.

writ[1] • n. **1** a form of written command in the name of a court or other legal authority, directing a person to act in a specified way. **2** (**one's writ**) one's power to enforce obedience.
– ORIGIN Old English.

writ[2] • v. archaic past part. of **WRITE**.
– PHRASES **writ large** in an obvious or exaggerated form.

write • v. (**writes**, **writing**, **wrote**; past part. **written**) **1** mark (letters, words, or other symbols) on a surface, with a pen, pencil, or similar implement. **2** write and send (a letter) to someone. **3** compose (a text or work) in writing. **4** compose (a musical work). **5** fill out (a cheque or similar document).
– PHRASES **write off 1** dismiss as insignificant. **2** cancel the record of (a bad debt); acknowledge the failure to recover (an asset). **3** Brit. damage (a vehicle) so badly that it cannot be repaired or is not worth repairing.
– ORIGIN Old English.

write-off • n. a vehicle that is too badly damaged to be repaired.

writer • n. a person who has written a particular text, or who writes books or articles as an occupation.

writerly • adj. **1** having to do with a professional author. **2** deliberately literary in style.

writer's block • n. the condition of being unable to think of what to write or how to proceed with writing.

writer's cramp • n. pain or stiffness in the hand caused by excessive writing.

write-up • n. a newspaper review of a recent event, performance, etc.

writhe /ryth/ • v. (**writhes**, **writhing**, **writhed**) twist or squirm in pain or as if in pain.
– ORIGIN Old English, 'make into coils, plait'.

writing • n. **1** the activity or skill of writing. **2** written work. **3** (**writings**) books or other written works. **4** a sequence of letters or symbols forming words.
– PHRASES **the writing is on the wall** there are clear signs that something unpleasant is going to happen. [ORIGIN with biblical reference to Belshazzar's feast (Book of Daniel, chapter 5), at which mysterious writing appeared on the wall foretelling Belshazzar's overthrow.]

written past part. of **WRITE**.

wrong • adj. **1** not correct or true; mistaken or in error. **2** unjust, dishonest, or immoral. **3** in a bad or abnormal condition: *something is wrong with the pump.* • adv. **1** in a mistaken or undesirable manner or direction. **2** with an incorrect result. • n. an unjust, dishonest, or immoral action. • v. **1** act unjustly or dishonestly towards. **2** mistakenly assert that (someone) has bad motives.
– PHRASES **get hold of the wrong end of the stick** misunderstand something. **in the**

wrong responsible for a mistake or offence. **on the wrong side of 1** out of favour with. **2** somewhat more than (a specified age).
– DERIVATIVES **wrongly** adv. **wrongness** n.
– ORIGIN Old Norse, 'awry, unjust'.

wrongdoing • n. illegal or dishonest behaviour.
– DERIVATIVES **wrongdoer** n.

wrong-foot • v. Brit. **1** (in a game) play so as to catch (an opponent) off balance. **2** place (someone) in a difficult or embarrassing situation by saying or doing something unexpected.

wrongful • adj. not fair, just, or legal.
– DERIVATIVES **wrongfully** adv.

wrong-headed • adj. having or showing bad judgement.

wrote past tense of **WRITE**.

wroth /rohth, roth/ • adj. archaic angry.
– ORIGIN Old English.

wrought /*rhymes with* bought/ • adj. **1** (of metals) beaten out or shaped by hammering. **2** (in combination) made in the specified way: *well-wrought*.
– ORIGIN archaic past and past participle of **WORK**.

wrought iron • n. a tough form of iron suitable for forging or rolling rather than casting.

wrung past and past part. of **WRING**.

wry /ry/ • adj. (**wryer**, **wryest** or **wrier**, **wriest**) **1** using or expressing dry, mocking humour. **2** (of a person's face) twisted into an expression of disgust, disappointment, or annoyance. **3** bending or twisted to one side.
– DERIVATIVES **wryly** adv.
– ORIGIN Old English, 'tend, incline'.

wryneck • n. a bird of the woodpecker family, with brown plumage and a habit of twisting its head backwards.

WSW • abbrev. west-south-west.

WTO • abbrev. World Trade Organization.

wunderkind /vuun-der-kind/ • n. (pl. **wunderkinds** or **wunderkinder** /vuun-der-kinder/) a person who achieves great success when young.
– ORIGIN German.

Wurlitzer /wer-lit-ser/ • n. trademark a large pipe organ or electric organ.
– ORIGIN named after the American instrument-maker Rudolf *Wurlitzer* (1831–1914).

wuss /*rhymes with* puss/ • n. N. Amer. informal a feeble person.
– ORIGIN unknown.

WWI • abbrev. World War I.

WWII • abbrev. World War II.

WWF • abbrev. **1** World Wide Fund for Nature. **2** World Wrestling Federation.

WWW • abbrev. World Wide Web.

Wyatt E
/wy-uht/, James (1746–1813), English architect. He was both a neoclassicist and a leading figure in the Gothic revival.

Wycherley E
/wich-er-li/, William (*c.*1640–1716), English dramatist, known for his comedy *The Country Wife*.

Wyclif E
/wik-lif/ (also **Wycliffe**), John (*c.*1330–84), English religious reformer. He initiated the first English translation of the complete Bible. He criticized the wealth and power of the Church and his teachings were spread by his followers, known as Lollards.

Wye E
a river which rises in the mountains of western Wales and flows generally south-eastwards to enter the Severn estuary.

Wyndham E
/wind-uhm/, John (1903–69; pen name of *John Wyndham Parkes Lucas Beynon Harris*), English science-fiction writer. His novels include *The Day of the Triffids* and *The Midwich Cuckoos*.

Wynette E
/wi-net/, Tammy (1942–98; born *Tammy Wynette Pugh*), American country singer. Her songs include 'Stand by Your Man'.

Wyoming E
/wy-**oh**-ming/ a state in the west central US; capital, Cheyenne.
– DERIVATIVES **Wyomingite** n.

X[1] (also **x**) • n. (pl. **Xs** or **X's**) **1** the twenty-fourth letter of the alphabet. **2** referring to an unknown or unspecified person or thing. **3** the first unknown quantity in an algebraic expression. **4** referring to the main or horizontal axis in a system of coordinates. **5** a cross-shaped written symbol, used to indicate an incorrect answer or to symbolize a kiss. **6** the Roman numeral for ten.

X[2] • symb. (formerly in the UK and US) a classification of films as suitable for adults only.

Xavier, St Francis E
/za-vi-er, zay-vi-er/ (1506–52), Spanish Catholic missionary. One of the original seven Jesuits, he travelled widely in the East, making thousands of converts. Feast day, 3 December.

X chromosome • n. Genetics (in humans and other mammals) a sex chromosome, two of which are normally present in female cells (designated XX) and only one in male cells (designated XY). Compare with **Y CHROMOSOME**.

xenon /zen-on, zee-non/ ● **n.** an inert gaseous chemical element, present in trace amounts in the air and used in some kinds of electric light.
– ORIGIN Greek *xenos* 'strange'.

xenophobia /zen-uh-foh-bi-uh/ ● **n.** strong dislike or fear of people from other countries.
– DERIVATIVES **xenophobe** n. **xenophobic** adj.
– ORIGIN Greek *xenos* 'stranger'.

Xenophon E
/zen-uh-fuhn/ (*c.*435–*c.*354 BC), Greek historian and general. From 401 he fought with the Persian prince Cyrus the Younger against Cyrus' elder brother, and led an army of Greek mercenaries in their retreat of about 1,500 km (900 miles) after Cyrus was killed; Xenophon recorded this in the *Anabasis*.

xerography /zeer-og-ruh-fi/ ● **n.** a dry copying process in which powder sticks to parts of a surface remaining electrically charged after being exposed to light from an image of the document to be copied.
– DERIVATIVES **xerographic** adj.
– ORIGIN Greek *xēros* 'dry'.

Xerox /zeer-oks, ze-roks/ ● **n.** trademark **1** a xerographic copying process. **2** a copy made using such a process. ● **v.** (**xerox**) copy (a document) by such a process.
– ORIGIN from **XEROGRAPHY**.

Xerxes I E
/zerk-seez/ (*c.*519–465 BC), son of Darius I, king of Persia 486–465. He invaded Greece in 480 BC, but following defeats at Salamis (480) and Plataea (479) was forced to withdraw.

Xian E
/shee-an/ (also **Hsian** or **Sian**) an industrial city in central China, capital of Shaanxi province. The city has been inhabited since the 11th century BC and was formerly the capital of China.

XL ● **abbrev.** extra large (as a clothes size).

Xmas /kriss-muhss, eks-muhss/ ● **n.** informal = **CHRISTMAS**.
– ORIGIN *X* representing the initial Greek character of Greek *Khristos* 'Christ'.

XML ● **abbrev.** Extensible Mark-up Language.

X-rated ● **adj. 1** pornographic or indecent. **2** (formerly) referring to a film given an X classification.

X-ray ● **n. 1** an electromagnetic wave of very short wavelength, able to pass through many solids and make it possible to see into or through them. **2** an image of the internal structure of an object produced by passing X-rays through it. ● **v.** photograph or examine with X-rays.
– ORIGIN from *X-* (because, when first discovered, the nature of the rays was unknown).

xylem /zy-luhm/ ● **n.** Bot. the tissue in plants which carries water and nutrients upwards from the root and also helps to form the woody part of the stem.
– ORIGIN Greek *xulon* 'wood'.

xylophone ● **n.** a musical instrument played by striking a row of wooden bars of graduated length with small beaters.
– ORIGIN Greek *xulon* 'wood'.

Y (also **y**) ● **n.** (pl. **Ys** or **Y's**) **1** the twenty-fifth letter of the alphabet. **2** referring to an unknown or unspecified person or thing. **3** (usu. ***y***) the second unknown quantity in an algebraic expression. **4** referring to the secondary or vertical axis in a system of coordinates.

y ● **abbrev.** year(s).

-y[1] ● **suffix** forming adjectives: **1** full of; having the quality of: *messy.* **2** inclined to; apt to: *sticky.*
– ORIGIN Old English.

-y[2] (also **-ey** or **-ie**) ● **suffix 1** forming diminutive nouns, pet names, etc.: *granny.* **2** forming verbs: *shinny.*
– ORIGIN Scots.

-y[3] ● **suffix** forming nouns: **1** referring to a state or quality: *jealousy.* **2** referring to an action or its result: *victory.*
– ORIGIN from Latin *-ia, -ium* or Greek *-eia, -ia*.

Y2K ● **abbrev.** year 2000 (with reference to the millennium bug).

yacht /yot/ ● **n. 1** a medium-sized sailing boat equipped for cruising or racing. **2** a powered boat equipped for cruising.
– DERIVATIVES **yachting** n.
– ORIGIN Dutch *jaghte.*

yack ● **n. & v.** var. of **YAK**[2].

yahoo /yah-hoo, yuh-hoo/ ● **n.** informal a rude, coarse, or violent person.
– ORIGIN the name of an imaginary people in Jonathan Swift's *Gulliver's Travels.*

Yahweh /yah-way/ ● **n.** a form of the Hebrew name of God used in the Bible.
– ORIGIN Hebrew.

yak[1] ● **n.** a large ox with shaggy hair and large horns, used in Tibet for carrying loads and for its milk, meat, and hide.
– ORIGIN Tibetan (the language of Tibet).

yak[2] (also **yack**) informal ● **v.** (**yaks, yakking, yakked**) talk at length about trivial or boring subjects. ● **n.** a trivial or lengthy conversation.

Yale ● **n.** trademark a type of lock with a latch bolt and a flat key with a serrated edge.

– ORIGIN named after the American locksmith Linus *Yale* Jr (1821–68).

Yale University E
a university at New Haven, Connecticut.

yam • n. **1** the starchy tuber of a tropical climbing plant, eaten as a vegetable. **2** N. Amer. a sweet potato.
– ORIGIN Portuguese *inhame* or former Spanish *iñame*.

Yamasaki E
/yam-uh-**sah**-ki/, Minoru (1912–86), American architect, who designed the St Louis Municipal Airport Terminal and the World Trade Center in New York.

yammer informal • v. (**yammers**, **yammering**, **yammered**) talk loudly and without pausing. • n. loud and sustained noise.
– ORIGIN Old English, 'to lament'.

Yamoussoukro E
/yam-oo-**soo**-kroh/ the capital of the Ivory Coast.

yang • n. (in Chinese philosophy) the active male principle of the universe. Contrasted with **YIN**.
– ORIGIN Chinese, 'male genitals, sun'.

Yangtze E
/**yang**-tsi/ the chief river of China, which rises in the Tibetan highlands and flows 6,380 km (3,964 miles) through central China, entering the East China Sea at Shanghai.

Yank • n. informal, usu. derog. an American.

yank informal • v. pull with a jerk. • n. a sudden hard pull.
– ORIGIN unknown.

Yankee • n. informal **1** usu. derog. an American. **2** US a person from New England or one of the northern states. **3** hist. a Federal soldier in the Civil War.
– ORIGIN perh. from Dutch *Jan* 'John'.

Yaoundé E
/ya-**uun**-day/ the capital of Cameroon.

yap • v. (**yaps**, **yapping**, **yapped**) **1** give a sharp, shrill bark. **2** informal talk at length in an irritating way. • n. a sharp, shrill bark.
– DERIVATIVES **yappy** adj.

yard[1] • n. **1** a unit of length equal to 3 feet (0.9144 metre). **2** a square or cubic yard, especially of sand or other building materials. **3** a long pole-like piece of wood slung across a ship's mast for a sail to hang from.
– ORIGIN Old English.

yard[2] • n. **1** esp. Brit. a piece of enclosed ground next to a building. **2** an area of land used for a particular purpose or business: *a builder's yard*. **3** N. Amer. the garden of a house.
– ORIGIN Old English, 'home, region'.

yardage • n. a distance or length measured in yards.

yardarm • n. either end of a ship's yard supporting a sail.

Yardie • n. informal **1** (among Jamaicans) a fellow Jamaican. **2** (in the UK) a member of a Jamaican or West Indian gang of criminals.
– ORIGIN Jamaican English *yard* 'house, home'.

yardstick • n. **1** a measuring rod a yard long. **2** a standard used for comparison.

yarmulke /**yar**-muul-kuh/ (also **yarmulka**) • n. a skullcap worn in public by Orthodox Jewish men or during prayer by other Jewish men.
– ORIGIN Yiddish.

yarn • n. **1** spun thread used for knitting, weaving, or sewing. **2** informal a long or rambling story.
– ORIGIN Old English.

yarrow • n. a plant with feathery leaves and heads of small white or pale pink flowers, used in herbal medicine.
– ORIGIN Old English.

yashmak /**yash**-mak/ • n. a veil concealing all of the face except the eyes, worn by some Muslim women in public.
– ORIGIN Turkish.

yaw • v. (of a moving ship or aircraft) turn to one side or from side to side. • n. yawing movement of a ship or aircraft.
– ORIGIN unknown.

yawl • n. a kind of sailing boat with two masts.
– ORIGIN German *jolle* or Dutch *jol*.

yawn • v. **1** open one's mouth wide and breathe in deeply due to tiredness or boredom. **2** (**yawning**) wide open: *a yawning chasm*. • n. **1** an act of yawning. **2** informal a boring event.
– ORIGIN Old English.

yawp • n. a harsh or hoarse cry or yelp. • v. shout or exclaim hoarsely.

yaws • n. a contagious tropical disease caused by a bacterium that enters cuts on the skin and causes small lesions which may develop into deep ulcers.
– ORIGIN prob. from Carib.

Y chromosome • n. Genetics (in humans and other mammals) a sex chromosome which is normally present only in male cells, which are designated XY. Compare with **X CHROMOSOME**.

yd • abbrev. yard (measure).

ye[1] • pron. (second person pl.) pl. of **THOU**[1].
– ORIGIN Old English.

ye[2] • det. archaic = **THE**.
– ORIGIN from a misunderstanding of the Old English letter þ (now written *th*), which could be written as y, so that *the* could be written *ye*.

yea • adv. archaic or formal yes.
– ORIGIN Old English.

Yeager E
/**yay**-ger/, Chuck (b.1923; full name *Charles Elwood Yeager*), American pilot. In 1947 he became the first person to break the sound barrier when he piloted the Bell X-1 rocket research aircraft to a speed of 670 mph.

yeah (also **yeh**) • exclam. & n. informal = **YES**.

year • n. **1** the time taken by the earth to make one revolution around the sun. **2** (also **calendar year**) the period of 365 days (or 366 days in leap years) starting from the first of January. **3** a period of the same length as this starting at a different point. **4** a similar period used for reckoning time according to other calendars. **5** (**one's years**) one's age or time of life. **6** (**years**) informal a very long time. **7** a set of students grouped together as being of roughly similar ages.
– PHRASES **year in, year out** continuously or repeatedly over a period of years.
– ORIGIN Old English.

yearbook • n. an annual publication giving current information about and listing events of the previous year.

yearling • n. an animal of a year old, or in its second year.

yearly • adj. & adv. happening or produced once a year or every year.

yearn /yern/ • v. have a strong feeling of loss and longing for something.
– ORIGIN Old English.

year-on-year • adj. (of figures, prices, etc.) as compared with the corresponding ones from a year earlier.

year-round • adj. happening or continuing throughout the year.

yeast • n. **1** a microscopic single-celled fungus capable of converting sugar into alcohol and carbon dioxide. **2** a greyish-yellow substance formed from this, used as a fermenting agent, to raise bread dough, and as a food supplement.
– DERIVATIVES **yeasty** adj.
– ORIGIN Old English.

Yeats E
/yayts/, W. B. (1865–1939; full name *William Butler Yeats*), Irish poet and dramatist, whose works stimulated Ireland's cultural and literary revival. His poetry includes 'Sailing to Byzantium' and 'Leda and the Swan'.

yell • n. a loud, sharp cry. • v. shout in a loud or piercing way.
– ORIGIN Old English.

yellow • adj. **1** of the colour of egg yolks or ripe lemons. **2** informal cowardly. • n. yellow colour. • v. become a yellow colour with age.
– DERIVATIVES **yellowish** adj.
– ORIGIN Old English.

yellow-belly • n. informal a coward.

yellow card • n. (in soccer) a yellow card shown by the referee to a player being cautioned.

yellow fever • n. a tropical disease caused by a virus transmitted by mosquitoes, causing fever and jaundice and often death.

yellowhammer • n. a common bunting, the male of which has a yellow head, neck, and breast.
– ORIGIN *-hammer* is perh. from Old English *amore* (a kind of bird).

Yellow Pages • pl. n. (trademark in the UK) a telephone directory printed on yellow paper and listing businesses and other organizations according to the goods or services they offer.

Yellow River E
the second-largest river in China, which rises in west central China and flows over 4,830 km (3,000 miles) before entering the Yellow Sea. Chinese name **Huang Ho**.

Yellow Sea E
an arm of the East China Sea, separating the Korean peninsula from the east coast of China. Chinese name **Huang Hai**.

Yellowstone National Park E
a national park in NW Wyoming and Montana. It contains many geysers and hot springs.

yelp • n. a short sharp cry. • v. make a yelp or yelps.
– ORIGIN Old English, 'to boast'.

Yeltsin E
/yelt-sin/, Boris (Nikolaevich) (b.1931), Russian statesman, President of the Russian Federation 1991–9. He faced opposition to his reforms and in 1993 survived an attempted coup; he resigned on 31 December 1999.

Yemen E
/ye-muhn/ a country in the south and southwest of Arabia; capital, Sana'a.
– DERIVATIVES **Yemeni** adj. & n.

yen[1] • n. (pl. **yen**) the basic unit of money of Japan.
– ORIGIN Japanese, 'round'.

yen[2] • n. informal a longing or yearning.
– ORIGIN Chinese.

Yenisei E
/yen-i-say/ a river in Siberia, which rises on the Mongolian border and flows generally northwards to the Arctic Ocean.

yeoman /yoh-muhn/ • n. hist. **1** a man owning a house and a small area of farming land. **2** a servant in a royal or noble household.
– ORIGIN prob. from YOUNG + MAN.

Yeoman of the Guard • n. a member of the British king or queen's bodyguard (now having only ceremonial duties).

yeomanry • n. hist. yeomen as a group.

Yeoman Warder • n. a warder at the Tower of London.

Yerevan E
/ye-ri-van/ the capital of Armenia.

yes • exclam. **1** used to give a response in favour of something. **2** used to reply to someone who is asking one something or attracting one's attention. **3** used to question a remark. **4** used to express delight. • n. (pl. **yeses** or **yesses**) an answer or vote in favour of something.
– ORIGIN Old English.

yes-man • n. informal a person who always agrees with their superiors.

yesterday • adv. on the day before today. • n. **1** the day before today. **2** the recent past.
– ORIGIN Old English.

yesteryear • n. literary last year or the recent past.

yet • adv. **1** up until now or then. **2** as soon as this: *wait, don't go yet.* **3** from now into the future for a specified length of time. **4** referring to something that will or may happen in the future. **5** still; even: *snow, snow, and yet more snow.* **6** in spite of that. • conj. but at the same time.
– ORIGIN Old English.

yeti /yet-i/ • n. a large hairy manlike creature said to live in the highest part of the Himalayas.
– ORIGIN Tibetan (the language of Tibet), 'little manlike animal'.

yew • n. a coniferous tree with poisonous red berry-like fruit and springy wood.
– ORIGIN Old English.

Y-fronts • pl. n. Brit. trademark men's or boys' underpants with a seam at the front in the shape of an upside-down Y.

YHA • abbrev. (in the UK) Youth Hostels Association.

Yid • n. informal, offens. a Jew.

Yiddish /yid-dish/ • n. a language used by

Jews from central and eastern Europe, originally a German dialect with words from Hebrew and several modern languages. ● **adj.** relating to this language.
– ORIGIN from Yiddish *yidish daytsh* 'Jewish German'.

yield ● **v. 1** produce or provide (a natural or industrial product). **2** produce (a result or gain). **3** give way to demands or pressure. **4** give up possession of. **5** (of a mass or structure) give way under force or pressure. ● **n.** an amount or result yielded.
– ORIGIN Old English, 'pay, repay'.

yin ● **n.** (in Chinese philosophy) the passive female principle of the universe. Contrasted with **YANG**.
– ORIGIN Chinese, 'feminine, moon'.

yippee ● **exclam.** expressing wild excitement or delight.

ylang-ylang /ee-lang-ee-lang/ ● **n.** a sweet-scented essential oil obtained from the flowers of a tropical tree, used in perfumery and aromatherapy.
– ORIGIN Tagalog (a language of the Philippines).

YMCA ● **abbrev.** Young Men's Christian Association.

Ynys Môn E
/uh-niss **mawn**/ Welsh name for **ANGLESEY**.

yob ● **n.** Brit. informal a rude and aggressive young man.
– DERIVATIVES **yobbery** n. **yobbish** adj.
– ORIGIN from **BOY** (spelt backwards).

yobbo ● **n.** (pl. **yobbos** or **yobboes**) Brit. informal a yob.

yodel /yoh-d'l/ ● **v.** (**yodels**, **yodelling**, **yodelled**; US **yodels**, **yodeling**, **yodeled**) practise a form of singing marked by rapid changes between the normal voice and falsetto. ● **n.** a song or call delivered in such a way.
– DERIVATIVES **yodeller** n.
– ORIGIN German *jodeln*.

yoga ● **n.** a Hindu spiritual discipline, a part of which, including simple meditation, breathing exercises, and specific body positions, is widely practised for health and relaxation.
– DERIVATIVES **yogic** adj.
– ORIGIN Sanskrit, 'union'.

yogi ● **n.** (pl. **yogis**) a person who is skilled in yoga.
– ORIGIN Sanskrit.

yogurt /yog-ert, yoh-gert/ (also **yoghurt** or **yoghourt**) ● **n.** a semi-solid slightly sour food prepared from milk with bacteria added.
– ORIGIN Turkish.

yoke ● **n. 1** a piece of wood fastened over the necks of two animals and attached to a plough or cart in order for them to pull it. **2** (pl. **yoke** or **yokes**) a pair of yoked animals. **3** a frame fitting over the neck and shoulders of a person, used for carrying pails or baskets. **4** something that restricts freedom or is a burden: *the yoke of imperialism.* **5** a part of a garment that fits over the shoulders and to which the main part of the garment is attached. ● **v.** (**yokes**, **yoking**, **yoked**) **1** join with a yoke. **2** bring (two people or things) into a close relationship: *we are yoked to the fates of others.*
– ORIGIN Old English.

yokel /yoh-k'l/ ● **n.** an unsophisticated country person.
– ORIGIN perh. from dialect *yokel* 'green woodpecker'.

Yokohama E
/yoh-koh-**hah**-muh/ a seaport on the island of Honshu, Japan. It is the country's second-largest city.

yolk /*rhymes with* poke/ ● **n.** the yellow inner part of a bird's egg, which is rich in protein and fat and nourishes the developing embryo.
– ORIGIN Old English.

Yom Kippur /yom kip-**poor**, yom **kip**-per/ ● **n.** the most solemn religious fast of the Jewish year, the last of the ten days of penitence that begin with Rosh Hashana (the Jewish New Year).
– ORIGIN Hebrew, 'day of atonement'.

yon literary or dialect ● **det. & adv.** yonder; that. ● **pron.** yonder person or thing.
– ORIGIN Old English.

yonder archaic or dialect ● **adv.** over there. ● **det.** that or those (referring to something situated at a distance).

yonks ● **pl. n.** Brit. informal a very long time.
– ORIGIN perh. from ***donkey's years*** (see **DONKEY**).

yore ● **n.** (in phr. **of yore**) literary of former times or long ago.
– ORIGIN Old English.

York E
a city in northern England, a unitary council formerly in Yorkshire.

York, House of E
the English royal house descended from Edmund of Langley (1341–1402), 1st Duke of York and 5th son of Edward III, that ruled England 1461–85, with a short break in 1470–1 (the restoration of Henry VI). With the white rose as its emblem it fought the Wars of the Roses with the House of Lancaster.

Yorkist ● **n.** a follower of the House of York in the Wars of the Roses. ● **adj.** relating to the House of York.

Yorks. ● **abbrev.** Yorkshire.

Yorkshire E
a former county of northern England. Since 1996 the northern part of the area has formed the county of North Yorkshire, while the rest of the Yorkshire area consists of unitary councils.

Yorkshire pudding ● **n.** a baked batter pudding typically eaten with roast beef.

Yorkshire terrier ● **n.** a small long-haired blue-grey and tan breed of terrier.

Yosemite National Park E
/yuh-**sem**-i-ti/ a national park in the Sierra Nevada range in central California. It includes Yosemite Falls, the highest waterfall in the US (739 m; 2,425 ft).

you ● **pron.** (second person sing. or pl.) **1** used to refer to the person or people that the speaker is addressing. **2** used to refer to the person being addressed together with other people of the same sort: *you Americans.* **3** used to refer to any person in general.
– ORIGIN Old English.

you'd • contr. **1** you had. **2** you would.

you'll • contr. you will; you shall.

Young[1], E
Brigham (1801–77), American Mormon leader. He succeeded Joseph Smith as the leader of the Mormons in 1844, and established their headquarters at Salt Lake City, Utah.

Young[2], E
Neil (Percival) (b.1945), Canadian singer, songwriter, and guitarist, known for such albums as *Harvest*.

Young[3], E
Thomas (1773–1829), English physicist, physician, and Egyptologist. His major work in physics concerned the wave theory of light and the elasticity of solids, and he investigated the optics of the eye.

young • adj. (**younger**, **youngest**) **1** having lived or existed for only a short time. **2** relating to or typical of young people. • pl. n. young children or animals; offspring.
– DERIVATIVES **youngish** adj.
– ORIGIN Old English.

young offender • n. Law (in the UK) a criminal between 14 and 17 years of age.

Young Pretender E
see **Stuart[1]**.

youngster • n. a child, young person, or young animal.

your • possess. det. **1** belonging to or associated with the person or people that the speaker is addressing. **2** belonging to or associated with any person in general. **3** (**Your**) used when addressing the holder of certain titles.
– ORIGIN Old English.

USAGE your
Do not confuse the possessive **your** meaning 'belonging to you' (as in *let me talk to your daughter*) with the form **you're**, which is short for **you are** (as in *you're a good cook*).

you're • contr. you are.

yours • possess. pron. used to refer to something belonging to or associated with the person or people that the speaker is addressing.

yourself • pron. (second person sing.) (pl. **yourselves**) **1** used as the object of a verb or preposition when this is the same as the subject of the clause and the subject is the person or people being addressed. **2** you personally.

youth • n. (pl. **youths**) **1** the period between childhood and adult age. **2** the qualities of energy, freshness, immaturity, etc. associated with being young. **3** young people. **4** a young man.
– ORIGIN Old English.

youth club (also **youth centre**) • n. a place or organization providing leisure activities for young people.

youthful • adj. **1** young or seeming young. **2** characteristic of young people.
– DERIVATIVES **youthfully** adv. **youthfulness** n.

youth hostel • n. a place providing cheap accommodation, aimed mainly at young people on holiday.

you've • contr. you have.

yowl /*rhymes with* fowl/ • n. a loud wailing cry of pain or distress. • v. make such a cry.

yo-yo • n. (pl. **yo-yos**) (trademark in the UK) a toy consisting of a pair of joined discs with a deep groove between them in which string is attached and wound, which can be spun down and up by its weight as the string unwinds and rewinds. • v. (**yo-yoes**, **yo-yoing**, **yo-yoed**) move up and down repeatedly.
– ORIGIN prob. from a language of the Philippines.

Ypres E
/ee-pruh/ a town in NW Belgium, near the border with France. Ypres was the scene of some of the bitterest fighting of the First World War.

Yr Wyddfa E
/ur wi*th*-va/ Welsh name for **Snowdon**.

YTS • abbrev. Youth Training Scheme.

ytterbium /it-ter-bi-uhm/ • n. a silvery-white metallic chemical element.
– ORIGIN from *Ytterby* in Sweden.

yttrium /it-tri-uhm/ • n. a greyish-white metallic chemical element.
– ORIGIN from *Ytterby* (see **ytterbium**).

yuan /yuu-ahn/ • n. (pl. **yuan**) the basic unit of money of China.
– ORIGIN Chinese, 'round'.

yucca /yuk-kuh/ • n. a plant with sword-like leaves, native to warm regions of the US and Mexico.
– ORIGIN Carib.

yuck (also **yuk**) • exclam. informal used to express strong distaste or disgust.
– DERIVATIVES **yucky** (also **yukky**) adj.

Yugoslavia E
/yoo-goh-**slah**-vi-uh/ a federation in SE Europe with two constituent republics, Serbia and Montenegro; federal capital, Belgrade.
– DERIVATIVES **Yugoslav** n. **Yugoslavian** adj. & n.

Yukon E
/yoo-kon/ a river of NW North America, which rises in Yukon Territory, NW Canada, and flows westwards through central Alaska to the Bering Sea.

Yukon Territory E
a territory of NW Canada, on the border with Alaska; capital, Whitehorse.

Yule (also **Yuletide**) • n. archaic Christmas.
– ORIGIN Old English or Old Norse.

yule log • n. **1** a large log traditionally burnt in the hearth on Christmas Eve. **2** a log-shaped chocolate cake eaten at Christmas.

yummy • adj. (**yummier**, **yummiest**) informal delicious.

yuppie (also **yuppy**) • n. (pl. **yuppies**) informal, derog. a well-paid young middle-class professional working in a city.
– ORIGIN from the acronym *young urban professional*.

YWCA • abbrev. Young Women's Christian Association.

Zz

Z /zed, US zee/ (also **z**) ● **n.** (pl. **Zs** or **Z's**) **1** the twenty-sixth letter of the alphabet. **2** (usu. ***z***) the third unknown quantity in an algebraic expression. **3** used in repeated form to represent buzzing or snoring.

zabaglione /za-ba-**lyoh**-ni/ ● **n.** an Italian dessert made of whipped egg yolks, sugar, and wine.
– ORIGIN Italian.

Zagreb E
/**zah**-greb/ the capital of Croatia.

Zaire E
/zy-**eer**/ (also **Zaïre**) a country in central Africa, with a short coastline on the Atlantic Ocean; capital, Kinshasa. Official name (from 1997) **DEMOCRATIC REPUBLIC OF CONGO**.
– DERIVATIVES **Zairean** /zy-eer-i-uhn/ (also **Zairian**) adj. & n.

Zaire River E
= **CONGO**[1].

Zakinthos E
/zak-in-thoss/ (also **Zakynthos**) one of the Ionian Islands, off the SW coast of mainland Greece. Also called **ZANTE**.

Zambezi E
/zam-**bee**-zi/ a river of East Africa, which rises in NW Zambia and flows for 2,560 km (1,600 miles) through Angola and Zambia to the Victoria Falls, turning eastwards to form the border between Zambia and Zimbabwe, before crossing Mozambique and entering the Indian Ocean.

Zambia E
/**zam**-bi-uh/ a country in central Africa; capital, Lusaka. Former name (until 1964) **NORTHERN RHODESIA**.
– DERIVATIVES **Zambian** adj. & n.

Zante E
/zan-ti/ = **ZAKINTHOS**.

zany ● **adj.** (**zanier**, **zaniest**) amusingly unconventional and individual.
– DERIVATIVES **zanily** adv. **zaniness** n.
– ORIGIN Italian *zani* or *zanni*, a form of *Gianni*, *Giovanni* 'John', name of a clown in traditional Italian comedy.

Zanzibar E
/zan-zi-**bar**/ an island off the coast of East Africa, part of Tanzania.
– DERIVATIVES **Zanzibari** adj. & n.

zap informal ● **v.** (**zaps**, **zapping**, **zapped**) **1** destroy. **2** move or propel suddenly and rapidly. **3** use a remote control to change television channels, operate a video recorder, etc. ● **n.** a sudden burst of energy or sound.

Zapata E
/zuh-**pah**-tuh/, Emiliano (1879–1919), Mexican revolutionary. Following the failure of successive regimes to redistribute land to the peasants, he joined with Pancho Villa and others to overthrow General Huerta (1914) and later fought against the regime of Venustiano Carranza.

Zappa E
/zap-puh/, Frank (1940–93), American rock singer, musician, and songwriter.

Zatopek E
/zat-uh-pek/, Emil (1922–2000), Czech long-distance runner. In the 1952 Olympic Games he won gold medals in the 5,000 metres, 10,000 metres, and marathon.

zeal /zeel/ ● **n.** great energy or enthusiasm for a cause or aim.
– ORIGIN Greek *zēlos*.

Zealand E
/zee-luhnd/ the chief island of Denmark, between the Jutland peninsula and the southern tip of Sweden.

zealot /zel-uht/ ● **n.** an excessively enthusiastic and strict follower of a religion or policy.
– DERIVATIVES **zealotry** n.

zealous /zel-uhss/ ● **adj.** having or showing zeal.
– DERIVATIVES **zealously** adv. **zealousness** n.

zebra /zeb-ruh, zee-bruh/ ● **n.** an African wild horse with black-and-white stripes and an erect mane.
– ORIGIN Italian, Spanish, or Portuguese, first meaning 'wild ass'.

zebra crossing ● **n.** Brit. a pedestrian street crossing marked with broad white stripes.

zebu /zee-boo/ ● **n.** a breed of domesticated ox with a humped back.
– ORIGIN French.

Zeebrugge E
/zay-bruug-guh/ a seaport on the coast of Belgium.

Zeffirelli E
/zef-fuh-**rel**-li/, Franco (b.1923; born *Gianfranco Corsi*), Italian film and theatre director. He directed the film *Romeo and Juliet* and is also known for his film versions of operas such as *La Traviata*.

zeitgeist /zyt-gysst/ ● **n.** the characteristic spirit or mood of a particular period of history.
– ORIGIN German.

Zen ● **n.** a type of Buddhism emphasizing the value of meditation and intuition.
– ORIGIN Japanese, 'meditation'.

zenith /zen-ith/ ● **n. 1** the point in the sky directly overhead. **2** the highest point in the sky

reached by the sun or moon. **3** the time at which something is most powerful or successful.
– ORIGIN Arabic, 'path over the head'.

Zeno E
/zee-noh/ (*c.*335–*c.*263 BC); known as **Zeno of Citium**, Greek philosopher. He founded the school of Stoic philosophy, teaching that virtue, the highest good, is based on knowledge, and that the vicissitudes of life are irrelevant to happiness.

zephyr /zef-fer/ ● **n.** literary a soft gentle breeze.
– ORIGIN Greek *zephuros* 'god of the west wind, west wind'.

Zeppelin /zep-puh-lin/ ● **n.** hist. a large German airship of the early 20th century.
– ORIGIN named after Ferdinand, Count von *Zeppelin*, German airship pioneer (1838–1917).

Zermatt E
/zer-mat/ an Alpine ski resort and mountaineering centre in southern Switzerland.

zero /*rhymes with* hero/ ● **cardinal number** (pl. **zeros**) **1** the figure 0; nought. **2** a temperature of 0°C (32°F), marking the freezing point of water. ● **v.** (**zeroes**, **zeroing**, **zeroed**) **1** adjust (an instrument) to zero. **2** set the sights of (a gun) for firing. **3** (**zero in on**) take aim at or focus attention on.
– ORIGIN Arabic, 'cipher'.

zero hour ● **n.** the time at which a military or other operation is set to begin.

zero tolerance ● **n.** strict enforcement of the law regarding any form of antisocial behaviour.

zest ● **n. 1** great enthusiasm and energy. **2** the quality of being exciting or interesting. **3** the outer coloured part of the peel of citrus fruit, used as flavouring.
– DERIVATIVES **zestful** adj. **zesty** adj.
– ORIGIN French *zeste*.

zester ● **n.** a kitchen utensil for scraping or peeling zest from citrus fruit.

zeugma /zyoog-muh/ ● **n.** a figure of speech in which a word applies to two others in different senses (e.g. *John and his driving licence expired last week*).
– ORIGIN Greek.

Zeus E
/zyooss/ the supreme Greek god and protector and ruler of humankind. Roman equivalent **JUPITER**[1].

Zhou Enlai E
/joh en-**ly**/ (also **Chou En-lai**) (1898–1976), Chinese Communist statesman, Prime Minister of China 1949–76. He was a founder of the Chinese Communist Party and supported Mao Zedong's rise to power. As Premier, he was a moderating influence during the Cultural Revolution.

Zhukov E
/*zh*oo-koff/, Georgi (Konstantinovich) (1896–1974), Soviet military leader. During the Second World War he defeated the Germans at Stalingrad (1943) and Leningrad (1944), and led the final assault on Germany and the capture of Berlin (1945).

Zia ul-Haq E
/zee-uh uul-**hak**/, Muhammad (1924–88), Pakistani general and statesman, President 1978–88. He led the coup which deposed President Zulfikar Bhutto in 1977. As President he maintained strict political control.

Ziegfeld E
/zeeg-feld/, Florenz (1869–1932), American theatre manager. He is best known for his spectacular revues, the *Ziegfeld Follies*, based on those of the Folies-Bergère in Paris.

zigzag ● **n.** a line or course having sharp alternate right and left turns. ● **adj. & adv.** veering to right and left alternately. ● **v.** (**zigzags**, **zigzagging**, **zigzagged**) take a zigzag course.
– ORIGIN German *Zickzack*.

zilch /zilch/ ● **pron.** informal, esp. N. Amer. nothing.
– ORIGIN perh. from a Mr *Zilch*, a character in a magazine.

zillion ● **cardinal number** informal an extremely large number of people or things.
– DERIVATIVES **zillionth** ordinal number.
– ORIGIN from *Z* + **MILLION**.

Zimbabwe E
/zim-**bahb**-wi, zim-**bahb**-way/ a country in SE Africa; capital, Harare. Former names **SOUTHERN RHODESIA** (until 1964), **RHODESIA** (1964–79).
– DERIVATIVES **Zimbabwean** /zim-**bahb**-wi-uhn, zim-**bahb**-way-uhn/ adj. & n.

Zimmer /zim-mer/ (also **Zimmer frame**) ● **n.** trademark a kind of walking frame.
– ORIGIN from *Zimmer* Orthopaedic Limited, the name of the manufacturer.

zinc /zingk/ ● **n.** a silvery-white metallic chemical element which is used in making brass and for coating iron and steel as a protection against corrosion.
– ORIGIN German *Zink*.

zing informal ● **n.** energy or excitement. ● **v.** move swiftly.
– DERIVATIVES **zingy** adj.

Zinnemann E
/**zin**-nuh-muhn/, Fred (1907–97), Austrian-born American film director. His films include *From Here to Eternity* and *A Man For All Seasons*.

zinnia /zin-ni-uh/ ● **n.** a plant of the daisy family with bright showy flowers.
– ORIGIN named after the German physician and botanist Johann G. *Zinn* (1727–59).

Zion /zy-uhn/ (also **Sion** /sy-uhn/) ● **n. 1** the hill of Jerusalem on which the city of David was built. **2** the Jewish people or religion. **3** (in Christian thought) the heavenly city or kingdom of heaven.
– ORIGIN Hebrew.

Zionism /zy-uh-ni-z'm/ ● **n.** a movement for the development and protection of a Jewish nation in Israel.
– DERIVATIVES **Zionist** n. & adj.

zip ● **n. 1** esp. Brit. a fastener consisting of two flexible strips of metal or plastic with interlocking projections that are closed or opened by pulling a slide along them. **2** informal energy; liveliness. ● **v.** (**zips**, **zipping**, **zipped**) **1** fasten with a zip. **2** informal move at high speed. **3** Computing compress (a file) so that it takes up less space.

zip code (also **ZIP code**) • n. US a postcode.
– ORIGIN acronym from *zone improvement plan*.

zipper esp. N. Amer. • n. a zip fastener. • v. (**zippers**, **zippering**, **zippered**) fasten with a zipper.

zippy • adj. (**zippier**, **zippiest**) informal **1** bright, fresh, or lively. **2** speedy.

zip-up • adj. esp. Brit. fastened with a zip.

zircon /zer-kuhn/ • n. a mineral that is brown or semi-transparent, used as a gem and in industry.
– ORIGIN German *Zirkon*.

zirconium /zer-**koh**-ni-uhm/ • n. a hard silver-grey metallic chemical element.

zit • n. informal, esp. N. Amer. a spot on the skin.
– ORIGIN unknown.

zither /zi-*th*er/ • n. a musical instrument with numerous strings stretched across a flat box, placed horizontally and played with the fingers and a plectrum.
– ORIGIN German.

zodiac /zoh-di-ak/ • n. an area of the sky in which the sun, moon, and planets appear to lie, divided by astrologers into twelve equal divisions or signs.
– DERIVATIVES **zodiacal** /zuh-**dy**-uh-k'l/ adj.
– ORIGIN Greek *zōidiakos*.

Zola E
/**zoh**-luh/, Émile (Édouard Charles Antoine) (1840–1902), French novelist and critic. A founder of literary naturalism, he is known for his series of twenty novels collectively entitled *Les Rougon-Macquart*.

zombie • n. **1** a corpse supposedly brought back to life by witchcraft. **2** informal a lifeless or completely unresponsive person.
– ORIGIN West African.

zone • n. **1** an area that has particular characteristics or a particular use. **2** (also **time zone**) an area where a common standard time is used. • v. (**zones**, **zoning**, **zoned**) divide into zones.
– DERIVATIVES **zonal** adj.
– ORIGIN Greek, 'girdle'.

zonk • v. informal **1** (**zonk out**) fall suddenly and heavily asleep. **2** (**zonked**) under the influence of drugs or alcohol.

zoo • n. **1** an establishment which keeps wild animals for study, conservation, or display to the public. **2** informal a confused or chaotic situation.
– ORIGIN short for *zoological garden*.

zookeeper • n. a person employed to look after the animals in a zoo.

zoology /zoo-**ol**-uh-ji, zoh-**ol**-uh-ji/ • n. **1** the scientific study of animals. **2** the animal life of a particular area or time.
– DERIVATIVES **zoological** adj. **zoologist** n.
– ORIGIN Greek *zōion* 'animal'.

zoom • v. **1** move or travel very quickly. **2** (of a camera) change smoothly from a long shot to a close-up or vice versa.

zoom lens • n. a lens allowing a camera to zoom by varying the distance between the centre of the lens and its focus.

Zoroastrianism /zo-roh-**ass**-tri-uh-ni-z'm/ • n. a religion of ancient Persia based on the worship of a single god, founded by the prophet Zoroaster (also called Zarathustra) in the 6th century BC.
– DERIVATIVES **Zoroastrian** adj. & n.

zucchini /zuu-**kee**-ni/ • n. (pl. **zucchini** or **zucchinis**) N. Amer. a courgette.
– ORIGIN Italian, 'little gourds'.

Zulu /**zoo**-loo/ • n. **1** a member of a South African people. **2** the language of this people.

Zurbarán E
/zoor-buh-**rahn**/, Francisco de (1598–1664), Spanish painter, known for his paintings of religious subjects.

Zurich E
/**zyoo**-rik/ a city in north central Switzerland, the country's largest city.

Zwingli E
/**tsving**-li/, Ulrich (1484–1531), Swiss Protestant reformer, the chief figure of the Swiss Reformation. His ideas gained strong support in Zurich but met with fierce resistance elsewhere; Zwingli was killed in the resulting civil war.

zygote /**zy**-goht/ • n. Biol. a cell resulting from the joining of two gametes.
– ORIGIN Greek *zugōtos* 'yoked'.

Appendix 1: **Countries of the World**

Country	Adjective/noun	Capital *see entry	Currency unit	Abbreviation (Olympics)
Afghanistan	Afghan	Kabul	afghani = 100 puls	AFG
Albania	Albanian	Tirana	lek = 100 qindarka	ALB
Algeria	Algerian	Algiers	dinar = 100 centimes	ALG
America (*see* United States of America)				
Andorra	Andorran	Andorra la Vella	euro = 100 cents	AND
Angola	Angolan	Luanda	kwanza = 100 lwei	ANG
Antigua and Barbuda	Antiguan, Barbudan	St John's	dollar = 100 cents	ANT
Argentina	Argentinian	Buenos Aires	peso = 100 centavos	ARG
Armenia	Armenian	Yerevan	dram = 100 luma	ARM
Australia	Australian	Canberra	dollar = 100 cents	AUS
Austria	Austrian	Vienna	euro = 100 cents	AUT
Azerbaijan	Azerbaijani	Baku	manat = 100 gopik	AZE
Bahamas	Bahamian	Nassau	dollar = 100 cents	BAH
Bahrain	Bahraini	Manama	dinar = 1,000 fils	BRN
Bangladesh	Bangladeshi	Dhaka	taka = 100 poisha	BAN
Barbados	Barbadian	Bridgetown	dollar = 100 cents	BAR
Belarus	Belarusian *or* Belarussian	Minsk	Belarusian rouble	BLR
Belgium	Belgian	Brussels	euro = 100 cents	BEL
Belize	Belizian	Belmopan	dollar = 100 cents	BIZ
Benin	Beninese	Porto Novo	African franc	BEN
Bhutan	Bhutanese	Thimphu	ngultrum = 100 chetrum, Indian rupee	BHU
Bolivia	Bolivian	La Paz	boliviano = 100 centavos	BOL
Bosnia-Herzegovina	Bosnian	Sarajevo	dinar = 100 paras	BIH
Botswana	Botswanan/Tswana	Gaborone	pula = 100 thebe	BOT
Brazil	Brazilian	Brasilia	real = 100 centavos	BRA
Brunei	Bruneian	Bandar Seri Begawan	dollar = 100 sen	BRU
Bulgaria	Bulgarian	Sofia	lev = 100 stotinki	BUL
Burkina Faso	Burkinese	Ouagadougou	African franc	BUR
Burma (officially called Myanmar)	Burmese	Rangoon	kyat = 100 pyas	MYA
Burundi	Burundian	Bujumbura	franc = 100 centimes	BDI
Cambodia	Cambodian	Phnom Penh	riel = 100 sen	CAM
Cameroon	Cameroonian	Yaoundé	African franc	CMR
Canada	Canadian	Ottawa	dollar = 100 cents	CAN
Cape Verde Islands	Cape Verdean	Praia	escudo = 100 centavos	CPV
Central African Republic	–	Bangui	African franc	CAF
Chad	Chadian	N'Djamena	African franc	CHA
Chile	Chilean	Santiago	peso = 100 centavos	CHI
China	Chinese	Beijing	yuan = 10 jiao *or* 100 fen	CHN
Colombia	Colombian	Bogotá	peso = 100 centavos	COL

Country	Adjective/noun	Capital *see entry	Currency unit	Abbreviation (Olympics)
Comoros	Comoran	Moroni	African franc	COM
Congo	Congolese	Brazzaville	African franc	CGO
Congo, Democratic Republic of (Zaire)	Congolese	Kinshasa	Congolese franc	COD
Costa Rica	Costa Rican	San José	colón = 100 centimos	CRC
Croatia	Croat *or* Croatian	Zagreb	kuna = 100 lipa	CRO
Cuba	Cuban	Havana	peso = 100 centavos	CUB
Cyprus	Cypriot	Nicosia	pound = 100 cents	CYP
Czech Republic	Czech	Prague	koruna = 100 haleru	CZE
Denmark	Danish/Dane	Copenhagen	krone = 100 øre	DEN
Djibouti	Djiboutian	Djibouti	franc = 100 centimes	DJI
Dominica	Dominican	Roseau	dollar = 100 cents	DMA
Dominican Republic	Dominican	Santo Domingo	peso = 100 centavos	DOM
Ecuador	Ecuadorean	Quito	sucre = 100 centavos	ECU
Egypt	Egyptian	Cairo	pound = 100 piastres *or* 1,000 milliemes	EGY
El Salvador	Salvadorean	San Salvador	colón = 100 centavos	ESA
Equatorial Guinea	Equatorial Guinean	Malabo	African franc	GEQ
Eritrea	Eritrean	Asmara	nakfa = 100 cents	ERI
Estonia	Estonian	Tallinn	kroon = 100 sents	EST
Ethiopia	Ethiopian	Addis Ababa	birr = 100 cents	ETH
Fiji	Fijian	Suva	dollar = 100 cents	FIJ
Finland	Finn	Helsinki	euro = 100 cents	FIN
France	French	Paris	euro = 100 cents	FRA
Gabon	Gabonese	Libreville	African franc	GAB
Gambia, the	Gambian	Banjul	dalasi = 100 butut	GAM
Georgia	Georgian	Tbilisi	lari = 100 tetri	GEO
Germany	German	Berlin*	euro = 100 cents	GER
Ghana	Ghanaian	Accra	cedi = 100 pesewas	GHA
Greece	Greek	Athens	euro = 100 cents	GRE
Grenada	Grenadian	St George's	dollar = 100 cents	GRN
Guatemala	Guatemalan	Guatemala City	quetzal = 100 centavos	GUA
Guinea	Guinean	Conakry	franc = 100 centimes	GUI
Guinea-Bissau	–	Bissau	peso = 100 centavos	GBS
Guyana	Guyanese	Georgetown	dollar = 100 cents	GUY
Haiti	Haitian	Port-au-Prince	gourde = 100 centimes	HAI
Holland (*see* Netherlands)				
Honduras	Honduran	Tegucigalpa	lempira = 100 centavos	HON
Hungary	Hungarian	Budapest	forint = 100 filler	HUN
Iceland	Icelandic/Icelander	Reykjavik	krona = 100 aurar	ISL
India	Indian	New Delhi	rupee = 100 paisa	IND
Indonesia	Indonesian	Djakarta	rupiah = 100 sen	INA
Iran	Iranian	Tehran	rial = 100 dinars	IRI
Iraq	Iraqi	Baghdad	dinar = 1,000 fils	IRQ
Ireland, Republic of	Irish	Dublin	euro = 100 cents	IRL
Israel	Israeli	Jerusalem	shekel = 100 agora	ISR
Italy	Italian	Rome	euro = 100 cents	ITA
Ivory Coast	Ivorian	Yamoussoukro	African franc	CIV

Country	Adjective/noun	Capital *see entry	Currency unit	Abbreviation (Olympics)
Jamaica	Jamaican	Kingston	dollar = 100 cents	JAM
Japan	Japanese	Tokyo	yen = 100 sen	JPN
Jordan	Jordanian	Amman	dinar = 1,000 fils	JOR
Kazakhstan	Kazakh	Astana	tenge = 100 teins	KAZ
Kenya	Kenyan	Nairobi	shilling = 100 cents	KEN
Kiribati	–	Bairiki	dollar = 100 cents	
Kuwait	Kuwaiti	Kuwait City	dinar = 1,000 fils	KUW
Kyrgyzstan	Kyrgyz	Bishkek	som = 100 tiyin	KGZ
Laos	Laotian	Vientiane	kip = 100 ats	LAO
Latvia	Latvian	Riga	lat = 100 santims	LAT
Lebanon	Lebanese	Beirut	pound = 100 piastres	LIB
Lesotho	Lesothan/Mosotho, *pl.* Basotho	Maseru	loti = 100 lisente	LES
Liberia	Liberian	Monrovia	dollar = 100 cents	LBR
Libya	Libyan	Tripoli	dinar = 1,000 dirhams	LBA
Liechtenstein	–/Liechtensteiner	Vaduz	franc = 100 centimes	LIE
Lithuania	Lithuanian	Vilnius	litas = 100 centas	LTU
Luxembourg	–/Luxembourger	Luxembourg	euro = 100 cents	LUX
Macedonia	Macedonian	Skopje	denar = 100 deni	MKD
Madagascar	Malagasay *or* Madagascan	Antananarivo	franc malgache = 100 centimes	MAD
Malawi	Malawian	Lilongwe	kwacha = 100 tambala	MAW
Malaysia	Malaysian	Kuala Lumpur	dollar (ringgit) = 100 sen	MAS
Maldives	Maldivian	Male	rufiyaa = 100 laris	MDV
Mali	Malian	Bamako	African franc	MLI
Malta	Maltese	Valletta	lira = 100 cents	MLT
Marshall Islands	Marshallese	Majuro	US dollar	
Mauritania	Mauritanian	Nouakchott	ouguiya = 5 khoums	MTN
Mauritius	Mauritian	Port Louis	rupee = 100 cents	MRI
Mexico	Mexican	Mexico City	peso = 100 centavos	MEX
Micronesia, Federated States of	Micronesian	Kolonia	US dollar	FSM
Moldova	Moldovan	Chişinău	leu = 100 bani	MDA
Monaco	Monégasque *or* Monacan	–	euro = 100 cents	MON
Mongolia	Mongolian	Ulan Bator	tugrik = 100 mongos	MGL
Montenegro (*see* Yugoslavia)				
Morocco	Moroccan	Rabat	dirham = 100 centimes	MAR
Mozambique	Mozambican	Maputo	mètical = 100 centavos	MOZ
Myanmar (*see* Burma)				
Namibia	Namibian	Windhoek	rand = 100 cents	NAM
Nauru	Nauruan	–	Australian dollar	NRU
Nepal	Nepalese	Kathmandu	rupee = 100 paisa	NEP
Netherlands, the	Dutch	Amsterdam*	euro = 100 cents	NED
New Zealand	–/New Zealander	Wellington	dollar = 100 cents	NZL
Nicaragua	Nicaraguan	Managua	cordoba = 100 centavos	NCA
Niger	Nigerien	Niamey	African franc	NIG
Nigeria	Nigerian	Abuja	naira = 100 kobo	NGR
North Korea	North Korean	Pyongyang	won = 100 jun	PRK
Norway	Norwegian	Oslo	krone = 100 øre	NOR

Country	Adjective/noun	Capital *see entry	Currency unit	Abbreviation (Olympics)
Oman	Omani	Muscat	rial = 1,000 baiza	OMA
Pakistan	Pakistani	Islamabad	rupee = 100 paisa	PAK
Panama	Panamanian	Panama City	balboa = 100 centésimos	PAN
Papua New Guinea	Papua New Guinean *or* Guinean	Port Moresby	kina = 100 toea	PNG
Paraguay	Paraguayan	Asunción	guarani = 100 centimos	PAR
Peru	Peruvian	Lima	nuevo sol = 100 cents	PER
Philippines	Filipino *or* Philippine	Manila	peso = 100 centavos	PHI
Poland	Polish/Pole	Warsaw	zloty = 100 groszy	POL
Portugal	Portuguese	Lisbon	euro = 100 cents	POR
Qatar	Qatari	Doha	riyal = 100 dirhams	QAT
Romania	Romanian	Bucharest	leu = 100 bani	ROM
Russia	Russian	Moscow	rouble = 100 copecks	RUS
Rwanda	Rwandan	Kigali	franc = 100 centimes	RWA
St Kitts and Nevis	–	Basseterre	dollar = 100 cents	SKN
St Lucia	St Lucian	Castries	dollar = 100 cents	LCA
St Vincent and the Grenadines	Vincentian, Grenadian	Kingstown	dollar = 100 cents	VIN
Samoa	Samoan	Apia	tala = 100 sene	SAM
San Marino	–	San Marino	euro = 100 cents	SMR
São Tomé and Príncipe	–	São Tomé	dobra = 100 centavos	STP
Saudi Arabia	Saudi Arabian *or* Saudi	Riyadh	riyal = 20 qursh *or* 100 halalas	KSA
Senegal	Senegalese	Dakar	African franc	SEN
Serbia (*see* Yugoslavia)				
Seychelles, the	Seychellois	Victoria	rupee = 100 cents	SEY
Sierra Leone	Sierra Leonean	Freetown	leone = 100 cents	SLE
Singapore	Singaporean	Singapore	dollar = 100 cents	SIN
Slovakia	Slovak	Bratislava	koruna = 100 haleru	SVK
Slovenia	Slovene *or* Slovenian	Ljubljana	tolar = 100 stotins	SLO
Solomon Islands	–/Solomon Islander	Honiara	dollar = 100 cents	SOL
Somalia	Somali	Mogadishu	shilling = 100 cents	SOM
South Africa	South African	Pretoria*	rand = 100 cents	RSA
South Korea	South Korean	Seoul	won = 100 jeon	KOR
Spain	Spanish/Spaniard	Madrid	euro = 100 cents	ESP
Sri Lanka	Sri Lankan	Colombo	rupee = 100 cents	SRI
Sudan	Sudanese	Khartoum	dinar = 10 pounds	SUD
Suriname	Surinamese	Paramaribo	guilder = 100 cents	SUR
Swaziland	Swazi	Mbabane	lilangeni = 100 cents	SWZ
Sweden	Swedish/Swede	Stockholm	krona = 100 öre	SWE
Switzerland	Swiss	Berne	franc = 100 centimes	SUI
Syria	Syrian	Damascus	pound = 100 piastres	SYR
Taiwan	Taiwanese	Taipei	New Taiwan dollar = 100 cents	TPE
Tajikistan	Tajik *or* Tadjik	Dushanbe	somoni = 100 dirams	TJK
Tanzania	Tanzanian	Dodoma	shilling = 100 cents	TAN
Thailand	Thai	Bangkok	baht = 100 satangs	THA
Togo	Togolese	Lomé	African franc	TOG
Tonga	Tongan	Nuku'alofa	pa'anga = 100 seniti	TGA
Trinidad and Tobago	Trinidadian, Tobagonian	Port-of-Spain	dollar = 100 cents	TRI
Tunisia	Tunisian	Tunis	dinar = 1,000 milliemes	TUN

Country	Adjective/noun	Capital *see entry	Currency unit	Abbreviation (Olympics)
Turkey	Turkish/Turk	Ankara	lira = 100 kurus	TUR
Turkmenistan	Turkmen *or* Turkoman	Ashgabat	manat = 100 tenge	TKM
Tuvalu	Tuvaluan	Funafuti	dollar = 100 cents	
Uganda	Ugandan	Kampala	shilling = 100 cents	UGA
Ukraine	Ukrainian	Kiev	hryvna = 100 kopiykas	UKR
United Arab Emirates	–	Abu Dhabi	dirham = 100 fils	UAE
United Kingdom	British/Briton	London	pound = 100 pence	GBR
United States of America	American	Washington, DC	dollar = 100 cents	USA
Uruguay	Uruguayan	Montevideo	peso = 100 centésimos	URU
Uzbekistan	Uzbek	Tashkent	som	UZB
Vanuatu	Vanuatuan	Vila	vatu = 100 centimes	VAN
Vatican City	–	–	euro = 100 cents	
Venezuela	Venezuelan	Caracas	bolivar = 100 centimos	VEN
Vietnam	Vietnamese	Hanoi	dong= 10 hao *or* 100 xu	VIE
Yemen	Yemeni	Sana'a	riyal = 100 fils	YEM
Yugoslavia (Montenegro, Serbia)	Yugoslav (Montenegrin, Serbian)	Belgrade	dinar = 100 paras	YUG
Zaire (*see* Congo, Democratic Republic of)				
Zambia	Zambian	Lusaka	kwacha = 100 ngwee	ZAM
Zimbabwe	Zimbabwean	Harare	dollar = 100 cents	ZIM

Principal dependencies

Country	Adjective/noun	Capital	Currency unit	Abbreviation
American Samoa (US)	American Samoan	Fagatogo	US dollar	ASA
Anguilla (UK)	Anguillan	The Valley	East Caribbean dollar	–
Aruba (Netherlands)	Aruban	Oranjestad	florin	ARU
Bermuda (UK)	Bermudan *or* Bermudian	Hamilton	dollar	BER
Cayman Islands (UK)	–	George Town	dollar	CAY
Christmas Island (Australia)	–	–	Australian dollar	–
Cocos Islands (Australia)	–	–	Australian dollar	
Cook Islands (NZ)	–	Avarua	NZ dollar	COK
Faeroe Islands (Denmark)	Faeroese *or* Faroese	Tórshavn	Danish krone	–
Falkland Islands (UK)	–/Falkland Islander	Stanley	pound	–
French Guiana (France)	–	Cayenne	euro = 100 cents	–
French Polynesia (France)	–	Papeete	Pacific franc	–
Gibraltar (UK)	Gibraltarian	Gibraltar	pound	–
Greenland (Denmark)	– /Greenlander	Nuuk	Danish krone	–
Guadeloupe (France)	Guadeloupian	Basse-Terre	euro = 100 cents	–
Guam (US)	Guamanian	Agaña	US dollar	GUM
Martinique (France)	French	Fort-de-France	euro = 100 cents	–
Mayotte (France)	–	Mamoutzu	euro = 100 cents	–
Montserrat (UK)	–	Plymouth	East Caribbean dollar	–
Netherlands Antilles (Netherlands)	–	Willemstad	guilder	AHO
New Caledonia (France)	New Caledonian	Nouméa	euro = 100 cents	–
Niue (NZ)	–	Alofi	NZ dollar	–
Norfolk Island (Australia)	–	–	Australian dollar	–
Northern Marianas (US)	–	Chalan Kanoa	US dollar	–
Palau (US)	–	Koror	US dollar	PLW
Pitcairn Islands (UK)	–/Pitcairn Islander	–	NZ dollar	–
Puerto Rico (US)	Puerto Rican	San Juan	US dollar	PUR
Réunion (France)	–	Saint-Denis	euro = 100 cents	–
St Helena and dependencies (UK)	–	Jamestown	pound	–
St Pierre and Miquelon (France)	–	St Pierre	euro = 100 cents	–
Svalbard (Norway)	–	Longyearbyen	Norwegian krone	–
Turks and Caicos Islands (UK)	–	Cockburn Town	US dollar	–
Virgin Islands (US)	–/Virgin Islander	Charlotte Amalie	US dollar	ISV
Virgin Islands, British (UK)	–/Virgin Islander	Road Town	US dollar	IVB
Wallis and Futuna Islands (France)	–	Mata-Utu	euro = 100 cents	–
Western Sahara (Morocco)	–	La'youn	Moroccan dirham	–

Appendix 2

The Commonwealth

Antigua and Barbuda
Australia
Bahamas
Bangladesh
Barbados
Belize
Botswana
Brunei
Cameroon
Canada
Cyprus
Dominica
Fiji
Gambia, the
Ghana
Grenada
Guyana
India
Jamaica
Kenya
Kiribati
Lesotho
Malawi
Malaysia
Maldives
Malta
Mauritius
Mozambique
Namibia
Nauru
New Zealand
Nigeria
Pakistan (suspended)
Papua New Guinea
St Kitts and Nevis
St Lucia
St Vincent and the Grenadines
Samoa
Seychelles, the
Sierra Leone (suspended)
Singapore
Solomon Islands
South Africa
Sri Lanka
Swaziland
Tanzania
Tonga
Trinidad and Tobago
Tuvalu
Uganda
United Kingdom
Vanuatu
Zambia
Zimbabwe

Provinces and territories of Canada (with postal abbreviations)

Province

Alberta (AB)
British Columbia (BC)
Manitoba (MB)
New Brunswick (NB)
Newfoundland and Labrador (NF)
Nova Scotia (NS)
Ontario (ON)
Prince Edward Island (PE)
Quebec (QC)
Saskatchewan (SK)
Northwest Territories (NT)
Nunavut (NT)
Yukon Territory (YT)

States and territories of Australia

State

New South Wales
Northern Territory
Queensland
South Australia
Tasmania
Victoria
Western Australia

Australian Capital Territory

States and Union Territories of India

State	Capital
Andhra Pradesh	Hyderabad
Arunachal Pradesh	Itanagar
Assam	Dispur
Bihar	Patna
Goa	Panaji
Chhattisgarh	Raipur
Gujarat	Gandhinagar
Haryana	Chandigarh
Himachal Pradesh	Shimla
Jammu and Kashmir	Srinagar (summer) Jammu (winter)
Jharkand	Ranchi
Karnataka	Bangalore
Kerala	Thiruvananthapuram
Madhya Pradesh	Bhopal
Maharashtra	Mumbai
Manipur	Imphal
Meghalaya	Shillong
Mizoram	Aizawl
Nagaland	Kohima
Orissa	Bhubaneswar
Punjab	Chandigarh
Rajasthan	Jaipur
Sikkim	Gangtok
Tamil Nadu	Chennai
Tripura	Agartala
Uttaranchal	Dehra Dun
Uttar Pradesh	Lucknow
West Bengal	Kolkata

Union Territory	
Andaman and Nicobar Islands	Port Blair
Chandigarh	Chandigarh
Dadra and Nagar Haveli	Silvassa
Daman and Diu	Daman
Delhi	Delhi
Lakshadweep	Kavaratti
Pondicherry	Pondicherry

Appendix 3: **States of the United States of America**

State	Capital	Popular name	Postal abbreviation
Alabama	Montgomery	Yellowhammer State, Heart of Dixie, Cotton State	AL
Alaska	Juneau	Great Land	AK
Arizona	Phoenix	Grand Canyon State	AZ
Arkansas	Little Rock	Land of Opportunity	AR
California	Sacramento	Golden State	CA
Colorado	Denver	Centennial State	CO
Connecticut	Hartford	Constitution State, Nutmeg State	CT
Delaware	Dover	First State, Diamond State	DE
Florida	Tallahassee	Sunshine State	FL
Georgia	Atlanta	Empire State of the South, Peach State	GA
Hawaii	Honolulu	Aloha State	HI
Idaho	Boise	Gem State	ID
Illinois	Springfield	Prairie State	IL
Indiana	Indianapolis	Hoosier State	IN
Iowa	Des Moines	Hawkeye State	IA
Kansas	Topeka	Sunflower State	KS
Kentucky	Frankfort	Bluegrass State	KY
Louisiana	Baton Rouge	Pelican State	LA
Maine	Augusta	Pine Tree State	ME
Maryland	Annapolis	Old Line State, Free State	MD
Massachusetts	Boston	Bay State, Old Colony	MA
Michigan	Lansing	Great Lake State, Wolverine State	MI
Minnesota	St Paul	North Star State, Gopher State	MN
Mississippi	Jackson	Magnolia State	MS
Missouri	Jefferson City	Show Me State	MO
Montana	Helena	Treasure State	MT
Nebraska	Lincoln	Cornhusker State, Sagebrush State	NE
Nevada	Carson City	Battleborn State, Silver State	NV
New Hampshire	Concord	Granite State	NH
New Jersey	Trenton	Garden State	NJ
New Mexico	Santa Fe	Land of Enchantment	NM
New York	Albany	Empire State	NY
North Carolina	Raleigh	Tar Heel State, Old North State	NC
North Dakota	Bismarck	Peace Garden State	ND
Ohio	Columbus	Buckeye State	OH
Oklahoma	Oklahoma City	Sooner State	OK
Oregon	Salem	Beaver State	OR
Pennsylvania	Harrisburg	Keystone State	PA
Rhode Island	Providence	Little Rhody, Ocean State	RI
South Carolina	Columbia	Palmetto State	SC
South Dakota	Pierre	Coyote State, Sunshine State	SD
Tennessee	Nashville	Volunteer State	TN
Texas	Austin	Lone Star State	TX
Utah	Salt Lake City	Beehive State	UT
Vermont	Montpelier	Green Mountain State	VT
Virginia	Richmond	Old Dominion	VA
Washington	Olympia	Evergreen State	WA
West Virginia	Charleston	Mountain State	WV
Wisconsin	Madison	Badger State	WI
Wyoming	Cheyenne	Equality State	WY

Appendix 4: **Prime Ministers and Presidents**

Prime Ministers of Great Britain and of the United Kingdom

[1721]–1742	Sir Robert Walpole	Whig
1742–1743	Earl of Wilmington	"
1743–1754	Henry Pelham	"
1754–1756	Duke of Newcastle	"
1756–1757	Duke of Devonshire	"
1757–1762	Duke of Newcastle	"
1762–1763	Earl of Bute	Tory
1763–1765	George Grenville	Whig
1765–1766	Marquess of Rockingham	"
1766–1768	William Pitt the Elder	"
1768–1770	Duke of Grafton	"
1770–1782	Lord North	Tory
1782	Marquess of Rockingham	Whig
1782–1783	Earl of Shelburne	"
1783	Duke of Portland	coalition
1783–1801	William Pitt the Younger	Tory
1801–1804	Henry Addington	"
1804–1806	William Pitt the Younger	"
1806–1807	Lord William Grenville	Whig
1807–1809	Duke of Portland	Tory
1809–1812	Spencer Perceval	"
1812–1827	Earl of Liverpool	"
1827	George Canning	"
1827–1828	Viscount Goderich	"
1828–1830	Duke of Wellington	"
1830–1834	Earl Grey	Whig
1834	Viscount Melbourne	"
1834	Duke of Wellington	Tory
1834–1835	Sir Robert Peel	Conservative
1835–1841	Viscount Melbourne	Whig
1841–1846	Sir Robert Peel	Conservative
1846–1852	Lord John Russell	Whig
1852	Earl of Derby	Conservative
1852–1855	Earl of Aberdeen	coalition
1855–1858	Viscount Palmerston	Whig
1858–1859	Earl of Derby	Conservative
1859–1865	Viscount Palmerston	Liberal
1865–1866	Earl Russell	Liberal
1866–1868	Earl of Derby	Conservative
1868	Benjamin Disraeli	"
1868–1874	William Ewart Gladstone	Liberal
1874–1880	Benjamin Disraeli	Conservative
1880–1885	William Ewart Gladstone	Liberal
1885–1886	Marquess of Salisbury	Conservative
1886	William Ewart Gladstone	Liberal
1886–1892	Marquess of Salisbury	Conservative
1892–1894	William Ewart Gladstone	Liberal
1894–1895	Earl of Rosebery	"
1895–1902	Marquess of Salisbury	Conservative
1902–1905	Arthur James Balfour	"
1905–1908	Sir Henry Campbell-Bannerman	Liberal
1908–1916	Herbert Henry Asquith	"
1916–1922	David Lloyd George	coalition
1922–1923	Andrew Bonar Law	Conservative
1923–1924	Stanley Baldwin	"
1924	James Ramsay MacDonald	Labour
1924–1929	Stanley Baldwin	Conservative
1929–1935	James Ramsay MacDonald	coalition
1935–1937	Stanley Baldwin	"
1937–1940	Neville Chamberlain	"
1940–1945	Winston Spencer Churchill	"
1945–1951	Clement Attlee	Labour
1951–1955	Sir Winston Spencer Churchill	Conservative
1955–1957	Sir Anthony Eden	"
1957–1963	Harold Macmillan	"
1963–1964	Sir Alec Douglas-Home	"
1964–1970	Harold Wilson	Labour
1970–1974	Edward Heath	Conservative
1974–1976	Harold Wilson	Labour
1976–1979	James Callaghan	"
1979–1990	Margaret Thatcher	Conservative
1990–1997	John Major	"
1997–	Tony Blair	Labour

Prime Ministers of Canada

1867–1873	John A. Macdonald	Conservative
1873–1878	Alexander Mackenzie	Liberal/Reform
1878–1891	John A. Macdonald	Conservative
1891–1892	John J. C. Abbot	Liberal-Conservative
1892–1894	John S. D. Thompson	Conservative
1894–1896	Mackenzie Bowell	"
1896	Charles Tupper	"
1896–1911	Wilfrid Laurier	Liberal
1911–1920	Robert L. Borden	Conservative
1920–1921	Arthur Meighen	Liberal
1921–1926	W. L. Mackenzie King	"
1926	Arthur Meighen	Conservative
1926–1930	W. L. Mackenzie King	Liberal
1930–1935	Richard B. Bennett	Conservative
1935–1948	W. L. Mackenzie King	Liberal
1948–1957	Louis Stephen St Laurent	"
1957–1963	John George Diefenbaker	Progessive Conservative
1963–1968	Lester B. Pearson	Liberal
1968–1979	Pierre Elliott Trudeau	"
1979–1980	Joseph Clark	Progressive Conservative
1980–1984	Pierre Elliott Trudeau	Liberal
1984	John Turner	"
1984–1993	Brian Mulroney	Progressive Conservative
1993	Kim Campbell	"
1993–2003	Jean Chrétien	Liberal

Prime Ministers of Australia

1901–1903	Edmund Barton	–
1903–1904	Alfred Deakin	Liberal
1904	John C. Watson	Labor
1904–1905	George Houstoun Reid	Free Trade
1905–1908	Alfred Deakin	Liberal
1908–1909	Andrew Fisher	Labor
1909–1910	Alfred Deakin	Liberal
1910–1913	Andrew Fisher	Labor
1913–1914	Joseph Cook	Liberal
1914–1915	Andrew Fisher	Labor
1915–1923	William M. Hughes	Nationalist
1923–1929	Stanley M. Bruce	"
1929–1932	James H. Scullin	Labor
1932–1939	Joseph A. Lyons	United Australia Party
1939–1941	Robert Gordon Menzies	Liberal
1941	Arthur William Fadden	Country Party
1941–1945	John Curtin	Labor
1945–1949	Joseph Benedict Chifley	"
1949–1966	Robert Gordon Menzies	Liberal
1966–1967	Harold Edward Holt	"
1967–1968 (Dec.–Jan.)	John McEwen	"
1968–1971	John Grey Gorton	"
1971–1972	William McMahon	"
1972–1975	Gough Whitlam	Labor
1975–1983	J. Malcolm Fraser	Liberal
1983–1991	Robert J. L. Hawke	Labor
1991–1996	Paul Keating	"
1996–	John Howard	Liberal

Prime Ministers of New Zealand

1891–1893	John Ballance	Liberal
1893–1906	Richard John Seddon	"
1906	William Hall-Jones	"
1906–1912	Joseph George Ward	"
1912	Thomas Mackenzie	"
1912–1925	William Ferguson Massey	Reform
1925	Francis Henry Dillon Bell	"
1925–1928	Joseph Gordon Coates	"
1928–1930	Joseph George Ward	Liberal
1930–1935	George William Forbes	"
1935–1940	Michael J. Savage	Labour
1940–1949	Peter Fraser	"
1949–1957	Sidney G. Holland	National Party
1957 (Aug.–Nov.)	Keith J. Holyoake	National Party
1957–1960	Walter Nash	Labour
1960–1972	Keith J. Holyoake	National Party
1972	John R. Marshall	"
1972–1974	Norman Kirk	Labour
1974–1975	Wallace Rowling	"
1975–1984	Robert D. Muldoon	National Party
1984–1989	David Lange	Labour
1989–1990	Geoffrey Palmer	"
1990 (Sept.–Oct.)	Mike Moore	"
1990–1997	James B. Bolger	National Party
1997–1999	Jenny Shipley	"
1999–	Helen Clark	Labour

Presidents of the United States of America

1789–1797	1. George Washington	Federalist
1797–1801	2. John Adams	"
1801–1809	3. Thomas Jefferson	Democratic Republican
1809–1817	4. James Madison	"
1817–1825	5. James Monroe	"
1825–1829	6. John Quincy Adams	Independent
1829–1837	7. Andrew Jackson	Democrat
1837–1841	8. Martin Van Buren	"
1841	9. William H. Harrison	Whig
1841–1845	10. John Tyler	Whig, then Democrat
1845–1849	11. James K. Polk	Democrat
1849–1850	12. Zachary Taylor	Whig
1850–1853	13. Millard Fillmore	"
1853–1857	14. Franklin Pierce	Democrat
1857–1861	15. James Buchanan	"
1861–1865	16. Abraham Lincoln	Republican
1865–1869	17. Andrew Johnson	Democrat
1869–1877	18. Ulysses S. Grant	Republican
1877–1881	19. Rutherford B. Hayes	"
1881	20. James A. Garfield	"
1881–1885	21. Chester A. Arthur	"
1885–1889	22. Grover Cleveland	Democrat
1889–1893	23. Benjamin Harrison	Republican
1893–1897	24. Grover Cleveland	Democrat
1897–1901	25. William McKinley	Republican
1901–1909	26. Theodore Roosevelt	"
1909–1913	27. William H. Taft	"
1913–1921	28. Woodrow Wilson	Democrat
1921–1923	29. Warren G. Harding	Republican
1923–1929	30. Calvin Collidge	"
1929–1933	31. Herbert Hoover	"
1933–1945	32. Franklin D. Roosevelt	Democrat
1945–1953	33. Harry S. Truman	"
1953–1961	34. Dwight D. Eisenhower	Republican
1961–1963	35. John F. Kennedy	Democrat
1963–1969	36. Lyndon B. Johnson	"
1969–1974	37. Richard M. Nixon	Republican
1974–1977	38. Gerald R. Ford	"
1977–1981	39. James Earl Carter	Democrat
1981–1989	40. Ronald W. Reagan	Republican
1989–1993	41. George H. W. Bush	"
1993–2001	42. William J. Clinton	Democrat
2001–	43. George W. Bush	Republican

Appendix 5: **Kings and Queens of England and the United Kingdom**

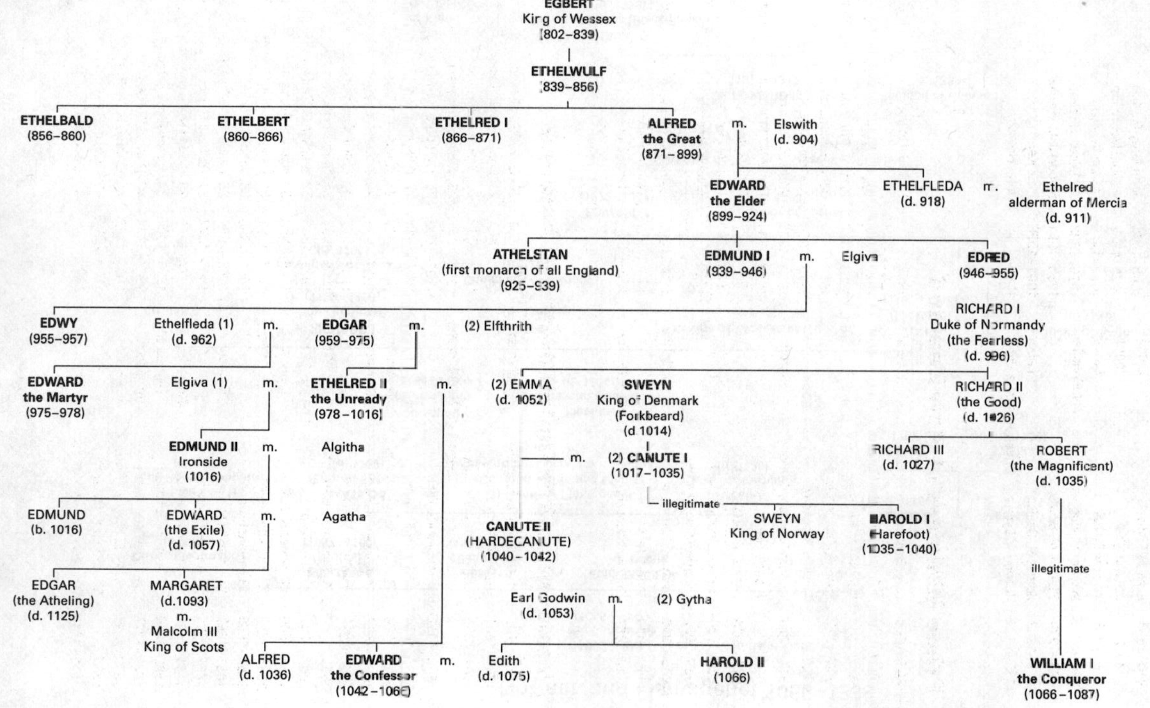

Norman and Plantagenet 1066–1399

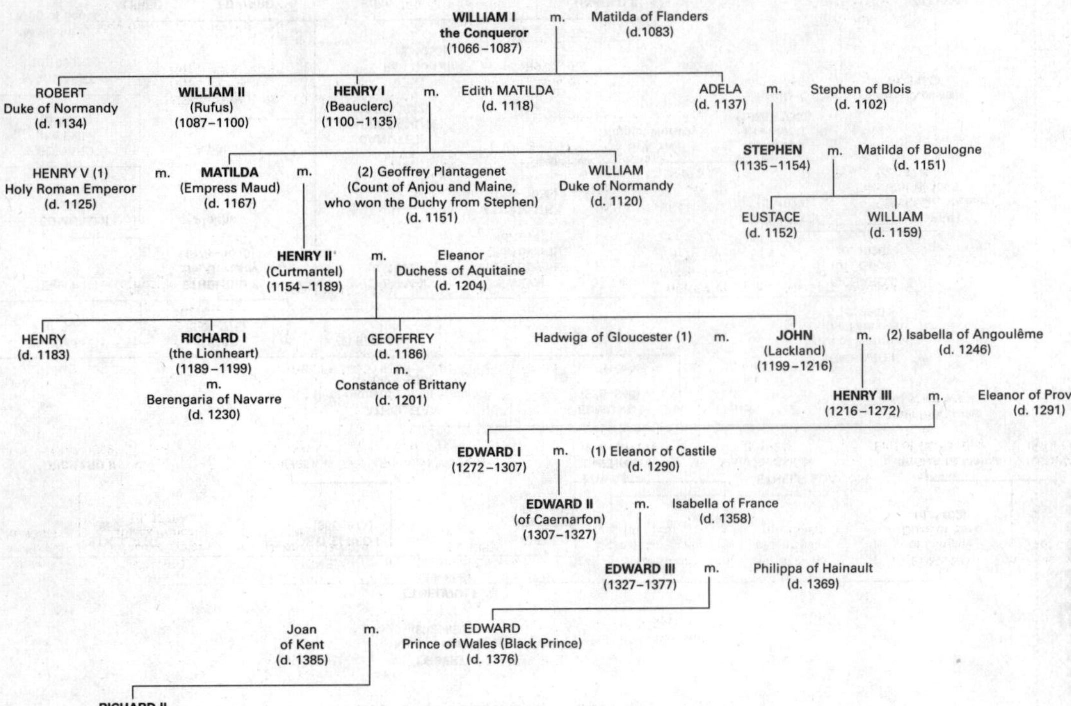

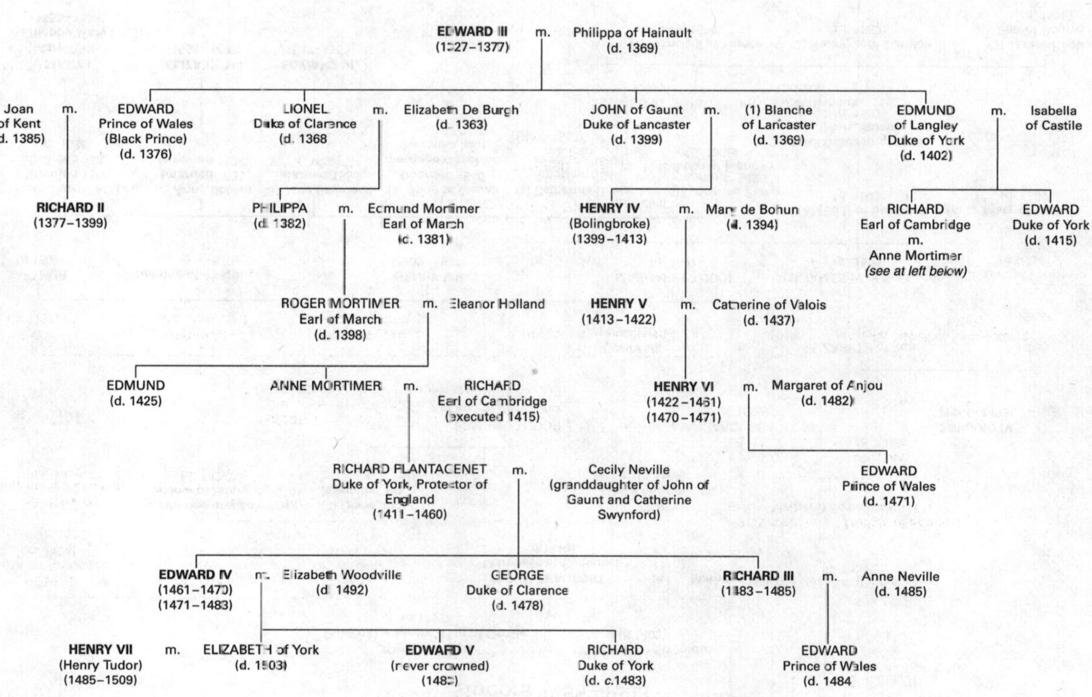
Lancaster and York 1399–1485
EDWARD III (1327–1377)
m.
Philippa of Hainault (d. 1369)
Joan of Kent (d. 1385)
m.
EDWARD Prince of Wales (Black Prince) (d. 1376)
LIONEL Duke of Clarence (d. 1368
m.
Elizabeth De Burgh (d. 1363)
JOHN of Gaunt Duke of Lancaster (d. 1399)
m.
(1) Blanche of Lancaster (d. 1369)
EDMUND of Langley Duke of York (d. 1402)
m.
Isabella of Castile
RICHARD II (1377–1399)
PHILIPPA (d. 1382)
m.
Edmund Mortimer Earl of March (d. 1381)
HENRY IV (Bolingbroke) (1399–1413)
m.
Mary de Bohun (d. 1394)
RICHARD Earl of Cambridge
m.
Anne Mortimer
(see at left below)
EDWARD Duke of York (d. 1415)
ROGER MORTIMER Earl of March (d. 1398)
m.
Eleanor Holland
HENRY V (1413–1422)
m.
Catherine of Valois (d. 1437)
EDMUND (d. 1425)
ANNE MORTIMER
m.
RICHARD Earl of Cambridge (executed 1415)
HENRY VI (1422–1461) (1470–1471)
m.
Margaret of Anjou (d. 1482)
RICHARD PLANTAGENET Duke of York, Protector of England (1411–1460)
m.
Cecily Neville (granddaughter of John of Gaunt and Catherine Swynford)
EDWARD Prince of Wales (d. 1471)
EDWARD IV (1461–1470) (1471–1483)
m.
Elizabeth Woodville (d. 1492)
GEORGE Duke of Clarence (d. 1478)
RICHARD III (1483–1485)
m.
Anne Neville (d. 1485)
HENRY VII (Henry Tudor) (1485–1509)
m.
ELIZABETH of York (d. 1503)
EDWARD V (never crowned) (1483)
RICHARD Duke of York (d. c.1483)
EDWARD Prince of Wales (d. 1484

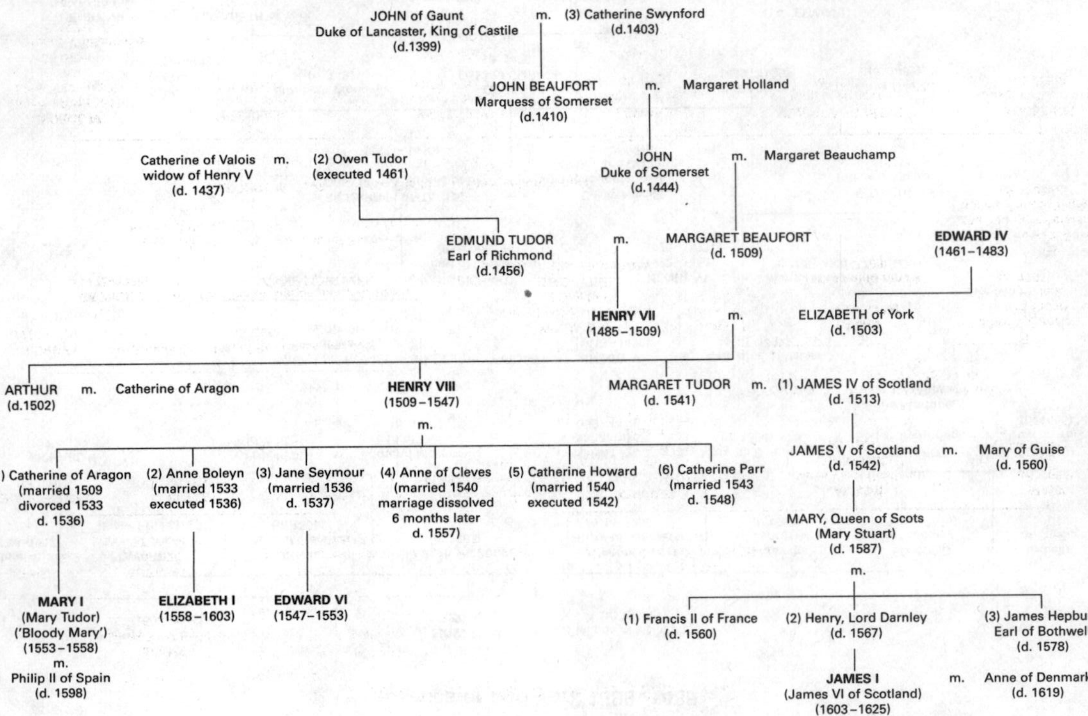
Tudors 1485–1603
JOHN of Gaunt
Duke of Lancaster, King of Castile
(d.1399)
m.
(3) Catherine Swynford
(d.1403)
JOHN BEAUFORT
Marquess of Somerset
(d.1410)
m.
Margaret Holland
Catherine of Valois
widow of Henry V
(d. 1437)
m.
(2) Owen Tudor
(executed 1461)
JOHN
Duke of Somerset
(d.1444)
m.
Margaret Beauchamp
EDMUND TUDOR
Earl of Richmond
(d.1456)
m.
MARGARET BEAUFORT
(d. 1509)
EDWARD IV
(1461–1483)
HENRY VII
(1485–1509)
m.
ELIZABETH of York
(d. 1503)
ARTHUR
(d.1502)
m.
Catherine of Aragon
HENRY VIII
(1509–1547)
m.
MARGARET TUDOR
(d. 1541)
m.
(1) JAMES IV of Scotland
(d. 1513)
(1) Catherine of Aragon
(married 1509
divorced 1533
d. 1536)
(2) Anne Boleyn
(married 1533
executed 1536)
(3) Jane Seymour
(married 1536
d. 1537)
(4) Anne of Cleves
(married 1540
marriage dissolved
6 months later
d. 1557)
(5) Catherine Howard
(married 1540
executed 1542)
(6) Catherine Parr
(married 1543
d. 1548)
JAMES V of Scotland
(d. 1542)
m.
Mary of Guise
(d. 1560)
MARY, Queen of Scots
(Mary Stuart)
(d. 1587)
m.
MARY I
(Mary Tudor)
('Bloody Mary')
(1553–1558)
m.
Philip II of Spain
(d. 1598)
ELIZABETH I
(1558–1603)
EDWARD VI
(1547–1553)
(1) Francis II of France
(d. 1560)
(2) Henry, Lord Darnley
(d. 1567)
(3) James Hepburn
Earl of Bothwell
(d. 1578)
JAMES I
(James VI of Scotland)
(1603–1625)
m.
Anne of Denmark
(d. 1619)

Stuarts and Hanoverians 1603–1837

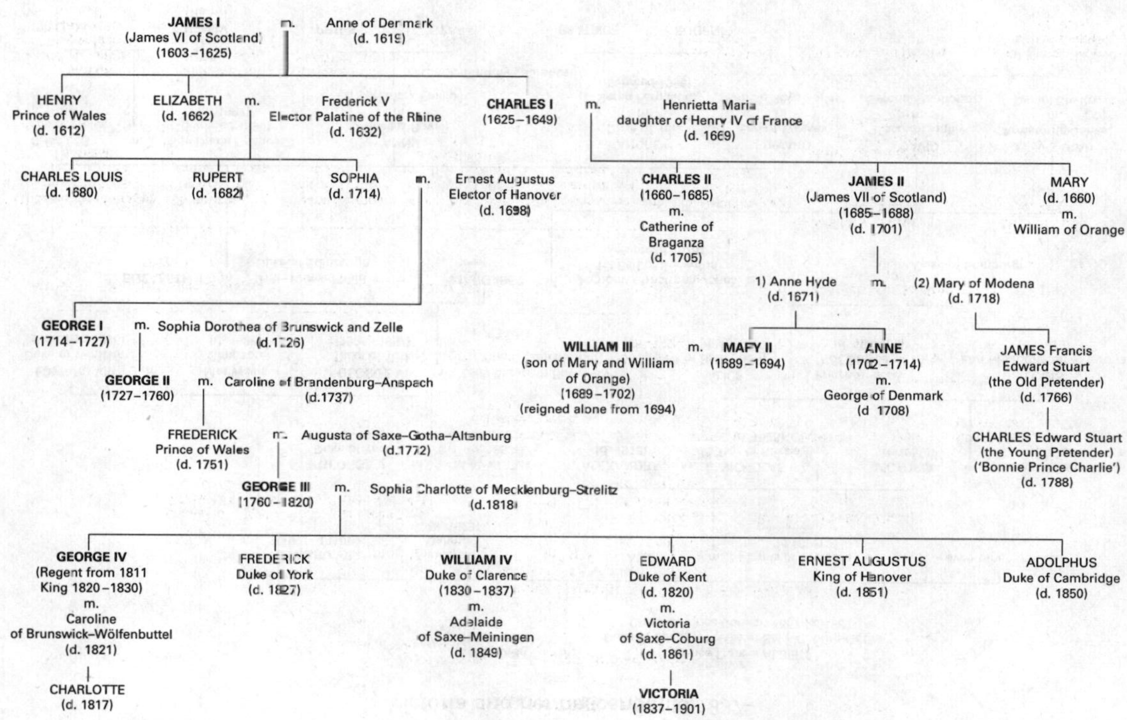

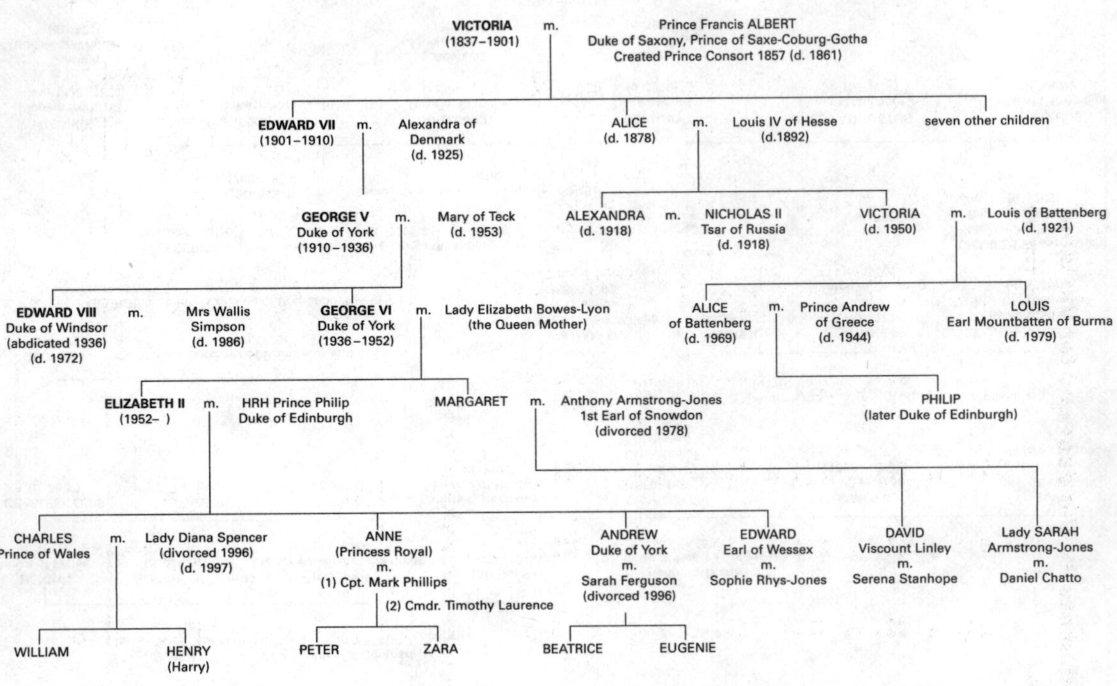

Victoria and her descendants 1837–
VICTORIA (1837–1901)
m.
Prince Francis ALBERT
Duke of Saxony, Prince of Saxe-Coburg-Gotha
Created Prince Consort 1857 (d. 1861)
EDWARD VII (1901–1910)
m.
Alexandra of Denmark (d. 1925)
ALICE (d. 1878)
m.
Louis IV of Hesse (d.1892)
seven other children
GEORGE V
Duke of York
(1910–1936)
m.
Mary of Teck (d. 1953)
ALEXANDRA (d. 1918)
m.
NICHOLAS II
Tsar of Russia
(d. 1918)
VICTORIA (d. 1950)
m.
Louis of Battenberg (d. 1921)
EDWARD VIII
Duke of Windsor
(abdicated 1936)
(d. 1972)
m.
Mrs Wallis Simpson (d. 1986)
GEORGE VI
Duke of York
(1936–1952)
m.
Lady Elizabeth Bowes-Lyon
(the Queen Mother)
ALICE
of Battenberg
(d. 1969)
m.
Prince Andrew
of Greece
(d. 1944)
LOUIS
Earl Mountbatten of Burma
(d. 1979)
ELIZABETH II
(1952–)
m.
HRH Prince Philip
Duke of Edinburgh
MARGARET
m.
Anthony Armstrong-Jones
1st Earl of Snowdon
(divorced 1978)
PHILIP
(later Duke of Edinburgh)
CHARLES
Prince of Wales
m.
Lady Diana Spencer
(divorced 1996)
(d. 1997)
ANNE
(Princess Royal)
m.
(1) Cpt. Mark Phillips
(2) Cmdr. Timothy Laurence
ANDREW
Duke of York
m.
Sarah Ferguson
(divorced 1996)
EDWARD
Earl of Wessex
m.
Sophie Rhys-Jones
DAVID
Viscount Linley
m.
Serena Stanhope
Lady SARAH
Armstrong-Jones
m.
Daniel Chatto
WILLIAM
HENRY
(Harry)
PETER
ZARA
BEATRICE
EUGENIE

Appendix 6: **Alphabets**

Alphabets for the deaf and for the blind

Braille

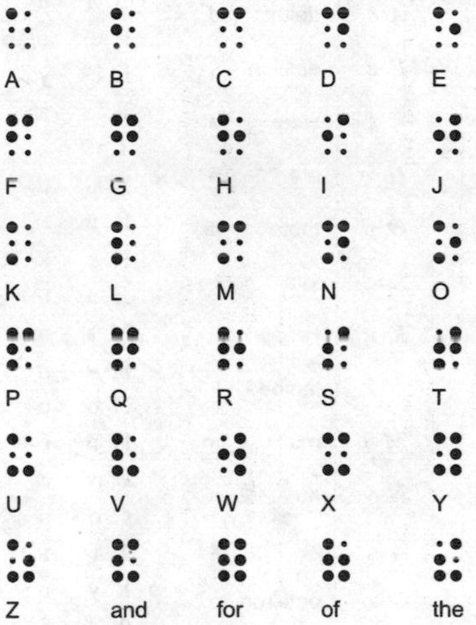

A B C D E
F G H I J
K L M N O
P Q R S T
U V W X Y
Z and for of the

Finger spelling

A B C D
E F G H
I J K L
M N O P
Q R S T
U V W X
Y Z good bad

Alphabets for signalling

Morse code

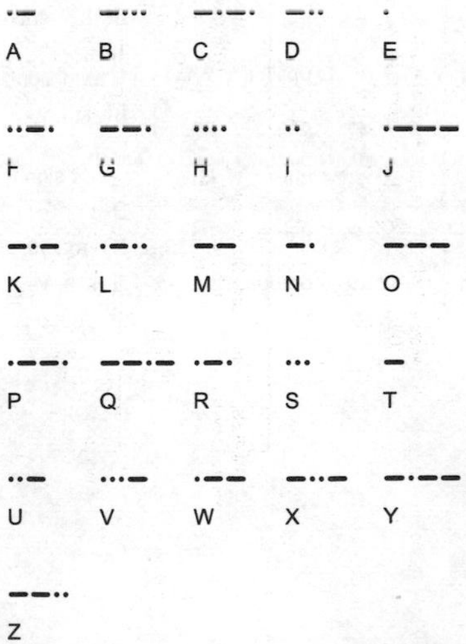

A	·—
B	—···
C	—·—·
D	—··
E	·
F	··—·
G	——·
H	····
I	··
J	·———
K	—·—
L	·—··
M	——
N	—·
O	———
P	·——·
Q	——·—
R	·—·
S	···
T	—
U	··—
V	···—
W	·——
X	—··—
Y	—·——
Z	——··

Semaphore

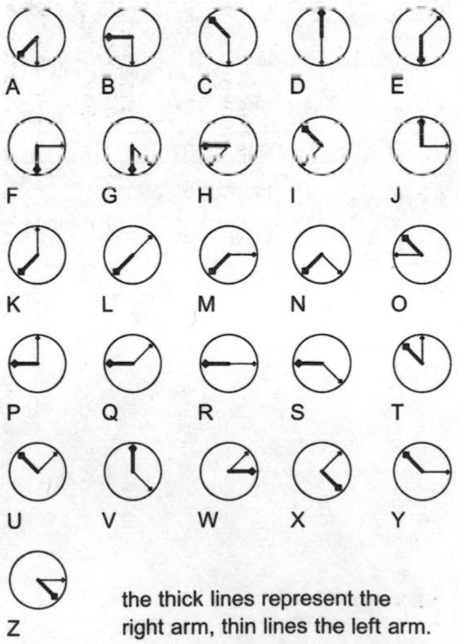

A B C D E
F G H I J
K L M N O
P Q R S T
U V W X Y
Z

the thick lines represent the right arm, thin lines the left arm.

Arabic, Hebrew, Greek, and Russian alphabets

Arabic

Alone	Final	Medial	Initial		
ا	ـا			'alif	'
ب	ـب	ـبـ	بـ	bā'	b
ت	ـت	ـتـ	تـ	tā'	t
ث	ـث	ـثـ	ثـ	thā'	th
ج	ـج	ـجـ	جـ	jīm	j
ح	ـح	ـحـ	حـ	ḥā'	ḥ
خ	ـخ	ـخـ	خـ	khā'	kh
د	ـد			dāl	d
ذ	ـذ			dhāl	dh
ر	ـر			rā'	r
ز	ـز			zāy	z
س	ـس	ـسـ	سـ	sīn	s
ش	ـش	ـشـ	شـ	shīn	sh
ص	ـص	ـصـ	صـ	ṣād	ṣ
ض	ـض	ـضـ	ضـ	ḍād	ḍ
ط	ـط	ـطـ	طـ	ṭā'	ṭ
ظ	ـظ	ـظـ	ظـ	ẓā'	ẓ
ع	ـع	ـعـ	عـ	'ayn	'
غ	ـغ	ـغـ	غـ	ghayn	gh
ف	ـف	ـفـ	فـ	fā'	f
ق	ـق	ـقـ	قـ	qāf	q
ك	ـك	ـكـ	كـ	kāf	k
ل	ـل	ـلـ	لـ	lām	l
م	ـم	ـمـ	مـ	mīm	m
ن	ـن	ـنـ	نـ	nūn	n
ه	ـه	ـهـ	هـ	hā'	h
و	ـو			wāw	w
ى	ـى	ـيـ	يـ	yā'	y

Hebrew

א		'aleph	'
ב		beth	b, bh
ג		gimel	g, gh
ד		daleth	d, dh
ה		he	h
ו		waw	w
ז		zayin	z
ח		ḥeth	ḥ
ט		ṭeth	ṭ
י		yodh	y
כ	ך	kaph	k, kh
ל		lamedh	l
מ	ם	mem	m
נ	ן	nun	n
ס		samekh	s
ע		'ayin	'
פ	ף	pe	p, ph
צ	ץ	ṣadhe	ṣ
ק		qoph	q
ר		resh	r
שׂ		śin	ś
שׁ		shin	sh
ת		taw	t, th

Greek

Α α	alpha	a
Β β	beta	b
Γ γ	gamma	g
Δ δ	delta	d
Ε ε	epsilon	e
Ζ ζ	zeta	z
Η η	eta	ē
Θ θ	theta	th
Ι ι	iota	i
Κ κ	kappa	k
Λ λ	lambda	l
Μ μ	mu	m
Ν ν	nu	n
Ξ ξ	xi	x
Ο ο	omicron	o
Π π	pi	p
Ρ ρ	rho	r, rh
Σ σ ς	sigma	s
Τ τ	tau	t
Υ υ	upsilon	u
Φ φ	phi	ph
Χ χ	chi	kh
Ψ ψ	psi	ps
Ω ω	omega	ō

Russian

А а	a
Б б	b
В в	v
Г г	g
Д д	d
Е е	e, ye
Ё ё	yo
Ж ж	zh
З з	z
И и	i
Й й	ĭ
К к	k
Л л	l
М м	m
Н н	n
О о	o
П п	p
Р р	r
С с	s
Т т	t
У у	u
Ф ф	f
Х х	kh
Ц ц	ts
Ч ч	ch
Ш ш	sh
Щ щ	shch
Ъ ъ	″ ('hard sign')
Ы ы	y
Ь ь	′ ('soft sign')
Э э	e
Ю ю	yu
Я я	ya

Punctuation marks

( )	brackets, parentheses
< >	angle brackets
[ ]	square brackets
{	brace
•	bullet
†	dagger, obelisk
‡	double dagger/diesis
*	asterisk/star
/	solidus/oblique/slash/virgule
§	section
~	swung dash
...	ellipsis/suspension points
¶	paragraph

Accents & diacritical marks

´	é	acute
°	å	bolle
˘	ŭ	breve
¸	ç	cedilla
^	ê	circumflex
¨	ö	umlaut/diaeresis
`	è	grave
ˇ	č	háček
¯	ō	macron
/	ø	streg
~	ñ	tilde

Phonetic alphabet

A	Alpha
B	Bravo
C	Charlie
D	Delta
E	Echo
F	Foxtrot
G	Golf
H	Hotel
I	India
J	Juliet
K	Kilo
L	Lima
M	Mike
N	November
O	Oscar
P	Papa
Q	Quebec
R	Romeo
S	Sierra
T	Tango
U	Uniform
V	Victor
W	Whisky
X	X-ray
Y	Yankee
Z	Zulu

Typefaces

	serif	sans serif	slab serif
roman	A	A	A
italic	*A*	*A*	*A*
bold face	**A**	**A**	**A**
light face	A	A	A

swash capitals	*ABCD*
upper case/ capital letters	ABCD
lower case/ small letters	abcde

ascenders

x-height — badge

descender

A selection of typefaces in 11pt size

American Typewriter

Bembo

Centaur

Gill Sans

Helvetica

Meta

Photina

Times

Walbaum

Appendix 7: Weights and measures

British and American, with metric equivalents

Linear measure

1 inch	= 25.4 millimetres exactly
1 foot = 12 inches	= 0.3048 metre exactly
1 yard = 3 feet	= 0.9144 metre exactly
1 (statute) mile = 1,760 yards	= 1.609 kilometres
1 int. nautical mile = 1.150779 miles	= 1.852 kilometres exactly

Square measure

1 square inch	= 6.45 sq. centimetres
1 square foot = 144 sq. in.	= 9.29 sq. decimetres
1 square yard = 9 sq. ft	= 0.836 sq. metre
1 acre = 4,840 sq. yd	= 0.405 hectare
1 square mile = 640 acres	= 259 hectares

Cubic measure

1 cubic inch	= 16.4 cu. centimetres
1 cubic foot = 1,728 cu. in.	= 0.0283 cu. metre
1 cubic yard = 27 cu. ft	= 0.765 cu. metre

Capacity measure

British

1 fluid oz = 1.7339 cu. in.	= 0.0284 litre
1 gill = 5 fluid oz	= 0.1421 litre
1 pint = 20 fluid oz = 34.68 cu. in.	= 0.568 litre
1 quart = 2 pints	= 1.136 litres
1 gallon = 4 quarts	= 4.546 litres
1 peck = 2 gallons	= 9.092 litres
1 bushel = 4 pecks	= 36.4 litres

American dry

1 pint = 33.60 cu. in.	= 0.550 litre
1 quart = 2 pints	= 1.101 litres
1 peck = 8 quarts	= 8.81 litres
1 bushel = 4 pecks	= 35.3 litres

American liquid

1 pint = 16 fluid oz = 28.88 cu. in.	= 0.473 litre
1 quart = 2 pints	= 0.946 litre
1 gallon = 4 quarts	= 3.785 litres

Avoirdupois weight

1 grain	= 0.065 gram
1 dram	= 1.772 grams
1 ounce = 16 drams	= 28.35 grams
1 pound = 16 ounces = 7,000 grains	= 0.4536 kilogram (0.45359237 exactly)
1 stone = 14 pounds	= 6.35 kilograms
1 hundredweight = 112 pounds	= 50.80 kilograms
1 short ton = 2,000 pounds	= 0.907 tonne
1 (long) ton = 20 hundredweight	= 1.016 tonnes

Metric, with British equivalents

Linear measure

1 millimetre	= 0.039 inch
1 centimetre = 10 mm	= 0.394 inch
1 decimetre = 10 cm	= 3.94 inches
1 metre = 100 cm	= 1.094 yards
1 kilometre = 1,000 m	= 0.6214 mile

Square measure

1 square centimetre	= 0.155 sq. inch
1 square metre = 10,000 sq. cm	= 1.196 sq. yards
1 are = 100 square metres	= 119.6 sq. yards
1 hectare = 100 ares	= 2.471 acres
1 square kilometre = 100 hectares	= 0.386 sq. mile

Cubic measure

1 cubic centimetre	= 0.061 cu. inch
1 cubic metre = 1,000,000 cu. cm	= 1.308 cu. yards

Capacity measure

1 millilitre	= 0.002 pint (British)
1 centilitre = 10 ml	= 0.018 pint
1 decilitre = 10 cl	= 0.176 pint
1 litre = 1000 ml	= 1.76 pints
1 decalitre = 10 l	= 2.20 gallons
1 hectolitre = 100 l	= 2.75 bushels
1 kilolitre = 1,000 l	= 3.44 quarters

Weight

1 milligram	= 0.015 grain
1 centigram = 10 mg	= 0.154 grain
1 decigram = 100 mg	= 1.543 grains
1 gram = 1000 mg	= 15.43 grains
1 decagram = 10 g	= 5.64 drams
1 hectogram = 100 g	= 3.527 ounces
1 kilogram = 1,000 g	= 2.205 pounds
1 tonne (metric ton) = 1,000 kg	= 0.984 (long) ton

Temperature

Fahrenheit water boils (under standard conditions) at 212° and freezes at 32°.

Celsius or Centigrade water boils at 100° and freezes at 0°.

Kelvin water boils at 373.15 K and freezes at 273.15 K.

To convert Celsius into Fahrenheit:
multiply by 9, divide by 5, and add 32.
To convert Fahrenheit into Celsius:
subtract 32, multiply by 5, and divide by 9.
To convert Celsius into Kelvin:
add 273.15.

°F	°C	°C	°F
–40	–40	–40	–40
–10	–23	–10	14
0	–18	0	32
10	–12	10	50
20	–7	20	68
30	–1	30	86
40	4	40	104
50	10	50	122
60	16	60	140
70	21	70	158
80	27	80	176
90	32	90	194
100	38	100	212
	(*approx.*)		(*exact*)

The Metric Prefixes

	Abbreviations	Factors
deca-	da	10
hecto-	h	10^2
kilo-	k	10^3
mega-	M	10^6
giga-	G	10^9
tera-	T	10^{12}
peta-	P	10^{15}
exa-	E	10^{18}
deci-	d	10^{-1}
centi-	c	10^{-2}
milli-	m	10^{-3}
micro-	μ	10^{-6}
nano-	n	10^{-9}
pico-	p	10^{-12}
femto-	f	10^{-15}
atto-	a	10^{-18}

These prefixes may be applied to any units of the metric system: hectogram (abbr. hg) = 100 grams; kilowatt (abbr. kW) = 1,000 watts; megahertz (MHz) = 1 million hertz; microvolt (μV) = one millionth of a volt; picofarad (pF) = 10^{-12} farad, and are sometimes applied to other units (megabit, microinch).

Power Notation

This expresses concisely any power of 10 (any number that is formed by multiplying or dividing ten by itself), and is sometimes used in the dictionary.

10^2 (ten squared) = $10 \times 10 = 100$
10^3 (ten cubed) = $10 \times 10 \times 10 = 1{,}000$
$10^4 = 10 \times 10 \times 10 \times 10 = 10{,}000$
$10^{10} = 10{,}000{,}000{,}000$ (1 followed by ten noughts)
$10^{-2} = 1/10^2 = 1/100 = 0.01$
$10^{-10} = 1/10^{10} = 1/10{,}000{,}000{,}000$
$6.2 \times 10^3 = 6{,}200$
$4.7 \times 10^{-2} = 0.047$

SI Units

Base units

Physical quantity	Name	Abbreviation or symbol
length	metre	m
mass	kilogram	kg
time	second	s
electric current	ampere	A
temperature	kelvin	K
amount of substance	mole	mol
luminous intensity	candela	cd

Supplementary units

Physical quantity	Name	Abbreviation or symbol
plane angle	radian	rad
solid angle	steradian	sr

Derived units with special names

Physical quantity	Name	Abbreviation or symbol
frequency	hertz	Hz
energy	joule	J
force	newton	N
power	watt	W
pressure	pascal	Pa
electric charge	coulomb	C
electromotive force	volt	V
electric resistance	ohm	Ω
electric conductance	siemens	S
electric capacitance	farad	F
magnetic flux	weber	Wb
inductance	henry	H
magnetic flux density	tesla	T
luminous flux	lumen	lm
illumination	lux	lx

Appendix 8: **Mathematical symbols and figures**

Mathematical symbols

$+$	plus or positive
$-$	minus or negative
$\pm$	plus or minus, positive or negative
$\times$	multiplied by
$\div$	divided by
$=$	equal to
$\equiv$	identically equal to
$\neq$	not equal to
$\not\equiv$	not identically equal to
$\approx$	approximately equal to
$\sim$	of the order of or similar to
$>$	greater than
$<$	less than
$\ngtr$	not greater than
$\nless$	not less than
$\geqslant$	greater than or equal to
$\leqslant$	less than or equal to
$\gg$	much greater than
$\ll$	much less than
$\sqrt{}$	square root
∞	infinity
$\propto$	proportional to
Σ	sum of
Π	product of
Δ	difference
$\therefore$	therefore
$\angle$	angle
$\parallel$	parallel to
$\perp$	perpendicular to
$:$	is to

Shapes and forms in mathematics

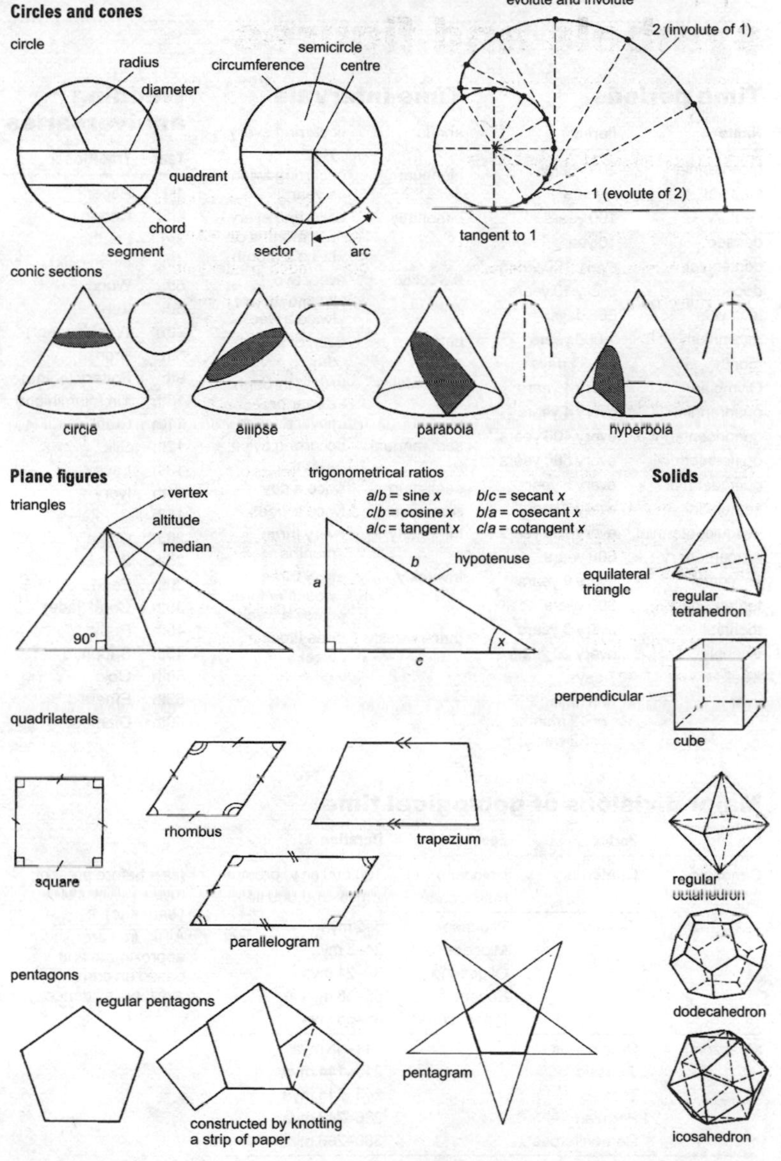

Appendix 9: **Time**

Time periods

Name	Period
bicentennial	200 years
biennial	2 years
century	100 years
decade	10 years
centennial	every 100 years
decennial	every 10 years
leap year	366 days
millennium	1,000 years
month	28–31 days
Olympiad	every 4 years
quadrennial	every 4 years
quadricentennial	every 400 years
quincentennial	every 500 years
quinquennial	every 5 years
septennial	every 7 years
sesquicentennial	every 150 years
sexcentenary	600 years
sexennial	every 6 years
tercentenary	300 years
triennial	every 3 years
vicennial	every 20 years
week	7 days
year	365 days *or* 12 months *or* 52 weeks

Time intervals

annual	occurring every year
biannual	occurring twice a year
bimonthly	occurring every two months *or* twice a month
biweekly	every two weeks *or* twice a week
diurnal	daily, of each day
perennial	lasting through a year *or* several years
semi-annual	occurring twice a year
semi-diurnal	twice a day
semi-weekly	twice a week
trimonthly	every three months
triweekly	every three weeks *or* three times a week
thrice weekly	three times a week

Wedding anniversaries

Year	Traditional
1st	Paper
2nd	Cotton
3rd	Leather
4th	Linen (silk)
5th	Wood
6th	Iron
7th	Wool (copper)
8th	Bronze
9th	Pottery (china)
10th	Tin (aluminium)
11th	Steel
12th	Silk
13th	Lace
14th	Ivory
15th	Crystal
20th	China
25th	Silver
30th	Pearl
35th	Coral (jade)
40th	Ruby
45th	Sapphire
50th	Gold
55th	Emerald
60th	Diamond

Major divisions of geological time

Era	Period	Epoch	Duration
Cenozoic	Quaternary	Holocene	100,000 BP to present
		Pleistocene	2 mya–100,000 BP
	Tertiary	Pliocene	5–2 mya
		Miocene	24–5 mya
		Oligocene	38–24 mya
		Eocene	55–38 mya
		Palaeocene	65–55 mya
Mesozoic	Cretaceous		144–65 mya
	Jurassic		213–144 mya
	Triassic		248–213 mya
	Permian		286–248 mya
	Carboniferous		360–286 mya
Palaeozoic	Devonian		408–360 mya
	Silurian		438–408 mya
	Ordovician		505–438 mya
	Cambrian		590–505 mya
	Precambrian		4,600–590 mya

(BP = before present; mya = millions of years ago)

All figures are approximate and based on currently available evidence.

Appendix 10: **Chemical Elements**

Element	Symbol	Atomic number	Description
Actinium	Ac	89	metal, radioactive
Aluminium	Al	13	metal
Americium	Am	95	metal, radioactive
Antimony	Sb	51	metal
Argon	Ar	18	noble gas
Arsenic	As	33	metal
Astatine	At	85	halogen, non-metal, radioactive
Barium	Ba	56	metal
Berkelium	Bk	97	metal, radioactive
Beryllium	Be	4	metal
Bismuth	Bi	83	metal
Bohrium	Bh	107	very unstable, radioactive
Boron	B	5	non-metal
Bromine	Br	35	halogen, liquid
Cadmium	Cd	48	metal
Caesium	Cs	55	alkali metal
Calcium	Ca	20	metal
Californium	Cf	98	metal, radioactive
Carbon	C	6	non-metal
Cerium	Ce	58	metal
Chlorine	Cl	17	halogen, gas
Chromium	Cr	24	metal
Cobalt	Co	27	metal
Copper	Cu	29	metal
Curium	Cm	96	metal, radioactive
Dubnium	Db	105	very unstable, radioactive
Dysprosium	Dy	66	metal
Einsteinium	Es	99	very unstable, radioactive
Erbium	Er	68	metal
Europium	Eu	63	metal
Fermium	Fm	100	very unstable, radioactive
Fluorine	F	9	halogen, gas
Francium	Fr	87	alkali metal, radioactive
Gadolinium	Gd	64	metal
Gallium	Ga	31	metal
Germanium	Ge	32	semiconductor
Gold	Au	79	metal
Hafnium	Hf	72	metal
Hassium	Hs	108	very unstable, radioactive
Helium	He	2	noble gas
Holmium	Ho	67	metal
Hydrogen	H	1	gas
Indium	In	49	metal
Iodine	I	53	halogen, non-metal
Iridium	Ir	77	metal
Iron	Fe	26	metal
Krypton	Kr	36	noble gas
Lanthanum	La	57	metal
Lawrencium	Lr	103	very unstable, radioactive
Lead	Pb	82	metal
Lithium	Li	3	alkali metal
Lutetium	Lu	71	metal
Magnesium	Mg	12	metal
Manganese	Mn	25	metal
Meitnerium	Mt	109	very unstable, radioactive
Mendelevium	Md	101	very unstable, radioactive
Mercury	Hg	80	metal, liquid
Molybdenum	Mo	42	metal
Neodymium	Nd	60	metal
Neon	Ne	10	noble gas
Neptunium	Np	93	metal, radioactive
Nickel	Ni	28	metal
Niobium	Nb	41	metal
Nitrogen	N	7	gas
Nobelium	No	102	very unstable, radioactive
Osmium	Os	76	metal
Oxygen	O	8	gas
Palladium	Pd	46	metal
Phosphorus	P	15	non-metal
Platinum	Pt	78	metal
Plutonium	Pu	94	metal, radioactive
Polonium	Po	84	metal, radioactive
Potassium	K	19	alkali metal
Praseodymium	Pr	59	metal
Promethium	Pm	61	metal, radioactive
Protactinium	Pa	91	metal, radioactive
Radium	Ra	88	metal, radioactive

Element	Symbol	Atomic number	Description
Radon	Rn	86	noble gas, radioactive
Rhenium	Re	75	metal
Rhodium	Rh	45	metal
Rubidium	Rb	37	alkali metal
Ruthenium	Ru	44	metal
Rutherfordium	Rf	104	very unstable, radioactive
Samarium	Sm	62	metal
Scandium	Sc	21	metal
Seaborgium	Sg	106	very unstable, radioactive
Selenium	Se	34	semiconductor
Silicon	Si	14	semiconductor
Silver	Ag	47	metal
Sodium	Na	11	alkali metal
Strontium	Sr	38	metal
Sulphur	S	16	non-metal
Tantalum	Ta	73	metal
Technetium	Tc	43	metal, radioactive
Tellurium	Te	52	semiconductor
Terbium	Tb	65	metal
Thallium	Tl	81	metal
Thorium	Th	90	metal, radioactive
Thulium	Tm	69	metal
Tin	Sn	50	metal
Titanium	Ti	22	metal
Tungsten	W	74	metal
Uranium	U	92	metal, radioactive
Vanadium	V	23	metal
Xenon	Xe	54	noble gas
Ytterbium	Yb	70	metal
Yttrium	Y	39	metal
Zinc	Zn	30	metal
Zirconium	Zr	40	metal

The periodic table

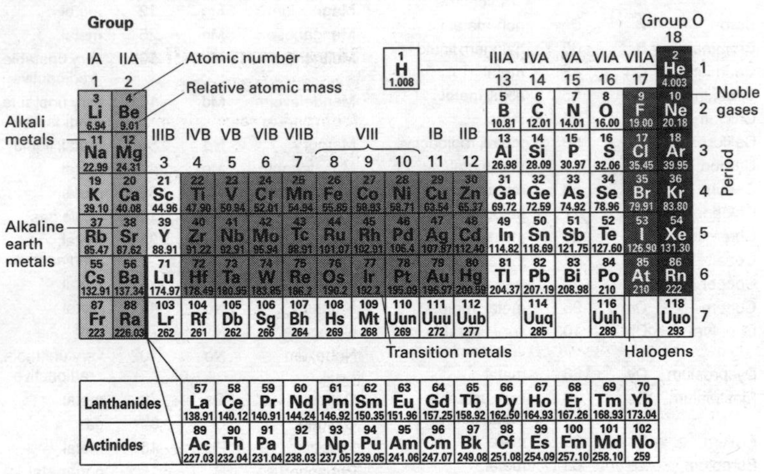

Pending agreement on their names, elements with atomic numbers above 109 are given the provisional designations ununnilium (110), unununium (111), ununbium (112), ununquadium (114), ununhexium (116), and ununoctium (118).

Appendix 11: **Planets, constellations, and star signs**

The Sun and Planets

Planet	Mean distance from sun (10^6 km)	Equatorial diameter (km)	Mass (earth = 1)	Volume (earth = 1)	Orbital period or 'year'	Rotation period or 'day'	Number of Satellites
Sun	–	1,400,000	330,000	1,300,000	–	25d*	–
Mercury	57.91	4,878	0.06	0.06	87.97d	58.65d	–
Venus	108.2	12,102	0.81	0.86	224.7d	243.0d(R)	–
Earth	149.6	12,756	1.00	1.00	365.3d	23.93h	1
Mars	227.9	6,786	0.11	0.15	687.0d	24.62h	2
Jupiter	778.3	142,980	318	1,323	11.86y	9.93h*	17
Saturn	1,427	120,540	95.2	752	29.46y	10.66h*	22
Uranus	2,871	51,120	14.5	64	84.01y	17.24h*(R)	21
Neptune	4,497	49,530	17.1	54	164.8y	16.11h*	8
Pluto	5,914	2,280	0.002	0.01	248.5y	6.39d(R)	1

* at equator (R) retrograde

Signs of the Zodiac

Aries Ram
(*March 21–April 20*)

Taurus Bull
(*April 21–May 20*)

Gemini Twins
(*May 21–June 20*)

Cancer Crab
(*June 21–July 21*)

Leo Lion
(*July 22–August 21*)

Virgo Virgin
(*August 22–September 21*)

Libra Scales
(*September 22–October 22*)

Scorpio Scorpion
(*October 23–November 21*)

Sagittarius Archer
(*November 22–December 20*)

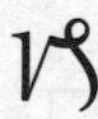

Capricorn Goat
(*December 21–January 19*)

Aquarius Water Bearer
(*January 20– February 18*)

Pisces Fish
(*February 19–March 20*)

Major non-Zodiac constellations

Astronomical name	Common name
Andromeda	—
Aquila	Eagle
Auriga	Charioteer
Boötes	Herdsman
Canis Major	Great Dog
Canis Minor	Little Dog
Carina	Keel
Cassiopeia	—
Centaurus	Centaur
Cepheus	—
Cetus	Whale
Crux (Australis)	Southern Cross
Cygnus	Swan
Draco	Dragon
Eridanus	River
Hercules	—
Hydra	Water Snake *or* Sea Monster
Lacerta	Lizard
Lyra	Lyre
Ophiuchus	Serpent Bearer
Orion	Hunter
Pegasus	—
Perseus	—
Puppis	Poop *or* Stern
Ursa Major	Great Bear
Ursa Minor	Little Bear
Vela	Sails

Appendix 12: **The Plant and Animal Kingdoms**

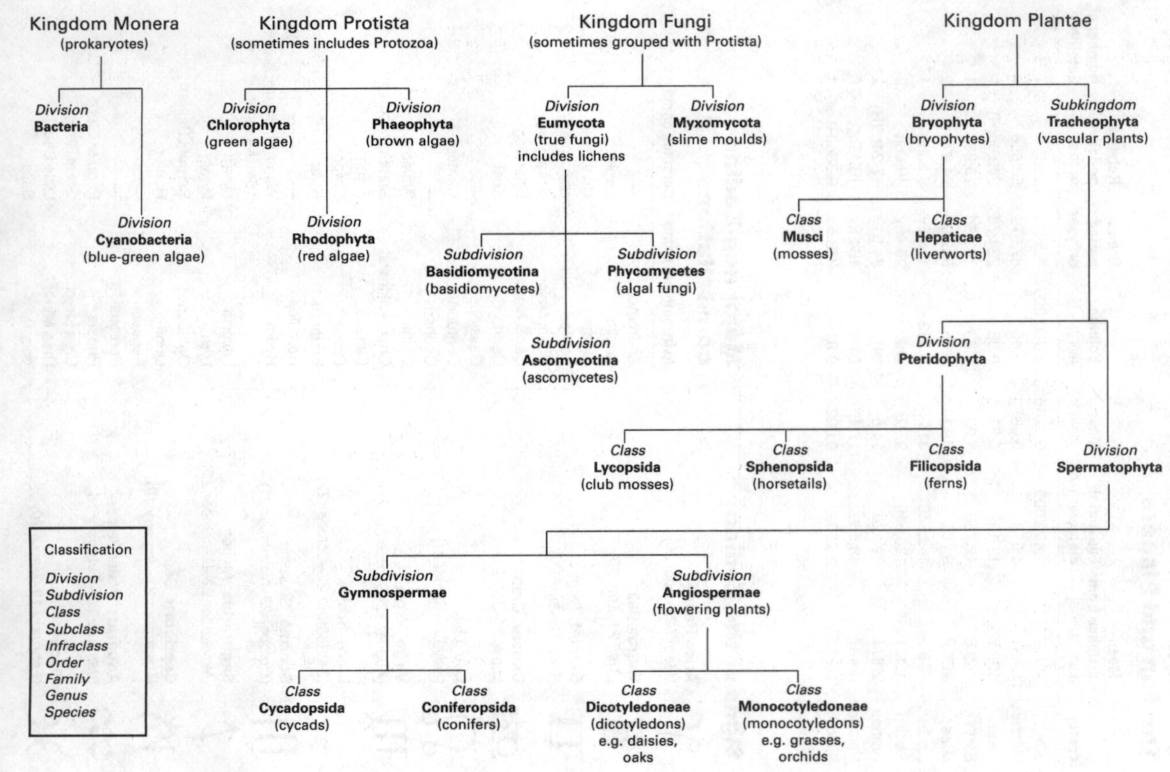

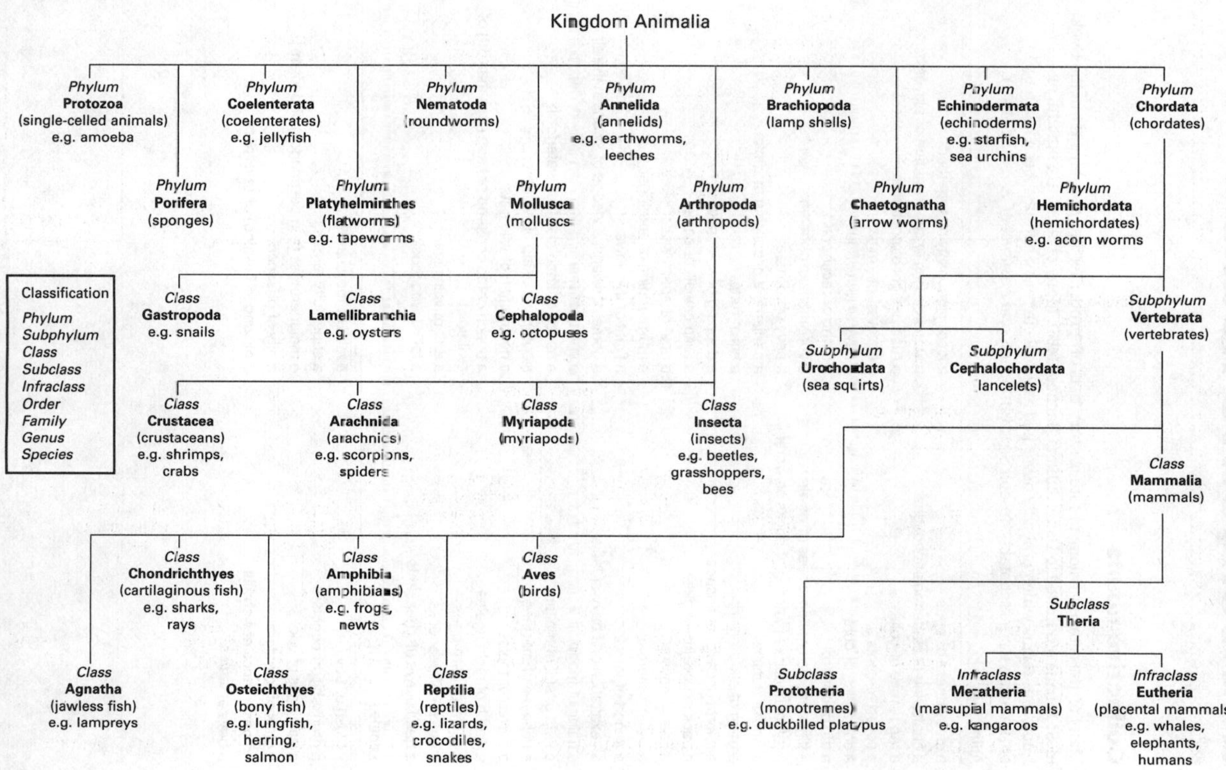
Kingdom Animalia
Phylum Protozoa (single-celled animals) e.g. amoeba
Phylum Porifera (sponges)
Phylum Coelenterata (coelenterates) e.g. jellyfish
Phylum Platyhelminthes (flatworms) e.g. tapeworms
Phylum Nematoda (roundworms)
Phylum Mollusca (molluscs)
Phylum Annelida (annelids) e.g. earthworms, leeches
Phylum Arthropoda (arthropods)
Phylum Brachiopoda (lamp shells)
Phylum Chaetognatha (arrow worms)
Phylum Echinodermata (echinoderms) e.g. starfish, sea urchins
Phylum Hemichordata (hemichordates) e.g. acorn worms
Phylum Chordata (chordates)
Classification
Phylum
Subphylum
Class
Subclass
Infraclass
Order
Family
Genus
Species
Class Gastropoda e.g. snails
Class Lamellibranchia e.g. oysters
Class Cephalopoda e.g. octopuses
Subphylum Vertebrata (vertebrates)
Subphylum Urochordata (sea squirts)
Subphylum Cephalochordata (lancelets)
Class Crustacea (crustaceans) e.g. shrimps, crabs
Class Arachnida (arachnids) e.g. scorpions, spiders
Class Myriapoda (myriapods)
Class Insecta (insects) e.g. beetles, grasshoppers, bees
Class Mammalia (mammals)
Class Chondrichthyes (cartilaginous fish) e.g. sharks, rays
Class Amphibia (amphibians) e.g. frogs, newts
Class Aves (birds)
Subclass Theria
Class Agnatha (jawless fish) e.g. lampreys
Class Osteichthyes (bony fish) e.g. lungfish, herring, salmon
Class Reptilia (reptiles) e.g. lizards, crocodiles, snakes
Subclass Prototheria (monotremes) e.g. duckbilled platypus
Infraclass Metatheria (marsupial mammals) e.g. kangaroos
Infraclass Eutheria (placental mammals) e.g. whales, elephants, humans

Appendix 13: **Animals and collective nouns**

Collective nouns

Many of these terms belong to 15th-century lists of 'proper terms', notably that in the Book of St Albans attributed to Dame Juliana Barnes (1486). Many of these are fanciful or humorous terms which probably never had any real currency, but have been taken up by antiquarian writers, notably Joseph Strutt in *Sports and Pastimes of England* (1801).

Animals

a shrewdness of apes
a chattering *or* clattering of choughs
a rag *or* rake of colts
a covert of coots
a cowardice of curs
a trip of dotterel
a flight *or* dole *or* piteousness of doves
a raft *or* bunch *or* paddling of ducks on water
a fling of dunlins
a gang of elk
a charm *or* chirm of finches
a pack *or* covey of grouse
a cast of hawks
a siege of herons
a desert of lapwing
an exaltation *or* a bevy of larks
a tiding of magpies
a sord *or* suit of mallard
a richesse of martens
a barren of mules
a watch of nightingales
a covey of partridges
a muster of peacocks
a head *or* nye of pheasants
a kit of pigeons flying together
a stand *or* wing *or* congregation of plovers
a rush *or* flight of pochards
a covey of ptarmigan
a bevy *or* drift of quail
a string of racehorses
an unkindness of ravens
a bevy of roe deer
a parliament *or* building of rooks
a hill of ruffs
a dopping of sheldrake
a wisp *or* walk of snipe
a host of sparrows
a murmuration of starlings
a flight of swallows
a game of swans; a wedge of swans in the air
a spring of teal
a bunch *or* knob *or* raft of waterfowl
a company *or* trip of wigeon
a destruction of wild cats
a bunch *or* trip *or* plump *or* knob (less than 30) of wildfowl
a drift of wild pigs
a fall of woodcock

People

a blush of boys
a drunkship of cobblers
a hastiness of cooks
a stalk of foresters
an observance of hermits
a bevy of ladies
a faith of merchants
a superfluity of nuns
a malapertness (= impertinence) of pedlars
a pity of prisoners
a glozing (= fawning) of taverners

Collective and other terms for animals

Animal	Group	Male	Female	Young	Related adjective	Home or menagerie
ass, donkey	herd, drove	jack, jackass, dicky	jenny	foal, colt (male), filly (female)	asinine	–
badger	cete*	boar	sow	cub	meline	sett (*or* set)
bee	swarm	–	–	–	apian	apiary, hive
bear	sloth*	–	–	cub	ursine	–
bird	flock	cock	hen	chick, fledgling	avian	nest, roost; aviary
cat	litter *or* kindle* (of kittens)	tom, gib-cat (usually castrated)	queen, tabby	kitten	feline	cattery; lair *or* den (wild cats)
cattle	herd, drove, drift; team *or* yoke (oxen)	bull, ox (castrated)	cow	calf, stirk, bullock (male), heifer (female), steer (castrated male)	bovine, taurine (bulls)	byre
chicken	brood, clutch	–	–	chick	–	–
deer	herd	buck, stag, hart	doe, hind	fawn, calf, kid; pricket *or* brocket (male)	cervine	–
dog	pack; kennel (of hounds); litter (of pups)	dog, hound	bitch	pup, puppy, whelp	canine	kennel
elephant	herd	bull	cow	calf	elephantine	–
ferret	business*	dog, buck, jack, hob	bitch, doe, jill	kit	musteline	–
fish	shoal	–	–	fry (pl.)	piscine	–
fox	skulk*	dog	vixen	cub	vulpine	earth, lair
frog	–	–	–	tadpole	ranine, batrachian, anuran, salientian	
goat	flock, herd, tribe	billy, buck	nanny, doe	kid	caprine, hircine	–
goose	gaggle, skein	gander	–	gosling	anserine	–
hare	down*, husk*, trip*	buck, jack	doe, puss	leveret	leporine	form
horse	herd, stable, team, troop; rag* *or* rake* (of colts)	stallion, horse, sire, gelding (castrated)	mare, dam	foal, colt (male), filly (female)	equine	stable, paddock, stall, stud
kangaroo	troop, herd, mob	buck, boomer	doe, blue flier	joey	maropine	–
leopard	leap*	leopard	leopardess	cub	pardine	–
lion	pride	lion	lioness	cub	leonine	den
mole	labour*	–	–	–	talpine	burrow, fortress, tunnel
monkey	troop, tribe	–	–	–	simian	–
otter	–	dog	bitch	cub	lutrine	holt, lodge
pig, boar	herd, sounder (of wild pigs), farrow (of piglets)	boar, hog (castrated)	sow, gilt	piglet, pigling, squeaker, shoat (N.Amer.), gilt (female)	porcine, suilline	pen, sty
polecat	–	hob	jill	kit	musteline	–

Animal	Group	Male	Female	Young	Related adjective	Home or menagerie
rabbit	–	buck	doe	kitten	oryctolagine	warren, burrow, coneygarth (historical)
rat	–	buck	doe	nestling	murine	–
rhinoceros	crash*	bull	cow	calf	rhinocerotic	–
seal	herd	bull	cow	pup, cub	phocine	rookery
sheep	flock, drove, trip, herd	ram, tup, wether (castrated)	ewe	lamb, teg, hog	ovine	fold
snake	–	–	–	–	anguine, ophidian	den, nest
squirrel	–	–	–	nestling	sciurine	drey
tiger	–	tiger	tigress	cub	tigrine	lair
whale	pod, school, herd	bull	cow	calf	cetacean	–
wolf	pack, rout*	dog	bitch	cub, whelp	lupine	lair, den
zebra	herd	stallion	mare	foal, colt (male), filly (female)	zebrine	–

Words marked * are obsolete or fanciful terms having little real currency, perhaps belonging more appropriately to the lists on p. 30.

Appendix 14: **Music**

Values of notes and rests

Some common symbols

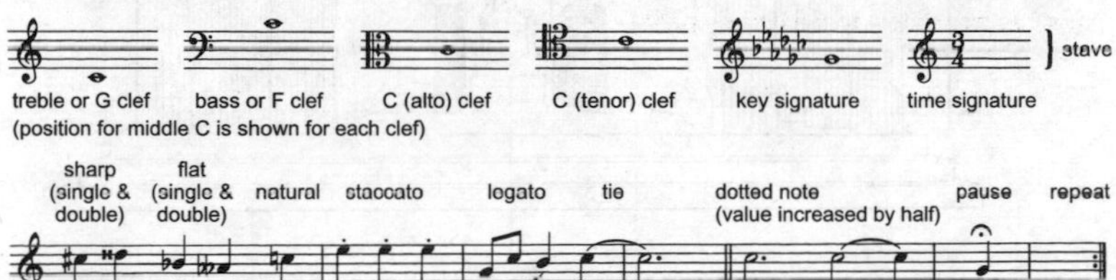

Tempo indicators

adagio	slow
largo	slow and dignified
andante	flowing, at a walking pace
allegro	quick and bright
allegretto	not as quick as allegro
vivace	fast and lively
presto	very quick
accelerando	getting faster
ritenuto (*rit.*)	holding back
rallentando (*rall.*)	getting slower
rubato	flexible tempo

Dynamics

<	*crescendo*	get louder
>	*diminuendo*	get quieter
ppp		very, very quiet
pp	*pianissimo*	very quiet
p	*piano*	quiet
mp	*mezzopiano*	quite quiet
mf	*mezzoforte*	quite loud
f	*forte*	loud
ff	*fortissimo*	very loud
fff		very, very loud
sf	*sforzando*	suddenly very loud

Interpretive indicators

cantabile	singing style
dolce	soft and sweet
espressivo	expressively
legato	smooth
staccato	detached

Appendix 15: **Architecture**

Classical

A Greek Doric temple

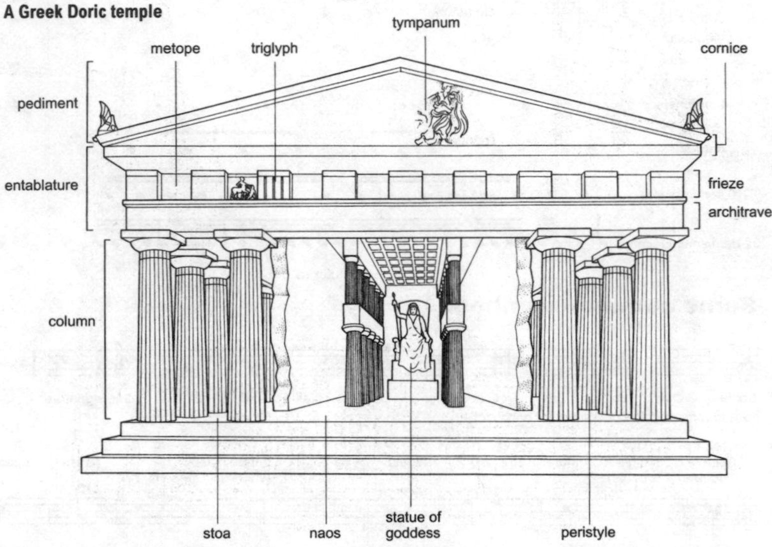

Orders of architecture: Greek origin

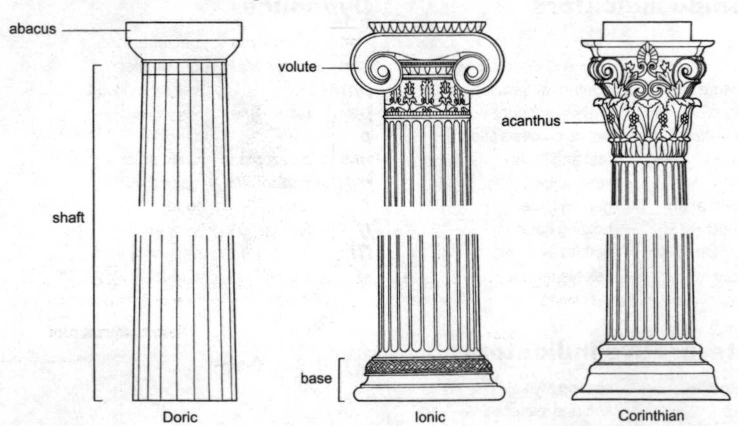

Medieval

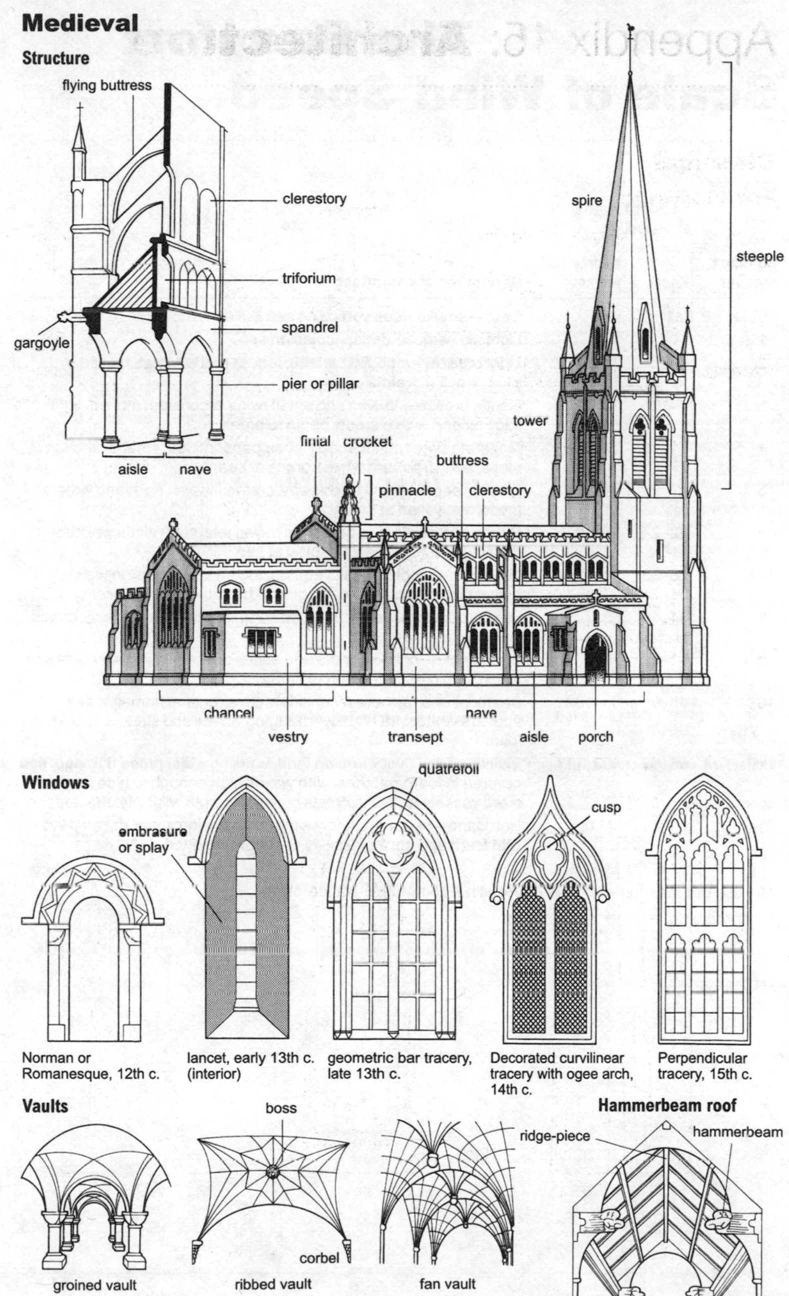

Norman or Romanesque, 12th c.

lancet, early 13th c. (interior)

geometric bar tracery, late 13th c.

Decorated curvilinear tracery with ogee arch, 14th c.

Perpendicular tracery, 15th c.

groined vault

ribbed vault

fan vault

Appendix 16: **The Beaufort Scale of Wind Speed**

Beaufort number	Equivalent speed at 10m above ground: Knots	Kilometres per hour	Description of conditions
0	<1	<1	Calm—smoke rises vertically; sea like a mirror.
1	1–3	1–6	Light air—smoke drifts; ripples on sea.
2	4–6	7–12	Light breeze—wind felt on face, leaves rustle, vanes moved by wind; small wavelets on sea.
3	7–10	13–19	Gentle breeze—leaves and small twigs in constant motion, light flags extend; wave crests begin to break.
4	11–16	20–30	Moderate breeze—dust and loose paper raised, small branches move; fairly frequent white horses at sea.
5	17–21	31–39	Fresh breeze—small trees sway, crested waves on inland waters; moderate waves at sea.
6	22–27	40–50	Strong breeze—large branches move, telegraph wires whistle; foaming crests and some spray at sea.
7	28–33	51–62	Near gale—whole trees in motion, inconvenience felt in walking against wind; foam at sea begins to be blown into streaks.
8	34–40	63–74	Gale—twigs broken off trees, walking upright difficult; wave crests break into spindrift.
9	41–47	75–87	Strong gale—chimney pots and slates removed; high waves at sea with rolling crests and dense spray.
10	48–55	88–102	Storm—trees uprooted, considerable structural damage; sea appears white with high overhanging waves and streaks of dense foam.
11	56–63	103–117	Violent storm—very rare on land, causing widespread damage; sea covered in foam patches, with waves high enough to hide medium-sized vessels and with crests blown into froth, visibility affected.
12	⩾64	⩾118	Hurricane—sea completely white, with driving spray, the air filled with foam and spray, visibility seriously impaired.

The use of the terms 'gale' and 'storm' is not completely standardized.